TO

FROM

ON

This is what the LORD says—

your Redeemer, the Holy One of Israel:

"I am the LORD your God, who teaches you what

is good for you and leads you along

the paths you should follow."

{ ISAIAH 48:17 }

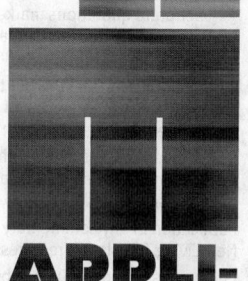

New Living
Translation®

TYNDALE HOUSE PUBLISHERS
CAROL STREAM, ILLINOIS

TEEN

APPLI-CATION® STUDY BIBLE

Visit Tyndale online at newlivingtranslation.com and tyndale.com.

The publisher gratefully acknowledges the role of Youth for Christ/USA in preparing the Life Application Notes and Bible Helps.

Adapted from *Student's Life Application Study Bible*, copyright © 1992, 1994, 1997, 2004 by Tyndale House Publishers, Carol Stream, IL 60188. All rights reserved.

Notes and Bible Helps copyright © 1988–1994, 1997, 2004, 2012 by Tyndale House Publishers. New Testament Notes and Bible Helps copyright © 1986 owned by assignment by Tyndale House Publishers. Maps copyright © 1996, 2004, 2013 by Tyndale House Publishers. All rights reserved.

Photograph of blurred sidewalk copyright © Asif Akbar/SXC. All rights reserved.
Steel City cover photograph copyright © Dan Shirley/rgbstock. All rights reserved.
Pink Fields cover photograph of grass copyright © Bert van 't Hul/SXC. All rights reserved.
Pink Fields cover photograph of birds copyright © Lesli Lundgren/SXC. All rights reserved.
Prison Fellowship cover art © Prison Fellowship Ministries.
Prison Fellowship cover illustration of friends copyright © Tetiana Garkusha/iStockphoto. All rights reserved.

Teen Life Application Study Bible is an edition of the *Holy Bible,* New Living Translation.

Holy Bible, New Living Translation, copyright © 1996, 2004, 2007 by Tyndale House Foundation. All rights reserved.

For information about special discounts for bulk purchases, please contact Tyndale House Publishers at csresponse@tyndale.com, or call 1-855-277-9400.

ISBN 978-1-4143-2462-3 Hardcover
ISBN 978-1-4143-2463-0 Softcover
ISBN 978-1-4143-2464-7 LeatherLike Pink Fields
ISBN 978-1-4964-1770-1 LeatherLike Pink Fields Indexed
ISBN 978-1-4143-2465-4 LeatherLike Steel City
ISBN 978-1-4964-1771-8 LeatherLike Steel City Indexed
ISBN 978-1-4143-7258-7 LeatherLike Black Pocket
ISBN 978-1-4964-3431-9 LeatherLike Teal
ISBN 978-1-4964-3432-6 LeatherLike Brown

Printed in the United States of America

27 26 25 24 23 22 21
19 18 17 16 15 14 13

Tyndale House Publishers and Wycliffe Bible Translators share the vision for an understandable, accurate translation of the Bible for every person in the world. Each sale of the *Holy Bible,* New Living Translation, benefits Wycliffe Bible Translators. Wycliffe is working with partners around the world to accomplish Vision 2025—an initiative to start a Bible translation program in every language group that needs it by the year 2025.

CONTENTS

A5   User's Guide: What You Can Expect
A8   A Look at the Book
A20 Finding Faith
A22 Help for New Believers
A24 14 Encounters with God
A29 A Note to Readers
A30 Introduction to the New Living Translation
A34 Contributors
A35 Photography Credits

OLD TESTAMENT

0003	Genesis	0469	2 Chronicles	0919	Daniel
0065	Exodus	0509	Ezra	0937	Hosea
0113	Leviticus	0523	Nehemiah	0951	Joel
0147	Numbers	0541	Esther	0957	Amos
0191	Deuteronomy	0553	Job	0969	Obadiah
0229	Joshua	0587	Psalms	0973	Jonah
0259	Judges	0671	Proverbs	0977	Micah
0289	Ruth	0703	Ecclesiastes	0987	Nahum
0295	1 Samuel	0715	Song of Songs	0991	Habakkuk
0331	2 Samuel	0723	Isaiah	0997	Zephaniah
0363	1 Kings	0791	Jeremiah	1003	Haggai
0399	2 Kings	0857	Lamentations	1007	Zechariah
0435	1 Chronicles	0867	Ezekiel	1019	Malachi

NEW TESTAMENT

1027	Matthew	1291	Ephesians	1347	Hebrews
1069	Mark	1301	Philippians	1363	James
1099	Luke	1307	Colossians	1369	1 Peter
1145	John	1315	1 Thessalonians	1377	2 Peter
1179	Acts	1321	2 Thessalonians	1383	1 John
1225	Romans	1325	1 Timothy	1391	2 John
1245	1 Corinthians	1333	2 Timothy	1393	3 John
1267	2 Corinthians	1339	Titus	1397	Jude
1281	Galatians	1343	Philemon	1401	Revelation

1423 Life Choices Index
1459 Features Index
1465 Where to Find It

USER'S GUIDE:
WHAT YOU CAN EXPECT

Welcome to the Teen Life Application Study Bible. *Most power tools come with a user's manual or instructions of some kind. This book is no exception! God gave us his Word to tell us about himself: how he operates, what he's done, and what his plans are for the people he created. This book is a "power tool" you can use. Wanna know more? Check this out: "All Scripture is inspired by God and is useful to teach us what is true and to make us realize what is wrong in our lives. It corrects us when we are wrong and teaches us to do what is right. God uses it to prepare and equip his people to do every good work" (2 Timothy 3:16-17).*

So, what're we to make of that? For starters, it reminds us to make Bible reading a priority. That's why the Teen Life Application Study Bible *was written—to help you understand and apply God's Word. It's easy to use and packed with helpful notes and other features. You'll find the notes within the text, at the beginnings and endings of books, and at the back of the Bible.*

At the back of the Bible you'll find . . .

LIFE CHOICES INDEX
You'll face many choices and questions in life—questions that need answers; choices that need wisdom. More than 100 topics are listed in this index. Each topic has a selection of relevant Bible passages and notes that relate.

INDEXES FOR "CHOICES," "I WONDER," ULTIMATE ISSUES, CHARTS, PERSONALITY PROFILES, MAPS, AND "MY STORY"
Again, Scripture references listed for these notes are to help you locate the notes easily. The notes may or may not actually relate to the Scripture listed.

"WHERE TO FIND IT"
More than 70 of the best-known Bible stories are listed in this index, along with Jesus' parables and miracles. Use either the Scripture references or the page numbers to quickly and easily find the story, parable, or miracle you want.

It's all here. Just about everything you'll need to understand and apply God's Word. The next step—actually taking time to read and study the Bible—is yours. So, what are you waiting for?

The following spread is a quick look at each of the special features.

EXPLANATION OF FEATURES

The Bible isn't a textbook; it's God's way of communicating himself to us. The Bible gives us hope and encouragement and shows us how to love and follow him. Sometimes God's Word can be hard to understand. The features in the Teen Life Application Study Bible *have been adapted from the best-selling* Life Application Study Bible *and connect to the stories and issues that real teens face. Each feature has been chosen to answer the question, "So what?"*

BOOK INTRODUCTIONS

Each introduction quickly introduces you to the who, what, when, where, and why of that book. Helpful background information about the author, audience, and purpose are found in the Stats section. The timeline will help you see how the events in the book connect to other related events, and Key Points will show you some of the book's important themes. Some books also include a map of major events.

LIFE APPLICATION NOTES

We've included 1,000 notes to help you understand what the Scriptures are saying and to help you apply them directly to your life. Look for them in the bottom corners of each page, below the dotted lines.

PERSONALITY PROFILE

The Bible is full of the stories of people and their interactions with God. We've included profiles of more than 50. Each profile gives some basic information on the person, the ups and downs of their life, and a practical look at why their life matters to us and what we can learn from them.

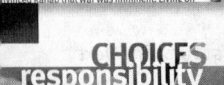

CHOICES

Over 60 Choices articles show teens in real-world situations that you have faced or will. Each one is anchored in a nearby Scripture passage, which you are asked to apply to your life. Topics include things like anger, friendship, sex, and serving God.

MAPS

Sometimes you need to know where you're at to get the most out of a passage or book. We've included maps in key places and in the introductions of Bible books that are filled with historical accounts to help you get a clearer picture of what's going on.

THE JUDGES OF ISRAEL

OTHNIEL (40 YEARS)	**EHUD (80 YEARS)**
He captured a powerful Canaanite city.	He killed Eglon and the Moabites.
Judges 3:7-11	Judges 3:12-30
DEBORAH (40 YEARS)	**GIDEON (40 YEARS)**
She defeated General Sisera and the Canaanites and later sang a victory song with Barak.	He used a fleece to God's will and defea Midianites with 300
Judges 4–5	Judges 6–8
JAIR (22 YEARS)	**JEPHTHAH (6 YEAR?**
He had 30 sons.	He made a rash vo

CHARTS

Nearly 70 charts throughout the Bible offer an easy and systematic way to understand how things fit together or to figure out the "so what?" of things like the various sacrifices, reasons to read the Psalms, or what Paul is talking about when he uses metaphors like the "armor of God."

THERE ARE "FRIENDS" WHO DESTROY EACH OTHER, BUT

A REAL FRIEND STICKS CLOSER THAN A BROTHER.

PROVERBS 18:24

⁴ Wise words are like deep waters;
wisdom flows from the wise like

KEY VERSES

Eighty-eight Key Verses throughout the Bible remind you of the hope and strength God provides.

MY STORY: Steve

When I was in first grade, I memorized Joshua 1:9: "This is my command—be strong and courageous! Do not be afraid or discouraged. For the LORD your God is with you wherever you go."

Recently I took part in a school play. I developed a bad case of stage fright before the performance. I didn't think I was going

MY STORY

Everyone has a story, but sometimes it's hard to see how our stories connect to the Bible. This Bible includes stories from real teens who are doing their best to follow God in the the real world. Their names have been changed, but their situations are real.

ULTIMATE ISSUES GOD'S

As you read the Old Testament, you may wonder, Why did God select the people of Israel as his chosen people? That's a good question, and one that's not easy to answer.

First, God singled out a man named Abram (later called Abraham) from the ancient city of Ur and promised to bless him and his descendants (Gen 12:1-3). But there was a condition attached: Abram had to remain faithful to God. Even though he had numerous lapses, Abram kept his end of the bargain, and God

ULTIMATE ISSUES

Some things that we think are important are really pretty minor. Others, not so much. Ultimate Issues deal with some of the big ones—hard questions about God, the Bible, and life.

I WONDER . . .

If Christ controls my life, where does my freedom of choice fit in?

One way that God demonstrated his love for us was by giving us freedom of choice. Someone once said, "Your heart has a door that can be opened only from the inside."

You make the choice to open the door of your heart to Jesus Christ when you receive him as Savior and Lord. Although his Spirit is at work prompting you to respond to his love, the choice is yours.

Picture your life as a house. Jesus Christ knocks o the front door and you decide to let him in (Rev 3:20

I WONDER

Is there a sin that God cannot forgive? Why should I go to church? Does God get tired of hearing about my problems? If you've ever asked a question like these, then the I Wonder articles are for you. We all struggle with questions about what it really means to follow after God. These articles will help you understand what the Bible says and then make it stick in your life.

A LOOK AT THE BOOK

INTRODUCTION

We usually think of the Bible as one book. That's logical because it looks like one book and comes from one Author. We also speak of it as God's Word. But when we read and study the Bible, we discover that it is actually an entire library between two covers. Not one book, but 66 (39 in the Old Testament; 27 in the New Testament)! Each book has its own style and uniqueness—yet each book contributes to the message God wants to get across with the whole Bible. What's more, though we use the word book, *some parts of the Bible are letters (like Paul's letter to the Romans) or collections (like the Psalms). Still, the overall message of the Bible is one message because it has one unifying Author—God. The reason the styles throughout the Bible vary is because God teamed up with dozens of people to write his Word.*

HOW THIS PLAN IS DIFFERENT

There are many plans to help you read through the Bible library. You can even start at page one and read straight through. The approach taken here, however, is designed to help you get a flavor of the whole Bible by reading selections from it throughout a year. You'll read the best-known stories and many important lessons. Some parts of the Bible offer so much help that they can be read every day. Among these are the Gospels, Psalms, and Proverbs.

BEFORE YOU BEGIN

Each day's reading has a title and a question. These application questions can help you as you read. So, get ready. You're about to start the awesome adventure of reading God's Word and getting to know him.

OLD TESTAMENT

Genesis 1:1–2:3 How It All Began
Why do human beings have value and worth?

Genesis 2:15–3:24 Adam and Eve
In what ways are you like those first humans?

Genesis 4:1-16 Cain and Abel
How do you handle anger?

Genesis 6:9-22 Noah Builds a Boat
What is the most difficult act that God has asked you to do?

Genesis 7:1-24 All Aboard?
If you were alive at this time, would you have been invited to get on the boat? Why or why not? Would you have accepted? Why or why not?

Genesis 8:1-22 A Long Wait
How would you have spent your time on the boat?

Genesis 9:1-17 Rules and Rainbows
What could you do the next time you see a rainbow to show that you take God's covenant seriously?

Genesis 11:1-9 The Tower of Babel
Is there anyone you trust more than God? Why or why not?

Genesis 12:1-9; 17:1-8, 15-16 God's Promises to Abraham and Sarah
How do you usually make decisions? How is God involved in those decisions?

Genesis 18:1-15 Unusual Visitors
How do you make guests feel welcome in your home? at school?

Genesis 19:1-29 Destruction of Sodom and Gomorrah
How does God feel about sin?

Genesis 21:8-21 Hagar and Ishmael
In what ways have you seen God work through the messes in your life?

Genesis 22:1-19 Abraham's Painful Decision
Could you have made the same decision as Abraham? Why or why not?

Genesis 24:1-27 A Faithful Servant
How do you approach difficult tasks?

Genesis 24:28-67 Isaac and Rebekah
How has God surprised you recently?

Genesis 25:19-34 Jacob and Esau
How do you treat your brothers or sisters?

Genesis 27:1-40 Jacob Tricks His Father
On a scale of 1 to 5 (with 5 being really important), how important is honesty in your relationship with your parents? Why?

Genesis 28:10-22 Jacob Meets God
In what places in your life has God seemed the most real?

Genesis 29:14-30 Jacob's Marriages
How do you show your love for others?

Genesis 32:1–33:18 Jacob Returns Home
What happens inside you when you try to avoid a problem?

Genesis 37 Jacob's Children
How are disagreements settled in your family?

Genesis 39 Joseph in Trouble
How do you react when you're treated unfairly?

Genesis 40 Dreams in Prison
When have you helped someone even though you had your own problems?

Genesis 41:1-36 Dreams in the Palace
Whom has God used to give you guidance?

Genesis 41:37-57 Joseph in Charge
How well do you handle big responsibilities?

Genesis 42 Joseph Sees His Brothers Again
If you had the chance to get back at someone who wronged you, would you take it? Why or why not?

Genesis 43 Back to Joseph
How quick are you to forgive? Why?

Genesis 44 Crisis in the Palace
How do you react when someone points out a mistake you've made? Why?

Genesis 45; 46:26-30 Finding a Lost Son
What do you appreciate about your parents? How do you show your appreciation?

Genesis 49 Jacob's Final Words
What legacies have your parents or grandparents passed on to you?

Exodus 1:8–2:10 Moses Is Born
How has God protected you from birth till now?

Exodus 2:11-25 Moses on the Run
When was the last time you found yourself running from God? Explain.

Exodus 3 God's Burning Bush
In what ways has God made himself known to you?

Exodus 4:1-17 Moses Isn't Sure
How willing are you to do what you feel God wants you to do? Explain.

Exodus 5 Resistance
How do you handle others' resistance toward doing what's right?

Exodus 6:1-13 Rejection
What would it cost you to do what God wants?

Exodus 7:1-14 A Stubborn Ruler
What decisions have you tried to resist that you knew God wanted you to make?

Exodus 7:15–9:7 Five out of Ten Plagues
When do you try to bargain with God? Why?

Exodus 9:8–10:29 Four More Plagues
What are the worst consequences you've seen that were a result of wrong actions?

Exodus 11; 12:29-36 The Ultimate Plague
In what amazing way has God rescued you from a problem?

Exodus 13:17–14:31 A Narrow Escape
When have you experienced God's protection?

Exodus 15:22-27; 17:1-7 God Provides Water
When are you most tempted to complain? Why?

Exodus 16 God's Unusual Food Supply
For what specific gift did you last thank God?

Exodus 18 Helpful Advice
Who are the dependable advisers in your life?

Exodus 19 An Appointment with God
How would you prepare to meet with God?

Exodus 20:1-21 The Ten Commandments
How important are these rules to you? Explain.

Exodus 32 The Gold Calf
What distracts you from obeying God?

Exodus 40 Instructions about God's Tent
When are you most aware of God's presence in your life?

Numbers 12 Trouble in the Family
What do you do when you find yourself feeling jealous of someone?

Numbers 13:1–14:4 Spying on the Promised Land
What do you usually do when you're faced with an impossible task?

Numbers 14:5-45 A Majority That Was Wrong
How often are your decisions based on peer pressure?

Numbers 21:4-9 Another Hard Lesson
What can you do to avoid repeating mistakes?

Numbers 22:5-35 Balaam and His Donkey
How do you avoid making a wrong choice when the right choice seems hard?

Deuteronomy 29 Moses Reviews God's Actions
How do you keep track of what God has done for you?

Deuteronomy 30 Moses Challenges the People
How do you show that you love God?

Deuteronomy 31:1-8 Moses Appoints New Leaders
In what ways have you been a leader?

Deuteronomy 34 The Death of Moses
How would you most like to be remembered?

Joshua 1 God Takes Over
Which of the qualities listed in this chapter would you most need to be like Joshua? Why?

Joshua 2 Spies Visit Jericho
What surprising individuals has God used in your life? Why do you think God chose them?

Joshua 3 The Invasion of Canaan
What instructions has God given you recently? How carefully did you follow them? Why?

Joshua 5:13–6:27 The Battle of Jericho
In what way has God worked through you to bring about something that would normally be impossible?

Joshua 7 Ultimate Consequences
What strongly negative or positive consequences have you experienced?

Joshua 10:1-15 The Longest Day
How do you know that God is powerful? Explain.

Joshua 23 Joshua Warns the Leaders
Which of Joshua's warnings do you most need to obey?

Joshua 24:1-31 Joshua's Last Words
How have the events of history provided hope for you?

Judges 4:4-24 Deborah Goes to War
What do you do to help suffering people?

Judges 6 Gideon Becomes a Judge
What examples of obedience can be found in your life?

Judges 7 Gideon and the Midianites
In what area of your life do you need to trust God more? Explain.

Judges 13 The Birth of Samson
In what part of your life do you need more discipline?

Judges 14 Samson's Riddle
How carefully do you consider the wisdom of your parents?

Judges 15 Samson and the Jawbone
What proof do you have that mistakes usually don't correct themselves?

Judges 16:1-21 Samson and Delilah
In what situations do you find yourself flirting with disaster?

Judges 16:22-31 Samson's Death
How well do you understand God's patience? Explain.

Ruth 1 Ruth and Naomi—A Friendship
How do difficulties affect your friendships?

Ruth 2 Ruth Meets Boaz
When have you found your reputation to be an advantage?

Ruth 3 Ruth Finds a Husband
What's the coolest thing that God has done for you lately?

Ruth 4 A Happy Ending
What future reasons could there be for obeying God today?

1 Samuel 1 A Serious Prayer
What promises have you made to God lately that you've kept?

1 Samuel 3 God Calls Samuel
When you read God's Word, what expectations do you have?

1 Samuel 8 Samuel's Disappointing Sons
What positive lessons have you learned from your parents' mistakes or the mistakes of other relatives?

1 Samuel 8 The People Want a King
What has God taught you about being responsible for your own choices?

1 Samuel 9:1-21 Saul and the Lost Donkeys
What is God's part in your daily decisions?

1 Samuel 10 Saul Becomes King
How do you evaluate people?

1 Samuel 14:1-23 Heroic Acts
What is the bravest thing you've ever done? Where did you find the courage to do it?

1 Samuel 16:1-13 Samuel Anoints David
Like God, do you choose to focus on a person's inner qualities? Why or why not?

1 Samuel 17:1-37 David Answers Goliath's Challenge
How does your confidence in God affect your decision to accept challenges?

1 Samuel 17:38-58 David Kills Goliath
What "giants" need to be defeated in your life?

1 Samuel 18 Trouble between Saul and David
How do you treat your friends who succeed?

1 Samuel 19:1-6; 20:1-42 David and Jonathan
How loyal are you to your friends? Would they agree? Why or why not?

1 Samuel 24:1-22 David Spares Saul's Life
Do you treat others the way you want to be treated? Why or why not?

1 Samuel 25:1-42 David and Abigail
How has God kept you from making big mistakes?

1 Samuel 28 Saul and the Occult
What kinds of things could be considered "occult practices"? How would God feel about your involvement in such things?

2 Samuel 5:1-12 David Becomes King over All Israel
How could you become a person who is more pleasing to God, as David was?

2 Samuel 9 The King's Kindness
How would you show kindness to an enemy?

2 Samuel 11 David and Bathsheba
How often are you tempted to correct one sin by committing another? Explain.

2 Samuel 12:1-25 David and Nathan
Which of your friends loves you enough to correct you?

2 Samuel 13:1-19 Family Problems
What steps do you take to avoid temptation?

2 Samuel 13:20-39 Revenge
Why do you think taking revenge never fully solves the problem?

2 Samuel 15 Betrayal
Who helps you keep your motives clear?

2 Samuel 18:1-18 The Death of Absalom
In what situations are you most likely to lose control?

1 Kings 1:5-27 Conflict over the Throne
What happens when you don't make good decisions?

1 Kings 1:28-53 Solomon Becomes King
When things in your world get confusing, how do you know God is still in control?

1 Kings 3:1-15 Solomon's Choice
If you were told that you could have anything you wanted, what would you ask for? Why?

1 Kings 3:16-28 Solomon Solves a Problem
In what situation in your life do you presently need God's wisdom?

1 Kings 6 Solomon Builds the Temple
What can you learn from Solomon about making and carrying out plans?

1 Kings 10:1-13 Solomon and the Queen of Sheba
When are you tempted to try to impress people?

1 Kings 12:1-24 Solomon's Unwise Son
Who are the people you count on for advice? How helpful is this advice usually? Explain.

1 Kings 17 God Takes Care of Elijah
How do obeying and trusting God go together in your life?

1 Kings 18:16-46 Elijah versus the Priests of Baal
How willing are you to take a stand for God? Explain.

1 Kings 19 Spiritual Burnout
When was the last time you felt depressed? How did you handle that?

1 Kings 21 The Stolen Vineyard
How important is justice in your life?

1 Kings 22:29-40 The Death of King Ahab
When are you tempted to think that you can hide from God?

2 Kings 2:1-12 Elijah's Chariot
When you make a commitment, how far will you go to carry it out?

2 Kings 2:13-25 Elisha's Miracles
How would someone else know that you have a deep respect for God?

2 Kings 5 The Healing of Naaman
What "small" things, if there have been any, have you refused to do for God? What happened as a result?

2 Kings 11 A Seven-Year-Old King
Who were your best examples in childhood?

2 Kings 22:1–23:3 Discovery of the Lost Book
If your Bible turned up missing, what effect would that have on your life? Explain.

Ezra 3:7-13 Rebuilding the Temple
How do you feel when you're working on a large, important project? Explain.

Nehemiah 2 Nehemiah Returns to Jerusalem
What relationships in your past need to be rebuilt? Why?

Nehemiah 5 Nehemiah's Concern for the Poor
How do you express your concern for the poor?

Nehemiah 8 Reading God's Word
How much of a priority for you is the reading of God's Word? Explain.

Esther 1 A Queen Is Replaced
Have you ever taken the important people in your life for granted? Why or why not?

Esther 2:1-18 Esther Is Chosen
When have difficult or confusing events in your life actually been a preparation for something you would later experience?

Esther 3 The Jews in Danger
In what situations are you tempted to compromise your faith? Why?

Esther 4 The Queen Decides to Help
What hard decisions have you had to make because of your faith in God?

Esther 5 Esther Risks Her Life
When was the last time you did something scary in obedience to God? What happened as a result?

Esther 6:1–7:10 God Protects His People
When is it helpful to remember that God is still in control of the world?

Job 1 The Testing of Job
In what situations do you most quickly question God's concern for you?

Job 2 Job and His Friends
How do you normally respond to someone else's pain? Is this a helpful response? Why or why not?

Job 38 God Speaks to Job
What things around you remind you of God's greatness?

Job 42 The Rest of Job's Story
When has God turned a disaster around for your good?

Psalm 1 Two Kinds of Lives
Which of the two kinds of people described in this passage do you really want to be? How do your actions reveal your choice?

Psalm 8 The Value of Humans
How do you know you have worth?

Psalm 23 A Sheep's Song
What is the most comforting phrase to you in this psalm?

Psalm 51 A Confession
How have your actions revealed your sorrow over a wrong choice?

Psalm 103 What God Is Like
Which picture in this psalm helps you understand God better?

Psalm 139 God Knows Us
What do you feel when you read this psalm?

Psalm 145 God for All People and Time
Which of God's qualities do you most need today?

Proverbs 4 Wise Words about Life
Is finding wisdom a priority for you? Why or why not?

Proverbs 5 Wise Words about Sex
How do these words compare with the messages you hear every day?

Ecclesiastes 12 A Summary of Life
In what way can you remember your Creator today?

Isaiah 6 God Chooses Isaiah
Can you relate to Isaiah's feelings in this chapter? If so, what did you do to express your need for forgiveness?

Isaiah 53 The Suffering Servant
How would you describe what Jesus did for you?

Jeremiah 1:1-9 God Calls a Prophet
If you were Jeremiah, how would you have responded to God's call? What do you think God wants to do through you?

Jeremiah 36 The Book Burning
How much risk is involved in your relationship with God?

Jeremiah 38:1-13 Jeremiah in the Well
What part of your life compares in any way with Jeremiah's time in the well?

Ezekiel 37:1-14 A Valley of Dry Bones
Have you ever experienced a time of spiritual "dryness"? Explain. How can you help people who are spiritually "dry"?

Daniel 1 Coping with Pressure to Conform
How do you usually respond when someone pressures you to go along with what everyone else is doing?

Daniel 2:1-24 A King's Dream
What qualities do seemingly hopeless situations bring out in you? Why?

Daniel 2:25-49 The Meaning of the Dream
Who gets the credit when things go right in your life? Why?

Daniel 3 Three Friends in a Furnace
What examples can you give of God's protection in your life?

Daniel 5 The Writing on the Wall
What message, if any, do you think God has for our society? Why?

Daniel 6 Daniel and the Lions
What do you do to spend time with God?

Jonah 1:1–2:10 Bending God's Directions
When did you last try to avoid doing what you knew God wanted you to do? What happened as a result?

Jonah 3:1–4:11 Wrong Motives
About what things do you complain to God? Why?

NEW TESTAMENT

You will read various parts of the four Gospels in order to have a fairly chronological biography of Jesus' life.

Luke 1:1-4; John 1:1-18 The Word Was God
What do you believe about Jesus?

Luke 1:5-25 The Angel and Zechariah
How would you react to an angel's visit?

Luke 1:26-56 Mary and Elizabeth
What makes you feel joyful?

Luke 1:57-80 John the Baptist Is Born
What hopes have your parents expressed to you about your life?

Matthew 1 A Family Tree
How has a family member's experience influenced your relationship with God?

Luke 2:1-20 Jesus Is Born!
What does Christmas mean to you?

Luke 2:21–3:8 Anna and Simeon See Jesus
What promise of God have you been waiting a long time to see fulfilled?

Matthew 2:1-12 Foreign Visitors
What gift would you offer to Jesus? Why?

Matthew 2:13-23 Escape and Return
How has knowing God brought excitement into your life?

Luke 2:41-52 Jesus in the Temple Again
What four words would summarize your teen years thus far? Why?

Mark 1:1-13 Baptism and Temptation
What are your most difficult temptations? How would they compare to Jesus' temptations? Explain.

John 1:19-34 John the Baptist and Jesus
To whom did you last talk about Christ? Why?

John 1:35-51 Jesus' First Disciples
How would someone know that you're a disciple of Jesus?

John 2 A Surprising Savior
How has Christ been unpredictable in your life?

John 3:1-21 Jesus and Nicodemus
How did you first meet Jesus?

John 3:22-36; Luke 3:19-20 John Gets into Trouble
When has knowing Christ gotten you into trouble?

John 4:1-42 Jesus Changes a Town
In what ways has Jesus affected your community?

John 4:43-54 Jesus' Ministry
In what practical ways has God met your needs recently?

Luke 4:16-30 Jesus Is Rejected
In what ways has Jesus been rejected by the people around you? Why?

Mark 1:16-39 Jesus Calls People to Follow
What specific things have you left behind to follow Christ?

Luke 5 Miracles and Questions
How do Jesus' miracles affect you today?

John 5 Honor for the Son
What do you find most attractive about Jesus? Why?

Mark 2:23–3:19 Jesus' Disciples
Based on what you know about Jesus' disciples, who do you most identify with? Why?

Matthew 5:1-16 The Beatitudes
Which of these attitudes do you struggle with most? Why?

Matthew 5:17-30 Rules for Living
How do Jesus' views on these subjects compare with yours?

Matthew 5:31-48 Jesus on Relationships
What part of your life could be most radically changed by these words? Why?

Matthew 6:1-18 The Pattern of Prayer
What do you find yourself praying for the most these days? Why?

Matthew 6:19-34 Money Matters
In what ways are money and worry related in your life?

Matthew 7:1-12 Judge or Pray?
Are you quicker to pray or to criticize? Why?

Matthew 7:13-29 Facts about Fruit and Foundations
What kind of fruit does your life show? What type of foundation is your life built on? Explain.

Luke 7:1-10 A Roman Centurion's Request
What is your attitude toward people from other cultures? How can you show them God's love?

Matthew 11 Jesus Describes John
How would you want Jesus to summarize your life? Why?

Luke 7:36–8:3 Expressions of Faith
How do you express your faith in Jesus?

Matthew 12:22-50 Troubles for Jesus
When are you tempted to have Jesus prove himself to you?

Mark 4:1-29 Jesus Seeks, Seeds, and Weeds
What kind of soil is your life right now? Why?

Matthew 13:24-43 More of Jesus' Parables
How concerned are you about where your friends and family will spend eternity? Explain.

Matthew 13:44-52 Even More Parables
How and where did you find the hidden treasure?

Luke 8:22-56 Jesus in Control
Which of the events in this passage gives you the greatest comfort? Why?

Matthew 9:27-38 The Compassion of Jesus
In what practical ways can you show Jesus' compassion to others?

Mark 6:1-13 The Mission
How clear an idea do you have of what God wants you to do? Explain.

Matthew 10:16-42 Jesus Prepares His Disciples
In what ways do Jesus' words speak to the fears you have?

Mark 6:14-29 Herod Kills John the Baptist
With which qualities of John the Baptist do you most identify? Why?

Matthew 14:13-36 Simply the Son of God
Would you have been more likely to step out with Peter or to stay in the boat? Why?

John 6:22-40 Bread from Heaven
How is Jesus "bread" to you?

John 6:41-71 Jesus Criticized and Deserted
How do you react when you hear critical comments about Jesus? Why do you react that way?

Mark 7 Purity
If God were to describe what you're like inside, what do you think he would say? Why?

Matthew 15:32–16:12 Jesus Feeds and Warns
How do you evaluate what you hear about God? Explain.

Mark 8:22-38 Who Is Jesus?
In what specific ways have you come to understand Jesus better in the last few weeks?

Luke 9:28-36 Jesus Is Transfigured
Would you rather leave the world and be with Christ or be with Christ in the world? Why?

Matthew 17:24–18:5 Who's the Greatest?
When do you worry about status? Why?

Mark 9:38-50 Who's on Our Side?
How do you respond to the beliefs of others?

Matthew 18:10-20 Dealing with Wrong Choices
How do you react to the failures of others? Why?

John 7:1-31 Reactions to Jesus' Teachings
Which of Jesus' teachings is the most difficult for you to accept? Why?

John 7:32-53 A Warrant for Jesus' Arrest
What does it mean to have "rivers of living water" flowing from within you?

John 8:1-20 Jesus: Forgiveness and Light
Who is the last person you had to forgive? How easy or hard was it for you to forgive? Why?

John 8:21-59 Jesus: Giver of Freedom
How has Christ made you free?

Luke 10:1-24 Jesus Sends Seventy Messengers
What would have been the most exciting part of this trip for you? Why?

Luke 10:25-42 A Friend in Need
Who has been a good Samaritan to you? Explain.

Luke 11:1-13 Jesus Teaches about Prayer
What is your prayer routine like?

Luke 11:14-32 Accusations and Unbelief
What are your strongest reasons for being a faithful follower of Christ?

Luke 11:33-54 Real Faith
What comments have you heard about your faith lately?

Luke 12:1-21 Treasure Talk
Whom or what do you treasure? Why?

Luke 12:22-48 Worry Warning
What worries you most these days? Why?

Luke 12:49-59 Troubles Ahead
What examples have you seen of the problems that Jesus mentions in this passage?

Luke 13:1-21 Turn Around
What does repentance mean to you?

John 9 Jesus and a Blind Man
What does "spiritual blindness" mean?

John 10:1-18 The Good Shepherd
How have you experienced God's guidance in your life?

Luke 13:22-35 Jesus: The King Who Grieves
How do you feel about those around you who don't know Christ?

Luke 14:1-14 Pride or Humility?
What actions would taking "the lowest place" involve in your life?

Luke 14:15-35 Following Jesus
What are you willing to leave behind in order to be a follower of Jesus?

Luke 15:1-10 Two Parables of Losing and Finding
How do these stories help you understand God's love for you?

Luke 15:11-32 A Lost Son
In what ways is this story like your life?

Luke 16:1-18 A Good Servant
How can you be a good steward of God's resources?

Luke 16:19-31 The Rich Man and Lazarus
How can you help the poor in your community?

John 11:1-37 Lazarus Dies
In what situations have you been disappointed with God?

John 11:38-57 Jesus Raises Lazarus
How would you have felt watching Lazarus walk out of the tomb? Why?

Luke 17:1-19 Jesus and Ten Lepers
For what are you thankful to God?

Luke 17:20-37 Jesus and the Kingdom of God
What difference would it make in your life if Jesus returned today?

Luke 18:1-14 Jesus Teaches about Prayer
What is the attitude of your prayers?

Mark 10:1-16 Jesus on Family Matters
How far will you go to keep your word?

Mark 10:17-31 Jesus and the Rich Man
What is the most difficult thing Jesus could ask you to give up?

Matthew 20:1-19 A Parable about Equal Pay
Would you have felt the same way as the first workers in this story? Why or why not?

Mark 10:35-52 Jesus on Serving Others
In what ways are you learning to be a servant?

Luke 19:1-10 Jesus and Zacchaeus
What physical characteristic has most affected how you feel about yourself?

John 12:1-11 A Woman Anoints Jesus
What have you ever "wasted" as an expression of love for Christ?

Matthew 21:1-17 Jesus Rides into Jerusalem
If you had been part of the crowd that day, what would have been your most lasting memory?

John 12:20-36 Why Jesus Must Die
How would you explain to someone why Jesus had to die on the cross?

John 12:37-50 Jesus and His Message
What kinds of pressures make you hesitant to tell others about your belief in Christ?

Mark 11:20-33 Ask for Anything
How bold is your prayer life? Why?

Matthew 21:28-46 Two Parables
In the first parable, which son's actions most resemble yours? Why?

Matthew 22:1-14 Wedding Feast
At what point in your life did you realize that you were invited to this feast? How did you respond?

Luke 20:20-40 Jesus Answers Questions
How do you really feel about living forever?

Mark 12:28-37 Questions Given and Taken
Whom do you know who is close to believing in Jesus?

Matthew 23 Warnings
Which of these seven warnings most directly relate to your life? Why?

Luke 21:1-24 Signs of the Times
What concerns you most about the future? Why?

Luke 21:25-38 Jesus on Being Prepared
How do your actions reflect your belief that Jesus will return someday?

Matthew 25:1-30 Ready for His Return
With which of the people in these two stories do you identify most? Why?

Matthew 25:31-46 Just Like Jesus
How can you treat people in ways you would want to treat Christ?

Luke 22:1-13 Preparing the Last Supper
How do you prepare yourself for Communion?

John 13:1-20 Jesus Washes His Disciples' Feet
What is the greatest service someone has done for you? How do you serve others?

John 13:21-38 A Sad Prediction
How well do you feel Christ knows you? Explain.

John 14:1-14 Jesus Is the Way
How would you rate your present level of understanding of Christ and his teachings? Explain.

John 14:15-31 The Comforter
How are you aware of the Holy Spirit's presence in your life?

John 15:1-17 The Vine and the Branches
What kind of fruit has the Gardener produced in you?

John 15:18–16:4 The Test of Troubles
How do Jesus' words about persecution make you feel? Why?

John 16:5-33 The Power of the Holy Spirit
Have you ever been persecuted for your faith? If so, how did God help you through that experience?

John 17 Jesus Prays
How do you think this prayer of Jesus affects your life?

Mark 14:27-52 A Passionate Prayer
What problem have you most persisted in praying about? What answer, if any, have you received?

John 18:1-26 Jesus Betrayed and Abandoned
How close have you come to Peter's denial of Christ? Explain.

Matthew 26:57-75 Trial and Denial
In what ways has being a follower of Jesus complicated your life?

Matthew 27:1-10 Judas's Death
When you think of the consequences of wrong actions, what personal examples come to mind? Explain.

Luke 23:1-12 Two Political Trials
In what ways did your family situation or culture prepare you to respond to Jesus?

Mark 15:6-24 Sentenced to Die
Was there a time when you chose to do the wrong thing on purpose? Why?

Luke 23:32-49 Jesus Crucified
What do you feel when you read the description of the Crucifixion? Explain.

Matthew 27:57-66 The Burial
What have you seen people do in their resistance to Christ?

John 20:1-18 Jesus Is Alive!
*What makes Easter an important
celebration in your life?*

Matthew 28:8-15 Reactions to the
Resurrection
*What would be your first words to Jesus if
he appeared to you? Why?*

Luke 24:13-43 Appearances of Jesus
*What convinced you that Jesus was who he
said he was—the promised Savior?*

John 20:24–21:14 More Appearances of Jesus
How has Jesus answered your doubts?

John 21:15-25 Jesus Talks with Peter
*What difference would it make to you to
read these verses with your name in place
of Peter's? Explain.*

Matthew 28:16-20 The Great Commission
What are you doing to fulfill this mission?

Luke 24:44-53 Jesus Says Farewell
*How have the Scriptures helped you
recently in your relationship with God?*

Acts 1:1-11 The Departure of Jesus
*What one thing would you be sure to do
if you knew that Jesus was coming back
today?*

Acts 1:12-26 First Things First
*What is your idea of the right amount of
time for prayer? Explain.*

Acts 2:1-13 An Amazing Gift
*What is the main purpose of any gift God
might have given you?*

Acts 2:14-40 Peter's First Sermon
*How would you put this sermon into your
own words?*

Acts 2:41–3:10 Daily Life in the Early Church
*What part of these early days would you
have enjoyed the most? Explain.*

Acts 3:11–4:4 Peter's Second Sermon
*If you were given three minutes to tell the
story of your relationship with Jesus, what
would you say?*

Acts 4:5-22 Hostile Reactions
*What excuses are you most likely to use to
avoid sharing your faith? Explain.*

Acts 4:23-37 Praying and Sharing
How is your church community like this one?

Acts 5:1-16 Strange Events
*How often are you tempted to take God
lightly?*

Acts 5:17-42 Arrested!
*How do you react when you are treated
unfairly?*

Acts 6 Stephen: Special Servant
*What responsibilities do you have in your
local church?*

Acts 7:1-50 Family History
*What events in your family history have
helped you to reach the point where you
are today?*

Acts 7:51-60 Just Like Stephen
*In what ways would you want to be more
like Stephen? Explain.*

Acts 8:1-25 Benefits of Persecution
*Which difficulties in your life has God used
to help you grow spiritually?*

Acts 8:26-40 An Unexpected Appointment
*What opportunities to share your faith have
you taken recently? What happened?*

Acts 9:1-19 Saul (Paul) Meets Jesus
*What unusual events has God used to catch
your attention?*

Acts 9:20-31 Paul's New Life
*What are some of the ways that Jesus has
changed your life?*

Acts 9:32-42 God Uses Peter
*This past week, what special ability did you
use to meet someone's need?*

Acts 10:1-23 God Speaks to Peter
*Who is the last person you would expect to
talk to about Jesus? Explain.*

Acts 10:24-48 Peter Learns a Lesson
*How has God helped you change your mind
about some attitudes?*

Acts 11:1-18 Gentiles Join the Family of God
*Why should all people be treated the same?
How do your actions show that you believe
this?*

Acts 11:19-29 Christians Helping One
Another
*What do you do when you hear stories
of extreme poverty or hardship among
Christians in other parts of the world?*

Acts 12 A Great Escape
*How do you react when God answers your
prayers?*

Acts 13:1-12 The Missionary Journey of Paul
and Barnabas
*What Christians do you know who might
help you discover more clearly how
God wants you to invest your time and
abilities?*

Acts 14 Response and Reaction
*What responses have you encountered
when you tried to share your faith?*

Acts 15:1-21 A Church Conference
How important is it for you to talk problems over with other Christians? Explain.

Acts 15:22-41 The Gentiles Are Accepted
In what ways is God affecting your life and the goals you've set?

Acts 16:1-15 Paul, Silas, and Timothy
In what ways have you cooperated with others recently in order to spread the Gospel?

Acts 16:16-40 Adventures in Jail
How have your reactions to hard times helped others to learn more about God?

Acts 17:1-15 Two Cities: Two Responses
What part does the Bible play in your evaluation of what you hear and read?

Acts 17:16-34 Paul in Athens
What aspects of God's presence do you notice in society?

Acts 19:1-20 Paul in Ephesus
In what situations are you most likely to become discouraged?

Acts 19:21-41 The Riot
When are you most likely to forget that God is in control? Explain.

Acts 20:1-12 Sleeping in Church
What does this story tell you about God's response to human weaknesses?

Acts 20:13-38 Saying Good-bye to Ephesus
When have painful good-byes worked for the best in your life?

Acts 21:1-14 Difficult Decision
What hard decisions do you have to make?

Acts 21:15-36 Paul in Jerusalem
What evidence do you see of God's leading in the lives of others (for example, friends or family members)?

Acts 21:37–22:29 Paul Speaks
How can you relate what Paul is saying to what God has done in your life?

Acts 22:30–23:22 A Plan to Kill Paul
How well do you know your rights and fulfill your responsibilities as a citizen of your country?

Acts 23:23–24:27 Paul in Prison
Which would be harder for you—persecution or prison? Why?

Acts 25 Paul Speaks to Festus
If Christianity were outlawed, what evidence could be brought against you to prove you are a Christian?

Acts 26 Paul Speaks to Agrippa
How comfortable are you in explaining your faith? Why?

Acts 27:1-26 The Storm at Sea
Have you ever been part of a group that experienced difficulties? (For example, you may have experienced persecution for your faith or because you're from a different culture.) What was your attitude as you went through this experience?

Acts 27:27-44 The Shipwreck
How has God brought good out of a bad situation in your life?

Acts 28:1-14 The Winter on Malta
How do you notice God in your daily routine?

Acts 28:15-31 Paul in Rome
What aspects of your daily routine show that you plan to persevere in your faith?

Romans 5:1-11 Faith Brings Joy
What has caused you to thank God recently?

Romans 8:1-17 Truly Free from Sin
In what areas are you still struggling with temptation?

Romans 8:18-39 The Love of Christ
What people or things do you sometimes fear might separate you from the love of Christ? Explain.

Romans 12 Spiritual Gifts
What is your spiritual gift? How are you using it?

1 Corinthians 13 Real Love
Which quality of love mentioned in this passage do you most need to ask God to increase in your life? Why?

1 Corinthians 15:1-19 The Gospel
What parts of the gospel are especially helpful to you in times of doubt or stress?

1 Corinthians 15:42-58 Victory at Last
How has this passage affected your ideas about life after death?

2 Corinthians 4 Weak Containers; Strong Contents
With which difficult situation mentioned in this passage do you most clearly identify?

Galatians 5:13-26 Two Radically Different Lives
How can you "live by the Spirit"?

Ephesians 1 God's Actions
In what ways has God marked your life?

Ephesians 2 God's Plan
When have you recently reminded yourself and God that you want your life to be used for his purposes?

Ephesians 4:1-16 The Church
What is your role in Christ's body?

Ephesians 6:10-20 Armor of God
How quick are you to use the Christian's only offensive weapon—the Word of God?

Philippians 2:1-18 The Mind of Jesus
In what ways would having Christ's attitude make you face this day differently?

Philippians 3 Learning Joy
What areas of your life could God be using to teach you joy? Explain.

Colossians 2:1-15 What We Have in Christ
What information, if any, have you heard recently that could affect your relationship with Christ? What will you do about it?

Colossians 3:1-17 Christian Characteristics
What do you envision when you think about heaven? How does that affect the way you live now?

1 Thessalonians 1 Spiritual Reputation
How do you think others would evaluate your spiritual life? Explain.

1 Thessalonians 4 Living for God
What specific action could you take today simply out of obedience to God?

2 Thessalonians 1 Encouragement
What other Christians could you encourage today? Why?

2 Thessalonians 3 Final Requests
How aware and involved are you in the worldwide spread of the gospel?

1 Timothy 4 Always Going Forward
Which of these positive commands would you choose to make a higher priority in your life?

1 Timothy 6:3-21 A Friend's Final Words
How does your attitude toward money match Paul's advice?

2 Timothy 1 The Importance of Examples
Who has been a good spiritual example for you? How can you thank him or her?

2 Timothy 3 Last Days
How many of these characteristics are part of your world today?

Titus 3:1-11; Philemon 1:4-7 Good Counsel
Which of these commands seems best suited to your life right now? Why?

Hebrews 10:19-39 The New Life
What do your prayer habits and church involvement reveal about the real importance of faith in your life?

Hebrews 11 A Review of Faith
How deep is your commitment to Christ? Explain.

Hebrews 12:1-13 Our Turn
What do you need to do to follow the advice in this passage? Why?

James 1 Tough Times
What difficulty are you facing right now? How could the suggestions in this passage help?

James 2 Faith and Actions
How have you shown your faith recently by your actions?

James 3:1-12 Words as Weapons
How do you tame your tongue?

1 Peter 2 Living Stones
Which would you choose as the biggest personal challenge in these verses? Why?

1 Peter 3 Relationships and Pain
How willing are you to carry out your relationships God's way, even in the face of difficulties?

2 Peter 1 Knowing God
How would you answer someone who asked you how a person can know God?

1 John 1 The Way of Forgiveness
What part does confession have in your life?

1 John 3 God Is Love
How do you put your love into action?

1 John 5 The Life God Gives
How do you know that you have eternal life? Explain.

2 John 1:4-6; 3 John 1:5-8; Jude 1:17-25 Family Matters
How often do you go out of your way to meet the needs of other Christians? Explain.

Revelation 1 Jesus the King
When you think of Jesus, what characteristics come to mind? Why?

Revelation 21 Everything Made New
What are you most looking forward to concerning the new world as described here? Why?

Revelation 22 Life in the New City
How eagerly do you await the return of Jesus? Explain.

FINDING FAITH

Whether you're new to Christianity or a veteran of following Jesus, it's important to "know your roots." How did you become a Christian? How has your salvation changed your life? What exactly does it mean to be "saved," anyway? When you're confident with the basics of your faith, you're like a tree with roots that reach deep into the earth: healthy and hard to topple. You'll also start to produce fruit for other people to see, and they'll start asking questions about how you got that way.

This is the second reason to know your roots: so that you can tell other people how to be saved. One of the last things Jesus told his disciples before he ascended to heaven was, "Preach the Good News to everyone" (Mark 16:15, page 1098). God wants us to be concerned with the salvation of everyone around us, and he uses us to plant the seeds of belief in their hearts. How exciting it is for us to be God's tools!

Don't get us wrong—sharing your faith can be intimidating sometimes. Maybe you're worried that you won't know what to say, or that the other person will laugh at you or get angry. If you suffer from such fears, always remember that God is with you. If you've prepared yourself to have this conversation, he will show you what to say. And even if some people don't listen, you are still obeying God by talking to them. Obedience is always a good thing.

MAKING YOUR FAITH YOUR OWN

All people are sinners who fall short of God's standard. Romans 3:23, page 1230
We all have sin engrained in our hearts. No matter how nice we think we are, no matter how many good things we do, we cannot fully eliminate sin from our lives by our own efforts. God's standard is perfection, and we simply can't live up to it.

The fair punishment for sin is eternal death. Romans 6:23, page 1233
Sin is a crime against an infinite God. The result of sin is death and eternal separation from him. An infinite offense demands an eternal punishment. Because we are sinful, we have earned this fate.

God sent Jesus Christ to pay the penalty for your sin. Romans 5:8, page 1232
Here's the thing: God loves us. He doesn't want anyone to be separated from him forever, so he offers a solution to this dire problem. God sent Jesus, his perfect Son, to die in our place. When he died on the cross, Jesus willingly took the blame for our sins. Every wrong thing you have ever done and ever will do has been paid for by Jesus.

Thanks to Jesus' death and resurrection, you too can have eternal life. John 11:25, page 1163
But the story doesn't end with Jesus' death! Three days later, he rose from the dead to show that we can have eternal life. Jesus not only paid the price for sin himself, he also permanently broke the power of death over us sinful humans.

To be saved, you need only acknowledge your need for Jesus and trust him completely for everything. Romans 10:9-10, page 1237

God offers all of us the chance to be saved through Jesus' power. If we want to be free of guilt and have eternal life, we must confess our sins to him and ask Jesus into our lives to stay forever. A short prayer like the following is often helpful when we do this:

> *"Dear God, I know that I'm a sinner who needs forgiveness. I know that Jesus Christ died for my sins, and I believe that he rose from the dead. I trust him alone as my Savior. Thank you so much for your gift of eternal life, and help me to live for you from now on. In Jesus' name, amen."*

Use this prayer as a starting point for expressing what is in your mind and heart. You may have a different way of praying, and that's okay. The important thing is that you believe in your heart that Jesus is your Savior and Lord.

SHARING YOUR FAITH WITH OTHERS

The first thing to remember when you start to talk to others about Jesus is that there is no one-size-fits-all method that will guarantee success every time. Everyone has his or her own story and a unique perspective on the world and belief. One person may never have heard the gospel, while another may have grown up with Christian parents and has since fallen away from faith. One of the exciting things about evangelism is the chance to become familiar with a broad spectrum of backgrounds. Learn to love people where they are in life, and they will be much more receptive than they would if you tried to stick to some sort of script.

Also, keep in mind that no one, not even the most experienced minister, is successful 100 percent of the time when sharing the gospel. If it seems that nobody is listening to you, don't be discouraged! You don't know how God is going to water the seeds you have planted. Often he will take years to soften people's hearts. In the meantime, pray. Ask God to strengthen you and show you if you could be approaching the conversation differently.

Here are a few tips to help you prepare for the wonderful experience of bringing Christ's love to others!

Seize the moment. Always be on the lookout for opportunities to talk about Jesus. When one presents itself, don't be afraid to dive in! It is good to plan and prepare, but don't be afraid to be spontaneous. Just remember: you should be sharing out of love and concern for the other person, not as a way to win an argument or prove something.

Know your stuff. Don't let yourself be caught off-guard when a faith-sharing opportunity arises. Make sure you know the basics of salvation ahead of time so that you can accurately address any questions or misconceptions your friends might bring up. If you think that more complicated topics will come into the conversation, investigate what the Bible says about those issues. And if you don't know how to answer a question, you can always tell the other person that you'll get back to him or her as you learn more. Often you'll find yourself having many conversations about faith with a person over time.

Ask questions, and listen to the answers. Most of the time, your evangelism will take the form of a conversation between you and other people. A conversation is a two-way street. Get to know the other person! Ask questions about her life story, her interests and hobbies, her hopes and fears. You may learn something, and you could find the conversation opening up doors that you would not have noticed otherwise.

Tell them your story. Sometimes it's easy to forget that some people feel uncomfortable being asked questions about their lives and beliefs. They may feel that they are making themselves too vulnerable by opening up to you. Sometimes you can put them a bit more at ease by sharing some of your personal history or struggles. Tell them about how you first came to Christ, or about some issues—faith-related or otherwise—that you struggle with. If you are willing to be vulnerable, they may be more willing to trust you.

Be humble. You may be very different from the person you're talking to, but you will always have one thing in common: You are both sinners who need Jesus. The only difference between you is that you've found Jesus, you've been forgiven, and you want to share that joy with other people!

HELP FOR NEW BELIEVERS

You know someone who's just started a relationship with Jesus Christ . . . so what can you do to help?

First of all, you can be excited about this opportunity. Second, you need to be serious about this responsibility. Read Romans 5:11. You have the privilege of helping someone grow in his or her new relationship with your friend Jesus Christ. Here are some ways you can help a new Christian and Jesus grow closer. Remember, we all need FRIENDS.

Follow up with your new Christian friend by getting together regularly.
Get together within 48 hours after your friend receives Christ, and at least once a week during the next six weeks (Matthew 28:20).

Reinforce what Christ has done in your friend's life.
Do this by looking at Scriptures that affirm God's commitment to Christians (John 14:20; Galatians 5:25; Colossians 2:13-14; Hebrews 13:5; 1 John 5:13).

Involve your friend in your church activities.
Take your friend with you and help answer any of his or her questions (Hebrews 10:24-25).

Exhibit Christ in your life through your actions and words.
You don't have to be perfect, just someone who wants to obey and please God (Colossians 3:17).

Nurture your friend's spiritual growth.
A new Christian is like a newborn baby who needs spiritual food and care. Try using the 14 encounters with God included in this section (1 Peter 2:2-3).

Do things together.
Spending time together will give you opportunities to encourage your friend and put your faith into practice (Acts 14:21-22).

Stand by your friend in both the good and bad times.
Your friend will fall down spiritually. Get ready to help him or her to get up and try again (Ephesians 4:11-16).

You have recently trusted Jesus Christ to be your Savior . . . so now what do you do?

First of all, you must know that through Christ you have become friends with God. Read Romans 5:11 again. Remember:

- You realized that your sin was keeping you from a relationship with God.
- You understood that Jesus Christ died on the cross to pay the penalty for your sin and that he rose again from the dead.
- You prayed, asking Jesus to forgive your sins and be your Savior.

"SO NOW WE CAN REJOICE IN OUR WONDERFUL NEW RELATIONSHIP WITH GOD BECAUSE OUR LORD JESUS CHRIST HAS MADE US FRIENDS OF GOD."

ROMANS 5:11

Next, please understand that you have begun an exciting and lasting friendship. As in any relationship, getting to know someone takes time—it doesn't just happen by itself. (Make sure you have a friend who has been a Christian for a while who can help you grow in your new faith. If no one has contacted you, you should go back to the person who helped you become a Christian and ask for help.)

You can grow closer to God just like you grow closer to people. God created you to have a relationship with him, to be his very own son or daughter. Now that you're his child and friend, he will patiently help you get to know him better and better.

Here are some ideas you can use to help you and God become close friends. Remember, all it takes is TIME.

Talk to God through prayer.
To help you learn how to talk to God, the "14 Encounters with God" include ideas for prayer. Give them a try. God will listen when you talk to him.

Investigate God's Word.
Decide on a time and place to read the Bible each day. The schedule for "14 Encounters with God" will help you know what to read. This will help you grow.

Make it practical.
One of the best ways to learn is by doing. The schedule includes action steps to help you make your friendship with God active and practical.

Express your thoughts.
You know how important it is to show appreciation to a friend. As you finish your daily time with God, thank him. During the next 14 encounters with God, try to keep a personal journal. Simply write down your thoughts, your questions, and, most important of all, why you're thankful to God!

Finally, to get to know God better, try using the following "14 Encounters with God" feature. These give you some great ways to spend time with God and find out more about who he is and who he wants you to be.

ENCOUNTERS WITH GOD

ASSURANCE

You recently became a Christian. Have you had any doubts about whether or not Jesus really came into your life? Do you wonder if you'll really go to heaven someday?

Talk to God: "Father, thank you for giving me a relationship with you. Jesus, thank you for giving me life. Please teach me and help me learn more about you. Amen."

Investigate God's Word: Read 1 John 5:11-13. Memorize verse 13.

Make it practical: Check out "I Wonder"—1 John 5:10-12, page 1389, or "My Story"—Matthew 7:24-27, page 1037. How can you put the ideas presented here into action in your own life?

Express your thoughts: In your journal, write a description of when, where, and how you became a Christian. Say thanks to God!

GOD, OUR FATHER

Everyone knows what it's like to not feel totally accepted by others. Did you know that when you became a Christian, God adopted you into his family and accepted you unconditionally?

Talk to God: "Dear God, thanks for making me part of your family. You accept me. That's awesome! Amen."

Investigate God's Word: Ephesians 1:3-8. Memorize verse 5.

Make it practical: "I Wonder"—Hebrews 1:1-3, page 1349, or "My Story"—Mark 9–10, page 1086.

Express your thoughts: In your journal, make a list of what you like about being part of God's family. Don't forget to thank him.

OK, now that you're a new Christian, what's next? Well, the best relationships are those that grow and deepen. It's the same way in your relationship with Jesus Christ. It's time for growth.

Talk to God: "Lord, help me to let my roots sink down into you. Thanks for helping me grow. Amen."

Investigate God's Word: Colossians 2:6-7. Memorize the first part of verse 7.

Make it practical: "I Wonder"—Colossians 2:6-7, page 1310, or "My Story"—2 Peter 1:5-8, page 1378.

Express your thoughts: Think of one way that you'd like to grow spiritually, share it with one friend, and write it in your journal. Then ask God to help you do what you've decided to do.

PRAYER

You know how good friends love to talk with each other. God, our heavenly Father, is ready for a heart-to-heart talk all the time. Conversation with God is a must!

Talk to God: "God, I'm so glad we can talk anytime. Thank you that you'll listen to my needs. Help me learn to listen to you. Amen."

Investigate God's Word: Philippians 4:6-7. Memorize verse 6.

Make it practical: "I Wonder"—1 Kings 3:3-14, page 369, or "My Story"—Ecclesiastes 5:1-7, page 707.

Express your thoughts: Commit yourself to spending at least three minutes in prayer every day. In your journal, keep a record of your prayer requests and answers. Tell God thanks for those answers.

BIBLE

When you get something new, you often receive an instruction manual. With your new life in Christ, you need God's instruction manual, the Bible. God communicates to us through his Word.

Talk to God: "Dear God, thank you for showing me what you're like through your Word. Help me to read it, study it, and obey it. Amen."

Investigate God's Word: 2 Timothy 3:14-17. Memorize verse 16.

Make it practical: "I Wonder"—John 20:31, page 1174, or "My Story"—Isaiah 41:10, page 764.

Express your thoughts: Commit yourself to spending five minutes a day reading the Bible. As a result of something you read, write down in your journal something you will do. Ask God to help you.

Friendships get stronger when you really get to know the other person. You have trusted Christ to be your Savior and to give you new life. Really get to know who he is and what he has done! It's incredible!

Talk to God: "Jesus, you are so powerful! I'm thankful that you hold everything together, including me! Amen."

Investigate God's Word: Colossians 1:15-23. Memorize verse 17.

Make it practical: "I Wonder"—Hebrews 1:1-3,5, page 1349.

Express your thoughts: Ask a friend to tell you what he or she really likes about Jesus. In your journal, write a note to Jesus about what you really appreciate about him.

OBEDIENCE

A good foundation is essential for a house to stand strong. Jesus wants you to realize that obeying God will give your life a solid foundation.

Talk to God: "Dear God, you know what's best for me. Help me to be strong and obey you in each area of my life. Amen."

Investigate God's Word: Luke 6:46-49. Memorize the first part of verse 47.

Make it practical: "I Wonder"—Joshua 24:14-15, page 256, or "My Story"—Ephesians 6:1-3, page 1297.

Express your thoughts: In your journal, list one area of your life where you are obeying God and one where you are not. Say thanks to God for helping you to want to obey.

HOLY SPIRIT

Nobody in this world knows you better than you know yourself. Nobody knows God like God's Spirit knows God. As a new Christian, you have been given God's Holy Spirit. He will give you insight into what God is like and what he wants you to do.

Talk to God: "Thank you, God, for giving me your Spirit. You know me so well, and I will trust your Spirit to help me know more about you. Amen."

Investigate God's Word: 1 Corinthians 2:9-16. Memorize verse 12.

Make it practical: "I Wonder"—Romans 7:15–8:2, page 1234, or "My Story"—Isaiah 7:9, page 732.

Express your thoughts: In your journal, write down one question that you'd like the Holy Spirit to help you with. Now take a couple of minutes and just listen to God. Tell him thanks.

The Bible says in 1 Peter 5:8 that our enemy Satan is like a lion that wants to rip us apart. Satan will tempt us to disobey God, but God will show us a way out!

Talk to God: "Dear God, you know the temptations I struggle with. Thank you that you have promised me a way to escape. Amen."

Investigate God's Word: 1 Corinthians 10:13. Memorize verse 13.

Make it practical: "My Story"—1 Peter 3:15, page 1373.

Express your thoughts: List the three temptations that Satan really uses on you. Now thank God ahead of time that he will show you how to not give in next time.

FORGIVENESS

As a child in God's family, you'll still mess up. But God's love for you is so great that he will forgive you! He can do that because he loves you!

Talk to God: "Dear God, I confess to you my sin of _____. I admit that it was wrong. Thank you that Jesus died on the cross to forgive me for this sin. Amen."

Investigate God's Word: 1 John 1:8-10. Memorize verse 9.

Make it practical: "I Wonder"—James 4:17, page 1367, or "My Story"—Lamentations 3:21-23, page 862.

Express your thoughts: Write down ways that you have disobeyed God recently. Look at each one and confess it through prayer. Cross out each sin. Let this remind you of God's loving forgiveness. Be sure to thank him!

CHURCH

Christians are part of the body of Christ, which is called his Church. Be sure you get together with other believers, members of the "body." It's an opportunity to love God and each other.

Talk to God: "Dear God, thank you for your body of believers, the Church. Teach me how to get involved with other Christians and really worship you. Amen."

Investigate God's Word: Hebrews 10:22-25. Memorize verse 25.

Make it practical: "I Wonder"—Hebrews 10:24-25, page 1353.

Express your thoughts: Go with some friends or family to church this week. List two ways you worshiped God.

If you have a close friend, you can't keep from talking about that person. When you love someone, you can hardly contain yourself! Let your love for Christ motivate you to tell others about him.

Talk to God: "Lord, you have changed my life. Give me the courage and opportunities to tell others about you. Amen."

Investigate God's Word: Romans 1:16-17. Memorize verse 16.

Make it practical: "I Wonder"—Luke 22:54-62, page 1139, or "My Story"—Acts 4:13, page 1187.

Express your thoughts: Write down the name of one person who needs to know Jesus Christ. Start praying for that person to become a Christian. Ask a Christian friend to pray with you for the person and to help you learn how to share your faith with him or her.

BIBLE MEMORY

To fight a battle you need powerful equipment. The Holy Spirit will use the power of God's Word like a sword to defeat Satan. So a great strategy is to memorize Scripture! What verses have you already learned?

Talk to God: "Lord, I need your power! Help me to memorize Scripture verses. I know this will help me live for you. Amen."

Investigate God's Word: Ephesians 6:10-17. Memorize verse 17.

Make it practical: "I Wonder"—Isaiah 46:4, page 771, or "My Story"—Philippians 4:13, page 1305.

Express your thoughts: Review your memory verses from the past 12 days. In your journal, write down your favorite verse.

SPIRITUAL GOAL

You've been a Christian for a short time now, and you're learning that you have a lifelong relationship with Christ. So what's your long-range plan? Becoming like Christ is the ultimate goal.

Talk to God: "Dear Jesus, more than anything else I want to become more like you. Thanks that you'll be patient and help me. Amen."

Investigate God's Word: Colossians 3:10-11. Memorize verse 10.

Make it practical: "I Wonder"—Jeremiah 29:11-13, page 827, or "My Story"—Micah 4:6-13, page 981.

Express your thoughts: Make a list of at least five ways you want to become more like Jesus. Spend time asking God to help you. Remind yourself to read this part of your journal in one month to check on your spiritual growth.

A NOTE TO READERS

The *Holy Bible*, New Living Translation, was first published in 1996. It quickly became one of the most popular Bible translations in the English-speaking world. While the NLT's influence was rapidly growing, the Bible Translation Committee determined that an additional investment in scholarly review and text refinement could make it even better. So shortly after its initial publication, the committee began an eight-year process with the purpose of increasing the level of the NLT's precision without sacrificing its easy-to-understand quality. This second-generation text was completed in 2004, with minor changes subsequently introduced in 2007.

The goal of any Bible translation is to convey the meaning and content of the ancient Hebrew, Aramaic, and Greek texts as accurately as possible to contemporary readers. The challenge for our translators was to create a text that would communicate as clearly and powerfully to today's readers as the original texts did to readers and listeners in the ancient biblical world. The resulting translation is easy to read and understand, while also accurately communicating the meaning and content of the original biblical texts. The NLT is a general-purpose text especially good for study, devotional reading, and reading aloud in worship services.

We believe that the New Living Translation—which combines the latest biblical scholarship with a clear, dynamic writing style—will communicate God's word powerfully to all who read it. We publish it with the prayer that God will use it to speak his timeless truth to the church and the world in a fresh, new way.

The Publishers
October 2007

INTRODUCTION TO
THE NEW LIVING TRANSLATION

Translation Philosophy and Methodology

English Bible translations tend to be governed by one of two general translation theories. The first theory has been called "formal-equivalence," "literal," or "word-for-word" translation. According to this theory, the translator attempts to render each word of the original language into English and seeks to preserve the original syntax and sentence structure as much as possible in translation. The second theory has been called "dynamic-equivalence," "functional-equivalence," or "thought-for-thought" translation. The goal of this translation theory is to produce in English the closest natural equivalent of the message expressed by the original-language text, both in meaning and in style.

Both of these translation theories have their strengths. A formal-equivalence translation preserves aspects of the original text—including ancient idioms, term consistency, and original-language syntax—that are valuable for scholars and professional study. It allows a reader to trace formal elements of the original-language text through the English translation. A dynamic-equivalence translation, on the other hand, focuses on translating the message of the original-language text. It ensures that the meaning of the text is readily apparent to the contemporary reader. This allows the message to come through with immediacy, without requiring the reader to struggle with foreign idioms and awkward syntax.

The translators of the New Living Translation set out to render the message of the original texts of Scripture into clear, contemporary English. As they did so, they kept the concerns of both formal-equivalence and dynamic-equivalence in mind. On the one hand, they translated as simply and literally as possible when that approach yielded an accurate, clear, and natural English text. Many words and phrases were rendered literally and consistently into English, preserving essential literary and rhetorical devices, ancient metaphors, and word choices that give structure to the text and provide echoes of meaning from one passage to the next.

On the other hand, the translators rendered the message more dynamically when the literal rendering was hard to understand, was misleading, or yielded archaic or foreign wording. They clarified difficult metaphors and terms to aid in the reader's understanding. The translators first struggled with the meaning of the words and phrases in the ancient context; then they rendered the message into clear, natural English. Their goal was to be both faithful to the ancient texts and eminently readable.

Translation Process and Team

To produce an accurate translation of the Bible into contemporary English, the translation team needed the skills necessary to enter into the thought patterns of the ancient authors and then to render their ideas, connotations, and effects into clear, contemporary English. To begin this process, qualified biblical scholars were needed to interpret the meaning of the original text and to check it against our base English translation. In order to guard against personal and theological biases, the scholars needed to represent a diverse group of evangelicals who would employ the best exegetical tools. Then to work alongside the scholars, skilled English stylists were needed to shape the text into clear, contemporary English.

With these concerns in mind, the Bible Translation Committee recruited teams of scholars that represented a broad spectrum of denominations, theological perspectives, and backgrounds within the worldwide evangelical community. Each book of the Bible was assigned to three different scholars with proven expertise in the book or group of books to be reviewed. Each of these scholars made a thorough review of a base translation and submitted suggested revisions to the appropriate Senior Translator. The Senior Translator then reviewed and summarized these suggestions and proposed a first-draft revision of the base text. This draft served as the basis for several additional phases of exegetical and stylistic committee review. Then the Bible Translation Committee jointly reviewed and approved every verse of the final translation.

The New Living Translation was first published in 1996. Shortly after its initial publication, the Bible Translation Committee began a process of further committee review and translation refinement. The purpose of this continued revision was to increase the level of precision without sacrificing the text's easy-to-understand quality. This second-edition text was completed in 2004, and an additional update with minor changes was subsequently introduced in 2007. This printing of the New Living Translation reflects the updated 2007 text.

The Texts behind the New Living Translation

The Old Testament translators used the Masoretic Text of the Hebrew Bible as represented in *Biblia Hebraica Stuttgartensia* (1977), with its extensive system of textual notes. The translators also took into account the Dead Sea Scrolls, the Septuagint and other Greek manuscripts, the Samaritan Pentateuch, the Syriac Peshitta, the Latin Vulgate, and any other versions or manuscripts that shed light on difficult passages.

The New Testament translators used the two standard editions of the Greek New Testament: the *Greek New Testament,* published by the United Bible Societies (UBS, fourth revised edition, 1993), and *Novum Testamentum Graece,* edited by Nestle and Aland (NA, twenty-seventh edition, 1993). These two editions, which have the same text but differ in punctuation and textual notes, represent, for the most part, the best in modern textual scholarship. However, in cases where strong textual or other scholarly evidence supported the decision, the translators sometimes chose to differ from the UBS and NA Greek texts and followed variant readings found in other ancient witnesses. Significant textual variants of this sort are always noted in the textual notes of the New Living Translation.

Translation Issues

The translators have made a conscious effort to provide a text that can be easily understood by the typical reader of modern English. To this end, we sought to use only vocabulary and language structures in common use today. We avoided using language likely to become quickly dated or that reflects only a narrow subdialect of English, with the goal of making the New Living Translation as broadly useful and timeless as possible.

But our concern for readability goes beyond the concerns of vocabulary and sentence structure. We are also concerned about historical and cultural barriers to understanding the Bible, and we have sought to translate terms shrouded in history and culture in ways that can be immediately understood. To this end:

- We have converted ancient weights and measures (for example, "ephah" [a unit of dry volume] or "cubit" [a unit of length]) to modern English (American) equivalents, since the ancient measures are not generally meaningful to today's readers. (In the textual footnotes we offer the literal Hebrew, Aramaic, or Greek measures, along with modern metric equivalents. The same general principle of giving the literal in a footnote was also applied to the other issues listed below.)
- Instead of translating ancient currency values literally, we have expressed them in common terms that communicate the message. For example, in the Old Testament, "ten shekels of silver" becomes "ten pieces of silver" to convey the intended message.
- Since the names of Hebrew months are unknown to most contemporary readers, and since the Hebrew lunar calendar fluctuates from year to year in relation to the solar calendar used today, we have looked for clear ways to communicate the time of year the Hebrew months (such as Abib) refer to. Where it is possible to define a specific ancient date in terms of our modern calendar, we use modern dates in the text. A textual footnote then gives the literal Hebrew date and states the rationale for our rendering. (See, for example, the text and note at Ezra 6:15.)
- Since ancient references to the time of day differ from our modern methods of denoting time, we have used renderings that are instantly understandable to the modern reader. Accordingly, we have rendered specific times of day by using approximate equivalents in terms of our common "o'clock" system.
- When the meaning of a proper name (or a wordplay inherent in a proper name) is relevant to the message of the text, its meaning is often illuminated with a textual footnote. For example, in Exodus 2:10 the text reads: "The princess named him Moses, for she explained, 'I lifted him out of the water.'" The accompanying footnote reads: *"Moses* sounds like a Hebrew term that means 'to lift out.'"
- Many words and phrases carry a great deal of cultural meaning that was obvious to the original readers but needs explanation in our own culture. For example, the phrase "they beat their breasts" (Luke 23:48) in ancient times meant that people were very upset, often in mourning. In our translation we chose to translate this phrase dynamically for clarity: "They went home *in deep sorrow.*"
- Metaphorical language is sometimes difficult for contemporary readers to understand, so at times we have chosen to translate or illuminate the meaning of a metaphor. For example, the ancient

poet writes, "Your neck is *like* the tower of David" (Song of Songs 4:4). We have rendered it "Your neck is *as beautiful as* the tower of David" to clarify the intended positive meaning of the simile.

- When the content of the original language text is poetic in character, we have rendered it in English poetic form. Hebrew poetry often uses parallelism, a literary form where a second phrase (or in some instances a third or fourth) echoes the initial phrase in some way. Whenever possible, we sought to represent these parallel phrases in natural poetic English.

- The Greek term *hoi Ioudaioi* is literally translated "the Jews" in many English translations. In the Gospel of John, however, this term doesn't always refer to the Jewish people generally. In some contexts, it refers more particularly to the Jewish religious leaders. We have attempted to capture the meaning in these different contexts by using terms such as "the people" (with a footnote: Greek *the Jewish people*) or "the Jewish leaders," where appropriate.

- One challenge we faced was how to translate accurately the ancient biblical text that was originally written in a context where male-oriented terms were used to refer to humanity generally. We needed to respect the nature of the ancient context while also trying to make the translation clear to a modern audience that tends to read male-oriented language as applying only to males. Often the original text, though using masculine terms, clearly intends that the message be applied to both men and women. A typical example is found in the New Testament letters, where the believers are called "brothers" (*adelphoi*). Yet it is clear from the content of these letters that they were addressed to all the believers—male and female. Thus, we have usually translated this Greek word as "brothers and sisters" in order to represent the historical situation more accurately.

We should emphasize that all masculine nouns and pronouns used to represent God (for example, "Father") have been maintained without exception. All decisions of this kind have been driven by the concern to reflect accurately the intended meaning of the original texts of Scripture.

Lexical Consistency in Terminology

For the sake of clarity, we have translated certain original-language terms consistently, especially within synoptic passages and for commonly repeated rhetorical phrases, and within certain word categories such as divine names and non-theological technical terminology (e.g., liturgical, legal, cultural, zoological, and botanical terms). For theological terms, we have allowed a greater semantic range of acceptable English words or phrases for a single Hebrew or Greek word. We have avoided some theological terms that are not readily understood by many modern readers. For example, we avoided using words such as "justification" and "sanctification," which are carryovers from Latin translations. In place of these words, we have provided renderings such as "made right with God" and "made holy."

Many individuals in the Bible, especially the Old Testament, are known by more than one name (e.g., Uzziah/Azariah). For the sake of clarity, we have tried to use a single spelling for any one individual, footnoting the literal spelling whenever we differ from it. This is especially helpful in delineating the kings of Israel and Judah. King Joash/Jehoash of Israel has been consistently called Jehoash, while King Joash/Jehoash of Judah is called Joash. A similar distinction has been used to distinguish between Joram/Jehoram of Israel and Joram/Jehoram of Judah. All such decisions were made with the goal of clarifying the text for the reader. When the ancient biblical writers clearly had a theological purpose in their choice of a variant name (e.g., Esh-baal/Ishbosheth), the different names have been maintained with an explanatory footnote.

The Rendering of Divine Names

In the Old Testament, all appearances of *'el, 'elohim,* or *'eloah* have been translated "God," except where the context demands the translation "god(s)." We have generally rendered the tetragrammaton (YHWH) consistently as "the LORD," utilizing a form with small capitals that is common among English translations. This will distinguish it from the name *'adonai,* which we render "Lord." When *'adonai* and YHWH appear together, we have rendered it "Sovereign LORD." When *'elohim* and YHWH appear together, we have rendered it "LORD God." When YH (the short form of YHWH) and YHWH appear together, we have rendered it "LORD GOD." When YHWH appears with the term *tseba'oth,* we have rendered it "LORD of Heaven's Armies" to translate the meaning of the name. In a few cases, we have utilized the transliteration, *Yahweh,* when the personal character of the name is being invoked in contrast to another divine name or the name of some other god (for example, see Exodus 3:15; 6:2-3).

In the Gospels and Acts, the Greek word *christos* has been translated as "Messiah" when the context assumes a Jewish audience. When a Gentile audience can be assumed (which is consistently the case in the Epistles and Revelation), *christos* has been translated as "Christ." The Greek word *kurios* is consistently translated "Lord," except that it is translated "LORD" wherever the New Testament text explicitly quotes from the Old Testament, and the text there has it in small capitals.

Textual Footnotes

The New Living Translation provides several kinds of textual footnotes, all designated in the text with an asterisk:

- When for the sake of clarity the NLT renders a difficult or potentially confusing phrase dynamically, we generally give the literal rendering in a textual footnote. This allows the reader to see the literal source of our dynamic rendering and how our translation relates to other more literal translations. These notes are prefaced with "Hebrew," "Aramaic," or "Greek," identifying the language of the underlying source text. For example, in Acts 2:42 we translated the literal "breaking of bread" (from the Greek) as "the Lord's Supper" to clarify that this verse refers to the ceremonial practice of the church rather than just an ordinary meal. Then we attached a footnote to "the Lord's Supper," which reads: "Greek *the breaking of bread.*"
- Textual footnotes are also used to show alternative renderings, prefaced with the word "Or." These normally occur for passages where an aspect of the meaning is debated. On occasion, we also provide notes on words or phrases that represent a departure from long-standing tradition. These notes are prefaced with "Traditionally rendered." For example, the footnote to the translation "serious skin disease" at Leviticus 13:2 says: "Traditionally rendered *leprosy.* The Hebrew word used throughout this passage is used to describe various skin diseases."
- When our translators follow a textual variant that differs significantly from our standard Hebrew or Greek texts (listed earlier), we document that difference with a footnote. We also footnote cases when the NLT excludes a passage that is included in the Greek text known as the *Textus Receptus* (and familiar to readers through its translation in the King James Version). In such cases, we offer a translation of the excluded text in a footnote, even though it is generally recognized as a later addition to the Greek text and not part of the original Greek New Testament.
- All Old Testament passages that are quoted in the New Testament are identified by a textual footnote at the New Testament location. When the New Testament clearly quotes from the Greek translation of the Old Testament, and when it differs significantly in wording from the Hebrew text, we also place a textual footnote at the Old Testament location. This note includes a rendering of the Greek version, along with a cross-reference to the New Testament passage(s) where it is cited (for example, see notes on Psalms 8:2; 53:3; Proverbs 3:12).
- Some textual footnotes provide cultural and historical information on places, things, and people in the Bible that are probably obscure to modern readers. Such notes should aid the reader in understanding the message of the text. For example, in Acts 12:1, "King Herod" is named in this translation as "King Herod Agrippa" and is identified in a footnote as being "the nephew of Herod Antipas and a grandson of Herod the Great."
- When the meaning of a proper name (or a wordplay inherent in a proper name) is relevant to the meaning of the text, it is either illuminated with a textual footnote or included within parentheses in the text itself. For example, the footnote concerning the name "Eve" at Genesis 3:20 reads: "*Eve* sounds like a Hebrew term that means 'to give life.' " This wordplay in the Hebrew illuminates the meaning of the text, which goes on to say that Eve "would be the mother of all who live."

As we submit this translation for publication, we recognize that any translation of the Scriptures is subject to limitations and imperfections. Anyone who has attempted to communicate the richness of God's Word into another language will realize it is impossible to make a perfect translation. Recognizing these limitations, we sought God's guidance and wisdom throughout this project. Now we pray that he will accept our efforts and use this translation for the benefit of the church and of all people.

We pray that the New Living Translation will overcome some of the barriers of history, culture, and language that have kept people from reading and understanding God's Word. We hope that readers unfamiliar with the Bible will find the words clear and easy to understand and that readers well versed in the Scriptures will gain a fresh perspective. We pray that readers will gain insight and wisdom for living, but most of all that they will meet the God of the Bible and be forever changed by knowing him.

The Bible Translation Committee

A full introduction to the NLT can be found at www.tyndale.com/sites/NLT/translation-process.
A complete list of the translators can be found at www.tyndale.com/sites/NLT/meet-the-team.

CONTRIBUTORS

DESIGN TEAM
Dr. Bruce B. Barton
Ron Beers
Dr. James Galvin
LaVonne Neff
David R. Veerman

SENIOR EDITOR
David R. Veerman

EDITORS
Karen Ball
Kathryn S. Olson
Linda Chaffee Taylor

REVISION EDITORS
Linda Washington
Leanne Rolland

GRAPHIC DESIGN
Dean H. Renninger

TYPESETTER
Kimberly D. Hutson

WRITERS:

DR. RICHARD R. DUNN
Lead Pastor, Fellowship Church
Knoxville, Tennessee

TERRY PRISK
Youth Communicator/Consultant
Executive Director of
    Contemporary Communication
Detroit, Michigan

KENT KELLER
Pastor, Redeemer Presbyterian
    Church
Miami, Florida

JARED REED
Pastor, Faith Presbyterian Church
Miami, Florida

LEN WOODS
Former Editor of *Youthwalk*
Minister to Students, Christ
    Community Church
Ruston, Louisiana

GREG JOHNSON
Former Editor of *Breakaway*

BYRON EMMERT
Speaker and seminar leader
Youth for Christ
Mt. Lake, Minnesota

DIANE EBLE
Freelance editor/writer
Wheaton, Illinois

NEIL WILSON
Pastor, Eureka United Methodist
    Church
Omro, Wisconsin

BILL SANDERS
Author and speaker
Kalamazoo, Michigan

DAVID R. VEERMAN
Veteran youth worker and
    author
The Livingstone Corporation
Carol Stream, Illinois

NOTES AND FEATURES:

BOOK INTRODUCTIONS
Jared Reed
Len Woods
David R. Veerman

PERSONALITY PROFILES
Neil Wilson

"CHOICES" NOTES
Len Woods

"I WONDER" NOTES
Greg Johnson

"MY STORY" NOTES
Terry Prisk
Diane Eble

ULTIMATE ISSUES
Kent Keller

LIFE CHOICES INDEX
Bill Sanders
Linda Chaffee Taylor

MAPS
Adapted from the *Life Application
    Study Bible*

CHARTS
Adapted from the *Life Application
    Study Bible*

A LOOK AT THE BOOK
Neil Wilson

HELP FOR NEW BELIEVERS/
14 ENCOUNTERS WITH GOD
Byron Emmert

LIFE APPLICATION NOTES
Adapted from the *Life Application
    Study Bible*
David R. Veerman
Thank you to the young people
    from the following youth
    groups for their invaluable
    assistance with this project:
Southern Gables Church,
    Denver, Colorado
Spring Hill Camps,
    Evart, Michigan
Pekin Bible Church,
    Pekin, Illinois
Ward Presbyterian Church,
    Livonia, Michigan
First Baptist Church,
    Holdrege, Nebraska
Naperville Presbyterian Church,
    Naperville, Illinois

PHOTOGRAPHY CREDITS

Stairs copyright © Chelsea Stover/SXC.

Pretty Flower in Pink; Mushrooms 1 copyright © Andrea Kratzenberg/SXC.

Remembrance; Fishermen Resource; Locked Behind; Wildflowers copyright © abcdz2000/SXC.

Skull X-ray; Prison at Robben Island copyright © Adam Ciesielski/SXC.

Life Is a Highway 1 copyright © Andrew Beierle/SXC.

Cans copyright © Alaa Hamed/SXC.

Upright Piano copyright © Aldo Cavini Benedetti/SXC.

Rotten Banana Leaf 2 copyright © Alessandro Paiva/SXC.

Autumn Morning Light copyright © Alfred Borchard/SXC.

Sunset copyright © amz1983/SXC.

The Honeycomb copyright © Andrei Ghergar/SXC.

Spiderweb copyright © Andrew Beierle/SXC.

World AIDS Day 2 copyright © Andrew Conn/SXC.

Wood Texture copyright © Andrew C. /SXC.

On the Move; Car copyright © Asif Akbar/SXC.

Wrinkled Crumpled Paper copyright © Alicia Solario/SXC.

Bokeh Texture 3 copyright © AssassinM/SXC.

Marijuana copyright © Mateusz Atroszko/SXC.

Slate Roof Tiles; Triangular Wood Texture; Ocher Metal Wall Texture; Grey Triangular Texture; Diamond Windows Texture; Abstract Blue Tiles Texture; Bull's Eye Pane-Glass Roundel Window Texture; Winter Ivy Texture; Futuristic Lift Interior; Leather Rainbow Curtain 2; Neon Lamp with Reflector; Green Metal Texture; Silver Metal Trefoil Texture copyright © Michael Richert-www.rgbstock.com/SXC.

Sheet Music 1; Vintage Paper 1; Watercolour 3; Grungy Paper 1 copyright © Billy Alexander/SXC.

Flashlight copyright © babs101525 /SXC.

Jesus Christ Crucified; Dome within a Church copyright © Fabio Medda/SXC.

Sailing Ropes copyright © Bart Groenhuizen/SXC.

Splashing Water 1 copyright © Bartlomiej Berczynski/SXC.

Fremantle copyright © bennoben/SXC.

Tropical Leaf; Golden Grass; Reaching copyright © Bert van 't Hul/SXC.

The Cross copyright © Craig Toron/SXC.

Mountain Lake Reflecting 3 copyright © Benjamin Earwicker/SXC.

Layers copyright © Brandon Bankston /SXC.

Helical Gear in Mono copyright © Philip MacKenzie/SXC.

Black_hole2 copyright © William Byrd/SXC.

Petals (close-up) copyright © Caltiva Creatividad/SXC.

Paris Airport copyright © Dave Hiebert /SXC.

La Defense copyright © Cecile Geng /SXC.

Olives copyright © Cisco p.a./SXC.

Money copyright © Cavell L. Blood /SXC.

Earth: Black Edition copyright © Sigurd Decroos/SXC.

Winter Street at Night copyright © Colin Brough/SXC.

New Forest copyright © Colin Hughes /SXC.

Eyes Peacock Feather copyright © Daniel Andres Forero/SXC.

Dry Plant; Lotus copyright © Ananya S. /SXC.

Wedding Gifts copyright © Gary Scott /SXC.

Cobblestone Street copyright © Christopher Mazzoli/SXC.

Gold Foil Texture copyright © Tamara Herrera/SXC.

Marathon; People copyright © Griszka Niewiadomski/SXC.

Zooming Texture copyright © dcubillas /SXC.

Building Detail copyright © John Lewis /SXC.

Water copyright © Dara Gallagher/SXC.

Eclectic Electric Light Nodes copyright © Dimitri Castrique/Scott Draves and the Electric Sheep/SXC.

Books; Candlelight copyright © Diane Miller/SXC.

Experimental 1 copyright © adam dworak/SXC.

Quail Hill Loop copyright © dlockeretz /SXC.

Steel Rebar; Metal Grate copyright © David Ritter/SXC.

Modern Architecture; Concrete Construction copyright © domiwo/SXC.

Mixed Numbers Texture copyright © D. Sharon Pruitt/SXC.

Playing with Light 2 and 3 copyright © Gabriella Fabbri/SXC.

X-plosion and E X O copyright © Thomas Boulvin/SXC.

Togetherness 3; Sea Water 1; Time Moves On 7; Sand Pattern 1 copyright © Stephen Eastop/SXC.

Flowers 5 copyright © Mark Flaherty-www.meandalan.co.uk/SXC.

Underneath the Foot copyright © Ginny Warner/SXC.

Group Picture copyright © Jenny W. /SXC.

Liquid Gold copyright © Enrica Bressan/SXC.

Waterfall Rainbow copyright © enriqedk/SXC.

Prayer copyright © Jesper Noer/SXC.

God copyright © Fabio Bertini/SXC.

Background (Circular) 1 copyright © firoz11/SXC.

Energy Links 1; Plasma Explosion 3 and 4; Shine Energy 6 copyright © Flávio Takemoto-www.takemoto.com.br/SXC.

All That Remains . . . copyright © Karen Barefoot/SXC.

Green Rug Texture copyright © foxumon/SXC.

Roof Tiles by Jan Vernee/SXC.

Sax Close-Up copyright © George Georgiades/SXC.

Water copyright © Juliane Riedl/SXC.

Glass Tiles copyright © Grethe Boe /SXC.

Silver Pheasant copyright © Atif Gulzar/SXC.

Construction; Out on the Streets copyright © Piotr Ciuchta/SXC.

Homeless copyright © H Dominique Abed/SXC.

Wood Texture 4 copyright © Hilde Torbjornsen-http://designer77 .com/SXC.

Sunset Sky copyright © Makio Kusahara/SXC.

Chain Texture 1; Broken Glass Texture 3; Old Window Glass Texture; Airplane Engine Detail 2 copyright © Kriss Szkurlatowski/SXC.

Journey to Myself by Peter Hostermann/SXC.

Chicago Train Tracks copyright © huntroo4/SXC.

Dark Doorway copyright © HybridSys /SXC.

Wooden Printing Block, Up Close copyright © Idac/SXC.

Background copyright © ilco/SXC.

Parts of the Old Watch copyright © Darko Skender/SXC.

Basketballs copyright © Janell Bargen /SXC.

OLD TESTAMENT

Ever turned on a TV show a few minutes after it began? Chances are, you turned it off before the show ended or flipped to a different channel because you couldn't figure out what was going on. To fully understand the plot, you needed to see the beginning of the show.

The same truth applies to the Bible. If you're having a hard time figuring out the plot, Genesis is the right place to begin your search for answers. Why? Because Genesis is the book of beginnings. In it you see the creation of the universe, the introduction of sin into the world, the beginning of God's plan to rescue his people from the sin habit, and the birth of the nation of Israel.

In Genesis we also get our first glimpse into God's character. Unlike everything else, God didn't have a beginning. He has always existed. Chapters 1 and 2 showcase his creativeness and power, while chapter 3 reveals his holiness and judgment of sin. Through the sad saga of Adam and Eve and their descendants, we view God's incredible love for his people even when they constantly disobey him.

As you read Genesis, what other beginnings do you see? How do they enlarge your view of God?

KEY POINTS

BEGINNINGS Genesis introduces God as Creator of all that exists, from planets to plants to people. All people were created in God's own image.

DISOBEDIENCE Sin results when people choose their own way instead of obeying God. Adam and Eve learned this the hard way. Only God can reverse the consequences of sinful choices.

PROMISES God promised to protect and provide for his people. He made specific promises known as *covenants*, which are binding agreements. God made a covenant with his people as a guarantee of what they could expect from him.

OBEDIENCE AND PROSPERITY Obedience to God keeps our relationship with him intact and causes us to prosper like Abraham. Prosperity doesn't necessarily mean wealth or other material possessions. Rather, true prosperity means living life as God created it to be lived—in the fullness of his blessings.

Modern names and boundaries are shown in gray.

KEY PLACES
God created the universe and the earth. Then he made man and woman, giving them a home in a beautiful garden. Unfortunately, Adam and Eve disobeyed God and were expelled from the garden (3:24).

❶ MOUNTAINS OF ARARAT

Adam and Eve's sin brought sin into the human race. Years later, sin had run rampant and God decided to destroy the earth with a great flood. He wiped out everything and everyone except for Noah, his family, and two of each animal, who were all safe in a huge boat. When the floods receded, the boat rested on the mountains of Ararat (8:4).

❷ BABEL

People never learn. Again sin abounded and the pride of the people led them to build a huge tower as a monument to their own greatness—obviously they had no thought of God. As punishment, God scattered the people by giving them different languages (11:8-9).

❸ UR OF THE CHALDEANS

Abram, a descendant of Shem, was born in this great city (11:27-28).

❹ HARAN

Terah, Lot, Abram, and Sarai left Ur and, following the fertile crescent of the Euphrates River, headed toward the land of Canaan. Along the way, they settled in the city of Haran for a while (11:31).

❺ SHECHEM

God urged Abram to leave Haran and go to a place where he would become the father of a great nation (12:1-2). So Abram, Sarai, and Lot traveled to the land of Canaan and settled near a city called Shechem (12:5-6).

❻ HEBRON

Abram (later known as Abraham) moved on to Hebron, to "the oak grove belonging to Mamre," where he put down his deepest roots (13:18). Abraham, Isaac, and Jacob all lived and were buried there.

❼ BEERSHEBA

After a dispute over ownership of the well here, Abraham made a covenant with Abimelech (21:23-31). Years later, as Isaac was moving from place to place, God appeared to him here and confirmed with him the covenant he had made with his father, Abraham (26:23-25).

❽ BETHEL

After deceiving his brother out of both his birthright and his blessing, Jacob left Beersheba and fled to Haran. Along the way God revealed himself to Jacob in a dream and again confirmed the covenant he had made with Abraham and Isaac (28:10-22). Jacob lived in Haran, worked for Laban, and married Leah and Rachel (29:15-28). After a tense meeting with his brother, Esau, Jacob returned to Bethel (35:1).

❾ EGYPT

Jacob had 12 sons, including Joseph, his favorite. Joseph's brothers grew jealous, until one day, out in the fields, they sold him to Ishmaelite traders who were going to Egypt. Eventually, Joseph was promoted from Egyptian slave to Pharaoh's "right-hand man," saving Egypt and the surrounding countries from famine. Joseph's entire family moved from Canaan to Egypt and settled there during the severe famine (46:5-7).

1 **THE ACCOUNT OF CREATION** In the beginning God created the heavens and the earth.* ²The earth was formless and empty, and darkness covered the deep waters. And the Spirit of God was hovering over the surface of the waters.

³Then God said, "Let there be light," and there was light. ⁴And God saw that the light was good. Then he separated the light from the darkness. ⁵God called the light "day" and the darkness "night."

And evening passed and morning came, marking the first day.

⁶Then God said, "Let there be a space between the waters, to separate the waters of the heavens from the waters of the earth." ⁷And that is what happened. God made this space to separate the waters of the earth from the waters of the heavens. ⁸God called the space "sky."

And evening passed and morning came, marking the second day.

⁹Then God said, "Let the waters beneath the sky flow together into one place, so dry ground may appear." And that is what happened. ¹⁰God called the dry ground "land" and the waters "seas." And God saw that it was good. ¹¹Then God said, "Let the land sprout with vegetation—every sort of seed-bearing plant, and trees that grow seed-bearing fruit. These seeds will then produce the kinds of plants and trees from which they came." And that is what happened. ¹²The land produced vegetation—all sorts of seed-bearing plants, and trees with seed-bearing fruit. Their seeds produced plants and trees of the same kind. And God saw that it was good.

¹³And evening passed and morning came, marking the third day.

¹⁴Then God said, "Let lights appear in the sky to separate the day from the night. Let them be signs to mark the seasons, days, and years. ¹⁵Let these lights in the sky shine down on the earth." And that is what happened. ¹⁶God made two great lights—the larger one to govern the day, and the smaller one to govern the night. He also made the stars. ¹⁷God set these lights in the sky to light the earth, ¹⁸to govern the day and night, and to separate the light from the darkness. And God saw that it was good.

¹⁹And evening passed and morning came, marking the fourth day.

²⁰Then God said, "Let the waters swarm with fish and other life. Let the skies be filled with birds of every kind." ²¹So God created great sea creatures and every living thing that scurries and swarms in the water, and every sort of bird—each producing offspring of the same kind. And God saw that it was good. ²²Then God blessed them, saying, "Be fruitful and multiply. Let the fish fill the seas, and let the birds multiply on the earth."

²³And evening passed and morning came, marking the fifth day.

²⁴Then God said, "Let the earth produce every sort of animal, each producing offspring of the same kind—livestock, small animals that scurry along the ground, and wild animals." And that is what happened. ²⁵God made all sorts of wild animals, livestock, and small animals, each able to produce offspring of the same kind. And God saw that it was good.

²⁶Then God said, "Let us make human beings* in our image, to be like us. They will reign over the fish in the sea, the birds in the sky, the livestock, all the wild animals on the earth, and the small animals that scurry along the ground."

²⁷ So God created human beings* in his
 own image.
 In the image of God he created them;
 male and female he created them.

²⁸Then God blessed them and said, "Be fruitful and multiply. Fill the earth and govern it. Reign over the fish in the sea, the

1:1 Or In the beginning when God created the heavens and the earth, . . . Or When God began to create the heavens and the earth, . . . 1:26 Or man; Hebrew reads adam. 1:27 Or the man; Hebrew reads ha-adam.

TRUE WORTH
(1:1-26) God created everything there is—the heavens, earth, plants, and animals. When God finished creating everything else, he then chose to make people in his image. The phrase "Let us make human beings in our image" in verse 26 does not mean that God created us exactly like himself, especially in a physical sense. Instead, we are reflections of God's glory. We can reflect his characteristics like love, patience, forgiveness, kindness, and faithfulness.

Our worth is not defined by possessions, achievements, physical attractiveness, or popularity. Instead, it is based on knowing that God created us in his likeness. Criticizing or downgrading ourselves is criticizing what God has made. Because we are like God, we can feel positive about ourselves and our abilities. Knowing that you are a person of infinite worth gives you the freedom to love God, know him personally, and make a valuable contribution to the lives of those around you.

birds in the sky, and all the animals that scurry along the ground."

²⁹Then God said, "Look! I have given you every seed-bearing plant throughout the earth and all the fruit trees for your food. ³⁰And I have given every green plant as food for all the wild animals, the birds in the sky, and the small animals that scurry along the ground—everything that has life." And that is what happened.

³¹Then God looked over all he had made, and he saw that it was very good!

And evening passed and morning came, marking the sixth day.

2 So the creation of the heavens and the earth and everything in them was completed. ²On the seventh day God had finished his work of creation, so he rested* from all his work. ³And God blessed the seventh day and declared it holy, because it was the day when he rested from all his work of creation.

⁴This is the account of the creation of the heavens and the earth.

THE MAN AND WOMAN IN EDEN When the LORD God made the earth and the heavens, ⁵neither wild plants nor grains were growing on the earth. For the LORD God had not yet sent rain to water the earth, and there were no people to cultivate the soil. ⁶Instead, springs* came up from the ground and watered all the land. ⁷Then the LORD God formed the man from the dust of the ground. He breathed the breath

2:2 Or *ceased;* also in 2:3. **2:6** Or *mist.*

ULTIMATE ISSUES *THE ORIGIN OF HUMANITY*

"It is now commonly accepted in scientific circles that human beings have become what they are today as a result of millions of years of evolution. Beginning as a one-celled animal. . . ." So reads the textbook used in biology classes in many public high schools.

"In the beginning God created the heavens and the earth. The earth was formless and empty. . . ." So begins the book of Genesis. The Christian student faces a conflict: whom to believe?

Probably no other issue has drawn a sharper dividing line between religious and nonreligious thought in our society than that of the origin of the human race. Were we, as Genesis 1 and 2 state, placed here by special divine creation? Or did we evolve from nothing into one-celled animals and on up the zoological chain into *Homo sapiens?* That's what we're told by proponents of Darwinian evolution, including many contemporary educators, philosophers, and others. Or perhaps there's a third option—God created people, using the process of evolution as his "laboratory."

Many young people feel the uneasy tension that exists among these views. Their spiritual authorities—the Bible, the church, the pastor, and the youth minister—stand firmly in the intentional design camp, while the public educational system, their biology teachers, and probably the majority of their peers lean heavily toward the evolutionist viewpoint. Who's right?

The Bible doesn't spell out in precise detail how human beings came to be. It does, however, give us some basic truths. First and foremost, human beings, like all the rest of the universe, are intentional creations of God. The Bible states that fact in the clearest of terms—God is mentioned performing some part of his creative work 31 times in Genesis 1 alone. The idea that we simply materialized out of nothingness is a logical and scientific impossibility. The first law of thermodynamics tells us that energy (and therefore, matter) can neither be created nor destroyed by natural causes. For the strict Darwinist/evolutionist, this is an impossible dilemma. If only natural causes were involved, how did nothing turn into something? Next, how did it become something animated—how does life evolve from one-celled organism to plant to animal? Then, how does that animated life-form become personal? And finally, how did that living, personal something develop intelligence, morality, personality, and spirituality? By chance? Impossible. Absolutely, scientifically, intellectually, and logically impossible.

The Christian, then, turns to the supernatural: God did it. It is a simple but utterly profound rationale. "In the beginning God created the heavens and the earth," and that sums it up. It does not rule out the possibility of some kind of God-directed evolution; neither does it give it any support. And honest Darwinists will admit that their beliefs involve as much faith and speculation—if not more—as the creationists'. Nobel Prize winner Ernst Chain said in 1970: "To postulate that the development and survival of the fittest is entirely a consequence of chance mutations seems to me a hypothesis based on no evidence and entirely irreconcilable with the facts. . . . It amazes me that [classical evolutionary theories] are swallowed so uncritically and readily, and for such a long time, by so many scientists without a murmur of protest."

So the Bible, and Genesis in particular, gives us one bedrock fact about the origin of humanity: God created us in his own image. Exactly how he did that remains a matter of faith, open to investigation by scientific inquiry. But the creationist position is as intellectually respectable as any of the alternatives. Every Christian can draw strength and confidence—and awe for his or her Creator—from knowing that. ■

of life into the man's nostrils, and the man became a living person.

⁸Then the LORD God planted a garden in Eden in the east, and there he placed the man he had made. ⁹The LORD God made all sorts of trees grow up from the ground—trees that were beautiful and that produced delicious fruit. In the middle of the garden he placed the tree of life and the tree of the knowledge of good and evil.

¹⁰A river flowed from the land of Eden, watering the garden and then dividing into four branches. ¹¹The first branch, called the Pishon, flowed around the entire land of Havilah, where gold is found. ¹²The gold of that land is exceptionally pure; aromatic resin and onyx stone are also found there. ¹³The second branch, called the Gihon, flowed around the entire land of Cush. ¹⁴The third branch, called the Tigris, flowed east of the land of Asshur. The fourth branch is called the Euphrates.

¹⁵The LORD God placed the man in the Garden of Eden to tend and watch over it. ¹⁶But the LORD God warned him, "You may freely eat the fruit of every tree in the garden—¹⁷except the tree of the knowledge of good and evil. If you eat its fruit, you are sure to die."

¹⁸Then the LORD God said, "It is not good for the man to be alone. I will make a helper who is just right for him." ¹⁹So the LORD God formed from the ground all the wild animals and all the birds of the sky. He brought them to the man* to see what he would call them, and the man chose a name for each one. ²⁰He gave names to all the livestock, all the birds of the sky, and all the wild animals. But still there was no helper just right for him.

²¹So the LORD God caused the man to fall into a deep sleep. While the man slept, the LORD God took out one of the man's ribs* and closed up the opening. ²²Then the LORD God made a woman from the rib, and he brought her to the man.

²³"At last!" the man exclaimed.

"This one is bone from my bone,
    and flesh from my flesh!
She will be called 'woman,'
    because she was taken from 'man.'"

²⁴This explains why a man leaves his father and mother and is joined to his wife, and the two are united into one.

²⁵Now the man and his wife were both naked, but they felt no shame.

3 **THE MAN AND WOMAN SIN** The serpent was the shrewdest of all the wild animals

DAYS OF CREATION

DAY 1: —LIGHT is created and separated from darkness

DAY 2—SKY AND WATER separated

DAY 3—SEA AND LAND distinguished

DAY 4—SUN, MOON, AND STARS preside over day and night; to mark off seasons, days, and years

DAY 5—FISH AND BIRDS fill the waters and the sky

DAY 6—ANIMALS fill the earth
MAN AND WOMAN care for the earth and commune with God

DAY 7—GOD rested and was pleased

the LORD God had made. One day he asked the woman, "Did God really say you must not eat the fruit from any of the trees in the garden?"

²"Of course we may eat fruit from the trees in the garden," the woman replied. ³"It's only the fruit from the tree in the middle of the garden that we are not allowed to eat. God said, 'You must not eat it or even touch it; if you do, you will die.'"

⁴"You won't die!" the serpent replied to the woman. ⁵"God knows that your eyes will be opened as soon as you eat it, and you will be like God, knowing both good and evil."

⁶The woman was convinced. She saw that the tree was beautiful and its fruit looked delicious, and she wanted the wisdom it would give her. So she took some of the fruit and ate it. Then she gave some to her husband, who was with her, and he ate it, too. ⁷At that moment their eyes were opened, and they suddenly felt shame at their nakedness. So they sewed fig leaves together to cover themselves.

⁸When the cool evening breezes were blowing, the man* and his wife heard the LORD God walking about in the garden. So they hid from

· ·

MARRIAGE
(2:18-24) God's creative work was not complete until he made woman. He could have made her from the dust of the ground, as he made man. God chose, however, to make her from the man's flesh and bone. In so doing, he illustrated that in marriage man and woman symbolically become one flesh. This is a mystical union of the couple's hearts and lives. Throughout the Bible, God treats this special partnership seriously. The goal in marriage should be more than friendship; it should be oneness. If you are planning to get married one day, are you willing to keep the commitment that makes the two of you one? What helpful habits can you begin to develop that will help you honor that commitment?

2:19 Or *Adam,* and so throughout the chapter.   **2:21** Or *took a part of the man's side.*   **3:8** Or *Adam,* and so throughout the chapter.

the LORD God among the trees. [9]Then the LORD God called to the man, "Where are you?"

[10]He replied, "I heard you walking in the garden, so I hid. I was afraid because I was naked."

[11]"Who told you that you were naked?" the LORD God asked. "Have you eaten from the tree whose fruit I commanded you not to eat?"

[12]The man replied, "It was the woman you gave me who gave me the fruit, and I ate it."

[13]Then the LORD God asked the woman, "What have you done?"

"The serpent deceived me," she replied. "That's why I ate it."

[14]Then the LORD God said to the serpent,

"Because you have done this, you are cursed
    more than all animals, domestic and wild.
You will crawl on your belly,
    groveling in the dust as long as you live.
[15] And I will cause hostility between you and the woman,
    and between your offspring and her offspring.
He will strike* your head,
    and you will strike his heel."

[16]Then he said to the woman,

"I will sharpen the pain of your pregnancy,
    and in pain you will give birth.
And you will desire to control your husband,
    but he will rule over you.*"

[17]And to the man he said,

"Since you listened to your wife and ate from the tree
    whose fruit I commanded you not to eat,
the ground is cursed because of you.
    All your life you will struggle to scratch a living from it.
[18] It will grow thorns and thistles for you,
    though you will eat of its grains.
[19] By the sweat of your brow
    will you have food to eat
until you return to the ground
    from which you were made.
For you were made from dust,
    and to dust you will return."

PARADISE LOST: GOD'S JUDGMENT [20]Then the man—Adam—named his wife Eve, because she would be the mother of all who live.* [21]And the LORD God made clothing from animal skins for Adam and his wife.

3:15 Or *bruise;* also in 3:15b. **3:16** Or *And though you will have desire for your husband, / he will rule over you.* **3:20** *Eve* sounds like a Hebrew term that means "to give life."

I WONDER . . .

When I read about creation and miracles in the Bible, I get confused. How do science and the Bible relate?

The Bible and science debate has raged for many years. Conflicts arise when we look for spiritual answers from science or for scientific answers in the Bible.

A former Vietnam POW told of the time he was allowed to send a tape home to his family. Realizing that this might be the last communication he would ever have with those he loved, the soldier took extensive notes on what he would cover before beginning to make the tape. His goal was to communicate the most important things that his family should know. To his wife, he talked of insurance, mortgage, child rearing, and relatives. To the kids, he personalized each message so that he touched on unique situations they would face the next few years as they grew up without him. To all of them he was careful to say how much he loved them.

That is the purpose behind the Bible. God put 66 books together to let his creation know the most important things about life, about what to do in certain situations, and especially about the extent of his love for them.

For some reason he chose to leave out dinosaurs,

fusion, and gravity (among other significant discoveries). Instead, God included stories of real people with real struggles who faced hardships and trials, many of whom conquered fears and circumstances because they realized that if God was for them, who could be against them! Many other stories are included of those who rejected God and then experienced tragic consequences.

Most of these biblical examples tell us much more about living, surviving, and prospering in a complicated society than science could ever hope to promise.

Your mind matters to God—he wants you to think. Never be afraid to ask tough questions about the Bible or the Christian faith. But also consider the appropriateness of each question. Is this the kind of question the Bible should answer? And do the same with science, asking the right questions.

Creation and the resurrection of Jesus Christ are two of the most important tenets of the Christian faith. Although neither can be duplicated in a laboratory, they also cannot be proven to be false by science.

If God can create life from nothing, as well as raise a man from the dead, he can lead us through this life and the next. We can trust him.

ADAM & EVE

UPS:
- *The first human male and female, husband and wife*
- *First to be made in the image of God*
- *First caretakers of creation*
- *First to know God personally*

DOWNS:
- *Both tended to handle mistakes and sin by excuses or blaming others*
- *Acted without considering consequences*
- *Together they brought sin into the creation*

STATS:
- *Where: Garden of Eden*
- *Occupation: Caretakers of Eden*
- *Relatives: Cain, Abel, Seth (sons); numerous other children*

KEY VERSE: *Genesis 1:27*

ADAM AND EVE were the only two humans who never experienced being young. Depending on how you feel, they may or may not have missed a lot! But try to imagine starting out life as an adult—no memories, no mistakes, no past little lessons to help you make adult decisions. . . . Most of us don't realize how much we learn or fail to learn during our growing years until it's too late.

For instance, we have many opportunities to learn as children that while there are some trustworthy people in our lives, not everyone can be trusted. We learn not to immediately trust new advice. Instead, we learn to compare it to wisdom we already have, or even to ask someone who has been trustworthy to evaluate the new advice.

Eve received some advice: "The fruit is great . . . God's being selfish . . . you will be like him if you try it." She trusted this advice even though it was contrary to what God had told her to do. She ate the fruit. She failed to trust the one who had never failed her. Adam made the same mistake. New advice, no questions, no checking—he ate the fruit. Both of them disobeyed God. They had to live with the painful consequences.

Like Adam and Eve, we often have to live with the painful consequences of accepting bad advice. But consequences are reminders of hard lessons. They are not excuses to give up or to repeat the same mistakes.

How do you evaluate the advice you receive? Why is it important to consider the source as well as the advice?

BOTTOM LINE: As Adam and Eve's descendants, we all reflect to some degree the image of God.

The basic tendency to sin goes back to the beginning of the human race. God wants people who are free to sin to choose instead to trust and love him. God's design for marriage was part of Creation.

Adam and Eve's story is told in Genesis 1:26–5:5. They also are mentioned in 1 Chronicles 1:1; Luke 3:38; Romans 5:12-19; 1 Corinthians 15:21-22, 45-49; 1 Timothy 2:13-14.

---

²²Then the Lord God said, "Look, the human beings* have become like us, knowing both good and evil. What if they reach out, take fruit from the tree of life, and eat it? Then they will live forever!" ²³So the Lord God banished them from the Garden of Eden, and he sent Adam out to cultivate the ground from which he had been made. ²⁴After sending them out, the Lord God stationed mighty cherubim to the east of the Garden of Eden. And he placed a flaming sword that flashed back and forth to guard the way to the tree of life.

4 **CAIN AND ABEL** Now Adam* had sexual relations with his wife, Eve, and she became pregnant. When she gave birth to Cain, she said, "With the Lord's help, I have produced* a man!" ²Later she gave birth to his brother and named him Abel.

When they grew up, Abel became a shepherd, while Cain cultivated the ground. ³When it was time for the harvest, Cain presented some of his crops as a gift to the Lord. ⁴Abel also brought a gift—the best of the firstborn lambs from his flock. The Lord accepted Abel and his gift, ⁵but he did not accept Cain and his gift. This made Cain very angry, and he looked dejected.

⁶"Why are you so angry?" the Lord asked Cain. "Why do you look so dejected? ⁷You will be accepted if you do what is right. But if you refuse to do what is right, then watch out! Sin is crouching at the door, eager to control you. But you must subdue it and be its master."

⁸One day Cain suggested to his brother, "Let's go out into the fields."* And while they were in the field, Cain attacked his brother, Abel, and killed him.

....

BIG MISTAKE

(4:3-10) Adam and Eve's disobedience (Gen 3) brought sin into the human race. They may have thought their sin (eating a "harmless" piece of fruit) wasn't very bad, but notice how quickly the sin habit developed in the lives of their children. Simple disobedience blossomed into outright murder. Adam and Eve acted only against God, but Cain acted against both God and a person. A small sin has a way of growing out of control. Feeling controlled by the sin habit? The best way to break free is to put yourself under God's control.

3:22 Or *the man;* Hebrew reads *ha-adam.* **4:1a** Or *the man;* also in 4:25. **4:1b** Or *I have acquired. Cain* sounds like a Hebrew term that can mean "produce" or "acquire." **4:8** As in Samaritan Pentateuch, Greek and Syriac versions, and Latin Vulgate; Masoretic Text lacks *"Let's go out into the fields."*

SATAN'S PLAN

Doubt—Makes you question God's Word and his goodness

Discouragement—Makes you look at your problems rather than at God

Diversion—Makes the wrong things seem attractive so you want them more than the right things

Defeat—Makes you feel like a failure, so you don't even try

Delay—Makes you put off doing something, so it never gets done

---

⁹Afterward the LORD asked Cain, "Where is your brother? Where is Abel?"

"I don't know," Cain responded. "Am I my brother's guardian?"

¹⁰But the LORD said, "What have you done? Listen! Your brother's blood cries out to me from the ground! ¹¹Now you are cursed and banished from the ground, which has swallowed your brother's blood. ¹²No longer will the ground yield good crops for you, no matter how hard you work! From now on you will be a homeless wanderer on the earth."

¹³Cain replied to the LORD, "My punishment* is too great for me to bear! ¹⁴You have banished me from the land and from your presence; you have made me a homeless wanderer. Anyone who finds me will kill me!"

¹⁵The LORD replied, "No, for I will give a sevenfold punishment to anyone who kills you." Then the LORD put a mark on Cain to warn anyone who might try to kill him. ¹⁶So Cain left the LORD's presence and settled in the land of Nod,* east of Eden.

THE DESCENDANTS OF CAIN

¹⁷Cain had sexual relations with his wife, and she became pregnant and gave birth to Enoch. Then Cain founded a city, which he named Enoch, after his son. ¹⁸Enoch had a son named Irad. Irad became the father of* Mehujael. Mehujael became the father of Methushael. Methushael became the father of Lamech.

¹⁹Lamech married two women. The first was named Adah, and the second was Zillah. ²⁰Adah gave birth to Jabal, who was the first of those who raise livestock and live in tents. ²¹His brother's name was Jubal, the first of all who play the harp and flute. ²²Lamech's other wife, Zillah, gave birth to a son named Tubal-cain. He became an expert in forging tools of bronze and iron. Tubal-cain had a sister named Naamah. ²³One day Lamech said to his wives,

"Adah and Zillah, hear my voice;
    listen to me, you wives of Lamech.
I have killed a man who attacked me,
    a young man who wounded me.
²⁴ If someone who kills Cain is punished seven
    times,

4:13 Or *My sin.*   4:16 *Nod* means "wandering."   4:18 Or *the ancestor of,* and so throughout the verse.

ABEL   *PERSONALITY PROFILE*

LET'S FACE IT. The first time you read Abel's story, maybe you thought you knew all about him. Maybe you had him pegged as the teacher's pet—the one who got all A's in class and always raised his hand with the right answer on his lips. Or maybe he's too close in personality to someone in your family who seems "perfect." Does that sound like your view of him?

Abel was the second child born into the world, but the first one to obey God. He worshiped in a way that pleased God. That really bothered his brother Cain. Maybe Abel suspected that Cain was angry with him. Brothers and sisters know things like that about each other. Yet Abel trusted his brother even when Cain suggested they go out to the field together.

The Bible doesn't tell us why God accepted Abel's gift and did not accept Cain's, but both brothers knew what God expected. Cain seemed to take a shortcut. Only Abel fully obeyed. He is remembered for his obedience and faith (Heb 11:4), and he is called "righteous" (Matt 23:35).

When it comes to obeying God, what's your style? Wholehearted like Abel? Halfhearted like Cain?

BOTTOM LINE: God hears those who come to him.
    God recognizes the innocent person, and sooner or later he judges the guilty.
    God prefers wholehearted, rather than halfhearted offerings.

Abel's story is told in Genesis 4:1-10. He also is mentioned in Matthew 23:35; Luke 11:51; Hebrews 11:4; 12:24.

UPS:
• *First member of the "Hall of Faith" in Hebrews 11:4*
• *First shepherd*
• *First martyr for truth (Matt 23:35)*

STATS:
• *Where: Just outside of Eden*
• *Occupation: Shepherd*
• *Relatives: Adam and Eve (parents); Cain (brother)*

KEY VERSE: *Hebrews 11:4*

then the one who kills me will be punished seventy-seven times!"

THE BIRTH OF SETH 25Adam had sexual relations with his wife again, and she gave birth to another son. She named him Seth,* for she said, "God has granted me another son in place of Abel, whom Cain killed." 26When Seth grew up, he had a son and named him Enosh. At that time people first began to worship the LORD by name.

5 **THE DESCENDANTS OF ADAM** This is the written account of the descendants of Adam. When God created human beings,* he made them to be like himself. 2He created them male and female, and he blessed them and called them "human."

3When Adam was 130 years old, he became the father of a son who was just like him—in his very image. He named his son Seth. 4After the birth of Seth, Adam lived another 800 years, and he had other sons and daughters. 5Adam lived 930 years, and then he died.

6When Seth was 105 years old, he became the father of* Enosh. 7After the birth of* Enosh, Seth lived another 807 years, and he had other sons and daughters. 8Seth lived 912 years, and then he died.

9When Enosh was 90 years old, he became the father of Kenan. 10After the birth of Kenan, Enosh lived another 815 years, and he had other sons and daughters. 11Enosh lived 905 years, and then he died.

12When Kenan was 70 years old, he became the father of Mahalalel. 13After the birth of Mahalalel, Kenan lived another 840 years, and he had other sons and daughters. 14Kenan lived 910 years, and then he died.

15When Mahalalel was 65 years old, he became the father of Jared. 16After the birth of Jared, Mahalalel lived another 830 years, and he had other sons and daughters. 17Mahalalel lived 895 years, and then he died.

18When Jared was 162 years old, he became the father of Enoch. 19After the birth of Enoch, Jared lived another 800 years, and he had other sons and daughters. 20Jared lived 962 years, and then he died.

21When Enoch was 65 years old, he became the father of Methuselah. 22After the birth of

---

MY STORY: Tynisha

I admit I want my own way most of the time. I'm not going to lie to you. And I want God to do things my way, rather than the other way around. Sometimes, I find myself reacting like Cain—you know, mad at God for not accepting my half-hearted efforts.

For me, submitting to God's will is the hardest part about being a Christian. I know it means giving up what I want and totally giving in to what God wants. It also means giving God my best instead of the least I can give. Sometimes, I want to say, "Cut me some slack, God!" But when I think about what God gave up for me and how much he keeps doing for me, I find myself wanting to do things his way.

Methuselah, Enoch lived in close fellowship with God for another 300 years, and he had other sons and daughters. 23Enoch lived 365 years, 24walking in close fellowship with God. Then one day he disappeared, because God took him.

25When Methuselah was 187 years old, he became the father of Lamech. 26After the birth of Lamech, Methuselah lived another 782 years, and he had other sons and daughters. 27Methuselah lived 969 years, and then he died.

28When Lamech was 182 years old, he became the father of a son. 29Lamech named his son Noah, for he said, "May he bring us relief* from our work and the painful labor of farming this ground that the LORD has cursed." 30After the birth of Noah, Lamech lived another 595 years, and he had other sons and daughters. 31Lamech lived 777 years, and then he died. 32By the time Noah was 500 years old, he was the father of Shem, Ham, and Japheth.

6 **A WORLD GONE WRONG** Then the people began to multiply on the earth, and daughters were born to them. 2The sons of God saw the beautiful women* and took any they wanted as their wives. 3Then the LORD said, "My Spirit will not put up with* humans for such a long time, for they are only mortal flesh. In the future, their normal lifespan will be no more than 120 years."

4In those days, and for some time after, giant

4:25 *Seth* probably means "granted"; the name may also mean "appointed." **5:1** Or *man;* Hebrew reads *adam;* similarly in 5:2. **5:6** Or *the ancestor of;* also in 5:9, 12, 15, 18, 21, 25. **5:7** Or *the birth of this ancestor of;* also in 5:10, 13, 16, 19, 22, 26. **5:29** *Noah* sounds like a Hebrew term that can mean "relief" or "comfort." **6:2** Hebrew *daughters of men;* also in 6:4. **6:3** Greek version reads *will not remain in.*

Nephilites lived on the earth, for whenever the sons of God had intercourse with women, they gave birth to children who became the heroes and famous warriors of ancient times.

⁵The LORD observed the extent of human wickedness on the earth, and he saw that everything they thought or imagined was consistently and totally evil. ⁶So the LORD was sorry he had ever made them and put them on the earth. It broke his heart. ⁷And the LORD said, "I will wipe this human race I have created from the face of the earth. Yes, and I will destroy every living thing—all the people, the large animals, the small animals that scurry along the ground, and even the birds of the sky. I am sorry I ever made them." ⁸But Noah found favor with the LORD.

THE STORY OF NOAH ⁹This is the account of Noah and his family. Noah was a righteous man, the only blameless person living on earth at the time, and he walked in close fellowship with God. ¹⁰Noah was the father of three sons: Shem, Ham, and Japheth.

¹¹Now God saw that the earth had become corrupt and was filled with violence. ¹²God observed all this corruption in the world, for everyone on earth was corrupt. ¹³So God said to Noah, "I have decided to destroy all living creatures, for they have filled the earth with violence. Yes, I will wipe them all out along with the earth!

¹⁴"Build a large boat* from cypress wood* and waterproof it with tar, inside and out. Then construct decks and stalls throughout its interior. ¹⁵Make the boat 450 feet long, 75 feet wide, and 45 feet high.* ¹⁶Leave an 18-inch opening* below the roof all the way around the boat. Put the door on the side, and build three decks inside the boat—lower, middle, and upper.

¹⁷"Look! I am about to cover the earth with a flood that will destroy every living thing that breathes. Everything on earth will die. ¹⁸But I will confirm my covenant with you. So enter

....

WHY WORRY?
(7:15-16) Many have wondered how this animal kingdom roundup happened. Did Noah and his sons spend years collecting them? Actually, God took care of that job while Noah and his sons were building the boat. They didn't have to worry about how the animals would arrive. Often we do just the opposite of Noah. We worry about details in our lives over which we have no control, while neglecting specific areas (such as attitudes, relationships, responsibilities) that are under our control. What task has God given you? What aspects of your life seem out of your control? Concentrate on what God has given you to do, and leave the rest to him.

the boat—you and your wife and your sons and their wives. ¹⁹Bring a pair of every kind of animal—a male and a female—into the boat with you to keep them alive during the flood. ²⁰Pairs of every kind of bird, and every kind of animal, and every kind of small animal that scurries along the ground, will come to you to be kept alive. ²¹And be sure to take on board enough food for your family and for all the animals."

²²So Noah did everything exactly as God had commanded him.

7 **THE FLOOD COVERS THE EARTH** When everything was ready, the LORD said to Noah, "Go into the boat with all your family, for among all the people of the earth, I can see that you alone are righteous. ²Take with you seven pairs—male and female—of each animal I have approved for eating and for sacrifice,* and take one pair of each of the others. ³Also take seven pairs of every kind of bird. There must be a male and a female in each pair to ensure that all life will survive on the earth after the flood. ⁴Seven days from now I will make the rains pour down on the earth. And it will rain for forty days and forty nights, until I have wiped from the earth all the living things I have created."

⁵So Noah did everything as the LORD commanded him.

⁶Noah was 600 years old when the flood covered the earth. ⁷He went on board the boat to escape the flood—he and his wife and his sons and their wives. ⁸With them were all the various kinds of animals—those approved for eating and for sacrifice and those that were not—along with all the birds and the small animals that scurry along the ground. ⁹They entered the boat in pairs, male and female, just as God had commanded Noah. ¹⁰After seven days, the waters of the flood came and covered the earth.

¹¹When Noah was 600 years old, on the seventeenth day of the second month, all the underground waters erupted from the earth, and the rain fell in mighty torrents from the sky. ¹²The rain continued to fall for forty days and forty nights.

¹³That very day Noah had gone into the boat with his wife and his sons—Shem, Ham, and Japheth—and their wives. ¹⁴With them in the boat were pairs of every kind of animal—domestic and wild, large and small—along with birds of every kind. ¹⁵Two by two they came into

6:14a Traditionally rendered *an ark.* **6:14b** Or *gopher wood.* **6:15** Hebrew *300 cubits* [138 meters] *long, 50 cubits* [23 meters] *wide, and 30 cubits* [13.8 meters] *high.* **6:16** Hebrew *an opening of 1 cubit* [46 centimeters]. **7:2** Hebrew *of each clean animal;* similarly in 7:8.

the boat, representing every living thing that breathes. ¹⁶A male and female of each kind entered, just as God had commanded Noah. Then the LORD closed the door behind them.

¹⁷For forty days the floodwaters grew deeper, covering the ground and lifting the boat high above the earth. ¹⁸As the waters rose higher and higher above the ground, the boat floated safely on the surface. ¹⁹Finally, the water covered even the highest mountains on the earth, ²⁰rising more than twenty-two feet* above the highest peaks. ²¹All the living things on earth died—birds, domestic animals, wild animals, small animals that scurry along the ground, and all the people. ²²Everything that breathed and lived on dry land died. ²³God wiped out every living thing on the earth—people, livestock, small animals that scurry along the ground, and the birds of the sky. All were destroyed. The only people who survived were Noah and those with him in the boat. ²⁴And the floodwaters covered the earth for 150 days.

8 THE FLOOD RECEDES

But God remembered Noah and all the wild animals and livestock with him in the boat. He sent a wind

7:20 Hebrew 15 cubits [6.9 meters]. 8:4 Hebrew on the seventeenth day of the seventh month; see 7:11. 8:5 Hebrew On the first day of the tenth month; see 7:11 and note on 8:4.

to blow across the earth, and the floodwaters began to recede. ²The underground waters stopped flowing, and the torrential rains from the sky were stopped. ³So the floodwaters gradually receded from the earth. After 150 days, ⁴exactly five months from the time the flood began,* the boat came to rest on the mountains of Ararat. ⁵Two and a half months later,* as the waters continued to go down, other mountain peaks became visible.

⁶After another forty days, Noah opened the window he had made in the boat ⁷and released a raven. The bird flew back and forth until the floodwaters on the earth had dried up. ⁸He also released a dove to see if the water had receded and it could find dry ground. ⁹But the dove could find no place to land because the water still covered the ground. So it returned to the boat, and Noah held out his hand and drew the dove back inside. ¹⁰After waiting another seven days, Noah released the dove again. ¹¹This time the dove returned to him in the evening with a fresh olive leaf in its beak. Then Noah knew that the floodwaters were almost gone. ¹²He waited another seven days and then released the dove again. This time it did not come back.

¹³Noah was now 601 years old. On the first day of the new year, ten and a half months after

the flood began,* the floodwaters had almost dried up from the earth. Noah lifted back the covering of the boat and saw that the surface of the ground was drying. ¹⁴Two more months went by,* and at last the earth was dry!

¹⁵Then God said to Noah, ¹⁶"Leave the boat, all of you—you and your wife, and your sons and their wives. ¹⁷Release all the animals—the birds, the livestock, and the small animals that scurry along the ground—so they can be fruitful and multiply throughout the earth."

¹⁸So Noah, his wife, and his sons and their wives left the boat. ¹⁹And all of the large and small animals and birds came out of the boat, pair by pair.

²⁰Then Noah built an altar to the LORD, and there he sacrificed as burnt offerings the animals and birds that had been approved for that purpose.* ²¹And the LORD was pleased with the aroma of the sacrifice and said to himself, "I will never again curse the ground because of the human race, even though everything they think or imagine is bent toward evil from childhood. I will never again destroy all living things. ²²As long as the earth remains, there will be

....

WHAT'S WRONG WITH MURDER?
(9:5-6) Here God explains why murder is so wrong: to kill a person is to kill someone made in God's image. All people possess the qualities that distinguish them from animals: morality, reason, creativity, and self-worth. When we interact with others, we interact with beings made by God, beings to whom God offers eternal life. In what ways do your actions show the value you place on human life?

planting and harvest, cold and heat, summer and winter, day and night."

9 GOD CONFIRMS HIS COVENANT Then God blessed Noah and his sons and told them, "Be fruitful and multiply. Fill the earth. ²All the animals of the earth, all the birds of the sky, all the small animals that scurry along the ground, and all the fish in the sea will look on you with fear and terror. I have placed them in your power. ³I have given them to you for food, just as I have given you grain and vegetables. ⁴But you must never eat any meat that still has the lifeblood in it.

⁵"And I will require the blood of anyone who takes another person's life. If a wild animal kills a person, it must die. And anyone who murders a fellow human must die. ⁶If anyone takes a human life, that person's life will also be taken by human hands. For God made human beings* in his own image. ⁷Now be fruitful and multiply, and repopulate the earth."

⁸Then God told Noah and his sons, ⁹"I hereby confirm my covenant with you and your descendants, ¹⁰and with all the animals that were on the boat with you—the birds, the livestock, and all the wild animals—every living creature on earth. ¹¹Yes, I am confirming my covenant with you. Never again will floodwaters kill all living creatures; never again will a flood destroy the earth."

¹²Then God said, "I am giving you a sign of my covenant with you and with all living creatures,

8:13 Hebrew On the first day of the first month; see 7:11.
8:14 Hebrew The twenty-seventh day of the second month arrived; see note on 8:13.   **8:20** Hebrew every clean animal and every clean bird.   **9:6** Or man; Hebrew reads ha-adam.

CHOICES
violence

On Friday nights at seven o'clock you're practically guaranteed to find Tyrice and Jordan in one of two places. Check first at Tyrice's. If they're not there, munching pizza and watching horror movies on DVD, try the mall. They probably will be standing in line at the movie theater, anxiously waiting for the chance to buy tickets for the newest cinematic tale of gore.

In the last couple of years, these guys have seen hundreds of violent movies and played video games that are even more violent. It doesn't matter what the plot is—deranged killers on the loose, murderous monsters on the rampage, the latest hit man role-play game—as long as there are some gruesome torture scenes, lots of mutilated bodies, and gallons of blood and guts, Tyrice and Jordan are satisfied.

"That one scene was so weak," Jordan complains as he ejects a DVD on Friday.

"Which one?" Tyrice responds.

"You know, the one where he shoved the girl into that giant meat grinder. I mean, the blood didn't even look real."

"Tell me about it!" Tyrice agrees. "Every scene in the whole movie was just ripped off from another movie."

"Want to watch *Shredded!* now?"

"Naw, let's play *Hit Man Heist*. I wanna try out your new game system. But let me go get some more cherry soda first."

Ever think that the violent scenes on the news, in movies, or in video games seem almost "tame"? That's what's known as being desensitized. It means you're so used to violence, it doesn't bother you anymore. Know what? Even though God has seen it all, he'll never be desensitized.

Check out God's response to violence in Genesis 6:11–13. What's your response?

for all generations to come. [13]I have placed my rainbow in the clouds. It is the sign of my covenant with you and with all the earth. [14]When I send clouds over the earth, the rainbow will appear in the clouds, [15]and I will remember my covenant with you and with all living creatures. Never again will the floodwaters destroy all life. [16]When I see the rainbow in the clouds, I will remember the eternal covenant between God and every living creature on earth." [17]Then God said to Noah, "Yes, this rainbow is the sign of the covenant I am confirming with all the creatures on earth."

NOAH'S SONS [18]The sons of Noah who came out of the boat with their father were Shem, Ham, and Japheth. (Ham is the father of Canaan.) [19]From these three sons of Noah came all the people who now populate the earth.

[20]After the flood, Noah began to cultivate the ground, and he planted a vineyard. [21]One day he drank some wine he had made, and he became drunk and lay naked inside his tent. [22]Ham, the father of Canaan, saw that his father was naked and went outside and told his brothers. [23]Then Shem and Japheth took a robe, held it over their shoulders, and backed into the tent to cover their father. As they did this, they looked the other way so they would not see him naked.

[24]When Noah woke up from his stupor, he learned what Ham, his youngest son, had done. [25]Then he cursed Canaan, the son of Ham:

"May Canaan be cursed!
    May he be the lowest of servants to his
        relatives."

[26]Then Noah said,

"May the LORD, the God of Shem, be
        blessed,
    and may Canaan be his servant!
[27] May God expand the territory of Japheth!
    May Japheth share the prosperity of Shem,*
        and may Canaan be his servant."

[28]Noah lived another 350 years after the great flood. [29]He lived 950 years, and then he died.

10 This is the account of the families of Shem, Ham, and Japheth, the three sons of Noah. Many children were born to them after the great flood.

DESCENDANTS OF JAPHETH [2]The descendants of Japheth were Gomer, Magog, Madai, Javan, Tubal, Meshech, and Tiras.

[3]The descendants of Gomer were Ashkenaz, Riphath, and Togarmah.

[4]The descendants of Javan were Elishah, Tarshish, Kittim, and Rodanim.* [5]Their descendants became the seafaring peoples that spread out to various lands, each identified by its own language, clan, and national identity.

DESCENDANTS OF HAM [6]The descendants of Ham were Cush, Mizraim, Put, and Canaan.

[7]The descendants of Cush were Seba, Havilah, Sabtah, Raamah, and Sabteca. The descendants of Raamah were Sheba and Dedan.

[8]Cush was also the ancestor of Nimrod, who was the first heroic warrior on earth. [9]Since he was the greatest hunter in the world,* his name became proverbial. People would say, "This man is like Nimrod, the greatest hunter in the world." [10]He built his kingdom in the land of Babylonia,* with the cities of Babylon, Erech, Akkad, and Calneh. [11]From there he expanded his territory to Assyria,* building the cities of Nineveh, Rehoboth-ir, Calah, [12]and Resen (the great city located between Nineveh and Calah).

[13]Mizraim was the ancestor of the Ludites, Anamites, Lehabites, Naphtuhites, [14]Pathrusites, Casluhites, and the Caphtorites, from whom the Philistines came.*

[15]Canaan's oldest son was Sidon, the ancestor of the Sidonians. Canaan was also the ancestor of the Hittites,* [16]Jebusites, Amorites, Girgashites, [17]Hivites, Arkites, Sinites, [18]Arvadites, Zemarites, and Hamathites. The Canaanite clans eventually spread out, [19]and the territory of Canaan extended from Sidon in the north to Gerar and Gaza in the south, and east as far as Sodom, Gomorrah, Admah, and Zeboiim, near Lasha.

[20]These were the descendants of Ham, identified by clan, language, territory, and national identity.

DESCENDANTS OF SHEM [21]Sons were also born to Shem, the older brother of Japheth.* Shem was the ancestor of all the descendants of Eber.

9:27 Hebrew *May he live in the tents of Shem.* **10:4** As in some Hebrew manuscripts and Greek version (see also 1 Chr 1:7); most Hebrew manuscripts read *Dodanim.* **10:9** Hebrew *a great hunter before the LORD;* also in 10:9b. **10:10** Hebrew *Shinar.* **10:11** Or *From that land Assyria went out.* **10:14** Hebrew *Casluhites, from whom the Philistines came, and Caphtorites.* Compare Jer 47:4; Amos 9:7. **10:15** Hebrew *ancestor of Heth.* **10:21** Or *Shem, whose older brother was Japheth.*

²²The descendants of Shem were Elam, Asshur, Arphaxad, Lud, and Aram.

²³The descendants of Aram were Uz, Hul, Gether, and Mash.

²⁴Arphaxad was the father of Shelah,* and Shelah was the father of Eber.

²⁵Eber had two sons. The first was named Peleg (which means "division"), for during his lifetime the people of the world were divided into different language groups. His brother's name was Joktan.

²⁶Joktan was the ancestor of Almodad, Sheleph, Hazarmaveth, Jerah, ²⁷Hadoram, Uzal, Diklah, ²⁸Obal, Abimael, Sheba, ²⁹Ophir, Havilah, and Jobab. All these were descendants of Joktan. ³⁰The territory they occupied extended from Mesha all the way to Sephar in the eastern mountains.

³¹These were the descendants of Shem, identified by clan, language, territory, and national identity.

CONCLUSION ³²These are the clans that descended from Noah's sons, arranged by nation according to their lines of descent. All the nations of the earth descended from these clans after the great flood.

11 THE TOWER OF BABEL

At one time all the people of the world spoke the same language and used the same words. ²As the people migrated to the east, they found a plain in the land of Babylonia* and settled there.

³They began saying to each other, "Let's make bricks and harden them with fire." (In this region bricks were used instead of stone, and tar was used for mortar.) ⁴Then they said, "Come, let's build a great city for ourselves with a tower that reaches into the sky. This will make us famous and keep us from being scattered all over the world."

⁵But the Lord came down to look at the city and the tower the people were building. ⁶"Look!" he said. "The people are united, and they all speak the same language. After this, nothing they set out to do will be impossible

for them! ⁷Come, let's go down and confuse the people with different languages. Then they won't be able to understand each other."

⁸In that way, the Lord scattered them all over the world, and they stopped building the city. ⁹That is why the city was called Babel,* because that is where the Lord confused the people with different languages. In this way he scattered them all over the world.

THE LINE OF DESCENT FROM SHEM TO ABRAM

¹⁰This is the account of Shem's family.

Two years after the great flood, when Shem was 100 years old, he became the father of* Arphaxad. ¹¹After the birth of* Arphaxad, Shem lived another 500 years and had other sons and daughters.

¹²When Arphaxad was 35 years old, he became the father of Shelah. ¹³After the birth of Shelah, Arphaxad lived another 403 years and had other sons and daughters.*

¹⁴When Shelah was 30 years old, he became the father of Eber. ¹⁵After the birth of Eber, Shelah lived another 403 years and had other sons and daughters.

¹⁶When Eber was 34 years old, he became the father of Peleg. ¹⁷After the birth of Peleg, Eber lived another 430 years and had other sons and daughters.

¹⁸When Peleg was 30 years old, he became the father of Reu. ¹⁹After the birth of Reu, Peleg lived another 209 years and had other sons and daughters.

²⁰When Reu was 32 years old, he became the father of Serug. ²¹After the birth of Serug, Reu lived another 207 years and had other sons and daughters.

²²When Serug was 30 years old, he became the father of Nahor. ²³After the birth of Nahor, Serug lived another 200 years and had other sons and daughters.

²⁴When Nahor was 29 years old, he became the father of Terah. ²⁵After the birth of Terah, Nahor lived another 119 years and had other sons and daughters.

²⁶After Terah was 70 years old, he became the father of Abram, Nahor, and Haran.

TOWERING PRIDE

(11:4) The tower of Babel was a great human achievement, a wonder of the ancient world. But it was a monument to the builders rather than to God. We still build monuments to ourselves (closets full of expensive clothes, the latest electronic gadget, a great music collection, shelves crammed with trophies) to call attention to our achievements. These may not be wrong in themselves, but when we find our identity and value in them, they take God's place in our lives. What "monuments" do you have?

10:24 Greek version reads *Arphaxad was the father of Cainan, Cainan was the father of Shelah.* Compare Luke 3:36. **11:2** Hebrew *Shinar.* **11:9** Or *Babylon. Babel* sounds like a Hebrew term that means "confusion." **11:10** Or *the ancestor of;* also in 11:12, 14, 16, 18, 20, 22, 24. **11:11** Or *the birth of this ancestor of;* also in 11:13, 15, 17, 19, 21, 23, 25. **11:12-13** Greek version reads ¹²*When Arphaxad was 135 years old, he became the father of Cainan.* ¹³*After the birth of Cainan, Arphaxad lived another 430 years and had other sons and daughters, and then he died. When Cainan was 130 years old, he became the father of Shelah. After the birth of Shelah, Cainan lived another 330 years and had other sons and daughters, and then he died.* Compare Luke 3:35-36.

THE FAMILY OF TERAH ²⁷This is the account of Terah's family. Terah was the father of Abram, Nahor, and Haran; and Haran was the father of Lot. ²⁸But Haran died in Ur of the Chaldeans, the land of his birth, while his father, Terah, was still living. ²⁹Meanwhile, Abram and Nahor both married. The name of Abram's wife was Sarai, and the name of Nahor's wife was Milcah. (Milcah and her sister Iscah were daughters of Nahor's brother Haran.) ³⁰But Sarai was unable to become pregnant and had no children.

³¹One day Terah took his son Abram, his daughter-in-law Sarai (his son Abram's wife), and his grandson Lot (his son Haran's child) and moved away from Ur of the Chaldeans. He was headed for the land of Canaan, but they stopped at Haran and settled there. ³²Terah lived for 205 years* and died while still in Haran.

12 **THE CALL OF ABRAM** The LORD had said to Abram, "Leave your native country, your relatives, and your father's family, and go to the land that I will show you. ²I will make you into a great nation. I will bless you and make you famous, and you will be a blessing to others. ³I will bless those who bless you and curse those who treat you with contempt. All the families on earth will be blessed through you."

⁴So Abram departed as the LORD had instructed, and Lot went with him. Abram was seventy-five years old when he left Haran. ⁵He took his wife, Sarai, his nephew Lot, and all his wealth—his livestock and all the people he had taken into his household at Haran—and headed for the land of Canaan. When they arrived in Canaan, ⁶Abram traveled through the land as far as Shechem. There he set up camp beside the oak of Moreh. At that time, the area was inhabited by Canaanites.

⁷Then the LORD appeared to Abram and said, "I will give this land to your descendants.*" And Abram built an altar there and dedicated it to the LORD, who had appeared to him. ⁸After that, Abram traveled south and set up camp in the hill country, with Bethel to the west and Ai to the east. There he built another altar and dedicated it to the LORD, and he worshiped the LORD. ⁹Then Abram continued traveling south by stages toward the Negev.

ABRAM AND SARAI IN EGYPT ¹⁰At that time a severe famine struck the land of Canaan, forcing Abram to go down to Egypt, where he lived as a foreigner. ¹¹As he was approaching the border of Egypt, Abram said to his wife, Sarai, "Look, you are a very beautiful woman. ¹²When the Egyptians see you, they will say, 'This is his wife. Let's kill him; then we can have her!' ¹³So please tell them you are my sister. Then they will spare my life and treat me well because of their interest in you."

¹⁴And sure enough, when Abram arrived in Egypt, everyone noticed Sarai's beauty. ¹⁵When the palace officials saw her, they sang her praises to Pharaoh, their king, and Sarai was taken into his palace. ¹⁶Then Pharaoh gave Abram many gifts because of her—sheep, goats, cattle, male and female donkeys, male and female servants, and camels.

¹⁷But the LORD sent terrible plagues upon Pharaoh and his household because of Sarai, Abram's wife. ¹⁸So Pharaoh summoned Abram and accused him sharply. "What have you done to me?" he demanded. "Why didn't you tell me she was your wife? ¹⁹Why did you say, 'She is my sister,' and allow me to take her as my wife? Now then, here is your wife. Take her and get out of here!" ²⁰Pharaoh ordered some of his men to escort them, and he sent Abram out of the country, along with his wife and all his possessions.

13 **ABRAM AND LOT SEPARATE** So Abram left Egypt and traveled north into the Negev, along with his wife and Lot and all that they owned. ²(Abram was very rich in livestock, silver, and gold.) ³From the Negev, they continued traveling by stages toward Bethel, and they pitched their tents between Bethel and Ai, where they had camped before. ⁴This was the same place where Abram had built the altar, and there he worshiped the LORD again.

⁵Lot, who was traveling with Abram, had also become very wealthy with flocks of sheep and goats, herds of cattle, and many tents. ⁶But the land could not support both Abram and Lot with all their flocks and herds living so close together. ⁷So disputes broke out between the herdsmen of Abram and Lot. (At that time

....

WILLING TO GO
(12:2) God promised to bless Abram by making him the father of a great nation; however, there was one condition. Abram had to do what God wanted him to do. This meant leaving his home and friends and traveling to a new land. Abram obeyed, leaving his home for God's promise of even greater blessings in the future. God may be trying to lead you to a place of greater service and usefulness for him. Don't let the comfort and security of your present position make you miss God's plan for you. Are you willing to go where he sends you?

11:32 Some ancient versions read *145 years*; compare 11:26 and 12:4.   **12:7** Hebrew *seed*.

Canaanites and Perizzites were also living in the land.)

⁸Finally Abram said to Lot, "Let's not allow this conflict to come between us or our herdsmen. After all, we are close relatives! ⁹The whole countryside is open to you. Take your choice of any section of the land you want, and we will separate. If you want the land to the left, then I'll take the land on the right. If you prefer the land on the right, then I'll go to the left."

¹⁰Lot took a long look at the fertile plains of the Jordan Valley in the direction of Zoar. The whole area was well watered everywhere, like the garden of the LORD or the beautiful land of Egypt. (This was before the LORD destroyed Sodom and Gomorrah.) ¹¹Lot chose for himself the whole Jordan Valley to the east of them. He went there with his flocks and servants and parted company with his uncle Abram. ¹²So Abram settled in the land of Canaan, and Lot moved his tents to a place near Sodom and

settled among the cities of the plain. ¹³But the people of this area were extremely wicked and constantly sinned against the LORD.

¹⁴After Lot had gone, the LORD said to Abram, "Look as far as you can see in every direction—north and south, east and west. ¹⁵I am giving all this land, as far as you can see, to you and your descendants* as a permanent possession. ¹⁶And I will give you so many descendants that, like the dust of the earth, they cannot be counted! ¹⁷Go and walk through the land in every direction, for I am giving it to you."

¹⁸So Abram moved his camp to Hebron and settled near the oak grove belonging to Mamre. There he built another altar to the LORD.

14 **ABRAM RESCUES LOT** About this time war broke out in the region. King Amraphel of Babylonia,* King Arioch of Ellasar, King Kedorlaomer of Elam, and King Tidal of Goiim ²fought against King Bera of Sodom, King Birsha of Gomorrah, King Shinab of Admah, King Shemeber of Zeboiim, and the king of Bela (also called Zoar).

³This second group of kings joined forces in Siddim Valley (that is, the valley of the Dead Sea*). ⁴For twelve years they had been subject to King Kedorlaomer, but in the thirteenth year they rebelled against him.

13:15 Hebrew *seed;* also in 13:16.   **14:1** Hebrew *Shinar;* also in 14:9.
14:3 Hebrew *Salt Sea.*

....

FAMILY FEUD

(13:5-9) Facing a potential conflict with his nephew Lot, Abram took the initiative in settling the dispute. He gave Lot the first choice of land and showed a willingness to risk being cheated. Abram's example shows us how to respond in difficult family situations: (1) take the initiative in resolving conflicts; (2) let others have first choice, even if that means not getting what we want; and (3) put family peace above personal desires.

LOT
PERSONALITY PROFILE

HAVE YOU NOTICED how some people simply drift through life? They don't really make choices; they just take the easiest way. Usually, that choice turns out to be the wrong way.

Lot, Abram's nephew, often took the easy way out. After his father died early on, Lot was cared for by his grandfather Terah and his uncle Abram. Though they were good role models, Lot's life was full of unwise decisions. Despite Abram's attention and God's help, Lot went his own way.

By the time Lot drifted away from Abram, his life had taken an ugly turn. He had become so blended into the culture of his day that he did not want to leave it. His wife was killed during the family's narrow escape from the destruction of Sodom and Gomorrah, and his daughters committed incest with him. His drifting finally led him to destruction.

But God brought good out of failure. The New Testament describes Lot as a righteous man (2 Pet 2:7-8). Even though he didn't do much about the evil surrounding him, it still bothered him deeply. And Ruth—a descendant of Moab, the child born from the incest between Lot and one of his daughters—was an ancestor of Jesus Christ.

Are you headed toward God or drifting away from him? What circumstances tempt you to drift?

BOTTOM LINE: God wants us to do more than drift through life; he wants people to be an influence for him.

Lot's story is told in Genesis 11:27; 12:5; 13–14; 19. He also is mentioned in Deuteronomy 2:9; Luke 17:28-32; 2 Peter 2:7-8.

UPS:
• *Successful businessman*
• *Called a righteous man by Peter (2 Pet 2:7-8)*

DOWNS:
• *Wishy-washy about decisions; usually chose the easy way out*
• *Usually thought of himself when decisions were made*

STATS:
• *Where: Lived first in Ur of the Chaldeans, then moved to Canaan with Abram*
• *Occupations: Wealthy sheep and cattle rancher, city official*
• *Relatives: Haran (father); Abram, later called Abraham (uncle who adopted him at Haran's death); wife (unnamed); two unnamed daughters*

KEY VERSE: *Genesis 19:16*

⁵One year later Kedorlaomer and his allies arrived and defeated the Rephaites at Ashteroth-karnaim, the Zuzites at Ham, the Emites at Shaveh-kiriathaim, ⁶and the Horites at Mount Seir, as far as El-paran at the edge of the wilderness. ⁷Then they turned back and came to En-mishpat (now called Kadesh) and conquered all the territory of the Amalekites, and also the Amorites living in Hazazon-tamar.

⁸Then the rebel kings of Sodom, Gomorrah, Admah, Zeboiim, and Bela (also called Zoar) prepared for battle in the valley of the Dead Sea.* ⁹They fought against King Kedorlaomer of Elam, King Tidal of Goiim, King Amraphel of Babylonia, and King Arioch of Ellasar—four kings against five. ¹⁰As it happened, the valley of the Dead Sea was filled with tar pits. And as the army of the kings of Sodom and Gomorrah fled, some fell into the tar pits, while the rest escaped into the mountains. ¹¹The victorious invaders then plundered Sodom and Gomorrah and headed for home, taking with them all the spoils of war and the food supplies. ¹²They also captured Lot—Abram's nephew who lived in Sodom—and carried off everything he owned.

¹³But one of Lot's men escaped and reported everything to Abram the Hebrew, who was living near the oak grove belonging to Mamre the Amorite. Mamre and his relatives, Eshcol and Aner, were Abram's allies. ¹⁴When Abram heard that his nephew Lot had been captured, he mobilized the 318 trained men who had been born into his household. Then he pursued Kedorlaomer's army until he caught up with them at Dan. ¹⁵There he divided his men and attacked during the night. Kedorlaomer's army fled, but Abram chased them as far as Hobah, north of Damascus. ¹⁶Abram recovered all the goods that had been taken, and he brought back his nephew Lot with his possessions and all the women and other captives.

MELCHIZEDEK BLESSES ABRAM
¹⁷After Abram returned from his victory over Kedorlaomer and all his allies, the king of Sodom went out to meet him in the valley of Shaveh (that is, the King's Valley).

¹⁸And Melchizedek, the king of Salem and a priest of God Most High,* brought Abram some bread and wine. ¹⁹Melchizedek blessed Abram with this blessing:

"Blessed be Abram by God Most High,
    Creator of heaven and earth.
²⁰ And blessed be God Most High,
    who has defeated your enemies for you."

14:8 Hebrew *Siddim Valley* (see 14:3); also in 14:10.   **14:18** Hebrew *El-Elyon*; also in 14:19, 20, 22.

Then Abram gave Melchizedek a tenth of all the goods he had recovered.

²¹The king of Sodom said to Abram, "Give back my people who were captured. But you may keep for yourself all the goods you have recovered."

²²Abram replied to the king of Sodom, "I solemnly swear to the LORD, God Most High, Creator of heaven and earth, ²³that I will not take so much as a single thread or sandal thong from what belongs to you. Otherwise you might say, 'I am the one who made Abram rich.' ²⁴I will accept only what my young warriors have already eaten, and I request that you give a fair share of the goods to my allies—Aner, Eshcol, and Mamre."

15 THE LORD'S COVENANT PROMISE TO ABRAM
Some time later, the LORD spoke to Abram in a vision and said to him, "Do not be afraid, Abram, for I will protect you, and your reward will be great."

²But Abram replied, "O Sovereign LORD, what good are all your blessings when I don't even have a son? Since you've given me no children, Eliezer of Damascus, a servant in my household, will inherit all my wealth. ³You have given me no descendants of my own, so one of my servants will be my heir."

⁴Then the LORD said to him, "No, your servant will not be your heir, for you will have a son of your own who will be your heir." ⁵Then the LORD took Abram outside and said to him, "Look up into the sky and count the stars if you can. That's how many descendants you will have!"

⁶And Abram believed the LORD, and the LORD counted him as righteous because of his faith.

⁷Then the LORD told him, "I am the LORD who brought you out of Ur of the Chaldeans to give you this land as your possession."

⁸But Abram replied, "O Sovereign LORD, how can I be sure that I will actually possess it?"

⁹The LORD told him, "Bring me a three-year-old heifer, a three-year-old female goat, a three-year-old ram, a turtledove, and a young pigeon." ¹⁰So Abram presented all these to him and killed them. Then he cut each animal down

....

GETTING IT RIGHT
(15:6) Although Abram had demonstrated his faith through his actions, his belief in the Lord made him right with God (Rom 4:1-5). We too can be right with God by trusting him with our lives. Church attendance, prayer, and good deeds will not make us right with God. A right relationship is based on faith—the heartfelt inner confidence that God is who he says he is and does what he says he will do. Obedience is a result of a good relationship with God.

the middle and laid the halves side by side; he did not, however, cut the birds in half. ¹¹Some vultures swooped down to eat the carcasses, but Abram chased them away.

¹²As the sun was going down, Abram fell into a deep sleep, and a terrifying darkness came down over him. ¹³Then the LORD said to Abram, "You can be sure that your descendants will be strangers in a foreign land, where they will be oppressed as slaves for 400 years. ¹⁴But I will punish the nation that enslaves them, and in the end they will come away with great wealth. ¹⁵(As for you, you will die in peace and be buried at a ripe old age.) ¹⁶After four generations your descendants will return here to this land, for the sins of the Amorites do not yet warrant their destruction."

¹⁷After the sun went down and darkness fell, Abram saw a smoking firepot and a flaming torch pass between the halves of the carcasses. ¹⁸So the LORD made a covenant with Abram that day and said, "I have given this land to your descendants, all the way from the border of Egypt* to the great Euphrates River—¹⁹the land now occupied by the Kenites, Kenizzites, Kadmonites, ²⁰Hittites, Perizzites, Rephaites, ²¹Amorites, Canaanites, Girgashites, and Jebusites."

16 THE BIRTH OF ISHMAEL

Now Sarai, Abram's wife, had not been able to bear children for him. But she had an Egyptian servant named Hagar. ²So Sarai said to Abram, "The LORD has prevented me from having children. Go and sleep with my servant. Perhaps I can have children through her." And Abram agreed with Sarai's proposal. ³So Sarai, Abram's wife, took Hagar the Egyptian servant and gave her to Abram as a wife. (This happened ten years after Abram had settled in the land of Canaan.)

⁴So Abram had sexual relations with Hagar, and she became pregnant. But when Hagar knew she was pregnant, she began to treat her mistress, Sarai, with contempt. ⁵Then Sarai said to Abram, "This is all your fault! I put my servant into your arms, but now that she's pregnant she treats me with contempt. The LORD will show who's wrong—you or me!"

⁶Abram replied, "Look, she is your servant, so deal with her as you see fit." Then Sarai treated Hagar so harshly that she finally ran away.

15:18 Hebrew *the river of Egypt,* referring either to an eastern branch of the Nile River or to the Brook of Egypt in the Sinai (see Num 34:5).

ABRAHAM
PERSONALITY PROFILE

AS YOU READ about Abraham's life, you might ask: "What on earth made God like this man so much?" Abraham made a lot of mistakes, and some of his mistakes had long-range consequences.

Yet what you will find if you read carefully is that in spite of his mistakes, Abraham trusted God with his life. This is the main fact the Bible tells us about him in both the Old and New Testaments (Gen 15:6; Rom 4:3).

Early in life, Abraham (then known as Abram) had to make an important decision. God asked him to choose between staying at home or following God's leading. It was a choice between doing what Abraham wanted to do or doing what God wanted Abraham to do.

Of course, Abraham couldn't know how his decision would affect the future, but God used Abraham's obedience to affect millions of people. Through Abraham the Jewish nation developed, and eventually Jesus Christ came into the world.

God gives us exactly the same choice he gave Abraham: go his way or the world's. Once Abraham gave his life to God, he never tried to take it back. He may have taken some wrong turns on the journey . . . but he never turned around. What about you? Is your basic desire to trust God and live his way, or is your goal to live life your way?

BOTTOM LINE: God desires dependence, trust, and faith in him—not faith in our ability to please him.

God's plan from the beginning has been to make himself known to all people.

Abraham's story is told in Genesis 11:27–25:11. He also is mentioned in Exodus 2:24; John 8:33-59; Acts 7:2-8, 32; Romans 4; Galatians 3:6-29; Hebrews 6:13–7:10; 11:8-18.

UPS:
- *Had a faith that pleased God*
- *Became the founder of the Jewish nation*
- *Was a successful and wealthy rancher*
- *Usually avoided conflicts, but when they happened, he let his opponent set the rules for settling the disputes*

DOWNS:
- *Had a lifelong tendency to lie when under pressure*

STATS:
- *Where: Born in Ur of the Chaldeans; spent most of his life in the land of Canaan*
- *Occupation: Wealthy livestock owner*
- *Relatives: Terah (father); Nahor and Haran (brothers); Sarah (wife); Ishmael and Isaac (sons); Lot (nephew)*
- *Contemporaries: Abimelech, Melchizedek*

KEY VERSE: *Genesis 15:6*

[7]The angel of the LORD found Hagar beside a spring of water in the wilderness, along the road to Shur. [8]The angel said to her, "Hagar, Sarai's servant, where have you come from, and where are you going?"

"I'm running away from my mistress, Sarai," she replied.

[9]The angel of the LORD said to her, "Return to your mistress, and submit to her authority." [10]Then he added, "I will give you more descendants than you can count."

[11]And the angel also said, "You are now pregnant and will give birth to a son. You are to name him Ishmael (which means 'God hears'), for the LORD has heard your cry of distress. [12]This son of yours will be a wild man, as untamed as a wild donkey! He will raise his fist against everyone, and everyone will be against him. Yes, he will live in open hostility against all his relatives."

[13]Thereafter, Hagar used another name to refer to the LORD, who had spoken to her. She said, "You are the God who sees me."* She also said, "Have I truly seen the One who sees me?" [14]So that well was named Beer-lahai-roi (which means "well of the Living One who sees me"). It can still be found between Kadesh and Bered.

[15]So Hagar gave Abram a son, and Abram named him Ishmael. [16]Abram was eighty-six years old when Ishmael was born.

17 ABRAM IS NAMED ABRAHAM When Abram was ninety-nine years old, the LORD appeared to him and said, "I am El-Shaddai—'God Almighty.' Serve me faithfully and live a blameless life. [2]I will make a covenant with you, by which I will guarantee to give you countless descendants."

[3]At this, Abram fell face down on the ground. Then God said to him, [4]"This is my covenant with you: I will make you the father of a multitude of nations! [5]What's more, I am changing your name. It will no longer be Abram. Instead, you will be called Abraham,* for you will be the father of many nations. [6]I will make you extremely fruitful. Your descendants will become many nations, and kings will be among them!

[7]"I will confirm my covenant with you and your descendants* after you, from generation to generation. This is the everlasting covenant: I will always be your God and the God of your descendants after you. [8]And I will give the entire land of Canaan, where you now live as a foreigner, to you and your descendants. It will be their possession forever, and I will be their God."

THE MARK OF THE COVENANT [9]Then God said to Abraham, "Your responsibility is to obey the terms of the covenant. You and all your descendants have this continual responsibility. [10]This is the covenant that you and your descendants must keep: Each male among you must be circumcised. [11]You must cut off the flesh of your foreskin as a sign of the covenant between me and you. [12]From generation to generation, every male child must be circumcised on the eighth day after his birth. This applies not only to members of your family but also to the servants born in your household and the foreign-born servants whom you have purchased. [13]All must be circumcised. Your bodies will bear the mark of my everlasting covenant. [14]Any male who fails to be circumcised will be cut off from the covenant family for breaking the covenant."

SARAI IS NAMED SARAH [15]Then God said to Abraham, "Regarding Sarai, your wife—her name will no longer be Sarai. From now on her name will be Sarah.* [16]And I will bless her and give you a son from her! Yes, I will bless her richly, and she will become the mother of many nations. Kings of nations will be among her descendants."

[17]Then Abraham bowed down to the ground, but he laughed to himself in disbelief. "How could I become a father at the age of 100?" he thought. "And how can Sarah have a baby when she is ninety years old?" [18]So Abraham said to God, "May Ishmael live under your special blessing!"

[19]But God replied, "No—Sarah, your wife, will give birth to a son for you. You will name him Isaac,* and I will confirm my covenant with him and his descendants as an everlasting covenant. [20]As for Ishmael, I will bless

....

RUNAWAY
(16:6-14) When Hagar ran away after a fight with her mistress Sarai, the angel of the Lord told her to return to her mistress. Hagar needed to work on her attitude toward Sarai, no matter how unfairly Sarai might have treated her. Running away from our problems rarely solves them. The wise person accepts God's help to face problems squarely.

REASON ENOUGH
(17:1) The Lord told Abram that he was "God Almighty." God has the same message for us today. We are to obey him because he is God—that is reason enough. Consider who God is—the only one with the power and ability to meet your every need.

16:13 Hebrew *El-roi.* **17:5** *Abram* means "exalted father"; *Abraham* sounds like a Hebrew term that means "father of many." **17:7** Hebrew *seed;* also in 17:7b, 8, 9, 10, 19. **17:15** *Sarai* and *Sarah* both mean "princess"; the change in spelling may reflect the difference in dialect between Ur and Canaan. **17:19** *Isaac* means "he laughs."

him also, just as you have asked. I will make him extremely fruitful and multiply his descendants. He will become the father of twelve princes, and I will make him a great nation. ²¹But my covenant will be confirmed with Isaac, who will be born to you and Sarah about this time next year." ²²When God had finished speaking, he left Abraham.

²³On that very day Abraham took his son, Ishmael, and every male in his household, including those born there and those he had bought. Then he circumcised them, cutting off their foreskins, just as God had told him. ²⁴Abraham was ninety-nine years old when he was circumcised, ²⁵and Ishmael, his son, was thirteen. ²⁶Both Abraham and his son, Ishmael, were circumcised on that same day, ²⁷along with all the other men and boys of the household, whether they were born there or bought as servants. All were circumcised with him.

18 A SON IS PROMISED TO SARAH The LORD appeared again to Abraham near the oak grove belonging to Mamre. One day Abraham was sitting at the entrance to his tent during the hottest part of the day. ²He looked up and noticed three men standing nearby. When he saw them, he ran to meet them and welcomed them, bowing low to the ground.

³"My lord," he said, "if it pleases you, stop here for a while. ⁴Rest in the shade of this tree while water is brought to wash your feet. ⁵And since you've honored your servant with this visit, let me prepare some food to refresh you before you continue on your journey."

"All right," they said. "Do as you have said."

⁶So Abraham ran back to the tent and said to Sarah, "Hurry! Get three large measures* of your best flour, knead it into dough, and bake some bread." ⁷Then Abraham ran out to the herd and chose a tender calf and gave it to his servant, who quickly prepared it. ⁸When the food was ready, Abraham took some yogurt and milk and the roasted meat, and he served it to the men. As they ate, Abraham waited on them in the shade of the trees.

···

LYING
(18:10-15) Sarah lied about her laughter at God's promise that she would have a son because she was afraid of being discovered. Fear is the most common motive for lying. We fear that our inner thoughts and emotions will be exposed or our wrongdoings discovered. Sometimes we fear that we'll look foolish if we're caught in a lie. But lying causes greater complications than telling the truth. If God can't be trusted with our thoughts and fears, we are in greater trouble than we first imagined.

⁹"Where is Sarah, your wife?" the visitors asked.

"She's inside the tent," Abraham replied.

¹⁰Then one of them said, "I will return to you about this time next year, and your wife, Sarah, will have a son!"

Sarah was listening to this conversation from the tent. ¹¹Abraham and Sarah were both very old by this time, and Sarah was long past the age of having children. ¹²So she laughed silently to herself and said, "How could a worn-out woman like me enjoy such pleasure, especially when my master—my husband—is also so old?"

¹³Then the LORD said to Abraham, "Why did Sarah laugh? Why did she say, 'Can an old woman like me have a baby?' ¹⁴Is anything too hard for the LORD? I will return about this time next year, and Sarah will have a son."

¹⁵Sarah was afraid, so she denied it, saying, "I didn't laugh."

But the LORD said, "No, you did laugh."

ABRAHAM INTERCEDES FOR SODOM ¹⁶Then the men got up from their meal and looked out toward Sodom. As they left, Abraham went with them to send them on their way.

¹⁷"Should I hide my plan from Abraham?" the LORD asked. ¹⁸"For Abraham will certainly become a great and mighty nation, and all the nations of the earth will be blessed through him. ¹⁹I have singled him out so that he will direct his sons and their families to keep the way of the LORD by doing what is right and just. Then I will do for Abraham all that I have promised."

²⁰So the LORD told Abraham, "I have heard a great outcry from Sodom and Gomorrah, because their sin is so flagrant. ²¹I am going down to see if their actions are as wicked as I have heard. If not, I want to know."

²²The other men turned and headed toward Sodom, but the LORD remained with Abraham. ²³Abraham approached him and said, "Will you sweep away both the righteous and the wicked? ²⁴Suppose you find fifty righteous people living there in the city—will you still sweep it away and not spare it for their sakes? ²⁵Surely you wouldn't do such a thing, destroying the righteous along with the wicked. Why, you would be treating the righteous and the wicked exactly the same! Surely you wouldn't do that! Should not the Judge of all the earth do what is right?"

²⁶And the LORD replied, "If I find fifty righteous people in Sodom, I will spare the entire city for their sake."

²⁷Then Abraham spoke again. "Since I have

18:6 Hebrew *3 seahs*, about half a bushel or 22 liters.

begun, let me speak further to my Lord, even though I am but dust and ashes. ²⁸Suppose there are only forty-five righteous people rather than fifty? Will you destroy the whole city for lack of five?"

And the LORD said, "I will not destroy it if I find forty-five righteous people there."

²⁹Then Abraham pressed his request further. "Suppose there are only forty?"

And the LORD replied, "I will not destroy it for the sake of the forty."

³⁰"Please don't be angry, my Lord," Abraham pleaded. "Let me speak—suppose only thirty righteous people are found?"

And the LORD replied, "I will not destroy it if I find thirty."

³¹Then Abraham said, "Since I have dared to speak to the Lord, let me continue—suppose there are only twenty?"

And the LORD replied, "Then I will not destroy it for the sake of the twenty."

³²Finally, Abraham said, "Lord, please don't be angry with me if I speak one more time. Suppose only ten are found there?"

And the LORD replied, "Then I will not destroy it for the sake of the ten."

³³When the LORD had finished his conversation with Abraham, he went on his way, and Abraham returned to his tent.

19 SODOM AND GOMORRAH DESTROYED

That evening the two angels came to the entrance of the city of Sodom. Lot was sitting there, and when he saw them, he stood up to meet them. Then he welcomed them and bowed with his face to the ground. ²"My lords," he said, "come to my home to wash your feet, and be my guests for the night. You may then get up early in the morning and be on your way again."

"Oh no," they replied. "We'll just spend the night out here in the city square."

³But Lot insisted, so at last they went home with him. Lot prepared a feast for them, complete with fresh bread made without yeast, and they ate. ⁴But before they retired for the night, all the men of Sodom, young and old, came from all over the city and surrounded the house. ⁵They shouted to Lot, "Where are the men who came to spend the night with you? Bring them out to us so we can have sex with them!"

⁶So Lot stepped outside to talk to them, shutting the door behind him. ⁷"Please, my brothers," he begged, "don't do such a wicked thing. ⁸Look, I have two virgin daughters. Let me bring them out to you, and you can do with

19:10 Hebrew *men;* also in 19:12, 16.

IS ANYTHING TOO HARD FOR THE LORD?

GENESIS 18:14

them as you wish. But please, leave these men alone, for they are my guests and are under my protection."

⁹"Stand back!" they shouted. "This fellow came to town as an outsider, and now he's acting like our judge! We'll treat you far worse than those other men!" And they lunged toward Lot to break down the door.

¹⁰But the two angels* reached out, pulled Lot into the house, and bolted the door. ¹¹Then they blinded all the men, young and old, who were at the door of the house, so they gave up trying to get inside.

¹²Meanwhile, the angels questioned Lot. "Do you have any other relatives here in the city?" they asked. "Get them out of this place—your sons-in-law, sons, daughters, or anyone else. ¹³For we are about to destroy this city completely. The outcry against this place is so great it has reached the LORD, and he has sent us to destroy it."

¹⁴So Lot rushed out to tell his daughters' fiancés, "Quick, get out of the city! The LORD is about to destroy it." But the young men thought he was only joking.

¹⁵At dawn the next morning the angels became insistent. "Hurry," they said to Lot. "Take your wife and your two daughters who are here. Get out right now, or you will be swept away in the destruction of the city!"

¹⁶When Lot still hesitated, the angels seized his hand and the hands of his wife and two daughters and rushed them to safety outside the city, for the LORD was merciful. ¹⁷When they

....

CHAMELEON OR CHAMPION?

(19:14) Lot had lived so long among ungodly people that he was no longer a believable witness for God. He had allowed his environment to shape him, rather than shaping his environment. Also, he had compromised to the point that he was almost useless to God. When Lot finally took a stand, nobody listened. Do those who know you see you as a follower of Christ? Or are you a chameleon like Lot—just one of the crowd, blending into your environment? If you want to make a difference, you must first decide to be different and take a stand for what's right.

were safely out of the city, one of the angels ordered, "Run for your lives! And don't look back or stop anywhere in the valley! Escape to the mountains, or you will be swept away!"

18"Oh no, my lord!" Lot begged. 19"You have been so gracious to me and saved my life, and you have shown such great kindness. But I cannot go to the mountains. Disaster would catch up to me there, and I would soon die. 20See, there is a small village nearby. Please let me go there instead; don't you see how small it is? Then my life will be saved."

21"All right," the angel said, "I will grant your request. I will not destroy the little village. 22But hurry! Escape to it, for I can do nothing until you arrive there." (This explains why that village was known as Zoar, which means "little place.")

23Lot reached the village just as the sun was rising over the horizon. 24Then the LORD rained down fire and burning sulfur from the sky on Sodom and Gomorrah. 25He utterly destroyed them, along with the other cities and villages of the plain, wiping out all the people and every bit of vegetation. 26But Lot's wife looked back as she was following behind him, and she turned into a pillar of salt.

27Abraham got up early that morning and hurried out to the place where he had stood in the LORD's presence. 28He looked out across the plain toward Sodom and Gomorrah and watched as columns of smoke rose from the cities like smoke from a furnace.

29But God had listened to Abraham's request and kept Lot safe, removing him from the disaster that engulfed the cities on the plain.

LOT AND HIS DAUGHTERS 30Afterward Lot left Zoar because he was afraid of the people there, and he went to live in a cave in the mountains with his two daughters. 31One day the older daughter said to her sister, "There are no men left anywhere in this entire area, so we can't get married like everyone else. And our father will soon be too old to have children. 32Come, let's get him drunk with wine, and then we will have sex with him. That way we will preserve our family line through our father."

33So that night they got him drunk with wine, and the older daughter went in and had intercourse with her father. He was unaware of her lying down or getting up again.

34The next morning the older daughter said to her younger sister, "I had sex with our father last night. Let's get him drunk with wine again tonight, and you go in and have sex with him. That way we will preserve our family line through our father." 35So that night they got him

SARAH *PERSONALITY PROFILE*

HAVE YOU EVER laughed out loud because you thought something was funny, only to discover that what you heard wasn't supposed to be funny? If so, you know how Sarah felt. When she overheard that she was going to have a baby, Sarah burst out laughing (Gen 18:10-12). After all, she was 90 years old and had not been able to conceive. The very idea of doing the impossible seemed . . . well, funny. But when God called her on that, she tried to fake her way out.

God promised to give Abraham a son through Sarah (Gen 17:16-21). Earlier, Sarah had taken matters into her own hands by giving her servant, Hagar, to Abraham to produce a son (see Gen 16). But that scheme had inspired anger and tears, rather than laughter.

God got the last laugh when Sarah's son was born. The impossible had become possible! God had her name the baby *Isaac*, which means "he laughs" (Gen 17:19 footnote).

Are you, like Sarah, tempted to laugh when faced with an impossible situation? God likes to do the impossible! Are you willing to trust him?

BOTTOM LINE: God responds to faith even in the midst of failure.
God is not bound by what usually happens. He can stretch the limits and cause unheard-of events to occur.

Sarah's story is told in Genesis 11:29–24:67. She also is mentioned in Isaiah 51:2; Romans 4:19; 9:9; Hebrews 11:11; 1 Peter 3:6.

UPS:
• *Was intensely loyal to her own child*
• *Became the mother of a nation and an ancestor of Jesus*
• *Was the first woman listed in the Hall of Faith in Hebrews 11*

DOWNS:
• *Had trouble believing God's promises to her*
• *Attempted to work problems out on her own, without consulting God*
• *Tried to cover her own faults by blaming others*

STATS:
• *Where: Married Abram in Ur of the Chaldeans, then moved with him to Canaan*
• *Occupation: Household manager*
• *Relatives: Terah (father); Abram, later called Abraham (husband); Nahor and Haran (half-brothers); Lot (nephew); Isaac (son)*

KEY VERSE: *Hebrews 11:11*

drunk with wine again, and the younger daughter went in and had intercourse with him. As before, he was unaware of her lying down or getting up again.

³⁶As a result, both of Lot's daughters became pregnant by their own father. ³⁷When the older daughter gave birth to a son, she named him Moab.* He became the ancestor of the nation now known as the Moabites. ³⁸When the younger daughter gave birth to a son, she named him Ben-ammi.* He became the ancestor of the nation now known as the Ammonites.

20 ABRAHAM DECEIVES ABIMELECH

Abraham moved south to the Negev and lived for a while between Kadesh and Shur, and then he moved on to Gerar. While living there as a foreigner, ²Abraham introduced his wife, Sarah, by saying, "She is my sister." So King Abimelech of Gerar sent for Sarah and had her brought to him at his palace.

³But that night God came to Abimelech in a dream and told him, "You are a dead man, for that woman you have taken is already married!"

⁴But Abimelech had not slept with her yet, so he said, "Lord, will you destroy an innocent nation? ⁵Didn't Abraham tell me, 'She is my sister'? And she herself said, 'Yes, he is my brother.' I acted in complete innocence! My hands are clean."

⁶In the dream God responded, "Yes, I know you are innocent. That's why I kept you from sinning against me, and why I did not let you touch her. ⁷Now return the woman to her husband, and he will pray for you, for he is a prophet. Then you will live. But if you don't return her to him, you can be sure that you and all your people will die."

⁸Abimelech got up early the next morning and quickly called all his servants together. When he told them what had happened, his men were terrified. ⁹Then Abimelech called for Abraham. "What have you done to us?" he demanded. "What crime have I committed that deserves treatment like this, making me and my kingdom guilty of this great sin? No one should ever do what you have done! ¹⁰Whatever possessed you to do such a thing?"

¹¹Abraham replied, "I thought, 'This is a godless place. They will want my wife and will kill me to get her.' ¹²And she really is my sister, for we both have the same father, but different mothers. And I married her. ¹³When God called

me to leave my father's home and to travel from place to place, I told her, 'Do me a favor. Wherever we go, tell the people that I am your brother.'"

¹⁴Then Abimelech took some of his sheep and goats, cattle, and male and female servants, and he presented them to Abraham. He also returned his wife, Sarah, to him. ¹⁵Then Abimelech said, "Look over my land and choose any place where you would like to live." ¹⁶And he said to Sarah, "Look, I am giving your 'brother' 1,000 pieces of silver* in the presence of all these witnesses. This is to compensate you for any wrong I may have done to you. This will settle any claim against me, and your reputation is cleared."

¹⁷Then Abraham prayed to God, and God healed Abimelech, his wife, and his female servants, so they could have children. ¹⁸For the LORD had caused all the women to be infertile because of what happened with Abraham's wife, Sarah.

21 THE BIRTH OF ISAAC

The LORD kept his word and did for Sarah exactly what he had promised. ²She became pregnant, and she gave birth to a son for Abraham in his old age. This happened at just the time God had said it would. ³And Abraham named their son Isaac. ⁴Eight days after Isaac was born, Abraham circumcised him as God had commanded. ⁵Abraham was 100 years old when Isaac was born.

⁶And Sarah declared, "God has brought me laughter.* All who hear about this will laugh with me. ⁷Who would have said to Abraham that Sarah would nurse a baby? Yet I have given Abraham a son in his old age!"

HAGAR AND ISHMAEL ARE SENT AWAY

⁸When Isaac grew up and was about to be weaned, Abraham prepared a huge feast to celebrate the occasion. ⁹But Sarah saw Ishmael—the son of Abraham and her Egyptian servant Hagar—making fun of her son, Isaac.* ¹⁰So she turned to Abraham and demanded, "Get rid of that slave woman and her son. He is not going to

....

SURPRISE!
(21:7) Even after repeated promises, a visit by two angels, and the appearance of the Lord himself, Sarah cried out with surprise and joy at the birth of her son. Because of her doubt, worry, and fear, she had forfeited the peace she could have felt in God's wonderful promise to her. The way to have peace of mind is to focus on God's promises, no matter what the circumstances are. Trust him to do what he says.

19:37 Moab sounds like a Hebrew term that means "from father." 19:38 Ben-ammi means "son of my kinsman." 20:16 Hebrew 1,000 [shekels] of silver, about 25 pounds or 11.4 kilograms in weight. 21:6 The name Isaac means "he laughs." 21:9 As in Greek version and Latin Vulgate; Hebrew lacks of her son, Isaac.

share the inheritance with my son, Isaac. I won't have it!"

¹¹This upset Abraham very much because Ishmael was his son. ¹²But God told Abraham, "Do not be upset over the boy and your servant. Do whatever Sarah tells you, for Isaac is the son through whom your descendants will be counted. ¹³But I will also make a nation of the descendants of Hagar's son because he is your son, too."

¹⁴So Abraham got up early the next morning, prepared food and a container of water, and strapped them on Hagar's shoulders. Then he sent her away with their son, and she wandered aimlessly in the wilderness of Beersheba.

¹⁵When the water was gone, she put the boy in the shade of a bush. ¹⁶Then she went and sat down by herself about a hundred yards* away. "I don't want to watch the boy die," she said, as she burst into tears.

¹⁷But God heard the boy crying, and the angel of God called to Hagar from heaven, "Hagar, what's wrong? Do not be afraid! God has heard the boy crying as he lies there. ¹⁸Go to him and comfort him, for I will make a great nation from his descendants."

¹⁹Then God opened Hagar's eyes, and she saw a well full of water. She quickly filled her water container and gave the boy a drink.

²⁰And God was with the boy as he grew up in the wilderness. He became a skillful archer, ²¹and he settled in the wilderness of Paran. His mother arranged for him to marry a woman from the land of Egypt.

ABRAHAM'S COVENANT WITH ABIMELECH

²²About this time, Abimelech came with Phicol, his army commander, to visit Abraham. "God is obviously with you, helping you in everything you do," Abimelech said. ²³"Swear to me in God's name that you will never deceive me, my children, or any of my descendants. I have been loyal to you, so now swear that you will be loyal to me and to this country where you are living as a foreigner."

²⁴Abraham replied, "Yes, I swear to it!" ²⁵Then Abraham complained to Abimelech about a well that Abimelech's servants had taken by force from Abraham's servants.

²⁶"This is the first I've heard of it," Abimelech

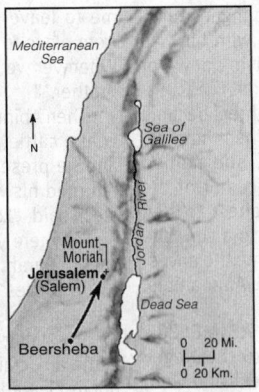

ABRAHAM'S TRIP TO MOUNT MORIAH
Abraham and Isaac traveled the 50 or 60 miles from Beersheba to Mount Moriah in about three days. This was a very difficult three days for Abraham, who was on his way to sacrifice his beloved son, Isaac.

answered. "I have no idea who is responsible. You have never complained about this before."

²⁷Abraham then gave some of his sheep, goats, and cattle to Abimelech, and they made a treaty. ²⁸But Abraham also took seven additional female lambs and set them off by themselves. ²⁹Abimelech asked, "Why have you set these seven apart from the others?"

³⁰Abraham replied, "Please accept these seven lambs to show your agreement that I dug this well." ³¹Then he named the place Beersheba (which means "well of the oath"), because that was where they had sworn the oath.

³²After making their covenant at Beersheba, Abimelech left with Phicol, the commander of his army, and they returned home to the land of the Philistines. ³³Then Abraham planted a tamarisk tree at Beersheba, and there he worshiped the LORD, the Eternal God.* ³⁴And Abraham lived as a foreigner in Philistine country for a long time.

22 ABRAHAM'S FAITH TESTED Some time later, God tested Abraham's faith. "Abraham!" God called.

"Yes," he replied. "Here I am."

²"Take your son, your only son—yes, Isaac, whom you love so much—and go to the land of Moriah. Go and sacrifice him as a burnt offering on one of the mountains, which I will show you."

³The next morning Abraham got up early. He saddled his donkey and took two of his servants with him, along with his son, Isaac. Then he chopped wood for a fire for a burnt offering and set out for the place God had told him about. ⁴On the third day of their journey, Abraham looked up and saw the place in the distance. ⁵"Stay here with the donkey," Abraham told the servants. "The boy and I will travel a little farther. We will worship there, and then we will come right back."

⁶So Abraham placed the wood for the burnt offering on Isaac's shoulders, while he himself carried the fire and the knife. As the two of them walked on together, ⁷Isaac turned to Abraham and said, "Father?"

"Yes, my son?" Abraham replied.

21:16 Hebrew *a bowshot.* **21:33** Hebrew *El-Olam.*

I WONDER...

What does God really expect from me? I hear so much from so many people that I almost feel overwhelmed. Do I have to be perfect to please him?

One essential quality about God is that he is very personal with each individual believer. Although he chooses not to treat everyone alike, he does have expectations of his kids. (Think of your parents' expectations for you.)

Some Christians may tell you about God's expectations based on where they are in their walk with him. If too many people are giving you advice, it could seem as though God expects way too much. If you are feeling overwhelmed, you might be listening to others' expectations, rather than God's.

So how can you please God?

The story of Cain and Abel (see Gen 4) gives a significant piece to the puzzle. Both of these men brought something to God, but only Abel's sacrifice pleased God. One reason was because Cain's heart was not really in his offering. He tried to please God out of obligation instead of love.

The first step in pleasing God is to examine our motivation for doing so. Do we really want to please him, or are we going through the motions because someone told us we should?

Obedience is the second step to pleasing God. It means loving him enough to listen to what he says, then following through on what we know he is telling us to do.

This is why reading the Bible every day is so important. We cannot obey what we do not know. All that God wants us to know is written very plainly in his Word.

Through the Holy Spirit, God speaks to us as we come to him with willing hearts. He gently shows us areas in our lives that we need to examine and change according to his timetable, not someone else's.

"We have the fire and the wood," the boy said, "but where is the sheep for the burnt offering?"

[8]"God will provide a sheep for the burnt offering, my son," Abraham answered. And they both walked on together.

[9]When they arrived at the place where God had told him to go, Abraham built an altar and arranged the wood on it. Then he tied his son, Isaac, and laid him on the altar on top of the wood. [10]And Abraham picked up the knife to kill his son as a sacrifice. [11]At that moment the angel of the LORD called to him from heaven, "Abraham! Abraham!"

"Yes," Abraham replied. "Here I am!"

[12]"Don't lay a hand on the boy!" the angel said. "Do not hurt him in any way, for now I know that you truly fear God. You have not withheld from me even your son, your only son."

[13]Then Abraham looked up and saw a ram caught by its horns in a thicket. So he took the ram and sacrificed it as a burnt offering in place of his son. [14]Abraham named the place Yahweh-Yireh (which means "the LORD will provide"). To this day, people still use that name as a proverb: "On the mountain of the LORD it will be provided."

[15]Then the angel of the LORD called again to Abraham from heaven. [16]"This is what the LORD says: Because you have obeyed me and have not withheld even your son, your only son, I swear by my own name that [17]I will certainly bless you. I will multiply your descendants*

22:17 Hebrew *seed;* also in 22:17b, 18.

beyond number, like the stars in the sky and the sand on the seashore. Your descendants will conquer the cities of their enemies. [18]And through your descendants all the nations of the earth will be blessed—all because you have obeyed me."

[19]Then they returned to the servants and traveled back to Beersheba, where Abraham continued to live.

[20]Soon after this, Abraham heard that Milcah, his brother Nahor's wife, had borne Nahor eight sons. [21]The oldest was named Uz, the next oldest was Buz, followed by Kemuel (the ancestor of the Arameans), [22]Kesed, Hazo, Pildash, Jidlaph, and Bethuel. [23](Bethuel became the father of Rebekah.) In addition to these eight sons from Milcah, [24]Nahor had four other children from his concubine Reumah. Their names were Tebah, Gaham, Tahash, and Maacah.

23 THE BURIAL OF SARAH
When Sarah was 127 years old, [2]she died at

....

PASSING THE TEST
(22:1-2) Why did God ask Abraham to sacrifice his son? Enemy nations practiced human sacrifice, but God condemned this as a terrible sin (Lev 20:1-5). God did not want Isaac to die; he wanted Abraham to prove that he loved God more than he loved his long-awaited son. Through this difficult experience, Abraham strengthened his commitment to God. He also learned about God's ability to provide. The purpose of testing is to strengthen our character and deepen our commitment to God. Are you feeling like you're being tested right now? How will you respond?

Kiriath-arba (now called Hebron) in the land of Canaan. There Abraham mourned and wept for her.

³Then, leaving her body, he said to the Hittite elders, ⁴"Here I am, a stranger and a foreigner among you. Please sell me a piece of land so I can give my wife a proper burial."

⁵The Hittites replied to Abraham, ⁶"Listen, my lord, you are an honored prince among us. Choose the finest of our tombs and bury her there. No one here will refuse to help you in this way."

⁷Then Abraham bowed low before the Hittites ⁸and said, "Since you are willing to help me in this way, be so kind as to ask Ephron son of Zohar ⁹to let me buy his cave at Machpelah, down at the end of his field. I will pay the full price in the presence of witnesses, so I will have a permanent burial place for my family."

¹⁰Ephron was sitting there among the others, and he answered Abraham as the others listened, speaking publicly before all the Hittite elders of the town. ¹¹"No, my lord," he said to Abraham, "please listen to me. I will give you the field and the cave. Here in the presence of my people, I give it to you. Go and bury your dead."

¹²Abraham again bowed low before the citizens of the land, ¹³and he replied to Ephron as everyone listened. "No, listen to me. I will buy it from you. Let me pay the full price for the field so I can bury my dead there."

¹⁴Ephron answered Abraham, ¹⁵"My lord, please listen to me. The land is worth 400 pieces* of silver, but what is that between friends? Go ahead and bury your dead."

¹⁶So Abraham agreed to Ephron's price and paid the amount he had suggested—400 pieces of silver, weighed according to the market standard. The Hittite elders witnessed the transaction.

¹⁷So Abraham bought the plot of land belonging to Ephron at Machpelah, near Mamre. This included the field itself, the cave that was in

23:15 Hebrew *400 shekels*, about 10 pounds or 4.6 kilograms in weight; also in 23:16.

ISAAC *PERSONALITY PROFILE*

LIKE IT OR NOT, your name is powerful. It sets you apart. It undoubtedly triggers some kind of reaction in people, based on the way you've treated them. When you hear your name spoken, you almost have to look. When people heard Isaac's name, they almost had to laugh!

Isaac's name means "he laughs." As with many Bible characters, there were several reasons Isaac got his name. Isaac's name reminded his parents of their first reaction of shocked laughter when God told them they would have a son though they were quite old. At other times, his name must have reminded them of the great joy they had when Isaac was born. His name was also a reminder of God's presence, for God had told Isaac's parents to give their child that name.

In a family of active leaders, Isaac was the quiet, "mind-my-own-business" type unless he had to be involved. He was the protected only child until Abraham arranged his marriage to Rebekah. Then Isaac allowed his wife to run their family. He rarely stood his ground and found it easier to compromise or lie than to confront.

In spite of these problems, Isaac was still a vital part of God's plan. Isaac learned the importance of faith in the one true God from his father. God's promise to Abraham to create a great nation through which he would bless the world was passed on to Isaac and to his twin sons.

Ever feel like Isaac—like you just go along with what your friends say or do, even though you believe otherwise? God works through people in spite of their weaknesses. Are you willing to tell God you're available to him, weaknesses and all? You will discover that his willingness to use you is even greater than your desire to be used.

BOTTOM LINE: Patience often brings rewards.
Both God's plans and his promises are larger than people.
God keeps his promises! He remains faithful though we are often faithless.

Isaac's story is told in Genesis 17:19; 21–22; 24–28; 35:27-29. He also is mentioned in Romans 9:7; Hebrews 11:17-20; James 2:21.

UPS:
• *Was the miracle child born to 90-year-old Sarah and 100-year-old Abraham*
• *The first descendant in fulfillment of God's promise to Abraham*
• *Seems to have been a caring and consistent husband, at least until his sons were born*
• *Demonstrated great patience*

DOWNS:
• *Tended to imitate his father and lie when under pressure*
• *Tried to avoid confrontation by bargaining*
• *Played favorites with his sons and alienated his wife*

STATS:
• *Where: The area called the Negev, in the southern part of Palestine, between Kadesh and Shur (Gen 20:1)*
• *Occupation: Wealthy livestock owner*
• *Relatives: Abraham and Sarah (parents); Ishmael (half-brother); Rebekah (wife); Esau and Jacob (twin sons)*

KEY VERSE: *Genesis 17:19*

it, and all the surrounding trees. ¹⁸It was transferred to Abraham as his permanent possession in the presence of the Hittite elders at the city gate. ¹⁹Then Abraham buried his wife, Sarah, there in Canaan, in the cave of Machpelah, near Mamre (also called Hebron). ²⁰So the field and the cave were transferred from the Hittites to Abraham for use as a permanent burial place.

24

A WIFE FOR ISAAC Abraham was now a very old man, and the LORD had blessed him in every way. ²One day Abraham said to his oldest servant, the man in charge of his household, "Take an oath by putting your hand under my thigh. ³Swear by the LORD, the God of heaven and earth, that you will not allow my son to marry one of these local Canaanite women. ⁴Go instead to my homeland, to my relatives, and find a wife there for my son Isaac."

⁵The servant asked, "But what if I can't find a young woman who is willing to travel so far from home? Should I then take Isaac there to live among your relatives in the land you came from?"

⁶"No!" Abraham responded. "Be careful never to take my son there. ⁷For the LORD, the God of heaven, who took me from my father's house and my native land, solemnly promised to give this land to my descendants.* He will send his angel ahead of you, and he will see to it that you find a wife there for my son. ⁸If she is unwilling to come back with you, then you are free from this oath of mine. But under no circumstances are you to take my son there."

⁹So the servant took an oath by putting his hand under the thigh of his master, Abraham. He swore to follow Abraham's instructions. ¹⁰Then he loaded ten of Abraham's camels with all kinds of expensive gifts from his master, and he traveled to distant Aram-naharaim. There he went to the town where Abraham's brother Nahor had settled. ¹¹He made the camels kneel beside a well just outside the town. It was evening, and the women were coming out to draw water.

¹²"O LORD, God of my master, Abraham," he prayed. "Please give me success today, and show unfailing love to my master, Abraham. ¹³See, I am standing here beside this spring, and the young women of the town are coming out to draw water. ¹⁴This is my request. I will ask one of them, 'Please give me a drink from your jug.' If she says, 'Yes, have a drink, and I will water your camels, too!'—let her be the one you have selected as Isaac's wife. This is how I will

24:7 Hebrew *seed*; also in 24:60.

WHAT THE BIBLE SAYS ABOUT MARRIAGE

Genesis 2:18-24—Marriage is God's idea.

Genesis 24:58-60—Commitment is essential to a successful marriage.

Genesis 29:18-20—Romance is important.

Jeremiah 33:10-11—Marriage holds times of great joy.

Malachi 2:14-15—Marriage creates the best environment for raising children.

Matthew 5:32—Unfaithfulness breaks the bond of trust, the foundation of all relationships.

Matthew 19:6—Marriage is permanent.

Romans 7:2-3—Ideally, only death should dissolve marriage.

Ephesians 5:21-33—Marriage is based on commitment, not just feelings.

Ephesians 5:23, 32—Marriage is a living symbol of Christ and the church.

Hebrews 13:4—Marriage is good and honorable.

---

know that you have shown unfailing love to my master."

¹⁵Before he had finished praying, he saw a young woman named Rebekah coming out with her water jug on her shoulder. She was the daughter of Bethuel, who was the son of Abraham's brother Nahor and his wife, Milcah. ¹⁶Rebekah was very beautiful and old enough to be married, but she was still a virgin. She went down to the spring, filled her jug, and came up again. ¹⁷Running over to her, the servant said, "Please give me a little drink of water from your jug."

¹⁸"Yes, my lord," she answered, "have a

....

HERE COMES THE BRIDE!
(24:4) Abraham wanted Isaac to marry a relative. This was a common and acceptable practice that had the added advantage of avoiding intermarriage with enemy nations. Also, parents usually would choose their sons' wives. Many of the chosen brides were teens! Are you thinking about getting married some day? What characteristics are you looking for in a future spouse? How much of a part will your parents play in your choice of a spouse?

INNER BEAUTY
(24:15-16) Rebekah had physical beauty, but Abraham's servant was looking for a sign of inner beauty. Our appearance is important to us, and we spend time and money to improve the way we look. But inner beauty is even more important. How do we develop inner beauty? Patience, kindness, and joy are the beauty treatments that help us become truly lovely on the inside.

drink." And she quickly lowered her jug from her shoulder and gave him a drink. ¹⁹When she had given him a drink, she said, "I'll draw water for your camels, too, until they have had enough to drink." ²⁰So she quickly emptied her jug into the watering trough and ran back to the well to draw water for all his camels.

²¹The servant watched her in silence, wondering whether or not the LORD had given him success in his mission. ²²Then at last, when the camels had finished drinking, he took out a gold ring for her nose and two large gold bracelets* for her wrists.

²³"Whose daughter are you?" he asked. "And please tell me, would your father have any room to put us up for the night?"

²⁴"I am the daughter of Bethuel," she replied. "My grandparents are Nahor and Milcah. ²⁵Yes, we have plenty of straw and feed for the camels, and we have room for guests."

²⁶The man bowed low and worshiped the LORD. ²⁷"Praise the LORD, the God of my master, Abraham," he said. "The LORD has shown unfailing love and faithfulness to my master, for he has led me straight to my master's relatives."

²⁸The young woman ran home to tell her family everything that had happened. ²⁹Now Rebekah had a brother named Laban, who ran out to meet the man at the spring. ³⁰He had seen the nose-ring and the bracelets on his sister's wrists, and had heard Rebekah tell what the man had said. So he rushed out to the spring, where the man was still standing beside his camels. ³¹Laban said to him, "Come and stay with us, you who are blessed by the LORD! Why are you standing here outside the town when I have a room all ready for you and a place prepared for the camels?"

³²So the man went home with Laban, and Laban unloaded the camels, gave him straw for their bedding, fed them, and provided water for the man and the camel drivers to wash their feet. ³³Then food was served. But Abraham's servant said, "I don't want to eat until I have told you why I have come."

"All right," Laban said, "tell us."

³⁴"I am Abraham's servant," he explained. ³⁵"And the LORD has greatly blessed my master; he has become a wealthy man. The LORD has given him flocks of sheep and goats, herds of cattle, a fortune in silver and gold, and many male and female servants and camels and donkeys.

³⁶"When Sarah, my master's wife, was very old, she gave birth to my master's son, and my master has given him everything he owns. ³⁷And my master made me take an oath. He said, 'Do not allow my son to marry one of these local Canaanite women. ³⁸Go instead to my father's house, to my relatives, and find a wife there for my son.'

³⁹"But I said to my master, 'What if I can't find a young woman who is willing to go back with me?' ⁴⁰He responded, 'The LORD, in whose presence I have lived, will send his angel with you and will make your mission successful. Yes, you must find a wife for my son from among my relatives, from my father's family. ⁴¹Then you will have fulfilled your obligation. But if you go to my relatives and they refuse to let her go with you, you will be free from my oath.'

⁴²"So today when I came to the spring, I prayed this prayer: 'O LORD, God of my master, Abraham, please give me success on this mission. ⁴³See, I am standing here beside this spring. This is my request. When a young woman comes to draw water, I will say to her, "Please give me a little drink of water from your jug." ⁴⁴If she says, "Yes, have a drink, and I will draw water for your camels, too," let her be the one you have selected to be the wife of my master's son.'

⁴⁵"Before I had finished praying in my heart, I saw Rebekah coming out with her water jug on her shoulder. She went down to the spring and drew water. So I said to her, 'Please give me a drink.' ⁴⁶She quickly lowered her jug from her shoulder and said, 'Yes, have a drink, and I will water your camels, too!' So I drank, and then she watered the camels.

⁴⁷"Then I asked, 'Whose daughter are you?' She replied, 'I am the daughter of Bethuel, and my grandparents are Nahor and Milcah.' So I put the ring on her nose, and the bracelets on her wrists.

⁴⁸"Then I bowed low and worshiped the LORD. I praised the LORD, the God of my master, Abraham, because he had led me straight to my master's niece to be his son's wife. ⁴⁹So tell me—will you or won't you show unfailing love and faithfulness to my master? Please tell me yes or no, and then I'll know what to do next."

⁵⁰Then Laban and Bethuel replied, "The LORD has obviously brought you here, so there is nothing we can say. ⁵¹Here is Rebekah; take her and go. Yes, let her be the wife of your master's son, as the LORD has directed."

⁵²When Abraham's servant heard their answer, he bowed down to the ground and worshiped the LORD. ⁵³Then he brought out silver and gold jewelry and clothing and presented

24:22 Hebrew *a gold nose-ring weighing a half shekel* [0.2 ounces or 6 grams] *and two gold bracelets weighing 10 shekels* [4 ounces or 114 grams].

them to Rebekah. He also gave expensive presents to her brother and mother. ⁵⁴Then they ate their meal, and the servant and the men with him stayed there overnight.

But early the next morning, Abraham's servant said, "Send me back to my master."

⁵⁵"But we want Rebekah to stay with us at least ten days," her brother and mother said. "Then she can go."

⁵⁶But he said, "Don't delay me. The LORD has made my mission successful; now send me back so I can return to my master."

⁵⁷"Well," they said, "we'll call Rebekah and ask her what she thinks." ⁵⁸So they called Rebekah. "Are you willing to go with this man?" they asked her.

And she replied, "Yes, I will go."

⁵⁹So they said good-bye to Rebekah and sent her away with Abraham's servant and his men. The woman who had been Rebekah's childhood nurse went along with her. ⁶⁰They gave her this blessing as she parted:

"Our sister, may you become
    the mother of many millions!
May your descendants be strong
    and conquer the cities of their enemies."

⁶¹Then Rebekah and her servant girls mounted the camels and followed the man. So Abraham's servant took Rebekah and went on his way.

⁶²Meanwhile, Isaac, whose home was in the Negev, had returned from Beer-lahai-roi. ⁶³One evening as he was walking and meditating in the fields, he looked up and saw the camels coming. ⁶⁴When Rebekah looked up and saw Isaac, she quickly dismounted from her camel. ⁶⁵"Who is that man walking through the fields to meet us?" she asked the servant.

And he replied, "It is my master." So Rebekah covered her face with her veil. ⁶⁶Then the servant told Isaac everything he had done.

⁶⁷And Isaac brought Rebekah into his mother Sarah's tent, and she became his wife. He loved her deeply, and she was a special comfort to him after the death of his mother.

25 **THE DEATH OF ABRAHAM** Abraham married another wife, whose name was Keturah. ²She gave birth to Zimran, Jokshan, Medan, Midian, Ishbak, and Shuah. ³Jokshan was the father of Sheba and Dedan. Dedan's descendants were the Asshurites, Letushites, and Leummites. ⁴Midian's sons were Ephah, Epher, Hanoch, Abida, and Eldaah. These were all descendants of Abraham through Keturah.

⁵Abraham gave everything he owned to his son Isaac. ⁶But before he died, he gave gifts to

---

PERSONALITY PROFILE **REBEKAH**

UPS:
- *Took immediate action when confronted with a need*
- *Persistent in her plans*

DOWNS:
- *Showed more initiative than wisdom*
- *Played favorites with her sons*
- *Deceived her husband*

STATS:
- *Where: Haran, Canaan*
- *Occupation: Household manager*
- *Relatives: Bethuel (father); Nahor and Milcah (grandparents); Isaac (husband); Laban (brother); Esau and Jacob (twin sons)*

KEY VERSE: *Genesis 24:67*

SOME PEOPLE KNOW how to get things started. They're initiators. They naturally make the first moves. Know anyone like this? Then you know what Rebekah was like.

When Rebekah saw something that needed to be done, she took action. Look at what she did at the well near her home. She gave a drink to Abraham's servant, who had come to find a wife for Isaac. That was kind. Then she offered to give a drink to his 10 thirsty camels. That really caught his attention—and led to a marriage between Isaac and Rebekah! Often a person's helpfulness makes a deeper impression than his or her appearance.

Other times, though, Rebekah acted without such good results. She found ways to help her favorite son, Jacob, do better than his brother, Esau. But Esau, an outdoorsy kind of guy, was Isaac's favorite. Rebekah later tricked her husband into giving to Jacob the special blessing that he meant to give Esau. She tried to accomplish God's plan *her* way and made a mess.

Most of us, if we're honest, will admit that we sometimes try to justify our actions in order to get our own way. (Sound like anyone you know?) Often we even want God's approval for our plans! Before we take action we need to be truthful about our real motives. Asking ourselves this question can help: "Am I sure God wants me to do this, or do I just want him to approve my plan?" The choice is up to you.

BOTTOM LINE: True followers of God are guided by his Word.
    God makes use of even our mistakes in his plan.
    Parental favoritism hurts a family.

Rebekah's story is told in Genesis 24–27. She also is mentioned in Romans 9:10-12.

the sons of his concubines and sent them off to a land in the east, away from Isaac.

7Abraham lived for 175 years, 8and he died at a ripe old age, having lived a long and satisfying life. He breathed his last and joined his ancestors in death. 9His sons Isaac and Ishmael buried him in the cave of Machpelah, near Mamre, in the field of Ephron son of Zohar the Hittite. 10This was the field Abraham had purchased from the Hittites and where he had buried his wife Sarah. 11After Abraham's death, God blessed his son Isaac, who settled near Beer-lahai-roi in the Negev.

ISHMAEL'S DESCENDANTS
12This is the account of the family of Ishmael, the son of Abraham through Hagar, Sarah's Egyptian servant. 13Here is a list, by their names and clans, of Ishmael's descendants: The oldest was Nebaioth, followed by Kedar, Adbeel, Mibsam, 14Mishma, Dumah, Massa, 15Hadad, Tema, Jetur, Naphish, and Kedemah. 16These twelve sons of Ishmael became the founders of twelve tribes named after them, listed according to the places they settled and camped. 17Ishmael lived for 137 years. Then he breathed his last and joined his ancestors in death. 18Ishmael's descendants occupied the region from Havilah to Shur, which is east of Egypt in the direction of Asshur. There they lived in open hostility toward all their relatives.*

THE BIRTHS OF ESAU AND JACOB
19This is the account of the family of Isaac, the son of Abraham. 20When Isaac was forty years old, he married Rebekah, the daughter of Bethuel the Aramean from Paddan-aram and the sister of Laban the Aramean.

21Isaac pleaded with the LORD on behalf of his wife, because she was unable to have children. The LORD answered Isaac's prayer, and Rebekah became pregnant with twins. 22But the two children struggled with each other in her womb. So she went to ask the LORD about it. "Why is this happening to me?" she asked.

23And the LORD told her, "The sons in your womb will become two nations. From the very beginning, the two nations will be rivals. One nation will be stronger than the other; and your older son will serve your younger son."

24And when the time came to give birth, Rebekah discovered that she did indeed have twins! 25The first one was very red at birth and covered with thick hair like a fur coat. So they named him Esau.* 26Then the other twin was born with his hand grasping Esau's heel. So they named him Jacob.* Isaac was sixty years old when the twins were born.

ESAU SELLS HIS BIRTHRIGHT
27As the boys grew up, Esau became a skillful hunter. He was an outdoorsman, but Jacob had a quiet temperament, preferring to stay at home. 28Isaac loved Esau because he enjoyed eating the wild game Esau brought home, but Rebekah loved Jacob.

29One day when Jacob was cooking some stew, Esau arrived home from the wilderness exhausted and hungry. 30Esau said to Jacob, "I'm starved! Give me some of that red stew!" (This is how Esau got his other name, Edom, which means "red.")

31"All right," Jacob replied, "but trade me your rights as the firstborn son."

32"Look, I'm dying of starvation!" said Esau. "What good is my birthright to me now?"

33But Jacob said, "First you must swear that your birthright is mine." So Esau swore an oath, thereby selling all his rights as the firstborn to his brother, Jacob.

34Then Jacob gave Esau some bread and lentil stew. Esau ate the meal, then got up and left. He showed contempt for his rights as the firstborn.

26 ISAAC DECEIVES ABIMELECH
A severe famine now struck the land, as had happened before in Abraham's time. So Isaac moved to Gerar, where Abimelech, king of the Philistines, lived.

2The LORD appeared to Isaac and said, "Do not go down to Egypt, but do as I tell you. 3Live here as a foreigner in this land, and I will be with you and bless you. I hereby confirm that I will give all these lands to you and your descendants,* just as I solemnly promised Abraham, your father. 4I will cause your descendants to become as numerous as the stars of the sky, and I will give them all these lands. And through your descendants all the nations of the earth will be blessed. 5I will do this because Abraham listened to me and obeyed all my requirements,

---

IMPULSE BUYING
(25:29-33) Esau traded the lasting benefits of his birthright for the immediate pleasure of food. The pressure of the moment distorted his perspective and made his decision seem urgent. Can you relate? When you see something you want, what's your first impulse? Do you have to have what you want right away? Or are you usually willing to wait? We can avoid making Esau's mistake by comparing the short-term satisfaction with its long-range consequences before we act.

25:18 The meaning of the Hebrew is uncertain. **25:25** *Esau* sounds like a Hebrew term that means "hair." **25:26** *Jacob* sounds like the Hebrew words for "heel" and "deceiver." **26:3** Hebrew *seed;* also in 26:4, 24.

commands, decrees, and instructions." ⁶So Isaac stayed in Gerar.

⁷When the men who lived there asked Isaac about his wife, Rebekah, he said, "She is my sister." He was afraid to say, "She is my wife." He thought, "They will kill me to get her, because she is so beautiful." ⁸But some time later, Abimelech, king of the Philistines, looked out his window and saw Isaac caressing Rebekah.

⁹Immediately, Abimelech called for Isaac and exclaimed, "She is obviously your wife! Why did you say, 'She is my sister'?"

"Because I was afraid someone would kill me to get her from me," Isaac replied.

¹⁰"How could you do this to us?" Abimelech exclaimed. "One of my people might easily have taken your wife and slept with her, and you would have made us guilty of great sin."

¹¹Then Abimelech issued a public proclamation: "Anyone who touches this man or his wife will be put to death!"

CONFLICT OVER WATER RIGHTS ¹²When Isaac planted his crops that year, he harvested a hundred times more grain than he planted, for the LORD blessed him. ¹³He became a very rich man, and his wealth continued to grow. ¹⁴He acquired so many flocks of sheep and goats, herds of cattle, and servants that the Philistines became jealous of him. ¹⁵So the Philistines filled up all of Isaac's wells with dirt. These were the wells that had been dug by the servants of his father, Abraham.

¹⁶Finally, Abimelech ordered Isaac to leave the country. "Go somewhere else," he said, "for you have become too powerful for us."

¹⁷So Isaac moved away to the Gerar Valley, where he set up their tents and settled down. ¹⁸He reopened the wells his father had dug, which the Philistines had filled in after Abraham's death. Isaac also restored the names Abraham had given them.

¹⁹Isaac's servants also dug in the Gerar Valley and discovered a well of fresh water. ²⁰But then the shepherds from Gerar came and claimed the spring. "This is our water," they said, and they argued over it with Isaac's herdsmen. So Isaac named the well Esek (which means "argument"). ²¹Isaac's men then dug another well, but again there was a dispute over it. So Isaac named it Sitnah (which means "hostility"). ²²Abandoning that one, Isaac moved on and dug another well. This time there was no dispute over it, so Isaac named the place Rehoboth (which means "open space"), for he said, "At last the LORD has created enough space for us to prosper in this land."

²³From there Isaac moved to Beersheba, ²⁴where the LORD appeared to him on the night of his arrival. "I am the God of your father, Abraham," he said. "Do not be afraid, for I am with you and will bless you. I will multiply your descendants, and they will become a great nation. I will do this because of my promise to Abraham, my servant." ²⁵Then Isaac built an altar there and worshiped the LORD. He set up his camp at that place, and his servants dug another well.

ISAAC'S COVENANT WITH ABIMELECH ²⁶One day King Abimelech came from Gerar with his adviser, Ahuzzath, and also Phicol, his army commander. ²⁷"Why have you come here?" Isaac asked. "You obviously hate me, since you kicked me off your land."

²⁸They replied, "We can plainly see that the LORD is with you. So we want to enter into a sworn treaty with you. Let's make a covenant. ²⁹Swear that you will not harm us, just as we have never troubled you. We have always treated you well, and we sent you away from us in peace. And now look how the LORD has blessed you!"

³⁰So Isaac prepared a covenant feast to celebrate the treaty, and they ate and drank together. ³¹Early the next morning, they each took a solemn oath not to interfere with each other. Then Isaac sent them home again, and they left him in peace.

³²That very day Isaac's servants came and told him about a new well they had dug. "We've found water!" they exclaimed. ³³So Isaac named the well Shibah (which means "oath"). And to this day the town that grew up there is called Beersheba (which means "well of the oath").

···

JEALOUSY
(26:12-16) God kept his promise to bless Isaac. The neighboring Philistines grew jealous because everything Isaac did seemed to go right. So they filled up his wells with dirt and tried to get rid of him. Jealousy is a dividing force strong enough to tear apart the mightiest of nations or the closest of friends. When you find yourself becoming jealous of others, try thanking God for their good fortune. And thank God for what he has already given you. A thankful attitude is a helpful way to keep jealousy and anger under control.

PARENTS AND CHOICES
(26:34-35) Esau's marriages to women from an enemy nation caused his parents grief. After all, he didn't allow them to have any say over his choice of brides. Since parents usually arranged marriages for their offspring, Esau's decision spoke volumes about his relationship with his folks. What do your decisions reveal about your relationship with your parent or parents? What could you do to improve that relationship?

34At the age of forty, Esau married two Hittite wives: Judith, the daughter of Beeri, and Basemath, the daughter of Elon. 35But Esau's wives made life miserable for Isaac and Rebekah.

27 JACOB STEALS ESAU'S BLESSING

One day when Isaac was old and turning blind, he called for Esau, his older son, and said, "My son."

"Yes, Father?" Esau replied.

2"I am an old man now," Isaac said, "and I don't know when I may die. 3Take your bow and a quiver full of arrows, and go out into the open country to hunt some wild game for me. 4Prepare my favorite dish, and bring it here for me to eat. Then I will pronounce the blessing that belongs to you, my firstborn son, before I die."

5But Rebekah overheard what Isaac had said to his son Esau. So when Esau left to hunt for the wild game, 6she said to her son Jacob, "Listen. I overheard your father say to Esau, 7'Bring me some wild game and prepare me a delicious meal. Then I will bless you in the LORD's presence before I die.' 8Now, my son, listen to me. Do exactly as I tell you. 9Go out to the flocks, and bring me two fine young goats. I'll use them to prepare your father's favorite dish. 10Then take the food to your father so he can eat it and bless you before he dies."

11"But look," Jacob replied to Rebekah, "my brother, Esau, is a hairy man, and my skin is smooth. 12What if my father touches me? He'll see that I'm trying to trick him, and then he'll curse me instead of blessing me."

13But his mother replied, "Then let the curse

GOING FOR THE GOAL?
(27:5-10) When Rebekah learned that Isaac was preparing to bless Esau, she quickly devised a plan to trick him into blessing Jacob instead. Although God had already told her that Jacob would become the family leader (25:23), Rebekah took matters into her own hands. She resorted to doing something wrong to try to bring about what God had already said would happen. For Rebekah, the end justified the means. Does that behavior sound familiar? Think about your goals. Are you, like Rebekah, tempted to take matters into your own hands in order to achieve those goals? Rebekah compromised her integrity to get what she wanted. No goal is worth that.

ESAU *PERSONALITY PROFILE*

AT SOME POINT in your life, you have probably had people tell you to use common sense. But did anyone ever explain what that meant? "Using common sense" means refusing to do something that you know will bring results you won't like.

Esau had a real problem with common sense. He made many wrong decisions because he didn't stop to think about what could happen. He wanted things right away without figuring out what he would have to pay later. Trading his birthright for a bowl of stew was one example of this problem. He also chose wives in direct opposition to his parents' wishes (see Gen 28:6-9).

What are you willing to trade for the things you want? Do you find yourself willing at times to give anything—even your relationships with family and friendships, reputation, body, or soul—to get what you feel you need *now?* Maybe, like Esau, you haven't been using common sense. If so, your first response, also like Esau, may be to get angry. That isn't necessarily wrong, as long as you direct the energy of that anger toward finding a solution and not toward punishing yourself or others.

Your greatest need probably is to find a new way to measure how important things are to you. Up until now, your only measurement may have been to ask, "Do I need this now?" But the best measurement of value comes from God and his Word. In other words, you could ask: "Is this what God wants?" A relationship with him will not only give an ultimate purpose to your life but will also be a daily guideline for real common sense living.

BOTTOM LINE: Although God allows certain events in our lives to accomplish his overall purposes, we are still responsible for our actions.

Consequences are important to consider.

It is possible to have great anger and yet not sin.

Esau's story is told in Genesis 25:19–28:9; 32–33; 36. He also is mentioned in Malachi 1:2-4; Romans 9:13; Hebrews 12:16-17.

UPS:
• *Ancestor of the Edomites*
• *Known for his archery skill*
• *Able to forgive after explosive anger*

DOWNS:
• *When faced with important decisions, tended to choose instant gratification rather than the long-range results*
• *Angered his parents by poor marriage choices*

STATS:
• *Where: Canaan*
• *Occupation: Skillful hunter*
• *Relatives: Isaac and Rebekah (parents); Jacob (twin brother); Judith, Basemath, and Mahalath (wives)*

KEY VERSE: *Hebrews 12:17*

fall on me, my son! Just do what I tell you. Go out and get the goats for me!"

¹⁴So Jacob went out and got the young goats for his mother. Rebekah took them and prepared a delicious meal, just the way Isaac liked it. ¹⁵Then she took Esau's favorite clothes, which were there in the house, and gave them to her younger son, Jacob. ¹⁶She covered his arms and the smooth part of his neck with the skin of the young goats. ¹⁷Then she gave Jacob the delicious meal, including freshly baked bread.

¹⁸So Jacob took the food to his father. "My father?" he said.

"Yes, my son," Isaac answered. "Who are you—Esau or Jacob?"

¹⁹Jacob replied, "It's Esau, your firstborn son. I've done as you told me. Here is the wild game. Now sit up and eat it so you can give me your blessing."

²⁰Isaac asked, "How did you find it so quickly, my son?"

"The LORD your God put it in my path!" Jacob replied.

²¹Then Isaac said to Jacob, "Come closer so I can touch you and make sure that you really are Esau." ²²So Jacob went closer to his father, and Isaac touched him. "The voice is Jacob's, but the hands are Esau's," Isaac said. ²³But he did not recognize Jacob, because Jacob's hands felt hairy just like Esau's. So Isaac prepared to bless Jacob. ²⁴"But are you really my son Esau?" he asked.

"Yes, I am," Jacob replied.

²⁵Then Isaac said, "Now, my son, bring me the wild game. Let me eat it, and then I will give you my blessing." So Jacob took the food to his father, and Isaac ate it. He also drank the wine that Jacob served him. ²⁶Then Isaac said to Jacob, "Please come a little closer and kiss me, my son."

²⁷So Jacob went over and kissed him. And when Isaac caught the smell of his clothes, he was finally convinced, and he blessed his son. He said, "Ah! The smell of my son is like the smell of the outdoors, which the LORD has blessed!

²⁸ "From the dew of heaven
    and the richness of the earth,
may God always give you abundant harvests
        of grain
    and bountiful new wine.
²⁹ May many nations become your servants,
    and may they bow down to you.
May you be the master over your brothers,

and may your mother's sons bow down to
        you.
All who curse you will be cursed,
    and all who bless you will be blessed."

³⁰As soon as Isaac had finished blessing Jacob, and almost before Jacob had left his father, Esau returned from his hunt. ³¹Esau prepared a delicious meal and brought it to his father. Then he said, "Sit up, my father, and eat my wild game so you can give me your blessing."

³²But Isaac asked him, "Who are you?"

Esau replied, "It's your son, your firstborn son, Esau."

³³Isaac began to tremble uncontrollably and said, "Then who just served me wild game? I have already eaten it, and I blessed him just before you came. And yes, that blessing must stand!"

³⁴When Esau heard his father's words, he let out a loud and bitter cry. "Oh my father, what about me? Bless me, too!" he begged.

³⁵But Isaac said, "Your brother was here, and he tricked me. He has taken away your blessing."

³⁶Esau exclaimed, "No wonder his name is Jacob, for now he has cheated me twice.* First he took my rights as the firstborn, and now he has stolen my blessing. Oh, haven't you saved even one blessing for me?"

³⁷Isaac said to Esau, "I have made Jacob your master and have declared that all his brothers will be his servants. I have guaranteed him an abundance of grain and wine—what is left for me to give you, my son?"

³⁸Esau pleaded, "But do you have only one blessing? Oh my father, bless me, too!" Then Esau broke down and wept.

³⁹Finally, his father, Isaac, said to him,

"You will live away from the richness of the
        earth,
    and away from the dew of the heaven
        above.
⁴⁰ You will live by your sword,
    and you will serve your brother.

27:36 *Jacob* sounds like the Hebrew words for "heel" and "deceiver."

WARNING!
(27:11-12) How we react to a moral problem or temptation often exposes our real attitudes or agendas. Sometimes we're more worried about getting caught than about doing what's right. Jacob did not seem concerned about the deceitfulness of his mother's plan; instead he feared getting in trouble while carrying it out. If you are worried about getting caught, you are probably in a position that is less than honest. The fear of getting caught is a warning to do right. Jacob paid a huge price for carrying out this dishonest plan. You can choose to do what is right!

But when you decide to break free,
  you will shake his yoke from your neck."

JACOB FLEES TO PADDAN-ARAM ⁴¹From that time on, Esau hated Jacob because their father had given Jacob the blessing. And Esau began to scheme: "I will soon be mourning my father's death. Then I will kill my brother, Jacob."

⁴²But Rebekah heard about Esau's plans. So she sent for Jacob and told him, "Listen, Esau is consoling himself by plotting to kill you. ⁴³So listen carefully, my son. Get ready and flee to my brother, Laban, in Haran. ⁴⁴Stay there with him until your brother cools off. ⁴⁵When he calms down and forgets what you have done to him, I will send for you to come back. Why should I lose both of you in one day?"

⁴⁶Then Rebekah said to Isaac, "I'm sick and tired of these local Hittite women! I would rather die than see Jacob marry one of them."

28 So Isaac called for Jacob, blessed him, and said, "You must not marry any of these Canaanite women. ²Instead, go at once to Paddan-aram, to the house of your grandfather Bethuel, and marry one of your uncle Laban's daughters. ³May God Almighty* bless you and give you many children. And may your descendants multiply and become many nations! ⁴May God pass on to you and your descendants* the blessings he promised to Abraham. May you own this land where you are now living as a foreigner, for God gave this land to Abraham."

⁵So Isaac sent Jacob away, and he went to Paddan-aram to stay with his uncle Laban, his mother's brother, the son of Bethuel the Aramean.

⁶Esau knew that his father, Isaac, had blessed Jacob and sent him to Paddan-aram to find a wife, and that he had warned Jacob, "You must not marry a Canaanite woman." ⁷He also knew that Jacob had obeyed his parents and gone to Paddan-aram. ⁸It was now very clear to Esau that his father did not like the local Canaanite women. ⁹So Esau visited his uncle Ishmael's family and married one of Ishmael's daughters, in addition to the wives he already had. His new wife's name was Mahalath. She

was the sister of Nebaioth and the daughter of Ishmael, Abraham's son.

JACOB'S DREAM AT BETHEL ¹⁰Meanwhile, Jacob left Beersheba and traveled toward Haran. ¹¹At sundown he arrived at a good place to set up camp and stopped there for the night. Jacob found a stone to rest his head against and lay down to sleep. ¹²As he slept, he dreamed of a stairway that reached from the earth up to heaven. And he saw the angels of God going up and down the stairway.

¹³At the top of the stairway stood the LORD, and he said, "I am the LORD, the God of your grandfather Abraham, and the God of your father, Isaac. The ground you are lying on belongs to you. I am giving it to you and your descendants. ¹⁴Your descendants will be as numerous as the dust of the earth! They will spread out in all directions—to the west and the east, to the north and the south. And all the families of the earth will be blessed through you and your descendants. ¹⁵What's more, I am with you, and I will protect you wherever you go. One day I will bring you back to this land. I will not leave you until I have finished giving you everything I have promised you."

¹⁶Then Jacob awoke from his sleep and said, "Surely the LORD is in this place, and I wasn't even aware of it!" ¹⁷But he was also afraid and said, "What an awesome place this is! It is none other than the house of God, the very gateway to heaven!"

¹⁸The next morning Jacob got up very early. He took the stone he had rested his head against, and he set it upright as a memorial pillar. Then he poured olive oil over it. ¹⁹He named that place Bethel (which means "house of God"), although it was previously called Luz.

²⁰Then Jacob made this vow: "If God will indeed be with me and protect me on this journey, and if he will provide me with food and clothing, ²¹and if I return safely to my father's home, then the LORD will certainly be my God. ²²And this memorial pillar I have set up will become a place for worshiping God, and I will present to God a tenth of everything he gives me."

29 **JACOB ARRIVES AT PADDAN-ARAM** Then Jacob hurried on, finally arriving in the land of the east. ²He saw a well in the distance. Three flocks of sheep and goats lay in an open field beside it, waiting to be watered. But a heavy stone covered the mouth of the well. ³It was the custom there to wait for all the

---

OWNING YOUR FAITH
(28:10-15) God's covenant promise to Abraham and Isaac was offered to Jacob as well. But it was not enough to be Abraham's grandson; Jacob had to establish his own relationship with God. God has no grandchildren; each of us must have a relationship with him. Hearing wonderful stories about Christians in your family is great, but you need to become part of the story yourself (see Gal 3:6-7).

28:3 Hebrew *El-Shaddai.*   28:4 Hebrew *seed;* also in 28:13, 14.

flocks to arrive before removing the stone and watering the animals. Afterward the stone would be placed back over the mouth of the well. ⁴Jacob went over to the shepherds and asked, "Where are you from, my friends?"

"We are from Haran," they answered.

⁵"Do you know a man there named Laban, the grandson of Nahor?" he asked.

"Yes, we do," they replied.

⁶"Is he doing well?" Jacob asked.

"Yes, he's well," they answered. "Look, here comes his daughter Rachel with the flock now."

⁷Jacob said, "Look, it's still broad daylight—too early to round up the animals. Why don't you water the sheep and goats so they can get back out to pasture?"

⁸"We can't water the animals until all the flocks have arrived," they replied. "Then the shepherds move the stone from the mouth of the well, and we water all the sheep and goats."

⁹Jacob was still talking with them when Rachel arrived with her father's flock, for she was a shepherd. ¹⁰And because Rachel was his cousin—the daughter of Laban, his mother's brother—and because the sheep and goats belonged to his uncle Laban, Jacob went over to the well and moved the stone from its mouth and watered his uncle's flock. ¹¹Then Jacob kissed Rachel, and he wept aloud. ¹²He explained to Rachel that he was her cousin on her father's side—the son of her aunt Rebekah. So Rachel quickly ran and told her father, Laban.

¹³As soon as Laban heard that his nephew Jacob had arrived, he ran out to meet him. He embraced and kissed him and brought him home. When Jacob had told him his story,

PERSONALITY PROFILE JACOB

KNOW ANYONE who's a born opportunist? You know—someone who makes the most of every opportunity to get what he or she wants. That's what Jacob was known for.

Jacob's name means "usurper," or "grabber," and he certainly lived up to it. He got the name by grabbing his twin brother Esau's heel while they were being born. Later, after he grabbed his brother's birthright and blessing, he had to run for his life.

When Jacob ran away from home, God appeared to him. God let Jacob know he was real and that he planned to work through Jacob despite Jacob's weakness. Shortly after this, Jacob had to live with his uncle Laban who was the king of opportunists!

Jacob agreed to seven years of labor for Laban in order to marry Laban's daughter, Rachel. But Laban pulled a fast one and gave his oldest daughter, Leah, to Jacob instead. To gain the woman he really wanted, Jacob was forced to work another seven years.

Although Jacob gained 20 years' worth of patience lessons through his uncle's schemes (see Gen 31:38), he realized that he was where God wanted him to be. When Jacob finally left Laban, he had become a different kind of grabber. This time, by the Jordan River, he grabbed on to God and wouldn't let go. He realized the value of God's presence and blessing.

Since God had changed Jacob, he changed his name as well. He would now be called Israel. By the time Jacob (Israel) was an old man, he wasn't so much a *grabber* as someone who had been *grabbed* by God. He no longer made plans without including God.

At what times and places has God made himself known to you? Are you more like the young Jacob, forcing God to track you down in the wilderness of your own plans and mistakes? Or are you more like the Jacob who placed his desires and plans before God for his approval before taking any action?

BOTTOM LINE: True security comes from God, rather than the material things you have.

All human intentions and actions—for good or for evil—are woven by God into his ongoing plan.

Jacob's story is told in Genesis 25:19–35:29; 37, 42–50. He also is mentioned in Hosea 12:2-13; Matthew 1:2; 22:31-32; Acts 3:13; 7:46; Romans 9:10-13; Hebrews 11:9, 20-21.

UPS:
- *Father of the 12 tribes of Israel*
- *Third in Abraham's line of God's plan*
- *Determined; willing to work long and hard for what he wanted*
- *Successful livestock owner*

DOWNS:
- *When faced with conflict, relied on his own resources rather than going to God for help*
- *Wanted to fill his life with things*

STATS:
- *Where: Canaan*
- *Occupations: Shepherd, livestock owner*
- *Relatives: Isaac and Rebekah (parents); Esau (twin brother); Laban (father-in-law); Rachel and Leah (wives); twelve sons and one daughter*

KEY VERSE: *Genesis 28:15*

14Laban exclaimed, "You really are my own flesh and blood!"

JACOB MARRIES LEAH AND RACHEL After Jacob had stayed with Laban for about a month, 15Laban said to him, "You shouldn't work for me without pay just because we are relatives. Tell me how much your wages should be."

16Now Laban had two daughters. The older daughter was named Leah, and the younger one was Rachel. 17There was no sparkle in Leah's eyes,* but Rachel had a beautiful figure and a lovely face. 18Since Jacob was in love with Rachel, he told her father, "I'll work for you for seven years if you'll give me Rachel, your younger daughter, as my wife."

19"Agreed!" Laban replied. "I'd rather give her to you than to anyone else. Stay and work with me." 20So Jacob worked seven years to pay for Rachel. But his love for her was so strong that it seemed to him but a few days.

21Finally, the time came for him to marry her. "I have fulfilled my agreement," Jacob said to Laban. "Now give me my wife so I can sleep with her."

22So Laban invited everyone in the neighborhood and prepared a wedding feast. 23But that night, when it was dark, Laban took Leah to Jacob, and he slept with her. 24(Laban had given Leah a servant, Zilpah, to be her maid.)

25But when Jacob woke up in the morning—it was Leah! "What have you done to me?" Jacob raged at Laban. "I worked seven years for Rachel! Why have you tricked me?"

26"It's not our custom here to marry off a younger daughter ahead of the firstborn," Laban replied. 27"But wait until the bridal week is over, then we'll give you Rachel, too—provided you promise to work another seven years for me."

28So Jacob agreed to work seven more years. A week after Jacob had married Leah, Laban gave him Rachel, too. 29(Laban gave Rachel a

---

WORTH THE WAIT

(29:20-28) Jacob waited seven years to marry Rachel. After being tricked into marrying her sister, he agreed to work seven more years after their father, Laban, allowed him to marry Rachel! People often wonder if a goal (saving money for college; abstaining from sex until marriage) is worth the wait. In our instant society, waiting for anything is seldom encouraged, and we can become very impatient. But the most important goals and desires are worth waiting for. Patience is hardest when we need it the most, but it is the key to achieving our goals.

29:17 Or *Leah had dull eyes,* or *Leah had soft eyes.* The meaning of the Hebrew is uncertain.

RACHEL *PERSONALITY PROFILE*

GOT ANY SIBLINGS? Ever feel a sense of competitiveness in regard to a brother or sister? Sometimes competitiveness is sparked by what you have in common. For example, maybe you felt you had to compete for the love of your mom or dad. Or, maybe you had to live up to the reputation of a stellar sib who was a legend at your school.

Rachel and her sister Leah had something in common. Not only did they share the same parents, they also shared the same husband—Jacob. But for Rachel, the urge to compete grew stronger when she found that Leah could easily provide their husband with something she could not: children.

Let's backtrack a bit. Rachel had been Jacob's choice for a wife in the first place. But through circumstances highly unforeseen, her sister beat her to the altar. Although she still retained Jacob's love and loyalty, she feared that her barrenness would soon eclipse her position as the number one wife. So when Leah had son after son, Rachel grew desperate enough to gain children by any means necessary. Her envy and competitiveness caused a rift in her relationship with her sister and her husband.

Ever think you have to earn the love and loyalty of the people in your life? Perhaps you've even thought that you can somehow earn God's love by what you do. But none of us can earn what God has already given us. He loves us! His love has no beginning and is incredibly patient. All we need to do is respond to God's love, which he has offered freely to us.

BOTTOM LINE: Loyalty must be controlled by what is true and right. Love is accepted, not earned.

Rachel's story is told in Genesis 29:6–35:20. She also is mentioned in Ruth 4:11.

UPS:
- *Showed great loyalty to her family*
- *Had two sons (Joseph and Benjamin) after being barren for many years*

DOWNS:
- *Envy and competitiveness spoiled her relationship with her sister, Leah*
- *Was capable of dishonesty by taking her loyalty too far*
- *Failed to recognize that Jacob's devotion was not dependent on her ability to have children*

STATS:
- *Where: Haran*
- *Occupations: Shepherdess, homemaker*
- *Relatives: Laban (father); Rebekah (aunt); Leah (sister); Jacob (husband); Joseph and Benjamin (sons)*

KEY VERSE: *Genesis 29:20*

servant, Bilhah, to be her maid.) ³⁰So Jacob slept with Rachel, too, and he loved her much more than Leah. He then stayed and worked for Laban the additional seven years.

JACOB'S MANY CHILDREN

³¹When the LORD saw that Leah was unloved, he enabled her to have children, but Rachel could not conceive. ³²So Leah became pregnant and gave birth to a son. She named him Reuben,* for she said, "The LORD has noticed my misery, and now my husband will love me."

³³She soon became pregnant again and gave birth to another son. She named him Simeon,* for she said, "The LORD heard that I was unloved and has given me another son."

³⁴Then she became pregnant a third time and gave birth to another son. She named him Levi,* for she said, "Surely this time my husband will feel affection for me, since I have given him three sons!"

³⁵Once again Leah became pregnant and gave birth to another son. She named him Judah,* for she said, "Now I will praise the LORD!" And then she stopped having children.

30 When Rachel saw that she wasn't having any children for Jacob, she became jealous of her sister. She pleaded with Jacob, "Give me children, or I'll die!"

²Then Jacob became furious with Rachel. "Am I God?" he asked. "He's the one who has kept you from having children!"

³Then Rachel told him, "Take my maid, Bilhah, and sleep with her. She will bear children for me,* and through her I can have a family, too." ⁴So Rachel gave her servant, Bilhah, to Jacob as a wife, and he slept with her. ⁵Bilhah became pregnant and presented him with a son. ⁶Rachel named him Dan,* for she said, "God has vindicated me! He has heard my request and given me a son." ⁷Then Bilhah became pregnant again and gave Jacob a second son. ⁸Rachel named him Naphtali,* for she said, "I have struggled hard with my sister, and I'm winning!"

⁹Meanwhile, Leah realized that she wasn't getting pregnant anymore, so she took her servant, Zilpah, and gave her to Jacob as a wife. ¹⁰Soon Zilpah presented him with a son. ¹¹Leah

named him Gad,* for she said, "How fortunate I am!" ¹²Then Zilpah gave Jacob a second son. ¹³And Leah named him Asher,* for she said, "What joy is mine! Now the other women will celebrate with me."

¹⁴One day during the wheat harvest, Reuben found some mandrakes growing in a field and brought them to his mother, Leah. Rachel begged Leah, "Please give me some of your son's mandrakes."

¹⁵But Leah angrily replied, "Wasn't it enough that you stole my husband? Now will you steal my son's mandrakes, too?"

Rachel answered, "I will let Jacob sleep with you tonight if you give me some of the mandrakes."

¹⁶So that evening, as Jacob was coming home from the fields, Leah went out to meet him. "You must come and sleep with me tonight!" she said. "I have paid for you with some mandrakes that my son found." So that night he slept with Leah. ¹⁷And God answered Leah's prayers. She became pregnant again and gave birth to a fifth son for Jacob. ¹⁸She named him Issachar,* for she said, "God has rewarded me for giving my servant to my husband as a wife." ¹⁹Then Leah became pregnant again and gave birth to a sixth son for Jacob. ²⁰She named him Zebulun,* for she said, "God has given me a good reward. Now my husband will treat me with respect, for I have given him six sons." ²¹Later she gave birth to a daughter and named her Dinah.

²²Then God remembered Rachel's plight and answered her prayers by enabling her to have children. ²³She became pregnant and gave birth to a son. "God has removed my disgrace," she said. ²⁴And she named him Joseph,* for she

....

WHAT'S RIGHT?
(30:1-12) Rachel and Leah were locked in a cruel contest. In their race to have children, they both gave their servant girls to Jacob as concubines. Although taking a concubine was an accepted custom of the day, God never delighted in this practice. He knew the potential heartache it could cause. Have you been wondering about a choice or lifestyle that everyone else seems to think is OK? Some socially acceptable practices might not be wise or right. Want to be wise? Base your choices on the truth of God's Word.

WAIT FOR GOD
(30:22-24) Eventually God answered Rachel's prayers and gave her a child of her own. In the meantime, however, she had given her servant girl to Jacob to gain children that way. The consequences of that decision were long lasting. Trusting God when nothing seems to happen is difficult. But it is harder still to live with the consequences of taking matters into our own hands. Feeling forgotten? Tired of waiting for God? Are you willing to wait just a little while longer for him to act? He may not act when you want him to, but he's always on time.

29:32 *Reuben* means "Look, a son!" It also sounds like the Hebrew for "He has seen my misery." **29:33** *Simeon* probably means "one who hears." **29:34** *Levi* sounds like a Hebrew term that means "being attached" or "feeling affection for." **29:35** *Judah* is related to the Hebrew term for "praise." **30:3** Hebrew *bear children on my knees.* **30:6** *Dan* means "he judged" or "he vindicated." **30:8** *Naphtali* means "my struggle." **30:11** *Gad* means "good fortune." **30:13** *Asher* means "happy." **30:18** *Issachar* sounds like a Hebrew term that means "reward." **30:20** *Zebulun* probably means "honor." **30:24** *Joseph* means "may he add."

said, "May the LORD add yet another son to my family."

JACOB'S WEALTH INCREASES
[25]Soon after Rachel had given birth to Joseph, Jacob said to Laban, "Please release me so I can go home to my own country. [26]Let me take my wives and children, for I have earned them by serving you, and let me be on my way. You certainly know how hard I have worked for you."

[27]"Please listen to me," Laban replied. "I have become wealthy, for* the LORD has blessed me because of you. [28]Tell me how much I owe you. Whatever it is, I'll pay it."

[29]Jacob replied, "You know how hard I've worked for you, and how your flocks and herds have grown under my care. [30]You had little indeed before I came, but your wealth has increased enormously. The LORD has blessed you through everything I've done. But now, what about me? When can I start providing for my own family?"

[31]"What wages do you want?" Laban asked again.

Jacob replied, "Don't give me anything. Just do this one thing, and I'll continue to tend and watch over your flocks. [32]Let me inspect your flocks today and remove all the sheep and goats that are speckled or spotted, along with all the black sheep. Give these to me as my wages. [33]In the future, when you check on the animals you have given me as my wages,

you'll see that I have been honest. If you find in my flock any goats without speckles or spots, or any sheep that are not black, you will know that I have stolen them from you."

[34]"All right," Laban replied. "It will be as you say." [35]But that very day Laban went out and removed the male goats that were streaked and spotted, all the female goats that were speckled and spotted or had white patches, and all the black sheep. He placed them in the care of his own sons, [36]who took them a three-days' journey from where Jacob was. Meanwhile, Jacob stayed and cared for the rest of Laban's flock.

[37]Then Jacob took some fresh branches from poplar, almond, and plane trees and peeled off strips of bark, making white streaks on them. [38]Then he placed these peeled branches in the watering troughs where the flocks came to drink, for that was where they mated. [39]And when they mated in front of the white-streaked branches, they gave birth to young that were streaked, speckled, and spotted. [40]Jacob separated those lambs from Laban's flock. And at mating time he turned the flock to face Laban's animals that were streaked or black. This is how he built his own flock instead of increasing Laban's.

[41]Whenever the stronger females were ready to mate, Jacob would place the peeled branches in the watering troughs in front of them. Then they would mate in front of the branches.

30:27 Or I have learned by divination that.

REUBEN *PERSONALITY PROFILE*

HOW WOULD YOUR MOM OR DAD describe your personality? Jacob summarized the personality of his son Reuben by comparing him to the unruliness of a flood. He knew that Reuben lacked stability. Reuben usually wanted to do the right thing, but seemed unable to stand against a crowd. His instability made him hard to trust. His private and public values contradicted each other. He went along with his brothers in their actions against Joseph while hoping he could do something helpful when they weren't looking. His plan failed.

Compromise has a way of destroying convictions. Without convictions, there is no direction. And lack of direction will destroy life. In Reuben's case, his early mistakes led to a real mess later on in life. Because of the decision he made in regard to his father's concubine, he lost the blessing and status usually given to the firstborn.

For many of us Jacob's description of his son, "unruly as a flood," is an accurate description of our lives. How about you? Are you the same person on the inside that you are on the outside? How do your actions show your integrity?

BOTTOM LINE: Public and private lives must show the same integrity, or one will destroy the other.

Punishment for sin may not be immediate, but it is certain.

Reuben's story is told in Genesis 29:31-32; 35:23; 37; 42–50.

UPS:
- *Saved Joseph's life by talking the other brothers out of murder*
- *Showed intense love for his father by offering his own sons as a guarantee that Benjamin's life would be safe*

DOWNS:
- *Gave in quickly to group pressure*
- *Did not directly protect Joseph from his brothers, although as eldest son he had the authority to do so*
- *Slept with his father's concubine*

STATS:
- *Where: Canaan, Egypt*
- *Occupation: Shepherd*
- *Relatives: Jacob and Leah (parents); eleven brothers, one sister*

KEY VERSE: *Genesis 49:4*

⁴²But he didn't do this with the weaker ones, so the weaker lambs belonged to Laban, and the stronger ones were Jacob's. ⁴³As a result, Jacob became very wealthy, with large flocks of sheep and goats, female and male servants, and many camels and donkeys.

31 JACOB FLEES FROM LABAN But Jacob soon learned that Laban's sons were grumbling about him. "Jacob has robbed our father of everything!" they said. "He has gained all his wealth at our father's expense." ²And Jacob began to notice a change in Laban's attitude toward him.

³Then the LORD said to Jacob, "Return to the land of your father and grandfather and to your relatives there, and I will be with you."

⁴So Jacob called Rachel and Leah out to the field where he was watching his flock. ⁵He said to them, "I have noticed that your father's attitude toward me has changed. But the God of my father has been with me. ⁶You know how hard I have worked for your father, ⁷but he has cheated me, changing my wages ten times. But God has not allowed him to do me any harm. ⁸For if he said, 'The speckled animals will be your wages,' the whole flock began to produce speckled young. And when he changed his mind and said, 'The striped animals will be your wages,' then the whole flock produced striped young. ⁹In this way, God has taken your father's animals and given them to me.

¹⁰"One time during the mating season, I had a dream and saw that the male goats mating with the females were streaked, speckled, and spotted. ¹¹Then in my dream, the angel of God said to me, 'Jacob!' And I replied, 'Yes, here I am.'

¹²"The angel said, 'Look up, and you will see that only the streaked, speckled, and spotted males are mating with the females of your flock. For I have seen how Laban has treated you. ¹³I am the God who appeared to you at Bethel,* the place where you anointed the pillar of stone and made your vow to me. Now get ready and leave this country and return to the land of your birth.'"

¹⁴Rachel and Leah responded, "That's fine with us! We won't inherit any of our father's wealth anyway. ¹⁵He has reduced our rights to those of foreign women. And after he sold us, he wasted the money you paid him for us. ¹⁶All the wealth God has given you from our father legally belongs to us and our children. So go ahead and do whatever God has told you."

¹⁷So Jacob put his wives and children on camels, ¹⁸and he drove all his livestock in front of him. He packed all the belongings he had acquired in Paddan-aram and set out for the land of Canaan, where his father, Isaac, lived. ¹⁹At the time they left, Laban was some distance away, shearing his sheep. Rachel stole her father's household idols and took them with her. ²⁰Jacob outwitted Laban the Aramean, for they set out secretly and never told Laban they were leaving. ²¹So Jacob took all his possessions with him and crossed the Euphrates River,* heading for the hill country of Gilead.

LABAN PURSUES JACOB ²²Three days later, Laban was told that Jacob had fled. ²³So he gathered a group of his relatives and set out in hot pursuit. He caught up with Jacob seven days later in the hill country of Gilead. ²⁴But the previous night God had appeared to Laban the Aramean in a dream and told him, "I'm warning you—leave Jacob alone!"

²⁵Laban caught up with Jacob as he was camped in the hill country of Gilead, and he set up his camp not far from Jacob's. ²⁶"What do you mean by deceiving me like this?" Laban demanded. "How dare you drag my daughters away like prisoners of war? ²⁷Why did you slip away secretly? Why did you deceive me? And why didn't you say you wanted to leave? I would have given you a farewell feast, with singing and music, accompanied by tambourines and harps. ²⁸Why didn't you let me kiss my daughters and grandchildren and tell them good-bye? You have acted very foolishly! ²⁹I could destroy you, but the God of your father appeared to me last night and warned me, 'Leave Jacob alone!' ³⁰I can understand your feeling that you must go, and your intense longing for your father's home. But why have you stolen my gods?"

³¹"I rushed away because I was afraid," Jacob answered. "I thought you would take your daughters from me by force. ³²But as for your gods, see if you can find them, and let the person who has taken them die! And if you find anything else that belongs to you, identify it before all these relatives of ours, and I will give it back!" But Jacob did not know that Rachel had stolen the household idols.

³³Laban went first into Jacob's tent to search there, then into Leah's, and then the tents of the two servant wives—but he found nothing. Finally, he went into Rachel's tent. ³⁴But Rachel had taken the household idols and hidden them in her camel saddle, and now she was sitting on them. When Laban had thoroughly searched her tent without finding them, ³⁵she said to her father, "Please, sir, forgive me if I

31:13 As in Greek version and an Aramaic Targum; Hebrew reads *the God of Bethel.*   31:21 Hebrew *the river.*

don't get up for you. I'm having my monthly period." So Laban continued his search, but he could not find the household idols.

³⁶Then Jacob became very angry, and he challenged Laban. "What's my crime?" he demanded. "What have I done wrong to make you chase after me as though I were a criminal? ³⁷You have rummaged through everything I own. Now show me what you found that belongs to you! Set it out here in front of us, before our relatives, for all to see. Let them judge between us!

³⁸"For twenty years I have been with you, caring for your flocks. In all that time your sheep and goats never miscarried. In all those years I never used a single ram of yours for food. ³⁹If any were attacked and killed by wild animals, I never showed you the carcass and asked you to reduce the count of your flock. No, I took the loss myself! You made me pay for every stolen animal, whether it was taken in broad daylight or in the dark of night.

⁴⁰"I worked for you through the scorching heat of the day and through cold and sleepless nights. ⁴¹Yes, for twenty years I slaved in your house! I worked for fourteen years earning your two daughters, and then six more years for your flock. And you changed my wages ten times! ⁴²In fact, if the God of my father had not been on my side—the God of Abraham and the fearsome God of Isaac*—you would have sent me away empty-handed. But God has seen your abuse and my hard work. That is why he appeared to you last night and rebuked you!"

JACOB'S TREATY WITH LABAN ⁴³Then Laban replied to Jacob, "These women are my daughters, these children are my grandchildren, and these flocks are my flocks—in fact, everything you see is mine. But what can I do now about my daughters and their children? ⁴⁴So come, let's make a covenant, you and I, and it will be a witness to our commitment."

⁴⁵So Jacob took a stone and set it up as a monument. ⁴⁶Then he told his family members, "Gather some stones." So they gathered stones and piled them in a heap. Then Jacob

and Laban sat down beside the pile of stones to eat a covenant meal. ⁴⁷To commemorate the event, Laban called the place Jegar-sahadutha (which means "witness pile" in Aramaic), and Jacob called it Galeed (which means "witness pile" in Hebrew).

⁴⁸Then Laban declared, "This pile of stones will stand as a witness to remind us of the covenant we have made today." This explains why it was called Galeed—"Witness Pile." ⁴⁹But it was also called Mizpah (which means "watchtower"), for Laban said, "May the LORD keep watch between us to make sure that we keep this covenant when we are out of each other's sight. ⁵⁰If you mistreat my daughters or if you marry other wives, God will see it even if no one else does. He is a witness to this covenant between us.

⁵¹"See this pile of stones," Laban continued, "and see this monument I have set between us. ⁵²They stand between us as witnesses of our vows. I will never pass this pile of stones to harm you, and you must never pass these stones or this monument to harm me. ⁵³I call on the God of our ancestors—the God of your grandfather Abraham and the God of my grandfather Nahor—to serve as a judge between us."

So Jacob took an oath before the fearsome God of his father, Isaac,* to respect the boundary line. ⁵⁴Then Jacob offered a sacrifice to God there on the mountain and invited everyone to a covenant feast. After they had eaten, they spent the night on the mountain.

⁵⁵*Laban got up early the next morning, and he kissed his grandchildren and his daughters and blessed them. Then he left and returned home.

32

¹*As Jacob started on his way again, angels of God came to meet him. ²When Jacob saw them, he exclaimed, "This is God's camp!" So he named the place Mahanaim.*

JACOB SENDS GIFTS TO ESAU ³Then Jacob sent messengers ahead to his brother, Esau, who was living in the region of Seir in the land of Edom. ⁴He told them, "Give this message to my master Esau: 'Humble greetings from your servant Jacob. Until now I have been living with Uncle Laban, ⁵and now I own cattle, donkeys, flocks of sheep and goats, and many servants, both men and women. I have sent these

....

THE DILIGENCE PAYOFF

(31:38-42) *Jacob had the habit of doing more than was expected of him. When his flocks were attacked, he took the losses rather than splitting them with Laban. He worked hard even after several pay cuts. His diligence eventually paid off—his flocks began to multiply. Diligence (1) pleases God, (2) earns recognition and advancement, (3) enhances your reputation, (4) builds others' confidence in you, (5) gives you more experience and knowledge, and (6) develops your spiritual maturity. Do you have the diligence habit?*

31:42 Or *and the Fear of Isaac.* **31:53** Or *the Fear of his father, Isaac.* **31:55** Verse 31:55 is numbered 32:1 in Hebrew text. **32:1** Verses 32:1-32 are numbered 32:2-33 in Hebrew text. **32:2** *Mahanaim* means "two camps."

messengers to inform my lord of my coming, hoping that you will be friendly to me.'"

[6]After delivering the message, the messengers returned to Jacob and reported, "We met your brother, Esau, and he is already on his way to meet you—with an army of 400 men!" [7]Jacob was terrified at the news. He divided his household, along with the flocks and herds and camels, into two groups. [8]He thought, "If Esau meets one group and attacks it, perhaps the other group can escape."

[9]Then Jacob prayed, "O God of my grandfather Abraham, and God of my father, Isaac—O Lord, you told me, 'Return to your own land and to your relatives.' And you promised me, 'I will treat you kindly.' [10]I am not worthy of all the unfailing love and faithfulness you have shown to me, your servant. When I left home and crossed the Jordan River, I owned nothing except a walking stick. Now my household fills two large camps! [11]O Lord, please rescue me from the hand of my brother, Esau. I am afraid that he is coming to attack me, along with my wives and children. [12]But you promised me, 'I will surely treat you kindly, and I will multiply your descendants until they become as numerous as the sands along the seashore—too many to count.'"

[13]Jacob stayed where he was for the night. Then he selected these gifts from his possessions to present to his brother, Esau: [14]200 female goats, 20 male goats, 200 ewes, 20 rams, [15]30 female camels with their young, 40 cows, 10 bulls, 20 female donkeys, and 10 male donkeys. [16]He divided these animals into herds and assigned each to different servants. Then he told his servants, "Go ahead of me with the animals, but keep some distance between the herds."

[17]He gave these instructions to the men leading the first group: "When my brother, Esau, meets you, he will ask, 'Whose servants are you? Where are you going? Who owns these animals?' [18]You must reply, 'They belong to your servant Jacob, but they are a gift for his master Esau. Look, he is coming right behind us.'"

[19]Jacob gave the same instructions to the second and third herdsmen and to all who followed behind the herds: "You must say the same thing to Esau when you meet him. [20]And be sure to say, 'Look, your servant Jacob is right behind us.'"

Jacob thought, "I will try to appease him by sending gifts ahead of me. When I see him in person, perhaps he will be friendly to me." [21]So the gifts were sent on ahead, while Jacob himself spent that night in the camp.

JACOB WRESTLES WITH GOD

[22]During the night Jacob got up and took his two wives, his two servant wives, and his eleven sons and crossed the Jabbok River with them. [23]After taking them to the other side, he sent over all his possessions.

[24]This left Jacob all alone in the camp, and a man came and wrestled with him until the dawn began to break. [25]When the man saw that he would not win the match, he touched Jacob's hip and wrenched it out of its socket. [26]Then the man said, "Let me go, for the dawn is breaking!"

But Jacob said, "I will not let you go unless you bless me."

[27]"What is your name?" the man asked.

He replied, "Jacob."

[28]"Your name will no longer be Jacob," the man told him. "From now on you will be called Israel,* because you have fought with God and with men and have won."

[29]"Please tell me your name," Jacob said.

"Why do you want to know my name?" the man replied. Then he blessed Jacob there.

[30]Jacob named the place Peniel (which means "face of God"), for he said, "I have seen God face to face, yet my life has been spared." [31]The sun was rising as Jacob left Peniel,* and he was limping because of the injury to his hip. [32](Even today the people of Israel don't eat the tendon near the hip socket because of what happened that night when the man strained the tendon of Jacob's hip.)

33 JACOB AND ESAU MAKE PEACE

Then Jacob looked up and saw Esau coming with his 400 men. So he divided the children among Leah, Rachel, and his two servant wives. [2]He put the servant wives and their children at the front, Leah and her children next, and Rachel and Joseph last. [3]Then Jacob went on ahead. As he approached his brother, he bowed to the ground seven times before him. [4]Then Esau ran to meet him and embraced him,

32:28 *Jacob* sounds like the Hebrew words for "heel" and "deceiver." *Israel* means "God fights."   32:31 Hebrew *Penuel,* a variant spelling of Peniel.

FRANTIC WITH FEAR

(32:6-12) How would you feel if you knew you were about to meet the person you had cheated out of his most precious possession? Jacob had taken Esau's birthright (25:33) and his blessings (27:27-40). Now that he was about to meet this brother for the first time in 20 years, he was frantic with fear. He collected his thoughts, however, and decided to pray. When we face a difficult conflict, we can run about frantically or we can pause to pray. Which approach will be more effective?

threw his arms around his neck, and kissed him. And they both wept.

⁵Then Esau looked at the women and children and asked, "Who are these people with you?"

"These are the children God has graciously given to me, your servant," Jacob replied. ⁶Then the servant wives came forward with their children and bowed before him. ⁷Next came Leah with her children, and they bowed before him. Finally, Joseph and Rachel came forward and bowed before him.

⁸"And what were all the flocks and herds I met as I came?" Esau asked.

Jacob replied, "They are a gift, my lord, to ensure your friendship."

⁹"My brother, I have plenty," Esau answered. "Keep what you have for yourself."

¹⁰But Jacob insisted, "No, if I have found favor with you, please accept this gift from me. And what a relief to see your friendly smile. It is like seeing the face of God! ¹¹Please take this gift I have brought you, for God has been very gracious to me. I have more than enough." And because Jacob insisted, Esau finally accepted the gift.

¹²"Well," Esau said, "let's be going. I will lead the way."

¹³But Jacob replied, "You can see, my lord, that some of the children are very young, and the flocks and herds have their young, too. If they are driven too hard, even for one day, all the animals could die. ¹⁴Please, my lord, go ahead of your servant. We will follow slowly, at a pace that is comfortable for the livestock and the children. I will meet you at Seir."

¹⁵"All right," Esau said, "but at least let me assign some of my men to guide and protect you."

· ·

BITTERNESS
(33:1-11) It is refreshing to see Esau's change of heart when the two brothers meet again. The bitterness over losing his birthright and blessing (27:32-38) seems gone. Instead Esau is content with what he has. Jacob even exclaims how great it is to see his brother's friendly smile (33:10). Ever feel the bite of bitterness after being cheated by someone? Many have. We can remove bitterness from our lives by honestly expressing our feelings to God, forgiving those who have wronged us, and being content with what we have.

PASSION
(34:1-4) Shechem may have been a victim of "love at first sight," but his actions were impulsive and evil. Not only did he sin against Dinah, he sinned against the entire family (34:6-7). The consequences of his deed were severe, both for his family and for Jacob's (34:25-31). His declared love for Dinah could not excuse the wrong that he did. Don't allow sexual passion to boil over into evil actions. Passion must be controlled.

Jacob responded, "That's not necessary. It's enough that you've received me warmly, my lord!"

¹⁶So Esau turned around and started back to Seir that same day. ¹⁷Jacob, on the other hand, traveled on to Succoth. There he built himself a house and made shelters for his livestock. That is why the place was named Succoth (which means "shelters").

¹⁸Later, having traveled all the way from Paddan-aram, Jacob arrived safely at the town of Shechem, in the land of Canaan. There he set up camp outside the town. ¹⁹Jacob bought the plot of land where he camped from the family of Hamor, the father of Shechem, for 100 pieces of silver.* ²⁰And there he built an altar and named it El-Elohe-Israel.*

34

REVENGE AGAINST SHECHEM One day Dinah, the daughter of Jacob and Leah, went to visit some of the young women who lived in the area. ²But when the local prince, Shechem son of Hamor the Hivite, saw Dinah, he seized her and raped her. ³But then he fell in love with her, and he tried to win her affection with tender words. ⁴He said to his father, Hamor, "Get me this young girl. I want to marry her."

⁵Soon Jacob heard that Shechem had defiled his daughter, Dinah. But since his sons were out in the fields herding his livestock, he said nothing until they returned. ⁶Hamor, Shechem's father, came to discuss the matter with Jacob. ⁷Meanwhile, Jacob's sons had come in from the field as soon as they heard what had happened. They were shocked and furious that their sister had been raped. Shechem had done a disgraceful thing against Jacob's family,* something that should never be done.

⁸Hamor tried to speak with Jacob and his sons. "My son Shechem is truly in love with your daughter," he said. "Please let him marry her. ⁹In fact, let's arrange other marriages, too. You give us your daughters for our sons, and we will give you our daughters for your sons. ¹⁰And you may live among us; the land is open to you! Settle here and trade with us. And feel free to buy property in the area."

¹¹Then Shechem himself spoke to Dinah's father and brothers. "Please be kind to me, and let me marry her," he begged. "I will give you whatever you ask. ¹²No matter what dowry or gift you demand, I will gladly pay it—just give me the girl as my wife."

33:19 Hebrew *100 kesitahs;* the value or weight of the kesitah is no longer known. **33:20** *El-Elohe-Israel* means "God, the God of Israel." **34:7** Hebrew *a disgraceful thing in Israel.*

¹³But since Shechem had defiled their sister, Dinah, Jacob's sons responded deceitfully to Shechem and his father, Hamor. ¹⁴They said to them, "We couldn't possibly allow this, because you're not circumcised. It would be a disgrace for our sister to marry a man like you! ¹⁵But here is a solution. If every man among you will be circumcised like we are, ¹⁶then we will give you our daughters, and we'll take your daughters for ourselves. We will live among you and become one people. ¹⁷But if you don't agree to be circumcised, we will take her and be on our way."

¹⁸Hamor and his son Shechem agreed to their proposal. ¹⁹Shechem wasted no time in acting on this request, for he wanted Jacob's daughter desperately. Shechem was a highly respected member of his family, ²⁰and he went with his father, Hamor, to present this proposal to the leaders at the town gate.

²¹"These men are our friends," they said. "Let's invite them to live here among us and trade freely. Look, the land is large enough to hold them. We can take their daughters as wives and let them marry ours. ²²But they will consider staying here and becoming one people with us only if all of our men are circumcised, just as they are. ²³But if we do this, all their livestock and possessions will eventually be ours. Come, let's agree to their terms and let them settle here among us."

²⁴So all the men in the town council agreed with Hamor and Shechem, and every male in the town was circumcised. ²⁵But three days later, when their wounds were still sore, two of Jacob's sons, Simeon and Levi, who were Dinah's full brothers, took their swords and entered the town without opposition. Then they slaughtered every male there, ²⁶including Hamor and his son Shechem. They killed them with their swords, then took Dinah from Shechem's house and returned to their camp.

²⁷Meanwhile, the rest of Jacob's sons arrived. Finding the men slaughtered, they plundered the town because their sister had been defiled there. ²⁸They seized all the flocks and herds and donkeys—everything they could lay their hands on, both inside the town and outside in the fields. ²⁹They looted all their wealth and plundered their houses. They also took all their little children and wives and led them away as captives.

³⁰Afterward Jacob said to Simeon and Levi, "You have ruined me! You've made me stink among all the people of this land—among all

35:10 *Jacob* sounds like the Hebrew words for "heel" and "deceiver." *Israel* means "God fights."

the Canaanites and Perizzites. We are so few that they will join forces and crush us. I will be ruined, and my entire household will be wiped out!"

³¹"But why should we let him treat our sister like a prostitute?" they retorted angrily.

35 JACOB'S RETURN TO BETHEL Then God said to Jacob, "Get ready and move to Bethel and settle there. Build an altar there to the God who appeared to you when you fled from your brother, Esau."

²So Jacob told everyone in his household, "Get rid of all your pagan idols, purify yourselves, and put on clean clothing. ³We are now going to Bethel, where I will build an altar to the God who answered my prayers when I was in distress. He has been with me wherever I have gone."

⁴So they gave Jacob all their pagan idols and earrings, and he buried them under the great tree near Shechem. ⁵As they set out, a terror from God spread over the people in all the towns of that area, so no one attacked Jacob's family.

⁶Eventually, Jacob and his household arrived at Luz (also called Bethel) in Canaan. ⁷Jacob built an altar there and named the place El-bethel (which means "God of Bethel"), because God had appeared to him there when he was fleeing from his brother, Esau.

⁸Soon after this, Rebekah's old nurse, Deborah, died. She was buried beneath the oak tree in the valley below Bethel. Ever since, the tree has been called Allon-bacuth (which means "oak of weeping").

⁹Now that Jacob had returned from Paddan-aram, God appeared to him again at Bethel. God blessed him, ¹⁰saying, "Your name is Jacob, but you will not be called Jacob any longer. From now on your name will be Israel."* So God renamed him Israel.

¹¹Then God said, "I am El-Shaddai—'God Almighty.' Be fruitful and multiply. You will become a great nation, even many nations. Kings will be among your descendants! ¹²And I will give you the land I once gave to Abraham and Isaac. Yes, I will give it to you and your descendants after you." ¹³Then God went up from the place where he had spoken to Jacob.

¹⁴Jacob set up a stone pillar to mark the place where God had spoken to him. Then he poured wine over it as an offering to God and anointed the pillar with olive oil. ¹⁵And Jacob named the place Bethel (which means "house of God"), because God had spoken to him there.

THE DEATHS OF RACHEL AND ISAAC ¹⁶Leaving Bethel, Jacob and his clan moved on toward Ephrath. But Rachel went into labor while they were still some distance away. Her labor pains were intense. ¹⁷After a very hard delivery, the midwife finally exclaimed, "Don't be afraid—you have another son!" ¹⁸Rachel was about to die, but with her last breath she named the baby Ben-oni (which means "son of my sorrow"). The baby's father, however, called him Benjamin (which means "son of my right hand"). ¹⁹So Rachel died and was buried on the way to Ephrath (that is, Bethlehem). ²⁰Jacob set up a stone monument over Rachel's grave, and it can be seen there to this day.

²¹Then Jacob* traveled on and camped beyond Migdal-eder. ²²While he was living there, Reuben had intercourse with Bilhah, his father's concubine, and Jacob soon heard about it.

These are the names of the twelve sons of Jacob:

²³The sons of Leah were Reuben (Jacob's oldest son), Simeon, Levi, Judah, Issachar, and Zebulun.

²⁴The sons of Rachel were Joseph and Benjamin.

²⁵The sons of Bilhah, Rachel's servant, were Dan and Naphtali.

²⁶The sons of Zilpah, Leah's servant, were Gad and Asher.

These are the names of the sons who were born to Jacob at Paddan-aram.

²⁷So Jacob returned to his father, Isaac, in Mamre, which is near Kiriath-arba (now called Hebron), where Abraham and Isaac had both lived as foreigners. ²⁸Isaac lived for 180 years. ²⁹Then he breathed his last and died at a ripe old age, joining his ancestors in death. And his sons, Esau and Jacob, buried him.

36 **DESCENDANTS OF ESAU** This is the account of the descendants of Esau (also known as Edom). ²Esau married two young women from Canaan: Adah, the daughter of Elon the Hittite; and Oholibamah, the daughter of Anah and granddaughter of Zibeon the Hivite. ³He also married his cousin Basemath, who was the daughter of Ishmael and the sister of Nebaioth. ⁴Adah gave birth to a son named Eliphaz for Esau. Basemath gave birth to a son named Reuel. ⁵Oholibamah gave birth to sons named Jeush, Jalam, and Korah. All these sons were born to Esau in the land of Canaan.

⁶Esau took his wives, his children, and his entire household, along with his livestock and cattle—all the wealth he had acquired in the land of Canaan—and moved away from his brother, Jacob. ⁷There was not enough land to support them both because of all the livestock and possessions they had acquired. ⁸So Esau (also known as Edom) settled in the hill country of Seir.

⁹This is the account of Esau's descendants, the Edomites, who lived in the hill country of Seir.

¹⁰These are the names of Esau's sons: Eliphaz, the son of Esau's wife Adah; and Reuel, the son of Esau's wife Basemath.

¹¹The descendants of Eliphaz were Teman, Omar, Zepho, Gatam, and Kenaz. ¹²Timna, the concubine of Esau's son Eliphaz, gave birth to a son named Amalek. These are the descendants of Esau's wife Adah.

¹³The descendants of Reuel were Nahath, Zerah, Shammah, and Mizzah. These are the descendants of Esau's wife Basemath.

¹⁴Esau also had sons through Oholibamah, the daughter of Anah and granddaughter of Zibeon. Their names were Jeush, Jalam, and Korah.

¹⁵These are the descendants of Esau who became the leaders of various clans:

The descendants of Esau's oldest son, Eliphaz, became the leaders of the clans of Teman, Omar, Zepho, Kenaz, ¹⁶Korah, Gatam, and Amalek. These are the clan leaders in the land of Edom who descended from Eliphaz. All these were descendants of Esau's wife Adah.

¹⁷The descendants of Esau's son Reuel became the leaders of the clans of Nahath, Zerah, Shammah, and Mizzah. These are the clan leaders in the land of Edom who descended from Reuel. All these were descendants of Esau's wife Basemath.

¹⁸The descendants of Esau and his wife Oholibamah became the leaders of the clans of Jeush, Jalam, and Korah. These are the

---

SIN'S CONSEQUENCES
(35:22) When Reuben slept with his father's concubine, he may have thought that he would get away with it. But on his deathbed, Jacob brought up Reuben's action. Instead of the double portion of the family inheritance that Reuben would have received as the oldest son, Jacob took away his status and gave it to someone else (49:4). Sin's consequences can plague us long after the sin is committed. We can run, but we can't hide from the consequences of wrong actions.

35:21 Hebrew *Israel;* also in 35:22a. The names "Jacob" and "Israel" are often interchanged throughout the Old Testament, referring sometimes to the individual patriarch and sometimes to the nation.

clan leaders who descended from Esau's wife Oholibamah, the daughter of Anah. ¹⁹These are the clans descended from Esau (also known as Edom), identified by their clan leaders.

ORIGINAL PEOPLES OF EDOM

²⁰These are the names of the tribes that descended from Seir the Horite. They lived in the land of Edom: Lotan, Shobal, Zibeon, Anah, ²¹Dishon, Ezer, and Dishan. These were the Horite clan leaders, the descendants of Seir, who lived in the land of Edom.

²²The descendants of Lotan were Hori and Hemam. Lotan's sister was named Timna.
²³The descendants of Shobal were Alvan, Manahath, Ebal, Shepho, and Onam.
²⁴The descendants of Zibeon were Aiah and Anah. (This is the Anah who discovered the hot springs in the wilderness while he was grazing his father's donkeys.)
²⁵The descendants of Anah were his son, Dishon, and his daughter, Oholibamah.
²⁶The descendants of Dishon* were Hemdan, Eshban, Ithran, and Keran.
²⁷The descendants of Ezer were Bilhan, Zaavan, and Akan.
²⁸The descendants of Dishan were Uz and Aran.
²⁹So these were the leaders of the Horite clans: Lotan, Shobal, Zibeon, Anah, ³⁰Dishon, Ezer, and Dishan. The Horite clans are named after their clan leaders, who lived in the land of Seir.

RULERS OF EDOM

³¹These are the kings who ruled in the land of Edom before any king ruled over the Israelites*:

³²Bela son of Beor, who ruled in Edom from his city of Dinhabah.
³³When Bela died, Jobab son of Zerah from Bozrah became king in his place.
³⁴When Jobab died, Husham from the land of the Temanites became king in his place.
³⁵When Husham died, Hadad son of Bedad became king in his place and ruled from the city of Avith. He was the one who defeated the Midianites in the land of Moab.
³⁶When Hadad died, Samlah from the city of Masrekah became king in his place.
³⁷When Samlah died, Shaul from the city of Rehoboth-on-the-River became king in his place.

36:26 Hebrew *Dishan*, a variant spelling of Dishon; compare 36:21, 28.   36:31 Or *before an Israelite king ruled over them.*   36:39 As in some Hebrew manuscripts, Samaritan Pentateuch, and Syriac version (see also 1 Chr 1:50); most Hebrew manuscripts read *Hadar.*
37:3a Hebrew *Israel;* also in 37:13. See note on 35:21.
37:3b Traditionally rendered *a coat of many colors.* The exact meaning of the Hebrew is uncertain.

³⁸When Shaul died, Baal-hanan son of Acbor became king in his place.
³⁹When Baal-hanan son of Acbor died, Hadad* became king in his place and ruled from the city of Pau. His wife was Mehetabel, the daughter of Matred and granddaughter of Me-zahab.

⁴⁰These are the names of the leaders of the clans descended from Esau, who lived in the places named for them: Timna, Alvah, Jetheth, ⁴¹Oholibamah, Elah, Pinon, ⁴²Kenaz, Teman, Mibzar, ⁴³Magdiel, and Iram. These are the leaders of the clans of Edom, listed according to their settlements in the land they occupied. They all descended from Esau, the ancestor of the Edomites.

37 JOSEPH'S DREAMS

So Jacob settled again in the land of Canaan, where his father had lived as a foreigner.

²This is the account of Jacob and his family. When Joseph was seventeen years old, he often tended his father's flocks. He worked for his half brothers, the sons of his father's wives Bilhah and Zilpah. But Joseph reported to his father some of the bad things his brothers were doing.

³Jacob* loved Joseph more than any of his other children because Joseph had been born to him in his old age. So one day Jacob had a special gift made for Joseph—a beautiful robe.* ⁴But his brothers hated Joseph because their father loved him more than the rest of them. They couldn't say a kind word to him.

⁵One night Joseph had a dream, and when he told his brothers about it, they hated him more than ever. ⁶"Listen to this dream," he said. ⁷"We were out in the field, tying up bundles of grain. Suddenly my bundle stood up, and your bundles all gathered around and bowed low before mine!"

⁸His brothers responded, "So you think you will be our king, do you? Do you actually think you will reign over us?" And they hated him all the more because of his dreams and the way he talked about them.

⁹Soon Joseph had another dream, and again he told his brothers about it. "Listen, I have had another dream," he said. "The sun, moon, and eleven stars bowed low before me!"

¹⁰This time he told the dream to his father as well as to his brothers, but his father scolded him. "What kind of dream is that?" he asked. "Will your mother and I and your brothers actually come and bow to the ground before you?" ¹¹But while his brothers were jealous of Joseph,

his father wondered what the dreams meant.

¹²Soon after this, Joseph's brothers went to pasture their father's flocks at Shechem. ¹³When they had been gone for some time, Jacob said to Joseph, "Your brothers are pasturing the sheep at Shechem. Get ready, and I will send you to them."

"I'm ready to go," Joseph replied.

¹⁴"Go and see how your brothers and the flocks are getting along," Jacob said. "Then come back and bring me a report." So Jacob sent him on his way, and Joseph traveled to Shechem from their home in the valley of Hebron.

¹⁵When he arrived there, a man from the area noticed him wandering around the countryside. "What are you looking for?" he asked.

¹⁶"I'm looking for my brothers," Joseph replied. "Do you know where they are pasturing their sheep?"

¹⁷"Yes," the man told him. "They have moved on from here, but I heard them say, 'Let's go on to Dothan.'" So Joseph followed his brothers to Dothan and found them there.

JOSEPH SOLD INTO SLAVERY

¹⁸When Joseph's brothers saw him coming, they recognized him in the distance. As he approached, they

JOSEPH GOES TO MEET HIS BROTHERS
Jacob asked Joseph to go find his brothers, who were grazing their flocks near Shechem. When Joseph arrived, he learned that his brothers had gone on to Dothan, which lay along a major trade route to Egypt. After he arrived at Dothan, the jealous brothers sold Joseph as a slave to a group of Ishmaelite traders who were on their way to Egypt.

made plans to kill him. ¹⁹"Here comes the dreamer!" they said. ²⁰"Come on, let's kill him and throw him into one of these cisterns. We can tell our father, 'A wild animal has eaten him.' Then we'll see what becomes of his dreams!"

²¹But when Reuben heard of their scheme, he came to Joseph's rescue. "Let's not kill him," he said. ²²"Why should we shed any blood? Let's just throw him into this empty cistern here in the wilderness. Then he'll die without our laying a hand on him." Reuben was secretly planning to rescue Joseph and return him to his father.

²³So when Joseph arrived, his brothers ripped off the beautiful robe he was wearing. ²⁴Then they grabbed him and threw him into the cistern. Now the cistern was empty; there was no water in it. ²⁵Then, just as they were sitting down to eat, they looked up and saw a caravan of camels in the distance coming toward them. It was a group of Ishmaelite traders taking a load of gum, balm, and aromatic resin from Gilead down to Egypt.

²⁶Judah said to his brothers, "What will we gain by killing our brother? We'd have to cover up the crime.* ²⁷Instead of hurting him, let's sell him to those Ishmaelite traders. After all, he is our brother—our own flesh and blood!" And his brothers agreed. ²⁸So when the Ishmaelites, who were Midianite traders, came by, Joseph's brothers pulled him out of the cistern and sold him to them for twenty pieces* of silver. And the traders took him to Egypt.

²⁹Some time later, Reuben returned to get Joseph out of the cistern. When he discovered that Joseph was missing, he tore his clothes in grief. ³⁰Then he went back to his brothers and lamented, "The boy is gone! What will I do now?"

³¹Then the brothers killed a young goat and dipped Joseph's robe in its blood. ³²They sent the beautiful robe to their father with this message: "Look at what we found. Doesn't this robe belong to your son?"

³³Their father recognized it immediately. "Yes," he said, "it is my son's robe. A wild animal must have eaten him. Joseph has

UGLY RAGE
(37:19-20) Could jealousy ever make you feel like killing someone? Before saying, "No way!" look at what happened in this story. Ten men were willing to kill their youngest brother because of his status as the favorite son. Their deep jealousy had grown into ugly rage, blinding them completely to what was right. Jealousy can be hard to recognize, because our reasons for it seem to make sense. But left unchecked, jealousy grows quickly and leads to serious sins. The longer you cultivate jealous feelings, the harder it is to uproot them. The time to deal with jealousy is when you notice yourself keeping score of what others have.

ME FIRST
(37:29-30) Reuben returned to the pit to find Joseph, but his little brother was gone. His first response, in effect, was "What is going to happen to me?" rather than "What is going to happen to Joseph?" In a tough situation, what's your first concern? Consider the person most affected by the problem, and you will be more likely to find a solution for it.

37:26 Hebrew *cover his blood.*   **37:28** Hebrew *20 shekels,* about 8 ounces or 228 grams in weight.

clearly been torn to pieces!" [34]Then Jacob tore his clothes and dressed himself in burlap. He mourned deeply for his son for a long time. [35]His family all tried to comfort him, but he refused to be comforted. "I will go to my grave* mourning for my son," he would say, and then he would weep.

[36]Meanwhile, the Midianite traders* arrived in Egypt, where they sold Joseph to Potiphar, an officer of Pharaoh, the king of Egypt. Potiphar was captain of the palace guard.

38 JUDAH AND TAMAR

About this time, Judah left home and moved to Adullam, where he stayed with a man named Hirah. [2]There he saw a Canaanite woman, the daughter of Shua, and he married her. When he slept with her, [3]she became pregnant and gave birth to a son, and he named the boy Er. [4]Then she became pregnant again and gave birth to another son, and she named him Onan. [5]And when she gave birth to a third son, she named him Shelah. At the time of Shelah's birth, they were living at Kezib.

[6]In the course of time, Judah arranged for his firstborn son, Er, to marry a young woman named Tamar. [7]But Er was a wicked man in the LORD's sight, so the LORD took his life. [8]Then Judah said to Er's brother Onan, "Go and marry Tamar, as our law requires of the brother of a man who has died. You must produce an heir for your brother."

[9]But Onan was not willing to have a child who would not be his own heir. So whenever he had intercourse with his brother's wife, he spilled the semen on the ground. This prevented her from having a child who would belong to his brother. [10]But the LORD considered it evil for Onan to deny a child to his dead brother. So the LORD took Onan's life, too.

[11]Then Judah said to Tamar, his daughter-in-law, "Go back to your parents' home and remain a widow until my son Shelah is old enough to marry you." (But Judah didn't really intend to do this because he was afraid Shelah would also die, like his two brothers.) So Tamar went back to live in her father's home.

[12]Some years later Judah's wife died. After the time of mourning was over, Judah and his friend Hirah the Adullamite went up to Timnah to supervise the shearing of his sheep. [13]Someone told Tamar, "Look, your father-in-law is going up to Timnah to shear his sheep."

37:35 Hebrew *go down to Sheol.*   37:36 Hebrew *the Medanites.* The relationship between the Midianites and Medanites is unclear; compare 37:28. See also 25:2.

PERSONALITY PROFILE JUDAH

UPS:
- *Was a natural leader— outspoken and decisive*
- *Thought clearly and took action in pressure situations*
- *Was willing to stand by his word and put himself on the line when necessary*
- *Was the fourth son of 12, and the one through whom God would eventually bring King David and Jesus, the Messiah*

DOWNS:
- *Suggested to his brothers that they sell Joseph into slavery*
- *Failed to keep his promise to his daughter-in-law, Tamar*

STATS:
- *Where: Canaan, Egypt*
- *Occupation: Shepherd*
- *Relatives: Jacob and Leah (parents); Bathshua (wife; 1 Chr 2:3); Tamar (daughter-in-law); eleven brothers, one sister, and five sons (Gen 38:3-5, 27-30)*

KEY VERSE: *Genesis 49:8-9*

PEOPLE WHO ARE LEADERS stand out at the right time. They don't necessarily act or look a certain way until the need for action comes along. Among their skills are the abilities to speak up, make decisions, take action, or take control. (Does that describe you?) Leaders can use their skills for great good or great evil.

Jacob's fourth son, Judah, was a natural leader. His life included many opportunities to exercise his skills. Unfortunately, Judah's decisions were often shaped more by the pressures of the moment than by a desire to cooperate with God's plan. But when he recognized his mistakes, he was willing to admit them. His experience with Tamar and the final confrontation with Joseph are both examples of his willingness to take responsibility for his sins when confronted. That quality was a strength Judah passed on to his descendant David.

Whether or not we have natural leadership qualities like Judah, we do have some of the same struggles. Taking responsibility for one's sins isn't always easy, but it's necessary. From Judah we can learn that it is not wise to avoid owning up to wrongdoing. It is better to openly admit our mistakes, shoulder the blame, and seek forgiveness. We may not avoid the consequences, but at least we won't keep going down the same destructive path.

BOTTOM LINE: God is in control far beyond the immediate situation.
Procrastination often brings about a worse result.
Judah's offer to substitute his life for Benjamin's is a picture of what his descendant Jesus would do for all people.

Judah's story is told in Genesis 29:35; 35:23; 37–50. He also is mentioned in 1 Chronicles 2:1-4.

WOMEN IN JESUS' FAMILY TREE

Tamar—Canaanite
Genesis 38:1-30

Rahab—Canaanite
Joshua 6:22-25

Ruth—Moabite
Ruth 4:13-22

Bathsheba—Israelite
2 Samuel 12:24-25

¹⁴Tamar was aware that Shelah had grown up, but no arrangements had been made for her to come and marry him. So she changed out of her widow's clothing and covered herself with a veil to disguise herself. Then she sat beside the road at the entrance to the village of Enaim, which is on the road to Timnah. ¹⁵Judah noticed her and thought she was a prostitute, since she had covered her face. ¹⁶So he stopped and propositioned her. "Let me have sex with you," he said, not realizing that she was his own daughter-in-law.

"How much will you pay to have sex with me?" Tamar asked.

¹⁷"I'll send you a young goat from my flock," Judah promised.

"But what will you give me to guarantee that you will send the goat?" she asked.

¹⁸"What kind of guarantee do you want?" he replied.

She answered, "Leave me your identification seal and its cord and the walking stick you are carrying." So Judah gave them to her. Then he had intercourse with her, and she became pregnant. ¹⁹Afterward she went back home, took off her veil, and put on her widow's clothing as usual.

²⁰Later Judah asked his friend Hirah the Adullamite to take the young goat to the woman and to pick up the things he had given her as his guarantee. But Hirah couldn't find her. ²¹So he asked the men who lived there, "Where can I find the shrine prostitute who was sitting beside the road at the entrance to Enaim?"

....

TURN AND RUN
(39:7-15) Joseph avoided Potiphar's wife as much as possible. He refused her sexual advances and finally ran from her. Sometimes merely trying to avoid temptation is not enough. We must turn and run, especially when the temptation seems very strong, as is often the case with sexual temptation. Running from sin isn't cowardly. It could save your life.

"We've never had a shrine prostitute here," they replied.

²²So Hirah returned to Judah and told him, "I couldn't find her anywhere, and the men of the village claim they've never had a shrine prostitute there."

²³"Then let her keep the things I gave her," Judah said. "I sent the young goat as we agreed, but you couldn't find her. We'd be the laughingstock of the village if we went back again to look for her."

²⁴About three months later, Judah was told, "Tamar, your daughter-in-law, has acted like a prostitute. And now, because of this, she's pregnant."

"Bring her out, and let her be burned!" Judah demanded.

²⁵But as they were taking her out to kill her, she sent this message to her father-in-law: "The man who owns these things made me pregnant. Look closely. Whose seal and cord and walking stick are these?"

²⁶Judah recognized them immediately and said, "She is more righteous than I am, because I didn't arrange for her to marry my son Shelah." And Judah never slept with Tamar again.

²⁷When the time came for Tamar to give birth, it was discovered that she was carrying twins. ²⁸While she was in labor, one of the babies reached out his hand. The midwife grabbed it and tied a scarlet string around the child's wrist, announcing, "This one came out first." ²⁹But then he pulled back his hand, and out came his brother! "What!" the midwife exclaimed. "How did you break out first?" So he was named Perez.* ³⁰Then the baby with the scarlet string on his wrist was born, and he was named Zerah.*

39 JOSEPH IN POTIPHAR'S HOUSE When Joseph was taken to Egypt by the Ishmaelite traders, he was purchased by Potiphar, an Egyptian officer. Potiphar was captain of the guard for Pharaoh, the king of Egypt.

²The LORD was with Joseph, so he succeeded in everything he did as he served in the home of his Egyptian master. ³Potiphar noticed this and realized that the LORD was with Joseph, giving him success in everything he did. ⁴This pleased Potiphar, so he soon made Joseph his personal attendant. He put him in charge of his entire household and everything he owned. ⁵From the day Joseph was put in charge of his master's household and property, the LORD began to bless Potiphar's household for Joseph's sake.

38:29 *Perez* means "breaking out." **38:30** *Zerah* means "scarlet" or "brightness."

All his household affairs ran smoothly, and his crops and livestock flourished. ⁶So Potiphar gave Joseph complete administrative responsibility over everything he owned. With Joseph there, he didn't worry about a thing—except what kind of food to eat!

Joseph was a very handsome and well-built young man, ⁷and Potiphar's wife soon began to look at him lustfully. "Come and sleep with me," she demanded.

⁸But Joseph refused. "Look," he told her, "my master trusts me with everything in his entire household. ⁹No one here has more authority than I do. He has held back nothing from me except you, because you are his wife. How could I do such a wicked thing? It would be a great sin against God."

¹⁰She kept putting pressure on Joseph day after day, but he refused to sleep with her, and he kept out of her way as much as possible. ¹¹One day, however, no one else was around when he went in to do his work. ¹²She came and grabbed him by his cloak, demanding, "Come on, sleep with me!" Joseph tore himself away, but he left his cloak in her hand as he ran from the house.

¹³When she saw that she was holding his cloak and he had fled, ¹⁴she called out to her servants. Soon all the men came running. "Look!" she said. "My husband has brought this Hebrew slave here to make fools of us! He came into my room to rape me, but I screamed. ¹⁵When he heard me scream, he ran outside and got away, but he left his cloak behind with me."

¹⁶She kept the cloak with her until her husband came home. ¹⁷Then she told him her story. "That Hebrew slave you've brought into our house tried to come in and fool around with me," she said. ¹⁸"But when I screamed, he ran outside, leaving his cloak with me!"

JOSEPH PUT IN PRISON

¹⁹Potiphar was furious when he heard his wife's story about how Joseph had treated her. ²⁰So he took Joseph and threw him into the prison where the king's prisoners were held, and there he remained. ²¹But the LORD was with Joseph in the prison and showed him his faithful love. And the LORD made Joseph a favorite with the prison warden. ²²Before long, the warden put Joseph in charge of all the other prisoners and over everything that happened in the prison. ²³The warden had no more worries, because Joseph took care of everything. The LORD was with him and caused everything he did to succeed.

40 JOSEPH INTERPRETS TWO DREAMS

Some time later, Pharaoh's chief cupbearer and chief baker offended their royal master. ²Pharaoh became angry with these two officials, ³and he put them in the prison where Joseph was, in the palace of the captain of the guard. ⁴They remained in prison for quite some time, and the captain of the guard assigned them to Joseph, who looked after them.

⁵While they were in prison, Pharaoh's cupbearer and baker each had a dream one night, and each dream had its own meaning. ⁶When Joseph saw them the next morning, he noticed that they both looked upset. ⁷"Why do you look so worried today?" he asked them.

⁸And they replied, "We both had dreams last night, but no one can tell us what they mean."

"Interpreting dreams is God's business," Joseph replied. "Go ahead and tell me your dreams."

⁹So the chief cup-bearer told Joseph his dream first. "In my dream," he said, "I saw a grapevine in front of me. ¹⁰The vine had three branches that began to bud and blossom, and soon it produced clusters of ripe grapes. ¹¹I was holding Pharaoh's wine cup in my hand, so I took a cluster of grapes and squeezed the juice into the cup. Then I placed the cup in Pharaoh's hand."

¹²"This is what the dream means," Joseph said. "The three branches represent three days. ¹³Within three days Pharaoh will lift you up and restore you to your position as his chief

---

SEDUCTION
(39:9) Potiphar's wife failed to seduce Joseph, who resisted this temptation by saying it would be a sin against God. Joseph didn't say, "I'd be hurting you," or "I'd be sinning against Potiphar," or "I'd be sinning against myself." Under pressure, such excuses are easily used. Remember that sexual sin is not just between two consenting adults. It is an act of disobedience to God.

POSITIVE ATTITUDE
(39:21-23) As a prisoner and slave, Joseph could have believed that his situation was hopeless. Instead, he did his best with each task given him. The chief jailer soon noticed his diligence and positive attitude and promoted him to prison administrator. Are you in a seemingly hopeless predicament? Ask God to help you recognize his presence, even in the middle of an impossibly difficult situation, and give you a positive attitude.

OPPORTUNITY
(40:8) When the subject of interpreting dreams came up, Joseph focused everyone's attention on God. Rather than using the situation to make himself look good, he turned it into a powerful witness for the Lord. One secret of effective witnessing is to recognize opportunities to relate God to the other person's experience. When the opportunity arises, we must have the courage to speak, as Joseph did. Go for it!

cup-bearer. ¹⁴And please remember me and do me a favor when things go well for you. Mention me to Pharaoh, so he might let me out of this place. ¹⁵For I was kidnapped from my homeland, the land of the Hebrews, and now I'm here in prison, but I did nothing to deserve it."

¹⁶When the chief baker saw that Joseph had given the first dream such a positive interpretation, he said to Joseph, "I had a dream, too. In my dream there were three baskets of white pastries stacked on my head. ¹⁷The top basket contained all kinds of pastries for Pharaoh, but the birds came and ate them from the basket on my head."

¹⁸"This is what the dream means," Joseph told him. "The three baskets also represent three days. ¹⁹Three days from now Pharaoh will lift you up and impale your body on a pole. Then birds will come and peck away at your flesh."

²⁰Pharaoh's birthday came three days later, and he prepared a banquet for all his officials and staff. He summoned* his chief cup-bearer and chief baker to join the other officials. ²¹He then restored the chief cup-bearer to his former position, so he could again hand Pharaoh his cup. ²²But Pharaoh impaled the chief baker, just as Joseph had predicted when he interpreted his dream. ²³Pharaoh's chief cup-bearer, however, forgot all about Joseph, never giving him another thought.

41 **PHARAOH'S DREAMS** Two full years later, Pharaoh dreamed that he was standing on the bank of the Nile River. ²In his dream he saw seven fat, healthy cows come up out of the river and begin grazing in the marsh grass. ³Then he saw seven more cows come up behind them from the Nile, but these were scrawny and thin. These cows stood beside the fat cows on the riverbank. ⁴Then the scrawny, thin cows ate the seven healthy, fat cows! At this point in the dream, Pharaoh woke up.

⁵But he fell asleep again and had a second dream. This time he saw seven heads of grain, plump and beautiful, growing on a single stalk. ⁶Then seven more heads of grain appeared,

but these were shriveled and withered by the east wind. ⁷And these thin heads swallowed up the seven plump, well-formed heads! Then Pharaoh woke up again and realized it was a dream.

⁸The next morning Pharaoh was very disturbed by the dreams. So he called for all the magicians and wise men of Egypt. When Pharaoh told them his dreams, not one of them could tell him what they meant.

⁹Finally, the king's chief cup-bearer spoke up. "Today I have been reminded of my failure," he told Pharaoh. ¹⁰"Some time ago, you were angry with the chief baker and me, and you imprisoned us in the palace of the captain of the guard. ¹¹One night the chief baker and I each had a dream, and each dream had its own meaning. ¹²There was a young Hebrew man with us in the prison who was a slave of the captain of the guard. We told him our dreams, and he told us what each of our dreams meant. ¹³And everything happened just as he had predicted. I was restored to my position as cup-bearer, and the chief baker was executed and impaled on a pole."

¹⁴Pharaoh sent for Joseph at once, and he was quickly brought from the prison. After he shaved and changed his clothes, he went in and stood before Pharaoh. ¹⁵Then Pharaoh said to Joseph, "I had a dream last night, and no one here can tell me what it means. But I have heard that when you hear about a dream you can interpret it."

¹⁶"It is beyond my power to do this," Joseph replied. "But God can tell you what it means and set you at ease."

¹⁷So Pharaoh told Joseph his dream. "In my dream," he said, "I was standing on the bank of the Nile River, ¹⁸and I saw seven fat, healthy cows come up out of the river and begin grazing in the marsh grass. ¹⁹But then I saw seven sick-looking cows, scrawny and thin, come up after them. I've never seen such sorry-looking animals in all the land of Egypt. ²⁰These thin, scrawny cows ate the seven fat cows. ²¹But afterward you wouldn't have known it, for they were still as thin and scrawny as before! Then I woke up.

²²"Then I fell asleep again, and I had another dream. This time I saw seven heads of grain, full and beautiful, growing on a single stalk. ²³Then seven more heads of grain appeared, but these were blighted, shriveled, and withered by the east wind. ²⁴And the shriveled heads swallowed the seven healthy heads. I told these dreams to

PREPARATION

(41:14) Our most important opportunities may come when we are least prepared for them. Joseph was brought hastily from the dungeon and pushed before Pharaoh. Did he have time to prepare? Yes and no. He had no warning that he suddenly would be pulled from prison and questioned by the king. Yet Joseph was ready for almost anything because of his right relationship with God. Are you and God tight? If not, what do you need to do to make things right? Keeping close to God can help you be prepared for anything that comes your way.

40:20 Hebrew *He lifted up the head of.*

the magicians, but no one could tell me what they mean."

²⁵Joseph responded, "Both of Pharaoh's dreams mean the same thing. God is telling Pharaoh in advance what he is about to do. ²⁶The seven healthy cows and the seven healthy heads of grain both represent seven years of prosperity. ²⁷The seven thin, scrawny cows that came up later and the seven thin heads of grain, withered by the east wind, represent seven years of famine.

²⁸"This will happen just as I have described it, for God has revealed to Pharaoh in advance what he is about to do. ²⁹The next seven years will be a period of great prosperity throughout the land of Egypt. ³⁰But afterward there will be seven years of famine so great that all the prosperity will be forgotten in Egypt. Famine will destroy the land. ³¹This famine will be so severe that even the memory of the good years will be erased. ³²As for having two similar dreams, it means that these events have been decreed by God, and he will soon make them happen.

³³"Therefore, Pharaoh should find an intelligent and wise man and put him in charge of the entire land of Egypt. ³⁴Then Pharaoh should appoint supervisors over the land and let them collect one-fifth of all the crops during the seven good years. ³⁵Have them gather all the food produced in the good years that are just ahead and bring it to Pharaoh's storehouses. Store it away, and guard it so there will be food in the cities. ³⁶That way there will be enough to eat when the seven years of famine come to the land of Egypt. Otherwise this famine will destroy the land."

JOSEPH MADE RULER OF EGYPT ³⁷Joseph's suggestions were well received by Pharaoh and his officials. ³⁸So Pharaoh asked his officials, "Can we find anyone else like this man so obviously filled with the spirit of God?" ³⁹Then Pharaoh said to Joseph, "Since God has revealed the meaning of the dreams to you, clearly no one else is as intelligent or wise as you are. ⁴⁰You will be in charge of my court, and all my people will take orders from you. Only I, sitting on my throne, will have a rank higher than yours."

⁴¹Pharaoh said to Joseph, "I hereby put you in charge of the entire land of Egypt." ⁴²Then

PERSONALITY PROFILE JOSEPH

UPS:
- Rose in power from slave to ruler of Egypt
- Was known for his personal integrity
- Was a man of spiritual sensitivity
- Prepared a nation to survive a famine

DOWNS:
- Youthful pride caused friction with his brothers

STATS:
- Where: Canaan, Egypt
- Occupations: Shepherd, slave, ruler
- Relatives: Jacob and Rachel (parents); eleven brothers, one sister; Asenath (wife); Manasseh and Ephraim (sons)

KEY VERSE: Genesis 41:38

EVER BEEN TOLD that you can be or do anything? Joseph believed that. He was naturally self-confident. He was also Jacob's favorite son. God had given Joseph hints of great plans for his life.

Sometimes, however, Joseph wasn't very sensitive of others' feelings. When he had dreams of greatness, he didn't hesitate to share them with his brothers and father. His dreams and status as the favorite of the family triggered his brothers' jealousy and anger. Eventually they tried to get rid of him.

As he grew, Joseph learned. The painful experiences in his life changed his self-confidence into a quiet but powerful confidence in God. He was able to survive and do well where most people would have failed. He added practical wisdom to his confidence and won the hearts of almost everyone who got to know him, including Potiphar, the jailer, other prisoners, the king, and after many years, even his 10 older brothers.

Perhaps you can identify with one or more of these hardships Joseph experienced: betrayal and desertion by family members, sexual temptation, punishment for doing the right thing, long imprisonment, and being forgotten by those he helped. As you read his story, note what Joseph did in each case. His positive response transformed each setback into a step forward. He didn't spend much time asking why. Instead, he kept doing what was right. Those who watched his life were aware that wherever Joseph went and whatever he did, God was with him.

What's your attitude when things go wrong? Are you tempted to complain? Or will you, like Joseph, let the hard times shape you?

BOTTOM LINE: How we respond to the circumstances in life shows our belief or unbelief.

With God's help, any situation can be used for good, even when others intend it for evil.

Joseph's story is told in Genesis 30:22-24; 35:24; 37; 39–50. He also is mentioned in Hebrews 11:21-22.

Pharaoh removed his signet ring from his hand and placed it on Joseph's finger. He dressed him in fine linen clothing and hung a gold chain around his neck. 43Then he had Joseph ride in the chariot reserved for his second-in-command. And wherever Joseph went, the command was shouted, "Kneel down!" So Pharaoh put Joseph in charge of all Egypt. 44And Pharaoh said to him, "I am Pharaoh, but no one will lift a hand or foot in the entire land of Egypt without your approval."

45Then Pharaoh gave Joseph a new Egyptian name, Zaphenath-paneah.* He also gave him a wife, whose name was Asenath. She was the daughter of Potiphera, the priest of On.* So Joseph took charge of the entire land of Egypt. 46He was thirty years old when he began serving in the court of Pharaoh, the king of Egypt. And when Joseph left Pharaoh's presence, he inspected the entire land of Egypt.

47As predicted, for seven years the land produced bumper crops. 48During those years, Joseph gathered all the crops grown in Egypt and stored the grain from the surrounding fields in the cities. 49He piled up huge amounts of grain like sand on the seashore. Finally, he stopped keeping records because there was too much to measure.

50During this time, before the first of the famine years, two sons were born to Joseph and his wife, Asenath, the daughter of Potiphera, the priest of On. 51Joseph named his older son Manasseh,* for he said, "God has made me forget all my troubles and everyone in my father's family." 52Joseph named his second son Ephraim,* for he said, "God has made me fruitful in this land of my grief."

53At last the seven years of bumper crops throughout the land of Egypt came to an end. 54Then the seven years of famine began, just as Joseph had predicted. The famine also struck all the surrounding countries, but throughout Egypt there was plenty of food. 55Eventually, however, the famine spread throughout the land of Egypt as well. And when the people cried out to Pharaoh for food, he told them, "Go to Joseph, and do whatever he tells you." 56So with severe famine everywhere, Joseph opened up the storehouses and distributed grain to the

Egyptians, for the famine was severe throughout the land of Egypt. 57And people from all around came to Egypt to buy grain from Joseph because the famine was severe throughout the world.

42 JOSEPH'S BROTHERS GO TO EGYPT

When Jacob heard that grain was available in Egypt, he said to his sons, "Why are you standing around looking at one another? 2I have heard there is grain in Egypt. Go down there, and buy enough grain to keep us alive. Otherwise we'll die."

3So Joseph's ten older brothers went down to Egypt to buy grain. 4But Jacob wouldn't let Joseph's younger brother, Benjamin, go with them, for fear some harm might come to him. 5So Jacob's* sons arrived in Egypt along with others to buy food, for the famine was in Canaan as well.

6Since Joseph was governor of all Egypt and in charge of selling grain to all the people, it was to him that his brothers came. When they arrived, they bowed before him with their faces to the ground. 7Joseph recognized his brothers instantly, but he pretended to be a stranger and spoke harshly to them. "Where are you from?" he demanded.

"From the land of Canaan," they replied. "We have come to buy food."

8Although Joseph recognized his brothers, they didn't recognize him. 9And he remembered the dreams he'd had about them many years before. He said to them, "You are spies! You have come to see how vulnerable our land has become."

10"No, my lord!" they exclaimed. "Your servants have simply come to buy food. 11We are all brothers—members of the same family. We are honest men, sir! We are not spies!"

12"Yes, you are!" Joseph insisted. "You have come to see how vulnerable our land has become."

13"Sir," they said, "there are actually twelve of us. We, your servants, are all brothers, sons of a man living in the land of Canaan. Our youngest brother is back there with our father right now, and one of our brothers is no longer with us."

14But Joseph insisted, "As I said, you are spies! 15This is how I will test your story. I swear by the life of Pharaoh that you will never leave Egypt unless your youngest brother comes here! 16One of you must go and get your brother.

TRAINING PROGRAM

(41:41) Joseph rose quickly to the top, from a prison cell to Pharaoh's palace. His training for this important position involved being first a slave and then a prisoner. In each situation he learned the importance of serving God and others. Whatever your situation, no matter how undesirable, consider it part of your training program for serving God.

41:45a Zaphenath-paneah probably means "God speaks and lives."
41:45b Greek version reads of Heliopolis; also in 41:50.   **41:51** Manasseh sounds like a Hebrew term that means "causing to forget."
41:52 Ephraim sounds like a Hebrew term that means "fruitful."
42:5 Hebrew Israel's. See note on 35:21.

I'll keep the rest of you here in prison. Then we'll find out whether or not your story is true. By the life of Pharaoh, if it turns out that you don't have a younger brother, then I'll know you are spies."

[17]So Joseph put them all in prison for three days. [18]On the third day Joseph said to them, "I am a God-fearing man. If you do as I say, you will live. [19]If you really are honest men, choose one of your brothers to remain in prison. The rest of you may go home with grain for your starving families. [20]But you must bring your youngest brother back to me. This will prove that you are telling the truth, and you will not die." To this they agreed.

[21]Speaking among themselves, they said, "Clearly we are being punished because of what we did to Joseph long ago. We saw his anguish when he pleaded for his life, but we wouldn't listen. That's why we're in this trouble."

[22]"Didn't I tell you not to sin against the boy?" Reuben asked. "But you wouldn't listen. And now we have to answer for his blood!"

[23]Of course, they didn't know that Joseph understood them, for he had been speaking to them through an interpreter. [24]Now he turned away from them and began to weep. When he regained his composure, he spoke to them again. Then he chose Simeon from among them and had him tied up right before their eyes.

[25]Joseph then ordered his servants to fill the men's sacks with grain, but he also gave secret instructions to return each brother's payment at the top of his sack. He also gave them supplies for their journey home. [26]So the brothers loaded their donkeys with the grain and headed for home.

[27]But when they stopped for the night and one of them opened his sack to get grain for his donkey, he found his money in the top of his sack. [28]"Look!" he exclaimed to his brothers. "My money has been returned; it's here in my sack!" Then their hearts sank. Trembling, they said to each other, "What has God done to us?"

[29]When the brothers came to their father, Jacob, in the land of Canaan, they told him everything that had happened to them. [30]"The man who is governor of the land spoke very harshly to us," they told him. "He accused us of being spies scouting the land. [31]But we said, 'We are honest men, not spies. [32]We are twelve brothers, sons of one father. One brother is no longer with us, and the youngest is at home with our father in the land of Canaan.'

[33]"Then the man who is governor of the land told us, 'This is how I will find out if you are honest men. Leave one of your brothers here with me, and take grain for your starving families and go on home. [34]But you must bring your youngest brother back to me. Then I will know you are honest men and not spies. Then I will give you back your brother, and you may trade freely in the land.'"

[35]As they emptied out their sacks, there in each man's sack was the bag of money he had paid for the grain! The brothers and their father were terrified when they saw the bags of money. [36]Jacob exclaimed, "You are robbing me of my children! Joseph is gone! Simeon is gone! And now you want to take Benjamin, too. Everything is going against me!"

[37]Then Reuben said to his father, "You may kill my two sons if I don't bring Benjamin back to you. I'll be responsible for him, and I promise to bring him back."

[38]But Jacob replied, "My son will not go down with you. His brother Joseph is dead, and he is all I have left. If anything should happen to him on your journey, you would send this grieving, white-haired man to his grave.*"

43 THE BROTHERS RETURN TO EGYPT

But the famine continued to ravage the land of Canaan. [2]When the grain they had brought from Egypt was almost gone, Jacob said to his sons, "Go back and buy us a little more food."

[3]But Judah said, "The man was serious when he warned us, 'You won't see my face again unless your brother is with you.' [4]If you send Benjamin with us, we will go down and buy more food. [5]But if you don't let Benjamin go, we won't go either. Remember, the man said, 'You won't see my face again unless your brother is with you.'"

[6]"Why were you so cruel to me?" Jacob* moaned. "Why did you tell him you had another brother?"

[7]"The man kept asking us questions about our family," they replied. "He asked, 'Is your father still alive? Do you have another brother?' So we answered his questions. How could we

42:38 Hebrew *to Sheol.*   43:6 Hebrew *Israel;* also in 43:11. See note on 35:21.

FULL RESPONSIBILITY
(43:8-9) Judah accepted full responsibility for Benjamin's safety. He did not know what that might mean for him, but he was determined to carry it out. In the end, Judah's stirring words caused Joseph to break down and reveal himself to his brothers (44:18–45:3). Accepting responsibility can be difficult at times. But it builds character and confidence, earns others' respect, and motivates us to complete our work. When you have been given an assignment to complete or a responsibility to fulfill, commit yourself to seeing it through.

know he would say, 'Bring your brother down here'?"

⁸Judah said to his father, "Send the boy with me, and we will be on our way. Otherwise we will all die of starvation—and not only we, but you and our little ones. ⁹I personally guarantee his safety. You may hold me responsible if I don't bring him back to you. Then let me bear the blame forever. ¹⁰If we hadn't wasted all this time, we could have gone and returned twice by now."

¹¹So their father, Jacob, finally said to them, "If it can't be avoided, then at least do this. Pack your bags with the best products of this land. Take them down to the man as gifts—balm, honey, gum, aromatic resin, pistachio nuts, and almonds. ¹²Also take double the money that was put back in your sacks, as it was probably someone's mistake. ¹³Then take your brother, and go back to the man. ¹⁴May God Almighty* give you mercy as you go before the man, so that he will release Simeon and let Benjamin return. But if I must lose my children, so be it."

¹⁵So the men packed Jacob's gifts and double the money and headed off with Benjamin. They finally arrived in Egypt and presented themselves to Joseph. ¹⁶When Joseph saw Benjamin with them, he said to the manager of his household, "These men will eat with me this noon. Take them inside the palace. Then go slaughter an animal, and prepare a big feast." ¹⁷So the man did as Joseph told him and took them into Joseph's palace.

¹⁸The brothers were terrified when they saw that they were being taken into Joseph's house. "It's because of the money someone put in our sacks last time we were here," they said. "He plans to pretend that we stole it. Then he will seize us, make us slaves, and take our donkeys."

A FEAST AT JOSEPH'S PALACE ¹⁹The brothers approached the manager of Joseph's household and spoke to him at the entrance to the palace. ²⁰"Sir," they said, "we came to Egypt once before to buy food. ²¹But as we were returning home, we stopped for the night and opened our sacks. Then we discovered that each man's money—the exact amount paid—was in the top of his sack! Here it is; we have brought it back with us. ²²We also have additional money to buy more food. We have no idea who put our money in our sacks."

²³"Relax. Don't be afraid," the household manager told them. "Your God, the God of your father, must have put this treasure into your sacks. I know I received your payment." Then

he released Simeon and brought him out to them.

²⁴The manager then led the men into Joseph's palace. He gave them water to wash their feet and provided food for their donkeys. ²⁵They were told they would be eating there, so they prepared their gifts for Joseph's arrival at noon. ²⁶When Joseph came home, they gave him the gifts they had brought him, then bowed low to the ground before him. ²⁷After greeting them, he asked, "How is your father, the old man you spoke about? Is he still alive?"

²⁸"Yes," they replied. "Our father, your servant, is alive and well." And they bowed low again.

²⁹Then Joseph looked at his brother Benjamin, the son of his own mother. "Is this your youngest brother, the one you told me about?" Joseph asked. "May God be gracious to you, my son." ³⁰Then Joseph hurried from the room because he was overcome with emotion for his brother. He went into his private room, where he broke down and wept. ³¹After washing his face, he came back out, keeping himself under control. Then he ordered, "Bring out the food!"

³²The waiters served Joseph at his own table, and his brothers were served at a separate table. The Egyptians who ate with Joseph sat at their own table, because Egyptians despise Hebrews and refuse to eat with them. ³³Joseph told each of his brothers where to sit, and to their amazement, he seated them according to age, from oldest to youngest. ³⁴And Joseph filled their plates with food from his own table, giving Benjamin five times as much as he gave the others. So they feasted and drank freely with him.

44

JOSEPH'S SILVER CUP When his brothers were ready to leave, Joseph gave these instructions to his palace manager: "Fill each of their sacks with as much grain as they can carry, and put each man's money back into his sack. ²Then put my personal silver cup at the top of the youngest brother's sack, along with the money for his grain." So the manager did as Joseph instructed him.

³The brothers were up at dawn and were sent on their journey with their loaded donkeys. ⁴But when they had gone only a short distance and were barely out of the city, Joseph said to his palace manager, "Chase after them and stop them. When you catch up with them, ask them, 'Why have you repaid my kindness with such evil? ⁵Why have you stolen my master's silver

43:14 Hebrew *El-Shaddai*.

cup,* which he uses to predict the future? What a wicked thing you have done!'"

⁶When the palace manager caught up with the men, he spoke to them as he had been instructed.

⁷"What are you talking about?" the brothers responded. "We are your servants and would never do such a thing! ⁸Didn't we return the money we found in our sacks? We brought it back all the way from the land of Canaan. Why would we steal silver or gold from your master's house? ⁹If you find his cup with any one of us, let that man die. And all the rest of us, my lord, will be your slaves."

¹⁰"That's fair," the man replied. "But only the one who stole the cup will be my slave. The rest of you may go free."

¹¹They all quickly took their sacks from the backs of their donkeys and opened them. ¹²The palace manager searched the brothers' sacks, from the oldest to the youngest. And the cup was found in Benjamin's sack! ¹³When the brothers saw this, they tore their clothing in despair. Then they loaded their donkeys again and returned to the city.

¹⁴Joseph was still in his palace when Judah and his brothers arrived, and they fell to the ground before him. ¹⁵"What have you done?" Joseph demanded. "Don't you know that a man like me can predict the future?"

¹⁶Judah answered, "Oh, my lord, what can we say to you? How can we explain this? How can we prove our innocence? God is punishing us for our sins. My lord, we have all returned to be your slaves—all of us, not just our brother who had your cup in his sack."

¹⁷"No," Joseph said. "I would never do such a thing! Only the man who stole the cup will be my slave. The rest of you may go back to your father in peace."

JUDAH SPEAKS FOR HIS BROTHERS

¹⁸Then Judah stepped forward and said, "Please, my lord, let your servant say just one word to you. Please, do not be angry with me, even though you are as powerful as Pharaoh himself.

¹⁹"My lord, previously you asked us, your servants, 'Do you have a father or a brother?' ²⁰And we responded, 'Yes, my lord, we have a father who is an old man, and his youngest son is a child of his old age. His full brother is dead, and he alone is left of his mother's children, and his father loves him very much.'

²¹"And you said to us, 'Bring him here so I can see him with my own eyes.' ²²But we said to you,

'My lord, the boy cannot leave his father, for his father would die.' ²³But you told us, 'Unless your youngest brother comes with you, you will never see my face again.'

²⁴"So we returned to your servant, our father, and told him what you had said. ²⁵Later, when he said, 'Go back again and buy us more food,' ²⁶we replied, 'We can't go unless you let our youngest brother go with us. We'll never get to see the man's face unless our youngest brother is with us.'

²⁷"Then my father said to us, 'As you know, my wife had two sons, ²⁸and one of them went away and never returned. Doubtless he was torn to pieces by some wild animal. I have never seen him since. ²⁹Now if you take his brother away from me, and any harm comes to him, you will send this grieving, white-haired man to his grave.*'

³⁰"And now, my lord, I cannot go back to my father without the boy. Our father's life is bound up in the boy's life. ³¹If he sees that the boy is not with us, our father will die. We, your servants, will indeed be responsible for sending that grieving, white-haired man to his grave. ³²My lord, I guaranteed to my father that I would take care of the boy. I told him, 'If I don't bring him back to you, I will bear the blame forever.'

³³"So please, my lord, let me stay here as a slave instead of the boy, and let the boy return with his brothers. ³⁴For how can I return to my father if the boy is not with me? I couldn't bear to see the anguish this would cause my father!"

45 JOSEPH REVEALS HIS IDENTITY

Joseph could stand it no longer. There were many people in the room, and he said to his attendants, "Out, all of you!" So he was alone with his brothers when he told them who he was. ²Then he broke down and wept. He wept so loudly the Egyptians could hear him, and word of it quickly carried to Pharaoh's palace.

³"I am Joseph!" he said to his brothers. "Is my father still alive?" But his brothers were speechless! They were stunned to realize that Joseph was standing there in front of them. ⁴"Please, come closer," he said to them. So they came

....

CHANGED LIFE

(44:16-34) When Judah was younger, he showed no regard for his brother Joseph or his father, Jacob. First, he convinced his brothers to sell Joseph as a slave (37:27). Second, he joined his brothers in lying to his father about Joseph's fate (37:32). But what a change had taken place in Judah! The man who sold one favored little brother into slavery now offered to become a slave himself to save another favored little brother. What are the evidences of your changed life? Would your family members agree?

44:5 As in Greek version; Hebrew lacks this phrase.　　**44:29** Hebrew *to Sheol*; also in 44:31.

closer. And he said again, "I am Joseph, your brother, whom you sold into slavery in Egypt. ⁵But don't be upset, and don't be angry with yourselves for selling me to this place. It was God who sent me here ahead of you to preserve your lives. ⁶This famine that has ravaged the land for two years will last five more years, and there will be neither plowing nor harvesting. ⁷God has sent me ahead of you to keep you and your families alive and to preserve many survivors.* ⁸So it was God who sent me here, not you! And he is the one who made me an adviser* to Pharaoh—the manager of his entire palace and the governor of all Egypt.

⁹"Now hurry back to my father and tell him, 'This is what your son Joseph says: God has made me master over all the land of Egypt. So come down to me immediately! ¹⁰You can live in the region of Goshen, where you can be near me with all your children and grandchildren, your flocks and herds, and everything you own. ¹¹I will take care of you there, for there are still five years of famine ahead of us. Otherwise you, your household, and all your animals will starve.'"

¹²Then Joseph added, "Look! You can see for yourselves, and so can my brother Benjamin, that I really am Joseph! ¹³Go tell my father of my honored position here in Egypt. Describe for him everything you have seen, and then bring my father here quickly." ¹⁴Weeping with joy, he embraced Benjamin, and Benjamin did the same. ¹⁵Then Joseph kissed each of his brothers and wept over them, and after that they began talking freely with him.

PHARAOH INVITES JACOB TO EGYPT ¹⁶The news soon reached Pharaoh's palace: "Joseph's brothers have arrived!" Pharaoh and his officials were all delighted to hear this.

¹⁷Pharaoh said to Joseph, "Tell your brothers, 'This is what you must do: Load your pack animals, and hurry back to the land of Canaan.

¹⁸Then get your father and all of your families, and return here to me. I will give you the very best land in Egypt, and you will eat from the best that the land produces.'"

¹⁹Then Pharaoh said to Joseph, "Tell your brothers, 'Take wagons from the land of Egypt to carry your little children and your wives, and bring your father here. ²⁰Don't worry about your personal belongings, for the best of all the land of Egypt is yours.'"

²¹So the sons of Jacob* did as they were told. Joseph provided them with wagons, as Pharaoh had commanded, and he gave them supplies for the journey. ²²And he gave each of them new clothes—but to Benjamin he gave five changes of clothes and 300 pieces* of silver. ²³He also sent his father ten male donkeys loaded with the finest products of Egypt, and ten female donkeys loaded with grain and bread and other supplies he would need on his journey.

²⁴So Joseph sent his brothers off, and as they left, he called after them, "Don't quarrel about all this along the way!" ²⁵And they left Egypt and returned to their father, Jacob, in the land of Canaan.

²⁶"Joseph is still alive!" they told him. "And he is governor of all the land of Egypt!" Jacob was stunned at the news—he couldn't believe it. ²⁷But when they repeated to Jacob everything Joseph had told them, and when he saw the wagons Joseph had sent to carry him, their father's spirits revived.

²⁸Then Jacob exclaimed, "It must be true! My son Joseph is alive! I must go and see him before I die."

46 JACOB'S JOURNEY TO EGYPT So Jacob* set out for Egypt with all his possessions. And when he came to Beersheba, he offered sacrifices to the God of his father, Isaac. ²During the night God spoke to him in a vision. "Jacob! Jacob!" he called.

"Here I am," Jacob replied.

³"I am God,* the God of your father," the voice said. "Do not be afraid to go down to Egypt, for there I will make your family into a great nation. ⁴I will go with you down to Egypt, and I will bring you back again. You will die in Egypt, but Joseph will be with you to close your eyes."

⁵So Jacob left Beersheba, and his sons took him to Egypt. They carried him and their little ones and their wives in the wagons Pharaoh had provided for them. ⁶They also took all their

---

INTENTIONS
(45:4-8) Although Joseph's brothers had wanted to get rid of him, God used even their evil actions to fulfill his ultimate plan. He sent Joseph ahead to preserve their lives, save Egypt, and prepare the way for the beginning of the nation of Israel. When people intend evil toward you, do you have trouble believing that God is still in control? God's plans are not dictated by human actions, and he can bring good out of evil.

STRANGE PLACES
(46:1-4) Before Jacob moved his household to Egypt, God promised to go with him and take care of his family. That reassurance probably helped Jacob to put aside his fear of change. Feeling fearful about the future? The same reassurance that God offered to Jacob is yours for the taking.

45:7 Or *and to save you with an extraordinary rescue.* The meaning of the Hebrew is uncertain. **45:8** Hebrew *a father.* **45:21** Hebrew *Israel;* also in 45:28. See note on 35:21. **45:22** Hebrew *300 shekels,* about 7.5 pounds or 3.4 kilograms in weight. **46:1** Hebrew *Israel;* also in 46:29, 30. See note on 35:21. **46:3** Hebrew *I am El.*

livestock and all the personal belongings they had acquired in the land of Canaan. So Jacob and his entire family went to Egypt—⁷sons and grandsons, daughters and granddaughters—all his descendants.

⁸These are the names of the descendants of Israel—the sons of Jacob—who went to Egypt:

Reuben was Jacob's oldest son. ⁹The sons of Reuben were Hanoch, Pallu, Hezron, and Carmi.

¹⁰The sons of Simeon were Jemuel, Jamin, Ohad, Jakin, Zohar, and Shaul. (Shaul's mother was a Canaanite woman.)

¹¹The sons of Levi were Gershon, Kohath, and Merari.

¹²The sons of Judah were Er, Onan, Shelah, Perez, and Zerah (though Er and Onan had died in the land of Canaan). The sons of Perez were Hezron and Hamul.

¹³The sons of Issachar were Tola, Puah,* Jashub,* and Shimron.

¹⁴The sons of Zebulun were Sered, Elon, and Jahleel.

¹⁵These were the sons of Leah and Jacob who were born in Paddan-aram, in addition to their daughter, Dinah. The number of Jacob's descendants (male and female) through Leah was thirty-three.

¹⁶The sons of Gad were Zephon,* Haggi, Shuni, Ezbon, Eri, Arodi, and Areli.

¹⁷The sons of Asher were Imnah, Ishvah, Ishvi, and Beriah. Their sister was Serah. Beriah's sons were Heber and Malkiel.

¹⁸These were the sons of Zilpah, the servant given to Leah by her father, Laban. The number of Jacob's descendants through Zilpah was sixteen.

¹⁹The sons of Jacob's wife Rachel were Joseph and Benjamin.

²⁰Joseph's sons, born in the land of Egypt, were Manasseh and Ephraim. Their mother was Asenath, daughter of Potiphera, the priest of On.*

²¹Benjamin's sons were Bela, Beker, Ashbel, Gera, Naaman, Ehi, Rosh, Muppim, Huppim, and Ard.

²²These were the sons of Rachel and Jacob. The number of Jacob's descendants through Rachel was fourteen.

²³The son of Dan was Hushim.

²⁴The sons of Naphtali were Jahzeel, Guni, Jezer, and Shillem.

²⁵These were the sons of Bilhah, the servant given to Rachel by her father, Laban. The number of Jacob's descendants through Bilhah was seven.

²⁶The total number of Jacob's direct descendants who went with him to Egypt, not counting his sons' wives, was sixty-six. ²⁷In addition, Joseph had two sons* who were born in Egypt. So altogether, there were seventy* members of Jacob's family in the land of Egypt.

JACOB'S FAMILY ARRIVES IN GOSHEN ²⁸As
they neared their destination, Jacob sent Judah ahead to meet Joseph and get directions to the region of Goshen. And when they finally arrived there, ²⁹Joseph prepared his chariot and traveled to Goshen to meet his father, Jacob. When Joseph arrived, he embraced his father and wept, holding him for a long time. ³⁰Finally, Jacob said to Joseph, "Now I am ready to die, since I have seen your face again and know you are still alive."

³¹And Joseph said to his brothers and to his father's entire family, "I will go to Pharaoh and tell him, 'My brothers and my father's entire family have come to me from the land of Canaan. ³²These men are shepherds, and they raise livestock. They have brought with them their flocks and herds and everything they own.'"

³³Then he said, "When Pharaoh calls for you and asks you about your occupation, ³⁴you must tell him, 'We, your servants, have raised livestock all our lives, as our ancestors have always done.' When you tell him this, he will let you live here in the region of Goshen, for the Egyptians despise shepherds."

47 JACOB BLESSES PHARAOH Then
Joseph went to see Pharaoh and told him, "My father and my brothers have arrived from the land of Canaan. They have come with all their flocks and herds and possessions, and they are now in the region of Goshen."

²Joseph took five of his brothers with him and presented them to Pharaoh. ³And Pharaoh asked the brothers, "What is your occupation?"

46:13a As in Syriac version and Samaritan Pentateuch (see also 1 Chr 7:1); Hebrew reads *Puvah*.   46:13b As in some Greek manuscripts and Samaritan Pentateuch (see also Num 26:24; 1 Chr 7:1); Hebrew reads *Iob*.   46:16 As in Greek version and Samaritan Pentateuch (see also Num 26:15); Hebrew reads *Ziphion*.   46:20 Greek version reads *of Heliopolis*.   46:27a Greek version reads *nine sons*, probably including Joseph's grandsons through Ephraim and Manasseh (see 1 Chr 7:14-20).   46:27b Greek version reads *seventy-five*; see note on Exod 1:5.

··

KEEP THE FAITH
(47:1-6) *The faithfulness of Joseph affected his entire family. When he was in prison, Joseph must have wondered about his future. Instead of despairing, he faithfully obeyed God and did what was right. Does that describe you? We may not always see the effects of our faith, but we can be sure that God will honor faithfulness.*

They replied, "We, your servants, are shepherds, just like our ancestors. 4We have come to live here in Egypt for a while, for there is no pasture for our flocks in Canaan. The famine is very severe there. So please, we request permission to live in the region of Goshen."

5Then Pharaoh said to Joseph, "Now that your father and brothers have joined you here, 6choose any place in the entire land of Egypt for them to live. Give them the best land of Egypt. Let them live in the region of Goshen. And if any of them have special skills, put them in charge of my livestock, too."

7Then Joseph brought in his father, Jacob, and presented him to Pharaoh. And Jacob blessed Pharaoh.

8"How old are you?" Pharaoh asked him.

9Jacob replied, "I have traveled this earth for 130 hard years. But my life has been short compared to the lives of my ancestors." 10Then Jacob blessed Pharaoh again before leaving his court.

11So Joseph assigned the best land of Egypt—the region of Rameses—to his father and his brothers, and he settled them there, just as Pharaoh had commanded. 12And Joseph provided food for his father and his brothers in amounts appropriate to the number of their dependents, including the smallest children.

JOSEPH'S LEADERSHIP IN THE FAMINE
13Meanwhile, the famine became so severe that all the food was used up, and people were starving throughout the lands of Egypt and Canaan. 14By selling grain to the people, Joseph eventually collected all the money in Egypt and Canaan, and he put the money in Pharaoh's treasury. 15When the people of Egypt and Canaan ran out of money, all the Egyptians came to Joseph. "Our money is gone!" they cried. "But please give us food, or we will die before your very eyes!"

16Joseph replied, "Since your money is gone, bring me your livestock. I will give you food in exchange for your livestock." 17So they brought their livestock to Joseph in exchange for food. In exchange for their horses, flocks of sheep and goats, herds of cattle, and donkeys,

Joseph provided them with food for another year.

18But that year ended, and the next year they came again and said, "We cannot hide the truth from you, my lord. Our money is gone, and all our livestock and cattle are yours. We have nothing left to give but our bodies and our land. 19Why should we die before your very eyes? Buy us and our land in exchange for food; we offer our land and ourselves as slaves for Pharaoh. Just give us grain so we may live and not die, and so the land does not become empty and desolate."

20So Joseph bought all the land of Egypt for Pharaoh. All the Egyptians sold him their fields because the famine was so severe, and soon all the land belonged to Pharaoh. 21As for the people, he made them all slaves,* from one end of Egypt to the other. 22The only land he did not buy was the land belonging to the priests. They received an allotment of food directly from Pharaoh, so they didn't need to sell their land.

23Then Joseph said to the people, "Look, today I have bought you and your land for Pharaoh. I will provide you with seed so you can plant the fields. 24Then when you harvest it, one-fifth of your crop will belong to Pharaoh. You may keep the remaining four-fifths as seed for your fields and as food for you, your households, and your little ones."

25"You have saved our lives!" they exclaimed. "May it please you, my lord, to let us be Pharaoh's servants." 26Joseph then issued a decree still in effect in the land of Egypt, that Pharaoh should receive one-fifth of all the crops grown on his land. Only the land belonging to the priests was not given to Pharaoh.

27Meanwhile, the people of Israel settled in the region of Goshen in Egypt. There they acquired property, and they were fruitful, and their population grew rapidly. 28Jacob lived for seventeen years after his arrival in Egypt, so he lived 147 years in all.

29As the time of his death drew near, Jacob* called for his son Joseph and said to him, "Please do me this favor. Put your hand under my thigh and swear that you will treat me with unfailing love by honoring this last request: Do not bury me in Egypt. 30When I die, please take my body out of Egypt and bury me with my ancestors."

So Joseph promised, "I will do as you ask."

31"Swear that you will do it," Jacob insisted.

47:21 As in Greek version and Samaritan Pentateuch; Hebrew reads *he moved them all into the towns.* 47:29 Hebrew *Israel;* also in 47:31b. See note on 35:21.

So Joseph gave his oath, and Jacob bowed humbly at the head of his bed.*

48 JACOB BLESSES MANASSEH AND EPHRAIM
One day not long after this, word came to Joseph, "Your father is failing rapidly." So Joseph went to visit his father, and he took with him his two sons, Manasseh and Ephraim.

²When Joseph arrived, Jacob was told, "Your son Joseph has come to see you." So Jacob* gathered his strength and sat up in his bed.

³Jacob said to Joseph, "God Almighty* appeared to me at Luz in the land of Canaan and blessed me. ⁴He said to me, 'I will make you fruitful, and I will multiply your descendants. I will make you a multitude of nations. And I will give this land of Canaan to your descendants* after you as an everlasting possession.'

⁵"Now I am claiming as my own sons these two boys of yours, Ephraim and Manasseh, who were born here in the land of Egypt before I arrived. They will be my sons, just as Reuben and Simeon are. ⁶But any children born to you in the future will be your own, and they will inherit land within the territories of their brothers Ephraim and Manasseh.

⁷"Long ago, as I was returning from Paddan-aram, Rachel died in the land of Canaan. We were still on the way, some distance from Ephrath (that is, Bethlehem). So with great sorrow I buried her there beside the road to Ephrath."

⁸Then Jacob looked over at the two boys. "Are these your sons?" he asked.

⁹"Yes," Joseph told him, "these are the sons God has given me here in Egypt."

And Jacob said, "Bring them closer to me, so I can bless them."

¹⁰Jacob was half blind because of his age and could hardly see. So Joseph brought the boys close to him, and Jacob kissed and embraced them. ¹¹Then Jacob said to Joseph, "I never thought I would see your face again, but now God has let me see your children, too!"

¹²Joseph moved the boys, who were at their grandfather's knees, and he bowed with his face to the ground. ¹³Then he positioned the

47:31 Greek version reads and Israel bowed in worship as he leaned on his staff. Compare Heb 11:21.   48:2 Hebrew Israel; also in 48:8, 10, 11, 13, 14, 21. See note on 35:21.   48:3 Hebrew El-Shaddai.   48:4 Hebrew seed; also in 48:19.

I WONDER...

Bad things seem to happen all the time. Does God care about what is happening in the world?

There are bad things that happen, and then there are tragedies. At some point in life everyone will experience both of these. Let's cover them one at a time.

The person who flunks a math test had something bad happen to him. Did he learn that it is important to keep up with assignments and study before a test? Hopefully.

A 10-year-old boy races out from behind a parked car and is almost hit by a car. He is scared to death, realizing that he could have been killed! Did he learn a lesson about not darting into the street? He better have; he may not get another chance!

In each case the person probably was not happy about what happened. But each situation in life, good or bad, is a learning experience.

Does God care that we learn important lessons about studying and safety? He cares very much!

Ask your folks about the five worst things that have happened to them. Then ask what they learned from these bad experiences. Finally, ask them if they were thankful that these occurred.

Going through tough times is bad only when you don't learn something when it's over.

Now let's discuss tragedy.

Unfortunately, no one is immune from what we believe is the ultimate tragedy—death. Even Jesus went through the loss of someone he loved (see John 11). It is the timing of death (especially when someone dies young), and how it occurs (like an innocent victim killed by a drunk driver), that makes us wonder if God really cares.

When Adam and Eve disobeyed God in the Garden of Eden, their punishment was separation from God. This incident also set in motion the life cycle, ending in death. But the good news is that Jesus Christ's death on the cross killed death! Not physical death, but spiritual death for all those who receive his gift of forgiveness.

One curse brought on the human race by Adam was physical death. Since that time people have discovered that death can happen in some pretty ugly ways (nuclear bombs, lung cancer, AIDS, and many others).

Still, as terrible as those may be, God knows that spiritual death is far worse than physical death. That's why he focused his attention on taking care of the real penalty for our sin—spiritual death (see Rom 6:23). God also knows how tragedy can point us to him and his purposes: "And we know that God causes everything to work together for the good of those who love God" (Rom 8:28).

No matter what tragedies or bad things occur, God can use any situation for good. And remember, whatever happens to you, God cares. He loves you and wants to work out his purposes in your life.

boys in front of Jacob. With his right hand he directed Ephraim toward Jacob's left hand, and with his left hand he put Manasseh at Jacob's right hand. ¹⁴But Jacob crossed his arms as he reached out to lay his hands on the boys' heads. He put his right hand on the head of Ephraim, though he was the younger boy, and his left hand on the head of Manasseh, though he was the firstborn. ¹⁵Then he blessed Joseph and said,

> "May the God before whom my grandfather
>   Abraham
> and my father, Isaac, walked—
> the God who has been my shepherd
>   all my life, to this very day,
> ¹⁶ the Angel who has redeemed me from
>   all harm—
>   may he bless these boys.
> May they preserve my name
>   and the names of Abraham and Isaac.
> And may their descendants multiply greatly
>   throughout the earth."

¹⁷But Joseph was upset when he saw that his father placed his right hand on Ephraim's head. So Joseph lifted it to move it from Ephraim's head to Manasseh's head. ¹⁸"No, my father," he said. "This one is the firstborn. Put your right hand on his head."

¹⁹But his father refused. "I know, my son; I know," he replied. "Manasseh will also become a great people, but his younger brother will become even greater. And his descendants will become a multitude of nations."

²⁰So Jacob blessed the boys that day with this blessing: "The people of Israel will use your names when they give a blessing. They will say, 'May God make you as prosperous as Ephraim and Manasseh.'" In this way, Jacob put Ephraim ahead of Manasseh.

....

NEVER SO BAD
(48:11) When Joseph became a slave, Jacob thought he was dead and wept in despair (37:34). But eventually God's plan allowed Jacob to regain not only his son, but his grandchildren as well. Circumstances are never so bad that they are beyond God's help. Because we belong to a loving God, we need never despair. We never know what good he will bring out of a seemingly hopeless situation.

FUTURE CHOICE
(49:3-28) Jacob blessed each of his sons and then made a prediction about each one's future. The way the men had lived played an important part in Jacob's blessing and prophecy. Our past affects our present and future. By sunrise tomorrow, our actions of today will have become part of the past. Yet they will already have begun to shape the future. What actions can you choose or avoid in order to positively shape your future?

²¹Then Jacob said to Joseph, "Look, I am about to die, but God will be with you and will take you back to Canaan, the land of your ancestors. ²²And beyond what I have given your brothers, I am giving you an extra portion of the land* that I took from the Amorites with my sword and bow."

49 JACOB'S LAST WORDS TO HIS SONS

Then Jacob called together all his sons and said, "Gather around me, and I will tell you what will happen to each of you in the days to come.

> ² "Come and listen, you sons of Jacob;
>   listen to Israel, your father.
>
> ³ "Reuben, you are my firstborn, my strength,
>   the child of my vigorous youth.
>   You are first in rank and first in power.
> ⁴ But you are as unruly as a flood,
>   and you will be first no longer.
> For you went to bed with my wife;
>   you defiled my marriage couch.
>
> ⁵ "Simeon and Levi are two of a kind;
>   their weapons are instruments of violence.
> ⁶ May I never join in their meetings;
>   may I never be a party to their plans.
> For in their anger they murdered men,
>   and they crippled oxen just for sport.
> ⁷ A curse on their anger, for it is fierce;
>   a curse on their wrath, for it is cruel.
> I will scatter them among the descendants
>   of Jacob;
>   I will disperse them throughout Israel.
>
> ⁸ "Judah, your brothers will praise you.
>   You will grasp your enemies by the neck.
>   All your relatives will bow before you.
> ⁹ Judah, my son, is a young lion
>   that has finished eating its prey.
> Like a lion he crouches and lies down;
>   like a lioness—who dares to rouse him?
> ¹⁰ The scepter will not depart from Judah,
>   nor the ruler's staff from his
>   descendants,*
> until the coming of the one to whom it
>   belongs,*
>   the one whom all nations will honor.
> ¹¹ He ties his foal to a grapevine,
>   the colt of his donkey to a choice vine.
> He washes his clothes in wine,
>   his robes in the blood of grapes.
> ¹² His eyes are darker than wine,
>   and his teeth are whiter than milk.

48:22 Or *an extra ridge of land.* The meaning of the Hebrew is uncertain. **49:10a** Hebrew *from between his feet.* **49:10b** Or *until tribute is brought to him and the peoples obey;* traditionally rendered *until Shiloh comes.*

¹³ "Zebulun will settle by the seashore
     and will be a harbor for ships;
     his borders will extend to Sidon.

¹⁴ "Issachar is a sturdy donkey,
     resting between two saddlepacks.*

¹⁵ When he sees how good the countryside is
     and how pleasant the land,
   he will bend his shoulder to the load
     and submit himself to hard labor.

¹⁶ "Dan will govern his people,
     like any other tribe in Israel.

¹⁷ Dan will be a snake beside the road,
     a poisonous viper along the path
   that bites the horse's hooves
     so its rider is thrown off.

¹⁸ I trust in you for salvation, O LORD!

¹⁹ "Gad will be attacked by marauding bands,
     but he will attack them when they retreat.

²⁰ "Asher will dine on rich foods
     and produce food fit for kings.

²¹ "Naphtali is a doe set free
     that bears beautiful fawns.

²² "Joseph is the foal of a wild donkey,
     the foal of a wild donkey at a spring—
     one of the wild donkeys on the ridge.*

²³ Archers attacked him savagely;
     they shot at him and harassed him.

²⁴ But his bow remained taut,
     and his arms were strengthened
   by the hands of the Mighty One of Jacob,
     by the Shepherd, the Rock of Israel.

²⁵ May the God of your father help you;
     may the Almighty bless you
   with the blessings of the heavens above,
     and blessings of the watery
        depths below,
     and blessings of the breasts
        and womb.

²⁶ May the blessings of your father
     surpass the blessings of the
        ancient mountains,*
     reaching to the heights of the eternal
        hills.
   May these blessings rest on the head
        of Joseph,
     who is a prince among his brothers.

²⁷ "Benjamin is a ravenous wolf,
     devouring his enemies in
        the morning
     and dividing his plunder in
        the evening."

²⁸These are the twelve tribes of Israel, and this is what their father said as he told his sons good-bye. He blessed each one with an appropriate message.

JACOB'S DEATH AND BURIAL ²⁹Then Jacob instructed them, "Soon I will die and join my ancestors. Bury me with my father and grandfather in the cave in the field of Ephron the Hittite. ³⁰This is the cave in the field of Machpelah, near Mamre in Canaan, that Abraham bought from Ephron the Hittite as a permanent burial site. ³¹There Abraham and his wife Sarah are buried. There Isaac and his wife, Rebekah, are buried. And there I buried Leah. ³²It is the plot of land and the cave that my grandfather Abraham bought from the Hittites."

³³When Jacob had finished this charge to his sons, he drew his feet into the bed, breathed his last, and joined his ancestors in death.

50 Joseph threw himself on his father and wept over him and kissed him. ²Then Joseph told the physicians who served him to embalm his father's body; so Jacob* was embalmed. ³The embalming process took the usual forty days. And the Egyptians mourned his death for seventy days.

⁴When the period of mourning was over, Joseph approached Pharaoh's advisers and said, "Please do me this favor and speak to Pharaoh on my behalf. ⁵Tell him that my father made me swear an oath. He said to me, 'Listen, I am about to die. Take my body back to the land of Canaan, and bury me in the tomb I prepared for myself.' So please allow me to go and bury my father. After his burial, I will return without delay."

⁶Pharaoh agreed to Joseph's request. "Go and bury your father, as he made you promise,"

....

GOOD GRIEF
(50:1-11) When Jacob died at the age of 147 (see also Gen 47:28), Joseph wept and mourned for months. Often we ostracize those who are grieving, especially if we think they have grieved too long. When someone close to us dies, we need a long period of time to work through our feelings. Crying and sharing what we feel with others helps us recover and go on with life. Allow yourself and others the freedom to grieve the loss of a loved one.

RELIABLE
(50:5-6) Joseph had proven himself trustworthy as Pharaoh's adviser. Because of his good record, Pharaoh was sure that he would return to Egypt as promised after burying his father in Canaan. Privileges and freedom often result when we have demonstrated our trustworthiness. Because trust must be built gradually over time, take every opportunity to prove your reliability, even in minor matters.

49:14 Or sheepfolds, or hearths.   **49:22** Or Joseph is a fruitful tree, / a fruitful tree beside a spring. / His branches reach over the wall. The meaning of the Hebrew is uncertain.   **49:26** Or of my ancestors.   **50:2** Hebrew Israel. See note on 35:21.

he said. 7So Joseph went up to bury his father. He was accompanied by all of Pharaoh's officials, all the senior members of Pharaoh's household, and all the senior officers of Egypt. 8Joseph also took his entire household and his brothers and their households. But they left their little children and flocks and herds in the land of Goshen. 9A great number of chariots and charioteers accompanied Joseph.

10When they arrived at the threshing floor of Atad, near the Jordan River, they held a very great and solemn memorial service, with a seven-day period of mourning for Joseph's father. 11The local residents, the Canaanites, watched them mourning at the threshing floor of Atad. Then they renamed that place (which is near the Jordan) Abel-mizraim,* for they said, "This is a place of deep mourning for these Egyptians."

12So Jacob's sons did as he had commanded them. 13They carried his body to the land of Canaan and buried him in the cave in the field of Machpelah, near Mamre. This is the cave that Abraham had bought as a permanent burial site from Ephron the Hittite.

JOSEPH REASSURES HIS BROTHERS 14After burying Jacob, Joseph returned to Egypt with his brothers and all who had accompanied him to his father's burial. 15But now that their father was dead, Joseph's brothers became fearful. "Now Joseph will show his anger and

pay us back for all the wrong we did to him," they said.

16So they sent this message to Joseph: "Before your father died, he instructed us 17to say to you: 'Please forgive your brothers for the great wrong they did to you—for their sin in treating you so cruelly.' So we, the servants of the God of your father, beg you to forgive our sin." When Joseph received the message, he broke down and wept. 18Then his brothers came and threw themselves down before Joseph. "Look, we are your slaves!" they said.

19But Joseph replied, "Don't be afraid of me. Am I God, that I can punish you? 20You intended to harm me, but God intended it all for good. He brought me to this position so I could save the lives of many people. 21No, don't be afraid. I will continue to take care of you and your children." So he reassured them by speaking kindly to them.

THE DEATH OF JOSEPH 22So Joseph and his brothers and their families continued to live in Egypt. Joseph lived to the age of 110. 23He lived to see three generations of descendants of his son Ephraim, and he lived to see the birth of the children of Manasseh's son Makir, whom he claimed as his own.*

24"Soon I will die," Joseph told his brothers, "but God will surely come to help you and lead you out of this land of Egypt. He will bring you back to the land he solemnly promised to give to Abraham, to Isaac, and to Jacob." 25Then Joseph made the sons of Israel swear an oath, and he said, "When God comes to help you and lead you back, you must take my bones with you." 26So Joseph died at the age of 110. The Egyptians embalmed him, and his body was placed in a coffin in Egypt.

50:11 *Abel-mizraim* means "mourning of the Egyptians."
50:23 Hebrew *who were born on Joseph's knees.*

··

MUSCLE BUILDING
(50:22-24) Joseph was ready to die. He believed that God would keep his promise and one day bring the Israelites back to their homeland. What a tremendous example! The secret for having that kind of faith is a lifetime of trusting God. Your faith is like a muscle—it grows with exercise, gaining strength over time. What are you doing to exercise your faith?

EXODUS

"I promise!" she exclaimed. But soon her words were forgotten in the rush and excitement of school.

Promises are an important part of life. Think about all of the promises made to you or by you recently. We promise to perform an action, be a certain place at a certain time, or give to a cause. Whether we keep those promises is another story! Yet when others make promises to us, we expect them to keep their word.

The book of Exodus is all about promises: God's promises to his people. We're invited to walk along with Moses and the people of Israel as they make their exodus from Egypt. We're also on the front row of the giving and receiving of the Ten Commandments—God's rules for living.

Knowing that God kept his promise to deliver the Israelites from slavery and lead them to a home of their own can increase our trust in him. Just as God was faithful to keep the promises he made to Israel, he will keep every promise he has made to us. He promises to love us no matter what, to care for and protect us, to help us overcome any temptation, to comfort and teach us, and to make us a new creation.

KEY POINTS

SLAVERY The Israelites were slaves for 400 years. Physical slavery is like slavery to sin. The longer you are a slave, the more difficult breaking free becomes. Gaining freedom from sin requires God's power.

RESCUE/REDEMPTION God rescued Israel through the leader Moses and through mighty miracles. God gave the Passover celebration as an annual reminder of their escape from slavery. Everyone needs to experience the deliverance from sin that God provides. Jesus Christ celebrated the Passover with his disciples at the Last Supper and then completed God's plan for our redemption by dying in our place.

GUIDANCE God guided Israel out of slavery by using the plagues, Moses' leadership, the miracle of the Red Sea, and the Ten Commandments. God demonstrates his power in our life through the guidance of wise leaders and the effort of Christian friends working together. He can be trusted to give us the guidance we need to follow his will.

TEN COMMANDMENTS Through the Ten Commandments, God taught Israel the importance of making the right choices and accepting responsibility for one's actions. Both are key to our growth as Christians.

THE NATION God established the nation of Israel to be the source of truth and salvation to all the world. Israel's newly formed nation models for us the need to depend upon God. Whether we are rebellious or obedient, God remains our only source of absolute, eternal truth and life.

STATS

PURPOSE
To record the events of Israel's deliverance from Egypt and development as a nation

AUTHOR
Moses

ORIGINAL AUDIENCE
The people of Israel

DATE WRITTEN
1450–1410 B.C.

WHERE WRITTEN
In the wilderness during Israel's wanderings, in the Sinai Peninsula

SETTING
Egypt. God's people, once highly favored in the land during the time of Joseph, are now slaves. God is about to set them free.

KEY PEOPLE
Moses, Moses' mother (Jochebed), Miriam, Pharaoh, Pharaoh's daughter, Jethro, Aaron, Joshua, Bezalel

KEY PLACES
Egypt, Goshen, the Nile River, the land of Midian, the Red Sea, the Sinai Peninsula, Mount Sinai

SPECIAL FEATURES
Exodus includes the Ten Commandments and more miracles than any other Old Testament book.

TIMELINE

1526 B.C.
Moses born

1446
Exodus from Egypt

1445
Ten Commandments

1406
Israel enters Canaan

1375
Judges begin to rule

Modern names and boundaries are shown in gray.

KEY PLACES

❶ LAND OF GOSHEN
This area was given to Jacob and his family when they moved to Egypt (Gen 47:5-6). It became the Hebrews' homeland for 400 years, and remained separate from the main Egyptian centers, for Egyptian culture looked down on shepherds and nomads. As the years passed, Jacob's family grew into a large nation (1:7).

❷ PITHOM AND RAMESES
After 400 years, a pharaoh came to the throne who had no respect for these descendants of Joseph and feared their large numbers. He forced them into slavery in order to oppress and subdue them. Out of their slave labor, the supply cities of Pithom and Rameses were built (1:11).

❸ LAND OF MIDIAN
Moses, a Hebrew who was raised as an Egyptian prince, killed an Egyptian taskmaster and fled for his life to the land

of Midian. There he became a shepherd and married a woman named Zipporah. It was while he was here that God commissioned him for the job of leading the Hebrew people out of Egypt (2:15–4:31).

❹ BAAL-ZEPHON
Slavery was not to last, because God planned to deliver his people. After choosing Moses and Aaron to be his spokesmen to Pharaoh, God worked a series of dramatic miracles in the land of Egypt to convince Pharaoh to let the Hebrews go (5:1–12:33). When finally freed, the entire nation set out with the riches of Egypt (12:34-36). One of their first stops was at Baal-zephon (14:2), where Pharaoh, who had changed his mind, chased the Hebrews and trapped them against the Red Sea. But God parted the waters and led the people through the sea on dry land. When Pharaoh's army tried

to pursue, the waters collapsed around them, and they were drowned (14:5-31).

❺ MARAH
Moses now led the people southward. The long trek across the desert brought hot tempers and parched throats to this mass of people. At Marah, the water they found was bitter, but God sweetened it (15:22-25).

❻ ELIM
As they continued their journey, the Hebrews (now called Israelites) came to Elim, an oasis with twelve springs (15:27).

❼ WILDERNESS OF SIN
Leaving Elim, the people headed into the Wilderness of Sin. Here the people became hungry, so God provided them with manna that came from heaven and covered the ground each morning (16:1, 13-15). The people ate this manna until they entered the Promised Land.

❽ REPHIDIM
Moses led the people to Rephidim, where they found no water. But God miraculously provided water from a rock (17:1, 5-6). Here the Israelites encountered their first test in battle: The Amalekites attacked and were defeated (17:8-13). Moses' father-in-law, Jethro, then arrived on the scene with some sound advice on delegating responsibilities (18).

❾ MOUNT SINAI
God had previously appeared to Moses on this mountain and commissioned him to lead Israel (3:1-10). Now Moses returned with the people God had asked him to lead. For almost a year the people camped at the foot of Mount Sinai. During this time God gave them his Ten Commandments as well as other laws for right living. He also provided the blueprint for building the Tabernacle (19–40). God was forging a holy nation that was prepared to live for and serve him alone.

1 THE ISRAELITES IN EGYPT

These are the names of the sons of Israel (that is, Jacob) who moved to Egypt with their father, each with his family: ²Reuben, Simeon, Levi, Judah, ³Issachar, Zebulun, Benjamin, ⁴Dan, Naphtali, Gad, and Asher. ⁵In all, Jacob had seventy* descendants in Egypt, including Joseph, who was already there.

⁶In time, Joseph and all of his brothers died, ending that entire generation. ⁷But their descendants, the Israelites, had many children and grandchildren. In fact, they multiplied so greatly that they became extremely powerful and filled the land.

⁸Eventually, a new king came to power in Egypt who knew nothing about Joseph or what he had done. ⁹He said to his people, "Look, the people of Israel now outnumber us and are stronger than we are. ¹⁰We must make a plan to keep them from growing even more. If we don't, and if war breaks out, they will join our enemies and fight against us. Then they will escape from the country.*"

¹¹So the Egyptians made the Israelites their slaves. They appointed brutal slave drivers over them, hoping to wear them down with crushing labor. They forced them to build the cities of Pithom and Rameses as supply centers for the king. ¹²But the more the Egyptians oppressed them, the more the Israelites multiplied and spread, and the more alarmed the Egyptians became. ¹³So the Egyptians worked the people of Israel without mercy. ¹⁴They made their lives bitter, forcing them to mix mortar and make bricks and do all the work in the fields. They were ruthless in all their demands.

¹⁵Then Pharaoh, the king of Egypt, gave this order to the Hebrew midwives, Shiphrah and Puah: ¹⁶"When you help the Hebrew women as they give birth, watch as they deliver.* If the baby is a boy, kill him; if it is a girl, let her live." ¹⁷But because the midwives feared God, they refused to obey the king's orders. They allowed the boys to live, too.

¹⁸So the king of Egypt called for the midwives. "Why have you done this?" he demanded. "Why have you allowed the boys to live?"

¹⁹"The Hebrew women are not like the Egyptian women," the midwives replied. "They are more vigorous and have their babies so quickly that we cannot get there in time."

²⁰So God was good to the midwives, and the Israelites continued to multiply, growing more and more powerful. ²¹And because the midwives feared God, he gave them families of their own.

²²Then Pharaoh gave this order to all his people: "Throw every newborn Hebrew boy into the Nile River. But you may let the girls live."

2 THE BIRTH OF MOSES

About this time, a man and woman from the tribe of Levi got married. ²The woman became pregnant and gave birth to a son. She saw that he was a special baby and kept him hidden for three months. ³But when she could no longer hide him, she got a basket made of papyrus reeds and waterproofed it with tar and pitch. She put the baby in the basket and laid it among the reeds along the bank of the Nile River. ⁴The baby's sister then stood at a distance, watching to see what would happen to him.

⁵Soon Pharaoh's daughter came down to bathe in the river, and her attendants walked along the riverbank. When the princess saw the basket among the reeds, she sent her maid to get it for her. ⁶When the princess opened it, she saw the baby. The little boy was crying, and she felt sorry for him. "This must be one of the Hebrew children," she said.

....

FOREIGNERS
(1:1) Jacob's family moved to Egypt at the invitation of Joseph, one of Jacob's sons, who had become a great ruler under Pharaoh. Jacob's family grew into a large nation. But as foreigners within the land, their lifestyle was quite different from that of the Egyptians. The Hebrews worshiped one God; the Egyptians worshiped many gods. The Hebrews were wanderers; the Egyptians had a deeply rooted culture. The Hebrews were shepherds; the Egyptians were builders. If you're a Christian, your lifestyle is "foreign" to those who lack your knowledge of Christ. Are you a foreigner or a chameleon—one who blends in with the crowd?

A LIE'S REWARD?
(1:15-21) God blessed the Hebrew midwives not because they lied to Pharaoh but because they saved the lives of innocent children. This story does not justify lying in most of the cases we face today. Protecting innocent lives honors God, and for doing that he blessed these women. In Acts 5:29, Peter and the apostles declare, "We must obey God rather than any human authority." In the same way, you will often have to choose between what God wants and what others are pressuring you to do. Be certain that God's way is best, even if it puts you in a tough position.

A SMALL FIGHT AGAINST EVIL
(2:1-3) Moses' mother wanted her child to live, but there was little she could do to change Pharaoh's new law. Her only alternative was to hide her son and later place him in a tiny basket on the river. God used her courageous act to place her son in the house of Pharaoh. Do you sometimes feel surrounded by evil and frustrated by how little you can do about it? With God, no effort, however small it may seem, will go to waste. He can turn a small act for good into a great triumph over evil.

1:5 Dead Sea Scrolls and Greek version read *seventy-five*; see notes on Gen 46:27. **1:10** Or *will take the country.* **1:16** Hebrew *look upon the two stones*; perhaps the reference is to a birthstool.

⁷Then the baby's sister approached the princess. "Should I go and find one of the Hebrew women to nurse the baby for you?" she asked.

⁸"Yes, do!" the princess replied. So the girl went and called the baby's mother.

⁹"Take this baby and nurse him for me," the princess told the baby's mother. "I will pay you for your help." So the woman took her baby home and nursed him.

¹⁰Later, when the boy was older, his mother brought him back to Pharaoh's daughter, who adopted him as her own son. The princess named him Moses,* for she explained, "I lifted him out of the water."

MOSES ESCAPES TO MIDIAN ¹¹Many years later, when Moses had grown up, he went out to visit his own people, the Hebrews, and he saw how hard they were forced to work. During his visit, he saw an Egyptian beating one of his fellow Hebrews. ¹²After looking in all directions to make sure no one was watching, Moses killed the Egyptian and hid the body in the sand.

¹³The next day, when Moses went out to visit his people again, he saw two Hebrew men fighting. "Why are you beating up your friend?" Moses said to the one who had started the fight.

¹⁴The man replied, "Who appointed you to be our prince and judge? Are you going to kill me as you killed that Egyptian yesterday?"

Then Moses was afraid, thinking, "Everyone knows what I did." ¹⁵And sure enough, Pharaoh heard what had happened, and he tried to kill Moses. But Moses fled from Pharaoh and went to live in the land of Midian.

When Moses arrived in Midian, he sat down beside a well. ¹⁶Now the priest of Midian had seven daughters who came as usual to draw water and fill the water troughs for their father's flocks. ¹⁷But some other shepherds came and chased them away. So Moses jumped up and rescued the girls from the shepherds. Then he drew water for their flocks.

¹⁸When the girls returned to Reuel, their father, he asked, "Why are you back so soon today?"

¹⁹"An Egyptian rescued us from the shepherds," they answered. "And then he drew water for us and watered our flocks."

²⁰"Then where is he?" their father asked. "Why did you leave him there? Invite him to come and eat with us."

²¹Moses accepted the invitation, and he settled there with him. In time, Reuel gave Moses his daughter Zipporah to be his wife. ²²Later she gave birth to a son, and Moses named him Gershom,* for he explained, "I have been a foreigner in a foreign land."

²³Years passed, and the king of Egypt died.

2:10 *Moses* sounds like a Hebrew term that means "to lift out."
2:22 *Gershom* sounds like a Hebrew term that means "a foreigner there."

MOSES *PERSONALITY PROFILE*

SOME PEOPLE can't stay out of trouble. (Know anyone like that?) Moses was that kind of person. He wasn't a troublemaker; he was usually trying to do the right thing. When he saw something wrong, he tried to make it right—and often ended up in trouble.

Moses was a reactor. When there was action, he reacted. Whether checking out a burning bush that didn't burn, defending a Hebrew slave, or trying to stop a fight, Moses reacted to the world around him.

Moses became a great leader because he learned to act, rather than react. He wasn't perfect—he even made a mistake that kept him out of the Promised Land. But God shaped and used his life anyway. God didn't change *who* or *what* Moses was; he worked on *how* Moses used what he'd been given.

God wants to change us in the same way. He will make the best version of us there could ever be, if we let him. When God changes us, he enhances the good qualities he gave us at the start. He also forgives us and straightens us out.

BOTTOM LINE: God first prepares his people, then uses them to do his work.

God does his greatest work through frail people.

UPS:
• Egyptian education; wilderness training
• Greatest Jewish leader; set the Exodus in motion
• Prophet and lawgiver; receiver of the Ten Commandments

DOWNS:
• Failed to enter the Promised Land because of disobedience to God
• Did not always recognize and use the talents of others

STATS:
• Where: Egypt, Midian, Wilderness of Sinai
• Occupation: Prince, shepherd, leader of the Israelites
• Relatives: Miriam (sister); Aaron (brother); Zipporah (wife); Gershom and Eliezer (sons)

KEY VERSES: *Matthew 17:3-4; Acts 7:20-44; Hebrews 11:23-28.*

But the Israelites continued to groan under their burden of slavery. They cried out for help, and their cry rose up to God. ²⁴God heard their groaning, and he remembered his covenant promise to Abraham, Isaac, and Jacob. ²⁵He looked down on the people of Israel and knew it was time to act.*

3 **MOSES AND THE BURNING BUSH** One day Moses was tending the flock of his father-in-law, Jethro,* the priest of Midian. He led the flock far into the wilderness and came to Sinai,* the mountain of God. ²There the angel of the LORD appeared to him in a blazing fire from the middle of a bush. Moses stared in amazement. Though the bush was engulfed in flames, it didn't burn up. ³"This is amazing," Moses said to himself. "Why isn't that bush burning up? I must go see it."

⁴When the LORD saw Moses coming to take a closer look, God called to him from the middle of the bush, "Moses! Moses!"

"Here I am!" Moses replied.

⁵"Do not come any closer," the LORD warned. "Take off your sandals, for you are standing on holy ground. ⁶I am the God of your father*—the God of Abraham, the God of Isaac, and the God of Jacob." When Moses heard this, he covered his face because he was afraid to look at God.

⁷Then the LORD told him, "I have certainly seen the oppression of my people in Egypt. I have heard their cries of distress because of their harsh slave drivers. Yes, I am aware of their suffering. ⁸So I have come down to rescue them from the power of the Egyptians and lead them out of Egypt into their own fertile and spacious land. It is a land flowing with milk and honey—the land where the Canaanites, Hittites, Amorites, Perizzites, Hivites, and Jebusites now live. ⁹Look! The cry of the people of Israel has reached me, and I have seen how harshly the Egyptians abuse them. ¹⁰Now go, for I am sending you to Pharaoh. You must lead my people Israel out of Egypt."

¹¹But Moses protested to God, "Who am I to appear before Pharaoh? Who am I to lead the people of Israel out of Egypt?"

¹²God answered, "I will be with you. And this is your sign that I am the one who has sent you: When you have brought the people out of Egypt, you will worship God at this very mountain."

¹³But Moses protested, "If I go to the people of Israel and tell them, 'The God of your ancestors has sent me to you,' they will ask me, 'What is his name?' Then what should I tell them?"

¹⁴God replied to Moses, "I AM WHO I AM.* Say this to the people of Israel: I AM has sent me to you." ¹⁵God also said to Moses, "Say this to the people of Israel: Yahweh,* the God of your ancestors—the God of Abraham, the God of Isaac, and the God of Jacob—has sent me to you.

This is my eternal name,
  my name to remember for all generations.

¹⁶"Now go and call together all the elders of Israel. Tell them, 'The LORD, the God of your ancestors—the God of Abraham, Isaac, and Jacob—has appeared to me. He told me, "I have been watching closely, and I see how the Egyptians are treating you. ¹⁷I have promised to rescue you from your oppression in Egypt. I will lead you to a land flowing with milk and honey—the land where the Canaanites, Hittites, Amorites, Perizzites, Hivites, and Jebusites now live."'

¹⁸"The elders of Israel will accept your message. Then you and the elders must go to the king of Egypt and tell him, 'The LORD, the God of the Hebrews, has met with us. So please let us take a three-day journey into the wilderness to offer sacrifices to the LORD, our God.'

¹⁹"But I know that the king of Egypt will not let you go unless a mighty hand forces him.* ²⁰So I will raise my hand and strike the Egyptians, performing all kinds of miracles among them. Then at last he will let you go. ²¹And I will cause the Egyptians to look favorably on you. They will give you gifts when you go so you will not leave empty-handed. ²²Every Israelite woman will ask for articles of silver and gold and fine clothing from her Egyptian neighbors and from the

2:25 Or *and acknowledged his obligation to help them.*
3:1a Moses' father-in-law went by two names, Jethro and Reuel. 3:1b Hebrew *Horeb,* another name for Sinai. 3:6 Greek version reads *your fathers.* 3:14 Or *I WILL BE WHAT I WILL BE.* 3:15 *Yahweh* is a transliteration of the proper name *YHWH* that is sometimes rendered "Jehovah"; in this translation it is usually rendered "the LORD" (note the use of small capitals). 3:19 As in Greek and Latin versions; Hebrew reads *will not let you go, not by a mighty hand.*

···

FROM ORDINARY TO EXTRAORDINARY
(4:2-4) A shepherd's staff was commonly a three- to six-foot wooden rod with a curved hook at the top. The shepherd used it for walking, guiding his sheep, killing snakes, and many other tasks. Still, it was just a stick. But with God's power, the ordinary shepherd's staff Moses carried became extraordinary. Think about the ordinary things in your life—your voice, a pen, a hammer, a broom, a musical instrument. It's easy to assume that God only uses special items and skills for his work. We assume that he only works with an artistic genius like Michelangelo or an amazingly gifted bass guitarist. But he takes delight in using ordinary items and skills for extraordinary purposes.

NOW GO!

I WILL BE WITH YOU AS YOU SPEAK, AND I WILL INSTRUCT YOU IN WHAT TO SAY.

EXODUS 4:12

foreign women in their houses. You will dress your sons and daughters with these, stripping the Egyptians of their wealth."

4 SIGNS OF THE LORD'S POWER But Moses protested again, "What if they won't believe me or listen to me? What if they say, 'The LORD never appeared to you'?"

²Then the LORD asked him, "What is that in your hand?"

"A shepherd's staff," Moses replied.

³"Throw it down on the ground," the LORD told him. So Moses threw down the staff, and it turned into a snake! Moses jumped back.

⁴Then the LORD told him, "Reach out and grab its tail." So Moses reached out and grabbed it, and it turned back into a shepherd's staff in his hand.

⁵"Perform this sign," the LORD told him. "Then they will believe that the LORD, the God of their ancestors—the God of Abraham, the God of Isaac, and the God of Jacob—really has appeared to you."

⁶Then the LORD said to Moses, "Now put your hand inside your cloak." So Moses put his hand inside his cloak, and when he took it out again, his hand was white as snow with a severe skin disease.* ⁷"Now put your hand back into your cloak," the LORD said. So Moses put his hand back in, and when he took it out again, it was as healthy as the rest of his body.

⁸The LORD said to Moses, "If they do not believe you and are not convinced by the first miraculous sign, they will be convinced by the second sign. ⁹And if they don't believe you or listen to you even after these two signs, then take some water from the Nile River and pour it out on the dry ground. When you do, the water from the Nile will turn to blood on the ground."

¹⁰But Moses pleaded with the LORD, "O Lord, I'm not very good with words. I never have been, and I'm not now, even though you have spoken to me. I get tongue-tied, and my words get tangled."

4:6 Or *with leprosy.* The Hebrew word used here can describe various skin diseases.

I WONDER...

I am having trouble letting other people know I am a Christian. I'm afraid they will laugh at me or ask a question I can't answer.

The Bible is filled with examples of people who faced the choice of either being courageous or letting their fears tell them how to act. Learning about the courage of people in the Bible is one good reason to read it every day. The examples we find in the Bible can give us the strength to step out in faith and do things that may at first seem very frightening.

In Exodus 3, God spoke with Moses through a burning bush. Although this was an incredible miracle, Exodus 4 relates how Moses was afraid people wouldn't believe that God had actually spoken to him! He had to choose between giving in to his fears or facing them head on. Eventually, Moses chose to draw courage from God and completed the task God had given him.

Character and skill are developed by repeating an action until you can do it well enough to enjoy it. This is true with everything from skiing to skateboarding, and it is true in telling your best friends on earth about your Friend in heaven.

God does not expect you to know all the answers. When the apostle Peter was confronted by the hostile religious leaders of the day who told him to stop talking about Jesus, he answered, "We cannot stop telling about everything we have seen and heard" (Acts 4:20). He had learned the joy of sharing his faith in Christ so much that he couldn't help but share what he knew!

You have the privilege and the responsibility of sharing what you have learned and what God has done in your life. If you don't know the answer, you can always say, "That's a good question. Can I find the answer and get back with you tomorrow?"

The key to Moses' decision to obey God's command to be his spokesman for the Israelites was remembering when God first spoke to him. The burning bush experience and God's continuing miracles gave Moses the courage to face incredible obstacles.

Rely on what God has done for you and daily lean on your growing relationship with Christ to strengthen you.

[11]Then the LORD asked Moses, "Who makes a person's mouth? Who decides whether people speak or do not speak, hear or do not hear, see or do not see? Is it not I, the LORD? [12]Now go! I will be with you as you speak, and I will instruct you in what to say."

[13]But Moses again pleaded, "Lord, please! Send anyone else."

[14]Then the LORD became angry with Moses. "All right," he said. "What about your brother, Aaron the Levite? I know he speaks well. And look! He is on his way to meet you now. He will be delighted to see you. [15]Talk to him, and put the words in his mouth. I will be with both of you as you speak, and I will instruct you both in what to do. [16]Aaron will be your spokesman to the people. He will be your mouthpiece, and you will stand in the place of God for him, telling him what to say. [17]And take your shepherd's staff with you, and use it to perform the miraculous signs I have shown you."

MOSES RETURNS TO EGYPT

[18]So Moses went back home to Jethro, his father-in-law. "Please let me return to my relatives in Egypt," Moses said. "I don't even know if they are still alive."

"Go in peace," Jethro replied.

[19]Before Moses left Midian, the LORD said to him, "Return to Egypt, for all those who wanted to kill you have died."

[20]So Moses took his wife and sons, put them on a donkey, and headed back to the land of Egypt. In his hand he carried the staff of God.

[21]And the LORD told Moses, "When you arrive back in Egypt, go to Pharaoh and perform all the miracles I have empowered you to do. But I will harden his heart so he will refuse to let the people go. [22]Then you will tell him, 'This is what the LORD says: Israel is my firstborn son. [23]I commanded you, "Let my son go, so he can worship me." But since you have refused, I will now kill your firstborn son!'"

[24]On the way to Egypt, at a place where Moses and his family had stopped for the night, the LORD confronted him and was about to kill him. [25]But Moses' wife, Zipporah, took a flint knife and circumcised her son. She touched his feet* with the foreskin and said, "Now you are a bridegroom of blood to me." [26](When she said "a bridegroom of blood," she was referring to the circumcision.) After that, the LORD left him alone.

[27]Now the LORD had said to Aaron, "Go out into the wilderness to meet Moses." So Aaron went and met Moses at the mountain of God,

4:25 The Hebrew word for "feet" may refer here to the male sex organ.

MY STORY: Richard

Whenever I get discouraged because I can't persuade a friend to believe the gospel, I remind myself that I can't convince someone who doesn't want to be convinced. See, there are some people that I wish were Christians. The fact that they don't believe has been tough for me to accept. But the story of Moses and Pharaoh helps me feel better. Nothing would convince Pharaoh that Moses represented the one true God—not plagues, not miracles, not even the deaths of all Egypt's firstborn sons and livestock. If this kind of stuff couldn't move Pharaoh to believe in God, then I'm not surprised that Christians today have trouble convincing people about God.

Maybe the best tactic is the slow, steady work of Christ in our lives, coupled with prayer and our attempts to live the Christian life. I'm learning to place the rest in God's hands.

and he embraced him. [28]Moses then told Aaron everything the LORD had commanded him to say. And he told him about the miraculous signs the LORD had commanded him to perform.

[29]Then Moses and Aaron returned to Egypt and called all the elders of Israel together. [30]Aaron told them everything the LORD had told Moses, and Moses performed the miraculous signs as they watched. [31]Then the people of Israel were convinced that the LORD had sent Moses and Aaron. When they heard that the LORD was concerned about them and had seen their misery, they bowed down and worshiped.

5 MOSES AND AARON SPEAK TO PHARAOH

After this presentation to Israel's leaders, Moses and Aaron went and spoke to Pharaoh. They told him, "This is what the LORD, the God

KEEP TALKING
(5:1-3) *Pharaoh would not listen to Moses and Aaron because he did not know the God of Israel. People who do not know God may choose to ignore his Word or his messengers. But that is no excuse to give up trying. Like Moses and Aaron, persistence counts. When others reject you or your faith, don't be surprised or discouraged. Instead, continue to tell them about God, trusting him to open closed minds and soften stubborn hearts.*

of Israel, says: Let my people go so they may hold a festival in my honor in the wilderness."

²"Is that so?" retorted Pharaoh. "And who is the LORD? Why should I listen to him and let Israel go? I don't know the LORD, and I will not let Israel go."

³But Aaron and Moses persisted. "The God of the Hebrews has met with us," they declared. "So let us take a three-day journey into the wilderness so we can offer sacrifices to the LORD our God. If we don't, he will kill us with a plague or with the sword."

⁴Pharaoh replied, "Moses and Aaron, why are you distracting the people from their tasks? Get back to work! ⁵Look, there are many of your people in the land, and you are stopping them from their work."

MAKING BRICKS WITHOUT STRAW
⁶That same day Pharaoh sent this order to the Egyptian slave drivers and the Israelite foremen: ⁷"Do not supply any more straw for making bricks. Make the people get it themselves! ⁸But still require them to make the same number of bricks as before. Don't reduce the quota. They are lazy. That's why they are crying out, 'Let us go and offer sacrifices to our God.' ⁹Load them down with more work. Make them sweat! That will teach them to listen to lies!"

¹⁰So the slave drivers and foremen went out and told the people: "This is what Pharaoh says: I will not provide any more straw for you. ¹¹Go and get it yourselves. Find it wherever you can. But you must produce just as many bricks as before!" ¹²So the people scattered throughout the land of Egypt in search of stubble to use as straw.

¹³Meanwhile, the Egyptian slave drivers continued to push hard. "Meet your daily quota of bricks, just as you did when we provided you with straw!" they demanded. ¹⁴Then they whipped the Israelite foremen they had put in charge of the work crews. "Why haven't you met your quotas either yesterday or today?" they demanded.

¹⁵So the Israelite foremen went to Pharaoh and pleaded with him. "Please don't treat your servants like this," they begged. ¹⁶"We are given no straw, but the slave drivers still demand, 'Make bricks!' We are being beaten, but it isn't our fault! Your own people are to blame!"

¹⁷But Pharaoh shouted, "You're just lazy! Lazy! That's why you're saying, 'Let us go and offer sacrifices to the LORD.' ¹⁸Now get back to work! No straw will be given to you, but you must still produce the full quota of bricks."

¹⁹The Israelite foremen could see that they were in serious trouble when they were told, "You must not reduce the number of bricks you make each day." ²⁰As they left Pharaoh's court, they confronted Moses and Aaron, who were waiting outside for them. ²¹The foremen said to them, "May the LORD judge and punish you for making us stink before Pharaoh and his officials. You have put a sword into their hands, an excuse to kill us!"

²²Then Moses went back to the LORD and protested, "Why have you brought all this trouble on your own people, Lord? Why did you send me? ²³Ever since I came to Pharaoh as your spokesman, he has been even more brutal to your people. And you have done nothing to rescue them!"

6 PROMISES OF DELIVERANCE Then the LORD told Moses, "Now you will see what I will do to Pharaoh. When he feels the force of my strong hand, he will let the people go. In fact, he will force them to leave his land!"

²And God said to Moses, "I am Yahweh—'the LORD.'* ³I appeared to Abraham, to Isaac, and to Jacob as El-Shaddai—'God Almighty'*—but I did not reveal my name, Yahweh, to them. ⁴And I reaffirmed my covenant with them. Under its terms, I promised to give them the land of Canaan, where they were living as foreigners. ⁵You can be sure that I have heard the groans of the people of Israel, who are now slaves to the Egyptians. And I am well aware of my covenant with them.

⁶"Therefore, say to the people of Israel: 'I am the LORD. I will free you from your oppression and will rescue you from your slavery in Egypt. I will redeem you with a powerful arm and great acts of judgment. ⁷I will claim you as my own people, and I will be your God. Then you will know that I am the LORD your God who has freed you from your oppression in Egypt. ⁸I will bring you into the land I swore to give to Abraham, Isaac, and Jacob. I will give it to you as your very own possession. I am the LORD!'"

⁹So Moses told the people of Israel what the LORD had said, but they refused to listen anymore. They had become too discouraged by the brutality of their slavery.

¹⁰Then the LORD said to Moses, ¹¹"Go back to Pharaoh, the king of Egypt, and tell him to let the people of Israel leave his country."

¹²"But LORD!" Moses objected. "My own people won't listen to me anymore. How can

6:2 *Yahweh* is a transliteration of the proper name *YHWH* that is sometimes rendered "Jehovah"; in this translation it is usually rendered "the LORD" (note the use of small capitals). 6:3 *El-Shaddai,* which means "God Almighty," is the name for God used in Gen 17:1; 28:3; 35:11; 43:14; 48:3.

I expect Pharaoh to listen? I'm such a clumsy speaker!*"

¹³But the LORD spoke to Moses and Aaron and gave them orders for the Israelites and for Pharaoh, the king of Egypt. The LORD commanded Moses and Aaron to lead the people of Israel out of Egypt.

THE ANCESTORS OF MOSES AND AARON

¹⁴These are the ancestors of some of the clans of Israel:

The sons of Reuben, Israel's oldest son, were Hanoch, Pallu, Hezron, and Carmi. Their descendants became the clans of Reuben.

¹⁵The sons of Simeon were Jemuel, Jamin, Ohad, Jakin, Zohar, and Shaul. (Shaul's mother was a Canaanite woman.) Their descendants became the clans of Simeon.

¹⁶These are the descendants of Levi, as listed in their family records: The sons of Levi were Gershon, Kohath, and Merari. (Levi lived to be 137 years old.)

¹⁷The descendants of Gershon included Libni and Shimei, each of whom became the ancestor of a clan.

¹⁸The descendants of Kohath included Amram, Izhar, Hebron, and Uzziel. (Kohath lived to be 133 years old.)

¹⁹The descendants of Merari included Mahli and Mushi.

These are the clans of the Levites, as listed in their family records.

²⁰Amram married his father's sister Jochebed, and she gave birth to his sons, Aaron and Moses. (Amram lived to be 137 years old.)

²¹The sons of Izhar were Korah, Nepheg, and Zicri.

²²The sons of Uzziel were Mishael, Elzaphan, and Sithri.

²³Aaron married Elisheba, the daughter of Amminadab and sister of Nahshon, and she gave birth to his sons, Nadab, Abihu, Eleazar, and Ithamar.

²⁴The sons of Korah were Assir, Elkanah, and Abiasaph. Their descendants became the clans of Korah.

²⁵Eleazar son of Aaron married one of the daughters of Putiel, and she gave birth to his son, Phinehas.

These are the ancestors of the Levite families, listed according to their clans.

²⁶The Aaron and Moses named in this list are the same ones to whom the LORD said, "Lead

6:12 Hebrew *I have uncircumcised lips;* also in 6:30.   7:9 Hebrew *tannin,* which elsewhere refers to a sea monster. Greek version translates it "dragon."

the people of Israel out of the land of Egypt like an army." ²⁷It was Moses and Aaron who spoke to Pharaoh, the king of Egypt, about leading the people of Israel out of Egypt.

²⁸When the LORD spoke to Moses in the land of Egypt, ²⁹he said to him, "I am the LORD! Tell Pharaoh, the king of Egypt, everything I am telling you." ³⁰But Moses argued with the LORD, saying, "I can't do it! I'm such a clumsy speaker! Why should Pharaoh listen to me?"

7 AARON'S STAFF BECOMES A SERPENT

Then the LORD said to Moses, "Pay close attention to this. I will make you seem like God to Pharaoh, and your brother, Aaron, will be your prophet. ²Tell Aaron everything I command you, and Aaron must command Pharaoh to let the people of Israel leave his country. ³But I will make Pharaoh's heart stubborn so I can multiply my miraculous signs and wonders in the land of Egypt. ⁴Even then Pharaoh will refuse to listen to you. So I will bring down my fist on Egypt. Then I will rescue my forces—my people, the Israelites—from the land of Egypt with great acts of judgment. ⁵When I raise my powerful hand and bring out the Israelites, the Egyptians will know that I am the LORD."

⁶So Moses and Aaron did just as the LORD had commanded them. ⁷Moses was eighty years old, and Aaron was eighty-three when they made their demands to Pharaoh.

⁸Then the LORD said to Moses and Aaron, ⁹"Pharaoh will demand, 'Show me a miracle.' When he does this, say to Aaron, 'Take your staff and throw it down in front of Pharaoh, and it will become a serpent.*'"

¹⁰So Moses and Aaron went to Pharaoh and did what the LORD had commanded them. Aaron threw down his staff before Pharaoh and his officials, and it became a serpent! ¹¹Then Pharaoh called in his own wise men and

---

GOD'S AMBASSADOR
(7:1) God made Moses his representative; he was "like God to Pharaoh." Christians are God's representatives, showing the world a lifestyle that differs from the world's. Much of the world knows little about God except what can be seen through the lives of God's people. What kind of God do they think you represent?

DOUBLE TROUBLE
(7:11) How were Pharaoh's wise men and magicians able to duplicate Moses' miracles? Some of their feats involved deception or illusions. But some may have used satanic power. Ironically, whenever the magicians duplicated one of Moses' plagues, it only made matters worse. If the magicians had been as powerful as God, they would have reversed the plagues, not added to them! Using deception and other tricks of Satan usually makes things go from bad to worse.

THE PLAGUES

BLOOD	Fish die, the river stinks, and the people are without water. Pharaoh's magicians duplicate the miracle by their magic, so Pharaoh is unmoved (7:14-24).
FROGS	Frogs come up from the water and completely cover the land. Again Pharaoh's magicians duplicate the miracle by sorcery, and Pharaoh is unmoved (8:1-15).
GNATS	All the dust of Egypt becomes a massive swarm of gnats. Magicians are unable to duplicate this and say it is the "finger of God," but Pharaoh's heart remains hard (8:16-19).
FLIES	Swarms of flies cover the land. Pharaoh promises to let the Hebrews go but then hardens his heart and refuses (8:20-32).
LIVESTOCK	All the Egyptians' livestock die—but none of Israel's is even sick. Pharaoh still refuses to let the people go (9:1-7).
BOILS	Horrible boils break out on everyone in Egypt. Magicians cannot respond as they are struck down with boils as well—Pharaoh refuses to listen (9:8-12).
HAIL	Hailstorms kill all the servants and animals left out or unprotected and strip or destroy almost every plant. Pharaoh admits his fault but then changes his mind and refuses to let the people go (9:13-35).
LOCUSTS	Locusts cover Egypt and eat everything left by the hail. Pharaoh confesses his sin but then becomes stubborn once again (10:1-20).
DARKNESS	Total darkness covers Egypt for three days so no one can even move—except the Hebrews, who have light as usual. Pharaoh again promises to let Israel go but again changes his mind (10:21-29).
DEATH OF FIRSTBORN	The firstborn of all the people and animals of Egypt die—but Israel is spared. Pharaoh urges Israel to leave but changes his mind and chases after them (11:1–12:33).

sorcerers, and these Egyptian magicians did the same thing with their magic. ¹²They threw down their staffs, which also became serpents! But then Aaron's staff swallowed up their staffs. ¹³Pharaoh's heart, however, remained hard. He still refused to listen, just as the LORD had predicted.

A PLAGUE OF BLOOD ¹⁴Then the LORD said to Moses, "Pharaoh's heart is stubborn,* and he still refuses to let the people go. ¹⁵So go to Pharaoh in the morning as he goes down to the river. Stand on the bank of the Nile and meet him there. Be sure to take along the staff that turned into a snake. ¹⁶Then announce to him, 'The LORD, the God of the Hebrews, has sent me to tell you, "Let my people go, so they can worship me in the wilderness." Until now, you have refused to listen to him. ¹⁷So this is what the LORD says: "I will show you that I am the LORD." Look! I will strike the water of the Nile with this staff in my hand, and the river will turn to blood. ¹⁸The fish in it will die, and the river

will stink. The Egyptians will not be able to drink any water from the Nile.'"

¹⁹Then the LORD said to Moses: "Tell Aaron, 'Take your staff and raise your hand over the waters of Egypt—all its rivers, canals, ponds, and all the reservoirs. Turn all the water to blood. Everywhere in Egypt the water will turn to blood, even the water stored in wooden bowls and stone pots.'"

²⁰So Moses and Aaron did just as the LORD commanded them. As Pharaoh and all of his officials watched, Aaron raised his staff and struck the water of the Nile. Suddenly, the whole river turned to blood! ²¹The fish in the river died, and the water became so foul that the Egyptians couldn't drink it. There was blood everywhere throughout the land of Egypt. ²²But again the magicians of Egypt used their magic, and they, too, turned water into blood. So Pharaoh's heart remained hard. He refused to listen to Moses and Aaron, just as the LORD had predicted. ²³Pharaoh returned to his palace and

7:14 Hebrew *heavy.*

put the whole thing out of his mind. ²⁴Then all the Egyptians dug along the riverbank to find drinking water, for they couldn't drink the water from the Nile.

²⁵Seven days passed from the time the LORD struck the Nile.

8 A PLAGUE OF FROGS

¹*Then the LORD said to Moses, "Go back to Pharaoh and announce to him, 'This is what the LORD says: Let my people go, so they can worship me. ²If you refuse to let them go, I will send a plague of frogs across your entire land. ³The Nile River will swarm with frogs. They will come up out of the river and into your palace, even into your bedroom and onto your bed! They will enter the houses of your officials and your people. They will even jump into your ovens and your kneading bowls. ⁴Frogs will jump on you, your people, and all your officials.'"

⁵*Then the LORD said to Moses, "Tell Aaron, 'Raise the staff in your hand over all the rivers, canals, and ponds of Egypt, and bring up frogs over all the land.'" ⁶So Aaron raised his hand over the waters of Egypt, and frogs came up and covered the whole land! ⁷But the magicians were able to do the same thing with their magic. They, too, caused frogs to come up on the land of Egypt.

⁸Then Pharaoh summoned Moses and Aaron and begged, "Plead with the LORD to take the frogs away from me and my people. I will let your people go, so they can offer sacrifices to the LORD."

⁹"You set the time!" Moses replied. "Tell me when you want me to pray for you, your officials, and your people. Then you and your houses will be rid of the frogs. They will remain only in the Nile River."

¹⁰"Do it tomorrow," Pharaoh said.

"All right," Moses replied, "it will be as you have said. Then you will know that there is no one like the LORD our God. ¹¹The frogs will leave you and your houses, your officials, and your people. They will remain only in the Nile River."

¹²So Moses and Aaron left Pharaoh's palace, and Moses cried out to the LORD about the frogs he had inflicted on Pharaoh. ¹³And the LORD did just what Moses had predicted. The frogs in the houses, the courtyards, and the fields all died. ¹⁴The Egyptians piled them into great heaps, and a terrible stench filled the land. ¹⁵But when Pharaoh saw that relief had come, he became

8:1 Verses 8:1-4 are numbered 7:26-29 in Hebrew text. **8:5** Verses 8:5-32 are numbered 8:1-28 in Hebrew text. **8:15** Hebrew *made his heart heavy;* also in 8:32. **8:23** As in Greek and Latin versions; Hebrew reads *I will set redemption between.*

stubborn.* He refused to listen to Moses and Aaron, just as the LORD had predicted.

A PLAGUE OF GNATS ¹⁶So the LORD said to Moses, "Tell Aaron, 'Raise your staff and strike the ground. The dust will turn into swarms of gnats throughout the land of Egypt.'" ¹⁷So Moses and Aaron did just as the LORD had commanded them. When Aaron raised his hand and struck the ground with his staff, gnats infested the entire land, covering the Egyptians and their animals. All the dust in the land of Egypt turned into gnats. ¹⁸Pharaoh's magicians tried to do the same thing with their secret arts, but this time they failed. And the gnats covered everyone, people and animals alike.

¹⁹"This is the finger of God!" the magicians exclaimed to Pharaoh. But Pharaoh's heart remained hard. He wouldn't listen to them, just as the LORD had predicted.

A PLAGUE OF FLIES ²⁰Then the LORD told Moses, "Get up early in the morning and stand in Pharaoh's way as he goes down to the river. Say to him, 'This is what the LORD says: Let my people go, so they can worship me. ²¹If you refuse, then I will send swarms of flies on you, your officials, your people, and all the houses. The Egyptian homes will be filled with flies, and the ground will be covered with them. ²²But this time I will spare the region of Goshen, where my people live. No flies will be found there. Then you will know that I am the LORD and that I am present even in the heart of your land. ²³I will make a clear distinction between* my people and your people. This miraculous sign will happen tomorrow.'"

²⁴And the LORD did just as he had said. A thick swarm of flies filled Pharaoh's palace and the houses of his officials. The whole land of Egypt was thrown into chaos by the flies.

²⁵Pharaoh called for Moses and Aaron. "All right! Go ahead and offer sacrifices to your God," he said. "But do it here in this land."

²⁶But Moses replied, "That wouldn't be right. The Egyptians detest the sacrifices that we offer to the LORD our God. Look, if we offer our sacrifices here where the Egyptians can see us, they will stone us. ²⁷We must take a three-day trip into the wilderness to offer sacrifices to the LORD our God, just as he has commanded us."

²⁸"All right, go ahead," Pharaoh replied. "I will let you go into the wilderness to offer sacrifices to the LORD your God. But don't go too far away. Now hurry and pray for me."

²⁹Moses answered, "As soon as I leave you, I will pray to the LORD, and tomorrow the swarms

of flies will disappear from you and your officials and all your people. But I am warning you, Pharaoh, don't lie to us again and refuse to let the people go to sacrifice to the LORD."

³⁰So Moses left Pharaoh's palace and pleaded with the LORD to remove all the flies. ³¹And the LORD did as Moses asked and caused the swarms of flies to disappear from Pharaoh, his officials, and his people. Not a single fly remained. ³²But Pharaoh again became stubborn and refused to let the people go.

9 A PLAGUE AGAINST LIVESTOCK "Go back to Pharaoh," the LORD commanded Moses. "Tell him, 'This is what the LORD, the God of the Hebrews, says: Let my people go, so they can worship me. ²If you continue to hold them and refuse to let them go, ³the hand of the LORD will strike all your livestock—your horses, donkeys, camels, cattle, sheep, and goats—with a deadly plague. ⁴But the LORD will again make a distinction between the livestock of the Israelites and that of the Egyptians. Not a single one of Israel's animals will die! ⁵The LORD has already set the time for the plague to begin. He has declared that he will strike the land tomorrow.'"

⁶And the LORD did just as he had said. The next morning all the livestock of the Egyptians died, but the Israelites didn't lose a single animal. ⁷Pharaoh sent his officials to investigate, and they discovered that the Israelites had not lost a single animal! But even so, Pharaoh's heart remained stubborn,* and he still refused to let the people go.

A PLAGUE OF FESTERING BOILS ⁸Then the LORD said to Moses and Aaron, "Take handfuls of soot from a brick kiln, and have Moses toss it into the air while Pharaoh watches. ⁹The ashes will spread like fine dust over the whole land of Egypt, causing festering boils to break out on people and animals throughout the land."

¹⁰So they took soot from a brick kiln and went and stood before Pharaoh. As Pharaoh watched, Moses threw the soot into the air, and boils broke out on people and animals alike. ¹¹Even the magicians were unable to stand before Moses, because the boils had broken out on them and all the Egyptians. ¹²But

the LORD hardened Pharaoh's heart, and just as the LORD had predicted to Moses, Pharaoh refused to listen.

A PLAGUE OF HAIL ¹³Then the LORD said to Moses, "Get up early in the morning and stand before Pharaoh. Tell him, 'This is what the LORD, the God of the Hebrews, says: Let my people go, so they can worship me. ¹⁴If you don't, I will send more plagues on you* and your officials and your people. Then you will know that there is no one like me in all the earth. ¹⁵By now I could have lifted my hand and struck you and your people with a plague to wipe you off the face of the earth. ¹⁶But I have spared you for a purpose—to show you my power* and to spread my fame throughout the earth. ¹⁷But you still lord it over my people and refuse to let them go. ¹⁸So tomorrow at this time I will send a hailstorm more devastating than any in all the history of Egypt. ¹⁹Quick! Order your livestock and servants to come in from the fields to find shelter. Any person or animal left outside will die when the hail falls.'"

²⁰Some of Pharaoh's officials were afraid because of what the LORD had said. They quickly brought their servants and livestock in from the fields. ²¹But those who paid no attention to the word of the LORD left theirs out in the open.

²²Then the LORD said to Moses, "Lift your hand toward the sky so hail may fall on the people, the livestock, and all the plants throughout the land of Egypt."

²³So Moses lifted his staff toward the sky, and the LORD sent thunder and hail, and lightning flashed toward the earth. The LORD sent a tremendous hailstorm against all the land of Egypt. ²⁴Never in all the history of Egypt had there been a storm like that, with such devastating hail and continuous lightning. ²⁵It left all of Egypt in ruins. The hail struck down everything in the open field—people, animals, and plants alike. Even the trees were destroyed. ²⁶The only place without hail was the region of Goshen, where the people of Israel lived.

²⁷Then Pharaoh quickly summoned Moses and Aaron. "This time I have sinned," he confessed. "The LORD is the righteous one, and my people and I are wrong. ²⁸Please beg the LORD to end this terrifying thunder and hail. We've had enough. I will let you go; you don't need to stay any longer."

²⁹"All right," Moses replied. "As soon as I leave the city, I will lift my hands and pray to

---

DON'T GIVE UP!
(9:1) God sent Moses a fifth time to Pharaoh with the demand to let his people go! Moses may have been tired and discouraged by this time, but he continued to obey. Is there a difficult conflict you must face again and again? As Moses discovered, persistence is rewarded. Don't give up!

9:7 Hebrew *heavy.*   **9:14** Hebrew *on your heart.*   **9:16** Greek version reads *to display my power in you;* compare Rom 9:17.

the LORD. Then the thunder and hail will stop, and you will know that the earth belongs to the LORD. ³⁰But I know that you and your officials still do not fear the LORD God."

³¹(All the flax and barley were ruined by the hail, because the barley had formed heads and the flax was budding. ³²But the wheat and the emmer wheat were spared, because they had not yet sprouted from the ground.)

³³So Moses left Pharaoh's court and went out of the city. When he lifted his hands to the LORD, the thunder and hail stopped, and the downpour ceased. ³⁴But when Pharaoh saw that the rain, hail, and thunder had stopped, he and his officials sinned again, and Pharaoh again became stubborn.* ³⁵Because his heart was hard, Pharaoh refused to let the people leave, just as the LORD had predicted through Moses.

10 A PLAGUE OF LOCUSTS Then the LORD said to Moses, "Return to Pharaoh and make your demands again. I have made him and his officials stubborn* so I can display my miraculous signs among them. ²I've also done it so you can tell your children and grandchildren about how I made a mockery of the Egyptians and about the signs I displayed among them—and so you will know that I am the LORD."

³So Moses and Aaron went to Pharaoh and said, "This is what the LORD, the God of the Hebrews, says: How long will you refuse to submit to me? Let my people go, so they can worship me. ⁴If you refuse, watch out! For tomorrow I will bring a swarm of locusts on your country. ⁵They will cover the land so that you won't be able to see the ground. They will devour what little is left of your crops after the hailstorm, including all the trees growing in the fields. ⁶They will overrun your palaces and the homes of your officials and all the houses in Egypt. Never in the history of Egypt have your ancestors seen a plague like this one!" And with that, Moses turned and left Pharaoh.

⁷Pharaoh's officials now came to Pharaoh and appealed to him. "How long will you let this man hold us hostage? Let the men go to worship the LORD their God! Don't you realize that Egypt lies in ruins?"

⁸So Moses and Aaron were brought back to Pharaoh. "All right," he told them, "go and worship the LORD your God. But who exactly will be going with you?"

⁹Moses replied, "We will all go—young and old, our sons and daughters, and our flocks and herds. We must all join together in celebrating a festival to the LORD."

¹⁰Pharaoh retorted, "The LORD will certainly need to be with you if I let you take your little ones! I can see through your evil plan. ¹¹Never! Only the men may go and worship the LORD, since that is what you requested." And Pharaoh threw them out of the palace.

¹²Then the LORD said to Moses, "Raise your hand over the land of Egypt to bring on the locusts. Let them cover the land and devour every plant that survived the hailstorm."

¹³So Moses raised his staff over Egypt, and the LORD caused an east wind to blow over the land all that day and through the night. When morning arrived, the east wind had brought the locusts. ¹⁴And the locusts swarmed over the whole land of Egypt, settling in dense swarms from one end of the country to the other. It was the worst locust plague in Egyptian history, and there has never been another one like it. ¹⁵For the locusts covered the whole country and darkened the land. They devoured every plant in the fields and all the fruit on the trees that had survived the hailstorm. Not a single leaf was left on the trees and plants throughout the land of Egypt.

¹⁶Pharaoh quickly summoned Moses and Aaron. "I have sinned against the LORD your God and against you," he confessed. ¹⁷"Forgive my sin, just this once, and plead with the LORD your God to take away this death from me."

¹⁸So Moses left Pharaoh's court and pleaded with the LORD. ¹⁹The LORD responded by shifting the wind, and the strong west wind blew the locusts into the Red Sea.* Not a single locust remained in all the land of Egypt. ²⁰But the LORD hardened Pharaoh's heart again, so he refused to let the people go.

A PLAGUE OF DARKNESS ²¹Then the LORD said to Moses, "Lift your hand toward heaven, and the land of Egypt will be covered with a darkness so thick you can feel it." ²²So Moses lifted his hand to the sky, and a deep darkness covered the entire land of Egypt for three days. ²³During all that time the people could not see each other, and no one moved. But there was light as usual where the people of Israel lived.

²⁴Finally, Pharaoh called for Moses. "Go and worship the LORD," he said. "But leave your flocks and herds here. You may even take your little ones with you."

²⁵"No," Moses said, "you must provide us with animals for sacrifices and burnt offerings to the LORD our God. ²⁶All our livestock must

9:34 Hebrew *made his heart heavy.* **10:1** Hebrew *have made his heart and his officials' hearts heavy.* **10:19** Hebrew *sea of reeds.*

go with us, too; not a hoof can be left behind. We must choose our sacrifices for the LORD our God from among these animals. And we won't know how we are to worship the LORD until we get there."

²⁷But the LORD hardened Pharaoh's heart once more, and he would not let them go. ²⁸"Get out of here!" Pharaoh shouted at Moses. "I'm warning you. Never come back to see me again! The day you see my face, you will die!"

²⁹"Very well," Moses replied. "I will never see your face again."

11 DEATH FOR EGYPT'S FIRSTBORN Then the LORD said to Moses, "I will strike Pharaoh and the land of Egypt with one more blow. After that, Pharaoh will let you leave this country. In fact, he will be so eager to get rid of you that he will force you all to leave. ²Tell all the Israelite men and women to ask their Egyptian neighbors for articles of silver and gold." ³(Now the LORD had caused the Egyptians to look favorably on the people of Israel. And Moses was considered a very great man in the land of Egypt, respected by Pharaoh's officials and the Egyptian people alike.)

⁴Moses had announced to Pharaoh, "This is what the LORD says: At midnight tonight I will pass through the heart of Egypt. ⁵All the firstborn sons will die in every family in Egypt, from the oldest son of Pharaoh, who sits on his throne, to the oldest son of his lowliest servant girl who grinds the flour. Even the firstborn of all the livestock will die. ⁶Then a loud wail will rise throughout the land of Egypt, a wail like no one has heard before or will ever hear again. ⁷But among the Israelites it will be so peaceful that not even a dog will bark. Then you

will know that the LORD makes a distinction between the Egyptians and the Israelites. ⁸All the officials of Egypt will run to me and fall to the ground before me. 'Please leave!' they will beg. 'Hurry! And take all your followers with you.' Only then will I go!" Then, burning with anger, Moses left Pharaoh.

⁹Now the LORD had told Moses earlier, "Pharaoh will not listen to you, but then I will do even more mighty miracles in the land of Egypt." ¹⁰Moses and Aaron performed these miracles in Pharaoh's presence, but the LORD hardened Pharaoh's heart, and he wouldn't let the Israelites leave the country.

12 THE FIRST PASSOVER While the Israelites were still in the land of Egypt, the LORD gave the following instructions to Moses and Aaron: ²"From now on, this month will be the first month of the year for you. ³Announce to the whole community of Israel that on the tenth day of this month each family must choose a lamb or a young goat for a sacrifice, one animal for each household. ⁴If a family is too small to eat a whole animal, let them share with another family in the neighborhood. Divide the animal according to the size of each family and how much they can eat. ⁵The animal you select must be a one-year-old male, either a sheep or a goat, with no defects.

⁶"Take special care of this chosen animal until the evening of the fourteenth day of this first month. Then the whole assembly of the community of Israel must slaughter their lamb or young goat at twilight. ⁷They are to take some of the blood and smear it on the sides and top of the doorframes of the houses where they eat the animal. ⁸That same night they must roast the meat over a fire and eat it along with bitter salad greens and bread made without yeast. ⁹Do not eat any of the meat raw or boiled in water. The whole animal—including the head, legs, and internal organs—must be roasted over a fire. ¹⁰Do not leave any of it until the next morning. Burn whatever is not eaten before morning.

¹¹"These are your instructions for eating this meal: Be fully dressed,* wear your sandals, and carry your walking stick in your hand. Eat the meal with urgency, for this is the LORD's Passover. ¹²On that night I will pass through the land of Egypt and strike down every firstborn son and firstborn male animal in the land of Egypt. I will execute judgment against all the gods of Egypt, for I am the LORD! ¹³But the blood on your doorposts will serve as a sign, marking

---

HARD-HEARTED
(11:10) Did God really harden Pharaoh's heart and force him to do wrong? Before the ten plagues began, Moses and Aaron announced what God would do if Pharaoh didn't let the people go. When it became evident that Pharaoh wouldn't change, God confirmed Pharaoh's prideful decision and set in motion the painful consequences of his actions. These days, are you tempted to say, "My will be done"? When God says, "Okay, your will be done," look out!

SUBSTITUTE
(12:1-30) While every firstborn child of the Egyptians died, the Israelite children were spared. Why? Because of the lambs' blood on the doorposts of their homes, the angel of death passed them by. This is a story of redemption, the central theme of the Bible. Redemption means "to buy back." But the Passover story is not the only redemption story. Jesus Christ redeemed us by his death on the cross. Our part is to trust him and accept his gift of eternal life (Titus 2:14; Heb 9:13-15, 23-28). Have you?

12:11 Hebrew *Bind up your loins.*

the houses where you are staying. When I see the blood, I will pass over you. This plague of death will not touch you when I strike the land of Egypt.

¹⁴"This is a day to remember. Each year, from generation to generation, you must celebrate it as a special festival to the LORD. This is a law for all time. ¹⁵For seven days the bread you eat must be made without yeast. On the first day of the festival, remove every trace of yeast from your homes. Anyone who eats bread made with yeast during the seven days of the festival will be cut off from the community of Israel. ¹⁶On the first day of the festival and again on the seventh day, all the people must observe an official day for holy assembly. No work of any kind may be done on these days except in the preparation of food.

¹⁷"Celebrate this Festival of Unleavened Bread, for it will remind you that I brought your forces out of the land of Egypt on this very day. This festival will be a permanent law for you; celebrate this day from generation to generation. ¹⁸The bread you eat must be made without yeast from the evening of the fourteenth day of the first month until the evening of the twenty-first day of that month. ¹⁹During those seven days, there must be no trace of yeast in your homes. Anyone who eats anything made with yeast during this week will be cut off from the community of Israel. These regulations apply both to the foreigners living among you and to the native-born Israelites. ²⁰During those days you must not eat anything made with yeast. Wherever you live, eat only bread made without yeast."

²¹Then Moses called all the elders of Israel together and said to them, "Go, pick out a lamb or young goat for each of your families, and slaughter the Passover animal. ²²Drain the blood into a basin. Then take a bundle of hyssop branches and dip it into the blood. Brush the hyssop across the top and sides of the doorframes of your houses. And no one may go out through the door until morning. ²³For the LORD will pass through the land to strike down the Egyptians. But when he sees the blood on the top and sides of the doorframe, the LORD will pass over your home. He will not permit his death angel to enter your house and strike you down.

²⁴"Remember, these instructions are a permanent law that you and your descendants must observe forever. ²⁵When you enter the land the LORD has promised to give you, you will continue to observe this ceremony. ²⁶Then your children will ask, 'What does this ceremony mean?' ²⁷And you will reply, 'It is the Passover sacrifice to the LORD, for he passed over the houses of the Israelites in Egypt. And though he struck the Egyptians, he spared our families.'" When Moses had finished speaking, all the people bowed down to the ground and worshiped.

²⁸So the people of Israel did just as the LORD had commanded through Moses and Aaron. ²⁹And that night at midnight, the LORD struck down all the firstborn sons in the land of Egypt, from the firstborn son of Pharaoh, who sat on his throne, to the firstborn son of the prisoner in the dungeon. Even the firstborn of their livestock were killed. ³⁰Pharaoh and all his officials and all the people of Egypt woke up during the night, and loud wailing was heard throughout the land of Egypt. There was not a single house where someone had not died.

ISRAEL'S EXODUS FROM EGYPT ³¹Pharaoh sent for Moses and Aaron during the night. "Get out!" he ordered. "Leave my people—and take the rest of the Israelites with you! Go and worship the LORD as you have requested. ³²Take your flocks and herds, as you said, and be gone. Go, but bless me as you leave." ³³All the Egyptians urged the people of Israel to get out of the land as quickly as possible, for they thought, "We will all die!"

³⁴The Israelites took their bread dough before yeast was added. They wrapped their kneading boards in their cloaks and carried them on their shoulders. ³⁵And the people of Israel did as Moses had instructed; they asked the Egyptians for clothing and articles of silver and gold. ³⁶The LORD caused the Egyptians to look favorably on the Israelites, and they gave the Israelites whatever they asked for. So they stripped the Egyptians of their wealth!

³⁷That night the people of Israel left Rameses and started for Succoth. There were about 600,000 men,* plus all the women and children. ³⁸A rabble of non-Israelites went with them, along with great flocks and herds of livestock. ³⁹For bread they baked flat cakes from the dough without yeast they had brought from Egypt. It was made without yeast because the people were driven out of Egypt in such a hurry that they had no time to prepare the bread or other food.

⁴⁰The people of Israel had lived in Egypt* for 430 years. ⁴¹In fact, it was on the last day of the 430th year that all the LORD's forces left the

12:37 Or *fighting men;* Hebrew reads *men on foot.*   **12:40** Samaritan Pentateuch reads *in Canaan and Egypt;* Greek version reads *in Egypt and Canaan.*

THE HEBREW CALENDAR

The Hebrew lunar months, based on the earth's position in relation to the moon, fluctuate on our modern calendar, which is based on the earth's position in relation to the sun. Thus, the Hebrew months often begin in the middle of the months of our modern calendar. Food crops in the ancient Near East were normally planted in the fall months of October and November and then harvested the next spring from March through June.

MONTH	TODAY'S CALENDAR	BIBLE REFERENCE	ISRAEL'S HOLIDAYS
1 Nisan (Abib)	March–April	Exodus 13:4; 23:15; 34:18; Deuteronomy 16:1; Esther 3:7	Passover (Lev 23:5); Unleavened Bread (Lev 23:6); Firstfruits (Lev 23:10)
2 Iyyar (Ziv)	April–May	1 Kings 6:1, 37	Second Passover (Num 9:10-11)
3 Sivan	May–June	Esther 8:9	Harvest/Pentecost (Lev 23:15)
4 Tammuz	June–July		
5 Ab	July–August		
6 Elul	August–September	Nehemiah 6:15	
7 Tishri (Ethanim)	September–October	1 Kings 8:2	Trumpets (Lev 23:24; Num 29:1); Day of Atonement (Lev 23:27); Shelters (Tabernacles) (Lev 23:34)
8 Marcheshvan (Bul)	October–November	1 Kings 6:38	
9 Kislev	November–December	Nehemiah 1:1	Hanukkah (John 10:22)
10 Tebeth	December–January	Esther 2:16	
11 Shebat	January–February	Zechariah 1:7	
12 Adar	February–March	Esther 3:7	Purim (Esth 9:24-32)

land. ⁴²On this night the LORD kept his promise to bring his people out of the land of Egypt. So this night belongs to him, and it must be commemorated every year by all the Israelites, from generation to generation.

INSTRUCTIONS FOR THE PASSOVER ⁴³Then the LORD said to Moses and Aaron, "These are the instructions for the festival of Passover. No outsiders are allowed to eat the Passover meal. ⁴⁴But any slave who has been purchased may eat it if he has been circumcised. ⁴⁵Temporary residents and hired servants may not eat it. ⁴⁶Each Passover lamb must be eaten in one house. Do not carry any of its meat outside, and do not break any of its bones. ⁴⁷The whole community of Israel must celebrate this Passover festival.

⁴⁸"If there are foreigners living among you who want to celebrate the LORD's Passover, let all their males be circumcised. Only then may

they celebrate the Passover with you like any native-born Israelite. But no uncircumcised male may ever eat the Passover meal. ⁴⁹This instruction applies to everyone, whether a native-born Israelite or a foreigner living among you."

⁵⁰So all the people of Israel followed all the LORD's commands to Moses and Aaron. ⁵¹On that very day the LORD brought the people of Israel out of the land of Egypt like an army.

13 **DEDICATION OF THE FIRSTBORN** Then the LORD said to Moses, ²"Dedicate to me every firstborn among the Israelites. The first offspring to be born, of both humans and animals, belongs to me."

³So Moses said to the people, "This is a day to remember forever—the day you left Egypt, the place of your slavery. Today the LORD has brought you out by the power of his mighty hand. (Remember, eat no food containing

yeast.) ⁴On this day in early spring, in the month of Abib,* you have been set free. ⁵You must celebrate this event in this month each year after the LORD brings you into the land of the Canaanites, Hittites, Amorites, Hivites, and Jebusites. (He swore to your ancestors that he would give you this land—a land flowing with milk and honey.) ⁶For seven days the bread you eat must be made without yeast. Then on the seventh day, celebrate a feast to the LORD. ⁷Eat bread without yeast during those seven days. In fact, there must be no yeast bread or any yeast at all found within the borders of your land during this time.

⁸"On the seventh day you must explain to your children, 'I am celebrating what the LORD did for me when I left Egypt.' ⁹This annual festival will be a visible sign to you, like a mark branded on your hand or your forehead. Let it remind you always to recite this teaching of the LORD: 'With a strong hand, the LORD rescued you from Egypt.'* ¹⁰So observe the decree of this festival at the appointed time each year.

¹¹"This is what you must do when the LORD fulfills the promise he swore to you and to your ancestors. When he gives you the land where the Canaanites now live, ¹²you must present all firstborn sons and firstborn male animals to the LORD, for they belong to him. ¹³A firstborn donkey may be bought back from the LORD by presenting a lamb or young goat in its place. But if you do not buy it back, you must break its neck. However, you must buy back every firstborn son.

¹⁴"And in the future, your children will ask you, 'What does all this mean?' Then you will tell them, 'With the power of his mighty hand, the LORD brought us out of Egypt, the place of our slavery. ¹⁵Pharaoh stubbornly refused to let us go, so the LORD killed all the firstborn males throughout the land of Egypt, both people and animals. That is why I now sacrifice all the firstborn males to the LORD—except that the firstborn sons are always bought back.' ¹⁶This ceremony will be like a mark branded on your hand or your forehead. It is a reminder that the power of the LORD's mighty hand brought us out of Egypt."

ISRAEL'S WILDERNESS DETOUR

¹⁷When Pharaoh finally let the people go, God did not lead them along the main road that runs through Philistine territory, even though that was the shortest route to the Promised Land. God said, "If the people are faced with a battle, they might change their minds and return to Egypt." ¹⁸So God led them in a roundabout way through the wilderness toward the Red Sea.* Thus the Israelites left Egypt like an army ready for battle.*

¹⁹Moses took the bones of Joseph with him, for Joseph had made the sons of Israel swear to do this. He said, "God will certainly come to help you. When he does, you must take my bones with you from this place."

²⁰The Israelites left Succoth and camped at Etham on the edge of the wilderness. ²¹The LORD went ahead of them. He guided them during the day with a pillar of cloud, and he provided light at night with a pillar of fire. This allowed them to travel by day or by night. ²²And the LORD did not remove the pillar of cloud or pillar of fire from its place in front of the people.

14 Then the LORD gave these instructions to Moses: ²"Order the Israelites to turn back and camp by Pi-hahiroth between Migdol and the sea. Camp there along the shore, across from Baal-zephon. ³Then Pharaoh will think, 'The Israelites are confused. They are trapped in the wilderness!' ⁴And once again I will harden Pharaoh's heart, and he will chase after you.* I have planned this in order to display my glory through Pharaoh and his whole army. After this the Egyptians will know that I am the LORD!" So the Israelites camped there as they were told.

THE EGYPTIANS PURSUE ISRAEL

⁵When word reached the king of Egypt that the Israelites had fled, Pharaoh and his officials changed

· ·

BRANDED

(13:9) The Festival of Unleavened Bread marked the Hebrews as a unique people—as though they were branded on their hands or foreheads. What actions or attitudes mark you as a follower of God? Think about the way you act at school, in the neighborhood, and at home. What you do in these areas will leave visible marks for all to see. Are you bearing the marks of God's love?

OBSTACLES

(13:17-18) God doesn't always work in the way that seems best to us. Instead of guiding the Israelites along the direct route from Egypt to the Promised Land, he decided to take them by a longer route. By going that way, they would avoid a conflict with the Philistines. When God doesn't lead you along the shortest path to your goal, are you tempted to complain or resist? If not, are you willing to trust him to lead you safely around unseen obstacles? Since he can see your whole journey from the beginning to the end, he knows the safest and best route to take you.

13:4 Hebrew *On this day in the month of Abib.* This first month of the ancient Hebrew lunar calendar usually occurs within the months of March and April. **13:9** Or *Let it remind you always to keep the instructions of the LORD on the tip of your tongue, because with a strong hand, the LORD rescued you from Egypt.* **13:18a** Hebrew *sea of reeds.* **13:18b** Greek version reads *left Egypt in the fifth generation.* **14:4** Hebrew *after them.*

DON'T BE AFRAID.
JUST STAND STILL AND
WATCH THE LORD RESCUE YOU TODAY.

their minds. "What have we done, letting all those Israelite slaves get away?" they asked. [6]So Pharaoh harnessed his chariot and called up his troops. [7]He took with him 600 of Egypt's best chariots, along with the rest of the chariots of Egypt, each with its commander. [8]The LORD hardened the heart of Pharaoh, the king of Egypt, so he chased after the people of Israel, who had left with fists raised in defiance. [9]The Egyptians chased after them with all the forces in Pharaoh's army—all his horses and chariots, his charioteers, and his troops. The Egyptians caught up with the people of Israel as they were camped beside the shore near Pi-hahiroth, across from Baal-zephon.

[10]As Pharaoh approached, the people of Israel looked up and panicked when they saw the Egyptians overtaking them. They cried out to the LORD, [11]and they said to Moses, "Why did you bring us out here to die in the wilderness? Weren't there enough graves for us in Egypt? What have you done to us? Why did you make us leave Egypt? [12]Didn't we tell you this would happen while we were still in Egypt? We said, 'Leave us alone! Let us be slaves to the Egyptians. It's better to be a slave in Egypt than a corpse in the wilderness!'"

[13]But Moses told the people, "Don't be afraid. Just stand still and watch the LORD rescue you today. The Egyptians you see today will never be seen again. [14]The LORD himself will fight for you. Just stay calm."

ESCAPE THROUGH THE RED SEA
[15]Then the LORD said to Moses, "Why are you crying out to me? Tell the people to get moving! [16]Pick up your staff and raise your hand over the sea. Divide the water so the Israelites can walk through the middle of the sea on dry ground. [17]And I will harden the hearts of the Egyptians, and they will charge in after the Israelites. My great glory will be displayed through Pharaoh and his troops, his chariots, and his charioteers. [18]When my glory is displayed through them, all Egypt will see my glory and know that I am the LORD!"

[19]Then the angel of God, who had been leading the people of Israel, moved to the rear of the camp. The pillar of cloud also moved from the front and stood behind them. [20]The cloud settled between the Egyptian and Israelite camps. As darkness fell, the cloud turned to fire, lighting up the night. But the Egyptians and Israelites did not approach each other all night.

[21]Then Moses raised his hand over the sea, and the LORD opened up a path through the water with a strong east wind. The wind blew all that night, turning the seabed into dry land. [22]So the people of Israel walked through the middle of the sea on dry ground, with walls of water on each side!

[23]Then the Egyptians—all of Pharaoh's horses, chariots, and charioteers—chased them into the middle of the sea. [24]But just before dawn the LORD looked down on the Egyptian army from the pillar of fire and cloud, and he threw their forces into total confusion. [25]He twisted* their chariot wheels, making their chariots difficult to drive. "Let's get out of here—away from these Israelites!" the Egyptians shouted. "The LORD is fighting for them against Egypt!"

[26]When all the Israelites had reached the other side, the LORD said to Moses, "Raise your hand over the sea again. Then the waters will rush back and cover the Egyptians and their chariots and charioteers." [27]So as the sun began to rise, Moses raised his hand over the sea, and the water rushed back into its usual place. The Egyptians tried to escape, but the LORD swept them into the sea. [28]Then the

14:25 As in Greek version, Samaritan Pentateuch, and Syriac version; Hebrew reads *He removed.*

GET MOVING!
(14:15) While the people of Israel grumbled at the Red Sea, God told Moses to stop praying and get moving! He promised to help the Israelites once they moved forward in faith. Although prayer deserves a vital place in our life, there also is a place for action. Sometimes we know what to do, but we pray for more guidance as an excuse to postpone a faith action. Got a Red Sea in your life? If you know what you need to do, what are you waiting for?

waters returned and covered all the chariots and charioteers—the entire army of Pharaoh. Of all the Egyptians who had chased the Israelites into the sea, not a single one survived.

²⁹But the people of Israel had walked through the middle of the sea on dry ground, as the water stood up like a wall on both sides. ³⁰That is how the Lord rescued Israel from the hand of the Egyptians that day. And the Israelites saw the bodies of the Egyptians washed up on the seashore. ³¹When the people of Israel saw the mighty power that the Lord had unleashed against the Egyptians, they were filled with awe before him. They put their faith in the Lord and in his servant Moses.

15 A SONG OF DELIVERANCE Then Moses and the people of Israel sang this song to the Lord:

"I will sing to the Lord,
    for he has triumphed gloriously;
he has hurled both horse and rider
    into the sea.
² The Lord is my strength and my song;
    he has given me victory.
This is my God, and I will praise him—
    my father's God, and I will exalt him!
³ The Lord is a warrior;
    Yahweh* is his name!
⁴ Pharaoh's chariots and army
    he has hurled into the sea.
The finest of Pharaoh's officers
    are drowned in the Red Sea.*
⁵ The deep waters gushed over them;
    they sank to the bottom like a stone.

⁶ "Your right hand, O Lord,
    is glorious in power.
Your right hand, O Lord,
    smashes the enemy.
⁷ In the greatness of your majesty,
    you overthrow those who rise against
        you.
You unleash your blazing fury;
    it consumes them like straw.
⁸ At the blast of your breath,
    the waters piled up!
The surging waters stood straight like a
      wall;
    in the heart of the sea the deep waters
      became hard.

⁹ "The enemy boasted, 'I will chase them
    and catch up with them.

I will plunder them
    and consume them.
I will flash my sword;
    my powerful hand will destroy them.'
¹⁰ But you blew with your breath,
    and the sea covered them.
They sank like lead
    in the mighty waters.

¹¹ "Who is like you among the gods, O Lord—
    glorious in holiness,
awesome in splendor,
    performing great wonders?
¹² You raised your right hand,
    and the earth swallowed our enemies.

¹³ "With your unfailing love you lead
    the people you have redeemed.
In your might, you guide them
    to your sacred home.
¹⁴ The peoples hear and tremble;
    anguish grips those who live in Philistia.
¹⁵ The leaders of Edom are terrified;
    the nobles of Moab tremble.
All who live in Canaan melt away;
¹⁶   terror and dread fall upon them.
The power of your arm
    makes them lifeless as stone
until your people pass by, O Lord,
    until the people you purchased pass by.
¹⁷ You will bring them in and plant them on
      your own mountain—
the place, O Lord, reserved for your own
      dwelling,
the sanctuary, O Lord, that your hands
      have established.
¹⁸ The Lord will reign forever and ever!"

¹⁹When Pharaoh's horses, chariots, and charioteers rushed into the sea, the Lord brought the water crashing down on them. But the people of Israel had walked through the middle of the sea on dry ground!

THE LORD HIMSELF WILL FIGHT FOR YOU.
EXODUS 14:14

[20]Then Miriam the prophet, Aaron's sister, took a tambourine and led all the women as they played their tambourines and danced. [21]And Miriam sang this song:

"Sing to the LORD,
for he has triumphed gloriously;
he has hurled both horse and rider
into the sea."

BITTER WATER AT MARAH

[22]Then Moses led the people of Israel away from the Red Sea, and they moved out into the desert of Shur.

....

PROTECTION FROM DISEASES
(15:26) *God promised that if the people obeyed him they would be free from the diseases that plagued the Egyptians. Little did they know that following his rules would help keep them free from diseases. For example, following God's law against prostitution would guard them against sexually transmitted diseases. Today, God's laws still keep us from harm. But he can't protect us if we don't submit to his directions for living.*

STRESSED OUT
(16:1-3) *It happened again. As the Israelites encountered danger, shortages, and inconvenience, they complained bitterly and longed to be back in Egypt. They didn't really want to be back in Egypt; they just wanted life to get a little easier. In the pressure of the moment, they couldn't focus on the cause of their stress (in this case, lack of trust in God). Instead, they could only think about the quickest way of escape. When you're in a tight spot, do you complain or carry on? Focusing on God's power and wisdom can help you deal with the cause of your stress and possibly overcome it.*

They traveled in this desert for three days without finding any water. [23]When they came to the oasis of Marah, the water was too bitter to drink. So they called the place Marah (which means "bitter").

[24]Then the people complained and turned against Moses. "What are we going to drink?" they demanded. [25]So Moses cried out to the LORD for help, and the LORD showed him a piece of wood. Moses threw it into the water, and this made the water good to drink.

It was there at Marah that the LORD set before them the following decree as a standard to test their faithfulness to him. [26]He said, "If you will listen carefully to the voice of the LORD your God and do what is right in his sight, obeying his commands and keeping all his decrees, then I will not make you suffer any of the diseases I sent on the Egyptians; for I am the LORD who heals you."

[27]After leaving Marah, the Israelites traveled on to the oasis of Elim, where they found twelve springs and seventy palm trees. They camped there beside the water.

16 MANNA AND QUAIL FROM HEAVEN

Then the whole community of Israel set out from Elim and journeyed into the wilderness of Sin,* between Elim and Mount Sinai. They arrived there on the fifteenth day of the second month, one month after leaving the

16:1a The geographical name *Sin* is related to *Sinai* and should not be confused with the English word *sin.*

MIRIAM *PERSONALITY PROFILE*

ASK OLDER BROTHERS OR SISTERS what their greatest test in life is and they will often answer, "My younger brother (or sister)!" Is that what you would say? This is especially true when the younger one seems more successful than the older. At such times, the bonds of family loyalty can be stretched to the breaking point.

When we first meet Miriam, she is involved in one of history's most unusual babysitting jobs: She watches her infant brother float down the Nile River in a waterproof cradle. When the baby is found, Miriam's quick thinking saves Moses and even allows him to be raised partially by his own mother. But it isn't long before the little brother she had protected grows into a great man—and their relationship changes. Moses needed her then; now, she needs him. The change probably wasn't easy for Miriam.

Instead of appreciating what God was doing in her brother's life, Miriam chose to criticize. Sound familiar? God had to teach Miriam and her other brother Aaron that each had a unique part in his plans. Being envious of one another was wrong.

The same lesson applies to our families. What difference would it make in your family if every criticism were changed into an encouraging or loving statement? Are you willing to model this new trend?

BOTTOM LINE: The motives behind criticism are often more important to deal with than the criticism itself.

UPS:
• *Quick thinker under pressure*
• *Able leader*
• *Songwriter*
• *Prophetess*

DOWNS:
• *Was envious of Moses' authority*
• *Openly criticized Moses' leadership*

STATS:
• *Where: Egypt, Sinai Peninsula*
• *Relatives: Aaron and Moses (brothers)*

KEY VERSES: *Exodus 2:1-25; 15:1-27; Numbers 12:1:1-16; 20:1; Deuteronomy 24:9; 1 Chronicles 6:3; Micah 6:4.*

FAMOUS SONGS IN THE BIBLE

WHERE	PURPOSE OF SONG
Exodus 15:1-21	Moses' song of victory and praise after God led Israel out of Egypt and saved them by parting the Red Sea; Miriam joined in the singing, too
Numbers 21:17-18	Israel's song of praise to God for giving them water in the wilderness
Deuteronomy 32:1-43	Moses' song of Israel's history with thanksgiving and praise as the Hebrews were about to enter the Promised Land
Judges 5:2-31	Deborah and Barak's song of praise thanking God for Israel's victory over King Jabin's army at Mount Tabor
2 Samuel 22:1-51	David's song of thanks and praise to God for rescuing him from Saul and his other enemies
Ezra 3:11	Israel's song of praise at the completion of the Temple's foundation
Song of Songs	Solomon's song of love celebrating the union of husband and wife
Isaiah 26:1-21	Isaiah's prophetic song about how the redeemed will sing in the new Jerusalem
Luke 1:46-55	Mary's song of praise to God for the conception of Jesus
Luke 1:68-79	Zechariah's song of praise for the promise of a son
Acts 16:25	Paul and Silas sang hymns in prison
Revelation 5:9-10	The "new song" of the 24 elders acclaiming Christ as worthy to break the seven seals of God's scroll
Revelation 14:3	The song of the 144,000 redeemed from the earth
Revelation 15:3-4	The song of all the redeemed in praise of the Lamb who redeemed them

land of Egypt.* ²There, too, the whole community of Israel complained about Moses and Aaron.

³"If only the Lord had killed us back in Egypt," they moaned. "There we sat around pots filled with meat and ate all the bread we wanted. But now you have brought us into this wilderness to starve us all to death."

⁴Then the Lord said to Moses, "Look, I'm going to rain down food from heaven for you. Each day the people can go out and pick up as much food as they need for that day. I will test them in this to see whether or not they will follow my instructions. ⁵On the sixth day they will gather food, and when they prepare it, there will be twice as much as usual."

⁶So Moses and Aaron said to all the people of Israel, "By evening you will realize it was the Lord who brought you out of the land of Egypt. ⁷In the morning you will see the glory of the Lord, because he has heard your complaints, which are against him, not against us. What have we done that you should complain about us?" ⁸Then Moses added, "The Lord will

give you meat to eat in the evening and bread to satisfy you in the morning, for he has heard all your complaints against him. What have we done? Yes, your complaints are against the Lord, not against us."

⁹Then Moses said to Aaron, "Announce this to the entire community of Israel: 'Present yourselves before the Lord, for he has heard your complaining.'" ¹⁰And as Aaron spoke to the whole community of Israel, they looked out toward the wilderness. There they could see the awesome glory of the Lord in the cloud.

¹¹Then the Lord said to Moses, ¹²"I have heard the Israelites' complaints. Now tell them, 'In the evening you will have meat to eat, and in the morning you will have all the bread you want. Then you will know that I am the Lord your God.'"

¹³That evening vast numbers of quail flew in and covered the camp. And the next morning the area around the camp was wet with dew. ¹⁴When the dew evaporated, a flaky substance as fine as frost blanketed the ground. ¹⁵The Israelites were puzzled when they saw it. "What is it?" they asked each other. They had no idea what it was.

16:1b The Exodus had occurred on the fifteenth day of the first month (see Num 33:3).

And Moses told them, "It is the food the LORD has given you to eat. ¹⁶These are the LORD's instructions: Each household should gather as much as it needs. Pick up two quarts* for each person in your tent."

¹⁷So the people of Israel did as they were told. Some gathered a lot, some only a little. ¹⁸But when they measured it out,* everyone had just enough. Those who gathered a lot had nothing left over, and those who gathered only a little had enough. Each family had just what it needed.

¹⁹Then Moses told them, "Do not keep any of it until morning." ²⁰But some of them didn't listen and kept some of it until morning. But by then it was full of maggots and had a terrible smell. Moses was very angry with them.

²¹After this the people gathered the food morning by morning, each family according to its need. And as the sun became hot, the flakes they had not picked up melted and disappeared. ²²On the sixth day, they gathered twice as much as usual—four quarts* for each person instead of two. Then all the leaders of the community came and asked Moses for an explanation. ²³He told them, "This is what the LORD commanded: Tomorrow will be a day of complete rest, a holy Sabbath day set apart for the LORD. So bake or boil as much as you want today, and set aside what is left for tomorrow."

²⁴So they put some aside until morning, just as Moses had commanded. And in the morning the leftover food was wholesome and good, without maggots or odor. ²⁵Moses said, "Eat this food today, for today is a Sabbath day dedicated to the LORD. There will be no food on the ground today. ²⁶You may gather the food for six days, but the seventh day is the Sabbath. There will be no food on the ground that day."

²⁷Some of the people went out anyway on the seventh day, but they found no food. ²⁸The LORD asked Moses, "How long will these people refuse to obey my commands and instructions? ²⁹They must realize that the Sabbath is the LORD's gift to you. That is why he gives you a two-day supply on the sixth day, so there will be enough for two days. On the Sabbath day you must each stay in your place. Do

not go out to pick up food on the seventh day." ³⁰So the people did not gather any food on the seventh day.

³¹The Israelites called the food manna.* It was white like coriander seed, and it tasted like honey wafers.

³²Then Moses said, "This is what the LORD has commanded: Fill a two-quart container with manna to preserve it for your descendants. Then later generations will be able to see the food I gave you in the wilderness when I set you free from Egypt."

³³Moses said to Aaron, "Get a jar and fill it with two quarts of manna. Then put it in a sacred place before the LORD to preserve it for all future generations." ³⁴Aaron did just as the LORD had commanded Moses. He eventually placed it in the Ark of the Covenant—in front of the stone tablets inscribed with the terms of the covenant.* ³⁵So the people of Israel ate manna for forty years until they arrived at the land where they would settle. They ate manna until they came to the border of the land of Canaan.

³⁶The container used to measure the manna was an omer, which was one-tenth of an ephah; it held about two quarts.*

17 **WATER FROM THE ROCK** At the LORD's command, the whole community of Israel left the wilderness of Sin* and moved from place to place. Eventually they camped at Rephidim, but there was no water there for the people to drink. ²So once more the people complained against Moses. "Give us water to drink!" they demanded.

"Quiet!" Moses replied. "Why are you complaining against me? And why are you testing the LORD?"

³But tormented by thirst, they continued to argue with Moses. "Why did you bring us out of Egypt? Are you trying to kill us, our children, and our livestock with thirst?"

⁴Then Moses cried out to the LORD, "What should I do with these people? They are ready to stone me!"

⁵The LORD said to Moses, "Walk out in front of the people. Take your staff, the one you used when you struck the water of the Nile, and call some of the elders of Israel to join you. ⁶I will stand before you on the rock at Mount Sinai.* Strike the rock, and water will come gushing out. Then the people will be able to drink." So

A TIME OUT WITH GOD
(16:23) The Israelites were not supposed to work on the Sabbath. Even cooking food was viewed as work. God knew that the busy routine of daily living could distract people from worshiping him. He wanted his people to rest from their labors and focus on him. It is so easy to let school, friends, and other activities crowd our schedules so tightly that we don't spend regular time with God. How do you guard your time with God?

16:16 Hebrew *1 omer* [2 liters]; also in 16:32, 33.   **16:18** Hebrew *measured it with an omer.*   **16:22** Hebrew *2 omers* [4 liters].
16:31 *Manna* means "What is it?" See 16:15.   **16:34** Hebrew *He placed it in front of the Testimony;* see note on 25:16.   **16:36** Hebrew *An omer is one-tenth of an ephah.*   **17:1** The geographical name *Sin* is related to *Sinai* and should not be confused with the English word *sin.*   **17:6** Hebrew *Horeb,* another name for Sinai.

Moses struck the rock as he was told, and water gushed out as the elders looked on.

⁷Moses named the place Massah (which means "test") and Meribah (which means "arguing") because the people of Israel argued with Moses and tested the LORD by saying, "Is the LORD here with us or not?"

ISRAEL DEFEATS THE AMALEKITES ⁸While the people of Israel were still at Rephidim, the warriors of Amalek attacked them. ⁹Moses commanded Joshua, "Choose some men to go out and fight the army of Amalek for us. Tomorrow, I will stand at the top of the hill, holding the staff of God in my hand."

¹⁰So Joshua did what Moses had commanded and fought the army of Amalek. Meanwhile, Moses, Aaron, and Hur climbed to the top of a nearby hill. ¹¹As long as Moses held up the staff in his hand, the Israelites had the advantage. But whenever he dropped his hand, the Amalekites gained the advantage. ¹²Moses' arms soon became so tired he could no longer hold them up. So Aaron and Hur found a stone for him to sit on. Then they stood on each side of Moses, holding up his hands. So his hands held steady until sunset. ¹³As a result, Joshua overwhelmed the army of Amalek in battle.

¹⁴After the victory, the LORD instructed Moses, "Write this down on a scroll as a permanent reminder, and read it aloud to Joshua: I will erase the memory of Amalek from under heaven." ¹⁵Moses built an altar there and named it Yahweh-Nissi (which means "the LORD is my banner"). ¹⁶He said, "They have raised their fist against the LORD's throne, so now* the LORD will be at war with Amalek generation after generation."

18

JETHRO'S VISIT TO MOSES Moses' father-in-law, Jethro, the priest of Midian, heard about everything God had done for Moses and his people, the Israelites. He heard especially about how the LORD had rescued them from Egypt.

²Earlier, Moses had sent his wife, Zipporah, and his two sons back to Jethro, who had taken them in. ³(Moses' first son was named Gershom,* for Moses had said when the boy was born, "I have been a foreigner in a foreign land." ⁴His second son was named Eliezer,* for Moses had said, "The God of my ancestors was my helper; he rescued me from the sword of Pharaoh.") ⁵Jethro, Moses' father-in-law,

now came to visit Moses in the wilderness. He brought Moses' wife and two sons with him, and they arrived while Moses and the people were camped near the mountain of God. ⁶Jethro had sent a message to Moses, saying, "I, Jethro, your father-in-law, am coming to see you with your wife and your two sons."

⁷So Moses went out to meet his father-in-law. He bowed low and kissed him. They asked about each other's welfare and then went into Moses' tent. ⁸Moses told his father-in-law everything the LORD had done to Pharaoh and Egypt on behalf of Israel. He also told about all the hardships they had experienced along the way and how the LORD had rescued his people from all their troubles. ⁹Jethro was delighted when he heard about all the good things the LORD had done for Israel as he rescued them from the hand of the Egyptians.

¹⁰"Praise the LORD," Jethro said, "for he has rescued you from the Egyptians and from Pharaoh. Yes, he has rescued Israel from the powerful hand of Egypt! ¹¹I know now that the LORD is greater than all other gods, because he rescued his people from the oppression of the proud Egyptians."

¹²Then Jethro, Moses' father-in-law, brought a burnt offering and sacrifices to God. Aaron and all the elders of Israel came out and joined him in a sacrificial meal in God's presence.

JETHRO'S WISE ADVICE ¹³The next day, Moses took his seat to hear the people's disputes against each other. They waited before him from morning till evening.

¹⁴When Moses' father-in-law saw all that Moses was doing for the people, he asked, "What are you really accomplishing here? Why are you trying to do all this alone while everyone stands around you from morning till evening?"

¹⁵Moses replied, "Because the people come to me to get a ruling from God. ¹⁶When a dispute arises, they come to me, and I am the one who settles the case between the quarreling parties. I inform the people of God's decrees and give them his instructions."

¹⁷"This is not good!" Moses' father-in-law

17:16 Or *Hands have been lifted up to the LORD's throne, and now.*
18:3 *Gershom* sounds like a Hebrew term that means "a foreigner there." 18:4 *Eliezer* means "God is my helper."

FAMILY TALK
(18:1-11) Moses told his father-in-law about the great deeds God performed to free the people of Israel from slavery in Egypt. Our relatives and friends often are the hardest people to talk with about God. Yet we can have an important influence over them. What are some opportunities you have to tell your friends and relatives about God? Do you take advantage of those opportunities?

HONOR YOUR FATHER AND MOTHER.

THEN YOU WILL LIVE A LONG, FULL LIFE IN THE LAND THE LORD YOUR GOD IS GIVING YOU.

EXODUS 20:12

exclaimed. [18]"You're going to wear yourself out—and the people, too. This job is too heavy a burden for you to handle all by yourself. [19]Now listen to me, and let me give you a word of advice, and may God be with you. You should continue to be the people's representative before God, bringing their disputes to him. [20]Teach them God's decrees, and give them his instructions. Show them how to conduct their lives. [21]But select from all the people some capable, honest men who fear God and hate bribes. Appoint them as leaders over groups of one thousand, one hundred, fifty, and ten. [22]They should always be available to solve the people's common disputes, but have them bring the major cases to you. Let the leaders decide the smaller matters themselves. They will help you carry the load, making the task easier for you. [23]If you follow this advice, and if God commands you to do so, then you will be able to endure the pressures, and all these people will go home in peace."

[24]Moses listened to his father-in-law's advice and followed his suggestions. [25]He chose capable men from all over Israel and appointed them as leaders over the people. He put them in charge of groups of one thousand, one hundred, fifty, and ten. [26]These men were always available to solve the people's common disputes. They brought the major cases to Moses, but they took care of the smaller matters themselves.

[27]Soon after this, Moses said good-bye to his father-in-law, who returned to his own land.

19 THE LORD REVEALS HIMSELF AT SINAI

Exactly two months after the Israelites left Egypt,* they arrived in the wilderness of Sinai. [2]After breaking camp at Rephidim, they came to the wilderness of Sinai and set up camp there at the base of Mount Sinai.

[3]Then Moses climbed the mountain to appear before God. The LORD called to him from the mountain and said, "Give these instructions to the family of Jacob; announce it to the descendants of Israel: [4]'You have seen what I did to the Egyptians. You know how I carried you on eagles' wings and brought you to myself. [5]Now if you will obey me and keep my covenant, you will be my own special treasure from among all the peoples on earth; for all the earth belongs to me. [6]And you will be my kingdom of priests, my holy nation.' This is the message you must give to the people of Israel."

[7]So Moses returned from the mountain and called together the elders of the people and told them everything the LORD had commanded him. [8]And all the people responded together, "We will do everything the LORD has commanded." So Moses brought the people's answer back to the LORD.

[9]Then the LORD said to Moses, "I will come to you in a thick cloud, Moses, so the people themselves can hear me when I speak with you. Then they will always trust you."

Moses told the LORD what the people had said. [10]Then the LORD told Moses, "Go down and prepare the people for my arrival. Consecrate them today and tomorrow, and have them wash their clothing. [11]Be sure they are ready on the third day, for on that day the LORD will come down on Mount Sinai as all the people watch. [12]Mark off a boundary all around the mountain. Warn the people, 'Be careful! Do not go up on the mountain or even touch its boundaries. Anyone who touches the mountain will certainly be put to death. [13]No hand may touch the person or animal that crosses the boundary; instead, stone them or shoot them with arrows. They must be put to death.' However, when the ram's horn sounds a long blast, then the people may go up on the mountain.*"

[14]So Moses went down to the people. He consecrated them for worship, and they washed their clothes. [15]He told them, "Get ready for the third day, and until then abstain from having sexual intercourse."

[16]On the morning of the third day, thunder roared and lightning flashed, and a dense cloud came down on the mountain. There was a long, loud blast from a ram's horn, and all the people trembled. [17]Moses led them out from the camp to meet with God, and they stood at the foot of the mountain. [18]All of Mount Sinai was covered with smoke because the LORD had descended on it in the form of fire. The smoke billowed into the sky like smoke from a brick

19:1 Hebrew *In the third month after the Israelites left Egypt, on that very day*, i.e., two lunar months to the day after leaving Egypt. Compare Num 33:3.   **19:13** Or *up to the mountain.*

kiln, and the whole mountain shook violently. ¹⁹As the blast of the ram's horn grew louder and louder, Moses spoke, and God thundered his reply. ²⁰The LORD came down on the top of Mount Sinai and called Moses to the top of the mountain. So Moses climbed the mountain.

²¹Then the LORD told Moses, "Go back down and warn the people not to break through the boundaries to see the LORD, or they will die. ²²Even the priests who regularly come near to the LORD must purify themselves so that the LORD does not break out and destroy them."

²³"But LORD," Moses protested, "the people cannot come up to Mount Sinai. You already warned us. You told me, 'Mark off a boundary all around the mountain to set it apart as holy.'"

²⁴But the LORD said, "Go down and bring Aaron back up with you. In the meantime, do not let the priests or the people break through to approach the LORD, or he will break out and destroy them."

²⁵So Moses went down to the people and told them what the LORD had said.

20 TEN COMMANDMENTS FOR THE COVENANT COMMUNITY
Then God gave the people all these instructions*:

²"I am the LORD your God, who rescued you from the land of Egypt, the place of your slavery.

³"You must not have any other god but me.

⁴"You must not make for yourself an idol of any kind or an image of anything in the heavens or on the earth or in the sea. ⁵You must not bow down to them or worship them, for I, the LORD your God, am a jealous God who will not tolerate your affection for any other gods. I lay the sins of the parents upon their children; the entire family is affected—even children in the third and fourth generations of those who reject me. ⁶But I lavish unfailing love for a thousand generations on those* who love me and obey my commands.

⁷"You must not misuse the name of the LORD your God. The LORD will not let you go unpunished if you misuse his name.

⁸"Remember to observe the Sabbath day by keeping it holy. ⁹You have six days each week for your ordinary work, ¹⁰but the seventh day is a Sabbath day of rest dedicated to the LORD your God. On that day no one in your household may do any work. This includes you, your sons and daughters, your male and female servants, your

20:1 Hebrew *all these words.*   **20:6** Hebrew *for thousands of those.*

MY STORY: Kristy

I loved ballet. I started ballet lessons when I was five years old and have been dancing ever since. In the past I practiced every day and took lessons at least once a week. I dreamed of someday joining the American Ballet Theatre.

By the time I got to high school, ballet had become my life. Everything revolved around my dancing—even my social life. If I had a recital, I dropped out of every other activity in order to practice. And I was obsessed with my weight, unwilling to gain even a few extra ounces.

When I became a Christian, I never dreamed that would affect my ballet. But one day in church the sermon was on the first commandment. The pastor talked about how certain things can become gods to us if we let them become more important than God. I compared the amount of time I spent practicing my ballet to the amount of time I spent reading the Bible and praying. Had ballet become my idol?

I began to pray about it. God showed me that I had allowed ballet to become more important than him. I decided to spend no more time practicing than I did reading the Bible and praying. I cut down on my dancing lessons and got involved in our church's youth group. It's been difficult to let up on dancing, but now it's OK that dancing is my second love. My first love is Jesus.

GOD'S NAME
(20:7) What's in a name? Everything, in God's case. His name reveals his character. Through the Ten Commandments, God reminded his people of the sacredness of his name. No one was to misuse it. Yet we often hear it used frivolously or in a curse today. The way we use God's name shows how we really feel about him. His name deserves respect. How do your conversations with others support this view?

livestock, and any foreigners living among you. ¹¹For in six days the LORD made the heavens, the earth, the sea, and everything in them; but on the seventh day he rested. That is why the LORD blessed the Sabbath day and set it apart as holy.

¹²"Honor your father and mother. Then you will live a long, full life in the land the LORD your God is giving you.

¹³"You must not murder.

¹⁴"You must not commit adultery.

¹⁵"You must not steal.

¹⁶"You must not testify falsely against your neighbor.

¹⁷"You must not covet your neighbor's house. You must not covet your neighbor's wife, male or female servant, ox or donkey, or anything else that belongs to your neighbor."

¹⁸When the people heard the thunder and the loud blast of the ram's horn, and when they saw the flashes of lightning and the smoke billowing from the mountain, they stood at a distance, trembling with fear.

¹⁹And they said to Moses, "You speak to us, and we will listen. But don't let God speak directly to us, or we will die!"

²⁰"Don't be afraid," Moses answered them, "for God has come in this way to test you, and so that your fear of him will keep you from sinning!"

²¹As the people stood in the distance, Moses approached the dark cloud where God was.

PROPER USE OF ALTARS ²²And the LORD said to Moses, "Say this to the people of Israel: You saw for yourselves that I spoke to you from heaven. ²³Remember, you must not make any idols of silver or gold to rival me.

²⁴"Build for me an altar made of earth, and offer your sacrifices to me—your burnt offerings and peace offerings, your sheep and goats, and your cattle. Build my altar wherever I cause my name to be remembered, and I will come to you and bless you. ²⁵If you use stones to build my altar, use only natural, uncut stones. Do not shape the stones with a tool, for that would make the altar unfit for holy use. ²⁶And do not approach my altar by going up steps. If you do, someone might look up under your clothing and see your nakedness.

21 **FAIR TREATMENT OF SLAVES** "These are the regulations you must present to Israel.

²"If you buy a Hebrew slave, he may serve for no more than six years. Set him free in the

. . . .

HONORING PARENTS
(20:12) This is the first commandment with a promise attached. To live in peace for generations in the Promised Land, the Israelites would need to respect authority and build strong families. But how is the command to "honor" parents lived out? Speaking well of them is one way. Showing them courtesy and respect—but not at the cost of disobeying God—also is a way to honor them. Parents have a special place in God's sight. The command to honor them is for everyone—even for those who find it difficult to get along with their parents. How do you honor yours?

ULTIMATE ISSUES *ABSOLUTE ANSWERS*

Have you ever heard anyone say that truth is relative? Maybe you've even heard someone say, "Your truth isn't necessarily my truth. What's true for you may not be true for me." Ever say that yourself?

Some people think that truth and standards of right and wrong change from decade to decade or from person to person. They make choices based on society's or their peers' definitions of right and wrong. As Judges 21:25 says, "The people [do] whatever seem[s] right in their own eyes." Does that describe anyone you know?

Magazines, newspapers, and the Internet carry story after story about lifestyle choices: an unmarried couple that lives together before marriage; a person who finally throws off the social pressures to explore his own homosexual identity; a teen who just wants to be free to express her sexuality; a pastor who leaves his wife for another woman—the list goes on. If you didn't catch those, just wait for the follow-up talk shows and movies. Many of these choices are made in the name of tolerance and other forms of political correctness. Those opposed to these lifestyle choices are viewed as intolerant, especially when society gives them the green light.

Wondering what's truly right or wrong? The Bible provides definite answers. The Ten Commandments and other laws reveal God's standards of right and wrong. Take lying, for example. God says no to that. What about adultery? Don't even think about it. Stealing? Nope. But honoring God and your parents are good moves.

Although times change, God's standards never do. "Your eternal word, O LORD, stands firm in heaven" (Ps 119:89). "The very essence of your words is truth; all your just regulations will stand forever" (Ps 119:160). Because God's standards always are the same, some are quick to describe the Bible as old-fashioned or lacking in relevance. Others might ignore it because they resent being measured by its standards. What's your view? ■

seventh year, and he will owe you nothing for his freedom. ³If he was single when he became your slave, he shall leave single. But if he was married before he became a slave, then his wife must be freed with him.

⁴"If his master gave him a wife while he was a slave and they had sons or daughters, then only the man will be free in the seventh year, but his wife and children will still belong to his master. ⁵But the slave may declare, 'I love my master, my wife, and my children. I don't want to go free.' ⁶If he does this, his master must present him before God.* Then his master must take him to the door or doorpost and publicly pierce his ear with an awl. After that, the slave will serve his master for life.

⁷"When a man sells his daughter as a slave, she will not be freed at the end of six years as the men are. ⁸If she does not satisfy her owner, he must allow her to be bought back again. But he is not allowed to sell her to foreigners, since he is the one who broke the contract with her. ⁹But if the slave's owner arranges for her to marry his son, he may no longer treat her as a slave but as a daughter.

¹⁰"If a man who has married a slave wife takes another wife for himself, he must not neglect the rights of the first wife to food, clothing, and sexual intimacy. ¹¹If he fails in any of these three obligations, she may leave as a free woman without making any payment.

CASES OF PERSONAL INJURY
¹²"Anyone who assaults and kills another person must be put to death. ¹³But if it was simply an accident permitted by God, I will appoint a place of refuge where the slayer can run for safety. ¹⁴However, if someone deliberately kills another person, then the slayer must be dragged even from my altar and be put to death.

¹⁵"Anyone who strikes father or mother must be put to death.

¹⁶"Kidnappers must be put to death, whether they are caught in possession of their victims or have already sold them as slaves.

¹⁷"Anyone who dishonors* father or mother must be put to death.

¹⁸"Now suppose two men quarrel, and one hits the other with a stone or fist, and the injured person does not die but is confined to bed. ¹⁹If he is later able to walk outside again, even with a crutch, the assailant will not be punished but must compensate his victim for lost wages and provide for his full recovery.

²⁰"If a man beats his male or female slave with a club and the slave dies as a result, the owner must be punished. ²¹But if the slave recovers within a day or two, then the owner shall not be punished, since the slave is his property.

²²"Now suppose two men are fighting, and in the process they accidentally strike a pregnant woman so she gives birth prematurely.* If no further injury results, the man who struck the woman must pay the amount of compensation the woman's husband demands and the judges approve. ²³But if there is further injury, the punishment must match the injury: a life for a life, ²⁴an eye for an eye, a tooth for a tooth, a hand for a hand, a foot for a foot, ²⁵a burn for a burn, a wound for a wound, a bruise for a bruise.

²⁶"If a man hits his male or female slave in the eye and the eye is blinded, he must let the slave go free to compensate for the eye. ²⁷And if a man knocks out the tooth of his male or female slave, he must let the slave go free to compensate for the tooth.

²⁸"If an ox* gores a man or woman to death, the ox must be stoned, and its flesh may not be eaten. In such a case, however, the owner will not be held liable. ²⁹But suppose the ox had a reputation for goring, and the owner had been informed but failed to keep it under control. If the ox then kills someone, it must be stoned, and the owner must also be put to death. ³⁰However, the dead person's relatives may accept payment to compensate for the loss of life. The owner of the ox may redeem his life by paying whatever is demanded.

³¹"The same regulation applies if the ox gores a boy or a girl. ³²But if the ox gores a slave, either male or female, the animal's owner must pay the slave's owner thirty silver coins,* and the ox must be stoned.

³³"Suppose someone digs or uncovers a pit and fails to cover it, and then an ox or a donkey falls into it. ³⁴The owner of the pit must pay full compensation to the owner of the animal, but then he gets to keep the dead animal.

³⁵"If someone's ox injures a neighbor's ox and the injured ox dies, then the two owners must sell the live ox and divide the price equally between them. They must also divide the dead animal. ³⁶But if the ox had a reputation for goring, yet its owner failed to keep it under control, he must pay full compensation—a live ox for the dead one—but he may keep the dead ox.

21:6 Or before the judges. **21:17** Greek version reads Anyone who speaks disrespectfully of. Compare Matt 15:4; Mark 7:10. **21:22** Or so she has a miscarriage; Hebrew reads so her children come out. **21:28** Or bull, or cow; also in 21:29-36. **21:32** Hebrew 30 shekels of silver, about 12 ounces or 342 grams in weight.

22 PROTECTION OF PROPERTY

¹*"If someone steals an ox* or sheep and then kills or sells it, the thief must pay back five oxen for each ox stolen, and four sheep for each sheep stolen.

²*"If a thief is caught in the act of breaking into a house and is struck and killed in the process, the person who killed the thief is not guilty of murder. ³But if it happens in daylight, the one who killed the thief is guilty of murder.

"A thief who is caught must pay in full for everything he stole. If he cannot pay, he must be sold as a slave to pay for his theft. ⁴If someone steals an ox or a donkey or a sheep and it is found in the thief's possession, then the thief must pay double the value of the stolen animal.

⁵"If an animal is grazing in a field or vineyard and the owner lets it stray into someone else's field to graze, then the animal's owner must pay compensation from the best of his own grain or grapes.

⁶"If you are burning thornbushes and the fire gets out of control and spreads into another person's field, destroying the sheaves or the uncut grain or the whole crop, the one who started the fire must pay for the lost crop.

⁷"Suppose someone leaves money or goods with a neighbor for safekeeping, and they are stolen from the neighbor's house. If the thief is caught, the compensation is double the value of what was stolen. ⁸But if the thief is not caught, the neighbor must appear before God,* who will determine if he stole the property.

⁹"Suppose there is a dispute between two people who both claim to own a particular ox, donkey, sheep, article of clothing, or any lost property. Both parties must come before God, and the person whom God declares* guilty must pay double compensation to the other.

....

RIGHTING WRONGS

(22:1-15) Throughout chapter 22, we find examples of the principle of restitution—making wrongs right. For example, if a man stole an animal, he had to repay up to four or five times its market value, depending on the circumstances. If you have done someone wrong, you should go beyond what is expected to make things right. This will help ease any pain you might have caused. It can also help the other person to be more forgiving and make you more likely to think before you do the same thing again.

STRANGERS

(22:21) God warned the Israelites not to treat foreigners unfairly, because they were once foreigners themselves in Egypt. It is not easy coming to a new environment where you feel alone and out of place. Are there newcomers in your corner of the world? Perhaps they're new to your school or newly arrived in this country. How can you show sensitivity to their struggles and express God's love by your kindness and generosity?

¹⁰"Now suppose someone leaves a donkey, ox, sheep, or any other animal with a neighbor for safekeeping, but it dies or is injured or gets away, and no one sees what happened. ¹¹The neighbor must then take an oath in the presence of the LORD. If the LORD confirms that the neighbor did not steal the property, the owner must accept the verdict, and no payment will be required. ¹²But if the animal was indeed stolen, the guilty person must pay compensation to the owner. ¹³If it was torn to pieces by a wild animal, the remains of the carcass must be shown as evidence, and no compensation will be required.

¹⁴"If someone borrows an animal from a neighbor and it is injured or dies when the owner is absent, the person who borrowed it must pay full compensation. ¹⁵But if the owner was present, no compensation is required. And no compensation is required if the animal was rented, for this loss is covered by the rental fee.

SOCIAL RESPONSIBILITY

¹⁶"If a man seduces a virgin who is not engaged to anyone and has sex with her, he must pay the customary bride price and marry her. ¹⁷But if her father refuses to let him marry her, the man must still pay him an amount equal to the bride price of a virgin.

¹⁸"You must not allow a sorceress to live.

¹⁹"Anyone who has sexual relations with an animal must certainly be put to death.

²⁰"Anyone who sacrifices to any god other than the LORD must be destroyed.*

²¹"You must not mistreat or oppress foreigners in any way. Remember, you yourselves were once foreigners in the land of Egypt.

²²"You must not exploit a widow or an orphan. ²³If you exploit them in any way and they cry out to me, then I will certainly hear their cry. ²⁴My anger will blaze against you, and I will kill you with the sword. Then your wives will be widows and your children fatherless.

²⁵"If you lend money to any of my people who are in need, do not charge interest as a money lender would. ²⁶If you take your neighbor's cloak as security for a loan, you must return it before sunset. ²⁷This coat may be the only blanket your neighbor has. How can a person sleep without it? If you do not return it and your neighbor cries out to me for help, then I will hear, for I am merciful.

22:1a Verse 22:1 is numbered 21:37 in Hebrew text. **22:1b** Or *bull,* or *cow;* also in 22:4, 9, 10. **22:2** Verses 22:2-31 are numbered 22:1-30 in Hebrew text. **22:8** Or *before the judges.* **22:9** Or *before the judges, and the person whom the judges declare.* **22:20** The Hebrew term used here refers to the complete consecration of things or people to the LORD, either by destroying them or by giving them as an offering.

²⁸"You must not dishonor God or curse any of your rulers.

²⁹"You must not hold anything back when you give me offerings from your crops and your wine.

"You must give me your firstborn sons.

³⁰"You must also give me the firstborn of your cattle, sheep, and goats. But leave the newborn animal with its mother for seven days; then give it to me on the eighth day.

³¹"You must be my holy people. Therefore, do not eat any animal that has been torn up and killed by wild animals. Throw it to the dogs.

23 A CALL FOR JUSTICE

"You must not pass along false rumors. You must not cooperate with evil people by lying on the witness stand.

²"You must not follow the crowd in doing wrong. When you are called to testify in a dispute, do not be swayed by the crowd to twist justice. ³And do not slant your testimony in favor of a person just because that person is poor.

⁴"If you come upon your enemy's ox or donkey that has strayed away, take it back to its owner. ⁵If you see that the donkey of someone who hates you has collapsed under its load, do not walk by. Instead, stop and help.

⁶"In a lawsuit, you must not deny justice to the poor.

⁷"Be sure never to charge anyone falsely with evil. Never sentence an innocent or blameless person to death, for I never declare a guilty person to be innocent.

⁸"Take no bribes, for a bribe makes you ignore something that you clearly see. A bribe makes even a righteous person twist the truth.

⁹"You must not oppress foreigners. You know what it's like to be a foreigner, for you yourselves were once foreigners in the land of Egypt.

¹⁰"Plant and harvest your crops for six years, ¹¹but let the land be renewed and lie uncultivated during the seventh year. Then let the poor among you harvest whatever grows on its own. Leave the rest for wild animals to eat. The same applies to your vineyards and olive groves.

¹²"You have six days each week for your ordinary work, but on the seventh day you must stop working. This gives your ox and your donkey a chance to rest. It also allows your slaves and the foreigners living among you to be refreshed.

¹³"Pay close attention to all my instructions. You must not call on the name of any other gods. Do not even speak their names.

THREE ANNUAL FESTIVALS

¹⁴"Each year you must celebrate three festivals in my honor. ¹⁵First, celebrate the Festival of Unleavened Bread. For seven days the bread you eat must be made without yeast, just as I commanded you. Celebrate this festival annually at the appointed time in early spring, in the month of

......

GOSSIP
(23:1-3) Making up or passing along false reports was strictly forbidden by God. Gossip/rumors, slander, and false witnessing undermine families, strain relationships, and add chaos to the justice system. Yet we often pass on unverified information in the form of prayer requests or "news." Even if you do not initiate a lie, you become responsible if you pass it along. What will you do the next time you hear a rumor?

CHOICES
peer pressure

Mike and Cody stare in horror at the wrecked family room in Mike's house. Stacks of greasy pizza boxes, mud and beer stains on the carpet, and a broken lamp meet their gaze. In the downstairs bathroom, Mike is sickened by the sight and smell of vomit. The toilet is clogged and overflowing.

The scene upstairs is even worse. There they find a leaking waterbed, beer spills and cans everywhere, a framed print lying broken beside a bed, and a trashed bathroom.

"I'm history!" Mike groans. "My parents will be back tomorrow!"

"Don't panic," Cody reassures him. "We can clean all night. Your folks will never know we had a party."

Mike gives his friend a you-must-be-brain-dead look. "Come on, Cody! It'll take a week to fix this mess!"

How did this disaster happen? Cody and some friends talked Mike into throwing a "Party for Profit" while his parents were away. They could get a couple of kegs, invite about 50 friends, and charge them each $15. It was a guaranteed success!

Mike refused at first, but soon changed his mind. "Okay," he finally said. "But only a few people!" Well, the "few" turned into more than 100, and the low-key party quickly turned into a wild nightmare.

Suppose Mike had listened to the advice of Exodus 23:2 instead of the counsel of his friends. How would this situation have changed?

When are you most tempted to give in to the crowd's wishes? After reading Exodus 23:2, what will you do the next time you're tempted?

Abib,* for that is the anniversary of your departure from Egypt. No one may appear before me without an offering.

16"Second, celebrate the Festival of Harvest,* when you bring me the first crops of your harvest.

"Finally, celebrate the Festival of the Final Harvest* at the end of the harvest season, when you have harvested all the crops from your fields. 17At these three times each year, every man in Israel must appear before the Sovereign, the LORD.

18"You must not offer the blood of my sacrificial offerings together with any baked goods containing yeast. And do not leave the fat from the festival offerings until the next morning.

19"As you harvest your crops, bring the very best of the first harvest to the house of the LORD your God.

"You must not cook a young goat in its mother's milk.

A PROMISE OF THE LORD'S PRESENCE 20"See, I am sending an angel before you to protect you on your journey and lead you safely to the place I have prepared for you. 21Pay close attention to him, and obey his instructions. Do not rebel against him, for he is my representative, and he will not forgive your rebellion. 22But if you are careful to obey him, following all my instructions, then I will be an enemy to your enemies, and I will oppose those who oppose you. 23For my angel will go before you and bring you into the land of the Amorites, Hittites, Perizzites, Canaanites, Hivites, and Jebusites, so you may live there. And I will destroy them completely. 24You must not worship the gods of these nations or serve them in any way or imitate their evil practices. Instead, you must utterly destroy them and smash their sacred pillars.

25"You must serve only the LORD your God. If you do, I* will bless you with food and water, and I will protect you from illness. 26There will be no miscarriages or infertility in your land, and I will give you long, full lives.

27"I will send my terror ahead of you and create panic among all the people whose lands you invade. I will make all your enemies turn and run. 28I will send terror* ahead of you to drive out the Hivites, Canaanites, and Hittites. 29But I will not drive them out in a single year, because the land would become desolate and the wild animals would multiply and threaten you. 30I will drive them out a little at a time until your population has increased enough to take possession of the land. 31And I will fix your

boundaries from the Red Sea to the Mediterranean Sea,* and from the eastern wilderness to the Euphrates River.* I will hand over to you the people now living in the land, and you will drive them out ahead of you.

32"Make no treaties with them or their gods. 33They must not live in your land, or they will cause you to sin against me. If you serve their gods, you will be caught in the trap of idolatry."

24 ISRAEL ACCEPTS THE LORD'S COVENANT Then the LORD instructed Moses: "Come up here to me, and bring along Aaron, Nadab, Abihu, and seventy of Israel's elders. All of you must worship from a distance. 2Only Moses is allowed to come near to the LORD. The others must not come near, and none of the other people are allowed to climb up the mountain with him."

3Then Moses went down to the people and repeated all the instructions and regulations the LORD had given him. All the people answered with one voice, "We will do everything the LORD has commanded."

4Then Moses carefully wrote down all the LORD's instructions. Early the next morning Moses got up and built an altar at the foot of the mountain. He also set up twelve pillars, one for each of the twelve tribes of Israel. 5Then he sent some of the young Israelite men to present burnt offerings and to sacrifice bulls as peace offerings to the LORD. 6Moses drained half the blood from these animals into basins. The other half he splattered against the altar.

7Then he took the Book of the Covenant and read it aloud to the people. Again they all responded, "We will do everything the LORD has commanded. We will obey."

8Then Moses took the blood from the basins and splattered it over the people, declaring, "Look, this blood confirms the covenant the LORD has made with you in giving you these instructions."

9Then Moses, Aaron, Nadab, Abihu, and the seventy elders of Israel climbed up the mountain. 10There they saw the God of Israel. Under his feet there seemed to be a surface of brilliant blue lapis lazuli, as clear as the sky itself. 11And though these nobles of Israel gazed upon

23:15 Hebrew *appointed time in the month of Abib.* This first month of the ancient Hebrew lunar calendar usually occurs within the months of March and April. **23:16a** Or *Festival of Weeks.* This was later called the Festival of Pentecost (see Acts 2:1). It is celebrated today as Shavuot (or Shabuoth). **23:16b** Or *Festival of Ingathering.* This was later called the Festival of Shelters or Festival of Tabernacles (see Lev 23:33-36). It is celebrated today as Sukkot (or Succoth). **23:25** As in Greek and Latin versions; Hebrew reads *he.* **23:28** Often rendered *the hornet.* The meaning of the Hebrew is uncertain. **23:31a** Hebrew *from the sea of reeds to the sea of the Philistines.* **23:31b** Hebrew *from the wilderness to the river.*

God, he did not destroy them. In fact, they ate a covenant meal, eating and drinking in his presence!

¹²Then the LORD said to Moses, "Come up to me on the mountain. Stay there, and I will give you the tablets of stone on which I have inscribed the instructions and commands so you can teach the people." ¹³So Moses and his assistant Joshua set out, and Moses climbed up the mountain of God.

¹⁴Moses told the elders, "Stay here and wait for us until we come back. Aaron and Hur are here with you. If anyone has a dispute while I am gone, consult with them."

¹⁵Then Moses climbed up the mountain, and the cloud covered it. ¹⁶And the glory of the LORD settled down on Mount Sinai, and the cloud covered it for six days. On the seventh day the LORD called to Moses from inside the cloud. ¹⁷To the Israelites at the foot of the mountain, the glory of the LORD appeared at the summit like a consuming fire. ¹⁸Then Moses disappeared into the cloud as he climbed higher up the mountain. He remained on the mountain forty days and forty nights.

25 OFFERINGS FOR THE TABERNACLE The LORD said to Moses, ²"Tell the people of Israel to bring me their sacred offerings. Accept the contributions from all whose hearts are moved to offer them. ³Here is a list of sacred offerings you may accept from them:

gold, silver, and bronze;
⁴ blue, purple, and scarlet thread;
fine linen and goat hair for cloth;
⁵ tanned ram skins and fine goatskin leather; acacia wood;
⁶ olive oil for the lamps;
spices for the anointing oil and the fragrant incense;
⁷ onyx stones, and other gemstones to be set in the ephod and the priest's chestpiece.

⁸"Have the people of Israel build me a holy sanctuary so I can live among them. ⁹You must build this Tabernacle and its furnishings exactly according to the pattern I will show you.

PLANS FOR THE ARK OF THE COVENANT
¹⁰"Have the people make an Ark of acacia wood—a sacred chest 45 inches long, 27 inches wide, and 27 inches high.* ¹¹Overlay it inside and outside with pure gold, and run a molding of gold all around it. ¹²Cast four gold rings and attach them to its four feet, two rings on each side. ¹³Make poles from acacia wood, and overlay them with gold. ¹⁴Insert the poles into the rings at the sides of the Ark to carry it. ¹⁵These carrying poles must stay inside the rings; never remove them. ¹⁶When the Ark is finished, place inside it the stone tablets inscribed with the terms of the covenant,* which I will give to you.

¹⁷"Then make the Ark's cover—the place of atonement—from pure gold. It must be 45 inches long and 27 inches wide.* ¹⁸Then make two cherubim from hammered gold, and place them on the two ends of the atonement cover. ¹⁹Mold the cherubim on each end of the atonement cover, making it all of one piece of gold. ²⁰The cherubim will face each other and look down on the atonement cover. With their wings spread above it, they will protect it. ²¹Place inside the Ark the stone tablets inscribed with the terms of the covenant, which I will give to you. Then put the atonement cover on top of the Ark. ²²I will meet with you there and talk to you from above the atonement cover between the gold cherubim that hover over the Ark of the Covenant.* From there I will give you my commands for the people of Israel.

PLANS FOR THE TABLE
²³"Then make a table of acacia wood, 36 inches long, 18 inches wide, and 27 inches high.* ²⁴Overlay it with pure gold and run a gold molding around the edge. ²⁵Decorate it with a 3-inch border* all around, and run a gold molding along the border. ²⁶Make four gold rings for the table and attach them at the four corners next to the four legs. ²⁷Attach the rings near the border to hold the poles that are used to carry the table. ²⁸Make these poles from acacia wood, and overlay them with gold. ²⁹Make special containers of pure gold for the table—bowls, pans, pitchers, and jars—to be used in pouring out liquid offerings. ³⁰Place the Bread of the Presence on the table to remain before me at all times.

PLANS FOR THE LAMPSTAND
³¹"Make a lampstand of pure, hammered gold. Make the entire lampstand and its decorations of one piece— the base, center stem, lamp cups, buds, and petals. ³²Make it with six branches going out from the center stem, three on each side. ³³Each of the six branches will have three lamp cups shaped like almond blossoms, complete with buds and petals. ³⁴Craft the center stem of the

25:10 Hebrew 2.5 cubits [115 centimeters] long, 1.5 cubits [69 centimeters] wide, and 1.5 cubits high. 25:16 Hebrew Place inside the Ark the Testimony; similarly in 25:21. The Hebrew word for "testimony" refers to the terms of the LORD's covenant with Israel as written on stone tablets, and also to the covenant itself. 25:17 Hebrew 2.5 cubits [115 centimeters] long and 1.5 cubits [69 centimeters] wide. 25:22 Or Ark of the Testimony. 25:23 Hebrew 2 cubits [92 centimeters] long, 1 cubit [46 centimeters] wide, and 1.5 cubits [69 centimeters] high. 25:25 Hebrew a border of a handbreadth [8 centimeters].

lampstand with four lamp cups shaped like almond blossoms, complete with buds and petals. ³⁵There will also be an almond bud beneath each pair of branches where the six branches extend from the center stem. ³⁶The almond buds and branches must all be of one piece with the center stem, and they must be hammered from pure gold. ³⁷Then make the seven lamps for the lampstand, and set them so they reflect their light forward. ³⁸The lamp snuffers and trays must also be made of pure gold. ³⁹You will need seventy-five pounds* of pure gold for the lampstand and its accessories.

⁴⁰"Be sure that you make everything according to the pattern I have shown you here on the mountain.

26 PLANS FOR THE TABERNACLE "Make the Tabernacle from ten curtains of finely woven linen. Decorate the curtains with blue, purple, and scarlet thread and with skillfully embroidered cherubim. ²These ten curtains must all be exactly the same size—42 feet long and 6 feet wide.* ³Join five of these curtains together to make one long curtain, then join the other five into a second long curtain. ⁴Put loops of blue yarn along the edge of the last curtain in each set. ⁵The fifty loops along the edge of one curtain are to match the fifty loops along the edge of the other curtain. ⁶Then make fifty gold clasps and fasten the long curtains together with the clasps. In this way, the Tabernacle will be made of one continuous piece.

⁷"Make eleven curtains of goat-hair cloth to serve as a tent covering for the Tabernacle. ⁸These eleven curtains must all be exactly the same size—45 feet long and 6 feet wide.* ⁹Join five of these curtains together to make one long curtain, and join the other six into a second long curtain. Allow 3 feet of material from the second set of curtains to hang over the front* of the sacred tent. ¹⁰Make fifty loops for one

edge of each large curtain. ¹¹Then make fifty bronze clasps, and fasten the loops of the long curtains with the clasps. In this way, the tent covering will be made of one continuous piece. ¹²The remaining 3 feet* of this tent covering will be left to hang over the back of the Tabernacle. ¹³Allow 18 inches* of remaining material to hang down over each side, so the Tabernacle is completely covered. ¹⁴Complete the tent covering with a protective layer of tanned ram skins and a layer of fine goatskin leather.

¹⁵"For the framework of the Tabernacle, construct frames of acacia wood. ¹⁶Each frame must be 15 feet high and 27 inches wide,* ¹⁷with two pegs under each frame. Make all the frames identical. ¹⁸Make twenty of these frames to support the curtains on the south side of the Tabernacle. ¹⁹Also make forty silver bases—two bases under each frame, with the pegs fitting securely into the bases. ²⁰For the north side of the Tabernacle, make another twenty frames, ²¹with their forty silver bases, two bases under each frame. ²²Make six frames for the rear—the west side of the Tabernacle—²³along with two additional frames to reinforce the rear corners of the Tabernacle. ²⁴These corner frames will be matched at the bottom and firmly attached at the top with a single ring, forming a single corner unit. Make both of these corner units the same way. ²⁵So there will be eight frames at the rear of the Tabernacle, set in sixteen silver bases—two bases under each frame.

²⁶"Make crossbars of acacia wood to link the frames, five crossbars for the north side of the Tabernacle ²⁷and five for the south side. Also make five crossbars for the rear of the Tabernacle, which will face west. ²⁸The middle crossbar, attached halfway up the frames, will run all the way from one end of the Tabernacle to the other. ²⁹Overlay the frames with gold, and make gold rings to hold the crossbars. Overlay the crossbars with gold as well.

³⁰"Set up this Tabernacle according to the pattern you were shown on the mountain.

³¹"For the inside of the Tabernacle, make a special curtain of finely woven linen. Decorate it with blue, purple, and scarlet thread and with skillfully embroidered cherubim. ³²Hang this curtain on gold hooks attached to four posts of acacia wood. Overlay the posts with gold, and set them in four silver bases. ³³Hang the inner curtain from clasps, and put the Ark of the

....

EASY ACCESS
(26:31) A linen curtain separated the two sacred rooms—the Holy Place and the Most Holy Place—in the Tabernacle. The priest entered the Holy Place each day to commune with God and tend to the altar of incense, the lampstand, and the table of the Bread of the Presence. The Most Holy Place housed the Ark of the Covenant. Only the high priest could enter the Most Holy Place. Even he could do so only once a year—on the Day of Atonement— to offer a sacrifice for the sins of the nation (see Lev 16).

When Jesus Christ later died on the cross, the curtain in the Temple (which had replaced the Tabernacle) tore from top to bottom (Mark 15:38), symbolizing our free access to God because of Jesus' death. We no longer need priests and sacrifices to approach God.

25:39 Hebrew *1 talent* [34 kilograms].   26:2 Hebrew *28 cubits* [12.9 meters] *long and 4 cubits* [1.8 meters] *wide.*   26:8 Hebrew *30 cubits* [13.8 meters] *long and 4 cubits* [1.8 meters] *wide.*
26:9 Hebrew *Double over the sixth sheet at the front.*
26:12 Hebrew *The half sheet that is left over.*   26:13 Hebrew *1 cubit* [46 centimeters].   26:16 Hebrew *10 cubits* [4.6 meters] *high and 1.5 cubits* [69 centimeters] *wide.*

Covenant* in the room behind it. This curtain will separate the Holy Place from the Most Holy Place.

³⁴"Then put the Ark's cover—the place of atonement—on top of the Ark of the Covenant inside the Most Holy Place. ³⁵Place the table outside the inner curtain on the north side of the Tabernacle, and place the lampstand across the room on the south side.

³⁶"Make another curtain for the entrance to the sacred tent. Make it of finely woven linen and embroider it with exquisite designs, using blue, purple, and scarlet thread. ³⁷Craft five posts from acacia wood. Overlay them with gold, and hang the curtain from them with gold hooks. Cast five bronze bases for the posts.

27 PLANS FOR THE ALTAR OF BURNT OFFERING "Using acacia wood, construct a square altar 7½ feet wide, 7½ feet long, and 4½ feet high.* ²Make horns for each of its four corners so that the horns and altar are all one piece. Overlay the altar with bronze. ³Make ash buckets, shovels, basins, meat forks, and firepans, all of bronze. ⁴Make a bronze grating for it, and attach four bronze rings at its four corners. ⁵Install the grating halfway down the side of the altar, under the ledge. ⁶For carrying the altar, make poles from acacia wood, and overlay them with bronze. ⁷Insert the poles through the rings on the two sides of the altar. ⁸The altar must be hollow, made from planks. Build it just as you were shown on the mountain.

PLANS FOR THE COURTYARD ⁹"Then make the courtyard for the Tabernacle, enclosed with curtains made of finely woven linen. On the south side, make the curtains 150 feet long.* ¹⁰They will be held up by twenty posts set securely in twenty bronze bases. Hang the curtains with silver hooks and rings. ¹¹Make the curtains the same on the north side—150 feet of curtains held up by twenty posts set securely in bronze bases. Hang the curtains with silver hooks and rings. ¹²The curtains on the west end of the courtyard will be 75 feet long,* supported by ten posts set into ten bases. ¹³The east end of the courtyard, the front, will also be 75 feet long. ¹⁴The courtyard entrance will

be on the east end, flanked by two curtains. The curtain on the right side will be 22½ feet long,* supported by three posts set into three bases. ¹⁵The curtain on the left side will also be 22½ feet long, supported by three posts set into three bases.

¹⁶"For the entrance to the courtyard, make a curtain that is 30 feet long.* Make it from finely woven linen, and decorate it with beautiful embroidery in blue, purple, and scarlet thread. Support it with four posts, each securely set in its own base. ¹⁷All the posts around the courtyard must have silver rings and hooks and bronze bases. ¹⁸So the entire courtyard will be 150 feet long and 75 feet wide, with curtain walls 7½ feet high,* made from finely woven linen. The bases for the posts will be made of bronze.

¹⁹"All the articles used in the rituals of the Tabernacle, including all the tent pegs used to support the Tabernacle and the courtyard curtains, must be made of bronze.

LIGHT FOR THE TABERNACLE ²⁰"Command the people of Israel to bring you pure oil of pressed olives for the light, to keep the lamps burning continually. ²¹The lampstand will stand in the Tabernacle, in front of the inner curtain that shields the Ark of the Covenant.* Aaron and his sons must keep the lamps burning in the LORD's presence all night. This is a permanent law for the people of Israel, and it must be observed from generation to generation.

28 CLOTHING FOR THE PRIESTS "Call for your brother, Aaron, and his sons, Nadab, Abihu, Eleazar, and Ithamar. Set them apart from the rest of the people of Israel so they may minister to me and be my priests. ²Make sacred garments for Aaron that are glorious and beautiful. ³Instruct all the skilled craftsmen whom I have filled with the spirit of wisdom. Have them make garments for Aaron that will distinguish him as a priest set apart for my service. ⁴These are the garments they are to make: a chestpiece, an ephod, a robe, a patterned tunic, a turban, and a sash. They are to make these sacred garments for your brother, Aaron, and his sons to wear when they serve me as priests. ⁵So give them fine linen cloth, gold thread, and blue, purple, and scarlet thread.

DESIGN OF THE EPHOD ⁶"The craftsmen must make the ephod of finely woven linen and skillfully embroider it with gold and with blue, purple, and scarlet thread. ⁷It will consist of

26:33 Or Ark of the Testimony; also in 26:34.   27:1 Hebrew 5 cubits [2.3 meters] wide, 5 cubits long, a square, and 3 cubits [1.4 meters] high.   27:9 Hebrew 100 cubits [46 meters]; also in 27:11.   27:12 Hebrew 50 cubits [23 meters]; also in 27:13.   27:14 Hebrew 15 cubits [6.9 meters]; also in 27:15.   27:16 Hebrew 20 cubits [9.2 meters].   27:18 Hebrew 100 cubits [46 meters] long and 50 by 50 [23 meters] wide and 5 cubits [2.3 meters] high.   27:21 Hebrew in the Tent of Meeting, outside the inner curtain that is in front of the Testimony. See note on 25:16.

two pieces, front and back, joined at the shoulders with two shoulder-pieces. ⁸The decorative sash will be made of the same materials: finely woven linen embroidered with gold and with blue, purple, and scarlet thread.

⁹"Take two onyx stones, and engrave on them the names of the tribes of Israel. ¹⁰Six names will be on each stone, arranged in the order of the births of the original sons of Israel. ¹¹Engrave these names on the two stones in the same way a jeweler engraves a seal. Then mount the stones in settings of gold filigree. ¹²Fasten the two stones on the shoulder-pieces of the ephod as a reminder that Aaron represents the people of Israel. Aaron will carry these names on his shoulders as a constant reminder whenever he goes before the Lord. ¹³Make the settings of gold filigree, ¹⁴then braid two cords of pure gold and attach them to the filigree settings on the shoulders of the ephod.

DESIGN OF THE CHESTPIECE ¹⁵"Then, with great skill and care, make a chestpiece to be worn for seeking a decision from God.* Make it to match the ephod, using finely woven linen embroidered with gold and with blue, purple, and scarlet thread. ¹⁶Make the chestpiece of a single piece of cloth folded to form a pouch nine inches* square. ¹⁷Mount four rows of gemstones* on it. The first row will contain a red carnelian, a pale-green peridot, and an emerald. ¹⁸The second row will contain a turquoise, a blue lapis lazuli, and a white moonstone. ¹⁹The third row will contain an orange jacinth, an agate, and a purple amethyst. ²⁰The fourth row will contain a blue-green beryl, an onyx, and a green jasper. All these stones will be set in gold filigree. ²¹Each stone will represent one of the twelve sons of Israel, and the name of that tribe will be engraved on it like a seal.

²²"To attach the chestpiece to the ephod, make braided cords of pure gold thread. ²³Then make two gold rings and attach them to the top corners of the chestpiece. ²⁴Tie the two gold cords to the two rings on the chestpiece. ²⁵Tie the other ends of the cords to the gold settings on the shoulder-pieces of the ephod. ²⁶Then make two more gold rings and attach them to the inside edges of the chestpiece next to the ephod. ²⁷And make two more gold rings and attach them to the front of the ephod, below the shoulder-pieces, just above the knot where the decorative sash is fastened to the ephod. ²⁸Then attach the bottom rings of the chestpiece to the rings on the ephod with blue cords. This will hold the chestpiece securely to the ephod above the decorative sash.

²⁹"In this way, Aaron will carry the names of the tribes of Israel on the sacred chestpiece* over his heart when he goes into the Holy Place. This will be a continual reminder that he represents the people when he comes before the Lord. ³⁰Insert the Urim and Thummim into the sacred chestpiece so they will be carried over Aaron's heart when he goes into the Lord's presence. In this way, Aaron will always carry over his heart the objects used to determine the Lord's will for his people whenever he goes in before the Lord.

ADDITIONAL CLOTHING FOR THE PRIESTS
³¹"Make the robe that is worn with the ephod from a single piece of blue cloth, ³²with an opening for Aaron's head in the middle of it. Reinforce the opening with a woven collar* so it will not tear. ³³Make pomegranates out of blue, purple, and scarlet yarn, and attach them to the hem of the robe, with gold bells between them. ³⁴The gold bells and pomegranates are to alternate all around the hem. ³⁵Aaron will wear this robe whenever he ministers before the Lord, and the bells will tinkle as he goes in and out of the Lord's presence in the Holy Place. If he wears it, he will not die.

³⁶"Next make a medallion of pure gold, and engrave it like a seal with these words: Holy to the Lord. ³⁷Attach the medallion with a blue cord to the front of Aaron's turban, where it must remain. ³⁸Aaron must wear it on his forehead so he may take on himself any guilt of the people of Israel when they consecrate their sacred offerings. He must always wear it on his forehead so the Lord will accept the people.

³⁹"Weave Aaron's patterned tunic from fine linen cloth. Fashion the turban from this linen as well. Also make a sash, and decorate it with colorful embroidery.

⁴⁰"For Aaron's sons, make tunics, sashes, and special head coverings that are glorious and beautiful. ⁴¹Clothe your brother, Aaron, and his sons with these garments, and then anoint and ordain them. Consecrate them so they can serve as my priests. ⁴²Also make linen undergarments for them, to be worn next to their bodies, reaching from their hips to their thighs. ⁴³These must be worn whenever Aaron and his sons enter the Tabernacle* or approach the altar in the Holy Place to perform their priestly duties. Then they will not incur

28:15 Hebrew *a chestpiece for decision.* **28:16** Hebrew *1 span* [23 centimeters]. **28:17** The identification of some of these gemstones is uncertain. **28:29** Hebrew *the chestpiece for decision;* also in 28:30. See 28:15. **28:32** The meaning of the Hebrew is uncertain. **28:43** Hebrew *Tent of Meeting.*

guilt and die. This is a permanent law for Aaron and all his descendants after him.

29 DEDICATION OF THE PRIESTS

"This is the ceremony you must follow when you consecrate Aaron and his sons to serve me as priests: Take a young bull and two rams with no defects. ²Then, using choice wheat flour and no yeast, make loaves of bread, thin cakes mixed with olive oil, and wafers spread with oil. ³Place them all in a single basket, and present them at the entrance of the Tabernacle, along with the young bull and the two rams.

⁴"Present Aaron and his sons at the entrance of the Tabernacle,* and wash them with water. ⁵Dress Aaron in his priestly garments—the tunic, the robe worn with the ephod, the ephod itself, and the chestpiece. Then wrap the decorative sash of the ephod around him. ⁶Place the turban on his head, and fasten the sacred medallion to the turban. ⁷Then anoint him by pouring the anointing oil over his head. ⁸Next present his sons, and dress them in their tunics. ⁹Wrap the sashes around the waists of Aaron and his sons, and put their special head coverings on them. Then the right to the priesthood will be theirs by law forever. In this way, you will ordain Aaron and his sons.

¹⁰"Bring the young bull to the entrance of the Tabernacle, where Aaron and his sons will lay their hands on its head. ¹¹Then slaughter the bull in the Lord's presence at the entrance of the Tabernacle. ¹²Put some of its blood on the horns of the altar with your finger, and pour out the rest at the base of the altar. ¹³Take all the fat around the internal organs, the long lobe of the liver, and the two kidneys and the fat around them, and burn it all on the altar. ¹⁴Then take the rest of the bull, including its hide, meat, and dung, and burn it outside the camp as a sin offering.

¹⁵"Next Aaron and his sons must lay their hands on the head of one of the rams. ¹⁶Then slaughter the ram, and splatter its blood against all sides of the altar. ¹⁷Cut the ram into pieces, and wash off the internal organs and the legs. Set them alongside the head and the other pieces of the body, ¹⁸then burn the entire animal on the altar. This is a burnt offering to the Lord; it is a pleasing aroma, a special gift presented to the Lord.

¹⁹"Now take the other ram, and have Aaron and his sons lay their hands on its head. ²⁰Then slaughter it, and apply some of its blood to the right earlobes of Aaron and his sons. Also put it on the thumbs of their right hands and the

29:4 Hebrew *Tent of Meeting;* also in 29:10, 11, 30, 32, 42, 44.

big toes of their right feet. Splatter the rest of the blood against all sides of the altar. ²¹Then take some of the blood from the altar and some of the anointing oil, and sprinkle it on Aaron and his sons and on their garments. In this way, they and their garments will be set apart as holy.

²²"Since this is the ram for the ordination of Aaron and his sons, take the fat of the ram, including the fat of the broad tail, the fat around the internal organs, the long lobe of the liver, and the two kidneys and the fat around them, along with the right thigh. ²³Then take one round loaf of bread, one thin cake mixed with olive oil, and one wafer from the basket of bread without yeast that was placed in the Lord's presence. ²⁴Put all these in the hands of Aaron and his sons to be lifted up as a special offering to the Lord. ²⁵Afterward take the various breads from their hands, and burn them on the altar along with the burnt offering. It is a pleasing aroma to the Lord, a special gift for him. ²⁶Then take the breast of Aaron's ordination ram, and lift it up in the Lord's presence as a special offering to him. Then keep it as your own portion.

²⁷"Set aside the portions of the ordination ram that belong to Aaron and his sons. This includes the breast and the thigh that were lifted up before the Lord as a special offering. ²⁸In the future, whenever the people of Israel lift up a peace offering, a portion of it must be set aside for Aaron and his descendants. This is their permanent right, and it is a sacred offering from the Israelites to the Lord.

²⁹"Aaron's sacred garments must be preserved for his descendants who succeed him, and they will wear them when they are anointed and ordained. ³⁰The descendant who succeeds him as high priest will wear these clothes for seven days as he ministers in the Tabernacle and the Holy Place.

³¹"Take the ram used in the ordination

....

RULES FOR WORSHIP

(29:10-46) *Ever wonder why there were so many rules for sacrifices? The rules were partially for quality control. A set standard of worship prevented problems from arising when individuals worshiped by their own rules. Also, following established patterns for worship separated the Hebrews from the pagan nations they would meet in the Promised Land. People from other nations performed sacrifices to their gods wherever, however, and whenever they wanted to. Lastly, the Hebrew form of worship showed Israel that they should be as serious about their relationship with God as he was about his relationship with them. Is serious a good description of your relationship with God?*

ceremony, and boil its meat in a sacred place. ³²Then Aaron and his sons will eat this meat, along with the bread in the basket, at the Tabernacle entrance. ³³They alone may eat the meat and bread used for their purification* in the ordination ceremony. No one else may eat them, for these things are set apart and holy. ³⁴If any of the ordination meat or bread remains until the morning, it must be burned. It may not be eaten, for it is holy.

³⁵"This is how you will ordain Aaron and his sons to their offices, just as I have commanded you. The ordination ceremony will go on for seven days. ³⁶Each day you must sacrifice a young bull as a sin offering to purify them, making them right with the LORD.* Afterward, cleanse the altar by purifying it*; make it holy by anointing it with oil. ³⁷Purify the altar, and consecrate it every day for seven days. After that, the altar will be absolutely holy, and whatever touches it will become holy.

³⁸"These are the sacrifices you are to offer regularly on the altar. Each day, offer two lambs that are a year old, ³⁹one in the morning and the other in the evening. ⁴⁰With one of them, offer two quarts of choice flour mixed with one quart of pure oil of pressed olives; also, offer one quart of wine* as a liquid offering. ⁴¹Offer the other lamb in the evening, along with the same offerings of flour and wine as in the morning. It will be a pleasing aroma, a special gift presented to the LORD.

⁴²"These burnt offerings are to be made each day from generation to generation. Offer them in the LORD's presence at the Tabernacle entrance; there I will meet with you and speak with you. ⁴³I will meet the people of Israel there, in the place made holy by my glorious presence. ⁴⁴Yes, I will consecrate the Tabernacle and the altar, and I will consecrate Aaron and his sons to serve me as priests. ⁴⁵Then I will live among the people of Israel and be their God, ⁴⁶and they will know that I am the LORD their God. I am the one who brought them out of the land of Egypt so that I could live among them. I am the LORD their God.

. . . .

A PAYMENT FOR SIN
(30:11-16) The atonement money was like a census tax. It illustrated the principle that all of the people of Israel belonged to God and therefore needed to be redeemed (bought) by the payment of a sacrifice. Whenever a census took place, everyone—rich and poor alike—was required to pay a tax that served as a ransom.

All of us need mercy and forgiveness because of our sinful thoughts and actions. God does not discriminate between people (see Acts 10:34-35; Gal 3:28). His offer of mercy through Jesus is for all.

30
PLANS FOR THE INCENSE ALTAR
"Then make another altar of acacia wood for burning incense. ²Make it 18 inches square and 36 inches high,* with horns at the corners carved from the same piece of wood as the altar itself. ³Overlay the top, sides, and horns of the altar with pure gold, and run a gold molding around the entire altar. ⁴Make two gold rings, and attach them on opposite sides of the altar below the gold molding to hold the carrying poles. ⁵Make the poles of acacia wood and overlay them with gold. ⁶Place the incense altar just outside the inner curtain that shields the Ark of the Covenant,* in front of the Ark's cover—the place of atonement—that covers the tablets inscribed with the terms of the covenant.* I will meet with you there.

⁷"Every morning when Aaron maintains the lamps, he must burn fragrant incense on the altar. ⁸And each evening when he lights the lamps, he must again burn incense in the LORD's presence. This must be done from generation to generation. ⁹Do not offer any unholy incense on this altar, or any burnt offerings, grain offerings, or liquid offerings.

¹⁰"Once a year Aaron must purify* the altar by smearing its horns with blood from the offering made to purify the people from their sin. This will be a regular, annual event from generation to generation, for this is the LORD's most holy altar."

MONEY FOR THE TABERNACLE
¹¹Then the LORD said to Moses, ¹²"Whenever you take a census of the people of Israel, each man who is counted must pay a ransom for himself to the LORD. Then no plague will strike the people as you count them. ¹³Each person who is counted must give a small piece of silver as a sacred offering to the LORD. (This payment is half a shekel,* based on the sanctuary shekel, which equals twenty gerahs.) ¹⁴All who have reached their twentieth birthday must give this sacred offering to the LORD. ¹⁵When this offering is given to the LORD to purify your lives, making you right with him,* the rich must not give more than the specified amount, and the poor must not give less. ¹⁶Receive this ransom money from the Israelites, and use it for the care of the

29:33 Or their atonement. 29:36a Or to make atonement. 29:36b Or by making atonement for it; similarly in 29:37. 29:40 Hebrew ¹⁄₁₀ of an ephah [2.2 liters] of choice flour . . . ¼ of a hin [1 liter] of pure oil . . . ¼ of a hin of wine. 30:2 Hebrew 1 cubit [46 centimeters] long and 1 cubit wide, a square, and 2 cubits [92 centimeters] high. 30:6a Or Ark of the Testimony; also in 30:26. 30:6b Hebrew that covers the Testimony; see note on 25:16. 30:10 Or make atonement for; also in 30:10b. 30:13 Or 0.2 ounces, or 6 grams. 30:15 Or to make atonement for your lives; similarly in 30:16.

Tabernacle.* It will bring the Israelites to the Lord's attention, and it will purify your lives."

PLANS FOR THE WASHBASIN ¹⁷Then the Lord said to Moses, ¹⁸"Make a bronze washbasin with a bronze stand. Place it between the Tabernacle and the altar, and fill it with water. ¹⁹Aaron and his sons will wash their hands and feet there. ²⁰They must wash with water whenever they go into the Tabernacle to appear before the Lord and when they approach the altar to burn up their special gifts to the Lord—or they will die! ²¹They must always wash their hands and feet, or they will die. This is a permanent law for Aaron and his descendants, to be observed from generation to generation."

THE ANOINTING OIL ²²Then the Lord said to Moses, ²³"Collect choice spices—12½ pounds of pure myrrh, 6¼ pounds of fragrant cinnamon, 6¼ pounds of fragrant calamus,* ²⁴and 12½ pounds of cassia*—as measured by the weight of the sanctuary shekel. Also get one gallon of olive oil.* ²⁵Like a skilled incense maker, blend these ingredients to make a holy anointing oil. ²⁶Use this sacred oil to anoint the Tabernacle, the Ark of the Covenant, ²⁷the table and all its utensils, the lampstand and all its accessories, the incense altar, ²⁸the altar of burnt offering and all its utensils, and the washbasin with its stand. ²⁹Consecrate them to make them absolutely holy. After this, whatever touches them will also become holy.

³⁰"Anoint Aaron and his sons also, consecrating them to serve me as priests. ³¹And say to the people of Israel, 'This holy anointing oil is reserved for me from generation to generation. ³²It must never be used to anoint anyone else, and you must never make any blend like it for yourselves. It is holy, and you must treat it as holy. ³³Anyone who makes a blend like it or anoints someone other than a priest will be cut off from the community.'"

THE INCENSE ³⁴Then the Lord said to Moses, "Gather fragrant spices—resin droplets, mollusk shell, and galbanum—and mix these fragrant spices with pure frankincense, weighed out in equal amounts. ³⁵Using the usual techniques of the incense maker, blend the spices together and sprinkle them with salt to produce a pure and holy incense. ³⁶Grind some of the

mixture into a very fine powder and put it in front of the Ark of the Covenant,* where I will meet with you in the Tabernacle. You must treat this incense as most holy. ³⁷Never use this formula to make this incense for yourselves. It is reserved for the Lord, and you must treat it as holy. ³⁸Anyone who makes incense like this for personal use will be cut off from the community."

31 CRAFTSMEN: BEZALEL AND OHOLIAB

Then the Lord said to Moses, ²"Look, I have specifically chosen Bezalel son of Uri, grandson of Hur, of the tribe of Judah. ³I have filled him with the Spirit of God, giving him great wisdom, ability, and expertise in all kinds of crafts. ⁴He is a master craftsman, expert in working with gold, silver, and bronze. ⁵He is skilled in engraving and mounting gemstones and in carving wood. He is a master at every craft!

⁶"And I have personally appointed Oholiab son of Ahisamach, of the tribe of Dan, to be his assistant. Moreover, I have given special skill to all the gifted craftsmen so they can make all the things I have commanded you to make:

⁷ the Tabernacle;*
   the Ark of the Covenant;*
   the Ark's cover—the place of atonement;
   all the furnishings of the Tabernacle;
⁸ the table and its utensils;
   the pure gold lampstand with all its
       accessories;
   the incense altar;
⁹ the altar of burnt offering with all its
       utensils;
   the washbasin with its stand;
¹⁰ the beautifully stitched garments—the
       sacred garments for Aaron the priest, and
       the garments for his sons to wear as they
       minister as priests;
¹¹ the anointing oil;
   the fragrant incense for the Holy Place.

The craftsmen must make everything as I have commanded you."

INSTRUCTIONS FOR THE SABBATH ¹²The Lord then gave these instructions to Moses: ¹³"Tell the people of Israel: 'Be careful to keep my Sabbath day, for the Sabbath is a sign of the covenant between me and you from generation to generation. It is given so you may know that I am the Lord, who makes you holy. ¹⁴You must keep the Sabbath day, for it is a holy day for you. Anyone who desecrates it must be put to death; anyone who works on that day will be cut off

---

30:16 Hebrew *Tent of Meeting;* also in 30:18, 20, 26, 36.
30:23 Hebrew *500 shekels* [5.7 kilograms] *of pure myrrh, 250 shekels* [2.9 kilograms] *of fragrant cinnamon, 250 shekels of fragrant calamus.* **30:24a** Hebrew *500 shekels* [5.7 kilograms] *of cassia.* **30:24b** Hebrew *1 hin* [3.8 liters] *of olive oil.* **30:36** Hebrew *in front of the Testimony;* see note on 25:16. **31:7a** Hebrew *the Tent of Meeting.* **31:7b** Hebrew *the Ark of the Testimony.*

from the community. ¹⁵You have six days each week for your ordinary work, but the seventh day must be a Sabbath day of complete rest, a holy day dedicated to the LORD. Anyone who works on the Sabbath must be put to death. ¹⁶The people of Israel must keep the Sabbath day by observing it from generation to generation. This is a covenant obligation for all time. ¹⁷It is a permanent sign of my covenant with the people of Israel. For in six days the LORD made heaven and earth, but on the seventh day he stopped working and was refreshed.'"

¹⁸When the LORD finished speaking with Moses on Mount Sinai, he gave him the two stone tablets inscribed with the terms of the covenant,* written by the finger of God.

32 **THE GOLD CALF** When the people saw how long it was taking Moses to come back down the mountain, they gathered around Aaron. "Come on," they said, "make us some gods who can lead us. We don't know what happened to this fellow Moses, who brought us here from the land of Egypt."

²So Aaron said, "Take the gold rings from the ears of your wives and sons and daughters, and bring them to me."

³All the people took the gold rings from their ears and brought them to Aaron. ⁴Then Aaron took the gold, melted it down, and molded it into the shape of a calf. When the people saw it, they exclaimed, "O Israel, these are the gods who brought you out of the land of Egypt!"

⁵Aaron saw how excited the people were, so he built an altar in front of the calf. Then he announced, "Tomorrow will be a festival to the LORD!"

⁶The people got up early the next morning to sacrifice burnt offerings and peace offerings. After this, they celebrated with feasting and drinking, and they indulged in pagan revelry.

⁷The LORD told Moses, "Quick! Go down the mountain! Your people whom you brought from the land of Egypt have corrupted themselves. ⁸How quickly they have turned away from the way I commanded them to live! They have melted down gold and made a calf, and they have bowed down and sacrificed to it. They are saying, 'These are your gods, O Israel, who brought you out of the land of Egypt.'"

⁹Then the LORD said, "I have seen how stubborn and rebellious these people are. ¹⁰Now leave me alone so my fierce anger can blaze against them, and I will destroy them. Then I will make you, Moses, into a great nation."

¹¹But Moses tried to pacify the LORD his God. "O LORD!" he said. "Why are you so angry with your own people whom you brought from the land of Egypt with such great power and such a strong hand? ¹²Why let the Egyptians say, 'Their God rescued them with the evil intention of slaughtering them in the mountains and wiping them from the face of the earth'? Turn away from your fierce anger. Change your mind about this terrible disaster you have threatened against your people! ¹³Remember your servants Abraham, Isaac, and Jacob.* You bound yourself with an oath to them, saying, 'I will make your descendants as numerous as the stars of heaven. And I will give them all of this land that I have promised to your descendants, and they will possess it forever.'"

¹⁴So the LORD changed his mind about the terrible disaster he had threatened to bring on his people.

¹⁵Then Moses turned and went down the mountain. He held in his hands the two stone tablets inscribed with the terms of the covenant.* They were inscribed on both sides, front and back. ¹⁶These tablets were God's work; the words on them were written by God himself.

¹⁷When Joshua heard the boisterous noise of the people shouting below them, he exclaimed to Moses, "It sounds like war in the camp!"

¹⁸But Moses replied, "No, it's not a shout of victory nor the wailing of defeat. I hear the sound of a celebration."

¹⁹When they came near the camp, Moses saw

IDOLS
(32:1-10) Idols again! Even though Israel had seen the invisible God in action, they still wanted the familiar gods they could see and shape into whatever image they desired. How like them we sometimes are! Our great temptation is still to shape God to our liking, to make him convenient to obey or ignore. God responds in great anger when his mercy is trampled on. The gods we create blind us to the love God wants to shower on us. God cannot work in us when we elevate anyone or anything above him. Are there any idols in your life? If so, what will you do about them?

PRAYER POWER
(32:9-14) God was ready to destroy the whole nation of Israel because they sinned. But when Moses pleaded for mercy, God spared them. This is one of the countless examples in Scripture of how prayer can make a difference. Many times, however, we neglect prayer because a situation seems irreversible. Can you relate? Knowing that God has the power to change the impossible into the possible can help you persist in the prayer habit.

31:18 Hebrew *the two tablets of the Testimony;* see note on 25:16. **32:13** Hebrew *Israel.* The names "Jacob" and "Israel" are often interchanged throughout the Old Testament, referring sometimes to the individual patriarch and sometimes to the nation. **32:15** Hebrew *the two tablets of the Testimony;* see note on 25:16.

the calf and the dancing, and he burned with anger. He threw the stone tablets to the ground, smashing them at the foot of the mountain. ²⁰He took the calf they had made and burned it. Then he ground it into powder, threw it into the water, and forced the people to drink it.

²¹Finally, he turned to Aaron and demanded, "What did these people do to you to make you bring such terrible sin upon them?"

²²"Don't get so upset, my lord," Aaron replied. "You yourself know how evil these people are. ²³They said to me, 'Make us gods who will lead us. We don't know what happened to this fellow Moses, who brought us here from the land of Egypt.' ²⁴So I told them, 'Whoever has gold jewelry, take it off.' When they brought it to me, I simply threw it into the fire—and out came this calf!"

²⁵Moses saw that Aaron had let the people get completely out of control, much to the amusement of their enemies.* ²⁶So he stood at the entrance to the camp and shouted, "All of you who are on the LORD's side, come here and join me." And all the Levites gathered around him.

²⁷Moses told them, "This is what the LORD, the God of Israel, says: Each of you, take your swords and go back and forth from one end of the camp to the other. Kill everyone—even your brothers, friends, and neighbors." ²⁸The Levites obeyed Moses' command, and about 3,000 people died that day.

²⁹Then Moses told the Levites, "Today you have ordained yourselves* for the service of the LORD, for you obeyed him even though it meant killing your own sons and brothers. Today you have earned a blessing."

MOSES INTERCEDES FOR ISRAEL ³⁰The next day Moses said to the people, "You have committed a terrible sin, but I will go back up to the LORD on the mountain. Perhaps I will be able to obtain forgiveness* for your sin."

³¹So Moses returned to the LORD and said, "Oh, what a terrible sin these people have committed. They have made gods of gold for themselves. ³²But now, if you will only forgive their sin—but if not, erase my name from the record you have written!"

³³But the LORD replied to Moses, "No, I will erase the name of everyone who has sinned against me. ³⁴Now go, lead the people to the

place I told you about. Look! My angel will lead the way before you. And when I come to call the people to account, I will certainly hold them responsible for their sins."

³⁵Then the LORD sent a great plague upon the people because they had worshiped the calf Aaron had made.

33 The LORD said to Moses, "Get going, you and the people you brought up from the land of Egypt. Go up to the land I swore to give to Abraham, Isaac, and Jacob. I told them, 'I will give this land to your descendants.' ²And I will send an angel before you to drive out the Canaanites, Amorites, Hittites, Perizzites, Hivites, and Jebusites. ³Go up to this land that flows with milk and honey. But I will not travel among you, for you are a stubborn and rebellious people. If I did, I would surely destroy you along the way."

⁴When the people heard these stern words, they went into mourning and stopped wearing their jewelry and fine clothes. ⁵For the LORD had told Moses to tell them, "You are a stubborn and rebellious people. If I were to travel with you for even a moment, I would destroy you. Remove your jewelry and fine clothes while I decide what to do with you." ⁶So from the time they left Mount Sinai,* the Israelites wore no more jewelry or fine clothes.

⁷It was Moses' practice to take the Tent of Meeting* and set it up some distance from the camp. Everyone who wanted to make a request of the LORD would go to the Tent of Meeting outside the camp.

⁸Whenever Moses went out to the Tent of Meeting, all the people would get up and stand in the entrances of their own tents. They would all watch Moses until he disappeared inside. ⁹As he went into the tent, the pillar of cloud would come down and hover at its entrance while the LORD spoke with Moses. ¹⁰When the people saw the cloud standing at the entrance of the tent, they would stand and bow down in front of their own tents. ¹¹Inside the Tent of Meeting, the LORD would speak to Moses face to face, as one speaks to a friend. Afterward Moses would return to the camp, but the young

---

32:25 Or out of control, and they mocked anyone who opposed them. The meaning of the Hebrew is unclear.   32:29 As in Greek and Latin versions; Hebrew reads Today ordain yourselves.   32:30 Or to make atonement.   33:6 Hebrew Horeb, another name for Sinai.   33:7 This "Tent of Meeting" is different from the Tabernacle described in chapters 26 and 36.

A FRIEND OF GOD
(33:11) God and Moses talked face to face, just as friends do. Moses relied on God's wisdom and direction. His personality and skills did not earn him God's friendship. God simply chose him as a friend. Thanks to Jesus, God chooses us to be his friends (see John 15:15). Have you accepted his friendship?

man who assisted him, Joshua son of Nun, would remain behind in the Tent of Meeting.

MOSES SEES THE LORD'S GLORY

¹²One day Moses said to the LORD, "You have been telling me, 'Take these people up to the Promised Land.' But you haven't told me whom you will send with me. You have told me, 'I know you by name, and I look favorably on you.' ¹³If it is true that you look favorably on me, let me know your ways so I may understand you more fully and continue to enjoy your favor. And remember that this nation is your very own people."

¹⁴The LORD replied, "I will personally go with you, Moses, and I will give you rest—everything will be fine for you."

¹⁵Then Moses said, "If you don't personally go with us, don't make us leave this place. ¹⁶How will anyone know that you look favorably on me—on me and on your people—if you don't go with us? For your presence among us sets your people and me apart from all other people on the earth."

¹⁷The LORD replied to Moses, "I will indeed do what you have asked, for I look favorably on you, and I know you by name."

¹⁸Moses responded, "Then show me your glorious presence."

¹⁹The LORD replied, "I will make all my goodness pass before you, and I will call out my name, Yahweh,* before you. For I will show mercy to anyone I choose, and I will show compassion to anyone I choose. ²⁰But you may not look directly at my face, for no one may see me and live." ²¹The LORD continued, "Look, stand near me on this rock. ²²As my glorious presence passes by, I will hide you in the crevice of the rock and cover you with my hand until I have passed by. ²³Then I will remove my hand and let you see me from behind. But my face will not be seen."

34 A NEW COPY OF THE COVENANT
Then the LORD told Moses, "Chisel out two stone tablets like the first ones. I will write on them the same words that were on the tablets you smashed. ²Be ready in the morning to climb up Mount Sinai and present yourself

to me on the top of the mountain. ³No one else may come with you. In fact, no one is to appear anywhere on the mountain. Do not even let the flocks or herds graze near the mountain."

⁴So Moses chiseled out two tablets of stone like the first ones. Early in the morning he climbed Mount Sinai as the LORD had commanded him, and he carried the two stone tablets in his hands.

⁵Then the LORD came down in a cloud and stood there with him; and he called out his own name, Yahweh.* ⁶The LORD passed in front of Moses, calling out,

"Yahweh!* The LORD!
     The God of compassion and mercy!
I am slow to anger
     and filled with unfailing love and
          faithfulness.
⁷ I lavish unfailing love to a thousand
          generations.*
     I forgive iniquity, rebellion, and sin.
But I do not excuse the guilty.
     I lay the sins of the parents upon their
          children and grandchildren;
the entire family is affected—
     even children in the third and fourth
          generations."

⁸Moses immediately threw himself to the ground and worshiped. ⁹And he said, "O Lord, if it is true that I have found favor with you, then please travel with us. Yes, this is a stubborn and rebellious people, but please forgive our iniquity and our sins. Claim us as your own special possession."

¹⁰The LORD replied, "Listen, I am making a covenant with you in the presence of all your people. I will perform miracles that have never been performed anywhere in all the earth or in any nation. And all the people around you will see the power of the LORD—the awesome power I will display for you. ¹¹But listen carefully to everything I command you today. Then I will go ahead of you and drive out the Amorites, Canaanites, Hittites, Perizzites, Hivites, and Jebusites.

¹²"Be very careful never to make a treaty with the people who live in the land where you are going. If you do, you will follow their evil ways and be trapped. ¹³Instead, you must break down their pagan altars, smash their sacred pillars,

---

GOD'S CHARACTER
(34:6-7) Moses had asked to see God's glorious presence (33:18), and this was God's response. He wanted to give Moses a brief overview of his character. Notice that God did not give Moses a vision of his power and majesty, but rather of his love. God's glory is revealed in his mercy, grace, compassion, faithfulness, forgiveness, and justice. We give glory to God when we show his characteristics. Do your actions resemble his?

33:19 *Yahweh* is a transliteration of the proper name *YHWH* that is sometimes rendered "Jehovah"; in this translation it is usually rendered "the LORD" (note the use of small capitals).   **34:5** *Yahweh* is a transliteration of the proper name *YHWH* that is sometimes rendered "Jehovah"; in this translation it is usually rendered "the LORD" (note the use of small capitals).   **34:6** See note on 34:5.   **34:7** Hebrew *for thousands.*

and cut down their Asherah poles. ¹⁴You must worship no other gods, for the LORD, whose very name is Jealous, is a God who is jealous about his relationship with you.

¹⁵"You must not make a treaty of any kind with the people living in the land. They lust after their gods, offering sacrifices to them. They will invite you to join them in their sacrificial meals, and you will go with them. ¹⁶Then you will accept their daughters, who sacrifice to other gods, as wives for your sons. And they will seduce your sons to commit adultery against me by worshiping other gods. ¹⁷You must not make any gods of molten metal for yourselves.

¹⁸"You must celebrate the Festival of Unleavened Bread. For seven days the bread you eat must be made without yeast, just as I commanded you. Celebrate this festival annually at the appointed time in early spring, in the month of Abib,* for that is the anniversary of your departure from Egypt.

¹⁹"The firstborn of every animal belongs to me, including the firstborn males from your herds of cattle and your flocks of sheep and goats. ²⁰A firstborn donkey may be bought back from the LORD by presenting a lamb or young goat in its place. But if you do not buy it back, you must break its neck. However, you must buy back every firstborn son.

"No one may appear before me without an offering.

²¹"You have six days each week for your ordinary work, but on the seventh day you must stop working, even during the seasons of plowing and harvest.

²²"You must celebrate the Festival of Harvest* with the first crop of the wheat harvest, and celebrate the Festival of the Final Harvest* at the end of the harvest season. ²³Three times each year every man in Israel must appear before the Sovereign, the LORD, the God of Israel. ²⁴I will drive out the other nations ahead of you and expand your territory, so no one will covet and conquer your land while you appear before the LORD your God three times each year.

²⁵"You must not offer the blood of my sacrificial offerings together with any baked goods containing yeast. And none of the meat of the

Passover sacrifice may be kept over until the next morning.

²⁶"As you harvest your crops, bring the very best of the first harvest to the house of the LORD your God.

"You must not cook a young goat in its mother's milk."

²⁷Then the LORD said to Moses, "Write down all these instructions, for they represent the terms of the covenant I am making with you and with Israel."

²⁸Moses remained there on the mountain with the LORD forty days and forty nights. In all that time he ate no bread and drank no water. And the LORD* wrote the terms of the covenant—the Ten Commandments*—on the stone tablets.

²⁹When Moses came down Mount Sinai carrying the two stone tablets inscribed with the terms of the covenant,* he wasn't aware that his face had become radiant because he had spoken to the LORD. ³⁰So when Aaron and the people of Israel saw the radiance of Moses' face, they were afraid to come near him.

³¹But Moses called out to them and asked Aaron and all the leaders of the community to come over, and he talked with them. ³²Then all the people of Israel approached him, and Moses gave them all the instructions the LORD had given him on Mount Sinai. ³³When Moses finished speaking with them, he covered his face with a veil. ³⁴But whenever he went into the Tent of Meeting to speak with the LORD, he would remove the veil until he came out again. Then he would give the people whatever instructions the LORD had given him, ³⁵and the people of Israel would see the radiant glow of his face. So he would put the veil over his face until he returned to speak with the LORD.

35 INSTRUCTIONS FOR THE SABBATH

Then Moses called together the whole community of Israel and told them, "These are the instructions the LORD has commanded you to follow. ²You have six days each week for your ordinary work, but the seventh day must be a Sabbath day of complete rest, a holy day dedicated to the LORD. Anyone who works on that day must be put to death. ³You must not even light a fire in any of your homes on the Sabbath."

OFFERINGS FOR THE TABERNACLE ⁴Then Moses said to the whole community of Israel, "This is what the LORD has commanded: ⁵Take a sacred offering for the LORD. Let those with

34:18 Hebrew *appointed time in the month of Abib.* This first month of the ancient Hebrew lunar calendar usually occurs within the months of March and April. 34:22a Hebrew *Festival of Weeks;* compare 23:16. This was later called the Festival of Pentecost. It is celebrated today as Shavuot (or Shabuoth). 34:22b Or *Festival of Ingathering.* This was later called the Festival of Shelters or Festival of Tabernacles (see Lev 23:33-36). It is celebrated today as Sukkot (or Succoth). 34:28a Hebrew *he.* 34:28b Hebrew *the ten words.* 34:29 Hebrew *the two tablets of the Testimony;* see note on 25:16.

generous hearts present the following gifts to the Lord:

gold, silver, and bronze;
⁶ blue, purple, and scarlet thread;
fine linen and goat hair for cloth;
⁷ tanned ram skins and fine goatskin leather;
acacia wood;
⁸ olive oil for the lamps;
spices for the anointing oil and the fragrant incense;
⁹ onyx stones, and other gemstones to be set in the ephod and the priest's chestpiece.

¹⁰"Come, all of you who are gifted craftsmen. Construct everything that the Lord has commanded:

¹¹ the Tabernacle and its sacred tent, its covering, clasps, frames, crossbars, posts, and bases;
¹² the Ark and its carrying poles;
the Ark's cover—the place of atonement;
the inner curtain to shield the Ark;
¹³ the table, its carrying poles, and all its utensils;
the Bread of the Presence;
¹⁴ for light, the lampstand, its accessories, the lamp cups, and the olive oil for lighting;
¹⁵ the incense altar and its carrying poles;
the anointing oil and fragrant incense;
the curtain for the entrance of the Tabernacle;
¹⁶ the altar of burnt offering;
the bronze grating of the altar and its carrying poles and utensils;
the washbasin with its stand;
¹⁷ the curtains for the walls of the courtyard;
the posts and their bases;
the curtain for the entrance to the courtyard;
¹⁸ the tent pegs of the Tabernacle and courtyard and their ropes;
¹⁹ the beautifully stitched garments for the priests to wear while ministering in the Holy Place—the sacred garments for Aaron the priest, and the garments for his sons to wear as they minister as priests."

²⁰So the whole community of Israel left Moses and returned to their tents. ²¹All whose hearts

· ·

CHEERFUL GIVING
(35:21) Those whose hearts were stirred by God gave cheerfully to the Tabernacle. They gave with great enthusiasm, because they knew how important their giving was to the completion of God's house. Their cheerful giving showed their level of commitment to God. Generous people aren't necessarily faithful to God. But faithful people are usually generous. Are you?

were stirred and whose spirits were moved came and brought their sacred offerings to the Lord. They brought all the materials needed for the Tabernacle,* for the performance of its rituals, and for the sacred garments. ²²Both men and women came, all whose hearts were willing. They brought to the Lord their offerings of gold—brooches, earrings, rings from their fingers, and necklaces. They presented gold objects of every kind as a special offering to the Lord. ²³All those who owned the following items willingly brought them: blue, purple, and scarlet thread; fine linen and goat hair for cloth; and tanned ram skins and fine goatskin leather. ²⁴And all who had silver and bronze objects gave them as a sacred offering to the Lord. And those who had acacia wood brought it for use in the project.

²⁵All the women who were skilled in sewing and spinning prepared blue, purple, and scarlet thread, and fine linen cloth. ²⁶All the women who were willing used their skills to spin the goat hair into yarn. ²⁷The leaders brought onyx stones and the special gemstones to be set in the ephod and the priest's chestpiece. ²⁸They also brought spices and olive oil for the light, the anointing oil, and the fragrant incense. ²⁹So the people of Israel—every man and woman who was eager to help in the work the Lord had given them through Moses—brought their gifts and gave them freely to the Lord.

³⁰Then Moses told the people of Israel, "The Lord has specifically chosen Bezalel son of Uri, grandson of Hur, of the tribe of Judah. ³¹The Lord has filled Bezalel with the Spirit of God, giving him great wisdom, ability, and expertise in all kinds of crafts. ³²He is a master craftsman, expert in working with gold, silver, and bronze. ³³He is skilled in engraving and mounting gemstones and in carving wood. He is a master at every craft. ³⁴And the Lord has given both him and Oholiab son of Ahisamach, of the tribe of Dan, the ability to teach their skills to others. ³⁵The Lord has given them special skills as engravers, designers, embroiderers in blue, purple, and scarlet thread on fine linen cloth, and weavers. They excel as craftsmen and as designers.

36 "The Lord has gifted Bezalel, Oholiab, and the other skilled craftsmen with wisdom and ability to perform any task involved in building the sanctuary. Let them construct and furnish the Tabernacle, just as the Lord has commanded."

²So Moses summoned Bezalel and Oholiab

35:21 Hebrew *Tent of Meeting.*

and all the others who were specially gifted by the LORD and were eager to get to work. ³Moses gave them the materials donated by the people of Israel as sacred offerings for the completion of the sanctuary. But the people continued to bring additional gifts each morning. ⁴Finally the craftsmen who were working on the sanctuary left their work. ⁵They went to Moses and reported, "The people have given more than enough materials to complete the job the LORD has commanded us to do!"

⁶So Moses gave the command, and this message was sent throughout the camp: "Men and women, don't prepare any more gifts for the sanctuary. We have enough!" So the people stopped bringing their sacred offerings. ⁷Their contributions were more than enough to complete the whole project.

BUILDING THE TABERNACLE ⁸The skilled craftsmen made ten curtains of finely woven linen for the Tabernacle. Then Bezalel* decorated the curtains with blue, purple, and scarlet thread and with skillfully embroidered cherubim. ⁹All ten curtains were exactly the same size—42 feet long and 6 feet wide.* ¹⁰Five of these curtains were joined together to make one long curtain, and the other five were joined to make a second long curtain. ¹¹He made fifty loops of blue yarn and put them along the edge of the last curtain in each set. ¹²The fifty loops along the edge of one curtain matched the fifty loops along the edge of the other curtain. ¹³Then he made fifty gold clasps and fastened the long curtains together with the clasps. In this way, the Tabernacle was made of one continuous piece.

¹⁴He made eleven curtains of goat-hair cloth to serve as a tent covering for the Tabernacle. ¹⁵These eleven curtains were all exactly the same size—45 feet long and 6 feet wide.* ¹⁶Bezalel joined five of these curtains together to make one long curtain, and the other six were joined to make a second long curtain. ¹⁷He made fifty loops for the edge of each large curtain. ¹⁸He also made fifty bronze clasps to fasten the long curtains together. In this way, the tent covering was made of one continuous piece. ¹⁹He completed the tent covering with a layer of tanned ram skins and a layer of fine goatskin leather.

²⁰For the framework of the Tabernacle, Bezalel constructed frames of acacia wood. ²¹Each frame was 15 feet high and 27 inches wide,*

²²with two pegs under each frame. All the frames were identical. ²³He made twenty of these frames to support the curtains on the south side of the Tabernacle. ²⁴He also made forty silver bases—two bases under each frame, with the pegs fitting securely into the bases. ²⁵For the north side of the Tabernacle, he made another twenty frames, ²⁶with their forty silver bases, two bases under each frame. ²⁷He made six frames for the rear—the west side of the Tabernacle—²⁸along with two additional frames to reinforce the rear corners of the Tabernacle. ²⁹These corner frames were matched at the bottom and firmly attached at the top with a single ring, forming a single corner unit. Both of these corner units were made the same way. ³⁰So there were eight frames at the rear of the Tabernacle, set in sixteen silver bases—two bases under each frame.

³¹Then he made crossbars of acacia wood to link the frames, five crossbars for the north side of the Tabernacle ³²and five for the south side. He also made five crossbars for the rear of the Tabernacle, which faced west. ³³He made the middle crossbar to attach halfway up the frames; it ran all the way from one end of the Tabernacle to the other. ³⁴He overlaid the frames with gold and made gold rings to hold the crossbars. Then he overlaid the crossbars with gold as well.

³⁵For the inside of the Tabernacle, Bezalel made a special curtain of finely woven linen. He decorated it with blue, purple, and scarlet thread and with skillfully embroidered cherubim. ³⁶For the curtain, he made four posts of acacia wood and four gold hooks. He overlaid the posts with gold and set them in four silver bases.

³⁷Then he made another curtain for the entrance to the sacred tent. He made it of finely woven linen and embroidered it with exquisite designs using blue, purple, and scarlet thread. ³⁸This curtain was hung on gold hooks attached to five posts. The posts with their decorated tops and hooks were overlaid with gold, and the five bases were cast from bronze.

36:8 Hebrew *he;* also in 36:16, 20, 35. See 37:1.   **36:9** Hebrew *28 cubits* [12.9 meters] *long and 4 cubits* [1.8 meters] *wide.*
36:15 Hebrew *30 cubits* [13.8 meters] *long and 4 cubits* [1.8 meters] *wide.*   **36:21** Hebrew *10 cubits* [4.6 meters] *high and 1.5 cubits* [69 centimeters] *wide.*

....

TEAMWORK
(36:8-9) *Making cloth (spinning and weaving) took a great deal of time in Moses' day. To own more than two or three changes of clothing was a sign of wealth! So you can imagine the huge effort involved in making enough cloth for the Tabernacle. It demonstrated a tremendous community effort. This same kind of teamwork is needed in churches and neighborhoods today. Without it, many essential services just wouldn't get done. Are you a team player? What part can you play in your church or community "team"?*

37 BUILDING THE ARK OF THE COVENANT

Next Bezalel made the Ark of acacia wood—a sacred chest 45 inches long, 27 inches wide, and 27 inches high.* ²He overlaid it inside and outside with pure gold, and he ran a molding of gold all around it. ³He cast four gold rings and attached them to its four feet, two rings on each side. ⁴Then he made poles from acacia wood and overlaid them with gold. ⁵He inserted the poles into the rings at the sides of the Ark to carry it.

⁶Then he made the Ark's cover—the place of atonement—from pure gold. It was 45 inches long and 27 inches wide.* ⁷He made two cherubim from hammered gold and placed them on the two ends of the atonement cover. ⁸He molded the cherubim on each end of the atonement cover, making it all of one piece of gold. ⁹The cherubim faced each other and looked down on the atonement cover. With their wings spread above it, they protected it.

BUILDING THE TABLE

¹⁰Then Bezalel* made the table of acacia wood, 36 inches long, 18 inches wide, and 27 inches high.* ¹¹He overlaid it with pure gold and ran a gold molding around the edge. ¹²He decorated it with a 3-inch border* all around, and he ran a gold molding along the border. ¹³Then he cast four gold rings for the table and attached them at the four corners next to the four legs. ¹⁴The rings were attached near the border to hold the poles that were used to carry the table. ¹⁵He made these poles from acacia wood and overlaid them with gold. ¹⁶Then he made special containers of pure gold for the table—bowls, pans, jars, and pitchers—to be used in pouring out liquid offerings.

BUILDING THE LAMPSTAND

¹⁷Then Bezalel made the lampstand of pure, hammered gold. He made the entire lampstand and its decorations of one piece—the base, center stem, lamp cups, buds, and petals. ¹⁸The lampstand had six branches going out from the center stem, three on each side. ¹⁹Each of the six branches had three lamp cups shaped like almond blossoms, complete with buds and petals. ²⁰The center stem of the lampstand was crafted with four lamp cups shaped like almond blossoms, complete with buds and petals. ²¹There was an almond bud beneath each pair of branches where the six branches extended from the center stem, all made of one piece. ²²The almond buds and branches were all of one piece with the center stem, and they were hammered from pure gold.

²³He also made seven lamps for the lamp-stand, lamp snuffers, and trays, all of pure gold. ²⁴The entire lampstand, along with its accessories, was made from seventy-five pounds* of pure gold.

BUILDING THE INCENSE ALTAR

²⁵Then Bezalel made the incense altar of acacia wood. It was 18 inches square and 36 inches high,* with horns at the corners carved from the same piece of wood as the altar itself. ²⁶He overlaid the top, sides, and horns of the altar with pure gold, and he ran a gold molding around the entire altar. ²⁷He made two gold rings and attached them on opposite sides of the altar below the gold molding to hold the carrying poles. ²⁸He made the poles of acacia wood and overlaid them with gold.

²⁹Then he made the sacred anointing oil and the fragrant incense, using the techniques of a skilled incense maker.

38 BUILDING THE ALTAR OF BURNT OFFERING

Next Bezalel* used acacia wood to construct the square altar of burnt offering. It was 7½ feet wide, 7½ feet long, and 4½ feet high.* ²He made horns for each of its four corners so that the horns and altar were all one piece. He overlaid the altar with bronze. ³Then he made all the altar utensils of bronze—the ash buckets, shovels, basins, meat forks, and firepans. ⁴Next he made a bronze grating and installed it halfway down the side of the altar, under the ledge. ⁵He cast four rings and attached them to the corners of the bronze grating to hold the carrying poles. ⁶He made the poles from acacia wood and overlaid them with bronze. ⁷He inserted the poles through the rings on the sides of the altar. The altar was hollow and was made from planks.

BUILDING THE WASHBASIN

⁸Bezalel made the bronze washbasin and its bronze stand from bronze mirrors donated by the women who served at the entrance of the Tabernacle.*

BUILDING THE COURTYARD

⁹Then Bezalel made the courtyard, which was enclosed with curtains made of finely woven linen. On the south side the curtains were 150 feet long.*

37:1 Hebrew 2.5 cubits [115 centimeters] long, 1.5 cubits [69 centimeters] wide, and 1.5 cubits high.   **37:6** Hebrew 2.5 cubits [115 centimeters] long and 1.5 cubits [69 centimeters] wide.
37:10a Hebrew he; also in 37:17, 25.   **37:10b** Hebrew 2 cubits [92 centimeters] long, 1 cubit [46 centimeters] wide, and 1.5 cubits [69 centimeters] high.   **37:12** Hebrew a border of a handbreadth [8 centimeters].   **37:24** Hebrew 1 talent [34 kilograms].
37:25 Hebrew 1 cubit [46 centimeters] long and 1 cubit wide, a square, and 2 cubits [92 centimeters] high.   **38:1a** Hebrew he; also in 38:8, 9.   **38:1b** Hebrew 5 cubits [2.3 meters] wide, 5 cubits long, a square, and 3 cubits [1.4 meters] high.   **38:8** Hebrew Tent of Meeting; also in 38:30.   **38:9** Hebrew 100 cubits [46 meters]; also in 38:11.

[10]They were held up by twenty posts set securely in twenty bronze bases. He hung the curtains with silver hooks and rings. [11]He made a similar set of curtains for the north side—150 feet of curtains held up by twenty posts set securely in bronze bases. He hung the curtains with silver hooks and rings. [12]The curtains on the west end of the courtyard were 75 feet long,* hung with silver hooks and rings and supported by ten posts set into ten bases. [13]The east end, the front, was also 75 feet long.

[14]The courtyard entrance was on the east end, flanked by two curtains. The curtain on the right side was 22½ feet long* and was supported by three posts set into three bases. [15]The curtain on the left side was also 22½ feet long and was supported by three posts set into three bases. [16]All the curtains used in the courtyard were made of finely woven linen. [17]Each post had a bronze base, and all the hooks and rings were silver. The tops of the posts of the courtyard were overlaid with silver, and the rings to hold up the curtains were made of silver.

[18]He made the curtain for the entrance to the courtyard of finely woven linen, and he decorated it with beautiful embroidery in blue, purple, and scarlet thread. It was 30 feet long, and its height was 7½ feet,* just like the curtains of the courtyard walls. [19]It was supported by four posts, each set securely in its own bronze base. The tops of the posts were overlaid with silver, and the hooks and rings were also made of silver.

[20]All the tent pegs used in the Tabernacle and courtyard were made of bronze.

INVENTORY OF MATERIALS [21]This is an inventory of the materials used in building the Tabernacle of the Covenant.* The Levites compiled the figures, as Moses directed, and Ithamar son of Aaron the priest served as recorder. [22]Bezalel son of Uri, grandson of Hur, of the tribe of Judah, made everything just as the Lord had commanded Moses. [23]He was assisted by Oholiab son of Ahisamach, of the tribe of Dan, a craftsman expert at engraving, designing, and embroidering with blue, purple, and scarlet thread on fine linen cloth.

38:12 Hebrew 50 cubits [23 meters]; also in 38:13.   38:14 Hebrew 15 cubits [6.9 meters]; also in 38:15.   38:18 Hebrew 20 cubits [9.2 meters] long and 5 cubits [2.3 meters] high.   38:21 Hebrew the Tabernacle, the Tabernacle of the Testimony.   38:24 Hebrew 29 talents and 730 shekels [994 kilograms]. Each shekel weighed about 0.4 ounces.   38:25 Hebrew 100 talents and 1,775 shekels [3,420 kilograms].   38:26 Or 0.2 ounces, or 6 grams.
38:27 Hebrew 100 talents [3,400 kilograms] of silver, 1 talent [34 kilograms] for each base.   38:28 Hebrew 1,775 shekels [20.2 kilograms].   38:29 Hebrew 70 talents and 2,400 shekels [2,407 kilograms].   39:2 Hebrew He; also in 39:8, 22.

[24]The people brought special offerings of gold totaling 2,193 pounds,* as measured by the weight of the sanctuary shekel. This gold was used throughout the Tabernacle.

[25]The whole community of Israel gave 7,545 pounds* of silver, as measured by the weight of the sanctuary shekel. [26]This silver came from the tax collected from each man registered in the census. (The tax is one beka, which is half a shekel,* based on the sanctuary shekel.) The tax was collected from 603,550 men who had reached their twentieth birthday. [27]The hundred bases for the frames of the sanctuary walls and for the posts supporting the inner curtain required 7,500 pounds of silver, about 75 pounds for each base.* [28]The remaining 45 pounds* of silver was used to make the hooks and rings and to overlay the tops of the posts.

[29]The people also brought as special offerings 5,310 pounds* of bronze, [30]which was used for casting the bases for the posts at the entrance to the Tabernacle, and for the bronze altar with its bronze grating and all the altar utensils. [31]Bronze was also used to make the bases for the posts that supported the curtains around the courtyard, the bases for the curtain at the entrance of the courtyard, and all the tent pegs for the Tabernacle and the courtyard.

39

CLOTHING FOR THE PRIESTS The craftsmen made beautiful sacred garments of blue, purple, and scarlet cloth—clothing for Aaron to wear while ministering in the Holy Place, just as the Lord had commanded Moses.

MAKING THE EPHOD [2]Bezalel* made the ephod of finely woven linen and embroidered it with gold and with blue, purple, and scarlet thread. [3]He made gold thread by hammering out thin sheets of gold and cutting it into fine strands. With great skill and care, he worked it into the fine linen with the blue, purple, and scarlet thread.

[4]The ephod consisted of two pieces, front and back, joined at the shoulders with two shoulder-pieces. [5]The decorative sash was made of the same materials: finely woven linen embroidered with gold and with blue, purple, and scarlet thread, just as the Lord had commanded Moses. [6]They mounted the two onyx stones in settings of gold filigree. The stones were engraved with the names of the tribes of Israel, just as a seal is engraved. [7]He fastened these stones on the shoulder-pieces of the ephod as a reminder that the priest represents

the people of Israel. All this was done just as the Lord had commanded Moses.

MAKING THE CHESTPIECE 8Bezalel made the chestpiece with great skill and care. He made it to match the ephod, using finely woven linen embroidered with gold and with blue, purple, and scarlet thread. 9He made the chestpiece of a single piece of cloth folded to form a pouch nine inches* square. 10They mounted four rows of gemstones* on it. The first row contained a red carnelian, a pale-green peridot, and an emerald. 11The second row contained a turquoise, a blue lapis lazuli, and a white moonstone. 12The third row contained an orange jacinth, an agate, and a purple amethyst. 13The fourth row contained a blue-green beryl, an onyx, and a green jasper. All these stones were set in gold filigree. 14Each stone represented one of the twelve sons of Israel, and the name of that tribe was engraved on it like a seal.

15To attach the chestpiece to the ephod, they made braided cords of pure gold thread. 16They also made two settings of gold filigree and two gold rings and attached them to the top corners of the chestpiece. 17They tied the two gold cords to the rings on the chestpiece. 18They tied the other ends of the cords to the gold settings on the shoulder-pieces of the ephod. 19Then they made two more gold rings and attached them to the inside edges of the chestpiece next to the ephod. 20Then they made two more gold rings and attached them to the front of the ephod, below the shoulder-pieces, just above the knot where the decorative sash was fastened to the ephod. 21They attached the bottom rings of the chestpiece to the rings on the ephod with blue cords. In this way, the chestpiece was held securely to the ephod above the decorative sash. All this was done just as the Lord had commanded Moses.

ADDITIONAL CLOTHING FOR THE PRIESTS 22Bezalel made the robe that is worn with the ephod from a single piece of blue woven cloth, 23with an opening for Aaron's head in the middle of it. The opening was reinforced with a woven collar* so it would not tear. 24They made pomegranates of blue, purple, and scarlet

yarn, and attached them to the hem of the robe. 25They also made bells of pure gold and placed them between the pomegranates along the hem of the robe, 26with bells and pomegranates alternating all around the hem. This robe was to be worn whenever the priest ministered before the Lord, just as the Lord had commanded Moses.

27They made tunics for Aaron and his sons from fine linen cloth. 28The turban and the special head coverings were made of fine linen, and the undergarments were also made of finely woven linen. 29The sashes were made of finely woven linen and embroidered with blue, purple, and scarlet thread, just as the Lord had commanded Moses.

30Finally, they made the sacred medallion—the badge of holiness—of pure gold. They engraved it like a seal with these words: Holy to the Lord. 31They attached the medallion with a blue cord to Aaron's turban, just as the Lord had commanded Moses.

MOSES INSPECTS THE WORK 32And so at last the Tabernacle* was finished. The Israelites had done everything just as the Lord had commanded Moses. 33And they brought the entire Tabernacle to Moses:

the sacred tent with all its furnishings, clasps, frames, crossbars, posts, and bases;
34 the tent coverings of tanned ram skins and fine goatskin leather;
the inner curtain to shield the Ark;
35 the Ark of the Covenant* and its carrying poles;
the Ark's cover—the place of atonement;
36 the table and all its utensils;
the Bread of the Presence;
37 the pure gold lampstand with its symmetrical lamp cups, all its accessories, and the olive oil for lighting;
38 the gold altar;
the anointing oil and fragrant incense;
the curtain for the entrance of the sacred tent;
39 the bronze altar;
the bronze grating and its carrying poles and utensils;
the washbasin with its stand;
40 the curtains for the walls of the courtyard;
the posts and their bases;
the curtain for the entrance to the courtyard;

....

SMALL DETAILS
(39:32) The Tabernacle was finally complete, down to the last detail. God was keenly interested in every detail—even the minor ones. Know what's cool? He cares infinitely more about you. You can talk with him about any of your concerns—no matter how small or unimportant they might seem.

39:9 Hebrew *1 span* [23 centimeters].   39:10 The identification of some of these gemstones is uncertain.   39:23 The meaning of the Hebrew is uncertain.   39:32 Hebrew *the Tabernacle, the Tent of Meeting;* also in 39:40.   39:35 Or *Ark of the Testimony.*

the ropes and tent pegs;

all the furnishings to be used in worship at the Tabernacle;

[41] the beautifully stitched garments for the priests to wear while ministering in the Holy Place—the sacred garments for Aaron the priest, and the garments for his sons to wear as they minister as priests.

[42] So the people of Israel followed all of the LORD's instructions to Moses. [43] Then Moses inspected all their work. When he found it had been done just as the LORD had commanded him, he blessed them.

40 THE TABERNACLE COMPLETED Then the LORD said to Moses, [2] "Set up the Tabernacle* on the first day of the new year.* [3] Place the Ark of the Covenant* inside, and install the inner curtain to enclose the Ark within the Most Holy Place. [4] Then bring in the table, and arrange the utensils on it. And bring in the lampstand, and set up the lamps.

[5] "Place the gold incense altar in front of the Ark of the Covenant. Then hang the curtain at the entrance of the Tabernacle. [6] Place the altar of burnt offering in front of the Tabernacle entrance. [7] Set the washbasin between the Tabernacle* and the altar, and fill it with water. [8] Then set up the courtyard around the outside of the tent, and hang the curtain for the courtyard entrance.

[9] "Take the anointing oil and anoint the Tabernacle and all its furnishings to consecrate them and make them holy. [10] Anoint the altar of burnt offering and its utensils to consecrate them. Then the altar will become absolutely holy. [11] Next anoint the washbasin and its stand to consecrate them.

[12] "Present Aaron and his sons at the entrance of the Tabernacle, and wash them with water. [13] Dress Aaron with the sacred garments and anoint him, consecrating him to serve me as a priest. [14] Then present his sons and dress them in their tunics. [15] Anoint them as you did their father, so they may also serve me as priests. With their anointing, Aaron's descendants are set apart for the priesthood forever, from generation to generation."

[16] Moses proceeded to do everything just as the LORD had commanded him. [17] So the Tabernacle was set up on the first day of the first month of the second year. [18] Moses erected the Tabernacle by setting down its bases, inserting the frames, attaching the crossbars, and setting up the posts. [19] Then he spread the coverings over the Tabernacle framework and put on the protective layers, just as the LORD had commanded him.

[20] He took the stone tablets inscribed with the terms of the covenant and placed them* inside the Ark. Then he attached the carrying poles to the Ark, and he set the Ark's cover—the place of atonement—on top of it. [21] Then he brought the Ark of the Covenant into the Tabernacle and hung the inner curtain to shield it from view, just as the LORD had commanded him.

[22] Next Moses placed the table in the Tabernacle, along the north side of the Holy Place, just outside the inner curtain. [23] And he arranged the Bread of the Presence on the table before the LORD, just as the LORD had commanded him.

[24] He set the lampstand in the Tabernacle across from the table on the south side of the Holy Place. [25] Then he lit the lamps in the LORD's presence, just as the LORD had commanded him. [26] He also placed the gold incense altar in the Tabernacle, in the Holy Place in front of the inner curtain. [27] On it he burned the fragrant incense, just as the LORD had commanded him.

[28] He hung the curtain at the entrance of the Tabernacle, [29] and he placed the altar of burnt offering near the Tabernacle entrance. On it he offered a burnt offering and a grain offering, just as the LORD had commanded him.

[30] Next Moses placed the washbasin between the Tabernacle and the altar. He filled it with water so the priests could wash themselves. [31] Moses and Aaron and Aaron's sons used water from it to wash their hands and feet. [32] Whenever they approached the altar and entered the Tabernacle, they washed themselves, just as the LORD had commanded Moses.

[33] Then he hung the curtains forming the courtyard around the Tabernacle and the altar. And he set up the curtain at the entrance of the courtyard. So at last Moses finished the work.

. . . .

BIG CHANGES
(40:38) Exodus began in gloom and ends in glory. The Israelites were once Egyptian slaves making bricks without straw. Now they're free and on their way to the land God promised them. This parallels our progress as Christians. We begin as slaves to sin, are bought at a price by God, and end our lives on earth with the promise of living with God forever. Is that a promise you're counting on?

40:2a Hebrew *the Tabernacle, the Tent of Meeting;* also in 40:6, 29. **40:2b** Hebrew *the first day of the first month.* This day of the ancient Hebrew lunar calendar occurred in March or April. **40:3** Or *Ark of the Testimony;* also in 40:5, 21. **40:7** Hebrew *Tent of Meeting;* also in 40:12, 22, 24, 26, 30, 32, 34, 35. **40:20** Hebrew *He placed the Testimony;* see note on 25:16.

THE LORD'S GLORY FILLS THE TABERNACLE

³⁴Then the cloud covered the Tabernacle, and the glory of the LORD filled the Tabernacle. ³⁵Moses could no longer enter the Tabernacle because the cloud had settled down over it, and the glory of the LORD filled the Tabernacle.

³⁶Now whenever the cloud lifted from the Tabernacle, the people of Israel would set out on their journey, following it. ³⁷But if the cloud did not rise, they remained where they were until it lifted. ³⁸The cloud of the LORD hovered over the Tabernacle during the day, and at night fire glowed inside the cloud so the whole family of Israel could see it. This continued throughout all their journeys.

LEVITICUS

Trey was one of the star players on the football team and also the coach's son. During the practices he usually tried hard to pay attention. But he knew he was doomed when Yolonda stopped by one day. As soon as he saw her, Trey could barely keep his mind on what the coach was saying. All he thought about was Yolonda.

But soon, Trey heard his father calling for his attention. "You need to stay focused, Trey," his dad advised. Trey remained attentive for the rest of the practice.

The coach expected Trey to listen during practice not because he was better than the other players but because Trey was his son. Trey's actions were a reflection of his relationship with his father.

The Israelites were in a similar situation. God demanded they "pay attention" because they were his chosen people, his children. God told them, "You must be holy because I, the LORD your God, am holy" (19:2). In the Bible, holy means set apart for God's service. That's why God gave them the laws recorded in the book of Leviticus. These laws would help them live holy lives. God also established the Day of Atonement (chapter 16) to allow them to come to him for forgiveness.

Leviticus is important to us, too. Our Day of Atonement is the day Jesus died. Because of him, we can be "holy" before God even though we disobey him. Jesus' death covers everything we do wrong.

As you read Leviticus, consider your relationship with God. Is living a life that pleases him your first priority?

STATS

PURPOSE
A handbook for the Levites outlining their priestly duties in worship; a guidebook of holy living for the Hebrews

AUTHOR
Moses

ORIGINAL AUDIENCE
The people of Israel

DATE OF EVENTS
1445–1444 B.C.

SETTING
At the foot of Mount Sinai, God teaches the Israelites how to live as holy people.

KEY PEOPLE
Moses, Aaron, Nadab, Abihu, Eleazar, Ithamar

SPECIAL FEATURE
Holiness is mentioned more often (152 times) than in any other book of the Bible.

TIMELINE

1446 B.C.
Exodus from Egypt

1445
Ten Commandments

1444
Israel camps at Mt. Sinai

1406
Moses dies, Canaan entered

1375
Judges begin to rule

1050
United kingdom under Saul

KEY POINTS

SACRIFICES The system of sacrifices that God established for Israel helps us understand the high cost of sin. An animal had to be sacrificed to pay the price for someone's sin. Jesus' death, however, did away with this temporary system by permanently paying the penalty for all sin.

HEALTH God established rules for all aspects of life. He wanted his people to be different from the surrounding nations. Through these rules, God preserved them from diseases and genetic problems while teaching them spiritual principles. Following his rules will make our lives different from those of unbelievers around us.

HOLINESS The word holy means "separated" or "devoted to God." God called his people to be committed to his ways and forsake the lifestyle they had in Egypt. God calls us to this level of commitment.

LEVITES The Levites and priests taught the people how to worship God. They regulated the moral, civil, and ceremonial laws of the people. Understanding their role enables us to better understand Jesus' role as our High Priest and our role as priestly believers.

1 PROCEDURES FOR THE BURNT OFFERING

The LORD called to Moses from the Tabernacle* and said to him, ²"Give the following instructions to the people of Israel. When you present an animal as an offering to the LORD, you may take it from your herd of cattle or your flock of sheep and goats.

³"If the animal you present as a burnt offering is from the herd, it must be a male with no defects. Bring it to the entrance of the Tabernacle so you* may be accepted by the LORD. ⁴Lay your hand on the animal's head, and the LORD will accept its death in your place to purify you, making you right with him.* ⁵Then slaughter the young bull in the LORD's presence, and Aaron's sons, the priests, will present the animal's blood by splattering it against all sides of the altar that stands at the entrance to the Tabernacle. ⁶Then skin the animal and cut it into pieces. ⁷The sons of Aaron the priest will build a wood fire on the altar. ⁸They will arrange the pieces of the offering, including the head and fat, on the wood burning on the altar. ⁹But the internal organs and the legs must first be washed with water. Then the priest will burn the entire sacrifice on the altar as a burnt offering. It is a special gift, a pleasing aroma to the LORD.

¹⁰"If the animal you present as a burnt offering is from the flock, it may be either a sheep or a goat, but it must be a male with no defects. ¹¹Slaughter the animal on the north side of the altar in the LORD's presence, and Aaron's sons, the priests, will splatter its blood against all sides of the altar. ¹²Then cut the animal in pieces, and the priests will arrange the pieces of the offering, including the head and fat, on the wood burning on the altar. ¹³But the internal organs and the legs must first be washed with water. Then the priest will burn the entire

THE ISRAELITES AT MOUNT SINAI
Throughout the book of Leviticus, the Israelites were camped at the foot of Mount Sinai. It was a time of regrouping as a nation and learning the importance of following God as they prepared to march toward the Promised Land.

sacrifice on the altar as a burnt offering. It is a special gift, a pleasing aroma to the LORD.

¹⁴"If you present a bird as a burnt offering to the LORD, choose either a turtledove or a young pigeon. ¹⁵The priest will take the bird to the altar, wring off its head, and burn it on the altar. But first he must drain its blood against the side of the altar. ¹⁶The priest must also remove the crop and the feathers* and throw them in the ashes on the east side of the altar. ¹⁷Then, grasping the bird by its wings, the priest will tear the bird open, but without tearing it apart. Then he will burn it as a burnt offering on the wood burning on the altar. It is a special gift, a pleasing aroma to the LORD.

2 PROCEDURES FOR THE GRAIN OFFERING

"When you present grain as an offering to the LORD, the offering must consist of choice flour. You are to pour olive oil on it, sprinkle it with frankincense, ²and bring it to Aaron's sons, the priests. The priest will scoop out a handful of the flour moistened with oil, together with all the frankincense, and burn this representative portion on the altar. It is a special gift, a pleasing aroma to the LORD. ³The rest of the grain offering will then be given to Aaron and his sons. This offering will be considered a most holy part of the special gifts presented to the LORD.

⁴"If your offering is a grain offering baked in an oven, it must be made of choice flour, but without any yeast. It may be presented in the form of thin cakes mixed with olive oil or wafers spread with olive oil. ⁵If your grain offering is cooked on a griddle, it must be made of choice flour mixed with olive oil but without any yeast. ⁶Break it in pieces and pour olive oil on it; it is a grain offering. ⁷If your grain offering is prepared in a pan, it must be made of choice flour and olive oil.

⁸"No matter how a grain offering for the LORD has been prepared, bring it to the priest, who will present it at the altar. ⁹The priest will take a representative portion of the grain offering and burn it on the altar. It is a special gift, a

---

THE HIGH COST OF SIN
(1:4) God used a system of sacrifices to teach his people about faith. The deaths of so many animals helped them see the high cost of their sin.

God's laws were intended to bring out true devotion of the heart. Our culture's casual attitude toward wrongdoing shows a forgetfulness of the cost of sin. Have you counted the cost? Jesus already paid it for you.

1:1 Hebrew Tent of Meeting; also in 1:3, 5.   1:3 Or it.   1:4 Or to make atonement for you.   1:16 Or the crop and its contents. The meaning of the Hebrew is uncertain.

pleasing aroma to the Lord. ¹⁰The rest of the grain offering will then be given to Aaron and his sons as their food. This offering will be considered a most holy part of the special gifts presented to the Lord.

¹¹"Do not use yeast in preparing any of the grain offerings you present to the Lord, because no yeast or honey may be burned as a special gift presented to the Lord. ¹²You may add yeast and honey to an offering of the first crops of your harvest, but these must never be offered on the altar as a pleasing aroma to the Lord. ¹³Season all your grain offerings with salt to remind you of God's eternal covenant. Never forget to add salt to your grain offerings.

¹⁴"If you present a grain offering to the Lord from the first portion of your harvest, bring fresh grain that is coarsely ground and roasted on a fire. ¹⁵Put olive oil on this grain offering, and sprinkle it with frankincense. ¹⁶The priest will take a representative portion of the grain moistened with oil, together with all the frankincense, and burn it as a special gift presented to the Lord.

3 PROCEDURES FOR THE PEACE OFFERING
"If you present an animal from the herd as a peace offering to the Lord, it may be a male or a female, but it must have no defects. ²Lay your hand on the animal's head, and slaughter it at the entrance of the Tabernacle.* Then Aaron's sons, the priests, will splatter its blood against all sides of the altar. ³The priest must present part of this peace offering as a special gift to the Lord. This includes all the fat around the internal organs, ⁴the two kidneys and the fat around them near the loins, and the long lobe of the liver. These must be removed with the kidneys, ⁵and Aaron's sons will burn them on top of the burnt offering on the wood burning on the altar. It is a special gift, a pleasing aroma to the Lord.

⁶"If you present an animal from the flock as a peace offering to the Lord, it may be a male or a female, but it must have no defects. ⁷If you present a sheep as your offering, bring it to the Lord, ⁸lay your hand on its head, and slaughter it in front of the Tabernacle. Aaron's sons will then splatter the sheep's blood against all sides of the altar. ⁹The priest must present the fat of this peace offering as a special gift to the Lord. This includes the fat of the broad tail cut off near the backbone, all the fat around the internal organs, ¹⁰the two kidneys and the fat

around them near the loins, and the long lobe of the liver. These must be removed with the kidneys, ¹¹and the priest will burn them on the altar. It is a special gift of food presented to the Lord.

¹²"If you present a goat as your offering, bring it to the Lord, ¹³lay your hand on its head, and slaughter it in front of the Tabernacle. Aaron's sons will then splatter the goat's blood against all sides of the altar. ¹⁴The priest must present part of this offering as a special gift to the Lord. This includes all the fat around the internal organs, ¹⁵the two kidneys and the fat around them near the loins, and the long lobe of the liver. These must be removed with the kidneys, ¹⁶and the priest will burn them on the altar. It is a special gift of food, a pleasing aroma to the Lord. All the fat belongs to the Lord.

¹⁷"You must never eat any fat or blood. This is a permanent law for you, and it must be observed from generation to generation, wherever you live."

4 PROCEDURES FOR THE SIN OFFERING
Then the Lord said to Moses, ²"Give the following instructions to the people of Israel. This is how you are to deal with those who sin unintentionally by doing anything that violates one of the Lord's commands.

³"If the high priest* sins, bringing guilt upon the entire community, he must give a sin offering for the sin he has committed. He must present to the Lord a young bull with no defects. ⁴He must bring the bull to the Lord at the entrance of the Tabernacle,* lay his hand on the bull's head, and slaughter it before the Lord. ⁵The high priest will then take some of the bull's blood into the Tabernacle, ⁶dip his finger in the blood, and sprinkle it seven times before the Lord in front of the inner curtain of

....

SALT
(2:13) The grain offerings were seasoned with salt as a reminder of the people's covenant (contract) with God. Salt symbolizes God's activity in a person's life—it penetrates, preserves, and acts as a healing agent. God wants to be "salt" in you—penetrating every aspect of your life, preserving you from the evil all around, and cleansing you when you sin.

I DIDN'T MEAN IT!
(4:1–5:19)) Have you ever done something wrong without realizing it until later? Although your sin was unintentional, it was still sin. One of the purposes of God's law was to make the Israelites aware of their unintentional sins so they would not repeat them. Leviticus 4 and 5 mention some of these unintentional sins and God's remedies for them. The Holy Spirit reminds us of our intentional and unintentional sins. Are you listening?

3:2 Hebrew *Tent of Meeting;* also in 3:8, 13.　**4:3** Hebrew *the anointed priest;* also in 4:5, 16.　**4:4** Hebrew *Tent of Meeting;* also in 4:5, 7, 14, 16, 18.

THE OFFERINGS

Listed here are the five key offerings the Israelites made to God. The Jews made these offerings in order to have their sins forgiven and to restore their fellowship with God. The death of Jesus Christ made these sacrifices unnecessary. Because of Jesus' death, our sins are completely forgiven and fellowship with God has been restored.

OFFERING	Burnt Offering (Lev 1— voluntary)	Grain Offering (Lev 2— voluntary)	Peace Offering (Lev 3— voluntary)	Sin Offering (Lev 4— required)	Guilt Offering (Lev 5— required)
PURPOSE	To make payment for sins in general	To show honor and respect to God in worship	To express gratitude to God	To make payment for unintentional sins of uncleanness, neglect, or thoughtlessness	To make payment for sins against God and others; a sacrifice was made to God and the injured person repaid or compensated
SIGNIFICANCE	Showed a person's devotion to God	Acknowledged that everything we have belongs to God	Symbolized peace and fellowship with God	Restored the sinner to fellowship with God; showed seriousness of sin	Provided compensation for injured parties
CHRIST, THE PERFECT OFFERING	Christ's death was the perfect offering.	Christ was the perfect man, who gave all of himself to God and others.	Christ is the only way to fellowship with God.	Christ's death restores our fellowship with God.	Christ's death takes away the deadly consequences of sin.

the sanctuary. ⁷The priest will then put some of the blood on the horns of the altar for fragrant incense that stands in the LORD's presence inside the Tabernacle. He will pour out the rest of the bull's blood at the base of the altar for burnt offerings at the entrance of the Tabernacle. ⁸Then the priest must remove all the fat of the bull to be offered as a sin offering. This includes all the fat around the internal organs, ⁹the two kidneys and the fat around them near the loins, and the long lobe of the liver. He must remove these along with the kidneys, ¹⁰just as he does with cattle offered as a peace offering, and burn them on the altar of burnt offerings. ¹¹But he must take whatever is left of the bull—its hide, meat, head, legs, internal organs, and dung—¹²and carry it away to a place outside the camp that is ceremonially clean, the place where the ashes are dumped. There, on the ash heap, he will burn it on a wood fire.

¹³"If the entire Israelite community sins by violating one of the LORD's commands, but the people don't realize it, they are still guilty.

¹⁴When they become aware of their sin, the people must bring a young bull as an offering for their sin and present it before the Tabernacle. ¹⁵The elders of the community must then lay their hands on the bull's head and slaughter it before the LORD. ¹⁶The high priest will then take some of the bull's blood into the Tabernacle, ¹⁷dip his finger in the blood, and sprinkle it seven times before the LORD in front of the inner curtain. ¹⁸He will then put some of the blood on the horns of the altar for fragrant incense that stands in the LORD's presence inside the Tabernacle. He will pour out the rest of the blood at the base of the altar for burnt offerings at the entrance of the Tabernacle. ¹⁹Then the priest must remove all the animal's fat and burn it on the altar, ²⁰just as he does with the bull offered as a sin offering for the high priest. Through this process, the priest will purify the people, making them right with the LORD,* and they will be forgiven. ²¹Then the priest must take what is left of the

4:20 Or *will make atonement for the people; similarly in 4:26, 31, 35.*

bull and carry it outside the camp and burn it there, just as is done with the sin offering for the high priest. This offering is for the sin of the entire congregation of Israel.

[22]"If one of Israel's leaders sins by violating one of the commands of the LORD his God but doesn't realize it, he is still guilty. [23]When he becomes aware of his sin, he must bring as his offering a male goat with no defects. [24]He must lay his hand on the goat's head and slaughter it at the place where burnt offerings are slaughtered before the LORD. This is an offering for his sin. [25]Then the priest will dip his finger in the blood of the sin offering and put it on the horns of the altar for burnt offerings. He will pour out the rest of the blood at the base of the altar. [26]Then he must burn all the goat's fat on the altar, just as he does with the peace offering. Through this process, the priest will purify the leader from his sin, making him right with the LORD, and he will be forgiven.

[27]"If any of the common people sin by violating one of the LORD's commands, but they don't realize it, they are still guilty. [28]When they become aware of their sin, they must bring as an offering for their sin a female goat with no defects. [29]They must lay a hand on the head of the sin offering and slaughter it at the place where burnt offerings are slaughtered. [30]Then the priest will dip his finger in the blood and put it on the horns of the altar for burnt offerings. He will pour out the rest of the blood at the base of the altar. [31]Then he must remove all the goat's fat, just as he does with the fat of the peace offering. He will burn the fat on the altar, and it will be a pleasing aroma to the LORD. Through this process, the priest will purify the people, making them right with the LORD, and they will be forgiven.

[32]"If the people bring a sheep as their sin offering, it must be a female with no defects. [33]They must lay a hand on the head of the sin offering and slaughter it at the place where burnt offerings are slaughtered. [34]Then the priest will dip his finger in the blood of the sin offering and put it on the horns of the altar for burnt offerings. He will pour out the rest of the blood at the base of the altar. [35]Then he must remove all the sheep's fat, just as he does with the fat of a sheep presented as a peace offering. He will burn the fat on the altar on top of the special gifts presented to the LORD. Through this process, the priest will purify the people from their sin, and they will be forgiven.

5:6 Or will make atonement for you for your sin; similarly in 5:10, 13, 16, 18.   5:11 Hebrew 1/10 of an ephah [2.2 liters].

5 **SINS REQUIRING A SIN OFFERING** "If you are called to testify about something you have seen or that you know about, it is sinful to refuse to testify, and you will be punished for your sin.

[2]"Or suppose you unknowingly touch something that is ceremonially unclean, such as the carcass of an unclean animal. When you realize what you have done, you must admit your defilement and your guilt. This is true whether it is a wild animal, a domestic animal, or an animal that scurries along the ground.

[3]"Or suppose you unknowingly touch something that makes a person unclean. When you realize what you have done, you must admit your guilt.

[4]"Or suppose you make a foolish vow of any kind, whether its purpose is for good or for bad. When you realize its foolishness, you must admit your guilt.

[5]"When you become aware of your guilt in any of these ways, you must confess your sin. [6]Then you must bring to the LORD as the penalty for your sin a female from the flock, either a sheep or a goat. This is a sin offering with which the priest will purify you from your sin, making you right with the LORD.*

[7]"But if you cannot afford to bring a sheep, you may bring to the LORD two turtledoves or two young pigeons as the penalty for your sin. One of the birds will be for a sin offering, and the other for a burnt offering. [8]You must bring them to the priest, who will present the first bird as the sin offering. He will wring its neck but without severing its head from the body. [9]Then he will sprinkle some of the blood of the sin offering against the sides of the altar, and the rest of the blood will be drained out at the base of the altar. This is an offering for sin. [10]The priest will then prepare the second bird as a burnt offering, following all the procedures that have been prescribed. Through this process the priest will purify you from your sin, making you right with the LORD, and you will be forgiven.

[11]"If you cannot afford to bring two turtledoves or two young pigeons, you may bring two quarts* of choice flour for your sin offering. Since it is an offering for sin, you must not moisten it with olive oil or put any frankincense

....

AVOID RASH VOWS
(5:4) Have you ever sworn to do or not do something and then wished you could take back that vow? God's people are called to keep their word, even when they make promises that are tough to keep. Our word should be enough. Strengthening a promise with a vow is not necessary. The wise person avoids making rash vows.

on it. 12Take the flour to the priest, who will scoop out a handful as a representative portion. He will burn it on the altar on top of the special gifts presented to the LORD. It is an offering for sin. 13Through this process, the priest will purify those who are guilty of any of these sins, making them right with the LORD, and they will be forgiven. The rest of the flour will belong to the priest, just as with the grain offering."

PROCEDURES FOR THE GUILT OFFERING

14Then the LORD said to Moses, 15"If one of you commits a sin by unintentionally defiling the LORD's sacred property, you must bring a guilt offering to the LORD. The offering must be your own ram with no defects, or you may buy one of equal value with silver, as measured by the weight of the sanctuary shekel.* 16You must make restitution for the sacred property you have harmed by paying for the loss, plus an additional 20 percent. When you give the payment to the priest, he will purify you with the ram sacrificed as a guilt offering, making you right with the LORD, and you will be forgiven.

17"Suppose you sin by violating one of the LORD's commands. Even if you are unaware of what you have done, you are guilty and will be punished for your sin. 18For a guilt offering, you must bring to the priest your own ram with no defects, or you may buy one of equal value. Through this process the priest will purify you from your unintentional sin, making you right with the LORD, and you will be forgiven. 19This is a guilt offering, for you have been guilty of an offense against the LORD."

6 SINS REQUIRING A GUILT OFFERING

1*Then the LORD said to Moses, 2"Suppose one of you sins against your associate and is unfaithful to the LORD. Suppose you cheat in a deal involving a security deposit, or you steal or commit fraud, 3or you find lost property and lie about it, or you lie while swearing to tell the truth, or you commit any other such sin. 4If you have sinned in any of these ways, you are guilty. You must give back whatever you stole, or the money you took by extortion, or the security

• •

STEALING

(6:1-7) Here we discover that stealing involves more than just taking from someone. Finding something and not returning it or refusing to return something borrowed are other forms of stealing. Both are sins against God and not just against a neighbor, a stranger, or a business. Instead of justifying our reason for keeping that overdue DVD from the video store or that library book we've had for five years, maybe we need to call it what it is: wrong.

deposit, or the lost property you found, 5or anything obtained by swearing falsely. You must make restitution by paying the full price plus an additional 20 percent to the person you have harmed. On the same day you must present a guilt offering. 6As a guilt offering to the LORD, you must bring to the priest your own ram with no defects, or you may buy one of equal value. 7Through this process, the priest will purify you before the LORD, making you right with him,* and you will be forgiven for any of these sins you have committed."

FURTHER INSTRUCTIONS FOR THE BURNT OFFERING
8*Then the LORD said to Moses, 9"Give Aaron and his sons the following instructions regarding the burnt offering. The burnt offering must be left on top of the altar until the next morning, and the fire on the altar must be kept burning all night. 10In the morning, after the priest on duty has put on his official linen clothing and linen undergarments, he must clean out the ashes of the burnt offering and put them beside the altar. 11Then he must take off these garments, change back into his regular clothes, and carry the ashes outside the camp to a place that is ceremonially clean. 12Meanwhile, the fire on the altar must be kept burning; it must never go out. Each morning the priest will add fresh wood to the fire and arrange the burnt offering on it. He will then burn the fat of the peace offerings on it. 13Remember, the fire must be kept burning on the altar at all times. It must never go out.

FURTHER INSTRUCTIONS FOR THE GRAIN OFFERING
14"These are the instructions regarding the grain offering. Aaron's sons must present this offering to the LORD in front of the altar. 15The priest on duty will take from the grain offering a handful of the choice flour moistened with olive oil, together with all the frankincense. He will burn this representative portion on the altar as a pleasing aroma to the LORD. 16Aaron and his sons may eat the rest of the flour, but it must be baked without yeast and eaten in a sacred place within the courtyard of the Tabernacle.* 17Remember, it must never be prepared with yeast. I have given it to the priests as their share of the special gifts presented to me. Like the sin offering and the guilt offering, it is most holy. 18Any of Aaron's male descendants may eat from the special

5:15 Each shekel was about 0.4 ounces or 11 grams in weight.
6:1 Verses 6:1-7 are numbered 5:20-26 in Hebrew text.   6:7 Or will make atonement for you before the LORD.   6:8 Verses 6:8-30 are numbered 6:1-23 in Hebrew text.   6:16 Hebrew Tent of Meeting; also in 6:26, 30.

gifts presented to the Lord. This is their permanent right from generation to generation. Anyone or anything that touches these offerings will become holy."

PROCEDURES FOR THE ORDINATION OFFERING
¹⁹Then the Lord said to Moses, ²⁰"On the day Aaron and his sons are anointed, they must present to the Lord a grain offering of two quarts* of choice flour, half to be offered in the morning and half to be offered in the evening. ²¹It must be carefully mixed with olive oil and cooked on a griddle. Then slice* this grain offering and present it as a pleasing aroma to the Lord. ²²In each generation, the high priest* who succeeds Aaron must prepare this same offering. It belongs to the Lord and must be burned up completely. This is a permanent law. ²³All such grain offerings of a priest must be burned up entirely. None of it may be eaten."

FURTHER INSTRUCTIONS FOR THE SIN OFFERING
²⁴Then the Lord said to Moses, ²⁵"Give Aaron and his sons the following instructions regarding the sin offering. The animal given as an offering for sin is a most holy offering, and it must be slaughtered in the Lord's presence at the place where the burnt offerings are slaughtered. ²⁶The priest who offers the sacrifice as a sin offering must eat his portion in a sacred place within the courtyard of the Tabernacle. ²⁷Anyone or anything that touches the sacrificial meat will become holy. If any of the sacrificial blood spatters on a person's clothing, the soiled garment must be washed in a sacred place. ²⁸If a clay pot is used to boil the sacrificial meat, it must then be broken. If a bronze pot is used, it must be scoured and thoroughly rinsed with water. ²⁹Any male from a priest's family may eat from this offering; it is most holy. ³⁰But the offering for sin may not be eaten if its blood was brought into the Tabernacle as an offering for purification* in the Holy Place. It must be completely burned with fire.

7 FURTHER INSTRUCTIONS FOR THE GUILT OFFERING
"These are the instructions for the guilt offering. It is most holy. ²The animal sacrificed as a guilt offering must be slaughtered at the place where the burnt offerings are slaughtered, and its blood must be splattered against all sides of the altar. ³The priest will then offer all its fat on the altar, including the fat of the broad tail, the fat around the internal

organs, ⁴the two kidneys and the fat around them near the loins, and the long lobe of the liver. These are to be removed with the kidneys, ⁵and the priests will burn them on the altar as a special gift presented to the Lord. This is the guilt offering. ⁶Any male from a priest's family may eat the meat. It must be eaten in a sacred place, for it is most holy.

⁷"The same instructions apply to both the guilt offering and the sin offering. Both belong to the priest who uses them to purify someone, making that person right with the Lord.* ⁸In the case of the burnt offering, the priest may keep the hide of the sacrificed animal. ⁹Any grain offering that has been baked in an oven, prepared in a pan, or cooked on a griddle belongs to the priest who presents it. ¹⁰All other grain offerings, whether made of dry flour or flour moistened with olive oil, are to be shared equally among all the priests, the descendants of Aaron.

FURTHER INSTRUCTIONS FOR THE PEACE OFFERING
¹¹"These are the instructions regarding the different kinds of peace offerings that may be presented to the Lord. ¹²If you present your peace offering as an expression of thanksgiving, the usual animal sacrifice must be accompanied by various kinds of bread made without yeast—thin cakes mixed with olive oil, wafers spread with oil, and cakes made of choice flour mixed with olive oil. ¹³This peace offering of thanksgiving must also be accompanied by loaves of bread made with yeast. ¹⁴One of each kind of bread must be presented as a gift to the Lord. It will then belong to the priest who splatters the blood of the peace offering against the altar. ¹⁵The meat of the peace offering of thanksgiving must be eaten on the same day it is offered. None of it may be saved for the next morning.

¹⁶"If you bring an offering to fulfill a vow or as a voluntary offering, the meat must be eaten on the same day the sacrifice is offered, but whatever is left over may be eaten on the second day. ¹⁷Any meat left over until the third day must be completely burned up. ¹⁸If any of the meat from the peace offering is eaten on the third day, the person who presented it will not be accepted by the Lord. You will receive no credit for offering it. By then the meat will be contaminated; if you eat it, you will be punished for your sin.

¹⁹"Meat that touches anything ceremonially unclean may not be eaten; it must be completely burned up. The rest of the meat may be eaten, but only by people who are ceremonially

6:20 Hebrew ¹⁄₁₀ of an ephah [2.2 liters].   6:21 The meaning of this Hebrew term is uncertain.   6:22 Hebrew the anointed priest.
6:30 Or an offering to make atonement.   7:7 Or to make atonement.

clean. ²⁰If you are ceremonially unclean and you eat meat from a peace offering that was presented to the LORD, you will be cut off from the community. ²¹If you touch anything that is unclean (whether it is human defilement or an unclean animal or any other unclean, detestable thing) and then eat meat from a peace offering presented to the LORD, you will be cut off from the community."

THE FORBIDDEN BLOOD AND FAT ²²Then the LORD said to Moses, ²³"Give the following instructions to the people of Israel. You must never eat fat, whether from cattle, sheep, or goats. ²⁴The fat of an animal found dead or torn to pieces by wild animals must never be eaten, though it may be used for any other purpose. ²⁵Anyone who eats fat from an animal presented as a special gift to the LORD will be cut off from the community. ²⁶No matter where you live, you must never consume the blood of any bird or animal. ²⁷Anyone who consumes blood will be cut off from the community."

A PORTION FOR THE PRIESTS ²⁸Then the LORD said to Moses, ²⁹"Give the following instructions to the people of Israel. When you present a peace offering to the LORD, bring part of it as a gift to the LORD. ³⁰Present it to the LORD with your own hands as a special gift to the LORD. Bring the fat of the animal, together with the breast, and lift up the breast as a special offering to the LORD. ³¹Then the priest will burn the fat on the altar, but the breast will belong to Aaron and his descendants. ³²Give the right thigh of your peace offering to the priest as a gift. ³³The right thigh must always be given to the priest who offers the blood and the fat of the peace offering. ³⁴For I have reserved the breast of the special offering and the right thigh of the sacred offering for the priests. It is the permanent right of Aaron and his descendants to share in the peace offerings brought by the people of Israel. ³⁵This is their rightful share. The special gifts presented to the LORD have been reserved for Aaron and his descendants from the time they were set apart to serve the LORD

as priests. ³⁶On the day they were anointed, the LORD commanded the Israelites to give these portions to the priests as their permanent share from generation to generation."

³⁷These are the instructions for the burnt offering, the grain offering, the sin offering, and the guilt offering, as well as the ordination offering and the peace offering. ³⁸The LORD gave these instructions to Moses on Mount Sinai when he commanded the Israelites to present their offerings to the LORD in the wilderness of Sinai.

8 ORDINATION OF THE PRIESTS Then the LORD said to Moses, ²"Bring Aaron and his sons, along with their sacred garments, the anointing oil, the bull for the sin offering, the two rams, and the basket of bread made without yeast, ³and call the entire community of Israel together at the entrance of the Tabernacle.*"

⁴So Moses followed the LORD's instructions, and the whole community assembled at the Tabernacle entrance. ⁵Moses announced to them, "This is what the LORD has commanded us to do!" ⁶Then he presented Aaron and his sons and washed them with water. ⁷He put the official tunic on Aaron and tied the sash around his waist. He dressed him in the robe, placed the ephod on him, and attached the ephod securely with its decorative sash. ⁸Then Moses placed the chestpiece on Aaron and put the Urim and the Thummim inside it. ⁹He placed the turban on Aaron's head and attached the gold medallion—the badge of holiness—to the front of the turban, just as the LORD had commanded him.

¹⁰Then Moses took the anointing oil and anointed the Tabernacle and everything in it, making them holy. ¹¹He sprinkled the oil on the altar seven times, anointing it and all its utensils, as well as the washbasin and its stand, making them holy. ¹²Then he poured some of the anointing oil on Aaron's head, anointing him and making him holy for his work. ¹³Next Moses presented Aaron's sons. He clothed them in their tunics, tied their sashes around them, and put their special head coverings on them, just as the LORD had commanded him.

¹⁴Then Moses presented the bull for the sin offering. Aaron and his sons laid their hands on the bull's head, ¹⁵and Moses slaughtered it. Moses took some of the blood, and with his finger he put it on the four horns of the altar to purify it. He poured out the rest of the

---

MEANINGLESS WORSHIP
(7:38) God gave his people many worship rules to follow. The rules and ceremonies in Leviticus were meant to teach the people valuable spiritual lessons. But over time, the people became indifferent to the meanings of these ceremonies. As a result, they began to lose touch with God. When you consider your response to worship these days, can you relate? Want worship to come alive once more? Start by admitting where you are. Don't worry. God can take it.

8:3 Hebrew *Tent of Meeting;* also in 8:4, 31, 33, 35.

blood at the base of the altar. Through this process, he made the altar holy by purifying it.* ¹⁶Then Moses took all the fat around the internal organs, the long lobe of the liver, and the two kidneys and the fat around them, and he burned it all on the altar. ¹⁷He took the rest of the bull, including its hide, meat, and dung, and burned it on a fire outside the camp, just as the LORD had commanded him.

¹⁸Then Moses presented the ram for the burnt offering. Aaron and his sons laid their hands on the ram's head, ¹⁹and Moses slaughtered it. Then Moses took the ram's blood and splattered it against all sides of the altar. ²⁰Then he cut the ram into pieces, and he burned the head, some of its pieces, and the fat on the altar. ²¹After washing the internal organs and the legs with water, Moses burned the entire ram on the altar as a burnt offering. It was a pleasing aroma, a special gift presented to the LORD, just as the LORD had commanded him.

²²Then Moses presented the other ram, which was the ram of ordination. Aaron and his sons laid their hands on the ram's head, ²³and Moses slaughtered it. Then Moses took some of its blood and applied it to the lobe of Aaron's right ear, the thumb of his right hand, and the big toe of his right foot. ²⁴Next Moses presented Aaron's sons and applied some of the blood to the lobes of their right ears, the thumbs of their right hands, and the big toes of their right feet. He then splattered the rest of the blood against all sides of the altar.

²⁵Next Moses took the fat, including the fat of the broad tail, the fat around the internal organs, the long lobe of the liver, and the two kidneys and the fat around them, along with the right thigh. ²⁶On top of these he placed a thin cake of bread made without yeast, a cake of bread mixed with olive oil, and a wafer spread with olive oil. All these were taken from the basket of bread made without yeast that was placed in the LORD's presence. ²⁷He put all these in the hands of Aaron and his sons, and he lifted them up as a special offering to the LORD. ²⁸Moses then took all the offerings back from them and burned them on the altar on top of the burnt offering. This was the ordination offering. It was a pleasing aroma, a special gift presented to the LORD. ²⁹Then Moses took the breast and lifted it up as a special offering to the LORD. This was Moses' portion of the ram of ordination, just as the LORD had commanded him.

³⁰Next Moses took some of the anointing oil and some of the blood that was on the altar, and he sprinkled them on Aaron and his garments and on his sons and their garments. In this way, he made Aaron and his sons and their garments holy.

³¹Then Moses said to Aaron and his sons, "Boil the remaining meat of the offerings at the Tabernacle entrance, and eat it there, along with the bread that is in the basket of offerings for the ordination, just as I commanded when I said, 'Aaron and his sons will eat it.' ³²Any meat or bread that is left over must then be burned up. ³³You must not leave the Tabernacle entrance for seven days, for that is when the ordination ceremony will be completed. ³⁴Everything we have done today was commanded by the LORD in order to purify you, making you right with him.* ³⁵Now stay at the entrance of the Tabernacle day and night for seven days, and do everything the LORD requires. If you fail to do this, you will die, for this is what the LORD has commanded." ³⁶So Aaron and his sons did everything the LORD had commanded through Moses.

9 THE PRIESTS BEGIN THEIR WORK After the ordination ceremony, on the eighth day, Moses called together Aaron and his sons and the elders of Israel. ²He said to Aaron, "Take a young bull for a sin offering and a ram for a burnt offering, both without defects, and present them to the LORD. ³Then tell the Israelites, 'Take a male goat for a sin offering, and take a calf and a lamb, both a year old and without defects, for a burnt offering. ⁴Also take a bull* and a ram for a peace offering and flour moistened with olive oil for a grain offering. Present all these offerings to the LORD because the LORD will appear to you today.'"

⁵So the people presented all these things at the entrance of the Tabernacle,* just as Moses had commanded. Then the whole community came forward and stood before the LORD. ⁶And Moses said, "This is what the LORD has commanded you to do so that the glory of the LORD may appear to you."

⁷Then Moses said to Aaron, "Come to the altar and sacrifice your sin offering and your

8:15 Or by making atonement for it; or that offerings for purification might be made on it.   8:34 Or to make atonement for you.   9:4 Or cow; also in 9:18, 19.   9:5 Hebrew Tent of Meeting; also in 9:23.

....

TOTALLY HOLY
(8:36) Aaron and his sons did all that the Lord told them to do. Considering the many lists of rules in Leviticus, that was a remarkable feat. They knew what God wanted, how he wanted it done, and with what attitude his instructions were to be carried out. God wants us to be thoroughly holy people with the same zealous attitude as Aaron and his sons. That's your attitude, right?

burnt offering to purify yourself and the people. Then present the offerings of the people to purify them, making them right with the LORD,* just as he has commanded."

8So Aaron went to the altar and slaughtered the calf as a sin offering for himself. 9His sons brought him the blood, and he dipped his finger in it and put it on the horns of the altar. He poured out the rest of the blood at the base of the altar. 10Then he burned on the altar the fat, the kidneys, and the long lobe of the liver from the sin offering, just as the LORD had commanded Moses. 11The meat and the hide, however, he burned outside the camp.

12Next Aaron slaughtered the animal for the burnt offering. His sons brought him the blood, and he splattered it against all sides of the altar. 13Then they handed him each piece of the burnt offering, including the head, and he burned them on the altar. 14Then he washed the internal organs and the legs and burned them on the altar along with the rest of the burnt offering.

15Next Aaron presented the offerings of the people. He slaughtered the people's goat and presented it as an offering for their sin, just as he had first done with the offering for his own sin. 16Then he presented the burnt offering and sacrificed it in the prescribed way. 17He also presented the grain offering, burning a handful of the flour mixture on the altar, in addition to the regular burnt offering for the morning.

18Then Aaron slaughtered the bull and the ram for the people's peace offering. His sons brought him the blood, and he splattered it against all sides of the altar. 19Then he took the fat of the bull and the ram—the fat of the broad tail and from around the internal organs—along with the kidneys and the long lobes of the livers. 20He placed these fat portions on top of the breasts of these animals and burned them on the altar. 21Aaron then lifted up the breasts and right thighs as a special offering to the LORD, just as Moses had commanded.

- -

A HOLY REMINDER
(10:2) Sadly, after the good report of Leviticus 8:36, we see how careless two of Aaron's sons had become about following the laws for sacrifices. In response, God destroyed them with a blast of fire. Performing the sacrifices was an act of obedience. Doing them correctly showed respect for God and reminded the Israelites of God's holiness.

We can easily grow careless about obeying God. At times, we want to do what we want instead of what he wants. Yet the punishment of Aaron's sons is a chilling reminder of how seriously God takes obedience. How serious are you about obeying God?

22After that, Aaron raised his hands toward the people and blessed them. Then, after presenting the sin offering, the burnt offering, and the peace offering, he stepped down from the altar. 23Then Moses and Aaron went into the Tabernacle, and when they came back out, they blessed the people again, and the glory of the LORD appeared to the whole community. 24Fire blazed forth from the LORD's presence and consumed the burnt offering and the fat on the altar. When the people saw this, they shouted with joy and fell face down on the ground.

10 THE SIN OF NADAB AND ABIHU Aaron's sons Nadab and Abihu put coals of fire in their incense burners and sprinkled incense over them. In this way, they disobeyed the LORD by burning before him the wrong kind of fire, different than he had commanded. 2So fire blazed forth from the LORD's presence and burned them up, and they died there before the LORD.

3Then Moses said to Aaron, "This is what the LORD meant when he said,

'I will display my holiness
    through those who come near me.
I will display my glory
    before all the people.'"

And Aaron was silent.

4Then Moses called for Mishael and Elzaphan, Aaron's cousins, the sons of Aaron's uncle Uzziel. He said to them, "Come forward and carry away the bodies of your relatives from in front of the sanctuary to a place outside the camp." 5So they came forward and picked them up by their garments and carried them out of the camp, just as Moses had commanded.

6Then Moses said to Aaron and his sons Eleazar and Ithamar, "Do not show grief by leaving your hair uncombed* or by tearing your clothes. If you do, you will die, and the LORD's anger will strike the whole community of Israel. However, the rest of the Israelites, your relatives, may mourn because of the LORD's fiery destruction of Nadab and Abihu. 7But you must not leave the entrance of the Tabernacle* or you will die, for you have been anointed with the LORD's anointing oil." So they did as Moses commanded.

INSTRUCTIONS FOR PRIESTLY CONDUCT

8Then the LORD said to Aaron, 9"You and your descendants must never drink wine or any other alcoholic drink before going into the

9:7 Or to make atonement for them.   10:6 Or by uncovering your heads.   10:7 Hebrew *Tent of Meeting*; also in 10:9.

Tabernacle. If you do, you will die. This is a permanent law for you, and it must be observed from generation to generation. ¹⁰You must distinguish between what is sacred and what is common, between what is ceremonially unclean and what is clean. ¹¹And you must teach the Israelites all the decrees that the Lord has given them through Moses."

¹²Then Moses said to Aaron and his remaining sons, Eleazar and Ithamar, "Take what is left of the grain offering after a portion has been presented as a special gift to the Lord, and eat it beside the altar. Make sure it contains no yeast, for it is most holy. ¹³You must eat it in a sacred place, for it has been given to you and your descendants as your portion of the special gifts presented to the Lord. These are the commands I have been given. ¹⁴But the breast and thigh that were lifted up as a special offering may be eaten in any place that is ceremonially clean. These parts have been given to you and your descendants as your portion of the peace offerings presented by the people of Israel. ¹⁵You must lift up the thigh and breast as a special offering to the Lord, along with the fat of the special gifts. These parts will belong to you and your descendants as your permanent right, just as the Lord has commanded."

¹⁶Moses then asked them what had happened to the goat of the sin offering. When he discovered it had been burned up, he became very angry with Eleazar and Ithamar, Aaron's remaining sons. ¹⁷"Why didn't you eat the sin offering in the sacred area?" he demanded. "It is a holy offering! The Lord has given it to you to remove the guilt of the community and to purify the people, making them right with the Lord.* ¹⁸Since the animal's blood was not brought into the Holy Place, you should have eaten the meat in the sacred area as I ordered you."

¹⁹Then Aaron answered Moses, "Today my sons presented both their sin offering and their burnt offering to the Lord. And yet this tragedy has happened to me. If I had eaten the people's sin offering on such a tragic day as this, would the Lord have been pleased?" ²⁰And when Moses heard this, he was satisfied.

11 CEREMONIALLY CLEAN AND UNCLEAN ANIMALS Then the Lord said to Moses and Aaron, ²"Give the following instructions to the people of Israel.

"Of all the land animals, these are the ones

10:17 Or *to make atonement for the people before the Lord.*
11:4 The identification of some of the animals, birds, and insects in this chapter is uncertain.   11:5 Or *coney,* or *rock badger.*

you may use for food. ³You may eat any animal that has completely split hooves and chews the cud. ⁴You may not, however, eat the following animals* that have split hooves or that chew the cud, but not both. The camel chews the cud but does not have split hooves, so it is ceremonially unclean for you. ⁵The hyrax* chews the cud but does not have split hooves, so it is unclean. ⁶The hare chews the cud but does not have split hooves, so it is unclean. ⁷The pig has evenly split hooves but does not chew the cud, so it is unclean. ⁸You may not eat the meat of these animals or even touch their carcasses. They are ceremonially unclean for you.

⁹"Of all the marine animals, these are ones you may use for food. You may eat anything from the water if it has both fins and scales, whether taken from salt water or from streams. ¹⁰But you must never eat animals from the sea or from rivers that do not have both fins and scales. They are detestable to you. This applies both to little creatures that live in shallow water and to all creatures that live in deep water. ¹¹They will always be detestable to you. You must never eat their meat or even touch their dead bodies. ¹²Any marine animal that does not have both fins and scales is detestable to you.

¹³"These are the birds that are detestable to you. You must never eat them: the griffon vulture, the bearded vulture, the black vulture, ¹⁴the kite, falcons of all kinds, ¹⁵ravens of all kinds, ¹⁶the eagle owl, the short-eared owl, the seagull, hawks of all kinds, ¹⁷the little owl, the cormorant, the great owl, ¹⁸the barn owl, the desert owl, the Egyptian vulture, ¹⁹the stork, herons of all kinds, the hoopoe, and the bat.

²⁰"You must not eat winged insects that walk along the ground; they are detestable to you. ²¹You may, however, eat winged insects that walk along the ground and have jointed legs so they can jump. ²²The insects you are permitted to eat include all kinds of locusts, bald locusts, crickets, and grasshoppers. ²³All other winged insects that walk along the ground are detestable to you.

²⁴"The following creatures will make you ceremonially unclean. If any of you touch their

....

KEEP AWAY
(11:8) God had strictly forbidden eating the meat of certain animals. The people of Israel were not even allowed to touch these dead animals. God wanted his people to keep away from forbidden items. Often we flirt with temptation, rationalizing that we haven't committed the sin . . . yet. But God wants us to separate ourselves from what he has forbidden. If necessary, that might mean running from temptation as Joseph did (see Gen 39:12).

carcasses, you will be defiled until evening. ²⁵If you pick up their carcasses, you must wash your clothes, and you will remain defiled until evening.

²⁶"Any animal that has split hooves that are not evenly divided or that does not chew the cud is unclean for you. If you touch the carcass of such an animal, you will be defiled. ²⁷Of the animals that walk on all fours, those that have paws are unclean. If you touch the carcass of such an animal, you will be defiled until evening. ²⁸If you pick up its carcass, you must wash your clothes, and you will remain defiled until evening. These animals are unclean for you.

²⁹"Of the small animals that scurry along the ground, these are unclean for you: the mole rat, the rat, large lizards of all kinds, ³⁰the gecko, the monitor lizard, the common lizard, the sand lizard, and the chameleon. ³¹All these small animals are unclean for you. If any of you touch the dead body of such an animal, you will be defiled until evening. ³²If such an animal dies and falls on something, that object will be unclean. This is true whether the object is made of wood, cloth, leather, or burlap. Whatever its use, you must dip it in water, and it will remain defiled until evening. After that, it will be ceremonially clean and may be used again.

BE PREPARED

(11:24-47) Leviticus contains rules the people of Israel used to prepare themselves for worship. Certain things could make a person ceremonially unclean and thus disqualified from worship. Similarly, we cannot live any way we want during the week and then rush into God's presence on Sunday. Our relationship with him must be one of constant repentance and cleansing so that we are prepared to worship him anytime.

HOLY DESIGN

(11:44-45) This chapter has more than rules for eating. These verses provide a key to understanding all of the laws in Leviticus. God wanted his people to be holy (set apart for a special purpose) to reflect his holiness. He established laws to help them remain separate—socially and spiritually—from the pagan nations they would encounter in Canaan.

Christians also are called to be holy (1 Pet 1:15-16). Like the Israelites, we have the task of maintaining God's standards, rather than the world's. Being holy in an unholy world isn't easy. But God doesn't expect you to accomplish this on your own. You can rely on the Holy Spirit's help.

A WORSHIP STOPPER

(12:1-8) Unclean did not mean "sinful," implying that sex or childbirth is dirty. Instead, it meant "not appropriate to make a sacrifice." In other words, the person could not worship at the tabernacle until a specified time had passed. Again, this doesn't mean that sex is unclean. It just means that there are appropriate (and inappropriate) times and places for everything.

³³"If such an animal falls into a clay pot, everything in the pot will be defiled, and the pot must be smashed. ³⁴If the water from such a container spills on any food, the food will be defiled. And any beverage in such a container will be defiled. ³⁵Any object on which the carcass of such an animal falls will be defiled. If it is an oven or hearth, it must be destroyed, for it is defiled, and you must treat it accordingly.

³⁶"However, if the carcass of such an animal falls into a spring or a cistern, the water will still be clean. But anyone who touches the carcass will be defiled. ³⁷If the carcass falls on seed grain to be planted in the field, the seed will still be considered clean. ³⁸But if the seed is wet when the carcass falls on it, the seed will be defiled.

³⁹"If an animal you are permitted to eat dies and you touch its carcass, you will be defiled until evening. ⁴⁰If you eat any of its meat or carry away its carcass, you must wash your clothes, and you will remain defiled until evening.

⁴¹"All small animals that scurry along the ground are detestable, and you must never eat them. ⁴²This includes all animals that slither along on their bellies, as well as those with four legs and those with many feet. All such animals that scurry along the ground are detestable, and you must never eat them. ⁴³Do not defile yourselves by touching them. You must not make yourselves ceremonially unclean because of them. ⁴⁴For I am the LORD your God. You must consecrate yourselves and be holy, because I am holy. So do not defile yourselves with any of these small animals that scurry along the ground. ⁴⁵For I, the LORD, am the one who brought you up from the land of Egypt, that I might be your God. Therefore, you must be holy because I am holy.

⁴⁶"These are the instructions regarding land animals, birds, marine creatures, and animals that scurry along the ground. ⁴⁷By these instructions you will know what is unclean and clean, and which animals may be eaten and which may not be eaten."

12 PURIFICATION AFTER CHILDBIRTH

The LORD said to Moses, ²"Give the following instructions to the people of Israel. If a woman becomes pregnant and gives birth to a son, she will be ceremonially unclean for seven days, just as she is unclean during her menstrual period. ³On the eighth day the boy's foreskin must be circumcised. ⁴After waiting thirty-three days, she will be purified from the bleeding of childbirth. During this time of purification, she must not touch anything that is set apart as holy. And she must not enter the sanctuary until her time of purification is over. [5]If a woman gives birth to a daughter, she will be ceremonially unclean for two weeks, just as she is unclean during her menstrual period. After waiting sixty-six days, she will be purified from the bleeding of childbirth.

[6]"When the time of purification is completed for either a son or a daughter, the woman must bring a one-year-old lamb for a burnt offering and a young pigeon or turtledove for a purification offering. She must bring her offerings to the priest at the entrance of the Tabernacle.* [7]The priest will then present them to the Lord to purify her.* Then she will be ceremonially clean again after her bleeding at childbirth. These are the instructions for a woman after the birth of a son or a daughter.

[8]"If a woman cannot afford to bring a lamb, she must bring two turtledoves or two young pigeons. One will be for the burnt offering and the other for the purification offering. The priest will sacrifice them to purify her, and she will be ceremonially clean."

13 SERIOUS SKIN DISEASES The Lord said to Moses and Aaron, [2]"If anyone has a swelling or a rash or discolored skin that might develop into a serious skin disease,* that person must be brought to Aaron the priest or to one of his sons.* [3]The priest will examine the affected area of the skin. If the hair in the affected area has turned white and the problem appears to be more than skin-deep, it is a serious skin disease, and the priest who examines it must pronounce the person ceremonially unclean.

[4]"But if the affected area of the skin is only a white discoloration and does not appear to be more than skin-deep, and if the hair on the spot has not turned white, the priest will quarantine the person for seven days. [5]On the seventh day the priest will make another examination. If he finds the affected area has not changed and the problem has not spread on the skin, the priest will quarantine the person for seven more days. [6]On the seventh day the priest will make another examination. If he finds the affected area has faded and has not spread, the priest will pronounce the person ceremonially clean. It was only a rash. The person's clothing must be washed, and the person will be ceremonially clean. [7]But if

the rash continues to spread after the person has been examined by the priest and has been pronounced clean, the infected person must return to be examined again. [8]If the priest finds that the rash has spread, he must pronounce the person ceremonially unclean, for it is indeed a skin disease.

[9]"Anyone who develops a serious skin disease must go to the priest for an examination. [10]If the priest finds a white swelling on the skin, and some hair on the spot has turned white, and there is an open sore in the affected area, [11]it is a chronic skin disease, and the priest must pronounce the person ceremonially unclean. In such cases the person need not be quarantined, for it is obvious that the skin is defiled by the disease.

[12]"Now suppose the disease has spread all over the person's skin, covering the body from head to foot. [13]When the priest examines the infected person and finds that the disease covers the entire body, he will pronounce the person ceremonially clean. Since the skin has turned completely white, the person is clean. [14]But if any open sores appear, the infected person will be pronounced ceremonially unclean. [15]The priest must make this pronouncement as soon as he sees an open sore, since open sores indicate the presence of a skin disease. [16]However, if the open sores heal and turn white like the rest of the skin, the person must return to the priest [17]for another examination. If the affected areas have indeed turned white, the priest will then pronounce the person ceremonially clean by declaring, 'You are clean!'

[18]"If anyone has a boil on the skin that has started to heal, [19]but a white swelling or a reddish white spot develops in its place, that person must go to the priest to be examined. [20]If the priest examines it and finds it to be more than skin-deep, and if the hair in the affected area has turned white, the priest must pronounce the person ceremonially unclean. The boil has become a serious skin disease. [21]But if the priest finds no white hair on the affected area and the problem appears to be no more than skin-deep and has faded, the priest must quarantine the person for seven days. [22]If during that time the affected area spreads on the skin, the priest must pronounce the person ceremonially unclean, because it is a serious disease. [23]But if the area grows no larger and does not spread, it is merely the scar from the boil, and the priest will pronounce the person ceremonially clean.

[24]"If anyone has suffered a burn on the skin and the burned area changes color, becoming

12:6 Hebrew Tent of Meeting.   12:7 Or to make atonement for her; also in 12:8.   13:2a Traditionally rendered leprosy. The Hebrew word used throughout this passage is used to describe various skin diseases.   13:2b Or one of his descendants.

either reddish white or shiny white, ²⁵the priest must examine it. If he finds that the hair in the affected area has turned white and the problem appears to be more than skin-deep, a skin disease has broken out in the burn. The priest must then pronounce the person ceremonially unclean, for it is clearly a serious skin disease. ²⁶But if the priest finds no white hair on the affected area and the problem appears to be no more than skin-deep and has faded, the priest must quarantine the infected person for seven days. ²⁷On the seventh day the priest must examine the person again. If the affected area has spread on the skin, the priest must pronounce that person ceremonially unclean, for it is clearly a serious skin disease. ²⁸But if the affected area has not changed or spread on the skin and has faded, it is simply a swelling from the burn. The priest will then pronounce the person ceremonially clean, for it is only the scar from the burn.

²⁹"If anyone, either a man or woman, has a sore on the head or chin, ³⁰the priest must examine it. If he finds it is more than skin-deep and has fine yellow hair on it, the priest must pronounce the person ceremonially unclean. It is a scabby sore of the head or chin. ³¹If the priest examines the scabby sore and finds that it is only skin-deep but there is no black hair on it, he must quarantine the person for seven days. ³²On the seventh day the priest must examine the sore again. If he finds that the scabby sore has not spread, and there is no yellow hair on it, and it appears to be only skin-deep, ³³the person must shave off all hair except the hair on the affected area. Then the priest must quarantine the person for another seven days. ³⁴On the seventh day he will examine the sore again. If it has not spread and appears to be no more than skin-deep, the priest will pronounce the person ceremonially clean. The person's clothing must be washed, and the person will be ceremonially clean. ³⁵But if the scabby sore begins to spread after the person is pronounced clean, ³⁶the priest must do another examination. If he finds that the sore has spread, the priest does not need to look for yellow hair. The infected person is ceremonially unclean. ³⁷But if the color of the scabby sore does not change and black hair has grown on it, it has healed. The priest will then pronounce the person ceremonially clean.

³⁸"If anyone, either a man or woman, has shiny white patches on the skin, ³⁹the priest must examine the affected area. If he finds that the shiny patches are only pale white, this is a harmless skin rash, and the person is ceremonially clean.

⁴⁰"If a man loses his hair and his head becomes bald, he is still ceremonially clean. ⁴¹And if he loses hair on his forehead, he simply has a bald forehead; he is still clean. ⁴²However, if a reddish white sore appears on the bald area at the top or back of his head, this is a skin disease. ⁴³The priest must examine him, and if he finds swelling around the reddish white sore anywhere on the man's head and it looks like a skin disease, ⁴⁴the man is indeed infected with a skin disease and is unclean. The priest must pronounce him ceremonially unclean because of the sore on his head.

⁴⁵"Those who suffer from a serious skin disease must tear their clothing and leave their hair uncombed.* They must cover their mouth and call out, 'Unclean! Unclean!' ⁴⁶As long as the serious disease lasts, they will be ceremonially unclean. They must live in isolation in their place outside the camp.

TREATMENT OF CONTAMINATED CLOTHING

⁴⁷"Now suppose mildew* contaminates some woolen or linen clothing, ⁴⁸woolen or linen fabric, the hide of an animal, or anything made of leather. ⁴⁹If the contaminated area in the clothing, the animal hide, the fabric, or the leather article has turned greenish or reddish, it is contaminated with mildew and must be shown to the priest. ⁵⁰After examining the affected spot, the priest will put the article in quarantine for seven days. ⁵¹On the seventh day the priest must inspect it again. If the contaminated area has spread, the clothing or fabric or leather is clearly contaminated by a serious mildew and is ceremonially unclean. ⁵²The priest must burn the item—the clothing, the woolen or linen fabric, or piece of leather—for it has been contaminated by a serious mildew. It must be completely destroyed by fire.

⁵³"But if the priest examines it and finds that the contaminated area has not spread in the clothing, the fabric, or the leather, ⁵⁴the priest will order the object to be washed and then quarantined for seven more days. ⁵⁵Then the priest must examine the object again. If he finds that the contaminated area has not changed color after being washed, even if it did not spread, the object is defiled. It must be completely burned up, whether the contaminated spot* is on the inside or outside. ⁵⁶But if the priest examines it and finds that

13:45 Or *and uncover their heads.*   **13:47** Traditionally rendered *leprosy.* The Hebrew term used throughout this passage is the same term used for the various skin diseases described in 13:1-46.
13:55 The meaning of the Hebrew is uncertain.

the contaminated area has faded after being washed, he must cut the spot from the clothing, the fabric, or the leather. ⁵⁷If the spot later reappears on the clothing, the fabric, or the leather article, the mildew is clearly spreading, and the contaminated object must be burned up. ⁵⁸But if the spot disappears from the clothing, the fabric, or the leather article after it has been washed, it must be washed again; then it will be ceremonially clean.

⁵⁹"These are the instructions for dealing with mildew that contaminates woolen or linen clothing or fabric or anything made of leather. This is how the priest will determine whether these items are ceremonially clean or unclean."

14 CLEANSING FROM SKIN DISEASES And the LORD said to Moses, ²"The following instructions are for those seeking ceremonial purification from a skin disease.* Those who have been healed must be brought to the priest, ³who will examine them at a place outside the camp. If the priest finds that someone has been healed of a serious skin disease, ⁴he will perform a purification ceremony, using two live birds that are ceremonially clean, a stick of cedar,* some scarlet yarn, and a hyssop branch. ⁵The priest will order that one bird be slaughtered over a clay pot filled with fresh water. ⁶He will take the live bird, the cedar stick, the scarlet yarn, and the hyssop branch, and dip them into the blood of the bird that was slaughtered over the fresh water. ⁷The priest will then sprinkle the blood of the dead bird seven times on the person being purified of the skin disease. When the priest has purified the person, he will release the live bird in the open field to fly away.

⁸"The persons being purified must then wash their clothes, shave off all their hair, and bathe themselves in water. Then they will be ceremonially clean and may return to the camp. However, they must remain outside their tents for seven days. ⁹On the seventh day they must again shave all the hair from their heads, including the hair of the beard and eyebrows. They must also wash their clothes and bathe themselves in water. Then they will be ceremonially clean.

¹⁰"On the eighth day each person being purified must bring two male lambs and a one-year-old female lamb, all with no defects, along with

a grain offering of six quarts* of choice flour moistened with olive oil, and a cup* of olive oil. ¹¹Then the officiating priest will present that person for purification, along with the offerings, before the LORD at the entrance of the Tabernacle.* ¹²The priest will take one of the male lambs and the olive oil and present them as a guilt offering, lifting them up as a special offering before the LORD. ¹³He will then slaughter the male lamb in the sacred area where sin offerings and burnt offerings are slaughtered. As with the sin offering, the guilt offering belongs to the priest. It is a most holy offering. ¹⁴The priest will then take some of the blood of the guilt offering and apply it to the lobe of the right ear, the thumb of the right hand, and the big toe of the right foot of the person being purified.

¹⁵"Then the priest will pour some of the olive oil into the palm of his own left hand. ¹⁶He will dip his right finger into the oil in his palm and sprinkle some of it with his finger seven times before the LORD. ¹⁷The priest will then apply some of the oil in his palm over the blood from the guilt offering that is on the lobe of the right ear, the thumb of the right hand, and the big toe of the right foot of the person being purified. ¹⁸The priest will apply the oil remaining in his hand to the head of the person being purified. Through this process, the priest will purify* the person before the LORD.

¹⁹"Then the priest must present the sin offering to purify the person who was cured of the skin disease. After that, the priest will slaughter the burnt offering ²⁰and offer it on the altar along with the grain offering. Through this process, the priest will purify the person who was healed, and the person will be ceremonially clean.

²¹"But anyone who is too poor and cannot afford these offerings may bring one male lamb for a guilt offering, to be lifted up as a special offering for purification. The person must also bring two quarts* of choice flour moistened with olive oil for the grain offering and a cup of olive oil. ²²The offering must also include two turtledoves or two young pigeons, whichever the person can afford. One of the pair must be used for the sin offering and the other for a burnt offering. ²³On the eighth day of the purification ceremony, the person being purified must bring the offerings to the priest in the LORD's presence at the entrance of the Tabernacle. ²⁴The priest will take the lamb for the guilt offering, along with the olive oil, and lift them up as a special offering to the LORD. ²⁵Then the priest will slaughter the lamb for the

14:2 Traditionally rendered *leprosy;* see note on 13:2a. 14:4 Or *juniper;* also in 14:6, 49, 51. 14:10a Hebrew *¾⁄₁₀ of an ephah* [6.6 liters]. 14:10b Hebrew *1 log* [0.3 liters]; also in 14:21. 14:11 Hebrew *Tent of Meeting;* also in 14:23. 14:18 Or *will make atonement for;* similarly in 14:19, 20, 21, 29, 31, 53. 14:21 Hebrew *¹⁄₁₀ of an ephah* [2.2 liters].

guilt offering. He will take some of its blood and apply it to the lobe of the right ear, the thumb of the right hand, and the big toe of the right foot of the person being purified.

²⁶"The priest will also pour some of the olive oil into the palm of his own left hand. ²⁷He will dip his right finger into the oil in his palm and sprinkle some of it seven times before the LORD. ²⁸The priest will then apply some of the oil in his palm over the blood from the guilt offering that is on the lobe of the right ear, the thumb of the right hand, and the big toe of the right foot of the person being purified. ²⁹The priest will apply the oil remaining in his hand to the head of the person being purified. Through this process, the priest will purify the person before the LORD.

³⁰"Then the priest will offer the two turtledoves or the two young pigeons, whichever the person can afford. ³¹One of them is for a sin offering and the other for a burnt offering, to be presented along with the grain offering. Through this process, the priest will purify the person before the LORD. ³²These are the instructions for purification for those who have recovered from a serious skin disease but who cannot afford to bring the offerings normally required for the ceremony of purification."

TREATMENT OF CONTAMINATED HOUSES

³³Then the LORD said to Moses and Aaron, ³⁴"When you arrive in Canaan, the land I am giving you as your own possession, I may contaminate some of the houses in your land with mildew.* ³⁵The owner of such a house must then go to the priest and say, 'It appears that my house has some kind of mildew.' ³⁶Before the priest goes in to inspect the house, he must have the house emptied so nothing inside will be pronounced ceremonially unclean. ³⁷Then the priest will go in and examine the mildew on the walls. If he finds greenish or reddish streaks and the contamination appears to go deeper than the wall's surface, ³⁸the priest will step outside the door and put the house in quarantine for seven days. ³⁹On the seventh day the priest must return for another inspection. If he finds that the mildew on the walls of the house has spread, ⁴⁰the priest must order

that the stones from those areas be removed. The contaminated material will then be taken outside the town to an area designated as ceremonially unclean. ⁴¹Next the inside walls of the entire house must be scraped thoroughly and the scrapings dumped in the unclean place outside the town. ⁴²Other stones will be brought in to replace the ones that were removed, and the walls will be replastered.

⁴³"But if the mildew reappears after all the stones have been replaced and the house has been scraped and replastered, ⁴⁴the priest must return and inspect the house again. If he finds that the mildew has spread, the walls are clearly contaminated with a serious mildew, and the house is defiled. ⁴⁵It must be torn down, and all its stones, timbers, and plaster must be carried out of town to the place designated as ceremonially unclean. ⁴⁶Those who enter the house during the period of quarantine will be ceremonially unclean until evening, ⁴⁷and all who sleep or eat in the house must wash their clothing.

⁴⁸"But if the priest returns for his inspection and finds that the mildew has not reappeared in the house after the fresh plastering, he will pronounce it clean because the mildew is clearly gone. ⁴⁹To purify the house the priest must take two birds, a stick of cedar, some scarlet yarn, and a hyssop branch. ⁵⁰He will slaughter one of the birds over a clay pot filled with fresh water. ⁵¹He will take the cedar stick, the hyssop branch, the scarlet yarn, and the live bird, and dip them into the blood of the slaughtered bird and into the fresh water. Then he will sprinkle the house seven times. ⁵²When the priest has purified the house in exactly this way, ⁵³he will release the live bird in the open fields outside the town. Through this process, the priest will purify the house, and it will be ceremonially clean.

⁵⁴"These are the instructions for dealing with serious skin diseases,* including scabby sores; ⁵⁵and mildew,* whether on clothing or in a house; ⁵⁶and a swelling on the skin, a rash, or discolored skin. ⁵⁷This procedure will determine whether a person or object is ceremonially clean or unclean."

"These are the instructions regarding skin diseases and mildew."

FUNGUS FACTS
(14:33-53) *Here are instructions concerning mildew on clothing or house walls. This was probably a mold, fungus, or bacteria. This kind of infection could spread rapidly and promote disease. Therefore checking its spread as soon as possible was important. What activity or relationship in your life has a similar, destructive effect on you or your faith?*

15 BODILY DISCHARGES
The LORD said to Moses and Aaron, ²"Give the following instructions to the people of Israel.

14:34 Traditionally rendered *leprosy;* see note on 13:47.
14:54 Traditionally rendered *leprosy;* see note on 13:2a.
14:55 Traditionally rendered *leprosy;* see note on 13:47.

"Any man who has a bodily discharge is ceremonially unclean. ³This defilement is caused by his discharge, whether the discharge continues or stops. In either case the man is unclean. ⁴Any bed on which the man with the discharge lies and anything on which he sits will be ceremonially unclean. ⁵So if you touch the man's bed, you must wash your clothes and bathe yourself in water, and you will remain unclean until evening. ⁶If you sit where the man with the discharge has sat, you must wash your clothes and bathe yourself in water, and you will remain unclean until evening. ⁷If you touch the man with the discharge, you must wash your clothes and bathe yourself in water, and you will remain unclean until evening. ⁸If the man spits on you, you must wash your clothes and bathe yourself in water, and you will remain unclean until evening. ⁹Any saddle blanket on which the man rides will be ceremonially unclean. ¹⁰If you touch anything that was under the man, you will be unclean until evening. You must wash your clothes and bathe yourself in water, and you will remain unclean until evening. ¹¹If the man touches you without first rinsing his hands, you must wash your clothes and bathe yourself in water, and you will remain unclean until evening. ¹²Any clay pot the man touches must be broken, and any wooden utensil he touches must be rinsed with water.

¹³"When the man with the discharge is healed, he must count off seven days for the period of purification. Then he must wash his clothes and bathe himself in fresh water, and he will be ceremonially clean. ¹⁴On the eighth day he must get two turtledoves or two young pigeons and come before the Lord at the entrance of the Tabernacle* and give his offerings to the priest. ¹⁵The priest will offer one bird for a sin offering and the other for a burnt offering. Through this process, the priest will purify* the man before the Lord for his discharge.

¹⁶"Whenever a man has an emission of semen, he must bathe his entire body in water, and he will remain ceremonially unclean until the next evening.* ¹⁷Any clothing or leather with semen on it must be washed in water, and it will remain unclean until evening. ¹⁸After a man and a woman have sexual intercourse, they must each bathe in water, and they will remain unclean until the next evening.

¹⁹"Whenever a woman has her menstrual period, she will be ceremonially unclean for seven days. Anyone who touches her during

15:14 Hebrew *Tent of Meeting;* also in 15:29.   **15:15** Or *will make atonement for;* also in 15:30.   **15:16** Hebrew *until evening;* also in 15:18.

SYSTEM OF SACRIFICE

OLD SYSTEM OF SACRIFICE	NEW SYSTEM OF SACRIFICE
Was temporary (Heb 8:13)	Is permanent (Heb 7:21)
Aaron first high priest (Lev 16:32)	Jesus only High Priest (Heb 4:14)
From tribe of Levi (Heb 7:16)	From tribe of Judah (Heb 7:14)
Ministered on earth (Heb 8:4)	Ministers in heaven (Heb 8:1-2)
Used blood of animals (Lev 16:15)	Uses blood of Christ (Heb 10:4-12)
Required many sacrifices (Heb 10:1-3)	Requires one sacrifice (Heb 9:28)
Needed perfect animals (Lev 22:19)	Needs perfect life (Heb 5:9)
Required careful approach to Tabernacle (Lev 16:2)	Encourages bold approach to throne (Heb 4:16)
Looked forward to new system (Heb 10:1)	Cancels old system (Heb 10:9)

that time will be unclean until evening. ²⁰Anything on which the woman lies or sits during the time of her period will be unclean. ²¹If any of you touch her bed, you must wash your clothes and bathe yourself in water, and you will remain unclean until evening. ²²If you touch any object she has sat on, you must wash your clothes and bathe yourself in water, and you will remain unclean until evening. ²³This includes her bed or any other object she has sat on; you will be unclean until evening if you touch it. ²⁴If a man has sexual intercourse with her and her blood touches him, her menstrual impurity will be transmitted to him. He will remain unclean for seven days, and any bed on which he lies will be unclean.

²⁵"If a woman has a flow of blood for many days that is unrelated to her menstrual period, or if the blood continues beyond the normal

....

SEX
(15:18) This verse is not implying that sex is dirty or disgusting. God created sex, both for the enjoyment of married couples and for continuing the race and the covenant. Everything must be seen and done with a view toward God's love and control. Sex is not separate from spirituality and God's care. God is concerned about our sexual habits. We tend to separate our physical and spiritual lives, but they are intertwined inseparably. God must be Lord over our whole selves—including our private lives.

period, she is ceremonially unclean. As during her menstrual period, the woman will be unclean as long as the discharge continues. ²⁶Any bed she lies on and any object she sits on during that time will be unclean, just as during her normal menstrual period. ²⁷If any of you touch these things, you will be ceremonially unclean. You must wash your clothes and bathe yourself in water, and you will remain unclean until evening.

²⁸"When the woman's bleeding stops, she must count off seven days. Then she will be ceremonially clean. ²⁹On the eighth day she must bring two turtledoves or two young pigeons and present them to the priest at the entrance of the Tabernacle. ³⁰The priest will offer one for a sin offering and the other for a burnt offering. Through this process, the priest will purify her before the LORD for the ceremonial impurity caused by her bleeding.

³¹"This is how you will guard the people of Israel from ceremonial uncleanness. Otherwise they would die, for their impurity would defile my Tabernacle that stands among them. ³²These are the instructions for dealing with anyone who has a bodily discharge—a man who is unclean because of an emission of semen ³³or a woman during her menstrual period. It applies to any man or woman who has a bodily discharge, and to a man who has sexual intercourse with a woman who is ceremonially unclean."

16 THE DAY OF ATONEMENT The LORD spoke to Moses after the death of Aaron's two sons, who died after they entered the LORD's presence and burned the wrong kind of fire before him. ²The LORD said to Moses, "Warn your brother, Aaron, not to enter the Most Holy Place behind the inner curtain whenever he chooses; if he does, he will die. For the Ark's cover—the place of atonement—is there, and I myself am present in the cloud above the atonement cover.

³"When Aaron enters the sanctuary area, he must follow these instructions fully. He must bring a young bull for a sin offering and a ram for a burnt offering. ⁴He must put on his linen

tunic and the linen undergarments worn next to his body. He must tie the linen sash around his waist and put the linen turban on his head. These are sacred garments, so he must bathe himself in water before he puts them on. ⁵Aaron must take from the community of Israel two male goats for a sin offering and a ram for a burnt offering.

⁶"Aaron will present his own bull as a sin offering to purify himself and his family, making them right with the LORD.* ⁷Then he must take the two male goats and present them to the LORD at the entrance of the Tabernacle.* ⁸He is to cast sacred lots to determine which goat will be reserved as an offering to the LORD and which will carry the sins of the people to the wilderness of Azazel. ⁹Aaron will then present as a sin offering the goat chosen by lot for the LORD. ¹⁰The other goat, the scapegoat chosen by lot to be sent away, will be kept alive, standing before the LORD. When it is sent away to Azazel in the wilderness, the people will be purified and made right with the LORD.*

¹¹"Aaron will present his own bull as a sin offering to purify himself and his family, making them right with the LORD. After he has slaughtered the bull as a sin offering, ¹²he will fill an incense burner with burning coals from the altar that stands before the LORD. Then he will take two handfuls of fragrant powdered incense and will carry the burner and the incense behind the inner curtain. ¹³There in the LORD's presence he will put the incense on the burning coals so that a cloud of incense will rise over the Ark's cover—the place of atonement—that rests on the Ark of the Covenant.* If he follows these instructions, he will not die. ¹⁴Then he must take some of the blood of the bull, dip his finger in it, and sprinkle it on the east side of the atonement cover. He must sprinkle blood seven times with his finger in front of the atonement cover.

¹⁵"Then Aaron must slaughter the first goat as a sin offering for the people and carry its blood behind the inner curtain. There he will sprinkle the goat's blood over the atonement cover and in front of it, just as he did with the bull's blood. ¹⁶Through this process, he will purify* the Most Holy Place, and he will do the same for the entire Tabernacle, because of the defiling sin and rebellion of the Israelites. ¹⁷No

16:6 Or *to make atonement for himself and his family;* similarly in 16:11, 17b, 24, 34.   16:7 Hebrew *Tent of Meeting;* also in 16:16, 17, 20, 23, 33.   16:10 Or *wilderness, it will make atonement for the people.*   16:13 Hebrew *that is above the Testimony.* The Hebrew word for "testimony" refers to the terms of the LORD's covenant with Israel as written on stone tablets, which were kept in the Ark, and also to the covenant itself.   16:16 Or *make atonement for;* similarly in 16:17a, 18, 20, 27, 33.

one else is allowed inside the Tabernacle when Aaron enters it for the purification ceremony in the Most Holy Place. No one may enter until he comes out again after purifying himself, his family, and all the congregation of Israel, making them right with the Lord.

18"Then Aaron will come out to purify the altar that stands before the Lord. He will do this by taking some of the blood from the bull and the goat and putting it on each of the horns of the altar. 19Then he must sprinkle the blood with his finger seven times over the altar. In this way, he will cleanse it from Israel's defilement and make it holy.

20"When Aaron has finished purifying the Most Holy Place and the Tabernacle and the altar, he must present the live goat. 21He will lay both of his hands on the goat's head and confess over it all the wickedness, rebellion, and sins of the people of Israel. In this way, he will transfer the people's sins to the head of the goat. Then a man specially chosen for the task will drive the goat into the wilderness. 22As the goat goes into the wilderness, it will carry all the people's sins upon itself into a desolate land.

23"When Aaron goes back into the Tabernacle, he must take off the linen garments he was wearing when he entered the Most Holy Place, and he must leave the garments there. 24Then he must bathe himself with water in a sacred place, put on his regular garments, and go out to sacrifice a burnt offering for himself and a burnt offering for the people. Through this process, he will purify himself and the people, making them right with the Lord. 25He must then burn all the fat of the sin offering on the altar.

26"The man chosen to drive the scapegoat into the wilderness of Azazel must wash his clothes and bathe himself in water. Then he may return to the camp.

27"The bull and the goat presented as sin offerings, whose blood Aaron takes into the Most Holy Place for the purification ceremony, will be carried outside the camp. The animals' hides, internal organs, and dung are all to be burned. 28The man who burns them must wash his clothes and bathe himself in water before returning to the camp.

29"On the tenth day of the appointed month in early autumn,* you must deny yourselves.* Neither native-born Israelites nor foreigners

ON THAT DAY OFFERINGS OF PURIFICATION WILL BE MADE FOR YOU, AND YOU WILL BE PURIFIED IN THE LORD'S PRESENCE FROM ALL YOUR SINS.

LEVITICUS 16:30

living among you may do any kind of work. This is a permanent law for you. 30On that day offerings of purification will be made for you,* and you will be purified in the Lord's presence from all your sins. 31It will be a Sabbath day of complete rest for you, and you must deny yourselves. This is a permanent law for you. 32In future generations, the purification* ceremony will be performed by the priest who has been anointed and ordained to serve as high priest in place of his ancestor Aaron. He will put on the holy linen garments 33and purify the Most Holy Place, the Tabernacle, the altar, the priests, and the entire congregation. 34This is a permanent law for you, to purify the people of Israel from their sins, making them right with the Lord once each year."

Moses followed all these instructions exactly as the Lord had commanded him.

17 PROHIBITIONS AGAINST EATING BLOOD Then the Lord said to Moses, 2"Give the following instructions to Aaron and his sons and all the people of Israel. This is what the Lord has commanded.

3"If any native Israelite sacrifices a bull* or a lamb or a goat anywhere inside or outside the camp 4instead of bringing it to the entrance of the Tabernacle* to present it as an offering to the Lord, that person will be as guilty as a murderer.* Such a person has shed blood and will be cut off from the community. 5The purpose of this rule is to stop the Israelites from sacrificing animals in the open fields. It will ensure that they bring their sacrifices to the priest at the entrance of the Tabernacle, so he can present them to the Lord as peace offerings. 6Then the priest will be able to splatter the blood against the Lord's altar at the entrance

16:29a Hebrew *On the tenth day of the seventh month.* This day in the ancient Hebrew lunar calendar occurred in September or October.   16:29b Or *must fast;* also in 16:31.   16:30 Or *atonement will be made for you, to purify you.*   16:32 Or *atonement.*   17:3 Or *cow.*   17:4a Hebrew *Tent of Meeting;* also in 17:5, 6, 9.   17:4b Hebrew *will be guilty of blood.*

of the Tabernacle, and he will burn the fat as a pleasing aroma to the LORD. 7The people must no longer be unfaithful to the LORD by offering sacrifices to the goat idols.* This is a permanent law for them, to be observed from generation to generation.

8"Give them this command as well. If any native Israelite or foreigner living among you offers a burnt offering or a sacrifice 9but does not bring it to the entrance of the Tabernacle to offer it to the LORD, that person will be cut off from the community.

10"And if any native Israelite or foreigner living among you eats or drinks blood in any form, I will turn against that person and cut him off from the community of your people, 11for the life of the body is in its blood. I have given you the blood on the altar to purify you, making you right with the LORD.* It is the blood, given in exchange for a life, that makes purification possible. 12That is why I have said to the people of Israel, 'You must never eat or drink blood—neither you nor the foreigners living among you.'

13"And if any native Israelite or foreigner living among you goes hunting and kills an animal or bird that is approved for eating, he must drain its blood and cover it with earth. 14The life of every creature is in its blood. That is why I have said to the people of Israel, 'You must never eat or drink blood, for the life of any creature is in its blood.' So whoever consumes blood will be cut off from the community.

15"And if any native-born Israelites or foreigners eat the meat of an animal that died naturally or was torn up by wild animals, they must wash their clothes and bathe themselves in water. They will remain ceremonially unclean until evening, but then they will be clean. 16But if they do not wash their clothes and bathe themselves, they will be punished for their sin."

18 FORBIDDEN SEXUAL PRACTICES Then the LORD said to Moses, 2"Give the following instructions to the people of Israel. I am the LORD your God. 3So do not act like the people in Egypt, where you used to live, or like the people of Canaan, where I am taking you. You must not imitate their way of life. 4You must obey all my regulations and be careful to obey my decrees, for I am the LORD your God. 5If you obey my decrees and my regulations, you will find life through them. I am the LORD.

6"You must never have sexual relations with a close relative, for I am the LORD.

7"Do not violate your father by having sexual relations with your mother. She is your mother; you must not have sexual relations with her.

8"Do not have sexual relations with any of your father's wives, for this would violate your father.

9"Do not have sexual relations with your sister or half sister, whether she is your father's daughter or your mother's daughter, whether she was born into your household or someone else's.

10"Do not have sexual relations with your granddaughter, whether she is your son's daughter or your daughter's daughter, for this would violate yourself.

11"Do not have sexual relations with your stepsister, the daughter of any of your father's wives, for she is your sister.

12"Do not have sexual relations with your father's sister, for she is your father's close relative.

13"Do not have sexual relations with your mother's sister, for she is your mother's close relative.

14"Do not violate your uncle, your father's brother, by having sexual relations with his wife, for she is your aunt.

15"Do not have sexual relations with your daughter-in-law; she is your son's wife, so you must not have sexual relations with her.

16"Do not have sexual relations with your brother's wife, for this would violate your brother.

17"Do not have sexual relations with both a woman and her daughter. And do not take* her granddaughter, whether her son's daughter or her daughter's daughter, and have sexual relations with them. They are close relatives, and this would be a wicked act.

18"While your wife is living, do not marry her sister and have sexual relations with her, for they would be rivals.

19"Do not have sexual relations with a woman during her period of menstrual impurity.

20"Do not defile yourself by having sexual intercourse with your neighbor's wife.

21"Do not permit any of your children to be

MOLDER OR MOLDED?
(18:3) The Israelites moved from one idol-infested region to another. As God helped them form a new culture, he warned them to stop imitating the people of Egypt. He also did not want his people to absorb the culture of Canaan. The same warning goes for us. Society may pressure us to conform to its way of life, but yielding to that pressure can eliminate our effectiveness in serving God. Don't be like gelatin—easily molded. Instead, help mold others by your strong faith.

17:7 Or goat demons.   **17:11** Or to make atonement for you.
18:17 Or do not marry.

offered as a sacrifice to Molech, for you must not bring shame on the name of your God. I am the LORD.

²²"Do not practice homosexuality, having sex with another man as with a woman. It is a detestable sin.

²³"A man must not defile himself by having sex with an animal. And a woman must not offer herself to a male animal to have intercourse with it. This is a perverse act.

²⁴"Do not defile yourselves in any of these ways, for the people I am driving out before you have defiled themselves in all these ways. ²⁵Because the entire land has become defiled, I am punishing the people who live there. I will cause the land to vomit them out. ²⁶You must obey all my decrees and regulations. You must not commit any of these detestable sins. This applies both to native-born Israelites and to the foreigners living among you.

²⁷"All these detestable activities are practiced by the people of the land where I am taking you, and this is how the land has become defiled. ²⁸So do not defile the land and give it a reason to vomit you out, as it will vomit out the people who live there now. ²⁹Whoever commits any of these detestable sins will be cut off from the community of Israel. ³⁰So obey my instructions, and do not defile yourselves by committing any of these detestable practices that were committed by the people who lived in the land before you. I am the LORD your God."

19:5 Or it.

19 HOLINESS IN PERSONAL CONDUCT

The LORD also said to Moses, ²"Give the following instructions to the entire community of Israel. You must be holy because I, the LORD your God, am holy.

³"Each of you must show great respect for your mother and father, and you must always observe my Sabbath days of rest. I am the LORD your God.

⁴"Do not put your trust in idols or make metal images of gods for yourselves. I am the LORD your God.

⁵"When you sacrifice a peace offering to the LORD, offer it properly so you* will be accepted by God. ⁶The sacrifice must be eaten on the same day you offer it or on the next day. Whatever is left over until the third day must be completely burned up. ⁷If any of the sacrifice is eaten on the third day, it will be contaminated, and I will not accept it. ⁸Anyone who eats it on the third day will be punished for defiling what is holy to the LORD and will be cut off from the community.

⁹"When you harvest the crops of your land, do not harvest the grain along the edges of your fields, and do not pick up what the harvesters drop. ¹⁰It is the same with your grape crop—do not strip every last bunch of grapes from the vines, and do not pick up the grapes that fall to the ground. Leave them for the poor and the foreigners living among you. I am the LORD your God.

¹¹"Do not steal.

ULTIMATE ISSUES *THE LAW*

It's universal: We see a sign that says *Wet Paint* and we want to touch it. We walk by a sign in a zoo that says *Do Not Feed the Animals* and what do we do? Slip the monkeys the rest of our jelly doughnut.

A law of human nature seems to be that rules are made to be broken. Something inside us makes us wonder, "What happens if I cross the line?"

God's people are not immune to this temptation. The Old Testament seems like a series of stories about God giving Israel rules—obedience meant blessing; disobedience meant punishment.

So what is the role of the law for Christians today? Are we, like the people of Moses' time, obligated to obey the law, or are we free of it?

First, the law can be divided into three branches: ceremonial, judicial, and moral. Ceremonial laws related to sacrifices, cleansing rituals, festivals, and so forth. Judicial laws dealt with the government— what kind of king Israel needed, criminal codes, and the like. The moral law concerned how people interacted with each other and with God. The Ten Commandments are the best-known section of the moral law.

Christian Bible scholars disagree as to how we are to view each branch, but the "majority opinion" is that the ceremonial laws were fulfilled in Christ; the judicial laws applied to the nation of Israel alone (although these principles form the foundation for laws in the United States and other Western nations); and the moral laws are true for all people, everywhere, at all times.

Now, what does the law do?

Think of the law as training wheels. Training wheels help beginning bike riders to stay upright until they "get the hang of riding." The law shows you how to walk uprightly before a holy God.

The law pointed the people of the Old Testament toward a coming Savior, who would fulfill the law and set his people free. We don't need to wait until the Savior comes. He has come already and written his law on our hearts (see Rom 2:15). ∎

"Do not deceive or cheat one another.

[12]"Do not bring shame on the name of your God by using it to swear falsely. I am the LORD.

[13]"Do not defraud or rob your neighbor.

"Do not make your hired workers wait until the next day to receive their pay.

[14]"Do not insult the deaf or cause the blind to stumble. You must fear your God; I am the LORD.

[15]"Do not twist justice in legal matters by favoring the poor or being partial to the rich and powerful. Always judge people fairly.

[16]"Do not spread slanderous gossip among your people.*

"Do not stand idly by when your neighbor's life is threatened. I am the LORD.

[17]"Do not nurse hatred in your heart for any of your relatives.* Confront people directly so you will not be held guilty for their sin.

[18]"Do not seek revenge or bear a grudge against a fellow Israelite, but love your neighbor as yourself. I am the LORD.

[19]"You must obey all my decrees.

"Do not mate two different kinds of animals.

· ·

TWO SIMPLE COMMANDS
(19:18) Don't, don't, don't. Some people think the Bible is nothing but a book of don'ts. But here we find two "dos" that sum up all of the other commandments. In Matthew 22:37-40, Jesus called these commandments—to love God and one's neighbors—the greatest commandments of all. Are these commandments high on your priorities list?

Do not plant your field with two different kinds of seed. Do not wear clothing woven from two different kinds of thread.

[20]"If a man has sex with a slave girl whose freedom has never been purchased but who is committed to become another man's wife, he must pay full compensation to her master. But since she is not a free woman, neither the man nor the woman will be put to death. [21]The man, however, must bring a ram as a guilt offering and present it to the LORD at the entrance of the Tabernacle.* [22]The priest will then purify him* before the LORD with the ram of the guilt offering, and the man's sin will be forgiven.

[23]"When you enter the land and plant fruit trees, leave the fruit unharvested for the first three years and consider it forbidden.* Do not eat it. [24]In the fourth year the entire crop must be consecrated to the LORD as a celebration of praise. [25]Finally, in the fifth year you may eat the fruit. If you follow this pattern, your harvest will increase. I am the LORD your God.

[26]"Do not eat meat that has not been drained of its blood.

"Do not practice fortune-telling or witchcraft.

[27]"Do not trim off the hair on your temples or trim your beards.

[28]"Do not cut your bodies for the dead, and

19:16 Hebrew *Do not act as a merchant toward your own people.*
19:17 Hebrew *for your brother.*   **19:21** Hebrew *Tent of Meeting.*
19:22 Or *make atonement for him.*   **19:23** Hebrew *consider it uncircumcised.*

I WONDER . . .

When I read a verse like Leviticus 19:28, I have to wonder: Is body piercing okay? What about tattoos?

Keep up with the latest trends? Although body piercing and tattoos have been around for centuries, they're really trendy these days. You can't go very far without seeing some form of piercing, from the more conventional one-hole in the earlobe to tongue piercing. And as for tattoos and other body decorations, well, let's just say that they're not confined to sailors and bikers. Suddenly, even your mom might consider getting a rose on her ankle!

But are tattoos and body piercing allowable, according to the Bible? Leviticus 19:28 says, "Do not cut your bodies for the dead, and do not mark your skin with tattoos. I am the LORD." Taking that verse at face value, one would assume that God says no to all piercing and tattoos. So, does that mean everyone with a tattoo needs to head to the nearest doctor to have it removed immediately? Does that mean no more earrings?

Actually, the best thing to do with a verse like this is to check out the context—the situation described in this passage. God knew that the nations in the land of Canaan used tattoos and body piercing as part of their religion. God vetoed both practices for Israel because he did not want his people to imitate the worship practices of these nations. In other words, he looked at the attitude behind the practice.

To sum up, the Bible does not say that body piercing and tattoos are wrong. Does that make either okay to do? A better question to ask yourself is *What's my reason for doing this?* Before you act, consider these questions: How carefully have you considered this issue? Have you weighed the pros and cons (the possible infection factor; the cost of removal if you grow bored with a tattoo)? Do you just want to do what everyone else is doing? If you've already made your choice, how does your decision show your desire to bring glory to God?

do not mark your skin with tattoos. I am the LORD.

²⁹"Do not defile your daughter by making her a prostitute, or the land will be filled with prostitution and wickedness.

³⁰"Keep my Sabbath days of rest, and show reverence toward my sanctuary. I am the LORD.

³¹"Do not defile yourselves by turning to mediums or to those who consult the spirits of the dead. I am the LORD your God.

³²"Stand up in the presence of the elderly, and show respect for the aged. Fear your God. I am the LORD.

³³"Do not take advantage of foreigners who live among you in your land. ³⁴Treat them like native-born Israelites, and love them as you love yourself. Remember that you were once foreigners living in the land of Egypt. I am the LORD your God.

³⁵"Do not use dishonest standards when measuring length, weight, or volume. ³⁶Your scales and weights must be accurate. Your containers for measuring dry materials or liquids must be accurate.* I am the LORD your God who brought you out of the land of Egypt.

³⁷"You must be careful to keep all of my decrees and regulations by putting them into practice. I am the LORD."

20 PUNISHMENTS FOR DISOBEDIENCE

The LORD said to Moses, ²"Give the people of Israel these instructions, which apply both to native Israelites and to the foreigners living in Israel.

"If any of them offer their children as a sacrifice to Molech, they must be put to death. The people of the community must stone them to death. ³I myself will turn against them and cut them off from the community, because they have defiled my sanctuary and brought shame on my holy name by offering their children to Molech. ⁴And if the people of the community ignore those who offer their children to Molech and refuse to execute them, ⁵I myself will turn against them and their families and will cut them off from the community. This will happen to all who commit spiritual prostitution by worshiping Molech.

⁶"I will also turn against those who commit spiritual prostitution by putting their trust in mediums or in those who consult the spirits of the dead. I will cut them off from the community. ⁷So set yourselves apart to be holy, for I am the LORD your God. ⁸Keep all my decrees

by putting them into practice, for I am the LORD who makes you holy.

⁹"Anyone who dishonors* father or mother must be put to death. Such a person is guilty of a capital offense.

¹⁰"If a man commits adultery with his neighbor's wife, both the man and the woman who have committed adultery must be put to death.

¹¹"If a man violates his father by having sex with one of his father's wives, both the man and the woman must be put to death, for they are guilty of a capital offense.

¹²"If a man has sex with his daughter-in-law, both must be put to death. They have committed a perverse act and are guilty of a capital offense.

¹³"If a man practices homosexuality, having sex with another man as with a woman, both men have committed a detestable act. They must both be put to death, for they are guilty of a capital offense.

¹⁴"If a man marries both a woman and her mother, he has committed a wicked act. The man and both women must be burned to death to wipe out such wickedness from among you.

¹⁵"If a man has sex with an animal, he must be put to death, and the animal must be killed.

¹⁶"If a woman presents herself to a male animal to have intercourse with it, she and the animal must both be put to death. You must kill both, for they are guilty of a capital offense.

¹⁷"If a man marries his sister, the daughter of either his father or his mother, and they have sexual relations, it is a shameful disgrace. They must be publicly cut off from the community. Since the man has violated his sister, he will be punished for his sin.

¹⁸"If a man has sexual relations with a woman during her menstrual period, both of them must be cut off from the community, for together they have exposed the source of her blood flow.

¹⁹"Do not have sexual relations with your aunt, whether your mother's sister or your father's sister. This would dishonor a close

....

JUST SAY NO TO THE OCCULT

(20:6) Everyone is interested in what the future holds. We often look to others for guidance. But God warned the Israelites against looking to the occult for advice. Mediums and psychics were outlawed because God was not the source of their information. At best, occult practitioners are fakes whose predictions cannot be trusted. At worst, they are in contact with evil spirits and are thus extremely dangerous. We don't need to look to the occult for information about the future. God has given us the Bible—a trustworthy source—for guidance. Is it your one-stop wisdom check?

19:36 Hebrew *Use an honest ephah* [a dry measure] *and an honest hin* [a liquid measure]. 20:9 Greek version reads *Anyone who speaks disrespectfully of.* Compare Matt 15:4; Mark 7:10.

I, THE LORD, AM HOLY,

relative. Both parties are guilty and will be punished for their sin.

²⁰"If a man has sex with his uncle's wife, he has violated his uncle. Both the man and woman will be punished for their sin, and they will die childless.

²¹"If a man marries his brother's wife, it is an act of impurity. He has violated his brother, and the guilty couple will remain childless.

²²"You must keep all my decrees and regulations by putting them into practice; otherwise the land to which I am bringing you as your new home will vomit you out. ²³Do not live according to the customs of the people I am driving out before you. It is because they do these shameful things that I detest them. ²⁴But I have promised you, 'You will possess their land because I will give it to you as your possession—a land flowing with milk and honey.' I am the LORD your God, who has set you apart from all other people.

²⁵"You must therefore make a distinction between ceremonially clean and unclean animals, and between clean and unclean birds. You must not defile yourselves by eating any unclean animal or bird or creature that scurries along the ground. I have identified them as being unclean for you. ²⁶You must be holy because I, the LORD, am holy. I have set you apart from all other people to be my very own.

²⁷"Men and women among you who act as mediums or who consult the spirits of the dead must be put to death by stoning. They are guilty of a capital offense."

21 INSTRUCTIONS FOR THE PRIESTS The LORD said to Moses, "Give the following instructions to the priests, the descendants of Aaron.

"A priest must not make himself ceremonially unclean by touching the dead body of a relative. ²The only exceptions are his closest relatives—his mother or father, son or daughter, brother, ³or his virgin sister who depends on him because she has no husband. ⁴But a priest must not defile himself and make himself unclean for someone who is related to him only by marriage.

⁵"The priests must not shave their heads or trim their beards or cut their bodies. ⁶They must be set apart as holy to their God and must never bring shame on the name of God. They must be holy, for they are the ones who present the special gifts to the LORD, gifts of food for their God.

SELF-DESTRUCTION
(20:22-23) God gave many rules to his people—but not without reason. He did not withhold good from them; he only prohibited those acts that would bring them to ruin. We understand God's physical laws of nature. For example, jumping off a 10-story building means death because of the law of gravity. But some don't understand how God's spiritual laws work. God forbids us to do certain things because he wants to keep us from self-destruction. It is in our own best interest to do things God's way.

CHOICES
stealing

Kelli and Cheyenne work together at Quackers, the newest fast-food restaurant in town. It's not such a bad job. The hours are good, the uniforms—surprise!—don't look like circus costumes, and the pay is more than minimum wage. Besides, the girls have great fun (and a lot of laughs) checking out the cute guys from a rival high school who frequent the place on weekends.

Today, however, when the girls come to work, they discover a terse note from the boss: *I want to talk to both of you. It's very important!*

Kelli's heart drops to her shoes, and Cheyenne's stomach does a cartwheel. What could it mean?

A raise? A promotion? Not likely. In fact, the girls are expecting the worst. See, they've been giving away free food and Quackers T-shirts to certain male customers. And Cheyenne took a whole box of burgers from the freezer late last Friday night to use at her Saturday pool party.

"We're dead!" Kelli moans. "We've done everything but actually take money out of the cash register!"

Cheyenne looks sheepish. "No—I even did that one night."

"Cheyenne! You didn't! How much did you take?"

"Fifty bucks."

"Oh no! What are we gonna say?"

Leviticus 19:11 could have helped Kelli and Cheyenne avoid this whole horrible headache. But God's command against stealing needs something else. It needs cooperation from people . . . like you.

AND I MAKE YOU HOLY.

⁷"Priests may not marry a woman defiled by prostitution, and they may not marry a woman who is divorced from her husband, for the priests are set apart as holy to their God. ⁸You must treat them as holy because they offer up food to your God. You must consider them holy because I, the LORD, am holy, and I make you holy.

⁹"If a priest's daughter defiles herself by becoming a prostitute, she also defiles her father's holiness, and she must be burned to death.

¹⁰"The high priest has the highest rank of all the priests. The anointing oil has been poured on his head, and he has been ordained to wear the priestly garments. He must never leave his hair uncombed* or tear his clothing. ¹¹He must not defile himself by going near a dead body. He may not make himself ceremonially unclean even for his father or mother. ¹²He must not defile the sanctuary of his God by leaving it to attend to a dead person, for he has been made holy by the anointing oil of his God. I am the LORD.

¹³"The high priest may marry only a virgin. ¹⁴He may not marry a widow, a woman who is divorced, or a woman who has defiled herself by prostitution. She must be a virgin from his own clan, ¹⁵so that he will not dishonor his descendants among his clan, for I am the LORD who makes him holy."

¹⁶Then the LORD said to Moses, ¹⁷"Give the following instructions to Aaron: In all future generations, none of your descendants who has any defect will qualify to offer food to his God. ¹⁸No one who has a defect qualifies, whether he is blind, lame, disfigured, deformed, ¹⁹or has a broken foot or arm, ²⁰or is hunchbacked or dwarfed, or has a defective eye, or skin sores or scabs, or damaged testicles. ²¹No descendant of Aaron who has a defect may approach the altar to present special gifts to the LORD. Since he has a defect, he may not approach the altar to offer food to his God. ²²However, he may eat from the food offered to God, including the holy offerings and the most holy offerings. ²³Yet because of his physical defect, he may not enter the room behind the inner curtain or approach the altar, for this would defile my holy places. I am the LORD who makes them holy."

21:10 Or *never uncover his head.*   **22:4** Traditionally rendered *leprosy;* see note on 13:2a.

²⁴So Moses gave these instructions to Aaron and his sons and to all the Israelites.

22
The LORD said to Moses, ²"Tell Aaron and his sons to be very careful with the sacred gifts that the Israelites set apart for me, so they do not bring shame on my holy name. I am the LORD. ³Give them the following instructions.

"In all future generations, if any of your descendants is ceremonially unclean when he approaches the sacred offerings that the people of Israel consecrate to the LORD, he must be cut off from my presence. I am the LORD.

⁴"If any of Aaron's descendants has a skin disease* or any kind of discharge that makes him ceremonially unclean, he may not eat from the sacred offerings until he has been pronounced clean. He also becomes unclean by touching a corpse, or by having an emission of semen, ⁵or by touching a small animal that is unclean, or by touching someone who is ceremonially unclean for any reason. ⁶The man who is defiled in any of these ways will remain unclean until evening. He may not eat from the sacred offerings until he has bathed himself in water. ⁷When the sun goes down, he will be ceremonially clean again and may eat from the sacred offerings, for this is his food. ⁸He may not eat an animal that has died a natural death or has been torn apart by wild animals, for this would defile him. I am the LORD.

⁹"The priests must follow my instructions carefully. Otherwise they will be punished for their sin and will die for violating my instructions. I am the LORD who makes them holy.

¹⁰"No one outside a priest's family may eat the sacred offerings. Even guests and hired workers in a priest's home are not allowed to eat them. ¹¹However, if the priest buys a slave for himself, the slave may eat from the sacred offerings. And if his slaves have children, they also may share his food. ¹²If a priest's daughter marries someone outside the priestly family, she may no longer eat the sacred offerings. ¹³But if she becomes a widow or is divorced and has no children to support her, and she returns to live in her father's home as in her youth, she may eat her father's food again. Otherwise, no one outside a priest's family may eat the sacred offerings.

¹⁴"Any such person who eats the sacred offerings without realizing it must pay the priest for the amount eaten, plus an additional 20 percent. ¹⁵The priests must not let the Israelites defile the sacred offerings brought to the LORD ¹⁶by allowing unauthorized people to eat them. This would bring guilt upon them and require them to pay compensation. I am the LORD who makes them holy."

WORTHY AND UNWORTHY OFFERINGS ¹⁷And the LORD said to Moses, ¹⁸"Give Aaron and his sons and all the Israelites these instructions, which apply both to native Israelites and to the foreigners living among you.

"If you present a gift as a burnt offering to the LORD, whether it is to fulfill a vow or is a voluntary offering, ¹⁹you* will be accepted only if your offering is a male animal with no defects. It may be a bull, a ram, or a male goat. ²⁰Do not present an animal with defects, because the LORD will not accept it on your behalf.

²¹"If you present a peace offering to the LORD from the herd or the flock, whether it is to fulfill a vow or is a voluntary offering, you must offer a perfect animal. It may have no defect of any kind. ²²You must not offer an animal that is blind, crippled, or injured, or that has a wart, a skin sore, or scabs. Such animals must never be offered on the altar as special gifts to the LORD. ²³If a bull* or lamb has a leg that is too long or too short, it may be offered as a voluntary offering, but it may not be offered to fulfill a vow. ²⁴If an animal has damaged testicles or is castrated, you may not offer it to the LORD. You must never do this in your own land, ²⁵and you must not accept such an animal from foreigners and then offer it as a sacrifice to your God. Such animals will not be accepted on your behalf, for they are mutilated or defective."

²⁶And the LORD said to Moses, ²⁷"When a calf or lamb or goat is born, it must be left with its mother for seven days. From the eighth day

on, it will be acceptable as a special gift to the LORD. ²⁸But you must not slaughter a mother animal and her offspring on the same day, whether from the herd or the flock. ²⁹When you bring a thanksgiving offering to the LORD, sacrifice it properly so you will be accepted. ³⁰Eat the entire sacrificial animal on the day it is presented. Do not leave any of it until the next morning. I am the LORD.

³¹"You must faithfully keep all my commands by putting them into practice, for I am the LORD. ³²Do not bring shame on my holy name, for I will display my holiness among the people of Israel. I am the LORD who makes you holy. ³³It was I who rescued you from the land of Egypt, that I might be your God. I am the LORD."

23 THE APPOINTED FESTIVALS The LORD said to Moses, ²"Give the following instructions to the people of Israel. These are the LORD's appointed festivals, which you are to proclaim as official days for holy assembly.

³"You have six days each week for your ordinary work, but the seventh day is a Sabbath day of complete rest, an official day for holy assembly. It is the LORD's Sabbath day, and it must be observed wherever you live.

⁴"In addition to the Sabbath, these are the LORD's appointed festivals, the official days for holy assembly that are to be celebrated at their proper times each year.

PASSOVER AND THE FESTIVAL OF UNLEAVENED BREAD ⁵"The LORD's Passover begins at sundown on the fourteenth day of the first month.* ⁶On the next day, the fifteenth day of the month, you must begin celebrating the Festival of Unleavened Bread. This festival to the LORD continues for seven days, and during that time the bread you eat must be made without yeast. ⁷On the first day of the festival, all the people must stop their ordinary work and observe an official day for holy assembly. ⁸For seven days you must present special gifts to the LORD. On the seventh day the people must again stop all their ordinary work to observe an official day for holy assembly."

CELEBRATION OF FIRST HARVEST ⁹Then the LORD said to Moses, ¹⁰"Give the following instructions to the people of Israel. When you enter the land I am giving you and you harvest its first crops, bring the priest a bundle of grain from the first cutting of your grain harvest. ¹¹On the day after the Sabbath, the priest will lift it

....

ONLY THE BEST
(22:19-25) Animals with defects were not acceptable as sacrifices because they did not represent God's holy nature. Only "perfect" animals were used. God also wants us to give our best with our time, talents, and treasures. When we offer our best, instead of the leftovers, we show the true meaning of worship and testify to God's supreme worth.

TRADITIONS
(23:1-4) God established several national holidays each year for celebration, fellowship, and worship. Much can be learned about people by observing the holidays they celebrate and the way they celebrate them. What do your holiday traditions say about your values?

22:19 Or *it*.   **22:23** Or *cow*.   **23:5** This day in the ancient Hebrew lunar calendar occurred in late March, April, or early May.

FESTIVALS

Besides enjoying one Sabbath day of rest each week, the Israelites also enjoyed 19 days when national holidays were celebrated.

FESTIVAL	WHAT IT CELEBRATED	ITS PURPOSE
Passover One day (Lev 23:5)	When God spared the lives of Israel's firstborn children in Egypt and freed the Hebrews from slavery	Reminded the people of God's deliverance
Unleavened Bread Seven days (Lev 23:6-8)	The Exodus from Egypt	Reminded the people they were leaving the old life behind and entering a new way of living
Firstfruits One day (Lev 23:9-14)	The first crops of the barley harvest	Reminded the people how God provided for them
Harvest (Pentecost) One day (Lev 23:15-22)	The end of the barley harvest and beginning of the wheat harvest	Showed joy and thanksgiving over the bountiful harvest
Trumpets One day (Lev 23:23-25)	The beginning of the seventh month (civil new year)	Restored fellowship with God
Day of Atonement One day (Lev 23:26-32)	The removal of sin from the people and the nation	Restored fellowship with God
Shelters Seven days (Lev 23:33-43)	God's protection and guidance in the wilderness	Renewed Israel's commitment to God and trust in his guidance and protection

up before the LORD so it may be accepted on your behalf. ¹²On that same day you must sacrifice a one-year-old male lamb with no defects as a burnt offering to the LORD. ¹³With it you must present a grain offering consisting of four quarts* of choice flour moistened with olive oil. It will be a special gift, a pleasing aroma to the LORD. You must also offer one quart* of wine as a liquid offering. ¹⁴Do not eat any bread or roasted grain or fresh kernels on that day until you bring this offering to your God. This is a permanent law for you, and it must be observed from generation to generation wherever you live.

THE FESTIVAL OF HARVEST ¹⁵"From the day after the Sabbath—the day you bring the bundle of grain to be lifted up as a special offering—count off seven full weeks. ¹⁶Keep counting until the day after the seventh Sabbath, fifty days later. Then present an offering of new grain to the LORD. ¹⁷From wherever you live, bring two loaves of bread to be lifted up before the LORD

as a special offering. Make these loaves from four quarts of choice flour, and bake them with yeast. They will be an offering to the LORD from the first of your crops. ¹⁸Along with the bread, present seven one-year-old male lambs with no defects, one young bull, and two rams as burnt offerings to the LORD. These burnt offerings, together with the grain offerings and liquid offerings, will be a special gift, a pleasing aroma to the LORD. ¹⁹Then you must offer one male goat as a sin offering and two one-year-old male lambs as a peace offering.

²⁰"The priest will lift up the two lambs as a special offering to the LORD, together with the loaves representing the first of your crops. These offerings, which are holy to the LORD, belong to the priests. ²¹That same day will be proclaimed an official day for holy assembly, a day on which you do no ordinary work. This is a permanent law for you, and it must be observed from generation to generation wherever you live.*

²²"When you harvest the crops of your land, do not harvest the grain along the edges of your fields, and do not pick up what the harvesters drop. Leave it for the poor and the foreigners living among you. I am the LORD your God."

23:13a Hebrew ²/₁₀ of an ephah [4.4 liters]; also in 23:17.
23:13b Hebrew ¼ of a hin [1 liter]. **23:21** This celebration, called the Festival of Harvest or the Festival of Weeks, was later called the Festival of Pentecost (see Acts 2:1). It is celebrated today as Shavuot (or Shabuoth).

THE FESTIVAL OF TRUMPETS ²³The Lord said to Moses, ²⁴"Give the following instructions to the people of Israel. On the first day of the appointed month in early autumn,* you are to observe a day of complete rest. It will be an official day for holy assembly, a day commemorated with loud blasts of a trumpet. ²⁵You must do no ordinary work on that day. Instead, you are to present special gifts to the Lord."

THE DAY OF ATONEMENT ²⁶Then the Lord said to Moses, ²⁷"Be careful to celebrate the Day of Atonement on the tenth day of that same month—nine days after the Festival of Trumpets.* You must observe it as an official day for holy assembly, a day to deny yourselves* and present special gifts to the Lord. ²⁸Do no work during that entire day because it is the Day of Atonement, when offerings of purification are made for you, making you right with* the Lord your God. ²⁹All who do not deny themselves that day will be cut off from God's people. ³⁰And I will destroy anyone among you who does any work on that day. ³¹You must not do any work at all! This is a permanent law for you, and it must be observed from generation to generation wherever you live. ³²This will be a Sabbath day of complete rest for you, and on that day you must deny yourselves. This day of rest will begin at sundown on the ninth day of the month and extend until sundown on the tenth day."

THE FESTIVAL OF SHELTERS ³³And the Lord said to Moses, ³⁴"Give the following instructions to the people of Israel. Begin celebrating the Festival of Shelters* on the fifteenth day of the appointed month—five days after the Day of Atonement.* This festival to the Lord will last for seven days. ³⁵On the first day of the festival you must proclaim an official day for holy assembly, when you do no ordinary work. ³⁶For seven days you must present special gifts to the Lord. The eighth day is another holy day on which you present your special gifts to the Lord. This will be a solemn occasion, and no ordinary work may be done that day.

³⁷("These are the Lord's appointed festivals. Celebrate them each year as official days for holy assembly by presenting special gifts to the Lord—burnt offerings, grain offerings, sacrifices, and liquid offerings—each on its proper day. ³⁸These festivals must be observed in addition to the Lord's regular Sabbath days, and the offerings are in addition to your personal gifts, the offerings you give to fulfill your vows, and the voluntary offerings you present to the Lord.)

³⁹"Remember that this seven-day festival to the Lord—the Festival of Shelters—begins on the fifteenth day of the appointed month,* after you have harvested all the produce of the land. The first day and the eighth day of the festival will be days of complete rest. ⁴⁰On the first day gather branches from magnificent trees*—palm fronds, boughs from leafy trees, and willows that grow by the streams. Then celebrate with joy before the Lord your God for seven days. ⁴¹You must observe this festival to the Lord for seven days every year. This is a permanent law for you, and it must be observed in the appointed month* from generation to generation. ⁴²For seven days you must live outside in little shelters. All native-born Israelites must live in shelters. ⁴³This will remind each new generation of Israelites that I made their ancestors live in shelters when I rescued them from the land of Egypt. I am the Lord your God."

⁴⁴So Moses gave the Israelites these instructions regarding the annual festivals of the Lord.

24

PURE OIL AND HOLY BREAD The Lord said to Moses, ²"Command the people of Israel to bring you pure oil of pressed olives for the light, to keep the lamps burning continually. ³This is the lampstand that stands in the Tabernacle, in front of the inner curtain that shields the Ark of the Covenant.* Aaron must keep the lamps burning in the Lord's presence all night. This is a permanent law for you, and it must be observed from generation to generation. ⁴Aaron and the priests must tend the lamps on the pure gold lampstand continually in the Lord's presence.

⁵"You must bake twelve loaves of bread from choice flour, using four quarts* of flour for each loaf. ⁶Place the bread before the Lord on the pure gold table, and arrange the loaves in two rows, with six loaves in each row. ⁷Put some pure frankincense near each row to serve as a representative offering, a special

23:24 Hebrew *On the first day of the seventh month.* This day in the ancient Hebrew lunar calendar occurred in September or October. This festival is celebrated today as Rosh Hashanah, the Jewish new year.   23:27a Hebrew *on the tenth day of the seventh month;* see 23:24 and the note there. This day in the ancient Hebrew lunar calendar occurred in September or October. It is celebrated today as Yom Kippur.   23:27b Or *to fast;* similarly in 23:29, 32.   23:28 Or *when atonement is made for you before.*   23:34a Or *Festival of Booths,* or *Festival of Tabernacles.* This was earlier called the Festival of the Final Harvest or Festival of Ingathering (see Exod 23:16b). It is celebrated today as Sukkot (or Succoth).   23:34b Hebrew *on the fifteenth day of the seventh month;* see 23:27a and the note there.   23:39 Hebrew *on the fifteenth day of the seventh month.*   23:40 Or *gather fruit from majestic trees.*   23:41 Hebrew *the seventh month.*   24:3 Hebrew *in the Tent of Meeting, outside the inner curtain of the Testimony;* see note on 16:13.   24:5 Hebrew ²⁄₁₀ *of an ephah* [4.4 liters].

gift presented to the LORD. [8]Every Sabbath day this bread must be laid out before the LORD. The bread is to be received from the people of Israel as a requirement of the eternal covenant. [9]The loaves of bread will belong to Aaron and his descendants, who must eat them in a sacred place, for they are most holy. It is the permanent right of the priests to claim this portion of the special gifts presented to the LORD."

AN EXAMPLE OF JUST PUNISHMENT

[10]One day a man who had an Israelite mother and an Egyptian father came out of his tent and got into a fight with one of the Israelite men. [11]During the fight, this son of an Israelite woman blasphemed the Name of the LORD* with a curse. So the man was brought to Moses for judgment. His mother was Shelomith, the daughter of Dibri of the tribe of Dan. [12]They kept the man in custody until the LORD's will in the matter should become clear to them.

[13]Then the LORD said to Moses, [14]"Take the blasphemer outside the camp, and tell all those who heard the curse to lay their hands on his head. Then let the entire community stone him to death. [15]Say to the people of Israel: Those who curse their God will be punished for their sin. [16]Anyone who blasphemes the Name of the LORD must be stoned to death by the whole community of Israel. Any native-born Israelite or foreigner among you who blasphemes the Name of the LORD must be put to death.

[17]"Anyone who takes another person's life must be put to death.

[18]"Anyone who kills another person's animal must pay for it in full—a live animal for the animal that was killed.

[19]"Anyone who injures another person must be dealt with according to the injury inflicted— [20]a fracture for a fracture, an eye for an eye, a tooth for a tooth. Whatever anyone does to injure another person must be paid back in kind.

[21]"Whoever kills an animal must pay for it in full, but whoever kills another person must be put to death.

[22]"This same standard applies both to native-born Israelites and to the foreigners living among you. I am the LORD your God."

[23]After Moses gave all these instructions to the Israelites, they took the blasphemer outside the camp and stoned him to death. The Israelites did just as the LORD had commanded Moses.

24:11 Hebrew *the Name*; also in 24:16b.   25:9 Hebrew *on the tenth day of the seventh month, on the Day of Atonement;* see 23:27a and the note there.

25

THE SABBATH YEAR

While Moses was on Mount Sinai, the LORD said to him, [2]"Give the following instructions to the people of Israel. When you have entered the land I am giving you, the land itself must observe a Sabbath rest before the LORD every seventh year. [3]For six years you may plant your fields and prune your vineyards and harvest your crops, [4]but during the seventh year the land must have a Sabbath year of complete rest. It is the LORD's Sabbath. Do not plant your fields or prune your vineyards during that year. [5]And don't store away the crops that grow on their own or gather the grapes from your unpruned vines. The land must have a year of complete rest. [6]But you may eat whatever the land produces on its own during its Sabbath. This applies to you, your male and female servants, your hired workers, and the temporary residents who live with you. [7]Your livestock and the wild animals in your land will also be allowed to eat what the land produces.

THE YEAR OF JUBILEE

[8]"In addition, you must count off seven Sabbath years, seven sets of seven years, adding up to forty-nine years in all. [9]Then on the Day of Atonement in the fiftieth year,* blow the ram's horn loud and long throughout the land. [10]Set this year apart as holy, a time to proclaim freedom throughout the land for all who live there. It will be a jubilee year for you, when each of you may return to the land that belonged to your ancestors and return to your own clan. [11]This fiftieth year will be a jubilee for you. During that year you must not plant your fields or store away any of the crops that grow on their own, and don't gather the grapes from your unpruned vines. [12]It will be a jubilee year for you, and you must keep it holy. But you may eat whatever the land produces on its own. [13]In the Year of Jubilee each of you may return to the land that belonged to your ancestors.

[14]"When you make an agreement with your neighbor to buy or sell property, you must not take advantage of each other. [15]When you buy land from your neighbor, the price you pay must be based on the number of years since the last jubilee. The seller must set the price by taking into account the number of years remaining until the next Year of Jubilee. [16]The more years until the next jubilee, the higher the price; the fewer years, the lower the price. After all, the person selling the land is actually selling you a certain number of harvests. [17]Show your fear of God by not taking advantage of each other. I am the LORD your God.

¹⁸"If you want to live securely in the land, follow my decrees and obey my regulations. ¹⁹Then the land will yield large crops, and you will eat your fill and live securely in it. ²⁰But you might ask, 'What will we eat during the seventh year, since we are not allowed to plant or harvest crops that year?' ²¹Be assured that I will send my blessing for you in the sixth year, so the land will produce a crop large enough for three years. ²²When you plant your fields in the eighth year, you will still be eating from the large crop of the sixth year. In fact, you will still be eating from that large crop when the new crop is harvested in the ninth year.

REDEMPTION OF PROPERTY ²³"The land must never be sold on a permanent basis, for the land belongs to me. You are only foreigners and tenant farmers working for me.

²⁴"With every purchase of land you must grant the seller the right to buy it back. ²⁵If one of your fellow Israelites falls into poverty and is forced to sell some family land, then a close relative should buy it back for him. ²⁶If there is no close relative to buy the land, but the person who sold it gets enough money to buy it back, ²⁷he then has the right to redeem it from the one who bought it. The price of the land will be discounted according to the number of years until the next Year of Jubilee. In this way the original owner can then return to the land. ²⁸But if the original owner cannot afford to buy back the land, it will remain with the new owner until the next Year of Jubilee. In the jubilee year, the land must be returned to the original owners so they can return to their family land.

²⁹"Anyone who sells a house inside a walled town has the right to buy it back for a full year after its sale. During that year, the seller retains the right to buy it back. ³⁰But if it is not bought back within a year, the sale of the house within the walled town cannot be reversed. It will become the permanent property of the buyer. It will not be returned to the original owner in the Year of Jubilee. ³¹But a house in a village—a settlement without fortified walls—will be treated like property in the countryside. Such a house may be bought back at any time, and it must be returned to the original owner in the Year of Jubilee.

³²"The Levites always have the right to buy back a house they have sold within the towns allotted to them. ³³And any property that is sold by the Levites—all houses within the Levitical towns—must be returned in the Year of Jubilee. After all, the houses in the towns reserved for the Levites are the only property they own in all Israel. ³⁴The open pastureland around the Levitical towns may never be sold. It is their permanent possession.

REDEMPTION OF THE POOR AND ENSLAVED
³⁵"If one of your fellow Israelites falls into poverty and cannot support himself, support him as you would a foreigner or a temporary resident and allow him to live with you. ³⁶Do not charge interest or make a profit at his expense. Instead, show your fear of God by letting him live with you as your relative. ³⁷Remember, do not charge interest on money you lend him or make a profit on food you sell him. ³⁸I am the LORD your God, who brought you out of the land of Egypt to give you the land of Canaan and to be your God.

³⁹"If one of your fellow Israelites falls into poverty and is forced to sell himself to you, do not treat him as a slave. ⁴⁰Treat him instead as a hired worker or as a temporary resident who lives with you, and he will serve you only until the Year of Jubilee. ⁴¹At that time he and his children will no longer be obligated to you, and they will return to their clans and go back to the land originally allotted to their ancestors. ⁴²The people of Israel are my servants, whom I brought out of the land of Egypt, so they must never be sold as slaves. ⁴³Show your fear of God by not treating them harshly.

⁴⁴"However, you may purchase male and female slaves from among the nations around you. ⁴⁵You may also purchase the children of temporary residents who live among you, including those who have been born in your land. You may treat them as your property, ⁴⁶passing them on to your children as a permanent inheritance. You may treat them as slaves, but you must never treat your fellow Israelites this way.

⁴⁷"Suppose a foreigner or temporary resident becomes rich while living among you. If any of your fellow Israelites fall into poverty and are forced to sell themselves to such a foreigner or to a member of his family, ⁴⁸they still retain the right to be bought back, even after they have been purchased. They may be bought back by a brother, ⁴⁹an uncle, or a cousin. In fact, anyone from the extended family may buy them back. They may also redeem themselves if they have prospered. ⁵⁰They will negotiate the price of their freedom with the person who bought them. The price will be based on the number of years from the time they were sold until the next Year of Jubilee—whatever it would cost to hire a worker for that period of time. ⁵¹If many years still remain until the

jubilee, they will repay the proper proportion of what they received when they sold themselves. ⁵²If only a few years remain until the Year of Jubilee, they will repay a small amount for their redemption. ⁵³The foreigner must treat them as workers hired on a yearly basis. You must not allow a foreigner to treat any of your fellow Israelites harshly. ⁵⁴If any Israelites have not been bought back by the time the Year of Jubilee arrives, they and their children must be set free at that time. ⁵⁵For the people of Israel belong to me. They are my servants, whom I brought out of the land of Egypt. I am the LORD your God.

26 BLESSINGS FOR OBEDIENCE
"Do not make idols or set up carved images, or sacred pillars, or sculptured stones in your land so you may worship them. I am the LORD your God. ²You must keep my Sabbath days of rest and show reverence for my sanctuary. I am the LORD.

³"If you follow my decrees and are careful to obey my commands, ⁴I will send you the seasonal rains. The land will then yield its crops, and the trees of the field will produce their fruit. ⁵Your threshing season will overlap with the grape harvest, and your grape harvest will overlap with the season of planting grain. You will eat your fill and live securely in your own land.

⁶"I will give you peace in the land, and you will be able to sleep with no cause for fear. I will rid the land of wild animals and keep your enemies out of your land. ⁷In fact, you will chase down your enemies and slaughter them with your swords. ⁸Five of you will chase a hundred, and a hundred of you will chase ten thousand! All your enemies will fall beneath your sword.

⁹"I will look favorably upon you, making you fertile and multiplying your people. And I will fulfill my covenant with you. ¹⁰You will have such a surplus of crops that you will need to clear out the old grain to make room for the new harvest! ¹¹I will live among you, and I will not despise you. ¹²I will walk among you; I will be your God, and you will be my people. ¹³I am the LORD your God, who brought you out of the land of Egypt so you would no longer be their slaves. I broke the yoke of slavery from your neck so you can walk with your heads held high.

PUNISHMENTS FOR DISOBEDIENCE
¹⁴"However, if you do not listen to me or obey all these commands, ¹⁵and if you break my covenant by rejecting my decrees, treating my regulations with contempt, and refusing to obey my

MY STORY: Kara

Okay, I know that most people don't usually read Leviticus unless they have to. I'm one of them. But since I was involved in a read-through-the-Bible-in-a-year program, I had to read every word of this book.

What hit me most as I read all this stuff about laws and sacrifices was how seriously God takes the way his people obey or disobey him. And he stated it so clearly for the Israelites. For example, in chapter 26 God says that obedience will bring prosperity in the Promised Land, but disobedience will bring nothing but trouble. How could the people be so stupid, I thought as I read. Why would they ever disobey? Easy for me to say, right? But even though I have more evidence of God's love than those people had, I still take God for granted and even disobey him on purpose at times.

Sometimes, what God wants me to do seems pretty clear. Like the time I needed to apologize to my mom for something I had said. I asked God to forgive me and went to talk with Mom.

God takes obedience seriously. That's what I need to do, too.

commands, ¹⁶I will punish you. I will bring sudden terrors upon you—wasting diseases and burning fevers that will cause your eyes to fail and your life to ebb away. You will plant your crops in vain because your enemies will eat them. ¹⁷I will turn against you, and you will be defeated by your enemies. Those who hate you will rule over you, and you will run even when no one is chasing you!

¹⁸"And if, in spite of all this, you still disobey me, I will punish you seven times over for your sins. ¹⁹I will break your proud spirit by making the skies as unyielding as iron and the earth as

....

WARNINGS
(26:1) The people of Israel were warned over and over against worshiping idols. We wonder how they could deceive themselves with these objects of wood and stone. Yet God could give us the same warning about the idols in our lives. An idol is anything more important to us than God. Money, looks, success, security, and popularity are just a few of today's idols. As you look at these false gods that promise everything you want but nothing you need, does idolatry seem so far removed from your experience?

hard as bronze. 20All your work will be for nothing, for your land will yield no crops, and your trees will bear no fruit.

21"If even then you remain hostile toward me and refuse to obey me, I will inflict disaster on you seven times over for your sins. 22I will send wild animals that will rob you of your children and destroy your livestock. Your numbers will dwindle, and your roads will be deserted.

23"And if you fail to learn the lesson and continue your hostility toward me, 24then I myself will be hostile toward you. I will personally strike you with calamity seven times over for your sins. 25I will send armies against you to carry out the curse of the covenant you have broken. When you run to your towns for safety, I will send a plague to destroy you there, and you will be handed over to your enemies. 26I will destroy your food supply, so that ten women will need only one oven to bake bread for their families. They will ration your food by weight, and though you have food to eat, you will not be satisfied.

27"If in spite of all this you still refuse to listen and still remain hostile toward me, 28then I will give full vent to my hostility. I myself will punish you seven times over for your sins. 29Then you will eat the flesh of your own sons and daughters. 30I will destroy your pagan shrines and knock down your places of worship. I will leave your lifeless corpses piled on top of your lifeless idols,* and I will despise you. 31I will make your cities desolate and destroy your places of pagan worship. I will take no pleasure in your offerings that should be a pleasing aroma to me. 32Yes, I myself will devastate your land, and your enemies who come to occupy it will be appalled at what they see. 33I will scatter you among the nations and bring out my sword against you. Your land will become desolate, and your cities will lie in ruins. 34Then at last the land will enjoy its neglected Sabbath years as it lies desolate while you are in exile in the land of your enemies. Then the land will finally rest and enjoy the Sabbaths it missed. 35As long as the land lies in ruins, it will enjoy the rest you never allowed it to take every seventh year while you lived in it.

36"And for those of you who survive, I will

demoralize you in the land of your enemies. You will live in such fear that the sound of a leaf driven by the wind will send you fleeing. You will run as though fleeing from a sword, and you will fall even when no one pursues you. 37Though no one is chasing you, you will stumble over each other as though fleeing from a sword. You will have no power to stand up against your enemies. 38You will die among the foreign nations and be devoured in the land of your enemies. 39Those of you who survive will waste away in your enemies' lands because of their sins and the sins of their ancestors.

40"But at last my people will confess their sins and the sins of their ancestors for betraying me and being hostile toward me. 41When I have turned their hostility back on them and brought them to the land of their enemies, then at last their stubborn hearts will be humbled, and they will pay for their sins. 42Then I will remember my covenant with Jacob and my covenant with Isaac and my covenant with Abraham, and I will remember the land. 43For the land must be abandoned to enjoy its years of Sabbath rest as it lies deserted. At last the people will pay for their sins, for they have continually rejected my regulations and despised my decrees.

44"But despite all this, I will not utterly reject or despise them while they are in exile in the land of their enemies. I will not cancel my covenant with them by wiping them out, for I am the LORD their God. 45For their sakes I will remember my ancient covenant with their ancestors, whom I brought out of the land of Egypt in the sight of all the nations, that I might be their God. I am the LORD."

46These are the decrees, regulations, and instructions that the LORD gave through Moses on Mount Sinai as evidence of the relationship between himself and the Israelites.

27 REDEMPTION OF GIFTS OFFERED TO THE LORD

The LORD said to Moses, 2"Give the following instructions to the people of Israel. If anyone makes a special vow to dedicate someone to the LORD by paying the value of that person, 3here is the scale of values to be used. A man between the ages of twenty and sixty is valued at fifty shekels* of silver, as measured by the sanctuary shekel. 4A woman of that age is valued at thirty shekels* of silver. 5A boy between the ages of five and twenty is valued at twenty shekels of silver; a girl of that age is valued at ten shekels* of silver. 6A

....

GROWTH
(26:40-45) In Exodus 34:6, God declared his mercy, grace, love, and faithfulness to Moses. This passage in Leviticus shows these characteristics in action. Even if the Israelites chose to disobey him, God refused to give up on them. He would still give them the opportunity to seek his forgiveness. God's purpose was not to destroy them but to help them grow. His faithfulness to Israel can provide encouragement for us today.

26:30 The Hebrew term (literally *round things*) probably alludes to dung.   27:3 Or *20 ounces* [570 grams].   27:4 Or *12 ounces* [342 grams].   27:5 Or *A boy . . . 8 ounces* [228 grams] *of silver; a girl . . . 4 ounces* [114 grams].

boy between the ages of one month and five years is valued at five shekels of silver; a girl of that age is valued at three shekels* of silver. ⁷A man older than sixty is valued at fifteen shekels of silver; a woman of that age is valued at ten shekels* of silver. ⁸If you desire to make such a vow but cannot afford to pay the required amount, take the person to the priest. He will determine the amount for you to pay based on what you can afford.

⁹"If your vow involves giving an animal that is acceptable as an offering to the LORD, any gift to the LORD will be considered holy. ¹⁰You may not exchange or substitute it for another animal—neither a good animal for a bad one nor a bad animal for a good one. But if you do exchange one animal for another, then both the original animal and its substitute will be considered holy. ¹¹If your vow involves an unclean animal—one that is not acceptable as an offering to the LORD—then you must bring the animal to the priest. ¹²He will assess its value, and his assessment will be final, whether high or low. ¹³If you want to buy back the animal, you must pay the value set by the priest, plus 20 percent.

¹⁴"If someone dedicates a house to the LORD, the priest will come to assess its value. The priest's assessment will be final, whether high or low. ¹⁵If the person who dedicated the house wants to buy it back, he must pay the value set by the priest, plus 20 percent. Then the house will again be his.

¹⁶"If someone dedicates to the LORD a piece of his family property, its value will be assessed according to the amount of seed required to plant it—fifty shekels of silver for a field planted with five bushels of barley seed.* ¹⁷If the field is dedicated to the LORD in the Year of Jubilee, then the entire assessment will apply. ¹⁸But if the field is dedicated after the Year of Jubilee, the priest will assess the land's value in proportion to the number of years left until the next Year of Jubilee. Its assessed value is reduced each year. ¹⁹If the person who dedicated the field wants to buy it back, he must pay the value set by the priest, plus 20 percent. Then the field will again be legally his. ²⁰But if he does not want to buy it back, and it is sold to someone else, the field can no longer be bought back. ²¹When the field is released in the Year of Jubilee, it will be holy, a field specially

set apart* for the LORD. It will become the property of the priests.

²²"If someone dedicates to the LORD a field he has purchased but which is not part of his family property, ²³the priest will assess its value based on the number of years left until the next Year of Jubilee. On that day he must give the assessed value of the land as a sacred donation to the LORD. ²⁴In the Year of Jubilee the field must be returned to the person from whom he purchased it, the one who inherited it as family property. ²⁵(All the payments must be measured by the weight of the sanctuary shekel,* which equals twenty gerahs.)

²⁶"You may not dedicate a firstborn animal to the LORD, for the firstborn of your cattle, sheep, and goats already belong to him. ²⁷However, you may buy back the firstborn of a ceremonially unclean animal by paying the priest's assessment of its worth, plus 20 percent. If you do not buy it back, the priest will sell it at its assessed value.

²⁸"However, anything specially set apart for the LORD—whether a person, an animal, or family property—must never be sold or bought back. Anything devoted in this way has been set apart as holy, and it belongs to the LORD. ²⁹No person specially set apart for destruction may be bought back. Such a person must be put to death.

³⁰"One-tenth of the produce of the land, whether grain from the fields or fruit from the trees, belongs to the LORD and must be set apart to him as holy. ³¹If you want to buy back the LORD's tenth of the grain or fruit, you must pay its value, plus 20 percent. ³²Count off every tenth animal from your herds and flocks and set them apart for the LORD as holy. ³³You may not pick and choose between good and bad animals, and you may not substitute one for another. But if you do exchange one animal for another, then both the original animal and its substitute will be considered holy and cannot be bought back."

³⁴These are the commands that the LORD gave through Moses on Mount Sinai for the Israelites.

···

ALWAYS THE SAME
(27:34) The book of Leviticus is filled with the commands God gave his people at the foot of Mount Sinai. From these commands we can learn much about God's nature. At first glance, Leviticus seems irrelevant to our high-tech world. But digging a little deeper, we realize that the book still speaks to us today. After all, God has not changed (see Heb 13:8). His principles are for all times. As people and society change, we need to continue to apply the principles of God's law to our present circumstances.

27:6 Or *A boy . . . 2 ounces* [57 grams] *of silver; a girl . . . 1.2 ounces* [34 grams].   27:7 Or *A man . . . 6 ounces* [171 grams] *of silver; a woman . . . 4 ounces* [114 grams].   27:16 Hebrew *50 shekels* [20 ounces, or 570 grams] *of silver for a homer* [182 liters] *of barley seed.*   27:21 The Hebrew term used here refers to the complete consecration of things or people to the LORD, either by destroying them or by giving them as an offering; also in 27:28, 29.   27:25 Each shekel was about 0.4 ounces [11 grams] in weight.

NUMBERS

At noon, a weary traveler who had been walking all day wanted to get out of the heat and rest. Thankfully he noticed a huge tree with branches forming a canopy of shade. He stumbled to the shade of the tree, threw down his pack, spread his blanket, and was soon blissfully asleep. He awoke feeling refreshed, gazed into the tree, and complained: "What a useless tree. There's no fruit!" He had forgotten about the tree's wonderful shade.

That traveler was a lot like the people of Israel. At the start of the book of Numbers, the Israelites seemed to be sitting in God's "shade." They were about to enter the Promised Land; the future looked great. But life took a bleak turn when the spies sent to Canaan returned. Instead of believing the good report of two of the spies, the people chose to focus on the negative report that the other ten brought back. They had forgotten God's promise to give them the land.

After hearing little but complaints from the people of Israel, God gave them a taste of his judgment. This generation would never enter the Promised Land. Only their children would.

Are we much different from the complaining Israelites? God has done, is doing, and will do so much for us. Yet we complain. "God, what are you doing?" "God, you don't care!" "God, how could you do this to me?" We don't trust him even though he proves himself to be trustworthy time after time. Are you trusting or complaining?

STATS

PURPOSE
To recount how Israel prepared to enter the Promised Land, how they sinned and were punished, and how they prepared to try again

AUTHOR
Moses

ORIGINAL AUDIENCE
The people of Israel

DATE WRITTEN
1450–1410 B.C.

SETTING
The Sinai wilderness, as well as lands just south and east of Canaan

KEY PEOPLE
Moses, Aaron, Miriam, Joshua, Caleb, Eleazar, Korah, Balaam

KEY PLACES
Mount Sinai, the Promised Land, Kadesh, Mount Hor, the plains of Moab

TIMELINE

1805 B.C.
Joseph dies

SLAVERY IN EGYPT
1446
Exodus from Egypt

1445
Ten Commandments

1444
First census

1443
First spy mission

WILDERNESS WANDERINGS
1407
Second census; Balaam prophesies

1406
Joshua appointed; Canaan entered

1375
Judges begin to rule

KEY POINTS

CENSUS Moses counted the Israelites twice for the defense of Israel as they entered the Promised Land. People have to be organized, trained, and led to be effective in making a difference in their world. Before beginning great tasks, it is always wise to count the cost of what lies ahead.

REBELLION At Kadesh the people of Israel rebelled, having accepted the negative report of 10 out of 12 spies. Rebellion against God is always serious. Usually rebellion is not an abrupt, radical departure from God; instead, it is the result of long-term drifting, often characterized by complaining and criticizing.

WANDERING Because they rebelled, the Israelites had a forty-year stay in the wilderness. During this time God trained a new generation to follow him while those who still had wrong attitudes died. He judges sin not just because he dislikes it but because he is holy and cannot tolerate it.

CANAAN Canaan was the Promised Land—the land God had promised to Abraham, Isaac, and Jacob. Canaan was to be the dwelling place of God's people, those set apart for true worship. Today, the place for true worship can be found in the human heart—the home of the Holy Spirit.

Modern names and boundaries are shown in gray.

KEY PLACES

❶ MOUNT SINAI

Numbers begins at Mount Sinai with Moses taking a census of the men eligible for battle. As the battle preparations began, the people also prepared for the spiritual warfare they would face. The Promised Land was full of wicked people who would try to entice the Israelites to sin. God, therefore, taught Moses and the Israelites how to live rightly (1:1–12:15).

❷ WILDERNESS OF PARAN

After a full year at Mount Sinai, the Israelites broke camp and began their march toward the Promised Land by moving into the wilderness of Paran. From there, one leader from each tribe was sent to explore the new land. After 40 days they

returned, and all but Joshua and Caleb were too afraid to enter. Because of their lack of faith, the Israelites were made to wander in the wilderness for 40 years (12:16–19:22).

❸ KADESH

With the years of wandering nearing an end, the Israelites set their sights once again on the Promised Land. Kadesh was the oasis where they spent most of their wilderness years. Miriam died here. And it was here that Moses angrily struck the rock, which kept him from entering the Promised Land (20).

❹ ARAD

When the king of Arad heard that Israel was on the move, he attacked, but he was soundly

defeated. Moses then led the people southward and eastward around the Dead Sea (21:1-3).

❺ EDOM

The Israelites wanted to travel through Edom, but the king of Edom refused them passage (20:14-22). So they traveled around Edom and became very discouraged. The people complained, and God sent poisonous snakes to punish them. Only by looking at a bronze snake on a pole could those bitten be healed (21:4-9).

❻ AMMON

Next, King Sihon of the Amorites refused Israel passage. When the Amorites attacked, Israel defeated them (21:21-32).

❼ BASHAN

After capturing the Amorite country, the Israelites moved up to Bashan. King Og attacked, but he was also defeated (21:33-35).

❽ PLAINS OF MOAB

The people camped on the plains of Moab, east of the Jordan River opposite Jericho. They were on the verge of entering the Promised Land (22:1).

❾ MOAB

King Balak of Moab, terrified of the Israelites, called upon Balaam, a famous sorcerer, to curse Israel from the mountains above where the Israelites camped. But the Lord caused Balaam to bless them instead (22:2–24:25).

❿ GILEAD

The tribes of Reuben and Gad decided to settle in the fertile country of Gilead east of the Jordan River because it was a good land for their sheep. But first they promised to help the other tribes conquer the land west of the Jordan River (32).

1 REGISTRATION OF ISRAEL'S TROOPS

A year after Israel's departure from Egypt, the LORD spoke to Moses in the Tabernacle* in the wilderness of Sinai. On the first day of the second month* of that year he said, ²"From the whole community of Israel, record the names of all the warriors by their clans and families. List all the men ³twenty years old or older who are able to go to war. You and Aaron must register the troops, ⁴and you will be assisted by one family leader from each tribe.

⁵"These are the tribes and the names of the leaders who will assist you:

Tribe	Leader
Reuben	Elizur son of Shedeur
⁶ Simeon	Shelumiel son of Zurishaddai
⁷ Judah	Nahshon son of Amminadab
⁸ Issachar	Nethanel son of Zuar
⁹ Zebulun	Eliab son of Helon
¹⁰ Ephraim son of Joseph	Elishama son of Ammihud
Manasseh son of Joseph	Gamaliel son of Pedahzur
¹¹ Benjamin	Abidan son of Gideoni
¹² Dan	Ahiezer son of Ammishaddai
¹³ Asher	Pagiel son of Ocran
¹⁴ Gad	Eliasaph son of Deuel
¹⁵ Naphtali	Ahira son of Enan

¹⁶These are the chosen leaders of the community, the leaders of their ancestral tribes, the heads of the clans of Israel."

¹⁷So Moses and Aaron called together these chosen leaders, ¹⁸and they assembled the whole community of Israel on that very day.* All the people were registered according to their ancestry by their clans and families. The men of Israel who were twenty years old or older were listed one by one, ¹⁹just as the LORD had commanded Moses. So Moses recorded their names in the wilderness of Sinai.

²⁰⁻²¹This is the number of men twenty years old or older who were able to go to war, as their names were listed in the records of their clans and families*:

Tribe	Number
Reuben (Jacob's* oldest son)	46,500
²²⁻²³ Simeon	59,300
²⁴⁻²⁵ Gad	45,650

²⁶⁻²⁷ Judah		74,600
²⁸⁻²⁹ Issachar		54,400
³⁰⁻³¹ Zebulun		57,400
³²⁻³³ Ephraim son of Joseph		40,500
³⁴⁻³⁵ Manasseh son of Joseph		32,200
³⁶⁻³⁷ Benjamin		35,400
³⁸⁻³⁹ Dan		62,700
⁴⁰⁻⁴¹ Asher		41,500
⁴²⁻⁴³ Naphtali		53,400

⁴⁴These were the men registered by Moses and Aaron and the twelve leaders of Israel, all listed according to their ancestral descent. ⁴⁵They were registered by families—all the men of Israel who were twenty years old or older and able to go to war. ⁴⁶The total number was 603,550.

⁴⁷But this total did not include the Levites. ⁴⁸For the LORD had said to Moses, ⁴⁹"Do not include the tribe of Levi in the registration; do not count them with the rest of the Israelites. ⁵⁰Put the Levites in charge of the Tabernacle of the Covenant,* along with all its furnishings and equipment. They must carry the Tabernacle and all its furnishings as you travel, and they must take care of it and camp around it. ⁵¹Whenever it is time for the Tabernacle to move, the Levites will take it down. And when it is time to stop, they will set it up again. But any unauthorized person who goes too near the Tabernacle must be put to death. ⁵²Each tribe of Israel will camp in a designated area with its own family banner. ⁵³But the Levites will camp around the Tabernacle of the Covenant to protect the community of Israel from the LORD's anger. The Levites are responsible to stand guard around the Tabernacle."

⁵⁴So the Israelites did everything just as the LORD had commanded Moses.

2 ORGANIZATION FOR ISRAEL'S CAMP

Then the LORD gave these instructions to Moses and Aaron: ²"When the Israelites set up camp, each tribe will be assigned its own area. The tribal divisions will camp beneath their family banners on all four sides of the Tabernacle,* but at some distance from it.

³⁻⁴"The divisions of Judah, Issachar, and Zebulun are to camp toward the sunrise on the east side of the Tabernacle, beneath their family banners. These are the names of the tribes, their leaders, and the numbers of their registered troops:

Tribe	Leader	Number
Judah	Nahshon son of Amminadab	74,600
⁵⁻⁶ Issachar	Nethanel son of Zuar	54,400
⁷⁻⁸ Zebulun	Eliab son of Helon	57,400

1:1a Hebrew the Tent of Meeting.   1:1b This day in the ancient Hebrew lunar calendar occurred in April or May.   1:18 Hebrew on the first day of the second month; see 1:1.   1:20-21a In the Hebrew text, this sentence (This is the number of men twenty years old or older who were able to go to war, as their names were listed in the records of their clans and families) is repeated in 1:22, 24, 26, 28, 30, 32, 34, 36, 38, 40, 42.   1:20-21b Hebrew Israel's. The names "Jacob" and "Israel" are often interchanged throughout the Old Testament, referring sometimes to the individual patriarch and sometimes to the nation.   1:50 Or Tabernacle of the Testimony; also in 1:53.   2:2 Hebrew the Tent of Meeting; also in 2:17.

⁹So the total of all the troops on Judah's side of the camp is 186,400. These three tribes are to lead the way whenever the Israelites travel to a new campsite.

¹⁰⁻¹¹"The divisions of Reuben, Simeon, and Gad are to camp on the south side of the Tabernacle, beneath their family banners. These are the names of the tribes, their leaders, and the numbers of their registered troops:

	Tribe	Leader	Number
	Reuben	Elizur son of Shedeur	46,500
¹²⁻¹³	Simeon	Shelumiel son of Zurishaddai	59,300
¹⁴⁻¹⁵	Gad	Eliasaph son of Deuel*	45,650

¹⁶So the total of all the troops on Reuben's side of the camp is 151,450. These three tribes will be second in line whenever the Israelites travel.

¹⁷"Then the Tabernacle, carried by the Levites, will set out from the middle of the camp. All the tribes are to travel in the same order that they camp, each in position under the appropriate family banner.

¹⁸⁻¹⁹"The divisions of Ephraim, Manasseh, and Benjamin are to camp on the west side of the Tabernacle, beneath their family banners. These are the names of the tribes, their leaders, and the numbers of their registered troops:

	Tribe	Leader	Number
	Ephraim	Elishama son of Ammihud	40,500
²⁰⁻²¹	Manasseh	Gamaliel son of Pedahzur	32,200
²²⁻²³	Benjamin	Abidan son of Gideoni	35,400

²⁴So the total of all the troops on Ephraim's side of the camp is 108,100. These three tribes will be third in line whenever the Israelites travel.

²⁵⁻²⁶"The divisions of Dan, Asher, and

Naphtali are to camp on the north side of the Tabernacle, beneath their family banners. These are the names of the tribes, their leaders, and the numbers of their registered troops:

	Tribe	Leader	Number
	Dan	Ahiezer son of Ammishaddai	62,700
²⁷⁻²⁸	Asher	Pagiel son of Ocran	41,500
²⁹⁻³⁰	Naphtali	Ahira son of Enan	53,400

³¹So the total of all the troops on Dan's side of the camp is 157,600. These three tribes will be last, marching under their banners whenever the Israelites travel."

³²In summary, the troops of Israel listed by their families totaled 603,550. ³³But as the LORD had commanded, the Levites were not included in this registration. ³⁴So the people of Israel did everything as the LORD had commanded Moses. Each clan and family set up camp and marched under their banners exactly as the LORD had instructed them.

3 LEVITES APPOINTED FOR SERVICE This is the family line of Aaron and Moses as it was recorded when the LORD spoke to Moses on Mount Sinai: ²The names of Aaron's sons were Nadab (the oldest), Abihu, Eleazar, and Ithamar. ³These sons of Aaron were anointed and ordained to minister as priests. ⁴But Nadab and Abihu died in the LORD's presence in the wilderness of Sinai when they burned before the LORD the wrong kind of fire, different than he had commanded. Since they had no sons, this left only Eleazar and Ithamar to serve as priests with their father, Aaron.

⁵Then the LORD said to Moses, ⁶"Call forward the tribe of Levi, and present them to Aaron the priest to serve as his assistants. ⁷They will serve Aaron and the whole community, performing their sacred duties in and around the Tabernacle.* ⁸They will also maintain all the furnishings of the sacred tent,* serving in the Tabernacle on behalf of all the Israelites. ⁹Assign the Levites to Aaron and his sons. They have been given from among all the people of Israel to serve as their assistants. ¹⁰Appoint Aaron and his sons to carry out the duties of the priesthood. But any unauthorized person who goes too near the sanctuary must be put to death."

¹¹And the LORD said to Moses, ¹²"Look, I have chosen the Levites from among the Israelites to serve as substitutes for all the firstborn sons of the people of Israel. The Levites belong to me,

---

CONTRAST
(2:34) This must have been one of the biggest campsites the world has ever seen! It would have taken about 12 square miles to set up tents for just the 600,000 fighting men—not to mention the women and children. Moses must have had a difficult time managing such a group. In the early stages of the journey and at Mount Sinai, the people were generally obedient to both God and Moses. But when the people left Mount Sinai and traveled across the rugged wilderness, they began to grumble and disobey. Soon problems erupted. The books of Exodus, Leviticus, and Numbers present a striking contrast between how much we can accomplish when we obey God, and how little we can accomplish when we don't.

2:14-15 As in many Hebrew manuscripts, Samaritan Pentateuch, and Latin Vulgate (see also 1:14); most Hebrew manuscripts read son of Reuel. **3:7** Hebrew around the Tent of Meeting, doing service at the Tabernacle. **3:8** Hebrew the Tent of Meeting; also in 3:25.

[13]for all the firstborn males are mine. On the day I struck down all the firstborn sons of the Egyptians, I set apart for myself all the firstborn in Israel, both of people and of animals. They are mine; I am the LORD."

REGISTRATION OF THE LEVITES

[14]The LORD spoke again to Moses in the wilderness of Sinai. He said, [15]"Record the names of the members of the tribe of Levi by their families and clans. List every male who is one month old or older." [16]So Moses listed them, just as the LORD had commanded.

[17]Levi had three sons, whose names were Gershon, Kohath, and Merari.
[18]The clans descended from Gershon were named after two of his descendants, Libni and Shimei.
[19]The clans descended from Kohath were named after four of his descendants, Amram, Izhar, Hebron, and Uzziel.
[20]The clans descended from Merari were named after two of his descendants, Mahli and Mushi.
These were the Levite clans, listed according to their family groups.

[21]The descendants of Gershon were composed of the clans descended from Libni and Shimei. [22]There were 7,500 males one month old or older among these Gershonite clans. [23]They were assigned the area to the west of the Tabernacle for their camp. [24]The leader of the Gershonite clans was Eliasaph son of Lael. [25]These two clans were responsible to care for the Tabernacle, including the sacred tent with its layers of coverings, the curtain at its entrance, [26]the curtains of the courtyard that surrounded the Tabernacle and altar, the curtain at the courtyard entrance, the ropes, and all the equipment related to their use.

[27]The descendants of Kohath were composed of the clans descended from Amram, Izhar, Hebron, and Uzziel. [28]There were 8,600* males one month old or older among these Kohathite clans. They were responsible for the care of the sanctuary, [29]and they were assigned the area south of the Tabernacle for their camp. [30]The leader of the Kohathite clans was Elizaphan son of Uzziel. [31]These four clans were responsible for the care of the Ark, the table, the lampstand, the altars, the various articles used in the sanctuary, the inner curtain, and all the equipment related to their use. [32]Eleazar, son

of Aaron the priest, was the chief administrator over all the Levites, with special responsibility for the oversight of the sanctuary.

[33]The descendants of Merari were composed of the clans descended from Mahli and Mushi. [34]There were 6,200 males one month old or older among these Merarite clans. [35]They were assigned the area north of the Tabernacle for their camp. The leader of the Merarite clans was Zuriel son of Abihail. [36]These two clans were responsible for the care of the frames supporting the Tabernacle, the crossbars, the pillars, the bases, and all the equipment related to their use. [37]They were also responsible for the posts of the courtyard and all their bases, pegs, and ropes.

[38]The area in front of the Tabernacle, in the east toward the sunrise,* was reserved for the tents of Moses and of Aaron and his sons, who had the final responsibility for the sanctuary on behalf of the people of Israel. Anyone other than a priest or Levite who went too near the sanctuary was to be put to death.

[39]When Moses and Aaron counted the Levite clans at the LORD's command, the total number was 22,000 males one month old or older.

REDEEMING THE FIRSTBORN SONS

[40]Then the LORD said to Moses, "Now count all the firstborn sons in Israel who are one month old or older, and make a list of their names. [41]The Levites must be reserved for me as substitutes for the firstborn sons of Israel; I am the LORD. And the Levites' livestock must be reserved for me as substitutes for the firstborn livestock of the whole nation of Israel."

[42]So Moses counted the firstborn sons of the people of Israel, just as the LORD had commanded. [43]The number of firstborn sons who were one month old or older was 22,273.

[44]Then the LORD said to Moses, [45]"Take the Levites as substitutes for the firstborn sons of the people of Israel. And take the livestock of the Levites as substitutes for the firstborn livestock of the people of Israel. The Levites belong to me; I am the LORD. [46]There are 273 more firstborn sons of Israel than there are Levites. To redeem these extra firstborn sons, [47]collect five pieces of silver* for each of them (each piece weighing the same as the sanctuary shekel, which equals twenty gerahs). [48]Give the silver to Aaron and his sons as the redemption price for the extra firstborn sons."

[49]So Moses collected the silver for redeeming the firstborn sons of Israel who exceeded the number of Levites. [50]He collected 1,365 pieces of silver* on behalf of these firstborn sons of

---

3:28 Some Greek manuscripts read *8,300;* see total in 3:39.
3:38 Hebrew *toward the sunrise, in front of the Tent of Meeting.*
3:47 Hebrew *5 shekels* [2 ounces or 57 grams].   **3:50** Hebrew *1,365 shekels* [34 pounds or 15.5 kilograms].

Israel (each piece weighing the same as the sanctuary shekel). ⁵¹And Moses gave the silver for the redemption to Aaron and his sons, just as the LORD had commanded.

4 DUTIES OF THE KOHATHITE CLAN Then the LORD said to Moses and Aaron, ²"Record the names of the members of the clans and families of the Kohathite division of the tribe of Levi. ³List all the men between the ages of thirty and fifty who are eligible to serve in the Tabernacle.*

⁴"The duties of the Kohathites at the Tabernacle will relate to the most sacred objects. ⁵When the camp moves, Aaron and his sons must enter the Tabernacle first to take down the inner curtain and cover the Ark of the Covenant* with it. ⁶Then they must cover the inner curtain with fine goatskin leather and spread over that a single piece of blue cloth. Finally, they must put the carrying poles of the Ark in place.

⁷"Next they must spread a blue cloth over the table where the Bread of the Presence is displayed, and on the cloth they will place the bowls, pans, jars, pitchers, and the special bread. ⁸They must spread a scarlet cloth over all of this, and finally a covering of fine goatskin leather on top of the scarlet cloth. Then they must insert the carrying poles into the table.

⁹"Next they must cover the lampstand with a blue cloth, along with its lamps, lamp snuffers, trays, and special jars of olive oil. ¹⁰Then they must cover the lampstand and its accessories with fine goatskin leather and place the bundle on a carrying frame.

¹¹"Next they must spread a blue cloth over the gold incense altar and cover this cloth with fine goatskin leather. Then they must attach the carrying poles to the altar. ¹²They must take all the remaining furnishings of the sanctuary and wrap them in a blue cloth, cover them with fine goatskin leather, and place them on the carrying frame.

¹³"They must remove the ashes from the altar for sacrifices and cover the altar with a purple cloth. ¹⁴All the altar utensils—the firepans, meat forks, shovels, basins, and all the containers—must be placed on the cloth, and a covering of fine goatskin leather must be spread over them. Finally, they must put the carrying poles in place. ¹⁵The camp will be ready to move when Aaron and his sons have finished covering the sanctuary and all the sacred articles. The Kohathites will come and carry these things to the next destination. But they must not touch the sacred objects, or they will die. So these are the things from the Tabernacle that the Kohathites must carry.

¹⁶"Eleazar son of Aaron the priest will be responsible for the oil of the lampstand, the fragrant incense, the daily grain offering, and the anointing oil. In fact, Eleazar will be responsible for the entire Tabernacle and everything in it, including the sanctuary and its furnishings."

¹⁷Then the LORD said to Moses and Aaron, ¹⁸"Do not let the Kohathite clans be destroyed from among the Levites! ¹⁹This is what you must do so they will live and not die when they approach the most sacred objects. Aaron and his sons must always go in with them and assign a specific duty or load to each person. ²⁰The Kohathites must never enter the sanctuary to look at the sacred objects for even a moment, or they will die."

DUTIES OF THE GERSHONITE CLAN ²¹And the LORD said to Moses, ²²"Record the names of the members of the clans and families of the Gershonite division of the tribe of Levi. ²³List all the men between the ages of thirty and fifty who are eligible to serve in the Tabernacle.

²⁴"These Gershonite clans will be responsible for general service and carrying loads. ²⁵They must carry the curtains of the Tabernacle, the Tabernacle itself with its coverings, the outer covering of fine goatskin leather, and the curtain for the Tabernacle entrance. ²⁶They are also to carry the curtains for the courtyard walls that surround the Tabernacle and altar, the curtain across the courtyard entrance, the ropes, and all the equipment related to their use. The Gershonites are responsible for all these items. ²⁷Aaron and his sons will direct the Gershonites regarding all their duties, whether it involves moving the equipment or doing other work. They must assign the Gershonites responsibility for the loads they are to carry. ²⁸So these are the duties assigned to the Gershonite clans at the Tabernacle. They will be directly responsible to Ithamar son of Aaron the priest.

DUTIES OF THE MERARITE CLAN ²⁹"Now record the names of the members of the clans and families of the Merarite division of the tribe of Levi. ³⁰List all the men between the ages of thirty and fifty who are eligible to serve in the Tabernacle.

³¹"Their only duty at the Tabernacle will be to carry loads. They will carry the frames of the Tabernacle, the crossbars, the posts, and the bases; ³²also the posts for the courtyard

4:3 Hebrew the Tent of Meeting; also in 4:4, 15, 23, 25, 28, 30, 31, 33, 35, 37, 39, 41, 43, 47. 4:5 Or Ark of the Testimony.

walls with their bases, pegs, and ropes; and all the accessories and everything else related to their use. Assign the various loads to each man by name. 33So these are the duties of the Merarite clans at the Tabernacle. They are directly responsible to Ithamar son of Aaron the priest."

SUMMARY OF THE REGISTRATION
34So Moses, Aaron, and the other leaders of the community listed the members of the Kohathite division by their clans and families. 35The list included all the men between thirty and fifty years of age who were eligible for service in the Tabernacle, 36and the total number came to 2,750. 37So this was the total of all those from the Kohathite clans who were eligible to serve at the Tabernacle. Moses and Aaron listed them, just as the LORD had commanded through Moses.

38The Gershonite division was also listed by its clans and families. 39The list included all the men between thirty and fifty years of age who were eligible for service in the Tabernacle, 40and the total number came to 2,630. 41So this was the total of all those from the Gershonite clans who were eligible to serve at the Tabernacle. Moses and Aaron listed them, just as the LORD had commanded.

42The Merarite division was also listed by its clans and families. 43The list included all the men between thirty and fifty years of age who were eligible for service in the Tabernacle, 44and the total number came to 3,200. 45So this was the total of all those from the Merarite clans who were eligible for service. Moses and Aaron listed them, just as the LORD had commanded through Moses.

46So Moses, Aaron, and the leaders of Israel listed all the Levites by their clans and families. 47All the men between thirty and fifty years of age who were eligible for service in the Tabernacle and for its transportation 48numbered 8,580. 49When their names were recorded, as the LORD had commanded through Moses, each man was assigned his task and told what to carry.

And so the registration was completed, just as the LORD had commanded Moses.

5 PURITY IN ISRAEL'S CAMP The LORD gave these instructions to Moses: 2"Command the people of Israel to remove from the camp anyone who has a skin disease* or a discharge, or who has become ceremonially unclean

by touching a dead person. 3This command applies to men and women alike. Remove them so they will not defile the camp in which I live among them." 4So the Israelites did as the LORD had commanded Moses and removed such people from the camp.

5Then the LORD said to Moses, 6"Give the following instructions to the people of Israel: If any of the people—men or women—betray the LORD by doing wrong to another person, they are guilty. 7They must confess their sin and make full restitution for what they have done, adding an additional 20 percent and returning it to the person who was wronged. 8But if the person who was wronged is dead, and there are no near relatives to whom restitution can be made, the payment belongs to the LORD and must be given to the priest. Those who are guilty must also bring a ram as a sacrifice, and they will be purified and made right with the LORD.* 9All the sacred offerings that the Israelites bring to a priest will belong to him. 10Each priest may keep all the sacred donations that he receives."

PROTECTING MARITAL FAITHFULNESS
11And the LORD said to Moses, 12"Give the following instructions to the people of Israel.

"Suppose a man's wife goes astray, and she is unfaithful to her husband 13and has sex with another man, but neither her husband nor anyone else knows about it. She has defiled herself, even though there was no witness and she was not caught in the act. 14If her husband becomes jealous and is suspicious of his wife and needs to know whether or not she has defiled herself, 15the husband must bring his wife to the priest. He must also bring an offering of two quarts* of barley flour to be presented on her behalf. Do not mix it with olive oil or frankincense, for it is a jealousy offering—an offering to prove whether or not she is guilty.

16"The priest will then present her to stand trial before the LORD. 17He must take some holy water in a clay jar and pour into it dust he has taken from the Tabernacle floor. 18When the priest has presented the woman before the LORD, he must unbind her hair and place in

....

SET THINGS RIGHT
(5:5-8) God included restitution, a unique concept for that day, as part of his law for Israel. When someone was robbed, the guilty person was required to restore to the victim what had been taken and pay an additional interest penalty. This can inspire us to look for ways to set things right when we have wronged someone.

5:2 Traditionally rendered *leprosy.* The Hebrew word used here describes various skin diseases. 5:8 Or *bring a ram for atonement, which will make atonement for them.* 5:15 Hebrew ⅒ *of an ephah* [2.2 liters].

her hands the offering of proof—the jealousy offering to determine whether her husband's suspicions are justified. The priest will stand before her, holding the jar of bitter water that brings a curse to those who are guilty. ¹⁹The priest will then put the woman under oath and say to her, 'If no other man has had sex with you, and you have not gone astray and defiled yourself while under your husband's authority, may you be immune from the effects of this bitter water that brings on the curse. ²⁰But if you have gone astray by being unfaithful to your husband, and have defiled yourself by having sex with another man—'

²¹"At this point the priest must put the woman under oath by saying, 'May the people know that the Lord's curse is upon you when he makes you infertile, causing your womb to shrivel* and your abdomen to swell. ²²Now may this water that brings the curse enter your body and cause your abdomen to swell and your womb to shrivel.*' And the woman will be required to say, 'Yes, let it be so.' ²³And the priest will write these curses on a piece of leather and wash them off into the bitter water. ²⁴He will make the woman drink the bitter water that brings on the curse. When the water enters her body, it will cause bitter suffering if she is guilty.

²⁵"The priest will take the jealousy offering from the woman's hand, lift it up before the Lord, and carry it to the altar. ²⁶He will take a handful of the flour as a token portion and burn it on the altar, and he will require the woman to drink the water. ²⁷If she has defiled herself by being unfaithful to her husband, the water that brings on the curse will cause bitter suffering. Her abdomen will swell and her womb will shrink,* and her name will become a curse among her people. ²⁸But if she has not defiled herself and is pure, then she will be unharmed and will still be able to have children.

²⁹"This is the ritual law for dealing with suspicion. If a woman goes astray and defiles herself while under her husband's authority, ³⁰or if a man becomes jealous and is suspicious that his wife has been unfaithful, the husband must present his wife before the Lord, and the priest will apply this entire ritual law to her. ³¹The husband will be innocent of any guilt in this matter, but his wife will be held accountable for her sin."

6 **NAZIRITE LAWS** Then the Lord said to Moses, ²"Give the following instructions to the people of Israel.

"If any of the people, either men or women, take the special vow of a Nazirite, setting themselves apart to the Lord in a special way, ³they must give up wine and other alcoholic drinks. They must not use vinegar made from wine or from other alcoholic drinks, they must not drink fresh grape juice, and they must not eat grapes or raisins. ⁴As long as they are bound by their Nazirite vow, they are not allowed to eat or drink anything that comes from a grapevine—not even the grape seeds or skins.

⁵"They must never cut their hair throughout the time of their vow, for they are holy and set apart to the Lord. Until the time of their vow has been fulfilled, they must let their hair grow long. ⁶And they must not go near a dead body during the entire period of their vow to the Lord. ⁷Even if the dead person is their own father, mother, brother, or sister, they must not defile themselves, for the hair on their head is the symbol of their separation to God. ⁸This requirement applies as long as they are set apart to the Lord.

⁹"If someone falls dead beside them, the hair they have dedicated will be defiled. They must wait for seven days and then shave their heads. Then they will be cleansed from their defilement. ¹⁰On the eighth day they must bring two turtledoves or two young pigeons to the priest at the entrance of the Tabernacle.* ¹¹The priest will offer one of the birds for a sin offering and the other for a burnt offering. In this way, he will purify them* from the guilt they incurred through contact with the dead body. Then they must reaffirm their commitment and let their hair begin to grow again. ¹²The days of their vow that were completed before their defilement no longer count. They must rededicate themselves to the Lord as a Nazirite for the full term of their vow, and each must bring a one-year-old male lamb for a guilt offering.

¹³"This is the ritual law for Nazirites. At the conclusion of their time of separation as Nazirites, they must each go to the entrance of the Tabernacle ¹⁴and offer their sacrifices to the Lord: a one-year-old male lamb without defect for a burnt offering, a one-year-old female lamb without defect for a sin offering, a ram without defect for a peace offering, ¹⁵a basket of bread made without yeast—cakes of choice flour mixed with olive oil and wafers spread with olive oil—along with their prescribed grain offerings and liquid offerings. ¹⁶The priest will present these offerings before the Lord: first the sin offering and the burnt offering; ¹⁷then

5:21 Hebrew *when he causes your thigh to waste away.*
5:22 Hebrew *and your thigh to waste away.*　**5:27** Hebrew *and her thigh will waste away.*　**6:10** Hebrew the *Tent of Meeting;* also in 6:13, 18.　**6:11** Or *make atonement for them.*

the ram for a peace offering, along with the basket of bread made without yeast. The priest must also present the prescribed grain offering and liquid offering to the Lord. ¹⁸"Then the Nazirites will shave their heads at the entrance of the Tabernacle. They will take the hair that had been dedicated and place it on the fire beneath the peace-offering sacrifice. ¹⁹After the Nazirite's head has been shaved, the priest will take for each of them the boiled shoulder of the ram, and he will take from the basket a cake and a wafer made without yeast. He will put them all into the Nazirite's hands. ²⁰Then the priest will lift them up as a special offering before the Lord. These are holy portions for the priest, along with the breast of the special offering and the thigh of the sacred offering that are lifted up before the Lord. After this ceremony the Nazirites may again drink wine.

²¹"This is the ritual law of the Nazirites, who vow to bring these offerings to the Lord. They may also bring additional offerings if they can afford it. And they must be careful to do whatever they vowed when they set themselves apart as Nazirites."

THE PRIESTLY BLESSING ²²Then the Lord said to Moses, ²³"Tell Aaron and his sons to bless the people of Israel with this special blessing:

²⁴ 'May the Lord bless you
      and protect you.
²⁵ May the Lord smile on you
      and be gracious to you.
²⁶ May the Lord show you his favor
      and give you his peace.'

²⁷Whenever Aaron and his sons bless the people of Israel in my name, I myself will bless them."

7 **OFFERINGS OF DEDICATION** On the day Moses set up the Tabernacle, he anointed it and set it apart as holy. He also anointed and set apart all its furnishings and the altar with its utensils. ²Then the leaders of Israel—tribal leaders who had registered the troops—came and brought their offerings. ³Together they brought six large wagons and twelve oxen. There was a wagon for every two leaders and an ox for each leader. They presented these to the Lord in front of the Tabernacle.

⁴Then the Lord said to Moses, ⁵"Receive

their gifts, and use these oxen and wagons for transporting the Tabernacle.* Distribute them among the Levites according to the work they have to do." ⁶So Moses took the wagons and oxen and presented them to the Levites. ⁷He gave two wagons and four oxen to the Gershonite division for their work, ⁸and he gave four wagons and eight oxen to the Merarite division for their work. All their work was done under the leadership of Ithamar son of Aaron the priest. ⁹But he gave none of the wagons or oxen to the Kohathite division, since they were required to carry the sacred objects of the Tabernacle on their shoulders.

¹⁰The leaders also presented dedication gifts for the altar at the time it was anointed. They each placed their gifts before the altar. ¹¹The Lord said to Moses, "Let one leader bring his gift each day for the dedication of the altar."

¹²On the first day Nahshon son of Amminadab, leader of the tribe of Judah, presented his offering.

¹³His offering consisted of a silver platter weighing 3¼ pounds and a silver basin weighing 1¾ pounds* (as measured by the weight of the sanctuary shekel). These were both filled with grain offerings of choice flour moistened with olive oil. ¹⁴He also brought a gold container weighing four ounces,* which was filled with incense. ¹⁵He brought a young bull, a ram, and a one-year-old male lamb for a burnt offering, ¹⁶and a male goat for a sin offering. ¹⁷For a peace offering he brought two bulls, five rams, five male goats, and five one-year-old male lambs. This was the offering brought by Nahshon son of Amminadab.

¹⁸On the second day Nethanel son of Zuar, leader of the tribe of Issachar, presented his offering.

¹⁹His offering consisted of a silver platter weighing 3¼ pounds and a silver basin weighing 1¾ pounds (as measured by the weight of the sanctuary shekel). These were both filled with grain offerings of choice flour moistened with olive oil. ²⁰He also brought a gold container weighing four ounces, which was filled with incense. ²¹He brought a young bull, a ram, and a one-year-old male lamb for a burnt offering, ²²and a male goat for a sin offering. ²³For a peace offering he brought two bulls, five rams, five male goats, and five one-year-old male lambs. This was the offering brought by Nethanel son of Zuar.

7:5 Hebrew *the Tent of Meeting;* also in 7:89. **7:13** Hebrew *silver platter weighing 130 shekels* [1.5 kilograms] *and a silver basin weighing 70 shekels* [800 grams]; also in 7:19, 25, 31, 37, 43, 49, 55, 61, 67, 73, 79, 85. **7:14** Hebrew *10 shekels* [114 grams]; also in 7:20, 26, 32, 38, 44, 50, 56, 62, 68, 74, 80, 86.

²⁴On the third day Eliab son of Helon, leader of the tribe of Zebulun, presented his offering. ²⁵His offering consisted of a silver platter weighing 3¼ pounds and a silver basin weighing 1¾ pounds (as measured by the weight of the sanctuary shekel). These were both filled with grain offerings of choice flour moistened with olive oil. ²⁶He also brought a gold container weighing four ounces, which was filled with incense. ²⁷He brought a young bull, a ram, and a one-year-old male lamb for a burnt offering, ²⁸and a male goat for a sin offering. ²⁹For a peace offering he brought two bulls, five rams, five male goats, and five one-year-old male lambs. This was the offering brought by Eliab son of Helon.

³⁰On the fourth day Elizur son of Shedeur, leader of the tribe of Reuben, presented his offering. ³¹His offering consisted of a silver platter weighing 3¼ pounds and a silver basin weighing 1¾ pounds (as measured by the weight of the sanctuary shekel). These were both filled with grain offerings of choice flour moistened with olive oil. ³²He also brought a gold container weighing four ounces, which was filled with incense. ³³He brought a young bull, a ram, and a one-year-old male lamb for a burnt offering, ³⁴and a male goat for a sin offering. ³⁵For a peace offering he brought two bulls, five rams, five male goats, and five one-year-old male lambs. This was the offering brought by Elizur son of Shedeur.

³⁶On the fifth day Shelumiel son of Zurishaddai, leader of the tribe of Simeon, presented his offering. ³⁷His offering consisted of a silver platter weighing 3¼ pounds and a silver basin weighing 1¾ pounds (as measured by the weight of the sanctuary shekel). These were both filled with grain offerings of choice flour moistened with olive oil. ³⁸He also brought a gold container weighing four ounces, which was filled with incense. ³⁹He brought a young bull, a ram, and a one-year-old male lamb for a burnt offering, ⁴⁰and a male goat for a sin offering. ⁴¹For a peace offering he brought two bulls, five rams, five male goats, and five one-year-old male lambs. This was the offering brought by Shelumiel son of Zurishaddai.

⁴²On the sixth day Eliasaph son of Deuel, leader of the tribe of Gad, presented his offering.

⁴³His offering consisted of a silver platter weighing 3¼ pounds and a silver basin weighing 1¾ pounds (as measured by the weight of the sanctuary shekel). These were both filled with grain offerings of choice flour moistened with olive oil. ⁴⁴He also brought a gold container weighing four ounces, which was filled with incense. ⁴⁵He brought a young bull, a ram, and a one-year-old male lamb for a burnt offering, ⁴⁶and a male goat for a sin offering. ⁴⁷For a peace offering he brought two bulls, five rams, five male goats, and five one-year-old male lambs. This was the offering brought by Eliasaph son of Deuel.

⁴⁸On the seventh day Elishama son of Ammihud, leader of the tribe of Ephraim, presented his offering. ⁴⁹His offering consisted of a silver platter weighing 3¼ pounds and a silver basin weighing 1¾ pounds (as measured by the weight of the sanctuary shekel). These were both filled with grain offerings of choice flour moistened with olive oil. ⁵⁰He also brought a gold container weighing four ounces, which was filled with incense. ⁵¹He brought a young bull, a ram, and a one-year-old male lamb for a burnt offering, ⁵²and a male goat for a sin offering. ⁵³For a peace offering he brought two bulls, five rams, five male goats, and five one-year-old male lambs. This was the offering brought by Elishama son of Ammihud.

⁵⁴On the eighth day Gamaliel son of Pedahzur, leader of the tribe of Manasseh, presented his offering. ⁵⁵His offering consisted of a silver platter weighing 3¼ pounds and a silver basin weighing 1¾ pounds (as measured by the weight of the sanctuary shekel). These were both filled with grain offerings of choice flour moistened with olive oil. ⁵⁶He also brought a gold container weighing four ounces, which was filled with incense. ⁵⁷He brought a young bull, a ram, and a one-year-old male lamb for a burnt offering, ⁵⁸and a male goat for a sin offering. ⁵⁹For a peace offering he brought two bulls, five rams, five male goats, and five one-year-old male lambs. This was the offering brought by Gamaliel son of Pedahzur.

⁶⁰On the ninth day Abidan son of Gideoni, leader of the tribe of Benjamin, presented his offering. ⁶¹His offering consisted of a silver platter

weighing 3¼ pounds and a silver basin weighing 1¾ pounds (as measured by the weight of the sanctuary shekel). These were both filled with grain offerings of choice flour moistened with olive oil. [62]He also brought a gold container weighing four ounces, which was filled with incense. [63]He brought a young bull, a ram, and a one-year-old male lamb for a burnt offering, [64]and a male goat for a sin offering. [65]For a peace offering he brought two bulls, five rams, five male goats, and five one-year-old male lambs. This was the offering brought by Abidan son of Gideoni.

[66]On the tenth day Ahiezer son of Ammishaddai, leader of the tribe of Dan, presented his offering.

[67]His offering consisted of a silver platter weighing 3¼ pounds and a silver basin weighing 1¾ pounds (as measured by the weight of the sanctuary shekel). These were both filled with grain offerings of choice flour moistened with olive oil. [68]He also brought a gold container weighing four ounces, which was filled with incense. [69]He brought a young bull, a ram, and a one-year-old male lamb for a burnt offering, [70]and a male goat for a sin offering. [71]For a peace offering he brought two bulls, five rams, five male goats, and five one-year-old male lambs. This was the offering brought by Ahiezer son of Ammishaddai.

[72]On the eleventh day Pagiel son of Ocran, leader of the tribe of Asher, presented his offering.

[73]His offering consisted of a silver platter weighing 3¼ pounds and a silver basin weighing 1¾ pounds (as measured by the weight of the sanctuary shekel). These were both filled with grain offerings of choice flour moistened with olive oil. [74]He also brought a gold container weighing four ounces, which was filled with incense. [75]He brought a young bull, a ram, and a one-year-old male lamb for a burnt offering, [76]and a male goat for a sin offering. [77]For a peace offering he brought two bulls, five rams, five male goats, and five one-year-old male lambs. This was the offering brought by Pagiel son of Ocran.

[78]On the twelfth day Ahira son of Enan, leader of the tribe of Naphtali, presented his offering.

[79]His offering consisted of a silver platter

weighing 3¼ pounds and a silver basin weighing 1¾ pounds (as measured by the weight of the sanctuary shekel). These were both filled with grain offerings of choice flour moistened with olive oil. [80]He also brought a gold container weighing four ounces, which was filled with incense. [81]He brought a young bull, a ram, and a one-year-old male lamb for a burnt offering, [82]and a male goat for a sin offering. [83]For a peace offering he brought two bulls, five rams, five male goats, and five one-year-old male lambs. This was the offering brought by Ahira son of Enan.

[84]So this was the dedication offering brought by the leaders of Israel at the time the altar was anointed: twelve silver platters, twelve silver basins, and twelve gold incense containers. [85]Each silver platter weighed 3¼ pounds, and each silver basin weighed 1¾ pounds. The total weight of the silver was 60 pounds* (as measured by the weight of the sanctuary shekel). [86]Each of the twelve gold containers that was filled with incense weighed four ounces (as measured by the weight of the sanctuary shekel). The total weight of the gold was three pounds.* [87]Twelve young bulls, twelve rams, and twelve one-year-old male lambs were donated for the burnt offerings, along with their prescribed grain offerings. Twelve male goats were brought for the sin offerings. [88]Twenty-four bulls, sixty rams, sixty male goats, and sixty one-year-old male lambs were donated for the peace offerings. This was the dedication offering for the altar after it was anointed.

[89]Whenever Moses went into the Tabernacle to speak with the Lord, he heard the voice speaking to him from between the two cherubim above the Ark's cover—the place of atonement—that rests on the Ark of the Covenant.* The Lord spoke to him from there.

8 PREPARING THE LAMPS The Lord said to Moses, [2]"Give Aaron the following instructions: When you set up the seven lamps in the lampstand, place them so their light shines

....

7:85 Hebrew 2,400 shekels [27.6 kilograms].   **7:86** Hebrew 120 shekels [1.4 kilograms].   **7:89** Or Ark of the Testimony.

HEARING GOD
(7:89) Imagine hearing the audible voice of God! Moses must have trembled at the sound. God sometimes spoke directly to his people to tell them the proper way to live. The Bible records these conversations to give us insights into God's character. Wondering what God sounds like? Check out his Word. Also, if you're a believer, the Holy Spirit lives within you. Have you paid attention to his "gentle whisper" (see 1 Kgs 19:12) recently?

forward in front of the lampstand." ³So Aaron did this. He set up the seven lamps so they reflected their light forward, just as the Lord had commanded Moses. ⁴The entire lampstand, from its base to its decorative blossoms, was made of beaten gold. It was built according to the exact design the Lord had shown Moses.

THE LEVITES DEDICATED ⁵Then the Lord said to Moses, ⁶"Now set the Levites apart from the rest of the people of Israel and make them ceremonially clean. ⁷Do this by sprinkling them with the water of purification, and have them shave their entire body and wash their clothing. Then they will be ceremonially clean. ⁸Have them bring a young bull and a grain offering of choice flour moistened with olive oil, along with a second young bull for a sin offering. ⁹Then assemble the whole community of Israel, and present the Levites at the entrance of the Tabernacle.* ¹⁰When you present the Levites before the Lord, the people of Israel must lay their hands on them. ¹¹Raising his hands, Aaron must then present the Levites to the Lord as a special offering from the people of Israel, thus dedicating them to the Lord's service.

¹²"Next the Levites will lay their hands on the heads of the young bulls. Present one as a sin offering and the other as a burnt offering to the Lord, to purify the Levites and make them right with the Lord.* ¹³Then have the Levites stand in front of Aaron and his sons, and raise your hands and present them as a special offering to the Lord. ¹⁴In this way, you will set the Levites apart from the rest of the people of Israel, and the Levites will belong to me. ¹⁵After this, they may go into the Tabernacle to do their work, because you have purified them and presented them as a special offering.

¹⁶"Of all the people of Israel, the Levites are reserved for me. I have claimed them for myself in place of all the firstborn sons of the Israelites; I have taken the Levites as their substitutes. ¹⁷For all the firstborn males among the people of Israel are mine, both of people and of animals. I set them apart for myself on the day I struck down all the firstborn sons of the Egyptians. ¹⁸Yes, I have claimed the Levites in place of all the firstborn sons of Israel. ¹⁹And of all the Israelites, I have assigned the Levites to Aaron and his sons. They will serve in the Tabernacle on behalf of the Israelites and make sacrifices to purify* the people so no plague will strike them when they approach the sanctuary."

²⁰So Moses, Aaron, and the whole community of Israel dedicated the Levites, carefully following all the Lord's instructions to Moses. ²¹The Levites purified themselves from sin and washed their clothes, and Aaron lifted them up and presented them to the Lord as a special offering. He then offered a sacrifice to purify them and make them right with the Lord.* ²²After that the Levites went into the Tabernacle to perform their duties, assisting Aaron and his sons. So they carried out all the commands that the Lord gave Moses concerning the Levites.

²³The Lord also instructed Moses, ²⁴"This is the rule the Levites must follow: They must begin serving in the Tabernacle at the age of twenty-five, ²⁵and they must retire at the age of fifty. ²⁶After retirement they may assist their fellow Levites by serving as guards at the Tabernacle, but they may not officiate in the service. This is how you must assign duties to the Levites."

9 **THE SECOND PASSOVER** A year after Israel's departure from Egypt, the Lord spoke to Moses in the wilderness of Sinai. In the first month* of that year he said, ²"Tell the Israelites to celebrate the Passover at the prescribed time, ³at twilight on the fourteenth day of the first month.* Be sure to follow all my decrees and regulations concerning this celebration."

⁴So Moses told the people to celebrate the Passover ⁵in the wilderness of Sinai as twilight fell on the fourteenth day of the month. And they celebrated the festival there, just as the Lord had commanded Moses. ⁶But some of the men had been ceremonially defiled by touching a dead body, so they could not celebrate the Passover that day. They came to Moses and Aaron that day ⁷and said, "We have become ceremonially unclean by touching a dead body. But why should we be prevented from presenting the Lord's offering at the proper time with the rest of the Israelites?"

⁸Moses answered, "Wait here until I have received instructions for you from the Lord."

⁹This was the Lord's reply to Moses. ¹⁰"Give the following instructions to the people of Israel: If any of the people now or in future generations are ceremonially unclean at Passover time because of touching a dead body, or if they are on a journey and cannot be present at the ceremony, they may still celebrate the Lord's Passover. ¹¹They must offer the

8:9 Hebrew *the Tent of Meeting;* also in 8:15, 19, 22, 24, 26. **8:12** Or *to make atonement for the Levites.* **8:19** Or *make atonement for.* **8:21** Or *then made atonement for them to purify them.* **9:1** The first month of the ancient Hebrew lunar calendar usually occurs within the months of March and April. **9:3** This day in the ancient Hebrew lunar calendar occurred in late March, April, or early May.

Passover sacrifice one month later, at twilight on the fourteenth day of the second month.* They must eat the Passover lamb at that time with bitter salad greens and bread made without yeast. [12]They must not leave any of the lamb until the next morning, and they must not break any of its bones. They must follow all the normal regulations concerning the Passover.

[13]"But those who neglect to celebrate the Passover at the regular time, even though they are ceremonially clean and not away on a trip, will be cut off from the community of Israel. If they fail to present the LORD's offering at the proper time, they will suffer the consequences of their guilt. [14]And if foreigners living among you want to celebrate the Passover to the LORD, they must follow these same decrees and regulations. The same laws apply both to native-born Israelites and to the foreigners living among you."

THE FIERY CLOUD [15]On the day the Tabernacle was set up, the cloud covered it.* But from evening until morning the cloud over the Tabernacle looked like a pillar of fire. [16]This was the regular pattern—at night the cloud that covered the Tabernacle had the appearance of fire. [17]Whenever the cloud lifted from over the sacred tent, the people of Israel would break camp and follow it. And wherever the cloud settled, the people of Israel would set up camp. [18]In this way, they traveled and camped at the LORD's command wherever he told them to go. Then they remained in their camp as long as the cloud stayed over the Tabernacle. [19]If the cloud remained over the Tabernacle for a long time, the Israelites stayed and performed their duty to the LORD. [20]Sometimes the cloud would stay over the Tabernacle for only a few days, so the people would stay for only a few days, as the LORD commanded. Then at the LORD's command they would break camp and move on. [21]Sometimes the cloud stayed only overnight and lifted the next morning. But day or night, when the cloud lifted, the people broke camp and moved on. [22]Whether the cloud stayed above the Tabernacle for two days, a month, or a year, the people of Israel stayed in camp and did not move on. But as soon as it lifted, they broke camp and moved on. [23]So they camped or traveled at the LORD's command, and they did whatever the LORD told them through Moses.

10 **THE SILVER TRUMPETS** Now the LORD said to Moses, [2]"Make two trumpets of hammered silver for calling the community to assemble and for signaling the breaking of camp. [3]When both trumpets are blown, everyone must gather before you at the entrance of the Tabernacle.* [4]But if only one trumpet is blown, then only the leaders—the heads of the clans of Israel—must present themselves to you.

[5]"When you sound the signal to move on, the tribes camped on the east side of the Tabernacle must break camp and move forward. [6]When you sound the signal a second time, the tribes camped on the south will follow. You must sound short blasts as the signal for moving on. [7]But when you call the people to an assembly, blow the trumpets with a different signal. [8]Only the priests, Aaron's descendants, are allowed to blow the trumpets. This is a permanent law for you, to be observed from generation to generation.

[9]"When you arrive in your own land and go to war against your enemies who attack you, sound the alarm with the trumpets. Then the LORD your God will remember you and rescue you from your enemies. [10]Blow the trumpets in times of gladness, too, sounding them at your annual festivals and at the beginning of each month. And blow the trumpets over your burnt offerings and peace offerings. The trumpets will remind the LORD your God of his covenant with you. I am the LORD your God."

THE ISRAELITES LEAVE SINAI [11]In the second year after Israel's departure from Egypt—on the twentieth day of the second month*—the cloud lifted from the Tabernacle of the Covenant.*

....

SAME LAWS FOR ALL
(9:14) Sometimes we are tempted to excuse non-Christians from following God's guidelines for worship. Yet foreigners at this time were expected to follow the same laws as the Israelites. God did not have a separate set of standards for unbelievers, and he still does not today. God's statement that "the same laws apply both to native-born Israelites and to the foreigners living among you" emphasizes this truth. Although God singled out Israel to be his people, his ultimate aim was to have all people obey and worship him.

IN THE RIGHT SPOT
(9:23) The Hebrews traveled and camped as God guided. When you follow God's guidance, you can be confident that you're where God wants you, whether you're moving or staying in one place. Instead of praying, "God, what do you want me to do next?" you might ask, "God, what do you want me to do while I'm right here?" Direction from God is not just for your next big move. He has a purpose in placing you where you are right now.

9:11 This day in the ancient Hebrew lunar calendar occurred in late April, May, or early June. **9:15** Hebrew *covered the Tabernacle, the Tent of the Testimony.* **10:3** Hebrew *Tent of Meeting.* **10:11a** This day in the ancient Hebrew lunar calendar occurred in late April, May, or early June. **10:11b** Or *Tabernacle of the Testimony.*

¹²So the Israelites set out from the wilderness of Sinai and traveled on from place to place until the cloud stopped in the wilderness of Paran.

¹³When the people set out for the first time, following the instructions the LORD had given through Moses, ¹⁴Judah's troops led the way. They marched behind their banner, and their leader was Nahshon son of Amminadab. ¹⁵They were joined by the troops of the tribe of Issachar, led by Nethanel son of Zuar, ¹⁶and the troops of the tribe of Zebulun, led by Eliab son of Helon.

¹⁷Then the Tabernacle was taken down, and the Gershonite and Merarite divisions of the Levites were next in the line of march, carrying the Tabernacle with them. ¹⁸Reuben's troops went next, marching behind their banner. Their leader was Elizur son of Shedeur. ¹⁹They were joined by the troops of the tribe of Simeon, led by Shelumiel son of Zurishaddai, ²⁰and the troops of the tribe of Gad, led by Eliasaph son of Deuel.

²¹Next came the Kohathite division of the Levites, carrying the sacred objects from the Tabernacle. Before they arrived at the next camp, the Tabernacle would already be set up at its new location. ²²Ephraim's troops went next, marching behind their banner. Their leader was Elishama son of Ammihud. ²³They were joined by the troops of the tribe of Manasseh, led by Gamaliel son of Pedahzur, ²⁴and the troops of the tribe of Benjamin, led by Abidan son of Gideoni.

²⁵Dan's troops went last, marching behind their banner and serving as the rear guard for all the tribal camps. Their leader was Ahiezer son of Ammishaddai. ²⁶They were joined by the troops of the tribe of Asher, led by Pagiel son of Ocran, ²⁷and the troops of the tribe of Naphtali, led by Ahira son of Enan.

²⁸This was the order in which the Israelites marched, division by division.

²⁹One day Moses said to his brother-in-law, Hobab son of Reuel the Midianite, "We are on our way to the place the LORD promised us, for he said, 'I will give it to you.' Come with us and we will treat you well, for the LORD has promised wonderful blessings for Israel!"

³⁰But Hobab replied, "No, I will not go. I must return to my own land and family."

³¹"Please don't leave us," Moses pleaded. "You know the places in the wilderness where we should camp. Come, be our guide. ³²If you do, we'll share with you all the blessings the LORD gives us."

³³They marched for three days after leaving the mountain of the LORD, with the Ark of the LORD's Covenant moving ahead of them to show them where to stop and rest. ³⁴As they moved on each day, the cloud of the LORD hovered over them. ³⁵And whenever the Ark set out, Moses would shout, "Arise, O LORD, and let your enemies be scattered! Let them flee before you!" ³⁶And when the Ark was set down, he would say, "Return, O LORD, to the countless thousands of Israel!"

11 THE PEOPLE COMPLAIN TO MOSES

Soon the people began to complain about their hardship, and the LORD heard everything they said. Then the LORD's anger blazed against them, and he sent a fire to rage among them, and he destroyed some of the people in the outskirts of the camp. ²Then the people screamed to Moses for help, and when he prayed to the LORD, the fire stopped. ³After that, the area was known as Taberah (which means "the place of burning"), because fire from the LORD had burned among them there.

⁴Then the foreign rabble who were traveling with the Israelites began to crave the good things of Egypt. And the people of Israel also began to complain. "Oh, for some meat!" they exclaimed. ⁵"We remember the fish we used to eat for free in Egypt. And we had all the cucumbers, melons, leeks, onions, and garlic we wanted. ⁶But now our appetites are gone. All we ever see is this manna!"

⁷The manna looked like small coriander seeds, and it was pale yellow like gum resin. ⁸The people would go out and gather it from the ground. They made flour by grinding it with

---

COMPLIMENTS

(10:29-32) By complimenting Hobab's wilderness skills, Moses let Hobab know that he was needed. The people in your life won't know that you appreciate them if you don't tell them. Complimenting the people in your life builds lasting relationships and helps them know their strengths and value. Think about those who have helped you this month. What can you do to let them know how much you need and appreciate them?

GRATITUDE ATTITUDE

(11:1-6) Dissatisfaction comes when our attention shifts from what we have to what we don't have. The people of Israel didn't seem to notice what God was doing for them—setting them free, making them a nation, giving them a new land—because they were so wrapped up in what God wasn't doing for them. They could think of nothing but the delicious Egyptian food they had left behind. Somehow they forgot that the brutal whip of Egyptian slavery was the cost of eating that food. Before we judge the Israelites too harshly, it's helpful to think about what occupies our attention most of the time. Are we grateful for what God has given us, or are we always thinking about what we would like to have?

hand mills or pounding it in mortars. Then they boiled it in a pot and made it into flat cakes. These cakes tasted like pastries baked with olive oil. ⁹The manna came down on the camp with the dew during the night.

¹⁰Moses heard all the families standing in the doorways of their tents whining, and the LORD became extremely angry. Moses was also very aggravated. ¹¹And Moses said to the LORD, "Why are you treating me, your servant, so harshly? Have mercy on me! What did I do to deserve the burden of all these people? ¹²Did I give birth to them? Did I bring them into the world? Why did you tell me to carry them in my arms like a mother carries a nursing baby? How can I carry them to the land you swore to give their ancestors? ¹³Where am I supposed to get meat for all these people? They keep whining to me, saying, 'Give us meat to eat!' ¹⁴I can't carry all these people by myself! The load is far too heavy! ¹⁵If this is how you intend to treat me, just go ahead and kill me. Do me a favor and spare me this misery!"

MOSES CHOOSES SEVENTY LEADERS ¹⁶Then the LORD said to Moses, "Gather before me seventy men who are recognized as elders and leaders of Israel. Bring them to the Tabernacle* to stand there with you. ¹⁷I will come down and talk to you there. I will take some of the Spirit that is upon you, and I will put the Spirit upon them also. They will bear the burden of the people along with you, so you will not have to carry it alone.

¹⁸"And say to the people, 'Purify yourselves, for tomorrow you will have meat to eat. You were whining, and the LORD heard you when you cried, "Oh, for some meat! We were better off in Egypt!" Now the LORD will give you meat, and you will have to eat it. ¹⁹And it won't be for just a day or two, or for five or ten or even twenty. ²⁰You will eat it for a whole month until you gag and are sick of it. For you have rejected the LORD, who is here among you, and you have whined to him, saying, "Why did we ever leave Egypt?"'"

²¹But Moses responded to the LORD, "There are 600,000 foot soldiers here with me, and yet you say, 'I will give them meat for a whole month!' ²²Even if we butchered all our flocks and herds, would that satisfy them? Even if we caught all the fish in the sea, would that be enough?"

²³Then the LORD said to Moses, "Has my arm lost its power? Now you will see whether or not my word comes true!"

²⁴So Moses went out and reported the LORD's words to the people. He gathered the seventy elders and stationed them around the Tabernacle.* ²⁵And the LORD came down in the cloud and spoke to Moses. Then he gave the seventy elders the same Spirit that was upon Moses. And when the Spirit rested upon them, they prophesied. But this never happened again.

²⁶Two men, Eldad and Medad, had stayed behind in the camp. They were listed among the elders, but they had not gone out to the Tabernacle. Yet the Spirit rested upon them as well, so they prophesied there in the camp. ²⁷A young man ran and reported to Moses, "Eldad and Medad are prophesying in the camp!"

²⁸Joshua son of Nun, who had been Moses' assistant since his youth, protested, "Moses, my master, make them stop!"

²⁹But Moses replied, "Are you jealous for my sake? I wish that all the LORD's people were prophets and that the LORD would put his Spirit upon them all!" ³⁰Then Moses returned to the camp with the elders of Israel.

THE LORD SENDS QUAIL ³¹Now the LORD sent a wind that brought quail from the sea and let them fall all around the camp. For miles in every direction there were quail flying about three feet above the ground.* ³²So the people went out and caught quail all that day and throughout the night and all the next day, too. No one gathered less than fifty bushels*! They spread the quail all around the camp to dry. ³³But while they were gorging themselves on the meat—while it was still in their mouths—the anger of the LORD blazed against the people, and he struck them with a severe plague. ³⁴So that place was called Kibroth-hattaavah (which means "graves of gluttony") because there they buried the people who had craved meat from Egypt. ³⁵From Kibroth-hattaavah the Israelites traveled to Hazeroth, where they stayed for some time.

12 **THE COMPLAINTS OF MIRIAM AND AARON** While they were at Hazeroth, Miriam and Aaron criticized Moses because he had married a Cushite woman. ²They said, "Has the LORD spoken only through Moses? Hasn't he spoken through us, too?" But the LORD heard them. ³(Now Moses was very humble—more humble than any other person on earth.)

⁴So immediately the LORD called to Moses, Aaron, and Miriam and said, "Go out to the Tabernacle,* all three of you!" So the three of

---

11:16 Hebrew *the Tent of Meeting.* **11:24** Hebrew *the tent;* also in 11:26. **11:31** Or *there were quail about 3 feet* [2 cubits or 92 centimeters] *deep on the ground.* **11:32** Hebrew *10 homers* [1.8 kiloliters]. **12:4** Hebrew *the Tent of Meeting.*

them went to the Tabernacle. ⁵Then the LORD descended in the pillar of cloud and stood at the entrance of the Tabernacle.* "Aaron and Miriam!" he called, and they stepped forward. ⁶And the LORD said to them, "Now listen to what I say:

"If there were prophets among you,
　I, the LORD, would reveal myself in
　　visions.
　I would speak to them in dreams.
⁷ But not with my servant Moses.
　Of all my house, he is the one I trust.
⁸ I speak to him face to face,
　clearly, and not in riddles!
　He sees the LORD as he is.
So why were you not afraid
　to criticize my servant Moses?"

⁹The LORD was very angry with them, and he departed. ¹⁰As the cloud moved from above the Tabernacle, there stood Miriam, her skin as white as snow from leprosy.* When Aaron saw what had happened to her, ¹¹he cried out to Moses, "Oh, my master! Please don't punish us for this sin we have so foolishly committed. ¹²Don't let her be like a stillborn baby, already decayed at birth."

¹³So Moses cried out to the LORD, "O God, I beg you, please heal her!"

¹⁴But the LORD said to Moses, "If her father had done nothing more than spit in her face, wouldn't she be defiled for seven days? So keep her outside the camp for seven days, and after that she may be accepted back."

¹⁵So Miriam was kept outside the camp for seven days, and the people waited until she was brought back before they traveled again. ¹⁶Then they left Hazeroth and camped in the wilderness of Paran.

13 TWELVE SCOUTS EXPLORE CANAAN

The LORD now said to Moses, ²"Send out men to explore the land of Canaan, the land I am giving to the Israelites. Send one leader from each of the twelve ancestral tribes." ³So Moses did as the LORD commanded him. He sent out twelve men, all tribal leaders of Israel,

from their camp in the wilderness of Paran. ⁴These were the tribes and the names of their leaders:

Tribe	Leader
Reuben	Shammua son of Zaccur
⁵ Simeon	Shaphat son of Hori
⁶ Judah	Caleb son of Jephunneh
⁷ Issachar	Igal son of Joseph
⁸ Ephraim	Hoshea son of Nun
⁹ Benjamin	Palti son of Raphu
¹⁰ Zebulun	Gaddiel son of Sodi
¹¹ Manasseh son of Joseph	Gaddi son of Susi
¹² Dan	Ammiel son of Gemalli
¹³ Asher	Sethur son of Michael
¹⁴ Naphtali	Nahbi son of Vophsi
¹⁵ Gad	Geuel son of Maki

¹⁶These are the names of the men Moses sent out to explore the land. (Moses called Hoshea son of Nun by the name Joshua.)

¹⁷Moses gave the men these instructions as he sent them out to explore the land: "Go north through the Negev into the hill country. ¹⁸See what the land is like, and find out whether the people living there are strong or weak, few or many. ¹⁹See what kind of land they live in. Is it good or bad? Do their towns have walls, or are they unprotected like open camps? ²⁰Is the soil fertile or poor? Are there many trees? Do your best to bring back samples of the crops you see." (It happened to be the season for harvesting the first ripe grapes.)

²¹So they went up and explored the land from the wilderness of Zin as far as Rehob, near Lebo-hamath. ²²Going north, they passed through the Negev and arrived at Hebron, where Ahiman, Sheshai, and Talmai— all descendants of Anak—lived. (The ancient town of Hebron was founded seven years before the Egyptian city of Zoan.) ²³When they came to the valley of Eshcol, they cut down a branch with a single cluster of grapes so large that it took two of them to carry it on a pole between them! They also brought back samples of the pomegranates and figs. ²⁴That place was called the valley of Eshcol (which means "cluster"), because of the cluster of grapes the Israelite men cut there.

THE SCOUTING REPORT ²⁵After exploring the land for forty days, the men returned ²⁶to Moses, Aaron, and the whole community of Israel at Kadesh in the wilderness of Paran. They reported to the whole community what they had seen and showed them the fruit they

---

FEAR OR FOCUS ON GOD?
(13:25-29) God told the Israelites that the rich and plentiful Promised Land would be theirs. But when the scouting party reported back to Moses, they couldn't stop focusing on their fears. God's promise to help had been forgotten. When facing tough decisions, do you tend to focus on the fear of potential difficulties or God's power to help? The Israelites wandered in the desert for 40 years because they chose to give in to fear. The consequences of disobedience can be far greater than any imagined fear.

12:5 Hebrew *the tent;* also in 12:10.　**12:10** Or *with a skin disease.* The Hebrew word used here can describe various skin diseases.

ISRAEL'S COMPLAINING

COMPLAINT	SIN	RESULT
11:1 About their hardships	Complained about their problems instead of praying to God	Thousands of people were destroyed when God sent fire to punish them.
11:4 About the lack of meat	Lusted after things they didn't have	God sent quail, but as the people began to eat, God struck them with a plague that killed many.
14:1-4 About being stuck in the wilderness, facing the giants of the Promised Land, and wishing to return to Egypt	Openly rebelled against God's leaders and failed to trust in his promises	All who complained were not allowed to enter the Promised Land; they were doomed to wander in the wilderness until they died.
16:3 About Moses' and Aaron's authority and leadership	Were greedy for more power and authority	The families, friends, and possessions of Korah, Dathan, and Abiram were swallowed up by the earth. Fire then burned up the 250 other men who rebelled.
16:41 That Moses and Aaron caused the deaths of Korah and his conspirators	Blamed others for their own troubles	God began to destroy Israel with a plague. Moses and Aaron made atonement for the people, but 14,700 of them were killed.
20:2-3 About the lack of water	Refused to believe that God would provide as he had promised	Moses sinned along with the people. For this he was barred from entering the Promised Land.
21:5 That God and Moses brought them into the wilderness	Failed to recognize that their problems were brought on by their own disobedience	God sent poisonous snakes that killed many people and seriously injured many others.

had taken from the land. ²⁷This was their report to Moses: "We entered the land you sent us to explore, and it is indeed a bountiful country—a land flowing with milk and honey. Here is the kind of fruit it produces. ²⁸But the people living there are powerful, and their towns are large and fortified. We even saw giants there, the descendants of Anak! ²⁹The Amalekites live in the Negev, and the Hittites, Jebusites, and Amorites live in the hill country. The Canaanites live along the coast of the Mediterranean Sea* and along the Jordan Valley."

³⁰But Caleb tried to quiet the people as they stood before Moses. "Let's go at once to take the land," he said. "We can certainly conquer it!"

³¹But the other men who had explored the land with him disagreed. "We can't go up against them! They are stronger than we are!" ³²So they spread this bad report about the land among the Israelites: "The land we traveled

13:29 Hebrew *the sea.*   13:33 Hebrew *nephilim.*

through and explored will devour anyone who goes to live there. All the people we saw were huge. ³³We even saw giants* there, the descendants of Anak. Next to them we felt like grasshoppers, and that's what they thought, too!"

14 **THE PEOPLE REBEL** Then the whole community began weeping aloud, and they cried all night. ²Their voices rose in a great chorus of protest against Moses and Aaron. "If only we had died in Egypt, or even here in the wilderness!" they complained. ³"Why is the LORD taking us to this country only to have us die in battle? Our wives and our little ones will be carried off as plunder! Wouldn't it be better for us to return to Egypt?" ⁴Then they plotted among themselves, "Let's choose a new leader and go back to Egypt!"

⁵Then Moses and Aaron fell face down on the ground before the whole community of Israel. ⁶Two of the men who had explored the land, Joshua son of Nun and Caleb son of Jephunneh,

THE LORD IS
SLOW TO ANGER
AND FILLED WITH
UNFAILING
LOVE,
FORGIVING EVERY KIND OF
SIN ═ REBELLION.

NUMBERS 14:18

tore their clothing. [7]They said to all the people of Israel, "The land we traveled through and explored is a wonderful land! [8]And if the LORD is pleased with us, he will bring us safely into that land and give it to us. It is a rich land flowing with milk and honey. [9]Do not rebel against the LORD, and don't be afraid of the people of the land. They are only helpless prey to us! They have no protection, but the LORD is with us! Don't be afraid of them!"

[10]But the whole community began to talk about stoning Joshua and Caleb. Then the glorious presence of the LORD appeared to all the Israelites at the Tabernacle.* [11]And the LORD said to Moses, "How long will these people treat me with contempt? Will they never believe me, even after all the miraculous signs I have done among them? [12]I will disown them and destroy them with a plague. Then I will make you into a nation greater and mightier than they are!"

MOSES INTERCEDES FOR THE PEOPLE [13]But Moses objected. "What will the Egyptians think when they hear about it?" he asked the LORD.

....

ADVICE
(14:6-10) Two wise men, Joshua and Caleb, encouraged the people to act on God's promise to give them the land of Canaan. But the people rejected their advice and even talked about killing them. Have you ever rejected advice that you didn't like? Next time you receive advice, why not evaluate it carefully and weigh it against God's Word. That advice could be God's message to you.

"They know full well the power you displayed in rescuing your people from Egypt. [14]Now if you destroy them, the Egyptians will send a report to the inhabitants of this land, who have already heard that you live among your people. They know, LORD, that you have appeared to your people face to face and that your pillar of cloud hovers over them. They know that you go before them in the pillar of cloud by day and the pillar of fire by night. [15]Now if you slaughter all these people with a single blow, the nations that have heard of your fame will say, [16]'The LORD was not able to bring them into the land he swore to give them, so he killed them in the wilderness.'

[17]"Please, Lord, prove that your power is as great as you have claimed. For you said, [18]'The LORD is slow to anger and filled with unfailing love, forgiving every kind of sin and rebellion. But he does not excuse the guilty. He lays the sins of the parents upon their children; the entire family is affected—even children in the third and fourth generations.' [19]In keeping with your magnificent, unfailing love, please pardon the sins of this people, just as you have forgiven them ever since they left Egypt."

[20]Then the LORD said, "I will pardon them as you have requested. [21]But as surely as I live, and as surely as the earth is filled with the LORD's glory, [22]not one of these people will ever enter that land. They have all seen my glorious presence and the miraculous signs I performed both in Egypt and in the wilderness, but again and again they have tested me by refusing to listen to my voice. [23]They will never even see the land I swore to give their ancestors. None of those who have treated me with contempt will ever see it. [24]But my servant Caleb has a different attitude than the others have. He has remained loyal to me, so I will bring him into the land he explored. His descendants will possess their full share of that land. [25]Now turn around, and don't go on toward the land where the Amalekites and Canaanites live. Tomorrow you must set out for the wilderness in the direction of the Red Sea.*"

THE LORD PUNISHES THE ISRAELITES [26]Then the LORD said to Moses and Aaron, [27]"How long must I put up with this wicked community and its complaints about me? Yes, I have heard the complaints the Israelites are making against me. [28]Now tell them this: 'As surely as I live, declares the LORD, I will do to you the very things I heard you say. [29]You will all drop dead in this wilderness! Because you

14:10 Hebrew *the Tent of Meeting.*   **14:25** Hebrew *sea of reeds.*

complained against me, every one of you who is twenty years old or older and was included in the registration will die. ³⁰You will not enter and occupy the land I swore to give you. The only exceptions will be Caleb son of Jephunneh and Joshua son of Nun.

³¹"'You said your children would be carried off as plunder. Well, I will bring them safely into the land, and they will enjoy what you have despised. ³²But as for you, you will drop dead in this wilderness. ³³And your children will be like shepherds, wandering in the wilderness for forty years. In this way, they will pay for your faithlessness, until the last of you lies dead in the wilderness.

³⁴"'Because your men explored the land for forty days, you must wander in the wilderness for forty years—a year for each day, suffering the consequences of your sins. Then you will discover what it is like to have me for an enemy.' ³⁵I, the LORD, have spoken! I will certainly do these things to every member of the community who has conspired against me. They will be destroyed here in this wilderness, and here they will die!"

³⁶The ten men Moses had sent to explore the land—the ones who incited rebellion against the LORD with their bad report—³⁷were struck dead with a plague before the LORD. ³⁸Of the twelve who had explored the land, only Joshua and Caleb remained alive.

³⁹When Moses reported the LORD's words to all the Israelites, the people were filled with grief. ⁴⁰Then they got up early the next morning and went to the top of the range of hills. "Let's go," they said. "We realize that we have sinned, but now we are ready to enter the land the LORD has promised us."

⁴¹But Moses said, "Why are you now disobeying the LORD's orders to return to the wilderness? It won't work. ⁴²Do not go up into the land now. You will only be crushed by your enemies because the LORD is not with you. ⁴³When you face the Amalekites and Canaanites in battle, you will be slaughtered. The LORD will abandon you because you have abandoned the LORD."

⁴⁴But the people defiantly pushed ahead toward the hill country, even though neither Moses nor the Ark of the LORD's Covenant left the camp. ⁴⁵Then the Amalekites and the Canaanites who lived in those hills came down and attacked them and chased them back as far as Hormah.

15:4a Hebrew ¹/₁₀ of an ephah [2.2 liters]. **15:4b** Hebrew ¼ of a hin [1 liter]; also in 15:5. **15:6a** Hebrew ²/₁₀ of an ephah [4.4 liters]. **15:6b** Hebrew ⅓ of a hin [1.3 liters]; also in 15:7. **15:9a** Hebrew ³/₁₀ of an ephah [6.6 liters]. **15:9b** Hebrew ½ of a hin [2 liters]; also in 15:10.

15 LAWS CONCERNING OFFERINGS

Then the LORD told Moses, ²"Give the following instructions to the people of Israel.

"When you finally settle in the land I am giving you, ³you will offer special gifts as a pleasing aroma to the LORD. These gifts may take the form of a burnt offering, a sacrifice to fulfill a vow, a voluntary offering, or an offering at any of your annual festivals, and they may be taken from your herds of cattle or your flocks of sheep and goats. ⁴When you present these offerings, you must also give the LORD a grain offering of two quarts* of choice flour mixed with one quart* of olive oil. ⁵For each lamb offered as a burnt offering or a special sacrifice, you must also present one quart of wine as a liquid offering.

⁶"If the sacrifice is a ram, give a grain offering of four quarts* of choice flour mixed with a third of a gallon* of olive oil, ⁷and give a third of a gallon of wine as a liquid offering. This will be a pleasing aroma to the LORD.

⁸"When you present a young bull as a burnt offering or as a sacrifice to fulfill a vow or as a peace offering to the LORD, ⁹you must also give a grain offering of six quarts* of choice flour mixed with two quarts* of olive oil, ¹⁰and give two quarts of wine as a liquid offering. This will be a special gift, a pleasing aroma to the LORD.

¹¹"Each sacrifice of a bull, ram, lamb, or young goat should be prepared in this way. ¹²Follow these instructions with each offering you present. ¹³All of you native-born Israelites must follow these instructions when you offer a special gift as a pleasing aroma to the LORD. ¹⁴And if any foreigners visit you or live among you and want to present a special gift as a pleasing aroma to the LORD, they must follow these same procedures. ¹⁵Native-born Israelites and foreigners are equal before the LORD and are subject to the same decrees. This is a permanent law for you, to be observed from generation to generation. ¹⁶The same instructions and regulations will apply both to you and to the foreigners living among you."

¹⁷Then the LORD said to Moses, ¹⁸"Give the following instructions to the people of Israel.

"When you arrive in the land where I am taking you, ¹⁹and you eat the crops that grow there, you must set some aside as a sacred offering to the LORD. ²⁰Present a cake from the first of the flour you grind, and set it aside as a sacred offering, as you do with the first grain from the threshing floor. ²¹Throughout the generations to come, you are to present a sacred offering to the LORD each year from the first of your ground flour.

²²"But suppose you unintentionally fail to carry out all these commands that the LORD has given you through Moses. ²³And suppose your descendants in the future fail to do everything the LORD has commanded through Moses. ²⁴If the mistake was made unintentionally, and the community was unaware of it, the whole community must present a young bull for a burnt offering as a pleasing aroma to the LORD. It must be offered along with its prescribed grain offering and liquid offering and with one male goat for a sin offering. ²⁵With it the priest will purify the whole community of Israel, making them right with the LORD,* and they will be forgiven. For it was an unintentional sin, and they have corrected it with their offerings to the LORD—the special gift and the sin offering. ²⁶The whole community of Israel will be forgiven, including the foreigners living among you, for all the people were involved in the sin.

²⁷"If one individual commits an unintentional sin, the guilty person must bring a one-year-old female goat for a sin offering. ²⁸The priest will sacrifice it to purify* the guilty person before the LORD, and that person will be forgiven. ²⁹These same instructions apply both to native-born Israelites and to the foreigners living among you.

³⁰"But those who brazenly violate the LORD's will, whether native-born Israelites or foreigners, have blasphemed the LORD, and they must be cut off from the community. ³¹Since they have treated the LORD's word with contempt and deliberately disobeyed his command, they must be completely cut off and suffer the punishment for their guilt."

PENALTY FOR BREAKING THE SABBATH ³²One day while the people of Israel were in the wilderness, they discovered a man gathering wood on the Sabbath day. ³³The people who found him doing this took him before Moses, Aaron, and the rest of the community. ³⁴They held him in custody because they did not know what to do with him. ³⁵Then the LORD said to Moses, "The man must be put to death! The whole community must stone him outside the camp." ³⁶So the whole community took the man outside the camp and stoned him to death, just as the LORD had commanded Moses.

TASSELS ON CLOTHING ³⁷Then the LORD said to Moses, ³⁸"Give the following instructions to the people of Israel: Throughout the generations to come you must make tassels for the hems of your clothing and attach them with a blue cord. ³⁹When you see the tassels, you will remember and obey all the commands of the LORD instead of following your own desires and defiling yourselves, as you are prone to do. ⁴⁰The tassels will help you remember that you must obey all my commands and be holy to your God. ⁴¹I am the LORD your God who brought you out of the land of Egypt that I might be your God. I am the LORD your God!"

16
KORAH'S REBELLION One day Korah son of Izhar, a descendant of Kohath son of Levi, conspired with Dathan and Abiram, the sons of Eliab, and On son of Peleth, from the tribe of Reuben. ²They incited a rebellion against Moses, along with 250 other leaders of the community, all prominent members of the assembly. ³They united against Moses and Aaron and said, "You have gone too far! The whole community of Israel has been set apart by the LORD, and he is with all of us. What right do you have to act as though you are greater than the rest of the LORD's people?"

⁴When Moses heard what they were saying, he fell face down on the ground. ⁵Then he said to Korah and his followers, "Tomorrow morning the LORD will show us who belongs to him* and who is holy. The LORD will allow only those whom he selects to enter his own presence. ⁶Korah, you and all your followers must prepare your incense burners. ⁷Light fires in them tomorrow, and burn incense before the LORD. Then we will see whom the LORD chooses as his holy one. You Levites are the ones who have gone too far!"

⁸Then Moses spoke again to Korah: "Now listen, you Levites! ⁹Does it seem insignificant to you that the God of Israel has chosen you from among all the community of Israel to be near him so you can serve in the LORD's Tabernacle and stand before the people to minister to them? ¹⁰Korah, he has already given this special ministry to you and your fellow Levites. Are you now demanding the priesthood as well?

A SELFISH AMBITION
(16:1-10) Korah wanted the special qualities God had given to Moses and other leaders, even though he had his own worthwhile abilities and responsibilities. In the end, his ambition caused him to lose everything. Sometimes we want the fame, power, or material possessions that someone else has. Trouble results when we try to gain what others have. If you've fallen into that trap, consider the chilling example of Korah, who gambled and lost.

15:25 Or will make atonement for the whole community of Israel.
15:28 Or to make atonement for.   **16:5** Greek version reads God has visited and knows those who are his. Compare 2 Tim 2:19.

¹¹The LORD is the one you and your followers are really revolting against! For who is Aaron that you are complaining about him?"

¹²Then Moses summoned Dathan and Abiram, the sons of Eliab, but they replied, "We refuse to come before you! ¹³Isn't it enough that you brought us out of Egypt, a land flowing with milk and honey, to kill us here in this wilderness, and that you now treat us like your subjects? ¹⁴What's more, you haven't brought us into another land flowing with milk and honey. You haven't given us a new homeland with fields and vineyards. Are you trying to fool these men?* We will not come."

¹⁵Then Moses became very angry and said to the LORD, "Do not accept their grain offerings! I have not taken so much as a donkey from them, and I have never hurt a single one of them." ¹⁶And Moses said to Korah, "You and all your followers must come here tomorrow and present yourselves before the LORD. Aaron will also be here. ¹⁷You and each of your 250 followers must prepare an incense burner and put incense on it, so you can all present them before the LORD. Aaron will also bring his incense burner."

¹⁸So each of these men prepared an incense burner, lit the fire, and placed incense on it. Then they all stood at the entrance of the Tabernacle* with Moses and Aaron. ¹⁹Meanwhile, Korah had stirred up the entire community against Moses and Aaron, and they all gathered at the Tabernacle entrance. Then the glorious presence of the LORD appeared to the whole community, ²⁰and the LORD said to Moses and Aaron, ²¹"Get away from all these people so that I may instantly destroy them!"

²²But Moses and Aaron fell face down on the ground. "O God," they pleaded, "you are the God who gives breath to all creatures. Must you be angry with all the people when only one man sins?"

²³And the LORD said to Moses, ²⁴"Then tell all the people to get away from the tents of Korah, Dathan, and Abiram."

²⁵So Moses got up and rushed over to the tents of Dathan and Abiram, followed by the elders of Israel. ²⁶"Quick!" he told the people. "Get away from the tents of these wicked men, and don't touch anything that belongs to them. If you do, you will be destroyed for their sins." ²⁷So all the people stood back from the tents of Korah, Dathan, and Abiram. Then Dathan and Abiram came out and stood at the entrances of

their tents, together with their wives and children and little ones.

²⁸And Moses said, "This is how you will know that the LORD has sent me to do all these things that I have done—for I have not done them on my own. ²⁹If these men die a natural death, or if nothing unusual happens, then the LORD has not sent me. ³⁰But if the LORD does something entirely new and the ground opens its mouth and swallows them and all their belongings, and they go down alive into the grave,* then you will know that these men have shown contempt for the LORD."

³¹He had hardly finished speaking the words when the ground suddenly split open beneath them. ³²The earth opened its mouth and swallowed the men, along with their households and all their followers who were standing with them, and everything they owned. ³³So they went down alive into the grave, along with all their belongings. The earth closed over them, and they all vanished from among the people of Israel. ³⁴All the people around them fled when they heard their screams. "The earth will swallow us, too!" they cried. ³⁵Then fire blazed forth from the LORD and burned up the 250 men who were offering incense.

³⁶*And the LORD said to Moses, ³⁷"Tell Eleazar son of Aaron the priest to pull all the incense burners from the fire, for they are holy. Also tell him to scatter the burning coals. ³⁸Take the incense burners of these men who have sinned at the cost of their lives, and hammer the metal into a thin sheet to overlay the altar. Since these burners were used in the LORD's presence, they have become holy. Let them serve as a warning to the people of Israel."

³⁹So Eleazar the priest collected the 250 bronze incense burners that had been used by the men who died in the fire, and he hammered them into a thin sheet to overlay the altar. ⁴⁰This would warn the Israelites that no unauthorized person—no one who was not a descendant of Aaron—should ever enter the LORD's presence to burn incense. If anyone did, the same thing would happen to him as happened to Korah and his followers. So the LORD's instructions to Moses were carried out.

⁴¹But the very next morning the whole

· ·

REVENGE
(16:22-27) *Moses and Aaron prayed for those with whom they were most angry and frustrated. Do you pray for those who hurt you or do you seek revenge? God promises to settle the score with wrongdoers. It is not our job to take revenge. God will make certain that, in the end, justice is done.*

16:14 Hebrew *Are you trying to put out the eyes of these men?* **16:18** Hebrew *the Tent of Meeting;* also in 16:19, 42, 43, 50. **16:30** Hebrew *into Sheol;* also in 16:33. **16:36** Verses 16:36-50 are numbered 17:1-15 in Hebrew text.

community of Israel began muttering again against Moses and Aaron, saying, "You have killed the LORD's people!" 42As the community gathered to protest against Moses and Aaron, they turned toward the Tabernacle and saw that the cloud had covered it, and the glorious presence of the LORD appeared.

43Moses and Aaron came and stood in front of the Tabernacle, 44and the LORD said to Moses, 45"Get away from all these people so that I can instantly destroy them!" But Moses and Aaron fell face down on the ground.

46And Moses said to Aaron, "Quick, take an incense burner and place burning coals on it from the altar. Lay incense on it, and carry it out among the people to purify them and make them right with the LORD.* The LORD's anger is blazing against them—the plague has already begun."

47Aaron did as Moses told him and ran out among the people. The plague had already begun to strike down the people, but Aaron burned the incense and purified* the people. 48He stood between the dead and the living, and the plague stopped. 49But 14,700 people died in that plague, in addition to those who had died in the affair involving Korah. 50Then because the plague had stopped, Aaron returned to Moses at the entrance of the Tabernacle.

17 THE BUDDING OF AARON'S STAFF

1*Then the LORD said to Moses, 2"Tell the people of Israel to bring you twelve wooden staffs, one from each leader of Israel's ancestral tribes, and inscribe each leader's name on his staff. 3Inscribe Aaron's name on the staff of the tribe of Levi, for there must be one staff for the leader of each ancestral tribe. 4Place these staffs in the Tabernacle in front of the Ark containing the tablets of the Covenant,* where I meet with you. 5Buds will sprout on the staff belonging to the man I choose. Then I will finally put an end to the people's murmuring and complaining against you."

6So Moses gave the instructions to the people of Israel, and each of the twelve tribal leaders,

··

REBELLION

(17:5, 10) *After witnessing spectacular miracles and experiencing the presence of God, the Israelites still rebelled. We wonder how they could be so blind and ignorant. But let's be honest—we often behave in the same way. We can escape this pattern only by paying attention to the signs of God's presence that we have been given. How has God guided and protected you in the past? How has he answered your prayers? If you focus your thoughts on these things, rebellion will become unthinkable.*

including Aaron, brought Moses a staff. 7Moses placed the staffs in the LORD's presence in the Tabernacle of the Covenant.* 8When he went into the Tabernacle of the Covenant the next day, he found that Aaron's staff, representing the tribe of Levi, had sprouted, budded, blossomed, and produced ripe almonds!

9When Moses brought all the staffs out from the LORD's presence, he showed them to the people. Each man claimed his own staff. 10And the LORD said to Moses: "Place Aaron's staff permanently before the Ark of the Covenant* to serve as a warning to rebels. This should put an end to their complaints against me and prevent any further deaths." 11So Moses did as the LORD commanded him.

12Then the people of Israel said to Moses, "Look, we are doomed! We are dead! We are ruined! 13Everyone who even comes close to the Tabernacle of the LORD dies. Are we all doomed to die?"

18 DUTIES OF PRIESTS AND LEVITES

Then the LORD said to Aaron: "You, your sons, and your relatives from the tribe of Levi will be held responsible for any offenses related to the sanctuary. But you and your sons alone will be held responsible for violations connected with the priesthood.

2"Bring your relatives of the tribe of Levi—your ancestral tribe—to assist you and your sons as you perform the sacred duties in front of the Tabernacle of the Covenant.* 3But as the Levites go about all their assigned duties at the Tabernacle, they must be careful not to go near any of the sacred objects or the altar. If they do, both you and they will die. 4The Levites must join you in fulfilling their responsibilities for the care and maintenance of the Tabernacle,* but no unauthorized person may assist you.

5"You yourselves must perform the sacred duties inside the sanctuary and at the altar. If you follow these instructions, the LORD's anger will never again blaze against the people of Israel. 6I myself have chosen your fellow Levites from among the Israelites to be your special assistants. They are a gift to you, dedicated to the LORD for service in the Tabernacle. 7But you and your sons, the priests, must personally handle all the priestly rituals associated with the altar and with everything

16:46 Or *to make atonement for them.*   **16:47** Or *and made atonement for.*   **17:1** Verses 17:1-13 are numbered 17:16-28 in Hebrew text.   **17:4** Hebrew *in the Tent of Meeting before the Testimony.* The Hebrew word for "testimony" refers to the terms of the LORD's covenant with Israel as written on stone tablets, which were kept in the Ark, and also to the covenant itself.   **17:7** Or *Tabernacle of the Testimony;* also in 17:8.   **17:10** Hebrew *before the Testimony;* see note on 17:4.   **18:2** Or *Tabernacle of the Testimony.*   **18:4** Hebrew *the Tent of Meeting;* also in 18:6, 21, 22, 23, 31.

behind the inner curtain. I am giving you the priesthood as your special privilege of service. Any unauthorized person who comes too near the sanctuary will be put to death."

SUPPORT FOR THE PRIESTS AND LEVITES ⁸The LORD gave these further instructions to Aaron: "I myself have put you in charge of all the holy offerings that are brought to me by the people of Israel. I have given all these consecrated offerings to you and your sons as your permanent share. ⁹You are allotted the portion of the most holy offerings that is not burned on the fire. This portion of all the most holy offerings—including the grain offerings, sin offerings, and guilt offerings—will be most holy, and it belongs to you and your sons. ¹⁰You must eat it as a most holy offering. All the males may eat of it, and you must treat it as most holy.

¹¹"All the sacred offerings and special offerings presented to me when the Israelites lift them up before the altar also belong to you. I have given them to you and to your sons and daughters as your permanent share. Any member of your family who is ceremonially clean may eat of these offerings.

¹²"I also give you the harvest gifts brought by the people as offerings to the LORD—the best of the olive oil, new wine, and grain. ¹³All the first crops of their land that the people present to the LORD belong to you. Any member of your family who is ceremonially clean may eat this food.

¹⁴"Everything in Israel that is specially set apart for the LORD* also belongs to you.

¹⁵"The firstborn of every mother, whether human or animal, that is offered to the LORD will be yours. But you must always redeem your firstborn sons and the firstborn of ceremonially unclean animals. ¹⁶Redeem them when they are one month old. The redemption price is five pieces of silver* (as measured by the weight of the sanctuary shekel, which equals twenty gerahs).

¹⁷"However, you may not redeem the firstborn of cattle, sheep, or goats. They are holy and have been set apart for the LORD. Sprinkle their blood on the altar, and burn their fat as a special gift, a pleasing aroma to the LORD. ¹⁸The meat of these animals will be yours, just like the breast and right thigh that are presented by lifting them up as a special offering before the altar. ¹⁹Yes, I am giving you all these holy offerings that the people of Israel bring to the LORD.

They are for you and your sons and daughters, to be eaten as your permanent share. This is an eternal and unbreakable covenant* between the LORD and you, and it also applies to your descendants."

²⁰And the LORD said to Aaron, "You priests will receive no allotment of land or share of property among the people of Israel. I am your share and your allotment. ²¹As for the tribe of Levi, your relatives, I will compensate them for their service in the Tabernacle. Instead of an allotment of land, I will give them the tithes from the entire land of Israel.

²²"From now on, no Israelites except priests or Levites may approach the Tabernacle. If they come too near, they will be judged guilty and will die. ²³Only the Levites may serve at the Tabernacle, and they will be held responsible for any offenses against it. This is a permanent law for you, to be observed from generation to generation. The Levites will receive no allotment of land among the Israelites, ²⁴because I have given them the Israelites' tithes, which have been presented as sacred offerings to the LORD. This will be the Levites' share. That is why I said they would receive no allotment of land among the Israelites."

²⁵The LORD also told Moses, ²⁶"Give these instructions to the Levites: When you receive from the people of Israel the tithes I have assigned as your allotment, give a tenth of the tithes you receive—a tithe of the tithe—to the LORD as a sacred offering. ²⁷The LORD will consider this offering to be your harvest offering, as though it were the first grain from your own threshing floor or wine from your own winepress. ²⁸You must present one-tenth of the tithe received from the Israelites as a sacred offering to the LORD. This is the LORD's sacred portion, and you must present it to Aaron the priest. ²⁹Be sure to give to the LORD the best portions of the gifts given to you.

³⁰"Also, give these instructions to the Levites: When you present the best part as your offering, it will be considered as though

....

GIVING TO GOD
(18:25-29) The Levites, who helped the priests, were required to tithe to support the work of the Tabernacle just like all of the other Israelites. No one was exempt from returning to God a portion of what was received from him. Though the Levites owned no land and operated no great enterprises, they were to treat their income the same as everyone else's by giving a portion to care for the needs of the other Levites and of the Tabernacle. The tithing principle is still relevant today. What can you give to help meet the needs of God's workers and to help build his kingdom?

18:14 The Hebrew term used here refers to the complete consecration of things or people to the LORD, either by destroying them or by giving them as an offering.   18:16 Hebrew 5 shekels [2 ounces or 57 grams] of silver.   18:19 Hebrew a covenant of salt.

it came from your own threshing floor or wine-press. ³¹You Levites and your families may eat this food anywhere you wish, for it is your compensation for serving in the Tabernacle. ³²You will not be considered guilty for accepting the LORD's tithes if you give the best portion to the priests. But be careful not to treat the holy gifts of the people of Israel as though they were common. If you do, you will die."

19 THE WATER OF PURIFICATION

The LORD said to Moses and Aaron, ²"Here is another legal requirement commanded by the LORD: Tell the people of Israel to bring you a red heifer, a perfect animal that has no defects and has never been yoked to a plow. ³Give it to Eleazar the priest, and it will be taken outside the camp and slaughtered in his presence. ⁴Eleazar will take some of its blood on his finger and sprinkle it seven times toward the front of the Tabernacle.* ⁵As Eleazar watches, the heifer must be burned—its hide, meat, blood, and dung. ⁶Eleazar the priest must then take a stick of cedar,* a hyssop branch, and some scarlet yarn and throw them into the fire where the heifer is burning.

⁷"Then the priest must wash his clothes and bathe himself in water. Afterward he may return to the camp, though he will remain ceremonially unclean until evening. ⁸The man who burns the animal must also wash his clothes and bathe himself in water, and he, too, will remain unclean until evening. ⁹Then someone who is ceremonially clean will gather up the ashes of the heifer and deposit them in a purified place outside the camp. They will be kept there for the community of Israel to use in the water for the purification ceremony. This ceremony is performed for the removal of sin. ¹⁰The man who gathers up the ashes of the heifer must also wash his clothes, and he will remain ceremonially unclean until evening. This is a permanent law for the people of Israel and any foreigners who live among them.

¹¹"All those who touch a dead human body will be ceremonially unclean for seven days. ¹²They must purify themselves on the third and seventh days with the water of purification; then they will be purified. But if they do not do this on the third and seventh days, they will continue to be unclean even after the seventh day. ¹³All those who touch a dead body and do not purify themselves in the proper way defile the LORD's Tabernacle, and they will be cut off from the community of Israel. Since the water of purification was not sprinkled on them, their defilement continues.

¹⁴"This is the ritual law that applies when someone dies inside a tent: All those who enter that tent and those who were inside when the death occurred will be ceremonially unclean for seven days. ¹⁵Any open container in the tent that was not covered with a lid is also defiled. ¹⁶And if someone in an open field touches the corpse of someone who was killed with a sword or who died a natural death, or if someone touches a human bone or a grave, that person will be defiled for seven days.

¹⁷"To remove the defilement, put some of the ashes from the burnt purification offering in a jar, and pour fresh water over them. ¹⁸Then someone who is ceremonially clean must take a hyssop branch and dip it into the water. That person must sprinkle the water on the tent, on all the furnishings in the tent, and on the people who were in the tent; also on the person who touched a human bone, or touched someone who was killed or who died naturally, or touched a grave. ¹⁹On the third and seventh days the person who is ceremonially clean must sprinkle the water on those who are defiled. Then on the seventh day the people being cleansed must wash their clothes and bathe themselves, and that evening they will be cleansed of their defilement.

²⁰"But those who become defiled and do not purify themselves will be cut off from the community, for they have defiled the sanctuary of the LORD. Since the water of purification has not been sprinkled on them, they remain defiled. ²¹This is a permanent law for the people. Those who sprinkle the water of purification must afterward wash their clothes, and anyone who then touches the water used for purification will remain defiled until evening. ²²Anything and anyone that a defiled person touches will be ceremonially unclean until evening."

20 MOSES STRIKES THE ROCK

In the first month of the year,* the whole community of Israel arrived in the wilderness of Zin and camped at Kadesh. While they were there, Miriam died and was buried.

²There was no water for the people to drink at that place, so they rebelled against Moses and Aaron. ³The people blamed Moses and said, "If only we had died in the LORD's presence with our brothers! ⁴Why have you brought the congregation of the LORD's people into this wilderness to die, along with all our livestock?

19:4 Hebrew *the Tent of Meeting.* **19:6** Or *juniper.* **20:1** The first month of the ancient Hebrew lunar calendar usually occurs within the months of March and April. The number of years since leaving Egypt is not specified.

⁵Why did you make us leave Egypt and bring us here to this terrible place? This land has no grain, no figs, no grapes, no pomegranates, and no water to drink!"

⁶Moses and Aaron turned away from the people and went to the entrance of the Tabernacle,* where they fell face down on the ground. Then the glorious presence of the LORD appeared to them, ⁷and the LORD said to Moses, ⁸"You and Aaron must take the staff and assemble the entire community. As the people watch, speak to the rock over there, and it will pour out its water. You will provide enough water from the rock to satisfy the whole community and their livestock."

⁹So Moses did as he was told. He took the staff from the place where it was kept before the LORD. ¹⁰Then he and Aaron summoned the people to come and gather at the rock. "Listen, you rebels!" he shouted. "Must we bring you water from this rock?" ¹¹Then Moses raised his hand and struck the rock twice with the staff, and water gushed out. So the entire community and their livestock drank their fill.

¹²But the LORD said to Moses and Aaron, "Because you did not trust me enough to demonstrate my holiness to the people of Israel, you will not lead them into the land I am giving them!" ¹³This place was known as the waters of Meribah (which means "arguing") because there the people of Israel argued with the LORD, and there he demonstrated his holiness among them.

EDOM REFUSES ISRAEL PASSAGE ¹⁴While Moses was at Kadesh, he sent ambassadors to the king of Edom with this message:

20:6 Hebrew *the Tent of Meeting.*

"This is what your relatives, the people of Israel, say: You know all the hardships we have been through. ¹⁵Our ancestors went down to Egypt, and we lived there a long time, and we and our ancestors were brutally mistreated by the Egyptians. ¹⁶But when we cried out to the LORD, he heard us and sent an angel who brought us out of Egypt. Now we are camped at Kadesh, a town on the border of your land. ¹⁷Please let us travel through your land. We will be careful not to go through your fields and vineyards. We won't even drink water from your wells. We will stay on the king's road and never leave it until we have passed through your territory."

¹⁸But the king of Edom said, "Stay out of my land, or I will meet you with an army!"

¹⁹The Israelites answered, "We will stay on the main road. If our livestock drink your water, we will pay for it. Just let us pass through your country. That's all we ask."

²⁰But the king of Edom replied, "Stay out! You may not pass through our land." With that he

---

CONFLICT

(20:14-21) *Moses negotiated and reasoned with the Edomite king. When nothing worked, he was left with two choices—force a conflict or avoid it. Moses knew there would be enough barriers in the days and months ahead. There was no point in adding another one unnecessarily. Sometimes conflict is unavoidable. At other times, however, it isn't worth the consequences. Open warfare may seem heroic, courageous, and even righteous, but it is not always the best choice. When we can find another way to solve our problems, even if it is harder for us to do, we should consider Moses' example.*

CHOICES
anger

Chad B's father always cautions him about his temper: "Son, someday your temper will get you into big trouble. Learn to express yourself without getting so mad. Go read Galatians 5:22-23 and pray about your attitude, OK?"

Each time Chad nods and apologizes. But the talks don't seem to accomplish much. Chad still blows up. And he ends up in at least one fistfight per month.

Finally, Mr. B's prediction came true. At a post-game party, some guys from a rival school showed up and started mouthing off. Words were exchanged. Tempers flared. Someone got shoved. A punch was thrown. Suddenly, the friendly get-together erupted into a small-scale riot!

As Chad squared off with one guy, another one came after him with a two-by-four. Chad turned into a wild man! Wrestling the board away from his surprised attacker, Chad chased both guys to their pickup truck. Before they could pull away, Chad smashed the truck's rear window and headlight, and put some major dents in the driver's door!

Minutes later, the police came to Chad's house. In his state of semi-shock, Chad heard words like *assault, lawyer,* and *arrest.*

Learn a lesson from Chad and from Moses in Numbers 20:1-12: A few minutes of unchecked anger can produce serious heartache! Moses learned that the hard way. You don't have to.

mobilized his army and marched out against them with an imposing force. [21]Because Edom refused to allow Israel to pass through their country, Israel was forced to turn around.

THE DEATH OF AARON
[22]The whole community of Israel left Kadesh and arrived at Mount Hor. [23]There, on the border of the land of Edom, the LORD said to Moses and Aaron, [24]"The time has come for Aaron to join his ancestors in death. He will not enter the land I am giving the people of Israel, because the two of you rebelled against my instructions concerning the water at Meribah. [25]Now take Aaron and his son Eleazar up Mount Hor. [26]There you will remove Aaron's priestly garments and put them on Eleazar, his son. Aaron will die there and join his ancestors."

[27]So Moses did as the LORD commanded. The three of them went up Mount Hor together as the whole community watched. [28]At the summit, Moses removed the priestly garments from Aaron and put them on Eleazar, Aaron's son. Then Aaron died there on top of the mountain, and Moses and Eleazar went back down. [29]When the people realized that Aaron had died, all Israel mourned for him thirty days.

21 VICTORY OVER THE CANAANITES
The Canaanite king of Arad, who lived in the Negev, heard that the Israelites were approaching on the road through Atharim. So he attacked the Israelites and took some of them as prisoners. [2]Then the people of Israel made this vow to the LORD: "If you will hand these people over to us, we will completely destroy* all their towns." [3]The LORD heard the Israelites' request and gave them victory over the Canaanites. The Israelites completely destroyed them and their towns, and the place has been called Hormah* ever since.

THE BRONZE SNAKE
[4]Then the people of Israel set out from Mount Hor, taking the road to the Red Sea* to go around the land of Edom. But the people grew impatient with the long journey, [5]and they began to speak against God and Moses. "Why have you brought us out of Egypt to die here in the wilderness?" they complained. "There is nothing to eat here and nothing to drink. And we hate this horrible manna!"

[6]So the LORD sent poisonous snakes among the people, and many were bitten and died. [7]Then the people came to Moses and cried out, "We have sinned by speaking against the LORD and against you. Pray that the LORD will take away the snakes." So Moses prayed for the people.

[8]Then the LORD told him, "Make a replica of a poisonous snake and attach it to a pole. All who are bitten will live if they simply look at it!" [9]So Moses made a snake out of bronze and attached it to a pole. Then anyone who was bitten by a snake could look at the bronze snake and be healed!

ISRAEL'S JOURNEY TO MOAB
[10]The Israelites traveled next to Oboth and camped there. [11]Then they went on to Iye-abarim, in the wilderness on the eastern border of Moab. [12]From there they traveled to the valley of Zered Brook and set up camp. [13]Then they moved out and camped on the far side of the Arnon River, in the wilderness adjacent to the territory of the Amorites. The Arnon is the boundary line between the Moabites and the Amorites. [14]For this reason *The Book of the Wars of the LORD* speaks of "the town of Waheb in the area of Suphah, and the ravines of the Arnon River, [15]and the ravines that extend as far as the settlement of Ar on the border of Moab."

[16]From there the Israelites traveled to Beer,* which is the well where the LORD said to Moses, "Assemble the people, and I will give them water." [17]There the Israelites sang this song:

"Spring up, O well!
    Yes, sing its praises!
[18] Sing of this well,
    which princes dug,
    which great leaders hollowed out
    with their scepters and staffs."

Then the Israelites left the wilderness and proceeded on through Mattanah, [19]Nahaliel, and Bamoth. [20]After that they went to the valley in Moab where Pisgah Peak overlooks the wasteland.*

VICTORY OVER SIHON AND OG
[21]The Israelites sent ambassadors to King Sihon of the Amorites with this message:

COMPLAINTS
(21:5) In Psalm 78, we learn the sources of Israel's complaining: (1) they forgot the miracles God did for them, (2) they demanded more than what God had given them, (3) their repentance was insincere, and (4) they were ungrateful for what God had done for them. Our complaining often has its roots in one of these actions and attitudes. It's like a weed. If we can cut off the source of complaining, it will not take hold and grow into bitterness or rebellion.

21:2 The Hebrew term used here refers to the complete consecration of things or people to the LORD, either by destroying them or by giving them as an offering; also in 21:3. **21:3** *Hormah* means "destruction." **21:4** Hebrew *sea of reeds.* **21:16** *Beer* means "well." **21:20** Or *overlooks Jeshimon.*

²²"Let us travel through your land. We will be careful not to go through your fields and vineyards. We won't even drink water from your wells. We will stay on the king's road until we have passed through your territory."

²³But King Sihon refused to let them cross his territory. Instead, he mobilized his entire army and attacked Israel in the wilderness, engaging them in battle at Jahaz. ²⁴But the Israelites slaughtered them with their swords and occupied their land from the Arnon River to the Jabbok River. They went only as far as the Ammonite border because the boundary of the Ammonites was fortified.*

²⁵So Israel captured all the towns of the Amorites and settled in them, including the city of Heshbon and its surrounding villages. ²⁶Heshbon had been the capital of King Sihon of the Amorites. He had defeated a former Moabite king and seized all his land as far as the Arnon River. ²⁷Therefore, the ancient poets wrote this about him:

"Come to Heshbon and let it be rebuilt!
    Let the city of Sihon be restored.
²⁸ A fire flamed forth from Heshbon,
    a blaze from the city of Sihon.
It burned the city of Ar in Moab;
    it destroyed the rulers of the Arnon
        heights.
²⁹ What sorrow awaits you, O people of Moab!
    You are finished, O worshipers of
        Chemosh!
Chemosh has left his sons as refugees,
    his daughters as captives of Sihon, the
        Amorite king.
³⁰ We have utterly destroyed them,
    from Heshbon to Dibon.
We have completely wiped them out
    as far away as Nophah and Medeba.*"

³¹So the people of Israel occupied the territory of the Amorites. ³²After Moses sent men to explore the Jazer area, they captured all the towns in the region and drove out the Amorites who lived there. ³³Then they turned and marched up the road to Bashan, but King Og of Bashan and all his people attacked them at Edrei. ³⁴The LORD said to Moses, "Do not be afraid of him, for I have handed him over to you, along with all his people and his land. Do the same to him as you did to King Sihon of the

Amorites, who ruled in Heshbon." ³⁵And Israel killed King Og, his sons, and all his subjects; not a single survivor remained. Then Israel occupied their land.

22 BALAK SENDS FOR BALAAM Then the people of Israel traveled to the plains of Moab and camped east of the Jordan River, across from Jericho. ²Balak son of Zippor, the Moabite king, had seen everything the Israelites did to the Amorites. ³And when the people of Moab saw how many Israelites there were, they were terrified. ⁴The king of Moab said to the elders of Midian, "This mob will devour everything in sight, like an ox devours grass in the field!"

So Balak, king of Moab, ⁵sent messengers to call Balaam son of Beor, who was living in his native land of Pethor* near the Euphrates River.* His message said:

"Look, a vast horde of people has arrived from Egypt. They cover the face of the earth and are threatening me. ⁶Please come and curse these people for me because they are too powerful for me. Then perhaps I will be able to conquer them and drive them from the land. I know that blessings fall on any people you bless, and curses fall on people you curse."

⁷Balak's messengers, who were elders of Moab and Midian, set out with money to pay Balaam to place a curse upon Israel.* They went to Balaam and delivered Balak's message to him. ⁸"Stay here overnight," Balaam said. "In the morning I will tell you whatever the LORD directs me to say." So the officials from Moab stayed there with Balaam.

⁹That night God came to Balaam and asked him, "Who are these men visiting you?"

¹⁰Balaam said to God, "Balak son of Zippor, king of Moab, has sent me this message: ¹¹'Look, a vast horde of people has arrived from Egypt, and they cover the face of the earth. Come and curse these people for me. Then perhaps I will be able to stand up to them and drive them from the land.'"

¹²But God told Balaam, "Do not go with them.

....

STEPS TO VICTORY
(21:34-35) *God assured Moses that Israel's enemy was conquered even before the battle began! God wants to give us victory over our enemies, which usually are problems related to sin, rather than armed soldiers. First, we must believe that he can help us. Second, we must trust him to help us. Third, we must take the steps he shows us.*

21:24 Or because the terrain of the Ammonite frontier was rugged; Hebrew reads because the boundary of the Ammonites was strong. 21:30 Or until fire spread to Medeba. The meaning of the Hebrew is uncertain.   22:5a Or who was at Pethor in the land of the Amavites. 22:5b Hebrew the river.   22:7 Hebrew set out with the money of divination in their hand.

You are not to curse these people, for they have been blessed!"

¹³The next morning Balaam got up and told Balak's officials, "Go on home! The LORD will not let me go with you."

¹⁴So the Moabite officials returned to King Balak and reported, "Balaam refused to come with us." ¹⁵Then Balak tried again. This time he sent a larger number of even more distinguished officials than those he had sent the first time. ¹⁶They went to Balaam and delivered this message to him:

"This is what Balak son of Zippor says: Please don't let anything stop you from coming to help me. ¹⁷I will pay you very well and do whatever you tell me. Just come and curse these people for me!"

¹⁸But Balaam responded to Balak's messengers, "Even if Balak were to give me his palace filled with silver and gold, I would be powerless to do anything against the will of the LORD my God. ¹⁹But stay here one more night, and I will see if the LORD has anything else to say to me."

²⁰That night God came to Balaam and told him, "Since these men have come for you, get up and go with them. But do only what I tell you to do."

BALAAM AND HIS DONKEY ²¹So the next morning Balaam got up, saddled his donkey, and started off with the Moabite officials. ²²But God was angry that Balaam was going, so he sent the angel of the LORD to stand in the road to block his way. As Balaam and two servants were riding along, ²³Balaam's donkey saw the angel of the LORD standing in the road with a drawn sword in his hand. The donkey bolted off the road into a field, but Balaam beat it and turned it back onto the road. ²⁴Then the angel of the LORD stood at a place where the road narrowed between two vineyard walls. ²⁵When the donkey saw the angel of the LORD, it tried to squeeze by and crushed Balaam's foot against the wall. So Balaam beat the donkey again. ²⁶Then the angel of the LORD moved farther down the road and stood in a place too narrow

for the donkey to get by at all. ²⁷This time when the donkey saw the angel, it lay down under Balaam. In a fit of rage Balaam beat the animal again with his staff.

²⁸Then the LORD gave the donkey the ability to speak. "What have I done to you that deserves your beating me three times?" it asked Balaam.

²⁹"You have made me look like a fool!" Balaam shouted. "If I had a sword with me, I would kill you!"

³⁰"But I am the same donkey you have ridden all your life," the donkey answered. "Have I ever done anything like this before?"

"No," Balaam admitted.

³¹Then the LORD opened Balaam's eyes, and he saw the angel of the LORD standing in the roadway with a drawn sword in his hand. Balaam bowed his head and fell face down on the ground before him.

³²"Why did you beat your donkey those three times?" the angel of the LORD demanded. "Look, I have come to block your way because you are stubbornly resisting me. ³³Three times the donkey saw me and shied away; otherwise, I would certainly have killed you by now and spared the donkey."

³⁴Then Balaam confessed to the angel of the LORD, "I have sinned. I didn't realize you were standing in the road to block my way. I will return home if you are against my going."

³⁵But the angel of the LORD told Balaam, "Go with these men, but say only what I tell you to say." So Balaam went on with Balak's officials. ³⁶When King Balak heard that Balaam was on the way, he went out to meet him at a Moabite town on the Arnon River at the farthest border of his land.

³⁷"Didn't I send you an urgent invitation? Why didn't you come right away?" Balak asked Balaam. "Didn't you believe me when I said I would reward you richly?"

³⁸Balaam replied, "Look, now I have come, but I have no power to say whatever I want. I will speak only the message that God puts in my mouth." ³⁹Then Balaam accompanied Balak to Kiriath-huzoth, ⁴⁰where the king sacrificed cattle and sheep. He sent portions of the meat to Balaam and the officials who were with him. ⁴¹The next morning Balak took Balaam up to Bamoth-baal. From there he could see some of the people of Israel spread out below him.

23 **BALAAM BLESSES ISRAEL** Then Balaam said to King Balak, "Build me seven altars here, and prepare seven young bulls and seven rams for me to sacrifice."

BLIND GREED
(22:20-23) Although God allowed Balaam to go with Balak's messengers, he was angry about Balaam's greedy attitude. The wealth offered by the king blinded Balaam to God's efforts to stop him. Though we may know what God wants us to do, we can become blinded by our desire for money, possessions, or prestige. We can avoid Balaam's mistake by looking past the allure of fame or fortune to the long-range benefits of following God.

[2]Balak followed his instructions, and the two of them sacrificed a young bull and a ram on each altar.

[3]Then Balaam said to Balak, "Stand here by your burnt offerings, and I will go to see if the LORD will respond to me. Then I will tell you whatever he reveals to me." So Balaam went alone to the top of a bare hill, [4]and God met him there. Balaam said to him, "I have prepared seven altars and have sacrificed a young bull and a ram on each altar."

[5]The LORD gave Balaam a message for King Balak. Then he said, "Go back to Balak and give him my message."

[6]So Balaam returned and found the king standing beside his burnt offerings with all the officials of Moab. [7]This was the message Balaam delivered:

> "Balak summoned me to come from Aram;
>   the king of Moab brought me from the
>   eastern hills.
> 'Come,' he said, 'curse Jacob for me!
>   Come and announce Israel's doom.'
> [8] But how can I curse those
>   whom God has not cursed?
> How can I condemn those
>   whom the LORD has not condemned?
> [9] I see them from the cliff tops;
>   I watch them from the hills.
> I see a people who live by themselves,
>   set apart from other nations.
> [10] Who can count Jacob's descendants, as
>   numerous as dust?
>   Who can count even a fourth of Israel's
>   people?
> Let me die like the righteous;
>   let my life end like theirs."

[11]Then King Balak demanded of Balaam, "What have you done to me? I brought you to curse my enemies. Instead, you have blessed them!"

[12]But Balaam replied, "I will speak only the message that the LORD puts in my mouth."

BALAAM'S SECOND MESSAGE [13]Then King Balak told him, "Come with me to another place. There you will see another part of the nation of Israel, but not all of them. Curse at least that many!" [14]So Balak took Balaam to the plateau of Zophim on Pisgah Peak. He built seven altars there and offered a young bull and a ram on each altar.

[15]Then Balaam said to the king, "Stand here by your burnt offerings while I go over there to meet the LORD."

[16]And the LORD met Balaam and gave him a message. Then he said, "Go back to Balak and give him my message."

[17]So Balaam returned and found the king standing beside his burnt offerings with all the officials of Moab. "What did the LORD say?" Balak asked eagerly.

[18]This was the message Balaam delivered:

> "Rise up, Balak, and listen!
>   Hear me, son of Zippor.
> [19] God is not a man, so he does not lie.
>   He is not human, so he does not change
>   his mind.
> Has he ever spoken and failed to act?
>   Has he ever promised and not carried it
>   through?
> [20] Listen, I received a command to bless;
>   God has blessed, and I cannot reverse it!
> [21] No misfortune is in his plan for Jacob;
>   no trouble is in store for Israel.
> For the LORD their God is with them;
>   he has been proclaimed their king.
> [22] God brought them out of Egypt;
>   for them he is as strong as a wild ox.
> [23] No curse can touch Jacob;
>   no magic has any power against Israel.
> For now it will be said of Jacob,
>   'What wonders God has done for Israel!'
> [24] These people rise up like a lioness,
>   like a majestic lion rousing itself.
> They refuse to rest
>   until they have feasted on prey,
>   drinking the blood of the slaughtered!"

[25]Then Balak said to Balaam, "Fine, but if you won't curse them, at least don't bless them!"

[26]But Balaam replied to Balak, "Didn't I tell you that I can do only what the LORD tells me?"

BALAAM'S THIRD MESSAGE [27]Then King Balak said to Balaam, "Come, I will take you to one more place. Perhaps it will please God to let you curse them from there." [28]So Balak took Balaam to the top of Mount Peor, overlooking the wasteland.* [29]Balaam again told Balak, "Build me seven altars, and prepare seven young bulls and seven rams for me to sacrifice." [30]So Balak did as Balaam

....

A NEW VIEW
(23:27) King Balak took Balaam to several places to entice him to curse the Israelites. He thought a change of scenery might help change Balaam's mind. But changing locations won't change God's will. Facing the source of our problems, especially if that source is an attitude we have, is a better choice. To make a change in geography or a change in jobs may only cloud the need for a change in heart.

23:28 Or *overlooking Jeshimon.*

ordered and offered a young bull and a ram on each altar.

24 By now Balaam realized that the LORD was determined to bless Israel, so he did not resort to divination as before. Instead, he turned and looked out toward the wilderness, ²where he saw the people of Israel camped, tribe by tribe. Then the Spirit of God came upon him, ³and this is the message he delivered:

"This is the message of Balaam son of Beor,
    the message of the man whose eyes see
        clearly,
⁴ the message of one who hears the words
        of God,
    who sees a vision from the Almighty,
    who bows down with eyes wide open:
⁵ How beautiful are your tents, O Jacob;
    how lovely are your homes, O Israel!
⁶ They spread before me like palm groves,*
    like gardens by the riverside.
They are like tall trees planted by the LORD,
    like cedars beside the waters.
⁷ Water will flow from their buckets;
    their offspring have all they need.
Their king will be greater than Agag;
    their kingdom will be exalted.
⁸ God brought them out of Egypt;
    for them he is as strong as a wild ox.
He devours all the nations that
        oppose him,
    breaking their bones in pieces,
    shooting them with arrows.
⁹ Like a lion, Israel crouches and lies down;
    like a lioness, who dares to arouse her?
Blessed is everyone who blesses you,
        O Israel,
    and cursed is everyone who curses you."

¹⁰King Balak flew into a rage against Balaam. He angrily clapped his hands and shouted, "I called you to curse my enemies! Instead, you have blessed them three times. ¹¹Now get out of here! Go back home! I promised to reward you richly, but the LORD has kept you from your reward."

¹²Balaam told Balak, "Don't you remember what I told your messengers? I said, ¹³'Even if Balak were to give me his palace filled with silver and gold, I would be powerless to do anything against the will of the LORD.' I told you that I could say only what the LORD says! ¹⁴Now I am returning to my own people. But first let me tell you what the Israelites will do to your people in the future."

BALAAM'S FINAL MESSAGES ¹⁵This is the message Balaam delivered:

"This is the message of Balaam son of Beor,
    the message of the man whose eyes see
        clearly,
¹⁶ the message of one who hears the words
        of God,
    who has knowledge from the Most High,
who sees a vision from the Almighty,
    who bows down with eyes wide open:
¹⁷ I see him, but not here and now.
    I perceive him, but far in the distant
        future.
A star will rise from Jacob;
    a scepter will emerge from Israel.
It will crush the foreheads of Moab's
        people,
    cracking the skulls of the people of Sheth.
¹⁸ Edom will be taken over,
    and Seir, its enemy, will be conquered,
    while Israel marches on in triumph.
¹⁹ A ruler will rise in Jacob
    who will destroy the survivors of Ir."

²⁰Then Balaam looked over toward the people of Amalek and delivered this message:

"Amalek was the greatest of nations,
    but its destiny is destruction!"

²¹Then he looked over toward the Kenites and delivered this message:

"Your home is secure;
    your nest is set in the rocks.
²² But the Kenites will be destroyed
    when Assyria* takes you captive."

²³Balaam concluded his messages by saying:

"Alas, who can survive
    unless God has willed it?
²⁴ Ships will come from the coasts of Cyprus*;
    they will oppress Assyria and afflict Eber,
    but they, too, will be utterly destroyed."

²⁵Then Balaam and Balak returned to their homes.

25 **MOAB SEDUCES ISRAEL** While the Israelites were camped at Acacia Grove,* some of the men defiled themselves by having* sexual relations with local Moabite women. ²These women invited them to attend sacrifices to their gods, so the Israelites feasted with them and worshiped the gods of Moab. ³In this way, Israel joined in the worship

24:6 Or *like a majestic valley.*   24:22 Hebrew *Asshur;* also in 24:24.
24:24 Hebrew *Kittim.*   25:1a Hebrew *Shittim.*   25:1b As in Greek version; Hebrew reads *some of the men began having.*

of Baal of Peor, causing the LORD's anger to blaze against his people.

⁴The LORD issued the following command to Moses: "Seize all the ringleaders and execute them before the LORD in broad daylight, so his fierce anger will turn away from the people of Israel."

⁵So Moses ordered Israel's judges, "Each of you must put to death the men under your authority who have joined in worshiping Baal of Peor."

⁶Just then one of the Israelite men brought a Midianite woman into his tent, right before the eyes of Moses and all the people, as everyone was weeping at the entrance of the Tabernacle.* ⁷When Phinehas son of Eleazar and grandson of Aaron the priest saw this, he jumped up and left the assembly. He took a spear ⁸and rushed after the man into his tent. Phinehas thrust the spear all the way through the man's body and into the woman's stomach. So the plague against the Israelites was stopped, ⁹but not before 24,000 people had died.

¹⁰Then the LORD said to Moses, ¹¹"Phinehas son of Eleazar and grandson of Aaron the priest has turned my anger away from the Israelites by being as zealous among them as I was. So I stopped destroying all Israel as I had intended to do in my zealous anger. ¹²Now tell him that I am making my special covenant of peace with him. ¹³In this covenant, I give him and his descendants a permanent right to the priesthood, for in his zeal for me, his God, he purified the people of Israel, making them right with me.*"

¹⁴The Israelite man killed with the Midianite woman was named Zimri son of Salu, the leader of a family from the tribe of Simeon. ¹⁵The woman's name was Cozbi; she was the daughter of Zur, the leader of a Midianite clan.

¹⁶Then the LORD said to Moses, ¹⁷"Attack the Midianites and destroy them, ¹⁸because they assaulted you with deceit and tricked you into worshiping Baal of Peor, and because of Cozbi, the daughter of a Midianite leader, who was killed at the time of the plague because of what happened at Peor."

26 THE SECOND REGISTRATION OF ISRAEL'S TROOPS

After the plague had ended, the LORD said to Moses and to Eleazar son of Aaron the priest, ²"From the whole community of Israel, record the names of all the warriors by their families. List all the men

twenty years old or older who are able to go to war."

³So there on the plains of Moab beside the Jordan River, across from Jericho, Moses and Eleazar the priest issued these instructions to the leaders of Israel: ⁴"List all the men of Israel twenty years old and older, just as the LORD commanded Moses."

This is the record of all the descendants of Israel who came out of Egypt.

THE TRIBE OF REUBEN ⁵These were the clans descended from the sons of Reuben, Jacob's* oldest son:

The Hanochite clan, named after their ancestor Hanoch.

The Palluite clan, named after their ancestor Pallu.

⁶ The Hezronite clan, named after their ancestor Hezron.

The Carmite clan, named after their ancestor Carmi.

⁷These were the clans of Reuben. Their registered troops numbered 43,730.

⁸Pallu was the ancestor of Eliab, ⁹and Eliab was the father of Nemuel, Dathan, and Abiram. This Dathan and Abiram are the same community leaders who conspired with Korah against Moses and Aaron, rebelling against the LORD. ¹⁰But the earth opened up its mouth and swallowed them with Korah, and fire devoured 250 of their followers. This served as a warning to the entire nation of Israel. ¹¹However, the sons of Korah did not die that day.

THE TRIBE OF SIMEON ¹²These were the clans descended from the sons of Simeon:

....

RIGHTEOUS ANGER
(25:6-11) It is clear from Phinehas's story that some anger is proper and justified. (Phinehas's case was unique, however.) But how can we know when our anger is appropriate and when it should be restrained? You might ask yourself these questions when you become angry: (1) Why am I angry? (2) Whose rights are being violated, mine or another's? (3) Is the truth (a principle of God) being violated? If only your rights are at stake, it may be wiser to keep angry feelings under control. But if the truth is at stake, anger often is justified, although violence and revenge are usually the wrong way to express it.

QUIET WORK
(26:1-65) Thirty-eight years had elapsed since the first great census in chapter 1 of Numbers. During that time, every Israelite man and woman over 20 years of age—except Caleb, Joshua, and Moses—had died; yet God's laws and the spiritual character of the nation were still intact. This quiet but powerful miracle is often overlooked. God often works in quiet ways in our day to bring about his long-range purposes.

25:6 Hebrew the Tent of Meeting. 25:13 Or he made atonement for the people of Israel. 26:5 Hebrew Israel's; see note on 1:20-21b.

The Jemuelite clan, named after their
   ancestor Jemuel.*

The Jaminite clan, named after their
   ancestor Jamin.

The Jakinite clan, named after their ancestor
   Jakin.

¹³ The Zoharite clan, named after their
   ancestor Zohar.*

The Shaulite clan, named after their
   ancestor Shaul.

¹⁴These were the clans of Simeon. Their registered troops numbered 22,200.

THE TRIBE OF GAD ¹⁵These were the clans
descended from the sons of Gad:

The Zephonite clan, named after their
   ancestor Zephon.

The Haggite clan, named after their ancestor
   Haggi.

The Shunite clan, named after their ancestor
   Shuni.

¹⁶ The Oznite clan, named after their ancestor
   Ozni.

The Erite clan, named after their ancestor Eri.

¹⁷ The Arodite clan, named after their ancestor
   Arodi.*

The Arelite clan, named after their ancestor
   Areli.

¹⁸These were the clans of Gad. Their registered
troops numbered 40,500.

THE TRIBE OF JUDAH ¹⁹Judah had two sons, Er
and Onan, who had died in the land of Canaan.
²⁰These were the clans descended from Judah's
surviving sons:

The Shelanite clan, named after their
   ancestor Shelah.

The Perezite clan, named after their
   ancestor Perez.

The Zerahite clan, named after their
   ancestor Zerah.

²¹These were the subclans descended from the
Perezites:

The Hezronites, named after their ancestor
   Hezron.

The Hamulites, named after their ancestor
   Hamul.

²²These were the clans of Judah. Their registered troops numbered 76,500.

THE TRIBE OF ISSACHAR ²³These were the
clans descended from the sons of Issachar:

The Tolaite clan, named after their ancestor
   Tola.

The Puite clan, named after their ancestor
   Puah.*

²⁴ The Jashubite clan, named after their
   ancestor Jashub.

The Shimronite clan, named after their
   ancestor Shimron.

²⁵These were the clans of Issachar. Their registered troops numbered 64,300.

THE TRIBE OF ZEBULUN ²⁶These were the clans
descended from the sons of Zebulun:

The Seredite clan, named after their
   ancestor Sered.

The Elonite clan, named after their ancestor
   Elon.

The Jahleelite clan, named after their
   ancestor Jahleel.

²⁷These were the clans of Zebulun. Their registered troops numbered 60,500.

THE TRIBE OF MANASSEH ²⁸Two clans were
descended from Joseph through Manasseh
and Ephraim.

²⁹These were the clans descended from
Manasseh:

The Makirite clan, named after their
   ancestor Makir.

The Gileadite clan, named after their
   ancestor Gilead, Makir's son.

³⁰These were the subclans descended from the
Gileadites:

The Iezerites, named after their ancestor
   Iezer.

The Helekites, named after their ancestor
   Helek.

³¹ The Asrielites, named after their ancestor
   Asriel.

The Shechemites, named after their
   ancestor Shechem.

³² The Shemidaites, named after their
   ancestor Shemida.

The Hepherites, named after their ancestor
   Hepher.

³³ (One of Hepher's descendants, Zelophehad,
   had no sons, but his daughters' names
   were Mahlah, Noah, Hoglah, Milcah,
   and Tirzah.)

³⁴These were the clans of Manasseh. Their registered troops numbered 52,700.

26:12 As in Syriac version (see also Gen 46:10; Exod 6:15); Hebrew
reads *Nemuelite . . . Nemuel.* **26:13** As in parallel texts at Gen
46:10 and Exod 6:15; Hebrew reads *Zerahite . . . Zerah.* **26:17** As in
Samaritan Pentateuch and Greek and Syriac versions (see also Gen
46:16); Hebrew reads *Arod.* **26:23** As in Samaritan Pentateuch,
Greek and Syriac versions, and Latin Vulgate (see also 1 Chr 7:1);
Hebrew reads *The Punite clan, named after its ancestor Puvah.*

THE TRIBE OF EPHRAIM [35]These were the clans descended from the sons of Ephraim:

The Shuthelahite clan, named after their ancestor Shuthelah.

The Bekerite clan, named after their ancestor Beker.

The Tahanite clan, named after their ancestor Tahan.

[36]This was the subclan descended from the Shuthelahites:

The Eranites, named after their ancestor Eran.

[37]These were the clans of Ephraim. Their registered troops numbered 32,500.

These clans of Manasseh and Ephraim were all descendants of Joseph.

THE TRIBE OF BENJAMIN [38]These were the clans descended from the sons of Benjamin:

The Belaite clan, named after their ancestor Bela.

The Ashbelite clan, named after their ancestor Ashbel.

The Ahiramite clan, named after their ancestor Ahiram.

[39] The Shuphamite clan, named after their ancestor Shupham.*

The Huphamite clan, named after their ancestor Hupham.

[40]These were the subclans descended from the Belaites:

The Ardites, named after their ancestor Ard.*

The Naamites, named after their ancestor Naaman.

[41]These were the clans of Benjamin. Their registered troops numbered 45,600.

THE TRIBE OF DAN [42]These were the clans descended from the sons of Dan:

The Shuhamite clan, named after their ancestor Shuham.

[43]These were the Shuhamite clans of Dan. Their registered troops numbered 64,400.

THE TRIBE OF ASHER [44]These were the clans descended from the sons of Asher:

The Imnite clan, named after their ancestor Imnah.

The Ishvite clan, named after their ancestor Ishvi.

The Beriite clan, named after their ancestor Beriah.

[45]These were the subclans descended from the Beriites:

The Heberites, named after their ancestor Heber.

The Malkielites, named after their ancestor Malkiel.

[46]Asher also had a daughter named Serah.

[47]These were the clans of Asher. Their registered troops numbered 53,400.

THE TRIBE OF NAPHTALI [48]These were the clans descended from the sons of Naphtali:

The Jahzeelite clan, named after their ancestor Jahzeel.

The Gunite clan, named after their ancestor Guni.

[49] The Jezerite clan, named after their ancestor Jezer.

The Shillemite clan, named after their ancestor Shillem.

[50]These were the clans of Naphtali. Their registered troops numbered 45,400.

RESULTS OF THE REGISTRATION [51]In summary, the registered troops of all Israel numbered 601,730.

[52]Then the LORD said to Moses, [53]"Divide the land among the tribes, and distribute the grants of land in proportion to the tribes' populations, as indicated by the number of names on the list. [54]Give the larger tribes more land and the smaller tribes less land, each group receiving a grant in proportion to the size of its population. [55]But you must assign the land by lot, and give land to each ancestral tribe according to the number of names on the list. [56]Each grant of land must be assigned by lot among the larger and smaller tribal groups."

THE TRIBE OF LEVI [57]This is the record of the Levites who were counted according to their clans:

The Gershonite clan, named after their ancestor Gershon.

The Kohathite clan, named after their ancestor Kohath.

The Merarite clan, named after their ancestor Merari.

[58]The Libnites, the Hebronites, the Mahlites, the Mushites, and the Korahites were all subclans of the Levites.

Now Kohath was the ancestor of Amram,

26:39 As in some Hebrew manuscripts, Samaritan Pentateuch, Greek and Syriac versions, and Latin Vulgate; most Hebrew manuscripts read *Shephupham*. 26:40 As in Samaritan Pentateuch, some Greek manuscripts, and Latin Vulgate; Hebrew lacks *named after their ancestor Ard*.

⁵⁹and Amram's wife was named Jochebed. She also was a descendant of Levi, born among the Levites in the land of Egypt. Amram and Jochebed became the parents of Aaron, Moses, and their sister, Miriam. ⁶⁰To Aaron were born Nadab, Abihu, Eleazar, and Ithamar. ⁶¹But Nadab and Abihu died when they burned before the LORD the wrong kind of fire, different than he had commanded.

⁶²The men from the Levite clans who were one month old or older numbered 23,000. But the Levites were not included in the registration of the rest of the people of Israel because they were not given an allotment of land when it was divided among the Israelites.

⁶³So these are the results of the registration of the people of Israel as conducted by Moses and Eleazar the priest on the plains of Moab beside the Jordan River, across from Jericho. ⁶⁴Not one person on this list had been among those listed in the previous registration taken by Moses and Aaron in the wilderness of Sinai. ⁶⁵For the LORD had said of them, "They will all die in the wilderness." Not one of them survived except Caleb son of Jephunneh and Joshua son of Nun.

27 THE DAUGHTERS OF ZELOPHEHAD

One day a petition was presented by the daughters of Zelophehad—Mahlah, Noah, Hoglah, Milcah, and Tirzah. Their father, Zelophehad, was a descendant of Hepher son of Gilead, son of Makir, son of Manasseh, son of Joseph. ²These women stood before Moses, Eleazar the priest, the tribal leaders, and the entire community at the entrance of the Tabernacle.* ³"Our father died in the wilderness," they said. "He was not among Korah's followers, who rebelled against the LORD; he died because of his own sin. But he had no sons. ⁴Why should the name of our father disappear from his clan just because he had no sons? Give us property along with the rest of our relatives."

⁵So Moses brought their case before the LORD. ⁶And the LORD replied to Moses, ⁷"The claim of the daughters of Zelophehad is legitimate. You must give them a grant of land along with their father's relatives. Assign them the property that would have been given to their father.

⁸"And give the following instructions to the people of Israel: If a man dies and has no son, then give his inheritance to his daughters. ⁹And if he has no daughter either, transfer his inheritance to his brothers. ¹⁰If he has no brothers, give his inheritance to his father's brothers. ¹¹But if his father has no brothers, give his inheritance to the nearest relative in his clan. This is a legal requirement for the people of Israel, just as the LORD commanded Moses."

JOSHUA CHOSEN TO LEAD ISRAEL

¹²One day the LORD said to Moses, "Climb one of the mountains east of the river,* and look out over the land I have given the people of Israel. ¹³After you have seen it, you will die like your brother, Aaron, ¹⁴for you both rebelled against my instructions in the wilderness of Zin. When the people of Israel rebelled, you failed to demonstrate my holiness to them at the waters." (These are the waters of Meribah at Kadesh* in the wilderness of Zin.)

¹⁵Then Moses said to the LORD, ¹⁶"O LORD, you are the God who gives breath to all creatures. Please appoint a new man as leader for the community. ¹⁷Give them someone who will guide them wherever they go and will lead them into battle, so the community of the LORD will not be like sheep without a shepherd."

¹⁸The LORD replied, "Take Joshua son of Nun, who has the Spirit in him, and lay your hands on him. ¹⁹Present him to Eleazar the priest before the whole community, and publicly commission him to lead the people. ²⁰Transfer some of your authority to him so the whole community of Israel will obey him. ²¹When direction from the LORD is needed, Joshua will stand before Eleazar the priest, who will use the Urim—one of the sacred lots cast before the LORD—to determine his will. This is how Joshua and the rest of the community of Israel will determine everything they should do."

²²So Moses did as the LORD commanded. He presented Joshua to Eleazar the priest and the whole community. ²³Moses laid his hands on him and commissioned him to lead the people, just as the LORD had commanded through Moses.

28 THE DAILY OFFERINGS

The LORD said to Moses, ²"Give these instructions to the people of Israel: The offerings you present as special gifts are a pleasing aroma to me;

GETTING READY FOR WORSHIP
(28:1-2) *Offerings had to be brought to the Tabernacle regularly and carried out in a certain way under the supervision of the priests. The people had to undergo a period of preparation to be sure they were ready for worship. During this time of preparation, they didn't have time to focus on idols or other distractions. God is pleased today when we allow nothing to come between him and us. How do you prepare to worship God?*

27:2 Hebrew *the Tent of Meeting.* **27:12** Or *the mountains of Abarim.* **27:14** Hebrew *waters of Meribath-kadesh.*

they are my food. See to it that they are brought at the appointed times and offered according to my instructions.

³"Say to the people: This is the special gift you must present to the LORD as your daily burnt offering. You must offer two one-year-old male lambs with no defects. ⁴Sacrifice one lamb in the morning and the other in the evening. ⁵With each lamb you must offer a grain offering of two quarts* of choice flour mixed with one quart* of pure oil of pressed olives. ⁶This is the regular burnt offering instituted at Mount Sinai as a special gift, a pleasing aroma to the LORD. ⁷Along with it you must present the proper liquid offering of one quart of alcoholic drink with each lamb, poured out in the Holy Place as an offering to the LORD. ⁸Offer the second lamb in the evening with the same grain offering and liquid offering. It, too, is a special gift, a pleasing aroma to the LORD.

THE SABBATH OFFERINGS ⁹"On the Sabbath day, sacrifice two one-year-old male lambs with no defects. They must be accompanied by a grain offering of four quarts* of choice flour moistened with olive oil, and a liquid offering. ¹⁰This is the burnt offering to be presented each Sabbath day, in addition to the regular burnt offering and its accompanying liquid offering.

THE MONTHLY OFFERINGS ¹¹"On the first day of each month, present an extra burnt offering to the LORD of two young bulls, one ram, and seven one-year-old male lambs, all with no defects. ¹²These must be accompanied by grain offerings of choice flour moistened with olive oil—six quarts* with each bull, four quarts with the ram, ¹³and two quarts with each lamb. This burnt offering will be a special gift, a pleasing aroma to the LORD. ¹⁴You must also present a liquid offering with each sacrifice: two quarts* of wine for each bull, a third of a gallon* for the ram, and one quart* for each lamb. Present this monthly burnt offering on the first day of each month throughout the year.

¹⁵"On the first day of each month, you must also offer one male goat for a sin offering to the LORD. This is in addition to the regular

burnt offering and its accompanying liquid offering.

OFFERINGS FOR THE PASSOVER ¹⁶"On the fourteenth day of the first month,* you must celebrate the LORD's Passover. ¹⁷On the following day—the fifteenth day of the month—a joyous, seven-day festival will begin, but no bread made with yeast may be eaten. ¹⁸The first day of the festival will be an official day for holy assembly, and no ordinary work may be done on that day. ¹⁹As a special gift you must present a burnt offering to the LORD—two young bulls, one ram, and seven one-year-old male lambs, all with no defects. ²⁰These will be accompanied by grain offerings of choice flour moistened with olive oil—six quarts with each bull, four quarts with the ram, ²¹and two quarts with each of the seven lambs. ²²You must also offer a male goat as a sin offering to purify yourselves and make yourselves right with the LORD.* ²³Present these offerings in addition to your regular morning burnt offering. ²⁴On each of the seven days of the festival, this is how you must prepare the food offering that is presented as a special gift, a pleasing aroma to the LORD. These will be offered in addition to the regular burnt offerings and liquid offerings. ²⁵The seventh day of the festival will be another official day for holy assembly, and no ordinary work may be done on that day.

OFFERINGS FOR THE FESTIVAL OF HARVEST ²⁶"At the Festival of Harvest,* when you present the first of your new grain to the LORD, you must call an official day for holy assembly, and you may do no ordinary work on that day. ²⁷Present a special burnt offering on that day as a pleasing aroma to the LORD. It will consist of two young bulls, one ram, and seven one-year-old male lambs. ²⁸These will be accompanied by grain offerings of choice flour moistened with olive oil—six quarts with each bull, four quarts with the ram, ²⁹and two quarts with each of the seven lambs. ³⁰Also, offer one male goat to purify yourselves and make yourselves right with the LORD. ³¹Prepare these special burnt offerings, along with their liquid offerings, in addition to the regular burnt offering and its accompanying grain offering. Be sure that all the animals you sacrifice have no defects.

29 OFFERINGS FOR THE FESTIVAL OF TRUMPETS "Celebrate the Festival of Trumpets each year on the first day of the appointed month in early autumn.* You must call an official day for holy assembly, and you

28:5a Hebrew ¹⁄₁₀ of an ephah [2.2 liters]; also in 28:13, 21, 29. 28:5b Hebrew ¼ of a hin [1 liter]; also in 28:7. 28:9 Hebrew ²⁄₁₀ of an ephah [4.4 liters]; also in 28:12, 20, 28. 28:12 Hebrew ³⁄₁₀ of an ephah [6.6 liters]; also in 28:20, 28. 28:14a Hebrew ½ of a hin [2 liters]. 28:14b Hebrew ⅓ of a hin [1.3 liters]. 28:14c Hebrew ¼ of a hin [1 liter]. 28:16 This day in the ancient Hebrew lunar calendar occurred in late March, April, or early May. 28:22 Or to make atonement for yourselves; also in 28:30. 28:26 Hebrew Festival of Weeks. This was later called the Festival of Pentecost (see Acts 2:1). It is celebrated today as Shavuot (or Shabuoth). 29:1 Hebrew the first day of the seventh month. This day in the ancient Hebrew lunar calendar occurred in September or October. This festival is celebrated today as Rosh Hashanah, the Jewish new year.

may do no ordinary work. ²On that day you must present a burnt offering as a pleasing aroma to the LORD. It will consist of one young bull, one ram, and seven one-year-old male lambs, all with no defects. ³These must be accompanied by grain offerings of choice flour moistened with olive oil—six quarts* with the bull, four quarts* with the ram, ⁴and two quarts* with each of the seven lambs. ⁵In addition, you must sacrifice a male goat as a sin offering to purify yourselves and make yourselves right with the LORD.* ⁶These special sacrifices are in addition to your regular monthly and daily burnt offerings, and they must be given with their prescribed grain offerings and liquid offerings. These offerings are given as a special gift to the LORD, a pleasing aroma to him.

OFFERINGS FOR THE DAY OF ATONEMENT

⁷"Ten days later, on the tenth day of the same month,* you must call another holy assembly. On that day, the Day of Atonement, the people must go without food and must do no ordinary work. ⁸You must present a burnt offering as a pleasing aroma to the LORD. It will consist of one young bull, one ram, and seven one-year-old male lambs, all with no defects. ⁹These offerings must be accompanied by the prescribed grain offerings of choice flour moistened with olive oil—six quarts of choice flour with the bull, four quarts of choice flour with the ram, ¹⁰and two quarts of choice flour with each of the seven lambs. ¹¹You must also sacrifice one male goat for a sin offering. This is in addition to the sin offering of atonement and the regular daily burnt offering with its grain offering, and their accompanying liquid offerings.

OFFERINGS FOR THE FESTIVAL OF SHELTERS

¹²"Five days later, on the fifteenth day of the same month,* you must call another holy assembly of all the people, and you may do no ordinary work on that day. It is the beginning of the Festival of Shelters,* a seven-day festival to

the LORD. ¹³On the first day of the festival, you must present a burnt offering as a special gift, a pleasing aroma to the LORD. It will consist of thirteen young bulls, two rams, and fourteen one-year-old male lambs, all with no defects. ¹⁴Each of these offerings must be accompanied by a grain offering of choice flour moistened with olive oil—six quarts for each of the thirteen bulls, four quarts for each of the two rams, ¹⁵and two quarts for each of the fourteen lambs. ¹⁶You must also sacrifice a male goat as a sin offering, in addition to the regular burnt offering with its accompanying grain offering and liquid offering.

¹⁷"On the second day of this seven-day festival, sacrifice twelve young bulls, two rams, and fourteen one-year-old male lambs, all with no defects. ¹⁸Each of these offerings of bulls, rams, and lambs must be accompanied by its prescribed grain offering and liquid offering. ¹⁹You must also sacrifice a male goat as a sin offering, in addition to the regular burnt offering with its accompanying grain offering and liquid offering.

²⁰"On the third day of the festival, sacrifice eleven young bulls, two rams, and fourteen one-year-old male lambs, all with no defects. ²¹Each of these offerings of bulls, rams, and lambs must be accompanied by its prescribed grain offering and liquid offering. ²²You must also sacrifice a male goat as a sin offering, in addition to the regular burnt offering with its accompanying grain offering and liquid offering.

²³"On the fourth day of the festival, sacrifice ten young bulls, two rams, and fourteen one-year-old male lambs, all with no defects. ²⁴Each of these offerings of bulls, rams, and lambs must be accompanied by its prescribed grain offering and liquid offering. ²⁵You must also sacrifice a male goat as a sin offering, in addition to the regular burnt offering with its accompanying grain offering and liquid offering.

²⁶"On the fifth day of the festival, sacrifice nine young bulls, two rams, and fourteen one-year-old male lambs, all with no defects. ²⁷Each of these offerings of bulls, rams, and lambs must be accompanied by its prescribed grain

---

WORSHIP TODAY
(29:1-2) The Festival of Trumpets demonstrated three important principles that we can follow as we worship God: (1) The people gathered together to celebrate and worship. There is something special about worshiping with other believers. (2) The normal daily routine was suspended and no hard work was done. Setting aside the time to worship without distractions allows us to prepare our hearts beforehand and reflect afterward. (3) The people sacrificed animals as burnt offerings to God. We show our commitment to God when we give something of value to him. The best gift, of course, is our complete loyalty to God.

29:3a Hebrew ³⁄₁₀ of an ephah [6.6 liters]; also in 29:9, 14.
29:3b Hebrew ²⁄₁₀ of an ephah [4.4 liters]; also in 29:9, 14.
29:4 Hebrew ¹⁄₁₀ of an ephah [2.2 liters]; also in 29:10, 15.   **29:5** Or to make atonement for yourselves.   **29:7** Hebrew On the tenth day of the seventh month; see 29:1 and the note there. This day in the ancient Hebrew lunar calendar occurred in September or October. It is celebrated today as Yom Kippur.   **29:12a** Hebrew On the fifteenth day of the seventh month; see 29:1, 7 and the notes there. This day in the ancient Hebrew lunar calendar occurred in late September, October, or early November.   **29:12b** Or Festival of Booths, or Festival of Tabernacles. This was earlier called the Festival of the Final Harvest or Festival of Ingathering (see Exod 23:16b). It is celebrated today as Sukkot (or Succoth).

offering and liquid offering. ²⁸You must also sacrifice a male goat as a sin offering, in addition to the regular burnt offering with its accompanying grain offering and liquid offering.

²⁹"On the sixth day of the festival, sacrifice eight young bulls, two rams, and fourteen one-year-old male lambs, all with no defects. ³⁰Each of these offerings of bulls, rams, and lambs must be accompanied by its prescribed grain offering and liquid offering. ³¹You must also sacrifice a male goat as a sin offering, in addition to the regular burnt offering with its accompanying grain offering and liquid offering.

³²"On the seventh day of the festival, sacrifice seven young bulls, two rams, and fourteen one-year-old male lambs, all with no defects. ³³Each of these offerings of bulls, rams, and lambs must be accompanied by its prescribed grain offering and liquid offering. ³⁴You must also sacrifice one male goat as a sin offering, in addition to the regular burnt offering with its accompanying grain offering and liquid offering.

³⁵"On the eighth day of the festival, proclaim another holy day. You must do no ordinary work on that day. ³⁶You must present a burnt offering as a special gift, a pleasing aroma to the LORD. It will consist of one young bull, one ram, and seven one-year-old male lambs, all with no defects. ³⁷Each of these offerings must be accompanied by its prescribed grain offering and liquid offering. ³⁸You must also sacrifice one male goat as a sin offering, in addition to the regular burnt offering with its accompanying grain offering and liquid offering.

³⁹"You must present these offerings to the LORD at your annual festivals. These are in addition to the sacrifices and offerings you present in connection with vows, or as voluntary offerings, burnt offerings, grain offerings, liquid offerings, or peace offerings."

⁴⁰*So Moses gave all of these instructions to the people of Israel as the LORD had commanded him.

30 LAWS CONCERNING VOWS ¹*Then Moses summoned the leaders of the tribes of Israel and told them, "This is what the LORD has commanded: ²A man who makes a vow to the LORD or makes a pledge under oath must never break it. He must do exactly what he said he would do.

³"If a young woman makes a vow to the LORD or a pledge under oath while she is still living at her father's home, ⁴and her father hears of the vow or pledge and does not object to it, then all her vows and pledges will stand. ⁵But if her father refuses to let her fulfill the vow or pledge on the day he hears of it, then all her vows and pledges will become invalid. The LORD will forgive her because her father would not let her fulfill them.

⁶"Now suppose a young woman makes a vow or binds herself with an impulsive pledge and later marries. ⁷If her husband learns of her vow or pledge and does not object on the day he hears of it, her vows and pledges will stand. ⁸But if her husband refuses to accept her vow or impulsive pledge on the day he hears of it, he nullifies her commitments, and the LORD will forgive her. ⁹If, however, a woman is a widow or is divorced, she must fulfill all her vows and pledges.

¹⁰"But suppose a woman is married and living in her husband's home when she makes a vow or binds herself with a pledge. ¹¹If her husband hears of it and does not object to it, her vow or pledge will stand. ¹²But if her husband refuses to accept it on the day he hears of it, her vow or pledge will be nullified, and the LORD will forgive her. ¹³So her husband may either confirm or nullify any vows or pledges she makes to deny herself. ¹⁴But if he does not object on the day he hears of it, then he is agreeing to all her vows and pledges. ¹⁵If he waits more than a day and then tries to nullify a vow or pledge, he will be punished for her guilt."

¹⁶These are the regulations the LORD gave Moses concerning relationships between a man and his wife, and between a father and a young daughter who still lives at home.

··

PROMISES
(30:1-2) Moses reminded the people that their promises to God and others must be kept. In ancient times, people did not sign written contracts. A person's word was as binding as a signature. To make a vow even more binding, an offering was given along with it. No one was forced by law to make a vow; but once made, vows had to be fulfilled. Breaking a vow meant a broken trust and a broken relationship. Trust is still the basis of our relationships with God and others. Thus a broken promise today is just as harmful as it was in Moses' day.

A PARENT'S ADVICE
(30:3-5) Under Israelite law, parents could overrule their children's vows. This helped young people avoid making foolish promises or costly commitments. From this law comes an important principle for both parents and children. A parent's advice is worth seeking. His or her experience could save you from making a serious mistake. Parents, however, are encouraged to exercise their authority with caution and grace. How have your parents helped you in your decision making recently?

29:40 Verse 29:40 is numbered 30:1 in Hebrew text.   30:1 Verses 30:1-16 are numbered 30:2-17 in Hebrew text.

31 CONQUEST OF THE MIDIANITES

Then the Lord said to Moses, ²"On behalf of the people of Israel, take revenge on the Midianites for leading them into idolatry. After that, you will die and join your ancestors."

³So Moses said to the people, "Choose some men, and arm them to fight the Lord's war of revenge against Midian. ⁴From each tribe of Israel, send 1,000 men into battle." ⁵So they chose 1,000 men from each tribe of Israel, a total of 12,000 men armed for battle. ⁶Then Moses sent them out, 1,000 men from each tribe, and Phinehas son of Eleazar the priest led them into battle. They carried along the holy objects of the sanctuary and the trumpets for sounding the charge. ⁷They attacked Midian as the Lord had commanded Moses, and they killed all the men. ⁸All five of the Midianite kings—Evi, Rekem, Zur, Hur, and Reba—died in the battle. They also killed Balaam son of Beor with the sword.

⁹Then the Israelite army captured the Midianite women and children and seized their cattle and flocks and all their wealth as plunder. ¹⁰They burned all the towns and villages where the Midianites had lived. ¹¹After they had gathered the plunder and captives, both people and animals, ¹²they brought them all to Moses and Eleazar the priest, and to the whole community of Israel, which was camped on the plains of Moab beside the Jordan River, across from Jericho. ¹³Moses, Eleazar the priest, and all the leaders of the community went to meet them outside the camp. ¹⁴But Moses was furious with all the generals and captains* who had returned from the battle.

31:14 Hebrew *the commanders of thousands, and the commanders of hundreds;* also in 31:48, 52, 54.

ULTIMATE ISSUES HOLY WAR?

The United States' involvement in Iraq has inspired many Internet polls about war and much posturing by politicians. While many people support the war (to gain justice for the human rights violations and acts of terrorism suffered by many, to punish the terrorists, and so forth), others seem doubtful. Some Christians have asked themselves, *Should a Christian ever go to war? Or should Christians be pacifists, refusing to take up arms no matter what the cause?* Perhaps you've thought or asked those questions.

This is a tough issue for believers today. It wasn't any simpler for our ancestors. Though warfare has changed dramatically—from swords and spears to nuclear warheads, stealth bombers, and smart bombs—the core issue remains the same: When, if ever, is it right for God's people to go into *physical* battle?

Let's examine God's orders for his chosen nation of Israel in the Old Testament. In Numbers 31, God told his people to go to war with the Midianites and to utterly destroy them. After crushing the Midianite army, the Israelites took all the Midianite women and children as captives, along with their possessions. God wasn't satisfied with that. Through Moses, his appointed leader, God commanded the soldiers to kill all the women who had ever had sex with a man and to kill all the boys. Only young, female virgins were to be spared. Why did God require such terrible punishment for Israel's enemies? Aren't Christians supposed to be loving and kind peacemakers?

To answer this, we have to understand some basic differences between the Old Testament nation of Israel and God's people today. In the Old Testament, God was leading his nation to their new home—Canaan. Along the way, they were opposed by numerous other nations, like the Midianites. (After all, who would voluntarily give up his or her home?)

The problem wasn't simply that these other people were in the way. They also worshiped idols and routinely sacrificed their children to these idols. No wonder God's anger burned against them, and he told Israel to cleanse Canaan of them. God didn't want their profane ways infecting his people.

For Christians today, however, the situation differs in some key aspects. God is leading us to our Promised Land, but ours is in heaven. We have no pagan nations to terminate; our war is a spiritual one. "For we are not fighting against flesh-and-blood enemies, but against evil rulers and authorities of the unseen world, against mighty powers in this dark world, and against evil spirits in the heavenly places" (Eph 6:12). God's people today are not determined by *nationality,* but by *spirituality.* Whereas God's blessings and promises before belonged to Abraham's physical descendants, they now belong to those who are spiritually "grafted" into Abraham's line (Rom 11:17). Therefore, when any nation goes to war today, its cause may be just, but it cannot be considered holy in the way Israel's wars were. Israel had God himself fighting battles for them, and he often gave Israel miraculous assistance and assurance of victory. No modern nation can make that claim.

So should a Christian go to war? Unfortunately, you won't find the final answer here. We see in God's Word that God has, at times, told his people to go to war with other people; therefore, those who believe war is never right should reconsider. Still, not all wars are fought for the cause of righteousness—some would say almost none of them are. Many wars can't even be considered justified, much less holy. ∎

¹⁵"Why have you let all the women live?" he demanded. ¹⁶"These are the very ones who followed Balaam's advice and caused the people of Israel to rebel against the LORD at Mount Peor. They are the ones who caused the plague to strike the LORD's people. ¹⁷So kill all the boys and all the women who have had intercourse with a man. ¹⁸Only the young girls who are virgins may live; you may keep them for yourselves. ¹⁹And all of you who have killed anyone or touched a dead body must stay outside the camp for seven days. You must purify yourselves and your captives on the third and seventh days. ²⁰Purify all your clothing, too, and everything made of leather, goat hair, or wood."

²¹Then Eleazar the priest said to the men who were in the battle, "The LORD has given Moses this legal requirement: ²²Anything made of gold, silver, bronze, iron, tin, or lead—²³that is, all metals that do not burn—must be passed through fire in order to be made ceremonially pure. These metal objects must then be further purified with the water of purification. But everything that burns must be purified by the water alone. ²⁴On the seventh day you must wash your clothes and be purified. Then you may return to the camp."

DIVISION OF THE PLUNDER ²⁵And the LORD said to Moses, ²⁶"You and Eleazar the priest and the family leaders of each tribe are to make a list of all the plunder taken in the battle, including the people and animals. ²⁷Then divide the plunder into two parts, and give half to the men who fought the battle and half to the rest of the people. ²⁸From the army's portion, first give the LORD his share of the plunder—one of every 500 of the prisoners and of the cattle, donkeys, sheep, and goats. ²⁹Give this share of the army's half to Eleazar the priest as an offering to the LORD. ³⁰From the half that belongs to the people of Israel, take one of every fifty of the prisoners and of the cattle, donkeys, sheep, goats, and other animals. Give this share to the Levites, who are in charge of maintaining the LORD's Tabernacle." ³¹So Moses and Eleazar the priest did as the LORD commanded Moses.

³²The plunder remaining from everything the fighting men had taken totaled 675,000 sheep and goats, ³³72,000 cattle, ³⁴61,000 donkeys, ³⁵and 32,000 virgin girls. ³⁶Half of the plunder was given to the fighting men. It totaled 337,500 sheep and goats, ³⁷of which 675 were the LORD's share; ³⁸36,000 cattle, of which 72 were the LORD's share; ³⁹30,500 donkeys, of which 61 were the LORD's share; ⁴⁰and 16,000 virgin girls, of whom 32 were the LORD's share. ⁴¹Moses gave all the LORD's share to Eleazar the priest, just as the LORD had directed him.

⁴²Half of the plunder belonged to the people of Israel, and Moses separated it from the half belonging to the fighting men. ⁴³It totaled 337,500 sheep and goats, ⁴⁴36,000 cattle, ⁴⁵30,500 donkeys, ⁴⁶and 16,000 virgin girls. ⁴⁷From the half-share given to the people, Moses took one of every fifty prisoners and animals and gave them to the Levites, who maintained the LORD's Tabernacle. All this was done as the LORD had commanded Moses.

⁴⁸Then all the generals and captains came to Moses ⁴⁹and said, "We, your servants, have accounted for all the men who went out to battle under our command; not one of us is missing! ⁵⁰So we are presenting the items of gold we captured as an offering to the LORD from our share of the plunder—armbands, bracelets, rings, earrings, and necklaces. This will purify our lives before the LORD and make us right with him.*"

⁵¹So Moses and Eleazar the priest received the gold from all the military commanders— all kinds of jewelry and crafted objects. ⁵²In all, the gold that the generals and captains presented as a gift to the LORD weighed about 420 pounds.* ⁵³All the fighting men had taken some of the plunder for themselves. ⁵⁴So Moses and Eleazar the priest accepted the gifts from the generals and captains and brought the gold to the Tabernacle* as a reminder to the LORD that the people of Israel belong to him.

32 **THE TRIBES EAST OF THE JORDAN** The tribes of Reuben and Gad owned vast numbers of livestock. So when they saw that the lands of Jazer and Gilead were ideally suited for their flocks and herds, ²they came to Moses, Eleazar the priest, and the other leaders of the community. They said, ³"Notice the towns of Ataroth, Dibon, Jazer, Nimrah, Heshbon, Elealeh, Sibmah,* Nebo, and Beon. ⁴The LORD has

31:50 Or will make atonement for our lives before the LORD. 31:52 Hebrew 16,750 shekels [191 kilograms]. 31:54 Hebrew the Tent of Meeting. 32:3 As in Samaritan Pentateuch and Greek version (see also 32:38); Hebrew reads Sebam.

....

DIVIDING THE SPOILS
(31:25-30) Moses told the Israelites to give God a portion of the spoils from the war with Midian. Another portion was to go to the soldiers and to the people who remained behind. Similarly, the money we earn is not ours alone. Everything we possess comes directly or indirectly from God and ultimately belongs to him. God is pleased when we return a portion to him and also share a portion with those in need.

YOU MAY BE SURE THAT YOUR SIN WILL FIND YOU OUT.

{ N U M B E R S   3 2 : 2 3 }

conquered this whole area for the community of Israel, and it is ideally suited for all our livestock. ⁵If we have found favor with you, please let us have this land as our property instead of giving us land across the Jordan River."

⁶"Do you intend to stay here while your brothers go across and do all the fighting?" Moses asked the men of Gad and Reuben. ⁷"Why do you want to discourage the rest of the people of Israel from going across to the land the LORD has given them? ⁸Your ancestors did the same thing when I sent them from Kadesh-barnea to explore the land. ⁹After they went up to the valley of Eshcol and explored the land, they discouraged the people of Israel from entering the land the LORD was giving them. ¹⁰Then the LORD was very angry with them, and he vowed, ¹¹'Of all those I rescued from Egypt, no one who is twenty years old or older will ever see the land I swore to give to Abraham, Isaac, and Jacob, for they have not obeyed me wholeheartedly. ¹²The only exceptions are Caleb son of Jephunneh the Kenizzite and Joshua son of Nun, for they have wholeheartedly followed the LORD.'

¹³"The LORD was angry with Israel and made them wander in the wilderness for forty years until the entire generation that sinned in the LORD's sight had died. ¹⁴But here you are, a brood of sinners, doing exactly the same thing! You are making the LORD even angrier with Israel. ¹⁵If you turn away from him like this and he abandons them again in the wilderness, you will be responsible for destroying this entire nation!"

¹⁶But they approached Moses and said, "We simply want to build pens for our livestock and fortified towns for our wives and children. ¹⁷Then we will arm ourselves and lead our fellow Israelites into battle until we have brought them safely to their land. Meanwhile, our families will stay in the fortified towns we build here, so they will be safe from any attacks by the local people. ¹⁸We will not return to our homes until all the people of Israel have received their portions of land. ¹⁹But we do not claim any of the land on the other side of the Jordan. We would rather live here on the east side and accept this as our grant of land."

²⁰Then Moses said, "If you keep your word and arm yourselves for the LORD's battles, ²¹and if your troops cross the Jordan and keep fighting until the LORD has driven out his enemies, ²²then you may return when the LORD has conquered the land. You will have fulfilled your duty to the LORD and to the rest of the people of Israel. And the land on the east side of the Jordan will be your property from the LORD. ²³But if you fail to keep your word, then you will have sinned against the LORD, and you may be sure that your sin will find you out. ²⁴Go ahead and build towns for your families and pens for your flocks, but do everything you have promised."

²⁵Then the men of Gad and Reuben replied, "We, your servants, will follow your instructions exactly. ²⁶Our children, wives, flocks, and cattle will stay here in the towns of Gilead. ²⁷But all who are able to bear arms will cross over to fight for the LORD, just as you have said."

²⁸So Moses gave orders to Eleazar the priest, Joshua son of Nun, and the leaders of the clans of Israel. ²⁹He said, "The men of Gad and Reuben who are armed for battle must cross the Jordan with you to fight for the LORD. If they do, give them the land of Gilead as their property when the land is conquered. ³⁰But if they refuse to arm themselves and cross over with you, then they must accept land with the rest of you in the land of Canaan."

³¹The tribes of Gad and Reuben said again, "We are your servants, and we will do as the LORD has commanded! ³²We will cross the Jordan into Canaan fully armed to fight for the LORD, but our property will be here on this side of the Jordan."

³³So Moses assigned land to the tribes of Gad, Reuben, and half the tribe of Manasseh son of Joseph. He gave them the territory of King Sihon of the Amorites and the land of King Og of Bashan—the whole land with its cities and surrounding lands.

³⁴The descendants of Gad built the towns of Dibon, Ataroth, Aroer, ³⁵Atroth-shophan, Jazer, Jogbehah, ³⁶Beth-nimrah, and Beth-haran.

. . . .

WRONG ASSUMPTIONS
(32:1-33) Three tribes (Reuben, Gad, and the half-tribe of Manasseh) wanted to live east of the Jordan River on land they had already conquered. Moses immediately assumed they had selfish motives and were trying to avoid helping the others fight for the land across the river. But Moses jumped to the wrong conclusion. Have you done something similar recently? In dealing with people, we must find out all the facts before making up our mind. We shouldn't automatically assume that their motives are wrong, even if their plans sound suspicious.

These were all fortified towns with pens for their flocks.

³⁷The descendants of Reuben built the towns of Heshbon, Elealeh, Kiriathaim, ³⁸Nebo, Baal-meon, and Sibmah. They changed the names of some of the towns they conquered and rebuilt.

³⁹Then the descendants of Makir of the tribe of Manasseh went to Gilead and conquered it, and they drove out the Amorites living there. ⁴⁰So Moses gave Gilead to the Makirites, descendants of Manasseh, and they settled there. ⁴¹The people of Jair, another clan of the tribe of Manasseh, captured many of the towns in Gilead and changed the name of that region to the Towns of Jair.* ⁴²Meanwhile, a man named Nobah captured the town of Kenath and its surrounding villages, and he renamed that area Nobah after himself.

33 REMEMBERING ISRAEL'S JOURNEY

This is the route the Israelites followed as they marched out of Egypt under the leadership of Moses and Aaron. ²At the LORD's direction, Moses kept a written record of their progress. These are the stages of their march, identified by the different places where they stopped along the way.

³They set out from the city of Rameses in early spring—on the fifteenth day of the first month*—on the morning after the first Passover celebration. The people of Israel left defiantly, in full view of all the Egyptians. ⁴Meanwhile, the Egyptians were burying all their firstborn sons, whom the LORD had killed the night before. The LORD had defeated the gods of Egypt that night with great acts of judgment!

⁵After leaving Rameses, the Israelites set up camp at Succoth.

⁶Then they left Succoth and camped at Etham on the edge of the wilderness.

⁷They left Etham and turned back toward Pi-hahiroth, opposite Baal-zephon, and camped near Migdol.

⁸They left Pi-hahiroth and crossed the Red Sea* into the wilderness beyond. Then they traveled for three days into the Etham wilderness and camped at Marah.

⁹They left Marah and camped at Elim, where there were twelve springs of water and seventy palm trees.

¹⁰They left Elim and camped beside the Red Sea.*

³²:⁴¹ Hebrew *Havvoth-jair.* **33:3** This day in the ancient Hebrew lunar calendar occurred in late March, April, or early May. **33:8** Hebrew *the sea.* **33:10** Hebrew *sea of reeds;* also in 33:11. **33:11** The geographical name *Sin* is related to *Sinai* and should not be confused with the English word *sin.*

¹¹They left the Red Sea and camped in the wilderness of Sin.*

¹²They left the wilderness of Sin and camped at Dophkah.

¹³They left Dophkah and camped at Alush.

¹⁴They left Alush and camped at Rephidim, where there was no water for the people to drink.

¹⁵They left Rephidim and camped in the wilderness of Sinai.

¹⁶They left the wilderness of Sinai and camped at Kibroth-hattaavah.

¹⁷They left Kibroth-hattaavah and camped at Hazeroth.

¹⁸They left Hazeroth and camped at Rithmah.

¹⁹They left Rithmah and camped at Rimmon-perez.

²⁰They left Rimmon-perez and camped at Libnah.

²¹They left Libnah and camped at Rissah.

²²They left Rissah and camped at Kehelathah.

²³They left Kehelathah and camped at Mount Shepher.

²⁴They left Mount Shepher and camped at Haradah.

²⁵They left Haradah and camped at Makheloth.

²⁶They left Makheloth and camped at Tahath.

²⁷They left Tahath and camped at Terah.

²⁸They left Terah and camped at Mithcah.

²⁹They left Mithcah and camped at Hashmonah.

³⁰They left Hashmonah and camped at Moseroth.

³¹They left Moseroth and camped at Bene-jaakan.

³²They left Bene-jaakan and camped at Hor-haggidgad.

³³They left Hor-haggidgad and camped at Jotbathah.

³⁴They left Jotbathah and camped at Abronah.

³⁵They left Abronah and camped at Ezion-geber.

³⁶They left Ezion-geber and camped at Kadesh in the wilderness of Zin.

³⁷They left Kadesh and camped at Mount Hor, at the border of Edom. ³⁸While they were at the foot of Mount Hor, Aaron the priest was directed by the LORD to go up the mountain,

....

A TRAVEL JOURNAL
(33:2) Moses recorded the Israelites' journey as God instructed him, providing a written record of their spiritual as well as geographic progress. Have you made spiritual progress lately? Recording your thoughts about God and lessons you have learned over a period of time can be a valuable aid to spiritual growth. A record of your spiritual pilgrimage will help you check up on your progress and avoid repeating past mistakes.

and there he died. This happened in midsummer, on the first day of the fifth month* of the fortieth year after Israel's departure from Egypt. 39Aaron was 123 years old when he died there on Mount Hor.

40At that time the Canaanite king of Arad, who lived in the Negev in the land of Canaan, heard that the people of Israel were approaching his land.

41Meanwhile, the Israelites left Mount Hor and camped at Zalmonah.

42Then they left Zalmonah and camped at Punon.

43They left Punon and camped at Oboth.

44They left Oboth and camped at Iye-abarim on -the border of Moab.

45They left Iye-abarim* and camped at Dibon-gad.

46They left Dibon-gad and camped at Almon-diblathaim.

47They left Almon-diblathaim and camped in the mountains east of the river,* near Mount Nebo.

48They left the mountains east of the river and camped on the plains of Moab beside the Jordan River, across from Jericho. 49Along the Jordan River they camped from Beth-jeshimoth as far as the meadows of Acacia* on the plains of Moab.

THE BORDERS OF THE PROMISED LAND
The borders of the Promised Land stretched from the wilderness of Zin and Kedesh-barnea in the south to Lebo-hamath and Riblah in the north, and from the Mediterranean seacoast on the west to the Jordan River on the east. The land of Gilead was also included.

50While they were camped near the Jordan River on the plains of Moab opposite Jericho, the LORD said to Moses, 51"Give the following instructions to the people of Israel: When you cross the Jordan River into the land of Canaan, 52you must drive out all the people living there. You must destroy all their carved and molten images and demolish all their pagan shrines. 53Take possession of the land and settle in it, because I have given it to you to occupy. 54You must distribute the land among the clans by sacred lot and in proportion to their size. A larger portion of land will be allotted to each of the larger clans, and a smaller portion will be allotted to each of the smaller clans. The decision of the sacred lot is final. In this way, the portions of land will be divided among your ancestral tribes. 55But if you fail to drive out the people who live in the land, those who remain will be like splinters in your eyes and thorns in your sides. They will harass you in the land where you live. 56And I will do to you what I had planned to do to them."

34 BOUNDARIES OF THE LAND
Then the LORD said to Moses, 2"Give these instructions to the Israelites: When you come into the land of Canaan, which I am giving you as your special possession, these will be the boundaries. 3The southern portion of your country will extend from the wilderness of Zin, along the edge of Edom. The southern boundary will begin on the east at the Dead Sea.* 4It will then run south past Scorpion Pass* in the direction of Zin. Its southernmost point will be Kadesh-barnea, from which it will go to Hazar-addar, and on to Azmon. 5From Azmon the boundary will turn toward the Brook of Egypt and end at the Mediterranean Sea.*

6"Your western boundary will be the coastline of the Mediterranean Sea.

7"Your northern boundary will begin at the Mediterranean Sea and run east to Mount Hor, 8then to Lebo-hamath, and on through Zedad 9and Ziphron to Hazar-enan. This will be your northern boundary.

10"The eastern boundary will start at Hazar-enan and run south to Shepham, 11then down to Riblah on the east side of Ain. From there the boundary will run down along the eastern edge of the Sea of Galilee,* 12and then along the Jordan River to the Dead Sea. These are the boundaries of your land."

13Then Moses told the Israelites, "This territory is the homeland you are to divide among yourselves by sacred lot. The LORD has commanded that the land be divided among the nine and a half remaining tribes. 14The families of the tribes of Reuben, Gad, and half the tribe of Manasseh have already received their grants of land 15on the east side of the Jordan River, across from Jericho toward the sunrise."

33:38 This day in the ancient Hebrew lunar calendar occurred in July or August.   **33:45** As in 33:44; Hebrew reads *Iyim*, another name for Iye-abarim.   **33:47** Or *the mountains of Abarim;* also in 33:48.   **33:49** Hebrew *as far as Abel-shittim.*   **34:3** Hebrew *Salt Sea;* also in 34:12.   **34:4** Or *the ascent of Akrabbim.*   **34:5** Hebrew *the sea;* also in 34:6, 7.   **34:11** Hebrew *Sea of Kinnereth.*

LEADERS TO DIVIDE THE LAND ¹⁶And the Lord said to Moses, ¹⁷"Eleazar the priest and Joshua son of Nun are the men designated to divide the grants of land among the people. ¹⁸Enlist one leader from each tribe to help them with the task. ¹⁹These are the tribes and the names of the leaders:

Tribe	Leader
Judah	Caleb son of Jephunneh
²⁰ Simeon	Shemuel son of Ammihud
²¹ Benjamin	Elidad son of Kislon
²² Dan	Bukki son of Jogli
²³ Manasseh son of Joseph	Hanniel son of Ephod
²⁴ Ephraim son of Joseph	Kemuel son of Shiphtan
²⁵ Zebulun	Elizaphan son of Parnach
²⁶ Issachar	Paltiel son of Azzan
²⁷ Asher	Ahihud son of Shelomi
²⁸ Naphtali	Pedahel son of Ammihud

²⁹These are the men the Lord has appointed to divide the grants of land in Canaan among the Israelites."

35 **TOWNS FOR THE LEVITES** While Israel was camped beside the Jordan on the plains of Moab across from Jericho, the Lord said to Moses, ²"Command the people of Israel to give to the Levites from their property certain towns to live in, along with the surrounding pasturelands. ³These towns will be for the Levites to live in, and the surrounding lands will provide pasture for their cattle, flocks, and other livestock. ⁴The pastureland assigned to the Levites around these towns will extend 1,500 feet* from the town walls in every direction. ⁵Measure off 3,000 feet* outside the town walls in every direction—east, south, west, north—with the town at the center. This area will serve as the larger pastureland for the towns.

⁶"Six of the towns you give the Levites will be cities of refuge, where a person who has accidentally killed someone can flee for safety. In addition, give them forty-two other towns. ⁷In all, forty-eight towns with the surrounding pastureland will be given to the Levites. ⁸These towns will come from the property of the people of Israel. The larger tribes will give more towns to the Levites, while the smaller tribes will give fewer. Each tribe will give property in proportion to the size of its land."

35:4 Hebrew *1,000 cubits* [460 meters].　**35:5** Hebrew *2,000 cubits* [920 meters].

CITIES OF REFUGE ⁹The Lord said to Moses, ¹⁰"Give the following instructions to the people of Israel.

"When you cross the Jordan into the land of Canaan, ¹¹designate cities of refuge to which people can flee if they have killed someone accidentally. ¹²These cities will be places of protection from a dead person's relatives who want to avenge the death. The slayer must not be put to death before being tried by the community. ¹³Designate six cities of refuge for yourselves, ¹⁴three on the east side of the Jordan River and three on the west in the land of Canaan. ¹⁵These cities are for the protection of Israelites, foreigners living among you, and traveling merchants. Anyone who accidentally kills someone may flee there for safety.

¹⁶"But if someone strikes and kills another person with a piece of iron, it is murder, and the murderer must be executed. ¹⁷Or if someone with a stone in his hand strikes and kills another person, it is murder, and the murderer must be put to death. ¹⁸Or if someone strikes and kills another person with a wooden object, it is murder, and the murderer must be put to death. ¹⁹The victim's nearest relative is responsible for putting the murderer to death. When they meet, the avenger must put the murderer to death. ²⁰So if someone hates another person and pushes him or throws a dangerous object at him and he dies, it is murder. ²¹Or if someone hates another person and hits him with a fist and he dies, it is murder. In such cases, the avenger must put the murderer to death when they meet.

²²"But suppose someone pushes another person without having shown previous

··

GETTING ORGANIZED GOD'S WAY
(34:16-29) In God's plan for settling the land, he explained to Moses what to do in a clear fashion and assigned specific people to oversee the division of the land. No plan is complete until each job is assigned and everyone understands his or her responsibilities. Need to organize some people for a task? God's method is a good one to follow.

TRUE JUSTICE
(35:9-28) At this time in Israel's history, if someone died because of violence, the murder suspect was not automatically considered guilty, even if murder was assumed. The people were to be intolerant of the sin, yet impartial to the accused so that he or she could have a fair trial. The cities of refuge represented God's concern for justice in a culture that did not always protect the innocent. It is unjust both to overlook wrongdoing and to jump to conclusions about guilt. When someone is accused of wrongdoing, are you willing to stand up for justice, protect those not yet proven guilty, and listen carefully to all sides of the story?

hostility, or throws something that unintentionally hits another person, ²³or accidentally drops a huge stone on someone, though they were not enemies, and the person dies. ²⁴If this should happen, the community must follow these regulations in making a judgment between the slayer and the avenger, the victim's nearest relative: ²⁵The community must protect the slayer from the avenger and must escort the slayer back to live in the city of refuge to which he fled. There he must remain until the death of the high priest, who was anointed with the sacred oil.

²⁶"But if the slayer ever leaves the limits of the city of refuge, ²⁷and the avenger finds him outside the city and kills him, it will not be considered murder. ²⁸The slayer should have stayed inside the city of refuge until the death of the high priest. But after the death of the high priest, the slayer may return to his own property. ²⁹These are legal requirements for you to observe from generation to generation, wherever you may live.

³⁰"All murderers must be put to death, but only if evidence is presented by more than one witness. No one may be put to death on the testimony of only one witness. ³¹Also, you must never accept a ransom payment for the life of someone judged guilty of murder and subject to execution; murderers must always be put to death. ³²And never accept a ransom payment from someone who has fled to a city of refuge, allowing a slayer to return to his property before the death of the high priest. ³³This will ensure that the land where you live will not be polluted, for murder pollutes the land. And no sacrifice except the execution of the murderer can purify the land from murder.* ³⁴You must not defile the land where you live, for I live

there myself. I am the LORD, who lives among the people of Israel."

36 WOMEN WHO INHERIT PROPERTY

Then the heads of the clans of Gilead—descendants of Makir, son of Manasseh, son of Joseph—came to Moses and the family leaders of Israel with a petition. ²They said, "Sir, the LORD instructed you to divide the land by sacred lot among the people of Israel. You were told by the LORD to give the grant of land owned by our brother Zelophehad to his daughters. ³But if they marry men from another tribe, their grants of land will go with them to the tribe into which they marry. In this way, the total area of our tribal land will be reduced. ⁴Then when the Year of Jubilee comes, their portion of land will be added to that of the new tribe, causing it to be lost forever to our ancestral tribe."

⁵So Moses gave the Israelites this command from the LORD: "The claim of the men of the tribe of Joseph is legitimate. ⁶This is what the LORD commands concerning the daughters of Zelophehad: Let them marry anyone they like, as long as it is within their own ancestral tribe. ⁷None of the territorial land may pass from tribe to tribe, for all the land given to each tribe must remain within the tribe to which it was first allotted. ⁸The daughters throughout the tribes of Israel who are in line to inherit property must marry within their tribe, so that all the Israelites will keep their ancestral property. ⁹No grant of land may pass from one tribe to another; each tribe of Israel must keep its allotted portion of land."

¹⁰The daughters of Zelophehad did as the LORD commanded Moses. ¹¹Mahlah, Tirzah, Hoglah, Milcah, and Noah all married cousins on their father's side. ¹²They married into the clans of Manasseh son of Joseph. Thus, their inheritance of land remained within their ancestral tribe.

¹³These are the commands and regulations that the LORD gave to the people of Israel through Moses while they were camped on the plains of Moab beside the Jordan River across from Jericho.

35:33 Or *can make atonement for murder.*

A CORRUPTING INFLUENCE
(35:33) According to God's law, murderers were to be executed because they corrupted the land. Murder and anger stem from the same root. While anger seems a lesser sin, it can often lead to more sin. Unchecked bitterness and anger will ultimately destroy us. We need to deal with these strong emotions in an appropriate way, before they get out of control.

DEUTERONOMY

Got a place where you keep various reminders from your past? Maybe you have a scrapbook or a box filled with mementos of happy occasions. Some people save flower petals. Others keep ticket stubs from movies, ball games, or concerts. Some store especially meaningful letters or old pictures.

If you're like most people, these treasures become even more meaningful to you when you are going through tough times. There is something comforting in remembering the good times you've had. Your keepsakes help you believe that everything is going to be OK.

The book of Deuteronomy is a book of memories. God had made a covenant, or promise, with the Israelites when they first came out of Egypt, pledging to take them into the Promised Land. But they refused to obey or trust God. So he let them wander in the wilderness until they died.

But since a new generation had grown up, God used Moses to remind them of the covenant. Moses first reviewed the mighty acts God had done for Israel. Then he let them know that, based on the past, they must trust, obey, and love God as they prepared to enter their new homeland. Only such an attitude would enable them to conquer the Promised Land.

As you read Deuteronomy, think about your "spiritual memories." How did God help you in the past? Are you willing to trust him for the future?

KEY POINTS

HISTORY Moses reviews God's efforts to set Israel free from slavery in Egypt. By reviewing God's promises and mighty acts, we can learn about his character and grow in faith.

LAWS The legal contract between God and his people had to be renewed for the new generation entering the Promised Land. Commitment to God and his truth cannot be taken for granted. Every person in each generation must respond anew to God's call.

LOVE God's faithful and patient love is portrayed more often than his punishment. His love forms the foundation for our trust in him. We can be confident that the one who loves us perfectly can be trusted with our lives.

CHOICES God reminded his people that in order to enjoy the blessings of his will for them, they would have to continue in obedience. Our choices make a difference. Choosing to follow God produces good results in our lives and in our relationships with others. Choosing to abandon God's ways brings harmful results to us and to others.

TEACHING God commanded the Israelites to teach their children his ways. God's truth must be passed on to future generations. It is not, however, just the traditions or commands that are to be passed on. Rather, we are to teach each new generation to know and love God personally.

STATS

PURPOSE
To remind the people of what God has done and encourage them to rededicate their lives to him

AUTHOR
Moses (except for the final summary, which Joshua probably wrote after Moses' death)

ORIGINAL AUDIENCE
Israel (the new generation entering the Promised Land)

DATE WRITTEN
About 1407/6 B.C.

SETTING
The east side of the Jordan River, within sight of the Promised Land

KEY PEOPLE
Moses, Joshua

KEY PLACE
The valley of Arabah in Moab, east of the Jordan River

TIMELINE

1805 B.C.
Joseph dies

SLAVERY IN EGYPT

1446
Exodus from Egypt

1445
Ten Commandments

WILDERNESS WANDERINGS

1406
Moses' death; Israelites enter Canaan

1375
Judges begin to rule

1050
United kingdom under Saul

1 INTRODUCTION TO MOSES' FIRST ADDRESS

These are the words that Moses spoke to all the people of Israel while they were in the wilderness east of the Jordan River. They were camped in the Jordan Valley* near Suph, between Paran on one side and Tophel, Laban, Hazeroth, and Di-zahab on the other.

²Normally it takes only eleven days to travel from Mount Sinai* to Kadesh-barnea, going by way of Mount Seir. ³But forty years after the Israelites left Egypt, on the first day of the eleventh month,* Moses addressed the people of Israel, telling them everything the LORD had commanded him to say. ⁴This took place after he had defeated King Sihon of the Amorites, who had ruled in Heshbon, and King Og of Bashan, who had ruled in Ashtaroth and Edrei.

⁵While the Israelites were in the land of Moab east of the Jordan River, Moses carefully explained the LORD's instructions as follows.

THE COMMAND TO LEAVE SINAI ⁶"When we were at Mount Sinai, the LORD our God said to us, 'You have stayed at this mountain long enough. ⁷It is time to break camp and move on. Go to the hill country of the Amorites and to all the neighboring regions—the Jordan Valley, the hill country, the western foothills,* the Negev, and the coastal plain. Go to the land of the Canaanites and to Lebanon, and all the way to the great Euphrates River. ⁸Look, I am giving all this land to you! Go in and occupy it, for it is the land the LORD swore to give to your ancestors Abraham, Isaac, and Jacob, and to all their descendants.'"

MOSES APPOINTS LEADERS FROM EACH TRIBE ⁹Moses continued, "At that time I told you, 'You are too great a burden for me to carry

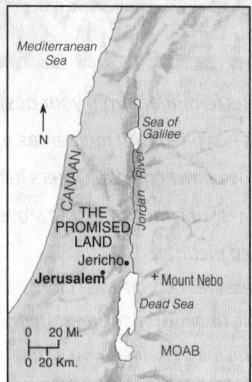

EVENTS IN DEUTERONOMY
The book of Deuteronomy opens with Israel camped east of the Jordan River in the land of Moab. Just before they crossed the river into the Promised Land, Moses prepared the people of Israel, teaching them how they were to live.

all by myself. ¹⁰The LORD your God has increased your population, making you as numerous as the stars! ¹¹And may the LORD, the God of your ancestors, multiply you a thousand times more and bless you as he promised! ¹²But you are such a heavy load to carry! How can I deal with all your problems and bickering? ¹³Choose some well-respected men from each tribe who are known for their wisdom and understanding, and I will appoint them as your leaders.'

¹⁴"Then you responded, 'Your plan is a good one.' ¹⁵So I took the wise and respected men you had selected from your tribes and appointed them to serve as judges and officials over you. Some were responsible for a thousand people, some for a hundred, some for fifty, and some for ten.

¹⁶"At that time I instructed the judges, 'You must hear the cases of your fellow Israelites and the foreigners living among you. Be perfectly fair in your decisions ¹⁷and impartial in your judgments. Hear the cases of those who are poor as well as those who are rich. Don't be afraid of anyone's anger, for the decision you make is God's decision. Bring me any cases that are too difficult for you, and I will handle them.'

¹⁸"At that time I gave you instructions about everything you were to do.

SCOUTS EXPLORE THE LAND ¹⁹"Then, just as the LORD our God commanded us, we left Mount Sinai and traveled through the great and terrifying wilderness, as you yourselves remember, and headed toward the hill country of the Amorites. When we arrived at Kadesh-barnea, ²⁰I said to you, 'You have now reached the hill country of the Amorites that the LORD our God is giving us. ²¹Look! He has placed the land in front of you. Go and occupy it as the LORD, the God of your ancestors, has promised you. Don't be afraid! Don't be discouraged!'

²²"But you all came to me and said, 'First, let's send out scouts to explore the land for us.

LEADERSHIP QUALITIES
(1:13-18) Moses identified some of the qualities of a good leader: wisdom, understanding, a good reputation, and fairness. These characteristics differ greatly from the ones that often help elect leaders today: good looks, wealth, popularity, and a willingness to do anything to get to the top. Think you've got what it takes to be a leader? Which set of qualities do you value most: the ones on Moses' list or the second list?

1:1 Hebrew *the Arabah;* also in 1:7. **1:2** Hebrew *Horeb,* another name for Sinai; also in 1:6, 19. **1:3** Hebrew *In the fortieth year, on the first day of the eleventh month.* This day in the ancient Hebrew lunar calendar occurred in January or February. **1:7** Hebrew *the Shephelah.*

They will advise us on the best route to take and which towns we should enter.'

²³"This seemed like a good idea to me, so I chose twelve scouts, one from each of your tribes. ²⁴They headed for the hill country and came to the valley of Eshcol and explored it. ²⁵They picked some of its fruit and brought it back to us. And they reported, 'The land the LORD our God has given us is indeed a good land.'

ISRAEL'S REBELLION AGAINST THE LORD

²⁶"But you rebelled against the command of the LORD your God and refused to go in. ²⁷You complained in your tents and said, 'The LORD must hate us. That's why he has brought us here from Egypt—to hand us over to the Amorites to be slaughtered. ²⁸Where can we go? Our brothers have demoralized us with their report. They tell us, "The people of the land are taller and more powerful than we are, and their towns are large, with walls rising high into the sky! We even saw giants there—the descendants of Anak!"'

²⁹"But I said to you, 'Don't be shocked or afraid of them! ³⁰The LORD your God is going ahead of you. He will fight for you, just as you saw him do in Egypt. ³¹And you saw how the LORD your God cared for you all along the way as you traveled through the wilderness, just as a father cares for his child. Now he has brought you to this place.'

³²"But even after all he did, you refused to trust the LORD your God, ³³who goes before you looking for the best places to camp, guiding you with a pillar of fire by night and a pillar of cloud by day.

³⁴"When the LORD heard your complaining, he became very angry. So he solemnly swore, ³⁵'Not one of you from this wicked generation will live to see the good land I swore to give your ancestors, ³⁶except Caleb son of Jephunneh. He will see this land because he has followed the LORD completely. I will give to him and his descendants some of the very land he explored during his scouting mission.'

³⁷"And the LORD was also angry with me because of you. He said to me, 'Moses, not even you will enter the Promised Land! ³⁸Instead, your assistant, Joshua son of Nun, will lead the people into the land. Encourage him, for he will lead Israel as they take possession of it. ³⁹I will give the land to your little ones—your innocent children. You were afraid they would be captured, but they will be the ones who occupy it. ⁴⁰As for you, turn around

now and go on back through the wilderness toward the Red Sea.*'

⁴¹"Then you confessed, 'We have sinned against the LORD! We will go into the land and fight for it, as the LORD our God has commanded us.' So your men strapped on their weapons, thinking it would be easy to attack the hill country.

⁴²"But the LORD told me to tell you, 'Do not attack, for I am not with you. If you go ahead on your own, you will be crushed by your enemies.'

⁴³"This is what I told you, but you would not listen. Instead, you again rebelled against the LORD's command and arrogantly went into the hill country to fight. ⁴⁴But the Amorites who lived there came out against you like a swarm of bees. They chased and battered you all the way from Seir to Hormah. ⁴⁵Then you returned and wept before the LORD, but he refused to listen. ⁴⁶So you stayed there at Kadesh for a long time.

2 REMEMBERING ISRAEL'S WANDERINGS

"Then we turned around and headed back across the wilderness toward the Red Sea,* just as the LORD had instructed me, and we wandered around in the region of Mount Seir for a long time.

²"Then at last the LORD said to me, ³'You have been wandering around in this hill country long enough; turn to the north. ⁴Give these orders to the people: "You will pass through the country belonging to your relatives the Edomites, the descendants of Esau, who live in Seir. The Edomites will feel threatened, so be careful. ⁵Do not bother them, for I have given them all the hill country around Mount Seir as their property, and I will not give you even one square foot of their land. ⁶If you need food to eat or water to drink, pay them for it. ⁷For the LORD your God has blessed you in everything you have done. He has watched your every step through this great wilderness. During these forty years, the LORD your God has been with you, and you have lacked nothing."'

⁸"So we bypassed the territory of our relatives, the descendants of Esau, who live in Seir. We avoided the road through the Arabah Valley that comes up from Elath and Ezion-geber.

"Then as we turned north along the desert route through Moab, ⁹the LORD warned us, 'Do not bother the Moabites, the descendants of Lot, or start a war with them. I have given them Ar as their property, and I will not give you any of their land.'"

¹⁰(A race of giants called the Emites had once lived in the area of Ar. They were as

1:40 Hebrew *sea of reeds.*   2:1 Hebrew *sea of reeds.*

strong and numerous and tall as the Anakites, another race of giants. ¹¹Both the Emites and the Anakites are also known as the Rephaites, though the Moabites call them Emites. ¹²In earlier times the Horites had lived in Seir, but they were driven out and displaced by the descendants of Esau, just as Israel drove out the people of Canaan when the LORD gave Israel their land.)

¹³Moses continued, "Then the LORD said to us, 'Get moving. Cross the Zered Brook.' So we crossed the brook.

¹⁴"Thirty-eight years passed from the time we first left Kadesh-barnea until we finally crossed the Zered Brook! By then, all the men old enough to fight in battle had died in the wilderness, as the LORD had vowed would happen. ¹⁵The LORD struck them down until they had all been eliminated from the community.

¹⁶"When all the men of fighting age had died, ¹⁷the LORD said to me, ¹⁸'Today you will cross the border of Moab at Ar ¹⁹and enter the land of the Ammonites, the descendants of Lot. But do not bother them or start a war with them. I have given the land of Ammon to them as their property, and I will not give you any of their land.'"

²⁰(That area was once considered the land of the Rephaites, who had lived there, though the Ammonites call them Zamzummites. ²¹They were also as strong and numerous and tall as the Anakites. But the LORD destroyed them so the Ammonites could occupy their land. ²²He had done the same for the descendants of Esau who lived in Seir, for he destroyed the Horites so they could settle there in their place. The descendants of Esau live there to this day. ²³A similar thing happened when the Caphtorites from Crete* invaded and destroyed the Avvites, who had lived in villages in the area of Gaza.)

²⁴Moses continued, "Then the LORD said, 'Now get moving! Cross the Arnon Gorge. Look, I will hand over to you Sihon the Amorite, king of Heshbon, and I will give you his land. Attack him and begin to occupy the land. ²⁵Beginning today I will make people throughout the earth terrified because of you. When they hear reports about you, they will tremble with dread and fear.'"

· ·

IMPOSSIBLE ODDS?
(3:1-3) The Israelites faced a big problem: the well-trained army of Og, the king of Bashan, was much stronger. But Israel defeated them because God fought for them. Facing a huge problem like the Israelites did? Maybe the obstacles you face seem impossible to beat. The same God who saw Og's army as no challenge at all is right there with you.

VICTORY OVER SIHON OF HESHBON   ²⁶Moses continued, "From the wilderness of Kedemoth I sent ambassadors to King Sihon of Heshbon with this proposal of peace:

²⁷'Let us travel through your land. We will stay on the main road and won't turn off into the fields on either side. ²⁸Sell us food to eat and water to drink, and we will pay for it. All we want is permission to pass through your land. ²⁹The descendants of Esau who live in Seir allowed us to go through their country, and so did the Moabites, who live in Ar. Let us pass through until we cross the Jordan into the land the LORD our God is giving us.'

³⁰"But King Sihon of Heshbon refused to allow us to pass through, because the LORD your God made Sihon stubborn and defiant so he could help you defeat him, as he has now done.

³¹"Then the LORD said to me, 'Look, I have begun to hand King Sihon and his land over to you. Begin now to conquer and occupy his land.'

³²"Then King Sihon declared war on us and mobilized his forces at Jahaz. ³³But the LORD our God handed him over to us, and we crushed him, his sons, and all his people. ³⁴We conquered all his towns and completely destroyed* everyone—men, women, and children. Not a single person was spared. ³⁵We took all the livestock as plunder for ourselves, along with anything of value from the towns we ransacked.

³⁶"The LORD our God also helped us conquer Aroer on the edge of the Arnon Gorge, and the town in the gorge, and the whole area as far as Gilead. No town had walls too strong for us. ³⁷However, we avoided the land of the Ammonites all along the Jabbok River and the towns in the hill country—all the places the LORD our God had commanded us to leave alone.

3 **VICTORY OVER OG OF BASHAN**   "Next we turned and headed for the land of Bashan, where King Og and his entire army attacked us at Edrei. ²But the LORD told me, 'Do not be afraid of him, for I have given you victory over Og and his entire army, and I will give you all his land. Treat him just as you treated King Sihon of the Amorites, who ruled in Heshbon.'

³"So the LORD our God handed King Og and all his people over to us, and we killed them all. Not a single person survived. ⁴We conquered

2:23 Hebrew *from Caphtor.*   **2:34** The Hebrew term used here refers to the complete consecration of things or people to the LORD, either by destroying them or by giving them as an offering.

all sixty of his towns—the entire Argob region in his kingdom of Bashan. Not a single town escaped our conquest. ⁵These towns were all fortified with high walls and barred gates. We also took many unwalled villages at the same time. ⁶We completely destroyed* the kingdom of Bashan, just as we had destroyed King Sihon of Heshbon. We destroyed all the people in every town we conquered—men, women, and children alike. ⁷But we kept all the livestock for ourselves and took plunder from all the towns.

⁸"So we took the land of the two Amorite kings east of the Jordan River—all the way from the Arnon Gorge to Mount Hermon. ⁹(Mount Hermon is called Sirion by the Sidonians, and the Amorites call it Senir.) ¹⁰We had now conquered all the cities on the plateau and all Gilead and Bashan, as far as the towns of Salecah and Edrei, which were part of Og's kingdom in Bashan. ¹¹(King Og of Bashan was the last survivor of the giant Rephaites. His bed was made of iron and was more than thirteen feet long and six feet wide.* It can still be seen in the Ammonite city of Rabbah.)

LAND DIVISION EAST OF THE JORDAN ¹²"When we took possession of this land, I gave to the tribes of Reuben and Gad the territory beyond Aroer along the Arnon Gorge, plus half of the hill country of Gilead with its towns. ¹³Then I gave the rest of Gilead and all of Bashan—Og's former kingdom—to the half-tribe of Manasseh. (This entire Argob region of Bashan used to be known as the land of the Rephaites. ¹⁴Jair, a leader from the tribe of Manasseh, conquered the whole Argob region in Bashan, all the way to the border of the Geshurites and Maacathites. Jair renamed this region after himself, calling it the Towns of Jair,* as it is still known today.) ¹⁵I gave Gilead to the clan of Makir. ¹⁶But I also gave part of Gilead to the tribes of Reuben and Gad. The area I gave them extended from the middle of the Arnon Gorge in the south to the Jabbok River on the Ammonite frontier. ¹⁷They also received the Jordan Valley, all the way from the Sea of Galilee down to the Dead Sea,* with the Jordan River serving as the western boundary. To the east were the slopes of Pisgah.

¹⁸"At that time I gave this command to the tribes that would live east of the Jordan:

'Although the Lord your God has given you this land as your property, all your fighting men must cross the Jordan ahead of your Israelite relatives, armed and ready to assist them. ¹⁹Your wives, children, and numerous livestock, however, may stay behind in the towns I have given you. ²⁰When the Lord has given security to the rest of the Israelites, as he has to you, and when they occupy the land the Lord your God is giving them across the Jordan River, then you may all return here to the land I have given you.'

MOSES FORBIDDEN TO ENTER THE LAND ²¹"At that time I gave Joshua this charge: 'You have seen for yourself everything the Lord your God has done to these two kings. He will do the same to all the kingdoms on the west side of the Jordan. ²²Do not be afraid of the nations there, for the Lord your God will fight for you.'

²³"At that time I pleaded with the Lord and said, ²⁴'O Sovereign Lord, you have only begun to show your greatness and the strength of your hand to me, your servant. Is there any god in heaven or on earth who can perform such great and mighty deeds as you do? ²⁵Please let me cross the Jordan to see the wonderful land on the other side, the beautiful hill country and the Lebanon mountains.'

²⁶"But the Lord was angry with me because of you, and he would not listen to me. 'That's enough!' he declared. 'Speak of it no more. ²⁷But go up to Pisgah Peak, and look over the land in every direction. Take a good look, but you may not cross the Jordan River. ²⁸Instead, commission Joshua and encourage and strengthen him, for he will lead the people across the Jordan. He will give them all the land you now see before you as their possession.' ²⁹So we stayed in the valley near Beth-peor.

4 MOSES URGES ISRAEL TO OBEY "And now, Israel, listen carefully to these decrees and regulations that I am about to teach you. Obey them so that you may live, so you may enter and occupy the land that the Lord, the God of your ancestors, is giving you. ²Do not add to or subtract from these

....

A SECRET WEAPON
(3:21-22) "The Lord your God will fight for you." What encouraging news for Joshua, who was to lead his men against army after army in the Promised Land! Since God promised to help him win every battle, he had nothing to fear. Our battles may not be against godless armies, but they are just as real as Joshua's. Whether we are trying to resist temptation or are battling fear, God has promised to fight with and for us as we obey him.

3:6 The Hebrew term used here refers to the complete consecration of things or people to the Lord, either by destroying them or by giving them as an offering; also in 3:6b. **3:11** Hebrew *9 cubits* [4.1 meters] *long and 4 cubits* [1.8 meters] *wide.* **3:14** Hebrew *Havvoth-jair.* **3:17** Hebrew *from Kinnereth to the Sea of the Arabah, the Salt Sea.*

commands I am giving you. Just obey the commands of the LORD your God that I am giving you.

³"You saw for yourself what the LORD did to you at Baal-peor. There the LORD your God destroyed everyone who had worshiped Baal, the god of Peor. ⁴But all of you who were faithful to the LORD your God are still alive today—every one of you.

⁵"Look, I now teach you these decrees and regulations just as the LORD my God commanded me, so that you may obey them in the land you are about to enter and occupy. ⁶Obey them completely, and you will display your wisdom and intelligence among the surrounding nations. When they hear all these decrees, they will exclaim, 'How wise and prudent are the people of this great nation!' ⁷For what great nation has a god as near to them as the LORD our God is near to us whenever we call on him? ⁸And what great nation has decrees and regulations as righteous and fair as this body of instructions that I am giving you today?

⁹"But watch out! Be careful never to forget what you yourself have seen. Do not let these memories escape from your mind as long as you live! And be sure to pass them on to your children and grandchildren. ¹⁰Never forget the day when you stood before the LORD your God

• •

DON'T FORGET
(4:9-10) Moses wanted to make sure that the people of Israel did not forget what God had accomplished for them. That's why he urged parents to tell their children about God's great miracles. You can keep God's great acts of faithfulness fresh in your mind by telling your friends what you have seen him do.

at Mount Sinai,* where he told me, 'Summon the people before me, and I will personally instruct them. Then they will learn to fear me as long as they live, and they will teach their children to fear me also.'

¹¹"You came near and stood at the foot of the mountain, while flames from the mountain shot into the sky. The mountain was shrouded in black clouds and deep darkness. ¹²And the LORD spoke to you from the heart of the fire. You heard the sound of his words but didn't see his form; there was only a voice. ¹³He proclaimed his covenant—the Ten Commandments*—which he commanded you to keep, and which he wrote on two stone tablets. ¹⁴It was at that time that the LORD commanded me to teach you his decrees and regulations so you would obey them in the land you are about to enter and occupy.

A WARNING AGAINST IDOLATRY ¹⁵"But be very careful! You did not see the LORD's form on the day he spoke to you from the heart of the fire at Mount Sinai. ¹⁶So do not corrupt yourselves by making an idol in any form—whether of a man or a woman, ¹⁷an animal on the ground, a bird in the sky, ¹⁸a small animal that scurries along the ground, or a fish in the deepest sea. ¹⁹And when you look up into the sky and see the sun, moon, and stars—all the forces of heaven—don't be seduced into worshiping them. The LORD your God gave them to all the peoples of the earth. ²⁰Remember that the LORD rescued you from the iron-smelting furnace of Egypt in order to make you his very own people and his special possession, which is what you are today.

4:10 Hebrew *Horeb,* another name for Sinai; also in 4:15.
4:13 Hebrew *the ten words.*

CHOICES
astrology

"What's that?" Kevin asks, pointing to a book in Kim's locker.

"Oh, that," Kim responds, picking up the skinny paperback. "That's a new book on astrology I got at a bookstore yesterday."

"Astrology?!" Kevin scoffs. "Don't tell me you believe all that junk!"

"Laugh if you want," Kim responds matter-of-factly. "But I've seen it come true in my life so many times it's scary! Besides, lots of people in this country believe in astrology. So really, Kevin, if you don't read your horoscope, you're the one who's out of it."

Lauren (the noisiest girl at school) walks up. "What

are you guys looking at? Oh, I have that book. It's so good! What sign are you, Kevin? . . . Or aren't you into astrology?"

Kevin hesitates before replying, "Well, it's not like I don't ever read my horoscope. I'm a Leo. Sometimes it's pretty accurate, I guess."

Kim smiles. "Well, you're welcome to borrow my copy. My mom has another one at home."

Kevin coughs nervously, "I don't know—I, uh . . ."

"Kevin, it's completely harmless!" Lauren urges. "Astrology is interesting . . . and a lot of fun. Take the book!"

Kim stands there offering the book. Kevin reluctantly takes it as the bell rings.

Is looking to the stars for guidance just an innocent diversion? Check out Deuteronomy 4:19 and 17:2-5. The next time someone suggests reading your horoscope, what will you say?

²¹"But the LORD was angry with me because of you. He vowed that I would not cross the Jordan River into the good land the LORD your God is giving you as your special possession. ²²You will cross the Jordan to occupy the land, but I will not. Instead, I will die here on the east side of the river. ²³So be careful not to break the covenant the LORD your God has made with you. Do not make idols of any shape or form, for the LORD your God has forbidden this. ²⁴The LORD your God is a devouring fire; he is a jealous God.

²⁵"In the future, when you have children and grandchildren and have lived in the land a long time, do not corrupt yourselves by making idols of any kind. This is evil in the sight of the LORD your God and will arouse his anger.

²⁶"Today I call on heaven and earth as witnesses against you. If you break my covenant, you will quickly disappear from the land you are crossing the Jordan to occupy. You will live there only a short time; then you will be utterly destroyed. ²⁷For the LORD will scatter you among the nations, where only a few of you will survive. ²⁸There, in a foreign land, you will worship idols made from wood and stone—gods that neither see nor hear nor eat nor smell. ²⁹But from there you will search again for the LORD your God. And if you search for him with all your heart and soul, you will find him.

³⁰"In the distant future, when you are suffering all these things, you will finally return to the LORD your God and listen to what he tells you. ³¹For the LORD your God is a merciful God; he will not abandon you or destroy you or forget the solemn covenant he made with your ancestors.

THERE IS ONLY ONE GOD ³²"Now search all of history, from the time God created people on the earth until now, and search from one end of the heavens to the other. Has anything as great as this ever been seen or heard before? ³³Has any nation ever heard the voice of God* speaking from fire—as you did—and survived? ³⁴Has any other god dared to take a nation for himself out of another nation by means of trials, miraculous signs, wonders, war, a strong hand, a powerful arm, and terrifying acts? Yet that is what the LORD your God did for you in Egypt, right before your eyes.

³⁵"He showed you these things so you would know that the LORD is God and there is no other. ³⁶He let you hear his voice from heaven so he

could instruct you. He let you see his great fire here on earth so he could speak to you from it. ³⁷Because he loved your ancestors, he chose to bless their descendants, and he personally brought you out of Egypt with a great display of power. ³⁸He drove out nations far greater than you, so he could bring you in and give you their land as your special possession, as it is today.

³⁹"So remember this and keep it firmly in mind: The LORD is God both in heaven and on earth, and there is no other. ⁴⁰If you obey all the decrees and commands I am giving you today, all will be well with you and your children. I am giving you these instructions so you will enjoy a long life in the land the LORD your God is giving you for all time."

EASTERN CITIES OF REFUGE ⁴¹Then Moses set apart three cities of refuge east of the Jordan River. ⁴²Anyone who killed another person unintentionally, without previous hostility, could flee there to live in safety. ⁴³These were the cities: Bezer on the wilderness plateau for the tribe of Reuben; Ramoth in Gilead for the tribe of Gad; Golan in Bashan for the tribe of Manasseh.

INTRODUCTION TO MOSES' SECOND ADDRESS ⁴⁴This is the body of instruction that Moses presented to the Israelites. ⁴⁵These are the laws, decrees, and regulations that Moses gave to the people of Israel when they left Egypt, ⁴⁶and as they camped in the valley near Beth-peor east of the Jordan River. (This land was formerly occupied by the Amorites under King Sihon, who ruled from Heshbon. But Moses and the Israelites destroyed him and his people when they came up from Egypt. ⁴⁷Israel took possession of his land and that of King Og of Bashan—the two Amorite kings east of the Jordan. ⁴⁸So Israel conquered the entire area from Aroer at the edge of the Arnon Gorge all the way to Mount Sirion,* also called Mount Hermon. ⁴⁹And they conquered the eastern bank of the Jordan River as far south as the Dead Sea,* below the slopes of Pisgah.)

5 **TEN COMMANDMENTS FOR THE COVENANT COMMUNITY** Moses called all the people of Israel together and said, "Listen carefully, Israel. Hear the decrees and regulations I am giving you today, so you may learn them and obey them!

²"The LORD our God made a covenant with us at Mount Sinai.* ³The LORD did not make this covenant with our ancestors, but with all of us who are alive today. ⁴At the mountain the

---

4:33 Or *voice of a god.*   **4:48** As in Syriac version (see also 3:9); Hebrew reads *Mount Sion.*   **4:49** Hebrew *took the Arabah on the east side of the Jordan as far as the sea of the Arabah.*   **5:2** Hebrew *Horeb,* another name for Sinai.

MY STORY: Amy

My parents are Christians, and even though they are stricter than I'd like, I have to admit they're good parents. One day while reading the Bible, I came across the fifth commandment, the one about honoring your parents. A note in the margin pointed out that there is a promise attached to this commandment: If you follow it, you will lead a long and happy life.

What struck me is that my parents are always saying things like, "We're only saying this for your own good. We want you to be happy." It seemed like God was saying, "Your parents love you. They are trying to help you lead a happy life, so if you listen to them, your life will go better." It all made sense. For a while I felt guilty that I didn't listen to them as much as I should, but I determined to consult them more.

A few nights later I decided to talk to them about a relationship I was having trouble with. I was surprised to find that they really understood, and my mom even had some helpful advice about what she had done in a similar situation. I hadn't realized before how much wisdom my parents really have to give me.

REMEMBERING THE COVENANT

(5:1) As the people of Israel reviewed their covenant with God, Moses commanded them to listen, learn, and obey God's laws and regulations. Moses' threefold command to the Israelites is excellent advice for all of God's followers. Listening means absorbing and accepting information about God. Learning means understanding the meaning and consequences of this information. Obeying means putting into action all we have learned and understood. All three parts are essential to a growing relationship with God. Which of the three is easiest for you? Which is hardest?

TEACHING CHILDREN

(6:4-9) This passage identifies a central theme of Deuteronomy. It sets a pattern that helps us relate the Word of God to daily life. We are to love God, obey his commandments, and teach them to our children. God emphasized the importance of teaching children about his commandments. Even if you don't have any children, you can still take part in a younger person's faith education. Maybe you have a niece or a younger cousin, or work with younger kids in a community center. How do you model your commitment to God's Word?

LORD spoke to you face to face from the heart of the fire. ⁵I stood as an intermediary between you and the LORD, for you were afraid of the fire and did not want to approach the mountain. He spoke to me, and I passed his words on to you. This is what he said:

⁶"I am the LORD your God, who rescued you from the land of Egypt, the place of your slavery.

⁷"You must not have any other god but me.

⁸"You must not make for yourself an idol of any kind, or an image of anything in the heavens or on the earth or in the sea. ⁹You must not bow down to them or worship them, for I, the LORD your God, am a jealous God who will not tolerate your affection for any other gods. I lay the sins of the parents upon their children; the entire family is affected—even children in the third and fourth generations of those who reject me. ¹⁰But I lavish unfailing love for a thousand generations on those* who love me and obey my commands.

¹¹"You must not misuse the name of the LORD your God. The LORD will not let you go unpunished if you misuse his name.

¹²"Observe the Sabbath day by keeping it holy, as the LORD your God has commanded you. ¹³You have six days each week for your ordinary work, ¹⁴but the seventh day is a Sabbath day of rest dedicated to the LORD your God. On that day no one in your household may do any work. This includes you, your sons and daughters, your male and female servants, your oxen and donkeys and other livestock, and any foreigners living among you. All your male and female servants must rest as you do. ¹⁵Remember that you were once slaves in Egypt, but the LORD your God brought you out with his strong hand and powerful arm. That is why the LORD your God has commanded you to rest on the Sabbath day.

¹⁶"Honor your father and mother, as the LORD your God commanded you. Then you will live a long, full life in the land the LORD your God is giving you.

¹⁷"You must not murder.

¹⁸"You must not commit adultery.

¹⁹"You must not steal.

²⁰"You must not testify falsely against your neighbor.

²¹"You must not covet your neighbor's wife. You must not covet your neighbor's house or land, male or female servant, ox or

5:10 Hebrew *for thousands of those.*

donkey, or anything else that belongs to your neighbor.

²²"The Lord spoke these words to all of you assembled there at the foot of the mountain. He spoke with a loud voice from the heart of the fire, surrounded by clouds and deep darkness. This was all he said at that time, and he wrote his words on two stone tablets and gave them to me.

²³"But when you heard the voice from the heart of the darkness, while the mountain was blazing with fire, all your tribal leaders and elders came to me. ²⁴They said, 'Look, the Lord our God has shown us his glory and greatness, and we have heard his voice from the heart of the fire. Today we have seen that God can speak to us humans, and yet we live! ²⁵But now, why should we risk death again? If the Lord our God speaks to us again, we will certainly die and be consumed by this awesome fire. ²⁶Can any living thing hear the voice of the living God from the heart of the fire as we did and yet survive? ²⁷Go yourself and listen to what the Lord our God says. Then come and tell us everything he tells you, and we will listen and obey.'

²⁸"The Lord heard the request you made to me. And he said, 'I have heard what the people said to you, and they are right. ²⁹Oh, that they would always have hearts like this, that they might fear me and obey all my commands! If they did, they and their descendants would prosper forever. ³⁰Go and tell them, "Return to your tents." ³¹But you stand here with me so I can give you all my commands, decrees, and regulations. You must teach them to the people so they can obey them in the land I am giving them as their possession.'"

³²So Moses told the people, "You must be careful to obey all the commands of the Lord your God, following his instructions in every detail. ³³Stay on the path that the Lord your God has commanded you to follow. Then you will live long and prosperous lives in the land you are about to enter and occupy.

6 **A CALL FOR WHOLEHEARTED COMMITMENT** "These are the commands, decrees, and regulations that the Lord your God commanded me to teach you. You must obey them in the land you are about to enter and occupy, ²and you and your children and grandchildren must fear the Lord your God as long as you live. If you obey all his decrees and commands, you will enjoy a long life. ³Listen closely, Israel, and be careful to obey. Then all will go well with you,

6:4 Or *The Lord our God is one Lord;* or *The Lord our God, the Lord is one;* or *The Lord is our God, the Lord is one.*

and you will have many children in the land flowing with milk and honey, just as the Lord, the God of your ancestors, promised you.

⁴"Listen, O Israel! The Lord is our God, the Lord alone.* ⁵And you must love the Lord your God with all your heart, all your soul, and all your strength. ⁶And you must commit yourselves wholeheartedly to these commands that I am giving you today. ⁷Repeat them again and again to your children. Talk about them when you are at home and when you are on the road, when you are going to bed and when you are getting up. ⁸Tie them to your hands and wear them on your forehead as reminders. ⁹Write them on the doorposts of your house and on your gates.

¹⁰"The Lord your God will soon bring you into the land he swore to give you when he made a vow to your ancestors Abraham, Isaac, and Jacob. It is a land with large, prosperous cities that you did not build. ¹¹The houses will be richly stocked with goods you did not produce. You will draw water from cisterns you did not dig, and you will eat from vineyards and olive trees you did not plant. When you have eaten your fill in this land, ¹²be careful not to forget the Lord, who rescued you from slavery in the land of Egypt. ¹³You must fear the Lord your God and serve him. When you take an oath, you must use only his name.

¹⁴"You must not worship any of the gods of neighboring nations, ¹⁵for the Lord your God, who lives among you, is a jealous God. His anger will flare up against you, and he will wipe you from the face of the earth. ¹⁶You must not test the Lord your God as you did when you complained at Massah. ¹⁷You must diligently obey the commands of the Lord your God—all the laws and decrees he has given you. ¹⁸Do what is right and good in the Lord's sight, so all will go well with you. Then you will enter and occupy the good land that the Lord swore to give your ancestors. ¹⁹You will drive out all the enemies living in the land, just as the Lord said you would.

²⁰"In the future your children will ask you, 'What is the meaning of these laws, decrees, and regulations that the Lord our God has commanded us to obey?'

²¹"Then you must tell them, 'We were Pharaoh's slaves in Egypt, but the Lord brought us out of Egypt with his strong hand. ²²The Lord did miraculous signs and wonders before our eyes, dealing terrifying blows against Egypt and Pharaoh and all his people. ²³He brought us out of Egypt so he could give us this land he had sworn to give our ancestors. ²⁴And the Lord our

THE LORD YOUR GOD.
IS INDEED GOD.

HE IS THE FAITHFUL GOD WHO KEEPS HIS COVENANT FOR A THOUSAND GENERATIONS.
DEUTERONOMY 7:9 |||||||

God commanded us to obey all these decrees and to fear him so he can continue to bless us and preserve our lives, as he has done to this day. ²⁵For we will be counted as righteous when we obey all the commands the LORD our God has given us.'

7 **THE PRIVILEGE OF HOLINESS** "When the LORD your God brings you into the land you are about to enter and occupy, he will clear away many nations ahead of you: the Hittites, Girgashites, Amorites, Canaanites, Perizzites, Hivites, and Jebusites. These seven nations are greater and more numerous than you. ²When the LORD your God hands these nations over to you and you conquer them, you must completely destroy* them. Make no treaties with them and show them no mercy. ³You must not intermarry with them. Do not let your daughters and sons marry their sons and daughters, ⁴for they will lead your children away from me to worship other gods. Then the anger of the LORD will burn against you, and he will quickly destroy you. ⁵This is what you must do. You must break down their pagan altars and shatter their sacred pillars. Cut down their Asherah poles and burn their idols. ⁶For you are a holy people, who belong to the LORD your God. Of all the people on

earth, the LORD your God has chosen you to be his own special treasure.

⁷"The LORD did not set his heart on you and choose you because you were more numerous than other nations, for you were the smallest of all nations! ⁸Rather, it was simply that the LORD loves you, and he was keeping the oath he had sworn to your ancestors. That is why the LORD rescued you with such a strong hand from your slavery and from the oppressive hand of Pharaoh, king of Egypt. ⁹Understand, therefore, that the LORD your God is indeed God. He is the faithful God who keeps his covenant for a thousand generations and lavishes his unfailing love on those who love him and obey his commands. ¹⁰But he does not hesitate to punish and destroy those who reject him. ¹¹Therefore, you must obey all these commands, decrees, and regulations I am giving you today.

¹²"If you listen to these regulations and faithfully obey them, the LORD your God will keep his covenant of unfailing love with you, as he promised with an oath to your ancestors. ¹³He will love you and bless you, and he will give you many children. He will give fertility to your land and your animals. When you arrive in the land he swore to give your ancestors, you will have large harvests of grain, new wine, and olive oil, and great herds of cattle, sheep, and goats. ¹⁴You will be blessed above all the nations of the earth. None of your men or women will be childless, and all your livestock will bear young. ¹⁵And the LORD will protect you from all sickness. He will not let you suffer from the terrible diseases you knew in Egypt, but he will inflict them on all your enemies!

¹⁶"You must destroy all the nations the LORD your God hands over to you. Show them no mercy, and do not worship their gods, or they will trap you. ¹⁷Perhaps you will think to yourselves, 'How can we ever conquer these nations that are so much more powerful than we are?' ¹⁸But don't be afraid of them! Just remember what the LORD your God did to Pharaoh and to all the land of Egypt. ¹⁹Remember the great terrors the LORD your God sent against them. You saw it all with your own eyes! And remember the miraculous signs and wonders, and the strong hand and powerful arm with which he brought you out of Egypt. The LORD your God will use this same power against all the people you fear. ²⁰And then the LORD your God will send terror* to drive out the few survivors still hiding from you!

7:2 The Hebrew term used here refers to the complete consecration of things or people to the LORD, either by destroying them or by giving them as an offering; also in 7:26. 7:20 Often rendered *the hornet.* The meaning of the Hebrew is uncertain.

²¹"No, do not be afraid of those nations, for the LORD your God is among you, and he is a great and awesome God. ²²The LORD your God will drive those nations out ahead of you little by little. You will not clear them away all at once, otherwise the wild animals would multiply too quickly for you. ²³But the LORD your God will hand them over to you. He will throw them into complete confusion until they are destroyed. ²⁴He will put their kings in your power, and you will erase their names from the face of the earth. No one will be able to stand against you, and you will destroy them all.

²⁵"You must burn their idols in fire, and you must not covet the silver or gold that covers them. You must not take it or it will become a trap to you, for it is detestable to the LORD your God. ²⁶Do not bring any detestable objects into your home, for then you will be destroyed, just like them. You must utterly detest such things, for they are set apart for destruction.

8 A CALL TO REMEMBER AND OBEY "Be careful to obey all the commands I am giving you today. Then you will live and multiply, and you will enter and occupy the land the LORD swore to give your ancestors. ²Remember how the LORD your God led you through the wilderness for these forty years, humbling you and testing you to prove your character, and to find out whether or not you would obey his commands. ³Yes, he humbled you by letting you go hungry and then feeding you with manna, a food previously unknown to you and your ancestors. He did it to teach you that people do not live by bread alone; rather, we live by every word that comes from the mouth of the LORD. ⁴For all these forty years your clothes didn't wear out, and your feet didn't blister or swell. ⁵Think about it: Just as a parent disciplines a child, the LORD your God disciplines you for your own good.

⁶"So obey the commands of the LORD your God by walking in his ways and fearing him. ⁷For the LORD your God is bringing you into a good land of flowing streams and pools of water, with fountains and springs that gush out in the valleys and hills. ⁸It is a land of wheat and barley; of grapevines, fig trees, and pomegranates; of olive oil and honey. ⁹It is a land where food is plentiful and nothing is lacking. It is a land where iron is as common as stone, and copper is abundant in the hills. ¹⁰When you have eaten your fill, be sure to praise the LORD your God for the good land he has given you.

¹¹"But that is the time to be careful! Beware that in your plenty you do not forget the LORD

OBEDIENCE

Deuteronomy 8:1 tells us to obey God's commands. We do this by obeying God with:

OUR HEART—By loving him more than any relationship, activity, achievement, or possession

OUR WILL—By committing ourselves completely to him

OUR MIND—By seeking to know him and his Word, so his principles and values form the foundation of all we think and do

OUR BODY—By recognizing that our strengths, talents, and sexuality are given to us by God to be used for fulfillment and pleasure according to his rules, not ours

OUR FINANCES—By realizing that all of the resources we have ultimately come from God, and that we are to be managers of them and not owners

OUR FUTURE—By choosing to make service to God and people the main purpose of our life's work

your God and disobey his commands, regulations, and decrees that I am giving you today. ¹²For when you have become full and prosperous and have built fine homes to live in, ¹³and when your flocks and herds have become very large and your silver and gold have multiplied along with everything else, be careful! ¹⁴Do not become proud at that time and forget the LORD your God, who rescued you from slavery in the land of Egypt. ¹⁵Do not forget that he led you through the great and terrifying wilderness with its poisonous snakes and scorpions, where it was so hot and dry. He gave you water from the rock! ¹⁶He fed you with manna in the wilderness, a food unknown to your ancestors. He did this to humble you and test you for your own good. ¹⁷He did all this so you would never say to yourself, 'I have achieved this wealth with my own strength and energy.' ¹⁸Remember the LORD your God. He is the one who gives you power to be successful, in order to fulfill the covenant he confirmed to your ancestors with an oath.

¹⁹"But I assure you of this: If you ever forget

ONE STEP AT A TIME
(7:21-24) Moses told the Israelites that God would destroy their enemies, but not all at once. God had the power to destroy those nations instantly, but he chose to do it in stages. In the same way and with the same power, God could miraculously and instantaneously change your life. Ever wish that? Many times God chooses to help people gradually, teaching them one lesson at a time. Are you willing to trust God's step-by-step process?

the LORD your God and follow other gods, worshiping and bowing down to them, you will certainly be destroyed. ²⁰Just as the LORD has destroyed other nations in your path, you also will be destroyed if you refuse to obey the LORD your God.

9 VICTORY BY GOD'S GRACE "Listen, O Israel! Today you are about to cross the Jordan River to take over the land belonging to nations much greater and more powerful than you. They live in cities with walls that reach to the sky! ²The people are strong and tall—descendants of the famous Anakite giants. You've heard the saying, 'Who can stand up to the Anakites?' ³But recognize today that the LORD your God is the one who will cross over ahead of you like a devouring fire to destroy them. He will subdue them so that you will quickly conquer them and drive them out, just as the LORD has promised.

⁴"After the LORD your God has done this for you, don't say in your hearts, 'The LORD has given us this land because we are such good people!' No, it is because of the wickedness of the other nations that he is pushing them out of your way. ⁵It is not because you are so good or have such integrity that you are about to occupy their land. The LORD your God will drive these nations out ahead of you only because of their wickedness, and to fulfill the oath he swore to your ancestors Abraham, Isaac, and Jacob. ⁶You must recognize that the LORD your God is not giving you this good land because you are good, for you are not—you are a stubborn people.

REMEMBERING THE GOLD CALF ⁷"Remember and never forget how angry you made the LORD your God out in the wilderness. From the day you left Egypt until now, you have been constantly rebelling against him. ⁸Even at Mount Sinai* you made the LORD so angry he was

∙∙∙

GOD'S MERCY

(9:1-6) If the Israelites were unrighteous and stubborn, why did God make such wonderful promises to them? There are two good reasons: (1) God and Israel had made a covenant (Gen 15; 17; Exod 19–20). God promised to be faithful to them and they promised to obey him. Even though the Israelites rarely held up their end of the bargain, God remained faithful. (2) God's unconditional mercy made him willing to restore his people no matter how many times they turned from him.

It is comforting to know that despite our inconsistencies and sins, God loves us unconditionally. Eternal life is not achieved on the merit system, but on the mercy system. God loves us no matter who we are or what we have done. Believe that?

ready to destroy you. ⁹This happened when I was on the mountain receiving the tablets of stone inscribed with the words of the covenant that the LORD had made with you. I was there for forty days and forty nights, and all that time I ate no food and drank no water. ¹⁰The LORD gave me the two tablets on which God had written with his own finger all the words he had spoken to you from the heart of the fire when you were assembled at the mountain.

¹¹"At the end of the forty days and nights, the LORD handed me the two stone tablets inscribed with the words of the covenant. ¹²Then the LORD said to me, 'Get up! Go down immediately, for the people you brought out of Egypt have corrupted themselves. How quickly they have turned away from the way I commanded them to live! They have melted gold and made an idol for themselves!'

¹³"The LORD also said to me, 'I have seen how stubborn and rebellious these people are. ¹⁴Leave me alone so I may destroy them and erase their name from under heaven. Then I will make a mighty nation of your descendants, a nation larger and more powerful than they are.'

¹⁵"So while the mountain was blazing with fire I turned and came down, holding in my hands the two stone tablets inscribed with the terms of the covenant. ¹⁶There below me I could see that you had sinned against the LORD your God. You had melted gold and made a calf idol for yourselves. How quickly you had turned away from the path the LORD had commanded you to follow! ¹⁷So I took the stone tablets and threw them to the ground, smashing them before your eyes.

¹⁸"Then, as before, I threw myself down before the LORD for forty days and nights. I ate no bread and drank no water because of the great sin you had committed by doing what the LORD hated, provoking him to anger. ¹⁹I feared that the furious anger of the LORD, which turned him against you, would drive him to destroy you. But again he listened to me. ²⁰The LORD was so angry with Aaron that he wanted to destroy him, too. But I prayed for Aaron, and the LORD spared him. ²¹I took your sin—the calf you had made—and I melted it down in the fire and ground it into fine dust. Then I threw the dust into the stream that flows down the mountain.

²²"You also made the LORD angry at Taberah,* Massah,* and Kibroth-hattaavah.* ²³And at Kadesh-barnea the LORD sent you out with

9:8 Hebrew Horeb, another name for Sinai.   9:22a Taberah means "place of burning." See Num 11:1-3.   9:22b Massah means "place of testing." See Exod 17:1-7.   9:22c Kibroth-hattaavah means "graves of gluttony." See Num 11:31-34.

this command: 'Go up and take over the land I have given you.' But you rebelled against the command of the LORD your God and refused to put your trust in him or obey him. ²⁴Yes, you have been rebelling against the LORD as long as I have known you.

²⁵"That is why I threw myself down before the LORD for forty days and nights—for the LORD said he would destroy you. ²⁶I prayed to the LORD and said, 'O Sovereign LORD, do not destroy them. They are your own people. They are your special possession, whom you redeemed from Egypt by your mighty power and your strong hand. ²⁷Please overlook the stubbornness and the awful sin of these people, and remember instead your servants Abraham, Isaac, and Jacob. ²⁸If you destroy these people, the Egyptians will say, "The Israelites died because the LORD wasn't able to bring them to the land he had promised to give them." Or they might say, "He destroyed them because he hated them; he deliberately took them into the wilderness to slaughter them." ²⁹But they are your people and your special possession, whom you brought out of Egypt by your great strength and powerful arm.'

10 A NEW COPY OF THE COVENANT "At that time the LORD said to me, 'Chisel out two stone tablets like the first ones. Also make a wooden Ark—a sacred chest to store them in. Come up to me on the mountain, ²and I will write on the tablets the same words that were on the ones you smashed. Then place the tablets in the Ark.'

³"So I made an Ark of acacia wood and cut two stone tablets like the first two. Then I went up the mountain with the tablets in my hand. ⁴Once again the LORD wrote the Ten Commandments* on the tablets and gave them to me. They were the same words the LORD had spoken to you from the heart of the fire on the day you were assembled at the foot of the mountain. ⁵Then I turned and came down the mountain and placed the tablets in the Ark of the Covenant, which I had made, just as the LORD commanded me. And the tablets are still there in the Ark."

⁶(The people of Israel set out from the wells of the people of Jaakan* and traveled to Moserah, where Aaron died and was buried. His son Eleazar ministered as high priest in his place. ⁷Then they journeyed to Gudgodah, and from there to Jotbathah, a land with many brooks and streams. ⁸At that time the LORD set apart

10:4 Hebrew the ten words.   10:6 Or set out from Beeroth of Bene-jaakan.   10:16 Hebrew circumcise the foreskin of your hearts.

the tribe of Levi to carry the Ark of the LORD's Covenant, and to stand before the LORD as his ministers, and to pronounce blessings in his name. These are their duties to this day. ⁹That is why the Levites have no share of property or possession of land among the other Israelite tribes. The LORD himself is their special possession, as the LORD your God told them.)

¹⁰"As for me, I stayed on the mountain in the LORD's presence for forty days and nights, as I had done the first time. And once again the LORD listened to my pleas and agreed not to destroy you. ¹¹Then the LORD said to me, 'Get up and resume the journey, and lead the people to the land I swore to give to their ancestors, so they may take possession of it.'

A CALL TO LOVE AND OBEDIENCE ¹²"And now, Israel, what does the LORD your God require of you? He requires only that you fear the LORD your God, and live in a way that pleases him, and love him and serve him with all your heart and soul. ¹³And you must always obey the LORD's commands and decrees that I am giving you today for your own good.

¹⁴"Look, the highest heavens and the earth and everything in it all belong to the LORD your God. ¹⁵Yet the LORD chose your ancestors as the objects of his love. And he chose you, their descendants, above all other nations, as is evident today. ¹⁶Therefore, change your hearts* and stop being stubborn.

¹⁷"For the LORD your God is the God of gods and Lord of lords. He is the great God, the mighty and awesome God, who shows no partiality and cannot be bribed. ¹⁸He ensures that orphans and widows receive justice. He shows love to the foreigners living among you and gives them food and clothing. ¹⁹So you, too, must show love to foreigners, for you yourselves were once foreigners in the land of Egypt. ²⁰You must fear the LORD your God and worship him and cling to him. Your oaths must be in his name alone. ²¹He alone is your God, the only one who is worthy of your praise, the one who has done these mighty miracles that

··

GREET EXPECTATIONS
(10:12-13) Often we ask, "What does God expect of me?" Here Moses gives a summary that's easy to remember. Here are the essentials: (1) Fear God (have a deep respect for his authority), (2) live according to his will, (3) love him, (4) serve him wholeheartedly, and (5) obey his commands. How often we complicate faith with man-made rules, regulations, and requirements. Are you feeling frustrated or burned out from trying hard to please God? You don't have to jump through hoops to please God. Just love and obey him.

you have seen with your own eyes. ²²When your ancestors went down into Egypt, there were only seventy of them. But now the Lord your God has made you as numerous as the stars in the sky!

11 "You must love the Lord your God and obey all his requirements, decrees, regulations, and commands. ²Keep in mind that I am not talking now to your children, who have never experienced the discipline of the Lord your God or seen his greatness and his strong hand and powerful arm. ³They didn't see the miraculous signs and wonders he performed in Egypt against Pharaoh and all his land. ⁴They didn't see what the Lord did to the armies of Egypt and to their horses and chariots—how he drowned them in the Red Sea* as they were chasing you. He destroyed them, and they have not recovered to this very day!

⁵"Your children didn't see how the Lord cared for you in the wilderness until you arrived here. ⁶They didn't see what he did to Dathan and Abiram (the sons of Eliab, a descendant of Reuben) when the earth opened its mouth in the Israelite camp and swallowed them, along with their households and tents and every living thing that belonged to them. ⁷But you have seen the Lord perform all these mighty deeds with your own eyes!

THE BLESSINGS OF OBEDIENCE

⁸"Therefore, be careful to obey every command I am giving you today, so you may have strength to go in and take over the land you are about to enter. ⁹If you obey, you will enjoy a long life in the land the Lord swore to give to your ancestors and to you, their descendants—a land flowing with milk and honey! ¹⁰For the land you are about to enter and take over is not like the land of Egypt from which you came, where you planted your seed and made irrigation ditches with your foot as in a vegetable garden. ¹¹Rather, the land you will soon take over is a land of hills and valleys with plenty of rain—¹²a land that the Lord your God cares for. He watches over it through each season of the year!

¹³"If you carefully obey all the commands I am giving you today, and if you love the Lord your God and serve him with all your heart and soul, ¹⁴then he will send the rains in their proper seasons—the early and late rains—so you can bring in your harvests of grain, new wine, and olive oil. ¹⁵He will give you lush pastureland for your livestock, and you yourselves will have all you want to eat.

¹⁶"But be careful. Don't let your heart be deceived so that you turn away from the Lord and serve and worship other gods. ¹⁷If you do,

11:4 Hebrew *sea of reeds.*

ULTIMATE ISSUES *COVENANTS*

You've seen it in the movies or maybe on the news—leaders of two warring countries decide to end the fighting and sign a peace treaty. The representative of the losing side agrees to terms of surrender, perhaps giving up contested land or paying back some money as a war debt. The winning country's spokesperson agrees to withdraw military forces, so long as the losing side keeps up its end of the agreement. Should they ever break their word and resume the hostilities, the conquering armies will come back in full force.

What we call a peace treaty was called a *covenant* in Old Testament times. It was used in situations where one kingdom defeated another in battle, or when a weaker empire wanted to avoid going to war with a more powerful one. In short, a covenant is an agreement between two parties that binds them to do certain things for each other. For example, the stronger party agrees not to destroy the weaker one; in return, the weaker one agrees to pay taxes or tribute. Also, the covenant agreement included sections explaining what would happen if the rules were kept and if they were broken. These sections were called "blessings" and "curses" (see Deut 11:26-32).

God's covenant with Israel started with Abram. God promised to give Abram many descendants and a wonderful land for their home. After establishing this covenant, God promised to take the curse on himself if he should ever break his part of the agreement.

You might be thinking, *That's a fascinating bit of historical trivia—but what does it have to do with me?* Just this: In Romans, Paul tells us that Christians will inherit the blessings promised to Abram (Abraham). Romans 11:17 says, "But some of these branches from Abraham's tree—some of the people of Israel—have been broken off. And you Gentiles, who were branches from a wild olive tree, have been grafted in. So now you also receive the blessing God has promised Abraham and his children, sharing in the rich nourishment from the root of God's special olive tree." So, if you're a Christian, this promise is for you!

No, that doesn't mean you can pick up and head to the Holy Land to stake out some prime real estate. Our Promised Land is in another place—a new heaven and a new earth. But as you read about God's covenant with Abram and with the nation of Israel, know with absolute certainty that God will keep his promises to you—all of them—just as he did with Israel. Your part is to enter into an agreement with him about your sin and his forgiveness through Jesus, the author of the new covenant. ∎

the LORD's anger will burn against you. He will shut up the sky and hold back the rain, and the ground will fail to produce its harvests. Then you will quickly die in that good land the LORD is giving you.

18"So commit yourselves wholeheartedly to these words of mine. Tie them to your hands and wear them on your forehead as reminders. 19Teach them to your children. Talk about them when you are at home and when you are on the road, when you are going to bed and when you are getting up. 20Write them on the doorposts of your house and on your gates, 21so that as long as the sky remains above the earth, you and your children may flourish in the land the LORD swore to give your ancestors.

22"Be careful to obey all these commands I am giving you. Show love to the LORD your God by walking in his ways and holding tightly to him. 23Then the LORD will drive out all the nations ahead of you, though they are much greater and stronger than you, and you will take over their land. 24Wherever you set foot, that land will be yours. Your frontiers will stretch from the wilderness in the south to Lebanon in the north, and from the Euphrates River in the east to the Mediterranean Sea in the west.* 25No one will be able to stand against you, for the LORD your God will cause the people to fear and dread you, as he promised, wherever you go in the whole land.

26"Look, today I am giving you the choice between a blessing and a curse! 27You will be blessed if you obey the commands of the LORD your God that I am giving you today. 28But you will be cursed if you reject the commands of the LORD your God and turn away from him and worship gods you have not known before.

29"When the LORD your God brings you into the land and helps you take possession of it, you must pronounce the blessing at Mount Gerizim and the curse at Mount Ebal. 30(These two mountains are west of the Jordan River in the land of the Canaanites who live in the Jordan Valley,* near the town of Gilgal, not far from the oaks of Moreh.) 31For you are about to cross the Jordan River to take over the land the LORD your God is giving you. When you take that land and are living in it, 32you must be careful to obey all the decrees and regulations I am giving you today.

12 THE LORD'S CHOSEN PLACE FOR WORSHIP "These are the decrees and regulations you must be careful to obey when you live in the land that the LORD, the God of

11:24 Hebrew *to the western sea.*   11:30 Hebrew *the Arabah.*

your ancestors, is giving you. You must obey them as long as you live.

2"When you drive out the nations that live there, you must destroy all the places where they worship their gods—high on the mountains, up on the hills, and under every green tree. 3Break down their altars and smash their sacred pillars. Burn their Asherah poles and cut down their carved idols. Completely erase the names of their gods!

4"Do not worship the LORD your God in the way these pagan peoples worship their gods. 5Rather, you must seek the LORD your God at the place of worship he himself will choose from among all the tribes—the place where his name will be honored. 6There you will bring your burnt offerings, your sacrifices, your tithes, your sacred offerings, your offerings to fulfill a vow, your voluntary offerings, and your offerings of the firstborn animals of your herds and flocks. 7There you and your families will feast in the presence of the LORD your God, and you will rejoice in all you have accomplished because the LORD your God has blessed you.

8"Your pattern of worship will change. Today all of you are doing as you please, 9because you have not yet arrived at the place of rest, the land the LORD your God is giving you as your special possession. 10But you will soon cross the Jordan River and live in the land the LORD your God is giving you. When he gives you rest from all your enemies and you're living safely in the land, 11you must bring everything I command you—your burnt offerings, your sacrifices, your tithes, your sacred offerings, and your offerings to fulfill a vow—to the designated place of worship, the place the LORD your God chooses for his name to be honored.

12"You must celebrate there in the presence of the LORD your God with your sons and daughters and all your servants. And remember to include the Levites who live in your towns, for they will receive no allotment of land among you. 13Be careful not to sacrifice your burnt offerings just anywhere you like. 14You may do so only at the place the LORD will choose within one of your tribal territories. There you must offer your burnt offerings and do everything I command you.

FAMILY WORSHIP
(12:12, 18) The Hebrews placed great emphasis on family worship, which often involved making sacrificial offerings or attending the required festivals. Worshiping as a family gave the children a healthy attitude toward worship and made it more meaningful for the adults. How have your family's worship traditions affected your view of worship?

I WONDER...

The Old Testament is long and sometimes boring. Why did God put it in the Bible?

Have you ever asked your grandmother to tell you her whole life story? You would probably receive an all-day talk, full of wonderful stories. Though it would be fun for your grandmother, you would likely be bored because you would hear too many facts that would not relate to your life!

If, however, you asked her to relate the top ten experiences that shaped her personality and helped her make it through life, it would only take an hour, it would be fascinating, and you would learn a lot.

The Old Testament is not a detailed day-by-day account of history. Instead it is the story of the Jewish people. Their history points to Jesus Christ. Through this story, we see God's plan of sending his Son, Jesus, to die on the cross to pay the penalty for our sin.

Living at the dawn of the twenty-first century limits our appreciation of the fact that for 3,000 years, the Old Testament has guided people from every walk of life. It was written not only for young people today, but also for people who needed to hear from God in A.D. 320 Rome or A.D. 1540 Germany. What this means is that not every story will affect you the way it has others through the years. But as you read through the Old Testament, you will be surprised at how many stories do relate to today. God's command to Moses and the Israelites to go into the Promised Land and possess it is the fulfillment of a promise to Abraham that God made long before Moses was even born. It shows that God has a plan for history and that he keeps his promises.

It is essential for you as a Christian to realize that your heavenly Father keeps his promises! We are able to give him control of our life because for centuries he has proven himself trustworthy. (See Hebrews 11 for a brief recap of God's faithfulness.)

The Old Testament tells us about the real-life struggles people experienced when faced with the choice of trusting God or doing things their own way.

Instead of giving us all of history to read, God has condensed his story into one book. He has even pointed out the most important lessons we need to pay attention to in order to live life to the fullest as his children.

¹⁵"But you may butcher your animals and eat their meat in any town whenever you want. You may freely eat the animals with which the LORD your God blesses you. All of you, whether ceremonially clean or unclean, may eat that meat, just as you now eat gazelle and deer. ¹⁶But you must not consume the blood. You must pour it out on the ground like water.

¹⁷"But you may not eat your offerings in your hometown—neither the tithe of your grain and new wine and olive oil, nor the firstborn of your flocks and herds, nor any offering to fulfill a vow, nor your voluntary offerings, nor your sacred offerings. ¹⁸You must eat these in the presence of the LORD your God at the place he will choose. Eat them there with your children, your servants, and the Levites who live in your towns, celebrating in the presence of the LORD your God in all you do. ¹⁹And be very careful never to neglect the Levites as long as you live in your land.

²⁰"When the LORD your God expands your territory as he has promised, and you have the urge to eat meat, you may freely eat meat whenever you want. ²¹It might happen that the designated place of worship—the place the LORD your God chooses for his name to be honored—is a long way from your home. If so, you may butcher any of the cattle, sheep, or goats the LORD has given you, and you may freely eat the meat in your hometown, as I have commanded you. ²²Anyone, whether ceremonially clean or unclean, may eat that meat, just as you do now with gazelle and deer. ²³But never consume the blood, for the blood is the life, and you must not consume the lifeblood with the meat. ²⁴Instead, pour out the blood on the ground like water. ²⁵Do not consume the blood, so that all may go well with you and your children after you, because you will be doing what pleases the LORD.

²⁶"Take your sacred gifts and your offerings given to fulfill a vow to the place the LORD chooses. ²⁷You must offer the meat and blood of your burnt offerings on the altar of the LORD your God. The blood of your other sacrifices must be poured out on the altar of the LORD your God, but you may eat the meat. ²⁸Be careful to obey all my commands, so that all will go well with you and your children after you, because you will be doing what is good and pleasing to the LORD your God.

²⁹"When the LORD your God goes ahead of you and destroys the nations and you drive them out and live in their land, ³⁰do not fall into the trap of following their customs and worshiping their gods. Do not inquire about their gods, saying, 'How do these nations worship their gods? I want to follow their example.' ³¹You must not worship the LORD your God the way the other nations worship their gods, for they perform for their gods every detestable act

that the LORD hates. They even burn their sons and daughters as sacrifices to their gods.

32*"So be careful to obey all the commands I give you. You must not add anything to them or subtract anything from them.

13 A WARNING AGAINST IDOLATRY

1*"Suppose there are prophets among you or those who dream dreams about the future, and they promise you signs or miracles, 2and the predicted signs or miracles occur. If they then say, 'Come, let us worship other gods'—gods you have not known before—3do not listen to them. The LORD your God is testing you to see if you truly love him with all your heart and soul. 4Serve only the LORD your God and fear him alone. Obey his commands, listen to his voice, and cling to him. 5The false prophets or visionaries who try to lead you astray must be put to death, for they encourage rebellion against the LORD your God, who redeemed you from slavery and brought you out of the land of Egypt. Since they try to lead you astray from the way the LORD your God commanded you to live, you must put them to death. In this way you will purge the evil from among you.

6"Suppose someone secretly entices you— even your brother, your son or daughter, your beloved wife, or your closest friend—and says, 'Let us go worship other gods'—gods that neither you nor your ancestors have known. 7They might suggest that you worship the gods of peoples who live nearby or who come from the ends of the earth. 8But do not give in or listen. Have no pity, and do not spare or protect them. 9You must put them to death! Strike the first blow yourself, and then all the people must join in. 10Stone the guilty ones to death because they have tried to draw you away from the LORD your God, who rescued you from the land of Egypt, the place of slavery. 11Then all Israel will hear about it and be afraid, and no one will act so wickedly again.

12"When you begin living in the towns the LORD your God is giving you, you may hear 13that scoundrels among you are leading their fellow citizens astray by saying, 'Let us go worship other gods'—gods you have not known before. 14In such cases, you must examine the facts carefully. If you find that the report is true and such a detestable act has been committed among you, 15you must attack that town and completely destroy* all its inhabitants, as well as all the livestock. 16Then you must pile all the plunder in the middle of the open square and burn it. Burn the entire town as a burnt offering to the LORD your God. That town must remain a ruin forever; it may never be rebuilt. 17Keep none of the plunder that has been set apart for destruction. Then the LORD will turn from his fierce anger and be merciful to you. He will have compassion on you and make you a large nation, just as he swore to your ancestors.

18"The LORD your God will be merciful only if you listen to his voice and keep all his commands that I am giving you today, doing what pleases him.

14 CEREMONIALLY CLEAN AND UNCLEAN ANIMALS

"Since you are the people of the LORD your God, never cut yourselves or shave the hair above your foreheads in mourning for the dead. 2You have been set apart as holy to the LORD your God, and he has chosen you from all the nations of the earth to be his own special treasure.

3"You must not eat any detestable animals that are ceremonially unclean. 4These are the animals* you may eat: the ox, the sheep, the goat, 5the deer, the gazelle, the roe deer, the wild goat, the addax, the antelope, and the mountain sheep.

6"You may eat any animal that has completely split hooves and chews the cud, 7but if the animal doesn't have both, it may not be eaten. So you may not eat the camel, the hare, or the hyrax.* They chew the cud but do not have split hooves, so they are ceremonially unclean for you. 8And you may not eat the pig. It has split hooves but does not chew the cud, so it is ceremonially unclean for you. You may not eat the meat of these animals or even touch their carcasses.

9"Of all the marine animals, you may eat whatever has both fins and scales. 10You may not, however, eat marine animals that do not

12:32 Verse 12:32 is numbered 13:1 in Hebrew text. 13:1 Verses 13:1-18 are numbered 13:2-19 in Hebrew text. 13:15 The Hebrew term used here refers to the complete consecration of things or people to the LORD, either by destroying them or by giving them as an offering; similarly in 13:17. 14:4 The identification of some of the animals and birds listed in this chapter is uncertain. 14:7 Or coney, or rock badger.

WHISPERED TEMPTATIONS

(13:1-11) The Israelites were warned not to listen to false prophets or anyone else who tried to get them to worship other gods. The temptation to abandon God's commands often sneaks up on us. It may come not with a loud shout, but in a whisper of doubt. Whispers can be very persuasive, especially if they come from loved ones. But not even love for relatives should take precedence over devotion to God. We can overcome whispered temptations by pouring out our feelings to God in prayer and by studying his Word.

have both fins and scales. They are ceremonially unclean for you.

[11]"You may eat any bird that is ceremonially clean. [12]These are the birds you may not eat: the griffon vulture, the bearded vulture, the black vulture, [13]the kite, the falcon, buzzards of all kinds, [14]ravens of all kinds, [15]the eagle owl, the short-eared owl, the seagull, hawks of all kinds, [16]the little owl, the great owl, the barn owl, [17]the desert owl, the Egyptian vulture, the cormorant, [18]the stork, herons of all kinds, the hoopoe, and the bat.

[19]"All winged insects that walk along the ground are ceremonially unclean for you and may not be eaten. [20]But you may eat any winged bird or insect that is ceremonially clean.

[21]"You must not eat anything that has died a natural death. You may give it to a foreigner living in your town, or you may sell it to a stranger. But do not eat it yourselves, for you are set apart as holy to the LORD your God.

"You must not cook a young goat in its mother's milk.

THE GIVING OF TITHES [22]"You must set aside a tithe of your crops—one-tenth of all the crops you harvest each year. [23]Bring this tithe to the designated place of worship—the place the LORD your God chooses for his name to be honored—and eat it there in his presence. This applies to your tithes of grain, new wine, olive oil, and the firstborn males of your flocks and herds. Doing this will teach you always to fear the LORD your God.

[24]"Now when the LORD your God blesses you with a good harvest, the place of worship he chooses for his name to be honored might be too far for you to bring the tithe. [25]If so, you may sell the tithe portion of your crops and herds, put the money in a pouch, and go to the place the LORD your God has chosen. [26]When you arrive, you may use the money to buy any kind of food you want—cattle, sheep, goats, wine, or other alcoholic drink. Then feast there in the presence of the LORD your God and celebrate with your household. [27]And do not neglect the Levites in your town, for they will receive no allotment of land among you.

[28]"At the end of every third year, bring the entire tithe of that year's harvest and store it in the nearest town. [29]Give it to the Levites, who will receive no allotment of land among you, as well as to the foreigners living among you, the orphans, and the widows in your towns, so they can eat and be satisfied. Then the LORD your God will bless you in all your work.

15 RELEASE FOR DEBTORS "At the end of every seventh year you must cancel the debts of everyone who owes you money. [2]This is how it must be done. Everyone must cancel the loans they have made to their fellow Israelites. They must not demand payment from their neighbors or relatives, for the LORD's time of release has arrived. [3]This release from debt, however, applies only to your fellow Israelites—not to the foreigners living among you.

[4]"There should be no poor among you, for the LORD your God will greatly bless you in the land he is giving you as a special possession. [5]You will receive this blessing if you are careful to obey all the commands of the LORD your God that I am giving you today. [6]The LORD your God will bless you as he has promised. You will lend money to many nations but will never need to borrow. You will rule many nations, but they will not rule over you.

[7]"But if there are any poor Israelites in your towns when you arrive in the land the LORD your God is giving you, do not be hard-hearted or tightfisted toward them. [8]Instead, be generous and lend them whatever they need. [9]Do not be mean-spirited and refuse someone a loan because the year for canceling debts is close at hand. If you refuse to make the loan and the needy person cries out to the LORD, you will be considered guilty of sin. [10]Give generously to the poor, not grudgingly, for the LORD your God will bless you in everything you do. [11]There will always be some in the land who are poor. That is why I am commanding you to share freely with the poor and with other Israelites in need.

RELEASE FOR HEBREW SLAVES [12]"If a fellow Hebrew sells himself or herself to be your servant* and serves you for six years, in the seventh year you must set that servant free.

[13]"When you release a male servant, do not send him away empty-handed. [14]Give him a

POVERTY
(15:7-11) God told the Israelites to help the poor among them when they arrived in the Promised Land. This was an important part of possessing the land (see also Deut 24:17-22). Some people make the assumption that people are poor through some fault of their own. Ever hear someone voice an opinion like that? This kind of reasoning makes it easy to close our hearts and hands against them. But we are not to invent reasons for ignoring the care of the poor. We are to respond to their needs no matter who or what was responsible for their condition. Who are the poor in your community? How will you help them?

15:12 Or *If a Hebrew man or woman is sold to you.*

generous farewell gift from your flock, your threshing floor, and your winepress. Share with him some of the bounty with which the LORD your God has blessed you. [15]Remember that you were once slaves in the land of Egypt and the LORD your God redeemed you! That is why I am giving you this command.

[16]"But suppose your servant says, 'I will not leave you,' because he loves you and your family, and he has done well with you. [17]In that case, take an awl and push it through his earlobe into the door. After that, he will be your servant for life. And do the same for your female servants.

[18]"You must not consider it a hardship when you release your servants. Remember that for six years they have given you services worth double the wages of hired workers, and the LORD your God will bless you in all you do.

SACRIFICING FIRSTBORN MALE ANIMALS

[19]"You must set aside for the LORD your God all the firstborn males from your flocks and herds. Do not use the firstborn of your herds to work your fields, and do not shear the firstborn of your flocks. [20]Instead, you and your family must eat these animals in the presence of the LORD your God each year at the place he chooses. [21]But if this firstborn animal has any defect, such as lameness or blindness, or if anything else is wrong with it, you must not sacrifice it to the LORD your God. [22]Instead, use it for food for your family in your hometown. Anyone, whether ceremonially clean or unclean, may eat it, just as anyone may eat a gazelle or deer. [23]But you must not consume the blood. You must pour it out on the ground like water.

16 PASSOVER AND THE FESTIVAL OF UNLEAVENED BREAD

"In honor of the LORD your God, celebrate the Passover each year in the early spring, in the month of Abib,* for that was the month in which the LORD your God brought you out of Egypt by night. [2]Your Passover sacrifice may be from either the flock or the herd, and it must be sacrificed to the LORD your God at the designated place of worship—the place he chooses for his name to be honored. [3]Eat it with bread made without yeast. For seven days the bread you eat must be made without yeast, as when you escaped from Egypt

in such a hurry. Eat this bread—the bread of suffering—so that as long as you live you will remember the day you departed from Egypt. [4]Let no yeast be found in any house throughout your land for those seven days. And when you sacrifice the Passover lamb on the evening of the first day, do not let any of the meat remain until the next morning.

[5]"You may not sacrifice the Passover in just any of the towns that the LORD your God is giving you. [6]You must offer it only at the designated place of worship—the place the LORD your God chooses for his name to be honored. Sacrifice it there in the evening as the sun goes down on the anniversary of your exodus from Egypt. [7]Roast the lamb and eat it in the place the LORD your God chooses. Then you may go back to your tents the next morning. [8]For the next six days you may not eat any bread made with yeast. On the seventh day proclaim another holy day in honor of the LORD your God, and no work may be done on that day.

THE FESTIVAL OF HARVEST

[9]"Count off seven weeks from when you first begin to cut the grain at the time of harvest. [10]Then celebrate the Festival of Harvest* to honor the LORD your God. Bring him a voluntary offering in proportion to the blessings you have received from him. [11]This is a time to celebrate before the LORD your God at the designated place of worship he will choose for his name to be honored. Celebrate with your sons and daughters, your male and female servants, the Levites from your towns, and the foreigners, orphans, and widows who live among you. [12]Remember that you were once slaves in Egypt, so be careful to obey all these decrees.

THE FESTIVAL OF SHELTERS

[13]"You must observe the Festival of Shelters* for seven days at the end of the harvest season, after the grain has been threshed and the grapes have been pressed. [14]This festival will be a happy time of celebrating with your sons and daughters, your male and female servants, and the Levites, foreigners, orphans, and widows from your towns. [15]For seven days you must celebrate this festival to honor the LORD your God at the place he chooses, for it is he who blesses you with bountiful harvests and gives you success in all your work. This festival will be a time of great joy for all.

[16]"Each year every man in Israel must celebrate these three festivals: the Festival of Unleavened Bread, the Festival of Harvest, and the Festival of Shelters. On each of these

16:1 Hebrew *Observe the month of Abib, and keep the Passover unto the LORD your God.* Abib, the first month of the ancient Hebrew lunar calendar, usually occurs within the months of March and April. **16:10** Hebrew *Festival of Weeks;* also in 16:16. This was later called the Festival of Pentecost (see Acts 2:1). It is celebrated today as Shavuot (or Shabuoth). **16:13** Or *Festival of Booths,* or *Festival of Tabernacles;* also in 16:16. This was earlier called the Festival of the Final Harvest or Festival of Ingathering (see Exod 23:16b). It is celebrated today as Sukkot (or Succoth).

occasions, all men must appear before the LORD your God at the place he chooses, but they must not appear before the LORD without a gift for him. 17All must give as they are able, according to the blessings given to them by the LORD your God.

JUSTICE FOR THE PEOPLE 18"Appoint judges and officials for yourselves from each of your tribes in all the towns the LORD your God is giving you. They must judge the people fairly. 19You must never twist justice or show partiality. Never accept a bribe, for bribes blind the eyes of the wise and corrupt the decisions of the godly. 20Let true justice prevail, so you may live and occupy the land that the LORD your God is giving you.

21"You must never set up a wooden Asherah pole beside the altar you build for the LORD your God. 22And never set up sacred pillars for worship, for the LORD your God hates them.

17 "Never sacrifice sick or defective cattle, sheep, or goats to the LORD your God, for he detests such gifts.

2"When you begin living in the towns the

. . . .

GIVING BACK TO GOD
(16:16-17) Each year every Hebrew male was required to attend three festivals wherever the Tabernacle happened to be (see also Exod 23:17; 34:23). At these festivals, each participant was encouraged to give what he could in proportion to what God had given him. Although God does not expect us to give more than we can, we are blessed when we give cheerfully. For some of us, 10 percent may be a burden. For most of us, it is far too little. If you were to give in proportion to what you have been given, what would you give?

A RULE FOR WITNESSES
(17:2-7) During this time in Israel's history, a law concerning capital punishment was established. A person accused of worshiping idols could not be stoned to death based on the testimony of only one witness. A death sentence required two or three witnesses. This system prevented angry individuals from giving false testimony (see Exod 20:16). Also, since the accusers threw the first stones, they thought twice about accusing unjustly. In the same way, we need to consider the consequences before we accuse someone of a wrongdoing.

A DANGEROUS FASCINATION
(18:9-14) Just as most of us are naturally curious about a magician's trick, the Israelites were curious about the occult practices of the Canaanites. Because Satan was involved in these practices, God warned Israel to avoid them. People today are still fascinated by horoscopes, fortune-telling, witchcraft, and cults. Often their interest comes from a desire to know and control the future. But the information Satan offers is likely to be distorted or completely false. With the trustworthy guidance of the Holy Spirit through the Scriptures and the church, we don't need to turn to occult sources for information.

LORD your God is giving you, a man or woman among you might do evil in the sight of the LORD your God and violate the covenant. 3For instance, they might serve other gods or worship the sun, the moon, or any of the stars—the forces of heaven—which I have strictly forbidden. 4When you hear about it, investigate the matter thoroughly. If it is true that this detestable thing has been done in Israel, 5then the man or woman who has committed such an evil act must be taken to the gates of the town and stoned to death. 6But never put a person to death on the testimony of only one witness. There must always be two or three witnesses. 7The witnesses must throw the first stones, and then all the people may join in. In this way, you will purge the evil from among you.

8"Suppose a case arises in a local court that is too hard for you to decide—for instance, whether someone is guilty of murder or only of manslaughter, or a difficult lawsuit, or a case involving different kinds of assault. Take such legal cases to the place the LORD your God will choose, 9and present them to the Levitical priests or the judge on duty at that time. They will hear the case and declare the verdict. 10You must carry out the verdict they announce and the sentence they prescribe at the place the LORD chooses. You must do exactly what they say. 11After they have interpreted the law and declared their verdict, the sentence they impose must be fully executed; do not modify it in any way. 12Anyone arrogant enough to reject the verdict of the judge or of the priest who represents the LORD your God must die. In this way you will purge the evil from Israel. 13Then everyone else will hear about it and be afraid to act so arrogantly.

GUIDELINES FOR A KING 14"You are about to enter the land the LORD your God is giving you. When you take it over and settle there, you may think, 'We should select a king to rule over us like the other nations around us.' 15If this happens, be sure to select as king the man the LORD your God chooses. You must appoint a fellow Israelite; he may not be a foreigner.

16"The king must not build up a large stable of horses for himself or send his people to Egypt to buy horses, for the LORD has told you, 'You must never return to Egypt.' 17The king must not take many wives for himself, because they will turn his heart away from the LORD. And he must not accumulate large amounts of wealth in silver and gold for himself.

18"When he sits on the throne as king, he

must copy for himself this body of instruction on a scroll in the presence of the Levitical priests. ¹⁹He must always keep that copy with him and read it daily as long as he lives. That way he will learn to fear the LORD his God by obeying all the terms of these instructions and decrees. ²⁰This regular reading will prevent him from becoming proud and acting as if he is above his fellow citizens. It will also prevent him from turning away from these commands in the smallest way. And it will ensure that he and his descendants will reign for many generations in Israel.

18 GIFTS FOR THE PRIESTS AND LEVITES
"Remember that the Levitical priests—that is, the whole of the tribe of Levi—will receive no allotment of land among the other tribes in Israel. Instead, the priests and Levites will eat from the special gifts given to the LORD, for that is their share. ²They will have no land of their own among the Israelites. The LORD himself is their special possession, just as he promised them.

³"These are the parts the priests may claim as their share from the cattle, sheep, and goats that the people bring as offerings: the shoulder, the cheeks, and the stomach. ⁴You must also give to the priests the first share of the grain, the new wine, the olive oil, and the wool at shearing time. ⁵For the LORD your God chose the tribe of Levi out of all your tribes to minister in the LORD's name forever.

⁶"Suppose a Levite chooses to move from his town in Israel, wherever he is living, to the place the LORD chooses for worship. ⁷He may minister there in the name of the LORD his God, just like all his fellow Levites who are serving the LORD there. ⁸He may eat his share of the sacrifices and offerings, even if he also receives support from his family.

A CALL TO HOLY LIVING ⁹"When you enter the land the LORD your God is giving you, be very careful not to imitate the detestable customs of the nations living there. ¹⁰For example, never sacrifice your son or daughter as a burnt offering.* And do not let your people practice fortune-telling, or use sorcery, or interpret omens, or engage in witchcraft, ¹¹or cast spells, or function as mediums or psychics, or call forth the spirits of the dead. ¹²Anyone who does these things is detestable to the LORD. It is because the other nations have done these detestable things that the LORD your God will drive them

18:10 Or *never make your son or daughter pass through the fire.*
18:16 Hebrew *Horeb*, another name for Sinai.

MY STORY: Meagan

It was strange how this one passage of Scripture—Ephesians 6:10-18, about putting on all of God's armor—kept coming up again and again in one week. First it came up in my quiet time. Then we studied the same passage in the youth Bible study. Finally, my pastor preached a sermon on spiritual warfare.

Later that week my friend brought out a Ouija board and asked me to try it with her. I felt uneasy about it, but it seemed like just a game, so I said yes. Some weird things happened; the piece that you put your fingers on really seemed to move of its own accord, and it spelled out some weird answers. I had a very creepy feeling that this was not of God. I told my friend I wanted to quit then and there, that I didn't think God wanted us to do this. That night I called my youth pastor and told him about it. He pointed out that Deuteronomy 18:9-14 warns us against trying to seek the future from means other than God. He reminded me that Satan is always trying to find a way to sneak into our lives. And he reminded me of Ephesians 6 and the armor God gives us to fight the devil. I realized that God had been trying to prepare me for the temptation to use the Ouija board, but I wasn't paying close enough attention at the time.

I learned from my mistake. I will never touch or mess with a Ouija board or horoscopes or anything like that again.

out ahead of you. ¹³But you must be blameless before the LORD your God. ¹⁴The nations you are about to displace consult sorcerers and fortune-tellers, but the LORD your God forbids you to do such things."

TRUE AND FALSE PROPHETS ¹⁵Moses continued, "The LORD your God will raise up for you a prophet like me from among your fellow Israelites. You must listen to him. ¹⁶For this is what you yourselves requested of the LORD your God when you were assembled at Mount Sinai.* You said, 'Don't let us hear the voice of the Lord our God anymore or see this blazing fire, for we will die.'

¹⁷"Then the Lord said to me, 'What they have said is right. ¹⁸I will raise up a prophet like you from among their fellow Israelites. I will put my words in his mouth, and he will tell the people everything I command him. ¹⁹I will personally deal with anyone who will not listen to the messages the prophet proclaims on my behalf. ²⁰But any prophet who falsely claims to speak in my name or who speaks in the name of another god must die.'

²¹"But you may wonder, 'How will we know whether or not a prophecy is from the Lord?' ²²If the prophet speaks in the Lord's name but his prediction does not happen or come true, you will know that the Lord did not give that message. That prophet has spoken without my authority and need not be feared.

19 CITIES OF REFUGE "When the Lord your God destroys the nations whose land he is giving you, you will take over their land and settle in their towns and homes. ²Then you must set apart three cities of refuge in the land the Lord your God is giving you. ³Survey the territory,* and divide the land the Lord your God is giving you into three districts, with one of these cities in each district. Then anyone who has killed someone can flee to one of the cities of refuge for safety.

⁴"If someone kills another person unintentionally, without previous hostility, the slayer may flee to any of these cities to live in safety. ⁵For example, suppose someone goes into the forest with a neighbor to cut wood. And suppose one of them swings an ax to chop down a tree, and the ax head flies off the handle, killing the other person. In such cases, the slayer may flee to one of the cities of refuge to live in safety.

⁶"If the distance to the nearest city of refuge is too far, an enraged avenger might be able to chase down and kill the person who caused the death. Then the slayer would die unfairly, since he had never shown hostility toward the person who died. ⁷That is why I am commanding you to set aside three cities of refuge.

⁸"And if the Lord your God enlarges your

territory, as he swore to your ancestors, and gives you all the land he promised them, ⁹you must designate three additional cities of refuge. (He will give you this land if you are careful to obey all the commands I have given you—if you always love the Lord your God and walk in his ways.) ¹⁰That way you will prevent the death of innocent people in the land the Lord your God is giving you as your special possession. You will not be held responsible for the death of innocent people.

¹¹"But suppose someone is hostile toward a neighbor and deliberately ambushes and murders him and then flees to one of the cities of refuge. ¹²In that case, the elders of the murderer's hometown must send agents to the city of refuge to bring him back and hand him over to the dead person's avenger to be put to death. ¹³Do not feel sorry for that murderer! Purge from Israel the guilt of murdering innocent people; then all will go well with you.

CONCERN FOR JUSTICE ¹⁴"When you arrive in the land the Lord your God is giving you as your special possession, you must never steal anyone's land by moving the boundary markers your ancestors set up to mark their property.

¹⁵"You must not convict anyone of a crime on the testimony of only one witness. The facts of the case must be established by the testimony of two or three witnesses.

¹⁶"If a malicious witness comes forward and accuses someone of a crime, ¹⁷then both the accuser and accused must appear before the Lord by coming to the priests and judges in office at that time. ¹⁸The judges must investigate the case thoroughly. If the accuser has brought false charges against his fellow Israelite, ¹⁹you must impose on the accuser the sentence he intended for the other person. In this way, you will purge such evil from among you. ²⁰Then the rest of the people will hear about it and be afraid to do such an evil thing. ²¹You must show no pity for the guilty! Your rule should be life for life, eye for eye, tooth for tooth, hand for hand, foot for foot.

20 REGULATIONS CONCERNING WAR "When you go out to fight your enemies and you face horses and chariots and an army greater than your own, do not be afraid. The Lord your God, who brought you out of the land of Egypt, is with you! ²When you prepare for battle, the priest must come forward to speak to the troops. ³He will say to them, 'Listen to me, all you men of Israel! Do not be afraid as you

GOD'S VICTORY EQUATION

(20:1) When the Israelites worried that powerful enemies outnumbered them, God reminded them that he was always with them. When big problems arise, many of us can relate to feelings of helplessness and hopelessness. Is that where you are now? If so, God wants you to consider a new equation: God + you = victory.

19:3 Or Keep the roads in good repair.

go out to fight your enemies today! Do not lose heart or panic or tremble before them. ⁴For the LORD your God is going with you! He will fight for you against your enemies, and he will give you victory!'

⁵"Then the officers of the army must address the troops and say, 'Has anyone here just built a new house but not yet dedicated it? If so, you may go home! You might be killed in the battle, and someone else would dedicate your house. ⁶Has anyone here just planted a vineyard but not yet eaten any of its fruit? If so, you may go home! You might die in battle, and someone else would eat the first fruit. ⁷Has anyone here just become engaged to a woman but not yet married her? Well, you may go home and get married! You might die in the battle, and someone else would marry her.'

⁸"Then the officers will also say, 'Is anyone here afraid or worried? If you are, you may go home before you frighten anyone else.' ⁹When the officers have finished speaking to their troops, they will appoint the unit commanders.

¹⁰"As you approach a town to attack it, you must first offer its people terms for peace. ¹¹If they accept your terms and open the gates to you, then all the people inside will serve you in forced labor. ¹²But if they refuse to make peace and prepare to fight, you must attack the town. ¹³When the LORD your God hands the town over to you, use your swords to kill every man in the town. ¹⁴But you may keep for yourselves all the women, children, livestock, and other plunder. You may enjoy the plunder from your enemies that the LORD your God has given you.

¹⁵"But these instructions apply only to distant towns, not to the towns of the nations in the land you will enter. ¹⁶In those towns that the LORD your God is giving you as a special possession, destroy every living thing. ¹⁷You must completely destroy* the Hittites, Amorites, Canaanites, Perizzites, Hivites, and Jebusites, just as the LORD your God has commanded you. ¹⁸This will prevent the people of the land from teaching you to imitate their detestable customs in the worship of their gods, which would cause you to sin deeply against the LORD your God.

¹⁹"When you are attacking a town and the war drags on, you must not cut down the trees with your axes. You may eat the fruit, but do not cut down the trees. Are the trees your enemies, that you should attack them? ²⁰You may only cut down trees that you know are not valuable

20:17 The Hebrew term used here refers to the complete consecration of things or people to the LORD, either by destroying them or by giving them as an offering.

for food. Use them to make the equipment you need to attack the enemy town until it falls.

21 CLEANSING FOR UNSOLVED MURDER

"When you are in the land the LORD your God is giving you, someone may be found murdered in a field, and you don't know who committed the murder. ²In such a case, your elders and judges must measure the distance from the site of the crime to the nearby towns. ³When the nearest town has been determined, that town's elders must select from the herd a young cow that has never been trained or yoked to a plow. ⁴They must lead it down to a valley that has not been plowed or planted and that has a stream running through it. There in the valley they must break the young cow's neck. ⁵Then the Levitical priests must step forward, for the LORD your God has chosen them to minister before him and to pronounce blessings in the LORD's name. They are to decide all legal and criminal cases.

⁶"The elders of the town must wash their hands over the young cow whose neck was broken. ⁷Then they must say, 'Our hands did not shed this person's blood, nor did we see it happen. ⁸O LORD, forgive your people Israel whom you have redeemed. Do not charge your people with the guilt of murdering an innocent person.' Then they will be absolved of the guilt of this person's blood. ⁹By following these instructions, you will do what is right in the LORD's sight and will cleanse the guilt of murder from your community.

MARRIAGE TO A CAPTIVE WOMAN ¹⁰"Suppose you go out to war against your enemies and the LORD your God hands them over to you, and you take some of them as captives. ¹¹And suppose you see among the captives a beautiful woman, and you are attracted to her and want to marry her. ¹²If this happens, you may take her to your home, where she must shave her head, cut her nails, ¹³and change the clothes she was wearing when she was captured. She will stay in your home, but let her mourn for her father and mother for a full month. Then you may marry her, and you will be her husband and she will be your wife. ¹⁴But if you marry her and she does not please you, you must let her go free. You may not sell her or treat her as a slave, for you have humiliated her.

RIGHTS OF THE FIRSTBORN ¹⁵"Suppose a man has two wives, but he loves one and not the other, and both have given him sons. And suppose the firstborn son is the son of the wife he does not love. [16]When the man divides his inheritance, he may not give the larger inheritance to his younger son, the son of the wife he loves, as if he were the firstborn son. [17]He must recognize the rights of his oldest son, the son of the wife he does not love, by giving him a double portion. He is the first son of his father's virility, and the rights of the firstborn belong to him.

DEALING WITH A REBELLIOUS SON

[18]"Suppose a man has a stubborn and rebellious son who will not obey his father or mother, even though they discipline him. [19]In such a case, the father and mother must take the son to the elders as they hold court at the town gate. [20]The parents must say to the elders, 'This son of ours is stubborn and rebellious and refuses to obey. He is a glutton and a drunkard.' [21]Then all the men of his town must stone him to death. In this way, you will purge this evil from among you, and all Israel will hear about it and be afraid.

VARIOUS REGULATIONS

[22]"If someone has committed a crime worthy of death and is executed and hung on a tree,* [23]the body must not remain hanging from the tree overnight. You must bury the body that same day, for anyone who is hung* is cursed in the sight of God. In this way, you will prevent the defilement of the land the LORD your God is giving you as your special possession.

22 "If you see your neighbor's ox or sheep or goat wandering away, don't ignore your responsibility.* Take it back to its owner. [2]If its owner does not live nearby or you don't know who the owner is, take it to your place and keep it until the owner comes looking for it. Then you must return it. [3]Do the same if you find your neighbor's donkey, clothing, or anything else your neighbor loses. Don't ignore your responsibility.

··

SEX ROLES

(22:5) This verse is not merely a discussion of Old Testament fashions. It describes a command to men and women to avoid reversing their sexual roles. Yet rejecting these roles is not uncommon today. Many talk shows feature the stories of individuals who feel "trapped" in the wrong kind of body and seek ways to make themselves "whole." Some of their paths to wholeness include homosexuality or sex-change operations. But neither path leads to the desired goal.

Ever struggle with questions about this issue? God had a purpose for making us uniquely male and female. He understands our struggles and wants us to trust that his plans for us are good.

[4]"If you see that your neighbor's donkey or ox has collapsed on the road, do not look the other way. Go and help your neighbor get it back on its feet!

[5]"A woman must not put on men's clothing, and a man must not wear women's clothing. Anyone who does this is detestable in the sight of the LORD your God.

[6]"If you happen to find a bird's nest in a tree or on the ground, and there are young ones or eggs in it with the mother sitting in the nest, do not take the mother with the young. [7]You may take the young, but let the mother go, so that you may prosper and enjoy a long life.

[8]"When you build a new house, you must build a railing around the edge of its flat roof. That way you will not be considered guilty of murder if someone falls from the roof.

[9]"You must not plant any other crop between the rows of your vineyard. If you do, you are forbidden to use either the grapes from the vineyard or the other crop.

[10]"You must not plow with an ox and a donkey harnessed together.

[11]"You must not wear clothing made of wool and linen woven together.

[12]"You must put four tassels on the hem of the cloak with which you cover yourself—on the front, back, and sides.

REGULATIONS FOR SEXUAL PURITY

[13]"Suppose a man marries a woman, but after sleeping with her, he turns against her [14]and publicly accuses her of shameful conduct, saying, 'When I married this woman, I discovered she was not a virgin.' [15]Then the woman's father and mother must bring the proof of her virginity to the elders as they hold court at the town gate. [16]Her father must say to them, 'I gave my daughter to this man to be his wife, and now he has turned against her. [17]He has accused her of shameful conduct, saying, "I discovered that your daughter was not a virgin." But here is the proof of my daughter's virginity.' Then they must spread her bed sheet before the elders. [18]The elders must then take the man and punish him. [19]They must also fine him 100 pieces of silver,* which he must pay to the woman's father because he publicly accused a virgin of Israel of shameful conduct. The woman will then remain the man's wife, and he may never divorce her.

[20]"But suppose the man's accusations are true, and he can show that she was not a virgin.

21:22 Or *impaled on a pole;* similarly in 21:23.   **21:23** Greek version reads *for everyone who is hung on a tree.* Compare Gal 3:13.
22:1 Hebrew *don't hide yourself;* similarly in 22:3.   **22:19** Hebrew *100 shekels of silver,* about 2.5 pounds or 1.1 kilograms in weight.

²¹The woman must be taken to the door of her father's home, and there the men of the town must stone her to death, for she has committed a disgraceful crime in Israel by being promiscuous while living in her parents' home. In this way, you will purge this evil from among you.

²²"If a man is discovered committing adultery, both he and the woman must die. In this way, you will purge Israel of such evil.

²³"Suppose a man meets a young woman, a virgin who is engaged to be married, and he has sexual intercourse with her. If this happens within a town, ²⁴you must take both of them to the gates of that town and stone them to death. The woman is guilty because she did not scream for help. The man must die because he violated another man's wife. In this way, you will purge this evil from among you.

²⁵"But if the man meets the engaged woman out in the country, and he rapes her, then only the man must die. ²⁶Do nothing to the young woman; she has committed no crime worthy of death. She is as innocent as a murder victim. ²⁷Since the man raped her out in the country, it must be assumed that she screamed, but there was no one to rescue her.

²⁸"Suppose a man has intercourse with a young woman who is a virgin but is not engaged to be married. If they are discovered, ²⁹he must pay her father fifty pieces of silver.* Then he must marry the young woman because he violated her, and he may never divorce her as long as he lives.

³⁰*"A man must not marry his father's former wife, for this would violate his father.

23 REGULATIONS CONCERNING WORSHIP

¹*"If a man's testicles are crushed or his penis is cut off, he may not be admitted to the assembly of the LORD.

²"If a person is illegitimate by birth, neither he nor his descendants for ten generations may be admitted to the assembly of the LORD.

³"No Ammonite or Moabite or any of their descendants for ten generations may be admitted to the assembly of the LORD. ⁴These nations did not welcome you with food and water when you came out of Egypt. Instead, they hired Balaam son of Beor from Pethor in distant Aram-naharaim to curse you. ⁵But the LORD your God refused to listen to Balaam. He turned the intended curse into a blessing because the LORD your God loves you. ⁶As long as you live, you must never promote the welfare and prosperity of the Ammonites or Moabites.

⁷"Do not detest the Edomites or the Egyptians, because the Edomites are your relatives and you lived as foreigners among the Egyptians. ⁸The third generation of Edomites and Egyptians may enter the assembly of the LORD.

MISCELLANEOUS REGULATIONS

⁹"When you go to war against your enemies, be sure to stay away from anything that is impure.

¹⁰"Any man who becomes ceremonially defiled because of a nocturnal emission must leave the camp and stay away all day. ¹¹Toward evening he must bathe himself, and at sunset he may return to the camp.

¹²"You must have a designated area outside the camp where you can go to relieve yourself. ¹³Each of you must have a spade as part of your equipment. Whenever you relieve yourself, dig a hole with the spade and cover the excrement. ¹⁴The camp must be holy, for the LORD your God moves around in your camp to protect you and to defeat your enemies. He must not see any shameful thing among you, or he will turn away from you.

¹⁵"If slaves should escape from their masters and take refuge with you, you must not hand them over to their masters. ¹⁶Let them live among you in any town they choose, and do not oppress them.

¹⁷"No Israelite, whether man or woman, may become a temple prostitute. ¹⁸When you are bringing an offering to fulfill a vow, you must not bring to the house of the LORD your God any offering from the earnings of a prostitute, whether a man* or a woman, for both are detestable to the LORD your God.

¹⁹"Do not charge interest on the loans you make to a fellow Israelite, whether you loan money, or food, or anything else. ²⁰You may charge interest to foreigners, but you may not charge interest to Israelites, so that the LORD your God may bless you in everything you do in the land you are about to enter and occupy.

²¹"When you make a vow to the LORD your

22:29 Hebrew 50 shekels of silver, about 1.25 pounds or 570 grams in weight.   22:30 Verse 22:30 is numbered 23:1 in Hebrew text.
23:1 Verses 23:1-25 are numbered 23:2-26 in Hebrew text.
23:18 Hebrew a dog.

··

GOD'S PURPOSE FOR SEX

(23:17-18) Although other nations in Canaan included prostitution in their worship rituals, this practice was forbidden for the Israelites. Prostitution makes a mockery of God's original plan for sex. It treats sex as an isolated physical act rather than an act of commitment within a marriage. Outside of marriage, sex destroys relationships. Within a marriage it can be a relationship builder, if approached with the right attitude. God frequently warned his people against indulging in sex outside of marriage. This warning still applies today.

God, be prompt in fulfilling whatever you promised him. For the LORD your God demands that you promptly fulfill all your vows, or you will be guilty of sin. ²²However, it is not a sin to refrain from making a vow. ²³But once you have voluntarily made a vow, be careful to fulfill your promise to the LORD your God.

²⁴"When you enter your neighbor's vineyard, you may eat your fill of grapes, but you must not carry any away in a basket. ²⁵And when you enter your neighbor's field of grain, you may pluck the heads of grain with your hand, but you must not harvest it with a sickle.

24 "Suppose a man marries a woman but she does not please him. Having discovered something wrong with her, he writes her a letter of divorce, hands it to her, and sends her away from his house. ²When she leaves his house, she is free to marry another man. ³But if the second husband also turns against her and divorces her, or if he dies, ⁴the first husband may not marry her again, for she has been defiled. That would be detestable to the LORD. You must not bring guilt upon the land the LORD your God is giving you as a special possession.

⁵"A newly married man must not be drafted into the army or be given any other official responsibilities. He must be free to spend one year at home, bringing happiness to the wife he has married.

⁶"It is wrong to take a set of millstones, or even just the upper millstone, as security for a loan, for the owner uses it to make a living.

⁷"If anyone kidnaps a fellow Israelite and treats him as a slave or sells him, the kidnapper must die. In this way, you will purge the evil from among you.

⁸"In all cases involving serious skin diseases,* be careful to follow the instructions of the Levitical priests; obey all the commands I have given them. ⁹Remember what the LORD your God did to Miriam as you were coming from Egypt.

¹⁰"If you lend anything to your neighbor, do not enter his house to pick up the item he is giving as security. ¹¹You must wait outside while he goes in and brings it out to you. ¹²If your neighbor is poor and gives you his cloak as security for a loan, do not keep the cloak overnight. ¹³Return the cloak to its owner by sunset so he can stay warm through the night and bless you, and the LORD your God will count you as righteous.

¹⁴"Never take advantage of poor and destitute laborers, whether they are fellow Israelites or foreigners living in your towns. ¹⁵You must pay them their wages each day before sunset because they are poor and are counting on it. If you don't, they might cry out to the LORD against you, and it would be counted against you as sin.

¹⁶"Parents must not be put to death for the sins of their children, nor children for the sins of their parents. Those deserving to die must be put to death for their own crimes.

¹⁷"True justice must be given to foreigners living among you and to orphans, and you must never accept a widow's garment as security for her debt. ¹⁸Always remember that you were slaves in Egypt and that the LORD your God redeemed you from your slavery. That is why I have given you this command.

¹⁹"When you are harvesting your crops and forget to bring in a bundle of grain from your field, don't go back to get it. Leave it for the foreigners, orphans, and widows. Then the LORD your God will bless you in all you do. ²⁰When you beat the olives from your olive trees, don't go over the boughs twice. Leave the remaining olives for the foreigners, orphans, and widows. ²¹When you gather the grapes in your vineyard, don't glean the vines after they are picked. Leave the remaining grapes for the foreigners, orphans, and widows. ²²Remember that you were slaves in the land of Egypt. That is why I am giving you this command.

25 "Suppose two people take a dispute to court, and the judges declare that one is right and the other is wrong. ²If the person in the wrong is sentenced to be flogged, the judge must command him to lie down and be beaten in his presence with the number of lashes appropriate to the crime. ³But never give more than forty lashes; more than forty lashes would publicly humiliate your neighbor.

⁴"You must not muzzle an ox to keep it from eating as it treads out the grain.

⁵"If two brothers are living together on the same property and one of them dies without a son, his widow may not be married to anyone from outside the family. Instead, her husband's brother should marry her and have intercourse with her to fulfill the duties of a brother-in-law. ⁶The first son she bears to him will be considered the son of the dead brother, so that his name will not be forgotten in Israel.

⁷"But if the man refuses to marry his brother's widow, she must go to the town gate and say to the elders assembled there, 'My husband's

24:8 Traditionally rendered *leprosy*. The Hebrew word used here can describe various skin diseases.

brother refuses to preserve his brother's name in Israel—he refuses to fulfill the duties of a brother-in-law by marrying me.' [8]The elders of the town will then summon him and talk with him. If he still refuses and says, 'I don't want to marry her,' [9]the widow must walk over to him in the presence of the elders, pull his sandal from his foot, and spit in his face. Then she must declare, 'This is what happens to a man who refuses to provide his brother with children.' [10]Ever afterward in Israel his family will be referred to as 'the family of the man whose sandal was pulled off'!

[11]"If two Israelite men get into a fight and the wife of one tries to rescue her husband by grabbing the testicles of the other man, [12]you must cut off her hand. Show her no pity.

[13]"You must use accurate scales when you weigh out merchandise, [14]and you must use full and honest measures. [15]Yes, always use honest weights and measures, so that you may enjoy a long life in the land the LORD your God is giving you. [16]All who cheat with dishonest weights and measures are detestable to the LORD your God.

[17]"Never forget what the Amalekites did to you as you came from Egypt. [18]They attacked you when you were exhausted and weary, and they struck down those who were straggling behind. They had no fear of God. [19]Therefore, when the LORD your God has given you rest from all your enemies in the land he is giving you as a special possession, you must destroy the Amalekites and erase their memory from under heaven. Never forget this!

26 HARVEST OFFERINGS AND TITHES

"When you enter the land the LORD your God is giving you as a special possession and you have conquered it and settled there, [2]put some of the first produce from each crop you harvest into a basket and bring it to the designated place of worship—the place the LORD your God chooses for his name to be honored. [3]Go to the priest in charge at that time and say to him, 'With this gift I acknowledge to the LORD your God that I have entered the land he swore to our ancestors he would give us.' [4]The priest will then take the basket from your hand and set it before the altar of the LORD your God.

[5]"You must then say in the presence of the LORD your God, 'My ancestor Jacob was a wandering Aramean who went to live as a foreigner in Egypt. His family arrived few in number, but in Egypt they became a large and mighty nation. [6]When the Egyptians oppressed and humiliated us by making us their slaves, [7]we cried out to the LORD, the God of our ancestors.

He heard our cries and saw our hardship, toil, and oppression. [8]So the LORD brought us out of Egypt with a strong hand and powerful arm, with overwhelming terror, and with miraculous signs and wonders. [9]He brought us to this place and gave us this land flowing with milk and honey! [10]And now, O LORD, I have brought you the first portion of the harvest you have given me from the ground.' Then place the produce before the LORD your God, and bow to the ground in worship before him. [11]Afterward you may go and celebrate because of all the good things the LORD your God has given to you and your household. Remember to include the Levites and the foreigners living among you in the celebration.

[12]"Every third year you must offer a special tithe of your crops. In this year of the special tithe you must give your tithes to the Levites, foreigners, orphans, and widows, so that they will have enough to eat in your towns. [13]Then you must declare in the presence of the LORD your God, 'I have taken the sacred gift from my house and have given it to the Levites, foreigners, orphans, and widows, just as you commanded me. I have not violated or forgotten any of your commands. [14]I have not eaten any of it while in mourning; I have not handled it while I was ceremonially unclean; and I have not offered any of it to the dead. I have obeyed the LORD my God and have done everything you commanded me. [15]Now look down from your holy dwelling place in heaven and bless your people Israel and the land you swore to our ancestors to give us—a land flowing with milk and honey.'

A CALL TO OBEY THE LORD'S COMMANDS

[16]"Today the LORD your God has commanded you to obey all these decrees and regulations. So be careful to obey them wholeheartedly. [17]You have declared today that the LORD is your God. And you have promised to walk in his ways, and to obey his decrees, commands, and regulations, and to do everything he tells you. [18]The LORD has declared today that you are his people, his own special treasure, just as he promised, and that you must obey all his commands. [19]And if you do, he will set you high

....

A SPIRITUAL JOURNEY

(26:1-11) The people of Israel were required to give an offering of thanks to God as soon as they settled in the Promised Land. They also were required to recite the history of God's dealings with his people. Who have you told about your spiritual journey? Talking about what God has done is a great way to tell him thanks.

above all the other nations he has made. Then you will receive praise, honor, and renown. You will be a nation that is holy to the LORD your God, just as he promised."

27 THE ALTAR ON MOUNT EBAL

Then Moses and the leaders of Israel gave this charge to the people: "Obey all these commands that I am giving you today. ²When you cross the Jordan River and enter the land the LORD your God is giving you, set up some large stones and coat them with plaster. ³Write this whole body of instruction on them when you cross the river to enter the land the LORD your God is giving you—a land flowing with milk and honey, just as the LORD, the God of your ancestors, promised you. ⁴When you cross the Jordan, set up these stones at Mount Ebal and coat them with plaster, as I am commanding you today.

⁵"Then build an altar there to the LORD your God, using natural, uncut stones. You must not shape the stones with an iron tool. ⁶Build the altar of uncut stones, and use it to offer burnt offerings to the LORD your God. ⁷Also sacrifice peace offerings on it, and celebrate by feasting there before the LORD your God. ⁸You must clearly write all these instructions on the stones coated with plaster."

⁹Then Moses and the Levitical priests addressed all Israel as follows: "O Israel, be quiet and listen! Today you have become the people of the LORD your God. ¹⁰So you must obey the LORD your God by keeping all these commands and decrees that I am giving you today."

CURSES FROM MOUNT EBAL ¹¹That same day Moses also gave this charge to the people: ¹²"When you cross the Jordan River, the tribes of Simeon, Levi, Judah, Issachar, Joseph, and Benjamin must stand on Mount Gerizim to proclaim a blessing over the people. ¹³And the tribes of Reuben, Gad, Asher, Zebulun, Dan, and Naphtali must stand on Mount Ebal to proclaim a curse.

¹⁴"Then the Levites will shout to all the people of Israel:

¹⁵'Cursed is anyone who carves or casts an idol and secretly sets it up. These idols, the work of craftsmen, are detestable to the LORD.'
And all the people will reply, 'Amen.'

¹⁶'Cursed is anyone who dishonors father or mother.'
And all the people will reply, 'Amen.'

¹⁷'Cursed is anyone who steals property from a neighbor by moving a boundary marker.'
And all the people will reply, 'Amen.'

¹⁸'Cursed is anyone who leads a blind person astray on the road.'
And all the people will reply, 'Amen.'

¹⁹'Cursed is anyone who denies justice to foreigners, orphans, or widows.'
And all the people will reply, 'Amen.'

²⁰'Cursed is anyone who has sexual intercourse with one of his father's wives, for he has violated his father.'
And all the people will reply, 'Amen.'

²¹'Cursed is anyone who has sexual intercourse with an animal.'
And all the people will reply, 'Amen.'

²²'Cursed is anyone who has sexual intercourse with his sister, whether she is the daughter of his father or his mother.'
And all the people will reply, 'Amen.'

²³'Cursed is anyone who has sexual intercourse with his mother-in-law.'
And all the people will reply, 'Amen.'

²⁴'Cursed is anyone who attacks a neighbor in secret.'
And all the people will reply, 'Amen.'

²⁵'Cursed is anyone who accepts payment to kill an innocent person.'
And all the people will reply, 'Amen.'

²⁶'Cursed is anyone who does not affirm and obey the terms of these instructions.'
And all the people will reply, 'Amen.'

28 BLESSINGS FOR OBEDIENCE

"If you fully obey the LORD your God and carefully keep all his commands that I am giving you today, the LORD your God will set you high above all the nations of the world. ²You will experience all these blessings if you obey the LORD your God:

CURSES AND BLESSINGS

(27:15-26) These curses were a series of oaths, spoken by the priests and affirmed by the people. The people promised to stay away from wrong actions by saying Amen ("So be it") and to take responsibility for their actions.

Looking at a list of curses like this might give us the idea that God is out to crush anyone who steps out of line. But that's not the case. Just as we warn children to stay away from hot stoves and busy streets, God warns us to stay away from dangerous actions. He does not leave us with only curses or consequences, however. Immediately following these curses, we discover the blessings that come from living for God (28:1-14). These give us extra incentive to obey his laws.

3 Your towns and your fields
　　will be blessed.
4 Your children and your crops
　　will be blessed.
The offspring of your herds and flocks
　　will be blessed.
5 Your fruit baskets and breadboards
　　will be blessed.
6 Wherever you go and whatever you do,
　　you will be blessed.

7"The LORD will conquer your enemies when they attack you. They will attack you from one direction, but they will scatter from you in seven! 8"The LORD will guarantee a blessing on everything you do and will fill your storehouses with grain. The LORD your God will bless you in the land he is giving you.

9"If you obey the commands of the LORD your God and walk in his ways, the LORD will establish you as his holy people as he swore he would do. 10Then all the nations of the world will see that you are a people claimed by the LORD, and they will stand in awe of you.

11"The LORD will give you prosperity in the land he swore to your ancestors to give you, blessing you with many children, numerous livestock, and abundant crops. 12The LORD will send rain at the proper time from his rich treasury in the heavens and will bless all the work you do. You will lend to many nations, but you will never need to borrow from them. 13If you listen to these commands of the LORD your God that I am giving you today, and if you carefully obey them, the LORD will make you the head and not the tail, and you will always be on top and never at the bottom. 14You must not turn away from any of the commands I am giving you today, nor follow after other gods and worship them.

CURSES FOR DISOBEDIENCE 15"But if you refuse to listen to the LORD your God and do not obey all the commands and decrees I am giving you today, all these curses will come and overwhelm you:

16 Your towns and your fields
　　will be cursed.
17 Your fruit baskets and breadboards
　　will be cursed.
18 Your children and your crops
　　will be cursed.
The offspring of your herds and flocks
　　will be cursed.
19 Wherever you go and whatever you do,
　　you will be cursed.

20"The LORD himself will send on you curses, confusion, and frustration in everything you do, until at last you are completely destroyed for doing evil and abandoning me. 21The LORD will afflict you with diseases until none of you are left in the land you are about to enter and occupy. 22The LORD will strike you with wasting diseases, fever, and inflammation, with scorching heat and drought, and with blight and mildew. These disasters will pursue you until you die. 23The skies above will be as unyielding as bronze, and the earth beneath will be as hard as iron. 24The LORD will change the rain that falls on your land into powder, and dust will pour down from the sky until you are destroyed.

25"The LORD will cause you to be defeated by your enemies. You will attack your enemies from one direction, but you will scatter from them in seven! You will be an object of horror to all the kingdoms of the earth. 26Your corpses will be food for all the scavenging birds and wild animals, and no one will be there to chase them away.

27"The LORD will afflict you with the boils of Egypt and with tumors, scurvy, and the itch, from which you cannot be cured. 28The LORD will strike you with madness, blindness, and panic. 29You will grope around in broad daylight like a blind person groping in the darkness, but you will not find your way. You will be oppressed and robbed continually, and no one will come to save you.

30"You will be engaged to a woman, but another man will sleep with her. You will build a house, but someone else will live in it. You will plant a vineyard, but you will never enjoy its fruit. 31Your ox will be butchered before your eyes, but you will not eat a single bite of the meat. Your donkey will be taken from you, never to be returned. Your sheep and goats will be given to your enemies, and no one will be there to help you. 32You will watch as your sons and daughters are taken away as slaves. Your heart will break for them, but you won't be able to help them. 33A foreign nation you have never heard about will eat the crops you worked so hard to grow. You will suffer under constant oppression and harsh treatment. 34You will go mad because of all the tragedy you see around you. 35The LORD will cover your knees and legs with incurable boils. In fact, you will be covered from head to foot.

36"The LORD will exile you and your king to a nation unknown to you and your ancestors. There in exile you will worship gods of wood and stone! 37You will become an object of horror, ridicule, and mockery among all the nations to which the LORD sends you.

38"You will plant much but harvest little, for locusts will eat your crops. 39You will plant vineyards and care for them, but you will not drink the wine or eat the grapes, for worms will destroy the vines. 40You will grow olive trees throughout your land, but you will never use the olive oil, for the fruit will drop before it ripens. 41You will have sons and daughters, but you will lose them, for they will be led away into captivity. 42Swarms of insects will destroy your trees and crops.

43"The foreigners living among you will become stronger and stronger, while you become weaker and weaker. 44They will lend money to you, but you will not lend to them. They will be the head, and you will be the tail!

45"If you refuse to listen to the LORD your God and to obey the commands and decrees he has given you, all these curses will pursue and overtake you until you are destroyed. 46These horrors will serve as a sign and warning among you and your descendants forever. 47If you do not serve the LORD your God with joy and enthusiasm for the abundant benefits you have received, 48you will serve your enemies whom the LORD will send against you. You will be left hungry, thirsty, naked, and lacking in everything. The LORD will put an iron yoke on your neck, oppressing you harshly until he has destroyed you.

49"The LORD will bring a distant nation against you from the end of the earth, and it will swoop down on you like a vulture. It is a nation whose language you do not understand, 50a fierce and heartless nation that shows no respect for the old and no pity for the young. 51Its armies will devour your livestock and crops, and you will be destroyed. They will leave you no grain, new wine, olive oil, calves, or lambs, and you will starve to death. 52They will attack your cities until all the fortified walls in your land—the walls you trusted to protect you—are knocked

. . . .

THE CURSE OF INSANITY
(28:34) Moses warned the people of Israel about the curses that resulted from rejecting God. One of these curses involved becoming mentally unhinged due to terrible hardships and tragedies. Do you ever feel that you will go crazy if you hear about one more rape, kidnapping, murder, or war? Much of the world's evil is a result of people's failure to acknowledge and serve God. When you hear bad news, don't groan helplessly as do unbelievers, who have no hope for the future. Remind yourself that in spite of it all, God has ultimate control and one day will come back to make everything right.

down. They will attack all the towns in the land the LORD your God has given you.

53"The siege and terrible distress of the enemy's attack will be so severe that you will eat the flesh of your own sons and daughters, whom the LORD your God has given you. 54The most tenderhearted man among you will have no compassion for his own brother, his beloved wife, and his surviving children. 55He will refuse to share with them the flesh he is devouring—the flesh of one of his own children—because he has nothing else to eat during the siege and terrible distress that your enemy will inflict on all your towns. 56The most tender and delicate woman among you—so delicate she would not so much as touch the ground with her foot—will be selfish toward the husband she loves and toward her own son or daughter. 57She will hide from them the afterbirth and the new baby she has borne, so that she herself can secretly eat them. She will have nothing else to eat during the siege and terrible distress that your enemy will inflict on all your towns.

58"If you refuse to obey all the words of instruction that are written in this book, and if you do not fear the glorious and awesome name of the LORD your God, 59then the LORD will overwhelm you and your children with indescribable plagues. These plagues will be intense and without relief, making you miserable and unbearably sick. 60He will afflict you with all the diseases of Egypt that you feared so much, and you will have no relief. 61The LORD will afflict you with every sickness and plague there is, even those not mentioned in this Book of Instruction, until you are destroyed. 62Though you become as numerous as the stars in the sky, few of you will be left because you would not listen to the LORD your God.

63"Just as the LORD has found great pleasure in causing you to prosper and multiply, the LORD will find pleasure in destroying you. You will be torn from the land you are about to enter and occupy. 64For the LORD will scatter you among all the nations from one end of the earth to the other. There you will worship foreign gods that neither you nor your ancestors have known, gods made of wood and stone! 65There among those nations you will find no peace or place to rest. And the LORD will cause your heart to tremble, your eyesight to fail, and your soul to despair. 66Your life will constantly hang in the balance. You will live night and day in fear, unsure if you will survive. 67In the morning you will say, 'If only it were night!' And in the evening you will say, 'If only it were morning!' For you will be terrified by the awful horrors you see around you. [68]Then the LORD will send you back to Egypt in ships, to a destination I promised you would never see again. There you will offer to sell yourselves to your enemies as slaves, but no one will buy you."

29
[1]*These are the terms of the covenant the LORD commanded Moses to make with the Israelites while they were in the land of Moab, in addition to the covenant he had made with them at Mount Sinai.*

MOSES REVIEWS THE COVENANT
[2]*Moses summoned all the Israelites and said to them, "You have seen with your own eyes everything the LORD did in the land of Egypt to Pharaoh and to all his servants and to his whole country—[3]all the great tests of strength, the miraculous signs, and the amazing wonders. [4]But to this day the LORD has not given you minds that understand, nor eyes that see, nor ears that hear! [5]For forty years I led you through the wilderness, yet your clothes and sandals did not wear out. [6]You ate no bread and drank no wine or other alcoholic drink, but he gave you food so you would know that he is the LORD your God.

[7]"When we came here, King Sihon of Heshbon and King Og of Bashan came out to fight against us, but we defeated them. [8]We took their land and gave it to the tribes of Reuben and Gad and to the half-tribe of Manasseh as their grant of land.

[9]"Therefore, obey the terms of this covenant so that you will prosper in everything you do. [10]All of you—tribal leaders, elders, officers, all the men of Israel—are standing today in the presence of the LORD your God. [11]Your little ones and your wives are with you, as well as the foreigners living among you who chop your wood and carry your water. [12]You are standing here today to enter into the covenant of the LORD your God. The LORD is making this covenant, including the curses. [13]By entering into the covenant today, he will establish you as his people and confirm that he is your God, just as he promised you and as he swore to your ancestors Abraham, Isaac, and Jacob.

[14]"But you are not the only ones with whom I am making this covenant with its curses. [15]I am making this covenant both with you who stand here today in the presence of the LORD our God, and also with the future generations who are not standing here today.

[16]"You remember how we lived in the land of Egypt and how we traveled through the lands of enemy nations as we left. [17]You have seen their detestable practices and their idols* made of wood, stone, silver, and gold. [18]I am making this covenant with you so that no one among you—no man, woman, clan, or tribe—will turn away from the LORD our God to worship these gods of other nations, and so that no root among you bears bitter and poisonous fruit.

[19]"Those who hear the warnings of this curse should not congratulate themselves, thinking, 'I am safe, even though I am following the desires of my own stubborn heart.' This would lead to utter ruin! [20]The LORD will never pardon such people. Instead his anger and jealousy will burn against them. All the curses written in this book will come down on them, and the LORD will erase their names from under heaven. [21]The LORD will separate them from all the tribes of Israel, to pour out on them all the curses of the covenant recorded in this Book of Instruction.

[22]"Then the generations to come, both your own descendants and the foreigners who come from distant lands, will see the devastation of the land and the diseases the LORD inflicts on it. [23]They will exclaim, 'The whole land is devastated by sulfur and salt. It is a wasteland with nothing planted and nothing growing, not even a blade of grass. It is like the cities of Sodom and Gomorrah, Admah and Zeboiim, which the LORD destroyed in his intense anger.'

[24]"And all the surrounding nations will ask, 'Why has the LORD done this to this land? Why was he so angry?'

[25]"And the answer will be, 'This happened because the people of the land abandoned the covenant that the LORD, the God of their ancestors, made with them when he brought them out of the land of Egypt. [26]Instead, they turned away to serve and worship gods they had not known before, gods that were not from the LORD. [27]That is why the LORD's anger has burned against this land, bringing down on it every curse recorded in this book. [28]In great

29:1a Verse 29:1 is numbered 28:69 in Hebrew text.   29:1b Hebrew Horeb, another name for Sinai.   29:2 Verses 29:2-29 are numbered 29:1-28 in Hebrew text.   29:17 The Hebrew term (literally round things) probably alludes to dung.

....

EVIL SEEDS
(29:18) Moses cautioned that the day the Hebrews chose to turn from God, a root would be planted that would produce bitter fruit. When we decide to do what we know is wrong, we plant an evil seed that begins to grow out of control—eventually yielding a crop of sorrow and pain. But we can prevent those seeds of sin from taking root. If you have done something wrong, confess it to God and others immediately. If the seed never finds fertile soil, its bitter fruit will never ripen.

OH, THAT YOU WOULD
CHOOSE LIFE,
SO THAT YOU AND YOUR
DESCENDANTS MIGHT LIVE!

=== DEUTERONOMY 30:19

anger and fury the LORD uprooted his people from their land and banished them to another land, where they still live today!'

[29]"The LORD our God has secrets known to no one. We are not accountable for them, but we and our children are accountable forever for all that he has revealed to us, so that we may obey all the terms of these instructions.

30 A CALL TO RETURN TO THE LORD

"In the future, when you experience all these blessings and curses I have listed for you, and when you are living among the nations to which the LORD your God has exiled you, take to heart all these instructions. [2]If at that time you and your children return to the LORD your God, and if you obey with all your heart and all your soul all the commands I have given you today, [3]then the LORD your God will restore your fortunes. He will have mercy on you and gather you back from all the nations where he has scattered you. [4]Even though you are banished to the ends of the earth, the LORD your God will gather you from there and bring you back again. [5]The LORD your God will return you to the land that belonged to your ancestors, and you will possess that land again. Then he will make you even more prosperous and numerous than your ancestors!

[6]"The LORD your God will change your heart* and the hearts of all your descendants, so that you will love him with all your heart and soul and so you may live! [7]The LORD your God will inflict all these curses on your enemies and on those who hate and persecute you. [8]Then you

....

FRESH START

(30:1-6) Moses told the Hebrews that when they were ready to return to God, he would be ready to receive them. God's mercy is unbelievable. It goes far beyond what we can imagine. Even if the Jews deliberately walked away from him and ruined their lives, God would still take them back. God wants to forgive us, too, and bring us back to himself. Some people don't learn this until their world has crashed in around them. Then the sorrow and pain seem to open their eyes to what God has been saying all along. Are you separated from God by sin? No matter how far you have wandered, God promises a fresh start if only you will turn to him.

will again obey the LORD and keep all his commands that I am giving you today.

[9]"The LORD your God will then make you successful in everything you do. He will give you many children and numerous livestock, and he will cause your fields to produce abundant harvests, for the LORD will again delight in being good to you as he was to your ancestors. [10]The LORD your God will delight in you if you obey his voice and keep the commands and decrees written in this Book of Instruction, and if you turn to the LORD your God with all your heart and soul.

THE CHOICE OF LIFE OR DEATH [11]"This command I am giving you today is not too difficult for you to understand, and it is not beyond your reach. [12]It is not kept in heaven, so distant that you must ask, 'Who will go up to heaven and bring it down so we can hear it and obey?' [13]It is not kept beyond the sea, so far away that you must ask, 'Who will cross the sea to bring it to us so we can hear it and obey?' [14]No, the message is very close at hand; it is on your lips and in your heart so that you can obey it.

[15]"Now listen! Today I am giving you a choice between life and death, between prosperity and disaster. [16]For I command you this day to love the LORD your God and to keep his commands, decrees, and regulations by walking in his ways. If you do this, you will live and multiply, and the LORD your God will bless you and the land you are about to enter and occupy.

[17]"But if your heart turns away and you refuse to listen, and if you are drawn away to serve and worship other gods, [18]then I warn you now that you will certainly be destroyed. You will not live a long, good life in the land you are crossing the Jordan to occupy.

[19]"Today I have given you the choice between life and death, between blessings and curses. Now I call on heaven and earth to witness the choice you make. Oh, that you would choose life, so that you and your descendants might live! [20]You can make this choice by loving the LORD your God, obeying him, and committing yourself firmly to him. This* is the key to your life. And if you love and obey the LORD, you will live long in the land the LORD swore to give your ancestors Abraham, Isaac, and Jacob."

31 JOSHUA BECOMES ISRAEL'S LEADER

When Moses had finished giving these instructions* to all the people of Israel, [2]he

30:6 Hebrew *circumcise your heart.* **30:20** Or *He.* **31:1** As in Dead Sea Scrolls and Greek version; Masoretic Text reads *Moses went and spoke.*

said, "I am now 120 years old, and I am no longer able to lead you. The LORD has told me, 'You will not cross the Jordan River.' ³But the LORD your God himself will cross over ahead of you. He will destroy the nations living there, and you will take possession of their land. Joshua will lead you across the river, just as the LORD promised.

⁴"The LORD will destroy the nations living in the land, just as he destroyed Sihon and Og, the kings of the Amorites. ⁵The LORD will hand over to you the people who live there, and you must deal with them as I have commanded you. ⁶So be strong and courageous! Do not be afraid and do not panic before them. For the LORD your God will personally go ahead of you. He will neither fail you nor abandon you."

⁷Then Moses called for Joshua, and as all Israel watched, he said to him, "Be strong and courageous! For you will lead these people into the land that the LORD swore to their ancestors he would give them. You are the one who will divide it among them as their grants of land. ⁸Do not be afraid or discouraged, for the LORD will personally go ahead of you. He will be with you; he will neither fail you nor abandon you."

PUBLIC READING OF THE BOOK OF INSTRUCTION
⁹So Moses wrote this entire body of instruction in a book and gave it to the priests, who carried the Ark of the LORD's Covenant, and to the elders of Israel. ¹⁰Then Moses gave them this command: "At the end of every seventh year, the Year of Release, during the Festival of Shelters, ¹¹you must read this Book of Instruction to all the people of Israel when they assemble before the LORD your God at the place he chooses. ¹²Call them all together—men, women, children, and the foreigners living in your towns—so they may hear this Book of Instruction and learn to fear the LORD your God and carefully obey all the terms of these instructions. ¹³Do this so that your children who have not known these instructions will hear them and will learn to fear the LORD your God. Do this as long as you live in the land you are crossing the Jordan to occupy."

ISRAEL'S DISOBEDIENCE PREDICTED
¹⁴Then the LORD said to Moses, "The time has come for you to die. Call Joshua and present yourselves at the Tabernacle,* so that I may commission him there." So Moses and Joshua went and presented themselves at the Tabernacle. ¹⁵And the LORD appeared to them in a pillar of cloud that stood at the entrance to the sacred tent.

31:14 Hebrew *Tent of Meeting*; also in 31:14b.

¹⁶The LORD said to Moses, "You are about to die and join your ancestors. After you are gone, these people will begin to worship foreign gods, the gods of the land where they are going. They will abandon me and break my covenant that I have made with them. ¹⁷Then my anger will blaze forth against them. I will abandon them, hiding my face from them, and they will be devoured. Terrible trouble will come down on them, and on that day they will say, 'These disasters have come down on us because God is no longer among us!' ¹⁸At that time I will hide my face from them on account of all the evil they commit by worshiping other gods.

¹⁹"So write down the words of this song, and teach it to the people of Israel. Help them learn it, so it may serve as a witness for me against them. ²⁰For I will bring them into the land I swore to give their ancestors—a land flowing with milk and honey. There they will become prosperous, eat all the food they want, and become fat. But they will begin to worship other gods; they will despise me and break my covenant. ²¹And when great disasters come down on them, this song will stand as evidence against them, for it will never be forgotten by their descendants. I know the intentions of these people, even now before they have entered the land I swore to give them."

²²So that very day Moses wrote down the words of the song and taught it to the Israelites.

²³Then the LORD commissioned Joshua son of Nun with these words: "Be strong and courageous, for you must bring the people of Israel into the land I swore to give them. I will be with you."

²⁴When Moses had finished writing this entire body of instruction in a book, ²⁵he gave this command to the Levites who carried the Ark of the LORD's Covenant: ²⁶"Take this Book of Instruction and place it beside the Ark of the Covenant of the LORD your God, so it may remain there as a witness against the people of Israel. ²⁷For I know how rebellious and stubborn you are. Even now, while I am still alive and am here with you, you have rebelled against the LORD. How much more rebellious will you be after my death!

....

REPENTANCE
(31:27-29) Moses knew that the Israelites, in spite of all they had seen of God's work, were rebellious at heart. They deserved God's punishment, although they often received his mercy instead. We, too, are stubborn and rebellious by nature. Throughout our lives we struggle with sin. Repentance once a month or once a week is not enough. We must constantly turn from our sins to God and let his mercy save us.

²⁸"Now summon all the elders and officials of your tribes, so that I can speak to them directly and call heaven and earth to witness against them. ²⁹I know that after my death you will become utterly corrupt and will turn from the way I have commanded you to follow. In the days to come, disaster will come down on you, for you will do what is evil in the LORD's sight, making him very angry with your actions."

THE SONG OF MOSES ³⁰So Moses recited this entire song publicly to the assembly of Israel:

32

¹"Listen, O heavens, and I will speak!
  Hear, O earth, the words that I say!
² Let my teaching fall on you like rain;
  let my speech settle like dew.
 Let my words fall like rain on tender grass,
  like gentle showers on young plants.
³ I will proclaim the name of the LORD;
  how glorious is our God!
⁴ He is the Rock; his deeds are perfect.
  Everything he does is just and fair.
 He is a faithful God who does no wrong;
  how just and upright he is!

⁵ "But they have acted corruptly toward him;
  when they act so perversely,
 are they really his children?*
  They are a deceitful and twisted
   generation.
⁶ Is this the way you repay the LORD,
  you foolish and senseless people?
 Isn't he your Father who created you?
  Has he not made you and established
   you?
⁷ Remember the days of long ago;
  think about the generations past.
 Ask your father, and he will inform you.
  Inquire of your elders, and they will tell
   you.
⁸ When the Most High assigned lands to the
   nations,
  when he divided up the human race,
 he established the boundaries of the
   peoples
  according to the number in his heavenly
   court.*

⁹ "For the people of Israel belong to
   the LORD;
  Jacob is his special possession.
¹⁰ He found them in a desert land,
  in an empty, howling wasteland.
 He surrounded them and watched over
   them;
  he guarded them as he would guard his
   own eyes.*

¹¹ Like an eagle that rouses her chicks
  and hovers over her young,
 so he spread his wings to take them up
  and carried them safely on his pinions.
¹² The LORD alone guided them;
  they followed no foreign gods.
¹³ He let them ride over the highlands
  and feast on the crops of the fields.
 He nourished them with honey from the rock
  and olive oil from the stony ground.
¹⁴ He fed them yogurt from the herd
  and milk from the flock,
  together with the fat of lambs.
 He gave them choice rams from Bashan,
   and goats,
  together with the choicest wheat.
 You drank the finest wine,
  made from the juice of grapes.

¹⁵ "But Israel* soon became fat and unruly;
  the people grew heavy, plump, and
   stuffed!
 Then they abandoned the God who had
   made them;
  they made light of the Rock of their
   salvation.
¹⁶ They stirred up his jealousy by worshiping
   foreign gods;
  they provoked his fury with detestable
   deeds.
¹⁷ They offered sacrifices to demons, which
   are not God,
  to gods they had not known before,
 to new gods only recently arrived,
  to gods their ancestors had never feared.
¹⁸ You neglected the Rock who had fathered
   you;
  you forgot the God who had given you
   birth.

¹⁹ "The LORD saw this and drew back,
  provoked to anger by his own sons and
   daughters.
²⁰ He said, 'I will abandon them;
  then see what becomes of them.
 For they are a twisted generation,
  children without integrity.
²¹ They have roused my jealousy by
   worshiping things that are not God;
  they have provoked my anger with their
   useless idols.
 Now I will rouse their jealousy through
   people who are not even a people;

32:5 The meaning of the Hebrew is uncertain. **32:8** As in Dead Sea Scrolls, which read *the number of the sons of God,* and Greek version, which reads *the number of the angels of God;* Masoretic Text reads *the number of the sons of Israel.* **32:10** Hebrew *as the pupil of his eye.* **32:15** Hebrew *Jeshurun,* a term of endearment for Israel.

I will provoke their anger through the
foolish Gentiles.
22 For my anger blazes forth like fire
and burns to the depths of the grave.*
It devours the earth and all its crops
and ignites the foundations of the
mountains.
23 I will heap disasters upon them
and shoot them down with my arrows.
24 I will weaken them with famine,
burning fever, and deadly disease.
I will send the fangs of wild beasts
and poisonous snakes that glide in
the dust.
25 Outside, the sword will bring death,
and inside, terror will strike
both young men and young women,
both infants and the aged.
26 I would have annihilated them,
wiping out even the memory of them.
27 But I feared the taunt of Israel's enemy,
who might misunderstand and say,
"Our own power has triumphed!
The LORD had nothing to do with this!'"

28 "But Israel is a senseless nation;
the people are foolish, without
understanding.
29 Oh, that they were wise and could
understand this!
Oh, that they might know their fate!
30 How could one person chase a thousand
of them,
and two people put ten thousand to
flight,
unless their Rock had sold them,
unless the LORD had given them up?
31 But the rock of our enemies is not like our
Rock,
as even they recognize.*
32 Their vine grows from the vine of Sodom,
from the vineyards of Gomorrah.
Their grapes are poison,
and their clusters are bitter.
33 Their wine is the venom of serpents,
the deadly poison of cobras.
34 "The LORD says, 'Am I not storing up these
things,
sealing them away in my treasury?
35 I will take revenge; I will pay them back.
In due time their feet will slip.
Their day of disaster will arrive,
and their destiny will overtake them.'

32:22 Hebrew *of Sheol.* 32:31 The meaning of the Hebrew is
uncertain. Greek version reads *our enemies are fools.* 32:36 Or *will
take revenge for.* 32:43a As in Dead Sea Scrolls and Greek version;
Masoretic Text lacks the first two lines. Compare Heb 1:6.
32:43b As in Greek version; Hebrew text lacks this line.

VARIETY IN WORSHIP

Israel's worship involved all of the senses. This reinforced the meaning of the ceremony and painted a
dramatic picture that worship touches all areas of life.

SIGHT—The beauty and symbolism of the Tabernacle;
every color and hue had a meaning.

HEARING—The use of music; there were instructions
for the use of a variety of instruments, and the Bible
records many songs.

SMELL—The incense and sacrifices were burned, emit-
ting familiar aromas.

TASTE—Israel's festivals were celebrations and memorials—much of the food had symbolic importance.

TOUCH—At the sacrifice, the one making the offering
touched the head of the animal to symbolize the fact
that it was taking his place.

36 "Indeed, the LORD will give justice to his
people,
and he will change his mind about* his
servants,
when he sees their strength is gone
and no one is left, slave or free.
37 Then he will ask, 'Where are their gods,
the rocks they fled to for refuge?
38 Where now are those gods,
who ate the fat of their sacrifices
and drank the wine of their offerings?
Let those gods arise and help you!
Let them provide you with shelter!
39 Look now; I myself am he!
There is no other god but me!
I am the one who kills and gives life;
I am the one who wounds and heals;
no one can be rescued from my powerful
hand!
40 Now I raise my hand to heaven
and declare, "As surely as I live,
41 when I sharpen my flashing sword
and begin to carry out justice,
I will take revenge on my enemies
and repay those who reject me.
42 I will make my arrows drunk with blood,
and my sword will devour flesh—
the blood of the slaughtered and the
captives,
and the heads of the enemy leaders.'"

43 "Rejoice with him, you heavens,
and let all of God's angels worship him.*
Rejoice with his people, you nations,
and let all the angels be strengthened
in him.*

For he will avenge the blood of his servants;
he will take revenge against his enemies.
He will repay those who hate him*
and cleanse the land for his people."

⁴⁴So Moses came with Joshua* son of Nun and recited all the words of this song to the people.

⁴⁵When Moses had finished reciting all these words to the people of Israel, ⁴⁶he added: "Take to heart all the words of warning I have given you today. Pass them on as a command to your children so they will obey every word of these instructions. ⁴⁷These instructions are not empty words—they are your life! By obeying them you will enjoy a long life in the land you will occupy when you cross the Jordan River."

MOSES' DEATH FORETOLD ⁴⁸That same day the LORD said to Moses, ⁴⁹"Go to Moab, to the mountains east of the river,* and climb Mount Nebo, which is across from Jericho. Look out across the land of Canaan, the land I am giving to the people of Israel as their own special possession. ⁵⁰Then you will die there on the mountain. You will join your ancestors, just as Aaron, your brother, died on Mount Hor and joined his ancestors. ⁵¹For both of you betrayed me with the Israelites at the waters of Meribah at Kadesh* in the wilderness of Zin. You failed to demonstrate my holiness to the people of Israel there. ⁵²So you will see the land from a distance, but you may not enter the land I am giving to the people of Israel."

33 **MOSES BLESSES THE PEOPLE** This is the blessing that Moses, the man of God, gave to the people of Israel before his death:

² "The LORD came from Mount Sinai
and dawned upon us* from Mount Seir;
he shone forth from Mount Paran
and came from Meribah-kadesh
with flaming fire at his right hand.*
³ Indeed, he loves his people;*
all his holy ones are in his hands.

They follow in his steps
and accept his teaching.
⁴ Moses gave us the LORD's instruction,
the special possession of the people
of Israel.*
⁵ The LORD became king in Israel*—
when the leaders of the people
assembled,
when the tribes of Israel gathered
as one."

⁶Moses said this about the tribe of Reuben:*

"Let the tribe of Reuben live and not
die out,
though they are few in number."

⁷Moses said this about the tribe of Judah:

"O LORD, hear the cry of Judah
and bring them together as a people.
Give them strength to defend their cause;
help them against their enemies!"

⁸Moses said this about the tribe of Levi:

"O LORD, you have given your Thummim
and Urim—the sacred lots—
to your faithful servants the Levites.*
You put them to the test at Massah
and struggled with them at the waters
of Meribah.
⁹ The Levites obeyed your word
and guarded your covenant.
They were more loyal to you
than to their own parents.
They ignored their relatives
and did not acknowledge their own
children.
¹⁰ They teach your regulations to Jacob;
they give your instructions to Israel.
They present incense before you
and offer whole burnt offerings on
the altar.
¹¹ Bless the ministry of the Levites, O LORD,
and accept all the work of their hands.
Hit their enemies where it hurts
the most;
strike down their foes so they
never rise again."

THE WAYS GOD BLESSES
(33:6-25) Note the difference in blessings God gave each tribe. To one he gave the best land, to another strength, to another safety. Too often we see someone with a particular blessing and think that God must love that person more than he loves us. But God chooses to equip each person in ways that he sees fit. We are not to compare ourselves with others (see 2 Cor 10:12). Instead, we are to work to build his kingdom. What gifts has God given you? How are you using them to help build his kingdom?

32:43c As in Dead Sea Scrolls and Greek version; Masoretic Text lacks this line.   **32:44** Hebrew *Hoshea,* a variant name for Joshua.   **32:49** Hebrew *the mountains of Abarim.*   **32:51** Hebrew *waters of Meribath-kadesh.*   **33:2a** As in Greek and Syriac versions; Hebrew reads *upon them.*   **33:2b** Or *came from myriads of holy ones, from the south, from his mountain slopes.* The meaning of the Hebrew is uncertain.   **33:3** As in Greek version; Hebrew reads *Indeed, lover of the peoples.*   **33:4** Hebrew *of Jacob.* The names "Jacob" and "Israel" are often interchanged throughout the Old Testament, referring sometimes to the individual patriarch and sometimes to the nation.   **33:5** Hebrew *in Jeshurun,* a term of endearment for Israel.   **33:6** Hebrew lacks *Moses said this about the tribe of Reuben.*   **33:8** As in Greek version; Hebrew lacks *the Levites.*

¹²Moses said this about the tribe of Benjamin:

"The people of Benjamin are loved by the LORD
    and live in safety beside him.
He surrounds them continuously
    and preserves them from every harm."

¹³Moses said this about the tribes of Joseph:

"May their land be blessed by the LORD
    with the precious gift of dew from the
        heavens
    and water from beneath the earth;
¹⁴ with the rich fruit that grows in the sun,
    and the rich harvest produced each
        month;
¹⁵ with the finest crops of the ancient
        mountains,
    and the abundance from the everlasting
        hills;
¹⁶ with the best gifts of the earth and its
        bounty,
    and the favor of the one who appeared in
        the burning bush.
May these blessings rest on Joseph's head,
    crowning the brow of the prince among
        his brothers.
¹⁷ Joseph has the majesty of a young bull;
    he has the horns of a wild ox.
He will gore distant nations,
    driving them to the ends of the earth.
This is my blessing for the multitudes of
        Ephraim
    and the thousands of Manasseh."

¹⁸Moses said this about the tribes of Zebulun
and Issachar*:

"May the people of Zebulun prosper in their
        travels.
    May the people of Issachar prosper at
        home in their tents.
¹⁹ They summon the people to the mountain
    to offer proper sacrifices there.
They benefit from the riches of the sea
    and the hidden treasures in the sand."

²⁰Moses said this about the tribe of Gad:

"Blessed is the one who enlarges Gad's
        territory!
    Gad is poised there like a lion
    to tear off an arm or a head.
²¹ The people of Gad took the best land for
        themselves;
    a leader's share was assigned to them.
When the leaders of the people were
        assembled,

33:18 Hebrew lacks and Issachar.   **33:26** Hebrew of Jeshurun,
a term of endearment for Israel.   **34:2** Hebrew the western sea.

they carried out the LORD's justice
    and obeyed his regulations for Israel."

²²Moses said this about the tribe of Dan:

"Dan is a lion's cub,
    leaping out from Bashan."

²³Moses said this about the tribe of Naphtali:

"O Naphtali, you are rich in favor
    and full of the LORD's blessings;
may you possess the west and the
        south."

²⁴Moses said this about the tribe of Asher:

"May Asher be blessed above other sons;
    may he be esteemed by his brothers;
    may he bathe his feet in olive oil.
²⁵ May the bolts of your gates be of iron and
        bronze;
    may you be secure all your days."

²⁶ "There is no one like the God of Israel.*
    He rides across the heavens to help you,
    across the skies in majestic splendor.
²⁷ The eternal God is your refuge,
    and his everlasting arms are under you.
He drives out the enemy before you;
    he cries out, 'Destroy them!'
²⁸ So Israel will live in safety,
    prosperous Jacob in security,
in a land of grain and new wine,
    while the heavens drop down dew.
²⁹ How blessed you are, O Israel!
    Who else is like you, a people saved by
        the LORD?
He is your protecting shield
    and your triumphant sword!
Your enemies will cringe before you,
    and you will stomp on their backs!"

34

THE DEATH OF MOSES Then Moses
went up to Mount Nebo from the plains
of Moab and climbed Pisgah Peak, which is
across from Jericho. And the LORD showed him
the whole land, from Gilead as far as Dan; ²all
the land of Naphtali; the land of Ephraim and
Manasseh; all the land of Judah, extending to
the Mediterranean Sea*; ³the Negev; the Jordan Valley with Jericho—the city of palms—as
far as Zoar. ⁴Then the LORD said to Moses,
"This is the land I promised on oath to Abraham, Isaac, and Jacob when I said, 'I will give it
to your descendants.' I have now allowed you
to see it with your own eyes, but you will not
enter the land."

⁵So Moses, the servant of the LORD, died
there in the land of Moab, just as the LORD

had said. ⁶The LORD buried him* in a valley near Beth-peor in Moab, but to this day no one knows the exact place. ⁷Moses was 120 years old when he died, yet his eyesight was clear, and he was as strong as ever. ⁸The people of Israel mourned for Moses on the plains of Moab for thirty days, until the customary period of mourning was over.

⁹Now Joshua son of Nun was full of the spirit of wisdom, for Moses had laid his hands on him. So the people of Israel obeyed him, doing just as the LORD had commanded Moses.

¹⁰There has never been another prophet in Israel like Moses, whom the LORD knew face to face. ¹¹The LORD sent him to perform all the miraculous signs and wonders in the land of Egypt against Pharaoh, and all his servants, and his entire land. ¹²With mighty power, Moses performed terrifying acts in the sight of all Israel.

34:6 Hebrew *He buried him;* Samaritan Pentateuch and some Greek manuscripts read *They buried him.*

FROM FAILURE TO SUCCESS

(34:10-12) Moses, the man who did not want to be sent to Egypt because he had trouble speaking in public (Exod 4:10), delivered the three addresses to Israel that make up the book of Deuteronomy. God changed this stuttering shepherd into a powerful speaker and national leader. Moses' success story is a great example for us. Ever wonder whether or not you'll be successful? Or maybe you've wondered whether past failures have doomed your chances for success. If so, take a lesson from Moses' life. God can turn failure into success.

JOSHUA

What characteristics do you think are important in a leader? If you were chosen as captain of the football or forensics team, head cheerleader, or class president, what would you need to be like? Strong? Smart? Clever? Good with people? Good-looking? Enthusiastic? Devoted?

God called Joshua to be the leader of Israel as they were about to enter the Promised Land. Joshua was unsure about his leadership capabilities. But God told him: "No one will be able to stand against you as long as you live. For I will be with you as I was with Moses. I will not fail you or abandon you" (1:5). Then God explained the qualities Joshua needed in order to be a good leader for his people.

The first quality was obedience to God and his law: "Be strong and very courageous. Be careful to obey all the instructions Moses gave you. Do not deviate from them, turning either to the right or to the left. Then you will be successful in everything you do" (1:7).

The second was total dependence on God for the victory. God had taken care of Israel in the past. He wanted Joshua to know that he would not win a single battle without God.

Have you been tapped to be a leader in your school or community? If so, take another look at Joshua's leadership. Are obedience and dependence on God apparent in your life? Remember that God does not require you to be strong, clever, efficient, or even good-looking to be an effective leader for him. Instead, God wants you to obey his Word and depend on his power. Then, if God has called you, he will use you.

STATS

PURPOSE
To give the history of Israel's conquest of the Promised Land

AUTHOR
Joshua, except for the ending, which may have been written by the high priest Phinehas, an eyewitness to the events recounted there

ORIGINAL AUDIENCE
The people of Israel

SETTING
Canaan, also called the Promised Land, which occupied the same general geographical territory as modern-day Israel

KEY PEOPLE
Joshua, Rahab, Achan, Phinehas, Eleazar

KEY PLACES
Jericho, Ai, Mount Ebal, Mount Gerizim, Gibeon, Gilgal, Shiloh, Shechem

SPECIAL FEATURE
Out of the original group of adults who had left Egypt, only Joshua and Caleb lived to enter the Promised Land.

KEY POINTS

SUCCESS God gave success to the Israelites when they obeyed his master plan, not when they followed their own desires. Likewise, we must adjust our mind to God's way of thinking in order to see his standard for success.

GOD'S FAITHFULNESS Remembering how God fulfilled his promises in the past assured the Israelites that he would be faithful in the future. In the same way, God's promises reassure us of his love, faithfulness, and guidance.

LEADERSHIP Joshua's dependence on God made him a strong and effective leader. To be a strong leader like Joshua, we must be ready to listen and act on God's commands.

CONQUEST God commanded his people to conquer the Canaanites and take their land. But Israel's commitment to the task didn't last. Commitment to God means more than being enthusiastic about him. We must complete all of the work he gives us and apply his instructions to every part of our lives.

TIMELINE

1446 B.C.
Exodus from Egypt

1406
Israelites enter Canaan

1375
Judges begin to rule

1050
United kingdom under Saul

1010
David becomes king

The broken lines (— · —) indicate modern boundaries.

KEY PLACES

❶ ACACIA GROVE
The story of Joshua begins with the Israelites camping at Acacia Grove. The Israelites under Joshua were ready to enter and conquer Canaan. But before the nation moved out, Joshua received instructions from God (1:1-18).

❷ JORDAN RIVER
The entire nation prepared to cross this river, which was swollen from spring rains. After the scouts returned from Jericho with a positive report, Joshua prepared the priests and people for a miracle. As the priests carried the Ark into the Jordan River, the water stopped flowing and the entire nation crossed on dry ground into the Promised Land (2:1–4:24).

❸ GILGAL
After crossing the Jordan River, the Israelites camped at Gilgal, where they renewed their commitment to God and celebrated the Passover. As Joshua made plans for the attack on Jericho, an angel appeared to him (5:1-15).

❹ JERICHO
The walled city of Jericho seemed a formidable enemy. But when Joshua followed God's plans, the great walls were no obstacle. The city was conquered with only the obedient marching of the people (6:1-27).

❺ AI
Victory could not continue without obedience to God. That is why the disobedience of one man, Achan, brought defeat to the entire nation in the first battle against Ai. But once the sin was recognized and punished, God told Joshua to take heart and go against Ai once again. This time the city was taken (7:1–8:29).

❻ MOUNT EBAL AND MOUNT GERIZIM
After the defeat of Ai, Joshua built an altar at Mount Ebal. Then the people divided themselves, half of them standing at the foot of Mount Ebal and half at the foot of Mount Gerizim. The priests stood between the mountains holding the Ark of the Covenant

as Joshua read God's laws to all the people (8:30-35).

❼ GIBEON
After reaffirming their covenant with God, the Israelites were tricked into making a peace treaty with the people of Gibeon. The Gibeonites asked the Israelites for a treaty, pretending that they had traveled a long distance. The Israelite leaders made the agreement without consulting God. The deception was soon discovered, but because the treaty had been made, Israel could not go back on its word. As a result, the Gibeonites saved their own lives, but they were forced to become Israel's slaves (9:1-27).

❽ VALLEY OF AIJALON
The king of Jerusalem was very angry at the Gibeonites for making a peace treaty with Israel. He gathered armies from four other cities to attack Gibeon. Gibeon summoned Joshua for help, and Joshua took immediate action. As the battle raged on and moved into the valley of Aijalon, Joshua prayed for the sun to stand still until the enemy could be destroyed (10:1-43).

❾ HAZOR
Up north in Hazor, King Jabin mobilized the kings of the surrounding cities to unite and crush Israel. But God gave Joshua and Israel victory (11:1-23).

❿ SHILOH
After the armies of Canaan were conquered, Israel gathered at Shiloh to set up the Tabernacle. The seven tribes who had not received land were given their allotments (18:1–19:51).

⓫ SHECHEM
Before Joshua died, he called the entire nation together at Shechem to remind them that it was God who had given them their land and that only with God's help could they keep it. The people vowed to follow God. As long as Joshua was alive, the land was at rest from war and trouble (24:1-33).

1 THE LORD'S CHARGE TO JOSHUA

After the death of Moses the LORD's servant, the LORD spoke to Joshua son of Nun, Moses' assistant. He said, ²"Moses my servant is dead. Therefore, the time has come for you to lead these people, the Israelites, across the Jordan River into the land I am giving them. ³I promise you what I promised Moses: 'Wherever you set foot, you will be on land I have given you—⁴from the Negev wilderness in the south to the Lebanon mountains in the north, from the Euphrates River in the east to the Mediterranean Sea* in the west, including all the land of the Hittites.' ⁵No one will be able to stand against you as long as you live. For I will be with you as I was with Moses. I will not fail you or abandon you.

⁶"Be strong and courageous, for you are the one who will lead these people to possess all the land I swore to their ancestors I would give them. ⁷Be strong and very courageous. Be careful to obey all the instructions Moses gave you. Do not deviate from them, turning either to the right or to the left. Then you will be successful in everything you do. ⁸Study this Book of Instruction continually. Meditate on it day and night so you will be sure to obey everything written in it. Only then will you prosper and succeed in all you do. ⁹This is my command—be strong and courageous! Do not be afraid or discouraged. For the LORD your God is with you wherever you go."

JOSHUA'S CHARGE TO THE ISRAELITES

¹⁰Joshua then commanded the officers of Israel, ¹¹"Go through the camp and tell the people to get their provisions ready. In three days you will cross the Jordan River and take

1:4 Hebrew *the Great Sea.*

possession of the land the LORD your God is giving you."

¹²Then Joshua called together the tribes of Reuben, Gad, and the half-tribe of Manasseh. He told them, ¹³"Remember what Moses, the servant of the LORD, commanded you: 'The LORD your God is giving you a place of rest. He has given you this land.' ¹⁴Your wives, children, and livestock may remain here in the land Moses assigned to you on the east side of the Jordan River. But your strong warriors, fully armed, must lead the other tribes across the Jordan to help them conquer their territory. Stay with them ¹⁵until the LORD gives them rest, as he has given you rest, and until they, too, possess the land the LORD your God is giving them. Only then may you return and settle here on the east side of the Jordan River in the land that Moses, the servant of the LORD, assigned to you."

¹⁶They answered Joshua, "We will do whatever you command us, and we will go wherever you send us. ¹⁷We will obey you just as we obeyed Moses. And may the LORD your God be with you as he was with Moses. ¹⁸Anyone who

••

CHALLENGE
(1:1-9) Joshua's new job consisted of leading more than two million people into a strange, new land and conquering it. What a challenge—even for a man of Joshua's capability! Every new job is a challenge. Without God, it can be frightening. With God, it can be a great adventure. Just as God assured Joshua that he would be with him, so God is with us as we face our new challenges. We may not conquer nations, but every day we face tough situations, difficult people, and temptations. God promises that he will never abandon us or fail to help us, regardless of how we feel. With God's help, we can conquer life's challenges.

CHOICES
responsibility

Carmen, a 16-year-old junior at Roberto Clemente High, is popular and always smiling. Although she seems to have it all together, appearances can be deceiving. Judge for yourself.

"Lupe, what am I going to do?" Carmen queries her best friend. "Eduardo asked me to be the girls' ministry leader this year."

"What does that mean?" Lupe asks.

"Well, I'd have to be involved in all of the campus ministry activities. You know—Bible studies, morning prayer group, outreaches—all that stuff. Ministry leaders are expected to talk a lot about their faith.... That's what's so weird. I mean, out of all the people Eduardo could have asked, he came to me! I've only been a Christian for three years."

"Sounds cool—"

"Sí. . . ."

"—and a lot of responsibility."

"That's what worries me! I've never had to plan everything and give everybody direction. I mean, I'd kinda like to do it; but what if I can't handle it? What if I do something stupid or let Eduardo down? What if I turn out to be a horrible leader and they fire me or something?"

"Oh, Carmen! You'll do great and you know it."

"*No sé* (I don't know). . . ."

Can you relate to how Carmen feels? Read Joshua 1:5-9. If you were Lupe, how would you share this comfort and encouragement with Carmen, or anyone facing big responsibilities?

MY STORY: Steve

When I was in first grade, I memorized Joshua 1:9: "This is my command—be strong and courageous! Do not be afraid or discouraged. For the LORD your God is with you wherever you go."

Recently I took part in a school play. I developed a bad case of stage fright before the performance. I didn't think I was going to make it through. I prayed, asking God to help me feel more comfortable with my part, and the verse came to mind gain. I was concentrating on this encouragement, straight from God's Word, and it dispelled my fear. I remembered my lines and even did pretty well in the play, according to several people.

There have been many other times when I've recalled this verse and gained courage from it. Whenever I feel scared and alone, I remember this verse. It always comforts me.

rebels against your orders and does not obey your words and everything you command will be put to death. So be strong and courageous!"

2 RAHAB PROTECTS THE SPIES

Then Joshua secretly sent out two spies from the Israelite camp at Acacia Grove.* He instructed them, "Scout out the land on the other side of the Jordan River, especially around Jericho." So the two men set out and came to the house of a prostitute named Rahab and stayed there that night.

²But someone told the king of Jericho, "Some Israelites have come here tonight to spy out the land." ³So the king of Jericho sent orders to Rahab: "Bring out the men who have come into

....

A NEW ROLE

(2:1) Why should the spies stop at the house of Rahab the prostitute? *Several reasons:* (1) it was a good place to gather information and have no questions asked in return, (2) Rahab's house was in an ideal location for a quick escape because it was built into the city wall, and (3) God directed the spies to Rahab's house because he knew that her heart was open to him and that she would be instrumental in the Israelite victory of Jericho. Rahab didn't allow her imperfect past to keep her from reaching out to God and helping his people. God often uses people with simple faith to accomplish his great purposes, no matter what kind of past they have or how insignificant they seem to be. Feeling like the mistakes you've made will keep you from being used by God? Remember Rahab!

your house, for they have come here to spy out the whole land."

⁴Rahab had hidden the two men, but she replied, "Yes, the men were here earlier, but I didn't know where they were from. ⁵They left the town at dusk, as the gates were about to close. I don't know where they went. If you hurry, you can probably catch up with them." ⁶(Actually, she had taken them up to the roof and hidden them beneath bundles of flax she had laid out.) ⁷So the king's men went looking for the spies along the road leading to the shallow crossings of the Jordan River. And as soon as the king's men had left, the gate of Jericho was shut.

⁸Before the spies went to sleep that night, Rahab went up on the roof to talk with them. ⁹"I know the LORD has given you this land," she told them. "We are all afraid of you. Everyone in the land is living in terror. ¹⁰For we have heard how the LORD made a dry path for you through the Red Sea* when you left Egypt. And we know what you did to Sihon and Og, the two Amorite kings east of the Jordan River, whose people you completely destroyed.* ¹¹No wonder our hearts have melted in fear! No one has the courage to fight after hearing such things. For the LORD your God is the supreme God of the heavens above and the earth below.

¹²"Now swear to me by the LORD that you will be kind to me and my family since I have helped you. Give me some guarantee that ¹³when Jericho is conquered, you will let me live, along with my father and mother, my brothers and sisters, and all their families."

¹⁴"We offer our own lives as a guarantee for your safety," the men agreed. "If you don't betray us, we will keep our promise and be kind to you when the LORD gives us the land."

¹⁵Then, since Rahab's house was built into the town wall, she let them down by a rope through the window. ¹⁶"Escape to the hill country," she told them. "Hide there for three days from the men searching for you. Then, when they have returned, you can go on your way."

¹⁷Before they left, the men told her, "We will be bound by the oath we have taken only if you follow these instructions. ¹⁸When we come into the land, you must leave this scarlet rope hanging from the window through which you let us down. And all your family members—your father, mother, brothers, and all your relatives—must be here inside the house. ¹⁹If they go out into the street and are killed, it will not be our

2:1 Hebrew *Shittim.* **2:10a** Hebrew *sea of reeds.* **2:10b** The Hebrew term used here refers to the complete consecration of things or people to the LORD, either by destroying them or by giving them as an offering.

fault. But if anyone lays a hand on people inside this house, we will accept the responsibility for their death. ²⁰If you betray us, however, we are not bound by this oath in any way."

²¹"I accept your terms," she replied. And she sent them on their way, leaving the scarlet rope hanging from the window.

²²The spies went up into the hill country and stayed there three days. The men who were chasing them searched everywhere along the road, but they finally returned without success. ²³Then the two spies came down from the hill country, crossed the Jordan River, and reported to Joshua all that had happened to them. ²⁴"The LORD has given us the whole land," they said, "for all the people in the land are terrified of us."

3 THE ISRAELITES CROSS THE JORDAN

Early the next morning Joshua and all the Israelites left Acacia Grove* and arrived at the banks of the Jordan River, where they camped before crossing. ²Three days later the Israelite officers went through the camp, ³giving these instructions to the people: "When you see the Levitical priests carrying the Ark of the Covenant of the LORD your God, move out from your positions and follow them. ⁴Since you have never traveled this way before, they will guide you. Stay about a half mile* behind them, keeping a

3:1 Hebrew *Shittim*.　**3:4** Hebrew *about 2,000 cubits* [920 meters].

clear distance between you and the Ark. Make sure you don't come any closer."

⁵Then Joshua told the people, "Purify yourselves, for tomorrow the LORD will do great wonders among you."

⁶In the morning Joshua said to the priests, "Lift up the Ark of the Covenant and lead the people across the river." And so they started out and went ahead of the people.

⁷The LORD told Joshua, "Today I will begin to make you a great leader in the eyes of all the Israelites. They will know that I am with you, just as I was with Moses. ⁸Give this command to the priests who carry the Ark of the Covenant: 'When you reach the banks of the Jordan River, take a few steps into the river and stop there.'"

⁹So Joshua told the Israelites, "Come and listen to what the LORD your God says. ¹⁰Today you will know that the living God is among you. He will surely drive out the Canaanites, Hittites, Hivites, Perizzites, Girgashites, Amorites, and Jebusites ahead of you. ¹¹Look, the Ark of the Covenant, which belongs to the Lord of the whole earth, will lead you across the Jordan River! ¹²Now choose twelve men from the tribes of Israel, one from each tribe. ¹³The priests will carry the Ark of the LORD, the Lord of all the earth. As soon as their feet touch the water, the flow of water will be cut off upstream, and the river will stand up like a wall."

PERSONALITY PROFILE — RAHAB

UPS:
- *Mother of Boaz, and thus an ancestor of David and Jesus (Matt 1:5)*
- *One of only two women listed in the Hall of Faith in Hebrews 11*
- *Resourceful, willing to help others at great risk to herself*

DOWNS:
- *Worked as a prostitute*

STATS:
- *Where: Jericho*
- *Occupation: Prostitute, innkeeper; later became a wife and mother*
- *Relatives: Salmon (husband); Boaz (son)*
- *Contemporaries: Joshua*

KEY VERSES: *Joshua 2:1-24; 6:1-27; Matthew 1:5; Hebrews 11:31; James 2:25.*

OUT OF ALL THE PEOPLE YOU KNOW, who is the most unlikely person you can think of to accomplish something great? Rahab was a surprise. She was one of those people we wouldn't expect God to use. But God looks at people differently than we do.

As a prostitute in the city of Jericho, Rahab lived on the edge of society. She was used in private and rejected in public. Her house, built right into the city wall, was a natural place for the Israelite spies to hide, since they would be mistaken for Rahab's customers.

Rumors about the coming Israelite invasion were all over the city, but having spies in her home convinced Rahab that war was imminent. Living on the city wall, Rahab probably felt especially vulnerable. Although she shared everyone's fears, she decided to do something about her own. She chose to trust the God of the Israelites. Although she didn't know much about God, she knew enough to recognize that he could be trusted. God saved Rahab's family because of her faith, not her profession!

Through Rahab's family line came the ultimate sign of God's mercy—his Son. If at times you feel like a failure, remember that Rahab overcame failure through her trust in God. You can do the same!

BOTTOM LINE: Rahab did not let fear affect her faith in God's ability to save her family from death.

Rahab's story is told in Joshua 2 and 6. She also is mentioned in Matthew 1:5; Hebrews 11:31; and James 2:25.

¹⁴So the people left their camp to cross the Jordan, and the priests who were carrying the Ark of the Covenant went ahead of them. ¹⁵It was the harvest season, and the Jordan was overflowing its banks. But as soon as the feet of the priests who were carrying the Ark touched the water at the river's edge, ¹⁶the water above that point began backing up a great distance away at a town called Adam, which is near Zarethan. And the water below that point flowed on to the Dead Sea* until the riverbed was dry. Then all the people crossed over near the town of Jericho.

¹⁷Meanwhile, the priests who were carrying the Ark of the LORD's Covenant stood on dry ground in the middle of the riverbed as the people passed by. They waited there until the whole nation of Israel had crossed the Jordan on dry ground.

4 MEMORIALS TO THE JORDAN CROSSING

When all the people had crossed the Jordan, the LORD said to Joshua, ²"Now choose twelve men, one from each tribe. ³Tell them, 'Take twelve stones from the very place where the priests are standing in the middle of the Jordan. Carry them out and pile them up at the place where you will camp tonight.'"

⁴So Joshua called together the twelve men he had chosen—one from each of the tribes of Israel. ⁵He told them, "Go into the middle of the Jordan, in front of the Ark of the LORD your God. Each of you must pick up one stone and carry it out on your shoulder—twelve stones in all, one for each of the twelve tribes of Israel. ⁶We will use these stones to build a memorial. In the future your children will ask you, 'What do these stones mean?' ⁷Then you can tell them, 'They remind us that the Jordan River stopped flowing when the Ark of the LORD's Covenant went across.' These stones will stand as a memorial among the people of Israel forever."

⁸So the men did as Joshua had commanded them. They took twelve stones from the middle of the Jordan River, one for each tribe, just as the LORD had told Joshua. They carried them to the place where they camped for the night and constructed the memorial there.

⁹Joshua also set up another pile of twelve stones in the middle of the Jordan, at the place where the priests who carried the Ark of the Covenant were standing. And they are there to this day.

¹⁰The priests who were carrying the Ark stood in the middle of the river until all of the LORD's commands that Moses had given to Joshua were carried out. Meanwhile, the people hurried across the riverbed. ¹¹And when everyone was safely on the other side, the priests crossed over with the Ark of the LORD as the people watched.

¹²The armed warriors from the tribes of Reuben, Gad, and the half-tribe of Manasseh led the Israelites across the Jordan, just as Moses had directed. ¹³These armed men—about 40,000 strong—were ready for battle, and the LORD was with them as they crossed over to the plains of Jericho.

¹⁴That day the LORD made Joshua a great leader in the eyes of all the Israelites, and for the rest of his life they revered him as much as they had revered Moses.

¹⁵The LORD had said to Joshua, ¹⁶"Command the priests carrying the Ark of the Covenant* to come up out of the riverbed." ¹⁷So Joshua gave the command. ¹⁸As soon as the priests carrying the Ark of the LORD's Covenant came up out of the riverbed and their feet were on high ground, the water of the Jordan returned and overflowed its banks as before.

¹⁹The people crossed the Jordan on the tenth day of the first month.* Then they camped at Gilgal, just east of Jericho. ²⁰It was there at Gilgal that Joshua piled up the twelve stones taken from the Jordan River.

²¹Then Joshua said to the Israelites, "In the future your children will ask, 'What do these stones mean?' ²²Then you can tell them, 'This is where the Israelites crossed the Jordan on dry ground.' ²³For the LORD your God dried up the river right before your eyes, and he kept it dry until you were all across, just as he did at the Red Sea* when he dried it up until we had all crossed over. ²⁴He did this so all the nations of the earth might know that the LORD's hand is powerful, and so you might fear the LORD your God forever."

5 When all the Amorite kings west of the Jordan and all the Canaanite kings who lived along the Mediterranean coast* heard how the LORD had dried up the Jordan River so the people of Israel could cross, they lost heart and were paralyzed with fear because of them.

ISRAEL REESTABLISHES COVENANT CEREMONIES

²At that time the LORD told Joshua, "Make flint knives and circumcise this second generation of Israelites.*" ³So Joshua made

3:16 Hebrew *the sea of the Arabah, the Salt Sea.* **4:16** Hebrew *Ark of the Testimony.* **4:19** This day in the ancient Hebrew lunar calendar occurred in late March, April, or early May. **4:23** Hebrew *sea of reeds.* **5:1** Hebrew *along the sea.* **5:2** Or *circumcise the Israelites a second time.*

flint knives and circumcised the entire male population of Israel at Gibeath-haaraloth.*

⁴Joshua had to circumcise them because all the men who were old enough to fight in battle when they left Egypt had died in the wilderness. ⁵Those who left Egypt had all been circumcised, but none of those born after the Exodus, during the years in the wilderness, had been circumcised. ⁶The Israelites had traveled in the wilderness for forty years until all the men who were old enough to fight in battle when they left Egypt had died. For they had disobeyed the LORD, and the LORD vowed he would not let them enter the land he had sworn to give us—a land flowing with milk and honey. ⁷So Joshua circumcised their sons—those who had grown up to take their fathers' places—for they had not been circumcised on the way to the Promised Land. ⁸After all the males had been circumcised, they rested in the camp until they were healed.

⁹Then the LORD said to Joshua, "Today I have rolled away the shame of your slavery in Egypt." So that place has been called Gilgal* to this day.

¹⁰While the Israelites were camped at Gilgal on the plains of Jericho, they celebrated Passover on the evening of the fourteenth day of the first month.* ¹¹The very next day they began to eat unleavened bread and roasted grain harvested from the land. ¹²No manna appeared on the day they first ate from the crops of the land, and it was never seen again. So from that time on the Israelites ate from the crops of Canaan.

THE LORD'S COMMANDER CONFRONTS JOSHUA
¹³When Joshua was near the town of Jericho, he looked up and saw a man standing in front of him with sword in hand. Joshua went up to him and demanded, "Are you friend or foe?"

¹⁴"Neither one," he replied. "I am the commander of the LORD's army."

At this, Joshua fell with his face to the ground in reverence. "I am at your command," Joshua said. "What do you want your servant to do?"

¹⁵The commander of the LORD's army replied, "Take off your sandals, for the place where you

5:3 *Gibeath-haaraloth* means "hill of foreskins." 5:9 *Gilgal* sounds like the Hebrew word *galal,* meaning "to roll." 5:10 This day in the ancient Hebrew lunar calendar occurred in late March, April, or early May.

ULTIMATE ISSUES *GOD'S CHOSEN PEOPLE*

As you read the Old Testament, you may wonder, Why did God select the people of Israel as his chosen people? That's a good question, and one that's not easy to answer.

First, God singled out a man named Abram (later called Abraham) from the ancient city of Ur and promised to bless him and his descendants (Gen 12:1-3). But there was a condition attached: Abram had to remain faithful to God. Even though he had numerous lapses, Abram kept his end of the bargain, and God was true to his word, making Abram's descendants into the nation of Israel. So God favored the Jews to keep his promise to Abram.

Second, God was setting the stage for his Son, the Messiah, to be ushered into the world many centuries later. Because God chose to have his Son born of a woman, he needed to provide an appropriate backdrop for the woman and her ancestry. He chose the people of Israel, the descendants of Abraham. Guiding them throughout their history, God made sure that the scene was prepared for Mary, a virgin engaged to be married, to be available to become the mother of the child, Jesus. At the right time, when God was ready to enter human space and time, he brought Mary and Joseph, descendants of Abraham, to the stable in Bethlehem. God's Son would be born a Jew.

Third, some have suggested that the people of Israel were the perfect "display case" for God's mercy and patient love. They were stubborn, rebellious, and unfaithful—just like many believers today. No one would have blamed God for giving up on them and starting over with a new nation. But God kept his word to Abraham and never abandoned Abraham's descendants. Although God punished them, scolded them, and sent them into exile, he never forgot them or his promise.

Many people today see the existence of the Jews as a powerful argument for the existence of God. In spite of overwhelming opposition throughout history, they are still here, while most of their enemies (at least from Old Testament times) are long gone. How else could they have survived, except for the protection of a powerful, loving God who refused to give up on them?

In the final analysis, we must remember that God is all-knowing, good, and sovereign. His reasons do not always make sense to us. While we cannot know with certainty why he chose to make the Jews his special people, we know that he did. Now, all who follow Christ are members of his chosen nation. They don't become Jews, but they become God's covenant people—Christ's church. As you continue to read the unfolding drama we call the Old Testament, watch for ways God shows his love for his people, and thank God for his kindness to them—and to you. ■

are standing is holy." And Joshua did as he was told.

6 THE FALL OF JERICHO

Now the gates of Jericho were tightly shut because the people were afraid of the Israelites. No one was allowed to go out or in. ²But the LORD said to Joshua, "I have given you Jericho, its king, and all its strong warriors. ³You and your fighting men should march around the town once a day for six days. ⁴Seven priests will walk ahead of the Ark, each carrying a ram's horn. On the seventh day you are to march around the town seven times, with the priests blowing the horns. ⁵When you hear the priests give one long blast on the rams' horns, have all the people shout as loud as they can. Then the walls of the town will collapse, and the people can charge straight into the town."

⁶So Joshua called together the priests and said, "Take up the Ark of the LORD's Covenant, and assign seven priests to walk in front of it, each carrying a ram's horn." ⁷Then he gave orders to the people: "March around the town, and the armed men will lead the way in front of the Ark of the LORD."

⁸After Joshua spoke to the people, the seven priests with the rams' horns started marching in the presence of the LORD, blowing the horns as they marched. And the Ark of the LORD's Covenant followed behind them. ⁹Some of the armed men marched in front of the priests with the horns and some behind the Ark, with the priests continually blowing the horns. ¹⁰"Do not shout; do not even talk," Joshua commanded. "Not a single word from any of you until I tell you to shout. Then shout!" ¹¹So the

---

A WAR ALREADY WON

(6:2-5) *Before the battle began, God told Joshua that the enemy had already been defeated! What confidence Joshua must have had as he went into battle! Christians also fight against a defeated enemy. Jesus defeated our enemy, Satan, when he died on the cross (Rom 8:37-39; Heb 2:14-15; 1 Jn 3:8). Although we still fight battles every day and evil continues in the world, we have the assurance that the war has already been won.*

JOSHUA *PERSONALITY PROFILE*

WHO IS THE LEADER you most admire? Being a good leader means more than being in charge. The best leaders are those who help others learn to lead. This is true for two reasons: (1) sometimes the job is too big for one person to do alone, so leadership has to be shared; and (2) some jobs take so long that they don't get done unless the first leader trains others to take over after he or she is gone. Joshua helped Moses with the huge job of leading the people of Israel. At the same time, he was being trained as the new leader.

Moses made an excellent decision when he chose Joshua as his assistant. Later, God told Moses that after his death, Joshua would take over as Israel's leader.

Joshua was an important part of the Exodus story. He led the army, and was the only person allowed to go with Moses partway up the mountain where Moses received the Ten Commandments. Of the 12 men sent as scouts into the Promised Land, only Joshua and Caleb reported that God could help them conquer the land. Joshua was always with Moses, like a shadow. His "basic training" involved watching and imitating everything his leader did and said.

Who is your Moses? Who is your Joshua? You are part of the unbroken chain of God's work in the world. What are you learning from these leaders? Can those who are watching you see how important God is to you? Why or why not? Ask God to lead you to a Moses worth following. Ask him also to make you a good Joshua.

BOTTOM LINE: Effective leadership is often the product of good preparation and encouragement.

The person we admire the most will have a definite effect on us and those who learn from us.

A person committed to God provides the best model for us.

Joshua is also mentioned in Exodus 17:9-14; 24:13; 32:17; 33:11; Numbers 11:28; 13–14; 26:65; 27:18-23; 32:12, 28; 34:17; Deuteronomy 1:38; 3:21-22, 28; 31:3, 14–15, 23; 34:9; Joshua; Judges 2:6-9; 1 Kings 16:34; and Hebrews 4:8.

UPS:
- *Moses' assistant and successor*
- *One of only two adults who experienced Egyptian slavery and lived to enter the Promised Land*
- *Led the Israelites into their God-given homeland*
- *Brilliant military strategist*
- *Faithful to ask God's direction in the challenges he faced*

DOWNS:
- *Was fooled by the Gibeonites*

STATS:
- *Where: Egypt, the wilderness of Sinai, and Canaan (the Promised Land)*
- *Occupation: Special assistant to Moses; warrior, leader*
- *Relatives: Nun (father)*
- *Contemporaries: Moses, Caleb, Miriam, Aaron*

KEY VERSES: *Exodus 17:9-14; Numbers 13–14; 26:65; 27:18-23; 32:12; Deuteronomy 34:9; Judges 2:6-9; 1 Kings 16:34; Hebrews 4:8.*

Ark of the LORD was carried around the town once that day, and then everyone returned to spend the night in the camp.

¹²Joshua got up early the next morning, and the priests again carried the Ark of the LORD. ¹³The seven priests with the rams' horns marched in front of the Ark of the LORD, blowing their horns. Again the armed men marched both in front of the priests with the horns and behind the Ark of the LORD. All this time the priests were blowing their horns. ¹⁴On the second day they again marched around the town once and returned to the camp. They followed this pattern for six days.

¹⁵On the seventh day the Israelites got up at dawn and marched around the town as they had done before. But this time they went around the town seven times. ¹⁶The seventh time around, as the priests sounded the long blast on their horns, Joshua commanded the people, "Shout! For the LORD has given you the town! ¹⁷Jericho and everything in it must be completely destroyed* as an offering to the LORD. Only Rahab the prostitute and the others in her house will be spared, for she protected our spies.

¹⁸"Do not take any of the things set apart for destruction, or you yourselves will be completely destroyed, and you will bring trouble on the camp of Israel. ¹⁹Everything made from silver, gold, bronze, or iron is sacred to the LORD and must be brought into his treasury."

²⁰When the people heard the sound of the rams' horns, they shouted as loud as they could. Suddenly, the walls of Jericho collapsed, and the Israelites charged straight into the town and captured it. ²¹They completely destroyed everything in it with their swords—men and women, young and old, cattle, sheep, goats, and donkeys.

²²Meanwhile, Joshua said to the two spies, "Keep your promise. Go to the prostitute's house and bring her out, along with all her family."

²³The men who had been spies went in and brought out Rahab, her father, mother, brothers, and all the other relatives who were with her. They moved her whole family to a safe place near the camp of Israel.

²⁴Then the Israelites burned the town and everything in it. Only the things made from sil-

ver, gold, bronze, or iron were kept for the treasury of the LORD's house. ²⁵So Joshua spared Rahab the prostitute and her relatives who were with her in the house, because she had hidden the spies Joshua sent to Jericho. And she lives among the Israelites to this day.

²⁶At that time Joshua invoked this curse:

"May the curse of the LORD fall on anyone
who tries to rebuild the town of Jericho.
At the cost of his firstborn son,
he will lay its foundation.
At the cost of his youngest son,
he will set up its gates."

²⁷So the LORD was with Joshua, and his reputation spread throughout the land.

7 **AI DEFEATS THE ISRAELITES** But Israel violated the instructions about the things set apart for the LORD.* A man named Achan had stolen some of these dedicated things, so the LORD was very angry with the Israelites. Achan was the son of Carmi, a descendant of Zimri* son of Zerah, of the tribe of Judah.

²Joshua sent some of his men from Jericho to spy out the town of Ai, east of Bethel, near Beth-aven. ³When they returned, they told Joshua, "There's no need for all of us to go up there; it won't take more than two or three thousand men to attack Ai. Since there are so few of them, don't make all our people struggle to go up there."

⁴So approximately 3,000 warriors were sent, but they were soundly defeated. The men of Ai ⁵chased the Israelites from the town gate as far as the quarries,* and they killed about thirty-six who were retreating down the slope. The Israelites were paralyzed with fear at this turn of events, and their courage melted away.

⁶Joshua and the elders of Israel tore their clothing in dismay, threw dust on their heads, and bowed face down to the ground before the Ark of the LORD until evening. ⁷Then Joshua cried out, "Oh, Sovereign LORD, why did you bring us across the Jordan River if you are

---

6:17 The Hebrew term used here refers to the complete consecration of things or people to the LORD, either by destroying them or by giving them as an offering; similarly in 6:18, 21.   7:1a The Hebrew term used here refers to the complete consecration of things or people to the LORD, either by destroying them or by giving them as an offering; similarly in 7:11, 12, 13, 15.   7:1b As in parallel text at 1 Chr 2:6; Hebrew reads *Zabdi*. Also in 7:17, 18.   7:5 Or *as far as Shebarim*.

LESSONS
(7:7) When Joshua first went against Ai, he did not consult God but relied on the strength of his army to defeat the small city (7:2-3). Only after Israel was defeated did they turn to God and ask, "What happened?" Too often we rely on our own skill and strength, especially when the task before us seems easy. We go to God only when the obstacles seem too great. However, only God knows what lies ahead. Consulting him, even when we are on a winning streak, may save us from grave mistakes or misjudgments. God may want us to learn lessons, get rid of pride, or consult others before he will work through us.

going to let the Amorites kill us? If only we had been content to stay on the other side! [8]Lord, what can I say now that Israel has fled from its enemies? [9]For when the Canaanites and all the other people living in the land hear about it, they will surround us and wipe our name off the face of the earth. And then what will happen to the honor of your great name?"

[10]But the LORD said to Joshua, "Get up! Why are you lying on your face like this? [11]Israel has sinned and broken my covenant! They have stolen some of the things that I commanded must be set apart for me. And they have not only stolen them but have lied about it and hidden the things among their own belongings. [12]That is why the Israelites are running from their enemies in defeat. For now Israel itself has been set apart for destruction. I will not remain with you any longer unless you destroy the things among you that were set apart for destruction.

[13]"Get up! Command the people to purify themselves in preparation for tomorrow. For this is what the LORD, the God of Israel, says: Hidden among you, O Israel, are things set apart for the LORD. You will never defeat your enemies until you remove these things from among you.

[14]"In the morning you must present yourselves by tribes, and the LORD will point out the tribe to which the guilty man belongs. That tribe must come forward with its clans, and the LORD will point out the guilty clan. That clan will then come forward, and the LORD will point out the guilty family. Finally, each member of the guilty family must come forward one by one. [15]The one who has stolen what was set apart for destruction will himself be burned with fire, along with everything he has, for he has broken the covenant of the LORD and has done a horrible thing in Israel."

ACHAN'S SIN [16]Early the next morning Joshua brought the tribes of Israel before the LORD, and the tribe of Judah was singled out. [17]Then the clans of Judah came forward, and the clan

of Zerah was singled out. Then the families of Zerah came forward, and the family of Zimri was singled out. [18]Every member of Zimri's family was brought forward person by person, and Achan was singled out.

[19]Then Joshua said to Achan, "My son, give glory to the LORD, the God of Israel, by telling the truth. Make your confession and tell me what you have done. Don't hide it from me."

[20]Achan replied, "It is true! I have sinned against the LORD, the God of Israel. [21]Among the plunder I saw a beautiful robe from Babylon,* 200 silver coins,* and a bar of gold weighing more than a pound.* I wanted them so much that I took them. They are hidden in the ground beneath my tent, with the silver buried deeper than the rest."

[22]So Joshua sent some men to make a search. They ran to the tent and found the stolen goods hidden there, just as Achan had said, with the silver buried beneath the rest. [23]They took the things from the tent and brought them to Joshua and all the Israelites. Then they laid them on the ground in the presence of the LORD.

[24]Then Joshua and all the Israelites took Achan, the silver, the robe, the bar of gold, his sons, daughters, cattle, donkeys, sheep, goats, tent, and everything he had, and they brought them to the valley of Achor. [25]Then Joshua said to Achan, "Why have you brought trouble on us? The LORD will now bring trouble on you." And all the Israelites stoned Achan and his family and burned their bodies. [26]They piled a great heap of stones over Achan, which remains to this day. That is why the place has been called the Valley of Trouble* ever since. So the LORD was no longer angry.

8 **THE ISRAELITES DEFEAT AI** Then the LORD said to Joshua, "Do not be afraid or discouraged. Take all your fighting men and attack Ai, for I have given you the king of Ai, his people, his town, and his land. [2]You will destroy them as you destroyed Jericho and its king. But this time you may keep the plunder and the livestock for yourselves. Set an ambush behind the town."

[3]So Joshua and all the fighting men set out to attack Ai. Joshua chose 30,000 of his best warriors and sent them out at night [4]with these orders: "Hide in ambush close behind the town and be ready for action. [5]When our main army attacks, the men of Ai will come out to

....

NO SMALL THING

(7:20-25) Achan underestimated God and didn't take his commands seriously (6:18-19). Taking a robe, some coins, and a bar of gold may have seemed a small matter to Achan, but the effects of his action were felt by the entire nation, especially his family. Israel lost a battle and the lives of thirty-six men because of Achan. Our actions, like Achan's, affect more people than just ourselves. Beware of the temptation to rationalize your sins by saying they are too small or too personal to hurt anyone but you. A small sin can have far-reaching consequences.

7:21a Hebrew *Shinar*. **7:21b** Hebrew *200 shekels of silver*, about 5 pounds or 2.3 kilograms in weight. **7:21c** Hebrew *50 shekels*, about 20 ounces or 570 grams in weight. **7:26** Hebrew *valley of Achor*.

fight as they did before, and we will run away from them. ⁶We will let them chase us until we have drawn them away from the town. For they will say, 'The Israelites are running away from us as they did before.' Then, while we are running from them, ⁷you will jump up from your ambush and take possession of the town, for the LORD your God will give it to you. ⁸Set the town on fire, as the LORD has commanded. You have your orders."

⁹So they left and went to the place of ambush between Bethel and the west side of Ai. But Joshua remained among the people in the camp that night. ¹⁰Early the next morning Joshua roused his men and started toward Ai, accompanied by the elders of Israel. ¹¹All the fighting men who were with Joshua marched in front of the town and camped on the north side of Ai, with a valley between them and the town. ¹²That night Joshua sent 5,000 men to lie in ambush between Bethel and Ai, on the west side of the town. ¹³So they stationed the main army north of the town and the ambush west of the town. Joshua himself spent that night in the valley.

¹⁴When the king of Ai saw the Israelites across the valley, he and all his army hurried out early in the morning and attacked the Israelites at a place overlooking the Jordan Valley.* But he didn't realize there was an ambush behind the town. ¹⁵Joshua and the Israelite army fled toward the wilderness as though they were badly beaten. ¹⁶Then all the men in the town were called out to chase after them. In this way, they were lured away from the town. ¹⁷There was not a man left in Ai or Bethel* who did not chase after the Israelites, and the town was left wide open.

¹⁸Then the LORD said to Joshua, "Point the spear in your hand toward Ai, for I will hand the town over to you." Joshua did as he was commanded. ¹⁹As soon as Joshua gave this signal, all the men in ambush jumped up from their position and poured into the town. They quickly captured it and set it on fire.

²⁰When the men of Ai looked behind them, smoke from the town was filling the sky, and they had nowhere to go. For the Israelites who had fled in the direction of the wilderness now turned on their pursuers. ²¹When Joshua and all the other Israelites saw that the ambush had succeeded and that smoke was rising from the town, they turned and attacked the men of

Ai. ²²Meanwhile, the Israelites who were inside the town came out and attacked the enemy from the rear. So the men of Ai were caught in the middle, with Israelite fighters on both sides. Israel attacked them, and not a single person survived or escaped. ²³Only the king of Ai was taken alive and brought to Joshua.

²⁴When the Israelite army finished chasing and killing all the men of Ai in the open fields, they went back and finished off everyone inside. ²⁵So the entire population of Ai, including men and women, was wiped out that day—12,000 in all. ²⁶For Joshua kept holding out his spear until everyone who had lived in Ai was completely destroyed.* ²⁷Only the livestock and the treasures of the town were not destroyed, for the Israelites kept these as plunder for themselves, as the LORD had commanded Joshua. ²⁸So Joshua burned the town of Ai,* and it became a permanent mound of ruins, desolate to this very day.

²⁹Joshua impaled the king of Ai on a sharpened pole and left him there until evening. At sunset the Israelites took down the body, as Joshua commanded, and threw it in front of the town gate. They piled a great heap of stones over him that can still be seen today.

THE LORD'S COVENANT RENEWED

³⁰Then Joshua built an altar to the LORD, the God of Israel, on Mount Ebal. ³¹He followed the commands that Moses the LORD's servant had written in the Book of Instruction: "Make me an altar from stones that are uncut and have not been shaped with iron tools."* Then on the altar they presented burnt offerings and peace offerings to the LORD. ³²And as the Israelites watched, Joshua copied onto the stones of the altar* the instructions Moses had given them.

³³Then all the Israelites—foreigners and native-born alike—along with the elders, officers, and judges, were divided into two groups. One group stood in front of Mount Gerizim, the other in front of Mount Ebal. Each group faced the other, and between them stood the Levitical priests carrying the Ark of the LORD's Covenant. This was all done according to the commands that Moses, the servant

8:14 Hebrew *the Arabah.*   8:17 Some manuscripts lack *or Bethel.*   8:26 The Hebrew term used here refers to the complete consecration of things or people to the LORD, either by destroying them or by giving them as an offering.   8:28 *Ai* means "ruin."   8:31 Exod 20:25; Deut 27:5-6.   8:32 Hebrew *onto the stones.*

....

REFRESHER COURSE
(8:33-35) After Israel's military victory at Ai, Joshua celebrated by thanking God and reading God's laws to the people of Israel. God knows how easily we forget. We, like the Israelites, constantly need to review what God says. Daily Bible reading can continually refresh our memory. We should read the Bible as a constant reminder of who God is and what we can become.

of the LORD, had previously given for blessing the people of Israel.

³⁴Joshua then read to them all the blessings and curses Moses had written in the Book of Instruction. ³⁵Every word of every command that Moses had ever given was read to the entire assembly of Israel, including the women and children and the foreigners who lived among them.

9 **THE GIBEONITES DECEIVE ISRAEL** Now all the kings west of the Jordan River heard about what had happened. These were the kings of the Hittites, Amorites, Canaanites, Perizzites, Hivites, and Jebusites, who lived in the hill country, in the western foothills,* and along the coast of the Mediterranean Sea* as far north as the Lebanon mountains. ²These kings combined their armies to fight as one against Joshua and the Israelites.

³But when the people of Gibeon heard what Joshua had done to Jericho and Ai, ⁴they resorted to deception to save themselves. They sent ambassadors to Joshua, loading their donkeys with weathered saddlebags and old, patched wineskins. ⁵They put on worn-out, patched sandals and ragged clothes. And the bread they took with them was dry and moldy. ⁶When they arrived at the camp of Israel at Gilgal, they told Joshua and the men of Israel, "We have come from a distant land to ask you to make a peace treaty with us."

⁷The Israelites replied to these Hivites, "How do we know you don't live nearby? For if you do, we cannot make a treaty with you."

⁸They replied, "We are your servants."

"But who are you?" Joshua demanded. "Where do you come from?"

⁹They answered, "Your servants have come from a very distant country. We have heard of the might of the LORD your God and of all he did in Egypt. ¹⁰We have also heard what he did to the two Amorite kings east of the Jordan River—King Sihon of Heshbon and King Og of Bashan (who lived in Ashtaroth). ¹¹So our elders and all our people instructed us, 'Take supplies for a long journey. Go meet with the people of Israel and tell them, "We are your servants; please make a treaty with us."'

¹²"This bread was hot from the ovens when we left our homes. But now, as you can see, it is dry and moldy. ¹³These wineskins were new when we filled them, but now they are old and split open. And our clothing and sandals are worn out from our very long journey."

¹⁴So the Israelites examined their food, but they did not consult the LORD. ¹⁵Then Joshua made a peace treaty with them and guaranteed their safety, and the leaders of the community ratified their agreement with a binding oath.

¹⁶Three days after making the treaty, they learned that these people actually lived nearby! ¹⁷The Israelites set out at once to investigate and reached their towns in three days. The names of these towns were Gibeon, Kephirah, Beeroth, and Kiriath-jearim. ¹⁸But the Israelites did not attack the towns, for the Israelite leaders had made a vow to them in the name of the LORD, the God of Israel.

The people of Israel grumbled against their leaders because of the treaty. ¹⁹But the leaders replied, "Since we have sworn an oath in the presence of the LORD, the God of Israel, we cannot touch them. ²⁰This is what we must do. We must let them live, for divine anger would come upon us if we broke our oath. ²¹Let them live." So they made them woodcutters and water carriers for the entire community, as the Israelite leaders directed.

²²Joshua called together the Gibeonites and said, "Why did you lie to us? Why did you say that you live in a distant land when you live right here among us? ²³May you be cursed! From now on you will always be servants who cut wood and carry water for the house of my God."

²⁴They replied, "We did it because we—your servants—were clearly told that the LORD your God commanded his servant Moses to give you this entire land and to destroy all the people living in it. So we feared greatly for our lives because of you. That is why we have done this. ²⁵Now we are at your mercy—do to us whatever you think is right."

²⁶So Joshua did not allow the people of Israel to kill them. ²⁷But that day he made the Gibeonites the woodcutters and water carriers for the community of Israel and for the altar of the LORD—wherever the LORD would choose to build it. And that is what they do to this day.

10 **ISRAEL DEFEATS THE SOUTHERN ARMIES** Adoni-zedek, king of Jerusalem, heard that Joshua had captured and completely destroyed* Ai and killed its king, just as he had destroyed the town of Jericho and killed its king. He also learned that the Gibeonites had made peace with Israel and were now their allies. ²He and his people became very afraid when they heard all this because Gibeon was

9:1a Hebrew *the Shephelah.*   **9:1b** Hebrew *the Great Sea.*   **10:1** The Hebrew term used here refers to the complete consecration of things or people to the LORD, either by destroying them or by giving them as an offering; also in 10:28, 35, 37, 39, 40.

a large town—as large as the royal cities and larger than Ai. And the Gibeonite men were strong warriors.

³So King Adoni-zedek of Jerusalem sent messengers to several other kings: Hoham of Hebron, Piram of Jarmuth, Japhia of Lachish, and Debir of Eglon. ⁴"Come and help me destroy Gibeon," he urged them, "for they have made peace with Joshua and the people of Israel." ⁵So these five Amorite kings combined their armies for a united attack. They moved all their troops into place and attacked Gibeon.

⁶The men of Gibeon quickly sent messengers to Joshua at his camp in Gilgal. "Don't abandon your servants now!" they pleaded. "Come at once! Save us! Help us! For all the Amorite kings who live in the hill country have joined forces to attack us."

⁷So Joshua and his entire army, including his best warriors, left Gilgal and set out for Gibeon. ⁸"Do not be afraid of them," the LORD said to Joshua, "for I have given you victory over them. Not a single one of them will be able to stand up to you."

⁹Joshua traveled all night from Gilgal and took the Amorite armies by surprise. ¹⁰The LORD threw them into a panic, and the Israelites slaughtered great numbers of them at Gibeon. Then the Israelites chased the enemy along the road to Beth-horon, killing them all along the way to Azekah and Makkedah. ¹¹As the Amorites retreated down the road from Beth-horon, the LORD destroyed them with a terrible hailstorm from heaven that continued until they reached Azekah. The hail killed more of the enemy than the Israelites killed with the sword.

¹²On the day the LORD gave the Israelites victory over the Amorites, Joshua prayed to the LORD in front of all the people of Israel. He said,

"Let the sun stand still over Gibeon,
and the moon over the valley of Aijalon."

¹³So the sun stood still and the moon stayed in place until the nation of Israel had defeated its enemies.

Is this event not recorded in *The Book of Jashar**? The sun stayed in the middle of the sky, and it did not set as on a normal day.* ¹⁴There has never been a day like this one before or since, when the LORD answered such a prayer. Surely the LORD fought for Israel that day!

¹⁵Then Joshua and the Israelite army returned to their camp at Gilgal.

10:13a Or *The Book of the Upright.* 10:13b Or *did not set for about a whole day.*

JOSHUA KILLS THE FIVE SOUTHERN KINGS

¹⁶During the battle the five kings escaped and hid in a cave at Makkedah. ¹⁷When Joshua heard that they had been found, ¹⁸he issued this command: "Cover the opening of the cave with large rocks, and place guards at the entrance to keep the kings inside. ¹⁹The rest of you continue chasing the enemy and cut them down from the rear. Don't give them a chance to get back to their towns, for the LORD your God has given you victory over them."

²⁰So Joshua and the Israelite army continued the slaughter and crushed the enemy. They totally wiped out the five armies except for a tiny remnant that managed to reach their fortified towns. ²¹Then the Israelites returned safely to Joshua in the camp at Makkedah. After that, no one dared to speak even a word against Israel.

²²Then Joshua said, "Remove the rocks covering the opening of the cave, and bring the five kings to me." ²³So they brought the five kings out of the cave—the kings of Jerusalem, Hebron, Jarmuth, Lachish, and Eglon. ²⁴When they brought them out, Joshua told the commanders of his army, "Come and put your feet on the kings' necks." And they did as they were told.

²⁵"Don't ever be afraid or discouraged," Joshua told his men. "Be strong and courageous, for the LORD is going to do this to all of your enemies." ²⁶Then Joshua killed each of the five kings and impaled them on five sharpened poles, where they hung until evening.

²⁷As the sun was going down, Joshua gave instructions for the bodies of the kings to be taken down from the poles and thrown into the cave where they had been hiding. Then they covered the opening of the cave with a pile of large rocks, which remains to this very day.

ISRAEL DESTROYS THE SOUTHERN TOWNS

²⁸That same day Joshua captured and destroyed the town of Makkedah. He killed everyone in it, including the king, leaving no survivors. He destroyed them all, and he killed the king of Makkedah as he had killed the king of Jericho. ²⁹Then Joshua and the Israelites went to Libnah and attacked it. ³⁰There, too,

HOPE FOR THE FUTURE
(10:25) With God's help, Israel won a battle against five Amorite armies (10:1-14). Joshua told his men never to be afraid, because God would give them similar victories over their remaining enemies. The same God who empowered Joshua and his troops and led us in the past will help us with our present and future needs. Reminding ourselves of God's past faithfulness will give us hope for the struggles that lie ahead.

the Lord gave them the town and its king. He killed everyone in it, leaving no survivors. Then Joshua killed the king of Libnah as he had killed the king of Jericho.

³¹From Libnah, Joshua and the Israelites went to Lachish and attacked it. ³²Here again, the Lord gave them Lachish. Joshua took it on the second day and killed everyone in it, just as he had done at Libnah. ³³During the attack on Lachish, King Horam of Gezer arrived with his army to help defend the town. But Joshua's men killed him and his army, leaving no survivors.

³⁴Then Joshua and the Israelite army went on to Eglon and attacked it. ³⁵They captured it that day and killed everyone in it. He completely destroyed everyone, just as he had done at Lachish. ³⁶From Eglon, Joshua and the Israelite army went up to Hebron and attacked it. ³⁷They captured the town and killed everyone in it, including its king, leaving no survivors. They did the same thing to all of its surrounding villages. And just as he had done at Eglon, he completely destroyed the entire population.

³⁸Then Joshua and the Israelites turned back and attacked Debir. ³⁹He captured the town, its king, and all of its surrounding villages. He completely destroyed everyone in it, leaving no survivors. He did to Debir and its king just what he had done to Hebron and to Libnah and its king.

⁴⁰So Joshua conquered the whole region—the kings and people of the hill country, the Negev, the western foothills,* and the mountain slopes. He completely destroyed everyone in the land, leaving no survivors, just as the Lord, the God of Israel, had commanded. ⁴¹Joshua slaughtered them from Kadesh-barnea to Gaza and from the region around the town of Goshen up to Gibeon. ⁴²Joshua conquered all these kings and their land in a single campaign, for the Lord, the God of Israel, was fighting for his people.

⁴³Then Joshua and the Israelite army returned to their camp at Gilgal.

11 ISRAEL DEFEATS THE NORTHERN ARMIES When King Jabin of Hazor

....

A THOROUGH RESPONSE
(10:40-43) God had commanded Joshua to conquer the people of Canaan to allow God's people to settle in this territory. Joshua did his part thoroughly. When God orders us to eliminate elements in our lives that cause us to do wrong (for example, Internet porn or TV shows that make us unsatisfied with our lives), we must not pause to debate, negotiate, or rationalize. Instead, like Joshua, our response must be swift and complete.

heard what had happened, he sent messages to the following kings: King Jobab of Madon; the king of Shimron; the king of Acshaph; ²all the kings of the northern hill country; the kings in the Jordan Valley south of Galilee*; the kings in the Galilean foothills*; the kings of Naphoth-dor on the west; ³the kings of Canaan, both east and west; the kings of the Amorites, the Hittites, the Perizzites, the Jebusites in the hill country, and the Hivites in the towns on the slopes of Mount Hermon in the land of Mizpah.

⁴All these kings came out to fight. Their combined armies formed a vast horde. And with all their horses and chariots, they covered the landscape like the sand on the seashore. ⁵The kings joined forces and established their camp around the water near Merom to fight against Israel.

⁶Then the Lord said to Joshua, "Do not be afraid of them. By this time tomorrow I will hand all of them over to Israel as dead men. Then you must cripple their horses and burn their chariots."

⁷So Joshua and all his fighting men traveled to the water near Merom and attacked suddenly. ⁸And the Lord gave them victory over their enemies. The Israelites chased them as far as Greater Sidon and Misrephoth-maim, and eastward into the valley of Mizpah, until not one enemy warrior was left alive. ⁹Then Joshua crippled the horses and burned all the chariots, as the Lord had instructed.

¹⁰Joshua then turned back and captured Hazor and killed its king. (Hazor had at one time been the capital of all these kingdoms.) ¹¹The Israelites completely destroyed* every living thing in the city, leaving no survivors. Not a single person was spared. And then Joshua burned the city.

¹²Joshua slaughtered all the other kings and their people, completely destroying them, just as Moses, the servant of the Lord, had commanded. ¹³But the Israelites did not burn any of the towns built on mounds except Hazor, which Joshua burned. ¹⁴And the Israelites took all the plunder and livestock of the ravaged towns for themselves. But they killed all the people, leaving no survivors. ¹⁵As the Lord had commanded his servant Moses, so Moses commanded Joshua. And Joshua did as he was told, carefully obeying all the commands that the Lord had given to Moses.

¹⁶So Joshua conquered the entire region—

10:40 Hebrew *the Shephelah.*   11:2a Hebrew *in the Arabah south of Kinnereth.*   11:2b Hebrew *the Shephelah;* also in 11:16.   11:11 The Hebrew term used here refers to the complete consecration of things or people to the Lord, either by destroying them or by giving them as an offering; also in 11:12, 20, 21.

the hill country, the entire Negev, the whole area around the town of Goshen, the western foothills, the Jordan Valley,* the mountains of Israel, and the Galilean foothills. ¹⁷The Israelite territory now extended all the way from Mount Halak, which leads up to Seir in the south, as far north as Baal-gad at the foot of Mount Hermon in the valley of Lebanon. Joshua killed all the kings of those territories, ¹⁸waging war for a long time to accomplish this. ¹⁹No one in this region made peace with the Israelites except the Hivites of Gibeon. All the others were defeated. ²⁰For the LORD hardened their hearts and caused them to fight the Israelites. So they were completely destroyed without mercy, as the LORD had commanded Moses.

²¹During this period Joshua destroyed all the descendants of Anak, who lived in the hill country of Hebron, Debir, Anab, and the entire hill country of Judah and Israel. He killed them all and completely destroyed their towns. ²²None of the descendants of Anak were left in all the land of Israel, though some still remained in Gaza, Gath, and Ashdod.

²³So Joshua took control of the entire land, just as the LORD had instructed Moses. He gave it to the people of Israel as their special possession, dividing the land among the tribes. So the land finally had rest from war.

12 KINGS DEFEATED EAST OF THE JORDAN

These are the kings east of the Jordan River who had been killed by the Israelites and whose land was taken. Their territory extended from the Arnon Gorge to Mount Hermon and included all the land east of the Jordan Valley.*

²King Sihon of the Amorites, who lived in Heshbon, was defeated. His kingdom included Aroer, on the edge of the Arnon Gorge, and extended from the middle of the Arnon Gorge to the Jabbok River, which serves as a border for the Ammonites. This territory included the southern half of the territory of Gilead. ³Sihon also controlled the Jordan Valley and regions to the east—from as far north as the Sea of Galilee to as far south as the Dead Sea,* including the road to Beth-jeshimoth and southward to the slopes of Pisgah.

⁴King Og of Bashan, the last of the Rephaites, lived at Ashtaroth and Edrei. ⁵He ruled a territory stretching from Mount Hermon to Salecah in the north and to all of Bashan in the east, and westward to the borders of the kingdoms of Geshur and Maacah. This territory included the northern half of Gilead, as far as the boundary of King Sihon of Heshbon.

⁶Moses, the servant of the LORD, and the Israelites had destroyed the people of King Sihon and King Og. And Moses gave their land as a possession to the tribes of Reuben, Gad, and the half-tribe of Manasseh.

KINGS DEFEATED WEST OF THE JORDAN ⁷The following is a list of the kings that Joshua and the Israelite armies defeated on the west side of the Jordan, from Baal-gad in the valley of Lebanon to Mount Halak, which leads up to Seir. (Joshua gave this land to the tribes of Israel as their possession, ⁸including the hill country, the western foothills,* the Jordan Valley, the mountain slopes, the Judean wilderness, and the Negev. The people who lived in this region were the Hittites, the Amorites, the Canaanites, the Perizzites, the Hivites, and the Jebusites.) These are the kings Israel defeated:

⁹ The king of Jericho
  The king of Ai, near Bethel
¹⁰ The king of Jerusalem
  The king of Hebron
¹¹ The king of Jarmuth
  The king of Lachish
¹² The king of Eglon
  The king of Gezer
¹³ The king of Debir
  The king of Geder
¹⁴ The king of Hormah
  The king of Arad
¹⁵ The king of Libnah
  The king of Adullam
¹⁶ The king of Makkedah
  The king of Bethel
¹⁷ The king of Tappuah
  The king of Hepher
¹⁸ The king of Aphek
  The king of Lasharon
¹⁹ The king of Madon
  The king of Hazor
²⁰ The king of Shimron-meron

....

PROGRESS
(11:16-23) Although the conquest of much of the land of Canaan seems to have happened quickly (we can read about it in one sitting), it actually took seven years. We often expect quick changes in our lives or quick victories over sin. But our journey with God is a lifelong process. Because changes and victories take time, many people grow impatient with God and feel like giving up. Are you wondering if you will ever make any progress in your life? Hold on to hope! One day you'll look back at this point in your life and be amazed at what God has done in you.

11:16 Hebrew *the Shephelah, the Arabah.*   **12:1** Hebrew *the Arabah;* also in 12:3, 8.   **12:3** Hebrew *from the Sea of Kinnereth to the Sea of the Arabah, which is the Salt Sea.*   **12:8** Hebrew *the Shephelah.*

THE CONQUERED LAND
Joshua displayed brilliant military strategy in the way he went about conquering the land of Canaan. He first captured the well-fortified (1) Jericho to gain a foothold in Canaan and to demonstrate the awesome might of the God of Israel. Then he gained the hill country around (2) Bethel. From there he subdued towns in the (3) lowlands. Then his army conquered important cities in the north, such as (4) Hazor. In all, Israel conquered land both east (12:1-6) and west (12:7-24) of the Jordan River, from (5) Mount Hermon in the north to (6) Mount Halak beyond the Negev in the south. Thirty-one kings and their cities had been defeated. The Israelites had overpowered the Hittites, the Amorites, the Canaanites, the Perizzites, the Hivites, and the Jebusites. Other people living in Canaan were yet to be conquered.

The broken lines (— · — ·) indicate modern boundaries.

The king of Acshaph
²¹ The king of Taanach
The king of Megiddo
²² The king of Kedesh
The king of Jokneam in Carmel
²³ The king of Dor in the town of Naphoth-dor*
The king of Goyim in Gilgal*
²⁴ The king of Tirzah.

In all, thirty-one kings were defeated.

13 THE LAND YET TO BE CONQUERED
When Joshua was an old man, the LORD said to him, "You are growing old, and much land remains to be conquered. ²This is the territory that remains: all the regions of the Philistines and the Geshurites, ³and the larger territory of the Canaanites, extending from the stream of Shihor on the border of Egypt, northward to the boundary of Ekron. It includes the territory of the five Philistine rulers of Gaza, Ashdod, Ashkelon, Gath, and Ekron. The land of the Avvites ⁴in the south also remains to be conquered. In the north, the following area has not yet been conquered: all the land of the Canaanites, including Mearah

12:23a Hebrew *Naphath-dor*, a variant spelling of Naphoth-dor.
12:23b Greek version reads *Goyim in Galilee*.

(which belongs to the Sidonians), stretching northward to Aphek on the border of the Amorites; 5the land of the Gebalites and all of the Lebanon mountain area to the east, from Baal-gad below Mount Hermon to Lebo-hamath; 6and all the hill country from Lebanon to Misrephoth-maim, including all the land of the Sidonians.

"I myself will drive these people out of the land ahead of the Israelites. So be sure to give this land to Israel as a special possession, just as I have commanded you. 7Include all this territory as Israel's possession when you divide this land among the nine tribes and the half-tribe of Manasseh."

THE LAND DIVIDED EAST OF THE JORDAN 8Half the tribe of Manasseh and the tribes of Reuben and Gad had already received their grants of land on the east side of the Jordan, for Moses, the servant of the LORD, had previously assigned this land to them.

9Their territory extended from Aroer on the edge of the Arnon Gorge (including the town in the middle of the gorge) to the plain beyond Medeba, as far as Dibon. 10It also included all the towns of King Sihon of the Amorites, who had reigned in Heshbon, and extended as far as the borders of Ammon. 11It included Gilead, the territory of the kingdoms of Geshur and Maacah, all of Mount Hermon, all of Bashan as far as Salecah, 12and all the territory of King Og of Bashan, who had reigned in Ashtaroth and Edrei. King Og was the last of the Rephaites, for Moses had attacked them and driven them out. 13But the Israelites failed to drive out the people of Geshur and Maacah, so they continue to live among the Israelites to this day.

AN ALLOTMENT FOR THE TRIBE OF LEVI 14Moses did not assign any allotment of land to the tribe of Levi. Instead, as the LORD had promised them, their allotment came from the offerings burned on the altar to the LORD, the God of Israel.

THE LAND GIVEN TO THE TRIBE OF REUBEN 15Moses had assigned the following area to the clans of the tribe of Reuben.

16Their territory extended from Aroer on the edge of the Arnon Gorge (including the

13:25 Hebrew *in front of.* 13:26 Hebrew *Li-debir,* apparently a variant spelling of Lo-debar (compare 2 Sam 9:4; 17:27; Amos 6:13). 13:27 Hebrew *Sea of Kinnereth.*

town in the middle of the gorge) to the plain beyond Medeba. 17It included Heshbon and the other towns on the plain—Dibon, Bamoth-baal, Beth-baal-meon, 18Jahaz, Kedemoth, Mephaath, 19Kiriathaim, Sibmah, Zereth-shahar on the hill above the valley, 20Beth-peor, the slopes of Pisgah, and Beth-jeshimoth.

21The land of Reuben also included all the towns of the plain and the entire kingdom of Sihon. Sihon was the Amorite king who had reigned in Heshbon and was killed by Moses along with the leaders of Midian—Evi, Rekem, Zur, Hur, and Reba—princes living in the region who were allied with Sihon. 22The Israelites had also killed Balaam son of Beor, who used magic to tell the future. 23The Jordan River marked the western boundary for the tribe of Reuben. The towns and their surrounding villages in this area were given as a homeland to the clans of the tribe of Reuben.

THE LAND GIVEN TO THE TRIBE OF GAD 24Moses had assigned the following area to the clans of the tribe of Gad.

25Their territory included Jazer, all the towns of Gilead, and half of the land of Ammon, as far as the town of Aroer just west of* Rabbah. 26It extended from Heshbon to Ramath-mizpeh and Betonim, and from Mahanaim to the territory of Lo-debar.* 27In the valley were Beth-haram, Beth-nimrah, Succoth, Zaphon, and the rest of the kingdom of King Sihon of Heshbon. The western boundary ran along the Jordan River, extended as far north as the tip of the Sea of Galilee,* and then turned eastward. 28The towns and their surrounding villages in this area were given as a homeland to the clans of the tribe of Gad.

THE LAND GIVEN TO THE HALF-TRIBE OF MANASSEH 29Moses had assigned the following area to the clans of the half-tribe of Manasseh.

....

THE AGE OF EXPERIENCE
(13:1) Joshua was 85 to 100 years old at this time. Yet God still had work for him to do. Our culture often glorifies the young and strong, and sets aside those who are older. But older people are filled with the wisdom that comes with experience. They are capable of serving if given the chance and should be encouraged to do so. Think about the older people you know. How can you learn from their experience?

30 Their territory extended from Mahanaim, including all of Bashan, all the former kingdom of King Og, and the sixty towns of Jair in Bashan. 31 It also included half of Gilead and King Og's royal cities of Ashtaroth and Edrei. All this was given to the clans of the descendants of Makir, who was Manasseh's son.

32 These are the allotments Moses had made while he was on the plains of Moab, across the Jordan River, east of Jericho. 33 But Moses gave no allotment of land to the tribe of Levi, for the Lord, the God of Israel, had promised that he himself would be their allotment.

14 THE LAND DIVIDED WEST OF THE JOR- DAN

The remaining tribes of Israel received land in Canaan as allotted by Eleazar the priest, Joshua son of Nun, and the tribal leaders. 2 These nine and a half tribes received their grants of land by means of sacred lots, in accordance with the Lord's command through Moses. 3 Moses had already given a grant of land to the two and a half tribes on the east side of the Jordan River, but he had given the Levites no such allotment. 4 The descendants of Joseph had become two separate tribes— Manasseh and Ephraim. And the Levites were given no land at all, only towns to live in with surrounding pasturelands for their livestock and all their possessions. 5 So the land was distributed in strict accordance with the Lord's commands to Moses.

CALEB REQUESTS HIS LAND 6 A delegation from the tribe of Judah, led by Caleb son of Jephunneh the Kenizzite, came to Joshua at Gilgal. Caleb said to Joshua, "Remember what the Lord said to Moses, the man of God, about you

and me when we were at Kadesh-barnea. 7 I was forty years old when Moses, the servant of the Lord, sent me from Kadesh-barnea to explore the land of Canaan. I returned and gave an honest report, 8 but my brothers who went with me frightened the people from entering the Promised Land. For my part, I wholeheartedly followed the Lord my God. 9 So that day Moses solemnly promised me, 'The land of Canaan on which you were just walking will be your grant of land and that of your descendants forever, because you wholeheartedly followed the Lord my God.'

10 "Now, as you can see, the Lord has kept me alive and well as he promised for all these forty-five years since Moses made this promise—even while Israel wandered in the wilderness. Today I am eighty-five years old. 11 I am as strong now as I was when Moses sent me on that journey, and I can still travel and fight as well as I could then. 12 So give me the hill country that the Lord promised me. You will remember that as scouts we found the descendants of Anak living there in great, walled towns. But if the Lord is with me, I will drive them out of the land, just as the Lord said."

13 So Joshua blessed Caleb son of Jephunneh and gave Hebron to him as his portion of land. 14 Hebron still belongs to the descendants of Caleb son of Jephunneh the Kenizzite because he wholeheartedly followed the Lord, the God of Israel. 15 (Previously Hebron had been called Kiriath-arba. It had been named after Arba, a great hero of the descendants of Anak.)

And the land had rest from war.

15 THE LAND GIVEN TO THE TRIBE OF JUDAH

The allotment for the clans of the tribe of Judah reached southward to the border of Edom, as far south as the wilderness of Zin.

2 The southern boundary began at the south bay of the Dead Sea,* 3 ran south of Scorpion Pass* into the wilderness of Zin, and then went south of Kadesh-barnea to Hezron. Then it went up to Addar, where it turned toward Karka. 4 From there it passed to Azmon until it finally reached the Brook of Egypt, which it followed to the Mediterranean Sea.* This was their* southern boundary.

5 The eastern boundary extended along the Dead Sea to the mouth of the Jordan River.

TOTAL OBEDIENCE
(14:1-5) The land was divided exactly as God had instructed Moses years earlier. Joshua followed God's commands precisely. Often we believe that "almost" is close enough. This idea can carry over into our spiritual lives. For example, we may follow God's Word as long as we agree with it but ignore it when the demands seem difficult. But God is looking for leaders who follow his instructions thoroughly. Does that describe you?

PROMISE KEEPER
(14:6-13) When Joshua gave Caleb his land, he was fulfilling a promise God had made to Caleb 45 years earlier. How about you? Are you this reliable? God is. Even today he honors promises he made thousands of years ago. In fact, some of his greatest promises are yet to be fulfilled. How does the knowledge of God's faithfulness make you feel? Let your faith grow as you understand how God keeps his word.

15:2 Hebrew *the Salt Sea;* also in 15:5. **15:3** Hebrew *Akrabbim.* **15:4a** Hebrew *the sea;* also in 15:11. **15:4b** Hebrew *your.*

The northern boundary began at the bay where the Jordan River empties into the Dead Sea, ⁶went up from there to Beth-hoglah, then proceeded north of Beth-arabah to the Stone of Bohan. (Bohan was Reuben's son.) ⁷From that point it went through the valley of Achor to Debir, turning north toward Gilgal, which is across from the slopes of Adummim on the south side of the valley. From there the boundary extended to the springs at En-shemesh and on to En-rogel. ⁸The boundary then passed through the valley of Ben-Hinnom, along the southern slopes of the Jebusites, where the city of Jerusalem is located. Then it went west to the top of the mountain above the valley of Hinnom, and on up to the northern end of the valley of Rephaim. ⁹From there the boundary extended from the top of the mountain to the spring at the waters of Nephtoah,* and from there to the towns on Mount Ephron. Then it turned toward Baalah (that is, Kiriath-jearim). ¹⁰The boundary circled west of Baalah to Mount Seir, passed along to the town of Kesalon on the northern slope of Mount Jearim, and went down to Beth-shemesh and on to Timnah. ¹¹The boundary then proceeded to the slope of the hill north of Ekron, where it turned toward Shikkeron and Mount Baalah. It passed Jabneel and ended at the Mediterranean Sea.

¹²The western boundary was the shoreline of the Mediterranean Sea.*

These are the boundaries for the clans of the tribe of Judah.

THE LAND GIVEN TO CALEB

¹³The LORD commanded Joshua to assign some of Judah's territory to Caleb son of Jephunneh. So Caleb was given the town of Kiriath-arba (that is, Hebron), which had been named after Anak's ancestor. ¹⁴Caleb drove out the three groups of Anakites—the descendants of Sheshai, Ahiman, and Talmai, the sons of Anak.

¹⁵From there he went to fight against the people living in the town of Debir (formerly called Kiriath-sepher). ¹⁶Caleb said, "I will give my daughter Acsah in marriage to the one who attacks and captures Kiriath-sepher." ¹⁷Othniel, the son of Caleb's brother Kenaz, was the one who conquered it, so Acsah became Othniel's wife.

¹⁸When Acsah married Othniel, she urged him* to ask her father for a field. As she got down off her donkey, Caleb asked her, "What's the matter?"

¹⁹She said, "Give me another gift. You have already given me land in the Negev; now please give me springs of water, too." So Caleb gave her the upper and lower springs.

THE TOWNS ALLOTTED TO JUDAH

²⁰This was the homeland allocated to the clans of the tribe of Judah.

²¹The towns of Judah situated along the borders of Edom in the extreme south were Kabzeel, Eder, Jagur, ²²Kinah, Dimonah, Adadah, ²³Kedesh, Hazor, Ithnan, ²⁴Ziph, Telem, Bealoth, ²⁵Hazor-hadattah, Kerioth-hezron (that is, Hazor), ²⁶Amam, Shema, Moladah, ²⁷Hazar-gaddah, Heshmon, Beth-pelet, ²⁸Hazar-shual, Beersheba, Biziothiah, ²⁹Baalah, Iim, Ezem, ³⁰Eltolad, Kesil, Hormah, ³¹Ziklag, Madmannah, Sansannah, ³²Lebaoth, Shilhim, Ain, and Rimmon—twenty-nine towns with their surrounding villages.

³³The following towns situated in the western foothills* were also given to Judah: Eshtaol, Zorah, Ashnah, ³⁴Zanoah, En-gannim, Tappuah, Enam, ³⁵Jarmuth, Adullam, Socoh, Azekah, ³⁶Shaaraim, Adithaim, Gederah, and Gederothaim—fourteen towns with their surrounding villages.

³⁷Also included were Zenan, Hadashah, Migdal-gad, ³⁸Dilean, Mizpeh, Joktheel, ³⁹Lachish, Bozkath, Eglon, ⁴⁰Cabbon, Lahmam, Kitlish, ⁴¹Gederoth, Beth-dagon, Naamah, and Makkedah—sixteen towns with their surrounding villages.

⁴²Besides these, there were Libnah, Ether, Ashan, ⁴³Iphtah, Ashnah, Nezib, ⁴⁴Keilah, Aczib, and Mareshah—nine towns with their surrounding villages.

⁴⁵The territory of the tribe of Judah also included Ekron and its surrounding settlements and villages. ⁴⁶From Ekron the boundary extended west and included the towns near Ashdod with their surrounding villages. ⁴⁷It also included Ashdod with its surrounding settlements and villages and Gaza with its settlements and villages, as far as the Brook of Egypt and along the coast of the Mediterranean Sea.

⁴⁸Judah also received the following towns in the hill country: Shamir, Jattir, Socoh, ⁴⁹Dannah, Kiriath-sannah (that is, Debir), ⁵⁰Anab, Eshtemoh, Anim, ⁵¹Goshen,

15:9 Or *the spring at Me-nephtoah.*   **15:12** Hebrew *the Great Sea;* also in 15:47.   **15:18** Some Greek manuscripts read *he urged her.* **15:33** Hebrew *the Shephelah.*

Holon, and Giloh—eleven towns with their surrounding villages.

⁵²Also included were the towns of Arab, Dumah, Eshan, ⁵³Janim, Beth-tappuah, Aphekah, ⁵⁴Humtah, Kiriath-arba (that is, Hebron), and Zior—nine towns with their surrounding villages.

⁵⁵Besides these, there were Maon, Carmel, Ziph, Juttah, ⁵⁶Jezreel, Jokdeam, Zanoah, ⁵⁷Kain, Gibeah, and Timnah—ten towns with their surrounding villages.

⁵⁸In addition, there were Halhul, Beth-zur, Gedor, ⁵⁹Maarath, Beth-anoth, and Eltekon—six towns with their surrounding villages.

⁶⁰There were also Kiriath-baal (that is, Kiriath-jearim) and Rabbah—two towns with their surrounding villages.

⁶¹In the wilderness there were the towns of Beth-arabah, Middin, Secacah, ⁶²Nibshan, the City of Salt, and En-gedi—six towns with their surrounding villages.

⁶³But the tribe of Judah could not drive out the Jebusites, who lived in the city of Jerusalem, so the Jebusites live there among the people of Judah to this day.

16 THE LAND GIVEN TO EPHRAIM AND WEST MANASSEH
The allotment for the descendants of Joseph extended from the Jordan River near Jericho, east of the springs of Jericho, through the wilderness and into the hill country of Bethel. ²From Bethel (that is, Luz)* it ran over to Ataroth in the territory of the Arkites. ³Then it

....

A DOUBLE PORTION
(16:1-10) *Though Joseph was one of Jacob's 12 sons, he did not have a tribe named after him. Yet his family group received a double portion of the land because Reuben had messed up years earlier (see Gen 49:3-4). Reuben's act of extreme disrespect for his father lost him the firstborn's traditional double-portion legacy. Instead, the double portion was given to Joseph's two sons, Ephraim and Manasseh, whom Jacob considered as his own (Gen 48:5). If you believe in Jesus, you are one of God's own. What "portions" of God's mercy have you received recently?*

UPDATING TRADITION
(17:3-4) *By giving land to the daughters of Zelophehad, Joshua honored a promise that Moses had made earlier (see Num 27:1-11). Although Israelite women did not traditionally inherit property, Moses put justice ahead of tradition and gave these five women the land they deserved.*

Ever allow a tradition to decide your actions? It's easy to refuse to honor a reasonable request because of tradition. But God sometimes calls us to break a tradition and replace it with a new one.

descended westward to the territory of the Japhletites as far as Lower Beth-horon, then to Gezer and over to the Mediterranean Sea.*

⁴This was the homeland allocated to the families of Joseph's sons, Manasseh and Ephraim.

THE LAND GIVEN TO EPHRAIM ⁵The following territory was given to the clans of the tribe of Ephraim.

The boundary of their homeland began at Ataroth-addar in the east. From there it ran to Upper Beth-horon, ⁶then on to the Mediterranean Sea. From Micmethath on the north, the boundary curved eastward past Taanath-shiloh to the east of Janoah. ⁷From Janoah it turned southward to Ataroth and Naarah, touched Jericho, and ended at the Jordan River. ⁸From Tappuah the boundary extended westward, following the Kanah Ravine to the Mediterranean Sea. This is the homeland allocated to the clans of the tribe of Ephraim.

⁹In addition, some towns with their surrounding villages in the territory allocated to the half-tribe of Manasseh were set aside for the tribe of Ephraim. ¹⁰They did not drive the Canaanites out of Gezer, however, so the people of Gezer live as slaves among the people of Ephraim to this day.

17 THE LAND GIVEN TO WEST MANASSEH
The next allotment of land was given to the half-tribe of Manasseh, the descendants of Joseph's older son. Makir, the firstborn son of Manasseh, was the father of Gilead. Because his descendants were experienced soldiers, the regions of Gilead and Bashan on the east side of the Jordan had already been given to them. ²So the allotment on the west side of the Jordan was for the remaining families within the clans of the tribe of Manasseh: Abiezer, Helek, Asriel, Shechem, Hepher, and Shemida. These clans represent the male descendants of Manasseh son of Joseph.

³However, Zelophehad, a descendant of Hepher son of Gilead, son of Makir, son of Manasseh, had no sons. He had only daughters, whose names were Mahlah, Noah, Hoglah, Milcah, and Tirzah. ⁴These women came to Eleazar the priest, Joshua son of Nun, and the Israelite leaders and said, "The LORD commanded Moses to give us a grant of land along with the men of our tribe."

16:2 As in Greek version (also see 18:13); Hebrew reads *From Bethel to Luz.* **16:3** Hebrew *the sea;* also in 16:6, 8.

So Joshua gave them a grant of land along with their uncles, as the LORD had commanded. ⁵As a result, Manasseh's total allocation came to ten parcels of land, in addition to the land of Gilead and Bashan across the Jordan River, ⁶because the female descendants of Manasseh received a grant of land along with the male descendants. (The land of Gilead was given to the rest of the male descendants of Manasseh.)

⁷The boundary of the tribe of Manasseh extended from the border of Asher to Micmethath, near Shechem. Then the boundary went south from Micmethath to the settlement near the spring of Tappuah. ⁸The land surrounding Tappuah belonged to Manasseh, but the town of Tappuah itself, on the border of Manasseh's territory, belonged to the tribe of Ephraim. ⁹From the spring of Tappuah, the boundary of Manasseh followed the Kanah Ravine to the Mediterranean Sea.* Several towns south of the ravine were inside Manasseh's territory, but they actually belonged to the tribe of Ephraim. ¹⁰In general, however, the land south of the ravine belonged to Ephraim, and the land north of the ravine belonged to Manasseh. Manasseh's boundary ran along the northern side of the ravine and ended at the Mediterranean Sea. North of Manasseh was the territory of Asher, and to the east was the territory of Issachar.

¹¹The following towns within the territory of Issachar and Asher, however, were given to Manasseh: Beth-shan,* Ibleam, Dor (that is, Naphoth-dor),* Endor, Taanach, and Megiddo, each with their surrounding settlements.

¹²But the descendants of Manasseh were unable to occupy these towns. They could not drive out the Canaanites who continued to live there. ¹³Later, however, when the Israelites became strong enough, they forced the Canaanites to work as slaves. But they did not drive them out of the land.

¹⁴The descendants of Joseph came to Joshua and asked, "Why have you given us only one portion of land as our homeland when the LORD has blessed us with so many people?"

¹⁵Joshua replied, "If there are so many of you, and if the hill country of Ephraim is not large enough for you, clear out land for yourselves in the forest where the Perizzites and Rephaites live."

¹⁶The descendants of Joseph responded, "It's true that the hill country is not large enough for us. But all the Canaanites in the lowlands have iron chariots, both those in Beth-shan and its surrounding settlements and those in the valley of Jezreel. They are too strong for us."

¹⁷Then Joshua said to the tribes of Ephraim and Manasseh, the descendants of Joseph, "Since you are so large and strong, you will be given more than one portion. ¹⁸The forests of the hill country will be yours as well. Clear as much of the land as you wish, and take possession of its farthest corners. And you will drive out the Canaanites from the valleys, too, even though they are strong and have iron chariots."

18 THE ALLOTMENTS OF THE REMAINING LAND

Now that the land was under Israelite control, the entire community of Israel gathered at Shiloh and set up the Tabernacle.* ²But there remained seven tribes who had not yet been allotted their grants of land.

³Then Joshua asked them, "How long are you going to wait before taking possession of the remaining land the LORD, the God of your ancestors, has given to you? ⁴Select three men from each tribe, and I will send them out to explore the land and map it out. They will then return to me with a written report of their proposed divisions of their new homeland. ⁵Let them divide the land into seven sections, excluding Judah's territory in the south and Joseph's territory in the north. ⁶And when you record the seven divisions of the land and bring them to me, I will cast sacred lots in the presence of the LORD our God to assign land to each tribe.

⁷"The Levites, however, will not receive any allotment of land. Their role as priests of the LORD is their allotment. And the tribes of Gad, Reuben, and the half-tribe of Manasseh won't receive any more land, for they have already received their grant of land, which Moses, the servant of the LORD, gave them on the east side of the Jordan River."

17:9 Hebrew *the sea;* also in 17:10.   17:11a Hebrew *Beth-shean,* a variant spelling of Beth-shan; also in 17:16.   17:11b The meaning of the Hebrew here is uncertain.   18:1 Hebrew *Tent of Meeting.*

....

PUTTING IT OFF
(18:3-6) Joshua wondered why some of the tribes were slow to claim their land. Like the Israelites, we sometimes delay doing jobs that seem large, difficult, boring, or disagreeable. Jobs we don't enjoy require concentration, teamwork, lots of encouragement, and accountability. Tempted to procrastinate? You might investigate the cause of the delay (fear; lack of confidence in your ability to finish the task). Then ask God to help you do what you need to do. Don't put it off!

⁸As the men started on their way to map out the land, Joshua commanded them, "Go and explore the land and write a description of it. Then return to me, and I will assign the land to the tribes by casting sacred lots here in the presence of the LORD at Shiloh." ⁹The men did as they were told and mapped the entire territory into seven sections, listing the towns in each section. They made a written record and then returned to Joshua in the camp at Shiloh. ¹⁰And there at Shiloh, Joshua cast sacred lots in the presence of the LORD to determine which tribe should have each section.

THE LAND GIVEN TO BENJAMIN ¹¹The first allotment of land went to the clans of the tribe of Benjamin. It lay between the territory assigned to the tribes of Judah and Joseph.

¹²The northern boundary of Benjamin's land began at the Jordan River, went north of the slope of Jericho, then west through the hill country and the wilderness of Beth-aven. ¹³From there the boundary went south to Luz (that is, Bethel) and proceeded down to Ataroth-addar on the hill that lies south of Lower Beth-horon.

¹⁴The boundary then made a turn and swung south along the western edge of the hill facing Beth-horon, ending at the village of Kiriath-baal (that is, Kiriath-jearim), a town belonging to the tribe of Judah. This was the western boundary.

¹⁵The southern boundary began at the outskirts of Kiriath-jearim. From that western point it ran* to the spring at the waters of Nephtoah,* ¹⁶and down to the base of the mountain beside the valley of Ben-Hinnom, at the northern end of the valley of Rephaim. From there it went down the valley of Hinnom, crossing south of the slope where the Jebusites lived, and continued down to En-rogel. ¹⁷From En-rogel the boundary proceeded in a northerly direction and came to En-shemesh and on to Geliloth (which is across from the slopes of Adummim). Then it went down to the Stone of Bohan. (Bohan was Reuben's son.) ¹⁸From there it passed along the north side of the slope overlooking the Jordan Valley.* The border then went down into the valley, ¹⁹ran past the north slope of Beth-hoglah, and ended at the north bay of the Dead Sea,* which is the southern end of the Jordan River. This was the southern boundary.

²⁰The eastern boundary was the Jordan River.

These were the boundaries of the homeland allocated to the clans of the tribe of Benjamin.

THE TOWNS GIVEN TO BENJAMIN ²¹These were the towns given to the clans of the tribe of Benjamin.

Jericho, Beth-hoglah, Emek-keziz, ²²Beth-arabah, Zemaraim, Bethel, ²³Avvim, Parah, Ophrah, ²⁴Kephar-ammoni, Ophni, and Geba—twelve towns with their surrounding villages. ²⁵Also Gibeon, Ramah, Beeroth, ²⁶Mizpah, Kephirah, Mozah, ²⁷Rekem, Irpeel, Taralah, ²⁸Zela, Haeleph, Jebus (that is, Jerusalem), Gibeah, and Kiriath*—fourteen towns with their surrounding villages.

This was the homeland allocated to the clans of the tribe of Benjamin.

19 **THE LAND GIVEN TO SIMEON** The second allotment of land went to the clans of the tribe of Simeon. Their homeland was surrounded by Judah's territory.

²Simeon's homeland included Beersheba, Sheba, Moladah, ³Hazar-shual, Balah, Ezem, ⁴Eltolad, Bethul, Hormah, ⁵Ziklag, Beth-marcaboth, Hazar-susah, ⁶Beth-lebaoth, and Sharuhen—thirteen towns with their surrounding villages. ⁷It also included Ain, Rimmon, Ether, and Ashan—four towns with their villages, ⁸including all the surrounding villages as far south as Baalath-beer (also known as Ramah of the Negev).

This was the homeland allocated to the clans of the tribe of Simeon. ⁹Their allocation of land came from part of what had been given to Judah because Judah's territory was too large for them. So the tribe of Simeon received an allocation within the territory of Judah.

THE LAND GIVEN TO ZEBULUN ¹⁰The third allotment of land went to the clans of the tribe of Zebulun.

The boundary of Zebulun's homeland started at Sarid. ¹¹From there it went west, going past Maralah, touching Dabbesheth, and proceeding to the brook east of Jokneam. ¹²In the other direction, the boundary went east from Sarid to the border of Kisloth-tabor, and from there

18:15a Or *From there it went to Mozah.* The meaning of the Hebrew is uncertain.   **18:15b** Or *the spring at Me-nephtoah.*   **18:18** Hebrew *overlooking the Arabah,* or *overlooking Beth-arabah.*   **18:19** Hebrew *Salt Sea.*   **18:28** Some Greek manuscripts read *Kiriath-jearim.*

to Daberath and up to Japhia. [13]Then it continued east to Gath-hepher, Eth-kazin, and Rimmon and turned toward Neah. [14]The northern boundary of Zebulun passed Hannathon and ended at the valley of Iphtah-el. [15]The towns in these areas included Kattath, Nahalal, Shimron, Idalah, and Bethlehem—twelve towns with their surrounding villages.

[16]The homeland allocated to the clans of the tribe of Zebulun included these towns and their surrounding villages.

THE LAND GIVEN TO ISSACHAR [17]The fourth allotment of land went to the clans of the tribe of Issachar.

[18]Its boundaries included the following towns: Jezreel, Kesulloth, Shunem, [19]Hapharaim, Shion, Anaharath, [20]Rabbith, Kishion, Ebez, [21]Remeth, En-gannim, En-haddah, and Beth-pazzez. [22]The boundary also touched Tabor, Shahazumah, and Beth-shemesh, ending at the Jordan River—sixteen towns with their surrounding villages.

[23]The homeland allocated to the clans of the tribe of Issachar included these towns and their surrounding villages.

THE LAND GIVEN TO ASHER [24]The fifth allotment of land went to the clans of the tribe of Asher.

[25]Its boundaries included these towns: Helkath, Hali, Beten, Acshaph, [26]Allammelech, Amad, and Mishal. The boundary on the west touched Carmel and Shihor-libnath, [27]then it turned east toward Beth-dagon, and ran as far as Zebulun in the valley of Iphtah-el, going north to Beth-emek and Neiel. It then continued north to Cabul, [28]Abdon,* Rehob, Hammon, Kanah, and as far as Greater Sidon. [29]Then the boundary turned toward Ramah and the fortress of Tyre, where it turned toward Hosah and came to the Mediterranean Sea.* The territory also included Mehebel, Aczib, [30]Ummah, Aphek, and Rehob—twenty-two towns with their surrounding villages.

[31]The homeland allocated to the clans of the tribe of Asher included these towns and their surrounding villages.

THE LAND GIVEN TO NAPHTALI [32]The sixth allotment of land went to the clans of the tribe of Naphtali.

[33]Its boundary ran from Heleph, from the oak at Zaanannim, and extended across to Adami-nekeb, Jabneel, and as far as Lakkum, ending at the Jordan River. [34]The western boundary ran past Aznoth-tabor, then to Hukkok, and touched the border of Zebulun in the south, the border of Asher on the west, and the Jordan River* on the east. [35]The fortified towns included in this territory were Ziddim, Zer, Hammath, Rakkath, Kinnereth, [36]Adamah, Ramah, Hazor, [37]Kedesh, Edrei, En-hazor, [38]Yiron, Migdal-el, Horem, Beth-anath, and Beth-shemesh—nineteen towns with their surrounding villages.

[39]The homeland allocated to the clans of the tribe of Naphtali included these towns and their surrounding villages.

THE LAND GIVEN TO DAN [40]The seventh allotment of land went to the clans of the tribe of Dan.

[41]The land allocated as their homeland included the following towns: Zorah, Eshtaol, Ir-shemesh, [42]Shaalabbin, Aijalon, Ithlah, [43]Elon, Timnah, Ekron, [44]Eltekeh, Gibbethon, Baalath, [45]Jehud, Bene-berak, Gath-rimmon, [46]Me-jarkon, Rakkon, and the territory across from Joppa.

[47]But the tribe of Dan had trouble taking possession of their land,* so they attacked the town of Laish.* They captured it, slaughtered its people, and settled there. They renamed the town Dan after their ancestor.

[48]The homeland allocated to the clans of the tribe of Dan included these towns and their surrounding villages.

THE LAND GIVEN TO JOSHUA [49]After all the land was divided among the tribes, the Israelites gave a piece of land to Joshua as his allocation. [50]For the LORD had said he

....

19:28 As in some Hebrew manuscripts (see also 21:30); most Hebrew manuscripts read *Ebron*.   **19:29** Hebrew *the sea*.   **19:34** Hebrew *and Judah at the Jordan River*.   **19:47a** Or *had trouble holding on to their land*.   **19:47b** Hebrew *Leshem*, a variant spelling of Laish.

WHEN THE GOING GETS TOUGH
(19:47-48) When the tribe of Dan decided that some of their land looked too difficult to conquer, they headed to Laish where a victory would be easier. Can you relate to that decision? Anyone can trust God when the going is easy. Our faith and courage are put to the test when things looks impossible. Do you believe that God is great enough to tackle your most difficult problem?

could have any town he wanted. He chose Timnath-serah in the hill country of Ephraim. He rebuilt the town and lived there.

⁵¹These are the territories that Eleazar the priest, Joshua son of Nun, and the tribal leaders allocated as grants of land to the tribes of Israel by casting sacred lots in the presence of the LORD at the entrance of the Tabernacle* at Shiloh. So the division of the land was completed.

20 THE CITIES OF REFUGE The LORD said to Joshua, ²"Now tell the Israelites to designate the cities of refuge, as I instructed Moses. ³Anyone who kills another person accidentally and unintentionally can run to one of these cities; they will be places of refuge from relatives seeking revenge for the person who was killed.

⁴"Upon reaching one of these cities, the one who caused the death will appear before the elders at the city gate and present his case. They must allow him to enter the city and give him a place to live among them. ⁵If the relatives of the victim come to avenge the killing, the leaders must not release the slayer to them, for he killed the other person unintentionally and without previous hostility. ⁶But the slayer must stay in that city and be tried by the local assembly, which will render a judgment. And he must continue to live in that city until the death of the high priest who was in office at the time of the accident. After that, he is free to return to his own home in the town from which he fled."

⁷The following cities were designated as cities of refuge: Kedesh of Galilee, in the hill country of Naphtali; Shechem, in the hill country of Ephraim; and Kiriath-arba (that is, Hebron), in the hill country of Judah. ⁸On the east side of the Jordan River, across from Jericho, the following cities were designated: Bezer, in the wilderness plain of the tribe of Reuben; Ramoth in Gilead, in the territory of the tribe of Gad; and Golan in Bashan, in the land of the tribe of Manasseh. ⁹These cities were set apart for all the Israelites as well as the foreigners living among them. Anyone who accidentally killed another person could take refuge in one of these cities. In this way, they could escape being killed in revenge prior to standing trial before the local assembly.

21 THE TOWNS GIVEN TO THE LEVITES Then the leaders of the tribe of Levi came to consult with Eleazar the priest, Joshua son of Nun, and the leaders of the other tribes of Israel. ²They came to them at

Shiloh in the land of Canaan and said, "The LORD commanded Moses to give us towns to live in and pasturelands for our livestock." ³So by the command of the LORD the people of Israel gave the Levites the following towns and pasturelands out of their own grants of land.

⁴The descendants of Aaron, who were members of the Kohathite clan within the tribe of Levi, were allotted thirteen towns that were originally assigned to the tribes of Judah, Simeon, and Benjamin. ⁵The other families of the Kohathite clan were allotted ten towns from the tribes of Ephraim, Dan, and the half-tribe of Manasseh.

⁶The clan of Gershon was allotted thirteen towns from the tribes of Issachar, Asher, Naphtali, and the half-tribe of Manasseh in Bashan. ⁷The clan of Merari was allotted twelve towns from the tribes of Reuben, Gad, and Zebulun.

⁸So the Israelites obeyed the LORD's command to Moses and assigned these towns and pasturelands to the Levites by casting sacred lots.

⁹The Israelites gave the following towns from the tribes of Judah and Simeon ¹⁰to the descendants of Aaron, who were members of the Kohathite clan within the tribe of Levi, since the sacred lot fell to them first: ¹¹Kiriath-arba (that is, Hebron), in the hill country of Judah, along with its surrounding pasturelands. (Arba was an ancestor of Anak.) ¹²But the open fields beyond the town and the surrounding villages were given to Caleb son of Jephunneh as his possession.

¹³The following towns with their pasturelands were given to the descendants of Aaron the priest: Hebron (a city of refuge for those who accidentally killed someone), Libnah, ¹⁴Jattir, Eshtemoa, ¹⁵Holon, Debir, ¹⁶Ain, Juttah, and Beth-shemesh—nine towns from these two tribes.

¹⁷From the tribe of Benjamin the priests were given the following towns with their pasturelands: Gibeon, Geba, ¹⁸Anathoth, and Almon—four towns. ¹⁹So in all, thirteen towns with their pasturelands were given to the priests, the descendants of Aaron.

²⁰The rest of the Kohathite clan from the tribe of Levi was allotted the following towns and pasturelands from the tribe of Ephraim: ²¹Shechem in the hill country of Ephraim (a city of refuge for those who accidentally killed someone), Gezer, ²²Kibzaim, and Beth-horon—four towns.

²³The following towns and pasturelands were allotted to the priests from the tribe of

19:51 Hebrew *Tent of Meeting.*

Dan: Eltekeh, Gibbethon, [24]Aijalon, and Gath-rimmon—four towns.

[25]The half-tribe of Manasseh allotted the following towns with their pasturelands to the priests: Taanach and Gath-rimmon—two towns. [26]So in all, ten towns with their pasturelands were given to the rest of the Kohathite clan.

[27]The descendants of Gershon, another clan within the tribe of Levi, received the following towns with their pasturelands from the half-tribe of Manasseh: Golan in Bashan (a city of refuge for those who accidentally killed someone) and Be-eshterah—two towns.

[28]From the tribe of Issachar they received the following towns with their pasturelands: Kishion, Daberath, [29]Jarmuth, and En-gannim—four towns.

[30]From the tribe of Asher they received the following towns with their pasturelands: Mishal, Abdon, [31]Helkath, and Rehob—four towns.

[32]From the tribe of Naphtali they received the following towns with their pasturelands: Kedesh in Galilee (a city of refuge for those who accidentally killed someone), Hammoth-dor, and Kartan—three towns. [33]So in all, thirteen towns with their pasturelands were allotted to the clan of Gershon.

[34]The rest of the Levites—the Merari clan—were given the following towns with their pasturelands from the tribe of Zebulun: Jokneam, Kartah, [35]Dimnah, and Nahalal—four towns.

[36]From the tribe of Reuben they received the following towns with their pasturelands: Bezer, Jahaz,* [37]Kedemoth, and Mephaath—four towns.

[38]From the tribe of Gad they received the following towns with their pasturelands: Ramoth in Gilead (a city of refuge for those who accidentally killed someone), Mahanaim, [39]Heshbon, and Jazer—four towns. [40]So in all, twelve towns were allotted to the clan of Merari.

[41]The total number of towns and pasturelands within Israelite territory given to the Levites came to forty-eight. [42]Every one of these towns had pasturelands surrounding it.

[43]So the LORD gave to Israel all the land he had sworn to give their ancestors, and they took possession of it and settled there. [44]And the LORD gave them rest on every side, just as he had solemnly promised their ancestors. None of their enemies could stand against them, for the LORD helped them conquer all their enemies. [45]Not a single one of all the good promises the LORD had given to the family of Israel was left unfulfilled; everything he had spoken came true.

22 THE EASTERN TRIBES RETURN HOME

Then Joshua called together the tribes of Reuben, Gad, and the half-tribe of Manasseh. [2]He told them, "You have done as Moses, the servant of the LORD, commanded you, and you have obeyed every order I have given you. [3]During all this time you have not deserted the other tribes. You have been careful to obey the commands of the LORD your God right up to the present day. [4]And now the LORD your God has given the other tribes rest, as he promised them. So go back home to the land that Moses, the servant of the LORD, gave you as your possession on the east side of the Jordan River. [5]But be very careful to obey all the commands and the instructions that Moses gave to you. Love the LORD your God, walk in all his ways, obey his commands, hold firmly to him, and serve him with all your heart and all your soul."

[6]So Joshua blessed them and sent them away, and they went home.

[7]Moses had given the land of Bashan, east of the Jordan River, to the half-tribe of Manasseh. (The other half of the tribe was given land west of the Jordan.) As Joshua sent them away and blessed them, [8]he said to them, "Go back to your homes with the great wealth you have taken from your enemies—the vast herds of livestock, the silver, gold, bronze, and iron, and the large supply of clothing. Share the plunder with your relatives."

[9]So the men of Reuben, Gad, and the half-tribe of Manasseh left the rest of Israel at Shiloh in the land of Canaan. They started the journey back to their own land of Gilead, the territory that belonged to them according to the LORD's command through Moses.

THE EASTERN TRIBES BUILD AN ALTAR

[10]But while they were still in Canaan, and when they came to a place called Geliloth* near the Jordan River, the men of Reuben, Gad, and the

···

FINISH THE JOB
(22:1-5) Before the conquest of Canaan had begun, the tribes of Reuben, Gad, and the half-tribe of Manasseh were given land on the east side of the Jordan River. But before they could settle down, they had to help the other tribes to conquer the land on the west side (Num 32:20-24). After they had carried out their duties, they were permitted to return to their families and build their cities. Follow-through is vital in God's work. How diligent are you to follow through on your promises?

21:36 Hebrew *Jahzah,* a variant spelling of Jahaz.   **22:10** Or *to the circle of stones;* similarly in 22:11.

half-tribe of Manasseh stopped to build a large and imposing altar.

[11]The rest of Israel heard that the people of Reuben, Gad, and the half-tribe of Manasseh had built an altar at Geliloth at the edge of the land of Canaan, on the west side of the Jordan River. [12]So the whole community of Israel gathered at Shiloh and prepared to go to war against them. [13]First, however, they sent a delegation led by Phinehas son of Eleazar, the priest, to talk with the tribes of Reuben, Gad, and the half-tribe of Manasseh. [14]In this delegation were ten leaders of Israel, one from each of the ten tribes, and each the head of his family within the clans of Israel.

[15]When they arrived in the land of Gilead, they said to the tribes of Reuben, Gad, and the half-tribe of Manasseh, [16]"The whole community of the LORD demands to know why you are betraying the God of Israel. How could you turn away from the LORD and build an altar for yourselves in rebellion against him? [17]Was our sin at Peor not enough? To this day we are not fully cleansed of it, even after the plague that struck the entire community of the LORD. [18]And yet today you are turning away from following the LORD. If you rebel against the LORD today, he will be angry with all of us tomorrow.

[19]"If you need the altar because the land you possess is defiled, then join us in the LORD's land, where the Tabernacle of the LORD is situated, and share our land with us. But do not rebel against the LORD or against us by building an altar other than the one true altar of the LORD our God. [20]Didn't divine anger fall on the entire community of Israel when Achan, a member of the clan of Zerah, sinned by stealing the things set apart for the LORD*? He was not the only one who died because of his sin."

[21]Then the people of Reuben, Gad, and the half-tribe of Manasseh answered the heads of the clans of Israel: [22]"The LORD, the Mighty One, is God! The LORD, the Mighty One, is God! He knows the truth, and may Israel know it, too! We have not built the altar in treacherous rebellion against the LORD. If we have done so, do not spare our lives this day. [23]If we have built an altar for ourselves to turn away from the LORD or to offer burnt offerings or grain offerings or peace offerings, may the LORD himself punish us.

[24]"The truth is, we have built this altar because we fear that in the future your descendants will say to ours, 'What right do you have to worship the LORD, the God of Israel? [25]The LORD has placed the Jordan River as a barrier between our people and you people of Reuben and Gad. You have no claim to the LORD.' So your descendants may prevent our descendants from worshiping the LORD.

[26]"So we decided to build the altar, not for burnt offerings or sacrifices, [27]but as a memorial. It will remind our descendants and your descendants that we, too, have the right to worship the LORD at his sanctuary with our burnt offerings, sacrifices, and peace offerings. Then your descendants will not be able to say to ours, 'You have no claim to the LORD.'

[28]"If they say this, our descendants can reply, 'Look at this copy of the LORD's altar that our ancestors made. It is not for burnt offerings or sacrifices; it is a reminder of the relationship both of us have with the LORD.' [29]Far be it from us to rebel against the LORD or turn away from him by building our own altar for burnt offerings, grain offerings, or sacrifices. Only the altar of the LORD our God that stands in front of the Tabernacle may be used for that purpose."

[30]When Phinehas the priest and the leaders of the community—the heads of the clans of Israel—heard this from the tribes of Reuben, Gad, and the half-tribe of Manasseh, they were satisfied. [31]Phinehas son of Eleazar, the priest, replied to them, "Today we know the LORD is among us because you have not committed this treachery against the LORD as we thought. Instead, you have rescued Israel from being destroyed by the hand of the LORD."

[32]Then Phinehas son of Eleazar, the priest, and the other leaders left the tribes of Reuben and Gad in Gilead and returned to the land of Canaan to tell the Israelites what had happened. [33]And all the Israelites were satisfied and praised God and spoke no more of war against Reuben and Gad.

[34]The people of Reuben and Gad named the altar "Witness,"* for they said, "It is a witness between us and them that the LORD is our God, too."

....

THE WHOLE STORY

(22:11-34) When the tribes of Reuben and Gad and the half-tribe of Manasseh built an altar at the Jordan River, the rest of Israel feared that these tribes were rebelling against God by worshiping idols. But before beginning an all-out war, a priest (Phinehas) led a delegation to learn the truth. When he learned that the altar was for a memorial rather than for heathen sacrifice, war was averted and unity restored. We would benefit from a similar approach to resolving conflicts. Assuming the worst about the intentions of others only brings trouble. Beware of reacting before you hear the whole story.

22:20 The Hebrew term used here refers to the complete consecration of things or people to the LORD, either by destroying them or by giving them as an offering. **22:34** Some manuscripts lack this word.

23 JOSHUA'S FINAL WORDS TO ISRAEL

The years passed, and the Lord had given the people of Israel rest from all their enemies. Joshua, who was now very old, ²called together all the elders, leaders, judges, and officers of Israel. He said to them, "I am now a very old man. ³You have seen everything the Lord your God has done for you during my lifetime. The Lord your God has fought for you against your enemies. ⁴I have allotted to you as your homeland all the land of the nations yet unconquered, as well as the land of those we have already conquered— from the Jordan River to the Mediterranean Sea* in the west. ⁵This land will be yours, for the Lord your God will himself drive out all the people living there now. You will take possession of their land, just as the Lord your God promised you.

⁶"So be very careful to follow everything Moses wrote in the Book of Instruction. Do not deviate from it, turning either to the right or to the left. ⁷Make sure you do not associate with the other people still remaining in the land. Do not even mention the names of their gods, much less swear by them or serve them or worship them. ⁸Rather, cling tightly to the Lord your God as you have done until now.

⁹"For the Lord has driven out great and powerful nations for you, and no one has yet been able to defeat you. ¹⁰Each one of you will put to flight a thousand of the enemy, for the Lord your God fights for you, just as he has promised. ¹¹So be very careful to love the Lord your God.

¹²"But if you turn away from him and cling to the customs of the survivors of these nations remaining among you, and if you intermarry with them, ¹³then know for certain that the Lord your God will no longer drive them out of your land. Instead, they will be a snare and a trap to you, a whip for your backs and thorny brambles in your eyes, and you will vanish from this good land the Lord your God has given you.

¹⁴"Soon I will die, going the way of everything on earth. Deep in your hearts you know that every promise of the Lord your God has come true. Not a single one has failed! ¹⁵But as surely as the Lord your God has given you the good things he promised, he will also bring disaster on you if you disobey him. He will completely destroy you from this good land he has given you. ¹⁶If you break the covenant of the Lord your God by worshiping and serving other gods, his anger will burn against you, and you will quickly vanish from the good land he has given you."

24 THE LORD'S COVENANT RENEWED

Then Joshua summoned all the tribes of Israel to Shechem, including their elders, leaders, judges, and officers. So they came and presented themselves to God.

²Joshua said to the people, "This is what the Lord, the God of Israel, says: Long ago your ancestors, including Terah, the father of Abraham and Nahor, lived beyond the Euphrates River,* and they worshiped other gods. ³But I took your ancestor Abraham from the land beyond the Euphrates and led him into the land of Canaan. I gave him many descendants through his son Isaac. ⁴To Isaac I gave Jacob and Esau. To Esau I gave the mountains of Seir, while Jacob and his children went down into Egypt.

⁵"Then I sent Moses and Aaron, and I brought terrible plagues on Egypt; and afterward I brought you out as a free people. ⁶But when your ancestors arrived at the Red Sea,* the Egyptians chased after you with chariots and charioteers. ⁷When your ancestors cried out to the Lord, I put darkness between you and the Egyptians. I brought the sea crashing down on the Egyptians, drowning them. With your very own eyes you saw what I did. Then you lived in the wilderness for many years.

⁸"Finally, I brought you into the land of the Amorites on the east side of the Jordan. They fought against you, but I destroyed them before you. I gave you victory over them, and you took possession of their land. ⁹Then Balak son of Zippor, king of Moab, started a war against Israel. He summoned Balaam son of Beor to curse you, ¹⁰but I would not listen to him. Instead, I made Balaam bless you, and so I rescued you from Balak.

¹¹"When you crossed the Jordan River and came to Jericho, the men of Jericho fought against you, as did the Amorites, the Perizzites, the Canaanites, the Hittites, the Girgashites, the Hivites, and the Jebusites. But I

··

CONSEQUENCES

(23:12-16) This chilling prediction about the consequences of intermarriage with Canaanite nations eventually became a reality. Numerous stories in the book of Judges show what Israel had to suffer because of their failure to follow God wholeheartedly. God was patient as usual with Israel, just as he is today with us. But his patience doesn't always mean that he approves of our plans. Tempted to demand your own way? Watch out! You may get your way—along with some painful consequences.

23:4 Hebrew *the Great Sea.*   **24:2** Hebrew *the river;* also in 24:3, 14, 15.   **24:6** Hebrew *sea of reeds.*

gave you victory over them. [12]And I sent terror* ahead of you to drive out the two kings of the Amorites. It was not your swords or bows that brought you victory. [13]I gave you land you had not worked on, and I gave you towns you did not build—the towns where you are now living. I gave you vineyards and olive groves for food, though you did not plant them.

[14]"So fear the LORD and serve him wholeheartedly. Put away forever the idols your ancestors worshiped when they lived beyond the Euphrates River and in Egypt. Serve the LORD alone. [15]But if you refuse to serve the LORD, then choose today whom you will serve. Would you prefer the gods your ancestors served beyond the Euphrates? Or will it be the gods of the Amorites in whose land you now live? But as for me and my family, we will serve the LORD."

[16]The people replied, "We would never abandon the LORD and serve other gods. [17]For the LORD our God is the one who rescued us and our ancestors from slavery in the land of Egypt. He performed mighty miracles before our very eyes. As we traveled through the wilderness among our enemies, he preserved us. [18]It was the LORD who drove out the Amorites and the other nations living here in the land. So we, too, will serve the LORD, for he alone is our God."

[19]Then Joshua warned the people, "You are not able to serve the LORD, for he is a holy and jealous God. He will not forgive your rebellion and your sins. [20]If you abandon the LORD and serve other gods, he will turn against you and destroy you, even though he has been so good to you."

[21]But the people answered Joshua, "No, we will serve the LORD!"

[22]"You are a witness to your own decision," Joshua said. "You have chosen to serve the LORD."

"Yes," they replied, "we are witnesses to what we have said."

[23]"All right then," Joshua said, "destroy the idols among you, and turn your hearts to the LORD, the God of Israel."

[24]The people said to Joshua, "We will serve the LORD our God. We will obey him alone."

[25]So Joshua made a covenant with the

24:12 Often rendered *the hornet*. The meaning of the Hebrew is uncertain.

IT'S YOUR CHOICE

(24:15) *The people had to decide whether they would obey the Lord, who had proven his trustworthiness, or obey the man-made idols of the people of Canaan. This is a decision each person faces today. That includes you. You can easily slip into a quiet rebellion—going about life in your own way. But the time will come when you have to choose who or what will control you. The choice is yours. Will you follow God's way or your own?*

I WONDER...

If Christ controls my life, where does my freedom of choice fit in?

One way that God demonstrated his love for us was by giving us freedom of choice. Someone once said, "Your heart has a door that can be opened only from the inside."

You make the choice to open the door of your heart to Jesus Christ when you receive him as Savior and Lord. Although his Spirit is at work prompting you to respond to his love, the choice is yours.

Picture your life as a house. Jesus Christ knocks on the front door and you decide to let him in (Rev 3:20). Where do you invite him next? Some Christians live their whole lives with Christ still standing in the entryway! Obviously this is not a very good way to treat an invited guest.

During your entire life as a Christian, you use your God-given freedom of choice to invite him into the rest of your house (your life) or to leave him at the front door.

Although your life is much more complicated than a house, let's take the illustration one step further.

In your house you probably have rooms that need repair. The living room, for example, could represent your relationships at home. How does the room look? When problems occur in this room, the solution is to ask the Master Carpenter, Jesus, for some renovation. Through his Word, other people, and the prodding of the Holy Spirit, God gently tells us how to make things right.

In his last recorded act of leadership, Joshua challenges the nation of Israel: "Put away forever the idols your ancestors worshiped when they lived beyond the Euphrates River and in Egypt. Serve the LORD alone" (Josh 24:14). The Israelites were faced with a choice of who they were going to serve. On this day, they confirmed their choice to serve the living God instead of idols made by human hands.

Every day you will be faced with the choice of serving God or something else. God loves you too much to take that choice away from you.

He has given to you the privilege of inviting him into every area of your life.

people that day at Shechem, committing them to follow the decrees and regulations of the LORD. ²⁶Joshua recorded these things in the Book of God's Instructions. As a reminder of their agreement, he took a huge stone and rolled it beneath the terebinth tree beside the Tabernacle of the LORD.

²⁷Joshua said to all the people, "This stone has heard everything the LORD said to us. It will be a witness to testify against you if you go back on your word to God."

²⁸Then Joshua sent all the people away to their own homelands.

LEADERS BURIED IN THE PROMISED LAND

²⁹After this, Joshua son of Nun, the servant of the LORD, died at the age of 110. ³⁰They bur-

ied him in the land he had been allocated, at Timnath-serah in the hill country of Ephraim, north of Mount Gaash.

³¹The people of Israel served the LORD throughout the lifetime of Joshua and of the elders who outlived him—those who had personally experienced all that the LORD had done for Israel.

³²The bones of Joseph, which the Israelites had brought along with them when they left Egypt, were buried at Shechem, in the parcel of ground Jacob had bought from the sons of Hamor for 100 pieces of silver.* This land was located in the territory allotted to the descendants of Joseph.

³³Eleazar son of Aaron also died. He was buried in the hill country of Ephraim, in the town of Gibeah, which had been given to his son Phinehas.

24:32 Hebrew *100 kesitahs;* the value or weight of the kesitah is no longer known.

JUDGES

Think about the superheroes you've read about or seen recently: the Justice League, Spider-Man, Batman, the X-Men. They always seem to arrive in the nick of time to save the day. The world longs for superheroes—extraordinary people who risk their lives for the common good. Unfortunately, superheroes like this don't exist. But that doesn't mean that the world lacks heroes. Think about that every time you pass a fire station.

The book of Judges is about heroes—12 people God used to deliver Israel. They were known as the judges. No way were they superheroes. None could qualify as perfect. One was even a murderer! But God used them to rescue Israel from some pretty tough enemies.

This book is all about the horrible results of sin but also about God's mercy. The people of Israel had become corrupt. The book of Judges describes them this way: "In those days Israel had no king; all the people did whatever seemed right in their own eyes" (17:6). Because of their actions God would allow a neighboring nation to conquer them. Then the people would turn back to God and he would send a "judge" to rescue them. Then, the people would follow God for a while until they became complacent, and the cycle would start again.

We can relate to such a cycle. We do our own thing for a while. But when trouble comes, we turn to God. When life seems good, we forget about God until we need help again. The book of Judges reminds us how much we depend on God and how we should obey him in good times and bad.

STATS

PURPOSE
To show that God's judgment against sin is certain, and that his forgiveness and restoration are also certain for those who repent

AUTHOR
Probably Samuel

ORIGINAL AUDIENCE
The people of Israel

SETTING
The land of Canaan, later called Israel. God had helped the Israelites conquer Canaan. But the people of Israel were in danger of losing this Promised Land because they had compromised and disobeyed God.

KEY PEOPLE
Othniel, Ehud, Deborah, Gideon, Abimelech, Jephthah, Samson, Delilah

SPECIAL FEATURE
Records Israel's first civil war

TIMELINE

1446 B.C.
Exodus from Egypt

1406
Israelites enter Canaan

1375
Period of the Judges begins

1367–1327
Othniel

1209–1169
Deborah

1162–1122
Gideon

1105
Samuel is born

1075–1055
Samson

KEY POINTS

DECLINE/COMPROMISE The people of Israel faced decline and failure because they compromised their principles and began living like the people of other nations. Society rewards those who compromise their faith: wealth, fame, power, and influence. But God calls his people to a higher standard.

DECAY/REBELLION Israel's compromises led them to rebel against God. Things will fall apart when we choose to go our own way, rather than God's.

DEFEAT/OPPRESSION God allowed foreign invaders to torment the Israelites when they rebelled. God sometimes uses "tough love" when his people rebel.

REPENTANCE Decline, decay, and defeat caused the people to cry out for help. They vowed to stop worshiping idols and obey God once more. In the same way, we must identify and renounce modern idols.

DELIVERANCE/HEROES Because Israel repented, God used ordinary people to deliver them from their enemies. Anyone who is dedicated to God can be used for his service.

The broken lines (— · — ·) indicate modern boundaries.

KEY PLACES

❶ BOKIM
The angel of the Lord appeared at Bokim, informing the Israelites that their sin and disobedience had broken their agreement with God. Their punishment would be oppression (1:1–3:11).

❷ JERICHO
King Eglon of Moab conquered and oppressed much of Israel. Ehud killed King Eglon, escaped, and then returned with an army that defeated the Moabites and freed Israel (3:12–31).

❸ HAZOR
King Jabin of Hazor conquered and oppressed Israel for 20 years. Then Deborah became Israel's leader (4:1–5:31).

❹ HILL OF MOREH
After 40 years of peace, the Midianites began harassing Israel. God chose Gideon to deliver Israel. Gideon attacked near the hill of Moreh and sent Midianites running in confusion (6:1–7:25).

❺ SHECHEM
Gideon's son Abimelech was treacherous and power hungry.

He killed 69 of his 70 half brothers so he could be king. The people of Shechem rebelled against Abimelech, but he gathered an army and defeated them. His lust for power led him to ransack two other cities (8:28–9:57).

❻ LAND OF AMMON
Again Israel turned away from God; so God turned away from them. But when the Ammonite army got ready to attack, Israel threw away her idols and called upon God. Jephthah had been run out of Israel but was asked to return and lead Israel's army. Later, Jephthah became involved in a war with the tribe of Ephraim (10:1–12:15).

❼ TIMNAH
God promised a barren couple they would have a son who would free Israel from the Philistines. Samson was to be a Nazirite—set apart for special service to God. But Samson did not take his responsibility seriously and even married a Philistine (13:1–14:20).

❽ VALLEY OF SOREK
Samson killed thousands of Philistines. The nation's leaders got their chance to stop him when Delilah, a Philistine woman from the valley of Sorek, stole Samson's heart (15:1–16:20).

❾ GAZA
The Philistines held a great festival in Gaza to celebrate Samson's imprisonment and to humiliate him before the crowds. When he was brought out as the entertainment, he collapsed the main pillars, causing the building to fall and kill thousands of Philistines. The prophecy about Samson was coming true (16:21-31).

❿ HILL COUNTRY OF EPHRAIM
A man named Micah lived here and hired his own priest to serve his idols. Micah assumed that God would support his own opinions of what was right (17:1-13).

⓫ DAN
The tribe of Dan migrated north to find new territory. Their warriors came upon the city of Laish and slaughtered the unarmed citizens, renaming the city Dan (18:1-31).

⓬ GIBEAH
A man and his concubine stopped in Gibeah, thinking they would be safe. But a crowd of perverts gathered outside the home of his host and demanded to have sex with him. Instead, the concubine was given to them. They raped and abused her all night. When the man found her dead the next morning, he cut her body into 12 pieces and sent a piece to each tribe of Israel, demonstrating that the nation had sunk to its lowest spiritual level (19:1-30).

⓭ MIZPAH
The leaders of Israel came to Mizpah to decide how to punish the evil men of Gibeah. But the city leaders refused to turn the criminals over, so Israel took vengeance upon the whole tribe of Benjamin, who lived there (20:1–21:25).

1 JUDAH AND SIMEON CONQUER THE LAND

After the death of Joshua, the Israelites asked the LORD, "Which tribe should go first to attack the Canaanites?"

²The LORD answered, "Judah, for I have given them victory over the land."

³The men of Judah said to their relatives from the tribe of Simeon, "Join with us to fight against the Canaanites living in the territory allotted to us. Then we will help you conquer your territory." So the men of Simeon went with Judah.

⁴When the men of Judah attacked, the LORD gave them victory over the Canaanites and Perizzites, and they killed 10,000 enemy warriors at the town of Bezek. ⁵While at Bezek they encountered King Adoni-bezek and fought against him, and the Canaanites and Perizzites were defeated. ⁶Adoni-bezek escaped, but the Israelites soon captured him and cut off his thumbs and big toes.

⁷Adoni-bezek said, "I once had seventy kings with their thumbs and big toes cut off, eating scraps from under my table. Now God has paid me back for what I did to them." They took him to Jerusalem, and he died there.

⁸The men of Judah attacked Jerusalem and captured it, killing all its people and setting the city on fire. ⁹Then they went down to fight the Canaanites living in the hill country, the Negev, and the western foothills.* ¹⁰Judah marched against the Canaanites in Hebron (formerly called Kiriath-arba), defeating the forces of Sheshai, Ahiman, and Talmai.

¹¹From there they went to fight against the people living in the town of Debir (formerly called Kiriath-sepher). ¹²Caleb said, "I will give my daughter Acsah in marriage to the one who attacks and captures Kiriath-sepher." ¹³Othniel, the son of Caleb's younger brother, Kenaz, was the one who conquered it, so Acsah became Othniel's wife.

¹⁴When Acsah married Othniel, she urged him* to ask her father for a field. As she got down off her donkey, Caleb asked her, "What's the matter?"

¹⁵She said, "Let me have another gift. You have already given me land in the Negev; now please give me springs of water, too." So Caleb gave her the upper and lower springs.

¹⁶When the tribe of Judah left Jericho—the city of palms—the Kenites, who were descendants of Moses' father-in-law, traveled with

them into the wilderness of Judah. They settled among the people there, near the town of Arad in the Negev.

¹⁷Then Judah joined with Simeon to fight against the Canaanites living in Zephath, and they completely destroyed* the town. So the town was named Hormah.* ¹⁸In addition, Judah captured the towns of Gaza, Ashkelon, and Ekron, along with their surrounding territories.

ISRAEL FAILS TO CONQUER THE LAND

¹⁹The LORD was with the people of Judah, and they took possession of the hill country. But they failed to drive out the people living in the plains, who had iron chariots. ²⁰The town of Hebron was given to Caleb as Moses had promised. And Caleb drove out the people living there, who were descendants of the three sons of Anak.

²¹The tribe of Benjamin, however, failed to drive out the Jebusites, who were living in Jerusalem. So to this day the Jebusites live in Jerusalem among the people of Benjamin.

²²The descendants of Joseph attacked the town of Bethel, and the LORD was with them. ²³They sent men to scout out Bethel (formerly known as Luz). ²⁴They confronted a man coming out of the town and said to him, "Show us a way into the town, and we will have mercy on you." ²⁵So he showed them a way in, and they killed everyone in the town except that man and his family. ²⁶Later the man moved to

....

A GREATER THREAT

(1:1-33) Canaan—the Promised Land—was filled with many different people groups. They lived in city-states where each city had its own government, army, and laws. One reason Canaan was so difficult to conquer was that each city had to be defeated individually. No single king could surrender the entire country to the Israelites. But Canaan's greatest threat to Israel was not its military but its religion. Canaanite religion idealized evil traits: cruelty in war, sexual immorality, selfish greed, and materialism. It was a "me first, anything goes" society. Does that sound familiar? We face the same challenges these days. How will you stand up to these challenges?

PERSEVERE

(1:19-36) Why didn't God's people follow through and completely obey his command to destroy the Canaanites? Here are a few of the possible reasons: (1) they had been fighting for a long time and were tired; (2) the enemy seemed too strong; (3) since Joshua's death, the tribes were no longer unified in purpose; or (4) they thought they could handle the temptation and be more prosperous by doing business with the Canaanites. Whatever the reason, they chose to compromise. Ever fall into that trap? Often we know what to do but just don't follow through. So, we gradually drift away from God. That is the time when we need to persevere the most. Tempted to compromise? Determine to persevere instead.

1:9 Hebrew *the Shephelah.* 1:14 Greek version and Latin Vulgate read *he urged her.* 1:17a The Hebrew term used here refers to the complete consecration of things or people to the LORD, either by destroying them or by giving them as an offering. 1:17b *Hormah* means "destruction."

the land of the Hittites, where he built a town. He named it Luz, which is is its name to this day. ²⁷The tribe of Manasseh failed to drive out the people living in Beth-shan,* Taanach, Dor, Ibleam, Megiddo, and all their surrounding settlements, because the Canaanites were determined to stay in that region. ²⁸When the Israelites grew stronger, they forced the Canaanites to work as slaves, but they never did drive them completely out of the land. ²⁹The tribe of Ephraim failed to drive out the Canaanites living in Gezer, so the Canaanites continued to live there among them. ³⁰The tribe of Zebulun failed to drive out the residents of Kitron and Nahalol, so the Canaanites continued to live among them. But the Canaanites were forced to work as slaves for the people of Zebulun. ³¹The tribe of Asher failed to drive out the residents of Acco, Sidon, Ahlab, Aczib, Helbah, Aphik, and Rehob. ³²Instead, the people of Asher moved in among the Canaanites, who controlled the land, for they failed to drive them out. ³³Likewise, the tribe of Naphtali failed to drive out the residents of Beth-shemesh and Beth-anath. Instead, they moved in among the Canaanites, who controlled the land. Nevertheless, the people of Beth-shemesh and Beth-anath were forced to work as slaves for the people of Naphtali. ³⁴As for the tribe of Dan, the Amorites forced them back into the hill country and would not let them come down into the plains. ³⁵The Amorites were determined to stay in Mount Heres, Aijalon, and Shaalbim, but when the descendants of Joseph became stronger, they forced the Amorites to work as slaves. ³⁶The boundary of the Amorites ran from Scorpion Pass* to Sela and continued upward from there.

2 THE LORD'S MESSENGER COMES TO BOKIM

The angel of the LORD went up from Gilgal to Bokim and said to the Israelites, "I brought you out of Egypt into this land that I swore to give your ancestors, and I said I would never break my covenant with you. ²For your part, you were not to make any covenants with the people living in this land; instead, you were to destroy their altars. But you disobeyed my command. Why did you do this? ³So now I declare that I will no longer drive out the people living in your land. They will be thorns in your sides,* and their gods will be a constant temptation to you."

⁴When the angel of the LORD finished speaking to all the Israelites, the people wept loudly. ⁵So they called the place Bokim (which means "weeping"), and they offered sacrifices there to the LORD.

THE DEATH OF JOSHUA ⁶After Joshua sent the people away, each of the tribes left to take possession of the land allotted to them. ⁷And the Israelites served the LORD throughout the lifetime of Joshua and the leaders who outlived him—those who had seen all the great things the LORD had done for Israel.

⁸Joshua son of Nun, the servant of the LORD, died at the age of 110. ⁹They buried him in the land he had been allocated, at Timnath-serah* in the hill country of Ephraim, north of Mount Gaash.

ISRAEL DISOBEYS THE LORD ¹⁰After that generation died, another generation grew up who did not acknowledge the LORD or remember the mighty things he had done for Israel.

¹¹The Israelites did evil in the LORD's sight and served the images of Baal. ¹²They abandoned the LORD, the God of their ancestors, who had brought them out of Egypt. They went after other gods, worshiping the gods of the people around them. And they angered the LORD. ¹³They abandoned the LORD to serve Baal and the images of Ashtoreth. ¹⁴This made the LORD burn with anger against Israel, so he handed them over to raiders who stole their possessions. He turned them over to their enemies all around, and they were no longer able to resist them. ¹⁵Every time Israel went out to battle, the LORD fought against them, causing them to be defeated, just as he had warned. And the people were in great distress.

THE LORD RESCUES HIS PEOPLE ¹⁶Then the LORD raised up judges to rescue the Israelites from their attackers. ¹⁷Yet Israel did not listen to the judges but prostituted themselves by worshiping other gods. How quickly they turned away from the path of their ancestors,

---

PEER PRESSURE
(2:11-15) This generation of Israelites abandoned the faith of their parents and began worshiping the false gods of their neighbors. Many things can tempt us to abandon what we know is right. The desire to be accepted by others can lead us into behavior that is unacceptable to God. But God wants us to stand firm. When someone tries to pressure you into disobedience, what will you do?

1:27 Hebrew *Beth-shean,* a variant spelling of Beth-shan. 1:36 Hebrew *Akrabbim.* 2:3 Hebrew *They will be in your sides;* compare Num 33:55. 2:9 As in parallel text at Josh 24:30; Hebrew reads *Timnath-heres,* a variant spelling of Timnath-serah.

who had walked in obedience to the LORD's commands.

[18]Whenever the LORD raised up a judge over Israel, he was with that judge and rescued the people from their enemies throughout the judge's lifetime. For the LORD took pity on his people, who were burdened by oppression and suffering. [19]But when the judge died, the people returned to their corrupt ways, behaving worse than those who had lived before them. They went after other gods, serving and worshiping them. And they refused to give up their evil practices and stubborn ways.

[20]So the LORD burned with anger against Israel. He said, "Because these people have violated my covenant, which I made with their ancestors, and have ignored my commands, [21]I will no longer drive out the nations that Joshua left unconquered when he died. [22]I did this to test Israel—to see whether or not they would follow the ways of the LORD as their ancestors did." [23]That is why the LORD left those nations in place. He did not quickly drive them out or allow Joshua to conquer them all.

3 **THE NATIONS LEFT IN CANAAN** These are the nations that the LORD left in the land to test those Israelites who had not experienced the wars of Canaan. [2]He did this to teach warfare to generations of Israelites who had no experience in battle. [3]These are the nations: the Philistines (those living under the

3:8 *Aram-naharaim* means "Aram of the two rivers," thought to have been located between the Euphrates and Balih Rivers in northwestern Mesopotamia.

THE LORD TOOK PITY ON HIS PEOPLE, WHO WERE BURDENED BY OPPRESSION AND SUFFERING. {JUDGES 2:18}

five Philistine rulers), all the Canaanites, the Sidonians, and the Hivites living in the mountains of Lebanon from Mount Baal-hermon to Lebo-hamath. [4]These people were left to test the Israelites—to see whether they would obey the commands the LORD had given to their ancestors through Moses.

[5]So the people of Israel lived among the Canaanites, Hittites, Amorites, Perizzites, Hivites, and Jebusites, [6]and they intermarried with them. Israelite sons married their daughters, and Israelite daughters were given in marriage to their sons. And the Israelites served their gods.

OTHNIEL BECOMES ISRAEL'S JUDGE [7]The Israelites did evil in the LORD's sight. They forgot about the LORD their God, and they served the images of Baal and the Asherah poles. [8]Then the LORD burned with anger against Israel, and he turned them over to King Cushan-rishathaim of Aram-naharaim.* And the Israelites served Cushan-rishathaim for eight years.

ULTIMATE ISSUES *OTHER RELIGIONS*

If you've been paying attention as you've read so far, you have noticed that God takes a dim view (to put it mildly) of other religions. One of the Ten Commandments spoke against "other gods." And whenever the people of Israel encountered foreigners who worshiped idols, God instructed them to use harsh measures when dealing with them.

As you read passages like Joshua 10–12, where Joshua and the people of Israel conquered city after city, killing all of the inhabitants, you may wonder, "Why is God so intolerant? Why is he so rough on lifeless idols and the people who believe in them?"

Admittedly, such harsh measures seem strange to us, unaccustomed as we are to these cultures and their worship rituals. But God had good reason for wanting Israel to avoid these religions. First, many of them, such as the followers of Molech, practiced detestable rituals—even child sacrifice—in their worship ceremonies (see Deut 12:31), a practice that disgusted God.

Second, God knew what prolonged contact with people who practiced these religions would do to his chosen people. It was like being exposed to a fatal virus. Because of God's concern for his people, his instructions to radically eliminate the source of the disease were as necessary as a surgeon removing a malignant tumor. Though painful and costly, it was necessary for survival. If they failed to remove the cancer—as they often did—it would grow back and threaten to destroy them. Then it would be up to God to do the "surgery" himself, which he did in the form of persecution and exile. It was far better for Israel to do it right in the first place.

While some Christians struggle with the temptation to try other religions (Buddhism; Hinduism), many more struggle with worshiping "idols." Our idols today—money, sex, status, alcohol, relationships—don't look much like the idols the Israelites encountered. But they are just as real and just as dangerous. Wouldn't you agree? ∎

⁹But when the people of Israel cried out to the Lord for help, the Lord raised up a rescuer to save them. His name was Othniel, the son of Caleb's younger brother, Kenaz. ¹⁰The Spirit of the Lord came upon him, and he became Israel's judge. He went to war against King Cushan-rishathaim of Aram, and the Lord gave Othniel victory over him. ¹¹So there was peace in the land for forty years. Then Othniel son of Kenaz died.

EHUD BECOMES ISRAEL'S JUDGE ¹²Once again the Israelites did evil in the Lord's sight, and the Lord gave King Eglon of Moab control over Israel because of their evil. ¹³Eglon enlisted the Ammonites and Amalekites as allies, and then he went out and defeated Israel, taking possession of Jericho, the city of palms. ¹⁴And the Israelites served Eglon of Moab for eighteen years.

¹⁵But when the people of Israel cried out to the Lord for help, the Lord again raised up a rescuer to save them. His name was Ehud son of Gera, a left-handed man of the tribe of Benjamin. The Israelites sent Ehud to deliver their tribute money to King Eglon of Moab. ¹⁶So Ehud made a double-edged dagger that was about a foot* long, and he strapped it to his right thigh, keeping it hidden under his clothing. ¹⁷He brought the tribute money to Eglon, who was very fat.

¹⁸After delivering the payment, Ehud started home with those who had helped carry the tribute. ¹⁹But when Ehud reached the stone idols near Gilgal, he turned back. He came to Eglon and said, "I have a secret message for you."

So the king commanded his servants, "Be quiet!" and he sent them all out of the room.

²⁰Ehud walked over to Eglon, who was sitting alone in a cool upstairs room. And Ehud said, "I have a message from God for you!" As King Eglon rose from his seat, ²¹Ehud reached with his left hand, pulled out the dagger strapped to his right thigh, and plunged it into the king's belly. ²²The dagger went so deep that the handle disappeared beneath the king's fat. So Ehud did not pull out the dagger, and the king's bowels emptied.* ²³Then Ehud closed and locked the doors of the room and escaped down the latrine.*

²⁴After Ehud was gone, the king's servants returned and found the doors to the upstairs room locked. They thought he might be using the latrine in the room, ²⁵so they waited. But when the king didn't come out after a long delay, they became concerned and got a key. And when they opened the doors, they found their master dead on the floor.

²⁶While the servants were waiting, Ehud escaped, passing the stone idols on his way to Seirah. ²⁷When he arrived in the hill country of Ephraim, Ehud sounded a call to arms. Then he led a band of Israelites down from the hills.

²⁸"Follow me," he said, "for the Lord has given you victory over Moab your enemy." So they followed him. And the Israelites took control of the shallow crossings of the Jordan River across from Moab, preventing anyone from crossing.

²⁹They attacked the Moabites and killed about 10,000 of their strongest and most able-bodied warriors. Not one of them escaped. ³⁰So Moab was conquered by Israel that day, and there was peace in the land for eighty years.

SHAMGAR BECOMES ISRAEL'S JUDGE ³¹After Ehud, Shamgar son of Anath rescued Israel. He once killed 600 Philistines with an ox goad.

4 **DEBORAH BECOMES ISRAEL'S JUDGE** After Ehud's death, the Israelites again did evil in the Lord's sight. ²So the Lord turned them over to King Jabin of Hazor, a Canaanite king. The commander of his army was Sisera, who lived in Harosheth-haggoyim. ³Sisera, who had 900 iron chariots, ruthlessly oppressed the Israelites for twenty years. Then the people of Israel cried out to the Lord for help.

⁴Deborah, the wife of Lappidoth, was a prophet who was judging Israel at that time. ⁵She would sit under the Palm of Deborah, between Ramah and Bethel in the hill country of Ephraim, and the Israelites would go to her for judgment. ⁶One day she sent for Barak son of Abinoam, who lived in Kedesh in the land of Naphtali. She said to him, "This is what the Lord, the God of Israel, commands you: Call out 10,000 warriors from the tribes of Naphtali and Zebulun at Mount Tabor. ⁷And I will call out

---

HURTING GOD
(4:1) *Israel hurt themselves and God when they did wrong. Everything we do wrong ultimately is against God because it shows a disregard for his commands and his authority over our lives. David prayed, "Against you, and you alone, have I sinned; I have done what is evil in your sight" (Ps 51:4). Recognizing the seriousness of sin is the first step toward removing it from our lives. Need to make things right with God? There's no time like the present.*

3:16 Hebrew *gomed*, the length of which is uncertain.   3:22 Or *and it came out behind*.   3:23 Or *and went out through the porch*; the meaning of the Hebrew is uncertain.

Sisera, commander of Jabin's army, along with his chariots and warriors, to the Kishon River. There I will give you victory over him."

[8]Barak told her, "I will go, but only if you go with me."

[9]"Very well," she replied, "I will go with you. But you will receive no honor in this venture, for the LORD's victory over Sisera will be at the hands of a woman." So Deborah went with Barak to Kedesh. [10]At Kedesh, Barak called together the tribes of Zebulun and Naphtali, and 10,000 warriors went up with him. Deborah also went with him.

[11]Now Heber the Kenite, a descendant of Moses' brother-in-law* Hobab, had moved away from the other members of his tribe and pitched his tent by the oak of Zaanannim near Kedesh.

[12]When Sisera was told that Barak son of Abinoam had gone up to Mount Tabor, [13]he called for all 900 of his iron chariots and all of his warriors, and they marched from Harosheth-haggoyim to the Kishon River.

[14]Then Deborah said to Barak, "Get ready! This is the day the LORD will give you victory over Sisera, for the LORD is marching ahead of you." So Barak led his 10,000 warriors down the slopes of Mount Tabor into battle. [15]When Barak attacked, the LORD threw Sisera and all his chariots and warriors into a panic. Sisera leaped down from his chariot and escaped on foot. [16]Then Barak chased the chariots and the enemy army all the way to Harosheth-haggoyim, killing all of Sisera's warriors. Not a single one was left alive.

[17]Meanwhile, Sisera ran to the tent of Jael, the wife of Heber the Kenite, because Heber's family was on friendly terms with King Jabin of Hazor. [18]Jael went out to meet Sisera and said to him, "Come into my tent, sir. Come in. Don't be afraid." So he went into her tent, and she covered him with a blanket.

[19]"Please give me some water," he said. "I'm thirsty." So she gave him some milk from a leather bag and covered him again.

[20]"Stand at the door of the tent," he told her. "If anybody comes and asks you if there is anyone here, say no."

[21]But when Sisera fell asleep from exhaustion, Jael quietly crept up to him with a hammer and tent peg in her hand. Then she drove the tent peg through his temple and into the ground, and so he died.

[22]When Barak came looking for Sisera, Jael went out to meet him. She said, "Come, and I will show you the man you are looking for." So

he followed her into the tent and found Sisera lying there dead, with the tent peg through his temple.

[23]So on that day Israel saw God defeat Jabin, the Canaanite king. [24]And from that time on Israel became stronger and stronger against King Jabin until they finally destroyed him.

5 THE SONG OF DEBORAH On that day Deborah and Barak son of Abinoam sang this song:

[2] "Israel's leaders took charge,
    and the people gladly followed.
Praise the LORD!

[3] "Listen, you kings!
    Pay attention, you mighty rulers!
For I will sing to the LORD.
    I will make music to the LORD, the God
    of Israel.

[4] "LORD, when you set out from Seir
    and marched across the fields of Edom,
the earth trembled,
    and the cloudy skies poured down rain.
[5] The mountains quaked in the presence of
    the LORD,
    the God of Mount Sinai—
in the presence of the LORD,
    the God of Israel.

[6] "In the days of Shamgar son of Anath,
    and in the days of Jael,
people avoided the main roads,
    and travelers stayed on winding
    pathways.
[7] There were few people left in the villages
    of Israel*—
until Deborah arose as a mother for Israel.
[8] When Israel chose new gods,
    war erupted at the city gates.
Yet not a shield or spear could be seen
    among forty thousand warriors in Israel!

....

A TRUE LEADER
(4:9) As a prophet and judge of Israel, Deborah guided the people on legal matters and told the soldiers when to go to battle. But more than that, she encouraged the people of Israel to live for God after the battle was over. Those who lead must not forget about the spiritual condition of those being led. A true leader is concerned for people, not just success. Does that describe you?

SONGS
(5:1-31) After the defeat of Sisera and the army of Jabin, Barak and Deborah sang a praise song to God. Songs of praise focus our attention on God by reminding us of his character and actions. Whether you are in the middle of a great victory or a difficult problem, singing praises to God can have a positive effect on your attitude.

4:11 Or *father-in-law*.   5:7 The meaning of the Hebrew is uncertain.

⁹ My heart is with the commanders of Israel,
    with those who volunteered for war.
Praise the LORD!

¹⁰ "Consider this, you who ride on fine
    donkeys,
    you who sit on fancy saddle blankets,
    and you who walk along the road.
¹¹ Listen to the village musicians*
    gathered at the watering holes.
They recount the righteous victories of the
    LORD
    and the victories of his villagers in Israel.
Then the people of the LORD
    marched down to the city gates.

¹² "Wake up, Deborah, wake up!
    Wake up, wake up, and sing a song!
Arise, Barak!
    Lead your captives away, son of Abinoam!

¹³ "Down from Tabor marched the few against
    the nobles.
The people of the LORD marched down
    against mighty warriors.
¹⁴ They came down from Ephraim—
    a land that once belonged to the
    Amalekites;
    they followed you, Benjamin, with your
    troops.
From Makir the commanders marched down;
    from Zebulun came those who carry a
    commander's staff.
¹⁵ The princes of Issachar were with Deborah
    and Barak.
    They followed Barak, rushing into the
    valley.
But in the tribe of Reuben
    there was great indecision.
¹⁶ Why did you sit at home among the
    sheepfolds—
    to hear the shepherds whistle for their
    flocks?
Yes, in the tribe of Reuben
    there was great indecision.
¹⁷ Gilead remained east of the Jordan.
    And why did Dan stay home?
Asher sat unmoved at the seashore,
    remaining in his harbors.
¹⁸ But Zebulun risked his life,
    as did Naphtali, on the heights of the
    battlefield.

¹⁹ "The kings of Canaan came and fought,
    at Taanach near Megiddo's springs,
    but they carried off no silver treasures.
²⁰ The stars fought from heaven.
    The stars in their orbits fought against
    Sisera.

²¹ The Kishon River swept them away—
    that ancient torrent, the Kishon.
March on with courage, my soul!
²² Then the horses' hooves hammered the
    ground,
    the galloping, galloping of Sisera's mighty
    steeds.
²³ 'Let the people of Meroz be cursed,'
    said the angel of the LORD.
    'Let them be utterly cursed,
because they did not come to help the LORD—
    to help the LORD against the mighty
    warriors.'

²⁴ "Most blessed among women is Jael,
    the wife of Heber the Kenite.
May she be blessed above all women
    who live in tents.
²⁵ Sisera asked for water,
    and she gave him milk.
In a bowl fit for nobles,
    she brought him yogurt.
²⁶ Then with her left hand she reached for a
    tent peg,
    and with her right hand for the workman's
    hammer.
She struck Sisera with the hammer,
    crushing his head.
With a shattering blow, she pierced his
    temples.
²⁷ He sank, he fell,
    he lay still at her feet.
And where he sank,
    there he died.

²⁸ "From the window Sisera's mother looked
    out.
    Through the window she watched for his
    return, saying,
'Why is his chariot so long in coming?
    Why don't we hear the sound of chariot
    wheels?'

²⁹ "Her wise women answer,
    and she repeats these words to herself:
³⁰ 'They must be dividing the captured plunder—
    with a woman or two for every man.
There will be colorful robes for Sisera,
    and colorful, embroidered robes for me.
Yes, the plunder will include
    colorful robes embroidered on both
    sides.'

³¹ "LORD, may all your enemies die like Sisera!
    But may those who love you rise like the
    sun in all its power!"

Then there was peace in the land for forty years.

5:11 The meaning of the Hebrew is uncertain.

6 GIDEON BECOMES ISRAEL'S JUDGE

The Israelites did evil in the LORD's sight. So the LORD handed them over to the Midianites for seven years. ²The Midianites were so cruel that the Israelites made hiding places for themselves in the mountains, caves, and strongholds. ³Whenever the Israelites planted their crops, marauders from Midian, Amalek, and the people of the east would attack Israel, ⁴camping in the land and destroying crops as far away as Gaza. They left the Israelites with nothing to eat, taking all the sheep, goats, cattle, and donkeys. ⁵These enemy hordes, coming with their livestock and tents, were as thick as locusts; they arrived on droves of camels too numerous to count. And they stayed until the land was stripped bare. ⁶So Israel was reduced to starvation by the Midianites. Then the Israelites cried out to the LORD for help.

⁷When they cried out to the LORD because of Midian, ⁸the LORD sent a prophet to the Israelites. He said, "This is what the LORD, the God of Israel, says: I brought you up out of slavery in Egypt. ⁹I rescued you from the Egyptians and from all who oppressed you. I drove out your enemies and gave you their land. ¹⁰I told you, 'I am the LORD your God. You must not worship the gods of the Amorites, in whose land you now live.' But you have not listened to me."

¹¹Then the angel of the LORD came and sat beneath the great tree at Ophrah, which belonged to Joash of the clan of Abiezer. Gideon son of Joash was threshing wheat at the bottom of a winepress to hide the grain from the Midianites. ¹²The angel of the LORD appeared to him and said, "Mighty hero, the LORD is with you!"

PERSONALITY PROFILE GIDEON

UPS:
- *Israel's fifth judge*
- *A military strategist who was an expert at surprise*
- *A member of the Hall of Faith in Hebrews 11*
- *Led a victorious Israelite army against the Midianite army*
- *Was offered the title of king by the people of Israel*
- *Though slow to be convinced, acted on his convictions*

DOWNS:
- *Feared that his own limitations would prevent God from working*
- *Collected Midianite gold and made a symbol which became an object of worship*
- *Through a sexual relationship outside marriage, fathered a son who would bring great grief to both Gideon's family and the nation of Israel*
- *Failed to influence the nation in God's ways; after his death, the people returned to worshiping idols*

STATS:
- *Where: Ophrah, the valley of Jezreel, the spring of Harod*
- *Occupation: Farmer, warrior, judge*
- *Relatives: Joash (father); Abimelech (son)*
- *Contemporaries: King Zebah, King Zalmunna*

KEY VERSES: *Judges 6:15-16*

MOST BELIEVERS want to know God's plan for their lives, but they're not always sure how to find it. We may think that God's will for our lives is hidden and that we might miss it if we're not watching. But if we're always looking around for God's next assignment, we probably won't do a very good job on what he has us doing now.

Fortunately, the Bible gives us a better way to understand God's guidance. In the Bible's descriptions of how God guided people, we can see that he usually showed people what he wanted next while they were completely involved in obeying him right where they were. A good example of this kind of guidance is seen in Gideon's life.

Times were hard, thanks to continual invasions by the Midianites. While Gideon tried his best to hide from the enemy the little bit of wheat his family had left, God's messenger showed up with an assignment. Gideon had been chosen to lead the Israelites against the Midianites. But Gideon had some questions that revealed his doubts. Was this really a task that God wanted him to do? Was he the right person for the job?

Sometimes we question God, because we want to be sure what he requires of us. But sometimes we ask questions because we really don't want to obey. God was patient with Gideon's questions and doubts—he knew Gideon wanted to obey. Gideon made mistakes, but he was still God's servant. You can be sure that God will guide you as long as your desire is to serve and obey him wherever you are.

BOTTOM LINE: God expands and uses the abilities he has already built into us.

God uses us in spite of our limitations and failures.

Even those who make great spiritual progress can easily fall into sin if they don't consistently follow God

Gideon's story is told in Judges 6–8. He also is mentioned in Hebrews 11:32-33.

[13]"Sir," Gideon replied, "if the LORD is with us, why has all this happened to us? And where are all the miracles our ancestors told us about? Didn't they say, 'The LORD brought us up out of Egypt'? But now the LORD has abandoned us and handed us over to the Midianites."

[14]Then the LORD turned to him and said, "Go with the strength you have, and rescue Israel from the Midianites. I am sending you!"

[15]"But Lord," Gideon replied, "how can I rescue Israel? My clan is the weakest in the whole tribe of Manasseh, and I am the least in my entire family!"

[16]The LORD said to him, "I will be with you. And you will destroy the Midianites as if you were fighting against one man."

[17]Gideon replied, "If you are truly going to help me, show me a sign to prove that it is really the LORD speaking to me. [18]Don't go away until I come back and bring my offering to you."

He answered, "I will stay here until you return."

[19]Gideon hurried home. He cooked a young goat, and with a basket* of flour he baked some bread without yeast. Then, carrying the meat in a basket and the broth in a pot, he brought them out and presented them to the angel, who was under the great tree.

[20]The angel of God said to him, "Place the meat and the unleavened bread on this rock, and pour the broth over it." And Gideon did as he was told. [21]Then the angel of the LORD touched the meat and bread with the tip of the staff in his hand, and fire flamed up from the rock and consumed all he had brought. And the angel of the LORD disappeared.

[22]When Gideon realized that it was the angel of the LORD, he cried out, "Oh, Sovereign LORD, I'm doomed! I have seen the angel of the LORD face to face!"

[23]"It is all right," the LORD replied. "Do not be afraid. You will not die." [24]And Gideon built an altar to the LORD there and named it Yahweh-Shalom (which means "the LORD is peace"). The altar remains in Ophrah in the land of the clan of Abiezer to this day.

[25]That night the LORD said to Gideon, "Take the second bull from your father's herd, the one that is seven years old. Pull down your father's altar to Baal, and cut down the Asherah pole standing beside it. [26]Then build an altar to the LORD your God here on this hilltop sanctuary, laying the stones carefully. Sacrifice the bull as a burnt offering on the altar, using as fuel the wood of the Asherah pole you cut down."

[27]So Gideon took ten of his servants and did as the LORD had commanded. But he did it at night because he was afraid of the other members of his father's household and the people of the town.

[28]Early the next morning, as the people of the town began to stir, someone discovered that the altar of Baal had been broken down and that the Asherah pole beside it had been cut down. In their place a new altar had been built, and on it were the remains of the bull that had been sacrificed. [29]The people said to each other, "Who did this?" And after asking around and making a careful search, they learned that it was Gideon, the son of Joash.

[30]"Bring out your son," the men of the town demanded of Joash. "He must die for destroying the altar of Baal and for cutting down the Asherah pole."

[31]But Joash shouted to the mob that confronted him, "Why are you defending Baal? Will you argue his case? Whoever pleads his case will be put to death by morning! If Baal truly is a god, let him defend himself and destroy the one who broke down his altar!" [32]From then on Gideon was called Jerub-baal, which means "Let Baal defend himself," because he broke down Baal's altar.

GIDEON ASKS FOR A SIGN

[33]Soon afterward the armies of Midian, Amalek, and the people of the east formed an alliance against Israel and crossed the Jordan, camping in the valley of Jezreel. [34]Then the Spirit of the LORD took possession of Gideon. He blew a ram's horn as a call to arms, and the men of the clan of Abiezer came to him. [35]He also sent messengers throughout Manasseh, Asher, Zebulun, and Naphtali, summoning their warriors, and all of them responded.

[36]Then Gideon said to God, "If you are truly going to use me to rescue Israel as you promised, [37]prove it to me in this way. I will put a

LAME EXCUSES

(6:14-16) God chose Gideon to lead the Israelites in battle against their enemies. He also promised to give Gideon the strength he needed to overcome the opposition. Yet Gideon made excuses, seeing only his limitations and weaknesses. As with Gideon, God calls us to serve him in specific ways, and he promises us the tools and strength we need. But we sometimes make excuses instead of serving him. Reminding God of our limitations only implies that he does not know all about us or that he has made a mistake in evaluating our character. Are you a Gideon—called to act on God's behalf? Instead of making excuses, step out in courage and do as he commands.

6:19 Hebrew *an ephah* [20 quarts or 22 liters].

wool fleece on the threshing floor tonight. If the fleece is wet with dew in the morning but the ground is dry, then I will know that you are going to help me rescue Israel as you promised." ³⁸And that is just what happened. When Gideon got up early the next morning, he squeezed the fleece and wrung out a whole bowlful of water.

³⁹Then Gideon said to God, "Please don't be angry with me, but let me make one more request. Let me use the fleece for one more test. This time let the fleece remain dry while the ground around it is wet with dew." ⁴⁰So that night God did as Gideon asked. The fleece was dry in the morning, but the ground was covered with dew.

7 GIDEON DEFEATS THE MIDIANITES So Jerub-baal (that is, Gideon) and his army got up early and went as far as the spring of Harod. The armies of Midian were camped north of them in the valley near the hill of Moreh. ²The Lord said to Gideon, "You have too many warriors with you. If I let all of you fight the Midianites, the Israelites will boast to me that they saved themselves by their own strength. ³Therefore, tell the people, 'Whoever is timid or afraid may leave this mountain* and go home.'" So 22,000 of them went home, leaving only 10,000 who were willing to fight.

⁴But the Lord told Gideon, "There are still too many! Bring them down to the spring, and I will test them to determine who will go with you and who will not." ⁵When Gideon took his warriors down to the water, the Lord told him, "Divide the men into two groups. In one group put all those who cup water in their hands and lap it up with their tongues like dogs. In the other group put all those who kneel down and drink with their mouths in the stream." ⁶Only 300 of the men drank from their hands. All the others got down on their knees and drank with their mouths in the stream.

⁷The Lord told Gideon, "With these 300 men I will rescue you and give you victory over the Midianites. Send all the others home." ⁸So Gideon collected the provisions and rams' horns of the other warriors and sent them home. But he kept the 300 men with him.

The Midianite camp was in the valley just below Gideon. ⁹That night the Lord said, "Get up! Go down into the Midianite camp, for I have given you victory over them! ¹⁰But if you are afraid to attack, go down to the camp with your

servant Purah. ¹¹Listen to what the Midianites are saying, and you will be greatly encouraged. Then you will be eager to attack."

So Gideon took Purah and went down to the edge of the enemy camp. ¹²The armies of Midian, Amalek, and the people of the east had settled in the valley like a swarm of locusts. Their camels were like grains of sand on the seashore—too many to count! ¹³Gideon crept up just as a man was telling his companion about a dream. The man said, "I had this dream, and in my dream a loaf of barley bread came tumbling down into the Midianite camp. It hit a tent, turned it over, and knocked it flat!"

¹⁴His companion answered, "Your dream can mean only one thing—God has given Gideon son of Joash, the Israelite, victory over Midian and all its allies!"

¹⁵When Gideon heard the dream and its interpretation, he bowed in worship before the Lord.* Then he returned to the Israelite camp and shouted, "Get up! For the Lord has given you victory over the Midianite hordes!" ¹⁶He divided the 300 men into three groups and gave each man a ram's horn and a clay jar with a torch in it.

¹⁷Then he said to them, "Keep your eyes on me. When I come to the edge of the camp, do just as I do. ¹⁸As soon as I and those with me blow the rams' horns, blow your horns, too, all around the entire camp, and shout, 'For the Lord and for Gideon!'"

¹⁹It was just after midnight,* after the changing of the guard, when Gideon and the 100 men with him reached the edge of

. . . .

WAITING FOR PROOF
(6:36-40) Was Gideon really testing God or was he simply asking God for more encouragement? In either case, though his motive was right (to obey God and defeat the enemy), his method was less than ideal. Gideon seems to have known that his requests might displease God (6:39), yet he demanded two miracles (6:37, 39) even after witnessing the miraculous fire from the rock (6:21). Certainly to make good decisions we need facts. But Gideon had all the facts and still hesitated. Instead of acting, he delayed his obedience because he wanted more proof. Can you relate? Like Gideon, fear sometimes makes us wait for more confirmation instead of taking action. Visible signs are unnecessary if they only confirm what we already know to be true. Do you know what God wants you to do? If so, are you acting or waiting?

THANK GOD
(7:15) Gideon stood just outside the enemy camp and thanked God. Rituals, motions, or loud praise would have announced his presence to the enemy, so Gideon's thanksgiving must have been a silent attitude of joy, worship, and praise to God. Similarly, we can thank God silently and constantly even in the middle of difficult situations.

7:3 Hebrew *may leave Mount Gilead.* The identity of Mount Gilead is uncertain in this context. It is perhaps used here as another name for Mount Gilboa. **7:15** As in Greek version; Hebrew reads *he bowed.* **7:19** Hebrew *at the beginning of the second watch.*

THE JUDGES OF ISRAEL

OTHNIEL (40 YEARS)
He captured a powerful
Canaanite city.
Judges 3:7-11

DEBORAH (40 YEARS)
She defeated General Sisera
and the Canaanites and later
sang a victory song with Barak.
Judges 4–5

JAIR (22 YEARS)
He had 30 sons.
Judges 10:3-5

ELON (10 YEARS)
Judges 12:11-12

EHUD (80 YEARS)
He killed Eglon and defeated
the Moabites.
Judges 3:12-30

GIDEON (40 YEARS)
He used a fleece to determine
God's will and defeated 135,000
Midianites with 300 men.
Judges 6–8

JEPHTHAH (6 YEARS)
He made a rash vow, defeated
the Ammonites, and later
battled Ephraim.
Judges 10:6–12:7

ABDON (8 YEARS)
He had 40 sons and 30 grandsons,
each of whom had his own donkey.
Judges 12:13-15

SHAMGAR
He killed 600 Philistines
with an ox goad.
Judges 3:31

TOLA (23 YEARS)
Judges 10:1-2

IBZAN (7 YEARS)
He had 30 sons and 30 daughters.
Judges 12:8-10

SAMSON (20 YEARS)
He was betrayed by Delilah but
destroyed thousands of Philistines.
Judges 13–16

SAMUEL (35 YEARS)
He provided godly leadership as
Israel transitioned to a monarchy.
1 Samuel 3–10

---

the Midianite camp. Suddenly, they blew the rams' horns and broke their clay jars. ²⁰Then all three groups blew their horns and broke their jars. They held the blazing torches in their left hands and the horns in their right hands, and they all shouted, "A sword for the LORD and for Gideon!"

²¹Each man stood at his position around the camp and watched as all the Midianites rushed around in a panic, shouting as they ran to escape. ²²When the 300 Israelites blew their rams' horns, the LORD caused the warriors in the camp to fight against each other with their swords. Those who were not killed fled to places as far away as Beth-shittah near Zererah and to the border of Abel-meholah near Tabbath.

²³Then Gideon sent for the warriors of Naphtali, Asher, and Manasseh, who joined in chasing the army of Midian. ²⁴Gideon also sent messengers throughout the hill country of Ephraim, saying, "Come down to attack the Midianites. Cut them off at the shallow crossings of the Jordan River at Beth-barah."

So all the men of Ephraim did as they were told. ²⁵They captured Oreb and Zeeb, the two Midianite commanders, killing Oreb at the rock of Oreb, and Zeeb at the winepress of Zeeb. And they continued to chase the Midianites. Afterward the Israelites brought the heads of Oreb and Zeeb to Gideon, who was by the Jordan River.

8 GIDEON KILLS ZEBAH AND ZALMUNNA

Then the people of Ephraim asked Gideon, "Why have you treated us this way? Why didn't you send for us when you first went out to fight the Midianites?" And they argued heatedly with Gideon.

²But Gideon replied, "What have I accomplished compared to you? Aren't even the left-over grapes of Ephraim's harvest better than the entire crop of my little clan of Abiezer? ³God gave you victory over Oreb and Zeeb, the commanders of the Midianite army. What have I accomplished compared to that?" When the men of Ephraim heard Gideon's answer, their anger subsided.

⁴Gideon then crossed the Jordan River with his 300 men, and though exhausted, they continued to chase the enemy. ⁵When they reached Succoth, Gideon asked the leaders of the town, "Please give my warriors some food. They are very tired. I am chasing Zebah and Zalmunna, the kings of Midian."

⁶But the officials of Succoth replied, "Catch Zebah and Zalmunna first, and then we will feed your army."

⁷So Gideon said, "After the LORD gives me victory over Zebah and Zalmunna, I will return and tear your flesh with the thorns and briers from the wilderness."

⁸From there Gideon went up to Peniel* and again asked for food, but he got the same an-

8:8 Hebrew *Penuel*, a variant spelling of Peniel; also in 8:9, 17.

swer. 9So he said to the people of Peniel, "After I return in victory, I will tear down this tower."

10By this time Zebah and Zalmunna were in Karkor with 15,000 warriors—all that remained of the allied armies of the east, for 120,000 had already been killed. 11Gideon circled around by the caravan route east of Nobah and Jogbehah, taking the Midianite army by surprise. 12Zebah and Zalmunna, the two Midianite kings, fled, but Gideon chased them down and captured all their warriors.

13After this, Gideon returned from the battle by way of Heres Pass. 14There he captured a young man from Succoth and demanded that he write down the names of all the seventy-seven officials and elders in the town. 15Gideon then returned to Succoth and said to the leaders, "Here are Zebah and Zalmunna. When we were here before, you taunted me, saying, 'Catch Zebah and Zalmunna first, and then we will feed your exhausted army.'" 16Then Gideon took the elders of the town and taught them a lesson, punishing them with thorns and briers from the wilderness. 17He also tore down the tower of Peniel and killed all the men in the town.

18Then Gideon asked Zebah and Zalmunna, "The men you killed at Tabor—what were they like?"

"Like you," they replied. "They all had the look of a king's son."

19"They were my brothers, the sons of my own mother!" Gideon exclaimed. "As surely as the LORD lives, I wouldn't kill you if you hadn't killed them."

20Turning to Jether, his oldest son, he said, "Kill them!" But Jether did not draw his sword, for he was only a boy and was afraid.

21Then Zebah and Zalmunna said to Gideon, "Be a man! Kill us yourself!" So Gideon killed them both and took the royal ornaments from the necks of their camels.

GIDEON'S SACRED EPHOD 22Then the Israelites said to Gideon, "Be our ruler! You and your son and your grandson will be our rulers, for you have rescued us from Midian."

23But Gideon replied, "I will not rule over you, nor will my son. The LORD will rule over you! 24However, I do have one request—that each of you give me an earring from the plunder you collected from your fallen enemies." (The enemies, being Ishmaelites, all wore gold earrings.)

I WONDER...

A friend says that my new faith in Christ is too narrow. He doesn't think that Jesus is the only way to God. Why can't God allow different ideas by other religions?

Suppose your history teacher told you that Columbus discovered America in 1492. Just then, four other people raised their hands and said, "I think he discovered America in 1454 (or 1678 or 1543 or 1733). What makes you the authority on history anyway? We are going to believe what we think is right."

Do these kids have the freedom to believe what they think is right? Of course they do.

A wise teacher would respond, "You may believe any date you choose to believe, but only one answer is correct, and I have told you what it is. If you put a different answer on the test at the end of the term, it will be marked wrong."

God has given people the freedom to choose what they want to believe about who he is and what his plan is for human beings. But when the test scores are graded at the end of the age, only one answer will be right.

During this period in Jewish history, the Israelites had no leader, so the Bible tells us that "all the people did whatever seemed right in their own eyes" (Judg 17:6). What this means is that not only did people choose to disobey God as their leader, but their actions were evil as well! Throughout history people have behaved according to what they believe about God.

If people believe that God does not exist or that God does not care how we live and treat each other, they will likely act accordingly. Usually, this means that they treat themselves or others like there will be no final exam when they pass on to the next life!

Jesus said, "I am the way, the truth, and the life. No one can come to the Father except through me" (John 14:6). This means that God grades on a pass/fail basis depending on what we have done with his Son, Jesus.

Many people would like to believe that God grades on a curve. In other words, if you do good things or go to church more than others or give more money than most people, you will get into heaven. Jesus makes it clear, however, that there is only one way to heaven.

God has given people the freedom to believe any religion they want. But the final authority is not their own beliefs. Only one answer is right. God's standard is faith in Jesus Christ, his death on the cross—so that our sin would not eternally separate us from God—and his resurrection.

²⁵"Gladly!" they replied. They spread out a cloak, and each one threw in a gold earring he had gathered from the plunder. ²⁶The weight of the gold earrings was forty-three pounds,* not including the royal ornaments and pendants, the purple clothing worn by the kings of Midian, or the chains around the necks of their camels.

²⁷Gideon made a sacred ephod from the gold and put it in Ophrah, his hometown. But soon all the Israelites prostituted themselves by worshiping it, and it became a trap for Gideon and his family.

²⁸That is the story of how the people of Israel defeated Midian, which never recovered. Throughout the rest of Gideon's lifetime—about forty years—there was peace in the land.

²⁹Then Gideon* son of Joash returned home. ³⁰He had seventy sons born to him, for he had many wives. ³¹He also had a concubine in Shechem, who gave birth to a son, whom he named Abimelech. ³²Gideon died when he was very old, and he was buried in the grave of his father, Joash, at Ophrah in the land of the clan of Abiezer.

³³As soon as Gideon died, the Israelites prostituted themselves by worshiping the images of Baal, making Baal-berith their god. ³⁴They forgot the LORD their God, who had rescued them from all their enemies surrounding them. ³⁵Nor did they show any loyalty to the family of Jerub-baal (that is, Gideon), despite all the good he had done for Israel.

9 ABIMELECH RULES OVER SHECHEM One day Gideon's* son Abimelech went to Shechem to visit his uncles—his mother's brothers. He said to them and to the rest of his mother's family, ²"Ask the leading citizens of Shechem whether they want to be ruled by all seventy of

Gideon's sons or by one man. And remember that I am your own flesh and blood!"

³So Abimelech's uncles gave his message to all the citizens of Shechem on his behalf. And after listening to this proposal, the people of Shechem decided in favor of Abimelech because he was their relative. ⁴They gave him seventy silver coins from the temple of Baal-berith, which he used to hire some reckless troublemakers who agreed to follow him. ⁵He went to his father's home at Ophrah, and there, on one stone, they killed all seventy of his half brothers, the sons of Gideon.* But the youngest brother, Jotham, escaped and hid.

⁶Then all the leading citizens of Shechem and Beth-millo called a meeting under the oak beside the pillar* at Shechem and made Abimelech their king.

JOTHAM'S PARABLE ⁷When Jotham heard about this, he climbed to the top of Mount Gerizim and shouted,

"Listen to me, citizens of Shechem!
    Listen to me if you want God to listen
        to you!
⁸ Once upon a time the trees decided to
        choose a king.
    First they said to the olive tree,
        'Be our king!'
⁹ But the olive tree refused, saying,
    'Should I quit producing the olive oil
        that blesses both God and people,
        just to wave back and forth over the trees?'
¹⁰ "Then they said to the fig tree,
        'You be our king!'
¹¹ But the fig tree also refused, saying,
    'Should I quit producing my sweet fruit
        just to wave back and forth over the trees?'
¹² "Then they said to the grapevine,
        'You be our king!'
¹³ But the grapevine also refused, saying,
    'Should I quit producing the wine
        that cheers both God and people,
        just to wave back and forth over the trees?'
¹⁴ "Then all the trees finally turned to the
        thornbush and said,
        'Come, you be our king!'
¹⁵ And the thornbush replied to the trees,
    'If you truly want to make me your king,
        come and take shelter in my shade.
    If not, let fire come out from me
        and devour the cedars of Lebanon.'"

• •

STAY ALERT
(8:31) The relationship between Gideon and his concubine (8:31) produced a son who tore apart Gideon's family and caused tragedy for the nation. Gideon may have won a battle for the nation, but he lost the war with his family. His story is a sad reminder of how temptation can creep in right after we have experienced a spiritual victory. That's why we need to stay alert and keep on praying when temptations come.

PRIORITIES
(9:7-21) Jotham told the story about the trees in order to help the people of Israel to set good priorities. He did not want them to appoint a leader of low character. As we serve in leadership positions, we also need to examine our motives. Do we just want praise, prestige, or power? In the parable, the thornbush chose to be a servant to the trees under its care. Is being a servant to others your first priority as a leader?

8:26 Hebrew *1,700 shekels* [19.4 kilograms]. 8:29 Hebrew *Jerub-baal*; see 6:32. 9:1 Hebrew *Jerub-baal's* (see 6:32); also in 9:2, 24. 9:5 Hebrew *Jerub-baal* (see 6:32); also in 9:16, 19, 28, 57. 9:6 The meaning of the Hebrew is uncertain.

[16]Jotham continued, "Now make sure you have acted honorably and in good faith by making Abimelech your king, and that you have done right by Gideon and all of his descendants. Have you treated him with the honor he deserves for all he accomplished? [17]For he fought for you and risked his life when he rescued you from the Midianites. [18]But today you have revolted against my father and his descendants, killing his seventy sons on one stone. And you have chosen his slave woman's son, Abimelech, to be your king just because he is your relative.

[19]"If you have acted honorably and in good faith toward Gideon and his descendants today, then may you find joy in Abimelech, and may he find joy in you. [20]But if you have not acted in good faith, then may fire come out from Abimelech and devour the leading citizens of Shechem and Beth-millo; and may fire come out from the citizens of Shechem and Beth-millo and devour Abimelech!"

[21]Then Jotham escaped and lived in Beer because he was afraid of his brother Abimelech.

SHECHEM REBELS AGAINST ABIMELECH

[22]After Abimelech had ruled over Israel for three years, [23]God sent a spirit that stirred up trouble between Abimelech and the leading citizens of Shechem, and they revolted. [24]God was punishing Abimelech for murdering Gideon's seventy sons, and the citizens of Shechem for supporting him in this treachery of murdering his brothers. [25]The citizens of Shechem set an ambush for Abimelech on the hilltops and robbed everyone who passed that way. But someone warned Abimelech about their plot.

[26]One day Gaal son of Ebed moved to Shechem with his brothers and gained the confidence of the leading citizens of Shechem. [27]During the annual harvest festival at Shechem, held in the temple of the local god, the wine flowed freely, and everyone began cursing Abimelech. [28]"Who is Abimelech?" Gaal shouted. "He's not a true son of Shechem,* so why should we be his servants? He's merely the son of Gideon, and this Zebul is merely his deputy. Serve the true sons of Hamor, the founder of Shechem. Why should we serve Abimelech? [29]If I were in charge here, I would get rid of Abimelech. I would say* to him, 'Get some soldiers, and come out and fight!'"

[30]But when Zebul, the leader of the city,

heard what Gaal was saying, he was furious. [31]He sent messengers to Abimelech in Arumah,* telling him, "Gaal son of Ebed and his brothers have come to live in Shechem, and now they are inciting the city to rebel against you. [32]Come by night with an army and hide out in the fields. [33]In the morning, as soon as it is daylight, attack the city. When Gaal and those who are with him come out against you, you can do with them as you wish."

[34]So Abimelech and all his men went by night and split into four groups, stationing themselves around Shechem. [35]Gaal was standing at the city gates when Abimelech and his army came out of hiding. [36]When Gaal saw them, he said to Zebul, "Look, there are people coming down from the hilltops!"

Zebul replied, "It's just the shadows on the hills that look like men."

[37]But again Gaal said, "No, people are coming down from the hills.* And another group is coming down the road past the Diviners' Oak.*"

[38]Then Zebul turned on him and asked, "Now where is that big mouth of yours? Wasn't it you that said, 'Who is Abimelech, and why should we be his servants?' The men you mocked are right outside the city! Go out and fight them!"

[39]So Gaal led the leading citizens of Shechem into battle against Abimelech. [40]But Abimelech chased him, and many of Shechem's men were wounded and fell along the road as they retreated to the city gate. [41]Abimelech returned to Arumah, and Zebul drove Gaal and his brothers out of Shechem.

[42]The next day the people of Shechem went out into the fields to battle. When Abimelech heard about it, [43]he divided his men into three groups and set an ambush in the fields. When Abimelech saw the people coming out of the city, he and his men jumped up from their hiding places and attacked them. [44]Abimelech and his group stormed the city gate to keep the men of Shechem from getting back in, while Abimelech's other two groups cut them down in the fields. [45]The battle went on all day before Abimelech finally captured the city. He killed the people, leveled the city, and scattered salt all over the ground.

[46]When the leading citizens who lived in the tower of Shechem heard what had happened, they ran and hid in the temple of Baal-berith.* [47]Someone reported to Abimelech that the citizens had gathered in the temple, [48]so he led his forces to Mount Zalmon. He took an ax and chopped some branches from a tree, then put them on his shoulder. "Quick, do as I have

9:28 Hebrew *Who is Shechem?* 9:29 As in Greek version; Hebrew reads *And he said.* 9:31 Or *in secret;* Hebrew reads *in Tormah;* compare 9:41. 9:37a Or *the center of the land.* 9:37b Hebrew *Elon-meonenim.* 9:46 Hebrew *El-berith,* another name for Baal-berith; compare 9:4.

done!" he told his men. ⁴⁹So each of them cut down some branches, following Abimelech's example. They piled the branches against the walls of the temple and set them on fire. So all the people who had lived in the tower of Shechem died—about 1,000 men and women.

⁵⁰Then Abimelech attacked the town of Thebez and captured it. ⁵¹But there was a strong tower inside the town, and all the men and women—the entire population—fled to it. They barricaded themselves in and climbed up to the roof of the tower. ⁵²Abimelech followed them to attack the tower. But as he prepared to set fire to the entrance, ⁵³a woman on the roof dropped a millstone that landed on Abimelech's head and crushed his skull.

⁵⁴He quickly said to his young armor bearer, "Draw your sword and kill me! Don't let it be said that a woman killed Abimelech!" So the young man ran him through with his sword, and he died. ⁵⁵When Abimelech's men saw that he was dead, they disbanded and returned to their homes.

⁵⁶In this way, God punished Abimelech for the evil he had done against his father by murdering his seventy brothers. ⁵⁷God also punished the men of Shechem for all their evil. So the curse of Jotham son of Gideon was fulfilled.

10 TOLA BECOMES ISRAEL'S JUDGE After Abimelech died, Tola son of Puah, son of Dodo, was the next person to rescue Israel. He was from the tribe of Issachar but lived in the town of Shamir in the hill country of Ephraim. ²He judged Israel for twenty-three years. When he died, he was buried in Shamir.

JAIR BECOMES ISRAEL'S JUDGE ³After Tola died, Jair from Gilead judged Israel for twenty-two years. ⁴His thirty sons rode around on thirty donkeys, and they owned thirty towns

NOTEWORTHY
(10:1-5) In five verses we read about two men who judged Israel for a total of 45 years. Yet all we know about them besides the length of their rules is that one had 30 sons who rode around on 30 donkeys. What are you doing for God that is worth noting? When your life is over, what will people remember about you? Will it be more than just the amount in your bank account or the number of years you lived?

PUNISHMENT
(10:7-10) God permitted enemy nations to oppress the Israelites because of their sin (2:1-3). When we turn away from God, sometimes he allows problems and pressures to plague us in order to move us back to him. When problems arise, before you ask, "Why me?" ask, "Is God trying to say something to me through this?"

in the land of Gilead, which are still called the Towns of Jair.* ⁵When Jair died, he was buried in Kamon.

THE AMMONITES OPPRESS ISRAEL ⁶Again the Israelites did evil in the LORD's sight. They served the images of Baal and Ashtoreth, and the gods of Aram, Sidon, Moab, Ammon, and Philistia. They abandoned the LORD and no longer served him at all. ⁷So the LORD burned with anger against Israel, and he turned them over to the Philistines and the Ammonites, ⁸who began to oppress them that year. For eighteen years they oppressed all the Israelites east of the Jordan River in the land of the Amorites (that is, in Gilead). ⁹The Ammonites also crossed to the west side of the Jordan and attacked Judah, Benjamin, and Ephraim.

The Israelites were in great distress. ¹⁰Finally, they cried out to the LORD for help, saying, "We have sinned against you because we have abandoned you as our God and have served the images of Baal."

¹¹The LORD replied, "Did I not rescue you from the Egyptians, the Amorites, the Ammonites, the Philistines, ¹²the Sidonians, the Amalekites, and the Maonites? When they oppressed you, you cried out to me for help, and I rescued you. ¹³Yet you have abandoned me and served other gods. So I will not rescue you anymore. ¹⁴Go and cry out to the gods you have chosen! Let them rescue you in your hour of distress!"

¹⁵But the Israelites pleaded with the LORD and said, "We have sinned. Punish us as you see fit, only rescue us today from our enemies." ¹⁶Then the Israelites put aside their foreign gods and served the LORD. And he was grieved by their misery.

¹⁷At that time the armies of Ammon had gathered for war and were camped in Gilead, and the people of Israel assembled and camped at Mizpah. ¹⁸The leaders of Gilead said to each other, "Whoever attacks the Ammonites first will become ruler over all the people of Gilead."

11 JEPHTHAH BECOMES ISRAEL'S JUDGE Now Jephthah of Gilead was a great warrior. He was the son of Gilead, but his mother was a prostitute. ²Gilead's wife also had several sons, and when these half brothers grew up, they chased Jephthah off the land. "You will not get any of our father's inheritance," they said, "for you are the son of a prostitute." ³So Jephthah fled from his

10:4 Hebrew *Havvoth-jair.*

GOD USES COMMON PEOPLE

God uses all sorts of people to do his work.

PERSON	KNOWN AS	TASK	REFERENCE
JACOB	A liar	To "father" the Israelite nation	Genesis 27
JOSEPH	A slave	To save his family	Genesis 39–47
MOSES	A shepherd in exile (and a murderer)	To lead Israel out of bondage into the Promised Land	Exodus 3
GIDEON	A farmer	To deliver Israel from Midian	Judges 6:11
JEPHTHAH	The son of a prostitute	To deliver Israel from the Ammonites	Judges 11:1
HANNAH	A housewife	To be the mother of Samuel	1 Samuel 1
DAVID	A shepherd boy and youngest of the family	To be Israel's greatest king	1 Samuel 16
EZRA	A scribe	To lead the return to Judah and to write some of the Bible	Ezra, Nehemiah
ESTHER	An orphan	To save her people from massacre	Esther
MARY	A peasant girl	To be the mother of Christ	Luke 1:27-38
MATTHEW	A tax collector	To be an apostle and Gospel writer	Matthew 9:9
LUKE	A Greek physician	To be a companion of Paul and a Gospel writer	Colossians 4:14
PETER	A fisherman	To be an apostle, a leader of the early church, and a writer of two New Testament letters	Matthew 4:18-20

brothers and lived in the land of Tob. Soon he had a band of worthless rebels following him.

⁴At about this time, the Ammonites began their war against Israel. ⁵When the Ammonites attacked, the elders of Gilead sent for Jephthah in the land of Tob. The elders said, ⁶"Come and be our commander! Help us fight the Ammonites!"

⁷But Jephthah said to them, "Aren't you the ones who hated me and drove me from my father's house? Why do you come to me now when you're in trouble?"

⁸"Because we need you," the elders replied. "If you lead us in battle against the Ammonites, we will make you ruler over all the people of Gilead."

⁹Jephthah said to the elders, "Let me get this straight. If I come with you and if the LORD gives me victory over the Ammonites, will you really make me ruler over all the people?"

¹⁰"The LORD is our witness," the elders replied. "We promise to do whatever you say."

¹¹So Jephthah went with the elders of Gilead, and the people made him their ruler and commander of the army. At Mizpah, in the presence of the LORD, Jephthah repeated what he had said to the elders.

....

REJECTION
(11:1-29) Jephthah, an illegitimate son of Gilead, was chased out of the country by his half brothers. His mistreatment came as a result of a decision made by others and not for any wrong he had done. But although his brothers rejected him, God chose to use him. When you're feeling rejected, blaming others and becoming discouraged might come naturally—but neither solves the problem. God, however, is able to make something good out of a bad situation. Are you willing to trust him?

¹²Then Jephthah sent messengers to the king of Ammon, asking, "Why have you come out to fight against my land?"

¹³The king of Ammon answered Jephthah's messengers, "When the Israelites came out of Egypt, they stole my land from the Arnon River to the Jabbok River and all the way to the Jordan. Now then, give back the land peaceably."

¹⁴Jephthah sent this message back to the Ammonite king:

¹⁵"This is what Jephthah says: Israel did not steal any land from Moab or Ammon. ¹⁶When the people of Israel arrived at Kadesh on their journey from Egypt after crossing the Red Sea,* ¹⁷they sent messengers to the king of Edom asking for permission to pass through his land. But their request was denied. Then they asked the king of Moab for similar permission, but he wouldn't let them pass through either. So the people of Israel stayed in Kadesh.

¹⁸"Finally, they went around Edom and Moab through the wilderness. They traveled along Moab's eastern border and camped on the other side of the Arnon River. But they never once crossed the Arnon River into Moab, for the Arnon was the border of Moab.

¹⁹"Then Israel sent messengers to King Sihon of the Amorites, who ruled from Heshbon, asking for permission to cross through his land to get to their destination. ²⁰But King Sihon didn't trust Israel to pass through his land. Instead, he mobilized his army at Jahaz and attacked them. ²¹But the LORD, the God of Israel, gave his people victory over King Sihon. So Israel took control of all the land of the Amorites, who lived in that region, ²²from the Arnon River to the Jabbok River, and from the eastern wilderness to the Jordan.

²³"So you see, it was the LORD, the God of Israel, who took away the land from the Amorites and gave it to Israel. Why, then, should we give it back to you? ²⁴You keep whatever your god Chemosh gives you, and we will keep whatever the LORD our God gives us. ²⁵Are you any better than Balak son of Zippor, king of Moab? Did he try to make a case against Israel for disputed land? Did he go to war against them?

²⁶"Israel has been living here for 300 years, inhabiting Heshbon and its surrounding settlements, all the way to Aroer and its settlements, and in all the towns along the Arnon River. Why have you made no effort to recover it before now? ²⁷Therefore, I have not sinned against you. Rather, you have wronged me by attacking me. Let the LORD, who is judge, decide today which of us is right—Israel or Ammon."

²⁸But the king of Ammon paid no attention to Jephthah's message.

JEPHTHAH'S VOW ²⁹At that time the Spirit of the LORD came upon Jephthah, and he went throughout the land of Gilead and Manasseh, including Mizpah in Gilead, and from there he led an army against the Ammonites. ³⁰And Jephthah made a vow to the LORD. He said, "If you give me victory over the Ammonites, ³¹I will give to the LORD whatever comes out of my house to meet me when I return in triumph. I will sacrifice it as a burnt offering."

³²So Jephthah led his army against the Ammonites, and the LORD gave him victory. ³³He crushed the Ammonites, devastating about twenty towns from Aroer to an area near Minnith and as far away as Abel-keramim. In this way Israel defeated the Ammonites.

³⁴When Jephthah returned home to Mizpah, his daughter came out to meet him, playing on a tambourine and dancing for joy. She was his one and only child; he had no other sons or daughters. ³⁵When he saw her, he tore his clothes in anguish. "Oh, my daughter!" he cried out. "You have completely destroyed me! You've brought disaster on me! For I have made a vow to the LORD, and I cannot take it back."

³⁶And she said, "Father, if you have made a vow to the LORD, you must do to me what you have vowed, for the LORD has given you a great victory over your enemies, the Ammonites. ³⁷But first let me do this one thing: Let me go up and roam in the hills and weep with my friends for two months, because I will die a virgin."

³⁸"You may go," Jephthah said. And he sent her away for two months. She and her friends went into the hills and wept because she would never have children. ³⁹When she re-

---

A RASH PROMISE

(11:30-40) Jephthah's rash vow brought him unspeakable grief. In the heat of emotion or personal turmoil it is easy to make foolish promises to God. These promises might sound very spiritual when we make them, but they often produce guilt and frustration when we are forced to fulfill them. Making spiritual "deals" only brings disappointment. God does not want promises for the future but obedience for today.

11:16 Hebrew *sea of reeds.*

turned home, her father kept the vow he had made, and she died a virgin.

So it has become a custom in Israel 40for young Israelite women to go away for four days each year to lament the fate of Jephthah's daughter.

12 EPHRAIM FIGHTS WITH JEPHTHAH
Then the people of Ephraim mobilized an army and crossed over the Jordan River to Zaphon. They sent this message to Jephthah: "Why didn't you call for us to help you fight against the Ammonites? We are going to burn down your house with you in it!"

2Jephthah replied, "I summoned you at the beginning of the dispute, but you refused to come! You failed to help us in our struggle against Ammon. 3So when I realized you weren't coming, I risked my life and went to battle without you, and the Lord gave me victory over the Ammonites. So why have you now come to fight me?"

4The people of Ephraim responded, "You men of Gilead are nothing more than fugitives from Ephraim and Manasseh." So Jephthah gathered all the men of Gilead and attacked the men of Ephraim and defeated them.

5Jephthah captured the shallow crossings of the Jordan River, and whenever a fugitive from Ephraim tried to go back across, the men of Gilead would challenge him. "Are you a member of the tribe of Ephraim?" they would ask. If the man said, "No, I'm not," 6they would tell him to say "Shibboleth." If he was from Ephraim, he would say "Sibboleth," because people from Ephraim cannot pronounce the word correctly. Then they would take him and kill him at the shallow crossings of the Jordan. In all, 42,000 Ephraimites were killed at that time.

7Jephthah judged Israel for six years. When he died, he was buried in one of the towns of Gilead.

IBZAN BECOMES ISRAEL'S JUDGE
8After Jephthah died, Ibzan from Bethlehem judged Israel. 9He had thirty sons and thirty daughters. He sent his daughters to marry men outside his clan, and he brought in thirty young women from outside his clan to marry his sons. Ibzan judged Israel for seven years. 10When he died, he was buried at Bethlehem.

ELON BECOMES ISRAEL'S JUDGE
11After Ibzan died, Elon from the tribe of Zebulun judged

Israel for ten years. 12When he died, he was buried at Aijalon in Zebulun.

ABDON BECOMES ISRAEL'S JUDGE
13After Elon died, Abdon son of Hillel, from Pirathon, judged Israel. 14He had forty sons and thirty grandsons, who rode on seventy donkeys. He judged Israel for eight years. 15When he died, he was buried at Pirathon in Ephraim, in the hill country of the Amalekites.

13 THE BIRTH OF SAMSON Again the
Israelites did evil in the Lord's sight, so the Lord handed them over to the Philistines, who oppressed them for forty years.

2In those days a man named Manoah from the tribe of Dan lived in the town of Zorah. His wife was unable to become pregnant, and they had no children. 3The angel of the Lord appeared to Manoah's wife and said, "Even though you have been unable to have children, you will soon become pregnant and give birth to a son. 4So be careful; you must not drink wine or any other alcoholic drink nor eat any forbidden food.* 5You will become pregnant and give birth to a son, and his hair must never be cut. For he will be dedicated to God as a Nazirite from birth. He will begin to rescue Israel from the Philistines."

6The woman ran and told her husband, "A man of God appeared to me! He looked like one of God's angels, terrifying to see. I didn't ask where he was from, and he didn't tell me his name. 7But he told me, 'You will become pregnant and give birth to a son. You must not drink wine or any other alcoholic drink nor eat any forbidden food. For your son will be dedicated to God as a Nazirite from the moment of his birth until the day of his death.'"

8Then Manoah prayed to the Lord, saying, "Lord, please let the man of God come back to us again and give us more instructions about this son who is to be born."

9God answered Manoah's prayer, and the angel of God appeared once again to his wife as she was sitting in the field. But her husband, Manoah, was not with her. 10So she

13:4 Hebrew any unclean thing; also in 13:7, 14.

A JOB TO DO
(13:5) Although Manoah's wife was told that her son would begin to rescue the Israelites from Philistine oppression, the job wasn't completed until David's day (2 Sam 8:1). Samson's part in subduing the Philistines was just the beginning, but it was important nonetheless. What task has God called you to do? Are you willing to be faithful in following God even if you don't see immediate results?

quickly ran and told her husband, "The man who appeared to me the other day is here again!"

11Manoah ran back with his wife and asked, "Are you the man who spoke to my wife the other day?"

"Yes," he replied, "I am."

12So Manoah asked him, "When your words come true, what kind of rules should govern the boy's life and work?"

13The angel of the LORD replied, "Be sure your wife follows the instructions I gave her. 14She must not eat grapes or raisins, drink wine or any other alcoholic drink, or eat any forbidden food."

15Then Manoah said to the angel of the LORD, "Please stay here until we can prepare a young goat for you to eat."

16"I will stay," the angel of the LORD replied, "but I will not eat anything. However, you may prepare a burnt offering as a sacrifice to the LORD." (Manoah didn't realize it was the angel of the LORD.)

17Then Manoah asked the angel of the LORD, "What is your name? For when all this comes true, we want to honor you."

18"Why do you ask my name?" the angel of the LORD replied. "It is too wonderful for you to understand."

19Then Manoah took a young goat and a grain offering and offered it on a rock as a sacrifice to the LORD. And as Manoah and his wife watched, the LORD did an amazing thing. 20As the flames from the altar shot up toward the sky, the angel of the LORD ascended in the fire. When Manoah and his wife saw this, they fell with their faces to the ground.

21The angel did not appear again to Manoah and his wife. Manoah finally realized it was the angel of the LORD, 22and he said to his wife, "We will certainly die, for we have seen God!"

23But his wife said, "If the LORD were going to kill us, he wouldn't have accepted our burnt offering and grain offering. He wouldn't have appeared to us and told us this wonderful thing and done these miracles."

24When her son was born, she named him Samson. And the LORD blessed him as he grew up. 25And the Spirit of the LORD began to stir

SAMSON
PERSONALITY PROFILE

IF IT HASN'T ALREADY HAPPENED, sooner or later someone is going to talk to you about your potential. Your "potential" is what you could realize if you keep developing an ability or working on some other goal set for your improvement. It is the plan God set in motion to make you the coolest *you* possible.

Samson had the potential to be a great servant of God. God planned to use him to lead the Israelites against their enemies the Philistines. To help him, God gave Samson incredible physical strength. Unfortunately, Samson became an example of what happens when a person doesn't live up to his or her potential.

Samson's life included many opportunities to help his people. But he wasted most of his chances and even wound up being made a fool of by a woman. Yet, despite his mistakes, God still worked with him. The last thing Samson did before he died was an act that started the work God had planned for him all along.

The New Testament does not mention Samson's failures or his great feats of strength. In Hebrews 11:32-33, he is simply called one who "by faith . . . received what God had promised." In the end, Samson recognized his dependence on God. God turned his failure into victory.

Want to reach your full potential? Why not start by putting your life in God's hands? If you've already done that, but feel that you've wasted too much of your potential, take heart. Samson's story teaches us that it is never too late to start over.

BOTTOM LINE: Great strength in one area of life does not make up for weaknesses in other areas.

God's presence does not overwhelm a person's will.

God can use people of faith despite their mistakes.

Samson's story is told in Judges 13–16. He also is mentioned in Hebrews 11:32-33.

UPS:
• Dedicated to God from birth as a Nazirite
• Known for his feats of strength
• Listed in the Hall of Faith in Hebrews 11
• Began to free Israel from Philistine oppression

DOWNS:
• Violated his vow and God's laws on many occasions
• Was controlled by his hormones
• Confided in the wrong people
• Used his gifts and abilities unwisely

STATS:
• Where: Zorah, Timnah, Ashkelon, Gaza, the valley of Sorek
• Occupation: Judge
• Relatives: Manoah (father)
• Contemporaries: Delilah, Samuel (who may have been born while Samson was a judge)

KEY VERSE: Judges 13:5

him while he lived in Mahaneh-dan, which is located between the towns of Zorah and Eshtaol.

14 SAMSON'S RIDDLE One day when Samson was in Timnah, one of the Philistine women caught his eye. ²When he returned home, he told his father and mother, "A young Philistine woman in Timnah caught my eye. I want to marry her. Get her for me."

³His father and mother objected. "Isn't there even one woman in our tribe or among all the Israelites you could marry?" they asked. "Why must you go to the pagan Philistines to find a wife?"

But Samson told his father, "Get her for me! She looks good to me." ⁴His father and mother didn't realize the LORD was at work in this, creating an opportunity to work against the Philistines, who ruled over Israel at that time.

⁵As Samson and his parents were going down to Timnah, a young lion suddenly attacked Samson near the vineyards of Timnah. ⁶At that moment the Spirit of the LORD came powerfully upon him, and he ripped the lion's jaws apart with his bare hands. He did it as easily as if it were a young goat. But he didn't tell his father or mother about it. ⁷When Samson arrived in Timnah, he talked with the woman and was very pleased with her.

⁸Later, when he returned to Timnah for the wedding, he turned off the path to look at the carcass of the lion. And he found that a swarm of bees had made some honey in the carcass. ⁹He scooped some of the honey into his hands and ate it along the way. He also gave some to his father and mother, and they ate it. But he didn't tell them he had taken the honey from the carcass of the lion.

¹⁰As his father was making final arrangements for the marriage, Samson threw a party at Timnah, as was the custom for elite young men. ¹¹When the bride's parents* saw him, they selected thirty young men from the town to be his companions.

¹²Samson said to them, "Let me tell you a riddle. If you solve my riddle during these seven days of the celebration, I will give you thirty fine linen robes and thirty sets of festive clothing. ¹³But if you can't solve it, then you must give me thirty fine linen robes and thirty sets of festive clothing."

"All right," they agreed, "let's hear your riddle."

¹⁴So he said:

"Out of the one who eats came something to eat;
out of the strong came something sweet."

Three days later they were still trying to figure it out. ¹⁵On the fourth* day they said to Samson's wife, "Entice your husband to explain the riddle for us, or we will burn down your father's house with you in it. Did you invite us to this party just to make us poor?"

¹⁶So Samson's wife came to him in tears and said, "You don't love me; you hate me! You have given my people a riddle, but you haven't told me the answer."

"I haven't even given the answer to my father or mother," he replied. "Why should I tell you?" ¹⁷So she cried whenever she was with him and kept it up for the rest of the celebration. At last, on the seventh day he told her the answer because she was tormenting him with her nagging. Then she explained the riddle to the young men.

¹⁸So before sunset of the seventh day, the men of the town came to Samson with their answer:

"What is sweeter than honey?
What is stronger than a lion?"

Samson replied, "If you hadn't plowed with my heifer, you wouldn't have solved my riddle!"

¹⁹Then the Spirit of the LORD came powerfully upon him. He went down to the town of Ashkelon, killed thirty men, took their belongings, and gave their clothing to the men who had solved his riddle. But Samson was furious about what had happened, and he went back home to live with his father and mother. ²⁰So his wife was given in marriage to the man who had been Samson's best man at the wedding.

15 SAMSON'S VENGEANCE ON THE PHILISTINES Later on, during the wheat harvest, Samson took a young goat as a present to his wife. He said, "I'm going into my wife's room to sleep with her," but her father wouldn't let him in.

²"I truly thought you must hate her," her father explained, "so I gave her in marriage to your best man. But look, her younger sister

14:11 Hebrew *they.* 14:15 As in Greek version; Hebrew reads *seventh.*

BOOMERANG
(15:1-20) Samson's reply in 15:11 is one to which many can relate: "I only did to them what they did to me." Revenge is an unending cycle. Each act of retaliation brings another. It is a boomerang that cannot be thrown without bringing damage to the thrower. Feeling the urge to "throw" revenge at someone? The revenge cycle can be halted only by forgiveness.

is even more beautiful than she is. Marry her instead."

³Samson said, "This time I cannot be blamed for everything I am going to do to you Philistines." ⁴Then he went out and caught 300 foxes. He tied their tails together in pairs, and he fastened a torch to each pair of tails. ⁵Then he lit the torches and let the foxes run through the grain fields of the Philistines. He burned all their grain to the ground, including the sheaves and the uncut grain. He also destroyed their vineyards and olive groves.

⁶"Who did this?" the Philistines demanded.

"Samson," was the reply, "because his father-in-law from Timnah gave Samson's wife to be married to his best man." So the Philistines went and got the woman and her father and burned them to death.

⁷"Because you did this," Samson vowed, "I won't rest until I take my revenge on you!" ⁸So he attacked the Philistines with great fury and killed many of them. Then he went to live in a cave in the rock of Etam.

⁹The Philistines retaliated by setting up camp in Judah and spreading out near the town of Lehi. ¹⁰The men of Judah asked the Philistines, "Why are you attacking us?"

The Philistines replied, "We've come to capture Samson. We've come to pay him back for what he did to us."

¹¹So 3,000 men of Judah went down to get Samson at the cave in the rock of Etam. They said to Samson, "Don't you realize the Philistines rule over us? What are you doing to us?"

But Samson replied, "I only did to them what they did to me."

¹²But the men of Judah told him, "We have come to tie you up and hand you over to the Philistines."

"All right," Samson said. "But promise that you won't kill me yourselves."

¹³"We will only tie you up and hand you over to the Philistines," they replied. "We won't kill you." So they tied him up with two new ropes and brought him up from the rock.

¹⁴As Samson arrived at Lehi, the Philistines

came shouting in triumph. But the Spirit of the LORD came powerfully upon Samson, and he snapped the ropes on his arms as if they were burnt strands of flax, and they fell from his wrists. ¹⁵Then he found the jawbone of a recently killed donkey. He picked it up and killed 1,000 Philistines with it. ¹⁶Then Samson said,

"With the jawbone of a donkey,
    I've piled them in heaps!
With the jawbone of a donkey,
    I've killed a thousand men!"

¹⁷When he finished his boasting, he threw away the jawbone; and the place was named Jawbone Hill.*

¹⁸Samson was now very thirsty, and he cried out to the LORD, "You have accomplished this great victory by the strength of your servant. Must I now die of thirst and fall into the hands of these pagans?" ¹⁹So God caused water to gush out of a hollow in the ground at Lehi, and Samson was revived as he drank. Then he named that place "The Spring of the One Who Cried Out,"* and it is still in Lehi to this day.

²⁰Samson judged Israel for twenty years during the period when the Philistines dominated the land.

16 SAMSON CARRIES AWAY GAZA'S GATES

One day Samson went to the Philistine town of Gaza and spent the night with a prostitute. ²Word soon spread* that Samson was there, so the men of Gaza gathered together and waited all night at the town gates. They kept quiet during the night, saying to themselves, "When the light of morning comes, we will kill him."

³But Samson stayed in bed only until midnight. Then he got up, took hold of the doors of the town gate, including the two posts, and lifted them up, bar and all. He put them on his shoulders and carried them all the way to the top of the hill across from Hebron.

SAMSON AND DELILAH ⁴Some time later Samson fell in love with a woman named Delilah, who lived in the valley of Sorek. ⁵The rulers of the Philistines went to her and said, "Entice Samson to tell you what makes him so strong and how he can be overpowered and tied up securely. Then each of us will give you 1,100 pieces* of silver."

⁶So Delilah said to Samson, "Please tell me

EXHAUSTION
(15:18) Samson was physically and emotionally exhausted. After a great personal victory, his attitude declined quickly into self-pity—"Must I now die of thirst?" Emotionally, we are most vulnerable after a great effort or when faced with real physical needs. That's why depression often follows great achievements. When you're feeling exhausted, let the message of Isaiah 40:31 renew your hope: "Those who trust in the LORD will find new strength." Concentrate on keeping your attitudes, actions, and words focused on God instead of yourself.

15:17 Hebrew *Ramath-lehi*. **15:19** Hebrew *En-hakkore*. **16:2** As in Greek and Syriac versions and Latin Vulgate; Hebrew lacks *Word soon spread.* **16:5** Hebrew *1,100 shekels*, about 28 pounds or 12.5 kilograms in weight.

what makes you so strong and what it would take to tie you up securely."

⁷Samson replied, "If I were tied up with seven new bowstrings that have not yet been dried, I would become as weak as anyone else."

⁸So the Philistine rulers brought Delilah seven new bowstrings, and she tied Samson up with them. ⁹She had hidden some men in one of the inner rooms of her house, and she cried out, "Samson! The Philistines have come to capture you!" But Samson snapped the bowstrings as a piece of string snaps when it is burned by a fire. So the secret of his strength was not discovered.

¹⁰Afterward Delilah said to him, "You've been making fun of me and telling me lies! Now please tell me how you can be tied up securely."

¹¹Samson replied, "If I were tied up with brand-new ropes that had never been used, I would become as weak as anyone else."

¹²So Delilah took new ropes and tied him up with them. The men were hiding in the inner room as before, and again Delilah cried out, "Samson! The Philistines have come to capture you!" But again Samson snapped the ropes from his arms as if they were thread.

¹³Then Delilah said, "You've been making fun of me and telling me lies! Now tell me how you can be tied up securely."

Samson replied, "If you were to weave the seven braids of my hair into the fabric on your

16:13-14 As in Greek version and Latin Vulgate; Hebrew lacks *I would become as weak as anyone else. / So while he slept, Delilah wove the seven braids of his hair into the fabric.* ¹⁴*Then she tightened it with the loom shuttle.*

loom and tighten it with the loom shuttle, I would become as weak as anyone else."

So while he slept, Delilah wove the seven braids of his hair into the fabric. ¹⁴Then she tightened it with the loom shuttle.* Again she cried out, "Samson! The Philistines have come to capture you!" But Samson woke up, pulled back the loom shuttle, and yanked his hair away from the loom and the fabric.

¹⁵Then Delilah pouted, "How can you tell me, 'I love you,' when you don't share your secrets with me? You've made fun of me three times now, and you still haven't told me what makes you so strong!" ¹⁶She tormented him with her nagging day after day until he was sick to death of it.

¹⁷Finally, Samson shared his secret with her. "My hair has never been cut," he confessed, "for I was dedicated to God as a Nazirite from birth. If my head were shaved, my strength would leave me, and I would become as weak as anyone else."

¹⁸Delilah realized he had finally told her

••

A FOOL FOR LOVE

(16:15) Samson allowed himself to be deceived by Delilah, because he didn't want to lose her. How can you avoid being deceived like this? (1) Use wisdom as you consider who to date. (The best way to gain wisdom is to ask God for it.) (2) Avoid compromising your principles. (3) Be patient. You'll soon discover your potential date's true colors.

NAGGING

(16:16-17) Delilah kept asking Samson for the secret of his strength until he finally grew tired of hearing her nagging and gave in. What a pitiful excuse for disobedience. Don't allow anyone, no matter how attractive or persuasive, talk you into doing wrong.

PERSONALITY PROFILE DELILAH

UPS:
• *Persistent when faced with obstacles*

DOWNS:
• *Valued money more than relationships*
• *Betrayed the man who trusted her*

STATS:
• *Where: Valley of Sorek*
• *Contemporary: Samson*

KEY VERSES: *Judges 16:16-17*

WHAT KIND OF REPUTATION do you have? A person can gain a reputation in two very different ways. One way is to help others do great things. Another is to keep others from doing great things. Delilah was only one person in Samson's life, but she almost completely ruined him. She persuaded Samson to go against what God wanted him to do. Because of what she thought she could get, Delilah used her persistence to wear Samson down. When others couldn't defeat Samson's strength or even discover its source, Delilah used deception to gain that information.

Delilah is never mentioned again in the Bible, but she is frequently remembered as an example of someone who betrayed a friend. That earned her a permanent reputation of the worst kind.

Are people helped by knowing you? Does your friendship encourage them to be the best they can be? Even more important, does knowing you help their relationship with God?

BOTTOM LINE: We can either help or hinder people to reach their potential.

Delilah's story is told in Judges 16.

the truth, so she sent for the Philistine rulers. "Come back one more time," she said, "for he has finally told me his secret." So the Philistine rulers returned with the money in their hands. [19]Delilah lulled Samson to sleep with his head in her lap, and then she called in a man to shave off the seven locks of his hair. In this way she began to bring him down,* and his strength left him.

[20]Then she cried out, "Samson! The Philistines have come to capture you!"

When he woke up, he thought, "I will do as before and shake myself free." But he didn't realize the LORD had left him.

[21]So the Philistines captured him and gouged out his eyes. They took him to Gaza, where he was bound with bronze chains and forced to grind grain in the prison.

[22]But before long, his hair began to grow back.

SAMSON'S FINAL VICTORY [23]The Philistine rulers held a great festival, offering sacrifices and praising their god, Dagon. They said, "Our god has given us victory over our enemy Samson!"

[24]When the people saw him, they praised their god, saying, "Our god has delivered our enemy to us! The one who killed so many of us is now in our power!"

[25]Half drunk by now, the people demanded, "Bring out Samson so he can amuse us!" So he was brought from the prison to amuse them, and they had him stand between the pillars supporting the roof.

[26]Samson said to the young servant who was leading him by the hand, "Place my hands against the pillars that hold up the temple. I want to rest against them." [27]Now the temple was completely filled with people. All the Philistine rulers were there, and there were about 3,000 men and women on the roof who were watching as Samson amused them.

[28]Then Samson prayed to the LORD, "Sovereign LORD, remember me again. O God, please strengthen me just one more time. With one blow let me pay back the Philistines for the loss of my two eyes." [29]Then Samson put his hands on the two center pillars that held up the temple. Pushing against them with both hands, [30]he prayed, "Let me die with the Philistines." And the temple crashed down on the Philistine rulers and all the people. So he killed more people when he died than he had during his entire lifetime.

[31]Later his brothers and other relatives went down to get his body. They took him back home and buried him between Zorah and Eshtaol, where his father, Manoah, was buried. Samson had judged Israel for twenty years.

17 **MICAH'S IDOLS** There was a man named Micah, who lived in the hill country of Ephraim. [2]One day he said to his mother, "I heard you place a curse on the person who stole 1,100 pieces* of silver from you. Well, I have the money. I was the one who took it."

16:19 Or *she began to torment him.* Greek version reads *He began to grow weak.*   **17:2** Hebrew *1,100 shekels,* about 28 pounds or 12.5 kilograms in weight.

SALVAGED
(16:28-30) Despite Samson's mistakes, God still answered his prayer and destroyed the Philistine temple and worshipers.

One of the effects of sin is that it keeps us from feeling like praying. But being good is not a prerequisite for prayer. Feeling distant from God lately? No matter how long you have been away from him, he is ready to hear from you and restore you to a right relationship.

CHOICES
compromise

Becca and her boyfriend James seem to have everything going for them:

- They are believers in Christ.
- They come from solid Christian homes.
- Friends constantly tease them by saying, "You guys are so good together. . . . You're just like an old married couple!"
- They are seniors at one of the best Christian schools in the state.
- They both have been accepted to one of the top Christian colleges in the country.
- They plan to marry after they finish college.
- They want to go to Guatemala as missionaries.

Amazing, isn't it? The relationship seems perfect. Proud parents, teachers, and church leaders agree that Becca and James each have been specially gifted by God, and they predict great things. Says Coach Acker, "Those two will be mightily used by the Lord."

Well, if the scenario seems too good to be true, it is. In just about two weeks, this perfect couple will see their dream world collapse right before their eyes.

See, Becca and James have let their physical relationship get out of hand. And now Becca is pregnant.

Check out Judges 16. How is Samson's story like Becca and James's situation? What would you do to avoid following the same path?

"The LORD bless you for admitting it," his mother replied. ³He returned the money to her, and she said, "I now dedicate these silver coins to the LORD. In honor of my son, I will have an image carved and an idol cast."

⁴So when he returned the money to his mother, she took 200 silver coins and gave them to a silversmith, who made them into an image and an idol. And these were placed in Micah's house. ⁵Micah set up a shrine for the idol, and he made a sacred ephod and some household idols. Then he installed one of his sons as his personal priest.

⁶In those days Israel had no king; all the people did whatever seemed right in their own eyes.

⁷One day a young Levite, who had been living in Bethlehem in Judah, arrived in that area. ⁸He had left Bethlehem in search of another place to live, and as he traveled, he came to the hill country of Ephraim. He happened to stop at Micah's house as he was traveling through. ⁹"Where are you from?" Micah asked him.

He replied, "I am a Levite from Bethlehem in Judah, and I am looking for a place to live."

¹⁰"Stay here with me," Micah said, "and you can be a father and priest to me. I will give you ten pieces* of silver a year, plus a change of clothes and your food." ¹¹The Levite agreed to this, and the young man became like one of Micah's sons.

¹²So Micah installed the Levite as his personal priest, and he lived in Micah's house. ¹³"I know the LORD will bless me now," Micah said, "because I have a Levite serving as my priest."

18 **IDOLATRY IN THE TRIBE OF DAN** Now in those days Israel had no king. And the tribe of Dan was trying to find a place where they could settle, for they had not yet moved into the land assigned to them when the land was divided among the tribes of Israel. ²So the men of Dan chose from their clans five capable warriors from the towns of Zorah and Eshtaol to scout out a land for them to settle in.

When these warriors arrived in the hill country of Ephraim, they came to Micah's house and spent the night there. ³While at Micah's house, they recognized the young Levite's accent, so they went over and asked him, "Who brought you here, and what are you doing in this place? Why are you here?" ⁴He told them

IN THOSE DAYS ISRAEL HAD NO KING;

ALL THE PEOPLE DID WHATEVER SEEMED RIGHT IN THEIR OWN EYES.

▪ ▪ ▪ ▪ ▪ ▪ ▪ ▪ ▪ ▪ ▪ JUDGES 17:6

about his agreement with Micah and that he had been hired as Micah's personal priest.

⁵Then they said, "Ask God whether or not our journey will be successful."

⁶"Go in peace," the priest replied. "For the LORD is watching over your journey."

⁷So the five men went on to the town of Laish, where they noticed the people living carefree lives, like the Sidonians; they were peaceful and secure.* The people were also wealthy because their land was very fertile. And they lived a great distance from Sidon and had no allies nearby.

⁸When the men returned to Zorah and Eshtaol, their relatives asked them, "What did you find?"

⁹The men replied, "Come on, let's attack them! We have seen the land, and it is very good. What are you waiting for? Don't hesitate to go and take possession of it. ¹⁰When you get there, you will find the people living carefree lives. God has given us a spacious and fertile land, lacking in nothing!"

¹¹So 600 men from the tribe of Dan, armed with weapons of war, set out from Zorah and Eshtaol. ¹²They camped at a place west of Kiriath-jearim in Judah, which is called Mahaneh-dan* to this day. ¹³Then they went on from there into the hill country of Ephraim and came to the house of Micah.

¹⁴The five men who had scouted out the land around Laish explained to the others, "These buildings contain a sacred ephod, as well as some household idols, a carved image, and a cast idol. What do you think you should do?" ¹⁵Then the five men turned off the road and went over to Micah's house, where the

....

17:10 Hebrew *10 shekels*, about 4 ounces or 114 grams in weight. **18:7** The meaning of the Hebrew is uncertain. **18:12** *Mahaneh-dan* means "the camp of Dan."

MOTIVES
(18:1-6) Through this entire incident, no one desired to worship God; instead, they wanted to use God for selfish gain. Today some people go to church to feel better, be accepted, relieve guilt, and gain friends. Beware of following God for selfish gains rather than selfless service.

young Levite lived, and greeted him kindly. [16]As the 600 armed warriors from the tribe of Dan stood at the entrance of the gate, [17]the five scouts entered the shrine and removed the carved image, the sacred ephod, the household idols, and the cast idol. Meanwhile, the priest was standing at the gate with the 600 armed warriors.

[18]When the priest saw the men carrying all the sacred objects out of Micah's shrine, he said, "What are you doing?"

[19]"Be quiet and come with us," they said. "Be a father and priest to all of us. Isn't it better to be a priest for an entire tribe and clan of Israel than for the household of just one man?"

[20]The young priest was quite happy to go with them, so he took along the sacred ephod, the household idols, and the carved image. [21]They turned and started on their way again, placing their children, livestock, and possessions in front of them.

[22]When the people from the tribe of Dan were quite a distance from Micah's house, the people who lived near Micah came chasing after them. [23]They were shouting as they caught up with them. The men of Dan turned around and said to Micah, "What's the matter? Why have you called these men together and chased after us like this?"

[24]"What do you mean, 'What's the matter?'" Micah replied. "You've taken away all the gods I have made, and my priest, and I have nothing left!"

[25]The men of Dan said, "Watch what you say! There are some short-tempered men around here who might get angry and kill you and your family." [26]So the men of Dan continued on their way. When Micah saw that there were too many of them for him to attack, he turned around and went home.

[27]Then, with Micah's idols and his priest, the men of Dan came to the town of Laish, whose people were peaceful and secure. They attacked with swords and burned the town to the ground. [28]There was no one to rescue the people, for they lived a great distance from Sidon and had no allies nearby. This happened in the valley near Beth-rehob.

Then the people of the tribe of Dan rebuilt the town and lived there. [29]They renamed the town Dan after their ancestor, Israel's son, but it had originally been called Laish. [30]Then they set up the carved image, and they appointed Jonathan son of Gershom, son of Moses,* as their priest. This family continued as priests for the tribe of Dan until the Exile. [31]So Micah's carved image was worshiped by the tribe of Dan as long as the Tabernacle of God remained at Shiloh.

19 THE LEVITE AND HIS CONCUBINE Now
in those days Israel had no king. There was a man from the tribe of Levi living in a remote area of the hill country of Ephraim. One day he brought home a woman from Bethlehem in Judah to be his concubine. [2]But she became angry with him* and returned to her father's home in Bethlehem.

After about four months, [3]her husband set out for Bethlehem to speak personally to her and persuade her to come back. He took with him a servant and a pair of donkeys. When he arrived at* her father's house, her father saw him and welcomed him. [4]Her father urged him to stay awhile, so he stayed three days, eating, drinking, and sleeping there.

[5]On the fourth day the man was up early, ready to leave, but the woman's father said to his son-in-law, "Have something to eat before you go." [6]So the two men sat down together and had something to eat and drink. Then the woman's father said, "Please stay another night and enjoy yourself." [7]The man got up to leave, but his father-in-law kept urging him to stay, so he finally gave in and stayed the night.

[8]On the morning of the fifth day he was up early again, ready to leave, and again the woman's father said, "Have something to eat; then you can leave later this afternoon." So they had another day of feasting. [9]Later, as the man and his concubine and servant were preparing to leave, his father-in-law said, "Look, it's almost evening. Stay the night and enjoy yourself. Tomorrow you can get up early and be on your way."

[10]But this time the man was determined to leave. So he took his two saddled donkeys and

---

CONCUBINES
(19:1-26) While polygamy was an accepted practice in Israel, it was not what God intended (see Gen 2:24). A concubine or secondary wife had the duties, but not the privileges, of being a wife. Her primary purposes were to give the man sexual pleasure, to bear additional children, and to contribute more help to the household or estate.

The man from the tribe of Levi clearly thought more about himself than about his concubine. This awful story illustrates the fact that unthinkable sin can result when we choose to fulfill our own desires rather than following God's design. God's plan is for one husband and one wife to be committed to each other with a sacrificial, lifelong love.

18:30 As in an ancient Hebrew tradition, some Greek manuscripts, and Latin Vulgate; Masoretic Text reads *son of Manasseh.* **19:2** Or *she was unfaithful to him.* **19:3** As in Greek version; Hebrew reads *When she brought him to.*

his concubine and headed in the direction of Jebus (that is, Jerusalem). ¹¹It was late in the day when they neared Jebus, and the man's servant said to him, "Let's stop at this Jebusite town and spend the night there."

¹²"No," his master said, "we can't stay in this foreign town where there are no Israelites. Instead, we will go on to Gibeah. ¹³Come on, let's try to get as far as Gibeah or Ramah, and we'll spend the night in one of those towns." ¹⁴So they went on. The sun was setting as they came to Gibeah, a town in the land of Benjamin, ¹⁵so they stopped there to spend the night. They rested in the town square, but no one took them in for the night.

¹⁶That evening an old man came home from his work in the fields. He was from the hill country of Ephraim, but he was living in Gibeah, where the people were from the tribe of Benjamin. ¹⁷When he saw the travelers sitting in the town square, he asked them where they were from and where they were going.

¹⁸"We have been in Bethlehem in Judah," the man replied. "We are on our way to a remote area in the hill country of Ephraim, which is my home. I traveled to Bethlehem, and now I'm returning home.* But no one has taken us in for the night, ¹⁹even though we have everything we need. We have straw and feed for our donkeys and plenty of bread and wine for ourselves."

²⁰"You are welcome to stay with me," the old man said. "I will give you anything you might need. But whatever you do, don't spend the night in the square." ²¹So he took them home with him and fed the donkeys. After they washed their feet, they ate and drank together.

²²While they were enjoying themselves, a crowd of troublemakers from the town surrounded the house. They began beating at the door and shouting to the old man, "Bring out the man who is staying with you so we can have sex with him."

²³The old man stepped outside to talk to them. "No, my brothers, don't do such an evil thing. For this man is a guest in my house, and such a thing would be shameful. ²⁴Here, take my virgin daughter and this man's concubine. I will bring them out to you, and you can abuse them and do whatever you like. But don't do such a shameful thing to this man."

²⁵But they wouldn't listen to him. So the Levite took hold of his concubine and pushed her out the door. The men of the town abused her all night, taking turns raping her until morning.

Finally, at dawn they let her go. ²⁶At daybreak the woman returned to the house where her husband was staying. She collapsed at the door of the house and lay there until it was light.

²⁷When her husband opened the door to leave, there lay his concubine with her hands on the threshold. ²⁸He said, "Get up! Let's go!" But there was no answer.* So he put her body on his donkey and took her home.

²⁹When he got home, he took a knife and cut his concubine's body into twelve pieces. Then he sent one piece to each tribe throughout all the territory of Israel.

³⁰Everyone who saw it said, "Such a horrible crime has not been committed in all the time since Israel left Egypt. Think about it! What are we going to do? Who's going to speak up?"

20 ISRAEL'S WAR WITH BENJAMIN Then all the Israelites were united as one man, from Dan in the north to Beersheba in the south, including those from across the Jordan in the land of Gilead. The entire community assembled in the presence of the LORD at Mizpah. ²The leaders of all the people and all the tribes of Israel—400,000 warriors armed with swords—took their positions in the assembly of the people of God. ³(Word soon reached the land of Benjamin that the other tribes had gone up to Mizpah.) The Israelites then asked how this terrible crime had happened.

⁴The Levite, the husband of the woman who had been murdered, said, "My concubine and I came to spend the night in Gibeah, a town that belongs to the people of Benjamin. ⁵That night some of the leading citizens of Gibeah surrounded the house, planning to kill me, and they raped my concubine until she was dead. ⁶So I cut her body into twelve pieces and sent the pieces throughout the territory assigned to Israel, for these men have committed a terrible and shameful crime. ⁷Now then, all of you—the entire community of Israel—must decide here and now what should be done about this!"

⁸And all the people rose to their feet in

19:18 As in Greek version (see also 19:29); Hebrew reads *now I'm going to the Tabernacle of the LORD.* **19:28** Greek version adds *for she was dead.*

DEFECTIVE GOVERNMENT
(19:30) The horrible crime described in this chapter wasn't Israel's worst offense. Even worse was the nation's failure to establish a government based upon God's laws. As a result, laws were usually not enforced. Sexual perversion and lawlessness were by-products of Israel's disobedience to God.

Whenever we drift away from God and his Word, all sorts of evil can follow. Our drifting away may be slow and almost imperceptible, but the effects can be long lasting. Want to know a sure cure for drifting? Return to God.

unison and declared, "None of us will return home! No, not even one of us! ⁹Instead, this is what we will do to Gibeah; we will draw lots to decide who will attack it. ¹⁰One-tenth of the men* from each tribe will be chosen to supply the warriors with food, and the rest of us will take revenge on Gibeah* of Benjamin for this shameful thing they have done in Israel." ¹¹So all the Israelites were completely united, and they gathered together to attack the town.

¹²The Israelites sent messengers to the tribe of Benjamin, saying, "What a terrible thing has been done among you! ¹³Give up those evil men, those troublemakers from Gibeah, so we can execute them and purge Israel of this evil."

But the people of Benjamin would not listen. ¹⁴Instead, they came from their towns and gathered at Gibeah to fight the Israelites. ¹⁵In all, 26,000 of their warriors armed with swords arrived in Gibeah to join the 700 elite troops who lived there. ¹⁶Among Benjamin's elite troops, 700 were left-handed, and each of them could sling a rock and hit a target within a hairsbreadth without missing. ¹⁷Israel had 400,000 experienced soldiers armed with swords, not counting Benjamin's warriors.

¹⁸Before the battle the Israelites went to Bethel and asked God, "Which tribe should go first to attack the people of Benjamin?"

The LORD answered, "Judah is to go first."

¹⁹So the Israelites left early the next morning and camped near Gibeah. ²⁰Then they advanced toward Gibeah to attack the men of Benjamin. ²¹But Benjamin's warriors, who were defending the town, came out and killed 22,000 Israelites on the battlefield that day.

²²But the Israelites encouraged each other and took their positions again at the same place they had fought the previous day. ²³For they had gone up to Bethel and wept in the presence of the LORD until evening. They had asked the LORD, "Should we fight against our relatives from Benjamin again?"

And the LORD had said, "Go out and fight against them."

²⁴So the next day they went out again to fight against the men of Benjamin, ²⁵but the men of Benjamin killed another 18,000 Israelites, all of whom were experienced with the sword.

²⁶Then all the Israelites went up to Bethel and wept in the presence of the LORD and fasted until evening. They also brought burnt offerings and peace offerings to the LORD. ²⁷The Israelites went up seeking direction from the LORD. (In those days the Ark of the Covenant of God was in Bethel, ²⁸and Phinehas son of Eleazar and grandson of Aaron was the

priest.) The Israelites asked the LORD, "Should we fight against our relatives from Benjamin again, or should we stop?"

The LORD said, "Go! Tomorrow I will hand them over to you."

²⁹So the Israelites set an ambush all around Gibeah. ³⁰They went out on the third day and took their positions at the same place as before. ³¹When the men of Benjamin came out to attack, they were drawn away from the town. And as they had done before, they began to kill the Israelites. About thirty Israelites died in the open fields and along the roads, one leading to Bethel and the other leading back to Gibeah.

³²Then the warriors of Benjamin shouted, "We're defeating them as we did before!" But the Israelites had planned in advance to run away so that the men of Benjamin would chase them along the roads and be drawn away from the town.

³³When the main group of Israelite warriors reached Baal-tamar, they turned and took up their positions. Meanwhile, the Israelites hiding in ambush to the west* of Gibeah jumped up to fight. ³⁴There were 10,000 elite Israelite troops who advanced against Gibeah. The fighting was so heavy that Benjamin didn't realize the impending disaster. ³⁵So the LORD helped Israel defeat Benjamin, and that day the Israelites killed 25,100 of Benjamin's warriors, all of whom were experienced swordsmen. ³⁶Then the men of Benjamin saw that they were beaten.

The Israelites had retreated from Benjamin's warriors in order to give those hiding in ambush more room to maneuver against Gibeah. ³⁷Then those who were hiding rushed in from all sides and killed everyone in the town. ³⁸They had arranged to send up a large cloud of smoke from the town as a signal. ³⁹When the Israelites saw the smoke, they turned and attacked Benjamin's warriors.

By that time Benjamin's warriors had killed about thirty Israelites, and they shouted, "We're defeating them as we did in the first battle!" ⁴⁰But when the warriors of Benjamin looked behind them and saw the smoke rising into the sky from every part of the town, ⁴¹the men of Israel turned and attacked. At this point the men of Benjamin became terrified, because they realized disaster was close at hand. ⁴²So they turned around and fled before

20:10a Hebrew *10 men from every hundred, 100 men from every thousand, and 1,000 men from every 10,000.* **20:10b** Hebrew *Geba,* in this case a variant spelling of Gibeah; also in 20:33. **20:33** As in Greek and Syriac versions and Latin Vulgate; Hebrew reads *hiding in the open space.*

the Israelites toward the wilderness. But they couldn't escape the battle, and the people who came out of the nearby towns were also killed.* ⁴³The Israelites surrounded the men of Benjamin and chased them relentlessly, finally overtaking them east of Gibeah.* ⁴⁴That day 18,000 of Benjamin's strongest warriors died in battle. ⁴⁵The survivors fled into the wilderness toward the rock of Rimmon, but Israel killed 5,000 of them along the road. They continued the chase until they had killed another 2,000 near Gidom.

⁴⁶So that day the tribe of Benjamin lost 25,000 strong warriors armed with swords, ⁴⁷leaving only 600 men who escaped to the rock of Rimmon, where they lived for four months. ⁴⁸And the Israelites returned and slaughtered every living thing in all the towns—the people, the livestock, and everything they found. They also burned down all the towns they came to.

21 ISRAEL PROVIDES WIVES FOR BENJAMIN

The Israelites had vowed at Mizpah, "We will never give our daughters in marriage to a man from the tribe of Benjamin." ²Now the people went to Bethel and sat in the presence of God until evening, weeping loudly and bitterly. ³"O Lord, God of Israel," they cried out, "why has this happened in Israel? Now one of our tribes is missing from Israel!"

⁴Early the next morning the people built an altar and presented their burnt offerings and peace offerings on it. ⁵Then they said, "Who among the tribes of Israel did not join us at Mizpah when we held our assembly in the presence of the Lord?" At that time they had taken a solemn oath in the Lord's presence, vowing that anyone who refused to come would be put to death.

⁶The Israelites felt sorry for their brother Benjamin and said, "Today one of the tribes of Israel has been cut off. ⁷How can we find wives for the few who remain, since we have sworn by the Lord not to give them our daughters in marriage?"

⁸So they asked, "Who among the tribes of Israel did not join us at Mizpah when we assembled in the presence of the Lord?" And they discovered that no one from Jabesh-gilead had attended the assembly. ⁹For after they counted all the people, no one from Jabesh-gilead was present.

¹⁰So the assembly sent 12,000 of their best warriors to Jabesh-gilead with orders to kill everyone there, including women and children. ¹¹"This is what you are to do," they said. "Completely destroy* all the males and every woman who is not a virgin." ¹²Among the residents of Jabesh-gilead they found 400 young virgins who had never slept with a man, and they brought them to the camp at Shiloh in the land of Canaan.

¹³The Israelite assembly sent a peace delegation to the remaining people of Benjamin who were living at the rock of Rimmon. ¹⁴Then the men of Benjamin returned to their homes, and the 400 women of Jabesh-gilead who had been spared were given to them as wives. But there were not enough women for all of them.

¹⁵The people felt sorry for Benjamin because the Lord had made this gap among the tribes of Israel. ¹⁶So the elders of the assembly asked, "How can we find wives for the few who remain, since the women of the tribe of Benjamin are dead? ¹⁷There must be heirs for the survivors so that an entire tribe of Israel is not wiped out. ¹⁸But we cannot give them our own daughters in marriage because we have sworn with a solemn oath that anyone who does this will fall under God's curse."

¹⁹Then they thought of the annual festival of the Lord held in Shiloh, south of Lebonah and north of Bethel, along the east side of the road that goes from Bethel to Shechem. ²⁰They told the men of Benjamin who still needed wives, "Go and hide in the vineyards. ²¹When you see the young women of Shiloh come out for their dances, rush out from the vineyards, and each of you can take one of them home to the land of Benjamin to be your wife! ²²And when their fathers and brothers come to us in protest, we will tell them, 'Please be sympathetic. Let them have your daughters, for we didn't find wives for all of them when we destroyed Jabesh-gilead. And you are not guilty of breaking the vow since you did not actually give your daughters to them in marriage.'"

· ·

QUICK ACTION
(20:46-48) The effects of the horrible rape and murder should never have been felt outside of the community where the crime happened. The local people should have brought the criminals to justice and corrected the negligence that originally permitted this crime. Instead, first the town and then the entire tribe defended this wickedness, even going to war over it. This war almost wiped out the fighting men of Benjamin. To prevent problems from turning into major conflicts, firm action must be taken quickly, wisely, and forcefully before the situation gets out of hand.

20:42 Or battle, for the people from the nearby towns also came out and killed them. **20:43** The meaning of the Hebrew is uncertain. **21:11** The Hebrew term used here refers to the complete consecration of things or people to the Lord, either by destroying them or by giving them as an offering.

HEROES
(21:25) During the time of the judges, the people of Israel experienced trouble because they became their own authority and acted on their own opinions of right and wrong. This produced horrendous results. Our world is similar. Many individuals and groups have made themselves the final authorities of what's right or wrong. But God calls his people to live by his rules. That is the act of a true hero.

To be truly heroic, we must go into battle each day in our home, school, church, and society to make God's kingdom a reality. Our weapons are the standards and truths we receive from God's Word. We will lose the battle if we gather the spoils of earthly treasures rather than seeking the treasures of heaven.

²³So the men of Benjamin did as they were told. Each man caught one of the women as she danced in the celebration and carried her off to be his wife. They returned to their own land, and they rebuilt their towns and lived in them.

²⁴Then the people of Israel departed by tribes and families, and they returned to their own homes.

²⁵In those days Israel had no king; all the people did whatever seemed right in their own eyes.

"Mom, that food looks awful!" "Dad, you always make me take out the garbage." "She's the worst teacher ever!" "My allowance isn't enough." "I hate the way I look." Sound familiar? Everyone likes to complain. When things don't go exactly as we think they should, we are quick to let others know we feel cheated and angry.

In the book of Ruth, we find Naomi's complaints. She blamed God for the deaths of her husband and two sons. She even wanted to be known as Mara, a name that means "bitter" (1:20).

But Naomi later learned that God wasn't to be blamed for her family members' deaths; instead, he was to be thanked for his kindness. His kindness was revealed through the love and loyalty of Ruth, one of Naomi's daughters-in-law.

We're like Naomi sometimes. If something in life is wrong, we conclude that it must be God's fault. The book of Ruth reminds us strongly and clearly that this is not the case. God is not to be blamed for our problems but praised for his goodness.

Read the book of Ruth—a story of relationships, rescue, and romance—and thank God for his goodness in your life.

KEY POINTS

FAITHFULNESS Ruth's faithfulness to Naomi as a daughter-in-law and friend is a great example of love and loyalty. We can imitate God's faithfulness by being loyal and loving in our relationships.

KINDNESS Ruth showed great kindness to Naomi and received kindness from Boaz, the redeemer of her family's inheritance. In a similar way, Christ showed his kindness by purchasing us to guarantee our eternal life.

INTEGRITY Ruth showed integrity by being loyal to Naomi, by her clean break from her former land and customs, and by her hard work in the field. God's faithfulness and kindness can encourage us to live lives characterized by integrity.

PROTECTION God protected Naomi and Ruth as they traveled to Bethlehem and while Ruth worked in the barley field. We can count on God's protection and mercy.

PROSPERITY/BLESSING Ruth and Naomi came to Bethlehem as poor widows, but soon became prosperous through Ruth's marriage to Boaz. Yet the greatest blessing was not material; it was the quality of love and respect between Ruth, Boaz, and Naomi. Relationships that God makes possible for us are one of his most special blessings.

1 ELIMELECH MOVES HIS FAMILY TO MOAB

In the days when the judges ruled in Israel, a severe famine came upon the land. So a man from Bethlehem in Judah left his home and went to live in the country of Moab, taking his wife and two sons with him. ²The man's name was Elimelech, and his wife was Naomi. Their two sons were Mahlon and Kilion. They were Ephrathites from Bethlehem in the land of Judah. And when they reached Moab, they settled there.

³Then Elimelech died, and Naomi was left with her two sons. ⁴The two sons married Moabite women. One married a woman named Orpah, and the other a woman named Ruth. But about ten years later, ⁵both Mahlon and Kilion died. This left Naomi alone, without her two sons or her husband.

NAOMI AND RUTH RETURN ⁶Then Naomi heard in Moab that the LORD had blessed his people in Judah by giving them good crops again. So Naomi and her daughters-in-law got ready to leave Moab to return to her homeland. ⁷With her two daughters-in-law she set out from the place where she had been living, and they took the road that would lead them back to Judah.

⁸But on the way, Naomi said to her two daughters-in-law, "Go back to your mothers' homes. And may the LORD reward you for your kindness to your husbands and to me. ⁹May the LORD bless you with the security of another marriage." Then she kissed them good-bye, and they all broke down and wept.

¹⁰"No," they said. "We want to go with you to your people."

¹¹But Naomi replied, "Why should you go on with me? Can I still give birth to other sons who could grow up to be your husbands? ¹²No, my daughters, return to your parents' homes, for I am too old to marry again. And even if it were possible, and I were to get married tonight and bear sons, then what? ¹³Would you wait for them to grow up and refuse to marry someone else? No, of course not, my daughters! Things are far more bitter for me than for you, because the LORD himself has raised his fist against me."

¹⁴And again they wept together, and Orpah kissed her mother-in-law good-bye. But Ruth clung tightly to Naomi. ¹⁵"Look," Naomi said to her, "your sister-in-law has gone back to her people and to her gods. You should do the same."

¹⁶But Ruth replied, "Don't ask me to leave you and turn back. Wherever you go, I will go; wherever you live, I will live. Your people will be my people, and your God will be my God. ¹⁷Wherever you die, I will die, and there I will be buried. May the LORD punish me severely if I allow anything but death to separate us!"

SETTING FOR THE STORY
Elimelech, Naomi, and their sons traveled from Bethlehem to the land of Moab because of a famine. After her husband and sons died, Naomi learned that the famine had ended, so she returned to Bethlehem with her daughter-in-law Ruth.

CHOICES
commitment

Aya and Kelsey have been friends ever since the third grade. Girl Scouts, softball, Sunday school—they've done it all together.

As they've grown older, however, the girls have developed vastly different interests. In fact, now, as teenagers, they couldn't be more opposite.

Aya is short and round. Extremely outgoing, she makes good grades and keeps everyone in the band in stitches. She's also very involved in the drama club. Kelsey is tall, pretty, and extremely shy. She's also an average student, dates quite a bit, and works at an expensive dress shop in the mall.

Since the two girls have such contrasting personalities, nobody can quite understand why they're still friends. But they are. They're best friends.

Just how close are they? Well, get this: Last week Aya and Kelsey made Saturday plans to go shopping. The very next day, Kelsey got a call from the hottest guy at school (a guy she's secretly liked all year). The call went like this:

"Kelsey? Hi, this is Eric. Listen, I was just wondering if you'd like to go horseback riding on Saturday?"

"This weekend?" Kelsey paused. "Um, Eric, I'd really like to, but I've kinda made plans already. Can we do it some other time?"

Would you have been that loyal to a friend? Read about another woman who understood the meaning of commitment in Ruth 1:1-18.

WHEREVER YOU GO, I WILL GO; WHEREVER YOU LIVE, I WILL LIVE. YOUR PEOPLE WILL BE MY PEOPLE, AND YOUR GOD WILL BE MY GOD.

[18]When Naomi saw that Ruth was determined to go with her, she said nothing more.

[19]So the two of them continued on their journey. When they came to Bethlehem, the entire town was excited by their arrival. "Is it really Naomi?" the women asked.

[20]"Don't call me Naomi," she responded. "Instead, call me Mara,* for the Almighty has made life very bitter for me. [21]I went away full, but the LORD has brought me home empty. Why call me Naomi when the LORD has caused me to suffer* and the Almighty has sent such tragedy upon me?"

[22]So Naomi returned from Moab, accompanied by her daughter-in-law Ruth, the young Moabite woman. They arrived in Bethlehem in late spring, at the beginning of the barley harvest.

2 RUTH WORKS IN BOAZ'S FIELD

Now there was a wealthy and influential man in Bethlehem named Boaz, who was a relative of Naomi's husband, Elimelech.

[2]One day Ruth the Moabite said to Naomi, "Let me go out into the harvest fields to pick up the stalks of grain left behind by anyone who is kind enough to let me do it."

Naomi replied, "All right, my daughter, go ahead." [3]So Ruth went out to gather grain behind the harvesters. And as it happened, she found herself working in a field that belonged to Boaz, the relative of her father-in-law, Elimelech.

[4]While she was there, Boaz arrived from Bethlehem and greeted the harvesters. "The LORD be with you!" he said.

"The LORD bless you!" the harvesters replied.

[5]Then Boaz asked his foreman, "Who is that young woman over there? Who does she belong to?"

[6]And the foreman replied, "She is the young woman from Moab who came back with Naomi. [7]She asked me this morning if she could gather grain behind the harvesters. She has been hard at work ever since, except for a few minutes' rest in the shelter."

[8]Boaz went over and said to Ruth, "Listen, my daughter. Stay right here with us when you gather grain; don't go to any other fields. Stay right behind the young women working in my field. [9]See which part of the field they are harvesting, and then follow them. I have warned the young men not to treat you roughly. And when you are thirsty, help yourself to the water they have drawn from the well."

[10]Ruth fell at his feet and thanked him warmly. "What have I done to deserve such kindness?" she asked. "I am only a foreigner."

[11]"Yes, I know," Boaz replied. "But I also know about everything you have done for your mother-in-law since the death of your husband. I have heard how you left your father and mother and your own land to live here among complete strangers. [12]May the LORD, the God of Israel, under whose wings you have come to take refuge, reward you fully for what you have done."

[13]"I hope I continue to please you, sir," she replied. "You have comforted me by speaking so kindly to me, even though I am not one of your workers."

[14]At mealtime Boaz called to her, "Come over here, and help yourself to some food. You can dip your bread in the sour wine." So she sat with his harvesters, and Boaz gave her some roasted grain to eat. She ate all she wanted and still had some left over.

[15]When Ruth went back to work again, Boaz ordered his young men, "Let her gather grain right among the sheaves without stopping her. [16]And pull out some heads of barley from the bundles and drop them on purpose for her. Let her pick them up, and don't give her a hard time!"

[17]So Ruth gathered barley there all day, and when she beat out the grain that evening, it filled an entire basket.* [18]She carried it back into town and showed it to her mother-in-law. Ruth also gave her the roasted grain that was left over from her meal.

[19]"Where did you gather all this grain today?" Naomi asked. "Where did you work? May the LORD bless the one who helped you!"

So Ruth told her mother-in-law about the

1:20 Naomi means "pleasant"; Mara means "bitter." 1:21 Or has testified against me. 2:17 Hebrew it was about an ephah [20 quarts or 22 liters].

man in whose field she had worked. She said, "The man I worked with today is named Boaz."

20"May the LORD bless him!" Naomi told her daughter-in-law. "He is showing his kindness to us as well as to your dead husband.* That man is one of our closest relatives, one of our family redeemers."

21Then Ruth* said, "What's more, Boaz even told me to come back and stay with his harvesters until the entire harvest is completed."

22"Good!" Naomi exclaimed. "Do as he said, my daughter. Stay with his young women right through the whole harvest. You might be harassed in other fields, but you'll be safe with him."

23So Ruth worked alongside the women in Boaz's fields and gathered grain with them until the end of the barley harvest. Then she continued working with them through the wheat harvest in early summer. And all the while she lived with her mother-in-law.

3 **RUTH AT THE THRESHING FLOOR** One day Naomi said to Ruth, "My daughter, it's time that I found a permanent home for you, so that you will be provided for. 2Boaz is a close relative of ours, and he's been very kind by letting you gather grain with his young women. Tonight he will be winnowing barley at the threshing floor. 3Now do as I tell you—take a bath and put on perfume and dress in your nicest clothes. Then go to the threshing floor, but don't let Boaz see you until he has finished eating and drinking. 4Be sure to notice where he lies down; then go and uncover his feet and lie down there. He will tell you what to do."

5"I will do everything you say," Ruth replied. 6So she went down to the threshing floor that night and followed the instructions of her mother-in-law.

7After Boaz had finished eating and drinking and was in good spirits, he lay down at the far end of the pile of grain and went to sleep. Then Ruth came quietly, uncovered his feet, and lay down. 8Around midnight Boaz suddenly woke up and turned over. He was surprised to find a woman lying at his feet! 9"Who are you?" he asked.

"I am your servant Ruth," she replied. "Spread the corner of your covering over me, for you are my family redeemer."

10"The LORD bless you, my daughter!" Boaz exclaimed. "You are showing even more family loyalty now than you did before, for you have not gone after a younger man, whether rich or poor. 11Now don't worry about a thing, my daughter. I will do what is necessary, for everyone in town knows you are a virtuous woman. 12But while it's true that I am one of your family redeemers, there is another man who is more closely related to you than I am. 13Stay here tonight, and in the morning I will talk to him. If he is willing to redeem you, very well. Let him marry you. But if he is not willing,

---

GOOD ADVICE
(3:5) As a foreigner, Ruth may have thought that Naomi's advice was odd. But Ruth followed the advice because she knew Naomi was kind and trustworthy. Each of us knows a parent, older friend, or relative who is always looking out for our best interests. The experience and knowledge of such a person can be invaluable. Imagine what Ruth's life would have been like had she ignored her mother-in-law. To whom do you go when you need good advice?

2:20 Hebrew *to the living and to the dead.*   2:21 Hebrew *Ruth the Moabite.*

then as surely as the LORD lives, I will redeem you myself! Now lie down here until morning."

[14] So Ruth lay at Boaz's feet until the morning, but she got up before it was light enough for people to recognize each other. For Boaz had said, "No one must know that a woman was here at the threshing floor." [15] Then Boaz said to her, "Bring your cloak and spread it out." He measured six scoops* of barley into the cloak and placed it on her back. Then he* returned to the town.

[16] When Ruth went back to her mother-in-law, Naomi asked, "What happened, my daughter?"

Ruth told Naomi everything Boaz had done for her, [17] and she added, "He gave me these six scoops of barley and said, 'Don't go back to your mother-in-law empty-handed.'"

[18] Then Naomi said to her, "Just be patient, my daughter, until we hear what happens. The man won't rest until he has settled things today."

4 BOAZ MARRIES RUTH

Boaz went to the town gate and took a seat there. Just then the family redeemer he had mentioned came by, so Boaz called out to him, "Come over here and sit down, friend. I want to talk to you."

3:15a Hebrew *six measures,* an unknown quantity. 3:15b Most Hebrew manuscripts read *he;* many Hebrew manuscripts, Syriac version, and Latin Vulgate read *she.*

So they sat down together. [2] Then Boaz called ten leaders from the town and asked them to sit as witnesses. [3] And Boaz said to the family redeemer, "You know Naomi, who came back from Moab. She is selling the land that belonged to our relative Elimelech. [4] I thought I should speak to you about it so that you can redeem it if you wish. If you want the land, then buy it here in the presence of these witnesses. But if you don't want it, let me know right away, because I am next in line to redeem it after you."

The man replied, "All right, I'll redeem it."

[5] Then Boaz told him, "Of course, your purchase of the land from Naomi also requires that you marry Ruth, the Moabite widow. That way she can have children who will carry on her husband's name and keep the land in the family."

[6] "Then I can't redeem it," the family redeemer replied, "because this might endanger my own estate. You redeem the land; I cannot do it."

[7] Now in those days it was the custom in Israel for anyone transferring a right of purchase to remove his sandal and hand it to the other party. This publicly validated the transaction. [8] So the other family redeemer drew off his sandal as he said to Boaz, "You buy the land."

ULTIMATE ISSUES SEXUAL MORALITY

Our society is like a department store window that a mischievous boy broke so he could switch all the items' price tags. The next day, people unknowingly paid the wrong amounts for items and walked out; some got great deals, some got ripped off—all were unaware of what had happened.

It's no secret. Our society's moral values are seriously out of order—especially in the area of sexual morality. Think about the last movie or TV show you saw. What view of sexuality did it portray? Would this viewpoint match up with what's in the Bible? Probably not, right?

Sex is often glorified in society. For some, it is the end all and be all. But what is God's opinion on the matter?

The place to begin searching for answers is God's Word. Genesis 1:26-27 tells us that God made us in his image, male and female. God created us to be sexual beings. He invented sex! But his good gift has been cheapened and exploited in society.

Ever hear the argument, "If it feels good, do it"? Some single people use that argument for sex: If it feels good, they do it whenever they want. This philosophy isn't new. The ancient Greeks called

it *hedonism.* What *is* new, though, is the widespread devastation it produces in countless lives: sexually transmitted diseases, a rise in teen pregnancy and abortions, and suicides as a result of broken relationships.

If ever there was a time to lift up the biblical standard of sexual morality, it's now. The Bible has some straightforward words about sexual behavior.

Hebrews 13:4 says, "Give honor to marriage, and remain faithful to one another in marriage. God will surely judge people who are immoral and those who commit adultery" (see also 1 Cor 6:13). Since God made sex to be part of the bond between a husband and wife, sex outside of marriage is wrong.

Of course, this leaves a sizable gray area of what is and isn't acceptable in God's eyes. The issue isn't "How much can I do before I'm considered sinning?" If you want to please God, a better question to ask is, "What would God have me do in my opposite-sex relationships? How can I best honor him and the other person?"

Navigating the waters of sexual morality can be challenging, but with the Bible, prayer, and other Christians' input as your compass, you can find your way without crashing on the rocks of sexual sin. ∎

⁹Then Boaz said to the elders and to the crowd standing around, "You are witnesses that today I have bought from Naomi all the property of Elimelech, Kilion, and Mahlon. ¹⁰And with the land I have acquired Ruth, the Moabite widow of Mahlon, to be my wife. This way she can have a son to carry on the family name of her dead husband and to inherit the family property here in his hometown. You are all witnesses today."

¹¹Then the elders and all the people standing in the gate replied, "We are witnesses! May the LORD make this woman who is coming into your home like Rachel and Leah, from whom all the nation of Israel descended! May you prosper in Ephrathah and be famous in Bethlehem. ¹²And may the LORD give you descendants by this young woman who will be like those of our ancestor Perez, the son of Tamar and Judah."

THE DESCENDANTS OF BOAZ ¹³So Boaz took Ruth into his home, and she became his wife. When he slept with her, the LORD enabled her to become pregnant, and she gave birth to a son. ¹⁴Then the women of the town said to Naomi, "Praise the LORD, who has now provided a redeemer for your family! May this child be famous in Israel. ¹⁵May he restore your youth and care for you in your old age. For he is the son of your daughter-in-law who loves you and has been better to you than seven sons!"

¹⁶Naomi took the baby and cuddled him to her breast. And she cared for him as if he were her own. ¹⁷The neighbor women said, "Now at last Naomi has a son again!" And they named him Obed. He became the father of Jesse and the grandfather of David.

¹⁸This is the genealogical record of their ancestor Perez:

Perez was the father of Hezron.
¹⁹ Hezron was the father of Ram.
Ram was the father of Amminadab.
²⁰ Amminadab was the father of Nahshon.
Nahshon was the father of Salmon.*
²¹ Salmon was the father of Boaz.
Boaz was the father of Obed.
²² Obed was the father of Jesse.
Jesse was the father of David.

4:20 As in some Greek manuscripts (see also 4:21); Hebrew reads *Salma.*

TOUGH TIMES

(4:15) God brought great blessings out of Naomi's tragedy, even greater than "seven sons" (indicating the great blessing of an abundance of heirs). Throughout her tough times, Naomi continued to trust God. And God, in his time, blessed her greatly. God can make something good happen even out of a hard situation. Be like Naomi, and don't turn your back on God when tragedy strikes. When hard times hit, trust God, instead of asking "How can God allow this to happen to me?" God is with you even in the hard times.

RUTH & NAOMI *PERSONALITY PROFILE*

WHO ARE YOUR TRUE FRIENDS? Real friends enjoy each other's company. Friendship weaves lives together. One of the greatest friendships described in the Bible was that of Ruth and Naomi. In fact, we know more about their friendship than we know about them as individuals.

Naomi and Ruth came from different cultures, families, and places. Naomi was older than Ruth. Ruth had been married to one of Naomi's sons. They had little but widowhood in common. Yet they forged a deep friendship.

Freedom was a key aspect of their friendship. Often in relationships people try to hold each other too tightly. Friendship can fade when there is no room to breathe. Naomi was willing to let Ruth return to her family. Ruth was willing to leave her homeland to go to Israel with Naomi. Naomi even helped arrange Ruth's marriage to Boaz although she knew Ruth's new role would change their relationship.

God was always part of Naomi and Ruth's friendship. Ruth met God through Naomi as the older woman allowed Ruth to see, hear, and feel all the joy and sorrow of her relationship with God. How much of your thoughts, feelings, and questions about God do you feel free to share with your best friends? God wants to be part of all of your friendships.

BOTTOM LINE: God's living presence in a relationship overcomes differences that might otherwise create division and disharmony.

Ruth and Naomi's story is told in the book of Ruth. Ruth also is mentioned in Matthew 1:5.

UPS:
• A relationship where the greatest bond was their faith in God
• A relationship of strong mutual commitment
• A relationship in which each person tried to do what was best for the other

STATS:
• Where: Moab, Bethlehem
• Occupation: Gleaner (Ruth)
• Relatives: Elimelech (Naomi's husband), Mahlon and Kilion (Naomi's sons), Orpah (Naomi's daughter-in-law and Ruth's sister-in-law), Boaz (Ruth's second husband)

KEY VERSE: Ruth 1:16

1 SAMUEL

"Hello? Is this Gia?" Gia had just answered her phone, even though she didn't recognize the number. The voice was unfamiliar.

"Yeah," she hesitated. "Who is this?"

"It's Adam from school."

Gia knew Adam, but never paid much attention to him. She was a popular senior at their high school and captain of the cheerleading squad.

"Why'd you call me?" she blurted out. She had never hung out with him. So far, she'd only dated popular guys: the class president, a guy with a new Mustang, and her latest ex was a star football player. "Popular" was not a word to describe Adam.

"I was hoping we could talk," Adam said. So they did—for an hour that night and for the next few weeks—about everything.

Gia found herself looking forward to Adam's calls. Soon Adam's status didn't matter. He had become a real friend. She began to realize that we often evaluate people by standards that ignore what's really important.

First Samuel shows how looks can be deceiving. Its stories feature Israel's first kings: Saul and David. Saul was tall, handsome, and brave. He looked like a king. But David was young and inexperienced. He didn't look like a leader, much less a king. Yet Saul proved to be a poor king. David, however, became a great one.

In 1 Samuel, watch Saul's rise and fall and David's ascent. Remember, people look at appearances, but God's standards are deeper

(1 Sam 16:7).

KEY POINTS

KING Because Israel had corrupt priests and judges, the people asked for a king like the other nations. God warned them that they would soon regret this request. God wants each person to be devoted to him more than to any leader.

GOD'S CONTROL Israel prospered as long as the people made God their true King. When the leaders disobeyed God, he overruled them. God is always at work in the world, even when we can't see what he is doing.

LEADERSHIP God guided his people using judges, priests, prophets, and kings. But when these leaders disobeyed God, they faced tragic consequences. Being a true leader means letting God guide you as you make decisions.

OBEDIENCE God wanted his people to follow him wholeheartedly, rather than maintaining a superficial commitment based on traditions or ceremonies. God wants our actions to be motivated by genuine, heartfelt devotion to him.

MERCY AND JUSTICE God responded to his people with tender mercy and swift justice. In showing mercy, he acted with his people's best interests in mind. In showing justice, he was faithful to his word and perfect moral nature. Because God is faithful, he can be counted on to show us mercy.

The broken lines (— · —) indicate modern boundaries.

named David was anointed to be Israel's next king. But it would be many years before David would sit upon the throne. In one particular battle in the valley of Elah, David killed Goliath, the Philistines' mightiest soldier. The Israelites praised David more than Saul, so Saul plotted to kill David (12:1–22:23).

❼ THE WILDERNESS

Even God's chosen kings face troubles. David ran for his life from Saul, hiding in the wildernesses of Ziph, Maon, and En-gedi. Though he had opportunities to kill Saul, David refused to do so because Saul was God's anointed king (23:1–26:25).

❽ GATH

David moved his men and family to Gath, the Philistine city where King Achish lived. Saul then stopped chasing him. The Philistines seemed to welcome this famous fugitive from Israel (27:1-4).

❾ ZIKLAG

In return for his pretended loyalty to King Achish, David asked for a city for his men and family. Achish gave him Ziklag. From there David raided the Geshurites, Girzites, and Amalekites, making sure no one escaped to tell the tale (27:5-12). Later David conquered the Amalekites after they raided Ziklag (30:1-31).

KEY PLACES

❶ RAMAH

Samuel was born in Ramah. Before his birth, Samuel's mother, Hannah, promised God that she would dedicate her son to serve God (1:1–2:11).

❷ SHILOH

Israel worshipped in Shiloh, where the Tabernacle and the Ark of the Covenant resided (2:12–3:21).

❸ KIRIATH-JEARIM

Hophni and Phinehas brought the Ark to the battlefield, believing that its mere presence would ensure victory. But the Philistines defeated the Israelites and captured the Ark. The Philistines found that the Ark was not the trophy they expected. God sent plagues upon every Philistine city the Ark entered. Finally, the Philistines sent the Ark back to Kiriath-jearim in Israel (4:1–7:1).

❹ MIZPAH

The Israelites' defeat made them realize that God was no longer blessing them. Samuel called the people together at Mizpah to fast and pray in sorrow for their sins. As Samuel grew old, the people came to him demanding a king so they could be like the other nations. At Mizpah, Saul was chosen by sacred lot to be Israel's first king (7:2–10:27).

❺ GILGAL

A battle with the Ammonites proved Saul's leadership abilities. Samuel and the people crowned Saul as king of Israel at Gilgal (11:1-15).

❻ VALLEY OF ELAH

Saul won many other battles, but over time he proved to be arrogant, sinful, and rebellious until God finally rejected him as king. Unknown to Saul, a young man

❿ MOUNT GILBOA

War with the Philistines broke out again in the north, near Mount Gilboa. Saul, who no longer relied on God, consulted a witch in a desperate attempt to contact Samuel for help. In the meantime, David was sent back to Ziklag because the Philistine commanders did not trust his loyalty in battle against Israel. The Philistines slaughtered the Israelites on Mount Gilboa, killing King Saul and his three sons, including David's loyal friend Jonathan. Without God, Saul had led a bitter and misguided life. His sinful actions affected not only himself, but also hurt his family and nation (28:1–31:13).

1 ELKANAH AND HIS FAMILY There was a man named Elkanah who lived in Ramah in the region of Zuph* in the hill country of Ephraim. He was the son of Jeroham, son of Elihu, son of Tohu, son of Zuph, of Ephraim. ²Elkanah had two wives, Hannah and Peninnah. Peninnah had children, but Hannah did not.

³Each year Elkanah would travel to Shiloh to worship and sacrifice to the Lord of Heaven's Armies at the Tabernacle. The priests of the Lord at that time were the two sons of Eli—Hophni and Phinehas. ⁴On the days Elkanah presented his sacrifice, he would give portions of the meat to Peninnah and each of her children. ⁵And though he loved Hannah, he would give her only one choice portion* because the Lord had given her no children. ⁶So Peninnah would taunt Hannah and make fun of her because the Lord had kept her from having children. ⁷Year after year it was the same—Peninnah would taunt Hannah as they went to the Tabernacle.* Each time, Hannah would be reduced to tears and would not even eat.

⁸"Why are you crying, Hannah?" Elkanah would ask. "Why aren't you eating? Why be downhearted just because you have no children? You have me—isn't that better than having ten sons?"

HANNAH'S PRAYER FOR A SON ⁹Once after a sacrificial meal at Shiloh, Hannah got up and went to pray. Eli the priest was sitting at his customary place beside the entrance of the Tabernacle.* ¹⁰Hannah was in deep anguish, crying bitterly as she prayed to the Lord. ¹¹And she made this vow: "O Lord of Heaven's Armies, if you will look upon my sorrow and answer my prayer and give me a son, then I will give him back to you. He will be yours for his entire lifetime, and as a sign that he has been dedicated to the Lord, his hair will never be cut.*"

¹²As she was praying to the Lord, Eli watched her. ¹³Seeing her lips moving but hearing no sound, he thought she had been drinking. ¹⁴"Must you come here drunk?" he demanded. "Throw away your wine!"

¹⁵"Oh no, sir!" she replied. "I haven't been drinking wine or anything stronger. But I am very discouraged, and I was pouring out my heart to the Lord. ¹⁶Don't think I am a wicked woman! For I have been praying out of great anguish and sorrow."

¹⁷"In that case," Eli said, "go in peace! May the God of Israel grant the request you have asked of him."

¹⁸"Oh, thank you, sir!" she exclaimed. Then she went back and began to eat again, and she was no longer sad.

SAMUEL'S BIRTH AND DEDICATION ¹⁹The entire family got up early the next morning and went to worship the Lord once more. Then they returned home to Ramah. When Elkanah slept with Hannah, the Lord remembered her plea, ²⁰and in due time she gave birth to a son. She named him Samuel,* for she said, "I asked the Lord for him."

²¹The next year Elkanah and his family went on their annual trip to offer a sacrifice to the Lord. ²²But Hannah did not go. She told her husband, "Wait until the boy is weaned. Then I will take him to the Tabernacle and leave him there with the Lord permanently.*"

²³"Whatever you think is best," Elkanah agreed. "Stay here for now, and may the Lord help you keep your promise." So she stayed home and nursed the boy until he was weaned.

²⁴When the child was weaned, Hannah took him to the Tabernacle in Shiloh. They brought along a three-year-old bull* for the sacrifice and a basket* of flour and some wine. ²⁵After sacrificing the bull, they brought the boy to Eli. ²⁶"Sir, do you remember me?" Hannah asked. "I am the woman who stood here several years ago praying to the Lord. ²⁷I asked the Lord to give me this boy, and he has granted my request. ²⁸Now I am giving him to the Lord, and he will belong to the Lord his whole life." And they* worshiped the Lord there.

....

STILL INVOLVED
(1:6-28) Part of God's plan for Hannah involved postponing her years of childbearing. While Peninnah and Elkanah looked at Hannah's seemingly dreary circumstances, God still had a plan. Know anyone who struggles with doubt about God's involvement in their life? How can you encourage them to believe that God still cares and is working out the best for them?

DISCOURAGED
(1:17-18) The change in Hannah's attitude may be attributed to three factors: (1) her honest prayer to God (1:10-11), (2) her resolve to leave the problem with God (1:18), and (3) the encouragement she received from Eli (1:17). Together, these factors make up the antidote for discouragement. When you feel discouraged, remember this antidote and change your attitude.

1:1 As in Greek version; Hebrew reads *in Ramathaim-zophim;* compare 1:19. 1:5 Or *And because he loved Hannah, he would give her a choice portion.* The meaning of the Hebrew is uncertain. 1:7 Hebrew *the house of the Lord;* also in 1:24. 1:9 Hebrew *the Temple of the Lord.* 1:11 Some manuscripts add *He will drink neither wine nor intoxicants.* 1:20 *Samuel* sounds like the Hebrew term for "asked of God" or "heard by God." 1:22 Some manuscripts add *I will offer him as a Nazirite for all time.* 1:24a As in Dead Sea Scrolls, Greek and Syriac versions; Masoretic Text reads *three bulls.* 1:24b Hebrew *and an ephah* [20 quarts or 22 liters]. 1:28 Hebrew *he.*

2 HANNAH'S PRAYER OF PRAISE Then Hannah prayed:

"My heart rejoices in the LORD!
  The LORD has made me strong.*
Now I have an answer for my enemies;
  I rejoice because you rescued me.
² No one is holy like the LORD!
  There is no one besides you;
  there is no Rock like our God.

³ "Stop acting so proud and haughty!
  Don't speak with such arrogance!
For the LORD is a God who knows what you
    have done;
  he will judge your actions.
⁴ The bow of the mighty is now broken,
  and those who stumbled are now strong.
⁵ Those who were well fed are now starving,
  and those who were starving are now full.
The childless woman now has seven
    children,
  and the woman with many children
    wastes away.
⁶ The LORD gives both death and life;
  he brings some down to the grave* but
    raises others up.
⁷ The LORD makes some poor and others rich;
  he brings some down and lifts others up.

2:1 Hebrew has exalted my horn.   2:6 Hebrew to Sheol.

HELP!
(2:2) Hannah praised God for being a "rock"—firm, strong, and unchanging. In our fast-paced world, friends come and go and circumstances change. Those who devote their lives to people, causes, possessions, or wealth are trusting things that will all pass away. None of them is a solid foundation for hope. But God is always present and ready to help, even when life seems to be falling apart. Is he the foundation of your hope?

ULTIMATE ISSUES WORSHIP

Think you could date someone for a while without ever telling that person how you feel about him or her? How about your family? Think they would be satisfied if you just grunted at them every once in a while and spared yourself the effort of letting them know that you love them? Nope. Most people want to be told now and then that they are loved.

God is like that, too. Although he's never insecure, like any good father God likes to hear his children express their love directly to him. This is the essence of what we call *worship*.

Israel had a lengthy list of instructions about worship (see Exod 35). These would have been familiar to people like Hannah who traveled regularly to worship at the Tabernacle (see 1 Sam 1). Many of these instructions may sound strange—involving lampstands, altars, sacrifices, priestly garments, and so forth. But we can draw principles from these instructions to help us worship the God who is the same yesterday, today, and forever. Here are some of the principles, listed according to the *who, what, when, where,* and *why* of worship.

Who: Easy, right? We worship God. But at times the focus of worship shifts from God to human beings. We don't necessarily "worship" ourselves, but often we zero in on what God does for us. Praising God for his goodness is OK. But danger lurks in thinking of God primarily in terms of how he can bless us, protect us, make us happy, and so forth. If we're not careful, we'll start thinking that he exists for our benefit, not the other way around. Remember: We worship God for who he is, not what he does for us.

What: Worship means giving God the glory and obedience he deserves. In a sense, all of life should be "worship"—obedience given out of love and respect to our great God. But we also need specified times of focused attention to praise, prayer, the teaching of God's Word, etc. Our "whole-life" worship is like a floodlight—unfocused. Special times of worship, especially on Sundays, are like a laser—much more intense and specific.

When: While any time is acceptable to worship God, the Scriptures teach us to set aside regular times for worship (Heb 10:24-25). The early church met on the first day of the week. Churches today often meet on Sunday and other days of the week.

Where: There are almost as many different places where Christians worship as there are Christians: church buildings, houses, schools, stores, shelters, tents, prisons, hospitals, ships, and on and on. The first Christians often gathered in secret places, like caves and catacombs. Jesus clearly taught that where a person worships God isn't as important as the worship itself (John 4:19-24). You can worship God anywhere.

The *why* of worship is simple and twofold: First, we worship because God wants us to. But worship is not just for us; it's for God. Much more important than whether *we* enjoy the music, sermon, and other worship elements is whether or not *God* is pleased with our offering of ourselves to him. Second, we worship because we need to. God is pleased when we bow before him and acknowledge his greatness, majesty, patience, and love toward us; and we are placed in the proper relationship to him. When we worship, we are reminded that he is God, and we are not.

So, are you ready to worship? Your Father is waiting for you. ∎

⁸ He lifts the poor from the dust
  and the needy from the garbage dump.
He sets them among princes,
  placing them in seats of honor.
For all the earth is the LORD's,
  and he has set the world in order.

⁹ "He will protect his faithful ones,
  but the wicked will disappear in darkness.
No one will succeed by strength alone.
¹⁰   Those who fight against the LORD will be
      shattered.
He thunders against them from heaven;
  the LORD judges throughout the earth.
He gives power to his king;
  he increases the strength* of his anointed
  one."

¹¹Then Elkanah returned home to Ramah
without Samuel. And the boy served the LORD
by assisting Eli the priest.

ELI'S WICKED SONS ¹²Now the sons of Eli were
scoundrels who had no respect for the LORD
¹³or for their duties as priests. Whenever anyone offered a sacrifice, Eli's sons would send
over a servant with a three-pronged fork. While
the meat of the sacrificed animal was still boiling, ¹⁴the servant would stick the fork into the
pot and demand that whatever it brought up
be given to Eli's sons. All the Israelites who
came to worship at Shiloh were treated this
way. ¹⁵Sometimes the servant would come
even before the animal's fat had been burned
on the altar. He would demand raw meat before it had been boiled so that it could be used
for roasting.

¹⁶The man offering the sacrifice might reply,
"Take as much as you want, but the fat must be
burned first." Then the servant would demand,
"No, give it to me now, or I'll take it by force."
¹⁷So the sin of these young men was very serious in the LORD's sight, for they treated the
LORD's offerings with contempt.

¹⁸But Samuel, though he was only a boy,
served the LORD. He wore a linen garment like
that of a priest.* ¹⁹Each year his mother made a
small coat for him and brought it to him when
she came with her husband for the sacrifice.
²⁰Before they returned home, Eli would bless
Elkanah and his wife and say, "May the LORD
give you other children to take the place of this
one she gave to the LORD.*" ²¹And the LORD

gave Hannah three sons and two daughters.
Meanwhile, Samuel grew up in the presence of
the LORD.

²²Now Eli was very old, but he was aware of
what his sons were doing to the people of Israel. He knew, for instance, that his sons were
seducing the young women who assisted at
the entrance of the Tabernacle.* ²³Eli said to
them, "I have been hearing reports from all
the people about the wicked things you are
doing. Why do you keep sinning? ²⁴You must
stop, my sons! The reports I hear among the
LORD's people are not good. ²⁵If someone sins
against another person, God* can mediate for
the guilty party. But if someone sins against
the LORD, who can intercede?" But Eli's sons
wouldn't listen to their father, for the LORD was
already planning to put them to death.

²⁶Meanwhile, the boy Samuel grew taller
and grew in favor with the LORD and with the
people.

A WARNING FOR ELI'S FAMILY ²⁷One day a
man of God came to Eli and gave him this message from the LORD: "I revealed myself* to
your ancestors when the people of Israel were
slaves in Egypt. ²⁸I chose your ancestor Aaron*
from among all the tribes of Israel to be my
priest, to offer sacrifices on my altar, to burn
incense, and to wear the priestly vest* as he
served me. And I assigned the sacrificial offerings to you priests. ²⁹So why do you scorn my
sacrifices and offerings? Why do you give your
sons more honor than you give me—for you
and they have become fat from the best offerings of my people Israel!

³⁰"Therefore, the LORD, the God of Israel,
says: I promised that your branch of the tribe
of Levi* would always be my priests. But I will
honor those who honor me, and I will despise
those who think lightly of me. ³¹The time is
coming when I will put an end to your family, so it will no longer serve as my priests.
All the members of your family will die before
their time. None will reach old age. ³²You will
watch with envy as I pour out prosperity on
the people of Israel. But no members of your
family will ever live out their days. ³³Those
who survive will live in sadness and grief, and

··

2:10 Hebrew *he exalts the horn.*   2:18 Hebrew *He wore a linen
ephod.*   2:20 As in Dead Sea Scrolls and Greek version; Masoretic
Text reads *this one he requested of the LORD.*   2:22 Hebrew *Tent of
Meeting.* Some manuscripts lack this entire sentence.   2:25 Or *the
judges.*   2:27 As in Greek and Syriac versions; Hebrew reads *Did I
reveal myself.*   2:28a Hebrew *your father.*   2:28b Hebrew *an
ephod.*   2:30 Hebrew *that your house and your father's house.*

YOUTH
*(2:18) Samuel was a young child, yet he "served the
LORD." Often children can serve God just as effectively
as adults. God will use anyone who is willing to learn
from him and serve him. He has no age limits. Don't
discount the faith of a child or let your age keep you from
serving God.*

their children will die a violent death.* ³⁴And to prove that what I have said will come true, I will cause your two sons, Hophni and Phinehas, to die on the same day!

³⁵"Then I will raise up a faithful priest who will serve me and do what I desire. I will establish his family, and they will be priests to my anointed kings forever. ³⁶Then all of your surviving family will bow before him, begging for money and food. 'Please,' they will say, 'give us jobs among the priests so we will have enough to eat.'"

··

LISTENING

(3:1-15) During the days of Eli, messages from God were rare. Why? Look at the attitude of Eli's sons (2:12-25). They refused to listen to God and allowed greed to get in the way of any communication with him.

Listening and responding are vital in a relationship with God. Although God may not speak audibly today, he speaks just as clearly through his Word. To receive his messages, we must be ready to listen and act upon what he tells us. Are you, like Samuel, ready to answer, "Speak, your servant is listening" (3:10) when God calls you to action?

3 THE LORD SPEAKS TO SAMUEL Meanwhile, the boy Samuel served the LORD by assisting Eli. Now in those days messages from the LORD were very rare, and visions were quite uncommon.

²One night Eli, who was almost blind by now, had gone to bed. ³The lamp of God had not yet gone out, and Samuel was sleeping in the Tabernacle* near the Ark of God. ⁴Suddenly the LORD called out, "Samuel!"

"Yes?" Samuel replied. "What is it?" ⁵He got up and ran to Eli. "Here I am. Did you call me?"

"I didn't call you," Eli replied. "Go back to bed." So he did.

⁶Then the LORD called out again, "Samuel!"

Again Samuel got up and went to Eli. "Here I am. Did you call me?"

"I didn't call you, my son," Eli said. "Go back to bed."

⁷Samuel did not yet know the LORD because he had never had a message from the LORD before. ⁸So the LORD called a third time, and once

2:33 As in Dead Sea Scrolls, which read *die by the sword;* Masoretic Text reads *die like mortals.*　**3:3** Hebrew *the Temple of the LORD.*

SAMUEL *PERSONALITY PROFILE*

EVER WONDER what your favorite celebrity was like when he or she was your age? We have little information about the early years of most of the people mentioned in the Bible. One delightful exception is Samuel, who was born as a result of God's answer to Hannah's prayer for a child. (In fact, the name "Samuel" comes from the Hebrew expression, "asked of God.") God had plans for Samuel from the start. He was able to use Samuel in many different and important ways for one big reason: Samuel was willing to be God's servant.

Samuel's life teaches us that those who are faithful to God in small things will be trusted with greater things. Little jobs like helping the high priest may not have seemed very important, but God used those tasks to train Samuel for bigger responsibilities.

Samuel moved ahead because he listened to God's directions. Too often we ask God to control our lives without being willing to give up the goals we've chosen. We ask God to help us get where *we* want to go. The first step in correcting this tendency is to give him both the control and the destination of our lives. The second step is to be obedient to what we already know God wants us to do. The third step is to watch for further direction from his Word—God's road map for life.

BOTTOM LINE: The significance of what people accomplish in life is directly related to their relationship with God.

Being a person of integrity is more important than anything we might do.

Samuel's story is told in 1 Samuel 1–16:13, 25:1; 28:3-20. He also is mentioned in Psalm 99:6; Jeremiah 15:1; Acts 3:24; 13:20; Hebrews 11:32.

UPS:

- Used by God to assist Israel's transition from a loosely governed tribal people to a monarchy
- Anointed the first two kings of Israel
- The last and most effective of Israel's judges
- Listed in the Hall of Faith in Hebrews 11

DOWNS:

- Unable to instill in his sons the same relationship he had with God

STATS:

- Where: Ephraim
- Occupation: Judge, prophet, priest
- Relatives: Hannah (mother); Elkanah (father); Joel and Abijah (sons)
- Contemporaries: Eli, Saul, David

KEY VERSES: 1 Samuel 1:1–16:13; 25:1; 28:3-20; Psalm 99:6; Jeremiah 15:1; Acts 3:24; 13:20; Hebrews 11:32.

more Samuel got up and went to Eli. "Here I am. Did you call me?"

Then Eli realized it was the LORD who was calling the boy. 9So he said to Samuel, "Go and lie down again, and if someone calls again, say, 'Speak, LORD, your servant is listening.'" So Samuel went back to bed.

10And the LORD came and called as before, "Samuel! Samuel!"

And Samuel replied, "Speak, your servant is listening."

11Then the LORD said to Samuel, "I am about to do a shocking thing in Israel. 12I am going to carry out all my threats against Eli and his family, from beginning to end. 13I have warned him that judgment is coming upon his family forever, because his sons are blaspheming God* and he hasn't disciplined them. 14So I have vowed that the sins of Eli and his sons will never be forgiven by sacrifices or offerings."

SAMUEL SPEAKS FOR THE LORD   15Samuel stayed in bed until morning, then got up and opened the doors of the Tabernacle* as usual. He was afraid to tell Eli what the LORD had said to him. 16But Eli called out to him, "Samuel, my son."

"Here I am," Samuel replied.

17"What did the LORD say to you? Tell me everything. And may God strike you and even kill you if you hide anything from me!" 18So Samuel told Eli everything; he didn't hold anything back. "It is the LORD's will," Eli replied. "Let him do what he thinks best."

19As Samuel grew up, the LORD was with him, and everything Samuel said proved to be reliable. 20And all Israel, from Dan in the north to Beersheba in the south, knew that Samuel was confirmed as a prophet of the LORD. 21The LORD continued to appear at Shiloh and gave messages to Samuel there at the Tabernacle. 4:1And Samuel's words went out to all the people of Israel.

4 **THE PHILISTINES CAPTURE THE ARK**   At that time Israel was at war with the Philistines. The Israelite army was camped near Ebenezer, and the Philistines were at Aphek. 2The Philistines attacked and defeated the army of Israel, killing 4,000 men. 3After the battle was over, the troops retreated to their camp, and the elders of Israel asked, "Why did the LORD allow us to be defeated by the Philistines?" Then they said, "Let's bring the Ark of the Covenant of the LORD from Shiloh. If we carry it into battle with us, it* will save us from our enemies."

4So they sent men to Shiloh to bring the Ark of the Covenant of the LORD of Heaven's Armies, who is enthroned between the cherubim. Hophni and Phinehas, the sons of Eli, were also there with the Ark of the Covenant of God. 5When all the Israelites saw the Ark of the Covenant of the LORD coming into the camp, their shout of joy was so loud it made the ground shake!

6"What's going on?" the Philistines asked. "What's all the shouting about in the Hebrew camp?" When they were told it was because the Ark of the LORD had arrived, 7they panicked. "The gods have* come into their camp!" they cried. "This is a disaster! We have never had to face anything like this before! 8Help! Who can save us from these mighty gods of Israel? They are the same gods who destroyed the Egyptians with plagues when Israel was in the wilderness. 9Fight as never before, Philistines! If you don't, we will become the Hebrews' slaves just as they have been ours! Stand up like men and fight!"

10So the Philistines fought desperately, and Israel was defeated again. The slaughter was great; 30,000 Israelite soldiers died that day. The survivors turned and fled to their tents. 11The Ark of God was captured, and Hophni and Phinehas, the two sons of Eli, were killed.

THE DEATH OF ELI   12A man from the tribe of Benjamin ran from the battlefield and arrived at Shiloh later that same day. He had torn his clothes and put dust on his head to show his grief. 13Eli was waiting beside the road to hear the news of the battle, for his heart trembled for the safety of the Ark of God. When the messenger arrived and told what had happened, an outcry resounded throughout the town.

14"What is all the noise about?" Eli asked.

The messenger rushed over to Eli, 15who was ninety-eight years old and blind. 16He said to

....

3:13 As in Greek version; Hebrew reads *his sons have made themselves contemptible.*   3:15 Hebrew *the house of the LORD.* 4:3 Or *he.*   4:7 Or *A god has.*

NEW AND FRESH
(4:5-8) The Philistines were frightened by stories of how God had helped the people of Israel when they left Egypt. But the Israelites had turned away from God and now were clinging only to a form of godliness.

Individuals, churches, and organizations often try to live on the memories of God's blessings. Israel wrongly assumed that because God had given them victory in the past, he would do it again, even though they had strayed far from him. Today, spiritual victories come when we stick with God, instead of taking him for granted. Don't live off the past. Keep your relationship with God new and fresh.

Eli, "I have just come from the battlefield—I was there this very day."

"What happened, my son?" Eli demanded.

[17]"Israel has been defeated by the Philistines," the messenger replied. "The people have been slaughtered, and your two sons, Hophni and Phinehas, were also killed. And the Ark of God has been captured."

[18]When the messenger mentioned what had happened to the Ark of God, Eli fell backward from his seat beside the gate. He broke his neck and died, for he was old and overweight. He had been Israel's judge for forty years.

[19]Eli's daughter-in-law, the wife of Phinehas, was pregnant and near her time of delivery. When she heard that the Ark of God had been captured and that her father-in-law and husband were dead, she went into labor and gave birth. [20]She died in childbirth, but before she passed away the midwives tried to encourage her. "Don't be afraid," they said. "You have a baby boy!" But she did not answer or pay attention to them.

[21]She named the child Ichabod (which means "Where is the glory?"), for she said, "Israel's glory is gone." She named him this because the Ark of God had been captured and because her father-in-law and husband were dead. [22]Then she said, "The glory has departed from Israel, for the Ark of God has been captured."

5 THE ARK IN PHILISTIA

After the Philistines captured the Ark of God, they took it from the battleground at Ebenezer to the town of Ashdod. [2]They carried the Ark of God into the temple of Dagon and placed it beside an idol of Dagon. [3]But when the citizens of Ashdod went to see it the next morning, Dagon had fallen with his face to the ground in front of the Ark of the LORD! So they took Dagon and put him in his place again. [4]But the next morning the same thing happened—Dagon had fallen face down before the Ark of the LORD again. This time his head and hands had broken off and were lying in the doorway. Only the trunk of his body was left intact. [5]That is why to this day

THE TRUTH HURTS
(5:1-7) After the Philistines stole the Ark of the Covenant, God showed them that he was the real God by breaking their idol, Dagon. But they didn't act upon that insight until they began suffering from tumors (probably boils). Similarly, many people don't respond to biblical truth until they experience pain and suddenly feel they have no place else to turn. Are you willing to listen to God for truth's sake, or do you turn to him only when you're suffering?

neither the priests of Dagon nor anyone who enters the temple of Dagon in Ashdod will step on its threshold.

[6]Then the LORD's heavy hand struck the people of Ashdod and the nearby villages with a plague of tumors.* [7]When the people realized what was happening, they cried out, "We can't keep the Ark of the God of Israel here any longer! He is against us! We will all be destroyed along with Dagon, our god." [8]So they called together the rulers of the Philistine towns and asked, "What should we do with the Ark of the God of Israel?"

The rulers discussed it and replied, "Move it to the town of Gath." So they moved the Ark of the God of Israel to Gath. [9]But when the Ark arrived at Gath, the LORD's heavy hand fell on its men, young and old; he struck them with a plague of tumors, and there was a great panic.

[10]So they sent the Ark of God to the town of Ekron, but when the people of Ekron saw it coming they cried out, "They are bringing the Ark of the God of Israel here to kill us, too!" [11]The people summoned the Philistine rulers again and begged them, "Please send the Ark of the God of Israel back to its own country, or it* will kill us all." For the deadly plague from God had already begun, and great fear was sweeping across the town. [12]Those who didn't die were afflicted with tumors; and the cry from the town rose to heaven.

6 THE PHILISTINES RETURN THE ARK

The Ark of the LORD remained in Philistine territory seven months in all. [2]Then the Philistines called in their priests and diviners and asked them, "What should we do about the Ark of the LORD? Tell us how to return it to its own country."

[3]"Send the Ark of the God of Israel back with a gift," they were told. "Send a guilt offering so the plague will stop. Then, if you are healed, you will know it was his hand that caused the plague."

[4]"What sort of guilt offering should we send?" they asked.

And they were told, "Since the plague has struck both you and your five rulers, make five gold tumors and five gold rats, just like those that have ravaged your land. [5]Make these things to show honor to the God of Israel. Perhaps then he will stop afflicting you, your gods, and your land. [6]Don't be stubborn and rebellious as Pharaoh and the Egyptians were.

5:6 Greek version and Latin Vulgate read *tumors; and rats appeared in their land, and death and destruction were throughout the city.* **5:11** Or *he.*

By the time God was finished with them, they were eager to let Israel go.

⁷"Now build a new cart, and find two cows that have just given birth to calves. Make sure the cows have never been yoked to a cart. Hitch the cows to the cart, but shut their calves away from them in a pen. ⁸Put the Ark of the Lord on the cart, and beside it place a chest containing the gold rats and gold tumors you are sending as a guilt offering. Then let the cows go wherever they want. ⁹If they cross the border of our land and go to Beth-shemesh, we will know it was the Lord who brought this great disaster upon us. If they don't, we will know it was not his hand that caused the plague. It came simply by chance."

¹⁰So these instructions were carried out. Two cows were hitched to the cart, and their newborn calves were shut up in a pen. ¹¹Then the Ark of the Lord and the chest containing the gold rats and gold tumors were placed on the cart. ¹²And sure enough, without veering off in other directions, the cows went straight along the road toward Beth-shemesh, lowing as they went. The Philistine rulers followed them as far as the border of Beth-shemesh.

¹³The people of Beth-shemesh were harvesting wheat in the valley, and when they saw the Ark, they were overjoyed! ¹⁴The cart came into the field of a man named Joshua and stopped beside a large rock. So the people broke up the wood of the cart for a fire and killed the cows and sacrificed them to the Lord as a burnt offering. ¹⁵Several men of the tribe of Levi lifted the Ark of the Lord and the chest containing the gold rats and gold tumors from the cart and placed them on the large rock. Many sacrifices and burnt offerings were offered to the Lord that day by the people of Beth-shemesh. ¹⁶The five Philistine rulers watched all this and then returned to Ekron that same day.

¹⁷The five gold tumors sent by the Philistines as a guilt offering to the Lord were gifts from the rulers of Ashdod, Gaza, Ashkelon, Gath, and Ekron. ¹⁸The five gold rats represented the five Philistine towns and their surrounding villages, which were controlled by the five rulers. The large rock at Beth-shemesh, where they set the Ark of the Lord, still stands in the field of Joshua as a witness to what happened there.

THE ARK MOVED TO KIRIATH-JEARIM ¹⁹But the Lord killed seventy men* from Beth-

shemesh because they looked into the Ark of the Lord. And the people mourned greatly because of what the Lord had done. ²⁰"Who is able to stand in the presence of the Lord, this holy God?" they cried out. "Where can we send the Ark from here?"

²¹So they sent messengers to the people at Kiriath-jearim and told them, "The Philistines have returned the Ark of the Lord. Come here and get it!"

7 So the men of Kiriath-jearim came to get the Ark of the Lord. They took it to the hillside home of Abinadab and ordained Eleazar, his son, to be in charge of it. ²The Ark remained in Kiriath-jearim for a long time—twenty years in all. During that time all Israel mourned because it seemed the Lord had abandoned them.

SAMUEL LEADS ISRAEL TO VICTORY ³Then

Samuel said to all the people of Israel, "If you are really serious about wanting to return to the Lord, get rid of your foreign gods and your images of Ashtoreth. Determine to obey only the Lord; then he will rescue you from the Philistines." ⁴So the Israelites got rid of their images of Baal and Ashtoreth and worshiped only the Lord.

⁵Then Samuel told them, "Gather all of Israel to Mizpah, and I will pray to the Lord for you." ⁶So they gathered at Mizpah and, in a great ceremony, drew water from a well and poured it out before the Lord. They also went without food all day and confessed that they had sinned against the Lord. (It was at Mizpah that Samuel became Israel's judge.)

⁷When the Philistine rulers heard that Israel

···

AN INGREDIENT OR THE SOURCE?

(6:9) The Philistines acknowledged the existence of the God of Israel but only as one of many so-called "gods" whose favor they sought. Thinking of God in this way made it easy for them to ignore God's demand that people worship him alone. Many people "worship" God this way. They see him as just one of many ingredients in a successful life. But God is not an ingredient—he is the source of life itself. Is that how you see God?

ABANDONED OR JUST INACTIVE?

(7:2-3) Sorrow gripped Israel for 20 years. The Ark was put away like an unwanted box in an attic. Many believed that the Lord had abandoned his people. But Samuel, now a grown man, roused them to action by calling them to do something, rather than complain.

We can easily complain about our problems to God, instead of doing what he requires. We don't even take the advice he has already given us. Do you ever feel as if God has abandoned you? Check to see what he has already told you to do. You might not receive new guidance until you have acted on his previous directions.

6:19 As in a few Hebrew manuscripts; most Hebrew manuscripts read *70 men, 50,000 men.* Perhaps the text should be understood to read *the Lord killed 70 men and 50 oxen.*

had gathered at Mizpah, they mobilized their army and advanced. The Israelites were badly frightened when they learned that the Philistines were approaching. [8]"Don't stop pleading with the LORD our God to save us from the Philistines!" they begged Samuel. [9]So Samuel took a young lamb and offered it to the LORD as a whole burnt offering. He pleaded with the LORD to help Israel, and the LORD answered him.

[10]Just as Samuel was sacrificing the burnt offering, the Philistines arrived to attack Israel. But the LORD spoke with a mighty voice of thunder from heaven that day, and the Philistines were thrown into such confusion that the Israelites defeated them. [11]The men of Israel chased them from Mizpah to a place below Beth-car, slaughtering them all along the way.

[12]Samuel then took a large stone and placed it between the towns of Mizpah and Jeshanah.* He named it Ebenezer (which means "the stone of help"), for he said, "Up to this point the LORD has helped us!"

[13]So the Philistines were subdued and didn't invade Israel again for some time. And throughout Samuel's lifetime, the LORD's powerful hand was raised against the Philistines. [14]The Israelite villages near Ekron and Gath that the Philistines had captured were restored to Israel, along with the rest of the territory that the Philistines had taken. And there was peace between Israel and the Amorites in those days.

[15]Samuel continued as Israel's judge for the rest of his life. [16]Each year he traveled around, setting up his court first at Bethel, then at Gilgal, and then at Mizpah. He judged the people of Israel at each of these places. [17]Then he would return to his home at Ramah, and he would hear cases there, too. And Samuel built an altar to the LORD at Ramah.

8 ISRAEL REQUESTS A KING

As Samuel grew old, he appointed his sons to be judges over Israel. [2]Joel and Abijah, his oldest sons, held court in Beersheba. [3]But they were not like their father, for they were greedy for money. They accepted bribes and perverted justice.

··

YOUR LIFE, HIS DESIGN
(9:1–10:16) Often we think that events just happen to us. But Saul's story illustrates that God often uses common occurrences to guide his people. Think of the good and bad circumstances that have affected you lately. Can you see God's purpose in them? Perhaps he is building a certain quality in your life or leading you to serve him in a new area.

[4]Finally, all the elders of Israel met at Ramah to discuss the matter with Samuel. [5]"Look," they told him, "you are now old, and your sons are not like you. Give us a king to judge us like all the other nations have."

[6]Samuel was displeased with their request and went to the LORD for guidance. [7]"Do everything they say to you," the LORD replied, "for it is me they are rejecting, not you. They don't want me to be their king any longer. [8]Ever since I brought them from Egypt they have continually abandoned me and followed other gods. And now they are giving you the same treatment. [9]Do as they ask, but solemnly warn them about the way a king will reign over them."

SAMUEL WARNS AGAINST A KINGDOM

[10]So Samuel passed on the LORD's warning to the people who were asking him for a king. [11]"This is how a king will reign over you," Samuel said. "The king will draft your sons and assign them to his chariots and his charioteers, making them run before his chariots. [12]Some will be generals and captains in his army,* some will be forced to plow in his fields and harvest his crops, and some will make his weapons and chariot equipment. [13]The king will take your daughters from you and force them to cook and bake and make perfumes for him. [14]He will take away the best of your fields and vineyards and olive groves and give them to his own officials. [15]He will take a tenth of your grain and your grape harvest and distribute it among his officers and attendants. [16]He will take your male and female slaves and demand the finest of your cattle* and donkeys for his own use. [17]He will demand a tenth of your flocks, and you will be his slaves. [18]When that day comes, you will beg for relief from this king you are demanding, but then the LORD will not help you."

[19]But the people refused to listen to Samuel's warning. "Even so, we still want a king," they said. [20]"We want to be like the nations around us. Our king will judge us and lead us into battle."

[21]So Samuel repeated to the LORD what the people had said, [22]and the LORD replied, "Do as they say, and give them a king." Then Samuel agreed and sent the people home.

9 SAUL MEETS SAMUEL

There was a wealthy, influential man named Kish from the tribe of Benjamin. He was the son of Abiel, son of Zeror, son of Becorath, son of Aphiah,

7:12 As in Greek and Syriac versions; Hebrew reads *Shen*.
8:12 Hebrew *commanders of thousands and commanders of fifties*.
8:16 As in Greek version; Hebrew reads *young men*.

of the tribe of Benjamin. ²His son Saul was the most handsome man in Israel—head and shoulders taller than anyone else in the land.

³One day Kish's donkeys strayed away, and he told Saul, "Take a servant with you, and go look for the donkeys." ⁴So Saul took one of the servants and traveled through the hill country of Ephraim, the land of Shalishah, the Shaalim area, and the entire land of Benjamin, but they couldn't find the donkeys anywhere.

⁵Finally, they entered the region of Zuph, and Saul said to his servant, "Let's go home. By now my father will be more worried about us than about the donkeys!"

⁶But the servant said, "I've just thought of something! There is a man of God who lives here in this town. He is held in high honor by all the people because everything he says comes true. Let's go find him. Perhaps he can tell us which way to go."

⁷"But we don't have anything to offer him," Saul replied. "Even our food is gone, and we don't have a thing to give him."

⁸"Well," the servant said, "I have one small silver piece.* We can at least offer it to the man of God and see what happens!" ⁹(In those days if people wanted a message from God, they would say, "Let's go and ask the seer," for prophets used to be called seers.)

¹⁰"All right," Saul agreed, "let's try it!" So

9:8 Hebrew ¼ *shekel of silver*, about 0.1 ounces or 3 grams in weight.

they started into the town where the man of God lived.

¹¹As they were climbing the hill to the town, they met some young women coming out to draw water. So Saul and his servant asked, "Is the seer here today?"

¹²"Yes," they replied. "Stay right on this road. He is at the town gates. He has just arrived to take part in a public sacrifice up at the place of worship. ¹³Hurry and catch him before he goes up there to eat. The guests won't begin eating until he arrives to bless the food."

¹⁴So they entered the town, and as they passed through the gates, Samuel was coming out toward them to go up to the place of worship.

¹⁵Now the LORD had told Samuel the previous day, ¹⁶"About this time tomorrow I will send you a man from the land of Benjamin. Anoint him to be the leader of my people, Israel. He will rescue them from the Philistines, for I have looked down on my people in mercy and have heard their cry."

¹⁷When Samuel saw Saul, the LORD said, "That's the man I told you about! He will rule my people."

¹⁸Just then Saul approached Samuel at the gateway and asked, "Can you please tell me where the seer's house is?"

¹⁹"I am the seer!" Samuel replied. "Go up to the place of worship ahead of me. We will

I WONDER . . .

So many things crowd God out of my life. How much of my time does God want?

God does not want to be just another addition to your life—he wants to be at the center of everything you do.

Check this out: Bike tires are only as strong as the hub of the wheel. If a tire consisted only of rim and spokes, the wheel would soon collapse under the constant pounding and pressure.

The spokes in our lives are those things that are important to us: family, friends, school, sports, entertainment, etc. If life revolves around any one of these "spokes," eventually the constant pounding and pressures of our world will wear us down and possibly cause us to collapse!

God knows this and has provided the strong central hub that will hold us together. When we ignore God and try to run our own lives, we are living as though we believe the spokes are strong enough to carry us.

The people of Israel chose to reject God as the hub of their lives by demanding a king to rule over them. What they were actually saying was, "God, since we can't see you, we can't trust you to take care of us. Give us someone we can see who will rule over us." Eventually God gave in to their request (see 1 Sam 8:7). The results, however, were devastating. Because they put their focus on what a mere human being could do for them (a weak spoke!), their enemies soon overpowered the entire nation until all of the people of Israel were forced out of the Promised Land.

The Old Testament graphically describes what happened when God's people rejected him as their leader.

Jesus Christ should be our hub. This means that we should make him central in our lives and consult his Word often.

When things begin to crowd out your relationship with God, try writing down a list of your priorities. Ask a trusted Christian friend to help you evaluate whether any one of these spokes is taking the place of God in your life.

eat there together, and in the morning I'll tell you what you want to know and send you on your way. 20And don't worry about those donkeys that were lost three days ago, for they have been found. And I am here to tell you that you and your family are the focus of all Israel's hopes."

21Saul replied, "But I'm only from the tribe of Benjamin, the smallest tribe in Israel, and my family is the least important of all the families of that tribe! Why are you talking like this to me?"

22Then Samuel brought Saul and his servant into the hall and placed them at the head of the table, honoring them above the thirty special guests. 23Samuel then instructed the cook to bring Saul the finest cut of meat, the piece that had been set aside for the guest of honor. 24So the cook brought in the meat and placed it before Saul. "Go ahead and eat it," Samuel said. "I was saving it for you even before I invited these others!" So Saul ate with Samuel that day.

25When they came down from the place of worship and returned to town, Samuel took Saul up to the roof of the house and prepared a bed for him there.* 26At daybreak the next morning, Samuel called to Saul, "Get up! It's time you were on your way." So Saul got ready,

and he and Samuel left the house together. 27When they reached the edge of town, Samuel told Saul to send his servant on ahead. After the servant was gone, Samuel said, "Stay here, for I have received a special message for you from God."

10 SAMUEL ANOINTS SAUL AS KING

Then Samuel took a flask of olive oil and poured it over Saul's head. He kissed Saul and said, "I am doing this because the LORD has appointed you to be the ruler over Israel, his special possession.* 2When you leave me today, you will see two men beside Rachel's tomb at Zelzah, on the border of Benjamin. They will tell you that the donkeys have been found and that your father has stopped worrying about them and is now worried about you. He is asking, 'Have you seen my son?'

3"When you get to the oak of Tabor, you will see three men coming toward you who are on their way to worship God at Bethel. One will be bringing three young goats, another will have three loaves of bread, and the third will be carrying a wineskin full of wine. 4They will greet

9:25 As in Greek version; Hebrew reads and talked with him there.
10:1 Greek version reads over Israel. And you will rule over the LORD's people and save them from their enemies around them. This will be the sign to you that the LORD has appointed you to be leader over his special possession.

SAUL — PERSONALITY PROFILE

FIRST IMPRESSIONS aren't always accurate. Sometimes a person with a great image looks very different when we discover his or her character, or lack thereof.

Saul made a good first impression—he looked like a king. But Saul lacked the traits that would have helped him be a good one. He often forgot or disobeyed God's directions. He was God's chosen leader, but God's choice did not mean that Saul was capable of being king on his own.

During his reign, Saul had his greatest successes when he obeyed God. His greatest failures resulted from acting on his own. Saul had the raw materials to be a good leader—appearance, courage, and action. Even his weaknesses could have been used by God if Saul had recognized them and left them in God's control. But Saul's choices alienated him from God and eventually from his own people.

While our strengths and abilities make us useful, our weaknesses often make us usable. Whatever we accomplish on our own is only a fraction of what God could do through us. Does he control your life?

BOTTOM LINE: God wants obedience from the heart, not empty rituals.
Obedience always involves sacrifice, but sacrifice does not always mean obedience.
God wants to make use of our strengths and weaknesses.
Our weaknesses can help us remember our need for God's guidance and help.

Saul's story is told in 1 Samuel 9–31. He also is mentioned in Acts 13:21-22.

UPS:
• First God-appointed king of Israel
• Known for his courage and generosity
• Stood tall, with a striking appearance

DOWNS:
• Lacked integrity
• Impulsive by nature, he tended to overstep his bounds
• Jealousy of David led to attempted murder
• Deliberately disobeyed God on several occasions

STATS:
• Where: The land of Benjamin
• Occupation: King of Israel
• Relatives: Kish (father); Ahinoam (wife); Jonathan, Ishbosheth, Abinadab, and Malkishua (sons); Merab and Michal (daughters)

KEY VERSES: 1 Samuel 9–31; Acts 13:21-22.

you and offer you two of the loaves, which you are to accept.

5"When you arrive at Gibeah of God,* where the garrison of the Philistines is located, you will meet a band of prophets coming down from the place of worship. They will be playing a harp, a tambourine, a flute, and a lyre, and they will be prophesying. 6At that time the Spirit of the LORD will come powerfully upon you, and you will prophesy with them. You will be changed into a different person. 7After these signs take place, do what must be done, for God is with you. 8Then go down to Gilgal ahead of me. I will join you there to sacrifice burnt offerings and peace offerings. You must wait for seven days until I arrive and give you further instructions."

SAMUEL'S SIGNS ARE FULFILLED
9As Saul turned and started to leave, God gave him a new heart, and all Samuel's signs were fulfilled that day. 10When Saul and his servant arrived at Gibeah, they saw a group of prophets coming toward them. Then the Spirit of God came powerfully upon Saul, and he, too, began to prophesy. 11When those who knew Saul heard about it, they exclaimed, "What? Is even Saul a prophet? How did the son of Kish become a prophet?"

12And one of those standing there said, "Can anyone become a prophet, no matter who his father is?"* So that is the origin of the saying "Is even Saul a prophet?"

13When Saul had finished prophesying, he went up to the place of worship. 14"Where have you been?" Saul's uncle asked him and his servant.

"We were looking for the donkeys," Saul replied, "but we couldn't find them. So we went to Samuel to ask him where they were."

15"Oh? And what did he say?" his uncle asked.

16"He told us that the donkeys had already been found," Saul replied. But Saul didn't tell his uncle what Samuel said about the kingdom.

SAUL IS ACCLAIMED KING
17Later Samuel called all the people of Israel to meet before the LORD at Mizpah. 18And he said, "This is what the LORD, the God of Israel, has declared: I brought you from Egypt and rescued you from the Egyptians and from all of the nations that were oppressing you. 19But though I have res-

cued you from your misery and distress, you have rejected your God today and have said, 'No, we want a king instead!' Now, therefore, present yourselves before the LORD by tribes and clans."

20So Samuel brought all the tribes of Israel before the LORD, and the tribe of Benjamin was chosen by lot. 21Then he brought each family of the tribe of Benjamin before the LORD, and the family of the Matrites was chosen. And finally Saul son of Kish was chosen from among them. But when they looked for him, he had disappeared! 22So they asked the LORD, "Where is he?"

And the LORD replied, "He is hiding among the baggage." 23So they found him and brought him out, and he stood head and shoulders above anyone else.

24Then Samuel said to all the people, "This is the man the LORD has chosen as your king. No one in all Israel is like him!"

And all the people shouted, "Long live the king!"

25Then Samuel told the people what the rights and duties of a king were. He wrote them down on a scroll and placed it before the LORD. Then Samuel sent the people home again.

26When Saul returned to his home at Gibeah, a group of men whose hearts God had touched went with him. 27But there were some scoundrels who complained, "How can this man save us?" And they scorned him and refused to bring him gifts. But Saul ignored them.

[Nahash, king of the Ammonites, had been grievously oppressing the people of Gad and Reuben who lived east of the Jordan River. He gouged out the right eye of each of the Israelites living there, and he didn't allow anyone to come and rescue them. In fact, of all the Israelites east of the Jordan, there wasn't a single one whose right eye Nahash had not gouged out. But there were 7,000 men who had escaped from the Ammonites, and they had settled in Jabesh-gilead.]*

11 SAUL DEFEATS THE AMMONITES
About a month later,* King Nahash of Ammon led his army against the Israelite town

....

10:5 Hebrew *Gibeath-elohim.*   10:12 Hebrew *said, "Who is their father?"*   10:27 This paragraph, which is not included in the Masoretic Text, is found in Dead Sea Scroll 4QSam³.   11:1 As in Greek version; Hebrew lacks *About a month later.*

HIDE AND SEEK
(10:22-24) When a king was to be chosen for Israel, Saul already knew that he was the one (10:1). Instead of coming forward, however, he hid. Often we hide from important responsibilities because we are afraid of failure, afraid of what others will think or perhaps unsure about how to proceed. Tempted to run from your responsibilities? You can run, but you can't hide from God. Why not seek him instead?

of Jabesh-gilead. But all the citizens of Jabesh asked for peace. "Make a treaty with us, and we will be your servants," they pleaded.

²"All right," Nahash said, "but only on one condition. I will gouge out the right eye of every one of you as a disgrace to all Israel!"

³"Give us seven days to send messengers throughout Israel!" replied the elders of Jabesh. "If no one comes to save us, we will agree to your terms."

⁴When the messengers came to Gibeah of Saul and told the people about their plight, everyone broke into tears. ⁵Saul had been plowing a field with his oxen, and when he returned to town, he asked, "What's the matter? Why is everyone crying?" So they told him about the message from Jabesh.

⁶Then the Spirit of God came powerfully upon Saul, and he became very angry. ⁷He took two oxen and cut them into pieces and sent the messengers to carry them throughout Israel with this message: "This is what will happen to the oxen of anyone who refuses to follow Saul and Samuel into battle!" And the Lord made the people afraid of Saul's anger, and all of them came out together as one. ⁸When Saul mobilized them at Bezek, he found that there were 300,000 men from Israel and 30,000* men from Judah.

⁹So Saul sent the messengers back to Jabesh-gilead to say, "We will rescue you by noontime tomorrow!" There was great joy throughout the town when that message arrived!

¹⁰The men of Jabesh then told their enemies, "Tomorrow we will come out to you, and you can do to us whatever you wish." ¹¹But before dawn the next morning, Saul arrived, having divided his army into three detachments. He launched a surprise attack against the Ammonites and slaughtered them the whole morning. The remnant of their army was so badly scattered that no two of them were left together.

¹²Then the people exclaimed to Samuel, "Now where are those men who said, 'Why should Saul rule over us?' Bring them here, and we will kill them!"

....

APPROPRIATE ANGER
(11:6) Anger is a powerful emotion. Often it is used wrongly to hurt others. But anger directed at sin and the mistreatment of others is not wrong. Saul was angered by the Ammonites' threat to humiliate and mistreat his fellow Israelites. God used Saul's anger to bring justice and freedom. When evil or injustice makes you angry, ask God to help you use that anger in constructive ways to bring about a positive change.

¹³But Saul replied, "No one will be executed today, for today the Lord has rescued Israel!"

¹⁴Then Samuel said to the people, "Come, let us all go to Gilgal to renew the kingdom." ¹⁵So they all went to Gilgal, and in a solemn ceremony before the Lord they made Saul king. Then they offered peace offerings to the Lord, and Saul and all the Israelites were filled with joy.

12 SAMUEL'S FAREWELL ADDRESS Then Samuel addressed all Israel: "I have done as you asked and given you a king. ²Your king is now your leader. I stand here before you—an old, gray-haired man—and my sons serve you. I have served as your leader from the time I was a boy to this very day. ³Now testify against me in the presence of the Lord and before his anointed one. Whose ox or donkey have I stolen? Have I ever cheated any of you? Have I ever oppressed you? Have I ever taken a bribe and perverted justice? Tell me and I will make right whatever I have done wrong."

⁴"No," they replied, "you have never cheated or oppressed us, and you have never taken even a single bribe."

⁵"The Lord and his anointed one are my witnesses today," Samuel declared, "that my hands are clean."

"Yes, he is a witness," they replied.

⁶"It was the Lord who appointed Moses and Aaron," Samuel continued. "He brought your ancestors out of the land of Egypt. ⁷Now stand here quietly before the Lord as I remind you of all the great things the Lord has done for you and your ancestors.

⁸"When the Israelites were* in Egypt and cried out to the Lord, he sent Moses and Aaron to rescue them from Egypt and to bring them into this land. ⁹But the people soon forgot about the Lord their God, so he handed them over to Sisera, the commander of Hazor's army, and also to the Philistines and to the king of Moab, who fought against them. ¹⁰Then they cried to the Lord again and confessed, 'We have sinned by turning away from the Lord and worshiping the images of Baal and Ashtoreth. But we will worship you and you alone if you will rescue us from our enemies.' ¹¹Then the Lord sent Gideon,* Bedan,* Jephthah, and Samuel* to save you, and you lived in safety.

11:8 Dead Sea Scrolls and Greek version read *70,000.*
12:8 Hebrew *When Jacob was.* The names "Jacob" and "Israel" are often interchanged throughout the Old Testament, referring sometimes to the individual patriarch and sometimes to the nation.
12:11a Hebrew *Jerub-baal,* another name for Gideon; see Judg 6:32.
12:11b Greek and Syriac versions read *Barak.*   **12:11c** Greek and Syriac versions read *Samson.*

¹²"But when you were afraid of Nahash, the king of Ammon, you came to me and said that you wanted a king to reign over you, even though the LORD your God was already your king. ¹³All right, here is the king you have chosen. You asked for him, and the LORD has granted your request.

¹⁴"Now if you fear and worship the LORD and listen to his voice, and if you do not rebel against the LORD's commands, then both you and your king will show that you recognize the LORD as your God. ¹⁵But if you rebel against the LORD's commands and refuse to listen to him, then his hand will be as heavy upon you as it was upon your ancestors.

¹⁶"Now stand here and see the great thing the LORD is about to do. ¹⁷You know that it does not rain at this time of the year during the wheat harvest. I will ask the LORD to send thunder and rain today. Then you will realize how wicked you have been in asking the LORD for a king!"

¹⁸So Samuel called to the LORD, and the LORD sent thunder and rain that day. And all the people were terrified of the LORD and of Samuel. ¹⁹"Pray to the LORD your God for us, or we will die!" they all said to Samuel. "For now we have added to our sins by asking for a king."

²⁰"Don't be afraid," Samuel reassured them. "You have certainly done wrong, but make sure now that you worship the LORD with all your heart, and don't turn your back on him. ²¹Don't go back to worshiping worthless idols that cannot help or rescue you—they are totally useless! ²²The LORD will not abandon his people, because that would dishonor his great name. For it has pleased the LORD to make you his very own people.

²³"As for me, I will certainly not sin against the LORD by ending my prayers for you. And I will continue to teach you what is good and right. ²⁴But be sure to fear the LORD and faithfully serve him. Think of all the wonderful things he has done for you. ²⁵But if you continue to sin, you and your king will be swept away."

13 CONTINUED WAR WITH PHILISTIA Saul was thirty* years old when he became king, and he reigned for forty-two years.*

²Saul selected 3,000 special troops from the army of Israel and sent the rest of the men home. He took 2,000 of the chosen men with

BE SURE TO FEAR THE LORD AND
FAITHFULLY SERVE HIM.
THINK OF ALL THE WONDERFUL THINGS HE HAS DONE FOR YOU.
1 SAMUEL 12:24

him to Micmash and the hill country of Bethel. The other 1,000 went with Saul's son Jonathan to Gibeah in the land of Benjamin.

³Soon after this, Jonathan attacked and defeated the garrison of Philistines at Geba. The news spread quickly among the Philistines. So Saul blew the ram's horn throughout the land, saying, "Hebrews, hear this! Rise up in revolt!" ⁴All Israel heard the news that Saul had destroyed the Philistine garrison at Geba and that the Philistines now hated the Israelites more than ever. So the entire Israelite army was summoned to join Saul at Gilgal.

⁵The Philistines mustered a mighty army of 3,000* chariots, 6,000 charioteers, and as many warriors as the grains of sand on the seashore! They camped at Micmash east of Beth-aven. ⁶The men of Israel saw what a tight spot they were in; and because they were hard pressed by the enemy, they tried to hide in caves, thickets, rocks, holes, and cisterns. ⁷Some of them crossed the Jordan River and escaped into the land of Gad and Gilead.

SAUL'S DISOBEDIENCE AND SAMUEL'S REBUKE
Meanwhile, Saul stayed at Gilgal, and his men were trembling with fear. ⁸Saul waited there seven days for Samuel, as Samuel had instructed him earlier, but Samuel still didn't come. Saul realized that his troops were rapidly slipping away. ⁹So he demanded, "Bring me the burnt offering and the peace offerings!" And Saul sacrificed the burnt offering himself.

¹⁰Just as Saul was finishing with the burnt

....

13:1a As in a few Greek manuscripts; the number is missing in the Hebrew.   13:1b Hebrew *reigned . . . and two*; the number is incomplete in the Hebrew. Compare Acts 13:21.   13:5 As in Greek and Syriac versions; Hebrew reads *30,000*.

EXCUSES, EXCUSES
(13:8-13) Saul had plenty of excuses for his disobedience. But Samuel zeroed in on the real issue: "You have not kept the command the LORD your God gave you" (13:13). By trying to hide his sins behind excuses, Saul lost his kingship (13:14). Like Saul, we sometimes gloss over our mistakes and sins, trying to justify and spiritualize our actions because of our "special" circumstances. But an excuse is just that—an excuse. God knows our true motives. He forgives, restores, and blesses only when we are honest about our actions.

offering, Samuel arrived. Saul went out to meet and welcome him, ¹¹but Samuel said, "What is this you have done?"

Saul replied, "I saw my men scattering from me, and you didn't arrive when you said you would, and the Philistines are at Micmash ready for battle. ¹²So I said, 'The Philistines are ready to march against us at Gilgal, and I haven't even asked for the LORD's help!' So I felt compelled to offer the burnt offering myself before you came."

¹³"How foolish!" Samuel exclaimed. "You have not kept the command the LORD your God gave you. Had you kept it, the LORD would have established your kingdom over Israel forever. ¹⁴But now your kingdom must end, for the LORD has sought out a man after his own heart. The LORD has already appointed him to be the leader of his people, because you have not kept the LORD's command."

ISRAEL'S MILITARY DISADVANTAGE ¹⁵Samuel then left Gilgal and went on his way, but the rest of the troops went with Saul to meet the army. They went up from Gilgal to Gibeah in the land of Benjamin.* When Saul counted the men who were still with him, he found only 600 were left! ¹⁶Saul and Jonathan and the troops with them were staying at Geba in the land of Benjamin. The Philistines set up their camp at Micmash. ¹⁷Three raiding parties soon left the camp of the Philistines. One went north toward Ophrah in the land of Shual, ¹⁸another went west to Beth-horon, and the third moved toward the border above the valley of Zeboim near the wilderness.

¹⁹There were no blacksmiths in the land of Israel in those days. The Philistines wouldn't allow them for fear they would make swords and spears for the Hebrews. ²⁰So whenever the Israelites needed to sharpen their plowshares, picks, axes, or sickles,* they had to take them to a Philistine blacksmith. ²¹(The charges were as follows: a quarter of an ounce of silver*

13:15 As in Greek version; Hebrew reads *Samuel then left Gilgal and went to Gibeah in the land of Benjamin.* **13:20** As in Greek version; Hebrew reads *or plowshares.* **13:21a** Hebrew *1 pim* [8 grams].

DAVID — PERSONALITY PROFILE

WHO IS THE COOLEST PERSON YOU KNOW? Does he or she have qualities like David? When we think of David, we think of a shepherd, poet, giant-killer, king, ancestor of Jesus—in short, we think of one of the greatest heroes in the Old Testament. But other words could also be used to describe David: betrayer, liar, adulterer, murderer.

The Bible makes no effort to hide David's failures. Yet he is remembered and respected as a godly man. Although David messed up many times, he was quick to confess his wrongdoings. His confessions were from the heart, and his repentance was real. David never took God's forgiveness lightly. In return, God never held back from David either his forgiveness or the consequences of his actions. David experienced the joy of forgiveness even when he had to suffer the consequences of wrong behavior.

David didn't make the same mistakes over and over. Rather, he learned from his mistakes. Is that how you are? Looking back at the list of David's good qualities, how many are true of your life?

BOTTOM LINE: Admitting our mistakes is the first step in dealing with them.

Forgiveness does not remove the consequences of sin.

God greatly desires our complete trust and worship.

David's story is told in 1 Samuel 16—1 Kings 2. He also is mentioned in Amos 6:5; Matthew 1:1, 6; 22:42-45; Luke 1:32; Romans 1:3; Hebrews 11:32.

UPS:
- Greatest king of Israel
- Ancestor of Jesus Christ
- Listed in the Hall of Faith in Hebrews 11
- Described by God as "a man after his own heart" (1 Sam 13:14; Acts 13:22)

DOWNS:
- Committed adultery with Bathsheba
- Arranged the murder of Uriah, Bathsheba's husband
- Disobeyed God by taking a census of the people

STATS:
- Where: Bethlehem, Jerusalem
- Occupation: Shepherd, musician, poet, soldier, king
- Relatives: Jesse (father); seven brothers; Michal, Ahinoam, Bathsheba, Abigail (wives); Absalom, Amnon, Solomon, Adonijah (sons); Tamar (daughter)
- Contemporaries: Saul, Jonathan, Samuel, Nathan

KEY VERSES: 1 Samuel 16—1 Kings 2; Amos 6:5; Matthew 1:1, 6; 22:43-45; Luke 1:32; Romans 1:3; Hebrews 11:32.

for sharpening a plowshare or a pick, and an eighth of an ounce* for sharpening an ax, a sickle, or an ox goad.) ²²So on the day of the battle none of the people of Israel had a sword or spear, except for Saul and Jonathan.

²³The pass at Micmash had meanwhile been secured by a contingent of the Philistine army.

14 JONATHAN'S DARING PLAN One day Jonathan said to his armor bearer, "Come on, let's go over to where the Philistines have their outpost." But Jonathan did not tell his father what he was doing.

²Meanwhile, Saul and his 600 men were camped on the outskirts of Gibeah, around the pomegranate tree* at Migron. ³Among Saul's men was Ahijah the priest, who was wearing the ephod, the priestly vest. Ahijah was the son of Ichabod's brother Ahitub, son of Phinehas, son of Eli, the priest of the Lord who had served at Shiloh.

No one realized that Jonathan had left the Israelite camp. ⁴To reach the Philistine outpost, Jonathan had to go down between two rocky cliffs that were called Bozez and Seneh. ⁵The cliff on the north was in front of Micmash, and the one on the south was in front of Geba. ⁶"Let's go across to the outpost of those pagans," Jonathan said to his armor bearer. "Perhaps the Lord will help us, for nothing can hinder the Lord. He can win a battle whether he has many warriors or only a few!"

⁷"Do what you think is best," the armor bearer replied. "I'm with you completely, whatever you decide."

⁸"All right then," Jonathan told him. "We will cross over and let them see us. ⁹If they say to us, 'Stay where you are or we'll kill you,' then we will stop and not go up to them. ¹⁰But if they say, 'Come on up and fight,' then we will go up. That will be the Lord's sign that he will help us defeat them."

¹¹When the Philistines saw them coming, they shouted, "Look! The Hebrews are crawling out of their holes!" ¹²Then the men from the outpost shouted to Jonathan, "Come on up here, and we'll teach you a lesson!"

"Come on, climb right behind me," Jonathan said to his armor bearer, "for the Lord will help us defeat them!"

¹³So they climbed up using both hands and feet, and the Philistines fell before Jonathan,

and his armor bearer killed those who came behind them. ¹⁴They killed some twenty men in all, and their bodies were scattered over about half an acre.*

¹⁵Suddenly, panic broke out in the Philistine army, both in the camp and in the field, including even the outposts and raiding parties. And just then an earthquake struck, and everyone was terrified.

ISRAEL DEFEATS THE PHILISTINES ¹⁶Saul's lookouts in Gibeah of Benjamin saw a strange sight—the vast army of Philistines began to melt away in every direction. ¹⁷"Call the roll and find out who's missing," Saul ordered. And when they checked, they found that Jonathan and his armor bearer were gone.

¹⁸Then Saul shouted to Ahijah, "Bring the ephod here!" For at that time Ahijah was wearing the ephod in front of the Israelites.* ¹⁹But while Saul was talking to the priest, the confusion in the Philistine camp grew louder and louder. So Saul said to the priest, "Never mind; let's get going!"*

²⁰Then Saul and all his men rushed out to the battle and found the Philistines killing each other. There was terrible confusion everywhere. ²¹Even the Hebrews who had previously gone over to the Philistine army revolted and joined in with Saul, Jonathan, and the rest of the Israelites. ²²Likewise, the men of Israel who were hiding in the hill country of Ephraim joined the chase when they saw the Philistines running away. ²³So the Lord saved Israel that day, and the battle continued to rage even beyond Beth-aven.

SAUL'S FOOLISH OATH ²⁴Now the men of Israel were pressed to exhaustion that day, because Saul had placed them under an oath, saying, "Let a curse fall on anyone who eats before evening—before I have full revenge on my enemies." So no one ate anything all day,

··

13:21b Hebrew ⅓ of a shekel [4 grams]. 14:2 Or around the rock of Rimmon; compare Judg 20:45, 47; 21:13. 14:14 Hebrew half a yoke; a "yoke" was the amount of land plowed by a pair of yoked oxen in one day. 14:18 As in some Greek manuscripts; Hebrew reads "Bring the Ark of God." For at that time the Ark of God was with the Israelites. 14:19 Hebrew Withdraw your hand.

OUTNUMBERED
(14:1-6) Jonathan and his armor bearer weren't much of a force to attack the huge Philistine army. But while everyone else was afraid, these men trusted God, knowing that the size of the enemy army had no relationship to God's ability to help them. God rewarded the faith and brave actions of these two men with a tremendous victory.

Have you ever faced an overwhelming problem? God is never intimidated by the size of an enemy or the complexity of a problem. With him, there are always enough resources to resist the pressures and win the battles. If God has called you to action, then bravely commit what few resources you have to God and rely on him to win the battle for you.

²⁵even though they had all found honeycomb on the ground in the forest. ²⁶They didn't dare touch the honey because they all feared the oath they had taken.

²⁷But Jonathan had not heard his father's command, and he dipped the end of his stick into a piece of honeycomb and ate the honey. After he had eaten it, he felt refreshed.* ²⁸But one of the men saw him and said, "Your father made the army take a strict oath that anyone who eats food today will be cursed. That is why everyone is weary and faint."

²⁹"My father has made trouble for us all!" Jonathan exclaimed. "A command like that only hurts us. See how refreshed I am now that I have eaten this little bit of honey. ³⁰If the men had been allowed to eat freely from the food they found among our enemies, think how many more Philistines we could have killed!"

³¹They chased and killed the Philistines all day from Micmash to Aijalon, growing more and more faint. ³²That evening they rushed for the battle plunder and butchered the sheep, goats, cattle, and calves, but they ate them without draining the blood. ³³Someone reported to Saul, "Look, the men are sinning against the LORD by eating meat that still has blood in it."

"That is very wrong," Saul said. "Find a large stone and roll it over here. ³⁴Then go out among the troops and tell them, 'Bring the cattle, sheep, and goats here to me. Kill them here, and drain the blood before you eat them. Do not sin against the LORD by eating meat with the blood still in it.'"

So that night all the troops brought their animals and slaughtered them there. ³⁵Then Saul built an altar to the LORD; it was the first of the altars he built to the LORD.

³⁶Then Saul said, "Let's chase the Philistines all night and plunder them until sunrise. Let's destroy every last one of them."

His men replied, "We'll do whatever you think is best."

But the priest said, "Let's ask God first."

³⁷So Saul asked God, "Should we go after the Philistines? Will you help us defeat them?" But God made no reply that day.

³⁸Then Saul said to the leaders, "Something's wrong! I want all my army commanders to come here. We must find out what sin was committed today. ³⁹I vow by the name of the LORD who rescued Israel that the sinner will surely die, even if it is my own son Jonathan!" But no one would tell him what the trouble was.

⁴⁰Then Saul said, "Jonathan and I will stand over here, and all of you stand over there."

And the people responded to Saul, "Whatever you think is best."

⁴¹Then Saul prayed, "O LORD, God of Israel, please show us who is guilty and who is innocent.*" Then they cast sacred lots, and Jonathan and Saul were chosen as the guilty ones, and the people were declared innocent.

⁴²Then Saul said, "Now cast lots again and choose between me and Jonathan." And Jonathan was shown to be the guilty one.

⁴³"Tell me what you have done," Saul demanded of Jonathan.

"I tasted a little honey," Jonathan admitted. "It was only a little bit on the end of my stick. Does that deserve death?"

⁴⁴"Yes, Jonathan," Saul said, "you must die! May God strike me and even kill me if you do not die for this."

⁴⁵But the people broke in and said to Saul, "Jonathan has won this great victory for Israel. Should he die? Far from it! As surely as the LORD lives, not one hair on his head will be touched, for God helped him do a great deed today." So the people rescued Jonathan, and he was not put to death.

⁴⁶Then Saul called back the army from chasing the Philistines, and the Philistines returned home.

SAUL'S MILITARY SUCCESSES
⁴⁷Now when Saul had secured his grasp on Israel's throne, he fought against his enemies in every direction—against Moab, Ammon, Edom, the kings of Zobah, and the Philistines. And wherever he turned, he was victorious.* ⁴⁸He performed great deeds and conquered the Amalekites, saving Israel from all those who had plundered them.

⁴⁹Saul's sons included Jonathan, Ishbosheth,* and Malkishua. He also had two

....

VOWS

(14:24-46) Saul made an oath without thinking through the implications. The results? Saul's men were too tired to fight. Also, they were so hungry they ate meat without draining the blood, which was against God's law (Lev 7:26). Not only that, Saul almost killed his own son because Jonathan broke the vow (14:42-44).

Saul's impulsive vow sounded heroic, but its disastrous side effects made it little more than "shooting off at the mouth." If you are in the middle of a conflict, guard against impulsive statements that you may be forced to honor.

14:27 Or *his eyes brightened;* similarly in 14:29.   14:41 Greek version adds *If the fault is with me or my son Jonathan, respond with Urim; but if the men of Israel are at fault, respond with Thummim.*   14:47 As in Greek version; Hebrew reads *he acted wickedly.*   14:49 Hebrew *Ishvi,* a variant name for Ishbosheth; also known as Esh-baal.

daughters: Merab, who was older, and Michal. [50]Saul's wife was Ahinoam, the daughter of Ahimaaz. The commander of Saul's army was Abner, the son of Saul's uncle Ner. [51]Saul's father, Kish, and Abner's father, Ner, were both sons of Abiel.

[52]The Israelites fought constantly with the Philistines throughout Saul's lifetime. So whenever Saul observed a young man who was brave and strong, he drafted him into his army.

15 SAUL DESTROYS THE AMALEKITES

One day Samuel said to Saul, "It was the LORD who told me to anoint you as king of his people, Israel. Now listen to this message from the LORD! [2]This is what the LORD of Heaven's Armies has declared: I have decided to settle accounts with the nation of Amalek for opposing Israel when they came from Egypt. [3]Now go and completely destroy* the entire Amalekite nation—men, women, children, babies, cattle, sheep, goats, camels, and donkeys."

[4]So Saul mobilized his army at Telaim. There were 200,000 soldiers from Israel and 10,000 men from Judah. [5]Then Saul and his army went to a town of the Amalekites and lay in wait in the valley. [6]Saul sent this warning to the Kenites: "Move away from where the Amalekites live, or you will die with them. For you showed kindness to all the people of Israel when they came up from Egypt." So the Kenites packed up and left.

[7]Then Saul slaughtered the Amalekites from Havilah all the way to Shur, east of Egypt. [8]He captured Agag, the Amalekite king, but completely destroyed everyone else. [9]Saul and his men spared Agag's life and kept the best of the sheep and goats, the cattle, the fat calves, and the lambs—everything, in fact, that appealed to them. They destroyed only what was worthless or of poor quality.

THE LORD REJECTS SAUL [10]Then the LORD said to Samuel, [11]"I am sorry that I ever made Saul king, for he has not been loyal to me and has refused to obey my command." Samuel was so deeply moved when he heard this that he cried out to the LORD all night.

[12]Early the next morning Samuel went to find Saul. Someone told him, "Saul went to the town of Carmel to set up a monument to himself; then he went on to Gilgal."

[13]When Samuel finally found him, Saul greeted him cheerfully. "May the LORD bless you," he said. "I have carried out the LORD's command!"

[14]"Then what is all the bleating of sheep and goats and the lowing of cattle I hear?" Samuel demanded.

15:3 The Hebrew term used here refers to the complete consecration of things or people to the LORD, either by destroying them or by giving them as an offering; also in 15:8, 9, 15, 18, 20, 21.

....

FAILURE
(15:13-14) Saul thought he had won a great victory over the Amalekites. God, however, saw it as a great failure because Saul had disobeyed him. Saul also lied to Samuel about the results of the battle. He may have thought that his lie wouldn't be detected, or that what he did wasn't wrong. He was mistaken.

Dishonest people soon begin to believe their own lies. This puts up a barrier between them and God. That's why honesty is so important in our relationships, both with God and with others.

CHOICES
living

On her way out the door for a company party, Mrs. Richards addresses her sophomore daughter, whom she has just grounded. "Alexis, remember—no visitors, and under no circumstances may you leave the house."

"OK, Mom," she mumbles.

After her mom leaves, Alexis grabs the phone and dials her best friend. "Katie, everything's cool." Ten minutes later Katie arrives.

"How 'bout checking the mall to see if Greg's there?" Alexis suggests.

"What if your mom calls?" Katie asks.

"Oh, I'll just tell her I was taking a bath."

The girls go to the mall. They shop, eat ice cream, and return home. Alexis slides into bed, thinking, "My mom is so out of it . . . I could have stayed out till midnight."

The next morning, Mrs. Richards, obviously angry, summons Alexis into the living room.

"Care to tell me about last night?" Mrs. Richards asks.

"Huh?" Alexis responds.

"Where did you go?"

"What are you talking about?" (It's an Oscar-winning performance.)

"Look, Alexis," Mrs. Richards says, "I know what you did. On my way to the party, I got a run in my hose. I stopped at the mall to get another pair. Guess who I saw there?"

Alexis sees her life flash before her eyes!

For a reminder of the high cost of dishonesty and disobedience, read 1 Samuel 15:1-23.

¹⁵"It's true that the army spared the best of the sheep, goats, and cattle," Saul admitted. "But they are going to sacrifice them to the LORD your God. We have destroyed everything else."

¹⁶Then Samuel said to Saul, "Stop! Listen to what the LORD told me last night!"

"What did he tell you?" Saul asked.

¹⁷And Samuel told him, "Although you may think little of yourself, are you not the leader of the tribes of Israel? The LORD has anointed you king of Israel. ¹⁸And the LORD sent you on a mission and told you, 'Go and completely destroy the sinners, the Amalekites, until they are all dead.' ¹⁹Why haven't you obeyed the LORD? Why did you rush for the plunder and do what was evil in the LORD's sight?"

²⁰"But I did obey the LORD," Saul insisted. "I carried out the mission he gave me. I brought back King Agag, but I destroyed everyone else. ²¹Then my troops brought in the best of the sheep, goats, cattle, and plunder to sacrifice to the LORD your God in Gilgal."

²²But Samuel replied,

"What is more pleasing to the LORD:
    your burnt offerings and sacrifices
    or your obedience to his voice?
Listen! Obedience is better than sacrifice,
    and submission is better than offering
        the fat of rams.
²³ Rebellion is as sinful as witchcraft,
    and stubbornness as bad as worshiping
        idols.
So because you have rejected the command
        of the LORD,
    he has rejected you as king."

SAUL PLEADS FOR FORGIVENESS

²⁴Then Saul admitted to Samuel, "Yes, I have sinned. I have disobeyed your instructions and the LORD's command, for I was afraid of the people and did what they demanded. ²⁵But now, please forgive my sin and come back with me so that I may worship the LORD."

²⁶But Samuel replied, "I will not go back with you! Since you have rejected the LORD's command, he has rejected you as king of Israel."

²⁷As Samuel turned to go, Saul tried to hold him back and tore the hem of his robe. ²⁸And Samuel said to him, "The LORD has torn the kingdom of Israel from you today and has given it to someone else—one who is better than you. ²⁹And he who is the Glory of Israel will not lie, nor will he change his mind, for he is not human that he should change his mind!"

³⁰Then Saul pleaded again, "I know I have sinned. But please, at least honor me before the elders of my people and before Israel by coming back with me so that I may worship the LORD your God." ³¹So Samuel finally agreed and went back with him, and Saul worshiped the LORD.

SAMUEL EXECUTES KING AGAG

³²Then Samuel said, "Bring King Agag to me." Agag arrived full of hope, for he thought, "Surely the worst is over, and I have been spared!"* ³³But Samuel said, "As your sword has killed the sons of many mothers, now your mother will be childless." And Samuel cut Agag to pieces before the LORD at Gilgal.

³⁴Then Samuel went home to Ramah, and Saul returned to his house at Gibeah of Saul. ³⁵Samuel never went to meet with Saul again, but he mourned constantly for him. And the LORD was sorry he had ever made Saul king of Israel.

16

SAMUEL ANOINTS DAVID AS KING

Now the LORD said to Samuel, "You have mourned long enough for Saul. I have rejected him as king of Israel, so fill your flask with olive oil and go to Bethlehem. Find a man named Jesse who lives there, for I have selected one of his sons to be my king."

²But Samuel asked, "How can I do that? If Saul hears about it, he will kill me."

"Take a heifer with you," the LORD replied, "and say that you have come to make a sacrifice to the LORD. ³Invite Jesse to the sacrifice, and I will show you which of his sons to anoint for me."

⁴So Samuel did as the LORD instructed. When he arrived at Bethlehem, the elders of the town came trembling to meet him. "What's wrong?" they asked. "Do you come in peace?"

⁵"Yes," Samuel replied. "I have come to sacrifice to the LORD. Purify yourselves and come with me to the sacrifice." Then Samuel performed the purification rite for Jesse and his sons and invited them to the sacrifice, too.

⁶When they arrived, Samuel took one look at Eliab and thought, "Surely this is the LORD's anointed!"

⁷But the LORD said to Samuel, "Don't judge by his appearance or height, for I have rejected him. The LORD doesn't see things the way you see them. People judge by outward appearance, but the LORD looks at the heart."

⁸Then Jesse told his son Abinadab to step

15:32 Dead Sea Scrolls and Greek version read *Agag arrived hesitantly, for he thought, "Surely this is the bitterness of death."*

PEOPLE JUDGE BY OUTWARD APPEARANCE, BUT THE LORD LOOKS AT THE HEART. 1 SAMUEL 16:7

forward and walk in front of Samuel. But Samuel said, "This is not the one the LORD has chosen." ⁹Next Jesse summoned Shimea,* but Samuel said, "Neither is this the one the LORD has chosen." ¹⁰In the same way all seven of Jesse's sons were presented to Samuel. But Samuel said to Jesse, "The LORD has not chosen any of these." ¹¹Then Samuel asked, "Are these all the sons you have?"

"There is still the youngest," Jesse replied. "But he's out in the fields watching the sheep and goats."

"Send for him at once," Samuel said. "We will not sit down to eat until he arrives."

¹²So Jesse sent for him. He was dark and handsome, with beautiful eyes.

And the LORD said, "This is the one; anoint him."

¹³So as David stood there among his brothers, Samuel took the flask of olive oil he had brought and anointed David with the oil. And the Spirit of the LORD came powerfully upon David from that day on. Then Samuel returned to Ramah.

DAVID SERVES IN SAUL'S COURT ¹⁴Now the Spirit of the LORD had left Saul, and the LORD sent a tormenting spirit* that filled him with depression and fear.

¹⁵Some of Saul's servants said to him, "A tormenting spirit from God is troubling you. ¹⁶Let us find a good musician to play the harp whenever the tormenting spirit troubles you. He will play soothing music, and you will soon be well again."

¹⁷"All right," Saul said. "Find me someone who plays well, and bring him here."

¹⁸One of the servants said to Saul, "One of Jesse's sons from Bethlehem is a talented harp player. Not only that—he is a brave warrior, a man of war, and has good judgment. He is also a fine-looking young man, and the LORD is with him."

¹⁹So Saul sent messengers to Jesse to say, "Send me your son David, the shepherd." ²⁰Jesse responded by sending David to Saul, along with a young goat, a donkey loaded with bread, and a wineskin full of wine.

²¹So David went to Saul and began serving him. Saul loved David very much, and David became his armor bearer.

²²Then Saul sent word to Jesse asking, "Please let David remain in my service, for I am very pleased with him."

²³And whenever the tormenting spirit from God troubled Saul, David would play the harp. Then Saul would feel better, and the tormenting spirit would go away.

17 GOLIATH CHALLENGES THE ISRAEL-ITES The Philistines now mustered their army for battle and camped between Socoh in Judah and Azekah at Ephes-dammim. ²Saul countered by gathering his Israelite troops near the valley of Elah. ³So the Philistines and Israelites faced each other on opposite hills, with the valley between them.

⁴Then Goliath, a Philistine champion from Gath, came out of the Philistine ranks to face the forces of Israel. He was over nine feet* tall! ⁵He wore a bronze helmet, and his bronze coat of mail weighed 125 pounds.* ⁶He also wore bronze leg armor, and he carried a bronze javelin on his shoulder. ⁷The shaft of his spear was as heavy and thick as a weaver's beam,

....

WHAT REALLY COUNTS
(16:7) Since Saul was tall and handsome, Samuel may have been trying to find someone who looked like Saul to be Israel's next king. But God warned Samuel against judging by appearance alone.

When people judge by appearance, they may overlook quality individuals who simply lack the particular physical characteristics that society currently admires. But appearance doesn't reveal what people are really like or what their true value is. Fortunately, God judges by character, not appearances. And because only God can see the inside, only he can accurately judge people. While we spend hours each week maintaining our outward appearance, we should do even more to develop our inner character. Everyone can see your face, but only you and God know what your heart really looks like. Integrity of heart is what counts with God. Is that what counts with you?

GROWTH
(16:19-21) When Saul asked David to join his palace staff, he obviously did not know that David had been secretly anointed king (16:12-13). Saul's invitation presented an excellent opportunity for the young, future king to gain firsthand information about leading a nation.

Sometimes our plans—even the ones we think God has approved—have to be put on hold indefinitely. Like David, we can use this waiting time profitably. How? By allowing our experiences to help us grow in wisdom.

16:9 Hebrew *Shammah,* a variant spelling of Shimea; compare 1 Chr 2:13; 20:7. **16:14** Or *an evil spirit;* also in 16:15, 16, 23. **17:4** Hebrew *6 cubits and 1 span* [which totals about 9.75 feet or 3 meters]; Dead Sea Scrolls and Greek version read *4 cubits and 1 span* [which totals about 6.75 feet or 2 meters]. **17:5** Hebrew *5,000 shekels* [57 kilograms].

SIMPLE OBJECTS

God often uses simple, ordinary objects to accomplish his tasks in the world. They only need to be dedicated to him for his use. What do you have that God can use? Anything and everything is a possible "instrument" for him.

OBJECT	REFERENCE	WHO USED IT?	HOW WAS IT USED?
A SHEPHERD'S STAFF	Exodus 4:2-4	Moses	To work miracles before Pharaoh
A RAM'S HORN	Joshua 6:3-5	Joshua	To flatten the walls of Jericho
A FLEECE	Judges 6:36-40	Gideon	To confirm God's will
HORNS, JARS, AND TORCHES	Judges 7:19-22	Gideon	To defeat the Midianites
A DONKEY'S JAWBONE	Judges 15:15	Samson	To kill 1,000 Philistines
A SMALL STONE	1 Samuel 17:49	David	To kill Goliath
OIL	2 Kings 4:1-7	Elisha	To demonstrate God's power to provide
A RIVER	2 Kings 5:9-14	Elisha	To heal a man of leprosy
A LINEN BELT	Jeremiah 13:1-11	Jeremiah	As an object lesson of God's wrath
POTTERY	Jeremiah 19:1-13	Jeremiah	As an object lesson of God's wrath
FOOD AND WATER	Ezekiel 4:9-17	Ezekiel	As an object lesson of judgment
FIVE LOAVES OF BREAD AND TWO FISH	Mark 6:30-44	Jesus	To feed a crowd of over 5,000 people

tipped with an iron spearhead that weighed 15 pounds.* His armor bearer walked ahead of him carrying a shield.

⁸Goliath stood and shouted a taunt across to the Israelites. "Why are you all coming out to fight?" he called. "I am the Philistine champion, but you are only the servants of Saul. Choose one man to come down here and fight me! ⁹If he kills me, then we will be your slaves. But if I kill him, you will be our slaves! ¹⁰I defy the armies of Israel today! Send me a man who will fight me!" ¹¹When Saul and the Israelites heard this, they were terrified and deeply shaken.

JESSE SENDS DAVID TO SAUL'S CAMP ¹²Now David was the son of a man named Jesse, an Ephrathite from Bethlehem in the land of Judah. Jesse was an old man at that time, and he had eight sons. ¹³Jesse's three oldest sons—Eliab, Abinadab, and Shimea*—had already joined Saul's army to fight the Philistines. ¹⁴David was the youngest son. David's three oldest brothers stayed with Saul's army, ¹⁵but David went back and forth so he could help his father with the sheep in Bethlehem.

¹⁶For forty days, every morning and evening, the Philistine champion strutted in front of the Israelite army.

¹⁷One day Jesse said to David, "Take this basket* of roasted grain and these ten loaves

of bread, and carry them quickly to your brothers. ¹⁸And give these ten cuts of cheese to their captain. See how your brothers are getting along, and bring back a report on how they are doing.*" ¹⁹David's brothers were with Saul and the Israelite army at the valley of Elah, fighting against the Philistines.

²⁰So David left the sheep with another shepherd and set out early the next morning with the gifts, as Jesse had directed him. He arrived at the camp just as the Israelite army was leaving for the battlefield with shouts and battle cries. ²¹Soon the Israelite and Philistine forces stood facing each other, army against army. ²²David left his things with the keeper of supplies and hurried out to the ranks to greet his brothers. ²³As he was talking with them, Goliath, the Philistine champion from Gath, came out from the Philistine ranks. Then David heard him shout his usual taunt to the army of Israel.

²⁴As soon as the Israelite army saw him, they began to run away in fright. ²⁵"Have you seen the giant?" the men asked. "He comes out each day to defy Israel. The king has offered a huge reward to anyone who kills him. He will give that man one of his daughters for a wife, and the man's entire family will be exempted from paying taxes!"

17:7 Hebrew *600 shekels* [6.8 kilograms].   **17:13** Hebrew *Shammah*, a variant spelling of Shimea; compare 1 Chr 2:13; 20:7.   **17:17** Hebrew *ephah* [20 quarts or 22 liters].   **17:18** Hebrew *and take their pledge.*

26David asked the soldiers standing nearby, "What will a man get for killing this Philistine and ending his defiance of Israel? Who is this pagan Philistine anyway, that he is allowed to defy the armies of the living God?"

27And these men gave David the same reply. They said, "Yes, that is the reward for killing him."

28But when David's oldest brother, Eliab, heard David talking to the men, he was angry. "What are you doing around here anyway?" he demanded. "What about those few sheep you're supposed to be taking care of? I know about your pride and deceit. You just want to see the battle!"

29"What have I done now?" David replied. "I was only asking a question!" 30He walked over to some others and asked them the same thing and received the same answer. 31Then David's question was reported to King Saul, and the king sent for him.

DAVID KILLS GOLIATH
32"Don't worry about this Philistine," David told Saul. "I'll go fight him!"

33"Don't be ridiculous!" Saul replied. "There's no way you can fight this Philistine and possibly win! You're only a boy, and he's been a man of war since his youth."

34But David persisted. "I have been taking care of my father's sheep and goats," he said. "When a lion or a bear comes to steal a lamb from the flock, 35I go after it with a club and rescue the lamb from its mouth. If the animal turns on me, I catch it by the jaw and club it to death. 36I have done this to both lions and bears, and I'll do it to this pagan Philistine, too, for he has defied the armies of the living God! 37The LORD who rescued me from the claws of the lion and the bear will rescue me from this Philistine!"

Saul finally consented. "All right, go ahead," he said. "And may the LORD be with you!"

38Then Saul gave David his own armor—a bronze helmet and a coat of mail. 39David put it on, strapped the sword over it, and took a step or two to see what it was like, for he had never worn such things before.

"I can't go in these," he protested to Saul. "I'm not used to them." So David took them off again. 40He picked up five smooth stones from a stream and put them into his shepherd's bag. Then, armed only with his shepherd's staff and sling, he started across the valley to fight the Philistine.

41Goliath walked out toward David with his shield bearer ahead of him, 42sneering in contempt at this ruddy-faced boy. 43"Am I a dog," he roared at David, "that you come at me with a stick?" And he cursed David by the names of his gods. 44"Come over here, and I'll give your flesh to the birds and wild animals!" Goliath yelled.

45David replied to the Philistine, "You come to me with sword, spear, and javelin, but I come to you in the name of the LORD of Heaven's Armies—the God of the armies of Israel, whom you have defied. 46Today the LORD will conquer you, and I will kill you and cut off your head. And then I will give the dead bodies of your men to the birds and wild animals, and the whole world will know that there is a God in Israel! 47And everyone assembled here will know that the LORD rescues his people, but not with sword and spear. This is the LORD's battle, and he will give you to us!"

48As Goliath moved closer to attack, David quickly ran out to meet him. 49Reaching into his shepherd's bag and taking out a stone, he hurled it with his sling and hit the Philistine in the forehead. The stone sank in, and Goliath stumbled and fell face down on the ground.

50So David triumphed over the Philistine with only a sling and a stone, for he had no sword. 51Then David ran over and pulled Goliath's sword from its sheath. David used it to kill him and cut off his head.

ISRAEL ROUTS THE PHILISTINES
When the Philistines saw that their champion was dead, they turned and ran. 52Then the men of Israel and Judah gave a great shout of triumph and rushed after the Philistines, chasing them as far as Gath* and the gates of Ekron. The bodies of the dead and wounded Philistines were strewn all along the road from Shaaraim, as far as Gath and Ekron. 53Then the Israelite army returned and plundered the deserted Philistine camp. 54(David took the Philistine's head to Jerusalem, but he stored the man's armor in his own tent.)

55As Saul watched David go out to fight the Philistine, he asked Abner, the commander

17:52 As in some Greek manuscripts; Hebrew reads *a valley.*

A CHANGE OF PERSPECTIVE
(17:26-37) Two people can have two different perspectives on the same event. As far as the fight with Goliath was concerned, Saul saw a huge giant and a young, insignificant-looking man. David, however, saw a mortal man defying an invincible God. David knew he would not be alone when he faced Goliath; God would fight with him. He looked at his situation from God's point of view. Seeing impossible situations from God's point of view helps us put giant problems in perspective.

of his army, "Abner, whose son is this young man?"

"I really don't know," Abner declared.

⁵⁶"Well, find out who he is!" the king told him.

⁵⁷As soon as David returned from killing Goliath, Abner brought him to Saul with the Philistine's head still in his hand. ⁵⁸"Tell me about your father, young man," Saul said.

··

TRUE FRIENDSHIP

(18:1-4) Soon after David and Jonathan met, they became close friends. Although Jonathan was probably somewhat older than David, their friendship is one of the deepest and closest recorded in the Bible because they (1) based their friendship on commitment to God, not just each other; (2) let nothing come between them—not even career or family problems; (3) drew closer together when their friendship was tested; and (4) were able to remain friends to the end.

Jonathan, the prince of Israel, later realized that David would become the next king (23:17), not Jonathan himself. But that did not weaken his love for David. Jonathan would much rather have lost the throne of Israel than his closest friend. How loyal are you to your friends?

POPULARITY

(18:5-18) While Saul's popularity made him arrogant, David remained humble even when the entire nation praised him. Although David succeeded in almost everything he tried and became famous throughout the land, he refused to allow his popularity to go to his head. Being called "most popular" can lead to an inflated sense of importance if a person isn't careful. Next time you do something cool, how will you react to praise?

And David replied, "His name is Jesse, and we live in Bethlehem."

18 SAUL BECOMES JEALOUS OF DAVID

After David had finished talking with Saul, he met Jonathan, the king's son. There was an immediate bond between them, for Jonathan loved David. ²From that day on Saul kept David with him and wouldn't let him return home. ³And Jonathan made a solemn pact with David, because he loved him as he loved himself. ⁴Jonathan sealed the pact by taking off his robe and giving it to David, together with his tunic, sword, bow, and belt.

⁵Whatever Saul asked David to do, David did it successfully. So Saul made him a commander over the men of war, an appointment that was welcomed by the people and Saul's officers alike.

⁶When the victorious Israelite army was returning home after David had killed the Philistine, women from all the towns of Israel came out to meet King Saul. They sang and danced for joy with tambourines and cymbals.* ⁷This was their song:

"Saul has killed his thousands,
    and David his ten thousands!"

⁸This made Saul very angry. "What's this?" he said. "They credit David with ten thousands

18:6 The type of instrument represented by the word *cymbals* is uncertain.

JONATHAN *PERSONALITY PROFILE*

LOYALTY is one of life's most costly qualities and is the most unselfish part of love. To be loyal, you cannot live only for yourself. Loyal people not only stand by their commitments, they are also willing to suffer for them. Jonathan is a shining example of loyalty. Sometimes he was forced to deal with a conflict between his loyalties to his father, Saul, and to his friend David. For Jonathan, truth always guided loyalty.

Jonathan found the source of truth in his relationship with God. He realized that no matter what, he must be loyal to him. Loyalty to God gave Jonathan the wisdom to deal effectively with the complicated situations in his life. He was loyal to Saul because Saul was his father and the king. He was loyal to David because David was his friend. But his loyalty to God helped him recognize the boundaries of his other relationships.

The conflicting demands of our relationships can challenge us as well. If we try to settle these conflicts only at the human level, we will constantly have to deal with a sense of betrayal. No other human can claim the loyalty that belongs to God. If we communicate to our friends that our number-one loyalty is to God and his truth, many of our choices will be much clearer. Do those closest to you know who has your greatest loyalty?

BOTTOM LINE: Loyalty is one of the strongest aspects of friendship.
    An allegiance to God puts all other relationships in perspective.
    Great friendships are costly.

Jonathan's story is told in 1 Samuel 13–15; 18–20; 31. He is also mentioned in 2 Samuel 9.

UPS:
• *Brave, loyal, and a natural leader*
• *Closest friend David ever had*
• *Did not put his personal well-being ahead of those he loved*
• *Depended on God*

STATS:
• *Occupation: Military leader*
• *Relatives: Saul (father); Ahinoam (mother); Abinadab, Malkishua, and Ishbosheth (brothers); Merab and Michal (sisters); Mephibosheth (son)*

KEY VERSES: *1 Samuel 13–14; 18–20; 31; 2 Samuel 9.*

and me with only thousands. Next they'll be making him their king!" ⁹So from that time on Saul kept a jealous eye on David.

¹⁰The very next day a tormenting spirit* from God overwhelmed Saul, and he began to rave in his house like a madman. David was playing the harp, as he did each day. But Saul had a spear in his hand, ¹¹and he suddenly hurled it at David, intending to pin him to the wall. But David escaped him twice.

¹²Saul was then afraid of David, for the LORD was with David and had turned away from Saul. ¹³Finally, Saul sent him away and appointed him commander over 1,000 men, and David faithfully led his troops into battle.

¹⁴David continued to succeed in everything he did, for the LORD was with him. ¹⁵When Saul recognized this, he became even more afraid of him. ¹⁶But all Israel and Judah loved David because he was so successful at leading his troops into battle.

DAVID MARRIES SAUL'S DAUGHTER ¹⁷One day Saul said to David, "I am ready to give you my older daughter, Merab, as your wife. But first you must prove yourself to be a real warrior by fighting the LORD's battles." For Saul thought, "I'll send him out against the Philistines and let them kill him rather than doing it myself."

¹⁸"Who am I, and what is my family in Israel that I should be the king's son-in-law?" David exclaimed. "My father's family is nothing!" ¹⁹So* when the time came for Saul to give his daughter Merab in marriage to David, he gave her instead to Adriel, a man from Meholah.

²⁰In the meantime, Saul's daughter Michal had fallen in love with David, and Saul was delighted when he heard about it. ²¹"Here's another chance to see him killed by the Philistines!" Saul said to himself. But to David he said, "Today you have a second chance to become my son-in-law!"

²²Then Saul told his men to say to David, "The king really likes you, and so do we. Why don't you accept the king's offer and become his son-in-law?"

²³When Saul's men said these things to David, he replied, "How can a poor man from a humble family afford the bride price for the daughter of a king?"

²⁴When Saul's men reported this back to the king, ²⁵he told them, "Tell David that all I want for the bride price is 100 Philistine foreskins! Vengeance on my enemies is all I really want." But what Saul had in mind was that David would be killed in the fight.

²⁶David was delighted to accept the offer. Before the time limit expired, ²⁷he and his men went out and killed 200 Philistines. Then David fulfilled the king's requirement by presenting all their foreskins to him. So Saul gave his daughter Michal to David to be his wife.

²⁸When Saul realized that the LORD was with David and how much his daughter Michal loved him, ²⁹Saul became even more afraid of him, and he remained David's enemy for the rest of his life.

³⁰Every time the commanders of the Philistines attacked, David was more successful against them than all the rest of Saul's officers. So David's name became very famous.

19 **SAUL TRIES TO KILL DAVID** Saul now urged his servants and his son Jonathan to assassinate David. But Jonathan, because of his strong affection for David, ²told him what his father was planning. "Tomorrow morning," he warned him, "you must find a hiding place out in the fields. ³I'll ask my father to go out there with me, and I'll talk to him about you. Then I'll tell you everything I can find out."

⁴The next morning Jonathan spoke with his father about David, saying many good things about him. "The king must not sin against his servant David," Jonathan said. "He's never done anything to harm you. He has always helped you in any way he could. ⁵Have you forgotten about the time he risked his life to kill the Philistine giant and how the LORD brought a great victory to all Israel as a result? You were certainly happy about it then. Why should you murder an innocent man like David? There is no reason for it at all!"

⁶So Saul listened to Jonathan and vowed, "As surely as the LORD lives, David will not be killed."

⁷Afterward Jonathan called David and told him what had happened. Then he brought David to Saul, and David served in the court as before.

⁸War broke out again after that, and David led his troops against the Philistines. He attacked them with such fury that they all ran away.

⁹But one day when Saul was sitting at home, with spear in hand, the tormenting spirit* from the LORD suddenly came upon him again. As David played his harp, ¹⁰Saul hurled his spear at David. But David dodged out of the way, and leaving the spear stuck in the wall, he fled and escaped into the night.

18:10 Or *an evil spirit.*   **18:19** Or *But.*   **19:9** Or *evil spirit.*

MICHAL SAVES DAVID'S LIFE

[11]Then Saul sent troops to watch David's house. They were told to kill David when he came out the next morning. But Michal, David's wife, warned him, "If you don't escape tonight, you will be dead by morning." [12]So she helped him climb out through a window, and he fled and escaped. [13]Then she took an idol* and put it in his bed, covered it with blankets, and put a cushion of goat's hair at its head.

[14]When the troops came to arrest David, she told them he was sick and couldn't get out of bed.

[15]But Saul sent the troops back to get David. He ordered, "Bring him to me in his bed so I can kill him!" [16]But when they came to carry David out, they discovered that it was only an idol in the bed with a cushion of goat's hair at its head.

[17]"Why have you betrayed me like this and let my enemy escape?" Saul demanded of Michal.

"I had to," Michal replied. "He threatened to kill me if I didn't help him."

[18]So David escaped and went to Ramah to see Samuel, and he told him all that Saul had done to him. Then Samuel took David with him to live at Naioth. [19]When the report reached Saul that David was at Naioth in Ramah, [20]he sent troops to capture him. But when they arrived and saw Samuel leading a group of prophets who were prophesying, the Spirit of God came upon Saul's men, and they also began to prophesy. [21]When Saul heard what had happened, he sent other troops, but they, too, prophesied! The same thing happened a third time. [22]Finally, Saul himself went to Ramah and arrived at the great well in Secu. "Where are Samuel and David?" he demanded.

"They are at Naioth in Ramah," someone told him.

[23]But on the way to Naioth in Ramah the Spirit of God came even upon Saul, and he, too, began to prophesy all the way to Naioth! [24]He tore off his clothes and lay naked on the ground all day and all night, prophesying in the presence of Samuel. The people who were watching exclaimed, "What? Is even Saul a prophet?"

· ·

GOD'S PROTECTION

(19:23) Jonathan spoke up for David (19:4). Michal helped him escape (19:11-17). Samuel gave him a place to hide (19:18). The Spirit of God interrupted Saul's manhunt (19:23). Each of these events was a demonstration of how God protected David from Saul. In what ways has God protected you recently?

20 JONATHAN HELPS DAVID

David now fled from Naioth in Ramah and found Jonathan. "What have I done?" he exclaimed. "What is my crime? How have I offended your father that he is so determined to kill me?"

[2]"That's not true!" Jonathan protested. "You're not going to die. He always tells me everything he's going to do, even the little things. I know my father wouldn't hide something like this from me. It just isn't so!"

[3]Then David took an oath before Jonathan and said, "Your father knows perfectly well about our friendship, so he has said to himself, 'I won't tell Jonathan—why should I hurt him?' But I swear to you that I am only a step away from death! I swear it by the LORD and by your own soul!"

[4]"Tell me what I can do to help you," Jonathan exclaimed.

[5]David replied, "Tomorrow we celebrate the new moon festival. I've always eaten with the king on this occasion, but tomorrow I'll hide in the field and stay there until the evening of the third day. [6]If your father asks where I am, tell him I asked permission to go home to Bethlehem for an annual family sacrifice. [7]If he says, 'Fine!' you will know all is well. But if he is angry and loses his temper, you will know he is determined to kill me. [8]Show me this loyalty as my sworn friend—for we made a solemn pact before the LORD—or kill me yourself if I have sinned against your father. But please don't betray me to him!"

[9]"Never!" Jonathan exclaimed. "You know that if I had the slightest notion my father was planning to kill you, I would tell you at once."

[10]Then David asked, "How will I know whether or not your father is angry?"

[11]"Come out to the field with me," Jonathan replied. And they went out there together.

[12]Then Jonathan told David, "I promise by the LORD, the God of Israel, that by this time tomorrow, or the next day at the latest, I will talk to my father and let you know at once how he feels about you. If he speaks favorably about you, I will let you know. [13]But if he is angry and wants you killed, may the LORD strike me and even kill me if I don't warn you so you can escape and live. May the LORD be with you as he used to be with my father. [14]And may you treat me with the faithful love of the LORD as long as I live. But if I die, [15]treat my family with this faithful love, even when the LORD destroys all your enemies from the face of the earth."

[16]So Jonathan made a solemn pact with Da-

19:13 Hebrew *teraphim;* also in 19:16.

vid,* saying, "May the LORD destroy all your enemies!" ¹⁷And Jonathan made David reaffirm his vow of friendship again, for Jonathan loved David as he loved himself.

¹⁸Then Jonathan said, "Tomorrow we celebrate the new moon festival. You will be missed when your place at the table is empty. ¹⁹The day after tomorrow, toward evening, go to the place where you hid before, and wait there by the stone pile.* ²⁰I will come out and shoot three arrows to the side of the stone pile as though I were shooting at a target. ²¹Then I will send a boy to bring the arrows back. If you hear me tell him, 'They're on this side,' then you will know, as surely as the LORD lives, that all is well, and there is no trouble. ²²But if I tell him, 'Go farther—the arrows are still ahead of you,' then it will mean that you must leave immediately, for the LORD is sending you away. ²³And may the LORD make us keep our promises to each other, for he has witnessed them."

²⁴So David hid himself in the field, and when the new moon festival began, the king sat down to eat. ²⁵He sat at his usual place against the wall, with Jonathan sitting opposite him* and Abner beside him. But David's place was empty. ²⁶Saul didn't say anything about it that day, for he said to himself, "Something must have made David ceremonially unclean." ²⁷But when David's place was empty again the next day, Saul asked Jonathan, "Why hasn't the son of Jesse been here for the meal either yesterday or today?"

²⁸Jonathan replied, "David earnestly asked me if he could go to Bethlehem. ²⁹He said, 'Please let me go, for we are having a family sacrifice. My brother demanded that I be there. So please let me get away to see my brothers.' That's why he isn't here at the king's table."

³⁰Saul boiled with rage at Jonathan. "You stupid son of a whore!"* he swore at him. "Do you think I don't know that you want him to be king in your place, shaming yourself and your mother? ³¹As long as that son of Jesse is alive, you'll never be king. Now go and get him so I can kill him!"

³²"But why should he be put to death?" Jonathan asked his father. "What has he done?" ³³Then Saul hurled his spear at Jonathan, intending to kill him. So at last Jonathan realized

that his father was really determined to kill David.

³⁴Jonathan left the table in fierce anger and refused to eat on that second day of the festival, for he was crushed by his father's shameful behavior toward David.

³⁵The next morning, as agreed, Jonathan went out into the field and took a young boy with him to gather his arrows. ³⁶"Start running," he told the boy, "so you can find the arrows as I shoot them." So the boy ran, and Jonathan shot an arrow beyond him. ³⁷When the boy had almost reached the arrow, Jonathan shouted, "The arrow is still ahead of you. ³⁸Hurry, hurry, don't wait." So the boy quickly gathered up the arrows and ran back to his master. ³⁹He, of course, suspected nothing; only Jonathan and David understood the signal. ⁴⁰Then Jonathan gave his bow and arrows to the boy and told him to take them back to town.

⁴¹As soon as the boy was gone, David came out from where he had been hiding near the stone pile.* Then David bowed three times to Jonathan with his face to the ground. Both of them were in tears as they embraced each other and said good-bye, especially David.

⁴²At last Jonathan said to David, "Go in peace, for we have sworn loyalty to each other in the LORD's name. The LORD is the witness of a bond between us and our children forever." Then David left, and Jonathan returned to the town.*

21 DAVID RUNS FROM SAUL ¹*David went to the town of Nob to see Ahimelech the priest. Ahimelech trembled when he saw him. "Why are you alone?" he asked. "Why is no one with you?"

²"The king has sent me on a private matter," David said. "He told me not to tell anyone why I am here. I have told my men where to meet me later. ³Now, what is there to eat? Give me five loaves of bread or anything else you have."

⁴"We don't have any regular bread," the priest replied. "But there is the holy bread, which you can have if your young men have not slept with any women recently."

....

LYING
(21:2) David lied to protect himself from Saul (21:10). Some may excuse this lie because David feared for his life. But nowhere in Scripture is David's lie condoned. In fact, his lie led to the deaths of 85 priests (22:9-23). The Bible makes it very clear that lying is wrong (Lev 19:11) and may lead to all sorts of harmful consequences. Is any lie worth that?

20:16 Hebrew *with the house of David.* **20:19** Hebrew *the stone Ezel.* The meaning of the Hebrew is uncertain. **20:25** As in Greek version; Hebrew reads *with Jonathan standing.* **20:30** Hebrew *You son of a perverse and rebellious woman.* **20:41** As in Greek version; Hebrew reads *near the south edge.* **20:42** This sentence is numbered 21:1 in Hebrew text. **21:1** Verses 21:1-15 are numbered 21:2-16 in Hebrew text.

5"Don't worry," David replied. "I never allow my men to be with women when they are on a campaign. And since they stay clean even on ordinary trips, how much more on this one!"

6Since there was no other food available, the priest gave him the holy bread—the Bread of the Presence that was placed before the LORD in the Tabernacle. It had just been replaced that day with fresh bread.

7Now Doeg the Edomite, Saul's chief herdsman, was there that day, having been detained before the LORD.*

8David asked Ahimelech, "Do you have a spear or sword? The king's business was so urgent that I didn't even have time to grab a weapon!"

9"I only have the sword of Goliath the Philistine, whom you killed in the valley of Elah," the priest replied. "It is wrapped in a cloth behind the ephod. Take that if you want it, for there is nothing else here."

"There is nothing like it!" David replied. "Give it to me!"

10So David escaped from Saul and went to King Achish of Gath. 11But the officers of Achish were unhappy about his being there. "Isn't this David, the king of the land?" they asked. "Isn't he the one the people honor with dances, singing,

'Saul has killed his thousands,
and David his ten thousands'?"

12David heard these comments and was very afraid of what King Achish of Gath might do to him. 13So he pretended to be insane, scratching on doors and drooling down his beard.

14Finally, King Achish said to his men, "Must you bring me a madman? 15We already have enough of them around here! Why should I let someone like this be my guest?"

22 DAVID AT THE CAVE OF ADULLAM So David left Gath and escaped to the cave of Adullam. Soon his brothers and all his other relatives joined him there. 2Then others began coming—men who were in trouble or in debt or who were just discontented—until David was the captain of about 400 men.

3Later David went to Mizpeh in Moab, where he asked the king, "Please allow my father and mother to live here with you until I know what God is going to do for me." 4So David's parents stayed in Moab with the king during the entire time David was living in his stronghold.

5One day the prophet Gad told David, "Leave the stronghold and return to the land of Judah." So David went to the forest of Hereth.

6The news of his arrival in Judah soon reached Saul. At the time, the king was sitting beneath the tamarisk tree on the hill at Gibeah, holding his spear and surrounded by his officers.

7"Listen here, you men of Benjamin!" Saul shouted to his officers when he heard the news. "Has that son of Jesse promised every one of you fields and vineyards? Has he promised to make you all generals and captains in his army?* 8Is that why you have conspired against me? For not one of you told me when my own son made a solemn pact with the son of Jesse. You're not even sorry for me. Think of it! My own son—encouraging him to kill me, as he is trying to do this very day!"

9Then Doeg the Edomite, who was standing there with Saul's men, spoke up. "When I was at Nob," he said, "I saw the son of Jesse talking to the priest, Ahimelech son of Ahitub. 10Ahimelech consulted the LORD for him. Then he gave him food and the sword of Goliath the Philistine."

THE SLAUGHTER OF THE PRIESTS 11King Saul immediately sent for Ahimelech and all his family, who served as priests at Nob. 12When they arrived, Saul shouted at him, "Listen to me, you son of Ahitub!"

"What is it, my king?" Ahimelech asked.

13"Why have you and the son of Jesse conspired against me?" Saul demanded. "Why did you give him food and a sword? Why have you consulted God for him? Why have you encouraged him to kill me, as he is trying to do this very day?"

14"But sir," Ahimelech replied, "is anyone among all your servants as faithful as David, your son-in-law? Why, he is the captain of your bodyguard and a highly honored member of your household! 15This was certainly not the first time I had consulted God for him! May the king not accuse me and my family in this matter, for I knew nothing at all of any plot against you."

16"You will surely die, Ahimelech, along with your entire family!" the king shouted. 17And he ordered his bodyguards, "Kill these priests of the LORD, for they are allies and conspirators with David! They knew he was running away from me, but they didn't tell me!" But Saul's men refused to kill the LORD's priests.

18Then the king said to Doeg, "You do it." So

21:7 The meaning of the Hebrew is uncertain. 22:7 Hebrew commanders of thousands and commanders of hundreds?

Doeg the Edomite turned on them and killed them that day, eighty-five priests in all, still wearing their priestly garments. ¹⁹Then he went to Nob, the town of the priests, and killed the priests' families—men and women, children and babies—and all the cattle, donkeys, sheep, and goats.

²⁰Only Abiathar, one of the sons of Ahimelech, escaped and fled to David. ²¹When he told David that Saul had killed the priests of the LORD, ²²David exclaimed, "I knew it! When I saw Doeg the Edomite there that day, I knew he was sure to tell Saul. Now I have caused the death of all your father's family. ²³Stay here with me, and don't be afraid. I will protect you with my own life, for the same person wants to kill us both."

23 DAVID PROTECTS THE TOWN OF KEILAH

One day news came to David that the Philistines were at Keilah stealing grain from the threshing floors. ²David asked the LORD, "Should I go and attack them?"

"Yes, go and save Keilah," the LORD told him.

³But David's men said, "We're afraid even here in Judah. We certainly don't want to go to Keilah to fight the whole Philistine army!"

⁴So David asked the LORD again, and again the LORD replied, "Go down to Keilah, for I will help you conquer the Philistines."

⁵So David and his men went to Keilah. They slaughtered the Philistines and took all their livestock and rescued the people of Keilah. ⁶Now when Abiathar son of Ahimelech fled to David at Keilah, he brought the ephod with him.

⁷Saul soon learned that David was at Keilah. "Good!" he exclaimed. "We've got him now! God has handed him over to me, for he has trapped himself in a walled town!" ⁸So Saul mobilized his entire army to march to Keilah and besiege David and his men.

⁹But David learned of Saul's plan and told Abiathar the priest to bring the ephod and ask the LORD what he should do. ¹⁰Then David prayed, "O LORD, God of Israel, I have heard that Saul is planning to come and destroy Keilah because I am here. ¹¹Will the leaders of Keilah betray me to him?* And will Saul actually come as I have heard? O LORD, God of Israel, please tell me."

And the LORD said, "He will come."

¹²Again David asked, "Will the leaders of Keilah betray me and my men to Saul?"

And the LORD replied, "Yes, they will betray you."

23:11 Some manuscripts lack the first sentence of 23:11.

DAVID HIDES IN THE WILDERNESS

¹³So David and his men—about 600 of them now—left Keilah and began roaming the countryside. Word soon reached Saul that David had escaped, so he didn't go to Keilah after all. ¹⁴David now stayed in the strongholds of the wilderness and in the hill country of Ziph. Saul hunted him day after day, but God didn't let Saul find him.

¹⁵One day near Horesh, David received the news that Saul was on the way to Ziph to search for him and kill him. ¹⁶Jonathan went to find David and encouraged him to stay strong in his faith in God. ¹⁷"Don't be afraid," Jonathan reassured him. "My father will never find you! You are going to be the king of Israel, and I will be next to you, as my father, Saul, is well aware." ¹⁸So the two of them renewed their solemn pact before the LORD. Then Jonathan returned home, while David stayed at Horesh.

¹⁹But now the men of Ziph went to Saul in Gibeah and betrayed David to him. "We know where David is hiding," they said. "He is in the strongholds of Horesh on the hill of Hakilah, which is in the southern part of Jeshimon. ²⁰Come down whenever you're ready, O king, and we will catch him and hand him over to you!"

²¹"The LORD bless you," Saul said. "At last someone is concerned about me! ²²Go and check again to be sure of where he is staying and who has seen him there, for I know that

....

GOOD WILL TRIUMPH
(22:18-19) Why did God allow 85 innocent priests to be killed? Scripture does not give a specific answer to this question, but it gives some insight into the issue.

Serving God does not guarantee that all will be well in this life. While God does not promise that good people will never be touched by the evil in this world, we can find comfort in his promise that ultimately all evil will be abolished. Those who remain faithful to God will be rewarded in the age to come (Matt 5:11-12; Rev 21:1-7; 22:1-21).

DECISIONS
(23:2) David asked God for advice before he took action. He listened to God's directions and then proceeded accordingly. Rather than trying to find God's will after the fact or having to ask God to undo the results of our hasty decisions, we should take time to discern God's will beforehand. We can hear him speak through the advice we receive from others, through his Word, and through the leading of his Spirit in our heart.

FRIENDS
(23:16-18) This may have been the last time David and Jonathan were together. As true friends, they were more than just companions who enjoyed each other's company. They encouraged each other's faith in God and trusted each other with their deepest thoughts and closest confidences. These are the marks of true friendship. How can you encourage your friends in their faith?

he is very crafty. [23]Discover his hiding places, and come back when you are sure. Then I'll go with you. And if he is in the area at all, I'll track him down, even if I have to search every hiding place in Judah!" [24]So the men of Ziph returned home ahead of Saul.

Meanwhile, David and his men had moved into the wilderness of Maon in the Arabah Valley south of Jeshimon. [25]When David heard that Saul and his men were searching for him, he went even farther into the wilderness to the great rock, and he remained there in the wilderness of Maon. But Saul kept after him in the wilderness.

[26]Saul and David were now on opposite sides of a mountain. Just as Saul and his men began to close in on David and his men, [27]an urgent message reached Saul that the Philistines were raiding Israel again. [28]So Saul quit chasing David and returned to fight the Philistines. Ever since that time, the place where David was camped has been called the Rock of Escape.* [29]*David then went to live in the strongholds of En-gedi.

24 DAVID SPARES SAUL'S LIFE

[1]*After Saul returned from fighting the Philistines, he was told that David had gone into the wilderness of En-gedi. [2]So Saul chose 3,000 elite troops from all Israel and went to search for David and his men near the rocks of the wild goats.

[3]At the place where the road passes some sheepfolds, Saul went into a cave to relieve himself. But as it happened, David and his men were hiding farther back in that very cave!

[4]"Now's your opportunity!" David's men whispered to him. "Today the LORD is telling you, 'I will certainly put your enemy into your power, to do with as you wish.'" So David crept forward and cut off a piece of the hem of Saul's robe.

[5]But then David's conscience began bothering him because he had cut Saul's robe. [6]"The LORD knows I shouldn't have done that to my lord the king," he said to his men. "The LORD forbid that I should do this to my lord the king and attack the LORD's anointed one, for the LORD himself has chosen him." [7]So David restrained his men and did not let them kill Saul.

After Saul had left the cave and gone on his way, [8]David came out and shouted after him, "My lord the king!" And when Saul looked around, David bowed low before him.

[9]Then he shouted to Saul, "Why do you listen to the people who say I am trying to harm you? [10]This very day you can see with your own eyes it isn't true. For the LORD placed you at my mercy back there in the cave. Some of my men told me to kill you, but I spared you. For I said, 'I will never harm the king—he is the LORD's anointed one.' [11]Look, my father, at what I have in my hand. It is a piece of the hem of your robe! I cut it off, but I didn't kill you. This proves that I am not trying to harm you and that I have not sinned against you, even though you have been hunting for me to kill me.

[12]"May the LORD judge between us. Perhaps the LORD will punish you for what you are trying to do to me, but I will never harm you. [13]As that old proverb says, 'From evil people come evil deeds.' So you can be sure I will never harm you. [14]Who is the king of Israel trying to catch anyway? Should he spend his time chasing one who is as worthless as a dead dog or a single flea? [15]May the LORD therefore judge which of us is right and punish the guilty one. He is my advocate, and he will rescue me from your power!"

[16]When David had finished speaking, Saul called back, "Is that really you, my son David?" Then he began to cry. [17]And he said to David, "You are a better man than I am, for you have repaid me good for evil. [18]Yes, you have been amazingly kind to me today, for when the LORD put me in a place where you could have killed me, you didn't do it. [19]Who else would let his enemy get away when he had him in his power? May the LORD reward you well for the kindness you have shown me today. [20]And now I realize that you are surely going to be king, and that the kingdom of Israel will flourish under your rule. [21]Now swear to me by the LORD that when that happens you will not kill my family and destroy my line of descendants!"

[22]So David promised this to Saul with an oath. Then Saul went home, but David and his men went back to their stronghold.

23:28 Hebrew *Sela-hammahlekoth*. 23:29 Verse 23:29 is numbered 24:1 in Hebrew text. 24:1 Verses 24:1-22 are numbered 24:2-23 in Hebrew text.

....

RESPECT
(24:5-7) *David had great respect for Saul, even though Saul continually tried to kill him. Although Saul was in a state of rebellion against God, David still respected the position he held as God's anointed king.*

Romans 13:1-7 reminds us that God places the government and its leaders in power. We may not know why, but like David, we are to respect the positions and roles of those to whom God has given authority. There is one exception, however. Because God is our highest authority, we should not allow a leader to force us to violate God's law.

25 THE DEATH OF SAMUEL
Now Samuel died, and all Israel gathered for his funeral. They buried him at his house in Ramah.

NABAL ANGERS DAVID
Then David moved down to the wilderness of Maon.* ²There was a wealthy man from Maon who owned property near the town of Carmel. He had 3,000 sheep and 1,000 goats, and it was sheep-shearing time. ³This man's name was Nabal, and his wife, Abigail, was a sensible and beautiful woman. But Nabal, a descendant of Caleb, was crude and mean in all his dealings.

⁴When David heard that Nabal was shearing his sheep, ⁵he sent ten of his young men to Carmel with this message for Nabal: ⁶"Peace and prosperity to you, your family, and everything you own! ⁷I am told that it is sheep-shearing time. While your shepherds stayed among us near Carmel, we never harmed them, and nothing was ever stolen from them. ⁸Ask your own men, and they will tell you this is true. So would you be kind to us, since we have come at a time of celebration? Please share any provisions you might have on hand with us and with our friend David." ⁹David's young men gave this message to Nabal in David's name, and they waited for a reply.

¹⁰"Who is this fellow David?" Nabal sneered to the young men. "Who does this son of Jesse think he is? There are lots of servants these days who run away from their masters. ¹¹Should I take my bread and my water and my meat that I've slaughtered for my shearers and give it to a band of outlaws who come from who knows where?"

¹²So David's young men returned and told him what Nabal had said. ¹³"Get your swords!" was David's reply as he strapped on his own. Then 400 men started off with David, and 200 remained behind to guard their equipment.

¹⁴Meanwhile, one of Nabal's servants went to Abigail and told her, "David sent messengers from the wilderness to greet our master, but he screamed insults at them. ¹⁵These men have been very good to us, and we never suffered any harm from them. Nothing was stolen from us the whole time they were with us. ¹⁶In fact, day and night they were like a wall of protection to us and the sheep. ¹⁷You need to know this and figure out what to do, for there is going to be trouble for our master and his

whole family. He's so ill-tempered that no one can even talk to him!"

¹⁸Abigail wasted no time. She quickly gathered 200 loaves of bread, two wineskins full of wine, five sheep that had been slaughtered, nearly a bushel* of roasted grain, 100 clusters of raisins, and 200 fig cakes. She packed them on donkeys ¹⁹and said to her servants, "Go on ahead. I will follow you shortly." But she didn't tell her husband Nabal what she was doing.

²⁰As she was riding her donkey into a mountain ravine, she saw David and his men coming toward her. ²¹David had just been saying, "A lot of good it did to help this fellow. We protected his flocks in the wilderness, and nothing he owned was lost or stolen. But he has repaid me evil for good. ²²May God strike me and kill me* if even one man of his household is still alive tomorrow morning!"

ABIGAIL INTERCEDES FOR NABAL
²³When Abigail saw David, she quickly got off her donkey and bowed low before him. ²⁴She fell at his feet and said, "I accept all blame in this matter, my lord. Please listen to what I have to say. ²⁵I know Nabal is a wicked and ill-tempered man; please don't pay any attention to him. He is a fool, just as his name suggests.* But I never even saw the young men you sent.

²⁶"Now, my lord, as surely as the LORD lives and you yourself live, since the LORD has kept you from murdering and taking vengeance into your own hands, let all your enemies and those who try to harm you be as cursed as Nabal is. ²⁷And here is a present that I, your servant, have brought to you and your young men. ²⁸Please forgive me if I have offended you in any way. The LORD will surely reward you with a lasting dynasty, for you are fighting the LORD's battles. And you have not done wrong throughout your entire life.

²⁹"Even when you are chased by those who seek to kill you, your life is safe in the care of the LORD your God, secure in his treasure pouch! But the lives of your enemies will disappear like stones shot from a sling! ³⁰When the LORD has done all he promised and has made

....

STOP AND LISTEN
(25:24) After Nabal refused his request for food, David was in no mood to listen when he set out for Nabal's property (25:13, 21-22). Nevertheless, he stopped to hear what Abigail had to say. If he had ignored her, he would have become guilty of taking vengeance into his own hands. No matter how right we think we are, we must always be careful to stop and listen to what others have to say. The extra time and effort can save us much pain and trouble in the long run.

25:1 As in Greek version (see also 25:2); Hebrew reads *Paran*.
25:18 Hebrew 5 *seahs* [30 liters].   25:22 As in Greek version; Hebrew reads *May God strike and kill the enemies of David*.
25:25 The name *Nabal* means "fool."

you leader of Israel, ³¹don't let this be a blemish on your record. Then your conscience won't have to bear the staggering burden of needless bloodshed and vengeance. And when the LORD has done these great things for you, please remember me, your servant!"

³²David replied to Abigail, "Praise the LORD, the God of Israel, who has sent you to meet me today! ³³Thank God for your good sense! Bless you for keeping me from murder and from carrying out vengeance with my own hands. ³⁴For I swear by the LORD, the God of Israel, who has kept me from hurting you, that if you had not hurried out to meet me, not one of Nabal's men would still be alive tomorrow morning." ³⁵Then David accepted her present and told her, "Return home in peace. I have heard what you said. We will not kill your husband."

³⁶When Abigail arrived home, she found that Nabal was throwing a big party and was celebrating like a king. He was very drunk, so she didn't tell him anything about her meeting with David until dawn the next day. ³⁷In the morning when Nabal was sober, his wife told him what had happened. As a result he had a stroke,* and he lay paralyzed on his bed like a stone. ³⁸About ten days later, the LORD struck him, and he died.

DAVID MARRIES ABIGAIL ³⁹When David heard that Nabal was dead, he said, "Praise the LORD, who has avenged the insult I received from Nabal and has kept me from doing it myself. Nabal has received the punishment for his sin." Then David sent messengers to Abigail to ask her to become his wife.

⁴⁰When the messengers arrived at Carmel,

· ·

CREATIVE IMPACT
(26:1-17) David could have killed Saul and Abner and made a point. But that action would have caused him to disobey God and set into motion unknown consequences. Instead, he took a water jug and a spear to show that he had had the opportunity to do evil, but chose not to do it. What are some creative, God-honoring ways you can make an impact in your school? Your neighborhood?

GOD FIRST
(26:8-11) The strongest moral decisions are the ones we make before temptation strikes. David was determined to follow God. This carried over into his decision not to kill God's chosen king, Saul, even when David's men and the circumstances presented the perfect opportunity. Who would you have been like in such a situation—David or David's men? To be like David and follow God, we must realize that we can't do wrong in order to execute justice. Even when our closest friends counsel us to do a certain action that seems right, we must always put God's commands first.

they told Abigail, "David has sent us to take you back to marry him."

⁴¹She bowed low to the ground and responded, "I, your servant, would be happy to marry David. I would even be willing to become a slave, washing the feet of his servants!" ⁴²Quickly getting ready, she took along five of her servant girls as attendants, mounted her donkey, and went with David's messengers. And so she became his wife. ⁴³David also married Ahinoam from Jezreel, making both of them his wives. ⁴⁴Saul, meanwhile, had given his daughter Michal, David's wife, to a man from Gallim named Palti son of Laish.

26 **DAVID SPARES SAUL AGAIN** Now some men from Ziph came to Saul at Gibeah to tell him, "David is hiding on the hill of Hakilah, which overlooks Jeshimon."

²So Saul took 3,000 of Israel's elite troops and went to hunt him down in the wilderness of Ziph. ³Saul camped along the road beside the hill of Hakilah, near Jeshimon, where David was hiding. When David learned that Saul had come after him into the wilderness, ⁴he sent out spies to verify the report of Saul's arrival.

⁵David slipped over to Saul's camp one night to look around. Saul and Abner son of Ner, the commander of his army, were sleeping inside a ring formed by the slumbering warriors. ⁶"Who will volunteer to go in there with me?" David asked Ahimelech the Hittite and Abishai son of Zeruiah, Joab's brother.

"I'll go with you," Abishai replied. ⁷So David and Abishai went right into Saul's camp and found him asleep, with his spear stuck in the ground beside his head. Abner and the soldiers were lying asleep around him.

⁸"God has surely handed your enemy over to you this time!" Abishai whispered to David. "Let me pin him to the ground with one thrust of the spear; I won't need to strike twice!"

⁹"No!" David said. "Don't kill him. For who can remain innocent after attacking the LORD's anointed one? ¹⁰Surely the LORD will strike Saul down someday, or he will die of old age or in battle. ¹¹The LORD forbid that I should kill the one he has anointed! But take his spear and that jug of water beside his head, and then let's get out of here!"

¹²So David took the spear and jug of water that were near Saul's head. Then he and Abishai got away without anyone seeing them or even waking up, because the LORD had put Saul's men into a deep sleep.

25:37 Hebrew *his heart failed him.*

¹³David climbed the hill opposite the camp until he was at a safe distance. ¹⁴Then he shouted down to the soldiers and to Abner son of Ner, "Wake up, Abner!"

"Who is it?" Abner demanded.

¹⁵"Well, Abner, you're a great man, aren't you?" David taunted. "Where in all Israel is there anyone as mighty? So why haven't you guarded your master the king when someone came to kill him? ¹⁶This isn't good at all! I swear by the LORD that you and your men deserve to die, because you failed to protect your master, the LORD's anointed! Look around! Where are the king's spear and the jug of water that were beside his head?"

¹⁷Saul recognized David's voice and called out, "Is that you, my son David?"

And David replied, "Yes, my lord the king. ¹⁸Why are you chasing me? What have I done? What is my crime? ¹⁹But now let my lord the king listen to his servant. If the LORD has stirred you up against me, then let him accept my offering. But if this is simply a human scheme, then may those involved be cursed by the LORD. For they have driven me from my home, so I can no longer live among the LORD's people, and they have said, 'Go, worship pagan gods.' ²⁰Must I die on foreign soil, far from the presence of the LORD? Why has the king of Israel come out to search for a single flea? Why does he hunt me down like a partridge on the mountains?"

²¹Then Saul confessed, "I have sinned. Come back home, my son, and I will no longer try to harm you, for you valued my life today. I have been a fool and very, very wrong."

²²"Here is your spear, O king," David replied. "Let one of your young men come over and get it. ²³The LORD gives his own reward for doing good and for being loyal, and I refused to kill you even when the LORD placed you in my power, for you are the LORD's anointed one. ²⁴Now may the LORD value my life, even as I have valued yours today. May he rescue me from all my troubles."

²⁵And Saul said to David, "Blessings on you, my son David. You will do many heroic deeds, and you will surely succeed." Then David went away, and Saul returned home.

27 DAVID AMONG THE PHILISTINES
But David kept thinking to himself, "Someday Saul is going to get me. The best thing I can do is escape to the Philistines. Then Saul will stop hunting for me in Israelite territory, and I will finally be safe."

²So David took his 600 men and went over

THE LORD GIVES HIS OWN REWARD FOR DOING GOOD AND FOR BEING LOYAL.

1 SAMUEL 26:23

and joined Achish son of Maoch, the king of Gath. ³David and his men and their families settled there with Achish at Gath. David brought his two wives along with him—Ahinoam from Jezreel and Abigail, Nabal's widow from Carmel. ⁴Word soon reached Saul that David had fled to Gath, so he stopped hunting for him.

⁵One day David said to Achish, "If it is all right with you, we would rather live in one of the country towns instead of here in the royal city."

⁶So Achish gave him the town of Ziklag (which still belongs to the kings of Judah to this day), ⁷and they lived there among the Philistines for a year and four months.

⁸David and his men spent their time raiding the Geshurites, the Girzites, and the Amalekites—people who had lived near Shur, toward the land of Egypt, since ancient times. ⁹David did not leave one person alive in the villages he attacked. He took the sheep, goats, cattle, donkeys, camels, and clothing before returning home to see King Achish.

¹⁰"Where did you make your raid today?" Achish would ask.

And David would reply, "Against the south of Judah, the Jerahmeelites, and the Kenites."

¹¹No one was left alive to come to Gath and tell where he had really been. This happened again and again while he was living among the Philistines. ¹²Achish believed David and thought to himself, "By now the people of Israel must hate him bitterly. Now he will have to stay here and serve me forever!"

....

PRETENSE
(27:10-12) Was David wrong in falsely reporting his activities to Achish? No doubt David was lying; however, he may have felt that lying was justified in a time of war against an enemy. The Philistines were still his enemies, but their territory was an excellent place to hide from Saul. When Achish asked David to go into battle against Israel, David agreed, once again pretending loyalty to the Philistines (29:2-3). Whether he would have actually fought Saul's army we can't know, but we can be sure that his ultimate loyalty was to God and not to Achish or Saul.

28

SAUL CONSULTS A MEDIUM About that time the Philistines mustered their armies for another war with Israel. King Achish told David, "You and your men will be expected to join me in battle."

[2]"Very well!" David agreed. "Now you will see for yourself what we can do."

Then Achish told David, "I will make you my personal bodyguard for life."

[3]Meanwhile, Samuel had died, and all Israel had mourned for him. He was buried in Ramah, his hometown. And Saul had banned from the land of Israel all mediums and those who consult the spirits of the dead.

[4]The Philistines set up their camp at Shunem, and Saul gathered all the army of Israel and camped at Gilboa. [5]When Saul saw the vast Philistine army, he became frantic with fear. [6]He asked the LORD what he should do, but the LORD refused to answer him, either by dreams or by sacred lots* or by the prophets. [7]Saul then said to his advisers, "Find a woman who is a medium, so I can go and ask her what to do."

His advisers replied, "There is a medium at Endor."

[8]So Saul disguised himself by wearing ordinary clothing instead of his royal robes. Then he went to the woman's home at night, accompanied by two of his men.

"I have to talk to a man who has died," he said. "Will you call up his spirit for me?"

[9]"Are you trying to get me killed?" the woman demanded. "You know that Saul has outlawed all the mediums and all who consult the spirits of the dead. Why are you setting a trap for me?"

[10]But Saul took an oath in the name of the LORD and promised, "As surely as the LORD lives, nothing bad will happen to you for doing this."

[11]Finally, the woman said, "Well, whose spirit do you want me to call up?"

"Call up Samuel," Saul replied.

[12]When the woman saw Samuel, she screamed, "You've deceived me! You are Saul!"

[13]"Don't be afraid!" the king told her. "What do you see?"

"I see a god* coming up out of the earth," she said.

[14]"What does he look like?" Saul asked.

"He is an old man wrapped in a robe," she replied. Saul realized it was Samuel, and he fell to the ground before him.

[15]"Why have you disturbed me by calling me back?" Samuel asked Saul.

"Because I am in deep trouble," Saul replied. "The Philistines are at war with me, and God has left me and won't reply by prophets or dreams. So I have called for you to tell me what to do."

[16]But Samuel replied, "Why ask me, since the LORD has left you and has become your enemy? [17]The LORD has done just as he said he would. He has torn the kingdom from you and given it to your rival, David. [18]The LORD has done this to you today because you refused to carry out his fierce anger against the Amalekites. [19]What's more, the LORD will hand you and the army of Israel over to the Philistines tomorrow, and you and your sons will be here with me. The LORD will bring down the entire army of Israel in defeat."

[20]Saul fell full length on the ground, paralyzed with fright because of Samuel's words. He was also faint with hunger, for he had eaten nothing all day and all night.

[21]When the woman saw how distraught he was, she said, "Sir, I obeyed your command at the risk of my life. [22]Now do what I say, and let me give you a little something to eat so you can regain your strength for the trip back."

[23]But Saul refused to eat anything. Then his advisers joined the woman in urging him to eat, so he finally yielded and got up from the ground and sat on the couch.

[24]The woman had been fattening a calf, so she hurried out and killed it. She took some flour, kneaded it into dough and baked unleavened bread. [25]She brought the meal to Saul and his advisers, and they ate it. Then they went out into the night.

29

THE PHILISTINES REJECT DAVID The entire Philistine army now mobilized at

---

KNOWING AND DOING WHAT'S RIGHT

(28:3-25) Although Saul had banned all mediums and psychics from Israel, he himself turned to one in desperation. Likewise, we may make a great show of denouncing something that we know is wrong. Yet if our heart doesn't change, we may find ourselves doing what we said was wrong. Knowing what is right and condemning what is wrong does not take the place of doing what is right.

DIRECTIONS

(28:15) God did not answer Saul's appeals for direction because Saul had not followed God's previous directions. Like Saul, many people wonder why their prayers seem unanswered. But if they don't fulfill the responsibilities God has already given them, they should not be surprised when he does not give further guidance. Tempted to ignore some previously given advice? Remember what happened to Saul!

28:6 Hebrew *by Urim.* **28:13** Or *gods.*

Aphek, and the Israelites camped at the spring in Jezreel. [2]As the Philistine rulers were leading out their troops in groups of hundreds and thousands, David and his men marched at the rear with King Achish. [3]But the Philistine commanders demanded, "What are these Hebrews doing here?"

And Achish told them, "This is David, the servant of King Saul of Israel. He's been with me for years, and I've never found a single fault in him from the day he arrived until today."

[4]But the Philistine commanders were angry. "Send him back to the town you've given him!" they demanded. "He can't go into the battle with us. What if he turns against us in battle and becomes our adversary? Is there any better way for him to reconcile himself with his master than by handing our heads over to him? [5]Isn't this the same David about whom the women of Israel sing in their dances,

'Saul has killed his thousands,
    and David his ten thousands'?"

[6]So Achish finally summoned David and said to him, "I swear by the LORD that you have been a trustworthy ally. I think you should go with me into battle, for I've never found a single flaw in you from the day you arrived until today. But the other Philistine rulers won't hear of it. [7]Please don't upset them, but go back quietly."

[8]"What have I done to deserve this treatment?" David demanded. "What have you ever found in your servant, that I can't go and fight the enemies of my lord the king?"

[9]But Achish insisted, "As far as I'm concerned, you're as perfect as an angel of God. But the Philistine commanders are afraid to have you with them in the battle. [10]Now get up early in the morning, and leave with your men as soon as it gets light."

[11]So David and his men headed back into the land of the Philistines, while the Philistine army went on to Jezreel.

30 DAVID DESTROYS THE AMALEKITES

Three days later, when David and his men arrived home at their town of Ziklag, they found that the Amalekites had made a raid into the Negev and Ziklag; they had crushed Ziklag and burned it to the ground. [2]They had carried off the women and children and everyone else but without killing anyone.

[3]When David and his men saw the ruins and realized what had happened to their families, [4]they wept until they could weep no more. [5]David's two wives, Ahinoam from Jezreel and Abigail, the widow of Nabal from Carmel, were among those captured. [6]David was now in great danger because all his men were very bitter about losing their sons and daughters, and they began to talk of stoning him. But David found strength in the LORD his God.

[7]Then he said to Abiathar the priest, "Bring me the ephod!" So Abiathar brought it. [8]Then David asked the LORD, "Should I chase after this band of raiders? Will I catch them?"

And the LORD told him, "Yes, go after them. You will surely recover everything that was taken from you!"

[9]So David and his 600 men set out, and they came to the brook Besor. [10]But 200 of the men were too exhausted to cross the brook, so David continued the pursuit with 400 men.

[11]Along the way they found an Egyptian man in a field and brought him to David. They gave him some bread to eat and water to drink. [12]They also gave him part of a fig cake and two clusters of raisins, for he hadn't had anything to eat or drink for three days and nights. Before long his strength returned.

[13]"To whom do you belong, and where do you come from?" David asked him.

"I am an Egyptian—the slave of an Amalekite," he replied. "My master abandoned me three days ago because I was sick. [14]We were on our way back from raiding the Kerethites in the Negev, the territory of Judah, and the land of Caleb, and we had just burned Ziklag."

[15]"Will you lead me to this band of raiders?" David asked.

The young man replied, "If you take an oath in God's name that you will not kill me or give me back to my master, then I will guide you to them."

[16]So he led David to them, and they found the Amalekites spread out across the fields, eating and drinking and dancing with joy because of

....

SCAPEGOAT
(30:1-9) Faced with the tragedy of losing their families, David's soldiers began to turn against him and even talked about killing him. Instead of planning a rescue, they looked for someone to blame. But David began looking for a solution rather than a scapegoat. When you're facing problems, will you look for a scapegoat or a solution?

KINDNESS
(30:11-15) The Amalekites cruelly left a servant to die, but David and his men treated the young man kindly. He returned their kindness by leading them to their enemy, the Amalekites. If you make a habit of treating those you meet with respect and dignity no matter how insignificant they may seem, you might find help in return. (Check out Luke 6:31—the "golden rule.")

the vast amount of plunder they had taken from the Philistines and the land of Judah. ¹⁷David and his men rushed in among them and slaughtered them throughout that night and the entire next day until evening. None of the Amalekites escaped except 400 young men who fled on camels. ¹⁸David got back everything the Amalekites had taken, and he rescued his two wives. ¹⁹Nothing was missing: small or great, son or daughter, nor anything else that had been taken. David brought everything back. ²⁰He also recovered all the flocks and herds, and his men drove them ahead of the other livestock. "This plunder belongs to David!" they said.

²¹Then David returned to the brook Besor and met up with the 200 men who had been left behind because they were too exhausted to go with him. They went out to meet David and his men, and David greeted them joyfully. ²²But some evil troublemakers among David's men said, "They didn't go with us, so they can't have any of the plunder we recovered. Give them their wives and children, and tell them to be gone."

²³But David said, "No, my brothers! Don't be selfish with what the LORD has given us. He has kept us safe and helped us defeat the band of raiders that attacked us. ²⁴Who will listen when you talk like this? We share and share alike—those who go to battle and those who guard the equipment." ²⁵From then on David made this a decree and regulation for Israel, and it is still followed today.

²⁶When he arrived at Ziklag, David sent part of the plunder to the elders of Judah, who were

. . . .

CHARACTER
(31:3-4) *Saul was tall, handsome, strong, rich, and powerful. But these qualities did not make him someone to imitate. He was tall physically, but he was small in God's eyes. He was handsome, but his sin made him ugly. He was strong, but his lack of faith made him weak. He was rich, but he was spiritually bankrupt. He could give orders to many, but he couldn't command their respect or allegiance. In other words, Saul looked good on the outside, but not so good on the inside. A good character is worth more than a face that could launch one thousand Teen People magazine covers. Would you agree?*

OBEDIENCE
(31:13) *Saul's death was also the death of an ideal. Israel could no longer believe that having a king like the other nations would solve their problems. The real problem was not the form of government, but the disobedience of the king. Like a brick, each obedient act is small in itself, but in time the acts pile up, building a huge wall of strong character—a great defense against temptation. Saul failed to build a wall of defense. What about you? Have you added a brick lately?*

his friends. "Here is a present for you, taken from the LORD's enemies," he said.

²⁷The gifts were sent to the people of the following towns David had visited: Bethel, Ramoth-negev, Jattir, ²⁸Aroer, Siphmoth, Eshtemoa, ²⁹Racal,* the towns of the Jerahmeelites, the towns of the Kenites, ³⁰Hormah, Bor-ashan, Athach, ³¹Hebron, and all the other places David and his men had visited.

31 THE DEATH OF SAUL Now the Philistines attacked Israel, and the men of Israel fled before them. Many were slaughtered on the slopes of Mount Gilboa. ²The Philistines closed in on Saul and his sons, and they killed three of his sons—Jonathan, Abinadab, and Malkishua. ³The fighting grew very fierce around Saul, and the Philistine archers caught up with him and wounded him severely.

⁴Saul groaned to his armor bearer, "Take your sword and kill me before these pagan Philistines come to run me through and taunt and torture me."

But his armor bearer was afraid and would not do it. So Saul took his own sword and fell on it. ⁵When his armor bearer realized that Saul was dead, he fell on his own sword and died beside the king. ⁶So Saul, his three sons, his armor bearer, and his troops all died together that same day.

⁷When the Israelites on the other side of the Jezreel Valley and beyond the Jordan saw that the Israelite army had fled and that Saul and his sons were dead, they abandoned their towns and fled. So the Philistines moved in and occupied their towns.

⁸The next day, when the Philistines went out to strip the dead, they found the bodies of Saul and his three sons on Mount Gilboa. ⁹So they cut off Saul's head and stripped off his armor. Then they proclaimed the good news of Saul's death in their pagan temple and to the people throughout the land of Philistia. ¹⁰They placed his armor in the temple of the Ashtoreths, and they fastened his body to the wall of the city of Beth-shan.

¹¹But when the people of Jabesh-gilead heard what the Philistines had done to Saul, ¹²all their mighty warriors traveled through the night to Beth-shan and took the bodies of Saul and his sons down from the wall. They brought them to Jabesh, where they burned the bodies. ¹³Then they took their bones and buried them beneath the tamarisk tree at Jabesh, and they fasted for seven days.

30:29 Greek version reads *Carmel.*

2 SAMUEL

Who do you look up to? Your youth leader? The lead singer of your favorite band? A political figure? The best basketball player at school? We usually admire heroes—those rare individuals who seem to do extraordinary things. The problem is they tend to fall off the pedestals we put them on.

That's the way it is with any human being. All of us make mistakes. But somehow we expect our heroes to be bigger than life—even perfect.

David was the essence of a hero: strong, brave, handsome, assertive, and committed. He was on top of the world—he was king, he had defeated his enemies, and the people loved him. But David was human, too. At the height of his success, he blew it and tried to cover up one wrong with another, from lust to adultery to murder (chs 11–12).

With most modern celebrities, that would be the end of the story— another one bites the dust. But with David, there was more. Recognizing his wrongdoing, David turned back to God and led the nation God's way. His comeback complete, he again proved himself to be a "man after [God's] own heart" (1 Sam 13:14).

Think David's life is cool enough to pattern your life after? Yeah, he had it all, or seemed to. But the most important thing that he had was his desire to make things right with God. That's a characteristic worth imitating.

KEY POINTS

KINGDOM GROWTH Under David's leadership, Israel grew rapidly. And through all of the changes, he continued to seek God's wisdom. David's example encourages us to stick with God no matter how much growth or how many changes we experience.

PERSONAL GREATNESS David's popularity and influence increased greatly. He realized that the Lord was behind his success. God does not regard personal greatness as something to be used selfishly but as an instrument to carry out his work among his people. The greatness we should desire is to love others as God loves us.

JUSTICE King David showed justice, mercy, and fairness to all. Although David was the most fair of all Israel's kings, he was still imperfect. His use of justice offered hope for a heavenly, ideal kingdom. This hope will never be satisfied until Christ, the Son of David, comes to rule in perfect justice forever.

CONSEQUENCES OF SIN David's sin with Bathsheba had consequences that affected his family and the nation for generations. Sin creates a cycle of suffering that is not worth the fleeting pleasure or "rush" it seems to offer.

STATS

PURPOSE
(1) To record the history of David's reign; (2) to demonstrate effective leadership under God; (3) to show the kinds of qualities that please God; (4) to depict David as a good leader of an imperfect kingdom; and (5) to foreshadow Christ, who will be the ideal leader of a new and perfect kingdom (see ch 7)

AUTHOR
Unknown. Some suggest Nathan's son Zabud may have been the author (1 Kgs 4:5). The book also includes the writings of Nathan and Gad (1 Chr 29:29).

ORIGINAL AUDIENCE
The people of Israel

DATE WRITTEN
930 B.C.

SETTING
The land of Israel under David's rule

SPECIAL FEATURE
This book was named after the prophet who anointed David and guided him in godly living.

TIMELINE

1050 B.C.
Saul becomes king

1010
Saul dies; David becomes king of Judah

1003
David becomes king of all Israel

991
Solomon is born

970
David dies; Solomon becomes king

930
The kingdom is divided

The broken lines (— · —) indicate modern boundaries.

KEY PLACES

❶ HEBRON
After Saul's death, David moved from the Philistine city of Ziklag to Hebron, where the tribe of Judah crowned him king. But the rest of Israel's tribes backed Saul's son Ishbosheth, and crowned him king at Mahanaim. As a result, there was war between Judah and the rest of the tribes of Israel until Ishbosheth was assassinated. Then all of Israel pledged loyalty to David as their king (1:1–5:5).

❷ JERUSALEM
One of David's first battles as king occurred at the fortress of Jerusalem. David and his troops took the city by surprise, and it became his capital. It was here that David brought the Ark of the Covenant and made a special covenant with God (5:6–7:29).

❸ GATH
The Philistines were Israel's constant enemy, though they did give David sanctuary when he was hiding from Saul (1 Sam 27). But when Saul died and David became king, the Philistines planned to defeat him. In a battle near Jerusalem, David and his troops routed the Philistines (5:17-25), but they were not completely subdued until David conquered Gath (8:1).

❹ MOAB
During the time of the judges, Moab controlled many cities in Israel and demanded heavy taxes (Judg 3:12-30). David conquered Moab and, in turn, levied tribute from them (8:2).

❺ EDOM
Though the Edomites and the Israelites traced their ancestry back to the same man, Isaac (Gen 25:19-23), they were long-standing enemies. David defeated the Edomites and forced them to pay tribute (8:14).

❻ RABBAH
The Ammonites insulted David's ambassadors and turned a peacemaking mission into angry warfare. The Ammonites called tens of thousands of mercenaries, but David defeated this alliance first at Helam, then at Rabbah, the capital city (10:1–12:31).

❼ MAHANAIM
David had victory in the field, but problems at home. His son, Absalom, incited a rebellion and declared himself king at Hebron. David and his men fled to Mahanaim. Acting on bad advice, Absalom mobilized his army to fight David (13:1–17:29).

❽ FOREST OF EPHRAIM
The armies of Absalom and David fought in the forest of Ephraim. Absalom's hair got caught in a tree, and Joab, David's general, found and killed him. With Absalom's death, the rebellion died (18:1–19:43).

❾ ABEL-BETH-MAACAH
A man named Sheba also incited a rebellion against David. He fled to Abel-beth-maacah, but Joab and a small troop besieged the city. The citizens of Abel-beth-maacah killed Sheba themselves (20:1-26). David's victories laid the foundation for the peaceful reign of his son Solomon.

1 DAVID LEARNS OF SAUL'S DEATH

DAVID LEARNS OF SAUL'S DEATH After the death of Saul, David returned from his victory over the Amalekites and spent two days in Ziklag. ²On the third day a man arrived from Saul's army camp. He had torn his clothes and put dirt on his head to show that he was in mourning. He fell to the ground before David in deep respect.

³"Where have you come from?" David asked.

"I escaped from the Israelite camp," the man replied.

⁴"What happened?" David demanded. "Tell me how the battle went."

The man replied, "Our entire army fled from the battle. Many of the men are dead, and Saul and his son Jonathan are also dead."

⁵"How do you know Saul and Jonathan are dead?" David demanded of the young man.

⁶The man answered, "I happened to be on Mount Gilboa, and there was Saul leaning on his spear with the enemy chariots and charioteers closing in on him. ⁷When he turned and saw me, he cried out for me to come to him. 'How can I help?' I asked him.

⁸"He responded, 'Who are you?'

"'I am an Amalekite,' I told him.

⁹"Then he begged me, 'Come over here and put me out of my misery, for I am in terrible pain and want to die.'

¹⁰"So I killed him," the Amalekite told David, "for I knew he couldn't live. Then I took his crown and his armband, and I have brought them here to you, my lord."

¹¹David and his men tore their clothes in sorrow when they heard the news. ¹²They mourned and wept and fasted all day for Saul and his son Jonathan, and for the LORD's army and the nation of Israel, because they had died by the sword that day.

¹³Then David said to the young man who had brought the news, "Where are you from?"

And he replied, "I am a foreigner, an Amalekite, who lives in your land."

¹⁴"Why were you not afraid to kill the LORD's anointed one?" David asked.

¹⁵Then David said to one of his men, "Kill him!" So the man thrust his sword into the Amalekite and killed him. ¹⁶"You have condemned yourself," David said, "for you yourself confessed that you killed the LORD's anointed one."

DAVID'S SONG FOR SAUL AND JONATHAN

¹⁷Then David composed a funeral song for Saul and Jonathan, ¹⁸and he commanded that it be taught to the people of Judah. It is known as the Song of the Bow, and it is recorded in *The Book of Jashar.**

¹⁹ Your pride and joy, O Israel, lies dead on the hills!
Oh, how the mighty heroes have fallen!
²⁰ Don't announce the news in Gath,
don't proclaim it in the streets of Ashkelon,
or the daughters of the Philistines will rejoice
and the pagans will laugh in triumph.

²¹ O mountains of Gilboa,
let there be no dew or rain upon you,
nor fruitful fields producing offerings of grain.*
For there the shield of the mighty heroes was defiled;
the shield of Saul will no longer be anointed with oil.

²² The bow of Jonathan was powerful,
and the sword of Saul did its mighty work.
They shed the blood of their enemies
and pierced the bodies of mighty heroes.

²³ How beloved and gracious were Saul and Jonathan!
They were together in life and in death.
They were swifter than eagles,
stronger than lions.

²⁴ O women of Israel, weep for Saul,
for he dressed you in luxurious scarlet clothing,
in garments decorated with gold.

²⁵ Oh, how the mighty heroes have fallen in battle!
Jonathan lies dead on the hills.

1:18 Or *The Book of the Upright.* *1:21* The meaning of the Hebrew is uncertain.

....

GRIEF
(1:1-12) David and his men were visibly shaken over Saul's death: "They mourned and wept and fasted all day." These actions revealed their genuine sorrow over the loss of their king, their friend Jonathan, and the other soldiers of Israel who had died that day. They were not ashamed to grieve. Today, expressing our emotions is considered by some to be a sign of weakness. Those who wish to appear strong try to hide their grief. But mourning can help us deal with our intense sorrow when a loved one dies.

SEEING GOOD INSTEAD OF EVIL
(1:17-27) Even though Saul had caused a ton of trouble for David, when he died, David still composed a funeral song for him and his son Jonathan. David had every reason to hate Saul, yet he chose not to. He chose to look at the good Saul had done and to forget the times when Saul had attacked him. Laying aside hatred and hurt in order to show respect for an enemy takes courage. Do you have that kind of courage and respect?

26 How I weep for you, my brother Jonathan!
     Oh, how much I loved you!
     And your love for me was deep,
         deeper than the love of women!

27 Oh, how the mighty heroes have fallen!
     Stripped of their weapons, they lie dead.

2 DAVID ANOINTED KING OF JUDAH After this, David asked the LORD, "Should I move back to one of the towns of Judah?"

"Yes," the LORD replied.

Then David asked, "Which town should I go to?"

"To Hebron," the LORD answered.

2David's two wives were Ahinoam from Jezreel and Abigail, the widow of Nabal from Carmel. So David and his wives 3and his men and their families all moved to Judah, and they settled in the villages near Hebron. 4Then the men of Judah came to David and anointed him king over the people of Judah.

When David heard that the men of Jabeshgilead had buried Saul, 5he sent them this message: "May the LORD bless you for being so loyal to your master Saul and giving him a decent burial. 6May the LORD be loyal to you in return and reward you with his unfailing love! And I, too, will reward you for what you have done. 7Now that Saul is dead, I ask you to be my strong and loyal subjects like the people of Judah, who have anointed me as their new king."

ISHBOSHETH PROCLAIMED KING OF ISRAEL

8But Abner son of Ner, the commander of Saul's army, had already gone to Mahanaim with Saul's son Ishbosheth.* 9There he proclaimed Ishbosheth king over Gilead, Jezreel, Ephraim, Benjamin, the land of the Ashurites, and all the rest of Israel.

10Ishbosheth, Saul's son, was forty years old when he became king, and he ruled from Mahanaim for two years. Meanwhile, the people of Judah remained loyal to David. 11David made Hebron his capital, and he ruled as king of Judah for seven and a half years.

STUBBORN

(2:21-24) Abner repeatedly warned Asahel to turn back or risk losing his life. Asahel, however, refused to turn from his self-imposed duty. Persistence is a good trait if it is for a worthy cause. But if the goal is only personal honor or gain, persistence may be no more than stubbornness. Asahel's stubbornness not only cost his life, but it also spurred unfortunate disunity in David's army for years to come (3:26-27; see also 1 Kgs 2:28-35). Before you decide to pursue a goal, make sure it is worth your devotion.

WAR BETWEEN ISRAEL AND JUDAH 12One day Abner led Ishbosheth's troops from Mahanaim to Gibeon. 13About the same time, Joab son of Zeruiah led David's troops out and met them at the pool of Gibeon. The two groups sat down there, facing each other from opposite sides of the pool.

14Then Abner suggested to Joab, "Let's have a few of our warriors fight hand to hand here in front of us."

"All right," Joab agreed. 15So twelve men were chosen to fight from each side—twelve men of Benjamin representing Ishbosheth son of Saul, and twelve representing David. 16Each one grabbed his opponent by the hair and thrust his sword into the other's side so that all of them died. So this place at Gibeon has been known ever since as the Field of Swords.*

17A fierce battle followed that day, and Abner and the men of Israel were defeated by the forces of David.

THE DEATH OF ASAHEL 18Joab, Abishai, and Asahel—the three sons of Zeruiah—were among David's forces that day. Asahel could run like a gazelle, 19and he began chasing Abner. He pursued him relentlessly, not stopping for anything. 20When Abner looked back and saw him coming, he called out, "Is that you, Asahel?"

"Yes, it is," he replied.

21"Go fight someone else!" Abner warned. "Take on one of the younger men, and strip him of his weapons." But Asahel kept right on chasing Abner.

22Again Abner shouted to him, "Get away from here! I don't want to kill you. How could I ever face your brother Joab again?"

23But Asahel refused to turn back, so Abner thrust the butt end of his spear through Asahel's stomach, and the spear came out through his back. He stumbled to the ground and died there. And everyone who came by that spot stopped and stood still when they saw Asahel lying there.

24When Joab and Abishai found out what had happened, they set out after Abner. The sun was just going down as they arrived at the hill of Ammah near Giah, along the road to the wilderness of Gibeon. 25Abner's troops from the tribe of Benjamin regrouped there at the top of the hill to take a stand.

26Abner shouted down to Joab, "Must we always be killing each other? Don't you realize that bitterness is the only result? When will you

2:8 *Ishbosheth* is another name for Esh-baal. 2:16 Hebrew *Helkath-hazzurim.*

call off your men from chasing their Israelite brothers?"

²⁷Then Joab said, "God only knows what would have happened if you hadn't spoken, for we would have chased you all night if necessary." ²⁸So Joab blew the ram's horn, and his men stopped chasing the troops of Israel.

²⁹All that night Abner and his men retreated through the Jordan Valley.* They crossed the Jordan River, traveling all through the morning,* and didn't stop until they arrived at Mahanaim.

³⁰Meanwhile, Joab and his men also returned home. When Joab counted his casualties, he discovered that only 19 men were missing in addition to Asahel. ³¹But 360 of Abner's men had been killed, all from the tribe of Benjamin. ³²Joab and his men took Asahel's body to Bethlehem and buried him there in his father's tomb. Then they traveled all night and reached Hebron at daybreak.

3 That was the beginning of a long war between those who were loyal to Saul and those loyal to David. As time passed David became stronger and stronger, while Saul's dynasty became weaker and weaker.

DAVID'S SONS BORN IN HEBRON ²These are the sons who were born to David in Hebron:

The oldest was Amnon, whose mother was Ahinoam from Jezreel.

³ The second was Daniel,* whose mother was Abigail, the widow of Nabal from Carmel.

The third was Absalom, whose mother was Maacah, the daughter of Talmai, king of Geshur.

⁴ The fourth was Adonijah, whose mother was Haggith.

The fifth was Shephatiah, whose mother was Abital.

⁵ The sixth was Ithream, whose mother was Eglah, David's wife.

These sons were all born to David in Hebron.

ABNER JOINS FORCES WITH DAVID ⁶As the war between the house of Saul and the house of David went on, Abner became a powerful leader among those loyal to Saul. ⁷One day Ishbosheth,* Saul's son, accused Abner of sleeping with one of his father's concubines, a woman named Rizpah, daughter of Aiah.

2:29a Hebrew *the Arabah.* **2:29b** Or *continued on through the Bithron.* The meaning of the Hebrew is uncertain. **3:3** As in parallel text at 1 Chr 3:1 (see also Greek version, which reads *Daluia,* and Dead Sea Scrolls, which read *Dan[iel]*); Hebrew reads *Kileab.* **3:7** *Ishbosheth* is another name for Esh-baal. **3:14** Hebrew *the foreskins.* **3:15** As in 1 Sam 25:44; Hebrew reads *Paltiel,* a variant spelling of Palti.

⁸Abner was furious. "Am I some Judean dog to be kicked around like this?" he shouted. "After all I have done for your father, Saul, and his family and friends by not handing you over to David, is this my reward—that you find fault with me about this woman? ⁹May God strike me and even kill me if I don't do everything I can to help David get what the LORD has promised him! ¹⁰I'm going to take Saul's kingdom and give it to David. I will establish the throne of David over Israel as well as Judah, all the way from Dan in the north to Beersheba in the south." ¹¹Ishbosheth didn't dare say another word because he was afraid of what Abner might do.

¹²Then Abner sent messengers to David, saying, "Doesn't the entire land belong to you? Make a solemn pact with me, and I will help turn over all of Israel to you."

¹³"All right," David replied, "but I will not negotiate with you unless you bring back my wife Michal, Saul's daughter, when you come."

¹⁴David then sent this message to Ishbosheth, Saul's son: "Give me back my wife Michal, for I bought her with the lives* of 100 Philistines."

¹⁵So Ishbosheth took Michal away from her husband, Palti* son of Laish. ¹⁶Palti followed along behind her as far as Bahurim, weeping as he went. Then Abner told him, "Go back home!" So Palti returned.

¹⁷Meanwhile, Abner had consulted with the elders of Israel. "For some time now," he told them, "you have wanted to make David your king. ¹⁸Now is the time! For the LORD has said, 'I have chosen David to save my people Israel from the hands of the Philistines and from all their other enemies.'" ¹⁹Abner also spoke with the men of Benjamin. Then he went to Hebron to tell David that all the people of Israel and Benjamin had agreed to support him.

²⁰When Abner and twenty of his men came to Hebron, David entertained them with a great feast. ²¹Then Abner said to David, "Let me go and call an assembly of all Israel to support my lord the king. They will make a covenant with you to make you their king, and you will rule

....

STAND FIRM
(3:7-11) Ishbosheth was right to speak out against Abner's behavior, but he didn't have the moral strength to maintain his authority (3:11). Lack of moral backbone became the root of Israel's troubles over the next four centuries. Only four of the next forty kings of Israel were called "good." Taking a stand for what you believe requires courage and conviction. When you believe something is wrong, what will you do to avoid allowing yourself be talked out of your position? How will you firmly attack the wrong and uphold the right?

over everything your heart desires." So David sent Abner safely on his way.

JOAB MURDERS ABNER
²²But just after David had sent Abner away in safety, Joab and some of David's troops returned from a raid, bringing much plunder with them. ²³When Joab arrived, he was told that Abner had just been there visiting the king and had been sent away in safety.

²⁴Joab rushed to the king and demanded, "What have you done? What do you mean by letting Abner get away? ²⁵You know perfectly well that he came to spy on you and find out everything you're doing!"

²⁶Joab then left David and sent messengers to catch up with Abner, asking him to return. They found him at the well of Sirah and brought him back, though David knew nothing about it. ²⁷When Abner arrived back at Hebron, Joab took him aside at the gateway as if to speak with him privately. But then he stabbed Abner in the stomach and killed him in revenge for killing his brother Asahel.

²⁸When David heard about it, he declared, "I vow by the LORD that I and my kingdom are forever innocent of this crime against Abner son of Ner. ²⁹Joab and his family are the guilty ones. May the family of Joab be cursed in every generation with a man who has open sores or leprosy* or who walks on crutches* or dies by the sword or begs for food!"

³⁰So Joab and his brother Abishai killed Abner because Abner had killed their brother Asahel at the battle of Gibeon.

DAVID MOURNS ABNER'S DEATH
³¹Then David said to Joab and all those who were with him, "Tear your clothes and put on burlap. Mourn for Abner." And King David himself walked behind the procession to the grave. ³²They buried Abner in Hebron, and the king and all the people wept at his graveside. ³³Then the king sang this funeral song for Abner:

"Should Abner have died as fools die?
³⁴ Your hands were not bound;
    your feet were not chained.
No, you were murdered—
    the victim of a wicked plot."

....

BE BOLD!
(4:1-7) Ishbosheth took his courage from another man (Abner) rather than from God. So when Abner died, Ishbosheth was left with nothing. In crisis and under pressure, he collapsed in fear. Fear can paralyze us, but faith and trust in God can overcome fear (2 Tim 1:6-8; Heb 13:6). If we trust in God, we will be free to respond boldly to the events around us.

All the people wept again for Abner. ³⁵David had refused to eat anything on the day of the funeral, and now everyone begged him to eat. But David had made a vow, saying, "May God strike me and even kill me if I eat anything before sundown."

³⁶This pleased the people very much. In fact, everything the king did pleased them! ³⁷So everyone in Judah and all Israel understood that David was not responsible for Abner's murder.

³⁸Then King David said to his officials, "Don't you realize that a great commander has fallen today in Israel? ³⁹And even though I am the anointed king, these two sons of Zeruiah—Joab and Abishai—are too strong for me to control. So may the LORD repay these evil men for their evil deeds."

4 THE MURDER OF ISHBOSHETH
When Ishbosheth,* Saul's son, heard about Abner's death at Hebron, he lost all courage, and all Israel became paralyzed with fear. ²Now there were two brothers, Baanah and Recab, who were captains of Ishbosheth's raiding parties. They were sons of Rimmon, a member of the tribe of Benjamin who lived in Beeroth. The town of Beeroth is now part of Benjamin's territory ³because the original people of Beeroth fled to Gittaim, where they still live as foreigners.

⁴(Saul's son Jonathan had a son named Mephibosheth,* who was crippled as a child. He was five years old when the report came from Jezreel that Saul and Jonathan had been killed in battle. When the child's nurse heard the news, she picked him up and fled. But as she hurried away, she dropped him, and he became crippled.)

⁵One day Recab and Baanah, the sons of Rimmon from Beeroth, went to Ishbosheth's house around noon as he was taking his midday rest. ⁶The doorkeeper, who had been sifting wheat, became drowsy and fell asleep. So Recab and Baanah slipped past her.* ⁷They went into the house and found Ishbosheth sleeping on his bed. They struck and killed him and cut off his head. Then, taking his head, they fled across the Jordan Valley* through the night. ⁸When they arrived at Hebron, they presented Ishbosheth's head

3:29a Or *or a contagious skin disease.* The Hebrew word used here can describe various skin diseases.   **3:29b** Or *who is effeminate;* Hebrew reads *who handles a spindle.*   **4:1** *Ishbosheth* is another name for Esh-baal.   **4:4** *Mephibosheth* is another name for Merib-baal.   **4:6** As in Greek version; Hebrew reads *So they went into the house pretending to fetch wheat, but they stabbed him in the stomach. Then Recab and Baanah escaped.*   **4:7** Hebrew *the Arabah.*

HIGHS AND LOWS OF DAVID'S LIFE

The Bible calls David a man after God's own heart (Acts 13:22), but that doesn't mean his life was free of troubles. David's life was full of highs and lows. Some of David's troubles were a result of his sins; some were a result of the sins of others. We can't always control our ups and downs, but we can trust God every day. We can be certain that he will help us through our trials, just as he helped David. In the end, he will reward us for our consistent faith.

Anointed as king (1 Sam 16)

Killed Goliath (1 Sam 17)

Crowned as king of all Israel (2 Sam 5)

Received God's covenant promise; conquered Israel's enemies (2 Sam 7–8)

Solomon born (2 Sam 12)

David restored as king (2 Sam 19)

David planned the Temple (1 Chr 22)

Fled from Saul (1 Sam 18–31)

Crowned as king of Judah (2 Sam 2)

Destroyed Ziklag; recovered kidnapped families (1 Sam 30)

Committed adultery and murder (2 Sam 11)

Absalom rebelled (2 Sam 15–18)

David sinned in taking the census (2 Sam 24)

---

to David. "Look!" they exclaimed to the king. "Here is the head of Ishbosheth, the son of your enemy Saul who tried to kill you. Today the LORD has given my lord the king revenge on Saul and his entire family!"

⁹But David said to Recab and Baanah, "The LORD, who saves me from all my enemies, is my witness. ¹⁰Someone once told me, 'Saul is dead,' thinking he was bringing me good news. But I seized him and killed him at Ziklag. That's the reward I gave him for his news! ¹¹How much more should I reward evil men who have killed an innocent man in his own house and on his own bed? Shouldn't I hold you responsible for his blood and rid the earth of you?"

¹²So David ordered his young men to kill them, and they did. They cut off their hands and feet and hung their bodies beside the pool in Hebron. Then they took Ishbosheth's head and buried it in Abner's tomb in Hebron.

5 **DAVID BECOMES KING OF ALL ISRAEL** Then all the tribes of Israel went to David at Hebron and told him, "We are your own flesh and blood. ²In the past,* when Saul was our king, you were the one who really led the forces of Israel. And the LORD told you, 'You will be the shepherd of my people Israel. You will be Israel's leader.'"

³So there at Hebron, King David made a cov-

enant before the LORD with all the elders of Israel. And they anointed him king of Israel.

⁴David was thirty years old when he began to reign, and he reigned forty years in all. ⁵He had reigned over Judah from Hebron for seven years and six months, and from Jerusalem he reigned over all Israel and Judah for thirty-three years.

DAVID CAPTURES JERUSALEM ⁶David then led his men to Jerusalem to fight against the Jebusites, the original inhabitants of the land who were living there. The Jebusites taunted David, saying, "You'll never get in here! Even the blind and lame could keep you out!" For the Jebusites thought they were safe. ⁷But David captured the fortress of Zion, which is now called the City of David.

⁸On the day of the attack, David said to his troops, "I hate those 'lame' and 'blind' Jebusites.* Whoever attacks them should strike by going into the city through the water tunnel.*" That is the origin of the saying, "The blind and the lame may not enter the house."*

....

PATIENCE
(5:4-5) Although he had been promised the kingship many years earlier, David did not become king of all Israel until he was 37 years old (1 Sam 16:13). During those years, David had to wait patiently for the fulfillment of God's promise. If you feel pressured to achieve instant results and success, remember David's patience. Just as his time of waiting prepared him for this important task, a waiting period may help prepare you by strengthening your spiritual character.

5:2 Or *For some time.*   5:8a Or *Those 'lame' and 'blind' Jebusites hate me.*   5:8b Or *with scaling hooks.* The meaning of the Hebrew is uncertain.   5:8c The meaning of this saying is uncertain.

⁹So David made the fortress his home, and he called it the City of David. He extended the city, starting at the supporting terraces* and working inward. ¹⁰And David became more and more powerful, because the LORD God of Heaven's Armies was with him.

¹¹Then King Hiram of Tyre sent messengers to David, along with cedar timber and carpenters and stonemasons, and they built David a palace. ¹²And David realized that the LORD had confirmed him as king over Israel and had blessed his kingdom for the sake of his people Israel.

¹³After moving from Hebron to Jerusalem, David married more concubines and wives, and they had more sons and daughters. ¹⁴These are the names of David's sons who were born in Jerusalem: Shammua, Shobab, Nathan, Solomon, ¹⁵Ibhar, Elishua, Nepheg, Japhia, ¹⁶Elishama, Eliada, and Eliphelet.

DAVID CONQUERS THE PHILISTINES

¹⁷When the Philistines heard that David had been anointed king of Israel, they mobilized all their forces to capture him. But David was told they were coming, so he went into the stronghold. ¹⁸The Philistines arrived and spread out across the valley of Rephaim. ¹⁹So David asked the LORD, "Should I go out to fight the Philistines? Will you hand them over to me?"

The LORD replied to David, "Yes, go ahead. I will certainly hand them over to you."

²⁰So David went to Baal-perazim and defeated the Philistines there. "The LORD did it!" David exclaimed. "He burst through my enemies like a raging flood!" So he named that place Baal-perazim (which means "the Lord who bursts through"). ²¹The Philistines had abandoned their idols there, so David and his men confiscated them.

²²But after a while the Philistines returned and again spread out across the valley of Rephaim. ²³And again David asked the LORD what to do. "Do not attack them straight on," the LORD replied. "Instead, circle around behind and at-

tack them near the poplar* trees. ²⁴When you hear a sound like marching feet in the tops of the poplar trees, be on the alert! That will be the signal that the LORD is moving ahead of you to strike down the Philistine army." ²⁵So David did what the LORD commanded, and he struck down the Philistines all the way from Gibeon* to Gezer.

6 MOVING THE ARK TO JERUSALEM

Then David again gathered all the elite troops in Israel, 30,000 in all. ²He led them to Baalah of Judah* to bring back the Ark of God, which bears the name of the LORD of Heaven's Armies,* who is enthroned between the cherubim. ³They placed the Ark of God on a new cart and brought it from Abinadab's house, which was on a hill. Uzzah and Ahio, Abinadab's sons, were guiding the cart as it left the house, ⁴carrying the Ark of God. Ahio walked in front of the Ark. ⁵David and all the people of Israel were celebrating before the LORD, singing songs* and playing all kinds of musical instruments—lyres, harps, tambourines, castanets, and cymbals.

⁶But when they arrived at the threshing floor of Nacon, the oxen stumbled, and Uzzah reached out his hand and steadied the Ark of God. ⁷Then the LORD's anger was aroused against Uzzah, and God struck him dead because of this.* So Uzzah died right there beside the Ark of God.

⁸David was angry because the LORD's anger had burst out against Uzzah. He named that place Perez-uzzah (which means "to burst out against Uzzah"), as it is still called today.

⁹David was now afraid of the LORD, and he asked, "How can I ever bring the Ark of the LORD back into my care?" ¹⁰So David decided not to move the Ark of the LORD into the City of David. Instead, he took it to the house of Obed-edom of Gath. ¹¹The Ark of the LORD remained there in Obed-edom's house for three months, and the LORD blessed Obed-edom and his entire household.

¹²Then King David was told, "The LORD has blessed Obed-edom's household and everything he has because of the Ark of God." So David went there and brought the Ark of God from the house of Obed-edom to the City of

....

BATTLES

(5:17-25) *David fought his battles the way God instructed him. In each instance he (1) asked if he should fight or not; (2) followed instructions carefully; and (3) gave God the glory. We can err in our "battles" by ignoring these steps and instead (1) doing what we want without considering God's will; (2) doing things our way and ignoring advice in the Bible or from other wise people; and (3) taking the glory ourselves or giving it to someone else without acknowledging the help we received from God. Next time you find yourself in the middle of a battle, what will you do?*

5:9 Hebrew *the millo*. The meaning of the Hebrew is uncertain.
5:23 Or *aspen*, or *balsam;* also in 5:24. The exact identification of this tree is uncertain.   5:25 As in Greek version (see also 1 Chr 14:16); Hebrew reads *Geba*.   6:2a *Baalah of Judah* is another name for Kiriath-jearim; compare 1 Chr 13:6.   6:2b *Or the Ark of God where the Name is proclaimed—the name of the LORD of Heaven's Armies.* Masoretic Text reads *before the LORD with all manner of cypress wood.*   6:7 As in Dead Sea Scrolls; Masoretic Text reads *because of his irreverence.*

David with a great celebration. [13]After the men who were carrying the Ark of the LORD had gone six steps, David sacrificed a bull and a fattened calf. [14]And David danced before the LORD with all his might, wearing a priestly garment.* [15]So David and all the people of Israel brought up the Ark of the LORD with shouts of joy and the blowing of rams' horns.

MICHAL'S CONTEMPT FOR DAVID

[16]But as the Ark of the LORD entered the City of David, Michal, the daughter of Saul, looked down from her window. When she saw King David leaping and dancing before the LORD, she was filled with contempt for him.

[17]They brought the Ark of the LORD and set it in its place inside the special tent David had prepared for it. And David sacrificed burnt

6:14 Hebrew *a linen ephod.* 6:19 Or *a portion of meat.* The meaning of the Hebrew is uncertain.

offerings and peace offerings to the LORD. [18]When he had finished his sacrifices, David blessed the people in the name of the LORD of Heaven's Armies. [19]Then he gave to every Israelite man and woman in the crowd a loaf of bread, a cake of dates,* and a cake of raisins. Then all the people returned to their homes.

[20]When David returned home to bless his own family, Michal, the daughter of Saul, came out to meet him. She said in disgust, "How distinguished the king of Israel looked today, shamelessly exposing himself to the servant girls like any vulgar person might do!"

[21]David retorted to Michal, "I was dancing before the LORD, who chose me above your father and all his family! He appointed me as the leader of Israel, the people of the LORD, so I celebrate before the LORD. [22]Yes, and I am willing to look even more foolish than this, even to be humiliated in my own eyes! But those servant

---

PERSONALITY PROFILE MICHAL

UPS:
- Loved David and became his first wife
- Saved David's life
- Could think and act quickly when necessary

DOWNS:
- Lied under pressure
- Allowed herself to become bitter over her circumstances
- Grew to hate David because of his love for God

STATS:
- Occupation: Daughter of one king (Saul) and wife of another (David)
- Relatives: Saul and Ahinoam (parents); Abinadab, Jonathan, Malkishua, and Ishbosheth (brothers); Merab (sister); David and Palti (husbands)

KEY VERSES: 1 Samuel 14:49-50; 18:20-29; 19:11-17; 25:44; 2 Samuel 3:13-14; 6:16-23; 1 Chronicles 15:29.

EVER WATCH A ROMANCE MOVIE where the couple vowed to love each other for all time? Sometimes what passes for "love" is little more than strong emotional attraction.

To Michal, King Saul's daughter, the courageous young David must have seemed like a dream come true. Her feelings for him gradually became obvious to others. Using this as an opportunity to get rid of his rival, Saul promised Michal's hand in marriage in exchange for David's success in the impossible mission of killing one hundred Philistines (1 Sam 18:21-25). But David was victorious. As a result, Saul had to allow Michal to marry David. David, meanwhile, became even more popular with the people.

Michal's love for David did not have time to be tested by the realities of marriage. Instead, she became involved in saving his life. Her quick thinking helped him escape, but the price was Saul's anger and Michal's separation from David (1 Sam 19:11-17). Her father gave her to another man, Palti, although David eventually took her back (1 Sam 25:44; 2 Sam 3:14-16).

Unlike her brother Jonathan, Michal did not have the kind of deep relationship with God that would have helped her cope with the difficulties in her life. She could not share David's joyful worship of God when the stolen Ark of the Lord was returned (2 Sam 6:16-23). Instead, she expressed bitterness and contempt for David. Sadly, Michal never bore David any children.

When a unified faith in God is not shared by a couple, the one who could hold them together sometimes seems to come between them. Beyond feeling sorry for Michal, we need to see her as a person like us. How quickly and easily we become bitter when life takes unexpected turns. But bitterness cannot change the bad things that have happened. Instead, it makes a bad situation worse. On the other hand, a willingness to turn to God gives him the opportunity to bring good out of our difficulties. That willingness has two parts: asking God for his guidance and looking for that guidance in his Word.

BOTTOM LINE: We are not as responsible for what happens to us as we are for how we respond to our circumstances.

Disobedience to God almost always harms us as well as others.

Michal's story is told in 1 Samuel 14:49-50; 18:20-29; 19:11-17; 25:44; 2 Samuel 3:13-14; 6:16-23. She also is mentioned in 1 Chronicles 15:29.

girls you mentioned will indeed think I am distinguished!" ²³So Michal, the daughter of Saul, remained childless throughout her entire life.

7 THE LORD'S COVENANT PROMISE TO DAVID

When King David was settled in his palace and the LORD had given him rest from all the surrounding enemies, ²the king summoned Nathan the prophet. "Look," David said, "I am living in a beautiful cedar palace,* but the Ark of God is out there in a tent!"

³Nathan replied to the king, "Go ahead and do whatever you have in mind, for the LORD is with you."

⁴But that same night the LORD said to Nathan,

⁵"Go and tell my servant David, 'This is what the LORD has declared: Are you the one to build a house for me to live in? ⁶I have never lived in a house, from the day I brought the Israelites out of Egypt until this very day. I have always moved from one place to another with a tent and a Tabernacle as my dwelling. ⁷Yet no matter where I have gone with the Israelites, I have never once complained to Israel's tribal leaders, the shepherds of my people Israel. I have never asked them, "Why haven't you built me a beautiful cedar house?"'

⁸"Now go and say to my servant David, 'This is what the LORD of Heaven's Armies has declared: I took you from tending sheep in the pasture and selected you to be the leader of my people Israel. ⁹I have been with you wherever you have gone, and I have destroyed all your enemies before your eyes. Now I will make your name as famous as anyone who has ever lived on the earth! ¹⁰And I will provide a homeland for my people Israel, planting them in a secure place where they will never be disturbed. Evil nations won't oppress them as they've done in the past, ¹¹starting from

the time I appointed judges to rule my people Israel. And I will give you rest from all your enemies.

"'Furthermore, the LORD declares that he will make a house for you—a dynasty of kings! ¹²For when you die and are buried with your ancestors, I will raise up one of your descendants, your own offspring, and I will make his kingdom strong. ¹³He is the one who will build a house—a temple—for my name. And I will secure his royal throne forever. ¹⁴I will be his father, and he will be my son. If he sins, I will correct and discipline him with the rod, like any father would do. ¹⁵But my favor will not be taken from him as I took it from Saul, whom I removed from your sight. ¹⁶Your house and your kingdom will continue before me* for all time, and your throne will be secure forever.'"

¹⁷So Nathan went back to David and told him everything the LORD had said in this vision.

DAVID'S PRAYER OF THANKS

¹⁸Then King David went in and sat before the LORD and prayed,

"Who am I, O Sovereign LORD, and what is my family, that you have brought me this far? ¹⁹And now, Sovereign LORD, in addition to everything else, you speak of giving your servant a lasting dynasty! Do you deal with everyone this way, O Sovereign LORD?*

²⁰"What more can I say to you? You know what your servant is really like, Sovereign LORD. ²¹Because of your promise and according to your will, you have done all these great things and have made them known to your servant.

²²"How great you are, O Sovereign LORD! There is no one like you. We have never even heard of another God like you! ²³What other nation on earth is like your people Israel? What other nation, O God, have you redeemed from slavery to be your own people? You made a great name for yourself when you redeemed your people from Egypt. You performed awesome miracles and drove out the nations and gods that stood in their way.* ²⁴You made Israel your very own people forever, and you, O LORD, became their God.

²⁵"And now, O LORD God, I am your

WHEN GOD SAYS NO
(7:1-16) David's request to build the Temple was good, but God said no. This does not mean that God rejected David. In fact, God was planning to do something even greater in David's life than allowing him the prestige of building Israel's first Temple. He promised that David's descendants would rule the kingdom forever. Although David's earthly dynasty ended four centuries later, Jesus Christ—a direct descendant of David—will be king forever (Acts 2:22-36). Christ will reign for eternity—first in his spiritual kingdom and ultimately on earth in the New Jerusalem (Luke 1:30-33; Rev 21).

Have you prayed with good intentions, only to have God say no? Realize that this is not rejection but God's way of fulfilling a greater purpose in your life.

7:2 Hebrew *a house of cedar.* **7:16** As in Greek version and some Hebrew manuscripts; Masoretic Text reads *before you.* **7:19** Or *This is your instruction for all humanity, O Sovereign LORD.* **7:23** As in Greek version (see also 1 Chr 17:21); Hebrew reads *You made a great name for yourself and performed awesome miracles for your land. You did this in the sight of your people, whom you redeemed from Egypt, from nations and their gods.*

servant; do as you have promised concerning me and my family. Confirm it as a promise that will last forever. ²⁶And may your name be honored forever so that everyone will say, 'The Lord of Heaven's Armies is God over Israel!' And may the house of your servant David continue before you forever.

²⁷"O Lord of Heaven's Armies, God of Israel, I have been bold enough to pray this prayer to you because you have revealed all this to your servant, saying, 'I will build a house for you—a dynasty of kings!' ²⁸For you are God, O Sovereign Lord. Your words are truth, and you have promised these good things to your servant. ²⁹And now, may it please you to bless the house of your servant, so that it may continue forever before you. For you have spoken, and when you grant a blessing to your servant, O Sovereign Lord, it is an eternal blessing!"

8 **DAVID'S MILITARY VICTORIES** After this, David defeated and subdued the Philistines by conquering Gath, their largest town.* ²David also conquered the land of Moab. He made the people lie down on the ground in a row, and he measured them off in groups with a length of rope. He measured off two groups to be executed for every one group to be spared. The Moabites who were spared became David's subjects and paid him tribute money.

³David also destroyed the forces of Hadadezer son of Rehob, king of Zobah, when Hadadezer marched out to strengthen his control along the Euphrates River. ⁴David captured 1,000 chariots, 7,000 charioteers,* and 20,000 foot soldiers. He crippled all the chariot horses except enough for 100 chariots.

⁵When Arameans from Damascus arrived to help King Hadadezer, David killed 22,000 of them. ⁶Then he placed several army garrisons in Damascus, the Aramean capital, and the Arameans became David's subjects and paid him tribute money. So the Lord made David victorious wherever he went.

⁷David brought the gold shields of Hadadezer's officers to Jerusalem, ⁸along with a large

THE LORD MADE DAVID VICTORIOUS WHEREVER HE WENT.

■ ■ ■ ■ ■ ■ ■ ■ ■ 2 SAMUEL 8:14

amount of bronze from Hadadezer's towns of Tebah* and Berothai.

⁹When King Toi of Hamath heard that David had destroyed the entire army of Hadadezer, ¹⁰he sent his son Joram to congratulate King David for his successful campaign. Hadadezer and Toi had been enemies and were often at war. Joram presented David with many gifts of silver, gold, and bronze.

¹¹King David dedicated all these gifts to the Lord, as he did with the silver and gold from the other nations he had defeated—¹²from Edom,* Moab, Ammon, Philistia, and Amalek—and from Hadadezer son of Rehob, king of Zobah.

¹³So David became even more famous when he returned from destroying 18,000 Edomites* in the Valley of Salt. ¹⁴He placed army garrisons throughout Edom, and all the Edomites became David's subjects. In fact, the Lord made David victorious wherever he went.

¹⁵So David reigned over all Israel and did what was just and right for all his people. ¹⁶Joab son of Zeruiah was commander of the army. Jehoshaphat son of Ahilud was the royal historian. ¹⁷Zadok son of Ahitub and Ahimelech son of Abiathar were the priests. Seraiah was the court secretary. ¹⁸Benaiah son of Jehoiada was captain of the king's bodyguard.* And David's sons served as priestly leaders.*

9 **DAVID'S KINDNESS TO MEPHIBOSHETH** One day David asked, "Is anyone in Saul's family still alive—anyone to whom I can show kindness for Jonathan's sake?" ²He summoned a man named Ziba, who had been one of Saul's servants. "Are you Ziba?" the king asked.

"Yes sir, I am," Ziba replied.

³The king then asked him, "Is anyone still

8:1 Hebrew *by conquering Metheg-ammah,* a name that means "the bridle," possibly referring to the size of the town or the tribute money taken from it. Compare 1 Chr 18:1. 8:4 As in Dead Sea Scrolls and Greek version (see also 1 Chr 18:4); Masoretic Text reads *captured 1,700 charioteers.* 8:8 As in some Greek manuscripts (see also 1 Chr 18:8); Hebrew reads *Betah.* 8:12 As in a few Hebrew manuscripts and Greek and Syriac versions (see also 8:14; 1 Chr 18:11); most Hebrew manuscripts read *Aram.* 8:13 As in a few Hebrew manuscripts and Greek and Syriac versions (see also 8:14; 1 Chr 18:12); most Hebrew manuscripts read *Arameans.* 8:18a Hebrew *of the Kerethites and Pelethites.* 8:18b Hebrew *David's sons were priests;* compare parallel text at 1 Chr 18:17.

THE PUBLIC EYE
(8:15) Everything David did pleased the people (3:36), not because he tried to please them, but because he tried to please God. Often those who try the hardest to become popular never make it. But the praise of people is not that important. Do you find yourself spending time trying to please others? Instead, strive to do what is right—and both God and people will respect your convictions.

alive from Saul's family? If so, I want to show God's kindness to them."

Ziba replied, "Yes, one of Jonathan's sons is still alive. He is crippled in both feet."

⁴"Where is he?" the king asked.

"In Lo-debar," Ziba told him, "at the home of Makir son of Ammiel."

⁵So David sent for him and brought him from Makir's home. ⁶His name was Mephibosheth*; he was Jonathan's son and Saul's grandson. When he came to David, he bowed low to the ground in deep respect. David said, "Greetings, Mephibosheth."

Mephibosheth replied, "I am your servant."

⁷"Don't be afraid!" David said. "I intend to show kindness to you because of my promise to your father, Jonathan. I will give you all the property that once belonged to your grandfather Saul, and you will eat here with me at the king's table!"

⁸Mephibosheth bowed respectfully and exclaimed, "Who is your servant, that you should show such kindness to a dead dog like me?"

⁹Then the king summoned Saul's servant Ziba and said, "I have given your master's grandson everything that belonged to Saul and his family. ¹⁰You and your sons and servants are to farm the land for him to produce food for your master's household.* But Mephibosheth, your master's grandson, will eat here at my table." (Ziba had fifteen sons and twenty servants.)

¹¹Ziba replied, "Yes, my lord the king; I am your servant, and I will do all that you have commanded." And from that time on, Mephibosheth ate regularly at David's table,* like one of the king's own sons.

¹²Mephibosheth had a young son named Mica. From then on, all the members of Ziba's household were Mephibosheth's servants. ¹³And Mephibosheth, who was crippled in both feet, lived in Jerusalem and ate regularly at the king's table.

10 DAVID DEFEATS THE AMMONITES

Some time after this, King Nahash* of the Ammonites died, and his son Hanun became king. ²David said, "I am going to show

loyalty to Hanun just as his father, Nahash, was always loyal to me." So David sent ambassadors to express sympathy to Hanun about his father's death.

But when David's ambassadors arrived in the land of Ammon, ³the Ammonite commanders said to Hanun, their master, "Do you really think these men are coming here to honor your father? No! David has sent them to spy out the city so they can come in and conquer it!" ⁴So Hanun seized David's ambassadors and shaved off half of each man's beard, cut off their robes at the buttocks, and sent them back to David in shame.

⁵When David heard what had happened, he sent messengers to tell the men, "Stay at Jericho until your beards grow out, and then come back." For they felt deep shame because of their appearance.

⁶When the people of Ammon realized how seriously they had angered David, they sent and hired 20,000 Aramean foot soldiers from the lands of Beth-rehob and Zobah, 1,000 from the king of Maacah, and 12,000 from the land of Tob. ⁷When David heard about this, he sent Joab and all his warriors to fight them. ⁸The Ammonite troops came out and drew up their battle lines at the entrance of the city gate, while the Arameans from Zobah and Rehob and the men from Tob and Maacah positioned themselves to fight in the open fields.

⁹When Joab saw that he would have to fight on both the front and the rear, he chose some of Israel's elite troops and placed them under his personal command to fight the Arameans in the fields. ¹⁰He left the rest of the army under the command of his brother Abishai, who was to attack the Ammonites. ¹¹"If the Arameans are too strong for me, then come over and help me," Joab told his brother. "And if the Ammonites are too strong for you, I will come and help you. ¹²Be courageous! Let us fight bravely for our people and the cities of our God. May the LORD's will be done."

¹³When Joab and his troops attacked, the Arameans began to run away. ¹⁴And when the Ammonites saw the Arameans running, they ran from Abishai and retreated into the city. After the battle was over, Joab returned to Jerusalem.

¹⁵The Arameans now realized that they were no match for Israel. So when they regrouped, ¹⁶they were joined by additional Aramean troops summoned by Hadadezer

---

BALANCE

(10:12) Our actions and our faith in God must be balanced. In this verse, Joab says, "Let us fight bravely for our people and the cities of our God." In other words, do what you can. Plan the battle strategy, use your mind to figure out the best techniques, and use your resources. But he also says, "May the LORD's will be done." Joab knew that the outcome was in God's hands. In the same way, we are to use our mind and our resources to obey God, while trusting him for the outcome.

9:6 Mephibosheth is another name for Merib-baal. **9:10** As in Greek version; Hebrew reads your master's grandson. **9:11** As in Greek version; Hebrew reads my table. **10:1** As in parallel text at 1 Chr 19:1; Hebrew reads the king.

from the other side of the Euphrates River.* These troops arrived at Helam under the command of Shobach, the commander of Hadadezer's forces.

17When David heard what was happening, he mobilized all Israel, crossed the Jordan River, and led the army to Helam. The Arameans positioned themselves in battle formation and fought against David. 18But again the Arameans fled from the Israelites. This time David's forces killed 700 charioteers and 40,000 foot soldiers,* including Shobach, the commander of their army. 19When all the kings allied with Hadadezer saw that they had been defeated by Israel, they surrendered to Israel and became their subjects. After that, the Arameans were afraid to help the Ammonites.

11 DAVID AND BATHSHEBA In the spring of the year,* when kings normally go out to war, David sent Joab and the Israelite army to fight the Ammonites. They destroyed the Ammonite army and laid siege to the city of Rabbah. However, David stayed behind in Jerusalem.

2Late one afternoon, after his midday rest, David got out of bed and was walking on the roof of the palace. As he looked out over the city, he noticed a woman of unusual beauty taking a bath. 3He sent someone to find out who she was, and he was told, "She is Bathsheba, the daughter of Eliam and the wife of Uriah the Hittite." 4Then David sent messen-

gers to get her; and when she came to the palace, he slept with her. She had just completed the purification rites after having her menstrual period. Then she returned home. 5Later, when Bathsheba discovered that she was pregnant, she sent David a message, saying, "I'm pregnant."

6Then David sent word to Joab: "Send me Uriah the Hittite." So Joab sent him to David. 7When Uriah arrived, David asked him how Joab and the army were getting along and how the war was progressing. 8Then he told Uriah, "Go on home and relax.*" David even sent a gift to Uriah after he had left the palace. 9But Uriah didn't go home. He slept that night at the palace entrance with the king's palace guard.

10When David heard that Uriah had not gone home, he summoned him and asked, "What's the matter? Why didn't you go home last night after being away for so long?"

11Uriah replied, "The Ark and the armies of Israel and Judah are living in tents,* and Joab

10:16 Hebrew *the river.* 10:18 As in some Greek manuscripts (see also 1 Chr 19:18); Hebrew reads *charioteers.* 11:1 Hebrew *At the turn of the year.* The first day of the year in the ancient Hebrew lunar calendar occurred in March or April. 11:8 Hebrew *and wash your feet,* an expression that may also have a connotation of ritualistic washing. 11:11 Or *at Succoth.*

....

TEMPTATION

(11:1-4) As David gazed from his palace roof, he saw a beautiful woman taking a bath, and lust filled his heart. He should have left the roof and fled from the temptation. Instead, he went further by asking about Bathsheba. The results of letting temptation stay in his heart were devastating.

At the root of most temptation is a real need or desire that God can fill. To flee temptation: (1) ask God in earnest prayer to help you stay away from people, places, and situations that offer temptation, (2) memorize and meditate on portions of Scripture that combat your specific weaknesses, and (3) find another believer with whom you can openly share your temptations and call this person for help when temptation strikes.

CHOICES
living for the moment

All winter, 17-year-old Traci thought about only one thing—spring break.

"It's gonna be so great!" she told anyone who would listen. "I'm going with my three best friends and my older sister. I had to, like, beg my mom for a year to get her permission, but she finally said I could. I can't wait to leave behind all this crummy weather and get away from my mom, seriously! Anyway, in just a few weeks I'll have it made—tons of rays, millions of guys, and no nosy mother!"

That was before. Now that spring break is history, it's not so much fun to get Traci talking about her trip. In fact, it's sad. See, the minute Traci hit the beach,

she forgot everything she stood for. She let herself get sucked up into the forget-your-troubles-and-party-till-you-puke mentality. And that attitude has left Traci with a lot of emotional scars.

"Why didn't I listen? My friends and my sister kept telling me to chill. But I just blew them off and went out by myself. The third night I met these college guys at a pool party and started hanging out with them. We started drinking and stuff. The next thing I knew, I was waking up in a motel room . . . in bed with some guy I'd never seen before. I don't even know what happened."

Ever know anyone who only lived for the moment? What were the consequences?
For another look at the consequences of living for the moment, read 2 Samuel 11–12.

and my master's men are camping in the open fields. How could I go home to wine and dine and sleep with my wife? I swear that I would never do such a thing."

¹²"Well, stay here today," David told him, "and tomorrow you may return to the army." So Uriah stayed in Jerusalem that day and the next. ¹³Then David invited him to dinner and got him drunk. But even then he couldn't get Uriah to go home to his wife. Again he slept at the palace entrance with the king's palace guard.

DAVID ARRANGES FOR URIAH'S DEATH ¹⁴So
the next morning David wrote a letter to Joab and gave it to Uriah to deliver. ¹⁵The letter instructed Joab, "Station Uriah on the front lines where the battle is fiercest. Then pull back so that he will be killed." ¹⁶So Joab assigned Uriah to a spot close to the city wall where he knew the enemy's strongest men were fighting. ¹⁷And when the enemy soldiers came out of the city to fight, Uriah the Hittite was killed along with several other Israelite soldiers.

¹⁸Then Joab sent a battle report to David. ¹⁹He told his messenger, "Report all the news of the battle to the king. ²⁰But he might get angry and ask, 'Why did the troops go so close to the city? Didn't they know there would be shooting from the walls? ²¹Wasn't Abimelech son of Gideon* killed at Thebez by a woman who threw a millstone down on him from the wall? Why would you get so close to the wall?' Then tell him, 'Uriah the Hittite was killed, too.'"

²²So the messenger went to Jerusalem and gave a complete report to David. ²³"The enemy came out against us in the open fields," he said. "And as we chased them back to the city gate, ²⁴the archers on the wall shot arrows at us. Some of the king's men were killed, including Uriah the Hittite."

²⁵"Well, tell Joab not to be discouraged," David said. "The sword devours this one today and that one tomorrow! Fight harder next time, and conquer the city!"

²⁶When Uriah's wife heard that her husband was dead, she mourned for him. ²⁷When the period of mourning was over, David sent for her and brought her to the palace, and she became

one of his wives. Then she gave birth to a son. But the LORD was displeased with what David had done.

12 NATHAN REBUKES DAVID So the LORD sent Nathan the prophet to tell David this story: "There were two men in a certain town. One was rich, and one was poor. ²The rich man owned a great many sheep and cattle. ³The poor man owned nothing but one little lamb he had bought. He raised that little lamb, and it grew up with his children. It ate from the man's own plate and drank from his cup. He cuddled it in his arms like a baby daughter. ⁴One day a guest arrived at the home of the rich man. But instead of killing an animal from his own flock or herd, he took the poor man's lamb and killed it and prepared it for his guest."

⁵David was furious. "As surely as the LORD lives," he vowed, "any man who would do such a thing deserves to die! ⁶He must repay four lambs to the poor man for the one he stole and for having no pity."

⁷Then Nathan said to David, "You are that man! The LORD, the God of Israel, says: I anointed you king of Israel and saved you from the power of Saul. ⁸I gave you your master's house and his wives and the kingdoms of Israel and Judah. And if that had not been enough, I would have given you much, much more. ⁹Why, then, have you despised the word of the LORD and done this horrible deed? For you have murdered Uriah the Hittite with the sword of the Ammonites and stolen his wife. ¹⁰From this time on, your family will live by the sword because you have despised me by taking Uriah's wife to be your own.

¹¹"This is what the LORD says: Because of what you have done, I will cause your own household to rebel against you. I will give your wives to another man before your very eyes, and he will go to bed with them in public view. ¹²You did it secretly, but I will make this happen to you openly in the sight of all Israel."

DAVID CONFESSES HIS GUILT ¹³Then David confessed to Nathan, "I have sinned against the LORD."

Nathan replied, "Yes, but the LORD has forgiven you, and you won't die for this sin. ¹⁴Nevertheless, because you have shown utter contempt for the LORD* by doing this, your child will die."

¹⁵After Nathan returned to his home, the

CONFRONT
(12:1-14) As a prophet, Nathan was required to confront sin—even the sin of a king. It took great courage, skill, and tact to speak to David in a way that would make him aware of his wrong actions. When you have to confront someone with unpleasant news, pray for courage, skill, and tact. How you present your message may be as important as what you say.

11:21 Hebrew *son of Jerub-besheth.* Jerub-besheth is a variation on the name Jerub-baal, which is another name for Gideon; see Judg 6:32. **12:14** As in Dead Sea Scrolls; Masoretic Text reads *the LORD's enemies.*

LORD sent a deadly illness to the child of David and Uriah's wife. ¹⁶David begged God to spare the child. He went without food and lay all night on the bare ground. ¹⁷The elders of his household pleaded with him to get up and eat with them, but he refused.

¹⁸Then on the seventh day the child died. David's advisers were afraid to tell him. "He wouldn't listen to reason while the child was ill," they said. "What drastic thing will he do when we tell him the child is dead?"

¹⁹When David saw them whispering, he realized what had happened. "Is the child dead?" he asked.

"Yes," they replied, "he is dead."

²⁰Then David got up from the ground, washed himself, put on lotions,* and changed his clothes. He went to the Tabernacle and worshiped the LORD. After that, he returned to the palace and was served food and ate.

²¹His advisers were amazed. "We don't understand you," they told him. "While the child was still living, you wept and refused to eat. But now that the child is dead, you have stopped your mourning and are eating again."

²²David replied, "I fasted and wept while the child was alive, for I said, 'Perhaps the LORD will be gracious to me and let the child live.' ²³But why should I fast when he is dead? Can I bring him back again? I will go to him one day, but he cannot return to me."

²⁴Then David comforted Bathsheba, his wife, and slept with her. She became pregnant and gave birth to a son, and David* named him Solomon. The LORD loved the child ²⁵and sent word through Nathan the prophet that they should name him Jedidiah (which means "beloved of the LORD"), as the LORD had commanded.*

DAVID CAPTURES RABBAH

²⁶Meanwhile, Joab was fighting against Rabbah, the capital of Ammon, and he captured the royal fortifications.* ²⁷Joab sent messengers to tell David, "I have fought against Rabbah and captured its water supply.* ²⁸Now bring the rest of the army and capture the city. Otherwise, I will capture it and get credit for the victory."

²⁹So David gathered the rest of the army and went to Rabbah, and he fought against it and

captured it. ³⁰David removed the crown from the king's head,* and it was placed on his own head. The crown was made of gold and set with gems, and it weighed seventy-five pounds.* David took a vast amount of plunder from the city. ³¹He also made slaves of the people of Rabbah and forced them to labor with* saws, iron picks, and iron axes, and to work in the brick kilns.* That is how he dealt with the people of all the Ammonite towns. Then David and all the army returned to Jerusalem.

13 THE RAPE OF TAMAR

Now David's son Absalom had a beautiful sister named Tamar. And Amnon, her half brother, fell desperately in love with her. ²Amnon became so obsessed with Tamar that he became ill. She was a virgin, and Amnon thought he could never have her.

³But Amnon had a very crafty friend—his cousin Jonadab. He was the son of David's brother Shimea.* ⁴One day Jonadab said to Amnon, "What's the trouble? Why should the son of a king look so dejected morning after morning?"

So Amnon told him, "I am in love with Tamar, my brother Absalom's sister."

⁵"Well," Jonadab said, "I'll tell you what to do. Go back to bed and pretend you are ill. When your father comes to see you, ask him to let Tamar come and prepare some food for you. Tell him you'll feel better if she prepares it as you watch and feeds you with her own hands."

⁶So Amnon lay down and pretended to be sick. And when the king came to see him, Amnon asked him, "Please let my sister Tamar come and cook my favorite dish* as I watch. Then I can eat it from her own hands." ⁷So David agreed and sent Tamar to Amnon's house to prepare some food for him.

⁸When Tamar arrived at Amnon's house, she went to the place where he was lying down so he could watch her mix some dough. Then she baked his favorite dish for him. ⁹But when she set the serving tray before him, he refused to eat. "Everyone get out of here," Amnon told his servants. So they all left.

....

12:20 Hebrew *anointed himself.* **12:24** Hebrew *he;* an alternate Hebrew reading and some Hebrew manuscripts read *she.*
12:25 As in Greek version; Hebrew reads *because of the LORD.*
12:26 Or *the royal city.* **12:27** Or *captured the city of water.*
12:30a Or *from the head of Milcom* (as in Greek version). Milcom, also called Molech, was the god of the Ammonites.
12:30b Hebrew *1 talent* [34 kilograms]. **12:31a** Or *He also brought out the people of Rabbah and put them under.* **12:31b** Or *and he made them pass through the brick kilns.* **13:3** Hebrew *Shimeah* (also in 13:32), a variant spelling of Shimea; compare 1 Chr 2:13.
13:6 Or *a couple of cakes;* also in 13:8, 10.

LOVE VS. LUST

(13:1-15) Love and lust are very different. After Amnon raped his half sister, his "love" turned to hate. Although he had claimed to be in love, he was actually overcome by lust. "Love is patient"; lust requires immediate sexual satisfaction. Love is "kind"; lust is harsh. Love "does not demand its own way"; lust does (see 1 Cor 13:4-5). In what ways do you show real love to the people in your life?

¹⁰Then he said to Tamar, "Now bring the food into my bedroom and feed it to me here." So Tamar took his favorite dish to him. ¹¹But as she was feeding him, he grabbed her and demanded, "Come to bed with me, my darling sister."

¹²"No, my brother!" she cried. "Don't be foolish! Don't do this to me! Such wicked things aren't done in Israel. ¹³Where could I go in my shame? And you would be called one of the greatest fools in Israel. Please, just speak to the king about it, and he will let you marry me."

¹⁴But Amnon wouldn't listen to her, and since he was stronger than she was, he raped her. ¹⁵Then suddenly Amnon's love turned to hate, and he hated her even more than he had loved her. "Get out of here!" he snarled at her.

¹⁶"No, no!" Tamar cried. "Sending me away now is worse than what you've already done to me."

But Amnon wouldn't listen to her. ¹⁷He shouted for his servant and demanded, "Throw this woman out, and lock the door behind her!"

¹⁸So the servant put her out and locked the door behind her. She was wearing a long, beautiful robe,* as was the custom in those days for the king's virgin daughters. ¹⁹But now Tamar tore her robe and put ashes on her head. And then, with her face in her hands, she went away crying.

²⁰Her brother Absalom saw her and asked,

13:18 Or *a robe with sleeves*, or *an ornamented robe*. The meaning of the Hebrew is uncertain.

ULTIMATE ISSUES DATE RAPE

Tamar's experience in chapter 13 is similar to that of many women today. Studies indicate the horrifying fact that as many as one out of every six women has been or will be raped. Date rape is the most common form of sexual abuse. One in eight female college students will experience rape or attempted rape, usually from a date or acquaintance. Even men are not immune: at least one out of every ten victims of sexual assault is male. (These figures do not include incest or other family-related sexual abuse.)

Most experts agree that these frightening numbers may reflect only a fraction of the reality. Only about 39 percent of sexual assaults are reported.

What should you do if you've been a victim of sexual abuse?

First, understand you *are* a victim of a crime. You did not "ask for it." What happened was not your fault. If you said no, and a man—boyfriend, stranger, father, acquaintance—forced himself on you, you were raped. The circumstances made no difference. Don't allow guilt to cause you to take responsibility for someone else's terrible decision. If you said no, no means no.

Second, realize that you are not alone and without resources. Unfortunately, countless women share your experience, and they understand your pain. Find one of those women—a counselor at a rape treatment center, a hospital staff worker, or someone you know—and tell your story. Talking about what happened helps break the power the incident has over you; not talking about it will keep you a victim forever. If you need help or information on counseling centers, contact the sexual assault hotline (1-800-656-HOPE) of RAINN (the Rape, Abuse & Incest National Network).

Third, understand that whatever guilt you experience—many women experience intense guilt—is false guilt. Regardless of what your conscience—or *he*—may tell you, you did nothing to deserve this.

If you have been a rape victim, seek help. And remember, the best source of help is God himself. He alone is able to heal your damaged body, emotions, and spirit. Turn to God and let him make you whole again. He can do it.

If you are a guy who is trying to help a female friend or family member work through this shattering experience, never tell a rape victim that she should "just get over it" or "get on with your life." Every woman who has been sexually violated wants to do just that, but it is impossible to "carry on" as though the rape never happened. Rape changes a woman's life. The inner anguish must be dealt with. Try to be patient, supportive, and loving.

If you are a guy who has committed rape, or if you consider it OK to force a girl to do anything sexually against her will, consider this: There is *no* excuse for rape or sexual abuse. NONE. The Bible has very harsh words for people who commit sexual immorality and for those who victimize others. Consider Galatians 6:7: "Don't be misled—you cannot mock the justice of God. You will always harvest what you plant." Don't think you can mock God's laws and abuse his image—which is what you do when you abuse any person—and get away with it. The thought of God's wrath waiting to be poured out on those who commit such sins should be enough to stop anyone in his tracks. And don't try to justify the act by saying, "She said no, but her body said yes," or "She wouldn't have gone out with me if she didn't want it, too." If a woman says no, she means no. Ignore this, and you are legally guilty of rape—and you can go to jail.

If you have committed this sin, cry out to God for mercy and forgiveness, and seek counseling. God is waiting—and willing—to help you. ∎

"Is it true that Amnon has been with you? Well, my sister, keep quiet for now, since he's your brother. Don't you worry about it." So Tamar lived as a desolate woman in her brother Absalom's house.

²¹When King David heard what had happened, he was very angry.* ²²And though Absalom never spoke to Amnon about this, he hated Amnon deeply because of what he had done to his sister.

ABSALOM'S REVENGE ON AMNON

²³Two years later, when Absalom's sheep were being sheared at Baal-hazor near Ephraim, Absalom invited all the king's sons to come to a feast. ²⁴He went to the king and said, "My sheep-shearers are now at work. Would the king and his servants please come to celebrate the occasion with me?"

²⁵The king replied, "No, my son. If we all came, we would be too much of a burden on you." Absalom pressed him, but the king would not come, though he gave Absalom his blessing.

²⁶"Well, then," Absalom said, "if you can't come, how about sending my brother Amnon with us?"

"Why Amnon?" the king asked. ²⁷But Absalom kept on pressing the king until he finally agreed to let all his sons attend, including Amnon. So Absalom prepared a feast fit for a king.*

²⁸Absalom told his men, "Wait until Amnon gets drunk; then at my signal, kill him! Don't be afraid. I'm the one who has given the command. Take courage and do it!" ²⁹So at Absalom's signal they murdered Amnon. Then the other sons of the king jumped on their mules and fled.

³⁰As they were on the way back to Jerusalem, this report reached David: "Absalom has killed all the king's sons; not one is left alive!" ³¹The king got up, tore his robe, and threw himself on the ground. His advisers also tore their clothes in horror and sorrow.

³²But just then Jonadab, the son of David's brother Shimea, arrived and said, "No, don't believe that all the king's sons have been killed! It was only Amnon! Absalom has been plotting this ever since Amnon raped his sister Tamar. ³³No, my lord the king, your sons aren't

all dead! It was only Amnon." ³⁴Meanwhile Absalom escaped.

Then the watchman on the Jerusalem wall saw a great crowd coming down the hill on the road from the west. He ran to tell the king, "I see a crowd of people coming from the Horonaim road along the side of the hill."*

³⁵"Look!" Jonadab told the king. "There they are now! The king's sons are coming, just as I said."

³⁶They soon arrived, weeping and sobbing, and the king and all his servants wept bitterly with them. ³⁷And David mourned many days for his son Amnon.

Absalom fled to his grandfather, Talmai son of Ammihud, the king of Geshur. ³⁸He stayed there in Geshur for three years. ³⁹And King David,* now reconciled to Amnon's death, longed to be reunited with his son Absalom.*

14 JOAB ARRANGES FOR ABSALOM'S RETURN

Joab realized how much the king longed to see Absalom. ²So he sent for a woman from Tekoa who had a reputation for great wisdom. He said to her, "Pretend you are in mourning; wear mourning clothes and don't put on lotions.* Act like a woman who has been mourning for the dead for a long time. ³Then go to the king and tell him the story I am about to tell you." Then Joab told her what to say.

⁴When the woman from Tekoa approached the king, she bowed with her face to the ground in deep respect and cried out, "O king! Help me!"

⁵"What's the trouble?" the king asked.

"Alas, I am a widow!" she replied. "My husband is dead. ⁶My two sons had a fight out in the field. And since no one was there to stop it, one of them was killed. ⁷Now the rest of the family is demanding, 'Let us have your son. We will execute him for murdering his brother. He doesn't deserve to inherit his family's property.' They want to extinguish the only coal I have left, and my husband's name and family will disappear from the face of the earth."

⁸"Leave it to me," the king told her. "Go home, and I'll see to it that no one touches him."

⁹"Oh, thank you, my lord the king," the woman from Tekoa replied. "If you are criticized for helping me, let the blame fall on me and on my father's house, and let the king and his throne be innocent."

¹⁰"If anyone objects," the king said, "bring him to me. I can assure you he will never complain again!"

¹¹Then she said, "Please swear to me by the

13:21 Dead Sea Scrolls and Greek version add *But he did not punish his son Amnon, because he loved him, for he was his firstborn.* 13:27 As in Greek and Latin versions (compare also Dead Sea Scrolls); the Hebrew text lacks this sentence. 13:34 As in Greek version; Hebrew lacks this sentence. 13:39a Dead Sea Scrolls and Greek version read *And the spirit of the king.* 13:39b Or *no longer felt a need to go out after Absalom.* 14:2 Hebrew *don't anoint yourself with oil.*

LORD your God that you won't let anyone take vengeance against my son. I want no more bloodshed."

"As surely as the LORD lives," he replied, "not a hair on your son's head will be disturbed!"

¹²"Please allow me to ask one more thing of my lord the king," she said.

"Go ahead and speak," he responded.

¹³She replied, "Why don't you do as much for the people of God as you have promised to do for me? You have convicted yourself in making this decision, because you have refused to bring home your own banished son. ¹⁴All of us must die eventually. Our lives are like water spilled out on the ground, which cannot be gathered up again. But God does not just sweep life away; instead, he devises ways to bring us back when we have been separated from him.

¹⁵"I have come to plead with my lord the king because people have threatened me. I said to myself, 'Perhaps the king will listen to me ¹⁶and rescue us from those who would cut us off from the inheritance* God has given us. ¹⁷Yes, my lord the king will give us peace of mind again.' I know that you are like an angel of God in discerning good from evil. May the LORD your God be with you."

¹⁸"I must know one thing," the king replied, "and tell me the truth."

"Yes, my lord the king," she responded.

¹⁹"Did Joab put you up to this?"

And the woman replied, "My lord the king, how can I deny it? Nobody can hide anything from you. Yes, Joab sent me and told me what to say. ²⁰He did it to place the matter before you in a different light. But you are as wise as an angel of God, and you understand everything that happens among us!"

²¹So the king sent for Joab and told him, "All right, go and bring back the young man Absalom."

²²Joab bowed with his face to the ground in deep respect and said, "At last I know that I have gained your approval, my lord the king, for you have granted me this request!"

²³Then Joab went to Geshur and brought Absalom back to Jerusalem. ²⁴But the king gave this order: "Absalom may go to his own house, but he must never come into my presence." So Absalom did not see the king.

ABSALOM RECONCILED TO DAVID ²⁵Now Absalom was praised as the most handsome man in all Israel. He was flawless from head to foot. ²⁶He cut his hair only once a year, and then only because it was so heavy. When he weighed it out, it came to five pounds!* ²⁷He had three

14:16 Or *the property*; or *the people*. **14:26** Hebrew *200 shekels* [2.3 kilograms] *by the royal standard.*

ABSALOM
PERSONALITY PROFILE

KNOW ANYONE WHO TALKS A GOOD GAME, but seems to lack character? Absalom was that kind of person. Although he looked like he would make the perfect king, his good looks could not make up for a lack of integrity.

The old saying that the apple doesn't fall far from the tree is true about Absalom. He made some of the same mistakes that David had made and often chose the wrong advice. He administered his own brand of justice for the rape of his sister, after watching his father's passive response. After running away and eventually being invited back to the kingdom, he decided that he deserved to be king more than David.

While David's sins took him away from God and back again, Absalom allowed his wrongdoings to keep him away from God. He was later killed after trying to take the kingdom by force.

Tempted to rebel like Absalom? Maybe you feel like your parents hassle you and don't give you the freedom you deserve. Or maybe you think you can make better decisions than your parents make. If so, take a cue from what happened to Absalom. Your life doesn't have to end in a tragedy. You can turn back. God is waiting.

BOTTOM LINE: The sins of parents are often repeated and amplified in their children.

A smart person gets a lot of advice; a wise person evaluates the advice he or she receives.

Sooner or later, actions against God's plans will fail.

Absalom's story is told in 2 Samuel 3:3; 13–18.

DOWNS:
• Avenged the rape of his sister Tamar by killing his half brother Amnon
• Plotted against his father to take over the throne of Israel
• Consistently listened to bad advice

STATS:
• Where: Hebron
• Occupation: Prince
• Relatives: David (father); Maacah (mother); Amnon, Adonijah, Solomon, and others (brothers); Tamar (sister)
• Contemporaries: Nathan, Jonadab, Joab, Ahithophel, Hushai

KEY VERSES: 2 Samuel 3:3; 13–18.

sons and one daughter. His daughter's name was Tamar, and she was very beautiful.

²⁸Absalom lived in Jerusalem for two years, but he never got to see the king. ²⁹Then Absalom sent for Joab to ask him to intercede for him, but Joab refused to come. Absalom sent for him a second time, but again Joab refused to come. ³⁰So Absalom said to his servants, "Go and set fire to Joab's barley field, the field next to mine." So they set his field on fire, as Absalom had commanded.

³¹Then Joab came to Absalom at his house and demanded, "Why did your servants set my field on fire?"

³²And Absalom replied, "Because I wanted you to ask the king why he brought me back from Geshur if he didn't intend to see me. I might as well have stayed there. Let me see the king; if he finds me guilty of anything, then let him kill me."

³³So Joab told the king what Absalom had said. Then at last David summoned Absalom, who came and bowed low before the king, and the king kissed him.

15 ABSALOM'S REBELLION After this, Absalom bought a chariot and horses, and he hired fifty bodyguards to run ahead of him. ²He got up early every morning and went out to the gate of the city. When people brought a case to the king for judgment, Absalom would ask where in Israel they were from, and they would tell him their tribe. ³Then Absalom would say, "You've really got a strong case here! It's too bad the king doesn't have anyone to hear it. ⁴I wish I were the judge. Then everyone could bring their cases to me for judgment, and I would give them justice!"

⁵When people tried to bow before him, Absalom wouldn't let them. Instead, he took them by the hand and kissed them. ⁶Absalom did this with everyone who came to the king for judgment, and so he stole the hearts of all the people of Israel.

⁷After four years,* Absalom said to the king, "Let me go to Hebron to offer a sacrifice to the LORD and fulfill a vow I made to him. ⁸For while your servant was at Geshur in Aram, I promised to sacrifice to the LORD in Hebron* if he would bring me back to Jerusalem."

⁹"All right," the king told him. "Go and fulfill your vow."

So Absalom went to Hebron. ¹⁰But while he was there, he sent secret messengers to all the

tribes of Israel to stir up a rebellion against the king. "As soon as you hear the ram's horn," his message read, "you are to say, 'Absalom has been crowned king in Hebron.'" ¹¹He took 200 men from Jerusalem with him as guests, but they knew nothing of his intentions. ¹²While Absalom was offering the sacrifices, he sent for Ahithophel, one of David's counselors who lived in Giloh. Soon many others also joined Absalom, and the conspiracy gained momentum.

DAVID ESCAPES FROM JERUSALEM ¹³A messenger soon arrived in Jerusalem to tell David, "All Israel has joined Absalom in a conspiracy against you!"

¹⁴"Then we must flee at once, or it will be too late!" David urged his men. "Hurry! If we get out of the city before Absalom arrives, both we and the city of Jerusalem will be spared from disaster."

¹⁵"We are with you," his advisers replied. "Do what you think is best."

¹⁶So the king and all his household set out at once. He left no one behind except ten of his concubines to look after the palace. ¹⁷The king and all his people set out on foot, pausing at the last house ¹⁸to let all the king's men move past to lead the way. There were 600 men from Gath who had come with David, along with the king's bodyguard.*

¹⁹Then the king turned and said to Ittai, a leader of the men from Gath, "Why are you coming with us? Go on back to King Absalom, for you are a guest in Israel, a foreigner in exile. ²⁰You arrived only recently, and should I force you today to wander with us? I don't even know where we will go. Go on back and take your

15:7 As in Greek and Syriac versions; Hebrew reads *forty years*.
15:8 As in some Greek manuscripts; Hebrew lacks *in Hebron*.
15:18 Hebrew *the Kerethites and Pelethites*.

INDECISIVE
(14:28) David made only halfhearted efforts to raise his children. In 13:21-39, David did not punish Amnon for his crime, nor did he deal decisively with Absalom's murder of Amnon. As a result, Absalom ran away to live with other relatives. When David finally allowed Absalom back, he did not speak to him for two years. Such indecisiveness became David's undoing. When bad behavior is ignored, it will bring greater pain than if it is dealt with immediately.

COURAGE
(15:14) Had David not escaped from Jerusalem, the resulting fight might have destroyed both him and the innocent inhabitants of the city. Some fights that we think are necessary may be costly and destructive to those around us. In such cases, it may be wise to back down and save the fight for another day—even if doing so hurts our pride. It takes courage to stand and fight, but it also takes courage to back down when you must for the sake of others.

kinsmen with you, and may the LORD show you his unfailing love and faithfulness.*"

²¹But Ittai said to the king, "I vow by the LORD and by your own life that I will go wherever my lord the king goes, no matter what happens—whether it means life or death."

²²David replied, "All right, come with us." So Ittai and all his men and their families went along.

²³Everyone cried loudly as the king and his followers passed by. They crossed the Kidron Valley and then went out toward the wilderness.

²⁴Zadok and all the Levites also came along, carrying the Ark of the Covenant of God. They set down the Ark of God, and Abiathar offered sacrifices* until everyone had passed out of the city.

²⁵Then the king instructed Zadok to take the Ark of God back into the city. "If the LORD sees fit," David said, "he will bring me back to see the Ark and the Tabernacle* again. ²⁶But if he is through with me, then let him do what seems best to him."

²⁷The king also told Zadok the priest, "Look,* here is my plan. You and Abiathar* should return quietly to the city with your son Ahimaaz and Abiathar's son Jonathan. ²⁸I will stop at the shallows of the Jordan River* and wait there for a report from you." ²⁹So Zadok and Abiathar took the Ark of God back to the city and stayed there.

³⁰David walked up the road to the Mount of Olives, weeping as he went. His head was covered and his feet were bare as a sign of mourning. And the people who were with him covered their heads and wept as they climbed the hill. ³¹When someone told David that his adviser Ahithophel was now backing Absalom, David prayed, "O LORD, let Ahithophel give Absalom foolish advice!"

³²When David reached the summit of the Mount of Olives where people worshiped God, Hushai the Arkite was waiting there for him. Hushai had torn his clothing and put dirt on his head as a sign of mourning. ³³But David told him, "If you go with me, you will only be a burden. ³⁴Return to Jerusalem and tell Absalom, 'I will now be your adviser, O king, just as I was your father's adviser in the past.' Then you can frustrate and counter Ahithophel's advice. ³⁵Zadok and Abiathar, the priests, will be there. Tell them about the plans being made in the king's palace, ³⁶and they will send their sons Ahimaaz and Jonathan to tell me what is going on."

³⁷So David's friend Hushai returned to Jerusalem, getting there just as Absalom arrived.

16 **DAVID AND ZIBA** When David had gone a little beyond the summit of the Mount of Olives, Ziba, the servant of Mephibosheth,* was waiting there for him. He had two donkeys loaded with 200 loaves of bread, 100 clusters of raisins, 100 bunches of summer fruit, and a wineskin full of wine.

15:20 As in Greek version; Hebrew reads *and may unfailing love and faithfulness go with you.* **15:24** Or *Abiathar went up.* **15:25** Hebrew *and his dwelling place.* **15:27a** As in Greek version; Hebrew reads *Are you a seer?* or *Do you see?* **15:27b** Hebrew lacks *and Abiathar;* compare 15:29. **15:28** Hebrew *at the crossing points of the wilderness.* **16:1** *Mephibosheth* is another name for Merib-baal.

I WONDER...

My older brother is always making fun of my new faith. How do I get him to stop?

People ridicule what they don't understand or what they wish they had themselves. It's really tough, however, when it comes from someone in your own family. David experienced this when his son Absalom tried to take his kingdom away (2 Sam 15).

Feeling the fire of opposition? Check out this advice from the apostle Peter.

Your best defense is a quiet offense: "Don't repay evil for evil. Don't retaliate with insults when people insult you. Instead, pay them back with a blessing. That is what God has called you to do, and he will bless you for it" (1 Pet 3:9).

When anyone makes fun of your faith, hold your tongue, pray for the person, be kind to him or her, and then wait for God's blessing. This verse ends with a promise directly from God. Though it doesn't say when or how God will bless you, it promises that he will.

Here are some steps to take when facing opposition for your faith (see 1 Pet 3:13-15):

First, check your attitude. If you understand that God is allowing you to experience this for a reason, you'll be able to thank him for it. It means that he believes in you enough to allow you to be tested!

Second, quietly trust yourself to Christ. You have trusted Christ to be Lord of your life; now allow him to be Lord over your circumstances. God is trying to develop your character.

Third, be real and be ready to explain your faith when opportunities arise. Don't be afraid to admit that you don't have all the answers.

Even doing all of this still may not relieve the tension. But "it is better to suffer for doing good, if that is what God wants, than to suffer for doing wrong!" (1 Pet 3:17).

²"What are these for?" the king asked Ziba.

Ziba replied, "The donkeys are for the king's people to ride on, and the bread and summer fruit are for the young men to eat. The wine is for those who become exhausted in the wilderness."

³"And where is Mephibosheth, Saul's grandson?" the king asked him.

"He stayed in Jerusalem," Ziba replied. "He said, 'Today I will get back the kingdom of my grandfather Saul.'"

⁴"In that case," the king told Ziba, "I give you everything Mephibosheth owns."

"I bow before you," Ziba replied. "May I always be pleasing to you, my lord the king."

SHIMEI CURSES DAVID ⁵As King David came to Bahurim, a man came out of the village cursing them. It was Shimei son of Gera, from the same clan as Saul's family. ⁶He threw stones at the king and the king's officers and all the mighty warriors who surrounded him. ⁷"Get out of here, you murderer, you scoundrel!" he shouted at David. ⁸"The LORD is paying you back for all the bloodshed in Saul's clan. You stole his throne, and now the LORD has given it to your son Absalom. At last you will taste some of your own medicine, for you are a murderer!"

⁹"Why should this dead dog curse my lord the king?" Abishai son of Zeruiah demanded. "Let me go over and cut off his head!"

¹⁰"No!" the king said. "Who asked your opinion, you sons of Zeruiah! If the LORD has told him to curse me, who are you to stop him?"

¹¹Then David said to Abishai and to all his servants, "My own son is trying to kill me. Doesn't this relative of Saul* have even more reason to do so? Leave him alone and let him curse, for the LORD has told him to do it. ¹²And perhaps the LORD will see that I am being wronged and will bless me because of these curses today." ¹³So David and his men continued down the road, and Shimei kept pace with them on a nearby hillside, cursing as he went and throwing stones at David and tossing dust into the air.

¹⁴The king and all who were with him grew weary along the way, so they rested when they reached the Jordan River.*

AHITHOPHEL ADVISES ABSALOM ¹⁵Meanwhile, Absalom and all the army of Israel arrived at Jerusalem, accompanied by Ahitho-

phel. ¹⁶When David's friend Hushai the Arkite arrived, he went immediately to see Absalom. "Long live the king!" he exclaimed. "Long live the king!"

¹⁷"Is this the way you treat your friend David?" Absalom asked him. "Why aren't you with him?"

¹⁸"I'm here because I belong to the man who is chosen by the LORD and by all the men of Israel," Hushai replied. ¹⁹"And anyway, why shouldn't I serve you? Just as I was your father's adviser, now I will be your adviser!"

²⁰Then Absalom turned to Ahithophel and asked him, "What should I do next?"

²¹Ahithophel told him, "Go and sleep with your father's concubines, for he has left them here to look after the palace. Then all Israel will know that you have insulted your father beyond hope of reconciliation, and they will throw their support to you." ²²So they set up a tent on the palace roof where everyone could see it, and Absalom went in and had sex with his father's concubines.

²³Absalom followed Ahithophel's advice, just as David had done. For every word Ahithophel spoke seemed as wise as though it had come directly from the mouth of God.

17 Now Ahithophel urged Absalom, "Let me choose 12,000 men to start out after David tonight. ²I will catch up with him while he is weary and discouraged. He and his troops will panic, and everyone will run away. Then I will kill only the king, ³and I will bring all the people back to you as a bride returns to her husband. After all, it is only one man's life that you seek.* Then you will be at peace with all the people." ⁴This plan seemed good to Absalom and to all the elders of Israel.

HUSHAI COUNTERS AHITHOPHEL'S ADVICE ⁵But then Absalom said, "Bring in Hushai the Arkite. Let's see what he thinks about this." ⁶When Hushai arrived, Absalom told him what Ahithophel had said. Then he asked, "What is your opinion? Should we follow Ahithophel's advice? If not, what do you suggest?"

⁷"Well," Hushai replied to Absalom, "this time Ahithophel has made a mistake. ⁸You know your father and his men; they are mighty

16:11 Hebrew *this Benjaminite.* **16:14** As in Greek version (see also 17:16); Hebrew reads *when they reached their destination.* **17:3** As in Greek version; Hebrew reads *like the return of all is the man whom you seek.*

....

CHECK IT OUT
(16:1-4) *David believed Ziba's charge against Mephibosheth without checking into it. Ever been hasty to accept a rumor or someone's condemnation of another person? The wise person always checks his or her sources.*

warriors. Right now they are as enraged as a mother bear who has been robbed of her cubs. And remember that your father is an experienced man of war. He won't be spending the night among the troops. [9]He has probably already hidden in some pit or cave. And when he comes out and attacks and a few of your men fall, there will be panic among your troops, and the word will spread that Absalom's men are being slaughtered. [10]Then even the bravest soldiers, though they have the heart of a lion, will be paralyzed with fear. For all Israel knows what a mighty warrior your father is and how courageous his men are.

[11]"I recommend that you mobilize the entire army of Israel, bringing them from as far away as Dan in the north and Beersheba in the south. That way you will have an army as numerous as the sand on the seashore. And I advise that you personally lead the troops. [12]When we find David, we'll fall on him like dew that falls on the ground. Then neither he nor any of his men will be left alive. [13]And if David were to escape into some town, you will have all Israel there at your command. Then we can take ropes and drag the walls of the town into the nearest valley until every stone is torn down."

[14]Then Absalom and all the men of Israel said, "Hushai's advice is better than Ahithophel's." For the LORD had determined to defeat the counsel of Ahithophel, which really was the better plan, so that he could bring disaster on Absalom!

HUSHAI WARNS DAVID TO ESCAPE
[15]Hushai told Zadok and Abiathar, the priests, what Ahithophel had said to Absalom and the elders of Israel and what he himself had advised instead. [16]"Quick!" he told them. "Find David and urge him not to stay at the shallows of the Jordan River* tonight. He must go across at once into the wilderness beyond. Otherwise he will die and his entire army with him."

[17]Jonathan and Ahimaaz had been staying at En-rogel so as not to be seen entering and leaving the city. Arrangements had been made for a servant girl to bring them the message they were to take to King David. [18]But a boy spotted them at En-rogel, and he told Absalom

about it. So they quickly escaped to Bahurim, where a man hid them down inside a well in his courtyard. [19]The man's wife put a cloth over the top of the well and scattered grain on it to dry in the sun; so no one suspected they were there.

[20]When Absalom's men arrived, they asked her, "Have you seen Ahimaaz and Jonathan?"

The woman replied, "They were here, but they crossed over the brook." Absalom's men looked for them without success and returned to Jerusalem.

[21]Then the two men crawled out of the well and hurried on to King David. "Quick!" they told him, "cross the Jordan tonight!" And they told him how Ahithophel had advised that he be captured and killed. [22]So David and all the people with him went across the Jordan River during the night, and they were all on the other bank before dawn.

[23]When Ahithophel realized that his advice had not been followed, he saddled his donkey, went to his hometown, set his affairs in order, and hanged himself. He died there and was buried in the family tomb.

[24]David soon arrived at Mahanaim. By now, Absalom had mobilized the entire army of Israel and was leading his troops across the Jordan River. [25]Absalom had appointed Amasa as commander of his army, replacing Joab, who had been commander under David. (Amasa was Joab's cousin. His father was Jether,* an Ishmaelite.* His mother, Abigail daughter of Nahash, was the sister of Joab's mother, Zeruiah.) [26]Absalom and the Israelite army set up camp in the land of Gilead.

[27]When David arrived at Mahanaim, he was warmly greeted by Shobi son of Nahash, who came from Rabbah of the Ammonites, and by Makir son of Ammiel from Lo-debar, and by Barzillai of Gilead from Rogelim. [28]They brought sleeping mats, cooking pots, serving bowls, wheat and barley, flour and roasted grain, beans, lentils, [29]honey, butter, sheep, goats, and cheese for David and those who were with him. For they said, "You must all be very hungry and tired and thirsty after your long march through the wilderness."

18 ABSALOM'S DEFEAT AND DEATH
David now mustered the men who were with him and appointed generals and captains* to lead them. [2]He sent the troops out in three

---

VANITY
(17:11) When Hushai appealed to Absalom through flattery, Absalom became trapped by his vanity. Hushai predicted great glory for Absalom if he personally would lead the entire army against David. "Pride goes before destruction" (Prov 16:18) is an appropriate comment on Absalom's ambitions. Tempted to let someone's flattery go to your head? Remember Absalom.

17:16 Hebrew *at the crossing points of the wilderness.*
17:25a Hebrew *Ithra,* a variant spelling of Jether.   17:25b As in some Greek manuscripts (see also 1 Chr 2:17); Hebrew reads *an Israelite.*
18:1 Hebrew *appointed commanders of thousands and commanders of hundreds.*

groups, placing one group under Joab, one under Joab's brother Abishai son of Zeruiah, and one under Ittai, the man from Gath. The king told his troops, "I am going out with you."

³But his men objected strongly. "You must not go," they urged. "If we have to turn and run—and even if half of us die—it will make no difference to Absalom's troops; they will be looking only for you. You are worth 10,000 of us,* and it is better that you stay here in the town and send help if we need it."

⁴"If you think that's the best plan, I'll do it," the king answered. So he stood alongside the gate of the town as all the troops marched out in groups of hundreds and of thousands.

⁵And the king gave this command to Joab, Abishai, and Ittai: "For my sake, deal gently with young Absalom." And all the troops heard the king give this order to his commanders.

⁶So the battle began in the forest of Ephraim, ⁷and the Israelite troops were beaten back by David's men. There was a great slaughter that day, and 20,000 men laid down their lives. ⁸The battle raged all across the countryside, and more men died because of the forest than were killed by the sword.

⁹During the battle, Absalom happened to come upon some of David's men. He tried to escape on his mule, but as he rode beneath the thick branches of a great tree, his hair* got caught in the tree. His mule kept going and left him dangling in the air. ¹⁰One of David's men saw what had happened and told Joab, "I saw Absalom dangling from a great tree."

¹¹"What?" Joab demanded. "You saw him there and didn't kill him? I would have rewarded you with ten pieces of silver* and a hero's belt!"

¹²"I would not kill the king's son for even a thousand pieces of silver,*" the man replied to Joab. "We all heard the king say to you and Abishai and Ittai, 'For my sake, please spare young Absalom.' ¹³And if I had betrayed the king by killing his son—and the king would certainly find out who did it—you yourself would be the first to abandon me."

¹⁴"Enough of this nonsense," Joab said. Then he took three daggers and plunged them into Absalom's heart as he dangled, still alive, in the great tree. ¹⁵Ten of Joab's young armor bearers then surrounded Absalom and killed him.

¹⁶Then Joab blew the ram's horn, and his men

returned from chasing the army of Israel. ¹⁷They threw Absalom's body into a deep pit in the forest and piled a great heap of stones over it. And all Israel fled to their homes.

¹⁸During his lifetime, Absalom had built a monument to himself in the King's Valley, for he said, "I have no son to carry on my name." He named the monument after himself, and it is known as Absalom's Monument to this day.

DAVID MOURNS ABSALOM'S DEATH ¹⁹Then Zadok's son Ahimaaz said, "Let me run to the king with the good news that the LORD has rescued him from his enemies."

²⁰"No," Joab told him, "it wouldn't be good news to the king that his son is dead. You can be my messenger another time, but not today."

²¹Then Joab said to a man from Ethiopia,* "Go tell the king what you have seen." The man bowed and ran off.

²²But Ahimaaz continued to plead with Joab, "Whatever happens, please let me go, too."

"Why should you go, my son?" Joab replied. "There will be no reward for your news."

²³"Yes, but let me go anyway," he begged.

Joab finally said, "All right, go ahead." So Ahimaaz took the less demanding route by way of the plain and ran to Mahanaim ahead of the Ethiopian.

²⁴While David was sitting between the inner and outer gates of the town, the watchman climbed to the roof of the gateway by the wall. As he looked, he saw a lone man running toward them. ²⁵He shouted the news down to David, and the king replied, "If he is alone, he has news."

As the messenger came closer, ²⁶the watchman saw another man running toward them. He shouted down, "Here comes another one!"

The king replied, "He also will have news."

²⁷"The first man runs like Ahimaaz son of Zadok," the watchman said.

"He is a good man and comes with good news," the king replied.

²⁸Then Ahimaaz cried out to the king, "Everything is all right!" He bowed before the king with his face to the ground and said, "Praise to the LORD your God, who has handed over the rebels who dared to stand against my lord the king."

²⁹"What about young Absalom?" the king demanded. "Is he all right?"

Ahimaaz replied, "When Joab told me to come, there was a lot of commotion. But I didn't know what was happening."

³⁰"Wait here," the king told him. So Ahimaaz stepped aside.

18:3 As in two Hebrew manuscripts and some Greek and Latin manuscripts; most Hebrew manuscripts read *Now there are 10,000 like us.* **18:9** Hebrew *his head.* **18:11** Hebrew *10 shekels of silver,* about 4 ounces or 114 grams in weight. **18:12** Hebrew *1,000 shekels,* about 25 pounds or 11.4 kilograms in weight. **18:21** Hebrew *from Cush;* similarly in 18:23, 31, 32.

³¹Then the man from Ethiopia arrived and said, "I have good news for my lord the king. Today the Lᴏʀᴅ has rescued you from all those who rebelled against you."

³²"What about young Absalom?" the king demanded. "Is he all right?"

And the Ethiopian replied, "May all of your enemies, my lord the king, both now and in the future, share the fate of that young man!"

³³*The king was overcome with emotion. He went up to the room over the gateway and burst into tears. And as he went, he cried, "O my son Absalom! My son, my son Absalom! If only I had died instead of you! O Absalom, my son, my son."

19 JOAB REBUKES THE KING

¹*Word soon reached Joab that the king was weeping and mourning for Absalom. ²As all the people heard of the king's deep grief for his son, the joy of that day's victory was turned into deep sadness. ³They crept back into the town that day as though they were ashamed and had deserted in battle. ⁴The king covered his face with his hands and kept on crying, "O my son Absalom! O Absalom, my son, my son!"

⁵Then Joab went to the king's room and said to him, "We saved your life today and the lives of your sons, your daughters, and your wives and concubines. Yet you act like this, making us feel ashamed of ourselves. ⁶You seem to love those who hate you and hate those who love you. You have made it clear today that your commanders and troops mean nothing to you. It seems that if Absalom had lived and

all of us had died, you would be pleased. ⁷Now go out there and congratulate your troops, for I swear by the Lᴏʀᴅ that if you don't go out, not a single one of them will remain here tonight. Then you will be worse off than ever before."

⁸So the king went out and took his seat at the town gate, and as the news spread throughout the town that he was there, everyone went to him.

Meanwhile, the Israelites who had supported Absalom fled to their homes. ⁹And throughout all the tribes of Israel there was much discussion and argument going on. The people were saying, "The king rescued us from our enemies and saved us from the Philistines, but Absalom chased him out of the country. ¹⁰Now Absalom, whom we anointed to rule over us, is dead. Why not ask David to come back and be our king again?"

¹¹Then King David sent Zadok and Abiathar, the priests, to say to the elders of Judah, "Why are you the last ones to welcome back the king into his palace? For I have heard that all Israel is ready. ¹²You are my relatives, my own tribe, my own flesh and blood! So why are you the last ones to welcome back the king?" ¹³And David told them to tell Amasa, "Since you are my own flesh and blood, like Joab, may God strike me and even kill me if I do not appoint you as commander of my army in his place."

¹⁴Then Amasa* convinced all the men of Judah, and they responded unanimously. They sent word to the king, "Return to us, and bring back all who are with you."

DAVID'S RETURN TO JERUSALEM

¹⁵So the king started back to Jerusalem. And when he arrived at the Jordan River, the people of Judah came to Gilgal to meet him and escort him across the river. ¹⁶Shimei son of Gera, the man from Bahurim in Benjamin, hurried across with the men of Judah to welcome King David. ¹⁷A thousand other men from the tribe of Benjamin were with him, including Ziba, the chief servant of the house of Saul, and Ziba's fifteen sons and twenty servants. They rushed down to the Jordan to meet the king. ¹⁸They crossed the shallows of the Jordan to bring the king's household across the river, helping him in every way they could.

DAVID'S MERCY TO SHIMEI

As the king was about to cross the river, Shimei fell down before him. ¹⁹"My lord the king, please forgive me," he pleaded. "Forget the terrible thing your

---

UNDESERVED

(18:33) Why was David so upset over the death of his rebel son? (1) David realized that he, in part, was responsible for Absalom's death. Nathan the prophet had said that because David had killed Uriah, the members of his household would rebel against him (12:11-12); (2) David was angry at Joab and his officers for killing Absalom, even though he had told them not to; (3) David truly loved his son and wanted to show mercy to him even though Absalom rebelled. Just as God bestows undeserved favor (grace) upon us when we rebel against him, David was gracious to Absalom. Is that how you are?

THE CROWD

(19:8-10) Just a few days before, Absalom had turned the hearts of Israel away from David. Here the people wanted David back as their king. Jesus would later experience this same kind of fickleness (compare Matt 21:1-11 with Matt 27:20-25). Because crowds are known to be fickle, we must have a higher moral code to follow than the pleasure of the majority. Following the moral principles given in God's Word will help you avoid being swayed by the crowd. Are you the kind of person who seeks to please the crowd no matter what the cost? Since a crowd's approval never lasts for long, is pleasing them worth the cost?

18:33 Verse 18:33 is numbered 19:1 in Hebrew text.   **19:1** Verses 19:1-43 are numbered 19:2-44 in Hebrew text.   **19:14** Or *David;* Hebrew reads *he.*

servant did when you left Jerusalem. May the king put it out of his mind. ²⁰I know how much I sinned. That is why I have come here today, the very first person in all Israel* to greet my lord the king."

²¹Then Abishai son of Zeruiah said, "Shimei should die, for he cursed the LORD's anointed king!"

²²"Who asked your opinion, you sons of Zeruiah!" David exclaimed. "Why have you become my adversary* today? This is not a day for execution but for celebration! Today I am once again the king of Israel!" ²³Then, turning to Shimei, David vowed, "Your life will be spared."

DAVID'S KINDNESS TO MEPHIBOSHETH
²⁴Now Mephibosheth,* Saul's grandson, came down from Jerusalem to meet the king. He had not cared for his feet, trimmed his beard, or washed his clothes since the day the king left Jerusalem. ²⁵"Why didn't you come with me, Mephibosheth?" the king asked him.

²⁶Mephibosheth replied, "My lord the king, my servant Ziba deceived me. I told him, 'Saddle my donkey* so I can go with the king.' For as you know I am crippled. ²⁷Ziba has slandered me by saying that I refused to come. But I know that my lord the king is like an angel of God, so do what you think is best. ²⁸All my relatives and I could expect only death from you, my lord, but instead you have honored me by allowing me to eat at your own table! What more can I ask?"

²⁹"You've said enough," David replied. "I've decided that you and Ziba will divide your land equally between you."

³⁰"Give him all of it," Mephibosheth said. "I am content just to have you safely back again, my lord the king!"

DAVID'S KINDNESS TO BARZILLAI
³¹Barzillai of Gilead had come down from Rogelim to escort the king across the Jordan. ³²He was very old, about eighty, and very wealthy. He was the one who had provided food for the king during his stay in Mahanaim. ³³"Come across with me and live in Jerusalem," the king said to Barzillai. "I will take care of you there."

³⁴"No," he replied, "I am far too old to go with the king to Jerusalem. ³⁵I am eighty years old today, and I can no longer enjoy anything. Food and wine are no longer tasty, and I cannot hear the singers as they sing. I would only be a

burden to my lord the king. ³⁶Just to go across the Jordan River with the king is all the honor I need! ³⁷Then let me return again to die in my own town, where my father and mother are buried. But here is your servant, my son Kimham. Let him go with my lord the king and receive whatever you want to give him."

³⁸"Good," the king agreed. "Kimham will go with me, and I will help him in any way you would like. And I will do for you anything you want." ³⁹So all the people crossed the Jordan with the king. After David had blessed Barzillai and kissed him, Barzillai returned to his own home.

⁴⁰The king then crossed over to Gilgal, taking Kimham with him. All the troops of Judah and half the troops of Israel escorted the king on his way.

AN ARGUMENT OVER THE KING
⁴¹But all the men of Israel complained to the king, "The men of Judah stole the king and didn't give us the honor of helping take you, your household, and all your men across the Jordan."

⁴²The men of Judah replied, "The king is one of our own kinsmen. Why should this make you angry? We haven't eaten any of the king's food or received any special favors!"

⁴³"But there are ten tribes in Israel," the others replied. "So we have ten times as much right to the king as you do. What right do you have to treat us with such contempt? Weren't we the first to speak of bringing him back to be our king again?" The argument continued back and forth, and the men of Judah spoke even more harshly than the men of Israel.

20 THE REVOLT OF SHEBA
There happened to be a troublemaker there named Sheba son of Bicri, a man from the tribe of Benjamin. Sheba blew a ram's horn and began to chant:

"Down with the dynasty of David!
    We have no interest in the son of Jesse.
Come on, you men of Israel,
    back to your homes!"

²So all the men of Israel deserted David and followed Sheba son of Bicri. But the men of Judah stayed with their king and escorted him from the Jordan River to Jerusalem.

³When David came to his palace in Jerusalem, he took the ten concubines he had left to look after the palace and placed them in seclusion. Their needs were provided for, but he no longer slept with them. So each of them lived like a widow until she died.

19:20 Hebrew *in the house of Joseph.* **19:22** Or *my prosecutor.* **19:24** *Mephibosheth* is another name for Merib-baal. **19:26** As in Greek, Syriac, and Latin versions; Hebrew reads *I will saddle a donkey for myself.*

⁴Then the king told Amasa, "Mobilize the army of Judah within three days, and report back at that time." ⁵So Amasa went out to notify Judah, but it took him longer than the time he had been given.

⁶Then David said to Abishai, "Sheba son of Bicri is going to hurt us more than Absalom did. Quick, take my troops and chase after him before he gets into a fortified town where we can't reach him."

⁷So Abishai and Joab,* together with the king's bodyguard* and all the mighty warriors, set out from Jerusalem to go after Sheba. ⁸As they arrived at the great stone in Gibeon, Amasa met them. Joab was wearing his military tunic with a dagger strapped to his belt. As he stepped forward to greet Amasa, he slipped the dagger from its sheath.*

⁹"How are you, my cousin?" Joab said and took him by the beard with his right hand as though to kiss him. ¹⁰Amasa didn't notice the dagger in his left hand, and Joab stabbed him in the stomach with it so that his insides gushed out onto the ground. Joab did not need to strike again, and Amasa soon died. Joab and his brother Abishai left him lying there and continued after Sheba.

¹¹One of Joab's young men shouted to Amasa's troops, "If you are for Joab and David, come and follow Joab." ¹²But Amasa lay in his blood in the middle of the road, and Joab's man saw that everyone was stopping to stare at him. So he pulled him off the road into a field and threw a cloak over him. ¹³With Amasa's body out of the way, everyone went on with Joab to capture Sheba son of Bicri.

¹⁴Meanwhile, Sheba traveled through all the tribes of Israel and eventually came to the town of Abel-beth-maacah. All the members of his own clan, the Bicrites,* assembled for battle and followed him into the town. ¹⁵When Joab's forces arrived, they attacked Abel-beth-maacah. They built a siege ramp against the town's fortifications and began battering down the wall. ¹⁶But a wise woman in the town called out to Joab, "Listen to me, Joab. Come over here so I can talk to you." ¹⁷As he approached, the woman asked, "Are you Joab?"

"I am," he replied.

So she said, "Listen carefully to your servant."

"I'm listening," he said.

¹⁸Then she continued, "There used to be a saying, 'If you want to settle an argument, ask advice at the town of Abel.' ¹⁹I am one who is peace loving and faithful in Israel. But you are destroying an important town in Israel.* Why do you want to devour what belongs to the LORD?"

²⁰And Joab replied, "Believe me, I don't want to devour or destroy your town! ²¹That's not my purpose. All I want is a man named Sheba son of Bicri from the hill country of Ephraim, who has revolted against King David. If you hand over this one man to me, I will leave the town in peace."

"All right," the woman replied, "we will throw his head over the wall to you." ²²Then the woman went to all the people with her wise advice, and they cut off Sheba's head and threw it out to Joab. So he blew the ram's horn and called his troops back from the attack. They all returned to their homes, and Joab returned to the king at Jerusalem.

²³Now Joab was the commander of the army of Israel. Benaiah son of Jehoiada was captain of the king's bodyguard. ²⁴Adoniram* was in charge of the labor force. Jehoshaphat son of Ahilud was the royal historian. ²⁵Sheva was the court secretary. Zadok and Abiathar were the priests. ²⁶And Ira, a descendant of Jair, was David's personal priest.

JUSTICE
(20:7-10) Once again Joab's murderous treachery went unpunished, just as it did when he killed Abner (3:26-30). Eventually, however, justice caught up with him (1 Kgs 2:28-35). It may seem that sin and treachery often go unpunished, but God's justice is not limited to this life's rewards. Are you worried that someone will get away with what he or she has done? "Don't worry about the wicked or envy those who do wrong. For like grass, they soon fade away. Like spring flowers, they soon wither" (Ps 37:1-2).

SPEAK UP
(20:16-22) Joab's men were on the brink of destroying the city of Abel-beth-maacah. Though women in that society were usually quiet in public, this woman spoke out. She stopped Joab's attack, not with weapons, but with wise words and a plan of action. Sometimes the courage to speak a few sensible words can prevent great disaster.

21 DAVID AVENGES THE GIBEONITES

There was a famine during David's reign that lasted for three years, so David asked the LORD about it. And the LORD said, "The famine has come because Saul and his family are guilty of murdering the Gibeonites."

²So the king summoned the Gibeonites. They were not part of Israel but were all that was left of the nation of the Amorites. The people of Israel had sworn not to kill them, but Saul, in his zeal for Israel and Judah, had tried

20:7a Hebrew *So Joab's men.* 20:7b Hebrew *the Kerethites and Pelethites;* also in 20:23. 20:8 Hebrew *As he stepped forward, it fell out.* 20:14 As in Greek and Latin versions; Hebrew reads *All the Berites.* 20:19 Hebrew *a town that is a mother in Israel.* 20:24 As in Greek version (see also 1 Kgs 4:6; 5:14); Hebrew reads *Adoram.*

to wipe them out. ³David asked them, "What can I do for you? How can I make amends so that you will bless the LORD's people again?"

⁴"Well, money can't settle this matter between us and the family of Saul," the Gibeonites replied. "Neither can we demand the life of anyone in Israel."

"What can I do then?" David asked. "Just tell me and I will do it for you."

⁵Then they replied, "It was Saul who planned to destroy us, to keep us from having any place at all in the territory of Israel. ⁶So let seven of Saul's sons be handed over to us, and we will execute them before the LORD at Gibeon, on the mountain of the LORD.*"

"All right," the king said, "I will do it." ⁷The king spared Jonathan's son Mephibosheth,* who was Saul's grandson, because of the oath David and Jonathan had sworn before the LORD. ⁸But he gave them Saul's two sons Armoni and Mephibosheth, whose mother was Rizpah daughter of Aiah. He also gave them the five sons of Saul's daughter Merab,* the wife of Adriel son of Barzillai from Meholah. ⁹The men of Gibeon executed them on the mountain before the LORD. So all seven of them died together at the beginning of the barley harvest.

¹⁰Then Rizpah daughter of Aiah, the mother of two of the men, spread burlap on a rock and stayed there the entire harvest season. She prevented the scavenger birds from tearing at their bodies during the day and stopped wild animals from eating them at night. ¹¹When David learned what Rizpah, Saul's concubine, had done, ¹²he went to the people of Jabesh-gilead and retrieved the bones of Saul and his son Jonathan. (When the Philistines had killed Saul and Jonathan on Mount Gilboa, the people of Jabesh-gilead stole their bodies from the public square of Beth-shan, where the Philistines had hung them.) ¹³So David obtained the bones of Saul and Jonathan, as well as the bones of the men the Gibeonites had executed.

¹⁴Then the king ordered that they bury the bones in the tomb of Kish, Saul's father, at the town of Zela in the land of Benjamin. After that, God ended the famine in the land.

21:6 As in Greek version (see also 21:9); Hebrew reads *at Gibeah of Saul, the chosen of the LORD.* 21:7 *Mephibosheth* is another name for Merib-baal. 21:8 As in a few Hebrew and Greek manuscripts and Syriac version (see also 1 Sam 18:19); most Hebrew manuscripts read *Michal.* 21:16a Or *a descendant of the Rapha;* also in 21:18, 20, 22. 21:16b Hebrew *300 shekels* [3.4 kilograms]. 21:19a As in parallel text at 1 Chr 20:5; Hebrew reads *son of Jaare-oregim.* 21:19b As in parallel text at 1 Chr 20:5; Hebrew reads *killed Goliath of Gath.* 21:21 As in parallel text at 1 Chr 20:7; Hebrew reads *Shimea,* a variant spelling of Shimea. 22:6 Hebrew *Sheol.*

BATTLES AGAINST PHILISTINE GIANTS ¹⁵Once again the Philistines were at war with Israel. And when David and his men were in the thick of battle, David became weak and exhausted. ¹⁶Ishbi-benob was a descendant of the giants*; his bronze spearhead weighed more than seven pounds,* and he was armed with a new sword. He had cornered David and was about to kill him. ¹⁷But Abishai son of Zeruiah came to David's rescue and killed the Philistine. Then David's men declared, "You are not going out to battle with us again! Why risk snuffing out the light of Israel?"

¹⁸After this, there was another battle against the Philistines at Gob. As they fought, Sibbecai from Hushah killed Saph, another descendant of the giants.

¹⁹During another battle at Gob, Elhanan son of Jair* from Bethlehem killed the brother of Goliath of Gath.* The handle of his spear was as thick as a weaver's beam!

²⁰In another battle with the Philistines at Gath, they encountered a huge man with six fingers on each hand and six toes on each foot, twenty-four in all, who was also a descendant of the giants. ²¹But when he defied and taunted Israel, he was killed by Jonathan, the son of David's brother Shimea.*

²²These four Philistines were descendants of the giants of Gath, but David and his warriors killed them.

22 DAVID'S SONG OF PRAISE

David sang this song to the LORD on the day the LORD rescued him from all his enemies and from Saul. ²He sang:

"The LORD is my rock, my fortress, and
　　my savior;
³　　my God is my rock, in whom I find
　　　protection.
He is my shield, the power that saves me,
　　and my place of safety.
He is my refuge, my savior,
　　the one who saves me from violence.
⁴ I called on the LORD, who is worthy of praise,
　　and he saved me from my enemies.

⁵ "The waves of death overwhelmed me;
　　floods of destruction swept over me.
⁶ The grave* wrapped its ropes around me;
　　death laid a trap in my path.
⁷ But in my distress I cried out to the LORD;
　　yes, I cried to my God for help.
He heard me from his sanctuary;
　　my cry reached his ears.

⁸ "Then the earth quaked and trembled.
　　The foundations of the heavens shook;

MY STORY: Mike

I was at a summer camp in Florida. Our group wanted to go swimming in the Gulf of Mexico, but we couldn't because there was a hurricane off the coast at the time and the riptides and undertow were too strong.

After dinner I walked down to the beach to look for a hat I had lost. A guy in my group noticed four boys—I couldn't tell how old they were—about 100 feet out in the water. They started swimming in, but one couldn't make it. He kept drifting farther out. The guy I was with ran into the water to save him. I stood on the shore for 10 seconds and then, without thinking, jumped in too.

When I was halfway to the boy, I met the guy from my group coming back; he couldn't make it so he had turned around. When I finally reached the boy, he was semiconscious. I grabbed him and tried to walk back to shore, but the water was over my head. I told the boy that every time there was a wave we would kick and try to ride it. I began to pray; I didn't know whether to just try to save my own life or hang on to the guy and keep trying to swim. I remembered 2 Samuel 22:17 and 2 Samuel 22:40 and kept on swimming. After five minutes I stopped swimming; I was able to stand up. Before long we were on the shore. I believe the only reason I made it was because God gave me the strength. I never saw the boy I rescued again.

....

FORGIVEN
(22:22-24) David was not saying that he had never sinned. Psalm 51 shows his tremendous anguish over his sin against Uriah and Bathsheba. But David understood God's faithfulness and wrote this song from God's perspective. He knew that God had made him clean again—"whiter than snow," with a "clean heart" (Ps 51:7, 10). Because of the death and resurrection of Jesus Christ, we also can be forgiven for anything wrong we have done or will do. Our guilt is replaced with his purity and forgiveness.

they quaked because of his anger.
9 Smoke poured from his nostrils;
   fierce flames leaped from his mouth.
   Glowing coals blazed forth from him.
10 He opened the heavens and came down;
   dark storm clouds were beneath his feet.
11 Mounted on a mighty angelic being,* he flew,
   soaring* on the wings of the wind.
12 He shrouded himself in darkness,
   veiling his approach with dense rain clouds.
13 A great brightness shone around him,
   and burning coals* blazed forth.
14 The LORD thundered from heaven;
   the voice of the Most High resounded.
15 He shot arrows and scattered his enemies;
   his lightning flashed, and they were confused.
16 Then at the command of the LORD,
   at the blast of his breath,
   the bottom of the sea could be seen,
   and the foundations of the earth were laid bare.

17 "He reached down from heaven and rescued me;
   he drew me out of deep waters.
18 He rescued me from my powerful enemies,
   from those who hated me and were too strong for me.
19 They attacked me at a moment when I was in distress,
   but the LORD supported me.
20 He led me to a place of safety;
   he rescued me because he delights in me.
21 The LORD rewarded me for doing right;
   he restored me because of my innocence.
22 For I have kept the ways of the LORD;
   I have not turned from my God to follow evil.
23 I have followed all his regulations;
   I have never abandoned his decrees.
24 I am blameless before God;
   I have kept myself from sin.
25 The LORD rewarded me for doing right.
   He has seen my innocence.

26 "To the faithful you show yourself faithful;
   to those with integrity you show integrity.
27 To the pure you show yourself pure,
   but to the wicked you show yourself hostile.
28 You rescue the humble,

22:11a Hebrew *a cherub.* **22:11b** As in some Hebrew manuscripts (see also Ps 18:10); other Hebrew manuscripts read *appearing.* **22:13** Or *and lightning bolts.*

but your eyes watch the proud and
humiliate them.
29 O LORD, you are my lamp.
The LORD lights up my darkness.
30 In your strength I can crush an army;
with my God I can scale any wall.

31 "God's way is perfect.
All the LORD's promises prove true.
He is a shield for all who look to him for
protection.
32 For who is God except the LORD?
Who but our God is a solid rock?
33 God is my strong fortress,
and he makes my way perfect.
34 He makes me as surefooted as a deer,
enabling me to stand on mountain
heights.
35 He trains my hands for battle;
he strengthens my arm to draw a bronze
bow.
36 You have given me your shield of victory;
your help* has made me great.
37 You have made a wide path for my feet
to keep them from slipping.

38 "I chased my enemies and destroyed them;
I did not stop until they were conquered.
39 I consumed them;
I struck them down so they did not get up;
they fell beneath my feet.
40 You have armed me with strength for the
battle;
you have subdued my enemies under
my feet.
41 You placed my foot on their necks.
I have destroyed all who hated me.
42 They looked for help, but no one came
to their rescue.
They even cried to the LORD, but he
refused to answer.
43 I ground them as fine as the dust of the
earth;
I trampled them* in the gutter like dirt.

44 "You gave me victory over my accusers.
You preserved me as the ruler over
nations;
people I don't even know now serve me.
45 Foreign nations cringe before me;
as soon as they hear of me, they submit.
46 They all lose their courage
and come trembling* from their
strongholds.

47 "The LORD lives! Praise to my Rock!
May God, the Rock of my salvation,
be exalted!
48 He is the God who pays back those who
harm me;
he brings down the nations under me
49 and delivers me from my enemies.
You hold me safe beyond the reach of my
enemies;
you save me from violent opponents.
50 For this, O LORD, I will praise you among the
nations;
I will sing praises to your name.
51 You give great victories to your king;
you show unfailing love to your anointed,
to David and all his descendants forever."

23 DAVID'S LAST WORDS These are the last words of David:

"David, the son of Jesse, speaks—
David, the man who was raised up
so high,
David, the man anointed by the God of
Jacob,
David, the sweet psalmist of Israel.*

2 "The Spirit of the LORD speaks through me;
his words are upon my tongue.
3 The God of Israel spoke.
The Rock of Israel said to me:
'The one who rules righteously,
who rules in the fear of God,
4 is like the light of morning at sunrise,
like a morning without clouds,
like the gleaming of the sun
on new grass after rain.'

5 "Is it not my family God has chosen?
Yes, he has made an everlasting covenant
with me.
His agreement is arranged and guaranteed
in every detail.
He will ensure my safety and success.
6 But the godless are like thorns to be thrown
away,

22:36 As in Dead Sea Scrolls (see also Ps 18:35); Masoretic Text
reads *your answering.*   22:43 As in Dead Sea Scrolls (see also
Ps 18:42); Masoretic Text reads *I crushed and trampled them.*
22:46 As in parallel text at Ps 18:45; Hebrew reads *come girding
themselves.*   23:1 Or *the favorite subject of the songs of Israel;*
or *the favorite of the Strong One of Israel.*

....

GOD'S MAN
(22:51) Ever since the Israelites first entered the Promised Land under Joshua, they had struggled to drive out
its wicked inhabitants. Now, more than 400 years later,
Israel had finally achieved peace. David had accomplished what no leader before him—judge or king—had
done. His administration was run on the principle of
dedication to God and to the well-being of the people.
Yet David wasn't perfect. Despite his offenses, however,
the Bible calls David a man after God's own heart (1 Sam
13:14; Acts 13:22). Is that the way your family and friends
would describe you?

for they tear the hand that touches them.
7 One must use iron tools to chop them down;
they will be totally consumed by fire."

DAVID'S MIGHTIEST WARRIORS
8These are the names of David's mightiest warriors. The first was Jashobeam the Hacmonite,* who was leader of the Three*—the three mightiest warriors among David's men. He once used his spear to kill 800 enemy warriors in a single battle.*

9Next in rank among the Three was Eleazar son of Dodai, a descendant of Ahoah. Once Eleazar and David stood together against the Philistines when the entire Israelite army had fled. 10He killed Philistines until his hand was too tired to lift his sword, and the LORD gave him a great victory that day. The rest of the army did not return until it was time to collect the plunder!

11Next in rank was Shammah son of Agee from Harar. One time the Philistines gathered at Lehi and attacked the Israelites in a field full of lentils. The Israelite army fled, 12but Shammah*

held his ground in the middle of the field and beat back the Philistines. So the LORD brought about a great victory.

13Once during the harvest, when David was at the cave of Adullam, the Philistine army was camped in the valley of Rephaim. The Three (who were among the Thirty—an elite group among David's fighting men) went down to meet him there. 14David was staying in the stronghold at the time, and a Philistine detachment had occupied the town of Bethlehem.

15David remarked longingly to his men, "Oh, how I would love some of that good water from the well by the gate in Bethlehem." 16So the Three broke through the Philistine lines, drew some water from the well by the gate in Bethlehem, and brought it back to David. But he refused to drink it. Instead, he poured it out as an offering to the LORD. 17"The LORD forbid that I should drink this!" he exclaimed. "This water

23:8a As in parallel text at 1 Chr 11:11; Hebrew reads *Josheb-basshebeth the Tahkemonite.* 23:8b As in Greek and Latin versions (see also 1 Chr 11:11); the meaning of the Hebrew is uncertain. 23:8c As in some Greek manuscripts (see also 1 Chr 11:11); the meaning of the Hebrew is uncertain, though it might be rendered *the Three. It was Adino the Eznite who killed 800 men at one time.* 23:12 Hebrew *he.*

DAVID'S MIGHTY MEN
PERSONALITY PROFILE

AS A KID, you might have played "Follow the Leader." But for many of us, that game blends into real life as we connect with the people in authority over us.

One way to understand David's success is to notice the kind of men who followed him. During the time he spent running from Saul, David built a fighting force of several hundred men. Some were relatives, others were outcasts of society. Many were in trouble with the law and probably seemed like gang members! But they all had at least one trait in common—complete devotion to David. He knew that he could count on them.

These guys were as close to superheroes as was humanly possible. Their achievements made them famous. Among these men were elite military groups like "the Thirty" and "the Three" (2 Sam 23:8-39).

Scripture gives the impression that these men were motivated to greatness by the qualities of their leader. David inspired them to achieve beyond their goals and meet their true potential. His effectiveness as a leader was clearly connected to his awareness of God's leading.

The leaders we follow and the causes to which we commit ourselves will affect our lives. Who are the leaders that you follow? Your answer can help you decide whether or not they deserve your loyalty. Do you also recognize God's leading in your life? No one can lead you to excellence the way your Creator can.

BOTTOM LINE: Greatness is often inspired by the quality and character of a leader.

Even a small force of able and loyal men can accomplish great feats.

Their stories are told in 1 Samuel 22–27; 29–30; 2 Samuel 1–5; 10–11; 21:15-22; 23:8-39. They also are mentioned in 1 Chronicles 11–12.

UPS:
- *Very capable*
- *Shared many special skills*
- *Though frequently outnumbered, were consistently victorious*
- *Loyal to David*

STATS:
- *Where: They came from all over Israel (primarily Judah and Benjamin), and from some of the other surrounding nations as well*
- *Occupations: Various backgrounds—almost all were fugitives*

KEY VERSES: *1 Samuel 22–27; 29–30 2 Samuel 1–5; 10–11; 15:12; 21:15-22; 23:8-39; 1 Chronicles 11–12.*

is as precious as the blood of these men* who risked their lives to bring it to me." So David did not drink it. These are examples of the exploits of the Three.

DAVID'S THIRTY MIGHTY MEN ¹⁸Abishai son of Zeruiah, the brother of Joab, was the leader of the Thirty.* He once used his spear to kill 300 enemy warriors in a single battle. It was by such feats that he became as famous as the Three. ¹⁹Abishai was the most famous of the Thirty* and was their commander, though he was not one of the Three.

²⁰There was also Benaiah son of Jehoiada, a valiant warrior* from Kabzeel. He did many heroic deeds, which included killing two champions* of Moab. Another time, on a snowy day, he chased a lion down into a pit and killed it. ²¹Once, armed only with a club, he killed a great Egyptian warrior who was armed with a spear. Benaiah wrenched the spear from the Egyptian's hand and killed him with it. ²²Deeds like these made Benaiah as famous as the Three mightiest warriors. ²³He was more honored than the other members of the Thirty, though he was not one of the Three. And David made him captain of his bodyguard.

²⁴Other members of the Thirty included:

Asahel, Joab's brother;
Elhanan son of Dodo from Bethlehem;
²⁵ Shammah from Harod;
Elika from Harod;
²⁶ Helez from Pelon*;
Ira son of Ikkesh from Tekoa;
²⁷ Abiezer from Anathoth;
Sibbecai* from Hushah;
²⁸ Zalmon from Ahoah;
Maharai from Netophah;
²⁹ Heled* son of Baanah from Netophah;
Ithai* son of Ribai from Gibeah (in the land of Benjamin);
³⁰ Benaiah from Pirathon;
Hurai* from Nahale-gaash*;
³¹ Abi-albon from Arabah;
Azmaveth from Bahurim;
³² Eliahba from Shaalbon;
the sons of Jashen;
Jonathan ³³son of Shagee* from Harar;
Ahiam son of Sharar from Harar;
³⁴ Eliphelet son of Ahasbai from Maacah;
Eliam son of Ahithophel from Giloh;
³⁵ Hezro from Carmel;
Paarai from Arba;
³⁶ Igal son of Nathan from Zobah;
Bani from Gad;
³⁷ Zelek from Ammon;
Naharai from Beeroth, Joab's armor bearer;
³⁸ Ira from Jattir;
Gareb from Jattir;
³⁹ Uriah the Hittite.

There were thirty-seven in all.

24 DAVID TAKES A CENSUS Once again the anger of the LORD burned against Israel, and he caused David to harm them by taking a census. "Go and count the people of Israel and Judah," the LORD told him.

²So the king said to Joab and the commanders* of the army, "Take a census of all the tribes of Israel—from Dan in the north to Beersheba in the south—so I may know how many people there are."

³But Joab replied to the king, "May the LORD your God let you live to see a hundred times as many people as there are now! But why, my lord the king, do you want to do this?"

⁴But the king insisted that they take the census, so Joab and the commanders of the army went out to count the people of Israel. ⁵First they crossed the Jordan and camped at Aroer, south of the town in the valley, in the direction of Gad. Then they went on to Jazer, ⁶then to Gilead in the land of Tahtim-hodshi* and to Dan-jaan and around to Sidon. ⁷Then they came to the fortress of Tyre, and all the towns of the Hivites and Canaanites. Finally, they went south to Judah* as far as Beersheba.

⁸Having gone through the entire land for nine months and twenty days, they returned to Jerusalem. ⁹Joab reported the number of people to the king. There were 800,000 capable warriors

23:17 Hebrew *Shall I drink the blood of these men?*   23:18 As in a few Hebrew manuscripts and Syriac version; most Hebrew manuscripts read *the Three.*   23:19 As in Syriac version; Hebrew reads *the Three.*   23:20a Or *son of Jehoiada, son of Ish-hai.*   23:20b Hebrew *two of Ariel.*   23:26 As in parallel text at 1 Chr 11:27 (see also 1 Chr 27:10); Hebrew reads *from Palti.*   23:27 As in some Greek manuscripts (see also 1 Chr 11:29); Hebrew reads *Mebunnai.*   23:29a As in some Hebrew manuscripts (see also 1 Chr 11:30); most Hebrew manuscripts read *Heleb.*   23:29b As in parallel text at 1 Chr 11:31; Hebrew reads *Ittai.*   23:30a As in some Greek manuscripts (see also 1 Chr 11:32); Hebrew reads *Hiddai.*   23:30b Or *from the ravines of Gaash.*   23:33 As in parallel text at 1 Chr 11:34; Hebrew reads *Jonathan, Shammah;* some Greek manuscripts read *Jonathan son of Shammah.*   24:2 As in Greek version (see also 24:4 and 1 Chr 21:2); Hebrew reads *Joab the commander.*   24:6 Greek version reads *to Gilead and to Kadesh in the land of the Hittites.*   24:7 Or *they went to the Negev of Judah.*

POURED OUT
(23:13-17) *David's mighty men risked their lives to get water for their thirsty leader. David poured out the water as an offering to God because he was so moved by the sacrifice it represented. When Hebrews offered animal sacrifices, they never consumed the blood. It represented life, so they would pour it out before God. David would not drink this water, which represented the lives of his soldiers. Instead, he offered it to God. What will you offer to God?*

in Israel who could handle a sword, and 500,000 in Judah.

JUDGMENT FOR DAVID'S SIN
¹⁰But after he had taken the census, David's conscience began to bother him. And he said to the LORD, "I have sinned greatly by taking this census. Please forgive my guilt, LORD, for doing this foolish thing."

¹¹The next morning the word of the LORD came to the prophet Gad, who was David's seer. This was the message: ¹²"Go and say to David, 'This is what the LORD says: I will give you three choices. Choose one of these punishments, and I will inflict it on you.'"

¹³So Gad came to David and asked him, "Will you choose three* years of famine throughout your land, three months of fleeing from your enemies, or three days of severe plague throughout your land? Think this over and decide what answer I should give the LORD who sent me."

¹⁴"I'm in a desperate situation!" David replied to Gad. "But let us fall into the hands of the LORD, for his mercy is great. Do not let me fall into human hands."

¹⁵So the LORD sent a plague upon Israel that morning, and it lasted for three days.* A total of 70,000 people died throughout the nation, from Dan in the north to Beersheba in the south. ¹⁶But as the angel was preparing to destroy Jerusalem, the LORD relented and said to the death angel, "Stop! That is enough!" At that moment the angel of the LORD was by the threshing floor of Araunah the Jebusite.

¹⁷When David saw the angel, he said to the LORD, "I am the one who has sinned and done wrong! But these people are as innocent as sheep—what have they done? Let your anger fall against me and my family."

DAVID BUILDS AN ALTAR
¹⁸That day Gad came to David and said to him, "Go up and build an altar to the LORD on the threshing floor of Araunah the Jebusite."

¹⁹So David went up to do what the LORD had commanded him. ²⁰When Araunah saw the king and his men coming toward him, he came and bowed before the king with his face to the ground. ²¹"Why have you come, my lord the king?" Araunah asked.

David replied, "I have come to buy your threshing floor and to build an altar to the LORD there, so that he will stop the plague."

²²"Take it, my lord the king, and use it as you wish," Araunah said to David. "Here are oxen for the burnt offering, and you can use the threshing boards and ox yokes for wood to build a fire on the altar. ²³I will give it all to you, Your Majesty, and may the LORD your God accept your sacrifice."

²⁴But the king replied to Araunah, "No, I insist on buying it, for I will not present burnt offerings to the LORD my God that have cost me nothing." So David paid him fifty pieces of silver* for the threshing floor and the oxen.

²⁵David built an altar there to the LORD and sacrificed burnt offerings and peace offerings. And the LORD answered his prayer for the land, and the plague on Israel was stopped.

24:13 As in Greek version (see also 1 Chr 21:12); Hebrew reads *seven*. **24:15** Hebrew *for the designated time.* **24:24** Hebrew *50 shekels of silver,* about 20 ounces or 570 grams in weight.

1 KINGS

Here's a quick quiz. What do you think of when you hear each of these names: Solomon . . . Elijah . . . Ahab . . . Jezebel . . . Nadab?

The usual response for Solomon would be "wisdom" or "the Temple." For Elijah, you might answer, "prophet" or "defeated the Baal worshipers on the mountain." Ahab and Jezebel are usually thought of as evil. As for Nadab, the usual response is "Nadab who?"

It's amazing what people remember about other people after they're gone. Whether good or evil, a person's reputation often remains long after his or her death.

First Kings tells the stories of many of the leaders of Israel. Some stories, like Solomon's, take several chapters to relate. Others, like Nadab's, just take a line or two. No matter what the length, when we read these accounts, we gain a snapshot of what these people were like—their character and their lives. As we read, we can learn what it takes to be someone who is remembered for good and not evil, for following God and not self. For Nadab, one choice line sums up his reputation: "He did what was evil in the LORD's sight and followed the example of his father, continuing the sins that Jeroboam had led Israel to commit" (15:26). That's some rep!

What would your friends and family say if they found your name in a similar quiz? What kind of a reputation are you building?

KEY POINTS

RULING THE RIGHT WAY All the kings of Israel and Judah were told to obey God and to govern according to his laws. But their tendency to abandon God's Word and to worship other gods led to their downfall. Having authority doesn't make us immune to the consequences of ignoring God's rules.

THE TEMPLE Solomon's Temple was a beautiful place of worship, prayer, and the presence of God. In the same way, the human heart is a place of worship, prayer, and the presence of God.

OTHER GODS Although the Israelites had God's law and had experienced his presence among them, they soon looked for other gods to worship. Although God has given us many things, many of us also find other gods (money, possessions, power) to worship.

PROPHETIC MESSAGE Elijah had the responsibility to confront the king and the people of Israel about their disobedience to God. Today, God uses the Bible and the wise counsel of believers to warn us to keep to his way.

SEEK FORGIVENESS Whenever the people of Israel owned up to their sin and returned to God, God heard their prayers and forgave them. We have the same assurance of forgiveness if we're willing to ask for it.

The broken lines (— · —) indicate modern boundaries.

KEY PLACES
David's son Solomon brought Israel into its golden age. His wealth and wisdom were acclaimed worldwide. But he ignored God in his later years (1:1–11:43).

❶ SHECHEM
After Solomon's death, Israel assembled at Shechem to inaugurate his son Rehoboam. However, Rehoboam threatened even higher taxes, which caused a revolt (12:1–12:19).

❷ ISRAEL
Jeroboam, leader of the rebels, was made king of Israel, now called the northern kingdom. Jeroboam made Shechem his capital city (12:20, 25).

❸ JUDAH
Only the tribes of Judah and Benjamin remained loyal to Rehoboam. These two tribes became the southern kingdom.

Rehoboam returned to Judah from Shechem and prepared to force the rebels into submission, but a prophet's message halted these plans (12:21-24).

❹ JERUSALEM
Jerusalem was the capital city of Judah. Its Temple, built by Solomon, was the focal point of Jewish worship. This worried Jeroboam. How could he keep his people loyal if they were constantly going to Rehoboam's capital to worship (12:26-27)?

❺ DAN
Jeroboam's solution was to set up his own worship centers. He had two calf idols made and

proclaimed them to be Israel's gods. One was placed in Dan, and the people were told that they could go there instead of going to Jerusalem to worship (12:28-29).

❻ BETHEL
The other idol made at Jeroboam's command was placed in Bethel. The people of the northern kingdom had two convenient locations for worship in their own country. But their sin displeased God. Meanwhile, in Jerusalem, Rehoboam was also allowing idolatry to creep in.

❼ TIRZAH
Baasha became king of Israel after assassinating Nadab. He moved the capital from Shechem to Tirzah (15:27–16:22).

❽ SAMARIA
Israel kings rose and fell through plots, assassinations, and warfare. When Omri became king, he bought a hill on which he built a new capital city, Samaria. Omri's son, Ahab, became the most wicked king of Israel. His wife, Jezebel, worshiped Baal. Ahab erected a temple to Baal in Samaria (16:23-34).

❾ MOUNT CARMEL
Elijah challenged the prophets of Baal and Asherah at Mount Carmel, where he proved that they were false prophets. There Elijah humiliated and then executed these prophets (18:1-46).

❿ JEZREEL
Elijah returned to Jezreel. But Queen Jezebel vowed to kill Elijah for killing her prophets. He ran for his life, but God cared for and encouraged him. During his travels, he anointed the future kings of Syria and Israel, as well as his own replacement, Elisha (19:1-21).

⓫ RAMOTH-GILEAD
The king of Aram declared war on Israel and was defeated in two battles. But the Arameans occupied Ramoth-gilead. Ahab and Jehoshaphat joined forces to recover the city. In this battle, Ahab was killed. Later, Jehoshaphat died (20:1–22:53).

1

DAVID IN HIS OLD AGE King David was now very old, and no matter how many blankets covered him, he could not keep warm. ²So his advisers told him, "Let us find a young virgin to wait on you and look after you, my lord. She will lie in your arms and keep you warm."

³So they searched throughout the land of Israel for a beautiful girl, and they found Abishag from Shunem and brought her to the king. ⁴The girl was very beautiful, and she looked after the king and took care of him. But the king had no sexual relations with her.

ADONIJAH CLAIMS THE THRONE ⁵About that time David's son Adonijah, whose mother was Haggith, began boasting, "I will make myself king." So he provided himself with chariots and charioteers and recruited fifty men to run in front of him. ⁶Now his father, King David, had never disciplined him at any time, even by asking, "Why are you doing that?" Adonijah had been born next after Absalom, and he was very handsome.

⁷Adonijah took Joab son of Zeruiah and Abiathar the priest into his confidence, and they agreed to help him become king. ⁸But Zadok the priest, Benaiah son of Jehoiada, Nathan the prophet, Shimei, Rei, and David's personal bodyguard refused to support Adonijah.

⁹Adonijah went to the Stone of Zoheleth* near the spring of En-rogel, where he sacrificed sheep, cattle, and fattened calves. He invited all his brothers—the other sons of King David—and all the royal officials of Judah. ¹⁰But he did not invite Nathan the prophet or Benaiah or the king's bodyguard or his brother Solomon.

¹¹Then Nathan went to Bathsheba, Solomon's mother, and asked her, "Haven't you heard that Haggith's son, Adonijah, has made himself king, and our lord David doesn't even know about it? ¹²If you want to save your own life and the life of your son Solomon, follow my advice. ¹³Go at once to King David and say to him, 'My lord the king, didn't you make a vow and say to me, "Your son Solomon will surely be the next king and will sit on my throne"? Why then has Adonijah become king?' ¹⁴And while you are still talking with him, I will come and confirm everything you have said."

¹⁵So Bathsheba went into the king's bedroom. (He was very old now, and Abishag was taking care of him.) ¹⁶Bathsheba bowed down before the king.

"What can I do for you?" he asked her.

¹⁷She replied, "My lord, you made a vow before the LORD your God when you said to me, 'Your son Solomon will surely be the next king and will sit on my throne.' ¹⁸But instead, Adonijah has made himself king, and my lord the king does not even know about it. ¹⁹He has sacrificed many cattle, fattened calves, and sheep, and he has invited all the king's sons to attend the celebration. He also invited Abiathar the priest and Joab, the commander of the army. But he did not invite your servant Solomon. ²⁰And now, my lord the king, all Israel is waiting for you to announce who will become king after you. ²¹If you do not act, my son Solomon and I will be treated as criminals as soon as my lord the king has died."

²²While she was still speaking with the king, Nathan the prophet arrived. ²³The king's officials told him, "Nathan the prophet is here to see you."

Nathan went in and bowed before the king with his face to the ground. ²⁴Nathan asked, "My lord the king, have you decided that Adonijah will be the next king and that he will sit on your throne? ²⁵Today he has sacrificed many cattle, fattened calves, and sheep, and he has invited all the king's sons to attend the celebration. He also invited the commanders of the army and Abiathar the priest. They are feasting and drinking with him and shouting, 'Long live King Adonijah!' ²⁶But he did not invite me or Zadok the priest or Benaiah or your servant Solomon. ²⁷Has my lord the king really done this without letting any of his officials know who should be the next king?"

DAVID MAKES SOLOMON KING ²⁸King David responded, "Call Bathsheba!" So she came back in and stood before the king. ²⁹And the king repeated his vow: "As surely as the LORD lives, who has rescued me from every danger, ³⁰your son Solomon will be the next king and will sit on my throne this very day, just as I vowed to you before the LORD, the God of Israel."

³¹Then Bathsheba bowed down with her face

....

TAKE ACTION

(1:5-14) When Nathan learned of Adonijah's conspiracy, he immediately tried to stop it. He was a man of both faith and action. Nathan knew the right course to take—that Solomon should be king—and moved quickly when he saw someone trying to block what was right. We often know what is right, but may not always act on it. Want to be a Nathan? Good intentions or angry feelings will only take you so far. Why not pray first; then take the action needed to correct the situation.

1:9 Or *to the Serpent's Stone;* Greek version supports reading *Zoheleth* as a proper name.

to the ground before the king and exclaimed, "May my lord King David live forever!"

³²Then King David ordered, "Call Zadok the priest, Nathan the prophet, and Benaiah son of Jehoiada." When they came into the king's presence, ³³the king said to them, "Take Solomon and my officials down to Gihon Spring. Solomon is to ride on my own mule. ³⁴There Zadok the priest and Nathan the prophet are to anoint him king over Israel. Blow the ram's horn and shout, 'Long live King Solomon!' ³⁵Then escort him back here, and he will sit on my throne. He will succeed me as king, for I have appointed him to be ruler over Israel and Judah."

³⁶"Amen!" Benaiah son of Jehoiada replied. "May the LORD, the God of my lord the king, decree that it happen. ³⁷And may the LORD be with Solomon as he has been with you, my lord the king, and may he make Solomon's reign even greater than yours!"

³⁸So Zadok the priest, Nathan the prophet, Benaiah son of Jehoiada, and the king's bodyguard* took Solomon down to Gihon Spring, with Solomon riding on King David's own mule. ³⁹There Zadok the priest took the flask of olive oil from the sacred tent and anointed Solomon with the oil. Then they sounded the ram's horn and all the people shouted, "Long live King Solomon!" ⁴⁰And all the people followed Solomon into Jerusalem, playing flutes and shouting for joy. The celebration was so joyous and noisy that the earth shook with the sound.

⁴¹Adonijah and his guests heard the celebrating and shouting just as they were finishing their banquet. When Joab heard the sound of the ram's horn, he asked, "What's going on? Why is the city in such an uproar?"

⁴²And while he was still speaking, Jonathan son of Abiathar the priest arrived. "Come in,"

1:38 Hebrew the Kerethites and Pelethites; also in 1:44.

SOLOMON
PERSONALITY PROFILE

GOT WISDOM? Having wisdom doesn't help unless you use it. Early in his life, Solomon had the sense to realize his need for wisdom. But although he asked God to give him wisdom to be a good king, he showed poor judgment in his private life. He married a woman from an enemy nation as part of a political deal. She was the first of several hundred wives he married. In doing this, Solomon went against not only his father's last words (see 1 Kgs 2:3-4), but also God's direct commands (see Deut 7:3-4). Solomon's actions remind us how easy it is to know what is right and yet not do it.

God's gift of wisdom to Solomon did not mean that he couldn't make mistakes. He had been given great opportunities as the king of God's chosen people, but with those opportunities came great responsibilities. Solomon took advantage of the opportunities, building a Temple for God and a huge palace for himself. Yet he became infamous as a king who charged high taxes and overworked his people.

Little is mentioned in the Bible about the last decade of Solomon's reign. Ecclesiastes probably records his final reflections on life. In that book, we observe a man proving through bitter experience that finding meaning in life apart from God doesn't work. Real security and contentment are only found in a trusting relationship with God.

The contentment we find in the opportunities and successes of this life is real, but temporary. The more we expect those feelings to last, the more quickly they are gone. Be sure to balance your pursuit of all the opportunities in life with keeping up with your responsibilities. Or, as Solomon put it, "Don't let the excitement of youth cause you to forget your Creator. Honor him in your youth before you grow old and say, 'Life is not pleasant anymore'" (Eccl 12:1).

BOTTOM LINE: A truly effective leader not only leads in public but at home as well.

Knowing what actions are required of us means little if we don't have the will to perform those actions.

Solomon's story is told in 2 Samuel 12:24-25; 1 Kings 1:10–11:43. He also is mentioned in 1 Chronicles 28–29; 2 Chronicles 1–9; Nehemiah 13:26; Psalm 72; and Matthew 6:29; 12:42.

UPS:
- *Third king of Israel, David's chosen heir*
- *The wisest man who ever lived*
- *Author of Ecclesiastes and Song of Solomon, as well as many of the proverbs and some of the psalms*
- *Built God's Temple in Jerusalem*
- *Diplomat, trader, collector, patron of the arts*

DOWNS:
- *Sealed many foreign agreements by marrying women from enemy nations*
- *Allowed his wives to draw him away from God*
- *Taxed his people excessively and drafted them into a labor force*

STATS:
- *Where: Jerusalem*
- *Occupation: King of Israel*
- *Relatives: David (father); Bathsheba (mother); Absalom, Adonijah (brothers); Tamar (half-sister); Rehoboam (son); 700 wives and 300 concubines*

KEY VERSE: *Nehemiah 13:26*

Adonijah said to him, "for you are a good man. You must have good news."

⁴³"Not at all!" Jonathan replied. "Our lord King David has just declared Solomon king! ⁴⁴The king sent him down to Gihon Spring with Zadok the priest, Nathan the prophet, and Benaiah son of Jehoiada, protected by the king's bodyguard. They had him ride on the king's own mule, ⁴⁵and Zadok and Nathan have anointed him at Gihon Spring as the new king. They have just returned, and the whole city is celebrating and rejoicing. That's what all the noise is about. ⁴⁶What's more, Solomon is now sitting on the royal throne as king. ⁴⁷And all the royal officials have gone to King David and congratulated him, saying, 'May your God make Solomon's fame even greater than your own, and may Solomon's reign be even greater than yours!' Then the king bowed his head in worship as he lay in his bed, ⁴⁸and he said, 'Praise the Lord, the God of Israel, who today has chosen a successor to sit on my throne while I am still alive to see it.'"

⁴⁹Then all of Adonijah's guests jumped up in panic from the banquet table and quickly scattered. ⁵⁰Adonijah was afraid of Solomon, so he rushed to the sacred tent and grabbed on to the horns of the altar. ⁵¹Word soon reached Solomon that Adonijah had seized the horns of the altar in fear, and that he was pleading, "Let King Solomon swear today that he will not kill me!"

⁵²Solomon replied, "If he proves himself to be loyal, not a hair on his head will be touched. But if he makes trouble, he will die." ⁵³So King Solomon summoned Adonijah, and they brought him down from the altar. He came and bowed respectfully before King Solomon, who dismissed him, saying, "Go on home."

2 DAVID'S FINAL INSTRUCTIONS TO SOLOMON

As the time of King David's death approached, he gave this charge to his son Solomon:

²"I am going where everyone on earth must someday go. Take courage and be a man. ³Observe the requirements of the Lord your God, and follow all his ways. Keep the decrees, commands, regulations, and laws written in the Law of Moses so that you will be successful in all you do and wherever you go. ⁴If you do this, then the Lord will keep the promise he made to me. He told me, 'If your descendants live as

they should and follow me faithfully with all their heart and soul, one of them will always sit on the throne of Israel.'

⁵"And there is something else. You know what Joab son of Zeruiah did to me when he murdered my two army commanders, Abner son of Ner and Amasa son of Jether. He pretended that it was an act of war, but it was done in a time of peace,* staining his belt and sandals with innocent blood.* ⁶Do with him what you think best, but don't let him grow old and go to his grave in peace.*

⁷"Be kind to the sons of Barzillai of Gilead. Make them permanent guests at your table, for they took care of me when I fled from your brother Absalom.

⁸"And remember Shimei son of Gera, the man from Bahurim in Benjamin. He cursed me with a terrible curse as I was fleeing to Mahanaim. When he came down to meet me at the Jordan River, I swore by the Lord that I would not kill him. ⁹But that oath does not make him innocent. You are a wise man, and you will know how to arrange a bloody death for him.*"

¹⁰Then David died and was buried with his ancestors in the City of David. ¹¹David had reigned over Israel for forty years, seven of them in Hebron and thirty-three in Jerusalem. ¹²Solomon became king and sat on the throne of David his father, and his kingdom was firmly established.

SOLOMON ESTABLISHES HIS RULE ¹³One day Adonijah, whose mother was Haggith, came to see Bathsheba, Solomon's mother. "Have you come with peaceful intentions?" she asked him.

....

SEEK GOD FIRST
(1:49-50) Sometimes it takes getting caught before someone is willing to give up his or her scheme. When Adonijah learned that his plans to usurp the throne of Israel had been exposed, he panicked and ran to the altar—the highest symbol of God's mercy and forgiveness. If Adonijah had first considered what God wanted, he might have avoided trouble. Do you check out what God has to say before you make plans or after? Don't wait until you have made a mess of things to run to God; it's much better to seek God's guidance before you act. Unlike Adonijah, you don't have to learn the hard way.

AN ALLIANCE WORTH MAKING
(2:13-25) This conspiracy to gain the throne of Israel was like an episode of Survivor. Adonijah tried to make an alliance with Solomon's mother. But Solomon knew that Adonijah wanted to use his mother to gain the throne for himself. Many people today try to form alliances to gain power or status. Consider your motives carefully before making alliances with others. If you want what God wants, you only need one ally—God.

2:5a Or He murdered them during a time of peace as revenge for deaths they had caused in time of war.   **2:5b** As in some Greek and Old Latin manuscripts; Hebrew reads with the blood of war.
2:6 Hebrew don't let his white head go down to Sheol in peace.
2:9 Hebrew how to bring his white head down to Sheol in blood.

"Yes," he said, "I come in peace. ¹⁴In fact, I have a favor to ask of you."

"What is it?" she asked.

¹⁵He replied, "As you know, the kingdom was rightfully mine; all Israel wanted me to be the next king. But the tables were turned, and the kingdom went to my brother instead; for that is the way the LORD wanted it. ¹⁶So now I have just one favor to ask of you. Please don't turn me down."

"What is it?" she asked.

¹⁷He replied, "Speak to King Solomon on my behalf, for I know he will do anything you request. Ask him to let me marry Abishag, the girl from Shunem."

¹⁸"All right," Bathsheba replied. "I will speak to the king for you."

¹⁹So Bathsheba went to King Solomon to speak on Adonijah's behalf. The king rose from his throne to meet her, and he bowed down before her. When he sat down on his throne again, the king ordered that a throne be brought for his mother, and she sat at his right hand.

²⁰"I have one small request to make of you," she said. "I hope you won't turn me down."

"What is it, my mother?" he asked. "You know I won't refuse you."

²¹"Then let your brother Adonijah marry Abishag, the girl from Shunem," she replied.

²²"How can you possibly ask me to give Abishag to Adonijah?" King Solomon demanded. "You might as well ask me to give him the kingdom! You know that he is my older brother, and that he has Abiathar the priest and Joab son of Zeruiah on his side."

²³Then King Solomon made a vow before the LORD: "May God strike me and even kill me if Adonijah has not sealed his fate with this request. ²⁴The LORD has confirmed me and placed me on the throne of my father, David; he has established my dynasty as he promised. So as surely as the LORD lives, Adonijah will die this very day!" ²⁵So King Solomon ordered Benaiah son of Jehoiada to execute him, and Adonijah was put to death.

²⁶Then the king said to Abiathar the priest, "Go back to your home in Anathoth. You deserve to die, but I will not kill you now, because you carried the Ark of the Sovereign LORD for David my father and you shared all his hardships." ²⁷So Solomon deposed Abiathar from his position as priest of the LORD, thereby fulfilling the prophecy the LORD had given at Shiloh concerning the descendants of Eli.

²⁸Joab had not joined Absalom's earlier rebellion, but he had joined Adonijah's rebellion. So when Joab heard about Adonijah's death, he ran to the sacred tent of the LORD and grabbed on to the horns of the altar. ²⁹When this was reported to King Solomon, he sent Benaiah son of Jehoiada to execute him.

³⁰Benaiah went to the sacred tent of the LORD and said to Joab, "The king orders you to come out!"

But Joab answered, "No, I will die here."

So Benaiah returned to the king and told him what Joab had said.

³¹"Do as he said," the king replied. "Kill him there beside the altar and bury him. This will remove the guilt of Joab's senseless murders from me and from my father's family. ³²The LORD will repay him* for the murders of two men who were more righteous and better than he. For my father knew nothing about the deaths of Abner son of Ner, commander of the army of Israel, and of Amasa son of Jether, commander of the army of Judah. ³³May their blood be on Joab and his descendants forever, and may the LORD grant peace forever to David, his descendants, his dynasty, and his throne."

³⁴So Benaiah son of Jehoiada returned to the sacred tent and killed Joab, and he was buried at his home in the wilderness. ³⁵Then the king appointed Benaiah to command the army in place of Joab, and he installed Zadok the priest to take the place of Abiathar.

³⁶The king then sent for Shimei and told him, "Build a house here in Jerusalem and live there. But don't step outside the city to go anywhere else. ³⁷On the day you so much as cross the Kidron Valley, you will surely die; and your blood will be on your own head."

³⁸Shimei replied, "Your sentence is fair; I will do whatever my lord the king commands." So Shimei lived in Jerusalem for a long time.

³⁹But three years later two of Shimei's slaves ran away to King Achish son of Maacah of Gath. When Shimei learned where they were, ⁴⁰he saddled his donkey and went to Gath to search for them. When he found them, he brought them back to Jerusalem.

⁴¹Solomon heard that Shimei had left Jerusalem and had gone to Gath and returned. ⁴²So the king sent for Shimei and demanded, "Didn't I make you swear by the LORD and warn you not to go anywhere else or you would surely die? And you replied, 'The sentence is fair; I will do as you say.' ⁴³Then why haven't you kept your oath to the LORD and obeyed my command?"

⁴⁴The king also said to Shimei, "You certainly remember all the wicked things you did to my father, David. May the LORD now bring that evil

2:32 Hebrew *will return his blood on his own head.*

on your own head. 45But may I, King Solomon, receive the LORD's blessings, and may one of David's descendants always sit on this throne in the presence of the LORD." 46Then, at the king's command, Benaiah son of Jehoiada took Shimei outside and killed him.

So the kingdom was now firmly in Solomon's grip.

3 **SOLOMON ASKS FOR WISDOM** Solomon made an alliance with Pharaoh, the king of Egypt, and married one of his daughters. He brought her to live in the City of David until he could finish building his palace and the Temple of the LORD and the wall around the city. 2At that time the people of Israel sacrificed their offerings at local places of worship, for a temple honoring the name of the LORD had not yet been built.

3Solomon loved the LORD and followed all the decrees of his father, David, except that Solomon, too, offered sacrifices and burned incense at the local places of worship. 4The most important of these places of worship was at Gibeon, so the king went there and sacrificed 1,000 burnt offerings. 5That night the LORD appeared to Solomon in a dream, and God said, "What do you want? Ask, and I will give it to you!"

6Solomon replied, "You showed faithful love to your servant my father, David, because he was honest and true and faithful to you. And you have continued your faithful love to him today by giving him a son to sit on his throne.

7"Now, O LORD my God, you have made me king instead of my father, David, but I am like a little child who doesn't know his way around. 8And here I am in the midst of your own chosen people, a nation so great and numerous they cannot be counted! 9Give me an understanding heart so that I can govern your people well and know the difference between right and wrong. For who by himself is able to govern this great people of yours?"

10The Lord was pleased that Solomon had asked for wisdom. 11So God replied, "Because you have asked for wisdom in governing my people with justice and have not asked for a long life or wealth or the death of your enemies—12I will give you what you asked for! I will give you a wise and understanding heart such as no one else has had or ever will have!

INROADS
(3:1) Marriage between royal families was a common practice in the ancient Near East because it secured peace. Although Solomon's marital alliances built friendships with surrounding nations, they were also the beginning of his downfall. These relationships became inroads for heathen ideas and practices. Solomon's foreign wives brought their idols to Jerusalem and eventually lured him into idolatry (11:1-8).

We can easily minimize religious differences in order to encourage the development of a friendship. But seemingly small differences can have an enormous impact upon a relationship. God gives us standards to follow for all our relationships, including marriage. If we follow God's will, we will not be lured away from our true focus.

WISE GUY
(3:5-9) When given a chance to have anything in the world, Solomon asked for wisdom to rule his people. God invites us to ask for wisdom and promises to give it (see Jas 1:5). But gaining wisdom won't guarantee that life will always be problem free. Having wisdom also won't mean that you automatically know everything. Notice that Solomon asked for wisdom to carry out his job; he did not ask God to do the job for him. We should not ask God to do for us what he wants to equip us to do ourselves. Instead, we should ask God to give us the wisdom to know what to do and the courage to follow through on it. Wisdom starts with the realization that God is the only one who truly knows all (see Prov 1:7).

I WONDER...

With so many things out there that I want and so many things I know I need, how do I know what to pray for?

Many people find themselves overwhelmed by what to pray for. They approach God like he's a department store: so much to choose from, so little time to shop. Does that describe you?

God told Solomon that he would give him anything he wanted. All he had to do was ask for it. Solomon's choice showed that the gift had already been given—he asked for wisdom. God not only gave him wisdom, he also added riches and honor as a bonus (see 1 Kgs 3:3-14).

Still wondering what to ask God for? You could follow Solomon's example. Choose a request that will honor God and help others. You might pray for character qualities (like patience, self-control, gentleness) that will help you get along better with other people and will help point others toward Christ. Another example is praying for the health of someone who is sick (Jas 5:14-16).

When you have needs you should never be afraid to ask God to meet them. He loves to answer the prayers of his children (see Luke 11:9-13)! As you pray, however, know that God has the right to answer whenever and however he chooses.

¹³And I will also give you what you did not ask for—riches and fame! No other king in all the world will be compared to you for the rest of your life! ¹⁴And if you follow me and obey my decrees and my commands as your father, David, did, I will give you a long life."

¹⁵Then Solomon woke up and realized it had been a dream. He returned to Jerusalem and stood before the Ark of the Lord's Covenant, where he sacrificed burnt offerings and peace offerings. Then he invited all his officials to a great banquet.

SOLOMON JUDGES WISELY ¹⁶Some time later two prostitutes came to the king to have an argument settled. ¹⁷"Please, my lord," one of them began, "this woman and I live in the same house. I gave birth to a baby while she was with me in the house. ¹⁸Three days later this woman also had a baby. We were alone; there were only two of us in the house.

¹⁹"But her baby died during the night when she rolled over on it. ²⁰Then she got up in the night and took my son from beside me while I was asleep. She laid her dead child in my arms and took mine to sleep beside her. ²¹And in the morning when I tried to nurse my son, he was dead! But when I looked more closely in the morning light, I saw that it wasn't my son at all."

²²Then the other woman interrupted, "It certainly was your son, and the living child is mine."

"No," the first woman said, "the living child is mine, and the dead one is yours." And so they argued back and forth before the king.

²³Then the king said, "Let's get the facts straight. Both of you claim the living child is yours, and each says that the dead one belongs to the other. ²⁴All right, bring me a sword." So a sword was brought to the king.

²⁵Then he said, "Cut the living child in two, and give half to one woman and half to the other!"

²⁶Then the woman who was the real mother of the living child, and who loved him very much, cried out, "Oh no, my lord! Give her the child—please do not kill him!"

But the other woman said, "All right, he will be neither yours nor mine; divide him between us!"

²⁷Then the king said, "Do not kill the child, but give him to the woman who wants him to live, for she is his mother!"

²⁸When all Israel heard the king's decision, the people were in awe of the king, for they saw the wisdom God had given him for rendering justice.

4 SOLOMON'S OFFICIALS AND GOVERNORS
King Solomon now ruled over all Israel, ²and these were his high officials:

Azariah son of Zadok was the priest.
³ Elihoreph and Ahijah, the sons of Shisha, were court secretaries.
Jehoshaphat son of Ahilud was the royal historian.
⁴ Benaiah son of Jehoiada was commander of the army.
Zadok and Abiathar were priests.
⁵ Azariah son of Nathan was in charge of the district governors.
Zabud son of Nathan, a priest, was a trusted adviser to the king.
⁶ Ahishar was manager of the palace property.
Adoniram son of Abda was in charge of the labor force.

⁷Solomon also had twelve district governors who were over all Israel. They were responsible for providing food for the king's household. Each of them arranged provisions for one month of the year. ⁸These are the names of the twelve governors:

Ben-hur, in the hill country of Ephraim.
⁹ Ben-deker, in Makaz, Shaalbim, Beth-shemesh, and Elon-bethhanan.
¹⁰ Ben-hesed, in Arubboth, including Socoh and all the land of Hepher.
¹¹ Ben-abinadab, in all of Naphoth-dor.* (He was married to Taphath, one of Solomon's daughters.)
¹² Baana son of Ahilud, in Taanach and Megiddo, all of Beth-shan* near Zarethan below Jezreel, and all the territory from Beth-shan to Abel-meholah and over to Jokmeam.
¹³ Ben-geber, in Ramoth-gilead, including the Towns of Jair (named for Jair of the tribe of Manasseh*) in Gilead, and in the Argob region of Bashan, including sixty large fortified towns with bronze bars on their gates.
¹⁴ Ahinadab son of Iddo, in Mahanaim.
¹⁵ Ahimaaz, in Naphtali. (He was married to Basemath, another of Solomon's daughters.)
¹⁶ Baana son of Hushai, in Asher and in Aloth.
¹⁷ Jehoshaphat son of Paruah, in Issachar.
¹⁸ Shimei son of Ela, in Benjamin.
¹⁹ Geber son of Uri, in the land of Gilead,*

4:11 Hebrew *Naphath-dor,* a variant spelling of Naphoth-dor. **4:12** Hebrew *Beth-shean,* a variant spelling of Beth-shan; also in 4:12b. **4:13** Hebrew *Jair son of Manasseh;* compare 1 Chr 2:22. **4:19a** Greek version reads *of Gad;* compare 4:13.

including the territories of King Sihon of the Amorites and King Og of Bashan. There was also one governor over the land of Judah.*

SOLOMON'S PROSPERITY AND WISDOM

²⁰The people of Judah and Israel were as numerous as the sand on the seashore. They were very contented, with plenty to eat and drink. ²¹*Solomon ruled over all the kingdoms from the Euphrates River* in the north to the land of the Philistines and the border of Egypt in the south. The conquered peoples of those lands sent tribute money to Solomon and continued to serve him throughout his lifetime.

²²The daily food requirements for Solomon's palace were 150 bushels of choice flour and 300 bushels of meal*; ²³also 10 oxen from the fattening pens, 20 pasture-fed cattle, 100 sheep or goats, as well as deer, gazelles, roe deer, and choice poultry.*

²⁴Solomon's dominion extended over all the kingdoms west of the Euphrates River, from Tiphsah to Gaza. And there was peace on all his borders. ²⁵During the lifetime of Solomon, all of Judah and Israel lived in peace and safety. And from Dan in the north to Beersheba in the south, each family had its own home and garden.*

²⁶Solomon had 4,000* stalls for his chariot horses, and he had 12,000 horses.*

²⁷The district governors faithfully provided food for King Solomon and his court; each made sure nothing was lacking during the month assigned to him. ²⁸They also brought the necessary barley and straw for the royal horses in the stables.

²⁹God gave Solomon very great wisdom and understanding, and knowledge as vast as the sands of the seashore. ³⁰In fact, his wisdom exceeded that of all the wise men of the East and the wise men of Egypt. ³¹He was wiser than anyone else, including Ethan the Ezrahite and the sons of Mahol—Heman, Calcol, and Darda. His fame spread throughout all the surrounding nations. ³²He composed some 3,000 proverbs and wrote 1,005 songs. ³³He could speak with authority about all kinds of plants, from

the great cedar of Lebanon to the tiny hyssop that grows from cracks in a wall. He could also speak about animals, birds, small creatures, and fish. ³⁴And kings from every nation sent their ambassadors to listen to the wisdom of Solomon.

5 PREPARATIONS FOR BUILDING THE TEMPLE

¹*King Hiram of Tyre had always been a loyal friend of David. When Hiram learned that David's son Solomon was the new king of Israel, he sent ambassadors to congratulate him.

²Then Solomon sent this message back to Hiram:

³"You know that my father, David, was not able to build a Temple to honor the name of the LORD his God because of the many wars waged against him by surrounding nations. He could not build until the LORD gave him victory over all his enemies. ⁴But now the LORD my God has given me peace on every side; I have no enemies, and all is well. ⁵So I am planning to build a Temple to honor the name of the LORD my God, just as he had instructed my father, David. For the LORD told him, 'Your son, whom I will place on your throne, will build the Temple to honor my name.'

⁶"Therefore, please command that cedars from Lebanon be cut for me. Let my men work alongside yours, and I will pay your men whatever wages you ask. As you know, there is no one among us who can cut timber like you Sidonians!"

⁷When Hiram received Solomon's message, he was very pleased and said, "Praise the LORD today for giving David a wise son to be king of the great nation of Israel." ⁸Then he sent this reply to Solomon:

"I have received your message, and I will supply all the cedar and cypress timber you need. ⁹My servants will bring the logs from the Lebanon mountains to the Mediterranean Sea* and make them into rafts and float them along the coast to whatever place you choose. Then we will break the rafts apart so you can carry the logs away. You can pay me by supplying me with food for my household."

¹⁰So Hiram supplied as much cedar and cypress timber as Solomon desired. ¹¹In return, Solomon sent him an annual payment of 100,000 bushels* of wheat for his household and 110,000 gallons* of pure olive oil. ¹²So the

4:19b As in some Greek manuscripts; Hebrew lacks *of Judah*. The meaning of the Hebrew is uncertain.   **4:21a** Verses 4:21-34 are numbered 5:1-14 in Hebrew text.   **4:21b** Hebrew *the river;* also in 4:24.   **4:22** Hebrew *30 cors* [5.5 kiloliters] *of choice flour and 60 cors* [11 kiloliters] *of meal.*   **4:23** Or *and fattened geese.*   **4:25** Hebrew *each family lived under its own grapevine and under its own fig tree.*   **4:26a** As in some Greek manuscripts (see also 2 Chr 9:25); Hebrew reads *40,000.*   **4:26b** Or *12,000 charioteers.*   **5:1** Verses 5:1-18 are numbered 5:15-32 in Hebrew text.   **5:9** Hebrew *the sea.*   **5:11a** Hebrew *20,000 cors* [3,640 kiloliters].   **5:11b** As in Greek version, which reads *20,000 baths* [420 kiloliters] (see also 2 Chr 2:10); Hebrew reads *20 cors,* about 800 gallons or 3.6 kiloliters in volume.

LORD gave wisdom to Solomon, just as he had promised. And Hiram and Solomon made a formal alliance of peace.

¹³Then King Solomon conscripted a labor force of 30,000 men from all Israel. ¹⁴He sent them to Lebanon in shifts, 10,000 every month, so that each man would be one month in Lebanon and two months at home. Adoniram was in charge of this labor force. ¹⁵Solomon also had 70,000 common laborers, 80,000 quarry workers in the hill country, ¹⁶and 3,600* foremen to supervise the work. ¹⁷At the king's command, they quarried large blocks of high-quality stone and shaped them to make the foundation of the Temple. ¹⁸Men from the city of Gebal helped Solomon's and Hiram's builders prepare the timber and stone for the Temple.

6 SOLOMON BUILDS THE TEMPLE It was in midspring, in the month of Ziv,* during the fourth year of Solomon's reign, that he began to construct the Temple of the LORD. This was 480 years after the people of Israel were rescued from their slavery in the land of Egypt.

²The Temple that King Solomon built for the LORD was 90 feet long, 30 feet wide, and 45 feet high.* ³The entry room at the front of the Temple was 30 feet* wide, running across the entire width of the Temple. It projected outward 15 feet* from the front of the Temple. ⁴Solomon also made narrow recessed windows throughout the Temple.

⁵He built a complex of rooms against the outer walls of the Temple, all the way around the sides and rear of the building. ⁶The complex

was three stories high, the bottom floor being 7½ feet wide, the second floor 9 feet wide, and the top floor 10½ feet wide.* The rooms were connected to the walls of the Temple by beams resting on ledges built out from the wall. So the beams were not inserted into the walls themselves.

⁷The stones used in the construction of the Temple were finished at the quarry, so there was no sound of hammer, ax, or any other iron tool at the building site.

⁸The entrance to the bottom floor* was on the south side of the Temple. There were winding stairs going up to the second floor, and another flight of stairs between the second and third floors. ⁹After completing the Temple structure, Solomon put in a ceiling made of cedar beams and planks. ¹⁰As already stated, he built a complex of rooms on three sides of the building, attached to the Temple walls by cedar timbers. Each story of the complex was 7½ feet* high.

¹¹Then the LORD gave this message to Solomon: ¹²"Concerning this Temple you are building, if you keep all my decrees and regulations and obey all my commands, I will fulfill through you the promise I made to your father, David. ¹³I will live among the Israelites and will never abandon my people Israel."

THE TEMPLE'S INTERIOR ¹⁴So Solomon finished building the Temple. ¹⁵The entire inside, from floor to ceiling, was paneled with wood. He paneled the walls and ceilings with cedar, and he used planks of cypress for the floors. ¹⁶He partitioned off an inner sanctuary—the Most Holy Place—at the far end of the Temple. It was 30 feet deep and was paneled with cedar from floor to ceiling. ¹⁷The main room of the Temple, outside the Most Holy Place, was 60 feet* long. ¹⁸Cedar paneling completely covered the stone walls throughout the Temple, and the paneling was decorated with carvings of gourds and open flowers.

¹⁹He prepared the inner sanctuary at the far end of the Temple, where the Ark of the LORD's Covenant would be placed. ²⁰This inner sanctuary was 30 feet long, 30 feet wide, and 30 feet high. He overlaid the inside with solid gold. He

....

FAMILY TIME

(5:13-14) Solomon drafted three times the number of workers needed for the Temple project and arranged their schedules so they wouldn't have to be away from home for long periods of time. This showed his concern for the welfare of his workers and the importance he placed on family life. The strength of a nation is in direct proportion to the strength of its families. Solomon wisely recognized that family time should be a top priority in the lives of his workers. Is spending time with your family one of your top priorities?

RESPECT

(6:7) The people's respect for God extended to every aspect of constructing the Temple. Not only were the best materials used, the sound of a hammer or any tool was not heard at the building site. Doing so required incredibly accurate measuring. It also meant cutting the stone miles away at the quarry. This detail is recorded not to teach how to build a church but to show the importance of demonstrating care, concern, honor, and respect for God and his sanctuary. Do you believe that God deserves this kind of respect? How do you show your respect for God?

5:16 As in some Greek manuscripts (see also 2 Chr 2:2, 18); Hebrew reads *3,300*. **6:1** Hebrew *It was in the month of Ziv, which is the second month.* This month of the ancient Hebrew lunar calendar usually occurs within the months of April and May. **6:2** Hebrew *60 cubits* [27.6 meters] *long, 20 cubits* [9.2 meters] *wide, and 30 cubits* [13.8 meters] *high.* **6:3a** Hebrew *20 cubits* [9.2 meters]; also in 6:16, 20. **6:3b** Hebrew *10 cubits* [4.6 meters]. **6:6** Hebrew *the bottom floor being 5 cubits* [2.3 meters] *wide, the second floor 6 cubits* [2.8 meters] *wide, and the top floor 7 cubits* [3.2 meters] *wide.* **6:8** As in Greek version; Hebrew reads *middle floor.* **6:10** Hebrew *5 cubits* [2.3 meters]. **6:17** Hebrew *40 cubits* [18.4 meters].

also overlaid the altar made of cedar.* ²¹Then Solomon overlaid the rest of the Temple's interior with solid gold, and he made gold chains to protect the entrance* to the Most Holy Place. ²²So he finished overlaying the entire Temple with gold, including the altar that belonged to the Most Holy Place.

²³He made two cherubim of wild olive* wood, each 15 feet* tall, and placed them in the inner sanctuary. ²⁴The wingspan of each of the cherubim was 15 feet, each wing being 7½ feet* long. ²⁵The two cherubim were identical in shape and size; ²⁶each was 15 feet tall. ²⁷He placed them side by side in the inner sanctuary of the Temple. Their outspread wings reached from wall to wall, while their inner wings touched at the center of the room. ²⁸He overlaid the two cherubim with gold.

²⁹He decorated all the walls of the inner sanctuary and the main room with carvings of cherubim, palm trees, and open flowers. ³⁰He overlaid the floor in both rooms with gold.

³¹For the entrance to the inner sanctuary, he made double doors of wild olive wood with five-sided doorposts.* ³²These double doors were decorated with carvings of cherubim, palm trees, and open flowers. The doors, including the decorations of cherubim and palm trees, were overlaid with gold.

³³Then he made four-sided doorposts of wild olive wood for the entrance to the Temple. ³⁴There were two folding doors of cypress wood, and each door was hinged to fold back upon itself. ³⁵These doors were decorated with carvings of cherubim, palm trees, and open flowers—all overlaid evenly with gold.

³⁶The walls of the inner courtyard were built so that there was one layer of cedar beams between every three layers of finished stone.

³⁷The foundation of the LORD's Temple was laid in midspring, in the month of Ziv,* during the fourth year of Solomon's reign. ³⁸The entire building was completed in every detail by midautumn, in the month of Bul,* during the eleventh year of his reign. So it took seven years to build the Temple.

7 SOLOMON BUILDS HIS PALACE Solomon also built a palace for himself, and it took him thirteen years to complete the construction.

²One of Solomon's buildings was called the Palace of the Forest of Lebanon. It was 150 feet long, 75 feet wide, and 45 feet high.* There were four rows of cedar pillars, and great cedar beams rested on the pillars. ³The hall had a cedar roof. Above the beams on the pillars were forty-five side rooms,* arranged in three tiers of fifteen each. ⁴On each end of the long hall were three rows of windows facing each other. ⁵All the doorways and doorposts* had rectangular frames and were arranged in sets of three, facing each other.

⁶Solomon also built the Hall of Pillars, which was 75 feet long and 45 feet wide.* There was a porch in front, along with a canopy supported by pillars.

⁷Solomon also built the throne room, known as the Hall of Justice, where he sat to hear legal matters. It was paneled with cedar from floor to ceiling.* ⁸Solomon's living quarters surrounded a courtyard behind this hall, and they were constructed the same way. He also built similar living quarters for Pharaoh's daughter, whom he had married.

⁹From foundation to eaves, all these buildings were built from huge blocks of high-quality stone, cut with saws and trimmed to exact measure on all sides. ¹⁰Some of the huge foundation stones were 15 feet long, and some were 12 feet* long. ¹¹The blocks of high-quality stone used in the walls were also cut to measure, and cedar beams were also used. ¹²The walls of the great courtyard were built so that there was one layer of cedar beams between every three layers of finished stone, just like the walls of the inner courtyard of the LORD's Temple with its entry room.

FURNISHINGS FOR THE TEMPLE ¹³King Solomon then asked for a man named Huram* to come from Tyre. ¹⁴He was half Israelite, since his mother was a widow from the tribe of Naphtali, and his father had been a craftsman in bronze from Tyre. Huram was extremely skillful and talented in any work in bronze, and he came to do all the metal work for King Solomon.

¹⁵Huram cast two bronze pillars, each 27 feet tall and 18 feet in circumference.* ¹⁶For the tops of the pillars he cast bronze

---

6:20 Or *overlaid the altar with cedar.* The meaning of the Hebrew is uncertain. **6:21** Or *to draw curtains across.* The meaning of the Hebrew is uncertain. **6:23a** Or *pine;* Hebrew reads *oil tree;* also in 6:31, 33. **6:23b** Hebrew *10 cubits* [4.6 meters]; also in 6:24, 26. **6:24** Hebrew *5 cubits* [2.3 meters]. **6:31** The meaning of the Hebrew is uncertain. **6:37** Hebrew *was laid in the month of Ziv.* This month of the ancient Hebrew lunar calendar usually occurs within the months of April and May. **6:38** Hebrew *by the month of Bul, which is the eighth month.* This month of the ancient Hebrew lunar calendar usually occurs within the months of October and November. **7:2** Hebrew *100 cubits* [46 meters] *long, 50 cubits* [23 meters] *wide, and 30 cubits* [13.5 meters] *high.* **7:3** Or *45 rafters,* or *45 beams,* or *45 pillars.* The architectural details in 7:2-6 can be interpreted in many different ways. **7:5** Greek version reads *windows.* **7:6** Hebrew *50 cubits* [23 meters] *long and 30 cubits* [13.8 meters] *wide.* **7:7** As in Syriac version and Latin Vulgate; Hebrew reads *from floor to floor.* **7:10** Hebrew *10 cubits* [4.6 meters] . . . *8 cubits* [3.7 meters]. **7:13** Hebrew *Hiram* (also in 7:40, 45); compare 2 Chr 2:13. This is not the same person mentioned in 5:1. **7:15** Hebrew *18 cubits* [8.3 meters] *tall and 12 cubits* [5.5 meters] *in circumference.*

capitals, each 7½ feet* tall. ¹⁷Each capital was decorated with seven sets of latticework and interwoven chains. ¹⁸He also encircled the latticework with two rows of pomegranates to decorate the capitals over the pillars. ¹⁹The capitals on the columns inside the entry room were shaped like water lilies, and they were six feet* tall. ²⁰The capitals on the two pillars had 200 pomegranates in two rows around them, beside the rounded surface next to the latticework. ²¹Huram set the pillars at the entrance of the Temple, one toward the south and one toward the north. He named the one on the south Jakin, and the one on the north Boaz.* ²²The capitals on the pillars were shaped like water lilies. And so the work on the pillars was finished.

²³Then Huram cast a great round basin, 15 feet across from rim to rim, called the Sea. It was 7½ feet deep and about 45 feet in circumference.* ²⁴It was encircled just below its rim by two rows of decorative gourds. There were about six gourds per foot* all the way around, and they were cast as part of the basin.

²⁵The Sea was placed on a base of twelve bronze oxen,* all facing outward. Three faced north, three faced west, three faced south, and three faced east, and the Sea rested on them. ²⁶The walls of the Sea were about three inches* thick, and its rim flared out like a cup and resembled a water lily blossom. It could hold about 11,000 gallons* of water.

²⁷Huram also made ten bronze water carts, each 6 feet long, 6 feet wide, and 4½ feet tall.* ²⁸They were constructed with side panels braced with crossbars. ²⁹Both the panels and the crossbars were decorated with carved lions, oxen, and cherubim. Above and below the lions and oxen were wreath decorations. ³⁰Each of these carts had four bronze wheels and bronze axles. There were supporting posts for the bronze basins at the corners of the carts; these supports were decorated on each side with carvings of wreaths. ³¹The top of each cart had a rounded frame for the basin. It projected 1½ feet* above the cart's top like a round pedestal, and its opening was 2¼ feet* across; it was decorated on the outside with carvings of wreaths. The panels of the carts were square,

not round. ³²Under the panels were four wheels that were connected to axles that had been cast as one unit with the cart. The wheels were 2¼ feet in diameter ³³and were similar to chariot wheels. The axles, spokes, rims, and hubs were all cast from molten bronze.

³⁴There were handles at each of the four corners of the carts, and these, too, were cast as one unit with the cart. ³⁵Around the top of each cart was a rim nine inches wide.* The corner supports and side panels were cast as one unit with the cart. ³⁶Carvings of cherubim, lions, and palm trees decorated the panels and corner supports wherever there was room, and there were wreaths all around. ³⁷All ten water carts were the same size and were made alike, for each was cast from the same mold.

³⁸Huram also made ten smaller bronze basins, one for each cart. Each basin was six feet across and could hold 220 gallons* of water. ³⁹He set five water carts on the south side of the Temple and five on the north side. The great bronze basin called the Sea was placed near the southeast corner of the Temple. ⁴⁰He also made the necessary washbasins, shovels, and bowls.

So at last Huram completed everything King Solomon had assigned him to make for the Temple of the LORD:

⁴¹ the two pillars;
the two bowl-shaped capitals on top of the pillars;
the two networks of interwoven chains that decorated the capitals;
⁴² the 400 pomegranates that hung from the chains on the capitals (two rows of pomegranates for each of the chain networks that decorated the capitals on top of the pillars);
⁴³ the ten water carts holding the ten basins;
⁴⁴ the Sea and the twelve oxen under it;
⁴⁵ the ash buckets, the shovels, and the bowls.

Huram made all these things of burnished bronze for the Temple of the LORD, just as King Solomon had directed. ⁴⁶The king had them cast in clay molds in the Jordan Valley between

7:16 Hebrew 5 cubits [2.3 meters].   7:19 Hebrew 4 cubits [1.8 meters]; also in 7:38.   7:21 Jakin probably means "he establishes"; Boaz probably means "in him is strength."   7:23 Hebrew 10 cubits [4.6 meters] across. . . . 5 cubits [2.3 meters] deep and 30 cubits [13.8 meters] in circumference.   7:24 Or 20 gourds per meter; Hebrew reads 10 per cubit.   7:25 Hebrew 12 oxen; compare 2 Kgs 16:17, which specifies bronze oxen.   7:26a Hebrew a handbreadth [8 centimeters].   7:26b Hebrew 2,000 baths [42 kiloliters].   7:27 Hebrew 4 cubits [1.8 meters] long, 4 cubits wide, and 3 cubits [1.4 meters] high.   7:31a Hebrew a cubit [46 centimeters].   7:31b Hebrew 1½ cubits [69 centimeters]; also in 7:32.   7:35 Hebrew half a cubit wide [23 centimeters].   7:38 Hebrew 40 baths [840 liters].

....

WORSHIP ITEMS
(7:38-46) Huram designed items of bronze for use in the Temple. Today's churches contain different items for worship: stained-glass windows, crosses, pulpits, hymnals, and Communion tables. While the instruments of worship may change, the purpose—to give honor and praise to God—never does.

Succoth and Zarethan. [47]Solomon did not weigh all these things because there were so many; the weight of the bronze could not be measured.

[48]Solomon also made all the furnishings of the Temple of the LORD:

the gold altar;

the gold table for the Bread of the Presence;
[49] the lampstands of solid gold, five on the south and five on the north, in front of the Most Holy Place;

the flower decorations, lamps, and tongs—all of gold;
[50] the small bowls, lamp snuffers, bowls, dishes, and incense burners—all of solid gold;

the doors for the entrances to the Most Holy Place and the main room of the Temple, with their fronts overlaid with gold.

[51]So King Solomon finished all his work on the Temple of the LORD. Then he brought all the gifts his father, David, had dedicated—the silver, the gold, and the various articles—and he stored them in the treasuries of the LORD's Temple.

8 THE ARK BROUGHT TO THE TEMPLE Solomon then summoned to Jerusalem the elders of Israel and all the heads of the tribes—the leaders of the ancestral families of the Israelites. They were to bring the Ark of the LORD's Covenant to the Temple from its location in the City of David, also known as Zion. [2]So all the men of Israel assembled before King Solomon at the annual Festival of Shelters, which is held in early autumn in the month of Ethanim.*

[3]When all the elders of Israel arrived, the priests picked up the Ark. [4]The priests and Levites brought up the Ark of the LORD along with the special tent* and all the sacred items that had been in it. [5]There, before the Ark, King Solomon and the entire community of Israel sacrificed so many sheep, goats, and cattle that no one could keep count!

[6]Then the priests carried the Ark of the LORD's Covenant into the inner sanctuary of the Temple—the Most Holy Place—and placed it beneath the wings of the cherubim. [7]The cherubim spread their wings over the Ark,

8:2 Hebrew *at the festival in the month Ethanim, which is the seventh month.* The Festival of Shelters began on the fifteenth day of the seventh month of the ancient Hebrew lunar calendar. This day occurred in late September, October, or early November. 8:4 Hebrew *the Tent of Meeting;* i.e., the tent mentioned in 2 Sam 6:17 and 1 Chr 16:1. 8:9 Hebrew *at Horeb,* another name for Sinai. 8:13 Some Greek texts add the line *Is this not written in the Book of Jashar?*

forming a canopy over the Ark and its carrying poles. [8]These poles were so long that their ends could be seen from the Temple's main room—the Holy Place—but not from the outside. They are still there to this day. [9]Nothing was in the Ark except the two stone tablets that Moses had placed in it at Mount Sinai,* where the LORD made a covenant with the people of Israel when they left the land of Egypt.

[10]When the priests came out of the Holy Place, a thick cloud filled the Temple of the LORD. [11]The priests could not continue their service because of the cloud, for the glorious presence of the LORD filled the Temple.

SOLOMON PRAISES THE LORD [12]Then Solomon prayed, "O LORD, you have said that you would live in a thick cloud of darkness. [13]Now I have built a glorious Temple for you, a place where you can live forever!*"

[14]Then the king turned around to the entire community of Israel standing before him and gave this blessing: [15]"Praise the LORD, the God of Israel, who has kept the promise he made to my father, David. For he told my father, [16]'From the day I brought my people Israel out of Egypt, I have never chosen a city among any of the tribes of Israel as the place where a Temple should be built to honor my name. But I have chosen David to be king over my people Israel.'"

[17]Then Solomon said, "My father, David, wanted to build this Temple to honor the name of the LORD, the God of Israel. [18]But the LORD told him, 'You wanted to build the Temple to honor my name. Your intention is good, [19]but you are not the one to do it. One of your own sons will build the Temple to honor me.'

[20]"And now the LORD has fulfilled the promise he made, for I have become king in my father's place, and I now sit on the throne of Israel, just as the LORD promised. I have built this Temple to honor the name of the LORD, the God of Israel. [21]And I have prepared a place there for the Ark, which contains the covenant that the LORD made with our ancestors when he brought them out of Egypt."

SOLOMON'S PRAYER OF DEDICATION [22]Then Solomon stood before the altar of the LORD in front of the entire community of Israel. He lifted his hands toward heaven, [23]and he prayed,

"O LORD, God of Israel, there is no God like you in all of heaven above or on the earth below. You keep your covenant and show unfailing love to all who walk before you in wholehearted devotion. ²⁴You have kept your promise to your servant David, my father. You made that promise with your own mouth, and with your own hands you have fulfilled it today.

²⁵"And now, O LORD, God of Israel, carry out the additional promise you made to your servant David, my father. For you said to him, 'If your descendants guard their behavior and faithfully follow me as you have done, one of them will always sit on the throne of Israel.' ²⁶Now, O God of Israel, fulfill this promise to your servant David, my father.

²⁷"But will God really live on earth? Why, even the highest heavens cannot contain you. How much less this Temple I have built! ²⁸Nevertheless, listen to my prayer and my plea, O LORD my God. Hear the cry and the prayer that your servant is making to you today. ²⁹May you watch over this Temple night and day, this place where you have said, 'My name will be there.' May you always hear the prayers I make toward this place. ³⁰May you hear the humble and earnest requests from me and your people Israel when we pray toward this place. Yes, hear us from heaven where you live, and when you hear, forgive.

³¹"If someone wrongs another person and is required to take an oath of innocence in front of your altar in this Temple, ³²then hear from heaven and judge between your servants—the accuser and the accused. Punish the guilty as they deserve. Acquit the innocent because of their innocence.

³³"If your people Israel are defeated by their enemies because they have sinned against you, and if they turn to you and acknowledge your name and pray to you here in this Temple, ³⁴then hear from heaven and forgive the sin of your people Israel and return them to this land you gave their ancestors.

³⁵"If the skies are shut up and there is no rain because your people have sinned against you, and if they pray toward this Temple and acknowledge your name and turn from their sins because you have punished them, ³⁶then hear from heaven

and forgive the sins of your servants, your people Israel. Teach them to follow the right path, and send rain on your land that you have given to your people as their special possession.

³⁷"If there is a famine in the land or a plague or crop disease or attacks of locusts or caterpillars, or if your people's enemies are in the land besieging their towns—whatever disaster or disease there is—³⁸and if your people Israel pray about their troubles, raising their hands toward this Temple, ³⁹then hear from heaven where you live, and forgive. Give your people what their actions deserve, for you alone know each human heart. ⁴⁰Then they will fear you as long as they live in the land you gave to our ancestors.

⁴¹"In the future, foreigners who do not belong to your people Israel will hear of you. They will come from distant lands because of your name, ⁴²for they will hear of your great name and your strong hand and your powerful arm. And when they pray toward this Temple, ⁴³then hear from heaven where you live, and grant what they ask of you. In this way, all the people of the earth will come to know and fear you, just as your own people Israel do. They, too, will know that this Temple I have built honors your name.

⁴⁴"If your people go out where you send them to fight their enemies, and if they pray to the LORD by turning toward this city you have chosen and toward this Temple I have built to honor your name, ⁴⁵then hear their prayers from heaven and uphold their cause.

⁴⁶"If they sin against you—and who has never sinned?—you might become angry with them and let their enemies conquer them and take them captive to their land far away or near. ⁴⁷But in that land of exile, they might turn to you in repentance and pray, 'We have sinned, done evil, and acted wickedly.' ⁴⁸If they turn to you with their whole heart and soul in the land of their enemies and pray toward the land you gave to their ancestors—toward this city you have chosen, and toward this Temple I have built to honor your name—⁴⁹then hear their prayers and their petition from heaven where you live, and uphold their cause. ⁵⁰Forgive your people who have sinned against you. Forgive all the offenses they have committed against you. Make their captors merciful to them, ⁵¹for they are your people—your special possession—whom

---

GOD'S HOME
(8:27) Solomon declared that even the highest heavens couldn't contain God. Although the heavens can't contain him, isn't it amazing that he's willing to take up residence in those who love him? If you're a believer, that includes you. What are you doing to welcome him home?

you brought out of the iron-smelting furnace of Egypt.

⁵²"May your eyes be open to my requests and to the requests of your people Israel. May you hear and answer them whenever they cry out to you. ⁵³For when you brought our ancestors out of Egypt, O Sovereign LORD, you told your servant Moses that you had set Israel apart from all the nations of the earth to be your own special possession."

THE DEDICATION OF THE TEMPLE
⁵⁴When Solomon finished making these prayers and petitions to the LORD, he stood up in front of the altar of the LORD, where he had been kneeling with his hands raised toward heaven. ⁵⁵He stood and in a loud voice blessed the entire congregation of Israel:

⁵⁶"Praise the LORD who has given rest to his people Israel, just as he promised. Not one word has failed of all the wonderful promises he gave through his servant Moses. ⁵⁷May the LORD our God be with us as he was with our ancestors; may he never leave us or abandon us. ⁵⁸May he give us the desire to do his will in everything and to obey all the commands, decrees, and regulations that he gave our ancestors. ⁵⁹And may these words that I have prayed in the presence of the LORD be before him constantly, day and night, so that the LORD our God may give justice to me and to his people Israel, according to each day's needs. ⁶⁰Then people all over the earth will know that the LORD alone is God and there is no other. ⁶¹And may you be completely faithful to the LORD our God. May you always obey his decrees and commands, just as you are doing today."

⁶²Then the king and all Israel with him offered sacrifices to the LORD. ⁶³Solomon offered to the LORD a peace offering of 22,000 cattle and 120,000 sheep and goats. And so the king and all the people of Israel dedicated the Temple of the LORD.

⁶⁴That same day the king consecrated the central area of the courtyard in front of the LORD's Temple. He offered burnt offerings, grain offerings, and the fat of peace offerings there, because the bronze altar in the LORD's presence was too small to hold all the burnt offerings, grain offerings, and the fat of the peace offerings.

⁶⁵Then Solomon and all Israel celebrated the Festival of Shelters* in the presence of the LORD our God. A large congregation had gathered from as far away as Lebo-hamath in the north and the Brook of Egypt in the south. The celebration went on for fourteen days in all—seven days for the dedication of the altar and seven days for the Festival of Shelters.* ⁶⁶After the festival was over,* Solomon sent the people home. They blessed the king and went to their homes joyful and glad because the LORD had been good to his servant David and to his people Israel.

9 THE LORD'S RESPONSE TO SOLOMON
So Solomon finished building the Temple of the LORD, as well as the royal palace. He completed everything he had planned to do. ²Then the LORD appeared to Solomon a second time, as he had done before at Gibeon. ³The LORD said to him,

"I have heard your prayer and your petition. I have set this Temple apart to be holy—this place you have built where my name will be honored forever. I will always watch over it, for it is dear to my heart.

⁴"As for you, if you will follow me with integrity and godliness, as David your father did, obeying all my commands, decrees, and regulations, ⁵then I will establish the throne of your dynasty over Israel forever. For I made this promise to your father, David: 'One of your descendants will always sit on the throne of Israel.'

⁶"But if you or your descendants abandon me and disobey the commands and decrees I have given you, and if you serve and worship other gods, ⁷then I will uproot Israel from this land that I have given them. I will reject this Temple that I have made holy to honor my name. I will make Israel an object of mockery and ridicule among the nations. ⁸And though this Temple is impressive now, all who pass by will be appalled and will shake their heads in amazement. They will ask, 'Why did the LORD do such terrible things to this land and to this Temple?' ⁹"And the answer will be, 'Because his people abandoned the LORD their God,

---

8:65a Hebrew *the festival;* see note on 8:2. **8:65b** Hebrew *seven days and seven days, fourteen days;* compare parallel text at 2 Chr 7:8-10. **8:66** Hebrew *On the eighth day,* probably referring to the day following the seven-day Festival of Shelters; compare parallel text at 2 Chr 7:9-10.

PRAYER REQUESTS
(8:54-61) Solomon blessed the people and prayed for them. He asked for (1) God's continued presence among his people (8:57); (2) the desire to do God's will in everything (8:58, 61); (3) help with daily needs (8:59); (4) the desire and ability to obey God's laws and commands (8:58); and (5) the spread of God's Kingdom to the entire world (8:60). Are these requests also yours?

who brought their ancestors out of Egypt, and they worshiped other gods instead and bowed down to them. That is why the LORD has brought all these disasters on them.'"

SOLOMON'S AGREEMENT WITH HIRAM

¹⁰It took Solomon twenty years to build the LORD's Temple and his own royal palace. At the end of that time, ¹¹he gave twenty towns in the land of Galilee to King Hiram of Tyre. (Hiram had previously provided all the cedar and cypress timber and gold that Solomon had requested.) ¹²But when Hiram came from Tyre to see the towns Solomon had given him, he was not at all pleased with them. ¹³"What kind of towns are these, my brother?" he asked. So Hiram called that area Cabul (which means "worthless"), as it is still known today. ¹⁴Nevertheless, Hiram paid* Solomon 9,000 pounds* of gold.

SOLOMON'S MANY ACHIEVEMENTS

¹⁵This is the account of the forced labor that King Solomon conscripted to build the LORD's Temple, the royal palace, the supporting terraces,* the wall of Jerusalem, and the cities of Hazor, Megiddo, and Gezer. ¹⁶(Pharaoh, the king of Egypt, had attacked and captured Gezer, killing the Canaanite population and burning it down. He gave the city to his daughter as a wedding gift when she married Solomon. ¹⁷So Solomon rebuilt the city of Gezer.) He also built up the towns of Lower Beth-horon, ¹⁸Baalath, and Tamar* in the wilderness within his land. ¹⁹He built towns as supply centers and constructed towns where his chariots and horses* could be stationed. He built everything he desired in Jerusalem and Lebanon and throughout his entire realm.

²⁰There were still some people living in the land who were not Israelites, including Amorites, Hittites, Perizzites, Hivites, and Jebusites. ²¹These were descendants of the nations whom the people of Israel had not completely destroyed.* So Solomon conscripted them for his labor force, and they serve in the labor force to this day. ²²But Solomon did not conscript any of the Israelites for forced labor. Instead,

he assigned them to serve as fighting men, government officials, officers and captains in his army, commanders of his chariots, and charioteers. ²³Solomon appointed 550 of them to supervise the people working on his various projects.

²⁴Solomon moved his wife, Pharaoh's daughter, from the City of David to the new palace he had built for her. Then he constructed the supporting terraces.

²⁵Three times each year Solomon presented burnt offerings and peace offerings on the altar he had built for the LORD. He also burned incense to the LORD. And so he finished the work of building the Temple.

²⁶King Solomon also built a fleet of ships at Ezion-geber, a port near Elath* in the land of Edom, along the shore of the Red Sea.* ²⁷Hiram sent experienced crews of sailors to sail the ships with Solomon's men. ²⁸They sailed to Ophir and brought back to Solomon some sixteen tons* of gold.

10 VISIT OF THE QUEEN OF SHEBA

When the queen of Sheba heard of Solomon's fame, which brought honor to the name of the LORD,* she came to test him with hard questions. ²She arrived in Jerusalem with a large group of attendants and a great caravan of camels loaded with spices, large quantities of gold, and precious jewels. When she met with Solomon, she talked with him about everything she had on her mind. ³Solomon had answers for all her questions; nothing was too hard for the king to explain to her. ⁴When the queen of Sheba realized how very wise Solomon was, and when she saw the palace he had built, ⁵she was overwhelmed. She was also amazed at the food on his tables, the organization of his officials and their splendid clothing, the cup-bearers, and the burnt offerings Solomon made at the Temple of the LORD.

⁶She exclaimed to the king, "Everything I heard in my country about your achievements* and wisdom is true! ⁷I didn't believe what was said until I arrived here and saw it with my own eyes. In fact, I had not heard the half of it! Your wisdom and prosperity are far beyond what I was told. ⁸How happy your people* must

---

WHATEVER IT TAKES?

(9:16) At this time, Israel and Egypt were the major powers in the area. During Solomon's reign, the Egyptian king captured the city of Gezer. To regain the city, Solomon married one of Pharaoh's daughters. Intermarriage among royal families was common but was not endorsed by God (see Deut 7:3-4; 17:17). Like Solomon, are you willing to do whatever it takes to get what you want, even if you have to do something wrong? Is any goal really worth that?

9:14a Or *For Hiram had paid.* **9:14b** Hebrew *120 talents* [4,000 kilograms]. **9:15** Hebrew *the millo*; also in 9:24. The meaning of the Hebrew is uncertain. **9:18** An alternate reading in the Masoretic Text reads *Tadmor.* **9:19** Or *and charioteers.* **9:21** The Hebrew term used here refers to the complete consecration of things or people to the LORD, either by destroying them or by giving them as an offering. **9:26a** As in Greek version (see also 2 Kgs 14:22; 16:6); Hebrew reads *Eloth*, a variant spelling of Elath. **9:26b** Hebrew *sea of reeds.* **9:28** Hebrew *420 talents* [14 metric tons]. **10:1** Or *which was due to the name of the LORD.* The meaning of the Hebrew is uncertain. **10:6** Hebrew *your words.* **10:8** Greek and Syriac versions and Latin Vulgate read *your wives.*

be! What a privilege for your officials to stand here day after day, listening to your wisdom! ⁹Praise the LORD your God, who delights in you and has placed you on the throne of Israel. Because of the LORD's eternal love for Israel, he has made you king so you can rule with justice and righteousness."

¹⁰Then she gave the king a gift of 9,000 pounds* of gold, great quantities of spices, and precious jewels. Never again were so many spices brought in as those the queen of Sheba gave to King Solomon.

¹¹(In addition, Hiram's ships brought gold from Ophir, and they also brought rich cargoes of red sandalwood* and precious jewels. ¹²The king used the sandalwood to make railings for the Temple of the LORD and the royal palace, and to construct lyres and harps for the musicians. Never before or since has there been such a supply of sandalwood.)

¹³King Solomon gave the queen of Sheba whatever she asked for, besides all the customary gifts he had so generously given. Then she and all her attendants returned to their own land.

SOLOMON'S WEALTH AND SPLENDOR ¹⁴Each year Solomon received about 25 tons* of gold. ¹⁵This did not include the additional revenue he received from merchants and traders, all the kings of Arabia, and the governors of the land.

¹⁶King Solomon made 200 large shields of hammered gold, each weighing more than fifteen pounds.* ¹⁷He also made 300 smaller shields of hammered gold, each weighing nearly four pounds.* The king placed these shields in the Palace of the Forest of Lebanon.

¹⁸Then the king made a huge throne, decorated with ivory and overlaid with fine gold. ¹⁹The throne had six steps and a rounded back. There were armrests on both sides of the seat, and the figure of a lion stood on each side of the throne. ²⁰There were also twelve other lions, one standing on each end of the six steps. No other throne in all the world could be compared with it!

²¹All of King Solomon's drinking cups were solid gold, as were all the utensils in the Palace of the Forest of Lebanon. They were not made of silver, for silver was considered worthless in Solomon's day!

²²The king had a fleet of trading ships* that sailed with Hiram's fleet. Once every three years the ships returned, loaded with gold, silver, ivory, apes, and peacocks.*

²³So King Solomon became richer and wiser than any other king on earth. ²⁴People from every nation came to consult him and to hear the wisdom God had given him. ²⁵Year after year everyone who visited brought him gifts of silver and gold, clothing, weapons, spices, horses, and mules.

²⁶Solomon built up a huge force of chariots and horses.* He had 1,400 chariots and 12,000 horses. He stationed some of them in the chariot cities and some near him in Jerusalem. ²⁷The king made silver as plentiful in Jerusalem as stone. And valuable cedar timber was as common as the sycamore-fig trees that grow in the foothills of Judah.* ²⁸Solomon's horses were imported from Egypt* and from Cilicia*; the king's traders acquired them from Cilicia at the standard price. ²⁹At that time chariots from Egypt could be purchased for 600 pieces of silver,* and horses for 150 pieces of silver.* They were then exported to the kings of the Hittites and the kings of Aram.

11 SOLOMON'S MANY WIVES Now King Solomon loved many foreign women. Besides Pharaoh's daughter, he married women from Moab, Ammon, Edom, Sidon, and from among the Hittites. ²The LORD had clearly instructed the people of Israel, "You must not marry them, because they will turn your hearts to their gods." Yet Solomon insisted on loving them anyway. ³He had 700 wives of royal birth and 300 concubines. And in fact, they did turn his heart away from the LORD.

⁴In Solomon's old age, they turned his heart to worship other gods instead of being completely faithful to the LORD his God, as his father, David, had been. ⁵Solomon worshiped Ashtoreth, the goddess of the Sidonians,

*****

KNOW IT AND APPLY IT
(11:1-12) Although Solomon had clear instructions from God not to marry women from foreign nations (see Deut 7:3-4; 17:17), he chose to disregard God's commands and married not one, but many heathen wives. These wives led him away from God. This disobedience later led to the kingdom dividing. Unfortunately, disobedience is usually the catalyst for many problems today. God knows our human strengths and weaknesses, and his commands are always for our good. Knowing God's Word or even believing it isn't enough; we must follow his Word and apply it in all of our activities and decisions.

10:10 Hebrew *120 talents* [4,000 kilograms].   **10:11** Hebrew *almug wood;* also in 10:12.   **10:14** Hebrew *666 shekels* [23 metric tons].
10:16 Hebrew *600* [*shekels*] *of gold* [6.8 kilograms].   **10:17** Hebrew *3 minas* [1.8 kilograms].   **10:22a** Hebrew *fleet of ships of Tarshish.*
10:22b Or *and baboons.*   **10:26** Or *charioteers;* also in 10:26b.
10:27 Hebrew *the Shephelah.*   **10:28a** Possibly *Muzur,* a district near Cilicia; also in 10:29.   **10:28b** Hebrew *Kue,* probably another name for Cilicia.   **10:29a** Hebrew *600* [*shekels*] *of silver,* about 15 pounds or 6.8 kilograms in weight.   **10:29b** Hebrew *150* [*shekels*], about 3.8 pounds or 1.7 kilograms in weight.

and Molech,* the detestable god of the Ammonites. [6]In this way, Solomon did what was evil in the LORD's sight; he refused to follow the LORD completely, as his father, David, had done.

[7]On the Mount of Olives, east of Jerusalem,* he even built a pagan shrine for Chemosh, the detestable god of Moab, and another for Molech, the detestable god of the Ammonites. [8]Solomon built such shrines for all his foreign wives to use for burning incense and sacrificing to their gods.

[9]The LORD was very angry with Solomon, for his heart had turned away from the LORD, the God of Israel, who had appeared to him twice. [10]He had warned Solomon specifically about worshiping other gods, but Solomon did not listen to the LORD's command. [11]So now the LORD said to him, "Since you have not kept my covenant and have disobeyed my decrees, I will surely tear the kingdom away from you and give it to one of your servants. [12]But for the sake of your father, David, I will not do this while you are still alive. I will take the kingdom away from your son. [13]And even so, I will not take away the entire kingdom; I will let him be king of one tribe, for the sake of my servant David and for the sake of Jerusalem, my chosen city."

SOLOMON'S ADVERSARIES
[14]Then the LORD raised up Hadad the Edomite, a member of Edom's royal family, to be Solomon's adversary. [15]Years before, David had defeated Edom. Joab, his army commander, had stayed to bury some of the Israelite soldiers who had died in battle. While there, they killed every male in Edom. [16]Joab and the army of Israel had stayed there for six months, killing them.

[17]But Hadad and a few of his father's royal officials escaped and headed for Egypt. (Hadad was just a boy at the time.) [18]They set out from Midian and went to Paran, where others joined them. Then they traveled to Egypt and went to Pharaoh, who gave them a home, food, and some land. [19]Pharaoh grew very fond of Hadad, and he gave him his wife's sister in marriage—the sister of Queen Tahpenes. [20]She bore him a son named Genubath. Tahpenes raised him* in Pharaoh's palace among Pharaoh's own sons.

[21]When the news reached Hadad in Egypt that David and his commander Joab were both dead, he said to Pharaoh, "Let me return to my own country."

[22]"Why?" Pharaoh asked him. "What do you lack here that makes you want to go home?"

"Nothing," he replied. "But even so, please let me return home."

11:5 Hebrew *Milcom,* a variant spelling of Molech; also in 11:33.
11:7 Hebrew *On the mountain east of Jerusalem.*   11:20 As in Greek version; Hebrew reads *weaned him.*

....

PRESSURE
(11:4) Solomon handled great pressures in running the government, but he could not handle the pressures from his wives who wanted him to worship their gods. In marriage and other close friendships, it is difficult to resist pressure to compromise. Our love leads us to identify with the desires of those we care about.

CHOICES
dating

"Matt is so hot. I'm soooo thankful he's in my life." That's what Claire (who prefers to be called C.J.) says, even after five months of going out with Matt. Here's the scoop on their relationship:

February—C.J. brought Matt to some youth group meetings and activities. He told her that her church friends were "OK." Maybe they could also hang out with his friends. (He had never attended a youth group meeting before.)

March—C.J. asked Matt to the spring youth retreat. He just smiled and said, "Hey, C. (He always calls her C.), that's not my thing. But if you decide to blow off that retreat, I can score us some tickets to the Amps concert." (The Amps are only the hottest band ever.)

April—C.J. missed a couple more youth events in favor of partying with Matt and his friends.

May—C.J.'s church/youth group attendance dropped drastically. She quit youth choir.

June—C.J. had her first cigarette and beer. She also slept with Matt for the first time. After all, they're "in love."

July—C.J. and her parents fought almost all month because she wouldn't break up with Matt.

August—C.J. has now gone 4 1/2 months without reading her Bible. (She isn't even sure where it is.)

"Wait a minute!" you say. "Do Christian/non-Christian relationships always turn out bad? Haven't Christians fallen in love with non-Christians and led them to the Lord?" Yes, but that is rare. It's a sad fact that healthy Christian/non-Christian dating situations are the exception—not the rule.

First Kings 11:1-13 shows how you can get burned through close relationships with those who don't share your beliefs and values. Based on Solomon's experiences and 2 Corinthians 6:14, what advice would you have for C.J.?

²³God also raised up Rezon son of Eliada as Solomon's adversary. Rezon had fled from his master, King Hadadezer of Zobah, ²⁴and had become the leader of a gang of rebels. After David conquered Hadadezer, Rezon and his men fled to Damascus, where he became king. ²⁵Rezon was Israel's bitter adversary for the rest of Solomon's reign, and he made trouble, just as Hadad did. Rezon hated Israel intensely and continued to reign in Aram.

JEROBOAM REBELS AGAINST SOLOMON

²⁶Another rebel leader was Jeroboam son of Nebat, one of Solomon's own officials. He came from the town of Zeredah in Ephraim, and his mother was Zeruah, a widow.

²⁷This is the story behind his rebellion. Solomon was rebuilding the supporting terraces* and repairing the walls of the city of his father, David. ²⁸Jeroboam was a very capable young man, and when Solomon saw how industrious he was, he put him in charge of the labor force from the tribes of Ephraim and Manasseh, the descendants of Joseph.

²⁹One day as Jeroboam was leaving Jerusalem, the prophet Ahijah from Shiloh met him along the way. Ahijah was wearing a new cloak. The two of them were alone in a field, ³⁰and Ahijah took hold of the new cloak he was wearing and tore it into twelve pieces. ³¹Then he said to Jeroboam, "Take ten of these pieces, for this is what the Lord, the God of Israel, says: 'I am about to tear the kingdom from the hand of Solomon, and I will give ten of the tribes to you! ³²But I will leave him one tribe for the sake of my servant David and for the sake of Jerusalem, which I have chosen out of all the tribes of Israel. ³³For Solomon has* abandoned me and worshiped Ashtoreth, the goddess of the Sidonians; Chemosh, the god of Moab; and Molech, the god of the Ammonites. He has not followed my ways and done what is pleasing in my sight. He has not obeyed my decrees and regulations as David his father did.

³⁴"'But I will not take the entire kingdom from Solomon at this time. For the sake of my servant David, the one whom I chose and who obeyed my commands and decrees, I will keep Solomon as leader for the rest of his life. ³⁵But I will take the kingdom away from his son and give ten of the tribes to you. ³⁶His son will have one tribe so that the descendants of David my servant will continue to reign, shining

like a lamp in Jerusalem, the city I have chosen to be the place for my name. ³⁷And I will place you on the throne of Israel, and you will rule over all that your heart desires. ³⁸If you listen to what I tell you and follow my ways and do whatever I consider to be right, and if you obey my decrees and commands, as my servant David did, then I will always be with you. I will establish an enduring dynasty for you as I did for David, and I will give Israel to you. ³⁹Because of Solomon's sin I will punish the descendants of David—though not forever.'"

⁴⁰Solomon tried to kill Jeroboam, but he fled to King Shishak of Egypt and stayed there until Solomon died.

SUMMARY OF SOLOMON'S REIGN ⁴¹The rest of the events in Solomon's reign, including all his deeds and his wisdom, are recorded in *The Book of the Acts of Solomon*. ⁴²Solomon ruled in Jerusalem over all Israel for forty years. ⁴³When he died, he was buried in the City of David, named for his father. Then his son Rehoboam became the next king.

12 THE NORTHERN TRIBES REVOLT

Rehoboam went to Shechem, where all Israel had gathered to make him king. ²When Jeroboam son of Nebat heard of this, he returned from Egypt,* for he had fled to Egypt to escape from King Solomon. ³The leaders of Israel summoned him, and Jeroboam and the whole assembly of Israel went to speak with Rehoboam. ⁴"Your father was a hard master," they said. "Lighten the harsh labor demands and heavy taxes that your father imposed on us. Then we will be your loyal subjects."

⁵Rehoboam replied, "Give me three days to think this over. Then come back for my answer." So the people went away.

⁶Then King Rehoboam discussed the matter with the older men who had counseled his father, Solomon. "What is your advice?" he asked. "How should I answer these people?"

⁷The older counselors replied, "If you are willing to be a servant to these people today and

11:27 Hebrew *the millo.* The meaning of the Hebrew is uncertain. 11:33 As in Greek, Syriac, and Latin Vulgate; Hebrew reads *For they have.* 12:2 As in Greek version and Latin Vulgate (see also 2 Chr 10:2); Hebrew reads *he lived in Egypt.*

···

GOOD ADVICE
(12:1-8) Rehoboam asked for advice, but he didn't carefully evaluate that advice. If he had, Rehoboam would have realized that the advice offered by the older men was wiser than that of his peers. Want some tips for evaluating advice? (1) Ask if it is realistic, workable, and consistent with the Bible. (2) Determine if the results of following the advice will be fair, make improvements, and give a positive solution or direction. (3) Seek counsel from those who are more experienced. Advice is helpful only if we evaluate it with God's standards in mind.

THE APPEAL OF IDOLS

On the surface, the lives of the kings don't make sense. How could they run to idolatry so fast when they had God's Word (at least some of it), the prophets, and the example of David? Below are some of the reasons for the enticement of idols. As societies change and evolve, they often throw out norms and values no longer considered necessary or acceptable. Believers must be careful not to follow society's example when it discards God's Word. When society does that, only godlessness and evil remain.

THE APPEAL OF IDOLS	POWER	PLEASURE	PASSION	PRAISE AND POPULARITY
	The people wanted freedom from the authority of both God and the priests. They wanted their religion to fit their lifestyle, not their lifestyle to fit their religion.	Idol worship exalted sensuality without responsibility or guilt. People acted out the vicious and sensuous personalities of the gods they worshiped, thus gaining approval for their degraded lives.	Humanity was reduced to little more than animals. The people did not have to be viewed as unique individuals but could be exploited sexually, politically, and economically.	The high and holy nature of God was replaced by gods who were more a reflection of human nature, thus more culturally suitable to the people. These gods no longer required sacrifice, just a token of appeasement.
MODERN PARALLEL	People do not want to answer to a greater authority. God gives us the Holy Spirit's power to help others not to have power over others.	People turn pleasure into a god, seeking it at the expense of everything else. God calls us to seek the kind of pleasure that leads to long-range rewards instead of seeking pleasure that leads to long-range disaster.	Like animals, people let physical drives and passions rule them. God calls us to redirect our passions to areas that build others up instead of seeking passion that exploits others.	Sacrifice is seen as a self-inflicted punishment, making no sense. Success is to be sought at all costs. But God calls us to praise him and to praise those who honor him.

give them a favorable answer, they will always be your loyal subjects."

⁸But Rehoboam rejected the advice of the older men and instead asked the opinion of the young men who had grown up with him and were now his advisers. ⁹"What is your advice?" he asked them. "How should I answer these people who want me to lighten the burdens imposed by my father?"

¹⁰The young men replied, "This is what you should tell those complainers who want a lighter burden: 'My little finger is thicker than my father's waist! ¹¹Yes, my father laid heavy burdens on you, but I'm going to make them even heavier! My father beat you with whips, but I will beat you with scorpions!'"

¹²Three days later Jeroboam and all the people returned to hear Rehoboam's decision, just as the king had ordered. ¹³But Rehoboam spoke harshly to the people, for he rejected the advice of the older counselors ¹⁴and followed the counsel of his younger advisers. He told the people, "My father laid heavy burdens on you, but I'm going to make them even heavier! My father beat you with whips, but I will beat you with scorpions!"

¹⁵So the king paid no attention to the people.

This turn of events was the will of the LORD, for it fulfilled the LORD's message to Jeroboam son of Nebat through the prophet Ahijah from Shiloh.

¹⁶When all Israel realized that the king had refused to listen to them, they responded,

"Down with the dynasty of David!
  We have no interest in the son of Jesse.
Back to your homes, O Israel!
  Look out for your own house, O David!"

So the people of Israel returned home. ¹⁷But Rehoboam continued to rule over the Israelites who lived in the towns of Judah.

¹⁸King Rehoboam sent Adoniram,* who was in charge of the labor force, to restore order, but the people of Israel stoned him to death. When this news reached King Rehoboam, he quickly jumped into his chariot and fled to Jerusalem. ¹⁹And to this day the northern tribes of Israel have refused to be ruled by a descendant of David.

²⁰When the people of Israel learned of Jeroboam's return from Egypt, they called an assembly and made him king over all Israel. So

12:18 As in some Greek manuscripts and Syriac version (see also 4:6; 5:14); Hebrew reads *Adoram.*

only the tribe of Judah remained loyal to the family of David.

SHEMAIAH'S PROPHECY

²¹When Rehoboam arrived at Jerusalem, he mobilized the men of Judah and the tribe of Benjamin—180,000 select troops—to fight against the men of Israel and to restore the kingdom to himself.

²²But God said to Shemaiah, the man of God, ²³"Say to Rehoboam son of Solomon, king of Judah, and to all the people of Judah and Benjamin, and to the rest of the people, ²⁴'This is what the LORD says: Do not fight against your relatives, the Israelites. Go back home, for what has happened is my doing!'" So they obeyed the message of the LORD and went home, as the LORD had commanded.

JEROBOAM MAKES GOLD CALVES

²⁵Jeroboam then built up the city of Shechem in the hill country of Ephraim, and it became his capital. Later he went and built up the town of Peniel.*

²⁶Jeroboam thought to himself, "Unless I am careful, the kingdom will return to the dynasty of David. ²⁷When these people go to Jerusalem to offer sacrifices at the Temple of the LORD, they will again give their allegiance to King Rehoboam of Judah. They will kill me and make him their king instead."

²⁸So on the advice of his counselors, the king made two gold calves. He said to the people,* "It is too much trouble for you to worship in Jerusalem. Look, Israel, these are the gods who brought you out of Egypt!"

²⁹He placed these calf idols in Bethel and in Dan—at either end of his kingdom. ³⁰But this became a great sin, for the people worshiped the idols, traveling as far north as Dan to worship the one there.

³¹Jeroboam also erected buildings at the pagan shrines and ordained priests from the common people—those who were not from the priestly tribe of Levi. ³²And Jeroboam instituted a religious festival in Bethel, held on the fifteenth day of the eighth month,* in imitation of the annual Festival of Shelters in Judah. There at Bethel he himself offered sacrifices to the calves he had made, and he appointed priests for the pagan shrines he had made. ³³So on the fifteenth day of the eighth month, a day that he himself had designated, Jeroboam offered sacrifices on the altar at Bethel. He instituted a religious festival for Israel, and he went up to the altar to burn incense.

12:25 Hebrew *Penuel*, a variant spelling of Peniel.   **12:28** Hebrew *to them.*   **12:32** This day of the ancient Hebrew lunar calendar occurred in late October or early November, exactly one month after the annual Festival of Shelters in Judah (see Lev 23:34).

13 A PROPHET DENOUNCES JEROBOAM

At the LORD's command, a man of God from Judah went to Bethel, arriving there just as Jeroboam was approaching the altar to burn incense. ²Then at the LORD's command, he shouted, "O altar, altar! This is what the LORD says: A child named Josiah will be born into the dynasty of David. On you he will sacrifice the priests from the pagan shrines who come here to burn incense, and human bones will be burned on you." ³That same day the man of God gave a sign to prove his message. He said, "The LORD has promised to give this sign: This altar will split apart, and its ashes will be poured out on the ground."

⁴When King Jeroboam heard the man of God speaking against the altar at Bethel, he pointed at him and shouted, "Seize that man!" But instantly the king's hand became paralyzed in that position, and he couldn't pull it back. ⁵At the same time a wide crack appeared in the altar, and the ashes poured out, just as the man of God had predicted in his message from the LORD.

⁶The king cried out to the man of God, "Please ask the LORD your God to restore my hand again!" So the man of God prayed to the LORD, and the king's hand was restored and he could move it again.

⁷Then the king said to the man of God, "Come to the palace with me and have something to eat, and I will give you a gift."

⁸But the man of God said to the king, "Even if you gave me half of everything you own, I would not go with you. I would not eat or drink anything in this place. ⁹For the LORD gave me this command: 'You must not eat or drink anything while you are there, and do not return to

....

DO WHAT'S RIGHT

(12:28) Israelite males were required to travel to the Temple in Jerusalem three times each year (see Deut 16:16). Jeroboam, however, set up his own worship centers and tried to convince the people of Israel to worship there instead. Those who obeyed Jeroboam disobeyed God. Likewise, some ideas, although practical, may lead you away from God. Don't let anyone talk you out of doing what is right by telling you that your actions are not worth the effort. Are you willing to do what God wants no matter what it may cost you in time, energy, reputation, or resources?

HARMFUL HEARSAY

(13:1-32) This prophet had been given strict orders from God to avoid eating or drinking anything while on his mission (13:9). He died because he listened to a man who claimed to have a message from God. The prophet should have followed God's word instead of hearsay. Which do you rely on: what your friends or others say or what you read in God's Word?

Judah by the same way you came.'" ¹⁰So he left Bethel and went home another way.

¹¹As it happened, there was an old prophet living in Bethel, and his sons* came home and told him what the man of God had done in Bethel that day. They also told their father what the man had said to the king. ¹²The old prophet asked them, "Which way did he go?" So they showed their father* which road the man of God had taken. ¹³"Quick, saddle the donkey," the old man said. So they saddled the donkey for him, and he mounted it.

¹⁴Then he rode after the man of God and found him sitting under a great tree. The old prophet asked him, "Are you the man of God who came from Judah?"

"Yes, I am," he replied.

¹⁵Then he said to the man of God, "Come home with me and eat some food."

¹⁶"No, I cannot," he replied. "I am not allowed to eat or drink anything here in this place. ¹⁷For the LORD gave me this command: 'You must not eat or drink anything while you are there, and do not return to Judah by the same way you came.'"

¹⁸But the old prophet answered, "I am a prophet, too, just as you are. And an angel gave me this command from the LORD: 'Bring him home with you so he can have something to eat and drink.'" But the old man was lying to him. ¹⁹So they went back together, and the man of God ate and drank at the prophet's home.

²⁰Then while they were sitting at the table, a command from the LORD came to the old prophet. ²¹He cried out to the man of God from Judah, "This is what the LORD says: You have defied the word of the LORD and have disobeyed the command the LORD your God gave you. ²²You came back to this place and ate and drank where he told you not to eat or drink. Because of this, your body will not be buried in the grave of your ancestors."

²³After the man of God had finished eating and drinking, the old prophet saddled his own donkey for him, ²⁴and the man of God started off again. But as he was traveling along, a lion came out and killed him. His body lay there on the road, with the donkey and the lion standing beside it. ²⁵People who passed by saw the body lying in the road and the lion standing beside it, and they went and reported it in Bethel, where the old prophet lived.

²⁶When the prophet heard the report, he said, "It is the man of God who disobeyed the LORD's command. The LORD has fulfilled his word by causing the lion to attack and kill him."

²⁷Then the prophet said to his sons, "Saddle a donkey for me." So they saddled a donkey, ²⁸and he went out and found the body lying in the road. The donkey and lion were still standing there beside it, for the lion had not eaten the body nor attacked the donkey. ²⁹So the prophet laid the body of the man of God on the donkey and took it back to the town to mourn over him and bury him. ³⁰He laid the body in his own grave, crying out in grief, "Oh, my brother!"

³¹Afterward the prophet said to his sons, "When I die, bury me in the grave where the man of God is buried. Lay my bones beside his bones. ³²For the message the LORD told him to proclaim against the altar in Bethel and against the pagan shrines in the towns of Samaria will certainly come true."

³³But even after this, Jeroboam did not turn from his evil ways. He continued to choose priests from the common people. He appointed anyone who wanted to become a priest for the pagan shrines. ³⁴This became a great sin and resulted in the utter destruction of Jeroboam's dynasty from the face of the earth.

14 AHIJAH'S PROPHECY AGAINST JEROBOAM

At that time Jeroboam's son Abijah became very sick. ²So Jeroboam told his wife, "Disguise yourself so that no one will recognize you as my wife. Then go to the prophet Ahijah at Shiloh—the man who told me I would become king. ³Take him a gift of ten loaves of bread, some cakes, and a jar of honey, and ask him what will happen to the boy."

⁴So Jeroboam's wife went to Ahijah's home at Shiloh. He was an old man now and could no longer see. ⁵But the LORD had told Ahijah, "Jeroboam's wife will come here, pretending to be someone else. She will ask you about her son, for he is very sick. Give her the answer I give you."

⁶So when Ahijah heard her footsteps at the door, he called out, "Come in, wife of Jeroboam! Why are you pretending to be someone else?" Then he told her, "I have bad news for you. ⁷Give your husband, Jeroboam, this message from the LORD, the God of Israel: 'I promoted you from the ranks of the common people and made you ruler over my people Israel. ⁸I ripped the kingdom away from the family of David and gave it to you. But you have not been like my servant David, who obeyed my commands and followed me with all his heart and always did whatever I wanted. ⁹You have done more evil than all who lived before you.

13:11 As in Greek version; Hebrew reads *son*. 13:12 As in Greek version; Hebrew reads *They had seen*.

You have made other gods for yourself and have made me furious with your gold calves. And since you have turned your back on me, ¹⁰I will bring disaster on your dynasty and will destroy every one of your male descendants, slave and free alike, anywhere in Israel. I will burn up your royal dynasty as one burns up trash until it is all gone. ¹¹The members of Jeroboam's family who die in the city will be eaten by dogs, and those who die in the field will be eaten by vultures. I, the Lord, have spoken.'"

¹²Then Ahijah said to Jeroboam's wife, "Go on home, and when you enter the city, the child will die. ¹³All Israel will mourn for him and bury him. He is the only member of your family who will have a proper burial, for this child is the only good thing that the Lord, the God of Israel, sees in the entire family of Jeroboam.

¹⁴"In addition, the Lord will raise up a king over Israel who will destroy the family of Jeroboam. This will happen today, even now! ¹⁵Then the Lord will shake Israel like a reed whipped about in a stream. He will uproot the people of Israel from this good land that he gave their ancestors and will scatter them beyond the Euphrates River,* for they have angered the Lord with the Asherah poles they have set up for worship. ¹⁶He will abandon Israel because Jeroboam sinned and made Israel sin along with him."

¹⁷So Jeroboam's wife returned to Tirzah, and the child died just as she walked through the door of her home. ¹⁸And all Israel buried him and mourned for him, as the Lord had promised through the prophet Ahijah.

¹⁹The rest of the events in Jeroboam's reign, including all his wars and how he ruled, are recorded in *The Book of the History of the Kings of Israel.* ²⁰Jeroboam reigned in Israel twenty-two years. When Jeroboam died, his son Nadab became the next king.

REHOBOAM RULES IN JUDAH
²¹Meanwhile, Rehoboam son of Solomon was king in Judah. He was forty-one years old when he became king, and he reigned seventeen years in Jerusalem, the city the Lord had chosen from among all the tribes of Israel as the place to honor his name. Rehoboam's mother was Naamah, an Ammonite woman.

²²During Rehoboam's reign, the people of Judah did what was evil in the Lord's sight, provoking his anger with their sin, for it was even worse than that of their ancestors. ²³For

they also built for themselves pagan shrines and set up sacred pillars and Asherah poles on every high hill and under every green tree. ²⁴There were even male and female shrine prostitutes throughout the land. The people imitated the detestable practices of the pagan nations the Lord had driven from the land ahead of the Israelites.

²⁵In the fifth year of King Rehoboam's reign, King Shishak of Egypt came up and attacked Jerusalem. ²⁶He ransacked the treasuries of the Lord's Temple and the royal palace; he stole everything, including all the gold shields Solomon had made. ²⁷King Rehoboam later replaced them with bronze shields as substitutes, and he entrusted them to the care of the commanders of the guard who protected the entrance to the royal palace. ²⁸Whenever the king went to the Temple of the Lord, the guards would also take the shields and then return them to the guardroom.

²⁹The rest of the events in Rehoboam's reign and everything he did are recorded in *The Book of the History of the Kings of Judah.* ³⁰There was constant war between Rehoboam and Jeroboam. ³¹When Rehoboam died, he was buried among his ancestors in the City of David. His mother was Naamah, an Ammonite woman. Then his son Abijam* became the next king.

15 ABIJAM RULES IN JUDAH
Abijam* began to rule over Judah in the eighteenth year of Jeroboam's reign in Israel. ²He reigned in Jerusalem three years. His mother was Maacah, the daughter of Absalom.*

³He committed the same sins as his father before him, and he was not faithful to the Lord his God, as his ancestor David had been. ⁴But for David's sake, the Lord his God allowed his descendants to continue ruling, shining like a lamp, and he gave Abijam a son to rule after him in Jerusalem. ⁵For David had done what was pleasing in the Lord's sight and had obeyed the Lord's commands throughout his

14:15 Hebrew *the river.* **14:31** Also known as *Abijah.* **15:1** Also known as *Abijah.* **15:2** Hebrew *Abishalom* (also in 15:10), a variant spelling of Absalom; compare 2 Chr 11:20.

....

ROBBED
(14:25-26) When the people of Israel became spiritually corrupt (14:24), they lost everything a short time later. Just five years after Solomon died, foreign invaders raided the Temple and palace. How quickly the glory, power, and money disappeared! The people's possessions and wealth had become more important to them than God. When we pay more attention to the "idols" of our lives (goals, money, relationships, status, possessions), we might find ourselves in the same situation as the people of Israel.

life, except in the affair concerning Uriah the Hittite.

⁶There was war between Abijam and Jeroboam* throughout Abijam's reign. ⁷The rest of the events in Abijam's reign and everything he did are recorded in *The Book of the History of the Kings of Judah*. There was constant war between Abijam and Jeroboam. ⁸When Abijam died, he was buried in the City of David. Then his son Asa became the next king.

ASA RULES IN JUDAH ⁹Asa began to rule over Judah in the twentieth year of Jeroboam's reign in Israel. ¹⁰He reigned in Jerusalem forty-one years. His grandmother* was Maacah, the daughter of Absalom.

¹¹Asa did what was pleasing in the LORD's sight, as his ancestor David had done. ¹²He banished the male and female shrine prostitutes from the land and got rid of all the idols* his ancestors had made. ¹³He even deposed his grandmother Maacah from her position as queen mother because she had made an obscene Asherah pole. He cut down her obscene pole and burned it in the Kidron Valley. ¹⁴Although the pagan shrines were not removed, Asa's heart remained completely faithful to the LORD throughout his life. ¹⁵He brought into the Temple of the LORD the silver and gold and the various items that he and his father had dedicated.

¹⁶There was constant war between King Asa of Judah and King Baasha of Israel. ¹⁷King Baasha of Israel invaded Judah and fortified Ramah in order to prevent anyone from entering or leaving King Asa's territory in Judah.

¹⁸Asa responded by removing all the silver and gold that was left in the treasuries of the Temple of the LORD and the royal palace. He sent it with some of his officials to Ben-hadad son of Tabrimmon, son of Hezion, the king of Aram, who was ruling in Damascus, along with this message:

¹⁹"Let there be a treaty* between you and me like the one between your father and my father. See, I am sending you a gift of silver and gold. Break your treaty with King Baasha of Israel so that he will leave me alone."

²⁰Ben-hadad agreed to King Asa's request and sent the commanders of his army to attack the towns of Israel. They conquered the towns of Ijon, Dan, Abel-beth-maacah, and all Kinnereth, and all the land of Naphtali. ²¹As soon as Baasha of Israel heard what was happening, he abandoned his project of fortifying

Ramah and withdrew to Tirzah. ²²Then King Asa sent an order throughout Judah, requiring that everyone, without exception, help to carry away the building stones and timbers that Baasha had been using to fortify Ramah. Asa used these materials to fortify the town of Geba in Benjamin and the town of Mizpah.

²³The rest of the events in Asa's reign—the extent of his power, everything he did, and the names of the cities he built—are recorded in *The Book of the History of the Kings of Judah*. In his old age his feet became diseased. ²⁴When Asa died, he was buried with his ancestors in the City of David.

Then Jehoshaphat, Asa's son, became the next king.

NADAB RULES IN ISRAEL ²⁵Nadab son of Jeroboam began to rule over Israel in the second year of King Asa's reign in Judah. He reigned in Israel two years. ²⁶But he did what was evil in the LORD's sight and followed the example of his father, continuing the sins that Jeroboam had led Israel to commit.

²⁷Then Baasha son of Ahijah, from the tribe of Issachar, plotted against Nadab and assassinated him while he and the Israelite army were laying siege to the Philistine town of Gibbethon. ²⁸Baasha killed Nadab in the third year of King Asa's reign in Judah, and he became the next king of Israel.

²⁹He immediately slaughtered all the descendants of King Jeroboam, so that not one of the royal family was left, just as the LORD had promised concerning Jeroboam by the prophet Ahijah from Shiloh. ³⁰This was done because Jeroboam had provoked the anger of the LORD, the God of Israel, by the sins he had committed and the sins he had led Israel to commit.

³¹The rest of the events in Nadab's reign and everything he did are recorded in *The Book of the History of the Kings of Israel*.

BAASHA RULES IN ISRAEL ³²There was constant war between King Asa of Judah and King Baasha of Israel. ³³Baasha son of Ahijah began to rule over all Israel in the third year of King Asa's reign in Judah. Baasha reigned in Tirzah twenty-four years. ³⁴But he did what was evil in the LORD's sight and followed the example of Jeroboam, continuing the sins that Jeroboam had led Israel to commit.

15:6 As in a few Hebrew and Greek manuscripts; most Hebrew manuscripts read *between Rehoboam and Jeroboam.* **15:10** Or *The queen mother;* Hebrew reads *His mother* (also in 15:13); compare 15:2. **15:12** The Hebrew term (literally *round things*) probably alludes to dung. **15:19** As in Greek version; Hebrew reads *There is a treaty.*

16 This message from the Lord was delivered to King Baasha by the prophet Jehu son of Hanani: [2]"I lifted you out of the dust to make you ruler of my people Israel, but you have followed the evil example of Jeroboam. You have provoked my anger by causing my people Israel to sin. [3]So now I will destroy you and your family, just as I destroyed the descendants of Jeroboam son of Nebat. [4]The members of Baasha's family who die in the city will be eaten by dogs, and those who die in the field will be eaten by vultures."

[5]The rest of the events in Baasha's reign and the extent of his power are recorded in *The Book of the History of the Kings of Israel.* [6]When Baasha died, he was buried in Tirzah. Then his son Elah became the next king.

[7]The message from the Lord against Baasha and his family came through the prophet Jehu son of Hanani. It was delivered because Baasha had done what was evil in the Lord's sight (just as the family of Jeroboam had done), and also because Baasha had destroyed the family of Jeroboam. The Lord's anger was provoked by Baasha's sins.

ELAH RULES IN ISRAEL [8]Elah son of Baasha began to rule over Israel in the twenty-sixth year of King Asa's reign in Judah. He reigned in the city of Tirzah for two years.

[9]Then Zimri, who commanded half of the royal chariots, made plans to kill him. One day in Tirzah, Elah was getting drunk at the home of Arza, the supervisor of the palace. [10]Zimri

LEARNING FROM MISTAKES
(16:1-7) Baasha did not learn from his ancestors' mistakes. So, God promised to destroy Baasha's family just as he had destroyed Jeroboam's family when they sinned. What have you learned from your past or through the experiences of others? How will you avoid repeating their mistakes or mistakes you made in the past?

PERSONALITY PROFILE AHAB

UPS:
- Eighth king of Israel
- Capable leader and military strategist

DOWNS:
- Considered the most evil of Israel's kings
- Married Jezebel, a woman from an enemy nation, and allowed her to promote Baal worship
- Desired land that belonged to another and allowed its owner to be killed
- Was used to getting his own way and got depressed when he didn't

STATS:
- Where: Northern kingdom of Israel
- Occupation: King
- Relatives: Jezebel (wife); Omri (father); Ahaziah, Jehoram (sons)
- Contemporaries: Elijah, Naboth, Jehu, Ben-hadad, Jehoshaphat

KEY VERSES: 1 Kings 16:30-33

WHEN SOMEONE GIVES YOU ADVICE, what do you do? Do you consider it or ignore it? Ahab consistently chose the latter.

The kings of Israel and Judah, both good and evil, had prophets sent by God to advise, confront, and aid them. King David had a faithful friend in God's prophet, Nathan; Ahab could have had an equally faithful friend in Elijah. But while David listened to Nathan and was willing to repent of his sins, Ahab saw Elijah as his enemy. Why? Because Elijah always brought bad news to Ahab, and Ahab refused to acknowledge that it was his disobedience to God and persistent idol worship, not Elijah's prophecies, that had earned the consequences. Instead, he blamed Elijah for bringing the prophecies of judgment, rather than taking Elijah's advice and changing his ways.

Ahab was trapped by his own choices, and he was unwilling to take the right action. As king, he was responsible to God and his prophet Elijah, but he was married to an evil woman who led him into idol worship. Ahab was a childish man who would brood for days if he did not get his way. He took his wife's destructive advice, listened only to the "prophets" who gave good news, and surrounded himself with people who encouraged him to do whatever he wanted. The wrong advice eventually led to his death.

If we're honest, we will admit to wanting someone to confirm our plans, rather than advising us to change them. But our plans aren't always right. That's why God encourages us to get advice from wise counselors. How can we test the advice we receive? Advice that agrees with the principles in God's Word is reliable. We must always separate advice from our own desires or whatever our friends say and weigh it against God's commands. God will never lead us to do what he has forbidden in his Word. Who is a wise counselor? Someone who follows God's rules.

BOTTOM LINE: The choice of a mate will have a significant effect on life—physically, spiritually, and emotionally.

Selfishness, left unchecked, can lead to great evil.

Wise counsel is invaluable.

Ahab's story is told in 1 Kings 16:28–22:40. He also is mentioned in 2 Chronicles 18:1-34 and Micah 6:16.

They step off the page like something out of a science fiction or a fantasy novel—wild individuals wearing strange clothes, seeing mind-boggling visions, hearing God's voice, and preaching a bone-chilling message: repent or you will pay. Who were they? They were the prophets—the men and women God sent to the nation of Israel (and occasionally to other nations) as his spokespeople.

Elijah was chosen as a prophet at a rough time in Israel's history—during Ahab's term as king. Elijah must have been a strange sight, walking around in black camel's hair and preaching against Israel's idolatries. Others, like Isaiah and Daniel, were powerful men in the life of the nation. They held important government positions or served as the king's advisers. Amos, on the other hand, was a shepherd and gardener, called from his simple life to be God's messenger. Hosea married a prostitute on God's orders. There is at least one prophetess—Huldah—whose story is in 2 Kings 22:14-20.

All the prophets were unique and preached to the nation of Israel under a variety of circumstances. So, what did they have in common?

First, they were God's appointed speakers. While the priests spoke to God for the people, the prophets spoke to the people for God. Often they would call on the people to stop doing wrong and return to God. Time after time their messages were ignored, and Israel suffered as a result.

Second, the prophets preached two kinds of messages: (1) a warning of the need to repent, and (2) a message about future events.

Many claimed to be prophets, and people could become confused over who to believe when the "prophets" disagreed. Tests were used, however, to determine who was a true prophet.

- True prophets spoke whenever and whatever God told them to. They didn't dream up prophecies and oracles and then claim that their messages came from God. In other religions, pagan prophets constantly tried to manipulate the gods into doing what they wanted. That's what the prophets of Baal tried to do (18:26-29). Israel's prophets were different. God took the initiative in speaking to them, telling them precisely what to say and do. Then these prophets spoke to the people, often beginning with, "The Lord says . . . ."

- Any prediction about the future had to come true or the prophet was considered false. The Old Testament contains many amazing predictions of events, sometimes several centuries into the future. An incredible number of those predictions, especially those concerning Israel and the coming Messiah, have come true with phenomenal accuracy. Others, particularly those concerning the end times, are now developing or still remain to be seen. But if ever a prophet could be shown to have made an error concerning a future event, he or she was considered a false prophet.

Christians disagree about whether or not we still have true prophets of God. Since certain people see their mission as calling the people of God to repentance for sin, it's hard to deny that many such prophets now live among us. But it is far more undecided whether we have people within the body of Christ who can describe the future because God has given them special revelation. A great many people have made fools of themselves (and their followers) by predicting future events, especially the second coming of Christ. Their "prophecies" crashed down around them. Evidently the wisest counsel regarding this kind of predictive prophesying is a good dose of godly skepticism.

Above all else, prophets pointed to the one who would come and who would be greater than all the prophets: Jesus Christ, the Messiah. ∎

---

walked in and struck him down and killed him. This happened in the twenty-seventh year of King Asa's reign in Judah. Then Zimri became the next king.

[11]Zimri immediately killed the entire royal family of Baasha, leaving him not even a single male child. He even destroyed distant relatives and friends. [12]So Zimri destroyed the dynasty of Baasha as the LORD had promised through the prophet Jehu. [13]This happened because of all the sins Baasha and his son Elah had committed, and because of the sins they led Israel to commit. They provoked the anger of the LORD, the God of Israel, with their worthless idols.

[14]The rest of the events in Elah's reign and everything he did are recorded in *The Book of the History of the Kings of Israel*.

ZIMRI RULES IN ISRAEL [15]Zimri began to rule over Israel in the twenty-seventh year of King Asa's reign in Judah, but his reign in Tirzah lasted only seven days. The army of Israel was then attacking the Philistine town of Gibbethon. [16]When they heard that Zimri had committed treason and had assassinated the king, that very day they chose Omri, commander of the army, as the new king of Israel. [17]So Omri led the entire army of Israel up from Gibbethon to attack Tirzah, Israel's capital. [18]When Zimri saw that the city had been taken, he went into the citadel of the palace and burned it down over himself and died in the flames. ¹⁹For he, too, had done what was evil in the LORD's sight. He followed the example of Jeroboam in all the sins he had committed and led Israel to commit.

²⁰The rest of the events in Zimri's reign and his conspiracy are recorded in *The Book of the History of the Kings of Israel.*

OMRI RULES IN ISRAEL ²¹But now the people of Israel were split into two factions. Half the people tried to make Tibni son of Ginath their king, while the other half supported Omri. ²²But Omri's supporters defeated the supporters of Tibni. So Tibni was killed, and Omri became the next king.

²³Omri began to rule over Israel in the thirty-first year of King Asa's reign in Judah. He reigned twelve years in all, six of them in Tirzah. ²⁴Then Omri bought the hill now known as Samaria from its owner, Shemer, for 150 pounds of silver.* He built a city on it and called the city Samaria in honor of Shemer.

²⁵But Omri did what was evil in the LORD's sight, even more than any of the kings before him. ²⁶He followed the example of Jeroboam son of Nebat in all the sins he had committed and led Israel to commit. The people provoked the anger of the LORD, the God of Israel, with their worthless idols.

²⁷The rest of the events in Omri's reign, the extent of his power, and everything he did are recorded in *The Book of the History of the Kings of Israel.* ²⁸When Omri died, he was buried in Samaria. Then his son Ahab became the next king.

AHAB RULES IN ISRAEL ²⁹Ahab son of Omri began to rule over Israel in the thirty-eighth year of King Asa's reign in Judah. He reigned in Samaria twenty-two years. ³⁰But Ahab son of Omri did what was evil in the LORD's sight, even more than any of the kings before him. ³¹And as though it were not enough to follow the example of Jeroboam, he married Jezebel, the daughter of King Ethbaal of the Sidonians, and he began to bow down in worship of Baal. ³²First Ahab built a temple and an altar for Baal in Samaria. ³³Then he set up an Asherah pole. He did more to provoke the anger of the LORD, the God of Israel, than any of the other kings of Israel before him.

³⁴It was during his reign that Hiel, a man from

Bethel, rebuilt Jericho. When he laid its foundations, it cost him the life of his oldest son, Abiram. And when he completed it and set up its gates, it cost him the life of his youngest son, Segub.* This all happened according to the message from the LORD concerning Jericho spoken by Joshua son of Nun.

17

ELIJAH FED BY RAVENS Now Elijah, who was from Tishbe in Gilead, told King Ahab, "As surely as the LORD, the God of Israel, lives—the God I serve—there will be no dew or rain during the next few years until I give the word!"

²Then the LORD said to Elijah, ³"Go to the east and hide by Kerith Brook, near where it enters the Jordan River. ⁴Drink from the brook and eat what the ravens bring you, for I have commanded them to bring you food."

⁵So Elijah did as the LORD told him and camped beside Kerith Brook, east of the Jordan. ⁶The ravens brought him bread and meat each morning and evening, and he drank from the brook. ⁷But after a while the brook dried up, for there was no rainfall anywhere in the land.

THE WIDOW AT ZAREPHATH ⁸Then the LORD said to Elijah, ⁹"Go and live in the village of Zarephath, near the city of Sidon. I have instructed a widow there to feed you."

¹⁰So he went to Zarephath. As he arrived at the gates of the village, he saw a widow gathering sticks, and he asked her, "Would you please bring me a little water in a cup?" ¹¹As she was going to get it, he called to her, "Bring me a bite of bread, too."

¹²But she said, "I swear by the LORD your God that I don't have a single piece of bread in the house. And I have only a handful of flour left in the jar and a little cooking oil in the bottom of the jug. I was just gathering a few sticks to cook this last meal, and then my son and I will die."

¹³But Elijah said to her, "Don't be afraid! Go ahead and do just what you've said, but make a little bread for me first. Then use what's left

···

GOD PROVIDES
(17:1-15) In a nation that was required by law to care for its prophets, it is ironic that God turned to ravens (unclean birds—see Lev 11:13-15) and a widow (a foreigner from Jezebel's home territory) to care for Elijah. God sometimes provides help where we least expect it in ways that go beyond our narrow definitions or expectations. No matter how bitter our trials or how seemingly hopeless our situation, we should look for God's hand of care. We may find his providence in some strange places! How has God provided for your needs lately?

16:24 Hebrew *for 2 talents* [68 kilograms] *of silver.* **16:34** An ancient Hebrew scribal tradition reads *He killed his oldest son when he laid its foundations, and he killed his youngest son when he set up its gates.*

to prepare a meal for yourself and your son. [14]For this is what the LORD, the God of Israel, says: There will always be flour and olive oil left in your containers until the time when the LORD sends rain and the crops grow again!"

[15]So she did as Elijah said, and she and Elijah and her family continued to eat for many days. [16]There was always enough flour and olive oil left in the containers, just as the LORD had promised through Elijah.

[17]Some time later the woman's son became sick. He grew worse and worse, and finally he died. [18]Then she said to Elijah, "O man of God, what have you done to me? Have you come here to point out my sins and kill my son?"

[19]But Elijah replied, "Give me your son." And he took the child's body from her arms, carried him up the stairs to the room where he was staying, and laid the body on his bed. [20]Then Elijah cried out to the LORD, "O LORD my God, why have you brought tragedy to this widow who has opened her home to me, causing her son to die?"

[21]And he stretched himself out over the child three times and cried out to the LORD, "O LORD my God, please let this child's life return to him." [22]The LORD heard Elijah's prayer, and the life of the child returned, and he revived! [23]Then Elijah brought him down from the upper room and gave him to his mother. "Look!" he said. "Your son is alive!"

[24]Then the woman told Elijah, "Now I know for sure that you are a man of God, and that the LORD truly speaks through you."

18 THE CONTEST ON MOUNT CARMEL

Later on, in the third year of the drought, the LORD said to Elijah, "Go and present yourself to King Ahab. Tell him that I will soon send rain!" [2]So Elijah went to appear before Ahab.

Meanwhile, the famine had become very severe in Samaria. [3]So Ahab summoned Obadiah, who was in charge of the palace. (Obadiah was a devoted follower of the LORD. [4]Once when Jezebel had tried to kill all the LORD's prophets, Obadiah had hidden 100 of them in two caves. He put fifty prophets in each cave and supplied them with food and water.)

TRIALS
(17:17) Even when God has done a miracle in our lives, our troubles may not be over. The famine was a terrible experience, but the worst was yet to come. But when the bigger trial hits us, we should recall God's faithfulness in our past. We are to depend on him again each time we face a new trial.

ELIJAH *PERSONALITY PROFILE*

ARE YOU A COMFORTER or a confronter? God made the prophet Elijah a confronter. He had to speak God's words to a king who often rejected his message. Elijah experienced depression and loneliness even though he worked for God.

It is interesting to read about the amazing miracles God accomplished through Elijah, but it is more helpful to think about the relationship they shared. All that happened in Elijah's life began when he responded to the miracle of being able to know God. This is a step we can take too.

In Elijah's life we really see the thrills of victory and the agonies of defeat. One huge victory was the defeat of the prophets of Baal (1 Kgs 18:17-40). But the agony of defeat came through Elijah's response to Jezebel's death threat. God used a gentle whisper to remind Elijah that the Almighty was still in control.

Elijah also had to learn that he wasn't alone. God reminded Elijah that 7,000 others in Israel were also faithful.

Like Elijah, do you fear that you're the only one still trying to be faithful to God? God always has more plans and people than we know about.

BOTTOM LINE: We are never as alone as we may feel; God is always there.

God speaks more frequently in persistent whispers than in shouts.

Elijah's story is told in 1 Kings 17:1—2 Kings 2:11. He is also mentioned in 2 Chronicles 21:12-15; Malachi 4:5-6; Matthew 11:14; 16:14; 17:3-13; 27:47-49; Luke 1:17; 4:25-26; John 1:21-25; Romans 11:2-4; James 5:17-18.

UPS:
- *The most famous and dramatic of Israel's prophets*
- *Predicted the beginning and end of a three-year drought*
- *Used by God to restore a dead child to his mother*
- *God's representative in a showdown with the priests of Baal and Asherah*
- *Appeared with Moses and Jesus during Jesus' transfiguration*

DOWNS:
- *Chose to work alone and paid for it through isolation*
- *Fled in fear from Jezebel when she threatened his life*

STATS:
- *Where: Gilead*
- *Occupation: Prophet*
- *Contemporaries: Ahab, Jezebel, Ahaziah, Obadiah, Jehu, Hazael*

KEY VERSES: *1 Kings 18:36, 38*

PROPHETS—FALSE AND TRUE

The false prophets were an obstacle to bringing God's word to the people. They would bring "messages" that contradicted the words of the true prophets. They gave messages that appealed to the people's sinful nature and comforted their fears. False prophets told people what they wanted to hear; true prophets told God's truth.

FALSE PROPHETS	TRUE PROPHETS
Worked for political purposes to benefit themselves	Worked for spiritual purposes to serve God and the people
Held positions of great wealth	Owned little to nothing
Gave false messages	Spoke only true messages
Spoke only what the people wanted to hear	Spoke only what God told them to say— no matter how unpopular

⁵Ahab said to Obadiah, "We must check every spring and valley in the land to see if we can find enough grass to save at least some of my horses and mules." ⁶So they divided the land between them. Ahab went one way by himself, and Obadiah went another way by himself.

⁷As Obadiah was walking along, he suddenly saw Elijah coming toward him. Obadiah recognized him at once and bowed low to the ground before him. "Is it really you, my lord Elijah?" he asked.

⁸"Yes, it is," Elijah replied. "Now go and tell your master, 'Elijah is here.'"

⁹"Oh, sir," Obadiah protested, "what harm have I done to you that you are sending me to my death at the hands of Ahab? ¹⁰For I swear by the LORD your God that the king has searched every nation and kingdom on earth from end to end to find you. And each time he was told, 'Elijah isn't here,' King Ahab forced the king of that nation to swear to the truth of his claim. ¹¹And now you say, 'Go and tell your master, "Elijah is here."' ¹²But as soon as I leave you, the Spirit of the LORD will carry you away to who knows where. When Ahab comes and cannot find you, he will kill me. Yet I have been a true servant of the LORD all my life. ¹³Has no one told you, my lord, about the time when Jezebel was trying to kill the LORD's prophets? I hid 100 of them in two caves and supplied them with food and water. ¹⁴And now you say, 'Go and tell your master, "Elijah is here."' Sir, if I do that, Ahab will certainly kill me."

¹⁵But Elijah said, "I swear by the LORD Almighty, in whose presence I stand, that I will present myself to Ahab this very day."

¹⁶So Obadiah went to tell Ahab that Elijah had come, and Ahab went out to meet Elijah.

18:19 Hebrew *who eat at Jezebel's table.*

¹⁷When Ahab saw him, he exclaimed, "So, is it really you, you troublemaker of Israel?"

¹⁸"I have made no trouble for Israel," Elijah replied. "You and your family are the troublemakers, for you have refused to obey the commands of the LORD and have worshiped the images of Baal instead. ¹⁹Now summon all Israel to join me at Mount Carmel, along with the 450 prophets of Baal and the 400 prophets of Asherah who are supported by Jezebel.*"

²⁰So Ahab summoned all the people of Israel and the prophets to Mount Carmel. ²¹Then Elijah stood in front of them and said, "How much longer will you waver, hobbling between two opinions? If the LORD is God, follow him! But if Baal is God, then follow him!" But the people were completely silent.

²²Then Elijah said to them, "I am the only prophet of the LORD who is left, but Baal has 450 prophets. ²³Now bring two bulls. The prophets of Baal may choose whichever one they wish and cut it into pieces and lay it on the wood of their altar, but without setting fire to it. I will prepare the other bull and lay it on the wood on the altar, but not set fire to it. ²⁴Then call on the name of your god, and I will call on the name of the LORD. The god who answers by setting fire to the wood is the true God!" And all the people agreed.

• •

MAKE A CHOICE
(18:21) Elijah challenged the people of Israel to take a stand—to follow God or Baal. Why did so many people waver between the two choices? Perhaps some were not sure what to believe. Many, however, probably went along with the crowd and worshiped a god they thought they could see—a god represented by a statue. How like many of us today! We might worship a god we can see—a god of money, status, or possessions. But God offers us the same choice he offered to the people of Israel: Will we worship him or an idol? What's your choice?

²⁵Then Elijah said to the prophets of Baal, "You go first, for there are many of you. Choose one of the bulls, and prepare it and call on the name of your god. But do not set fire to the wood."

²⁶So they prepared one of the bulls and placed it on the altar. Then they called on the name of Baal from morning until noontime, shouting, "O Baal, answer us!" But there was no reply of any kind. Then they danced, hobbling around the altar they had made.

²⁷About noontime Elijah began mocking them. "You'll have to shout louder," he scoffed, "for surely he is a god! Perhaps he is daydreaming, or is relieving himself.* Or maybe he is away on a trip, or is asleep and needs to be wakened!"

²⁸So they shouted louder, and following their normal custom, they cut themselves with knives and swords until the blood gushed out. ²⁹They raved all afternoon until the time of the evening sacrifice, but still there was no sound, no reply, no response.

³⁰Then Elijah called to the people, "Come over here!" They all crowded around him as he repaired the altar of the Lord that had been torn down. ³¹He took twelve stones, one to represent each of the tribes of Israel,* ³²and he used the stones to rebuild the altar in the name of the Lord. Then he dug a trench around the altar large enough to hold about three gallons.* ³³He piled wood on the altar, cut the bull into pieces, and laid the pieces on the wood.

Then he said, "Fill four large jars with water, and pour the water over the offering and the wood."

³⁴After they had done this, he said, "Do the same thing again!" And when they were finished, he said, "Now do it a third time!" So they did as he said, ³⁵and the water ran around the altar and even filled the trench.

³⁶At the usual time for offering the evening sacrifice, Elijah the prophet walked up to the altar and prayed, "O Lord, God of Abraham, Isaac, and Jacob,* prove today that you are God in Israel and that I am your servant.

Prove that I have done all this at your command. ³⁷O Lord, answer me! Answer me so these people will know that you, O Lord, are God and that you have brought them back to yourself."

³⁸Immediately the fire of the Lord flashed down from heaven and burned up the young bull, the wood, the stones, and the dust. It even licked up all the water in the trench! ³⁹And when all the people saw it, they fell face down on the ground and cried out, "The Lord—he is God! Yes, the Lord is God!"

⁴⁰Then Elijah commanded, "Seize all the prophets of Baal. Don't let a single one escape!" So the people seized them all, and Elijah took them down to the Kishon Valley and killed them there.

ELIJAH PRAYS FOR RAIN ⁴¹Then Elijah said to Ahab, "Go get something to eat and drink, for I hear a mighty rainstorm coming!"

⁴²So Ahab went to eat and drink. But Elijah climbed to the top of Mount Carmel and bowed low to the ground and prayed with his face between his knees.

⁴³Then he said to his servant, "Go and look out toward the sea."

The servant went and looked, then returned to Elijah and said, "I didn't see anything."

Seven times Elijah told him to go and look. ⁴⁴Finally the seventh time, his servant told him, "I saw a little cloud about the size of a man's hand rising from the sea."

Then Elijah shouted, "Hurry to Ahab and tell him, 'Climb into your chariot and go back home. If you don't hurry, the rain will stop you!'"

⁴⁵And soon the sky was black with clouds. A heavy wind brought a terrific rainstorm, and Ahab left quickly for Jezreel. ⁴⁶Then the Lord gave special strength to Elijah. He tucked his cloak into his belt* and ran ahead of Ahab's chariot all the way to the entrance of Jezreel.

19 **ELIJAH FLEES TO SINAI** When Ahab got home, he told Jezebel everything Elijah had done, including the way he had killed all the prophets of Baal. ²So Jezebel sent this message to Elijah: "May the gods strike me and even kill me if by this time tomorrow I have not killed you just as you killed them."

³Elijah was afraid and fled for his life. He went to Beersheba, a town in Judah, and he

---

GOD'S HELP

(18:36-38) *God answered Elijah's request by sending fire from heaven. He also promises to help us accomplish what he commands us to do. The proof may not be as dramatic in our life as in Elijah's, but God will make resources available to us in creative ways to accomplish his purposes. He might give us the wisdom to live a life that's pleasing to him, the courage to take a stand for truth, or the means to provide help for someone in need. Like Elijah, we can have faith that, whatever God commands us to do, he will provide what we need to carry it through.*

18:27 Or *is busy somewhere else,* or *is engaged in business.*
18:31 Hebrew *each of the tribes of the sons of Jacob to whom the Lord had said, "Your name will be Israel."* **18:32** Hebrew *2 seahs* [12 liters] *of seed.* **18:36** Hebrew *and Israel.* The names "Jacob" and "Israel" are often interchanged throughout the Old Testament, referring sometimes to the individual patriarch and sometimes to the nation. **18:46** Hebrew *He bound up his loins.*

left his servant there. ⁴Then he went on alone into the wilderness, traveling all day. He sat down under a solitary broom tree and prayed that he might die. "I have had enough, LORD," he said. "Take my life, for I am no better than my ancestors who have already died."

⁵Then he lay down and slept under the broom tree. But as he was sleeping, an angel touched him and told him, "Get up and eat!" ⁶He looked around and there beside his head was some bread baked on hot stones and a jar of water! So he ate and drank and lay down again.

⁷Then the angel of the LORD came again and touched him and said, "Get up and eat some more, or the journey ahead will be too much for you."

⁸So he got up and ate and drank, and the food gave him enough strength to travel forty days and forty nights to Mount Sinai,* the mountain of God. ⁹There he came to a cave, where he spent the night.

THE LORD SPEAKS TO ELIJAH But the LORD said to him, "What are you doing here, Elijah?"

¹⁰Elijah replied, "I have zealously served the LORD God Almighty. But the people of Israel have broken their covenant with you, torn down your altars, and killed every one of your prophets. I am the only one left, and now they are trying to kill me, too."

¹¹"Go out and stand before me on the mountain," the LORD told him. And as Elijah stood there, the LORD passed by, and a mighty windstorm hit the mountain. It was such a terrible blast that the rocks were torn loose, but the LORD was not in the wind. After the wind there was an earthquake, but the LORD was not in the earthquake. ¹²And after the earthquake there was a fire, but the LORD was not in the fire. And after the fire there was the sound of a gentle whisper. ¹³When Elijah heard it, he wrapped his face in his cloak and went out and stood at the entrance of the cave.

And a voice said, "What are you doing here, Elijah?"

¹⁴He replied again, "I have zealously served the LORD God Almighty. But the people of Israel have broken their covenant with you, torn down your altars, and killed every one of your prophets. I am the only one left, and now they are trying to kill me, too."

¹⁵Then the LORD told him, "Go back the same way you came, and travel to the wilderness of Damascus. When you arrive there, anoint Hazael to be king of Aram. ¹⁶Then anoint Jehu

19:8 Hebrew *to Horeb,* another name for Sinai.   **19:16** Hebrew *descendant of Nimshi;* compare 2 Kgs 9:2, 14.

AFTER THE EARTHQUAKE THERE WAS A FIRE, BUT THE LORD WAS NOT IN THE FIRE. AND AFTER THE FIRE THERE WAS THE SOUND OF A GENTLE WHISPER. {1 KINGS 19:12}

grandson of Nimshi* to be king of Israel, and anoint Elisha son of Shaphat from the town of Abel-meholah to replace you as my prophet. ¹⁷Anyone who escapes from Hazael will be killed by Jehu, and those who escape Jehu will be killed by Elisha! ¹⁸Yet I will preserve 7,000 others in Israel who have never bowed down to Baal or kissed him!"

THE CALL OF ELISHA ¹⁹So Elijah went and found Elisha son of Shaphat plowing a field. There were twelve teams of oxen in the field, and Elisha was plowing with the twelfth team. Elijah went over to him and threw his cloak across his shoulders and then walked away. ²⁰Elisha left the oxen standing there, ran after Elijah, and said to him, "First let me go and kiss my father and mother good-bye, and then I will go with you!"

Elijah replied, "Go on back, but think about what I have done to you."

²¹So Elisha returned to his oxen and slaughtered them. He used the wood from the plow to build a fire to roast their flesh. He passed around the meat to the townspeople, and they all ate. Then he went with Elijah as his assistant.

⸱⸱⸱

FROM A HIGH TO A LOW

(19:3-4) Elijah experienced the depths of fatigue and discouragement just after his two great spiritual victories: the defeat of the prophets of Baal and the answered prayer for rain. But God took care of him in practical ways. First, God let Elijah rest and eat. Then God confronted him with the need to return to his mission in life—to be God's prophet. Often discouragement sets in after great spiritual experiences, especially those requiring physical effort or producing emotional excitement. When the blues hit after a great spiritual experience, remember that God's purpose for your life is not over yet.

WHISPERS

(19:11-13) Elijah knew that the gentle whisper was God's voice. He realized that God didn't reveal himself only in powerful, miraculous ways. Many of us look for God only at retreats, conferences, or through the powerful messages of leaders. Yet God often gently whispers in the quietness of a humbled heart. Are you listening for him? You might need to take a step back from the noise and activity of your busy life. His guidance may come when you least expect it.

20 BEN-HADAD ATTACKS SAMARIA

About that time King Ben-hadad of Aram mobilized his army, supported by the chariots and horses of thirty-two allied kings. They went to besiege Samaria, the capital of Israel, and launched attacks against it. ²Ben-hadad sent messengers into the city to relay this message to King Ahab of Israel: "This is what Ben-hadad says: ³'Your silver and gold are mine, and so are your wives and the best of your children!'"

⁴"All right, my lord the king," Israel's king replied. "All that I have is yours!"

⁵Soon Ben-hadad's messengers returned again and said, "This is what Ben-hadad says: 'I have already demanded that you give me your silver, gold, wives, and children. ⁶But about this time tomorrow I will send my officials to search your palace and the homes of your people. They will take away everything you consider valuable!'"

⁷Then Ahab summoned all the elders of the land and said to them, "Look how this man is stirring up trouble! I already agreed with his demand that I give him my wives and children and silver and gold."

⁸"Don't give in to any more demands," all the elders and the people advised.

⁹So Ahab told the messengers from Ben-hadad, "Say this to my lord the king: 'I will give you everything you asked for the first time, but I cannot accept this last demand of yours.'" So the messengers returned to Ben-hadad with that response.

¹⁰Then Ben-hadad sent this message to Ahab: "May the gods strike me and even kill me if there remains enough dust from Samaria to provide even a handful for each of my soldiers."

¹¹The king of Israel sent back this answer: "A warrior putting on his sword for battle should not boast like a warrior who has already won."

¹²Ahab's reply reached Ben-hadad and the other kings as they were drinking in their tents.* "Prepare to attack!" Ben-hadad commanded his officers. So they prepared to attack the city.

AHAB'S VICTORY OVER BEN-HADAD

¹³Then a certain prophet came to see King Ahab of Israel and told him, "This is what the LORD says: Do you see all these enemy forces? Today I will hand them all over to you. Then you will know that I am the LORD."

¹⁴Ahab asked, "How will he do it?"

And the prophet replied, "This is what the LORD says: The troops of the provincial commanders will do it."

"Should we attack first?" Ahab asked.

"Yes," the prophet answered.

¹⁵So Ahab mustered the troops of the 232 provincial commanders. Then he called out the rest of the army of Israel, some 7,000 men. ¹⁶About noontime, as Ben-hadad and the thirty-two allied kings were still in their tents drinking themselves into a stupor, ¹⁷the troops of the provincial commanders marched out of the city as the first contingent.

As they approached, Ben-hadad's scouts reported to him, "Some troops are coming from Samaria."

¹⁸"Take them alive," Ben-hadad commanded, "whether they have come for peace or for war."

¹⁹But Ahab's provincial commanders and the entire army had now come out to fight. ²⁰Each Israelite soldier killed his Aramean opponent, and suddenly the entire Aramean army panicked and fled. The Israelites chased them, but King Ben-hadad and a few of his charioteers escaped on horses. ²¹However, the king of Israel destroyed the other horses and chariots and slaughtered the Arameans.

²²Afterward the prophet said to King Ahab, "Get ready for another attack. Begin making plans now, for the king of Aram will come back next spring.*"

BEN-HADAD'S SECOND ATTACK

²³After their defeat, Ben-hadad's officers said to him, "The Israelite gods are gods of the hills; that is why they won. But we can beat them easily on the plains. ²⁴Only this time replace the kings with field commanders! ²⁵Recruit another army like the one you lost. Give us the same number of horses, chariots, and men, and we will fight against them on the plains. There's no doubt that we will beat them." So King Ben-hadad did as they suggested.

²⁶The following spring he called up the Aramean army and marched out against Israel, this time at Aphek. ²⁷Israel then mustered its army, set up supply lines, and marched out for

A SECRET WEAPON
(20:23) *Since the days of Joshua, Israel's soldiers had a reputation for being superior fighters in the hills. Yet they were ineffective in the open plains and valleys because they didn't use chariots in battle. This was the assessment of Ben-hadad's officers. What they didn't understand was that God was the one who made all of the difference in battle, not the chariots. When faced with emotional or spiritual battles, remember that victory doesn't come from how you fight, but from having God at your side.*

20:12 Or *in Succoth;* also in 20:16.   20:22 Hebrew *at the turn of the year;* similarly in 20:26. The first day of the year in the ancient Hebrew lunar calendar occurred in March or April.

battle. But the Israelite army looked like two little flocks of goats in comparison to the vast Aramean forces that filled the countryside!

28Then the man of God went to the king of Israel and said, "This is what the LORD says: The Arameans have said, 'The LORD is a god of the hills and not of the plains.' So I will defeat this vast army for you. Then you will know that I am the LORD."

29The two armies camped opposite each other for seven days, and on the seventh day the battle began. The Israelites killed 100,000 Aramean foot soldiers in one day. 30The rest fled into the town of Aphek, but the wall fell on them and killed another 27,000. Ben-hadad fled into the town and hid in a secret room.

31Ben-hadad's officers said to him, "Sir, we have heard that the kings of Israel are merciful. So let's humble ourselves by wearing burlap around our waists and putting ropes on our heads, and surrender to the king of Israel. Then perhaps he will let you live."

32So they put on burlap and ropes, and they went to the king of Israel and begged, "Your servant Ben-hadad says, 'Please let me live!'"

The king of Israel responded, "Is he still alive? He is my brother!"

33The men took this as a good sign and quickly picked up on his words. "Yes," they said, "your brother Ben-hadad!"

"Go and get him," the king of Israel told them. And when Ben-hadad arrived, Ahab invited him up into his chariot.

34Ben-hadad told him, "I will give back the towns my father took from your father, and you may establish places of trade in Damascus, as my father did in Samaria."

Then Ahab said, "I will release you under these conditions." So they made a new treaty, and Ben-hadad was set free.

A PROPHET CONDEMNS AHAB

35Meanwhile, the LORD instructed one of the group of prophets to say to another man, "Hit me!" But the man refused to hit the prophet. 36Then the prophet told him, "Because you have not obeyed the voice of the LORD, a lion will kill you as soon as you leave me." And when he had gone, a lion did attack and kill him.

37Then the prophet turned to another man and said, "Hit me!" So he struck the prophet and wounded him.

38The prophet placed a bandage over his eyes to disguise himself and then waited be-

side the road for the king. 39As the king passed by, the prophet called out to him, "Sir, I was in the thick of battle, and suddenly a man brought me a prisoner. He said, 'Guard this man; if for any reason he gets away, you will either die or pay a fine of seventy-five pounds* of silver!' 40But while I was busy doing something else, the prisoner disappeared!"

"Well, it's your own fault," the king replied. "You have brought the judgment on yourself."

41Then the prophet quickly pulled the bandage from his eyes, and the king of Israel recognized him as one of the prophets. 42The prophet said to him, "This is what the LORD says: Because you have spared the man I said must be destroyed,* now you must die in his place, and your people will die instead of his people." 43So the king of Israel went home to Samaria angry and sullen.

21 NABOTH'S VINEYARD

Now there was a man named Naboth, from Jezreel, who owned a vineyard in Jezreel beside the palace of King Ahab of Samaria. 2One day Ahab said to Naboth, "Since your vineyard is so convenient to my palace, I would like to buy it to use as a vegetable garden. I will give you a better vineyard in exchange, or if you prefer, I will pay you for it."

3But Naboth replied, "The LORD forbid that I should give you the inheritance that was passed down by my ancestors."

4So Ahab went home angry and sullen because of Naboth's answer. The king went to bed with his face to the wall and refused to eat!

5"What's the matter?" his wife Jezebel asked him. "What's made you so upset that you're not eating?"

6"I asked Naboth to sell me his vineyard or trade it, but he refused!" Ahab told her.

7"Are you the king of Israel or not?" Jezebel demanded. "Get up and eat something, and don't worry about it. I'll get you Naboth's vineyard!"

8So she wrote letters in Ahab's name, sealed them with his seal, and sent them to the elders and other leaders of the town where Naboth lived. 9In her letters she commanded: "Call the citizens together for fasting and prayer, and give Naboth a place of honor. 10And then seat two scoundrels across from him who will accuse him of cursing God and the king. Then take him out and stone him to death."

11So the elders and other town leaders followed the instructions Jezebel had written in the letters. 12They called for a fast and put Naboth at a prominent place before the people.

20:39 Hebrew 1 talent [34 kilograms].   20:42 The Hebrew term used here refers to the complete consecration of things or people to the LORD, either by destroying them or by giving them as an offering.

¹³Then the two scoundrels came and sat down across from him. And they accused Naboth before all the people, saying, "He cursed God and the king." So he was dragged outside the town and stoned to death. ¹⁴The town leaders then sent word to Jezebel, "Naboth has been stoned to death."

¹⁵When Jezebel heard the news, she said to Ahab, "You know the vineyard Naboth wouldn't sell you? Well, you can have it now! He's dead!" ¹⁶So Ahab immediately went down to the vineyard of Naboth to claim it.

¹⁷But the LORD said to Elijah,* ¹⁸"Go down to meet King Ahab of Israel, who rules in Samaria. He will be at Naboth's vineyard in Jezreel, claiming it for himself. ¹⁹Give him this message: 'This is what the LORD says: Wasn't it enough that you killed Naboth? Must you rob him, too? Because you have done this, dogs will lick your blood at the very place where they licked the blood of Naboth!'"

²⁰"So, my enemy, you have found me!" Ahab exclaimed to Elijah.

"Yes," Elijah answered, "I have come because you have sold yourself to what is evil in the LORD's sight. ²¹So now the LORD says, 'I will bring disaster on you and consume you. I will destroy every one of your male descendants, slave and free alike, anywhere in Israel! ²²I am going to destroy your family as I did the family of Jeroboam son of Nebat and the family of Baasha son of Ahijah, for you have made me very angry and have led Israel into sin.'

²³"And regarding Jezebel, the LORD says, 'Dogs will eat Jezebel's body at the plot of land in Jezreel.*'

²⁴"The members of Ahab's family who die in the city will be eaten by dogs, and those who die in the field will be eaten by vultures."

²⁵(No one else so completely sold himself to what was evil in the LORD's sight as Ahab did under the influence of his wife Jezebel. ²⁶His worst outrage was worshiping idols* just as the Amorites had done—the people whom the

LORD had driven out from the land ahead of the Israelites.)

²⁷But when Ahab heard this message, he tore his clothing, dressed in burlap, and fasted. He even slept in burlap and went about in deep mourning.

²⁸Then another message from the LORD came to Elijah: ²⁹"Do you see how Ahab has humbled himself before me? Because he has done this, I will not do what I promised during his lifetime. It will happen to his sons; I will destroy his dynasty."

22 JEHOSHAPHAT AND AHAB For three years there was no war between Aram and Israel. ²Then during the third year, King Jehoshaphat of Judah went to visit King Ahab of Israel. ³During the visit, the king of Israel said to his officials, "Do you realize that the town of Ramoth-gilead belongs to us? And yet we've done nothing to recapture it from the king of Aram!"

⁴Then he turned to Jehoshaphat and asked, "Will you join me in battle to recover Ramoth-gilead?"

Jehoshaphat replied to the king of Israel, "Why, of course! You and I are as one. My troops are your troops, and my horses are your horses." ⁵Then Jehoshaphat added, "But first let's find out what the LORD says."

⁶So the king of Israel summoned the prophets, about 400 of them, and asked them, "Should I go to war against Ramoth-gilead, or should I hold back?"

They all replied, "Yes, go right ahead! The Lord will give the king victory."

⁷But Jehoshaphat asked, "Is there not also a prophet of the LORD here? We should ask him the same question."

⁸The king of Israel replied to Jehoshaphat, "There is one more man who could consult the LORD for us, but I hate him. He never prophesies anything but trouble for me! His name is Micaiah son of Imlah."

Jehoshaphat replied, "That's not the way a king should talk! Let's hear what he has to say."

⁹So the king of Israel called one of his officials and said, "Quick! Bring Micaiah son of Imlah."

MICAIAH PROPHESIES AGAINST AHAB ¹⁰King Ahab of Israel and King Jehoshaphat of Judah, dressed in their royal robes, were sitting on thrones at the threshing floor near the gate of Samaria. All of Ahab's prophets were

···

BLINDNESS
(21:20) Ahab still refused to admit his sin against God. Instead, he accused Elijah of being his enemy. When we are blinded by envy and hatred, it is almost impossible to see our own sin.

NEVER TOO LATE
(21:29) Ahab was more wicked than any other king of Israel (16:30; 21:25), but when he repented in deep humility, God took notice and reduced his punishment. The same Lord who was merciful to Ahab wants to be merciful to you. It's never too late to humble yourself, turn to God, and ask for forgiveness.

21:17 Hebrew *Elijah the Tishbite;* also in 21:28.   21:23 As in several Hebrew manuscripts, Syriac, and Latin Vulgate (see also 2 Kgs 9:26, 36); most Hebrew manuscripts read *at the city wall.*   21:26 The Hebrew term (literally *round things*) probably alludes to dung.

prophesying there in front of them. ¹¹One of them, Zedekiah son of Kenaanah, made some iron horns and proclaimed, "This is what the LORD says: With these horns you will gore the Arameans to death!"

¹²All the other prophets agreed. "Yes," they said, "go up to Ramoth-gilead and be victorious, for the LORD will give the king victory!"

¹³Meanwhile, the messenger who went to get Micaiah said to him, "Look, all the prophets are promising victory for the king. Be sure that you agree with them and promise success."

¹⁴But Micaiah replied, "As surely as the LORD lives, I will say only what the LORD tells me to say."

¹⁵When Micaiah arrived before the king, Ahab asked him, "Micaiah, should we go to war against Ramoth-gilead, or should we hold back?"

Micaiah replied sarcastically, "Yes, go up and be victorious, for the LORD will give the king victory!"

¹⁶But the king replied sharply, "How many times must I demand that you speak only the truth to me when you speak for the LORD?"

¹⁷Then Micaiah told him, "In a vision I saw all Israel scattered on the mountains, like sheep without a shepherd. And the LORD said, 'Their master has been killed.* Send them home in peace.'"

¹⁸"Didn't I tell you?" the king of Israel exclaimed to Jehoshaphat. "He never prophesies anything but trouble for me."

¹⁹Then Micaiah continued, "Listen to what the LORD says! I saw the LORD sitting on his throne with all the armies of heaven around him, on his right and on his left. ²⁰And the LORD said, 'Who can entice Ahab to go into battle against Ramoth-gilead so he can be killed?'

"There were many suggestions, ²¹and finally a spirit approached the LORD and said, 'I can do it!'

²²"'How will you do this?' the LORD asked.

"And the spirit replied, 'I will go out and inspire all of Ahab's prophets to speak lies.'

"'You will succeed,' said the LORD. 'Go ahead and do it.'

²³"So you see, the LORD has put a lying spirit in the mouths of all your prophets. For the LORD has pronounced your doom."

²⁴Then Zedekiah son of Kenaanah walked up to Micaiah and slapped him across the face. "Since when did the Spirit of the LORD leave me to speak to you?" he demanded.

²⁵And Micaiah replied, "You will find out soon enough when you are trying to hide in some secret room!"

²⁶"Arrest him!" the king of Israel ordered. "Take him back to Amon, the governor of the city, and to my son Joash. ²⁷Give them this order from the king: 'Put this man in prison, and feed him nothing but bread and water until I return safely from the battle!'"

²⁸But Micaiah replied, "If you return safely, it will mean that the LORD has not spoken through me!" Then he added to those standing around, "Everyone mark my words!"

THE DEATH OF AHAB ²⁹So King Ahab of Israel and King Jehoshaphat of Judah led their armies against Ramoth-gilead. ³⁰The king of Israel said to Jehoshaphat, "As we go into battle, I will disguise myself so no one will recognize me, but you wear your royal robes." So the king of Israel disguised himself, and they went into battle.

³¹Meanwhile, the king of Aram had issued these orders to his thirty-two chariot commanders: "Attack only the king of Israel. Don't bother with anyone else!" ³²So when the Aramean chariot commanders saw Jehoshaphat in his royal robes, they went after him. "There is the king of Israel!" they shouted. But when Jehoshaphat called out, ³³the chariot commanders realized he was not the king of Israel, and they stopped chasing him.

³⁴An Aramean soldier, however, randomly shot an arrow at the Israelite troops and hit the king of Israel between the joints of his armor. "Turn the horses* and get me out of here!" Ahab groaned to the driver of his chariot. "I'm badly wounded!"

³⁵The battle raged all that day, and the king remained propped up in his chariot facing the Arameans. The blood from his wound ran down to the floor of his chariot, and as evening arrived he died. ³⁶Just as the sun was setting, the cry ran through his troops: "We're done for! Run for your lives!"

³⁷So the king died, and his body was taken to Samaria and buried there. ³⁸Then his chariot was washed beside the pool of Samaria, and dogs came and licked his blood at the place

22:17 Hebrew *These people have no master.*   22:34 Hebrew *Turn your hand.*

··

A FUTILE ESCAPE

(22:29-34) Ahab could not escape God's judgment. Ben-hadad, the king of Aram, sent his 32 charioteers with the sole purpose of killing Ahab. Thinking he could escape, Ahab tried a disguise; but a random shot struck him while the chariots chased the wrong king—Jehoshaphat. Sometimes people today try to escape reality by disguising themselves. They act differently, change schools, or move to a new town. Yet no one can escape the consequences of wrong actions.

where the prostitutes bathed,* just as the LORD had promised.

³⁹The rest of the events in Ahab's reign and everything he did, including the story of the ivory palace and the towns he built, are recorded in *The Book of the History of the Kings of Israel.* ⁴⁰So Ahab died, and his son Ahaziah became the next king.

JEHOSHAPHAT RULES IN JUDAH
⁴¹Jehoshaphat son of Asa began to rule over Judah in the fourth year of King Ahab's reign in Israel. ⁴²Jehoshaphat was thirty-five years old when he became king, and he reigned in Jerusalem twenty-five years. His mother was Azubah, the daughter of Shilhi.

⁴³Jehoshaphat was a good king, following the example of his father, Asa. He did what was pleasing in the LORD's sight. *During his reign, however, he failed to remove all the pagan shrines, and the people still offered sacrifices and burned incense there. ⁴⁴Jehoshaphat also made peace with the king of Israel.

....

ULTIMATELY DEFEATED
(22:52-53) The book of 1 Kings began with a united nation under King David—the greatest king in Israel's history. It ends, however, with a divided kingdom and the death of Ahab, the king with the worst reputation of all. What happened? The people stopped acknowledging God as their ultimate leader. Instead, they conformed to the lifestyles of evil leaders. So, God allowed enemy nations to arise and defeat Israel and Judah as punishment for their sins. Failing to acknowledge God as the ultimate leader of our lives is the first step toward ultimate defeat.

⁴⁵The rest of the events in Jehoshaphat's reign, the extent of his power, and the wars he waged are recorded in *The Book of the History of the Kings of Judah.* ⁴⁶He banished from the land the rest of the male and female shrine prostitutes, who still continued their practices from the days of his father, Asa.

⁴⁷(There was no king in Edom at that time, only a deputy.)

⁴⁸Jehoshaphat also built a fleet of trading ships* to sail to Ophir for gold. But the ships never set sail, for they met with disaster in their home port of Ezion-geber. ⁴⁹At one time Ahaziah son of Ahab had proposed to Jehoshaphat, "Let my men sail with your men in the ships." But Jehoshaphat refused the request.

⁵⁰When Jehoshaphat died, he was buried with his ancestors in the City of David. Then his son Jehoram became the next king.

AHAZIAH RULES IN ISRAEL
⁵¹Ahaziah son of Ahab began to rule over Israel in the seventeenth year of King Jehoshaphat's reign in Judah. He reigned in Samaria two years. ⁵²But he did what was evil in the LORD's sight, following the example of his father and mother and the example of Jeroboam son of Nebat, who had led Israel to sin. ⁵³He served Baal and worshiped him, provoking the anger of the LORD, the God of Israel, just as his father had done.

22:38 Or *his blood, and the prostitutes bathed [in it];* or *his blood, and they washed his armor.*   **22:43** Verses 22:43b-53 are numbered 22:44-54 in Hebrew text.   **22:48** Hebrew *fleet of ships of Tarshish.*

2 KINGS

"He used to be cool. But since he became class president, he thinks he owns the school!"

"We used to be friends. But she turned into a snob about a week after making cheerleader!"

Maybe you've heard, thought, or even spoken lines like that. It's amazing, isn't it, how some people change when they get a little power or an important position? Suddenly they're in the spotlight, and you're not good enough or popular enough or rich enough to be seen with them.

Of course, it doesn't always happen that way. Now and then someone who has made it to the top avoids being corrupted by power. But with so many examples on the other side (politicians, business men and women, athletes, entertainment stars, and even clergy), clearly such people are the exceptions.

Second Kings tells about the leaders of the two nations of Israel and Judah. These kings could have used their power to help their people and lead them God's way. But of the 28 kings in Israel and Judah who appear in 2 Kings, only two—Hezekiah and Josiah—are called "good."

Many people seek power, but fail to use it for good. If power were within your grasp—the power to influence others—what would you do with it? As you read, learn from the negative examples of the kings and determine to be God's person—even if you win the race, get elected, or gain the prize.

KEY POINTS

A LONE VOICE Elisha was a lone voice against the evil practices of the kings of Israel. Likewise we're called to take a stand against wrong, even if it means standing alone. Yet we're not really alone. God stands with us.

WORSHIPING IDOLS Every evil king in both Israel and Judah encouraged the worship of idols. An idol is any idea, ability, possession, or person that we regard more highly than God. Idols today are power, money, physical attractiveness, and so on. Those who believe in God must resist the allure of these idols.

A CORRUPTING INFLUENCE Only 20 percent of all the kings of both kingdoms followed God. That means corrupt leaders had control of the kingdom for the majority of the time. We are still responsible to God, even if a leader chooses to disobey him.

JUDGMENT After repeated warnings to his people, God used enemy nations to punish his disobedient people. When we reject God's commands and purpose for our life, the consequences can be severe. But God offers forgiveness if we ask for it.

STATS

PURPOSE
To demonstrate the consequences of refusing to make God their true leader

AUTHOR
Unknown; possibly Jeremiah or a group of prophets

ORIGINAL AUDIENCE
The people of Israel

SETTING
Israel has been divided into two kingdoms, Israel and Judah, for over a century.

KEY PEOPLE
Elijah, Elisha, Jezebel, Athaliah, Joash, Hezekiah, Sennacherib, Isaiah, Josiah

SPECIAL FEATURE
The 17 prophetic books parallel the events of 2 Kings.

TIMELINE

848 B.C.
Elijah's ministry transfers to Elisha
835
Joash, king of Judah
760
Amos's ministry begins
753
Hosea's ministry begins
742
Micah's ministry begins
740
Isaiah's ministry begins
722
Israel (northern kingdom) falls
715
Hezekiah, king of Judah
640
Josiah, king of Judah
627
Jeremiah's ministry begins
605
First captivity of Judah— Daniel taken
597
Second captivity of Judah— Ezekiel taken
586
Judah (southern kingdom) falls

The broken lines (— · — ·) indicate modern boundaries.

KEY PLACES
The history of both Israel and Judah was greatly affected by the prophet Elisha's ministry. He served Israel for 50 years, fighting the idolatry of its kings and calling its people back to God.

the city, hoping to kill him. But Elisha prayed that the Arameans would be blinded—and they were! Then he led the blinded army into Samaria, Israel's capital city (6:8-23).

❻ SAMARIA
The Arameans later besieged Samaria. Ironically, Israel's king thought it was Elisha's fault, but Elisha said food would be available in abundance the next day. True to Elisha's word, the Lord caused panic in the Aramean camp and they ran, leaving their supplies to Samaria's starving people (6:24–7:20).

❼ DAMASCUS
Elisha obeyed God and traveled to Damascus, the capital of Aram. King Ben-hadad was sick and sent Hazael to ask Elisha if he would recover. Elisha knew the king would die, and told this to Hazael. Hazael then murdered Ben-hadad, making himself king (8:7-29).

❽ RAMOTH-GILEAD
Elisha sent a young prophet to Ramoth-gilead to anoint Jehu as Israel's next king. Jehu set out to destroy the wicked dynasties of Israel and Judah, killing Kings Joram and Ahaziah and wicked Queen Jezebel. He then destroyed King Ahab's family and all the Baal worshipers in Israel (9:1–10:36).

❾ JERUSALEM
Power-hungry Athaliah became queen of Judah when her son Ahaziah was killed. She had all her grandsons killed but Joash was saved by his aunt. Joash was crowned king at the age of seven and overthrew Athaliah. Meanwhile in Samaria, the Arameans continued to harass Israel. Elisha told Israel's new king that he would be victorious over Aram three times (11:1–13:19).

A series of evil kings in Israel followed Elisha's death. Their idolatry and rejection of God caused their downfall. The Assyrian Empire captured Samaria and took most of the Israelites into captivity (13:20–17:41). Jerusalem fell to the next world power, Babylon, and its people were taken captive (18:1–25:30).

❶ JERICHO
Elijah's ministry had come to an end. Elijah was taken by God in a whirlwind, and Elisha returned alone with Elijah's cloak. The prophets in Jericho realized that Elisha replaced Elijah (1:1–2:25).

❷ WILDERNESS OF EDOM
The king of Moab rebelled against Israel, so the nations of Israel, Judah, and Edom decided to attack from the wilderness of Edom, but ran out of water. The kings consulted Elisha, who said that God would send both water and victory (3:1-27).

❸ SHUNEM
Elijah helped a woman clear a debt by giving her a miraculous supply of olive oil to sell. For another family in Shunem, he raised a son from the dead (4:1-37).

❹ GILGAL
Elisha cared for the prophets in Gilgal—he removed poison from a stew, fed many with a small amount of food, and caused an ax head to float so someone could retrieve it (4:38–6:7).

❺ DOTHAN
The Aramean king tracked Elisha down in Dothan and surrounded

1 ELIJAH CONFRONTS KING AHAZIAH After King Ahab's death, the land of Moab rebelled against Israel.

²One day Israel's new king, Ahaziah, fell through the latticework of an upper room at his palace in Samaria and was seriously injured. So he sent messengers to the temple of Baal-zebub, the god of Ekron, to ask whether he would recover.

³But the angel of the LORD told Elijah, who was from Tishbe, "Go and confront the messengers of the king of Samaria and ask them, 'Is there no God in Israel? Why are you going to Baal-zebub, the god of Ekron, to ask whether the king will recover? ⁴Now, therefore, this is what the LORD says: You will never leave the bed you are lying on; you will surely die.'" So Elijah went to deliver the message.

⁵When the messengers returned to the king, he asked them, "Why have you returned so soon?"

⁶They replied, "A man came up to us and told us to go back to the king and give him this message. 'This is what the LORD says: Is there no God in Israel? Why are you sending men to Baal-zebub, the god of Ekron, to ask whether you will recover? Therefore, because you have done this, you will never leave the bed you are lying on; you will surely die.'"

⁷"What sort of man was he?" the king demanded. "What did he look like?"

⁸They replied, "He was a hairy man,* and he wore a leather belt around his waist."

"Elijah from Tishbe!" the king exclaimed.

⁹Then he sent an army captain with fifty soldiers to arrest him. They found him sitting on top of a hill. The captain said to him, "Man of God, the king has commanded you to come down with us."

¹⁰But Elijah replied to the captain, "If I am a man of God, let fire come down from heaven and destroy you and your fifty men!" Then fire fell from heaven and killed them all.

¹¹So the king sent another captain with fifty men. The captain said to him, "Man of God, the king demands that you come down at once."

¹²Elijah replied, "If I am a man of God, let fire come down from heaven and destroy you and your fifty men!" And again the fire of God fell from heaven and killed them all.

¹³Once more the king sent a third captain with fifty men. But this time the captain went up the hill and fell to his knees before Elijah. He pleaded with him, "O man of God, please spare my life and the lives of these, your fifty

servants. ¹⁴See how the fire from heaven came down and destroyed the first two groups. But now please spare my life!"

¹⁵Then the angel of the LORD said to Elijah, "Go down with him, and don't be afraid of him." So Elijah got up and went with him to the king.

¹⁶And Elijah said to the king, "This is what the LORD says: Why did you send messengers to Baal-zebub, the god of Ekron, to ask whether you will recover? Is there no God in Israel to answer your question? Therefore, because you have done this, you will never leave the bed you are lying on; you will surely die."

¹⁷So Ahaziah died, just as the LORD had promised through Elijah. Since Ahaziah did not have a son to succeed him, his brother Joram* became the next king. This took place in the second year of the reign of Jehoram son of Jehoshaphat, king of Judah.

¹⁸The rest of the events in Ahaziah's reign are recorded in *The Book of the History of the Kings of Israel.*

2 ELIJAH TAKEN INTO HEAVEN When the LORD was about to take Elijah up to heaven in a whirlwind, Elijah and Elisha were traveling from Gilgal. ²And Elijah said to Elisha, "Stay here, for the LORD has told me to go to Bethel."

But Elisha replied, "As surely as the LORD lives and you yourself live, I will never leave you!" So they went down together to Bethel.

³The group of prophets from Bethel came to Elisha and asked him, "Did you know that the LORD is going to take your master away from you today?"

"Of course I know," Elisha answered. "But be quiet about it."

⁴Then Elijah said to Elisha, "Stay here, for the LORD has told me to go to Jericho."

But Elisha replied again, "As surely as the LORD lives and you yourself live, I will never leave you." So they went on together to Jericho.

⁵Then the group of prophets from Jericho came to Elisha and asked him, "Did you know that the LORD is going to take your master away from you today?"

"Of course I know," Elisha answered. "But be quiet about it."

⁶Then Elijah said to Elisha, "Stay here, for the LORD has told me to go to the Jordan River."

But again Elisha replied, "As surely as the LORD lives and you yourself live, I will never leave you." So they went on together.

⁷Fifty men from the group of prophets also went and watched from a distance as Elijah and Elisha stopped beside the Jordan River. ⁸Then

1:8 Or *He was wearing clothing made of hair.* **1:17** Hebrew *Jehoram,* a variant spelling of Joram.

Elijah folded his cloak together and struck the water with it. The river divided, and the two of them went across on dry ground!

⁹When they came to the other side, Elijah said to Elisha, "Tell me what I can do for you before I am taken away."

And Elisha replied, "Please let me inherit a double share of your spirit and become your successor."

¹⁰"You have asked a difficult thing," Elijah replied. "If you see me when I am taken from you, then you will get your request. But if not, then you won't."

¹¹As they were walking along and talking, suddenly a chariot of fire appeared, drawn by horses of fire. It drove between the two men, separating them, and Elijah was carried by a whirlwind into heaven. ¹²Elisha saw it and cried out, "My father! My father! I see the chariots and charioteers of Israel!" And as they disappeared from sight, Elisha tore his clothes in distress.

¹³Elisha picked up Elijah's cloak, which had fallen when he was taken up. Then Elisha returned to the bank of the Jordan River. ¹⁴He struck the water with Elijah's cloak and cried out, "Where is the LORD, the God of Elijah?" Then the river divided, and Elisha went across.

¹⁵When the group of prophets from Jericho saw from a distance what happened, they exclaimed, "Elijah's spirit rests upon Elisha!" And they went to meet him and bowed to the ground before him. ¹⁶"Sir," they said, "just say the word and fifty of our strongest men will search the wilderness for your master. Perhaps the Spirit of the LORD has left him on some mountain or in some valley."

"No," Elisha said, "don't send them." ¹⁷But they kept urging him until they shamed him into agreeing, and he finally said, "All right, send them." So fifty men searched for three days but did not find Elijah. ¹⁸Elisha was still

PURE MOTIVES

(2:9) Elisha asked to become Elijah's successor. He literally asked Elijah for "a double share of your spirit." This was a bold request, but God granted it. Why? Because Elisha's motives were pure. His goal was not to be better or more powerful than Elijah, but to accomplish more for God. If our motives are pure, we don't have to be afraid to ask for big things from God. What's your request?

ELISHA   *PERSONALITY PROFILE*

EVER HAD TO REPLACE SOMEONE? Maybe you were second string but got called into the game. Some talented people can be difficult to replace.

The great prophet Elijah was a tough act to follow. But Elisha had been handpicked by God as a replacement for the job as God's voice. Elisha carefully observed Elijah's example in order to learn the knowledge and wisdom he needed for the work to which God had called him.

Though Elijah and Elisha were both prophets, each had his own style. Because Elijah did a good job of confronting evil and idol worship, Elisha was able to be a comforter. He showed people how much God cared. The Bible records 18 encounters between Elisha and people who needed help.

Elisha saw more in life than most people because he recognized that with God there was more to life. He knew that all we are and have comes from God. The miracles done through Elisha put people in touch with the personal and all-powerful God. Elijah would have been proud of his replacement's work.

We, too, have great examples to follow—both people in the Bible and those today who have positively influenced our lives. We must resist the tendency to think about the limitations that our family background or environment create for us. Instead, we should ask God to use us for his purpose—perhaps, like Elijah, to win great conflicts, or like Elisha, to compassionately care for the daily needs of those around us. Ask God to use you as only he can. The person you will become and the work you will do are being shaped by the people you follow today. Are they worth following?

BOTTOM LINE: One measure of greatness is the willingness to serve the poor as well as the powerful.

An effective replacement not only learns from his or her master, but also builds upon his or her master's achievements.

Elisha's story is told in 1 Kings 19:16-21; 2 Kings 2:1–13:20. He is also mentioned in Luke 4:27.

UPS:
- *Elijah's successor as a prophet of God*
- *Had a ministry that lasted over 50 years*
- *Had a major impact on four nations: Israel, Judah, Moab, and Syria*
- *A man of integrity who did not try to enrich himself at others' expense*
- *Did many miracles to help those in need*

STATS:
- *Where: From the tribe of Issachar, prophesied to northern kingdom*
- *Occupations: Farmer, prophet*
- *Relatives: Shaphat (father)*
- *Contemporaries: Elijah, Ahab, Jezebel, Jehu*

KEY VERSE: *2 Kings 2:9*

at Jericho when they returned. "Didn't I tell you not to go?" he asked.

ELISHA'S FIRST MIRACLES
[19] One day the leaders of the town of Jericho visited Elisha. "We have a problem, my lord," they told him. "This town is located in pleasant surroundings, as you can see. But the water is bad, and the land is unproductive."

[20] Elisha said, "Bring me a new bowl with salt in it." So they brought it to him. [21] Then he went out to the spring that supplied the town with water and threw the salt into it. And he said, "This is what the LORD says: I have purified this water. It will no longer cause death or infertility.*" [22] And the water has remained pure ever since, just as Elisha said.

[23] Elisha left Jericho and went up to Bethel. As he was walking along the road, a group of boys from the town began mocking and making fun of him. "Go away, baldy!" they chanted. "Go away, baldy!" [24] Elisha turned around and looked at them, and he cursed them in the name of the LORD. Then two bears came out of the woods and mauled forty-two of them. [25] From there Elisha went to Mount Carmel and finally returned to Samaria.

3 WAR BETWEEN ISRAEL AND MOAB
Ahab's son Joram* began to rule over Israel in the eighteenth year of King Jehoshaphat's reign in Judah. He reigned in Samaria twelve years. [2] He did what was evil in the LORD's sight, but not to the same extent as his father and mother. He at least tore down the sacred pillar of Baal that his father had set up. [3] Nevertheless, he continued in the sins that Jeroboam son of Nebat had committed and led the people of Israel to commit.

[4] King Mesha of Moab was a sheep breeder. He used to pay the king of Israel an annual tribute of 100,000 lambs and the wool of 100,000 rams. [5] But after Ahab's death, the king of Moab rebelled against the king of Israel. [6] So King Joram promptly mustered the army of Israel and marched from Samaria. [7] On the way, he sent this message to King Jehoshaphat of Judah: "The king of Moab has rebelled against me. Will you join me in battle against him?"

And Jehoshaphat replied, "Why, of course! You and I are as one. My troops are your troops, and my horses are your horses." [8] Then Jehoshaphat asked, "What route will we take?"

"We will attack from the wilderness of Edom," Joram replied.

[9] The king of Edom and his troops joined them, and all three armies traveled along a roundabout route through the wilderness for seven days. But there was no water for the men or their animals.

[10] "What should we do?" the king of Israel cried out. "The LORD has brought the three of us here to let the king of Moab defeat us."

[11] But King Jehoshaphat of Judah asked, "Is there no prophet of the LORD with us? If there is, we can ask the LORD what to do through him."

One of King Joram's officers replied, "Elisha son of Shaphat is here. He used to be Elijah's personal assistant.*"

[12] Jehoshaphat said, "Yes, the LORD speaks through him." So the kings of Israel, Judah, and Edom went to consult with Elisha.

[13] "Why are you coming to me?"* Elisha asked the king of Israel. "Go to the pagan prophets of your father and mother!"

But King Joram of Israel said, "No! For it was the LORD who called us three kings here—only to be defeated by the king of Moab!"

[14] Elisha replied, "As surely as the LORD Almighty lives, whom I serve, I wouldn't even bother with you except for my respect for King Jehoshaphat of Judah. [15] Now bring me someone who can play the harp."

While the harp was being played, the power* of the LORD came upon Elisha, [16] and he said, "This is what the LORD says: This dry valley will be filled with pools of water! [17] You will see neither wind nor rain, says the LORD,

....

ZERO TOLERANCE
(2:23-25) These boys made fun of God's messenger, Elisha, and paid for it with their lives. Sound harsh? God had a reason for allowing this. He wanted to show a zero-tolerance policy toward anyone who rejected his messenger. Making fun of religious leaders has been a popular sport through the ages. Sometimes we express cynicism or disrespect toward leaders whom we feel "deserve" our contempt. But instead of mocking them, maybe we could pray for them instead. True leaders, those who follow God, need to be heard with respect and encouraged in their ministry.

FAITH DECLINE
(3:1-20) Jehoshaphat's request for a "prophet of the LORD" (3:11) shows how true worship of God in both Israel and Judah had declined. The decline usually started in the heart of each person and worked its way out. If your heart could be examined, what would be found: a decline or a rise in worship? In David's day, both the high priest and the prophets gave the king advice. But most of the priests had left Israel and God's prophets were seen as messengers of doom (1 Kgs 22:18). This miracle predicted by Elisha affirmed God's power and authority and validated Elisha's ministry.

2:21 Or *or make the land unproductive;* Hebrew reads *or barrenness.*   3:1 Hebrew *Jehoram,* a variant spelling of Joram; also in 3:6.   3:11 Hebrew *He used to pour water on the hands of Elijah.*
3:13 Hebrew *What is there in common between you and me?*
3:15 Hebrew *the hand.*

but this valley will be filled with water. You will have plenty for yourselves and your cattle and other animals. ¹⁸But this is only a simple thing for the LORD, for he will make you victorious over the army of Moab! ¹⁹You will conquer the best of their towns, even the fortified ones. You will cut down all their good trees, stop up all their springs, and ruin all their good land with stones."

²⁰The next day at about the time when the morning sacrifice was offered, water suddenly appeared! It was flowing from the direction of Edom, and soon there was water everywhere.

²¹Meanwhile, when the people of Moab heard about the three armies marching against them, they mobilized every man who was old enough to strap on a sword, and they stationed themselves along their border. ²²But when they got up the next morning, the sun was shining across the water, making it appear red to the Moabites—like blood. ²³"It's blood!" the Moabites exclaimed. "The three armies must have

ULTIMATE ISSUES *MIRACLES*

"I can't believe that!" said Alice.

"Can't you?" the Queen said in a pitying tone. "Try again: draw a long breath and shut your eyes."

Alice laughed. "There's no use trying," she said: "One can't believe impossible things."

"I daresay you haven't had much practice," said the Queen. "When I was your age, I did it for half an hour a day. Why, sometimes I've believed as many as six impossible things before breakfast." (From *Through the Looking Glass,* Lewis Carroll, [New York: Penguin Books, 1985], chapter 5.)

Do you sometimes feel as if you're being asked to believe the impossible as you read the Bible? Fire from heaven . . . flaming chariots . . . little boys coming back to life . . . floating ax heads . . . and many other incredible stories. Sometimes it seems you're looking at an issue of *Tales of the Supernatural* instead of God's Word.

Is the Bible all true, or is it full of myths and fairy tales? Do miracles really happen?

First we need to define what a miracle is. You hear the word a lot. Perhaps this definition will help: A miracle is any outwardly observable event that breaks the normal laws of nature. This includes miracles of nature (the parting of the Red Sea in Exod 14); healings (Naaman in 2 Kgs 5); and supernatural displays (appearances of angels or the writing on the wall in Dan 5). By definition, miracles take place by God's initiative, not a human being's. They aren't predictable. And that's one of the problems.

We tend to be skeptical of anything that cannot be photographed, documented, or otherwise objectively "proven." Often, our first response to accounts of something unusual is, "Right. Prove it." When no proof is offered, we are (often rightly) unconvinced. The miracles recorded in the Bible, however, are different from an Elvis sighting or an encounter with Bigfoot.

The miracles in the Bible often were witnessed by more than one or two people. The plagues in Egypt were experienced by thousands. Faking that kind of testimony would be impossible. The parting of the Red Sea would have been tough to fake, too—either the water rolled back or it didn't. When that many people see and experience something miraculous, it's hard to laugh it off as the story of a couple of crazies. As someone has said in regard to the resurrection of Christ, if one person tells you a dead man got out of his grave, you lock him up. If two people say it, it's a conspiracy. If five hundred people say it, you go down to the cemetery and check it out. So it is with many of the miracles recorded in the Scriptures. There are too many eyewitnesses to discount them.

Another argument to consider is the logical one. If God exists and he created the universe and set up the laws that govern it, why would it be inconsistent or unbelievable for him to bend or break the rules he made in the first place? The answer is simple: it's not. It is logical that the one who made natural law can act in ways that go beyond it.

Still it's hard to believe something like that unless you see it for yourself. Unfortunately, most of us have never seen anything we could legitimately call a miracle. The great Christian writer C. S. Lewis puts it like this:

"You are probably quite right in thinking that you will never see a miracle done. . . . They come on great occasions. . . . If we were heroic missionaries, apostles or martyrs, it would be different. But why you or I? . . . How likely is it that you or I will be present when a peace treaty is signed, when a dictator commits suicide? That we should see a miracle is even less likely" (C. S. Lewis, *Miracles* [New York: Macmillan, 1978], pp. 167–168).

Just as we believe in other world-changing events without the benefit of being there, so the biblical writers ask us to believe their testimonies of God's supernatural actions in human history. These writings are just one more way God demonstrates his sovereign control and his intense personal involvement in our lives. ■

attacked and killed each other! Let's go, men of Moab, and collect the plunder!"

²⁴But when the Moabites arrived at the Israelite camp, the army of Israel rushed out and attacked them until they turned and ran. The army of Israel chased them into the land of Moab, destroying everything as they went.* ²⁵They destroyed the towns, covered their good land with stones, stopped up all the springs, and cut down all the good trees. Finally, only Kir-hareseth and its stone walls were left, but men with slings surrounded and attacked it.

²⁶When the king of Moab saw that he was losing the battle, he led 700 of his swordsmen in a desperate attempt to break through the enemy lines near the king of Edom, but they failed. ²⁷Then the king of Moab took his oldest son, who would have been the next king, and sacrificed him as a burnt offering on the wall. So there was great anger against Israel,* and the Israelites withdrew and returned to their own land.

4 **ELISHA HELPS A POOR WIDOW** One day the widow of a member of the group of prophets came to Elisha and cried out, "My husband who served you is dead, and you know how he feared the LORD. But now a creditor has come, threatening to take my two sons as slaves."

²"What can I do to help you?" Elisha asked. "Tell me, what do you have in the house?"

"Nothing at all, except a flask of olive oil," she replied.

³And Elisha said, "Borrow as many empty jars as you can from your friends and neighbors. ⁴Then go into your house with your sons and shut the door behind you. Pour olive oil from your flask into the jars, setting each one aside when it is filled."

⁵So she did as she was told. Her sons kept bringing jars to her, and she filled one after another. ⁶Soon every container was full to the brim!

"Bring me another jar," she said to one of her sons.

"There aren't any more!" he told her. And then the olive oil stopped flowing.

⁷When she told the man of God what had happened, he said to her, "Now sell the olive oil and pay your debts, and you and your sons can live on what is left over."

ELISHA AND THE WOMAN FROM SHUNEM

⁸One day Elisha went to the town of Shunem.

3:24 The meaning of the Hebrew is uncertain. 3:27 Or *So Israel's anger was great.* The meaning of the Hebrew is uncertain.

A wealthy woman lived there, and she urged him to come to her home for a meal. After that, whenever he passed that way, he would stop there for something to eat.

⁹She said to her husband, "I am sure this man who stops in from time to time is a holy man of God. ¹⁰Let's build a small room for him on the roof and furnish it with a bed, a table, a chair, and a lamp. Then he will have a place to stay whenever he comes by."

¹¹One day Elisha returned to Shunem, and he went up to this upper room to rest. ¹²He said to his servant Gehazi, "Tell the woman from Shunem I want to speak to her." When she appeared, ¹³Elisha said to Gehazi, "Tell her, 'We appreciate the kind concern you have shown us. What can we do for you? Can we put in a good word for you to the king or to the commander of the army?'"

"No," she replied, "my family takes good care of me."

¹⁴Later Elisha asked Gehazi, "What can we do for her?"

Gehazi replied, "She doesn't have a son, and her husband is an old man."

¹⁵"Call her back again," Elisha told him. When the woman returned, Elisha said to her as she stood in the doorway, ¹⁶"Next year at this time you will be holding a son in your arms!"

"No, my lord!" she cried. "O man of God, don't deceive me and get my hopes up like that."

¹⁷But sure enough, the woman soon became pregnant. And at that time the following year she had a son, just as Elisha had said.

¹⁸One day when her child was older, he went out to help his father, who was working with the harvesters. ¹⁹Suddenly he cried out, "My head hurts! My head hurts!"

His father said to one of the servants, "Carry him home to his mother."

²⁰So the servant took him home, and his mother held him on her lap. But around noontime he died. ²¹She carried him up and laid him on the bed of the man of God, then shut the door and left him there. ²²She sent a message to her husband: "Send one of the servants and

EMPTY JARS, FULL FAITH
(4:1-7) The widow and her sons collected empty jars from their neighbors, and they began to pour oil into them from their one small jar. The oil stopped pouring only when they ran out of containers. The large number of jars they gathered indicated that they had great faith. God's provision was as large as their willingness to obey. Beware of limiting God's blessings by a lack of faith and obedience.

a donkey so that I can hurry to the man of God and come right back."

²³"Why go today?" he asked. "It is neither a new moon festival nor a Sabbath."

But she said, "It will be all right."

²⁴So she saddled the donkey and said to the servant, "Hurry! Don't slow down unless I tell you to."

²⁵As she approached the man of God at Mount Carmel, Elisha saw her in the distance. He said to Gehazi, "Look, the woman from Shunem is coming. ²⁶Run out to meet her and ask her, 'Is everything all right with you, your husband, and your child?'"

"Yes," the woman told Gehazi, "everything is fine."

²⁷But when she came to the man of God at the mountain, she fell to the ground before him and caught hold of his feet. Gehazi began to push her away, but the man of God said, "Leave her alone. She is deeply troubled, but the LORD has not told me what it is."

²⁸Then she said, "Did I ask you for a son, my lord? And didn't I say, 'Don't deceive me and get my hopes up'?"

²⁹Then Elisha said to Gehazi, "Get ready to travel*; take my staff and go! Don't talk to anyone along the way. Go quickly and lay the staff on the child's face."

³⁰But the boy's mother said, "As surely as the LORD lives and you yourself live, I won't go home unless you go with me." So Elisha returned with her.

³¹Gehazi hurried on ahead and laid the staff on the child's face, but nothing happened. There was no sign of life. He returned to meet Elisha and told him, "The child is still dead."

³²When Elisha arrived, the child was indeed dead, lying there on the prophet's bed. ³³He went in alone and shut the door behind him and prayed to the LORD. ³⁴Then he lay down on the child's body, placing his mouth on the child's mouth, his eyes on the child's eyes, and his hands on the child's hands. And as he stretched out on him, the child's body began to grow warm again! ³⁵Elisha got up, walked back and forth across the room once, and then

stretched himself out again on the child. This time the boy sneezed seven times and opened his eyes!

³⁶Then Elisha summoned Gehazi. "Call the child's mother!" he said. And when she came in, Elisha said, "Here, take your son!" ³⁷She fell at his feet and bowed before him, overwhelmed with gratitude. Then she took her son in her arms and carried him downstairs.

MIRACLES DURING A FAMINE ³⁸Elisha now returned to Gilgal, and there was a famine in the land. One day as the group of prophets was seated before him, he said to his servant, "Put a large pot on the fire, and make some stew for the rest of the group."

³⁹One of the young men went out into the field to gather herbs and came back with a pocketful of wild gourds. He shredded them and put them into the pot without realizing they were poisonous. ⁴⁰Some of the stew was served to the men. But after they had eaten a bite or two they cried out, "Man of God, there's poison in this stew!" So they would not eat it.

⁴¹Elisha said, "Bring me some flour." Then he threw it into the pot and said, "Now it's all right; go ahead and eat." And then it did not harm them.

⁴²One day a man from Baal-shalishah brought the man of God a sack of fresh grain and twenty loaves of barley bread made from the first grain of his harvest. Elisha said, "Give it to the people so they can eat."

⁴³"What?" his servant exclaimed. "Feed a hundred people with only this?"

But Elisha repeated, "Give it to the people so they can eat, for this is what the LORD says: Everyone will eat, and there will even be some left over!" ⁴⁴And when they gave it to the people, there was plenty for all and some left over, just as the LORD had promised.

5 **THE HEALING OF NAAMAN** The king of Aram had great admiration for Naaman, the commander of his army, because through him the LORD had given Aram great victories. But though Naaman was a mighty warrior, he suffered from leprosy.*

²At this time Aramean raiders had invaded the land of Israel, and among their captives was a young girl who had been given to Naaman's wife as a maid. ³One day the girl said to her mistress, "I wish my master would go to see the prophet in Samaria. He would heal him of his leprosy."

LEPROSY

(5:1) Leprosy, much like cancer today, was one of the most feared diseases of the time. It was extremely contagious and, in many cases, incurable. In its worst forms, leprosy led to death. Many lepers were forced out of the cities into quarantine camps. Since Naaman still held his post, he probably had a mild form of the disease, or perhaps it was in the early stages. In either case, Naaman's career would be tragically shortened by his disease.

4:29 Hebrew *Bind up your loins.* **5:1** Or *from a contagious skin disease.* The Hebrew word used here and throughout this passage can describe various skin diseases.

⁴So Naaman told the king what the young girl from Israel had said. ⁵"Go and visit the prophet," the king of Aram told him. "I will send a letter of introduction for you to take to the king of Israel." So Naaman started out, carrying as gifts 750 pounds of silver, 150 pounds of gold,* and ten sets of clothing. ⁶The letter to the king of Israel said: "With this letter I present my servant Naaman. I want you to heal him of his leprosy."

⁷When the king of Israel read the letter, he tore his clothes in dismay and said, "This man sends me a leper to heal! Am I God, that I can give life and take it away? I can see that he's just trying to pick a fight with me."

⁸But when Elisha, the man of God, heard that the king of Israel had torn his clothes in dismay, he sent this message to him: "Why are you so upset? Send Naaman to me, and he will learn that there is a true prophet here in Israel."

⁹So Naaman went with his horses and chariots and waited at the door of Elisha's house. ¹⁰But Elisha sent a messenger out to him with this message: "Go and wash yourself seven times in the Jordan River. Then your skin will be restored, and you will be healed of your leprosy."

¹¹But Naaman became angry and stalked away. "I thought he would certainly come out to meet me!" he said. "I expected him to wave his hand over the leprosy and call on the name of the LORD his God and heal me! ¹²Aren't the rivers of Damascus, the Abana and the Pharpar, better than any of the rivers of Israel? Why shouldn't I wash in them and be healed?" So Naaman turned and went away in a rage.

¹³But his officers tried to reason with him and said, "Sir,* if the prophet had told you to do something very difficult, wouldn't you have done it? So you should certainly obey him when he says simply, 'Go and wash and be cured!'" ¹⁴So Naaman went down to the Jordan River and dipped himself seven times, as the man of God had instructed him. And his skin became as healthy as the skin of a young child, and he was healed!

¹⁵Then Naaman and his entire party went back to find the man of God. They stood before him, and Naaman said, "Now I know that there is no God in all the world except in Israel. So please accept a gift from your servant."

¹⁶But Elisha replied, "As surely as the LORD lives, whom I serve, I will not accept any gifts."

And though Naaman urged him to take the gift, Elisha refused.

¹⁷Then Naaman said, "All right, but please allow me to load two of my mules with earth from this place, and I will take it back home with me. From now on I will never again offer burnt offerings or sacrifices to any other god except the LORD. ¹⁸However, may the LORD pardon me in this one thing: When my master the king goes into the temple of the god Rimmon to worship there and leans on my arm, may the LORD pardon me when I bow, too."

¹⁹"Go in peace," Elisha said. So Naaman started home again.

THE GREED OF GEHAZI ²⁰But Gehazi, the servant of Elisha, the man of God, said to himself, "My master should not have let this Aramean get away without accepting any of his gifts. As surely as the LORD lives, I will chase after him and get something from him." ²¹So Gehazi set off after Naaman.

When Naaman saw Gehazi running after him, he climbed down from his chariot and went to meet him. "Is everything all right?" Naaman asked.

²²"Yes," Gehazi said, "but my master has sent me to tell you that two young prophets from the hill country of Ephraim have just arrived. He would like 75 pounds* of silver and two sets of clothing to give to them."

²³"By all means, take twice as much* silver," Naaman insisted. He gave him two sets of clothing, tied up the money in two bags, and sent two of his servants to carry the gifts for Gehazi. ²⁴But when they arrived at the citadel,*

··

HUMILITY
(5:9-15) Naaman, a great hero, was used to getting respect, so he was outraged when Elisha treated him like an ordinary person. To wash in a great river would be one thing, but the Jordan was small and dirty. To wash in the Jordan, Naaman thought, was beneath a man of his position. But Naaman had to humble himself and obey Elisha's commands in order to be healed. Have you ever felt that one of God's rules was too embarrassing to follow? Obedience to God often begins with humility. It also involves loving God more than our pride.

WHAT'S MORE IMPORTANT: GAIN OR GOD?
(5:20-27) Gehazi saw a perfect opportunity to get rich by selfishly asking for the reward Elisha had refused. His plan had three fatal flaws: (1) He willingly accepted money for what he didn't do; (2) he wrongly implied that money could be exchanged for God's free gift of healing and mercy; and (3) he lied and tried to cover up his motives for accepting money. Although Gehazi had been a helpful servant, personal gain had become more important to him than serving God. True service is motivated by love for God and seeks no personal gain. Is that a good description of your motives for serving God?

5:5 Hebrew *10 talents* [340 kilograms] *of silver, 6,000 shekels* [68 kilograms] *of gold.* **5:13** Hebrew *My father.* **5:22** Hebrew *1 talent* [34 kilograms]. **5:23** Hebrew *take 2 talents* [68 kilograms]. **5:24** Hebrew *the Ophel.*

Gehazi took the gifts from the servants and sent the men back. Then he went and hid the gifts inside the house.

²⁵When he went in to his master, Elisha asked him, "Where have you been, Gehazi?"

"I haven't been anywhere," he replied.

²⁶But Elisha asked him, "Don't you realize that I was there in spirit when Naaman stepped down from his chariot to meet you? Is this the time to receive money and clothing, olive groves and vineyards, sheep and cattle, and male and female servants? ²⁷Because you have done this, you and your descendants will suffer from Naaman's leprosy forever." When Gehazi left the room, he was covered with leprosy; his skin was white as snow.

6

THE FLOATING AX HEAD One day the group of prophets came to Elisha and told him, "As you can see, this place where we meet with you is too small. ²Let's go down to the Jordan River, where there are plenty of logs. There we can build a new place for us to meet."

"All right," he told them, "go ahead."

³"Please come with us," someone suggested.

"I will," he said. ⁴So he went with them.

When they arrived at the Jordan, they began cutting down trees. ⁵But as one of them was cutting a tree, his ax head fell into the river. "Oh, sir!" he cried. "It was a borrowed ax!"

⁶"Where did it fall?" the man of God asked. When he showed him the place, Elisha cut a stick and threw it into the water at that spot. Then the ax head floated to the surface. ⁷"Grab it," Elisha said. And the man reached out and grabbed it.

ELISHA TRAPS THE ARAMEANS ⁸When the king of Aram was at war with Israel, he would confer with his officers and say, "We will mobilize our forces at such and such a place."

⁹But immediately Elisha, the man of God, would warn the king of Israel, "Do not go near that place, for the Arameans are planning to mobilize their troops there." ¹⁰So the king of Israel would send word to the place indicated by the man of God. Time and again Elisha warned the king, so that he would be on the alert there.

¹¹The king of Aram became very upset over this. He called his officers together and demanded, "Which of you is the traitor? Who has been informing the king of Israel of my plans?"

¹²"It's not us, my lord the king," one of the officers replied. "Elisha, the prophet in Israel, tells the king of Israel even the words you speak in the privacy of your bedroom!"

¹³"Go and find out where he is," the king commanded, "so I can send troops to seize him."

And the report came back: "Elisha is at Dothan." ¹⁴So one night the king of Aram sent a great army with many chariots and horses to surround the city.

¹⁵When the servant of the man of God got up early the next morning and went outside, there were troops, horses, and chariots everywhere. "Oh, sir, what will we do now?" the young man cried to Elisha.

¹⁶"Don't be afraid!" Elisha told him. "For there are more on our side than on theirs!" ¹⁷Then Elisha prayed, "O LORD, open his eyes and let him see!" The LORD opened the young man's eyes, and when he looked up, he saw that the hillside around Elisha was filled with horses and chariots of fire.

¹⁸As the Aramean army advanced toward him, Elisha prayed, "O LORD, please make them

CHOICES
outspoken

Are you sitting down? Sixteen-year-old David H. not only went to a church youth retreat this past weekend (unbelievable), but he also asked Jesus Christ to be his Lord and Savior (major shock)! It's not a joke; I was there. David was dead serious.

Remember now, this is the same guy who stayed wasted for almost his whole freshman year. We're talking about the most outspoken enemy of the Christian students at Lanier High School.

At school on Monday, word quickly got around about David's surprising decision. When David's wild partying buds approached him to find out what really happened, David brushed them off, saying, "Hey, it's kind of private. I'd rather not talk about it now."

Puzzled, David's best friend, Randy, dropped by after school.

"C'mon, Dave," he urged. "I'm curious . . . Tell me the deal."

David froze. He knew he made the right decision at the retreat. He'd felt liberated, closer to God, and a whole lot happier inside. Yet he didn't want to be abused by his cynical, definitely non-Christian friends.

What do you think? Should he tell Randy what happened—and risk catching a lot of grief? Or should he just hope his friends find God on their own?

Can you relate to David's fear of sharing the Good News? Read 2 Kings 6:24–7:11 (and take special note of 7:9). What advice would you give David?

blind." So the LORD struck them with blindness as Elisha had asked.

¹⁹Then Elisha went out and told them, "You have come the wrong way! This isn't the right city! Follow me, and I will take you to the man you are looking for." And he led them to the city of Samaria.

²⁰As soon as they had entered Samaria, Elisha prayed, "O LORD, now open their eyes and let them see." So the LORD opened their eyes, and they discovered that they were in the middle of Samaria.

²¹When the king of Israel saw them, he shouted to Elisha, "My father, should I kill them? Should I kill them?"

²²"Of course not!" Elisha replied. "Do we kill prisoners of war? Give them food and drink and send them home again to their master."

²³So the king made a great feast for them and then sent them home to their master. After that, the Aramean raiders stayed away from the land of Israel.

BEN-HADAD BESIEGES SAMARIA ²⁴Some time later, however, King Ben-hadad of Aram mustered his entire army and besieged Samaria. ²⁵As a result, there was a great famine in the city. The siege lasted so long that a donkey's head sold for eighty pieces of silver, and a cup of dove's dung sold for five pieces* of silver.

²⁶One day as the king of Israel was walking along the wall of the city, a woman called to him, "Please help me, my lord the king!"

²⁷He answered, "If the LORD doesn't help you, what can I do? I have neither food from the threshing floor nor wine from the press to give you." ²⁸But then the king asked, "What is the matter?"

She replied, "This woman said to me: 'Come on, let's eat your son today, then we will eat my son tomorrow.' ²⁹So we cooked my son and ate him. Then the next day I said to her, 'Kill your son so we can eat him,' but she has hidden her son."

³⁰When the king heard this, he tore his clothes in despair. And as the king walked along the wall, the people could see that he was wearing burlap under his robe next to his skin. ³¹"May God strike me and even kill me if I don't separate Elisha's head from his shoulders this very day," the king vowed.

³²Elisha was sitting in his house with the elders of Israel when the king sent a messenger to summon him. But before the messenger arrived, Elisha said to the elders, "A murderer has sent a man to cut off my head. When he arrives, shut the door and keep him out. We will soon hear his master's steps following him."

³³While Elisha was still saying this, the messenger arrived. And the king* said, "All this misery is from the LORD! Why should I wait for the LORD any longer?"

7 Elisha replied, "Listen to this message from the LORD! This is what the LORD says: By this time tomorrow in the markets of Samaria, five quarts of choice flour will cost only one piece of silver,* and ten quarts of barley grain will cost only one piece of silver.*"

²The officer assisting the king said to the man of God, "That couldn't happen even if the LORD opened the windows of heaven!"

But Elisha replied, "You will see it happen with your own eyes, but you won't be able to eat any of it!"

LEPERS VISIT THE ENEMY CAMP ³Now there were four men with leprosy* sitting at the entrance of the city gates. "Why should we sit here waiting to die?" they asked each other. ⁴"We will starve if we stay here, but with the famine in the city, we will starve if we go back there. So we might as well go out and surrender to the Aramean army. If they let us live, so

· ·

HIDDEN RESOURCES
(6:16-17) Elisha's servant was no longer afraid when he saw God's mighty heavenly army. Faith reveals that God is doing more for his people than we could ever realize through human understanding alone. When you face situations that seem overwhelming, God can give you the faith to see his plan in action.

A FATAL FOCUS
(7:1-2) When Elisha prophesied God's deliverance, the king's officer didn't believe Elisha's message concerning the end of the famine. Yet God's words came true anyway (7:14-16). Like the officer, we're sometimes preoccupied with problems instead of looking for the solutions that God offers. When a problem comes your way, will you focus on it or on God?

SHARING THE NEWS
(7:3-10) The lepers discovered the deserted camp and realized that their lives had been spared. At first they kept the wonderful news to themselves, forgetting their fellow citizens who were starving inside the city walls. The Good News about Jesus Christ must be shared, too, for no news is more important than that. We must remember those who are dying without it. We must not become so preoccupied with our own faith that we neglect sharing it with those around us. Our "wonderful news," like that of the lepers, will not wait until morning.

6:25 Hebrew *sold for 80 shekels* [2 pounds, or 0.9 kilograms] *of silver, and ¼ of a cab* [0.3 liters] *of dove's dung sold for 5 shekels* [2 ounces, or 57 grams]. *Dove's dung* may be a variety of wild vegetable.   **6:33** Hebrew *he.*   **7:1a** Hebrew *1 seah* [6 liters] *of choice flour will cost 1 shekel* [0.4 ounces, or 11 grams]; also in 7:16, 18.   **7:1b** Hebrew *2 seahs* [12 liters] *of barley grain will cost 1 shekel* [0.4 ounces, or 11 grams]; also in 7:16, 18.   **7:3** Or *with a contagious skin disease.* The Hebrew word used here and throughout this passage can describe various skin diseases.

much the better. But if they kill us, we would have died anyway."

⁵So at twilight they set out for the camp of the Arameans. But when they came to the edge of the camp, no one was there! ⁶For the Lord had caused the Aramean army to hear the clatter of speeding chariots and the galloping of horses and the sounds of a great army approaching. "The king of Israel has hired the Hittites and Egyptians* to attack us!" they cried to one another. ⁷So they panicked and ran into the night, abandoning their tents, horses, donkeys, and everything else, as they fled for their lives.

⁸When the lepers arrived at the edge of the camp, they went into one tent after another, eating and drinking wine; and they carried off silver and gold and clothing and hid it. ⁹Finally, they said to each other, "This is not right. This is a day of good news, and we aren't sharing it with anyone! If we wait until morning, some calamity will certainly fall upon us. Come on, let's go back and tell the people at the palace."

¹⁰So they went back to the city and told the gatekeepers what had happened. "We went out to the Aramean camp," they said, "and no one was there! The horses and donkeys were tethered and the tents were all in order, but there wasn't a single person around!" ¹¹Then the gatekeepers shouted the news to the people in the palace.

ISRAEL PLUNDERS THE CAMP ¹²The king got out of bed in the middle of the night and told his officers, "I know what has happened. The Arameans know we are starving, so they have left their camp and have hidden in the fields. They are expecting us to leave the city, and then they will take us alive and capture the city."

¹³One of his officers replied, "We had better send out scouts to check into this. Let them take five of the remaining horses. If something happens to them, it will be no worse than if they stay here and die with the rest of us."

¹⁴So two chariots with horses were prepared, and the king sent scouts to see what had happened to the Aramean army. ¹⁵They went all the way to the Jordan River, following a trail of clothing and equipment that the Arameans had thrown away in their mad rush to escape. The scouts returned and told the king about it. ¹⁶Then the people of Samaria rushed out and plundered the Aramean camp. So it was true that five quarts of choice flour were sold that day for one piece of silver, and ten quarts of barley grain were sold for one piece of silver, just as the LORD had promised. ¹⁷The king appointed his officer to control the traffic at the gate, but he was knocked down and trampled to death as the people rushed out.

So everything happened exactly as the man of God had predicted when the king came to his house. ¹⁸The man of God had said to the king, "By this time tomorrow in the markets of Samaria, five quarts of choice flour will cost one piece of silver, and ten quarts of barley grain will cost one piece of silver."

¹⁹The king's officer had replied, "That couldn't happen even if the LORD opened the windows of heaven!" And the man of God had said, "You will see it happen with your own

7:6 Possibly *and the people of Muzur,* a district near Cilicia.

I WONDER...

Why should I tell others what I believe about God?

Try to remember the best gift you ever received. What did you do after you opened it? More than likely, you called your best friend to tell him or her about it.

Forgiveness from sin is the greatest gift you will ever receive! It is impossible to keep quiet about it if you truly recognize how important this free gift really is.

Check out the story of the four men with leprosy who discovered an empty camp (2 Kgs 7:3-15). All of their enemies were gone! The joy and amazement the lepers experienced was beyond their wildest dreams. God had given them something that was simply too wonderful to keep to themselves. They couldn't wait to share the good news with everyone.

The choice for the four men with leprosy—keeping their discovery a secret or telling others about it—probably was tough to make because their disease separated them from other people. But they didn't hesitate to make the right choice.

Our sin is like leprosy. We cannot always tell its effects, but left unchecked, the "disease" gets progressively worse. But forgiveness is the antidote for this disease. Our thankful response to God could cause us to tell all who will listen!

Unfortunately, some people take for granted the gift of salvation through Jesus Christ. These are often the people who say little about their faith. For others, having Christ as Savior is the most exciting gift they have ever received! Of course, having a present doesn't automatically mean that others will know about it. We must tell them.

eyes, but you won't be able to eat any of it!" [20]And so it was, for the people trampled him to death at the gate!

8 THE WOMAN FROM SHUNEM RETURNS HOME
Elisha had told the woman whose son he had brought back to life, "Take your family and move to some other place, for the LORD has called for a famine on Israel that will last for seven years." [2]So the woman did as the man of God instructed. She took her family and settled in the land of the Philistines for seven years.

[3]After the famine ended she returned from the land of the Philistines, and she went to see the king about getting back her house and land. [4]As she came in, the king was talking with Gehazi, the servant of the man of God. The king had just said, "Tell me some stories about the great things Elisha has done." [5]And Gehazi was telling the king about the time Elisha had brought a boy back to life. At that very moment, the mother of the boy walked in to make her appeal to the king about her house and land.

"Look, my lord the king!" Gehazi exclaimed. "Here is the woman now, and this is her son— the very one Elisha brought back to life!"

[6]"Is this true?" the king asked her. And she told him the story. So he directed one of his officials to see that everything she had lost was restored to her, including the value of any crops that had been harvested during her absence.

HAZAEL MURDERS BEN-HADAD
[7]Elisha went to Damascus, the capital of Aram, where King Ben-hadad lay sick. When someone told the king that the man of God had come, [8]the king said to Hazael, "Take a gift to the man of God. Then tell him to ask the LORD, 'Will I recover from this illness?'"

[9]So Hazael loaded down forty camels with the finest products of Damascus as a gift for Elisha. He went to him and said, "Your servant Ben-hadad, the king of Aram, has sent me to ask, 'Will I recover from this illness?'"

[10]And Elisha replied, "Go and tell him, 'You will surely recover.' But actually the LORD has shown me that he will surely die!" [11]Elisha stared at Hazael* with a fixed gaze until Hazael became uneasy.* Then the man of God started weeping.

[12]"What's the matter, my lord?" Hazael asked him.

Elisha replied, "I know the terrible things you will do to the people of Israel. You will burn their fortified cities, kill their young men with the sword, dash their little children to the ground, and rip open their pregnant women!"

[13]Hazael responded, "How could a nobody like me* ever accomplish such great things?"

Elisha answered, "The LORD has shown me that you are going to be the king of Aram."

[14]When Hazael left Elisha and went back, the king asked him, "What did Elisha tell you?"

And Hazael replied, "He told me that you will surely recover."

[15]But the next day Hazael took a blanket, soaked it in water, and held it over the king's face until he died. Then Hazael became the next king of Aram.

JEHORAM RULES IN JUDAH
[16]Jehoram son of King Jehoshaphat of Judah began to rule over Judah in the fifth year of the reign of Joram son of Ahab, king of Israel. [17]Jehoram was thirty-two years old when he became king, and he reigned in Jerusalem eight years. [18]But Jehoram followed the example of the kings of Israel and was as wicked as King Ahab, for he had married one of Ahab's daughters. So Jehoram did what was evil in the LORD's sight. [19]But the LORD did not want to destroy Judah, for he had made a covenant with David and promised that his descendants would continue to rule, shining like a lamp forever.

[20]During Jehoram's reign, the Edomites revolted against Judah and crowned their own king. [21]So Jehoram* went with all his chariots to attack the town of Zair.* The Edomites surrounded him and his chariot commanders, but he went out at night and attacked them* under cover of darkness. But Jehoram's army deserted him and fled to their homes. [22]So Edom has been independent from Judah to this day. The town of Libnah also revolted about that same time.

[23]The rest of the events in Jehoram's reign and everything he did are recorded in *The Book of the History of the Kings of Judah.* [24]When Jehoram died, he was buried with his ancestors in the City of David. Then his son Ahaziah became the next king.

AHAZIAH RULES IN JUDAH
[25]Ahaziah son of Jehoram began to rule over Judah in the twelfth year of the reign of Joram son of Ahab, king of Israel.

[26]Ahaziah was twenty-two years old when

8:11a Hebrew *He stared at him.* **8:11b** The meaning of the Hebrew is uncertain. **8:13** Hebrew *a dog.* **8:21a** Hebrew *Joram,* a variant spelling of Jehoram; also in 8:23, 24. **8:21b** Greek version reads *Seir.* **8:21c** Or *he went out and escaped.* The meaning of the Hebrew is uncertain.

he became king, and he reigned in Jerusalem one year. His mother was Athaliah, a granddaughter of King Omri of Israel. [27]Ahaziah followed the evil example of King Ahab's family. He did what was evil in the LORD's sight, just as Ahab's family had done, for he was related by marriage to the family of Ahab.

[28]Ahaziah joined Joram son of Ahab, the king of Israel, in his war against King Hazael of Aram at Ramoth-gilead. When the Arameans wounded King Joram in the battle, [29]he returned to Jezreel to recover from the wounds he had received at Ramoth.* Because Joram was wounded, King Ahaziah of Judah went to Jezreel to visit him.

9 JEHU ANOINTED KING OF ISRAEL

Meanwhile, Elisha the prophet had summoned a member of the group of prophets. "Get ready to travel,"* he told him, "and take this flask of olive oil with you. Go to Ramoth-gilead, [2]and find Jehu son of Jehoshaphat, son of Nimshi. Call him into a private room away from his friends, [3]and pour the oil over his head. Say to him, 'This is what the LORD says: I anoint you to be the king over Israel.' Then open the door and run for your life!"

[4]So the young prophet did as he was told and went to Ramoth-gilead. [5]When he arrived there, he found Jehu sitting around with the other army officers. "I have a message for you, Commander," he said.

"For which one of us?" Jehu asked.

"For you, Commander," he replied.

[6]So Jehu left the others and went into the house. Then the young prophet poured the oil over Jehu's head and said, "This is what the LORD, the God of Israel, says: I anoint you king over the LORD's people, Israel. [7]You are to destroy the family of Ahab, your master. In this way, I will avenge the murder of my prophets and all the LORD's servants who were killed by Jezebel. [8]The entire family of Ahab must be wiped out. I will destroy every one of his male descendants, slave and free alike, anywhere in Israel. [9]I will destroy the family of Ahab as I destroyed the families of Jeroboam son of Nebat

and of Baasha son of Ahijah. [10]Dogs will eat Ahab's wife Jezebel at the plot of land in Jezreel, and no one will bury her." Then the young prophet opened the door and ran.

[11]Jehu went back to his fellow officers, and one of them asked him, "What did that madman want? Is everything all right?"

"You know how a man like that babbles on," Jehu replied.

[12]"You're hiding something," they said. "Tell us."

So Jehu told them, "He said to me, 'This is what the LORD says: I have anointed you to be king over Israel.'"

[13]Then they quickly spread out their cloaks on the bare steps and blew the ram's horn, shouting, "Jehu is king!"

JEHU KILLS JORAM AND AHAZIAH

[14]So Jehu son of Jehoshaphat, son of Nimshi, led a conspiracy against King Joram. (Now Joram had been with the army at Ramoth-gilead, defending Israel against the forces of King Hazael of Aram. [15]But King Joram* was wounded in the fighting and returned to Jezreel to recover from his wounds.) So Jehu told the men with him, "If you want me to be king, don't let anyone leave town and go to Jezreel to report what we have done."

[16]Then Jehu got into a chariot and rode to Jezreel to find King Joram, who was lying there wounded. King Ahaziah of Judah was there, too, for he had gone to visit him. [17]The watchman on the tower of Jezreel saw Jehu and his company approaching, so he shouted to Joram, "I see a company of troops coming!"

"Send out a rider to ask if they are coming in peace," King Joram ordered.

[18]So a horseman went out to meet Jehu and said, "The king wants to know if you are coming in peace."

Jehu replied, "What do you know about peace? Fall in behind me!"

The watchman called out to the king, "The messenger has met them, but he's not returning."

[19]So the king sent out a second horseman. He rode up to them and said, "The king wants to know if you come in peace."

Again Jehu answered, "What do you know about peace? Fall in behind me!"

[20]The watchman exclaimed, "The messenger has met them, but he isn't returning either! It must be Jehu son of Nimshi, for he's driving like a madman."

....

PEACE

(9:18-19) The riders met Jehu and asked if he came in peace and friendship. But Jehu responded, "What do you know about peace?" Jehu scoffed, because he knew that the men represented a cruel king. Friendship and peace are genuine when they are rooted in a relationship with God. Don't seek friendship with those who are enemies of the good and the true King. Lasting peace and genuine friendship can come only from knowing the God who gives them to us.

8:29 Hebrew *Ramah*, a variant spelling of Ramoth.   **9:1** Hebrew *Bind up your loins*.   **9:15** Hebrew *Jehoram*, a variant spelling of Joram; also in 9:17, 21, 22, 23, 24.

²¹"Quick! Get my chariot ready!" King Joram commanded.

Then King Joram of Israel and King Ahaziah of Judah rode out in their chariots to meet Jehu. They met him at the plot of land that had belonged to Naboth of Jezreel. ²²King Joram demanded, "Do you come in peace, Jehu?"

Jehu replied, "How can there be peace as long as the idolatry and witchcraft of your mother, Jezebel, are all around us?"

²³Then King Joram turned the horses around* and fled, shouting to King Ahaziah, "Treason, Ahaziah!" ²⁴But Jehu drew his bow and shot Joram between the shoulders. The arrow pierced his heart, and he sank down dead in his chariot.

²⁵Jehu said to Bidkar, his officer, "Throw him into the plot of land that belonged to Naboth of Jezreel. Do you remember when you and I were riding along behind his father, Ahab? The LORD pronounced this message against him: ²⁶'I solemnly swear that I will repay him here on this plot of land, says the LORD, for the murder of Naboth and his sons that I saw yesterday.' So throw him out on Naboth's property, just as the LORD said."

²⁷When King Ahaziah of Judah saw what was happening, he fled along the road to Beth-haggan. Jehu rode after him, shouting, "Shoot him, too!" So they shot Ahaziah in his chariot at the Ascent of Gur, near Ibleam. He was able to go on as far as Megiddo, but he died there. ²⁸His servants took him by chariot to Jerusalem, where they buried him with his ancestors in the City of David. ²⁹Ahaziah had become king over Judah in the eleventh year of the reign of Joram son of Ahab.

THE DEATH OF JEZEBEL ³⁰When Jezebel, the queen mother, heard that Jehu had come to Jezreel, she painted her eyelids and fixed her hair and sat at a window. ³¹When Jehu entered the gate of the palace, she shouted at him, "Have you come in peace, you murderer? You're just like Zimri, who murdered his master!"*

³²Jehu looked up and saw her at the window and shouted, "Who is on my side?" And two or three eunuchs looked out at him. ³³"Throw her down!" Jehu yelled. So they threw her out the window, and her blood spattered against the wall and on the horses. And Jehu trampled her body under his horses' hooves.

³⁴Then Jehu went into the palace and ate and drank. Afterward he said, "Someone go and bury this cursed woman, for she is the daughter of a king." ³⁵But when they went out to bury her, they found only her skull, her feet, and her hands.

³⁶When they returned and told Jehu, he stated, "This fulfills the message from the LORD, which he spoke through his servant Elijah from Tishbe: 'At the plot of land in Jezreel, dogs will eat Jezebel's body. ³⁷Her remains will be scattered like dung on the plot of land in Jezreel, so that no one will be able to recognize her.'"

10 JEHU KILLS AHAB'S FAMILY Ahab had seventy sons living in the city of Samaria. So Jehu wrote letters and sent them to Samaria, to the elders and officials of the city,* and to the guardians of King Ahab's sons. He said, ²"The king's sons are with you, and you have at your disposal chariots, horses, a fortified city, and weapons. As soon as you receive this letter, ³select the best qualified of your master's sons to be your king, and prepare to fight for Ahab's dynasty."

⁴But they were paralyzed with fear and said, "We've seen that two kings couldn't stand against this man! What can we do?"

⁵So the palace and city administrators, together with the elders and the guardians of the king's sons, sent this message to Jehu: "We are your servants and will do anything you tell us. We will not make anyone king; do whatever you think is best."

⁶Jehu responded with a second letter: "If you are on my side and are going to obey me, bring the heads of your master's sons to me at Jezreel by this time tomorrow." Now the seventy sons of the king were being cared for by the leaders of Samaria, where they had been raised since childhood. ⁷When the letter arrived, the leaders killed all seventy of the king's sons. They placed their heads in baskets and presented them to Jehu at Jezreel.

⁸A messenger went to Jehu and said, "They have brought the heads of the king's sons."

So Jehu ordered, "Pile them in two heaps at the entrance of the city gate, and leave them there until morning."

⁹In the morning he went out and spoke to the crowd that had gathered around them. "You are not to blame," he told them. "I am the one who conspired against my master and killed him. But who killed all these? ¹⁰You can be sure that the message of the LORD that was spoken concerning Ahab's family will not fail. The LORD declared through his servant Elijah that this would happen." ¹¹Then Jehu killed all who were left of Ahab's relatives living in

9:23 Hebrew *turned his hands.* **9:31** See 1 Kgs 16:9-10, where Zimri killed his master, King Elah. **10:1** As in some Greek manuscripts and Latin Vulgate (see also 10:6); Hebrew reads *of Jezreel.*

Jezreel and all his important officials, his personal friends, and his priests. So Ahab was left without a single survivor.

[12] Then Jehu set out for Samaria. Along the way, while he was at Beth-eked of the Shepherds, [13] he met some relatives of King Ahaziah of Judah. "Who are you?" he asked them.

And they replied, "We are relatives of King Ahaziah. We are going to visit the sons of King Ahab and the sons of the queen mother."

[14] "Take them alive!" Jehu shouted to his men. And they captured all forty-two of them and killed them at the well of Beth-eked. None of them escaped.

[15] When Jehu left there, he met Jehonadab son of Recab, who was coming to meet him. After they had greeted each other, Jehu said to him, "Are you as loyal to me as I am to you?"

"Yes, I am," Jehonadab replied.

"If you are," Jehu said, "then give me your hand." So Jehonadab put out his hand, and Jehu helped him into the chariot. [16] Then Jehu said, "Now come with me, and see how devoted I am to the LORD." So Jehonadab rode along with him.

[17] When Jehu arrived in Samaria, he killed everyone who was left there from Ahab's family, just as the LORD had promised through Elijah.

JEHU KILLS THE PRIESTS OF BAAL [18] Then Jehu called a meeting of all the people of the city and said to them, "Ahab's worship of Baal was nothing compared to the way I will worship him! [19] Therefore, summon all the prophets and worshipers of Baal, and call together all his priests. See to it that every one of them comes, for I am going to offer a great sacrifice to Baal. Anyone who fails to come will be put to death." But Jehu's cunning plan was to destroy all the worshipers of Baal.

[20] Then Jehu ordered, "Prepare a solemn assembly to worship Baal!" So they did. [21] He sent messengers throughout all Israel summoning those who worshiped Baal. They all came—not a single one remained behind—and they filled the temple of Baal from one end to the other. [22] And Jehu instructed the keeper of the wardrobe, "Be sure that every worshiper of Baal wears one of these robes." So robes were given to them.

[23] Then Jehu went into the temple of Baal with Jehonadab son of Recab. Jehu said to the worshipers of Baal, "Make sure no one who worships the LORD is here—only those who worship Baal." [24] So they were all inside the temple to offer sacrifices and burnt offerings. Now Jehu had stationed eighty of his men outside the building and had warned them, "If you let anyone escape, you will pay for it with your own life."

[25] As soon as Jehu had finished sacrificing the burnt offering, he commanded his guards and officers, "Go in and kill all of them. Don't let a single one escape!" So they killed them all with their swords, and the guards and officers dragged their bodies outside.* Then Jehu's men went into the innermost fortress* of the temple of Baal. [26] They dragged out the sacred pillar* used in the worship of Baal and burned it. [27] They smashed the sacred pillar and wrecked the temple of Baal, converting it into a public toilet, as it remains to this day.

[28] In this way, Jehu destroyed every trace of Baal worship from Israel. [29] He did not, however, destroy the gold calves at Bethel and Dan, with which Jeroboam son of Nebat had caused Israel to sin.

[30] Nonetheless the LORD said to Jehu, "You have done well in following my instructions to destroy the family of Ahab. Therefore, your descendants will be kings of Israel down to the fourth generation." [31] But Jehu did not obey the Law of the LORD, the God of Israel, with all his heart. He refused to turn from the sins that Jeroboam had led Israel to commit.

THE DEATH OF JEHU [32] At about this time the LORD began to cut down the size of Israel's territory. King Hazael conquered several sections of the country [33] east of the Jordan River, includ-

---

TOLERANCE
(10:23-29) Israel was supposed to be intolerant of any religion that did not worship the true God. The religions of surrounding nations were evil and corrupt, based on sexual promiscuity, political favors, greed, and materialism. They were designed to destroy life, not uphold it. Israel was God's special nation, chosen to be an example of what was right, true, and fair. But Israel's kings, priests, and elders, contaminated by surrounding pagan beliefs, had become tolerant and apathetic. We are to be completely intolerant of sin and remove it from our lives. It is one thing to be tolerant of others' views, but we should not condone actions that lead people away from God's standards of living.

LIP SERVICE
(10:30-31) Jehu did much of what the Lord told him to, but he did not fully obey God. Jehu had become God's instrument for carrying out justice, rather than God's servant. As a result, Jehu gave only lip service to God while he worshiped the golden calves. In the same way we can be very active in our work for God and still not give the heartfelt obedience he desires. Are you a servant or an instrument?

10:25a Or *they left their bodies lying there;* or *they threw them out into the outermost court.* **10:25b** Hebrew *city.* **10:26** As in Greek and Syriac versions and Latin Vulgate; Hebrew reads *sacred pillars.*

GOD OR IDOLS

Why did people continually turn to idols instead of to God?

IDOLS WERE:	GOD IS:
Tangible	Intangible—no physical form
Morally similar—had human characteristics	Morally dissimilar—has divine characteristics
Comprehensible	Incomprehensible
Able to be manipulated	Not able to be manipulated

WORSHIPING IDOLS INVOLVED:	WORSHIPING GOD INVOLVES:
Materialism	Sacrifice
Sexual immorality	Purity and commitment
Doing whatever a person wanted	Doing what God wants
Focusing on self	Focusing on others

ing all of Gilead, Gad, Reuben, and Manasseh. He conquered the area from the town of Aroer by the Arnon Gorge to as far north as Gilead and Bashan.

34The rest of the events in Jehu's reign— everything he did and all his achievements— are recorded in *The Book of the History of the Kings of Israel*.

35When Jehu died, he was buried in Samaria. Then his son Jehoahaz became the next king. 36In all, Jehu reigned over Israel from Samaria for twenty-eight years.

11 QUEEN ATHALIAH RULES IN JUDAH

When Athaliah, the mother of King Ahaziah of Judah, learned that her son was dead, she began to destroy the rest of the royal family. 2But Ahaziah's sister Jehosheba, the daughter of King Jehoram,* took Ahaziah's infant son, Joash, and stole him away from among the rest of the king's children, who were about to be killed. She put Joash and his nurse in a bedroom to hide him from Athaliah, so the child was not murdered. 3Joash remained hidden in the Temple of the LORD for six years while Athaliah ruled over the land.

REVOLT AGAINST ATHALIAH 4In the seventh year of Athaliah's reign, Jehoiada the priest summoned the commanders, the Carite mercenaries, and the palace guards to come to the Temple of the LORD. He made a solemn pact with them and made them swear an oath of loyalty there in the LORD's Temple; then he showed them the king's son.

5Jehoiada told them, "This is what you must

11:2 Hebrew *Joram*, a variant spelling of Jehoram. 11:12 Or *a copy of the covenant.*

do. A third of you who are on duty on the Sabbath are to guard the royal palace itself. 6Another third of you are to stand guard at the Sur Gate. And the final third must stand guard behind the palace guard. These three groups will all guard the palace. 7The other two units who are off duty on the Sabbath must stand guard for the king at the LORD's Temple. 8Form a bodyguard around the king and keep your weapons in hand. Kill anyone who tries to break through. Stay with the king wherever he goes."

9So the commanders did everything as Jehoiada the priest ordered. The commanders took charge of the men reporting for duty that Sabbath, as well as those who were going off duty. They brought them all to Jehoiada the priest, 10and he supplied them with the spears and small shields that had once belonged to King David and were stored in the Temple of the LORD. 11The palace guards stationed themselves around the king, with their weapons ready. They formed a line from the south side of the Temple around to the north side and all around the altar.

12Then Jehoiada brought out Joash, the king's son, placed the crown on his head, and presented him with a copy of God's laws.* They anointed him and proclaimed him king, and everyone clapped their hands and shouted, "Long live the king!"

THE DEATH OF ATHALIAH 13When Athaliah heard all the noise made by the palace guards and the people, she hurried to the LORD's Temple to see what was happening. 14When she arrived, she saw the newly crowned king standing in his place of authority by the pillar, as was the custom at times of coronation. The commanders and trumpeters were surrounding him, and people from all over the land were rejoicing and blowing trumpets. When Athaliah saw all this, she tore her clothes in despair and shouted, "Treason! Treason!"

¹⁵Then Jehoiada the priest ordered the commanders who were in charge of the troops, "Take her to the soldiers in front of the Temple,* and kill anyone who tries to rescue her." For the priest had said, "She must not be killed in the Temple of the LORD." ¹⁶So they seized her and led her out to the gate where horses enter the palace grounds, and she was killed there.

JEHOIADA'S RELIGIOUS REFORMS
¹⁷Then Jehoiada made a covenant between the LORD and the king and the people that they would be the LORD's people. He also made a covenant between the king and the people. ¹⁸And all the people of the land went over to the temple of Baal and tore it down. They demolished the altars and smashed the idols to pieces, and they killed Mattan the priest of Baal in front of the altars.

Jehoiada the priest stationed guards at the Temple of the LORD. ¹⁹Then the commanders, the Carite mercenaries, the palace guards, and all the people of the land escorted the king from the Temple of the LORD. They went through the gate of the guards and into the palace, and the king took his seat on the royal throne. ²⁰So all the people of the land rejoiced, and the city was peaceful because Athaliah had been killed at the king's palace.

²¹*Joash* was seven years old when he became king.

12
JOASH REPAIRS THE TEMPLE ¹*Joash* began to rule over Judah in the seventh year of King Jehu's reign in Israel. He reigned in Jerusalem forty years. His mother was Zibiah

from Beersheba. ²All his life Joash did what was pleasing in the LORD's sight because Jehoiada the priest instructed him. ³Yet even so, he did not destroy the pagan shrines, and the people still offered sacrifices and burned incense there.

⁴One day King Joash said to the priests, "Collect all the money brought as a sacred offering to the LORD's Temple, whether it is a regular assessment, a payment of vows, or a voluntary gift. ⁵Let the priests take some of that money to pay for whatever repairs are needed at the Temple."

⁶But by the twenty-third year of Joash's reign, the priests still had not repaired the Temple. ⁷So King Joash called for Jehoiada and the other priests and asked them, "Why haven't you repaired the Temple? Don't use any more money for your own needs. From now on, it must all be spent on Temple repairs." ⁸So the priests agreed not to accept any more money from the people, and they also agreed to let others take responsibility for repairing the Temple.

⁹Then Jehoiada the priest bored a hole in the lid of a large chest and set it on the right-hand side of the altar at the entrance of the Temple of the LORD. The priests guarding the entrance put all of the people's contributions into the chest. ¹⁰Whenever the chest became full, the court secretary and the high priest counted the money that had been brought to the LORD's Temple and put it into bags. ¹¹Then they gave the money to the construction supervisors, who used it to pay the people working on the LORD's Temple—the carpenters, the builders, ¹²the masons, and the stonecutters. They also used the money to buy the timber and the finished stone needed for repairing the LORD's Temple, and they paid any other expenses related to the Temple's restoration.

¹³The money brought to the Temple was not used for making silver bowls, lamp snuffers, basins, trumpets, or other articles of gold or silver for the Temple of the LORD. ¹⁴It was paid to the workmen, who used it for the Temple repairs. ¹⁵No accounting of this money was required from the construction supervisors, because they were honest and trustworthy men. ¹⁶However, the money that was contributed for guilt offerings and sin offerings was not brought into the LORD's Temple. It was given to the priests for their own use.

A GOOD INFLUENCE
(12:1-2) Jehoiada, the high priest, was a good influence over Joash, the young king of Judah. As long as Joash heeded Jehoiada's good instruction, he fulfilled God's plan for his life. Who offers you wise advice? Do you follow that advice?

EVALUATE ACTIONS
(12:3) Like Jehu (see 10:30-31), Joash didn't go far enough in his plan to reform the nation, but he did a lot of good. When we aren't sure if we've gone far enough in correcting our actions, we can ask ourselves these questions: (1) Does the Bible prohibit this action? (2) Does this action take me away from loving, worshiping, or serving God? (3) Does this action bring out the best in me, consistent with God's purpose? (4) Does this action benefit other believers?

11:15 Or *Bring her out from between the ranks;* or *Take her out of the Temple precincts.* The meaning of the Hebrew is uncertain. **11:21a** Verse 11:21 is numbered 12:1 in Hebrew text. **11:21b** Hebrew *Jehoash,* a variant spelling of Joash. **12:1a** Verses 12:1-21 are numbered 12:2-22 in Hebrew text. **12:1b** Hebrew *Jehoash,* a variant spelling of Joash; also in 12:2, 4, 6, 7, 18.

THE END OF JOASH'S REIGN ¹⁷About this time King Hazael of Aram went to war against Gath and captured it. Then he turned to attack Jerusalem. ¹⁸King Joash collected all the sacred objects that Jehoshaphat, Jehoram, and Ahaziah, the previous kings of Judah, had dedicated, along with what he himself had dedicated. He sent them all to Hazael, along with all the gold in the treasuries of the LORD's Temple and the royal palace. So Hazael called off his attack on Jerusalem.

¹⁹The rest of the events in Joash's reign and everything he did are recorded in *The Book of the History of the Kings of Judah.*

²⁰Joash's officers plotted against him and assassinated him at Beth-millo on the road to Silla. ²¹The assassins were Jozacar* son of Shimeath and Jehozabad son of Shomer—both trusted advisers. Joash was buried with his ancestors in the City of David. Then his son Amaziah became the next king.

13 **JEHOAHAZ RULES IN ISRAEL** Jehoahaz son of Jehu began to rule over Israel in the twenty-third year of King Joash's reign in Judah. He reigned in Samaria seventeen years. ²But he did what was evil in the LORD's sight. He followed the example of Jeroboam son of Nebat, continuing the sins that Jeroboam had led Israel to commit. ³So the LORD was very angry with Israel, and he allowed King Hazael of Aram and his son Ben-hadad to defeat them repeatedly.

⁴Then Jehoahaz prayed for the LORD's help, and the LORD heard his prayer, for he could see how severely the king of Aram was oppressing Israel. ⁵So the LORD provided someone to rescue the Israelites from the tyranny of the Arameans. Then Israel lived in safety again as they had in former days.

⁶But they continued to sin, following the evil example of Jeroboam. They also allowed the Asherah pole in Samaria to remain standing. ⁷Finally, Jehoahaz's army was reduced to 50 charioteers, 10 chariots, and 10,000 foot soldiers. The king of Aram had killed the others, trampling them like dust under his feet.

⁸The rest of the events in Jehoahaz's reign—everything he did and the extent of his power—are recorded in *The Book of the History of the Kings of Israel.* ⁹When Jehoahaz died, he was buried in Samaria. Then his son Jehoash* became the next king.

JEHOASH RULES IN ISRAEL ¹⁰Jehoash son of Jehoahaz began to rule over Israel in the thirty-seventh year of King Joash's reign in Judah. He reigned in Samaria sixteen years. ¹¹But he did what was evil in the LORD's sight. He refused to turn from the sins that Jeroboam son of Nebat had led Israel to commit.

¹²The rest of the events in Jehoash's reign and everything he did, including the extent of his power and his war with King Amaziah of Judah, are recorded in *The Book of the History of the Kings of Israel.* ¹³When Jehoash died, he was buried in Samaria with the kings of Israel. Then his son Jeroboam II became the next king.

ELISHA'S FINAL PROPHECY ¹⁴When Elisha was in his last illness, King Jehoash of Israel visited him and wept over him. "My father! My father! I see the chariots and charioteers of Israel!" he cried.

¹⁵Elisha told him, "Get a bow and some arrows." And the king did as he was told. ¹⁶Elisha told him, "Put your hand on the bow," and Elisha laid his own hands on the king's hands.

¹⁷Then he commanded, "Open that eastern window," and he opened it. Then he said, "Shoot!" So he shot an arrow. Elisha proclaimed, "This is the LORD's arrow, an arrow of victory over Aram, for you will completely conquer the Arameans at Aphek."

¹⁸Then he said, "Now pick up the other arrows and strike them against the ground." So the king picked them up and struck the ground three times. ¹⁹But the man of God was angry with him. "You should have struck the ground five or six times!" he exclaimed. "Then you would have beaten Aram until it was entirely destroyed. Now you will be victorious only three times."

²⁰Then Elisha died and was buried.

Groups of Moabite raiders used to invade the land each spring. ²¹Once when some Israelites were burying a man, they spied a band of these

YES!
(13:4-6) Although God rescued Israel from their enemies, they didn't stick with him for long. Pretty soon, they were back to worshiping idols. Saying no to wrong actions isn't enough; we must also say yes to a life of commitment to God. Have you said yes lately?

PARTIAL VICTORY
(13:14-19) When Jehoash was told to strike the ground with arrows, he halfheartedly obeyed. As a result, Elisha told him that his victory over Aram would not be complete. Receiving the full benefits of God's plan for our life requires wholehearted obedience to God's commands. Want to fully experience the "full" life God offers (see John 10:10)? Love him wholeheartedly.

12:21 As in Greek and Syriac versions; Hebrew reads *Jozabad.* **13:9** Hebrew *Joash,* a variant spelling of Jehoash; also in 13:10, 12, 13, 14, 25.

MY STORY: Amanda

I've always been a leader: class president, a member of the leadership team in our youth group, vice president of the Key Club. And I always assumed that leadership meant enjoying certain privileges: respect, being treated well, people listening to me when I made suggestions or comments, and even a certain amount of special consideration when decisions were made.

Then I read 2 Kings and saw how the different kinds of leaders affected their people. Good kings led their people in ways that pleased the Lord, and that resulted in them being blessed. Evil kings led their people into disaster and destruction. So much seemed to depend on the leaders!

One day not long after that, I read Matthew 20:25-28, and I finally realized that my idea of leadership was all wrong. I usually thought only of myself; here Jesus was saying that leaders must be servants. After being in the habit of serving myself, it was difficult to serve, as Jesus said. Putting others first made leadership harder, not easier.

I talked about it with my youth leader. She encouraged me to look at a few other verses—Romans 5:3-4 and 8:18. These verses talk about how difficulties have a purpose: to strengthen our faith. Serving others doesn't come naturally, and sometimes it hurts to give up my own rights. But I'm finding that following Jesus' way is helping my faith to grow—and some people even think I'm a better leader!

raiders. So they hastily threw the corpse into the tomb of Elisha and fled. But as soon as the body touched Elisha's bones, the dead man revived and jumped to his feet!

²²King Hazael of Aram had oppressed Israel during the entire reign of King Jehoahaz. ²³But the LORD was gracious and merciful to the people of Israel, and they were not totally destroyed. He pitied them because of his covenant with Abraham, Isaac, and Jacob. And to

this day he still has not completely destroyed them or banished them from his presence.

²⁴King Hazael of Aram died, and his son Ben-hadad became the next king. ²⁵Then Jehoash son of Jehoahaz recaptured from Ben-hadad son of Hazael the towns that had been taken from Jehoash's father, Jehoahaz. Jehoash defeated Ben-hadad on three occasions, and he recovered the Israelite towns.

14 **AMAZIAH RULES IN JUDAH** Amaziah son of Joash began to rule over Judah in the second year of the reign of King Jehoash* of Israel. ²Amaziah was twenty-five years old when he became king, and he reigned in Jerusalem twenty-nine years. His mother was Jehoaddin from Jerusalem. ³Amaziah did what was pleasing in the LORD's sight, but not like his ancestor David. Instead, he followed the example of his father, Joash. ⁴Amaziah did not destroy the pagan shrines, and the people still offered sacrifices and burned incense there.

⁵When Amaziah was well established as king, he executed the officials who had assassinated his father. ⁶However, he did not kill the children of the assassins, for he obeyed the command of the LORD as written by Moses in the Book of the Law: "Parents must not be put to death for the sins of their children, nor children for the sins of their parents. Those deserving to die must be put to death for their own crimes."*

⁷Amaziah also killed 10,000 Edomites in the Valley of Salt. He also conquered Sela and changed its name to Joktheel, as it is called to this day.

⁸One day Amaziah sent messengers with this challenge to Israel's king Jehoash, the son of Jehoahaz and grandson of Jehu: "Come and meet me in battle!"*

⁹But King Jehoash of Israel replied to King Amaziah of Judah with this story: "Out in the Lebanon mountains, a thistle sent a message to a mighty cedar tree: 'Give your daughter in marriage to my son.' But just then a wild animal of Lebanon came by and stepped on the thistle, crushing it!

¹⁰"You have indeed defeated Edom, and you are very proud of it. But be content with your victory and stay at home! Why stir up trouble that will only bring disaster on you and the people of Judah?"

¹¹But Amaziah refused to listen, so King Je-

14:1 Hebrew *Joash*, a variant spelling of Jehoash; also in 14:13, 23, 27. **14:6** Deut 24:16. **14:8** Hebrew *Come, let us look one another in the face.*

hoash of Israel mobilized his army against King Amaziah of Judah. The two armies drew up their battle lines at Beth-shemesh in Judah. ¹²Judah was routed by the army of Israel, and its army scattered and fled for home. ¹³King Jehoash of Israel captured Judah's king, Amaziah son of Joash and grandson of Ahaziah, at Beth-shemesh. Then he marched to Jerusalem, where he demolished 600 feet* of Jerusalem's wall, from the Ephraim Gate to the Corner Gate. ¹⁴He carried off all the gold and silver and all the articles from the Temple of the Lord. He also seized the treasures from the royal palace, along with hostages, and then returned to Samaria.

¹⁵The rest of the events in Jehoash's reign and everything he did, including the extent of his power and his war with King Amaziah of Judah, are recorded in *The Book of the History of the Kings of Israel.* ¹⁶When Jehoash died, he was buried in Samaria with the kings of Israel. And his son Jeroboam II became the next king.

¹⁷King Amaziah of Judah lived for fifteen years after the death of King Jehoash of Israel. ¹⁸The rest of the events in Amaziah's reign are recorded in *The Book of the History of the Kings of Judah.*

¹⁹There was a conspiracy against Amaziah's life in Jerusalem, and he fled to Lachish. But his enemies sent assassins after him, and they killed him there. ²⁰They brought his body back to Jerusalem on a horse, and he was buried with his ancestors in the City of David.

²¹All the people of Judah had crowned Amaziah's sixteen-year-old son, Uzziah,* as king in place of his father, Amaziah. ²²After his father's death, Uzziah rebuilt the town of Elath and restored it to Judah.

JEROBOAM II RULES IN ISRAEL
²³Jeroboam II, the son of Jehoash, began to rule over Israel in the fifteenth year of King Amaziah's reign in Judah. Jeroboam reigned in Samaria forty-one years. ²⁴He did what was evil in the Lord's sight. He refused to turn from the sins that Jeroboam son of Nebat had led Israel to commit. ²⁵Jeroboam II recovered the territories of Israel between Lebo-hamath and the Dead Sea,* just as the Lord, the God of Israel, had promised through Jonah son of Amittai, the prophet from Gath-hepher.

²⁶For the Lord saw the bitter suffering of everyone in Israel, and that there was no one in Israel, slave or free, to help them. ²⁷And because the Lord had not said he would blot out the name of Israel completely, he used Jeroboam II, the son of Jehoash, to save them.

²⁸The rest of the events in the reign of Jeroboam II and everything he did—including the extent of his power, his wars, and how he recovered for Israel both Damascus and Hamath, which had belonged to Judah*—are recorded in *The Book of the History of the Kings of Israel.* ²⁹When Jeroboam II died, he was buried in Samaria* with the kings of Israel. Then his son Zechariah became the next king.

15 UZZIAH RULES IN JUDAH
Uzziah* son of Amaziah began to rule over Judah in the twenty-seventh year of the reign of King Jeroboam II of Israel. ²He was sixteen years old when he became king, and he reigned in Jerusalem fifty-two years. His mother was Jecoliah from Jerusalem.

³He did what was pleasing in the Lord's sight, just as his father, Amaziah, had done. ⁴But he did not destroy the pagan shrines, and the people still offered sacrifices and burned incense there. ⁵The Lord struck the king with leprosy,* which lasted until the day he died. He lived in isolation in a separate house. The king's son Jotham was put in charge of the royal palace, and he governed the people of the land.

⁶The rest of the events in Uzziah's reign and everything he did are recorded in *The Book of the History of the Kings of Judah.* ⁷When Uzziah died, he was buried with his ancestors in the City of David. And his son Jotham became the next king.

14:13 Hebrew *400 cubits* [180 meters]. **14:21** Hebrew *Azariah,* a variant spelling of Uzziah. **14:25** Hebrew *the sea of the Arabah.* **14:28** Or *to Yaudi.* The meaning of the Hebrew is uncertain. **14:29** As in some Greek manuscripts; Hebrew lacks *he was buried in Samaria.* **15:1** Hebrew *Azariah,* a variant spelling of Uzziah; also in 15:6, 7, 8, 17, 23, 27. **15:5** Or *with a contagious skin disease.* The Hebrew word used here and throughout this passage can describe various skin diseases.

....

A WISE USE OF RESOURCES
(14:23-28) Although Jeroboam II had no regard for God, Israel enjoyed power and prosperity under his warlike policies and skillful administration. Yet his administration ignored policies of justice and mercy. The rich people grew self-centered; the poor grew discouraged. Jesus once said that to those who are given much, much will be required (Luke 12:48). We have a responsibility to use our resources wisely and mercifully.

THE BEST ROLE MODEL
(15:1-5) Although Uzziah accomplished a great deal, he failed to destroy the centers of idol worship, just as his father (Amaziah) and grandfather (Joash) had failed to do. Uzziah's father and grandfather were basically good kings, but they were poor models in some important areas. Looking for a good role model to imitate? You can't find a better one than Jesus.

ZECHARIAH RULES IN ISRAEL ⁸Zechariah son of Jeroboam II began to rule over Israel in the thirty-eighth year of King Uzziah's reign in Judah. He reigned in Samaria six months. ⁹Zechariah did what was evil in the LORD's sight, as his ancestors had done. He refused to turn from the sins that Jeroboam son of Nebat had led Israel to commit. ¹⁰Then Shallum son of Jabesh conspired against Zechariah, assassinated him in public,* and became the next king.

¹¹The rest of the events in Zechariah's reign are recorded in *The Book of the History of the Kings of Israel.* ¹²So the LORD's message to Jehu came true: "Your descendants will be kings of Israel down to the fourth generation."

SHALLUM RULES IN ISRAEL ¹³Shallum son of Jabesh began to rule over Israel in the thirty-ninth year of King Uzziah's reign in Judah. Shallum reigned in Samaria only one month. ¹⁴Then Menahem son of Gadi went to Samaria from Tirzah and assassinated him, and he became the next king.

¹⁵The rest of the events in Shallum's reign, including his conspiracy, are recorded in *The Book of the History of the Kings of Israel.*

MENAHEM RULES IN ISRAEL ¹⁶At that time Menahem destroyed the town of Tappuah* and all the surrounding countryside as far as Tirzah, because its citizens refused to surrender the town. He killed the entire population and ripped open the pregnant women.

¹⁷Menahem son of Gadi began to rule over Israel in the thirty-ninth year of King Uzziah's reign in Judah. He reigned in Samaria ten years. ¹⁸But Menahem did what was evil in the LORD's sight. During his entire reign, he refused to turn from the sins that Jeroboam son of Nebat had led Israel to commit.

¹⁹Then King Tiglath-pileser* of Assyria invaded the land. But Menahem paid him thirty-seven tons* of silver to gain his support in tightening his grip on royal power. ²⁰Menahem extorted the money from the rich of Israel, demanding that each of them pay fifty pieces* of silver to the king of Assyria. So the king of Assyria turned from attacking Israel and did not stay in the land.

²¹The rest of the events in Menahem's reign and everything he did are recorded in *The Book of the History of the Kings of Israel.* ²²When Menahem died, his son Pekahiah became the next king.

PEKAHIAH RULES IN ISRAEL ²³Pekahiah son of Menahem began to rule over Israel in the fiftieth year of King Uzziah's reign in Judah. He reigned in Samaria two years. ²⁴But Pekahiah did what was evil in the LORD's sight. He refused to turn from the sins that Jeroboam son of Nebat had led Israel to commit.

²⁵Then Pekah son of Remaliah, the commander of Pekahiah's army, conspired against him. With fifty men from Gilead, Pekah assassinated the king, along with Argob and Arieh, in the citadel of the palace at Samaria. And Pekah reigned in his place.

²⁶The rest of the events in Pekahiah's reign and everything he did are recorded in *The Book of the History of the Kings of Israel.*

PEKAH RULES IN ISRAEL ²⁷Pekah son of Remaliah began to rule over Israel in the fifty-second year of King Uzziah's reign in Judah. He reigned in Samaria twenty years. ²⁸But Pekah did what was evil in the LORD's sight. He refused to turn from the sins that Jeroboam son of Nebat had led Israel to commit.

²⁹During Pekah's reign, King Tiglath-pileser of Assyria attacked Israel again, and he captured the towns of Ijon, Abel-beth-maacah, Janoah, Kedesh, and Hazor. He also conquered the regions of Gilead, Galilee, and all of Naphtali, and he took the people to Assyria as captives. ³⁰Then Hoshea son of Elah conspired against Pekah and assassinated him. He began to rule over Israel in the twentieth year of Jotham son of Uzziah.

³¹The rest of the events in Pekah's reign and everything he did are recorded in *The Book of the History of the Kings of Israel.*

JOTHAM RULES IN JUDAH ³²Jotham son of Uzziah began to rule over Judah in the second year of King Pekah's reign in Israel. ³³He was twenty-five years old when he became king, and he reigned in Jerusalem sixteen years. His mother was Jerusha, the daughter of Zadok.

³⁴Jotham did what was pleasing in the LORD's sight. He did everything his father, Uzziah, had done. ³⁵But he did not destroy the pagan

---

INFLUENCE
(15:8-9) *Zechariah encouraged Israel (the northern kingdom) to disobey God by worshiping idols. The wrong things we do become doubly worse when we encourage others to disobey God. We are responsible for the way we influence others. What would your friends say about your influence over them?*

15:10 Or *at Ibleam.* **15:16** As in some Greek manuscripts; other Greek manuscripts read *at Ibleam.* Hebrew reads *Tiphsah.*
15:19a Hebrew *Pul,* another name for Tiglath-pileser.
15:19b Hebrew *1,000 talents* [34 metric tons]. **15:20** Hebrew *50 shekels* [20 ounces, or 570 grams].

shrines, and the people still offered sacrifices and burned incense there. He rebuilt the upper gate of the Temple of the LORD.

³⁶The rest of the events in Jotham's reign and everything he did are recorded in *The Book of the History of the Kings of Judah.* ³⁷In those days the LORD began to send King Rezin of Aram and King Pekah of Israel to attack Judah. ³⁸When Jotham died, he was buried with his ancestors in the City of David. And his son Ahaz became the next king.

16 AHAZ RULES IN JUDAH Ahaz son of Jotham began to rule over Judah in the seventeenth year of King Pekah's reign in Israel. ²Ahaz was twenty years old when he became king, and he reigned in Jerusalem sixteen years. He did not do what was pleasing in the sight of the LORD his God, as his ancestor David had done. ³Instead, he followed the example of the kings of Israel, even sacrificing his own son in the fire.* In this way, he followed the detestable practices of the pagan nations the LORD had driven from the land ahead of the Israelites. ⁴He offered sacrifices and burned incense at the pagan shrines and on the hills and under every green tree.

⁵Then King Rezin of Aram and King Pekah of Israel came up to attack Jerusalem. They besieged Ahaz but could not conquer him. ⁶At that time the king of Edom* recovered the town of Elath for Edom.* He drove out the people of Judah and sent Edomites* to live there, as they do to this day.

⁷King Ahaz sent messengers to King Tiglath-pileser of Assyria with this message: "I am your servant and your vassal.* Come up and rescue me from the attacking armies of Aram and Israel." ⁸Then Ahaz took the silver and gold from the Temple of the LORD and the palace treasury and sent it as a payment to the Assyrian king. ⁹So the king of Assyria attacked the Aramean capital of Damascus and led its population away as captives, resettling them in Kir. He also killed King Rezin.

¹⁰King Ahaz then went to Damascus to meet with King Tiglath-pileser of Assyria. While he was there, he took special note of the altar. Then he sent a model of the altar to Uriah the priest, along with its design in full detail. ¹¹Uriah followed the king's instructions and built an altar just like it, and it was ready before

the king returned from Damascus. ¹²When the king returned, he inspected the altar and made offerings on it. ¹³He presented a burnt offering and a grain offering, he poured out a liquid offering, and he sprinkled the blood of peace offerings on the altar.

¹⁴Then King Ahaz removed the old bronze altar from its place in front of the LORD's Temple, between the entrance and the new altar, and placed it on the north side of the new altar. ¹⁵He told Uriah the priest, "Use the new altar* for the morning sacrifices of burnt offering, the evening grain offering, the king's burnt offering and grain offering, and the burnt offerings of all the people, as well as their grain offerings and liquid offerings. Sprinkle the blood from all the burnt offerings and sacrifices on the new altar. The bronze altar will be for my personal use only." ¹⁶Uriah the priest did just as King Ahaz commanded him.

¹⁷Then the king removed the side panels and basins from the portable water carts. He also removed the great bronze basin called the Sea from the backs of the bronze oxen and placed it on the stone pavement. ¹⁸In deference to the king of Assyria, he also removed the canopy that had been constructed inside the palace for use on the Sabbath day,* as well as the king's outer entrance to the Temple of the LORD.

¹⁹The rest of the events in Ahaz's reign and everything he did are recorded in *The Book of the History of the Kings of Judah.* ²⁰When Ahaz died, he was buried with his ancestors in the City of David. Then his son Hezekiah became the next king.

17 HOSHEA RULES IN ISRAEL Hoshea son of Elah began to rule over Israel in the twelfth year of King Ahaz's reign in Judah. He

16:3 Or *even making his son pass through the fire.* **16:6a** As in Latin Vulgate; Hebrew reads *Rezin king of Aram.* **16:6b** As in Latin Vulgate; Hebrew reads *Aram.* **16:6c** As in Greek version, Latin Vulgate, and an alternate reading of the Masoretic Text; the other alternate reads *Arameans.* **16:7** Hebrew *your son.* **16:15** Hebrew *the great altar.* **16:18** The meaning of the Hebrew is uncertain.

FIRST PRIORITY
(15:34-35) Although Jotham was a decent king of Judah, he failed in a most critical area: he didn't destroy the pagan shrines where the people worshiped idols. Like Jotham, we may live a basically good life and yet miss doing what is most important. A lifetime of doing good is not enough if we make the crucial mistake of not fully obeying God. A true follower of God puts him first in all areas of life. That's what you do, right?

BLATANT DISREGARD
(16:1-16) Evil King Ahaz copied pagan religious customs, changed the Temple services, and used the Temple altar for his personal use. In so doing, he demonstrated a blatant disregard for God's commands. We condemn Ahaz for his action, but we do the same thing if we try to mold God's message to fit our preferences. God wants to be worshiped for who he is, not what we would like him to be.

reigned in Samaria nine years. ²He did what was evil in the LORD's sight, but not to the same extent as the kings of Israel who ruled before him.

³King Shalmaneser of Assyria attacked King Hoshea, so Hoshea was forced to pay heavy tribute to Assyria. ⁴But Hoshea stopped paying the annual tribute and conspired against the king of Assyria by asking King So of Egypt* to help him shake free of Assyria's power. When the king of Assyria discovered this treachery, he seized Hoshea and put him in prison.

SAMARIA FALLS TO ASSYRIA
⁵Then the king of Assyria invaded the entire land, and for three years he besieged the city of Samaria. ⁶Finally, in the ninth year of King Hoshea's reign, Samaria fell, and the people of Israel were exiled to Assyria. They were settled in colonies in Halah, along the banks of the Habor River in Gozan, and in the cities of the Medes.

⁷This disaster came upon the people of Israel because they worshiped other gods. They sinned against the LORD their God, who had brought them safely out of Egypt and had rescued them from the power of Pharaoh, the king of Egypt. ⁸They had followed the practices of the pagan nations the LORD had driven from the land ahead of them, as well as the practices the kings of Israel had introduced. ⁹The people of Israel had also secretly done many things that were not pleasing to the LORD their God. They built pagan shrines for themselves in all their towns, from the smallest outpost to the largest walled city. ¹⁰They set up sacred pillars and Asherah poles at the top of every hill and under every green tree. ¹¹They offered sacrifices on all the hilltops, just like the nations the LORD had driven from the land ahead of them. So the people of Israel had done many evil things, arousing the LORD's anger. ¹²Yes,

they worshiped idols,* despite the LORD's specific and repeated warnings.

¹³Again and again the LORD had sent his prophets and seers to warn both Israel and Judah: "Turn from all your evil ways. Obey my commands and decrees—the entire law that I commanded your ancestors to obey, and that I gave you through my servants the prophets."

¹⁴But the Israelites would not listen. They were as stubborn as their ancestors who refused to believe in the LORD their God. ¹⁵They rejected his decrees and the covenant he had made with their ancestors, and they despised all his warnings. They worshiped worthless idols, so they became worthless themselves. They followed the example of the nations around them, disobeying the LORD's command not to imitate them.

¹⁶They rejected all the commands of the LORD their God and made two calves from metal. They set up an Asherah pole and worshiped Baal and all the forces of heaven. ¹⁷They even sacrificed their own sons and daughters in the fire.* They consulted fortune-tellers and practiced sorcery and sold themselves to evil, arousing the LORD's anger.

¹⁸Because the LORD was very angry with Israel, he swept them away from his presence. Only the tribe of Judah remained in the land. ¹⁹But even the people of Judah refused to obey the commands of the LORD their God, for they followed the evil practices that Israel had introduced. ²⁰The LORD rejected all the descendants of Israel. He punished them by handing them over to their attackers until he had banished Israel from his presence.

²¹For when the LORD* tore Israel away from the kingdom of David, they chose Jeroboam son of Nebat as their king. But Jeroboam drew Israel away from following the LORD and made them commit a great sin. ²²And the people of Israel persisted in all the evil ways of Jeroboam. They did not turn from these sins ²³until the LORD finally swept them away from his presence, just as all his prophets had warned. So Israel was exiled from their land to Assyria, where they remain to this day.

FOREIGNERS SETTLE IN ISRAEL
²⁴The king of Assyria transported groups of people from Babylon, Cuthah, Avva, Hamath, and Sepharvaim and resettled them in the towns of Samaria, replacing the people of Israel. They took possession of Samaria and lived in its towns. ²⁵But

---

COPYING

(17:7-17) The Lord judged the people of Israel because they copied the bad habits of the surrounding nations, worshiping false gods, accommodating heathen customs, and following their own desires. We do the same when we follow the crowd instead of obeying God. How do your actions show your willingness to imitate God (see Eph 5:1)?

PART OF THE COLLECTION?

(17:24-29) The new settlers in Israel worshiped God without giving up their pagan customs. They treated God as a good luck charm or like one of the gods in their collection. A similar attitude is common today. Many people claim to believe in God while refusing to give up attitudes and actions that displease him. God prefers to be first in your life, rather than used as a back-up plan.

17:4 Or by asking the king of Egypt at Sais.   17:12 The Hebrew term (literally round things) probably alludes to dung.   17:17 Or They even made their sons and daughters pass through the fire.
17:21 Hebrew he; compare 1 Kgs 11:31-32.

since these foreign settlers did not worship the LORD when they first arrived, the LORD sent lions among them, which killed some of them. ²⁶So a message was sent to the king of Assyria: "The people you have sent to live in the towns of Samaria do not know the religious customs of the God of the land. He has sent lions among them to destroy them because they have not worshiped him correctly." ²⁷The king of Assyria then commanded, "Send one of the exiled priests back to Samaria. Let him live there and teach the new residents the religious customs of the God of the land." ²⁸So one of the priests who had been exiled from Samaria returned to Bethel and taught the new residents how to worship the LORD.

²⁹But these various groups of foreigners also continued to worship their own gods. In town after town where they lived, they placed their idols at the pagan shrines that the people of Samaria had built. ³⁰Those from Babylon worshiped idols of their god Succoth-benoth. Those from Cuthah worshiped their god Nergal. And those from Hamath worshiped Ashima. ³¹The Avvites worshiped their gods Nibhaz and Tartak. And the people from Sepharvaim even burned their own children as sacrifices to their gods Adrammelech and Anammelech.

³²These new residents worshiped the LORD, but they also appointed from among themselves all sorts of people as priests to offer sacrifices at their places of worship. ³³And though they worshiped the LORD, they continued to follow their own gods according to the religious customs of the nations from which they came. ³⁴And this is still going on today. They continue to follow their former practices instead of truly worshiping the LORD and obeying the decrees, regulations, instructions, and commands he gave the descendants of Jacob, whose name he changed to Israel.

³⁵For the LORD had made a covenant with the descendants of Jacob and commanded them: "Do not worship any other gods or bow before them or serve them or offer sacrifices to them. ³⁶But worship only the LORD, who brought you out of Egypt with great strength and a powerful arm. Bow down to him alone, and offer sacrifices only to him. ³⁷Be careful at all times to obey the decrees, regulations, instructions, and commands that he wrote for you. You must not worship other gods. ³⁸Do not forget the covenant I made with you, and do not worship

ISRAEL TAKEN CAPTIVE
Finally the sins of Israel's people caught up with them. God allowed Assyria to defeat and disperse the people. They were led into captivity, swallowed up by the mighty, evil Assyrian Empire. Sin always brings discipline, and the consequences of that sin are sometimes inescapable.

other gods. ³⁹You must worship only the LORD your God. He is the one who will rescue you from all your enemies."

⁴⁰But the people would not listen and continued to follow their former practices. ⁴¹So while these new residents worshiped the LORD, they also worshiped their idols. And to this day their descendants do the same.

18 HEZEKIAH RULES IN JUDAH Hezekiah son of Ahaz began to rule over Judah in the third year of King Hoshea's reign in Israel. ²He was twenty-five years old when he became king, and he reigned in Jerusalem twenty-nine years. His mother was Abijah,* the daughter of Zechariah. ³He did what was pleasing in the LORD's sight, just as his ancestor David had done. ⁴He removed the pagan shrines, smashed the sacred pillars, and cut down the Asherah poles. He broke up the bronze serpent that Moses had made, because the people of Israel had been offering sacrifices to it. The bronze serpent was called Nehushtan.*

⁵Hezekiah trusted in the LORD, the God of Israel. There was no one like him among all the kings of Judah, either before or after his time. ⁶He remained faithful to the LORD in everything, and he carefully obeyed all the commands the LORD had given Moses. ⁷So the LORD was with him, and Hezekiah was successful in everything he did. He revolted against the king of

....

AN OBJECT OF WORSHIP
(18:4) The bronze serpent had been made to cure the Israelites of a deadly plague (see Num 21:4-9). It demonstrated God's presence, power, and mercy. But when this sculpture became an object of worship instead of a reminder of whom to worship, Hezekiah was forced to destroy it. We must be careful that the things we use to aid our worship don't become objects of worship themselves.

18:2 As in parallel text at 2 Chr 29:11; Hebrew reads *Abi,* a variant spelling of Abijah.   18:4 *Nehushtan* sounds like the Hebrew terms that mean "snake," "bronze," and "unclean thing."

HEZEKIAH TRUSTED IN THE LORD, THE GOD OF ISRAEL.
THERE WAS NO ONE LIKE HIM AMONG ALL THE KINGS OF JUDAH. 2 KINGS 18:5

Assyria and refused to pay him tribute. [8]He also conquered the Philistines as far distant as Gaza and its territory, from their smallest outpost to their largest walled city.

[9]During the fourth year of Hezekiah's reign, which was the seventh year of King Hoshea's reign in Israel, King Shalmaneser of Assyria attacked the city of Samaria and began a siege against it. [10]Three years later, during the sixth year of King Hezekiah's reign and the ninth year of King Hoshea's reign in Israel, Samaria fell. [11]At that time the king of Assyria exiled the Israelites to Assyria and placed them in colonies in Halah, along the banks of the Habor River in Gozan, and in the cities of the Medes. [12]For they refused to listen to the LORD their God and obey him. Instead, they violated his covenant—all the laws that Moses the LORD's servant had commanded them to obey.

ASSYRIA INVADES JUDAH [13]In the fourteenth year of King Hezekiah's reign,* King Sennacherib of Assyria came to attack the fortified towns of Judah and conquered them. [14]King Hezekiah sent this message to the king of Assyria at Lachish: "I have done wrong. I will pay whatever tribute money you demand if you will only withdraw." The king of Assyria then demanded a settlement of more than eleven tons of silver and one ton of gold.* [15]To gather this amount, King Hezekiah used all the silver stored in the Temple of the LORD and in the palace treasury. [16]Hezekiah even stripped the gold from the doors of the LORD's Temple and from the doorposts he had overlaid with gold, and he gave it all to the Assyrian king.

[17]Nevertheless, the king of Assyria sent his commander in chief, his field commander, and his chief of staff* from Lachish with a huge army to confront King Hezekiah in Jerusalem. The Assyrians took up a position beside the aqueduct that feeds water into the upper pool, near the road leading to the field where cloth is washed.* [18]They summoned King Hezekiah, but the king sent these officials to meet with them: Eliakim son of Hilkiah, the palace administrator; Shebna the court secretary; and Joah son of Asaph, the royal historian.

SENNACHERIB THREATENS JERUSALEM [19]Then the Assyrian king's chief of staff told them to give this message to Hezekiah:

"This is what the great king of Assyria says: What are you trusting in that makes you so confident? [20]Do you think that mere words can substitute for military skill and strength? Who are you counting on, that you have rebelled against me? [21]On Egypt? If you lean on Egypt, it will be like a reed that splinters beneath your weight and pierces your hand. Pharaoh, the king of Egypt, is completely unreliable!

[22]"But perhaps you will say to me, 'We are trusting in the LORD our God!' But isn't he the one who was insulted by Hezekiah? Didn't Hezekiah tear down his shrines and altars and make everyone in Judah and Jerusalem worship only at the altar here in Jerusalem?

[23]"I'll tell you what! Strike a bargain with my master, the king of Assyria. I will give you 2,000 horses if you can find that many men to ride on them! [24]With your tiny army, how can you think of challenging even the weakest contingent of my master's troops, even with the help of Egypt's chariots and charioteers? [25]What's more, do you think we have invaded your land without the LORD's direction? The LORD himself told us, 'Attack this land and destroy it!'"

[26]Then Eliakim son of Hilkiah, Shebna, and Joah said to the Assyrian chief of staff, "Please speak to us in Aramaic, for we understand it well. Don't speak in Hebrew,* for the people on the wall will hear."

[27]But Sennacherib's chief of staff replied, "Do you think my master sent this message only to you and your master? He wants all the people to hear it, for when we put this city under siege, they will suffer along with you. They will be so hungry and thirsty that they will eat their own dung and drink their own urine."

[28]Then the chief of staff stood and shouted in Hebrew to the people on the wall, "Listen to this message from the great king of Assyria! [29]This is what the king says: Don't let Hezekiah deceive you. He will never be able to rescue you from my power. [30]Don't let him fool you into trusting in the LORD by saying, 'The LORD will surely rescue us. This city will never fall into the hands of the Assyrian king!'

18:13 The fourteenth year of Hezekiah's reign was 701 B.C.
18:14 Hebrew *300 talents* [10 metric tons] *of silver and 30 talents* [1 metric ton] *of gold.*   18:17a Or *the rabshakeh;* also in 18:19, 26, 27, 28, 37.   18:17b Or *bleached.*   18:26 Hebrew *in the dialect of Judah;* also in 18:28.

³¹"Don't listen to Hezekiah! These are the terms the king of Assyria is offering: Make peace with me—open the gates and come out. Then each of you can continue eating from your own grapevine and fig tree and drinking from your own well. ³²Then I will arrange to take you to another land like this one—a land of grain and new wine, bread and vineyards, olive groves and honey. Choose life instead of death!

"Don't listen to Hezekiah when he tries to mislead you by saying, 'The LORD will rescue us!' ³³Have the gods of any other nations ever saved their people from the king of Assyria? ³⁴What happened to the gods of Hamath and Arpad? And what about the gods of Sepharvaim, Hena, and Ivvah? Did any god rescue Samaria from my power? ³⁵What god of any nation has ever been able to save its people from my power? So what makes you think that the LORD can rescue Jerusalem from me?"

³⁶But the people were silent and did not utter a word because Hezekiah had commanded them, "Do not answer him."

³⁷Then Eliakim son of Hilkiah, the palace administrator; Shebna the court secretary; and Joah son of Asaph, the royal historian, went back to Hezekiah. They tore their clothes in despair, and they went in to see the king and told him what the Assyrian chief of staff had said.

19 HEZEKIAH SEEKS THE LORD'S HELP
When King Hezekiah heard their report, he tore his clothes and put on burlap and went into the Temple of the LORD. ²And he sent

---

Eliakim the palace administrator, Shebna the court secretary, and the leading priests, all dressed in burlap, to the prophet Isaiah son of Amoz. ³They told him, "This is what King Hezekiah says: Today is a day of trouble, insults, and disgrace. It is like when a child is ready to be born, but the mother has no strength to deliver the baby. ⁴But perhaps the LORD your God has heard the Assyrian chief of staff,* sent by the king to defy the living God, and will punish him for his words. Oh, pray for those of us who are left!"

⁵After King Hezekiah's officials delivered the king's message to Isaiah, ⁶the prophet replied, "Say to your master, 'This is what the LORD says: Do not be disturbed by this blasphemous speech against me from the Assyrian king's messengers. ⁷Listen! I myself will move against him,* and the king will receive a message that he is needed at home. So he will return to his land, where I will have him killed with a sword.'"

⁸Meanwhile, the Assyrian chief of staff left Jerusalem and went to consult the king of Assyria, who had left Lachish and was attacking Libnah.

⁹Soon afterward King Sennacherib received word that King Tirhakah of Ethiopia* was leading an army to fight against him. Before leaving to meet the attack, he sent messengers back to Hezekiah in Jerusalem with this message:

¹⁰"This message is for King Hezekiah of Judah. Don't let your God, in whom you trust, deceive you with promises that Jerusalem will not be captured by the king of Assyria. ¹¹You know perfectly well what the kings of Assyria have done wherever they have gone. They have completely destroyed everyone who stood in their way! Why should you be any different? ¹²Have the gods of other nations rescued them—such nations as Gozan, Haran, Rezeph, and the people of Eden who were in Tel-assar? My predecessors destroyed them all! ¹³What happened to the king of Hamath and the king of Arpad? What happened to the kings of Sepharvaim, Hena, and Ivvah?"

··

PRAYER
(19:1-37) Sennacherib, whose armies had captured the fortified cities of Judah, sent a message telling Hezekiah to surrender (18:13-35). Having realized that the situation was hopeless, Hezekiah asked God for help. God answered by defeating this seemingly invincible army. Is prayer your first response in a crisis?

¹⁴After Hezekiah received the letter from the messengers and read it, he went up to the LORD's Temple and spread it out before the LORD. ¹⁵And Hezekiah prayed this prayer before the LORD: "O LORD, God of Israel, you are enthroned between the mighty cherubim! You alone are God of all the kingdoms of the earth. You alone created the heavens and the earth. ¹⁶Bend down, O LORD, and listen! Open your eyes, O LORD, and see! Listen to Sennacherib's words of defiance against the living God.

¹⁷"It is true, LORD, that the kings of Assyria have destroyed all these nations. ¹⁸And they have thrown the gods of these nations into the fire and burned them. But of course the Assyrians could destroy them! They were not gods at all—only idols of wood and stone shaped by human hands. ¹⁹Now, O LORD our God, rescue us from his power; then all the kingdoms of the earth will know that you alone, O LORD, are God."

ISAIAH PREDICTS JUDAH'S DELIVERANCE

²⁰Then Isaiah son of Amoz sent this message to Hezekiah: "This is what the LORD, the God of Israel, says: I have heard your prayer about King Sennacherib of Assyria. ²¹And the LORD has spoken this word against him:

"The virgin daughter of Zion
⠀⠀despises you and laughs at you.
The daughter of Jerusalem
⠀⠀shakes her head in derision as you flee.

²² "Whom have you been defying and
⠀⠀⠀ridiculing?
⠀⠀Against whom did you raise your voice?
At whom did you look with such haughty
⠀⠀⠀eyes?
⠀⠀It was the Holy One of Israel!
²³ By your messengers you have defied
⠀⠀⠀the Lord.
⠀⠀You have said, 'With my many chariots
I have conquered the highest mountains—
⠀⠀yes, the remotest peaks of Lebanon.
I have cut down its tallest cedars
⠀⠀and its finest cypress trees.
I have reached its farthest corners
⠀⠀and explored its deepest forests.
²⁴ I have dug wells in many foreign lands
⠀⠀and refreshed myself with their water.
With the sole of my foot
⠀⠀I stopped up all the rivers of Egypt!'

²⁵ "But have you not heard?
⠀⠀I decided this long ago.

19:4 Or the *rabshakeh*; also in 19:8. 19:7 Hebrew *I will put a spirit in him.* 19:9 Hebrew *of Cush.*

Long ago I planned it,
   and now I am making it happen.
I planned for you to crush fortified cities
   into heaps of rubble.
26 That is why their people have so little power
   and are so frightened and confused.
They are as weak as grass,
   as easily trampled as tender green
      shoots.
They are like grass sprouting on a housetop,
   scorched before it can grow lush and tall.

27 "But I know you well—
   where you stay
and when you come and go.
   I know the way you have raged against
      me.
28 And because of your raging against me
   and your arrogance, which I have heard
      for myself,
I will put my hook in your nose
   and my bit in your mouth.
I will make you return
   by the same road on which you came."

29Then Isaiah said to Hezekiah, "Here is the proof that what I say is true:

"This year you will eat only what grows up by
   itself,
and next year you will eat what springs up
   from that.
But in the third year you will plant crops and
   harvest them;
   you will tend vineyards and eat their fruit.
30 And you who are left in Judah,
   who have escaped the ravages of the
      siege,
will put roots down in your own soil
   and will grow up and flourish.
31 For a remnant of my people will spread out
   from Jerusalem,
   a group of survivors from Mount Zion.
The passionate commitment of the LORD
   of Heaven's Armies*
   will make this happen!

32"And this is what the LORD says about the king of Assyria:

"His armies will not enter Jerusalem.
   They will not even shoot an arrow at it.
They will not march outside its gates with
   their shields

nor build banks of earth against its walls.
33 The king will return to his own country
   by the same road on which he came.
He will not enter this city,
   says the LORD.
34 For my own honor and for the sake of my
      servant David,
   I will defend this city and protect it."

35That night the angel of the LORD went out to the Assyrian camp and killed 185,000 Assyrian soldiers. When the surviving Assyrians* woke up the next morning, they found corpses everywhere. 36Then King Sennacherib of Assyria broke camp and returned to his own land. He went home to his capital of Nineveh and stayed there.

37One day while he was worshiping in the temple of his god Nisroch, his sons* Adrammelech and Sharezer killed him with their swords. They then escaped to the land of Ararat, and another son, Esarhaddon, became the next king of Assyria.

20 HEZEKIAH'S SICKNESS AND RECOVERY

About that time Hezekiah became deathly ill, and the prophet Isaiah son of Amoz went to visit him. He gave the king this message: "This is what the LORD says: Set your affairs in order, for you are going to die. You will not recover from this illness."

2When Hezekiah heard this, he turned his face to the wall and prayed to the LORD, 3"Remember, O LORD, how I have always been faithful to you and have served you single-mindedly, always doing what pleases you." Then he broke down and wept bitterly.

4But before Isaiah had left the middle courtyard,* this message came to him from the LORD: 5"Go back to Hezekiah, the leader of my people. Tell him, 'This is what the LORD, the God of your ancestor David, says: I have heard your prayer and seen your tears. I will heal you, and three days from now you will get out of bed and go to the Temple of the LORD. 6I will add fifteen years to your life, and I will rescue you and this city from the king of Assyria. I will defend this city for my own honor and for the sake of my servant David.'"

19:31 As in Greek and Syriac versions, Latin Vulgate, and an alternate reading of the Masoretic Text (see also Isa 37:32); the other alternate reads the LORD.   19:35 Hebrew When they.
19:37 As in Greek version and an alternate reading of the Masoretic Text (see also Isa 37:38); the other alternate reading lacks his sons.
20:4 As in Greek version and an alternate reading in the Masoretic Text; the other alternate reads the middle of the city.

THE POWER OF ONE
(20:1-11) Over a 100-year period of Judah's history (732–640 B.C.), Hezekiah was the only faithful king—but what a difference he made! Because of Hezekiah's faith and prayer, God healed him and saved his city from the Assyrians. You can make a difference, too, even if your faith puts you in the minority. Faith in the power of the one true God can bring about change in any situation.

⁷Then Isaiah said, "Make an ointment from figs." So Hezekiah's servants spread the ointment over the boil, and Hezekiah recovered!

⁸Meanwhile, Hezekiah had said to Isaiah, "What sign will the LORD give to prove that he will heal me and that I will go to the Temple of the LORD three days from now?"

⁹Isaiah replied, "This is the sign from the LORD to prove that he will do as he promised. Would you like the shadow on the sundial to go forward ten steps or backward ten steps?*"

¹⁰"The shadow always moves forward," Hezekiah replied, "so that would be easy. Make it go ten steps backward instead." ¹¹So Isaiah the prophet asked the LORD to do this, and he caused the shadow to move ten steps backward on the sundial* of Ahaz!

ENVOYS FROM BABYLON ¹²Soon after this, Merodach-baladan son of Baladan, king of Babylon, sent Hezekiah his best wishes and a gift, for he had heard that Hezekiah had been very sick. ¹³Hezekiah received the Babylonian envoys and showed them everything in his treasure-houses—the silver, the gold, the spices, and the aromatic oils. He also took them to see his armory and showed them everything in his royal treasuries! There was nothing in his palace or kingdom that Hezekiah did not show them.

¹⁴Then Isaiah the prophet went to King Hezekiah and asked him, "What did those men want? Where were they from?"

Hezekiah replied, "They came from the distant land of Babylon."

¹⁵"What did they see in your palace?" Isaiah asked.

"They saw everything," Hezekiah replied. "I showed them everything I own—all my royal treasuries."

¹⁶Then Isaiah said to Hezekiah, "Listen to this message from the LORD: ¹⁷The time is coming when everything in your palace—all the treasures stored up by your ancestors until now—will be carried off to Babylon. Nothing will be left, says the LORD. ¹⁸Some of your very own sons will be taken away into exile. They will become eunuchs who will serve in the palace of Babylon's king."

¹⁹Then Hezekiah said to Isaiah, "This message you have given me from the LORD is good." For the king was thinking, "At least there will be peace and security during my lifetime."

²⁰The rest of the events in Hezekiah's reign, including the extent of his power and how he built a pool and dug a tunnel* to bring water into the city, are recorded in *The Book of the History of the Kings of Judah*. ²¹Hezekiah died, and his son Manasseh became the next king.

21 **MANASSEH RULES IN JUDAH** Manasseh was twelve years old when he became king, and he reigned in Jerusalem fifty-five years. His mother was Hephzibah. ²He did what was evil in the LORD's sight, following the detestable practices of the pagan nations that the LORD had driven from the land ahead of the Israelites. ³He rebuilt the pagan shrines his father, Hezekiah, had destroyed. He constructed altars for Baal and set up an Asherah pole, just as King Ahab of Israel had done. He also bowed before all the powers of the heavens and worshiped them.

⁴He built pagan altars in the Temple of the LORD, the place where the LORD had said, "My name will remain in Jerusalem forever." ⁵He built these altars for all the powers of the heavens in both courtyards of the LORD's Temple. ⁶Manasseh also sacrificed his own son in the fire.* He practiced sorcery and divination, and he consulted with mediums and psychics. He did much that was evil in the LORD's sight, arousing his anger.

⁷Manasseh even made a carved image of Asherah and set it up in the Temple, the very place where the LORD had told David and his son Solomon: "My name will be honored forever in this Temple and in Jerusalem—the city I have chosen from among all the tribes of Israel. ⁸If the Israelites will be careful to obey my commands—all the laws my servant Moses gave them—I will not send them into exile from this land that I gave their ancestors." ⁹But the people refused to listen, and Manasseh led them to do even more evil than the pagan nations that the LORD had destroyed when the people of Israel entered the land.

¹⁰Then the LORD said through his servants the prophets: ¹¹"King Manasseh of Judah has done many detestable things. He is even more wicked than the Amorites, who lived in this

---

OCCULT
(21:1-18) Manasseh, the king of Judah, angered God by dabbling in the occult. His actions showed his disregard for God's laws (Lev 19:31; Deut 18:9-14). Today, many books, television shows, and games emphasize the "harmlessness" of consulting psychics or attending séances in order to discover the truth about the future. But dabbling in the occult is far from harmless. Want to be assured of a good future? Don't mess up in the present by doing what you know is wrong.

20:9 Or *The shadow on the sundial has gone forward ten steps; do you want it to go backward ten steps?* **20:11** Hebrew *the steps.* **20:20** Hebrew *watercourse.* **21:6** Or *also made his son pass through the fire.*

land before Israel. He has caused the people of Judah to sin with his idols.* ¹²So this is what the LORD, the God of Israel, says: I will bring such disaster on Jerusalem and Judah that the ears of those who hear about it will tingle with horror. ¹³I will judge Jerusalem by the same standard I used for Samaria and the same measure* I used for the family of Ahab. I will wipe away the people of Jerusalem as one wipes a dish and turns it upside down. ¹⁴Then I will reject even the remnant of my own people who are left, and I will hand them over as plunder for their enemies. ¹⁵For they have done great evil in my sight and have angered me ever since their ancestors came out of Egypt."

¹⁶Manasseh also murdered many innocent people until Jerusalem was filled from one end to the other with innocent blood. This was in addition to the sin that he caused the people of Judah to commit, leading them to do evil in the LORD's sight.

¹⁷The rest of the events in Manasseh's reign and everything he did, including the sins he committed, are recorded in *The Book of the History of the Kings of Judah.* ¹⁸When Manas-

seh died, he was buried in the palace garden, the garden of Uzza. Then his son Amon became the next king.

AMON RULES IN JUDAH ¹⁹Amon was twenty-two years old when he became king, and he reigned in Jerusalem two years. His mother was Meshullemeth, the daughter of Haruz from Jotbah. ²⁰He did what was evil in the LORD's sight, just as his father, Manasseh, had done. ²¹He followed the example of his father, worshiping the same idols his father had worshiped. ²²He abandoned the LORD, the God of his ancestors, and he refused to follow the LORD's ways.

²³Then Amon's own officials conspired against him and assassinated him in his palace. ²⁴But the people of the land killed all those who had conspired against King Amon, and they made his son Josiah the next king.

²⁵The rest of the events in Amon's reign and what he did are recorded in *The Book of the History of the Kings of Judah.* ²⁶He was buried in his tomb in the garden of Uzza. Then his son Josiah became the next king.

22 **JOSIAH RULES IN JUDAH** Josiah was eight years old when he became king,

21:11 The Hebrew term (literally *round things*) probably alludes to dung; also in 21:21.   21:13 Hebrew *the same plumb line I used for Samaria and the same plumb bob.*

PERSONALITY PROFILE JOSIAH

UPS:
- King of Judah
- Wanted to know God and obey him
- A reformer like his great-grandfather, Hezekiah
- Cleaned out the Temple and revived obedience to God's laws

DOWNS:
- Became involved in a military conflict that he had been warned against

STATS:
- Where: Jerusalem
- Occupation: Sixteenth king of Judah, the southern kingdom
- Relatives: Amon (father); Jedidah (mother); Jehoahaz (son)
- Contemporaries: Jeremiah, Huldah, Hilkiah, Zephaniah

KEY VERSES: Jeremiah 22:15-16

THINK WAAAAYYY BACK to the time when you were eight. What were your responsibilities? Josiah had a huge one: he was king of Judah. Oh sure, he had advisers to help him. But he also had something else going for him: a close relationship with God, like that of his great-grandfather Hezekiah.

At a young age, Josiah became aware of the spiritual sickness in his land. In a sense, Josiah began his search for God by destroying and cleaning up whatever he found that didn't belong to the worship of the true God. Along the way, a scroll containing God's law was rediscovered in the Temple. For Josiah, the discovery of the scroll was better than finding a hidden treasure map.

As the scroll of God's law was read to Josiah, he was shocked, frightened, and humbled. He realized that he and the nation had a long way to go to get right with God. He tried everything he could to help his people return to God. Although he changed many things, he couldn't change hearts. On the outside, the people cooperated with Josiah, but they made few changes on the inside.

How would you describe your relationship with God? Would you have to admit that you usually just "go along" with God like the people of Judah? Or are you, like Josiah, deeply humbled by God's Word and anxious to do what he wants? Humble obedience pleases God. Outside changes aren't enough. God wants to change lives inside and out.

BOTTOM LINE: God consistently responds to those who turn from their sins with a humble heart.

Even sweeping outward reforms are of little lasting value if there are no changes in people's lives.

Josiah's story is told in 2 Kings 21:24; 22:1–23:30; 2 Chronicles 33:25–35:27. He also is mentioned in Jeremiah 1:3; 22:11, 15-16.

and he reigned in Jerusalem thirty-one years. His mother was Jedidah, the daughter of Adaiah from Bozkath. ²He did what was pleasing in the LORD's sight and followed the example of his ancestor David. He did not turn away from doing what was right.

³In the eighteenth year of his reign, King Josiah sent Shaphan son of Azaliah and grandson of Meshullam, the court secretary, to the Temple of the LORD. He told him, ⁴"Go to Hilkiah the high priest and have him count the money the gatekeepers have collected from the people at the LORD's Temple. ⁵Entrust this money to the men assigned to supervise the Temple's restoration. Then they can use it to pay workers to repair the Temple of the LORD. ⁶They will need to hire carpenters, builders, and masons. Also have them buy the timber and the finished stone needed to repair the Temple. ⁷But don't require the construction supervisors to keep account of the money they receive, for they are honest and trustworthy men."

HILKIAH DISCOVERS GOD'S LAW
⁸Hilkiah the high priest said to Shaphan the court secretary, "I have found the Book of the Law in the LORD's Temple!" Then Hilkiah gave the scroll to Shaphan, and he read it.

⁹Shaphan went to the king and reported, "Your officials have turned over the money collected at the Temple of the LORD to the workers and supervisors at the Temple." ¹⁰Shaphan also told the king, "Hilkiah the priest has given me a scroll." So Shaphan read it to the king.

¹¹When the king heard what was written in the Book of the Law, he tore his clothes in despair. ¹²Then he gave these orders to Hilkiah the priest, Ahikam son of Shaphan, Acbor son of Micaiah, Shaphan the court secretary, and Asaiah the king's personal adviser: ¹³"Go to the Temple and speak to the LORD for me and for the people and for all Judah. Inquire about the words written in this scroll that has been found. For the LORD's great anger is burning against us because our ancestors have not obeyed the words in this scroll. We have not been doing everything it says we must do."

¹⁴So Hilkiah the priest, Ahikam, Acbor, Shaphan, and Asaiah went to the New Quarter* of Jerusalem to consult with the prophet Huldah. She was the wife of Shallum son of Tikvah, son of Harhas, the keeper of the Temple wardrobe.

¹⁵She said to them, "The LORD, the God of Israel, has spoken! Go back and tell the man who sent you, ¹⁶'This is what the LORD says: I am going to bring disaster on this city* and its people. All the words written in the scroll that the king of Judah has read will come true. ¹⁷For my people have abandoned me and offered sacrifices to pagan gods, and I am very angry with them for everything they have done. My anger will burn against this place, and it will not be quenched.'

¹⁸"But go to the king of Judah who sent you to seek the LORD and tell him: 'This is what the LORD, the God of Israel, says concerning the message you have just heard: ¹⁹You were sorry and humbled yourself before the LORD when you heard what I said against this city and its people—that this land would be cursed and become desolate. You tore your clothing in despair and wept before me in repentance. And I have indeed heard you, says the LORD. ²⁰So I will not send the promised disaster until after you have died and been buried in peace. You will not see the disaster I am going to bring on this city.'"

So they took her message back to the king.

23 JOSIAH'S RELIGIOUS REFORMS
Then the king summoned all the elders of Judah and Jerusalem. ²And the king went up to the Temple of the LORD with all the people of Judah and Jerusalem, along with the priests and the prophets—all the people from the least to the greatest. There the king read to them the entire Book of the Covenant that had been found in the LORD's Temple. ³The king took his place of authority beside the pillar

....

FOUNDATION OF OBEDIENCE
(22:1-2) In reading the biblical lists of kings, it is rare to find one who obeyed God completely. Josiah was such a person. For 18 years he reigned obediently; then, when he was 26, he began reforms based on God's laws. You're never too young to begin learning the discipline of obedience. The foundation of obedience that you establish now can lead to greater responsibilities in your adulthood.

SORROW OVER SIN
(22:3-19) When Josiah realized how corrupt his nation had become, he tore his clothes and wept before God. Josiah used the customs of his day to show his sorrow over the nation's wrongdoing. We are unlikely to tear our clothing these days, but we can find other ways to demonstrate how sorry we are when we do wrong things. How do you show your sorrow?

JUST DO IT!
(23:1-7) Josiah didn't just cry about his people's wrongdoings; he also took action. It is not enough to say we believe what is right; we must respond with action, doing what faith requires. This is what James meant when he said that "faith without good deeds is useless" (Jas 2:20). How active is your faith?

22:14 Or *the Second Quarter,* a newer section of Jerusalem. Hebrew reads *the Mishneh.*   22:16 Hebrew *this place;* also in 22:19, 20.

and renewed the covenant in the LORD's presence. He pledged to obey the LORD by keeping all his commands, laws, and decrees with all his heart and soul. In this way, he confirmed all the terms of the covenant that were written in the scroll, and all the people pledged themselves to the covenant.

⁴Then the king instructed Hilkiah the high priest and the priests of the second rank and the Temple gatekeepers to remove from the LORD's Temple all the articles that were used to worship Baal, Asherah, and all the powers of the heavens. The king had all these things burned outside Jerusalem on the terraces of the Kidron Valley, and he carried the ashes away to Bethel. ⁵He did away with the idolatrous priests, who had been appointed by the previous kings of Judah, for they had offered sacrifices at the pagan shrines throughout Judah and even in the vicinity of Jerusalem. They had also offered sacrifices to Baal, and to the sun, the moon, the constellations, and to all the powers of the heavens. ⁶The king removed the Asherah pole from the LORD's Temple and took it outside Jerusalem to the Kidron Valley, where he burned it. Then he ground the ashes of the pole to dust and threw the dust over the graves of the people. ⁷He also tore down the living quarters of the male and female shrine prostitutes that were inside the Temple of the LORD, where the women wove coverings for the Asherah pole.

⁸Josiah brought to Jerusalem all the priests who were living in other towns of Judah. He also defiled the pagan shrines, where they had offered sacrifices—all the way from Geba to Beersheba. He destroyed the shrines at the entrance to the gate of Joshua, the governor of Jerusalem. This gate was located to the left of the city gate as one enters the city. ⁹The priests who had served at the pagan shrines were not allowed* to serve at the LORD's altar in Jerusalem, but they were allowed to eat unleavened bread with the other priests.

¹⁰Then the king defiled the altar of Topheth in the valley of Ben-Hinnom, so no one could ever again use it to sacrifice a son or daughter in the fire* as an offering to Molech. ¹¹He removed from the entrance of the LORD's Temple the horse statues that the former kings of Judah had dedicated to the sun. They were near

the quarters of Nathan-melech the eunuch, an officer of the court.* The king also burned the chariots dedicated to the sun.

¹²Josiah tore down the altars that the kings of Judah had built on the palace roof above the upper room of Ahaz. The king destroyed the altars that Manasseh had built in the two courtyards of the LORD's Temple. He smashed them to bits* and scattered the pieces in the Kidron Valley. ¹³The king also desecrated the pagan shrines east of Jerusalem, to the south of the Mount of Corruption, where King Solomon of Israel had built shrines for Ashtoreth, the detestable goddess of the Sidonians; and for Chemosh, the detestable god of the Moabites; and for Molech,* the vile god of the Ammonites. ¹⁴He smashed the sacred pillars and cut down the Asherah poles. Then he desecrated these places by scattering human bones over them.

¹⁵The king also tore down the altar at Bethel—the pagan shrine that Jeroboam son of Nebat had made when he caused Israel to sin. He burned down the shrine and ground it to dust, and he burned the Asherah pole. ¹⁶Then Josiah turned around and noticed several tombs in the side of the hill. He ordered that the bones be brought out, and he burned them on the altar at Bethel to desecrate it. (This happened just as the LORD had promised through the man of God when Jeroboam stood beside the altar at the festival.)

Then Josiah turned and looked up at the tomb of the man of God* who had predicted these things. ¹⁷"What is that monument over there?" Josiah asked.

And the people of the town told him, "It is the tomb of the man of God who came from Judah and predicted the very things that you have just done to the altar at Bethel!"

¹⁸Josiah replied, "Leave it alone. Don't disturb his bones." So they did not burn his bones or those of the old prophet from Samaria.

¹⁹Then Josiah demolished all the buildings at the pagan shrines in the towns of Samaria, just as he had done at Bethel. They had been built by the various kings of Israel and had made the LORD* very angry. ²⁰He executed the priests of the pagan shrines on their own altars, and he burned human bones on the altars to desecrate them. Finally, he returned to Jerusalem.

JOSIAH CELEBRATES PASSOVER ²¹King Josiah then issued this order to all the people: "You must celebrate the Passover to the LORD your God, as required in this Book of the Covenant."

23:9 Hebrew *did not come up.* **23:10** Or *to make a son or daughter pass through the fire.* **23:11** The meaning of the Hebrew is uncertain. **23:12** Or *He quickly removed them.* **23:13** Hebrew *Milcom,* a variant spelling of Molech. **23:16** As in Greek version; Hebrew lacks *when Jeroboam stood beside the altar at the festival. Then Josiah turned and looked up at the tomb of the man of God.* **23:19** As in Greek and Syriac versions and Latin Vulgate; Hebrew lacks *the LORD.*

²²There had not been a Passover celebration like that since the time when the judges ruled in Israel, nor throughout all the years of the kings of Israel and Judah. ²³This Passover was celebrated to the LORD in Jerusalem in the eighteenth year of King Josiah's reign.

²⁴Josiah also got rid of the mediums and psychics, the household gods, the idols,* and every other kind of detestable practice, both in Jerusalem and throughout the land of Judah. He did this in obedience to the laws written in the scroll that Hilkiah the priest had found in the LORD's Temple. ²⁵Never before had there been a king like Josiah, who turned to the LORD with all his heart and soul and strength, obeying all the laws of Moses. And there has never been a king like him since.

²⁶Even so, the LORD was very angry with Judah because of all the wicked things Manasseh had done to provoke him. ²⁷For the LORD said, "I will also banish Judah from my presence just as I have banished Israel. And I will reject my chosen city of Jerusalem and the Temple where my name was to be honored."

²⁸The rest of the events in Josiah's reign and all his deeds are recorded in *The Book of the History of the Kings of Judah.*

²⁹While Josiah was king, Pharaoh Neco, king of Egypt, went to the Euphrates River to help the king of Assyria. King Josiah and his army marched out to fight him,* but King Neco* killed him when they met at Megiddo. ³⁰Josiah's officers took his body back in a chariot from Megiddo to Jerusalem and buried him in his own tomb. Then the people of the land anointed Josiah's son Jehoahaz and made him the next king.

JEHOAHAZ RULES IN JUDAH

³¹Jehoahaz was twenty-three years old when he became king, and he reigned in Jerusalem three months. His mother was Hamutal, the daughter of Jeremiah from Libnah. ³²He did what was evil in the LORD's sight, just as his ancestors had done.

³³Pharaoh Neco put Jehoahaz in prison at Riblah in the land of Hamath to prevent him from ruling* in Jerusalem. He also demanded that Judah pay 7,500 pounds of silver and 75 pounds of gold* as tribute.

JEHOIAKIM RULES IN JUDAH

³⁴Pharaoh Neco then installed Eliakim, another of Josiah's sons, to reign in place of his father, and he changed Eliakim's name to Jehoiakim. Jehoahaz was taken to Egypt as a prisoner, where he died.

³⁵In order to get the silver and gold demanded as tribute by Pharaoh Neco, Jehoiakim collected a tax from the people of Judah, requiring them to pay in proportion to their wealth.

³⁶Jehoiakim was twenty-five years old when he became king, and he reigned in Jerusalem eleven years. His mother was Zebidah, the daughter of Pedaiah from Rumah. ³⁷He did what was evil in the LORD's sight, just as his ancestors had done.

24 During Jehoiakim's reign, King Nebuchadnezzar of Babylon invaded the land of Judah. Jehoiakim surrendered and paid him tribute for three years but then rebelled. ²Then the LORD sent bands of Babylonian,* Aramean, Moabite, and Ammonite raiders against Judah to destroy it, just as the LORD had promised through his prophets. ³These disasters happened to Judah because of the LORD's command. He had decided to banish Judah from his presence because of the many sins of Manasseh, ⁴who had filled Jerusalem with innocent blood. The LORD would not forgive this.

⁵The rest of the events in Jehoiakim's reign and all his deeds are recorded in *The Book of the History of the Kings of Judah.* ⁶When Jehoiakim died, his son Jehoiachin became the next king.

⁷The king of Egypt did not venture out of his country after that, for the king of Babylon captured the entire area formerly claimed by Egypt—from the Brook of Egypt to the Euphrates River.

JEHOIACHIN RULES IN JUDAH

⁸Jehoiachin was eighteen years old when he became king, and he reigned in Jerusalem three months. His mother was Nehushta, the daughter of Elnathan from Jerusalem. ⁹Jehoiachin did what was evil in the LORD's sight, just as his father had done.

¹⁰During Jehoiachin's reign, the officers of King Nebuchadnezzar of Babylon came up against Jerusalem and besieged it. ¹¹Nebuchadnezzar himself arrived at the city during the siege. ¹²Then King Jehoiachin, along with the queen mother, his advisers, his commanders, and his officials, surrendered to the Babylonians.

In the eighth year of Nebuchadnezzar's reign, he took Jehoiachin prisoner. ¹³As the LORD had said beforehand, Nebuchadnezzar carried away all the treasures from the LORD's Temple and the royal palace. He stripped away* all the

23:24 The Hebrew term (literally *round things*) probably alludes to dung.   **23:29a** Or *Josiah went out to meet him.*   **23:29b** Hebrew *he.*   **23:33a** The meaning of the Hebrew is uncertain.   **23:33b** Hebrew *100 talents* [3,400 kilograms] *of silver and 1 talent* [34 kilograms] *of gold.*   **24:2** Or *Chaldean.*   **24:13** Or *He cut apart.*

gold objects that King Solomon of Israel had placed in the Temple. ¹⁴King Nebuchadnezzar took all of Jerusalem captive, including all the commanders and the best of the soldiers, craftsmen, and artisans—10,000 in all. Only the poorest people were left in the land.

¹⁵Nebuchadnezzar led King Jehoiachin away as a captive to Babylon, along with the queen mother, his wives and officials, and all Jerusalem's elite. ¹⁶He also exiled 7,000 of the best troops and 1,000 craftsmen and artisans, all of whom were strong and fit for war. ¹⁷Then the king of Babylon installed Mattaniah, Jehoiachin's* uncle, as the next king, and he changed Mattaniah's name to Zedekiah.

ZEDEKIAH RULES IN JUDAH

¹⁸Zedekiah was twenty-one years old when he became king, and he reigned in Jerusalem eleven years. His mother was Hamutal, the daughter of Jeremiah from Libnah. ¹⁹But Zedekiah did what was evil in the LORD's sight, just as Jehoiakim had done. ²⁰These things happened because of the LORD's anger against the people of Jerusalem and Judah, until he finally banished them from his presence and sent them into exile.

THE FALL OF JERUSALEM

Zedekiah rebelled against the king of Babylon.

25 So on January 15,* during the ninth year of Zedekiah's reign, King Nebuchadnezzar of Babylon led his entire army against Jerusalem. They surrounded the city and built siege ramps against its walls. ²Jerusalem was kept under siege until the eleventh year of King Zedekiah's reign.

³By July 18 in the eleventh year of Zedekiah's reign,* the famine in the city had become very severe, and the last of the food was entirely gone. ⁴Then a section of the city wall was broken down, and all the soldiers fled. Since the city was surrounded by the Babylonians,* they waited for nightfall. Then they slipped through the gate between the two walls behind the king's garden and headed toward the Jordan Valley.*

⁵But the Babylonian* troops chased the king

JUDAH EXILED
Evil permeated Judah, and God's anger flared against his rebellious people. Babylon conquered Assyria and became the new world power. The Babylonian army marched into Jerusalem, burned the Temple, tore down the city's massive walls, and carried off the people into captivity.

and caught him on the plains of Jericho, for his men had all deserted him and scattered. ⁶They took him to the king of Babylon at Riblah, where they pronounced judgment upon Zedekiah. ⁷They made Zedekiah watch as they slaughtered his sons. Then they gouged out Zedekiah's eyes, bound him in bronze chains, and led him away to Babylon.

THE TEMPLE DESTROYED

⁸On August 14 of that year,* which was the nineteenth year of King Nebuchadnezzar's reign, Nebuzaradan, the captain of the guard and an official of the Babylonian king, arrived in Jerusalem. ⁹He burned down the Temple of the LORD, the royal palace, and all the houses of Jerusalem. He destroyed all the important buildings* in the city. ¹⁰Then he supervised the entire Babylonian army as they tore down the walls of Jerusalem on every side. ¹¹Nebuzaradan, the captain of the guard, then took as exiles the rest of the people who remained in the city, the defectors who had declared their allegiance to the king of Babylon, and the rest of the population. ¹²But the captain of the guard allowed some of the poorest people to stay behind in Judah to care for the vineyards and fields.

¹³The Babylonians broke up the bronze pillars in front of the LORD's Temple, the bronze water carts, and the great bronze basin called

24:17 Hebrew *his.*   **25:1** Hebrew *on the tenth day of the tenth month,* of the ancient Hebrew lunar calendar. A number of events in 2 Kings can be cross-checked with dates in surviving Babylonian records and related accurately to our modern calendar. This day was January 15, 588 B.C.   **25:3** Hebrew *By the ninth day of the [fourth] month* [in the eleventh year of Zedekiah's reign] (compare Jer 52:6 and the note there). This day was July 18, 586 B.C.; also see note on 25:1.   **25:4a** Or *the Chaldeans;* also in 25:13, 25, 26.   **25:4b** Hebrew *the Arabah.*   **25:5** Or *Chaldean;* also in 25:10, 24.   **25:8** Hebrew *On the seventh day of the fifth month,* of the ancient Hebrew lunar calendar. This day was August 14, 586 B.C.; also see note on 25:1.   **25:9** Or *destroyed the houses of all the important people.*

···

EARLY WARNINGS
(25:1-21) Judah, like Israel (the northern kingdom), was unfaithful to God. So God, as he had warned, allowed the people of Judah to be exiled. The book of Lamentations records the prophet Jeremiah's sorrow at seeing Jerusalem destroyed (see, for example, Lam 1:1-3).

God will fulfill his promises and carry out his warnings. Have you received any warnings in your life lately? How will you respond to them?

the Sea, and they carried all the bronze away to Babylon. ¹⁴They also took all the ash buckets, shovels, lamp snuffers, dishes, and all the other bronze articles used for making sacrifices at the Temple. ¹⁵Nebuzaradan, the captain of the guard, also took the incense burners and basins, and all the other articles made of pure gold or silver.

¹⁶The weight of the bronze from the two pillars, the Sea, and the water carts was too great to be measured. These things had been made for the LORD's Temple in the days of King Solomon. ¹⁷Each of the pillars was 27 feet* tall. The bronze capital on top of each pillar was 7½ feet* high and was decorated with a network of bronze pomegranates all the way around.

¹⁸Nebuzaradan, the captain of the guard, took with him as prisoners Seraiah the high priest, Zephaniah the priest of the second rank, and the three chief gatekeepers. ¹⁹And from among the people still hiding in the city, he took an officer who had been in charge of the Judean army; five of the king's personal advisers; the army commander's chief secretary, who was in charge of recruitment; and sixty other citizens. ²⁰Nebuzaradan, the captain of the guard, took them all to the king of Babylon at Riblah. ²¹And there at Riblah, in the land of Hamath, the king of Babylon had them all put to death. So the people of Judah were sent into exile from their land.

GEDALIAH GOVERNS IN JUDAH ²²Then King Nebuchadnezzar appointed Gedaliah son of Ahikam and grandson of Shaphan as governor over the people he had left in Judah. ²³When all the army commanders and their men learned that the king of Babylon had appointed Gedaliah as governor, they went to see him at Mizpah. These included Ishmael son of Nethaniah, Johanan son of Kareah, Seraiah son of Tanhumeth the Netophathite, and Jezaniah* son of the Maacathite, and all their men.

²⁴Gedaliah vowed to them that the Babylonian officials meant them no harm. "Don't be afraid of them. Live in the land and serve the king of Babylon, and all will go well for you," he promised.

²⁵But in midautumn of that year,* Ishmael son of Nethaniah and grandson of Elishama, who was of the royal family, went to Mizpah with ten men and killed Gedaliah. He also killed all the Judeans and Babylonians who were with Gedaliah at Mizpah.

²⁶Then all the people of Judah, from the least to the greatest, as well as the army commanders, fled in panic to Egypt, for they were afraid of what the Babylonians would do to them.

HOPE FOR ISRAEL'S ROYAL LINE ²⁷In the thirty-seventh year of the exile of King Jehoiachin of Judah, Evil-merodach ascended to the Babylonian throne. He was kind to* Jehoiachin and released him from prison on April 2 of that year.* ²⁸He spoke kindly to Jehoiachin and gave him a higher place than all the other exiled kings in Babylon. ²⁹He supplied Jehoiachin with new clothes to replace his prison garb and allowed him to dine in the king's presence for the rest of his life. ³⁰So the Babylonian king gave him a regular food allowance as long as he lived.

AN UNHAPPY ENDING

(25:26) The book of 2 Kings opened with Elijah being carried to heaven—the destination awaiting those who follow God. But the book ends with the people of Judah being driven away from their land—the result of failing to follow God.

Second Kings is an illustration of what happens when disobedience becomes a way of life. An unhappy ending is a guarantee for those who adopt that lifestyle. Is any momentary thrill worth that?

25:17a Hebrew *18 cubits* [8.1 meters]. **25:17b** As in parallel texts at 1 Kgs 7:16, 2 Chr 3:15, and Jer 52:22, all of which read *5 cubits* [2.3 meters]; Hebrew reads *3 cubits*, which is 4.5 feet or 1.4 meters. **25:23** As in parallel text at Jer 40:8; Hebrew reads *Jaazaniah*, a variant spelling of Jezaniah. **25:25** Hebrew *in the seventh month*, of the ancient Hebrew lunar calendar. This month occurred within the months of October and November 586 B.C.; also see note on 25:1. **25:27a** Hebrew *He raised the head of.* **25:27b** Hebrew *on the twenty-seventh day of the twelfth month*, of the ancient Hebrew lunar calendar. This day was April 2, 561 B.C.; also see note on 25:1.

CHRONICLES

"That team will be toast tonight!" The coach's voice booms over the PA in the packed gymnasium. With those words the student body begins to clap and yell wildly. Somewhere in the back a few people start screaming their school team's name. Others join in. Soon everyone is standing and screaming in unison.

Pep rallies can draw a school together. And for those few moments, all differences are forgotten as the crowd focuses on one objective—winning the big game.

First Chronicles can be considered a written pep rally. Writing for the Jews who had returned to their homeland, the author attempts to form a sense of national conscience and awaken national pride and unity.

Beginning with Adam, 1 Chronicles relates the exciting history of Israel. By recalling the past, the author hoped to spur the Israelites on to a great future. But 1 Chronicles is more than a history lesson. It shows the spiritual strength of the nation. Only by uniting in worship of God could the nation regain the importance and vitality it once had.

We, too, have a great spiritual heritage that has been passed on to us by the people in the Bible and in our families. As you read 1 Chronicles, why not commit to doing your part to pass on God's truth to the next generation?

STATS

PURPOSE
To unify God's people, to trace the Davidic line, and to teach that worship ought to be the center of individual and national life

AUTHOR
Ezra, according to Jewish tradition

ORIGINAL AUDIENCE
The exiles who had returned from captivity

DATE WRITTEN
Approximately 430 B.C.; recording events that occurred about 1000–960 B.C.

SETTING
First Chronicles parallels 2 Samuel and comments on it. Written after the Exile from a priestly point of view, 1 Chronicles emphasizes the religious history of Judah and Israel.

KEY PLACES
Hebron, Jerusalem, the Temple

TIMELINE

1050 B.C.
Saul becomes king

1010
Saul dies; David becomes king of Judah

1003
David becomes king of all Israel

1000
David captures Jerusalem

980(?)
David's census

KEY POINTS

A SPIRITUAL FOUNDATION By retelling Israel's history in the family histories of the kings, the writer showed the spiritual foundation of the nation. The Bible provides a spiritual foundation upon which we can build our lives.

A PERFECT KING Although the story of David's life and relationship with God show that he was a great king, he was still imperfect. His descendant, Jesus Christ, is the only totally perfect king who will someday rule over all the earth.

AN ENCOURAGEMENT TO WORSHIP David brought the Ark of the Covenant to the Tabernacle at Jerusalem to encourage the people to worship God. In the same way, we are to encourage each other to worship God.

The broken lines (–·–·–) indicate modern boundaries.

KEY PLACES
The genealogies of 1 Chronicles present an overview of Israel's history. The first nine chapters are filled with genealogies tracing the lineages of people from the Creation to the Exile in Babylon. Saul's death is recorded in chapter 10. Chapter 11 begins the history of David's reign over Israel.

❶ HEBRON
Although David had been anointed king years earlier, his reign began when the leaders of Israel accepted him as king at Hebron (11:1-3).

❷ JERUSALEM
David set out to complete the conquest of the land begun by Joshua. He attacked Jerusalem, captured it, and made it his capital (11:4–12:40).

❸ KIRIATH-JEARIM
The Ark of the Covenant, which had been captured by the Philistines in battle and then returned (1 Sam 4–6), was in safekeeping in Kiriath-jearim. David summoned all Israel to this city to join together in bringing the Ark to Jerusalem. Unfortunately, it was not moved according to God's instructions, and as a result one man died. David left the Ark in the home of Obed-edom until he could discover how to transport it correctly (1 Chr 13:1-14).

❹ TYRE
David did much building in Jerusalem. King Hiram of Tyre sent workers and supplies to help build David's palace. Cedar, abundant in the mountains north of Israel, was a valuable and hardy wood for the beautiful buildings in Jerusalem (14:1–17:27).

❺ BAAL-PERAZIM
David was not very popular with the Philistines because he had killed Goliath, one of their greatest warriors (1 Sam 17). When David began to rule over a united Israel, the Philistines set out to capture him. But David and his army attacked the Philistines at Baal-perazim as they approached Jerusalem. David's army defeated the mighty Philistines twice, causing all the surrounding nations to fear his power (1 Chr 14:11-17). After this battle, David moved the Ark to Jerusalem, this time following God's instructions for its transportation. There was great celebration as the Ark was brought into Jerusalem (15:1–17:27). David spent the remainder of his life making preparations for the building of the Temple, a central place for the worship of God (18:1–29:30).

1 FROM ADAM TO NOAH'S SONS

The descendants of Adam were Seth, Enosh, ²Kenan, Mahalalel, Jared, ³Enoch, Methuselah, Lamech, ⁴and Noah.

The sons of Noah were* Shem, Ham, and Japheth.

DESCENDANTS OF JAPHETH

⁵The descendants of Japheth were Gomer, Magog, Madai, Javan, Tubal, Meshech, and Tiras.

⁶The descendants of Gomer were Ashkenaz, Riphath,* and Togarmah.

⁷The descendants of Javan were Elishah, Tarshish, Kittim, and Rodanim.

DESCENDANTS OF HAM

⁸The descendants of Ham were Cush, Mizraim,* Put, and Canaan.

⁹The descendants of Cush were Seba, Havilah, Sabtah, Raamah, and Sabteca. The descendants of Raamah were Sheba and Dedan. ¹⁰Cush was also the ancestor of Nimrod, who was the first heroic warrior on earth.

¹¹Mizraim was the ancestor of the Ludites, Anamites, Lehabites, Naphtuhites, ¹²Pathrusites, Casluhites, and the Caphtorites, from whom the Philistines came.*

¹³Canaan's oldest son was Sidon, the ancestor of the Sidonians. Canaan was also the ancestor of the Hittites,* ¹⁴Jebusites, Amorites, Girgashites, ¹⁵Hivites, Arkites, Sinites, ¹⁶Arvadites, Zemarites, and Hamathites.

DESCENDANTS OF SHEM

¹⁷The descendants of Shem were Elam, Asshur, Arphaxad, Lud, and Aram.

The descendants of Aram were* Uz, Hul, Gether, and Mash.*

¹⁸Arphaxad was the father of Shelah. Shelah was the father of Eber.

¹⁹Eber had two sons. The first was named Peleg (which means "division"), for during his lifetime the people of the world were divided into different language groups. His brother's name was Joktan.

²⁰Joktan was the ancestor of Almodad, Sheleph, Hazarmaveth, Jerah, ²¹Hadoram, Uzal, Diklah, ²²Obal,* Abimael, Sheba, ²³Ophir, Havilah, and Jobab. All these were descendants of Joktan.

²⁴So this is the family line descended from Shem: Arphaxad, Shelah,* ²⁵Eber, Peleg, Reu, ²⁶Serug, Nahor, Terah, ²⁷and Abram, later known as Abraham.

DESCENDANTS OF ABRAHAM

²⁸The sons of Abraham were Isaac and Ishmael. ²⁹These are their genealogical records:

The sons of Ishmael were Nebaioth (the oldest), Kedar, Adbeel, Mibsam, ³⁰Mishma, Dumah, Massa, Hadad, Tema, ³¹Jetur, Naphish, and Kedemah. These were the sons of Ishmael.

³²The sons of Keturah, Abraham's concubine, were Zimran, Jokshan, Medan, Midian, Ishbak, and Shuah.

The sons of Jokshan were Sheba and Dedan.

³³The sons of Midian were Ephah, Epher, Hanoch, Abida, and Eldaah.

All these were descendants of Abraham through his concubine Keturah.

DESCENDANTS OF ISAAC

³⁴Abraham was the father of Isaac. The sons of Isaac were Esau and Israel.*

DESCENDANTS OF ESAU

³⁵The sons of Esau were Eliphaz, Reuel, Jeush, Jalam, and Korah.

³⁶The descendants of Eliphaz were Teman, Omar, Zepho,* Gatam, Kenaz, and Amalek, who was born to Timna.*

³⁷The descendants of Reuel were Nahath, Zerah, Shammah, and Mizzah.

ORIGINAL PEOPLES OF EDOM

³⁸The descendants of Seir were Lotan, Shobal, Zibeon, Anah, Dishon, Ezer, and Dishan.

³⁹The descendants of Lotan were Hori and Hemam.* Lotan's sister was named Timna.

1:4 As in Greek version (see also Gen 5:3-32); Hebrew lacks *The sons of Noah were.* **1:6** As in some Hebrew manuscripts and Greek version (see also Gen 10:3); most Hebrew manuscripts read *Diphath.* **1:8** Or *Egypt;* also in 1:11. **1:12** Hebrew *Casluhites, from whom the Philistines came, Caphtorites.* See Jer 47:4; Amos 9:7. **1:13** Hebrew *ancestor of Heth.* **1:17a** As in one Hebrew manuscript and some Greek manuscripts (see also Gen 10:23); most Hebrew manuscripts lack *The descendants of Aram were.* **1:17b** As in parallel text at Gen 10:23; Hebrew reads *and Meshech.* **1:22** As in some Hebrew manuscripts and Syriac version (see also Gen 10:28); most Hebrew manuscripts read *Ebal.* **1:24** Some Greek manuscripts read *Arphaxad, Cainan, Shelah.* See notes on Gen 10:24; 11:12-13. **1:34** *Israel* is the name that God gave to Jacob. **1:36a** As in many Hebrew manuscripts and a few Greek manuscripts (see also Gen 36:11); most Hebrew manuscripts read *Zephi.* **1:36b** As in some Greek manuscripts (see also Gen 36:12); Hebrew reads *Kenaz, Timna, and Amalek.* **1:39** As in parallel text at Gen 36:22; Hebrew reads *and Homam.*

. . . .

A FAMILY HISTORY

(1:1) The family histories of 1 Chronicles, beginning with this verse, demonstrate God's interest in nations and individuals. Although billions of people have lived since Adam, none is a stranger to God. He works through people to bring about his plans. Each individual is more than a name on a list. He or she is a special person whom God knows and loves. These family histories can remind us of our place in God's plans and in his family.

⁴⁰The descendants of Shobal were Alvan,* Manahath, Ebal, Shepho,* and Onam.

The descendants of Zibeon were Aiah and Anah.

⁴¹The son of Anah was Dishon.

The descendants of Dishon were Hemdan,* Eshban, Ithran, and Keran.

⁴²The descendants of Ezer were Bilhan, Zaavan, and Akan.*

The descendants of Dishan* were Uz and Aran.

RULERS OF EDOM ⁴³These are the kings who ruled in the land of Edom before any king ruled over the Israelites*:

Bela son of Beor, who ruled from his city of Dinhabah.

⁴⁴When Bela died, Jobab son of Zerah from Bozrah became king in his place.

⁴⁵When Jobab died, Husham from the land of the Temanites became king in his place.

⁴⁶When Husham died, Hadad son of Bedad became king in his place and ruled from the city of Avith. He was the one who destroyed the Midianite army in the land of Moab.

⁴⁷When Hadad died, Samlah from the city of Masrekah became king in his place.

⁴⁸When Samlah died, Shaul from the city of Rehoboth-on-the-River became king in his place.

⁴⁹When Shaul died, Baal-hanan son of Acbor became king in his place.

⁵⁰When Baal-hanan died, Hadad became king in his place and ruled from the city of Pau.* His wife was Mehetabel, the daughter of Matred and granddaughter of Me-zahab. ⁵¹Then Hadad died.

The clan leaders of Edom were Timna, Alvah,* Jetheth, ⁵²Oholibamah, Elah, Pinon, ⁵³Kenaz, Teman, Mibzar, ⁵⁴Magdiel, and Iram. These are the clan leaders of Edom.

2 DESCENDANTS OF ISRAEL
The sons of Israel* were Reuben, Simeon, Levi, Judah, Issachar, Zebulun, ²Dan, Joseph, Benjamin, Naphtali, Gad, and Asher.

DESCENDANTS OF JUDAH ³Judah had three sons from Bathshua, a Canaanite woman. Their names were Er, Onan, and Shelah. But the LORD saw that the oldest son, Er, was a

1:40a As in many Hebrew manuscripts and a few Greek manuscripts (see also Gen 36:23); most Hebrew manuscripts read *Alian.* **1:40b** As in some Hebrew manuscripts (see also Gen 36:23); most Hebrew manuscripts read *Shephi.* **1:41** As in many Hebrew manuscripts and some Greek manuscripts (see also Gen 36:26); most Hebrew manuscripts read *Hamran.* **1:42a** As in many Hebrew and Greek manuscripts (see also Gen 36:27); most Hebrew manuscripts read *Jaakan.* **1:42b** Hebrew *Dishon;* compare 1:38 and parallel text at Gen 36:28. **1:43** Or *before an Israelite king ruled over them.* **1:50** As in many Hebrew manuscripts, some Greek manuscripts, Syriac version, and Latin Vulgate (see also Gen 36:39); most Hebrew manuscripts read *Pai.* **1:51** As in parallel text at Gen 36:40; Hebrew reads *Aliah.* **2:1** *Israel* is the name that God gave to Jacob.

ISHMAEL

HAVE YOU EVER WONDERED whether you were born into the wrong family? That question must have haunted Ishmael at times. He might have felt trapped in a conflict between two jealous women: Sarah and Hagar.

Sarah's impatience with God led her to use Hagar as a surrogate mother. Since Hagar was a servant, she allowed herself to be used in this way. But Hagar's pregnancy gave birth to strong feelings of superiority toward Sarah. Into this tense atmosphere, Ishmael was born.

Much of what happened to Ishmael cannot be blamed on him. He was caught in a process much bigger than himself. But his actions showed that he chose to become part of the problem, not the solution. He chose to live in his circumstances instead of living above them.

The choice Ishmael had is one we all must make. There are circumstances over which we have no control (heredity, for instance), but there are others over which we do have control (our decisions). We all have inherited a nature that desires to do wrong. It can be partly controlled—but not overcome—by human effort. Ishmael's life is a picture of the mess we make when we don't try to change those things that we can change.

The God of the Bible has offered us a solution. His answer is not control, but a changed life freely given by God. To begin a changed life, trust God to forgive your sinful past, and to help you change your attitude toward him and others.

BOTTOM LINE: God's plans even allow for people's mistakes.

Ishmael's story is told in Genesis 16; 17:24-25; 21; 25:9-18. He also is mentioned in 1 Chronicles 1:28-31; Galatians 4:29-30.

UPS:
- *One of the first to experience circumcision—the physical sign of God's covenant*
- *Known for his ability as an archer and hunter*
- *Fathered twelve sons who became leaders of warrior tribes*

DOWNS:
- *Failed to recognize the place of his half brother, Isaac, and mocked him*

STATS:
- *Where: Canaan and Egypt*
- *Occupations: Archer, hunter, warrior*
- *Relatives: Hagar and Abraham (parents); Isaac (half brother)*

KEY VERSES: *Genesis 21:17-18*

wicked man, so he killed him. ⁴Later Judah had twin sons from Tamar, his widowed daughter-in-law. Their names were Perez and Zerah. So Judah had five sons in all.

⁵The sons of Perez were Hezron and Hamul.

⁶The sons of Zerah were Zimri, Ethan, Heman, Calcol, and Darda*—five in all.

⁷The son of Carmi (a descendant of Zimri) was Achan,* who brought disaster on Israel by taking plunder that had been set apart for the LORD.*

⁸The son of Ethan was Azariah.

FROM JUDAH'S GRANDSON HEZRON TO DAVID
⁹The sons of Hezron were Jerahmeel, Ram, and Caleb.*

¹⁰ Ram was the father of Amminadab. Amminadab was the father of Nahshon, a leader of Judah.

¹¹ Nahshon was the father of Salmon.* Salmon was the father of Boaz.

¹² Boaz was the father of Obed. Obed was the father of Jesse.

¹³Jesse's first son was Eliab, his second was Abinadab, his third was Shimea, ¹⁴his fourth was Nethanel, his fifth was Raddai, ¹⁵his sixth was Ozem, and his seventh was David.

¹⁶Their sisters were named Zeruiah and Abigail. Zeruiah had three sons named Abishai, Joab, and Asahel. ¹⁷Abigail married a man named Jether, an Ishmaelite, and they had a son named Amasa.

OTHER DESCENDANTS OF HEZRON
¹⁸Hezron's son Caleb had sons from his wife Azubah and from Jerioth.* Her sons were named Jesher, Shobab, and Ardon. ¹⁹After Azubah died, Caleb married Ephrathah,* and they had a son named Hur. ²⁰Hur was the father of Uri. Uri was the father of Bezalel.

²¹When Hezron was sixty years old, he married Gilead's sister, the daughter of Makir. They had a son named Segub. ²²Segub was the father of Jair, who ruled twenty-three towns in the land of Gilead. ²³(But Geshur and Aram captured the Towns of Jair* and also took Kenath and its sixty surrounding villages.) All these were descendants of Makir, the father of Gilead.

²⁴Soon after Hezron died in the town of Caleb-ephrathah, his wife Abijah gave birth to a son named Ashhur (the father of* Tekoa).

DESCENDANTS OF HEZRON'S SON JERAHMEEL
²⁵The sons of Jerahmeel, the oldest son of Hezron, were Ram (the firstborn), Bunah, Oren, Ozem, and Ahijah. ²⁶Jerahmeel had a second wife named Atarah. She was the mother of Onam.

²⁷The sons of Ram, the oldest son of Jerahmeel, were Maaz, Jamin, and Eker.

²⁸The sons of Onam were Shammai and Jada. The sons of Shammai were Nadab and Abishur.

²⁹The sons of Abishur and his wife Abihail were Ahban and Molid.

³⁰The sons of Nadab were Seled and Appaim. Seled died without children, ³¹but Appaim had a son named Ishi. The son of Ishi was Sheshan. Sheshan had a descendant named Ahlai.

³²The sons of Jada, Shammai's brother, were Jether and Jonathan. Jether died without children, ³³but Jonathan had two sons named Peleth and Zaza.

These were all descendants of Jerahmeel.

³⁴Sheshan had no sons, though he did have daughters. He also had an Egyptian servant named Jarha. ³⁵Sheshan gave one of his daughters to be the wife of Jarha, and they had a son named Attai.

³⁶ Attai was the father of Nathan. Nathan was the father of Zabad.

³⁷ Zabad was the father of Ephlal. Ephlal was the father of Obed.

³⁸ Obed was the father of Jehu. Jehu was the father of Azariah.

³⁹ Azariah was the father of Helez. Helez was the father of Eleasah.

⁴⁰ Eleasah was the father of Sismai. Sismai was the father of Shallum.

⁴¹ Shallum was the father of Jekamiah. Jekamiah was the father of Elishama.

DESCENDANTS OF HEZRON'S SON CALEB
⁴²The descendants of Caleb, the brother of Jerahmeel, included Mesha (the firstborn), who became the father of Ziph. Caleb's

---

2:6 As in many Hebrew manuscripts, some Greek manuscripts, and Syriac version (see also 1 Kgs 4:31); Hebrew reads *Dara*.
2:7a Hebrew *Achar*; compare Josh 7:1. *Achar* means "disaster."
2:7b The Hebrew term used here refers to the complete consecration of things or people to the LORD, either by destroying them or by giving them as an offering.   2:9 Hebrew *Kelubai*, a variant spelling of Caleb; compare 2:18.   2:11 As in Greek version (see also Ruth 4:20); Hebrew reads *Salma*.   2:18 Or *Caleb had a daughter named Jerioth from his wife, Azubah.* The meaning of the Hebrew is uncertain.   2:19 Hebrew *Ephrath*, a variant spelling of Ephrathah; compare 2:50 and 4:4.   2:23 Or *captured Havvoth-jair*.   2:24 Or *the founder of*; also in 2:42, 45, 49.

descendants also included the sons of Mareshah, the father of Hebron.*

⁴³The sons of Hebron were Korah, Tappuah, Rekem, and Shema. ⁴⁴Shema was the father of Raham. Raham was the father of Jorkeam. Rekem was the father of Shammai. ⁴⁵The son of Shammai was Maon. Maon was the father of Beth-zur.

⁴⁶Caleb's concubine Ephah gave birth to Haran, Moza, and Gazez. Haran was the father of Gazez.

⁴⁷The sons of Jahdai were Regem, Jotham, Geshan, Pelet, Ephah, and Shaaph.

⁴⁸Another of Caleb's concubines, Maacah, gave birth to Sheber and Tirhanah. ⁴⁹She also gave birth to Shaaph (the father of Madmannah) and Sheva (the father of Macbenah and Gibea). Caleb also had a daughter named Acsah.

⁵⁰These were all descendants of Caleb.

DESCENDANTS OF CALEB'S SON HUR The sons of Hur, the oldest son of Caleb's wife Ephrathah, were Shobal (the founder of Kiriath-jearim), ⁵¹Salma (the founder of Bethlehem), and Hareph (the founder of Beth-gader).

⁵²The descendants of Shobal (the founder of Kiriath-jearim) were Haroeh, half the Manahathites, ⁵³and the families of Kiriath-jearim—the Ithrites, Puthites, Shumathites, and Mishraites, from whom came the people of Zorah and Eshtaol.

⁵⁴The descendants of Salma were the people of Bethlehem, the Netophathites, Atroth-beth-joab, the other half of the Manahathites, the Zorites, ⁵⁵and the families of scribes living at Jabez—the Tirathites, Shimeathites, and Sucathites. All these were Kenites who descended from Hammath, the father of the family of Recab.*

3 **DESCENDANTS OF DAVID** These are the sons of David who were born in Hebron:

The oldest was Amnon, whose mother was Ahinoam from Jezreel.

The second was Daniel, whose mother was Abigail from Carmel.

² The third was Absalom, whose mother was Maacah, the daughter of Talmai, king of Geshur.

The fourth was Adonijah, whose mother was Haggith.

³ The fifth was Shephatiah, whose mother was Abital.

The sixth was Ithream, whose mother was Eglah, David's wife.

⁴These six sons were born to David in Hebron, where he reigned seven and a half years.

Then David reigned another thirty-three years in Jerusalem. ⁵The sons born to David in Jerusalem included Shammua,* Shobab, Nathan, and Solomon. Their mother was Bathsheba,* the daughter of Ammiel. ⁶David also had nine other sons: Ibhar, Elishua,* Elpelet,* ⁷Nogah, Nepheg, Japhia, ⁸Elishama, Eliada, and Eliphelet.

⁹These were the sons of David, not including his sons born to his concubines. Their sister was named Tamar.

DESCENDANTS OF SOLOMON ¹⁰The descendants of Solomon were Rehoboam, Abijah, Asa, Jehoshaphat, ¹¹Jehoram,* Ahaziah, Joash, ¹²Amaziah, Uzziah,* Jotham, ¹³Ahaz, Hezekiah, Manasseh, ¹⁴Amon, and Josiah.

¹⁵The sons of Josiah were Johanan (the oldest), Jehoiakim (the second), Zedekiah (the third), and Jehoahaz* (the fourth).

¹⁶The successors of Jehoiakim were his son Jehoiachin and his brother Zedekiah.*

DESCENDANTS OF JEHOIACHIN ¹⁷The sons of Jehoiachin,* who was taken prisoner by the Babylonians, were Shealtiel, ¹⁸Malkiram, Pedaiah, Shenazzar, Jekamiah, Hoshama, and Nedabiah.

¹⁹The sons of Pedaiah were Zerubbabel and Shimei.

The sons of Zerubbabel were Meshullam and Hananiah. (Their sister was Shelomith.) ²⁰His five other sons were Hashubah, Ohel, Berekiah, Hasadiah, and Jushab-hesed.

²¹The sons of Hananiah were Pelatiah and Jeshaiah. Jeshaiah's son was Rephaiah. Rephaiah's son was Arnan. Arnan's son was Obadiah. Obadiah's son was Shecaniah.

²²The descendants of Shecaniah were Shemaiah and his sons, Hattush, Igal, Bariah, Neariah, and Shaphat—six in all.

²³The sons of Neariah were Elioenai, Hizkiah, and Azrikam—three in all.

²⁴The sons of Elioenai were Hodaviah,

2:42 Or *who founded Hebron.* The meaning of the Hebrew is uncertain. **2:55** Or *the founder of Beth-recab.* **3:5a** As in Syriac version (see also 14:4; 2 Sam 5:14); Hebrew reads *Shimea.* **3:5b** Hebrew *Bathshua,* a variant spelling of Bathsheba. **3:6a** As in some Hebrew and Greek manuscripts (see also 14:5-7 and 2 Sam 5:15); most Hebrew manuscripts read *Elishama.* **3:6b** Hebrew *Eliphelet;* compare parallel text at 14:5-7. **3:11** Hebrew *Joram,* a variant spelling of Jehoram. **3:12** Hebrew *Azariah,* a variant spelling of Uzziah. **3:15** Hebrew *Shallum,* another name for Jehoahaz. **3:16** Hebrew *The sons of Jehoiakim were his son Jeconiah* [a variant spelling of Jehoiachin] *and his son Zedekiah.* **3:17** Hebrew *Jeconiah,* a variant spelling of Jehoiachin.

Eliashib, Pelaiah, Akkub, Johanan, Delaiah, and Anani—seven in all.

4 OTHER DESCENDANTS OF JUDAH The descendants of Judah were Perez, Hezron, Carmi, Hur, and Shobal.

2Shobal's son Reaiah was the father of Jahath. Jahath was the father of Ahumai and Lahad. These were the families of the Zorathites.

3The descendants of* Etam were Jezreel, Ishma, Idbash, their sister Hazzelelponi, 4Penuel (the father of* Gedor), and Ezer (the father of Hushah). These were the descendants of Hur (the firstborn of Ephrathah), the ancestor of Bethlehem.

5Ashhur (the father of Tekoa) had two wives, named Helah and Naarah. 6Naarah gave birth to Ahuzzam, Hepher, Temeni, and Haahashtari. 7Helah gave birth to Zereth, Izhar,* Ethnan, 8and Koz, who became the ancestor of Anub, Zobebah, and all the families of Aharhel son of Harum.

9There was a man named Jabez who was more honorable than any of his brothers. His mother named him Jabez* because his birth had been so painful. 10He was the one who prayed to the God of Israel, "Oh, that you would bless me and expand my territory! Please be with me in all that I do, and keep me from all trouble and pain!" And God granted him his request.

11Kelub (the brother of Shuhah) was the father of Mehir. Mehir was the father of Eshton. 12Eshton was the father of Beth-rapha, Paseah, and Tehinnah. Tehinnah was the father of Ir-nahash. These were the descendants of Recah.

13The sons of Kenaz were Othniel and Seraiah. Othniel's sons were Hathath and Meonothai.* 14Meonothai was the father of Ophrah. Seraiah was the father of Joab, the founder of the Valley of Craftsmen,* so called because they were craftsmen.

15The sons of Caleb son of Jephunneh were Iru, Elah, and Naam. The son of Elah was Kenaz.

16The sons of Jehallelel were Ziph, Ziphah, Tiria, and Asarel.

17The sons of Ezrah were Jether, Mered, Epher, and Jalon. One of Mered's wives

became* the mother of Miriam, Shammai, and Ishbah (the father of Eshtemoa). 18He married a woman from Judah, who became the mother of Jered (the father of Gedor), Heber (the father of Soco), and Jekuthiel (the father of Zanoah). Mered also married Bithia, a daughter of Pharaoh, and she bore him children.

19Hodiah's wife was the sister of Naham. One of her sons was the father of Keilah the Garmite, and another was the father of Eshtemoa the Maacathite.

20The sons of Shimon were Amnon, Rinnah, Ben-hanan, and Tilon.

The descendants of Ishi were Zoheth and Ben-zoheth.

DESCENDANTS OF JUDAH'S SON SHELAH

21Shelah was one of Judah's sons. The descendants of Shelah were Er (the father of Lecah); Laadah (the father of Mareshah); the families of linen workers at Beth-ashbea; 22Jokim; the men of Cozeba; and Joash and Saraph, who ruled over Moab and Jashubi-lehem. These names all come from ancient records. 23They were the pottery makers who lived in Netaim and Gederah. They lived there and worked for the king.

DESCENDANTS OF SIMEON 24The sons of Simeon were Jemuel,* Jamin, Jarib, Zohar,* and Shaul.

25The descendants of Shaul were Shallum, Mibsam, and Mishma.

26The descendants of Mishma were Hammuel, Zaccur, and Shimei.

27Shimei had sixteen sons and six daughters, but none of his brothers had large families. So Simeon's tribe never grew as large as the tribe of Judah.

28They lived in Beersheba, Moladah, Hazar-shual, 29Bilhah, Ezem, Tolad, 30Bethuel, Hormah, Ziklag, 31Beth-marcaboth, Hazar-susim, Beth-biri, and Shaaraim. These

---

4:3 As in Greek version; Hebrew reads *father of.* The meaning of the Hebrew is uncertain. 4:4 Or *the founder of;* also in 4:5, 12, 14, 17, 18, and perhaps other instances where the text reads *the father of.* 4:7 As in an alternate reading in the Masoretic Text (see also Latin Vulgate); the other alternate and the Greek version read *Zohar.* 4:9 *Jabez* sounds like a Hebrew word meaning "distress" or "pain." 4:13 As in some Greek manuscripts and Latin Vulgate; Hebrew lacks *and Meonothai.* 4:14 Or *Joab, the father of Ge-harashim.* 4:17 Or *Jether's wife became;* Hebrew reads *She became.* 4:24a As in Syriac version (see also Gen 46:10; Exod 6:15); Hebrew reads *Nemuel.* 4:24b As in parallel texts at Gen 46:10 and Exod 6:15; Hebrew reads *Zerah.*

A MEMORABLE PRAYER
(4:10) Jabez is remembered as "the one who prayed to the God of Israel." It is significant that he is remembered for a prayer rather than a heroic act. This is quite a contrast to what Er is remembered for (see note at 2:3). Jabez wasn't afraid to ask for something huge from God. Jabez asked God to (1) bless him, (2) expand his territory, (3) be with him in all he did, and (4) keep him from all trouble and pain. Jabez acknowledged God as the true center of his work and life. When we pray for God's blessing, we should also pray that he will take his rightful position as Lord over all areas of our lives. Then we, too, may be remembered for more than just a heroic deed.

towns were under their control until the time of King David. ³²Their descendants also lived in Etam, Ain, Rimmon, Token, and Ashan—five towns ³³and their surrounding villages as far away as Baalath.* This was their territory, and these names are listed in their genealogical records.

³⁴Other descendants of Simeon included Meshobab, Jamlech, Joshah son of Amaziah, ³⁵Joel, Jehu son of Joshibiah, son of Seraiah, son of Asiel, ³⁶Elioenai, Jaakobah, Jeshohaiah, Asaiah, Adiel, Jesimiel, Benaiah, ³⁷and Ziza son of Shiphi, son of Allon, son of Jedaiah, son of Shimri, son of Shemaiah.

³⁸These were the names of some of the leaders of Simeon's wealthy clans. Their families grew, ³⁹and they traveled to the region of Gerar,* in the east part of the valley, seeking pastureland for their flocks. ⁴⁰They found lush pastures there, and the land was quiet and peaceful.

Some of Ham's descendants had been living in that region. ⁴¹But during the reign of King Hezekiah of Judah, these leaders of Simeon invaded the region and completely destroyed* the homes of the descendants of Ham and of the Meunites. No trace of them remains today. They killed everyone who lived there and took the land for themselves, because they wanted its good pastureland for their flocks. ⁴²Five hundred of these invaders from the tribe of Simeon went to Mount Seir, led by Pelatiah, Neariah, Rephaiah, and Uzziel—all sons of Ishi. ⁴³They destroyed the few Amalekites who had survived, and they have lived there ever since.

5 **DESCENDANTS OF REUBEN** The oldest son of Israel* was Reuben. But since he dishonored his father by sleeping with one of his father's concubines, his birthright was given to the sons of his brother Joseph. For this reason, Reuben is not listed in the genealogical records as the firstborn son. ²The descendants of Judah became the most powerful tribe and provided a ruler for the nation,* but the birthright belonged to Joseph.

CONSEQUENCES
(5:1) *This record of Reuben's sin of incest shows the lasting consequences of sin. As the oldest son, Reuben would have inherited a double portion of his father's estate. But he lost everything—rights, privileges, and family—because of one act. Every wrong action has consequences, either now or in the future. When temptation comes, consider the possible consequences.*

³The sons of Reuben, the oldest son of Israel, were Hanoch, Pallu, Hezron, and Carmi. ⁴The descendants of Joel were Shemaiah, Gog, Shimei, ⁵Micah, Reaiah, Baal, ⁶and Beerah. Beerah was the leader of the Reubenites when they were taken into captivity by King Tiglath-pileser* of Assyria.

⁷Beerah's* relatives are listed in their genealogical records by their clans: Jeiel (the leader), Zechariah, ⁸and Bela son of Azaz, son of Shema, son of Joel.

The Reubenites lived in the area that stretches from Aroer to Nebo and Baal-meon. ⁹And since they had so many livestock in the land of Gilead, they spread east toward the edge of the desert that stretches to the Euphrates River.

¹⁰During the reign of Saul, the Reubenites defeated the Hagrites in battle. Then they moved into the Hagrite settlements all along the eastern edge of Gilead.

DESCENDANTS OF GAD ¹¹Next to the Reubenites, the descendants of Gad lived in the land of Bashan as far east as Salecah. ¹²Joel was the leader in the land of Bashan, and Shapham was second-in-command, followed by Janai and Shaphat.

¹³Their relatives, the leaders of seven other clans, were Michael, Meshullam, Sheba, Jorai, Jacan, Zia, and Eber. ¹⁴These were all descendants of Abihail son of Huri, son of Jaroah, son of Gilead, son of Michael, son of Jeshishai, son of Jahdo, son of Buz. ¹⁵Ahi son of Abdiel, son of Guni, was the leader of their clans.

¹⁶The Gadites lived in the land of Gilead, in Bashan and its villages, and throughout all the pasturelands of Sharon. ¹⁷All of these were listed in the genealogical records during the days of King Jotham of Judah and King Jeroboam of Israel.

THE TRIBES EAST OF THE JORDAN ¹⁸There were 44,760 capable warriors in the armies of Reuben, Gad, and the half-tribe of Manasseh. They were all skilled in combat and armed with shields, swords, and bows. ¹⁹They waged war against the Hagrites, the Jeturites, the Naphishites, and the Nodabites. ²⁰They cried out to God during the battle, and he answered

4:33 As in some Greek manuscripts (see also Josh 19:8); Hebrew reads *Baal*. **4:39** As in Greek version; Hebrew reads *Gedor*. **4:41** The Hebrew term used here refers to the complete consecration of things or people to the LORD, either by destroying them or by giving them as an offering. **5:1** *Israel* is the name that God gave to Jacob. **5:2** Or *and from Judah came a prince*. **5:6** Hebrew *Tilgath-pilneser*, a variant spelling of Tiglath-pileser; also in 5:26. **5:7** Hebrew *His*.

their prayer because they trusted in him. So the Hagrites and all their allies were defeated. ²¹The plunder taken from the Hagrites included 50,000 camels, 250,000 sheep and goats, 2,000 donkeys, and 100,000 captives. ²²Many of the Hagrites were killed in the battle because God was fighting against them. The people of Reuben, Gad, and Manasseh lived in their land until they were taken into exile.

²³The half-tribe of Manasseh was very large and spread through the land from Bashan to Baal-hermon, Senir, and Mount Hermon. ²⁴These were the leaders of their clans: Epher,* Ishi, Eliel, Azriel, Jeremiah, Hodaviah, and Jahdiel. These men had a great reputation as mighty warriors and leaders of their clans.

²⁵But these tribes were unfaithful to the God of their ancestors. They worshiped the gods of the nations that God had destroyed. ²⁶So the God of Israel caused King Pul of Assyria (also known as Tiglath-pileser) to invade the land and take away the people of Reuben, Gad, and the half-tribe of Manasseh as captives. The Assyrians exiled them to Halah, Habor, Hara, and the Gozan River, where they remain to this day.

6 THE PRIESTLY LINE

¹*The sons of Levi were Gershon, Kohath, and Merari. ²The descendants of Kohath included Amram, Izhar, Hebron, and Uzziel. ³The children of Amram were Aaron, Moses, and Miriam.

The sons of Aaron were Nadab, Abihu, Eleazar, and Ithamar.

⁴ Eleazar was the father of Phinehas.
Phinehas was the father of Abishua.
⁵ Abishua was the father of Bukki.
Bukki was the father of Uzzi.
⁶ Uzzi was the father of Zerahiah.
Zerahiah was the father of Meraioth.
⁷ Meraioth was the father of Amariah.
Amariah was the father of Ahitub.
⁸ Ahitub was the father of Zadok.
Zadok was the father of Ahimaaz.
⁹ Ahimaaz was the father of Azariah.
Azariah was the father of Johanan.
¹⁰ Johanan was the father of Azariah, the high priest at the Temple* built by Solomon in Jerusalem.

¹¹ Azariah was the father of Amariah.
Amariah was the father of Ahitub.
¹² Ahitub was the father of Zadok.
Zadok was the father of Shallum.
¹³ Shallum was the father of Hilkiah.
Hilkiah was the father of Azariah.
¹⁴ Azariah was the father of Seraiah.
Seraiah was the father of Jehozadak, ¹⁵who went into exile when the LORD sent the people of Judah and Jerusalem into captivity under Nebuchadnezzar.

THE LEVITE CLANS

¹⁶*The sons of Levi were Gershon,* Kohath, and Merari.
¹⁷The descendants of Gershon included Libni and Shimei.
¹⁸The descendants of Kohath included Amram, Izhar, Hebron, and Uzziel.
¹⁹The descendants of Merari included Mahli and Mushi.

The following were the Levite clans, listed according to their ancestral descent:

²⁰The descendants of Gershon included Libni, Jahath, Zimmah, ²¹Joah, Iddo, Zerah, and Jeatherai.
²²The descendants of Kohath included Amminadab, Korah, Assir, ²³Elkanah, Abiasaph,* Assir, ²⁴Tahath, Uriel, Uzziah, and Shaul.
²⁵The descendants of Elkanah included Amasai, Ahimoth, ²⁶Elkanah, Zophai, Nahath, ²⁷Eliab, Jeroham, Elkanah, and Samuel.*
²⁸The sons of Samuel were Joel* (the older) and Abijah (the second).
²⁹The descendants of Merari included Mahli, Libni, Shimei, Uzzah, ³⁰Shimea, Haggiah, and Asaiah.

THE TEMPLE MUSICIANS

³¹David assigned the following men to lead the music at the house of the LORD after the Ark was placed there. ³²They ministered with music at the Tabernacle* until Solomon built the Temple of the LORD in Jerusalem. They carried out their work, following all the regulations handed down to

5:24 As in Greek version and Latin Vulgate; Hebrew reads and Epher. 6:1 Verses 6:1-15 are numbered 5:27-41 in Hebrew text. 6:10 Hebrew the house. 6:16a Verses 6:16-81 are numbered 6:1-66 in Hebrew text. 6:16b Hebrew Gershom, a variant spelling of Gershon (see 6:1); also in 6:17, 20, 43, 62, 71. 6:23 Hebrew Ebiasaph, a variant spelling of Abiasaph (also in 6:37); compare parallel text at Exod 6:24. 6:27 As in some Greek manuscripts (see also 6:33-34); Hebrew lacks and Samuel. 6:28 As in some Greek manuscripts and the Syriac version (see also 6:33 and 1 Sam 8:2); Hebrew lacks Joel. 6:32 Hebrew the Tabernacle, the Tent of Meeting.

SUCCESSFUL FAILURES
(5:23-26) As warriors and leaders, these men seemed successful. They were numerous and powerful. But they failed in the most important quality—putting God first in their lives. In a way, they were "successful failures." They followed the world's standard of success but not God's. Do your standards for success match God's standards or the world's?

them. ³³These are the men who served, along with their sons:

Heman the musician was from the clan of Kohath. His genealogy was traced back through Joel, Samuel, ³⁴Elkanah, Jeroham, Eliel, Toah, ³⁵Zuph, Elkanah, Mahath, Amasai, ³⁶Elkanah, Joel, Azariah, Zephaniah, ³⁷Tahath, Assir, Abiasaph, Korah, ³⁸Izhar, Kohath, Levi, and Israel.*

³⁹Heman's first assistant was Asaph from the clan of Gershon.* Asaph's genealogy was traced back through Berekiah, Shimea, ⁴⁰Michael, Baaseiah, Malkijah, ⁴¹Ethni, Zerah, Adaiah, ⁴²Ethan, Zimmah, Shimei, ⁴³Jahath, Gershon, and Levi.

⁴⁴Heman's second assistant was Ethan from the clan of Merari. Ethan's genealogy was traced back through Kishi, Abdi, Malluch, ⁴⁵Hashabiah, Amaziah, Hilkiah, ⁴⁶Amzi, Bani, Shemer, ⁴⁷Mahli, Mushi, Merari, and Levi.

⁴⁸Their fellow Levites were appointed to various other tasks in the Tabernacle, the house of God.

AARON'S DESCENDANTS ⁴⁹Only Aaron and his descendants served as priests. They presented the offerings on the altar of burnt offering and the altar of incense, and they performed all the other duties related to the Most Holy Place. They made atonement for Israel by doing everything that Moses, the servant of God, had commanded them.

⁵⁰The descendants of Aaron were Eleazar, Phinehas, Abishua, ⁵¹Bukki, Uzzi, Zerahiah, ⁵²Meraioth, Amariah, Ahitub, ⁵³Zadok, and Ahimaaz.

··

TALENTS
(6:31-32) The builders and craftsmen had completed the Temple, and the priests and the Levites had been assigned their responsibilities for taking care of it. Now it was time for another group of people—the musicians—to use their talents for God. Some of the musicians' names are recorded here, showing that a person doesn't have to be an ordained minister to serve God. Builders, craftsmen, worship assistants, choir members, and song leaders all made significant contributions. God has given you a unique combination of talents and gifts. Use them to serve him.

SELECTIVE OR THOROUGH?
(6:49) Aaron and his descendants strictly followed the details of worship that God commanded through Moses. They did not choose only those commands they wanted to obey. This is a sharp contrast to what happened to Uzzah when important details in handling the Ark of the Covenant were neglected (13:6-10). When it comes to obeying God's rules, are you selective or thorough?

TERRITORY FOR THE LEVITES ⁵⁴This is a record of the towns and territory assigned by means of sacred lots to the descendants of Aaron, who were from the clan of Kohath. ⁵⁵This territory included Hebron and its surrounding pasturelands in Judah, ⁵⁶but the fields and outlying areas belonging to the city were given to Caleb son of Jephunneh. ⁵⁷So the descendants of Aaron were given the following towns, each with its pasturelands: Hebron (a city of refuge),* Libnah, Jattir, Eshtemoa, ⁵⁸Holon,* Debir, ⁵⁹Ain,* Juttah,* and Beth-shemesh. ⁶⁰And from the territory of Benjamin they were given Gibeon,* Geba, Alemeth, and Anathoth, each with its pasturelands. So thirteen towns were given to the descendants of Aaron. ⁶¹The remaining descendants of Kohath received ten towns from the territory of the half-tribe of Manasseh by means of sacred lots.

⁶²The descendants of Gershon received by sacred lots thirteen towns from the territories of Issachar, Asher, Naphtali, and from the Bashan area of Manasseh, east of the Jordan.

⁶³The descendants of Merari received by sacred lots twelve towns from the territories of Reuben, Gad, and Zebulun.

⁶⁴So the people of Israel assigned all these towns and pasturelands to the Levites. ⁶⁵The towns in the territories of Judah, Simeon, and Benjamin, mentioned above, were assigned to them by means of sacred lots.

⁶⁶The descendants of Kohath were given the following towns from the territory of Ephraim, each with its pasturelands: ⁶⁷Shechem (a city of refuge in the hill country of Ephraim),* Gezer, ⁶⁸Jokmeam, Beth-horon, ⁶⁹Aijalon, and Gath-rimmon. ⁷⁰The remaining descendants of Kohath were assigned the towns of Aner and Bileam from the territory of the half-tribe of Manasseh, each with its pasturelands.

⁷¹The descendants of Gershon received the towns of Golan (in Bashan) and Ashtaroth from the territory of the half-tribe of Manasseh, each with its pasturelands. ⁷²From the territory of Issachar, they were given Kedesh, Daberath, ⁷³Ramoth, and Anem, each with its pasturelands. ⁷⁴From the territory of Asher, they received Mashal, Abdon, ⁷⁵Hukok, and Rehob, each with its pasturelands. ⁷⁶From the

6:38 *Israel* is the name that God gave to Jacob.   **6:39** Hebrew lacks *from the clan of Gershon;* see 6:43.   **6:57** As in parallel text at Josh 21:13; Hebrew reads *were given the cities of refuge: Hebron, and the following towns, each with its pasturelands.*   **6:58** As in parallel text at Josh 21:15; Masoretic Text reads *Hilez;* other manuscripts read *Hilen.*   **6:59a** As in parallel text at Josh 21:16; Hebrew reads *Ashan.*   **6:59b** As in Syriac version (see also Josh 21:16); Hebrew lacks *Juttah.*   **6:60** As in parallel text at Josh 21:17; Hebrew lacks *Gibeon.*   **6:66-67** As in parallel text at Josh 21:21. Hebrew text reads *were given the cities of refuge: Shechem in the hill country of Ephraim, and the following towns, each with its pasturelands.*

territory of Naphtali, they were given Kedesh in Galilee, Hammon, and Kiriathaim, each with its pasturelands.

⁷⁷The remaining descendants of Merari received the towns of Jokneam, Kartah,* Rimmon,* and Tabor from the territory of Zebulun, each with its pasturelands. ⁷⁸From the territory of Reuben, east of the Jordan River opposite Jericho, they received Bezer (a desert town), Jahaz,* ⁷⁹Kedemoth, and Mephaath, each with its pasturelands. ⁸⁰And from the territory of Gad, they received Ramoth in Gilead, Mahanaim, ⁸¹Heshbon, and Jazer, each with its pasturelands.

7 DESCENDANTS OF ISSACHAR The four sons of Issachar were Tola, Puah, Jashub, and Shimron.

²The sons of Tola were Uzzi, Rephaiah, Jeriel, Jahmai, Ibsam, and Shemuel. Each of them was the leader of an ancestral clan. At the time of King David, the total number of mighty warriors listed in the records of these clans was 22,600.

³The son of Uzzi was Izrahiah. The sons of Izrahiah were Michael, Obadiah, Joel, and Isshiah. These five became the leaders of clans. ⁴All of them had many wives and many sons, so the total number of men available for military service among their descendants was 36,000.

⁵The total number of mighty warriors from all the clans of the tribe of Issachar was 87,000. All of them were listed in their genealogical records.

DESCENDANTS OF BENJAMIN ⁶Three of Benjamin's sons were Bela, Beker, and Jediael.

⁷The five sons of Bela were Ezbon, Uzzi, Uzziel, Jerimoth, and Iri. Each of them was the leader of an ancestral clan. The total number of mighty warriors from these clans was 22,034, as listed in their genealogical records.

⁸The sons of Beker were Zemirah, Joash, Eliezer, Elioenai, Omri, Jeremoth, Abijah, Anathoth, and Alemeth. ⁹Each of them was the leader of an ancestral clan. The total number of mighty warriors and leaders from

these clans was 20,200, as listed in their genealogical records.

¹⁰The son of Jediael was Bilhan. The sons of Bilhan were Jeush, Benjamin, Ehud, Kenaanah, Zethan, Tarshish, and Ahishahar. ¹¹Each of them was the leader of an ancestral clan. From these clans the total number of mighty warriors ready for war was 17,200.

¹²The sons of Ir were Shuppim and Huppim. Hushim was the son of Aher.

DESCENDANTS OF NAPHTALI ¹³The sons of Naphtali were Jahzeel,* Guni, Jezer, and Shillem.* They were all descendants of Jacob's concubine Bilhah.

DESCENDANTS OF MANASSEH ¹⁴The descendants of Manasseh through his Aramean concubine included Asriel. She also bore Makir, the father of Gilead. ¹⁵Makir found wives for* Huppim and Shuppim. Makir had a sister named Maacah. One of his descendants was Zelophehad, who had only daughters.

¹⁶Makir's wife, Maacah, gave birth to a son whom she named Peresh. His brother's name was Sheresh. The sons of Peresh were Ulam and Rakem. ¹⁷The son of Ulam was Bedan. All these were considered Gileadites, descendants of Makir son of Manasseh.

¹⁸Makir's sister Hammoleketh gave birth to Ishhod, Abiezer, and Mahlah.

¹⁹The sons of Shemida were Ahian, Shechem, Likhi, and Aniam.

DESCENDANTS OF EPHRAIM ²⁰The descendants of Ephraim were Shuthelah, Bered, Tahath, Eleadah, Tahath, ²¹Zabad, Shuthelah, Ezer, and Elead. These two were killed trying to steal livestock from the local farmers near Gath. ²²Their father, Ephraim, mourned for them a long time, and his relatives came to comfort him. ²³Afterward Ephraim slept with his wife, and she became pregnant and gave birth to a son. Ephraim named him Beriah* because of the tragedy his family had suffered. ²⁴He had a daughter named Sheerah. She built the towns of Lower and Upper Beth-horon and Uzzen-sheerah.

²⁵The descendants of Ephraim included Rephah, Resheph, Telah, Tahan, ²⁶Ladan, Ammihud, Elishama, ²⁷Nun, and Joshua.

²⁸The descendants of Ephraim lived in the territory that included Bethel and its surrounding towns to the south, Naaran to the east,

---

6:77a As in Greek version (see also Josh 21:34); Hebrew lacks *Jokneam, Kartah*. 6:77b As in Greek version (see also Josh 19:13); Hebrew reads *Rimmono*. 6:78 Hebrew *Jahzah*, a variant spelling of Jahaz. 7:13a As in parallel text at Gen 46:24; Hebrew reads *Jahziel*, a variant spelling of Jahzeel. 7:13b As in some Hebrew and Greek manuscripts (see also Gen 46:24; Num 26:49); most Hebrew manuscripts read *Shallum*. 7:15 Or *Makir took a wife from*. The meaning of the Hebrew is uncertain. 7:23 *Beriah* sounds like a Hebrew term meaning "tragedy" or "misfortune."

Gezer and its villages to the west, and Shechem and its surrounding villages to the north as far as Ayyah and its towns. ²⁹Along the border of Manasseh were the towns of Beth-shan,* Taanach, Megiddo, Dor, and their surrounding villages. The descendants of Joseph son of Israel* lived in these towns.

DESCENDANTS OF ASHER ³⁰The sons of Asher were Imnah, Ishvah, Ishvi, and Beriah. They had a sister named Serah.

³¹The sons of Beriah were Heber and Malkiel (the father of Birzaith).

³²The sons of Heber were Japhlet, Shomer, and Hotham. They had a sister named Shua.

³³The sons of Japhlet were Pasach, Bimhal, and Ashvath.

³⁴The sons of Shomer were Ahi,* Rohgah, Hubbah, and Aram.

³⁵The sons of his brother Helem* were Zophah, Imna, Shelesh, and Amal.

³⁶The sons of Zophah were Suah, Harnepher, Shual, Beri, Imrah, ³⁷Bezer, Hod, Shamma, Shilshah, Ithran,* and Beera.

³⁸The sons of Jether were Jephunneh, Pispah, and Ara.

³⁹The sons of Ulla were Arah, Hanniel, and Rizia.

⁴⁰Each of these descendants of Asher was the head of an ancestral clan. They were all select men—mighty warriors and outstanding leaders. The total number of men available for military service was 26,000, as listed in their genealogical records.

8 **DESCENDANTS OF BENJAMIN** Benjamin's first son was Bela, the second was Ashbel, the third was Aharah, ²the fourth was Nohah, and the fifth was Rapha.

³The sons of Bela were Addar, Gera, Abihud,* ⁴Abishua, Naaman, Ahoah, ⁵Gera, Shephuphan, and Huram.

⁶The sons of Ehud, leaders of the clans living at Geba, were exiled to Manahath. ⁷Ehud's sons were Naaman, Ahijah, and Gera. Gera, who led them into exile, was the father of Uzza and Ahihud.*

⁸After Shaharaim divorced his wives Hushim and Baara, he had children in the land of Moab. ⁹His wife Hodesh gave birth to Jobab, Zibia, Mesha, Malcam, ¹⁰Jeuz, Sakia, and Mirmah. These sons all became the leaders of clans.

¹¹Shaharaim's wife Hushim had already given birth to Abitub and Elpaal. ¹²The sons of Elpaal were Eber, Misham, Shemed (who built the towns of Ono and Lod and their nearby villages), ¹³Beriah, and Shema. They were the leaders of the clans living in Aijalon, and they drove out the inhabitants of Gath.

¹⁴Ahio, Shashak, Jeremoth, ¹⁵Zebadiah, Arad, Eder, ¹⁶Michael, Ishpah, and Joha were the sons of Beriah.

¹⁷Zebadiah, Meshullam, Hizki, Heber, ¹⁸Ishmerai, Izliah, and Jobab were the sons of Elpaal.

¹⁹Jakim, Zicri, Zabdi, ²⁰Elienai, Zillethai, Eliel, ²¹Adaiah, Beraiah, and Shimrath were the sons of Shimei.

²²Ishpan, Eber, Eliel, ²³Abdon, Zicri, Hanan, ²⁴Hananiah, Elam, Anthothijah, ²⁵Iphdeiah, and Penuel were the sons of Shashak.

²⁶Shamsherai, Shehariah, Athaliah, ²⁷Jaareshiah, Elijah, and Zicri were the sons of Jeroham.

²⁸These were the leaders of the ancestral clans; they were listed in their genealogical records, and they all lived in Jerusalem.

THE FAMILY OF SAUL ²⁹Jeiel* (the father of* Gibeon) lived in the town of Gibeon. His wife's name was Maacah, ³⁰and his oldest son was named Abdon. Jeiel's other sons were Zur, Kish, Baal, Ner,* Nadab, ³¹Gedor, Ahio, Zechariah,* ³²and Mikloth, who was the father of Shimeam.* All these families lived near each other in Jerusalem.

³³ Ner was the father of Kish. Kish was the father of Saul. Saul was the father of Jonathan, Malkishua, Abinadab, and Esh-baal.

³⁴ Jonathan was the father of Merib-baal. Merib-baal was the father of Micah.

³⁵ Micah was the father of Pithon, Melech, Tahrea,* and Ahaz.

7:29a Hebrew Beth-shean, a variant spelling of Beth-shan. 7:29b Israel is the name that God gave to Jacob. 7:34 Or The sons of Shomer, his brother, were. 7:35 Possibly another name for Hotham; compare 7:32. 7:37 Possibly another name for Jether; compare 7:38. 8:3 Possibly Gera the father of Ehud; compare 8:6. 8:7 Or Gera, that is Heglam, was the father of Uzza and Ahihud. 8:29a As in some Greek manuscripts (see also 9:35); Hebrew lacks Jeiel. 8:29b Or the founder of. 8:30 As in some Greek manuscripts (see also 9:36); Hebrew lacks Ner. 8:31 As in parallel text at 9:37; Hebrew reads Zeker, a variant spelling of Zechariah. 8:32 As in parallel text at 9:38; Hebrew reads Shimeah, a variant spelling of Shimeam. 8:35 As in parallel text at 9:41; Hebrew reads Tarea, a variant spelling of Tahrea.

36 Ahaz was the father of Jadah.*
  Jadah was the father of Alemeth, Azmaveth,
    and Zimri.
  Zimri was the father of Moza.
37 Moza was the father of Binea.
  Binea was the father of Rephaiah.*
  Rephaiah was the father of Eleasah.
  Eleasah was the father of Azel.
38 Azel had six sons: Azrikam, Bokeru, Ishmael,
  Sheariah, Obadiah, and Hanan. These were
  the sons of Azel.
39 Azel's brother Eshek had three sons: the first
  was Ulam, the second was Jeush, and the
  third was Eliphelet. 40 Ulam's sons were all
  mighty warriors and expert archers. They
  had many sons and grandsons—150 in all.

All these were descendants of Benjamin.

9 So all Israel was listed in the genealogical
  records in *The Book of the Kings of Israel.*

THE RETURNING EXILES The people of Judah
were exiled to Babylon because they were unfaithful to the LORD. 2 The first of the exiles to
return to their property in their former towns
were priests, Levites, Temple servants, and
other Israelites. 3 Some of the people from the
tribes of Judah, Benjamin, Ephraim, and Manasseh came and settled in Jerusalem.

4 One family that returned was that of Uthai son
  of Ammihud, son of Omri, son of Imri, son of
  Bani, a descendant of Perez son of Judah.
5 Others returned from the Shilonite clan,
  including Asaiah (the oldest) and his sons.
6 From the Zerahite clan, Jeuel returned with his
  relatives.
In all, 690 families from the tribe of Judah
returned.

7 From the tribe of Benjamin came Sallu son
  of Meshullam, son of Hodaviah, son of
  Hassenuah; 8 Ibneiah son of Jeroham; Elah
  son of Uzzi, son of Micri; and Meshullam
  son of Shephatiah, son of Reuel, son of
  Ibnijah.
9 These men were all leaders of clans, and
  they were listed in their genealogical records.
In all, 956 families from the tribe of Benjamin
returned.

THE RETURNING PRIESTS 10 Among the
  priests who returned were Jedaiah,
  Jehoiarib, Jakin, 11 Azariah son of Hilkiah,
son of Meshullam, son of Zadok, son of
Meraioth, son of Ahitub. Azariah was the
chief officer of the house of God.
12 Other returning priests were Adaiah son of
Jeroham, son of Pashhur, son of Malkijah,
and Maasai son of Adiel, son of Jahzerah,
son of Meshullam, son of Meshillemith, son
of Immer.
13 In all, 1,760 priests returned. They were heads
of clans and very able men. They were responsible for ministering at the house of God.

THE RETURNING LEVITES 14 The Levites who
returned were Shemaiah son of Hasshub,
son of Azrikam, son of Hashabiah, a
descendant of Merari; 15 Bakbakkar; Heresh;
Galal; Mattaniah son of Mica, son of Zicri,
son of Asaph; 16 Obadiah son of Shemaiah,
son of Galal, son of Jeduthun; and
Berekiah son of Asa, son of Elkanah, who
lived in the area of Netophah.

17 The gatekeepers who returned were Shallum,
Akkub, Talmon, Ahiman, and their relatives.
Shallum was the chief gatekeeper. 18 Prior
to this time, they were responsible for the
King's Gate on the east side. These men
served as gatekeepers for the camps of the
Levites. 19 Shallum was the son of Kore, a
descendant of Abiasaph,* from the clan of
Korah. He and his relatives, the Korahites,
were responsible for guarding the entrance
to the sanctuary, just as their ancestors
had guarded the Tabernacle in the camp
of the LORD.
20 Phinehas son of Eleazar had been in
charge of the gatekeepers in earlier times,
and the LORD had been with him. 21 And
later Zechariah son of Meshelemiah was
responsible for guarding the entrance to
the Tabernacle.*

22 In all, there were 212 gatekeepers in
those days, and they were listed according to
the genealogies in their villages. David and
Samuel the seer had appointed their ancestors because they were reliable men. 23 These
gatekeepers and their descendants, by their
divisions, were responsible for guarding the
entrance to the house of the LORD when that
house was a tent. 24 The gatekeepers were

8:36 As in parallel text at 9:42; Hebrew reads *Jehoaddah*, a variant
spelling of Jadah.   8:37 As in parallel text at 9:43; Hebrew reads
Raphah, a variant spelling of Rephaiah.   9:19 Hebrew *Ebiasaph*,
a variant spelling of Abiasaph; compare Exod 6:24.   9:21 Hebrew
Tent of Meeting.

A MAJOR EFFECT
*(9:1) Although every person in Judah did not worship
idols, the entire nation had been driven away from their
homeland. At this point they were allowed to return. The
wrongdoings of a few can have a huge effect on everyone.
Rather than think,* I'm not hurting anyone but me, *think of
the impact one isolated incident can have on others.*

stationed on all four sides—east, west, north, and south. ²⁵Their relatives in the villages came regularly to share their duties for seven-day periods.

²⁶The four chief gatekeepers, all Levites, were trusted officials, for they were responsible for the rooms and treasuries at the house of God. ²⁷They would spend the night around the house of God, since it was their duty to guard it and to open the gates every morning.

²⁸Some of the gatekeepers were assigned to care for the various articles used in worship. They checked them in and out to avoid any loss. ²⁹Others were responsible for the furnishings, the items in the sanctuary, and the supplies, such as choice flour, wine, olive oil, frankincense, and spices. ³⁰But it was the priests who blended the spices. ³¹Mattithiah, a Levite and the oldest son of Shallum the Korahite, was entrusted with baking the bread used in the offerings. ³²And some members of the clan of Kohath were in charge of preparing the bread to be set on the table each Sabbath day.

³³The musicians, all prominent Levites, lived at the Temple. They were exempt from other responsibilities since they were on duty at all hours. ³⁴All these men lived in Jerusalem. They were the heads of Levite families and were listed as prominent leaders in their genealogical records.

KING SAUL'S FAMILY TREE ³⁵Jeiel (the father of* Gibeon) lived in the town of Gibeon. His wife's name was Maacah, ³⁶and his oldest son was named Abdon. Jeiel's other sons were Zur, Kish, Baal, Ner, Nadab, ³⁷Gedor, Ahio, Zechariah, and Mikloth. ³⁸Mikloth was the father of Shimeam. All these families lived near each other in Jerusalem.

³⁹ Ner was the father of Kish.
Kish was the father of Saul.
Saul was the father of Jonathan, Malkishua, Abinadab, and Esh-baal.

⁴⁰ Jonathan was the father of Merib-baal.
Merib-baal was the father of Micah.

⁴¹ The sons of Micah were Pithon, Melech, Tahrea, and Ahaz.*

⁴² Ahaz was the father of Jadah.*
Jadah was the father of Alemeth, Azmaveth, and Zimri.
Zimri was the father of Moza.

⁴³ Moza was the father of Binea.
Binea's son was Rephaiah.
Rephaiah's son was Eleasah.
Eleasah's son was Azel.

⁴⁴Azel had six sons, whose names were Azrikam, Bokeru, Ishmael, Sheariah, Obadiah, and Hanan. These were the sons of Azel.

10 THE DEATH OF KING SAUL Now the Philistines attacked Israel, and the men of Israel fled before them. Many were slaughtered on the slopes of Mount Gilboa. ²The Philistines closed in on Saul and his sons, and they killed three of his sons—Jonathan, Abinadab, and Malkishua. ³The fighting grew very fierce around Saul, and the Philistine archers caught up with him and wounded him.

⁴Saul groaned to his armor bearer, "Take your sword and kill me before these pagan Philistines come to taunt and torture me."

But his armor bearer was afraid and would not do it. So Saul took his own sword and fell on it. ⁵When his armor bearer realized that Saul was dead, he fell on his own sword and died. ⁶So Saul and his three sons died there together, bringing his dynasty to an end.

⁷When all the Israelites in the Jezreel Valley saw that their army had fled and that Saul and his sons were dead, they abandoned their towns and fled. So the Philistines moved in and occupied their towns.

⁸The next day, when the Philistines went out to strip the dead, they found the bodies of Saul and his sons on Mount Gilboa. ⁹So they stripped off Saul's armor and cut off his head. Then they proclaimed the good news of Saul's death before their idols and to the people throughout the land of Philistia. ¹⁰They placed his armor in the temple of their gods, and they fastened his head to the temple of Dagon.

¹¹But when everyone in Jabesh-gilead heard about everything the Philistines had done to Saul, ¹²all their mighty warriors brought the bodies of Saul and his sons back to Jabesh. Then they buried their bones beneath the great tree at Jabesh, and they fasted for seven days.

¹³So Saul died because he was unfaithful to

9:35 Or *the founder of.* **9:41** As in Syriac version and Latin Vulgate (see also 8:35); Hebrew lacks *and Ahaz.* **9:42** As in some Hebrew manuscripts and Greek version (see also 8:36); Hebrew reads *Jarah.*

BE PREPARED
(9:22-32) *The priests and Levites put a lot of time and effort into worship. Not only did they perform rather complicated tasks (described in Lev 1–9), they also took care of many pieces of equipment. Their maintenance of the Tabernacle allowed the people to worship without worry. Think of the many people who work behind the scenes at your church. Their dedication allows you to worship without worry. The preparations they make also serve as a reminder to be prepared for worship. How do you prepare for worship?*

the LORD. He failed to obey the LORD's command, and he even consulted a medium [14]instead of asking the LORD for guidance. So the LORD killed him and turned the kingdom over to David son of Jesse.

11 DAVID BECOMES KING OF ALL ISRAEL

Then all Israel gathered before David at Hebron and told him, "We are your own flesh and blood. [2]In the past,* even when Saul was king, you were the one who really led the forces of Israel. And the LORD your God told you, 'You will be the shepherd of my people Israel. You will be the leader of my people Israel.'"

[3]So there at Hebron, David made a covenant before the LORD with all the elders of Israel. And they anointed him king of Israel, just as the LORD had promised through Samuel.

DAVID CAPTURES JERUSALEM [4]Then David and all Israel went to Jerusalem (or Jebus, as it used to be called), where the Jebusites, the original inhabitants of the land, were living. [5]The people of Jebus taunted David, saying, "You'll never get in here!" But David captured the fortress of Zion, which is now called the City of David.

[6]David had said to his troops, "Whoever is first to attack the Jebusites will become the commander of my armies!" And Joab, the son of David's sister Zeruiah, was first to attack, so he became the commander of David's armies.

[7]David made the fortress his home, and that is why it is called the City of David. [8]He extended the city from the supporting terraces* to the surrounding area, while Joab rebuilt the rest of Jerusalem. [9]And David became more and more powerful, because the LORD of Heaven's Armies was with him.

DAVID'S MIGHTIEST WARRIORS [10]These are the leaders of David's mighty warriors. Together with all Israel, they decided to make David their king, just as the LORD had promised concerning Israel.

[11]Here is the record of David's mightiest warriors: The first was Jashobeam the Hacmonite, who was leader of the Three—the mightiest warriors among David's men.* He once used his spear to kill 300 enemy warriors in a single battle.

[12]Next in rank among the Three was Eleazar son of Dodai,* a descendant of Ahoah. [13]He was with David in the battle against the Philistines at Pas-dammim. The battle took place in a field full of barley, and the Israelite army fled. [14]But Eleazar and David* held their ground in the middle of the field and beat back the Philistines. So the LORD saved them by giving them a great victory.

[15]Once when David was at the rock near the cave of Adullam, the Philistine army was camped in the valley of Rephaim. The Three (who were among the Thirty—an elite group among David's fighting men) went down to meet him there. [16]David was staying in the stronghold at the time, and a Philistine detachment had occupied the town of Bethlehem.

[17]David remarked longingly to his men, "Oh, how I would love some of that good water from the well by the gate in Bethlehem." [18]So the Three broke through the Philistine lines, drew some water from the well by the gate in Bethlehem, and brought it back to David. But David refused to drink it. Instead, he poured it out as an offering to the LORD. [19]"God forbid that I should drink this!" he exclaimed. "This water is as precious as the blood of these men* who risked their lives to bring it to me." So David did not drink it. These are examples of the exploits of the Three.

DAVID'S THIRTY MIGHTY MEN [20]Abishai, the brother of Joab, was the leader of the Thirty.* He once used his spear to kill 300 enemy warriors in a single battle. It was by such feats that he became as famous as the Three. [21]Abishai was the most famous of the Thirty and was their commander, though he was not one of the Three.

[22]There was also Benaiah son of Jehoiada, a

....

IN PURSUIT
(10:13-14) Saul's unfaithfulness was both active and passive; he not only did wrong, he also failed to do right. He actively disobeyed by attempting murder, ignoring God's instructions, and seeking guidance from a witch. He passively disobeyed by neglecting to ask God for guidance as he ran the kingdom. Obedience, too, is both passive and active. It is not enough just to avoid what is wrong; we need to actively pursue what is right. Is that what you seek?

FAME
(11:9) King David's power and fame increased as a result of his consistent trust in God. In contrast, King Saul's power and fame decreased because he wanted all the credit for himself and ignored God (1 Sam 15:1-26; 1 Chr 10:13-14). Those who are concerned about building a name for themselves risk losing the very recognition they crave. Are you a David or a Saul?

11:2 Or *For some time.*   **11:8** Hebrew *the millo.* The meaning of the Hebrew is uncertain.   **11:11** As in some Greek manuscripts (see also 2 Sam 23:8); Hebrew reads *leader of the Thirty,* or *leader of the captains.*   **11:12** As in parallel text at 2 Sam 23:9 (see also 1 Chr 27:4); Hebrew reads *Dodo,* a variant spelling of Dodai. **11:14** Hebrew *they.*   **11:19** Hebrew *Shall I drink the lifeblood of these men?*   **11:20** As in Syriac version; Hebrew reads *the Three;* also in 11:21.

valiant warrior from Kabzeel. He did many heroic deeds, which included killing two champions* of Moab. Another time, on a snowy day, he chased a lion down into a pit and killed it. ²³Once, armed only with a club, he killed an Egyptian warrior who was 7½ feet* tall and whose spear was as thick as a weaver's beam. Benaiah wrenched the spear from the Egyptian's hand and killed him with it. ²⁴Deeds like these made Benaiah as famous as the three mightiest warriors. ²⁵He was more honored than the other members of the Thirty, though he was not one of the Three. And David made him captain of his bodyguard.

²⁶David's mighty warriors also included:

Asahel, Joab's brother;
Elhanan son of Dodo from Bethlehem;
²⁷ Shammah from Harod;*
Helez from Pelon;
²⁸ Ira son of Ikkesh from Tekoa;
Abiezer from Anathoth;
²⁹ Sibbecai from Hushah;
Zalmon* from Ahoah;
³⁰ Maharai from Netophah;
Heled son of Baanah from Netophah;
³¹ Ithai son of Ribai from Gibeah (in the land of Benjamin);
Benaiah from Pirathon;
³² Hurai from near Nahale-gaash*;
Abi-albon* from Arabah;
³³ Azmaveth from Bahurim*;
Eliahba from Shaalbon;
³⁴ the sons of Jashen* from Gizon;
Jonathan son of Shagee from Harar;
³⁵ Ahiam son of Sharar* from Harar;
Eliphal son of Ur;
³⁶ Hepher from Mekerah;
Ahijah from Pelon;
³⁷ Hezro from Carmel;
Paarai* son of Ezbai;
³⁸ Joel, the brother of Nathan;
Mibhar son of Hagri;
³⁹ Zelek from Ammon;
Naharai from Beeroth, Joab's armor bearer;
⁴⁰ Ira from Jattir;
Gareb from Jattir;
⁴¹ Uriah the Hittite;
Zabad son of Ahlai;
⁴² Adina son of Shiza, the Reubenite leader who had thirty men with him;
⁴³ Hanan son of Maacah;
Joshaphat from Mithna;
⁴⁴ Uzzia from Ashtaroth;
Shama and Jeiel, the sons of Hotham, from Aroer;
⁴⁵ Jediael son of Shimri;

Joha, his brother, from Tiz;
⁴⁶ Eliel from Mahavah;
Jeribai and Joshaviah, the sons of Elnaam;
Ithmah from Moab;
⁴⁷ Eliel and Obed;
Jaasiel from Zobah.*

12 WARRIORS JOIN DAVID'S ARMY The following men joined David at Ziklag while he was hiding from Saul son of Kish. They were among the warriors who fought beside David in battle. ²All of them were expert archers, and they could shoot arrows or sling stones with their left hand as well as their right. They were all relatives of Saul from the tribe of Benjamin. ³Their leader was Ahiezer son of Shemaah from Gibeah; his brother Joash was second-in-command. These were the other warriors:

Jeziel and Pelet, sons of Azmaveth;
Beracah;
Jehu from Anathoth;
⁴ Ishmaiah from Gibeon, a famous warrior and leader among the Thirty;
*Jeremiah, Jahaziel, Johanan, and Jozabad from Gederah;
⁵ Eluzai, Jerimoth, Bealiah, Shemariah, and Shephatiah from Haruph;
⁶ Elkanah, Isshiah, Azarel, Joezer, and Jashobeam, who were Korahites;
⁷ Joelah and Zebadiah, sons of Jeroham from Gedor.

⁸Some brave and experienced warriors from the tribe of Gad also defected to David while he was at the stronghold in the wilderness. They were expert with both shield and spear, as fierce as lions and as swift as deer on the mountains.

⁹ Ezer was their leader.
Obadiah was second.
Eliab was third.
¹⁰ Mishmannah was fourth.
Jeremiah was fifth.
¹¹ Attai was sixth.
Eliel was seventh.
¹² Johanan was eighth.
Elzabad was ninth.

11:22 Or *two sons of Ariel.* **11:23** Hebrew 5 *cubits* [2.3 meters]. **11:27** As in parallel text at 2 Sam 23:25; Hebrew reads *Shammoth from Haror.* **11:29** As in parallel text at 2 Sam 23:28; Hebrew reads *Ilai.* **11:32a** Or *from the ravines of Gaash.* **11:32b** As in parallel text at 2 Sam 23:31; Hebrew reads *Abiel.* **11:33** As in parallel text at 2 Sam 23:31; Hebrew reads *Baharum.* **11:34** As in parallel text at 2 Sam 23:32; Hebrew reads *sons of Hashem.* **11:35** As in parallel text at 2 Sam 23:33; Hebrew reads *son of Sacar.* **11:37** As in parallel text at 2 Sam 23:35; Hebrew reads *Naarai.* **11:47** Or *the Mezobaite.* **12:4** Verses 12:4b-40 are numbered 12:5-41 in Hebrew text.

¹³ Jeremiah was tenth.
Macbannai was eleventh.

¹⁴These warriors from Gad were army commanders. The weakest among them could take on a hundred regular troops, and the strongest could take on a thousand! ¹⁵These were the men who crossed the Jordan River during its seasonal flooding at the beginning of the year and drove out all the people living in the lowlands on both the east and west banks.

¹⁶Others from Benjamin and Judah came to David at the stronghold. ¹⁷David went out to meet them and said, "If you have come in peace to help me, we are friends. But if you have come to betray me to my enemies when I am innocent, then may the God of our ancestors see it and punish you."

¹⁸Then the Spirit came upon Amasai, the leader of the Thirty, and he said,

"We are yours, David!
We are on your side, son of Jesse.
Peace and prosperity be with you,
and success to all who help you,
for your God is the one who
helps you."

So David let them join him, and he made them officers over his troops.

¹⁹Some men from Manasseh defected from the Israelite army and joined David when he set out with the Philistines to fight against Saul. But as it turned out, the Philistine rulers refused to let David and his men go with them. After much discussion, they sent them back, for they said, "It will cost us our heads if David switches loyalties to Saul and turns against us."

²⁰Here is a list of the men from Manasseh who defected to David as he was returning to Ziklag: Adnah, Jozabad, Jediael, Michael, Jozabad, Elihu, and Zillethai. Each commanded 1,000 troops from the tribe of Manasseh. ²¹They helped David chase down bands of raiders, for they were all brave and able warriors who became commanders in his army. ²²Day after day more men joined David until he had a great army, like the army of God.

²³These are the numbers of armed warriors who joined David at Hebron. They were all eager to see David become king instead of Saul, just as the LORD had promised.

²⁴From the tribe of Judah, there were 6,800 warriors armed with shields and spears.
²⁵From the tribe of Simeon, there were 7,100 brave warriors.
²⁶From the tribe of Levi, there were 4,600 warriors. ²⁷This included Jehoiada, leader of the family of Aaron, who had 3,700 under his command. ²⁸This also included Zadok, a brave young warrior, with 22 members of his family who were all officers.
²⁹From the tribe of Benjamin, Saul's relatives, there were 3,000 warriors. Most of the men from Benjamin had remained loyal to Saul until this time.
³⁰From the tribe of Ephraim, there were 20,800 brave warriors, each highly respected in his own clan.
³¹From the half-tribe of Manasseh west of the Jordan, 18,000 men were designated by name to help David become king.
³²From the tribe of Issachar, there were 200 leaders of the tribe with their relatives. All these men understood the signs of the times and knew the best course for Israel to take.
³³From the tribe of Zebulun, there were 50,000 skilled warriors. They were fully armed and prepared for battle and completely loyal to David.
³⁴From the tribe of Naphtali, there were 1,000 officers and 37,000 warriors armed with shields and spears.
³⁵From the tribe of Dan, there were 28,600 warriors, all prepared for battle.
³⁶From the tribe of Asher, there were 40,000 trained warriors, all prepared for battle.
³⁷From the east side of the Jordan River— where the tribes of Reuben and Gad and the half-tribe of Manasseh lived—there were 120,000 troops armed with every kind of weapon.

³⁸All these men came in battle array to Hebron with the single purpose of making David the king over all Israel. In fact, everyone in Israel agreed that David should be their king. ³⁹They feasted and drank with David for three days, for preparations had been made by their relatives for their arrival. ⁴⁰And people from as far away as Issachar, Zebulun, and Naphtali brought food on donkeys, camels, mules, and oxen. Vast supplies of flour, fig cakes, clusters of raisins, wine, olive oil, cattle, sheep, and

....

HOLY SPIRIT
(12:18) How did the Holy Spirit work in Old Testament times? When God chose a person to do a task, the Spirit would give that person the ability to do it. The Spirit gave artistic ability to Bezalel (Exod 31:1-5), military prowess to Jephthah (Judg 11:29), and a word of prophecy to Zechariah (2 Chr 24:20). Here the Holy Spirit came upon Amasai, one of David's warriors. Beginning at Pentecost, however, the Spirit came upon all believers (Acts 2:1-21). That same Spirit is ready to equip you for any task.

DAVID REALIZED THAT THE LORD HAD CONFIRMED HIM AS KING OVER ISRAEL AND HAD GREATLY BLESSED HIS KINGDOM FOR THE SAKE OF HIS PEOPLE ISRAEL. |||||||| 1 CHRONICLES 14:2

goats were brought to the celebration. There was great joy throughout the land of Israel.

13 DAVID ATTEMPTS TO MOVE THE ARK

David consulted with all his officials, including the generals and captains of his army.* ²Then he addressed the entire assembly of Israel as follows: "If you approve and if it is the will of the LORD our God, let us send messages to all the Israelites throughout the land, including the priests and Levites in their towns and pasturelands. Let us invite them to come and join us. ³It is time to bring back the Ark of our God, for we neglected it during the reign of Saul."

⁴The whole assembly agreed to this, for the people could see it was the right thing to do. ⁵So David summoned all Israel, from the Shihor Brook of Egypt in the south all the way to the town of Lebo-hamath in the north, to join in bringing the Ark of God from Kiriath-jearim. ⁶Then David and all Israel went to Baalah of Ju-

dah (also called Kiriath-jearim) to bring back the Ark of God, which bears the name* of the LORD who is enthroned between the cherubim. ⁷They placed the Ark of God on a new cart and brought it from Abinadab's house. Uzzah and Ahio were guiding the cart. ⁸David and all Israel were celebrating before God with all their might, singing songs and playing all kinds of musical instruments—lyres, harps, tambourines, cymbals, and trumpets.

⁹But when they arrived at the threshing floor of Nacon,* the oxen stumbled, and Uzzah reached out his hand to steady the Ark. ¹⁰Then the LORD's anger was aroused against Uzzah, and he struck him dead because he had laid his hand on the Ark. So Uzzah died there in the presence of God.

¹¹David was angry because the LORD's anger had burst out against Uzzah. He named that place Perez-uzzah (which means "to burst out against Uzzah"), as it is still called today. ¹²David was now afraid of God, and he asked, "How can I ever bring the Ark of God back into my care?" ¹³So David did not move the Ark into the City of David. Instead, he took it to the house of Obed-edom of Gath. ¹⁴The Ark of God remained there in Obed-edom's house for three months, and the LORD blessed the household of Obed-edom and everything he owned.

14 DAVID'S PALACE AND FAMILY

Then King Hiram of Tyre sent messengers to David, along with cedar timber, and stonemasons and carpenters to build him a palace. ²And David realized that the LORD had confirmed him as king over Israel and had greatly blessed his kingdom for the sake of his people Israel.

³Then David married more wives in Jerusalem, and they had more sons and daughters. ⁴These are the names of David's sons who were born in Jerusalem: Shammua, Shobab, Nathan, Solomon, ⁵Ibhar, Elishua, Elpelet, ⁶Nogah, Nepheg, Japhia, ⁷Elishama, Eliada,* and Eliphelet.

DAVID CONQUERS THE PHILISTINES

⁸When the Philistines heard that David had been anointed king over all Israel, they mobilized all their forces to capture him. But David was told they were coming, so he marched out to meet them. ⁹The Philistines arrived and made a raid in the valley of Rephaim. ¹⁰So David asked God, "Should I go out to fight the Philistines? Will you hand them over to me?"

THE ARK
(13:3) The "Ark of our God" is also called the Ark of the Covenant. It rested in the Most Holy Place in the Temple and was the most sacred artifact of the Hebrew faith. The Ark was a large box containing the stone tablet on which God had written the Ten Commandments (Exod 25:10-22). David had already made Jerusalem his political capital (1 Chr 11:4-9). At this time, he brought the Ark there in hopes of making it the nation's center for worship, too.

ASK GOD FIRST
(14:10) Before David went to battle, he first asked God for his opinion. When do you ask for God's help? Do you seek him firsthand or as a last resort? Too often we wait until we are in the middle of trouble before turning to God. By then the consequences of our actions are already unfolding.

13:1 Hebrew *the commanders of thousands and of hundreds.*
13:6 Or *the Ark of God, where the Name is proclaimed—the name.*
13:9 As in parallel text at 2 Sam 6:6; Hebrew reads *Kidon.*
14:7 Hebrew *Beeliada,* a variant spelling of Eliada; compare 3:8 and parallel text at 2 Sam 5:16.

The LORD replied, "Yes, go ahead. I will hand them over to you."

[11]So David and his troops went up to Baal-perazim and defeated the Philistines there. "God did it!" David exclaimed. "He used me to burst through my enemies like a raging flood!" So they named that place Baal-perazim (which means "the Lord who bursts through"). [12]The Philistines had abandoned their gods there, so David gave orders to burn them.

[13]But after a while the Philistines returned and raided the valley again. [14]And once again David asked God what to do. "Do not attack them straight on," God replied. "Instead, circle around behind and attack them near the poplar* trees. [15]When you hear a sound like marching feet in the tops of the poplar trees, go out and attack! That will be the signal that God is moving ahead of you to strike down the Philistine army." [16]So David did what God commanded, and they struck down the Philistine army all the way from Gibeon to Gezer.

[17]So David's fame spread everywhere, and the LORD caused all the nations to fear David.

15 PREPARING TO MOVE THE ARK David now built several buildings for himself in the City of David. He also prepared a place for the Ark of God and set up a special tent for it. [2]Then he commanded, "No one except the Levites may carry the Ark of God. The LORD has chosen them to carry the Ark of the LORD and to serve him forever."

[3]Then David summoned all Israel to Jerusalem to bring the Ark of the LORD to the place he had prepared for it. [4]This is the number of the descendants of Aaron (the priests) and the Levites who were called together:

[5]From the clan of Kohath, 120, with Uriel as their leader.

[6]From the clan of Merari, 220, with Asaiah as their leader.

[7]From the clan of Gershon,* 130, with Joel as their leader.

[8]From the descendants of Elizaphan, 200, with Shemaiah as their leader.

[9]From the descendants of Hebron, 80, with Eliel as their leader.

[10]From the descendants of Uzziel, 112, with Amminadab as their leader.

14:14 Or *aspen,* or *balsam;* also in 14:15. The exact identification of this tree is uncertain.   15:7 Hebrew *Gershom,* a variant spelling of Gershon.   15:18 As in several Hebrew manuscripts and Greek version (see also parallel lists in 15:20; 16:5); Masoretic Text reads *Zechariah ben Jaaziel.*   15:20 Hebrew adds *according to Alamoth,* which is probably a musical term. The meaning of the Hebrew is uncertain.   15:21 Hebrew adds *according to the Sheminith,* which is probably a musical term. The meaning of the Hebrew is uncertain.   15:23 Hebrew *chosen as gatekeepers for;* also in 15:24.   15:25 Hebrew *the commanders of thousands.*

[11]Then David summoned the priests, Zadok and Abiathar, and these Levite leaders: Uriel, Asaiah, Joel, Shemaiah, Eliel, and Amminadab. [12]He said to them, "You are the leaders of the Levite families. You must purify yourselves and all your fellow Levites, so you can bring the Ark of the LORD, the God of Israel, to the place I have prepared for it. [13]Because you Levites did not carry the Ark the first time, the anger of the LORD our God burst out against us. We failed to ask God how to move it properly." [14]So the priests and the Levites purified themselves in order to bring the Ark of the LORD, the God of Israel, to Jerusalem. [15]Then the Levites carried the Ark of God on their shoulders with its carrying poles, just as the LORD had instructed Moses.

[16]David also ordered the Levite leaders to appoint a choir of Levites who were singers and musicians to sing joyful songs to the accompaniment of harps, lyres, and cymbals. [17]So the Levites appointed Heman son of Joel along with his fellow Levites: Asaph son of Berekiah, and Ethan son of Kushaiah from the clan of Merari. [18]The following men were chosen as their assistants: Zechariah, Jaaziel,* Shemiramoth, Jehiel, Unni, Eliab, Benaiah, Maaseiah, Mattithiah, Eliphelehu, Mikneiah, and the gatekeepers—Obed-edom and Jeiel.

[19]The musicians Heman, Asaph, and Ethan were chosen to sound the bronze cymbals. [20]Zechariah, Aziel, Shemiramoth, Jehiel, Unni, Eliab, Maaseiah, and Benaiah were chosen to play the harps.* [21]Mattithiah, Eliphelehu, Mikneiah, Obed-edom, Jeiel, and Azaziah were chosen to play the lyres.* [22]Kenaniah, the head Levite, was chosen as the choir leader because of his skill.

[23]Berekiah and Elkanah were chosen to guard* the Ark. [24]Shebaniah, Joshaphat, Nethanel, Amasai, Zechariah, Benaiah, and Eliezer—all of whom were priests—were chosen to blow the trumpets as they marched in front of the Ark of God. Obed-edom and Jehiah were chosen to guard the Ark.

MOVING THE ARK TO JERUSALEM [25]Then David and the elders of Israel and the generals of the army* went to the house of Obed-edom to

....

EXACT INSTRUCTIONS
(15:13-15) When David's first attempt to move the Ark failed (13:8-14), he learned an important lesson: always follow God's instructions precisely. This time David saw to it that the Levites carried the Ark as Numbers 4:5-15 instructed. We may not fully understand the reasons behind God's instructions, but we can choose to believe that his judgment is perfect. Is that what you believe?

bring the Ark of the LORD's Covenant up to Jerusalem with a great celebration. ²⁶And because God was clearly helping the Levites as they carried the Ark of the LORD's Covenant, they sacrificed seven bulls and seven rams.

²⁷David was dressed in a robe of fine linen, as were all the Levites who carried the Ark, and also the singers, and Kenaniah the choir leader. David was also wearing a priestly garment.* ²⁸So all Israel brought up the Ark of the LORD's Covenant with shouts of joy, the blowing of rams' horns and trumpets, the crashing of cymbals, and loud playing on harps and lyres.

²⁹But as the Ark of the LORD's Covenant entered the City of David, Michal, the daughter of Saul, looked down from her window. When she saw King David skipping about and laughing with joy, she was filled with contempt for him.

16

They brought the Ark of God and placed it inside the special tent David had prepared for it. And they presented burnt offerings and peace offerings to God. ²When he had finished his sacrifices, David blessed the people in the name of the LORD. ³Then he gave to every man and woman in all Israel a loaf of bread, a cake of dates,* and a cake of raisins.

⁴David appointed the following Levites to lead the people in worship before the Ark of the LORD—to invoke his blessings, to give thanks, and to praise the LORD, the God of Israel. ⁵Asaph, the leader of this group, sounded the cymbals. Second to him was Zechariah, followed by Jeiel, Shemiramoth, Jehiel, Mattithiah, Eliab, Benaiah, Obed-edom, and Jeiel. They played the harps and lyres. ⁶The priests, Benaiah and Jahaziel, played the trumpets regularly before the Ark of God's Covenant.

DAVID'S SONG OF PRAISE ⁷On that day David gave to Asaph and his fellow Levites this song of thanksgiving to the LORD:

⁸ Give thanks to the LORD and proclaim his greatness.
   Let the whole world know what he has done.
⁹ Sing to him; yes, sing his praises.
   Tell everyone about his wonderful deeds.
¹⁰ Exult in his holy name;

rejoice, you who worship the LORD.
¹¹ Search for the LORD and for his strength;
   continually seek him.
¹² Remember the wonders he has performed,
   his miracles, and the rulings he has given,
¹³ you children of his servant Israel,
   you descendants of Jacob, his chosen ones.

¹⁴ He is the LORD our God.
   His justice is seen throughout the land.
¹⁵ Remember his covenant forever—
   the commitment he made to a thousand generations.
¹⁶ This is the covenant he made with Abraham
   and the oath he swore to Isaac.
¹⁷ He confirmed it to Jacob as a decree,
   and to the people of Israel as a never-ending covenant:
¹⁸ "I will give you the land of Canaan
   as your special possession."

¹⁹ He said this when you were few in number,
   a tiny group of strangers in Canaan.
²⁰ They wandered from nation to nation,
   from one kingdom to another.
²¹ Yet he did not let anyone oppress them.
   He warned kings on their behalf:
²² "Do not touch my chosen people,
   and do not hurt my prophets."

²³ Let the whole earth sing to the LORD!
   Each day proclaim the good news that he saves.
²⁴ Publish his glorious deeds among the nations.
   Tell everyone about the amazing things he does.
²⁵ Great is the LORD! He is most worthy of praise!
   He is to be feared above all gods.
²⁶ The gods of other nations are mere idols,
   but the LORD made the heavens!
²⁷ Honor and majesty surround him;
   strength and joy fill his dwelling.

²⁸ O nations of the world, recognize the LORD,
   recognize that the LORD is glorious and strong.
²⁹ Give to the LORD the glory he deserves!
   Bring your offering and come into his presence.
   Worship the LORD in all his holy splendor.
³⁰ Let all the earth tremble before him.
   The world stands firm and cannot be shaken.

THANK YOU
(16:7-36) David used a psalm to express his gratitude to God. In that psalm he recalled what God had done for him and why God always deserved praise. Many of David's psalms (see the book of Psalms) have inspired generations of people to offer praise to God. How do you express thanks to God?

15:27 Hebrew *a linen ephod.*   **16:3** Or *a portion of meat.* The meaning of the Hebrew is uncertain.

MUSIC IN BIBLE TIMES

Paul clearly puts forth the Christian's view that things are not good or bad in and of themselves (see Rom 14 and 1 Cor 14:7-8, 26). The point always should be to worship the Lord or help others by means of the things of this world, including music. Music was created by God and can be returned to him in praise. Does the music you play or listen to have a negative impact upon your relationship with God or a positive one?

HIGHLIGHTS OF MUSICAL USE IN SCRIPTURE	REFERENCES
Jubal was the first musician	Genesis 4:21
Miriam and other women sang and danced to praise God	Exodus 15:1-21
Jericho fell to the sound of rams' horns	Joshua 6:4-20
Saul experienced the soothing effect of music	1 Samuel 16:14-23
The king's coronation was accompanied by music	1 Kings 1:39-40
David organized the use of music for worship	1 Chronicles 16:4-7
The Ark of the Covenant was accompanied by trumpeters	1 Chronicles 16:6
Everything was to be used by everyone to praise the Lord	Psalm 150
There were musicians for the king's court	Ecclesiastes 2:8
Jesus and the disciples sang a hymn	Matthew 26:30
Paul and Silas sang in jail	Acts 16:25
We are to sing to the Lord with thankful hearts	Colossians 3:16

In the New Testament, worship continued in the synagogues until the Christians became unwelcome there, so there was a rich musical heritage already established. The fact that music is mentioned less often in the New Testament does not mean it was less important.

---

³¹ Let the heavens be glad, and the earth
    rejoice!
  Tell all the nations, "The LORD reigns!"
³² Let the sea and everything in it shout his
    praise!
  Let the fields and their crops burst out
    with joy!
³³ Let the trees of the forest rustle with praise,
    for the LORD is coming to judge
    the earth.
³⁴ Give thanks to the LORD, for he is good!
    His faithful love endures forever.
³⁵ Cry out, "Save us, O God of our salvation!
    Gather and rescue us from among the
    nations,
  so we can thank your holy name
    and rejoice and praise you."
³⁶ Praise the LORD, the God of Israel,
    who lives from everlasting to
    everlasting!

And all the people shouted "Amen!" and praised the LORD.

WORSHIP AT JERUSALEM AND GIBEON ³⁷Da-
vid arranged for Asaph and his fellow Levites to serve regularly before the Ark of the LORD's Covenant, doing whatever needed to be done each day. ³⁸This group included Obed-edom (son of

16:42 Or to accompany the sacred music; or to accompany singing to God. 17:1 Hebrew a house of cedar.

Jeduthun), Hosah, and sixty-eight other Levites as gatekeepers.

³⁹Meanwhile, David stationed Zadok the priest and his fellow priests at the Tabernacle of the LORD at the place of worship in Gibeon, where they continued to minister before the LORD. ⁴⁰They sacrificed the regular burnt offerings to the LORD each morning and evening on the altar set aside for that purpose, obeying everything written in the Law of the LORD, as he had commanded Israel. ⁴¹David also appointed Heman, Jeduthun, and the others chosen by name to give thanks to the LORD, for "his faithful love endures forever." ⁴²They used their trumpets, cymbals, and other instruments to accompany their songs of praise to God.* And the sons of Jeduthun were appointed as gatekeepers.

⁴³Then all the people returned to their homes, and David turned and went home to bless his own family.

17 THE LORD'S COVENANT PROMISE TO DAVID
When David was settled in his palace, he summoned Nathan the prophet. "Look," David said, "I am living in a beautiful cedar palace,* but the Ark of the LORD's Covenant is out there under a tent!"

²Nathan replied to David, "Do whatever you have in mind, for God is with you."

³But that same night God said to Nathan,

[4]"Go and tell my servant David, 'This is what the LORD has declared: You are not the one to build a house for me to live in. [5]I have never lived in a house, from the day I brought the Israelites out of Egypt until this very day. My home has always been a tent, moving from one place to another in a Tabernacle. [6]Yet no matter where I have gone with the Israelites, I have never once complained to Israel's leaders,* the shepherds of my people. I have never asked them, "Why haven't you built me a beautiful cedar house?"'

[7]"Now go and say to my servant David, 'This is what the LORD of Heaven's Armies has declared: I took you from tending sheep in the pasture and selected you to be the leader of my people Israel. [8]I have been with you wherever you have gone, and I have destroyed all your enemies before your eyes. Now I will make your name as famous as anyone who has ever lived on the earth! [9]And I will provide a homeland for my people Israel, planting them in a secure place where they will never be disturbed. Evil nations won't oppress them as they've done in the past, [10]starting from the time I appointed judges to rule my people Israel. And I will defeat all your enemies.

"'Furthermore, I declare that the LORD will build a house for you—a dynasty of kings! [11]For when you die and join your ancestors, I will raise up one of your descendants, one of your sons, and I will make his kingdom strong. [12]He is the one who will build a house—a temple—for me. And I will secure his throne forever. [13]I will be his father, and he will be my son. I will never take my favor from him as I took it from the one who ruled before you. [14]I will confirm him as king over my house and my kingdom for all time, and his throne will be secure forever.'"

- -

A HUMBLE RESPONSE
(17:16-27) When God said no to David's request to build a Temple, David responded with humility, rather than resentment. He recognized that the true King, God, had a right to say yes or no to any request. What's your response when God says no?

GOD ON OUR SIDE
(18:1-14) God helped David to be victorious over his enemies. In the same way, God promises to see us through the battles that we fight here on earth: battles over temptation, and attitudes of the heart, and against spiritual or physical enemies. As Paul once said, "If God is for us, who can ever be against us?" (Rom 8:31).

[15]So Nathan went back to David and told him everything the LORD had said in this vision.

DAVID'S PRAYER OF THANKS [16]Then King David went in and sat before the LORD and prayed,

"Who am I, O LORD God, and what is my family, that you have brought me this far? [17]And now, O God, in addition to everything else, you speak of giving your servant a lasting dynasty! You speak as though I were someone very great,* O LORD God!

[18]"What more can I say to you about the way you have honored me? You know what your servant is really like. [19]For the sake of your servant, O LORD, and according to your will, you have done all these great things and have made them known.

[20]"O LORD, there is no one like you. We have never even heard of another God like you! [21]What other nation on earth is like your people Israel? What other nation, O God, have you redeemed from slavery to be your own people? You made a great name for yourself when you redeemed your people from Egypt. You performed awesome miracles and drove out the nations that stood in their way. [22]You chose Israel to be your very own people forever, and you, O LORD, became their God.

[23]"And now, O LORD, I am your servant; do as you have promised concerning me and my family. May it be a promise that will last forever. [24]And may your name be established and honored forever so that everyone will say, 'The LORD of Heaven's Armies, the God of Israel, is Israel's God!' And may the house of your servant David continue before you forever.

[25]"O my God, I have been bold enough to pray to you because you have revealed to your servant that you will build a house for him—a dynasty of kings! [26]For you are God, O LORD. And you have promised these good things to your servant. [27]And now, it has pleased you to bless the house of your servant, so that it will continue forever before you. For when you grant a blessing, O LORD, it is an eternal blessing!"

18 **DAVID'S MILITARY VICTORIES** After this, David defeated and subdued the Philistines by conquering Gath and its surrounding towns. [2]David also conquered the land of Moab, and the Moabites who were

17:6 As in Greek version (see also 2 Sam 7:7); Hebrew reads *judges.*
17:17 The meaning of the Hebrew is uncertain.

spared became David's subjects and paid him tribute money.

³David also destroyed the forces of Hadadezer, king of Zobah, as far as Hamath,* when Hadadezer marched out to strengthen his control along the Euphrates River. ⁴David captured 1,000 chariots, 7,000 charioteers, and 20,000 foot soldiers. He crippled all the chariot horses except enough for 100 chariots.

⁵When Arameans from Damascus arrived to help King Hadadezer, David killed 22,000 of them. ⁶Then he placed several army garrisons* in Damascus, the Aramean capital, and the Arameans became David's subjects and paid him tribute money. So the LORD made David victorious wherever he went.

⁷David brought the gold shields of Hadadezer's officers to Jerusalem, ⁸along with a large amount of bronze from Hadadezer's towns of Tebah* and Cun. Later Solomon melted the bronze and molded it into the great bronze basin called the Sea, the pillars, and the various bronze articles used at the Temple.

⁹When King Toi* of Hamath heard that David had destroyed the entire army of King Hadadezer of Zobah, ¹⁰he sent his son Joram* to congratulate King David for his successful campaign. Hadadezer and Toi had been enemies and were often at war. Joram presented David with many gifts of gold, silver, and bronze.

¹¹King David dedicated all these gifts to the LORD, along with the silver and gold he had taken from the other nations—from Edom, Moab, Ammon, Philistia, and Amalek.

¹²Abishai son of Zeruiah destroyed 18,000 Edomites in the Valley of Salt. ¹³He placed army garrisons in Edom, and all the Edomites became David's subjects. In fact, the LORD made David victorious wherever he went.

¹⁴So David reigned over all Israel and did what was just and right for all his people. ¹⁵Joab son of Zeruiah was commander of the army. Jehoshaphat son of Ahilud was the royal historian. ¹⁶Zadok son of Ahitub and Ahimelech* son of Abiathar were the priests. Seraiah* was the court secretary. ¹⁷Benaiah son of Jehoiada was captain of the king's bodyguard.* And David's sons served as the king's chief assistants.

18:3 The meaning of the Hebrew is uncertain. 18:6 As in Greek version and Latin Vulgate (see also 2 Sam 8:6); Hebrew lacks several army garrisons. 18:8 Hebrew reads Tibhath, a variant spelling of Tebah; compare parallel text at 2 Sam 8:8. 18:9 As in parallel text at 2 Sam 8:9; Hebrew reads Tou; also in 18:10. 18:10 As in parallel text at 2 Sam 8:10; Hebrew reads Hadoram, a variant spelling of Joram. 18:16a As in some Hebrew manuscripts, Syriac version, and Latin Vulgate (see also 2 Sam 8:17); most Hebrew manuscripts read Abimelech. 18:16b As in parallel text at 2 Sam 8:17; Hebrew reads Shavsha. 18:17 Hebrew of the Kerethites and Pelethites. 19:1 As in parallel text at 2 Sam 10:1; Hebrew lacks Hanun. 19:6 Hebrew 1,000 talents [34,000 kilograms].

19 DAVID DEFEATS THE AMMONITES

Some time after this, King Nahash of the Ammonites died, and his son Hanun* became king. ²David said, "I am going to show loyalty to Hanun because his father, Nahash, was always loyal to me." So David sent messengers to express sympathy to Hanun about his father's death.

But when David's ambassadors arrived in the land of Ammon, ³the Ammonite commanders said to Hanun, "Do you really think these men are coming here to honor your father? No! David has sent them to spy out the land so they can come in and conquer it!" ⁴So Hanun seized David's ambassadors and shaved them, cut off their robes at the buttocks, and sent them back to David in shame.

⁵When David heard what had happened to the men, he sent messengers to tell them, "Stay at Jericho until your beards grow out, and then come back." For they felt deep shame because of their appearance.

⁶When the people of Ammon realized how seriously they had angered David, Hanun and the Ammonites sent 75,000 pounds* of silver to hire chariots and charioteers from Aram-naharaim, Aram-maacah, and Zobah. ⁷They also hired 32,000 chariots and secured the support of the king of Maacah and his army. These forces camped at Medeba, where they were joined by the Ammonite troops that Hanun had recruited from his own towns. ⁸When David heard about this, he sent Joab and all his warriors to fight them. ⁹The Ammonite troops came out and drew up their battle lines at the entrance of the city, while the other kings positioned themselves to fight in the open fields.

¹⁰When Joab saw that he would have to fight on both the front and the rear, he chose some of Israel's elite troops and placed them under his personal command to fight the Arameans in the fields. ¹¹He left the rest of the army under the command of his brother Abishai, who was to attack the Ammonites. ¹²"If the Arameans are too strong for me, then come over and help me," Joab told his brother. "And if the Ammonites are too strong for you, I will help you. ¹³Be courageous! Let us fight bravely for our people and the cities of our God. May the LORD's will be done."

¹⁴When Joab and his troops attacked, the Arameans began to run away. ¹⁵And when the Ammonites saw the Arameans running, they also ran from Abishai and retreated into the city. Then Joab returned to Jerusalem.

¹⁶The Arameans now realized that they were no match for Israel, so they sent messengers

and summoned additional Aramean troops from the other side of the Euphrates River.* These troops were under the command of Shobach,* the commander of Hadadezer's forces. [17]When David heard what was happening, he mobilized all Israel, crossed the Jordan River, and positioned his troops in battle formation. Then David engaged the Arameans in battle, and they fought against him. [18]But again the Arameans fled from the Israelites. This time David's forces killed 7,000 charioteers and 40,000 foot soldiers, including Shobach, the commander of their army. [19]When Hadadezer's allies saw that they had been defeated by Israel, they surrendered to David and became his subjects. After that, the Arameans were no longer willing to help the Ammonites.

20 DAVID CAPTURES RABBAH In the spring of the year,* when kings normally go out to war, Joab led the Israelite army in successful attacks against the land of the Ammonites. In the process he laid siege to the city of Rabbah. However, David stayed behind in Jerusalem.

[2]When David arrived at Rabbah, he removed the crown from the king's head,* and it was placed on his own head. The crown was made of gold and set with gems, and he found that it weighed seventy-five pounds.* David took a vast amount of plunder from the city. [3]He also made slaves of the people of Rabbah and forced them to labor with saws, iron picks, and iron axes.* That is how David dealt with the people of all the Ammonite towns. Then David and all the army returned to Jerusalem.

BATTLES AGAINST PHILISTINE GIANTS [4]After this, war broke out with the Philistines at Gezer. As they fought, Sibbecai from Hushah killed

Saph,* a descendant of the giants,* and so the Philistines were subdued.

[5]During another battle with the Philistines, Elhanan son of Jair killed Lahmi, the brother of Goliath of Gath. The handle of Lahmi's spear was as thick as a weaver's beam!

[6]In another battle with the Philistines at Gath, they encountered a huge man with six fingers on each hand and six toes on each foot, twenty-four in all, who was also a descendant of the giants. [7]But when he defied and taunted Israel, he was killed by Jonathan, the son of David's brother Shimea.

[8]These Philistines were descendants of the giants of Gath, but David and his warriors killed them.

21 DAVID TAKES A CENSUS Satan rose up against Israel and caused David to take a census of the people of Israel. [2]So David said to Joab and the commanders of the army, "Take a census of all the people of Israel—from Beersheba in the south to Dan in the north—and bring me a report so I may know how many there are."

[3]But Joab replied, "May the LORD increase the number of his people a hundred times over! But why, my lord the king, do you want to do this? Are they not all your servants? Why must you cause Israel to sin?"

[4]But the king insisted that they take the census, so Joab traveled throughout all Israel to count the people. Then he returned to Jerusalem [5]and reported the number of people to David. There were 1,100,000 warriors in all Israel who could handle a sword, and 470,000 in Judah. [6]But Joab did not include the tribes of Levi and Benjamin in the census because he was so distressed at what the king had made him do.

JUDGMENT FOR DAVID'S SIN [7]God was very displeased with the census, and he punished Israel for it. [8]Then David said to God, "I have sinned greatly by taking this census. Please forgive my guilt for doing this foolish thing."

[9]Then the LORD spoke to Gad, David's seer. This was the message: [10]"Go and say to David, 'This is what the LORD says: I will give you three choices. Choose one of these punishments, and I will inflict it on you.'"

SPRING INTO WAR
(20:1) Why was spring the season when wars usually began? During the winter, opposing kings planned future conquests. Then, when the fair weather permitted it, their pent-up rage and energy broke forth into war. What are the "springs" in your life—times when you are most sensitive to the conflicts around you? You can "diffuse" them by confessing any fear, bitterness, or anger to God, allowing him to deal with it.

CLEANING HOUSE
(21:1-16) When David realized his sin, he took full responsibility, admitted he was wrong, and asked God to forgive him. Many people want the "perks" of a relationship with God but not the hard stuff, such as owning up to wrongs done. But admitting our sins is a necessary part of a relationship with God. It's like brushing your teeth or cleaning out your locker—you've got to do it regularly.

19:16a Hebrew *the river.*   **19:16b** As in parallel text at 2 Sam 10:16; Hebrew reads *Shophach;* also in 19:18.   **20:1** Hebrew *At the turn of the year.* The first day of the year in the ancient Hebrew lunar calendar occurred in March or April.   **20:2a** Or *from the head of Milcom* (as in Greek version and Latin Vulgate). Milcom, also called *Molech,* was the god of the Ammonites.   **20:2b** Hebrew *1 talent* [34 kilograms].   **20:3** As in parallel text at 2 Sam 12:31; Hebrew reads *and cut them with saws, iron picks, and saws.*   **20:4a** As in parallel text at 2 Sam 21:18; Hebrew reads *Sippai.*   **20:4b** Hebrew *descendant of the Rephaites;* also in 20:6, 8.

¹¹So Gad came to David and said, "These are the choices the LORD has given you. ¹²You may choose three years of famine, three months of destruction by the sword of your enemies, or three days of severe plague as the angel of the LORD brings devastation throughout the land of Israel. Decide what answer I should give the LORD who sent me."

¹³"I'm in a desperate situation!" David replied to Gad. "But let me fall into the hands of the LORD, for his mercy is very great. Do not let me fall into human hands."

¹⁴So the LORD sent a plague upon Israel, and 70,000 people died as a result. ¹⁵And God sent an angel to destroy Jerusalem. But just as the angel was preparing to destroy it, the LORD relented and said to the death angel, "Stop! That is enough!" At that moment the angel of the LORD was standing by the threshing floor of Araunah* the Jebusite.

¹⁶David looked up and saw the angel of the LORD standing between heaven and earth with his sword drawn, reaching out over Jerusalem. So David and the leaders of Israel put on burlap to show their deep distress and fell face down on the ground. ¹⁷And David said to God, "I am the one who called for the census! I am the one who has sinned and done wrong! But these people are as innocent as sheep—what have they done? O LORD my God, let your anger fall against me and my family, but do not destroy your people."

DAVID BUILDS AN ALTAR ¹⁸Then the angel of the LORD told Gad to instruct David to go up and build an altar to the LORD on the threshing floor of Araunah the Jebusite. ¹⁹So David went up to do what the LORD had commanded him through Gad. ²⁰Araunah, who was busy threshing wheat at the time, turned and saw the angel there. His four sons, who were with him, ran away and hid. ²¹When Araunah saw David approaching, he left his threshing floor and bowed before David with his face to the ground.

²²David said to Araunah, "Let me buy this threshing floor from you at its full price. Then I will build an altar to the LORD there, so that he will stop the plague."

²³"Take it, my lord the king, and use it as you wish," Araunah said to David. "I will give the oxen for the burnt offerings, and the threshing boards for wood to build a fire on the altar, and the wheat for the grain offering. I will give it all to you."

21:15 As in parallel text at 2 Sam 24:16; Hebrew reads *Ornan*, another name for Araunah; also in 21:18-28.　**21:25** Hebrew *600 shekels of gold*, about 15 pounds or 6.8 kilograms in weight.

²⁴But King David replied to Araunah, "No, I insist on buying it for the full price. I will not take what is yours and give it to the LORD. I will not present burnt offerings that have cost me nothing!" ²⁵So David gave Araunah 600 pieces of gold* in payment for the threshing floor.

²⁶David built an altar there to the LORD and sacrificed burnt offerings and peace offerings. And when David prayed, the LORD answered him by sending fire from heaven to burn up the offering on the altar. ²⁷Then the LORD spoke to the angel, who put the sword back into its sheath.

²⁸When David saw that the LORD had answered his prayer, he offered sacrifices there at Araunah's threshing floor. ²⁹At that time the Tabernacle of the LORD and the altar of burnt offering that Moses had made in the wilderness were located at the place of worship in Gibeon. ³⁰But David was not able to go there to inquire of God, because he was terrified by the drawn sword of the angel of the LORD.

22 Then David said, "This will be the location for the Temple of the LORD God and the place of the altar for Israel's burnt offerings!"

PREPARATIONS FOR THE TEMPLE ²So David gave orders to call together the foreigners living in Israel, and he assigned them the task of preparing finished stone for building the Temple of God. ³David provided large amounts of iron for the nails that would be needed for the doors in the gates and for the clamps, and he gave more bronze than could be weighed. ⁴He also provided innumerable cedar logs, for the men of Tyre and Sidon had brought vast amounts of cedar to David.

⁵David said, "My son Solomon is still young and inexperienced. And since the Temple to be built for the LORD must be a magnificent structure, famous and glorious throughout the world, I will begin making preparations for it now." So David collected vast amounts of building materials before his death.

⁶Then David sent for his son Solomon and instructed him to build a Temple for the LORD, the God of Israel. ⁷"My son, I wanted to build a Temple to honor the name of the LORD my God," David told him. ⁸"But the LORD said to me, 'You have killed many men in the battles you have fought. And since you have shed so much blood in my sight, you will not be the one to build a Temple to honor my name. ⁹But you will have a son who will be a man of peace. I will give him peace with his enemies in all the

surrounding lands. His name will be Solomon,* and I will give peace and quiet to Israel during his reign. ¹⁰He is the one who will build a Temple to honor my name. He will be my son, and I will be his father. And I will secure the throne of his kingdom over Israel forever.'

¹¹"Now, my son, may the LORD be with you and give you success as you follow his directions in building the Temple of the LORD your God. ¹²And may the LORD give you wisdom and understanding, that you may obey the Law of the LORD your God as you rule over Israel. ¹³For you will be successful if you carefully obey the decrees and regulations that the LORD gave to Israel through Moses. Be strong and courageous; do not be afraid or lose heart!

¹⁴"I have worked hard to provide materials for building the Temple of the LORD—nearly 4,000 tons of gold, 40,000 tons of silver,* and so much iron and bronze that it cannot be weighed. I have also gathered timber and stone for the walls, though you may need to add more. ¹⁵You have a large number of skilled stonemasons and carpenters and craftsmen of every kind. ¹⁶You have expert goldsmiths and silversmiths and workers of bronze and iron. Now begin the work, and may the LORD be with you!"

¹⁷Then David ordered all the leaders of Israel to assist Solomon in this project. ¹⁸"The LORD your God is with you," he declared. "He has given you peace with the surrounding nations. He has handed them over to me, and they are now subject to the LORD and his people. ¹⁹Now seek the LORD your God with all your heart and soul. Build the sanctuary of the LORD God so that you can bring the Ark of the LORD's Covenant and the holy vessels of God into the Temple built to honor the LORD's name."

23 DUTIES OF THE LEVITES

When David was an old man, he appointed his son Solomon to be king over Israel. ²David summoned all the leaders of Israel, together with the priests and Levites. ³All the Levites who were thirty years old or older were counted, and the total came to 38,000. ⁴Then David said, "From all the Levites, 24,000 will supervise the work at the Temple of the LORD. Another 6,000 will serve as officials and judges.

⁵Another 4,000 will work as gatekeepers, and 4,000 will praise the LORD with the musical instruments I have made." ⁶Then David divided the Levites into divisions named after the clans descended from the three sons of Levi—Gershon, Kohath, and Merari.

THE GERSHONITES ⁷The Gershonite family units were defined by their lines of descent from Libni* and Shimei, the sons of Gershon. ⁸Three of the descendants of Libni were Jehiel (the family leader), Zetham, and Joel. ⁹These were the leaders of the family of Libni.

Three of the descendants of Shimei were Shelomoth, Haziel, and Haran. ¹⁰Four other descendants of Shimei were Jahath, Ziza,* Jeush, and Beriah. ¹¹Jahath was the family leader, and Ziza was next. Jeush and Beriah were counted as a single family because neither had many sons.

THE KOHATHITES ¹²Four of the descendants of Kohath were Amram, Izhar, Hebron, and Uzziel.

¹³The sons of Amram were Aaron and Moses. Aaron and his descendants were set apart to dedicate the most holy things, to offer sacrifices in the LORD's presence, to serve the LORD, and to pronounce blessings in his name forever.

¹⁴As for Moses, the man of God, his sons were included with the tribe of Levi. ¹⁵The sons of Moses were Gershom and Eliezer. ¹⁶The descendants of Gershom included Shebuel, the family leader. ¹⁷Eliezer had only one son, Rehabiah, the family leader. Rehabiah had numerous descendants.

¹⁸The descendants of Izhar included Shelomith, the family leader.

¹⁹The descendants of Hebron included Jeriah (the family leader), Amariah (the second), Jahaziel (the third), and Jekameam (the fourth).

²⁰The descendants of Uzziel included Micah (the family leader) and Isshiah (the second).

THE MERARITES ²¹The descendants of Merari included Mahli and Mushi.

The sons of Mahli were Eleazar and Kish. ²²Eleazar died with no sons, only daughters. His daughters married their cousins, the sons of Kish.

....

WHOLEHEARTEDLY
(22:11-19) David wanted his son Solomon to understand the value of wholeheartedly obeying God. This kind of obedience involves using good judgment and having the right attitudes (strength, courage, and enthusiasm). Is that an accurate description of your dedication to God?

22:9 Solomon sounds like and is probably derived from the Hebrew word for "peace." 22:14 Hebrew 100,000 talents [3,400 metric tons] of gold, 1,000,000 talents [34,000 metric tons] of silver. 23:7 Hebrew Ladan (also in 23:8, 9), a variant spelling of Libni; compare 6:17. 23:10 As in Greek version and Latin Vulgate (see also 23:11); Hebrew reads Zina.

²³Three of the descendants of Mushi were Mahli, Eder, and Jerimoth.

²⁴These were the descendants of Levi by clans, the leaders of their family groups, registered carefully by name. Each had to be twenty years old or older to qualify for service in the house of the LORD. ²⁵For David said, "The LORD, the God of Israel, has given us peace, and he will always live in Jerusalem. ²⁶Now the Levites will no longer need to carry the Tabernacle and its furnishings from place to place." ²⁷In accordance with David's final instructions, all the Levites twenty years old or older were registered for service.

²⁸The work of the Levites was to assist the priests, the descendants of Aaron, as they served at the house of the LORD. They also took care of the courtyards and side rooms, helped perform the ceremonies of purification, and served in many other ways in the house of God. ²⁹They were in charge of the sacred bread that was set out on the table, the choice flour for the grain offerings, the wafers made without yeast, the cakes cooked in olive oil, and the other mixed breads. They were also responsible to check all the weights and measures. ³⁰And each morning and evening they stood before the LORD to sing songs of thanks and praise to him. ³¹They assisted with the burnt offerings that were presented to the LORD on Sabbath days, at new moon celebrations, and at all the appointed festivals. The required number of Levites served in the LORD's presence at all times, following all the procedures they had been given.

³²And so, under the supervision of the priests, the Levites watched over the Tabernacle and the Temple* and faithfully carried out their duties of service at the house of the LORD.

24 DUTIES OF THE PRIESTS This is how
Aaron's descendants, the priests, were divided into groups for service. The sons of Aaron were Nadab, Abihu, Eleazar, and Ithamar. ²But Nadab and Abihu died before their father, and they had no sons. So only Eleazar and Ithamar were left to carry on as priests.

³With the help of Zadok, who was a descendant of Eleazar, and of Ahimelech, who was a descendant of Ithamar, David divided Aaron's descendants into groups according to their various duties. ⁴Eleazar's descendants were divided into sixteen groups and Ithamar's

into eight, for there were more family leaders among the descendants of Eleazar.

⁵All tasks were assigned to the various groups by means of sacred lots so that no preference would be shown, for there were many qualified officials serving God in the sanctuary from among the descendants of both Eleazar and Ithamar. ⁶Shemaiah son of Nethanel, a Levite, acted as secretary and wrote down the names and assignments in the presence of the king, the officials, Zadok the priest, Ahimelech son of Abiathar, and the family leaders of the priests and Levites. The descendants of Eleazar and Ithamar took turns casting lots.

⁷ The first lot fell to Jehoiarib.
  The second lot fell to Jedaiah.
⁸ The third lot fell to Harim.
  The fourth lot fell to Seorim.
⁹ The fifth lot fell to Malkijah.
  The sixth lot fell to Mijamin.
¹⁰ The seventh lot fell to Hakkoz.
  The eighth lot fell to Abijah.
¹¹ The ninth lot fell to Jeshua.
  The tenth lot fell to Shecaniah.
¹² The eleventh lot fell to Eliashib.
  The twelfth lot fell to Jakim.
¹³ The thirteenth lot fell to Huppah.
  The fourteenth lot fell to Jeshebeab.
¹⁴ The fifteenth lot fell to Bilgah.
  The sixteenth lot fell to Immer.
¹⁵ The seventeenth lot fell to Hezir.
  The eighteenth lot fell to Happizzez.
¹⁶ The nineteenth lot fell to Pethahiah.
  The twentieth lot fell to Jehezkel.
¹⁷ The twenty-first lot fell to Jakin.
  The twenty-second lot fell to Gamul.
¹⁸ The twenty-third lot fell to Delaiah.
  The twenty-fourth lot fell to Maaziah.

¹⁹Each group carried out its appointed duties in the house of the LORD according to the procedures established by their ancestor Aaron in obedience to the commands of the LORD, the God of Israel.

FAMILY LEADERS AMONG THE LEVITES ²⁰These were the other family leaders descended from Levi:

From the descendants of Amram, the leader was Shebuel.*
From the descendants of Shebuel, the leader was Jehdeiah.
²¹ From the descendants of Rehabiah, the leader was Isshiah.
²² From the descendants of Izhar, the leader was Shelomith.*

23:32 Hebrew *the Tent of Meeting and the sanctuary.*
24:20 Hebrew *Shubael* (also in 24:20b), a variant spelling of Shebuel; compare 23:16 and 26:24.   **24:22** Hebrew *Shelomoth* (also in 24:22b), a variant spelling of Shelomith; compare 23:18.

From the descendants of Shelomith, the leader was Jahath. [23] From the descendants of Hebron, Jeriah was the leader,* Amariah was second, Jahaziel was third, and Jekameam was fourth. [24] From the descendants of Uzziel, the leader was Micah.

From the descendants of Micah, the leader was Shamir, [25]along with Isshiah, the brother of Micah.

From the descendants of Isshiah, the leader was Zechariah. [26] From the descendants of Merari, the leaders were Mahli and Mushi.

From the descendants of Jaaziah, the leader was Beno. [27] From the descendants of Merari through Jaaziah, the leaders were Beno, Shoham, Zaccur, and Ibri. [28] From the descendants of Mahli, the leader was Eleazar, though he had no sons. [29] From the descendants of Kish, the leader was Jerahmeel. [30] From the descendants of Mushi, the leaders were Mahli, Eder, and Jerimoth.

These were the descendants of Levi in their various families. [31]Like the descendants of Aaron, they were assigned to their duties by means of sacred lots, without regard to age or rank. Lots were drawn in the presence of King David, Zadok, Ahimelech, and the family leaders of the priests and the Levites.

25 DUTIES OF THE MUSICIANS David and the army commanders then appointed men from the families of Asaph, Heman, and Jeduthun to proclaim God's messages to the accompaniment of lyres, harps, and cymbals. Here is a list of their names and their work:

[2]From the sons of Asaph, there were Zaccur, Joseph, Nethaniah, and Asarelah. They worked under the direction of their father, Asaph, who proclaimed God's messages by the king's orders.

[3]From the sons of Jeduthun, there were Gedaliah, Zeri, Jeshaiah, Shimei,* Hashabiah, and Mattithiah, six in all. They worked under the direction of their father, Jeduthun, who proclaimed God's messages to the accompaniment of the lyre, offering thanks and praise to the LORD.

[4]From the sons of Heman, there were Bukkiah, Mattaniah, Uzziel, Shubael,* Jerimoth, Hananiah, Hanani, Eliathah, Giddalti, Romamti-ezer, Joshbekashah, Mallothi, Hothir, and Mahazioth. [5]All these were the sons of Heman, the king's seer, for God had honored him with fourteen sons and three daughters.

[6]All these men were under the direction of their fathers as they made music at the house of the LORD. Their responsibilities included the playing of cymbals, harps, and lyres at the house of God. Asaph, Jeduthun, and Heman reported directly to the king. [7]They and their families were all trained in making music before the LORD, and each of them—288 in all—was an accomplished musician. [8]The musicians were appointed to their term of service by means of sacred lots, without regard to whether they were young or old, teacher or student.

[9] The first lot fell to Joseph of the Asaph clan and twelve of his sons and relatives.*

The second lot fell to Gedaliah and twelve of his sons and relatives. [10] The third lot fell to Zaccur and twelve of his sons and relatives. [11] The fourth lot fell to Zeri* and twelve of his sons and relatives. [12] The fifth lot fell to Nethaniah and twelve of his sons and relatives. [13] The sixth lot fell to Bukkiah and twelve of his sons and relatives. [14] The seventh lot fell to Asarelah* and twelve of his sons and relatives. [15] The eighth lot fell to Jeshaiah and twelve of his sons and relatives. [16] The ninth lot fell to Mattaniah and twelve of his sons and relatives. [17] The tenth lot fell to Shimei and twelve of his sons and relatives. [18] The eleventh lot fell to Uzziel* and twelve of his sons and relatives. [19] The twelfth lot fell to Hashabiah and twelve of his sons and relatives.

PITCH IN

(25:1-7) There were many ways to contribute to worship in the Tabernacle. Some proclaimed God's messages (25:1), some led in prayer (25:3), and others played instruments and sang (25:6-7). Because God has given everyone an ability of some kind (see Rom 12:3-11; 1 Cor 12:12-31), everyone has a significant contribution to make in the church. How will you use your talents?

24:23 Hebrew *From the descendants of Jeriah;* compare 23:19. **25:3** As in one Hebrew manuscript and some Greek manuscripts (see also 25:17); most Hebrew manuscripts lack *Shimei.* **25:4** Hebrew *Shebuel,* a variant spelling of Shubael; compare 25:20. **25:9** As in Greek version; Hebrew lacks *and twelve of his sons and relatives.* **25:11** Hebrew *Izri,* a variant spelling of Zeri; compare 25:3. **25:14** Hebrew *Jesarelah,* a variant spelling of Asarelah; compare 25:2. **25:18** Hebrew *Azarel,* a variant spelling of Uzziel; compare 25:4.

20 The thirteenth lot fell to Shubael and twelve of his sons and relatives.
21 The fourteenth lot fell to Mattithiah and twelve of his sons and relatives.
22 The fifteenth lot fell to Jerimoth* and twelve of his sons and relatives.
23 The sixteenth lot fell to Hananiah and twelve of his sons and relatives.
24 The seventeenth lot fell to Joshbekashah* and twelve of his sons and relatives.
25 The eighteenth lot fell to Hanani and twelve of his sons and relatives.
26 The nineteenth lot fell to Mallothi and twelve of his sons and relatives.
27 The twentieth lot fell to Eliathah and twelve of his sons and relatives.
28 The twenty-first lot fell to Hothir and twelve of his sons and relatives.
29 The twenty-second lot fell to Giddalti and twelve of his sons and relatives.
30 The twenty-third lot fell to Mahazioth and twelve of his sons and relatives.
31 The twenty-fourth lot fell to Romamti-ezer and twelve of his sons and relatives.

26 DUTIES OF THE GATEKEEPERS These are the divisions of the gatekeepers:

From the Korahites, there was Meshelemiah son of Kore, of the family of Abiasaph.* 2The sons of Meshelemiah were Zechariah (the oldest), Jediael (the second), Zebadiah (the third), Jathniel (the fourth), 3Elam (the fifth), Jehohanan (the sixth), and Eliehoenai (the seventh).
4The sons of Obed-edom, also gatekeepers, were Shemaiah (the oldest), Jehozabad (the second), Joah (the third), Sacar (the fourth), Nethanel (the fifth), 5Ammiel (the sixth), Issachar (the seventh), and Peullethai (the eighth). God had richly blessed Obed-edom.

6Obed-edom's son Shemaiah had sons with great ability who earned positions of great authority in the clan. 7Their names were Othni, Rephael, Obed, and Elzabad. Their relatives, Elihu and Semakiah, were also very capable men.

8All of these descendants of Obed-edom, including their sons and grandsons—sixty-two of them in all—were very capable men, well qualified for their work.
9Meshelemiah's eighteen sons and relatives were also very capable men.

10Hosah, of the Merari clan, appointed Shimri as the leader among his sons, though he was not the oldest. 11His other sons included Hilkiah (the second), Tebaliah (the third), and Zechariah (the fourth). Hosah's sons and relatives, who served as gatekeepers, numbered thirteen in all.

12These divisions of the gatekeepers were named for their family leaders, and like the other Levites, they served at the house of the LORD. 13They were assigned by families for guard duty at the various gates, without regard to age or training, for it was all decided by means of sacred lots.

14The responsibility for the east gate went to Meshelemiah* and his group. The north gate was assigned to his son Zechariah, a man of unusual wisdom. 15The south gate went to Obed-edom, and his sons were put in charge of the storehouse. 16Shuppim and Hosah were assigned the west gate and the gateway leading up to the Temple.* Guard duties were divided evenly. 17Six Levites were assigned each day to the east gate, four to the north gate, four to the south gate, and two pairs at the storehouse. 18Six were assigned each day to the west gate, four to the gateway leading up to the Temple, and two to the courtyard.*

19These were the divisions of the gatekeepers from the clans of Korah and Merari.

TREASURERS AND OTHER OFFICIALS
20Other Levites, led by Ahijah, were in charge of the treasuries of the house of God and the treasuries of the gifts dedicated to the LORD. 21From the family of Libni* in the clan of Gershon, Jehiel* was the leader. 22The sons of Jehiel, Zetham and his brother Joel, were in charge of the treasuries of the house of the LORD.

23These are the leaders that descended from Amram, Izhar, Hebron, and Uzziel:

24From the clan of Amram, Shebuel was a descendant of Gershom son of Moses. He was the chief officer of the treasuries. 25His relatives through Eliezer were Rehabiah, Jeshaiah, Joram, Zicri, and Shelomoth.

26Shelomoth and his relatives were in charge of the treasuries containing the gifts that King David, the family leaders, and the generals and captains* and other officers of the army had dedicated to the LORD. 27These

25:22 Hebrew *Jeremoth,* a variant spelling of Jerimoth; compare 25:4. 25:24 Hebrew *Joshbekasha,* a variant spelling of Joshbekashah; compare 25:4. 26:1 As in Greek version (see also Exod 6:24); Hebrew reads *Asaph.* 26:14 Hebrew *Shelemiah,* a variant spelling of Meshelemiah; compare 26:2. 26:16 Or *the gate of Shalleketh on the upper road* (also in 26:18). The meaning of the Hebrew is uncertain. 26:18 Or *the colonnade.* The meaning of the Hebrew is uncertain. 26:21a Hebrew *Ladan,* a variant spelling of Libni; compare 6:17. 26:21b Hebrew *Jehieli* (also in 26:22), a variant spelling of Jehiel; compare 23:8. 26:26 Hebrew *the commanders of thousands and of hundreds.*

PRINCIPLES TO LIVE BY

David gave his son Solomon principles to guide him through life (see 1 Chr 28:9-10). These same ideas are ones that any Christian can learn and follow.

1	2	3	4	5	6
Get to know God personally.	Learn God's commands and discover what he wants you to do.	Worship God with a clean heart.	Serve God with a willing mind.	Be faithful.	Don't become discouraged.

men dedicated some of the plunder they had gained in battle to maintain the house of the LORD. ²⁸Shelomoth* and his relatives also cared for the gifts dedicated to the LORD by Samuel the seer, Saul son of Kish, Abner son of Ner, and Joab son of Zeruiah. All the other dedicated gifts were in their care, too.

²⁹From the clan of Izhar came Kenaniah. He and his sons were given administrative responsibilities* over Israel as officials and judges.

³⁰From the clan of Hebron came Hashabiah. He and his relatives—1,700 capable men—were put in charge of the Israelite lands west of the Jordan River. They were responsible for all matters related to the things of the LORD and the service of the king in that area.

³¹Also from the clan of Hebron came Jeriah,* who was the leader of the Hebronites according to the genealogical records. (In the fortieth year of David's reign, a search was made in the records, and capable men from the clan of Hebron were found at Jazer in the land of Gilead.) ³²There were 2,700 capable men among the relatives of Jeriah. King David sent them to the east side of the Jordan River and put them in charge of the tribes of Reuben and Gad and the half-tribe of Manasseh. They were responsible for all matters related to God and to the king.

27 MILITARY COMMANDERS AND DI-VISIONS This is the list of Israelite generals and captains,* and their officers,

····································

JOYFUL GIVING
(26:27) The spoils of war rightfully belonged to the victorious army. These soldiers, however, gave their portion of all the battle plunder to the Temple to express their dedication to God. Many times, we give out of obligation, rather than out of joy. Is your giving a matter of rejoicing rather than duty?

who served the king by supervising the army divisions that were on duty each month of the year. Each division served for one month and had 24,000 troops.

²Jashobeam son of Zabdiel was commander of the first division of 24,000 troops, which was on duty during the first month. ³He was a descendant of Perez and was in charge of all the army officers for the first month.

⁴Dodai, a descendant of Ahoah, was commander of the second division of 24,000 troops, which was on duty during the second month. Mikloth was his chief officer.

⁵Benaiah son of Jehoiada the priest was commander of the third division of 24,000 troops, which was on duty during the third month. ⁶This was the Benaiah who commanded David's elite military group known as the Thirty. His son Ammizabad was his chief officer.

⁷Asahel, the brother of Joab, was commander of the fourth division of 24,000 troops, which was on duty during the fourth month. Asahel was succeeded by his son Zebadiah.

⁸Shammah* the Izrahite was commander of the fifth division of 24,000 troops, which was on duty during the fifth month.

⁹Ira son of Ikkesh from Tekoa was commander of the sixth division of 24,000 troops, which was on duty during the sixth month.

¹⁰Helez, a descendant of Ephraim from Pelon, was commander of the seventh division of 24,000 troops, which was on duty during the seventh month.

¹¹Sibbecai, a descendant of Zerah from Hushah, was commander of the eighth division of 24,000 troops, which was on duty during the eighth month.

¹²Abiezer from Anathoth in the territory of

26:28 Hebrew *Shelomith,* a variant spelling of Shelomoth.
26:29 Or *were given outside work;* or *were given work away from the Temple area.* **26:31** Hebrew *Jerijah,* a variant spelling of Jeriah; compare 23:19. **27:1** Hebrew *commanders of thousands and of hundreds.* **27:8** Hebrew *Shamhuth,* a variant spelling of Shammah; compare 11:27 and 2 Sam 23:25.

Benjamin was commander of the ninth division of 24,000 troops, which was on duty during the ninth month. [13]Maharai, a descendant of Zerah from Netophah, was commander of the tenth division of 24,000 troops, which was on duty during the tenth month. [14]Benaiah from Pirathon in Ephraim was commander of the eleventh division of 24,000 troops, which was on duty during the eleventh month. [15]Heled,* a descendant of Othniel from Netophah, was commander of the twelfth division of 24,000 troops, which was on duty during the twelfth month.

LEADERS OF THE TRIBES [16]The following were the tribes of Israel and their leaders:

Tribe	Leader
Reuben	Eliezer son of Zicri
Simeon	Shephatiah son of Maacah
[17]Levi	Hashabiah son of Kemuel
Aaron (the priests)	Zadok
[18]Judah	Elihu (a brother of David)
Issachar	Omri son of Michael
[19]Zebulun	Ishmaiah son of Obadiah
Naphtali	Jeremoth son of Azriel
[20]Ephraim	Hoshea son of Azaziah
Manasseh (west)	Joel son of Pedaiah
[21]Manasseh in Gilead (east)	Iddo son of Zechariah
Benjamin	Jaasiel son of Abner
[22]Dan	Azarel son of Jeroham

These were the leaders of the tribes of Israel. [23]When David took his census, he did not count those who were younger than twenty years of age, because the LORD had promised to make the Israelites as numerous as the stars in heaven. [24]Joab son of Zeruiah began the census but never finished it because* the anger of God fell on Israel. The total number was never recorded in King David's official records.

OFFICIALS OF DAVID'S KINGDOM [25]Azmaveth son of Adiel was in charge of the palace treasuries.

Jonathan son of Uzziah was in charge of the regional treasuries throughout the towns, villages, and fortresses of Israel. [26]Ezri son of Kelub was in charge of the field workers who farmed the king's lands. [27]Shimei from Ramah was in charge of the king's vineyards.

Zabdi from Shepham was responsible for the grapes and the supplies of wine. [28]Baal-hanan from Geder was in charge of the king's olive groves and sycamore-fig trees in the foothills of Judah.*

Joash was responsible for the supplies of olive oil. [29]Shitrai from Sharon was in charge of the cattle on the Sharon Plain.

Shaphat son of Adlai was responsible for the cattle in the valleys. [30]Obil the Ishmaelite was in charge of the camels.

Jehdeiah from Meronoth was in charge of the donkeys. [31]Jaziz the Hagrite was in charge of the king's flocks of sheep and goats.

All these officials were overseers of King David's property.

[32]Jonathan, David's uncle, was a wise counselor to the king, a man of great insight, and a scribe. Jehiel the Hacmonite was responsible for teaching the king's sons. [33]Ahithophel was the royal adviser. Hushai the Arkite was the king's friend. [34]Ahithophel was succeeded by Jehoiada son of Benaiah and by Abiathar. Joab was commander of the king's army.

28 DAVID'S INSTRUCTIONS TO SOLOMON

David summoned all the officials of Israel to Jerusalem—the leaders of the tribes, the commanders of the army divisions, the other generals and captains,* the overseers of the royal property and livestock, the palace officials, the mighty men, and all the other brave warriors in the kingdom. [2]David rose to his feet and said: "My brothers and my people! It was my desire to build a Temple where the Ark of the LORD's Covenant, God's footstool, could rest permanently. I made the necessary preparations for building it, [3]but God said to me, 'You must not build a Temple to honor my name, for you are a warrior and have shed much blood.'

[4]"Yet the LORD, the God of Israel, has chosen me from among all my father's family to be king over Israel forever. For he has chosen the tribe of Judah to rule, and from among the families

27:15 Hebrew *Heldai*, a variant spelling of Heled; compare 11:30 and 2 Sam 23:29.   **27:24** Or *never finished it, and yet.*   **27:28** Hebrew *the Shephelah.*   **28:1** Hebrew *the commanders of thousands and commanders of hundreds.*

....

TAKE HIM SERIOUSLY
(28:1-10) David encouraged Solomon to obey all of God's commands. He wanted Solomon to take God seriously. Maybe you don't have to run a country, but as you grow closer to adulthood, perhaps you're already considering the decisions you'll need to make for yourself. Like Solomon, are you willing to take God seriously? He's your best hope for the future.

of Judah he chose my father's family. And from among my father's sons the LORD was pleased to make me king over all Israel. [5]And from among my sons—for the LORD has given me many—he chose Solomon to succeed me on the throne of Israel and to rule over the LORD's kingdom. [6]He said to me, 'Your son Solomon will build my Temple and its courtyards, for I have chosen him as my son, and I will be his father. [7]And if he continues to obey my commands and regulations as he does now, I will make his kingdom last forever.'

[8]"So now, with God as our witness, and in the sight of all Israel—the LORD's assembly—I give you this charge. Be careful to obey all the commands of the LORD your God, so that you may continue to possess this good land and leave it to your children as a permanent inheritance.

[9]"And Solomon, my son, learn to know the God of your ancestors intimately. Worship and serve him with your whole heart and a willing mind. For the LORD sees every heart and knows every plan and thought. If you seek him, you will find him. But if you forsake him, he will reject you forever. [10]So take this seriously. The

· ·

ALL KNOWING

(28:9) Nothing can be hidden from God. He sees and understands everything in our hearts. David found this out the hard way when God sent Nathan to expose David's sins of adultery and murder (2 Sam 12). David told Solomon to be completely open with God and dedicated to him. It makes no sense to try to hide any thoughts and actions from an all-knowing God. This should cause you joy, not fear, because God knows even the worst things about you and loves you anyway.

LORD has chosen you to build a Temple as his sanctuary. Be strong, and do the work."

[11]Then David gave Solomon the plans for the Temple and its surroundings, including the entry room, the storerooms, the upstairs rooms, the inner rooms, and the inner sanctuary—which was the place of atonement. [12]David also gave Solomon all the plans he had in mind* for the courtyards of the LORD's Temple, the outside rooms, the treasuries, and the rooms for the gifts dedicated to the LORD. [13]The king also gave Solomon the instructions concerning the work of the various divisions of priests and Levites in the Temple of the LORD. And he gave specifications for the items in the Temple that were to be used for worship.

[14]David gave instructions regarding how much gold and silver should be used to make the items needed for service. [15]He told Solomon the amount of gold needed for the gold lampstands and lamps, and the amount of silver for the silver lampstands and lamps, depending on how each would be used. [16]He designated the amount of gold for the table on which the Bread of the Presence would be placed and the amount of silver for other tables.

[17]David also designated the amount of gold for the solid gold meat hooks used to handle the sacrificial meat and for the basins, pitchers, and dishes, as well as the amount of silver for every dish. [18]He designated the amount of refined gold for the altar of incense. Finally, he gave him a plan for the LORD's "chariot"—the gold cherubim* whose wings were stretched out over the Ark of the LORD's Covenant.

28:12 Or *the plans of the spirit that was with him.* **28:18** Hebrew for the gold cherub chariot.

CHOICES
the boss

"I just wish God would leave me alone. It's like I can't get away from him."

"What do you mean, Reed?"

"Well, my parents go to church all the time and they make me go—to everything."

"And you don't like that?"

"I'd rather do almost anything else—even homework. But with my parents, attendance isn't open for discussion."

"Your older brother is a missionary, isn't he?"

"Yeah."

"Do you stay in touch?"

"He sends me these thick letters every month—they're like handwritten sermons telling me to make Jesus the Lord of my life. I wish he'd let me live the way I want to live."

"How is that?"

"Well, I don't want to *totally* forget God, but I think it's extreme to think and talk about him all the time. I want to live my life without having to think about God every single day."

"Reed, are you a Christian? Have you ever really trusted Christ?"

"Yeah. When I was eleven."

"But now you're saying you want to live for God on your terms? Whenever you feel like it?"

"I guess so."

Like Reed, a lot of Christians don't want Christ to be their Master and Boss. They want to control their own lives. They believe they can do whatever they desire and still find fulfillment.

See 1 Chronicles 28:9 for the real secret to satisfaction in life.

I just realized that I have been living off of the faith of my parents. How do I make my faith my own?

This may be the most significant realization of your life. Some young people never understand that God wants us to know him personally. Living off of someone else's faith is like borrowing something from a friend. No matter what you borrow—a car, a cell phone, clothes, a skateboard, CDs, or faith—it isn't yours and must be returned.

Solomon was challenged to "learn to know the God of your ancestors intimately" (1 Chr 28:9). In other words, he wasn't to settle for hearing how someone else trusted God. He needed to find out for himself.

During these years, your faith will be tested. Friends who do not believe in Christ may see nothing wrong with doing things that would cause your conscience to start screaming in protest. That's when you will have to make a choice: Will you go along with your friends, or will you stand on what you believe? If your faith is strong (if it is yours and not your parents' or your youth leader's), no amount of pressure from friends will be able to blow you away (see Matt 7:24-27).

Consider taking these steps to help develop your faith. First, make sure you have asked Jesus Christ to forgive your sin and come into your life. Second, begin to ask questions about the Bible. God wants you to understand it as well as believe and obey it. Third, look for other Christians who are excited about developing their faith in God—people who do not want to settle for second best. What you learn from them can convince you that being a Christian is worth the work and is 100 percent right for you!

¹⁹"Every part of this plan," David told Solomon, "was given to me in writing from the hand of the LORD.*"

²⁰Then David continued, "Be strong and courageous, and do the work. Don't be afraid or discouraged, for the LORD God, my God, is with you. He will see to it that all the work related to the Temple of the LORD is finished correctly. ²¹The various divisions of priests and Levites will serve in the Temple of God. Others with skills of every kind will volunteer, and the officials and the entire nation are at your command."

29 GIFTS FOR BUILDING THE TEMPLE

Then King David turned to the entire assembly and said, "My son Solomon, whom God has clearly chosen as the next king of Israel, is still young and inexperienced. The work ahead of him is enormous, for the Temple he will build is not for mere mortals—it is for the LORD God himself! ²Using every resource at my command, I have gathered as much as I could for building the Temple of my God. Now there is enough gold, silver, bronze, iron, and wood, as well as great quantities of onyx, other precious stones, costly jewels, and all kinds of fine stone and marble.

³"And now, because of my devotion to the Temple of my God, I am giving all of my own private treasures of gold and silver to help in the construction. This is in addition to the building materials I have already collected for his holy Temple. ⁴I am donating more than 112 tons of gold* from Ophir and 262 tons of refined silver* to be used for overlaying the walls of the buildings ⁵and for the other gold and silver work to be done by the craftsmen. Now then, who will follow my example and give offerings to the LORD today?"

⁶Then the family leaders, the leaders of the tribes of Israel, the generals and captains of the army,* and the king's administrative officers all gave willingly. ⁷For the construction of the Temple of God, they gave about 188 tons of gold,* 10,000 gold coins,* 375 tons of silver,* 675 tons of bronze,* and 3,750 tons of iron.* ⁸They also contributed numerous precious stones, which were deposited in the treasury of the house of the LORD under the care of Jehiel, a descendant of Gershon. ⁹The people rejoiced over the offerings, for they had given freely and wholeheartedly to the LORD, and King David was filled with joy.

DAVID'S PRAYER OF PRAISE ¹⁰Then David praised the LORD in the presence of the whole assembly:

"O LORD, the God of our ancestor Israel,*
may you be praised forever and ever!
¹¹Yours, O LORD, is the greatness, the power,
the glory, the victory, and the majesty.
Everything in the heavens and on earth is
yours, O LORD, and this is your kingdom.
We adore you as the one who is over all
things. ¹²Wealth and honor come from you

28:19 Or *was written under the direction of the LORD.* **29:4a** Hebrew *3,000 talents* [102 metric tons] *of gold.* **29:4b** Hebrew *7,000 talents* [238 metric tons] *of silver.* **29:6** Hebrew *the commanders of thousands and commanders of hundreds.* **29:7a** Hebrew *5,000 talents* [170 metric tons] *of gold.* **29:7b** Hebrew *10,000 darics* [a Persian coin] *of gold,* about 185 pounds or 84 kilograms in weight. **29:7c** Hebrew *10,000 talents* [340 metric tons] *of silver.* **29:7d** Hebrew *18,000 talents* [612 metric tons] *of bronze.* **29:7e** Hebrew *100,000 talents* [3,400 metric tons] *of iron.* **29:10** *Israel* is the name that God gave to Jacob.

alone, for you rule over everything. Power and might are in your hand, and at your discretion people are made great and given strength.

¹³"O our God, we thank you and praise your glorious name! ¹⁴But who am I, and who are my people, that we could give anything to you? Everything we have has come from you, and we give you only what you first gave us! ¹⁵We are here for only a moment, visitors and strangers in the land as our ancestors were before us. Our days on earth are like a passing shadow, gone so soon without a trace.

¹⁶"O LORD our God, even this material we have gathered to build a Temple to honor your holy name comes from you! It all belongs to you! ¹⁷I know, my God, that you examine our hearts and rejoice when you find integrity there. You know I have done all this with good motives, and I have watched your people offer their gifts willingly and joyously.

¹⁸"O LORD, the God of our ancestors Abraham, Isaac, and Israel, make your people always want to obey you. See to it that their love for you never changes. ¹⁹Give my son Solomon the wholehearted desire to obey all your commands, laws, and decrees,

and to do everything necessary to build this Temple, for which I have made these preparations."

²⁰Then David said to the whole assembly, "Give praise to the LORD your God!" And the entire assembly praised the LORD, the God of their ancestors, and they bowed low and knelt before the LORD and the king.

SOLOMON NAMED AS KING ²¹The next day they brought 1,000 bulls, 1,000 rams, and 1,000 male lambs as burnt offerings to the LORD. They also brought liquid offerings and many other sacrifices on behalf of all Israel. ²²They feasted and drank in the LORD's presence with great joy that day.

And again they crowned David's son Solomon as their new king. They anointed him before the LORD as their leader, and they anointed Zadok as priest. ²³So Solomon took the throne of the LORD in place of his father, David, and he succeeded in everything, and all Israel obeyed him. ²⁴All the officials, the warriors, and the sons of King David pledged their loyalty to King Solomon. ²⁵And the LORD exalted Solomon in the sight of all Israel, and he gave Solomon greater royal splendor than any king in Israel before him.

SUMMARY OF DAVID'S REIGN ²⁶So David son of Jesse reigned over all Israel. ²⁷He reigned over Israel for forty years, seven of them in Hebron and thirty-three in Jerusalem. ²⁸He died at a ripe old age, having enjoyed long life, wealth, and honor. Then his son Solomon ruled in his place.

²⁹All the events of King David's reign, from beginning to end, are written in *The Record of Samuel the Seer, The Record of Nathan the Prophet,* and *The Record of Gad the Seer.* ³⁰These accounts include the mighty deeds of his reign and everything that happened to him and to Israel and to all the surrounding kingdoms.

SECURITY
(29:11-12) David acknowledged God's greatness. Our constantly changing world is controlled by a constant and unchanging God. As we see life's events come and go, objects fade, materials decay, and friends change, the only thing on which we can truly depend is God's control. His love and purpose for us never change. Only when we understand this can we have real peace and security.

A DESIRE TO SERVE
(29:19) David wanted Solomon to have a heart that desired, above all else, to serve God. Do you find it difficult to do what God wants or even harder to want to do it? God can give you a loyal heart that desires to do his will. If you trust Jesus as your Savior, this is already happening in you. Paul wrote, "God is working in you, giving you the desire and the power to do what pleases him" (Phil 2:13).

"You can't drive the car for two weeks." "Detention for five days." "No parties for two weeks." "You're grounded for a week." "No cell phone for a month."

So what do those statements have in common? They're punishments. Have you experienced one lately?

Many times during Israel's history, God sent messengers to the divided country's leaders threatening punishment for their disobedience. Each time, the leaders would beg for one more chance, but they never kept their promises. Finally God allowed them to be conquered (the northern kingdom by Assyria, and the southern kingdom by Babylon) and taken into captivity.

Second Chronicles was written after some of the Jews returned to their homeland from their exile. The author reminded these people of their forefathers' sin and its results. Only by truly submitting to God could Israel regain its strength as a nation. As God told Solomon, "If my people who are called by my name will humble themselves and pray and seek my face and turn from their wicked ways, I will hear from heaven and will forgive their sins and restore their land" (7:14).

Second Chronicles is a reminder for you, too. God never takes wrongdoing lightly. But he's always ready to forgive those who ask.

KEY POINTS

TEMPLE The Temple was the symbol of God's presence and the place set aside for worship and prayer. Although we attend church in a physical building, the human heart is the main center of God's presence today.

PEACE While Solomon and his descendants were faithful to God, they experienced victory in battle, success in government, and peace with other nations. Peace was, and is, the result of loyalty to God and his law. Only God can bring true peace. He's greater than any enemy, army, or national alliance.

PRAYER When the king and his people prayed for help in defeating their enemies, God helped them. Likewise, if we seek God with humility, God will answer our prayers.

CHANGE FOR THE BETTER Although idol worship and injustice were common, some kings led the people back to God and reformed their society. We can be instruments of change as we remind people of God's standards.

CONSEQUENCE OF CASUAL COMMITMENT When the people of Israel refused to stop doing wrong, God allowed them to be conquered by their enemies. Although our disobedience may not be as obvious as Israel's, quite often our commitment to God is casual or even phony. God wants his people to be fully committed to him.

The broken lines (— ·—·—) indicate modern boundaries.

KEY PLACES

❶ GIBEON

King Solomon summoned the nation's leaders to a ceremony in Gibeon. Here God told Solomon to ask for whatever he desired. Solomon asked for wisdom and knowledge to rule Israel (1:1-12).

❷ JERUSALEM

Solomon returned to the capital city, Jerusalem. His reign began a golden age for Israel. Solomon implemented plans for the Temple that had been drawn up by his father, David. The magnificent building symbolized Solomon's wealth and wisdom (1:13–9:31).

❸ SHECHEM

After Solomon's death, his son Rehoboam was ready to be crowned in Shechem. However, his promise of higher taxes and harder work for the people led to rebellion. Everyone but the tribes of Judah and Benjamin deserted Rehoboam and set up their own kingdom to the north called Israel. Rehoboam returned to Jerusalem as ruler over the southern kingdom, called Judah (10:1–12:16). The rest of 2 Chronicles records Judah's history.

❹ HILL COUNTRY OF EPHRAIM

Abijah became the next king of Judah, and soon war broke out between Israel and Judah. When the armies of the two nations arrived for battle in the hill country of Ephraim, Israel had twice as many troops as Judah.

It looked like Judah's defeat was certain. But they cried out to God, and God gave them victory over Israel. (13:1-22).

❺ ARAM

Asa, a godly king, removed every trace of idol worship from Judah and renewed the people's covenant with God in Jerusalem. But King Baasha of Israel built a fortress to control traffic into Judah. Instead of looking to God for guidance, Asa sent silver and gold from the Temple to the king of Aram, requesting his help against King Baasha. As a result, God became angry with Judah (14:1–16:14).

❻ SAMARIA

Although Jehoshaphat was a godly king, he allied himself with Israel's most evil king, Ahab. Ahab's capital was in Samaria. Ahab wanted help fighting for control of Ramoth-gilead. Jehoshaphat didn't listen to God's prophet who had promised defeat, and instead joined Ahab in battle (17:1–18:27).

❼ RAMOTH-GILEAD

The alliance with Israel against Ramoth-gilead ended in defeat and Ahab's death. Although shaken by his defeat, Jehoshaphat returned to Jerusalem and to God. But his son Jehoram was a wicked king, as was his son, Ahaziah. And history repeated itself. Ahaziah formed an alliance with Israel's King Jehoram to fight the Arameans at Ramoth-gilead where both kings died (18:28–22:9).

❷ JERUSALEM

The rest of Judah's history recorded in 2 Chronicles centers on Jerusalem. Some kings caused Judah to sin by promoting idol worship. Others cleaned up the idol worship, reopened and restored the Temple, and, in the case of Josiah, tried to follow God's laws nonetheless, a series of evil kings sent Judah into a downward spiral that ended with the Babylonian empire overrunning the country. The Temple was burned, the walls of the city were broken down, and the people were deported to Babylon.

1

SOLOMON ASKS FOR WISDOM Solomon son of David took firm control of his kingdom, for the LORD his God was with him and made him very powerful.

²Solomon called together all the leaders of Israel—the generals and captains of the army,* the judges, and all the political and clan leaders. ³Then he led the entire assembly to the place of worship in Gibeon, for God's Tabernacle* was located there. (This was the Tabernacle that Moses, the LORD's servant, had made in the wilderness.)

⁴David had already moved the Ark of God from Kiriath-jearim to the tent he had prepared for it in Jerusalem. ⁵But the bronze altar made by Bezalel son of Uri and grandson of Hur was there* at Gibeon in front of the Tabernacle of the LORD. So Solomon and the people gathered in front of it to consult the LORD.* ⁶There in front of the Tabernacle, Solomon went up to the bronze altar in the LORD's presence and sacrificed 1,000 burnt offerings on it.

⁷That night God appeared to Solomon and said, "What do you want? Ask, and I will give it to you!"

⁸Solomon replied to God, "You showed faithful love to David, my father, and now you have made me king in his place. ⁹O LORD God, please continue to keep your promise to David my father, for you have made me king over a people as numerous as the dust of the earth! ¹⁰Give me the wisdom and knowledge to lead them properly,* for who could possibly govern this great people of yours?"

¹¹God said to Solomon, "Because your greatest desire is to help your people, and you did not ask for wealth, riches, fame, or even the death of your enemies or a long life, but rather you asked for wisdom and knowledge to properly govern my people—¹²I will certainly give you the wisdom and knowledge you requested. But I will also give you wealth, riches, and fame such as no other king has had before you or will ever have in the future!"

¹³Then Solomon returned to Jerusalem from the Tabernacle at the place of worship in Gibeon, and he reigned over Israel.

¹⁴Solomon built up a huge force of chariots and horses.* He had 1,400 chariots and 12,000 horses. He stationed some of them in the chariot cities and some near him in Jerusalem. ¹⁵The king made silver and gold as plentiful in Jerusalem as stone. And valuable cedar timber was as common as the sycamore-fig trees that grow in the foothills of Judah.* ¹⁶Solomon's horses were imported from Egypt* and from Cilicia*; the king's traders acquired them from Cilicia at the standard price. ¹⁷At that time chariots from Egypt could be purchased for 600 pieces of silver,* and horses for 150 pieces of silver.* They were then exported to the kings of the Hittites and the kings of Aram.

2

PREPARATIONS FOR BUILDING THE TEMPLE ¹*Solomon decided to build a Temple to honor the name of the LORD, and also a royal palace for himself. ²*He enlisted a force of 70,000 laborers, 80,000 men to quarry stone in the hill country, and 3,600 foremen.

³Solomon also sent this message to King Hiram* at Tyre:

"Send me cedar logs as you did for my father, David, when he was building his palace. ⁴I am about to build a Temple to honor the name of the LORD my God. It will be a place set apart to burn fragrant incense before him, to display the special sacrificial bread, and to sacrifice burnt offerings each morning and evening, on the Sabbaths, at new moon celebrations, and at the other appointed festivals of the LORD our God. He has commanded Israel to do these things forever.

PRIORITIES
(1:11-13) Although Solomon could have asked for anything, he asked for wisdom to rule the nation. Because God approved of the way Solomon ordered his priorities, he gave Solomon the wisdom he asked for and money to spare. Jesus also spoke about priorities. He said that when we put God first, everything we need will be provided (Matt 6:33). This isn't a guarantee that we will be wealthy and famous like Solomon. Instead, it means that when we wisely put God first, the wisdom he gives us will enable us to live a rich, rewarding life.

CELEBRATE
(2:4) A celebration is an occasion of joy, and remembering God's goodness to his people was certainly a reason to be joyful. God wanted Israel to celebrate certain occasions regularly because the people were quick to forget and to turn to other gods. We also have special celebrations to commemorate and help us recall God's goodness. We also have short memories, so Christmas, Easter, and other celebrations help us remember what God has done for us. What new celebration tradition can you begin? How about a party to celebrate your spiritual birth?

1:2 Hebrew *the commanders of thousands and of hundreds.*
1:3 Hebrew *Tent of Meeting;* also in 1:6, 13. **1:5a** As in Greek version and Latin Vulgate, and some Hebrew manuscripts. Masoretic Text reads *he placed.* **1:5b** Hebrew *to consult him.* **1:10** Hebrew *to go out and come in before this people.* **1:14** Or *charioteers;* also in 1:14b. **1:15** Hebrew *the Shephelah.* **1:16a** Possibly *Muzur,* a district near Cilicia; also in 1:17. **1:16b** Hebrew *Kue,* probably another name for Cilicia. **1:17a** Hebrew *600 [shekels] of silver,* about 15 pounds or 6.8 kilograms in weight. **1:17b** Hebrew *150 [shekels],* about 3.8 pounds or 1.7 kilograms in weight.
2:1 Verse 2:1 is numbered 1:18 in Hebrew text. **2:2** Verses 2:2-18 are numbered 2:1-17 in Hebrew text. **2:3** Hebrew *Huram,* a variant spelling of Hiram; also in 2:11.

⁵"This must be a magnificent Temple because our God is greater than all other gods. ⁶But who can really build him a worthy home? Not even the highest heavens can contain him! So who am I to consider building a Temple for him, except as a place to burn sacrifices to him?

⁷"So send me a master craftsman who can work with gold, silver, bronze, and iron, as well as with purple, scarlet, and blue cloth. He must be a skilled engraver who can work with the craftsmen of Judah and Jerusalem who were selected by my father, David.

⁸"Also send me cedar, cypress, and red sandalwood* logs from Lebanon, for I know that your men are without equal at cutting timber in Lebanon. I will send my men to help them. ⁹An immense amount of timber will be needed, for the Temple I am going to build will be very large and magnificent. ¹⁰In payment for your woodcutters, I will send 100,000 bushels of crushed wheat, 100,000 bushels of barley,* 110,000 gallons of wine, and 110,000 gallons of olive oil.*"

¹¹King Hiram sent this letter of reply to Solomon:

"It is because the LORD loves his people that he has made you their king! ¹²Praise the LORD, the God of Israel, who made the heavens and the earth! He has given King David a wise son, gifted with skill and understanding, who will build a Temple for the LORD and a royal palace for himself.

¹³"I am sending you a master craftsman named Huram-abi, who is extremely talented. ¹⁴His mother is from the tribe of Dan in Israel, and his father is from Tyre. He is skillful at making things from gold, silver, bronze, and iron, and he also works with stone and wood. He can work with purple, blue, and scarlet cloth and fine linen. He is also an engraver and can follow any design given to him. He will work with your craftsmen and those appointed by my lord David, your father.

¹⁵"Send along the wheat, barley, olive oil, and wine that my lord has mentioned. ¹⁶We will cut whatever timber you need from the Lebanon mountains and will float the logs in rafts down the coast of the Mediterranean Sea* to Joppa. From there you can transport the logs up to Jerusalem."

¹⁷Solomon took a census of all foreigners in the land of Israel, like the census his father had taken, and he counted 153,600. ¹⁸He assigned 70,000 of them as common laborers, 80,000 as quarry workers in the hill country, and 3,600 as foremen.

3 **SOLOMON BUILDS THE TEMPLE** So Solomon began to build the Temple of the LORD in Jerusalem on Mount Moriah, where the LORD had appeared to David, his father. The Temple was built on the threshing floor of Araunah* the Jebusite, the site that David had selected. ²The construction began in midspring,* during the fourth year of Solomon's reign.

³These are the dimensions Solomon used for the foundation of the Temple of God (using the old standard of measurement).* It was 90 feet long and 30 feet wide.* ⁴The entry room at the front of the Temple was 30 feet* wide, running across the entire width of the Temple, and 30 feet* high. He overlaid the inside with pure gold.

⁵He paneled the main room of the Temple with cypress wood, overlaid it with fine gold, and decorated it with carvings of palm trees and chains. ⁶He decorated the walls of the Temple with beautiful jewels and with gold from the land of Parvaim. ⁷He overlaid the beams, thresholds, walls, and doors throughout the Temple with gold, and he carved figures of cherubim on the walls.

⁸He made the Most Holy Place 30 feet wide, corresponding to the width of the Temple, and 30 feet deep. He overlaid its interior with 23 tons* of fine gold. ⁹The gold nails that were used weighed 20 ounces* each. He also overlaid the walls of the upper rooms with gold.

¹⁰He made two figures shaped like cherubim, overlaid them with gold, and placed them in the Most Holy Place. ¹¹The total wingspan of the two cherubim standing side by side was 30 feet. One wing of the first figure was 7½ feet* long, and it touched the Temple wall. The other wing, also 7½ feet long, touched one of the wings of the second figure. ¹²In the same way, the second figure had one wing 7½ feet

2:8 Or *juniper;* Hebrew reads *algum,* perhaps a variant spelling of *almug;* compare 9:10-11 and parallel text at 1 Kgs 10:11-12. 2:10a Hebrew *20,000 cors* [3,640 kiloliters] *of crushed wheat, 20,000 cors of barley.* 2:10b Hebrew *20,000 baths* [420 kiloliters] *of wine, and 20,000 baths of olive oil.* 2:16 Hebrew *the sea.* 3:1 Hebrew reads *Ornan,* a variant spelling of Araunah; compare 2 Sam 24:16. 3:2 Hebrew *on the second day of the second month.* This day of the ancient Hebrew lunar calendar occurred in April or May. 3:3a The "old standard of measurement" was a cubit equal to 18 inches [46 centimeters]. The new standard was a cubit of approximately 21 inches [53 centimeters]. 3:3b Hebrew *60 cubits* [27.6 meters] *long and 20 cubits* [9.2 meters] *wide.* 3:4a Hebrew *20 cubits* [9.2 meters]; also in 3:8, 11, 13. 3:4b As in some Greek and Syriac manuscripts, which read *20 cubits* [9.2 meters]; Hebrew reads *120 [cubits],* which is 180 feet or 55 meters. 3:8 Hebrew *600 talents* [20.4 metric tons]. 3:9 Hebrew *50 shekels* [570 grams]. 3:11 Hebrew *5 cubits* [2.3 meters]; also in 3:11b, 12, 15.

long that touched the opposite wall. The other wing, also 7½ feet long, touched the wing of the first figure. ¹³So the wingspan of the two cherubim side by side was 30 feet. They stood on their feet and faced out toward the main room of the Temple.

¹⁴Across the entrance of the Most Holy Place he hung a curtain made of fine linen, decorated with blue, purple, and scarlet thread and embroidered with figures of cherubim.

¹⁵For the front of the Temple, he made two pillars that were 27 feet* tall, each topped by a capital extending upward another 7½ feet. ¹⁶He made a network of interwoven chains and used them to decorate the tops of the pillars. He also made 100 decorative pomegranates and attached them to the chains. ¹⁷Then he set up the two pillars at the entrance of the Temple, one to the south of the entrance and the other to the north. He named the one on the south Jakin, and the one on the north Boaz.*

4

FURNISHINGS FOR THE TEMPLE Solomon* also made a bronze altar 30 feet long, 30 feet wide, and 15 feet high.* ²Then he cast a great round basin, 15 feet across from rim to rim, called the Sea. It was 7½ feet deep and about 45 feet in circumference.* ³It was encircled just below its rim by two rows of figures that resembled oxen. There were about six oxen per foot* all the way around, and they were cast as part of the basin.

⁴The Sea was placed on a base of twelve bronze oxen, all facing outward. Three faced north, three faced west, three faced south, and three faced east, and the Sea rested on them. ⁵The walls of the Sea were about three inches* thick, and its rim flared out like a cup and resembled a water lily blossom. It could hold about 16,500 gallons* of water.

⁶He also made ten smaller basins for washing the utensils for the burnt offerings. He set five on the south side and five on the north. But the priests washed themselves in the Sea.

⁷He then cast ten gold lampstands according to the specifications that had been given, and he put them in the Temple. Five were placed against the south wall, and five were placed against the north wall.

⁸He also built ten tables and placed them in the Temple, five along the south wall and five along the north wall. Then he molded 100 gold basins.

⁹He then built a courtyard for the priests, and also the large outer courtyard. He made doors for the courtyard entrances and overlaid them with bronze. ¹⁰The great bronze basin called the Sea was placed near the southeast corner of the Temple.

¹¹Huram-abi also made the necessary washbasins, shovels, and bowls.

So at last Huram-abi completed everything King Solomon had assigned him to make for the Temple of God:

¹² the two pillars;
   the two bowl-shaped capitals on top of the pillars;
   the two networks of interwoven chains that decorated the capitals;
¹³ the 400 pomegranates that hung from the chains on the capitals (two rows of pomegranates for each of the chain networks that decorated the capitals on top of the pillars);
¹⁴ the water carts holding the basins;
¹⁵ the Sea and the twelve oxen under it;
¹⁶ the ash buckets, the shovels, the meat hooks, and all the related articles.

Huram-abi made all these things of burnished bronze for the Temple of the LORD, just as King Solomon had directed. ¹⁷The king had them cast in clay molds in the Jordan Valley between Succoth and Zarethan.* ¹⁸Solomon used such great quantities of bronze that its weight could not be determined.

¹⁹Solomon also made all the furnishings for the Temple of God:

   the gold altar;
   the tables for the Bread of the Presence;
²⁰ the lampstands and their lamps of solid gold, to burn in front of the Most Holy Place as prescribed;
²¹ the flower decorations, lamps, and tongs— all of the purest gold;
²² the lamp snuffers, bowls, dishes, and incense burners—all of solid gold;

3:15 As in Syriac version (see also 1 Kgs 7:15; 2 Kgs 25:17; Jer 52:21), which reads 18 cubits [8.3 meters]; Hebrew reads 35 cubits, which is 52.5 feet or 16.5 meters.   3:17 Jakin probably means "he establishes"; Boaz probably means "in him is strength."   4:1a Or Huram-abi; Hebrew reads He.   4:1b Hebrew 20 cubits [9.2 meters] long, 20 cubits wide, and 10 cubits [4.6 meters] high.   4:2 Hebrew 10 cubits [4.6 meters] across . . . 5 cubits [2.3 meters] deep and 30 cubits [13.8 meters] in circumference.   4:3 Or 20 oxen per meter; Hebrew reads 10 per cubit.   4:5a Hebrew a handbreadth [8 centimeters].   4:5b Hebrew 3,000 baths [63 kiloliters].   4:17 As in parallel text at 1 Kgs 7:46; Hebrew reads Zeredah.

· ·

WORSHIP TOOLS
(4:11-16) Pots, shovels, and basins—these were implements of worship and quite different from what we use today. Although the worship implements have changed, the purpose of worship remains the same: to give honor and praise to God. We must never confuse our worship of God with the things we use to help us worship him.

the doors for the entrances to the Most Holy Place and the main room of the Temple, overlaid with gold.

5 So Solomon finished all his work on the Temple of the Lord. Then he brought all the gifts his father, David, had dedicated—the silver, the gold, and the various articles—and he stored them in the treasuries of the Temple of God.

THE ARK BROUGHT TO THE TEMPLE ²Solomon then summoned to Jerusalem the elders of Israel and all the heads of tribes—the leaders of the ancestral families of Israel. They were to bring the Ark of the Lord's Covenant to the Temple from its location in the City of David, also known as Zion. ³So all the men of Israel assembled before the king at the annual Festival of Shelters, which is held in early autumn.*

⁴When all the elders of Israel arrived, the Levites picked up the Ark. ⁵The priests and Levites brought up the Ark along with the special tent* and all the sacred items that had been in it. ⁶There, before the Ark, King Solomon and the entire community of Israel sacrificed so many sheep, goats, and cattle that no one could keep count!

⁷Then the priests carried the Ark of the Lord's Covenant into the inner sanctuary of the Temple—the Most Holy Place—and placed it beneath the wings of the cherubim. ⁸The cherubim spread their wings over the Ark, forming a canopy over the Ark and its carrying poles. ⁹These poles were so long that their ends could be seen from the Temple's main room—the Holy Place*—but not from the outside. They are still there to this day. ¹⁰Nothing was in the Ark except the two stone tablets that Moses had placed in it at Mount Sinai,* where the Lord made a covenant with the people of Israel when they left Egypt.

¹¹Then the priests left the Holy Place. All the priests who were present had purified themselves, whether or not they were on duty that day. ¹²And the Levites who were musicians—Asaph, Heman, Jeduthun, and all their sons

and brothers—were dressed in fine linen robes and stood at the east side of the altar playing cymbals, lyres, and harps. They were joined by 120 priests who were playing trumpets. ¹³The trumpeters and singers performed together in unison to praise and give thanks to the Lord. Accompanied by trumpets, cymbals, and other instruments, they raised their voices and praised the Lord with these words:

"He is good!
    His faithful love endures forever!"

At that moment a thick cloud filled the Temple of the Lord. ¹⁴The priests could not continue their service because of the cloud, for the glorious presence of the Lord filled the Temple of God.

6 **SOLOMON PRAISES THE LORD** Then Solomon prayed, "O Lord, you have said that you would live in a thick cloud of darkness. ²Now I have built a glorious Temple for you, a place where you can live forever!"

³Then the king turned around to the entire community of Israel standing before him and gave this blessing: ⁴"Praise the Lord, the God of Israel, who has kept the promise he made to my father, David. For he told my father, ⁵'From the day I brought my people out of the land of Egypt, I have never chosen a city among any of the tribes of Israel as the place where a Temple should be built to honor my name. Nor have I chosen a king to lead my people Israel. ⁶But now I have chosen Jerusalem as the place for my name to be honored, and I have chosen David to be king over my people Israel.'"

⁷Then Solomon said, "My father, David, wanted to build this Temple to honor the name of the Lord, the God of Israel. ⁸But the Lord told him, 'You wanted to build the Temple to honor my name. Your intention is good, ⁹but you are not the one to do it. One of your own sons will build the Temple to honor me.'

¹⁰"And now the Lord has fulfilled the promise he made, for I have become king in my father's place, and now I sit on the throne of Israel, just as the Lord promised. I have built this Temple to honor the name of the Lord, the God of Israel. ¹¹There I have placed the Ark, which contains the covenant that the Lord made with the people of Israel."

··

LIVING WORSHIP
(5:2-14) *The first service at the Temple began with honoring God and acknowledging his presence and goodness. In the same way, our worship should begin by recognizing who God is and what he has done for us. Praise God first; then you will be prepared to present your needs to him. Recalling God's love and mercy will bring daily worship to life. Psalm 107 is an example of how David recalled God's loving-kindness.*

5:3 Hebrew *at the festival that is in the seventh month.* The Festival of Shelters began on the fifteenth day of the seventh month of the ancient Hebrew lunar calendar. This day occurred in late September, October, or early November.   **5:5** Hebrew *the Tent of Meeting;* i.e., the tent mentioned in 2 Sam 6:17 and 1 Chr 16:1.   **5:9** As in some Hebrew manuscripts and Greek version (see also 1 Kgs 8:8); Masoretic Text reads *from the Ark in front of the Most Holy Place.*   **5:10** Hebrew *Horeb,* another name for Sinai.

SOLOMON'S PRAYER OF DEDICATION

[12]Then Solomon stood before the altar of the LORD in front of the entire community of Israel, and he lifted his hands in prayer. [13]Now Solomon had made a bronze platform 7½ feet long, 7½ feet wide, and 4½ feet high* and had placed it at the center of the Temple's outer courtyard. He stood on the platform, and then he knelt in front of the entire community of Israel and lifted his hands toward heaven. [14]He prayed,

"O LORD, God of Israel, there is no God like you in all of heaven and earth. You keep your covenant and show unfailing love to all who walk before you in wholehearted devotion. [15]You have kept your promise to your servant David, my father. You made that promise with your own mouth, and with your own hands you have fulfilled it today.

[16]"And now, O LORD, God of Israel, carry out the additional promise you made to your servant David, my father. For you said to him, 'If your descendants guard their behavior and faithfully follow my Law as you have done, one of them will always sit on the throne of Israel.' [17]Now, O LORD, God of Israel, fulfill this promise to your servant David.

[18]"But will God really live on earth among people? Why, even the highest heavens cannot contain you. How much less this Temple I have built! [19]Nevertheless, listen to my prayer and my plea, O LORD my God. Hear the cry and the prayer that your servant is making to you. [20]May you watch over this Temple day and night, this place where you have said you would put your name. May you always hear the prayers I make toward this place. [21]May you hear the humble and earnest requests from me and your people Israel when we pray toward this place. Yes, hear us from heaven where you live, and when you hear, forgive.

[22]"If someone wrongs another person and is required to take an oath of innocence in front of your altar at this Temple, [23]then hear from heaven and judge between your servants—the accuser and the accused. Pay back the guilty as they deserve. Acquit the innocent because of their innocence.

[24]"If your people Israel are defeated by their enemies because they have sinned against you, and if they turn back and acknowledge your name and pray to you here in this Temple, [25]then hear from heaven and forgive the sin of your people Israel and return them to this land you gave to them and to their ancestors.

[26]"If the skies are shut up and there is no rain because your people have sinned against you, and if they pray toward this Temple and acknowledge your name and turn from their sins because you have punished them, [27]then hear from heaven and forgive the sins of your servants, your people Israel. Teach them to follow the right path, and send rain on your land that you have given to your people as their special possession.

[28]"If there is a famine in the land or a plague or crop disease or attacks of locusts or caterpillars, or if your people's enemies are in the land besieging their towns—whatever disaster or disease there is—[29]and if your people Israel pray about their troubles or sorrow, raising their hands toward this Temple, [30]then hear from heaven where you live, and forgive. Give your people what their actions deserve, for you alone know each human heart. [31]Then they will fear you and walk in your ways as long as they live in the land you gave to our ancestors.

[32]"In the future, foreigners who do not belong to your people Israel will hear of you. They will come from distant lands when they hear of your great name and your strong hand and your powerful arm. And when they pray toward this Temple, [33]then hear from heaven where you live, and grant what they ask of you. In this way, all the people of the earth will come to know and fear you, just as your own people Israel do. They, too, will

6:13 Hebrew *5 cubits* [2.3 meters] *long, 5 cubits wide, and 3 cubits* [1.4 meters] *high.*

AMAZING GRACE
(6:18) Solomon was amazed that God was willing to live on earth among sinful people. What's even more amazing is the fact that Jesus, the Son of God, chose to live on earth as a man. Some would call that amazing grace. What would you call it?

FAR AWAY
(6:21-39) In his prayer, Solomon acknowledged God's willingness to forgive his people when they admitted their wrongdoing. Have you ever felt far away from God—separated by personal problems and feelings of failure? Romans 8:38 says that "nothing can ever separate us from God's love." That's true because Jesus made forgiveness an open door we can always walk through. God is waiting and listening for our confessions of guilt and our willingness to obey him. He is ready to forgive us and to restore us to fellowship with him. Don't wait to experience this loving forgiveness.

know that this Temple I have built honors your name.

³⁴"If your people go out where you send them to fight their enemies, and if they pray to you by turning toward this city you have chosen and toward this Temple I have built to honor your name, ³⁵then hear their prayers from heaven and uphold their cause.

³⁶"If they sin against you—and who has never sinned?—you might become angry with them and let their enemies conquer them and take them captive to a foreign land far away or near. ³⁷But in that land of exile, they might turn to you in repentance and pray, 'We have sinned, done evil, and acted wickedly.' ³⁸If they turn to you with their whole heart and soul in the land of their captivity and pray toward the land you gave to their ancestors—toward this city you have chosen, and toward this Temple I have built to honor your name—³⁹then hear their prayers and their petitions from heaven where you live, and uphold their cause. Forgive your people who have sinned against you.

⁴⁰"O my God, may your eyes be open and your ears attentive to all the prayers made to you in this place.

⁴¹ "And now arise, O Lord God, and enter your resting place,
along with the Ark, the symbol of your power.
May your priests, O Lord God, be clothed with salvation;
may your loyal servants rejoice in your goodness.
⁴² O Lord God, do not reject the king you have anointed.
Remember your unfailing love for your servant David."

7 THE DEDICATION OF THE TEMPLE
When Solomon finished praying, fire flashed down from heaven and burned up the burnt offerings and sacrifices, and the glorious presence of the Lord filled the Temple. ²The priests could not enter the Temple of the Lord be-

cause the glorious presence of the Lord filled it. ³When all the people of Israel saw the fire coming down and the glorious presence of the Lord filling the Temple, they fell face down on the ground and worshiped and praised the Lord, saying,

"He is good!
His faithful love endures forever!"

⁴Then the king and all the people offered sacrifices to the Lord. ⁵King Solomon offered a sacrifice of 22,000 cattle and 120,000 sheep and goats. And so the king and all the people dedicated the Temple of God. ⁶The priests took their assigned positions, and so did the Levites who were singing, "His faithful love endures forever!" They accompanied the singing with music from the instruments King David had made for praising the Lord. Across from the Levites, the priests blew the trumpets, while all Israel stood.

⁷Solomon then consecrated the central area of the courtyard in front of the Lord's Temple. He offered burnt offerings and the fat of peace offerings there, because the bronze altar he had built could not hold all the burnt offerings, grain offerings, and sacrificial fat.

⁸For the next seven days Solomon and all Israel celebrated the Festival of Shelters.* A large congregation had gathered from as far away as Lebo-hamath in the north and the Brook of Egypt in the south. ⁹On the eighth day they had a closing ceremony, for they had celebrated the dedication of the altar for seven days and the Festival of Shelters for seven days. ¹⁰Then at the end of the celebration,* Solomon sent the people home. They were all joyful and glad because the Lord had been so good to David and to Solomon and to his people Israel.

THE LORD'S RESPONSE TO SOLOMON
¹¹So Solomon finished the Temple of the Lord, as well as the royal palace. He completed everything he had planned to do in the construction of the Temple and the palace. ¹²Then one night the Lord appeared to Solomon and said,

"I have heard your prayer and have chosen this Temple as the place for making sacrifices. ¹³At times I might shut up the heavens so that no rain falls, or command grasshoppers to devour your crops, or send plagues among you. ¹⁴Then if my people who are called by my name will humble

7:8 Hebrew *the festival* (also in 7:9); see note on 5:3. 7:10 Hebrew *Then on the twenty-third day of the seventh month.* This day of the ancient Hebrew lunar calendar occurred in October or early November.

STEPS TO FORGIVENESS
(7:12-22) In chapter 6, Solomon asked God to forgive his people when they messed up. God answered with three conditions for forgiveness: (1) Humble yourself by admitting what you did wrong, (2) ask God to forgive you, and (3) reject harmful habits. Owning up to a wrong is more than talk—it's changed behavior and a commitment to doing what's right. Are you committed?

IF MY PEOPLE...WILL HUMBLE THEMSELVES... AND TURN FROM THEIR WICKED WAYS, I WILL... FORGIVE THEIR SINS AND RESTORE THEIR LAND.

2 CHRONICLES 7:14

themselves and pray and seek my face and turn from their wicked ways, I will hear from heaven and will forgive their sins and restore their land. ¹⁵My eyes will be open and my ears attentive to every prayer made in this place. ¹⁶For I have chosen this Temple and set it apart to be holy—a place where my name will be honored forever. I will always watch over it, for it is dear to my heart.

¹⁷"As for you, if you faithfully follow me as David your father did, obeying all my commands, decrees, and regulations, ¹⁸then I will establish the throne of your dynasty. For I made this covenant with your father, David, when I said, 'One of your descendants will always rule over Israel.'

¹⁹"But if you or your descendants abandon me and disobey the decrees and commands I have given you, and if you serve and worship other gods, ²⁰then I will uproot the people from this land that I have given them. I will reject this Temple that I have made holy to honor my name. I will make it an object of mockery and ridicule among the nations. ²¹And though this Temple is impressive now, all who pass by will be appalled. They will ask, 'Why did the LORD do such terrible things to this land and to this Temple?'

²²"And the answer will be, 'Because his people abandoned the LORD, the God of their ancestors, who brought them out of Egypt, and they worshiped other gods instead and bowed down to them. That is why he has brought all these disasters on them.'"

8 **SOLOMON'S MANY ACHIEVEMENTS** It took Solomon twenty years to build the LORD's Temple and his own royal palace. At the end of that time, ²Solomon turned his attention to rebuilding the towns that King Hiram* had given him, and he settled Israelites in them. ³Solomon also fought against the town of Hamath-zobah and conquered it. ⁴He rebuilt Tadmor in the wilderness and built towns in

the region of Hamath as supply centers. ⁵He fortified the towns of Upper Beth-horon and Lower Beth-horon, rebuilding their walls and installing barred gates. ⁶He also rebuilt Baalath and other supply centers and constructed towns where his chariots and horses* could be stationed. He built everything he desired in Jerusalem and Lebanon and throughout his entire realm.

⁷There were still some people living in the land who were not Israelites, including the Hittites, Amorites, Perizzites, Hivites, and Jebusites. ⁸These were descendants of the nations whom the people of Israel had not destroyed. So Solomon conscripted them for his labor force, and they serve in the labor force to this day. ⁹But Solomon did not conscript any of the Israelites for his labor force. Instead, he assigned them to serve as fighting men, officers in his army, commanders of his chariots, and charioteers. ¹⁰King Solomon appointed 250 of them to supervise the people.

¹¹Solomon moved his wife, Pharaoh's daughter, from the City of David to the new palace he had built for her. He said, "My wife must not live in King David's palace, for the Ark of the LORD has been there, and it is holy ground."

¹²Then Solomon presented burnt offerings to the LORD on the altar he had built for him in front of the entry room of the Temple. ¹³He offered the sacrifices for the Sabbaths, the new moon festivals, and the three annual festivals—the Passover celebration, the Festival of Harvest,* and the Festival of Shelters—as Moses had commanded.

¹⁴In assigning the priests to their duties, Solomon followed the regulations of his father, David. He also assigned the Levites to lead the people in praise and to assist the priests in their daily duties. And he assigned the gatekeepers to their gates by their divisions, following the commands of David, the man of God. ¹⁵Solomon did not deviate in any way from David's commands concerning the priests and Levites and the treasuries. ¹⁶So Solomon made sure that all the work related to building the Temple of the LORD was carried out, from the day its foundation was laid to the day of its completion.

8:2 Hebrew *Huram,* a variant spelling of Hiram; also in 8:18.
8:6 Or *and charioteers.*   8:13 Or *Festival of Weeks.*

¹⁷Later Solomon went to Ezion-geber and Elath,* ports along the shore of the Red Sea* in the land of Edom. ¹⁸Hiram sent him ships commanded by his own officers and manned by experienced crews of sailors. These ships sailed to Ophir with Solomon's men and brought back to Solomon almost seventeen tons* of gold.

9 VISIT OF THE QUEEN OF SHEBA When the queen of Sheba heard of Solomon's fame, she came to Jerusalem to test him with hard questions. She arrived with a large group of attendants and a great caravan of camels loaded with spices, large quantities of gold, and precious jewels. When she met with Solomon, she talked with him about everything she had on her mind. ²Solomon had answers for all her questions; nothing was too hard for him to explain to her. ³When the queen of Sheba realized how wise Solomon was, and when she saw the palace he had built, ⁴she was overwhelmed. She was also amazed at the food on his tables, the organization of his officials and their splendid clothing, the cup-bearers and their robes, and the burnt offerings Solomon made at the Temple of the LORD.

⁵She exclaimed to the king, "Everything I heard in my country about your achievements* and wisdom is true! ⁶I didn't believe what was said until I arrived here and saw it with my own eyes. In fact, I had not heard the half of your great wisdom! It is far beyond what I was told. ⁷How happy your people must be! What a privilege for your officials to stand here day after day, listening to your wisdom! ⁸Praise the LORD your God, who delights in you and has placed you on the throne as king to rule for him. Because God loves Israel and desires this kingdom to last forever, he has made you king over them so you can rule with justice and righteousness."

⁹Then she gave the king a gift of 9,000 pounds* of gold, great quantities of spices, and precious jewels. Never before had there been spices as fine as those the queen of Sheba gave to King Solomon.

¹⁰(In addition, the crews of Hiram and Solomon brought gold from Ophir, and they also brought red sandalwood* and precious jewels. ¹¹The king used the sandalwood to make steps* for the Temple of the LORD and the royal palace, and to construct lyres and harps for the musicians. Never before had such beautiful things been seen in Judah.)

¹²King Solomon gave the queen of Sheba whatever she asked for—gifts of greater value than the gifts she had given him. Then she and all her attendants returned to their own land.

SOLOMON'S WEALTH AND SPLENDOR ¹³Each year Solomon received about 25 tons* of gold. ¹⁴This did not include the additional revenue he received from merchants and traders. All the kings of Arabia and the governors of the provinces also brought gold and silver to Solomon.

¹⁵King Solomon made 200 large shields of hammered gold, each weighing more than 15 pounds.* ¹⁶He also made 300 smaller shields of hammered gold, each weighing more than 7½ pounds.* The king placed these shields in the Palace of the Forest of Lebanon.

¹⁷Then the king made a huge throne, decorated with ivory and overlaid with pure gold. ¹⁸The throne had six steps, with a footstool of gold. There were armrests on both sides of the seat, and the figure of a lion stood on each side of the throne. ¹⁹There were also twelve other lions, one standing on each end of the six steps. No other throne in all the world could be compared with it!

²⁰All of King Solomon's drinking cups were solid gold, as were all the utensils in the Palace of the Forest of Lebanon. They were not made of silver, for silver was considered worthless in Solomon's day!

²¹The king had a fleet of trading ships* manned by the sailors sent by Hiram.* Once every three years the ships returned, loaded with gold, silver, ivory, apes, and peacocks.*

²²So King Solomon became richer and wiser than any other king on earth. ²³Kings from every nation came to consult him and to hear the wisdom God had given him. ²⁴Year after year everyone who visited brought him gifts of silver and gold, clothing, weapons, spices, horses, and mules.

THE GOD BEHIND IT ALL
(9:1-8) The queen of Sheba had heard about Solomon's wisdom, but she was overwhelmed when she saw for herself the proof of that wisdom. The queen could see the God behind Solomon's incredible wisdom and wealth. As people get to know you, do they catch a glimpse of the God behind you and in you? Your life is your most powerful witness.

8:17a As in Greek version (see also 2 Kgs 14:22; 16:6); Hebrew reads *Eloth*, a variant spelling of Elath. **8:17b** As in parallel text at 1 Kgs 9:26; Hebrew reads *the sea*. **8:18** Hebrew *450 talents* [15.3 metric tons]. **9:5** Hebrew *your words*. **9:9** Hebrew *120 talents* [4,000 kilograms]. **9:10** Hebrew *algum wood* (also in 9:11); perhaps a variant spelling of *almug*. Compare parallel text at 1 Kgs 10:11-12. **9:11** Or *gateways*. The meaning of the Hebrew is uncertain. **9:13** Hebrew *666 talents* [23 metric tons]. **9:15** Hebrew *600 [shekels] of hammered gold* [6.8 kilograms]. **9:16** Hebrew *300 [shekels] of gold* [3.4 kilograms]. **9:21a** Hebrew *fleet of ships that could sail to Tarshish*. **9:21b** Hebrew *Huram*, a variant spelling of Hiram. **9:21c** Or *and baboons*.

²⁵Solomon had 4,000 stalls for his horses and chariots, and he had 12,000 horses.* He stationed some of them in the chariot cities, and some near him in Jerusalem. ²⁶He ruled over all the kings from the Euphrates River* in the north to the land of the Philistines and the border of Egypt in the south. ²⁷The king made silver as plentiful in Jerusalem as stone. And valuable cedar timber was as common as the sycamore-fig trees that grow in the foothills of Judah.* ²⁸Solomon's horses were imported from Egypt* and many other countries.

SUMMARY OF SOLOMON'S REIGN ²⁹The rest of the events of Solomon's reign, from beginning to end, are recorded in *The Record of Nathan the Prophet,* and *The Prophecy of Ahijah from Shiloh,* and also in *The Visions of Iddo the Seer,* concerning Jeroboam son of Nebat. ³⁰Solomon ruled in Jerusalem over all Israel for forty years. ³¹When he died, he was buried in the City of David, named for his father. Then his son Rehoboam became the next king.

10 **THE NORTHERN TRIBES REVOLT** Rehoboam went to Shechem, where all Israel had gathered to make him king. ²When Jeroboam son of Nebat heard of this, he returned from Egypt, for he had fled to Egypt to escape from King Solomon. ³The leaders of Israel summoned him, and Jeroboam and all Israel went to speak with Rehoboam. ⁴"Your father was a hard master," they said. "Lighten the harsh labor demands and heavy taxes that your father imposed on us. Then we will be your loyal subjects."

⁵Rehoboam replied, "Come back in three days for my answer." So the people went away. ⁶Then King Rehoboam discussed the matter with the older men who had counseled his father, Solomon. "What is your advice?" he asked. "How should I answer these people?"

⁷The older counselors replied, "If you are good to these people and do your best to please them and give them a favorable answer, they will always be your loyal subjects."

⁸But Rehoboam rejected the advice of the older men and instead asked the opinion of the young men who had grown up with him and were now his advisers. ⁹"What is your advice?" he asked them. "How should I answer these

people who want me to lighten the burdens imposed by my father?"

¹⁰The young men replied, "This is what you should tell those complainers who want a lighter burden: 'My little finger is thicker than my father's waist! ¹¹Yes, my father laid heavy burdens on you, but I'm going to make them even heavier! My father beat you with whips, but I will beat you with scorpions!'"

¹²Three days later Jeroboam and all the people returned to hear Rehoboam's decision, just as the king had ordered. ¹³But Rehoboam spoke harshly to them, for he rejected the advice of the older counselors ¹⁴and followed the counsel of his younger advisers. He told the people, "My father laid* heavy burdens on you, but I'm going to make them even heavier! My father beat you with whips, but I will beat you with scorpions!"

¹⁵So the king paid no attention to the people. This turn of events was the will of God, for it fulfilled the Lᴏʀᴅ's message to Jeroboam son of Nebat through the prophet Ahijah from Shiloh.

¹⁶When all Israel realized* that the king had refused to listen to them, they responded,

"Down with the dynasty of David!
 We have no interest in the son of Jesse.
Back to your homes, O Israel!
 Look out for your own house, O David!"

So all the people of Israel returned home. ¹⁷But Rehoboam continued to rule over the Israelites who lived in the towns of Judah. ¹⁸King Rehoboam sent Adoniram,* who was

....

PEERS
(10:1-14) Following bad advice can lead to disaster. Rehoboam lost his chance to rule a peaceful, united kingdom because he rejected the advice of his father's older counselors, preferring the counsel of his peers. Rehoboam made two errors in seeking advice: (1) he did not give extra consideration to the suggestions of those who knew the situation better than he, and (2) he did not ask God for wisdom to discern which was better. Like Rehoboam, many live by the philosophy: If I can't trust my friends, who can I trust? Is that how you feel? But friends don't always see the big picture. The best advice often comes from people with the most experience. Are you willing to listen?

GREEDY
(10:16-19) In trying to have it all, Rehoboam lost almost everything. Motivated by greed and power, he pressed too hard and divided the kingdom. He didn't need more money or power because he had inherited the richest kingdom in the world. He didn't need more control because the land was at peace. His demands were based on selfishness rather than reason or spiritual discernment. Those who selfishly insist on having it all often wind up with little or nothing.

9:25 Or *12,000 charioteers.*   **9:26** Hebrew *the river.*   **9:27** Hebrew *the Shephelah.*   **9:28** Possibly *Muzur,* a district near Cilicia. **10:14** As in Greek version and many Hebrew manuscripts (see also 1 Kgs 12:14); Masoretic Text reads *I will lay.*   **10:16** As in Syriac version, Latin Vulgate, and many Hebrew manuscripts (see also 1 Kgs 12:16); Masoretic Text lacks *realized.*   **10:18** Hebrew *Hadoram,* a variant spelling of Adoniram; compare 1 Kgs 4:6; 5:14; 12:18.

in charge of the labor force, to restore order, but the people of Israel stoned him to death. When this news reached King Rehoboam, he quickly jumped into his chariot and fled to Jerusalem. [19]And to this day the northern tribes of Israel have refused to be ruled by a descendant of David.

11 SHEMAIAH'S PROPHECY When Rehoboam arrived at Jerusalem, he mobilized the men of Judah and Benjamin—180,000 select troops—to fight against Israel and to restore the kingdom to himself.

[2]But the LORD said to Shemaiah, the man of God, [3]"Say to Rehoboam son of Solomon, king of Judah, and to all the Israelites in Judah and Benjamin: [4]'This is what the LORD says: Do not fight against your relatives. Go back home, for what has happened is my doing!'" So they obeyed the message of the LORD and did not fight against Jeroboam.

REHOBOAM FORTIFIES JUDAH [5]Rehoboam remained in Jerusalem and fortified various towns for the defense of Judah. [6]He built up Bethlehem, Etam, Tekoa, [7]Beth-zur, Soco, Adullam, [8]Gath, Mareshah, Ziph, [9]Adoraim, Lachish, Azekah, [10]Zorah, Aijalon, and Hebron. These became the fortified towns of Judah and Benjamin. [11]Rehoboam strengthened their defenses and stationed commanders in them, and he stored supplies of food, olive oil, and wine. [12]He also put shields and spears in these towns as a further safety measure. So only Judah and Benjamin remained under his control.

[13]But all the priests and Levites living among the northern tribes of Israel sided with Rehoboam. [14]The Levites even abandoned their pasturelands and property and moved to Judah and Jerusalem, because Jeroboam and his sons would not allow them to serve the LORD as priests. [15]Jeroboam appointed his own priests to serve at the pagan shrines, where they worshiped the goat and calf idols he had made. [16]From all the tribes of Israel, those who sincerely wanted to worship the LORD, the God of Israel, followed the Levites to Jerusalem, where they could offer sacrifices to the LORD, the God of their ancestors. [17]This strengthened

the kingdom of Judah, and for three years they supported Rehoboam son of Solomon, for during those years they faithfully followed in the footsteps of David and Solomon.

REHOBOAM'S FAMILY [18]Rehoboam married his cousin Mahalath, the daughter of David's son Jerimoth and of Abihail, the daughter of Eliab son of Jesse. [19]Mahalath had three sons—Jeush, Shemariah, and Zaham. [20]Later Rehoboam married another cousin, Maacah, the daughter of Absalom. Maacah gave birth to Abijah, Attai, Ziza, and Shelomith. [21]Rehoboam loved Maacah more than any of his other wives and concubines. In all, he had eighteen wives and sixty concubines, and they gave birth to twenty-eight sons and sixty daughters.

[22]Rehoboam appointed Maacah's son Abijah as leader among the princes, making it clear that he would be the next king. [23]Rehoboam also wisely gave responsibilities to his other sons and stationed some of them in the fortified towns throughout the land of Judah and Benjamin. He provided them with generous provisions, and he found many wives for them.

12 EGYPT INVADES JUDAH But when Rehoboam was firmly established and strong, he abandoned the Law of the LORD, and all Israel followed him in this sin. [2]Because they were unfaithful to the LORD, King Shishak of Egypt came up and attacked Jerusalem in the fifth year of King Rehoboam's reign. [3]He came with 1,200 chariots, 60,000 horses,* and a countless army of foot soldiers, including Libyans, Sukkites, and Ethiopians.* [4]Shishak conquered Judah's fortified towns and then advanced to attack Jerusalem.

[5]The prophet Shemaiah then met with Rehoboam and Judah's leaders, who had all fled to Jerusalem because of Shishak. Shemaiah told them, "This is what the LORD says: You have abandoned me, so I am abandoning you to Shishak."

[6]Then the leaders of Israel and the king humbled themselves and said, "The LORD is right in doing this to us!"

[7]When the LORD saw their change of heart, he gave this message to Shemaiah: "Since the people have humbled themselves, I will not completely destroy them and will soon give them some relief. I will not use Shishak to pour out my anger on Jerusalem. [8]But they will become his subjects, so they will know the differ-

---

GOOD TIMES
(12:1) At the height of his popularity and power, Rehoboam started ignoring God. What happened? Often it is more difficult to be a believer in good times than in bad. Tough times push us toward God, but success can make us feel self-sufficient and self-satisfied. When everything is going right, how will you guard your faith?

12:3a Or *charioteers,* or *horsemen.*   12:3b Hebrew *and Cushites.*

ence between serving me and serving earthly rulers."

⁹So King Shishak of Egypt came up and attacked Jerusalem. He ransacked the treasuries of the LORD's Temple and the royal palace; he stole everything, including all the gold shields Solomon had made. ¹⁰King Rehoboam later replaced them with bronze shields as substitutes, and he entrusted them to the care of the commanders of the guard who protected the entrance to the royal palace. ¹¹Whenever the king went to the Temple of the LORD, the guards would also take the shields and then return them to the guardroom. ¹²Because Rehoboam humbled himself, the LORD's anger was turned away, and he did not destroy him completely. There were still some good things in the land of Judah.

SUMMARY OF REHOBOAM'S REIGN ¹³King
Rehoboam firmly established himself in Jerusalem and continued to rule. He was forty-one years old when he became king, and he reigned seventeen years in Jerusalem, the city the LORD had chosen from among all the tribes of Israel as the place to honor his name. Rehoboam's mother was Naamah, a woman from Ammon. ¹⁴But he was an evil king, for he did not seek the LORD with all his heart.

¹⁵The rest of the events of Rehoboam's reign, from beginning to end, are recorded in *The Record of Shemaiah the Prophet* and *The Record of Iddo the Seer,* which are part of the genealogical record. Rehoboam and Jeroboam were continually at war with each other. ¹⁶When Rehoboam died, he was buried in the City of David. Then his son Abijah became the next king.

13 **ABIJAH'S WAR WITH JEROBOAM** Abijah began to rule over Judah in the eighteenth year of Jeroboam's reign in Israel. ²He reigned in Jerusalem three years. His mother was Maacah,* the daughter of Uriel from Gibeah.

Then war broke out between Abijah and Jeroboam. ³Judah, led by King Abijah, fielded 400,000 select warriors, while Jeroboam mustered 800,000 select troops from Israel.

⁴When the army of Judah arrived in the hill country of Ephraim, Abijah stood on Mount Zemaraim and shouted to Jeroboam and all Israel: "Listen to me! ⁵Don't you realize that the LORD, the God of Israel, made a lasting

covenant* with David, giving him and his descendants the throne of Israel forever? ⁶Yet Jeroboam son of Nebat, a mere servant of David's son Solomon, rebelled against his master. ⁷Then a whole gang of scoundrels joined him, defying Solomon's son Rehoboam when he was young and inexperienced and could not stand up to them.

⁸"Do you really think you can stand against the kingdom of the LORD that is led by the descendants of David? You may have a vast army, and you have those gold calves that Jeroboam made as your gods. ⁹But you have chased away the priests of the LORD (the descendants of Aaron) and the Levites, and you have appointed your own priests, just like the pagan nations. You let anyone become a priest these days! Whoever comes to be dedicated with a young bull and seven rams can become a priest of these so-called gods of yours!

¹⁰"But as for us, the LORD is our God, and we have not abandoned him. Only the descendants of Aaron serve the LORD as priests, and the Levites alone may help them in their work. ¹¹They present burnt offerings and fragrant incense to the LORD every morning and evening. They place the Bread of the Presence on the holy table, and they light the gold lampstand every evening. We are following the instructions of the LORD our God, but you have abandoned him. ¹²So you see, God is with us. He is our leader. His priests blow their trumpets and lead us into battle against you. O people of Israel, do not fight against the LORD, the God of your ancestors, for you will not succeed!"

¹³Meanwhile, Jeroboam had secretly sent part of his army around behind the men of Judah to ambush them. ¹⁴When Judah realized that they were being attacked from the front and the rear, they cried out to the LORD for help. Then the priests blew the trumpets, ¹⁵and the men of Judah began to shout. At the sound of their battle cry, God defeated Jeroboam and all Israel and routed them before Abijah and the army of Judah.

¹⁶The Israelite army fled from Judah, and God handed them over to Judah in defeat. ¹⁷Abijah and his army inflicted heavy losses on them; 500,000 of Israel's select troops were killed that day. ¹⁸So Judah defeated Israel on that occasion because they trusted in the LORD, the God of their ancestors. ¹⁹Abijah and his army pursued Jeroboam's troops and captured some of his towns, including Bethel, Jeshanah, and Ephron, along with their surrounding villages.

²⁰So Jeroboam of Israel never regained his

13:2 As in most Greek manuscripts and Syriac version (see also 2 Chr 11:20-21; 1 Kgs 15:2); Hebrew reads *Micaiah,* a variant spelling of Maacah.   **13:5** Hebrew *a covenant of salt.*

power during Abijah's lifetime, and finally the LORD struck him down and he died. ²¹Meanwhile, Abijah of Judah grew more and more powerful. He married fourteen wives and had twenty-two sons and sixteen daughters.

²²The rest of the events of Abijah's reign, including his words and deeds, are recorded in *The Commentary of Iddo the Prophet.*

14 EARLY YEARS OF ASA'S REIGN ¹*When Abijah died, he was buried in the City of David. Then his son Asa became the next king. There was peace in the land for ten years. ²*Asa did what was pleasing and good in the sight of the LORD his God. ³He removed the foreign altars and the pagan shrines. He smashed the sacred pillars and cut down the Asherah poles. ⁴He commanded the people of Judah to seek the LORD, the God of their ancestors, and to obey his law and his commands. ⁵Asa also removed the pagan shrines, as well as the incense altars from every one of Judah's towns. So Asa's kingdom enjoyed a period of peace. ⁶During those peaceful years, he was able to build up the fortified towns throughout Judah. No one tried to make war against him at this time, for the LORD was giving him rest from his enemies.

⁷Asa told the people of Judah, "Let us build towns and fortify them with walls, towers, gates, and bars. The land is still ours because we sought the LORD our God, and he has given us peace on every side." So they went ahead with these projects and brought them to completion.

⁸King Asa had an army of 300,000 warriors from the tribe of Judah, armed with large shields and spears. He also had an army of 280,000 warriors from the tribe of Benjamin, armed with small shields and bows. Both armies were composed of well-trained fighting men.

⁹Once an Ethiopian* named Zerah attacked Judah with an army of 1,000,000 men* and 300 chariots. They advanced to the town of Mareshah, ¹⁰so Asa deployed his armies for battle in the valley north of Mareshah.* ¹¹Then Asa cried out to the LORD his God, "O LORD, no

one but you can help the powerless against the mighty! Help us, O LORD our God, for we trust in you alone. It is in your name that we have come against this vast horde. O LORD, you are our God; do not let mere men prevail against you!"

¹²So the LORD defeated the Ethiopians* in the presence of Asa and the army of Judah, and the enemy fled. ¹³Asa and his army pursued them as far as Gerar, and so many Ethiopians fell that they were unable to rally. They were destroyed by the LORD and his army, and the army of Judah carried off a vast amount of plunder.

¹⁴While they were at Gerar, they attacked all the towns in that area, and terror from the LORD came upon the people there. As a result, a vast amount of plunder was taken from these towns, too. ¹⁵They also attacked the camps of herdsmen and captured many sheep, goats, and camels before finally returning to Jerusalem.

15 ASA'S RELIGIOUS REFORMS Then the Spirit of God came upon Azariah son of Oded, ²and he went out to meet King Asa as he was returning from the battle. "Listen to me, Asa!" he shouted. "Listen, all you people of Judah and Benjamin! The LORD will stay with you as long as you stay with him! Whenever you seek him, you will find him. But if you abandon him, he will abandon you. ³For a long time Israel was without the true God, without a priest to teach them, and without the Law to instruct them. ⁴But whenever they were in trouble and turned to the LORD, the God of Israel, and sought him out, they found him.

⁵"During those dark times, it was not safe to travel. Problems troubled the people of every land. ⁶Nation fought against nation, and city against city, for God was troubling them with every kind of problem. ⁷But as for you, be strong and courageous, for your work will be rewarded."

⁸When Asa heard this message from Azariah the prophet,* he took courage and removed all the detestable idols from the land of Judah and Benjamin and in the towns he had captured in the hill country of Ephraim. And he repaired the altar of the LORD, which stood in front of the entry room of the LORD's Temple.

⁹Then Asa called together all the people of

BE PREPARED

(14:1-8) King Asa chose to build up Judah's defenses during a time of peace. Times of peace are not just for resting. They allow us to prepare for times of trouble. The same is true for temptation. The best decisions about what to do when temptations arise are made with a cool head, long before the heat of temptation is upon us. What are you doing now to build your defenses?

14:1 Verse 14:1 is numbered 13:23 in Hebrew text.   **14:2** Verses 14:2-15 are numbered 14:1-14 in Hebrew text.   **14:9a** Hebrew *a Cushite.*   **14:9b** Or *an army of thousands and thousands;* Hebrew reads *an army of a thousand thousands.*   **14:10** Or *in the Zephathah Valley near Mareshah.*   **14:12** Hebrew *Cushites;* also in 14:13.   **15:8** As in Syriac version and Latin Vulgate (see also 15:1); Hebrew reads *from Oded the prophet.*

Judah and Benjamin, along with the people of Ephraim, Manasseh, and Simeon who had settled among them. For many from Israel had moved to Judah during Asa's reign when they saw that the LORD his God was with him. [10]The people gathered at Jerusalem in late spring,* during the fifteenth year of Asa's reign.

[11]On that day they sacrificed to the LORD 700 cattle and 7,000 sheep and goats from the plunder they had taken in the battle. [12]Then they entered into a covenant to seek the LORD, the God of their ancestors, with all their heart and soul. [13]They agreed that anyone who refused to seek the LORD, the God of Israel, would be put to death—whether young or old, man or woman. [14]They shouted out their oath of loyalty to the LORD with trumpets blaring and rams' horns sounding. [15]All in Judah were happy about this covenant, for they had entered into it with all their heart. They earnestly sought after God, and they found him. And the LORD gave them rest from their enemies on every side.

[16]King Asa even deposed his grandmother* Maacah from her position as queen mother because she had made an obscene Asherah pole. He cut down her obscene pole, broke it up, and burned it in the Kidron Valley. [17]Although the pagan shrines were not removed from Israel, Asa's heart remained completely faithful throughout his life. [18]He brought into the Temple of God the silver and gold and the various items that he and his father had dedicated.

[19]So there was no more war until the thirty-fifth year of Asa's reign.

16 FINAL YEARS OF ASA'S REIGN In the thirty-sixth year of Asa's reign, King Baasha of Israel invaded Judah and fortified Ramah in order to prevent anyone from entering or leaving King Asa's territory in Judah.

[2]Asa responded by removing the silver and gold from the treasuries of the Temple of the LORD and the royal palace. He sent it to King Ben-hadad of Aram, who was ruling in Damascus, along with this message:

[3]"Let there be a treaty* between you and me like the one between your father and my father. See, I am sending you silver and gold. Break your treaty with King Baasha of Israel so that he will leave me alone."

> THE EYES OF THE LORD SEARCH THE WHOLE EARTH IN ORDER TO STRENGTHEN THOSE WHOSE HEARTS ARE FULLY COMMITTED TO HIM.
> (2 CHRONICLES 16:9)

[4]Ben-hadad agreed to King Asa's request and sent the commanders of his army to attack the towns of Israel. They conquered the towns of Ijon, Dan, Abel-beth-maacah,* and all the store cities in Naphtali. [5]As soon as Baasha of Israel heard what was happening, he abandoned his project of fortifying Ramah and stopped all work on it. [6]Then King Asa called out all the men of Judah to carry away the building stones and timbers that Baasha had been using to fortify Ramah. Asa used these materials to fortify the towns of Geba and Mizpah.

[7]At that time Hanani the seer came to King Asa and told him, "Because you have put your trust in the king of Aram instead of in the LORD your God, you missed your chance to destroy the army of the king of Aram. [8]Don't you remember what happened to the Ethiopians* and Libyans and their vast army, with all of their chariots and charioteers?* At that time you relied on the LORD, and he handed them over to you. [9]The eyes of the LORD search the whole earth in order to strengthen those whose hearts are fully committed to him. What a fool you have been! From now on you will be at war."

[10]Asa became so angry with Hanani for saying this that he threw him into prison and put him in stocks. At that time Asa also began to oppress some of his people.

SUMMARY OF ASA'S REIGN [11]The rest of the events of Asa's reign, from beginning to end, are recorded in *The Book of the Kings of Judah and Israel*. [12]In the thirty-ninth year of his reign, Asa developed a serious foot disease. Yet even with the severity of his disease, he did not seek

....

THE TRUTH
(16:1-10) Asa, the king of Judah, blew it when he chose to trust the king of Aram rather than God. So, God sent a prophet—Hanani—with a message of woe for Asa. But Asa threw the prophet in jail. Ever know someone who reacted angrily when told the truth about a wrong he or she committed? How well do you accept the truth when you hear it? Jesus once said that the truth, God's truth, can set a person free (see John 8:32). But it has to be accepted before it can do that.

15:10 Hebrew *in the third month*. This month of the ancient Hebrew lunar calendar usually occurs within the months of May and June. 15:16 Hebrew *his mother*. 16:3 As in Greek version; Hebrew reads *There is a treaty*. 16:4 As in parallel text at 1 Kgs 15:20; Hebrew reads *Abel-maim*, another name for Abel-beth-maacah. 16:8a Hebrew *Cushites*. 16:8b Or *and horsemen?*

the LORD's help but turned only to his physicians. ¹³So he died in the forty-first year of his reign. ¹⁴He was buried in the tomb he had carved out for himself in the City of David. He was laid on a bed perfumed with sweet spices and fragrant ointments, and the people built a huge funeral fire in his honor.

17 JEHOSHAPHAT RULES IN JUDAH Then Jehoshaphat, Asa's son, became the next king. He strengthened Judah to stand against any attack from Israel. ²He stationed troops in all the fortified towns of Judah, and he assigned additional garrisons to the land of Judah and to the towns of Ephraim that his father, Asa, had captured.

³The LORD was with Jehoshaphat because he followed the example of his father's early years* and did not worship the images of Baal. ⁴He sought his father's God and obeyed his commands instead of following the evil practices of the kingdom of Israel. ⁵So the LORD established Jehoshaphat's control over the kingdom of Judah. All the people of Judah brought gifts to Jehoshaphat, so he became very wealthy and highly esteemed. ⁶He was deeply committed to* the ways of the LORD. He removed the pagan shrines and Asherah poles from Judah.

⁷In the third year of his reign Jehoshaphat sent his officials to teach in all the towns of Judah. These officials included Ben-hail, Obadiah, Zechariah, Nethanel, and Micaiah. ⁸He sent Levites along with them, including Shemaiah, Nethaniah, Zebadiah, Asahel, Shemiramoth, Jehonathan, Adonijah, Tobijah, and Tob-adonijah. He also sent out the priests Elishama and Jehoram. ⁹They took copies of the Book of the Law of the LORD and traveled around through all the towns of Judah, teaching the people.

¹⁰Then the fear of the LORD fell over all the surrounding kingdoms so that none of them wanted to declare war on Jehoshaphat. ¹¹Some of the Philistines brought him gifts and silver

as tribute, and the Arabs brought 7,700 rams and 7,700 male goats.

¹²So Jehoshaphat became more and more powerful and built fortresses and storage cities throughout Judah. ¹³He stored numerous supplies in Judah's towns and stationed an army of seasoned troops at Jerusalem. ¹⁴His army was enrolled according to ancestral clans.

From Judah there were 300,000 troops organized in units of 1,000, under the command of Adnah. ¹⁵Next in command was Jehohanan, who commanded 280,000 troops. ¹⁶Next was Amasiah son of Zicri, who volunteered for the LORD's service, with 200,000 troops under his command.

¹⁷From Benjamin there were 200,000 troops equipped with bows and shields. They were under the command of Eliada, a veteran soldier. ¹⁸Next in command was Jehozabad, who commanded 180,000 armed men.

¹⁹These were the troops stationed in Jerusalem to serve the king, besides those Jehoshaphat stationed in the fortified towns throughout Judah.

18 JEHOSHAPHAT AND AHAB Jehoshaphat enjoyed great riches and high esteem, and he made an alliance with Ahab of Israel by having his son marry Ahab's daughter. ²A few years later he went to Samaria to visit Ahab, who prepared a great banquet for him and his officials. They butchered great numbers of sheep, goats, and cattle for the feast. Then Ahab enticed Jehoshaphat to join forces with him to recover Ramoth-gilead.

³"Will you go with me to Ramoth-gilead?" King Ahab of Israel asked King Jehoshaphat of Judah.

Jehoshaphat replied, "Why, of course! You and I are as one, and my troops are your troops. We will certainly join you in battle." ⁴Then Jehoshaphat added, "But first let's find out what the LORD says."

⁵So the king of Israel summoned the prophets, 400 of them, and asked them, "Should we go to war against Ramoth-gilead, or should I hold back?"

They all replied, "Yes, go right ahead! God will give the king victory."

⁶But Jehoshaphat asked, "Is there not also a prophet of the LORD here? We should ask him the same question."

⁷The king of Israel replied to Jehoshaphat, "There is one more man who could consult the

---

GOD'S UNSTOPPABLE WILL
(18:1-32) After Micaiah prophesied death for King Ahab (18:16, 27), Ahab disguised himself to fool the enemy. Although the disguise worked, it didn't fool God and stop the prophecy from coming to pass. A random Aramean arrow found an opening between the joints in his armor and killed him. God's will is always fulfilled despite the defenses people try to erect. God can use anything, even an error, to bring his will to pass. That means we can trust him to work his plans and keep his promises, no matter what.

17:3 Some Hebrew manuscripts read the example of his father, David.   17:6 Hebrew His heart was courageous in.

Lᴏʀᴅ for us, but I hate him. He never prophesies anything but trouble for me! His name is Micaiah son of Imlah."

Jehoshaphat replied, "That's not the way a king should talk! Let's hear what he has to say." ⁸So the king of Israel called one of his officials and said, "Quick! Bring Micaiah son of Imlah."

MICAIAH PROPHESIES AGAINST AHAB
⁹King Ahab of Israel and King Jehoshaphat of Judah, dressed in their royal robes, were sitting on thrones at the threshing floor near the gate of Samaria. All of Ahab's prophets were prophesying there in front of them. ¹⁰One of them, Zedekiah son of Kenaanah, made some iron horns and proclaimed, "This is what the Lᴏʀᴅ says: With these horns you will gore the Arameans to death!"

¹¹All the other prophets agreed. "Yes," they said, "go up to Ramoth-gilead and be victorious, for the Lᴏʀᴅ will give the king victory!"

¹²Meanwhile, the messenger who went to get Micaiah said to him, "Look, all the prophets are promising victory for the king. Be sure that you agree with them and promise success."

¹³But Micaiah replied, "As surely as the Lᴏʀᴅ lives, I will say only what my God says."

¹⁴When Micaiah arrived before the king, Ahab asked him, "Micaiah, should we go to war against Ramoth-gilead, or should I hold back?"

Micaiah replied sarcastically, "Yes, go up and be victorious, for you will have victory over them!"

¹⁵But the king replied sharply, "How many times must I demand that you speak only the truth to me when you speak for the Lᴏʀᴅ?"

¹⁶Then Micaiah told him, "In a vision I saw all Israel scattered on the mountains, like sheep without a shepherd. And the Lᴏʀᴅ said, 'Their master has been killed.* Send them home in peace.'"

¹⁷"Didn't I tell you?" the king of Israel exclaimed to Jehoshaphat. "He never prophesies anything but trouble for me."

¹⁸Then Micaiah continued, "Listen to what the Lᴏʀᴅ says! I saw the Lᴏʀᴅ sitting on his throne with all the armies of heaven around him, on his right and on his left. ¹⁹And the Lᴏʀᴅ said, 'Who can entice King Ahab of Israel to go into battle against Ramoth-gilead so he can be killed?'

"There were many suggestions, ²⁰and finally a spirit approached the Lᴏʀᴅ and said, 'I can do it!'

"'How will you do this?' the Lᴏʀᴅ asked.

²¹"And the spirit replied, 'I will go out and inspire all of Ahab's prophets to speak lies.'

"'You will succeed,' said the Lᴏʀᴅ. 'Go ahead and do it.'

²²"So you see, the Lᴏʀᴅ has put a lying spirit in the mouths of your prophets. For the Lᴏʀᴅ has pronounced your doom."

²³Then Zedekiah son of Kenaanah walked up to Micaiah and slapped him across the face. "Since when did the Spirit of the Lᴏʀᴅ leave me to speak to you?" he demanded.

²⁴And Micaiah replied, "You will find out soon enough when you are trying to hide in some secret room!"

²⁵"Arrest him!" the king of Israel ordered. "Take him back to Amon, the governor of the city, and to my son Joash. ²⁶Give them this order from the king: 'Put this man in prison, and feed him nothing but bread and water until I return safely from the battle!'"

²⁷But Micaiah replied, "If you return safely, it will mean that the Lᴏʀᴅ has not spoken through me!" Then he added to those standing around, "Everyone mark my words!"

THE DEATH OF AHAB
²⁸So King Ahab of Israel and King Jehoshaphat of Judah led their armies against Ramoth-gilead. ²⁹The king of Israel said to Jehoshaphat, "As we go into battle, I will disguise myself so no one will recognize me, but you wear your royal robes." So the king of Israel disguised himself, and they went into battle.

³⁰Meanwhile, the king of Aram had issued these orders to his chariot commanders: "Attack only the king of Israel! Don't bother with anyone else." ³¹So when the Aramean chariot commanders saw Jehoshaphat in his royal robes, they went after him. "There is the king of Israel!" they shouted. But Jehoshaphat called out, and the Lᴏʀᴅ saved him. God helped him by turning the attackers away from him. ³²As soon as the chariot commanders realized he was not the king of Israel, they stopped chasing him.

³³An Aramean soldier, however, randomly shot an arrow at the Israelite troops and hit the king of Israel between the joints of his armor. "Turn the horses* and get me out of here!" Ahab groaned to the driver of the chariot. "I'm badly wounded!"

³⁴The battle raged all that day, and the king of Israel propped himself up in his chariot facing the Arameans. In the evening, just as the sun was setting, he died.

18:16 Hebrew *These people have no master.* 18:33 Hebrew *Turn your hand.*

19 JEHOSHAPHAT APPOINTS JUDGES

When King Jehoshaphat of Judah arrived safely home in Jerusalem, ²Jehu son of Hanani the seer went out to meet him. "Why should you help the wicked and love those who hate the LORD?" he asked the king. "Because of what you have done, the LORD is very angry with you. ³Even so, there is some good in you, for you have removed the Asherah poles throughout the land, and you have committed yourself to seeking God."

⁴Jehoshaphat lived in Jerusalem, but he went out among the people, traveling from Beersheba to the hill country of Ephraim, encouraging the people to return to the LORD, the God of their ancestors. ⁵He appointed judges throughout the nation in all the fortified towns, ⁶and he said to them, "Always think carefully before pronouncing judgment. Remember that you do not judge to please people but to please the LORD. He will be with you when you render the verdict in each case. ⁷Fear the LORD and judge with integrity, for the LORD our God does not tolerate perverted justice, partiality, or the taking of bribes."

⁸In Jerusalem, Jehoshaphat appointed some of the Levites and priests and clan leaders in Israel to serve as judges for cases involving the LORD's regulations and for civil disputes. ⁹These were his instructions to them: "You must always act in the fear of the LORD, with faithfulness and an undivided heart. ¹⁰Whenever a case comes to you from fellow citizens in an outlying town, whether a murder case or some other violation of God's laws, commands, decrees, or regulations, you must warn

• •

INTEGRITY
(19:5-10) Jehoshaphat delegated some of his authority to a group of judges. His advice for the judges is helpful for all leaders: (1) Think carefully before you make a decision (19:6); (2) be fair (19:7); and (3) act with integrity (19:9). A person acts with integrity by depending on God. Have you taken that first step?

BATTLES
(20:1-15) When faced with an unstoppable enemy, Jehoshaphat turned to God. Through the prophet Jahaziel, God promised to fight for Judah. We may not fight an enemy army, but we daily battle temptation, pressure, and "mighty powers in this dark world, and against evil spirits in the heavenly places" (Eph 6:12). We must remember that, as believers, we have God's Spirit in us and that God promises to fight for us. How do we let God fight for us? (1) By realizing the battle is not ours but God's; (2) by recognizing human limitations and allowing God's strength and power to work through our fears and weaknesses; (3) by making sure our battle is for God and not just our own selfish desires; and (4) by asking God for help.

them not to sin against the LORD, so that he will not be angry with you and them. Do this and you will not be guilty.

¹¹"Amariah the high priest will have final say in all cases involving the LORD. Zebadiah son of Ishmael, a leader from the tribe of Judah, will have final say in all civil cases. The Levites will assist you in making sure that justice is served. Take courage as you fulfill your duties, and may the LORD be with those who do what is right."

20 WAR WITH SURROUNDING NATIONS

After this, the armies of the Moabites, Ammonites, and some of the Meunites* declared war on Jehoshaphat. ²Messengers came and told Jehoshaphat, "A vast army from Edom* is marching against you from beyond the Dead Sea.* They are already at Hazazon-tamar." (This was another name for En-gedi.)

³Jehoshaphat was terrified by this news and begged the LORD for guidance. He also ordered everyone in Judah to begin fasting. ⁴So people from all the towns of Judah came to Jerusalem to seek the LORD's help.

⁵Jehoshaphat stood before the community of Judah and Jerusalem in front of the new courtyard at the Temple of the LORD. ⁶He prayed, "O LORD, God of our ancestors, you alone are the God who is in heaven. You are ruler of all the kingdoms of the earth. You are powerful and mighty; no one can stand against you! ⁷O our God, did you not drive out those who lived in this land when your people Israel arrived? And did you not give this land forever to the descendants of your friend Abraham? ⁸Your people settled here and built this Temple to honor your name. ⁹They said, 'Whenever we are faced with any calamity such as war,* plague, or famine, we can come to stand in your presence before this Temple where your name is honored. We can cry out to you to save us, and you will hear us and rescue us.'

¹⁰"And now see what the armies of Ammon, Moab, and Mount Seir are doing. You would not let our ancestors invade those nations when Israel left Egypt, so they went around them and did not destroy them. ¹¹Now see how they reward us! For they have come to throw us out of your land, which you gave us as an inheritance. ¹²O our God, won't you stop them? We are powerless against this mighty army that is about to attack us. We do not know what to do, but we are looking to you for help."

¹³As all the men of Judah stood before the

20:1 As in some Greek manuscripts (see also 26:7); Hebrew repeats *Ammonites.* 20:2a As in one Hebrew manuscript; most Hebrew manuscripts and ancient versions read *Aram.* 20:2b Hebrew *the sea.* 20:9 Or *sword of judgment;* or *sword, judgment.*

LORD with their little ones, wives, and children, [14]the Spirit of the LORD came upon one of the men standing there. His name was Jahaziel son of Zechariah, son of Benaiah, son of Jeiel, son of Mattaniah, a Levite who was a descendant of Asaph.

[15]He said, "Listen, all you people of Judah and Jerusalem! Listen, King Jehoshaphat! This is what the LORD says: Do not be afraid! Don't be discouraged by this mighty army, for the battle is not yours, but God's. [16]Tomorrow, march out against them. You will find them coming up through the ascent of Ziz at the end of the valley that opens into the wilderness of Jeruel. [17]But you will not even need to fight. Take your positions; then stand still and watch the LORD's victory. He is with you, O people of Judah and Jerusalem. Do not be afraid or discouraged. Go out against them tomorrow, for the LORD is with you!"

[18]Then King Jehoshaphat bowed low with his face to the ground. And all the people of Judah and Jerusalem did the same, worshiping the LORD. [19]Then the Levites from the clans of Kohath and Korah stood to praise the LORD, the God of Israel, with a very loud shout.

[20]Early the next morning the army of Judah went out into the wilderness of Tekoa. On the way Jehoshaphat stopped and said, "Listen to me, all you people of Judah and Jerusalem! Believe in the LORD your God, and you will be able to stand firm. Believe in his prophets, and you will succeed."

20:25 As in some Hebrew manuscripts and Latin Vulgate; most Hebrew manuscripts read *corpses*.   20:26 Hebrew *valley of Beracah*.

[21]After consulting the people, the king appointed singers to walk ahead of the army, singing to the LORD and praising him for his holy splendor. This is what they sang:

"Give thanks to the LORD;
    his faithful love endures forever!"

[22]At the very moment they began to sing and give praise, the LORD caused the armies of Ammon, Moab, and Mount Seir to start fighting among themselves. [23]The armies of Moab and Ammon turned against their allies from Mount Seir and killed every one of them. After they had destroyed the army of Seir, they began attacking each other. [24]So when the army of Judah arrived at the lookout point in the wilderness, all they saw were dead bodies lying on the ground as far as they could see. Not a single one of the enemy had escaped.

[25]King Jehoshaphat and his men went out to gather the plunder. They found vast amounts of equipment, clothing,* and other valuables—more than they could carry. There was so much plunder that it took them three days just to collect it all! [26]On the fourth day they gathered in the Valley of Blessing,* which got its name that day because the people praised and thanked the LORD there. It is still called the Valley of Blessing today.

[27]Then all the men returned to Jerusalem, with Jehoshaphat leading them, overjoyed that the LORD had given them victory over their enemies. [28]They marched into Jerusalem to the music of harps, lyres, and trumpets, and they proceeded to the Temple of the LORD.

I WONDER...

Church seems boring and confusing sometimes. Are all of the songs, readings, and rituals necessary?

Worshiping God keeps us connected to him. In worship, we recognize God as the one who is in control and who has the power to change our circumstances and life (see 2 Chr 20:20-22).

Jehoshaphat discovered this fact very graphically as he sent the worshipers out with his army. As the worshipers were singing, God miraculously provided a victory!

Worship takes many forms. Most of the songs and readings come right from Scripture. If you concentrate on the meaning behind what is being sung or read, you will see that the words communicate very important facts about God.

Music helps us remember. When we sing a song

many times, we will memorize it more easily. You can probably sing every word of your favorite popular songs.

Another purpose of worship is to encourage us to grow in our faith. It can encourage us to go out to face a world of collapsed morals.

Worship is also the time for us to praise God for who he is and to thank him for all he has done. Being in church with our brothers and sisters in Christ is like a family reunion—worshiping together.

Ephesians 5:19 was written during a time when Christians were put in prison for their faith. It says that believers should always be "singing psalms and hymns and spiritual songs among yourselves, and making music to the Lord in your hearts." By doing what this verse talks about, believers were able to encourage each other as they reminded themselves of the faithfulness, goodness, and strength of God.

²⁹When all the surrounding kingdoms heard that the LORD himself had fought against the enemies of Israel, the fear of God came over them. ³⁰So Jehoshaphat's kingdom was at peace, for his God had given him rest on every side.

SUMMARY OF JEHOSHAPHAT'S REIGN ³¹So Jehoshaphat ruled over the land of Judah. He was thirty-five years old when he became king, and he reigned in Jerusalem twenty-five years. His mother was Azubah, the daughter of Shilhi.

³²Jehoshaphat was a good king, following the ways of his father, Asa. He did what was pleasing in the LORD's sight. ³³During his reign, however, he failed to remove all the pagan shrines, and the people never fully committed themselves to follow the God of their ancestors.

³⁴The rest of the events of Jehoshaphat's reign, from beginning to end, are recorded in The Record of Jehu Son of Hanani, which is included in The Book of the Kings of Israel.

³⁵Some time later King Jehoshaphat of Judah made an alliance with King Ahaziah of Israel, who was very wicked.* ³⁶Together they built a fleet of trading ships* at the port of Ezion-geber. ³⁷Then Eliezer son of Dodavahu from Mareshah prophesied against Jehoshaphat. He said, "Because you have allied yourself with King Ahaziah, the LORD will destroy your work." So the ships met with disaster and never put out to sea.*

21 **JEHORAM RULES IN JUDAH** When Jehoshaphat died, he was buried with his ancestors in the City of David. Then his son Jehoram became the next king.

²Jehoram's brothers—the other sons of Jehoshaphat—were Azariah, Jehiel, Zechariah, Azariahu, Michael, and Shephatiah; all these

20:35 Or who made him do what was wicked. **20:36** Hebrew fleet of ships that could go to Tarshish. **20:37** Hebrew never set sail for Tarshish.

JEHOSHAPHAT PERSONALITY PROFILE

WHAT DO YOU THINK: Do children usually learn from their parents' mistakes or just repeat them? Are you a product of your environment? Some would argue that they are. "Hey, I grew up in the projects, man. I can't help it." Or, "I'm from a dysfunctional family."

Jehoshaphat's life illustrates the power of a person's environment. His father, Asa, had served God for a while during his time as king of Judah, but he eventually forgot about God. Jehoshaphat didn't seem to want to make the same mistake.

To avoid idolatry, Jehoshaphat "followed the example of his father's early years and did not worship the images of Baal" (2 Chr 17:3). He even went so far as to destroy the pagan shrines and Asherah poles from the land (2 Chr 17:6). The presence of these idols tempted people to worship them, so Jehoshaphat destroyed them. He changed his environment.

Jehoshaphat did this and many other good things. But he made some mistakes too. He made an alliance with the evil king Ahab and married Ahab's daughter, Athaliah. As a result, their son Jehoram was influenced by Ahab and Jezebel. They turned Jehoram and his son Ahaziah toward idolatry. The whole nation of Judah followed their example. Because of these things, the environment of idolatry took hold once again.

Jehoshaphat's story and those of other kings of Israel and Judah are examples of the need for God's help to rise above one's environment. We can only fall back on that excuse for so long. Sooner or later, a bigger life change is needed. To what degree have you allowed God to make that kind of life change in you?

BOTTOM LINE: God is pleased when his people are consistent in their relationship with him.

Jehoshaphat's story is told in 1 Kings 15:24; 22; and 2 Chronicles 17:1–21:1. He also is mentioned in 2 Kings 3:1-14 and Joel 3:2, 12.

UPS:
- A bold follower of God, he reminded the people of the early years with his father, Asa
- Carried out a national program of religious education
- Had many military victories
- Developed an extensive legal structure throughout the kingdom

DOWNS:
- Failed to recognize the long-term results of his decisions
- Did not completely destroy idols and idol worship in the land
- Became entangled with evil King Ahab through alliances
- Became Ahaziah's business partner in a disastrous shipping venture

STATS:
- Where: Jerusalem
- Occupation: King of Judah
- Relatives: Asa (father); Azubah (mother); Jehoram (son); Athaliah (daughter-in-law)
- Contemporaries: Ahab, Jezebel, Micaiah, Ahaziah, Jehu

KEY VERSES: 2 Chronicles 20:32-33

were the sons of Jehoshaphat king of Judah.* ³Their father had given each of them valuable gifts of silver, gold, and costly items, and also some of Judah's fortified towns. However, he designated Jehoram as the next king because he was the oldest. ⁴But when Jehoram had become solidly established as king, he killed all his brothers and some of the other leaders of Judah.

⁵Jehoram was thirty-two years old when he became king, and he reigned in Jerusalem eight years. ⁶But Jehoram followed the example of the kings of Israel and was as wicked as King Ahab, for he had married one of Ahab's daughters. So Jehoram did what was evil in the LORD's sight. ⁷But the LORD did not want to destroy David's dynasty, for he had made a covenant with David and promised that his descendants would continue to rule, shining like a lamp forever.

⁸During Jehoram's reign, the Edomites revolted against Judah and crowned their own king. ⁹So Jehoram went out with his full army and all his chariots. The Edomites surrounded him and his chariot commanders, but he went out at night and attacked them* under cover of darkness. ¹⁰Even so, Edom has been independent from Judah to this day. The town of Libnah also revolted about that same time. All this happened because Jehoram had abandoned the LORD, the God of his ancestors. ¹¹He had built pagan shrines in the hill country of Judah and had led the people of Jerusalem and Judah to give themselves to pagan gods and to go astray.

¹²Then Elijah the prophet wrote Jehoram this letter:

"This is what the LORD, the God of your ancestor David, says: You have not followed the good example of your father, Jehoshaphat, or your grandfather King Asa of Judah. ¹³Instead, you have been as evil as the kings of Israel. You have led the people of Jerusalem and Judah to worship idols, just as King Ahab did in Israel. And you have even killed your own brothers, men who were better than you. ¹⁴So now the LORD is about to strike you, your people, your children, your wives, and all that is yours with a heavy blow. ¹⁵You yourself will suffer with a severe intestinal disease that will get worse each day until your bowels come out."

¹⁶Then the LORD stirred up the Philistines and the Arabs, who lived near the Ethiopians,* to attack Jehoram. ¹⁷They marched against Judah, broke down its defenses, and carried away everything of value in the royal palace, including the king's sons and his wives. Only his youngest son, Ahaziah,* was spared.

¹⁸After all this, the LORD struck Jehoram with the severe intestinal disease. ¹⁹The disease grew worse and worse, and at the end of two years it caused his bowels to come out, and he died in agony. His people did not build a great funeral fire to honor him as they had done for his ancestors.

²⁰Jehoram was thirty-two years old when he became king, and he reigned in Jerusalem eight years. No one was sorry when he died. They buried him in the City of David, but not in the royal cemetery.

22 AHAZIAH RULES IN JUDAH Then the people of Jerusalem made Ahaziah, Jehoram's youngest son, their next king, since the marauding bands who came with the Arabs* had killed all the older sons. So Ahaziah son of Jehoram reigned as king of Judah.

²Ahaziah was twenty-two* years old when he became king, and he reigned in Jerusalem one year. His mother was Athaliah, a granddaughter of King Omri. ³Ahaziah also followed the evil example of King Ahab's family, for his mother encouraged him in doing wrong. ⁴He did what was evil in the LORD's sight, just as Ahab's family had done. They even became his advisers after the death of his father, and they led him to ruin.

••

NOT INDIFFERENT
(21:6-11) Jehoram "abandoned the LORD, the God of his ancestors." He married a woman who worshiped idols; he killed his six brothers; he allowed and even promoted idol worship. Yet he wasn't killed in battle or by treachery; instead, he died by a lingering and painful disease (21:18-19). Worried that someone will get away with something he or she did wrong just as Jehoram seemed to? Sometimes God waits for just the right time to allow a person to reap the consequences of his or her actions (see also Ps 37:1-2, 12-13).

GOOD ADVICE
(22:4-5) Like Rehoboam before him (see 10:1-14), Ahaziah chose to listen to bad advice and paid for it with his life. A person who seeks advice needs to consider the source, then carefully weigh what is said. Looking for advice? You can use God's Word to "test everything that is said. Hold on to what is good" (1 Thes 5:21).

21:2 Masoretic Text reads *of Israel;* also in 21:4. The author of Chronicles sees Judah as representative of the true Israel. (Some Hebrew manuscripts, Greek and Syriac versions, and Latin Vulgate read *of Judah.*) 21:9 Or *he went out and escaped.* The meaning of the Hebrew is uncertain. 21:16 Hebrew *the Cushites.* 21:17 Hebrew *Jehoahaz,* a variant spelling of Ahaziah; compare 22:1. 22:1 Or *marauding bands of Arabs.* 22:2 As in some Greek manuscripts and Syriac version (see also 2 Kgs 8:26); Hebrew reads *forty-two.*

⁵Following their evil advice, Ahaziah joined King Joram,* the son of King Ahab of Israel, in his war against King Hazael of Aram at Ramoth-gilead. When the Arameans wounded Joram in the battle, ⁶he returned to Jezreel to recover from the wounds he had received at Ramoth.* Because Joram was wounded, King Ahaziah* of Judah went to Jezreel to visit him.

⁷But God had decided that this visit would be Ahaziah's downfall. While he was there, Ahaziah went out with Joram to meet Jehu grandson of Nimshi,* whom the LORD had appointed to destroy the dynasty of Ahab.

⁸While Jehu was executing judgment against the family of Ahab, he happened to meet some of Judah's officials and Ahaziah's relatives* who were traveling with Ahaziah. So Jehu killed them all. ⁹Then Jehu's men searched for Ahaziah, and they found him hiding in the city of Samaria. They brought him to Jehu, who killed him. Ahaziah was given a decent burial because the people said, "He was the grandson of Jehoshaphat—a man who sought the LORD with all his heart." But none of the surviving members of Ahaziah's family was capable of ruling the kingdom.

QUEEN ATHALIAH RULES IN JUDAH ¹⁰When Athaliah, the mother of King Ahaziah of Judah, learned that her son was dead, she began to destroy the rest of Judah's royal family. ¹¹But Ahaziah's sister Jehosheba,* the daughter of King Jehoram, took Ahaziah's infant son, Joash, and stole him away from among the rest of the king's children, who were about to be killed. She put Joash and his nurse in a bedroom. In this way, Jehosheba, wife of Jehoiada the priest and sister of Ahaziah, hid the child so that Athaliah could not murder him. ¹²Joash remained hidden in the Temple of God for six years while Athaliah ruled over the land.

23 **REVOLT AGAINST ATHALIAH** In the seventh year of Athaliah's reign, Jehoiada the priest decided to act. He summoned his courage and made a pact with five army commanders: Azariah son of Jeroham, Ish-

22:5 Hebrew *Jehoram,* a variant spelling of Joram; also in 22:6, 7. **22:6a** Hebrew *Ramah,* a variant spelling of Ramoth. **22:6b** As in some Hebrew manuscripts, Greek and Syriac versions, and Latin Vulgate (see also 2 Kgs 8:29); most Hebrew manuscripts read *Azariah.* **22:7** Hebrew *descendant of Nimshi;* compare 2 Kgs 9:2, 14. **22:8** As in Greek version (see also 2 Kgs 10:13); Hebrew reads *and sons of the brothers of Ahaziah.* **22:11** As in parallel text at 2 Kgs 11:2; Hebrew lacks *Ahaziah's sister* and reads *Jehoshabeath* [a variant spelling of Jehosheba].

JOASH *PERSONALITY PROFILE*

EVER KNOW SOMEONE who seemed to have had it rough all of his or her life? Maybe you feel that life couldn't be more unfair.

Joash could've felt like that. Although he was a prince, his life was hardly easy. After his father (Ahaziah) was killed, his grandmother tried to kill Joash so that *she* could rule the kingdom. But an aunt and uncle (Jehosheba and Jehoiada) protected and raised him.

When Joash became king at age seven, his uncle Jehoiada made most of the decisions for him. Jehoiada was a good man, but he never taught Joash how to be a good king. After Jehoiada died, it only took Joash a short time to make a mess of his life and his kingdom. Joash had depended on Jehoiada, but he never really learned to depend on Jehoiada's God.

Like many children, Joash's knowledge of God was secondhand. He worshiped his uncle's God instead of having his own relationship with God. Is God your parents' God or yours as well? Your view of life is usually affected by your view of God. Make sure you know him.

BOTTOM LINE: A good and hopeful beginning can be ruined by an evil ending. Even the best counsel is ineffective if it doesn't help us make wise decisions.

All of us are responsible for what we do.

Joash's story is told in 2 Kings 11:1–12:21 and 2 Chronicles 22:11–24:27.

UPS:
• *Carried out extensive repairs on the Temple*
• *Was faithful to God as long as Jehoiada, a priest, lived*

DOWNS:
• *Allowed his people to continue worshiping idols*
• *Used the Temple treasures to bribe King Hazael of Syria*
• *Killed Jehoiada's son, Zechariah*
• *Allowed his advisers to lead the people away from God*

STATS:
• *Where: Jerusalem*
• *Occupation: King of Judah*
• *Relatives: Ahaziah (father); Zibiah (mother); Athaliah (grandmother); Jehosheba (aunt); Jehoiada (uncle); Amaziah (son); Zechariah (cousin)*
• *Contemporaries: Jehu, Hazael*

KEY VERSES: *2 Chronicles 24:17-18*

mael son of Jehohanan, Azariah son of Obed, Maaseiah son of Adaiah, and Elishaphat son of Zicri. ²These men traveled secretly throughout Judah and summoned the Levites and clan leaders in all the towns to come to Jerusalem. ³They all gathered at the Temple of God, where they made a solemn pact with Joash, the young king.

Jehoiada said to them, "Here is the king's son! The time has come for him to reign! The LORD has promised that a descendant of David will be our king. ⁴This is what you must do. When you priests and Levites come on duty on the Sabbath, a third of you will serve as gatekeepers. ⁵Another third will go over to the royal palace, and the final third will be at the Foundation Gate. Everyone else should stay in the courtyards of the LORD's Temple. ⁶Remember, only the priests and Levites on duty may enter the Temple of the LORD, for they are set apart as holy. The rest of the people must obey the LORD's instructions and stay outside. ⁷You Levites, form a bodyguard around the king and keep your weapons in hand. Kill anyone who tries to enter the Temple. Stay with the king wherever he goes."

⁸So the Levites and all the people of Judah did everything as Jehoiada the priest ordered. The commanders took charge of the men reporting for duty that Sabbath, as well as those who were going off duty. Jehoiada the priest did not let anyone go home after their shift ended. ⁹Then Jehoiada supplied the commanders with the spears and the large and small shields that had once belonged to King David and were stored in the Temple of God. ¹⁰He stationed all the people around the king, with their weapons ready. They formed a line from the south side of the Temple around to the north side and all around the altar.

¹¹Then Jehoiada and his sons brought out Joash, the king's son, placed the crown on his head, and presented him with a copy of God's laws.* They anointed him and proclaimed him king, and everyone shouted, "Long live the king!"

THE DEATH OF ATHALIAH
¹²When Athaliah heard the noise of the people running and the shouts of praise to the king, she hurried to the LORD's Temple to see what was happening. ¹³When she arrived, she saw the newly crowned king standing in his place of authority by the pillar at the Temple entrance. The com-

manders and trumpeters were surrounding him, and people from all over the land were rejoicing and blowing trumpets. Singers with musical instruments were leading the people in a great celebration. When Athaliah saw all this, she tore her clothes in despair and shouted, "Treason! Treason!"

¹⁴Then Jehoiada the priest ordered the commanders who were in charge of the troops, "Take her to the soldiers in front of the Temple,* and kill anyone who tries to rescue her." For the priest had said, "She must not be killed in the Temple of the LORD." ¹⁵So they seized her and led her out to the entrance of the Horse Gate on the palace grounds, and they killed her there.

JEHOIADA'S RELIGIOUS REFORMS
¹⁶Then Jehoiada made a covenant between himself and the king and the people that they would be the LORD's people. ¹⁷And all the people went over to the temple of Baal and tore it down. They demolished the altars and smashed the idols, and they killed Mattan the priest of Baal in front of the altars.

¹⁸Jehoiada now put the priests and Levites in charge of the Temple of the LORD, following all the directions given by David. He also commanded them to present burnt offerings to the LORD, as prescribed by the Law of Moses, and to sing and rejoice as David had instructed. ¹⁹He also stationed gatekeepers at the gates of the LORD's Temple to keep out those who for any reason were ceremonially unclean.

²⁰Then the commanders, nobles, rulers, and all the people of the land escorted the king from the Temple of the LORD. They went through the upper gate and into the palace, and they seated the king on the royal throne. ²¹So all the people of the land rejoiced, and the city was peaceful because Athaliah had been killed.

24 JOASH REPAIRS THE TEMPLE Joash was seven years old when he became king, and he reigned in Jerusalem forty years. His mother was Zibiah from Beersheba. ²Joash did what was pleasing in the LORD's sight throughout the lifetime of Jehoiada the priest.

23:11 Or a copy of the covenant. 23:14 Or Bring her out from between the ranks; or Take her out of the Temple precincts. The meaning of the Hebrew is uncertain.

TAKE A STAND
(23:1-11) Although the act could have cost him his life, Jehoiada gathered up his courage and did what was right, restoring Temple worship and anointing the new king. At times we must correct a wrong or speak out for what is right. When such a situation arises, what will you do?

³Jehoiada chose two wives for Joash, and he had sons and daughters.

⁴At one point Joash decided to repair and restore the Temple of the LORD. ⁵He summoned the priests and Levites and gave them these instructions: "Go to all the towns of Judah and collect the required annual offerings, so that we can repair the Temple of your God. Do not delay!" But the Levites did not act immediately.

⁶So the king called for Jehoiada the high priest and asked him, "Why haven't you demanded that the Levites go out and collect the Temple taxes from the towns of Judah and from Jerusalem? Moses, the servant of the LORD, levied this tax on the community of Israel in order to maintain the Tabernacle of the Covenant.*"

⁷Over the years the followers of wicked Athaliah had broken into the Temple of God, and they had used all the dedicated things from the Temple of the LORD to worship the images of Baal.

⁸So now the king ordered a chest to be made and set outside the gate leading to the Temple of the LORD. ⁹Then a proclamation was sent throughout Judah and Jerusalem, telling the people to bring to the LORD the tax that Moses, the servant of God, had required of the Israelites in the wilderness. ¹⁰This pleased all the leaders and the people, and they gladly brought their money and filled the chest with it.

¹¹Whenever the chest became full, the Levites would carry it to the king's officials. Then the court secretary and an officer of the high priest would come and empty the chest and take it back to the Temple again. This went on day after day, and a large amount of money was collected. ¹²The king and Jehoiada gave the money to the construction supervisors, who hired masons and carpenters to restore the Temple of the LORD. They also hired metalworkers, who made articles of iron and bronze for the LORD's Temple.

¹³The men in charge of the renovation worked hard and made steady progress. They restored the Temple of God according to its original design and strengthened it. ¹⁴When all the repairs were finished, they brought the remaining money to the king and Jehoiada. It was used to make various articles for the Temple of the LORD—articles for worship services and for burnt offerings, including ladles and other articles made of gold and silver. And the burnt offerings were sacrificed continually in the Temple of the LORD during the lifetime of Jehoiada the priest.

¹⁵Jehoiada lived to a very old age, finally dying at 130. ¹⁶He was buried among the kings in the City of David, because he had done so much good in Israel for God and his Temple.

JEHOIADA'S REFORMS REVERSED ¹⁷But after Jehoiada's death, the leaders of Judah came and bowed before King Joash and persuaded him to listen to their advice. ¹⁸They decided to abandon the Temple of the LORD, the God of their ancestors, and they worshiped Asherah poles and idols instead! Because of this sin, divine anger fell on Judah and Jerusalem. ¹⁹Yet the LORD sent prophets to bring them back to him. The prophets warned them, but still the people would not listen.

²⁰Then the Spirit of God came upon Zechariah son of Jehoiada the priest. He stood before the people and said, "This is what God says: Why do you disobey the LORD's commands and keep yourselves from prospering? You have abandoned the LORD, and now he has abandoned you!"

²¹Then the leaders plotted to kill Zechariah, and King Joash ordered that they stone him to death in the courtyard of the LORD's Temple. ²²That was how King Joash repaid Jehoiada for his loyalty—by killing his son. Zechariah's last words as he died were, "May the LORD see what they are doing and avenge my death!"

THE END OF JOASH'S REIGN ²³In the spring of the year* the Aramean army marched against Joash. They invaded Judah and Jerusalem and killed all the leaders of the nation. Then they sent all the plunder back to their king in Damascus. ²⁴Although the Arameans attacked with only a small army, the LORD helped them conquer the much larger army of Judah. The people of Judah had abandoned the LORD, the God of their ancestors, so judgment was carried out against Joash.

²⁵The Arameans withdrew, leaving Joash severely wounded. But his own officials plotted to kill him for murdering the son* of Jehoiada

....

PROSPERITY
(24:17-18) *If everything went so well in Judah when the people worshiped God, why did they turn away from him? Prosperity is both a blessing and a curse. While it can be a sign of God's blessing to those who follow him, it carries with it the potential for moral and spiritual decline. Rich people are tempted to become self-sufficient and proud—to take God for granted. In times of prosperity, we must not lose sight of the fact that God is the source of our blessings.*

24:6 Hebrew *Tent of the Testimony.*   24:23 Hebrew *At the turn of the year.* The first day of the year in the ancient Hebrew lunar calendar occurred in March or April.   24:25 As in Greek version and Latin Vulgate; Hebrew reads *sons.*

the priest. They assassinated him as he lay in bed. Then he was buried in the City of David, but not in the royal cemetery. ²⁶The assassins were Jozacar,* the son of an Ammonite woman named Shimeath, and Jehozabad, the son of a Moabite woman named Shomer.*

²⁷The account of the sons of Joash, the prophecies about him, and the record of his restoration of the Temple of God are written in *The Commentary on the Book of the Kings*. His son Amaziah became the next king.

25 **AMAZIAH RULES IN JUDAH** Amaziah was twenty-five years old when he became king, and he reigned in Jerusalem twenty-nine years. His mother was Jehoaddin* from Jerusalem. ²Amaziah did what was pleasing in the LORD's sight, but not wholeheartedly.

³When Amaziah was well established as king, he executed the officials who had assassinated his father. ⁴However, he did not kill the children of the assassins, for he obeyed the command of the LORD as written by Moses in the Book of the Law: "Parents must not be put to death for the sins of their children, nor children for the sins of their parents. Those deserving to die must be put to death for their own crimes."*

⁵Then Amaziah organized the army, assigning generals and captains* for all Judah and Benjamin. He took a census and found that he had an army of 300,000 select troops, twenty years old and older, all trained in the use of spear and shield. ⁶He also paid about 7,500 pounds* of silver to hire 100,000 experienced fighting men from Israel.

⁷But a man of God came to him and said, "Your Majesty, do not hire troops from Israel, for the LORD is not with Israel. He will not help those people of Ephraim! ⁸If you let them go with your troops into battle, you will be defeated by the enemy no matter how well you fight. God will overthrow you, for he has the power to help you or to trip you up."

⁹Amaziah asked the man of God, "But what about all that silver I paid to hire the army of Israel?"

The man of God replied, "The LORD is able to give you much more than this!" ¹⁰So Amaziah discharged the hired troops and sent them

back to Ephraim. This made them very angry with Judah, and they returned home in a great rage.

¹¹Then Amaziah summoned his courage and led his army to the Valley of Salt, where they killed 10,000 Edomite troops from Seir. ¹²They captured another 10,000 and took them to the top of a cliff and threw them off, dashing them to pieces on the rocks below.

¹³Meanwhile, the hired troops that Amaziah had sent home raided several of the towns of Judah between Samaria and Beth-horon. They killed 3,000 people and carried off great quantities of plunder.

¹⁴When King Amaziah returned from slaughtering the Edomites, he brought with him idols taken from the people of Seir. He set them up as his own gods, bowed down in front of them, and offered sacrifices to them! ¹⁵This made the LORD very angry, and he sent a prophet to ask, "Why do you turn to gods who could not even save their own people from you?"

¹⁶But the king interrupted him and said, "Since when have I made you the king's counselor? Be quiet now before I have you killed!"

So the prophet stopped with this warning: "I know that God has determined to destroy you because you have done this and have refused to accept my counsel."

¹⁷After consulting with his advisers, King Amaziah of Judah sent this challenge to Israel's king Jehoash,* the son of Jehoahaz and grandson of Jehu: "Come and meet me in battle!"*

¹⁸But King Jehoash of Israel replied to King Amaziah of Judah with this story: "Out in the Lebanon mountains, a thistle sent a message to a mighty cedar tree: 'Give your daughter in marriage to my son.' But just then a wild animal of Lebanon came by and stepped on the thistle, crushing it!

¹⁹"You are saying, 'I have defeated Edom,'

24:26a As in parallel text at 2 Kgs 12:21; Hebrew reads *Zabad*. 24:26b As in parallel text at 2 Kgs 12:21; Hebrew reads *Shimrith*, a variant spelling of Shomer.   25:1 As in parallel text at 2 Kgs 14:2; Hebrew reads *Jehoaddan*, a variant spelling of Jehoaddin.   25:4 Deut 24:16.   25:5 Hebrew *commanders of thousands and commanders of hundreds*.   25:6 Hebrew *100 talents* [3,400 kilograms].   25:17a Hebrew *Joash*, a variant spelling of Jehoash; also in 25:18, 21, 23, 25.   25:17b Hebrew *Come, let us look one another in the face*.

....

A COSTLY DECISION
(25:5-10) Amaziah made a financial agreement with mercenaries, offering to pay them to fight for him (25:6). But before they could go to battle, Amaziah received the prophet's warning. Although sending the soldiers home with pay cost him plenty, Amaziah wisely realized that the money was not worth the ruin the alliance could cause. Sometimes we pay a price in order to do what's right. What would you have chosen to do?

WATCH OUT
(25:14) After the victory, Amaziah returned and burned incense to idols. We are very susceptible to sin after great victories. That's when we feel confident and prideful. We lower our defenses, and Satan attacks with all sorts of temptations. When you win, watch out. After mountain peaks come the valleys.

and you are very proud of it. But my advice is to stay at home. Why stir up trouble that will only bring disaster on you and the people of Judah?"

²⁰But Amaziah refused to listen, for God was determined to destroy him for turning to the gods of Edom. ²¹So King Jehoash of Israel mobilized his army against King Amaziah of Judah. The two armies drew up their battle lines at Beth-shemesh in Judah. ²²Judah was routed by the army of Israel, and its army scattered and fled for home. ²³King Jehoash of Israel captured Judah's king, Amaziah son of Joash and grandson of Ahaziah, at Beth-shemesh. Then he brought him to Jerusalem, where he demolished 600 feet* of Jerusalem's wall, from the Ephraim Gate to the Corner Gate. ²⁴He carried off all the gold and silver and all the articles from the Temple of God that had been in the care of Obed-edom. He also seized the treasures of the royal palace, along with hostages, and then returned to Samaria.

²⁵King Amaziah of Judah lived on for fifteen years after the death of King Jehoash of Israel. ²⁶The rest of the events in Amaziah's reign, from beginning to end, are recorded in *The Book of the Kings of Judah and Israel.*

²⁷After Amaziah turned away from the LORD, there was a conspiracy against his life in Jerusalem, and he fled to Lachish. But his enemies sent assassins after him, and they killed him there. ²⁸They brought his body back on a horse, and he was buried with his ancestors in the City of David.*

26 UZZIAH RULES IN JUDAH

All the people of Judah had crowned Amaziah's sixteen-year-old son, Uzziah, as king in place of his father. ²After his father's death, Uzziah rebuilt the town of Elath* and restored it to Judah.

³Uzziah was sixteen years old when he became king, and he reigned in Jerusalem fifty-two years. His mother was Jecoliah from Jerusalem. ⁴He did what was pleasing in the LORD's sight, just as his father, Amaziah, had done. ⁵Uzziah sought God during the days of Zechariah, who taught him to fear God.* And

as long as the king sought guidance from the LORD, God gave him success.

⁶Uzziah declared war on the Philistines and broke down the walls of Gath, Jabneh, and Ashdod. Then he built new towns in the Ashdod area and in other parts of Philistia. ⁷God helped him in his wars against the Philistines, his battles with the Arabs of Gur,* and his wars with the Meunites. ⁸The Meunites* paid annual tribute to him, and his fame spread even to Egypt, for he had become very powerful.

⁹Uzziah built fortified towers in Jerusalem at the Corner Gate, at the Valley Gate, and at the angle in the wall. ¹⁰He also constructed forts in the wilderness and dug many water cisterns, because he kept great herds of livestock in the foothills of Judah* and on the plains. He was also a man who loved the soil. He had many workers who cared for his farms and vineyards, both on the hillsides and in the fertile valleys.

¹¹Uzziah had an army of well-trained warriors, ready to march into battle, unit by unit. This army had been mustered and organized by Jeiel, the secretary of the army, and his assistant, Maaseiah. They were under the direction of Hananiah, one of the king's officials. ¹²These regiments of mighty warriors were commanded by 2,600 clan leaders. ¹³The army consisted of 307,500 men, all elite troops. They were prepared to assist the king against any enemy.

¹⁴Uzziah provided the entire army with shields, spears, helmets, coats of mail, bows, and sling stones. ¹⁵And he built structures on the walls of Jerusalem, designed by experts to protect those who shot arrows and hurled large stones* from the towers and the corners of the wall. His fame spread far and wide, for the LORD gave him marvelous help, and he became very powerful.

UZZIAH'S SIN AND PUNISHMENT

¹⁶But when he had become powerful, he also became proud, which led to his downfall. He sinned against the LORD his God by entering the sanctuary of the LORD's Temple and personally burning incense on the incense altar. ¹⁷Azariah the high priest went in after him with eighty other priests of the LORD, all brave men. ¹⁸They confronted King Uzziah and said, "It is not for you, Uzziah, to burn incense to the LORD. That

---

THE PULL OF PRIDE
(26:1-16) After God gave Uzziah great power as king of Judah, he became proud and corrupt. God hates pride. In fact, "pride goes before destruction, and haughtiness before a fall" (Prov 16:18). What do you have or want that sparks your pride? Talent? Money? Popularity? Power? Don't forget Proverbs 16:18. How will you give God credit for what you have?

25:23 Hebrew *400 cubits* [180 meters]. **25:28** As in some Hebrew manuscripts and other ancient versions (see also 2 Kgs 14:20); most Hebrew manuscripts read *the city of Judah.* **26:2** As in Greek version (see also 2 Kgs 14:22; 16:6); Hebrew reads *Eloth,* a variant spelling of Elath. **26:5** As in Syriac and Greek versions; Hebrew reads *who instructed him in divine visions.* **26:7** As in Greek version; Hebrew reads *Gur-baal.* **26:8** As in Greek version; Hebrew reads *Ammonites.* Compare 26:7. **26:10** Hebrew *the Shephelah.* **26:15** Or *to shoot arrows and hurl large stones.*

CAREFUL OBEDIENCE

Solomon and his workers carefully followed God's instructions (4:7). As a result, the Temple work was blessed by God and completed in every detail. Here are a few examples of (1) people in the Bible who did not carefully follow one of God's instructions, and (2) the resulting consequences. It is not enough to obey God halfheartedly.

WHO	GOD'S INSTRUCTION	DISOBEDIENCE	RESULT
Adam and Eve	Don't eat fruit from the tree of the knowledge of good and evil (Gen 2:16-17).	Satan tempted them and they ate (Gen 3:1-6).	They were banished from the Garden of Eden; pain and death were inflicted on all humanity (Gen 3:24; Rom 5:12).
Nadab and Abihu	Fire for the sacrifice must come from the proper source (Lev 6:12-13).	They used a different kind of fire for their sacrifice (Lev 10:1).	They were struck dead (Lev 10:2).
Moses	"Speak to the rock over there, and it will pour out its water" (Num 20:8).	He struck the rock twice with his staff (Num 20:11).	He was not allowed to enter the Promised Land (Num 20:12).
Saul	Completely destroy the evil Amalekites (1 Sam 15:3).	He spared the king and kept some of the plunder (1 Sam 15:8-9).	God promised to end his reign (1 Sam 15:16-26).
Uzzah	Only a priest can touch the Tabernacle's furnishings and articles (Num 4:15).	He touched the Ark of the Covenant (2 Sam 6:6).	He died instantly (2 Sam 6:7).
Uzziah	Only the priests can offer incense in the Temple or Tabernacle sanctuary (Num 16:39-40; 18:7).	He entered the sanctuary in the Temple, where only priests were allowed to go (2 Chr 26:16-18).	He became a leper (2 Chr 26:19).

is the work of the priests alone, the descendants of Aaron who are set apart for this work. Get out of the sanctuary, for you have sinned. The LORD God will not honor you for this!"

¹⁹Uzziah, who was holding an incense burner, became furious. But as he was standing there raging at the priests before the incense altar in the LORD's Temple, leprosy* suddenly broke out on his forehead. ²⁰When Azariah the high priest and all the other priests saw the leprosy, they rushed him out. And the king himself was eager to get out because the LORD had struck him. ²¹So King Uzziah had leprosy until the day he died. He lived in isolation in a separate house, for he was excluded from the Temple of the LORD. His son Jotham was put in charge of the royal palace, and he governed the people of the land.

²²The rest of the events of Uzziah's reign, from beginning to end, are recorded by the prophet Isaiah son of Amoz. ²³When Uzziah died, he was buried with his ancestors; his grave was in a nearby burial field belonging to the kings, for the people said, "He had leprosy." And his son Jotham became the next king.

27 JOTHAM RULES IN JUDAH Jotham was twenty-five years old when he became king, and he reigned in Jerusalem sixteen years. His mother was Jerusha, the daughter of Zadok.

²Jotham did what was pleasing in the LORD's sight. He did everything his father, Uzziah, had done, except that Jotham did not sin by entering the Temple of the LORD. But the people continued in their corrupt ways.

³Jotham rebuilt the upper gate of the Temple of the LORD. He also did extensive rebuilding on the wall at the hill of Ophel. ⁴He built towns in the hill country of Judah and constructed fortresses and towers in the wooded areas. ⁵Jotham went to war against the Ammonites and conquered them. Over the next three years he received from them an annual tribute of 7,500 pounds* of silver, 50,000 bushels of wheat, and 50,000 bushels of barley.*

26:19 Or a contagious skin disease. The Hebrew word used here and throughout this passage can describe various skin diseases. 27:5a Hebrew 100 talents [3,400 kilograms]. 27:5b Hebrew 10,000 cors [1,820 kiloliters] of wheat, and 10,000 cors of barley.

⁶King Jotham became powerful because he was careful to live in obedience to the LORD his God.

⁷The rest of the events of Jotham's reign, including all his wars and other activities, are recorded in *The Book of the Kings of Israel and Judah*. ⁸He was twenty-five years old when he became king, and he reigned in Jerusalem sixteen years. ⁹When Jotham died, he was buried in the City of David. And his son Ahaz became the next king.

28 **AHAZ RULES IN JUDAH** Ahaz was twenty years old when he became king, and he reigned in Jerusalem sixteen years. He did not do what was pleasing in the sight of the LORD, as his ancestor David had done. ²Instead, he followed the example of the kings of Israel. He cast metal images for the worship of Baal. ³He offered sacrifices in the valley of Ben-Hinnom, even sacrificing his own sons in the fire.* In this way, he followed the detestable practices of the pagan nations the LORD had driven from the land ahead of the Israelites. ⁴He offered sacrifices and burned incense at the pagan shrines and on the hills and under every green tree.

⁵Because of all this, the LORD his God allowed the king of Aram to defeat Ahaz and to exile large numbers of his people to Damascus. The armies of the king of Israel also defeated Ahaz and inflicted many casualties on his army. ⁶In a single day Pekah son of Remaliah, Israel's king, killed 120,000 of Judah's troops, all of them experienced warriors, because they had abandoned the LORD, the God of their ancestors. ⁷Then Zicri, a warrior from Ephraim, killed Maaseiah, the king's son; Azrikam, the king's palace commander; and Elkanah, the

28:3 Or *even making his sons pass through the fire.*

ULTIMATE ISSUES *ABORTION*

"Keep your laws off my body!" scream the words on one placard. A sign held by a woman in an opposing group shows a picture of an aborted baby and reads "Who imposed their morality on this little one?" The news programs run story after story, pro-life and pro-abortion forces hold endless debates, and courts and legislatures are all but paralyzed over this most heated social issue: Abortion.

Obviously, this is not a simple, one-dimensional issue. Besides the central problem of whether or not it is ever right to take the life of an unborn person, other, related issues are significant: obtaining parental consent for girls under 18 who want to have an abortion; legalizing abortion up to a certain age of the fetus (for example, three months); "harvesting" fetal tissues to help people with diseases like Parkinson's disease; and many more. While these concerns complicate the situation, one question cuts across all of them: who can say what's right?

If a person (a judge, a doctor, or a legislator) or a human institution (the Supreme Court or the Senate) makes a decision in this matter, another person or institution may overturn that decision later on. This has happened countless times. What is needed, it would seem, is a judgment or a ruling from a source higher than human opinion. That's why for many centuries Christians have turned to the Bible for just such input. Believing the Bible to be God's own words on matters such as this, Jesus' followers have historically looked to the Scriptures for answers to life's most important—and most difficult—questions.

Unfortunately, no verse of Scripture simply states, "Thus saith the Lord: abortion is wrong [or right]." If we had such a verse, it would be an open-and-shut case for believers. Certain passages, however, give principles that apply to this difficult topic. In Psalm 139, David praises God for overseeing his life, starting before he was born. David thanks God first for the fantastic way the human body is designed and constructed and then for the fact that every day of his life is scheduled and "recorded in [God's] book" (139:16).

Since God is the Creator and Designer of life, we can logically conclude that no one should treat any life lightly. If we are God's workmanship, who has the right to tamper with or destroy that workmanship? (Another verse, 2 Chronicles 28:3, shows how evil one king was by saying that he even sacrificed his own children to idols.) Yet, tragically, that is what happens on a daily basis. Abortion is used as a means of birth control, of removing an unwanted complication. For those who take seriously the sanctity of life as an expression of God's handiwork, this can be seen only as an abomination, a sin of the most serious kind. As such, we as a society desperately need to cry out to God in repentance and ask his forgiveness for what we have allowed to be done to millions of his little ones.

A number of topics in the Bible (being made in the image of God, sexual morality, etc.) and Scripture passages (e.g., Exod 21:22-25; Lev 24:17-22; Jer 1:4-5) closely relate to the abortion issue. Concerned Christians should think through their stand on the rights of the unborn in relation to these other issues and in light of the whole counsel of God, not just one passage. (One principle that should always be kept in mind when considering abortion or any other moral problem is forgiveness.) Psalm 139 is a good place to start. ∎

king's second-in-command. ⁸The armies of Israel captured 200,000 women and children from Judah and seized tremendous amounts of plunder, which they took back to Samaria.

⁹But a prophet of the LORD named Oded was there in Samaria when the army of Israel returned home. He went out to meet them and said, "The LORD, the God of your ancestors, was angry with Judah and let you defeat them. But you have gone too far, killing them without mercy, and all heaven is disturbed. ¹⁰And now you are planning to make slaves of these people from Judah and Jerusalem. What about your own sins against the LORD your God? ¹¹Listen to me and return these prisoners you have taken, for they are your own relatives. Watch out, because now the LORD's fierce anger has been turned against you!"

¹²Then some of the leaders of Israel*— Azariah son of Jehohanan, Berekiah son of Meshillemoth, Jehizkiah son of Shallum, and Amasa son of Hadlai—agreed with this and confronted the men returning from battle. ¹³"You must not bring the prisoners here!" they declared. "We cannot afford to add to our sins and guilt. Our guilt is already great, and the LORD's fierce anger is already turned against Israel."

¹⁴So the warriors released the prisoners and handed over the plunder in the sight of the leaders and all the people. ¹⁵Then the four men just mentioned by name came forward and distributed clothes from the plunder to the prisoners who were naked. They provided clothing and sandals to wear, gave them enough food and drink, and dressed their wounds with olive oil. They put those who were weak on donkeys and took all the prisoners back to their own people in Jericho, the city of palms. Then they returned to Samaria.

AHAZ CLOSES THE TEMPLE ¹⁶At that time King Ahaz of Judah asked the king of Assyria for help. ¹⁷The armies of Edom had again invaded Judah and taken captives. ¹⁸And the Philistines had raided towns located in the foothills of Judah* and in the Negev of Judah. They had already captured and occupied Bethshemesh, Aijalon, Gederoth, Soco with its villages, Timnah with its villages, and Gimzo with its villages. ¹⁹The LORD was humbling Judah because of King Ahaz of Judah,* for he had

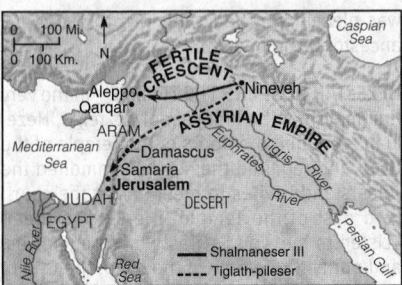

THE ASSYRIAN EMPIRE
The mighty Assyrian Empire extended north from the Persian Gulf, across the Fertile Crescent, and south to Egypt. Shalmaneser III extended the empire toward the Mediterranean Sea by conquering cities as far west as Qarqar. Tiglath-pileser extended the empire south into Aram, Judah, and Philistia. It was Shalmaneser V who destroyed Samaria, Israel's capital.

encouraged his people to sin and had been utterly unfaithful to the LORD.

²⁰So when King Tiglath-pileser* of Assyria arrived, he attacked Ahaz instead of helping him. ²¹Ahaz took valuable items from the LORD's Temple, the royal palace, and from the homes of his officials and gave them to the king of Assyria as tribute. But this did not help him.

²²Even during this time of trouble, King Ahaz continued to reject the LORD. ²³He offered sacrifices to the gods of Damascus who had defeated him, for he said, "Since these gods helped the kings of Aram, they will help me, too, if I sacrifice to them." But instead, they led to his ruin and the ruin of all Judah.

²⁴The king took the various articles from the Temple of God and broke them into pieces. He shut the doors of the LORD's Temple so that no one could worship there, and he set up altars to pagan gods in every corner of Jerusalem. ²⁵He made pagan shrines in all the towns of Judah for offering sacrifices to other gods. In this way, he aroused the anger of the LORD, the God of his ancestors.

²⁶The rest of the events of Ahaz's reign and everything he did, from beginning to end, are recorded in *The Book of the Kings of Judah and Israel.* ²⁷When Ahaz died, he was buried in Jerusalem but not in the royal cemetery of the kings of Judah. Then his son Hezekiah became the next king.

29 HEZEKIAH RULES IN JUDAH Hezekiah was twenty-five years old when he became the king of Judah, and he reigned in Jerusalem twenty-nine years. His mother was Abijah, the daughter of Zechariah. ²He did what

---

28:12 Hebrew *Ephraim,* referring to the northern kingdom of Israel. 28:18 Hebrew *the Shephelah.* 28:19 Masoretic Text reads *of Israel;* also in 28:23, 27. The author of Chronicles sees Judah as representative of the true Israel. (Some Hebrew manuscripts and Greek version read *of Judah.*) 28:20 Hebrew *Tilgath-pileser,* a variant spelling of Tiglath-pileser.

was pleasing in the LORD's sight, just as his ancestor David had done.

HEZEKIAH REOPENS THE TEMPLE

³In the very first month of the first year of his reign, Hezekiah reopened the doors of the Temple of the LORD and repaired them. ⁴He summoned the priests and Levites to meet him at the courtyard east of the Temple. ⁵He said to them, "Listen to me, you Levites! Purify yourselves, and purify the Temple of the LORD, the God of your ancestors. Remove all the defiled things from the sanctuary. ⁶Our ancestors were unfaithful and did what was evil in the sight of the LORD our God. They abandoned the LORD and his dwelling place; they turned their backs on him. ⁷They also shut the doors to the Temple's entry room, and they snuffed out the lamps. They stopped burning incense and presenting burnt offerings at the sanctuary of the God of Israel.

⁸"That is why the LORD's anger has fallen upon Judah and Jerusalem. He has made them an object of dread, horror, and ridicule, as you can see with your own eyes. ⁹Because of this, our fathers have been killed in battle, and our sons and daughters and wives have been captured. ¹⁰But now I will make a covenant with the LORD, the God of Israel, so that his fierce anger will turn away from us. ¹¹My sons, do not neglect your duties any longer! The LORD has chosen you to stand in his presence, to minister to him, and to lead the people in worship and present offerings to him."

¹²Then these Levites got right to work:

From the clan of Kohath: Mahath son of Amasai and Joel son of Azariah.
From the clan of Merari: Kish son of Abdi and Azariah son of Jehallelel.
From the clan of Gershon: Joah son of Zimmah and Eden son of Joah.
¹³ From the family of Elizaphan: Shimri and Jeiel.
From the family of Asaph: Zechariah and Mattaniah.
¹⁴ From the family of Heman: Jehiel and Shimei.

From the family of Jeduthun: Shemaiah and Uzziel.

¹⁵These men called together their fellow Levites, and they all purified themselves. Then they began to cleanse the Temple of the LORD, just as the king had commanded. They were careful to follow all the LORD's instructions in their work. ¹⁶The priests went into the sanctuary of the Temple of the LORD to cleanse it, and they took out to the Temple courtyard all the defiled things they found. From there the Levites carted it all out to the Kidron Valley.

¹⁷They began the work in early spring, on the first day of the new year,* and in eight days they had reached the entry room of the LORD's Temple. Then they purified the Temple of the LORD itself, which took another eight days. So the entire task was completed in sixteen days.

THE TEMPLE REDEDICATION

¹⁸Then the Levites went to King Hezekiah and gave him this report: "We have cleansed the entire Temple of the LORD, the altar of burnt offering with all its utensils, and the table of the Bread of the Presence with all its utensils. ¹⁹We have also recovered all the items discarded by King Ahaz when he was unfaithful and closed the Temple. They are now in front of the altar of the LORD, purified and ready for use."

²⁰Early the next morning King Hezekiah gathered the city officials and went to the Temple of the LORD. ²¹They brought seven bulls, seven rams, and seven male lambs as a burnt offering, together with seven male goats as a sin offering for the kingdom, for the Temple, and for Judah. The king commanded the priests, who were descendants of Aaron, to sacrifice the animals on the altar of the LORD.

²²So they killed the bulls, and the priests took the blood and sprinkled it on the altar. Next they killed the rams and sprinkled their blood on the altar. And finally, they did the same with the male lambs. ²³The male goats for the sin offering were then brought before the king and the assembly of people, who laid their hands on them. ²⁴The priests then killed the goats as a sin offering and sprinkled their blood on the altar to make atonement for the sins of all Israel. The king had specifically commanded that this burnt offering and sin offering should be made for all Israel.

²⁵King Hezekiah then stationed the Levites at the Temple of the LORD with cymbals, lyres, and harps. He obeyed all the commands that

---

BACK IN THE GAME
(29:11) The Levites had been kept from their Temple duties by Ahaz (28:24). But Hezekiah called them back into service. Feeling inactive like the Levites due to pressure or responsibilities? If you're serious about getting back in the game, your "life coach"—God—will send opportunities your way. Then, like the Levites, be ready for action (29:12-15).

29:17 Hebrew *on the first day of the first month.* This day in the ancient Hebrew lunar calendar occurred in March or early April, 715 B.C.

the LORD had given to King David through Gad, the king's seer, and the prophet Nathan. ²⁶The Levites then took their positions around the Temple with the instruments of David, and the priests took their positions with the trumpets.

²⁷Then Hezekiah ordered that the burnt offering be placed on the altar. As the burnt offering was begun, songs of praise to the LORD were begun, accompanied by the trumpets and other instruments of David, the former king of Israel. ²⁸The entire assembly worshiped the LORD as the singers sang and the trumpets blew, until all the burnt offerings were finished. ²⁹Then the king and everyone with him bowed down in worship. ³⁰King Hezekiah and the officials ordered the Levites to praise the LORD with the psalms written by David and by Asaph the seer. So they offered joyous praise and bowed down in worship.

³¹Then Hezekiah declared, "Now that you have consecrated yourselves to the LORD, bring your sacrifices and thanksgiving offerings to the Temple of the LORD." So the people brought their sacrifices and thanksgiving offerings, and all whose hearts were willing brought burnt offerings, too. ³²The people brought to the LORD 70 bulls, 100 rams, and 200 male lambs for burnt offerings. ³³They also brought 600 cattle and 3,000 sheep and goats as sacred offerings.

³⁴But there were too few priests to prepare all the burnt offerings. So their relatives the Levites helped them until the work was finished and more priests had been purified, for the Levites had been more conscientious about purifying themselves than the priests had been. ³⁵There was an abundance of burnt offerings, along with the usual liquid offerings, and a great deal of fat from the many peace offerings.

So the Temple of the LORD was restored to service. ³⁶And Hezekiah and all the people rejoiced because of what God had done for the people, for everything had been accomplished so quickly.

30 PREPARATIONS FOR PASSOVER King
Hezekiah now sent word to all Israel and Judah, and he wrote letters of invitation to the people of Ephraim and Manasseh. He asked everyone to come to the Temple of the LORD at Jerusalem to celebrate the Passover of the LORD, the God of Israel. ²The king, his officials, and all the community of Jerusalem de-

30:2 Hebrew *in the second month.* Passover was normally observed in the first month (of the ancient Hebrew lunar calendar).
30:6 *Israel* is the name that God gave to Jacob.

cided to celebrate Passover a month later than usual.* ³They were unable to celebrate it at the prescribed time because not enough priests could be purified by then, and the people had not yet assembled at Jerusalem.

⁴This plan for keeping the Passover seemed right to the king and all the people. ⁵So they sent a proclamation throughout all Israel, from Beersheba in the south to Dan in the north, inviting everyone to come to Jerusalem to celebrate the Passover of the LORD, the God of Israel. The people had not been celebrating it in great numbers as required in the Law.

⁶At the king's command, runners were sent throughout Israel and Judah. They carried letters that said:

"O people of Israel, return to the LORD, the God of Abraham, Isaac, and Israel,* so that he will return to the few of us who have survived the conquest of the Assyrian kings. ⁷Do not be like your ancestors and relatives who abandoned the LORD, the God of their ancestors, and became an object of derision, as you yourselves can see. ⁸Do not be stubborn, as they were, but submit yourselves to the LORD. Come to his Temple, which he has set apart as holy forever. Worship the LORD your God so that his fierce anger will turn away from you.

⁹"For if you return to the LORD, your relatives and your children will be treated mercifully by their captors, and they will be able to return to this land. For the LORD your God is gracious and merciful. If you return to him, he will not continue to turn his face from you."

CELEBRATION OF PASSOVER ¹⁰The runners
went from town to town throughout Ephraim and Manasseh and as far as the territory of Zebulun. But most of the people just laughed at the runners and made fun of them. ¹¹However, some people from Asher, Manasseh, and Zebulun humbled themselves and went to Jerusalem.

¹²At the same time, God's hand was on the

RUNNING THE SHOW
(30:1-9) *King Hezekiah was dedicated to God and to making his people right with God. In letters to the people of Judah and Israel, he urged everyone to return to God. He knew that his people could be stubborn in their refusal to let God run their lives. Running our own lives is a habit we like to hold on to. We might let God make a decision or two, while we make the majority of them. But God is an all-or-nothing God. Either he runs the whole show or we do. Who's running your show?*

people in the land of Judah, giving them all one heart to obey the orders of the king and his officials, who were following the word of the LORD. ¹³So a huge crowd assembled at Jerusalem in midspring* to celebrate the Festival of Unleavened Bread. ¹⁴They set to work and removed the pagan altars from Jerusalem. They took away all the incense altars and threw them into the Kidron Valley.

¹⁵On the fourteenth day of the second month, one month later than usual,* the people slaughtered the Passover lamb. This shamed the priests and Levites, so they purified themselves and brought burnt offerings to the Temple of the LORD. ¹⁶Then they took their places at the Temple as prescribed in the Law of Moses, the man of God. The Levites brought the sacrificial blood to the priests, who then sprinkled it on the altar.

¹⁷Since many of the people had not purified themselves, the Levites had to slaughter their Passover lamb for them, to set them apart for the LORD. ¹⁸Most of those who came from Ephraim, Manasseh, Issachar, and Zebulun had not purified themselves. But King Hezekiah prayed for them, and they were allowed to eat the Passover meal anyway, even though this was contrary to the requirements of the Law. For Hezekiah said, "May the LORD, who is good, pardon those ¹⁹who decide to follow the LORD, the God of their ancestors, even though they are not properly cleansed for the ceremony." ²⁰And the LORD listened to Hezekiah's prayer and healed the people.

²¹So the people of Israel who were present in Jerusalem joyously celebrated the Festival of Unleavened Bread for seven days. Each day the Levites and priests sang to the LORD, accompanied by loud instruments.* ²²Hezekiah encouraged all the Levites regarding the skill they displayed as they served the LORD. The celebration continued for seven days. Peace offerings were sacrificed, and the people gave thanks to the LORD, the God of their ancestors.

²³The entire assembly then decided to continue the festival another seven days, so they celebrated joyfully for another week. ²⁴King

Hezekiah gave the people 1,000 bulls and 7,000 sheep and goats for offerings, and the officials donated 1,000 bulls and 10,000 sheep and goats. Meanwhile, many more priests purified themselves.

²⁵The entire assembly of Judah rejoiced, including the priests, the Levites, all who came from the land of Israel, the foreigners who came to the festival, and all those who lived in Judah. ²⁶There was great joy in the city, for Jerusalem had not seen a celebration like this one since the days of Solomon, King David's son. ²⁷Then the priests and Levites stood and blessed the people, and God heard their prayer from his holy dwelling in heaven.

31 HEZEKIAH'S RELIGIOUS REFORMS

When the festival ended, the Israelites who attended went to all the towns of Judah, Benjamin, Ephraim, and Manasseh, and they smashed all the sacred pillars, cut down the Asherah poles, and removed the pagan shrines and altars. After this, the Israelites returned to their own towns and homes.

²Hezekiah then organized the priests and Levites into divisions to offer the burnt offerings and peace offerings, and to worship and give thanks and praise to the LORD at the gates of the Temple. ³The king also made a personal contribution of animals for the daily morning and evening burnt offerings, the weekly Sabbath festivals, the monthly new moon festivals, and the annual festivals as prescribed in the Law of the LORD. ⁴In addition, he required the people in Jerusalem to bring a portion of their goods to the priests and Levites, so they could devote themselves fully to the Law of the LORD.

⁵When the people of Israel heard these requirements, they responded generously by bringing the first share of their grain, new wine, olive oil, honey, and all the produce of their fields. They brought a large quantity—a tithe of all they produced. ⁶The people who had moved to Judah from Israel, and the people of Judah themselves, brought in the tithes of their cattle, sheep, and goats and a tithe of the things that had been dedicated to the LORD their God, and they piled them up in great heaps. ⁷They began piling them up in late spring, and the heaps continued to grow until early autumn.* ⁸When Hezekiah and his

---

GENEROSITY

(31:4-12) Hezekiah re-established the practice of tithing—giving the first portion of one's income—to the priests and Levites to allow them to serve God in the Temple. The people responded immediately and generously. God's work needs the support of his people. Do you give him the first portion of your income or your time? Generosity makes our giving delightful to God (2 Cor 8–9). How different the church would be today if all believers consistently followed this pattern.

30:13 Hebrew *in the second month.* The second month of the ancient Hebrew lunar calendar usually occurs within the months of April and May.   **30:15** Hebrew *On the fourteenth day of the second month.* Passover normally began on the fourteenth day of the first month (see Lev 23:5).   **30:21** Or *sang to the LORD with all their strength.*   **31:7** Hebrew *in the third month . . . until the seventh month.* The third month of the ancient Hebrew lunar calendar usually occurs within the months of May and June; the seventh month usually occurs within September and October.

officials came and saw these huge piles, they thanked the LORD and his people Israel!

⁹"Where did all this come from?" Hezekiah asked the priests and Levites.

¹⁰And Azariah the high priest, from the family of Zadok, replied, "Since the people began bringing their gifts to the LORD's Temple, we have had enough to eat and plenty to spare. The LORD has blessed his people, and all this is left over."

¹¹Hezekiah ordered that storerooms be prepared in the Temple of the LORD. When this was done, ¹²the people faithfully brought all the tithes and gifts to the Temple. Conaniah the Levite was put in charge, assisted by his brother Shimei. ¹³The supervisors under them were Jehiel, Azaziah, Nahath, Asahel, Jerimoth, Jozabad, Eliel, Ismakiah, Mahath, and Benaiah. These appointments were made by King Hezekiah and Azariah, the chief official in the Temple of God.

¹⁴Kore son of Imnah the Levite, who was the gatekeeper at the East Gate, was put in charge of distributing the voluntary offerings given to God, the gifts, and the things that had been dedicated to the LORD. ¹⁵His faithful assistants were Eden, Miniamin, Jeshua, Shemaiah, Amariah, and Shecaniah. They distributed the gifts among the families of priests in their towns by their divisions, dividing the gifts fairly among old and young alike. ¹⁶They distributed the gifts to all males three years old or older, regardless of their place in the genealogical records. The distribution went to all who would come to the LORD's Temple to perform their daily duties according to their divisions. ¹⁷They distributed gifts to the priests who were listed by their families in the genealogical records, and to the Levites twenty years old or older who were listed according to their jobs and their divisions. ¹⁸Food allotments were also given to the families of all those listed in the genealogical records, including their little babies, wives, sons, and daughters. For they had all been faithful in purifying themselves.

¹⁹As for the priests, the descendants of Aaron, who were living in the open villages around the towns, men were appointed by name to distribute portions to every male among the priests and to all the Levites listed in the genealogical records.

²⁰In this way, King Hezekiah handled the distribution throughout all Judah, doing what was pleasing and good in the sight of the LORD his God. ²¹In all that he did in the service of the Temple of God and in his efforts to follow

God's laws and commands, Hezekiah sought his God wholeheartedly. As a result, he was very successful.

32 ASSYRIA INVADES JUDAH

After Hezekiah had faithfully carried out this work, King Sennacherib of Assyria invaded Judah. He laid siege to the fortified towns, giving orders for his army to break through their walls. ²When Hezekiah realized that Sennacherib also intended to attack Jerusalem, ³he consulted with his officials and military advisers, and they decided to stop the flow of the springs outside the city. ⁴They organized a huge work crew to stop the flow of the springs, cutting off the brook that ran through the fields. For they said, "Why should the kings of Assyria come here and find plenty of water?"

⁵Then Hezekiah worked hard at repairing all the broken sections of the wall, erecting towers, and constructing a second wall outside the first. He also reinforced the supporting terraces* in the City of David and manufactured large numbers of weapons and shields. ⁶He appointed military officers over the people and assembled them before him in the square at the city gate. Then Hezekiah encouraged them by saying: ⁷"Be strong and courageous! Don't be afraid or discouraged because of the king of Assyria or his mighty army, for there is a power far greater on our side! ⁸He may have a great army, but they are merely men. We have the LORD our God to help us and to fight our battles for us!" Hezekiah's words greatly encouraged the people.

SENNACHERIB THREATENS JERUSALEM

⁹While King Sennacherib of Assyria was still besieging the town of Lachish, he sent his officers to Jerusalem with this message for Hezekiah and all the people in the city:

¹⁰"This is what King Sennacherib of Assyria says: What are you trusting in that makes you think you can survive my siege of Jerusalem? ¹¹Hezekiah has said, 'The LORD our God will rescue us from the king of Assyria.' Surely Hezekiah is misleading you, sentencing you to death by famine and thirst! ¹²Don't you realize that Hezekiah

32:5 Hebrew the millo. The meaning of the Hebrew is uncertain.

TRUSTING GOD
(32:1-8) When King Hezekiah was confronted with an Assyrian invasion, he made two important decisions: (1) He did everything he could to deal with the situation, and (2) he trusted God for the outcome. When you're faced with difficult or frightening situations, is this your pattern of action?

is the very person who destroyed all the LORD's shrines and altars? He commanded Judah and Jerusalem to worship only at the altar at the Temple and to offer sacrifices on it alone.

¹³"Surely you must realize what I and the other kings of Assyria before me have done to all the people of the earth! Were any of the gods of those nations able to rescue their people from my power? ¹⁴Which of their gods was able to rescue its people from the destructive power of my predecessors? What makes you think your God can rescue you from me? ¹⁵Don't let Hezekiah deceive you! Don't let him fool you like this! I say it again—no god of any nation or kingdom has ever yet been able to rescue his people from me or my ancestors. How much less will your God rescue you from my power!"

¹⁶And Sennacherib's officers further mocked the LORD God and his servant Hezekiah, heaping insult upon insult. ¹⁷The king also sent letters scorning the LORD, the God of Israel. He wrote, "Just as the gods of all the other nations failed to rescue their people from my power, so the God of Hezekiah will also fail." ¹⁸The Assyrian officials who brought the letters shouted this in Hebrew* to the people gathered on the walls of the city, trying to terrify them so it would be easier to capture the city. ¹⁹These officers talked about the God of Jerusalem as though he were one of the pagan gods, made by human hands.

²⁰Then King Hezekiah and the prophet Isaiah son of Amoz cried out in prayer to God in heaven. ²¹And the LORD sent an angel who destroyed the Assyrian army with all its commanders and officers. So Sennacherib was forced to return home in disgrace to his own land. And when he entered the temple of his god, some of his own sons killed him there with a sword.

²²That is how the LORD rescued Hezekiah and the people of Jerusalem from King Sennacherib of Assyria and from all the others who threatened them. So there was peace throughout the land. ²³From then on King Hezekiah became highly respected among all the surrounding nations, and many gifts for the LORD arrived at Jerusalem, with valuable presents for King Hezekiah, too.

HEZEKIAH'S SICKNESS AND RECOVERY

²⁴About that time Hezekiah became deathly ill. He prayed to the LORD, who healed him and gave him a miraculous sign. ²⁵But Hezekiah did not respond appropriately to the kind-

32:18 Hebrew *in the dialect of Judah.*

MANASSEH   *PERSONALITY PROFILE*

IN YOUR OPINION, what's the worst thing that a person could do? Got a list in mind? If you take a good look at Manasseh's life, you might find an action or two from your list. Manasseh made evil an art form.

Just how bad was this guy? Not only did he rebuild altars dedicated to pagan gods in Solomon's Temple, he also sacrificed his children to them! Child sacrifice is a vile act of heathen idolatry, an act against both God and people. Such blatant sins require severe correction. In addition, Manasseh had a few hobbies that angered God, namely sorcery, divination, and witchcraft. He also frequented the psychic hotline of the day.

But God showed justice to Manasseh by warning him and then allowing him to be conquered and captured.

Something amazing happened as a result: Manasseh asked God to forgive his sins! Given the nature of Manasseh's rebellion, we are not surprised by God's punishment. But Manasseh's repentance and God's forgiveness are unexpected. When God said yes to his request, Manasseh was given a new start.

Still got that list in your head of the worse things that a person could do? Maybe your name is on that list as the doer of one of those terrible actions. If so, take a minute to reread Manasseh's story. God is still ready to forgive even the worst things that a person could do.

BOTTOM LINE: Forgiveness is limited not by the amount of sin but by our willingness to repent.

Manasseh's story is told in 2 Kings 21:1-18 and 2 Chronicles 32:33–33:20. He also is mentioned in Jeremiah 15:4.

UPS:
- *Despite the bitter consequences of his sins, he learned from them*
- *Humbly repented of his sins before God*

DOWNS:
- *Challenged God's authority and was defeated*
- *Reversed many of the positive effects of his father Hezekiah's rule*
- *Sacrificed his children to idols*

STATS:
- *Occupation: King of Judah*
- *Relatives: Hezekiah (father); Hephzibah (mother); Amon (son)*

KEY VERSES: *2 Chronicles 33:12-13*

ness shown him, and he became proud. So the Lord's anger came against him and against Judah and Jerusalem. ²⁶Then Hezekiah humbled himself and repented of his pride, as did the people of Jerusalem. So the Lord's anger did not fall on them during Hezekiah's lifetime.

²⁷Hezekiah was very wealthy and highly honored. He built special treasury buildings for his silver, gold, precious stones, and spices, and for his shields and other valuable items. ²⁸He also constructed many storehouses for his grain, new wine, and olive oil; and he made many stalls for his cattle and pens for his flocks of sheep and goats. ²⁹He built many towns and acquired vast flocks and herds, for God had given him great wealth. ³⁰He blocked up the upper spring of Gihon and brought the water down through a tunnel to the west side of the City of David. And so he succeeded in everything he did.

³¹However, when ambassadors arrived from Babylon to ask about the remarkable events that had taken place in the land, God withdrew from Hezekiah in order to test him and to see what was really in his heart.

SUMMARY OF HEZEKIAH'S REIGN ³²The rest of the events in Hezekiah's reign and his acts of devotion are recorded in *The Vision of the Prophet Isaiah Son of Amoz,* which is included in *The Book of the Kings of Judah and Israel.* ³³When Hezekiah died, he was buried in the upper area of the royal cemetery, and all Judah and Jerusalem honored him at his death. And his son Manasseh became the next king.

33 **MANASSEH RULES IN JUDAH** Manasseh was twelve years old when he became king, and he reigned in Jerusalem fifty-five years. ²He did what was evil in the Lord's sight, following the detestable practices of the pagan nations that the Lord had driven from the land ahead of the Israelites. ³He rebuilt the pagan shrines his father, Hezekiah, had broken down. He constructed altars for the images of Baal and set up Asherah poles. He also bowed before all the powers of the heavens and worshiped them.

⁴He built pagan altars in the Temple of the Lord, the place where the Lord had said, "My name will remain in Jerusalem forever." ⁵He built these altars for all the powers of the heavens in both courtyards of the Lord's Temple. ⁶Manasseh also sacrificed his own sons in the fire* in the valley of Ben-Hinnom. He practiced sorcery, divination, and witchcraft, and he

33:6 Or *also made his sons pass through the fire.*

consulted with mediums and psychics. He did much that was evil in the Lord's sight, arousing his anger.

⁷Manasseh even took a carved idol he had made and set it up in God's Temple, the very place where God had told David and his son Solomon: "My name will be honored forever in this Temple and in Jerusalem—the city I have chosen from among all the tribes of Israel. ⁸If the Israelites will be careful to obey my commands—all the laws, decrees, and regulations given through Moses—I will not send them into exile from this land that I set aside for your ancestors." ⁹But Manasseh led the people of Judah and Jerusalem to do even more evil than the pagan nations that the Lord had destroyed when the people of Israel entered the land.

¹⁰The Lord spoke to Manasseh and his people, but they ignored all his warnings. ¹¹So the Lord sent the commanders of the Assyrian armies, and they took Manasseh prisoner. They put a ring through his nose, bound him in bronze chains, and led him away to Babylon. ¹²But while in deep distress, Manasseh sought the Lord his God and sincerely humbled himself before the God of his ancestors. ¹³And when he prayed, the Lord listened to him and was moved by his request. So the Lord brought Manasseh back to Jerusalem and to his kingdom. Then Manasseh finally realized that the Lord alone is God!

¹⁴After this Manasseh rebuilt the outer wall of the City of David, from west of the Gihon Spring in the Kidron Valley to the Fish Gate, and continuing around the hill of Ophel. He built the wall very high. And he stationed his military officers in all of the fortified towns of Judah. ¹⁵Manasseh also removed the foreign gods and the idol from the Lord's Temple. He tore down all the altars he had built on the hill where the Temple stood and all the altars that were in Jerusalem, and he dumped them outside the city. ¹⁶Then he restored the altar of the Lord and sacrificed peace offerings and thanksgiving offerings on it. He also encouraged the people of Judah to worship the Lord, the God of Israel. ¹⁷However, the people still

....

BEYOND FORGIVENESS?
(33:1-13) *In the list of corrupt kings, Manasseh would rank near the top. His life is a catalog of evil deeds including idol worship, sacrificing his own children, and Temple desecration. But after being captured by the Assyrians, he asked God to forgive him for his wrongs. And, incredibly, God forgave him. Even after reading that story, do you still doubt that anyone could forgive what you have done? Take heart—no one is beyond God's forgiveness.*

sacrificed at the pagan shrines, though only to the LORD their God.

¹⁸The rest of the events of Manasseh's reign, his prayer to God, and the words the seers spoke to him in the name of the LORD, the God of Israel, are recorded in *The Book of the Kings of Israel.* ¹⁹Manasseh's prayer, the account of the way God answered him, and an account of all his sins and unfaithfulness are recorded in *The Record of the Seers.** It includes a list of the locations where he built pagan shrines and set up Asherah poles and idols before he humbled himself and repented. ²⁰When Manasseh died, he was buried in his palace. Then his son Amon became the next king.

AMON RULES IN JUDAH ²¹Amon was twenty-two years old when he became king, and he reigned in Jerusalem two years. ²²He did what was evil in the LORD's sight, just as his father, Manasseh, had done. He worshiped and sacrificed to all the idols his father had made. ²³But unlike his father, he did not humble himself before the LORD. Instead, Amon sinned even more.

²⁴Then Amon's own officials conspired against him and assassinated him in his palace. ²⁵But the people of the land killed all those who had conspired against King Amon, and they made his son Josiah the next king.

34 **JOSIAH RULES IN JUDAH** Josiah was eight years old when he became king, and he reigned in Jerusalem thirty-one years. ²He did what was pleasing in the LORD's sight and followed the example of his ancestor David. He did not turn away from doing what was right.

³During the eighth year of his reign, while he was still young, Josiah began to seek the God of his ancestor David. Then in the twelfth year he began to purify Judah and Jerusalem, destroying all the pagan shrines, the Asherah poles, and the carved idols and cast images. ⁴He ordered that the altars of Baal be demolished and that the incense altars which stood above them be broken down. He also made sure that the Asherah poles, the carved idols, and the cast images were smashed and scattered over the graves of those who had sacrificed to them. ⁵He burned the bones of the pagan priests on their own altars, and so he purified Judah and Jerusalem.

⁶He did the same thing in the towns of Manasseh, Ephraim, and Simeon, even as far as Naphtali, and in the regions* all around them. ⁷He destroyed the pagan altars and the Ashe-

rah poles, and he crushed the idols into dust. He cut down all the incense altars throughout the land of Israel. Finally, he returned to Jerusalem.

⁸In the eighteenth year of his reign, after he had purified the land and the Temple, Josiah appointed Shaphan son of Azaliah, Maaseiah the governor of Jerusalem, and Joah son of Joahaz, the royal historian, to repair the Temple of the LORD his God. ⁹They gave Hilkiah the high priest the money that had been collected by the Levites who served as gatekeepers at the Temple of God. The gifts were brought by people from Manasseh, Ephraim, and from all the remnant of Israel, as well as from all Judah, Benjamin, and the people of Jerusalem.

¹⁰He entrusted the money to the men assigned to supervise the restoration of the LORD's Temple. Then they paid the workers who did the repairs and renovation of the Temple. ¹¹They hired carpenters and builders, who purchased finished stone for the walls and timber for the rafters and beams. They restored what earlier kings of Judah had allowed to fall into ruin.

¹²The workers served faithfully under the leadership of Jahath and Obadiah, Levites of the Merarite clan, and Zechariah and Meshullam, Levites of the Kohathite clan. Other Levites, all of whom were skilled musicians, ¹³were put in charge of the laborers of the various trades. Still others assisted as secretaries, officials, and gatekeepers.

HILKIAH DISCOVERS GOD'S LAW ¹⁴While they were bringing out the money collected at the LORD's Temple, Hilkiah the priest found the Book of the Law of the LORD that was written by Moses. ¹⁵Hilkiah said to Shaphan the court secretary, "I have found the Book of the Law in the LORD's Temple!" Then Hilkiah gave the scroll to Shaphan.

¹⁶Shaphan took the scroll to the king and reported, "Your officials are doing everything they were assigned to do. ¹⁷The money that was collected at the Temple of the LORD has been turned over to the supervisors and workmen." ¹⁸Shaphan also told the king, "Hilkiah the priest has given me a scroll." So Shaphan read it to the king.

¹⁹When the king heard what was written in the Law, he tore his clothes in despair. ²⁰Then he gave these orders to Hilkiah, Ahikam son of Shaphan, Acbor son of Micaiah,* Shaphan the

33:19 Or *The Record of Hozai.* **34:6** As in Syriac version; Hebrew reads *in their temples,* or *in their ruins.* The meaning of the Hebrew is uncertain. **34:20** As in parallel text at 2 Kgs 22:12; Hebrew reads *Abdon son of Micah.*

court secretary, and Asaiah the king's personal adviser: [21]"Go to the Temple and speak to the LORD for me and for all the remnant of Israel and Judah. Inquire about the words written in the scroll that has been found. For the LORD's great anger has been poured out on us because our ancestors have not obeyed the word of the LORD. We have not been doing everything this scroll says we must do."

[22]So Hilkiah and the other men went to the New Quarter* of Jerusalem to consult with the prophet Huldah. She was the wife of Shallum son of Tikvah, son of Harhas,* the keeper of the Temple wardrobe.

[23]She said to them, "The LORD, the God of Israel, has spoken! Go back and tell the man who sent you, [24]'This is what the LORD says: I am going to bring disaster on this city* and its people. All the curses written in the scroll that was read to the king of Judah will come true. [25]For my people have abandoned me and offered sacrifices to pagan gods, and I am very angry with them for everything they have done. My anger will be poured out on this place, and it will not be quenched.'

[26]"But go to the king of Judah who sent you to seek the LORD and tell him: 'This is what the LORD, the God of Israel, says concerning the message you have just heard: [27]You were sorry and humbled yourself before God when you heard his words against this city and its people. You humbled yourself and tore your clothing in despair and wept before me in repentance. And I have indeed heard you, says the LORD. [28]So I will not send the promised

34:22a Or the Second Quarter, a newer section of Jerusalem. Hebrew reads the Mishneh.   34:22b As in parallel text at 2 Kgs 22:14; Hebrew reads son of Tokhath, son of Hasrah.   34:24 Hebrew this place; also in 34:27, 28.

disaster until after you have died and been buried in peace. You yourself will not see the disaster I am going to bring on this city and its people.'"

So they took her message back to the king.

JOSIAH'S RELIGIOUS REFORMS

[29]Then the king summoned all the elders of Judah and Jerusalem. [30]And the king went up to the Temple of the LORD with all the people of Judah and Jerusalem, along with the priests and the Levites—all the people from the greatest to the least. There the king read to them the entire Book of the Covenant that had been found in the LORD's Temple. [31]The king took his place of authority beside the pillar and renewed the covenant in the LORD's presence. He pledged to obey the LORD by keeping all his commands, laws, and decrees with all his heart and soul. He promised to obey all the terms of the covenant that were written in the scroll. [32]And he required everyone in Jerusalem and the people of Benjamin to make a similar pledge. The people of Jerusalem did so, renewing their covenant with God, the God of their ancestors.

[33]So Josiah removed all detestable idols from the entire land of Israel and required

....

GOTTA READ IT
(34:31) *When Josiah read the Book of the Law that Hilkiah discovered (34:14), he repented and humbly promised to follow God's commandments. Not much is different between a book hidden in the Temple and a Bible hidden on the bookshelf. We can't know what God wants us to do if we don't read it. And reading God's Word isn't enough; we need to be willing to do what it says. Are you willing?*

CHOICES
american idols

Tim normally uses anthropology class to snooze or do algebra homework. Not today. Mr. Mariano spent the hour talking about the religious beliefs of certain tribes indigenous to the rainforests of the Amazon. The discussion of human sacrifices and strange rituals had Tim paying extra special attention.

After school, he continued to rattle on about what he had heard. "Lindsay, can you believe people would actually worship a piece of wood or stone? Don't you think that's weird?"

"Like we're any better in this country?" Lindsay scoffed.

"What are you talking about?"

"We worship idols here, too."

"Aw, come on! Nobody worships statues or rocks around here."

"Well, no. We don't come right out and bow down in front of a statue. We're too sophisticated for that. But think about it. Think about the people who build their lives around the American dream—getting more stuff or a bigger house, gaining more status. Or think about the people who spend all of their time, energy, and money on sports or getting good grades, or—"

"Hey! What's wrong with sports?"

"Nothing . . . unless a sport takes over your whole life. Tim, anything that becomes more important than God is an idol."

Lindsay is right. The Bible repeatedly warns us not to let things or people replace God in our lives. Not sure? Check out the story of King Josiah in 2 Chronicles 34.

everyone to worship the LORD their God. And throughout the rest of his lifetime, they did not turn away from the LORD, the God of their ancestors.

35 **JOSIAH CELEBRATES PASSOVER** Then Josiah announced that the Passover of the LORD would be celebrated in Jerusalem, and so the Passover lamb was slaughtered on the fourteenth day of the first month.* ²Josiah also assigned the priests to their duties and encouraged them in their work at the Temple of the LORD. ³He issued this order to the Levites, who were to teach all Israel and who had been set apart to serve the LORD: "Put the holy Ark in the Temple that was built by Solomon son of David, the king of Israel. You no longer need to carry it back and forth on your shoulders. Now spend your time serving the LORD your God and his people Israel. ⁴Report for duty according to the family divisions of your ancestors, following the directions of King David of Israel and the directions of his son Solomon.

⁵"Then stand in the sanctuary at the place appointed for your family division and help the families assigned to you as they bring their offerings to the Temple. ⁶Slaughter the Passover lambs, purify yourselves, and prepare to help those who come. Follow all the directions that the LORD gave through Moses."

⁷Then Josiah provided 30,000 lambs and young goats for the people's Passover offerings, along with 3,000 cattle, all from the king's own flocks and herds. ⁸The king's officials also made willing contributions to the people, priests, and Levites. Hilkiah, Zechariah, and Jehiel, the administrators of God's Temple, gave the priests 2,600 lambs and young goats and 300 cattle as Passover offerings. ⁹The Levite leaders—Conaniah and his brothers Shemaiah and Nethanel, as well as Hashabiah, Jeiel, and Jozabad—gave 5,000 lambs and young goats and 500 cattle to the Levites for their Passover offerings.

¹⁰When everything was ready for the Passover celebration, the priests and the Levites took their places, organized by their divisions, as the king had commanded. ¹¹The Levites then slaughtered the Passover lambs and presented the blood to the priests, who sprinkled the blood on the altar while the Levites prepared the animals. ¹²They divided the burnt offerings among the people by their family groups, so they could offer them to the LORD as prescribed in the Book of Moses. They did the same with the cattle. ¹³Then they roasted the Passover lambs as prescribed; and they boiled the holy offerings in pots, kettles, and pans, and brought them out quickly so the people could eat them.

¹⁴Afterward the Levites prepared Passover offerings for themselves and for the priests—the descendants of Aaron—because the priests had been busy from morning till night offering the burnt offerings and the fat portions. The Levites took responsibility for all these preparations.

¹⁵The musicians, descendants of Asaph, were in their assigned places, following the commands that had been given by David, Asaph, Heman, and Jeduthun, the king's seer. The gatekeepers guarded the gates and did not need to leave their posts of duty, for their Passover offerings were prepared for them by their fellow Levites.

¹⁶The entire ceremony for the LORD's Passover was completed that day. All the burnt offerings were sacrificed on the altar of the LORD, as King Josiah had commanded. ¹⁷All the Israelites present in Jerusalem celebrated Passover and the Festival of Unleavened Bread for seven days. ¹⁸Never since the time of the prophet Samuel had there been such a Passover. None of the kings of Israel had ever kept a Passover as Josiah did, involving all the priests and Levites, all the people of Jerusalem, and people from all over Judah and Israel. ¹⁹This Passover celebration took place in the eighteenth year of Josiah's reign.

JOSIAH DIES IN BATTLE ²⁰After Josiah had finished restoring the Temple, King Neco of Egypt led his army up from Egypt to do battle at Carchemish on the Euphrates River, and Josiah and his army marched out to fight him.* ²¹But King Neco sent messengers to Josiah with this message:

"What do you want with me, king of Judah? I have no quarrel with you today! I am on my way to fight another nation, and God has told me to hurry! Do not interfere with God, who is with me, or he will destroy you."

²²But Josiah refused to listen to Neco, to whom God had indeed spoken, and he would not turn back. Instead, he disguised himself and led his army into battle on the plain of Megiddo. ²³But the enemy archers hit King Josiah with their arrows and wounded him. He cried out to his men, "Take me from the battle, for I am badly wounded!"

²⁴So they lifted Josiah out of his chariot

35:1 This day in the ancient Hebrew lunar calendar was April 5, 622 B.C. **35:20** Or *Josiah went out to meet him.*

and placed him in another chariot. Then they brought him back to Jerusalem, where he died. He was buried there in the royal cemetery. And all Judah and Jerusalem mourned for him. ²⁵The prophet Jeremiah composed funeral songs for Josiah, and to this day choirs still sing these sad songs about his death. These songs of sorrow have become a tradition and are recorded in *The Book of Laments*.

²⁶The rest of the events of Josiah's reign and his acts of devotion (carried out according to what was written in the Law of the LORD), ²⁷from beginning to end—all are recorded in *The Book of the Kings of Israel and Judah*.

36 JEHOAHAZ RULES IN JUDAH
Then the people of the land took Josiah's son Jehoahaz and made him the next king in Jerusalem.

²Jehoahaz* was twenty-three years old when he became king, and he reigned in Jerusalem three months.

³Then he was deposed by the king of Egypt, who demanded that Judah pay 7,500 pounds of silver and 75 pounds of gold* as tribute.

JEHOIAKIM RULES IN JUDAH
⁴The king of Egypt then installed Eliakim, the brother of Jehoahaz, as the next king of Judah and Jerusalem, and he changed Eliakim's name to Jehoiakim. Then Neco took Jehoahaz to Egypt as a prisoner.

⁵Jehoiakim was twenty-five years old when he became king, and he reigned in Jerusalem eleven years. He did what was evil in the sight of the LORD his God.

⁶Then King Nebuchadnezzar of Babylon came to Jerusalem and captured it, and he bound Jehoiakim in bronze chains and led him away to Babylon. ⁷Nebuchadnezzar also took some of the treasures from the Temple of the LORD, and he placed them in his palace* in Babylon.

⁸The rest of the events in Jehoiakim's reign, including all the evil things he did and everything found against him, are recorded in *The Book of the Kings of Israel and Judah*. Then his son Jehoiachin became the next king.

JEHOIACHIN RULES IN JUDAH
⁹Jehoiachin was eighteen* years old when he became king,

EXILE TO BABYLON
Despite Judah's few good kings and timely reforms, the people never truly changed. Their evil continued, and finally God used the Babylonian Empire under Nebuchadnezzar to conquer Judah, destroy Jerusalem, and take the people captive to Babylon.

and he reigned in Jerusalem three months and ten days. Jehoiachin did what was evil in the LORD's sight.

¹⁰In the spring of the year* King Nebuchadnezzar took Jehoiachin to Babylon. Many treasures from the Temple of the LORD were also taken to Babylon at that time. And Nebuchadnezzar installed Jehoiachin's uncle,* Zedekiah, as the next king in Judah and Jerusalem.

ZEDEKIAH RULES IN JUDAH
¹¹Zedekiah was twenty-one years old when he became king, and he reigned in Jerusalem eleven years. ¹²He did what was evil in the sight of the LORD his God, and he refused to humble himself when the prophet Jeremiah spoke to him directly from the LORD. ¹³He also rebelled against King Nebuchadnezzar, even though he had taken an oath of loyalty in God's name. Zedekiah was a hard and stubborn man, refusing to turn to the LORD, the God of Israel.

¹⁴Likewise, all the leaders of the priests and the people became more and more unfaithful. They followed all the pagan practices of the surrounding nations, desecrating the Temple of the LORD that had been consecrated in Jerusalem.

¹⁵The LORD, the God of their ancestors, repeatedly sent his prophets to warn them, for he had compassion on his people and his Temple. ¹⁶But the people mocked these messengers of God and despised their words. They scoffed at the prophets until the LORD's anger could no longer be restrained and nothing could be done.

THE FALL OF JERUSALEM
¹⁷So the LORD brought the king of Babylon against them. The Babylonians* killed Judah's young men,

36:2 Hebrew *Joahaz*, a variant spelling of Jehoahaz; also in 36:4. 36:3 Hebrew *100 talents* [3,400 kilograms] *of silver and 1 talent* [34 kilograms] *of gold*. 36:7 Or *temple*. 36:9 As in one Hebrew manuscript, some Greek manuscripts, and Syriac version (see also 2 Kgs 24:8); most Hebrew manuscripts read *eight*. 36:10a Hebrew *At the turn of the year*. The first day of this year in the ancient Hebrew lunar calendar was April 13, 597 B.C. 36:10b As in parallel text at 2 Kgs 24:17; Hebrew reads *brother*, or *relative*. 36:17 Or *Chaldeans*.

even chasing after them into the Temple. They had no pity on the people, killing both young men and young women, the old and the infirm. God handed all of them over to Nebuchadnezzar. [18]The king took home to Babylon all the articles, large and small, used in the Temple of God, and the treasures from both the LORD's Temple and from the palace of the king and his officials. [19]Then his army burned the Temple of God, tore down the walls of Jerusalem, burned all the palaces, and completely destroyed everything of value.* [20]The few who survived were taken as exiles to Babylon, and they became servants to the king and his sons until the kingdom of Persia came to power.

[21]So the message of the LORD spoken through Jeremiah was fulfilled. The land finally enjoyed its Sabbath rest, lying desolate until the seventy years were fulfilled, just as the prophet had said.

BEYOND CURE

(36:16) God continually warned the people of Judah about their wrongs and offered his forgiveness. But the people constantly returned to their bad habits. Eventually the situation was beyond cure. Wondering why? After a time God allows people who constantly reject him to go their own way (see Rom 1:18-32). When that happens, judgment follows. As Romans 1:18 tells us, "God shows his anger from heaven against all sinful, wicked people who suppress the truth by their wickedness." Don't want that? Don't reject him.

STRIPPED

(36:20) Second Chronicles started off on a high note, with the people gladly worshiping in the newly built Temple. But after ignoring God, they found themselves stripped of everything, divided up, and carried off to exile. Even though they lost it all, God was still with them. Like the people of Israel, are you feeling like you've been left with nothing? When everything in life seems stripped away from us, we also can be assured that God will never abandon us.

CYRUS ALLOWS THE EXILES TO RETURN

[22]In the first year of King Cyrus of Persia,* the LORD fulfilled the prophecy he had given through Jeremiah.* He stirred the heart of Cyrus to put this proclamation in writing and to send it throughout his kingdom:

[23]"This is what King Cyrus of Persia says:

"The LORD, the God of heaven, has given me all the kingdoms of the earth. He has appointed me to build him a Temple at Jerusalem, which is in Judah. Any of you who are the LORD's people may go there for this task. And may the LORD your God be with you!"

36:19 Or destroyed all the valuable articles from the Temple. **36:22a** The first year of Cyrus's reign over Babylon was 538 B.C. **36:22b** See Jer 25:11-12; 29:10.

EZRA

Ever look at someone who seems to have everything and think, Man, she's got it made. What more could she want? *On the surface, her life seems perfect. But looks can be deceiving.*

The same held true in the lives of the people of Israel. Years earlier, under Zerubbabel's leadership, some of the people from Israel had been given permission to leave Babylon and return to build the Temple. Although the returnees had met with some opposition, eventually they had been successful. The Temple was completed and dedicated. Everything looked good on the outside.

But when Ezra, a priest and scribe, reached Jerusalem, he wept. The people looked obedient because they had rebuilt the Temple. Yet their lives were a mess. Ezra knew that they needed a spiritual shake-up. The book of Ezra shows his commitment to helping his people to make things right with God.

In need of a spiritual tune-up or shake-up? As you read Ezra you can make Ezra's commitment yours.

KEY POINTS

RESTORATION By returning to the land of Israel from Babylon, the Jews showed their belief in God's promise to restore them. God promises to forgive and restore us when we return to him.

OPPOSITION Opposition came soon after the people of Israel built the altar and the Temple foundation was laid. Opposition always comes whenever anyone does anything for God. But God can overcome all opposition.

GOD'S WORD When the people of Israel returned to their homeland, they also returned to the influence of God's Word. The Bible also can be a powerful influence in our lives.

FAITH/ACTION The urging of Israel's leaders motivated the people to complete the Temple. But over the years, many of them had intermarried with idol worshipers and adopted their heathen practices. Only when their faith was tested and strengthened did they remove these sins from their lives. As we trust God with our heart and mind, we also must put our faith into action.

1 CYRUS ALLOWS THE EXILES TO RETURN

In the first year of King Cyrus of Persia,* the LORD fulfilled the prophecy he had given through Jeremiah.* He stirred the heart of Cyrus to put this proclamation in writing and to send it throughout his kingdom:

....

CAPTIVES

(1:1-7) The book of Ezra opens in 538 B.C., 48 years after Nebuchadnezzar destroyed Jerusalem, defeated the southern kingdom of Judah, and carried the Jews away to Babylon as captives (2 Kgs 25; 2 Chr 36). Nebuchadnezzar died in 562, and because his successor was not strong, Babylon was overthrown by Persia in 539, just prior to the events recorded in this book. Both the Babylonians and the Persians had a relaxed policy toward their captives, allowing them to own land and homes and to take ordinary jobs. Many of the Jews—like Daniel, Mordecai, and Esther—rose to prominent positions within the nation. King Cyrus of Persia went a step further: He allowed many of the people of Israel to return to their homeland. By doing this, he hoped to win their loyalty and thus provide buffer zones around the borders of his empire. What he didn't realize, however, was that he was the means of fulfilling God's promise to return the people to their land. As Proverbs 21:1 says, "The king's heart is like a stream of water directed by the LORD; he guides it wherever he pleases." God's plans are never overthrown. Are you willing to trust that he will fulfill any promise he's made to you?

²"This is what King Cyrus of Persia says:

"The LORD, the God of heaven, has given me all the kingdoms of the earth. He has appointed me to build him a Temple at Jerusalem, which is in Judah. ³Any of you who are his people may go to Jerusalem in Judah to rebuild this Temple of the LORD, the God of Israel, who lives in Jerusalem. And may your God be with you! ⁴Wherever this Jewish remnant is found, let their neighbors contribute toward their expenses by giving them silver and gold, supplies for the journey, and livestock, as well as a voluntary offering for the Temple of God in Jerusalem."

⁵Then God stirred the hearts of the priests and Levites and the leaders of the tribes of Judah and Benjamin to go to Jerusalem to rebuild the Temple of the LORD. ⁶And all their neighbors assisted by giving them articles of silver and gold, supplies for the journey, and livestock. They gave them many valuable gifts in addition to all the voluntary offerings.

⁷King Cyrus himself brought out the ar-

1:1a The first year of Cyrus's reign over Babylon was 538 B.C.
1:1b See Jer 25:11-12; 29:10.

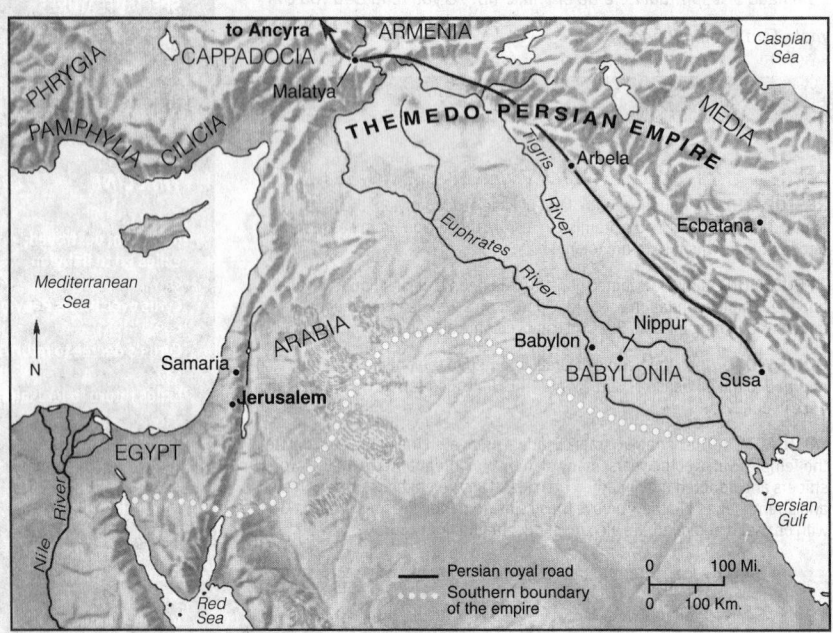

THE MEDO-PERSIAN EMPIRE

The Medo-Persian Empire included much of the area shown on this map and more. The Jewish exiles were concentrated in the area around Nippur in the Babylonian province. King Cyrus's decree, which allowed the Israelites to return to their homeland and rebuild the Temple, was discovered in the palace of Achmetha (also called Ecbatana).

ticles that King Nebuchadnezzar had taken from the LORD's Temple in Jerusalem and had placed in the temple of his own gods. 8Cyrus directed Mithredath, the treasurer of Persia, to count these items and present them to Sheshbazzar, the leader of the exiles returning to Judah.* 9This is a list of the items that were returned:

gold basins	30
silver basins	1,000
silver incense burners*	29
10 gold bowls	30
silver bowls	410
other items	1,000

11In all, there were 5,400 articles of gold and silver. Sheshbazzar brought all of these along when the exiles went from Babylon to Jerusalem.

2 EXILES WHO RETURNED WITH ZERUBBABEL

Here is the list of the Jewish exiles of the provinces who returned from their captivity. King Nebuchadnezzar had deported them to Babylon, but now they returned to Jerusalem and the other towns in Judah where they originally lived. 2Their leaders were Zerubbabel, Jeshua, Nehemiah, Seraiah, Reelaiah, Mordecai, Bilshan, Mispar, Bigvai, Rehum, and Baanah.

This is the number of the men of Israel who returned from exile:

3	The family of Parosh	2,172
4	The family of Shephatiah	372
5	The family of Arah	775
6	The family of Pahath-moab (descendants of Jeshua and Joab)	2,812
7	The family of Elam	1,254
8	The family of Zattu	945
9	The family of Zaccai	760
10	The family of Bani	642
11	The family of Bebai	623
12	The family of Azgad	1,222
13	The family of Adonikam	666
14	The family of Bigvai	2,056
15	The family of Adin	454
16	The family of Ater (descendants of Hezekiah)	98
17	The family of Bezai	323
18	The family of Jorah	112
19	The family of Hashum	223

1:8 Hebrew Sheshbazzar, the prince of Judah. 1:9 The meaning of this Hebrew word is uncertain. 2:24 As in parallel text at Neh 7:28; Hebrew reads Azmaveth. 2:25 As in some Hebrew manuscripts and Greek version (see also Neh 7:29); Hebrew reads Kiriath-arim. 2:31 Or of the other Elam. 2:46 As in an alternate reading of the Masoretic Text (see also Neh 7:48); the other alternate reads Shamlai.

20	The family of Gibbar	95
21	The people of Bethlehem	123
22	The people of Netophah	56
23	The people of Anathoth	128
24	The people of Beth-azmaveth*	42
25	The people of Kiriath-jearim,* Kephirah, and Beeroth	743
26	The people of Ramah and Geba	621
27	The people of Micmash	122
28	The people of Bethel and Ai	223
29	The citizens of Nebo	52
30	The citizens of Magbish	156
31	The citizens of West Elam*	1,254
32	The citizens of Harim	320
33	The citizens of Lod, Hadid, and Ono	725
34	The citizens of Jericho	345
35	The citizens of Senaah	3,630

36These are the priests who returned from exile:

	The family of Jedaiah (through the line of Jeshua)	973
37	The family of Immer	1,052
38	The family of Pashhur	1,247
39	The family of Harim	1,017

40These are the Levites who returned from exile:

	The families of Jeshua and Kadmiel (descendants of Hodaviah)	74
41	The singers of the family of Asaph	128
42	The gatekeepers of the families of Shallum, Ater, Talmon, Akkub, Hatita, and Shobai	139

43The descendants of the following Temple servants returned from exile:

Ziha, Hasupha, Tabbaoth,
44 Keros, Siaha, Padon,
45 Lebanah, Hagabah, Akkub,
46 Hagab, Shalmai,* Hanan,
47 Giddel, Gahar, Reaiah,
48 Rezin, Nekoda, Gazzam,
49 Uzza, Paseah, Besai,
50 Asnah, Meunim, Nephusim,
51 Bakbuk, Hakupha, Harhur,
52 Bazluth, Mehida, Harsha,
53 Barkos, Sisera, Temah,
54 Neziah, and Hatipha.

55The descendants of these servants of King Solomon returned from exile:

Sotai, Hassophereth, Peruda,
56 Jaalah, Darkon, Giddel,
57 Shephatiah, Hattil, Pokereth-hazzebaim, and Ami.

58In all, the Temple servants and the descendants of Solomon's servants numbered 392.

59Another group returned at this time from the towns of Tel-melah, Tel-harsha, Kerub, Addan, and Immer. However, they could not prove that they or their families were descendants of Israel. ⁶⁰This group included the families of Delaiah, Tobiah, and Nekoda—a total of 652 people.

⁶¹Three families of priests—Hobaiah, Hakkoz, and Barzillai—also returned. (This Barzillai had married a woman who was a descendant of Barzillai of Gilead, and he had taken her family name.) ⁶²They searched for their names in the genealogical records, but they were not found, so they were disqualified from serving as priests. ⁶³The governor told them not to eat the priests' share of food from the sacrifices until a priest could consult the Lord about the matter by using the Urim and Thummim—the sacred lots.

⁶⁴So a total of 42,360 people returned to Judah, ⁶⁵in addition to 7,337 servants and 200 singers, both men and women. ⁶⁶They took with them 736 horses, 245 mules, ⁶⁷435 camels, and 6,720 donkeys.

⁶⁸When they arrived at the Temple of the Lord in Jerusalem, some of the family leaders made voluntary offerings toward the rebuilding of God's Temple on its original site, ⁶⁹and each leader gave as much as he could. The total of their gifts came to 61,000 gold coins,* 6,250 pounds* of silver, and 100 robes for the priests.

⁷⁰So the priests, the Levites, the singers, the gatekeepers, the Temple servants, and some of the common people settled in villages near Jerusalem. The rest of the people returned to their own towns throughout Israel.

3 **THE ALTAR IS REBUILT** In early autumn,* when the Israelites had settled in their towns, all the people assembled in Jerusalem with a unified purpose. ²Then Jeshua son of Jehozadak* joined his fellow priests and Zerubbabel son of Shealtiel with his family in rebuilding the altar of the God of Israel. They wanted to sacrifice burnt offerings on it, as instructed in the Law of Moses, the man of God. ³Even though the people were afraid of the local residents, they rebuilt the altar at its old site. Then they began to sacrifice burnt of-

ferings on the altar to the Lord each morning and evening.

⁴They celebrated the Festival of Shelters as prescribed in the Law, sacrificing the number of burnt offerings specified for each day of the festival. ⁵They also offered the regular burnt offerings and the offerings required for the new moon celebrations and the annual festivals as prescribed by the Lord. The people also gave voluntary offerings to the Lord. ⁶Fifteen days before the Festival of Shelters began,* the priests had begun to sacrifice burnt offerings to the Lord. This was even before they had started to lay the foundation of the Lord's Temple.

THE PEOPLE BEGIN TO REBUILD THE TEMPLE
⁷Then the people hired masons and carpenters and bought cedar logs from the people of Tyre and Sidon, paying them with food, wine, and olive oil. The logs were brought down from the Lebanon mountains and floated along the coast of the Mediterranean Sea* to Joppa, for King Cyrus had given permission for this.

⁸The construction of the Temple of God began in midspring,* during the second year after they arrived in Jerusalem. The work force was made up of everyone who had returned from exile, including Zerubbabel son of Shealtiel, Jeshua son of Jehozadak and his fellow priests, and all the Levites. The Levites who were twenty years old or older were put in charge of rebuilding the Lord's Temple. ⁹The workers at the Temple of God were supervised by Jeshua with his sons and relatives, and Kadmiel and his sons, all descendants of Hodaviah.* They were helped in this task by the Levites of the family of Henadad.

¹⁰When the builders completed the foundation of the Lord's Temple, the priests put on their robes and took their places to blow their trumpets. And the Levites, descendants of Asaph, clashed their cymbals to praise the Lord, just as King David had prescribed. ¹¹With praise and thanks, they sang this song to the Lord:

2:69a Hebrew *61,000 darics of gold*, about 1,100 pounds or 500 kilograms in weight.   2:69b Hebrew *5,000 minas* [3,000 kilograms].   3:1 Hebrew *In the seventh month*. The year is not specified, so it may have been during Cyrus's first year (538 B.C.) or second year (537 B.C.). The seventh month of the ancient Hebrew lunar calendar occurred within the months of September/October 538 B.C. and October/November 537 B.C.   3:2 Hebrew *Jozadak*, a variant spelling of Jehozadak; also in 3:8.   3:6 Hebrew *On the first day of the seventh month*. This day in the ancient Hebrew lunar calendar occurred in September or October. The Festival of Shelters began on the fifteenth day of the seventh month.   3:7 Hebrew *the sea*.   3:8 Hebrew *in the second month*. This month in the ancient Hebrew lunar calendar occurred within the months of April and May 536 B.C.   3:9 Hebrew *sons of Judah* (i.e., *bene Yehudah*). *Bene* might also be read here as the proper name Binnui; *Yehudah* is probably another name for Hodaviah. Compare 2:40; Neh 7:43; 1 Esdras 5:58.

TIME TO PREPARE
(3:1-8) The people of Israel spent months just preparing to build the Temple. During this time, the altar was built, materials were ordered and collected, and workers were hired. How much prep time do you take before doing a project? Most of us would rather do a job than prepare for it. Preparation time may not feel heroic or spiritual, but it is vital to any project you want to do well.

"He is so good!
His faithful love for Israel endures
    forever!"

Then all the people gave a great shout, praising the LORD because the foundation of the LORD's Temple had been laid. ¹²But many of the older priests, Levites, and other leaders who had seen the first Temple wept aloud when they saw the new Temple's foundation. The others, however, were shouting for joy. ¹³The joyful shouting and weeping mingled together in a loud noise that could be heard far in the distance.

4 ENEMIES OPPOSE THE REBUILDING The enemies of Judah and Benjamin heard that the exiles were rebuilding a Temple to the LORD, the God of Israel. ²So they approached Zerubbabel and the other leaders and said, "Let us build with you, for we worship your God just as you do. We have sacrificed to him ever since King Esarhaddon of Assyria brought us here."

³But Zerubbabel, Jeshua, and the other leaders of Israel replied, "You may have no part in this work. We alone will build the Temple for the LORD, the God of Israel, just as King Cyrus of Persia commanded us."

⁴Then the local residents tried to discourage and frighten the people of Judah to keep them from their work. ⁵They bribed agents to work against them and to frustrate their plans. This went on during the entire reign of King Cyrus of Persia and lasted until King Darius of Persia took the throne.*

LATER OPPOSITION UNDER XERXES AND ARTAXERXES ⁶Years later when Xerxes* began his reign, the enemies of Judah wrote a letter of accusation against the people of Judah and Jerusalem.

⁷Even later, during the reign of King Artaxerxes of Persia,* the enemies of Judah, led by Bishlam, Mithredath, and Tabeel, sent a letter to Artaxerxes in the Aramaic language, and it was translated for the king.

⁸*Rehum the governor and Shimshai the court secretary wrote the letter, telling King Artaxerxes about the situation in Jerusalem. ⁹They greeted the king for all their colleagues— the judges and local leaders, the people of Tarpel, the Persians, the Babylonians, and

the people of Erech and Susa (that is, Elam). ¹⁰They also sent greetings from the rest of the people whom the great and noble Ashurbanipal* had deported and relocated in Samaria and throughout the neighboring lands of the province west of the Euphrates River.* ¹¹This is a copy of their letter:

"To King Artaxerxes, from your loyal subjects in the province west of the Euphrates River.

¹²"The king should know that the Jews who came here to Jerusalem from Babylon are rebuilding this rebellious and evil city. They have already laid the foundation and will soon finish its walls. ¹³And the king should know that if this city is rebuilt and its walls are completed, it will be much to your disadvantage, for the Jews will then refuse to pay their tribute, customs, and tolls to you.

¹⁴"Since we are your loyal subjects* and do not want to see the king dishonored in this way, we have sent the king this information. ¹⁵We suggest that a search be made in your ancestors' records, where you will discover what a rebellious city this has been in the past. In fact, it was destroyed because of its long and troublesome history of revolt against the kings and countries who controlled it. ¹⁶We declare to the king that if this city is rebuilt and its walls are completed, the province west of the Euphrates River will be lost to you."

¹⁷Then King Artaxerxes sent this reply:

"To Rehum the governor, Shimshai the court secretary, and their colleagues living in Samaria and throughout the province west of the Euphrates River. Greetings.

¹⁸"The letter you sent has been translated and read to me. ¹⁹I ordered a search of the records and have found that Jerusalem has indeed been a hotbed of insurrection against many kings. In fact, rebellion and revolt are normal there! ²⁰Powerful kings have ruled over Jerusalem and the entire province west of the Euphrates River,

---

4:5 Darius reigned 521–486 B.C. 4:6 Hebrew *Ahasuerus*, another name for Xerxes. He reigned 486–465 B.C. 4:7 Artaxerxes reigned 465–424 B.C. 4:8 The original text of 4:8–6:18 is in Aramaic. 4:10a Aramaic *Osnappar*, another name for Ashurbanipal. 4:10b Aramaic *the province beyond the river;* also in 4:11, 16, 17, 20. 4:14 Aramaic *Since we eat the salt of the palace.*

SPIRITUAL TROUBLE
(4:1-6) Enemies of the people of Israel interfered with the building project. In the same way, believers can expect opposition as they do God's work (2 Tim 3:12). The opposition may involve offers of friendships that only lead to distractions (Ezra 4:2), attempts to discourage or intimidate (4:4-5), or unjust accusations (4:6). If you learn to expect opposition, you won't be stopped by it. Move ahead with the work God has planned for you, and trust him to overcome the obstacles.

receiving tribute, customs, and tolls.
²¹Therefore, issue orders to have these
men stop their work. That city must not
be rebuilt except at my express command.
²²Be diligent, and don't neglect this matter,
for we must not permit the situation to harm
the king's interests."

²³When this letter from King Artaxerxes was
read to Rehum, Shimshai, and their colleagues,
they hurried to Jerusalem. Then, with a show of
strength, they forced the Jews to stop building.

THE REBUILDING RESUMES ²⁴So the work on
the Temple of God in Jerusalem had stopped,
and it remained at a standstill until the second
year of the reign of King Darius of Persia.*

5 At that time the prophets Haggai and Zechariah son of Iddo prophesied to the Jews
in Judah and Jerusalem. They prophesied in the
name of the God of Israel who was over them.
²Zerubbabel son of Shealtiel and Jeshua son of
Jehozadak* responded by starting again to rebuild the Temple of God in Jerusalem. And the
prophets of God were with them and helped
them.

³But Tattenai, governor of the province west
of the Euphrates River,* and Shethar-bozenai
and their colleagues soon arrived in Jerusalem
and asked, "Who gave you permission to rebuild this Temple and restore this structure?"
⁴They also asked for the names of all the men
working on the Temple. ⁵But because their God
was watching over them, the leaders of the
Jews were not prevented from building until a
report was sent to Darius and he returned his
decision.

TATTENAI'S LETTER TO KING DARIUS ⁶This is
a copy of the letter that Tattenai the governor,
Shethar-bozenai, and the other officials of the
province west of the Euphrates River sent to
King Darius:

⁷"To King Darius. Greetings.
⁸"The king should know that we went
to the construction site of the Temple of

the great God in the province of Judah. It
is being rebuilt with specially prepared
stones, and timber is being laid in its walls.
The work is going forward with great energy
and success.

⁹"We asked the leaders, 'Who gave you
permission to rebuild this Temple and
restore this structure?' ¹⁰And we demanded
their names so that we could tell you who
the leaders were.

¹¹"This was their answer: 'We are the
servants of the God of heaven and earth,
and we are rebuilding the Temple that
was built here many years ago by a great
king of Israel. ¹²But because our ancestors
angered the God of heaven, he abandoned
them to King Nebuchadnezzar of Babylon,*
who destroyed this Temple and exiled
the people to Babylonia. ¹³However, King
Cyrus of Babylon,* during the first year
of his reign, issued a decree that the
Temple of God should be rebuilt. ¹⁴King
Cyrus returned the gold and silver cups
that Nebuchadnezzar had taken from
the Temple of God in Jerusalem and had
placed in the temple of Babylon. These
cups were taken from that temple and
presented to a man named Sheshbazzar,
whom King Cyrus appointed as governor
of Judah. ¹⁵The king instructed him to return
the cups to their place in Jerusalem and
to rebuild the Temple of God there on its
original site. ¹⁶So this Sheshbazzar came
and laid the foundations of the Temple of
God in Jerusalem. The people have been
working on it ever since, though it is not yet
completed.'

¹⁷"Therefore, if it pleases the king, we
request that a search be made in the royal
archives of Babylon to discover whether
King Cyrus ever issued a decree to rebuild
God's Temple in Jerusalem. And then let the
king send us his decision in this matter."

6 **DARIUS APPROVES THE REBUILDING** So
King Darius issued orders that a search be
made in the Babylonian archives, which were
stored in the treasury. ²But it was at the fortress
at Ecbatana in the province of Media that a
scroll was found. This is what it said:

"Memorandum:
³"In the first year of King Cyrus's reign,

A BOLD RESPONSE
*(5:3-11) While rebuilding the Temple, the workers were
confronted by the governor, who demanded to know
who had given permission for their construction project
(5:3). The people boldly replied, "We are the servants of
the God of heaven and earth." They knew that God was
on their side. Is this bold response your response when
you face opposition? Like the people of Israel, you can be
assured that God is on your side when you take a stand
for what's right.*

4:24 The second year of Darius's reign was 520 B.C. The narrative
started in 4:1-5 is resumed at verse 24.   **5:2** Aramaic *Jozadak*, a
variant spelling of Jehozadak.   **5:3** Aramaic *the province beyond
the river*; also in 5:6.   **5:12** Aramaic *Nebuchadnezzar the Chaldean.*
5:13 King Cyrus of Persia is here identified as the king of Babylon
because Persia had conquered the Babylonian Empire.

a decree was sent out concerning the Temple of God at Jerusalem.

"Let the Temple be rebuilt on the site where Jews used to offer their sacrifices, using the original foundations. Its height will be ninety feet, and its width will be ninety feet.* ⁴Every three layers of specially prepared stones will be topped by a layer of timber. All expenses will be paid by the royal treasury. ⁵Furthermore, the gold and silver cups, which were taken to Babylon by Nebuchadnezzar from the Temple of God in Jerusalem, must be returned to Jerusalem and put back where they belong. Let them be taken back to the Temple of God."

⁶So King Darius sent this message:

"Now therefore, Tattenai, governor of the province west of the Euphrates River,* and Shethar-bozenai, and your colleagues and other officials west of the Euphrates River— stay away from there! ⁷Do not disturb the construction of the Temple of God. Let it be rebuilt on its original site, and do not hinder the governor of Judah and the elders of the Jews in their work.

⁸"Moreover, I hereby decree that you are to help these elders of the Jews as they rebuild this Temple of God. You must pay the full construction costs, without delay, from my taxes collected in the province west of the Euphrates River so that the work will not be interrupted.

⁹"Give the priests in Jerusalem whatever is needed in the way of young bulls, rams, and male lambs for the burnt offerings presented to the God of heaven. And without fail, provide them with as much wheat, salt, wine, and olive oil as they need each day. ¹⁰Then they will be able to offer acceptable sacrifices to the God of heaven and pray for the welfare of the king and his sons.

¹¹"Those who violate this decree in any way will have a beam pulled from their house. Then they will be tied to it and flogged, and their house will be reduced

THERE WAS GREAT JOY THROUGHOUT THE LAND.

to a pile of rubble.* ¹²May the God who has chosen the city of Jerusalem as the place to honor his name destroy any king or nation that violates this command and destroys this Temple.

"I, Darius, have issued this decree. Let it be obeyed with all diligence."

THE TEMPLE'S DEDICATION ¹³Tattenai, governor of the province west of the Euphrates River, and Shethar-bozenai and their colleagues complied at once with the command of King Darius. ¹⁴So the Jewish elders continued their work, and they were greatly encouraged by the preaching of the prophets Haggai and Zechariah son of Iddo. The Temple was finally finished, as had been commanded by the God of Israel and decreed by Cyrus, Darius, and Artaxerxes, the kings of Persia. ¹⁵The Temple was completed on March 12,* during the sixth year of King Darius's reign.

¹⁶The Temple of God was then dedicated with great joy by the people of Israel, the priests, the Levites, and the rest of the people who had returned from exile. ¹⁷During the dedication ceremony for the Temple of God, 100 young bulls, 200 rams, and 400 male lambs were sacrificed. And 12 male goats were presented as a sin offering for the twelve tribes of Israel. ¹⁸Then the priests and Levites were divided into their various divisions to serve at the Temple of God in Jerusalem, as prescribed in the Book of Moses.

CELEBRATION OF PASSOVER ¹⁹On April 21* the returned exiles celebrated Passover. ²⁰The priests and Levites had purified themselves and were ceremonially clean. So they slaughtered the Passover lamb for all the returned exiles, for their fellow priests, and for themselves.

....

6:3 Aramaic *Its height will be 60 cubits* [27.6 meters], *and its width will be 60 cubits.* It is commonly held that this verse should be emended to read: "Its height will be 30 cubits [45 feet, or 13.8 meters], its length will be 60 cubits [90 feet, or 27.6 meters], and its width will be 20 cubits [30 feet, or 9.2 meters]"; compare 1 Kgs 6:2. The emendation regarding the width is supported by the Syriac version.   **6:6** Aramaic *the province beyond the river;* also in 6:6b, 8, 13.   **6:11** Aramaic *a dunghill.*   **6:15** Aramaic *on the third day of the month Adar,* of the ancient Hebrew lunar calendar. A number of events in Ezra can be cross-checked with dates in surviving Persian records and related accurately to our modern calendar. This day was March 12, 515 B.C.   **6:19** Hebrew *On the fourteenth day of the first month,* of the ancient Hebrew lunar calendar. This day was April 21, 515 B.C.; also see note on 6:15.

TIMING
(6:16-22) Feasting and celebration were on the menu at the great Temple dedication. But that also was the time when the priests and Levites "were divided into their various divisions to serve at the Temple." There is a time to celebrate and a time to work. Both, in their time, are proper and necessary when worshiping and serving God, and God is evident in both.

²¹The Passover meal was eaten by the people of Israel who had returned from exile and by the others in the land who had turned from their immoral customs to worship the LORD, the God of Israel. ²²Then they celebrated the Festival of Unleavened Bread for seven days. There was great joy throughout the land because the LORD had caused the king of Assyria* to be favorable to them, so that he helped them to rebuild the Temple of God, the God of Israel.

7 **EZRA ARRIVES IN JERUSALEM** Many years later, during the reign of King Artaxerxes of Persia,* there was a man named Ezra. He was the son* of Seraiah, son of Azariah, son of Hilkiah, ²son of Shallum, son of Zadok, son of Ahitub, ³son of Amariah, son of Azariah, son* of Meraioth, ⁴son of Zerahiah, son of Uzzi, son of Bukki, ⁵son of Abishua, son of Phinehas, son of Eleazar, son of Aaron the high priest.* ⁶This Ezra was a scribe who was well versed in the Law of Moses, which the LORD, the God of Israel, had given to the people of Israel. He came up to Jerusalem from Babylon, and the king gave him everything he asked for, because the gracious hand of the LORD his God was on him. ⁷Some of the people of Israel, as well as some of the priests, Levites, singers, gatekeepers, and Temple servants, traveled up to Jerusalem with him in the seventh year of King Artaxerxes' reign.

⁸Ezra arrived in Jerusalem in August* of that year. ⁹He had arranged to leave Babylon on April 8, the first day of the new year,* and he arrived at Jerusalem on August 4,* for the gracious hand of his God was on him. ¹⁰This was because Ezra had determined to study and obey the Law of the LORD and to teach those decrees and regulations to the people of Israel.

ARTAXERXES' LETTER TO EZRA ¹¹King Artaxerxes had given a copy of the following letter to Ezra, the priest and scribe who studied and taught the commands and decrees of the LORD to Israel:

¹²*"From Artaxerxes, the king of kings, to Ezra the priest, the teacher of the law of the God of heaven. Greetings.

¹³"I decree that any of the people of Israel in my kingdom, including the priests and Levites, may volunteer to return to Jerusalem with you. ¹⁴I and my council of seven hereby instruct you to conduct an inquiry into the situation in Judah and Jerusalem, based on your God's law, which is in your hand. ¹⁵We also commission you to take with you silver and gold, which we are freely presenting as an offering to the God of Israel who lives in Jerusalem.

¹⁶"Furthermore, you are to take any silver and gold that you may obtain from the province of Babylon, as well as the voluntary offerings of the people and the priests that are presented for the Temple of their God in Jerusalem. ¹⁷These donations are to be used specifically for the purchase of bulls, rams, male lambs, and the appropriate grain offerings and liquid offerings, all of which

6:22 King Darius of Persia is here identified as the king of Assyria because Persia had conquered the Babylonian Empire, which included the earlier Assyrian Empire. **7:1a** Artaxerxes reigned 465–424 B.C. **7:1b** Or *descendant*; see 1 Chr 6:14. **7:3** Or *descendant*; see 1 Chr 6:6-10. **7:5** Or *the first priest*. **7:8** Hebrew *in the fifth month*. This month in the ancient Hebrew lunar calendar occurred within the months of August and September 458 B.C. **7:9a** Hebrew *on the first day of the first month*, of the ancient Hebrew lunar calendar. This day was April 8, 458 B.C.; also see note on 6:15. **7:9b** Hebrew *on the first day of the fifth month*, of the ancient Hebrew lunar calendar. This day was August 4, 458 B.C.; also see note on 6:15. **7:12** The original text of 7:12-26 is in Aramaic.

will be offered on the altar of the Temple of your God in Jerusalem. ¹⁸Any silver and gold that is left over may be used in whatever way you and your colleagues feel is the will of your God.

¹⁹"But as for the cups we are entrusting to you for the service of the Temple of your God, deliver them all to the God of Jerusalem. ²⁰If you need anything else for your God's Temple or for any similar needs, you may take it from the royal treasury.

²¹"I, Artaxerxes the king, hereby send this decree to all the treasurers in the province west of the Euphrates River*: 'You are to give Ezra, the priest and teacher of the law of the God of heaven, whatever he requests of you. ²²You are to give him up to 7,500 pounds* of silver, 500 bushels* of wheat, 550 gallons of wine, 550 gallons of olive oil,* and an unlimited supply of salt. ²³Be careful to provide whatever the God of heaven demands for his Temple, for why should we risk bringing God's anger against the realm of the king and his sons? ²⁴I also decree that no priest, Levite, singer, gatekeeper, Temple servant, or other worker in this Temple of God will be required to pay tribute, customs, or tolls of any kind.'

²⁵"And you, Ezra, are to use the wisdom your God has given you to appoint magistrates and judges who know your God's laws to govern all the people in the province west of the Euphrates River. Teach the law to anyone who does not know it. ²⁶Anyone who refuses to obey the law of your God and the law of the king will be punished immediately, either by death, banishment, confiscation of goods, or imprisonment."

EZRA PRAISES THE LORD ²⁷Praise the LORD, the God of our ancestors, who made the king want to beautify the Temple of the LORD in Jerusalem! ²⁸And praise him for demonstrating such unfailing love to me by honoring me before the king, his council, and all his mighty nobles! I felt encouraged because the gracious hand of the LORD my God was on me. And I gathered some of the leaders of Israel to return with me to Jerusalem.

8 **EXILES WHO RETURNED WITH EZRA** Here is a list of the family leaders and the genealogies of those who came with me from Babylon during the reign of King Artaxerxes:

² From the family of Phinehas: Gershom.
From the family of Ithamar: Daniel.
From the family of David: Hattush, ³a descendant of Shecaniah.
From the family of Parosh: Zechariah and 150 other men were registered.
⁴ From the family of Pahath-moab: Eliehoenai son of Zerahiah and 200 other men.
⁵ From the family of Zattu*: Shecaniah son of Jahaziel and 300 other men.
⁶ From the family of Adin: Ebed son of Jonathan and 50 other men.
⁷ From the family of Elam: Jeshaiah son of Athaliah and 70 other men.
⁸ From the family of Shephatiah: Zebadiah son of Michael and 80 other men.
⁹ From the family of Joab: Obadiah son of Jehiel and 218 other men.
¹⁰ From the family of Bani*: Shelomith son of Josiphiah and 160 other men.
¹¹ From the family of Bebai: Zechariah son of Bebai and 28 other men.
¹² From the family of Azgad: Johanan son of Hakkatan and 110 other men.
¹³ From the family of Adonikam, who came later*: Eliphelet, Jeuel, Shemaiah, and 60 other men.
¹⁴ From the family of Bigvai: Uthai, Zaccur,* and 70 other men.

EZRA'S JOURNEY TO JERUSALEM ¹⁵I assembled the exiles at the Ahava Canal, and we camped there for three days while I went over the lists of the people and the priests who had arrived. I found that not one Levite had volunteered to come along. ¹⁶So I sent for Eliezer, Ariel, Shemaiah, Elnathan, Jarib, Elnathan,

7:21 Aramaic *the province beyond the river;* also in 7:25.
7:22a Aramaic *100 talents* [3,400 kilograms]. 7:22b Aramaic *100 cors* [18.2 kiloliters]. 7:22c Aramaic *100 baths* [2.1 kiloliters] *of wine, 100 baths of olive oil.* 8:5 As in some Greek manuscripts (see also 1 Esdras 8:32); Hebrew lacks *Zattu.* 8:10 As in some Greek manuscripts (see also 1 Esdras 8:36); Hebrew lacks *Bani.* 8:13 Or *who were the last of his family.* 8:14 As in Greek and Syriac versions and an alternate reading of the Masoretic Text; the other alternate reads *Zabbud.*

SUPPORT FOR LEADERS
(7:24) Why did Artaxerxes exempt Temple workers from paying taxes? He recognized that the priests and Levites filled an important role in society as spiritual leaders, so he freed them from paying taxes. When we give money to support the work of our local churches, we free our leaders and their staff to do what they're called to do. In what ways do you support your church leaders?

A DANGEROUS JOURNEY
(8:15-36) Ezra and the people traveled approximately nine hundred miles on foot. The trip took them through dangerous and difficult territory and lasted about four months. They prayed that God would protect them and give them a good journey. We may never have to travel that far (on foot at least), but we still need guidance and protection. Have you asked God for either lately?

Nathan, Zechariah, and Meshullam, who were leaders of the people. I also sent for Joiarib and Elnathan, who were men of discernment. [17]I sent them to Iddo, the leader of the Levites at Casiphia, to ask him and his relatives and the Temple servants to send us ministers for the Temple of God at Jerusalem.

[18]Since the gracious hand of our God was on us, they sent us a man named Sherebiah, along with eighteen of his sons and brothers. He was a very astute man and a descendant of Mahli, who was a descendant of Levi son of Israel.* [19]They also sent Hashabiah, together with Jeshaiah from the descendants of Merari, and twenty of his sons and brothers, [20]and 220 Temple servants. The Temple servants were assistants to the Levites—a group of Temple workers first instituted by King David and his officials. They were all listed by name.

[21]And there by the Ahava Canal, I gave orders for all of us to fast and humble ourselves before our God. We prayed that he would give us a safe journey and protect us, our children, and our goods as we traveled. [22]For I was ashamed to ask the king for soldiers and horsemen* to accompany us and protect us from enemies along the way. After all, we had told the king, "Our God's hand of protection is on all who worship him, but his fierce anger rages against those who abandon him." [23]So we fasted and earnestly prayed that our God would take care of us, and he heard our prayer.

[24]I appointed twelve leaders of the priests—Sherebiah, Hashabiah, and ten other priests—[25]to be in charge of transporting the silver, the gold, the gold bowls, and the other items that the king, his council, his officials, and all the people of Israel had presented for the Temple of God. [26]I weighed the treasure as I gave it to them and found the totals to be as follows:

24 tons* of silver,
7,500 pounds* of silver articles,
7,500 pounds of gold,

[27]20 gold bowls, equal in value to 1,000 gold coins,*
2 fine articles of polished bronze, as precious as gold.

[28]And I said to these priests, "You and these treasures have been set apart as holy to the LORD. This silver and gold is a voluntary offering to the LORD, the God of our ancestors. [29]Guard these treasures well until you present them to the leading priests, the Levites, and the leaders of Israel, who will weigh them at the storerooms of the LORD's Temple in Jerusalem." [30]So the priests and the Levites accepted the task of transporting these treasures of silver and gold to the Temple of our God in Jerusalem.

[31]We broke camp at the Ahava Canal on April 19* and started off to Jerusalem. And the gracious hand of our God protected us and saved us from enemies and bandits along the way. [32]So we arrived safely in Jerusalem, where we rested for three days.

[33]On the fourth day after our arrival, the silver, gold, and other valuables were weighed at the Temple of our God and entrusted to Meremoth son of Uriah the priest and to Eleazar son of Phinehas, along with Jozabad son of Jeshua and Noadiah son of Binnui—both of whom were Levites. [34]Everything was accounted for by number and weight, and the total weight was officially recorded.

[35]Then the exiles who had come out of captivity sacrificed burnt offerings to the God of Israel. They presented twelve bulls for all the people of Israel, as well as ninety-six rams and seventy-seven male lambs. They also offered twelve male goats as a sin offering. All this was given as a burnt offering to the LORD. [36]The king's decrees were delivered to his highest officers and the governors of the province west of the Euphrates River,* who then cooperated by supporting the people and the Temple of God.

9 EZRA'S PRAYER CONCERNING INTERMARRIAGE
When these things had been done, the Jewish leaders came to me and said, "Many of the people of Israel, and even some of the priests and Levites, have not kept themselves separate from the other peoples living in the land. They have taken up the detestable practices of the Canaanites, Hittites,

---

MARRIAGE LAWS
(9:1-15) Marriages between the people of Israel and the people of other nations were forbidden by law (see Deut 7:3-4). Opposition to mixed marriage was not racial prejudice because Jews and non-Jews of this area were of the same Semitic background. The reasons were strictly spiritual. God knew that people from other nations would encourage his people to worship their gods. Although we're not forbidden to marry people from other nations today, problems occur when believers marry unbelievers (see 2 Cor 6:14-15). Such marriages cannot have unity in the most important issue in life—commitment to God. If you're thinking that who you marry doesn't matter, think again!

8:18 Israel is the name that God gave to Jacob.   **8:22** Or charioteers.   **8:26a** Hebrew 650 talents [22 metric tons].   **8:26b** Hebrew 100 talents [3,400 kilograms]; also in 8:26c.   **8:27** Hebrew 1,000 darics, about 19 pounds or 8.6 kilograms in weight.   **8:31** Hebrew on the twelfth day of the first month, of the ancient Hebrew lunar calendar. This day was April 19, 458 B.C.; also see note on 6:15.   **8:36** Hebrew the province beyond the river.

Perizzites, Jebusites, Ammonites, Moabites, Egyptians, and Amorites. ²For the men of Israel have married women from these people and have taken them as wives for their sons. So the holy race has become polluted by these mixed marriages. Worse yet, the leaders and officials have led the way in this outrage."

³When I heard this, I tore my cloak and my shirt, pulled hair from my head and beard, and sat down utterly shocked. ⁴Then all who trembled at the words of the God of Israel came and sat with me because of this outrage committed by the returned exiles. And I sat there utterly appalled until the time of the evening sacrifice.

⁵At the time of the sacrifice, I stood up from where I had sat in mourning with my clothes torn. I fell to my knees and lifted my hands to the LORD my God. ⁶I prayed,

"O my God, I am utterly ashamed; I blush to lift up my face to you. For our sins are piled higher than our heads, and our guilt has reached to the heavens. ⁷From the days of our ancestors until now, we have been steeped in sin. That is why we and our kings and our priests have been at the mercy of the pagan kings of the land. We have been killed, captured, robbed, and disgraced, just as we are today.

⁸"But now we have been given a brief moment of grace, for the LORD our God has allowed a few of us to survive as a remnant. He has given us security in this holy place. Our God has brightened our eyes and granted us some relief from our slavery. ⁹For we were slaves, but in his unfailing love our God did not abandon us in our slavery. Instead, he caused the kings of Persia to treat us favorably. He revived us so we could rebuild the Temple of our God and repair its ruins. He has given us a protective wall in Judah and Jerusalem.

¹⁰"And now, O our God, what can we say after all of this? For once again we have abandoned your commands! ¹¹Your servants the prophets warned us when they said, 'The land you are entering to possess is totally defiled by the detestable practices of the people living there. From one end to the other, the land is filled with corruption. ¹²Don't let your daughters marry their sons! Don't take their daughters as wives for your sons. Don't ever promote the peace and prosperity of those nations. If you follow these instructions, you will be strong and will enjoy the good things the land produces, and you will leave this prosperity to your children forever.'

¹³"Now we are being punished because of our wickedness and our great guilt. But we have actually been punished far less than we deserve, for you, our God, have allowed some of us to survive as a remnant. ¹⁴But even so, we are again breaking your commands and intermarrying with people who do these detestable things. Won't your anger be enough to destroy us, so that even this little remnant no longer survives? ¹⁵O LORD, God of Israel, you are just. We come before you in our guilt as nothing but an escaped remnant, though in such a condition none of us can stand in your presence."

10 THE PEOPLE CONFESS THEIR SIN While Ezra prayed and made this confession, weeping and lying face down on the ground in front of the Temple of God, a very large crowd of people from Israel—men, women, and children—gathered and wept bitterly with him. ²Then Shecaniah son of Jehiel, a descendant of Elam, said to Ezra, "We have been unfaithful to our God, for we have married these pagan women of the land. But in spite of this there is hope for Israel. ³Let us now make a covenant

....

ON HIS KNEES
(9:5-15) After learning about the sins of the people, Ezra fell to his knees in prayer. His heartfelt prayer provides a good perspective on sin. He recognized (1) that sin is serious (9:6); (2) that no one sins without affecting others (9:7); (3) that he was not sinless although he didn't have a heathen wife (9:10); and (4) that God's love and mercy had spared the nation when they did nothing to deserve it (9:9, 15). It is easy to view sin lightly in a world that sees it as inconsequential, but we should view sin as seriously as Ezra did.

OBEDIENCE
(10:1-3) The men who married women from other nations agreed to divorce their wives and send away their children. Sounds cruel, right? Yet this act was necessary to preserve Israel as a nation committed to God. So, the disobedient Israelites were forced to choose between two painful options: continue in these marriages and risk God's wrath or divorce their wives. Does this mean that God approves of divorce? No! Elsewhere in Scripture, God makes it clear that he hates divorce (Mal 2:15-16; Matt 19:8-9). Obeying God's commands can keep us from facing a no-win situation as the Israelites did here.

FROM SORROW TO ACTION
(10:1-11) Following Ezra's earnest prayer, the people owned up to their wrong actions and asked for help to make things right with God. Making things right doesn't just involve an apology. It also involves a change in attitude and actions. If you've blown it with God or with someone else, what are you going to do about it?

with our God to divorce our pagan wives and to send them away with their children. We will follow the advice given by you and by the others who respect the commands of our God. Let it be done according to the Law of God. ⁴Get up, for it is your duty to tell us how to proceed in setting things straight. We are behind you, so be strong and take action."

⁵So Ezra stood up and demanded that the leaders of the priests and the Levites and all the people of Israel swear that they would do as Shecaniah had said. And they all swore a solemn oath. ⁶Then Ezra left the front of the Temple of God and went to the room of Jehohanan son of Eliashib. He spent the night* there without eating or drinking anything. He was still in mourning because of the unfaithfulness of the returned exiles.

⁷Then a proclamation was made throughout Judah and Jerusalem that all the exiles should come to Jerusalem. ⁸Those who failed to come within three days would, if the leaders and elders so decided, forfeit all their property and be expelled from the assembly of the exiles.

⁹Within three days, all the people of Judah and Benjamin had gathered in Jerusalem. This took place on December 19,* and all the people were sitting in the square before the Temple of God. They were trembling both because of the seriousness of the matter and because it was raining. ¹⁰Then Ezra the priest stood and said to them: "You have committed a terrible sin. By marrying pagan women, you have increased Israel's guilt. ¹¹So now confess your sin to the LORD, the God of your ancestors, and do what he demands. Separate yourselves from the people of the land and from these pagan women."

¹²Then the whole assembly raised their voices and answered, "Yes, you are right; we must do as you say!" ¹³Then they added, "This isn't something that can be done in a day or two, for many of us are involved in this extremely sinful affair. And this is the rainy season, so we cannot stay out here much longer. ¹⁴Let our leaders act on behalf of us all. Let everyone who has a pagan wife come at a scheduled time, accompanied by the leaders and judges of his city, so that the fierce anger of our God concerning this affair may be turned away from us."

¹⁵Only Jonathan son of Asahel and Jahzeiah son of Tikvah opposed this course of action, and they were supported by Meshullam and Shabbethai the Levite.

¹⁶So this was the plan they followed. Ezra selected leaders to represent their families, designating each of the representatives by name. On December 29,* the leaders sat down to investigate the matter. ¹⁷By March 27, the first day of the new year,* they had finished dealing with all the men who had married pagan wives.

THOSE GUILTY OF INTERMARRIAGE ¹⁸These are the priests who had married pagan wives:

From the family of Jeshua son of Jehozadak* and his brothers: Maaseiah, Eliezer, Jarib, and Gedaliah. ¹⁹They vowed to divorce their wives, and they each acknowledged their guilt by offering a ram as a guilt offering.

²⁰From the family of Immer: Hanani and Zebadiah.

²¹From the family of Harim: Maaseiah, Elijah, Shemaiah, Jehiel, and Uzziah.

²²From the family of Pashhur: Elioenai, Maaseiah, Ishmael, Nethanel, Jozabad, and Elasah.

²³These are the Levites who were guilty: Jozabad, Shimei, Kelaiah (also called Kelita), Pethahiah, Judah, and Eliezer.

²⁴This is the singer who was guilty: Eliashib.

These are the gatekeepers who were guilty: Shallum, Telem, and Uri.

²⁵These are the other people of Israel who were guilty:

From the family of Parosh: Ramiah, Izziah, Malkijah, Mijamin, Eleazar, Hashabiah,* and Benaiah.

²⁶From the family of Elam: Mattaniah, Zechariah, Jehiel, Abdi, Jeremoth, and Elijah.

²⁷From the family of Zattu: Elioenai, Eliashib, Mattaniah, Jeremoth, Zabad, and Aziza.

²⁸From the family of Bebai: Jehohanan, Hananiah, Zabbai, and Athlai.

²⁹From the family of Bani: Meshullam, Malluch, Adaiah, Jashub, Sheal, and Jeremoth.

³⁰From the family of Pahath-moab: Adna, Kelal, Benaiah, Maaseiah, Mattaniah, Bezalel, Binnui, and Manasseh.

³¹From the family of Harim: Eliezer, Ishijah, Malkijah, Shemaiah, Shimeon, ³²Benjamin, Malluch, and Shemariah.

10:6 As in parallel text at 1 Esdras 9:2; Hebrew reads *He went.* **10:9** Hebrew *on the twentieth day of the ninth month,* of the ancient Hebrew lunar calendar. This day was December 19, 458 B.C.; also see note on 6:15. **10:16** Hebrew *On the first day of the tenth month,* of the ancient Hebrew lunar calendar. This day was December 29, 458 B.C.; also see note on 6:15. **10:17** Hebrew *By the first day of the first month,* of the ancient Hebrew lunar calendar. This day was March 27, 457 B.C.; also see note on 6:15. **10:18** Hebrew *Jozadak,* a variant spelling of Jehozadak. **10:25** As in parallel text at 1 Esdras 9:26; Hebrew reads *Malkijah.*

³³From the family of Hashum: Mattenai, Mattattah, Zabad, Eliphelet, Jeremai, Manasseh, and Shimei.
³⁴From the family of Bani: Maadai, Amram, Uel, ³⁵Benaiah, Bedeiah, Keluhi, ³⁶Vaniah, Meremoth, Eliashib, ³⁷Mattaniah, Mattenai, and Jaasu.
³⁸From the family of Binnui*: Shimei, ³⁹Shelemiah, Nathan, Adaiah, ⁴⁰Macnadebai, Shashai, Sharai, ⁴¹Azarel, Shelemiah, Shemariah, ⁴²Shallum, Amariah, and Joseph.

10:37-38 As in Greek version; Hebrew reads *Jaasu,* ³⁸*Bani, Binnui.*
10:44 Or *and they sent them away with their children.* The meaning of the Hebrew is uncertain.

⁴³From the family of Nebo: Jeiel, Mattithiah, Zabad, Zebina, Jaddai, Joel, and Benaiah.

⁴⁴Each of these men had a pagan wife, and some even had children by these wives.*

....

REBUILT
(10:44) The book of Ezra opens with God's Temple in ruins and the people of Judah captive in Babylon. Ezra tells of the return of God's people, the rebuilding of the Temple, and the restoration of the sacrificial worship system. Similarly, God is able to restore and rebuild the lives of people today. No one is so far away from God that he or she cannot be restored. Repentance is all that is required. No matter how far we have strayed, or how long it has been since we have worshiped God, he is able to restore our relationship to him and rebuild our lives.

NEHEMIAH

Are you a leader? Maybe you're the one people count on the most for input ("Where do you think we should go this Friday?") or motivation to do a task ("You really help the team to focus"). But real leadership often is shown by the way a person handles tough problems and painful situations.

Nehemiah was a proven leader. He left a secure position in the government of Persia to return to his homeland and rebuild the walls of Jerusalem. He succeeded, too, despite incredible obstacles and opposition. The book of Nehemiah tells his story.

Let's face it: the glory and the praise of leadership can seem pretty sweet. But how many want the difficulties that come with being a leader? Yet those God chooses to be leaders can be assured that he also will equip them for the job ahead. Think you have what it takes to be a leader? The book of Nehemiah provides a picture of leadership in action. Do you see yourself in that picture? As you read this book, ask God to help you become a leader like Nehemiah.

KEY POINTS

VISION God put the desire in Nehemiah's heart to rebuild the walls, giving him a vision for the work. Likewise, God can give us the vision and desire to work toward the building of his kingdom.

PRAYER Nehemiah and Ezra responded to problems with prayer. When Nehemiah began his work he recognized the problem, prayed right away, and then acted on the problem. Prayer and action go hand in hand. Through prayer, God guides our preparation, teamwork, and efforts to carry out his will.

LEADERSHIP Nehemiah used careful planning, teamwork, problem solving, and courage to get the work done. These same qualities are needed in leaders today.

PROBLEMS After the work began, Nehemiah faced threats from enemies and the discouragement of his own workers. But he didn't give up. When problems arise, we must face them squarely and press on to complete God's work.

A COMPLETE CHANGE Although God had enabled them to build the wall, the work wasn't complete until the people rebuilt their lives spiritually. Recognizing and admitting sin is not enough. Being serious about God must result in a changed life.

STATS

PURPOSE
To record the history of the third return to Jerusalem after captivity, telling how the walls were rebuilt and faith of the former exiles was renewed

AUTHOR
Nehemiah probably wrote the book, with Ezra serving as editor.

ORIGINAL AUDIENCE
The exiles who had returned from captivity

DATE WRITTEN
Approximately 445– 432 B.C.

SETTING
Jerusalem. Three returns were led by Zerubbabel (537 B.C.), Ezra (458), and Nehemiah (445).

KEY PEOPLE
Nehemiah, Ezra, Sanballat, Tobiah

KEY PLACE
Jerusalem

SPECIAL FEATURE
This book shows the fulfillment of the prophecies of Zechariah and Daniel concerning the rebuilding of Jerusalem's walls.

TIMELINE

586 B.C.
Jerusalem destroyed; exiles go to Babylon

537
First exiles return to Jerusalem

516
Temple completed

458
Ezra comes to Jerusalem

445
Nehemiah comes to Jerusalem; wall completed

430 (?)
Malachi begins his ministry

1

These are the memoirs of Nehemiah son of Hacaliah.

NEHEMIAH'S CONCERN FOR JERUSALEM

In late autumn, in the month of Kislev, in the twentieth year of King Artaxerxes' reign,* I was at the fortress of Susa. ²Hanani, one of my brothers, came to visit me with some other men who had just arrived from Judah. I asked them about the Jews who had returned there from captivity and about how things were going in Jerusalem.

³They said to me, "Things are not going well for those who returned to the province of Judah. They are in great trouble and disgrace. The wall of Jerusalem has been torn down, and the gates have been destroyed by fire."

⁴When I heard this, I sat down and wept. In fact, for days I mourned, fasted, and prayed to the God of heaven. ⁵Then I said,

"O LORD, God of heaven, the great and awesome God who keeps his covenant of unfailing love with those who love him and obey his commands, ⁶listen to my prayer! Look down and see me praying night and day for your people Israel. I confess that we have sinned against you. Yes, even my own family and I have sinned! ⁷We have sinned terribly by not obeying the commands, decrees, and regulations that you gave us through your servant Moses.

⁸"Please remember what you told your servant Moses: 'If you are unfaithful to me, I will scatter you among the nations. ⁹But if you return to me and obey my commands and live by them, then even if you are exiled to the ends of the earth, I will bring you back

to the place I have chosen for my name to be honored.'

¹⁰"The people you rescued by your great power and strong hand are your servants. ¹¹O Lord, please hear my prayer! Listen to the prayers of those of us who delight in honoring you. Please grant me success today by making the king favorable to me.* Put it into his heart to be kind to me."

In those days I was the king's cup-bearer.

2

NEHEMIAH GOES TO JERUSALEM

Early the following spring, in the month of Nisan,* during the twentieth year of King Artaxerxes' reign, I was serving the king his wine. I had never before appeared sad in his presence. ²So the king asked me, "Why are you looking so sad? You don't look sick to me. You must be deeply troubled."

Then I was terrified, ³but I replied, "Long live the king! How can I not be sad? For the city where my ancestors are buried is in ruins, and the gates have been destroyed by fire."

⁴The king asked, "Well, how can I help you?"

With a prayer to the God of heaven, ⁵I replied, "If it please the king, and if you are pleased with me, your servant, send me to Judah to rebuild the city where my ancestors are buried."

⁶The king, with the queen sitting beside him, asked, "How long will you be gone? When will you return?" After I told him how long I would be gone, the king agreed to my request.

⁷I also said to the king, "If it please the king, let me have letters addressed to the governors of the province west of the Euphrates River,* instructing them to let me travel safely through their territories on my way to Judah. ⁸And please give me a letter addressed to Asaph, the manager of the king's forest, instructing him to give me timber. I will need it to make beams for the gates of the Temple fortress, for the city walls, and for a house for myself." And the king granted these requests, because the gracious hand of God was on me.

⁹When I came to the governors of the province west of the Euphrates River, I delivered the king's letters to them. The king, I should add, had sent along army officers and horsemen* to protect me. ¹⁰But when Sanballat the Horonite

······································

TAKE ACTION

(1:4-11) Although Nehemiah was upset about the condition of Jerusalem, he didn't just brood about it. After his initial grief, he poured his heart out to God and looked for ways to improve the situation, putting all his resources of knowledge, experience, and organization into determining what should be done. Is that what you do when you're faced with a problem? If they're honest, many will admit that they might whine first ("Why me?") before any thought of action comes to mind. Asking God for help is the part of the equation that we sometimes leave out. But God can offer solutions we've never even dreamed of. Do you trust him enough to ask for his help?

HAVE NO FEAR!

(2:3) Nehemiah wasn't ashamed to admit his fear; he just refused to be ruled by it. When we focus on our fears instead of on God, we give them power to keep us from accomplishing anything. Is fear keeping you from doing something for God? God is greater than our fears. Recognizing your fear is the first step in committing it to God. If God has given you an assignment, he will help you accomplish it.

1:1 Hebrew *In the month of Kislev of the twentieth year.* A number of dates in the book of Nehemiah can be cross-checked with dates in surviving Persian records and related accurately to our modern calendar. This month of the ancient Hebrew lunar calendar occurred within the months of November and December 446 B.C. The *twentieth year* probably refers to the reign of King Artaxerxes I; compare 2:1; 5:14. **1:11** Hebrew *today in the sight of this man.* **2:1** Hebrew *In the month of Nisan.* This month of the ancient Hebrew lunar calendar occurred within the months of April and May 445 B.C. **2:7** Hebrew *the province beyond the river;* also in 2:9. **2:9** Or *charioteers.*

and Tobiah the Ammonite official heard of my arrival, they were very displeased that someone had come to help the people of Israel.

NEHEMIAH INSPECTS JERUSALEM'S WALL

[11]So I arrived in Jerusalem. Three days later, [12]I slipped out during the night, taking only a few others with me. I had not told anyone about the plans God had put in my heart for Jerusalem. We took no pack animals with us except the donkey I was riding. [13]After dark I went out through the Valley Gate, past the Jackal's Well,* and over to the Dung Gate to inspect the broken walls and burned gates. [14]Then I went to the Fountain Gate and to the King's Pool, but my donkey couldn't get through the rubble. [15]So, though it was still dark, I went up the Kidron Valley* instead, inspecting the wall before I turned back and entered again at the Valley Gate.

[16]The city officials did not know I had been out there or what I was doing, for I had not yet said anything to anyone about my plans. I had not yet spoken to the Jewish leaders—the priests, the nobles, the officials, or anyone else in the administration. [17]But now I said to them, "You know very well what trouble we are in. Jerusalem lies in ruins, and its gates have been destroyed by fire. Let us rebuild the wall of Jerusalem and end this disgrace!" [18]Then I told them about how the gracious hand of God had been on me, and about my conversation with the king.

They replied at once, "Yes, let's rebuild the wall!" So they began the good work.

[19]But when Sanballat, Tobiah, and Geshem the Arab heard of our plan, they scoffed contemptuously. "What are you doing? Are you rebelling against the king?" they asked.

[20]I replied, "The God of heaven will help us succeed. We, his servants, will start rebuilding this wall. But you have no share, legal right, or historic claim in Jerusalem."

3 REBUILDING THE WALL OF JERUSALEM

Then Eliashib the high priest and the other priests started to rebuild at the Sheep Gate. They dedicated it and set up its doors, building the wall as far as the Tower of the Hundred, which they dedicated, and the Tower of Hananel. [2]People from the town of Jericho worked next to them, and beyond them was Zaccur son of Imri.

[3]The Fish Gate was built by the sons of Has-

2:13 Or *Serpent's Well.* 2:15 Hebrew *the valley.* 3:6 Or *The Mishneh Gate,* or *The Jeshanah Gate.* 3:7 Hebrew *the province beyond the river.* 3:8 Or *They fortified Jerusalem up to the Broad Wall.*

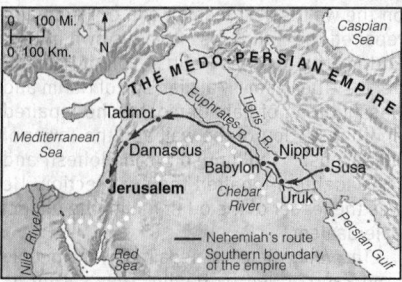

NEHEMIAH GOES TO JERUSALEM
Nehemiah worked in Susa as a personal assistant for the king of the vast Medo-Persian Empire. When he heard that the rebuilding projects in Jerusalem were progressing slowly, he asked the king if he could go there to help his people complete the task of rebuilding their city's walls. The king agreed to let him go; so he left as soon as possible, traveling along much the same route Ezra had taken.

senaah. They laid the beams, set up its doors, and installed its bolts and bars. [4]Meremoth son of Uriah and grandson of Hakkoz repaired the next section of wall. Beside him were Meshullam son of Berekiah and grandson of Meshezabel, and then Zadok son of Baana. [5]Next were the people from Tekoa, though their leaders refused to work with the construction supervisors.

[6]The Old City Gate* was repaired by Joiada son of Paseah and Meshullam son of Besodeiah. They laid the beams, set up its doors, and installed its bolts and bars. [7]Next to them were Melatiah from Gibeon, Jadon from Meronoth, people from Gibeon, and people from Mizpah, the headquarters of the governor of the province west of the Euphrates River.* [8]Next was Uzziel son of Harhaiah, a goldsmith by trade, who also worked on the wall. Beyond him was Hananiah, a manufacturer of perfumes. They left out a section of Jerusalem as they built the Broad Wall.*

[9]Rephaiah son of Hur, the leader of half the district of Jerusalem, was next to them

....

SHARING THE VISION
(2:16-18) Spiritual renewal often begins with one person's vision. Nehemiah had a vision, and shared it with enthusiasm, inspiring Jerusalem's leaders to rebuild the wall.

We frequently underestimate people and don't challenge them with our dreams for God's work in the world. When God plants an idea in your mind to accomplish something for him, share it with others and trust the Holy Spirit to impress them with similar thoughts. Don't see yourself as the only one through whom God is working. Often God uses one person to express the vision and others to turn it into reality. When you inspire others, you put teamwork into action to accomplish God's goals.

on the wall. ¹⁰Next Jedaiah son of Harumaph repaired the wall across from his own house, and next to him was Hattush son of Hashab-neiah. ¹¹Then came Malkijah son of Harim and Hasshub son of Pahath-moab, who repaired another section of the wall and the Tower of the Ovens. ¹²Shallum son of Hallohesh and his daughters repaired the next section. He was the leader of the other half of the district of Jerusalem.

¹³The Valley Gate was repaired by the people from Zanoah, led by Hanun. They set up its doors and installed its bolts and bars. They also repaired the 1,500 feet* of wall to the Dung Gate.

¹⁴The Dung Gate was repaired by Malkijah son of Recab, the leader of the Beth-hakkerem district. He rebuilt it, set up its doors, and in-stalled its bolts and bars.

¹⁵The Fountain Gate was repaired by Shal-lum* son of Col-hozeh, the leader of the Miz-pah district. He rebuilt it, roofed it, set up its doors, and installed its bolts and bars. Then he repaired the wall of the pool of Siloam* near the king's garden, and he rebuilt the wall as far as the stairs that descend from the City of David. ¹⁶Next to him was Nehemiah son of Azbuk, the leader of half the district of Beth-zur. He rebuilt the wall from a place across from the tombs of David's family as far as the water reservoir and the House of the Warriors.

¹⁷Next to him, repairs were made by a group of Levites working under the supervision of Rehum son of Bani. Then came Hashabiah, the leader of half the district of Keilah, who supervised the building of the wall on behalf of his own district. ¹⁸Next down the line were his countrymen led by Binnui* son of Hena-dad, the leader of the other half of the district of Keilah.

¹⁹Next to them, Ezer son of Jeshua, the leader of Mizpah, repaired another section of wall across from the ascent to the armory near the angle in the wall. ²⁰Next to him was Baruch son of Zabbai, who zealously repaired an ad-ditional section from the angle to the door of the house of Eliashib the high priest. ²¹Mer-emoth son of Uriah and grandson of Hakkoz rebuilt another section of the wall extending from the door of Eliashib's house to the end of the house.

²²The next repairs were made by the priests from the surrounding region. ²³After them, Benjamin and Hasshub repaired the section across from their house, and Azariah son of Maaseiah and grandson of Ananiah repaired the section across from his house. ²⁴Next was Binnui son of Henadad, who rebuilt another section of the wall from Azariah's house to the angle and the corner. ²⁵Palal son of Uzai carried on the work from a point opposite the angle and the tower that projects up from the king's upper house beside the court of the guard. Next to him were Pedaiah son of Parosh, ²⁶with the Temple servants living on the hill of Ophel, who repaired the wall as far as a point across from the Water Gate to the east and the projecting tower. ²⁷Then came the people of Tekoa, who repaired another section across from the great projecting tower and over to the wall of Ophel.

²⁸Above the Horse Gate, the priests repaired the wall. Each one repaired the section im-mediately across from his own house. ²⁹Next Zadok son of Immer also rebuilt the wall across from his own house, and beyond him was She-maiah son of Shecaniah, the gatekeeper of the East Gate. ³⁰Next Hananiah son of Shelemiah and Hanun, the sixth son of Zalaph, repaired another section, while Meshullam son of Ber-ekiah rebuilt the wall across from where he lived. ³¹Malkijah, one of the goldsmiths, re-paired the wall as far as the housing for the Temple servants and merchants, across from the Inspection Gate. Then he continued as far as the upper room at the corner. ³²The other goldsmiths and merchants repaired the wall from that corner to the Sheep Gate.

4 ENEMIES OPPOSE THE REBUILDING

¹*Sanballat was very angry when he learned that we were rebuilding the wall. He flew into a rage and mocked the Jews, ²saying in front of his friends and the Samarian army officers, "What does this bunch of poor, feeble Jews think they're doing? Do they think they can build the wall in a single day by just of-fering a few sacrifices?* Do they actually think they can make something of stones from a rub-bish heap—and charred ones at that?"

³Tobiah the Ammonite, who was standing beside him, remarked, "That stone wall would collapse if even a fox walked along the top of it!"

⁴Then I prayed, "Hear us, our God, for we are being mocked. May their scoffing fall back on their own heads, and may they themselves be-come captives in a foreign land! ⁵Do not ignore their guilt. Do not blot out their sins, for they

3:13 Hebrew 1,000 cubits [450 meters].   3:15a As in Syriac version; Hebrew reads Shallun.   3:15b Hebrew pool of Shelah, another name for the pool of Siloam.   3:18 As in a few Hebrew manuscripts, some Greek manuscripts, and Syriac version (see also 3:24; 10:9); most Hebrew manuscripts read Bavvai.   4:1 Verses 4:1-6 are numbered 3:33-38 in Hebrew text.   4:2 The meaning of the Hebrew is uncertain.

have provoked you to anger here in front of* the builders."

⁶At last the wall was completed to half its height around the entire city, for the people had worked with enthusiasm.

⁷*But when Sanballat and Tobiah and the Arabs, Ammonites, and Ashdodites heard that the work was going ahead and that the gaps in the wall of Jerusalem were being repaired, they were furious. ⁸They all made plans to come and fight against Jerusalem and throw us into confusion. ⁹But we prayed to our God and guarded the city day and night to protect ourselves.

¹⁰Then the people of Judah began to complain, "The workers are getting tired, and there is so much rubble to be moved. We will never be able to build the wall by ourselves."

¹¹Meanwhile, our enemies were saying, "Before they know what's happening, we will swoop down on them and kill them and end their work."

¹²The Jews who lived near the enemy came and told us again and again, "They will come from all directions and attack us!"* ¹³So I placed armed guards behind the lowest parts of the wall in the exposed areas. I stationed the people to stand guard by families, armed with swords, spears, and bows.

¹⁴Then as I looked over the situation, I called together the nobles and the rest of the people and said to them, "Don't be afraid of the enemy! Remember the Lord, who is great and glorious, and fight for your brothers, your sons, your daughters, your wives, and your homes!"

¹⁵When our enemies heard that we knew of their plans and that God had frustrated them, we all returned to our work on the wall. ¹⁶But from then on, only half my men worked while the other half stood guard with spears, shields, bows, and coats of mail. The leaders stationed themselves behind the people of Judah ¹⁷who were building the wall. The laborers carried on their work with one hand supporting their load and one hand holding a weapon. ¹⁸All the builders had a sword belted to their side. The trumpeter stayed with me to sound the alarm.

¹⁹Then I explained to the nobles and officials and all the people, "The work is very spread out, and we are widely separated from each other along the wall. ²⁰When you hear the blast of the trumpet, rush to wherever it is sounding. Then our God will fight for us!"

²¹We worked early and late, from sunrise to sunset. And half the men were always on guard. ²²I also told everyone living outside the walls to stay in Jerusalem. That way they and their servants could help with guard duty at night and work during the day. ²³During this time, none of us—not I, nor my relatives, nor my servants, nor the guards who were with me—ever took off our clothes. We carried our weapons with us at all times, even when we went for water.*

4:5 Or *for they have thrown insults in the face of.* **4:7** Verses 4:7-23 are numbered 4:1-17 in Hebrew text. **4:12** The meaning of the Hebrew is uncertain. **4:23** Or *Each his weapon in his right hand.* Hebrew reads *Each his weapon the water.* The meaning of the Hebrew is uncertain.

....

A CURE FOR DISCOURAGEMENT
(4:10-14) When the builders of the wall grew discouraged, Nehemiah reminded them of their goal and of God's protection. Feeling overwhelmed and discouraged by an assignment? The only cure for fatigue and discouragement is focusing on God and his purposes. He will remind you of what you're working toward and give you the strength to do it.

CHOICES
opposition

At church camp, Tyson was challenged to start a Bible study at his school.

That's an awesome idea! Tyson thought. So he started praying about it and, in time, became convinced that God wanted him to do it. And that's when all of the trouble began. He never dreamed that such a simple plan would become such a big deal. Here are some of the highlights:

• The principal doesn't want to give him a room (even though Tyson keeps assuring him that the Bible study would not take place during school hours).

• No faculty members would agree to sponsor the group.

• A few Christian friends are urging him to forget it.

• Some of Tyson's classmates have nicknamed him "Holy Roller" and "Jesus Freak."

• One huge senior (who's very anti-Christian) has been trying to pick a fight during gym class.

With these obstacles, Tyson wonders whether it's worth the effort after all. "I don't have to start a Bible study to be a good Christian. Besides, I can do without all this grief." Dumping the plan has started to sound good. Would you agree?

Read Nehemiah 4. The people of Israel were no strangers to opposition. They found plenty as they tried to rebuild the walls of Jerusalem. What would you say to Tyson, based on their experience? And what's the secret to hanging in there when people mock your faith?

5 NEHEMIAH DEFENDS THE OPPRESSED

About this time some of the men and their wives raised a cry of protest against their fellow Jews. [2]They were saying, "We have such large families. We need more food to survive."

[3]Others said, "We have mortgaged our fields, vineyards, and homes to get food during the famine."

[4]And others said, "We have had to borrow money on our fields and vineyards to pay our taxes. [5]We belong to the same family as those who are wealthy, and our children are just like theirs. Yet we must sell our children into slavery just to get enough money to live. We have already sold some of our daughters, and we are helpless to do anything about it, for our fields and vineyards are already mortgaged to others."

[6]When I heard their complaints, I was very angry. [7]After thinking it over, I spoke out against these nobles and officials. I told them, "You are hurting your own relatives by charging interest when they borrow money!" Then I called a public meeting to deal with the problem.

[8]At the meeting I said to them, "We are doing all we can to redeem our Jewish relatives who have had to sell themselves to pagan foreigners, but you are selling them back into slavery again. How often must we redeem them?" And they had nothing to say in their defense.

[9]Then I pressed further, "What you are doing is not right! Should you not walk in the fear of our God in order to avoid being mocked by enemy nations? [10]I myself, as well as my brothers and my workers, have been lending the people money and grain, but now let us stop this business of charging interest. [11]You must restore their fields, vineyards, olive groves, and homes to them this very day. And repay the interest you charged when you lent them money, grain, new wine, and olive oil."

[12]They replied, "We will give back everything and demand nothing more from the people. We will do as you say." Then I called the priests and made the nobles and officials swear to do what they had promised.

[13]I shook out the folds of my robe and said, "If you fail to keep your promise, may God shake you like this from your homes and from your property!"

The whole assembly responded, "Amen," and they praised the LORD. And the people did as they had promised.

[14]For the entire twelve years that I was governor of Judah—from the twentieth year to the thirty-second year of the reign of King Artaxerxes*—neither I nor my officials drew on our official food allowance. [15]The former governors, in contrast, had laid heavy burdens on the people, demanding a daily ration of food and wine, besides forty pieces* of silver. Even their assistants took advantage of the people. But because I feared God, I did not act that way.

[16]I also devoted myself to working on the wall and refused to acquire any land. And I required all my servants to spend time working on the wall. [17]I asked for nothing, even though I regularly fed 150 Jewish officials at my table, besides all the visitors from other lands! [18]The provisions I paid for each day included one ox, six choice sheep or goats, and a large number of poultry. And every ten days we needed a large supply of all kinds of wine. Yet I refused to claim the governor's food allowance because the people already carried a heavy burden.

[19]Remember, O my God, all that I have done for these people, and bless me for it.

6 CONTINUED OPPOSITION TO REBUILDING

Sanballat, Tobiah, Geshem the Arab, and the rest of our enemies found out that I had finished rebuilding the wall and that no gaps remained—though we had not yet set up the doors in the gates. [2]So Sanballat and Geshem sent a message asking me to meet them at one of the villages* in the plain of Ono.

But I realized they were plotting to harm me, [3]so I replied by sending this message to them: "I am engaged in a great work, so I can't come. Why should I stop working to come and meet with you?"

[4]Four times they sent the same message, and each time I gave the same reply. [5]The fifth time, Sanballat's servant came with an open letter in his hand, [6]and this is what it said:

"There is a rumor among the surrounding nations, and Geshem* tells me it is true, that you and the Jews are planning to rebel and that is why you are building the wall. According to his reports, you plan to be their king. [7]He also reports that you have appointed prophets in Jerusalem to proclaim about you, 'Look! There is a king in Judah!'

"You can be very sure that this report will get back to the king, so I suggest that you come and talk it over with me."

[8]I replied, "There is no truth in any part of your story. You are making up the whole thing."

5:14 That is, 445–433 B.C.　**5:15** Hebrew *40 shekels* [1 pound, or 456 grams].　**6:2** As in Greek version; Hebrew reads *at Kephirim.*　**6:6** Hebrew *Gashmu,* a variant spelling of Geshem.

⁹They were just trying to intimidate us, imagining that they could discourage us and stop the work. So I continued the work with even greater determination.*

¹⁰Later I went to visit Shemaiah son of Delaiah and grandson of Mehetabel, who was confined to his home. He said, "Let us meet together inside the Temple of God and bolt the doors shut. Your enemies are coming to kill you tonight."

¹¹But I replied, "Should someone in my position run from danger? Should someone in my position enter the Temple to save his life? No, I won't do it!" ¹²I realized that God had not spoken to him, but that he had uttered this prophecy against me because Tobiah and Sanballat had hired him. ¹³They were hoping to intimidate me and make me sin. Then they would be able to accuse and discredit me.

¹⁴Remember, O my God, all the evil things that Tobiah and Sanballat have done. And remember Noadiah the prophet and all the prophets like her who have tried to intimidate me.

THE BUILDERS COMPLETE THE WALL

¹⁵So on October 2* the wall was finished—just fifty-two days after we had begun. ¹⁶When our enemies and the surrounding nations heard about it, they were frightened and humiliated. They realized this work had been done with the help of our God.

¹⁷During those fifty-two days, many letters went back and forth between Tobiah and the nobles of Judah. ¹⁸For many in Judah had sworn allegiance to him because his father-in-law was Shecaniah son of Arah, and his son Jehohanan was married to the daughter of Meshullam son of Berekiah. ¹⁹They kept telling me about Tobiah's good deeds, and then they told him everything I said. And Tobiah kept sending threatening letters to intimidate me.

7 After the wall was finished and I had set up the doors in the gates, the gatekeepers, singers, and Levites were appointed. ²I gave the responsibility of governing Jerusalem to my brother Hanani, along with Hananiah, the commander of the fortress, for he was a faithful man who feared God more than most. ³I said

to them, "Do not leave the gates open during the hottest part of the day.* And even while the gatekeepers are on duty, have them shut and bar the doors. Appoint the residents of Jerusalem to act as guards, everyone on a regular watch. Some will serve at sentry posts and some in front of their own homes."

NEHEMIAH REGISTERS THE PEOPLE

⁴At that time the city was large and spacious, but the population was small, and none of the houses had been rebuilt. ⁵So my God gave me the idea to call together all the nobles and leaders of the city, along with the ordinary citizens, for registration. I had found the genealogical record of those who had first returned to Judah. This is what was written there:

⁶Here is the list of the Jewish exiles of the provinces who returned from their captivity. King Nebuchadnezzar had deported them to Babylon, but now they returned to Jerusalem and the other towns in Judah where they originally lived. ⁷Their leaders were Zerubbabel, Jeshua, Nehemiah, Seraiah,* Reelaiah,* Nahamani, Mordecai, Bilshan, Mispar,* Bigvai, Rehum,* and Baanah.

This is the number of the men of Israel who returned from exile:

⁸ The family of Parosh	2,172
⁹ The family of Shephatiah	372
¹⁰ The family of Arah	652
¹¹ The family of Pahath-moab (descendants of Jeshua and Joab)	2,818
¹² The family of Elam	1,254
¹³ The family of Zattu	845
¹⁴ The family of Zaccai	760
¹⁵ The family of Bani*	648

COURAGE
(6:10-13) When enemies threatened Nehemiah, he refused to give in to fear and flee to the Temple. Since Nehemiah wasn't a priest, he wasn't allowed to hide in the Temple (see Num 18:22). If he had run for his life, he would have undermined the courage he wanted to instill in the people.

Leaders often are targets for attacks. Maybe that's why Paul later encouraged believers to pray for those in authority (1 Tim 2:2). Have you developed that habit?

PROJECT FOLLOW-UP
(7:1-4) The wall was complete, but the work wasn't finished. Nehemiah assigned each family the task of protecting the section of wall next to their home. Ever been tempted to relax your guard and rest on past accomplishments after you've completed a large task? According to Nehemiah, you still have work to do! Following through after a project is completed is as vital as doing the project itself.

6:9 As in Greek version; Hebrew reads *But now to strengthen my hands.* 6:15 Hebrew *on the twenty-fifth day of the month Elul,* of the ancient Hebrew lunar calendar. This day was October 2, 445 B.C.; also see note on 1:1. 7:3 Or *Keep the gates of Jerusalem closed until the sun is hot.* 7:7a As in parallel text at Ezra 2:2; Hebrew reads *Azariah.* 7:7b As in parallel text at Ezra 2:2; Hebrew reads *Raamiah.* 7:7c As in parallel text at Ezra 2:2; Hebrew reads *Mispereth.* 7:7d As in parallel text at Ezra 2:2; Hebrew reads *Nehum.* 7:15 As in parallel text at Ezra 2:10; Hebrew reads *Binnui.*

16 The family of Bebai 628
17 The family of Azgad 2,322
18 The family of Adonikam 667
19 The family of Bigvai 2,067
20 The family of Adin 655
21 The family of Ater (descendants
    of Hezekiah) 98
22 The family of Hashum 328
23 The family of Bezai 324
24 The family of Jorah* 112
25 The family of Gibbar* 95
26 The people of Bethlehem
    and Netophah 188
27 The people of Anathoth 128
28 The people of Beth-azmaveth 42
29 The people of Kiriath-jearim,
    Kephirah, and Beeroth 743
30 The people of Ramah and Geba 621
31 The people of Micmash 122
32 The people of Bethel and Ai 123
33 The people of West Nebo* 52
34 The citizens of West Elam* 1,254
35 The citizens of Harim 320
36 The citizens of Jericho 345
37 The citizens of Lod, Hadid,
    and Ono 721
38 The citizens of Senaah 3,930

39These are the priests who returned from
exile:

The family of Jedaiah (through the line
    of Jeshua) 973
40 The family of Immer 1,052
41 The family of Pashhur 1,247
42 The family of Harim 1,017

43These are the Levites who returned from
exile:

The families of Jeshua and Kadmiel
    (descendants of Hodaviah*) 74
44 The singers of the family of Asaph . . . 148
45 The gatekeepers of the families of
    Shallum, Ater, Talmon, Akkub,
    Hatita, and Shobai 138

46The descendants of the following Temple
servants returned from exile:
    Ziha, Hasupha, Tabbaoth,
47 Keros, Siaha,* Padon,
48 Lebanah, Hagabah, Shalmai,
49 Hanan, Giddel, Gahar,
50 Reaiah, Rezin, Nekoda,
51 Gazzam, Uzza, Paseah,
52 Besai, Meunim, Nephusim,*
53 Bakbuk, Hakupha, Harhur,
54 Bazluth,* Mehida, Harsha,
55 Barkos, Sisera, Temah,
56 Neziah, and Hatipha.

57The descendants of these servants of King
Solomon returned from exile:
    Sotai, Hassophereth, Peruda,*
58 Jaalah,* Darkon, Giddel,
59 Shephatiah, Hattil, Pokereth-hazzebaim,
    and Ami.*

60In all, the Temple servants and the
descendants of Solomon's servants
numbered 392.

61Another group returned at this time
from the towns of Tel-melah, Tel-harsha,
Kerub, Addan,* and Immer. However, they
could not prove that they or their families
were descendants of Israel. 62This group
included the families of Delaiah, Tobiah,
and Nekoda—a total of 642 people.
63Three families of priests—Hobaiah,
Hakkoz, and Barzillai—also returned.
(This Barzillai had married a woman who
was a descendant of Barzillai of Gilead,
and he had taken her family name.)
64They searched for their names in the
genealogical records, but they were not
found, so they were disqualified from
serving as priests. 65The governor told them
not to eat the priests' share of food from the
sacrifices until a priest could consult the
LORD about the matter by using the Urim
and Thummim—the sacred lots.

66So a total of 42,360 people returned to
Judah, 67in addition to 7,337 servants and
245 singers, both men and women. 68They
took with them 736 horses, 245 mules,*
69435 camels, and 6,720 donkeys.
70Some of the family leaders gave
gifts for the work. The governor gave to
the treasury 1,000 gold coins,* 50 gold
basins, and 530 robes for the priests. 71The
other leaders gave to the treasury a total
of 20,000 gold coins* and some 2,750
pounds* of silver for the work. 72The rest of
the people gave 20,000 gold coins, about
2,500 pounds* of silver, and 67 robes for
the priests.

7:24 As in parallel text at Ezra 2:18; Hebrew reads *Hariph.* **7:25** As
in parallel text at Ezra 2:20; Hebrew reads *Gibeon.* **7:33** Or *of the
other Nebo.* **7:34** Or *of the other Elam.* **7:43** As in parallel
text at Ezra 2:40; Hebrew reads *Hodevah.* **7:47** As in parallel text
at Ezra 2:44; Hebrew reads *Sia.* **7:52** As in parallel text at Ezra
2:50; Hebrew reads *Nephushesim.* **7:54** As in parallel text at Ezra
2:52; Hebrew reads *Bazlith.* **7:57** As in parallel text at Ezra 2:55;
Hebrew reads *Sotai, Sophereth, Perida.* **7:58** As in parallel text
at Ezra 2:56; Hebrew reads *Jaala.* **7:59** As in parallel text at Ezra
2:57; Hebrew reads *Amon.* **7:61** As in parallel text at Ezra 2:59;
Hebrew reads *Addon.* **7:68** As in some Hebrew manuscripts (see
also Ezra 2:66); most Hebrew manuscripts lack this verse. Verses
7:69-73 are numbered 7:68-72 in Hebrew text. **7:70** Hebrew *1,000
darics of gold,* about 19 pounds or 8.6 kilograms in weight.
7:71a Hebrew *20,000 darics of gold,* about 375 pounds or
170 kilograms in weight; also in 7:72. **7:71b** Hebrew *2,200 minas*
[1,300 kilograms]. **7:72** Hebrew *2,000 minas* [1,200 kilograms].

[73]So the priests, the Levites, the gatekeepers, the singers, the Temple servants, and some of the common people settled near Jerusalem. The rest of the people returned to their own towns throughout Israel.

8 EZRA READS THE LAW

In October,* when the Israelites had settled in their towns, [8:1]all the people assembled with a unified purpose at the square just inside the Water Gate. They asked Ezra the scribe to bring out the Book of the Law of Moses, which the Lord had given for Israel to obey.

[2]So on October 8* Ezra the priest brought the Book of the Law before the assembly, which included the men and women and all the children old enough to understand. [3]He faced the square just inside the Water Gate from early morning until noon and read aloud to everyone who could understand. All the people listened closely to the Book of the Law.

[4]Ezra the scribe stood on a high wooden platform that had been made for the occasion. To his right stood Mattithiah, Shema, Anaiah, Uriah, Hilkiah, and Maaseiah. To his left stood Pedaiah, Mishael, Malkijah, Hashum, Hash-baddanah, Zechariah, and Meshullam. [5]Ezra stood on the platform in full view of all the people. When they saw him open the book, they all rose to their feet.

[6]Then Ezra praised the Lord, the great God, and all the people chanted, "Amen! Amen!" as they lifted their hands. Then they bowed down and worshiped the Lord with their faces to the ground.

[7]The Levites—Jeshua, Bani, Sherebiah, Jamin, Akkub, Shabbethai, Hodiah, Maaseiah, Kelita, Azariah, Jozabad, Hanan, and Pelaiah—then instructed the people in the Law while everyone remained in their places. [8]They read from the Book of the Law of God and clearly explained the meaning of what was being read, helping the people understand each passage.

[9]Then Nehemiah the governor, Ezra the priest and scribe, and the Levites who were interpreting for the people said to them, "Don't mourn or weep on such a day as this! For today is a sacred day before the Lord your God." For

the people had all been weeping as they listened to the words of the Law.

[10]And Nehemiah* continued, "Go and celebrate with a feast of rich foods and sweet drinks, and share gifts of food with people who have nothing prepared. This is a sacred day before our Lord. Don't be dejected and sad, for the joy of the Lord is your strength!"

[11]And the Levites, too, quieted the people, telling them, "Hush! Don't weep! For this is a sacred day." [12]So the people went away to eat and drink at a festive meal, to share gifts of food, and to celebrate with great joy because they had heard God's words and understood them.

THE FESTIVAL OF SHELTERS

[13]On October 9* the family leaders of all the people, together with the priests and Levites, met with Ezra the scribe to go over the Law in greater detail. [14]As they studied the Law, they discovered that the Lord had commanded through Moses that the Israelites should live in shelters during the festival to be held that month.* [15]He had said that a proclamation should be made throughout their towns and in Jerusalem, telling the people to go to the hills to get branches from olive, wild olive,* myrtle, palm, and other leafy trees. They were to use these branches to make shelters in which they would live during the festival, as prescribed in the Law.

[16]So the people went out and cut branches and used them to build shelters on the roofs of their houses, in their courtyards, in the courtyards of God's Temple, or in the squares just

THE JOY OF THE LORD IS YOUR STRENGTH!
NEHEMIAH 8:10

7:73 Hebrew *In the seventh month.* This month of the ancient Hebrew lunar calendar occurred within the months of October and November 445 B.C. 8:2 Hebrew *on the first day of the seventh month,* of the ancient Hebrew lunar calendar. This day was October 8, 445 B.C.; also see note on 1:1. 8:10 Hebrew *he.* 8:13 Hebrew *On the second day,* of the seventh month of the ancient Hebrew lunar calendar. This day was October 9, 445 B.C.; also see notes on 1:1 and 8:2. 8:14 Hebrew *in the seventh month.* This month of the ancient Hebrew lunar calendar usually occurs within the months of September and October. See Lev 23:39-43. 8:15 Or *pine;* Hebrew reads *oil tree.*

APPLY IT
(8:1-5) The people paid close attention to Ezra as he read God's Word, and their lives were changed. Because we hear and read the Bible so often, we can become dulled to its words and immune to its teachings. Instead, we should listen carefully to every verse and ask the Holy Spirit to help us answer the question, "How does this apply to my life?"

ACT ON IT!
(8:1-14) After Ezra read God's laws to the people, they studied them further and then acted upon them. A careful reading of a Scripture passage always calls for a response to these questions: "What should I do with this knowledge?" and "How should my life change?" Action is the fruit of belief.

inside the Water Gate and the Ephraim Gate. [17]So everyone who had returned from captivity lived in these shelters during the festival, and they were all filled with great joy! The Israelites had not celebrated like this since the days of Joshua* son of Nun.

[18]Ezra read from the Book of the Law of God on each of the seven days of the festival. Then on the eighth day they held a solemn assembly, as was required by law.

9 THE PEOPLE CONFESS THEIR SINS On October 31* the people assembled again, and this time they fasted and dressed in burlap and sprinkled dust on their heads. [2]Those of Israelite descent separated themselves from all foreigners as they confessed their own sins and the sins of their ancestors. [3]They remained standing in place for three hours* while the Book of the Law of the LORD their God was read aloud to them. Then for three more hours they confessed their sins and worshiped the LORD their God. [4]The Levites—Jeshua, Bani, Kadmiel, Shebaniah, Bunni, Sherebiah, Bani, and Kenani—stood on the stairway of the Levites and cried out to the LORD their God with loud voices.

[5]Then the leaders of the Levites—Jeshua, Kadmiel, Bani, Hashabneiah, Sherebiah, Hodiah, Shebaniah, and Pethahiah—called out to the people: "Stand up and praise the LORD your God, for he lives from everlasting to everlasting!" Then they prayed:

"May your glorious name be praised! May it be exalted above all blessing and praise!

[6]"You alone are the LORD. You made the skies and the heavens and all the stars. You made the earth and the seas and everything in them. You preserve them all, and the angels of heaven worship you.

[7]"You are the LORD God, who chose Abram and brought him from Ur of the Chaldeans and renamed him Abraham. [8]When he had proved himself faithful, you made a covenant with him to give him and his descendants the land of the Canaanites, Hittites, Amorites, Perizzites, Jebusites, and Girgashites. And you have done what you

promised, for you are always true to your word.

[9]"You saw the misery of our ancestors in Egypt, and you heard their cries from beside the Red Sea.* [10]You displayed miraculous signs and wonders against Pharaoh, his officials, and all his people, for you knew how arrogantly they were treating our ancestors. You have a glorious reputation that has never been forgotten. [11]You divided the sea for your people so they could walk through on dry land! And then you hurled their enemies into the depths of the sea. They sank like stones beneath the mighty waters. [12]You led our ancestors by a pillar of cloud during the day and a pillar of fire at night so that they could find their way.

[13]"You came down at Mount Sinai and spoke to them from heaven. You gave them regulations and instructions that were just, and decrees and commands that were good. [14]You instructed them concerning your holy Sabbath. And you commanded them, through Moses your servant, to obey all your commands, decrees, and instructions.

[15]"You gave them bread from heaven when they were hungry and water from the rock when they were thirsty. You commanded them to go and take possession of the land you had sworn to give them.

[16]"But our ancestors were proud and stubborn, and they paid no attention to your commands. [17]They refused to obey and did not remember the miracles you had done for them. Instead, they became stubborn and appointed a leader to take them back to their slavery in Egypt! But you are a God of forgiveness, gracious and merciful, slow to become angry, and rich in unfailing love. You did not abandon them, [18]even when they made an idol shaped like a calf and said, 'This is your god who brought you out of Egypt!' They committed terrible blasphemies.

[19]"But in your great mercy you did not abandon them to die in the wilderness. The pillar of cloud still led them forward by day, and the pillar of fire showed them the way through the night. [20]You sent your good Spirit to instruct them, and you did not stop giving them manna from heaven or water for their thirst. [21]For forty years you sustained

....

TRUTH HURTS
(9:1-3) After hearing the word of God (see 8:18), the people of Israel admitted their wrongs to one another. As we study God's Word, God sometimes shows us attitudes and actions to change in our lives. That's why the Bible is considered "sharper than the sharpest two-edged sword" (Heb 4:12). The truth hurts sometimes. But Jesus promised that "the truth will set you free" (John 8:32).

8:17 Hebrew *Jeshua,* a variant spelling of Joshua. **9:1** Hebrew *On the twenty-fourth day of that same month,* the seventh month of the ancient Hebrew lunar calendar. This day was October 31, 445 B.C.; also see notes on 1:1 and 8:2. **9:3** Hebrew *for a quarter of a day.* **9:9** Hebrew *sea of reeds.*

them in the wilderness, and they lacked nothing. Their clothes did not wear out, and their feet did not swell!

²²"Then you helped our ancestors conquer kingdoms and nations, and you placed your people in every corner of the land.* They took over the land of King Sihon of Heshbon and the land of King Og of Bashan. ²³You made their descendants as numerous as the stars in the sky and brought them into the land you had promised to their ancestors.

²⁴"They went in and took possession of the land. You subdued whole nations before them. Even the Canaanites, who inhabited the land, were powerless! Your people could deal with these nations and their kings as they pleased. ²⁵Our ancestors captured fortified cities and fertile land. They took over houses full of good things, with cisterns already dug and vineyards and olive groves and fruit trees in abundance. So they ate until they were full and grew fat and enjoyed themselves in all your blessings.

²⁶"But despite all this, they were disobedient and rebelled against you. They turned their backs on your Law, they killed your prophets who warned them to return to you, and they committed terrible blasphemies. ²⁷So you handed them over to their enemies, who made them suffer. But in their time of trouble they cried to you, and you heard them from heaven. In your great mercy, you sent them liberators who rescued them from their enemies.

²⁸"But as soon as they were at peace, your people again committed evil in your sight, and once more you let their enemies conquer them. Yet whenever your people turned and cried to you again for help, you listened once more from heaven. In your wonderful mercy, you rescued them many times!

²⁹"You warned them to return to your Law, but they became proud and obstinate and disobeyed your commands. They did not follow your regulations, by which people will find life if only they obey. They stubbornly turned their backs on you and refused to listen. ³⁰In your love, you were patient with them for many years. You sent your Spirit, who warned them through the prophets. But still they wouldn't listen! So

once again you allowed the peoples of the land to conquer them. ³¹But in your great mercy, you did not destroy them completely or abandon them forever. What a gracious and merciful God you are!

³²"And now, our God, the great and mighty and awesome God, who keeps his covenant of unfailing love, do not let all the hardships we have suffered seem insignificant to you. Great trouble has come upon us and upon our kings and leaders and priests and prophets and ancestors—all of your people—from the days when the kings of Assyria first triumphed over us until now. ³³Every time you punished us you were being just. We have sinned greatly, and you gave us only what we deserved. ³⁴Our kings, leaders, priests, and ancestors did not obey your Law or listen to the warnings in your commands and laws. ³⁵Even while they had their own kingdom, they did not serve you, though you showered your goodness on them. You gave them a large, fertile land, but they refused to turn from their wickedness.

³⁶"So now today we are slaves in the land of plenty that you gave our ancestors for their enjoyment! We are slaves here in this good land. ³⁷The lush produce of this land piles up in the hands of the kings whom you have set over us because of our sins. They have power over us and our livestock. We serve them at their pleasure, and we are in great misery."

THE PEOPLE AGREE TO OBEY

³⁸*The people responded, "In view of all this,* we are making a solemn promise and putting it in writing. On this sealed document are the names of our leaders and Levites and priests."

10

¹*The document was ratified and sealed with the following names:

The governor:
    Nehemiah son of Hacaliah, and also Zedekiah.
²The following priests:
    Seraiah, Azariah, Jeremiah, ³Pashhur,

9:22 The meaning of the Hebrew is uncertain.   9:38a Verse 9:38 is numbered 10:1 in Hebrew text.   9:38b Or *In spite of all this.*
10:1 Verses 10:1-39 are numbered 10:2-40 in Hebrew text.

SHOWERED
(9:35-36) Sometimes the very blessings God has showered on us makes us forget him. We often are tempted to rely on money for security rather than on God. As you see what happened to the Israelites, look at your own life. Do your blessings make you thankful to God and draw you closer to him, or do they make you feel independent and forgetful of God?

Amariah, Malkijah, [4]Hattush, Shebaniah, Malluch, [5]Harim, Meremoth, Obadiah, [6]Daniel, Ginnethon, Baruch, [7]Meshullam, Abijah, Mijamin, [8]Maaziah, Bilgai, and Shemaiah. These were the priests.

[9]The following Levites:

Jeshua son of Azaniah, Binnui from the family of Henadad, Kadmiel, [10]and their fellow Levites: Shebaniah, Hodiah, Kelita, Pelaiah, Hanan, [11]Mica, Rehob, Hashabiah, [12]Zaccur, Sherebiah, Shebaniah, [13]Hodiah, Bani, and Beninu.

[14]The following leaders:

Parosh, Pahath-moab, Elam, Zattu, Bani, [15]Bunni, Azgad, Bebai, [16]Adonijah, Bigvai, Adin, [17]Ater, Hezekiah, Azzur, [18]Hodiah, Hashum, Bezai, [19]Hariph, Anathoth, Nebai, [20]Magpiash, Meshullam, Hezir, [21]Meshezabel, Zadok, Jaddua, [22]Pelatiah, Hanan, Anaiah, [23]Hoshea, Hananiah, Hasshub, [24]Hallohesh, Pilha, Shobek, [25]Rehum, Hashabnah, Maaseiah, [26]Ahiah, Hanan, Anan, [27]Malluch, Harim, and Baanah.

THE VOW OF THE PEOPLE [28]Then the rest of the people—the priests, Levites, gatekeepers, singers, Temple servants, and all who had separated themselves from the pagan people of the land in order to obey the Law of God, together with their wives, sons, daughters, and all who were old enough to understand— [29]joined their leaders and bound themselves with an oath. They swore a curse on themselves if they failed to obey the Law of God as issued by his servant Moses. They solemnly promised to carefully follow all the commands, regulations, and decrees of the LORD our Lord:

[30]"We promise not to let our daughters marry the pagan people of the land, and not to let our sons marry their daughters.

COMMITTED
(10:28-39) The wall was completed, and the covenant God made with his people in the days of Moses (see Deut 8) was restored. This covenant includes principles that are important for us today. Our relationship with God goes far beyond church attendance and regular quiet times. It affects our relationships (Neh 10:30), our time (10:31), and our resources (10:32-39). How committed are you?

GIFTS
(10:36) We, too, need to remember that everything we have—possessions, talents, money, friends, etc.—is from God. We should dedicate all that we have to his use. Don't withhold anything from God. Instead, ask him to show you how to honor him with your time, talents, relationships, and possessions.

[31]"We also promise that if the people of the land should bring any merchandise or grain to be sold on the Sabbath or on any other holy day, we will refuse to buy it. Every seventh year we will let our land rest, and we will cancel all debts owed to us.

[32]"In addition, we promise to obey the command to pay the annual Temple tax of one-eighth of an ounce of silver* for the care of the Temple of our God. [33]This will provide for the Bread of the Presence; for the regular grain offerings and burnt offerings; for the offerings on the Sabbaths, the new moon celebrations, and the annual festivals; for the holy offerings; and for the sin offerings to make atonement for Israel. It will provide for everything necessary for the work of the Temple of our God.

[34]"We have cast sacred lots to determine when—at regular times each year—the families of the priests, Levites, and the common people should bring wood to God's Temple to be burned on the altar of the LORD our God, as is written in the Law.

[35]"We promise to bring the first part of every harvest to the LORD's Temple year after year—whether it be a crop from the soil or from our fruit trees. [36]We agree to give God our oldest sons and the firstborn of all our herds and flocks, as prescribed in the Law. We will present them to the priests who minister in the Temple of our God. [37]We will store the produce in the storerooms of the Temple of our God. We will bring the best of our flour and other grain offerings, the best of our fruit, and the best of our new wine and olive oil. And we promise to bring to the Levites a tenth of everything our land produces, for it is the Levites who collect the tithes in all our rural towns.

[38]"A priest—a descendant of Aaron—will be with the Levites as they receive these tithes. And a tenth of all that is collected as tithes will be delivered by the Levites to the Temple of our God and placed in the storerooms. [39]The people and the Levites must bring these offerings of grain, new wine, and olive oil to the storerooms and place them in the sacred containers near the ministering priests, the gatekeepers, and the singers.

"We promise together not to neglect the Temple of our God."

11 **THE PEOPLE OCCUPY JERUSALEM** The leaders of the people were living in Je-

10:32 Hebrew tax of ⅓ of a shekel [4 grams].

rusalem, the holy city. A tenth of the people from the other towns of Judah and Benjamin were chosen by sacred lots to live there, too, while the rest stayed where they were. ²And the people commended everyone who volunteered to resettle in Jerusalem.

³Here is a list of the names of the provincial officials who came to live in Jerusalem. (Most of the people, priests, Levites, Temple servants, and descendants of Solomon's servants continued to live in their own homes in the various towns of Judah, ⁴but some of the people from Judah and Benjamin resettled in Jerusalem.)

From the tribe of Judah:

Athaiah son of Uzziah, son of Zechariah, son of Amariah, son of Shephatiah, son of Mahalalel, of the family of Perez. ⁵Also Maaseiah son of Baruch, son of Col-hozeh, son of Hazaiah, son of Adaiah, son of Joiarib, son of Zechariah, of the family of Shelah.* ⁶There were 468 descendants of Perez who lived in Jerusalem—all outstanding men.

⁷From the tribe of Benjamin:

Sallu son of Meshullam, son of Joed, son of Pedaiah, son of Kolaiah, son of Maaseiah, son of Ithiel, son of Jeshaiah. ⁸After him were Gabbai and Sallai and a total of 928 relatives. ⁹Their chief officer was Joel son of Zicri, who was assisted by Judah son of Hassenuah, second-in-command over the city.

¹⁰From the priests:

Jedaiah son of Joiarib; Jakin; ¹¹and Seraiah son of Hilkiah, son of Meshullam, son of Zadok, son of Meraioth, son of Ahitub, the supervisor of the Temple of God. ¹²Also 822 of their associates, who worked at the Temple. Also Adaiah son of Jeroham, son of Pelaliah, son of Amzi, son of Zechariah, son of Pashhur, son of Malkijah, ¹³along with 242 of his associates, who were heads of their families. Also Amashsai son of Azarel, son of Ahzai, son of Meshillemoth, son of Immer, ¹⁴and 128 of his* outstanding associates. Their chief officer was Zabdiel son of Haggedolim.

¹⁵From the Levites:

Shemaiah son of Hasshub, son of Azrikam, son of Hashabiah, son of Bunni. ¹⁶Also Shabbethai and Jozabad, who were in charge of the work outside the Temple of God. ¹⁷Also Mattaniah son of Mica, son of Zabdi, a descendant of Asaph, who led in thanksgiving and prayer. Also Bakbukiah, who was Mattaniah's assistant, and Abda son of Shammua, son of Galal, son of Jeduthun. ¹⁸In all, there were 284 Levites in the holy city.

¹⁹From the gatekeepers:

Akkub, Talmon, and 172 of their associates, who guarded the gates.

²⁰The other priests, Levites, and the rest of the Israelites lived wherever their family inheritance was located in any of the towns of Judah. ²¹The Temple servants, however, whose leaders were Ziha and Gishpa, all lived on the hill of Ophel.

²²The chief officer of the Levites in Jerusalem was Uzzi son of Bani, son of Hashabiah, son of Mattaniah, son of Mica, a descendant of Asaph, whose family served as singers at God's Temple. ²³Their daily responsibilities were carried out according to the terms of a royal command.

²⁴Pethahiah son of Meshezabel, a descendant of Zerah son of Judah, was the royal adviser in all matters of public administration.

²⁵As for the surrounding villages with their open fields, some of the people of Judah lived in Kiriath-arba with its settlements, Dibon with its settlements, and Jekabzeel with its villages. ²⁶They also lived in Jeshua, Moladah, Beth-pelet, ²⁷Hazar-shual, Beersheba with its settlements, ²⁸Ziklag, and Meconah with its settlements. ²⁹They also lived in En-rimmon, Zorah, Jarmuth, ³⁰Zanoah, and Adullam with their surrounding villages. They also lived in Lachish with its nearby fields and Azekah with its surrounding villages. So the people of Judah were living all the way from Beersheba in the south to the valley of Hinnom.

³¹Some of the people of Benjamin lived at Geba, Micmash, Aija, and Bethel with its settlements. ³²They also lived in Anathoth, Nob,

....

VOLUNTEER

(11:1) The exiles who returned were few in number compared to Jerusalem's population in the days of the kings. Because the walls had been rebuilt on their original foundations, the city seemed sparsely populated. Nehemiah asked one-tenth of the people from the outlying areas to move inside the city walls to keep large areas of the city from being vacant. Apparently these people did not want to move into the city. Only a few volunteered. Finally, Nehemiah cast lots to determine who among the remaining people would have to move.

How do you respond when God calls you to action? Do you resist or grumble about what you are being asked to do, or are you a willing volunteer? Ask God to help you become someone who is willing to follow his call, no matter where it may lead.

11:5 Hebrew *son of the Shilonite.* 11:14 As in Greek version; Hebrew reads *their.*

Ananiah, [33]Hazor, Ramah, Gittaim, [34]Hadid, Zeboim, Neballat, [35]Lod, Ono, and the Valley of Craftsmen.* [36]Some of the Levites who lived in Judah were sent to live with the tribe of Benjamin.

12 A HISTORY OF THE PRIESTS AND LEVITES Here is the list of the priests and Levites who returned with Zerubbabel son of Shealtiel and Jeshua the high priest:

Seraiah, Jeremiah, Ezra,
[2] Amariah, Malluch, Hattush,
[3] Shecaniah, Harim,* Meremoth,
[4] Iddo, Ginnethon,* Abijah,
[5] Miniamin, Moadiah,* Bilgah,
[6] Shemaiah, Joiarib, Jedaiah,
[7] Sallu, Amok, Hilkiah, and Jedaiah.

These were the leaders of the priests and their associates in the days of Jeshua.

[8]The Levites who returned with them were Jeshua, Binnui, Kadmiel, Sherebiah, Judah, and Mattaniah, who with his associates was in charge of the songs of thanksgiving. [9]Their associates, Bakbukiah and Unni, stood opposite them during the service.

[10] Jeshua the high priest was the father of Joiakim.
Joiakim was the father of Eliashib.
Eliashib was the father of Joiada.
[11] Joiada was the father of Johanan.*
Johanan was the father of Jaddua.

[12]Now when Joiakim was high priest, the family leaders of the priests were as follows:

Meraiah was leader of the family of Seraiah.
Hananiah was leader of the family of Jeremiah.
[13] Meshullam was leader of the family of Ezra.
Jehohanan was leader of the family of Amariah.
[14] Jonathan was leader of the family of Malluch.*
Joseph was leader of the family of Shecaniah.*
[15] Adna was leader of the family of Harim.
Helkai was leader of the family of Meremoth.*
[16] Zechariah was leader of the family of Iddo.
Meshullam was leader of the family of Ginnethon.
[17] Zicri was leader of the family of Abijah.
There was also a* leader of the family of Miniamin.
Piltai was leader of the family of Moadiah.

[18] Shammua was leader of the family of Bilgah.
Jehonathan was leader of the family of Shemaiah.
[19] Mattenai was leader of the family of Joiarib.
Uzzi was leader of the family of Jedaiah.
[20] Kallai was leader of the family of Sallu.*
Eber was leader of the family of Amok.
[21] Hashabiah was leader of the family of Hilkiah.
Nethanel was leader of the family of Jedaiah.

[22]A record of the Levite families was kept during the years when Eliashib, Joiada, Johanan, and Jaddua served as high priest. Another record of the priests was kept during the reign of Darius the Persian.* [23]A record of the heads of the Levite families was kept in *The Book of History* down to the days of Johanan, the grandson* of Eliashib.

[24]These were the family leaders of the Levites: Hashabiah, Sherebiah, Jeshua, Binnui,* Kadmiel, and other associates, who stood opposite them during the ceremonies of praise and thanksgiving, one section responding to the other, as commanded by David, the man of God. [25]This included Mattaniah, Bakbukiah, and Obadiah.

Meshullam, Talmon, and Akkub were the gatekeepers in charge of the storerooms at the gates. [26]These all served in the days of Joiakim son of Jeshua, son of Jehozadak,* and in the days of Nehemiah the governor and of Ezra the priest and scribe.

DEDICATION OF JERUSALEM'S WALL [27]For the dedication of the new wall of Jerusalem, the Levites throughout the land were asked to come to Jerusalem to assist in the ceremonies. They were to take part in the joyous occasion with their songs of thanksgiving and with the music of cymbals, harps, and lyres. [28]The singers were brought together from the region around Jerusalem and from the villages of the Netophathites. [29]They also came from

11:35 Or *and Ge-harashim.* 12:3 Hebrew *Rehum;* compare 7:42; 12:15; Ezra 2:39. 12:4 As in some Hebrew manuscripts and Latin Vulgate (see also 12:16); most Hebrew manuscripts read *Ginnethoi.* 12:5 Hebrew *Mijamin, Maadiah;* compare 12:17. 12:11 Hebrew *Jonathan;* compare 12:22. 12:14a As in Greek version (see also 10:4; 12:2); Hebrew reads *Malluchi.* 12:14b As in many Hebrew manuscripts, some Greek manuscripts, and Syriac version (see also 12:3); most Hebrew manuscripts read *Shebaniah.* 12:15 As in some Greek manuscripts (see also 12:3); Hebrew reads *Meraioth.* 12:17 Hebrew lacks the name of this family leader. 12:20 Hebrew *Sallai;* compare 12:7. 12:22 *Darius the Persian* is probably Darius II, who reigned 423–404 B.C., or possibly Darius III, who reigned 336–331 B.C. 12:23 Hebrew *descendant;* compare 12:10-11. 12:24 Hebrew *son of* (i.e., *ben*), which should probably be read here as the proper name Binnui; compare Ezra 3:9 and the note there. 12:26 Hebrew *Jozadak,* a variant spelling of Jehozadak.

Beth-gilgal and the rural areas near Geba and Azmaveth, for the singers had built their own settlements around Jerusalem. ³⁰The priests and Levites first purified themselves; then they purified the people, the gates, and the wall.

³¹I led the leaders of Judah to the top of the wall and organized two large choirs to give thanks. One of the choirs proceeded southward* along the top of the wall to the Dung Gate. ³²Hoshaiah and half the leaders of Judah followed them, ³³along with Azariah, Ezra, Meshullam, ³⁴Judah, Benjamin, Shemaiah, and Jeremiah. ³⁵Then came some priests who played trumpets, including Zechariah son of Jonathan, son of Shemaiah, son of Mattaniah, son of Micaiah, son of Zaccur, a descendant of Asaph. ³⁶And Zechariah's colleagues were Shemaiah, Azarel, Milalai, Gilalai, Maai, Nethanel, Judah, and Hanani. They used the musical instruments prescribed by David, the man of God. Ezra the scribe led this procession. ³⁷At the Fountain Gate they went straight up the steps on the ascent of the city wall toward the City of David. They passed the house of David and then proceeded to the Water Gate on the east.

³⁸The second choir giving thanks went northward* around the other way to meet them. I followed them, together with the other half of the people, along the top of the wall past the Tower of the Ovens to the Broad Wall, ³⁹then past the Ephraim Gate to the Old City Gate,* past the Fish Gate and the Tower of Hananel, and on to the Tower of the Hundred. Then we continued on to the Sheep Gate and stopped at the Guard Gate.

⁴⁰The two choirs that were giving thanks then proceeded to the Temple of God, where they took their places. So did I, together with the group of leaders who were with me. ⁴¹We went together with the trumpet-playing priests— Eliakim, Maaseiah, Miniamin, Micaiah, Elioenai, Zechariah, and Hananiah—⁴²and the singers—Maaseiah, Shemaiah, Eleazar, Uzzi, Jehohanan, Malkijah, Elam, and Ezer. They played and sang loudly under the direction of Jezrahiah the choir director.

⁴³Many sacrifices were offered on that joyous day, for God had given the people cause for great joy. The women and children also participated in the celebration, and the joy of the people of Jerusalem could be heard far away.

PROVISIONS FOR TEMPLE WORSHIP ⁴⁴On

that day men were appointed to be in charge

of the storerooms for the offerings, the first part of the harvest, and the tithes. They were responsible to collect from the fields outside the towns the portions required by the Law for the priests and Levites. For all the people of Judah took joy in the priests and Levites and their work. ⁴⁵They performed the service of their God and the service of purification, as commanded by David and his son Solomon, and so did the singers and the gatekeepers. ⁴⁶The custom of having choir directors to lead the choirs in hymns of praise and thanksgiving to God began long ago in the days of David and Asaph. ⁴⁷So now, in the days of Zerubbabel and of Nehemiah, all Israel brought a daily supply of food for the singers, the gatekeepers, and the Levites. The Levites, in turn, gave a portion of what they received to the priests, the descendants of Aaron.

13 NEHEMIAH'S VARIOUS REFORMS On
that same day, as the Book of Moses was being read to the people, the passage was found that said no Ammonite or Moabite should ever be permitted to enter the assembly of God.* ²For they had not provided the Israelites with food and water in the wilderness. Instead, they hired Balaam to curse them, though our God turned the curse into a blessing. ³When this passage of the Law was read, all those of foreign descent were immediately excluded from the assembly.

⁴Before this had happened, Eliashib the priest, who had been appointed as supervisor of the storerooms of the Temple of our God and who was also a relative of Tobiah, ⁵had converted a large storage room and placed it at Tobiah's disposal. The room had previously been used for storing the grain offerings, the

....

TUNE IN
(12:31-42) Music was an important part of the dedication of the city wall. It still is an important part of worship today. But sometimes, we tune out God and are more in tune with how much we like a song. But praise still delights God when it comes from the right spirit, even if the song isn't that great. He wants our full focus as we worship. Does he have your attention?

PROTECTION FROM A BAD INFLUENCE
(13:1-3) "Those of foreign descent" refers to the Moabites and Ammonites, two enemies of Israel. They were not allowed in the Temple (see Deut 23:3-5). This rule wasn't about prejudice; it was to protect the people of Israel, who were easily led astray. In the same way, God warns believers to be wise about relationships (Prov 16:29; 24:1; 2 Tim 2:22). Think about the people who influence you the most. Do they bring out the best or the worst in you?

12:31 Hebrew *to the right.* **12:38** Hebrew *to the left.* **12:39** *Or the Mishneh Gate,* or *the Jeshanah Gate.* **13:1** See Deut 23:3-6.

frankincense, various articles for the Temple, and the tithes of grain, new wine, and olive oil (which were prescribed for the Levites, the singers, and the gatekeepers), as well as the offerings for the priests.

⁶I was not in Jerusalem at that time, for I had returned to King Artaxerxes of Babylon in the thirty-second year of his reign,* though I later asked his permission to return. ⁷When I arrived back in Jerusalem, I learned about Eliashib's evil deed in providing Tobiah with a room in the courtyards of the Temple of God. ⁸I became very upset and threw all of Tobiah's belongings out of the room. ⁹Then I demanded that the rooms be purified, and I brought back the articles for God's Temple, the grain offerings, and the frankincense.

¹⁰I also discovered that the Levites had not been given their prescribed portions of food, so they and the singers who were to conduct the worship services had all returned to work their fields. ¹¹I immediately confronted the leaders and demanded, "Why has the Temple of God been neglected?" Then I called all the Levites back again and restored them to their proper duties. ¹²And once more all the people of Judah began bringing their tithes of grain, new wine, and olive oil to the Temple storerooms.

¹³I assigned supervisors for the storerooms: Shelemiah the priest, Zadok the scribe, and Pedaiah, one of the Levites. And I appointed Hanan son of Zaccur and grandson of Mattaniah as their assistant. These men had an excellent reputation, and it was their job to make honest distributions to their fellow Levites.

···

LEADERSHIP
(13:31) Nehemiah's life story provides many principles of effective leadership that still apply. (1) Have a clear purpose and keep evaluating it in light of God's will. Nothing prevented Nehemiah from staying on track. (2) Be straightforward and honest. Everyone knew exactly what Nehemiah needed, and he spoke the truth even when it made his goal harder to achieve. (3) Live above reproach. The accusations against Nehemiah were empty and false. (4) Be a person of constant prayer, deriving power and wisdom from your contact with God. Everything Nehemiah did glorified God.

Leadership appears glamorous at times, but it often is lonely, thankless, and filled with pressures to compromise values and standards. Nehemiah was able to accomplish a huge task against incredible odds because he learned that there is no success without risk of failure, no reward without hard work, no opportunity without criticism, and no true leadership without trust in God.

¹⁴Remember this good deed, O my God, and do not forget all that I have faithfully done for the Temple of my God and its services.

¹⁵In those days I saw men of Judah treading out their winepresses on the Sabbath. They were also bringing in grain, loading it on donkeys, and bringing their wine, grapes, figs, and all sorts of produce to Jerusalem to sell on the Sabbath. So I rebuked them for selling their produce on that day. ¹⁶Some men from Tyre, who lived in Jerusalem, were bringing in fish and all kinds of merchandise. They were selling it on the Sabbath to the people of Judah—and in Jerusalem at that!

¹⁷So I confronted the nobles of Judah. "Why are you profaning the Sabbath in this evil way?" I asked. ¹⁸"Wasn't it just this sort of thing that your ancestors did that caused our God to bring all this trouble upon us and our city? Now you are bringing even more wrath upon Israel by permitting the Sabbath to be desecrated in this way!"

¹⁹Then I commanded that the gates of Jerusalem should be shut as darkness fell every Friday evening,* not to be opened until the Sabbath ended. I sent some of my own servants to guard the gates so that no merchandise could be brought in on the Sabbath day. ²⁰The merchants and tradesmen with a variety of wares camped outside Jerusalem once or twice. ²¹But I spoke sharply to them and said, "What are you doing out here, camping around the wall? If you do this again, I will arrest you!" And that was the last time they came on the Sabbath. ²²Then I commanded the Levites to purify themselves and to guard the gates in order to preserve the holiness of the Sabbath.

Remember this good deed also, O my God! Have compassion on me according to your great and unfailing love.

²³About the same time I realized that some of the men of Judah had married women from Ashdod, Ammon, and Moab. ²⁴Furthermore, half their children spoke the language of Ashdod or of some other people and could not speak the language of Judah at all. ²⁵So I confronted them and called down curses on them. I beat some of them and pulled out their hair. I made them swear in the name of God that they would not let their children intermarry with the pagan people of the land. ²⁶"Wasn't this exactly what led King Solomon

13:6 King Artaxerxes of Persia is here identified as the king of Babylon because Persia had conquered the Babylonian Empire. The thirty-second year of Artaxerxes was 433 B.C. **13:19** Hebrew *on the day before the Sabbath.*

of Israel into sin?" I demanded. "There was no king from any nation who could compare to him, and God loved him and made him king over all Israel. But even he was led into sin by his foreign wives. 27How could you even think of committing this sinful deed and acting unfaithfully toward God by marrying foreign women?"

28One of the sons of Joiada son of Eliashib the high priest had married a daughter of Sanballat the Horonite, so I banished him from my presence.

29Remember them, O my God, for they have defiled the priesthood and the solemn vows of the priests and Levites.

30So I purged out everything foreign and assigned tasks to the priests and Levites, making certain that each knew his work. 31I also made sure that the supply of wood for the altar and the first portions of the harvest were brought at the proper times.

Remember this in my favor, O my God.

Overflowing with fans, the gymnasium rocks with excitement. It's the crucial moment—the one anticipated all season—and joy mixes with fear and tension. Only one point behind, the team could find its season ending abruptly. But two seconds remain in the game, and their player is at the free throw line. Cheers erupt as the ball swishes through the hoop. But then silence engulfs the stands as she approaches for her second shot. Everything is on the line—the play-offs, the dreams, the season. But the shooter's practice pays off. The basket is made, the game is won, and a hero is made. She came through when it counted.

In Persia, Esther similarly faced a crucial moment—but thousands of lives were at stake. All the Jews in Persia were to be killed. As the queen, Esther, who also was a Jew, was the only one who could save them. She could have looked for an easy way out, but Esther knew that God had placed her in an influential position "for just such a time as this" (4:14). She seized the moment and took action, regardless of the consequences (4:16). Because of Esther, lives were saved.

As you read Esther, consider your willingness to act for God if you have the opportunity. Remember, he places you where you can make a difference "for just such a time as this."

KEY POINTS

IN CONTROL The book of Esther tells of the circumstances that were essential for the survival of God's people in Persia. The "circumstances" were not the result of chance but of God's grand design. God is in control of every area of life. With God in charge, we can take courage. He can guide us through the circumstances we face in our lives.

RACISM Haman was a descendant of King Agag, an enemy of the Jews. Lust for power and pride drove Haman to hate Mordecai, Esther's cousin. Racial hatred is always wrong. We must learn to see others the way that God does, rather than through the often cloudy lenses of our own cultural "glasses."

ACTION Faced with death, Esther and Mordecai set aside their fear and took action. Believing that God is in control sometimes isn't enough; we also must courageously follow God's guidance.

RESCUE The Feast of Purim symbolized God's rescue of the Jews from death. God is able to rescue us when we're in trouble.

WISDOM Mordecai took steps to understand and work within the Persian law, yet he did not compromise his integrity. Surviving in an unbelieving world takes great wisdom. We demonstrate wisdom by respecting what's true and good and by taking a stand against whatever is wrong.

STATS

PURPOSE
To demonstrate God's sovereignty and his concern for his people

AUTHOR
Unknown; possibly Mordecai (9:29)

ORIGINAL AUDIENCE
The people of Israel

DATE WRITTEN
Around 483–471 B.C.

SETTING
The Persian empire, mostly in the king's palace; about 30 years prior to the events in Nehemiah

KEY PEOPLE
Esther, Mordecai, King Xerxes, Haman

KEY PLACE
The king's palace in Susa, Persia

SPECIAL FEATURES
Esther is one of only two books named for a woman. In the original version of Esther no name, title, or pronoun for God appears in it. Some early church leaders questioned its inclusion in the Bible. But God's presence is clear throughout the book.

TIMELINE

586 B.C.
Jerusalem destroyed; exiles go to Babylon

537
First exiles return to Jerusalem

486
Xerxes I becomes king of Persia

479
Esther becomes queen

474
Haman's decree to destroy the Jews

473
First Feast of Purim

THE WORLD OF ESTHER'S DAY
Esther lived in the capital of the vast Medo-Persian Empire, which incorporated the provinces of Media and Persia, as well as the previous empires of Assyria and Babylon. Esther, a Jewess, was chosen by King Xerxes to be his queen. The story of how she saved her people takes place in the palace in Susa.

1

THE KING'S BANQUET These events happened in the days of King Xerxes,* who reigned over 127 provinces stretching from India to Ethiopia.* ²At that time Xerxes ruled his empire from his royal throne at the fortress of Susa. ³In the third year of his reign, he gave a banquet for all his nobles and officials. He invited all the military officers of Persia and Media as well as the princes and nobles of the provinces. ⁴The celebration lasted 180 days—a tremendous display of the opulent wealth of his empire and the pomp and splendor of his majesty.

⁵When it was all over, the king gave a banquet for all the people, from the greatest to the least, who were in the fortress of Susa. It lasted for seven days and was held in the courtyard of the palace garden. ⁶The courtyard was beautifully decorated with white cotton curtains and blue hangings, which were fastened with white linen cords and purple ribbons to silver rings embedded in marble pillars. Gold and silver couches stood on a mosaic pavement of porphyry, marble, mother-of-pearl, and other costly stones.

⁷Drinks were served in gold goblets of many designs, and there was an abundance of royal wine, reflecting the king's generosity. ⁸By edict of the king, no limits were placed on the drinking, for the king had instructed all his palace officials to serve each man as much as he wanted.

⁹At the same time, Queen Vashti gave a banquet for the women in the royal palace of King Xerxes.

QUEEN VASHTI DEPOSED ¹⁰On the seventh day of the feast, when King Xerxes was in high spirits because of the wine, he told the seven eunuchs who attended him—Mehuman, Biztha, Harbona, Bigtha, Abagtha, Zethar, and Carcas—¹¹to bring Queen Vashti to him with the royal crown on her head. He wanted the nobles and all the other men to gaze on her beauty,

---

DECISIONS
(1:10-11) Half drunk, Xerxes made a rash decision—one that he later regretted (2:1). Poor decisions often are made in the heat of the moment, when a person isn't thinking clearly. When do you make decisions: on impulse or after careful thought?

1:1a Hebrew *Ahasuerus,* another name for Xerxes; also throughout the book of Esther. Xerxes reigned 486–465 B.C. **1:1b** Hebrew *to Cush.*

for she was a very beautiful woman. ¹²But when they conveyed the king's order to Queen Vashti, she refused to come. This made the king furious, and he burned with anger.

¹³He immediately consulted with his wise advisers, who knew all the Persian laws and customs, for he always asked their advice. ¹⁴The names of these men were Carshena, Shethar, Admatha, Tarshish, Meres, Marsena, and Memucan—seven nobles of Persia and Media. They met with the king regularly and held the highest positions in the empire.

¹⁵"What must be done to Queen Vashti?" the king demanded. "What penalty does the law provide for a queen who refuses to obey the king's orders, properly sent through his eunuchs?"

¹⁶Memucan answered the king and his nobles, "Queen Vashti has wronged not only the king but also every noble and citizen throughout your empire. ¹⁷Women everywhere will begin to despise their husbands when they learn that Queen Vashti has refused to appear before the king. ¹⁸Before this day is out, the wives of all the king's nobles throughout Persia and Media will hear what the queen did and will start treating their husbands the same way. There will be no end to their contempt and anger.

¹⁹"So if it please the king, we suggest that you issue a written decree, a law of the Persians and Medes that cannot be revoked. It should order that Queen Vashti be forever banished from the presence of King Xerxes, and that the king should choose another queen more worthy than she. ²⁰When this decree is published throughout the king's vast empire, husbands everywhere, whatever their rank, will receive proper respect from their wives!"

²¹The king and his nobles thought this made good sense, so he followed Memucan's counsel. ²²He sent letters to all parts of the empire, to each province in its own script and language, proclaiming that every man should be the ruler of his own home and should say whatever he pleases.*

2 ESTHER BECOMES QUEEN

But after Xerxes' anger had subsided, he began thinking about Vashti and what she had done and the decree he had made. ²So his personal attendants suggested, "Let us search the empire to find beautiful young virgins for the king. ³Let the king appoint agents in each province to bring these beautiful young women into the royal harem at the fortress of Susa. Hegai, the king's eunuch in charge of the harem, will see that they are all given beauty treatments. ⁴After that, the young woman who most pleases the king will be made queen instead of Vashti." This advice was very appealing to the king, so he put the plan into effect.

⁵At that time there was a Jewish man in the fortress of Susa whose name was Mordecai son of Jair. He was from the tribe of Benjamin and was a descendant of Kish and Shimei. ⁶His family* had been among those who, with King Jehoiachin* of Judah, had been exiled from Jerusalem to Babylon by King Nebuchadnezzar. ⁷This man had a very beautiful and lovely young cousin, Hadassah, who was also called Esther. When her father and mother died, Mordecai adopted her into his family and raised her as his own daughter.

⁸As a result of the king's decree, Esther, along with many other young women, was brought to the king's harem at the fortress of Susa and placed in Hegai's care. ⁹Hegai was very impressed with Esther and treated her kindly. He quickly ordered a special menu for her and provided her with beauty treatments. He also assigned her seven maids specially chosen from the king's palace, and he moved her and her maids into the best place in the harem.

¹⁰Esther had not told anyone of her nationality and family background, because Mordecai had directed her not to do so. ¹¹Every day Mordecai would take a walk near the courtyard of the harem to find out about Esther and what was happening to her.

¹²Before each young woman was taken to the king's bed, she was given the prescribed twelve months of beauty treatments—six months with oil of myrrh, followed by six months with special perfumes and ointments. ¹³When it was time for her to go to the king's palace, she was given her choice of whatever clothing or jewelry she wanted to take from the harem. ¹⁴That evening she was taken to the king's private rooms, and the next morning she was brought to the second harem,*

1:22 Or and should speak in the language of his own people.
2:6a Hebrew He. 2:6b Hebrew Jeconiah, a variant spelling of Jehoiachin. 2:14 Or to another part of the harem.

RESPECT
(1:20-21) One way to rule a nation is to issue edicts that force people to comply. King Xerxes and his advisers responded this way. But in Matthew 20:25-26, Jesus spoke against the way some leaders "flaunt their authority over those under them." As believers, we are to act differently. God encourages us to treat each other with respect and love (1 Cor 13). How do you show your respect toward others?

where the king's wives lived. There she would be under the care of Shaashgaz, the king's eunuch in charge of the concubines. She would never go to the king again unless he had especially enjoyed her and requested her by name.

¹⁵Esther was the daughter of Abihail, who was Mordecai's uncle. (Mordecai had adopted his younger cousin Esther.) When it was Esther's turn to go to the king, she accepted the advice of Hegai, the eunuch in charge of the harem. She asked for nothing except what he suggested, and she was admired by everyone who saw her.

¹⁶Esther was taken to King Xerxes at the royal palace in early winter* of the seventh year of his reign. ¹⁷And the king loved Esther more than any of the other young women. He was so delighted with her that he set the royal crown on her head and declared her queen instead of Vashti. ¹⁸To celebrate the occasion, he gave a great banquet in Esther's honor for all his nobles and officials, declaring a public holiday for the provinces and giving generous gifts to everyone.

¹⁹Even after all the young women had been transferred to the second harem* and Mordecai had become a palace official,* ²⁰Esther continued to keep her family background and nationality a secret. She was still following Mordecai's directions, just as she did when she lived in his home.

MORDECAI'S LOYALTY TO THE KING ²¹One day as Mordecai was on duty at the king's gate, two of the king's eunuchs, Bigthana* and Teresh—who were guards at the door of the king's private quarters—became angry at King Xerxes and plotted to assassinate him. ²²But

2:16 Hebrew *in the tenth month, the month of Tebeth.* A number of dates in the book of Esther can be cross-checked with dates in surviving Persian records and related accurately to our modern calendar. This month of the ancient Hebrew lunar calendar occurred within the months of December 479 B.C. and January 478 B.C. **2:19a** The meaning of the Hebrew is uncertain. **2:19b** Hebrew *and Mordecai was sitting in the gate of the king.* **2:21** Hebrew *Bigthan;* compare 6:2.

ESTHER *PERSONALITY PROFILE*

CINDERELLA. SLEEPING BEAUTY. BEAUTY AND THE BEAST. You could probably name a hundred fairy tales off the top of your head. Fairy tales are just entertaining stories you read when you were a kid. Surely this kind of thing couldn't happen in real life, right?

Wrong. The story of Esther is a fairy tale come true. You know the saga. A poor, but beautiful young woman catches the eye of and marries a king. You've read or seen that scenario tons of times. But this is one fairy tale with some bite. Esther's story isn't just a romance. It's a story of survival—the survival of the people of Israel—because of the courage of one woman.

Esther just happened to be in the right place at the right time. Although her beauty and character won her the notice of King Xerxes, God ultimately was the one who placed her in that position. When Esther's cousin, Mordecai, told her of the plot to kill the Jews—her people—she had to risk her own security to help them. After all, her family heritage wasn't known. If the king disapproved of her request to appear before him, he could have sent her away or put her to death. (The former queen had been banished in disgrace.)

Esther's story has a happy ending. Her quick thinking allowed her people to be saved and the villain of the story punished. And thus a new holiday—Purim—was born in honor of the risk-taking young queen who saved the lives of her people.

Ever wish that your life could be a fairy tale with a guaranteed happy ending? If you're a believer, you're in the same situation as Esther. You've caught the eye of the King of the Universe. The defeat of the villain of the story (Satan) has already been accomplished because of the death and resurrection of this King. But even a guaranteed happy ending doesn't mean that you'll never have to take a risk for your faith. You might have to. The reality of your relationship with God can make all the difference when the pressure is on.

BOTTOM LINE: Serving God sometimes involves risking our own security.
    God has a purpose for the situations in which he places us.
    Courage, while often vital, does not replace careful planning.

Esther's story is told in the book of Esther.

UPS:
- *Won the heart of Persia's king with her beauty and character*
- *Combined courage with careful planning*
- *Open to advice and willing to act*
- *More concerned for others than for her own security*

STATS:
- *Where: Persian Empire*
- *Occupation: Queen of Persia*
- *Relatives: Mordecai (cousin); Xerxes (husband); Abihail (father)*

KEY VERSE: *Esther 4:16*

Mordecai heard about the plot and gave the information to Queen Esther. She then told the king about it and gave Mordecai credit for the report. ²³When an investigation was made and Mordecai's story was found to be true, the two men were impaled on a sharpened pole. This was all recorded in *The Book of the History of King Xerxes' Reign*.

3 HAMAN'S PLOT AGAINST THE JEWS Some time later King Xerxes promoted Haman son of Hammedatha the Agagite over all the other nobles, making him the most powerful official in the empire. ²All the king's officials would bow down before Haman to show him respect whenever he passed by, for so the king had commanded. But Mordecai refused to bow down or show him respect.

³Then the palace officials at the king's gate asked Mordecai, "Why are you disobeying the king's command?" ⁴They spoke to him day after day, but still he refused to comply with the order. So they spoke to Haman about this to see if he would tolerate Mordecai's conduct, since Mordecai had told them he was a Jew.

⁵When Haman saw that Mordecai would not bow down or show him respect, he was filled with rage. ⁶He had learned of Mordecai's nationality, so he decided it was not enough to lay hands on Mordecai alone. Instead, he looked for a way to destroy all the Jews throughout the entire empire of Xerxes.

⁷So in the month of April,* during the twelfth year of King Xerxes' reign, lots were cast in Haman's presence (the lots were called *purim*) to determine the best day and month to take action. And the day selected was March 7, nearly a year later.*

⁸Then Haman approached King Xerxes and said, "There is a certain race of people scattered through all the provinces of your empire who keep themselves separate from everyone else. Their laws are different from those of any other people, and they refuse to obey the laws of the king. So it is not in the king's interest to let them live. ⁹If it please the king, issue a decree that they be destroyed, and I will give 10,000 large sacks* of silver to the government

administrators to be deposited in the royal treasury."

¹⁰The king agreed, confirming his decision by removing his signet ring from his finger and giving it to Haman son of Hammedatha the Agagite, the enemy of the Jews. ¹¹The king said, "The money and the people are both yours to do with as you see fit."

¹²So on April 17* the king's secretaries were summoned, and a decree was written exactly as Haman dictated. It was sent to the king's highest officers, the governors of the respective provinces, and the nobles of each province in their own scripts and languages. The decree was written in the name of King Xerxes and sealed with the king's signet ring. ¹³Dispatches were sent by swift messengers into all the provinces of the empire, giving the order that all Jews—young and old, including women and children—must be killed, slaughtered, and annihilated on a single day. This was scheduled to happen on March 7 of the next year.* The property of the Jews would be given to those who killed them.

¹⁴A copy of this decree was to be issued as law in every province and proclaimed to all peoples, so that they would be ready to do their duty on the appointed day. ¹⁵At the king's command, the decree went out by swift messengers, and it was also proclaimed in the fortress of Susa. Then the king and Haman sat down to drink, but the city of Susa fell into confusion.

4 MORDECAI REQUESTS ESTHER'S HELP When Mordecai learned about all that had been done, he tore his clothes, put on burlap and ashes, and went out into the city, crying with a loud and bitter wail. ²He went as far as the gate of the palace, for no one was allowed to enter the palace gate while wearing clothes of mourning. ³And as news of the king's decree reached all the provinces, there was great mourning among the Jews. They fasted, wept, and wailed, and many people lay in burlap and ashes.

⁴When Queen Esther's maids and eunuchs came and told her about Mordecai, she was deeply distressed. She sent clothing to him to replace the burlap, but he refused it. ⁵Then

3:7a Hebrew *in the first month, the month of Nisan.* This month of the ancient Hebrew lunar calendar occurred within the months of April and May 474 B.C.; also see note on 2:16. **3:7b** As in 3:13, which reads *the thirteenth day of the twelfth month, the month of Adar;* Hebrew reads *in the twelfth month,* of the ancient Hebrew lunar calendar. The date selected was March 7, 473 B.C.; also see note on 2:16. **3:9** Hebrew *10,000 talents,* about 375 tons or 340 metric tons in weight. **3:12** Hebrew *On the thirteenth day of the first month,* of the ancient Hebrew lunar calendar. This day was April 17, 474 B.C.; also see note on 2:16. **3:13** Hebrew *on the thirteenth day of the twelfth month, the month of Adar,* of the ancient Hebrew lunar calendar. The date selected was March 7, 473 B.C.; also see note on 2:16.

CONVICTION
(3:2) Mordecai's faith was based on conviction. He didn't first take a poll to determine the safest or most popular course of action; he had the courage to stand alone. Doing what's right is not always popular, and those who do right will often be in the minority. But to obey God is more important than obeying people (see Acts 5:29).

IF I MUST DIE, I MUST DIE.

ESTHER 4:16

Esther sent for Hathach, one of the king's eunuchs who had been appointed as her attendant. She ordered him to go to Mordecai and find out what was troubling him and why he was in mourning. [6]So Hathach went out to Mordecai in the square in front of the palace gate.

[7]Mordecai told him the whole story, including the exact amount of money Haman had promised to pay into the royal treasury for the destruction of the Jews. [8]Mordecai gave Hathach a copy of the decree issued in Susa that called for the death of all Jews. He asked Hathach to show it to Esther and explain the situation to her. He also asked Hathach to direct her to go to the king to beg for mercy and plead for her people. [9]So Hathach returned to Esther with Mordecai's message.

[10]Then Esther told Hathach to go back and relay this message to Mordecai: [11]"All the king's officials and even the people in the provinces know that anyone who appears before the king in his inner court without being invited is doomed to die unless the king holds out his gold scepter. And the king has not called for me to come to him for thirty days." [12]So Hathach* gave Esther's message to Mordecai.

[13]Mordecai sent this reply to Esther: "Don't think for a moment that because you're in the palace you will escape when all other Jews are killed. [14]If you keep quiet at a time like this, deliverance and relief for the Jews will arise from some other place, but you and your relatives will die. Who knows if perhaps you were made queen for just such a time as this?"

[15]Then Esther sent this reply to Mordecai: [16]"Go and gather together all the Jews of Susa and fast for me. Do not eat or drink for three days, night or day. My maids and I will do the same. And then, though it is against the law, I will go in to see the king. If I must die, I must die." [17]So Mordecai went away and did everything as Esther had ordered him.

5 **ESTHER'S REQUEST TO THE KING** On the third day of the fast, Esther put on her royal robes and entered the inner court of the palace, just across from the king's hall. The king was sitting on his royal throne, facing the entrance. [2]When he saw Queen Esther standing there in the inner court, he welcomed her and held out the gold scepter to her. So Esther approached and touched the end of the scepter.

[3]Then the king asked her, "What do you want, Queen Esther? What is your request? I will give it to you, even if it is half the kingdom!"

[4]And Esther replied, "If it please the king, let the king and Haman come today to a banquet I have prepared for the king."

[5]The king turned to his attendants and said, "Tell Haman to come quickly to a banquet, as Esther has requested." So the king and Haman went to Esther's banquet.

[6]And while they were drinking wine, the king said to Esther, "Now tell me what you really want. What is your request? I will give it to you, even if it is half the kingdom!"

[7]Esther replied, "This is my request and deepest wish. [8]If I have found favor with the king, and if it pleases the king to grant my request and do what I ask, please come with Haman

4:12 As in Greek version; Hebrew reads *they.*

CHOICES
taking a stand

You wouldn't want to be in Ryan's shoes. He's in a jam, and none of his options are very appealing.

See, in just a few minutes, Ryan and K.D. will be face-to-face with one of Mrs. Seal's infamous geometry exams. But K.D. just announced, "Hey, Ryan! You've got to help me out, dude. I didn't have time to study last night. I don't know any of the theorems. So look, just write big and when I tap you on the shoulder, lean to your left, OK?"

Lunch is almost over. The bell will be ringing any minute. Ryan's mind is racing:

"Do I let K.D. copy off me just this once? But what if I get accused of cheating? I probably should tell him no now—before class starts. But then he'll tell everyone I wouldn't help him out, and I'll never hear the end of it. Man, what am I gonna do?

"It ticks me off the way he uses people. . . . It's not my fault if he fails. He should've studied, instead of being so lazy. Still, I don't want everybody thinking I'm a loser. Maybe I should—"

BBBBRRRIIIINNNNNGGGGG!!!

What would you do in Ryan's shoes?

Chapters 3 and 4 of the exciting book of Esther are about taking a stand for what is right, no matter what. Read about the young queen who made tough decisions when the stakes were—literally—life and death.

Depending on your point of view, you may be thrilled, irritated, intrigued, or just surprised to see a book of the Bible—two, in fact—named for a woman. The Bible is, admittedly, a male-dominated work. After all, Israel's society was a patriarchal one. But, as the books of Ruth and Esther point out, women were very important in the story of God's redemption of humanity.

Ruth is the story of a young widow who, out of loyalty, follows her mother-in-law back to Bethlehem to live. In the midst of tough times for the two of them, Ruth shows she is a hard worker and a woman of integrity and high moral character. God rewards her faithfulness by providing her with a new husband, Boaz, a good man who had attained some measure of wealth and could, therefore, provide for both women. In addition, Ruth and Boaz become the great-grandparents of David, the king of Israel, and ancestors of Jesus, the Jewish Messiah. Ruth is an excellent role model for young believers today, female or male.

Esther is the story of another faithful woman in radically different circumstances. A young Jewish girl in exile in Babylon, Esther, by virtue of her good looks, catches the eye of King Xerxes and is made queen. Even as queen, however, she has to watch her step, being careful not to displease her husband and risk being banished or even killed. The day arrives, however, where she must risk the king's displeasure to save her people, the Jews, from mass destruction. Although afraid at first to stick her neck out, she finally decides to risk it, saying, "Though it is against the law, I will go in to see the king. If I must die, I must die" (Esth 4:16). That's gutsy, courageous faith, the kind that Christian women—and men—today would do well to imitate.

Although these are the only two books named for women, Scripture contains many other stories of important women—some good, some bad. If you're interested, look at the accounts of Rahab (Josh 2; 6); Deborah (Judg 4–5); Jezebel (1 Kgs 16:31; 19; 21; 2 Kgs 9:30-37); Mary and Martha (Luke 10:38-42); and, of course, Mary, Jesus' mother (Luke 1–2; John 19:25-27).

For a number of reasons, cultural and otherwise, most of the prominent characters in the Bible are men. But women play a vital role in the unfolding drama of both the Old and New Testaments, just as they do in God's work in the world today. ■

tomorrow to the banquet I will prepare for you. Then I will explain what this is all about."

HAMAN'S PLAN TO KILL MORDECAI 9Haman was a happy man as he left the banquet! But when he saw Mordecai sitting at the palace gate, not standing up or trembling nervously before him, Haman became furious. 10However, he restrained himself and went on home.

Then Haman gathered together his friends and Zeresh, his wife, 11and boasted to them about his great wealth and his many children. He bragged about the honors the king had given him and how he had been promoted over all the other nobles and officials.

12Then Haman added, "And that's not all! Queen Esther invited only me and the king himself to the banquet she prepared for us. And she has invited me to dine with her and the king again tomorrow!" 13Then he added, "But this is all worth nothing as long as I see Mordecai the Jew just sitting there at the palace gate."

14So Haman's wife, Zeresh, and all his friends suggested, "Set up a sharpened pole that stands seventy-five feet* tall, and in the morning ask the king to impale Mordecai on it. When this is done, you can go on your merry way to the banquet with the king." This pleased Haman, and he ordered the pole set up.

5:14 Hebrew 50 cubits [22.5 meters].

6 **THE KING HONORS MORDECAI** That night the king had trouble sleeping, so he ordered an attendant to bring the book of the history of his reign so it could be read to him. 2In those records he discovered an account of how Mordecai had exposed the plot of Bigthana and Teresh, two of the eunuchs who guarded the door to the king's private quarters. They had plotted to assassinate King Xerxes.

3"What reward or recognition did we ever give Mordecai for this?" the king asked.

His attendants replied, "Nothing has been done for him."

4"Who is that in the outer court?" the king inquired. As it happened, Haman had just arrived in the outer court of the palace to ask the king to impale Mordecai on the pole he had prepared.

5So the attendants replied to the king, "Haman is out in the court."

"Bring him in," the king ordered. 6So Haman came in, and the king said, "What should I do to honor a man who truly pleases me?"

Haman thought to himself, "Whom would the king wish to honor more than me?" 7So he replied, "If the king wishes to honor someone, 8he should bring out one of the king's own royal robes, as well as a horse that the king himself has ridden—one with a royal emblem on its head. 9Let the robes and the horse be handed

HOW GOD WORKS IN THE WORLD

GOD'S ACTION	Natural Order	Miracles	Providence
	God set into action through creation a normal working of his universe. He also revealed his expectations of people through his Word and people's consciences.	God breaks into the natural order to respond to the expressed needs of people.	God overrules the natural order to accomplish an act that people may or may not have requested.
EXAMPLES FROM ESTHER	Natural Order	Miracles	Providence
	God gave Esther natural beauty. Esther planned a way to save her people.	God allowed Esther to speak to the king. The people prayed and fasted.	God allowed Mordecai to overhear a plot. Mordecai trusted God to accomplish what was impossible in human terms.
ACTION WE CAN TAKE	Plan	Pray	Trust & Obey
	Can make plans based on the order and dependability of God's creation. Know and obey his words.	Can ask God to intervene in certain affairs while realizing that our knowledge and perspective are limited.	Can trust that God is in control even when the circumstances may not seem to indicate that he is.
MISTAKES WE CAN MAKE	Disobey	Demand	Despair
	Can violate the natural order, disobey God's commands.	Can assume that we understand what is needed and expect God to agree and answer our prayers that way.	Can assume God doesn't answer prayer or respond to our needs and live as though there is nothing but the natural order.

over to one of the king's most noble officials. And let him see that the man whom the king wishes to honor is dressed in the king's robes and led through the city square on the king's horse. Have the official shout as they go, 'This is what the king does for someone he wishes to honor!'"

[10]"Excellent!" the king said to Haman. "Quick! Take the robes and my horse, and do just as you have said for Mordecai the Jew, who sits at the gate of the palace. Leave out nothing you have suggested!"

[11]So Haman took the robes and put them on Mordecai, placed him on the king's own horse, and led him through the city square, shouting, "This is what the king does for someone he wishes to honor!" [12]Afterward Mordecai re-

....

BRAGGING
(6:6-12) Just the night before (5:9-14), Haman had boasted about his position and the honor he was about to receive. Now he was humiliated and later marked for death (7:8-10). How quickly the course of life can change! Maybe that's why James 4:13-16 warns us to avoid bragging. Got a skill or something else you think is worth bragging about? What will you do instead?

turned to the palace gate, but Haman hurried home dejected and completely humiliated.

[13]When Haman told his wife, Zeresh, and all his friends what had happened, his wise advisers and his wife said, "Since Mordecai—this man who has humiliated you—is of Jewish birth, you will never succeed in your plans against him. It will be fatal to continue opposing him."

[14]While they were still talking, the king's eunuchs arrived and quickly took Haman to the banquet Esther had prepared.

7 THE KING EXECUTES HAMAN So the king and Haman went to Queen Esther's banquet. [2]On this second occasion, while they were drinking wine, the king again said to Esther, "Tell me what you want, Queen Esther. What is your request? I will give it to you, even if it is half the kingdom!"

[3]Queen Esther replied, "If I have found favor with the king, and if it pleases the king to grant my request, I ask that my life and the lives of my people will be spared. [4]For my people and I have been sold to those who would kill, slaugh-

ter, and annihilate us. If we had merely been sold as slaves, I could remain quiet, for that would be too trivial a matter to warrant disturbing the king."

⁵"Who would do such a thing?" King Xerxes demanded. "Who would be so presumptuous as to touch you?"

⁶Esther replied, "This wicked Haman is our adversary and our enemy." Haman grew pale with fright before the king and queen. ⁷Then the king jumped to his feet in a rage and went out into the palace garden.

Haman, however, stayed behind to plead for his life with Queen Esther, for he knew that the king intended to kill him. ⁸In despair he fell on the couch where Queen Esther was reclining, just as the king was returning from the palace garden.

The king exclaimed, "Will he even assault the queen right here in the palace, before my very eyes?" And as soon as the king spoke, his attendants covered Haman's face, signaling his doom.

⁹Then Harbona, one of the king's eunuchs, said, "Haman has set up a sharpened pole that stands seventy-five feet* tall in his own courtyard. He intended to use it to impale Mordecai, the man who saved the king from assassination."

"Then impale Haman on it!" the king ordered. ¹⁰So they impaled Haman on the pole he had set up for Mordecai, and the king's anger subsided.

8 A DECREE TO HELP THE JEWS

On that same day King Xerxes gave the property of Haman, the enemy of the Jews, to Queen Esther. Then Mordecai was brought before the king, for Esther had told the king how they were related. ²The king took off his signet ring—which he had taken back from Haman—and gave it to Mordecai. And Esther appointed Mordecai to be in charge of Haman's property.

³Then Esther went again before the king, falling down at his feet and begging him with tears to stop the evil plot devised by Haman the Agagite against the Jews. ⁴Again the king held out the gold scepter to Esther. So she rose and stood before him.

⁵Esther said, "If it please the king, and if I have found favor with him, and if he thinks it is right, and if I am pleasing to him, let there

be a decree that reverses the orders of Haman son of Hammedatha the Agagite, who ordered that Jews throughout all the king's provinces should be destroyed. ⁶For how can I endure to see my people and my family slaughtered and destroyed?"

⁷Then King Xerxes said to Queen Esther and Mordecai the Jew, "I have given Esther the property of Haman, and he has been impaled on a pole because he tried to destroy the Jews. ⁸Now go ahead and send a message to the Jews in the king's name, telling them whatever you want, and seal it with the king's signet ring. But remember that whatever has already been written in the king's name and sealed with his signet ring can never be revoked."

⁹So on June 25* the king's secretaries were summoned, and a decree was written exactly as Mordecai dictated. It was sent to the Jews and to the highest officers, the governors, and the nobles of all the 127 provinces stretching from India to Ethiopia.* The decree was written in the scripts and languages of all the peoples of the empire, including that of the Jews. ¹⁰The decree was written in the name of King Xerxes and sealed with the king's signet ring. Mordecai sent the dispatches by swift messengers, who rode fast horses especially bred for the king's service.

¹¹The king's decree gave the Jews in every city authority to unite to defend their lives. They were allowed to kill, slaughter, and annihilate anyone of any nationality or province who might attack them or their children and wives, and to take the property of their enemies. ¹²The day chosen for this event throughout all the provinces of King Xerxes was March 7 of the next year.*

¹³A copy of this decree was to be issued as law in every province and proclaimed to all peoples, so that the Jews would be ready to take revenge on their enemies on the appointed day. ¹⁴So urged on by the king's command, the messengers rode out swiftly on fast horses bred for the king's service. The same decree was also proclaimed in the fortress of Susa.

¹⁵Then Mordecai left the king's presence,

7:9 Hebrew 50 cubits [22.5 meters]. **8:9a** Hebrew on the twenty-third day of the third month, the month of Sivan, of the ancient Hebrew lunar calendar. This day was June 25, 474 B.C.; also see note on 2:16. **8:9b** Hebrew to Cush. **8:12** Hebrew the thirteenth day of the twelfth month, the month of Adar, of the ancient Hebrew lunar calendar. The date selected was March 7, 473 B.C.; also see note on 2:16.

....

THE PRICE OF HEROISM

(8:15-17) Everyone wants to be a hero and receive praise, honor, and wealth, but few are willing to pay the price of heroism. Mordecai served the government faithfully for years, put up with Haman's hatred and oppression, and risked his life for his people. The price to be paid by God's heroes is long-term commitment. Are you ready and willing to pay the price?

wearing the royal robe of blue and white, the great crown of gold, and an outer cloak of fine linen and purple. And the people of Susa celebrated the new decree. [16]The Jews were filled with joy and gladness and were honored everywhere. [17]In every province and city, wherever the king's decree arrived, the Jews rejoiced and had a great celebration and declared a public festival and holiday. And many of the people of the land became Jews themselves, for they feared what the Jews might do to them.

9 THE VICTORY OF THE JEWS So on March 7*

the two decrees of the king were put into effect. On that day, the enemies of the Jews had hoped to overpower them, but quite the opposite happened. It was the Jews who overpowered their enemies. [2]The Jews gathered in their cities throughout all the king's provinces to attack anyone who tried to harm them. But no one could make a stand against them, for everyone was afraid of them. [3]And all the nobles of the provinces, the highest officers, the governors, and the royal officials helped the Jews for fear of Mordecai. [4]For Mordecai had been promoted in the king's palace, and his fame spread throughout all the provinces as he became more and more powerful.

[5]So the Jews went ahead on the appointed day and struck down their enemies with the sword. They killed and annihilated their enemies and did as they pleased with those who hated them. [6]In the fortress of Susa itself, the Jews killed 500 men. [7]They also killed Parshandatha, Dalphon, Aspatha, [8]Poratha, Adalia, Aridatha, [9]Parmashta, Arisai, Aridai, and Vaizatha—[10]the ten sons of Haman son of Hammedatha, the enemy of the Jews. But they did not take any plunder.

[11]That very day, when the king was informed of the number of people killed in the fortress of Susa, [12]he called for Queen Esther. He said, "The Jews have killed 500 men in the fortress of Susa alone, as well as Haman's ten sons. If they have done that here, what has happened in the rest of the provinces? But now, what more do you want? It will be granted to you; tell me and I will do it."

[13]Esther responded, "If it please the king, give the Jews in Susa permission to do again tomorrow as they have done today, and let the bodies of Haman's ten sons be impaled on a pole."

[14]So the king agreed, and the decree was announced in Susa. And they impaled the bodies of Haman's ten sons. [15]Then the Jews at Susa gathered together on March 8* and killed 300 more men, and again they took no plunder.

[16]Meanwhile, the other Jews throughout the king's provinces had gathered together to defend their lives. They gained relief from all their enemies, killing 75,000 of those who hated them. But they did not take any plunder. [17]This was done throughout the provinces on March 7, and on March 8 they rested,* celebrating their victory with a day of feasting and gladness. [18](The Jews at Susa killed their enemies on March 7 and again on March 8, then rested on March 9,* making that their day of feasting and gladness.) [19]So to this day, rural Jews living in remote villages celebrate an annual festival and holiday on the appointed day in late winter,* when they rejoice and send gifts of food to each other.

THE FESTIVAL OF PURIM [20]Mordecai recorded these events and sent letters to the Jews near and far, throughout all the provinces of King Xerxes, [21]calling on them to celebrate an annual festival on these two days.* [22]He told them to celebrate these days with feasting and gladness and by giving gifts of food to each other and presents to the poor. This would commemorate a time when the Jews gained relief from their enemies, when their sorrow was turned into gladness and their mourning into joy.

[23]So the Jews accepted Mordecai's proposal and adopted this annual custom. [24]Haman son of Hammedatha the Agagite, the enemy of the Jews, had plotted to crush and destroy them on the date determined by casting lots (the lots were called *purim*). [25]But when Esther came before the king, he issued a decree causing Haman's evil plot to backfire, and Haman and his sons were impaled on a sharpened pole. [26]That is why this celebration is called Purim, because it is the ancient word for casting lots.

So because of Mordecai's letter and because of what they had experienced, [27]the Jews throughout the realm agreed to inaugurate this tradition and to pass it on to their descendants and to all who became Jews. They declared they would never fail to celebrate these two prescribed days at the appointed

9:1 Hebrew *on the thirteenth day of the twelfth month, the month of Adar,* of the ancient Hebrew lunar calendar. This day was March 7, 473 B.C.; also see note on 2:16. **9:15** Hebrew *the fourteenth day of the month of Adar,* of the ancient Hebrew lunar calendar. This day was March 8, 473 B.C.; also see note on 2:16. **9:17** Hebrew *on the thirteenth day of the month of Adar, and on the fourteenth day they rested.* These days were March 7 and 8, 473 B.C.; also see note on 2:16. **9:18** Hebrew *killed their enemies on the thirteenth day and the fourteenth day, and then rested on the fifteenth day,* of the Hebrew month of Adar. **9:19** Hebrew *on the fourteenth day of the month of Adar.* This day of the ancient Hebrew lunar calendar occurs in February or March. **9:21** Hebrew *on the fourteenth and fifteenth days of Adar,* of the ancient Hebrew lunar calendar.

time each year. [28]These days would be remembered and kept from generation to generation and celebrated by every family throughout the provinces and cities of the empire. This Festival of Purim would never cease to be celebrated among the Jews, nor would the memory of what happened ever die out among their descendants.

[29]Then Queen Esther, the daughter of Abihail, along with Mordecai the Jew, wrote another letter putting the queen's full authority behind Mordecai's letter to establish the Festival of Purim. [30]Letters wishing peace and security were sent to the Jews throughout the 127 provinces of the empire of Xerxes. [31]These letters established the Festival of Purim—an annual celebration of these days at the appointed time, decreed by both Mordecai the Jew and Queen Esther. (The people decided to observe this festival, just as they had decided for themselves and their descendants to establish the times of fasting and mourning.) [32]So the command of Esther confirmed the practices of Purim, and it was all written down in the records.

10 THE GREATNESS OF XERXES AND MORDECAI
King Xerxes imposed a tribute throughout his empire, even to the distant coastlands. [2]His great achievements and the full account of the greatness of Mordecai, whom the king had promoted, are recorded in *The Book of the History of the Kings of Media and Persia.* [3]Mordecai the Jew became the prime minister, with authority next to that of King Xerxes himself. He was very great among the Jews, who held him in high esteem, because he continued to work for the good of his people and to speak up for the welfare of all their descendants.

AVAILABLE
(9:29-31) Jewish women were expected to be quiet, to serve in the home, and to stay on the fringe of religious and political life. But Esther was a Jewish woman who broke through the cultural norms, stepping outside her expected role to risk her life to help God's people. Whatever your place in life, God can use you. Be open, available, and ready—God may use you to do what others are afraid even to consider.

IN CONTROL
(10:1-3) In the book of Esther, we clearly see God at work in the lives of individuals and in the affairs of a nation, even though he's not mentioned directly. Esther's story reminds us of the need to look for God's behind-the-scenes work in our lives. Even when it looks as if the world is in the hands of evil people, God is still in control, protecting those who belong to him. Do you trust him enough to let him tackle the most hopeless situation you face?

"Why me, God?" Have you ever thought, whispered, or screamed that question? Maybe you've even thought that God was against you.

At one time or another, everyone does . . . even people in the Bible. That is not surprising. What is surprising is God's answer to their questions.

Job loved God, and everything was going great in his life. He had money, land, possessions, and a large family. But one day his world fell apart. He lost everything . . . except his life, a bitter wife, and accusing "friends." As you might imagine, Job asked why. Why him? Why now? The book of Job tells this story, and it gives God's reply. And after God spoke, Job was silent. Job is a book about success, tragedy, friends, and faith. As you read Job, allow God to begin changing your ideas about suffering. Learn to trust God even when you don't understand.

KEY POINTS

SUFFERING Job's greatest trial was not the pain or loss; it was his inability to understand why God allowed him to suffer. Many of us who suffer have the same question. Although we may not be able to understand fully the pain we experience, it can lead us to rediscover God. He's always present, even when we suffer.

SATAN'S ATTACKS Satan tried to drive a wedge between Job and God. Satan was limited to what God allowed. We must learn to recognize Satan's attacks, but we should not fear them. Although we can't control how or when Satan may attack, we can always choose how we will respond when trouble comes.

TRUST Satan tried to drive a wedge between Job and God by getting Job to doubt God's love and justice. When life seems unfair, we're sometimes tempted to believe that God is unfair. Like Job, we can choose to trust instead of doubt.

PRIDE Job's friends thought they had all of the right answers concerning Job's suffering. But they were dead wrong. We must be careful not to judge others who are suffering, because we may fall into the same pride pit.

STATS

PURPOSE
To demonstrate God's sovereignty and the meaning of true faith. It addresses the question, Why does God allow bad things to happen?

AUTHOR
Possibly Job. Some have suggested Moses, Solomon, or Elihu.

ORIGINAL AUDIENCE
The people of Israel

DATE WRITTEN
Unknown. Records events that probably occurred during the time of the patriarchs (approximately 2000–1800 B.C.)

SETTING
The land of Uz, probably northeast of Palestine

KEY PEOPLE
Job, Job's wife (unnamed), Eliphaz the Temanite, Bildad the Shuhite, Zophar the Naamathite, Elihu the Buzite

SPECIAL FEATURES
Job is the first of the poetic books in the Hebrew Bible. Many consider it to be the oldest book in the Bible. The book gives us insights into the work of Satan. Ezekiel 14:14, 20 and James 5:11 mention Job as a historical character.

1 **PROLOGUE** There once was a man named Job who lived in the land of Uz. He was blameless—a man of complete integrity. He feared God and stayed away from evil. ²He had seven sons and three daughters. ³He owned 7,000 sheep, 3,000 camels, 500 teams of oxen, and 500 female donkeys. He also had many servants. He was, in fact, the richest person in that entire area.

⁴Job's sons would take turns preparing feasts in their homes, and they would also invite their three sisters to celebrate with them. ⁵When these celebrations ended—sometimes after several days—Job would purify his children. He would get up early in the morning and offer a burnt offering for each of them. For Job said to himself, "Perhaps my children have sinned and have cursed God in their hearts." This was Job's regular practice.

JOB'S FIRST TEST ⁶One day the members of the heavenly court* came to present themselves before the Lord, and the Accuser, Satan,* came with them. ⁷"Where have you come from?" the Lord asked Satan.

Satan answered the Lord, "I have been patrolling the earth, watching everything that's going on."

⁸Then the Lord asked Satan, "Have you noticed my servant Job? He is the finest man in all the earth. He is blameless—a man of complete integrity. He fears God and stays away from evil."

⁹Satan replied to the Lord, "Yes, but Job has good reason to fear God. ¹⁰You have always put

a wall of protection around him and his home and his property. You have made him prosper in everything he does. Look how rich he is! ¹¹But reach out and take away everything he has, and he will surely curse you to your face!"

¹²"All right, you may test him," the Lord said to Satan. "Do whatever you want with everything he possesses, but don't harm him physically." So Satan left the Lord's presence.

¹³One day when Job's sons and daughters were feasting at the oldest brother's house, ¹⁴a messenger arrived at Job's home with this news: "Your oxen were plowing, with the donkeys feeding beside them, ¹⁵when the Sabeans raided us. They stole all the animals and killed all the farmhands. I am the only one who escaped to tell you."

¹⁶While he was still speaking, another messenger arrived with this news: "The fire of God has fallen from heaven and burned up your sheep and all the shepherds. I am the only one who escaped to tell you."

¹⁷While he was still speaking, a third messenger arrived with this news: "Three bands of Chaldean raiders have stolen your camels and killed your servants. I am the only one who escaped to tell you."

¹⁸While he was still speaking, another messenger arrived with this news: "Your sons and daughters were feasting in their oldest brother's home. ¹⁹Suddenly, a powerful wind swept in from the wilderness and hit the house on all sides. The house collapsed, and all your children are dead. I am the only one who escaped to tell you."

²⁰Job stood up and tore his robe in grief. Then he shaved his head and fell to the ground to worship. ²¹He said,

"I came naked from my mother's womb,
    and I will be naked when I leave.
The Lord gave me what I had,
    and the Lord has taken it away.
Praise the name of the Lord!"

²²In all of this, Job did not sin by blaming God.

2 **JOB'S SECOND TEST** One day the members of the heavenly court* came again to present themselves before the Lord, and the Accuser, Satan,* came with them. ²"Where have you come from?" the Lord asked Satan.

Satan answered the Lord, "I have been patrolling the earth, watching everything that's going on."

WHY ME?
(1:1) When reading the book of Job, we have information that the characters in the story do not. Job lost all he had through no fault of his own. As he struggled to understand why all this was happening to him, it became clear that he was not meant to know the reasons. He would have to face life with the answers and explanations held back. Only then would his faith fully develop. Like Job, you may not have the answers to why you suffer. But you can choose to either trust God no matter what or be frustrated and bitter. What will you choose?

A TIME TO GRIEVE
(1:20-22) Job did not hide his overwhelming grief. This emotional display did not mean he had lost his faith in God; instead, it showed that he was human and that he loved his family. God created our emotions, and it is not sinful to express them as Job did. Often we try to hold in our feelings in an attempt to appear unaffected. Or, we fear that our friends can't handle such emotions. If you have experienced deep loss, disappointment, or heartbreak, admit your feelings to yourself and others, and grieve. God understands what we're going through, our feelings and our need to grieve. And best of all, he's always willing to listen.

1:6a Hebrew *the sons of God.*   **1:6b** Hebrew *and the satan;* similarly throughout this chapter.   **2:1a** Hebrew *the sons of God.*
2:1b Hebrew *and the satan;* similarly throughout this chapter.

³Then the LORD asked Satan, "Have you noticed my servant Job? He is the finest man in all the earth. He is blameless—a man of complete integrity. He fears God and stays away from evil. And he has maintained his integrity, even though you urged me to harm him without cause."

⁴Satan replied to the LORD, "Skin for skin! A man will give up everything he has to save his life. ⁵But reach out and take away his health, and he will surely curse you to your face!"

⁶"All right, do with him as you please," the LORD said to Satan. "But spare his life." ⁷So Satan left the LORD's presence, and he struck Job with terrible boils from head to foot.

⁸Job scraped his skin with a piece of broken pottery as he sat among the ashes. ⁹His wife said to him, "Are you still trying to maintain your integrity? Curse God and die."

¹⁰But Job replied, "You talk like a foolish woman. Should we accept only good things from the hand of God and never anything bad?" So in all this, Job said nothing wrong.

JOB'S THREE FRIENDS SHARE HIS ANGUISH

¹¹When three of Job's friends heard of the tragedy he had suffered, they got together and traveled from their homes to comfort and console him. Their names were Eliphaz the Temanite, Bildad the Shuhite, and Zophar the Naamathite. ¹²When they saw Job from a distance, they scarcely recognized him. Wailing loudly, they tore their robes and threw dust into the air over their heads to show their grief. ¹³Then they sat on the ground with him for seven days and nights. No one said a word to Job, for they saw that his suffering was too great for words.

3 **JOB'S FIRST SPEECH** At last Job spoke, and he cursed the day of his birth. ²He said:

³ "Let the day of my birth be erased,
and the night I was conceived.
⁴ Let that day be turned to darkness.
Let it be lost even to God on high,
and let no light shine on it.
⁵ Let the darkness and utter gloom claim that
day for its own.
Let a black cloud overshadow it,
and let the darkness terrify it.
⁶ Let that night be blotted off the calendar,
never again to be counted among the
days of the year,
never again to appear among the months.

3:8 The identification of Leviathan is disputed, ranging from an earthly creature to a mythical sea monster in ancient literature.

⁷ Let that night be childless.
Let it have no joy.
⁸ Let those who are experts at cursing—
whose cursing could rouse Leviathan*—
curse that day.
⁹ Let its morning stars remain dark.
Let it hope for light, but in vain;
may it never see the morning light.
¹⁰ Curse that day for failing to shut my
mother's womb,
for letting me be born to see all this
trouble.

¹¹ "Why wasn't I born dead?
Why didn't I die as I came from the
womb?
¹² Why was I laid on my mother's lap?
Why did she nurse me at her breasts?
¹³ Had I died at birth, I would now be at peace.
I would be asleep and at rest.
¹⁴ I would rest with the world's kings and
prime ministers,
whose great buildings now lie in ruins.
¹⁵ I would rest with princes, rich in gold,
whose palaces were filled with silver.
¹⁶ Why wasn't I buried like a stillborn child,
like a baby who never lives to see the
light?
¹⁷ For in death the wicked cause no trouble,
and the weary are at rest.
¹⁸ Even captives are at ease in death,
with no guards to curse them.
¹⁹ Rich and poor are both there,
and the slave is free from his master.

²⁰ "Oh, why give light to those in misery,
and life to those who are bitter?
²¹ They long for death, and it won't come.
They search for death more eagerly than
for hidden treasure.
²² They're filled with joy when they finally die,
and rejoice when they find the grave.
²³ Why is life given to those with no future,
those God has surrounded with
difficulties?

·····································

SILENT COMFORT
(2:11-13) *Why did Job's friends arrive and then just sit quietly? According to Jewish tradition, people who came to comfort someone in mourning were not to speak until the mourner spoke. Job's friends realized that his pain was too deep to be healed with mere words, so they said nothing. (If only they had continued to just sit quietly!) Often, we feel we must say something spiritual and insightful to a hurting friend. But silence often is the best response to another person's suffering. Want to help a grieving friend? Just be there for him or her. Pat answers and trite quotations say much less than caring silence and loving companionship.*

24 I cannot eat for sighing;
  my groans pour out like water.
25 What I always feared has happened to me.
  What I dreaded has come true.
26 I have no peace, no quietness.
  I have no rest; only trouble comes."

4 ELIPHAZ'S FIRST RESPONSE TO JOB Then
Eliphaz the Temanite replied to Job:

2 "Will you be patient and let me say a word?
  For who could keep from speaking out?

3 "In the past you have encouraged many
    people;
  you have strengthened those who were
    weak.
4 Your words have supported those who were
    falling;
  you encouraged those with shaky knees.
5 But now when trouble strikes, you lose
    heart.
  You are terrified when it touches you.
6 Doesn't your reverence for God give you
    confidence?

Doesn't your life of integrity give you
  hope?

7 "Stop and think! Do the innocent die?
  When have the upright been destroyed?
8 My experience shows that those who plant
    trouble
  and cultivate evil will harvest
    the same.
9 A breath from God destroys them.
  They vanish in a blast of his anger.
10 The lion roars and the wildcat snarls,
  but the teeth of strong lions will be
    broken.
11 The fierce lion will starve for lack of prey,
  and the cubs of the lioness will be
    scattered.

12 "This truth was given to me in secret,
  as though whispered in my ear.
13 It came to me in a disturbing vision
    at night,
  when people are in a deep sleep.
14 Fear gripped me,
  and my bones trembled.

JOB *PERSONALITY PROFILE*

THINK ABOUT THE WORST TRAGEDY you've ever faced: the death of a parent; the breakup of your family due to divorce; the end of a treasured relationship; a terminal illness; the loss of all your possessions. Now imagine all of that happening in one day.

Job faced a day of unbelievable sorrow as loss after loss occurred. As we read his story, our minds reel. This isn't supposed to happen, we think. Job was a good man. Good things should happen to people who do good things, and bad things should happen to people who do bad things, right? Life can work out that way—but not always. Job's life can teach us what God wants us to do when we don't understand what's happening to us.

When knowing why becomes important, we can use the letters of that word "why" to remind us of Job's lessons. Like Job, we need to wait, hope, and yield.

Waiting is difficult. Our "instant" age has taught us to expect answers and help fast. Job wanted to know why. When God finally spoke, he didn't offer Job an answer. He showed Job that knowing God is better than knowing all of the answers.

That's why hoping is important. When we remember that God loves us, that he has good plans for us, and that he is more powerful than any situation we might encounter, we have hope. Hope means we trust God even if we never find out why something happened.

Yielding means wanting to do whatever God wants. It means praying like this: "God, I'm willing to wait and hope, because you are my God." Are there some areas in your life that need this prayer?

Asking why can be more than a question when it points us to God.

BOTTOM LINE: Knowing God is better than knowing the answers.
  God is not arbitrary or uncaring.
  Pain is not always punishment.

Job's story is told in the book of Job. He also is mentioned in Ezekiel 14:14, 20 and James 5:11.

UPS:
• *A man of faith, patience, and endurance*
• *Known as a generous and caring person*
• *Very wealthy*

DOWNS:
• *Allowed his suffering to overwhelm him and make him question God*

STATS:
• *Where: Land of Uz*
• *Occupation: Wealthy land and livestock owner*
• *Relatives: His wife and first ten children not named. Daughters from the second set of children: Jemimah, Keziah, Keren-happuch*
• *Contemporaries: Eliphaz, Bildad, Zophar, Elihu*

KEY VERSES: *James 5:10-11*

15 A spirit* swept past my face,
   and my hair stood on end.*
16 The spirit stopped, but I couldn't see its
      shape.
   There was a form before my eyes.
   In the silence I heard a voice say,
17 'Can a mortal be innocent before God?
      Can anyone be pure before
      the Creator?'

18 "If God does not trust his own angels
      and has charged his messengers with
      foolishness,
19 how much less will he trust people made
      of clay!
   They are made of dust, crushed as easily
      as a moth.
20 They are alive in the morning but dead by
      evening,
   gone forever without a trace.
21 Their tent-cords are pulled and the tent
      collapses,
   and they die in ignorance.

5 ELIPHAZ'S RESPONSE CONTINUES

1 "Cry for help, but will anyone answer you?
   Which of the angels* will help you?
2 Surely resentment destroys the fool,
   and jealousy kills the simple.
3 I have seen that fools may be successful
      for the moment,
   but then comes sudden disaster.
4 Their children are abandoned far from help;
   they are crushed in court with no one to
      defend them.
5 The hungry devour their harvest,
   even when it is guarded by brambles.*
   The thirsty pant after their wealth.
6 But evil does not spring from the soil,
   and trouble does not sprout from
      the earth.
7 People are born for trouble
   as readily as sparks fly up from a fire.

8 "If I were you, I would go to God
   and present my case to him.
9 He does great things too marvelous to
      understand.
   He performs countless miracles.
10 He gives rain for the earth
   and water for the fields.
11 He gives prosperity to the poor
   and protects those who suffer.
12 He frustrates the plans of schemers

FROM SIX DISASTERS HE WILL RESCUE YOU; EVEN IN THE SEVENTH, HE WILL KEEP YOU FROM EVIL.

JOB 5:19

so the work of their hands will not
      succeed.
13 He traps the wise in their own cleverness
   so their cunning schemes are thwarted.
14 They find it is dark in the daytime,
   and they grope at noon as if it were night.
15 He rescues the poor from the cutting words
      of the strong,
   and rescues them from the clutches of
      the powerful.
16 And so at last the poor have hope,
   and the snapping jaws of the wicked
      are shut.

17 "But consider the joy of those corrected
      by God!
   Do not despise the discipline of the
      Almighty when you sin.
18 For though he wounds, he also bandages.
   He strikes, but his hands also heal.
19 From six disasters he will rescue you;
   even in the seventh, he will keep you
      from evil.
20 He will save you from death in time
      of famine,
   from the power of the sword in time
      of war.
21 You will be safe from slander
   and have no fear when destruction
      comes.
22 You will laugh at destruction and famine;
   wild animals will not terrify you.
23 You will be at peace with the stones of the
      field,
   and its wild animals will be at peace
      with you.

....

GOOD ADVICE
(5:17) Eliphaz was right—being "corrected" by God when
we do wrong is a blessing. His advice, however, did not
apply to Job. As we know from the beginning of the book,
Job's suffering was not a result of wrong actions on his
part. Like Eliphaz, we sometimes give people excellent
advice only to learn that it doesn't apply to them and is
therefore not very helpful. Those who offer counsel from
God's Word should take care to thoroughly understand
a person's situation before giving advice.

4:15a Or *wind;* also in 4:16.   4:15b Or *its wind sent shivers up my
spine.*   5:1 Hebrew *the holy ones.*   5:5 The meaning of the Hebrew
for this phrase is uncertain.

24 You will know that your home is safe.
   When you survey your possessions,
      nothing will be missing.
25 You will have many children;
   your descendants will be as plentiful
      as grass!
26 You will go to the grave at a ripe old age,
   like a sheaf of grain harvested at the
      proper time!

27 "We have studied life and found all this
      to be true.
   Listen to my counsel, and apply it to
      yourself."

6 JOB'S SECOND SPEECH: A RESPONSE TO ELIPHAZ Then Job spoke again:

2 "If my misery could be weighed
   and my troubles be put on the scales,
3 they would outweigh all the sands of
      the sea.
   That is why I spoke impulsively.
4 For the Almighty has struck me down with
      his arrows.
   Their poison infects my spirit.
   God's terrors are lined up against me.
5 Don't I have a right to complain?
   Don't wild donkeys bray when they find
      no grass,
   and oxen bellow when they have no food?
6 Don't people complain about unsalted
      food?
   Does anyone want the tasteless white
      of an egg?*
7 My appetite disappears when I look at it;
   I gag at the thought of eating it!

8 "Oh, that I might have my request,
   that God would grant my desire.
9 I wish he would crush me.
   I wish he would reach out his hand and
      kill me.
10 At least I can take comfort in this:
   Despite the pain,
   I have not denied the words of the Holy
      One.
11 But I don't have the strength to endure.

STRUGGLES
(6:8-13) In his grief, Job wanted to give in, to be freed from his discomfort, and to die. But God did not grant Job's request. He had a greater plan for him. When the going gets tough, are you tempted to give up? To trust God in the good times is commendable, but to trust him during the difficult times tests us to our limits and exercises our faith. In your struggles, large or small, are you willing to trust that God is in control as Romans 8:28 suggests?

   I have nothing to live for.
12 Do I have the strength of a stone?
   Is my body made of bronze?
13 No, I am utterly helpless,
   without any chance of success.

14 "One should be kind to a fainting friend,
   but you accuse me without any fear of the
      Almighty.*
15 My brothers, you have proved as unreliable
      as a seasonal brook
   that overflows its banks in the spring
16 when it is swollen with ice and melting
      snow.
17 But when the hot weather arrives, the water
      disappears.
   The brook vanishes in the heat.
18 The caravans turn aside to be refreshed,
   but there is nothing to drink, so they die.
19 The caravans from Tema search for this
      water;
   the travelers from Sheba hope to find it.
20 They count on it but are disappointed.
   When they arrive, their hopes are dashed.
21 You, too, have given no help.
   You have seen my calamity, and you
      are afraid.
22 But why? Have I ever asked you for a gift?
   Have I begged for anything of yours
      for myself?
23 Have I asked you to rescue me from my
      enemies,
   or to save me from ruthless people?
24 Teach me, and I will keep quiet.
   Show me what I have done wrong.
25 Honest words can be painful,
   but what do your criticisms amount to?
26 Do you think your words are convincing
   when you disregard my cry of
      desperation?
27 You would even send an orphan into
      slavery*
   or sell a friend.
28 Look at me!
   Would I lie to your face?
29 Stop assuming my guilt,
   for I have done no wrong.
30 Do you think I am lying?
   Don't I know the difference between right
      and wrong?

7 1 "Is not all human life a struggle?
   Our lives are like that of a hired hand,
2 like a worker who longs for the shade,
   like a servant waiting to be paid.

6:6 Or the tasteless juice of the mallow plant? **6:14** Or friend, / or he might lose his fear of the Almighty. **6:27** Hebrew even gamble over an orphan.

³ I, too, have been assigned months of
  futility,
  long and weary nights of misery.
⁴ Lying in bed, I think, 'When will it be
  morning?'
  But the night drags on, and I toss till
  dawn.
⁵ My body is covered with maggots and
  scabs.
  My skin breaks open, oozing with pus.

JOB CRIES OUT TO GOD

⁶ "My days fly faster than a weaver's shuttle.
  They end without hope.
⁷ O God, remember that my life is but a
  breath,
  and I will never again feel happiness.
⁸ You see me now, but not for long.
  You will look for me, but I will be gone.
⁹ Just as a cloud dissipates and vanishes,
  those who die* will not come back.
¹⁰ They are gone forever from their home—
  never to be seen again.

¹¹ "I cannot keep from speaking.
  I must express my anguish.
  My bitter soul must complain.
¹² Am I a sea monster or a dragon
  that you must place me under guard?
¹³ I think, 'My bed will comfort me,
  and sleep will ease my misery,'
¹⁴ but then you shatter me with dreams
  and terrify me with visions.
¹⁵ I would rather be strangled—
  rather die than suffer like this.
¹⁶ I hate my life and don't want to go on living.
  Oh, leave me alone for my few remaining
  days.

¹⁷ "What are people, that you should make so
  much of us,
  that you should think of us so often?
¹⁸ For you examine us every morning
  and test us every moment.
¹⁹ Why won't you leave me alone,
  at least long enough for me to swallow!
²⁰ If I have sinned, what have I done to you,
  O watcher of all humanity?
  Why make me your target?
  Am I a burden to you?
²¹ Why not just forgive my sin
  and take away my guilt?
  For soon I will lie down in the dust and die.
  When you look for me, I will be gone."

8 BILDAD'S FIRST RESPONSE TO JOB
Then Bildad the Shuhite replied to Job:

7:9 Hebrew *who go down to Sheol.*

² "How long will you go on like this?
  You sound like a blustering wind.
³ Does God twist justice?
  Does the Almighty twist what is right?
⁴ Your children must have sinned against
  him,
  so their punishment was well deserved.
⁵ But if you pray to God
  and seek the favor of the Almighty,
⁶ and if you are pure and live with integrity,
  he will surely rise up and restore your
  happy home.
⁷ And though you started with little,
  you will end with much.

⁸ "Just ask the previous generation.
  Pay attention to the experience of our
  ancestors.
⁹ For we were born but yesterday and know
  nothing.
  Our days on earth are as fleeting as
  a shadow.
¹⁰ But those who came before us will
  teach you.
  They will teach you the wisdom of old.

¹¹ "Can papyrus reeds grow tall without a
  marsh?
  Can marsh grass flourish without water?
¹² While they are still flowering, not ready to
  be cut,
  they begin to wither more quickly than
  grass.
¹³ The same happens to all who forget God.
  The hopes of the godless evaporate.
¹⁴ Their confidence hangs by a thread.
  They are leaning on a spider's web.
¹⁵ They cling to their home for security, but
  it won't last.
  They try to hold it tight, but it will not
  endure.
¹⁶ The godless seem like a lush plant growing
  in the sunshine,
  its branches spreading across the garden.
¹⁷ Its roots grow down through a pile of
  stones;
  it takes hold on a bed of rocks.
¹⁸ But when it is uprooted,
  it's as though it never existed!

···

FEELING SECURE
(8:14-15) *Bildad wrongly assumed that Job failed to
trust God for his security. Everyone has a need to feel
secure. But sometimes our security is based on money,
possessions, knowledge, or relationships. All of these are
temporary. Only God can give lasting security. What have
you trusted for your security? How lasting is it? A secure
foundation with God keeps feelings of insecurity at bay.*

¹⁹ That's the end of its life,
    and others spring up from the earth
        to replace it.

²⁰ "But look, God will not reject a person
        of integrity,
    nor will he lend a hand to the wicked.
²¹ He will once again fill your mouth with
        laughter
    and your lips with shouts of joy.
²² Those who hate you will be clothed with
        shame,
    and the home of the wicked will be
        destroyed."

9 JOB'S THIRD SPEECH: A RESPONSE TO BILDAD Then Job spoke again:

² "Yes, I know all this is true in principle.
    But how can a person be declared
        innocent in God's sight?
³ If someone wanted to take God to court,*

would it be possible to answer him even
        once in a thousand times?
⁴ For God is so wise and so mighty.
    Who has ever challenged him
        successfully?

⁵ "Without warning, he moves the mountains,
    overturning them in his anger.
⁶ He shakes the earth from its place,
    and its foundations tremble.
⁷ If he commands it, the sun won't rise
    and the stars won't shine.
⁸ He alone has spread out the heavens
    and marches on the waves of the sea.
⁹ He made all the stars—the Bear and Orion,
    the Pleiades and the constellations of the
        southern sky.
¹⁰ He does great things too marvelous to
        understand.
    He performs countless miracles.

9:3 Or *If God wanted to take someone to court.*

ULTIMATE ISSUES SUFFERING AND EVIL

Sooner or later, every Christian faces this question: Why does God allow suffering and evil? Why does God allow bad things to happen? Philosophers express it like this: "If God is good, he must not be all-powerful, otherwise he wouldn't allow evil. If he *is* all-powerful, he must not be good."

Does God see what's going on here? Does he care? If so, why doesn't he intervene?

The book of Job addresses this question more than any portion of Scripture. For reasons unknown to Job, a series of crushing catastrophes hit him, leaving him to ask, "Why me, God?" And God responds (chs 38–41) with his longest unbroken speech in the Bible—but he never explains why. He basically tells Job that as God he can do whatever he wants, and that's all the answer Job needs.

Big help, right?

The fact that God doesn't answer Job's question is somewhat disturbing. But the following perspectives may help when you are faced with suffering and evil.

First, remember that though God never answered Job directly, he didn't condemn Job for asking. He just reminded Job who he was talking to. It seems that "why?" is a question we are free to ask, but God is not bound to answer. Sometimes he will; sometimes he won't.

Second, remember that we live in a broken world of sinful people. It is a planet in rebellion against its Creator; we shouldn't be surprised, then, that believers are caught in the cross fire. When you are tempted to blame God for your suffering, think of it like this: Imagine giving a fragile, priceless family heirloom to a child. He looks it over and then smashes it to the

floor. As he stands in the middle of the shattered pieces of what you gave him, he shakes his clenched fist in your face and says, "Look what you've done! Look at this piece of junk you gave me!" The child is wrong; you gave him a wonderful, treasured possession, and he ruined it. In the same way, God gave us a perfect world; we've turned it into the chaos it is today.

Third, remember that being a Christian does not exempt you from pain and suffering. Jesus even guaranteed us that we would experience hard times (John 16:33). But we can be comforted: Jesus overcame suffering and we can, too. Serving God is easy when life is sunny; the test is how we respond when the storm washes over us. And if you're serious about following Jesus, brace yourself: storms will come.

Fourth, contrary to what a lot of Christians believe, God does not promise his children happiness. He's much more concerned with our holiness, and that involves pain and sacrifice. Worthwhile things seldom, if ever, come without great cost. Following Jesus is no exception. Of course, God isn't a cosmic killjoy, getting his kicks out of watching us squirm. He just wants us to imitate his Son—even when it isn't all fun and games.

Finally, when nothing else helps, remember this: When you or someone you love suffers, no one hurts more than God. He's a good Father, and it pains him deeply to see his children hurt. He feels with us so genuinely that he got personally involved in our struggle—he became a man and suffered and died for us. So when you hurt, remember: you never cry alone. God knows, God sees, and God cares. ■

¹¹ "Yet when he comes near, I cannot see him.
When he moves by, I do not see him go.
¹² If he snatches someone in death, who can
stop him?
Who dares to ask, 'What are you doing?'
¹³ And God does not restrain his anger.
Even the monsters of the sea* are
crushed beneath his feet.

¹⁴ "So who am I, that I should try to answer
God
or even reason with him?
¹⁵ Even if I were right, I would have no defense.
I could only plead for mercy.
¹⁶ And even if I summoned him and he
responded,
I'm not sure he would listen to me.
¹⁷ For he attacks me with a storm
and repeatedly wounds me without
cause.
¹⁸ He will not let me catch my breath,
but fills me instead with bitter sorrows.
¹⁹ If it's a question of strength, he's the
strong one.
If it's a matter of justice, who dares to
summon him to court?
²⁰ Though I am innocent, my own mouth would
pronounce me guilty.
Though I am blameless, it* would prove
me wicked.

²¹ "I am innocent,
but it makes no difference to me—
I despise my life.
²² Innocent or wicked, it is all the same to God.
That's why I say, 'He destroys both the
blameless and the wicked.'
²³ When a plague* sweeps through,
he laughs at the death of the innocent.
²⁴ The whole earth is in the hands of the
wicked,
and God blinds the eyes of the judges.
If he's not the one who does it, who is?

²⁵ "My life passes more swiftly than a runner.
It flees away without a glimpse of
happiness.
²⁶ It disappears like a swift papyrus boat,
like an eagle swooping down on its prey.
²⁷ If I decided to forget my complaints,
to put away my sad face and be cheerful,
²⁸ I would still dread all the pain,
for I know you will not find me innocent,
O God.
²⁹ Whatever happens, I will be found guilty.
So what's the use of trying?

³⁰ Even if I were to wash myself with soap
and clean my hands with lye,
³¹ you would plunge me into a muddy ditch,
and my own filthy clothing would
hate me.

³² "God is not a mortal like me,
so I cannot argue with him or take him
to trial.
³³ If only there were a mediator between us,
someone who could bring us together.
³⁴ The mediator could make God stop
beating me,
and I would no longer live in terror of his
punishment.
³⁵ Then I could speak to him without fear,
but I cannot do that in my own strength.

10 JOB FRAMES HIS PLEA TO GOD

¹ "I am disgusted with my life.
Let me complain freely.
My bitter soul must complain.
² I will say to God, 'Don't simply condemn me—
tell me the charge you are bringing
against me.
³ What do you gain by oppressing me?
Why do you reject me, the work of your
own hands,
while smiling on the schemes of the
wicked?
⁴ Are your eyes like those of a human?
Do you see things only as people see
them?
⁵ Is your lifetime only as long as ours?
Is your life so short
⁶ that you must quickly probe for my guilt
and search for my sin?
⁷ Although you know I am not guilty,
no one can rescue me from your hands.

⁸ "'You formed me with your hands; you
made me,
yet now you completely destroy me.
⁹ Remember that you made me from dust—
will you turn me back to dust so soon?
¹⁰ You guided my conception
and formed me in the womb.*

....

HOW UNFAIR!
(10:1) Job complained to his friends about his misery.
When life seems unfair, self-pity is a natural response. At
that point, we are only one step from self-righteousness,
where we keep track of life's injustices and say, "Look
what happened to me; how unfair it is!" What we really
mean is, "God is unfair." But hard times can help us
mature in our faith. When facing difficult situations, ask,
"What can I learn and how can I grow?" rather than "Who
did this to me and how can I get out of it?"

9:13 Hebrew *the helpers of Rahab,* the name of a mythical sea
monster that represents chaos in ancient literature.   **9:20** Or *he.*
9:23 Or *disaster.*   **10:10** Hebrew *You poured me out like milk / and
curdled me like cheese.*

¹¹ You clothed me with skin and flesh,
   and you knit my bones and sinews
      together.
¹² You gave me life and showed me your
      unfailing love.
   My life was preserved by your care.

¹³ "'Yet your real motive—
      your true intent—
¹⁴ was to watch me, and if I sinned,
      you would not forgive my guilt.
¹⁵ If I am guilty, too bad for me;
      and even if I'm innocent, I can't hold my
         head high,
      because I am filled with shame and
         misery.
¹⁶ And if I hold my head high, you hunt me like
         a lion
      and display your awesome power
         against me.
¹⁷ Again and again you witness against me.
      You pour out your growing anger on me
      and bring fresh armies against me.

¹⁸ "'Why, then, did you deliver me from my
         mother's womb?
      Why didn't you let me die at birth?
¹⁹ It would be as though I had never existed,
      going directly from the womb to the
         grave.
²⁰ I have only a few days left, so leave me
         alone,
      that I may have a moment of comfort
²¹ before I leave—never to return—
      for the land of darkness and utter gloom.
²² It is a land as dark as midnight,
      a land of gloom and confusion,
      where even the light is dark as
         midnight.'"

11 ZOPHAR'S FIRST RESPONSE TO JOB
Then Zophar the Naamathite replied to
Job:

² "Shouldn't someone answer this torrent of
      words?
   Is a person proved innocent just by a lot
      of talking?

....

NO HIDING FROM GOD
(11:1-11) Zophar incorrectly assumed that Job was being
punished because of hidden wrongdoings. Although his
assumption was wrong, he explained quite accurately
that God knows and sees everything. Ever think, No one
will ever know in regard to something you've done? We
can hide some wrongs from others, but we can do nothing
without God knowing about it. Our lives are an open book
to him. Job understood this as well as Zophar, but it didn't
apply to his dilemma.

³ Should I remain silent while you babble on?
   When you mock God, shouldn't someone
      make you ashamed?
⁴ You claim, 'My beliefs are pure,'
   and 'I am clean in the sight of God.'
⁵ If only God would speak;
   if only he would tell you what he thinks!
⁶ If only he would tell you the secrets of
      wisdom,
   for true wisdom is not a simple matter.
   Listen! God is doubtless punishing you
      far less than you deserve!

⁷ "Can you solve the mysteries of God?
   Can you discover everything about the
      Almighty?
⁸ Such knowledge is higher than the heavens—
      and who are you?
   It is deeper than the underworld*—
      what do you know?
⁹ It is broader than the earth
      and wider than the sea.
¹⁰ If God comes and puts a person in prison
      or calls the court to order, who can
         stop him?
¹¹ For he knows those who are false,
      and he takes note of all their sins.
¹² An empty-headed person won't become
         wise
      any more than a wild donkey can bear
         a human child.*

¹³ "If only you would prepare your heart
      and lift up your hands to him in prayer!
¹⁴ Get rid of your sins,
      and leave all iniquity behind you.
¹⁵ Then your face will brighten with innocence.
      You will be strong and free of fear.
¹⁶ You will forget your misery;
      it will be like water flowing away.
¹⁷ Your life will be brighter than the noonday.
      Even darkness will be as bright as
         morning.
¹⁸ Having hope will give you courage.
      You will be protected and will rest in
         safety.
¹⁹ You will lie down unafraid,
      and many will look to you for help.
²⁰ But the wicked will be blinded.
      They will have no escape.
      Their only hope is death."

12 JOB'S FOURTH SPEECH: A RESPONSE
TO ZOPHAR Then Job spoke again:

² "You people really know everything,
      don't you?

11:8 Hebrew *than Sheol.*   **11:12** Or *than a wild male donkey can*
bear a tame colt.

And when you die, wisdom will die
　　with you!

3 Well, I know a few things myself—
　　and you're no better than I am.
　　Who doesn't know these things you've
　　　been saying?

4 Yet my friends laugh at me,
　　for I call on God and expect an answer.
　I am a just and blameless man,
　　yet they laugh at me.

5 People who are at ease mock those in
　　trouble.
　　They give a push to people who are
　　　stumbling.

6 But robbers are left in peace,
　　and those who provoke God live in safety—
　　though God keeps them in his power.

7 "Just ask the animals, and they will
　　teach you.
　　Ask the birds of the sky, and they will
　　　tell you.

8 Speak to the earth, and it will instruct you.
　　Let the fish in the sea speak to you.

9 For they all know
　　that my disaster* has come from the hand
　　　of the LORD.

10 For the life of every living thing is in his
　　hand,
　　and the breath of every human being.

11 The ear tests the words it hears
　　just as the mouth distinguishes between
　　　foods.

12 Wisdom belongs to the aged,
　　and understanding to the old.

13 "But true wisdom and power are found
　　in God;
　　counsel and understanding are his.

14 What he destroys cannot be rebuilt.
　　When he puts someone in prison, there
　　　is no escape.

15 If he holds back the rain, the earth becomes
　　a desert.
　　If he releases the waters, they flood
　　　the earth.

16 Yes, strength and wisdom are his;
　　deceivers and deceived are both in his
　　　power.

17 He leads counselors away, stripped of good
　　judgment;
　　wise judges become fools.

18 He removes the royal robe of kings.
　　They are led away with ropes around
　　　their waist.

19 He leads priests away, stripped of status;

12:9 Hebrew *that this.*

he overthrows those with long years
　　in power.

20 He silences the trusted adviser
　　and removes the insight of the elders.

21 He pours disgrace upon princes
　　and disarms the strong.

22 "He uncovers mysteries hidden in darkness;
　　he brings light to the deepest gloom.

23 He builds up nations, and he destroys them.
　　He expands nations, and he abandons
　　　them.

24 He strips kings of understanding
　　and leaves them wandering in a pathless
　　　wasteland.

25 They grope in the darkness without a light.
　　He makes them stagger like drunkards.

13 JOB WANTS TO ARGUE HIS CASE WITH GOD

1 "Look, I have seen all this with my own eyes
　　and heard it with my own ears, and now I
　　　understand.

2 I know as much as you do.
　　You are no better than I am.

3 As for me, I would speak directly to the
　　Almighty.
　　I want to argue my case with God himself.

4 As for you, you smear me with lies.
　　As physicians, you are worthless quacks.

5 If only you could be silent!
　　That's the wisest thing you could do.

6 Listen to my charge;
　　pay attention to my arguments.

7 "Are you defending God with lies?
　　Do you make your dishonest arguments
　　　for his sake?

8 Will you slant your testimony in his favor?
　　Will you argue God's case for him?

9 What will happen when he finds out what
　　you are doing?
　　Can you fool him as easily as you fool
　　　people?

10 No, you will be in trouble with him
　　if you secretly slant your testimony in his
　　　favor.

11 Doesn't his majesty terrify you?
　　Doesn't your fear of him overwhelm you?

12 Your platitudes are as valuable as ashes.
　　Your defense is as fragile as a clay pot.

GUIDANCE
*(12:13-25) Job acknowledged that real wisdom comes
from God. Many leaders brag about their intelligence and
wisdom, but human wisdom is child's play compared to
God's wisdom. His wisdom is 100 percent trustworthy.
Who do you trust for advice?*

HOW SUFFERING AFFECTS US

SUFFERING IS HELPFUL WHEN:	SUFFERING IS HARMFUL WHEN:
We turn to God for understanding, endurance, and deliverance	We become hardened and reject God
We ask important questions we might not take time to think about in our normal routine	We refuse to ask any questions and miss any lessons that might be good for us
We let it prepare us to identify with and comfort others who suffer	We allow it to make us self-centered and selfish
We are open to being helped by others who are obeying God	We withdraw from the help others can give
We realize we can identify with the suffering Christ endured on the cross	We accuse God of being unjust and perhaps lead others to reject him
We are sensitized to the amount of suffering in the world	We refuse to be open to any changes in our lives

13 "Be silent now and leave me alone.
    Let me speak, and I will face the
       consequences.
14 Yes, I will take my life in my hands
    and say what I really think.
15 God might kill me, but I have no other
       hope.*
    I am going to argue my case with him.
16 But this is what will save me—I am not
       godless.
    If I were, I could not stand before him.

17 "Listen closely to what I am about to say.
    Hear me out.
18 I have prepared my case;
    I will be proved innocent.
19 Who can argue with me over this?
    And if you prove me wrong, I will remain
       silent and die.

JOB ASKS HOW HE HAS SINNED

20 "O God, grant me these two things,
    and then I will be able to face you.
21 Remove your heavy hand from me,
    and don't terrify me with your awesome
       presence.
22 Now summon me, and I will answer!
    Or let me speak to you, and you reply.
23 Tell me, what have I done wrong?
    Show me my rebellion and my sin.

24 Why do you turn away from me?
    Why do you treat me as your enemy?
25 Would you terrify a leaf blown by the wind?
    Would you chase dry straw?

26 "You write bitter accusations against me
    and bring up all the sins of my youth.
27 You put my feet in stocks.
    You examine all my paths.
    You trace all my footprints.
28 I waste away like rotting wood,
    like a moth-eaten coat.

14
1 "How frail is humanity!
    How short is life, how full of trouble!
2 We blossom like a flower and then wither.
    Like a passing shadow, we quickly
       disappear.
3 Must you keep an eye on such a frail
       creature
    and demand an accounting from me?
4 Who can bring purity out of an impure
       person?
    No one!
5 You have decided the length of our lives.
    You know how many months we will live,
    and we are not given a minute longer.
6 So leave us alone and let us rest!
    We are like hired hands, so let us finish
       our work in peace.

7 "Even a tree has more hope!
    If it is cut down, it will sprout again
    and grow new branches.
8 Though its roots have grown old in the earth
    and its stump decays,

UNENDING LIFE
(14:1-15) Although Job realized that life is brief and full of trouble, he held on to the hope of life after death. God's solution to an unfair world is to guarantee life with him forever. No matter how unfair your present world seems, God offers the hope of being in his presence forever.

13:15 An alternate reading in the Masoretic Text reads *God might kill me, but I hope in him.*

9 at the scent of water it will bud
    and sprout again like a new seedling.
10 "But when people die, their strength
      is gone.
    They breathe their last, and then where
      are they?
11 As water evaporates from a lake
    and a river disappears in drought,
12 people are laid to rest and do not rise again.
    Until the heavens are no more, they will
      not wake up
    nor be roused from their sleep.

13 "I wish you would hide me in the grave*
    and forget me there until your anger has
      passed.
    But mark your calendar to think of me
      again!
14 Can the dead live again?
    If so, this would give me hope through all
      my years of struggle,
    and I would eagerly await the release
      of death.
15 You would call and I would answer,
    and you would yearn for me, your
      handiwork.
16 For then you would guard my steps,
    instead of watching for my sins.
17 My sins would be sealed in a pouch,
    and you would cover my guilt.

18 "But instead, as mountains fall and crumble
    and as rocks fall from a cliff,
19 as water wears away the stones
    and floods wash away the soil,
    so you destroy people's hope.
20 You always overpower them, and they pass
      from the scene.
    You disfigure them in death and send
      them away.
21 They never know if their children grow up
      in honor
    or sink to insignificance.
22 They suffer painfully;
    their life is full of trouble."

15 ELIPHAZ'S SECOND RESPONSE TO JOB
Then Eliphaz the Temanite replied:

2 "A wise man wouldn't answer with such
      empty talk!
    You are nothing but a windbag.
3 The wise don't engage in empty chatter.
    What good are such words?
4 Have you no fear of God,

14:13 Hebrew in Sheol.   15:12 Or Why do your eyes flash with anger;
Hebrew reads Why do your eyes blink.   15:15 Hebrew the holy ones.
15:23 Greek version reads He is appointed to be food for a vulture.

no reverence for him?
5 Your sins are telling your mouth what to say.
    Your words are based on clever
      deception.
6 Your own mouth condemns you, not I.
    Your own lips testify against you.

7 "Were you the first person ever born?
    Were you born before the hills were
      made?
8 Were you listening at God's secret council?
    Do you have a monopoly on wisdom?
9 What do you know that we don't?
    What do you understand that we do not?
10 On our side are aged, gray-haired men
    much older than your father!

11 "Is God's comfort too little for you?
    Is his gentle word not enough?
12 What has taken away your reason?
    What has weakened your vision,*
13 that you turn against God
    and say all these evil things?
14 Can any mortal be pure?
    Can anyone born of a woman be just?
15 Look, God does not even trust the angels.*
    Even the heavens are not absolutely pure
      in his sight.
16 How much less pure is a corrupt and sinful
      person
    with a thirst for wickedness!

17 "If you will listen, I will show you.
    I will answer you from my own experience.
18 And it is confirmed by the reports of
      wise men
    who have heard the same thing from
      their fathers—
19 from those to whom the land was given
    long before any foreigners arrived.

20 "The wicked writhe in pain throughout
      their lives.
    Years of trouble are stored up for the
      ruthless.
21 The sound of terror rings in their ears,
    and even on good days they fear the
      attack of the destroyer.
22 They dare not go out into the darkness
    for fear they will be murdered.
23 They wander around, saying, 'Where can
      I find bread?'*
    They know their day of destruction
      is near.
24 That dark day terrifies them.
    They live in distress and anguish,
    like a king preparing for battle.
25 For they shake their fists at God,
    defying the Almighty.

26 Holding their strong shields,
   they defiantly charge against him.

27 "These wicked people are heavy and
   prosperous;
   their waists bulge with fat.

28 But their cities will be ruined.
   They will live in abandoned houses
   that are ready to tumble down.

29 Their riches will not last,
   and their wealth will not endure.
   Their possessions will no longer spread
   across the horizon.

30 "They will not escape the darkness.
   The burning sun will wither their shoots,
   and the breath of God will destroy them.

31 Let them no longer fool themselves by
   trusting in empty riches,
   for emptiness will be their only reward.

32 Like trees, they will be cut down in the
   prime of life;
   their branches will never again be green.

33 They will be like a vine whose grapes are
   harvested too early,
   like an olive tree that loses its blossoms
   before the fruit can form.

34 For the godless are barren.
   Their homes, enriched through bribery,
   will burn.

35 They conceive trouble and give birth to evil.
   Their womb produces deceit."

16 JOB'S FIFTH SPEECH: A RESPONSE TO ELIPHAZ Then Job spoke again:

2 "I have heard all this before.
   What miserable comforters you are!

3 Won't you ever stop blowing hot air?
   What makes you keep on talking?

4 I could say the same things if you were
   in my place.
   I could spout off criticism and shake
   my head at you.

5 But if it were me, I would encourage you.
   I would try to take away your grief.

6 Instead, I suffer if I defend myself,
   and I suffer no less if I refuse to speak.

COMFORT 101
(16:1-5) Instead of comforting Job, his friends blamed him for his suffering. Job began his reply to Eliphaz by calling him and his friends "miserable comforters" (16:2). Want to avoid that label as you offer comfort to someone in pain? Job offers some advice: (1) Don't talk just for the sake of talking; (2) don't give pat answers; (3) don't criticize; (4) put yourself in the other person's place; and (5) offer sincere help and encouragement. The best comforters are those who know something about suffering.

7 "O God, you have ground me down
   and devastated my family.

8 As if to prove I have sinned, you've reduced
   me to skin and bones.
   My gaunt flesh testifies against me.

9 God hates me and angrily tears me apart.
   He snaps his teeth at me
   and pierces me with his eyes.

10 People jeer and laugh at me.
   They slap my cheek in contempt.
   A mob gathers against me.

11 God has handed me over to sinners.
   He has tossed me into the hands of the
   wicked.

12 "I was living quietly until he shattered me.
   He took me by the neck and broke me in
   pieces.
   Then he set me up as his target,

13 and now his archers surround me.
   His arrows pierce me without mercy.
   The ground is wet with my blood.*

14 Again and again he smashes against me,
   charging at me like a warrior.

15 I wear burlap to show my grief.
   My pride lies in the dust.

16 My eyes are red with weeping;
   dark shadows circle my eyes.

17 Yet I have done no wrong,
   and my prayer is pure.

18 "O earth, do not conceal my blood.
   Let it cry out on my behalf.

19 Even now my witness is in heaven.
   My advocate is there on high.

20 My friends scorn me,
   but I pour out my tears to God.

21 I need someone to mediate between God
   and me,
   as a person mediates between friends.

22 For soon I must go down that road
   from which I will never return.

17 JOB CONTINUES TO DEFEND HIS INNOCENCE

1 "My spirit is crushed,
   and my life is nearly snuffed out.
   The grave is ready to receive me.

2 I am surrounded by mockers.
   I watch how bitterly they taunt me.

3 "You must defend my innocence, O God,
   since no one else will stand up for me.

4 You have closed their minds to
   understanding,
   but do not let them triumph.

16:13 Hebrew *my gall.*

⁵ They betray their friends for their own
　　advantage,
　　so let their children faint with hunger.

⁶ "God has made a mockery of me among
　　the people;
　　they spit in my face.
⁷ My eyes are swollen with weeping,
　　and I am but a shadow of my former self.
⁸ The virtuous are horrified when they see me.
　　The innocent rise up against the ungodly.
⁹ The righteous keep moving forward,
　　and those with clean hands become
　　stronger and stronger.

¹⁰ "As for all of you, come back with a better
　　argument,
　　though I still won't find a wise man
　　among you.
¹¹ My days are over.
　　My hopes have disappeared.
　　My heart's desires are broken.
¹² These men say that night is day;
　　they claim that the darkness is light.
¹³ What if I go to the grave*
　　and make my bed in darkness?
¹⁴ What if I call the grave my father,
　　and the maggot my mother or my sister?
¹⁵ Where then is my hope?
　　Can anyone find it?
¹⁶ No, my hope will go down with me to
　　the grave.
　　We will rest together in the dust!"

18 BILDAD'S SECOND RESPONSE TO JOB
Then Bildad the Shuhite replied:

² "How long before you stop talking?
　　Speak sense if you want us to answer!
³ Do you think we are mere animals?
　　Do you think we are stupid?
⁴ You may tear out your hair in anger,
　　but will that destroy the earth?
　　Will it make the rocks tremble?

⁵ "Surely the light of the wicked will be
　　snuffed out.
　　The sparks of their fire will not glow.
⁶ The light in their tent will grow dark.
　　The lamp hanging above them will be
　　quenched.
⁷ The confident stride of the wicked will be
　　shortened.
　　Their own schemes will be their downfall.
⁸ The wicked walk into a net.
　　They fall into a pit.
⁹ A trap grabs them by the heel.

17:13 Hebrew *to Sheol*; also in 17:16.　**19:6** Or *for I am like a city under siege.*

A snare holds them tight.
¹⁰ A noose lies hidden on the ground.
　　A rope is stretched across their path.

¹¹ "Terrors surround the wicked
　　and trouble them at every step.
¹² Hunger depletes their strength,
　　and calamity waits for them to stumble.
¹³ Disease eats their skin;
　　death devours their limbs.
¹⁴ They are torn from the security of their
　　homes
　　and are brought down to the king of
　　terrors.
¹⁵ The homes of the wicked will burn down;
　　burning sulfur rains on their houses.
¹⁶ Their roots will dry up,
　　and their branches will wither.
¹⁷ All memory of their existence will fade from
　　the earth;
　　no one will remember their names.
¹⁸ They will be thrust from light into darkness,
　　driven from the world.
¹⁹ They will have neither children nor
　　grandchildren,
　　nor any survivor in the place where they
　　lived.
²⁰ People in the west are appalled at their fate;
　　people in the east are horrified.
²¹ They will say, 'This was the home of a
　　wicked person,
　　the place of one who rejected God.'"

19 JOB'S SIXTH SPEECH: A RESPONSE TO BILDAD
Then Job spoke again:

² "How long will you torture me?
　　How long will you try to crush me with
　　your words?
³ You have already insulted me ten times.
　　You should be ashamed of treating me so
　　badly.
⁴ Even if I have sinned,
　　that is my concern, not yours.
⁵ You think you're better than I am,
　　using my humiliation as evidence
　　of my sin.
⁶ But it is God who has wronged me,
　　capturing me in his net.*

NEVER-ENDING HOPE
(17:15) Job gave up hope of future restoration of wealth and family, and he wrapped himself in thoughts of death and the rest from grief and pain that death promised. The rewards that Job's friends mentioned all were related to this present life. The friends were silent about the possibility of life after death. We must be careful to avoid viewing life only in terms of this present world because God promises the faithful a never-ending future.

{JOB 19:25}

I KNOW THAT MY REDEEMER LIVES, AND HE WILL STAND UPON THE EARTH AT LAST.

7 "I cry out, 'Help!' but no one answers me.
I protest, but there is no justice.
8 God has blocked my way so I cannot move.
He has plunged my path into darkness.
9 He has stripped me of my honor
and removed the crown from my head.
10 He has demolished me on every side, and
I am finished.
He has uprooted my hope like a fallen
tree.
11 His fury burns against me;
he counts me as an enemy.
12 His troops advance.
They build up roads to attack me.
They camp all around my tent.

13 "My relatives stay far away,
and my friends have turned against me.
14 My family is gone,
and my close friends have forgotten me.
15 My servants and maids consider me a
stranger.
I am like a foreigner to them.
16 When I call my servant, he doesn't come;
I have to plead with him!
17 My breath is repulsive to my wife.
I am rejected by my own family.
18 Even young children despise me.
When I stand to speak, they turn their
backs on me.
19 My close friends detest me.
Those I loved have turned against me.
20 I have been reduced to skin and bones
and have escaped death by the skin
of my teeth.

....

PAYBACK

(20:1-7) Although Zophar was wrong in his assumptions about Job, he was correct in his opinions about the final end of evil people. Ever been burned by someone who seemed to get away with hurting you? Maybe you've wondered if crime really does pay, especially when lying, stealing, and oppressing others brings temporary gain to those who practice them. But in the end, God's justice will prevail (see Ps 37).

21 "Have mercy on me, my friends, have mercy,
for the hand of God has struck me.
22 Must you also persecute me, like God does?
Haven't you chewed me up enough?

23 "Oh, that my words could be recorded.
Oh, that they could be inscribed on a
monument,
24 carved with an iron chisel and filled with
lead,
engraved forever in the rock.

25 "But as for me, I know that my Redeemer
lives,
and he will stand upon the earth at last.
26 And after my body has decayed,
yet in my body I will see God!*
27 I will see him for myself.
Yes, I will see him with my own eyes.
I am overwhelmed at the thought!

28 "How dare you go on persecuting me,
saying, 'It's his own fault'?
29 You should fear punishment yourselves,
for your attitude deserves punishment.
Then you will know that there is indeed
a judgment."

20 ZOPHAR'S SECOND RESPONSE TO JOB
Then Zophar the Naamathite replied:

2 "I must reply
because I am greatly disturbed.
3 I've had to endure your insults,
but now my spirit prompts me to reply.

4 "Don't you realize that from the beginning
of time,
ever since people were first placed on
the earth,
5 the triumph of the wicked has been short
lived
and the joy of the godless has been only
temporary?
6 Though the pride of the godless reaches to
the heavens
and their heads touch the clouds,
7 yet they will vanish forever,
thrown away like their own dung.
Those who knew them will ask,
'Where are they?'
8 They will fade like a dream and not
be found.
They will vanish like a vision in the night.
9 Those who once saw them will see them
no more.
Their families will never see them again.

19:26 Or *without my body I will see God.* The meaning of the Hebrew is uncertain.

10 Their children will beg from the poor,
   for they must give back their stolen
   riches.
11 Though they are young,
   their bones will lie in the dust.

12 "They enjoyed the sweet taste of
   wickedness,
   letting it melt under their tongue.
13 They savored it,
   holding it long in their mouths.
14 But suddenly the food in their bellies turns
   sour,
   a poisonous venom in their stomach.
15 They will vomit the wealth they swallowed.
   God won't let them keep it down.
16 They will suck the poison of cobras.
   The viper will kill them.
17 They will never again enjoy streams
   of olive oil
   or rivers of milk and honey.
18 They will give back everything they
   worked for.
   Their wealth will bring them no joy.
19 For they oppressed the poor and left them
   destitute.
   They foreclosed on their homes.
20 They were always greedy and never
   satisfied.
   Nothing remains of all the things they
   dreamed about.
21 Nothing is left after they finish gorging
   themselves.
   Therefore, their prosperity will not endure.

22 "In the midst of plenty, they will run into
   trouble
   and be overcome by misery.
23 May God give them a bellyful of trouble.
   May God rain down his anger upon them.
24 When they try to escape an iron weapon,
   a bronze-tipped arrow will pierce them.
25 The arrow is pulled from their back,
   and the arrowhead glistens with blood.*
   The terrors of death are upon them.
26   Their treasures will be thrown into
   deepest darkness.
   A wildfire will devour their goods,
   consuming all they have left.
27 The heavens will reveal their guilt,
   and the earth will testify against them.
28 A flood will sweep away their house.
   God's anger will descend on them in
   torrents.
29 This is the reward that God gives the wicked.
   It is the inheritance decreed by God."

20:25 Hebrew *with gall.*   21:13 Hebrew *to Sheol.*

21 JOB'S SEVENTH SPEECH: A RESPONSE TO ZOPHAR   Then Job spoke again:

2 "Listen closely to what I am saying.
   That's one consolation you can give me.
3 Bear with me, and let me speak.
   After I have spoken, you may resume
   mocking me.

4 "My complaint is with God, not with people.
   I have good reason to be so impatient.
5 Look at me and be stunned.
   Put your hand over your mouth in shock.
6 When I think about what I am saying,
   I shudder.
   My body trembles.

7 "Why do the wicked prosper,
   growing old and powerful?
8 They live to see their children grow up and
   settle down,
   and they enjoy their grandchildren.
9 Their homes are safe from every fear,
   and God does not punish them.
10 Their bulls never fail to breed.
   Their cows bear calves and never
   miscarry.
11 They let their children frisk about
   like lambs.
   Their little ones skip and dance.
12 They sing with tambourine and harp.
   They celebrate to the sound of the flute.
13 They spend their days in prosperity,
   then go down to the grave* in peace.
14 And yet they say to God, 'Go away.
   We want no part of you and your ways.
15 Who is the Almighty, and why should we
   obey him?
   What good will it do us to pray?'
16 (They think their prosperity is of their own
   doing,
   but I will have nothing to do with that
   kind of thinking.)

17 "Yet the light of the wicked never seems
   to be extinguished.
   Do they ever have trouble?
   Does God distribute sorrows to them
   in anger?

SUCCESS
*(21:7-18) Job refuted Zophar's idea that evil people never
experience wealth and happiness, pointing out that in
the real world the wicked do indeed prosper. God does
what he wants to individuals (21:22-25), and people
should not use their circumstances to measure their own
goodness or God's—prosperity and goodness are not
necessarily related. To Job's friends, success was based
on outward performance; to God, however, success is
based on a person's heart.*

¹⁸ Are they driven before the wind like straw?
  Are they carried away by the storm
    like chaff?
  Not at all!

¹⁹ "'Well,' you say, 'at least God will punish
    their children!'
  But I say he should punish the ones
    who sin,
  so that they understand his judgment.
²⁰ Let them see their destruction with their
    own eyes.
  Let them drink deeply of the anger of the
    Almighty.
²¹ For they will not care what happens to their
    family
  after they are dead.

²² "But who can teach a lesson to God,
  since he judges even the most
    powerful?
²³ One person dies in prosperity,
  completely comfortable and secure,
²⁴ the picture of good health,
  vigorous and fit.
²⁵ Another person dies in bitter poverty,
  never having tasted the good life.
²⁶ But both are buried in the same dust,
  both eaten by the same maggots.

²⁷ "Look, I know what you're thinking.
  I know the schemes you plot against me.
²⁸ You will tell me of rich and wicked people
  whose houses have vanished because
    of their sins.
²⁹ But ask those who have been around,
  and they will tell you the truth.
³⁰ Evil people are spared in times of calamity
  and are allowed to escape disaster.
³¹ No one criticizes them openly
  or pays them back for what they
    have done.
³² When they are carried to the grave,
  an honor guard keeps watch at their
    tomb.
³³ A great funeral procession goes to the
    cemetery.

....

A RIGHT ATTITUDE
(21:22) In the middle of Job's confusion about his suffering, he asked, "But who can teach God, since he judges
even the most powerful?" He refused to allow his suffering to cause him to turn his back on God. Can you say the
same? Even if your struggles seem as great and difficult
as Job's, your response will indicate your current attitude
toward God. Rather than becoming angry with God, are
you willing to continue to trust him, no matter what your
circumstances may be? Although it's sometimes difficult
to believe, God is in control.

Many pay their respects as the body
  is laid to rest,
and the earth gives sweet repose.

³⁴ "How can your empty clichés comfort me?
  All your explanations are lies!"

22 ELIPHAZ'S THIRD RESPONSE TO JOB
Then Eliphaz the Temanite replied:

² "Can a person do anything to help God?
  Can even a wise person be helpful
    to him?
³ Is it any advantage to the Almighty if you
    are righteous?
  Would it be any gain to him if you were
    perfect?
⁴ Is it because you're so pious that he
    accuses you
  and brings judgment against you?
⁵ No, it's because of your wickedness!
  There's no limit to your sins.

⁶ "For example, you must have lent money
    to your friend
  and demanded clothing as security.
  Yes, you stripped him to the bone.
⁷ You must have refused water for the thirsty
  and food for the hungry.
⁸ You probably think the land belongs to the
    powerful
  and only the privileged have a right to it!
⁹ You must have sent widows away
    empty-handed
  and crushed the hopes of orphans.
¹⁰ That is why you are surrounded by traps
  and tremble from sudden fears.
¹¹ That is why you cannot see in the darkness,
  and waves of water cover you.

¹² "God is so great—higher than the heavens,
  higher than the farthest stars.
¹³ But you reply, 'That's why God can't see
    what I am doing!
  How can he judge through the thick
    darkness?
¹⁴ For thick clouds swirl about him, and he
    cannot see us.
  He is way up there, walking on the vault
    of heaven.'

¹⁵ "Will you continue on the old paths
  where evil people have walked?
¹⁶ They were snatched away in the prime
    of life,
  the foundations of their lives washed
    away.
¹⁷ For they said to God, 'Leave us alone!
  What can the Almighty do to us?'

¹⁸ Yet he was the one who filled their homes
       with good things,
    so I will have nothing to do with that kind
       of thinking.

¹⁹ "The righteous will be happy to see the
       wicked destroyed,
    and the innocent will laugh in contempt.
²⁰ They will say, 'See how our enemies have
       been destroyed.
    The last of them have been consumed
       in the fire.'

²¹ "Submit to God, and you will have peace;
    then things will go well for you.
²² Listen to his instructions,
    and store them in your heart.
²³ If you return to the Almighty, you will
       be restored—
    so clean up your life.
²⁴ If you give up your lust for money
    and throw your precious gold into
       the river,
²⁵ the Almighty himself will be your treasure.
    He will be your precious silver!

²⁶ "Then you will take delight in the Almighty
    and look up to God.
²⁷ You will pray to him, and he will hear you,
    and you will fulfill your vows to him.
²⁸ You will succeed in whatever you choose
       to do,
    and light will shine on the road ahead
       of you.
²⁹ If people are in trouble and you say, 'Help
       them,'
    God will save them.
³⁰ Even sinners will be rescued;
    they will be rescued because your hands
       are pure."

23 JOB'S EIGHTH SPEECH: A RESPONSE TO ELIPHAZ Then Job spoke again:

² "My complaint today is still a bitter one,
    and I try hard not to groan aloud.
³ If only I knew where to find God,
    I would go to his court.
⁴ I would lay out my case
    and present my arguments.
⁵ Then I would listen to his reply
    and understand what he says to me.
⁶ Would he use his great power to argue
       with me?
    No, he would give me a fair hearing.
⁷ Honest people can reason with him,
    so I would be forever acquitted by
       my judge.
⁸ I go east, but he is not there.

I go west, but I cannot find him.
⁹ I do not see him in the north, for he
       is hidden.
    I look to the south, but he is concealed.

¹⁰ "But he knows where I am going.
    And when he tests me, I will come out
       as pure as gold.
¹¹ For I have stayed on God's paths;
    I have followed his ways and not turned
       aside.
¹² I have not departed from his commands,
    but have treasured his words more than
       daily food.
¹³ But once he has made his decision, who
       can change his mind?
    Whatever he wants to do, he does.
¹⁴ So he will do to me whatever he has
       planned.
    He controls my destiny.
¹⁵ No wonder I am so terrified in his presence.
    When I think of it, terror grips me.
¹⁶ God has made me sick at heart;
    the Almighty has terrified me.
¹⁷ Darkness is all around me;
    thick, impenetrable darkness is
       everywhere.

24 JOB ASKS WHY THE WICKED ARE NOT PUNISHED

¹ "Why doesn't the Almighty bring the wicked
       to judgment?
    Why must the godly wait for him in vain?
² Evil people steal land by moving the
       boundary markers.
    They steal livestock and put them in their
       own pastures.
³ They take the orphan's donkey
    and demand the widow's ox as security
       for a loan.
⁴ The poor are pushed off the path;
    the needy must hide together for safety.
⁵ Like wild donkeys in the wilderness,
    the poor must spend all their time looking
       for food,
    searching even in the desert for food for
       their children.

DEEP PURPOSES
(23:8-14) Job wavered back and forth, first proclaiming loyalty to God and then expressing his terror of him. His friends' words and his own suspicions undermined his confidence in God. When hard times come, we sometimes blame God or think he's punishing us. But God's purposes go deeper than our ability to grasp what's really happening. While that might sound like a pat answer, it is the same answer God gave Job in chapters 38–41. Often we cannot know, or are not meant to know, why God allows us to suffer.

⁶ They harvest a field they do not own,
and they glean in the vineyards of the
wicked.
⁷ All night they lie naked in the cold,
without clothing or covering.
⁸ They are soaked by mountain showers,
and they huddle against the rocks for
want of a home.

⁹ "The wicked snatch a widow's child from
her breast,
taking the baby as security for a loan.
¹⁰ The poor must go about naked, without any
clothing.
They harvest food for others while they
themselves are starving.
¹¹ They press out olive oil without being
allowed to taste it,
and they tread in the winepress as they
suffer from thirst.
¹² The groans of the dying rise from the city,
and the wounded cry for help,
yet God ignores their moaning.

¹³ "Wicked people rebel against the light.
They refuse to acknowledge its ways
or stay in its paths.
¹⁴ The murderer rises in the early dawn
to kill the poor and needy;
at night he is a thief.
¹⁵ The adulterer waits for the twilight,
saying, 'No one will see me then.'
He hides his face so no one will
know him.
¹⁶ Thieves break into houses at night
and sleep in the daytime.
They are not acquainted with the light.
¹⁷ The black night is their morning.
They ally themselves with the terrors
of the darkness.

¹⁸ "But they disappear like foam down
a river.
Everything they own is cursed,
and they are afraid to enter their own
vineyards.
¹⁹ The grave* consumes sinners
just as drought and heat consume snow.
²⁰ Their own mothers will forget them.
Maggots will find them sweet to eat.

No one will remember them.
Wicked people are broken like a tree in
the storm.
²¹ They cheat the woman who has no son to
help her.
They refuse to help the needy widow.

²² "God, in his power, drags away the rich.
They may rise high, but they have no
assurance of life.
²³ They may be allowed to live in security,
but God is always watching them.
²⁴ And though they are great now,
in a moment they will be gone like all
others,
cut off like heads of grain.
²⁵ Can anyone claim otherwise?
Who can prove me wrong?"

25 BILDAD'S THIRD RESPONSE TO JOB
Then Bildad the Shuhite replied:

² "God is powerful and dreadful.
He enforces peace in the heavens.
³ Who is able to count his heavenly army?
Doesn't his light shine on all the earth?
⁴ How can a mortal be innocent before God?
Can anyone born of a woman be pure?
⁵ God is more glorious than the moon;
he shines brighter than the stars.
⁶ In comparison, people are maggots;
we mortals are mere worms."

26 JOB'S NINTH SPEECH: A RESPONSE
TO BILDAD Then Job spoke again:

² "How you have helped the powerless!
How you have saved the weak!
³ How you have enlightened my stupidity!
What wise advice you have offered!
⁴ Where have you gotten all these wise
sayings?
Whose spirit speaks through you?

⁵ "The dead tremble—
those who live beneath the waters.
⁶ The underworld* is naked in God's
presence.
The place of destruction* is uncovered.
⁷ God stretches the northern sky over empty
space
and hangs the earth on nothing.
⁸ He wraps the rain in his thick clouds,
and the clouds don't burst with the
weight.
⁹ He covers the face of the moon,*
shrouding it with his clouds.

GREATER RESULTS
(26:1-4) With great sarcasm, Job attacked his friends'
comments. Their theological explanations failed to bring
any relief because they were unable to turn their knowledge into helpful counsel. When dealing with people,
loving and understanding them is more important than
analyzing them or giving advice. Compassion produces
greater results than criticism or blame.

24:19 Hebrew *Sheol.* **26:6a** Hebrew *Sheol.* **26:6b** Hebrew
Abaddon. **26:9** Or *covers his throne.*

¹⁰ He created the horizon when he separated
the waters;
he set the boundary between day and
night.
¹¹ The foundations of heaven tremble;
they shudder at his rebuke.
¹² By his power the sea grew calm.
By his skill he crushed the great sea
monster.*
¹³ His Spirit made the heavens beautiful,
and his power pierced the gliding
serpent.
¹⁴ These are just the beginning of all that he
does,
merely a whisper of his power.
Who, then, can comprehend the thunder
of his power?"

27 JOB'S FINAL SPEECH Job continued speaking:

² "I vow by the living God, who has taken
away my rights,
by the Almighty who has embittered
my soul—
³ As long as I live,
while I have breath from God,
⁴ my lips will speak no evil,
and my tongue will speak no lies.
⁵ I will never concede that you are right;
I will defend my integrity until I die.
⁶ I will maintain my innocence without
wavering.
My conscience is clear for as long as I live.
⁷ "May my enemy be punished like the
wicked,
my adversary like those who do evil.
⁸ For what hope do the godless have when
God cuts them off
and takes away their life?
⁹ Will God listen to their cry
when trouble comes upon them?
¹⁰ Can they take delight in the Almighty?
Can they call to God at any time?
¹¹ I will teach you about God's power.
I will not conceal anything concerning
the Almighty.
¹² But you have seen all this,
yet you say all these useless things to me.
¹³ "This is what the wicked will receive
from God;
this is their inheritance from the
Almighty.
¹⁴ They may have many children,

26:12 Hebrew *Rahab*, the name of a mythical sea monster that
represents chaos in ancient literature. **27:18** As in Greek and
Syriac versions (see also 8:14); Hebrew reads *a moth.*

but the children will die in war or starve
to death.
¹⁵ Those who survive will die of a plague,
and not even their widows will mourn
them.
¹⁶ "Evil people may have piles of money
and may store away mounds of clothing.
¹⁷ But the righteous will wear that clothing,
and the innocent will divide that money.
¹⁸ The wicked build houses as fragile as a
spider's web,*
as flimsy as a shelter made of branches.
¹⁹ The wicked go to bed rich
but wake to find that all their wealth is
gone.
²⁰ Terror overwhelms them like a flood,
and they are blown away in the storms
of the night.
²¹ The east wind carries them away, and they
are gone.
It sweeps them away.
²² It whirls down on them without mercy.
They struggle to flee from its power.
²³ But everyone jeers at them
and mocks them.

28 JOB SPEAKS OF WISDOM AND UNDERSTANDING

¹ "People know where to mine silver
and how to refine gold.
² They know where to dig iron from the earth
and how to smelt copper from rock.
³ They know how to shine light in the
darkness
and explore the farthest regions of the
earth
as they search in the dark for ore.
⁴ They sink a mine shaft into the earth
far from where anyone lives.

··

CLEAR CONSCIENCE
*(27:1-6) In the face of his friends' accusations, Job
declared that his conscience was clear. Only right living
can cause a person to have a clear conscience. Like Job,
we can't claim perfect lives, but we can claim forgiven
lives. When we confess our sins to God, we are forgiven
and can live our lives with clear consciences (1 Jn 1:9).*

WISE WITHOUT GOD?
*(28:1-28) Job knew that the search for wisdom began
and ended with God. People can perform all kinds of
technological wonders. They can find stars invisible to
the eye; they can travel through space; they can store
volumes of information on a microchip. But even the
greatest scientists, on their own, are at a loss to discover
wisdom for their daily lives. God is the true source of
wisdom. True wisdom is having God's perspective on life.
As the Creator of life, only God knows what is best for his
creation. Do you have his perspective?*

They descend on ropes, swinging back
and forth.
⁵ Food is grown on the earth above,
but down below, the earth is melted as
by fire.
⁶ Here the rocks contain precious lapis lazuli,
and the dust contains gold.
⁷ These are treasures no bird of prey can see,
no falcon's eye observe.
⁸ No wild animal has walked upon these
treasures;
no lion has ever set his paw there.
⁹ People know how to tear apart flinty rocks
and overturn the roots of mountains.
¹⁰ They cut tunnels in the rocks
and uncover precious stones.
¹¹ They dam up the trickling streams
and bring to light the hidden treasures.

¹² "But do people know where to find wisdom?
Where can they find understanding?
¹³ No one knows where to find it,
for it is not found among the living.
¹⁴ 'It is not here,' says the ocean.
'Nor is it here,' says the sea.
¹⁵ It cannot be bought with gold.
It cannot be purchased with silver.
¹⁶ It's worth more than all the gold of Ophir,
greater than precious onyx or lapis lazuli.
¹⁷ Wisdom is more valuable than gold and
crystal.
It cannot be purchased with jewels
mounted in fine gold.
¹⁸ Coral and jasper are worthless in trying
to get it.
The price of wisdom is far above rubies.
¹⁹ Precious peridot from Ethiopia* cannot be
exchanged for it.
It's worth more than the purest gold.

²⁰ "But do people know where to find wisdom?
Where can they find understanding?
²¹ It is hidden from the eyes of all humanity.
Even the sharp-eyed birds in the sky
cannot discover it.
²² Destruction* and Death say,
'We've heard only rumors of where
wisdom can be found.'

²³ "God alone understands the way to wisdom;
he knows where it can be found,
²⁴ for he looks throughout the whole earth
and sees everything under the heavens.
²⁵ He decided how hard the winds should
blow
and how much rain should fall.
²⁶ He made the laws for the rain
and laid out a path for the lightning.

²⁷ Then he saw wisdom and evaluated it.
He set it in place and examined it
thoroughly.
²⁸ And this is what he says to all humanity:
'The fear of the Lord is true wisdom;
to forsake evil is real understanding.'"

29 JOB SPEAKS OF HIS FORMER BLESSINGS Job continued speaking:

² "I long for the years gone by
when God took care of me,
³ when he lit up the way before me
and I walked safely through the darkness.
⁴ When I was in my prime,
God's friendship was felt in my home.
⁵ The Almighty was still with me,
and my children were around me.
⁶ My cows produced milk in abundance,
and my groves poured out streams of
olive oil.

⁷ "Those were the days when I went to the
city gate
and took my place among the honored
leaders.
⁸ The young stepped aside when they
saw me,
and even the aged rose in respect at my
coming.
⁹ The princes stood in silence
and put their hands over their mouths.
¹⁰ The highest officials of the city stood
quietly,
holding their tongues in respect.

¹¹ "All who heard me praised me.
All who saw me spoke well of me.
¹² For I assisted the poor in their need
and the orphans who required help.
¹³ I helped those without hope, and they
blessed me.
And I caused the widows' hearts to sing
for joy.
¹⁴ Everything I did was honest.
Righteousness covered me like a robe,
and I wore justice like a turban.
¹⁵ I served as eyes for the blind
and feet for the lame.
¹⁶ I was a father to the poor
and assisted strangers who needed help.
¹⁷ I broke the jaws of godless oppressors
and plucked their victims from their teeth.

¹⁸ "I thought, 'Surely I will die surrounded by
my family
after a long, good life.*

28:19 Hebrew *from Cush.*   28:22 Hebrew *Abaddon.*
29:18 Hebrew *after I have counted my days like sand.*

19 For I am like a tree whose roots reach
   the water,
      whose branches are refreshed with
      the dew.
20 New honors are constantly bestowed on me,
   and my strength is continually renewed.'

21 "Everyone listened to my advice.
   They were silent as they waited for me to
      speak.
22 And after I spoke, they had nothing to add,
   for my counsel satisfied them.
23 They longed for me to speak as people long
      for rain.
   They drank my words like a refreshing
      spring rain.
24 When they were discouraged, I smiled
      at them.
   My look of approval was precious
      to them.
25 Like a chief, I told them what to do.
   I lived like a king among his troops
   and comforted those who mourned.

30 JOB SPEAKS OF HIS ANGUISH

1 "But now I am mocked by people younger
      than I,
   by young men whose fathers are not
      worthy to run with my sheepdogs.
2 A lot of good they are to me—
   those worn-out wretches!
3 They are gaunt with hunger
   and flee to the deserts,
      to desolate and gloomy wastelands.
4 They pluck wild greens from among the
      bushes
   and eat from the roots of broom trees.
5 They are driven from human society,
   and people shout at them as if they were
      thieves.
6 So now they live in frightening ravines,
   in caves and among the rocks.
7 They sound like animals howling among the
      bushes,
   huddled together beneath the nettles.
8 They are nameless fools,
   outcasts from society.

9 "And now they mock me with vulgar songs!
   They taunt me!
10 They despise me and won't come near me,
   except to spit in my face.
11 For God has cut my bowstring.
   He has humbled me,
      so they have thrown off all restraint.
12 These outcasts oppose me to my face.
   They send me sprawling

and lay traps in my path.
13 They block my road
   and do everything they can to destroy me.
   They know I have no one to help me.
14 They come at me from all directions.
   They jump on me when I am down.
15 I live in terror now.
   My honor has blown away in the wind,
      and my prosperity has vanished like
      a cloud.

16 "And now my life seeps away.
   Depression haunts my days.
17 At night my bones are filled with pain,
   which gnaws at me relentlessly.
18 With a strong hand, God grabs my shirt.
   He grips me by the collar of my coat.
19 He has thrown me into the mud.
   I'm nothing more than dust and ashes.

20 "I cry to you, O God, but you don't answer.
   I stand before you, but you don't
      even look.
21 You have become cruel toward me.
   You use your power to persecute me.
22 You throw me into the whirlwind
   and destroy me in the storm.
23 And I know you are sending me to my death—
   the destination of all who live.

24 "Surely no one would turn against the
      needy
   when they cry for help in their trouble.
25 Did I not weep for those in trouble?
   Was I not deeply grieved for the needy?
26 So I looked for good, but evil came instead.
   I waited for the light, but darkness fell.
27 My heart is troubled and restless.
   Days of suffering torment me.
28 I walk in gloom, without sunlight.
   I stand in the public square and cry
      for help.
29 Instead, I am considered a brother to jackals
   and a companion to owls.
30 My skin has turned dark,
   and my bones burn with fever.
31 My harp plays sad music,
   and my flute accompanies those who
      weep.

31 JOB'S FINAL PROTEST OF INNOCENCE

1 "I made a covenant with my eyes
   not to look with lust at a young woman.
2 For what has God above chosen for us?
   What is our inheritance from the Almighty
      on high?
3 Isn't it calamity for the wicked
   and misfortune for those who do evil?

⁴ Doesn't he see everything I do
  and every step I take?

⁵ "Have I lied to anyone
  or deceived anyone?
⁶ Let God weigh me on the scales of justice,
  for he knows my integrity.
⁷ If I have strayed from his pathway,
  or if my heart has lusted for what my eyes
    have seen,
  or if I am guilty of any other sin,
⁸ then let someone else eat the crops I have
    planted.
  Let all that I have planted be uprooted.

⁹ "If my heart has been seduced by a woman,
  or if I have lusted for my neighbor's wife,
¹⁰ then let my wife belong to* another man;
  let other men sleep with her.
¹¹ For lust is a shameful sin,
  a crime that should be punished.
¹² It is a fire that burns all the way to hell.*
  It would wipe out everything I own.

¹³ "If I have been unfair to my male or female
    servants
  when they brought their complaints
    to me,
¹⁴ how could I face God?
  What could I say when he questioned me?
¹⁵ For God created both me and my servants.
  He created us both in the womb.

¹⁶ "Have I refused to help the poor,
  or crushed the hopes of widows?
¹⁷ Have I been stingy with my food
  and refused to share it with orphans?
¹⁸ No, from childhood I have cared for orphans
    like a father,
  and all my life I have cared for widows.
¹⁹ Whenever I saw the homeless without
    clothes
  and the needy with nothing to wear,
²⁰ did they not praise me
  for providing wool clothing to keep them
    warm?

²¹ "If I raised my hand against an orphan,
  knowing the judges would take my side,
²² then let my shoulder be wrenched out
    of place!

- -

COVER UP
*(31:33-34) Job declared that he did not try to hide his
sin as people normally do. The fear that our sins will be
discovered leads us to patterns of deception. We cover
up with lies so that we will appear good to others. But
we cannot hide from God. Do you try to keep people from
seeing the real you? Acknowledge your sins and free
yourself to receive forgiveness and a new life.*

  Let my arm be torn from its socket!
²³ That would be better than facing God's
    judgment.
  For if the majesty of God opposes me,
    what hope is there?

²⁴ "Have I put my trust in money
  or felt secure because of my gold?
²⁵ Have I gloated about my wealth
  and all that I own?

²⁶ "Have I looked at the sun shining in the
    skies,
  or the moon walking down its silver
    pathway,
²⁷ and been secretly enticed in my heart
  to throw kisses at them in worship?
²⁸ If so, I should be punished by the judges,
  for it would mean I had denied the God
    of heaven.

²⁹ "Have I ever rejoiced when disaster struck
    my enemies,
  or become excited when harm came
    their way?
³⁰ No, I have never sinned by cursing anyone
  or by asking for revenge.

³¹ "My servants have never said,
  'He let others go hungry.'
³² I have never turned away a stranger
  but have opened my doors to everyone.

³³ "Have I tried to hide my sins like other
    people do,
  concealing my guilt in my heart?
³⁴ Have I feared the crowd
  or the contempt of the masses,
  so that I kept quiet and stayed indoors?

³⁵ "If only someone would listen to me!
  Look, I will sign my name to my defense.
  Let the Almighty answer me.
  Let my accuser write out the charges
    against me.
³⁶ I would face the accusation proudly.
  I would wear it like a crown.
³⁷ For I would tell him exactly what I have
    done.
  I would come before him like a prince.

³⁸ "If my land accuses me
  and all its furrows cry out together,
³⁹ or if I have stolen its crops
  or murdered its owners,
⁴⁰ then let thistles grow on that land instead
    of wheat,
  and weeds instead of barley."

Job's words are ended.

31:10 Hebrew *grind for.*   **31:12** Hebrew *to Abaddon.*

32 ELIHU RESPONDS TO JOB'S FRIENDS

Job's three friends refused to reply further to reply to Job because he kept insisting on his innocence.

2 Then Elihu son of Barakel the Buzite, of the clan of Ram, became angry. He was angry because Job refused to admit that he had sinned and that God was right in punishing him. 3 He was also angry with Job's three friends, for they made God* appear to be wrong by their inability to answer Job's arguments. 4 Elihu had waited for the others to speak to Job because they were older than he. 5 But when he saw that they had no further reply, he spoke out angrily. 6 Elihu son of Barakel the Buzite said,

"I am young and you are old,
    so I held back from telling you what
        I think.
7 I thought, 'Those who are older should
        speak,
    for wisdom comes with age.'
8 But there is a spirit* within people,
    the breath of the Almighty within them,
        that makes them intelligent.
9 Sometimes the elders are not wise.
    Sometimes the aged do not understand
        justice.
10 So listen to me,
    and let me tell you what I think.

11 "I have waited all this time,
    listening very carefully to your arguments,
    listening to you grope for words.
12 I have listened,
    but not one of you has refuted Job
    or answered his arguments.

32:3 As in ancient Hebrew scribal tradition; the Masoretic Text
reads *Job.* 32:8 Or *Spirit;* also in 32:18.

13 And don't tell me, 'He is too wise for us.
    Only God can convince him.'
14 If Job had been arguing with me,
    I would not answer with your kind of logic!
15 You sit there baffled,
    with nothing more to say.
16 Should I continue to wait, now that you
        are silent?
    Must I also remain silent?
17 No, I will say my piece.
    I will speak my mind.
18 For I am full of pent-up words,
    and the spirit within me urges me on.
19 I am like a cask of wine without a vent,
    like a new wineskin ready to burst!
20 I must speak to find relief,
    so let me give my answers.
21 I won't play favorites
    or try to flatter anyone.
22 For if I tried flattery,
    my Creator would soon destroy me.

33 ELIHU PRESENTS HIS CASE AGAINST JOB

1 "Listen to my words, Job;
    pay attention to what I have to say.

···

WISDOM LIVED OUT
(32:8-9) *Merely recognizing a great truth is not enough; the truth must be lived out in our lives. Elihu recognized the truth that God was the only source of real wisdom, but he did not use God's wisdom to help Job. While Elihu recognized the source of wisdom, he did not seek to acquire it. Becoming wise is an ongoing, lifelong pursuit. Don't be content just to know about wisdom; make it part of your life.*

CHOICES
pornography

Jared's problem started three years ago while surfing the Net with some friends. As they looked for a game site, they suddenly stumbled across a porn site. Jared was 12.

Pretty soon, Jared and his friends had moved on to downloading pictures. None of their parents suspected a thing since one of Jared's friends had his own laptop—and no firewalls.

After a while, Jared's friends moved on to other things. But by then, Jared was hooked on porn. At first he didn't think much about it. *I'm not really hurting anyone,* he decided. *It's just a little harmless fun.* Yet he wanted to see more and more. Jared was almost totally controlled by his desire to see some skin.

Not only did Jared's obsession bring him great frustration (because pornography is such a lie),

but it also caused him unbelievable guilt. He couldn't even glance at a woman without mentally undressing her. And no matter how hard he tried, he couldn't get the dirty images out of his mind. Not only that, Christ's warning about lust (Matt 5:28) haunted him.

Finally, Jared realized, *I've got a problem. But I can't handle it on my own.* After talking with his parents, Jared decided to talk to Jeff, his youth leader. After praying with him, Jeff got Jared into a good Bible study. Jeff also helped Jared to find a prayer partner who would pray with him each week and hold him accountable for his Internet visits.

By the way, Jared doesn't surf the Net much anymore.

Pornography addiction is one hard habit to break. Check out Job 31:1. Why would this be good advice for someone like Jared?

2 Now that I have begun to speak,
   let me continue.
3 I speak with all sincerity;
   I speak the truth.
4 For the Spirit of God has made me,
   and the breath of the Almighty gives
   me life.
5 Answer me, if you can;
   make your case and take your stand.
6 Look, you and I both belong to God.
   I, too, was formed from clay.
7 So you don't need to be afraid of me.
   I won't come down hard on you.

8 "You have spoken in my hearing,
   and I have heard your very words.
9 You said, 'I am pure; I am without sin;
   I am innocent; I have no guilt.
10 God is picking a quarrel with me,
   and he considers me his enemy.
11 He puts my feet in the stocks
   and watches my every move.'

12 "But you are wrong, and I will show you why.
   For God is greater than any human being.
13 So why are you bringing a charge
      against him?
   Why say he does not respond to people's
      complaints?
14 For God speaks again and again,
   though people do not recognize it.
15 He speaks in dreams, in visions of the night,
   when deep sleep falls on people
   as they lie in their beds.
16 He whispers in their ears
   and terrifies them with warnings.
17 He makes them turn from doing wrong;
   he keeps them from pride.
18 He protects them from the grave,
   from crossing over the river of death.

19 "Or God disciplines people with pain on
      their sickbeds,
   with ceaseless aching in their bones.
20 They lose their appetite
   for even the most delicious food.
21 Their flesh wastes away,
   and their bones stick out.
22 They are at death's door;
   the angels of death wait for them.

23 "But if an angel from heaven appears—
   a special messenger to intercede for
      a person
   and declare that he is upright—
24 he will be gracious and say,
   'Rescue him from the grave,
      for I have found a ransom for his life.'

25 Then his body will become as healthy
      as a child's,
   firm and youthful again.
26 When he prays to God,
   he will be accepted.
   And God will receive him with joy
   and restore him to good standing.
27 He will declare to his friends,
   'I sinned and twisted the truth,
      but it was not worth it.*
28 God rescued me from the grave,
   and now my life is filled with light.'

29 "Yes, God does these things
   again and again for people.
30 He rescues them from the grave
   so they may enjoy the light of life.
31 Mark this well, Job. Listen to me,
   for I have more to say.
32 But if you have anything to say, go ahead.
   Speak, for I am anxious to see you
      justified.
33 But if not, then listen to me.
   Keep silent and I will teach you wisdom!"

34 ELIHU ACCUSES JOB OF ARROGANCE
Then Elihu said:

2 "Listen to me, you wise men.
   Pay attention, you who have knowledge.
3 Job said, 'The ear tests the words it hears
   just as the mouth distinguishes between
      foods.'
4 So let us discern for ourselves what is right;
   let us learn together what is good.
5 For Job also said, 'I am innocent,
   but God has taken away my rights.
6 I am innocent, but they call me a liar.
   My suffering is incurable, though I have
      not sinned.'

7 "Tell me, has there ever been a man like Job,
   with his thirst for irreverent talk?
8 He chooses evil people as companions.
   He spends his time with wicked men.
9 He has even said, 'Why waste time
   trying to please God?'

10 "Listen to me, you who have understanding.
   Everyone knows that God doesn't sin!
   The Almighty can do no wrong.
11 He repays people according to their deeds.
   He treats people as they deserve.
12 Truly, God will not do wrong.
   The Almighty will not twist justice.
13 Did someone else put the world in his care?
   Who set the whole world in place?

33:27 Greek version reads *but he* [God] *did not punish me as my sin deserved.*

14 If God were to take back his spirit
    and withdraw his breath,
15 all life would cease,
    and humanity would turn again to dust.

16 "Now listen to me if you are wise.
    Pay attention to what I say.
17 Could God govern if he hated justice?
    Are you going to condemn the almighty
    judge?
18 For he says to kings, 'You are wicked,'
    and to nobles, 'You are unjust.'
19 He doesn't care how great a person may be,
    and he pays no more attention to the rich
    than to the poor.
    He made them all.
20 In a moment they die.
    In the middle of the night they pass away;
    the mighty are removed without human
    hand.

21 "For God watches how people live;
    he sees everything they do.
22 No darkness is thick enough
    to hide the wicked from his eyes.
23 We don't set the time
    when we will come before God in
    judgment.
24 He brings the mighty to ruin without asking
    anyone,
    and he sets up others in their place.
25 He knows what they do,
    and in the night he overturns and
    destroys them.
26 He strikes them down because they are
    wicked,
    doing it openly for all to see.
27 For they turned away from following him.
    They have no respect for any of his ways.
28 They cause the poor to cry out, catching
    God's attention.
    He hears the cries of the needy.
29 But if he chooses to remain quiet,
    who can criticize him?
    When he hides his face, no one can find him,
    whether an individual or a nation.
30 He prevents the godless from ruling
    so they cannot be a snare to the people.

31 "Why don't people say to God, 'I have
    sinned,
    but I will sin no more'?
32 Or 'I don't know what evil I have
    done—tell me.
    If I have done wrong, I will stop at once'?

35:13-14 These verses can also be translated as follows: 13Indeed,
God doesn't listen to their empty plea; / the Almighty is not
concerned. / 14How much less will he listen when you say you don't
see him, / and that your case is before him and you're waiting for
justice.

33 "Must God tailor his justice to your
    demands?
    But you have rejected him!
    The choice is yours, not mine.
    Go ahead, share your wisdom with us.
34 After all, bright people will tell me,
    and wise people will hear me say,
35 'Job speaks out of ignorance;
    his words lack insight.'
36 Job, you deserve the maximum penalty
    for the wicked way you have talked.
37 For you have added rebellion to your sin;
    you show no respect,
    and you speak many angry words
    against God."

35 ELIHU REMINDS JOB OF GOD'S JUSTICE   Then Elihu said:

2 "Do you think it is right for you to claim,
    'I am righteous before God'?
3 For you also ask, 'What's in it for me?
    What's the use of living a righteous life?'

4 "I will answer you
    and all your friends, too.
5 Look up into the sky,
    and see the clouds high above you.
6 If you sin, how does that affect God?
    Even if you sin again and again,
    what effect will it have on him?
7 If you are good, is this some great gift
    to him?
    What could you possibly give him?
8 No, your sins affect only people like
    yourself,
    and your good deeds also affect only
    humans.

9 "People cry out when they are oppressed.
    They groan beneath the power of the
    mighty.
10 Yet they don't ask, 'Where is God my
    Creator,
    the one who gives songs in the night?
11 Where is the one who makes us smarter
    than the animals
    and wiser than the birds of the sky?'
12 And when they cry out, God does not
    answer
    because of their pride.
13 But it is wrong to say God doesn't listen,
    to say the Almighty isn't concerned.
14 You say you can't see him,
    but he will bring justice if you will
    only wait.*
15 You say he does not respond to sinners
    with anger

and is not greatly concerned about
wickedness.*
¹⁶ But you are talking nonsense, Job.
You have spoken like a fool."

36 Elihu continued speaking:

² "Let me go on, and I will show you the truth.
For I have not finished defending God!
³ I will present profound arguments
for the righteousness of my Creator.
⁴ I am telling you nothing but the truth,
for I am a man of great knowledge.

⁵ "God is mighty, but he does not despise
anyone!
He is mighty in both power and
understanding.
⁶ He does not let the wicked live
but gives justice to the afflicted.
⁷ He never takes his eyes off the innocent,
but he sets them on thrones with kings
and exalts them forever.
⁸ If they are bound in chains
and caught up in a web of trouble,
⁹ he shows them the reason.
He shows them their sins of pride.
¹⁰ He gets their attention
and commands that they turn from evil.

¹¹ "If they listen and obey God,
they will be blessed with prosperity
throughout their lives.
All their years will be pleasant.
¹² But if they refuse to listen to him,
they will be killed by the sword*
and die from lack of understanding.
¹³ For the godless are full of resentment.
Even when he punishes them,
they refuse to cry out to him for help.
¹⁴ They die when they are young,
after wasting their lives in immoral living.
¹⁵ But by means of their suffering, he rescues
those who suffer.
For he gets their attention through
adversity.

¹⁶ "God is leading you away from danger, Job,
to a place free from distress.
He is setting your table with the best food.
¹⁷ But you are obsessed with whether the
godless will be judged.
Don't worry, judgment and justice will
be upheld.
¹⁸ But watch out, or you may be seduced
by wealth.*
Don't let yourself be bribed into sin.
¹⁹ Could all your wealth*
or all your mighty efforts
keep you from distress?
²⁰ Do not long for the cover of night,
for that is when people will be
destroyed.*
²¹ Be on guard! Turn back from evil,
for God sent this suffering
to keep you from a life of evil.

ELIHU REMINDS JOB OF GOD'S POWER
²² "Look, God is all-powerful.
Who is a teacher like him?
²³ No one can tell him what to do,
or say to him, 'You have done wrong.'
²⁴ Instead, glorify his mighty works,
singing songs of praise.
²⁵ Everyone has seen these things,
though only from a distance.

²⁶ "Look, God is greater than we can
understand.
His years cannot be counted.
²⁷ He draws up the water vapor
and then distills it into rain.
²⁸ The rain pours down from the clouds,
and everyone benefits.
²⁹ Who can understand the spreading of
the clouds
and the thunder that rolls forth from
heaven?
³⁰ See how he spreads the lightning
around him
and how it lights up the depths of the sea.
³¹ By these mighty acts he nourishes* the
people,
giving them food in abundance.
³² He fills his hands with lightning bolts
and hurls each at its target.
³³ The thunder announces his presence;
the storm announces his indignant
anger.*

....

NEVER ENOUGH KNOWLEDGE
(36:26) *One theme in the poetic literature of the Bible is
that we cannot know God completely. This doesn't mean
that we can't have any knowledge about God. In fact, the
Bible is full of details about who God is, how we can know
him, and how we can have an eternal relationship with
him. What it means is that we can never know enough to
answer all of life's questions (Eccl 3:11), to predict our
own future, or to manipulate God for our own ends. Life
sometimes inspires more questions than answers. But
God provides fresh insights into life's dilemmas (see Job
37:19-24).*

35:15 As in Greek and Latin versions; the meaning of this Hebrew
word is uncertain.　**36:12** Or *they will cross the river* [of death].
36:18 Or *But don't let your anger lead you to mockery.*　**36:19** Or
Could all your cries for help.　**36:16-20** The meaning of the Hebrew
in this passage is uncertain.　**36:31** Or *He governs.*　**36:33** Or *even
the cattle know when a storm is coming.* The meaning of the Hebrew
is uncertain.

37

¹ "My heart pounds as I think of this.
  It trembles within me.
² Listen carefully to the thunder of God's
    voice
  as it rolls from his mouth.
³ It rolls across the heavens,
  and his lightning flashes in every
    direction.
⁴ Then comes the roaring of the thunder—
  the tremendous voice of his majesty.
  He does not restrain it when he speaks.
⁵ God's voice is glorious in the thunder.
  We can't even imagine the greatness of
    his power.

⁶ "He directs the snow to fall on the earth
  and tells the rain to pour down.
⁷ Then everyone stops working
  so they can watch his power.
⁸ The wild animals take cover
  and stay inside their dens.
⁹ The stormy wind comes from its chamber,
  and the driving winds bring the cold.
¹⁰ God's breath sends the ice,
  freezing wide expanses of water.
¹¹ He loads the clouds with moisture,
  and they flash with his lightning.
¹² The clouds churn about at his direction.
  They do whatever he commands
    throughout the earth.
¹³ He makes these things happen either to
    punish people
  or to show his unfailing love.

¹⁴ "Pay attention to this, Job.
  Stop and consider the wonderful miracles
    of God!
¹⁵ Do you know how God controls the storm
  and causes the lightning to flash from his
    clouds?
¹⁶ Do you understand how he moves the
    clouds
  with wonderful perfection and skill?
¹⁷ When you are sweltering in your clothes
  and the south wind dies down and
    everything is still,
¹⁸ he makes the skies reflect the heat like
  a bronze mirror.
  Can you do that?

¹⁹ "So teach the rest of us what to say to God.
  We are too ignorant to make our own
    arguments.
²⁰ Should God be notified that I want to
    speak?
  Can people even speak when they are
    confused?*

²¹ We cannot look at the sun,
  for it shines brightly in the sky
  when the wind clears away the clouds.
²² So also, golden splendor comes from the
    mountain of God.*
  He is clothed in dazzling splendor.
²³ We cannot imagine the power of the
    Almighty;
  but even though he is just and
    righteous,
  he does not destroy us.
²⁴ No wonder people everywhere fear him.
  All who are wise show him reverence."

38

THE LORD CHALLENGES JOB

Then the LORD answered Job from
the whirlwind:

² "Who is this that questions my wisdom
  with such ignorant words?
³ Brace yourself like a man,
  because I have some questions for you,
  and you must answer them.

⁴ "Where were you when I laid the
    foundations of the earth?
  Tell me, if you know so much.
⁵ Who determined its dimensions
  and stretched out the surveying line?
⁶ What supports its foundations,
  and who laid its cornerstone
⁷ as the morning stars sang together
  and all the angels* shouted for joy?

⁸ "Who kept the sea inside its boundaries
  as it burst from the womb,
⁹ and as I clothed it with clouds
  and wrapped it in thick darkness?
¹⁰ For I locked it behind barred gates,
  limiting its shores.
¹¹ I said, 'This far and no farther will you come.
  Here your proud waves must stop!'

¹² "Have you ever commanded the morning
    to appear
  and caused the dawn to rise in the east?
¹³ Have you made daylight spread to the ends
    of the earth,
  to bring an end to the night's
    wickedness?

···

ALL ABOUT GOD
*(38:1) God didn't answer any of Job's questions. They
weren't the heart of the issue. Instead, God used Job's
ignorance of the earth's natural order to reveal his ignorance of God's moral order. If Job didn't understand the
workings of God's physical creation, how could he possibly understand God's mind and character? Only God has
that understanding. Our only option is to submit to his
authority and care.*

37:20 Or speak without being swallowed up? **37:22** Or from the
north; or from the abode. **38:7** Hebrew the sons of God.

¹⁴ As the light approaches,
the earth takes shape like clay pressed
beneath a seal;
it is robed in brilliant colors.*
¹⁵ The light disturbs the wicked
and stops the arm that is raised in
violence.

¹⁶ "Have you explored the springs from which
the seas come?
Have you explored their depths?
¹⁷ Do you know where the gates of death are
located?
Have you seen the gates of utter gloom?
¹⁸ Do you realize the extent of the earth?
Tell me about it if you know!

¹⁹ "Where does light come from,
and where does darkness go?
²⁰ Can you take each to its home?
Do you know how to get there?
²¹ But of course you know all this!
For you were born before it was
all created,
and you are so very experienced!

²² "Have you visited the storehouses of the
snow
or seen the storehouses of hail?
²³ (I have reserved them as weapons for the
time of trouble,
for the day of battle and war.)
²⁴ Where is the path to the source of light?
Where is the home of the east wind?

²⁵ "Who created a channel for the torrents
of rain?
Who laid out the path for the lightning?
²⁶ Who makes the rain fall on barren land,
in a desert where no one lives?
²⁷ Who sends rain to satisfy the parched
ground
and make the tender grass spring up?

²⁸ "Does the rain have a father?
Who gives birth to the dew?
²⁹ Who is the mother of the ice?
Who gives birth to the frost from the
heavens?
³⁰ For the water turns to ice as hard as rock,
and the surface of the water freezes.

LIMITED KNOWLEDGE
*(39:1-30) God asked Job several questions about the ani-
mal kingdom in order to demonstrate how limited Job's
knowledge really was. God was not seeking answers from
Job. Instead, he was getting Job to recognize and submit
to God's power and sovereignty. Only then would he be
able to hear what God was really saying to him.*

³¹ "Can you direct the movement of the stars—
binding the cluster of the Pleiades
or loosening the cords of Orion?
³² Can you direct the sequence of the seasons
or guide the Bear with her cubs across the
heavens?
³³ Do you know the laws of the universe?
Can you use them to regulate the earth?

³⁴ "Can you shout to the clouds
and make it rain?
³⁵ Can you make lightning appear
and cause it to strike as you direct?
³⁶ Who gives intuition to the heart
and instinct to the mind?
³⁷ Who is wise enough to count all the clouds?
Who can tilt the water jars of heaven
³⁸ when the parched ground is dry
and the soil has hardened into clods?

³⁹ "Can you stalk prey for a lioness
and satisfy the young lions' appetites
⁴⁰ as they lie in their dens
or crouch in the thicket?
⁴¹ Who provides food for the ravens
when their young cry out to God
and wander about in hunger?

39 THE LORD'S CHALLENGE CONTINUES

¹ "Do you know when the wild goats give
birth?
Have you watched as deer are born in the
wild?
² Do you know how many months they carry
their young?
Are you aware of the time of their
delivery?
³ They crouch down to give birth to their
young
and deliver their offspring.
⁴ Their young grow up in the open fields,
then leave home and never return.

⁵ "Who gives the wild donkey its freedom?
Who untied its ropes?
⁶ I have placed it in the wilderness;
its home is the wasteland.
⁷ It hates the noise of the city
and has no driver to shout at it.
⁸ The mountains are its pastureland,
where it searches for every blade of grass.

⁹ "Will the wild ox consent to being tamed?
Will it spend the night in your stall?
¹⁰ Can you hitch a wild ox to a plow?
Will it plow a field for you?
¹¹ Given its strength, can you trust it?

38:14 Or *its features stand out like folds in a robe.*

Can you leave and trust the ox to do your
work?
12 Can you rely on it to bring home your grain
and deliver it to your threshing floor?

13 "The ostrich flaps her wings grandly,
but they are no match for the feathers
of the stork.
14 She lays her eggs on top of the earth,
letting them be warmed in the dust.
15 She doesn't worry that a foot might crush
them
or a wild animal might destroy them.
16 She is harsh toward her young,
as if they were not her own.
She doesn't care if they die.
17 For God has deprived her of wisdom.
He has given her no understanding.
18 But whenever she jumps up to run,
she passes the swiftest horse with
its rider.

19 "Have you given the horse its strength
or clothed its neck with a flowing mane?
20 Did you give it the ability to leap like a
locust?
Its majestic snorting is terrifying!
21 It paws the earth and rejoices in its strength
when it charges out to battle.
22 It laughs at fear and is unafraid.
It does not run from the sword.
23 The arrows rattle against it,
and the spear and javelin flash.
24 It paws the ground fiercely
and rushes forward into battle when the
ram's horn blows.
25 It snorts at the sound of the horn.
It senses the battle in the distance.
It quivers at the captain's commands and
the noise of battle.

26 "Is it your wisdom that makes the hawk soar
and spread its wings toward the south?
27 Is it at your command that the eagle rises
to the heights to make its nest?
28 It lives on the cliffs,
making its home on a distant, rocky crag.
29 From there it hunts its prey,
keeping watch with piercing eyes.
30 Its young gulp down blood.
Where there's a carcass, there you'll
find it."

40

Then the LORD said to Job,

2 "Do you still want to argue with the
Almighty?

40:15 The identification of Behemoth is disputed, ranging from an
earthly creature to a mythical sea monster in ancient literature.

You are God's critic, but do you have the
answers?"

JOB RESPONDS TO THE LORD 3Then Job replied to the LORD,

4 "I am nothing—how could I ever find the
answers?
I will cover my mouth with my hand.
5 I have said too much already.
I have nothing more to say."

THE LORD CHALLENGES JOB AGAIN 6Then the
LORD answered Job from the whirlwind:

7 "Brace yourself like a man,
because I have some questions for you,
and you must answer them.

8 "Will you discredit my justice
and condemn me just to prove you
are right?
9 Are you as strong as God?
Can you thunder with a voice like his?
10 All right, put on your glory and splendor,
your honor and majesty.
11 Give vent to your anger.
Let it overflow against the proud.
12 Humiliate the proud with a glance;
walk on the wicked where they stand.
13 Bury them in the dust.
Imprison them in the world of the dead.
14 Then even I would praise you,
for your own strength would save you.

15 "Take a look at Behemoth,*
which I made, just as I made you.
It eats grass like an ox.
16 See its powerful loins
and the muscles of its belly.
17 Its tail is as strong as a cedar.
The sinews of its thighs are knit tightly
together.
18 Its bones are tubes of bronze.
Its limbs are bars of iron.
19 It is a prime example of God's handiwork,
and only its Creator can threaten it.

....

ARGUING WITH GOD
(40:1-5) Job realized the futility of arguing with God.
In what ways do you argue with the Almighty? Do you
demand answers when things don't go your way, when
you get cut from a team, when someone close to you is ill
or dies, when money is tight, when you fail, or when unexpected changes occur? The next time you are tempted
to complain to God, consider how much he loves you
and remember Job's reaction when he had his chance to
speak. Are you willing to give God a chance to reveal his
greater purposes for you? His plans may unfold over the
course of your life and not at any given moment.

²⁰ The mountains offer it their best food,
  where all the wild animals play.
²¹ It lies under the lotus plants,*
  hidden by the reeds in the marsh.
²² The lotus plants give it shade
  among the willows beside the stream.
²³ It is not disturbed by the raging river,
  not concerned when the swelling Jordan
    rushes around it.
²⁴ No one can catch it off guard
  or put a ring in its nose and lead it away.

41 THE LORD'S CHALLENGE CONTINUES

¹*"Can you catch Leviathan* with a hook
  or put a noose around its jaw?
² Can you tie it with a rope through the nose
  or pierce its jaw with a spike?
³ Will it beg you for mercy
  or implore you for pity?
⁴ Will it agree to work for you,
  to be your slave for life?
⁵ Can you make it a pet like a bird,
  or give it to your little girls to play with?
⁶ Will merchants try to buy it
  to sell it in their shops?
⁷ Will its hide be hurt by spears
  or its head by a harpoon?
⁸ If you lay a hand on it,
  you will certainly remember the battle
    that follows.
  You won't try that again!
⁹*No, it is useless to try to capture it.
  The hunter who attempts it will be
    knocked down.
¹⁰ And since no one dares to disturb it,
  who then can stand up to me?
¹¹ Who has given me anything that I need to
    pay back?
  Everything under heaven is mine.

¹² "I want to emphasize Leviathan's limbs
  and its enormous strength and graceful
    form.
¹³ Who can strip off its hide,
  and who can penetrate its double layer
    of armor?*
¹⁴ Who could pry open its jaws?
  For its teeth are terrible!
¹⁵ Its scales are like rows of shields
  tightly sealed together.
¹⁶ They are so close together
  that no air can get between them.
¹⁷ Each scale sticks tight to the next.
  They interlock and cannot be penetrated.

¹⁸ "When it sneezes, it flashes light!
  Its eyes are like the red of dawn.

¹⁹ Lightning leaps from its mouth;
  flames of fire flash out.
²⁰ Smoke streams from its nostrils
  like steam from a pot heated over burning
    rushes.
²¹ Its breath would kindle coals,
  for flames shoot from its mouth.

²² "The tremendous strength in Leviathan's
    neck
  strikes terror wherever it goes.
²³ Its flesh is hard and firm
  and cannot be penetrated.
²⁴ Its heart is hard as rock,
  hard as a millstone.
²⁵ When it rises, the mighty are afraid,
  gripped by terror.
²⁶ No sword can stop it,
  no spear, dart, or javelin.
²⁷ Iron is nothing but straw to that creature,
  and bronze is like rotten wood.
²⁸ Arrows cannot make it flee.
  Stones shot from a sling are like bits
    of grass.
²⁹ Clubs are like a blade of grass,
  and it laughs at the swish of javelins.
³⁰ Its belly is covered with scales as sharp
    as glass.
  It plows up the ground as it drags through
    the mud.

³¹ "Leviathan makes the water boil with its
    commotion.
  It stirs the depths like a pot
    of ointment.
³² The water glistens in its wake,
  making the sea look white.
³³ Nothing on earth is its equal,
  no other creature so fearless.
³⁴ Of all the creatures, it is the proudest.
  It is the king of beasts."

42 JOB RESPONDS TO THE LORD

Then Job replied to the LORD:

² "I know that you can do anything,
  and no one can stop you.
³ You asked, 'Who is this that questions my
    wisdom with such ignorance?'
  It is I—and I was talking about things
    I knew nothing about,
  things far too wonderful for me.
⁴ You said, 'Listen and I will speak!
  I have some questions for you,

40:21 Or *bramble bushes;* also in 40:22. **41:1a** Verses 41:1-8 are
numbered 40:25-32 in Hebrew text. **41:1b** The identification of
Leviathan is disputed, ranging from an earthly creature to a mythical
sea monster in ancient literature. **41:9** Verses 41:9-34 are
numbered 41:1-26 in Hebrew text. **41:13** As in Greek version;
Hebrew reads *its bridle?*

and you must answer them.'
⁵ I had only heard about you
before,
but now I have seen you with
my own eyes.
⁶ I take back everything I said,
and I sit in dust and ashes to show
my repentance."

CONCLUSION: THE LORD BLESSES JOB

⁷After the LORD had finished speaking to Job, he said to Eliphaz the Temanite: "I am angry with you and your two friends, for you have not spoken accurately about me, as my servant Job has. ⁸So take seven bulls and seven rams and go to my servant Job and offer a burnt offering for yourselves. My servant Job will pray for you, and I will accept his prayer on your behalf. I will not treat you as you deserve, for you have not spoken accurately about me, as my servant Job has." ⁹So Eliphaz the Temanite, Bildad the Shuhite, and Zophar the Naamathite did as the LORD commanded them, and the LORD accepted Job's prayer.

¹⁰When Job prayed for his friends, the LORD restored his fortunes. In fact, the LORD gave him twice as much as before! ¹¹Then all his brothers, sisters, and former friends came and feasted with him in his home. And they consoled him and comforted him because of all the trials the LORD had brought against him.

42:11 Hebrew *a kesitah;* the value or weight of the kesitah is no longer known.

And each of them brought him a gift of money* and a gold ring.

¹²So the LORD blessed Job in the second half of his life even more than in the beginning. For now he had 14,000 sheep, 6,000 camels, 1,000 teams of oxen, and 1,000 female donkeys. ¹³He also gave Job seven more sons and three more daughters. ¹⁴He named his first daughter Jemimah, the second Keziah, and the third Keren-happuch. ¹⁵In all the land no women were as lovely as the daughters of Job. And their father put them into his will along with their brothers.

¹⁶Job lived 140 years after that, living to see four generations of his children and grandchildren. ¹⁷Then he died, an old man who had lived a long, full life.

....

UNANSWERED QUESTIONS
(42:1-6) Throughout the book, we see Job's friends demanding that Job admit his sins and ask for forgiveness. Although Job made things right with God, his repentance was not the kind called for by his friends. Instead, he repented of his attitude and acknowledged God's great power and perfect justice. Like Job, we can't know the reasons for everything that happens. Thus we often must choose between anger and trust. Will you trust God with your unanswered questions?

WILLING TO FORGIVE
(42:7-10) After receiving much criticism, Job was still able to pray for his three friends. Forgiving someone who wrongly accused you of something you didn't do can be difficult, but Job did it. During New Testament times, Jesus advised his followers to offer forgiveness to those who wronged them (see Matt 6:14-15; 18:35). Are you willing?

PSALMS

Emotions. We experience countless feelings every day, ranging from exuberant joy to deep grief. We feel pain when someone we love dies. We feel anger when things go wrong. We feel confusion when we don't understand something. And we feel joy when something good happens. Emotions add spice and color to life.

The book of Psalms is about emotions. The pages are filled with them: anger, confusion, joy, pain, humility, bewilderment, contentment—all directed toward God. God created us with emotions, and he knows they will be part of our dealings with him.

Many people read the book of Psalms because of its honesty. Rather than ignoring the "negative" emotions or condemning them as sinful, the writers faced their feelings and continued to talk with God.

Psalms is also loved because of the clear picture of God it presents. Our emotions change constantly, but God is constant. While we fret, worry, and shout about injustice, God remains calm. When we come to him, embarrassed because of something we did wrong, he doesn't express surprise or anger. Instead, he is gentle and ready to forgive. Psalms reminds us that God is exalted, the Creator and Ruler of the world, and worthy of worship. He alone is God.

How are you feeling today? Angry? Afraid? Frustrated? Or are you joyful, happy, and excited? Read Psalms and express yourself honestly to God.

KEY POINTS

PRAISE Psalms are songs of praise to God as our Creator, Savior, and provider. Reading the Psalms can encourage us to praise him.

GOD'S POWER God is all-powerful and always in control of every situation. Believing in God's power can overcome the despair of any pain or trial.

FORGIVENESS Many psalms are intense prayers asking God for forgiveness. Because God forgives us, we can pray to him honestly and directly. When we receive God's forgiveness, we move from being separated from him to being close to him, from feeling guilty to feeling loved.

GRATITUDE God protects, guides, forgives, and provides everything we need. When we realize how much we benefit from knowing God, we can fully express our thanks to him.

TRUST God's faithfulness and justice has been proven throughout history. Knowing him intimately drives away doubt, fear, and loneliness.

STATS

PURPOSE
To provide a collection of songs expressing praise, thanksgiving, and confession to God

AUTHORS
David (73 psalms); Asaph (12); the descendants of Korah (10); Solomon (2); Heman, Ethan, and Moses (1 each). Anonymous (51), but see Acts 4:25-26 and Hebrews 4:7.

ORIGINAL AUDIENCE
The people of Israel

DATE WRITTEN
Between the time of Moses and the Babylonian captivity (ca. 1440–586 B.C.)

SETTING
For the most part, the psalms do not recount historical events; however, they often parallel events in history (see Pss 18; 51).

KEY PERSON
David

KEY PLACE
God's holy Temple

SPECIAL FEATURES
Although Psalms has a unified plan, each psalm can be read and understood alone. Psalms is probably the most widely read book of the Bible because it is easy to relate to the writers' emotions.

BOOK ONE (Psalms 1–41)

1 ¹ Oh, the joys of those who do not
     follow the advice of the wicked,
   or stand around with sinners,
   or join in with mockers.
² But they delight in the law of
     the LORD,
   meditating on it day and night.
³ They are like trees planted along the
     riverbank,
   bearing fruit each season.
Their leaves never wither,
   and they prosper in all they do.

⁴ But not the wicked!
   They are like worthless chaff, scattered
     by the wind.
⁵ They will be condemned at the time
     of judgment.
   Sinners will have no place among
     the godly.
⁶ For the LORD watches over the path
     of the godly,
   but the path of the wicked leads
     to destruction.

....

FREEDOM

(2:3) Some people think they can experience freedom away from God and his rules. Ever feel that way? Yet we all serve somebody or something, whether a person in authority, the wishes of friends, or our own desires. Just as a fish is not free when it leaves the water and a tree is not free when it leaves the soil, we aren't really free if we try to live our lives without God. The one sure route to freedom is wholeheartedly serving God the Creator. He can set you free to be the person he created you to be.

2 ¹ Why are the nations so angry?
     Why do they waste their time with futile
     plans?
² The kings of the earth prepare for battle;
   the rulers plot together
against the LORD
   and against his anointed one.
³ "Let us break their chains," they cry,
   "and free ourselves from slavery
     to God."

⁴ But the one who rules in heaven laughs.
   The Lord scoffs at them.
⁵ Then in anger he rebukes them,
   terrifying them with his fierce fury.
⁶ For the Lord declares, "I have placed my
     chosen king on the throne
in Jerusalem,* on my holy
     mountain."

⁷ The king proclaims the LORD's decree:
   "The LORD said to me, 'You are my son.*
   Today I have become your Father.*
⁸ Only ask, and I will give you the nations as
     your inheritance,
   the whole earth as your possession.
⁹ You will break* them with an iron rod
   and smash them like clay pots.'"

¹⁰ Now then, you kings, act wisely!
   Be warned, you rulers of the earth!
¹¹ Serve the LORD with reverent fear,
   and rejoice with trembling.
¹² Submit to God's royal son,* or he will
     become angry,
   and you will be destroyed in the midst
     of all your activities—

2:6 Hebrew on Zion.   **2:7a** Or Son; also in 2:12.   **2:7b** Or Today I reveal you as my son.   **2:9** Greek version reads rule. Compare Rev 2:27.   **2:12** The meaning of the Hebrew is uncertain.

CHOICES
friendship

Last year Chelsea moved from a small Midwest town to Chicago. She didn't want to leave her hometown, but her dad got a job offer he'd wanted for years. Chelsea left behind close friends, a great youth group, a good school, and 14 years' worth of memories.

Chicago was a brand-new world. In Baxter, everybody knew everybody else (not to mention everybody else's business). In Chicago, Chelsea felt invisible. The first month she cried almost every night.

Even when Chelsea's family found a church with a big youth group, things didn't improve. Nobody in the group really made an effort to include her. They were so into their own little cliques, they barely noticed Chelsea.

At about that same time, however, a group of kids at school began reaching out to "the new girl." One guy called himself an agnostic. Two of the girls claimed to have had abortions. Another guy had a police record. None of them went to church.

When Chelsea's parents expressed concern about her choice of friends, Chelsea retorted, "Well, they may be a little bit on the wild side, but at least they treat me like a person. I'd rather hang out with them than with those fakes at the church!"

What would you do in Chelsea's situation? Do friends really affect the direction of your life? Read Psalm 1, noting especially the first verse.

for his anger flares up in an instant.
But what joy for all who take refuge
in him!

3 A psalm of David, regarding the time David fled
from his son Absalom.

1 O Lord, I have so many enemies;
so many are against me.
2 So many are saying,
"God will never rescue him!" Interlude*

3 But you, O Lord, are a shield around me;
you are my glory, the one who holds my
head high.
4 I cried out to the Lord,
and he answered me from his holy
mountain. Interlude

5 I lay down and slept,
yet I woke up in safety,
for the Lord was watching over me.
6 I am not afraid of ten thousand enemies
who surround me on every side.

7 Arise, O Lord!
Rescue me, my God!
Slap all my enemies in the face!
Shatter the teeth of the wicked!
8 Victory comes from you, O Lord.
May you bless your people. Interlude

4 For the choir director: A psalm of David, to be
accompanied by stringed instruments.

1 Answer me when I call to you,
O God who declares me innocent.
Free me from my troubles.
Have mercy on me and hear my prayer.

2 How long will you people ruin my
reputation?
How long will you make groundless
accusations?
How long will you continue your lies?
Interlude

3 You can be sure of this:
The Lord set apart the godly for himself.
The Lord will answer when I call to him.

4 Don't sin by letting anger control you.
Think about it overnight and remain
silent. Interlude
5 Offer sacrifices in the right spirit,
and trust the Lord.

6 Many people say, "Who will show us better
times?"

Let your face smile on us, Lord.
7 You have given me greater joy
than those who have abundant harvests
of grain and new wine.
8 In peace I will lie down and sleep,
for you alone, O Lord, will keep me safe.

5 For the choir director: A psalm of David, to be
accompanied by the flute.

1 O Lord, hear me as I pray;
pay attention to my groaning.
2 Listen to my cry for help, my King and
my God,
for I pray to no one but you.
3 Listen to my voice in the morning, Lord.
Each morning I bring my requests to you
and wait expectantly.

4 O God, you take no pleasure in wickedness;
you cannot tolerate the sins of the
wicked.
5 Therefore, the proud may not stand in your
presence,
for you hate all who do evil.
6 You will destroy those who tell lies.
The Lord detests murderers and
deceivers.

7 Because of your unfailing love, I can enter
your house;
I will worship at your Temple with
deepest awe.
8 Lead me in the right path, O Lord,
or my enemies will conquer me.
Make your way plain for me to follow.

9 My enemies cannot speak a truthful word.
Their deepest desire is to destroy others.
Their talk is foul, like the stench from an
open grave.
Their tongues are filled with flattery.*
10 O God, declare them guilty.
Let them be caught in their own traps.
Drive them away because of their many
sins,
for they have rebelled against you.

11 But let all who take refuge in you rejoice;
let them sing joyful praises forever.
Spread your protection over them,

3:2 Hebrew Selah. The meaning of this word is uncertain, though it
is probably a musical or literary term. It is rendered Interlude
throughout the Psalms. **5:9** Greek version reads with lies.
Compare Rom 3:13.

HE ALWAYS LISTENS
(4:1-3) David knew God heard his prayers and would
answer him. Ever doubt that God listens to your prayers?
Sometimes we fear that God will ignore us because we've
messed up somehow. But God is still willing to listen
to us. When you feel that your prayers are bouncing off
the ceiling, remember that God loves you. He hears and
answers.

MY STORY: Jenna

There was a time a couple of years ago when I was really down on myself and very confused. I couldn't do anything to make myself feel better. So, I prayed about it.

One night I opened my Bible looking for help. I leafed through the Psalms, remembering that a friend had once told me that whenever he felt bad, reading the Psalms helped.

Psalm 6 sort of jumped off the page at me—especially verse 3: "I am sick at heart. How long, O LORD, until you restore me?" That's how I felt—totally distressed. I read and reread that psalm. It spoke straight to my heart, and it showed me that God was there for me, as always.

Now whenever I'm in doubt about God's love and care, I turn to that psalm. It reminds me that God is always there and that he will lead me through any dark time I experience, just as he did on the night when I first read Psalm 6.

that all who love your name may be filled
   with joy.
¹² For you bless the godly, O LORD;
   you surround them with your shield
      of love.

6 *For the choir director: A psalm of David, to be accompanied by an eight-stringed instrument.* *

¹ O LORD, don't rebuke me in your anger
   or discipline me in your rage.
² Have compassion on me, LORD, for I am
      weak.
   Heal me, LORD, for my bones
      are in agony.
³ I am sick at heart.
   How long, O LORD, until you restore me?

....

REVENGE
(7:1-6) Have you ever been falsely accused by someone and wanted revenge? David wrote this psalm when he was falsely accused of trying to kill King Saul to gain the throne (1 Sam 24:9-11). Instead of seeking revenge, David cried out to God for justice. The proper response to false accusations is prayer, not revenge. God says, "I will take revenge; I will pay them back" (Deut 32:35; see also Rom 12:19). Instead of striking back, ask God to right your wrong and restore your reputation.

⁴ Return, O LORD, and rescue me.
   Save me because of your unfailing love.
⁵ For the dead do not remember you.
   Who can praise you from the grave?*

⁶ I am worn out from sobbing.
   All night I flood my bed with weeping,
      drenching it with my tears.
⁷ My vision is blurred by grief;
   my eyes are worn out because of all my
      enemies.

⁸ Go away, all you who do evil,
   for the LORD has heard my weeping.
⁹ The LORD has heard my plea;
   the LORD will answer my prayer.
¹⁰ May all my enemies be disgraced and
      terrified.
   May they suddenly turn back in shame.

7 *A psalm of David, which he sang to the LORD concerning Cush of the tribe of Benjamin.*

¹ I come to you for protection, O LORD
      my God.
   Save me from my persecutors—
      rescue me!
² If you don't, they will maul me like a lion,
      tearing me to pieces with no one to
         rescue me.
³ O LORD my God, if I have done wrong
   or am guilty of injustice,
⁴ if I have betrayed a friend
   or plundered my enemy without cause,
⁵ then let my enemies capture me.
   Let them trample me into the ground
   and drag my honor in the dust.   *Interlude*

⁶ Arise, O LORD, in anger!
   Stand up against the fury of my enemies!
   Wake up, my God, and bring justice!
⁷ Gather the nations before you.
   Rule over them from on high.
⁸ The LORD judges the nations.
   Declare me righteous, O LORD,
   for I am innocent, O Most High!
⁹ End the evil of those who are wicked,
   and defend the righteous.
   For you look deep within the mind
      and heart,
   O righteous God.

¹⁰ God is my shield,
   saving those whose hearts are true
      and right.
¹¹ God is an honest judge.
   He is angry with the wicked every day.

6:TITLE Hebrew *with stringed instruments; according to the* sheminith. **6:5** Hebrew *from Sheol?*

¹² If a person does not repent,
God* will sharpen his sword;
he will bend and string his bow.
¹³ He will prepare his deadly weapons
and shoot his flaming arrows.

¹⁴ The wicked conceive evil;
they are pregnant with trouble
and give birth to lies.
¹⁵ They dig a deep pit to trap others,
then fall into it themselves.
¹⁶ The trouble they make for others backfires
on them.
The violence they plan falls on their own
heads.

¹⁷ I will thank the LORD because he is just;
I will sing praise to the name of the LORD
Most High.

8 For the choir director: A psalm of David, to be
accompanied by a stringed instrument.*

¹ O LORD, our Lord, your majestic name fills
the earth!
Your glory is higher than the heavens.
² You have taught children and infants
to tell of your strength,*
silencing your enemies
and all who oppose you.

³ When I look at the night sky and see the
work of your fingers—
the moon and the stars you set in place—

⁴ what are mere mortals that you should think
about them,
human beings that you should care
for them?*
⁵ Yet you made them only a little lower
than God*
and crowned them* with glory and honor.
⁶ You gave them charge of everything you
made,
putting all things under their authority—
⁷ the flocks and the herds
and all the wild animals,
⁸ the birds in the sky, the fish in the sea,
and everything that swims the ocean
currents.

⁹ O LORD, our Lord, your majestic name fills
the earth!

9 For the choir director: A psalm of David, to be
sung to the tune "Death of the Son."

¹ I will praise you, LORD, with all my heart;
I will tell of all the marvelous things you
have done.
² I will be filled with joy because of you.
I will sing praises to your name,
O Most High.

³ My enemies retreated;
they staggered and died when you
appeared.
⁴ For you have judged in my favor;

7:12 Hebrew *he.*   8:TITLE Hebrew *according to the gittith.*
8:2 Greek version reads *to give you praise.* Compare Matt 21:16.
8:4 Hebrew *what is man that you should think of him, / the son of
man that you should care for him?*   8:5a Or *Yet you made them only
a little lower than the angels;* Hebrew reads *Yet you made him* [i.e.,
man] *a little lower than Elohim.*   8:5b Hebrew *him* [i.e., man];
similarly in 8:6.

· ·

NATURALLY
*(9:1-2) One of the natural results of praising God is wit-
nessing. When we know God is wonderful, we naturally
want to tell others and have them praise God with us.*

ULTIMATE ISSUES MADE IN THE IMAGE OF GOD

Got a coin handy? Good. Whose face is on it? More
than likely, you're looking at the image of a former
president or a well-known woman from history
(Susan B. Anthony or Sacagawea). If you check out
a set of stamps, you might see the image of another
well-known person from history.

Imagine having millions of coins or stamps
bearing your image. (Unfortunately, you usually
have to be dead before you can appear on either.)
Although God has never been on a stamp or
a coin, all people bear his image. According
to Psalm 8, we were made in his image. We're
"stamped" with his likeness. This doesn't mean
that we have his chin or his eyebrows. We have
his characteristics.

It's easy to believe this truth when we think about
kind, attractive, thoughtful people. But it's just as

true of the murderer on death row or the terrorist
bomber. We're God's image-bearers not because
we're good but because he created us. Our worth
is based on his work, not on our goodness—which
is a good thing because we are full of sinfulness.
We're like a masterpiece caked with mud and filth.
Underneath the dirt, we still bear the Master's signature. That should help guide how we treat each
other—even the people we don't like.

When you're confronted by people who seem to
exist only to make your life unpleasant—the classmate who majors in being obnoxious, the relative
who constantly criticizes you, the teacher who seems
to take pleasure in humiliating you—remember: that
person was made in God's image just as you were.
Regardless of our sinfulness, we are all of great
value to God. ■

from your throne you have judged with
    fairness.
⁵ You have rebuked the nations and
        destroyed the wicked;
    you have erased their names forever.
⁶ The enemy is finished, in endless ruins;
    the cities you uprooted are now forgotten.

⁷ But the Lord reigns forever,
    executing judgment from his throne.
⁸ He will judge the world with justice
    and rule the nations with fairness.
⁹ The Lord is a shelter for the oppressed,
    a refuge in times of trouble.
¹⁰ Those who know your name trust in you,
    for you, O Lord, do not abandon those
        who search for you.

¹¹ Sing praises to the Lord who reigns in
        Jerusalem.*
    Tell the world about his unforgettable
        deeds.
¹² For he who avenges murder cares for the
        helpless.
    He does not ignore the cries of those
        who suffer.

¹³ Lord, have mercy on me.
    See how my enemies torment me.
    Snatch me back from the jaws of death.
¹⁴ Save me so I can praise you publicly at
        Jerusalem's gates,
    so I can rejoice that you have rescued me.

¹⁵ The nations have fallen into the pit they dug
        for others.
    Their own feet have been caught in the
        trap they set.
¹⁶ The Lord is known for his justice.
    The wicked are trapped by their own
        deeds.   *Quiet Interlude**

¹⁷ The wicked will go down to the grave.*
    This is the fate of all the nations who
        ignore God.
¹⁸ But the needy will not be ignored forever;
    the hopes of the poor will not always be
        crushed.

¹⁹ Arise, O Lord!
    Do not let mere mortals defy you!

- -

KEEP ON PRAYING
*(10:1) To the psalm writer, God seemed far away. "Why
do you hide when I am in trouble?" he asked God. But
though the writer had honest doubts, he kept praying.
He also didn't assume that God no longer cared. Would
you have the same reaction in a moment of doubt? During
those times when you feel alone or forgotten are you
willing to stick with God?*

Judge the nations!
²⁰ Make them tremble in fear, O Lord.
    Let the nations know they are merely
        human.   *Interlude*

10
¹O Lord, why do you stand so far
        away?
    Why do you hide when I am in trouble?
² The wicked arrogantly hunt down the poor.
    Let them be caught in the evil they plan
        for others.
³ For they brag about their evil desires;
    they praise the greedy and curse the Lord.

⁴ The wicked are too proud to seek God.
    They seem to think that God is dead.
⁵ Yet they succeed in everything they do.
    They do not see your punishment
        awaiting them.
    They sneer at all their enemies.
⁶ They think, "Nothing bad will ever happen
        to us!
    We will be free of trouble forever!"

⁷ Their mouths are full of cursing, lies, and
        threats.*
    Trouble and evil are on the tips of their
        tongues.
⁸ They lurk in ambush in the villages,
    waiting to murder innocent people.
    They are always searching for helpless
        victims.
⁹ Like lions crouched in hiding,
    they wait to pounce on the helpless.
    Like hunters they capture the helpless
    and drag them away in nets.
¹⁰ Their helpless victims are crushed;
    they fall beneath the strength of the
        wicked.
¹¹ The wicked think, "God isn't watching us!
    He has closed his eyes and won't even
        see what we do!"

¹² Arise, O Lord!
    Punish the wicked, O God!
    Do not ignore the helpless!
¹³ Why do the wicked get away with despising
        God?
    They think, "God will never call us to
        account."
¹⁴ But you see the trouble and grief they
        cause.
    You take note of it and punish them.
    The helpless put their trust in you.
    You defend the orphans.

9:11 Hebrew *Zion;* also in 9:14.   9:16 Hebrew *Higgaion Selah.* The
meaning of this phrase is uncertain.   9:17 Hebrew *to Sheol.*
10:7 Greek version reads *cursing and bitterness.* Compare Rom 3:14.

¹⁵ Break the arms of these wicked, evil people!
    Go after them until the last one is
    destroyed.
¹⁶ The LORD is king forever and ever!
    The godless nations will vanish from
    the land.
¹⁷ LORD, you know the hopes of the helpless.
    Surely you will hear their cries and
    comfort them.
¹⁸ You will bring justice to the orphans and the
    oppressed,
    so mere people can no longer terrify
    them.

11
For the choir director: A psalm of David.

¹ I trust in the LORD for protection.
  So why do you say to me,
    "Fly like a bird to the mountains for
    safety!
² The wicked are stringing their bows
    and fitting their arrows on the
    bowstrings.
  They shoot from the shadows
    at those whose hearts are right.
³ The foundations of law and order have
    collapsed.
  What can the righteous do?"

⁴ But the LORD is in his holy Temple;
    the LORD still rules from heaven.
  He watches everyone closely,
    examining every person on earth.
⁵ The LORD examines both the righteous and
    the wicked.
  He hates those who love violence.
⁶ He will rain down blazing coals and burning
    sulfur on the wicked,
    punishing them with scorching winds.
⁷ For the righteous LORD loves justice.
    The virtuous will see his face.

12
*For the choir director: A psalm of David,
to be accompanied by an eight-stringed
instrument.**

¹ Help, O LORD, for the godly are fast
    disappearing!
  The faithful have vanished from the earth!
² Neighbors lie to each other,
    speaking with flattering lips and deceitful
    hearts.
³ May the LORD cut off their flattering lips
    and silence their boastful tongues.
⁴ They say, "We will lie to our hearts' content.
    Our lips are our own—who can stop us?"

12:TITLE Hebrew *according to the sheminith.*

MY STORY: Eric

*I couldn't get what my friend had told me
out of my mind. She said that when she was
eight years old her oldest brother sexually
abused her—more than once.*

*This really bothered me for a long time.
I felt angry, mainly at God. I just couldn't
understand it. How could God let such a
terrible thing happen to such a wonderful
person? Why hadn't he done anything to
stop it—like have the phone ring, or someone come to the door, or someone come
home? Anything!*

*One day I was reading in the Psalms and
came across Psalm 13. I saw that the psalmist was angry at God, too—he was actually
complaining to God! That gave me the
freedom to spill out my heart to God. I told
God all my bitter and confused thoughts
concerning what happened to my friend.
I cried. I even lashed out at God. And the
result of telling God what was on my mind
and my heart was an incredible peace. Psalm
13 showed me that God always wants to hear
what's on my mind, even when I'm angry
with him. In the end, I found that God is there
for me—even if I don't always understand all
his ways.*

⁵ The LORD replies, "I have seen violence
    done to the helpless,
    and I have heard the groans of the poor.
  Now I will rise up to rescue them,
    as they have longed for me to do."
⁶ The LORD's promises are pure,
    like silver refined in a furnace,
    purified seven times over.
⁷ Therefore, LORD, we know you will protect
    the oppressed,
    preserving them forever from this lying
    generation,
⁸ even though the wicked strut about,
    and evil is praised throughout the land.

....

LYING LIPS
(12:2-4) We may be tempted to believe that lies are
relatively harmless, even useful at times. But God doesn't
ignore deceit, flattery, or boasting. Each action originates
from an attitude expressed in our speech. The tongue can
be our greatest enemy because, though small, it can do
great damage (Jas 3:2-12). Be careful how you use yours.

13
For the choir director: A psalm of David.

¹ O LORD, how long will you forget me?
    Forever?
  How long will you look the other way?
² How long must I struggle with anguish in
    my soul,
  with sorrow in my heart every day?
  How long will my enemy have the upper
    hand?

³ Turn and answer me, O LORD my God!
  Restore the sparkle to my eyes,
    or I will die.
⁴ Don't let my enemies gloat, saying, "We
    have defeated him!"
  Don't let them rejoice at my downfall.

⁵ But I trust in your unfailing love.
  I will rejoice because you have
    rescued me.
⁶ I will sing to the LORD
    because he is good to me.

14
For the choir director: A psalm of David.

¹ Only fools say in their hearts,
  "There is no God."
  They are corrupt, and their actions are evil;
    not one of them does good!

² The LORD looks down from heaven
    on the entire human race;
  he looks to see if anyone is truly wise,
    if anyone seeks God.
³ But no, all have turned away;
    all have become corrupt.*

No one does good,
    not a single one!

⁴ Will those who do evil never learn?
  They eat up my people like bread
  and wouldn't think of praying to the LORD.
⁵ Terror will grip them,
    for God is with those who obey him.
⁶ The wicked frustrate the plans of the
    oppressed,
  but the LORD will protect his people.

⁷ Who will come from Mount Zion to rescue
    Israel?
  When the LORD restores his people,
  Jacob will shout with joy, and Israel will
    rejoice.

15
A psalm of David.

¹ Who may worship in your sanctuary, LORD?
  Who may enter your presence on your
    holy hill?
² Those who lead blameless lives and do
    what is right,
  speaking the truth from sincere hearts.
³ Those who refuse to gossip
    or harm their neighbors
    or speak evil of their friends.
⁴ Those who despise flagrant sinners,
  and honor the faithful followers of the
    LORD,
  and keep their promises even when
    it hurts.
⁵ Those who lend money without charging
    interest,

14:3 Greek version reads *have become useless.* Compare Rom 3:12.

I WONDER...

A friend of mine is convinced that being good will get him into heaven. I'm starting to agree with him. God won't send people to hell who live good lives, will he?

Most people would like to believe that God grades on a curve. In other words, if they're better than others, it will be all right with God. All they have to do to pass is not kill anyone or steal, mind their own business, and wait for heaven.

But God has a better plan. God's way makes it possible for anyone to live with him forever—not just those who are good enough.

But there's a catch: No one is good enough. Psalm 14:1-3 is clear. There isn't anyone who is good. Not one! All of us have strayed away. This doesn't mean we're all murderers. It does mean our hearts are stained with the sin of Adam—the desire to be good in our own lives and to run them ourselves. No one has a pure heart. This means that none of us are good enough to be with God. (See Luke 18:18-26 for a great illustration.)

God has one method of salvation: Jesus. In Jesus, every person has the opportunity to be with God for eternity—even murderers and thieves. The Bible says, "If you confess with your mouth that Jesus is Lord and believe in your heart that God raised him from the dead, you will be saved" (Rom 10:9).

Most people say this is too simple. But God isn't trying to make it tough on us. He wants us to be with him forever!

REASONS TO READ PSALMS

God's Word was written to be studied, understood, and applied, and the book of Psalms lends itself most directly to application. We may turn to Psalms looking for something, but sooner or later we will meet Someone. As we read and memorize the psalms, we will discover how much they are already part of us. They put our deepest hurts, longings, thoughts, and prayers into words. They gently push us toward being what God designed us to be—people who love and live for him.

To find comfort *Psalm 23*	To learn a new prayer *Psalm 136*	To give thanks to God *Psalm 136*	To please God *Psalm 15*
To meet God intimately *Psalm 103*	To learn a new song *Psalm 92*	To give praise to God *Psalm 145*	To feel worthwhile *Psalm 139*
To understand why you should read the Bible *Psalm 119*	To know that God is in control *Psalm 146*	To know how to come to God each day *Psalm 5*	To know why you should worship God *Psalm 104*
To understand yourself more clearly *Psalm 8*	To be forgiven for your sins *Psalm 51*		

and who cannot be bribed to lie about
the innocent.
Such people will stand firm forever.

16 *A psalm* of David.*

¹ Keep me safe, O God,
for I have come to you for refuge.

² I said to the LORD, "You are my Master!
Every good thing I have comes from you."
³ The godly people in the land
are my true heroes!
I take pleasure in them!
⁴ Troubles multiply for those who chase after
other gods.
I will not take part in their sacrifices of
blood
or even speak the names of their gods.

⁵ LORD, you alone are my inheritance, my cup
of blessing.
You guard all that is mine.
⁶ The land you have given me is a pleasant
land.
What a wonderful inheritance!

⁷ I will bless the LORD who guides me;
even at night my heart instructs me.
⁸ I know the LORD is always with me.
I will not be shaken, for he is right
beside me.

16:TITLE Hebrew *miktam*. This may be a literary or musical term.
16:9 Greek version reads *and my tongue shouts his praises.*
Compare Acts 2:26. **16:10a** Hebrew *in Sheol.* **16:10b** Or *your
Holy One.* **16:11** Greek version reads *You have shown me the way
of life, / and you will fill me with the joy of your presence.* Compare
Acts 2:28.

⁹ No wonder my heart is glad, and I rejoice.*
My body rests in safety.
¹⁰ For you will not leave my soul among the
dead*
or allow your holy one* to rot in the grave.
¹¹ You will show me the way of life,
granting me the joy of your presence
and the pleasures of living with you
forever.*

17 *A prayer of David.*

¹ O LORD, hear my plea for justice.
Listen to my cry for help.
Pay attention to my prayer,
for it comes from honest lips.
² Declare me innocent,
for you see those who do right.

³ You have tested my thoughts and examined
my heart in the night.
You have scrutinized me and found
nothing wrong.
I am determined not to sin in what I say.
⁴ I have followed your commands,
which keep me from following cruel and
evil people.
⁵ My steps have stayed on your path;
I have not wavered from following you.

⁶ I am praying to you because I know you will
answer, O God.
Bend down and listen as I pray.
⁷ Show me your unfailing love in wonderful
ways.
By your mighty power you rescue

those who seek refuge from their
    enemies.
8 Guard me as you would guard your
    own eyes.*
  Hide me in the shadow of your wings.
9 Protect me from wicked people who
    attack me,
  from murderous enemies who
    surround me.
10 They are without pity.
  Listen to their boasting!
11 They track me down and surround me,
  watching for the chance to throw me
    to the ground.
12 They are like hungry lions, eager to tear
    me apart—
  like young lions hiding in ambush.

13 Arise, O Lord!
  Stand against them, and bring them
    to their knees!
  Rescue me from the wicked with your
    sword!
14 By the power of your hand, O Lord,
  destroy those who look to this world for
    their reward.
  But satisfy the hunger of your treasured
    ones.
  May their children have plenty,
  leaving an inheritance for their
    descendants.
15 Because I am righteous, I will see you.
  When I awake, I will see you face to face
    and be satisfied.

18

*For the choir director: A psalm of David,
the servant of the Lord. He sang this
song to the Lord on the day the Lord rescued him
from all his enemies and from Saul. He sang:*

1 I love you, Lord;
  you are my strength.
2 The Lord is my rock, my fortress, and my
    savior;
  my God is my rock, in whom I find
    protection.
  He is my shield, the power that saves me,
    and my place of safety.
3 I called on the Lord, who is worthy of
    praise,
  and he saved me from my enemies.

4 The ropes of death entangled me;
  floods of destruction swept over me.
5 The grave* wrapped its ropes around me;
  death laid a trap in my path.
6 But in my distress I cried out to the Lord;
  yes, I prayed to my God for help.

He heard me from his sanctuary;
  my cry to him reached his ears.

7 Then the earth quaked and trembled.
  The foundations of the mountains shook;
  they quaked because of his anger.
8 Smoke poured from his nostrils;
  fierce flames leaped from his mouth.
  Glowing coals blazed forth from him.
9 He opened the heavens and came down;
  dark storm clouds were beneath his feet.
10 Mounted on a mighty angelic being,*
    he flew,
  soaring on the wings of the wind.
11 He shrouded himself in darkness,
  veiling his approach with dark rain
    clouds.
12 Thick clouds shielded the brightness
    around him
  and rained down hail and burning coals.*
13 The Lord thundered from heaven;
  the voice of the Most High resounded
    amid the hail and burning coals.
14 He shot his arrows and scattered his
    enemies;
  his lightning flashed, and they were
    greatly confused.
15 Then at your command, O Lord,
  at the blast of your breath,
  the bottom of the sea could be seen,
  and the foundations of the earth were
    laid bare.

16 He reached down from heaven and
    rescued me;
  he drew me out of deep waters.
17 He rescued me from my powerful enemies,
  from those who hated me and were too
    strong for me.
18 They attacked me at a moment when I was
    in distress,
  but the Lord supported me.
19 He led me to a place of safety;
  he rescued me because he delights
    in me.

20 The Lord rewarded me for doing right;
  he restored me because of my innocence.
21 For I have kept the ways of the Lord;
  I have not turned from my God to
    follow evil.
22 I have followed all his regulations;
  I have never abandoned his decrees.
23 I am blameless before God;
  I have kept myself from sin.
24 The Lord rewarded me for doing right.
  He has seen my innocence.

17:8 Hebrew *as the pupil of your eye.*   18:5 Hebrew *Sheol.*
18:10 Hebrew *a cherub.*   18:12 Or *and lightning bolts;* also in 18:13.

²⁵ To the faithful you show yourself faithful;
   to those with integrity you show integrity.
²⁶ To the pure you show yourself pure,
   but to the wicked you show yourself
      hostile.
²⁷ You rescue the humble,
   but you humiliate the proud.
²⁸ You light a lamp for me.
   The LORD, my God, lights up my darkness.
²⁹ In your strength I can crush an army;
   with my God I can scale any wall.

³⁰ God's way is perfect.
   All the LORD's promises prove true.
   He is a shield for all who look to him
      for protection.
³¹ For who is God except the LORD?
   Who but our God is a solid rock?
³² God arms me with strength,
   and he makes my way perfect.
³³ He makes me as surefooted as a deer,
   enabling me to stand on mountain
      heights.
³⁴ He trains my hands for battle;
   he strengthens my arm to draw a
      bronze bow.
³⁵ You have given me your shield of victory.
   Your right hand supports me;
   your help has made me great.
³⁶ You have made a wide path for my feet
   to keep them from slipping.

³⁷ I chased my enemies and caught them;
   I did not stop until they were conquered.
³⁸ I struck them down so they could not get up;
   they fell beneath my feet.
³⁹ You have armed me with strength for the
      battle;
   you have subdued my enemies under
      my feet.
⁴⁰ You placed my foot on their necks.
   I have destroyed all who hated me.
⁴¹ They called for help, but no one came to
      their rescue.
   They even cried to the LORD, but he
      refused to answer.
⁴² I ground them as fine as dust in the wind.
   I swept them into the gutter like dirt.
⁴³ You gave me victory over my accusers.
   You appointed me ruler over nations;
   people I don't even know now serve me.
⁴⁴ As soon as they hear of me, they submit;
   foreign nations cringe before me.
⁴⁵ They all lose their courage
   and come trembling from their
      strongholds.

19:3 Or *There is no speech or language where their voice is not heard.*

THE HEAVENS PROCLAIM THE GLORY OF GOD. THE SKIES DISPLAY HIS CRAFTSMANSHIP.

PSALM 19:1

⁴⁶ The LORD lives! Praise to my Rock!
   May the God of my salvation be exalted!
⁴⁷ He is the God who pays back those who
      harm me;
   he subdues the nations under me
⁴⁸   and rescues me from my enemies.
   You hold me safe beyond the reach of my
      enemies;
   you save me from violent opponents.
⁴⁹ For this, O LORD, I will praise you among the
      nations;
   I will sing praises to your name.
⁵⁰ You give great victories to your king;
   you show unfailing love to your anointed,
   to David and all his descendants forever.

19

For the choir director: A psalm of David.

¹ The heavens proclaim the glory of God.
   The skies display his craftsmanship.
² Day after day they continue to speak;
   night after night they make him known.
³ They speak without a sound or word;
   their voice is never heard.*
⁴ Yet their message has gone throughout
      the earth,
   and their words to all the world.

   God has made a home in the heavens for
      the sun.

....

SHIELD
(18:30) Ever hear someone say that belief in God is a crutch for weak people? Although David was a mighty warrior who fought with highly trained soldiers, he still knew that only God could protect him. God is indeed a shield to protect us because we are too weak to face problems by ourselves. He strengthens, protects, and guides us.

HIS GENTLENESS
(18:35) David offers an interesting twist to the concept of greatness by admitting that God's gentleness made him great. Our society believes that greatness is attained through a combination of opportunity, talent, and aggressiveness. But Jesus once described himself as "gentle at heart" (Matt 11:29). True greatness comes from living according to God's laws and standards and recognizing that all we have comes from the gentleness of God's mercy.

⁵ It bursts forth like a radiant bridegroom
  after his wedding.
  It rejoices like a great athlete eager to run
  the race.
⁶ The sun rises at one end of the heavens
  and follows its course to the other end.
  Nothing can hide from its heat.

⁷ The instructions of the LORD are perfect,
  reviving the soul.
  The decrees of the LORD are trustworthy,
  making wise the simple.
⁸ The commandments of the LORD are right,
  bringing joy to the heart.
  The commands of the LORD are clear,
  giving insight for living.
⁹ Reverence for the LORD is pure,
  lasting forever.
  The laws of the LORD are true;
  each one is fair.
¹⁰ They are more desirable than gold,
   even the finest gold.
   They are sweeter than honey,
   even honey dripping from the comb.
¹¹ They are a warning to your servant,
   a great reward for those who obey them.

¹² How can I know all the sins lurking in my
   heart?
   Cleanse me from these hidden faults.
¹³ Keep your servant from deliberate sins!
   Don't let them control me.
   Then I will be free of guilt
   and innocent of great sin.

¹⁴ May the words of my mouth
   and the meditation of my heart
   be pleasing to you,
   O LORD, my rock and my redeemer.

20 For the choir director: A psalm of David.

¹ In times of trouble, may the LORD answer
  your cry.
  May the name of the God of Jacob keep
  you safe from all harm.
² May he send you help from his sanctuary
  and strengthen you from Jerusalem.*
³ May he remember all your gifts
  and look favorably on your burnt
  offerings.   *Interlude*

GUILT
*(19:12-13) Many believers are plagued by guilt. Guilt
can play an important role in bringing us to Christ and in
keeping us behaving properly, but it should not cripple us
or make us feel fearful. God fully and completely forgives
us—even for those sins that we do unknowingly.*

⁴ May he grant your heart's desires
  and make all your plans succeed.
⁵ May we shout for joy when we hear of your
  victory
  and raise a victory banner in the name
  of our God.
  May the LORD answer all your prayers.

⁶ Now I know that the LORD rescues his
  anointed king.
  He will answer him from his holy heaven
  and rescue him by his great power.
⁷ Some nations boast of their chariots and
  horses,
  but we boast in the name of the LORD
  our God.
⁸ Those nations will fall down and collapse,
  but we will rise up and stand firm.

⁹ Give victory to our king, O LORD!
  Answer our cry for help.

21 For the choir director: A psalm of David.

¹ How the king rejoices in your strength,
  O LORD!
  He shouts with joy because you give him
  victory.
² For you have given him his heart's desire;
  you have withheld nothing he requested.
                                      Interlude

³ You welcomed him back with success and
  prosperity.
  You placed a crown of finest gold on his
  head.
⁴ He asked you to preserve his life,
  and you granted his request.
  The days of his life stretch on forever.
⁵ Your victory brings him great honor,
  and you have clothed him with splendor
  and majesty.
⁶ You have endowed him with eternal
  blessings
  and given him the joy of your presence.
⁷ For the king trusts in the LORD.
  The unfailing love of the Most High will
  keep him from stumbling.

⁸ You will capture all your enemies.
  Your strong right hand will seize all who
  hate you.
⁹ You will throw them in a flaming furnace
  when you appear.
  The LORD will consume them in his anger;
  fire will devour them.

20:2 Hebrew *Zion.*

¹⁰ You will wipe their children from the face of
the earth;
they will never have descendants.
¹¹ Although they plot against you,
their evil schemes will never succeed.
¹² For they will turn and run
when they see your arrows aimed at
them.
¹³ Rise up, O Lord, in all your power.
With music and singing we celebrate your
mighty acts.

22 *For the choir director: A psalm of David, to
be sung to the tune "Doe of the Dawn."*

¹ My God, my God, why have you
abandoned me?
Why are you so far away when I groan for
help?
² Every day I call to you, my God, but you do
not answer.
Every night you hear my voice, but I find
no relief.

³ Yet you are holy,
enthroned on the praises of Israel.
⁴ Our ancestors trusted in you,
and you rescued them.
⁵ They cried out to you and were saved.
They trusted in you and were never
disgraced.

⁶ But I am a worm and not a man.
I am scorned and despised by all!
⁷ Everyone who sees me mocks me.
They sneer and shake their heads, saying,
⁸ "Is this the one who relies on the Lord?
Then let the Lord save him!
If the Lord loves him so much,
let the Lord rescue him!"

⁹ Yet you brought me safely from my mother's
womb
and led me to trust you at my mother's
breast.
¹⁰ I was thrust into your arms at my birth.
You have been my God from the moment
I was born.

¹¹ Do not stay so far from me,
for trouble is near,
and no one else can help me.
¹² My enemies surround me like a herd of
bulls;
fierce bulls of Bashan have hemmed
me in!
¹³ Like lions they open their jaws against me,
roaring and tearing into their prey.

22:18 Hebrew *cast lots.*   **22:22** Hebrew *my brothers.*

¹⁴ My life is poured out like water,
and all my bones are out of joint.
My heart is like wax,
melting within me.
¹⁵ My strength has dried up like sunbaked
clay.
My tongue sticks to the roof of my mouth.
You have laid me in the dust and left me
for dead.
¹⁶ My enemies surround me like a pack
of dogs;
an evil gang closes in on me.
They have pierced my hands and feet.
¹⁷ I can count all my bones.
My enemies stare at me and gloat.
¹⁸ They divide my garments among themselves
and throw dice* for my clothing.

¹⁹ O Lord, do not stay far away!
You are my strength; come quickly to
my aid!
²⁰ Save me from the sword;
spare my precious life from these dogs.
²¹ Snatch me from the lion's jaws
and from the horns of these wild oxen.

²² I will proclaim your name to my brothers and
sisters.*
I will praise you among your assembled
people.
²³ Praise the Lord, all you who fear him!
Honor him, all you descendants of Jacob!
Show him reverence, all you descendants
of Israel!
²⁴ For he has not ignored or belittled the
suffering of the needy.
He has not turned his back on them,
but has listened to their cries for help.

²⁵ I will praise you in the great assembly.
I will fulfill my vows in the presence of
those who worship you.
²⁶ The poor will eat and be satisfied.
All who seek the Lord will praise him.
Their hearts will rejoice with
everlasting joy.
²⁷ The whole earth will acknowledge the Lord
and return to him.
All the families of the nations will bow
down before him.
²⁸ For royal power belongs to the Lord.
He rules all the nations.
²⁹ Let the rich of the earth feast and worship.
Bow before him, all who are mortal,
all whose lives will end as dust.
³⁰ Our children will also serve him.
Future generations will hear about the
wonders of the Lord.

THE LORD IS MY SHEPHERD; I HAVE ALL THAT I NEED.

{ PSALM 23:1}

³¹ His righteous acts will be told to those not
yet born.
They will hear about everything he has
done.

23 *A psalm of David.*

¹ The LORD is my shepherd;
I have all that I need.
² He lets me rest in green meadows;
he leads me beside peaceful streams.
³ He renews my strength.
He guides me along right paths,
bringing honor to his name.
⁴ Even when I walk
through the darkest valley,*
I will not be afraid,
for you are close beside me.
Your rod and your staff
protect and comfort me.
⁵ You prepare a feast for me
in the presence of my enemies.
You honor me by anointing my head
with oil.
My cup overflows with blessings.
⁶ Surely your goodness and unfailing love will
pursue me
all the days of my life,
and I will live in the house of the LORD
forever.

BEST INTERESTS
*(23:1-3) David compares God's concern for his people to
that of a shepherd. When we allow God, our Shepherd, to
guide us, we experience peace and contentment. When
we choose to sin, however, we are choosing to go our own
way, and we cannot blame God for the environment in
which we find ourselves. Our Shepherd knows the "green
meadows" and "peaceful streams" that will renew us. We
will reach these places only by sticking close to him like
sheep would to a shepherd. How close are you?*

ENEMIES
*(25:2) David asked God to keep his enemies from over-
coming him because they opposed what God stood for.
Seventy-two psalms—almost half the book—speak about
enemies. Enemies are those who not only oppose us but
also oppose God's way of living. A less tangible enemy
can be a temptation like money, success, prestige, or lust.
And our greatest enemy is Satan. Although these enemies
may seem huge, they are no match for God.*

24 *A psalm of David.*

¹ The earth is the LORD's, and everything in it.
The world and all its people belong
to him.
² For he laid the earth's foundation on
the seas
and built it on the ocean depths.
³ Who may climb the mountain of the LORD?
Who may stand in his holy place?
⁴ Only those whose hands and hearts
are pure,
who do not worship idols
and never tell lies.
⁵ They will receive the LORD's blessing
and have a right relationship with God
their savior.
⁶ Such people may seek you
and worship in your presence, O God
of Jacob.   *Interlude*
⁷ Open up, ancient gates!
Open up, ancient doors,
and let the King of glory enter.
⁸ Who is the King of glory?
The LORD, strong and mighty;
the LORD, invincible in battle.
⁹ Open up, ancient gates!
Open up, ancient doors,
and let the King of glory enter.
¹⁰ Who is the King of glory?
The LORD of Heaven's Armies—
he is the King of glory.   *Interlude*

25* *A psalm of David.*

¹ O LORD, I give my life to you.
²   I trust in you, my God!
Do not let me be disgraced,
or let my enemies rejoice in my defeat.
³ No one who trusts in you will ever be
disgraced,
but disgrace comes to those who try to
deceive others.

⁴ Show me the right path, O LORD;
point out the road for me to follow.

23:4 Or *the dark valley of death.* 25 This psalm is a Hebrew
acrostic poem; each verse begins with a successive letter of the
Hebrew alphabet.

⁵ Lead me by your truth and teach me,
for you are the God who saves me.
All day long I put my hope in you.
⁶ Remember, O Lord, your compassion and
unfailing love,
which you have shown from long
ages past.
⁷ Do not remember the rebellious sins
of my youth.
Remember me in the light of your
unfailing love,
for you are merciful, O Lord.

⁸ The Lord is good and does what is right;
he shows the proper path to those who
go astray.
⁹ He leads the humble in doing right,
teaching them his way.
¹⁰ The Lord leads with unfailing love and
faithfulness
all who keep his covenant and obey his
demands.

¹¹ For the honor of your name, O Lord,
forgive my many, many sins.
¹² Who are those who fear the Lord?
He will show them the path they should
choose.
¹³ They will live in prosperity,
and their children will inherit the land.
¹⁴ The Lord is a friend to those who fear him.
He teaches them his covenant.
¹⁵ My eyes are always on the Lord,
for he rescues me from the traps of my
enemies.

¹⁶ Turn to me and have mercy,
for I am alone and in deep distress.
¹⁷ My problems go from bad to worse.
Oh, save me from them all!
¹⁸ Feel my pain and see my trouble.
Forgive all my sins.
¹⁹ See how many enemies I have
and how viciously they hate me!
²⁰ Protect me! Rescue my life from them!
Do not let me be disgraced, for in you
I take refuge.
²¹ May integrity and honesty protect me,
for I put my hope in you.

²² O God, ransom Israel
from all its troubles.

26 *A psalm of David.*

¹ Declare me innocent, O Lord,
for I have acted with integrity;
I have trusted in the Lord without
wavering.

² Put me on trial, Lord, and
cross-examine me.
Test my motives and my heart.
³ For I am always aware of your unfailing love,
and I have lived according to your truth.
⁴ I do not spend time with liars
or go along with hypocrites.
⁵ I hate the gatherings of those who do evil,
and I refuse to join in with the wicked.
⁶ I wash my hands to declare my innocence.
I come to your altar, O Lord,
⁷ singing a song of thanksgiving
and telling of all your wonders.
⁸ I love your sanctuary, Lord,
the place where your glorious presence
dwells.

⁹ Don't let me suffer the fate of sinners.
Don't condemn me along with murderers.
¹⁰ Their hands are dirty with evil schemes,
and they constantly take bribes.
¹¹ But I am not like that; I live with integrity.
So redeem me and show me mercy.
¹² Now I stand on solid ground,
and I will publicly praise the Lord.

27 *A psalm of David.*

¹ The Lord is my light and my salvation—
so why should I be afraid?
The Lord is my fortress, protecting me from
danger,
so why should I tremble?
² When evil people come to devour me,
when my enemies and foes attack me,
they will stumble and fall.
³ Though a mighty army surrounds me,
my heart will not be afraid.
Even if I am attacked,
I will remain confident.

⁴ The one thing I ask of the Lord—
the thing I seek most—
is to live in the house of the Lord all the
days of my life,
delighting in the Lord's perfections
and meditating in his Temple.
⁵ For he will conceal me there when troubles
come;

ALREADY PREPARED
(27:1-14) *David sought God's guidance every day. So,
when troubles came his way, he was already prepared
to handle any test. We often run to God when we are
experiencing difficulties. Many of our problems could be
avoided or handled far more easily by constantly relying
on God's help and direction. Do you seek God daily or
only during emergencies?*

he will hide me in his sanctuary.
  He will place me out of reach on a high
    rock.
6 Then I will hold my head high
  above my enemies who surround me.
At his sanctuary I will offer sacrifices with
    shouts of joy,
  singing and praising the LORD with music.

7 Hear me as I pray, O LORD.
  Be merciful and answer me!
8 My heart has heard you say, "Come and talk
    with me."
  And my heart responds, "LORD, I am
    coming."
9 Do not turn your back on me.
  Do not reject your servant in anger.
  You have always been my helper.
Don't leave me now; don't abandon me,
  O God of my salvation!
10 Even if my father and mother abandon me,
  the LORD will hold me close.

11 Teach me how to live, O LORD.
  Lead me along the right path,
  for my enemies are waiting for me.
12 Do not let me fall into their hands.
  For they accuse me of things I've never
    done;
  with every breath they threaten me with
    violence.
13 Yet I am confident I will see the LORD's
    goodness
  while I am here in the land of the living.

14 Wait patiently for the LORD.
  Be brave and courageous.
  Yes, wait patiently for the LORD.

28 *A psalm of David.*

1 I pray to you, O LORD, my rock.
  Do not turn a deaf ear to me.
For if you are silent,
  I might as well give up and die.
2 Listen to my prayer for mercy
  as I cry out to you for help,

as I lift my hands toward your holy
    sanctuary.

3 Do not drag me away with the wicked—
  with those who do evil—
those who speak friendly words to their
    neighbors
  while planning evil in their hearts.
4 Give them the punishment they so richly
    deserve!
  Measure it out in proportion to their
    wickedness.
Pay them back for all their evil deeds!
  Give them a taste of what they have
    done to others.
5 They care nothing for what the LORD
    has done
  or for what his hands have made.
So he will tear them down,
  and they will never be rebuilt!

6 Praise the LORD!
  For he has heard my cry for mercy.
7 The LORD is my strength and shield.
  I trust him with all my heart.
He helps me, and my heart is filled with joy.
  I burst out in songs of thanksgiving.

8 The LORD gives his people strength.
  He is a safe fortress for his anointed king.
9 Save your people!
  Bless Israel, your special possession.*
Lead them like a shepherd,
  and carry them in your arms forever.

29 *A psalm of David.*

1 Honor the LORD, you heavenly beings*;
  honor the LORD for his glory and strength.
2 Honor the LORD for the glory of his name.
  Worship the LORD in the splendor of his
    holiness.

3 The voice of the LORD echoes above the sea.
  The God of glory thunders.
  The LORD thunders over the mighty sea.
4 The voice of the LORD is powerful;
  the voice of the LORD is majestic.
5 The voice of the LORD splits the mighty
    cedars;
  the LORD shatters the cedars
    of Lebanon.
6 He makes Lebanon's mountains skip like
    a calf;
  he makes Mount Hermon* leap like
    a young wild ox.

FAKE FRIENDSHIP
(28:3-5) As king of Israel, David may have met many who pretended friendship for selfish reasons. David knew God would punish them accordingly, but he prayed that their punishment would come swiftly. Faking friendship is easy. Deceitful people often pretend to be kind or offer a false sort of friendship to gain their own ends. True believers live honest lives before God and others. They don't offer friendship only for what they can get out of it. How would your friends describe your brand of friendship?

28:9 Hebrew *Bless your inheritance.*   29:1 Hebrew *you sons of God.*
29:6 Hebrew *Sirion,* another name for Mount Hermon.

7 The voice of the LORD strikes
   with bolts of lightning.
8 The voice of the LORD makes the barren
   wilderness quake;
   the LORD shakes the wilderness of
   Kadesh.
9 The voice of the LORD twists mighty oaks*
   and strips the forests bare.
   In his Temple everyone shouts, "Glory!"

10 The LORD rules over the floodwaters.
   The LORD reigns as king forever.
11 The LORD gives his people strength.
   The LORD blesses them with peace.

30

A psalm of David. A song for the dedication of the Temple.

1 I will exalt you, LORD, for you rescued me.
   You refused to let my enemies triumph
   over me.
2 O LORD my God, I cried to you for help,
   and you restored my health.
3 You brought me up from the grave,* O LORD.
   You kept me from falling into the pit of
   death.

4 Sing to the LORD, all you godly ones!
   Praise his holy name.
5 For his anger lasts only a moment,
   but his favor lasts a lifetime!
   Weeping may last through the night,
   but joy comes with the morning.

6 When I was prosperous, I said,
   "Nothing can stop me now!"
7 Your favor, O LORD, made me as secure as
   a mountain.
   Then you turned away from me, and I was
   shattered.

8 I cried out to you, O LORD.
   I begged the Lord for mercy, saying,
9 "What will you gain if I die,
   if I sink into the grave?
   Can my dust praise you?
   Can it tell of your faithfulness?
10 Hear me, LORD, and have mercy on me.
   Help me, O LORD."

11 You have turned my mourning into joyful
   dancing.
   You have taken away my clothes of
   mourning and clothed me with joy,
12 that I might sing praises to you and not be
   silent.
   O LORD my God, I will give you thanks
   forever!

29:9 Or *causes the deer to writhe in labor.*   30:3 Hebrew *from Sheol.*

31

For the choir director: A psalm of David.

1 O LORD, I have come to you for protection;
   don't let me be disgraced.
   Save me, for you do what is right.
2 Turn your ear to listen to me;
   rescue me quickly.
   Be my rock of protection,
   a fortress where I will be safe.
3 You are my rock and my fortress.
   For the honor of your name, lead me
   out of this danger.
4 Pull me from the trap my enemies set
   for me,
   for I find protection in you alone.
5 I entrust my spirit into your hand.
   Rescue me, LORD, for you are a
   faithful God.

6 I hate those who worship worthless idols.
   I trust in the LORD.
7 I will be glad and rejoice in your unfailing
   love,
   for you have seen my troubles,
   and you care about the anguish of
   my soul.
8 You have not handed me over to my
   enemies
   but have set me in a safe place.

9 Have mercy on me, LORD, for I am in
   distress.
   Tears blur my eyes.
   My body and soul are withering away.
10 I am dying from grief;
   my years are shortened by sadness.
   Sin has drained my strength;
   I am wasting away from within.
11 I am scorned by all my enemies
   and despised by my neighbors—
   even my friends are afraid to come
   near me.
   When they see me on the street,
   they run the other way.
12 I am ignored as if I were dead,
   as if I were a broken pot.
13 I have heard the many rumors about me,

....

FALSE SECURITY
(30:6-7) Wealth and power had made David feel invincible. Although he knew that both came from God, he felt a certain pride in them. Wealth, power, and fame can have an intoxicating effect on people, making them feel self-reliant and independent from God. But this is a false security that is shattered easily. Feeling secure because of what you have (popularity, money, high GPA)? Don't be fooled by the false security of prosperity or status. Unlike God, these won't last forever.

and I am surrounded by terror.
My enemies conspire against me,
plotting to take my life.

14 But I am trusting in you, O Lord,
saying, "You are my God!"
15 My future is in your hands.
Rescue me from those who hunt me
down relentlessly.
16 Let your favor shine on your servant.
In your unfailing love, rescue me.
17 Don't let me be disgraced, O Lord,
for I call out to you for help.
Let the wicked be disgraced;
let them lie silent in the grave.*
18 Silence their lying lips—
those proud and arrogant lips that
accuse the godly.

19 How great is the goodness
you have stored up for those who
fear you.
You lavish it on those who come to you for
protection,
blessing them before the watching world.
20 You hide them in the shelter of your
presence,
safe from those who conspire against
them.
You shelter them in your presence,
far from accusing tongues.

21 Praise the Lord,
for he has shown me the wonders of his
unfailing love.
He kept me safe when my city was under
attack.
22 In panic I cried out,
"I am cut off from the Lord!"
But you heard my cry for mercy
and answered my call for help.

23 Love the Lord, all you godly ones!
For the Lord protects those who are loyal
to him,
but he harshly punishes the arrogant.
24 So be strong and courageous,
all you who put your hope in
the Lord!

32

A psalm* of David.

1 Oh, what joy for those
whose disobedience is forgiven,
whose sin is put out of sight!
2 Yes, what joy for those
whose record the Lord has cleared
of guilt,*

whose lives are lived in complete
honesty!
3 When I refused to confess my sin,
my body wasted away,
and I groaned all day long.
4 Day and night your hand of discipline was
heavy on me.
My strength evaporated like water in the
summer heat.   *Interlude*

5 Finally, I confessed all my sins to you
and stopped trying to hide my guilt.
I said to myself, "I will confess my rebellion
to the Lord."
And you forgave me! All my guilt is gone.
Interlude

6 Therefore, let all the godly pray to you while
there is still time,
that they may not drown in the
floodwaters of judgment.
7 For you are my hiding place;
you protect me from trouble.
You surround me with songs of victory.
Interlude

8 The Lord says, "I will guide you along the
best pathway for your life.
I will advise you and watch over you.
9 Do not be like a senseless horse or mule
that needs a bit and bridle to keep it
under control."

10 Many sorrows come to the wicked,
but unfailing love surrounds those who
trust the Lord.
11 So rejoice in the Lord and be glad, all you
who obey him!
Shout for joy, all you whose hearts
are pure!

33

1 Let the godly sing for joy to the Lord;
it is fitting for the pure to praise
him.
2 Praise the Lord with melodies on the lyre;
make music for him on the ten-stringed
harp.
3 Sing a new song of praise to him;
play skillfully on the harp, and sing
with joy.
4 For the word of the Lord holds true,
and we can trust everything he does.
5 He loves whatever is just and good;
the unfailing love of the Lord fills the
earth.

31:17 Hebrew *in Sheol.*   **32:TITLE** Hebrew *maskil.* This may
be a literary or musical term.   **32:2** Greek version reads *of sin.*
Compare Rom 4:7.

6 The Lord merely spoke,
and the heavens were created.
He breathed the word,
and all the stars were born.
7 He assigned the sea its boundaries
and locked the oceans in vast reservoirs.
8 Let the whole world fear the Lord,
and let everyone stand in awe of him.
9 For when he spoke, the world began!
It appeared at his command.

10 The Lord frustrates the plans of the nations
and thwarts all their schemes.
11 But the Lord's plans stand firm forever;
his intentions can never be shaken.

12 What joy for the nation whose God is the
Lord,
whose people he has chosen as his
inheritance.

13 The Lord looks down from heaven
and sees the whole human race.
14 From his throne he observes
all who live on the earth.
15 He made their hearts,
so he understands everything they do.
16 The best-equipped army cannot save a king,
nor is great strength enough to save a
warrior.
17 Don't count on your warhorse to give you
victory—
for all its strength, it cannot save you.

18 But the Lord watches over those who fear
him,
those who rely on his unfailing love.
19 He rescues them from death
and keeps them alive in times of famine.

20 We put our hope in the Lord.
He is our help and our shield.
21 In him our hearts rejoice,
for we trust in his holy name.
22 Let your unfailing love surround us, Lord,
for our hope is in you alone.

34

*A psalm of David, regarding the time he
pretended to be insane in front of
Abimelech, who sent him away.*

1 I will praise the Lord at all times.
I will constantly speak his praises.
2 I will boast only in the Lord;
let all who are helpless take heart.
3 Come, let us tell of the Lord's greatness;
let us exalt his name together.

4 I prayed to the Lord, and he answered me.
He freed me from all my fears.

34 This psalm is a Hebrew acrostic poem; each verse begins with
a successive letter of the Hebrew alphabet.

5 Those who look to him for help will be
radiant with joy;
no shadow of shame will darken their
faces.
6 In my desperation I prayed, and the Lord
listened;
he saved me from all my troubles.
7 For the angel of the Lord is a guard;
he surrounds and defends all who
fear him.

8 Taste and see that the Lord is good.
Oh, the joys of those who take refuge
in him!
9 Fear the Lord, you his godly people,
for those who fear him will have all
they need.
10 Even strong young lions sometimes go
hungry,
but those who trust in the Lord will lack
no good thing.

11 Come, my children, and listen to me,
and I will teach you to fear the Lord.
12 Does anyone want to live a life
that is long and prosperous?
13 Then keep your tongue from speaking evil
and your lips from telling lies!
14 Turn away from evil and do good.
Search for peace, and work to
maintain it.

15 The eyes of the Lord watch over those who
do right;
his ears are open to their cries for help.
16 But the Lord turns his face against those
who do evil;
he will erase their memory from the earth.
17 The Lord hears his people when they call to
him for help.
He rescues them from all their troubles.
18 The Lord is close to the brokenhearted;

....

IN GOD WE TRUST?
*(33:4) A person's words are measured by the quality of
his or her character. If your friends trust what you say, it
is because they trust you. If you trust what God says, it
is because you trust him to be the God he claims to be.
If you doubt his words, you doubt the integrity of God
himself. Would you say, like the psalmist, "We can trust
everything he does"?*

ALL WE NEED
*(34:9-10) "Those who fear him will have all they need."
This is not a blanket promise that all Christians will be
rich. After all, many Christians face unbearable poverty
and hardship. It reflects David's belief in God's goodness—all those who call upon God will be answered,
sometimes in unexpected ways. In what unusual ways
have you seen God act in your life? How do these experiences help you to trust him in other situations?*

MY STORY: Anita

There are two Scriptures that help me daily. Because I have a disease called Epstein-Barr Virus, I am always tired and often in pain. Psalm 34 reminds me that I can rely on God constantly for every ounce of strength I need. It also reminds me that God hears the cry of those who trust him. I rely on these verses constantly.

Jeremiah 29:11 is my source of hope for the future. It reminds me that my constant worry about college and about ever getting over my illness is totally unnecessary; everything that happens is part of God's plan for my life. His plan is for good, not disaster, and he intends to give me a future and a hope. He truly will take care of everything as I trust him.

I have memorized these passages, and I remind myself of the words whenever I need to—which is almost every day! They are a great source of comfort to me.

    he rescues those whose spirits are crushed.

19 The righteous person faces many troubles, but the LORD comes to the rescue each time.
20 For the LORD protects the bones of the righteous;
    not one of them is broken!

21 Calamity will surely overtake the wicked, and those who hate the righteous will be punished.
22 But the LORD will redeem those who serve him.
    No one who takes refuge in him will be condemned.

35 *A psalm of David.*

1 O LORD, oppose those who oppose me. Fight those who fight against me.
2 Put on your armor, and take up your shield. Prepare for battle, and come to my aid.
3 Lift up your spear and javelin against those who pursue me.
    Let me hear you say,
    "I will give you victory!"
4 Bring shame and disgrace on those trying to kill me;

turn them back and humiliate those who want to harm me.
5 Blow them away like chaff in the wind—a wind sent by the angel of the LORD.
6 Make their path dark and slippery, with the angel of the LORD pursuing them.
7 I did them no wrong, but they laid a trap for me.
    I did them no wrong, but they dug a pit to catch me.
8 So let sudden ruin come upon them!
    Let them be caught in the trap they set for me!
    Let them be destroyed in the pit they dug for me.

9 Then I will rejoice in the LORD.
    I will be glad because he rescues me.
10 With every bone in my body I will praise him:
    "LORD, who can compare with you?
    Who else rescues the helpless from the strong?
    Who else protects the helpless and poor from those who rob them?"

11 Malicious witnesses testify against me.
    They accuse me of crimes I know nothing about.
12 They repay me evil for good.
    I am sick with despair.
13 Yet when they were ill, I grieved for them.
    I denied myself by fasting for them, but my prayers returned unanswered.
14 I was sad, as though they were my friends or family,
    as if I were grieving for my own mother.
15 But they are glad now that I am in trouble; they gleefully join together against me.
    I am attacked by people I don't even know; they slander me constantly.
16 They mock me and call me names; they snarl at me.

17 How long, O Lord, will you look on and do nothing?
    Rescue me from their fierce attacks.
    Protect my life from these lions!
18 Then I will thank you in front of the great assembly.
    I will praise you before all the people.
19 Don't let my treacherous enemies rejoice over my defeat.
    Don't let those who hate me without cause gloat over my sorrow.
20 They don't talk of peace;
    they plot against innocent people who mind their own business.

²¹ They shout, "Aha! Aha!
  With our own eyes we saw him do it!"

²² O LORD, you know all about this.
  Do not stay silent.
  Do not abandon me now, O Lord.
²³ Wake up! Rise to my defense!
  Take up my case, my God and my Lord.
²⁴ Declare me not guilty, O LORD my God, for
     you give justice.
  Don't let my enemies laugh about me in
     my troubles.
²⁵ Don't let them say, "Look, we got what we
     wanted!
  Now we will eat him alive!"

²⁶ May those who rejoice at my troubles
     be humiliated and disgraced.
  May those who triumph over me
     be covered with shame and dishonor.
²⁷ But give great joy to those who came to my
     defense.
  Let them continually say, "Great is the
     LORD,
  who delights in blessing his servant with
     peace!"
²⁸ Then I will proclaim your justice,
  and I will praise you all day long.

36 For the choir director: A psalm of David, the
      servant of the LORD.

¹ Sin whispers to the wicked, deep within
     their hearts.
  They have no fear of God at all.
² In their blind conceit,
  they cannot see how wicked they
     really are.
³ Everything they say is crooked and
     deceitful.
  They refuse to act wisely or do good.
⁴ They lie awake at night, hatching sinful
     plots.
  Their actions are never good.
  They make no attempt to turn from evil.

⁵ Your unfailing love, O LORD, is as vast as the
     heavens;
  your faithfulness reaches beyond the
     clouds.
⁶ Your righteousness is like the mighty
     mountains,
  your justice like the ocean depths.
  You care for people and animals alike,
     O LORD.
⁷ How precious is your unfailing love,
     O God!

37 This psalm is a Hebrew acrostic poem; each stanza begins with
a successive letter of the Hebrew alphabet.

All humanity finds shelter
  in the shadow of your wings.
⁸ You feed them from the abundance of your
     own house,
  letting them drink from your river of
     delights.
⁹ For you are the fountain of life,
  the light by which we see.

¹⁰ Pour out your unfailing love on those who
     love you;
  give justice to those with honest hearts.
¹¹ Don't let the proud trample me
  or the wicked push me around.
¹² Look! Those who do evil have fallen!
  They are thrown down, never to rise
     again.

37 * A psalm of David.

¹ Don't worry about the wicked
  or envy those who do wrong.
² For like grass, they soon fade away.
  Like spring flowers, they soon wither.

³ Trust in the LORD and do good.
  Then you will live safely in the land and
     prosper.
⁴ Take delight in the LORD,
  and he will give you your heart's desires.

⁵ Commit everything you do to the LORD.
  Trust him, and he will help you.
⁶ He will make your innocence radiate like
     the dawn,
  and the justice of your cause will shine
     like the noonday sun.

⁷ Be still in the presence of the LORD,
  and wait patiently for him to act.
  Don't worry about evil people who prosper
  or fret about their wicked schemes.

⁸ Stop being angry!
  Turn from your rage!
  Do not lose your temper—
  it only leads to harm.
⁹ For the wicked will be destroyed,

··

SHORT-TERM AND LONG-TERM REWARDS
*(37:1-40) Like David, have you ever worried when people
seem to prosper by their evil acts while kind people
suffer? Maybe you're wondering what the advantage
of being good is when you see bad behavior rewarded.
The rewards for those who do evil are short lived while
those who stick with God have long-term rewards. In
other words, they're getting theirs now, but you'll get
yours later. An eternal reward awaits you, but only eternal
destruction awaits those who do evil.*

but those who trust in the Lord will
    possess the land.

10 Soon the wicked will disappear.
    Though you look for them, they will
    be gone.
11 The lowly will possess the land
    and will live in peace and prosperity.

12 The wicked plot against the godly;
    they snarl at them in defiance.
13 But the Lord just laughs,
    for he sees their day of judgment coming.

14 The wicked draw their swords
    and string their bows
to kill the poor and the oppressed,
    to slaughter those who do right.
15 But their swords will stab their
    own hearts,
    and their bows will be broken.

16 It is better to be godly and have little
    than to be evil and rich.
17 For the strength of the wicked will be
    shattered,
    but the Lord takes care of the godly.

18 Day by day the Lord takes care of the
    innocent,
    and they will receive an inheritance that
    lasts forever.
19 They will not be disgraced in hard times;
    even in famine they will have more than
    enough.

20 But the wicked will die.
    The Lord's enemies are like flowers in
    a field—
    they will disappear like smoke.

21 The wicked borrow and never repay,
    but the godly are generous givers.
22 Those the Lord blesses will possess
    the land,
    but those he curses will die.

23 The Lord directs the steps of the godly.
    He delights in every detail of their lives.
24 Though they stumble, they will never fall,
    for the Lord holds them by the hand.

25 Once I was young, and now I am old.
    Yet I have never seen the godly
    abandoned
    or their children begging for bread.
26 The godly always give generous loans
    to others,
    and their children are a blessing.

27 Turn from evil and do good,
    and you will live in the land forever.

28 For the Lord loves justice,
    and he will never abandon the godly.

He will keep them safe forever,
    but the children of the wicked will die.
29 The godly will possess the land
    and will live there forever.

30 The godly offer good counsel;
    they teach right from wrong.
31 They have made God's law their own,
    so they will never slip from his path.

32 The wicked wait in ambush for the godly,
    looking for an excuse to kill them.
33 But the Lord will not let the wicked succeed
    or let the godly be condemned when they
    are put on trial.

34 Put your hope in the Lord.
    Travel steadily along his path.
He will honor you by giving you the land.
    You will see the wicked destroyed.

35 I have seen wicked and ruthless people
    flourishing like a tree in its native soil.
36 But when I looked again, they were gone!
    Though I searched for them, I could not
    find them!

37 Look at those who are honest and good,
    for a wonderful future awaits those who
    love peace.
38 But the rebellious will be destroyed;
    they have no future.

39 The Lord rescues the godly;
    he is their fortress in times of trouble.
40 The Lord helps them,
    rescuing them from the wicked.
He saves them,
    and they find shelter in him.

38

*A psalm of David, asking God to
remember him.*

1 O Lord, don't rebuke me in your anger
    or discipline me in your rage!
2 Your arrows have struck deep,
    and your blows are crushing me.
3 Because of your anger, my whole body is
    sick;
    my health is broken because of my sins.
4 My guilt overwhelms me—
    it is a burden too heavy to bear.
5 My wounds fester and stink
    because of my foolish sins.
6 I am bent over and racked with pain.
    All day long I walk around filled with grief.
7 A raging fever burns within me,
    and my health is broken.

8 I am exhausted and completely crushed.
   My groans come from an anguished
      heart.

9 You know what I long for, Lord;
   you hear my every sigh.
10 My heart beats wildly, my strength fails,
   and I am going blind.
11 My loved ones and friends stay away,
      fearing my disease.
   Even my own family stands at a distance.
12 Meanwhile, my enemies lay traps to kill me.
   Those who wish me harm make plans to
      ruin me.
   All day long they plan their treachery.

13 But I am deaf to all their threats.
   I am silent before them as one who
      cannot speak.
14 I choose to hear nothing,
   and I make no reply.
15 For I am waiting for you, O Lord.
   You must answer for me, O Lord my God.
16 I prayed, "Don't let my enemies gloat
      over me
   or rejoice at my downfall."

17 I am on the verge of collapse,
   facing constant pain.
18 But I confess my sins;
   I am deeply sorry for what I have done.
19 I have many aggressive enemies;
   they hate me without reason.
20 They repay me evil for good
   and oppose me for pursuing good.
21 Do not abandon me, O Lord.
   Do not stand at a distance, my God.
22 Come quickly to help me,
   O Lord my savior.

39 *For Jeduthun, the choir director: A psalm of David.*

1 I said to myself, "I will watch what I do
   and not sin in what I say.
   I will hold my tongue
      when the ungodly are around me."
2 But as I stood there in silence—
   not even speaking of good things—
   the turmoil within me grew worse.
3 The more I thought about it,
   the hotter I got,
      igniting a fire of words:
4 "Lord, remind me how brief my time on
      earth will be.
   Remind me that my days are numbered—
      how fleeting my life is.
5 You have made my life no longer than the
      width of my hand.

My entire lifetime is just a moment to you;
   at best, each of us is but a breath."
                                          Interlude

6 We are merely moving shadows,
   and all our busy rushing ends in nothing.
   We heap up wealth,
      not knowing who will spend it.
7 And so, Lord, where do I put my hope?
   My only hope is in you.
8 Rescue me from my rebellion.
   Do not let fools mock me.
9 I am silent before you; I won't say a word,
   for my punishment is from you.
10 But please stop striking me!
   I am exhausted by the blows from
      your hand.
11 When you discipline us for our sins,
   you consume like a moth what is
      precious to us.
   Each of us is but a breath.   *Interlude*

12 Hear my prayer, O Lord!
   Listen to my cries for help!
   Don't ignore my tears.
   For I am your guest—
      a traveler passing through,
   as my ancestors were before me.
13 Leave me alone so I can smile again
   before I am gone and exist no more.

40 *For the choir director: A psalm of David.*

1 I waited patiently for the Lord to help me,
   and he turned to me and heard my cry.
2 He lifted me out of the pit of despair,
   out of the mud and the mire.
   He set my feet on solid ground
   and steadied me as I walked along.
3 He has given me a new song to sing,
   a hymn of praise to our God.
   Many will see what he has done and be
      amazed.
   They will put their trust in the Lord.

4 Oh, the joys of those who trust the Lord,
   who have no confidence in the proud
   or in those who worship idols.

· ·

DON'T PUT IT OFF
(39:4) David acknowledged the brevity of life. Life is
short no matter how long we live. Maybe that's why
procrastination is such a thief of time. We put off telling
people how much they matter to us. We put off doing that
research paper until the day before it's due. Some of us
realize too late how short life is. But David's warning
about the brevity of life is an antidote to the virus of procrastination. What decisions or other important actions
are you putting off? Life is short. Time is running out.

⁵ O LORD my God, you have performed many
        wonders for us.
      Your plans for us are too numerous to list.
      You have no equal.
    If I tried to recite all your wonderful deeds,
      I would never come to the end of them.

⁶ You take no delight in sacrifices or offerings.
      Now that you have made me listen,
        I finally understand*—
      you don't require burnt offerings or sin
        offerings.
⁷ Then I said, "Look, I have come.
      As is written about me in the Scriptures:
⁸ I take joy in doing your will, my God,
      for your instructions are written on my
        heart."

⁹ I have told all your people about your
        justice.
      I have not been afraid to speak out,
        as you, O LORD, well know.
¹⁰ I have not kept the good news of your
        justice hidden in my heart;
      I have talked about your faithfulness
        and saving power.
    I have told everyone in the great
        assembly
      of your unfailing love and
        faithfulness.

¹¹ LORD, don't hold back your tender mercies
        from me.
      Let your unfailing love and faithfulness
        always protect me.
¹² For troubles surround me—
        too many to count!
    My sins pile up so high
      I can't see my way out.
    They outnumber the hairs on my head.
      I have lost all courage.

¹³ Please, LORD, rescue me!
      Come quickly, LORD, and help me.
¹⁴ May those who try to destroy me
      be humiliated and put to shame.
    May those who take delight in my trouble
      be turned back in disgrace.
¹⁵ Let them be horrified by their shame,
      for they said, "Aha! We've got him now!"

¹⁶ But may all who search for you
      be filled with joy and gladness in you.
    May those who love your salvation
      repeatedly shout, "The LORD is great!"
¹⁷ As for me, since I am poor and needy,
      let the Lord keep me in his thoughts.
    You are my helper and my savior.
      O my God, do not delay.

41
For the choir director: A psalm of David.

¹ Oh, the joys of those who are kind to the
        poor!
      The LORD rescues them when they are in
        trouble.
² The LORD protects them
      and keeps them alive.
    He gives them prosperity in the land
      and rescues them from their enemies.
³ The LORD nurses them when they are sick
      and restores them to health.

⁴ "O LORD," I prayed, "have mercy on me.
      Heal me, for I have sinned against you."
⁵ But my enemies say nothing but evil
        about me.
      "How soon will he die and be forgotten?"
        they ask.
⁶ They visit me as if they were my friends,
      but all the while they gather gossip,
      and when they leave, they spread it
        everywhere.
⁷ All who hate me whisper about me,
      imagining the worst.
⁸ "He has some fatal disease," they say.
      "He will never get out of that bed!"
⁹ Even my best friend, the one I trusted
        completely,
      the one who shared my food, has turned
        against me.

¹⁰ LORD, have mercy on me.
      Make me well again, so I can pay them
        back!
¹¹ I know you are pleased with me,
      for you have not let my enemies triumph
        over me.
¹² You have preserved my life because I am
        innocent;
      you have brought me into your presence
        forever.

¹³ Praise the LORD, the God of Israel,
      who lives from everlasting to everlasting.
    Amen and amen!

BOOK TWO (Psalms 42–72)

42
For the choir director: A psalm of the
descendants of Korah.*

¹ As the deer longs for streams of water,
      so I long for you, O God.
² I thirst for God, the living God.
      When can I go and stand before him?
³ Day and night I have only tears for food,

40:6 Greek version reads *You have given me a body.* Compare Heb 10:5.
42:TITLE Hebrew *maskil.* This may be a literary or musical term.

while my enemies continually taunt me,
  saying,
  "Where is this God of yours?"

⁴ My heart is breaking
  as I remember how it used to be:
I walked among the crowds of worshipers,
  leading a great procession to the house
    of God,
singing for joy and giving thanks
  amid the sound of a great celebration!

⁵ Why am I discouraged?
  Why is my heart so sad?
I will put my hope in God!
  I will praise him again—
  my Savior and ⁶my God!

Now I am deeply discouraged,
  but I will remember you—
even from distant Mount Hermon, the
    source of the Jordan,
  from the land of Mount Mizar.
⁷ I hear the tumult of the raging seas
  as your waves and surging tides sweep
    over me.
⁸ But each day the LORD pours his unfailing
    love upon me,
  and through each night I sing his songs,
    praying to God who gives me life.

⁹ "O God my rock," I cry,
  "why have you forgotten me?
Why must I wander around in grief,
  oppressed by my enemies?"
¹⁰ Their taunts break my bones.
  They scoff, "Where is this God of yours?"

¹¹ Why am I discouraged?
  Why is my heart so sad?
I will put my hope in God!
  I will praise him again—
  my Savior and my God!

43

¹Declare me innocent, O God!
  Defend me against these ungodly
    people.
  Rescue me from these unjust liars.
² For you are God, my only safe haven.
  Why have you tossed me aside?
Why must I wander around in grief,
  oppressed by my enemies?
³ Send out your light and your truth;
  let them guide me.
Let them lead me to your holy mountain,
  to the place where you live.

⁴ There I will go to the altar of God,
  to God—the source of all my joy.
I will praise you with my harp,
  O God, my God!

⁵ Why am I discouraged?
  Why is my heart so sad?
I will put my hope in God!
  I will praise him again—
  my Savior and my God!

44

For the choir director: A psalm* of the
descendants of Korah.

¹ O God, we have heard it with our
    own ears—
  our ancestors have told us
of all you did in their day,
  in days long ago:
² You drove out the pagan nations by your
    power
  and gave all the land to our ancestors.
You crushed their enemies
  and set our ancestors free.
³ They did not conquer the land with their
    swords;
  it was not their own strong arm that gave
    them victory.
It was your right hand and strong arm
  and the blinding light from your face that
    helped them,
  for you loved them.

⁴ You are my King and my God.
  You command victories for Israel.*
⁵ Only by your power can we push back our
    enemies;
  only in your name can we trample our
    foes.
⁶ I do not trust in my bow;
  I do not count on my sword to save me.
⁷ You are the one who gives us victory over
    our enemies;
  you disgrace those who hate us.
⁸ O God, we give glory to you all day long
  and constantly praise your name.
  Interlude

44:TITLE Hebrew *maskil*. This may be a literary or musical term.
44:4 Hebrew *for Jacob*. The names "Jacob" and "Israel" are often
interchanged throughout the Old Testament, referring sometimes
to the individual patriarch and sometimes to the nation.

··

DEPRESSION
*(42:1-11) After being carried away from Jerusalem by
an invading army, the psalm writer was understandably
depressed. Many of us can relate to feelings of depression. One cure for the blues is to think about what God
has done in the past for his people. This will take your
mind off the present negative situation and give hope that
it will improve. It will focus your thoughts on God's ability
to help you rather than on your ability to help yourself.
When you feel depressed, take advantage of this psalm's
antidepressant. It's a sure cure for the blues.*

⁹ But now you have tossed us aside in
      dishonor.
   You no longer lead our armies to battle.
¹⁰ You make us retreat from our enemies
      and allow those who hate us to plunder
      our land.
¹¹ You have butchered us like sheep
      and scattered us among the nations.
¹² You sold your precious people for a
      pittance,
   making nothing on the sale.
¹³ You let our neighbors mock us.
   We are an object of scorn and derision to
      those around us.
¹⁴ You have made us the butt of their jokes;
   they shake their heads at us in scorn.
¹⁵ We can't escape the constant humiliation;
   shame is written across our faces.
¹⁶ All we hear are the taunts of our mockers.
   All we see are our vengeful enemies.

¹⁷ All this has happened though we have not
      forgotten you.
   We have not violated your covenant.
¹⁸ Our hearts have not deserted you.
   We have not strayed from your path.
¹⁹ Yet you have crushed us in the jackal's
      desert home.
   You have covered us with darkness
      and death.

²⁰ If we had forgotten the name of our God
      or spread our hands in prayer to
      foreign gods,
²¹ God would surely have known it,
   for he knows the secrets of every heart.
²² But for your sake we are killed every day;
   we are being slaughtered like sheep.

²³ Wake up, O Lord! Why do you sleep?
   Get up! Do not reject us forever.
²⁴ Why do you look the other way?

Why do you ignore our suffering and
   oppression?
²⁵ We collapse in the dust,
   lying face down in the dirt.
²⁶ Rise up! Help us!
   Ransom us because of your unfailing
      love.

45 *For the choir director: A love song to be
     sung to the tune "Lilies." A psalm* of the
descendants of Korah.*

¹ Beautiful words stir my heart.
   I will recite a lovely poem about the king,
   for my tongue is like the pen of a skillful
      poet.

² You are the most handsome of all.
   Gracious words stream from your lips.
   God himself has blessed you forever.
³ Put on your sword, O mighty warrior!
   You are so glorious, so majestic!
⁴ In your majesty, ride out to victory,
   defending truth, humility, and justice.
   Go forth to perform awe-inspiring deeds!
⁵ Your arrows are sharp, piercing your
      enemies' hearts.
   The nations fall beneath your feet.

⁶ Your throne, O God,* endures forever
      and ever.
   You rule with a scepter of justice.
⁷ You love justice and hate evil.
   Therefore God, your God, has
      anointed you,
   pouring out the oil of joy on you more
      than on anyone else.
⁸ Myrrh, aloes, and cassia perfume your
      robes.
   In ivory palaces the music of strings
      entertains you.
⁹ Kings' daughters are among your noble
      women.
   At your right side stands the queen,
   wearing jewelry of finest gold from Ophir!

¹⁰ Listen to me, O royal daughter; take to heart
      what I say.
   Forget your people and your family far
      away.
¹¹ For your royal husband delights in your
      beauty;
   honor him, for he is your lord.
¹² The princess of Tyre* will shower you with
      gifts.
   The wealthy will beg your favor.
¹³ The bride, a princess, looks glorious

CONSTANT LOVE
*(44:22-26) After a defeat by Israel's enemies, the writer
cried to God to save his people by his constant love. When
you're in trouble, what truths do you hold on to? Like the
psalmist, you can hold on to the fact that God's love will
never change. Nothing can separate us from God's love,
not even death (see Rom 8:35-39).*

CONFIDENCE
*(46:1-3) Even in the face of utter destruction, the psalm-
ist expressed a quiet confidence in God's ability to save
him. The fear of mountains or cities suddenly crumbling
because of a nuclear blast haunts many people today.
Facing destruction or terrorism without fear seems impossible. Yet the Bible is clear: God is our eternal refuge,
even in the face of total destruction. Like the psalm writer,
would you confidently say, "[I] will not fear," even if the
world seems to crumble around you?*

45:TITLE Hebrew *maskil*. This may be a literary or musical term.
45:6 Or *Your divine throne.*   45:12 Hebrew *The daughter of Tyre.*

in her golden gown.

¹⁴ In her beautiful robes, she is led to the king,
accompanied by her bridesmaids.

¹⁵ What a joyful and enthusiastic procession
as they enter the king's palace!

¹⁶ Your sons will become kings like their
father.
You will make them rulers over many
lands.

¹⁷ I will bring honor to your name in every
generation.
Therefore, the nations will praise you
forever and ever.

46

For the choir director: A song of the descendants of Korah, to be sung by soprano voices.*

¹ God is our refuge and strength,
always ready to help in times of trouble.

² So we will not fear when earthquakes come
and the mountains crumble into the sea.

³ Let the oceans roar and foam.
Let the mountains tremble as the waters
surge!
Interlude

⁴ A river brings joy to the city of our God,
the sacred home of the Most High.

⁵ God dwells in that city; it cannot be
destroyed.
From the very break of day, God will
protect it.

⁶ The nations are in chaos,
and their kingdoms crumble!
God's voice thunders,
and the earth melts!

⁷ The LORD of Heaven's Armies is here
among us;
the God of Israel* is our fortress.
Interlude

⁸ Come, see the glorious works of the LORD:
See how he brings destruction upon the
world.

⁹ He causes wars to end throughout the
earth.
He breaks the bow and snaps the spear;
he burns the shields with fire.

¹⁰ "Be still, and know that I am God!
I will be honored by every nation.
I will be honored throughout the world."

¹¹ The LORD of Heaven's Armies is here
among us;
the God of Israel is our fortress. *Interlude*

46:TITLE Hebrew *according to alamoth.* **46:7** Hebrew *of Jacob;* also
in 46:11. See note on 44:4. **47:7** Hebrew *maskil.* This may be a
literary or musical term.

MY STORY: Jodi

Everything was going wrong in my life. My parents were getting a divorce. My boyfriend broke up with me. I couldn't concentrate in school, so my grades started going down.

My faith was affected, too. I couldn't understand why God was allowing all this to happen to me. When I prayed, I felt like I was talking to myself. I guess I was mad at God, blaming him in my heart for the things that were happening.

I tried to read the Bible anyway, even though I was struggling spiritually. One day I read Psalm 46. Verse 10 really made me stop and think. This verse seemed to say, "Stop looking at your problems and look at me. Look at who I am." I realized God was in charge—he knew exactly what he was doing and had a purpose in mind for what I was going through. I just needed to accept it and believe he is a loving God who would never deliberately hurt me.

That changed my perspective. Instead of blaming God, I asked him to help me through my struggles. And he has. Things are still rough sometimes, but now I know that God is for me, and he will work things out for good. As Romans 8:31 says, "If God is for us, who can ever be against us?"

47

For the choir director: A psalm of the descendants of Korah.

¹ Come, everyone! Clap your hands!
Shout to God with joyful praise!

² For the LORD Most High is awesome.
He is the great King of all the earth.

³ He subdues the nations before us,
putting our enemies beneath our feet.

⁴ He chose the Promised Land as our
inheritance,
the proud possession of Jacob's
descendants, whom he loves.
Interlude

⁵ God has ascended with a mighty shout.
The LORD has ascended with trumpets
blaring.

⁶ Sing praises to God, sing praises;
sing praises to our King, sing praises!

⁷ For God is the King over all the earth.
Praise him with a psalm.*

⁸ God reigns above the nations,
    sitting on his holy throne.
⁹ The rulers of the world have gathered
        together
    with the people of the God of Abraham.
For all the kings of the earth belong to God.
    He is highly honored everywhere.

48

A song. A psalm of the descendants of Korah.

¹ How great is the LORD,
    how deserving of praise,
in the city of our God,
    which sits on his holy mountain!
² It is high and magnificent;
    the whole earth rejoices to see it!
Mount Zion, the holy mountain,*
    is the city of the great King!
³ God himself is in Jerusalem's towers,
    revealing himself as its defender.

⁴ The kings of the earth joined forces
    and advanced against the city.
⁵ But when they saw it, they were stunned;
    they were terrified and ran away.
⁶ They were gripped with terror
    and writhed in pain like a woman in labor.
⁷ You destroyed them like the mighty ships of
        Tarshish
    shattered by a powerful east wind.

⁸ We had heard of the city's glory,
    but now we have seen it ourselves—
    the city of the LORD of Heaven's Armies.
It is the city of our God;
    he will make it safe forever.   *Interlude*

⁹ O God, we meditate on your unfailing love
    as we worship in your Temple.
¹⁰ As your name deserves, O God,
    you will be praised to the ends of the
        earth.
    Your strong right hand is filled with
        victory.
¹¹ Let the people on Mount Zion rejoice.
    Let all the towns of Judah be glad
    because of your justice.

¹² Go, inspect the city of Jerusalem.*
    Walk around and count the many towers.

¹³ Take note of the fortified walls,
    and tour all the citadels,
that you may describe them
    to future generations.
¹⁴ For that is what God is like.
    He is our God forever and ever,
    and he will guide us until we die.

49

For the choir director: A psalm of the descendants of Korah.

¹ Listen to this, all you people!
    Pay attention, everyone in the world!
² High and low,
    rich and poor—listen!
³ For my words are wise,
    and my thoughts are filled with insight.
⁴ I listen carefully to many proverbs
    and solve riddles with inspiration from
        a harp.

⁵ Why should I fear when trouble comes,
    when enemies surround me?
⁶ They trust in their wealth
    and boast of great riches.
⁷ Yet they cannot redeem themselves from
        death*
    by paying a ransom to God.
⁸ Redemption does not come so easily,
    for no one can ever pay enough
⁹ to live forever
    and never see the grave.

¹⁰ Those who are wise must finally die,
    just like the foolish and senseless,
    leaving all their wealth behind.
¹¹ The grave is their eternal home,
    where they will stay forever.
They may name their estates after
        themselves,
¹²   but their fame will not last.
    They will die, just like animals.
¹³ This is the fate of fools,
    though they are remembered
    as being wise.*   *Interlude*

¹⁴ Like sheep, they are led to the grave,*
    where death will be their shepherd.
In the morning the godly will rule over them.
    Their bodies will rot in the grave,
    far from their grand estates.
¹⁵ But as for me, God will redeem my life.
    He will snatch me from the power
    of the grave.   *Interlude*

¹⁶ So don't be dismayed when the wicked
        grow rich

THE GUIDE
(48:14) *We often pray for God's guidance as we struggle with decisions. What we need is both guidance and a guide—a map that gives us landmarks and directions and a constant companion who has an intimate knowledge of the way. A guide can also make sure that we interpret the map correctly. The Bible is just such a map, and God is a constant companion and guide. Is he yours?*

48:2 Or *Mount Zion, in the far north;* Hebrew reads *Mount Zion, the heights of Zaphon.*   **48:12** Hebrew *Zion.*   **49:7** Or *no one can redeem the life of another.*   **49:13** The meaning of the Hebrew is uncertain.   **49:14** Hebrew *Sheol;* also in 49:14b, 15.

and their homes become ever more
   splendid.
¹⁷ For when they die, they take nothing with
      them.
   Their wealth will not follow them into
      the grave.
¹⁸ In this life they consider themselves
      fortunate
   and are applauded for their success.
¹⁹ But they will die like all before them
   and never again see the light of day.
²⁰ People who boast of their wealth don't
      understand;
   they will die, just like animals.

50 *A psalm of Asaph.*

¹ The Lord, the Mighty One, is God,
   and he has spoken;
   he has summoned all humanity
      from where the sun rises to where
      it sets.
² From Mount Zion, the perfection of beauty,
   God shines in glorious radiance.
³ Our God approaches,
   and he is not silent.
   Fire devours everything in his way,
   and a great storm rages around him.
⁴ He calls on the heavens above and earth
      below
   to witness the judgment of his people.
⁵ "Bring my faithful people to me—
   those who made a covenant with me by
      giving sacrifices."
⁶ Then let the heavens proclaim his justice,
   for God himself will be the judge.

                                        Interlude

⁷ "O my people, listen as I speak.
   Here are my charges against you, O Israel:
   I am God, your God!
⁸ I have no complaint about your sacrifices
   or the burnt offerings you constantly offer.
⁹ But I do not need the bulls from your barns
   or the goats from your pens.
¹⁰ For all the animals of the forest are mine,
   and I own the cattle on a thousand hills.
¹¹ I know every bird on the mountains,
   and all the animals of the field are mine.
¹² If I were hungry, I would not tell you,
   for all the world is mine and everything
      in it.
¹³ Do I eat the meat of bulls?
   Do I drink the blood of goats?
¹⁴ Make thankfulness your sacrifice to God,

and keep the vows you made to the
   Most High.
¹⁵ Then call on me when you are in trouble,
   and I will rescue you,
   and you will give me glory."

¹⁶ But God says to the wicked:
   "Why bother reciting my decrees
   and pretending to obey my covenant?
¹⁷ For you refuse my discipline
   and treat my words like trash.
¹⁸ When you see thieves, you approve of them,
   and you spend your time with adulterers.
¹⁹ Your mouth is filled with wickedness,
   and your tongue is full of lies.
²⁰ You sit around and slander your brother—
   your own mother's son.
²¹ While you did all this, I remained silent,
   and you thought I didn't care.
   But now I will rebuke you,
   listing all my charges against you.
²² Repent, all of you who forget me,
   or I will tear you apart,
   and no one will help you.
²³ But giving thanks is a sacrifice that truly
      honors me.
   If you keep to my path,
   I will reveal to you the salvation of God."

51 *For the choir director: A psalm of David,
    regarding the time Nathan the prophet
came to him after David had committed adultery
with Bathsheba.*

¹ Have mercy on me, O God,
   because of your unfailing love.
   Because of your great compassion,
   blot out the stain of my sins.
² Wash me clean from my guilt.
   Purify me from my sin.
³ For I recognize my rebellion;
   it haunts me day and night.
⁴ Against you, and you alone, have I sinned;
   I have done what is evil in your sight.
   You will be proved right in what you say,
   and your judgment against me is just.*
⁵ For I was born a sinner—

51:4 Greek version reads *and you will win your case in court.*
Compare Rom 3:4.

AN ISOLATED INCIDENT?
(51:4) Although David sinned with Bathsheba, he said he
had sinned against God. When someone steals, murders,
or lies, he or she hurts someone else. According to the
world's standards today, sex between two consenting
adults is acceptable because nobody gets hurt. But
people do get hurt. In David's case, a man was murdered
and a baby died. When we blow it, we hurt ourselves,
God, and others. Makes you want to think before you act,
doesn't it?

yes, from the moment my mother
  conceived me.
6 But you desire honesty from the womb,*
  teaching me wisdom even there.

7 Purify me from my sins,* and I will be clean;
  wash me, and I will be whiter than snow.
8 Oh, give me back my joy again;
  you have broken me—
  now let me rejoice.
9 Don't keep looking at my sins.
  Remove the stain of my guilt.
10 Create in me a clean heart, O God.
  Renew a loyal spirit within me.
11 Do not banish me from your presence,
  and don't take your Holy Spirit* from me.

12 Restore to me the joy of your salvation,
  and make me willing to obey you.
13 Then I will teach your ways to rebels,
  and they will return to you.
14 Forgive me for shedding blood, O God who
  saves;
  then I will joyfully sing of your
  forgiveness.
15 Unseal my lips, O Lord,
  that my mouth may praise you.

16 You do not desire a sacrifice, or I would
  offer one.
  You do not want a burnt offering.
17 The sacrifice you desire is a broken spirit.
  You will not reject a broken and repentant
  heart, O God.
18 Look with favor on Zion and help her;
  rebuild the walls of Jerusalem.
19 Then you will be pleased with sacrifices
  offered in the right spirit—

with burnt offerings and whole burnt
  offerings.
Then bulls will again be sacrificed on
  your altar.

52 *For the choir director: A psalm* of David,
regarding the time Doeg the Edomite said to
Saul, "David has gone to see Ahimelech."*

1 Why do you boast about your crimes, great
  warrior?
  Don't you realize God's justice continues
  forever?
2 All day long you plot destruction.
  Your tongue cuts like a sharp razor;
  you're an expert at telling lies.
3 You love evil more than good
  and lies more than truth.   *Interlude*

4 You love to destroy others with your words,
  you liar!
5 But God will strike you down once and
  for all.
  He will pull you from your home
  and uproot you from the land of the living.
                                      Interlude

6 The righteous will see it and be amazed.
  They will laugh and say,
7 "Look what happens to mighty warriors
  who do not trust in God.
  They trust their wealth instead
  and grow more and more bold in their
  wickedness."

51:6 Or *from the heart;* Hebrew reads *in the inward parts.*
51:7 Hebrew *Purify me with the hyssop branch.*   **51:11** Or *your spirit
of holiness.*   **52:TITLE** Hebrew *maskil.* This may be a literary or
musical term.

I WONDER...

Is there any sin that God will not forgive?

Second Samuel 12:1-23 records the incident that
caused King David to pray the prayer of Psalm 51.
David not only committed adultery, but he had the
woman's husband murdered so he could marry
her! That's pretty bad behavior for anyone, let alone
a king.

  When confronted with his sin a year after those
events, David repented. He asked God to forgive him
and to renew their relationship once again.

  Though David's sins were great, God forgave him.
God is always willing to forgive those who admit their
mistakes and who genuinely try not to repeat them.

  The only sin that cannot be forgiven is when someone refuses to receive Christ, ignoring or rejecting the
Holy Spirit's work in his or her life. This is referred to

as blasphemy against the Holy Spirit. It is rejection of
God and refusal to accept his forgiveness. Jesus talks
about this in Matthew 12:31-32.

  The good news is God did not leave us on our
own. He sent Jesus to pay the penalty for us and
to die in our place. This way he killed sin forever. All
who receive Christ into their lives and accept his gift
of forgiveness are forgiven—period (John 1:12).

  By daily coming to God in humility, trust, and
dependence, we show him that we mean business in
keeping our relationship with him clean and growing.
This daily turning to God is the opposite of blaspheming the Holy Spirit. We're inviting the Holy Spirit into
our lives.

  David's prayer is the perfect example of a humble
heart seeking after the only thing in life that really
matters: God.

8 But I am like an olive tree, thriving in the
   house of God.
  I will always trust in God's unfailing love.
9 I will praise you forever, O God,
   for what you have done.
  I will trust in your good name
   in the presence of your faithful people.

53

*For the choir director: A meditation;
a psalm* of David.*

1 Only fools say in their hearts,
   "There is no God."
  They are corrupt, and their actions are evil;
   not one of them does good!

2 God looks down from heaven
   on the entire human race;
  he looks to see if anyone is truly wise,
   if anyone seeks God.
3 But no, all have turned away;
   all have become corrupt.*
  No one does good,
   not a single one!

4 Will those who do evil never learn?
   They eat up my people like bread
   and wouldn't think of praying to God.
5 Terror will grip them,
   terror like they have never known before.
  God will scatter the bones of your enemies.
   You will put them to shame, for God has
   rejected them.

6 Who will come from Mount Zion to rescue
   Israel?
  When God restores his people,
   Jacob will shout with joy, and Israel will
   rejoice.

54

For the choir director: A psalm of David,
regarding the time the Ziphites came and
said to Saul, "We know where David is hiding."
To be accompanied by stringed instruments.*

1 Come with great power, O God, and rescue
   me!
  Defend me with your might.
2 Listen to my prayer, O God.
   Pay attention to my plea.
3 For strangers are attacking me;
   violent people are trying to kill me.
  They care nothing for God.   *Interlude*

4 But God is my helper.
  The Lord keeps me alive!

5 May the evil plans of my enemies be turned
   against them.
  Do as you promised and put an end to
   them.
6 I will sacrifice a voluntary offering to you;
   I will praise your name, O LORD,
   for it is good.
7 For you have rescued me from my troubles
   and helped me to triumph over my
   enemies.

55

For the choir director: A psalm of David, to
be accompanied by stringed instruments.*

1 Listen to my prayer, O God.
   Do not ignore my cry for help!
2 Please listen and answer me,
   for I am overwhelmed by my troubles.
3 My enemies shout at me,
   making loud and wicked threats.
  They bring trouble on me
   and angrily hunt me down.

4 My heart pounds in my chest.
   The terror of death assaults me.
5 Fear and trembling overwhelm me,
   and I can't stop shaking.
6 Oh, that I had wings like a dove;
   then I would fly away and rest!
7 I would fly far away
   to the quiet of the wilderness.   *Interlude*
8 How quickly I would escape—
   far from this wild storm of hatred.

9 Confuse them, Lord, and frustrate their
   plans,
  for I see violence and conflict in the city.
10 Its walls are patrolled day and night against
   invaders,
  but the real danger is wickedness within
   the city.
11 Everything is falling apart;
   threats and cheating are rampant in the
   streets.

12 It is not an enemy who taunts me—
   I could bear that.

....

FOOLS

(53:1) Echoing the message of Psalm 14, David proclaimed that "only fools say in their hearts, 'There is no
God.'" People may say there is no God in order to hide
what they do, to have an excuse to continue doing what
they're doing, or to ignore the Judge and avoid the judgment. A "fool" is not necessarily lacking intelligence;
many atheists have some seriously high IQs. They believe
that Christians are foolish in their beliefs. But according
to God, fools are people who reject God, the only one who
can save them.

53:TITLE Hebrew *According to mahalath; a maskil*. These may be
literary or musical terms.   53:3 Greek version reads *have become
useless*. Compare Rom 3:12.   54:TITLE Hebrew *maskil*. This may be
a literary or musical term.   55:TITLE Hebrew *maskil*. This may
be a literary or musical term.

It is not my foes who so arrogantly
    insult me—
I could have hidden from them.
[13] Instead, it is you—my equal,
    my companion and close friend.
[14] What good fellowship we once enjoyed
    as we walked together to the house
        of God.

[15] Let death stalk my enemies;
    let the grave* swallow them alive,
    for evil makes its home within them.

[16] But I will call on God,
    and the LORD will rescue me.
[17] Morning, noon, and night
    I cry out in my distress,
    and the LORD hears my voice.
[18] He ransoms me and keeps me safe
    from the battle waged against me,
    though many still oppose me.
[19] God, who has ruled forever,
    will hear me and humble them.   *Interlude*
For my enemies refuse to change their ways;
    they do not fear God.

[20] As for my companion, he betrayed his
        friends;
    he broke his promises.
[21] His words are as smooth as butter,
    but in his heart is war.
His words are as soothing as lotion,
    but underneath are daggers!

[22] Give your burdens to the LORD,
    and he will take care of you.
He will not permit the godly to slip
    and fall.

[23] But you, O God, will send the wicked
    down to the pit of destruction.
Murderers and liars will die young,
    but I am trusting you to save me.

56 *For the choir director: A psalm* of David,
regarding the time the Philistines seized
him in Gath. To be sung to the tune "Dove on
Distant Oaks."*

[1] O God, have mercy on me,
    for people are hounding me.
    My foes attack me all day long.

REAL FRIENDS
*(55:12-14) Nothing hurts as much as a wound from a
friend. Real friends, however, stick by you in times of
trouble and offer love, acceptance, and understanding. At
times our friends will lovingly confront us, but their motive
will be to help. Would your friends describe you as faithful
or fickle?*

[2] I am constantly hounded by those who
        slander me,
    and many are boldly attacking me.
[3] But when I am afraid,
    I will put my trust in you.
[4] I praise God for what he has promised.
    I trust in God, so why should I be afraid?
    What can mere mortals do to me?

[5] They are always twisting what I say;
    they spend their days plotting to
        harm me.
[6] They come together to spy on me—
    watching my every step, eager to kill me.
[7] Don't let them get away with their
        wickedness;
    in your anger, O God, bring them down.

[8] You keep track of all my sorrows.*
    You have collected all my tears in your
        bottle.
    You have recorded each one in
        your book.

[9] My enemies will retreat when I call to you
        for help.
    This I know: God is on my side!
[10] I praise God for what he has promised;
    yes, I praise the LORD for what he has
        promised.
[11] I trust in God, so why should I be afraid?
    What can mere mortals do to me?

[12] I will fulfill my vows to you, O God,
    and will offer a sacrifice of thanks for
        your help.
[13] For you have rescued me from death;
    you have kept my feet from slipping.
So now I can walk in your presence, O God,
    in your life-giving light.

57 *For the choir director: A psalm* of David,
regarding the time he fled from Saul and
went into the cave. To be sung to the tune "Do Not
Destroy!"*

[1] Have mercy on me, O God, have mercy!
    I look to you for protection.
    I will hide beneath the shadow of
        your wings
    until the danger passes by.
[2] I cry out to God Most High,*
    to God who will fulfill his purpose for me.
[3] He will send help from heaven to rescue me,
    disgracing those who hound me.
                                    Interlude

55:15 Hebrew *let Sheol.*   **56:TITLE** Hebrew *miktam.* This may
be a literary or musical term.   **56:8** Or *my wanderings.*
57:TITLE Hebrew *miktam.* This may be a literary or musical term.
57:2 Hebrew *Elohim-Elyon.*

My God will send forth his unfailing love and
faithfulness.

⁴ I am surrounded by fierce lions
who greedily devour human prey—
whose teeth pierce like spears and arrows,
and whose tongues cut like swords.

⁵ Be exalted, O God, above the highest
heavens!
May your glory shine over all the earth.

⁶ My enemies have set a trap for me.
I am weary from distress.
They have dug a deep pit in my path,
but they themselves have fallen into it.
Interlude

⁷ My heart is confident in you, O God;
my heart is confident.
No wonder I can sing your praises!
⁸ Wake up, my heart!
Wake up, O lyre and harp!
I will wake the dawn with my song.
⁹ I will thank you, Lord, among all the people.
I will sing your praises among
the nations.
¹⁰ For your unfailing love is as high as
the heavens.
Your faithfulness reaches to the clouds.

¹¹ Be exalted, O God, above the highest
heavens.
May your glory shine over all the earth.

58

For the choir director: A psalm of David,
to be sung to the tune "Do Not Destroy!"*

¹ Justice—do you rulers* know the meaning
of the word?
Do you judge the people fairly?
² No! You plot injustice in your hearts.
You spread violence throughout
the land.
³ These wicked people are born sinners;
even from birth they have lied and
gone their own way.
⁴ They spit venom like deadly snakes;
they are like cobras that refuse to listen,
⁵ ignoring the tunes of the snake charmers,
no matter how skillfully they play.

⁶ Break off their fangs, O God!
Smash the jaws of these lions, O LORD!
⁷ May they disappear like water into thirsty
ground.
Make their weapons useless in their
hands.*

58:TITLE Hebrew *miktam*. This may be a literary or musical term.
58:1 Or *you gods.*   **58:7** Or *Let them be trodden down and wither
like grass.* The meaning of the Hebrew is uncertain.

MY STORY: David

*I'll never forget the day my father collapsed
and was rushed to the hospital. The doctor
told my mother and me that he'd suffered a
severe heart attack and was now teetering
between life and death; it could go either
way. I was really scared! Standing with my
mother by his bed, I prayed harder than I'd
ever prayed before. I didn't want to lose my
dad! I thought about how my father loved
Jesus and always reached out to others, and
I couldn't believe that God would be done
with him yet. It almost seemed that God was
reassuring me of this, but I asked him for a
promise from his Word. The verse he brought
to mind was Psalm 57:1: "Have mercy on me,
O God, have mercy! I look to you for protection. I will hide beneath the shadow of your
wings until the danger passes by."*

*Through that verse, I knew that whatever
happened, God would take care of my mom
and me. I was to leave everything absolutely in God's hands and trust him for the
outcome.*

*That's what I did. And I discovered that
God is so faithful: my father did recover.
God has continued to use Dad in marvelous
ways to bring others to trust in Christ. And
I learned something invaluable about trusting God and leaving everything in his hands
when I'm facing life's storms.*

⁸ May they be like snails that dissolve into
slime,
like a stillborn child who will never see
the sun.
⁹ God will sweep them away, both young
and old,
faster than a pot heats over burning
thorns.
¹⁰ The godly will rejoice when they see
injustice avenged.
They will wash their feet in the blood
of the wicked.
¹¹ Then at last everyone will say,
"There truly is a reward for those who live
for God;
surely there is a God who judges justly
here on earth."

59

For the choir director: A psalm* of David, regarding the time Saul sent soldiers to watch David's house in order to kill him. To be sung to the tune "Do Not Destroy!"

1 Rescue me from my enemies, O God.
    Protect me from those who have come
      to destroy me.
2 Rescue me from these criminals;
    save me from these murderers.
3 They have set an ambush for me.
    Fierce enemies are out there waiting,
      Lord,
    though I have not sinned or offended
      them.
4 I have done nothing wrong,
    yet they prepare to attack me.
    Wake up! See what is happening and
      help me!
5 O Lord God of Heaven's Armies, the God
      of Israel,
    wake up and punish those hostile
      nations.
    Show no mercy to wicked traitors.
                                                    Interlude

6 They come out at night,
    snarling like vicious dogs
      as they prowl the streets.
7 Listen to the filth that comes from their
      mouths;
    their words cut like swords.
    "After all, who can hear us?" they sneer.
8 But Lord, you laugh at them.
    You scoff at all the hostile nations.
9 You are my strength; I wait for you to
      rescue me,
    for you, O God, are my fortress.
10 In his unfailing love, my God will stand
      with me.
    He will let me look down in triumph on all
      my enemies.

11 Don't kill them, for my people soon forget
      such lessons;
    stagger them with your power, and bring
      them to their knees,
    O Lord our shield.
12 Because of the sinful things they say,
    because of the evil that is on their lips,
    let them be captured by their pride,

their curses, and their lies.
13 Destroy them in your anger!
    Wipe them out completely!
    Then the whole world will know
      that God reigns in Israel.*
                                                    Interlude

14 My enemies come out at night,
    snarling like vicious dogs
      as they prowl the streets.
15 They scavenge for food
    but go to sleep unsatisfied.*

16 But as for me, I will sing about your power.
    Each morning I will sing with joy about
      your unfailing love.
    For you have been my refuge,
    a place of safety when I am in distress.
17 O my Strength, to you I sing praises,
    for you, O God, are my refuge,
    the God who shows me unfailing love.

60

For the choir director: A psalm* of David useful for teaching, regarding the time David fought Aram-naharaim and Aram-zobah, and Joab returned and killed 12,000 Edomites in the Valley of Salt. To be sung to the tune "Lily of the Testimony."

1 You have rejected us, O God, and broken
      our defenses.
    You have been angry with us; now restore
      us to your favor.
2 You have shaken our land and split it open.
    Seal the cracks, for the land trembles.
3 You have been very hard on us,
    making us drink wine that sent us reeling.
4 But you have raised a banner for those who
      fear you—
    a rallying point in the face of attack.
                                                    Interlude

5 Now rescue your beloved people.
    Answer and save us by your power.
6 God has promised this by his holiness*:
    "I will divide up Shechem with joy.
    I will measure out the valley of Succoth.
7 Gilead is mine,
    and Manasseh, too.
    Ephraim, my helmet, will produce my
      warriors,
    and Judah, my scepter, will produce
      my kings.
8 But Moab, my washbasin, will become my
      servant,
    and I will wipe my feet on Edom
    and shout in triumph over Philistia."

....

UNCHANGING
(59:1-11) While David was hunted by enemies, changes occurred daily as he ran from place to place. But David knew that he could count on God for stability even with all the changes swirling around him. Ever feel like your life is in a constant state of flux? One thing won't ever change: God's love for you. Like David, you can count on that.

59:TITLE Hebrew *miktam*. This may be a literary or musical term. **59:13** Hebrew *in Jacob*. See note on 44:4. **59:15** Or *and growl if they don't get enough.* **60:TITLE** Hebrew *miktam*. This may be a literary or musical term. **60:6** Or *in his sanctuary.*

9 Who will bring me into the fortified city?
  Who will bring me victory over Edom?
10 Have you rejected us, O God?
  Will you no longer march with our armies?
11 Oh, please help us against our enemies,
  for all human help is useless.
12 With God's help we will do mighty things,
  for he will trample down our foes.

61

For the choir director: A psalm of David, to be accompanied by stringed instruments.

1 O God, listen to my cry!
  Hear my prayer!
2 From the ends of the earth,
  I cry to you for help
  when my heart is overwhelmed.
  Lead me to the towering rock of safety,
3   for you are my safe refuge,
  a fortress where my enemies cannot
  reach me.
4 Let me live forever in your sanctuary,
  safe beneath the shelter of your wings!
                                    Interlude

5 For you have heard my vows, O God.
  You have given me an inheritance
  reserved for those who fear your name.
6 Add many years to the life of the king!
  May his years span the generations!
7 May he reign under God's protection
  forever.
  May your unfailing love and faithfulness
  watch over him.
8 Then I will sing praises to your name forever
  as I fulfill my vows each day.

62

For Jeduthun, the choir director: A psalm of David.

1 I wait quietly before God,
  for my victory comes from him.
2 He alone is my rock and my salvation,
  my fortress where I will never be shaken.

3 So many enemies against one man—
  all of them trying to kill me.
  To them I'm just a broken-down wall
  or a tottering fence.
4 They plan to topple me from my high
  position.
  They delight in telling lies about me.
  They praise me to my face
  but curse me in their hearts.   *Interlude*

5 Let all that I am wait quietly before God,
  for my hope is in him.
6 He alone is my rock and my salvation,
  my fortress where I will not be shaken.

7 My victory and honor come from God alone.
  He is my refuge, a rock where no enemy
  can reach me.
8 O my people, trust in him at all times.
  Pour out your heart to him,
  for God is our refuge.   *Interlude*

9 Common people are as worthless as a puff
  of wind,
  and the powerful are not what they
  appear to be.
  If you weigh them on the scales,
  together they are lighter than a breath
  of air.

10 Don't make your living by extortion
  or put your hope in stealing.
  And if your wealth increases,
  don't make it the center of your life.

11 God has spoken plainly,
  and I have heard it many times:
  Power, O God, belongs to you;
12   unfailing love, O Lord, is yours.
  Surely you repay all people
  according to what they have done.

63

A psalm of David, regarding a time when David was in the wilderness of Judah.

1 O God, you are my God;
  I earnestly search for you.
  My soul thirsts for you;
  my whole body longs for you
  in this parched and weary land
  where there is no water.
2 I have seen you in your sanctuary
  and gazed upon your power and glory.
3 Your unfailing love is better than life itself;
  how I praise you!
4 I will praise you as long as I live,
  lifting up my hands to you in prayer.
5 You satisfy me more than the richest feast.
  I will praise you with songs of joy.
6 I lie awake thinking of you,
  meditating on you through the night.
7 Because you are my helper,
  I sing for joy in the shadow of your wings.
8 I cling to you;
  your strong right hand holds me securely.

9 But those plotting to destroy me will come
  to ruin.

....

A COMMITMENT TO PRAISE
(61:8) David continually praised God through both the good and difficult times of his life. His commitment to praise God every day showed his respect for God. Do you have the same commitment to praise? How do you show your respect for God?

They will go down into the depths
of the earth.
¹⁰ They will die by the sword
and become the food of jackals.
¹¹ But the king will rejoice in God.
All who trust in him will praise him,
while liars will be silenced.

64 *For the choir director: A psalm of David.*

¹ O God, listen to my complaint.
Protect my life from my enemies' threats.
² Hide me from the plots of this evil mob,
from this gang of wrongdoers.
³ They sharpen their tongues like swords
and aim their bitter words like arrows.
⁴ They shoot from ambush at the innocent,
attacking suddenly and fearlessly.
⁵ They encourage each other to do evil
and plan how to set their traps in secret.
"Who will ever notice?" they ask.
⁶ As they plot their crimes, they say,
"We have devised the perfect plan!"
Yes, the human heart and mind are
cunning.

⁷ But God himself will shoot them with his
arrows,
suddenly striking them down.
⁸ Their own tongues will ruin them,
and all who see them will shake their
heads in scorn.
⁹ Then everyone will be afraid;
they will proclaim the mighty acts of God
and realize all the amazing things he
does.
¹⁰ The godly will rejoice in the LORD
and find shelter in him.
And those who do what is right
will praise him.

65 *For the choir director: A song. A psalm of David.*

¹ What mighty praise, O God,
belongs to you in Zion.
We will fulfill our vows to you,
² for you answer our prayers.
All of us must come to you.

FORGIVEN
(65:3) Although sins fill our hearts, minds, and actions, God will forgive them all if we ask sincerely. Do you feel as though God could never forgive you, that you've done too much wrong, or some of your sins are too big? Don't worry—God can and will forgive them all. Nobody is beyond redemption, and nobody is so full of sin that he or she cannot be made clean.

³ Though we are overwhelmed by our sins,
you forgive them all.
⁴ What joy for those you choose to bring near,
those who live in your holy courts.
What festivities await us
inside your holy Temple.

⁵ You faithfully answer our prayers with
awesome deeds,
O God our savior.
You are the hope of everyone on earth,
even those who sail on distant seas.
⁶ You formed the mountains by your power
and armed yourself with mighty strength.
⁷ You quieted the raging oceans
with their pounding waves
and silenced the shouting of the nations.
⁸ Those who live at the ends of the earth
stand in awe of your wonders.
From where the sun rises to where it sets,
you inspire shouts of joy.

⁹ You take care of the earth and water it,
making it rich and fertile.
The river of God has plenty of water;
it provides a bountiful harvest of grain,
for you have ordered it so.
¹⁰ You drench the plowed ground with rain,
melting the clods and leveling the ridges.
You soften the earth with showers
and bless its abundant crops.
¹¹ You crown the year with a bountiful harvest;
even the hard pathways overflow with
abundance.
¹² The grasslands of the wilderness become
a lush pasture,
and the hillsides blossom with joy.
¹³ The meadows are clothed with flocks of
sheep,
and the valleys are carpeted with grain.
They all shout and sing for joy!

66 *For the choir director: A song. A psalm.*

¹ Shout joyful praises to God, all the earth!
² Sing about the glory of his name!
Tell the world how glorious he is.
³ Say to God, "How awesome are your deeds!
Your enemies cringe before your mighty
power.
⁴ Everything on earth will worship you;
they will sing your praises,
shouting your name in glorious songs."
Interlude

⁵ Come and see what our God has done,
what awesome miracles he performs for
people!

⁶ He made a dry path through the Red Sea,*
and his people went across on foot.
There we rejoiced in him.
⁷ For by his great power he rules forever.
He watches every movement of the
nations;
let no rebel rise in defiance.   *Interlude*

⁸ Let the whole world bless our God
and loudly sing his praises.
⁹ Our lives are in his hands,
and he keeps our feet from stumbling.
¹⁰ You have tested us, O God;
you have purified us like silver.
¹¹ You captured us in your net
and laid the burden of slavery on our
backs.
¹² Then you put a leader over us.*
We went through fire and flood,
but you brought us to a place of great
abundance.

¹³ Now I come to your Temple with burnt
offerings
to fulfill the vows I made to you—
¹⁴ yes, the sacred vows that I made
when I was in deep trouble.
¹⁵ That is why I am sacrificing burnt offerings
to you—
the best of my rams as a pleasing aroma,
and a sacrifice of bulls and male goats.
Interlude

¹⁶ Come and listen, all you who fear God,
and I will tell you what he did for me.
¹⁷ For I cried out to him for help,
praising him as I spoke.
¹⁸ If I had not confessed the sin in my heart,
the Lord would not have listened.
¹⁹ But God did listen!
He paid attention to my prayer.
²⁰ Praise God, who did not ignore my prayer
or withdraw his unfailing love from me.

67 *For the choir director: A song. A psalm, to be
accompanied by stringed instruments.*

¹ May God be merciful and bless us.
May his face smile with favor on us.
Interlude

² May your ways be known throughout
the earth,
your saving power among people
everywhere.
³ May the nations praise you, O God.
Yes, may all the nations praise you.

66:6 Hebrew *the sea.*   **66:12** Or *You made people ride over our
heads.*

⁴ Let the whole world sing for joy,
because you govern the nations with
justice
and guide the people of the whole world.
Interlude

⁵ May the nations praise you, O God.
Yes, may all the nations praise you.
⁶ Then the earth will yield its harvests,
and God, our God, will richly bless us.
⁷ Yes, God will bless us,
and people all over the world will
fear him.

68 *For the choir director: A song. A psalm
of David.*

¹ Rise up, O God, and scatter your enemies.
Let those who hate God run for their lives.
² Blow them away like smoke.
Melt them like wax in a fire.
Let the wicked perish in the presence
of God.
³ But let the godly rejoice.
Let them be glad in God's presence.
Let them be filled with joy.
⁴ Sing praises to God and to his name!
Sing loud praises to him who rides the
clouds.
His name is the LORD—
rejoice in his presence!

⁵ Father to the fatherless, defender
of widows—
this is God, whose dwelling is holy.
⁶ God places the lonely in families;
he sets the prisoners free and gives
them joy.
But he makes the rebellious live in
a sun-scorched land.

⁷ O God, when you led your people out
from Egypt,
when you marched through the
dry wasteland,   *Interlude*
⁸ the earth trembled, and the heavens poured
down rain
before you, the God of Sinai,
before God, the God of Israel.

A PROMISE REMEMBERED
*(66:13-15) People sometimes make bargains with God,
saying, "If you heal me (or get me out of this mess), I'll
obey you for the rest of my life." Soon after they recover,
however, they often forget their vow and resume their old
lifestyle. This writer remembered his promise and fulfilled
it. God always keeps his promises, and wants us to follow
his example. How careful are you to follow through on
whatever you promise to do?*

9 You sent abundant rain, O God,
    to refresh the weary land.
10 There your people finally settled,
    and with a bountiful harvest, O God,
    you provided for your needy people.

11 The Lord gives the word,
    and a great army* brings the good news.
12 Enemy kings and their armies flee,
    while the women of Israel divide the
    plunder.
13 Even those who lived among the sheepfolds
    found treasures—
    doves with wings of silver
    and feathers of gold.
14 The Almighty scattered the enemy kings
    like a blowing snowstorm on Mount
    Zalmon.

15 The mountains of Bashan are majestic,
    with many peaks stretching high into
    the sky.
16 Why do you look with envy, O rugged
    mountains,
    at Mount Zion, where God has chosen
    to live,
    where the LORD himself will live
    forever?

17 Surrounded by unnumbered thousands
    of chariots,
    the Lord came from Mount Sinai into his
    sanctuary.
18 When you ascended to the heights,
    you led a crowd of captives.
    You received gifts from the people,
    even from those who rebelled
    against you.
    Now the LORD God will live among
    us there.

19 Praise the Lord; praise God our savior!
    For each day he carries us in his arms.
                  Interlude
20 Our God is a God who saves!
    The Sovereign LORD rescues us from
    death.
21 But God will smash the heads of his
    enemies,
    crushing the skulls of those who love
    their guilty ways.
22 The Lord says, "I will bring my enemies
    down from Bashan;
    I will bring them up from the depths
    of the sea.
23 You, my people, will wash your feet in their
    blood,
    and even your dogs will get their share!"

24 Your procession has come into view,
    O God—
    the procession of my God and King as he
    goes into the sanctuary.
25 Singers are in front, musicians behind;
    between them are young women playing
    tambourines.
26 Praise God, all you people of Israel;
    praise the LORD, the source of Israel's life.
27 Look, the little tribe of Benjamin leads
    the way.
    Then comes a great throng of rulers from
    Judah
    and all the rulers of Zebulun and
    Naphtali.

28 Summon your might, O God.
    Display your power, O God, as you have
    in the past.
29 The kings of the earth are bringing tribute
    to your Temple in Jerusalem.
30 Rebuke these enemy nations—
    these wild animals lurking in the reeds,
    this herd of bulls among the weaker
    calves.
    Make them bring bars of silver in humble
    tribute.
    Scatter the nations that delight in war.
31 Let Egypt come with gifts of precious
    metals*;
    let Ethiopia* bow in submission to God.
32 Sing to God, you kingdoms of the earth.
    Sing praises to the Lord.   *Interlude*
33 Sing to the one who rides across the ancient
    heavens,
    his mighty voice thundering from the sky.
34 Tell everyone about God's power.
    His majesty shines down on Israel;
    his strength is mighty in the heavens.
35 God is awesome in his sanctuary.
    The God of Israel gives power and
    strength to his people.

    Praise be to God!

69

For the choir director: A psalm of David, to be sung to the tune "Lilies."

1 Save me, O God,
    for the floodwaters are up to my neck.
2 Deeper and deeper I sink into the mire;
    I can't find a foothold.
    I am in deep water,
    and the floods overwhelm me.
3 I am exhausted from crying for help;
    my throat is parched.
    My eyes are swollen with weeping,

68:11 Or *a host of women.*   **68:31a** Or *of rich cloth.*
68:31b Hebrew *Cush.*

waiting for my God to help me.

⁴ Those who hate me without cause
    outnumber the hairs on my head.
Many enemies try to destroy me with lies,
    demanding that I give back what I didn't
    steal.

⁵ O God, you know how foolish I am;
    my sins cannot be hidden from you.
⁶ Don't let those who trust in you be ashamed
    because of me,
    O Sovereign LORD of Heaven's Armies.
Don't let me cause them to be humiliated,
    O God of Israel.

⁷ For I endure insults for your sake;
    humiliation is written all over my face.
⁸ Even my own brothers pretend they don't
    know me;
    they treat me like a stranger.

⁹ Passion for your house has consumed me,
    and the insults of those who insult you
    have fallen on me.
¹⁰ When I weep and fast,
    they scoff at me.
¹¹ When I dress in burlap to show sorrow,
    they make fun of me.
¹² I am the favorite topic of town gossip,
    and all the drunks sing about me.

¹³ But I keep praying to you, LORD,
    hoping this time you will show me favor.
In your unfailing love, O God,
    answer my prayer with your sure
    salvation.
¹⁴ Rescue me from the mud;
    don't let me sink any deeper!
Save me from those who hate me,
    and pull me from these deep waters.
¹⁵ Don't let the floods overwhelm me,
    or the deep waters swallow me,
    or the pit of death devour me.

¹⁶ Answer my prayers, O LORD,
    for your unfailing love is wonderful.
Take care of me,
    for your mercy is so plentiful.
¹⁷ Don't hide from your servant;
    answer me quickly, for I am in deep
    trouble!
¹⁸ Come and redeem me;
    free me from my enemies.

¹⁹ You know of my shame, scorn, and disgrace.
    You see all that my enemies are doing.

²⁰ Their insults have broken my heart,
    and I am in despair.
If only one person would show some pity;
    if only one would turn and comfort me.
²¹ But instead, they give me poison* for food;
    they offer me sour wine for my thirst.

²² Let the bountiful table set before them
    become a snare
    and their prosperity become a trap.*
²³ Let their eyes go blind so they cannot see,
    and make their bodies shake
    continually.*
²⁴ Pour out your fury on them;
    consume them with your burning anger.
²⁵ Let their homes become desolate
    and their tents be deserted.
²⁶ To the one you have punished, they add
    insult to injury;
    they add to the pain of those you have
    hurt.
²⁷ Pile their sins up high,
    and don't let them go free.
²⁸ Erase their names from the Book of Life;
    don't let them be counted among the
    righteous.

²⁹ I am suffering and in pain.
    Rescue me, O God, by your saving power.

³⁰ Then I will praise God's name with singing,
    and I will honor him with thanksgiving.
³¹ For this will please the LORD more than
    sacrificing cattle,
    more than presenting a bull with its horns
    and hooves.
³² The humble will see their God at work and
    be glad.
Let all who seek God's help be
    encouraged.
³³ For the LORD hears the cries of the needy;
    he does not despise his imprisoned
    people.

³⁴ Praise him, O heaven and earth,
    the seas and all that move in them.
³⁵ For God will save Jerusalem*
    and rebuild the towns of Judah.
His people will live there
    and settle in their own land.
³⁶ The descendants of those who obey him
    will inherit the land,
    and those who love him will live there
    in safety.

69:21 Or *gall.*   **69:22** Greek version reads *Let their bountiful table
set before them become a snare, / a trap that makes them think all is
well. / Let their blessings cause them to stumble, / and let them get
what they deserve.* Compare Rom 11:9.   **69:23** Greek version reads
and let their backs be bent forever. Compare Rom 11:10.
69:35 Hebrew *Zion.*

70 *For the choir director: A psalm of David,
asking God to remember him.*

¹ Please, God, rescue me!
    Come quickly, LORD, and help me.

2 May those who try to kill me
    be humiliated and put to shame.
May those who take delight in my trouble
    be turned back in disgrace.
3 Let them be horrified by their shame,
    for they said, "Aha! We've got him now!"
4 But may all who search for you
    be filled with joy and gladness in you.
May those who love your salvation
    repeatedly shout, "God is great!"
5 But as for me, I am poor and needy;
    please hurry to my aid, O God.
You are my helper and my savior;
    O Lord, do not delay.

71 ¹ O Lord, I have come to you for
        protection;
    don't let me be disgraced.
² Save me and rescue me,
    for you do what is right.
Turn your ear to listen to me,
    and set me free.
³ Be my rock of safety
    where I can always hide.
Give the order to save me,
    for you are my rock and my fortress.
⁴ My God, rescue me from the power of the
        wicked,
    from the clutches of cruel oppressors.
⁵ O Lord, you alone are my hope.
    I've trusted you, O Lord, from childhood.
⁶ Yes, you have been with me from birth;
    from my mother's womb you have cared
        for me.
    No wonder I am always praising you!

⁷ My life is an example to many,
    because you have been my strength and
        protection.
⁸ That is why I can never stop praising you;
    I declare your glory all day long.
⁹ And now, in my old age, don't set
        me aside.
    Don't abandon me when my strength
        is failing.
¹⁰ For my enemies are whispering
        against me.
    They are plotting together to kill me.

PANIC AND PRAISE

(70:1-5) This short psalm was David's plea for God to rush to his aid. Yet even in this moment of panic, he remembered to praise. Often our prayers are filled with requests for others and ourselves. Consequently, we forget to thank God for what he has done or to worship him for who he is. Adding a praise postscript to a prayer is important because it helps us remember who God is. How much of a priority is praise in your prayers?

¹¹ They say, "God has abandoned him.
    Let's go and get him,
    for no one will help him now."
¹² O God, don't stay away.
    My God, please hurry to help me.
¹³ Bring disgrace and destruction on my
        accusers.
    Humiliate and shame those who want
        to harm me.
¹⁴ But I will keep on hoping for your help;
    I will praise you more and more.
¹⁵ I will tell everyone about your
        righteousness.
    All day long I will proclaim your saving
        power,
    though I am not skilled with words.*
¹⁶ I will praise your mighty deeds,
        O Sovereign Lord.
    I will tell everyone that you alone
        are just.

¹⁷ O God, you have taught me from my earliest
        childhood,
    and I constantly tell others about the
        wonderful things you do.
¹⁸ Now that I am old and gray,
    do not abandon me, O God.
Let me proclaim your power to this new
        generation,
    your mighty miracles to all who come
        after me.

¹⁹ Your righteousness, O God, reaches to the
        highest heavens.
    You have done such wonderful things.
    Who can compare with you, O God?
²⁰ You have allowed me to suffer much
        hardship,
    but you will restore me to life again
    and lift me up from the depths of the
        earth.
²¹ You will restore me to even greater honor
    and comfort me once again.

²² Then I will praise you with music on the
        harp,
    because you are faithful to your promises,
        O my God.
I will sing praises to you with a lyre,
    O Holy One of Israel.
²³ I will shout for joy and sing your praises,
    for you have ransomed me.
²⁴ I will tell about your righteous deeds
    all day long,
    for everyone who tried to hurt me
    has been shamed and humiliated.

71:15 Or *though I cannot count it.*

72 *A psalm of Solomon.*

1 Give your love of justice to the king, O God,
    and righteousness to the king's son.
2 Help him judge your people in the right way;
    let the poor always be treated fairly.
3 May the mountains yield prosperity
        for all,
    and may the hills be fruitful.
4 Help him to defend the poor,
    to rescue the children of the needy,
    and to crush their oppressors.
5 May they fear you* as long as the sun
        shines,
    as long as the moon remains in the sky.
    Yes, forever!

6 May the king's rule be refreshing like spring
        rain on freshly cut grass,
    like the showers that water the earth.
7 May all the godly flourish during his reign.
    May there be abundant prosperity until
        the moon is no more.
8 May he reign from sea to sea,
    and from the Euphrates River* to the
        ends of the earth.
9 Desert nomads will bow before him;
    his enemies will fall before him in the
        dust.
10 The western kings of Tarshish and other
        distant lands
    will bring him tribute.
    The eastern kings of Sheba and Seba
    will bring him gifts.
11 All kings will bow before him,
    and all nations will serve him.

12 He will rescue the poor when they cry
        to him;
    he will help the oppressed, who have
        no one to defend them.
13 He feels pity for the weak and the needy,
    and he will rescue them.
14 He will redeem them from oppression and
        violence,
    for their lives are precious to him.

15 Long live the king!
    May the gold of Sheba be given to him.
    May the people always pray for him
    and bless him all day long.
16 May there be abundant grain throughout
        the land,
    flourishing even on the hilltops.
    May the fruit trees flourish like the trees
        of Lebanon,

72:5 Greek version reads *May they endure.*   72:8 Hebrew *the river.*

and may the people thrive like grass in
    a field.
17 May the king's name endure forever;
    may it continue as long as the
        sun shines.
    May all nations be blessed through him
    and bring him praise.

18 Praise the LORD God, the God of Israel,
    who alone does such wonderful things.
19 Praise his glorious name forever!
    Let the whole earth be filled with
        his glory.
    Amen and amen!

20 (This ends the prayers of David son
    of Jesse.)

BOOK THREE (Psalms 73–89)

73 *A psalm of Asaph.*

1 Truly God is good to Israel,
    to those whose hearts are pure.
2 But as for me, I almost lost my footing.
    My feet were slipping, and I was almost
        gone.
3 For I envied the proud
    when I saw them prosper despite their
        wickedness.
4 They seem to live such painless lives;
    their bodies are so healthy and strong.
5 They don't have troubles like other people;
    they're not plagued with problems like
        everyone else.
6 They wear pride like a jeweled necklace
    and clothe themselves with cruelty.
7 These fat cats have everything
    their hearts could ever wish for!
8 They scoff and speak only evil;
    in their pride they seek to crush others.
9 They boast against the very heavens,
    and their words strut throughout the
        earth.
10 And so the people are dismayed and
        confused,
    drinking in all their words.
11 "What does God know?" they ask.
    "Does the Most High even know what's
        happening?"
12 Look at these wicked people—

....

REACHING OUT TO THOSE IN NEED
(72:12-14) Solomon acknowledged God's concern for
the poor and those who are mistreated. God encourages
us to show the same compassion. What are you doing to
reach out with God's love to the poor, weak, and needy in
the world?

enjoying a life of ease while their riches
multiply.

13 Did I keep my heart pure for nothing?
Did I keep myself innocent for no reason?
14 I get nothing but trouble all day long;
every morning brings me pain.

15 If I had really spoken this way to others,
I would have been a traitor to your
people.
16 So I tried to understand why the wicked
prosper.
But what a difficult task it is!
17 Then I went into your sanctuary, O God,
and I finally understood the destiny of the
wicked.
18 Truly, you put them on a slippery path
and send them sliding over the cliff to
destruction.
19 In an instant they are destroyed,
completely swept away by terrors.
20 When you arise, O Lord,
you will laugh at their silly ideas
as a person laughs at dreams in the
morning.

21 Then I realized that my heart was bitter,
and I was all torn up inside.
22 I was so foolish and ignorant—
I must have seemed like a senseless
animal to you.
23 Yet I still belong to you;
you hold my right hand.
24 You guide me with your counsel,
leading me to a glorious destiny.
25 Whom have I in heaven but you?
I desire you more than anything on earth.
26 My health may fail, and my spirit may grow
weak,
but God remains the strength of my heart;
he is mine forever.

27 Those who desert him will perish,
for you destroy those who abandon you.
28 But as for me, how good it is to be near God!
I have made the Sovereign LORD my
shelter,
and I will tell everyone about the
wonderful things you do.

....

TRACES OF GOD
*(74:1-8) When enemy armies defeated Israel, they
destroyed Jerusalem, trying to wipe out every trace of
God. This has often been the response of people who
hate God. Today many continually try to erase all traces of
God from our society and in our schools. Yet the strongest
traces of God can be found in the lives of believers. Is that
true of you? How do your actions show "traces of God"?*

74 *A psalm* of Asaph.*

1 O God, why have you rejected us so long?
Why is your anger so intense against the
sheep of your own pasture?
2 Remember that we are the people you
chose long ago,
the tribe you redeemed as your own
special possession!
And remember Jerusalem,* your home
here on earth.
3 Walk through the awful ruins of the city;
see how the enemy has destroyed your
sanctuary.

4 There your enemies shouted their victorious
battle cries;
there they set up their battle standards.
5 They swung their axes
like woodcutters in a forest.
6 With axes and picks,
they smashed the carved paneling.
7 They burned your sanctuary to the ground.
They defiled the place that bears your
name.
8 Then they thought, "Let's destroy
everything!"
So they burned down all the places where
God was worshiped.

9 We no longer see your miraculous signs.
All the prophets are gone,
and no one can tell us when it will end.
10 How long, O God, will you allow our enemies
to insult you?
Will you let them dishonor your name
forever?
11 Why do you hold back your strong right hand?
Unleash your powerful fist and destroy
them.

12 You, O God, are my king from ages past,
bringing salvation to the earth.
13 You split the sea by your strength
and smashed the heads of the sea
monsters.
14 You crushed the heads of Leviathan*
and let the desert animals eat him.
15 You caused the springs and streams to gush
forth,
and you dried up rivers that never run dry.
16 Both day and night belong to you;
you made the starlight* and the sun.
17 You set the boundaries of the earth,
and you made both summer and winter.

74:TITLE Hebrew *maskil.* This may be a literary or musical term.
74:2 Hebrew *Mount Zion.*   **74:14** The identification of Leviathan
is disputed, ranging from an earthly creature to a mythical sea
monster in ancient literature.   **74:16** Or *moon;* Hebrew reads *light.*

18 See how these enemies insult you, LORD.
  A foolish nation has dishonored your
    name.
19 Don't let these wild beasts destroy your
    turtledoves.
  Don't forget your suffering people forever.

20 Remember your covenant promises,
    for the land is full of darkness and
      violence!
21 Don't let the downtrodden be humiliated
    again.
  Instead, let the poor and needy praise
    your name.

22 Arise, O God, and defend your cause.
  Remember how these fools insult you all
    day long.
23 Don't overlook what your enemies have said
    or their growing uproar.

75 For the choir director: A psalm of Asaph. A
    song to be sung to the tune "Do Not Destroy!"

1 We thank you, O God!
  We give thanks because you are near.
  People everywhere tell of your wonderful
    deeds.

2 God says, "At the time I have planned,
    I will bring justice against the wicked.
3 When the earth quakes and its people live
      in turmoil,
  I am the one who keeps its foundations
    firm.   *Interlude*

4 "I warned the proud, 'Stop your boasting!'
  I told the wicked, 'Don't raise your fists!
5 Don't raise your fists in defiance at the
    heavens

75:6 Hebrew *should lift.*   **76:2** Hebrew *Salem,* another name
for Jerusalem.

  or speak with such arrogance.'"
6 For no one on earth—from east or west,
    or even from the wilderness—
  should raise a defiant fist.*
7 It is God alone who judges;
  he decides who will rise and who will fall.
8 For the LORD holds a cup in his hand
    that is full of foaming wine mixed with
      spices.
  He pours out the wine in judgment,
    and all the wicked must drink it,
      draining it to the dregs.

9 But as for me, I will always proclaim what
      God has done;
  I will sing praises to the God of Jacob.
10 For God says, "I will break the strength of
      the wicked,
  but I will increase the power
    of the godly."

76 For the choir director: A psalm of Asaph.
    A song to be accompanied by stringed
instruments.

1 God is honored in Judah;
  his name is great in Israel.
2 Jerusalem* is where he lives;
  Mount Zion is his home.

....

GOD'S TIMING
(75:2) Children have difficulty grasping the concept of
time. "It's not time yet" is not a reason they easily understand. They only comprehend the present. As limited
human beings, we can't comprehend God's perspective
on time. God's time frame is a mystery to most of us.
Sometimes he seems to move much too slowly. We want
everything now, not recognizing that God's timing is perfect. Think about the last time God came through. Are you
willing to trust that his timing is just right for you?

CHOICES
injustice

"It isn't fair!" Joy sobs. "I really try hard to live for the
Lord. I go to church, read my Bible, pray every day, try
to tell my friends about God—everything! But does
it do any good? No way! My life is still the worst. My
family is awful, my fat body is a wreck, I never get
asked out, I have only two friends, and I can't even
pass geometry! You'd think God would at least reward
me a little bit.

"On the other hand, Renita has it made! All the
guys think she's so hot. She goes out every weekend.
She makes straight As without even trying. Her family
is rich—I mean, how many other kids get their own

MX-5 Miata? She never has any problems. Her life is
totally perfect . . . and get this: she's not even a Christian! In fact, she couldn't care less about God.

"It doesn't make any sense. Why do I get hassled
for doing what's right, and she gets rewarded for
doing whatever she wants whenever she wants? You
know what I'm saying?

"Doesn't God see what's going on? Doesn't he
care? I'm serious . . . there is absolutely no justice in
this world. I might as well live like a heathen for all
the good it does me."

*Ever feel like Joy? Ever wonder why some non-Christians seem to have perfect lives, while so
many of God's people struggle and have lives full of pain? A follower of God named Asaph once
asked some of the very same questions. Psalm 73 describes the answers he found.*

³ There he has broken the fiery arrows of the
enemy,
the shields and swords and weapons
of war.   *Interlude*

⁴ You are glorious and more majestic
than the everlasting mountains.*
⁵ Our boldest enemies have been plundered.
They lie before us in the sleep of death.
No warrior could lift a hand against us.
⁶ At the blast of your breath, O God of Jacob,
their horses and chariots lay still.

⁷ No wonder you are greatly feared!
Who can stand before you when your
anger explodes?
⁸ From heaven you sentenced your enemies;
the earth trembled and stood silent
before you.
⁹ You stand up to judge those who do evil,
O God,
and to rescue the oppressed of the earth.
Interlude

¹⁰ Human defiance only enhances your glory,
for you use it as a weapon.*

¹¹ Make vows to the LORD your God, and keep
them.
Let everyone bring tribute to the
Awesome One.
¹² For he breaks the pride of princes,
and the kings of the earth fear him.

77
*For Jeduthun, the choir director: A psalm
of Asaph.*

¹ I cry out to God; yes, I shout.
Oh, that God would listen to me!
² When I was in deep trouble,
I searched for the Lord.
All night long I prayed, with hands lifted
toward heaven,
but my soul was not comforted.
³ I think of God, and I moan,
overwhelmed with longing for his help.
Interlude

⁴ You don't let me sleep.
I am too distressed even to pray!
⁵ I think of the good old days,
long since ended,
⁶ when my nights were filled with joyful
songs.
I search my soul and ponder the
difference now.
⁷ Has the Lord rejected me forever?
Will he never again be kind to me?
⁸ Is his unfailing love gone forever?
Have his promises permanently failed?

⁹ Has God forgotten to be gracious?
Has he slammed the door on his
compassion?   *Interlude*

¹⁰ And I said, "This is my fate;
the Most High has turned his hand
against me."
¹¹ But then I recall all you have done,
O LORD;
I remember your wonderful deeds
of long ago.
¹² They are constantly in my thoughts.
I cannot stop thinking about your
mighty works.

¹³ O God, your ways are holy.
Is there any god as mighty as you?
¹⁴ You are the God of great wonders!
You demonstrate your awesome power
among the nations.
¹⁵ By your strong arm, you redeemed your
people,
the descendants of Jacob and Joseph.
Interlude

¹⁶ When the Red Sea* saw you, O God,
its waters looked and trembled!
The sea quaked to its very depths.
¹⁷ The clouds poured down rain;
the thunder rumbled in the sky.
Your arrows of lightning flashed.
¹⁸ Your thunder roared from the whirlwind;
the lightning lit up the world!
The earth trembled and shook.
¹⁹ Your road led through the sea,
your pathway through the mighty
waters—
a pathway no one knew was there!
²⁰ You led your people along that road like
a flock of sheep,
with Moses and Aaron as their
shepherds.

78
A psalm of Asaph.*

¹ O my people, listen to my instructions.
Open your ears to what I am saying,
² for I will speak to you in a parable.
I will teach you hidden lessons from
our past—
³ stories we have heard and known,
stories our ancestors handed down to us.
⁴ We will not hide these truths from our
children;
we will tell the next generation

76:4 As in Greek version; Hebrew reads *than mountains filled with
beasts of prey.*   **76:10** The meaning of the Hebrew is uncertain.
77:16 Hebrew *the waters.*   **78:TITLE** Hebrew *maskil.* This may be
a literary or musical term.

about the glorious deeds of the LORD,
  about his power and his mighty wonders.
⁵ For he issued his laws to Jacob;
  he gave his instructions to Israel.
He commanded our ancestors
  to teach them to their children,
⁶ so the next generation might know them—
  even the children not yet born—
  and they in turn will teach their own
  children.
⁷ So each generation should set its hope
  anew on God,
  not forgetting his glorious miracles
  and obeying his commands.
⁸ Then they will not be like their ancestors—
  stubborn, rebellious, and unfaithful,
  refusing to give their hearts to God.

⁹ The warriors of Ephraim, though armed
  with bows,
  turned their backs and fled on the day
  of battle.
¹⁰ They did not keep God's covenant
  and refused to live by his instructions.
¹¹ They forgot what he had done—
  the great wonders he had shown them,
¹² the miracles he did for their ancestors
  on the plain of Zoan in the land of Egypt.
¹³ For he divided the sea and led them
  through,
  making the water stand up like walls!
¹⁴ In the daytime he led them by a cloud,
  and all night by a pillar of fire.
¹⁵ He split open the rocks in the wilderness
  to give them water, as from a gushing
  spring.
¹⁶ He made streams pour from the rock,
  making the waters flow down like a river!

¹⁷ Yet they kept on sinning against him,
  rebelling against the Most High in the
  desert.
¹⁸ They stubbornly tested God in their hearts,
  demanding the foods they craved.
¹⁹ They even spoke against God himself,
  saying,
  "God can't give us food in the wilderness.
²⁰ Yes, he can strike a rock so water
  gushes out,
  but he can't give his people bread
  and meat."
²¹ When the LORD heard them, he was furious.
  The fire of his wrath burned against Jacob.
  Yes, his anger rose against Israel,
²² for they did not believe God
  or trust him to care for them.
²³ But he commanded the skies to open;

78:35 Hebrew *El-Elyon*.

he opened the doors of heaven.
²⁴ He rained down manna for them to eat;
  he gave them bread from heaven.
²⁵ They ate the food of angels!
  God gave them all they could hold.
²⁶ He released the east wind in the heavens
  and guided the south wind by his mighty
  power.
²⁷ He rained down meat as thick as dust—
  birds as plentiful as the sand on the
  seashore!
²⁸ He caused the birds to fall within their camp
  and all around their tents.
²⁹ The people ate their fill.
  He gave them what they craved.
³⁰ But before they satisfied their craving,
  while the meat was yet in their mouths,
³¹ the anger of God rose against them,
  and he killed their strongest men.
  He struck down the finest of Israel's
  young men.

³² But in spite of this, the people kept sinning.
  Despite his wonders, they refused to
  trust him.
³³ So he ended their lives in failure,
  their years in terror.
³⁴ When God began killing them,
  they finally sought him.
  They repented and took God seriously.
³⁵ Then they remembered that God was
  their rock,
  that God Most High* was their redeemer.
³⁶ But all they gave him was lip service;
  they lied to him with their tongues.
³⁷ Their hearts were not loyal to him.
  They did not keep his covenant.
³⁸ Yet he was merciful and forgave their sins
  and did not destroy them all.
  Many times he held back his anger
  and did not unleash his fury!
³⁹ For he remembered that they were merely
  mortal,
  gone like a breath of wind that never
  returns.

⁴⁰ Oh, how often they rebelled against him
  in the wilderness
  and grieved his heart in that dry
  wasteland.

···

ALL TALK, NO ACTION
*(78:1-72) Over and over the people of Israel promised
that they would follow God; yet they turned away from
him again and again. The problem was that they followed
God with words and not with their hearts, thus their
repentance was empty. Talk is cheap. God wants our
words and actions to match. Do yours?*

⁴¹ Again and again they tested God's patience
     and provoked the Holy One of Israel.
⁴² They did not remember his power
     and how he rescued them from their
       enemies.
⁴³ They did not remember his miraculous signs
       in Egypt,
     his wonders on the plain of Zoan.
⁴⁴ For he turned their rivers into blood,
     so no one could drink from the streams.
⁴⁵ He sent vast swarms of flies to consume
       them
     and hordes of frogs to ruin them.
⁴⁶ He gave their crops to caterpillars;
     their harvest was consumed by locusts.
⁴⁷ He destroyed their grapevines with hail
     and shattered their sycamore-figs with
       sleet.
⁴⁸ He abandoned their cattle to the hail,
     their livestock to bolts of lightning.
⁴⁹ He loosed on them his fierce anger—
     all his fury, rage, and hostility.
     He dispatched against them
     a band of destroying angels.
⁵⁰ He turned his anger against them;
     he did not spare the Egyptians' lives
     but ravaged them with the plague.
⁵¹ He killed the oldest son in each Egyptian
       family,
     the flower of youth throughout the land
       of Egypt.*
⁵² But he led his own people like a flock of
       sheep,
     guiding them safely through the
       wilderness.
⁵³ He kept them safe so they were not afraid;
     but the sea covered their enemies.
⁵⁴ He brought them to the border of his holy
       land,
     to this land of hills he had won for them.
⁵⁵ He drove out the nations before them;
     he gave them their inheritance by lot.

· ·

BASIC TRAINING
*(78:71-72) Although David had already assumed
the throne of Israel when this psalm was written, he
was called a shepherd and not a king. Shepherding,
a common profession in biblical times, was a highly
responsible job. The flocks were completely dependent
upon shepherds for guidance, provision, and protection.
David had spent his early years as a shepherd (1 Sam
16:10-11). Being a shepherd trained David for the responsibilities God had in store for him. When he was ready,
God took him from caring for sheep to caring for Israel,
God's people. God is shaping you right now for future
responsibilities. Maybe you can't see how doing those
same dull chores day after day can prepare you for a cool
purpose. But God can.*

     He settled the tribes of Israel into their
       homes.
⁵⁶ But they kept testing and rebelling against
       God Most High.
     They did not obey his laws.
⁵⁷ They turned back and were as faithless
       as their parents.
     They were as undependable as
       a crooked bow.
⁵⁸ They angered God by building shrines
       to other gods;
     they made him jealous with their idols.
⁵⁹ When God heard them, he was very angry,
     and he completely rejected Israel.
⁶⁰ Then he abandoned his dwelling
       at Shiloh,
     the Tabernacle where he had lived
       among the people.
⁶¹ He allowed the Ark of his might to be
       captured;
     he surrendered his glory into enemy
       hands.
⁶² He gave his people over to be butchered by
       the sword,
     because he was so angry with his own
       people—his special possession.
⁶³ Their young men were killed by fire;
     their young women died before singing
       their wedding songs.
⁶⁴ Their priests were slaughtered,
     and their widows could not mourn their
       deaths.

⁶⁵ Then the Lord rose up as though waking
       from sleep,
     like a warrior aroused from a drunken
       stupor.
⁶⁶ He routed his enemies
     and sent them to eternal shame.
⁶⁷ But he rejected Joseph's descendants;
     he did not choose the tribe of
       Ephraim.
⁶⁸ He chose instead the tribe of Judah,
     and Mount Zion, which he loved.
⁶⁹ There he built his sanctuary as high as the
       heavens,
     as solid and enduring as the earth.
⁷⁰ He chose his servant David,
     calling him from the sheep pens.
⁷¹ He took David from tending the ewes and
       lambs
     and made him the shepherd of Jacob's
       descendants—
     God's own people, Israel.
⁷² He cared for them with a true heart
     and led them with skillful hands.

78:51 Hebrew *in the tents of Ham.*

79

A psalm of Asaph.

[1] O God, pagan nations have conquered
    your land,
    your special possession.
They have defiled your holy Temple
    and made Jerusalem a heap of ruins.
[2] They have left the bodies of your servants
    as food for the birds of heaven.
The flesh of your godly ones
    has become food for the wild animals.
[3] Blood has flowed like water all around
    Jerusalem;
    no one is left to bury the dead.
[4] We are mocked by our neighbors,
    an object of scorn and derision to those
    around us.

[5] O LORD, how long will you be angry with us?
    Forever?
    How long will your jealousy burn like fire?
[6] Pour out your wrath on the nations that
    refuse to acknowledge you—
    on kingdoms that do not call upon your
    name.
[7] For they have devoured your people Israel,*
    making the land a desolate wilderness.
[8] Do not hold us guilty for the sins of our
    ancestors!
    Let your compassion quickly meet our
    needs,
    for we are on the brink of despair.

[9] Help us, O God of our salvation!
    Help us for the glory of your name.
Save us and forgive our sins
    for the honor of your name.
[10] Why should pagan nations be allowed
    to scoff,
    asking, "Where is their God?"
Show us your vengeance against the
    nations,
    for they have spilled the blood of your
    servants.
[11] Listen to the moaning of the prisoners.
    Demonstrate your great power by saving
    those condemned to die.
[12] O Lord, pay back our neighbors seven times
    for the scorn they have hurled at you.
[13] Then we your people, the sheep of your
    pasture,
    will thank you forever and ever,
    praising your greatness from generation
    to generation.

79:7 Hebrew *devoured Jacob.* See note on 44:4.   **80:6** As in Syriac
version; Hebrew reads *the strife.*   **80:11** Hebrew *west to the sea, . . .
east to the river.*

80

*For the choir director: A psalm of Asaph, to
be sung to the tune "Lilies of the Covenant."*

[1] Please listen, O Shepherd of Israel,
    you who lead Joseph's descendants like
    a flock.
O God, enthroned above the cherubim,
    display your radiant glory
[2] to Ephraim, Benjamin, and Manasseh.
Show us your mighty power.
    Come to rescue us!

[3] Turn us again to yourself, O God.
    Make your face shine down upon us.
    Only then will we be saved.
[4] O LORD God of Heaven's Armies,
    how long will you be angry with our
    prayers?
[5] You have fed us with sorrow
    and made us drink tears by the bucketful.
[6] You have made us the scorn* of
    neighboring nations.
    Our enemies treat us as a joke.

[7] Turn us again to yourself, O God of Heaven's
    Armies.
    Make your face shine down upon us.
    Only then will we be saved.
[8] You brought us from Egypt like a grapevine;
    you drove away the pagan nations and
    transplanted us into your land.
[9] You cleared the ground for us,
    and we took root and filled the land.
[10] Our shade covered the mountains;
    our branches covered the mighty cedars.
[11] We spread our branches west to the
    Mediterranean Sea;
    our shoots spread east to the
    Euphrates River.*
[12] But now, why have you broken down
    our walls
    so that all who pass by may steal
    our fruit?
[13] The wild boar from the forest devours it,
    and the wild animals feed on it.

[14] Come back, we beg you, O God of Heaven's
    Armies.
    Look down from heaven and see our
    plight.

....

BE PREPARED

*(79:10) The psalmist acknowledged how enemies mocked
the beliefs of Israel. Christians have always endured terrible treatment because of their faith. Some have given
up because the persecution seemed too great. If you're
a Christian, you can expect to face persecution. As Jesus
said, "Here on earth you will have many trials and sorrows. But take heart, because I have overcome the world"
(John 16:33). His words are a warning to be prepared.*

Take care of this grapevine
15   that you yourself have planted,
     this son you have raised for yourself.
16 For we are chopped up and burned by our
     enemies.
     May they perish at the sight of your frown.
17 Strengthen the man you love,
     the son of your choice.
18 Then we will never abandon you again.
     Revive us so we can call on your name
        once more.

19 Turn us again to yourself, O Lord God
        of Heaven's Armies.
     Make your face shine down upon us.
     Only then will we be saved.

81

*For the choir director: A psalm of Asaph, to
be accompanied by a stringed instrument.**

1   Sing praises to God, our strength.
     Sing to the God of Jacob.
2   Sing! Beat the tambourine.
     Play the sweet lyre and the harp.
3   Blow the ram's horn at new moon,
     and again at full moon to call a festival!
4   For this is required by the decrees of Israel;
     it is a regulation of the God of Jacob.
5   He made it a law for Israel*
     when he attacked Egypt to set us free.

     I heard an unknown voice say,
6   "Now I will take the load from your
        shoulders;
     I will free your hands from their heavy
        tasks.
7   You cried to me in trouble, and I saved you;
     I answered out of the thundercloud
     and tested your faith when there was
        no water at Meribah.   *Interlude*

8   "Listen to me, O my people, while I give you
        stern warnings.
     O Israel, if you would only listen to me!
9   You must never have a foreign god;
     you must not bow down before
        a false god.
10 For it was I, the Lord your God,
     who rescued you from the land of Egypt.

Open your mouth wide, and I will fill it
     with good things.
11 "But no, my people wouldn't listen.
     Israel did not want me around.
12 So I let them follow their own stubborn
        desires,
     living according to their own ideas.
13 Oh, that my people would listen to me!
     Oh, that Israel would follow me, walking
        in my paths!
14 How quickly I would then subdue their
        enemies!
     How soon my hands would be upon
        their foes!
15 Those who hate the Lord would cringe
        before him;
     they would be doomed forever.
16 But I would feed you with the finest wheat.
     I would satisfy you with wild honey from
        the rock."

82

A psalm of Asaph.

1   God presides over heaven's court;
     he pronounces judgment on the
        heavenly beings:
2   "How long will you hand down unjust
        decisions
     by favoring the wicked?   *Interlude*

3   "Give justice to the poor and the orphan;
     uphold the rights of the oppressed and
        the destitute.
4   Rescue the poor and helpless;
     deliver them from the grasp of evil
        people.
5   But these oppressors know nothing;
     they are so ignorant!
     They wander about in darkness,
        while the whole world is shaken
        to the core.
6   I say, 'You are gods;
     you are all children of the Most High.
7   But you will die like mere mortals
     and fall like every other ruler.'"

8   Rise up, O God, and judge the earth,
     for all the nations belong to you.

83

A song. A psalm of Asaph.

1   O God, do not be silent!
     Do not be deaf.
     Do not be quiet, O God.
2   Don't you hear the uproar of your enemies?

HOLIDAYS
*(81:1-5) Israel's sacred feasts were times of celebration
to remind the nation of God's amazing help throughout
the years. Thanksgiving, Christmas, and Easter are times
of celebration for our nation. But for many, those holidays
have little meaning beyond presents, food, and football.
Yet each holiday presents an opportunity to worship God
for what he has done for us—especially for sending his
Son to die in our place. As each holiday approaches, how
will you acknowledge the spiritual significance of the day?*

81:TITLE Hebrew *according to the gittith.*   **81:5** Hebrew *for Joseph.*

Don't you see that your arrogant enemies
    are rising up?
3 They devise crafty schemes against your
    people;
   they conspire against your precious ones.
4 "Come," they say, "let us wipe out Israel as
    a nation.
   We will destroy the very memory of its
    existence."
5 Yes, this was their unanimous decision.
   They signed a treaty as allies
    against you—
6 these Edomites and Ishmaelites;
   Moabites and Hagrites;
7 Gebalites, Ammonites, and Amalekites;
   and people from Philistia and Tyre.
8 Assyria has joined them, too,
   and is allied with the descendants of Lot.
                    Interlude

9 Do to them as you did to the Midianites
   and as you did to Sisera and Jabin at the
    Kishon River.
10 They were destroyed at Endor,
   and their decaying corpses fertilized
    the soil.
11 Let their mighty nobles die as Oreb and
    Zeeb did.
   Let all their princes die like Zebah and
    Zalmunna,
12 for they said, "Let us seize for our own use
   these pasturelands of God!"
13 O my God, scatter them like tumbleweed,
   like chaff before the wind!
14 As a fire burns a forest
   and as a flame sets mountains ablaze,
15 chase them with your fierce storm;
   terrify them with your tempest.
16 Utterly disgrace them
   until they submit to your name, O LORD.
17 Let them be ashamed and terrified forever.
   Let them die in disgrace.
18 Then they will learn that you alone are
    called the LORD,
   that you alone are the Most High,
    supreme over all the earth.

84

*For the choir director: A psalm of the
descendants of Korah, to be accompanied
by a stringed instrument.**

1 How lovely is your dwelling place,
   O LORD of Heaven's Armies.
2 I long, yes, I faint with longing
   to enter the courts of the LORD.
   With my whole being, body and soul,

I will shout joyfully to the living God.
3 Even the sparrow finds a home,
   and the swallow builds her nest and
    raises her young
 at a place near your altar,
   O LORD of Heaven's Armies, my King and
    my God!
4 What joy for those who can live in your
    house,
   always singing your praises.   *Interlude*

5 What joy for those whose strength comes
    from the LORD,
   who have set their minds on a pilgrimage
    to Jerusalem.
6 When they walk through the Valley of
    Weeping,*
   it will become a place of refreshing
    springs.
   The autumn rains will clothe it with
    blessings.
7 They will continue to grow stronger,
   and each of them will appear before God
    in Jerusalem.*
8 O LORD God of Heaven's Armies, hear
    my prayer.
   Listen, O God of Jacob.   *Interlude*

9 O God, look with favor upon the king, our
    shield!
   Show favor to the one you have anointed.

10 A single day in your courts
   is better than a thousand anywhere else!
 I would rather be a gatekeeper in the house
    of my God
   than live the good life in the homes of the
    wicked.
11 For the LORD God is our sun and our shield.
   He gives us grace and glory.
   The LORD will withhold no good thing
    from those who do what is right.
12 O LORD of Heaven's Armies,
   what joy for those who trust in you.

85

*For the choir director: A psalm of the
descendants of Korah.*

1 LORD, you poured out blessings on your land!
   You restored the fortunes of Israel.*

84:TITLE Hebrew *according to the gittith.* 84:6 Or *Valley of Poplars;*
Hebrew reads *valley of Baca.* 84:7 Hebrew *Zion.* 85:1 Hebrew of
Jacob. See note on 44:4.

BLOWN AWAY
*(83:1-18) Surrounding Judah were enemy nations that
sought its downfall. Asaph prayed that God would blow
these nations away like chaff before the wind until, in
their defeat, they would recognize the greatness of God.
Sometimes we must be defeated before we turn to God
for help. Wouldn't it be better to seek the Lord in times
of prosperity than to wait until his judgment is upon us?*

² You forgave the guilt of your people—
    yes, you covered all their sins.   *Interlude*
³ You held back your fury.
    You kept back your blazing anger.

⁴ Now restore us again, O God of our
        salvation.
    Put aside your anger against us once
        more.
⁵ Will you be angry with us always?
    Will you prolong your wrath to all
        generations?
⁶ Won't you revive us again,
    so your people can rejoice in you?
⁷ Show us your unfailing love, O LORD,
    and grant us your salvation.

⁸ I listen carefully to what God the LORD is
        saying,
    for he speaks peace to his faithful people.
    But let them not return to their foolish
        ways.
⁹ Surely his salvation is near to those who
        fear him,
    so our land will be filled with his glory.

¹⁰ Unfailing love and truth have met together.
    Righteousness and peace have kissed!
¹¹ Truth springs up from the earth,
    and righteousness smiles down from
        heaven.
¹² Yes, the LORD pours down his blessings.
    Our land will yield its bountiful harvest.
¹³ Righteousness goes as a herald before him,
    preparing the way for his steps.

86 *A prayer of David.*

¹ Bend down, O LORD, and hear my prayer;
    answer me, for I need your help.
² Protect me, for I am devoted to you.
    Save me, for I serve you and trust you.
    You are my God.
³ Be merciful to me, O Lord,
    for I am calling on you constantly.
⁴ Give me happiness, O Lord,
    for I give myself to you.
⁵ O Lord, you are so good, so ready to forgive,
    so full of unfailing love for all who ask for
        your help.
⁶ Listen closely to my prayer, O LORD;

....

WHOLEHEARTED
(86:11-12) *Praising God with all our heart means appreciating him and honoring him in all areas of life. If we're pursuing God wholeheartedly, then our work, relationships, use of money, and desires will be in keeping with his will.*

hear my urgent cry.
⁷ I will call to you whenever I'm in trouble,
    and you will answer me.

⁸ No pagan god is like you, O Lord.
    None can do what you do!
⁹ All the nations you made
    will come and bow before you, Lord;
    they will praise your holy name.
¹⁰ For you are great and perform wonderful
        deeds.
    You alone are God.

¹¹ Teach me your ways, O LORD,
    that I may live according to your truth!
Grant me purity of heart,
    so that I may honor you.
¹² With all my heart I will praise you, O Lord
        my God.
    I will give glory to your name forever,
¹³ for your love for me is very great.
    You have rescued me from the depths
        of death.*

¹⁴ O God, insolent people rise up against me;
    a violent gang is trying to kill me.
    You mean nothing to them.
¹⁵ But you, O Lord,
    are a God of compassion and mercy,
slow to get angry
    and filled with unfailing love and
        faithfulness.
¹⁶ Look down and have mercy on me.
    Give your strength to your servant;
    save me, the son of your servant.
¹⁷ Send me a sign of your favor.
    Then those who hate me will be put to
        shame,
    for you, O LORD, help and comfort me.

87 *A song. A psalm of the descendants of Korah.*

¹ On the holy mountain
    stands the city founded by the LORD.
² He loves the city of Jerusalem
    more than any other city in Israel.*
³ O city of God,
    what glorious things are said of you!
                                                Interlude

⁴ I will count Egypt* and Babylon among
        those who know me—
    also Philistia and Tyre, and even distant
        Ethiopia.*

86:13 Hebrew *of Sheol.*   87:2 Hebrew *He loves the gates of Zion more than all the dwellings of Jacob.* See note on 44:4.
87:4a Hebrew *Rahab,* the name of a mythical sea monster that represents chaos in ancient literature. The name is used here as a poetic name for Egypt.   87:4b Hebrew *Cush.*

In the movie *The Accidental Tourist*, the main characters are a husband and wife named Macon and Sarah Leary. Their son, Ethan has died tragically, leaving them in despair, struggling to pull their lives back together. In one particularly touching scene, Sarah says to Macon:

"I should have agreed to teach summer school or something. I open my eyes in the morning and I think, *Why bother getting up? Why bother eating? Why bother breathing?*"

This isn't just a scene from a movie—it is, unfortunately, an experience common to many people. Life can be terribly unfair, terribly tragic. When we're in the depths of despair, we feel like Sarah Leary: why bother going on at all?

Some believe that being a Christian makes a person somehow immune to depression. If you happen to fall into the pit of despair, well, you're not very "spiritual" are you? Such judgments add a load of guilt to a person who is already miserable.

For those who struggle with feelings of depression, there's good news and bad news.

The bad news is that such feelings are a fact of life in this broken world. Some disappointments or tragedies can leave a person depressed. Now the good news: you are not alone. As Psalm 88 (and many other passages) clearly shows, even God's chosen people experience anxiety, despair, and darkness in their soul. If Psalm 88 doesn't convince you, check out Elijah's story (1 Kgs 19) and Jesus' experience in Gethsemane. Matthew 26:38 speaks of Jesus' soul being "crushed with grief to the point of death."

Obviously, depression that lasts for a long time indicates a need for counseling; but nothing is unusual or unspiritual about going "through the darkest valley" (Ps 23:4) from time to time.

So when you are caught in one of those unpleasant times, don't add guilt to your load. Just trust that God knows what's up and will help you through this. ∎

They have all become citizens of
   Jerusalem!
5 Regarding Jerusalem* it will be said,
   "Everyone enjoys the rights of citizenship
      there."
   And the Most High will personally bless
      this city.
6 When the LORD registers the nations,
   he will say,
   "They have all become citizens of
      Jerusalem."   *Interlude*
7 The people will play flutes* and sing,
   "The source of my life springs from
      Jerusalem!"

88 *For the choir director: A psalm of the descendants of Korah. A song to be sung to the tune "The Suffering of Affliction." A psalm* of Heman the Ezrahite.*

1 O LORD, God of my salvation,
   I cry out to you by day.
   I come to you at night.
2 Now hear my prayer;
   listen to my cry.
3 For my life is full of troubles,
   and death* draws near.
4 I am as good as dead,
   like a strong man with no strength left.
5 They have left me among the dead,
   and I lie like a corpse in a grave.

I am forgotten,
   cut off from your care.
6 You have thrown me into the lowest pit,
   into the darkest depths.
7 Your anger weighs me down;
   with wave after wave you have
      engulfed me.   *Interlude*
8 You have driven my friends away
   by making me repulsive to them.
   I am in a trap with no way of escape.
9   My eyes are blinded by my tears.
   Each day I beg for your help, O LORD;
   I lift my hands to you for mercy.
10 Are your wonderful deeds of any use
      to the dead?
   Do the dead rise up and praise you?
                                     Interlude
11 Can those in the grave declare your
      unfailing love?
   Can they proclaim your faithfulness in the
      place of destruction?*
12 Can the darkness speak of your wonderful
      deeds?
   Can anyone in the land of forgetfulness
      talk about your righteousness?
13 O LORD, I cry out to you.
   I will keep on pleading day by day.
14 O LORD, why do you reject me?
   Why do you turn your face from me?
15 I have been sick and close to death since
      my youth.
   I stand helpless and desperate before
      your terrors.

87:5 Hebrew *Zion*. 87:7 Or *will dance*. 88:TITLE Hebrew *maskil*. This may be a literary or musical term. 88:3 Hebrew *Sheol*. 88:11 Hebrew *in Abaddon?*

16 Your fierce anger has overwhelmed me.
    Your terrors have paralyzed me.
17 They swirl around me like floodwaters all
    day long.
    They have engulfed me completely.
18 You have taken away my companions and
    loved ones.
    Darkness is my closest friend.

89

A psalm* of Ethan the Ezrahite.

1 I will sing of the LORD's unfailing love
    forever!
    Young and old will hear of your
    faithfulness.
2 Your unfailing love will last forever.
    Your faithfulness is as enduring as the
    heavens.

3 The LORD said, "I have made a covenant
    with David, my chosen servant.
    I have sworn this oath to him:
4 'I will establish your descendants as kings
    forever;
    they will sit on your throne from now
    until eternity.'"   *Interlude*
5 All heaven will praise your great
    wonders, LORD;
    myriads of angels will praise you for your
    faithfulness.
6 For who in all of heaven can compare with
    the LORD?
    What mightiest angel is anything like the
    LORD?
7 The highest angelic powers stand in awe
    of God.
    He is far more awesome than all who
    surround his throne.
8 O LORD God of Heaven's Armies!
    Where is there anyone as mighty as you,
    O LORD?
    You are entirely faithful.

9 You rule the oceans.
    You subdue their storm-tossed waves.
10 You crushed the great sea monster.*
    You scattered your enemies with your
    mighty arm.

11 The heavens are yours, and the earth
    is yours;
    everything in the world is yours—you
    created it all.
12 You created north and south.
    Mount Tabor and Mount Hermon praise
    your name.
13 Powerful is your arm!
    Strong is your hand!
    Your right hand is lifted high in glorious
    strength.
14 Righteousness and justice are the
    foundation of your throne.
    Unfailing love and truth walk before you
    as attendants.
15 Happy are those who hear the joyful call to
    worship,
    for they will walk in the light of your
    presence, LORD.
16 They rejoice all day long in your wonderful
    reputation.
    They exult in your righteousness.
17 You are their glorious strength.
    It pleases you to make us strong.
18 Yes, our protection comes from the LORD,
    and he, the Holy One of Israel, has given
    us our king.

19 Long ago you spoke in a vision to your
    faithful people.
    You said, "I have raised up a warrior.
    I have selected him from the common
    people to be king.
20 I have found my servant David.
    I have anointed him with my holy oil.
21 I will steady him with my hand;
    with my powerful arm I will make him
    strong.
22 His enemies will not defeat him,
    nor will the wicked overpower him.
23 I will beat down his adversaries before him
    and destroy those who hate him.
24 My faithfulness and unfailing love will be
    with him,
    and by my authority he will grow in power.
25 I will extend his rule over the sea,
    his dominion over the rivers.
26 And he will call out to me, 'You are my
    Father,
    my God, and the Rock of my salvation.'
27 I will make him my firstborn son,
    the mightiest king on earth.
28 I will love him and be kind to him forever;
    my covenant with him will never end.
29 I will preserve an heir for him;

HIS REPRESENTATIVES

*(89:14-15) God's throne is pictured with a foundation of
righteousness and justice, and he is attended by love and
truth. These describe fundamental aspects of the way God
deals with people. As God's representatives, we have the
responsibility of treating people the same way that God
treats them. Would a friend or family member describe
your actions as righteous, fair, loving, and truthful?*

89:TITLE Hebrew *maskil.* This may be a literary or musical term.
89:10 Hebrew *Rahab,* the name of a mythical sea monster that
represents chaos in ancient literature.

his throne will be as endless as the days
of heaven.
³⁰ But if his descendants forsake my
instructions
and fail to obey my regulations,
³¹ if they do not obey my decrees
and fail to keep my commands,
³² then I will punish their sin with the rod,
and their disobedience with beating.
³³ But I will never stop loving him
nor fail to keep my promise to him.
³⁴ No, I will not break my covenant;
I will not take back a single word I said.
³⁵ I have sworn an oath to David,
and in my holiness I cannot lie:
³⁶ His dynasty will go on forever;
his kingdom will endure as the sun.
³⁷ It will be as eternal as the moon,
my faithful witness in the sky!"   *Interlude*

³⁸ But now you have rejected him and cast
him off.
You are angry with your anointed king.
³⁹ You have renounced your covenant
with him;
you have thrown his crown in the dust.
⁴⁰ You have broken down the walls
protecting him
and ruined every fort defending him.
⁴¹ Everyone who comes along has robbed him,
and he has become a joke to his
neighbors.
⁴² You have strengthened his enemies
and made them all rejoice.
⁴³ You have made his sword useless
and refused to help him in battle.
⁴⁴ You have ended his splendor
and overturned his throne.
⁴⁵ You have made him old before his time
and publicly disgraced him.   *Interlude*

⁴⁶ O Lᴏʀᴅ, how long will this go on?
Will you hide yourself forever?
How long will your anger burn like fire?
⁴⁷ Remember how short my life is,
how empty and futile this human
existence!
⁴⁸ No one can live forever; all will die.
No one can escape the power
of the grave.*   *Interlude*

⁴⁹ Lord, where is your unfailing love?
You promised it to David with a faithful
pledge.
⁵⁰ Consider, Lord, how your servants are
disgraced!

89:48 Hebrew *of Sheol.*

I carry in my heart the insults of so many
people.
⁵¹ Your enemies have mocked me, O Lᴏʀᴅ;
they mock your anointed king wherever
he goes.

⁵² Praise the Lᴏʀᴅ forever!
Amen and amen!

BOOK FOUR (Psalms 90–106)

90 *A prayer of Moses, the man of God.*

¹ Lord, through all the generations
you have been our home!
² Before the mountains were born,
before you gave birth to the earth and
the world,
from beginning to end, you are God.

³ You turn people back to dust, saying,
"Return to dust, you mortals!"
⁴ For you, a thousand years are as
a passing day,
as brief as a few night hours.
⁵ You sweep people away like dreams that
disappear.
They are like grass that springs up in the
morning.
⁶ In the morning it blooms and flourishes,
but by evening it is dry and withered.
⁷ We wither beneath your anger;
we are overwhelmed by your fury.
⁸ You spread out our sins before you—
our secret sins—and you see them all.
⁹ We live our lives beneath your wrath,
ending our years with a groan.

¹⁰ Seventy years are given to us!
Some even live to eighty.
But even the best years are filled with pain
and trouble;
soon they disappear, and we fly away.
¹¹ Who can comprehend the power of your
anger?
Your wrath is as awesome as the fear you
deserve.
¹² Teach us to realize the brevity of life,
so that we may grow in wisdom.

¹³ O Lᴏʀᴅ, come back to us!
How long will you delay?
Take pity on your servants!
¹⁴ Satisfy us each morning with your
unfailing love,
so we may sing for joy to the end
of our lives.
¹⁵ Give us gladness in proportion to our
former misery!

Replace the evil years with good.
¹⁶ Let us, your servants, see you work again;
let our children see your glory.
¹⁷ And may the Lord our God show us his approval
and make our efforts successful.
Yes, make our efforts successful!

91

¹ Those who live in the shelter of the Most High
will find rest in the shadow of the Almighty.
² This I declare about the LORD:
He alone is my refuge, my place of safety;
he is my God, and I trust him.
³ For he will rescue you from every trap
and protect you from deadly disease.
⁴ He will cover you with his feathers.
He will shelter you with his wings.
His faithful promises are your armor and protection.
⁵ Do not be afraid of the terrors of the night,
nor the arrow that flies in the day.
⁶ Do not dread the disease that stalks in darkness,
nor the disaster that strikes at midday.
⁷ Though a thousand fall at your side,
though ten thousand are dying around you,
these evils will not touch you.
⁸ Just open your eyes,
and see how the wicked are punished.

⁹ If you make the LORD your refuge,
if you make the Most High your shelter,
¹⁰ no evil will conquer you;
no plague will come near your home.
¹¹ For he will order his angels
to protect you wherever you go.
¹² They will hold you up with their hands
so you won't even hurt your foot on a stone.

···

A SHELTER
(91:1-16) *When bad weather strikes, everyone immediately heads for shelter. When hard times come, the psalm writer encourages everyone to head to shelter—God. The protection he offers is tailor made to fit any kind of trouble. Is God your first option for shelter when trouble comes?*

FOR A LIFETIME
(92:14-15) *A person can honor God his or her entire life. Honoring God is not limited to young people who still have physical strength and vitality. Even in old age, devoted believers can produce spiritual fruit. Many faithful older people have much to share and teach others based on their long relationship with God. Seek out an elderly friend or relative to tell you about life experiences with the Lord and challenge you to new heights of spiritual living. Are you willing to listen?*

¹³ You will trample upon lions and cobras;
you will crush fierce lions and serpents under your feet!
¹⁴ The LORD says, "I will rescue those who love me.
I will protect those who trust in my name.
¹⁵ When they call on me, I will answer;
I will be with them in trouble.
I will rescue and honor them.
¹⁶ I will reward them with a long life
and give them my salvation."

92

A psalm. A song to be sung on the Sabbath Day.

¹ It is good to give thanks to the LORD,
to sing praises to the Most High.
² It is good to proclaim your unfailing love in the morning,
your faithfulness in the evening,
³ accompanied by the ten-stringed harp
and the melody of the lyre.

⁴ You thrill me, LORD, with all you have done for me!
I sing for joy because of what you have done.
⁵ O LORD, what great works you do!
And how deep are your thoughts.
⁶ Only a simpleton would not know,
and only a fool would not understand this:
⁷ Though the wicked sprout like weeds
and evildoers flourish,
they will be destroyed forever.

⁸ But you, O LORD, will be exalted forever.
⁹ Your enemies, LORD, will surely perish;
all evildoers will be scattered.
¹⁰ But you have made me as strong as a wild ox.
You have anointed me with the finest oil.
¹¹ My eyes have seen the downfall of my enemies;
my ears have heard the defeat of my wicked opponents.
¹² But the godly will flourish like palm trees
and grow strong like the cedars of Lebanon.
¹³ For they are transplanted to the LORD's own house.
They flourish in the courts of our God.
¹⁴ Even in old age they will still produce fruit;
they will remain vital and green.
¹⁵ They will declare, "The LORD is just!
He is my rock!
There is no evil in him!"

93

¹The Lord is king! He is robed in
majesty.
Indeed, the Lord is robed in majesty and
armed with strength.
The world stands firm
and cannot be shaken.

² Your throne, O Lord, has stood from time
immemorial.
You yourself are from the everlasting past.
³ The floods have risen up, O Lord.
The floods have roared like thunder;
the floods have lifted their pounding
waves.
⁴ But mightier than the violent raging of the
seas,
mightier than the breakers on the shore—
the Lord above is mightier than these!
⁵ Your royal laws cannot be changed.
Your reign, O Lord, is holy forever and
ever.

94

¹O Lord, the God of vengeance,
O God of vengeance, let your
glorious justice shine forth!
² Arise, O judge of the earth.
Give the proud what they deserve.
³ How long, O Lord?
How long will the wicked be allowed to
gloat?
⁴ How long will they speak with arrogance?
How long will these evil people boast?
⁵ They crush your people, Lord,
hurting those you claim as your own.
⁶ They kill widows and foreigners
and murder orphans.
⁷ "The Lord isn't looking," they say,
"and besides, the God of Israel* doesn't
care."

⁸ Think again, you fools!
When will you finally catch on?
⁹ Is he deaf—the one who made your ears?
Is he blind—the one who formed your
eyes?
¹⁰ He punishes the nations—won't he also
punish you?
He knows everything—doesn't he also
know what you are doing?
¹¹ The Lord knows people's thoughts;
he knows they are worthless!

¹² Joyful are those you discipline, Lord,
those you teach with your instructions.
¹³ You give them relief from troubled times
until a pit is dug to capture the wicked.
¹⁴ The Lord will not reject his people;

94:7 Hebrew *of Jacob.* See note on 44:4.

he will not abandon his special
possession.
¹⁵ Judgment will again be founded on justice,
and those with virtuous hearts will
pursue it.

¹⁶ Who will protect me from the wicked?
Who will stand up for me against
evildoers?
¹⁷ Unless the Lord had helped me,
I would soon have settled in the silence
of the grave.
¹⁸ I cried out, "I am slipping!"
but your unfailing love, O Lord,
supported me.
¹⁹ When doubts filled my mind,
your comfort gave me renewed hope and
cheer.

²⁰ Can unjust leaders claim that God is on
their side—
leaders whose decrees permit injustice?
²¹ They gang up against the righteous
and condemn the innocent to death.
²² But the Lord is my fortress;
my God is the mighty rock where I hide.
²³ God will turn the sins of evil people back on
them.
He will destroy them for their sins.
The Lord our God will destroy them.

95

¹Come, let us sing to the Lord!
Let us shout joyfully to the Rock
of our salvation.
² Let us come to him with thanksgiving.
Let us sing psalms of praise to him.
³ For the Lord is a great God,
a great King above all gods.
⁴ He holds in his hands the depths of the
earth
and the mightiest mountains.
⁵ The sea belongs to him, for he made it.
His hands formed the dry land, too.

⁶ Come, let us worship and bow down.
Let us kneel before the Lord our maker,
⁷ for he is our God.
We are the people he watches over,
the flock under his care.

If only you would listen to his voice today!
⁸ The Lord says, "Don't harden your hearts
as Israel did at Meribah,
as they did at Massah in the wilderness.
⁹ For there your ancestors tested and tried my
patience,
even though they saw everything I did.
¹⁰ For forty years I was angry with them, and
I said,

'They are a people whose hearts turn away
  from me.
They refuse to do what I tell them.'
11 So in my anger I took an oath:
  'They will never enter my place of rest.'"

96
¹Sing a new song to the LORD!
  Let the whole earth sing to the
  LORD!
² Sing to the LORD; praise his name.
  Each day proclaim the good news that he
  saves.
³ Publish his glorious deeds among the
  nations.
  Tell everyone about the amazing things
  he does.
⁴ Great is the LORD! He is most worthy of
  praise!
  He is to be feared above all gods.
⁵ The gods of other nations are mere idols,
  but the LORD made the heavens!
⁶ Honor and majesty surround him;
  strength and beauty fill his sanctuary.

⁷ O nations of the world, recognize the LORD;
  recognize that the LORD is glorious and
  strong.
⁸ Give to the LORD the glory he deserves!
  Bring your offering and come into his
  courts.
⁹ Worship the LORD in all his holy splendor.
  Let all the earth tremble before him.
¹⁰ Tell all the nations, "The LORD reigns!"
  The world stands firm and cannot be
  shaken.
  He will judge all peoples fairly.

¹¹ Let the heavens be glad, and the earth
  rejoice!
  Let the sea and everything in it shout
  his praise!
¹² Let the fields and their crops burst out
  with joy!
  Let the trees of the forest rustle with
  praise
¹³ before the LORD, for he is coming!
  He is coming to judge the earth.

....

WANTING WHAT HE WANTS
*(97:10) A sincere desire to please God will result in an
alignment of your desires with God's desires. You will
love what God loves and hate what God hates. If you do
not despise the actions of people who take advantage
of others, if you admire people who look out only for
themselves, or if you envy those who get ahead using
any means to accomplish their ends, then your primary
desire in life is not aligned with God's desires. In need
of a realignment? Just by acknowledging your need,
you're halfway there!*

He will judge the world with justice,
  and the nations with his truth.

97
¹The LORD is king!
  Let the earth rejoice!
  Let the farthest coastlands be glad.
² Dark clouds surround him.
  Righteousness and justice are the
  foundation of his throne.
³ Fire spreads ahead of him
  and burns up all his foes.
⁴ His lightning flashes out across the world.
  The earth sees and trembles.
⁵ The mountains melt like wax before
  the LORD,
  before the Lord of all the earth.
⁶ The heavens proclaim his righteousness;
  every nation sees his glory.
⁷ Those who worship idols are disgraced—
  all who brag about their worthless gods—
  for every god must bow to him.
⁸ Jerusalem* has heard and rejoiced,
  and all the towns of Judah are glad
  because of your justice, O LORD!
⁹ For you, O LORD, are supreme over all the
  earth;
  you are exalted far above all gods.

¹⁰ You who love the LORD, hate evil!
  He protects the lives of his godly people
  and rescues them from the power of the
  wicked.
¹¹ Light shines on the godly,
  and joy on those whose hearts are right.
¹² May all who are godly rejoice in the LORD
  and praise his holy name!

98
A psalm.

¹ Sing a new song to the LORD,
  for he has done wonderful deeds.
  His right hand has won a mighty victory;
  his holy arm has shown his saving
  power!
² The LORD has announced his victory
  and has revealed his righteousness
  to every nation!
³ He has remembered his promise to love
  and be faithful to Israel.
  The ends of the earth have seen the
  victory of our God.

⁴ Shout to the LORD, all the earth;
  break out in praise and sing for joy!
⁵ Sing your praise to the LORD with the harp,
  with the harp and melodious song,

97:8 Hebrew *Zion.*

6 with trumpets and the sound of the ram's
horn.
Make a joyful symphony before the LORD,
the King!

7 Let the sea and everything in it shout his
praise!
Let the earth and all living things join in.
8 Let the rivers clap their hands in glee!
Let the hills sing out their songs of joy
9 before the LORD.
For the LORD is coming to judge the earth.
He will judge the world with justice,
and the nations with fairness.

99

1 The LORD is king!
Let the nations tremble!
He sits on his throne between the cherubim.
Let the whole earth quake!
2 The LORD sits in majesty in Jerusalem,*
exalted above all the nations.
3 Let them praise your great and awesome
name.
Your name is holy!
4 Mighty King, lover of justice,
you have established fairness.
You have acted with justice
and righteousness throughout Israel.*
5 Exalt the LORD our God!
Bow low before his feet, for he is holy!

6 Moses and Aaron were among his priests;
Samuel also called on his name.
They cried to the LORD for help,
and he answered them.
7 He spoke to Israel from the pillar of cloud,
and they followed the laws and decrees
he gave them.
8 O LORD our God, you answered them.
You were a forgiving God to them,
but you punished them when they went
wrong.

9 Exalt the LORD our God,
and worship at his holy mountain in
Jerusalem,
for the LORD our God is holy!

100

A psalm of thanksgiving.

1 Shout with joy to the LORD, all the earth!
2 Worship the LORD with gladness.
Come before him, singing with joy.
3 Acknowledge that the LORD is God!
He made us, and we are his.*

99:2 Hebrew *Zion.* 99:4 Hebrew *Jacob.* See note on 44:4.
100:3 As in an alternate reading in the Masoretic Text; the other
alternate and some ancient versions read *and not we ourselves.*

ENTER HIS GATES WITH THANKSGIVING; GO INTO HIS COURTS WITH PRAISE. GIVE THANKS TO HIM AND PRAISE HIS NAME.

We are his people, the sheep of his
pasture.
4 Enter his gates with thanksgiving;
go into his courts with praise.
Give thanks to him and praise his name.
5 For the LORD is good.
His unfailing love continues forever,
and his faithfulness continues to each
generation.

101

A psalm of David.

1 I will sing of your love and justice, LORD.
I will praise you with songs.
2 I will be careful to live a blameless life—
when will you come to help me?
I will lead a life of integrity
in my own home.
3 I will refuse to look at
anything vile and vulgar.
I hate all who deal crookedly;
I will have nothing to do with them.
4 I will reject perverse ideas
and stay away from every evil.
5 I will not tolerate people who slander their
neighbors.
I will not endure conceit and pride.

6 I will search for faithful people
to be my companions.
Only those who are above reproach
will be allowed to serve me.

....

FAMILY NAME
(99:3) God's name symbolizes his nature and his reputation. Unfortunately the name of God is often misused or
treated lightly by those who don't understand its significance. How can you honor God's name by your words and
your life?

COMPANIONS
(101:3-8) David set different standards for associates
than most. He said that he would only have "faithful
people" as his companions and that he would avoid
wrongdoers. What standards do you have for your associates? Who do you hang out with?

7 I will not allow deceivers to serve in my
    house,
    and liars will not stay in my presence.
8 My daily task will be to ferret out the wicked
    and free the city of the LORD from
        their grip.

102

*A prayer of one overwhelmed with
trouble, pouring out problems before
the LORD.*

1 LORD, hear my prayer!
    Listen to my plea!
2 Don't turn away from me
    in my time of distress.
    Bend down to listen,
    and answer me quickly when I call to you.
3 For my days disappear like smoke,
    and my bones burn like red-hot coals.
4 My heart is sick, withered like grass,
    and I have lost my appetite.
5 Because of my groaning,
    I am reduced to skin and bones.
6 I am like an owl in the desert,
    like a little owl in a far-off wilderness.
7 I lie awake,
    lonely as a solitary bird on the roof.
8 My enemies taunt me day after day.
    They mock and curse me.
9 I eat ashes for food.
    My tears run down into my drink
10 because of your anger and wrath.
    For you have picked me up and thrown
        me out.
11 My life passes as swiftly as the evening
        shadows.
    I am withering away like grass.

12 But you, O LORD, will sit on your throne
        forever.
    Your fame will endure to every generation.
13 You will arise and have mercy on
        Jerusalem*—
    and now is the time to pity her,
    now is the time you promised to help.
14 For your people love every stone in her walls
    and cherish even the dust in her streets.
15 Then the nations will tremble before
        the LORD.

PRAISE LIST
*(103:3-18) David praised God for his glorious acts. Here's
his list of reasons to praise God: for his love, forgiveness,
salvation, kindness, mercy, justice, patience, and tenderness. We receive all of these freely, without having to earn
any of them. No matter how difficult your life seems, you
can always find something to be grateful for. When you
feel as though you have nothing to praise God for, read
David's list.*

The kings of the earth will tremble before
        his glory.
16 For the LORD will rebuild Jerusalem.
    He will appear in his glory.
17 He will listen to the prayers of the destitute.
    He will not reject their pleas.

18 Let this be recorded for future generations,
    so that a people not yet born will praise
        the LORD.
19 Tell them the LORD looked down
    from his heavenly sanctuary.
    He looked down to earth from heaven
20 to hear the groans of the prisoners,
    to release those condemned to die.
21 And so the LORD's fame will be celebrated
        in Zion,
    his praises in Jerusalem,
22 when multitudes gather together
    and kingdoms come to worship
        the LORD.

23 He broke my strength in midlife,
    cutting short my days.
24 But I cried to him, "O my God, who lives
        forever,
    don't take my life while I am so young!
25 Long ago you laid the foundation of the
        earth
    and made the heavens with your hands.
26 They will perish, but you remain forever;
    they will wear out like old clothing.
    You will change them like a garment
    and discard them.
27 But you are always the same;
    you will live forever.
28 The children of your people
    will live in security.
    Their children's children
    will thrive in your presence."

103

A psalm of David.

1 Let all that I am praise the LORD;
    with my whole heart, I will praise his holy
        name.
2 Let all that I am praise the LORD;
    may I never forget the good things he
        does for me.
3 He forgives all my sins
    and heals all my diseases.
4 He redeems me from death
    and crowns me with love and tender
        mercies.
5 He fills my life with good things.
    My youth is renewed like the eagle's!

102:13 Hebrew *Zion;* also in 102:16.

⁶ The LORD gives righteousness
   and justice to all who are treated unfairly.

⁷ He revealed his character to Moses
   and his deeds to the people of Israel.
⁸ The LORD is compassionate and merciful,
   slow to get angry and filled with
      unfailing love.
⁹ He will not constantly accuse us,
   nor remain angry forever.
¹⁰ He does not punish us for all our sins;
   he does not deal harshly with us, as we
      deserve.
¹¹ For his unfailing love toward those who
      fear him
   is as great as the height of the heavens
      above the earth.
¹² He has removed our sins as far from us
   as the east is from the west.
¹³ The LORD is like a father to his children,
   tender and compassionate to those who
      fear him.
¹⁴ For he knows how weak we are;
   he remembers we are only dust.
¹⁵ Our days on earth are like grass;
   like wildflowers, we bloom and die.
¹⁶ The wind blows, and we are gone—
   as though we had never been here.
¹⁷ But the love of the LORD remains forever
   with those who fear him.
   His salvation extends to the children's
      children
¹⁸ of those who are faithful to his covenant,
   of those who obey his commandments!

¹⁹ The LORD has made the heavens his throne;
   from there he rules over everything.

²⁰ Praise the LORD, you angels,
   you mighty ones who carry out his plans,
   listening for each of his commands.
²¹ Yes, praise the LORD, you armies of angels
   who serve him and do his will!
²² Praise the LORD, everything he has created,
   everything in all his kingdom.

   Let all that I am praise the LORD.

104 ¹Let all that I am praise the LORD.

O LORD my God, how great you are!
   You are robed with honor and majesty.
²   You are dressed in a robe of light.
   You stretch out the starry curtain of the
      heavens;

³   you lay out the rafters of your home in the
      rain clouds.
   You make the clouds your chariot;
      you ride upon the wings of the wind.
⁴ The winds are your messengers;
   flames of fire are your servants.*

⁵ You placed the world on its foundation
   so it would never be moved.
⁶ You clothed the earth with floods of water,
   water that covered even the mountains.
⁷ At your command, the water fled;
   at the sound of your thunder, it hurried
      away.
⁸ Mountains rose and valleys sank
   to the levels you decreed.
⁹ Then you set a firm boundary for the seas,
   so they would never again cover the
      earth.

¹⁰ You make springs pour water into the
      ravines,
   so streams gush down from the
      mountains.
¹¹ They provide water for all the animals,
   and the wild donkeys quench their thirst.
¹² The birds nest beside the streams
   and sing among the branches of the
      trees.
¹³ You send rain on the mountains from your
      heavenly home,
   and you fill the earth with the fruit of your
      labor.
¹⁴ You cause grass to grow for the livestock
   and plants for people to use.
   You allow them to produce food from the
      earth—
¹⁵   wine to make them glad,
   olive oil to soothe their skin,
      and bread to give them strength.
¹⁶ The trees of the LORD are well cared for—
   the cedars of Lebanon that he planted.
¹⁷ There the birds make their nests,
   and the storks make their homes in the
      cypresses.
¹⁸ High in the mountains live the wild goats,
   and the rocks form a refuge for the
      hyraxes.*
¹⁹ You made the moon to mark the seasons,
   and the sun knows when to set.
²⁰ You send the darkness, and it becomes
      night,
   when all the forest animals prowl about.
²¹ Then the young lions roar for their prey,
   stalking the food provided by God.
²² At dawn they slink back
   into their dens to rest.

104:4 Greek version reads *He sends his angels like the winds, / his servants like flames of fire.* Compare Heb 1:7.   **104:18** Or *coneys,* or *rock badgers.*

²³ Then people go off to their work,
    where they labor until evening.

²⁴ O Lord, what a variety of things you have
        made!
    In wisdom you have made them all.
    The earth is full of your creatures.
²⁵ Here is the ocean, vast and wide,
    teeming with life of every kind,
    both large and small.
²⁶ See the ships sailing along,
    and Leviathan,* which you made to play
        in the sea.

²⁷ They all depend on you
    to give them food as they need it.
²⁸ When you supply it, they gather it.
    You open your hand to feed them,
    and they are richly satisfied.
²⁹ But if you turn away from them, they panic.
    When you take away their breath,
    they die and turn again to dust.
³⁰ When you give them your breath,* life is
        created,
    and you renew the face of the earth.

³¹ May the glory of the Lord continue forever!
    The Lord takes pleasure in all he has
        made!
³² The earth trembles at his glance;
    the mountains smoke at his touch.

³³ I will sing to the Lord as long as I live.
    I will praise my God to my last breath!
³⁴ May all my thoughts be pleasing to him,
    for I rejoice in the Lord.
³⁵ Let all sinners vanish from the face of the
        earth;
    let the wicked disappear forever.

Let all that I am praise the Lord.

Praise the Lord!

A RICH VARIETY
*(104:24) The earth is filled with an amazing variety
of plants and creatures. Such a variety reveals the rich
creativity, goodness, and wisdom of God. As you observe
your surroundings, what's the first thing you notice? Take
a fresh look at people, seeing each one as his unique creation, each with his or her own special talents, abilities,
and gifts. Like the psalmist, you'll probably be inspired
to praise God.*

KEEP SEARCHING
*(105:1-5) If God seems far away, keep searching for him.
God rewards "those who sincerely seek him" (Heb 11:6).
Jesus promised, "Keep on seeking, and you will find"
(Matt 7:7). This psalm suggests a valuable way to search
out God—become familiar with the way he has helped his
people in the past. The Bible records the history of God's
people. In searching its pages we will discover a loving
God who is waiting for us to find him.*

105

¹ Give thanks to the Lord and
        proclaim his greatness.
    Let the whole world know what he has
        done.
² Sing to him; yes, sing his praises.
    Tell everyone about his wonderful deeds.
³ Exult in his holy name;
    rejoice, you who worship the Lord.
⁴ Search for the Lord and for his strength;
    continually seek him.
⁵ Remember the wonders he has performed,
    his miracles, and the rulings he has
        given,
⁶ you children of his servant Abraham,
    you descendants of Jacob, his chosen
        ones.

⁷ He is the Lord our God.
    His justice is seen throughout the land.
⁸ He always stands by his covenant—
    the commitment he made to a thousand
        generations.
⁹ This is the covenant he made with Abraham
    and the oath he swore to Isaac.
¹⁰ He confirmed it to Jacob as a decree,
    and to the people of Israel as a never-
        ending covenant:
¹¹ "I will give you the land of Canaan
    as your special possession."

¹² He said this when they were few in number,
    a tiny group of strangers in Canaan.
¹³ They wandered from nation to nation,
    from one kingdom to another.
¹⁴ Yet he did not let anyone oppress them.
    He warned kings on their behalf:
¹⁵ "Do not touch my chosen people,
    and do not hurt my prophets."

¹⁶ He called for a famine on the land of
        Canaan,
    cutting off its food supply.
¹⁷ Then he sent someone to Egypt ahead of
        them—
    Joseph, who was sold as a slave.
¹⁸ They bruised his feet with fetters
    and placed his neck in an iron collar.
¹⁹ Until the time came to fulfill his dreams,*
    the Lord tested Joseph's character.
²⁰ Then Pharaoh sent for him and set him free;
    the ruler of the nation opened his prison
        door.
²¹ Joseph was put in charge of all the king's
        household;
    he became ruler over all the king's
        possessions.

104:26 The identification of Leviathan is disputed, ranging from
an earthly creature to a mythical sea monster in ancient literature.
104:30 Or *When you send your Spirit.*   105:19 Hebrew *his word.*

²² He could instruct the king's aides as he
    pleased
    and teach the king's advisers.

²³ Then Israel arrived in Egypt;
    Jacob lived as a foreigner in the land of
    Ham.

²⁴ And the LORD multiplied the people of Israel
    until they became too mighty for their
    enemies.

²⁵ Then he turned the Egyptians against the
    Israelites,
    and they plotted against the LORD's
    servants.

²⁶ But the LORD sent his servant Moses,
    along with Aaron, whom he had chosen.

²⁷ They performed miraculous signs among
    the Egyptians,
    and wonders in the land of Ham.

²⁸ The LORD blanketed Egypt in darkness,
    for they had defied his commands to let
    his people go.

²⁹ He turned their water into blood,
    poisoning all the fish.

³⁰ Then frogs overran the land
    and even invaded the king's bedrooms.

³¹ When the LORD spoke, flies descended on
    the Egyptians,
    and gnats swarmed across Egypt.

³² He sent them hail instead of rain,
    and lightning flashed over the land.

³³ He ruined their grapevines and fig trees
    and shattered all the trees.

³⁴ He spoke, and hordes of locusts came—
    young locusts beyond number.

³⁵ They ate up everything green in the land,
    destroying all the crops in their fields.

³⁶ Then he killed the oldest son in each
    Egyptian home,
    the pride and joy of each family.

³⁷ The LORD brought his people out of Egypt,
    loaded with silver and gold;
    and not one among the tribes of Israel
    even stumbled.

³⁸ Egypt was glad when they were gone,
    for they feared them greatly.

³⁹ The LORD spread a cloud above them as
    a covering
    and gave them a great fire to light the
    darkness.

⁴⁰ They asked for meat, and he sent them
    quail;
    he satisfied their hunger with manna—
    bread from heaven.

⁴¹ He split open a rock, and water gushed out
    to form a river through the dry wasteland.

⁴² For he remembered his sacred promise
    to his servant Abraham.

⁴³ So he brought his people out of Egypt
    with joy,
    his chosen ones with rejoicing.

⁴⁴ He gave his people the lands of pagan
    nations,
    and they harvested crops that others had
    planted.

⁴⁵ All this happened so they would follow his
    decrees
    and obey his instructions.

Praise the LORD!

106

¹ Praise the LORD!

Give thanks to the LORD, for he is good!
    His faithful love endures forever.
² Who can list the glorious miracles of the
    LORD?
    Who can ever praise him enough?
³ There is joy for those who deal justly with
    others
    and always do what is right.

⁴ Remember me, LORD, when you show favor
    to your people;
    come near and rescue me.
⁵ Let me share in the prosperity of your
    chosen ones.
    Let me rejoice in the joy of your people;
    let me praise you with those who are your
    heritage.

⁶ Like our ancestors, we have sinned.
    We have done wrong! We have acted
    wickedly!
⁷ Our ancestors in Egypt
    were not impressed by the LORD's
    miraculous deeds.
    They soon forgot his many acts of kindness
    to them.
    Instead, they rebelled against him at the
    Red Sea.*
⁸ Even so, he saved them—
    to defend the honor of his name
    and to demonstrate his mighty power.
⁹ He commanded the Red Sea* to dry up.
    He led Israel across the sea as if it were
    a desert.
¹⁰ So he rescued them from their enemies
    and redeemed them from their foes.
¹¹ Then the water returned and covered their
    enemies;
    not one of them survived.

106:7 Hebrew at the sea, the sea of reeds.   106:9 Hebrew sea
of reeds; also in 106:22.

12 Then his people believed his promises.
  Then they sang his praise.

13 Yet how quickly they forgot what he had
    done!
  They wouldn't wait for his counsel!
14 In the wilderness their desires ran wild,
    testing God's patience in that dry
    wasteland.
15 So he gave them what they asked for,
    but he sent a plague along with it.
16 The people in the camp were jealous of
    Moses
  and envious of Aaron, the LORD's holy
    priest.
17 Because of this, the earth opened up;
    it swallowed Dathan
  and buried Abiram and the other rebels.
18 Fire fell upon their followers;
    a flame consumed the wicked.

19 The people made a calf at Mount Sinai*;
    they bowed before an image made of gold.
20 They traded their glorious God
    for a statue of a grass-eating bull.
21 They forgot God, their savior,
    who had done such great things in
    Egypt—
22 such wonderful things in the land of Ham,
    such awesome deeds at the Red Sea.
23 So he declared he would destroy them.
  But Moses, his chosen one, stepped
    between the LORD and the people.
  He begged him to turn from his anger
    and not destroy them.

24 The people refused to enter the pleasant
    land,
  for they wouldn't believe his promise
    to care for them.
25 Instead, they grumbled in their tents
    and refused to obey the LORD.
26 Therefore, he solemnly swore
    that he would kill them in the wilderness,
27 that he would scatter their descendants
    among the nations,
  exiling them to distant lands.

....

TROUBLES
(106:40-42) *God allowed trouble to come to the Israelites to help them. Some of our troubles can be helpful
because they (1) humble us, (2) allow us to experience
more of God's faithfulness, (3) make us more dependent
upon God, (4) encourage us to submit to God's purpose
for our lives, and (5) make us more compassionate to
others in trouble. Of course, believing that hard times can
be helpful doesn't come naturally! But as Romans 8:28
states, "God causes everything to work together for the
good of those who love God and are called according to
his purpose for them."*

28 Then our ancestors joined in the worship
    of Baal at Peor;
  they even ate sacrifices offered to the
    dead!
29 They angered the LORD with all these things,
    so a plague broke out among them.
30 But Phinehas had the courage to intervene,
    and the plague was stopped.
31 So he has been regarded as a righteous man
    ever since that time.

32 At Meribah, too, they angered the LORD,
    causing Moses serious trouble.
33 They made Moses angry,*
    and he spoke foolishly.

34 Israel failed to destroy the nations in
    the land,
  as the LORD had commanded them.
35 Instead, they mingled among the pagans
    and adopted their evil customs.
36 They worshiped their idols,
    which led to their downfall.
37 They even sacrificed their sons
    and their daughters to the demons.
38 They shed innocent blood,
    the blood of their sons and daughters.
  By sacrificing them to the idols of Canaan,
    they polluted the land with murder.
39 They defiled themselves by their evil deeds,
    and their love of idols was adultery in the
    LORD's sight.

40 That is why the LORD's anger burned against
    his people,
  and he abhorred his own special
    possession.
41 He handed them over to pagan nations,
    and they were ruled by those who hated
    them.
42 Their enemies crushed them
    and brought them under their cruel
    power.
43 Again and again he rescued them,
    but they chose to rebel against him,
  and they were finally destroyed by
    their sin.
44 Even so, he pitied them in their distress
    and listened to their cries.
45 He remembered his covenant with them
    and relented because of his unfailing
    love.
46 He even caused their captors
    to treat them with kindness.

47 Save us, O LORD our God!
    Gather us back from among the nations,

106:19 Hebrew *at Horeb,* another name for Sinai.   **106:33** Hebrew
They embittered his spirit.

so we can thank your holy name
and rejoice and praise you.

48 Praise the LORD, the God of Israel,
who lives from everlasting to everlasting!
Let all the people say, "Amen!"

Praise the LORD!

BOOK FIVE (Psalms 107–150)

107 1 Give thanks to the LORD, for he
is good!
His faithful love endures forever.
2 Has the LORD redeemed you? Then
speak out!
Tell others he has redeemed you from
your enemies.
3 For he has gathered the exiles from many
lands,
from east and west,
from north and south.

4 Some wandered in the wilderness,
lost and homeless.
5 Hungry and thirsty,
they nearly died.
6 "LORD, help!" they cried in their trouble,
and he rescued them from their distress.
7 He led them straight to safety,
to a city where they could live.
8 Let them praise the LORD for his great love
and for the wonderful things he has done
for them.
9 For he satisfies the thirsty
and fills the hungry with good things.

10 Some sat in darkness and deepest gloom,
imprisoned in iron chains of misery.
11 They rebelled against the words of God,
scorning the counsel of the Most High.
12 That is why he broke them with hard labor;
they fell, and no one was there to help
them.
13 "LORD, help!" they cried in their trouble,
and he saved them from their distress.
14 He led them from the darkness and deepest
gloom;
he snapped their chains.
15 Let them praise the LORD for his great love
and for the wonderful things he has done
for them.
16 For he broke down their prison gates
of bronze;
he cut apart their bars of iron.

17 Some were fools; they rebelled
and suffered for their sins.
18 They couldn't stand the thought of food,
and they were knocking on death's door.

19 "LORD, help!" they cried in their trouble,
and he saved them from their distress.
20 He sent out his word and healed them,
snatching them from the door of death.
21 Let them praise the LORD for his great love
and for the wonderful things he has done
for them.
22 Let them offer sacrifices of thanksgiving
and sing joyfully about his glorious acts.

23 Some went off to sea in ships,
plying the trade routes of the world.
24 They, too, observed the LORD's power in
action,
his impressive works on the deepest
seas.
25 He spoke, and the winds rose,
stirring up the waves.
26 Their ships were tossed to the heavens
and plunged again to the depths;
the sailors cringed in terror.
27 They reeled and staggered like drunkards
and were at their wits' end.
28 "LORD, help!" they cried in their trouble,
and he saved them from their distress.
29 He calmed the storm to a whisper
and stilled the waves.
30 What a blessing was that stillness
as he brought them safely into harbor!
31 Let them praise the LORD for his great love
and for the wonderful things he has done
for them.
32 Let them exalt him publicly before the
congregation
and before the leaders of the nation.

33 He changes rivers into deserts,
and springs of water into dry, thirsty land.
34 He turns the fruitful land into salty
wastelands,
because of the wickedness of those who
live there.
35 But he also turns deserts into pools
of water,
the dry land into springs of water.
36 He brings the hungry to settle there
and to build their cities.
37 They sow their fields, plant their vineyards,
and harvest their bumper crops.
38 How he blesses them!
They raise large families there,
and their herds of livestock increase.

39 When they decrease in number and become
impoverished
through oppression, trouble, and sorrow,
40 the LORD pours contempt on
their princes,

causing them to wander in trackless
wastelands.
41 But he rescues the poor from trouble
and increases their families like flocks of
sheep.
42 The godly will see these things and be glad,
while the wicked are struck silent.
43 Those who are wise will take all this to
heart;
they will see in our history the faithful
love of the LORD.

108 *A song. A psalm of David.*

1 My heart is confident in you, O God;
no wonder I can sing your praises with all
my heart!
2 Wake up, lyre and harp!
I will wake the dawn with my song.
3 I will thank you, LORD, among all the people.
I will sing your praises among the nations.
4 For your unfailing love is higher than the
heavens.
Your faithfulness reaches to the clouds.
5 Be exalted, O God, above the highest
heavens.
May your glory shine over all the earth.

6 Now rescue your beloved people.
Answer and save us by your power.
7 God has promised this by his holiness*:
"I will divide up Shechem with joy.
I will measure out the valley of Succoth.
8 Gilead is mine,
and Manasseh, too.
Ephraim, my helmet, will produce my
warriors,
and Judah, my scepter, will produce
my kings.
9 But Moab, my washbasin, will become
my servant,
and I will wipe my feet on Edom
and shout in triumph over Philistia."

10 Who will bring me into the fortified city?
Who will bring me victory over Edom?
11 Have you rejected us, O God?
Will you no longer march with our armies?
12 Oh, please help us against our enemies,
for all human help is useless.

BEYOND SURVIVAL
*(108:12-13) David prayed not just for rescue, but for vic-
tory. Ever pray for just enough strength to make it through
a stressful situation? With God's help we can claim more
than just survival, we can claim victory! Look for ways
God can use your distress as an opportunity to show his
mighty power.*

13 With God's help we will do mighty things,
for he will trample down our foes.

109 *For the choir director: A psalm of David.*

1 O God, whom I praise,
don't stand silent and aloof
2 while the wicked slander me
and tell lies about me.
3 They surround me with hateful words
and fight against me for no reason.
4 I love them, but they try to destroy me with
accusations
even as I am praying for them!
5 They repay evil for good,
and hatred for my love.

6 They say,* "Get an evil person to turn
against him.
Send an accuser to bring him to trial.
7 When his case comes up for judgment,
let him be pronounced guilty.
Count his prayers as sins.
8 Let his years be few;
let someone else take his position.
9 May his children become fatherless,
and his wife a widow.
10 May his children wander as beggars
and be driven from their ruined homes.
11 May creditors seize his entire estate,
and strangers take all he has earned.
12 Let no one be kind to him;
let no one pity his fatherless children.
13 May all his offspring die.
May his family name be blotted out in
a single generation.
14 May the LORD never forget the sins of his
fathers;
may his mother's sins never be erased
from the record.
15 May the LORD always remember
these sins,
and may his name disappear from
human memory.
16 For he refused all kindness to others;
he persecuted the poor and needy,
and he hounded the brokenhearted
to death.
17 He loved to curse others;
now you curse him.
He never blessed others;
now don't you bless him.
18 Cursing is as natural to him as his
clothing,
or the water he drinks,
or the rich food he eats.

108:7 Or *in his sanctuary.*   **109:6** Hebrew lacks *They say.*

¹⁹ Now may his curses return and cling to him
like clothing;
may they be tied around him like a belt."
²⁰ May those curses become the LORD's
punishment
for my accusers who speak evil of me.
²¹ But deal well with me, O Sovereign LORD,
for the sake of your own reputation!
Rescue me
because you are so faithful and good.
²² For I am poor and needy,
and my heart is full of pain.
²³ I am fading like a shadow at dusk;
I am brushed off like a locust.
²⁴ My knees are weak from fasting,
and I am skin and bones.
²⁵ I am a joke to people everywhere;
when they see me, they shake their
heads in scorn.

²⁶ Help me, O LORD my God!
Save me because of your unfailing love.
²⁷ Let them see that this is your doing,
that you yourself have done it, LORD.
²⁸ Then let them curse me if they like,
but you will bless me!
When they attack me, they will be
disgraced!
But I, your servant, will go right on
rejoicing!
²⁹ May my accusers be clothed with disgrace;
may their humiliation cover them like a
cloak.
³⁰ But I will give repeated thanks to the LORD,
praising him to everyone.
³¹ For he stands beside the needy,
ready to save them from those who
condemn them.

110 *A psalm of David.*

¹ The LORD said to my Lord,
"Sit in the place of honor at my right hand
until I humble your enemies,
making them a footstool under your feet."

² The LORD will extend your powerful kingdom
from Jerusalem*;
you will rule over your enemies.
³ When you go to war,
your people will serve you willingly.
You are arrayed in holy garments,
and your strength will be renewed each
day like the morning dew.

⁴ The LORD has taken an oath and will not
break his vow:
"You are a priest forever in the order
of Melchizedek."
⁵ The Lord stands at your right hand to
protect you.
He will strike down many kings when his
anger erupts.
⁶ He will punish the nations
and fill their lands with corpses;
he will shatter heads over the whole earth.
⁷ But he himself will be refreshed from brooks
along the way.
He will be victorious.

111 * ¹Praise the LORD!

I will thank the LORD with all my heart
as I meet with his godly people.
² How amazing are the deeds of the LORD!
All who delight in him should ponder
them.
³ Everything he does reveals his glory and
majesty.
His righteousness never fails.
⁴ He causes us to remember his wonderful
works.
How gracious and merciful is our LORD!
⁵ He gives food to those who fear him;
he always remembers his covenant.
⁶ He has shown his great power to his people
by giving them the lands of other nations.
⁷ All he does is just and good,
and all his commandments are
trustworthy.
⁸ They are forever true,
to be obeyed faithfully and with integrity.
⁹ He has paid a full ransom for his people.
He has guaranteed his covenant with
them forever.
What a holy, awe-inspiring name he has!
¹⁰ Fear of the LORD is the foundation of true
wisdom.
All who obey his commandments will
grow in wisdom.

Praise him forever!

••

ON THE FENCE?
(110:1-7) *This psalm shows God's promise of sending the
Messiah. Both the Old and New Testaments proclaim the
characteristics of the Savior. The New Testament clearly
shows that Jesus is the promised Messiah. Many people
have a vague belief in God, but refuse to accept Jesus as
anything more than a great human teacher. But the Bible
does not allow that option. Are you on the fence concerning your beliefs about Jesus? Do you believe that he's God
or just a great teacher?*

110:2 Hebrew *Zion.* **111** This psalm is a Hebrew acrostic poem;
after the introductory note of praise, each line begins with a
successive letter of the Hebrew alphabet.

112 [*] ¹Praise the LORD!

How joyful are those who fear the LORD
and delight in obeying his commands.
² Their children will be successful
everywhere;
an entire generation of godly people will
be blessed.
³ They themselves will be wealthy,
and their good deeds will last forever.
⁴ Light shines in the darkness for the godly.
They are generous, compassionate, and
righteous.
⁵ Good comes to those who lend money
generously
and conduct their business fairly.
⁶ Such people will not be overcome by evil.
Those who are righteous will be long
remembered.
⁷ They do not fear bad news;
they confidently trust the LORD to care
for them.
⁸ They are confident and fearless
and can face their foes triumphantly.
⁹ They share freely and give generously to
those in need.
Their good deeds will be remembered
forever.
They will have influence and honor.
¹⁰ The wicked will see this and be infuriated.
They will grind their teeth in anger;
they will slink away, their hopes thwarted.

113 ¹Praise the LORD!

Yes, give praise, O servants of the LORD.
Praise the name of the LORD!
² Blessed be the name of the LORD
now and forever.
³ Everywhere—from east to west—
praise the name of the LORD.
⁴ For the LORD is high above the nations;
his glory is higher than the heavens.

⁵ Who can be compared with the LORD
our God,
who is enthroned on high?
⁶ He stoops to look down

....

FEARLESS
*(112:1, 7-8) Everyone wants to live without fear. We
admire people who face dangers and overcome them. The
psalm writer teaches us that fear of God can lead to a fearless life. To fear God means to respect and revere him as
the almighty Lord. When we trust God completely to take
care of us, we will find that our other fears—even of death
itself—will subside.*

on heaven and on earth.
⁷ He lifts the poor from the dust
and the needy from the garbage dump.
⁸ He sets them among princes,
even the princes of his own people!
⁹ He gives the childless woman a family,
making her a happy mother.

Praise the LORD!

114 ¹When the Israelites escaped
from Egypt—
when the family of Jacob left that
foreign land—
² the land of Judah became God's sanctuary,
and Israel became his kingdom.

³ The Red Sea* saw them coming and hurried
out of their way!
The water of the Jordan River turned away.
⁴ The mountains skipped like rams,
the hills like lambs!
⁵ What's wrong, Red Sea, that made you hurry
out of their way?
What happened, Jordan River, that you
turned away?
⁶ Why, mountains, did you skip like rams?
Why, hills, like lambs?

⁷ Tremble, O earth, at the presence of the
Lord,
at the presence of the God of Jacob.
⁸ He turned the rock into a pool of water;
yes, a spring of water flowed from solid
rock.

115 ¹Not to us, O LORD, not to us,
but to your name goes all the
glory
for your unfailing love and
faithfulness.
² Why let the nations say,
"Where is their God?"
³ Our God is in the heavens,
and he does as he wishes.
⁴ Their idols are merely things of silver
and gold,
shaped by human hands.
⁵ They have mouths but cannot speak,
and eyes but cannot see.
⁶ They have ears but cannot hear,
and noses but cannot smell.
⁷ They have hands but cannot feel,
and feet but cannot walk,
and throats but cannot make
a sound.

112 This psalm is a Hebrew acrostic poem; after the introductory
note of praise, each line begins with a successive letter of the
Hebrew alphabet. **114:3** Hebrew *the sea;* also in 114:5.

8 And those who make idols are just like
  them,
    as are all who trust in them.

9 O Israel, trust the LORD!
    He is your helper and your shield.
10 O priests, descendants of Aaron, trust
    the LORD!
    He is your helper and your shield.
11 All you who fear the LORD, trust the LORD!
    He is your helper and your shield.

12 The LORD remembers us and will bless us.
    He will bless the people of Israel
    and bless the priests, the descendants
      of Aaron.
13 He will bless those who fear the LORD,
    both great and lowly.

14 May the LORD richly bless
    both you and your children.
15 May you be blessed by the LORD,
    who made heaven and earth.
16 The heavens belong to the LORD,
    but he has given the earth to all
      humanity.
17 The dead cannot sing praises to the LORD,
    for they have gone into the silence
      of the grave.
18 But we can praise the LORD
    both now and forever!

Praise the LORD!

116

1 I love the LORD because he hears
    my voice
    and my prayer for mercy.
2 Because he bends down to listen,
    I will pray as long as I have breath!
3 Death wrapped its ropes around me;
    the terrors of the grave* overtook me.
    I saw only trouble and sorrow.
4 Then I called on the name of the LORD:
    "Please, LORD, save me!"
5 How kind the LORD is! How good he is!
    So merciful, this God of ours!
6 The LORD protects those of childlike faith;
    I was facing death, and he saved me.
7 Let my soul be at rest again,
    for the LORD has been good to me.
8 He has saved me from death,
    my eyes from tears,
    my feet from stumbling.
9 And so I walk in the LORD's presence
    as I live here on earth!
10 I believed in you, so I said,
    "I am deeply troubled, LORD."
11 In my anxiety I cried out to you,

116:3 Hebrew *of Sheol.*

    "These people are all liars!"
12 What can I offer the LORD
    for all he has done for me?
13 I will lift up the cup of salvation
    and praise the LORD's name for saving me.
14 I will keep my promises to the LORD
    in the presence of all his people.

15 The LORD cares deeply
    when his loved ones die.
16 O LORD, I am your servant;
    yes, I am your servant, born into your
      household;
    you have freed me from my chains.
17 I will offer you a sacrifice of thanksgiving
    and call on the name of the LORD.
18 I will fulfill my vows to the LORD
    in the presence of all his people—
19 in the house of the LORD
    in the heart of Jerusalem.

Praise the LORD!

117

1 Praise the LORD, all you nations.
    Praise him, all you people of the
      earth.
2 For he loves us with unfailing love;
    the LORD's faithfulness endures forever.

Praise the LORD!

118

1 Give thanks to the LORD, for he
    is good!
    His faithful love endures forever.

2 Let all Israel repeat:
    "His faithful love endures forever."
3 Let Aaron's descendants, the priests,
      repeat:
    "His faithful love endures forever."
4 Let all who fear the LORD repeat:
    "His faithful love endures forever."

5 In my distress I prayed to the LORD,
    and the LORD answered me and set
      me free.
6 The LORD is for me, so I will have no fear.
    What can mere people do to me?
7 Yes, the LORD is for me; he will help me.
    I will look in triumph at those who
      hate me.
8 It is better to take refuge in the LORD

....

THINKING OF YOU
*(115:12) "The LORD remembers us" says the psalm writer.
What a fantastic truth! Many times we can feel isolated,
alone, and abandoned—even by God. In reality, he sees,
understands, and thinks about us. When depressed or
struggling, be encouraged that God keeps you in his
thoughts. If he thinks about you, surely his help is near.*

than to trust in people.
⁹ It is better to take refuge in the LORD
　　than to trust in princes.

¹⁰ Though hostile nations surrounded me,
　　I destroyed them all with the authority
　　　of the LORD.
¹¹ Yes, they surrounded and attacked me,
　　but I destroyed them all with the authority
　　　of the LORD.
¹² They swarmed around me like bees;
　　they blazed against me like a crackling
　　　fire.
　　But I destroyed them all with the authority
　　　of the LORD.
¹³ My enemies did their best to kill me,
　　but the LORD rescued me.
¹⁴ The LORD is my strength and my song;
　　he has given me victory.
¹⁵ Songs of joy and victory are sung in the
　　　camp of the godly.
　　The strong right arm of the LORD has done
　　　glorious things!
¹⁶ The strong right arm of the LORD is raised in
　　　triumph.
　　The strong right arm of the LORD has done
　　　glorious things!
¹⁷ I will not die; instead, I will live
　　to tell what the LORD has done.
¹⁸ The LORD has punished me severely,
　　but he did not let me die.

¹⁹ Open for me the gates where the righteous
　　　enter,
　　and I will go in and thank the LORD.
²⁰ These gates lead to the presence of the
　　　LORD,
　　and the godly enter there.
²¹ I thank you for answering my prayer
　　and giving me victory!

²² The stone that the builders rejected
　　has now become the cornerstone.

²³ This is the LORD's doing,
　　and it is wonderful to see.
²⁴ This is the day the LORD has made.
　　We will rejoice and be glad in it.
²⁵ Please, LORD, please save us.
　　Please, LORD, please give us success.
²⁶ Bless the one who comes in the name
　　　of the LORD.
　　We bless you from the house of the LORD.
²⁷ The LORD is God, shining upon us.
　　Take the sacrifice and bind it with cords
　　　on the altar.
²⁸ You are my God, and I will praise you!
　　You are my God, and I will exalt you!

²⁹ Give thanks to the LORD, for he is good!
　　His faithful love endures forever.

119 *

Aleph
¹ Joyful are people of integrity,
　　who follow the instructions of the LORD.
² Joyful are those who obey his laws
　　and search for him with all their hearts.
³ They do not compromise with evil,
　　and they walk only in his paths.
⁴ You have charged us
　　to keep your commandments carefully.
⁵ Oh, that my actions would consistently
　　reflect your decrees!
⁶ Then I will not be ashamed
　　when I compare my life with your
　　　commands.
⁷ As I learn your righteous regulations,
　　I will thank you by living as I should!
⁸ I will obey your decrees.
　　Please don't give up on me!

Beth
⁹ How can a young person stay pure?
　　By obeying your word.
¹⁰ I have tried hard to find you—
　　don't let me wander from your
　　　commands.
¹¹ I have hidden your word in my heart,
　　that I might not sin against you.
¹² I praise you, O LORD;
　　teach me your decrees.
¹³ I have recited aloud
　　all the regulations you have given us.
¹⁴ I have rejoiced in your laws
　　as much as in riches.
¹⁵ I will study your commandments

DETERRENT
(119:11) *Hiding God's Word in our heart and mind is a deterrent to sin. This alone should motivate us to memorize Scripture. But memorization alone will not keep us from doing wrong; we must also put God's Word to work in our lives, making it a vital guide to everything we do.*

RULES
(119:12-18) *Most people don't like rules because they keep us from doing what we want, or so we think. We may find it strange, therefore, to hear the psalm writer talk of rejoicing in God's laws as much as in riches (119:14). But God's laws were given to free us to be all he wants us to be. They restrict us from doing those things that will cripple us and keep us from being our best. God's laws are guidelines to help us follow in his path and not wander onto paths that lead to destruction.*

119 This psalm is a Hebrew acrostic poem; there are twenty-two stanzas, one for each successive letter of the Hebrew alphabet. Each of the eight verses within each stanza begins with the Hebrew letter named in its heading.

and reflect on your ways.
¹⁶ I will delight in your decrees
and not forget your word.

Gimel

¹⁷ Be good to your servant,
that I may live and obey your word.
¹⁸ Open my eyes to see
the wonderful truths in your instructions.
¹⁹ I am only a foreigner in the land.
Don't hide your commands from me!
²⁰ I am always overwhelmed
with a desire for your regulations.
²¹ You rebuke the arrogant;
those who wander from your commands
are cursed.
²² Don't let them scorn and insult me,
for I have obeyed your laws.
²³ Even princes sit and speak against me,
but I will meditate on your decrees.
²⁴ Your laws please me;
they give me wise advice.

Daleth

²⁵ I lie in the dust;
revive me by your word.
²⁶ I told you my plans, and you answered.
Now teach me your decrees.
²⁷ Help me understand the meaning of your
commandments,
and I will meditate on your wonderful
deeds.
²⁸ I weep with sorrow;
encourage me by your word.
²⁹ Keep me from lying to myself;
give me the privilege of knowing your
instructions.
³⁰ I have chosen to be faithful;
I have determined to live by your
regulations.
³¹ I cling to your laws.
LORD, don't let me be put to shame!
³² I will pursue your commands,
for you expand my understanding.

He

³³ Teach me your decrees, O LORD;
I will keep them to the end.
³⁴ Give me understanding and I will obey your
instructions;
I will put them into practice with all my
heart.
³⁵ Make me walk along the path of your
commands,
for that is where my happiness is found.
³⁶ Give me an eagerness for your laws

rather than a love for money!
³⁷ Turn my eyes from worthless things,
and give me life through your word.*
³⁸ Reassure me of your promise,
made to those who fear you.
³⁹ Help me abandon my shameful ways;
for your regulations are good.
⁴⁰ I long to obey your commandments!
Renew my life with your goodness.

Waw

⁴¹ LORD, give me your unfailing love,
the salvation that you promised me.
⁴² Then I can answer those who taunt me,
for I trust in your word.
⁴³ Do not snatch your word of truth from me,
for your regulations are my only hope.
⁴⁴ I will keep on obeying your instructions
forever and ever.
⁴⁵ I will walk in freedom,
for I have devoted myself to your
commandments.
⁴⁶ I will speak to kings about your laws,
and I will not be ashamed.
⁴⁷ How I delight in your commands!
How I love them!
⁴⁸ I honor and love your commands.
I meditate on your decrees.

Zayin

⁴⁹ Remember your promise to me;
it is my only hope.
⁵⁰ Your promise revives me;
it comforts me in all my troubles.
⁵¹ The proud hold me in utter contempt,
but I do not turn away from your
instructions.
⁵² I meditate on your age-old regulations;
O LORD, they comfort me.
⁵³ I become furious with the wicked,
because they reject your instructions.
⁵⁴ Your decrees have been the theme of my
songs
wherever I have lived.
⁵⁵ I reflect at night on who you are, O LORD;
therefore, I obey your instructions.
⁵⁶ This is how I spend my life:
obeying your commandments.

Heth

⁵⁷ LORD, you are mine!
I promise to obey your words!
⁵⁸ With all my heart I want your blessings.
Be merciful as you promised.
⁵⁹ I pondered the direction of my life,
and I turned to follow your laws.
⁶⁰ I will hurry, without delay,

119:37 Some manuscripts read *in your ways.*

to obey your commands.
61 Evil people try to drag me into sin,
    but I am firmly anchored to your
      instructions.
62 I rise at midnight to thank you
    for your just regulations.
63 I am a friend to anyone who fears you—
    anyone who obeys your commandments.
64 O Lord, your unfailing love fills the earth;
    teach me your decrees.

Teth

65 You have done many good things for me,
    Lord,
    just as you promised.
66 I believe in your commands;
    now teach me good judgment and
      knowledge.
67 I used to wander off until you
    disciplined me;
    but now I closely follow your word.
68 You are good and do only good;
    teach me your decrees.
69 Arrogant people smear me with lies,
    but in truth I obey your commandments
      with all my heart.
70 Their hearts are dull and stupid,
    but I delight in your instructions.
71 My suffering was good for me,
    for it taught me to pay attention to your
      decrees.
72 Your instructions are more valuable to me
    than millions in gold and silver.

Yodh

73 You made me; you created me.
    Now give me the sense to follow your
      commands.
74 May all who fear you find in me a cause
    for joy,
    for I have put my hope in your word.
75 I know, O Lord, that your regulations are
    fair;
    you disciplined me because I needed it.
76 Now let your unfailing love comfort me,
    just as you promised me, your servant.
77 Surround me with your tender mercies so I
    may live,
    for your instructions are my delight.
78 Bring disgrace upon the arrogant people
    who lied about me;
    meanwhile, I will concentrate on your
      commandments.
79 Let me be united with all who fear you,
    with those who know your laws.
80 May I be blameless in keeping your decrees;
    then I will never be ashamed.

Kaph

81 I am worn out waiting for your rescue,
    but I have put my hope in your word.
82 My eyes are straining to see your promises
    come true.
    When will you comfort me?
83 I am shriveled like a wineskin in
    the smoke,
    but I have not forgotten to obey
      your decrees.
84 How long must I wait?
    When will you punish those who
      persecute me?
85 These arrogant people who hate your
    instructions
    have dug deep pits to trap me.
86 All your commands are trustworthy.
    Protect me from those who hunt
      me down without cause.
87 They almost finished me off,
    but I refused to abandon your
      commandments.
88 In your unfailing love, spare my life;
    then I can continue to obey your laws.

Lamedh

89 Your eternal word, O Lord,
    stands firm in heaven.
90 Your faithfulness extends to every
    generation,
    as enduring as the earth you created.
91 Your regulations remain true to this day,
    for everything serves your plans.
92 If your instructions hadn't sustained me
    with joy,
    I would have died in my misery.
93 I will never forget your commandments,
    for by them you give me life.
94 I am yours; rescue me!
    For I have worked hard at obeying your
      commandments.
95 Though the wicked hide along the way to
    kill me,
    I will quietly keep my mind on your laws.
96 Even perfection has its limits,
    but your commands have no limit.

Mem

97 Oh, how I love your instructions!
    I think about them all day long.
98 Your commands make me wiser than my
    enemies,
    for they are my constant guide.
99 Yes, I have more insight than my teachers,
    for I am always thinking of your laws.
100 I am even wiser than my elders,
    for I have kept your commandments.

101 I have refused to walk on any evil path,
   so that I may remain obedient to your
   word.
102 I haven't turned away from your
   regulations,
   for you have taught me well.
103 How sweet your words taste to me;
   they are sweeter than honey.
104 Your commandments give me
   understanding;
   no wonder I hate every false way
   of life.

Nun

105 Your word is a lamp to guide my feet
   and a light for my path.
106 I've promised it once, and I'll promise
   it again:
   I will obey your righteous regulations.
107 I have suffered much, O LORD;
   restore my life again as you promised.
108 LORD, accept my offering of praise,
   and teach me your regulations.
109 My life constantly hangs in the balance,
   but I will not stop obeying your
   instructions.
110 The wicked have set their traps for me,
   but I will not turn from your
   commandments.
111 Your laws are my treasure;
   they are my heart's delight.
112 I am determined to keep your
   decrees
   to the very end.

Samekh

113 I hate those with divided loyalties,
   but I love your instructions.
114 You are my refuge and my shield;
   your word is my source of hope.
115 Get out of my life, you evil-minded people,
   for I intend to obey the commands
   of my God.
116 LORD, sustain me as you promised, that
   I may live!
   Do not let my hope be crushed.
117 Sustain me, and I will be rescued;
   then I will meditate continually on your
   decrees.
118 But you have rejected all who stray from
   your decrees.
   They are only fooling themselves.
119 You skim off the wicked of the earth like
   scum;
   no wonder I love to obey your laws!
120 I tremble in fear of you;
   I stand in awe of your regulations.

Ayin

121 Don't leave me to the mercy of my enemies,
   for I have done what is just and right.
122 Please guarantee a blessing for me.
   Don't let the arrogant oppress me!
123 My eyes strain to see your rescue,
   to see the truth of your promise fulfilled.
124 I am your servant; deal with me in
   unfailing love,
   and teach me your decrees.
125 Give discernment to me, your servant;
   then I will understand your laws.
126 LORD, it is time for you to act,
   for these evil people have violated your
   instructions.
127 Truly, I love your commands
   more than gold, even the finest gold.
128 Each of your commandments is right.
   That is why I hate every false way.

Pe

129 Your laws are wonderful.
   No wonder I obey them!
130 The teaching of your word gives light,
   so even the simple can understand.
131 I pant with expectation,
   longing for your commands.
132 Come and show me your mercy,
   as you do for all who love your name.
133 Guide my steps by your word,
   so I will not be overcome by evil.
134 Ransom me from the oppression of evil
   people;
   then I can obey your
   commandments.
135 Look upon me with love;
   teach me your decrees.
136 Rivers of tears gush from my eyes
   because people disobey your
   instructions.

....

WISER
*(119:97-104) God's Word makes us wise—wiser than
our enemies and wiser than any teachers who ignore
God's Word. True wisdom does not come from amassing
knowledge but in applying knowledge in a life-changing
way. Intelligent or experienced people aren't necessarily
wise. Wise people are those who allow what God teaches
to make a difference in their lives. What are you doing to
grow in wisdom?*

MEDICINE FOR LIFE
*(119:125) Faith comes alive at the points where we apply
Scripture to our lives. The Bible is similar to medicine—it
goes to work when it is applied to the areas where it is
most needed. As you read the Bible, be on the alert for
lessons, commands, or examples that you can apply to
situations in your life.*

Tsadhe

137 O LORD, you are righteous,
    and your regulations are fair.
138 Your laws are perfect
    and completely trustworthy.
139 I am overwhelmed with indignation,
    for my enemies have disregarded your
        words.
140 Your promises have been thoroughly
        tested;
    that is why I love them so much.
141 I am insignificant and despised,
    but I don't forget your commandments.
142 Your justice is eternal,
    and your instructions are perfectly true.
143 As pressure and stress bear down on me,
    I find joy in your commands.
144 Your laws are always right;
    help me to understand them
        so I may live.

Qoph

145 I pray with all my heart; answer me, LORD!
    I will obey your decrees.
146 I cry out to you; rescue me,
    that I may obey your laws.
147 I rise early, before the sun is up;
    I cry out for help and put my hope in your
        words.
148 I stay awake through the night,
    thinking about your promise.
149 In your faithful love, O LORD, hear my cry;
    let me be revived by following your
        regulations.
150 Lawless people are coming to attack me;
    they live far from your instructions.
151 But you are near, O LORD,
    and all your commands are true.
152 I have known from my earliest days
    that your laws will last forever.

Resh

153 Look upon my suffering and rescue me,
    for I have not forgotten your instructions.
154 Argue my case; take my side!
    Protect my life as you promised.
155 The wicked are far from rescue,
    for they do not bother with your decrees.
156 LORD, how great is your mercy;
    let me be revived by following your
        regulations.
157 Many persecute and trouble me,
    yet I have not swerved from your laws.
158 Seeing these traitors makes me sick at
        heart,
    because they care nothing for your word.
159 See how I love your commandments, LORD.

Give back my life because of your
    unfailing love.
160 The very essence of your words is truth;
    all your just regulations will stand
        forever.

Shin

161 Powerful people harass me without cause,
    but my heart trembles only at your word.
162 I rejoice in your word
    like one who discovers a great treasure.
163 I hate and abhor all falsehood,
    but I love your instructions.
164 I will praise you seven times a day
    because all your regulations are just.
165 Those who love your instructions have
        great peace
    and do not stumble.
166 I long for your rescue, LORD,
    so I have obeyed your commands.
167 I have obeyed your laws,
    for I love them very much.
168 Yes, I obey your commandments and laws
    because you know everything I do.

Taw

169 O LORD, listen to my cry;
    give me the discerning mind you
        promised.
170 Listen to my prayer;
    rescue me as you promised.
171 Let praise flow from my lips,
    for you have taught me your decrees.
172 Let my tongue sing about your word,
    for all your commands are right.
173 Give me a helping hand,
    for I have chosen to follow your
        commandments.
174 O LORD, I have longed for your rescue,
    and your instructions are my delight.
175 Let me live so I can praise you,
    and may your regulations help me.
176 I have wandered away like a lost sheep;
    come and find me,
    for I have not forgotten your commands.

120

*A song for pilgrims ascending to
Jerusalem.*

1 I took my troubles to the LORD;
    I cried out to him, and he answered my
        prayer.
2 Rescue me, O LORD, from liars
    and from all deceitful people.
3 O deceptive tongue, what will God do
        to you?
    How will he increase your punishment?

⁴ You will be pierced with sharp arrows
  and burned with glowing coals.

⁵ How I suffer in far-off Meshech.
  It pains me to live in distant Kedar.
⁶ I am tired of living
  among people who hate peace.
⁷ I search for peace;
  but when I speak of peace,
    they want war!

121

A song for pilgrims ascending to Jerusalem.

¹ I look up to the mountains—
  does my help come from there?
² My help comes from the LORD,
  who made heaven and earth!

³ He will not let you stumble;
  the one who watches over you will not
    slumber.
⁴ Indeed, he who watches over Israel
  never slumbers or sleeps.

⁵ The LORD himself watches over you!
  The LORD stands beside you as your
    protective shade.
⁶ The sun will not harm you by day,
  nor the moon at night.

⁷ The LORD keeps you from all harm
  and watches over your life.
⁸ The LORD keeps watch over you as you come
    and go,
  both now and forever.

122

A song for pilgrims ascending to Jerusalem. A psalm of David.

¹ I was glad when they said to me,
  "Let us go to the house of the LORD."
² And now here we are,
  standing inside your gates, O Jerusalem.
³ Jerusalem is a well-built city;
  its seamless walls cannot be breached.
⁴ All the tribes of Israel—the LORD's people—
  make their pilgrimage here.
  They come to give thanks to the name of
    the LORD,
  as the law requires of Israel.
⁵ Here stand the thrones where judgment
    is given,
  the thrones of the dynasty of David.

⁶ Pray for peace in Jerusalem.
  May all who love this city prosper.
⁷ O Jerusalem, may there be peace within
    your walls
  and prosperity in your palaces.

HE WILL NOT LET YOU STUMBLE; THE ONE WHO WATCHES OVER YOU WILL NOT SLUMBER.

PSALM 121:3

⁸ For the sake of my family and friends,
  I will say,
    "May you have peace."
⁹ For the sake of the house of the LORD
    our God,
  I will seek what is best for you,
    O Jerusalem.

123

A song for pilgrims ascending to Jerusalem.

¹ I lift my eyes to you,
  O God, enthroned in heaven.
² We keep looking to the LORD our God for his
    mercy,
  just as servants keep their eyes on their
    master,
  as a slave girl watches her mistress for
    the slightest signal.
³ Have mercy on us, LORD, have mercy,
  for we have had our fill of contempt.
⁴ We have had more than our fill of the
    scoffing of the proud
  and the contempt of the arrogant.

124

A song for pilgrims ascending to Jerusalem. A psalm of David.

¹ What if the LORD had not been on our side?
  Let all Israel repeat:
² What if the LORD had not been on our side
    when people attacked us?
³ They would have swallowed us alive
  in their burning anger.
⁴ The waters would have engulfed us;

....

PEACEMAKER
(120:6-7) Peacemaking is not very popular because
human nature wants a winner. But then, someone must
be a loser. The glory of peacemaking is that it may produce two winners. Peacemaking is God's way; in fact,
Jesus said, "God blesses those who work for peace, for
they will be called the children of God" (Matt 5:9). In what
ways can you work for peace?

PRAYING FOR OTHERS
(122:6-9) The psalm writer was not praying for his own
peace and prosperity but for his fellow citizens of Jerusalem. Prayer on the behalf of others is usually unselfish.
So, are you ready to pray for someone today?

a torrent would have overwhelmed us.
⁵ Yes, the raging waters of their fury
   would have overwhelmed our very lives.

⁶ Praise the LORD,
   who did not let their teeth tear us apart!
⁷ We escaped like a bird from a hunter's trap.
   The trap is broken, and we are free!
⁸ Our help is from the LORD,
   who made heaven and earth.

125
A song for pilgrims ascending to Jerusalem.

¹ Those who trust in the LORD are as secure
      as Mount Zion;
   they will not be defeated but will endure
      forever.
² Just as the mountains surround Jerusalem,
   so the LORD surrounds his people, both
      now and forever.
³ The wicked will not rule the land of the
      godly,
   for then the godly might be tempted
      to do wrong.
⁴ O LORD, do good to those who are good,
   whose hearts are in tune with you.
⁵ But banish those who turn to crooked ways,
      O LORD.
   Take them away with those who do evil.

   May Israel have peace!

126
A song for pilgrims ascending to Jerusalem.

¹ When the LORD brought back his exiles to
      Jerusalem,*
   it was like a dream!
² We were filled with laughter,
   and we sang for joy.
   And the other nations said,
      "What amazing things the LORD has
         done for them."
³ Yes, the LORD has done amazing things
      for us!
   What joy!

⁴ Restore our fortunes, LORD,
   as streams renew the desert.
⁵ Those who plant in tears
   will harvest with shouts of joy.

⁶ They weep as they go to plant their seed,
   but they sing as they return with the
      harvest.

127
A song for pilgrims ascending to Jerusalem. A psalm of Solomon.

¹ Unless the LORD builds a house,
   the work of the builders is wasted.
   Unless the LORD protects a city,
      guarding it with sentries will do no good.
² It is useless for you to work so hard
   from early morning until late at night,
anxiously working for food to eat;
   for God gives rest to his loved ones.

³ Children are a gift from the LORD;
   they are a reward from him.
⁴ Children born to a young man
   are like arrows in a warrior's hands.
⁵ How joyful is the man whose quiver is full
      of them!
   He will not be put to shame when he
      confronts his accusers at the city gates.

128
A song for pilgrims ascending to Jerusalem.

¹ How joyful are those who fear the LORD—
   all who follow his ways!
² You will enjoy the fruit of your labor.
   How joyful and prosperous you will be!
³ Your wife will be like a fruitful grapevine,
   flourishing within your home.
   Your children will be like vigorous young
      olive trees
      as they sit around your table.
⁴ That is the LORD's blessing
   for those who fear him.

⁵ May the LORD continually bless you from
      Zion.
   May you see Jerusalem prosper as long as
      you live.
⁶ May you live to enjoy your grandchildren.
   May Israel have peace!

129
A song for pilgrims ascending to Jerusalem.

¹ From my earliest youth my enemies have
      persecuted me.
   Let all Israel repeat this:
² From my earliest youth my enemies have
      persecuted me,
   but they have never defeated me.
³ My back is covered with cuts,
   as if a farmer had plowed long furrows.

126:1 Hebrew *Zion.*

··

GOD'S FOUNDATION
*(127:1) Families establish homes and sentries guard
cities, but both of these activities are futile unless God
does the work. A family without God can never experience
the true sense of community that God brings to relationships. Are your relationships built on the foundation God
established?*

⁴ But the LORD is good;
  he has cut me free from the ropes of the
    ungodly.

⁵ May all who hate Jerusalem*
  be turned back in shameful defeat.
⁶ May they be as useless as grass on a
    rooftop,
  turning yellow when only half grown,
⁷ ignored by the harvester,
  despised by the binder.
⁸ And may those who pass by
  refuse to give them this blessing:
  "The LORD bless you;
    we bless you in the LORD's name."

130
A song for pilgrims ascending to Jerusalem.

¹ From the depths of despair, O LORD,
  I call for your help.
² Hear my cry, O Lord.
  Pay attention to my prayer.

³ LORD, if you kept a record of our sins,
  who, O Lord, could ever survive?
⁴ But you offer forgiveness,
  that we might learn to fear you.

⁵ I am counting on the LORD;
  yes, I am counting on him.
  I have put my hope in his word.
⁶ I long for the Lord
  more than sentries long for the dawn,
  yes, more than sentries long for
    the dawn.

⁷ O Israel, hope in the LORD;
  for with the LORD there is unfailing love.
  His redemption overflows.
⁸ He himself will redeem Israel
  from every kind of sin.

131
A song for pilgrims ascending to Jerusalem. A psalm of David.

¹ LORD, my heart is not proud;
  my eyes are not haughty.
  I don't concern myself with matters too great
    or too awesome for me to grasp.
² Instead, I have calmed and quieted myself,
  like a weaned child who no longer cries
    for its mother's milk.
  Yes, like a weaned child is my soul
    within me.

³ O Israel, put your hope in the LORD—
  now and always.

129:5 Hebrew *Zion.* **132:2** Hebrew *of Jacob;* also in 132:5. See note on 44:4. **132:13** Hebrew *Zion.*

132
A song for pilgrims ascending to Jerusalem.

¹ LORD, remember David
  and all that he suffered.
² He made a solemn promise to the LORD.
  He vowed to the Mighty One of Israel,*
³ "I will not go home;
  I will not let myself rest.
⁴ I will not let my eyes sleep
  nor close my eyelids in slumber
⁵ until I find a place to build a house for the
    LORD,
  a sanctuary for the Mighty One of Israel."

⁶ We heard that the Ark was in Ephrathah;
  then we found it in the distant
    countryside of Jaar.
⁷ Let us go to the sanctuary of the LORD;
  let us worship at the footstool of his
    throne.
⁸ Arise, O LORD, and enter your resting place,
  along with the Ark, the symbol of your
    power.
⁹ May your priests be clothed in godliness;
  may your loyal servants sing for joy.
¹⁰ For the sake of your servant David,
  do not reject the king you have anointed.

¹¹ The LORD swore an oath to David
  with a promise he will never take back:
  "I will place one of your descendants
    on your throne.
¹² If your descendants obey the terms of my
    covenant
  and the laws that I teach them,
  then your royal line
    will continue forever and ever."

¹³ For the LORD has chosen Jerusalem*;
  he has desired it for his home.
¹⁴ "This is my resting place forever," he said.
  "I will live here, for this is the home I
    desired.
¹⁵ I will bless this city and make it prosperous;
  I will satisfy its poor with food.
¹⁶ I will clothe its priests with godliness;
  its faithful servants will sing for joy.
¹⁷ Here I will increase the power of David;
  my anointed one will be a light for my
    people.
¹⁸ I will clothe his enemies with shame,
  but he will be a glorious king."

133
A song for pilgrims ascending to Jerusalem. A psalm of David.

¹ How wonderful and pleasant it is
  when brothers live together in harmony!

WHERE TO GET HELP IN THE BOOK OF PSALMS

WHEN YOU FEEL . . .

Afraid 3, 4, 27, 46, 49, 56, 91, 118
Alone 9, 10, 12, 13, 27, 40, 43
Burned Out 6, 63
Cheated 41
Confused 10, 12, 73
Depressed 27, 34, 42, 43, 88, 143
Distressed 13, 25, 31, 40, 107
Elated 19, 96
Guilty 19, 32, 38, 51
Hateful 11
Impatient 13, 27, 37, 40
Insecure 3, 5, 12, 91
Insulted 41, 70
Jealous 37
Like Quitting 29, 43, 145
Lost 23, 139
Overwhelmed 25, 69, 142
Penitent/Sorry 32, 51, 66
Proud 14, 30, 49
Purposeless 14, 25, 39, 49, 90
Sad 13
Self-confident 24
Tense 4
Thankful 118, 136, 138
Threatened 3, 11, 17
Tired/Weak 6, 13, 18, 28, 29, 40, 86
Trapped 7, 17, 42, 88, 142
Unimportant 8, 90, 139
Vengeful 3, 7, 109
Worried 37
Worshipful 8, 19, 27, 29, 150

WHEN YOU'RE FACING . . .

Atheists 10, 14, 19, 52, 53, 115
Competition 133
Criticism 35, 56, 120
Danger 11
Death 6, 71, 90
Decisions 1, 119
Discrimination 54
Doubts 34, 37, 94
Evil people 10, 35, 36, 49, 52, 109, 140
Enemies 3, 25, 35, 41, 56, 59
Handicap/Illness 6, 139
Heresy 14
Hypocrisy 26, 28, 40, 50
Lies 5, 12, 120
Old Age 71, 92
Persecution 1, 3, 7, 56
Poverty 9, 10, 12
Punishment 6, 38, 39
Slander/Insults 7, 15, 35, 43, 120
Slaughter 6, 46, 83
Sorrow 23, 34
Success 18, 112, 127, 128
Temptation 38, 141
Troubles 34, 55, 86, 102, 142, 145
Verbal Cruelty 35, 120

WHEN YOU WANT . . .

Acceptance 139
Answers 4, 17
Confidence 46, 71
Courage 11, 42
Fellowship with God 5, 16, 25, 27, 37, 133
Forgiveness 32, 38, 40, 51, 69, 86, 103, 130
Friendship 16
Godliness 15, 25
Guidance 1, 5, 15, 19, 25, 32, 48
Healing 6, 41
Hope 16, 17, 18, 23, 27
Humility 19, 147
Illumination 19
Integrity 24, 25
Joy 9, 16, 28, 126
Justice 2, 7, 14, 26, 37, 49, 58, 82
Knowledge 2, 8, 18, 19, 25, 29, 97, 103
Leadership 72
Miracles 60, 111
Money 15, 16, 17, 49
Peace 3, 4
Perspective 2, 11
Prayer 5, 17, 27, 61
Protection 3, 4, 7, 16, 17, 18, 23, 27, 31, 91, 121, 125
Provision 23
Rest 23, 27
Salvation 26, 37, 49, 126
Stability 11, 33, 46
Vindication 9, 14, 28, 35, 109
Wisdom 1, 16, 19, 64, 111

² For harmony is as precious as the
   anointing oil
   that was poured over Aaron's head,
   that ran down his beard
   and onto the border of his robe.
³ Harmony is as refreshing as the dew from
      Mount Hermon
   that falls on the mountains of Zion.
   And there the LORD has pronounced his
      blessing,
   even life everlasting.

134 *A song for pilgrims ascending to Jerusalem.*

¹ Oh, praise the LORD, all you servants
      of the LORD,

you who serve at night in the house
      of the LORD.
² Lift up holy hands in prayer,
   and praise the LORD.

³ May the LORD, who made heaven and earth,
   bless you from Jerusalem.*

135 ¹Praise the LORD!

Praise the name of the LORD!
Praise him, you who serve the LORD,
² you who serve in the house of the LORD,
   in the courts of the house of our God.

³ Praise the LORD, for the LORD is good;
   celebrate his lovely name with music.

134:3 Hebrew *Zion.*

⁴ For the LORD has chosen Jacob for himself,
  Israel for his own special treasure.

⁵ I know the greatness of the LORD—
  that our Lord is greater than any
    other god.
⁶ The LORD does whatever pleases him
  throughout all heaven and earth,
  and on the seas and in their depths.
⁷ He causes the clouds to rise over the whole
    earth.
  He sends the lightning with the rain
  and releases the wind from his
    storehouses.

⁸ He destroyed the firstborn in each Egyptian
    home,
  both people and animals.
⁹ He performed miraculous signs and
    wonders in Egypt
  against Pharaoh and all his people.
¹⁰ He struck down great nations
  and slaughtered mighty kings—
¹¹ Sihon king of the Amorites,
  Og king of Bashan,
  and all the kings of Canaan.
¹² He gave their land as an inheritance,
  a special possession to his people Israel.

¹³ Your name, O LORD, endures forever;
  your fame, O LORD, is known to every
    generation.
¹⁴ For the LORD will give justice to his people
  and have compassion on his servants.

¹⁵ The idols of the nations are merely things
    of silver and gold,
  shaped by human hands.
¹⁶ They have mouths but cannot speak,
  and eyes but cannot see.
¹⁷ They have ears but cannot hear,
  and noses but cannot smell.
¹⁸ And those who make idols are just like
    them,
  as are all who trust in them.

¹⁹ O Israel, praise the LORD!
  O priests—descendants of Aaron—praise
    the LORD!
²⁰ O Levites, praise the LORD!
  All you who fear the LORD, praise the LORD!
²¹ The LORD be praised from Zion,
  for he lives here in Jerusalem.

  Praise the LORD!

136

¹Give thanks to the LORD, for he
  is good!
  His faithful love endures forever.

136:13 Hebrew *sea of reeds;* also in 136:15.

² Give thanks to the God of gods.
  His faithful love endures forever.
³ Give thanks to the Lord of lords.
  His faithful love endures forever.
⁴ Give thanks to him who alone does mighty
    miracles.
  His faithful love endures forever.
⁵ Give thanks to him who made the heavens
    so skillfully.
  His faithful love endures forever.
⁶ Give thanks to him who placed the earth
    among the waters.
  His faithful love endures forever.
⁷ Give thanks to him who made the heavenly
    lights—
  His faithful love endures forever.
⁸ the sun to rule the day,
  His faithful love endures forever.
⁹ and the moon and stars to rule the night.
  His faithful love endures forever.

¹⁰ Give thanks to him who killed the firstborn
    of Egypt.
  His faithful love endures forever.
¹¹ He brought Israel out of Egypt.
  His faithful love endures forever.
¹² He acted with a strong hand and
    powerful arm.
  His faithful love endures forever.
¹³ Give thanks to him who parted the
    Red Sea.*
  His faithful love endures forever.
¹⁴ He led Israel safely through,
  His faithful love endures forever.
¹⁵ but he hurled Pharaoh and his army into the
    Red Sea.
  His faithful love endures forever.
¹⁶ Give thanks to him who led his people
    through the wilderness.
  His faithful love endures forever.

¹⁷ Give thanks to him who struck down
    mighty kings.
  His faithful love endures forever.
¹⁸ He killed powerful kings—
  His faithful love endures forever.
¹⁹ Sihon king of the Amorites,
  His faithful love endures forever.
²⁰ and Og king of Bashan.
  His faithful love endures forever.
²¹ God gave the land of these kings as an
    inheritance—
  His faithful love endures forever.
²² a special possession to his servant Israel.
  His faithful love endures forever.

²³ He remembered us in our weakness.
  His faithful love endures forever.

²⁴ He saved us from our enemies.
His faithful love endures forever.
²⁵ He gives food to every living thing.
His faithful love endures forever.
²⁶ Give thanks to the God of heaven.
His faithful love endures forever.

137

¹ Beside the rivers of Babylon, we
sat and wept
as we thought of Jerusalem.*
² We put away our harps,
hanging them on the branches of poplar
trees.
³ For our captors demanded a song from us.
Our tormentors insisted on a joyful hymn:
"Sing us one of those songs of
Jerusalem!"
⁴ But how can we sing the songs of the LORD
while in a pagan land?

⁵ If I forget you, O Jerusalem,
let my right hand forget how to play
the harp.
⁶ May my tongue stick to the roof of my mouth
if I fail to remember you,
if I don't make Jerusalem my greatest joy.

⁷ O LORD, remember what the Edomites did
on the day the armies of Babylon
captured Jerusalem.
"Destroy it!" they yelled.
"Level it to the ground!"
⁸ O Babylon, you will be destroyed.
Happy is the one who pays you back
for what you have done to us.
⁹ Happy is the one who takes your babies
and smashes them against the rocks!

138 *A psalm of David.*

¹ I give you thanks, O LORD, with all my heart;
I will sing your praises before the gods.
² I bow before your holy Temple as I worship.
I praise your name for your unfailing love
and faithfulness;
for your promises are backed
by all the honor of your name.
³ As soon as I pray, you answer me;
you encourage me by giving me strength.

....

PLANS
*(138:8) David counted on God's plan for his life. We make
plans for our future and work hard to see those dreams
come true. But to truly make the most of life, we must
include God's plans in our plans. He alone knows what is
best for us. How willing are you to submit your plans and
dreams to God?*

⁴ Every king in all the earth will thank you,
LORD,
for all of them will hear your words.
⁵ Yes, they will sing about the LORD's ways,
for the glory of the LORD is very great.
⁶ Though the LORD is great, he cares for the
humble,
but he keeps his distance from the proud.

⁷ Though I am surrounded by troubles,
you will protect me from the anger of my
enemies.
You reach out your hand,
and the power of your right hand
saves me.
⁸ The LORD will work out his plans for my life—
for your faithful love, O LORD, endures
forever.
Don't abandon me, for you made me.

139 *For the choir director: A psalm of David.*

¹ O LORD, you have examined my heart
and know everything about me.
² You know when I sit down or stand up.
You know my thoughts even when I'm
far away.
³ You see me when I travel
and when I rest at home.
You know everything I do.
⁴ You know what I am going to say
even before I say it, LORD.
⁵ You go before me and follow me.
You place your hand of blessing
on my head.
⁶ Such knowledge is too wonderful for me,
too great for me to understand!

⁷ I can never escape from your Spirit!
I can never get away from your presence!
⁸ If I go up to heaven, you are there;
if I go down to the grave,* you are there.
⁹ If I ride the wings of the morning,
if I dwell by the farthest oceans,
¹⁰ even there your hand will guide me,
and your strength will support me.
¹¹ I could ask the darkness to hide me
and the light around me to become
night—
¹² but even in darkness I cannot hide
from you.
To you the night shines as bright as day.
Darkness and light are the same to you.

¹³ You made all the delicate, inner parts
of my body

137:1 Hebrew *Zion*; also in 137:3.   **139:8** Hebrew *to Sheol.*

and knit me together in my mother's womb.
¹⁴ Thank you for making me so wonderfully complex!
    Your workmanship is marvelous—how well I know it.
¹⁵ You watched me as I was being formed in utter seclusion,
    as I was woven together in the dark of the womb.
¹⁶ You saw me before I was born.
    Every day of my life was recorded in your book.
    Every moment was laid out
    before a single day had passed.
¹⁷ How precious are your thoughts about me,*
    O God.
    They cannot be numbered!
¹⁸ I can't even count them;
    they outnumber the grains of sand!
    And when I wake up,
    you are still with me!
¹⁹ O God, if only you would destroy the wicked!
    Get out of my life, you murderers!
²⁰ They blaspheme you;
    your enemies misuse your name.
²¹ O Lord, shouldn't I hate those who hate you?
    Shouldn't I despise those who oppose you?
²² Yes, I hate them with total hatred,
    for your enemies are my enemies.

²³ Search me, O God, and know my heart;
    test me and know my anxious thoughts.
²⁴ Point out anything in me that offends you,
    and lead me along the path of everlasting life.

139:17 Or *How precious to me are your thoughts.*

140 *For the choir director: A psalm of David.*

¹ O Lord, rescue me from evil people.
    Protect me from those who are violent,
² those who plot evil in their hearts
    and stir up trouble all day long.
³ Their tongues sting like a snake;
    the venom of a viper drips from their lips.
                                Interlude

⁴ O Lord, keep me out of the hands of the wicked.
    Protect me from those who are violent,
    for they are plotting against me.
⁵ The proud have set a trap to catch me;
    they have stretched out a net;
    they have placed traps all along the way.
                                Interlude

⁶ I said to the Lord, "You are my God!"
    Listen, O Lord, to my cries for mercy!
⁷ O Sovereign Lord, the strong one who rescued me,
    you protected me on the day of battle.
⁸ Lord, do not let evil people have their way.
    Do not let their evil schemes succeed,
    or they will become proud.   *Interlude*

⁹ Let my enemies be destroyed
    by the very evil they have planned for me.

AMAZING WORKMANSHIP
(139:13-15) *God created each human being unique, special, and wonderful. When you feel worthless or even begin to hate yourself, remember that God made you "wonderfully complex," made you for a purpose, and constantly thinks about you (139:14, 17). Have as much respect for yourself as your Creator has for you.*

CHOICES
abortion

"Sarah, maybe you made a mistake—maybe the test is wrong."

"I don't think so. . . . Oh, Kris, what am I gonna do?" The tears begin to roll down Sarah's face. "I'm pregnant!"

Kris hugs her friend. "Look, don't panic. Everything's gonna work out. My sister will help us. She knows about this clinic. The doctors are good, and nobody else has to find out."

Sarah is shocked. "You mean an abortion?"

"C'mon, Sarah, you're only 17. What are you gonna do with a kid? And what would you tell your mom?"

"I don't know . . . I'm so confused." Sarah sighs,

wiping her eyes on her sleeve. "What would you do? I mean, could you kill your own baby?"

"What do you mean, 'kill'? It's just a bunch of cells! It's not a person yet. If you were six or seven months pregnant, I'd say no. But you're only a few weeks. I don't see what else you can do."

"You really think it's okay?"

"Well, do you have any better ideas?"

Sarah sighs again. "How soon can you call your sister?"

Kris picks up the phone. "I bet she's at her dorm right now."

Is Sarah making the right decision? Is Kris right about when life begins? See Psalm 139:13-18. What would you tell Sarah?

MY STORY: Melinda

I had an unusually frightening experience at the beginning of my sophomore year: I ate an apple that some disturbed person had tampered with. It wasn't poisonous—not like it would have killed me—but it did make me pretty sick. Most of all, the experience scared me. For about a year and a half, I wouldn't eat anything unless I shared it with someone, or someone else tried a bite first and was okay.

Finally, I talked to my youth leader about my fear. She encouraged me to read Psalm 140 and to realize that God was there to help and protect me—no matter what! Then she pointed out that God didn't want me to give in to a spirit of fear, and she showed me 2 Timothy 1:7. That verse became very meaningful to me. I memorized it and reminded myself of it over and over, until eventually I began to believe that most people could be trusted, that most people weren't out to hurt me.

I'm so glad God used the Psalms and 2 Timothy to remind me that he cares for me.

10 Let burning coals fall down on
  their heads.
  Let them be thrown into the fire
  or into watery pits from which they can't
   escape.
11 Don't let liars prosper here in our land.
  Cause great disasters to fall on the
   violent.

12 But I know the LORD will help those they
   persecute;
  he will give justice to the poor.
13 Surely righteous people are praising your
   name;
  the godly will live in your presence.

THE TONGUE
(141:3) David wisely asked God to help him keep his mouth shut. James wrote that the tongue is small but can do enormous damage (Jas 3:5). On the average, a person opens his or her mouth approximately 700 times a day to speak. So keeping silent takes great self-control—God control. We should ask God to help us guard what we say so that our words will bring honor to him.

141 *A psalm of David.*

1 O LORD, I am calling to you. Please hurry!
  Listen when I cry to you for help!
2 Accept my prayer as incense offered to you,
  and my upraised hands as an evening
   offering.

3 Take control of what I say, O LORD,
  and guard my lips.
4 Don't let me drift toward evil
  or take part in acts of wickedness.
  Don't let me share in the delicacies
  of those who do wrong.

5 Let the godly strike me!
  It will be a kindness!
If they correct me, it is soothing
   medicine.
  Don't let me refuse it.

But I pray constantly
  against the wicked and their deeds.
6 When their leaders are thrown down from
  a cliff,
  the wicked will listen to my words and
   find them true.
7 Like rocks brought up by a plow,
  the bones of the wicked will lie scattered
   without burial.*

8 I look to you for help, O Sovereign LORD.
  You are my refuge; don't let them
   kill me.
9 Keep me from the traps they have set
   for me,
  from the snares of those who do wrong.
10 Let the wicked fall into their own nets,
  but let me escape.

142 *A psalm* of David, regarding his experience in the cave. A prayer.*

1 I cry out to the LORD;
  I plead for the LORD's mercy.
2 I pour out my complaints before him
  and tell him all my troubles.
3 When I am overwhelmed,
  you alone know the way I should turn.
Wherever I go,
  my enemies have set traps for me.
4 I look for someone to come and help me,
  but no one gives me a passing thought!
No one will help me;
  no one cares a bit what happens
   to me.
5 Then I pray to you, O LORD.

141:7 Hebrew *scattered at the mouth of Sheol.*   **142:TITLE** Hebrew *maskil.* This may be a literary or musical term.

I say, "You are my place of refuge.
  You are all I really want in life.
[6] Hear my cry,
  for I am very low.
Rescue me from my persecutors,
  for they are too strong for me.
[7] Bring me out of prison
  so I can thank you.
The godly will crowd around me,
  for you are good to me."

143 *A psalm of David.*

[1] Hear my prayer, O LORD;
  listen to my plea!
  Answer me because you are faithful
    and righteous.
[2] Don't put your servant on trial,
  for no one is innocent before you.
[3] My enemy has chased me.
  He has knocked me to the ground
  and forces me to live in darkness like
    those in the grave.
[4] I am losing all hope;
  I am paralyzed with fear.
[5] I remember the days of old.
  I ponder all your great works
  and think about what you have done.
[6] I lift my hands to you in prayer.
  I thirst for you as parched land thirsts
    for rain.   *Interlude*

[7] Come quickly, LORD, and answer me,
  for my depression deepens.
Don't turn away from me,
  or I will die.
[8] Let me hear of your unfailing love each
    morning,
  for I am trusting you.
Show me where to walk,
  for I give myself to you.
[9] Rescue me from my enemies, LORD;
  I run to you to hide me.
[10] Teach me to do your will,
  for you are my God.
May your gracious Spirit lead me forward
  on a firm footing.
[11] For the glory of your name, O LORD, preserve
    my life.
  Because of your faithfulness, bring me
    out of this distress.
[12] In your unfailing love, silence all my
    enemies
  and destroy all my foes,
  for I am your servant.

144:2 Some manuscripts read *my people.*

144 *A psalm of David.*

[1] Praise the LORD, who is my rock.
  He trains my hands for war
  and gives my fingers skill for battle.
[2] He is my loving ally and my fortress,
  my tower of safety, my rescuer.
He is my shield, and I take refuge in him.
  He makes the nations* submit to me.

[3] O LORD, what are human beings that you
    should notice them,
  mere mortals that you should think about
    them?
[4] For they are like a breath of air;
  their days are like a passing shadow.

[5] Open the heavens, LORD, and come down.
  Touch the mountains so they billow
    smoke.
[6] Hurl your lightning bolts and scatter your
    enemies!
  Shoot your arrows and confuse them!
[7] Reach down from heaven and rescue me;
  rescue me from deep waters,
  from the power of my enemies.
[8] Their mouths are full of lies;
  they swear to tell the truth, but they lie
    instead.

[9] I will sing a new song to you, O God!
  I will sing your praises with a ten-stringed
    harp.
[10] For you grant victory to kings!
  You rescued your servant David from the
    fatal sword.
[11] Save me!
  Rescue me from the power of my
    enemies.
Their mouths are full of lies;
  they swear to tell the truth, but they lie
    instead.

[12] May our sons flourish in their youth
  like well-nurtured plants.
May our daughters be like graceful pillars,
  carved to beautify a palace.
[13] May our barns be filled
  with crops of every kind.
May the flocks in our fields multiply by the
    thousands,
  even tens of thousands,
[14] and may our oxen be loaded down with
    produce.
May there be no enemy breaking through
    our walls,
  no going into captivity,
  no cries of alarm in our town squares.

15 Yes, joyful are those who live like this!
   Joyful indeed are those whose God
      is the LORD.

145 *
A psalm of praise of David.

1 I will exalt you, my God and King,
   and praise your name forever and ever.
2 I will praise you every day;
   yes, I will praise you forever.
3 Great is the LORD! He is most worthy of
      praise!
   No one can measure his greatness.

4 Let each generation tell its children of your
      mighty acts;
   let them proclaim your power.
5 I will meditate* on your majestic, glorious
      splendor
   and your wonderful miracles.
6 Your awe-inspiring deeds will be on every
      tongue;
   I will proclaim your greatness.
7 Everyone will share the story of your
      wonderful goodness;
   they will sing with joy about your
      righteousness.

8 The LORD is merciful and compassionate,
   slow to get angry and filled with unfailing
      love.
9 The LORD is good to everyone.
   He showers compassion on all his
      creation.

10 All of your works will thank you, LORD,
   and your faithful followers will praise you.
11 They will speak of the glory of your kingdom;
   they will give examples of your power.
12 They will tell about your mighty deeds
   and about the majesty and glory of your
      reign.
13 For your kingdom is an everlasting kingdom.
   You rule throughout all generations.

   The LORD always keeps his promises;
      he is gracious in all he does.*
14 The LORD helps the fallen
   and lifts those bent beneath their loads.
15 The eyes of all look to you in hope;
   you give them their food as they need it.
16 When you open your hand,
   you satisfy the hunger and thirst of every
      living thing.
17 The LORD is righteous in everything he does;
   he is filled with kindness.
18 The LORD is close to all who call on him,
   yes, to all who call on him in truth.
19 He grants the desires of those who fear him;

he hears their cries for help and rescues
   them.
20 The LORD protects all those who love him,
   but he destroys the wicked.

21 I will praise the LORD,
   and may everyone on earth bless his holy
      name
   forever and ever.

146 1 Praise the LORD!

   Let all that I am praise the LORD.
2   I will praise the LORD as long as I live.
   I will sing praises to my God with my
      dying breath.

3 Don't put your confidence in powerful
      people;
   there is no help for you there.
4 When they breathe their last, they return
      to the earth,
   and all their plans die with them.
5 But joyful are those who have the God
      of Israel* as their helper,
   whose hope is in the LORD their God.
6 He made heaven and earth,
   the sea, and everything in them.
   He keeps every promise forever.
7 He gives justice to the oppressed
   and food to the hungry.
   The LORD frees the prisoners.
8   The LORD opens the eyes of the blind.
   The LORD lifts up those who are weighed
      down.
   The LORD loves the godly.
9 The LORD protects the foreigners among us.
   He cares for the orphans and widows,
   but he frustrates the plans of the wicked.

10 The LORD will reign forever.
   He will be your God, O Jerusalem,*
      throughout the generations.

   Praise the LORD!

147 1 Praise the LORD!

   How good to sing praises to our God!
   How delightful and how fitting!
2 The LORD is rebuilding Jerusalem
   and bringing the exiles back to Israel.
3 He heals the brokenhearted
   and bandages their wounds.

145 This psalm is a Hebrew acrostic poem; each verse (including
13b) begins with a successive letter of the Hebrew alphabet.
145:5 Some manuscripts read *They will speak.* 145:13 The last two
lines of 145:13 are not found in many of the ancient manuscripts.
146:5 Hebrew *of Jacob.* See note on 44:4. 146:10 Hebrew *Zion.*

4 He counts the stars
and calls them all by name.
5 How great is our Lord! His power is absolute!
His understanding is beyond
comprehension!
6 The LORD supports the humble,
but he brings the wicked down into
the dust.

7 Sing out your thanks to the LORD;
sing praises to our God with a harp.
8 He covers the heavens with clouds,
provides rain for the earth,
and makes the grass grow in mountain
pastures.
9 He gives food to the wild animals
and feeds the young ravens when
they cry.
10 He takes no pleasure in the strength
of a horse
or in human might.
11 No, the LORD's delight is in those who
fear him,
those who put their hope in his
unfailing love.

12 Glorify the LORD, O Jerusalem!
Praise your God, O Zion!
13 For he has strengthened the bars of
your gates
and blessed your children within your
walls.
14 He sends peace across your nation
and satisfies your hunger with the finest
wheat.
15 He sends his orders to the world—
how swiftly his word flies!
16 He sends the snow like white wool;
he scatters frost upon the ground like
ashes.
17 He hurls the hail like stones.*
Who can stand against his freezing cold?
18 Then, at his command, it all melts.
He sends his winds, and the ice thaws.
19 He has revealed his words to Jacob,
his decrees and regulations to Israel.
20 He has not done this for any other nation;
they do not know his regulations.

Praise the LORD!

148 ¹Praise the LORD!

Praise the LORD from the heavens!
Praise him from the skies!
2 Praise him, all his angels!

Praise him, all the armies of heaven!
3 Praise him, sun and moon!
Praise him, all you twinkling stars!
4 Praise him, skies above!
Praise him, vapors high above
the clouds!
5 Let every created thing give praise to the
LORD,
for he issued his command, and they
came into being.
6 He set them in place forever and ever.
His decree will never be revoked.

7 Praise the LORD from the earth,
you creatures of the ocean depths,
8 fire and hail, snow and clouds,*
wind and weather that obey him,
9 mountains and all hills,
fruit trees and all cedars,
10 wild animals and all livestock,
small scurrying animals and birds,
11 kings of the earth and all people,
rulers and judges of the earth,
12 young men and young women,
old men and children.

13 Let them all praise the name of the LORD.
For his name is very great;
his glory towers over the earth and
heaven!
14 He has made his people strong,
honoring his faithful ones—
the people of Israel who are close
to him.

Praise the LORD!

149 ¹Praise the LORD!

Sing to the LORD a new song.
Sing his praises in the assembly of the
faithful.

2 O Israel, rejoice in your Maker.
O people of Jerusalem,* exult in your
King.
3 Praise his name with dancing,
accompanied by tambourine and harp.

....

UNLIMITED
*(147:5) We can sometimes feel as though we don't under-
stand ourselves at all—what we want, how we feel, what's
wrong with us. But God's understanding is unlimited;
therefore, he knows us completely. If you feel troubled
and are filled with self-doubts and questions, remember
that God knows and understands you perfectly. Take your
mind off yourself and focus, instead, on him. And the
more you learn about God and his ways, the better you
will understand yourself.*

147:17 Hebrew *like bread crumbs.* 148:8 Or *mist,* or *smoke.*
149:2 Hebrew *Zion.*

⁴ For the LORD delights in his people;
  he crowns the humble with victory.
⁵ Let the faithful rejoice that he
    honors them.
  Let them sing for joy as they lie on their
    beds.

⁶ Let the praises of God be in their mouths,
  and a sharp sword in their hands—
⁷ to execute vengeance on the nations
  and punishment on the peoples,
⁸ to bind their kings with shackles
  and their leaders with iron chains,
⁹ to execute the judgment written against
  them.

....

WAYS TO PRAISE
(149:3-5) Although the Bible invites us to praise God, we often aren't sure how to go about it. Here, several ways are suggested: with your voice, in music, in your actions. What is your favorite way to offer praise?

This is the glorious privilege of his
  faithful ones.

Praise the LORD!

150 ¹ Praise the LORD!

Praise God in his sanctuary;
  praise him in his mighty heaven!
² Praise him for his mighty works;
  praise his unequaled greatness!
³ Praise him with a blast of the ram's horn;
  praise him with the lyre and harp!
⁴ Praise him with the tambourine and
    dancing;
  praise him with strings and flutes!
⁵ Praise him with a clash of cymbals;
  praise him with loud clanging cymbals.
⁶ Let everything that breathes sing praises
    to the LORD!

Praise the LORD!

PROVERBS

What do you think you need to get by in life? Your good looks or sparkling personality? A good bank account? Friends in high places? Incredible grades? You probably have a list of "needs." But is wisdom on your list?

Many people confuse wisdom with intelligence. Wisdom is an intelligence of a different sort. According to the American Heritage Dictionary, it means "1. The ability to discern what is true, right, or lasting; insight. 2. Common sense; good judgment." In other words, wisdom is the ability to make good (wise) decisions. Lots of people are smart (book knowledge), but only a few are wise.

Proverbs was written by Solomon, the king who asked for and received wisdom from God (see 1 Kgs 3). In this book he provides proverbs—wise sayings—about money, marriage, family life, discipline, friends, laziness, speech, relationships, temptation, and leadership. Solomon's purpose was "to teach people wisdom and discipline, to help them understand the insights of the wise. . . . to teach people to live disciplined and successful lives, to help them do what is right, just, and fair" (1:2-3).

Proverbs is a book of answers—answers to our questions about life. Most people would like to have more wisdom in many areas. As you read, ask God to make the wisdom of Solomon your wisdom, too. In what areas could you use more wisdom?

STATS

PURPOSE
To teach people how to be understanding, just, and fair in everything they do

AUTHOR
Solomon wrote most of this book; Agur and Lemuel contributed some of the later sections.

ORIGINAL AUDIENCE
The people of Israel

DATE WRITTEN
Solomon wrote and compiled most of these proverbs early in his reign.

SETTING
The book of Proverbs reflects the poetic style of the era. It is a book of wise sayings to teach people how to live godly lives.

SPECIAL FEATURES
The book uses varied literary forms: poems, brief parables, pointed questions, and couplets. Other literary devices include antithesis, comparison, and personification.

KEY POINTS

WISDOM God wants his people to be wise. He helps us gain wisdom through the rules and advice in the Bible and through making right decisions.

RELATIONSHIPS Proverbs gives us advice for developing our relationships with friends, family members, and co-workers. To relate to people, we need consistency, sensitivity, and discipline.

WISE WORDS What we say shows our real attitude toward others. To be wise in our speech we need to use self-control. What we say affects others.

WORK God controls the final outcome of all we do; however, we must carry out our work with diligence and discipline, not laziness. Because God evaluates how we live, we should work purposefully, doing our best with what God has given us.

SUCCESS Although people work very hard for money and fame, God considers a good reputation, faith, and obedience to be the true measures of success. A successful relationship with God counts for eternity. Everything else is only temporary.

1 THE PURPOSE OF PROVERBS These are the proverbs of Solomon, David's son, king of Israel.

2 Their purpose is to teach people wisdom
   and discipline,
      to help them understand the insights
         of the wise.
3 Their purpose is to teach people to live
   disciplined and successful lives,
      to help them do what is right, just,
         and fair.
4 These proverbs will give insight to the
   simple,
      knowledge and discernment to the young.
5 Let the wise listen to these proverbs and
   become even wiser.

Let those with understanding receive
   guidance
6 by exploring the meaning in these proverbs
   and parables,
      the words of the wise and their riddles.

7 Fear of the LORD is the foundation of true
   knowledge,
      but fools despise wisdom and discipline.

A FATHER'S EXHORTATION: ACQUIRE WISDOM

8 My child,* listen when your father
   corrects you.
      Don't neglect your mother's instruction.
9 What you learn from them will crown you
   with grace
      and be a chain of honor around
         your neck.

10 My child, if sinners entice you,
    turn your back on them!
11 They may say, "Come and join us.
    Let's hide and kill someone!
       Just for fun, let's ambush the innocent!
12 Let's swallow them alive, like the grave*;
       let's swallow them whole, like those who
          go down to the pit of death.
13 Think of the great things we'll get!
    We'll fill our houses with all the stuff
       we take.

1:8 Hebrew *My son;* also in 1:10, 15.   1:12 Hebrew *like Sheol.*

TURN AND RUN
(1:10-19) *Sin is attractive because it offers a quick route to prosperity and makes us feel like one of the crowd. When we go along with others and refuse to listen to the truth, our own appetites become our masters. We'll do anything to satisfy them. But sin is deadly. We must learn to make choices not on the basis of flashy appeal or short-range pleasure, but in view of the long-range effects. Sometimes this means steering clear of people who want to draw us into activities we know are wrong. We can't be friendly with sin and expect our lives to remain unaffected. Turn and run—this is not cowardly; it is both brave and wise.*

I WONDER . . .

I'm always giving in to my friends. Lots of times this goes against what I think a Christian should do. How do I withstand the pressure?

If every young person had a dollar for every time friends asked him or her to "come along," most could pay for four years of college!

Being included feels great, and everyone needs friends. But friends don't always have our welfare at heart. In fact, sometimes they only want us to join them so they can feel better about doing whatever it is they want to do.

But is this really pressure?

When someone invites you to go along with a questionable (or bad) situation and you give in, you haven't succumbed to peer pressure. You have chosen to do something wrong and have concealed your true identity.

Too often we hide our real character, hoping to be liked by a group or person. We want to be accepted. Unfortunately, this often works. If it didn't, people wouldn't do it!

All are tempted to bend their rules or beliefs in order for someone to like them. During the teenage years, this kind of pressure can be intense, and it can generate a hungry urge to do what others are doing in order to fit in.

But God wants to provide the inner muscle you'll need to combat the outer pressure you feel. Ask him to give you the courage and strength to say no.

He also wants to teach you what to do. Remember when Mom or Dad taught you to do something like bake cookies or start a lawnmower? They didn't just tell you to do it, they showed you how.

God shows us how to act through the teachings and stories in the Bible.

Commands like "Don't copy the behavior and customs of this world, but let God transform you into a new person by changing the way you think" (Rom 12:2) need to be read to understand God's heart. But examples from throughout the Bible can help.

Consider these: Joseph ran from temptation (Gen 39:12), and Daniel prayed his way through it (Dan 6:10). And like the counsel in Proverbs 1:10, sometimes we just have to realize that the consequences are not worth the risk.

¹⁴ Come, throw in your lot with us;
  we'll all share the loot."

¹⁵ My child, don't go along with them!
  Stay far away from their paths.
¹⁶ They rush to commit evil deeds.
  They hurry to commit murder.
¹⁷ If a bird sees a trap being set,
  it knows to stay away.
¹⁸ But these people set an ambush for
  themselves;
  they are trying to get themselves killed.
¹⁹ Such is the fate of all who are greedy for
  money;
  it robs them of life.

WISDOM SHOUTS IN THE STREETS

²⁰ Wisdom shouts in the streets.
  She cries out in the public square.
²¹ She calls to the crowds along the main
  street,
  to those gathered in front of the city gate:
²² "How long, you simpletons,
  will you insist on being simpleminded?
  How long will you mockers relish your
  mocking?
  How long will you fools hate knowledge?
²³ Come and listen to my counsel.
  I'll share my heart with you
  and make you wise.

²⁴ "I called you so often, but you wouldn't
  come.
  I reached out to you, but you paid no
  attention.
²⁵ You ignored my advice
  and rejected the correction I offered.
²⁶ So I will laugh when you are in trouble!
  I will mock you when disaster overtakes
  you—
²⁷ when calamity overtakes you like a storm,
  when disaster engulfs you like a cyclone,
  and anguish and distress overwhelm you.

²⁸ "When they cry for help, I will not answer.
  Though they anxiously search for me,
  they will not find me.
²⁹ For they hated knowledge
  and chose not to fear the LORD.
³⁰ They rejected my advice
  and paid no attention when I corrected
  them.
³¹ Therefore, they must eat the bitter fruit
  of living their own way,
  choking on their own schemes.
³² For simpletons turn away from me—
  to death.

2:1 Hebrew *My son.*

Fools are destroyed by their own
  complacency.
³³ But all who listen to me will live in peace,
  untroubled by fear of harm."

2 THE BENEFITS OF WISDOM

¹ My child,* listen to what I say,
  and treasure my commands.
² Tune your ears to wisdom,
  and concentrate on understanding.
³ Cry out for insight,
  and ask for understanding.
⁴ Search for them as you would for silver;
  seek them like hidden treasures.
⁵ Then you will understand what it means
  to fear the LORD,
  and you will gain knowledge of God.
⁶ For the LORD grants wisdom!
  From his mouth come knowledge and
  understanding.
⁷ He grants a treasure of common sense
  to the honest.
  He is a shield to those who walk with
  integrity.
⁸ He guards the paths of the just
  and protects those who are faithful
  to him.

⁹ Then you will understand what is right, just,
  and fair,
  and you will find the right way to go.
¹⁰ For wisdom will enter your heart,
  and knowledge will fill you with joy.
¹¹ Wise choices will watch over you.
  Understanding will keep you safe.

¹² Wisdom will save you from evil people,
  from those whose words are twisted.
¹³ These men turn from the right way
  to walk down dark paths.
¹⁴ They take pleasure in doing wrong,
  and they enjoy the twisted ways of evil.
¹⁵ Their actions are crooked,
  and their ways are wrong.

¹⁶ Wisdom will save you from the immoral
  woman,

....

CHOICES
*(2:9-10) Wisdom comes through a constant process of
growth. First, we must trust and honor God. Second, we
must realize that the Bible reveals God's wisdom to us.
Third, we must learn to make the right choices. Fourth,
when we make sinful or mistaken choices, we must learn
from our errors. People don't develop all aspects of
wisdom at once. For example, some people seem to have
more insight than discretion; others have more knowledge than common sense. But the source of wisdom is
still God. Want to be wise? Start at the source.*

TRUST IN THE LORD WITH ALL YOUR HEART; . . . SEEK HIS WILL IN ALL YOU DO, AND HE WILL SHOW YOU WHICH PATH TO TAKE. PROVERBS 3:5-6

from the seductive words of the
promiscuous woman.
¹⁷ She has abandoned her husband
and ignores the covenant she made
before God.
¹⁸ Entering her house leads to death;
it is the road to the grave.*
¹⁹ The man who visits her is doomed.
He will never reach the paths of life.

²⁰ Follow the steps of good men instead,
and stay on the paths of the righteous.
²¹ For only the godly will live in the land,
and those with integrity will remain in it.
²² But the wicked will be removed from the
land,
and the treacherous will be uprooted.

3 TRUSTING IN THE LORD

¹ My child,* never forget the things I have
taught you.
Store my commands in your heart.
² If you do this, you will live many years,
and your life will be satisfying.
³ Never let loyalty and kindness leave you!
Tie them around your neck as a reminder.
Write them deep within your heart.
⁴ Then you will find favor with both God and
people,
and you will earn a good reputation.

⁵ Trust in the LORD with all your heart;
do not depend on your own
understanding.
⁶ Seek his will in all you do,
and he will show you which path to take.

⁷ Don't be impressed with your own wisdom.
Instead, fear the LORD and turn away
from evil.
⁸ Then you will have healing for your body
and strength for your bones.

⁹ Honor the LORD with your wealth
and with the best part of everything you
produce.
¹⁰ Then he will fill your barns with grain,
and your vats will overflow with good
wine.

¹¹ My child, don't reject the LORD's discipline,
and don't be upset when he corrects you.
¹² For the LORD corrects those he loves,
just as a father corrects a child in whom
he delights.*

¹³ Joyful is the person who finds wisdom,
the one who gains understanding.
¹⁴ For wisdom is more profitable than silver,
and her wages are better than gold.
¹⁵ Wisdom is more precious than rubies;
nothing you desire can compare with her.
¹⁶ She offers you long life in her right hand,
and riches and honor in her left.
¹⁷ She will guide you down delightful paths;
all her ways are satisfying.
¹⁸ Wisdom is a tree of life to those who
embrace her;
happy are those who hold her tightly.

¹⁹ By wisdom the LORD founded the earth;
by understanding he created the
heavens.
²⁰ By his knowledge the deep fountains of the
earth burst forth,
and the dew settles beneath the
night sky.

²¹ My child, don't lose sight of common sense
and discernment.
Hang on to them,
²² for they will refresh your soul.
They are like jewels on a necklace.
²³ They keep you safe on your way,
and your feet will not stumble.
²⁴ You can go to bed without fear;
you will lie down and sleep soundly.
²⁵ You need not be afraid of sudden disaster
or the destruction that comes upon the
wicked,
²⁶ for the LORD is your security.
He will keep your foot from being caught
in a trap.

²⁷ Do not withhold good from those who
deserve it
when it's in your power to help them.
²⁸ If you can help your neighbor now,
don't say,
"Come back tomorrow, and then I'll
help you."

²⁹ Don't plot harm against your neighbor,
for those who live nearby trust you.
³⁰ Don't pick a fight without reason,
when no one has done you harm.

³¹ Don't envy violent people
or copy their ways.

2:18 Hebrew *to the spirits of the dead.*   **3:1** Hebrew *My son;* also
in 3:11, 21.   **3:12** Greek version reads *And he punishes those he
accepts as his children.* Compare Heb 12:6.

32 Such wicked people are detestable to the
LORD,
but he offers his friendship to the godly.

33 The LORD curses the house of the wicked,
but he blesses the home of the upright.

34 The LORD mocks the mockers
but is gracious to the humble.*

35 The wise inherit honor,
but fools are put to shame!

4 A FATHER'S WISE ADVICE

1 My children,* listen when your father
corrects you.
Pay attention and learn good judgment,
2 for I am giving you good guidance.
Don't turn away from my instructions.
3 For I, too, was once my father's son,
tenderly loved as my mother's only child.

4 My father taught me,
"Take my words to heart.
Follow my commands, and you will live.
5 Get wisdom; develop good judgment.
Don't forget my words or turn away from
them.
6 Don't turn your back on wisdom, for she will
protect you.
Love her, and she will guard you.
7 Getting wisdom is the wisest thing you
can do!
And whatever else you do, develop good
judgment.
8 If you prize wisdom, she will make you
great.
Embrace her, and she will honor you.
9 She will place a lovely wreath on your head;
she will present you with a beautiful
crown."

10 My child,* listen to me and do as I say,
and you will have a long, good life.
11 I will teach you wisdom's ways
and lead you in straight paths.
12 When you walk, you won't be held back;
when you run, you won't stumble.
13 Take hold of my instructions; don't let
them go.
Guard them, for they are the key to life.

14 Don't do as the wicked do,
and don't follow the path of evildoers.
15 Don't even think about it; don't go that way.
Turn away and keep moving.

16 For evil people can't sleep until they've
done their evil deed for the day.
They can't rest until they've caused
someone to stumble.
17 They eat the food of wickedness
and drink the wine of violence!

18 The way of the righteous is like the first
gleam of dawn,
which shines ever brighter until the full
light of day.
19 But the way of the wicked is like total
darkness.
They have no idea what they are
stumbling over.

20 My child, pay attention to what I say.
Listen carefully to my words.
21 Don't lose sight of them.
Let them penetrate deep into your heart,
22 for they bring life to those who find them,
and healing to their whole body.

23 Guard your heart above all else,
for it determines the course of your life.

24 Avoid all perverse talk;
stay away from corrupt speech.
25 Look straight ahead,
and fix your eyes on what lies before you.
26 Mark out a straight path for your feet;
stay on the safe path.
27 Don't get sidetracked;
keep your feet from following evil.

5 AVOID IMMORAL WOMEN

1 My son, pay attention to my wisdom;
listen carefully to my wise counsel.
2 Then you will show discernment,
and your lips will express what you've
learned.
3 For the lips of an immoral woman are as
sweet as honey,
and her mouth is smoother than oil.
4 But in the end she is as bitter as poison,
as dangerous as a double-edged sword.
5 Her feet go down to death;
her steps lead straight to the grave.*

....

GUARD YOUR HEART
*(4:23-27) According to Solomon, wise people guard their
hearts. Our hearts—our feelings of love and desire—dic-
tate to a great extent how we live because we always
find time to do what we enjoy. So, how do we guard our
hearts? By concentrating on those desires that will keep
us on the right path. This will involve discipline and a
commitment to God's purposes. It will also mean watching out for detours that lead to temptation.*

3:34 Greek version reads *The LORD opposes the proud / but favors
the humble.* Compare Jas 4:6; 1 Pet 5:5. **4:1** Hebrew *My sons.*
4:10 Hebrew *My son;* also in 4:20. **5:5** Hebrew *to Sheol.*

MY STORY: John

Sometimes reading Scripture is like getting a good swift kick in the pants! That's what happened to me, anyway.

I've had this problem with procrastination and laziness. Basically, I just don't make an effort with things that bore me (like school or chores my parents want me to do). One day, as I was reading along in Proverbs 6:6-11, which describes what a lazy person is like, I knew that it was talking about me! Those verses taught me that putting things off isn't just a bad habit, it's a sin that can lead to some pretty bad consequences. This passage helped motivate me to quit sitting around and to take some action—even if I don't feel like it.

6 For she cares nothing about the path to life.
   She staggers down a crooked trail and
      doesn't realize it.

7 So now, my sons, listen to me.
   Never stray from what I am about to say:
8 Stay away from her!
   Don't go near the door of her house!
9 If you do, you will lose your honor
   and will lose to merciless people all you
      have achieved.
10 Strangers will consume your wealth,
   and someone else will enjoy the fruit of
      your labor.
11 In the end you will groan in anguish
   when disease consumes your body.
12 You will say, "How I hated discipline!
   If only I had not ignored all the warnings!
13 Oh, why didn't I listen to my teachers?
   Why didn't I pay attention to my
      instructors?
14 I have come to the brink of utter ruin,
   and now I must face public disgrace."

15 Drink water from your own well—
   share your love only with your wife.*
16 Why spill the water of your springs in the
      streets,
   having sex with just anyone?*
17 You should reserve it for yourselves.
   Never share it with strangers.
18 Let your wife be a fountain of blessing
      for you.
   Rejoice in the wife of your youth.
19 She is a loving deer, a graceful doe.

Let her breasts satisfy you always.
   May you always be captivated by her love.
20 Why be captivated, my son, by an immoral
      woman,
   or fondle the breasts of a promiscuous
      woman?

21 For the LORD sees clearly what a man does,
   examining every path he takes.
22 An evil man is held captive by his own sins;
   they are ropes that catch and hold him.
23 He will die for lack of self-control;
   he will be lost because of his great
      foolishness.

6 LESSONS FOR DAILY LIFE

1 My child,* if you have put up security for
      a friend's debt
   or agreed to guarantee the debt of
      a stranger—
2 if you have trapped yourself by your
      agreement
   and are caught by what you said—
3 follow my advice and save yourself,
   for you have placed yourself at your
      friend's mercy.
   Now swallow your pride;
      go and beg to have your name erased.
4 Don't put it off; do it now!
   Don't rest until you do.
5 Save yourself like a gazelle escaping from
      a hunter,
   like a bird fleeing from a net.

6 Take a lesson from the ants, you lazybones.
   Learn from their ways and become wise!
7 Though they have no prince
   or governor or ruler to make them work,
8 they labor hard all summer,
   gathering food for the winter.
9 But you, lazybones, how long will you
      sleep?
   When will you wake up?
10 A little extra sleep, a little more slumber,
   a little folding of the hands to rest—
11 then poverty will pounce on you like a
      bandit;
   scarcity will attack you like an armed
      robber.

12 What are worthless and wicked people like?
   They are constant liars,
13 signaling their deceit with a wink of the eye,
   a nudge of the foot, or the wiggle of
      fingers.

5:15 Hebrew *Drink water from your own cistern, / flowing water from your own well.*   **5:16** Hebrew *Why spill your springs in the streets, / your streams in the city squares?*   **6:1** Hebrew *My son.*

¹⁴ Their perverted hearts plot evil,
and they constantly stir up trouble.
¹⁵ But they will be destroyed suddenly,
broken in an instant beyond all hope of
healing.

¹⁶ There are six things the LORD hates—
no, seven things he detests:
¹⁷ haughty eyes,
a lying tongue,
hands that kill the innocent,
¹⁸ a heart that plots evil,
feet that race to do wrong,
¹⁹ a false witness who pours out lies,
a person who sows discord in a family.

²⁰ My son, obey your father's commands,
and don't neglect your mother's
instruction.
²¹ Keep their words always in your heart.
Tie them around your neck.
²² When you walk, their counsel will lead you.
When you sleep, they will protect you.
When you wake up, they will advise you.
²³ For their command is a lamp
and their instruction a light;
their corrective discipline
is the way to life.
²⁴ It will keep you from the immoral woman,
from the smooth tongue of a promiscuous
woman.
²⁵ Don't lust for her beauty.
Don't let her coy glances seduce you.
²⁶ For a prostitute will bring you to poverty,*
but sleeping with another man's wife will
cost you your life.
²⁷ Can a man scoop a flame into his lap
and not have his clothes catch on fire?
²⁸ Can he walk on hot coals
and not blister his feet?
²⁹ So it is with the man who sleeps with
another man's wife.
He who embraces her will not go
unpunished.

³⁰ Excuses might be found for a thief
who steals because he is starving.
³¹ But if he is caught, he must pay back seven
times what he stole,
even if he has to sell everything in his
house.
³² But the man who commits adultery is an
utter fool,
for he destroys himself.
³³ He will be wounded and disgraced.
His shame will never be erased.

³⁴ For the woman's jealous husband will be
furious,
and he will show no mercy when he takes
revenge.
³⁵ He will accept no compensation,
nor be satisfied with a payoff of any size.

7 ANOTHER WARNING ABOUT IMMORAL WOMEN

¹ Follow my advice, my son;
always treasure my commands.
² Obey my commands and live!
Guard my instructions as you guard your
own eyes.*
³ Tie them on your fingers as a reminder.
Write them deep within your heart.

⁴ Love wisdom like a sister;
make insight a beloved member of your
family.
⁵ Let them protect you from an affair with an
immoral woman,
from listening to the flattery of a
promiscuous woman.

⁶ While I was at the window of my house,
looking through the curtain,
⁷ I saw some naive young men,
and one in particular who lacked common
sense.
⁸ He was crossing the street near the house
of an immoral woman,
strolling down the path by her house.
⁹ It was at twilight, in the evening,
as deep darkness fell.
¹⁰ The woman approached him,
seductively dressed and sly of heart.
¹¹ She was the brash, rebellious type,
never content to stay at home.
¹² She is often in the streets and markets,
soliciting at every corner.
¹³ She threw her arms around him and
kissed him,
and with a brazen look she said,
¹⁴ "I've just made my peace offerings
and fulfilled my vows.
¹⁵ You're the one I was looking for!
I came out to find you, and here you are!
¹⁶ My bed is spread with beautiful blankets,
with colored sheets of Egyptian linen.

6:26 Hebrew *to a loaf of bread.*   7:2 Hebrew *as the pupil
of your eye.*

···

LISTEN UP!
*(6:20-24) "My son, obey your father's commands, and
don't neglect your mother's instruction" (6:20). Have you
ever heard a parent give this advice? Even if we believe it,
many of us turn a deaf ear to a parent's advice at times.
But the wise person can gain wisdom by seeking the
advice of a godly parent or another adult.*

17 I've perfumed my bed
  with myrrh, aloes, and cinnamon.
18 Come, let's drink our fill of love until
  morning.
  Let's enjoy each other's caresses,
19 for my husband is not home.
  He's away on a long trip.
20 He has taken a wallet full of money with him
  and won't return until later this month.*"

21 So she seduced him with her pretty speech
  and enticed him with her flattery.
22 He followed her at once,
  like an ox going to the slaughter.
  He was like a stag caught in a trap,
23   awaiting the arrow that would pierce
  its heart.
  He was like a bird flying into a snare,
  little knowing it would cost him his life.

24 So listen to me, my sons,
  and pay attention to my words.
25 Don't let your hearts stray away toward her.
  Don't wander down her wayward path.
26 For she has been the ruin of many;
  many men have been her victims.
27 Her house is the road to the grave.*
  Her bedroom is the den of death.

8 WISDOM CALLS FOR A HEARING

1 Listen as Wisdom calls out!
  Hear as understanding raises her voice!
2 On the hilltop along the road,
  she takes her stand at the crossroads.
3 By the gates at the entrance to the town,
  on the road leading in, she cries aloud,
4 "I call to you, to all of you!
  I raise my voice to all people.
5 You simple people, use good judgment.
  You foolish people, show some
  understanding.
6 Listen to me! For I have important things
  to tell you.
  Everything I say is right,
7 for I speak the truth
  and detest every kind of deception.
8 My advice is wholesome.
  There is nothing devious or crooked in it.
9 My words are plain to anyone with
  understanding,
  clear to those with knowledge.
10 Choose my instruction rather than silver,
  and knowledge rather than pure gold.
11 For wisdom is far more valuable than rubies.
  Nothing you desire can compare with it.

12 "I, Wisdom, live together with good
  judgment.

I know where to discover knowledge and
  discernment.
13 All who fear the LORD will hate evil.
  Therefore, I hate pride and arrogance,
  corruption and perverse speech.
14 Common sense and success belong to me.
  Insight and strength are mine.
15 Because of me, kings reign,
  and rulers make just decrees.
16 Rulers lead with my help,
  and nobles make righteous judgments.*

17 "I love all who love me.
  Those who search will surely find me.
18 I have riches and honor,
  as well as enduring wealth and justice.
19 My gifts are better than gold, even the
  purest gold,
  my wages better than sterling silver!
20 I walk in righteousness,
  in paths of justice.
21 Those who love me inherit wealth.
  I will fill their treasuries.

22 "The LORD formed me from the beginning,
  before he created anything else.
23 I was appointed in ages past,
  at the very first, before the earth began.
24 I was born before the oceans were created,
  before the springs bubbled forth their
  waters.
25 Before the mountains were formed,
  before the hills, I was born—
26 before he had made the earth and fields
  and the first handfuls of soil.
27 I was there when he established the
  heavens,
  when he drew the horizon on the oceans.
28 I was there when he set the clouds above,
  when he established springs deep in the
  earth.
29 I was there when he set the limits of the
  seas,
  so they would not spread beyond their
  boundaries.
  And when he marked off the earth's
  foundations,
30   I was the architect at his side.
  I was his constant delight,
  rejoicing always in his presence.
31 And how happy I was with the world he
  created;
  how I rejoiced with the human family!

32 "And so, my children,* listen to me,
  for all who follow my ways are joyful.

7:20 Hebrew *until the moon is full.*   **7:27** Hebrew *to Sheol.*
8:16 Some Hebrew manuscripts and Greek version read *and nobles
are judges over the earth.*   **8:32** Hebrew *my sons.*

³³ Listen to my instruction and be wise.
　　Don't ignore it.
³⁴ Joyful are those who listen to me,
　　watching for me daily at my gates,
　　waiting for me outside my home!
³⁵ For whoever finds me finds life
　　and receives favor from the LORD.
³⁶ But those who miss me injure themselves.
　　All who hate me love death."

9

¹ Wisdom has built her house;
　　she has carved its seven columns.
² She has prepared a great banquet,
　　mixed the wines, and set the table.
³ She has sent her servants to invite everyone
　　to come.
　She calls out from the heights
　　overlooking the city.
⁴ "Come in with me," she urges the simple.
　To those who lack good judgment,
　　she says,
⁵ "Come, eat my food,
　　and drink the wine I have mixed.
⁶ Leave your simple ways behind, and begin
　　to live;
　learn to use good judgment."

⁷ Anyone who rebukes a mocker will get an
　　insult in return.
　Anyone who corrects the wicked will
　　get hurt.
⁸ So don't bother correcting mockers;
　　they will only hate you.
　But correct the wise,
　　and they will love you.
⁹ Instruct the wise,
　　and they will be even wiser.
　Teach the righteous,
　　and they will learn even more.

¹⁰ Fear of the LORD is the foundation
　　of wisdom.
　Knowledge of the Holy One results
　　in good judgment.
¹¹ Wisdom will multiply your days
　　and add years to your life.
¹² If you become wise, you will be the one
　　to benefit.
　If you scorn wisdom, you will be the one
　　to suffer.

FOLLY CALLS FOR A HEARING
¹³ The woman named Folly is brash.
　　She is ignorant and doesn't know it.
¹⁴ She sits in her doorway
　　on the heights overlooking the city.

¹⁵ She calls out to men going by
　　who are minding their own business.
¹⁶ "Come in with me," she urges the simple.
　To those who lack good judgment,
　　she says,
¹⁷ "Stolen water is refreshing;
　　food eaten in secret tastes the best!"
¹⁸ But little do they know that the dead are
　　there.
　Her guests are in the depths of the
　　grave.*

10 THE PROVERBS OF SOLOMON
The proverbs of Solomon:

A wise child* brings joy to a father;
　a foolish child brings grief to
　　a mother.

² Tainted wealth has no lasting value,
　　but right living can save your life.

³ The LORD will not let the godly go hungry,
　　but he refuses to satisfy the craving
　　of the wicked.

⁴ Lazy people are soon poor;
　　hard workers get rich.

⁵ A wise youth harvests in the summer,
　　but one who sleeps during harvest
　　is a disgrace.

⁶ The godly are showered with blessings;
　　the words of the wicked conceal violent
　　intentions.

⁷ We have happy memories of the godly,
　　but the name of a wicked person rots
　　away.

⁸ The wise are glad to be instructed,
　　but babbling fools fall flat on
　　their faces.

⁹ People with integrity walk safely,
　　but those who follow crooked paths will
　　slip and fall.

· ·

STOLEN FOOD
(9:1-17) Some sins can be hypnotic and intoxicating. That's why many people put aside all thought of wisdom's banquet (9:1-6) in order to eat the stolen food of foolishness (9:5, 17). Before reaching for forbidden fruit, take a long look at what happens to those who eat it.

WASTED TIME
(10:4-5) Every day has 24 hours filled with opportunities to grow, serve, and be productive. Wasting time is easy, letting life slip from our grasp. Yet we can choose to be productive in our use of time. See time as God's gift, and seize the opportunity to live for him. How will you use your time?

9:18 Hebrew *in Sheol.*　**10:1** Hebrew *son;* also in 10:1b.

¹⁰ People who wink at wrong cause trouble,
  but a bold reproof promotes peace.*

¹¹ The words of the godly are a life-giving
    fountain;
  the words of the wicked conceal violent
    intentions.

¹² Hatred stirs up quarrels,
  but love makes up for all offenses.

¹³ Wise words come from the lips of people
    with understanding,
  but those lacking sense will be beaten
    with a rod.

¹⁴ Wise people treasure knowledge,
  but the babbling of a fool invites disaster.

¹⁵ The wealth of the rich is their fortress;
  the poverty of the poor is their
    destruction.

¹⁶ The earnings of the godly enhance their
    lives,
  but evil people squander their money
    on sin.

¹⁷ People who accept discipline are on the
    pathway to life,
  but those who ignore correction will
    go astray.

¹⁸ Hiding hatred makes you a liar;
  slandering others makes you a fool.

¹⁹ Too much talk leads to sin.
  Be sensible and keep your mouth shut.

²⁰ The words of the godly are like sterling
    silver;
  the heart of a fool is worthless.

²¹ The words of the godly encourage many,
  but fools are destroyed by their lack of
    common sense.

²² The blessing of the Lord makes a person
    rich,
  and he adds no sorrow with it.

²³ Doing wrong is fun for a fool,
  but living wisely brings pleasure to the
    sensible.

²⁴ The fears of the wicked will be fulfilled;
  the hopes of the godly will be granted.

²⁵ When the storms of life come, the wicked
    are whirled away,
  but the godly have a lasting foundation.

²⁶ Lazy people irritate their employers,
  like vinegar to the teeth or smoke in
    the eyes.

²⁷ Fear of the Lord lengthens one's life,
  but the years of the wicked are cut short.

²⁸ The hopes of the godly result in happiness,
  but the expectations of the wicked come
    to nothing.

²⁹ The way of the Lord is a stronghold to those
    with integrity,
  but it destroys the wicked.

³⁰ The godly will never be disturbed,
  but the wicked will be removed from the
    land.

³¹ The mouth of the godly person gives wise
    advice,
  but the tongue that deceives will be
    cut off.

³² The lips of the godly speak helpful words,
  but the mouth of the wicked speaks
    perverse words.

11

¹ The Lord detests the use of dishonest
    scales,
  but he delights in accurate weights.

² Pride leads to disgrace,
  but with humility comes wisdom.

³ Honesty guides good people;
  dishonesty destroys treacherous people.

⁴ Riches won't help on the day of judgment,
  but right living can save you from death.

⁵ The godly are directed by honesty;
  the wicked fall beneath their load of sin.

⁶ The godliness of good people rescues them;
  the ambition of treacherous people traps
    them.

⁷ When the wicked die, their hopes die with
    them,
  for they rely on their own feeble strength.

⁸ The godly are rescued from trouble,
  and it falls on the wicked instead.

⁹ With their words, the godless destroy their
    friends,
  but knowledge will rescue the righteous.

¹⁰ The whole city celebrates when the godly
    succeed;
  they shout for joy when the wicked die.

¹¹ Upright citizens are good for a city and make
    it prosper,
  but the talk of the wicked tears it apart.

10:10 As in Greek version; Hebrew reads *but babbling fools fall flat
on their faces.*

¹² It is foolish to belittle one's neighbor;
　　a sensible person keeps quiet.

¹³ A gossip goes around telling secrets,
　　but those who are trustworthy can keep
　　　a confidence.

¹⁴ Without wise leadership, a nation falls;
　　there is safety in having many advisers.

¹⁵ There's danger in putting up security for
　　　a stranger's debt;
　　it's safer not to guarantee another
　　　person's debt.

¹⁶ A gracious woman gains respect,
　　but ruthless men gain only wealth.

¹⁷ Your kindness will reward you,
　　but your cruelty will destroy you.

¹⁸ Evil people get rich for the moment,
　　but the reward of the godly will last.

¹⁹ Godly people find life;
　　evil people find death.

²⁰ The LORD detests people with crooked
　　　hearts,
　　but he delights in those with integrity.

²¹ Evil people will surely be punished,
　　but the children of the godly will go free.

²² A beautiful woman who lacks discretion
　　is like a gold ring in a pig's snout.

²³ The godly can look forward to a reward,
　　while the wicked can expect only
　　　judgment.

²⁴ Give freely and become more wealthy;
　　be stingy and lose everything.

11:30 Or *and those who win souls are wise.*　**11:31** Greek version reads *If the righteous are barely saved, / what will happen to godless sinners?* Compare 1 Pet 4:18.

²⁵ The generous will prosper;
　　those who refresh others will themselves
　　　be refreshed.

²⁶ People curse those who hoard their grain,
　　but they bless the one who sells in time
　　　of need.

²⁷ If you search for good, you will find favor;
　　but if you search for evil, it will find you!

²⁸ Trust in your money and down you go!
　　But the godly flourish like leaves in
　　　spring.

²⁹ Those who bring trouble on their families
　　　inherit the wind.
　　The fool will be a servant to the wise.

³⁰ The seeds of good deeds become a tree
　　　of life;
　　a wise person wins friends.*

³¹ If the righteous are rewarded here
　　　on earth,
　　what will happen to wicked sinners?*

12 ¹ To learn, you must love discipline;
　　it is stupid to hate correction.

² The LORD approves of those who are good,
　　but he condemns those who plan
　　　wickedness.

· ·

REWARDS AND PUNISHMENT
(11:31) Contrary to popular opinion, no one will ever completely get away with wrongdoing. Ultimately, the faithful are rewarded for their faith while those who do evil acts are punished (see also 1 Pet 4:17-18). Tempted to think that what you do doesn't matter? News flash: it does.

CHOICES
cheating

When it comes to ditching schoolwork, Tucker has always been the man with the plan. If he spent half as much time actually studying as he does trying to invent new ways to avoid doing his schoolwork, he probably could make straight As. Check this out:

- Through the Internet, Tucker found a company that sells term papers. For thirty bucks and an hour's worth of editing, he can turn in a top-notch report on almost any subject.
- He gets his friends to divide the daily algebra assignments. In study hall they each spend about 15 minutes doing a part of the homework (instead of an hour or more doing the whole thing by themselves). Tucker makes photocopies of the

pages on his family's scanner/copier for everyone, and passes them out first thing in the morning.
- Tucker has never read an assigned book for English class. Between the movie versions and CliffsNotes™, he can always fake it.
- Two of his teachers use the exact same tests from last year. Tucker bought old copies from two college freshmen.
- He has a programmable watch that can store up to 100 facts and dates. On exam days, the watch gets a mean workout!

　Tucker laughs at how stupid his teachers are and at how many people get away with cheating.

Now check out Proverbs 11:1. How do you think God views Tucker's lifestyle?

3 Wickedness never brings stability,
  but the godly have deep roots.

4 A worthy wife is a crown for her husband,
  but a disgraceful woman is like cancer in
    his bones.

5 The plans of the godly are just;
  the advice of the wicked is treacherous.

6 The words of the wicked are like a
    murderous ambush,
  but the words of the godly save lives.

7 The wicked die and disappear,
  but the family of the godly stands firm.

8 A sensible person wins admiration,
  but a warped mind is despised.

9 Better to be an ordinary person with a
    servant
  than to be self-important but have
    no food.

10 The godly care for their animals,
   but the wicked are always cruel.

11 A hard worker has plenty of food,
   but a person who chases fantasies has
     no sense.

12 Thieves are jealous of each other's loot,
   but the godly are well rooted and bear
     their own fruit.

13 The wicked are trapped by their own words,
   but the godly escape such trouble.

14 Wise words bring many benefits,
   and hard work brings rewards.

15 Fools think their own way is right,
   but the wise listen to others.

16 A fool is quick-tempered,
   but a wise person stays calm when
     insulted.

17 An honest witness tells the truth;
   a false witness tells lies.

18 Some people make cutting remarks,
   but the words of the wise bring healing.

19 Truthful words stand the test of time,
   but lies are soon exposed.

20 Deceit fills hearts that are plotting evil;
   joy fills hearts that are planning peace!

21 No harm comes to the godly,
   but the wicked have their fill of trouble.

22 The LORD detests lying lips,
   but he delights in those who tell the truth.

23 The wise don't make a show of their
     knowledge,
   but fools broadcast their foolishness.

24 Work hard and become a leader;
   be lazy and become a slave.

25 Worry weighs a person down;
   an encouraging word cheers a person up.

26 The godly give good advice to their friends;*
   the wicked lead them astray.

27 Lazy people don't even cook the game they
     catch,
   but the diligent make use of everything
     they find.

28 The way of the godly leads to life;
   that path does not lead to death.

13 ¹A wise child accepts a parent's
         discipline;*
   a mocker refuses to listen to correction.

2 Wise words will win you a good meal,
  but treacherous people have an appetite
    for violence.

3 Those who control their tongue will have
    a long life;
  opening your mouth can ruin everything.

4 Lazy people want much but get little,
  but those who work hard will prosper.

5 The godly hate lies;
  the wicked cause shame and disgrace.

6 Godliness guards the path of the blameless,
  but the evil are misled by sin.

7 Some who are poor pretend to be rich;
  others who are rich pretend to be poor.

8 The rich can pay a ransom for their lives,
  but the poor won't even get threatened.

9 The life of the godly is full of light and joy,
  but the light of the wicked will be
    snuffed out.

10 Pride leads to conflict;
   those who take advice are wise.

. . . .

KEEP YOUR COOL
(12:16) When someone insults you, do you immediately
think of an insult in return? Many do—it's only natural.
But this solves nothing and only encourages trouble.
That's why the writer suggests that a better reaction is to
stay calm and answer slowly and quietly. Your positive
response can achieve positive results.

12:26 Or *The godly are cautious in friendship;* or *The godly are freed
from evil. The meaning of the Hebrew is uncertain.*   **13:1** Hebrew *A
wise son accepts his father's discipline.*

¹¹ Wealth from get-rich-quick schemes quickly disappears;
     wealth from hard work grows over time.

¹² Hope deferred makes the heart sick,
     but a dream fulfilled is a tree of life.

¹³ People who despise advice are asking for trouble;
     those who respect a command will succeed.

¹⁴ The instruction of the wise is like a life-giving fountain;
     those who accept it avoid the snares of death.

¹⁵ A person with good sense is respected;
     a treacherous person is headed for destruction.*

¹⁶ Wise people think before they act;
     fools don't—and even brag about their foolishness.

¹⁷ An unreliable messenger stumbles into trouble,
     but a reliable messenger brings healing.

¹⁸ If you ignore criticism, you will end in poverty and disgrace;
     if you accept correction, you will be honored.

¹⁹ It is pleasant to see dreams come true,
     but fools refuse to turn from evil to attain them.

²⁰ Walk with the wise and become wise;
     associate with fools and get in trouble.

²¹ Trouble chases sinners,
     while blessings reward the righteous.

²² Good people leave an inheritance to their grandchildren,
     but the sinner's wealth passes to the godly.

²³ A poor person's farm may produce much food,
     but injustice sweeps it all away.

²⁴ Those who spare the rod of discipline hate their children.
     Those who love their children care enough to discipline them.

²⁵ The godly eat to their hearts' content,
     but the belly of the wicked goes hungry.

13:15 As in Greek version; Hebrew reads *the way of the treacherous is lasting.*

14 ¹ A wise woman builds her home,
     but a foolish woman tears it down with her own hands.

² Those who follow the right path fear the LORD;
     those who take the wrong path despise him.

³ A fool's proud talk becomes a rod that beats him,
     but the words of the wise keep them safe.

⁴ Without oxen a stable stays clean,
     but you need a strong ox for a large harvest.

⁵ An honest witness does not lie;
     a false witness breathes lies.

⁶ A mocker seeks wisdom and never finds it,
     but knowledge comes easily to those with understanding.

⁷ Stay away from fools,
     for you won't find knowledge on their lips.

⁸ The prudent understand where they are going,
     but fools deceive themselves.

⁹ Fools make fun of guilt,
     but the godly acknowledge it and seek reconciliation.

¹⁰ Each heart knows its own bitterness,
     and no one else can fully share its joy.

¹¹ The house of the wicked will be destroyed,
     but the tent of the godly will flourish.

¹² There is a path before each person that seems right,
     but it ends in death.

¹³ Laughter can conceal a heavy heart,
     but when the laughter ends, the grief remains.

¹⁴ Backsliders get what they deserve;
     good people receive their reward.

¹⁵ Only simpletons believe everything they're told!
     The prudent carefully consider their steps.

MAKE THINGS RIGHT
(14:9) Siblings argue. Husbands and wives part ways. People continue to hold on to past bitterness. But God wants his people to forgive each other. When you know you have wronged someone, are you willing to own up to it or to ask yourself, "How can I make things right with this person?"

A GENTLE ANSWER DEFLECTS ANGER,

BUT HARSH WORDS MAKE TEMPERS FLARE.

¹⁶ The wise are cautious* and avoid danger;
fools plunge ahead with reckless confidence.

¹⁷ Short-tempered people do foolish things,
and schemers are hated.

¹⁸ Simpletons are clothed with foolishness,*
but the prudent are crowned with knowledge.

¹⁹ Evil people will bow before good people;
the wicked will bow at the gates of the godly.

²⁰ The poor are despised even by their neighbors,
while the rich have many "friends."

²¹ It is a sin to belittle one's neighbor;
blessed are those who help the poor.

²² If you plan to do evil, you will be lost;
if you plan to do good, you will receive unfailing love and faithfulness.

²³ Work brings profit,
but mere talk leads to poverty!

²⁴ Wealth is a crown for the wise;
the effort of fools yields only foolishness.

²⁵ A truthful witness saves lives,
but a false witness is a traitor.

²⁶ Those who fear the LORD are secure;
he will be a refuge for their children.

²⁷ Fear of the LORD is a life-giving fountain;
it offers escape from the snares of death.

²⁸ A growing population is a king's glory;
a prince without subjects has nothing.

²⁹ People with understanding control their anger;
a hot temper shows great foolishness.

³⁰ A peaceful heart leads to a healthy body;
jealousy is like cancer in the bones.

....

A QUIET RESPONSE
(15:1) Have you ever tried to argue in a whisper? It's difficult to argue with someone who insists on answering softly. On the other hand, a rising voice almost always triggers an angry response. Want to seek peace instead of arguing? A quiet response is your best choice.

³¹ Those who oppress the poor insult their Maker,
but helping the poor honors him.

³² The wicked are crushed by disaster,
but the godly have a refuge when they die.

³³ Wisdom is enshrined in an understanding heart;
wisdom is not* found among fools.

³⁴ Godliness makes a nation great,
but sin is a disgrace to any people.

³⁵ A king rejoices in wise servants
but is angry with those who disgrace him.

15 ¹ A gentle answer deflects anger,
but harsh words make tempers flare.

² The tongue of the wise makes knowledge appealing,
but the mouth of a fool belches out foolishness.

³ The LORD is watching everywhere,
keeping his eye on both the evil and the good.

⁴ Gentle words are a tree of life;
a deceitful tongue crushes the spirit.

⁵ Only a fool despises a parent's* discipline;
whoever learns from correction is wise.

⁶ There is treasure in the house of the godly,
but the earnings of the wicked bring trouble.

⁷ The lips of the wise give good advice;
the heart of a fool has none to give.

⁸ The LORD detests the sacrifice of the wicked,
but he delights in the prayers of the upright.

⁹ The LORD detests the way of the wicked,
but he loves those who pursue godliness.

¹⁰ Whoever abandons the right path will be severely disciplined;
whoever hates correction will die.

¹¹ Even Death and Destruction* hold no secrets from the LORD.
How much more does he know the human heart!

¹² Mockers hate to be corrected,
so they stay away from the wise.

14:16 Hebrew *The wise fear.*   **14:18** Or *inherit foolishness.*
14:33 As in Greek and Syriac versions; Hebrew lacks *not.*
15:5 Hebrew *father's.*   **15:11** Hebrew *Sheol and Abaddon.*

¹³ A glad heart makes a happy face;
a broken heart crushes the spirit.

¹⁴ A wise person is hungry for knowledge,
while the fool feeds on trash.

¹⁵ For the despondent, every day brings
trouble;
for the happy heart, life is a continual
feast.

¹⁶ Better to have little, with fear for the LORD,
than to have great treasure and inner
turmoil.

¹⁷ A bowl of vegetables with someone you love
is better than steak with someone you
hate.

¹⁸ A hot-tempered person starts fights;
a cool-tempered person stops them.

¹⁹ A lazy person's way is blocked with briers,
but the path of the upright is an open
highway.

²⁰ Sensible children bring joy to their father;
foolish children despise their mother.

²¹ Foolishness brings joy to those with no
sense;
a sensible person stays on the right path.

²² Plans go wrong for lack of advice;
many advisers bring success.

²³ Everyone enjoys a fitting reply;
it is wonderful to say the right thing at the
right time!

²⁴ The path of life leads upward for the wise;
they leave the grave* behind.

²⁵ The LORD tears down the house of the
proud,
but he protects the property of widows.

²⁶ The LORD detests evil plans,
but he delights in pure words.

²⁷ Greed brings grief to the whole family,
but those who hate bribes will live.

²⁸ The heart of the godly thinks carefully
before speaking;
the mouth of the wicked overflows with
evil words.

²⁹ The LORD is far from the wicked,
but he hears the prayers of the
righteous.

³⁰ A cheerful look brings joy to the heart;
good news makes for good health.

15:24 Hebrew *Sheol.*

³¹ If you listen to constructive criticism,
you will be at home among the wise.

³² If you reject discipline, you only harm
yourself;
but if you listen to correction, you grow
in understanding.

³³ Fear of the LORD teaches wisdom;
humility precedes honor.

16

¹ We can make our own plans,
but the LORD gives the right answer.

² People may be pure in their own eyes,
but the LORD examines their motives.

³ Commit your actions to the LORD,
and your plans will succeed.

⁴ The LORD has made everything for his own
purposes,
even the wicked for a day
of disaster.

⁵ The LORD detests the proud;
they will surely be punished.

⁶ Unfailing love and faithfulness make
atonement for sin.
By fearing the LORD, people
avoid evil.

⁷ When people's lives please the LORD,
even their enemies are at peace with
them.

⁸ Better to have little, with godliness,
than to be rich and dishonest.

⁹ We can make our plans,
but the LORD determines our steps.

¹⁰ The king speaks with divine wisdom;
he must never judge unfairly.

¹¹ The LORD demands accurate scales
and balances;
he sets the standards for
fairness.

¹² A king detests wrongdoing,
for his rule is built on justice.

NEW IDEAS
*(15:22) Those with tunnel vision, people who are locked
into one way of thinking, are likely to miss the right road
because they have closed their minds to any new options.
We need the help of those who can enlarge our vision and
broaden our perspective. Seek the advice of those who
know you and who have a wealth of experience. Build a
network of counselors. Then be willing to weigh their suggestions carefully. Your plans will be strengthened and
your chances for success increased.*

¹³ The king is pleased with words from
    righteous lips;
  he loves those who speak honestly.

¹⁴ The anger of the king is a deadly threat;
  the wise will try to appease it.

¹⁵ When the king smiles, there is life;
  his favor refreshes like a spring rain.

¹⁶ How much better to get wisdom than gold,
  and good judgment than silver!

¹⁷ The path of the virtuous leads away
    from evil;
  whoever follows that path is safe.

¹⁸ Pride goes before destruction,
  and haughtiness before a fall.

¹⁹ Better to live humbly with the poor
  than to share plunder with the proud.

²⁰ Those who listen to instruction will prosper;
  those who trust the LORD will be joyful.

²¹ The wise are known for their understanding,
  and pleasant words are persuasive.

²² Discretion is a life-giving fountain to those
    who possess it,
  but discipline is wasted on fools.

²³ From a wise mind comes wise speech;
  the words of the wise are persuasive.

²⁴ Kind words are like honey—
  sweet to the soul and healthy for the
    body.

²⁵ There is a path before each person that
    seems right,
  but it ends in death.

²⁶ It is good for workers to have an appetite;
  an empty stomach drives them on.

²⁷ Scoundrels create trouble;
  their words are a destructive blaze.

²⁸ A troublemaker plants seeds of strife;
  gossip separates the best of friends.

²⁹ Violent people mislead their companions,
  leading them down a harmful path.

³⁰ With narrowed eyes, people plot evil;
  with a smirk, they plan their
    mischief.

³¹ Gray hair is a crown of glory;
  it is gained by living a godly life.

³² Better to be patient than powerful;
  better to have self-control than to
    conquer a city.

³³ We may throw the dice,*
  but the LORD determines how they fall.

16:33 Hebrew *We may cast lots.*

I WONDER...

*I hear Christians talk a lot about God's will.
Has God planned out everything I'll ever do?*

Follow these instructions: Put your right hand straight up in the air. Next place your index finger in your left ear (come on, your left ear). Now clap your hands.

Who controlled your hands and fingers?

Tough question. Especially if you were silly enough to do what was asked. But we know from experience that when people give us instructions, *we* choose whether or not we obey.

The question, however, is who has ultimate control—you or God. This question has been debated for centuries, and the discussion can get quite complicated. For now, let's keep it as simple as possible.

We each have a will, a part within our brains that is the "chooser." Because we are human, the things we do sometimes don't match up with what God wants us to do. It isn't God's will for us to sin.

Of course, God is strong enough to force his will on us. But because he loves us, he allows us to have choices. What loving, earthly father would force his child to say, "I love you, Daddy"? He would find no satisfaction at all in a forced expression of love.

God does not force us to follow him. And it is obvious that many use their will to reject Christ. In essence, they choose to go to hell!

Putting all of these facts together points to the conclusion that God has allowed us to use our wills to sometimes go against his will. One of the highest acts of love you can give someone is the opportunity to reject you. This is exactly what God has done.

So what *is* God's will for us?

First, it is to know him.

Second, it is to help others. "For we are God's masterpiece. He has created us anew in Christ Jesus, so we can do the good things he planned for us long ago" (Eph 2:10).

Third, it is to be filled with the Holy Spirit. "So be careful how you live. Don't live like fools, but like those who are wise. Make the most of every opportunity in these evil days. Don't act thoughtlessly, but understand what the Lord wants you to do. Don't be drunk with wine, because that will ruin your life. Instead, be filled with the Holy Spirit" (Eph 5:15-18).

By allowing God to fill you, you are really saying, "God, take my will and help me do what you want." You are following the wisdom of Proverbs 16:9.

17

¹ Better a dry crust eaten in peace
than a house filled with feasting—
and conflict.

² A wise servant will rule over the master's
disgraceful son
and will share the inheritance of the
master's children.

³ Fire tests the purity of silver and gold,
but the LORD tests the heart.

⁴ Wrongdoers eagerly listen to gossip;
liars pay close attention to slander.

⁵ Those who mock the poor insult their
Maker;
those who rejoice at the misfortune
of others will be punished.

⁶ Grandchildren are the crowning glory
of the aged;
parents* are the pride of their children.

⁷ Eloquent words are not fitting for a fool;
even less are lies fitting for a ruler.

⁸ A bribe is like a lucky charm;
whoever gives one will prosper!

⁹ Love prospers when a fault is forgiven,
but dwelling on it separates close friends.

¹⁰ A single rebuke does more for a person
of understanding
than a hundred lashes on the back
of a fool.

¹¹ Evil people are eager for rebellion,
but they will be severely punished.

¹² It is safer to meet a bear robbed of her cubs
than to confront a fool caught in
foolishness.

¹³ If you repay good with evil,
evil will never leave your house.

¹⁴ Starting a quarrel is like opening a
floodgate,
so stop before a dispute breaks out.

¹⁵ Acquitting the guilty and condemning
the innocent—
both are detestable to the LORD.

¹⁶ It is senseless to pay tuition to educate
a fool,
since he has no heart for learning.

¹⁷ A friend is always loyal,
and a brother is born to help in time
of need.

17:6 Hebrew *fathers.*   **17:25** Hebrew *A foolish son.*

¹⁸ It's poor judgment to guarantee another
person's debt
or put up security for a friend.

¹⁹ Anyone who loves to quarrel loves sin;
anyone who trusts in high walls invites
disaster.

²⁰ The crooked heart will not prosper;
the lying tongue tumbles into trouble.

²¹ It is painful to be the parent of a fool;
there is no joy for the father
of a rebel.

²² A cheerful heart is good medicine,
but a broken spirit saps a person's
strength.

²³ The wicked take secret bribes
to pervert the course of justice.

²⁴ Sensible people keep their eyes glued
on wisdom,
but a fool's eyes wander to the ends
of the earth.

²⁵ Foolish children* bring grief to their father
and bitterness to the one who gave
them birth.

²⁶ It is wrong to punish the godly for being
good
or to flog leaders for being honest.

²⁷ A truly wise person uses few words;
a person with understanding is
even-tempered.

²⁸ Even fools are thought wise when they
keep silent;
with their mouths shut, they seem
intelligent.

18

¹ Unfriendly people care only about
themselves;
they lash out at common sense.

² Fools have no interest in understanding;
they only want to air their own opinions.

³ Doing wrong leads to disgrace,
and scandalous behavior brings
contempt.

A MAJOR INSULT
(17:5) *Few acts are as cruel as making fun of those who
are less fortunate, but many people do it because it
makes them feel good to be better off or more successful
than someone else. But God takes personally any insults
leveled at the poor, the weak, those who are different, or
anyone who is an easy target. Making fun of them is the
same as making fun of him.*

THERE ARE "FRIENDS" WHO DESTROY EACH OTHER, BUT A REAL FRIEND STICKS CLOSER THAN A BROTHER.

PROVERBS 18:24

4 Wise words are like deep waters;
 wisdom flows from the wise like
 a bubbling brook.

5 It is not right to acquit the guilty
 or deny justice to the innocent.

6 Fools' words get them into constant
 quarrels;
 they are asking for a beating.

7 The mouths of fools are their ruin;
 they trap themselves with their lips.

8 Rumors are dainty morsels
 that sink deep into one's heart.

9 A lazy person is as bad as
 someone who destroys things.

10 The name of the LORD is a strong fortress;
 the godly run to him and are safe.

11 The rich think of their wealth as a strong
 defense;
 they imagine it to be a high wall of safety.

12 Haughtiness goes before destruction;
 humility precedes honor.

13 Spouting off before listening to the facts
 is both shameful and foolish.

14 The human spirit can endure a sick body,
 but who can bear a crushed spirit?

15 Intelligent people are always ready to learn.
 Their ears are open for knowledge.

16 Giving a gift can open doors;
 it gives access to important people!

17 The first to speak in court sounds right—
 until the cross-examination begins.

18 Flipping a coin* can end arguments;
 it settles disputes between powerful
 opponents.

19 An offended friend is harder to win back
 than a fortified city.
 Arguments separate friends like a gate
 locked with bars.

20 Wise words satisfy like a good meal;
 the right words bring satisfaction.

21 The tongue can bring death or life;
 those who love to talk will reap the
 consequences.

22 The man who finds a wife finds a treasure,
 and he receives favor from the LORD.

23 The poor plead for mercy;
 the rich answer with insults.

24 There are "friends" who destroy each other,
 but a real friend sticks closer than a
 brother.

19

1 Better to be poor and honest
 than to be dishonest and a fool.

2 Enthusiasm without knowledge is no good;
 haste makes mistakes.

3 People ruin their lives by their own
 foolishness
 and then are angry at the LORD.

4 Wealth makes many "friends";
 poverty drives them all away.

5 A false witness will not go unpunished,
 nor will a liar escape.

6 Many seek favors from a ruler;
 everyone is the friend of a person who
 gives gifts!

7 The relatives of the poor despise them;
 how much more will their friends avoid
 them!
Though the poor plead with them,
 their friends are gone.

8 To acquire wisdom is to love oneself;
 people who cherish understanding will
 prosper.

9 A false witness will not go unpunished,
 and a liar will be destroyed.

TRUE FRIENDSHIP
*(18:24) Many people today feel isolated from others.
Ever feel that way? Being in a crowd might make you more
aware of your isolation. Lonely people don't need to hear
"Have a nice day." They need friends who will stick close,
listen, care, and offer help when it is needed—in good and
bad times. Having one such friend is better than having
dozens of superficial acquaintances. Instead of wishing
you could find a true friend, why not seek to become one
yourself. There are people who need your friendship. Ask
God to reveal them to you, and then take on the challenge
of being a true friend.*

18:18 Hebrew *Casting lots.*

¹⁰ It isn't right for a fool to live in luxury
or for a slave to rule over princes!

¹¹ Sensible people control their temper;
they earn respect by overlooking wrongs.

¹² The king's anger is like a lion's roar,
but his favor is like dew on the grass.

¹³ A foolish child* is a calamity to a father;
a quarrelsome wife is as annoying as
constant dripping.

¹⁴ Fathers can give their sons an inheritance
of houses and wealth,
but only the Lord can give an
understanding wife.

¹⁵ Lazy people sleep soundly,
but idleness leaves them hungry.

¹⁶ Keep the commandments and keep
your life;
despising them leads to death.

¹⁷ If you help the poor, you are lending to the
Lord—
and he will repay you!

¹⁸ Discipline your children while there is hope.
Otherwise you will ruin their lives.

¹⁹ Hot-tempered people must pay the penalty.
If you rescue them once, you will have to
do it again.

²⁰ Get all the advice and instruction you can,
so you will be wise the rest of your life.

²¹ You can make many plans,
but the Lord's purpose will prevail.

²² Loyalty makes a person attractive.
It is better to be poor than dishonest.

²³ Fear of the Lord leads to life,
bringing security and protection from
harm.

²⁴ Lazy people take food in their hand
but don't even lift it to their mouth.

²⁵ If you punish a mocker, the simpleminded
will learn a lesson;
if you correct the wise, they will be all the
wiser.

²⁶ Children who mistreat their father or chase
away their mother
are an embarrassment and a public
disgrace.

²⁷ If you stop listening to instruction, my child,
you will turn your back on knowledge.

19:13 Hebrew *son;* also in 19:27.   **20:10** Hebrew *A stone and
a stone, an ephah and an ephah.*

TO ACQUIRE WISDOM IS TO LOVE ONESELF; PEOPLE WHO CHERISH UNDERSTANDING WILL PROSPER. {PROVERBS 19:8}

²⁸ A corrupt witness makes a mockery of
justice;
the mouth of the wicked gulps down evil.

²⁹ Punishment is made for mockers,
and the backs of fools are made to be
beaten.

20 ¹Wine produces mockers; alcohol
leads to brawls.
Those led astray by drink cannot be wise.

² The king's fury is like a lion's roar;
to rouse his anger is to risk your life.

³ Avoiding a fight is a mark of honor;
only fools insist on quarreling.

⁴ Those too lazy to plow in the right season
will have no food at the harvest.

⁵ Though good advice lies deep within the
heart,
a person with understanding will draw
it out.

⁶ Many will say they are loyal friends,
but who can find one who is truly reliable?

⁷ The godly walk with integrity;
blessed are their children who follow
them.

⁸ When a king sits in judgment, he weighs all
the evidence,
distinguishing the bad from the good.

⁹ Who can say, "I have cleansed my heart;
I am pure and free from sin"?

¹⁰ False weights and unequal measures*—
the Lord detests double standards of
every kind.

¹¹ Even children are known by the way
they act,

....

INNER BEAUTY
(19:22) *Many people spend tons of money trying to
improve the way they look outside. Unfortunately, they
sometimes neglect their inner appearance. Inwardly, you
can be as attractive as you want to be. You can have kindness, for example, in any amount you choose. Or, as this
verse suggests, you can be loyal. You can control your
most important asset: the attractiveness of your character.*

STRATEGY FOR EFFECTIVE LIVING

BEGINS WITH GOD'S WISDOM	REQUIRES MORAL APPLICATION	REQUIRES PRACTICAL APPLICATION	RESULTS IN EFFECTIVE LIVING
Respecting and appreciating who God is. Reverence and awe in recognizing the almighty God.	Trusting in God and his Word. Allowing his Word to speak to us personally. Being willing to obey.	Acting on God's direction in daily devotions.	Experiencing what God does with our obedience.

whether their conduct is pure, and
   whether it is right.

¹² Ears to hear and eyes to see—
   both are gifts from the LORD.

¹³ If you love sleep, you will end in poverty.
   Keep your eyes open, and there will be
      plenty to eat!

¹⁴ The buyer haggles over the price, saying,
      "It's worthless,"
   then brags about getting a bargain!

¹⁵ Wise words are more valuable
   than much gold and many rubies.

¹⁶ Get security from someone who guarantees
      a stranger's debt.
   Get a deposit if he does it for foreigners.*

¹⁷ Stolen bread tastes sweet,
   but it turns to gravel in the mouth.

¹⁸ Plans succeed through good counsel;
   don't go to war without wise advice.

¹⁹ A gossip goes around telling secrets,
   so don't hang around with chatterers.

²⁰ If you insult your father or mother,
   your light will be snuffed out in total
      darkness.

²¹ An inheritance obtained too early in life
   is not a blessing in the end.

²² Don't say, "I will get even for this wrong."
   Wait for the LORD to handle the matter.

²³ The LORD detests double standards;
   he is not pleased by dishonest scales.

²⁴ The LORD directs our steps,
   so why try to understand everything along
      the way?

²⁵ Don't trap yourself by making a rash
      promise to God
   and only later counting the cost.

²⁶ A wise king scatters the wicked like wheat,
   then runs his threshing wheel over them.

²⁷ The LORD's light penetrates the human
      spirit,*
   exposing every hidden motive.

²⁸ Unfailing love and faithfulness protect the
      king;
   his throne is made secure through love.

²⁹ The glory of the young is their strength;
   the gray hair of experience is the splendor
      of the old.

³⁰ Physical punishment cleanses away evil;*
   such discipline purifies the heart.

21 ¹The king's heart is like a stream of
      water directed by the LORD;
   he guides it wherever he pleases.

² People may be right in their own eyes,
   but the LORD examines their heart.

³ The LORD is more pleased when we do what
      is right and just
   than when we offer him sacrifices.

⁴ Haughty eyes, a proud heart,
   and evil actions are all sin.

⁵ Good planning and hard work lead to
      prosperity,
   but hasty shortcuts lead to poverty.

⁶ Wealth created by a lying tongue
   is a vanishing mist and a deadly trap.*

⁷ The violence of the wicked sweeps them
      away,
   because they refuse to do what is just.

MOTIVES

(21:2) People can find an excuse for doing almost any-thing, but God looks behind the excuse to the motives, the real reasons for our actions. We often have to make difficult choices in areas of life where the right action is hard to discern. A good first step to making such a decision is to identify our motives. For example, are we serving others in order to gain attention? Identifying our motives can help us avoid phony actions.

20:16 An alternate reading in the Masoretic Text is *for a promiscuous woman.* **20:27** Or *The human spirit is the LORD's light.* **20:30** The meaning of the Hebrew is uncertain. **21:6** As in Greek version; Hebrew reads *mist for those who seek death.*

⁸ The guilty walk a crooked path;
  the innocent travel a straight road.

⁹ It's better to live alone in the corner
    of an attic
  than with a quarrelsome wife in a lovely
    home.

¹⁰ Evil people desire evil;
  their neighbors get no mercy from them.

¹¹ If you punish a mocker, the simpleminded
    become wise;
  if you instruct the wise, they will be all the
    wiser.

¹² The Righteous One* knows what is going
    on in the homes of the wicked;
  he will bring disaster on them.

¹³ Those who shut their ears to the cries
    of the poor
  will be ignored in their own time
    of need.

¹⁴ A secret gift calms anger;
  a bribe under the table pacifies fury.

¹⁵ Justice is a joy to the godly,
  but it terrifies evildoers.

¹⁶ The person who strays from common sense
  will end up in the company of the dead.

¹⁷ Those who love pleasure become poor;
  those who love wine and luxury will never
    be rich.

¹⁸ The wicked are punished in place of the
    godly,
  and traitors in place of the honest.

¹⁹ It's better to live alone in the desert
  than with a quarrelsome, complaining
    wife.

²⁰ The wise have wealth and luxury,
  but fools spend whatever they get.

²¹ Whoever pursues righteousness and
    unfailing love
  will find life, righteousness, and honor.

²² The wise conquer the city of the strong
  and level the fortress in which they trust.

²³ Watch your tongue and keep your mouth
    shut,
  and you will stay out of trouble.

²⁴ Mockers are proud and haughty;
  they act with boundless arrogance.

21:12 Or *The righteous man.*   **22:8** The Greek version includes an
additional proverb: *God blesses a man who gives cheerfully, / but
his worthless deeds will come to an end.* Compare 2 Cor 9:7.

²⁵ Despite their desires, the lazy will come
    to ruin,
  for their hands refuse to work.

²⁶ Some people are always greedy for more,
  but the godly love to give!

²⁷ The sacrifice of an evil person is detestable,
  especially when it is offered with wrong
    motives.

²⁸ A false witness will be cut off,
  but a credible witness will be allowed
    to speak.

²⁹ The wicked bluff their way through,
  but the virtuous think before they act.

³⁰ No human wisdom or understanding or plan
  can stand against the Lord.

³¹ The horse is prepared for the day of battle,
  but the victory belongs to the Lord.

22

¹ Choose a good reputation over great
    riches;
  being held in high esteem is better than
    silver or gold.

² The rich and poor have this in common:
  The Lord made them both.

³ A prudent person foresees danger and takes
    precautions.
  The simpleton goes blindly on and suffers
    the consequences.

⁴ True humility and fear of the Lord
  lead to riches, honor, and long life.

⁵ Corrupt people walk a thorny, treacherous
    road;
  whoever values life will avoid it.

⁶ Direct your children onto the right path,
  and when they are older, they will not
    leave it.

⁷ Just as the rich rule the poor,
  so the borrower is servant to the lender.

⁸ Those who plant injustice will harvest
    disaster,
  and their reign of terror will come to
    an end.*

⁹ Blessed are those who are generous,
  because they feed the poor.

¹⁰ Throw out the mocker, and fighting
    goes, too.
  Quarrels and insults will disappear.

¹¹ Whoever loves a pure heart and gracious
    speech
  will have the king as a friend.

¹² The LORD preserves those with knowledge,
　　but he ruins the plans of the treacherous.

¹³ The lazy person claims, "There's a lion out
　　there!
　If I go outside, I might be killed!"

¹⁴ The mouth of an immoral woman is a
　　dangerous trap;
　those who make the LORD angry will fall
　　into it.

¹⁵ A youngster's heart is filled with
　　foolishness,
　but physical discipline will drive it far
　　away.

¹⁶ A person who gets ahead by oppressing
　　the poor
　or by showering gifts on the rich will end
　　in poverty.

SAYINGS OF THE WISE

¹⁷ Listen to the words of the wise;
　　apply your heart to my instruction.
¹⁸ For it is good to keep these sayings in your
　　heart
　and always ready on your lips.
¹⁹ I am teaching you today—yes, you—
　　so you will trust in the LORD.
²⁰ I have written thirty sayings* for you,
　　filled with advice and knowledge.
²¹ In this way, you may know the truth
　　and take an accurate report to those who
　　sent you.

CHOOSING FRIENDS
(22:24-25) *People tend to become like those around them. Even the negative characteristics sometimes rub off. The Bible exhorts us to be cautious in our choice of companions. When it comes to your friends, how choosy are you?*

²² Don't rob the poor just because you can,
　　or exploit the needy in court.
²³ For the LORD is their defender.
　He will ruin anyone who ruins them.

²⁴ Don't befriend angry people
　　or associate with hot-tempered
　　people,
²⁵ or you will learn to be like them
　　and endanger your soul.

²⁶ Don't agree to guarantee another person's
　　debt
　or put up security for someone else.
²⁷ If you can't pay it,
　　even your bed will be snatched from
　　under you.

²⁸ Don't cheat your neighbor by moving the
　　ancient boundary markers
　set up by previous generations.

²⁹ Do you see any truly competent workers?
　They will serve kings
　rather than working for ordinary people.

23

¹ While dining with a ruler,
　　pay attention to what is put before
　　you.
² If you are a big eater,
　　put a knife to your throat;
³ don't desire all the delicacies,
　　for he might be trying to trick you.

⁴ Don't wear yourself out trying to get rich.
　Be wise enough to know when to quit.
⁵ In the blink of an eye wealth disappears,
　　for it will sprout wings
　　and fly away like an eagle.

⁶ Don't eat with people who are stingy;
　　don't desire their delicacies.

22:20 Or *excellent sayings;* the meaning of the Hebrew is uncertain.

CHOICES
drinking

The first time 13-year-old Paul drank with his friends, Mario and Antoine, it was kind of exciting. With the help of a college student, the three guys managed to get a six-pack—two beers each. It wasn't enough to get smashed, but it was enough to get a slight buzz. Sipping slowly as they sat around a campfire, the boys laughed for several hours. The next day Mario suggested, "We should do that more often!"

So each weekend they played the game, always coming up with a new scheme to acquire alcohol. Once they stumbled upon a block party where there were three "unguarded" kegs just sitting there.

Another time they swiped a bottle of vodka from a neighbor's liquor cabinet. Another time a high school senior bought them some tequila and showed them how to shoot it.

Every now and then one of the guys would overdo it and end up with a mean hangover. But they never got caught. It didn't affect their grades at school since they only did it on weekends. Yeah, they thought everything was cool . . . until Paul went on a church retreat one weekend.

Now Paul won't go with Mario and Antoine anymore. He thinks they're headed for trouble. And they think he's turned into a religious fanatic.

See one of the passages that changed Paul's mind about drinking. Read Proverbs 23:29-35.

7 They are always thinking about how much
it costs.*
"Eat and drink," they say, but they don't
mean it.
8 You will throw up what little you've eaten,
and your compliments will be wasted.

9 Don't waste your breath on fools,
for they will despise the wisest advice.

10 Don't cheat your neighbor by moving the
ancient boundary markers;
don't take the land of defenseless
orphans.
11 For their Redeemer* is strong;
he himself will bring their charges
against you.

12 Commit yourself to instruction;
listen carefully to words of knowledge.

13 Don't fail to discipline your children.
They won't die if you spank them.
14 Physical discipline
may well save them from death.*

15 My child,* if your heart is wise,
my own heart will rejoice!
16 Everything in me will celebrate
when you speak what is right.

17 Don't envy sinners,
but always continue to fear the LORD.
18 You will be rewarded for this;
your hope will not be disappointed.

19 My child, listen and be wise:
Keep your heart on the right course.
20 Do not carouse with drunkards
or feast with gluttons,
21 for they are on their way to poverty,
and too much sleep clothes them in rags.

22 Listen to your father, who gave you life,
and don't despise your mother when she
is old.
23 Get the truth and never sell it;
also get wisdom, discipline, and good
judgment.
24 The father of godly children has cause
for joy.
What a pleasure to have children who
are wise.*
25 So give your father and mother joy!
May she who gave you birth be happy.

26 O my son, give me your heart.
May your eyes take delight in following
my ways.

23:7 The meaning of the Hebrew is uncertain.   23:11 Or redeemer.
23:14 Hebrew from Sheol.   23:15 Hebrew My son; also in 23:19.
23:24 Hebrew to have a wise son.   24:5 As in Greek version;
Hebrew reads A wise man is strength.

27 A prostitute is a dangerous trap;
a promiscuous woman is as dangerous as
falling into a narrow well.
28 She hides and waits like a robber,
eager to make more men unfaithful.

29 Who has anguish? Who has sorrow?
Who is always fighting? Who is always
complaining?
Who has unnecessary bruises? Who has
bloodshot eyes?
30 It is the one who spends long hours in the
taverns,
trying out new drinks.
31 Don't gaze at the wine, seeing how red it is,
how it sparkles in the cup, how smoothly
it goes down.
32 For in the end it bites like a poisonous
snake;
it stings like a viper.
33 You will see hallucinations,
and you will say crazy things.
34 You will stagger like a sailor tossed at sea,
clinging to a swaying mast.
35 And you will say, "They hit me, but I didn't
feel it.
I didn't even know it when they beat
me up.
When will I wake up
so I can look for another drink?"

24

1 Don't envy evil people
or desire their company.
2 For their hearts plot violence,
and their words always stir up trouble.

3 A house is built by wisdom
and becomes strong through good sense.
4 Through knowledge its rooms are filled
with all sorts of precious riches and
valuables.

5 The wise are mightier than the strong,*
and those with knowledge grow stronger
and stronger.
6 So don't go to war without wise guidance;
victory depends on having many advisers.

7 Wisdom is too lofty for fools.
Among leaders at the city gate, they have
nothing to say.

....

THE STING OF DRINKING
*(23:29-35) Some people drink in order to seem cool.
Others imbibe to find relief from their problems. But the
"comfort" of alcohol is only temporary. Real relief comes
from dealing with the cause of anguish and sorrow, and
turning to God for peace. Getting drunk leads to more
problems. As this passage states, "in the end it bites like
a poisonous snake; it stings like a viper" (23:32).*

8 A person who plans evil
    will get a reputation as a troublemaker.
9 The schemes of a fool are sinful;
    everyone detests a mocker.

10 If you fail under pressure,
    your strength is too small.

11 Rescue those who are unjustly sentenced
    to die;
    save them as they stagger to their death.
12 Don't excuse yourself by saying, "Look, we
    didn't know."
    For God understands all hearts, and he
    sees you.
    He who guards your soul knows you knew.
    He will repay all people as their actions
    deserve.

13 My child,* eat honey, for it is good,
    and the honeycomb is sweet to the taste.
14 In the same way, wisdom is sweet to your
    soul.
    If you find it, you will have a bright future,
    and your hopes will not be cut short.

15 Don't wait in ambush at the home of
    the godly,
    and don't raid the house where the
    godly live.
16 The godly may trip seven times, but they will
    get up again.
    But one disaster is enough to overthrow
    the wicked.

17 Don't rejoice when your enemies fall;
    don't be happy when they stumble.
18 For the LORD will be displeased with you
    and will turn his anger away from them.

19 Don't fret because of evildoers;
    don't envy the wicked.
20 For evil people have no future;
    the light of the wicked will be snuffed out.

21 My child, fear the LORD and the king.
    Don't associate with rebels,
22   for disaster will hit them suddenly.
    Who knows what punishment will come
    from the LORD and the king?

MORE SAYINGS OF THE WISE 23Here are some
further sayings of the wise:

It is wrong to show favoritism when passing
    judgment.
24 A judge who says to the wicked, "You are
    innocent,"
    will be cursed by many people and
    denounced by the nations.

25 But it will go well for those who convict the
    guilty;
    rich blessings will be showered on them.

26 An honest answer
    is like a kiss of friendship.

27 Do your planning and prepare your fields
    before building your house.

28 Don't testify against your neighbors without
    cause;
    don't lie about them.
29 And don't say, "Now I can pay them back for
    what they've done to me!
    I'll get even with them!"

30 I walked by the field of a lazy person,
    the vineyard of one with no common
    sense.
31 I saw that it was overgrown with nettles.
    It was covered with weeds,
    and its walls were broken down.
32 Then, as I looked and thought about it,
    I learned this lesson:
33 A little extra sleep, a little more slumber,
    a little folding of the hands to rest—
34 then poverty will pounce on you like a
    bandit;
    scarcity will attack you like an armed
    robber.

25 **MORE PROVERBS OF SOLOMON**
These are more proverbs of Solomon,
collected by the advisers of King Hezekiah
of Judah.

2 It is God's privilege to conceal things
    and the king's privilege to discover them.

3 No one can comprehend the height of
    heaven, the depth of the earth,
    or all that goes on in the king's mind!

4 Remove the impurities from silver,
    and the sterling will be ready for the
    silversmith.
5 Remove the wicked from the king's court,
    and his reign will be made secure by
    justice.

6 Don't demand an audience with the king
    or push for a place among the great.
7 It's better to wait for an invitation to the
    head table
    than to be sent away in public disgrace.

Just because you've seen something,
8   don't be in a hurry to go to court.
    For what will you do in the end

24:13 Hebrew *My son;* also in 24:21.

if your neighbor deals you a shameful
defeat?

9 When arguing with your neighbor,
don't betray another person's secret.

10 Others may accuse you of gossip,
and you will never regain your good
reputation.

11 Timely advice is lovely,
like golden apples in a silver basket.

12 To one who listens, valid criticism
is like a gold earring or other gold jewelry.

13 Trustworthy messengers refresh like snow in
summer.
They revive the spirit of their employer.

14 A person who promises a gift but doesn't
give it
is like clouds and wind that bring no rain.

15 Patience can persuade a prince,
and soft speech can break bones.

16 Do you like honey?
Don't eat too much, or it will make
you sick!

17 Don't visit your neighbors too often,
or you will wear out your welcome.

18 Telling lies about others
is as harmful as hitting them with an ax,
wounding them with a sword,
or shooting them with a sharp arrow.

19 Putting confidence in an unreliable person
in times of trouble
is like chewing with a broken tooth or
walking on a lame foot.

20 Singing cheerful songs to a person with
a heavy heart
is like taking someone's coat in cold
weather
or pouring vinegar in a wound.*

21 If your enemies are hungry, give them food
to eat.
If they are thirsty, give them water to
drink.

22 You will heap burning coals of shame on
their heads,
and the Lord will reward you.

23 As surely as a north wind brings rain,
so a gossiping tongue causes anger!

24 It's better to live alone in the corner
of an attic

25:20 As in Greek version; Hebrew reads *pouring vinegar on soda.*

than with a quarrelsome wife in a lovely
home.

25 Good news from far away
is like cold water to the thirsty.

26 If the godly give in to the wicked,
it's like polluting a fountain or muddying
a spring.

27 It's not good to eat too much honey,
and it's not good to seek honors for
yourself.

28 A person without self-control
is like a city with broken-down walls.

26 ¹ Honor is no more associated
with fools
than snow with summer or rain with
harvest.

² Like a fluttering sparrow or a darting
swallow,
an undeserved curse will not land on its
intended victim.

³ Guide a horse with a whip, a donkey with
a bridle,
and a fool with a rod to his back!

⁴ Don't answer the foolish arguments of fools,
or you will become as foolish as
they are.

⁵ Be sure to answer the foolish arguments
of fools,
or they will become wise in their own
estimation.

⁶ Trusting a fool to convey a message
is like cutting off one's feet or drinking
poison!

⁷ A proverb in the mouth of a fool
is as useless as a paralyzed leg.

⁸ Honoring a fool
is as foolish as tying a stone to a
slingshot.

⁹ A proverb in the mouth of a fool
is like a thorny branch brandished by
a drunk.

....

LYING
(25:18) The effects of lying can be as permanent as those
of a stab wound. Yet sometimes, we don't call our actions
lies. Instead, we might pass on information or "stretch the
truth" a little. A lie by any other name is still a lie. The next
time you are tempted to share a bit of gossip, imagine
yourself striking the victim of your remarks with a sword.
This image may shock you into silence.

¹⁰ An employer who hires a fool or a bystander
is like an archer who shoots at random.

¹¹ As a dog returns to its vomit,
so a fool repeats his foolishness.

¹² There is more hope for fools
than for people who think they are wise.

¹³ The lazy person claims, "There's a lion on
the road!
Yes, I'm sure there's a lion out there!"

¹⁴ As a door swings back and forth on its
hinges,
so the lazy person turns over in bed.

¹⁵ Lazy people take food in their hand
but don't even lift it to their mouth.

¹⁶ Lazy people consider themselves smarter
than seven wise counselors.

¹⁷ Interfering in someone else's argument
is as foolish as yanking a dog's ears.

¹⁸ Just as damaging
as a madman shooting a deadly weapon
¹⁹ is someone who lies to a friend
and then says, "I was only joking."

²⁰ Fire goes out without wood,
and quarrels disappear when gossip
stops.

²¹ A quarrelsome person starts fights
as easily as hot embers light charcoal or
fire lights wood.

²² Rumors are dainty morsels
that sink deep into one's heart.

²³ Smooth* words may hide a wicked heart,
just as a pretty glaze covers a clay pot.

²⁴ People may cover their hatred with pleasant
words,
but they're deceiving you.
²⁵ They pretend to be kind, but don't believe
them.
Their hearts are full of many evils.*
²⁶ While their hatred may be concealed by
trickery,

•••

LAZINESS

*(26:13-16) If a person is not willing to work, he or she
can find endless excuses to avoid it. But laziness is more
dangerous than a fierce lion. The less you do, the less
you want to do, and the more useless you become. You
can overcome laziness or procrastination by taking these
small steps toward change: (1) Set a concrete, realistic
goal; (2) figure out the steps needed to reach it; and
(3) pray for strength and persistence.*

their wrongdoing will be exposed in
public.

²⁷ If you set a trap for others,
you will get caught in it yourself.
If you roll a boulder down on others,
it will crush you instead.

²⁸ A lying tongue hates its victims,
and flattering words cause ruin.

27 ¹Don't brag about tomorrow,
since you don't know what the day
will bring.

² Let someone else praise you, not your own
mouth—
a stranger, not your own lips.

³ A stone is heavy and sand is weighty,
but the resentment caused by a fool is
even heavier.

⁴ Anger is cruel, and wrath is like a flood,
but jealousy is even more dangerous.

⁵ An open rebuke
is better than hidden love!

⁶ Wounds from a sincere friend
are better than many kisses from an
enemy.

⁷ A person who is full refuses honey,
but even bitter food tastes sweet to the
hungry.

⁸ A person who strays from home
is like a bird that strays from its nest.

⁹ The heartfelt counsel of a friend
is as sweet as perfume and incense.

¹⁰ Never abandon a friend—
either yours or your father's.
When disaster strikes, you won't have to ask
your brother for assistance.
It's better to go to a neighbor than to a
brother who lives far away.

¹¹ Be wise, my child,* and make my heart glad.
Then I will be able to answer my critics.

¹² A prudent person foresees danger and takes
precautions.
The simpleton goes blindly on and suffers
the consequences.

¹³ Get security from someone who guarantees
a stranger's debt.
Get a deposit if he does it for foreigners.*

26:23 As in Greek version; Hebrew reads *Burning.*   **26:25** Hebrew
seven evils.   **27:11** Hebrew *my son.*   **27:13** As in Greek and Latin
versions (see also 20:16); Hebrew reads *for a promiscuous woman.*

¹⁴ A loud and cheerful greeting early in the
   morning
     will be taken as a curse!

¹⁵ A quarrelsome wife is as annoying
     as constant dripping on a rainy day.
¹⁶ Stopping her complaints is like trying to
   stop the wind
     or trying to hold something with greased
     hands.

¹⁷ As iron sharpens iron,
     so a friend sharpens a friend.

¹⁸ As workers who tend a fig tree are allowed
   to eat the fruit,
     so workers who protect their employer's
     interests will be rewarded.

¹⁹ As a face is reflected in water,
     so the heart reflects the real person.

²⁰ Just as Death and Destruction* are never
   satisfied,
     so human desire is never satisfied.

²¹ Fire tests the purity of silver and gold,
     but a person is tested by being praised.*

²² You cannot separate fools from their
   foolishness,
     even though you grind them like grain
     with mortar and pestle.

²³ Know the state of your flocks,
     and put your heart into caring for your
     herds,
²⁴ for riches don't last forever,
     and the crown might not be passed to the
     next generation.
²⁵ After the hay is harvested and the new crop
   appears
     and the mountain grasses are
     gathered in,
²⁶ your sheep will provide wool for clothing,
     and your goats will provide the price of
     a field.
²⁷ And you will have enough goats' milk for
   yourself,
     your family, and your servant girls.

28

¹ The wicked run away when no one is
     chasing them,
     but the godly are as bold as lions.

² When there is moral rot within a nation, its
   government topples easily.
     But wise and knowledgeable leaders
     bring stability.

27:20 Hebrew *Sheol and Abaddon.*   27:21 Or *by flattery.*
28:7 Hebrew *their father.*   28:14 Or *those who fear the LORD;*
Hebrew reads *those who fear.*

³ A poor person who oppresses the poor
     is like a pounding rain that destroys
     the crops.

⁴ To reject the law is to praise the wicked;
     to obey the law is to fight them.

⁵ Evil people don't understand justice,
     but those who follow the LORD
     understand completely.

⁶ Better to be poor and honest
     than to be dishonest and rich.

⁷ Young people who obey the law are wise;
     those with wild friends bring shame to
     their parents.*

⁸ Income from charging high interest rates
     will end up in the pocket of someone who
     is kind to the poor.

⁹ God detests the prayers
     of a person who ignores the law.

¹⁰ Those who lead good people along an
   evil path
     will fall into their own trap,
     but the honest will inherit good things.

¹¹ Rich people may think they are wise,
     but a poor person with discernment can
     see right through them.

¹² When the godly succeed, everyone is glad.
     When the wicked take charge, people go
     into hiding.

¹³ People who conceal their sins will not
   prosper,
     but if they confess and turn from them,
     they will receive mercy.

¹⁴ Blessed are those who fear to do wrong,*
     but the stubborn are headed for serious
     trouble.

....

NAGGING
*(27:15-16) People nag because they think they're not
getting through to the person to whom they're talking. Yet
nagging sometimes hinders communication more than it
helps. When tempted to engage in this destructive habit,
stop and examine your motives. Are you more concerned
about yourself—about getting your way or being right—
than about the person you are "helping"? If you truly are
concerned about other people, here is a more effective
way to get through to them: surprise them with words
of love and with patience and see what happens.*

INTENTIONS
*(28:9) God does not listen to our prayers if we intend
to go back to what we did wrong as soon as we get off
our knees. If we want to forsake our sin and follow him,
however, he willingly listens—no matter how bad our
wrongdoing has been. What closes his ears is not the
depth of our sin but the shallowness of our "repentance."*

MY STORY: Kristen

I went to England with a missions group to do street evangelism right after I graduated from high school. Once I got out on the street, supposedly ready to talk to someone, I froze. I was struck with fear and couldn't say a word.

It really bothered me. That evening I looked up fear in a Bible concordance, and read through several Scriptures. The verse that helped me most was Proverbs 29:25: "Fearing people is a dangerous trap, but trusting the LORD means safety." I realized that I had fallen into Satan's trap because I was afraid of people—what they would think of me, even what they might do to me, if I tried to share the gospel. I vowed that I would trust God.

The next day I was still nervous. So, I asked God to keep me from falling into the trap of fear and to help me know what to say. Things went much better. As I trusted God to help and protect me during that mission trip, I grew more and more bold in sharing my faith. I actually came to enjoy it! But I might have stayed stuck in fear if I hadn't found that verse and really applied it to my situation.

¹⁵ A wicked ruler is as dangerous to the poor as a roaring lion or an attacking bear.

¹⁶ A ruler with no understanding will oppress his people,
but one who hates corruption will have a long life.

¹⁷ A murderer's tormented conscience will drive him into the grave.
Don't protect him!

¹⁸ The blameless will be rescued from harm,
but the crooked will be suddenly destroyed.

¹⁹ A hard worker has plenty of food,
but a person who chases fantasies ends up in poverty.

²⁰ The trustworthy person will get a rich reward,
but a person who wants quick riches will get into trouble.

²¹ Showing partiality is never good,
yet some will do wrong for a mere piece of bread.

²² Greedy people try to get rich quick
but don't realize they're headed for poverty.

²³ In the end, people appreciate honest criticism
far more than flattery.

²⁴ Anyone who steals from his father and mother
and says, "What's wrong with that?"
is no better than a murderer.

²⁵ Greed causes fighting;
trusting the LORD leads to prosperity.

²⁶ Those who trust their own insight are foolish,
but anyone who walks in wisdom is safe.

²⁷ Whoever gives to the poor will lack nothing,
but those who close their eyes to poverty will be cursed.

²⁸ When the wicked take charge, people go into hiding.
When the wicked meet disaster, the godly flourish.

29

¹ Whoever stubbornly refuses to accept criticism
will suddenly be destroyed beyond recovery.

² When the godly are in authority, the people rejoice.
But when the wicked are in power, they groan.

³ The man who loves wisdom brings joy to his father,
but if he hangs around with prostitutes, his wealth is wasted.

⁴ A just king gives stability to his nation,
but one who demands bribes destroys it.

⁵ To flatter friends
is to lay a trap for their feet.

⁶ Evil people are trapped by sin,
but the righteous escape, shouting for joy.

⁷ The godly care about the rights of the poor;
the wicked don't care at all.

⁸ Mockers can get a whole town agitated,
but the wise will calm anger.

⁹ If a wise person takes a fool to court,
  there will be ranting and ridicule but no
  satisfaction.

¹⁰ The bloodthirsty hate blameless people,
  but the upright seek to help them.*

¹¹ Fools vent their anger,
  but the wise quietly hold it back.

¹² If a ruler pays attention to liars,
  all his advisers will be wicked.

¹³ The poor and the oppressor have this in
  common—
  the LORD gives sight to the eyes of both.

¹⁴ If a king judges the poor fairly,
  his throne will last forever.

¹⁵ To discipline a child produces wisdom,
  but a mother is disgraced by an
  undisciplined child.

¹⁶ When the wicked are in authority, sin
  flourishes,
  but the godly will live to see their
  downfall.

¹⁷ Discipline your children, and they will give
  you peace of mind
  and will make your heart glad.

¹⁸ When people do not accept divine
  guidance, they run wild.
  But whoever obeys the law is joyful.

¹⁹ Words alone will not discipline a servant;
  the words may be understood, but they
  are not heeded.

²⁰ There is more hope for a fool
  than for someone who speaks without
  thinking.

²¹ A servant pampered from childhood
  will become a rebel.

²² An angry person starts fights;
  a hot-tempered person commits all kinds
  of sin.

²³ Pride ends in humiliation,
  while humility brings honor.

²⁴ If you assist a thief, you only hurt yourself.
  You are sworn to tell the truth, but you
  dare not testify.

²⁵ Fearing people is a dangerous trap,
  but trusting the LORD means safety.

²⁶ Many seek the ruler's favor,
  but justice comes from the LORD.

²⁷ The righteous despise the unjust;
  the wicked despise the godly.

30 THE SAYINGS OF AGUR The sayings of Agur son of Jakeh contain this message.*

I am weary, O God;
  I am weary and worn out, O God.*
² I am too stupid to be human,
  and I lack common sense.
³ I have not mastered human wisdom,
  nor do I know the Holy One.

⁴ Who but God goes up to heaven and comes
  back down?
  Who holds the wind in his fists?
Who wraps up the oceans in his cloak?
  Who has created the whole wide world?
What is his name—and his son's name?
  Tell me if you know!

⁵ Every word of God proves true.
  He is a shield to all who come to him for
  protection.
⁶ Do not add to his words,
  or he may rebuke you and expose you
  as a liar.

⁷ O God, I beg two favors from you;
  let me have them before I die.
⁸ First, help me never to tell a lie.
  Second, give me neither poverty nor
  riches!
  Give me just enough to satisfy my needs.
⁹ For if I grow rich, I may deny you and say,
  "Who is the LORD?"
  And if I am too poor, I may steal and thus
  insult God's holy name.

¹⁰ Never slander a worker to the employer,
  or the person will curse you, and you will
  pay for it.

¹¹ Some people curse their father
  and do not thank their mother.
¹² They are pure in their own eyes,
  but they are filthy and unwashed.
¹³ They look proudly around,
  casting disdainful glances.
¹⁴ They have teeth like swords
  and fangs like knives.
  They devour the poor from the earth
  and the needy from among humanity.

¹⁵ The leech has two suckers
  that cry out, "More, more!"*

29:10 Or *The bloodthirsty hate blameless people, / and they seek to kill the upright;* Hebrew reads *The bloodthirsty hate blameless people; / as for the upright, they seek their life.* **30:1a** Or *son of Jakeh from Massa;* or *son of Jakeh, an oracle.* **30:1b** The Hebrew can also be translated *The man declares this to Ithiel, / to Ithiel and to Ucal.* **30:15** Hebrew *two daughters who cry out, "Give, give!"*

HOW GOD IS DESCRIBED IN PROVERBS

Proverbs is a book about wise living. It often focuses on a person's response and attitude toward God, who is the source of wisdom. A number of proverbs point out aspects of God's character. Knowing God helps us on the way to wisdom.

GOD . . .

Is aware of all that happens—15:3
Knows all people—15:11; 16:2; 21:2
Is the maker of all things—16:4
Controls all things—16:33; 21:30
Is a strong fortress—18:10
Rescues good people from danger—11:8, 21
Rewards the godly—11:31
Blesses good people, condemns the wicked—12:2
Delights in our prayers—15:8, 29
Loves those who obey him—11:27; 15:9-10; 16:20; 22:12
Cares for the poor, sick, and widows—15:25; 22:22-23
Purifies hearts—17:3
Hates evil—17:5; 21:27; 28:9

OUR RESPONSE SHOULD BE . . .

To reverence God—10:27; 14:26-27; 15:16; 16:6; 19:23; 28:14
To obey God's Word—13:13; 19:16
To please God—16:7; 21:3
To trust God—22:17-19; 29:25

There are three things that are never satisfied—
   no, four that never say, "Enough!":
16 the grave,*
   the barren womb,
   the thirsty desert,
   the blazing fire.

17 The eye that mocks a father
   and despises a mother's instructions
will be plucked out by ravens of the valley
   and eaten by vultures.

18 There are three things that amaze me—
   no, four things that I don't understand:
19 how an eagle glides through the sky,
   how a snake slithers on a rock,
   how a ship navigates the ocean,
   how a man loves a woman.

20 An adulterous woman consumes a man,
   then wipes her mouth and says, "What's wrong with that?"

21 There are three things that make the earth tremble—

no, four it cannot endure:
22 a slave who becomes a king,
   an overbearing fool who prospers,
23 a bitter woman who finally gets a husband,
   a servant girl who supplants her mistress.

24 There are four things on earth that are small but unusually wise:
25 Ants—they aren't strong,
   but they store up food all summer.
26 Hyraxes*—they aren't powerful,
   but they make their homes among the rocks.
27 Locusts—they have no king,
   but they march in formation.
28 Lizards—they are easy to catch,
   but they are found even in kings' palaces.

29 There are three things that walk with stately stride—
   no, four that strut about:
30 the lion, king of animals, who won't turn aside for anything,
31 the strutting rooster,
   the male goat,
   a king as he leads his army.

32 If you have been a fool by being proud
   or plotting evil,
   cover your mouth in shame.

33 As the beating of cream yields butter
   and striking the nose causes bleeding,
   so stirring up anger causes quarrels.

31 THE SAYINGS OF KING LEMUEL The sayings of King Lemuel contain this message,* which his mother taught him.

2 O my son, O son of my womb,
   O son of my vows,
3 do not waste your strength on women,
   on those who ruin kings.

4 It is not for kings, O Lemuel, to guzzle wine.
   Rulers should not crave alcohol.
5 For if they drink, they may forget the law
   and not give justice to the oppressed.
6 Alcohol is for the dying,
   and wine for those in bitter distress.
7 Let them drink to forget their poverty
   and remember their troubles no more.

8 Speak up for those who cannot speak for themselves;

30:16 Hebrew *Sheol.*   **30:26** Or *Coneys,* or *Rock badgers.*   **31:1** Or *of Lemuel, king of Massa;* or *of King Lemuel, an oracle.*

ensure justice for those being crushed.
⁹ Yes, speak up for the poor and helpless,
　　and see that they get justice.

A WIFE OF NOBLE CHARACTER

¹⁰*Who can find a virtuous and capable wife?
　　She is more precious than rubies.
¹¹ Her husband can trust her,
　　and she will greatly enrich his life.

31:10 Verses 10-31 comprise a Hebrew acrostic poem; each verse begins with a successive letter of the Hebrew alphabet.

¹² She brings him good, not harm,
　　all the days of her life.

¹³ She finds wool and flax
　　and busily spins it.
¹⁴ She is like a merchant's ship,
　　bringing her food from afar.
¹⁵ She gets up before dawn to prepare
　　breakfast for her household
　　and plan the day's work for her
　　servant girls.

ULTIMATE ISSUES *LOOKING FOR A PERFECT 10*

WANTED: LIFE PARTNER. Must have a body that can stop traffic, money to last two lifetimes (mine and yours), hair that looks like it belongs in a shampoo commercial, great sense of humor, high IQ (just below mine), well-paying job, your own car. Must love my kind of music (loud), sports, and everything about me. Send resume and photo to: Is That Too Much to Ask? Inc., P.O. Box 101010, FantasyLand, U.S.A. 12345.

Sound familiar? Everybody seems to have an image of the perfect guy or girl. Perfect looks, perfect personality, perfect relationship. . . . But think about it. What *really* makes someone a perfect 10? Looks? Most of our views come from being bombarded daily by images of actors and supermodels who have made the "hot" list. The message is as subtle as a sledge-hammer: Use our product and you will not only look as good as our models do, but you will find yourself surrounded by other beautiful people. You will be happy, popular, and adored.

Nothing is wrong with wanting to look your best, or with being attracted to good-looking people. But when looking good becomes an obsession—when you have to wear certain clothes, spend hours getting ready for school or a date, throw down a small fortune on cosmetics, colognes, hair products, etc.—you've bought into the Madison Avenue lie. You are more than your looks. You're *beautiful,* not because of your physical appearance, but because you were made in the image of God!

Next to looks, we might think that having a great personality is another key contributor to the hottie sweepstakes. Can't be Miss America? Maybe you can settle for Miss Congeniality. Everybody knows the joke. You've been set up for a blind date, you ask what he (or she) looks like and they say, "He (or she) has a *great* personality." Which tells you one thing: you're going to the movies with either Godzilla or Frankenstein's Bride.

But there's another side: an attractive guy or girl who has the personality of a dead squid. If you've encountered this, you know personality *is* important. You can only spend so much time looking at each

other. Looks may draw attention, but personality keeps it. Or kills it.

Spirituality: *Hmmm,* you may be thinking. *Looks and personality, OK. But what is "spirituality"?* Everyone has a spiritual nature. That's what makes you more than a mass of oxygen-absorbing molecules, glands, and hormones. If you belong to Christ, you are spiritually alive. If not, you're spiritually dead. (For more on this, see Rom 3; Gal 5:16-26; Eph 2:1-10.) When you're thinking about spending the rest of your life with someone, you need to look for more than looks and personality. You need to be spiritually compatible, too.

Proverbs 31:10-31 gives a vivid, lively picture of what a truly spiritual woman is like. And she's no plastic saint, sitting home reading the Bible until her husband shows up. She's strong, intelligent, industrious, compassionate, wise: "She is clothed with strength and dignity" (31:25). (When you get right down to it, that's a good description of a godly man, too.)

Sure, good looks are great. But *everyone* grows old, gets wrinkles, and adds a few pounds. A relationship based on looks or personality is doomed to failure. Don't believe it? Try to find a successful, faithful marriage in Hollywood, *Body Beautiful capital of the world.*

The only cement that can bond two people together for life is mutual commitment to God and to each other. So, instead of wondering whether you're hot or not, consider whether you're hot—on fire for God—or not. That's one question he'd rather have you answer.

And when you're ready to find a partner for life, make the spiritual dimension your primary requirement. Nothing's wrong with looking for a perfect 10. Just remember, it takes more than beauty or a pleasant temperament to add up to someone whose love will last. So take a look at Proverbs 31, a great snapshot image of a person who has that something more. (For more on the subject of marriage itself, see the Ultimate Issue on marriage in 1 Corinthians.) ■

¹⁶ She goes to inspect a field and buys it;
   with her earnings she plants a vineyard.
¹⁷ She is energetic and strong,
   a hard worker.
¹⁸ She makes sure her dealings are profitable;
   her lamp burns late into the night.
¹⁹ Her hands are busy spinning thread,
   her fingers twisting fiber.
²⁰ She extends a helping hand to the poor
   and opens her arms to the needy.
²¹ She has no fear of winter for her household,
   for everyone has warm* clothes.

···

AN IDEAL WOMAN

(31:10-31) Proverbs has a lot to say about women. How fitting that the book ends with a picture of a woman of strong character, great wisdom, many skills, and great compassion.

Some people have the mistaken idea that the ideal woman in the Bible is shy and totally domestic. Not so! This woman is an excellent wife and mother. She also is a manufacturer, importer, manager, realtor, farmer, seamstress, upholsterer, and merchant. Her strength and dignity do not come from her amazing achievements, however. They are a result of her reverence for God. In our society where physical appearance counts for so much, it may surprise us to realize that her appearance is never mentioned. Her attractiveness comes entirely from her character. How does this description of her character inspire you?

²² She makes her own bedspreads.
   She dresses in fine linen and purple
   gowns.
²³ Her husband is well known at the city gates,
   where he sits with the other civic leaders.
²⁴ She makes belted linen garments
   and sashes to sell to the merchants.
²⁵ She is clothed with strength and dignity,
   and she laughs without fear of the future.
²⁶ When she speaks, her words are wise,
   and she gives instructions with kindness.
²⁷ She carefully watches everything in her
   household
   and suffers nothing from laziness.

²⁸ Her children stand and bless her.
   Her husband praises her:
²⁹ "There are many virtuous and capable
   women in the world,
   but you surpass them all!"

³⁰ Charm is deceptive, and beauty does
   not last;
   but a woman who fears the LORD will be
   greatly praised.
³¹ Reward her for all she has done.
   Let her deeds publicly declare
   her praise.

31:21 As in Greek and Latin versions; Hebrew reads *scarlet*.

ECCLESIASTES

"Be true to yourself." "All I wanna do is have some fun." "What's right for me is right for me." You've probably heard expressions like these, or know people who live life this way. This philosophy isn't new. In fact, essentially the same message appears in the Bible.

Centuries ago, King Solomon wrote, *"People should eat and drink and enjoy the fruits of their labor, for these are gifts from God"* (Eccl 3:13). Solomon knew what he was talking about. As a very wise and wealthy king, he had spent a lifetime experiencing and analyzing everything the world had to offer. Building homes, being served, partying, spending money, playing music, having sex . . . Solomon had done it all. His conclusion? Life is brief, boring, and empty, so enjoy pleasure while you can!

Yes, the Bible says that life is meaningless, so we should just party and do what we want.

But there's a catch. Solomon's last word is that we need to keep God at the center of our lives to enjoy life as God meant for us to live (see Eccl 12:1-7). Without God, people merely exist, moving quickly from the excitement of youth to the bitterness of old age. But with God, we can enjoy each moment, relationship, and experience along the way.

Read Ecclesiastes, Solomon's analysis of life, and then have a real party!

STATS

PURPOSE
To spare future generations the bitterness of learning through their own experiences that life is meaningless apart from God

AUTHOR
Solomon, although he is not mentioned by name in the text

ORIGINAL AUDIENCE
Solomon's subjects in particular and all people in general

DATE WRITTEN
Probably around 935 B.C., late in Solomon's life

SETTING
Solomon looks back on his life, much of which was lived apart from God.

KEY POINTS

SEARCHING Solomon searched for satisfaction almost as though he conducted a scientific experiment. As he gained pleasure, wealth, and success, he discovered that life without God was meaningless. Like Solomon, our search for meaning ultimately will end with the same conclusion.

WORK Solomon tried to shake people's confidence in their own efforts, abilities, and wisdom. He did this to direct them to faith in God as the only sound basis for living. Without God, there is no lasting reward or benefit in hard work.

LIFE AND DEATH The reality of aging and dying reminds us of the end to come, when God will judge each person's life. Because life is so short, we need wisdom greater than this world can offer. We need the wisdom of God. If we listen to him, we will be spared from the bitterness of a meaningless life.

WISDOM Human wisdom doesn't provide all the answers. To understand life, we need the wisdom that can be found only in God's Word to us—the Bible. When we realize that God will evaluate all we do, we should learn to live wisely, remembering that God is with us at each moment. We can have God's wisdom only when we obey him.

1

These are the words of the Teacher,* King David's son, who ruled in Jerusalem.

EVERYING IS MEANINGLESS [2]"Everything is meaningless," says the Teacher, "completely meaningless!"

[3]What do people get for all their hard work under the sun? [4]Generations come and generations go, but the earth never changes. [5]The sun rises and the sun sets, then hurries around to rise again. [6]The wind blows south, and then turns north. Around and around it goes, blowing in circles. [7]Rivers run into the sea, but the sea is never full. Then the water returns again to the rivers and flows out again to the sea. [8]Everything is wearisome beyond description. No matter how much we see, we are never satisfied. No matter how much we hear, we are not content.

[9]History merely repeats itself. It has all been done before. Nothing under the sun is truly new. [10]Sometimes people say, "Here is something new!" But actually it is old; nothing is ever truly new. [11]We don't remember what happened in the past, and in future generations, no one will remember what we are doing now.

THE TEACHER SPEAKS: THE FUTILITY OF WISDOM [12]I, the Teacher, was king of Israel, and I lived in Jerusalem. [13]I devoted myself to search for understanding and to explore by wisdom everything being done under heaven. I soon discovered that God has dealt a tragic existence to the human race. [14]I observed everything going on under the sun, and really, it is all meaningless—like chasing the wind.

[15] What is wrong cannot be made right.
    What is missing cannot be recovered.

[16]I said to myself, "Look, I am wiser than any of the kings who ruled in Jerusalem before me. I have greater wisdom and knowledge than any of them." [17]So I set out to learn everything from wisdom to madness and folly. But I learned firsthand that pursuing all this is like chasing the wind.

[18] The greater my wisdom, the greater my grief.
    To increase knowledge only increases sorrow.

2

THE FUTILITY OF PLEASURE I said to myself, "Come on, let's try pleasure. Let's look for the 'good things' in life." But I found that this, too, was meaningless. [2]So I said, "Laughter is silly. What good does it do to seek pleasure?" [3]After much thought, I decided to cheer myself with wine. And while still seeking wisdom, I clutched at foolishness. In this way, I tried to experience the only happiness most people find during their brief life in this world.

[4]I also tried to find meaning by building huge homes for myself and by planting beautiful vineyards. [5]I made gardens and parks, filling them with all kinds of fruit trees. [6]I built reservoirs to collect the water to irrigate my many flourishing groves. [7]I bought slaves, both men and women, and others were born into my household. I also owned large herds and flocks, more than any of the kings who had lived in Jerusalem before me. [8]I collected great sums of silver and gold, the treasure of many kings and provinces. I hired wonderful singers, both men and women, and had many beautiful concubines. I had everything a man could desire!

[9]So I became greater than all who had lived in Jerusalem before me, and my wisdom never failed me. [10]Anything I wanted, I would take. I denied myself no pleasure. I even found great pleasure in hard work, a reward for all my labors. [11]But as I looked at everything I had worked so hard to accomplish, it was all so meaningless—like chasing the wind. There was nothing really worthwhile anywhere.

THE WISE AND THE FOOLISH [12]So I decided to compare wisdom with foolishness and madness (for who can do this better than I, the king?*). [13]I thought, "Wisdom is better than foolishness, just as light is better than darkness. [14]For the wise can see where they are going, but fools walk in the dark." Yet I saw that the wise and the foolish share the same fate. [15]Both will die. So I said to myself, "Since I will end up the same as the fool, what's the value of all my wisdom? This is all so meaningless!" [16]For the wise and the foolish both die. The wise will not be remembered any longer than the fool. In the days to come, both will be forgotten.

THE MEANING OF LIFE
(1:8-11) Solomon expressed his weariness and discontentment with life. Many people feel restless and dissatisfied. They wonder if their lives have a purpose. In this book, Solomon tests our faith, challenging us to find true and lasting meaning in God alone. Have you taken a hard look at your life lately? Does it seem filled with purpose or is it daily drudgery? If it is the latter, perhaps God is challenging you to rethink your direction in life.

1:1 Hebrew *Qoheleth;* this term is rendered "the Teacher" throughout this book.   **2:12** The meaning of the Hebrew is uncertain.

¹⁷So I came to hate life because everything done here under the sun is so troubling. Everything is meaningless—like chasing the wind.

THE FUTILITY OF WORK ¹⁸I came to hate all my hard work here on earth, for I must leave to others everything I have earned. ¹⁹And who can tell whether my successors will be wise or foolish? Yet they will control everything I have gained by my skill and hard work under the sun. How meaningless! ²⁰So I gave up in despair, questioning the value of all my hard work in this world.

²¹Some people work wisely with knowledge and skill, then must leave the fruit of their efforts to someone who hasn't worked for it. This, too, is meaningless, a great tragedy. ²²So what do people get in this life for all their hard work and anxiety? ²³Their days of labor are filled with pain and grief; even at night their minds cannot rest. It is all meaningless.

²⁴So I decided there is nothing better than to enjoy food and drink and to find satisfaction in work. Then I realized that these pleasures are from the hand of God. ²⁵For who can eat or enjoy anything apart from him?* ²⁶God gives wisdom, knowledge, and joy to those who please him. But if a sinner becomes wealthy, God takes the wealth away and gives it to those who please him. This, too, is meaningless—like chasing the wind.

3 A TIME FOR EVERYTHING

¹ For everything there is a season,
   a time for every activity under heaven.
² A time to be born and a time to die.
   A time to plant and a time to harvest.
³ A time to kill and a time to heal.
   A time to tear down and a time to
      build up.
⁴ A time to cry and a time to laugh.
   A time to grieve and a time to dance.
⁵ A time to scatter stones and a time to
      gather stones.
   A time to embrace and a time to turn
      away.
⁶ A time to search and a time to quit
      searching.
   A time to keep and a time to throw away.
⁷ A time to tear and a time to mend.
   A time to be quiet and a time to speak.
⁸ A time to love and a time to hate.
   A time for war and a time for peace.

2:25 As in Greek and Syriac versions; Hebrew reads *apart from me?*

MY STORY: Rick

When I graduated from junior high school, I was popular and had good grades and stuff. I had everything going for me. During the summer before senior high school, though, I realized things would be different. Most of my friends wouldn't be going to the same high school with me. I'd have to start over.

I decided to live it up that summer. I partied with my friends and had a blast. But in between these times I felt depressed. I was living for the moment. Somehow that felt lonely.

One day I was flipping through the Bible, ya know, just messing around, and decided to read the book of Ecclesiastes. The whole book really spoke to me. Here was a dude I could identify with. He too seemed to be living for the moment, and found it just as empty as I did! One verse especially expressed my feelings: "But as I looked at everything I had worked so hard to accomplish, it was all so meaningless—like chasing the wind. There was nothing really worthwhile anywhere" (2:11). My whole summer to that point had been consumed with pleasure—chasing the wind.

Although that verse may sound depressing, it actually made me feel better. Here was someone who knew how I was feeling, and expressed it perfectly.

After reading Ecclesiastes, I realized how futile it is to strive after material possessions, money, fame, and even popularity. They are all temporary. But what God gives us (love, joy, and other stuff) is more permanent.

AN ENDLESS PARTY?
(2:24-26) Is Solomon recommending that we party until we drop? No, he is encouraging us to take pleasure in what we're doing now and to enjoy life because it comes from God's hand. True enjoyment in life comes only as we follow God's guidelines for living. Those who really know how to enjoy life are the ones who consider each day to be a gift from God, thanking him for it and serving him in it. That's what you do, right?

⁹What do people really get for all their hard work? ¹⁰I have seen the burden God has placed on us all. ¹¹Yet God has made everything beautiful for its own time. He has planted eternity in the human heart, but even so, people cannot see the whole scope of God's work from beginning to end. ¹²So I concluded there is nothing better than to be happy and enjoy ourselves as long as we can. ¹³And people should eat and drink and enjoy the fruits of their labor, for these are gifts from God.

¹⁴And I know that whatever God does is final. Nothing can be added to it or taken from it. God's purpose is that people should fear him. ¹⁵What is happening now has happened before, and what will happen in the future has happened before, because God makes the same things happen over and over again.

THE INJUSTICES OF LIFE ¹⁶I also noticed that under the sun there is evil in the courtroom. Yes, even the courts of law are corrupt! ¹⁷I said to myself, "In due season God will judge everyone, both good and bad, for all their deeds."

¹⁸I also thought about the human condition—how God proves to people that they are like animals. ¹⁹For people and animals share the same fate—both breathe* and both must die. So people have no real advantage over the animals. How meaningless! ²⁰Both go to the same place—they came from dust and they return to dust. ²¹For who can prove that the human spirit goes up and the spirit of animals goes down into the earth? ²²So I saw that there is nothing better for people than to be happy in their work. That is why we are here! No one will bring us back from death to enjoy life after we die.

4 Again, I observed all the oppression that takes place under the sun. I saw the tears of the oppressed, with no one to comfort them. The oppressors have great power, and their victims are helpless. ²So I concluded that the dead are better off than the living. ³But most fortunate of all are those who are not yet born. For they have not seen all the evil that is done under the sun.

⁴Then I observed that most people are motivated to success because they envy their neighbors. But this, too, is meaningless—like chasing the wind.

5 "Fools fold their idle hands,
　　leading them to ruin."

⁶And yet,

"Better to have one handful with quietness
　　than two handfuls with hard work
　　and chasing the wind."

THE ADVANTAGES OF COMPANIONSHIP ⁷I observed yet another example of something meaningless under the sun. ⁸This is the case of a man who is all alone, without a child or a brother, yet who works hard to gain as much wealth as he can. But then he asks himself, "Who am I working for? Why am I giving up so much pleasure now?" It is all so meaningless and depressing.

⁹Two people are better off than one, for they can help each other succeed. ¹⁰If one person falls, the other can reach out and help. But someone who falls alone is in real trouble. ¹¹Likewise, two people lying close together can keep each other warm. But how can one be warm alone? ¹²A person standing alone can be attacked and defeated, but two can stand

3:19 Or *both have the same spirit.*

CHOICES
pleasure

At a youth rally, the speaker is pleading with the students—begging them not to make the mistakes he made.

"Please hear what I'm saying. When I was your age, I was empty inside. I came from a broken home. I hated myself and everybody else. I tried everything to fill the hole inside: drugs, alcohol, sleeping around, partying.

"I tried to convince myself I was having a good time. And those things did feel good . . . for a while. But the feeling was only temporary. No matter what I did, I couldn't shake that inner loneliness and hurt.

"Everything I did to try to ease my pain only made my hurt increase. Listen to me: You will never find what you're really looking for until you accept the love of Jesus Christ. Coming to know him—the Lord of life—will bring you the peace you so desperately need. There is life nowhere else."

As the speaker concludes, Carin thinks, "Yeah, he says all this after he's had all his fun. Maybe I'll just have a good time now . . . and get serious about God later."

The book of Ecclesiastes describes King Solomon's frantic search for satisfaction. Chapters 1 and 2 relate all the different ways he tried to find fulfillment apart from God. His conclusion is in 12:13-14.

Will you listen to the voices of experience and save yourself a lot of heartache? Or will you be stubborn and learn the hard way?

back-to-back and conquer. Three are even better, for a triple-braided cord is not easily broken.

THE FUTILITY OF POLITICAL POWER ¹³It is better to be a poor but wise youth than an old and foolish king who refuses all advice. ¹⁴Such a youth could rise from poverty and succeed. He might even become king, though he has been in prison. ¹⁵But then everyone rushes to the side of yet another youth* who replaces him. ¹⁶Endless crowds stand around him,* but then another generation grows up and rejects him, too. So it is all meaningless—like chasing the wind.

5 **APPROACHING GOD WITH CARE** ¹*As you enter the house of God, keep your ears open and your mouth shut. It is evil to make mindless offerings to God. ²*Don't make rash promises, and don't be hasty in bringing matters before God. After all, God is in heaven, and you are here on earth. So let your words be few.

³Too much activity gives you restless dreams; too many words make you a fool.

⁴When you make a promise to God, don't delay in following through, for God takes no pleasure in fools. Keep all the promises you make to him. ⁵It is better to say nothing than to make a promise and not keep it. ⁶Don't let your mouth make you sin. And don't defend yourself by telling the Temple messenger that the promise you made was a mistake. That would make God angry, and he might wipe out everything you have achieved.

⁷Talk is cheap, like daydreams and other useless activities. Fear God instead.

THE FUTILITY OF WEALTH ⁸Don't be surprised if you see a poor person being oppressed by the powerful and if justice is being miscarried throughout the land. For every official is under orders from higher up, and matters of justice get lost in red tape and bureaucracy. ⁹Even the king milks the land for his own profit!*

¹⁰Those who love money will never have enough. How meaningless to think that wealth brings true happiness! ¹¹The more you have, the more people come to help you spend it. So what good is wealth—except perhaps to watch it slip through your fingers!

4:15 Hebrew *the second youth.* 4:16 Hebrew *There is no end to all the people, to all those who are before them.* 5:1 Verse 5:1 is numbered 4:17 in Hebrew text. 5:2 Verses 5:2-20 are numbered 5:1-19 in Hebrew text. 5:9 The meaning of the Hebrew in verses 8 and 9 is uncertain.

MY STORY: Kelsey

I really wanted to grow in my walk with God, so I vowed that I would have a quiet time every night. For a while everything went very well. I felt I understood what I read, and as I tried to apply the Bible to my daily life, I began to see changes in myself. That excited me.

But then I went through a period of time when I didn't seem to be getting anything out of the Bible. For some reason, one night I started reading Ecclesiastes. I felt stressed—in a rush to get to my homework so I could get to bed at a decent hour. When I came across chapter 5, verses 1-7, I suddenly woke up! I remembered that I had vowed to spend time with God every day and that it was God I was treating so rudely by rushing through my time with him. My attitude was all wrong. Having a quiet time wasn't like some chore I had to do; it was a privilege to meet with the awesome God of the universe! I asked God to forgive me for my attitude and thanked him for speaking to me through his Word.

¹²People who work hard sleep well, whether they eat little or much. But the rich seldom get a good night's sleep.

¹³There is another serious problem I have seen under the sun. Hoarding riches harms the saver. ¹⁴Money is put into risky investments that turn sour, and everything is lost. In the end, there is nothing left to pass on to one's children. ¹⁵We all come to the end of our lives as naked and empty-handed as on the day we were born. We can't take our riches with us.

¹⁶And this, too, is a very serious problem. People leave this world no better off than when they came. All their hard work is for nothing—like working for the wind. ¹⁷Throughout their lives, they live under a cloud—frustrated, discouraged, and angry.

¹⁸Even so, I have noticed one thing, at least, that is good. It is good for people to eat, drink, and enjoy their work under the sun during the short life God has given them, and to accept their lot in life. ¹⁹And it is a good thing to receive wealth from God and the good health to

enjoy it. To enjoy your work and accept your lot in life—this is indeed a gift from God. [20]God keeps such people so busy enjoying life that they take no time to brood over the past.

6 There is another serious tragedy I have seen under the sun, and it weighs heavily on humanity. [2]God gives some people great wealth and honor and everything they could ever want, but then he doesn't give them the chance to enjoy these things. They die, and someone else, even a stranger, ends up enjoying their wealth! This is meaningless—a sickening tragedy.

[3]A man might have a hundred children and live to be very old. But if he finds no satisfaction in life and doesn't even get a decent burial, it would have been better for him to be born dead. [4]His birth would have been meaningless, and he would have ended in darkness. He wouldn't even have had a name, [5]and he would never have seen the sun or known of its existence. Yet he would have had more peace than in growing up to be an unhappy man. [6]He might live a thousand years twice over but still not find contentment. And since he must die like everyone else—well, what's the use?

[7]All people spend their lives scratching for food, but they never seem to have enough. [8]So are wise people really better off than fools? Do poor people gain anything by being wise and knowing how to act in front of others?

[9]Enjoy what you have rather than desiring what you don't have. Just dreaming about nice things is meaningless—like chasing the wind.

THE FUTURE—DETERMINED AND UNKNOWN
[10]Everything has already been decided. It was known long ago what each person would be. So there's no use arguing with God about your destiny.

[11]The more words you speak, the less they mean. So what good are they?

[12]In the few days of our meaningless lives, who knows how our days can best be spent? Our lives are like a shadow. Who can tell what will happen on this earth after we are gone?

··

FLATTERY
(7:5-6) Have you ever been paid a compliment when you knew it was inappropriate or merely an attempt to flatter you? Some people would rather feel good than know the truth. Too often, pleasant compliments are valued above helpful information (Prov 27:6). Solomon reminds us that facing honest criticism is far better than wallowing in the compliments of fools.

7 WISDOM FOR LIFE
[1] A good reputation is more valuable than
    costly perfume.
    And the day you die is better than the day
        you are born.
[2] Better to spend your time at funerals than
        at parties.
    After all, everyone dies—
        so the living should take this to heart.
[3] Sorrow is better than laughter,
        for sadness has a refining influence
            on us.
[4] A wise person thinks a lot about death,
        while a fool thinks only about having
            a good time.

[5] Better to be criticized by a wise person
        than to be praised by a fool.
[6] A fool's laughter is quickly gone,
        like thorns crackling in a fire.
    This also is meaningless.

[7] Extortion turns wise people into fools,
        and bribes corrupt the heart.

[8] Finishing is better than starting.
    Patience is better than pride.

[9] Control your temper,
        for anger labels you a fool.

[10] Don't long for "the good old days."
    This is not wise.

[11] Wisdom is even better when you have
        money.
    Both are a benefit as you go through life.
[12] Wisdom and money can get you almost
        anything,
    but only wisdom can save your life.

[13] Accept the way God does things,
        for who can straighten what he has made
            crooked?
[14] Enjoy prosperity while you can,
        but when hard times strike, realize that
            both come from God.
    Remember that nothing is certain in this
        life.

THE LIMITS OF HUMAN WISDOM
[15]I have seen everything in this meaningless life, including the death of good young people and the long life of wicked people. [16]So don't be too good or too wise! Why destroy yourself? [17]On the other hand, don't be too wicked either. Don't be a fool! Why die before your time? [18]Pay attention to these instructions, for anyone who fears God will avoid both extremes.*

7:18 Or *will follow them both.*

¹⁹One wise person is stronger than ten leading citizens of a town!

²⁰Not a single person on earth is always good and never sins.

²¹Don't eavesdrop on others—you may hear your servant curse you. ²²For you know how often you yourself have cursed others.

²³I have always tried my best to let wisdom guide my thoughts and actions. I said to myself, "I am determined to be wise." But it didn't work. ²⁴Wisdom is always distant and difficult to find. ²⁵I searched everywhere, determined to find wisdom and to understand the reason for things. I was determined to prove to myself that wickedness is stupid and that foolishness is madness.

²⁶I discovered that a seductive woman* is a trap more bitter than death. Her passion is a snare, and her soft hands are chains. Those who are pleasing to God will escape her, but sinners will be caught in her snare.

²⁷"This is my conclusion," says the Teacher. "I discovered this after looking at the matter from every possible angle. ²⁸Though I have searched repeatedly, I have not found what I was looking for. Only one out of a thousand men is virtuous, but not one woman! ²⁹But I did find this: God created people to be virtuous, but they have each turned to follow their own downward path."

8 ¹How wonderful to be wise,
      to analyze and interpret things.
Wisdom lights up a person's face,
      softening its harshness.

OBEDIENCE TO THE KING

²Obey the king since you vowed to God that you would. ³Don't try to avoid doing your duty, and don't stand with those who plot evil, for the king can do whatever he wants. ⁴His command is backed by great power. No one can resist or question it. ⁵Those who obey him will not be punished. Those who are wise will find a time and a way to do what is right, ⁶for there is a time and a way for everything, even when a person is in trouble.

⁷Indeed, how can people avoid what they don't know is going to happen? ⁸None of us can hold back our spirit from departing. None of us has the power to prevent the day of our death. There is no escaping that obligation, that dark battle. And in the face of death, wickedness will certainly not rescue the wicked.

7:26 Hebrew *a woman.*   8:10 As in some Hebrew manuscripts and Greek version; many Hebrew manuscripts read *and are forgotten.*
9:2 As in Greek and Syriac versions and Latin Vulgate; Hebrew lacks *or bad.*

THE WICKED AND THE RIGHTEOUS

⁹I have thought deeply about all that goes on here under the sun, where people have the power to hurt each other. ¹⁰I have seen wicked people buried with honor. Yet they were the very ones who frequented the Temple and are now praised* in the same city where they committed their crimes! This, too, is meaningless. ¹¹When a crime is not punished quickly, people feel it is safe to do wrong. ¹²But even though a person sins a hundred times and still lives a long time, I know that those who fear God will be better off. ¹³The wicked will not prosper, for they do not fear God. Their days will never grow long like the evening shadows.

¹⁴And this is not all that is meaningless in our world. In this life, good people are often treated as though they were wicked, and wicked people are often treated as though they were good. This is so meaningless!

¹⁵So I recommend having fun, because there is nothing better for people in this world than to eat, drink, and enjoy life. That way they will experience some happiness along with all the hard work God gives them under the sun.

¹⁶In my search for wisdom and in my observation of people's burdens here on earth, I discovered that there is ceaseless activity, day and night. ¹⁷I realized that no one can discover everything God is doing under the sun. Not even the wisest people discover everything, no matter what they claim.

9 DEATH COMES TO ALL This, too, I carefully explored: Even though the actions of godly and wise people are in God's hands, no one knows whether God will show them favor. ²The same destiny ultimately awaits everyone, whether righteous or wicked, good or bad,* ceremonially clean or unclean, religious or irreligious. Good people receive the same treatment as sinners, and people who make promises to God are treated like people who don't.

³It seems so tragic that everyone under the sun suffers the same fate. That is why people

· ·

CONSEQUENCES
(8:11) Like Solomon, have you ever noticed others doing the same wrong thing that they saw someone else get away with? We should never assume that God doesn't care if we have sinned, or that sin has no consequences, simply because he hasn't punished us immediately. Unfortunately, doing what someone else did wrong is easier when we don't see that person suffer consequences immediately. But God knows every wrong we commit. One day we will have to answer for everything we have done *(12:14).*

MY STORY: Amanda

One time, my best friend and I had an argument and stopped speaking to each other. I was bummed for a while over some of the things she had said to me. I wasn't going to let her get away with treating me like she had!

Then I came across two verses: Ecclesiastes 10:12, "Wise words bring approval, but fools are destroyed by their own words" and 1 Peter 4:8, "Most important of all, continue to show deep love for each other, for love covers a multitude of sins." As I read these verses over and over, whatever we had argued about became less and less important. Maintaining a friendship with someone who also knew God's love became very important. I also realized that there were some faults in me that needed her forgiveness.

I didn't waste any time. I called my friend on the phone, read her the passages, and told her I was sorry for letting something petty come between us. She cried a little and said that she was so glad I had called, and that she didn't feel right either about us fighting.

These verses clearly showed me how precious Christian friendship is; it's something to be guarded and treasured. I'm really thankful that God helped me to work things out with my friend.

are not more careful to be good. Instead, they choose their own mad course, for they have no hope. There is nothing ahead but death anyway. 4There is hope only for the living. As they say, "It's better to be a live dog than a dead lion!"

5The living at least know they will die, but the dead know nothing. They have no further reward, nor are they remembered. 6Whatever they did in their lifetime—loving, hating, envying—is all long gone. They no longer play a part in anything here on earth. 7So go ahead. Eat your food with joy, and drink your wine with a happy heart, for God approves of this! 8Wear fine clothes, with a splash of cologne!

9Live happily with the woman you love through all the meaningless days of life that God has given you under the sun. The wife God gives you is your reward for all your earthly toil. 10Whatever you do, do well. For when you go to the grave,* there will be no work or planning or knowledge or wisdom.

11I have observed something else under the sun. The fastest runner doesn't always win the race, and the strongest warrior doesn't always win the battle. The wise sometimes go hungry, and the skillful are not necessarily wealthy. And those who are educated don't always lead successful lives. It is all decided by chance, by being in the right place at the right time.

12People can never predict when hard times might come. Like fish in a net or birds in a trap, people are caught by sudden tragedy.

THOUGHTS ON WISDOM AND FOLLY 13Here is another bit of wisdom that has impressed me as I have watched the way our world works. 14There was a small town with only a few people, and a great king came with his army and besieged it. 15A poor, wise man knew how to save the town, and so it was rescued. But afterward no one thought to thank him. 16So even though wisdom is better than strength, those who are wise will be despised if they are poor. What they say will not be appreciated for long.

17 Better to hear the quiet words of a wise person
    than the shouts of a foolish king.
18 Better to have wisdom than weapons of war,
    but one sinner can destroy much that is good.

10

1As dead flies cause even a bottle of perfume to stink,
    so a little foolishness spoils great wisdom and honor.

2 A wise person chooses the right road;
    a fool takes the wrong one.

3 You can identify fools
    just by the way they walk down the street!

4 If your boss is angry at you, don't quit!
    A quiet spirit can overcome even great mistakes.

THE IRONIES OF LIFE 5There is another evil I have seen under the sun. Kings and rulers make a grave mistake 6when they give great authority to foolish people and low positions to people of proven worth. 7I have even seen

9:10 Hebrew *to Sheol.*

servants riding horseback like princes—and princes walking like servants!

⁸ When you dig a well,
  you might fall in.
  When you demolish an old wall,
  you could be bitten by a snake.

⁹ When you work in a quarry,
  stones might fall and crush you.
  When you chop wood,
  there is danger with each stroke of
  your ax.

¹⁰ Using a dull ax requires great strength,
  so sharpen the blade.
  That's the value of wisdom;
  it helps you succeed.

¹¹ If a snake bites before you charm it,
  what's the use of being a snake charmer?

¹² Wise words bring approval,
  but fools are destroyed by their own
  words.

¹³ Fools base their thoughts on foolish
  assumptions,
  so their conclusions will be wicked
  madness;
¹⁴ they chatter on and on.

  No one really knows what is going to
  happen;
  no one can predict the future.

10:16 Or *a child.*

¹⁵ Fools are so exhausted by a little work
  that they can't even find their way home.

¹⁶ What sorrow for the land ruled by a
  servant,*
  the land whose leaders feast in the
  morning.

¹⁷ Happy is the land whose king is a noble
  leader
  and whose leaders feast at the proper
  time
  to gain strength for their work, not to get
  drunk.

¹⁸ Laziness leads to a sagging roof;
  idleness leads to a leaky house.

¹⁹ A party gives laughter,
  wine gives happiness,
  and money gives everything!

²⁰ Never make light of the king, even in your
  thoughts.

···

MONEY MATTERS

(10:19) *Many people believe that money is the answer to every problem. But just as the effects of alcohol are only temporary, the soothing effect of the last purchase soon wears off. Although some verses in the Bible mention the necessity of money for survival, others warn against the love of money (see Matt 6:24; 1 Tim 6:10; Heb 13:5). The love of money is a problem because we trust it, rather than God, to solve our problems. Those who pursue money's empty promises will discover one day that they are spiritually bankrupt.*

I WONDER...

I recently became a Christian, but I'm afraid I'll miss out on a lot of fun during my teenage years. Can't I wait until later to live for Christ?

A speaker once related a dream he'd had. The location was hell, and the demons were trying to think of ways to stop people from accepting Christ.

The ideas they came up with included the usual ones: drugs, sexual temptations, intellectualism, money, fame, status, and so forth.

All of these strategies were tried, but they weren't very effective.

Finally, one demon suggested a plan that surprised everyone. "Let's tell people that believing the Bible and following Christ are the right things to do and that being a committed believer is the only way to live life. But," he concluded, "let's tell them to do it *tomorrow!*"

That has become Satan's strategy—and for many people tomorrow never comes!

This delay tactic works like Novocain. It numbs people and keeps them from turning to the truth when they hear it.

We are creatures of habit. We've learned almost everything—reading, writing, math, speech—by doing the same thing over and over. Our thoughts about God are the same way. Believing we can live the way we want to now and commit our lives to God later fulfills Satan's strategy.

Thought patterns become habits; habits become beliefs; beliefs become actions; and actions determine our eternity!

You may be afraid you'll miss out on the fun, but those "good times" don't last. Ecclesiastes 11:9–12:8 makes it clear that to live life to the fullest, we must follow God—not in fear that he wants to take away our fun, but in faith that he wants to make our life into something wonderful.

Life begins the moment we realize that the world doesn't revolve around us, but around God, who made the world and all that is in it.

And don't make fun of the powerful, even
in your own bedroom.
For a little bird might deliver your message
and tell them what you said.

11 THE UNCERTAINTIES OF LIFE

1 Send your grain across the seas,
and in time, profits will flow back to you.*
2 But divide your investments among many
places,*
for you do not know what risks might lie
ahead.

3 When clouds are heavy, the rains come
down.

Whether a tree falls north or south, it
stays where it falls.

4 Farmers who wait for perfect weather never
plant.
If they watch every cloud, they never
harvest.

5 Just as you cannot understand the path of
the wind or the mystery of a tiny baby growing
in its mother's womb,* so you cannot understand the activity of God, who does all things.

11:1 Or Give generously, / for your gifts will return to you later.
Hebrew reads Throw your bread on the waters, / for after many days
you will find it again.   **11:2** Hebrew among seven or even eight.
11:5 Some manuscripts read Just as you cannot understand how
breath comes to a tiny baby in its mother's womb.

ULTIMATE ISSUES IS THERE MEANING TO LIFE?

What do you do when you're bored? A recent Associated Press News Service story mentioned the recre-
ational choice of two teens. Having used the video
game Grand Theft Auto as "a means of escaping the
monotony of teenage life," they decided to act it out
by shooting at cars. They wound up killing one person and injuring others.

Some choices reveal a sad lack of meaning to a
life. Many people wonder if life has a purpose. The
sad fact is that suicide is always listed as a leading cause of death among teenagers. Many people,
including young people, struggle to find meaning for
their lives, a reason for living. If this describes you at
all, the book of Ecclesiastes was written for you.

The message of Ecclesiastes is brutally straightforward. Solomon, the writer, tells us that he has tried
everything life has to offer—wine, women, and song
(the ancient equivalent of sex, drugs, and rock 'n'
roll). His conclusion is this: "Fear God and obey his
commands, for this is everyone's duty" (12:13). In
other words, God gives meaning to our lives. No God,
no meaning.

Think of it this way: without God, you are just a
bunch of molecules thrown together by chance. If
there is no God, you came from—and are headed
toward—impersonal nothingness. Any attempt at
finding purpose is utterly doomed to failure. You
might just as well be a lizard, or a rock, or nothing
at all . . . if God doesn't exist.

Sounds pretty bleak, doesn't it? It is bleak, if we
subtract God from the equation. This belief that there
is no God and therefore no meaning is what has
driven many, including some of the greatest minds in
history, to despair, alcoholism, and even suicide. The
noted historian Will Durant put it this way: "The greatest question of our time is not communism versus
individualism, not Europe versus America, not even
the East versus the West; it is whether men can live
without God."

Trina Paulus examines this question from another,
wonderfully creative angle in her book Hope for
the Flowers. The book tells the story of a caterpillar
named Stripe and his quest for meaning. One day
Stripe sees a giant column made up of caterpillars
standing on top of other caterpillars. All of them are
trying to climb over the others to get to the top. So
Stripe begins to climb, too, until he gets near the
top—where he finds he can go no higher. Then someone says that to get any farther, they'd have to get rid
of some of the other caterpillars. The column begins
to shake, and Stripe sees caterpillars fall and hears
them scream.

Then—silence.

Frustration surges through Stripe at the thought
that this was the only way up. Then he hears a tiny
whisper from the top: "There's nothing here at all!"
It's answered by another: "Quiet, fool! They'll hear
you down the pillar. We're where they want to get.
That's what's here!"

Stripe feels frozen. The top isn't so high after
all! It only looks good from the bottom. There's
another whisper: "Look over there—another pillar—and there, too—everywhere!" Angry and
frustrated, Stripe moans, "My pillar, only one
of thousands. Millions of caterpillars climbing
nowhere! Something is really wrong, but . . . what
else is there?"

The good news is, there is something more. We
don't have to run pointlessly after illusions like a
slightly more sophisticated version of a hamster on
a treadmill. There is a personal God who created
you, knows you by name, loves you, and wants you
to know him intimately. He gives purpose and meaning to life as he calls us to follow him in his grand
adventure.

If you're searching for meaning, follow the writer of
Ecclesiastes to its source: a lifelong personal encounter with God. ■

⁶Plant your seed in the morning and keep busy all afternoon, for you don't know if profit will come from one activity or another—or maybe both.

ADVICE FOR YOUNG AND OLD ⁷Light is sweet; how pleasant to see a new day dawning.

⁸When people live to be very old, let them rejoice in every day of life. But let them also remember there will be many dark days. Everything still to come is meaningless.

⁹Young people,* it's wonderful to be young! Enjoy every minute of it. Do everything you want to do; take it all in. But remember that you must give an account to God for everything you do. ¹⁰So refuse to worry, and keep your body healthy. But remember that youth, with a whole life before you, is meaningless.

12 Don't let the excitement of youth cause you to forget your Creator. Honor him in your youth before you grow old and say, "Life is not pleasant anymore." ²Remember him before the light of the sun, moon, and stars is dim to your old eyes, and rain clouds continually darken your sky. ³Remember him before your legs—the guards of your house—start to tremble; and before your shoulders—the strong men—stoop. Remember him before your teeth—your few remaining servants—stop grinding; and before your eyes—the women looking through the windows—see dimly.

⁴Remember him before the door to life's opportunities is closed and the sound of work fades. Now you rise at the first chirping of the birds, but then all their sounds will grow faint.

⁵Remember him before you become fearful of falling and worry about danger in the streets; before your hair turns white like an almond tree in bloom, and you drag along without energy like a dying grasshopper, and the caperberry no longer inspires sexual desire. Remember him before you near the grave, your everlasting home, when the mourners will weep at your funeral.

⁶Yes, remember your Creator now while you are young, before the silver cord of life snaps and the golden bowl is broken. Don't wait until the water jar is smashed at the spring and the pulley is broken at the well. ⁷For then the dust will return to the earth, and the spirit will return to God who gave it.

11:9 Hebrew *Young man.*   12:10 Or *sought to write what was upright and true.*   12:11 Or *one shepherd.*   12:12 Hebrew *my son.*

FEAR GOD AND OBEY HIS COMMANDS,

FOR THIS IS EVERYONE'S DUTY. GOD WILL JUDGE US FOR EVERYTHING WE DO, INCLUDING EVERY SECRET THING.

■ ■ ■ E C C L E S I A S T E S   1 2 : 1 3 - 1 4

CONCLUDING THOUGHTS ABOUT THE TEACHER ⁸"Everything is meaningless," says the Teacher, "completely meaningless."

⁹Keep this in mind: The Teacher was considered wise, and he taught the people everything he knew. He listened carefully to many proverbs, studying and classifying them. ¹⁰The Teacher sought to find just the right words to express truths clearly.*

¹¹The words of the wise are like cattle prods—painful but helpful. Their collected sayings are like a nail-studded stick with which a shepherd* drives the sheep.

¹²But, my child,* let me give you some further advice: Be careful, for writing books is endless, and much study wears you out.

¹³That's the whole story. Here now is my final conclusion: Fear God and obey his commands, for this is everyone's duty. ¹⁴God will judge us for everything we do, including every secret thing, whether good or bad.

CHOICES
(11:10) Often people say, "It doesn't matter." But many of our choices will be irreversible—they will stay with us for a lifetime. What you do when you're young does matter. Enjoy life now, but don't do anything—physically, morally, or spiritually—that will prevent you from enjoying life when you are old.

SOLOMON'S ADVICE
(12:1-14) Solomon presents his antidotes for the two main ailments presented in this book: Those who lack purpose and direction in life should respect God and follow his principles for living; those who think life is unfair should remember that God will review every person's life to determine how he or she has responded to him. Have you committed your life to him, both present and future? Does your life measure up to his standards?

SONG OF SONGS

Check out some of the songs on the Billboard Hot 100, and you'll probably find a mix of I-gotta-have-you-now lyrics. Or glance at the steadily growing list of reality TV shows or reruns of prime-time soaps and you'll find stories of "instant love" or a paint-by-the-numbers view of relationships. The message comes through loud and clear: Love is a formula, lust is in, and marriage isn't necessary for a couple to experience sex.

That's not what God had in mind for love, sex, and marriage. Sex is meant to be an exciting, fulfilling physical union of a man and a woman who are protected by the commitment of marriage—not an act of conquest and self-gratification. Love is meant to be a self-giving action, not a self-centered emotion.

Nowhere are the true meanings of love and sex more beautifully portrayed than in the Song of Songs. Here we get an intimate glimpse into the relationship between the king (Solomon) and his bride. Love, sex, and marriage are celebrated in the context of living the way God designed us to live.

Confused about the messages you hear about love and marriage? The Song of Songs may have the answers you need.

STATS

PURPOSE
To tell of the love between a bridegroom (King Solomon) and his bride, to affirm the value of marriage, and to picture God's love for his people

AUTHOR
Solomon

ORIGINAL AUDIENCE
The people of Israel

DATE WRITTEN
Probably early in Solomon's reign

SETTING
Israel—the bride's garden and the king's palace

KEY PEOPLE
King Solomon, his chosen bride, and the young women of Jerusalem

KEY POINTS

LOVE As the beauty and wonder of romance unfolded between Solomon and his bride, the intense power of love affected the two lovers. Love is a powerful expression of feeling and commitment between two people; it is not to be regarded casually. We should not try to manipulate others into loving us.

COMMITMENT Solomon and his bride celebrated their commitment to each other. The decision to commit yourself to your spouse alone is one that needs to be reaffirmed daily. But it can begin even before marriage as you flee from sexual temptation.

SEX God wants sex to be a product of the love and commitment of two married people. God is glorified by sex within a godly marriage—for mutual pleasure, not selfish enjoyment.

BEAUTY The two lovers praise the beauty they see in each other. The language they use shows the spontaneity and mystery of love. The love one feels for a husband or wife reveals that person's inner beauty—qualities that keep love alive.

PROBLEMS Over time, feelings of loneliness, indifference, and isolation came between Solomon and his bride. During those times, love grew cold and barriers arose. Through careful communication, lovers can be reconciled, a commitment renewed, and romance refreshed.

1

This is Solomon's song of songs, more wonderful than any other.

*Young Woman**

² Kiss me and kiss me again,
 for your love is sweeter than wine.
³ How fragrant your cologne;
 your name is like its spreading fragrance.
 No wonder all the young women love you!
⁴ Take me with you; come, let's run!
 The king has brought me into his bedroom.

Young Women of Jerusalem

How happy we are for you, O king.
 We praise your love even more than wine.

Young Woman

How right they are to adore you.

⁵ I am dark but beautiful,
 O women of Jerusalem—
 dark as the tents of Kedar,
 dark as the curtains of Solomon's tents.
⁶ Don't stare at me because I am dark—
 the sun has darkened my skin.
 My brothers were angry with me;
 they forced me to care for their vineyards,
 so I couldn't care for myself—my own vineyard.

⁷ Tell me, my love, where are you leading your flock today?
 Where will you rest your sheep at noon?
 For why should I wander like a prostitute*
 among your friends and their flocks?

Young Man

⁸ If you don't know, O most beautiful woman,
 follow the trail of my flock,
 and graze your young goats by the shepherds' tents.
⁹ You are as exciting, my darling,
 as a mare among Pharaoh's stallions.
¹⁰ How lovely are your cheeks;
 your earrings set them afire!
 How lovely is your neck,
 enhanced by a string of jewels.
¹¹ We will make for you earrings of gold
 and beads of silver.

Young Woman

¹² The king is lying on his couch,
 enchanted by the fragrance of my perfume.
¹³ My lover is like a sachet of myrrh
 lying between my breasts.
¹⁴ He is like a bouquet of sweet henna blossoms
 from the vineyards of En-gedi.

Young Man

¹⁵ How beautiful you are, my darling,
 how beautiful!
 Your eyes are like doves.

Young Woman

¹⁶ You are so handsome, my love,
 pleasing beyond words!
 The soft grass is our bed;
¹⁷ fragrant cedar branches are the beams of our house,
 and pleasant smelling firs are the rafters.

2

Young Woman

¹ I am the spring crocus blooming on the Sharon Plain,*
 the lily of the valley.

Young Man

² Like a lily among thistles
 is my darling among young women.

Young Woman

³ Like the finest apple tree in the orchard
 is my lover among other young men.
 I sit in his delightful shade
 and taste his delicious fruit.
⁴ He escorts me to the banquet hall;
 it's obvious how much he loves me.
⁵ Strengthen me with raisin cakes,
 refresh me with apples,
 for I am weak with love.
⁶ His left arm is under my head,
 and his right arm embraces me.

⁷ Promise me, O women of Jerusalem,
 by the gazelles and wild deer,
 not to awaken love until the time is right.*

⁸ Ah, I hear my lover coming!
 He is leaping over the mountains,
 bounding over the hills.
⁹ My lover is like a swift gazelle

A TREAT
(1:1-4) This vivid description of a love relationship begins with a picture of love itself. Love is "sweeter than wine." We can enjoy love. God created it as a gift to us and a treat for all our senses.

1:1 The headings identifying the speakers are not in the original text, though the Hebrew usually gives clues by means of the gender of the person speaking.   1:7 Hebrew *like a veiled woman.* 2:1 Traditionally rendered *I am the rose of Sharon.* Sharon Plain is a region in the coastal plain of Palestine.   2:7 Or *not to awaken love until it is ready.*

or a young stag.
Look, there he is behind the wall,
    looking through the window,
    peering into the room.
¹⁰ My lover said to me,
    "Rise up, my darling!
    Come away with me, my fair one!
¹¹ Look, the winter is past,
    and the rains are over and gone.
¹² The flowers are springing up,
    the season of singing birds* has come,
    and the cooing of turtledoves fills the air.
¹³ The fig trees are forming young fruit,
    and the fragrant grapevines are
        blossoming.
    Rise up, my darling!
    Come away with me, my fair one!"

Young Man
¹⁴ My dove is hiding behind the rocks,
    behind an outcrop on the cliff.
    Let me see your face;
    let me hear your voice.
    For your voice is pleasant,
    and your face is lovely.

Young Women of Jerusalem
¹⁵ Catch all the foxes,
    those little foxes,
    before they ruin the vineyard of love,
    for the grapevines are blossoming!

Young Woman
¹⁶ My lover is mine, and I am his.
    He browses among the lilies.
¹⁷ Before the dawn breezes blow
    and the night shadows flee,
    return to me, my love, like a gazelle
    or a young stag on the rugged
        mountains.*

3

Young Woman
¹ One night as I lay in bed, I yearned for my
        lover.
    I yearned for him, but he did not come.
² So I said to myself, "I will get up and roam
        the city,
    searching in all its streets and squares.
    I will search for the one I love."
    So I searched everywhere but did not
        find him.
³ The watchmen stopped me as they made
        their rounds,

and I asked, "Have you seen the one
    I love?"
⁴ Then scarcely had I left them
    when I found my love!
    I caught and held him tightly,
    then I brought him to my mother's house,
    into my mother's bed, where I had been
        conceived.

⁵ Promise me, O women of Jerusalem,
    by the gazelles and wild deer,
    not to awaken love until the time is right.*

Young Women of Jerusalem
⁶ Who is this sweeping in from the wilderness
    like a cloud of smoke?
    Who is it, fragrant with myrrh and
        frankincense
    and every kind of spice?
⁷ Look, it is Solomon's carriage,
    surrounded by sixty heroic men,
    the best of Israel's soldiers.
⁸ They are all skilled swordsmen,
    experienced warriors.
    Each wears a sword on his thigh,
    ready to defend the king against an attack
        in the night.
⁹ King Solomon's carriage is built
    of wood imported from Lebanon.
¹⁰ Its posts are silver,
    its canopy gold;
    its cushions are purple.
    It was decorated with love
    by the young women of Jerusalem.

Young Woman
¹¹ Come out to see King Solomon,
    young women of Jerusalem.*
    He wears the crown his mother gave him on
        his wedding day,
    his most joyous day.

4

Young Man
¹ You are beautiful, my darling,
    beautiful beyond words.
    Your eyes are like doves
    behind your veil.

....

OVERPOWERED
(2:7; 3:5) Feelings of love can create intimacy that over-powers reason. Ever feel like that? Many couples too often are in a hurry to develop an intimate relationship based on their strong feelings. But feelings aren't enough to support a lasting relationship. This verse encourages us to avoid forcing romance lest the feelings of love grow faster than the commitment needed to make love last. Want to be wise? Wait for feelings of love and commitment to develop together.

2:12 Or *the season of pruning vines.*   **2:17** Or *on the hills of Bether.*
3:5 Or *not to awaken love until it is ready.*   **3:11** Hebrew of *Zion.*

Your hair falls in waves,
   like a flock of goats winding down the
     slopes of Gilead.
² Your teeth are as white as sheep,
   recently shorn and freshly washed.
Your smile is flawless,
   each tooth matched with its twin.*
³ Your lips are like scarlet ribbon;
   your mouth is inviting.
Your cheeks are like rosy pomegranates
   behind your veil.
⁴ Your neck is as beautiful as the tower
   of David,
   jeweled with the shields of a thousand
     heroes.
⁵ Your breasts are like two fawns,
   twin fawns of a gazelle grazing among
     the lilies.
⁶ Before the dawn breezes blow
   and the night shadows flee,
I will hurry to the mountain of myrrh
   and to the hill of frankincense.
⁷ You are altogether beautiful, my darling,
   beautiful in every way.

⁸ Come with me from Lebanon, my bride,
   come with me from Lebanon.

Come down* from Mount Amana,
   from the peaks of Senir and Hermon,
where the lions have their dens
   and leopards live among the hills.

⁹ You have captured my heart,
   my treasure,* my bride.
You hold it hostage with one glance
   of your eyes,
   with a single jewel of your necklace.
¹⁰ Your love delights me,
   my treasure, my bride.
Your love is better than wine,
   your perfume more fragrant than spices.
¹¹ Your lips are as sweet as nectar,
   my bride.
Honey and milk are under
   your tongue.
Your clothes are scented
   like the cedars of Lebanon.

¹² You are my private garden, my treasure,
   my bride,
   a secluded spring, a hidden fountain.
¹³ Your thighs shelter a paradise of
     pomegranates
   with rare spices—
henna with nard,
¹⁴   nard and saffron,
   fragrant calamus and cinnamon,
with all the trees of frankincense, myrrh,
     and aloes,
   and every other lovely spice.
¹⁵ You are a garden fountain,
   a well of fresh water
   streaming down from Lebanon's
     mountains.

4:2 Hebrew *Not one is missing; each has a twin.*   4:8 Or *Look down.*
4:9 Hebrew *my sister;* also in 4:10, 12.

WHY WAIT?

(4:12) In comparing his bride to a private garden, Solomon praised her virginity. On many talk shows and sitcoms, and in magazines, people often picture their virginity as something they need to get rid of as soon as possible. Yet abstinence has always been God's plan for unmarried people—and with good reason. Sex without marriage is cheap. It cannot compare with the joy of giving yourself completely to the one who is totally committed to you.

CHOICES
virginity

Cassie's sixteenth birthday tomorrow promises to be awesome. She'll finally get her driver's license, and she finally can officially date!

   She and her boyfriend, Paul, will be able to leave . . . in a car . . . by themselves . . . for a whole evening! No more brothers barging into the living room. No more being dropped off at parties. Privacy at last!

   Today, Cassie got a package from her older sister Beth, who got married last month. Enclosed was a long letter—one of those that you keep forever. It said a lot of things, but maybe the best part was this advice: "Cass, I know how much you love Paul, and

I know it will be hard for you two to stay pure now that you're officially dating. Take it from someone who waited: Sex is best when you save it for marriage! I promise you—virgins get the last (and the loudest and longest) laugh.

   "Most of my friends—even my Christian friends—didn't wait. They traded short-term pleasure for long-term pain. Don't make that mistake! Make the commitment to God that you won't let your physical relationship get out of control!

   "Give Paul a hug from me. And know that Mike and I pray for you two every single day. I love you, Cass.

   "Beth"

What a great letter! Read another beautiful description of a virgin bride on her wedding night in Song of Solomon 4. Note especially verse 12.

Young Woman

¹⁶ Awake, north wind!
  Rise up, south wind!
Blow on my garden
  and spread its fragrance all around.
Come into your garden, my love;
  taste its finest fruits.

5

Young Man

¹ I have entered my garden, my treasure,*
  my bride!
  I gather myrrh with my spices
and eat honeycomb with my honey.
  I drink wine with my milk.

Young Women of Jerusalem

Oh, lover and beloved, eat and drink!
  Yes, drink deeply of your love!

Young Woman

² I slept, but my heart was awake,
  when I heard my lover knocking and
    calling:
"Open to me, my treasure, my darling,
  my dove, my perfect one.
My head is drenched with dew,
  my hair with the dampness of the night."

³ But I responded,
"I have taken off my robe.
  Should I get dressed again?
I have washed my feet.
  Should I get them soiled?"

⁴ My lover tried to unlatch the door,
  and my heart thrilled within me.
⁵ I jumped up to open the door for my love,
  and my hands dripped with perfume.
My fingers dripped with lovely myrrh
  as I pulled back the bolt.
⁶ I opened to my lover,
  but he was gone!
  My heart sank.
I searched for him
  but could not find him anywhere.
I called to him,
  but there was no reply.
⁷ The night watchmen found me
  as they made their rounds.
They beat and bruised me
  and stripped off my veil,
  those watchmen on the walls.

⁸ Make this promise, O women of Jerusalem—
  If you find my lover,
  tell him I am weak with love.

5:1 Hebrew *my sister;* also in 5:2.

Young Women of Jerusalem

⁹ Why is your lover better than
    all others,
  O woman of rare beauty?
What makes your lover so special
  that we must promise this?

Young Woman

¹⁰ My lover is dark and dazzling,
  better than ten thousand others!
¹¹ His head is finest gold,
  his wavy hair is black as a raven.
¹² His eyes sparkle like doves
  beside springs of water;
they are set like jewels
  washed in milk.
¹³ His cheeks are like gardens of spices
  giving off fragrance.
His lips are like lilies,
  perfumed with myrrh.
¹⁴ His arms are like rounded bars of gold,
  set with beryl.
His body is like bright ivory,
  glowing with lapis lazuli.
¹⁵ His legs are like marble pillars
  set in sockets of finest gold.
His posture is stately,
  like the noble cedars of Lebanon.
¹⁶ His mouth is sweetness itself;
  he is desirable in every way.
Such, O women of Jerusalem,
  is my lover, my friend.

6

Young Women of Jerusalem

¹ Where has your lover gone,
  O woman of rare beauty?
Which way did he turn
  so we can help you find him?

Young Woman

² My lover has gone down to his garden,
  to his spice beds,
to browse in the gardens
  and gather the lilies.
³ I am my lover's, and my lover is mine.
  He browses among the lilies.

Young Man

⁴ You are beautiful, my darling,
  like the lovely city of Tirzah.
Yes, as beautiful as Jerusalem,
  as majestic as an army with billowing
    banners.
⁵ Turn your eyes away,
  for they overpower me.
Your hair falls in waves,

like a flock of goats winding down the
slopes of Gilead.
⁶ Your teeth are as white as sheep
that are freshly washed.
Your smile is flawless,
each tooth matched with its twin.*
⁷ Your cheeks are like rosy pomegranates
behind your veil.

⁸ Even among sixty queens
and eighty concubines
and countless young women,
⁹ I would still choose my dove, my perfect
one—
the favorite of her mother,
dearly loved by the one who bore her.
The young women see her and praise her;
even queens and royal concubines sing
her praises:
¹⁰ "Who is this, arising like the dawn,
as fair as the moon,
as bright as the sun,
as majestic as an army with billowing
banners?"

Young Woman
¹¹ I went down to the grove of walnut trees
and out to the valley to see the new
spring growth,
to see whether the grapevines had budded
or the pomegranates were in bloom.
¹² Before I realized it,
my strong desires had taken me to the
chariot of a noble man.*

Young Women of Jerusalem
¹³*Return, return to us, O maid of Shulam.
Come back, come back, that we may see
you again.

Young Man
Why do you stare at this young woman of
Shulam,
as she moves so gracefully between two
lines of dancers?*

7

¹* How beautiful are your sandaled feet,
O queenly maiden.

Your rounded thighs are like jewels,
the work of a skilled craftsman.
² Your navel is perfectly formed
like a goblet filled with mixed wine.
Between your thighs lies a mound of wheat
bordered with lilies.
³ Your breasts are like two fawns,
twin fawns of a gazelle.
⁴ Your neck is as beautiful as an ivory tower.
Your eyes are like the sparkling pools in
Heshbon
by the gate of Bath-rabbim.
Your nose is as fine as the tower
of Lebanon
overlooking Damascus.
⁵ Your head is as majestic as Mount Carmel,
and the sheen of your hair radiates
royalty.
The king is held captive by its tresses.
⁶ Oh, how beautiful you are!
How pleasing, my love, how full of
delights!
⁷ You are slender like a palm tree,
and your breasts are like its clusters
of fruit.
⁸ I said, "I will climb the palm tree
and take hold of its fruit."
May your breasts be like grape clusters,
and the fragrance of your breath like
apples.
⁹ May your kisses be as exciting as the best
wine,
flowing gently over lips and teeth.*

Young Woman
¹⁰ I am my lover's,
and he claims me as his own.
¹¹ Come, my love, let us go out to the fields
and spend the night among the
wildflowers.*
¹² Let us get up early and go to the vineyards
to see if the grapevines have budded,
if the blossoms have opened,
and if the pomegranates have bloomed.
There I will give you my love.
¹³ There the mandrakes give off their
fragrance,
and the finest fruits are at our door,
new delights as well as old,
which I have saved for you,
my lover.

MORE LOVE
(7:1-13) Solomon and his bride confidently expressed
their love for each other. When marriage partners are
secure in their love and relationship, they find the freedom to initiate and enjoy acts of love. In your dating
relationships, have you ever doubted God's plan for sex?
Many people have. Don't accept anything less than the
kind of love he wants for you: the secure, freeing love that
you will find only in marriage.

6:6 Hebrew *Not one is missing; each has a twin.* 6:12 Or *to the
royal chariots of my people,* or *to the chariots of Amminadab.* The
meaning of the Hebrew is uncertain. 6:13a Verse 6:13 is numbered
7:1 in Hebrew text. 6:13b Or *as you would at the movements of two
armies?* or *as you would at the dance of Mahanaim?* The meaning of
the Hebrew is uncertain. 7:1 Verses 7:1-13 are numbered 7:2-14 in
Hebrew text. 7:9 As in Greek and Syriac versions and Latin
Vulgate; Hebrew reads *over lips of sleepers.* 7:11 Or *in the villages.*

8

Young Woman

¹ Oh, I wish you were my brother,
who nursed at my mother's breasts.
Then I could kiss you no matter who was watching,
and no one would criticize me.
² I would bring you to my childhood home,
and there you would teach me.*
I would give you spiced wine to drink,
my sweet pomegranate wine.
³ Your left arm would be under my head,
and your right arm would embrace me.

⁴ Promise me, O women of Jerusalem,
not to awaken love until the time is right.*

Young Women of Jerusalem

⁵ Who is this sweeping in from the desert,
leaning on her lover?

8:2 Or *there she will teach me; or there she bore me.* **8:4** Or *not to awaken love until it is ready.* **8:6a** Or *its passion.* **8:6b** Hebrew as *Sheol.*

Young Woman

I aroused you under the apple tree,
where your mother gave you birth,
where in great pain she delivered you.
⁶ Place me like a seal over your heart,
like a seal on your arm.
For love is as strong as death,
its jealousy* as enduring as the grave.*
Love flashes like fire,
the brightest kind of flame.
⁷ Many waters cannot quench love,
nor can rivers drown it.
If a man tried to buy love

···

PRICELESS LOVE

(8:6-7) In this final description of their love, the bride includes some of its significant characteristics (see also 1 Cor 13). Love is as strong as death; it cannot be killed by time or disaster; and it cannot be bought for any price because it is freely given. Love is priceless. Even the richest king cannot buy it. It must be accepted as a gift from God and then shared within the guidelines God provides.

ULTIMATE ISSUES *THE TRUTH ABOUT SEX*

"Your rounded thighs are like jewels, the work of a skilled craftsman. Your navel is perfectly formed. . . . Your breasts are like . . . clusters of fruit . . . May your kisses be as exciting as the best wine." Where would you expect to find this kind of writing? A steamy romance novel? The Internet? How about your local Bible—namely Song of Songs 7:1-9!

Wow! What is writing like this doing in the Bible? No wonder the Song of Songs has caused so much confusion, controversy, and even embarrassment.

Song of Songs is not the only place where the Bible talks about sex (see, for example, 1 Cor 6; Gal 5:16-25; Eph 5:1-3; Heb 13:4). But here the Scriptures reach their highest, most beautiful, frank, and poetic view of sex. Sex was invented by God, not by Hollywood or the average music video producer. So, what can we conclude from this?

- Sex is *good*. Unfortunately, some have treated this aspect of God's creation as if it were shameful or to be avoided. But God created sex, and he created us as sexual creatures; therefore, sex is good. Regardless of the dangers and trouble surrounding sex, this fact remains: Sex is part of God's creative plan for men and women.

- Sex is *powerful*. Of all the ways people have of expressing themselves to one another, sex is the most powerful. It involves a person's total being. When sex is kept in its proper context—marriage—it is a powerful vehicle for good, for bringing a husband and wife together as one. Unfortunately,

when sex is expressed before or outside of marriage, it can be powerfully destructive.

Think of it like this: Would you give a seven-year-old the keys to a new Ferrari and send him or her out to drive it in the Grand Prix? No way, right? A seven-year-old isn't physically, mentally, or emotionally prepared to handle the car or the course. He or she will crash and burn and be hurt badly. The same is true with people who are young and not married—they are not prepared mentally, emotionally, or spiritually for the experience of sex. They think they're ready, but sex requires a strong structure to support and contain it. Get the picture?

- Sex is *made for marriage*. Period. Sex is such an explosive force between two people that it must be expressed in an environment of love, support, and commitment. Especially commitment. That's what is missing in sex outside of marriage—commitment. Sex is 100 percent physical commitment. Unless there is 100 percent emotional, financial, social, and spiritual commitment, the relationship will be unbalanced and will probably collapse, leading to pain, anger, shame, and much more. Those who decide to become sexually involved despite God's instructions shouldn't be surprised when, like our young Ferrari driver, they crash and burn.

Sex, as the Song of Songs says so beautifully, is God's idea. If you follow his leading—including waiting until marriage to have sex—you'll experience one of God's greatest gifts in a way that is fulfilling to you and pleasing to him. ■

with all his wealth,
his offer would be utterly scorned.

The Young Woman's Brothers

⁸ We have a little sister
too young to have breasts.
What will we do for our sister
if someone asks to marry her?
⁹ If she is a virgin, like a wall,
we will protect her with a silver tower.
But if she is promiscuous, like a swinging
door,
we will block her door with a cedar bar.

Young Woman

¹⁰ I was a virgin, like a wall;
now my breasts are like towers.
When my lover looks at me,
he is delighted with what he sees.

¹¹ Solomon has a vineyard at Baal-hamon,
which he leases out to tenant farmers.
Each of them pays a thousand pieces
of silver*
for harvesting its fruit.
¹² But my vineyard is mine to give,
and Solomon need not pay a thousand
pieces of silver.
But I will give two hundred pieces
to those who care for its vines.

Young Man

¹³ O my darling, lingering in the gardens,
your companions are fortunate to hear
your voice.
Let me hear it, too!

Young Woman

¹⁴ Come away, my love! Be like
a gazelle
or a young stag on the mountains
of spices.

8:11 Hebrew *1,000 shekels of silver.*

ISAIAH

On shaky legs, Matt slowly walked to the front of the room. The fluttering in his stomach grew with every step. As he turned to face the class, he was sure everyone could hear his heart pounding. Wiping his sweaty palms on his pants, he pulled out his note cards and began to speak.

Stage fright. We know it all too well. You're in front of everyone, exposed and vulnerable.

Now, if you think that's tough, imagine being a prophet like Isaiah. Not only would you have to speak in public, but usually your messages would not be what people wanted to hear. As a prophet, you would have to speak of sin, judgment, and changes that had to be made. And often you would have to confront kings, men who could have you put to death on a whim. Sometimes, to really make a point, you would have to act out your messages. That wouldn't be too much fun either; yet true prophets spoke out for God, regardless of how they felt.

Isaiah was one of the greatest prophets who ever lived, and the book of Isaiah contains his messages. This book is the Bible's first major prophetic book. It has often been called a "little Bible," since it has 66 chapters, just as the Bible has 66 books. As you read, you'll see Isaiah in action as he stays close to God and speaks to the people. Some of the most well-known prophecies about the Messiah are in Isaiah. The book of Isaiah encourages us all to faithfully take God's message wherever he sends us.

KEY POINTS

HOLINESS God's moral perfection stands in contrast to evil people and nations. Because he is without sin, he alone can help us when we mess up.

PUNISHMENT God promised to punish Israel and other nations for their wrongdoings. Likewise, we won't be shielded from the consequences of our wrongdoing if we boldly choose to disobey God.

SALVATION/MESSIAH The Savior's perfect sacrifice, his servant life, and his coming kingdom are all foretold by Isaiah. Through Christ, the promise of redemption and restoration is fulfilled.

HOPE God promises comfort, deliverance, and restoration in his future kingdom. No matter how bleak our current situation, or how evil the world becomes, we have the hope that God will keep his promises.

STATS

PURPOSE
To call Judah back to God and to tell of God's salvation through the Messiah

AUTHOR
Isaiah, son of Amoz

ORIGINAL AUDIENCE
The people of Israel

DATE WRITTEN
Chs 1–39, during Isaiah's ministry, about 700 B.C. Chs 40–66, near the end of Isaiah's life, about 681 B.C.

SETTING
Jerusalem

KEY PEOPLE
Isaiah; his two sons, Shear-jashub and Maher-shalal-hash-baz

SPECIAL FEATURES
Many of the prophecies in Isaiah predict both soon-to-occur events and distant, future events at the same time.

TIMELINE

760 B.C.
Amos becomes a prophet

753
Hosea becomes a prophet

742
Micah becomes a prophet

740
Isaiah becomes a prophet

735
Ahaz, king of Judah

732
Hoshea, king of Israel

722
Israel falls to Assyria

715
Hezekiah, king of Judah

701
Sennacherib besieges Jerusalem

697
Manasseh, king of Judah

681
Isaiah's ministry ends

640
Josiah, king of Judah

1 These are the visions that Isaiah son of Amoz saw concerning Judah and Jerusalem. He saw these visions during the years when Uzziah, Jotham, Ahaz, and Hezekiah were kings of Judah.*

A MESSAGE FOR REBELLIOUS JUDAH

² Listen, O heavens! Pay attention, earth!
This is what the LORD says:
"The children I raised and cared for
have rebelled against me.
³ Even an ox knows its owner,
and a donkey recognizes its master's
care—
but Israel doesn't know its master.
My people don't recognize my care for
them."
⁴ Oh, what a sinful nation they are—
loaded down with a burden of guilt.
They are evil people,
corrupt children who have rejected the
LORD.
They have despised the Holy One of Israel
and turned their backs on him.

⁵ Why do you continue to invite punishment?
Must you rebel forever?
Your head is injured,
and your heart is sick.
⁶ You are battered from head to foot—
covered with bruises, welts, and infected
wounds—
without any soothing ointments or
bandages.
⁷ Your country lies in ruins,
and your towns are burned.
Foreigners plunder your fields before your
eyes
and destroy everything they see.
⁸ Beautiful Jerusalem* stands abandoned
like a watchman's shelter in a vineyard,

like a lean-to in a cucumber field after the
harvest,
like a helpless city under siege.
⁹ If the LORD of Heaven's Armies
had not spared a few of us,*
we would have been wiped out like Sodom,
destroyed like Gomorrah.

¹⁰ Listen to the LORD, you leaders of "Sodom."
Listen to the law of our God, people of
"Gomorrah."
¹¹ "What makes you think I want all your
sacrifices?"
says the LORD.
"I am sick of your burnt offerings of rams
and the fat of fattened cattle.
I get no pleasure from the blood
of bulls and lambs and goats.
¹² When you come to worship me,
who asked you to parade through my
courts with all your ceremony?
¹³ Stop bringing me your meaningless gifts;
the incense of your offerings disgusts me!
As for your celebrations of the new moon
and the Sabbath
and your special days for fasting—
they are all sinful and false.
I want no more of your pious meetings.
¹⁴ I hate your new moon celebrations and your
annual festivals.
They are a burden to me. I cannot stand
them!
¹⁵ When you lift up your hands in prayer, I will
not look.
Though you offer many prayers, I will not
listen,
for your hands are covered with the blood
of innocent victims.
¹⁶ Wash yourselves and be clean!
Get your sins out of my sight.
Give up your evil ways.
¹⁷ Learn to do good.
Seek justice.
Help the oppressed.
Defend the cause of orphans.
Fight for the rights of widows.

¹⁸ "Come now, let's settle this,"
says the LORD.
"Though your sins are like scarlet,
I will make them as white as snow.
Though they are red like crimson,
I will make them as white as wool.
¹⁹ If you will only obey me,
you will have plenty to eat.

ISOLATED
(1:1-9) As long as the people of Judah continued to sin, they isolated themselves from God's help (see also 54:6-8). Have you ever felt separated from God because of something you've done? Remember, God does not abandon you—your sin is what has blocked communication with him. The only sure cure for this kind of isolation is to own up to what you've done and admit that you want to change (see Isa 1:16-19; 1 Jn 1:9). Are you willing?

STAINS
(1:18) Some stains are virtually impossible to remove from clothing. The "stain" of sin seems equally permanent. But God can remove this stain from our lives just as he promised to do for the Israelites. Through prayer we can be assured that Christ has forgiven all our sins, even the worst ones, and has removed our most indelible stains. All we have to do is ask (see Ps 51:1-10).

1:1 These kings reigned from 792 to 686 B.C.   **1:8** Hebrew *The daughter of Zion.*   **1:9** Greek version reads *a few of our children.* Compare Rom 9:29.

²⁰ But if you turn away and refuse to
        listen,
    you will be devoured by the sword
        of your enemies.
    I, the LORD, have spoken!"

UNFAITHFUL JERUSALEM

²¹ See how Jerusalem, once so faithful,
        has become a prostitute.
    Once the home of justice and
        righteousness,
    she is now filled with murderers.
²² Once like pure silver,
        you have become like worthless slag.
    Once so pure,
        you are now like watered-down wine.
²³ Your leaders are rebels,
        the companions of thieves.
    All of them love bribes
        and demand payoffs,
    but they refuse to defend the cause
        of orphans
    or fight for the rights of widows.

²⁴ Therefore, the Lord, the LORD of Heaven's
        Armies,
    the Mighty One of Israel, says,
    "I will take revenge on my enemies
        and pay back my foes!
²⁵ I will raise my fist against you.
    I will melt you down and skim off your
        slag.
    I will remove all your impurities.
²⁶ Then I will give you good judges again
        and wise counselors like you used to
        have.
    Then Jerusalem will again be called the
        Home of Justice
        and the Faithful City."

²⁷ Zion will be restored by justice;
        those who repent will be revived by
        righteousness.
²⁸ But rebels and sinners will be completely
        destroyed,
    and those who desert the LORD will
        be consumed.

²⁹ You will be ashamed of your idol worship
        in groves of sacred oaks.
    You will blush because you worshiped
        in gardens dedicated to idols.
³⁰ You will be like a great tree with withered
        leaves,
    like a garden without water.
³¹ The strongest among you will disappear like
        straw;
    their evil deeds will be the spark that sets
        it on fire.
    They and their evil works will burn up
        together,
    and no one will be able to put out the fire.

2 THE LORD'S FUTURE REIGN
This is a vision that Isaiah son of Amoz saw concerning Judah and Jerusalem:

² In the last days, the mountain of the LORD's
        house
    will be the highest of all—
    the most important place on earth.
    It will be raised above the other hills,
        and people from all over the world will
        stream there to worship.
³ People from many nations will come
        and say,
    "Come, let us go up to the mountain of the
        LORD,

CHOICES
so religious

If there were a contest for being religious, Terri probably would take home first prize. Just look: She . . .

- rarely misses church.
- sings in the choir (and sometimes even does solos!).
- serves as an officer in her youth group.
- puts 10 percent of all she earns in the offering plate.
- reads two chapters in her Bible every night.
- says a blessing before every meal she eats.

Yes, you would assume that Terri is a deeply spiritual person. Anyone involved in all those religious activities must be a great Christian, right?

Well, look again. If Terri is so close to God, then why does she use the language she uses? And why does she rip her classmates to shreds the way she does? And how come she's so mean to her little brothers and to her grandmother?

If Terri's so together spiritually, why does she talk back to her parents almost every day? If she is such an example of a mature child of God, why does she go to some of the parties she goes to? (And how in the world does she justify doing what she does at those parties?)

"Religious" people can brag about their religious activities all they want—God isn't impressed. In fact, he says that when our lives are full of sin, our religious activities are worthless. To please him, our lives must be consistent in every way. Check out God's reaction to his people's religious activities in Isaiah 1:10-17.

to the house of Jacob's God.
There he will teach us his ways,
  and we will walk in his paths."
For the LORD's teaching will go out from
    Zion;
  his word will go out from Jerusalem.
⁴ The LORD will mediate between nations
  and will settle international disputes.
They will hammer their swords into
    plowshares
  and their spears into pruning hooks.
Nation will no longer fight against nation,
  nor train for war anymore.

A WARNING OF JUDGMENT
⁵ Come, descendants of Jacob,
  let us walk in the light of the LORD!
⁶ For the LORD has rejected his people,
  the descendants of Jacob,
because they have filled their land with
    practices from the East
  and with sorcerers, as the
    Philistines do.
  They have made alliances with pagans.
⁷ Israel is full of silver and gold;
  there is no end to its treasures.
Their land is full of warhorses;
  there is no end to its chariots.
⁸ Their land is full of idols;
  the people worship things they have
    made
  with their own hands.
⁹ So now they will be humbled,
  and all will be brought low—
  do not forgive them.
¹⁰ Crawl into caves in the rocks.
  Hide in the dust
from the terror of the LORD
  and the glory of his majesty.
¹¹ Human pride will be brought down,
  and human arrogance will be humbled.
Only the LORD will be exalted
  on that day of judgment.

¹² For the LORD of Heaven's Armies
  has a day of reckoning.
He will punish the proud and mighty
  and bring down everything that is exalted.
¹³ He will cut down the tall cedars of Lebanon
  and all the mighty oaks of Bashan.

¹⁴ He will level all the high mountains
  and all the lofty hills.
¹⁵ He will break down every high tower
  and every fortified wall.
¹⁶ He will destroy all the great trading ships*
  and every magnificent vessel.
¹⁷ Human pride will be humbled,
  and human arrogance will be brought
    down.
Only the LORD will be exalted
  on that day of judgment.

¹⁸ Idols will completely disappear.
¹⁹ When the LORD rises to shake the earth,
  his enemies will crawl into holes in the
    ground.
They will hide in caves in the rocks
  from the terror of the LORD
  and the glory of his majesty.
²⁰ On that day of judgment they will abandon
    the gold and silver idols
  they made for themselves to worship.
They will leave their gods to the rodents
    and bats,
²¹   while they crawl away into caverns
  and hide among the jagged rocks in the
    cliffs.
They will try to escape the terror of the LORD
  and the glory of his majesty
  as he rises to shake the earth.
²² Don't put your trust in mere humans.
  They are as frail as breath.
  What good are they?

3 JUDGMENT AGAINST JUDAH
¹ The Lord, the LORD of Heaven's Armies,
  will take away from Jerusalem
    and Judah
everything they depend on:
  every bit of bread
  and every drop of water,
² all their heroes and soldiers,
  judges and prophets,
  fortune-tellers and elders,
³ army officers and high officials,
  advisers, skilled craftsmen, and
    astrologers.

⁴ I will make boys their leaders,
  and toddlers their rulers.
⁵ People will oppress each other—
  man against man,
  neighbor against neighbor.
Young people will insult their elders,
  and vulgar people will sneer at the
    honorable.

2:16 Hebrew *every ship of Tarshish.*

RELIABLE
(2:22) Isaiah warned the people of Judah to stop put-
ting all of their trust in other people. People are "frail as
breath" compared to God. They are undependable, sinful,
and mortal. Often we trust our fellow humans instead of
trusting the all-knowing God. But only God is completely
reliable.

6 In those days a man will say to his brother,
"Since you have a coat, you be our leader!
Take charge of this heap of ruins!"
7 But he will reply,
"No! I can't help.
I don't have any extra food or clothes.
Don't put me in charge!"

8 For Jerusalem will stumble,
and Judah will fall,
because they speak out against the LORD
and refuse to obey him.
They provoke him to his face.
9 The very look on their faces gives them
away.
They display their sin like the people
of Sodom
and don't even try to hide it.
They are doomed!
They have brought destruction upon
themselves.

10 Tell the godly that all will be well for them.
They will enjoy the rich reward they have
earned!
11 But the wicked are doomed,
for they will get exactly what they deserve.

12 Childish leaders oppress my people,
and women rule over them.
O my people, your leaders mislead you;
they send you down the wrong road.

13 The LORD takes his place in court
and presents his case against his people!
14 The LORD comes forward to pronounce
judgment
on the elders and rulers of his people:
"You have ruined Israel, my vineyard.
Your houses are filled with things stolen
from the poor.
15 How dare you crush my people,
grinding the faces of the poor into the
dust?"
demands the Lord, the LORD of Heaven's
Armies.

A WARNING TO JERUSALEM

16 The LORD says, "Beautiful Zion* is haughty:
craning her elegant neck,
flirting with her eyes,
walking with dainty steps,
tinkling her ankle bracelets.
17 So the Lord will send scabs on her head;
the LORD will make beautiful Zion bald."

3:16 Or The women of Zion (with corresponding changes to plural
forms through verse 24); Hebrew reads The daughters of Zion; also
in 3:17. 3:24 As in Dead Sea Scrolls; Masoretic Text reads robes /
because instead of beauty. 4:2 Or the Branch. 4:4 Or from the
women of Zion; Hebrew reads from the daughters of Zion.

18 On that day of judgment
the Lord will strip away everything
that makes her beautiful:
ornaments, headbands, crescent
necklaces,
19 earrings, bracelets, and veils;
20 scarves, ankle bracelets, sashes,
perfumes, and charms;
21 rings, jewels,
22 party clothes, gowns, capes, and purses;
23 mirrors, fine linen garments,
head ornaments, and shawls.

24 Instead of smelling of sweet perfume, she
will stink.
She will wear a rope for a sash,
and her elegant hair will fall out.
She will wear rough burlap instead of rich
robes.
Shame will replace her beauty.*
25 The men of the city will be killed with the
sword,
and her warriors will die in battle.
26 The gates of Zion will weep and mourn.
The city will be like a ravaged woman,
huddled on the ground.

4 In that day so few men will be left that
seven women will fight for each man, saying, "Let us all marry you! We will provide our
own food and clothing. Only let us take your
name so we won't be mocked as old maids."

A PROMISE OF RESTORATION

2 But in that day, the branch* of the LORD
will be beautiful and glorious;
the fruit of the land will be the pride and
glory
of all who survive in Israel.
3 All who remain in Zion
will be a holy people—
those who survive the destruction of
Jerusalem
and are recorded among the living.
4 The Lord will wash the filth from beautiful
Zion*
and cleanse Jerusalem of its bloodstains
with the hot breath of fiery judgment.

SELF-CENTERED THINKING
*(3:16-26) The women of Judah had placed their empha-
sis on clothing and jewelry rather than on God. They
thought only of themselves instead of the mistreated poor
people around them (3:14-15). (Remind you of anyone
you know?) Does this mean that God has a problem with
clothing and jewelry? No. But self-centered thinking
of any kind disturbs him. How observant are you of the
needs of those around you?*

ISAIAH

SERVED AS A PROPHET TO JUDAH FROM 740 TO 681 B.C.

Climate of the times	Society was in a great upheaval. Under King Ahaz and King Manasseh, the people reverted to idolatry, and even child sacrifice.
Main message	Although judgment from other nations was inevitable, the people could still have a special relationship with God.
Importance of message	Sometimes we must suffer judgment and discipline before we are restored to God.
Contemporary prophets	Hosea (753–715 B.C.) Micah (742–687 B.C.)

5 Then the LORD will provide shade for
    Mount Zion
and all who assemble there.
He will provide a canopy of cloud during
    the day
and smoke and flaming fire at night,
    covering the glorious land.
6 It will be a shelter from daytime heat
    and a hiding place from storms and rain.

5 A SONG ABOUT THE LORD'S VINEYARD

1 Now I will sing for the one I love
    a song about his vineyard:
My beloved had a vineyard
    on a rich and fertile hill.
2 He plowed the land, cleared its stones,
    and planted it with the best vines.
In the middle he built a watchtower
    and carved a winepress in the nearby
    rocks.
Then he waited for a harvest of sweet
    grapes,
    but the grapes that grew were bitter.

3 Now, you people of Jerusalem and Judah,
    you judge between me and my vineyard.
4 What more could I have done for my
    vineyard
    that I have not already done?
When I expected sweet grapes,

HUMAN IDOLS
(5:1-13) God planned to punish the people of Israel by sending them into exile. The nation's heroes—the great and honored among them—would suffer the same humiliation as the common people. Why? Because they lived by their own values rather than God's. God wanted the people of Israel to see that their human idols fall. Many of today's heroes in TV, movies, sports, entertainment, and books are idolized because of their ability to live as they please. Are your heroes those who defy God, or those who defy the world in order to serve God?

why did my vineyard give me bitter
    grapes?

5 Now let me tell you
    what I will do to my vineyard:
I will tear down its hedges
    and let it be destroyed.
I will break down its walls
    and let the animals trample it.
6 I will make it a wild place
    where the vines are not pruned and the
    ground is not hoed,
    a place overgrown with briers and thorns.
I will command the clouds
    to drop no rain on it.

7 The nation of Israel is the vineyard of the
    LORD of Heaven's Armies.
The people of Judah are his pleasant
    garden.
He expected a crop of justice,
    but instead he found oppression.
He expected to find righteousness,
    but instead he heard cries of violence.

JUDAH'S GUILT AND JUDGMENT

8 What sorrow for you who buy up house after
    house and field after field,
    until everyone is evicted and you live
    alone in the land.
9 But I have heard the LORD of Heaven's
    Armies
    swear a solemn oath:
"Many houses will stand deserted;
    even beautiful mansions will be empty.
10 Ten acres* of vineyard will not produce even
    six gallons* of wine.
Ten baskets of seed will yield only one
    basket* of grain."

5:10a Hebrew *A ten yoke,* that is, the area of land plowed by ten teams of oxen in one day.   **5:10b** Hebrew *a bath* [21 liters]. **5:10c** Hebrew *A homer* [5 bushels or 182 liters] *of seed will yield only an ephah* [20 quarts or 22 liters].

11 What sorrow for those who get up early in
the morning
looking for a drink of alcohol
and spend long evenings drinking wine
to make themselves flaming drunk.
12 They furnish wine and lovely music at their
grand parties—
lyre and harp, tambourine and flute—
but they never think about the LORD
or notice what he is doing.

13 So my people will go into exile far away
because they do not know me.
Those who are great and honored will starve,
and the common people will die of thirst.
14 The grave* is licking its lips in anticipation,
opening its mouth wide.
The great and the lowly
and all the drunken mob will be
swallowed up.
15 Humanity will be destroyed, and people
brought down;
even the arrogant will lower their eyes in
humiliation.
16 But the LORD of Heaven's Armies will be
exalted by his justice.
The holiness of God will be displayed by
his righteousness.
17 In that day lambs will find good pastures,
and fattened sheep and young goats* will
feed among the ruins.

18 What sorrow for those who drag their sins
behind them
with ropes made of lies,
who drag wickedness behind them like
a cart!
19 They even mock God and say,
"Hurry up and do something!
We want to see what you can do.
Let the Holy One of Israel carry out his plan,
for we want to know what it is."

20 What sorrow for those who say
that evil is good and good is evil,
that dark is light and light is dark,
that bitter is sweet and sweet is bitter.
21 What sorrow for those who are wise in their
own eyes
and think themselves so clever.
22 What sorrow for those who are heroes at
drinking wine
and boast about all the alcohol they can
hold.
23 They take bribes to let the wicked go free,
and they punish the innocent.

24 Therefore, just as fire licks up stubble
and dry grass shrivels in the flame,
so their roots will rot
and their flowers wither.
For they have rejected the law of the LORD
of Heaven's Armies;
they have despised the word of the Holy
One of Israel.
25 That is why the LORD's anger burns against
his people,
and why he has raised his fist to crush
them.
The mountains tremble,
and the corpses of his people litter the
streets like garbage.
But even then the LORD's anger is not
satisfied.
His fist is still poised to strike!

26 He will send a signal to distant nations
far away
and whistle to those at the ends of the
earth.
They will come racing toward Jerusalem.
27 They will not get tired or stumble.
They will not stop for rest or sleep.
Not a belt will be loose,
not a sandal strap broken.
28 Their arrows will be sharp
and their bows ready for battle.
Sparks will fly from their horses' hooves,
and the wheels of their chariots will spin
like a whirlwind.
29 They will roar like lions,
like the strongest of lions.
Growling, they will pounce on their victims
and carry them off,
and no one will be there to rescue them.
30 They will roar over their victims on that day
of destruction
like the roaring of the sea.
If someone looks across the land,
only darkness and distress will be seen;
even the light will be darkened by clouds.

6 ISAIAH'S CLEANSING AND CALL

It was in
the year King Uzziah died* that I saw the
Lord. He was sitting on a lofty throne, and the
train of his robe filled the Temple. 2Attending

5:14 Hebrew *Sheol.* 5:17 As in Greek version; Hebrew reads *and strangers.* 6:1 King Uzziah died in 740 B.C.

GREATNESS
*(6:1-7) Isaiah's lofty view of God in 6:1-4 gives us a sense
of God's greatness, mystery, and power. Isaiah's recognition of his sinfulness reminds us that no one is without
fault. When we recognize how great God is, and how
desperately we need his forgiveness, we will be energized
to do his work. How does your concept of the greatness of
God measure up to Isaiah's?*

him were mighty seraphim, each having six wings. With two wings they covered their faces, with two they covered their feet, and with two they flew. ³They were calling out to each other,

"Holy, holy, holy is the LORD of Heaven's Armies!
The whole earth is filled with his glory!"

⁴Their voices shook the Temple to its foundations, and the entire building was filled with smoke.

⁵Then I said, "It's all over! I am doomed, for I am a sinful man. I have filthy lips, and I live among a people with filthy lips. Yet I have seen the King, the LORD of Heaven's Armies."

⁶Then one of the seraphim flew to me with a burning coal he had taken from the altar with a pair of tongs. ⁷He touched my lips with it and said, "See, this coal has touched your lips. Now your guilt is removed, and your sins are forgiven."

⁸Then I heard the Lord asking, "Whom should I send as a messenger to this people? Who will go for us?"

I said, "Here I am. Send me."

⁹And he said, "Yes, go, and say to this people,

ULTIMATE ISSUES — WHO IS GOD?

Is there really a God? If so, what's he really like? Have you been asked those questions lately? Maybe you've *asked* those questions yourself because of conflicting information you've heard.

The Eastern sage says, "God is within you" or "God is illusion."

The New Ager says, "I am God. You are God. Everyone is a part of God, and God is a part of everyone."

The philosopher says, "God is the ultimate concept."

The atheist says, "There is no God."

The Christian says, "There is a God, and he is not you or me. God is different and separate from his creation. We are made in God's image, and we can know him."

So who's right? Who is God?

"It was in the year King Uzziah died that I saw the Lord. He was sitting on a lofty throne, and the train of his robe filled the Temple." So writes the prophet Isaiah in the sixth chapter of the book named for him. Isaiah also wondered what God was like. Isaiah had received messages from God for Israel, and he had delivered them faithfully. But around the time of King Uzziah's death (approximately 740 B.C.), Isaiah not only heard a message, he got a glimpse of God! Understandably, Isaiah was overwhelmed. What does the Bible say about what Isaiah saw?

Any study of what God is like should begin with a look at the names given for him in Scripture. Each name—Elohim, Adonai, El Shaddai, Yahweh (or Jehovah), Abba—reveals an aspect of God's nature and character.

The Bible puts God's characteristics into basically two categories: the "incommunicable" ones, those he does not share with his creation; and the "communicable" ones, those he does share with us.

The incommunicable attributes include these:

EXISTENCE—Before anything else existed, God was. The idea that something or some*one* exists outside of time is mind-boggling. Still, it is a logical necessity that something had to come first, and that first something had to always exist. The Bible's answer to this mystery is straightforward: "Before the mountains were born, before you gave birth to the earth and the world, from beginning to end, you are God" (Ps 90:2).

IMMUTABILITY—This means God never changes; he is the same yesterday, today, and forever (Mal 3:6). You never have to worry about God's actions from one day to the next—he is forever consistent. Unlike the "gods" of other religions—moody, fickle, often cruel, and all-too-human—the One True God is eternally the same. In a constantly changing world, it is comforting to know we always have one source of stability.

INFINITY—God is beyond all boundaries. He is limitless. This infinity is expressed in different ways. In regard to *time,* God is eternal; he always was, is, and will be. In regard to *space,* he is omnipresent, or everywhere at once. No corner of the universe lacks his presence. In regard to *power,* he is omnipotent, or all-powerful. God can do anything that is consistent with his character. (Some things God cannot do—he cannot lie, break a promise, be less than God, and so forth.) God alone is the power of creation: he spoke, and the universe was created. God will someday speak another kind of word and bring the curtain down. In regard to knowledge, he is omniscient, or all-knowing. Nothing and no one exists that God does not know completely. He knows everything about you.

We can comprehend God's communicable attributes because he shares them with us to some degree. These include the abilities to think, to love, to make moral judgments and wise choices, to communicate, to work, and so on. Though God's ability in these areas is light-years beyond ours, he has given us some capacity to resemble him in certain areas. Remember, we are made in the image of God.

Many different ideas and belief systems center around the question, Who is God? Christianity is based on the confident assertion that the real God, the God of Isaiah and of the Bible, has revealed himself to us, and we can know him. ∎

'Listen carefully, but do not understand.
Watch closely, but learn nothing.'
10 Harden the hearts of these people.
Plug their ears and shut their eyes.
That way, they will not see with their eyes,
nor hear with their ears,
nor understand with their hearts
and turn to me for healing."*

11 Then I said, "Lord, how long will this go on?"
And he replied,

"Until their towns are empty,
their houses are deserted,
and the whole country is a wasteland;
12 until the Lord has sent everyone away,
and the entire land of Israel lies
deserted.
13 If even a tenth—a remnant—survive,
it will be invaded again and burned.
But as a terebinth or oak tree leaves a
stump when it is cut down,
so Israel's stump will be a holy seed."

7 A MESSAGE FOR AHAZ When Ahaz, son of
Jotham and grandson of Uzziah, was king
of Judah, King Rezin of Syria* and Pekah son of
Remaliah, the king of Israel, set out to attack
Jerusalem. However, they were unable to carry
out their plan.

2 The news had come to the royal court of Judah: "Syria is allied with Israel* against us!"
So the hearts of the king and his people trembled with fear, like trees shaking in a storm.

3 Then the Lord said to Isaiah, "Take your
son Shear-jashub* and go out to meet King
Ahaz. You will find him at the end of the aqueduct that feeds water into the upper pool,
near the road leading to the field where cloth
is washed.* 4 Tell him to stop worrying. Tell
him he doesn't need to fear the fierce anger
of those two burned-out embers, King Rezin
of Syria and Pekah son of Remaliah. 5 Yes, the
kings of Syria and Israel are plotting against
him, saying, 6 "We will attack Judah and capture
it for ourselves. Then we will install the son of
Tabeel as Judah's king.' 7 But this is what the
Sovereign Lord says:

6:9-10 Greek version reads And he said, "Go and say to this
people, / 'When you hear what I say, you will not understand. /
When you see what I do, you will not comprehend.' / For the hearts
of these people are hardened, / and their ears cannot hear, and they
have closed their eyes— / so their eyes cannot see, / and their ears
cannot hear, / and their hearts cannot understand, / and they cannot
turn to me and let me heal them." Compare Matt 13:14-15; Mark
4:12; Luke 8:10; Acts 28:26-27.   7:1 Hebrew Aram; also in 7:2, 4,
5, 8.   7:2 Hebrew Ephraim, referring to the northern kingdom of
Israel; also in 7:5, 8, 9, 17.   7:3a Shear-jashub means "A remnant
will return."   7:3b Or bleached.   7:11 Hebrew as deep as Sheol.
7:14 Or young woman.   7:15 Or curds; also in 7:22.   7:20a Hebrew
the river.   7:20b Hebrew shave off the head, the hair of the legs,
and the beard.

"This invasion will never happen;
it will never take place;
8 for Syria is no stronger than its capital,
Damascus,
and Damascus is no stronger than its
king, Rezin.
As for Israel, within sixty-five years
it will be crushed and completely
destroyed.
9 Israel is no stronger than its capital,
Samaria,
and Samaria is no stronger than its king,
Pekah son of Remaliah.
Unless your faith is firm,
I cannot make you stand firm."

THE SIGN OF IMMANUEL 10 Later, the Lord
sent this message to King Ahaz: 11 "Ask the
Lord your God for a sign of confirmation,
Ahaz. Make it as difficult as you want—as
high as heaven or as deep as the place of the
dead.*"

12 But the king refused. "No," he said, "I will
not test the Lord like that."

13 Then Isaiah said, "Listen well, you royal
family of David! Isn't it enough to exhaust
human patience? Must you exhaust the patience of my God as well? 14 All right then, the
Lord himself will give you the sign. Look! The
virgin* will conceive a child! She will give birth
to a son and will call him Immanuel (which
means 'God is with us'). 15 By the time this child
is old enough to choose what is right and reject what is wrong, he will be eating yogurt*
and honey. 16 For before the child is that old,
the lands of the two kings you fear so much
will both be deserted.

17 "Then the Lord will bring things on you,
your nation, and your family unlike anything
since Israel broke away from Judah. He will
bring the king of Assyria upon you!"

18 In that day the Lord will whistle for the
army of southern Egypt and for the army of
Assyria. They will swarm around you like flies
and bees. 19 They will come in vast hordes and
settle in the fertile areas and also in the desolate valleys, caves, and thorny places. 20 In that
day the Lord will hire a "razor" from beyond
the Euphrates River*—the king of Assyria—
and use it to shave off everything: your land,
your crops, and your people.*

21 In that day a farmer will be fortunate
to have a cow and two sheep or goats left.
22 Nevertheless, there will be enough milk for
everyone because so few people will be left in
the land. They will eat their fill of yogurt and
honey. 23 In that day the lush vineyards, now

MY STORY: Jason

I always had problems with peer pressure. I became a Christian in seventh grade, but had trouble really living like one. I was good at putting people down, for one thing. And I swore a lot. But probably the biggest weakness I had was partying.

When someone asked me to go to a party, it was like I couldn't say no. Then when I got there, if there was drinking, I couldn't resist. I tried to a couple of times, but people would ask why I wasn't having a beer. Once I even tried to tell them it was because I was a Christian. I shouldn't have said that. They joked about my being too "holy" for them, and I felt so bad I gave in and even drank too much that night. After that, I was afraid to say anything about my faith because I thought it would be worse if I said something and then didn't act at all like a Christian.

Still, I read my Bible. And I started going to youth group in our church. That helped me change some, but I continued to feel like a hypocrite.

One day I was reading in Isaiah, and for some reason Isaiah 7:9 leaped out at me: "Unless your faith is firm, I cannot make you stand firm." I had been praying that God would make me a stronger Christian. This verse seemed to be saying to me that I hadn't really believed that God would help me take a stand and that I needed to choose to stand firm rather than give in to pressure.

Reading that verse was a turning point for me. I decided that I had to learn more about my faith and God's promises, and more about how God's Holy Spirit is working in my life. I spent more time with my church friends and less with my school friends. At first that was difficult, but it later turned out to be easier than I thought. The youth group often had things planned for the weekend, so when someone invited me to a party, I could honestly say I had other plans. I still struggle with saying no to my friends, but it's less of a struggle now. The more I learn about God, the more I see how he works in me through his Holy Spirit, and the more I believe God, the more he really does protect me.

---

worth 1,000 pieces of silver,* will become patches of briers and thorns. ²⁴The entire land will become a vast expanse of briers and thorns, a hunting ground overrun by wildlife. ²⁵No one will go to the fertile hillsides where the gardens once grew, for briers and thorns will cover them. Cattle, sheep, and goats will graze there.

8 **THE COMING ASSYRIAN INVASION** Then the LORD said to me, "Make a large sign-board and clearly write this name on it: Maher-shalal-hash-baz.*" ²I asked Uriah the priest and Zechariah son of Jeberekiah, both known as honest men, to witness my doing this.

³Then I slept with my wife, and she became pregnant and gave birth to a son. And the LORD said, "Call him Maher-shalal-hash-baz. ⁴For before this child is old enough to say 'Papa' or 'Mama,' the king of Assyria will carry away both the abundance of Damascus and the riches of Samaria."

⁵Then the LORD spoke to me again and said,

⁶"My care for the people of Judah is like the gently flowing waters of Shiloah, but they have rejected it. They are rejoicing over what will happen to* King Rezin and King Pekah.* ⁷Therefore, the Lord will overwhelm them with a mighty flood from the Euphrates River*—the king of Assyria and all his glory. This flood will overflow all its channels ⁸and sweep into Judah until it is chin deep. It will spread its wings, submerging your land from one end to the other, O Immanuel.

⁹ "Huddle together, you nations, and be terrified.
   Listen, all you distant lands.
Prepare for battle, but you will be crushed!
   Yes, prepare for battle, but you will be crushed!
¹⁰ Call your councils of war, but they will be worthless.

7:23 Hebrew *1,000 shekels of silver,* about 25 pounds or 11.4 kilograms in weight.   **8:1** *Maher-shalal-hash-baz* means "Swift to plunder and quick to carry away."   **8:6a** Or *They are rejoicing because of.*   **8:6b** Hebrew *and the son of Remaliah.*   **8:7** Hebrew *the river.*

Develop your strategies, but they will not
succeed.
For God is with us!*"

A CALL TO TRUST THE LORD

[11]The LORD has given me a strong warning not to think like everyone else does. He said,

[12] "Don't call everything a conspiracy, like
they do,
and don't live in dread of what frightens
them.
[13] Make the LORD of Heaven's Armies holy in
your life.
He is the one you should fear.
He is the one who should make you tremble.
[14]   He will keep you safe.
But to Israel and Judah
he will be a stone that makes people
stumble,
a rock that makes them fall.
And for the people of Jerusalem
he will be a trap and a snare.
[15] Many will stumble and fall,
never to rise again.
They will be snared and captured."

[16] Preserve the teaching of God;
entrust his instructions to those who
follow me.
[17] I will wait for the LORD,
who has turned away from the
descendants of Jacob.
I will put my hope in him.

[18]I and the children the LORD has given me serve as signs and warnings to Israel from the LORD of Heaven's Armies who dwells in his Temple on Mount Zion.

[19]Someone may say to you, "Let's ask the mediums and those who consult the spirits of the dead. With their whisperings and mutterings, they will tell us what to do." But shouldn't people ask God for guidance? Should the living seek guidance from the dead?

[20]Look to God's instructions and teachings! People who contradict his word are completely in the dark. [21]They will go from one place to another, weary and hungry. And because they are hungry, they will rage and curse their king and their God. They will look up to heaven [22]and down at the earth, but wherever they look, there will be trouble and anguish and dark despair. They will be thrown out into the darkness.

9 HOPE IN THE MESSIAH [1]*Nevertheless, that time of darkness and despair will not go on forever. The land of Zebulun and Naphtali will be humbled, but there will be a time in the future when Galilee of the Gentiles, which lies along the road that runs between the Jordan and the sea, will be filled with glory.

[2]*The people who walk in darkness
will see a great light.
For those who live in a land of deep
darkness,*
a light will shine.
[3] You will enlarge the nation of Israel,
and its people will rejoice.
They will rejoice before you
as people rejoice at the harvest
and like warriors dividing the plunder.
[4] For you will break the yoke of their slavery
and lift the heavy burden from their
shoulders.
You will break the oppressor's rod,
just as you did when you destroyed the
army of Midian.
[5] The boots of the warrior
and the uniforms bloodstained by war
will all be burned.
They will be fuel for the fire.

[6] For a child is born to us,
a son is given to us.
The government will rest on his
shoulders.
And he will be called:
Wonderful Counselor,* Mighty God,
Everlasting Father, Prince of Peace.
[7] His government and its peace
will never end.
He will rule with fairness and justice from
the throne of his ancestor David
for all eternity.

....

CHOICES
(8:5-15) Because the people of Judah rejected God's gentle care in favor of seeking help from other nations, God planned to punish them. Here we see two distinct attributes of God—his love and his wrath. Continually ignoring God's love and guidance often leads us into trouble, which invites his wrath. We must recognize the consequences of our choices. God seeks to protect us from bad choices, but he still gives us the freedom to make them.

BLAME
(8:21-22) After rejecting God's plan for their lives, the people of Judah blamed him for their trials. People continually blame God for their self-induced problems. How do you respond to the unpleasant consequences of poor choices? Where do you place the blame? If you've been tempted to blame God, consider instead the ways you can grow even through your failures.

8:10 Hebrew *Immanuel!*   **9:1** Verse 9:1 is numbered 8:23 in Hebrew text.   **9:2a** Verses 9:2-21 are numbered 9:1-20 in Hebrew text.   **9:2b** Greek version reads *a land where death casts its shadow.* Compare Matt 4:16.   **9:6** Or *Wonderful, Counselor.*

NAMES FOR THE MESSIAH

ISAIAH USES FIVE NAMES TO DESCRIBE THE MESSIAH (9:6). THESE NAMES HAVE SPECIAL MEANING TO US.

WONDERFUL—He is exceptional, distinguished, and without equal.

COUNSELOR—He gives the right advice.

MIGHTY GOD—He is God himself.

EVERLASTING FATHER—He is timeless; he is God our Father.

PRINCE OF PEACE—His government is one of justice and peace.

The passionate commitment of the LORD
   of Heaven's Armies
   will make this happen!

THE LORD'S ANGER AGAINST ISRAEL
⁸ The Lord has spoken out against Jacob;
   his judgment has fallen upon Israel.
⁹ And the people of Israel* and Samaria,
   who spoke with such pride and
      arrogance,
   will soon know it.
¹⁰ They said, "We will replace the broken
      bricks of our ruins with finished stone,
   and replant the felled sycamore-fig trees
      with cedars."

¹¹ But the LORD will bring Rezin's enemies
      against Israel
   and stir up all their foes.
¹² The Syrians* from the east and the
      Philistines from the west
   will bare their fangs and devour Israel.
   But even then the LORD's anger will not be
      satisfied.
   His fist is still poised to strike.

¹³ For after all this punishment, the people will
      still not repent.
   They will not seek the LORD of Heaven's
      Armies.
¹⁴ Therefore, in a single day the LORD will
      destroy both the head and the tail,
   the noble palm branch and the lowly reed.
¹⁵ The leaders of Israel are the head,

and the lying prophets are the tail.
¹⁶ For the leaders of the people have misled
      them.
   They have led them down the path of
      destruction.
¹⁷ That is why the Lord takes no pleasure in the
      young men
   and shows no mercy even to the widows
      and orphans.
   For they are all wicked hypocrites,
      and they all speak foolishness.
   But even then the LORD's anger will not be
      satisfied.
   His fist is still poised to strike.

¹⁸ This wickedness is like a brushfire.
   It burns not only briers and thorns
   but also sets the forests ablaze.
   Its burning sends up clouds of smoke.
¹⁹ The land will be blackened
   by the fury of the LORD of Heaven's
      Armies.
   The people will be fuel for the fire,
   and no one will spare even his own
      brother.
²⁰ They will attack their neighbor on the right
   but will still be hungry.
   They will devour their neighbor on the left
   but will not be satisfied.
   In the end they will even eat their own
      children.*
²¹ Manasseh will feed on Ephraim,
   Ephraim will feed on Manasseh,
   and both will devour Judah.
   But even then the LORD's anger will not be
      satisfied.
   His fist is still poised to strike.

10 ¹What sorrow awaits the unjust judges
         and those who issue unfair laws.
² They deprive the poor of justice
   and deny the rights of the needy among
      my people.

THE PROBLEM OF PRIDE
*(9:8-10) Israel was called arrogant for saying, in essence,
"We've faced a temporary setback, but by our own
strength we will rebuild our city." Though God made
Israel a nation and gave them the land they occupied,
the people trusted themselves rather than God. Too often
we take pride in our accomplishments or possessions,
forgetting that God has given us all our abilities. We even
become proud of our status as Christians. God is not
pleased with any pride or attitudes of self-sufficiency.
Tempted to think you're all that? Watch out!*

9:9 Hebrew *of Ephraim*, referring to the northern kingdom of Israel.
9:12 Hebrew *Arameans.*   **9:20** Or *eat their own arms.*

They prey on widows
and take advantage of orphans.
³ What will you do when I punish you,
when I send disaster upon you from
a distant land?
To whom will you turn for help?
Where will your treasures be safe?
⁴ You will stumble along as prisoners
or lie among the dead.
But even then the LORD's anger will not be
satisfied.
His fist is still poised to strike.

JUDGMENT AGAINST ASSYRIA

⁵ "What sorrow awaits Assyria, the rod of my
anger.
I use it as a club to express my anger.
⁶ I am sending Assyria against a godless
nation,
against a people with whom I am angry.
Assyria will plunder them,
trampling them like dirt beneath its feet.
⁷ But the king of Assyria will not understand
that he is my tool;
his mind does not work that way.
His plan is simply to destroy,
to cut down nation after nation.
⁸ He will say,
'Each of my princes will soon be a king.
⁹ We destroyed Calno just as we did
Carchemish.
Hamath fell before us as Arpad did.
And we destroyed Samaria just as we did
Damascus.
¹⁰ Yes, we have finished off many a kingdom
whose gods were greater than those in
Jerusalem and Samaria.
¹¹ So we will defeat Jerusalem and her gods,
just as we destroyed Samaria with hers.'"

¹²After the Lord has used the king of Assyria
to accomplish his purposes on Mount Zion and
in Jerusalem, he will turn against the king of
Assyria and punish him—for he is proud and
arrogant. ¹³He boasts,

"By my own powerful arm I have done this.
With my own shrewd wisdom I planned it.
I have broken down the defenses of nations
and carried off their treasures.
I have knocked down their kings like a
bull.
¹⁴ I have robbed their nests of riches
and gathered up kingdoms as a farmer
gathers eggs.

No one can even flap a wing against me
or utter a peep of protest."

¹⁵ But can the ax boast greater power than the
person who uses it?
Is the saw greater than the person who
saws?
Can a rod strike unless a hand moves it?
Can a wooden cane walk by itself?
¹⁶ Therefore, the Lord, the LORD of Heaven's
Armies,
will send a plague among Assyria's proud
troops,
and a flaming fire will consume its glory.
¹⁷ The LORD, the Light of Israel, will be a fire;
the Holy One will be a flame.
He will devour the thorns and briers with
fire,
burning up the enemy in a single night.
¹⁸ The LORD will consume Assyria's glory
like a fire consumes a forest in a fruitful
land;
it will waste away like sick people in a
plague.
¹⁹ Of all that glorious forest, only a few trees
will survive—
so few that a child could count them!

HOPE FOR THE LORD'S PEOPLE

²⁰ In that day the remnant left in Israel,
the survivors in the house of Jacob,
will no longer depend on allies
who seek to destroy them.
But they will faithfully trust the LORD,
the Holy One of Israel.
²¹ A remnant will return;*
yes, the remnant of Jacob will return to
the Mighty God.
²² But though the people of Israel are as
numerous
as the sand of the seashore,
only a remnant of them will return.
The LORD has rightly decided to destroy
his people.
²³ Yes, the Lord, the LORD of Heaven's Armies,
has already decided to destroy the entire
land.*

....

10:21 Hebrew *Shear-jashub;* see 7:3; 8:18.   **10:22-23** Greek version
reads *only a remnant of them will be saved. / For he will carry out his
sentence quickly and with finality and righteousness; / for God will
carry out his sentence upon all the world with finality.* Compare Rom
9:27-28.

THE REMNANT
(10:20-22) *Those who remained faithful to God despite
the horrors of the promised enemy invasion were called
"the remnant." The key to being a part of this group
was faith. Being a descendant of Abraham, living in the
Promised Land, having trusted God at one time—none of
these characteristics were good enough. Are you relying
on your Christian heritage, the rituals of worship, or past
experiences to put you in a right relationship with God?
The key to being set apart by God is faith in him.*

²⁴So this is what the Lord, the LORD of Heaven's Armies, says: "O my people in Zion, do not be afraid of the Assyrians when they oppress you with rod and club as the Egyptians did long ago. ²⁵In a little while my anger against you will end, and then my anger will rise up to destroy them." ²⁶The LORD of Heaven's Armies will lash them with his whip, as he did when Gideon triumphed over the Midianites at the rock of Oreb, or when the LORD's staff was raised to drown the Egyptian army in the sea.

²⁷ In that day the LORD will end the bondage
        of his people.
    He will break the yoke of slavery
        and lift it from their shoulders.*

²⁸ Look, the Assyrians are now at Aiath.
        They are passing through Migron
        and are storing their equipment at
            Micmash.
²⁹ They are crossing the pass
        and are camping at Geba.
    Fear strikes the town of Ramah.
        All the people of Gibeah, the hometown
            of Saul,
        are running for their lives.
³⁰ Scream in terror,
        you people of Gallim!
    Shout out a warning to Laishah.
        Oh, poor Anathoth!
³¹ There go the people of Madmenah, all
        fleeing.
    The citizens of Gebim are trying to hide.
³² The enemy stops at Nob for the rest of
        that day.
    He shakes his fist at beautiful Mount
        Zion, the mountain of Jerusalem.

³³ But look! The Lord, the LORD of Heaven's
        Armies,
    will chop down the mighty tree of Assyria
        with great power!
    He will cut down the proud.
        That lofty tree will be brought down.
³⁴ He will cut down the forest trees with
        an ax.
    Lebanon will fall to the Mighty One.*

··

FAIR TREATMENT
(11:1-5) Isaiah prophesied about a perfect leader who would judge everyone fairly. We all long for fair treatment from others, but do we give it? We hate being judged based on appearance, false evidence, or hearsay, but we can be quick to judge others using those same criteria. Only Christ—the promised perfect leader—is totally fair. And only as he governs our hearts can we learn to be as fair in our treatment of others as we expect them to be with us (see also Luke 6:31).

11 A BRANCH FROM DAVID'S LINE

¹ Out of the stump of David's family* will grow
        a shoot—
    yes, a new Branch bearing fruit from the
        old root.

² And the Spirit of the LORD will rest on him—
        the Spirit of wisdom and understanding,
    the Spirit of counsel and might,
        the Spirit of knowledge and the fear of
            the LORD.
³ He will delight in obeying the LORD.
        He will not judge by appearance
        nor make a decision based on hearsay.
⁴ He will give justice to the poor
        and make fair decisions for the exploited.
    The earth will shake at the force of his word,
        and one breath from his mouth will
            destroy the wicked.
⁵ He will wear righteousness like a belt
        and truth like an undergarment.

⁶ In that day the wolf and the lamb will live
        together;
    the leopard will lie down with the baby
        goat.
    The calf and the yearling will be safe with
        the lion,
    and a little child will lead them all.
⁷ The cow will graze near the bear.
        The cub and the calf will lie down
            together.
    The lion will eat hay like a cow.
⁸ The baby will play safely near the hole of
        a cobra.
    Yes, a little child will put its hand in a nest
        of deadly snakes without harm.
⁹ Nothing will hurt or destroy in all my holy
        mountain,
    for as the waters fill the sea,
        so the earth will be filled with people who
            know the LORD.

¹⁰ In that day the heir to David's throne*
        will be a banner of salvation to all the
            world.
    The nations will rally to him,
        and the land where he lives will be
            a glorious place.*
¹¹ In that day the Lord will reach out his
        hand a second time
    to bring back the remnant of his
        people—

10:27 As in Greek version; Hebrew reads *The yoke will be broken, / for you have grown so fat.*   **10:34** Or *with an ax / as even the mighty trees of Lebanon fall.*   **11:1** Hebrew *the stump of the line of Jesse.* Jesse was King David's father.   **11:10a** Hebrew *the root of Jesse.* **11:10b** Greek version reads *In that day the heir to David's throne* [literally *the root of Jesse*] *will come, / and he will rule over the Gentiles. / They will place their hopes on him.* Compare Rom 15:12.

those who remain in Assyria and northern
Egypt;
in southern Egypt, Ethiopia,* and Elam;
in Babylonia,* Hamath, and all the
distant coastlands.
¹² He will raise a flag among the nations
and assemble the exiles of Israel.
He will gather the scattered people of Judah
from the ends of the earth.
¹³ Then at last the jealousy between Israel*
and Judah will end.
They will not be rivals anymore.
¹⁴ They will join forces to swoop down on
Philistia to the west.
Together they will attack and plunder the
nations to the east.
They will occupy the lands of Edom and
Moab,
and Ammon will obey them.
¹⁵ The LORD will make a dry path through the
gulf of the Red Sea.*
He will wave his hand over the Euphrates
River,*
sending a mighty wind to divide it into
seven streams
so it can easily be crossed on foot.
¹⁶ He will make a highway for the remnant
of his people,
the remnant coming from Assyria,
just as he did for Israel long ago
when they returned from Egypt.

12 SONGS OF PRAISE FOR SALVATION
¹ In that day you will sing:
"I will praise you, O LORD!
You were angry with me, but not anymore.
Now you comfort me.
² See, God has come to save me.
I will trust in him and not be afraid.
The LORD GOD is my strength and my song;
he has given me victory."

³ With joy you will drink deeply
from the fountain of salvation!
⁴ In that wonderful day you will sing:
"Thank the LORD! Praise his name!
Tell the nations what he has done.
Let them know how mighty he is!
⁵ Sing to the LORD, for he has done wonderful
things.
Make known his praise around the world.
⁶ Let all the people of Jerusalem* shout his
praise with joy!

11:11a Hebrew *in Pathros, Cush.*   11:11b Hebrew *in Shinar.*
11:13 Hebrew *Ephraim,* referring to the northern kingdom of Israel.
11:15a Hebrew *will destroy the tongue of the sea of Egypt.*
11:15b Hebrew *the river.*   12:6 Hebrew *Zion.*

For great is the Holy One of Israel who
lives among you."

13 A MESSAGE ABOUT BABYLON Isaiah son of Amoz received this message concerning the destruction of Babylon:

² "Raise a signal flag on a bare hilltop.
Call up an army against Babylon.
Wave your hand to encourage them
as they march into the palaces of the high
and mighty.
³ I, the LORD, have dedicated these soldiers
for this task.
Yes, I have called mighty warriors to
express my anger,
and they will rejoice when I am exalted."

⁴ Hear the noise on the mountains!
Listen, as the vast armies march!
It is the noise and shouting of many nations.
The LORD of Heaven's Armies has called
this army together.
⁵ They come from distant countries,
from beyond the farthest horizons.
They are the LORD's weapons to carry out
his anger.
With them he will destroy the
whole land.

⁶ Scream in terror, for the day of the LORD has
arrived—
the time for the Almighty to destroy.
⁷ Every arm is paralyzed with fear.
Every heart melts,
⁸ and people are terrified.
Pangs of anguish grip them,
like those of a woman in labor.
They look helplessly at one another,
their faces aflame with fear.

⁹ For see, the day of the LORD is coming—
the terrible day of his fury and fierce
anger.
The land will be made desolate,
and all the sinners destroyed with it.
¹⁰ The heavens will be black above them;
the stars will give no light.
The sun will be dark when it rises,
and the moon will provide no light.

¹¹ "I, the LORD, will punish the world for its evil
and the wicked for their sin.
I will crush the arrogance of the proud
and humble the pride of the mighty.
¹² I will make people scarcer than gold—
more rare than the fine gold of Ophir.
¹³ For I will shake the heavens.
The earth will move from its place

when the LORD of Heaven's Armies displays
his wrath
in the day of his fierce anger."

¹⁴ Everyone in Babylon will run about like a
hunted gazelle,
like sheep without a shepherd.
They will try to find their own people
and flee to their own land.
¹⁵ Anyone who is captured will be cut down—
run through with a sword.
¹⁶ Their little children will be dashed to death
before their eyes.
Their homes will be sacked, and their
wives will be raped.

¹⁷ "Look, I will stir up the Medes against
Babylon.
They cannot be tempted by silver
or bribed with gold.
¹⁸ The attacking armies will shoot down the
young men with arrows.
They will have no mercy on helpless
babies
and will show no compassion for
children."

¹⁹ Babylon, the most glorious of kingdoms,
the flower of Chaldean pride,
will be devastated like Sodom and
Gomorrah
when God destroyed them.
²⁰ Babylon will never be inhabited again.
It will remain empty for generation after
generation.
Nomads will refuse to camp there,
and shepherds will not bed down their
sheep.
²¹ Desert animals will move into the ruined
city,
and the houses will be haunted by
howling creatures.
Owls will live among the ruins,
and wild goats will go there to dance.
²² Hyenas will howl in its fortresses,

and jackals will make dens in its luxurious
palaces.
Babylon's days are numbered;
its time of destruction will soon arrive.

14 **A TAUNT FOR BABYLON'S KING** But
the LORD will have mercy on the descendants of Jacob. He will choose Israel as
his special people once again. He will bring
them back to settle once again in their own
land. And people from many different nations
will come and join them there and unite with
the people of Israel.* ²The nations of the world
will help the LORD's people to return, and those
who come to live in their land will serve them.
Those who captured Israel will themselves be
captured, and Israel will rule over its enemies.
³In that wonderful day when the LORD gives
his people rest from sorrow and fear, from slavery and chains, ⁴you will taunt the king of Babylon. You will say,

"The mighty man has been destroyed.
Yes, your insolence* is ended.
⁵ For the LORD has crushed your wicked
power
and broken your evil rule.
⁶ You struck the people with endless blows
of rage
and held the nations in your angry grip
with unrelenting tyranny.
⁷ But finally the earth is at rest and quiet.
Now it can sing again!
⁸ Even the trees of the forest—
the cypress trees and the cedars
of Lebanon—
sing out this joyous song:
'Since you have been cut down,
no one will come now to cut us down!'

⁹ "In the place of the dead* there is
excitement
over your arrival.
The spirits of world leaders and mighty
kings long dead
stand up to see you.
¹⁰ With one voice they all cry out,
'Now you are as weak as we are!
¹¹ Your might and power were buried
with you.*
The sound of the harp in your palace has
ceased.
Now maggots are your sheet,
and worms your blanket.'

....

UTTER RUIN
*(13:20) Even before Babylon became a world power, Isa-
iah prophesied that its destruction would be so complete
that it would never rise again. The city was conquered in
539 B.C. by Cyrus. The details of Isaiah's prophecy may
not be fulfilled until the end times.*

POWER FAILURE
*(14:1-6) God permitted Babylon to have power for a pur-
pose—to chastise his wayward people (see 47:1-9). When
that purpose ended, so did the power. Earthly power is
temporary. If you don't believe that, consider the ex-pol-
iticians you read about in the news. Is your confidence in
human power or in God? Only God's power is everlasting.*

14:1 Hebrew *the house of Jacob.* The names "Jacob" and "Israel"
are often interchanged throughout the Old Testament, referring
sometimes to the individual patriarch and sometimes to the nation.
14:4 As in Dead Sea Scrolls; the meaning of the Masoretic Text is
uncertain.   **14:9** Hebrew *Sheol;* also in 14:15.   **14:11** Hebrew *were
brought down to Sheol.*

¹² "How you are fallen from heaven,
O shining star, son of the morning!
You have been thrown down to the earth,
you who destroyed the nations of the
world.
¹³ For you said to yourself,
'I will ascend to heaven and set my throne
above God's stars.
I will preside on the mountain of the gods
far away in the north.*
¹⁴ I will climb to the highest heavens
and be like the Most High.'
¹⁵ Instead, you will be brought down to the
place of the dead,
down to its lowest depths.
¹⁶ Everyone there will stare at you and ask,
'Can this be the one who shook the earth
and made the kingdoms of the world
tremble?
¹⁷ Is this the one who destroyed the world
and made it into a wasteland?
Is this the king who demolished the world's
greatest cities
and had no mercy on his prisoners?'

¹⁸ "The kings of the nations lie in
stately glory,
each in his own tomb,
¹⁹ but you will be thrown out of your grave
like a worthless branch.
Like a corpse trampled underfoot,
you will be dumped into a mass grave
with those killed in battle.
You will descend to the pit.
²⁰ You will not be given a proper burial,
for you have destroyed your nation
and slaughtered your people.
The descendants of such an evil person
will never again receive honor.
²¹ Kill this man's children!
Let them die because of their father's
sins!
They must not rise and conquer the earth,
filling the world with their cities."

²² This is what the Lord of Heaven's Armies
says:
"I, myself, have risen against Babylon!
I will destroy its children and its children's
children,"
says the Lord.
²³ "I will make Babylon a desolate place
of owls,
filled with swamps and marshes.
I will sweep the land with the broom
of destruction.

I, the Lord of Heaven's Armies, have
spoken!"

A MESSAGE ABOUT ASSYRIA ²⁴The Lord of Heaven's Armies has sworn this oath:

"It will all happen as I have planned.
It will be as I have decided.
²⁵ I will break the Assyrians when they are in
Israel;
I will trample them on my mountains.
My people will no longer be their slaves
nor bow down under their heavy loads.
²⁶ I have a plan for the whole earth,
a hand of judgment upon all the nations.
²⁷ The Lord of Heaven's Armies has spoken—
who can change his plans?
When his hand is raised,
who can stop him?"

A MESSAGE ABOUT PHILISTIA ²⁸This message came to me the year King Ahaz died:*

²⁹ Do not rejoice, you Philistines,
that the rod that struck you is broken—
that the king who attacked you is dead.
For from that snake a more poisonous snake
will be born,
a fiery serpent to destroy you!
³⁰ I will feed the poor in my pasture;
the needy will lie down in peace.
But as for you, I will wipe you out with famine
and destroy the few who remain.
³¹ Wail at the gates! Weep in the cities!
Melt with fear, you Philistines!
A powerful army comes like smoke from the
north.
Each soldier rushes forward eager to
fight.

³²What should we tell the Philistine messengers? Tell them,

"The Lord has built Jerusalem*;
its walls will give refuge to his oppressed
people."

15 A MESSAGE ABOUT MOAB This message came to me concerning Moab:

In one night the town of Ar will be leveled,
and the city of Kir will be destroyed.
² Your people will go to their temple in Dibon
to mourn.
They will go to their sacred shrines to
weep.
They will wail for the fate of Nebo and
Medeba,
shaving their heads in sorrow and cutting
off their beards.

14:13 Or *on the heights of Zaphon.*   **14:28** King Ahaz died in 715 B.C.
14:32 Hebrew *Zion.*

³ They will wear burlap as they wander the
streets.
From every home and public square will
come the sound of wailing.
⁴ The people of Heshbon and Elealeh will
cry out;
their voices will be heard as far away as
Jahaz!
The bravest warriors of Moab will cry out in
utter terror.
They will be helpless with fear.

⁵ My heart weeps for Moab.
Its people flee to Zoar and
Eglath-shelishiyah.
Weeping, they climb the road to Luhith.
Their cries of distress can be heard all
along the road to Horonaim.
⁶ Even the waters of Nimrim are dried up!
The grassy banks are scorched.
The tender plants are gone;
nothing green remains.
⁷ The people grab their possessions
and carry them across the Ravine
of Willows.
⁸ A cry of distress echoes through the land
of Moab
from one end to the other—
from Eglaim to Beer-elim.
⁹ The stream near Dibon* runs red with blood,
but I am still not finished with Dibon!
Lions will hunt down the survivors—
both those who try to escape
and those who remain behind.

16

¹ Send lambs from Sela as tribute
to the ruler of the land.
Send them through the desert
to the mountain of beautiful Zion.
² The women of Moab are left like homeless
birds
at the shallow crossings of the Arnon
River.
³ "Help us," they cry.
"Defend us against our enemies.

Protect us from their relentless attack.
Do not betray us now that we have
escaped.
⁴ Let our refugees stay among you.
Hide them from our enemies until the
terror is past."

When oppression and destruction have
ended
and enemy raiders have disappeared,
⁵ then God will establish one of David's
descendants as king.
He will rule with mercy and truth.
He will always do what is just
and be eager to do what is right.

⁶ We have heard about proud Moab—
about its pride and arrogance and rage.
But all that boasting has disappeared.
⁷ The entire land of Moab weeps.
Yes, everyone in Moab mourns
for the cakes of raisins from Kir-hareseth.
They are all gone now.
⁸ The farms of Heshbon are abandoned;
the vineyards at Sibmah are deserted.
The rulers of the nations have broken down
Moab—
that beautiful grapevine.
Its tendrils spread north as far as the town
of Jazer
and trailed eastward into the
wilderness.
Its shoots reached so far west
that they crossed over the Dead Sea.*

⁹ So now I weep for Jazer and the vineyards
of Sibmah;
my tears will flow for Heshbon and
Elealeh.
There are no more shouts of joy
over your summer fruits and harvest.
¹⁰ Gone now is the gladness,
gone the joy of harvest.
There will be no singing in the vineyards,
no more happy shouts,
no treading of grapes in the winepresses.
I have ended all their harvest joys.
¹¹ My heart's cry for Moab is like a lament
on a harp.
I am filled with anguish for
Kir-hareseth.*
¹² The people of Moab will worship at their
pagan shrines,
but it will do them no good.
They will cry to the gods in their temples,
but no one will be able to save them.

THE ENEMY

*(15:1-9) Ever know someone who seemed to constantly
make trouble for you or someone else? The nation of
Moab was like that. The Moabites were descendants
of Lot through his incestuous relationship with his older
daughter (Gen 19:31-38). They invaded Israel (Judg
3:12-14) and fought against the armies of Saul (1 Sam
14:47) and David (2 Sam 8:2, 11-12). They were like
mosquitoes—persistently annoying. But Isaiah prophesied that Moab would be punished for its harsh treatment
of Israel. If you've despaired over the persistence of an
enemy, consider the example of Moab. Sooner or later,
God will bring all evil to an end.*

15:9 As in Dead Sea Scrolls, some Greek manuscripts, and Latin
Vulgate; Masoretic Text reads *Dimon;* also in 15:9b.   16:8 Hebrew
the sea.   16:11 Hebrew *Kir-heres,* a variant spelling of Kir-hareseth.

¹³The LORD has already said these things about Moab in the past. ¹⁴But now the LORD says, "Within three years, counting each day,* the glory of Moab will be ended. From its great population, only a few of its people will be left alive."

17 A MESSAGE ABOUT DAMASCUS AND ISRAEL This message came to me concerning Damascus:

"Look, the city of Damascus will disappear!
    It will become a heap of ruins.
² The towns of Aroer will be deserted.
    Flocks will graze in the streets and lie
        down undisturbed,
    with no one to chase them away.
³ The fortified towns of Israel* will also be
        destroyed,
    and the royal power of Damascus will
        end.
All that remains of Syria*
    will share the fate of Israel's departed
        glory,"
    declares the LORD of Heaven's Armies.

⁴ "In that day Israel's* glory will grow dim;
    its robust body will waste away.
⁵ The whole land will look like a grainfield
    after the harvesters have gathered the
        grain.
It will be desolate,
    like the fields in the valley of Rephaim
        after the harvest.
⁶ Only a few of its people will be left,
    like stray olives left on a tree after the
        harvest.
Only two or three remain in the highest
        branches,
    four or five scattered here and there
        on the limbs,"
    declares the LORD, the God of Israel.

⁷ Then at last the people will look to their
        Creator
    and turn their eyes to the Holy One of
        Israel.
⁸ They will no longer look to their idols for
        help
    or worship what their own hands have
        made.
They will never again bow down to their
        Asherah poles

or worship at the pagan shrines they have
        built.
⁹ Their largest cities will be like a deserted
        forest,
    like the land the Hivites and Amorites
        abandoned*
when the Israelites came here so long ago.
    It will be utterly desolate.
¹⁰ Why? Because you have turned from the
        God who can save you.
    You have forgotten the Rock who can
        hide you.
So you may plant the finest grapevines
    and import the most expensive seedlings.
¹¹ They may sprout on the day you set them
        out;
    yes, they may blossom on the very
        morning you plant them,
but you will never pick any grapes from
        them.
    Your only harvest will be a load of grief
        and unrelieved pain.

¹² Listen! The armies of many nations
    roar like the roaring of the sea.
Hear the thunder of the mighty forces
    as they rush forward like thundering
        waves.
¹³ But though they thunder like breakers on
        a beach,
    God will silence them, and they will run
        away.
They will flee like chaff scattered by the
        wind,
    like a tumbleweed whirling before a
        storm.
¹⁴ In the evening Israel waits in terror,
    but by dawn its enemies are dead.
This is the just reward of those who
        plunder us,
    a fitting end for those who destroy us.

18 A MESSAGE ABOUT ETHIOPIA

¹ Listen, Ethiopia*—land of fluttering sails*
    that lies at the headwaters of the Nile,
² that sends ambassadors
    in swift boats down the river.

Go, swift messengers!
Take a message to a tall, smooth-skinned
        people,
    who are feared far and wide
for their conquests and destruction,
    and whose land is divided by rivers.

³ All you people of the world,
    everyone who lives on the earth—

16:14 Hebrew *Within three years, as a servant bound by contract would count them.* 17:3a Hebrew *of Ephraim,* referring to the northern kingdom of Israel. 17:3b Hebrew *Aram.* 17:4 Hebrew *Jacob's.* See note on 14:1. 17:9 As in Greek version; Hebrew reads *like places of the wood and the highest bough.* 18:1a Hebrew *Cush.* 18:1b Or *land of many locusts;* Hebrew reads *land of whirring wings.*

when I raise my battle flag on the mountain,
　look!
When I blow the ram's horn, listen!
⁴ For the LORD has told me this:
"I will watch quietly from my dwelling
　place—
　as quietly as the heat rises on a summer
　　day,
　or as the morning dew forms during the
　　harvest."
⁵ Even before you begin your attack,
　while your plans are ripening like
　　grapes,
the LORD will cut off your new growth with
　pruning shears.
He will snip off and discard your
　spreading branches.
⁶ Your mighty army will be left dead in the
　fields
for the mountain vultures and wild
　animals.
The vultures will tear at the corpses all
　summer.
The wild animals will gnaw at the bones
　all winter.

⁷ At that time the LORD of Heaven's Armies
　will receive gifts
from this land divided by rivers,
from this tall, smooth-skinned people,
　who are feared far and wide for their
　　conquests and destruction.
They will bring the gifts to Jerusalem,*
　where the LORD of Heaven's Armies
　　dwells.

19 A MESSAGE ABOUT EGYPT This message came to me concerning Egypt:

Look! The LORD is advancing against Egypt,
　riding on a swift cloud.
The idols of Egypt tremble.
　The hearts of the Egyptians melt
　　with fear.

² "I will make Egyptian fight against
　Egyptian—
　brother against brother,
neighbor against neighbor,
　city against city,
　province against province.
³ The Egyptians will lose heart,
　and I will confuse their plans.
They will plead with their idols for wisdom
　and call on spirits, mediums, and those
　who consult the spirits of the dead.
⁴ I will hand Egypt over
　to a hard, cruel master.

A fierce king will rule them,"
　says the Lord, the LORD of Heaven's
　　Armies.

⁵ The waters of the Nile will fail to rise and
　flood the fields.
The riverbed will be parched and dry.
⁶ The canals of the Nile will dry up,
　and the streams of Egypt will stink
　with rotting reeds and rushes.
⁷ All the greenery along the riverbank
　and all the crops along the river
　will dry up and blow away.
⁸ The fishermen will lament for lack of work.
　Those who cast hooks into the Nile will
　　groan,
　and those who use nets will lose heart.
⁹ There will be no flax for the harvesters,
　no thread for the weavers.
¹⁰ They will be in despair,
　and all the workers will be sick at heart.

¹¹ What fools are the officials of Zoan!
　Their best counsel to the king of Egypt
　　is stupid and wrong.
Will they still boast to Pharaoh of their
　wisdom?
Will they dare brag about all their wise
　ancestors?
¹² Where are your wise counselors, Pharaoh?
　Let them tell you what God plans,
　what the LORD of Heaven's Armies is
　　going to do to Egypt.
¹³ The officials of Zoan are fools,
　and the officials of Memphis* are
　　deluded.
The leaders of the people
　have led Egypt astray.
¹⁴ The LORD has sent a spirit of foolishness
　on them,
　so all their suggestions are wrong.
They cause Egypt to stagger
　like a drunk in his vomit.
¹⁵ There is nothing Egypt can do.
　All are helpless—
the head and the tail,
　the noble palm branch and the lowly
　　reed.

¹⁶In that day the Egyptians will be as weak
as women. They will cower in fear beneath the
upraised fist of the LORD of Heaven's Armies.
¹⁷Just to speak the name of Israel will terrorize
them, for the LORD of Heaven's Armies has laid
out his plans against them.

¹⁸In that day five of Egypt's cities will follow
the LORD of Heaven's Armies. They will even

18:7 Hebrew *to Mount Zion.*　**19:13** Hebrew *Noph.*

begin to speak Hebrew, the language of Canaan. One of these cities will be Heliopolis, the City of the Sun.*

19In that day there will be an altar to the LORD in the heart of Egypt, and there will be a monument to the LORD at its border. 20It will be a sign and a witness that the LORD of Heaven's Armies is worshiped in the land of Egypt. When the people cry to the LORD for help against those who oppress them, he will send them a savior who will rescue them. 21The LORD will make himself known to the Egyptians. Yes, they will know the LORD and will give their sacrifices and offerings to him. They will make a vow to the LORD and will keep it. 22The LORD will strike Egypt, and then he will bring healing. For the Egyptians will turn to the LORD, and he will listen to their pleas and heal them.

23In that day Egypt and Assyria will be connected by a highway. The Egyptians and Assyrians will move freely between their lands, and they will both worship God. 24And Israel will be their ally. The three will be together, and Israel will be a blessing to them. 25For the LORD of Heaven's Armies will say, "Blessed be Egypt, my people. Blessed be Assyria, the land I have made. Blessed be Israel, my special possession!"

20 A MESSAGE ABOUT EGYPT AND ETHIOPIA

In the year when King Sargon of Assyria sent his commander in chief to capture the Philistine city of Ashdod,* 2the LORD told Isaiah son of Amoz, "Take off the burlap you have been wearing, and remove your sandals." Isaiah did as he was told and walked around naked and barefoot.

3Then the LORD said, "My servant Isaiah has been walking around naked and barefoot for the last three years. This is a sign—a symbol of the terrible troubles I will bring upon Egypt and Ethiopia.* 4For the king of Assyria will take away the Egyptians and Ethiopians* as prisoners. He will make them walk naked and barefoot, both young and old, their buttocks bared, to the shame of Egypt. 5Then the Philistines will be thrown into panic, for they counted on the power of Ethiopia and boasted of their allies in Egypt! 6They will say, 'If this can happen to Egypt, what chance do we have? We were counting on Egypt to protect us from the king of Assyria.'"

19:18 Or will be the City of Destruction.   20:1 Ashdod was captured by Assyria in 711 B.C.   20:3 Hebrew Cush; also in 20:5.   20:4 Hebrew Cushites.   21:1 Hebrew concerning the desert by the sea.   21:8 As in Dead Sea Scrolls and Syriac version; Masoretic Text reads a lion.

21 A MESSAGE ABOUT BABYLON

This message came to me concerning Babylon—the desert by the sea*:

Disaster is roaring down on you from the
    desert,
    like a whirlwind sweeping in from the
        Negev.
2 I see a terrifying vision:
    I see the betrayer betraying,
    the destroyer destroying.
Go ahead, you Elamites and Medes,
    attack and lay siege.
I will make an end
    to all the groaning Babylon caused.
3 My stomach aches and burns with pain.
    Sharp pangs of anguish are upon me,
    like those of a woman in labor.
I grow faint when I hear what God is
        planning;
    I am too afraid to look.
4 My mind reels and my heart races.
    I longed for evening to come,
    but now I am terrified of the dark.

5 Look! They are preparing a great feast.
    They are spreading rugs for people to
        sit on.
    Everyone is eating and drinking.
But quick! Grab your shields and prepare
        for battle.
    You are being attacked!

6 Meanwhile, the Lord said to me,
    "Put a watchman on the city wall.
    Let him shout out what he sees.
7 He should look for chariots
    drawn by pairs of horses,
and for riders on donkeys and camels.
    Let the watchman be fully alert."

8 Then the watchman* called out,
    "Day after day I have stood on the
        watchtower, my lord.
    Night after night I have remained at my
        post.
9 Now at last—look!
Here comes a man in a chariot
    with a pair of horses!"

....

UNITY
(19:21-25) Isaiah prophesied that at some future time, the people of Egypt and Assyria would unite and turn to God. That prophecy probably sounded utterly impossible to the people of Israel. After all, Egypt and Assyria were bitter enemies. Yet Jesus breaks down every barrier that threatens relationships. In Christ, people and nations who are poles apart politically will bow at his feet as brothers and sisters. Is there someone you can't imagine ever getting along with? Believe in the Barrier Breaker—Jesus.

Then the watchman said,
"Babylon is fallen, fallen!
All the idols of Babylon
   lie broken on the ground!"
10 O my people, threshed and winnowed,
   I have told you everything the LORD
      of Heaven's Armies has said,
   everything the God of Israel has
      told me.

A MESSAGE ABOUT EDOM
11This message came to me concerning Edom*:

Someone from Edom* keeps calling to me,
   "Watchman, how much longer until
      morning?
   When will the night be over?"
12 The watchman replies,
   "Morning is coming, but night will soon
      return.
   If you wish to ask again, then come back
      and ask."

A MESSAGE ABOUT ARABIA
13This message came to me concerning Arabia:

O caravans from Dedan,
   hide in the deserts of Arabia.
14 O people of Tema,
   bring water to these thirsty people,
   food to these weary refugees.
15 They have fled from the sword,
   from the drawn sword,
from the bent bow
   and the terrors of battle.

16The Lord said to me, "Within a year, counting each day,* all the glory of Kedar will come to an end. 17Only a few of its courageous archers will survive. I, the LORD, the God of Israel, have spoken!"

....

THE NEWS
(21:11-12) *Everyone wants to hear the good news that all troubles are over and that prosperity lies ahead. The watchman tells how to get that good news—turn to God and seek him with all your heart. Without God, the news of world events and the world's future is anything but good. Without God, our personal future is bad news. Spread the good news.*

CONSEQUENCES
(22:4) *Isaiah mourned because of the punishment his people experienced due to their rebellion against God. Sometimes people we care for ignore our attempts to help them. Then we feel helpless as we watch them suffer the consequences of actions we tried to stop. God expects us to be involved with others—this may cause us to suffer with them. Is someone you know experiencing the consequences of wrong actions? You can do one thing for them: Pray for God's mercy.*

22 A MESSAGE ABOUT JERUSALEM
This message came to me concerning Jerusalem—the Valley of Vision*:

What is happening?
   Why is everyone running to the rooftops?
2 The whole city is in a terrible uproar.
   What do I see in this reveling city?
Bodies are lying everywhere,
   killed not in battle but by famine and
      disease.
3 All your leaders have fled.
   They surrendered without resistance.
The people tried to slip away,
   but they were captured, too.
4 That's why I said, "Leave me alone
      to weep;
   do not try to comfort me.
Let me cry for my people
   as I watch them being destroyed."

5 Oh, what a day of crushing defeat!
   What a day of confusion and terror
brought by the Lord, the LORD of Heaven's
      Armies,
   upon the Valley of Vision!
The walls of Jerusalem have been broken,
   and cries of death echo from the
      mountainsides.
6 Elamites are the archers,
   with their chariots and charioteers.
The men of Kir hold up the shields.
7 Chariots fill your beautiful valleys,
   and charioteers storm your gates.
8 Judah's defenses have been stripped away.
   You run to the armory* for your weapons.
9 You inspect the breaks in the walls of
      Jerusalem.*
   You store up water in the lower pool.
10 You survey the houses and tear some down
      for stone to strengthen the walls.
11 Between the city walls, you build a reservoir
      for water from the old pool.
But you never ask for help from the One who
      did all this.
   You never considered the One who
      planned this long ago.

12 At that time the Lord, the LORD of Heaven's
      Armies,
   called you to weep and mourn.
He told you to shave your heads in sorrow
      for your sins

21:11a Hebrew *Dumah*, which means "silence" or "stillness." It is a wordplay on the word *Edom*. 21:11b Hebrew *Seir*, another name for Edom. 21:16 Hebrew *Within a year, as a servant bound by contract would count it.* Some ancient manuscripts read *Within three years*, as in 16:14. 22:1 Hebrew *concerning the Valley of Vision.* 22:8 Hebrew *to the House of the Forest;* see 1 Kgs 7:2-5. 22:9 Hebrew *the city of David.*

and to wear clothes of burlap to show
 your remorse.
¹³ But instead, you dance and play;
 you slaughter cattle and kill sheep.
 You feast on meat and drink wine.
 You say, "Let's feast and drink,
 for tomorrow we die!"

¹⁴The LORD of Heaven's Armies has revealed
this to me: "Till the day you die, you will never
be forgiven for this sin." That is the judgment
of the Lord, the LORD of Heaven's Armies.

A MESSAGE FOR SHEBNA

¹⁵This is what the
Lord, the LORD of Heaven's Armies, said to me:
"Confront Shebna, the palace administrator,
and give him this message:

¹⁶ "Who do you think you are,
 and what are you doing here,
 building a beautiful tomb for yourself—
 a monument high up in the rock?
¹⁷ For the LORD is about to hurl you away,
 mighty man.
 He is going to grab you,
¹⁸ crumple you into a ball,
 and toss you away into a distant, barren
 land.
 There you will die,
 and your glorious chariots will be broken
 and useless.
 You are a disgrace to your master!

¹⁹"Yes, I will drive you out of office," says the
LORD. "I will pull you down from your high position. ²⁰And then I will call my servant Eliakim
son of Hilkiah to replace you. ²¹I will dress him
in your royal robes and will give him your title
and your authority. And he will be a father to
the people of Jerusalem and Judah. ²²I will give
him the key to the house of David—the high-
est position in the royal court. When he opens
doors, no one will be able to close them; when
he closes doors, no one will be able to open
them. ²³He will bring honor to his family name,
for I will drive him firmly in place like a nail in
the wall. ²⁴They will give him great responsibility, and he will bring honor to even the lowliest
members of his family.*"

²⁵But the LORD of Heaven's Armies also says:
"The time will come when I will pull out the nail
that seemed so firm. It will come out and fall to
the ground. Everything it supports will fall with
it. I, the LORD, have spoken!"

^{22:24} Hebrew *They will hang on him all the glory of his father's
house: its offspring and offshoots, all its lesser vessels, from the
bowls to all the jars.* **23:1** Hebrew *Kittim;* also in 23:12.
23:3 Hebrew *from Shihor,* a branch of the Nile River. **23:10** The
meaning of the Hebrew in this verse is uncertain. **23:11** Hebrew
Canaan.

23 A MESSAGE ABOUT TYRE This mes-
sage came to me concerning Tyre:

Weep, O ships of Tarshish,
 for the harbor and houses of Tyre are
 gone!
The rumors you heard in Cyprus*
 are all true.
² Mourn in silence, you people of the coast
 and you merchants of Sidon.
Your traders crossed the sea,
³   sailing over deep waters.
They brought you grain from Egypt*
 and harvests from along the Nile.
You were the marketplace of the world.

⁴ But now you are put to shame, city of Sidon,
 for Tyre, the fortress of the sea, says,
 "Now I am childless;
 I have no sons or daughters."
⁵ When Egypt hears the news about Tyre,
 there will be great sorrow.
⁶ Send word now to Tarshish!
 Wail, you people who live in distant
 lands!
⁷ Is this silent ruin all that is left of your once
 joyous city?
 What a long history was yours!
 Think of all the colonists you sent to
 distant places.

⁸ Who has brought this disaster on Tyre,
 that great creator of kingdoms?
Her traders were all princes,
 her merchants were nobles.
⁹ The LORD of Heaven's Armies has done it
 to destroy your pride
 and bring low all earth's nobility.
¹⁰ Come, people of Tarshish,
 sweep over the land like the flooding
 Nile,
 for Tyre is defenseless.*
¹¹ The LORD held out his hand over the sea
 and shook the kingdoms of the earth.
He has spoken out against Phoenicia,*
 ordering that her fortresses be destroyed.
¹² He says, "Never again will you rejoice,
 O daughter of Sidon, for you have been
 crushed.
Even if you flee to Cyprus,
 you will find no rest."

HOPE
(22:13-14) *The people of Israel said that they might as
well "feast and drink" because they had given up hope.
Today, people who have given up hope usually respond in
one of two ways: despair or self-indulgence. But neither
response helps the person or the situation. A more helpful response is to turn to God and trust in his promises.*

¹³ Look at the land of Babylonia*—
    the people of that land are gone!
The Assyrians have handed Babylon over
    to the wild animals of the desert.
They have built siege ramps against its
    walls,
    torn down its palaces,
    and turned it to a heap of rubble.

¹⁴ Wail, O ships of Tarshish,
    for your harbor is destroyed!

¹⁵For seventy years, the length of a king's life, Tyre will be forgotten. But then the city will come back to life as in the song about the prostitute:

¹⁶ Take a harp and walk the streets,
    you forgotten harlot.
Make sweet melody and sing your songs
    so you will be remembered again.

¹⁷Yes, after seventy years the LORD will revive Tyre. But she will be no different than she was before. She will again be a prostitute to all kingdoms around the world. ¹⁸But in the end her profits will be given to the LORD. Her wealth will not be hoarded but will provide good food and fine clothing for the LORD's priests.

24 DESTRUCTION OF THE EARTH

¹ Look! The LORD is about to destroy the earth
    and make it a vast wasteland.
He devastates the surface of the earth
    and scatters the people.
² Priests and laypeople,
    servants and masters,
    maids and mistresses,
    buyers and sellers,
    lenders and borrowers,
    bankers and debtors—none will be
    spared.
³ The earth will be completely emptied and
    looted.
    The LORD has spoken!

⁴ The earth mourns and dries up,
    and the crops waste away and wither.

Even the greatest people on earth waste
    away.
⁵ The earth suffers for the sins of its people,
    for they have twisted God's instructions,
    violated his laws,
    and broken his everlasting covenant.
⁶ Therefore, a curse consumes the earth.
    Its people must pay the price for
    their sin.
They are destroyed by fire,
    and only a few are left alive.
⁷ The grapevines waste away,
    and there is no new wine.
All the merrymakers sigh and mourn.
⁸ The cheerful sound of tambourines is
    stilled;
    the happy cries of celebration are heard
    no more.
The melodious chords of the harp are
    silent.
⁹ Gone are the joys of wine and song;
    alcoholic drink turns bitter in the mouth.
¹⁰ The city writhes in chaos;
    every home is locked to keep out
    intruders.
¹¹ Mobs gather in the streets, crying out
    for wine.
Joy has turned to gloom.
Gladness has been banished from
    the land.
¹² The city is left in ruins,
    its gates battered down.
¹³ Throughout the earth the story is the
    same—
    only a remnant is left,
like the stray olives left on the tree
    or the few grapes left on the vine after
    harvest.

¹⁴ But all who are left shout and sing for joy.
    Those in the west praise the LORD's
    majesty.
¹⁵ In eastern lands, give glory to the LORD.
    In the lands beyond the sea, praise the
    name of the LORD, the God of Israel.
¹⁶ We hear songs of praise from the ends of
    the earth,
    songs that give glory to the Righteous
    One!

But my heart is heavy with grief.
    Weep for me, for I wither away.
Deceit still prevails,
    and treachery is everywhere.
¹⁷ Terror and traps and snares will be
    your lot,
    you people of the earth.

23:13 Or *Chaldea.*

DETER DETERIORATION
(24:1-13) *The land of Israel reflected the consequences of the nation's rebellion. Crops withered or wouldn't grow. Today we see the results of sin in our own land—pollution, crime, poverty, and more. Sin affects every aspect of society so extensively that even those faithful to God suffer. We cannot blame God for these conditions because we humans have brought them on ourselves. Yet we believers can slow our society's deterioration by our examples of faithfulness toward God and others. Are you ready to make a difference?*

18 Those who flee in terror will fall into a trap,
    and those who escape the trap will be
        caught in a snare.

    Destruction falls like rain from the heavens;
        the foundations of the earth shake.
19 The earth has broken up.
    It has utterly collapsed;
        it is violently shaken.
20 The earth staggers like a drunk.
    It trembles like a tent in a storm.
    It falls and will not rise again,
        for the guilt of its rebellion is very heavy.

21 In that day the LORD will punish the gods
    in the heavens
        and the proud rulers of the nations on
            earth.
22 They will be rounded up and put in prison.
    They will be shut up in prison
        and will finally be punished.
23 Then the glory of the moon will wane,
    and the brightness of the sun will fade,
        for the LORD of Heaven's Armies will rule
            on Mount Zion.
        He will rule in great glory in Jerusalem,
            in the sight of all the leaders of his
                people.

25 PRAISE FOR JUDGMENT AND SALVATION

1 O LORD, I will honor and praise your name,
    for you are my God.
    You do such wonderful things!
        You planned them long ago,
            and now you have accomplished them.
2 You turn mighty cities into heaps of ruins.
    Cities with strong walls are turned to
        rubble.
    Beautiful palaces in distant lands disappear
        and will never be rebuilt.
3 Therefore, strong nations will declare your
    glory;
        ruthless nations will fear you.

4 But you are a tower of refuge to the poor,
    O LORD,
        a tower of refuge to the needy in distress.
    You are a refuge from the storm
        and a shelter from the heat.
    For the oppressive acts of ruthless people
        are like a storm beating against a wall,
5   or like the relentless heat of the desert.
    But you silence the roar of foreign nations.
        As the shade of a cloud cools relentless
            heat,

25:6 Hebrew *On this mountain;* also in 25:10.   **25:8** Greek version
reads *Death is swallowed up in victory.* Compare 1 Cor 15:54.

so the boastful songs of ruthless people
    are stilled.

6 In Jerusalem,* the LORD of Heaven's Armies
    will spread a wonderful feast
    for all the people of the world.
    It will be a delicious banquet
        with clear, well-aged wine and choice
            meat.
7 There he will remove the cloud of gloom,
    the shadow of death that hangs over the
        earth.
8 He will swallow up death forever!*
    The Sovereign LORD will wipe away all
        tears.
    He will remove forever all insults and
        mockery
        against his land and people.
    The LORD has spoken!

9 In that day the people will proclaim,
    "This is our God!
    We trusted in him, and he saved us!
    This is the LORD, in whom we trusted.
        Let us rejoice in the salvation he brings!"
10 For the LORD's hand of blessing will rest on
    Jerusalem.
    But Moab will be crushed.
        It will be like straw trampled down and
            left to rot.
11 God will push down Moab's people
    as a swimmer pushes down water with
        his hands.
    He will end their pride
        and all their evil works.
12 The high walls of Moab will be demolished.
    They will be brought down to the ground,
        down into the dust.

26 A SONG OF PRAISE TO THE LORD   In
that day, everyone in the land of Judah
will sing this song:

Our city is strong!
    We are surrounded by the walls of God's
        salvation.
2 Open the gates to all who are righteous;
    allow the faithful to enter.
3 You will keep in perfect peace

....

FIX YOUR EYES
*(26:3) Here's an experiment for you: Try not to think
about rabbits. Ready? Go. You're thinking of them, aren't
you? Essentially this is Isaiah's message. (No, not rabbits.
Forget about them.) Whatever you "fix" your mind on
affects your life. If you're fixated on problems, you'll be
filled with fear. If you focus on God, as Isaiah suggests,
you will be kept "in perfect peace" (see Phil 4:8 also).
Okay. You can stop thinking about rabbits now.*
....

YOU WILL KEEP IN PERFECT PEACE
ALL WHO TRUST IN YOU,
ALL WHOSE THOUGHTS
ARE FIXED ON YOU! { ISAIAH 26:3 }

all who trust in you,
  all whose thoughts are fixed on you!
4 Trust in the LORD always,
  for the LORD GOD is the eternal Rock.
5 He humbles the proud
  and brings down the arrogant city.
  He brings it down to the dust.
6 The poor and oppressed trample it
    underfoot,
  and the needy walk all over it.

7 But for those who are righteous,
  the way is not steep and rough.
You are a God who does what is right,
  and you smooth out the path ahead
    of them.
8 LORD, we show our trust in you by obeying
    your laws;
  our heart's desire is to glorify your name.
9 All night long I search for you;
  in the morning I earnestly seek for God.
For only when you come to judge the earth
  will people learn what is right.
10 Your kindness to the wicked
  does not make them do good.
Although others do right, the wicked keep
    doing wrong
  and take no notice of the LORD's majesty.
11 O LORD, they pay no attention to your
    upraised fist.
  Show them your eagerness to defend
    your people.
Then they will be ashamed.
  Let your fire consume your enemies.

12 LORD, you will grant us peace;
  all we have accomplished is really
    from you.
13 O LORD our God, others have ruled us,
  but you alone are the one we worship.
14 Those we served before are dead and gone.

- -

SECRET PLOTS
(26:21) When God comes to judge the earth, the guilty
will find no place to hide. Jesus said that secret plots will
become public information because his truth, like a light
shining in a dark corner, will reveal them (Matt 10:26).
Instead of trying to hide your shameful thoughts and
actions from God, confess them to him and receive his
forgiveness.

Their departed spirits will never return!
You attacked them and destroyed them,
  and they are long forgotten.
15 O LORD, you have made our nation great;
  yes, you have made us great.
You have extended our borders,
  and we give you the glory!

16 LORD, in distress we searched for you.
  We prayed beneath the burden of your
    discipline.
17 Just as a pregnant woman
  writhes and cries out in pain as she gives
    birth,
  so were we in your presence, LORD.
18 We, too, writhe in agony,
  but nothing comes of our suffering.
We have not given salvation to the earth,
  nor brought life into the world.
19 But those who die in the LORD will live;
  their bodies will rise again!
Those who sleep in the earth
  will rise up and sing for joy!
For your life-giving light will fall like dew
  on your people in the place of the dead!

RESTORATION FOR ISRAEL
20 Go home, my people,
  and lock your doors!
Hide yourselves for a little while
  until the LORD's anger has passed.
21 Look! The LORD is coming from heaven
  to punish the people of the earth for
    their sins.
The earth will no longer hide those who
  have been killed.
  They will be brought out for all to see.

27 In that day the LORD will take his terrible, swift sword and punish Leviathan,* the swiftly moving serpent, the coiling,
writhing serpent. He will kill the dragon of the
sea.

2 "In that day,
  sing about the fruitful vineyard.
3 I, the LORD, will watch over it,
  watering it carefully.
Day and night I will watch so no one can
  harm it.
4   My anger will be gone.
If I find briers and thorns growing,
  I will attack them;
I will burn them up—
5   unless they turn to me for help.
Let them make peace with me;

27:1 The identification of Leviathan is disputed, ranging from an
earthly creature to a mythical sea monster in ancient literature.

yes, let them make peace with me."
6 The time is coming when Jacob's
    descendants will take root.
  Israel will bud and blossom
    and fill the whole earth with fruit!

7 Has the LORD struck Israel
    as he struck her enemies?
  Has he punished her
    as he punished them?
8 No, but he exiled Israel to call her to
    account.
  She was exiled from her land
    as though blown away in a storm from
    the east.
9 The LORD did this to purge Israel's*
    wickedness,
    to take away all her sin.
  As a result, all the pagan altars will be
    crushed to dust.
    No Asherah pole or pagan shrine will be
    left standing.
10 The fortified towns will be silent and empty,
    the houses abandoned, the streets
    overgrown with weeds.
  Calves will graze there,
    chewing on twigs and branches.
11 The people are like the dead branches
    of a tree,
    broken off and used for kindling beneath
    the cooking pots.
  Israel is a foolish and stupid nation,
    for its people have turned away from God.
  Therefore, the one who made them
    will show them no pity or mercy.

12 Yet the time will come when the LORD will
gather them together like handpicked grain.
One by one he will gather them—from the
Euphrates River* in the east to the Brook of
Egypt in the west. 13 In that day the great trumpet will sound. Many who were dying in exile
in Assyria and Egypt will return to Jerusalem to
worship the LORD on his holy mountain.

28 A MESSAGE ABOUT SAMARIA
1 What sorrow awaits the proud city
    of Samaria—
  the glorious crown of the drunks
    of Israel.*
  It sits at the head of a fertile valley,
    but its glorious beauty will fade like
    a flower.

27:9 Hebrew *Jacob's.* See note on 14:1.   27:12 Hebrew *the river.*
28:1 Hebrew *What sorrow awaits the crowning glory of the drunks
of Ephraim,* referring to Samaria, capital of the northern kingdom
of Israel.   28:3 Hebrew *The crowning glory of the drunks of
Ephraim;* see note on 28:1.

It is the pride of a people
    brought down by wine.
2 For the Lord will send a mighty army
    against it.
  Like a mighty hailstorm and a torrential
    rain,
  they will burst upon it like a surging flood
    and smash it to the ground.
3 The proud city of Samaria—
    the glorious crown of the drunks
    of Israel*—
  will be trampled beneath its enemies'
    feet.
4 It sits at the head of a fertile valley,
    but its glorious beauty will fade like
    a flower.
  Whoever sees it will snatch it up,
    as an early fig is quickly picked and
    eaten.

5 Then at last the LORD of Heaven's Armies
    will himself be Israel's glorious crown.
  He will be the pride and joy
    of the remnant of his people.
6 He will give a longing for justice
    to their judges.
  He will give great courage
    to their warriors who stand at the gates.

7 Now, however, Israel is led by drunks
    who reel with wine and stagger with
    alcohol.
  The priests and prophets stagger with
    alcohol
    and lose themselves in wine.
  They reel when they see visions
    and stagger as they render decisions.
8 Their tables are covered with vomit;
    filth is everywhere.
9 "Who does the LORD think we are?"
    they ask.
  "Why does he speak to us like this?
  Are we little children,
    just recently weaned?
10 He tells us everything over and over—
    one line at a time,
    one line at a time,

AGAIN AND AGAIN
(28:1-13) God used repetition and simple words to get
his messages through to the people. Do you find that God
has to teach you the same lessons over and over? The
simplicity of God's message can be a stumbling block for
some (28:9-10), leading them to think it must have little
value. But some of the simplest messages (for example,
Jesus loves you) can have a profound impact. What messages have you heard again and again? Maybe it's time
you listened.

a little here,
  and a little there!"

¹¹ So now God will have to speak to his people
    through foreign oppressors who speak a
    strange language!
¹² God has told his people,
  "Here is a place of rest;
    let the weary rest here.
  This is a place of quiet rest."
    But they would not listen.
¹³ So the Lord will spell out his message for
    them again,
  one line at a time,
    one line at a time,
  a little here,
    and a little there,
  so that they will stumble and fall.
    They will be injured, trapped, and
    captured.

¹⁴ Therefore, listen to this message from
    the Lord,
  you scoffing rulers in Jerusalem.
¹⁵ You boast, "We have struck a bargain to
    cheat death
  and have made a deal to dodge the
    grave.*
  The coming destruction can never touch us,
    for we have built a strong refuge made of
    lies and deception."

¹⁶ Therefore, this is what the Sovereign Lord
    says:
  "Look! I am placing a foundation stone in
    Jerusalem,*
  a firm and tested stone.
  It is a precious cornerstone that is safe to
    build on.
    Whoever believes need never be
    shaken.*
¹⁷ I will test you with the measuring line of
    justice
  and the plumb line of righteousness.
  Since your refuge is made of lies,
    a hailstorm will knock it down.
  Since it is made of deception,
    a flood will sweep it away.
¹⁸ I will cancel the bargain you made to cheat
    death,
  and I will overturn your deal to dodge the
    grave.
  When the terrible enemy sweeps through,
    you will be trampled into the ground.
¹⁹ Again and again that flood will come,
    morning after morning,
  day and night,
    until you are carried away."

This message will bring terror to your
    people.
²⁰ The bed you have made is too short to
    lie on.
  The blankets are too narrow to cover you.
²¹ The Lord will come as he did against the
    Philistines at Mount Perazim
  and against the Amorites at Gibeon.
  He will come to do a strange thing;
    he will come to do an unusual deed:
²² For the Lord, the Lord of Heaven's Armies,
    has plainly said that he is determined to
    crush the whole land.
  So scoff no more,
    or your punishment will be even greater.

²³ Listen to me;
    listen, and pay close attention.
²⁴ Does a farmer always plow and never sow?
  Is he forever cultivating the soil and never
    planting?
²⁵ Does he not finally plant his seeds—
    black cumin, cumin, wheat, barley, and
    emmer wheat—
  each in its proper way,
    and each in its proper place?
²⁶ The farmer knows just what to do,
    for God has given him understanding.
²⁷ A heavy sledge is never used to thresh
    black cumin;
  rather, it is beaten with a light stick.
  A threshing wheel is never rolled on cumin;
    instead, it is beaten lightly with a flail.
²⁸ Grain for bread is easily crushed,
    so he doesn't keep on pounding it.
  He threshes it under the wheels of a cart,
    but he doesn't pulverize it.
²⁹ The Lord of Heaven's Armies is a wonderful
    teacher,
  and he gives the farmer great wisdom.

29 A MESSAGE ABOUT JERUSALEM

¹ "What sorrow awaits Ariel,* the City of
    David.
  Year after year you celebrate your feasts.
² Yet I will bring disaster upon you,
    and there will be much weeping and
    sorrow.
  For Jerusalem will become what her name
    Ariel means—
    an altar covered with blood.
³ I will be your enemy,

28:15 Hebrew Sheol; also in 28:18. 28:16a Hebrew in Zion.
28:16b Greek version reads Look! I am placing a stone in the
foundation of Jerusalem [literally Zion], / a precious cornerstone for
its foundation, chosen for great honor. / Anyone who trusts in him
will never be disgraced. Compare Rom 9:33; 1 Pet 2:6. 29:1 Ariel
sounds like a Hebrew term that means "hearth" or "altar."

surrounding Jerusalem and attacking its
    walls.
I will build siege towers
    and destroy it.
⁴ Then deep from the earth you will speak;
    from low in the dust your words will come.
Your voice will whisper from the ground
    like a ghost conjured up from the grave.

⁵ "But suddenly, your ruthless enemies will
        be crushed
    like the finest of dust.
Your many attackers will be driven away
    like chaff before the wind.
Suddenly, in an instant,
⁶ I, the LORD of Heaven's Armies, will act
        for you
with thunder and earthquake and great
        noise,
    with whirlwind and storm and
        consuming fire.
⁷ All the nations fighting against Jerusalem*
    will vanish like a dream!
Those who are attacking her walls
    will vanish like a vision in the night.
⁸ A hungry person dreams of eating
    but wakes up still hungry.
A thirsty person dreams of drinking

but is still faint from thirst when morning
    comes.
So it will be with your enemies,
    with those who attack Mount Zion."

⁹ Are you amazed and incredulous?
    Don't you believe it?
Then go ahead and be blind.
    You are stupid, but not from wine!
    You stagger, but not from liquor!
¹⁰ For the LORD has poured out on you a spirit
        of deep sleep.
    He has closed the eyes of your prophets
        and visionaries.

¹¹All the future events in this vision are like a
sealed book to them. When you give it to those
who can read, they will say, "We can't read it
because it is sealed." ¹²When you give it to
those who cannot read, they will say, "We don't
know how to read."

¹³ And so the Lord says,
    "These people say they are mine.
They honor me with their lips,
    but their hearts are far from me.
And their worship of me
    is nothing but man-made rules learned
        by rote.*
¹⁴ Because of this, I will once again astound
        these hypocrites
    with amazing wonders.

29:7 Hebrew *Ariel*.   **29:13** Greek version reads *Their worship is
a farce, / for they teach man-made ideas as commands from God.*
Compare Mark 7:7.

I WONDER . . .

*It seems as though every other month my
dad is complaining about hearing of another
TV preacher getting into trouble or a local
pastor or priest who molested someone.
What do I say to people who point to the
hypocrites in this world as their reason
for giving God the cold shoulder?*

Unfortunately, even some of God's children act
shamefully. In fact, probably every Christian, at one
time or another, has betrayed God by his or her
actions.

The word "hypocrite" means "playact," to claim to
be a certain type of person while acting like someone
else. God is pretty upset at hypocrites, those who
claim to be his followers but really aren't.

Jesus said, "Beware of the yeast of the Pharisees—
their hypocrisy. The time is coming when everything
that is covered up will be revealed, and all that is
secret will be made known to all. Whatever you have
said in the dark will be heard in the light, and what you
have whispered behind closed doors will be shouted
from the housetops for all to hear!" (Luke 12:1-3).

When our world's final act draws to a close,
some of the first to receive God's wrath will be
those who have been playacting with God (see Isa
29:13-14). He is not amused or impressed; they will
be judged.

Unfortunately, you can do nothing to prevent
strangers from misrepresenting Christ. The only
person you can prevent from being a hypocrite is
you. Here are some ways to keep from becoming
a hypocrite:

First, watch your own actions closely. Though
God reads your heart, other people see your actions
first (see 2 Cor 13:5). If what you say doesn't match
what you say you believe, get ready to be called a
hypocrite.

Second, don't come down on other people too
hard. Remember, the only difference between
you and those who aren't Christians is that you've
received the gift of forgiveness.

Third, be quick to admit when you make a mistake.
True humility is rare in our culture. For some reason,
people are drawn to those who can readily admit their
mistakes. It's called being genuine.

The wisdom of the wise will pass away,
   and the intelligence of the intelligent will
      disappear."

¹⁵ What sorrow awaits those who try to hide
      their plans from the LORD,
   who do their evil deeds in the dark!
   "The LORD can't see us," they say.
      "He doesn't know what's going on!"
¹⁶ How foolish can you be?
   He is the Potter, and he is certainly
      greater than you, the clay!
   Should the created thing say of the one
      who made it,
   "He didn't make me"?
   Does a jar ever say,
      "The potter who made me
         is stupid"?

¹⁷ Soon—and it will not be very long—
   the forests of Lebanon will become a
      fertile field,
   and the fertile field will yield bountiful
      crops.
¹⁸ In that day the deaf will hear words read
      from a book,
   and the blind will see through the gloom
      and darkness.
¹⁹ The humble will be filled with fresh joy from
      the LORD.
   The poor will rejoice in the Holy One of
      Israel.
²⁰ The scoffer will be gone,
   the arrogant will disappear,
   and those who plot evil will be killed.
²¹ Those who convict the innocent
   by their false testimony will
      disappear.

· ·

HYPOCRISY
*(29:13-14) Isaiah condemned the people of Judah for
being hypocrites. They claimed to belong to God. Yet
because they were disobedient and merely went through
the motions, God punished them. Religion had become
routine instead of real. That's why Jesus quoted this
passage (Matt 15:8-9; Mark 7:6-7) when he spoke to the
Pharisees, the religious leaders of his day. Like the Pharisees, we fall into the same pit of hypocrisy when worship
becomes merely a ritual, rather than heartfelt and sincere.
God wants people to worship him honestly and wholeheartedly. Is that your desire as well?*

HIDING
*(29:15-16) The people of Jerusalem tried to hide their
plans from God. They thought God couldn't see them and
didn't know what was happening. It's strange that so
many people think they can hide from God. In Psalm 139
we learn that God has examined us and knows everything
about us. Would you be embarrassed if your best friends
knew your personal thoughts? Remember that God knows
all of them.*

A similar fate awaits those who use trickery
      to pervert justice
   and who tell lies to destroy the innocent.

²²That is why the LORD, who redeemed Abra-
ham, says to the people of Israel,*

   "My people will no longer be ashamed
      or turn pale with fear.
²³ For when they see their many children
      and all the blessings I have given them,
   they will recognize the holiness of the Holy
      One of Israel.
   They will stand in awe of the God
      of Jacob.
²⁴ Then the wayward will gain
      understanding,
   and complainers will accept
      instruction.

30 JUDAH'S WORTHLESS TREATY WITH EGYPT

¹ "What sorrow awaits my rebellious
      children,"
   says the LORD.
   "You make plans that are contrary to mine.
      You make alliances not directed by my
         Spirit,
      thus piling up your sins.
² For without consulting me,
   you have gone down to Egypt for help.
   You have put your trust in Pharaoh's
      protection.
   You have tried to hide in his shade.
³ But by trusting Pharaoh, you will be
      humiliated,
   and by depending on him, you will be
      disgraced.
⁴ For though his power extends to Zoan
      and his officials have arrived in Hanes,
⁵ all who trust in him will be ashamed.
   He will not help you.
   Instead, he will disgrace you."

⁶This message came to me concerning the ani-
mals in the Negev:

   The caravan moves slowly
      across the terrible desert to Egypt—
   donkeys weighed down with riches
      and camels loaded with treasure—
   all to pay for Egypt's protection.
   They travel through the wilderness,
      a place of lionesses and lions,
      a place where vipers and poisonous
         snakes live.
   All this, and Egypt will give you nothing
      in return.

29:22 Hebrew *of Jacob.* See note on 14:1.

ALLIANCES TODAY

Isaiah warned Judah not to ally with Egypt (30:1-7; 31:1-3). He knew that trust in any nation or military might was futile. Judah's only hope was to trust in God. Although we don't consciously put our hope for deliverance in political alliances in quite the same way, we often put our hope in other forces.

GOVERNMENT	SCIENCE	EDUCATION	FINANCIAL SYSTEMS	MEDICAL CARE
We rely on governments to legislate morality, but laws cannot change people's hearts.	We enjoy the benefits of science and technology. We look to scientific predictions and analysis before we look to the Bible.	We act as though education and degrees can guarantee our future and success without considering what God plans for our future.	We place our faith in financial "security," making as much money as we can for ourselves and forgetting that, while being wise with our money, we must trust God for our needs.	We regard medicine as the way to prolong life and preserve its quality—quite apart from faith and moral living.

7 Egypt's promises are worthless!
  Therefore, I call her Rahab—
    the Harmless Dragon.*

A WARNING FOR REBELLIOUS JUDAH

8 Now go and write down these words.
    Write them in a book.
  They will stand until the end of time
    as a witness
9 that these people are stubborn rebels
    who refuse to pay attention to the LORD's
      instructions.
10 They tell the seers,
    "Stop seeing visions!"
  They tell the prophets,
    "Don't tell us what is right.
  Tell us nice things.
  Tell us lies.
11 Forget all this gloom.
  Get off your narrow path.
  Stop telling us about your
    'Holy One of Israel.'"

12This is the reply of the Holy One of Israel:

  "Because you despise what I tell you
    and trust instead in oppression and lies,
13 calamity will come upon you suddenly—
    like a bulging wall that bursts and falls.
  In an instant it will collapse
    and come crashing down.
14 You will be smashed like a piece of pottery—
    shattered so completely that
  there won't be a piece big enough
    to carry coals from a fireplace
    or a little water from the well."

30:7 Hebrew *Rahab who sits still.* Rahab is the name of a mythical sea monster that represents chaos in ancient literature. The name is used here as a poetic name for Egypt.

15 This is what the Sovereign LORD,
    the Holy One of Israel, says:
  "Only in returning to me
    and resting in me will you be saved.
  In quietness and confidence is your
    strength.
  But you would have none of it.
16 You said, 'No, we will get our help from
    Egypt.
  They will give us swift horses for riding
    into battle.'
  But the only swiftness you are going to see
    is the swiftness of your enemies
      chasing you!
17 One of them will chase a thousand of you.
    Five of them will make all of you flee.
  You will be left like a lonely flagpole on a hill
    or a tattered banner on a distant
      mountaintop."

BLESSINGS FOR THE LORD'S PEOPLE

18 So the LORD must wait for you to come
    to him
  so he can show you his love and
    compassion.
  For the LORD is a faithful God.
    Blessed are those who wait for his help.

19 O people of Zion, who live in Jerusalem,
    you will weep no more.
  He will be gracious if you ask for help.
  He will surely respond to the sound of
    your cries.
20 Though the Lord gave you adversity for food
    and suffering for drink,
  he will still be with you to teach you.
    You will see your teacher with your
      own eyes.

²¹ Your own ears will hear him.
Right behind you a voice will say,
"This is the way you should go,"
whether to the right or to the left.
²² Then you will destroy all your silver idols
and your precious gold images.
You will throw them out like filthy rags,
saying to them, "Good riddance!"

²³Then the LORD will bless you with rain at planting time. There will be wonderful harvests and plenty of pastureland for your livestock. ²⁴The oxen and donkeys that till the ground will eat good grain, its chaff blown away by the wind. ²⁵In that day, when your enemies are slaughtered and the towers fall, there will be streams of water flowing down every mountain and hill. ²⁶The moon will be as bright as the sun, and the sun will be seven times brighter— like the light of seven days in one! So it will be when the LORD begins to heal his people and cure the wounds he gave them.

²⁷ Look! The LORD is coming from far away,
burning with anger,
surrounded by thick, rising smoke.
His lips are filled with fury;
his words consume like fire.
²⁸ His hot breath pours out like a flood
up to the neck of his enemies.
He will sift out the proud nations for
destruction.
He will bridle them and lead them away
to ruin.

²⁹ But the people of God will sing a song of joy,
like the songs at the holy festivals.
You will be filled with joy,
as when a flutist leads a group of pilgrims
to Jerusalem, the mountain of the LORD—
to the Rock of Israel.
³⁰ And the LORD will make his majestic voice
heard.
He will display the strength of his mighty
arm.
It will descend with devouring flames,
with cloudbursts, thunderstorms, and
huge hailstones.
³¹ At the LORD's command, the Assyrians will
be shattered.
He will strike them down with his royal
scepter.
³² And as the LORD strikes them with his rod
of punishment,
his people will celebrate with
tambourines and harps.
Lifting his mighty arm, he will fight the
Assyrians.

³³ Topheth—the place of burning—
has long been ready for the Assyrian king;
the pyre is piled high with wood.
The breath of the LORD, like fire from a
volcano,
will set it ablaze.

31 THE FUTILITY OF RELYING ON EGYPT

¹ What sorrow awaits those who look to Egypt
for help,
trusting their horses, chariots, and
charioteers
and depending on the strength of human
armies
instead of looking to the LORD,
the Holy One of Israel.
² In his wisdom, the LORD will send great
disaster;
he will not change his mind.
He will rise against the wicked
and against their helpers.
³ For these Egyptians are mere humans, not
God!
Their horses are puny flesh, not mighty
spirits!
When the LORD raises his fist against them,
those who help will stumble,
and those being helped will fall.
They will all fall down and die together.

⁴But this is what the LORD has told me:

"When a strong young lion
stands growling over a sheep it has killed,
it is not frightened by the shouts and noise
of a whole crowd of shepherds.
In the same way, the LORD of Heaven's
Armies
will come down and fight on Mount Zion.
⁵ The LORD of Heaven's Armies will hover over
Jerusalem
and protect it like a bird protecting its
nest.
He will defend and save the city;
he will pass over it and rescue it."

⁶Though you are such wicked rebels, my people, come and return to the LORD. ⁷I know the glorious day will come when each of you will throw away the gold idols and silver images your sinful hands have made.

⁸ "The Assyrians will be destroyed,
but not by the swords of men.
The sword of God will strike them,
and they will panic and flee.
The strong young Assyrians
will be taken away as captives.

⁹ Even the strongest will quake with terror,
    and princes will flee when they see your
        battle flags,"
says the LORD, whose fire burns in Zion,
    whose flame blazes from Jerusalem.

32 ISRAEL'S ULTIMATE DELIVERANCE

¹ Look, a righteous king is coming!
    And honest princes will rule under him.
² Each one will be like a shelter from the wind
    and a refuge from the storm,
like streams of water in the desert
    and the shadow of a great rock in a
        parched land.
³ Then everyone who has eyes will be able to
    see the truth,
    and everyone who has ears will be able
        to hear it.
⁴ Even the hotheads will be full of sense and
    understanding.
    Those who stammer will speak out
        plainly.
⁵ In that day ungodly fools will not be heroes.
    Scoundrels will not be respected.
⁶ For fools speak foolishness
    and make evil plans.
They practice ungodliness
    and spread false teachings about the
        LORD.
They deprive the hungry of food
    and give no water to the thirsty.
⁷ The smooth tricks of scoundrels are evil.
    They plot crooked schemes.
They lie to convict the poor,
    even when the cause of the poor is just.
⁸ But generous people plan to do what is
    generous,
    and they stand firm in their generosity.

⁹ Listen, you women who lie around in ease.
    Listen to me, you who are so smug.
¹⁰ In a short time—just a little more than
    a year—
    you careless ones will suddenly begin
        to care.
For your fruit crops will fail,
    and the harvest will never take place.
¹¹ Tremble, you women of ease;
    throw off your complacency.
Strip off your pretty clothes,
    and put on burlap to show your grief.
¹² Beat your breasts in sorrow for your
    bountiful farms

and your fruitful grapevines.
¹³ For your land will be overgrown with thorns
    and briers.
    Your joyful homes and happy towns will
        be gone.
¹⁴ The palace and the city will be deserted,
    and busy towns will be empty.
    Wild donkeys will frolic and flocks will graze
        in the empty forts* and watchtowers
¹⁵ until at last the Spirit is poured out
    on us from heaven.
Then the wilderness will become a fertile
    field,
    and the fertile field will yield bountiful
        crops.

¹⁶ Justice will rule in the wilderness
    and righteousness in the fertile field.
¹⁷ And this righteousness will bring peace.
    Yes, it will bring quietness and confidence
        forever.
¹⁸ My people will live in safety, quietly at
    home.
    They will be at rest.
¹⁹ Even if the forest should be destroyed
    and the city torn down,
²⁰ the LORD will greatly bless his people.
    Wherever they plant seed, bountiful crops
        will spring up.
    Their cattle and donkeys will graze freely.

33 A MESSAGE ABOUT ASSYRIA

¹ What sorrow awaits you Assyrians, who
        have destroyed others*
    but have never been destroyed
        yourselves.
    You betray others,

....

IDOLS
(31:7) *Someday the people of Israel would get rid of their idols, recognizing that the idols were nothing but wood or stone. Today, idols such as money, fame, or success seem more difficult to toss. Instead of contributing to our spiritual development, they rob us of our thoughts, time, energy, and devotion to God. At first they seem exciting and promise to take us places, but in the end we will find that we have become their slaves. What idols, if any, do you need to throw away?*

AT EASE
(32:9-13) *The people turned their backs on God and concentrated on their own best interests. This warning was not just to the women of Israel, but it applied to all who chose to concentrate on their own comfort, little knowing that an enemy approached. Wealth and luxury bring false security, lulling us into thinking all is well when disaster could lurk around the corner. By abandoning God's purpose for our lives, we also abandon his help. Are you at ease or at work for his kingdom?*

32:14 Hebrew *the Ophel.*   **33:1** Hebrew *What sorrow awaits you, O destroyer.* The Hebrew text does not specifically name Assyria as the object of the prophecy in this chapter.

but you have never been betrayed.
When you are done destroying,
  you will be destroyed.
When you are done betraying,
  you will be betrayed.

2 But LORD, be merciful to us,
  for we have waited for you.
Be our strong arm each day
  and our salvation in times of trouble.
3 The enemy runs at the sound of your voice.
  When you stand up, the nations flee!
4 Just as caterpillars and locusts strip the
    fields and vines,
  so the fallen army of Assyria will be
    stripped!

5 Though the LORD is very great and lives in
    heaven,
  he will make Jerusalem* his home of
    justice and righteousness.
6 In that day he will be your sure foundation,
  providing a rich store of salvation,
    wisdom, and knowledge.
  The fear of the LORD will be your treasure.

7 But now your brave warriors weep in public.
  Your ambassadors of peace cry in bitter
    disappointment.
8 Your roads are deserted;
  no one travels them anymore.
The Assyrians have broken their peace
    treaty
  and care nothing for the promises they
    made before witnesses.*
  They have no respect for anyone.
9 The land of Israel wilts in mourning.
  Lebanon withers with shame.
The plain of Sharon is now a wilderness.
  Bashan and Carmel have been plundered.

10 But the LORD says: "Now I will stand up.
  Now I will show my power and might.
11 You Assyrians produce nothing but dry grass
    and stubble.
  Your own breath will turn to fire and
    consume you.
12 Your people will be burned up completely,

. . . .

PROMISES
*(33:1) The Assyrians continually broke their promises
but demanded that others keep theirs. Does that sound
familiar? Maybe you know someone who recently broke
a promise. Maybe that someone was you. (Be honest.)
Broken promises shatter trust and destroy relationships.
Determine to make no promises that you can't keep, and
ask forgiveness for past promises that you have broken.
Are you willing to exercise the same fairness with others
that you demand for yourself?*

like thornbushes cut down and tossed in
    a fire.
13 Listen to what I have done, you nations far
    away!
  And you that are near, acknowledge my
    might!"

14 The sinners in Jerusalem shake with fear.
  Terror seizes the godless.
"Who can live with this devouring fire?"
    they cry.
  "Who can survive this all-consuming
    fire?"
15 Those who are honest and fair,
  who refuse to profit by fraud,
  who stay far away from bribes,
who refuse to listen to those who plot
    murder,
  who shut their eyes to all enticement to
    do wrong—
16 these are the ones who will dwell on high.
  The rocks of the mountains will be their
    fortress.
Food will be supplied to them,
  and they will have water in abundance.

17 Your eyes will see the king in all his
    splendor,
  and you will see a land that stretches into
    the distance.
18 You will think back to this time of terror,
    asking,
"Where are the Assyrian officers
  who counted our towers?
Where are the bookkeepers
  who recorded the plunder taken from our
    fallen city?"
19 You will no longer see these fierce, violent
    people
  with their strange, unknown language.

20 Instead, you will see Zion as a place of holy
    festivals.
  You will see Jerusalem, a city quiet and
    secure.
It will be like a tent whose ropes are taut
  and whose stakes are firmly fixed.
21 The LORD will be our Mighty One.
  He will be like a wide river of protection
that no enemy can cross,
  that no enemy ship can sail upon.
22 For the LORD is our judge,
  our lawgiver, and our king.
  He will care for us and save us.
23 The enemies' sails hang loose
  on broken masts with useless tackle.

33:5 Hebrew *Zion;* also in 33:14.   **33:8** As in Dead Sea Scrolls;
Masoretic Text reads *care nothing for the cities.*

Their treasure will be divided by the people
of God.
Even the lame will take their share!
24 The people of Israel will no longer say,
"We are sick and helpless,"
for the Lord will forgive their sins.

34 A MESSAGE FOR THE NATIONS

1 Come here and listen, O nations of the
earth.
Let the world and everything in it hear my
words.
2 For the Lord is enraged against the nations.
His fury is against all their armies.
He will completely destroy* them,
dooming them to slaughter.
3 Their dead will be left unburied,
and the stench of rotting bodies will fill
the land.
The mountains will flow with their blood.
4 The heavens above will melt away
and disappear like a rolled-up scroll.
The stars will fall from the sky
like withered leaves from a grapevine,
or shriveled figs from a fig tree.

5 And when my sword has finished its work in
the heavens,
it will fall upon Edom,
the nation I have marked for destruction.
6 The sword of the Lord is drenched with
blood
and covered with fat—
with the blood of lambs and goats,
with the fat of rams prepared for sacrifice.
Yes, the Lord will offer a sacrifice in the city
of Bozrah.
He will make a mighty slaughter in Edom.
7 Even men as strong as wild oxen will die—
the young men alongside the veterans.
The land will be soaked with blood
and the soil enriched with fat.

8 For it is the day of the Lord's revenge,
the year when Edom will be paid back for
all it did to Israel.*
9 The streams of Edom will be filled with
burning pitch,
and the ground will be covered with fire.
10 This judgment on Edom will never end;
the smoke of its burning will
rise forever.

34:2 The Hebrew term used here refers to the complete
consecration of things or people to the Lord, either by destroying
them or by giving them as an offering; similarly in 34:5.
34:8 Hebrew *to Zion*.   34:11 The identification of some of these
birds is uncertain.   34:12 The meaning of the Hebrew is uncertain.
34:14 Hebrew *Lilith*, possibly a reference to a mythical demon of
the night.

The land will lie deserted from generation to
generation.
No one will live there anymore.
11 It will be haunted by the desert owl and the
screech owl,
the great owl and the raven.*
For God will measure that land carefully;
he will measure it for chaos and
destruction.
12 It will be called the Land of Nothing,
and all its nobles will soon be gone.*
13 Thorns will overrun its palaces;
nettles and thistles will grow in its forts.
The ruins will become a haunt for jackals
and a home for owls.
14 Desert animals will mingle there with
hyenas,
their howls filling the night.
Wild goats will bleat at one another among
the ruins,
and night creatures* will come there to
rest.
15 There the owl will make her nest and lay her
eggs.
She will hatch her young and cover them
with her wings.
And the buzzards will come,
each one with its mate.

16 Search the book of the Lord,
and see what he will do.
Not one of these birds and animals will be
missing,
and none will lack a mate,
for the Lord has promised this.
His Spirit will make it all come true.
17 He has surveyed and divided the land
and deeded it over to those creatures.
They will possess it forever,
from generation to generation.

35 HOPE FOR RESTORATION

1 Even the wilderness and desert will be glad
in those days.
The wasteland will rejoice and blossom
with spring crocuses.
2 Yes, there will be an abundance of flowers
and singing and joy!
The deserts will become as green as the
mountains of Lebanon,
as lovely as Mount Carmel or the plain
of Sharon.
There the Lord will display his glory,
the splendor of our God.
3 With this news, strengthen those who have
tired hands,

and encourage those who have weak
knees.
⁴ Say to those with fearful hearts,
"Be strong, and do not fear,
for your God is coming to destroy your
enemies.
He is coming to save you."

⁵ And when he comes, he will open the eyes
of the blind
and unplug the ears of the deaf.
⁶ The lame will leap like a deer,
and those who cannot speak will sing
for joy!
Springs will gush forth in the wilderness,
and streams will water the wasteland.
⁷ The parched ground will become a pool,
and springs of water will satisfy the
thirsty land.
Marsh grass and reeds and rushes will
flourish
where desert jackals once lived.

⁸ And a great road will go through that once
deserted land.
It will be named the Highway of Holiness.
Evil-minded people will never travel on it.
It will be only for those who walk in God's
ways;
fools will never walk there.
⁹ Lions will not lurk along its course,
nor any other ferocious beasts.
There will be no other dangers.
Only the redeemed will walk on it.

···

VISIONS
*(35:1-10) In chapters 1–34, Isaiah delivered a message
of judgment on all nations, including the divided nation
of Israel (Israel, the northern kingdom, and Judah, the
southern kingdom), for rejecting God. Although God
gave glimpses of relief and restoration for the remnant
of faithful believers, the climate of wrath, fury, judgment,
and destruction prevailed. Now Isaiah breaks through
with a vision of beauty and encouragement. God is just
as complete in his mercy as he is severe in his judgment.
God's complete moral perfection is revealed by his hatred
of all sin, and this leads to judgment. This same moral
perfection is revealed in his love for all he has created.
We can trust that God's judgment will always be balanced
by his love.*

DECEIT
*(36:7) The representative of the Assyrian king claimed
that Hezekiah insulted God by tearing down his altars in
the hills and making the people worship in Jerusalem.
Either the Assyrians didn't understand how God was worshiped, or they wanted to deceive the people into thinking
they had angered God. In the same way, Satan tries to
confuse or deceive us. People don't necessarily need
to be sinful to be ineffective for God; they need only be
confused about what God wants. A careful study of God's
Word can help us avoid Satan's deceit.*

¹⁰ Those who have been ransomed by the
LORD will return.
They will enter Jerusalem* singing,
crowned with everlasting joy.
Sorrow and mourning will disappear,
and they will be filled with joy and
gladness.

36 **ASSYRIA INVADES JUDAH** In the fourteenth year of King Hezekiah's reign,*
King Sennacherib of Assyria came to attack the
fortified towns of Judah and conquered them.
²Then the king of Assyria sent his chief of staff*
from Lachish with a huge army to confront King
Hezekiah in Jerusalem. The Assyrians took up
a position beside the aqueduct that feeds
water into the upper pool, near the road leading to the field where cloth is washed.*
³These are the officials who went out to meet
with them: Eliakim son of Hilkiah, the palace
administrator; Shebna the court secretary;
and Joah son of Asaph, the royal historian.

SENNACHERIB THREATENS JERUSALEM ⁴Then
the Assyrian king's chief of staff told them to
give this message to Hezekiah:

"This is what the great king of Assyria
says: What are you trusting in that makes
you so confident? ⁵Do you think that mere
words can substitute for military skill and
strength? Who are you counting on, that
you have rebelled against me? ⁶On Egypt? If
you lean on Egypt, it will be like a reed that
splinters beneath your weight and pierces
your hand. Pharaoh, the king of Egypt, is
completely unreliable!
⁷"But perhaps you will say to me, 'We
are trusting in the LORD our God!' But isn't
he the one who was insulted by Hezekiah?
Didn't Hezekiah tear down his shrines and
altars and make everyone in Judah and
Jerusalem worship only at the altar here
in Jerusalem?
⁸"I'll tell you what! Strike a bargain with
my master, the king of Assyria. I will give
you 2,000 horses if you can find that many
men to ride on them! ⁹With your tiny army,
how can you think of challenging even the
weakest contingent of my master's troops,
even with the help of Egypt's chariots and
charioteers? ¹⁰What's more, do you think
we have invaded your land without the
LORD's direction? The LORD himself told us,
'Attack this land and destroy it!'"

35:10 Hebrew *Zion.* **36:1** The fourteenth year of Hezekiah's reign
was 701 B.C. **36:2a** Or *the rabshakeh;* also in 36:4, 11, 12, 22.
36:2b Or *bleached.*

¹¹Then Eliakim, Shebna, and Joah said to the Assyrian chief of staff, "Please speak to us in Aramaic, for we understand it well. Don't speak in Hebrew,* for the people on the wall will hear."

¹²But Sennacherib's chief of staff replied, "Do you think my master sent this message only to you and your master? He wants all the people to hear it, for when we put this city under siege, they will suffer along with you. They will be so hungry and thirsty that they will eat their own dung and drink their own urine."

¹³Then the chief of staff stood and shouted in Hebrew to the people on the wall, "Listen to this message from the great king of Assyria! ¹⁴This is what the king says: Don't let Hezekiah deceive you. He will never be able to rescue you. ¹⁵Don't let him fool you into trusting in the Lord by saying, 'The Lord will surely rescue us. This city will never fall into the hands of the Assyrian king!'

¹⁶"Don't listen to Hezekiah! These are the terms the king of Assyria is offering: Make peace with me—open the gates and come out. Then each of you can continue eating from your own grapevine and fig tree and drinking from your own well. ¹⁷Then I will arrange to take you to another land like this one—a land of grain and new wine, bread and vineyards.

¹⁸"Don't let Hezekiah mislead you by saying, 'The Lord will rescue us!' Have the gods of any other nations ever saved their people from the king of Assyria? ¹⁹What happened to the gods of Hamath and Arpad? And what about the gods of Sepharvaim? Did any god rescue Samaria from my power? ²⁰What god of any nation has ever been able to save its people from my power? So what makes you think that the Lord can rescue Jerusalem from me?"

²¹But the people were silent and did not utter a word because Hezekiah had commanded them, "Do not answer him."

²²Then Eliakim son of Hilkiah, the palace administrator; Shebna the court secretary; and Joah son of Asaph, the royal historian, went back to Hezekiah. They tore their clothes in despair, and they went in to see the king and told him what the Assyrian chief of staff had said.

37 HEZEKIAH SEEKS THE LORD'S HELP

When King Hezekiah heard their report, he tore his clothes and put on burlap and went into the Temple of the Lord. ²And he sent Eliakim the palace administrator, Shebna the court secretary, and the leading priests, all dressed in burlap, to the prophet Isaiah son of Amoz. ³They told him, "This is what King Hezekiah says: Today is a day of trouble, insults, and disgrace. It is like when a child is ready to be born, but the mother has no strength to deliver the baby. ⁴But perhaps the Lord your God has heard the Assyrian chief of staff,* sent by the king to defy the living God, and will punish him for his words. Oh, pray for those of us who are left!"

⁵After King Hezekiah's officials delivered the king's message to Isaiah, ⁶the prophet replied, "Say to your master, 'This is what the Lord says: Do not be disturbed by this blasphemous speech against me from the Assyrian king's messengers. ⁷Listen! I myself will move against him,* and the king will receive a message that he is needed at home. So he will return to his land, where I will have him killed with a sword.'"

⁸Meanwhile, the Assyrian chief of staff left Jerusalem and went to consult the king of Assyria, who had left Lachish and was attacking Libnah.

⁹Soon afterward King Sennacherib received word that King Tirhakah of Ethiopia* was leading an army to fight against him. Before leaving to meet the attack, he sent messengers back to Hezekiah in Jerusalem with this message:

¹⁰"This message is for King Hezekiah of Judah. Don't let your God, in whom you trust, deceive you with promises that Jerusalem will not be captured by the king of Assyria. ¹¹You know perfectly well what the kings of Assyria have done wherever they have gone. They have completely destroyed everyone who stood in their way! Why should you be any different? ¹²Have the gods of other nations rescued them—such nations as Gozan, Haran, Rezeph, and the people of Eden who were in Tel-assar? My predecessors destroyed them all! ¹³What happened to the king of Hamath and the king of Arpad? What happened to the kings of Sepharvaim, Hena, and Ivvah?"

¹⁴After Hezekiah received the letter from the messengers and read it, he went up to the

36:11 Hebrew *in the dialect of Judah;* also in 36:13.   37:4 Or *the rabshakeh;* also in 37:8.   37:7 Hebrew *I will put a spirit in him.* 37:9 Hebrew *of Cush.*

....

THE ANSWER
(37:8-20) Although the answer to Hezekiah's prayer was already in motion, Hezekiah wasn't aware of it. He persisted in prayer and faith even though he couldn't see the answer coming. Sometimes, we can't see the answer to our prayers right away. Still, our task is to ask in faith and wait.

LORD's Temple and spread it out before the LORD. ¹⁵And Hezekiah prayed this prayer before the LORD: ¹⁶"O LORD of Heaven's Armies, God of Israel, you are enthroned between the mighty cherubim! You alone are God of all the kingdoms of the earth. You alone created the heavens and the earth. ¹⁷Bend down, O LORD, and listen! Open your eyes, O LORD, and see! Listen to Sennacherib's words of defiance against the living God.

¹⁸"It is true, LORD, that the kings of Assyria have destroyed all these nations. ¹⁹And they have thrown the gods of these nations into the fire and burned them. But of course the Assyrians could destroy them! They were not gods at all—only idols of wood and stone shaped by human hands. ²⁰Now, O LORD our God, rescue us from his power; then all the kingdoms of the earth will know that you alone, O LORD, are God.*"

ISAIAH PREDICTS JUDAH'S DELIVERANCE

²¹Then Isaiah son of Amoz sent this message to Hezekiah: "This is what the LORD, the God of Israel, says: Because you prayed about King Sennacherib of Assyria, ²²the LORD has spoken this word against him:

"The virgin daughter of Zion
    despises you and laughs at you.
The daughter of Jerusalem
    shakes her head in derision as you flee.

²³ "Whom have you been defying and
        ridiculing?
    Against whom did you raise your voice?
At whom did you look with such haughty
        eyes?
    It was the Holy One of Israel!
²⁴ By your messengers you have defied the
        Lord.
    You have said, 'With my many chariots
I have conquered the highest mountains—
    yes, the remotest peaks of Lebanon.
I have cut down its tallest cedars
    and its finest cypress trees.
I have reached its farthest heights
    and explored its deepest forests.
²⁵ I have dug wells in many foreign lands*
    and refreshed myself with their water.
With the sole of my foot,
    I stopped up all the rivers of Egypt!'

²⁶ "But have you not heard?
    I decided this long ago.
Long ago I planned it,
    and now I am making it happen.
I planned for you to crush fortified cities
    into heaps of rubble.
²⁷ That is why their people have so little power
    and are so frightened and confused.
They are as weak as grass,
    as easily trampled as tender green
        shoots.
They are like grass sprouting on a housetop,
    scorched* before it can grow lush and
        tall.

²⁸ "But I know you well—
    where you stay
and when you come and go.
    I know the way you have raged against
        me.
²⁹ And because of your raging against me
    and your arrogance, which I have heard
        for myself,
I will put my hook in your nose
    and my bit in your mouth.
I will make you return
    by the same road on which you came."

³⁰Then Isaiah said to Hezekiah, "Here is the proof that what I say is true:

"This year you will eat only what grows up
        by itself,
    and next year you will eat what springs up
        from that.
But in the third year you will plant crops and
        harvest them;
    you will tend vineyards and eat their fruit.
³¹ And you who are left in Judah,
    who have escaped the ravages of the
        siege,
will put roots down in your own soil
    and grow up and flourish.
³² For a remnant of my people will spread out
        from Jerusalem,
    a group of survivors from Mount Zion.
The passionate commitment of the LORD
        of Heaven's Armies
    will make this happen!

³³"And this is what the LORD says about the king of Assyria:

"'His armies will not enter Jerusalem.
    They will not even shoot an arrow at it.
They will not march outside its gates with
        their shields
    nor build banks of earth against its walls.
³⁴ The king will return to his own country
    by the same road on which he came.

37:20 As in Dead Sea Scrolls (see also 2 Kgs 19:19); Masoretic Text reads *you alone are the LORD.* **37:25** As in Dead Sea Scrolls (see also 2 Kgs 19:24); Masoretic Text lacks *in many foreign lands.* **37:27** As in Dead Sea Scrolls and some Greek manuscripts (see also 2 Kgs 19:26); most Hebrew manuscripts read *like a terraced field.*

He will not enter this city,'
   says the LORD.
35 'For my own honor and for the sake of my
     servant David,
   I will defend this city and protect it.'"

36That night the angel of the LORD went out to the Assyrian camp and killed 185,000 Assyrian soldiers. When the surviving Assyrians* woke up the next morning, they found corpses everywhere. 37Then King Sennacherib of Assyria broke camp and returned to his own land. He went home to his capital of Nineveh and stayed there.

38One day while he was worshiping in the temple of his god Nisroch, his sons Adrammelech and Sharezer killed him with their swords. They then escaped to the land of Ararat, and another son, Esarhaddon, became the next king of Assyria.

38 HEZEKIAH'S SICKNESS AND RECOVERY

About that time Hezekiah became deathly ill, and the prophet Isaiah son of Amoz went to visit him. He gave the king this message: "This is what the LORD says: 'Set your affairs in order, for you are going to die. You will not recover from this illness.'"

2When Hezekiah heard this, he turned his face to the wall and prayed to the LORD, 3"Remember, O LORD, how I have always been faithful to you and have served you singlemindedly, always doing what pleases you." Then he broke down and wept bitterly.

4Then this message came to Isaiah from the LORD: 5"Go back to Hezekiah and tell him, 'This is what the LORD, the God of your ancestor David, says: I have heard your prayer and seen your tears. I will add fifteen years to your life, 6and I will rescue you and this city from the king of Assyria. Yes, I will defend this city.

7"'And this is the sign from the LORD to prove that he will do as he promised: 8I will cause the sun's shadow to move ten steps backward on the sundial* of Ahaz!'" So the shadow on the sundial moved backward ten steps.

HEZEKIAH'S POEM OF PRAISE

9When King Hezekiah was well again, he wrote this poem:

10 I said, "In the prime of my life,
   must I now enter the place of the dead?*
   Am I to be robbed of the rest of my
     years?"
11 I said, "Never again will I see the LORD GOD
   while still in the land of the living.

Never again will I see my friends
   or be with those who live in this world.
12 My life has been blown away
   like a shepherd's tent in a storm.
It has been cut short,
   as when a weaver cuts cloth from a loom.
   Suddenly, my life was over.
13 I waited patiently all night,
   but I was torn apart as though by lions.
   Suddenly, my life was over.
14 Delirious, I chattered like a swallow or
    a crane,
   and then I moaned like a
    mourning dove.
My eyes grew tired of looking to
    heaven for help.
   I am in trouble, Lord. Help me!"

15 But what could I say?
   For he himself sent this sickness.
Now I will walk humbly throughout my years
   because of this anguish I have felt.
16 Lord, your discipline is good,
   for it leads to life and health.
You restore my health
   and allow me to live!
17 Yes, this anguish was good for me,
   for you have rescued me from death
   and forgiven all my sins.
18 For the dead* cannot praise you;
   they cannot raise their voices in praise.
Those who go down to the grave
   can no longer hope in your faithfulness.
19 Only the living can praise you as I do today.
   Each generation tells of your faithfulness
    to the next.
20 Think of it—the LORD is ready to heal me!
   I will sing his praises with instruments
every day of my life
   in the Temple of the LORD.

....

RADICAL CHANGE
(38:1-8) When Isaiah told Hezekiah of his impending death, Hezekiah immediately turned to God. God responded to Hezekiah's prayer, allowing him to live another 15 years. In response to fervent prayer, God may change the course of our lives, too. Don't hesitate to ask God for radical changes if you will honor him with those changes. So, what's your prayer?

GOD AT WORK
(38:9-20) Hezekiah, one of Judah's most faithful kings, worked hard throughout his reign to stamp out idol worship and to purify the worship of the true God at the Temple in Jerusalem. Nevertheless, he knew his kingdom was not completely pure. Only God's miraculous interventions preserved Judah from its enemies. Many times we're tempted to grumble about what we think God isn't doing, instead of thanking him for what he is doing. How is God at work around you? Have you thanked him lately?

37:36 Hebrew *When they.* 38:8 Hebrew *the steps.* 38:10 Hebrew *enter the gates of Sheol?* 38:18 Hebrew *Sheol.*

²¹Isaiah had said to Hezekiah's servants, "Make an ointment from figs and spread it over the boil, and Hezekiah will recover."

²²And Hezekiah had asked, "What sign will prove that I will go to the Temple of the LORD?"

39 ENVOYS FROM BABYLON

Soon after this, Merodach-baladan son of Baladan, king of Babylon, sent Hezekiah his best wishes and a gift. He had heard that Hezekiah had been very sick and that he had recovered. ²Hezekiah was delighted with the Babylonian envoys and showed them everything in his treasure-houses—the silver, the gold, the spices, and the aromatic oils. He also took them to see his armory and showed them everything in his royal treasuries! There was nothing in his palace or kingdom that Hezekiah did not show them.

³Then Isaiah the prophet went to King Hezekiah and asked him, "What did those men want? Where were they from?"

Hezekiah replied, "They came from the distant land of Babylon."

⁴"What did they see in your palace?" asked Isaiah.

"They saw everything," Hezekiah replied. "I showed them everything I own—all my royal treasuries."

⁵Then Isaiah said to Hezekiah, "Listen to this message from the LORD of Heaven's Armies: ⁶'The time is coming when everything in your palace—all the treasures stored up by your ancestors until now—will be carried off to Babylon. Nothing will be left,' says the LORD. ⁷'Some of your very own sons will be taken away into exile. They will become eunuchs who will serve in the palace of Babylon's king.'"

⁸Then Hezekiah said to Isaiah, "This message you have given me from the LORD is good." For the king was thinking, "At least there will be peace and security during my lifetime."

40 COMFORT FOR GOD'S PEOPLE

¹ "Comfort, comfort my people,"
    says your God.
² "Speak tenderly to Jerusalem.

....

COMFORT
(40:1) God's people still had 100 years of trouble before Jerusalem would fall. After that would come 70 years of exile. So God told Isaiah to speak tenderly and to comfort Jerusalem. When your life seems to be falling apart, ask God to comfort you. You may not escape hard times, but you can find God's comfort during them.

Tell her that her sad days are gone
    and her sins are pardoned.
Yes, the LORD has punished her twice over
    for all her sins."

³ Listen! It's the voice of someone shouting,
"Clear the way through the wilderness
    for the LORD!
Make a straight highway through the
    wasteland
    for our God!
⁴ Fill in the valleys,
    and level the mountains and hills.
Straighten the curves,
    and smooth out the rough places.
⁵ Then the glory of the LORD will be revealed,
    and all people will see it together.
    The LORD has spoken!"*

⁶ A voice said, "Shout!"
    I asked, "What should I shout?"

"Shout that people are like the grass.
    Their beauty fades as quickly
    as the flowers in a field.
⁷ The grass withers and the flowers fade
    beneath the breath of the LORD.
    And so it is with people.
⁸ The grass withers and the flowers fade,
    but the word of our God stands forever."

⁹ O Zion, messenger of good news,
    shout from the mountaintops!
Shout it louder, O Jerusalem.*
    Shout, and do not be afraid.
Tell the towns of Judah,
    "Your God is coming!"
¹⁰ Yes, the Sovereign LORD is coming in power.
    He will rule with a powerful arm.
    See, he brings his reward with him as he
        comes.
¹¹ He will feed his flock like a shepherd.
    He will carry the lambs in his arms,
holding them close to his heart.
    He will gently lead the mother sheep with
        their young.

THE LORD HAS NO EQUAL

¹² Who else has held the oceans in his hand?
    Who has measured off the heavens with
        his fingers?
Who else knows the weight of the earth
    or has weighed the mountains and hills
        on a scale?

40:3-5 Greek version reads *He is a voice shouting in the wilderness, / "Prepare the way for the LORD's coming! / Clear a road for our God! / Fill in the valleys, / and level the mountains and hills. / And then the glory of the LORD will be revealed, / and all people will see the salvation sent from God. / The LORD has spoken!"* Compare Matt 3:3; Mark 1:3; Luke 3:4-6.   40:9 Or *O messenger of good news, shout to Zion from the mountaintops! Shout it louder to Jerusalem.*

¹³ Who is able to advise the Spirit of the
    Lord?*
    Who knows enough to give him advice or
        teach him?
¹⁴ Has the Lord ever needed anyone's advice?
    Does he need instruction about what is
        good?
    Did someone teach him what is right
        or show him the path of justice?

¹⁵ No, for all the nations of the world
    are but a drop in the bucket.
    They are nothing more
        than dust on the scales.
    He picks up the whole earth
        as though it were a grain of sand.
¹⁶ All the wood in Lebanon's forests
    and all Lebanon's animals would not be
        enough
    to make a burnt offering worthy of our
        God.
¹⁷ The nations of the world are worth nothing
        to him.
    In his eyes they count for less than
        nothing—
    mere emptiness and froth.

¹⁸ To whom can you compare God?
    What image can you find to resemble
        him?
¹⁹ Can he be compared to an idol formed in
        a mold,
    overlaid with gold, and decorated with
        silver chains?
²⁰ Or if people are too poor for that,
    they might at least choose wood that
        won't decay
    and a skilled craftsman
        to carve an image that won't fall down!

²¹ Haven't you heard? Don't you understand?
    Are you deaf to the words of God—
    the words he gave before the world began?
    Are you so ignorant?
²² God sits above the circle of the earth.
    The people below seem like grasshoppers
        to him!
    He spreads out the heavens like a curtain
        and makes his tent from them.
²³ He judges the great people of the world
        and brings them all to nothing.
²⁴ They hardly get started, barely taking root,
    when he blows on them and they wither.
    The wind carries them off like chaff.

²⁵ "To whom will you compare me?
    Who is my equal?" asks the Holy One.

40:13 Greek version reads *Who can know the Lord's thoughts?*
Compare Rom 11:34; 1 Cor 2:16.

²⁶ Look up into the heavens.
    Who created all the stars?
    He brings them out like an army, one after
        another,
    calling each by its name.
    Because of his great power and
        incomparable strength,
    not a single one is missing.
²⁷ O Jacob, how can you say the Lord does not
        see your troubles?
    O Israel, how can you say God ignores
        your rights?
²⁸ Have you never heard?
    Have you never understood?
    The Lord is the everlasting God,
        the Creator of all the earth.
    He never grows weak or weary.
    No one can measure the depths of his
        understanding.
²⁹ He gives power to the weak
        and strength to the powerless.
³⁰ Even youths will become weak and tired,
        and young men will fall in exhaustion.
³¹ But those who trust in the Lord will find
        new strength.
    They will soar high on wings like eagles.
    They will run and not grow weary.
    They will walk and not faint.

41 GOD'S HELP FOR ISRAEL

¹ "Listen in silence before me, you lands
        beyond the sea.
    Bring your strongest arguments.
    Come now and speak.
    The court is ready for your case.

² "Who has stirred up this king from the east,
        rightly calling him to God's service?
    Who gives this man victory over many
        nations
    and permits him to trample their kings
        underfoot?
    With his sword, he reduces armies to dust.
    With his bow, he scatters them like chaff
        before the wind.
³ He chases them away and goes on safely,
        though he is walking over unfamiliar
        ground.
⁴ Who has done such mighty deeds,

STRENGTH
*(40:29-31) Even the strongest people get tired at times,
but God's power and strength never diminish. He is never
too busy to help and listen. His strength is our source of
strength. When you feel all of life crushing you and you
can't go another step, remember that you can ask God to
renew your strength.*

MY STORY: Maia

I recently switched schools. In my old school, I knew everyone. In this new, much larger school, I knew no one. The situation forced me to depend on God. I knew that I really needed God's help and guidance to make it through those first few months.

During this time, I memorized Isaiah 41:10 and Philippians 4:13. Whenever I felt unnoticed or afraid to talk to someone, I would repeat these verses to myself. I remembered that God was with me, that he would strengthen me, and that he had already won the victory for me. These two verses became a lifeline for me. They helped me make the adjustments, so that I now do have friends and I feel pretty comfortable at my new school.

summoning each new generation from the beginning of time?
It is I, the LORD, the First and the Last.
I alone am he."

5 The lands beyond the sea watch in fear.
Remote lands tremble and mobilize for war.
6 The idol makers encourage one another, saying to each other, "Be strong!"
7 The carver encourages the goldsmith, and the molder helps at the anvil.
"Good," they say. "It's coming along fine."
Carefully they join the parts together, then fasten the thing in place so it won't fall over.

8 "But as for you, Israel my servant, Jacob my chosen one, descended from Abraham my friend,
9 I have called you back from the ends of the earth,

saying, 'You are my servant.'
For I have chosen you and will not throw you away.
10 Don't be afraid, for I am with you.
Don't be discouraged, for I am your God.
I will strengthen you and help you.
I will hold you up with my victorious right hand.

11 "See, all your angry enemies lie there, confused and humiliated.
Anyone who opposes you will die and come to nothing.
12 You will look in vain for those who tried to conquer you.
Those who attack you will come to nothing.
13 For I hold you by your right hand— I, the LORD your God.
And I say to you, 'Don't be afraid. I am here to help you.
14 Though you are a lowly worm, O Jacob, don't be afraid, people of Israel, for I will help you.
I am the LORD, your Redeemer.
I am the Holy One of Israel.'
15 You will be a new threshing instrument with many sharp teeth.
You will tear your enemies apart, making chaff of mountains.
16 You will toss them into the air, and the wind will blow them all away; a whirlwind will scatter them.
Then you will rejoice in the LORD.
You will glory in the Holy One of Israel.

17 "When the poor and needy search for water and there is none, and their tongues are parched from thirst,
then I, the LORD, will answer them.
I, the God of Israel, will never abandon them.
18 I will open up rivers for them on the high plateaus.
I will give them fountains of water in the valleys.
I will fill the desert with pools of water.
Rivers fed by springs will flow across the parched ground.
19 I will plant trees in the barren desert— cedar, acacia, myrtle, olive, cypress, fir, and pine.
20 I am doing this so all who see this miracle will understand what it means—
that it is the LORD who has done this, the Holy One of Israel who created it.

THE FUTURE
(41:4) Each generation gets caught up in its own problems, but God's plan embraces all generations. When your great-grandparents lived, God worked personally in the lives of his people. When your great-grandchildren live, God will still work personally in the lives of his people. He is the only One who sees as clearly a hundred years from now as he saw a hundred years ago. When you are concerned about the future, talk with God—he knows the generations of the future as well as he knows the generations of the past.

²¹ "Present the case for your idols,"
  says the LORD.
"Let them show what they can do,"
  says the King of Israel.*
²² "Let them try to tell us what happened
    long ago
  so that we may consider the evidence.
Or let them tell us what the future holds,
  so we can know what's going to happen.
²³ Yes, tell us what will occur in the days
    ahead.
  Then we will know you are gods.
In fact, do anything—good or bad!
  Do something that will amaze and
    frighten us.
²⁴ But no! You are less than nothing and can
    do nothing at all.
  Those who choose you pollute
    themselves.

²⁵ "But I have stirred up a leader who will
    come from the north.
  I have called him by name from the east.
I will give him victory over kings and princes.
  He will trample them as a potter treads
    on clay.
²⁶ "Who told you from the beginning
    that this would happen?
Who predicted this,
  making you admit that he was right?
  No one said a word!
²⁷ I was the first to tell Zion,
  'Look! Help is on the way!'*
I will send Jerusalem a messenger with
  good news.
²⁸ Not one of your idols told you this.
  Not one gave any answer when I asked.
²⁹ See, they are all foolish, worthless things.
  All your idols are as empty as
    the wind.

42 THE LORD'S CHOSEN SERVANT

¹ "Look at my servant, whom I strengthen.
  He is my chosen one, who pleases me.
I have put my Spirit upon him.
  He will bring justice to the nations.
² He will not shout
  or raise his voice in public.
³ He will not crush the weakest reed
  or put out a flickering candle.
  He will bring justice to all who have been
    wronged.
⁴ He will not falter or lose heart

41:21 Hebrew *the King of Jacob.* See note on 14:1.   41:27 Or *'Look! They are coming home.'*   42:4 Greek version reads *And his name will be the hope of all the world.* Compare Matt 12:21.

until justice prevails throughout the
    earth.
  Even distant lands beyond the sea will
    wait for his instruction.*"

⁵ God, the LORD, created the heavens and
    stretched them out.
  He created the earth and everything in it.
He gives breath to everyone,
  life to everyone who walks the earth.
And it is he who says,
⁶ "I, the LORD, have called you to demonstrate
    my righteousness.
  I will take you by the hand and guard you,
and I will give you to my people, Israel,
  as a symbol of my covenant with them.
And you will be a light to guide the nations.
⁷ You will open the eyes of the blind.
You will free the captives from prison,
  releasing those who sit in dark dungeons.

⁸ "I am the LORD; that is my name!
  I will not give my glory to anyone else,
    nor share my praise with carved idols.
⁹ Everything I prophesied has come true,
  and now I will prophesy again.
I will tell you the future before it happens."

A SONG OF PRAISE TO THE LORD

¹⁰ Sing a new song to the LORD!
  Sing his praises from the ends of the
    earth!
Sing, all you who sail the seas,
  all you who live in distant coastlands.
¹¹ Join in the chorus, you desert towns;
  let the villages of Kedar rejoice!
Let the people of Sela sing for joy;
  shout praises from the mountaintops!
¹² Let the whole world glorify the LORD;
  let it sing his praise.
¹³ The LORD will march forth like a mighty hero;
  he will come out like a warrior, full of fury.
He will shout his battle cry
  and crush all his enemies.

¹⁴ He will say, "I have long been silent;
  yes, I have restrained myself.
But now, like a woman in labor,
  I will cry and groan and pant.
¹⁵ I will level the mountains and hills
  and blight all their greenery.
I will turn the rivers into dry land
  and will dry up all the pools.
¹⁶ I will lead blind Israel down a new path,
  guiding them along an unfamiliar way.
I will brighten the darkness before them
  and smooth out the road ahead of them.
Yes, I will indeed do these things;

I will not forsake them.
¹⁷ But those who trust in idols,
who say, 'You are our gods,'
will be turned away in shame.

ISRAEL'S FAILURE TO LISTEN AND SEE

¹⁸ "Listen, you who are deaf!
Look and see, you blind!
¹⁹ Who is as blind as my own people, my
servant?
Who is as deaf as my messenger?
Who is as blind as my chosen people,
the servant of the LORD?
²⁰ You see and recognize what is right
but refuse to act on it.
You hear with your ears,
but you don't really listen."

²¹ Because he is righteous,
the LORD has exalted his glorious law.
²² But his own people have been robbed and
plundered,
enslaved, imprisoned, and trapped.
They are fair game for anyone
and have no one to protect them,
no one to take them back home.

²³ Who will hear these lessons from the past
and see the ruin that awaits you in the
future?
²⁴ Who allowed Israel to be robbed and hurt?
It was the LORD, against whom we sinned,
for the people would not walk in his path,
nor would they obey his law.
²⁵ Therefore, he poured out his fury on them
and destroyed them in battle.
They were enveloped in flames,
but they still refused to understand.
They were consumed by fire,
but they did not learn their lesson.

43 THE SAVIOR OF ISRAEL

¹ But now, O Jacob, listen to the LORD who
created you.
O Israel, the one who formed you says,
"Do not be afraid, for I have ransomed you.
I have called you by name; you are mine.
² When you go through deep waters,
I will be with you.

When you go through rivers of difficulty,
you will not drown.
When you walk through the fire of
oppression,
you will not be burned up;
the flames will not consume you.
³ For I am the LORD, your God,
the Holy One of Israel, your Savior.
I gave Egypt as a ransom for your freedom;
I gave Ethiopia* and Seba in your place.
⁴ Others were given in exchange for you.
I traded their lives for yours
because you are precious to me.
You are honored, and I love you.

⁵ "Do not be afraid, for I am with you.
I will gather you and your children from
east and west.
⁶ I will say to the north and south,
'Bring my sons and daughters back to
Israel
from the distant corners of the earth.
⁷ Bring all who claim me as their God,
for I have made them for my glory.
It was I who created them.'"

⁸ Bring out the people who have eyes but are
blind,
who have ears but are deaf.
⁹ Gather the nations together!
Assemble the peoples of the world!
Which of their idols has ever foretold such
things?
Which can predict what will happen
tomorrow?
Where are the witnesses of such
predictions?
Who can verify that they spoke the truth?

¹⁰ "But you are my witnesses, O Israel!" says
the LORD.
"You are my servant.
You have been chosen to know me, believe
in me,
and understand that I alone am God.
There is no other God—
there never has been, and there never
will be.
¹¹ I, yes I, am the LORD,
and there is no other Savior.
¹² First I predicted your rescue,
then I saved you and proclaimed it to the
world.
No foreign god has ever done this.
You are witnesses that I am the only
God,"
says the LORD.

^{43:3} Hebrew *Cush.*

SEEING GOD THROUGH YOUR EYES
*(43:10-11) Israel's task was to be a witness, telling the
world who God is and what he has done. Believers today
share the responsibility of being God's witnesses. How do
your words and example reveal to others what God is like?
Although they can't see God directly, they can see him
reflected in you.*

13 "From eternity to eternity I am God.
    No one can snatch anyone out of my
        hand.
    No one can undo what I have done."

THE LORD'S PROMISE OF VICTORY

14This is what the LORD says—your Redeemer, the Holy One of Israel:

"For your sakes I will send an army against
    Babylon,
    forcing the Babylonians* to flee in those
        ships they are so proud of.
15 I am the LORD, your Holy One,
    Israel's Creator and King.
16 I am the LORD, who opened a way through
        the waters,
    making a dry path through the sea.
17 I called forth the mighty army of Egypt
        with all its chariots and horses.
    I drew them beneath the waves, and they
        drowned,
        their lives snuffed out like a smoldering
            candlewick.

18 "But forget all that—
    it is nothing compared to what I am going
        to do.
19 For I am about to do something new.
    See, I have already begun! Do you not
        see it?
    I will make a pathway through the
        wilderness.
    I will create rivers in the dry wasteland.
20 The wild animals in the fields will thank me,
        the jackals and owls, too,
    for giving them water in the desert.
    Yes, I will make rivers in the dry wasteland
        so my chosen people can be refreshed.
21 I have made Israel for myself,
    and they will someday honor me before
        the whole world.

22 "But, dear family of Jacob, you refuse to ask
        for my help.
    You have grown tired of me, O Israel!
23 You have not brought me sheep or goats for
        burnt offerings.
    You have not honored me with sacrifices,
        though I have not burdened and wearied
            you
        with requests for grain offerings and
            frankincense.
24 You have not brought me fragrant calamus
        or pleased me with the fat from sacrifices.

Instead, you have burdened me with your
        sins
    and wearied me with your faults.

25 "I—yes, I alone—will blot out your sins for
        my own sake
    and will never think of them again.
26 Let us review the situation together,
    and you can present your case to prove
        your innocence.
27 From the very beginning, your first ancestor
        sinned against me;
    all your leaders broke my laws.
28 That is why I have disgraced your priests;
    I have decreed complete destruction* for
        Jacob
    and shame for Israel.

44

1"But now, listen to me, Jacob my
        servant,
    Israel my chosen one.
2 The LORD who made you and helps you
        says:
    Do not be afraid, O Jacob, my servant,
    O dear Israel,* my chosen one.
3 For I will pour out water to quench your thirst
        and to irrigate your parched fields.
    And I will pour out my Spirit on your
        descendants,
    and my blessing on your children.
4 They will thrive like watered grass,
    like willows on a riverbank.
5 Some will proudly claim, 'I belong to the
        LORD.'
    Others will say, 'I am a descendant of
        Jacob.'
    Some will write the LORD's name on their
        hands
    and will take the name of Israel as their
        own."

THE FOOLISHNESS OF IDOLS

6This is what the LORD says—Israel's King and Redeemer, the LORD of Heaven's Armies:

"I am the First and the Last;
    there is no other God.
7 Who is like me?
    Let him step forward and prove to you his
        power.
    Let him do as I have done since ancient
        times
    when I established a people and
        explained its future.
8 Do not tremble; do not be afraid.
    Did I not proclaim my purposes for you
        long ago?

43:14 Or *Chaldeans.* 43:28 The Hebrew term used here refers to the complete consecration of things or people to the LORD, either by destroying them or by giving them as an offering. 44:2 Hebrew *Jeshurun,* a term of endearment for Israel.

TODAY'S IDOLATRY

God asks, "Who but a fool would make his own god—an idol that cannot help him one bit?" (44:10). We think of idols as statues of wood or stone, but in reality an idol is anything that is given sacred value and power. If your answer to any of the following questions is anyone other than God, you need to check out who you are ultimately worshiping.

Who created me?

Whom do I ultimately trust?

To whom do I look for security and happiness?

To whom do I look for ultimate truth?

Who is in charge of my future?

> You are my witnesses—is there any other God?
> No! There is no other Rock—not one!"

9 How foolish are those who manufacture idols.
These prized objects are really worthless.
The people who worship idols don't know this,
so they are all put to shame.
10 Who but a fool would make his own god—
an idol that cannot help him one bit?
11 All who worship idols will be disgraced
along with all these craftsmen—mere humans—
who claim they can make a god.
They may all stand together,
but they will stand in terror and shame.

12 The blacksmith stands at his forge to make a sharp tool,
pounding and shaping it with all his might.
His work makes him hungry and weak.
It makes him thirsty and faint.
13 Then the wood-carver measures a block of wood
and draws a pattern on it.
He works with chisel and plane
and carves it into a human figure.
He gives it human beauty
and puts it in a little shrine.
14 He cuts down cedars;
he selects the cypress and the oak;
he plants the pine in the forest
to be nourished by the rain.
15 Then he uses part of the wood to make a fire.
With it he warms himself and bakes his bread.
Then—yes, it's true—he takes the rest of it

and makes himself a god to worship!
He makes an idol
and bows down in front of it!
16 He burns part of the tree to roast his meat
and to keep himself warm.
He says, "Ah, that fire feels good."
17 Then he takes what's left
and makes his god: a carved idol!
He falls down in front of it,
worshiping and praying to it.
"Rescue me!" he says.
"You are my god!"

18 Such stupidity and ignorance!
Their eyes are closed, and they cannot see.
Their minds are shut, and they cannot think.
19 The person who made the idol never stops to reflect,
"Why, it's just a block of wood!
I burned half of it for heat
and used it to bake my bread and roast my meat.
How can the rest of it be a god?
Should I bow down to worship a piece of wood?"
20 The poor, deluded fool feeds on ashes.
He trusts something that can't help him at all.
Yet he cannot bring himself to ask,
"Is this idol that I'm holding in my hand a lie?"

RESTORATION FOR JERUSALEM

21 "Pay attention, O Jacob,
for you are my servant, O Israel.
I, the LORD, made you,
and I will not forget you.
22 I have swept away your sins like a cloud.
I have scattered your offenses like the morning mist.
Oh, return to me,
for I have paid the price to set you free."

23 Sing, O heavens, for the LORD has done this wondrous thing.
Shout for joy, O depths of the earth!
Break into song,
O mountains and forests and every tree!
For the LORD has redeemed Jacob
and is glorified in Israel.

24 This is what the LORD says—
your Redeemer and Creator:
"I am the LORD, who made all things.
I alone stretched out the heavens.
Who was with me

when I made the earth?

25 I expose the false prophets as liars
   and make fools of fortune-tellers.
I cause the wise to give bad advice,
   thus proving them to be fools.
26 But I carry out the predictions of my
      prophets!
   By them I say to Jerusalem, 'People will
      live here again,'
   and to the towns of Judah, 'You will be
      rebuilt;
   I will restore all your ruins!'
27 When I speak to the rivers and say, 'Dry up!'
      they will be dry.
28 When I say of Cyrus, 'He is my shepherd,'
      he will certainly do as I say.
He will command, 'Rebuild Jerusalem';
      he will say, 'Restore the Temple.'"

45 CYRUS, THE LORD'S CHOSEN ONE

1 This is what the LORD says to Cyrus, his
      anointed one,
   whose right hand he will empower.
Before him, mighty kings will be paralyzed
      with fear.
   Their fortress gates will be opened,
      never to shut again.
2 This is what the LORD says:

"I will go before you, Cyrus,
   and level the mountains.*
I will smash down gates of bronze
   and cut through bars of iron.
3 And I will give you treasures hidden in the
      darkness—
   secret riches.
I will do this so you may know that I am the
      LORD,
   the God of Israel, the one who calls you
      by name.

4 "And why have I called you for this work?
   Why did I call you by name when you did
      not know me?
It is for the sake of Jacob my servant,
   Israel my chosen one.
5 I am the LORD;
   there is no other God.
I have equipped you for battle,
   though you don't even know me,
6 so all the world from east to west
   will know there is no other God.
I am the LORD, and there is no other.
7   I create the light and make the darkness.
I send good times and bad times.

45:2 As in Dead Sea Scrolls and Greek version; Masoretic Text reads
the swellings.

I, the LORD, am the one who does these
      things.

8 "Open up, O heavens,
   and pour out your righteousness.
Let the earth open wide
   so salvation and righteousness can
      sprout up together.
I, the LORD, created them.

9 "What sorrow awaits those who argue with
      their Creator.
Does a clay pot argue with its maker?
Does the clay dispute with the one who
      shapes it, saying,
   'Stop, you're doing it wrong!'
Does the pot exclaim,
   'How clumsy can you be?'
10 How terrible it would be if a newborn baby
      said to its father,
   'Why was I born?'
or if it said to its mother,
   'Why did you make me this way?'"

11 This is what the LORD says—
   the Holy One of Israel and your Creator:
"Do you question what I do for my children?
   Do you give me orders about the work of
      my hands?
12 I am the one who made the earth
   and created people to live on it.
With my hands I stretched out the heavens.
   All the stars are at my command.
13 I will raise up Cyrus to fulfill my righteous
      purpose,
   and I will guide his actions.
He will restore my city and free my captive
      people—
   without seeking a reward!
I, the LORD of Heaven's Armies, have
      spoken!"

....

PROPHECIES
*(44:28) Isaiah, who lived from about 740 to 681 B.C.,
called Cyrus by name almost 150 years before he ruled
(559–530 B.C.)! Later historians said that Cyrus read this
prophecy and was so moved that he carried it out. Isaiah
also had predicted the fall of Jerusalem more than 100
years before it happened (586 B.C.), and the rebuilding
of the Temple about 200 years before it happened. Obviously, these prophecies came from a God who knows the
future. Knowing this, are you willing to let him have your
biggest concerns?*

BAD TIMES
*(45:7) God tells us that he sends the good times and
the bad. Life is sprinkled with both types of experiences,
and both are needed for us to grow spiritually. We might
complain to God about the bad and forget to thank him
for the good. But good and bad experiences can build
up our trust in God.*

MY STORY: Julio

When my family moved from Mexico to the United States, everything familiar to me was gone. I had to learn a new language, adjust to totally different ways of doing things, and make friends with people who seemed to have grown up on a different planet rather than in a different country. I was very, very lonely for a long time.

I turned often to the Bible. So many verses were meaningful to me. But Isaiah 46:4 especially helped because it spoke of God's tender care and how he would be with me always, even when I'm old. I would imagine God right there with me in this strange school, and I'd talk to him in my heart, telling him how I felt. It was a great comfort to know that he was right there with me and that he cared. I knew he heard my prayers and understood—and I could speak to him in Spanish! This experience has brought me closer to God as I depend on him every day for the understanding and help I need to make this adjustment.

FUTURE CONVERSION OF GENTILES

¹⁴This is what the LORD says:

"You will rule the Egyptians,
 the Ethiopians,* and the Sabeans.
They will come to you with all their
 merchandise,
 and it will all be yours.
They will follow you as prisoners in chains.
 They will fall to their knees in front of you
 and say,
'God is with you, and he is the only God.
 There is no other.'"

¹⁵ Truly, O God of Israel, our Savior,
 you work in mysterious ways.
¹⁶ All craftsmen who make idols will be
 humiliated.
 They will all be disgraced together.
¹⁷ But the LORD will save the people of Israel
 with eternal salvation.
Throughout everlasting ages,
 they will never again be humiliated and
 disgraced.
¹⁸ For the LORD is God,
 and he created the heavens and earth
 and put everything in place.

He made the world to be lived in,
 not to be a place of empty chaos.
"I am the LORD," he says,
 "and there is no other.
¹⁹ I publicly proclaim bold promises.
 I do not whisper obscurities in some dark
 corner.
I would not have told the people of Israel*
 to seek me
 if I could not be found.
I, the LORD, speak only what is true
 and declare only what is right.

²⁰ "Gather together and come,
 you fugitives from surrounding nations.
What fools they are who carry around their
 wooden idols
 and pray to gods that cannot save!
²¹ Consult together, argue your case.
 Get together and decide what to say.
Who made these things known so long ago?
 What idol ever told you they would
 happen?
Was it not I, the LORD?
 For there is no other God but me,
a righteous God and Savior.
 There is none but me.
²² Let all the world look to me for salvation!
 For I am God; there is no other.
²³ I have sworn by my own name;
 I have spoken the truth,
 and I will never go back on my word:
Every knee will bend to me,
 and every tongue will confess allegiance
 to me.*"
²⁴ The people will declare,
 "The LORD is the source of all my
 righteousness and strength."
And all who were angry with him
 will come to him and be ashamed.
²⁵ In the LORD all the generations of Israel will
 be justified,
 and in him they will boast.

46 BABYLON'S FALSE GODS

¹ Bel and Nebo, the gods of Babylon,
 bow as they are lowered to the ground.
They are being hauled away on ox carts.
 The poor beasts stagger under the weight.
² Both the idols and their owners are bowed
 down.
 The gods cannot protect the people,
and the people cannot protect the gods.
 They go off into captivity together.

45:14 Hebrew *Cushites.*   **45:19** Hebrew *of Jacob.* See note on 14:1.
45:23 Hebrew *will confess;* Greek version reads *will confess and give praise to God.* Compare Rom 14:11.

³ "Listen to me, descendants of Jacob,
  all you who remain in Israel.
I have cared for you since you were born.
  Yes, I carried you before you were born.
⁴ I will be your God throughout your lifetime—
  until your hair is white with age.
I made you, and I will care for you.
  I will carry you along and save you.

⁵ "To whom will you compare me?
  Who is my equal?
⁶ Some people pour out their silver
    and gold
  and hire a craftsman to make
    a god from it.
  Then they bow down and worship it!
⁷ They carry it around on their shoulders,
  and when they set it down, it stays there.
  It can't even move!
And when someone prays to it, there is no
    answer.
  It can't rescue anyone from trouble.

⁸ "Do not forget this! Keep it in mind!
  Remember this, you guilty ones.
⁹ Remember the things I have done in the
    past.
  For I alone am God!
I am God, and there is none like me.
¹⁰ Only I can tell you the future
  before it even happens.
Everything I plan will come to pass,
  for I do whatever I wish.
¹¹ I will call a swift bird of prey from the east—
  a leader from a distant land to come and
    do my bidding.

46:13 Hebrew *Zion.* **47:1** Or *Chaldea;* also in 47:5.

I have said what I would do,
  and I will do it.

¹² "Listen to me, you stubborn people
  who are so far from doing right.
¹³ For I am ready to set things right,
  not in the distant future, but right now!
I am ready to save Jerusalem*
  and show my glory to Israel.

47 PREDICTION OF BABYLON'S FALL

¹ "Come down, virgin daughter of Babylon,
  and sit in the dust.
For your days of sitting on a throne have
    ended.
O daughter of Babylonia,* never again will
    you be
  the lovely princess, tender and delicate.
² Take heavy millstones and grind flour.
  Remove your veil, and strip off your robe.
  Expose yourself to public view.
³ You will be naked and burdened with
    shame.
  I will take vengeance against you
    without pity."

. . . .

POWER
*(47:1-9) Caught up in the pursuit of power and pleasure,
Babylon believed in its own greatness and claimed to be
the only power on earth. Nebuchadnezzar, its king, called
himself "god," but the true God taught him a powerful
lesson by taking everything away from him (Dan 4:27-37).
Isaiah predicted the fall of this seemingly invincible
nation, just as he prophesied about the destruction of
other nations. Only God is truly invincible. Does he have
your complete trust?*

I WONDER...

**What's so wrong about horoscopes?
They're just harmless entertainment, right?**

Many activities that seem harmless unfortunately
lead to more harmful activities like those of the
occult.

The Bible mentions several examples of occult
activity among the people of Israel and other nations.
When King Saul of Israel wanted information about
an upcoming battle, he consulted someone who
claimed to be able to speak to the dead (see 1 Sam
28). Other passages deal with astrology, divination,
wizards, and sorcery (see Deut 18:10-14; 2 Chr 33:6;
Isa 47:12-15; Dan 2:1-2; Acts 8:9-13; 16:16-19). God
always condemned these activities.

If Satan can get people to tolerate evil in small

doses at a time, eventually they may become
desensitized and not recognize that they are
being fed something that will dull their interest
in God.

Satan would never get anyone to follow him if
he revealed all his evil. Instead, he slowly gives us
small doses of evil until we're so desensitized to it
that it seems a normal part of life.

This is the strategy: to capture our minds through
one small compromise into darkness after another.

Our best defense is to know the truth of the Word
of God, so we can discern when we are being tempted
by evil. God knows it is real. And Jesus came to
destroy the works of the devil. Remember, "the Spirit
who lives in you is greater than the spirit who lives in
the world" (1 Jn 4:4).

⁴ Our Redeemer, whose name is the Lord of
    Heaven's Armies,
    is the Holy One of Israel.

⁵ "O beautiful Babylon, sit now in darkness
    and silence.
    Never again will you be known as the
      queen of kingdoms.
⁶ For I was angry with my chosen people
    and punished them by letting them fall
      into your hands.
But you, Babylon, showed them no mercy.
    You oppressed even the elderly.
⁷ You said, 'I will reign forever as queen of the
    world!'
    You did not reflect on your actions
    or think about their consequences.

⁸ "Listen to this, you pleasure-loving
    kingdom,
    living at ease and feeling secure.
You say, 'I am the only one, and there is no
    other.
    I will never be a widow or lose my
      children.'
⁹ Well, both these things will come upon you
    in a moment:
    widowhood and the loss of your children.
Yes, these calamities will come upon you,
    despite all your witchcraft and magic.

¹⁰ "You felt secure in your wickedness.
    'No one sees me,' you said.
But your 'wisdom' and 'knowledge' have led
    you astray,
    and you said, 'I am the only one, and
      there is no other.'
¹¹ So disaster will overtake you,
    and you won't be able to charm it away.
Calamity will fall upon you,
    and you won't be able to buy your way
      out.
A catastrophe will strike you suddenly,
    one for which you are not prepared.

¹² "Now use your magical charms!
    Use the spells you have worked at all
      these years!
Maybe they will do you some good.
    Maybe they can make someone afraid
      of you.
¹³ All the advice you receive has made you
    tired.
    Where are all your astrologers,
those stargazers who make predictions
    each month?
    Let them stand up and save you from
    what the future holds.
¹⁴ But they are like straw burning in a fire;

they cannot save themselves from the
    flame.
You will get no help from them at all;
    their hearth is no place to sit for warmth.
¹⁵ And all your friends,
    those with whom you've done business
      since childhood,
will go their own ways,
    turning a deaf ear to your cries.

48 GOD'S STUBBORN PEOPLE

¹ "Listen to me, O family of Jacob,
    you who are called by the name of Israel
    and born into the family of Judah.
Listen, you who take oaths in the name of
    the Lord
    and call on the God of Israel.
You don't keep your promises,
²   even though you call yourself the holy city
and talk about depending on the God of
    Israel,
    whose name is the Lord of Heaven's
      Armies.
³ Long ago I told you what was going to
    happen.
    Then suddenly I took action,
    and all my predictions came true.
⁴ For I know how stubborn and obstinate
    you are.
    Your necks are as unbending as iron.
    Your heads are as hard as bronze.
⁵ That is why I told you what would happen;
    I told you beforehand what I was going
      to do.
Then you could never say, 'My idols did it.
    My wooden image and metal god
      commanded it to happen!'
⁶ You have heard my predictions and seen
    them fulfilled,
    but you refuse to admit it.
Now I will tell you new things,
    secrets you have not yet heard.
⁷ They are brand new, not things from the
    past.
    So you cannot say, 'We knew that all the
      time!'

⁸ "Yes, I will tell you of things that are entirely
    new,
    things you never heard of before.
For I know so well what traitors you are.
    You have been rebels from birth.
⁹ Yet for my own sake and for the honor of my
    name,
    I will hold back my anger and not wipe
    you out.

¹⁰ I have refined you, but not as silver is
refined.
Rather, I have refined you in the furnace
of suffering.
¹¹ I will rescue you for my sake—
yes, for my own sake!
I will not let my reputation be tarnished,
and I will not share my glory with idols!

FREEDOM FROM BABYLON

¹² "Listen to me, O family of Jacob,
Israel my chosen one!
I alone am God,
the First and the Last.
¹³ It was my hand that laid the foundations of
the earth,
my right hand that spread out the
heavens above.
When I call out the stars,
they all appear in order."

¹⁴ Have any of your idols ever told you this?
Come, all of you, and listen:
The LORD has chosen Cyrus as his ally.
He will use him to put an end to the
empire of Babylon
and to destroy the Babylonian* armies.

¹⁵ "I have said it: I am calling Cyrus!
I will send him on this errand and will
help him succeed.
¹⁶ Come closer, and listen to this.
From the beginning I have told you plainly
what would happen."

And now the Sovereign LORD and his Spirit
have sent me with this message.
¹⁷ This is what the LORD says—
your Redeemer, the Holy One of Israel:
"I am the LORD your God,
who teaches you what is good for you
and leads you along the paths you should
follow.
¹⁸ Oh, that you had listened to my commands!
Then you would have had peace flowing
like a gentle river
and righteousness rolling over you like
waves in the sea.
¹⁹ Your descendants would have been like the
sands along the seashore—
too many to count!
There would have been no need for your
destruction,
or for cutting off your family name."

²⁰ Yet even now, be free from your captivity!
Leave Babylon and the Babylonians.*

Sing out this message!
Shout it to the ends of the earth!
The LORD has redeemed his servants,
the people of Israel.*
²¹ They were not thirsty
when he led them through the desert.
He divided the rock,
and water gushed out for them to drink.
²² "But there is no peace for the wicked,"
says the LORD.

49 THE LORD'S SERVANT COMMISSIONED

¹ Listen to me, all you in distant lands!
Pay attention, you who are far away!
The LORD called me before my birth;
from within the womb he called me by
name.
² He made my words of judgment as sharp
as a sword.
He has hidden me in the shadow of
his hand.
I am like a sharp arrow in his quiver.
³ He said to me, "You are my servant, Israel,
and you will bring me glory."

⁴ I replied, "But my work seems so useless!
I have spent my strength for nothing and
to no purpose.
Yet I leave it all in the LORD's hand;
I will trust God for my reward."

⁵ And now the LORD speaks—
the one who formed me in my mother's
womb to be his servant,
who commissioned me to bring Israel
back to him.
The LORD has honored me,
and my God has given me strength.
⁶ He says, "You will do more than restore the
people of Israel to me.
I will make you a light to the Gentiles,
and you will bring my salvation to the
ends of the earth."

⁷ The LORD, the Redeemer
and Holy One of Israel,
says to the one who is despised and
rejected by the nations,
to the one who is the servant
of rulers:

....

PLAIN
(48:16) *God's message has been told plainly and clearly,
not in secret. We have a tendency to complicate God's
message. When God talks through his messenger, whomever he has chosen, our job is to listen. The closer we
come to God, the better we can listen to what he is saying.*

48:14 Or *Chaldean.* **48:20a** Or *the Chaldeans.* **48:20b** Hebrew
his servant, Jacob. See note on 14:1.

"Kings will stand at attention when you
    pass by.
Princes will also bow low
because of the LORD, the faithful one,
    the Holy One of Israel, who has
    chosen you."

PROMISES OF ISRAEL'S RESTORATION
8This
is what the LORD says:

"At just the right time, I will respond to you.*
    On the day of salvation I will help you.
I will protect you and give you to the people
    as my covenant with them.
Through you I will reestablish the land of
    Israel
    and assign it to its own people again.
9 I will say to the prisoners, 'Come out in
    freedom,'
    and to those in darkness, 'Come into the
    light.'
They will be my sheep, grazing in green
    pastures
    and on hills that were previously bare.
10 They will neither hunger nor thirst.
    The searing sun will not reach them
    anymore.
For the LORD in his mercy will lead them;
    he will lead them beside cool waters.
11 And I will make my mountains into level
    paths for them.
    The highways will be raised above the
    valleys.
12 See, my people will return from far away,
    from lands to the north and west,
    and from as far south as Egypt.*"

13 Sing for joy, O heavens!
    Rejoice, O earth!
    Burst into song, O mountains!
For the LORD has comforted his people
    and will have compassion on them in
    their suffering.

14 Yet Jerusalem* says, "The LORD has
    deserted us;
    the Lord has forgotten us."

15 "Never! Can a mother forget her nursing
    child?

Can she feel no love for the child she has
    borne?
But even if that were possible,
    I would not forget you!
16 See, I have written your name on the palms
    of my hands.
    Always in my mind is a picture of
    Jerusalem's walls in ruins.
17 Soon your descendants will come back,
    and all who are trying to destroy you will
    go away.
18 Look around you and see,
    for all your children will come back to you.
As surely as I live," says the LORD,
    "they will be like jewels or bridal
    ornaments for you to display.

19 "Even the most desolate parts of your
    abandoned land
    will soon be crowded with your people.
Your enemies who enslaved you
    will be far away.
20 The generations born in exile will return
    and say,
    'We need more room! It's crowded here!'
21 Then you will think to yourself,
    'Who has given me all these
    descendants?
For most of my children were killed,
    and the rest were carried away into exile.
I was left here all alone.
    Where did all these people come from?
Who bore these children?
    Who raised them for me?'"

22 This is what the Sovereign LORD says:
    "See, I will give a signal to the godless
    nations.
They will carry your little sons back to you in
    their arms;
    they will bring your daughters on their
    shoulders.
23 Kings and queens will serve you
    and care for all your needs.
They will bow to the earth before you
    and lick the dust from your feet.
Then you will know that I am the LORD.
    Those who trust in me will never be put
    to shame."

24 Who can snatch the plunder of war from the
    hands of a warrior?
    Who can demand that a tyrant* let his
    captives go?

....

DESERTED
(49:14-15) Isaiah prophesied that the people of Israel
would feel deserted by God after their land was invaded.
Isaiah pointed out that God would never leave them, just
as a mother wouldn't leave her little child. Yet hard times
can make us feel unloved or abandoned. This passage in
Isaiah is a good reminder that God will never forsake us
(see also Heb 13:5).

49:8 Greek version reads *I heard you.* Compare 2 Cor 6:2.   49:12 As
in Dead Sea Scrolls, which read *from the region of Aswan,* which is
in southern Egypt. Masoretic Text reads *from the region of Sinim.*
49:14 Hebrew *Zion.*   49:24 As in Dead Sea Scrolls, Syriac version,
and Latin Vulgate (also see 49:25); Masoretic Text reads *a righteous
person.*

²⁵ But the LORD says,
"The captives of warriors will be released,
and the plunder of tyrants will be
retrieved.
For I will fight those who fight you,
and I will save your children.
²⁶ I will feed your enemies with their own flesh.
They will be drunk with rivers of their own
blood.
All the world will know that I, the LORD,
am your Savior and your Redeemer,
the Mighty One of Israel.*"

50 This is what the LORD says:

"Was your mother sent away because I
divorced her?
Did I sell you as slaves to my creditors?
No, you were sold because of your sins.
And your mother, too, was taken because
of your sins.
² Why was no one there when I came?
Why didn't anyone answer when I called?
Is it because I have no power to rescue?
No, that is not the reason!
For I can speak to the sea and make it
dry up!
I can turn rivers into deserts covered with
dying fish.
³ I dress the skies in darkness,
covering them with clothes of mourning."

THE LORD'S OBEDIENT SERVANT

⁴ The Sovereign LORD has given me his words
of wisdom,
so that I know how to comfort the weary.
Morning by morning he wakens me
and opens my understanding to his will.
⁵ The Sovereign LORD has spoken to me,
and I have listened.
I have not rebelled or turned away.
⁶ I offered my back to those who beat me
and my cheeks to those who pulled out
my beard.
I did not hide my face
from mockery and spitting.
⁷ Because the Sovereign LORD helps me,
I will not be disgraced.
Therefore, I have set my face like a stone,
determined to do his will.
And I know that I will not be put to shame.
⁸ He who gives me justice is near.
Who will dare to bring charges against
me now?

49:26 Hebrew *of Jacob*. See note on 14:1.   **51:3** Hebrew *Zion*; also
in 51:16.

Where are my accusers?
Let them appear!
⁹ See, the Sovereign LORD is on my side!
Who will declare me guilty?
All my enemies will be destroyed
like old clothes that have been eaten
by moths!

¹⁰ Who among you fears the LORD
and obeys his servant?
If you are walking in darkness,
without a ray of light,
trust in the LORD
and rely on your God.
¹¹ But watch out, you who live in your own
light
and warm yourselves by your own fires.
This is the reward you will receive from me:
You will soon fall down in great torment.

51 A CALL TO TRUST THE LORD

¹ "Listen to me, all who hope for
deliverance—
all who seek the LORD!
Consider the rock from which you were cut,
the quarry from which you were mined.
² Yes, think about Abraham, your ancestor,
and Sarah, who gave birth to your nation.
Abraham was only one man when I called
him.
But when I blessed him, he became a
great nation."

³ The LORD will comfort Israel* again
and have pity on her ruins.
Her desert will blossom like Eden,
her barren wilderness like the garden
of the LORD.
Joy and gladness will be found there.
Songs of thanksgiving will fill the air.

⁴ "Listen to me, my people.
Hear me, Israel,
for my law will be proclaimed,
and my justice will become a light to the
nations.
⁵ My mercy and justice are coming soon.
My salvation is on the way.
My strong arm will bring justice to the
nations.
All distant lands will look to me
and wait in hope for my powerful arm.
⁶ Look up to the skies above,
and gaze down on the earth below.
For the skies will disappear like smoke,
and the earth will wear out like a piece
of clothing.

The people of the earth will die like flies,
  but my salvation lasts forever.
  My righteous rule will never end!

7 "Listen to me, you who know right from
    wrong,
  you who cherish my law in your hearts.
Do not be afraid of people's scorn,
  nor fear their insults.
8 For the moth will devour them as it devours
    clothing.
  The worm will eat at them as it eats wool.
But my righteousness will last forever.
  My salvation will continue from
    generation to generation."

9 Wake up, wake up, O LORD! Clothe yourself
    with strength!
  Flex your mighty right arm!
Rouse yourself as in the days of old
  when you slew Egypt, the dragon of the
    Nile.*
10 Are you not the same today,
  the one who dried up the sea,
making a path of escape through the depths
  so that your people could cross over?
11 Those who have been ransomed by the
    LORD will return.
  They will enter Jerusalem* singing,
    crowned with everlasting joy.
Sorrow and mourning will disappear,
  and they will be filled with joy and
    gladness.

12 "I, yes I, am the one who comforts you.
  So why are you afraid of mere humans,
  who wither like the grass and disappear?
13 Yet you have forgotten the LORD, your
    Creator,
  the one who stretched out the sky like
    a canopy
  and laid the foundations of the earth.
Will you remain in constant dread of human
    oppressors?
Will you continue to fear the anger of your
    enemies?
Where is their fury and anger now?
  It is gone!

RIDICULED
*(51:7) Isaiah encouraged those who served God to
discern right from wrong and to follow God's laws. He
also gave them hope when they faced people's scorn
or slander because of their faith. We need not fear when
people ridicule us for our faith because God is with us,
and truth will prevail. If people make fun of you or dislike
you because you believe in God, remember that they are
not against you personally, but against God. He'll deal
with them.*

14 Soon all you captives will be released!
  Imprisonment, starvation, and death will
    not be your fate!
15 For I am the LORD your God,
  who stirs up the sea, causing its waves
    to roar.
  My name is the LORD of Heaven's Armies.
16 And I have put my words in your mouth
  and hidden you safely in my hand.
I stretched out* the sky like a canopy
  and laid the foundations of the earth.
I am the one who says to Israel,
  'You are my people!'"

17 Wake up, wake up, O Jerusalem!
  You have drunk the cup of the LORD's fury.
You have drunk the cup of terror,
  tipping out its last drops.
18 Not one of your children is left alive
  to take your hand and guide you.
19 These two calamities have fallen on you:
  desolation and destruction, famine
    and war.
And who is left to sympathize with you?
  Who is left to comfort you?*
20 For your children have fainted and lie in the
    streets,
  helpless as antelopes caught in a net.
The LORD has poured out his fury;
  God has rebuked them.

21 But now listen to this, you afflicted ones
  who sit in a drunken stupor,
  though not from drinking wine.
22 This is what the Sovereign LORD,
  your God and Defender, says:
"See, I have taken the terrible cup from your
    hands.
  You will drink no more of my fury.
23 Instead, I will hand that cup to your
    tormentors,
  those who said, 'We will trample you into
    the dust
  and walk on your backs.'"

52 DELIVERANCE FOR JERUSALEM

1 Wake up, wake up, O Zion!
  Clothe yourself with strength.
Put on your beautiful clothes, O holy city
  of Jerusalem,
  for unclean and godless people will enter
    your gates no longer.

51:9 Hebrew *You slew Rahab; you pierced the dragon.* Rahab is the
name of a mythical sea monster that represents chaos in ancient
literature. The name is used here as a poetic name for Egypt.
51:11 Hebrew *Zion.*   **51:16** As in Syriac version (see also 51:13);
Hebrew reads *planted.*   **51:19** As in Dead Sea Scrolls and Greek,
Latin, and Syriac versions; Masoretic Text reads *How can
I comfort you?*

² Rise from the dust, O Jerusalem.
  Sit in a place of honor.
Remove the chains of slavery from your
  neck,
  O captive daughter of Zion.
³ For this is what the LORD says:
"When I sold you into exile,
  I received no payment.
Now I can redeem you
  without having to pay for you."

⁴This is what the Sovereign LORD says: "Long ago my people chose to live in Egypt. Now they are oppressed by Assyria. ⁵What is this?" asks the LORD. "Why are my people enslaved again? Those who rule them shout in exultation. My name is blasphemed all day long.* ⁶But I will reveal my name to my people, and they will come to know its power. Then at last they will recognize that I am the one who speaks to them."

⁷ How beautiful on the mountains
  are the feet of the messenger who brings
    good news,
  the good news of peace and salvation,
  the news that the God of Israel* reigns!
⁸ The watchmen shout and sing with joy,
  for before their very eyes
  they see the LORD returning to
    Jerusalem.*
⁹ Let the ruins of Jerusalem break into joyful
    song,
  for the LORD has comforted his people.
  He has redeemed Jerusalem.
¹⁰ The LORD has demonstrated his holy power
  before the eyes of all the nations.
All the ends of the earth will see
  the victory of our God.

¹¹ Get out! Get out and leave your captivity,
  where everything you touch is unclean.
Get out of there and purify yourselves,
  you who carry home the sacred objects
    of the LORD.
¹² You will not leave in a hurry,
  running for your lives.
For the LORD will go ahead of you;
  yes, the God of Israel will protect you
    from behind.

THE LORD'S SUFFERING SERVANT

¹³ See, my servant will prosper;
  he will be highly exalted.

¹⁴ But many were amazed when they
    saw him.*
  His face was so disfigured he seemed
    hardly human,
  and from his appearance, one would
    scarcely know he was a man.
¹⁵ And he will startle* many nations.
  Kings will stand speechless in his
    presence.
For they will see what they had not been
    told;
  they will understand what they had not
    heard about.*

53 ¹Who has believed our message?
  To whom has the LORD revealed his
    powerful arm?
² My servant grew up in the LORD's presence
  like a tender green shoot,
  like a root in dry ground.
There was nothing beautiful or majestic
  about his appearance,
  nothing to attract us to him.
³ He was despised and rejected—
  a man of sorrows, acquainted with
    deepest grief.
We turned our backs on him and looked the
    other way.
  He was despised, and we did not care.

⁴ Yet it was our weaknesses he carried;
  it was our sorrows* that weighed him
    down.
And we thought his troubles were a
    punishment from God,
  a punishment for his own sins!
⁵ But he was pierced for our rebellion,
  crushed for our sins.
He was beaten so we could be whole.
  He was whipped so we could be healed.
⁶ All of us, like sheep, have strayed away.
  We have left God's paths to follow our
    own.
Yet the LORD laid on him
  the sins of us all.

⁷ He was oppressed and treated harshly,
  yet he never said a word.

52:5 Greek version reads *The Gentiles continually blaspheme my name because of you.* Compare Rom 2:24.   52:7 Hebrew *of Zion.*   52:8 Hebrew *to Zion.*   52:14 As in Syriac version; Hebrew reads *you.*   52:15a Or *cleanse.*   52:15b Greek version reads *Those who have never been told about him will see, / and those who have never heard of him will understand.* Compare Rom 15:21.   53:4 Or *Yet it was our sicknesses he carried; / it was our diseases.*

HE'S IN CONTROL
(52:13–53:12) The servant, as the term is used here, is the Messiah—Jesus. This prophecy occurred hundreds of years before Jesus arrived and is one among many in the book of Isaiah (see also 7:14; 9:6-7; 42:1-4). Think of the coordination necessary to bring everything to pass! This just goes to show the incredible control God has over everything. Yet for all of his control, he never forces himself into someone's life. He waits to be invited. Does he have control over your life?

BUT HE WAS PIERCED FOR OUR REBELLION, CRUSHED FOR OUR SINS.
HE WAS BEATEN SO WE COULD BE WHOLE.
HE WAS WHIPPED SO WE COULD BE HEALED.
ISAIAH 53:5

He was led like a lamb to the slaughter.
And as a sheep is silent before the
shearers,
he did not open his mouth.
8 Unjustly condemned,
he was led away.*
No one cared that he died without
descendants,
that his life was cut short in midstream.*
But he was struck down
for the rebellion of my people.
9 He had done no wrong
and had never deceived anyone.
But he was buried like a criminal;
he was put in a rich man's grave.

10 But it was the LORD's good plan to crush
him
and cause him grief.
Yet when his life is made an offering for sin,
he will have many descendants.
He will enjoy a long life,
and the LORD's good plan will prosper in
his hands.
11 When he sees all that is accomplished by
his anguish,
he will be satisfied.
And because of his experience,
my righteous servant will make it possible
for many to be counted righteous,
for he will bear all their sins.
12 I will give him the honors of a victorious
soldier,
because he exposed himself to death.
He was counted among the rebels.
He bore the sins of many and interceded
for rebels.

54 FUTURE GLORY FOR JERUSALEM

1 "Sing, O childless woman,
you who have never given birth!
Break into loud and joyful song,
O Jerusalem,
you who have never been in labor.
For the desolate woman now has more
children
than the woman who lives with her
husband,"
says the LORD.

2 "Enlarge your house; build an addition.
Spread out your home, and spare no
expense!
3 For you will soon be bursting at the seams.
Your descendants will occupy other
nations
and resettle the ruined cities.

4 "Fear not; you will no longer live in shame.
Don't be afraid; there is no more disgrace
for you.
You will no longer remember the shame
of your youth
and the sorrows of widowhood.
5 For your Creator will be your husband;
the LORD of Heaven's Armies is his name!
He is your Redeemer, the Holy One of Israel,
the God of all the earth.
6 For the LORD has called you back from your
grief—
as though you were a young wife
abandoned by her husband,"
says your God.
7 "For a brief moment I abandoned you,
but with great compassion I will take you
back.
8 In a burst of anger I turned my face away for
a little while.
But with everlasting love I will have
compassion on you,"
says the LORD, your Redeemer.

9 "Just as I swore in the time of Noah
that I would never again let a flood cover
the earth,
so now I swear
that I will never again be angry and
punish you.
10 For the mountains may move
and the hills disappear,
but even then my faithful love for you will
remain.
My covenant of blessing will never be
broken,"
says the LORD, who has mercy on you.

11 "O storm-battered city,
troubled and desolate!

53:8a Greek version reads *He was humiliated and received no justice.* Compare Acts 8:33.   **53:8b** Or *As for his contemporaries, / who cared that his life was cut short in midstream?* Greek version reads *Who can speak of his descendants? / For his life was taken from the earth.* Compare Acts 8:33.

I will rebuild you with precious jewels
and make your foundations from lapis
lazuli.

¹² I will make your towers of sparkling rubies,
your gates of shining gems,
and your walls of precious stones.

¹³ I will teach all your children,
and they will enjoy great peace.

¹⁴ You will be secure under a government that
is just and fair.
Your enemies will stay far away.
You will live in peace,
and terror will not come near.

¹⁵ If any nation comes to fight you,
it is not because I sent them.
Whoever attacks you will go down in
defeat.

¹⁶ "I have created the blacksmith
who fans the coals beneath the forge
and makes the weapons of destruction.
And I have created the armies that
destroy.

¹⁷ But in that coming day
no weapon turned against you will
succeed.
You will silence every voice
raised up to accuse you.
These benefits are enjoyed by the servants
of the LORD;
their vindication will come from me.
I, the LORD, have spoken!

55 INVITATION TO THE LORD'S SALVATION

¹ "Is anyone thirsty?
Come and drink—
even if you have no money!
Come, take your choice of wine or milk—
it's all free!

² Why spend your money on food that does
not give you strength?
Why pay for food that does you no good?
Listen to me, and you will eat what is good.
You will enjoy the finest food.

³ "Come to me with your ears wide open.
Listen, and you will find life.
I will make an everlasting covenant
with you.
I will give you all the unfailing love
I promised to David.

⁴ See how I used him to display my power
among the peoples.
I made him a leader among the
nations.

⁵ You also will command nations you
do not know,

and peoples unknown to you will come
running to obey,
because I, the LORD your God,
the Holy One of Israel, have made you
glorious."

⁶ Seek the LORD while you can find him.
Call on him now while he is near.

⁷ Let the wicked change their ways
and banish the very thought of doing
wrong.
Let them turn to the LORD that he may have
mercy on them.
Yes, turn to our God, for he will forgive
generously.

⁸ "My thoughts are nothing like your
thoughts," says the LORD.
"And my ways are far beyond anything
you could imagine.

⁹ For just as the heavens are higher than the
earth,
so my ways are higher than your ways
and my thoughts higher than your
thoughts.

¹⁰ "The rain and snow come down from the
heavens
and stay on the ground to water the earth.
They cause the grain to grow,
producing seed for the farmer
and bread for the hungry.

¹¹ It is the same with my word.
I send it out, and it always produces fruit.
It will accomplish all I want it to,
and it will prosper everywhere I send it.

¹² You will live in joy and peace.
The mountains and hills will burst into
song,
and the trees of the field will clap their
hands!

¹³ Where once there were thorns, cypress trees
will grow.
Where nettles grew, myrtles will
sprout up.
These events will bring great honor to the
LORD's name;
they will be an everlasting sign of his
power and love."

....

CALL NOW
*(55:6) Isaiah encouraged the people of Israel to call upon
the Lord while he is near. Sometimes we might think
that God has moved away from us. Often the truth is that
we're the ones who have drifted away. We do that when
we decide to go our own way, rather than his. But God is
always close by and will hear us whenever we call, even
if we're not sure he'll listen. Feeling far away? Don't be
afraid to call now!*

56 BLESSINGS FOR ALL NATIONS This is
what the Lord says:

"Be just and fair to all.
    Do what is right and good,
for I am coming soon to rescue you
    and to display my righteousness among
        you.
² Blessed are all those
    who are careful to do this.
Blessed are those who honor my Sabbath
        days of rest
    and keep themselves from doing wrong.

³ "Don't let foreigners who commit
        themselves to the Lord say,
    'The Lord will never let me be part of his
        people.'
And don't let the eunuchs say,
    'I'm a dried-up tree with no children and
        no future.'
⁴ For this is what the Lord says:
I will bless those eunuchs
    who keep my Sabbath days holy
and who choose to do what pleases me
    and commit their lives to me.
⁵ I will give them—within the walls of my
        house—
    a memorial and a name
    far greater than sons and daughters could
        give.
For the name I give them is an everlasting
        one.
    It will never disappear!

⁶ "I will also bless the foreigners who commit
        themselves to the Lord,
    who serve him and love his name,
who worship him and do not desecrate the
        Sabbath day of rest,
    and who hold fast to my covenant.
⁷ I will bring them to my holy mountain of
        Jerusalem
    and will fill them with joy in my house of
        prayer.
I will accept their burnt offerings and
        sacrifices,
    because my Temple will be called a house
        of prayer for all nations.
⁸ For the Sovereign Lord,
    who brings back the outcasts of Israel,
        says:
I will bring others, too,
    besides my people Israel."

SINFUL LEADERS CONDEMNED
⁹ Come, wild animals of the field!
    Come, wild animals of the forest!
Come and devour my people!
¹⁰ For the leaders of my people—
    the Lord's watchmen, his shepherds—
    are blind and ignorant.
They are like silent watchdogs
    that give no warning when danger comes.
They love to lie around, sleeping and
        dreaming.
¹¹ Like greedy dogs, they are never satisfied.
They are ignorant shepherds,
    all following their own path
    and intent on personal gain.
¹² "Come," they say, "let's get some wine and
        have a party.
    Let's all get drunk.
Then tomorrow we'll do it again
    and have an even bigger party!"

57 ¹Good people pass away;
    the godly often die before their
        time.
But no one seems to care or wonder why.
No one seems to understand
    that God is protecting them from the evil
        to come.
² For those who follow godly paths
    will rest in peace when they die.

IDOLATROUS WORSHIP CONDEMNED
³ "But you—come here, you witches' children,
    you offspring of adulterers and
        prostitutes!
⁴ Whom do you mock,
    making faces and sticking out your
        tongues?
    You children of sinners and liars!
⁵ You worship your idols with great passion
    beneath the oaks and under every green
        tree.
You sacrifice your children down in the
        valleys,
    among the jagged rocks in the cliffs.
⁶ Your gods are the smooth stones in the
        valleys.
    You worship them with liquid offerings
        and grain offerings.
They, not I, are your inheritance.
    Do you think all this makes me happy?
⁷ You have committed adultery on every high
        mountain.
    There you have worshiped idols
    and have been unfaithful to me.
⁸ You have put pagan symbols
    on your doorposts and behind your
        doors.
You have left me

and climbed into bed with these
detestable gods.
You have committed yourselves to them.
You love to look at their naked bodies.
⁹ You have given olive oil to Molech*
with many gifts of perfume.
You have traveled far,
even into the world of the dead,*
to find new gods to love.
¹⁰ You grew weary in your search,
but you never gave up.
Desire gave you renewed strength,
and you did not grow weary.

¹¹ "Are you afraid of these idols?
Do they terrify you?
Is that why you have lied to me
and forgotten me and my words?
Is it because of my long silence
that you no longer fear me?
¹² Now I will expose your so-called good
deeds.
None of them will help you.
¹³ Let's see if your idols can save you
when you cry to them for help.
Why, a puff of wind can knock them down!
If you just breathe on them, they fall over!
But whoever trusts in me will inherit the
land
and possess my holy mountain."

GOD FORGIVES THE REPENTANT

¹⁴ God says, "Rebuild the road!
Clear away the rocks and stones
so my people can return from captivity."

¹⁵ The high and lofty one who lives in eternity,
the Holy One, says this:
"I live in the high and holy place
with those whose spirits are contrite and
humble.
I restore the crushed spirit of the humble
and revive the courage of those with
repentant hearts.
¹⁶ For I will not fight against you forever;
I will not always be angry.
If I were, all people would pass away—
all the souls I have made.
¹⁷ I was angry,
so I punished these greedy people.
I withdrew from them,
but they kept going on their own
stubborn way.
¹⁸ I have seen what they do,
but I will heal them anyway!
I will lead them.

I will comfort those who mourn,
¹⁹ bringing words of praise to their lips.
May they have abundant peace, both near
and far,"
says the LORD, who heals them.
²⁰ "But those who still reject me are like the
restless sea,
which is never still
but continually churns up mud and dirt.
²¹ There is no peace for the wicked,"
says my God.

58 TRUE AND FALSE WORSHIP

¹ "Shout with the voice of a trumpet blast.
Shout aloud! Don't be timid.
Tell my people Israel* of their sins!
² Yet they act so pious!
They come to the Temple every day
and seem delighted to learn all about me.
They act like a righteous nation
that would never abandon the laws of its
God.
They ask me to take action on their behalf,
pretending they want to be near me.
³ 'We have fasted before you!' they say.
'Why aren't you impressed?
We have been very hard on ourselves,
and you don't even notice it!'

"I will tell you why!" I respond.
"It's because you are fasting to please
yourselves.
Even while you fast,
you keep oppressing your workers.
⁴ What good is fasting
when you keep on fighting and
quarreling?
This kind of fasting
will never get you anywhere with me.

....

GOOD DEEDS
*(57:12-13) Isaiah warned the idol worshipers of Judah
that their attempts at right living wouldn't save them any
more than their weak, worthless idols could. We cannot
be saved through good deeds because our best deeds
aren't good enough to outweigh the bad things we've
done (see Isa 64:6). Salvation is a gift from God (Eph
2:10). Like any gift, we can either accept it or reject it. So,
your choice is . . . ?*

TRUE WORSHIP
*(58:1-14) Isaiah warned the people against hypocritical
actions. He wanted them to know that true worship was
more than religious ritual, going to the Temple every day,
and listening to Scripture readings. It involved authentic-
ity and an honest confession of wrongdoing. But having
a genuine compassion for the poor, the helpless, and the
oppressed was also an aspect of worship. That's still the
case today. How "true" is your worship of God?*

57:9a Or *to the king.*   **57:9b** Hebrew *into Sheol.*   **58:1** Hebrew
Jacob. See note on 14:1.

⁵ You humble yourselves
   by going through the motions of penance,
bowing your heads
   like reeds bending in the wind.
You dress in burlap
   and cover yourselves with ashes.
Is this what you call fasting?
   Do you really think this will please the
      LORD?

⁶ "No, this is the kind of fasting I want:
Free those who are wrongly imprisoned;
   lighten the burden of those who work
      for you.
Let the oppressed go free,
   and remove the chains that bind people.
⁷ Share your food with the hungry,
   and give shelter to the homeless.
Give clothes to those who need them,
   and do not hide from relatives who need
      your help.

⁸ "Then your salvation will come like the
      dawn,
   and your wounds will quickly heal.
Your godliness will lead you forward,
   and the glory of the LORD will protect you
      from behind.
⁹ Then when you call, the LORD will answer.
   'Yes, I am here,' he will quickly reply.

"Remove the heavy yoke of oppression.
   Stop pointing your finger and spreading
      vicious rumors!
¹⁰ Feed the hungry,
   and help those in trouble.
Then your light will shine out from the
      darkness,
   and the darkness around you will be as
      bright as noon.
¹¹ The LORD will guide you continually,
   giving you water when you are dry
   and restoring your strength.
You will be like a well-watered garden,
   like an ever-flowing spring.
¹² Some of you will rebuild the deserted ruins
      of your cities.
   Then you will be known as a rebuilder
      of walls
   and a restorer of homes.

¹³ "Keep the Sabbath day holy.
   Don't pursue your own interests on that
      day,
   but enjoy the Sabbath
      and speak of it with delight as the LORD's
         holy day.
   Honor the Sabbath in everything you do on
      that day,

and don't follow your own desires or talk
      idly.
¹⁴ Then the LORD will be your delight.
   I will give you great honor
and satisfy you with the inheritance
   I promised to your ancestor Jacob.
I, the LORD, have spoken!"

59 WARNINGS AGAINST SIN

¹ Listen! The LORD's arm is not too weak to
      save you,
   nor is his ear too deaf to hear you call.
² It's your sins that have cut you off from God.
   Because of your sins, he has turned away
      and will not listen anymore.
³ Your hands are the hands of murderers,
   and your fingers are filthy with sin.
Your lips are full of lies,
   and your mouth spews corruption.

⁴ No one cares about being fair and honest.
   The people's lawsuits are based on lies.
They conceive evil deeds
   and then give birth to sin.
⁵ They hatch deadly snakes
   and weave spiders' webs.
Whoever falls into their webs will die,
   and there's danger even in getting near
      them.
⁶ Their webs can't be made into clothing,
   and nothing they do is productive.
All their activity is filled with sin,
   and violence is their trademark.
⁷ Their feet run to do evil,
   and they rush to commit murder.
They think only about sinning.
   Misery and destruction always follow
      them.
⁸ They don't know where to find peace
   or what it means to be just and good.
They have mapped out crooked roads,
   and no one who follows them knows
      a moment's peace.

⁹ So there is no justice among us,
   and we know nothing about right living.
We look for light but find only darkness.
   We look for bright skies but walk in
      gloom.
¹⁰ We grope like the blind along a wall,
   feeling our way like people without eyes.
Even at brightest noontime,
   we stumble as though it were dark.
Among the living,
   we are like the dead.
¹¹ We growl like hungry bears;
   we moan like mournful doves.

We look for justice, but it never comes.
We look for rescue, but it is far away
from us.
[12] For our sins are piled up before God
and testify against us.
Yes, we know what sinners we are.
[13] We know we have rebelled and have denied
the LORD.
We have turned our backs on our God.
We know how unfair and oppressive we
have been,
carefully planning our deceitful lies.
[14] Our courts oppose the righteous,
and justice is nowhere to be found.
Truth stumbles in the streets,
and honesty has been outlawed.
[15] Yes, truth is gone,
and anyone who renounces evil is
attacked.

The LORD looked and was displeased
to find there was no justice.
[16] He was amazed to see that no one
intervened
to help the oppressed.
So he himself stepped in to save them with
his strong arm,
and his justice sustained him.
[17] He put on righteousness as his body armor
and placed the helmet of salvation on his
head.
He clothed himself with a robe of vengeance
and wrapped himself in a cloak of divine
passion.
[18] He will repay his enemies for their evil
deeds.
His fury will fall on his foes.
He will pay them back even to the ends
of the earth.
[19] In the west, people will respect the name
of the LORD;
in the east, they will glorify him.
For he will come like a raging flood tide
driven by the breath of the LORD.*

[20] "The Redeemer will come to Jerusalem
to buy back those in Israel
who have turned from their sins,"*
says the LORD.

[21]"And this is my covenant with them," says
the LORD. "My Spirit will not leave them, and
neither will these words I have given you. They
will be on your lips and on the lips of your chil-

dren and your children's children forever. I, the
LORD, have spoken!

60 FUTURE GLORY FOR JERUSALEM
[1] "Arise, Jerusalem! Let your light shine for all
to see.
For the glory of the LORD rises to shine
on you.
[2] Darkness as black as night covers all the
nations of the earth,
but the glory of the LORD rises and
appears over you.
[3] All nations will come to your light;
mighty kings will come to see your
radiance.

[4] "Look and see, for everyone is coming
home!
Your sons are coming from distant lands;
your little daughters will be carried home.
[5] Your eyes will shine,
and your heart will thrill with joy,
for merchants from around the world will
come to you.
They will bring you the wealth of many
lands.
[6] Vast caravans of camels will converge
on you,
the camels of Midian and Ephah.
The people of Sheba will bring gold and
frankincense
and will come worshiping the LORD.
[7] The flocks of Kedar will be given to you,
and the rams of Nebaioth will be brought
for my altars.
I will accept their offerings,
and I will make my Temple glorious.

[8] "And what do I see flying like clouds to
Israel,
like doves to their nests?
[9] They are ships from the ends of the earth,
from lands that trust in me,
led by the great ships of Tarshish.
They are bringing the people of Israel home
from far away,
carrying their silver and gold.
They will honor the LORD your God,
the Holy One of Israel,
for he has filled you with splendor.

....

PATIENCE
*(60:1-22) What are you longing for these days? As we
read these promises of a future period, we long for their
fulfillment. But we must patiently wait for God's timing.
God is in control of history, and he weaves all of our lives
together into his plan.*

59:19 Or When the enemy comes like a raging flood tide, / the Spirit
of the LORD will drive him back.   59:20 Hebrew The Redeemer will
come to Zion / to buy back those in Jacob / who have turned from
their sins. Greek version reads The one who rescues will come on
behalf of Zion, / and he will turn Jacob away from ungodliness.
Compare Rom 11:26.

10 "Foreigners will come to rebuild your towns,
     and their kings will serve you.
 For though I have destroyed you in my
     anger,
   I will now have mercy on you through my
     grace.
11 Your gates will stay open day and night
     to receive the wealth of many lands.
 The kings of the world will be led as captives
     in a victory procession.
12 For the nations that refuse to serve you
     will be destroyed.

13 "The glory of Lebanon will be yours—
     the forests of cypress, fir, and pine—
 to beautify my sanctuary.
   My Temple will be glorious!
14 The descendants of your tormentors
     will come and bow before you.
 Those who despised you
     will kiss your feet.
 They will call you the City of the LORD,
     and Zion of the Holy One of Israel.

15 "Though you were once despised and
     hated,
     with no one traveling through you,
 I will make you beautiful forever,
     a joy to all generations.
16 Powerful kings and mighty nations
     will satisfy your every need,
 as though you were a child
     nursing at the breast of a queen.
 You will know at last that I, the LORD,
     am your Savior and your Redeemer,
     the Mighty One of Israel.*
17 I will exchange your bronze for gold,
     your iron for silver,
 your wood for bronze,
     and your stones for iron.
 I will make peace your leader
     and righteousness your ruler.
18 Violence will disappear from your land;
     the desolation and destruction of war
     will end.
 Salvation will surround you like city walls,
     and praise will be on the lips of all who
     enter there.

19 "No longer will you need the sun to shine
     by day,
     nor the moon to give its light by night,
 for the LORD your God will be your
     everlasting light,
   and your God will be your glory.
20 Your sun will never set;
     your moon will not go down.
 For the LORD will be your everlasting light.
   Your days of mourning will come to
     an end.
21 All your people will be righteous.
     They will possess their land forever,
 for I will plant them there with my own
     hands
   in order to bring myself glory.
22 The smallest family will become a thousand
     people,
   and the tiniest group will become a
     mighty nation.
 At the right time, I, the LORD, will make
     it happen."

61 GOOD NEWS FOR THE OPPRESSED

1 The Spirit of the Sovereign LORD is upon me,
     for the LORD has anointed me
     to bring good news to the poor.
 He has sent me to comfort the
     brokenhearted
   and to proclaim that captives will be
     released
   and prisoners will be freed.*
2 He has sent me to tell those who mourn
     that the time of the LORD's favor has
     come,*
   and with it, the day of God's anger
     against their enemies.
3 To all who mourn in Israel,*
     he will give a crown of beauty for ashes,
 a joyous blessing instead of mourning,
     festive praise instead of despair.
 In their righteousness, they will be like
     great oaks
   that the LORD has planted for his own
     glory.

4 They will rebuild the ancient ruins,
     repairing cities destroyed long ago.
 They will revive them,
     though they have been deserted for many
     generations.
5 Foreigners will be your servants.
     They will feed your flocks
     and plow your fields

JUSTICE FOR THE SUFFERING
(61:1-3) Isaiah assured the people of Judah that a Savior would someday make things right for his suffering people. Centuries after Isaiah, Jesus quoted this very passage (see Luke 4:16-22) as a sign that he had come to fulfill this passage. Some periods of suffering seem to go on forever. We long for relief, but also for justice when we're treated unjustly. Wondering when God will make things right for you? He may not act as quickly as we would like him to act. But he's never late.

60:16 Hebrew *of Jacob.* See note on 14:1.   **61:1** Greek version reads *and the blind will see.* Compare Luke 4:18.   **61:2** Or *to proclaim the acceptable year of the LORD.*   **61:3** Hebrew *in Zion.*

and tend your vineyards.
⁶ You will be called priests of the LORD,
   ministers of our God.
You will feed on the treasures of the nations
   and boast in their riches.
⁷ Instead of shame and dishonor,
   you will enjoy a double share of honor.
You will possess a double portion of
      prosperity in your land,
   and everlasting joy will be yours.

⁸ "For I, the LORD, love justice.
   I hate robbery and wrongdoing.
I will faithfully reward my people for their
      suffering
   and make an everlasting covenant with
      them.
⁹ Their descendants will be recognized
   and honored among the nations.
Everyone will realize that they are a people
   the LORD has blessed."

¹⁰ I am overwhelmed with joy in the LORD
      my God!
   For he has dressed me with the clothing
      of salvation
   and draped me in a robe of
      righteousness.
I am like a bridegroom in his wedding suit
   or a bride with her jewels.
¹¹ The Sovereign LORD will show his justice to
      the nations of the world.
   Everyone will praise him!
His righteousness will be like a garden in
      early spring,
   with plants springing up everywhere.

62 ISAIAH'S PRAYER FOR JERUSALEM

¹ Because I love Zion,
   I will not keep still.
Because my heart yearns for Jerusalem,
   I cannot remain silent.
I will not stop praying for her
   until her righteousness shines like the
      dawn,
   and her salvation blazes like a burning
      torch.
² The nations will see your righteousness.
   World leaders will be blinded by your
      glory.
And you will be given a new name
   by the LORD's own mouth.
³ The LORD will hold you in his hand for all
      to see—

62:4a Hebrew *Azubah*, which means "forsaken." 62:4b Hebrew
Shemamah, which means "desolate." 62:4c Hebrew *Hephzibah*,
which means "my delight is in her." 62:4d Hebrew *Beulah*, which
means "married." 62:11 Hebrew *Tell the daughter of Zion*.

a splendid crown in the hand of God.
⁴ Never again will you be called "The Forsaken
      City"*
   or "The Desolate Land."*
Your new name will be "The City of God's
      Delight"*
   and "The Bride of God,"*
for the LORD delights in you
   and will claim you as his bride.
⁵ Your children will commit themselves
      to you, O Jerusalem,
   just as a young man commits himself
      to his bride.
Then God will rejoice over you
   as a bridegroom rejoices over his bride.

⁶ O Jerusalem, I have posted watchmen on
      your walls;
   they will pray day and night, continually.
   Take no rest, all you who pray to the LORD.
⁷ Give the LORD no rest until he completes
      his work,
   until he makes Jerusalem the pride of the
      earth.
⁸ The LORD has sworn to Jerusalem by his own
      strength:
   "I will never again hand you over to your
      enemies.
Never again will foreign warriors come
   and take away your grain and new wine.
⁹ You raised the grain, and you will eat it,
      praising the LORD.
Within the courtyards of the Temple,
   you yourselves will drink the wine you
      have pressed."

¹⁰ Go out through the gates!
   Prepare the highway for my people to
      return!
Smooth out the road; pull out the boulders;
   raise a flag for all the nations to see.
¹¹ The LORD has sent this message to every
      land:
   "Tell the people of Israel,*
   'Look, your Savior is coming.

···

DETERMINATION

(62:1-7) *Isaiah's zeal for his country and his desire to see
the work of salvation completed caused him to pray continually, hoping that Israel would be saved. What are you
most determined to do? Get into a good college? Break
a sports record? Get straight A's? Do you share Isaiah's
determination to see God's will done? When we pray,
"May your Kingdom come soon. May your will be done
on earth, as it is in heaven" (Matt 6:10), we're saying, in
a sense, "Go for it God—whatever you want to do." How
much zeal do you have in regard to praying for others and
doing Kingdom work?*

See, he brings his reward with him as
   he comes.'"
¹² They will be called "The Holy People"
   and "The People Redeemed by the LORD."
And Jerusalem will be known as "The
   Desirable Place"
   and "The City No Longer Forsaken."

63 JUDGMENT AGAINST THE LORD'S ENEMIES

¹ Who is this who comes from Edom,
   from the city of Bozrah,
   with his clothing stained red?
Who is this in royal robes,
   marching in his great strength?

"It is I, the LORD, announcing your salvation!
   It is I, the LORD, who has the power to
   save!"

² Why are your clothes so red,
   as if you have been treading out grapes?

³ "I have been treading the winepress alone;
   no one was there to help me.
In my anger I have trampled my enemies
   as if they were grapes.
In my fury I have trampled my foes.
   Their blood has stained my clothes.
⁴ For the time has come for me to avenge my
   people,
   to ransom them from their oppressors.
⁵ I was amazed to see that no one intervened
   to help the oppressed.
So I myself stepped in to save them with my
   strong arm,
   and my wrath sustained me.
⁶ I crushed the nations in my anger
   and made them stagger and fall to the
   ground,
   spilling their blood upon the earth."

PRAISE FOR DELIVERANCE

⁷ I will tell of the LORD's unfailing love.
   I will praise the LORD for all he has done.
I will rejoice in his great goodness to Israel,
   which he has granted according to his
   mercy and love.
⁸ He said, "They are my very own people.
   Surely they will not betray me again."
And he became their Savior.
⁹ In all their suffering he also suffered,
   and he personally* rescued them.
In his love and mercy he redeemed them.
   He lifted them up and carried them
   through all the years.
¹⁰ But they rebelled against him
   and grieved his Holy Spirit.

So he became their enemy
   and fought against them.

¹¹ Then they remembered those days of old
   when Moses led his people out
   of Egypt.
They cried out, "Where is the one who
   brought Israel through the sea,
   with Moses as their shepherd?
Where is the one who sent his Holy Spirit
   to be among his people?
¹² Where is the one whose power was
   displayed
   when Moses lifted up his hand—
the one who divided the sea before them,
   making himself famous forever?
¹³ Where is the one who led them through the
   bottom of the sea?
They were like fine stallions
   racing through the desert, never
   stumbling.
¹⁴ As with cattle going down into a peaceful
   valley,
   the Spirit of the LORD gave them rest.
You led your people, LORD,
   and gained a magnificent reputation."

PRAYER FOR MERCY AND PARDON

¹⁵ LORD, look down from heaven;
   look from your holy, glorious home, and
   see us.
Where is the passion and the might
   you used to show on our behalf?
   Where are your mercy and compassion
   now?
¹⁶ Surely you are still our Father!
   Even if Abraham and Jacob* would
   disown us,
LORD, you would still be our Father.
   You are our Redeemer from ages past.
¹⁷ LORD, why have you allowed us to turn from
   your path?
Why have you given us stubborn hearts
   so we no longer fear you?
Return and help us, for we are your
   servants,
   the tribes that are your special
   possession.
¹⁸ How briefly your holy people possessed
   your holy place,
   and now our enemies have destroyed it.
¹⁹ Sometimes it seems as though we never
   belonged to you,
   as though we had never been known as
   your people.

63:9 Hebrew *and the angel of his presence.*   **63:16** Hebrew *Israel.*
See note on 14:1.

64

¹*Oh, that you would burst from the
heavens and come down!
How the mountains would quake in your
presence!
²*As fire causes wood to burn
and water to boil,
your coming would make the nations
tremble.
Then your enemies would learn the
reason for your fame!
³ When you came down long ago,
you did awesome deeds beyond our
highest expectations.
And oh, how the mountains quaked!
⁴ For since the world began,
no ear has heard
and no eye has seen a God like you,
who works for those who wait for him!
⁵ You welcome those who gladly do good,
who follow godly ways.
But you have been very angry with us,
for we are not godly.
We are constant sinners;
how can people like us be saved?
⁶ We are all infected and impure with sin.
When we display our righteous deeds,
they are nothing but filthy rags.
Like autumn leaves, we wither and fall,
and our sins sweep us away like the wind.
⁷ Yet no one calls on your name
or pleads with you for mercy.
Therefore, you have turned away from us
and turned us over* to our sins.

⁸ And yet, O LORD, you are our Father.
We are the clay, and you are the potter.
We all are formed by your hand.
⁹ Don't be so angry with us, LORD.
Please don't remember our sins forever.
Look at us, we pray,
and see that we are all your people.
¹⁰ Your holy cities are destroyed.
Zion is a wilderness;
yes, Jerusalem is a desolate ruin.
¹¹ The holy and beautiful Temple
where our ancestors praised you
has been burned down,
and all the things of beauty are
destroyed.
¹² After all this, LORD, must you still refuse
to help us?

Will you continue to be silent and
punish us?

65

JUDGMENT AND FINAL SALVATION The
LORD says,

"I was ready to respond, but no one asked
for help.
I was ready to be found, but no one was
looking for me.
I said, 'Here I am, here I am!'
to a nation that did not call on my name.*
² All day long I opened my arms to a
rebellious people.*
But they follow their own evil paths
and their own crooked schemes.
³ All day long they insult me to my face
by worshiping idols in their sacred
gardens.
They burn incense on pagan altars.
⁴ At night they go out among the graves,
worshiping the dead.
They eat the flesh of pigs
and make stews with other forbidden
foods.
⁵ Yet they say to each other,
'Don't come too close or you will
defile me!
I am holier than you!'
These people are a stench in my nostrils,
an acrid smell that never goes away.

⁶ "Look, my decree is written out* in front
of me:
I will not stand silent;
I will repay them in full!
Yes, I will repay them—
⁷ both for their own sins
and for those of their ancestors,"
says the LORD.
"For they also burned incense on the
mountains
and insulted me on the hills.
I will pay them back in full!

⁸ "But I will not destroy them all,"
says the LORD.
"For just as good grapes are found among
a cluster of bad ones
(and someone will say, 'Don't throw them
all away—
some of those grapes are good!'),

64:1 In the Hebrew text this verse is included in 63:19. **64:2** Verses
64:2-12 are numbered 64:1-11 in Hebrew text. **64:7** As in Greek,
Syriac, and Aramaic versions; Hebrew reads *melted us.* **65:1** Or *to
a nation that did not bear my name.* **65:1-2** Greek version reads *I
was found by people who were not looking for me. / I showed myself
to those who were not asking for me. / All day long I opened my
arms to them, / but they were disobedient and rebellious.* Compare
Rom 10:20-21. **65:6** Or *their sins are written out;* Hebrew reads *it
stands written.*

··

REPAY
*(65:6) God said he would repay the people for their sins.
Judgment is not our job but his because he alone is just.
Who else knows our hearts and minds? Who else knows
what is a completely fair reward or punishment?*

so I will not destroy all Israel.
For I still have true servants there.
⁹ I will preserve a remnant of the people
of Israel*
and of Judah to possess my land.
Those I choose will inherit it,
and my servants will live there.
¹⁰ The plain of Sharon will again be filled with
flocks
for my people who have searched for me,
and the valley of Achor will be a place to
pasture herds.

¹¹ "But because the rest of you have forsaken
the LORD
and have forgotten his Temple,
and because you have prepared feasts to
honor the god of Fate
and have offered mixed wine to the god
of Destiny,
¹² now I will 'destine' you for the sword.
All of you will bow down before the
executioner.
For when I called, you did not answer.
When I spoke, you did not listen.
You deliberately sinned—before my very
eyes—
and chose to do what you know I
despise."

¹³ Therefore, this is what the Sovereign LORD
says:
"My servants will eat,
but you will starve.
My servants will drink,
but you will be thirsty.
My servants will rejoice,
but you will be sad and ashamed.
¹⁴ My servants will sing for joy,
but you will cry in sorrow and despair.
¹⁵ Your name will be a curse word among my
people,
for the Sovereign LORD will destroy you
and will call his true servants by another
name.
¹⁶ All who invoke a blessing or take an oath
will do so by the God of truth.
For I will put aside my anger
and forget the evil of earlier days.

¹⁷ "Look! I am creating new heavens and a
new earth,
and no one will even think about the old
ones anymore.
¹⁸ Be glad; rejoice forever in my creation!
And look! I will create Jerusalem as a
place of happiness.
Her people will be a source of joy.

¹⁹ I will rejoice over Jerusalem
and delight in my people.
And the sound of weeping and crying
will be heard in it no more.

²⁰ "No longer will babies die when only a few
days old.
No longer will adults die before they have
lived a full life.
No longer will people be considered old at
one hundred!
Only the cursed will die that young!
²¹ In those days people will live in the houses
they build
and eat the fruit of their own vineyards.
²² Unlike the past, invaders will not take their
houses
and confiscate their vineyards.
For my people will live as long as trees,
and my chosen ones will have time to
enjoy their hard-won gains.
²³ They will not work in vain,
and their children will not be doomed to
misfortune.
For they are people blessed by the LORD,
and their children, too, will be blessed.
²⁴ I will answer them before they even call to
me.
While they are still talking about their
needs,
I will go ahead and answer their prayers!
²⁵ The wolf and the lamb will feed together.
The lion will eat hay like a cow.
But the snakes will eat dust.
In those days no one will be hurt or
destroyed on my holy mountain.
I, the LORD, have spoken!"

66

This is what the LORD says:

"Heaven is my throne,
and the earth is my footstool.
Could you build me a temple as good as
that?
Could you build me such a resting place?
² My hands have made both heaven and
earth;
they and everything in them are mine.*
I, the LORD, have spoken!

"I will bless those who have humble and
contrite hearts,
who tremble at my word.
³ But those who choose their own ways—
delighting in their detestable sins—

65:9 Hebrew *remnant of Jacob.* See note on 14:1.   66:2 As in Greek,
Latin, and Syriac versions; Hebrew reads *these things are.*

will not have their offerings accepted.
When such people sacrifice a bull,
it is no more acceptable than a human
sacrifice.
When they sacrifice a lamb,
it's as though they had sacrificed a dog!
When they bring an offering of grain,
they might as well offer the blood of a pig.
When they burn frankincense,
it's as if they had blessed an idol.
⁴ I will send them great trouble—
all the things they feared.
For when I called, they did not answer.
When I spoke, they did not listen.
They deliberately sinned before my
very eyes
and chose to do what they know
I despise."

⁵ Hear this message from the LORD,
all you who tremble at his words:
"Your own people hate you
and throw you out for being loyal to my
name.
'Let the LORD be honored!' they scoff.
'Be joyful in him!'
But they will be put to shame.
⁶ What is all the commotion in the city?
What is that terrible noise from the
Temple?
It is the voice of the LORD
taking vengeance against his enemies.

⁷ "Before the birth pains even begin,
Jerusalem gives birth to a son.
⁸ Who has ever seen anything as strange as
this?
Who ever heard of such a thing?
Has a nation ever been born in a single day?
Has a country ever come forth in a mere
moment?
But by the time Jerusalem's* birth pains
begin,
her children will be born.
⁹ Would I ever bring this nation to the point
of birth
and then not deliver it?" asks the LORD.
"No! I would never keep this nation from
being born,"
says your God.

¹⁰ "Rejoice with Jerusalem!
Be glad with her, all you who love her
and all you who mourn for her.
¹¹ Drink deeply of her glory

even as an infant drinks at its mother's
comforting breasts."

¹² This is what the LORD says:
"I will give Jerusalem a river of peace and
prosperity.
The wealth of the nations will flow to her.
Her children will be nursed at her breasts,
carried in her arms, and held on her lap.
¹³ I will comfort you there in Jerusalem
as a mother comforts her child."

¹⁴ When you see these things, your heart will
rejoice.
You will flourish like the grass!
Everyone will see the LORD's hand of
blessing on his servants—
and his anger against his enemies.
¹⁵ See, the LORD is coming with fire,
and his swift chariots roar like a
whirlwind.
He will bring punishment with the fury
of his anger
and the flaming fire of his hot rebuke.
¹⁶ The LORD will punish the world by fire
and by his sword.
He will judge the earth,
and many will be killed by him.

¹⁷"Those who 'consecrate' and 'purify' themselves in a sacred garden with its idol in the center—feasting on pork and rats and other detestable meats—will come to a terrible end," says the LORD.

¹⁸"I can see what they are doing, and I know what they are thinking. So I will gather all nations and peoples together, and they will see my glory. ¹⁹I will perform a sign among them. And I will send those who survive to be messengers to the nations—to Tarshish, to the Libyans* and Lydians* (who are famous as archers), to Tubal and Greece,* and to all the lands beyond the sea that have not heard of my fame or seen my glory. There they will declare my glory to the nations. ²⁰They will bring the remnant of your people back from every nation. They will bring them to my holy mountain in Jerusalem as an offering to the LORD. They will ride on horses, in chariots and

....

DRAMA
(66:22-24) Isaiah brings his book to a close with great drama. For the faithless, there is a sobering portrayal of judgment. For the faithful, there is a glorious picture of a rich reward to come—"As surely as my new heavens and earth will remain, so will you always be my people, with a name that will never disappear." Is that what you're looking forward to? Your faithfulness now can assure that bright future.

66:8 Hebrew *Zion's.* **66:19a** As in some Greek manuscripts, which read *Put* [that is, *Libya*]; Hebrew reads *Pul.* **66:19b** Hebrew *Lud.* **66:19c** Hebrew *Javan.*

wagons, and on mules and camels," says the
LORD. ²¹"And I will appoint some of them to
be my priests and Levites. I, the LORD, have
spoken!

²² "As surely as my new heavens and earth will
    remain,
      so will you always be my people,
    with a name that will never disappear,"
    says the LORD.
²³ "All humanity will come to worship me

from week to week
    and from month to month.
²⁴ And as they go out, they will see
    the dead bodies of those who have
      rebelled against me.
For the worms that devour them will
    never die,
    and the fire that burns them will never
      go out.
All who pass by
    will view them with utter horror."

"You big crybaby. Stop your blubbering!"

Tears can seem embarrassing and awkward—even a sign of weakness. When we were young, tears came easily over a broken toy, a skinned knee, and other assorted real or imagined hurts. As we grew older, we learned to hide our feelings, especially our sadness. We tried to look tough or put on a happy face. That's a shame, really, because tears are important. In fact, tears can tell us a lot about people, allowing us to see what affects them deeply, what they care about . . . what breaks their hearts.

Jeremiah is called the weeping prophet. In his books (Jeremiah and Lamentations), it seems as though all he did was cry. Jeremiah cried because he loved deeply, and because he knew the truth, that God planned to punish his beloved nation because of their long history of rebellion. He tried to help the people of Israel see the need to return to God, but they wouldn't listen. So he cried.

What brings tears to your eyes? Have you ever cried over the consequences of someone's poor choice? A heart filled with compassion can't help but cry over the trouble in the world. Is that the kind of heart you have?

KEY POINTS

SIN Judah's deterioration and disaster stemmed from disobedience to God. When we refuse to listen to God's warnings and go our own way, we invite disaster.

PUNISHMENT The people of Judah could only blame themselves for their suffering because they refused to listen to God. Likewise, we must answer to God for how we live.

FAITHFUL TO FULFILL God brought the events prophesied by Micah, Isaiah, and Zephaniah to pass according to his timetable. We can trust God to faithfully fulfill his promises.

HOPE Jeremiah predicted that after the destruction of the nation, God would send a new Shepherd, the Messiah. The Messiah would lead them into a new future, a new covenant, and a new day of hope. God still renews the hope of his suffering people with the promise of eternal life with him.

FAITHFUL SERVICE Jeremiah served God faithfully for over 40 years. During that time the people ignored, rejected, and persecuted him. Jeremiah's preaching was unsuccessful by human standards, yet he did not fail. People's acceptance or rejection of us is not the measure of our success. God's approval is our standard for service.

STATS

PURPOSE
To urge God's people to turn from their sins and to turn back to God

AUTHOR
Jeremiah

ORIGINAL AUDIENCE
Judah (the southern kingdom) and its capital city, Jerusalem

DATE WRITTEN
Around 627–586 B.C.

SETTING
During the reigns of Judah's last five kings. The nation was sliding quickly toward destruction and exile (586 B.C.; see 2 Kgs 21–25).

KEY PEOPLE
Josiah, Jehoahaz, Jehoiakim, Jehoiachin, Zedekiah, Baruch, Nebuchadnezzar

KEY PLACES
Anathoth, Jerusalem, Ramah, Egypt

SPECIAL FEATURES
The book is a combination of history, poetry, and biography.

TIMELINE

640 B.C.
Zephaniah becomes a prophet

627
Jeremiah becomes a prophet

612
Habakkuk becomes a prophet

609
King Josiah killed in battle

605
Daniel taken captive

597
Ezekiel taken captive

593
Ezekiel prophesies in Babylon

586
Judah falls; Jerusalem destroyed; Jeremiah's ministry ends

537
First exiles return to Judah

1 These are the words of Jeremiah son of Hilkiah, one of the priests from the town of Anathoth in the land of Benjamin. ²The LORD first gave messages to Jeremiah during the thirteenth year of the reign of Josiah son of Amon, king of Judah.* ³The LORD's messages continued throughout the reign of King Jehoiakim, Josiah's son, until the eleventh year of the reign of King Zedekiah, another of Josiah's sons. In August* of that eleventh year the people of Jerusalem were taken away as captives.

JEREMIAH'S CALL AND FIRST VISIONS
⁴The LORD gave me this message:

⁵ "I knew you before I formed you in your
      mother's womb.
    Before you were born I set you apart
      and appointed you as my prophet to the
      nations."

⁶"O Sovereign LORD," I said, "I can't speak for you! I'm too young!"

⁷The LORD replied, "Don't say, 'I'm too young,' for you must go wherever I send you and say whatever I tell you. ⁸And don't be afraid of the people, for I will be with you and will protect you. I, the LORD, have spoken!" ⁹Then the LORD reached out and touched my mouth and said,

"Look, I have put my words in your mouth!
¹⁰ Today I appoint you to stand up
      against nations and kingdoms.
    Some you must uproot and tear down,
      destroy and overthrow.
    Others you must build up
      and plant."

¹¹Then the LORD said to me, "Look, Jeremiah! What do you see?"

And I replied, "I see a branch from an almond tree."

¹²And the LORD said, "That's right, and it means that I am watching,* and I will certainly carry out all my plans."

¹³Then the LORD spoke to me again and asked, "What do you see now?"

And I replied, "I see a pot of boiling water, spilling from the north."

¹⁴"Yes," the LORD said, "for terror from the north will boil out on the people of this land. ¹⁵Listen! I am calling the armies of the kingdoms of the north to come to Jerusalem. I, the LORD, have spoken!

"They will set their thrones
      at the gates of the city.
    They will attack its walls
      and all the other towns of Judah.
¹⁶ I will pronounce judgment
      on my people for all their evil—
    for deserting me and burning incense to
      other gods.
    Yes, they worship idols made with their
      own hands!

¹⁷ "Get up and prepare for action.
      Go out and tell them everything I tell you
      to say.
    Do not be afraid of them,
      or I will make you look foolish in front
      of them.
¹⁸ For see, today I have made you strong
      like a fortified city that cannot be
      captured,
    like an iron pillar or a bronze wall.
    You will stand against the whole land—
      the kings, officials, priests, and people
      of Judah.
¹⁹ They will fight you, but they will fail.
      For I am with you, and I will take care
      of you.
    I, the LORD, have spoken!"

2 THE LORD'S CASE AGAINST HIS PEOPLE
The LORD gave me another message. He said, ²"Go and shout this message to Jerusalem. This is what the LORD says:

"I remember how eager you were to
      please me
    as a young bride long ago,
    how you loved me and followed me

TOO YOUNG TO SERVE?
(1:1-8) Jeremiah tried to use his youth as an excuse to avoid being God's spokesman. But God overruled any excuse that he came up with. Have you ever thought that your age exempted you from doing anything for God? Maybe you've thought that you could wait until after you've finished college to get serious about God. How does knowing that God doesn't accept the age excuse change your view of what you can do for God?

STAY TRUE
(1:16; 2:1-3) The people of Israel obeyed God initially but failed to be faithful to their commitment. Think about how you feel when someone fails to keep a promise. Yet we can do that with God, letting other relationships and involvements take first priority. Are you just as serious about your commitment to him? Remember your commitment and keep God in first place.

1:2 The thirteenth year of Josiah's reign was 627 B.C.   **1:3** Hebrew *In the fifth month*, of the ancient Hebrew lunar calendar. A number of events in Jeremiah can be cross-checked with dates in surviving Babylonian records and related accurately to our modern calendar. The fifth month in the eleventh year of Zedekiah's reign occurred within the months of August and September 586 B.C. Also see 52:12 and the note there.   **1:12** The Hebrew word for "watching" *(shoqed)* sounds like the word for "almond tree" *(shaqed)*.

MY STORY: Lori

The topic of abortion comes up often in school, among friends and elsewhere. I had thought through my position in theory, but when my best friend told me she was pregnant and was going to get an abortion, it wasn't theoretical anymore.

When Lee called me on the phone one night and asked me to come talk, I knew something was wrong. As soon as we were alone, she blurted out: "I'm pregnant. And I have an appointment at an abortion clinic tomorrow."

I couldn't believe my ears. Lee was a Christian. We had discussed abortion often and had agreed on our stance: It was wrong. Now Lee was telling me she was going to have one tomorrow!

Trying to keep calm, I told her I realized it was her decision. Then I said, "You know I don't believe in abortion. You always said you didn't either. It doesn't make it any more right now that you're pregnant. It's still a baby we're talking about.

"This is your decision. But as your friend, I want to make sure you've thought this through. Can we read a few passages of Scripture and pray together? Then I promise, I'll stick by you, whatever you decide."

We read Jeremiah 1:4-5 and Psalm 139. I told her, "Whenever I read these passages, they say to me that God knows us from the very beginning, and that he has a plan for each person. That's why I think you should have this baby, Lee. God will take care of your baby because he already loves the baby. And he'll take care of you, too."

We cried together, but I really believed what I said. I asked Lee if I could pray for the baby. She nodded, crying. So I prayed that God would give Lee the courage to make the right choice, and that he would take care of her baby.

Lee didn't promise she wouldn't have the abortion. I prayed hard all the next day. That evening, she called and said she hadn't gone through with it. I told her I was very happy and thought she made the right choice.

Lee will tell you that she believes she made the right choice, too. She had a beautiful girl whom she placed for adoption with a loving Christian couple. It hurts her to think about the baby, but she knows she did the right thing.

---

even through the barren wilderness.
³ In those days Israel was holy to the LORD,
    the first of his children.*
All who harmed his people were declared
        guilty,
    and disaster fell on them.
    I, the LORD, have spoken!"

⁴Listen to the word of the LORD, people of Jacob—all you families of Israel! ⁵This is what the LORD says:

"What did your ancestors find wrong
        with me
    that led them to stray so far from me?
They worshiped worthless idols,
    only to become worthless themselves.
⁶ They did not ask, 'Where is the LORD
    who brought us safely out of Egypt
and led us through the barren wilderness—

a land of deserts and pits,
a land of drought and death,
    where no one lives or even travels?'

⁷ "And when I brought you into a fruitful land
    to enjoy its bounty and goodness,
you defiled my land
    and corrupted the possession I had
        promised you.
⁸ The priests did not ask,
    'Where is the LORD?'
Those who taught my word ignored me,
    the rulers turned against me,
and the prophets spoke in the name of Baal,
    wasting their time on worthless idols.
⁹ Therefore, I will bring my case against you,"
    says the LORD.
"I will even bring charges against your
        children's children
    in the years to come.

2:3 Hebrew *the firstfruits of his harvest.*

¹⁰ "Go west and look in the land of Cyprus*;
 go east and search through the land of
 Kedar.
 Has anyone ever heard of anything
 as strange as this?
¹¹ Has any nation ever traded its gods for
 new ones,
 even though they are not gods at all?
Yet my people have exchanged their
 glorious God*
 for worthless idols!
¹² The heavens are shocked at such a thing
 and shrink back in horror and dismay,"
 says the LORD.
¹³ "For my people have done two evil things:
 They have abandoned me—

the fountain of living water.
And they have dug for themselves cracked
 cisterns
 that can hold no water at all!

THE RESULTS OF ISRAEL'S SIN
¹⁴ "Why has Israel become a slave?
 Why has he been carried away as plunder?
¹⁵ Strong lions have roared against him,
 and the land has been destroyed.
The towns are now in ruins,
 and no one lives in them anymore.
¹⁶ Egyptians, marching from their cities of
 Memphis* and Tahpanhes,
 have destroyed Israel's glory and power.
¹⁷ And you have brought this upon yourselves
 by rebelling against the LORD your God,
 even though he was leading you on
 the way!

¹⁸ "What have you gained by your alliances
 with Egypt
 and your covenants with Assyria?
What good to you are the streams of
 the Nile*
 or the waters of the Euphrates River?*

CRACKED CISTERNS
(2:13) Who would set aside a sparkling fountain of water for a cistern, a pit that collected rainwater? God used Jeremiah to remind the Israelites that they had turned from him, the fountain of living water, to idols. Not only that, the cisterns they chose were cracked and empty. The people had built religious systems for storing truth, but they were worthless. Today's "cracked cisterns" include money, power/status, other relationships, popularity— the list goes on. Are you clinging to any of these? None can compare with God's promise of living water (see John 4:10). Drink and be refreshed.

2:10 Hebrew *Kittim.* **2:11** Hebrew *their glory.* **2:16** Hebrew *Noph.* **2:18a** Hebrew *of Shihor,* a branch of the Nile River. **2:18b** Hebrew *the river.*

I WONDER...

My mom used to go to church a lot, but she doesn't anymore. What can I do to get her to give God more attention?

Going from a close relationship with Christ to total neglect is like going from a two-wheel bike to one with training wheels. It seems safer, but it's not half the fun.

You may see many people who start out strong in their walk with God, but for some reason they begin to fade and eventually drop off.

Remember, the Christian life is not a sprint—it's a long-distance race, a marathon! How you start is not nearly as important as how you finish.

In a long race, many people get weary of waiting for the prize and decide to drop out. Your mother may be an example of that. She seems to have turned her attention elsewhere, forgetting about the race altogether.

As Jeremiah 2:13 says, when people reject God, they need other things to hold life together. But those other things are just "cracked cisterns" that don't hold anything of value.

And like the person who goes back to the bike with training wheels because it's safer, some people allow distractions to push God aside.

Some people believe that the Christian life means having their problems solved immediately, always being treated right by people, never having doubts about the future, always having prayers answered right away, and always feeling good about church. Those people are pursuing the wrong goals! They will be disappointed, grow tired, and tend to drop out.

Our goal should be to get to know the God who created us and loved us enough to die on a cross to save us from sin—then we'll never get tired of the faith. There's always something new to discover about the richness and depth of God's love for us. If we work to let God change our selfish characters into selfless characters, the race will never seem too long.

Don't try to change your mom. She'll likely not appreciate it, no matter how good your motives are. Instead, give God permission to change you! Focus on how well *you* are doing, and let God take care of your mom.

Become more diligent in doing your chores and homework. Begin to treat your brothers and sisters better than you have. Pray for your mom to see these changes. Then give God time to work. Remember, he wants her to have a right relationship with him even more than you do!

¹⁹ Your wickedness will bring its own
punishment.
Your turning from me will shame you.
You will see what an evil, bitter thing it is
to abandon the LORD your God and not to
fear him.
I, the Lord, the LORD of Heaven's Armies,
have spoken!

²⁰ "Long ago I broke the yoke that
oppressed you
and tore away the chains of your slavery,
but still you said,
'I will not serve you.'
On every hill and under every green tree,
you have prostituted yourselves by
bowing down to idols.
²¹ But I was the one who planted you,
choosing a vine of the purest stock—
the very best.
How did you grow into this corrupt wild
vine?
²² No amount of soap or lye can make you
clean.
I still see the stain of your guilt.
I, the Sovereign LORD, have spoken!

ISRAEL, AN UNFAITHFUL WIFE

²³ "You say, 'That's not true!
I haven't worshiped the images of Baal!'
But how can you say that?
Go and look in any valley in the land!
Face the awful sins you have done.
You are like a restless female camel
desperately searching for a mate.
²⁴ You are like a wild donkey,
sniffing the wind at mating time.
Who can restrain her lust?
Those who desire her don't need to
search,
for she goes running to them!
²⁵ When will you stop running?
When will you stop panting after other
gods?
But you say, 'Save your breath.
I'm in love with these foreign gods,
and I can't stop loving them now!'

²⁶ "Israel is like a thief
who feels shame only when he gets
caught.
They, their kings, officials, priests, and
prophets—
all are alike in this.
²⁷ To an image carved from a piece of wood
they say,
'You are my father.'

> **YOU WILL SEE WHAT AN
> EVIL, BITTER THING IT IS
> TO ABANDON THE LORD
> YOUR GOD AND NOT
> TO FEAR HIM.**
>
> *JEREMIAH 2:19*

To an idol chiseled from a block of stone
they say,
'You are my mother.'
They turn their backs on me,
but in times of trouble they cry out to me,
'Come and save us!'
²⁸ But why not call on these gods you have
made?
When trouble comes, let them save you
if they can!
For you have as many gods
as there are towns in Judah.
²⁹ Why do you accuse me of doing wrong?
You are the ones who have rebelled,"
says the LORD.
³⁰ "I have punished your children,
but they did not respond to my discipline.
You yourselves have killed your prophets
as a lion kills its prey.

³¹ "O my people, listen to the words of the
LORD!
Have I been like a desert to Israel?
Have I been to them a land of darkness?
Why then do my people say, 'At last we are
free from God!
We don't need him anymore!'
³² Does a young woman forget her jewelry?
Does a bride hide her wedding dress?
Yet for years on end
my people have forgotten me.

³³ "How you plot and scheme to win your
lovers.
Even an experienced prostitute could
learn from you!
³⁴ Your clothing is stained with the blood
of the innocent and the poor,
though you didn't catch them breaking
into your houses!
³⁵ And yet you say,
'I have done nothing wrong.

....

FORGETTING
*(2:31-32) Forgetting can be dangerous, whether it is
intentional or an oversight. Israel forgot God by focusing
its affections on the allurements of the world. The more
we focus on the world's pleasures, the easier we will forget God's care, love, dependability, guidance, and, most
of all, God himself. What pleases you most? Have you
been forgetting God lately?*

Surely God isn't angry with me!'
But now I will punish you severely
    because you claim you have not sinned.
³⁶ First here, then there—
    you flit from one ally to another asking
        for help.
But your new friends in Egypt will let you
        down,
    just as Assyria did before.
³⁷ In despair, you will be led into exile
    with your hands on your heads,
for the LORD has rejected the nations you
        trust.
    They will not help you at all.

3

¹ "If a man divorces a woman
        and she goes and marries someone
            else,
he will not take her back again,
    for that would surely corrupt the land.
But you have prostituted yourself with many
        lovers,
    so why are you trying to come back to
        me?"
    says the LORD.
² "Look at the shrines on every hilltop.
    Is there any place you have not been
        defiled
    by your adultery with other gods?
You sit like a prostitute beside the road
    waiting for a customer.
    You sit alone like a nomad in the desert.
You have polluted the land with your
        prostitution
    and your wickedness.
³ That's why even the spring rains have failed.
    For you are a brazen prostitute and
        completely shameless.
⁴ Yet you say to me,
    'Father, you have been my guide since
        my youth.
⁵ Surely you won't be angry forever!
    Surely you can forget about it!'
So you talk,
    but you keep on doing all the evil
        you can."

....

DOWNPLAY IT?

(3:1-5) The people of Israel tried to minimize their wrongs. When we know we've done something wrong, we want to downplay the error by saying, "It wasn't so bad!" In that way, we relieve some of the guilt we feel. But if we view every wrong attitude and action as a serious offense to God, we'll begin to understand what living for God is all about. Is there an action in your life that you've written off as too small to worry about? God wants us to confess every sin and turn from it.

JUDAH FOLLOWS ISRAEL'S EXAMPLE ⁶During the reign of King Josiah, the LORD said to me, "Have you seen what fickle Israel has done? Like a wife who commits adultery, Israel has worshiped other gods on every hill and under every green tree. ⁷I thought, 'After she has done all this, she will return to me.' But she did not return, and her faithless sister Judah saw this. ⁸She saw that I divorced faithless Israel because of her adultery. But that treacherous sister Judah had no fear, and now she, too, has left me and given herself to prostitution. ⁹Israel treated it all so lightly—she thought nothing of committing adultery by worshiping idols made of wood and stone. So now the land has been polluted. ¹⁰But despite all this, her faithless sister Judah has never sincerely returned to me. She has only pretended to be sorry. I, the LORD, have spoken!"

HOPE FOR WAYWARD ISRAEL ¹¹Then the LORD said to me, "Even faithless Israel is less guilty than treacherous Judah! ¹²Therefore, go and give this message to Israel.* This is what the LORD says:

"O Israel, my faithless people,
    come home to me again,
for I am merciful.
    I will not be angry with you forever.
¹³ Only acknowledge your guilt.
    Admit that you rebelled against the LORD
        your God
and committed adultery against him
    by worshiping idols under every green
        tree.
Confess that you refused to listen to my
        voice.
    I, the LORD, have spoken!

¹⁴ "Return home, you wayward children,"
    says the LORD,
    "for I am your master.
I will bring you back to the land of Israel*—
    one from this town and two from that
        family—
from wherever you are scattered.
¹⁵ And I will give you shepherds after my own
        heart,
    who will guide you with knowledge and
        understanding.

¹⁶"And when your land is once more filled with people," says the LORD, "you will no longer wish for 'the good old days' when you possessed the Ark of the LORD's Covenant. You will not miss those days or even remember them,

3:12 Hebrew *toward the north.*   **3:14** Hebrew *to Zion.*

and there will be no need to rebuild the Ark. ¹⁷In that day Jerusalem will be known as 'The Throne of the Lord.' All nations will come there to honor the Lord. They will no longer stubbornly follow their own evil desires. ¹⁸In those days the people of Judah and Israel will return together from exile in the north. They will return to the land I gave their ancestors as an inheritance forever.

19 "I thought to myself,
    'I would love to treat you as my own
        children!'
I wanted nothing more than to give you this
        beautiful land—
    the finest possession in the world.
I looked forward to your calling me 'Father,'
    and I wanted you never to turn from me.
20 But you have been unfaithful to me, you
        people of Israel!
    You have been like a faithless wife who
        leaves her husband.
    I, the Lord, have spoken."

21 Voices are heard high on the windswept
        mountains,
    the weeping and pleading of Israel's
        people.
For they have chosen crooked paths
    and have forgotten the Lord their God.

22 "My wayward children," says the Lord,
    "come back to me, and I will heal your
        wayward hearts."

"Yes, we're coming," the people reply,
    "for you are the Lord our God.
23 Our worship of idols on the hills
    and our religious orgies on the mountains
        are a delusion.
Only in the Lord our God
    will Israel ever find salvation.
24 From childhood we have watched
    as everything our ancestors worked for—
their flocks and herds, their sons and
        daughters—
    was squandered on a delusion.
25 Let us now lie down in shame
    and cover ourselves with dishonor,
for we and our ancestors have sinned
    against the Lord our God.
From our childhood to this day
    we have never obeyed him."

4 ¹"O Israel," says the Lord,
    "if you wanted to return to me, you
        could.

4:4 Hebrew *Circumcise yourselves to the Lord, and take away the foreskins of your heart.* 4:6 Hebrew *Zion.*

JEREMIAH

Served as a prophet to Judah from 627 B.C. until the Exile in 586 B.C.

CLIMATE OF THE TIMES
Society was deteriorating economically, politically, and spiritually. Wars and captivity threatened the people. God's Word was outlawed.

MAIN MESSAGE
Repentance from sin would postpone Judah's coming judgment at the hands of Babylon.

IMPORTANCE OF MESSAGE
Repentance is one of the greatest needs in our immoral world. God's promises to the faithful shine brightly by bringing hope for tomorrow and strength for today.

CONTEMPORARY PROPHETS
Habakkuk (612–589 B.C.)
Zephaniah (640–621 B.C.)

You could throw away your detestable idols
    and stray away no more.
² Then when you swear by my name,
        saying,
    'As surely as the Lord lives,'
you could do so
    with truth, justice, and righteousness.
Then you would be a blessing to the nations
        of the world,
    and all people would come and praise
        my name."

COMING JUDGMENT AGAINST JUDAH ³This is what the Lord says to the people of Judah and Jerusalem:

"Plow up the hard ground of your hearts!
    Do not waste your good seed among
        thorns.
4 O people of Judah and Jerusalem,
    surrender your pride and power.
Change your hearts before the Lord,*
    or my anger will burn like an
        unquenchable fire
    because of all your sins.

5 "Shout to Judah, and broadcast to
        Jerusalem!
    Tell them to sound the alarm throughout
        the land:
'Run for your lives!
    Flee to the fortified cities!'
6 Raise a signal flag as a warning for
        Jerusalem*:
    'Flee now! Do not delay!'

For I am bringing terrible destruction
    upon you
    from the north."

⁷ A lion stalks from its den,
    a destroyer of nations.
It has left its lair and is headed your way.
    It's going to devastate your land!
Your towns will lie in ruins,
    with no one living in them anymore.
⁸ So put on clothes of mourning
    and weep with broken hearts,
for the fierce anger of the LORD
    is still upon us.

⁹ "In that day," says the LORD,
    "the king and the officials will tremble
      in fear.
The priests will be struck with horror,
    and the prophets will be appalled."

¹⁰ Then I said, "O Sovereign LORD,
    the people have been deceived by what
      you said,
for you promised peace for Jerusalem.
    But the sword is held at their throats!"

¹¹ The time is coming when the LORD will say
    to the people of Jerusalem,
"My dear people, a burning wind is blowing
    in from the desert,
    and it's not a gentle breeze useful for
      winnowing grain.
¹² It is a roaring blast sent by me!
    Now I will pronounce your destruction!"

¹³ Our enemy rushes down on us like storm
      clouds!
    His chariots are like whirlwinds.
His horses are swifter than eagles.
    How terrible it will be, for we are doomed!
¹⁴ O Jerusalem, cleanse your heart
    that you may be saved.
How long will you harbor
    your evil thoughts?
¹⁵ Your destruction has been announced
    from Dan and the hill country of Ephraim.

¹⁶ "Warn the surrounding nations
    and announce this to Jerusalem:
The enemy is coming from a distant land,
    raising a battle cry against the towns of
      Judah.

. . . .

FAITHFUL
*(4:27) God warned that destruction was certain, but he
also promised that a remnant would remain faithful to
him and would be spared, even though the nation would
be wiped out. God is committed to preserving those who
are faithful to him.*

¹⁷ They surround Jerusalem like watchmen
    around a field,
    for my people have rebelled against me,"
says the LORD.
¹⁸ "Your own actions have brought this
    upon you.
This punishment is bitter, piercing you
    to the heart!"

JEREMIAH WEEPS FOR HIS PEOPLE

¹⁹ My heart, my heart—I writhe in pain!
    My heart pounds within me! I cannot
      be still.
For I have heard the blast of enemy trumpets
    and the roar of their battle cries.
²⁰ Waves of destruction roll over the land,
    until it lies in complete desolation.
Suddenly my tents are destroyed;
    in a moment my shelters are crushed.
²¹ How long must I see the battle flags
    and hear the trumpets of war?

²² "My people are foolish
    and do not know me," says the LORD.
"They are stupid children
    who have no understanding.
They are clever enough at doing wrong,
    but they have no idea how to do right!"

JEREMIAH'S VISION OF COMING DISASTER

²³ I looked at the earth, and it was empty and
      formless.
    I looked at the heavens, and there was
      no light.
²⁴ I looked at the mountains and hills,
    and they trembled and shook.
²⁵ I looked, and all the people were gone.
    All the birds of the sky had flown away.
²⁶ I looked, and the fertile fields had become
    a wilderness.
    The towns lay in ruins,
    crushed by the LORD's fierce anger.

²⁷ This is what the LORD says:
"The whole land will be ruined,
    but I will not destroy it completely.
²⁸ The earth will mourn
    and the heavens will be draped in black
because of my decree against my people.
    I have made up my mind and will not
      change it."

²⁹ At the noise of charioteers and archers,
    the people flee in terror.
They hide in the bushes
    and run for the mountains.
All the towns have been abandoned—
    not a person remains!
³⁰ What are you doing,

you who have been plundered?
Why do you dress up in beautiful clothing
    and put on gold jewelry?
Why do you brighten your eyes with
    mascara?
Your primping will do you no good!
The allies who were your lovers
    despise you and seek to kill you.

³¹ I hear a cry, like that of a woman in labor,
    the groans of a woman giving birth to her
    first child.
It is beautiful Jerusalem*
    gasping for breath and crying out,
    "Help! I'm being murdered!"

5 THE SINS OF JUDAH

¹ "Run up and down every street in
    Jerusalem," says the LORD.
    "Look high and low; search throughout
    the city!
If you can find even one just and honest
    person,
    I will not destroy the city.
² But even when they are under oath,
    saying, 'As surely as the LORD lives,'
    they are still telling lies!"

³ LORD, you are searching for honesty.
You struck your people,
    but they paid no attention.
You crushed them,
    but they refused to be corrected.
They are determined, with faces set like
    stone;
    they have refused to repent.

⁴ Then I said, "But what can we expect from
    the poor?
    They are ignorant.
They don't know the ways of the LORD.
    They don't understand God's laws.
⁵ So I will go and speak to their leaders.
    Surely they know the ways of the LORD
    and understand God's laws."
But the leaders, too, as one man,
    had thrown off God's yoke
    and broken his chains.
⁶ So now a lion from the forest will attack
    them;
    a wolf from the desert will pounce on
    them.
A leopard will lurk near their towns,
    tearing apart any who dare to venture out.
For their rebellion is great,
    and their sins are many.

4:31 Hebrew *the daughter of Zion*.

⁷ "How can I pardon you?
    For even your children have turned from
    me.
They have sworn by gods that are not gods
    at all!
I fed my people until they were full.
But they thanked me by committing adultery
    and lining up at the brothels.
⁸ They are well-fed, lusty stallions,
    each neighing for his neighbor's wife.
⁹ Should I not punish them for this?" says
    the LORD.
    "Should I not avenge myself against
    such a nation?

¹⁰ "Go down the rows of the vineyards and
    destroy the grapevines,
    leaving a scattered few alive.
Strip the branches from the vines,
    for these people do not belong to the
    LORD.
¹¹ The people of Israel and Judah
    are full of treachery against me,"
    says the LORD.
¹² "They have lied about the LORD
    and said, 'He won't bother us!
No disasters will come upon us.
    There will be no war or famine.
¹³ God's prophets are all windbags
    who don't really speak for him.
    Let their predictions of disaster fall
    on themselves!'"

¹⁴Therefore, this is what the LORD God of Heaven's Armies says:

"Because the people are talking like this,
    my messages will flame out of your mouth
    and burn the people like kindling wood.
¹⁵ O Israel, I will bring a distant nation
    against you,"
    says the LORD.
"It is a mighty nation,
    an ancient nation,
a people whose language you do not know,
    whose speech you cannot understand.
¹⁶ Their weapons are deadly;
    their warriors are mighty.
¹⁷ They will devour the food of your harvest;
    they will devour your sons and daughters.
They will devour your flocks and herds;
    they will devour your grapes and figs.
And they will destroy your fortified towns,
    which you think are so safe.

¹⁸"Yet even in those days I will not blot you
out completely," says the LORD. ¹⁹"And when
your people ask, 'Why did the LORD our God
do all this to us?' you must reply, 'You rejected

him and gave yourselves to foreign gods in your own land. Now you will serve foreigners in a land that is not your own.'

A WARNING FOR GOD'S PEOPLE

20 "Make this announcement to Israel,*
  and say this to Judah:
21 Listen, you foolish and senseless people,
    with eyes that do not see
    and ears that do not hear.
22 Have you no respect for me?
    Why don't you tremble in my presence?
  I, the LORD, define the ocean's sandy
    shoreline
    as an everlasting boundary that the
      waters cannot cross.
  The waves may toss and roar,
    but they can never pass the boundaries
      I set.
23 But my people have stubborn and rebellious
    hearts.
  They have turned away and abandoned
    me.
24 They do not say from the heart,
  'Let us live in awe of the LORD our God,
  for he gives us rain each spring and fall,
    assuring us of a harvest when the time
      is right.'
25 Your wickedness has deprived you of these
    wonderful blessings.
  Your sin has robbed you of all these good
    things.

26 "Among my people are wicked men
    who lie in wait for victims like a hunter
      hiding in a blind.
  They continually set traps
    to catch people.
27 Like a cage filled with birds,
    their homes are filled with evil plots.
  And now they are great and rich.
28 They are fat and sleek,
    and there is no limit to their wicked
      deeds.
  They refuse to provide justice to orphans
    and deny the rights of the poor.
29 Should I not punish them for this?" says
    the LORD.

"Should I not avenge myself against such
  a nation?
30 A horrible and shocking thing
    has happened in this land—
31 the prophets give false prophecies,
    and the priests rule with an iron hand.
  Worse yet, my people like it that way!
    But what will you do when the end
      comes?

6 JERUSALEM'S LAST WARNING

1 "Run for your lives, you people of Benjamin!
    Get out of Jerusalem!
  Sound the alarm in Tekoa!
    Send up a signal at Beth-hakkerem!
  A powerful army is coming from the north,
    coming with disaster and destruction.
2 O Jerusalem,* you are my beautiful and
      delicate daughter—
    but I will destroy you!
3 Enemies will surround you, like shepherds
      camped around the city.
  Each chooses a place for his troops to
      devour.
4 They shout, 'Prepare for battle!
    Attack at noon!'
  'No, it's too late; the day is fading,
    and the evening shadows are falling.'
5 'Well then, let's attack at night
    and destroy her palaces!'"

6 This is what the LORD of Heaven's Armies
      says:
  "Cut down the trees for battering rams.
    Build siege ramps against the walls of
      Jerusalem.
  This is the city to be punished,
    for she is wicked through and through.
7 She spouts evil like a fountain.
    Her streets echo with the sounds of
      violence and destruction.
  I always see her sickness and sores.
8 Listen to this warning, Jerusalem,
    or I will turn from you in disgust.
  Listen, or I will turn you into a heap of ruins,
    a land where no one lives."

9 This is what the LORD of Heaven's Armies
      says:
  "Even the few who remain in Israel
    will be picked over again,
  as when a harvester checks each vine a
      second time
    to pick the grapes that were missed."

RESPECT
(5:20-24) The people of the divided nation of Israel had lost their awe of God. God had to strip away the things that Israel had grown to respect more than him. For many people today, respect for God isn't a priority. Some even have the attitude that God has yet to do something to earn their respect. Does God have your respect? If so, how do your actions reveal your level of respect?

5:20 Hebrew *to the house of Jacob.* The names "Jacob" and "Israel" are often interchanged throughout the Old Testament, referring sometimes to the individual patriarch and sometimes to the nation. **6:2** Hebrew *Daughter of Zion.*

JUDAH'S CONSTANT REBELLION

¹⁰ To whom can I give warning?
    Who will listen when I speak?
Their ears are closed,
    and they cannot hear.
They scorn the word of the LORD.
    They don't want to listen at all.
¹¹ So now I am filled with the LORD's fury.
    Yes, I am tired of holding it in!

"I will pour out my fury on children playing
    in the streets
    and on gatherings of young men,
on husbands and wives
    and on those who are old and gray.
¹² Their homes will be turned over to their
    enemies,
    as will their fields and their wives.
For I will raise my powerful fist
    against the people of this land,"
    says the LORD.
¹³ "From the least to the greatest,
    their lives are ruled by greed.
From prophets to priests,
    they are all frauds.
¹⁴ They offer superficial treatments
    for my people's mortal wound.
They give assurances of peace
    when there is no peace.
¹⁵ Are they ashamed of their disgusting
    actions?
    Not at all—they don't even know how to
    blush!
Therefore, they will lie among the
    slaughtered.
    They will be brought down when I punish
    them,"
    says the LORD.

JUDAH REJECTS THE LORD'S WAY

¹⁶ This is what the LORD says:
    "Stop at the crossroads and look around.
    Ask for the old, godly way, and walk in it.
Travel its path, and you will find rest for your
    souls.
    But you reply, 'No, that's not the road we
    want!'
¹⁷ I posted watchmen over you who said,
    'Listen for the sound of the alarm.'
But you replied,
    'No! We won't pay attention!'

¹⁸ "Therefore, listen to this, all you nations.
    Take note of my people's situation.
¹⁹ Listen, all the earth!
    I will bring disaster on my people.

It is the fruit of their own schemes,
    because they refuse to listen to me.
They have rejected my word.
²⁰ There's no use offering me sweet
    frankincense from Sheba.
    Keep your fragrant calamus imported
    from distant lands!
I will not accept your burnt offerings.
    Your sacrifices have no pleasing aroma
    for me."

²¹ Therefore, this is what the LORD says:
    "I will put obstacles in my people's path.
Fathers and sons will both fall over them.
    Neighbors and friends will die together."

AN INVASION FROM THE NORTH

²² This is what the LORD says:
    "Look! A great army coming from the north!
    A great nation is rising against you from
    far-off lands.
²³ They are armed with bows and spears.
    They are cruel and show no mercy.
They sound like a roaring sea
    as they ride forward on horses.
They are coming in battle formation,
    planning to destroy you, beautiful
    Jerusalem.*"

²⁴ We have heard reports about the enemy,
    and we wring our hands in fright.
Pangs of anguish have gripped us,
    like those of a woman in labor.
²⁵ Don't go out to the fields!
    Don't travel on the roads!
The enemy's sword is everywhere
    and terrorizes us at every turn!
²⁶ Oh, my people, dress yourselves in burlap
    and sit among the ashes.
Mourn and weep bitterly, as for the loss of
    an only son.
    For suddenly the destroying armies will
    be upon you!

²⁷ "Jeremiah, I have made you a tester of
    metals,*
    that you may determine the quality of my
    people.
²⁸ They are the worst kind of rebel,

6:23 Hebrew *daughter of Zion.*   **6:27** As in Greek version; Hebrew reads *a tester of my people a fortress.*

SAY IT ANYWAY
(6:10-11) Jeremiah's job as prophet was to remind the people of Judah to obey God, even though they didn't want to listen to him. Being obedient wasn't very exciting to them. Does that sound familiar? Maybe you've heard people say that being a Christian doesn't seem "fun." As unsettling as people's responses might be, God still wants us to share his truth. Regardless of how others might respond, say it anyway.

full of slander.
They are as hard as bronze and iron,
     and they lead others into corruption.
29 The bellows fiercely fan the flames
     to burn out the corruption.
But it does not purify them,
     for the wickedness remains.
30 I will label them 'Rejected Silver,'
     for I, the LORD, am discarding them."

7 JEREMIAH SPEAKS AT THE TEMPLE The LORD gave another message to Jeremiah. He said, 2"Go to the entrance of the LORD's Temple, and give this message to the people: 'O Judah, listen to this message from the LORD! Listen to it, all of you who worship here! 3This is what the LORD of Heaven's Armies, the God of Israel, says:

"'Even now, if you quit your evil ways, I will let you stay in your own land. 4But don't be fooled by those who promise you safety simply because the LORD's Temple is here. They chant, "The LORD's Temple is here! The LORD's Temple is here!" 5But I will be merciful only if you stop your evil thoughts and deeds and start treating each other with justice; 6only if you stop exploiting foreigners, orphans, and widows; only if you stop your murdering; and only if you stop harming yourselves by worshiping idols. 7Then I will let you stay in this land that I gave to your ancestors to keep forever.

8"'Don't be fooled into thinking that you will never suffer because the Temple is here. It's a lie! 9Do you really think you can steal, murder, commit adultery, lie, and burn incense to Baal and all those other new gods of yours, 10and then come here and stand before me in my Temple and chant, "We are safe!"—only to go right back to all those evils again? 11Don't you

yourselves admit that this Temple, which bears my name, has become a den of thieves? Surely I see all the evil going on there. I, the LORD, have spoken!

12"'Go now to the place at Shiloh where I once put the Tabernacle that bore my name. See what I did there because of all the wickedness of my people, the Israelites. 13While you were doing these wicked things, says the LORD, I spoke to you about it repeatedly, but you would not listen. I called out to you, but you refused to answer. 14So just as I destroyed Shiloh, I will now destroy this Temple that bears my name, this Temple that you trust in for help, this place that I gave to you and your ancestors. 15And I will send you out of my sight into exile, just as I did your relatives, the people of Israel.*'

JUDAH'S PERSISTENT IDOLATRY 16"Pray no more for these people, Jeremiah. Do not weep or pray for them, and don't beg me to help them, for I will not listen to you. 17Don't you see what they are doing throughout the towns of Judah and in the streets of Jerusalem? 18No wonder I am so angry! Watch how the children gather wood and the fathers build sacrificial fires. See how the women knead dough and make cakes to offer to the Queen of Heaven. And they pour out liquid offerings to their other idol gods! 19Am I the one they are hurting?" asks the LORD. "Most of all, they hurt themselves, to their own shame."

20So this is what the Sovereign LORD says: "I will pour out my terrible fury on this place. Its people, animals, trees, and crops will be consumed by the unquenchable fire of my anger."

21This is what the LORD of Heaven's Armies, the God of Israel, says: "Take your burnt offerings and your other sacrifices and eat them yourselves! 22When I led your ancestors out of Egypt, it was not burnt offerings and sacrifices I wanted from them. 23This is what I told them: 'Obey me, and I will be your God, and you will be my people. Do everything as I say, and all will be well!'

24"But my people would not listen to me. They kept doing whatever they wanted, following the stubborn desires of their evil hearts. They went backward instead of forward. 25From the day your ancestors left Egypt until now, I have continued to send my servants, the prophets—day in and day out. 26But my people have not listened to me or even tried to hear. They have been stubborn and sinful—even worse than their ancestors.

....

AN EMPTY RITUAL
(7:1-8) The people of Judah thought that their temple attendance would keep them from being punished by God. They were "religious" rather than committed to God. We can easily fall into this trap if we go through the motions of attending church or youth group without a real heart connection. Sometimes, we even think that God demands that we participate in these activities, regardless of how we feel. But empty rituals never impress God. He desires a true heart connection with his people. Does he have a connection to your heart?

HURT
(7:19) This verse answers the question, "Who gets hurt when we turn away from God?" We do! Separating oneself from God is like keeping a green plant away from soil or water, or cutting off its food supply. God is our only source of spiritual strength. Want to keep spiritually alive? Stay connected to the source (see also John 15:1-8). Cut yourself off from the Source, and you cut off life itself.

7:15 Hebrew *of Ephraim,* referring to the northern kingdom of Israel.

²⁷"Tell them all this, but do not expect them to listen. Shout out your warnings, but do not expect them to respond. ²⁸Say to them, 'This is the nation whose people will not obey the LORD their God and who refuse to be taught. Truth has vanished from among them; it is no longer heard on their lips. ²⁹Shave your head in mourning, and weep alone on the mountains. For the LORD has rejected and forsaken this generation that has provoked his fury.'

THE VALLEY OF SLAUGHTER
³⁰"The people of Judah have sinned before my very eyes," says the LORD. "They have set up their abominable idols right in the Temple that bears my name, defiling it. ³¹They have built pagan shrines at Topheth, the garbage dump in the valley of Ben-Hinnom, and there they burn their sons and daughters in the fire. I have never commanded such a horrible deed; it never even crossed my mind to command such a thing! ³²So beware, for the time is coming," says the LORD, "when that garbage dump will no longer be called Topheth or the valley of Ben-Hinnom, but the Valley of Slaughter. They will bury the bodies in Topheth until there is no more room for them. ³³The bodies of my people will be food for the vultures and wild animals, and no one will be left to scare them away. ³⁴I will put an end to the happy singing and laughter in the streets of Jerusalem. The joyful voices of bridegrooms and brides will no longer be heard in the towns of Judah. The land will lie in complete desolation.

8 "In that day," says the LORD, "the enemy will break open the graves of the kings and officials of Judah, and the graves of the priests, prophets, and common people of Jerusalem. ²They will spread out their bones on the ground before the sun, moon, and stars—the gods my people have loved, served, and worshiped. Their bones will not be gathered up again or buried but will be scattered on the ground like manure. ³And the people of this evil nation who survive will wish to die rather than live where I will send them. I, the LORD of Heaven's Armies, have spoken!

DECEPTION BY FALSE PROPHETS
⁴"Jeremiah, say to the people, 'This is what the LORD says:

"'When people fall down, don't they get up again?
When they discover they're on the wrong road, don't they turn back?

8:7 The identification of some of these birds is uncertain.

⁵ Then why do these people stay on their self-destructive path?
Why do the people of Jerusalem refuse to turn back?
They cling tightly to their lies and will not turn around.
⁶ I listen to their conversations and don't hear a word of truth.
Is anyone sorry for doing wrong?
Does anyone say, "What a terrible thing I have done"?
No! All are running down the path of sin as swiftly as a horse galloping into battle!
⁷ Even the stork that flies across the sky knows the time of her migration,
as do the turtledove, the swallow, and the crane.*
They all return at the proper time each year.
But not my people!
They do not know the LORD's laws.

⁸ "'How can you say, "We are wise because we have the word of the LORD,"
when your teachers have twisted it by writing lies?
⁹ These wise teachers will fall into the trap of their own foolishness,
for they have rejected the word of the LORD.
Are they so wise after all?
¹⁰ I will give their wives to others and their farms to strangers.
From the least to the greatest, their lives are ruled by greed.
Yes, even my prophets and priests are like that.
They are all frauds.
¹¹ They offer superficial treatments for my people's mortal wound.
They give assurances of peace when there is no peace.
¹² Are they ashamed of these disgusting actions?
Not at all—they don't even know how to blush!
Therefore, they will lie among the slaughtered.
They will be brought down when I punish them,

··

BEWARE
(8:8-13) The prophets and priests were giving false assurances rather than correction. How can we correct a fault or turn from a sin if our leaders tell us that all is well? Beware of people who are always agreeable. At best, they give you no help; at worst, they may be trying to manipulate you. Your best defense is to know the truth for yourself.

says the LORD.

¹³ I will surely consume them.
There will be no more harvests of figs and
grapes.
Their fruit trees will all die.
Whatever I gave them will soon be gone.
I, the LORD, have spoken!'

¹⁴ "Then the people will say,
'Why should we wait here to die?
Come, let's go to the fortified towns and die
there.
For the LORD our God has decreed our
destruction
and has given us a cup of poison to drink
because we sinned against the LORD.
¹⁵ We hoped for peace, but no peace came.
We hoped for a time of healing, but found
only terror.'

¹⁶ "The snorting of the enemies' warhorses
can be heard
all the way from the land of Dan in the
north!
The neighing of their stallions makes the
whole land tremble.
They are coming to devour the land and
everything in it—
cities and people alike.

¹⁷ I will send these enemy troops among you
like poisonous snakes you cannot charm.
They will bite you, and you will die.
I, the LORD, have spoken!"

JEREMIAH WEEPS FOR SINFUL JUDAH

¹⁸ My grief is beyond healing;
my heart is broken.
¹⁹ Listen to the weeping of my people;
it can be heard all across the land.
"Has the LORD abandoned Jerusalem?*" the
people ask.
"Is her King no longer there?"

"Oh, why have they provoked my anger with
their carved idols
and their worthless foreign gods?" says
the LORD.

²⁰ "The harvest is finished,
and the summer is gone," the people cry,
"yet we are not saved!"

....

SO MOVED
(8:18-22) These verses provide a vivid picture of Jer-
emiah's emotions as he watched his people reject God.
He responded with anguish to a world dying in sin. How
often do we respond this way for friends and neighbors
who reject God? Only when we have Jeremiah's kind of
concern will we be moved to help.

²¹ I hurt with the hurt of my people.
I mourn and am overcome with grief.
²² Is there no medicine in Gilead?
Is there no physician there?
Why is there no healing
for the wounds of my people?

9 ¹*If only my head were a pool of water
and my eyes a fountain of tears,
I would weep day and night
for all my people who have been
slaughtered.
²*Oh, that I could go away and forget my
people
and live in a travelers' shack in the
desert.
For they are all adulterers—
a pack of treacherous liars.

JUDGMENT FOR DISOBEDIENCE

³ "My people bend their tongues like bows
to shoot out lies.
They refuse to stand up for the truth.
They only go from bad to worse.
They do not know me,"
says the LORD.

⁴ "Beware of your neighbor!
Don't even trust your brother!
For brother takes advantage of brother,
and friend slanders friend.
⁵ They all fool and defraud each other;
no one tells the truth.
With practiced tongues they tell lies;
they wear themselves out with all their
sinning.
⁶ They pile lie upon lie
and utterly refuse to acknowledge me,"
says the LORD.

⁷ Therefore, this is what the LORD of Heaven's
Armies says:
"See, I will melt them down in a crucible
and test them like metal.
What else can I do with my people?*
⁸ For their tongues shoot lies like poisoned
arrows.
They speak friendly words to their neighbors
while scheming in their heart to kill them.
⁹ Should I not punish them for this?" says the
LORD.
"Should I not avenge myself against
such a nation?"

¹⁰ I will weep for the mountains
and wail for the wilderness pastures.

8:19 Hebrew *Zion?* **9:1** Verse 9:1 is numbered 8:23 in Hebrew text.
9:2 Verses 9:2-26 are numbered 9:1-25 in Hebrew text. **9:7** Hebrew
with the daughter of my people? Greek version reads *with the evil
daughter of my people?*

For they are desolate and empty of life;
   the lowing of cattle is heard no more;
   the birds and wild animals have all fled.

11 "I will make Jerusalem into a heap of ruins,"
   says the LORD.
"It will be a place haunted by jackals.
The towns of Judah will be ghost towns,
   with no one living in them."

12 Who is wise enough to understand all this? Who has been instructed by the LORD and can explain it to others? Why has the land been so ruined that no one dares to travel through it?

13 The LORD replies, "This has happened because my people have abandoned my instructions; they have refused to obey what I said. 14 Instead, they have stubbornly followed their own desires and worshiped the images of Baal, as their ancestors taught them. 15 So now, this is what the LORD of Heaven's Armies, the God of Israel, says: Look! I will feed them with bitterness and give them poison to drink. 16 I will scatter them around the world, in places they and their ancestors never heard of, and even there I will chase them with the sword until I have destroyed them completely."

WEEPING IN JERUSALEM

17 This is what the LORD of Heaven's Armies says:
"Consider all this, and call for the
   mourners.
   Send for the women who mourn at
   funerals.
18 Quick! Begin your weeping!
   Let the tears flow from your eyes.

9:19 Hebrew *Zion*.

19 Hear the people of Jerusalem* crying in
   despair,
   'We are ruined! We are completely
     humiliated!
We must leave our land,
   because our homes have been torn
     down.'"

20 Listen, you women, to the words of the
   LORD;
   open your ears to what he has to say.
Teach your daughters to wail;
   teach one another how to lament.
21 For death has crept in through our windows
   and has entered our mansions.
It has killed off the flower of our youth:
   Children no longer play in the streets,
   and young men no longer gather in the
     squares.

22 This is what the LORD says:
"Bodies will be scattered across the fields
   like clumps of manure,
   like bundles of grain after the harvest.
   No one will be left to bury them."

23 This is what the LORD says:
"Don't let the wise boast in their wisdom,
   or the powerful boast in their power,
   or the rich boast in their riches.
24 But those who wish to boast
   should boast in this alone:
that they truly know me and understand
   that I am the LORD
who demonstrates unfailing love
and who brings justice and righteousness
   to the earth,

CHOICES
priorities

In August, some guys from Adams High are sitting around discussing their summers:

Brandon: "Get this—my dad is paying me twelve bucks an hour to make deliveries! Counting that and my afternoon lawn business, I'm gonna clear $4,500 easy!"

Devin: "That's great, but money ain't gonna help you block on the football field. I've been in the gym every day. So far, I've increased my bench press from 200 to 250 pounds! I'll be all-district this year."

Alejandro: "Too bad you didn't work on your brain muscle! I've had the best of all possible summers. I've biked most of the summer, I earned a little money, I hung out and had a blast, and I just got back from computer camp—"

Brandon (laughing): "Computer camp?! Dude, you're kidding!"

Alejandro: "Hey, laugh all you want. We'll see who's laughing next spring when I get a scholarship to Princeton or Harvard, and you're stuck at some junior college."

Devin: "Not likely, bro! What about you, Josiah? Didn't you just go on some church trip?"

Josiah's kind of embarrassed. He did just return from a mission trip to Mexico. It was incredible, but compared to making tons of money, building the perfect athletic body, or getting a scholarship, it doesn't seem like much. Or does it?

Can you relate to Josiah's feelings? What does this scene show us about priorities?
See Jeremiah 9:23-24 for a clear look at what really matters.

and that I delight in these things.
I, the LORD, have spoken!

²⁵"A time is coming," says the LORD, "when I will punish all those who are circumcised in body but not in spirit—²⁶the Egyptians, Edomites, Ammonites, Moabites, the people who live in the desert in remote places,* and yes, even the people of Judah. And like all these pagan nations, the people of Israel also have uncircumcised hearts."

10 IDOLATRY BRINGS DESTRUCTION

Hear the word that the LORD speaks to you, O Israel! ²This is what the LORD says:

"Do not act like the other nations,
who try to read their future in the stars.
Do not be afraid of their predictions,
even though other nations are terrified
by them.
³ Their ways are futile and foolish.
They cut down a tree, and a craftsman
carves an idol.
⁴ They decorate it with gold and silver
and then fasten it securely with hammer
and nails
so it won't fall over.
⁵ Their gods are like
helpless scarecrows in a cucumber
field!
They cannot speak,
and they need to be carried because they
cannot walk.
Do not be afraid of such gods,
for they can neither harm you nor do you
any good."

⁶ LORD, there is no one like you!
For you are great, and your name is full
of power.
⁷ Who would not fear you, O King of nations?
That title belongs to you alone!
Among all the wise people of the earth
and in all the kingdoms of the world,
there is no one like you.

⁸ People who worship idols are stupid and
foolish.

• •

STAR CHARTS
(10:1-5) Everyone would like to know the future. Decisions would be easier, failures avoided, and success assured. The people of Judah tried to figure out the future by reading signs in the sky (like horoscopes). Jeremiah's response applies today: God made the stars that people consult. God, who promises to guide you, knows your future and will be with you all the way. Don't trust the stars; trust the One who made them.

The things they worship are made of
wood!
⁹ They bring beaten sheets of silver from
Tarshish
and gold from Uphaz,
and they give these materials to skillful
craftsmen
who make their idols.
Then they dress these gods in royal blue
and purple robes
made by expert tailors.
¹⁰ But the LORD is the only true God.
He is the living God and the everlasting
King!
The whole earth trembles at his anger.
The nations cannot stand up to his wrath.

¹¹Say this to those who worship other gods: "Your so-called gods, who did not make the heavens and earth, will vanish from the earth and from under the heavens."*

¹² But God made the earth by his power,
and he preserves it by his wisdom.
With his own understanding
he stretched out the heavens.
¹³ When he speaks in the thunder,
the heavens roar with rain.
He causes the clouds to rise over the earth.
He sends the lightning with the rain
and releases the wind from his
storehouses.
¹⁴ The whole human race is foolish and has
no knowledge!
The craftsmen are disgraced by the idols
they make,
for their carefully shaped works are a fraud.
These idols have no breath or power.
¹⁵ Idols are worthless; they are ridiculous lies!
On the day of reckoning they will all be
destroyed.
¹⁶ But the God of Israel* is no idol!
He is the Creator of everything that exists,
including Israel, his own special
possession.
The LORD of Heaven's Armies is his name!

THE COMING DESTRUCTION

¹⁷ Pack your bags and prepare to leave;
the siege is about to begin.
¹⁸ For this is what the LORD says:
"Suddenly, I will fling out
all you who live in this land.
I will pour great troubles upon you,
and at last you will feel my anger."

9:26 Or *in the desert and clip the corners of their hair.*   **10:11** The original text of this verse is in Aramaic.   **10:16** Hebrew *the Portion of Jacob.* See note on 5:20.

¹⁹ My wound is severe,
  and my grief is great.
My sickness is incurable,
  but I must bear it.
²⁰ My home is gone,
  and no one is left to help me rebuild it.
My children have been taken away,
  and I will never see them again.
²¹ The shepherds of my people have lost their
  senses.
They no longer seek wisdom from the
  LORD.
Therefore, they fail completely,
  and their flocks are scattered.
²² Listen! Hear the terrifying roar of great
  armies
  as they roll down from the north.
The towns of Judah will be destroyed
  and become a haunt for jackals.

JEREMIAH'S PRAYER

²³ I know, LORD, that our lives are not
  our own.
We are not able to plan our own course.
²⁴ So correct me, LORD, but please be gentle.
  Do not correct me in anger, for I would
  die.
²⁵ Pour out your wrath on the nations that
  refuse to acknowledge you—
  on the peoples that do not call upon your
  name.
For they have devoured your people Israel*;
  they have devoured and consumed
  them,
  making the land a desolate
  wilderness.

11 JUDAH'S BROKEN COVENANT The
LORD gave another message to Jeremiah. He said, ²"Remind the people of Judah
and Jerusalem about the terms of my covenant
with them. ³Say to them, 'This is what the LORD,
the God of Israel, says: Cursed is anyone who
does not obey the terms of my covenant! ⁴For
I said to your ancestors when I brought them
out of the iron-smelting furnace of Egypt, "If
you obey me and do whatever I command you,
then you will be my people, and I will be your
God." ⁵I said this so I could keep my promise to
your ancestors to give you a land flowing with
milk and honey—the land you live in today.'"
  Then I replied, "Amen, LORD! May it be so."
  ⁶Then the LORD said, "Broadcast this message in the streets of Jerusalem. Go from town
to town throughout the land and say, 'Remember the ancient covenant, and do every-

10:25 Hebrew *devoured Jacob.* See note on 5:20.

thing it requires. ⁷For I solemnly warned your
ancestors when I brought them out of Egypt,
"Obey me!" I have repeated this warning over
and over to this day, ⁸but your ancestors did
not listen or even pay attention. Instead, they
stubbornly followed their own evil desires.
And because they refused to obey, I brought
upon them all the curses described in this
covenant.'"

⁹Again the LORD spoke to me and said, "I
have discovered a conspiracy against me
among the people of Judah and Jerusalem.
¹⁰They have returned to the sins of their forefathers. They have refused to listen to me and
are worshiping other gods. Israel and Judah
have both broken the covenant I made with
their ancestors. ¹¹Therefore, this is what the
LORD says: I am going to bring calamity upon
them, and they will not escape. Though they
beg for mercy, I will not listen to their cries.
¹²Then the people of Judah and Jerusalem will
pray to their idols and burn incense before
them. But the idols will not save them when
disaster strikes! ¹³Look now, people of Judah;
you have as many gods as you have towns.
You have as many altars of shame—altars for
burning incense to your god Baal—as there are
streets in Jerusalem.

¹⁴"Pray no more for these people, Jeremiah.
Do not weep or pray for them, for I will not listen
to them when they cry out to me in distress.

¹⁵ "What right do my beloved people have to
  come to my Temple,
  when they have done so many immoral
  things?
Can their vows and sacrifices prevent their
  destruction?
  They actually rejoice in doing evil!
¹⁶ I, the LORD, once called them a thriving
  olive tree,
  beautiful to see and full of good fruit.
But now I have sent the fury of their
  enemies
  to burn them with fire,
  leaving them charred and broken.

¹⁷"I, the LORD of Heaven's Armies, who
planted this olive tree, have ordered it destroyed. For the people of Israel and Judah
have done evil, arousing my anger by burning
incense to Baal."

A PLOT AGAINST JEREMIAH
¹⁸Then the LORD
told me about the plots my enemies were making against me. ¹⁹I was like a lamb being led
to the slaughter. I had no idea that they were
planning to kill me! "Let's destroy this man

and all his words," they said. "Let's cut him down, so his name will be forgotten forever."

20 O LORD of Heaven's Armies,
you make righteous judgments,
and you examine the deepest thoughts
and secrets.
Let me see your vengeance against them,
for I have committed my cause to you.

21 This is what the LORD says about the men of Anathoth who wanted me dead. They had said, "We will kill you if you do not stop prophesying in the LORD's name." 22 So this is what the LORD of Heaven's Armies says about them: "I will punish them! Their young men will die in battle, and their boys and girls will starve to death. 23 Not one of these plotters from Anathoth will survive, for I will bring disaster upon them when their time of punishment comes."

....

TOUGH TIMES
(12:1-6) Life was difficult for Jeremiah despite his love for and obedience to God. When he asked God for relief, God's reply in effect was, "If you think this is bad, how are you going to cope when life gets really tough?" Not all of God's answers to prayer are easy to accept. Any Christian who has experienced war, grief, or a serious illness knows this. But we are to be committed to God even when the going gets tough or when he doesn't answer our prayers with immediate relief.

12 JEREMIAH QUESTIONS THE LORD'S JUSTICE

1 LORD, you always give me justice
when I bring a case before you.
So let me bring you this complaint:
Why are the wicked so prosperous?
Why are evil people so happy?
2 You have planted them,
and they have taken root and
prospered.
Your name is on their lips,
but you are far from their hearts.
3 But as for me, LORD, you know my heart.
You see me and test my thoughts.
Drag these people away like sheep to be
butchered!
Set them aside to be slaughtered!

4 How long must this land mourn?
Even the grass in the fields has
withered.
The wild animals and birds have
disappeared
because of the evil in the land.
For the people have said,
"The LORD doesn't see what's ahead
for us!"

THE LORD'S REPLY TO JEREMIAH

5 "If racing against mere men makes you
tired,

ULTIMATE ISSUES *MODERN-DAY IDOLS*

A drunken orgy around a golden calf . . . the latest sports car . . . offering sacrifices to Baal . . . teens screaming their adoration of their favorite band at a concert . . .

What do these scenes have in common? They all represent forms of idol worship.

"Wait a minute," you say. "The golden calf and Baal are definitely idols. But why bring up a car and a concert?"

Glad you asked. An idol is *anything* we desire above God and his will for our lives. Ouch!

Idols in Jeremiah's day were statues representing pagan gods. Idolatry comes in more subtle forms these days. Instead of a golden calf, we're enticed by a "golden" or "platinum" credit card. Instead of Baal, we "worship" ball players and rock stars, imitating them, from their hairstyles and shoes to their lifestyles. Instead of temple prostitutes, we're seduced by Internet porn. So is having a credit card or liking a band or thinking about sex wrong? Of course not. The problem comes in using them the wrong way or in loving things (or people) more than we love God.

So, why is idolatry so bad? Why does God hate it so much?

First, worshiping a false god (anything that comes before the *real* God is a *false* god) degrades us. It makes us less than what we are intended to be. We are made in the image of God, with the opportunity through Christ to know him and, in some ways, to be like him. When we worship an idol—a lesser god—we aim much lower and, all too often, hit our target.

Second, idolatry often is subtle and hard to detect. Think about your latest crush or one you used to have. (Okay—one you wish you had.) Maybe you wanted to hang out with him or her all of the time—more than with anyone else. But some relationships involve an unhealthy dependence; the couple puts each other before God. This can be disastrous for a relationship with each other and with God.

Finally, idol worship steals from God. When we love someone or something else more than God, we rob him of the worship and loyalty that rightly belong only to him (see Exod 20:4-5).

Idolatry has a way of creeping in and destroying parts of your life, just as cancer destroys parts of your body. That's why it needs a radical cure, just as cancer does. What's that radical cure? Give up the idol. ■

how will you race against horses?
If you stumble and fall on open ground,
what will you do in the thickets near the
Jordan?

⁶ Even your brothers, members of your own
family,
have turned against you.
They plot and raise complaints against
you.
Do not trust them,
no matter how pleasantly they speak.

⁷ "I have abandoned my people, my special
possession.
I have surrendered my dearest ones to
their enemies.
⁸ My chosen people have roared at me like
a lion of the forest,
so I have treated them with contempt.
⁹ My chosen people act like speckled
vultures,*
but they themselves are surrounded by
vultures.
Bring on the wild animals to pick their
corpses clean!

¹⁰ "Many rulers have ravaged my vineyard,
trampling down the vines
and turning all its beauty into a barren
wilderness.
¹¹ They have made it an empty wasteland;
I hear its mournful cry.
The whole land is desolate,
and no one even cares.
¹² On all the bare hilltops,
destroying armies can be seen.
The sword of the LORD devours people
from one end of the nation to the other.
No one will escape!
¹³ My people have planted wheat
but are harvesting thorns.
They have worn themselves out,
but it has done them no good.
They will harvest a crop of shame
because of the fierce anger of the LORD."

A MESSAGE FOR ISRAEL'S NEIGHBORS ¹⁴Now
this is what the LORD says: "I will uproot from
their land all the evil nations reaching out for
the possession I gave my people Israel. And
I will uproot Judah from among them. ¹⁵But
afterward I will return and have compassion
on all of them. I will bring them home to their
own lands again, each nation to its own possession. ¹⁶And if these nations truly learn the
ways of my people, and if they learn to swear
by my name, saying, 'As surely as the LORD

lives' (just as they taught my people to swear
by the name of Baal), then they will be given a
place among my people. ¹⁷But any nation who
refuses to obey me will be uprooted and destroyed. I, the LORD, have spoken!"

13 JEREMIAH'S LINEN LOINCLOTH This
is what the LORD said to me: "Go and
buy a linen loincloth and put it on, but do not
wash it." ²So I bought the loincloth as the LORD
directed me, and I put it on.

³Then the LORD gave me another message:
⁴"Take the linen loincloth you are wearing, and
go to the Euphrates River.* Hide it there in a
hole in the rocks." ⁵So I went and hid it by the
Euphrates as the LORD had instructed me.

⁶A long time afterward the LORD said to me,
"Go back to the Euphrates and get the loincloth I told you to hide there." ⁷So I went to the
Euphrates and dug it out of the hole where I
had hidden it. But now it was rotting and falling apart. The loincloth was good for nothing.

⁸Then I received this message from the LORD:
⁹"This is what the LORD says: This shows how
I will rot away the pride of Judah and Jerusalem. ¹⁰These wicked people refuse to listen to
me. They stubbornly follow their own desires
and worship other gods. Therefore, they will
become like this loincloth—good for nothing!
¹¹As a loincloth clings to a man's waist, so I created Judah and Israel to cling to me, says the
LORD. They were to be my people, my pride, my
glory—an honor to my name. But they would
not listen to me.

¹²"So tell them, 'This is what the LORD, the
God of Israel, says: May all your jars be filled
with wine.' And they will reply, 'Of course! Jars
are made to be filled with wine!'

¹³"Then tell them, 'No, this is what the LORD
means: I will fill everyone in this land with
drunkenness—from the king sitting on David's
throne to the priests and the prophets, right
down to the common people of Jerusalem.
¹⁴I will smash them against each other, even
parents against children, says the LORD. I will
not let my pity or mercy or compassion keep
me from destroying them.'"

....

USELESS
*(13:1-11) Actions speak louder than words. Jeremiah
often used vivid object lessons to arouse the people's
curiosity and get his point across. The linen belt represented Judah. Although the people had once been close
to God, their pride made them as useless as Jeremiah's
belt. How do you think God would describe your actions
lately? Useful? Useless? If you want to be useful or even
more so, actions speak louder than words.*

12:9 Or *speckled hyenas.* **13:4** Hebrew *Perath;* also in 13:5, 6, 7.

A WARNING AGAINST PRIDE

¹⁵ Listen and pay attention!
  Do not be arrogant, for the LORD has
    spoken.
¹⁶ Give glory to the LORD your God
    before it is too late.
  Acknowledge him before he brings darkness
    upon you,
      causing you to stumble and fall on the
        darkening mountains.
  For then, when you look for light,
    you will find only terrible darkness and
      gloom.
¹⁷ And if you still refuse to listen,
  I will weep alone because of your pride.
  My eyes will overflow with tears,
    because the LORD's flock will be led away
      into exile.

¹⁸ Say to the king and his mother,
  "Come down from your thrones
    and sit in the dust,
  for your glorious crowns
    will soon be snatched from
      your heads."
¹⁹ The towns of the Negev will close
    their gates,
  and no one will be able to open them.
  The people of Judah will be taken away as
    captives.
  All will be carried into exile.

²⁰ Open up your eyes and see
    the armies marching down from the
      north!
  Where is your flock—
    your beautiful flock—
  that he gave you to care for?
²¹ What will you say when the LORD takes the
    allies you have cultivated
  and appoints them as your rulers?
  Pangs of anguish will grip you,
    like those of a woman in labor!
²² You may ask yourself,
  "Why is all this happening to me?"
    It is because of your many sins!
  That is why you have been stripped
    and raped by invading armies.

· ·

DANGER
*(13:15) While it is good to respect our nation and
our church, our loyalties always carry a hidden danger—pride. When is pride harmful? When it causes us
(1) to look down on others; (2) to be selfish with our
resources; (3) to force our solutions on others' problems;
(4) to think God is blessing us because of our own merits;
(5) to be content with our plans rather than seeking
God's plans.*

²³ Can an Ethiopian* change the color of his
    skin?
  Can a leopard take away its spots?
  Neither can you start doing good,
    for you have always done evil.
²⁴ "I will scatter you like chaff
    that is blown away by the desert winds.
²⁵ This is your allotment,
    the portion I have assigned to you,"
      says the LORD,
  "for you have forgotten me,
    putting your trust in false gods.
²⁶ I myself will strip you
    and expose you to shame.
²⁷ I have seen your adultery and lust,
    and your disgusting idol worship out in
      the fields and on the hills.
  What sorrow awaits you, Jerusalem!
    How long before you are pure?"

14 JUDAH'S TERRIBLE DROUGHT This
message came to Jeremiah from the
LORD, explaining why he was holding back the
rain:

² "Judah wilts;
    commerce at the city gates grinds to a
      halt.
  All the people sit on the ground in
    mourning,
    and a great cry rises from Jerusalem.
³ The nobles send servants to get water,
    but all the wells are dry.
  The servants return with empty pitchers,
    confused and desperate,
      covering their heads in grief.
⁴ The ground is parched
    and cracked for lack of rain.
  The farmers are deeply troubled;
    they, too, cover their heads.
⁵ Even the doe abandons her newborn fawn
    because there is no grass in the field.
⁶ The wild donkeys stand on the bare hills
    panting like thirsty jackals.
  They strain their eyes looking for grass,
    but there is none to be found."

⁷ The people say, "Our wickedness has
    caught up with us, LORD,
  but help us for the sake of your own
    reputation.
  We have turned away from you
    and sinned against you again and again.
⁸ O Hope of Israel, our Savior in times of
    trouble,
  why are you like a stranger to us?

14:23 Hebrew *a Cushite.*

Why are you like a traveler passing through
the land,
stopping only for the night?
⁹ Are you also confused?
Is our champion helpless to save us?
You are right here among us, LORD.
We are known as your people.
Please don't abandon us now!"

¹⁰ So this is what the LORD says to his people:
"You love to wander far from me
and do not restrain yourselves.
Therefore, I will no longer accept you as my
people.
Now I will remember all your wickedness
and will punish you for your sins."

THE LORD FORBIDS JEREMIAH TO INTERCEDE

¹¹Then the LORD said to me, "Do not pray for
these people anymore. ¹²When they fast, I
will pay no attention. When they present their
burnt offerings and grain offerings to me, I will
not accept them. Instead, I will devour them
with war, famine, and disease."

¹³Then I said, "O Sovereign LORD, their prophets are telling them, 'All is well—no war or famine will come. The LORD will surely send you
peace.'"

¹⁴Then the LORD said, "These prophets are
telling lies in my name. I did not send them
or tell them to speak. I did not give them any
messages. They prophesy of visions and revelations they have never seen or heard. They
speak foolishness made up in their own lying
hearts. ¹⁵Therefore, this is what the LORD says:
I will punish these lying prophets, for they have
spoken in my name even though I never sent
them. They say that no war or famine will come,
but they themselves will die by war and famine!
¹⁶As for the people to whom they prophesy—
their bodies will be thrown out into the streets
of Jerusalem, victims of famine and war. There
will be no one left to bury them. Husbands,
wives, sons, and daughters—all will be gone.
For I will pour out their own wickedness on
them. ¹⁷Now, Jeremiah, say this to them:

"Night and day my eyes overflow with tears.
I cannot stop weeping,
for my virgin daughter—my precious
people—
has been struck down
and lies mortally wounded.
¹⁸ If I go out into the fields,
I see the bodies of people slaughtered by
the enemy.
If I walk the city streets,

14:19 Hebrew *Zion?*

I see people who have died of starvation.
The prophets and priests continue with
their work,
but they don't know what they're doing."

A PRAYER FOR HEALING

¹⁹ LORD, have you completely rejected Judah?
Do you really hate Jerusalem?*
Why have you wounded us past all hope of
healing?
We hoped for peace, but no peace came.
We hoped for a time of healing, but found
only terror.
²⁰ LORD, we confess our wickedness
and that of our ancestors, too.
We all have sinned against you.
²¹ For the sake of your reputation, LORD, do not
abandon us.
Do not disgrace your own glorious throne.
Please remember us,
and do not break your covenant with us.

²² Can any of the worthless foreign gods send
us rain?
Does it fall from the sky by itself?
No, you are the one, O LORD our God!
Only you can do such things.
So we will wait for you to help us.

15 JUDAH'S INEVITABLE DOOM Then the
LORD said to me, "Even if Moses and
Samuel stood before me pleading for these
people, I wouldn't help them. Away with them!
Get them out of my sight! ²And if they say to
you, 'But where can we go?' tell them, 'This is
what the LORD says:

"'Those who are destined for death,
to death;
those who are destined for war, to war;
those who are destined for famine,
to famine;
those who are destined for captivity,
to captivity.'

³"I will send four kinds of destroyers against
them," says the LORD. "I will send the sword to
kill, the dogs to drag away, the vultures to devour, and the wild animals to finish up what is
left. ⁴Because of the wicked things Manasseh

....

HIS WILL OR YOURS?
(14:11-12) *Because of the continual false repentance of
the people of Judah, God turned deaf ears to their cries.
He left them to wallow in the mess of their own making.
God will allow only so much rebellion to take place before
he tells a person, "Your will be done." Although God is
infinitely patient, he doesn't force anyone to obey him.
Do you want his will or your will to be done?*

son of Hezekiah, king of Judah, did in Jerusalem, I will make my people an object of horror to all the kingdoms of the earth.

5 "Who will feel sorry for you, Jerusalem?
   Who will weep for you?
   Who will even bother to ask how you are?
6 You have abandoned me
   and turned your back on me,"
   says the LORD.
"Therefore, I will raise my fist to destroy you.
   I am tired of always giving you another
     chance.
7 I will winnow you like grain at the gates of
     your cities
   and take away the children you hold dear.
I will destroy my own people,
   because they refuse to change their evil
     ways.
8 There will be more widows
   than the grains of sand on the seashore.
At noontime I will bring a destroyer
   against the mothers of young men.
I will cause anguish and terror
   to come upon them suddenly.
9 The mother of seven grows faint and gasps
     for breath;
   her sun has gone down while it is still
     day.
She sits childless now,
   disgraced and humiliated.
And I will hand over those who are left
   to be killed by the enemy.
   I, the LORD, have spoken!"

JEREMIAH'S COMPLAINT   10 Then I said,

"What sorrow is mine, my mother.
   Oh, that I had died at birth!
   I am hated everywhere I go.
I am neither a lender who threatens to
     foreclose
   nor a borrower who refuses to pay—
   yet they all curse me."

11 The LORD replied,

"I will take care of you, Jeremiah.

Your enemies will ask you to plead on
     their behalf
   in times of trouble and distress.
12 Can a man break a bar of iron from the
     north,
   or a bar of bronze?
13 At no cost to them,
   I will hand over your wealth and treasures
as plunder to your enemies,
   for sin runs rampant in your land.
14 I will tell your enemies to take you
   as captives to a foreign land.
For my anger blazes like a fire
   that will burn forever.*"

15 Then I said,

"LORD, you know what's happening to me.
   Please step in and help me. Punish my
     persecutors!
Please give me time; don't let me die young.
   It's for your sake that I am suffering.
16 When I discovered your words, I devoured
     them.
   They are my joy and my heart's delight,
for I bear your name,
   O LORD God of Heaven's Armies.
17 I never joined the people in their merry
     feasts.
   I sat alone because your hand was on me.
   I was filled with indignation at their sins.
18 Why then does my suffering continue?
   Why is my wound so incurable?
Your help seems as uncertain as a seasonal
     brook,
   like a spring that has gone dry."

19 This is how the LORD responds:

"If you return to me, I will restore you
   so you can continue to serve me.
If you speak good words rather than
     worthless ones,
   you will be my spokesman.
You must influence them;
   do not let them influence you!
20 They will fight against you like an attacking
     army,
   but I will make you as secure as a fortified
     wall of bronze.
They will not conquer you,
   for I am with you to protect and rescue
     you.
   I, the LORD, have spoken!
21 Yes, I will certainly keep you safe from these
     wicked men.
   I will rescue you from their cruel hands."

INFLUENCE
(15:17-21) *Jeremiah accused God of not helping him when he really needed it. Jeremiah had taken his eyes off God's purposes and was feeling sorry for himself. He was angry, hurt, and afraid. In response, God didn't get angry at Jeremiah; he answered by reminding Jeremiah of his promise—"You will be my spokesman." So, what does that tell us? Namely: (1) We can reveal our deepest thoughts to God. (2) God expects us to trust no matter what. (3) We are here to influence others for God.*

15:14 As in some Hebrew manuscripts (see also 17:4); most Hebrew manuscripts read *will burn against you.*

16 JEREMIAH FORBIDDEN TO MARRY

The LORD gave me another message. He said, [2]"Do not get married or have children in this place. [3]For this is what the LORD says about the children born here in this city and about their mothers and fathers: [4]They will die from terrible diseases. No one will mourn for them or bury them, and they will lie scattered on the ground like manure. They will die from war and famine, and their bodies will be food for the vultures and wild animals."

JUDAH'S COMING PUNISHMENT

[5]This is what the LORD says: "Do not go to funerals to mourn and show sympathy for these people, for I have removed my protection and peace from them. I have taken away my unfailing love and my mercy. [6]Both the great and the lowly will die in this land. No one will bury them or mourn for them. Their friends will not cut themselves in sorrow or shave their heads in sadness. [7]No one will offer a meal to comfort those who mourn for the dead—not even at the death of a mother or father. No one will send a cup of wine to console them.

[8]"And do not go to their feasts and parties. Do not eat and drink with them at all. [9]For this is what the LORD of Heaven's Armies, the God of Israel, says: In your own lifetime, before your very eyes, I will put an end to the happy singing and laughter in this land. The joyful voices of bridegrooms and brides will no longer be heard.

[10]"When you tell the people all these things, they will ask, 'Why has the LORD decreed such terrible things against us? What have we done to deserve such treatment? What is our sin against the LORD our God?'

[11]"Then you will give them the LORD's reply: 'It is because your ancestors were unfaithful to me. They worshiped other gods and served them. They abandoned me and did not obey my word. [12]And you are even worse than your ancestors! You stubbornly follow your own evil desires and refuse to listen to me. [13]So I will throw you out of this land and send you into a foreign land where you and your ancestors have never been. There you can worship idols day and night—and I will grant you no favors!'

HOPE DESPITE THE DISASTER

[14]"But the time is coming," says the LORD, "when people who are taking an oath will no longer say, 'As surely as the LORD lives, who rescued the people of Israel from the land of Egypt.' [15]Instead, they will say, 'As surely as the LORD lives, who brought the people of Israel back to their own land from the land of the north and from all the countries to which he had exiled them.' For I will bring them back to this land that I gave their ancestors.

[16]"But now I am sending for many fishermen who will catch them," says the LORD. "I am sending for hunters who will hunt them down in the mountains, hills, and caves. [17]I am watching them closely, and I see every sin. They cannot hope to hide from me. [18]I will double their punishment for all their sins, because they have defiled my land with lifeless images of their detestable gods and have filled my territory with their evil deeds."

JEREMIAH'S PRAYER OF CONFIDENCE

[19] LORD, you are my strength and fortress,
   my refuge in the day of trouble!
Nations from around the world
   will come to you and say,
"Our ancestors left us a foolish heritage,
   for they worshiped worthless idols.
[20] Can people make their own gods?
   These are not real gods at all!"

[21] The LORD says,
"Now I will show them my power;
   now I will show them my might.
At last they will know and understand
   that I am the LORD."

17 JUDAH'S SIN AND PUNISHMENT

[1] "The sin of Judah
   is inscribed with an iron chisel—
engraved with a diamond point on their
      stony hearts
   and on the corners of their altars.
[2] Even their children go to worship
   at their pagan altars and Asherah poles,
beneath every green tree
   and on every high hill.
[3] So I will hand over my holy mountain—
   along with all your wealth and treasures
   and your pagan shrines—
as plunder to your enemies,
   for sin runs rampant in your land.

....

HIDE-AND-SEEK

(16:17) Small children think that if they can't see you, then you can't see them. The people of Judah may have wished that hiding from God was as simple as closing their eyes. Although they closed their eyes to their wrongs, everything was revealed to God. Ever been tempted to play hide-and-seek with God, thinking that maybe he won't notice a sinful attitude or action? News flash: He knows everything. You already knew that, right? So, instead of hiding, why not seek him?

⁴ The wonderful possession I have reserved
  for you
  will slip from your hands.
I will tell your enemies to take you
  as captives to a foreign land.
For my anger blazes like a fire
  that will burn forever."

WISDOM FROM THE LORD

⁵ This is what the LORD says:
"Cursed are those who put their trust in
  mere humans,
  who rely on human strength
  and turn their hearts away from the LORD.
⁶ They are like stunted shrubs in the desert,
  with no hope for the future.
They will live in the barren wilderness,
  in an uninhabited salty land.

⁷ "But blessed are those who trust in the
  LORD
  and have made the LORD their hope and
  confidence.
⁸ They are like trees planted along a
  riverbank,
  with roots that reach deep into the water.
Such trees are not bothered by the heat
  or worried by long months of drought.
Their leaves stay green,
  and they never stop producing fruit.

⁹ "The human heart is the most deceitful of all
  things,
  and desperately wicked.
  Who really knows how bad it is?
¹⁰ But I, the LORD, search all hearts
  and examine secret motives.

I give all people their due rewards,
  according to what their actions deserve."

JEREMIAH'S TRUST IN THE LORD

¹¹ Like a partridge that hatches eggs she has
  not laid,
  so are those who get their wealth by
  unjust means.
At midlife they will lose their riches;
  in the end, they will become poor old
  fools.
¹² But we worship at your throne—
  eternal, high, and glorious!
¹³ O LORD, the hope of Israel,
  all who turn away from you will be
  disgraced.
They will be buried in the dust of the earth,
  for they have abandoned the LORD, the
  fountain of living water.

¹⁴ O LORD, if you heal me, I will be truly healed;
  if you save me, I will be truly saved.
  My praises are for you alone!
¹⁵ People scoff at me and say,
  "What is this 'message from the LORD' you
  talk about?
  Why don't your predictions come true?"

¹⁶ LORD, I have not abandoned my job
  as a shepherd for your people.
I have not urged you to send disaster.
  You have heard everything I've said.
¹⁷ LORD, don't terrorize me!
  You alone are my hope in the day of
  disaster.
¹⁸ Bring shame and dismay on all who
  persecute me,

I WONDER...

I've done some pretty awful things in my life. How could God forgive me for what I've done?

Recognizing that you've done wrong is 90 percent of the battle.

Usually people who build up years of wrong actions also have built a shell around their hearts. This shell protects them from feeling guilty about what they've done. As the shell gets harder and thicker, they continue a downward spiral, doing more and more wrong things.

Jeremiah, God's prophet, looked at the human tendency to sin and came to this conclusion: "The human heart is the most deceitful of all things, and desperately wicked. Who really knows how

bad it is? But I, the LORD, search all hearts and examine secret motives. I give all people their due rewards, according to what their actions deserve" (Jer 17:9-10).

As you'll notice, this passage doesn't say that some people's hearts are more wicked than others'. All of us have the potential for destructive actions.

But there's good news. Check out Isaiah 1:18: "'Come now, let's settle this,' says the LORD. 'Though your sins are like scarlet, I will make them as white as snow. Though they are red like crimson, I will make them as white as wool.'"

God isn't shocked by anything you've done. He's willing to forgive you if you let him.

So, don't give up—give in . . . to God. Ask him to forgive you and help you start over.

but don't let me experience shame and
dismay.
Bring a day of terror on them.
Yes, bring double destruction upon them!

OBSERVING THE SABBATH ¹⁹This is what the
LORD said to me: "Go and stand in the gates of
Jerusalem, first in the gate where the king goes
in and out, and then in each of the other gates.
²⁰Say to all the people, 'Listen to this message
from the LORD, you kings of Judah and all you
people of Judah and everyone living in Jerusalem. ²¹This is what the LORD says: Listen to my
warning! Stop carrying on your trade at Jerusalem's gates on the Sabbath day. ²²Do not do
your work on the Sabbath, but make it a holy
day. I gave this command to your ancestors,
²³but they did not listen or obey. They stubbornly refused to pay attention or accept my
discipline.

²⁴"'But if you obey me, says the LORD, and
do not carry on your trade at the gates or work
on the Sabbath day, and if you keep it holy,
²⁵then kings and their officials will go in and
out of these gates forever. There will always
be a descendant of David sitting on the throne
here in Jerusalem. Kings and their officials will
always ride in and out among the people of
Judah in chariots and on horses, and this city
will remain forever. ²⁶And from all around Jerusalem, from the towns of Judah and Benjamin,
from the western foothills* and the hill country
and the Negev, the people will come with their
burnt offerings and sacrifices. They will bring
their grain offerings, frankincense, and thanksgiving offerings to the LORD's Temple.

²⁷"'But if you do not listen to me and refuse to keep the Sabbath holy, and if on the
Sabbath day you bring loads of merchandise
through the gates of Jerusalem just as on other
days, then I will set fire to these gates. The fire
will spread to the palaces, and no one will be
able to put out the roaring flames.'"

18 THE POTTER AND THE CLAY The LORD
gave another message to Jeremiah. He
said, ²"Go down to the potter's shop, and I will
speak to you there." ³So I did as he told me
and found the potter working at his wheel. ⁴But
the jar he was making did not turn out as he
had hoped, so he crushed it into a lump of clay
again and started over.

⁵Then the LORD gave me this message:
⁶"O Israel, can I not do to you as this potter has
done to his clay? As the clay is in the potter's
hand, so are you in my hand. ⁷If I announce

17:26 Hebrew *the Shephelah.*

that a certain nation or kingdom is to be uprooted, torn down, and destroyed, ⁸but then
that nation renounces its evil ways, I will not
destroy it as I had planned. ⁹And if I announce
that I will plant and build up a certain nation
or kingdom, ¹⁰but then that nation turns to evil
and refuses to obey me, I will not bless it as I
said I would.

¹¹"Therefore, Jeremiah, go and warn all Judah and Jerusalem. Say to them, 'This is what
the LORD says: I am planning disaster for you
instead of good. So turn from your evil ways,
each of you, and do what is right.'"

¹²But the people replied, "Don't waste your
breath. We will continue to live as we want to,
stubbornly following our own evil desires."

¹³So this is what the LORD says:

"Has anyone ever heard of such a thing,
    even among the pagan nations?
My virgin daughter Israel
    has done something terrible!
¹⁴ Does the snow ever disappear from the
        mountaintops of Lebanon?
    Do the cold streams flowing from those
        distant mountains ever run dry?
¹⁵ But my people are not so reliable, for they
        have deserted me;
    they burn incense to worthless idols.
    They have stumbled off the ancient
        highways
    and walk in muddy paths.
¹⁶ Therefore, their land will become desolate,
        a monument to their stupidity.
    All who pass by will be astonished
        and will shake their heads in amazement.
¹⁷ I will scatter my people before their enemies
        as the east wind scatters dust.
    And in all their trouble I will turn my back
        on them
        and refuse to notice their distress."

A PLOT AGAINST JEREMIAH ¹⁸Then the
people said, "Come on, let's plot a way to stop

....

OPPOSITION
*(18:18) Jeremiah's words and actions challenged the
people of Judah's social and moral behavior. So, they
spread false rumors about him to shut him up. Jeremiah
wasn't afraid to give unpopular criticism. The people
could either obey his message or silence him. They
chose the latter. Have you ever been mistreated because
you told people about God? Many people have been
so discouraged by persecution that they gave up even
speaking about God. God never promised to keep his
faithful servants from experiencing persecution. But he
does promise that he will be with them and will give them
strength to endure (2 Cor 1:3-7). Knowing this, are you
willing to persevere even through persecution?*

Jeremiah. We have plenty of priests and wise men and prophets. We don't need him to teach the word and give us advice and prophecies. Let's spread rumors about him and ignore what he says."

¹⁹ LORD, hear me and help me!
　　Listen to what my enemies are saying.
²⁰ Should they repay evil for good?
　　They have dug a pit to kill me,
　　　though I pleaded for them
　　　　and tried to protect them from
　　　　　your anger.
²¹ So let their children starve!
　　Let them die by the sword!
　　Let their wives become childless
　　　widows.
　　Let their old men die in a plague,
　　　and let their young men be killed in
　　　　battle!
²² Let screaming be heard from their homes
　　　as warriors come suddenly upon them.
　　For they have dug a pit for me
　　　and have hidden traps along my path.
²³ LORD, you know all about their murderous
　　　plots against me.
　　Don't forgive their crimes and blot out
　　　their sins.
　　Let them die before you.
　　Deal with them in your anger.

19 JEREMIAH'S SHATTERED JAR This is what the LORD said to me: "Go and buy a clay jar. Then ask some of the leaders of the people and of the priests to follow you. ²Go out through the Gate of Broken Pots to the garbage dump in the valley of Ben-Hinnom, and give them this message. ³Say to them, 'Listen to this message from the LORD, you kings of Judah and citizens of Jerusalem! This is what the LORD of Heaven's Armies, the God of Israel, says: I will bring a terrible disaster on this place, and the ears of those who hear about it will ring!

⁴"For Israel has forsaken me and turned this valley into a place of wickedness. The people burn incense to foreign gods—idols never before acknowledged by this generation, by their ancestors, or by the kings of Judah. And they have filled this place with the blood of inno-cent children. ⁵They have built pagan shrines to Baal, and there they burn their sons as sacrifices to Baal. I have never commanded such a horrible deed; it never even crossed my mind to command such a thing! ⁶So beware, for the time is coming, says the LORD, when this garbage dump will no longer be called Topheth or the valley of Ben-Hinnom, but the Valley of Slaughter.

⁷"'For I will upset the careful plans of Judah and Jerusalem. I will allow the people to be slaughtered by invading armies, and I will leave their dead bodies as food for the vultures and wild animals. ⁸I will reduce Jerusalem to ruins, making it a monument to their stupidity. All who pass by will be astonished and will gasp at the destruction they see there. ⁹I will see to it that your enemies lay siege to the city until all the food is gone. Then those trapped inside will eat their own sons and daughters and friends. They will be driven to utter despair.'

¹⁰"As these men watch you, Jeremiah, smash the jar you brought. ¹¹Then say to them, 'This is what the LORD of Heaven's Armies says: As this jar lies shattered, so I will shatter the people of Judah and Jerusalem beyond all hope of repair. They will bury the bodies here in Topheth, the garbage dump, until there is no more room for them. ¹²This is what I will do to this place and its people, says the LORD. I will cause this city to become defiled like Topheth. ¹³Yes, all the houses in Jerusalem, including the palace of Judah's kings, will become like Topheth—all the houses where you burned incense on the rooftops to your star gods, and where liquid offerings were poured out to your idols.'"

¹⁴Then Jeremiah returned from Topheth, the garbage dump where he had delivered this message, and he stopped in front of the Temple of the LORD. He said to the people there, ¹⁵"This is what the LORD of Heaven's Armies, the God of Israel, says: 'I will bring disaster upon this city and its surrounding towns as I promised, because you have stubbornly refused to listen to me.'"

20 JEREMIAH AND PASHHUR Now Pashhur son of Immer, the priest in charge of the Temple of the LORD, heard what Jeremiah was prophesying. ²So he arrested Jeremiah the prophet and had him whipped and put in stocks at the Benjamin Gate of the LORD's Temple.

³The next day, when Pashhur finally released him, Jeremiah said, "Pashhur, the LORD has changed your name. From now on you are to

TAKE TRUTH TO HEART
(20:1-3) Pashhur heard Jeremiah's words and, because of his guilt, locked Jeremiah up instead of taking his message to heart and acting on it. The truth sometimes stings, but our reaction to the truth shows what we are made of. Pashhur's actions proved that he didn't value truth. How do you react to truth?

be called 'The Man Who Lives in Terror.'* [4]For this is what the LORD says: 'I will send terror upon you and all your friends, and you will watch as they are slaughtered by the swords of the enemy. I will hand the people of Judah over to the king of Babylon. He will take them captive to Babylon or run them through with the sword. [5]And I will let your enemies plunder Jerusalem. All the famed treasures of the city—the precious jewels and gold and silver of your kings—will be carried off to Babylon. [6]As for you, Pashhur, you and all your household will go as captives to Babylon. There you will die and be buried, you and all your friends to whom you prophesied that everything would be all right.'"

20:3 Hebrew *Magor-missabib*, which means "surrounded by terror"; also in 20:10.

JEREMIAH'S COMPLAINT

[7] O LORD, you misled me,
 and I allowed myself to be misled.
You are stronger than I am,
 and you overpowered me.
Now I am mocked every day;
 everyone laughs at me.
[8] When I speak, the words burst out.
 "Violence and destruction!" I shout.
So these messages from the LORD
 have made me a household joke.
[9] But if I say I'll never mention the LORD
 or speak in his name,
his word burns in my heart like a fire.
 It's like a fire in my bones!
I am worn out trying to hold it in!
 I can't do it!

ULTIMATE ISSUES SUICIDE

"I curse the day I was born! . . . Why was I ever born? My entire life has been filled with trouble, sorrow, and shame."

This doesn't sound like one of God's greatest prophets. Yet it is! It's Jeremiah, pouring his heart out to God (see Jer 20:14, 18), wishing he'd never been born.

Have you ever felt this kind of despair? Problems like broken relationships, misunderstandings, abuse, or changes in family life (for example, divorce) can trigger feelings of despair or helplessness. For some, though, these feelings become so intense that death seems more desirable than life.

Statistics show that suicide is the second- or third-leading cause of death among American teens. Everyone occasionally faces despair, but why does one person struggle through while another ends his or her life? The critical factor is loss of hope.

A suicidal person looks at his or her problems and says, "I am powerless to change things. What's more, I have no hope that things will get better."

What does God think about suicide? Unfortunately, the Bible does not give a simple here's-what-God-says-about-the-issue answer. But it does give us some helpful principles.

We aren't the author of life; God is. No "self-made" men or women exist. You're here because God made you in his image; because he loves you, he wants to know you, and he wants you to know him. When someone commits suicide, that person is saying, in effect, "Look, God, you goofed when you let me slip into this world. So I'm going to correct your mistake." But life—and death—are God's territory. To trespass on that holy ground means you've decided to play God. God does not look on it lightly. However, suicide is not an unforgivable sin. Jesus only named one of those, and it isn't suicide.

This doesn't mean that suicide is okay. Actually, suicide is one of the most selfish, cowardly, and hateful acts anyone can commit. Those who have ever had to deal with someone's suicide know: The emotional devastation for those left behind is unbelievable. Suicide doesn't solve problems. It dumps them on someone else, multiplied many times over. Don't believe the lie that "everyone will be better off without me." They won't. You'll just cause overwhelming pain and heartbreak.

So what do you do when you decide—or someone you care about decides—to simply end it all?

First, remember you're not alone. Everyone has felt that way. If others can deal with it, you can, too.

Second, don't lose hope. Don't believe the lie that your circumstances will never change. They can. Sometimes all you need is time. Suicide is a permanent solution to a temporary problem.

Third, know the danger signals that indicate someone might be considering suicide: withdrawal; decreased academic performance; going through a family crisis; being the victim of abuse or neglect; drug abuse (yours or a family member's); death of a friend or family member; approaching the anniversary date of a significant loss or death; previous suicide attempts; family history of suicide; preoccupation with death or talk of suicide. If you or a friend are experiencing one or more of these signals, get help from someone you can trust— someone trained to help you with your problems. Counseling is extremely important. You might also contact the National Suicide Hotline: 1-800-SUICIDE or 1-800-784-2433.

Finally, remember, even if it seems no one else cares about you and your pain, God cares. You can trust him with your deepest fears or sorrows. ■

¹⁰ I have heard the many rumors about me.
They call me "The Man Who Lives in
Terror."
They threaten, "If you say anything, we will
report it."
Even my old friends are watching me,
waiting for a fatal slip.
"He will trap himself," they say,
"and then we will get our revenge on
him."

¹¹ But the LORD stands beside me like a great
warrior.
Before him my persecutors will stumble.
They cannot defeat me.
They will fail and be thoroughly humiliated.
Their dishonor will never be forgotten.

¹² O LORD of Heaven's Armies,
you test those who are righteous,
and you examine the deepest thoughts
and secrets.
Let me see your vengeance against them,
for I have committed my cause to you.

¹³ Sing to the LORD!
Praise the LORD!
For though I was poor and needy,
he rescued me from my oppressors.

¹⁴ Yet I curse the day I was born!
May no one celebrate the day of my birth.

¹⁵ I curse the messenger who told my father,
"Good news—you have a son!"

¹⁶ Let him be destroyed like the cities of old
that the LORD overthrew without mercy.
Terrify him all day long with battle shouts,

¹⁷ because he did not kill me at birth.
Oh, that I had died in my mother's womb,
that her body had been my grave!

¹⁸ Why was I ever born?
My entire life has been filled
with trouble, sorrow, and shame.

21 NO DELIVERANCE FROM BABYLON

The LORD spoke through Jeremiah
when King Zedekiah sent Pashhur son of Malkijah and Zephaniah son of Maaseiah, the
priest, to speak with him. They begged Jeremiah, ²"Please speak to the LORD for us and
ask him to help us. King Nebuchadnezzar* of
Babylon is attacking Judah. Perhaps the LORD
will be gracious and do a mighty miracle as
he has done in the past. Perhaps he will force
Nebuchadnezzar to withdraw his armies."

³Jeremiah replied, "Go back to King Zedekiah and tell him, ⁴'This is what the LORD, the
God of Israel, says: I will make your weapons
useless against the king of Babylon and the
Babylonians* who are outside your walls attacking you. In fact, I will bring your enemies
right into the heart of this city. ⁵I myself will
fight against you with a strong hand and a
powerful arm, for I am very angry. You have
made me furious! ⁶I will send a terrible plague
upon this city, and both people and animals
will die. ⁷And after all that, says the LORD, I will
hand over King Zedekiah, his staff, and everyone else in the city who survives the disease,
war, and famine. I will hand them over to King
Nebuchadnezzar of Babylon and to their other
enemies. He will slaughter them and show
them no mercy, pity, or compassion.'

⁸"Tell all the people, 'This is what the
LORD says: Take your choice of life or death!
⁹Everyone who stays in Jerusalem will die from
war, famine, or disease, but those who go out
and surrender to the Babylonians will live.
Their reward will be life! ¹⁰For I have decided
to bring disaster and not good upon this city,
says the LORD. It will be handed over to the
king of Babylon, and he will reduce it to ashes.'

JUDGMENT ON JUDAH'S KINGS ¹¹"Say to the
royal family of Judah, 'Listen to this message
from the LORD! ¹²This is what the LORD says to
the dynasty of David:

"'Give justice each morning to the people
you judge!
Help those who have been robbed;
rescue them from their oppressors.
Otherwise, my anger will burn like an
unquenchable fire
because of all your sins.

¹³ I will personally fight against the people
in Jerusalem,
that mighty fortress—
the people who boast, "No one can touch
us here.
No one can break in here."

¹⁴ And I myself will punish you for your
sinfulness,
says the LORD.
I will light a fire in your forests
that will burn up everything around you.'"

22 A MESSAGE FOR JUDAH'S KINGS

This is what the LORD said to me: "Go
over and speak directly to the king of Judah.
Say to him, ²'Listen to this message from the
LORD, you king of Judah, sitting on David's
throne. Let your attendants and your people
listen, too. ³This is what the LORD says: Be fair-
minded and just. Do what is right! Help those

21:2 Hebrew *Nebuchadrezzar,* a variant spelling of Nebuchadnezzar;
also in 21:7.   21:4 Or *Chaldeans;* also in 21:9.

who have been robbed; rescue them from their oppressors. Quit your evil deeds! Do not mistreat foreigners, orphans, and widows. Stop murdering the innocent! ⁴If you obey me, there will always be a descendant of David sitting on the throne here in Jerusalem. The king will ride through the palace gates in chariots and on horses, with his parade of attendants and subjects. ⁵But if you refuse to pay attention to this warning, I swear by my own name, says the LORD, that this palace will become a pile of rubble.'"

A MESSAGE ABOUT THE PALACE

⁶Now this is what the LORD says concerning Judah's royal palace:

"I love you as much as fruitful Gilead
    and the green forests of Lebanon.
But I will turn you into a desert,
    with no one living within your walls.
⁷ I will call for wreckers,
    who will bring out their tools to dismantle
        you.
They will tear out all your fine cedar beams
    and throw them on the fire.

⁸"People from many nations will pass by the ruins of this city and say to one another, 'Why did the LORD destroy such a great city?' ⁹And the answer will be, 'Because they violated their covenant with the LORD their God by worshiping other gods.'"

A MESSAGE ABOUT JEHOAHAZ

¹⁰ Do not weep for the dead king or mourn his
        loss.
    Instead, weep for the captive king being
        led away!
    For he will never return to see his native
        land again.

¹¹For this is what the LORD says about Jehoahaz,* who succeeded his father, King Josiah, and was taken away as a captive: "He will never return. ¹²He will die in a distant land and will never again see his own country."

A MESSAGE ABOUT JEHOIAKIM

¹³ And the LORD says, "What sorrow awaits
        Jehoiakim,*
    who builds his palace with forced labor.*
He builds injustice into its walls,
    for he makes his neighbors work for
        nothing.
    He does not pay them for their labor.

22:11 Hebrew *Shallum,* another name for Jehoahaz.   22:13a The brother and successor of the exiled Jehoahaz. See 22:18.
22:13b Hebrew *by unrighteousness.*   22:20 Or *in Abarim.*

¹⁴ He says, 'I will build a magnificent palace
        with huge rooms and many windows.
    I will panel it throughout with fragrant cedar
        and paint it a lovely red.'
¹⁵ But a beautiful cedar palace does not make
        a great king!
    Your father, Josiah, also had plenty to eat
        and drink.
    But he was just and right in all his dealings.
        That is why God blessed him.
¹⁶ He gave justice and help to the poor and
        needy,
    and everything went well for him.
    Isn't that what it means to know me?"
        says the LORD.
¹⁷ "But you! You have eyes only for greed and
        dishonesty!
    You murder the innocent,
        oppress the poor, and reign ruthlessly."

¹⁸Therefore, this is what the LORD says about Jehoiakim, son of King Josiah:

"The people will not mourn for him, crying
        to one another,
    'Alas, my brother! Alas, my sister!'
His subjects will not mourn for him, crying,
    'Alas, our master is dead! Alas, his
        splendor is gone!'
¹⁹ He will be buried like a dead donkey—
        dragged out of Jerusalem and dumped
        outside the gates!
²⁰ Weep for your allies in Lebanon.
        Shout for them in Bashan.
    Search for them in the regions east of the
        river.*
    See, they are all destroyed.
        Not one is left to help you.
²¹ I warned you when you were prosperous,
        but you replied, 'Don't bother me.'
    You have been that way since childhood—
        you simply will not obey me!
²² And now the wind will blow away your allies.
    All your friends will be taken away as
        captives.
    Surely then you will see your wickedness
        and be ashamed.
²³ It may be nice to live in a beautiful palace
        paneled with wood from the cedars of
        Lebanon,

....

YOUR OWN FAITH
(22:15-16) King Jehoiakim's father, Josiah, had been faithful to God. Unfortunately, Jehoiakim was unfaithful. He refused to follow his father's example of faith. Are you relying on the faith of your fathers? Faith cannot be inherited from parents or grandparents like money can. We must have our own faith in God.

but soon you will groan with pangs of
    anguish—
    anguish like that of a woman in labor.

A MESSAGE FOR JEHOIACHIN ²⁴"As surely
as I live," says the LORD, "I will abandon you,
Jehoiachin* son of Jehoiakim, king of Judah.
Even if you were the signet ring on my right
hand, I would pull you off. ²⁵I will hand you
over to those who seek to kill you, those you
so desperately fear—to King Nebuchadnezzar* of Babylon and the mighty Babylonian*
army. ²⁶I will expel you and your mother from
this land, and you will die in a foreign country,
not in your native land. ²⁷You will never again
return to the land you yearn for.

²⁸ "Why is this man Jehoiachin like a
    discarded, broken jar?
    Why are he and his children to be exiled
        to a foreign land?
²⁹ O earth, earth, earth!
    Listen to this message from the LORD!
³⁰ This is what the LORD says:
'Let the record show that this man
    Jehoiachin was childless.
He is a failure,
for none of his children will succeed him
    on the throne of David
    to rule over Judah.'

23

THE RIGHTEOUS DESCENDANT "What
sorrow awaits the leaders of my
people—the shepherds of my sheep—for they
have destroyed and scattered the very ones
they were expected to care for," says the LORD.
²Therefore, this is what the LORD, the God
of Israel, says to these shepherds: "Instead of
caring for my flock and leading them to safety,
you have deserted them and driven them to
destruction. Now I will pour out judgment on
you for the evil you have done to them. ³But
I will gather together the remnant of my flock
from the countries where I have driven them.
I will bring them back to their own sheepfold,

....

CORRUPTION
(23:9-14) How did the nation become so corrupt? A major
factor was false prophecy. The false prophets were very
popular because they made the people of Judah believe
that all was well. By contrast, Jeremiah's message from
God was unpopular because it showed the people how
bad their actions were. Check out these three charac-
teristics of false prophets: (1) They fail to speak God's
message or water it down to make it more "acceptable."
(2) They encourage their listeners, often subtly, to dis-
obey God. (3) They tend to be arrogant and self-serving,
appealing to the desires of their audience instead of being
true to God's Word. Don't be fooled.

and they will be fruitful and increase in number. ⁴Then I will appoint responsible shepherds
who will care for them, and they will never be
afraid again. Not a single one will be lost or
missing. I, the LORD, have spoken!

⁵ "For the time is coming,"
    says the LORD,
"when I will raise up a righteous
    descendant*
    from King David's line.
He will be a King who rules with
    wisdom.
He will do what is just and right
    throughout the land.
⁶ And this will be his name:
    'The LORD Is Our Righteousness.'*
In that day Judah will be saved,
    and Israel will live in safety.

⁷"In that day," says the LORD, "when people
are taking an oath, they will no longer say,
'As surely as the LORD lives, who rescued the
people of Israel from the land of Egypt.' ⁸Instead, they will say, 'As surely as the LORD
lives, who brought the people of Israel back to
their own land from the land of the north and
from all the countries to which he had exiled
them.' Then they will live in their own land."

JUDGMENT ON FALSE PROPHETS
⁹ My heart is broken because of the false
        prophets,
    and my bones tremble.
I stagger like a drunkard,
    like someone overcome by wine,
because of the holy words
    the LORD has spoken against them.
¹⁰ For the land is full of adultery,
    and it lies under a curse.
The land itself is in mourning—
    its wilderness pastures are dried up.
For they all do evil
    and abuse what power they have.

¹¹ "Even the priests and prophets
    are ungodly, wicked men.
I have seen their despicable acts
    right here in my own Temple,"
    says the LORD.
¹² "Therefore, the paths they take
    will become slippery.
They will be chased through the dark,
    and there they will fall.
For I will bring disaster upon them

22:24 Hebrew *Coniah,* a variant spelling of Jehoiachin; also
in 22:28. **22:25a** Hebrew *Nebuchadrezzar,* a variant spelling of
Nebuchadnezzar. **22:25b** Or *Chaldean.* **23:5** Hebrew *a righteous
branch.* **23:6** Hebrew *Yahweh Tsidqenu.*

at the time fixed for their punishment.
I, the LORD, have spoken!

13 "I saw that the prophets of Samaria were
terribly evil,
for they prophesied in the name of Baal
and led my people of Israel into sin.
14 But now I see that the prophets of Jerusalem
are even worse!
They commit adultery and love
dishonesty.
They encourage those who are doing evil
so that no one turns away from their sins.
These prophets are as wicked
as the people of Sodom and Gomorrah
once were."

15Therefore, this is what the LORD of Heaven's
Armies says concerning the prophets:

"I will feed them with bitterness
and give them poison to drink.
For it is because of Jerusalem's prophets
that wickedness has filled this land."

16This is what the LORD of Heaven's Armies says
to his people:

"Do not listen to these prophets when they
prophesy to you,
filling you with futile hopes.
They are making up everything they say.
They do not speak for the LORD!
17 They keep saying to those who despise
my word,
'Don't worry! The LORD says you will have
peace!'
And to those who stubbornly follow their
own desires,
they say, 'No harm will come your way!'

18 "Have any of these prophets been in the
LORD's presence
to hear what he is really saying?
Has even one of them cared enough
to listen?
19 Look! The LORD's anger bursts out like
a storm,
a whirlwind that swirls down on the
heads of the wicked.
20 The anger of the LORD will not diminish
until it has finished all he has planned.
In the days to come
you will understand all this very clearly.

21 "I have not sent these prophets,
yet they run around claiming to speak
for me.
I have given them no message,
yet they go on prophesying.

22 If they had stood before me and listened
to me,
they would have spoken my words,
and they would have turned my people
from their evil ways and deeds.
23 Am I a God who is only close at hand?" says
the LORD.
"No, I am far away at the same time.
24 Can anyone hide from me in a secret place?
Am I not everywhere in all the heavens
and earth?"
says the LORD.

25"I have heard these prophets say, 'Listen to
the dream I had from God last night.' And then
they proceed to tell lies in my name. 26How long
will this go on? If they are prophets, they are
prophets of deceit, inventing everything they
say. 27By telling these false dreams, they are
trying to get my people to forget me, just as
their ancestors did by worshiping the idols of
Baal.

28 "Let these false prophets tell their dreams,
but let my true messengers faithfully
proclaim my every word.
There is a difference between straw and
grain!
29 Does not my word burn like fire?"
says the LORD.
"Is it not like a mighty hammer
that smashes a rock to pieces?

30"Therefore," says the LORD, "I am against
these prophets who steal messages from
each other and claim they are from me. 31I am
against these smooth-tongued prophets who
say, 'This prophecy is from the LORD!' 32I am
against these false prophets. Their imaginary
dreams are flagrant lies that lead my people
into sin. I did not send or appoint them, and
they have no message at all for my people.
I, the LORD, have spoken!

FALSE PROPHECIES AND FALSE PROPHETS
33"Suppose one of the people or one of the

....

LIVE IT!
*(23:28) True and false prophets are as different as chaff
and wheat. Worthless chaff blows away with the wind,
while wheat remains to nourish many. To share God's
Word is a great responsibility because the way we present
it and live it will encourage people either to accept it or
reject it. Whether we speak from a pulpit, teach in a class,
or share with friends, our responsibility is to accurately
communicate and live out God's truth. As you share his
Word with friends and neighbors, they will look for its
effectiveness in your life. Unless it has changed you, why
should they expect it to change them? If you don't live
it, don't preach it.*

prophets or priests asks you, 'What prophecy has the LORD burdened you with now?' You must reply, 'You are the burden!* The LORD says he will abandon you!'

³⁴"If any prophet, priest, or anyone else says, 'I have a prophecy from the LORD,' I will punish that person along with his entire family. ³⁵You should keep asking each other, 'What is the LORD's answer?' or 'What is the LORD saying?' ³⁶But stop using this phrase, 'prophecy from the LORD.' For people are using it to give authority to their own ideas, turning upside down the words of our God, the living God, the LORD of Heaven's Armies.

³⁷"This is what you should say to the prophets: 'What is the LORD's answer?' or 'What is the LORD saying?' ³⁸But suppose they respond, 'This is a prophecy from the LORD!' Then you should say, 'This is what the LORD says: Because you have used this phrase, "prophecy from the LORD," even though I warned you not to use it, ³⁹I will forget you completely.* I will expel you from my presence, along with this city that I gave to you and your ancestors. ⁴⁰And I will make you an object of ridicule, and your name will be infamous throughout the ages.'"

24 GOOD AND BAD FIGS
After King Nebuchadnezzar* of Babylon exiled Jehoiachin* son of Jehoiakim, king of Judah, to Babylon along with the officials of Judah and all the craftsmen and artisans, the LORD gave me this vision. I saw two baskets of figs placed in front of the LORD's Temple in Jerusalem. ²One basket was filled with fresh, ripe figs, while the other was filled with bad figs that were too rotten to eat.

³Then the LORD said to me, "What do you see, Jeremiah?"

. . . .

THE BLESSING OF TROUBLE
(24:1-10) The good figs represented the exiles to Babylon—not because they were good, but because the captivity would cause them to turn back to God. The bad figs represented those who remained in Judah or ran away to Egypt. Trouble can be a blessing if it makes us stronger, while prosperity can be a curse if it entices us away from God. God can use any event of your life to help you grow stronger and closer to him.

DON'T QUIT!
(25:1-6) Imagine preaching the same message for 23 years and continually being rejected! Even though he was rejected, Jeremiah continued to proclaim the same message: "Turn from the evil road you are traveling and from the evil things you are doing." God is even more faithful to us. He never stops loving us, even when we reject him. Are you that faithful?

I replied, "Figs, some very good and some very bad, too rotten to eat."

⁴Then the LORD gave me this message: ⁵"This is what the LORD, the God of Israel, says: The good figs represent the exiles I sent from Judah to the land of the Babylonians.* ⁶I will watch over and care for them, and I will bring them back here again. I will build them up and not tear them down. I will plant them and not uproot them. ⁷I will give them hearts that recognize me as the LORD. They will be my people, and I will be their God, for they will return to me wholeheartedly.

⁸"But the bad figs," the LORD said, "represent King Zedekiah of Judah, his officials, all the people left in Jerusalem, and those who live in Egypt. I will treat them like bad figs, too rotten to eat. ⁹I will make them an object of horror and a symbol of evil to every nation on earth. They will be disgraced and mocked, taunted and cursed, wherever I scatter them. ¹⁰And I will send war, famine, and disease until they have vanished from the land of Israel, which I gave to them and their ancestors."

25 SEVENTY YEARS OF CAPTIVITY
This message for all the people of Judah came to Jeremiah from the LORD during the fourth year of Jehoiakim's reign over Judah.* This was the year when King Nebuchadnezzar* of Babylon began his reign.

²Jeremiah the prophet said to all the people in Judah and Jerusalem, ³"For the past twenty-three years—from the thirteenth year of the reign of Josiah son of Amon,* king of Judah, until now—the LORD has been giving me his messages. I have faithfully passed them on to you, but you have not listened.

⁴"Again and again the LORD has sent you his servants, the prophets, but you have not listened or even paid attention. ⁵Each time the message was this: 'Turn from the evil road you are traveling and from the evil things you are doing. Only then will I let you live in this land that the LORD gave to you and your ancestors forever. ⁶Do not provoke my anger by worshiping idols you made with your own hands. Then I will not harm you.'

⁷"But you would not listen to me," says the LORD. "You made me furious by worshiping

23:33 As in Greek version and Latin Vulgate; Hebrew reads *What burden?* 23:39 Some Hebrew manuscripts and Greek version read *I will surely lift you up.* 24:1a Hebrew *Nebuchadrezzar,* a variant spelling of Nebuchadnezzar. 24:1b Hebrew *Jeconiah,* a variant spelling of Jehoiachin. 24:5 Or *Chaldeans.* 25:1a The fourth year of Jehoiakim's reign and the accession year of Nebuchadnezzar's reign was 605 B.C. 25:1b Hebrew *Nebuchadrezzar,* a variant spelling of Nebuchadnezzar; also in 25:9. 25:3 The thirteenth year of Josiah's reign was 627 B.C.

idols you made with your own hands, bringing on yourselves all the disasters you now suffer. 8And now the LORD of Heaven's Armies says: Because you have not listened to me, 9I will gather together all the armies of the north under King Nebuchadnezzar of Babylon, whom I have appointed as my deputy. I will bring them all against this land and its people and against the surrounding nations. I will completely destroy* you and make you an object of horror and contempt and a ruin forever. 10I will take away your happy singing and laughter. The joyful voices of bridegrooms and brides will no longer be heard. Your millstones will fall silent, and the lights in your homes will go out. 11This entire land will become a desolate wasteland. Israel and her neighboring lands will serve the king of Babylon for seventy years.

12"Then, after the seventy years of captivity are over, I will punish the king of Babylon and his people for their sins," says the LORD. "I will make the country of the Babylonians* a wasteland forever. 13I will bring upon them all the terrors I have promised in this book—all the penalties announced by Jeremiah against the nations. 14Many nations and great kings will enslave the Babylonians, just as they enslaved my people. I will punish them in proportion to the suffering they cause my people."

THE CUP OF THE LORD'S ANGER 15This is what the LORD, the God of Israel, said to me: "Take from my hand this cup filled to the brim with my anger, and make all the nations to whom I send you drink from it. 16When they drink from it, they will stagger, crazed by the warfare I will send against them."

17So I took the cup of anger from the LORD and made all the nations drink from it—every nation to which the LORD sent me. 18I went to Jerusalem and the other towns of Judah, and their kings and officials drank from the cup. From that day until this, they have been a desolate ruin, an object of horror, contempt, and cursing. 19I gave the cup to Pharaoh, king of Egypt, his attendants, his officials, and all his people, 20along with all the foreigners living in that land. I also gave it to all the kings of the land of Uz and the kings of the Philistine cities of Ashkelon, Gaza, Ekron, and what remains of Ashdod. 21Then I gave the cup to the nations of Edom, Moab, and Ammon, 22and the kings of Tyre and Sidon, and the kings of the regions

across the sea. 23I gave it to Dedan, Tema, and Buz, and to the people who live in distant places.* 24I gave it to the kings of Arabia, the kings of the nomadic tribes of the desert, 25and to the kings of Zimri, Elam, and Media. 26And I gave it to the kings of the northern countries, far and near, one after the other—all the kingdoms of the world. And finally, the king of Babylon* himself drank from the cup of the LORD's anger.

27Then the LORD said to me, "Now tell them, 'This is what the LORD of Heaven's Armies, the God of Israel, says: Drink from this cup of my anger. Get drunk and vomit; fall to rise no more, for I am sending terrible wars against you.' 28And if they refuse to accept the cup, tell them, 'The LORD of Heaven's Armies says: You have no choice but to drink from it. 29I have begun to punish Jerusalem, the city that bears my name. Now should I let you go unpunished? No, you will not escape disaster. I will call for war against all the nations of the earth. I, the LORD of Heaven's Armies, have spoken!'

30"Now prophesy all these things, and say to them,

"'The LORD will roar against his own land
      from his holy dwelling in heaven.
He will shout like those who tread grapes;
      he will shout against everyone on earth.
31 His cry of judgment will reach the ends of
         the earth,
      for the LORD will bring his case against all
         the nations.
He will judge all the people of the earth,
      slaughtering the wicked with the sword.
      I, the LORD, have spoken!'"

32 This is what the LORD of Heaven's Armies
         says:
      "Look! Disaster will fall upon nation after
         nation!
A great whirlwind of fury is rising
      from the most distant corners of the
         earth!"

33In that day those the LORD has slaughtered will fill the earth from one end to the other. No one will mourn for them or gather up their bodies to bury them. They will be scattered on the ground like manure.

34 Weep and moan, you evil shepherds!
      Roll in the dust, you leaders of the flock!
The time of your slaughter has arrived;
      you will fall and shatter like a fragile vase.
35 You will find no place to hide;
      there will be no way to escape.
36 Listen to the frantic cries of the shepherds.

25:9 The Hebrew term used here refers to the complete consecration of things or people to the LORD, either by destroying them or by giving them as an offering.   25:12 Or *Chaldeans.*
25:23 Or *who clip the corners of their hair.*   25:26 Hebrew of *Sheshach,* a code name for Babylon.

The leaders of the flock are wailing in
despair,
    for the LORD is ruining their pastures.
³⁷ Peaceful meadows will be turned into a
wasteland
    by the LORD's fierce anger.
³⁸ He has left his den like a strong lion seeking
its prey,
    and their land will be made desolate
    by the sword of the enemy
    and the LORD's fierce anger.

26 JEREMIAH'S ESCAPE FROM DEATH

This message came to Jeremiah from
the LORD early in the reign of Jehoiakim son of
Josiah,* king of Judah. ²"This is what the LORD
says: Stand in the courtyard in front of the Temple of the LORD, and make an announcement
to the people who have come there to worship
from all over Judah. Give them my entire message; include every word. ³Perhaps they will
listen and turn from their evil ways. Then I will
change my mind about the disaster I am ready
to pour out on them because of their sins.

⁴"Say to them, 'This is what the LORD says:
If you will not listen to me and obey my word I
have given you, ⁵and if you will not listen to my
servants, the prophets—for I sent them again
and again to warn you, but you would not listen to them—⁶then I will destroy this Temple as
I destroyed Shiloh, the place where the Tabernacle was located. And I will make Jerusalem
an object of cursing in every nation on earth.'"

⁷The priests, the prophets, and all the
people listened to Jeremiah as he spoke in
front of the LORD's Temple. ⁸But when Jeremiah had finished his message, saying everything the LORD had told him to say, the priests
and prophets and all the people at the Temple
mobbed him. "Kill him!" they shouted. ⁹"What
right do you have to prophesy in the LORD's
name that this Temple will be destroyed like
Shiloh? What do you mean, saying that Jerusalem will be destroyed and left with no inhabitants?" And all the people threatened him as
he stood in front of the Temple.

¹⁰When the officials of Judah heard what
was happening, they rushed over from the

palace and sat down at the New Gate of the
Temple to hold court. ¹¹The priests and prophets presented their accusations to the officials
and the people. "This man should die!" they
said. "You have heard with your own ears what
a traitor he is, for he has prophesied against
this city."

¹²Then Jeremiah spoke to the officials and
the people in his own defense. "The LORD sent
me to prophesy against this Temple and this
city," he said. "The LORD gave me every word
that I have spoken. ¹³But if you stop your sinning and begin to obey the LORD your God, he
will change his mind about this disaster that
he has announced against you. ¹⁴As for me,
I am in your hands—do with me as you think
best. ¹⁵But if you kill me, rest assured that you
will be killing an innocent man! The responsibility for such a deed will lie on you, on this
city, and on every person living in it. For it is
absolutely true that the LORD sent me to speak
every word you have heard."

¹⁶Then the officials and the people said to
the priests and prophets, "This man does not
deserve the death sentence, for he has spoken
to us in the name of the LORD our God."

¹⁷Then some of the wise old men stood and
spoke to all the people assembled there.
¹⁸They said, "Remember when Micah of Mo-
resheth prophesied during the reign of King
Hezekiah of Judah. He told the people of
Judah,

'This is what the LORD of Heaven's Armies
    says:
Mount Zion will be plowed like an open
    field;
    Jerusalem will be reduced to ruins!
A thicket will grow on the heights
    where the Temple now stands.'*

¹⁹But did King Hezekiah and the people kill him
for saying this? No, they turned from their sins
and worshiped the LORD. They begged him
for mercy. Then the LORD changed his mind
about the terrible disaster he had pronounced
against them. So we are about to do ourselves
great harm."

²⁰At this time Uriah son of Shemaiah from
Kiriath-jearim was also prophesying for the
LORD. And he predicted the same terrible disaster against the city and nation as Jeremiah
did. ²¹When King Jehoiakim and the army officers and officials heard what he was saying,
the king sent someone to kill him. But Uriah
heard about the plan and escaped in fear to
Egypt. ²²Then King Jehoiakim sent Elnathan

....

WITH US

(26:16-17, 24) *Jeremiah's life was in serious danger,
but God used officials and wise men to protect him. God
spared Jeremiah because his work was not done. Believers, even some of God's prophets, die painful deaths at
times. God does not promise to keep every follower from
suffering. But he promises to be with us in the middle
of trials.*

26:1 The first year of Jehoiakim's reign was 608 B.C.   **26:18** Mic 3:12.

son of Acbor to Egypt along with several other men to capture Uriah. ²³They took him prisoner and brought him back to King Jehoiakim. The king then killed Uriah with a sword and had him buried in an unmarked grave.

²⁴Nevertheless, Ahikam son of Shaphan stood up for Jeremiah and persuaded the court not to turn him over to the mob to be killed.

27 JEREMIAH WEARS AN OX YOKE This message came to Jeremiah from the LORD early in the reign of Zedekiah* son of Josiah, king of Judah.

²This is what the LORD said to me: "Make a yoke, and fasten it on your neck with leather straps. ³Then send messages to the kings of Edom, Moab, Ammon, Tyre, and Sidon through their ambassadors who have come to see King Zedekiah in Jerusalem. ⁴Give them this message for their masters: 'This is what the LORD of Heaven's Armies, the God of Israel, says: ⁵With my great strength and powerful arm I made the earth and all its people and every animal. I can give these things of mine to anyone I choose. ⁶Now I will give your countries to King Nebuchadnezzar of Babylon, who is my servant. I have put everything, even the wild animals, under his control. ⁷All the nations will serve him, his son, and his grandson until his time is up. Then many nations and great kings will conquer and rule over Babylon. ⁸So you must submit to Babylon's king and serve him; put your neck under Babylon's yoke! I will punish any nation that refuses to be his slave, says the LORD. I will send war, famine, and disease upon that nation until Babylon has conquered it.

⁹"Do not listen to your false prophets, fortune-tellers, interpreters of dreams, mediums, and sorcerers who say, "The king of Babylon will not conquer you." ¹⁰They are all liars, and their lies will lead to your being driven out of your land. I will drive you out and send you far away to die. ¹¹But the people of any nation that submits to the king of Babylon will be allowed to stay in their own country to farm the land as usual. I, the LORD, have spoken!'"

¹²Then I repeated this same message to King Zedekiah of Judah. "If you want to live, submit to the yoke of the king of Babylon and his people. ¹³Why do you insist on dying—you and your people? Why should you choose war,

famine, and disease, which the LORD will bring against every nation that refuses to submit to Babylon's king? ¹⁴Do not listen to the false prophets who keep telling you, 'The king of Babylon will not conquer you.' They are liars. ¹⁵This is what the LORD says: 'I have not sent these prophets! They are telling you lies in my name, so I will drive you from this land. You will all die—you and all these prophets, too.'"

¹⁶Then I spoke to the priests and the people and said, "This is what the LORD says: 'Do not listen to your prophets who claim that soon the gold articles taken from my Temple will be returned from Babylon. It is all a lie! ¹⁷Do not listen to them. Surrender to the king of Babylon, and you will live. Why should this whole city be destroyed? ¹⁸If they really are prophets and speak the LORD's messages, let them pray to the LORD of Heaven's Armies. Let them pray that the articles remaining in the LORD's Temple and in the king's palace and in the palaces of Jerusalem will not be carried away to Babylon!'

¹⁹"For the LORD of Heaven's Armies has spoken about the pillars in front of the Temple, the great bronze basin called the Sea, the water carts, and all the other ceremonial articles. ²⁰King Nebuchadnezzar of Babylon left them here when he exiled Jehoiachin* son of Jehoiakim, king of Judah, to Babylon, along with all the other nobles of Judah and Jerusalem. ²¹Yes, this is what the LORD of Heaven's Armies, the God of Israel, says about the precious things still in the Temple and in the palace of Judah's king: ²²'They will all be carried away to Babylon and will stay there until I send for them,' says the LORD. 'Then I will bring them back to Jerusalem again.'"

28 JEREMIAH CONDEMNS HANANIAH One day in late summer* of that same year—the fourth year of the reign of Zedekiah, king of Judah—Hananiah son of Azzur, a prophet from Gibeon, addressed me publicly in the Temple while all the priests and people listened. He said, ²"This is what the LORD of Heaven's Armies, the God of Israel, says: 'I will

27:1 As in some Hebrew manuscripts and Syriac version (see also 27:3, 12); most Hebrew manuscripts read *Jehoiakim.* 27:20 Hebrew *Jeconiah,* a variant spelling of Jehoiachin. 28:1 Hebrew *In the fifth month,* of the ancient Hebrew lunar calendar. The fifth month in the fourth year of Zedekiah's reign occurred within the months of August and September 593 B.C. Also see note on 1:3.

....

TRUE FRIEND
(27:9-11) The false prophets told the people what they wanted to hear, even though these "prophets" knew the message was not true. The people in Jeremiah's day needed a true friend like Jeremiah, who brought God's painful, corrective word. A true friend speaks the truth no matter how much it hurts. Seek friends who speak truthfully, even though their correction is painful. Someone who flatters you by telling you lies is not a true friend.

"FOR I KNOW THE PLANS I HAVE FOR YOU," SAYS THE LORD.
"THEY ARE PLANS FOR GOOD
AND NOT FOR DISASTER, TO GIVE YOU A FUTURE AND A HOPE."

JEREMIAH 29:11

remove the yoke of the king of Babylon from your necks. ³Within two years I will bring back all the Temple treasures that King Nebuchadnezzar carried off to Babylon. ⁴And I will bring back Jehoiachin* son of Jehoiakim, king of Judah, and all the other captives that were taken to Babylon. I will surely break the yoke that the king of Babylon has put on your necks. I, the LORD, have spoken!'"

⁵Jeremiah responded to Hananiah as they stood in front of all the priests and people at the Temple. ⁶He said, "Amen! May your prophecies come true! I hope the LORD does everything you say. I hope he does bring back from Babylon the treasures of this Temple and all the captives. ⁷But listen now to the solemn words I speak to you in the presence of all these people. ⁸The ancient prophets who preceded you and me spoke against many nations, always warning of war, disaster, and disease. ⁹So a prophet who predicts peace must show he is right. Only when his predictions come true can we know that he is really from the LORD."

¹⁰Then Hananiah the prophet took the yoke off Jeremiah's neck and broke it in pieces. ¹¹And Hananiah said again to the crowd that had gathered, "This is what the LORD says: 'Just as this yoke has been broken, within two years I will break the yoke of oppression from all the nations now subject to King Nebuchadnezzar of Babylon.'" With that, Jeremiah left the Temple area.

¹²Soon after this confrontation with Hananiah, the LORD gave this message to Jeremiah: ¹³"Go and tell Hananiah, 'This is what the LORD says: You have broken a wooden yoke, but you have replaced it with a yoke of

iron. ¹⁴The LORD of Heaven's Armies, the God of Israel, says: I have put a yoke of iron on the necks of all these nations, forcing them into slavery under King Nebuchadnezzar of Babylon. I have put everything, even the wild animals, under his control.'"

¹⁵Then Jeremiah the prophet said to Hananiah, "Listen, Hananiah! The LORD has not sent you, but the people believe your lies. ¹⁶Therefore, this is what the LORD says: 'You must die. Your life will end this very year because you have rebelled against the LORD.'"

¹⁷Two months later* the prophet Hananiah died.

29 **A LETTER TO THE EXILES** Jeremiah wrote a letter from Jerusalem to the elders, priests, prophets, and all the people who had been exiled to Babylon by King Nebuchadnezzar. ²This was after King Jehoiachin,* the queen mother, the court officials, the other officials of Judah, and all the craftsmen and artisans had been deported from Jerusalem. ³He sent the letter with Elasah son of Shaphan and Gemariah son of Hilkiah when they went to Babylon as King Zedekiah's ambassadors to Nebuchadnezzar. This is what Jeremiah's letter said:

⁴This is what the LORD of Heaven's Armies, the God of Israel, says to all the captives he has exiled to Babylon from Jerusalem: ⁵"Build homes, and plan to stay. Plant gardens, and eat the food they produce. ⁶Marry and have children. Then find spouses for them so that you may have many grandchildren. Multiply! Do not dwindle away! ⁷And work for the peace and prosperity of the city where I sent you into exile. Pray to the LORD for it, for its welfare will determine your welfare."

⁸This is what the LORD of Heaven's Armies, the God of Israel, says: "Do not let your prophets and fortune-tellers who are with you in the land of Babylon trick you. Do not listen to their dreams, ⁹because they are telling you lies in my name. I have not sent them," says the LORD.

···

THE TRUTH HURTS
(28:1-17) Jeremiah spoke the truth, but was unpopular. Hananiah spoke lies, but his deceitful words brought false hope and comfort to the people. God had already outlined the marks of a true prophet: The predictions always come true and never contradict previous revelations (Deut 13; 18:15-22; Jer 23:9-14). Even though Jeremiah's predictions came true, the people still preferred to listen to comforting lies rather than painful truth. Which would you prefer: a comforting lie or a painful truth? Are you open to God's words to you, even if you don't particularly like what he has to say?

28:4 Hebrew *Jeconiah,* a variant spelling of Jehoiachin.
28:17 Hebrew *In the seventh month of that same year.* See 28:1 and the note there.   29:2 Hebrew *Jeconiah,* a variant spelling of Jehoiachin.

¹⁰This is what the LORD says: "You will be in Babylon for seventy years. But then I will come and do for you all the good things I have promised, and I will bring you home again. ¹¹For I know the plans I have for you," says the LORD. "They are plans for good and not for disaster, to give you a future and a hope. ¹²In those days when you pray, I will listen. ¹³If you look for me wholeheartedly, you will find me. ¹⁴I will be found by you," says the LORD. "I will end your captivity and restore your fortunes. I will gather you out of the nations where I sent you and will bring you home again to your own land."

¹⁵You claim that the LORD has raised up prophets for you in Babylon. ¹⁶But this is what the LORD says about the king who sits on David's throne and all those still living here in Jerusalem—your relatives who were not exiled to Babylon. ¹⁷This is what the LORD of Heaven's Armies says: "I will send war, famine, and disease upon them and make them like bad figs, too rotten to eat. ¹⁸Yes, I will pursue them with war, famine, and disease, and I will scatter them around the world. In every nation where I send them, I will make them an object of

29:21 Hebrew *Nebuchadrezzar*, a variant spelling of Nebuchadnezzar.

damnation, horror, contempt, and mockery. ¹⁹For they refuse to listen to me, though I have spoken to them repeatedly through the prophets I sent. And you who are in exile have not listened either," says the LORD.

²⁰Therefore, listen to this message from the LORD, all you captives there in Babylon. ²¹This is what the LORD of Heaven's Armies, the God of Israel, says about your prophets—Ahab son of Kolaiah and Zedekiah son of Maaseiah—who are telling you lies in my name: "I will turn them over to Nebuchadnezzar* for execution before your eyes. ²²Their terrible fate will become proverbial, so that the Judean exiles will curse someone by saying, 'May the LORD make you like Zedekiah and Ahab, whom the king of Babylon burned alive!' ²³For these men have done terrible things among my people. They have committed adultery with their neighbors' wives and have lied in my name, saying things I did not command. I am a witness to this. I, the LORD, have spoken."

A MESSAGE FOR SHEMAIAH ²⁴The LORD sent this message to Shemaiah the Nehelamite in Babylon: ²⁵"This is what the LORD of Heaven's

I WONDER...

I'm afraid to give my whole life to God because I think he'll tell me to do something I don't want to do. What happens if I hold back part of my life from God?

Imagine going out for basketball and telling the coach that you only want to practice, not play in the games. Or that you only want to play in the first half of each game. How do you think your coach or teammates would react?

Undoubtedly, they would be a little put off by your selfish attitude. After all, if you're going to be on the team, you should play in the games. And if you play, you shouldn't avoid the last half when your team might need you the most.

Unfortunately, many people have that attitude about their relationship with God. They want it on their terms—with benefits and no hassles. By their attitudes and their actions, they tell the Coach (God) two messages: They don't really want the benefits and fun of playing on the team (except heaven, of course), and they don't want to contribute during the times when other people might need them the most!

God wants your whole life, so he can make some-

thing extraordinary out of it. Jesus told his followers, "The thief's purpose is to steal and kill and destroy. My purpose is to give them a rich and satisfying life" (John 10:10). That's a level of trust you may not have yet.

The Christian life was never meant to be done halfway. You're either sold out to God or sold out to the world. For God to give you "a rich and satisfying life," you must give your life in full to God. Jesus said, "If you cling to your life, you will lose it; but if you give up your life for me, you will find it" (Matt 10:39).

And don't worry about what God will ask of you. He knows you better than anyone else does. He made you, and he loves you more than you'll ever know. Because God put you together, he knows what it will take to make you the happiest and most fulfilled in life. If you choose any other direction, you'll be settling for second best.

God's goal isn't to make his kids miserable. Just take a look at Jeremiah 29:11-13. You'll see that God wants to lead us in a direction that will cause us to say, "The game wasn't easy, God, especially the last quarter. But thanks for believing in me enough to put me in—I really had fun."

Armies, the God of Israel, says: You wrote a letter on your own authority to Zephaniah son of Maaseiah, the priest, and you sent copies to the other priests and people in Jerusalem. You wrote to Zephaniah,

²⁶"The LORD has appointed you to replace Jehoiada as the priest in charge of the house of the LORD. You are responsible to put into stocks and neck irons any crazy man who claims to be a prophet. ²⁷So why have you done nothing to stop Jeremiah from Anathoth, who pretends to be a prophet among you? ²⁸Jeremiah sent a letter here to Babylon, predicting that our captivity will be a long one. He said, 'Build homes, and plan to stay. Plant gardens, and eat the food they produce.'"

²⁹But when Zephaniah the priest received Shemaiah's letter, he took it to Jeremiah and read it to him. ³⁰Then the LORD gave this message to Jeremiah: ³¹"Send an open letter to all the exiles in Babylon. Tell them, 'This is what the LORD says concerning Shemaiah the Nehelamite: Since he has prophesied to you when I did not send him and has tricked you into believing his lies, ³²I will punish him and his family. None of his descendants will see the good things I will do for my people, for he has incited you to rebel against me. I, the LORD, have spoken!'"

30 PROMISES OF DELIVERANCE The LORD gave another message to Jeremiah. He said, ²"This is what the LORD, the God of Israel, says: Write down for the record everything I have said to you, Jeremiah. ³For the time is coming when I will restore the fortunes of my people of Israel and Judah. I will bring them home to this land that I gave to their ancestors, and they will possess it again. I, the LORD, have spoken!"

⁴This is the message the LORD gave concerning Israel and Judah. ⁵This is what the LORD says:

"I hear cries of fear;
    there is terror and no peace.
⁶ Now let me ask you a question:
    Do men give birth to babies?
Then why do they stand there, ashen-faced,
    hands pressed against their sides
    like a woman in labor?
⁷ In all history there has never been such a
        time of terror.
    It will be a time of trouble for my people
        Israel.*

Yet in the end they will be saved!
⁸ For in that day,"
    says the LORD of Heaven's Armies,
"I will break the yoke from their necks
    and snap their chains.
Foreigners will no longer be their masters.
⁹   For my people will serve the LORD their
        God
and their king descended from David—
    the king I will raise up for them.

¹⁰ "So do not be afraid, Jacob, my servant;
    do not be dismayed, Israel,"
    says the LORD.
"For I will bring you home again from
        distant lands,
    and your children will return from their
        exile.
Israel will return to a life of peace and quiet,
    and no one will terrorize them.
¹¹ For I am with you and will save you,"
    says the LORD.
"I will completely destroy the nations where
        I have scattered you,
    but I will not completely destroy you.
I will discipline you, but with justice;
    I cannot let you go unpunished."

¹² This is what the LORD says:
"Your injury is incurable—
    a terrible wound.
¹³ There is no one to help you
    or to bind up your injury.
No medicine can heal you.
¹⁴ All your lovers—your allies—have left you
    and do not care about you anymore.
I have wounded you cruelly,
    as though I were your enemy.
For your sins are many,
    and your guilt is great.
¹⁵ Why do you protest your punishment—
    this wound that has no cure?
I have had to punish you
    because your sins are many
    and your guilt is great.

¹⁶ "But all who devour you will be devoured,
    and all your enemies will be sent into
        exile.
All who plunder you will be plundered,
    and all who attack you will be attacked.
¹⁷ I will give you back your health
    and heal your wounds," says the LORD.
"For you are called an outcast—
    'Jerusalem* for whom no
        one cares.'"

30:7 Hebrew *Jacob;* also in 30:10b, 18. See note on 5:20.
30:17 Hebrew *Zion.*

¹⁸ This is what the LORD says:
"When I bring Israel home again from
        captivity
    and restore their fortunes,
Jerusalem will be rebuilt on its ruins,
    and the palace reconstructed as before.
¹⁹ There will be joy and songs of thanksgiving,
    and I will multiply my people, not
        diminish them;
I will honor them, not despise them.
²⁰   Their children will prosper as they did
        long ago.
I will establish them as a nation before me,
    and I will punish anyone who hurts them.
²¹ They will have their own ruler again,
    and he will come from their own people.
I will invite him to approach me," says the
    LORD,
    "for who would dare to come unless
        invited?
²² You will be my people,
    and I will be your God."

²³ Look! The LORD's anger bursts out like
        a storm,
    a driving wind that swirls down on the
        heads of the wicked.
²⁴ The fierce anger of the LORD will not
        diminish
    until it has finished all he has planned.
In the days to come
    you will understand all this.

31 HOPE FOR RESTORATION "In that
day," says the LORD, "I will be the God
of all the families of Israel, and they will be my
people. ²This is what the LORD says:

"Those who survive the coming destruction
    will find blessings even in the barren
        land,
    for I will give rest to the people of Israel."

³ Long ago the LORD said to Israel:
"I have loved you, my people, with an
        everlasting love.
    With unfailing love I have drawn you to
        myself.
⁴ I will rebuild you, my virgin Israel.
    You will again be happy
    and dance merrily with your tambourines.
⁵ Again you will plant your vineyards on the
        mountains of Samaria
    and eat from your own gardens there.
⁶ The day will come when watchmen will
        shout
    from the hill country of Ephraim,

'Come, let us go up to Jerusalem*
    to worship the LORD our God.'"

⁷ Now this is what the LORD says:
"Sing with joy for Israel.*
    Shout for the greatest of nations!
Shout out with praise and joy:
'Save your people, O LORD,
    the remnant of Israel!'
⁸ For I will bring them from the north
    and from the distant corners of the earth.
I will not forget the blind and lame,
    the expectant mothers and women in
        labor.
A great company will return!
⁹ Tears of joy will stream down their faces,
    and I will lead them home with great care.
They will walk beside quiet streams
    and on smooth paths where they will not
        stumble.
For I am Israel's father,
    and Ephraim is my oldest child.

¹⁰ "Listen to this message from the LORD,
        you nations of the world;
    proclaim it in distant coastlands:
The LORD, who scattered his people,
    will gather them and watch over them
        as a shepherd does his flock.
¹¹ For the LORD has redeemed Israel
    from those too strong for them.
¹² They will come home and sing songs of joy
        on the heights of Jerusalem.
    They will be radiant because of the LORD's
        good gifts—
    the abundant crops of grain, new wine, and
        olive oil,
    and the healthy flocks and herds.
Their life will be like a watered garden,
    and all their sorrows will be gone.
¹³ The young women will dance for joy,
    and the men—old and young—will join in
        the celebration.
I will turn their mourning into joy.
    I will comfort them and exchange their
        sorrow for rejoicing.
¹⁴ The priests will enjoy abundance,
    and my people will feast on my good gifts.
    I, the LORD, have spoken!"

....

MAGNIFICENT LOVE
*(31:3) God reaches toward his people with kindness
motivated by deep and everlasting love. God is eager to
do the best for his people if they will only let him. After
many words of warning about sin, this reminder of God's
magnificent love is refreshing. We may often think of
God with dread or fear; but if we look carefully, we can
see him lovingly drawing us toward himself.*

31:6 Hebrew *Zion;* also in 31:12.   **31:7** Hebrew *Jacob;* also in 31:11.
See note on 5:20.

RACHEL'S SADNESS TURNS TO JOY

¹⁵This is what the LORD says:

"A cry is heard in Ramah—
deep anguish and bitter weeping.
Rachel weeps for her children,
refusing to be comforted—
for her children are gone."

¹⁶ But now this is what the LORD says:
"Do not weep any longer,
for I will reward you," says the LORD.
"Your children will come back to you
from the distant land of the enemy.
¹⁷ There is hope for your future," says the
LORD.
"Your children will come again to their
own land.
¹⁸ I have heard Israel* saying,
'You disciplined me severely,
like a calf that needs training for the yoke.
Turn me again to you and restore me,
for you alone are the LORD my God.
¹⁹ I turned away from God,
but then I was sorry.
I kicked myself for my stupidity!
I was thoroughly ashamed of all I did in
my younger days.'
²⁰ "Is not Israel still my son,
my darling child?" says the LORD.
"I often have to punish him,
but I still love him.
That's why I long for him
and surely will have mercy on him.
²¹ Set up road signs;
put up guideposts.
Mark well the path
by which you came.

Come back again, my virgin Israel;
return to your towns here.
²² How long will you wander,
my wayward daughter?
For the LORD will cause something new to
happen—
Israel will embrace her God.*"

²³This is what the LORD of Heaven's Armies, the God of Israel, says: "When I bring them back from captivity, the people of Judah and its towns will again say, 'The LORD bless you, O righteous home, O holy mountain!' ²⁴Townspeople and farmers and shepherds alike will live together in peace and happiness. ²⁵For I have given rest to the weary and joy to the sorrowing."

²⁶At this, I woke up and looked around. My sleep had been very sweet.

²⁷"The day is coming," says the LORD, "when I will greatly increase the human population and the number of animals here in Israel and Judah. ²⁸In the past I deliberately uprooted and tore down this nation. I overthrew it, destroyed it, and brought disaster upon it. But in the future I will just as deliberately plant it and build it up. I, the LORD, have spoken!

²⁹"The people will no longer quote this proverb:

'The parents have eaten sour grapes,
but their children's mouths pucker at the
taste.'

³⁰All people will die for their own sins—those who eat the sour grapes will be the ones whose mouths will pucker.

³¹"The day is coming," says the LORD, "when I will make a new covenant with the people of Israel and Judah. ³²This covenant will not be like the one I made with their ancestors when I took them by the hand and brought them out of the land of Egypt. They broke that covenant, though I loved them as a husband loves his wife," says the LORD.

³³"But this is the new covenant I will make with the people of Israel on that day," says the LORD. "I will put my instructions deep within them, and I will write them on their hearts. I will be their God, and they will be my people. ³⁴And they will not need to teach their neighbors, nor will they need to teach their relatives, saying, 'You should know the LORD.' For everyone, from the least to the greatest, will know me already," says the LORD. "And I will forgive their wickedness, and I will never again remember their sins."

....

RETURN
(31:18-20) These verses describe grief and mourning. Ephraim was one of the major tribes of the northern kingdom (Israel). Although the northern kingdom had sunk into the most degrading sins, God still loved the people. A remnant would turn to God, repenting of their sins, and God would forgive them. God still loves you, despite what you have done. He will forgive you if you will return to him.

REVOLUTION
(31:33) The old covenant, broken by the people, would be replaced by a new covenant. The foundation of this new covenant is the promised Messiah. It's revolutionary, involving not only Israel, but also the Gentiles. It also involves a personal relationship with God, with his laws inscribed on the human heart instead of on stone tablets. Jeremiah looked forward to the day when the Messiah would come to establish this covenant. This covenant is already established through Christ (see Heb 8:6). He makes a relationship with God possible. Is this an offer you've accepted?

31:18 Hebrew *Ephraim*, referring to the northern kingdom of Israel; also in 31:20. **31:22** Hebrew *a woman will surround a man.*

35 It is the Lord who provides the sun to light
　　the day
　and the moon and stars to light the night,
　　and who stirs the sea into roaring waves.
　His name is the Lord of Heaven's Armies,
　　and this is what he says:
36 "I am as likely to reject my people Israel
　　as I am to abolish the laws of nature!"
37 This is what the Lord says:
　"Just as the heavens cannot be measured
　　and the foundations of the earth cannot
　　　be explored,
　so I will not consider casting them away
　　for the evil they have done.
　I, the Lord, have spoken!

38 "The day is coming," says the Lord, "when
all Jerusalem will be rebuilt for me, from the
Tower of Hananel to the Corner Gate. 39 A measuring line will be stretched out over the hill
of Gareb and across to Goah. 40 And the entire
area—including the graveyard and ash dump
in the valley, and all the fields out to the Kidron
Valley on the east as far as the Horse Gate—will
be holy to the Lord. The city will never again be
captured or destroyed."

32 JEREMIAH'S LAND PURCHASE The
following message came to Jeremiah
from the Lord in the tenth year of the reign
of Zedekiah,* king of Judah. This was also the
eighteenth year of the reign of King Nebuchadnezzar.* 2 Jerusalem was then under siege from
the Babylonian army, and Jeremiah was imprisoned in the courtyard of the guard in the royal
palace. 3 King Zedekiah had put him there, asking why he kept giving this prophecy: "This is
what the Lord says: 'I am about to hand this
city over to the king of Babylon, and he will
take it. 4 King Zedekiah will be captured by the
Babylonians* and taken to meet the king of
Babylon face to face. 5 He will take Zedekiah
to Babylon, and I will deal with him there,' says
the Lord. 'If you fight against the Babylonians,
you will never succeed.'"

6 At that time the Lord sent me a message.
He said, 7 "Your cousin Hanamel son of Shallum will come and say to you, 'Buy my field at
Anathoth. By law you have the right to buy it
before it is offered to anyone else.'"

8 Then, just as the Lord had said he would,
my cousin Hanamel came and visited me in
the prison. He said, "Please buy my field at
Anathoth in the land of Benjamin. By law you

have the right to buy it before it is offered to
anyone else, so buy it for yourself." Then I
knew that the message I had heard was from
the Lord.

9 So I bought the field at Anathoth, paying
Hanamel seventeen pieces* of silver for it. 10 I
signed and sealed the deed of purchase before witnesses, weighed out the silver, and
paid him. 11 Then I took the sealed deed and an
unsealed copy of the deed, which contained
the terms and conditions of the purchase,
12 and I handed them to Baruch son of Neriah
and grandson of Mahseiah. I did all this in
the presence of my cousin Hanamel, the witnesses who had signed the deed, and all the
men of Judah who were there in the courtyard
of the guardhouse.

13 Then I said to Baruch as they all listened,
14 "This is what the Lord of Heaven's Armies,
the God of Israel, says: 'Take both this sealed
deed and the unsealed copy, and put them
into a pottery jar to preserve them for a long
time.' 15 For this is what the Lord of Heaven's
Armies, the God of Israel, says: 'Someday
people will again own property here in this
land and will buy and sell houses and vineyards and fields.'"

JEREMIAH'S PRAYER 16 Then after I had given
the papers to Baruch, I prayed to the Lord:

17 "O Sovereign Lord! You made the heavens
and earth by your strong hand and powerful
arm. Nothing is too hard for you! 18 You show
unfailing love to thousands, but you also
bring the consequences of one generation's
sin upon the next. You are the great and
powerful God, the Lord of Heaven's Armies.
19 You have all wisdom and do great and
mighty miracles. You see the conduct of
all people, and you give them what they
deserve. 20 You performed miraculous signs
and wonders in the land of Egypt—things
still remembered to this day! And you have
continued to do great miracles in Israel and
all around the world. You have made your
name famous to this day.

....

TRUST
*(32:6-12) Trust doesn't come easy. It wasn't easy for
Jeremiah to buy land already captured by the enemy.
But he trusted God. It wasn't easy for David to think that
he would become king, even after he was anointed. But
he trusted God (1 Sam 16–30). It wasn't easy for Moses
to believe that he and his people would escape Egypt,
even after God spoke to him from a burning bush. But he
trusted God (Exod 3:1–4:20). How about you? You can
choose to trust or choose to doubt.*

32:1a The tenth year of Zedekiah's reign and the eighteenth year of
Nebuchadnezzar's reign was 587 B.C.　**32:1b** Hebrew
Nebuchadrezzar, a variant spelling of Nebuchadnezzar; also in
32:28.　**32:4** Or *Chaldeans;* also in 32:5, 24, 25, 28, 29, 43.
32:9 Hebrew *17 shekels,* about 7 ounces or 194 grams in weight.

²¹"You brought Israel out of Egypt with mighty signs and wonders, with a strong hand and powerful arm, and with overwhelming terror. ²²You gave the people of Israel this land that you had promised their ancestors long before—a land flowing with milk and honey. ²³Our ancestors came and conquered it and lived in it, but they refused to obey you or follow your word. They have not done anything you commanded. That is why you have sent this terrible disaster upon them.

²⁴"See how the siege ramps have been built against the city walls! Through war, famine, and disease, the city will be handed over to the Babylonians, who will conquer it. Everything has happened just as you said. ²⁵And yet, O Sovereign LORD, you have told me to buy the field—paying good money for it before these witnesses—even though the city will soon be handed over to the Babylonians."

A PREDICTION OF JERUSALEM'S FALL ²⁶Then this message came to Jeremiah from the LORD: ²⁷"I am the LORD, the God of all the peoples of the world. Is anything too hard for me? ²⁸Therefore, this is what the LORD says: I will hand this city over to the Babylonians and to Nebuchadnezzar, king of Babylon, and he will capture it. ²⁹The Babylonians outside the walls will come in and set fire to the city. They will burn down all these houses where the people provoked my anger by burning incense to Baal on the rooftops and by pouring out liquid offerings to other gods. ³⁰Israel and Judah have done nothing but wrong since their earliest days. They have infuriated me with all their evil deeds," says the LORD. ³¹"From the time this city was built until now, it has done nothing but anger me, so I am determined to get rid of it.

³²"The sins of Israel and Judah—the sins of the people of Jerusalem, the kings, the officials, the priests, and the prophets—have stirred up my anger. ³³My people have turned their backs on me and have refused to return. Even though I diligently taught them, they would not receive instruction or obey. ³⁴They have set up their abominable idols right in my own Temple, defiling it. ³⁵They have built pagan shrines to Baal in the valley of Ben-Hinnom, and there they sacrifice their sons and daughters to Molech. I have never commanded such a horrible deed; it never even crossed my mind to command such a thing. What an incredible evil, causing Judah to sin so greatly!

A PROMISE OF RESTORATION ³⁶"Now I want to say something more about this city. You have been saying, 'It will fall to the king of Babylon through war, famine, and disease.' But this is what the LORD, the God of Israel, says: ³⁷I will certainly bring my people back again from all the countries where I will scatter them in my fury. I will bring them back to this very city and let them live in peace and safety. ³⁸They will be my people, and I will be their God. ³⁹And I will give them one heart and one purpose: to worship me forever, for their own good and for the good of all their descendants. ⁴⁰And I will make an everlasting covenant with them: I will never stop doing good for them. I will put a desire in their hearts to worship me, and they will never leave me. ⁴¹I will find joy doing good for them and will faithfully and wholeheartedly replant them in this land.

⁴²"This is what the LORD says: Just as I have brought all these calamities on them, so I will do all the good I have promised them. ⁴³Fields will again be bought and sold in this land about which you now say, 'It has been ravaged by the Babylonians, a desolate land where people and animals have all disappeared.' ⁴⁴Yes, fields will once again be bought and sold—deeds signed and sealed and witnessed—in the land of Benjamin and here in Jerusalem, in the towns of Judah and in the hill country, in the foothills of Judah* and in the Negev, too. For someday I will restore prosperity to them. I, the LORD, have spoken!"

33 **PROMISES OF PEACE AND PROSPERITY** While Jeremiah was still confined in the courtyard of the guard, the LORD gave him this second message: ²"This is what the LORD says—the LORD who made the earth, who formed and established it, whose name is the LORD: ³Ask me and I will tell you remarkable secrets you do not know about things to come. ⁴For this is what the LORD, the God of Israel, says: You have torn down the houses of this city and even the king's palace to get materials to strengthen the walls against the siege ramps and swords of the enemy. ⁵You expect to fight the Babylonians,* but the men of this city are already as good as dead, for I have determined to destroy them in my terrible anger. I have abandoned them because of all their wickedness.

⁶"Nevertheless, the time will come when I will heal Jerusalem's wounds and give it prosperity and true peace. ⁷I will restore the fortunes of Judah and Israel and rebuild their

32:44 Hebrew *the Shephelah.*   **33:5** Or *Chaldeans.*

towns. ⁸I will cleanse them of their sins against me and forgive all their sins of rebellion. ⁹Then this city will bring me joy, glory, and honor before all the nations of the earth! The people of the world will see all the good I do for my people, and they will tremble with awe at the peace and prosperity I provide for them.

¹⁰"This is what the LORD says: You have said, 'This is a desolate land where people and animals have all disappeared.' Yet in the empty streets of Jerusalem and Judah's other towns, there will be heard once more ¹¹the sounds of joy and laughter. The joyful voices of bridegrooms and brides will be heard again, along with the joyous songs of people bringing thanksgiving offerings to the LORD. They will sing,

'Give thanks to the LORD of Heaven's
    Armies,
for the LORD is good.
His faithful love endures forever!'

For I will restore the prosperity of this land to what it was in the past, says the LORD.

¹²"This is what the LORD of Heaven's Armies says: This land—though it is now desolate and has no people and animals—will once more have pastures where shepherds can lead their flocks. ¹³Once again shepherds will count their flocks in the towns of the hill country, the foothills of Judah,* the Negev, the land of Benjamin, the vicinity of Jerusalem, and all the towns of Judah. I, the LORD, have spoken!

¹⁴"The day will come, says the LORD, when I will do for Israel and Judah all the good things I have promised them.

¹⁵ "In those days and at that time
    I will raise up a righteous descendant*
        from King David's line.
    He will do what is just and right
        throughout the land.
¹⁶ In that day Judah will be saved,
    and Jerusalem will live in safety.
And this will be its name:
    'The LORD Is Our Righteousness.'*

¹⁷For this is what the LORD says: David will have a descendant sitting on the throne of Israel forever. ¹⁸And there will always be Levitical priests to offer burnt offerings and grain offerings and sacrifices to me."

¹⁹Then this message came to Jeremiah from the LORD: ²⁰"This is what the LORD says: If you can break my covenant with the day and the night so that one does not follow the other,

²¹only then will my covenant with my servant David be broken. Only then will he no longer have a descendant to reign on his throne. The same is true for my covenant with the Levitical priests who minister before me. ²²And as the stars of the sky cannot be counted and the sand on the seashore cannot be measured, so I will multiply the descendants of my servant David and the Levites who minister before me."

²³The LORD gave another message to Jeremiah. He said, ²⁴"Have you noticed what people are saying?—'The LORD chose Judah and Israel and then abandoned them!' They are sneering and saying that Israel is not worthy to be counted as a nation. ²⁵But this is what the LORD says: I would no more reject my people than I would change my laws that govern night and day, earth and sky. ²⁶I will never abandon the descendants of Jacob or David, my servant, or change the plan that David's descendants will rule the descendants of Abraham, Isaac, and Jacob. Instead, I will restore them to their land and have mercy on them."

34 A WARNING FOR ZEDEKIAH
King Nebuchadnezzar of Babylon came with all the armies from the kingdoms he ruled, and he fought against Jerusalem and the towns of Judah. At that time this message came to Jeremiah from the LORD: ²"Go to King Zedekiah of Judah, and tell him, 'This is what the LORD, the God of Israel, says: I am about to hand this city over to the king of Babylon, and he will burn it down. ³You will not escape his grasp but will be captured and taken to meet the king of Babylon face to face. Then you will be exiled to Babylon.

⁴"'But listen to this promise from the LORD, O Zedekiah, king of Judah. This is what the LORD says: You will not be killed in war ⁵but will die peacefully. People will burn incense in your memory, just as they did for your ancestors, the kings who preceded you. They will mourn for you, crying, "Alas, our master is dead!" This I have decreed, says the LORD.'"

⁶So Jeremiah the prophet delivered the message to King Zedekiah of Judah. ⁷At this time the Babylonian army was besieging Jerusalem, Lachish, and Azekah—the only fortified cities of Judah not yet captured.

FREEDOM FOR HEBREW SLAVES
⁸This message came to Jeremiah from the LORD after King Zedekiah made a covenant with the people, proclaiming freedom for the slaves. ⁹He had ordered all the people to free their

33:13 Hebrew *the Shephelah.*   33:15 Hebrew *a righteous branch.*
33:16 Hebrew *Yahweh Tsidqenu.*

Hebrew slaves—both men and women. No one was to keep a fellow Judean in bondage. ¹⁰The officials and all the people had obeyed the king's command, ¹¹but later they changed their minds. They took back the men and women they had freed, forcing them to be slaves again.

¹²So the LORD gave them this message through Jeremiah: ¹³"This is what the LORD, the God of Israel, says: I made a covenant with your ancestors long ago when I rescued them from their slavery in Egypt. ¹⁴I told them that every Hebrew slave must be freed after serving six years. But your ancestors paid no attention to me. ¹⁵Recently you repented and did what was right, following my command. You freed your slaves and made a solemn covenant with me in the Temple that bears my name. ¹⁶But now you have shrugged off your oath and defiled my name by taking back the men and women you had freed, forcing them to be slaves once again.

¹⁷"Therefore, this is what the LORD says: Since you have not obeyed me by setting your countrymen free, I will set you free to be destroyed by war, disease, and famine. You will be an object of horror to all the nations of the earth. ¹⁸Because you have broken the terms of our covenant, I will cut you apart just as you cut apart the calf when you walked between its halves to solemnize your vows. ¹⁹Yes, I will cut you apart, whether you are officials of Judah or Jerusalem, court officials, priests, or common people—for you have broken your oath. ²⁰I will give you to your enemies, and they will kill you. Your bodies will be food for the vultures and wild animals.

· ·

PROMISES
(34:15-16) The people of Israel had a difficult time keeping their promises to God. In the Temple, they would solemnly promise to obey God, but back in their homes and at work they wouldn't do it. God expressed his great displeasure. If you want to please God, make sure you keep your promises. God wants promises lived out, not just piously made.

WHY OBEY?
(35:1-17) Consider the contrast between the Recabites and the other Israelites: (1) The Recabites kept their vows to a fallible human leader; Israel broke their covenant with their infallible divine Leader. (2) Jehonadab told his family once not to drink and they didn't; God continually commanded Israel to turn from sin and they refused. (3) The Recabites obeyed laws dealing with temporal issues; Israel disobeyed God's laws dealing with eternal issues. (4) The Recabites would be rewarded; Israel would be punished. Often we observe customs because of tradition. But God's Word is eternal. Isn't it worth believing and obeying?

²¹"I will hand over King Zedekiah of Judah and his officials to the army of the king of Babylon. And although Babylon's king has left Jerusalem for a while, ²²I will call the Babylonian armies back again. They will fight against this city and will capture it and burn it down. I will see to it that all the towns of Judah are destroyed, with no one living there."

35 **THE FAITHFUL RECABITES** This is the message the LORD gave Jeremiah when Jehoiakim son of Josiah was king of Judah: ²"Go to the settlement where the families of the Recabites live, and invite them to the LORD's Temple. Take them into one of the inner rooms, and offer them some wine."

³So I went to see Jaazaniah son of Jeremiah and grandson of Habazziniah and all his brothers and sons—representing all the Recabite families. ⁴I took them to the Temple, and we went into the room assigned to the sons of Hanan son of Igdaliah, a man of God. This room was located next to the one used by the Temple officials, directly above the room of Maaseiah son of Shallum, the Temple gatekeeper.

⁵I set cups and jugs of wine before them and invited them to have a drink, ⁶but they refused. "No," they said, "we don't drink wine, because our ancestor Jehonadab* son of Recab gave us this command: 'You and your descendants must never drink wine. ⁷And do not build houses or plant crops or vineyards, but always live in tents. If you follow these commands, you will live long, good lives in the land.' ⁸So we have obeyed him in all these things. We have never had a drink of wine to this day, nor have our wives, our sons, or our daughters. ⁹We haven't built houses or owned vineyards or farms or planted crops. ¹⁰We have lived in tents and have fully obeyed all the commands of Jehonadab, our ancestor. ¹¹But when King Nebuchadnezzar* of Babylon attacked this country, we were afraid of the Babylonian and Syrian* armies. So we decided to move to Jerusalem. That is why we are here."

¹²Then the LORD gave this message to Jeremiah: ¹³"This is what the LORD of Heaven's Armies, the God of Israel, says: Go and say to the people in Judah and Jerusalem, 'Come and learn a lesson about how to obey me. ¹⁴The Recabites do not drink wine to this day because their ancestor Jehonadab told them not to. But I have spoken to you again and again,

35:6 Hebrew *Jonadab,* a variant spelling of Jehonadab; also in 35:10, 14, 16, 18, 19. See 2 Kgs 10:15. **35:11a** Hebrew *Nebuchadrezzar,* a variant spelling of Nebuchadnezzar. **35:11b** Or *Chaldean and Aramean.*

and you refuse to obey me. ¹⁵Time after time I sent you prophets, who told you, "Turn from your wicked ways, and start doing things right. Stop worshiping other gods so that you might live in peace here in the land I have given to you and your ancestors." But you would not listen to me or obey me. ¹⁶The descendants of Jehonadab son of Recab have obeyed their ancestor completely, but you have refused to listen to me.'

¹⁷"Therefore, this is what the LORD God of Heaven's Armies, the God of Israel, says: 'Because you refuse to listen or answer when I call, I will send upon Judah and Jerusalem all the disasters I have threatened.'"

¹⁸Then Jeremiah turned to the Recabites and said, "This is what the LORD of Heaven's Armies, the God of Israel, says: 'You have obeyed your ancestor Jehonadab in every respect, following all his instructions.' ¹⁹Therefore, this is what the LORD of Heaven's Armies, the God of Israel, says: 'Jehonadab son of Recab will always have descendants who serve me.'"

36 BARUCH READS THE LORD'S MESSAGES

During the fourth year that Jehoiakim son of Josiah was king in Judah,* the LORD gave this message to Jeremiah: ²"Get a scroll, and write down all my messages against Israel, Judah, and the other nations. Begin with the first message back in the days of Josiah, and write down every message, right up to the present time. ³Perhaps the people of Judah will repent when they hear again all the terrible things I have planned for them. Then I will be able to forgive their sins and wrongdoings."

⁴So Jeremiah sent for Baruch son of Neriah, and as Jeremiah dictated all the prophecies that the LORD had given him, Baruch wrote them on a scroll. ⁵Then Jeremiah said to Baruch, "I am a prisoner here and unable to go to the Temple. ⁶So you go to the Temple on the next day of fasting, and read the messages from the LORD that I have had you write on this scroll. Read them so the people who are there from all over Judah will hear them. ⁷Perhaps even yet they will turn from their evil ways and ask the LORD's forgiveness before it is too late. For the LORD has threatened them with his terrible anger."

⁸Baruch did as Jeremiah told him and read these messages from the LORD to the people at the Temple. ⁹He did this on a day of sacred

fasting held in late autumn,* during the fifth year of the reign of Jehoiakim son of Josiah. People from all over Judah had come to Jerusalem to attend the services at the Temple on that day. ¹⁰Baruch read Jeremiah's words on the scroll to all the people. He stood in front of the Temple room of Gemariah, son of Shaphan the secretary. This room was just off the upper courtyard of the Temple, near the New Gate entrance.

¹¹When Micaiah son of Gemariah and grandson of Shaphan heard the messages from the LORD, ¹²he went down to the secretary's room in the palace where the administrative officials were meeting. Elishama the secretary was there, along with Delaiah son of Shemaiah, Elnathan son of Acbor, Gemariah son of Shaphan, Zedekiah son of Hananiah, and all the other officials. ¹³When Micaiah told them about the messages Baruch was reading to the people, ¹⁴the officials sent Jehudi son of Nethaniah, grandson of Shelemiah and great-grandson of Cushi, to ask Baruch to come and read the messages to them, too. So Baruch took the scroll and went to them. ¹⁵"Sit down and read the scroll to us," the officials said, and Baruch did as they requested.

¹⁶When they heard all the messages, they looked at one another in alarm. "We must tell the king what we have heard," they said to Baruch. ¹⁷"But first, tell us how you got these messages. Did they come directly from Jeremiah?"

¹⁸So Baruch explained, "Jeremiah dictated them, and I wrote them down in ink, word for word, on this scroll."

¹⁹"You and Jeremiah should both hide," the officials told Baruch. "Don't tell anyone where you are!" ²⁰Then the officials left the scroll for safekeeping in the room of Elishama the secretary and went to tell the king what had happened.

KING JEHOIAKIM BURNS THE SCROLL

²¹The king sent Jehudi to get the scroll. Jehudi brought it from Elishama's room and read it to the king as all his officials stood by. ²²It was late autumn, and the king was in a winterized

36:1 The fourth year of Jehoiakim's reign was 605 B.C.
36:9 Hebrew *in the ninth month,* of the ancient Hebrew lunar calendar (also in 36:22). The ninth month in the fifth year of Jehoiakim's reign occurred within the months of November and December 604 B.C. Also see note on 1:3.

FASTING TO FOCUS
(36:9) Days of fasting often were called at times of national emergency. At such times, the people abstained from eating food and concentrated on prayer and worship. Fasting is one of the spiritual disciplines—a way to deny self and concentrate on God. It is also a time of preparation. Moses fasted for 40 days while God talked with him on Mt. Sinai (Exod 24:18). Jesus fasted 40 days at the beginning of his ministry (Matt 4:1-2). In what ways do you deny self in order to focus on God?

part of the palace, sitting in front of a fire to keep warm. ²³Each time Jehudi finished reading three or four columns, the king took a knife and cut off that section of the scroll. He then threw it into the fire, section by section, until the whole scroll was burned up. ²⁴Neither the king nor his attendants showed any signs of fear or repentance at what they heard. ²⁵Even when Elnathan, Delaiah, and Gemariah begged the king not to burn the scroll, he wouldn't listen.

²⁶Then the king commanded his son Jerahmeel, Seraiah son of Azriel, and Shelemiah son of Abdeel to arrest Baruch and Jeremiah. But the LORD had hidden them.

JEREMIAH REWRITES THE SCROLL

²⁷After the king had burned the scroll on which Baruch had written Jeremiah's words, the LORD gave Jeremiah another message. He said, ²⁸"Get another scroll, and write everything again just as you did on the scroll King Jehoiakim burned. ²⁹Then say to the king, 'This is what the LORD says: You burned the scroll because it said the king of Babylon would destroy this land and empty it of people and animals. ³⁰Now this is what the LORD says about King Jehoiakim of Judah: He will have no heirs to sit on the throne of David. His dead body will be thrown out to lie unburied—exposed to the heat of the day and the frost of the night. ³¹I will punish him and his family and his attendants for their sins. I will pour out on them and on all the people of Jerusalem and Judah all the disasters I promised, for they would not listen to my warnings.'"

³²So Jeremiah took another scroll and dictated again to his secretary, Baruch. He wrote everything that had been on the scroll King Jehoiakim had burned in the fire. Only this time he added much more!

37 ZEDEKIAH CALLS FOR JEREMIAH

Zedekiah son of Josiah succeeded Jehoiachin* son of Jehoiakim as the king of Judah.

He was appointed by King Nebuchadnezzar* of Babylon. ²But neither King Zedekiah nor his attendants nor the people who were left in the land listened to what the LORD said through Jeremiah.

³Nevertheless, King Zedekiah sent Jehucal son of Shelemiah, and Zephaniah the priest, son of Maaseiah, to ask Jeremiah, "Please pray to the LORD our God for us." ⁴Jeremiah had not yet been imprisoned, so he could come and go among the people as he pleased.

⁵At this time the army of Pharaoh Hophra* of Egypt appeared at the southern border of Judah. When the Babylonian* army heard about it, they withdrew from their siege of Jerusalem.

⁶Then the LORD gave this message to Jeremiah: ⁷"This is what the LORD, the God of Israel, says: The king of Judah sent you to ask me what is going to happen. Tell him, 'Pharaoh's army is about to return to Egypt, though he came here to help you. ⁸Then the Babylonians* will come back and capture this city and burn it to the ground.'

⁹"This is what the LORD says: Do not fool yourselves into thinking that the Babylonians are gone for good. They aren't! ¹⁰Even if you were to destroy the entire Babylonian army, leaving only a handful of wounded survivors, they would still stagger from their tents and burn this city to the ground!"

JEREMIAH IS IMPRISONED

¹¹When the Babylonian army left Jerusalem because of Pharaoh's approaching army, ¹²Jeremiah started to leave the city on his way to the territory of Benjamin, to claim his share of the property among his relatives there.* ¹³But as he was walking through the Benjamin Gate, a sentry arrested him and said, "You are defecting to the Babylonians!" The sentry making the arrest was Irijah son of Shelemiah, grandson of Hananiah.

¹⁴"That's not true!" Jeremiah protested. "I had no intention of doing any such thing." But Irijah wouldn't listen, and he took Jeremiah before the officials. ¹⁵They were furious with Jeremiah and had him flogged and imprisoned in the house of Jonathan the secretary. Jonathan's house had been converted into a prison. ¹⁶Jeremiah was put into a dungeon cell, where he remained for many days.

¹⁷Later King Zedekiah secretly requested that Jeremiah come to the palace, where the king

GOD'S WORD

(36:21-32) God told Jeremiah to write his words on a scroll. Because he was not allowed to go to the Temple, Jeremiah asked his scribe, Baruch, to whom he had dictated the message, to read the scroll to the people gathered there. Baruch then read it to the officials, and, finally, Jehudi read it to the king himself. Although King Jehoiakim burned Jeremiah's scroll, he couldn't destroy God's Word. Today many people try to put God's Word aside, or say that it contains errors and cannot be trusted. People may reject God's Word, but they cannot destroy it. God's Word will stand forever (Ps 119:89).

37:1a Hebrew *Coniah*, a variant spelling of Jehoiachin.
37:1b Hebrew *Nebuchadrezzar*, a variant spelling of Nebuchadnezzar.
37:5a Hebrew *army of Pharaoh*; see 44:30. 37:5b Or *Chaldean*; also in 37:10, 11. 37:8 Or *Chaldeans*; also in 37:9, 13. 37:12 Hebrew *to separate from there in the midst of the people.*

asked him, "Do you have any messages from the LORD?"

"Yes, I do!" said Jeremiah. "You will be defeated by the king of Babylon."

[18]Then Jeremiah asked the king, "What crime have I committed? What have I done against you, your attendants, or the people that I should be imprisoned like this? [19]Where are your prophets now who told you the king of Babylon would not attack you or this land? [20]Listen, my lord the king, I beg you. Don't send me back to the dungeon in the house of Jonathan the secretary, for I will die there."

[21]So King Zedekiah commanded that Jeremiah not be returned to the dungeon. Instead, he was imprisoned in the courtyard of the guard in the royal palace. The king also commanded that Jeremiah be given a loaf of fresh bread every day as long as there was any left in the city. So Jeremiah was put in the palace prison.

38 JEREMIAH IN A CISTERN Now Shephatiah son of Mattan, Gedaliah son of Pashhur, Jehucal* son of Shelemiah, and Pashhur son of Malkijah heard what Jeremiah had been telling the people. He had been saying, [2]"This is what the LORD says: 'Everyone who stays in Jerusalem will die from war, famine, or disease, but those who surrender to the Babylonians* will live. Their reward will be life. They will live!' [3]The LORD also says: 'The city of Jerusalem will certainly be handed over to the army of the king of Babylon, who will capture it.'"

[4]So these officials went to the king and said, "Sir, this man must die! That kind of talk will undermine the morale of the few fighting men we have left, as well as that of all the people. This man is a traitor!"

[5]King Zedekiah agreed. "All right," he said. "Do as you like. I can't stop you."

[6]So the officials took Jeremiah from his cell and lowered him by ropes into an empty cistern in the prison yard. It belonged to Malkijah, a member of the royal family. There was no water in the cistern, but there was a thick layer of mud at the bottom, and Jeremiah sank down into it.

[7]But Ebed-melech the Ethiopian,* an important court official, heard that Jeremiah was in the cistern. At that time the king was holding court at the Benjamin Gate, [8]so Ebed-melech rushed from the palace to speak with him. [9]"My lord the king," he said, "these men have

38:1 Hebrew *Jucal,* a variant spelling of Jehucal; see 37:3.   38:2 Or *Chaldeans;* also in 38:18, 19, 23.   38:7 Hebrew *the Cushite.*

done a very evil thing in putting Jeremiah the prophet into the cistern. He will soon die of hunger, for almost all the bread in the city is gone."

[10]So the king told Ebed-melech, "Take thirty of my men with you, and pull Jeremiah out of the cistern before he dies."

[11]So Ebed-melech took the men with him and went to a room in the palace beneath the treasury, where he found some old rags and discarded clothing. He carried these to the cistern and lowered them to Jeremiah on a rope. [12]Ebed-melech called down to Jeremiah, "Put these rags under your armpits to protect you from the ropes." Then when Jeremiah was ready, [13]they pulled him out. So Jeremiah was returned to the courtyard of the guard—the palace prison—where he remained.

ZEDEKIAH QUESTIONS JEREMIAH   [14]One day King Zedekiah sent for Jeremiah and had him brought to the third entrance of the LORD's Temple. "I want to ask you something," the king said. "And don't try to hide the truth."

[15]Jeremiah said, "If I tell you the truth, you will kill me. And if I give you advice, you won't listen to me anyway."

[16]So King Zedekiah secretly promised him, "As surely as the LORD our Creator lives, I will not kill you or hand you over to the men who want you dead."

[17]Then Jeremiah said to Zedekiah, "This is what the LORD God of Heaven's Armies, the God of Israel, says: 'If you surrender to the Babylonian officers, you and your family will live, and the city will not be burned down. [18]But if you refuse to surrender, you

....

REWARDS
(38:6) Judah's leaders persecuted Jeremiah repeatedly for faithfully proclaiming God's messages. For 40 years of faithful ministry, Jeremiah received no acclaim, no love, no popular following. He was beaten, jailed, threatened, and even forced to leave his homeland. Only the heathen Babylonians showed him any respect. God does not guarantee that his faithful servants will escape persecution. But he does promise that he will be with them and will give them strength to endure (2 Cor 1:3-7). As you minister to others, recognize that your service is for God, not for human approval. God's rewards often don't come in this life.

THE COURAGE TO STAND ALONE
(38:9-13) Ebed-melech feared God more than man. He alone among the palace officials stood up against the murder plot. His obedience could have cost him his life. Because he risked his life to save Jeremiah, he was spared when Jerusalem fell (39:15-18). Would you do the same? Standing alone can be difficult. But God willingly provides the courage to do what's right. Just ask him for it.

will not escape! This city will be handed over to the Babylonians, and they will burn it to the ground.'"

[19]"But I am afraid to surrender," the king said, "for the Babylonians may hand me over to the Judeans who have defected to them. And who knows what they will do to me!"

[20]Jeremiah replied, "You won't be handed over to them if you choose to obey the LORD. Your life will be spared, and all will go well for you. [21]But if you refuse to surrender, this is what the LORD has revealed to me: [22]All the women left in your palace will be brought out and given to the officers of the Babylonian army. Then the women will taunt you, saying,

'What fine friends you have!
    They have betrayed and misled you.
When your feet sank in the mud,
    they left you to your fate!'

[23]All your wives and children will be led out to the Babylonians, and you will not escape. You will be seized by the king of Babylon, and this city will be burned down."

[24]Then Zedekiah said to Jeremiah, "Don't tell anyone you told me this, or you will die! [25]My officials may hear that I spoke to you, and they may say, 'Tell us what you and the king were talking about. If you don't tell us, we will kill you.' [26]If this happens, just tell them you

ULTIMATE ISSUES *SEXUAL ABUSE*

Seventeen-year-old Shelly sat on the couch in her youth pastor's office, sobbing quietly. "I've never told anyone this," she choked out. "I feel so dirty. . . . When I was younger, my father made me have sex with him . . . lots of times . . . over several years. He said if I ever told anyone, I'd regret it. He said it was 'our little secret.' Besides, he's an elder in the church—who would believe me?"

Unfortunately, this is not an isolated incident. Sexual abuse is happening more and more. It is the secret, unspoken pain of countless hearts.

Sexual abuse may be defined as any contact or interaction (visual, verbal, psychological, or physical) between a child or adolescent and an adult when the younger person is being used for the sexual gratification of the older person (or anyone else).* A recent survey indicates that 38 percent of the women in this country have been sexually abused by age 18. The actual percentage may be even higher. The percentage of sexually abused males, though lower, is still shockingly high. Sexual abuse is like some huge, silent tidal wave that has reached unbelievable proportions, threatening to destroy countless lives.

Surprisingly enough, victims of sexual abuse don't always know they've been abused. Some victims believe it wasn't abuse because the perpetrator was a family member or a friend, not a total stranger. Others believe they must somehow have invited the offense. Regardless of the relationship or the form the abuse takes, it still is abuse and it is wrong.

Common results of sexual abuse include feelings of betrayal, fear, anger, powerlessness, shame, depression, and, later on, difficulty in having healthy relationships, especially with the opposite sex. Having been betrayed so devastatingly, many victims have an overwhelming fear of letting anyone get close enough to hurt them again. Often they keep others at arm's length emotionally, or they just shut down their emotions altogether. They become little more than empty shells who spend their time trying to keep anyone from breaking through their protective front. It is a miserable way to live.

So what should a person do who has been, or is now being, sexually abused?

First, remember you are not alone.

A staggering number of people, male and female, have been sexually abused. There are people who understand and can help you.

Second, talk to someone about what has happened or about what you are going through. The abuser's greatest weapon over you is your silence. Regardless of what you've been told, you must share your pain with someone else. If possible, talk with your youth pastor, Campus Life or Young Life director, school counselor, or a psychologist or psychiatrist you trust. If that person is unable or unwilling to help, don't give up. Find someone who will listen and understand. There may be a hotline or agency in your area designed specifically to help victims of sexual abuse.

Third, remember that if you have been sexually abused in any way, it is not your fault. You are not responsible for what happened to you. You are a victim. Do not give in to feelings that you somehow "asked for it" or brought the abuse on yourself. Seek counsel from someone who can help you understand this and can help you work through your pain.

Finally, remember that you are made in the image of God. Sexual abuse is a serious crime against that image, and God will deal with those who inflict such damage on others. But there is great comfort in knowing that the same God who judges sin was once a victim of sin himself. Christ knows, he cares, and he understands. ■

*This definition is based on one given by Dr. Dan Allender in his excellent book *The Wounded Heart* (NavPress, 1990), p. 30.

begged me not to send you back to Jonathan's dungeon, for fear you would die there."

²⁷Sure enough, it wasn't long before the king's officials came to Jeremiah and asked him why the king had called for him. But Jeremiah followed the king's instructions, and they left without finding out the truth. No one had overheard the conversation between Jeremiah and the king. ²⁸And Jeremiah remained a prisoner in the courtyard of the guard until the day Jerusalem was captured.

39 THE FALL OF JERUSALEM

In January* of the ninth year of King Zedekiah's reign, King Nebuchadnezzar* came with his army to besiege Jerusalem. ²Two and a half years later, on July 18* in the eleventh year of Zedekiah's reign, the Babylonians broke through the wall, and the city fell. ³All the officers of the Babylonian army came in and sat in triumph at the Middle Gate: Nergal-sharezer of Samgar, and Nebo-sarsekim,* a chief officer, and Nergal-sharezer, the king's adviser, and all the other officers.

⁴When King Zedekiah and all the soldiers saw that the Babylonians had broken into the city, they fled. They waited for nightfall and then slipped through the gate between the two walls behind the king's garden and headed toward the Jordan Valley.*

⁵But the Babylonian* troops chased the king and caught him on the plains of Jericho. They took him to King Nebuchadnezzar of Babylon, who was at Riblah in the land of Hamath. There the king of Babylon pronounced judgment upon Zedekiah. ⁶He made Zedekiah watch as they slaughtered his sons and all the nobles of Judah. ⁷Then they gouged out Zedekiah's eyes, bound him in bronze chains, and led him away to Babylon.

⁸Meanwhile, the Babylonians burned Jerusalem, including the palace, and tore down the walls of the city. ⁹Then Nebuzaradan, the captain of the guard, sent to Babylon the rest of the people who remained in the city as well as those who had defected to him. ¹⁰But Nebuzaradan left a few of the poorest people in Judah, and he assigned them vineyards and fields to care for.

JEREMIAH REMAINS IN JUDAH ¹¹King Nebuchadnezzar had told Nebuzaradan, the captain of the guard, to find Jeremiah. ¹²"See that he isn't hurt," he said. "Look after him well, and give him anything he wants." ¹³So Nebuzaradan, the captain of the guard; Nebushazban, a chief officer; Nergal-sharezer, the king's adviser; and the other officers of Babylon's king ¹⁴sent messengers to bring Jeremiah out of the prison. They put him under the care of Gedaliah son of Ahikam and grandson of Shaphan, who took him back to his home. So Jeremiah stayed in Judah among his own people.

¹⁵The LORD had given the following message to Jeremiah while he was still in prison: ¹⁶"Say to Ebed-melech the Ethiopian,* 'This is what the LORD of Heaven's Armies, the God of Israel, says: I will do to this city everything I have threatened. I will send disaster, not prosperity. You will see its destruction, ¹⁷but I will rescue you from those you fear so much. ¹⁸Because you trusted me, I will give you your life as a reward. I will rescue you and keep you safe. I, the LORD, have spoken!'"

40

The LORD gave a message to Jeremiah after Nebuzaradan, the captain of the guard, had released him at Ramah. He had found Jeremiah bound in chains among all the other captives of Jerusalem and Judah who were being sent to exile in Babylon.

²The captain of the guard called for Jeremiah and said, "The LORD your God has brought this disaster on this land, ³just as he said he would. For these people have sinned against the LORD and disobeyed him. That is why it happened. ⁴But I am going to take off your chains and let you go. If you want to come with me to Babylon, you are welcome. I will see that you are well cared for. But if you don't want to come, you may stay here. The whole land is before you—go wherever you like. ⁵If you decide to stay, then return to Gedaliah son of Ahikam and grandson of Shaphan. He has been appointed governor of Judah by the king of Babylon. Stay there with the people he rules. But it's up to you; go wherever you like."

Then Nebuzaradan, the captain of the guard, gave Jeremiah some food and money and let him go. ⁶So Jeremiah returned to Gedaliah son

---

39:1a Hebrew *In the tenth month,* of the ancient Hebrew lunar calendar. A number of events in Jeremiah can be cross-checked with dates in surviving Babylonian records and related accurately to our modern calendar. This event occurred on January 15, 588 B.C.; see 52:4a and the note there. **39:1b** Hebrew *Nebuchadrezzar,* a variant spelling of Nebuchadnezzar; also in 39:11. **39:2** Hebrew *On the ninth day of the fourth month.* This day was July 18, 586 B.C.; also see note on 39:1a. **39:3** Or *Nergal-sharezer, Samgar-nebo, Sarsekim.* **39:4** Hebrew *the Arabah.* **39:5** Or *Chaldean;* similarly in 39:8. **39:16** Hebrew *the Cushite.*

KNOW HIM
(40:1-3) The Babylonian captain, who did not know God, acknowledged that God had given the Babylonians victory. Many people recognize that God exists and does miracles, yet fail to have a relationship with him. Do you know God or know about him? There's a big difference!

of Ahikam at Mizpah, and he lived in Judah with the few who were still left in the land.

GEDALIAH GOVERNS IN JUDAH 7The leaders of the Judean guerrilla bands in the countryside heard that the king of Babylon had appointed Gedaliah son of Ahikam as governor over the poor people who were left behind in Judah—the men, women, and children who hadn't been exiled to Babylon. 8So they went to see Gedaliah at Mizpah. These included: Ishmael son of Nethaniah, Johanan and Jonathan sons of Kareah, Seraiah son of Tanhumeth, the sons of Ephai the Netophathite, Jezaniah son of the Maacathite, and all their men.

9Gedaliah vowed to them that the Babylonians* meant them no harm. "Don't be afraid to serve them. Live in the land and serve the king of Babylon, and all will go well for you," he promised. 10"As for me, I will stay at Mizpah to represent you before the Babylonians who come to meet with us. Settle in the towns you have taken, and live off the land. Harvest the grapes and summer fruits and olives, and store them away."

11When the Judeans in Moab, Ammon, Edom, and the other nearby countries heard that the king of Babylon had left a few people in Judah and that Gedaliah was the governor, 12they began to return to Judah from the places to which they had fled. They stopped at Mizpah to meet with Gedaliah and then went into the Judean countryside to gather a great harvest of grapes and other crops.

A PLOT AGAINST GEDALIAH 13Soon after this, Johanan son of Kareah and the other guerrilla leaders came to Gedaliah at Mizpah. 14They said to him, "Did you know that Baalis, king of Ammon, has sent Ishmael son of Nethaniah to assassinate you?" But Gedaliah refused to believe them.

15Later Johanan had a private conference with Gedaliah and volunteered to kill Ishmael secretly. "Why should we let him come and murder you?" Johanan asked. "What will happen then to the Judeans who have returned? Why should the few of us who are still left be scattered and lost?"

16But Gedaliah said to Johanan, "I forbid you to do any such thing, for you are lying about Ishmael."

41 **THE MURDER OF GEDALIAH** But in midautumn,* Ishmael son of Nethaniah and grandson of Elishama, who was a member of the royal family and had been one of the king's high officials, went to Mizpah with ten men to meet Gedaliah. While they were eating together, 2Ishmael and his ten men suddenly jumped up, drew their swords, and killed Gedaliah, whom the king of Babylon had appointed governor. 3Ishmael also killed all the Judeans and the Babylonian* soldiers who were with Gedaliah at Mizpah.

4The next day, before anyone had heard about Gedaliah's murder, 5eighty men arrived from Shechem, Shiloh, and Samaria to worship at the Temple of the LORD. They had shaved off their beards, torn their clothes, and cut themselves, and had brought along grain offerings and frankincense. 6Ishmael left Mizpah to meet them, weeping as he went. When he reached them, he said, "Oh, come and see what has happened to Gedaliah!"

7But as soon as they were all inside the town, Ishmael and his men killed all but ten of them and threw their bodies into a cistern. 8The other ten had talked Ishmael into letting them go by promising to bring him their stores of wheat, barley, olive oil, and honey that they had hidden away. 9The cistern where Ishmael dumped the bodies of the men he murdered was the large one dug by King Asa when he fortified Mizpah to protect himself against King Baasha of Israel. Ishmael son of Nethaniah filled it with corpses.

10Then Ishmael made captives of the king's daughters and the other people who had been left under Gedaliah's care in Mizpah by Nebuzaradan, the captain of the guard. Taking them with him, he started back toward the land of Ammon.

11But when Johanan son of Kareah and the other guerrilla leaders heard about Ishmael's crimes, 12they took all their men and set out to stop him. They caught up with him at the large pool near Gibeon. 13The people Ishmael had captured shouted for joy when they saw Johanan and the other guerrilla leaders. 14And all the captives from Mizpah escaped and began to help Johanan. 15Meanwhile, Ishmael and eight of his men escaped from Johanan into the land of Ammon.

16Then Johanan son of Kareah and the other guerrilla leaders took all the people they had rescued in Gibeon—the soldiers, women, children, and court officials* whom Ishmael had captured after he killed Gedaliah. 17They took them all to the village of Geruth-kimham near Bethlehem, where they prepared to

40:9 Or *Chaldeans;* also in 40:10.   **41:1** Hebrew *in the seventh month,* of the ancient Hebrew lunar calendar. This month occurred within the months of October and November 586 B.C.; also see note on 39:1a.   **41:3** Or *Chaldean.*   **41:16** Or *eunuchs.*

leave for Egypt. ¹⁸They were afraid of what the Babylonians* would do when they heard that Ishmael had killed Gedaliah, the governor appointed by the Babylonian king.

42 WARNING TO STAY IN JUDAH

Then all the guerrilla leaders, including Johanan son of Kareah and Jezaniah* son of Hoshaiah, and all the people, from the least to the greatest, approached ²Jeremiah the prophet. They said, "Please pray to the LORD your God for us. As you can see, we are only a tiny remnant compared to what we were before. ³Pray that the LORD your God will show us what to do and where to go."

⁴"All right," Jeremiah replied. "I will pray to the LORD your God, as you have asked, and I will tell you everything he says. I will hide nothing from you."

⁵Then they said to Jeremiah, "May the LORD your God be a faithful witness against us if we refuse to obey whatever he tells us to do! ⁶Whether we like it or not, we will obey the LORD our God to whom we are sending you with our plea. For if we obey him, everything will turn out well for us."

⁷Ten days later the LORD gave his reply to Jeremiah. ⁸So he called for Johanan son of Kareah and the other guerrilla leaders, and for all the people, from the least to the greatest. ⁹He said to them, "You sent me to the LORD, the God of Israel, with your request, and this is his reply: ¹⁰'Stay here in this land. If you do, I will build you up and not tear you down; I will plant you and not uproot you. For I am sorry about all the punishment I have had to bring upon you. ¹¹Do not fear the king of Babylon anymore,' says the LORD. 'For I am with you and will save you and rescue you from his power. ¹²I will be merciful to you by making him kind, so he will let you stay here in your land.'

¹³"But if you refuse to obey the LORD your God, and if you say, 'We will not stay here; ¹⁴instead, we will go to Egypt where we will be free from war, the call to arms, and hunger,' ¹⁵then hear the LORD's message to the remnant of Judah. This is what the LORD of Heaven's Armies, the God of Israel, says: 'If you are determined to go to Egypt and live there, ¹⁶the very war and famine you fear will catch up to you, and you will die there. ¹⁷That is the fate awaiting every one of you who insists on going to live in Egypt. Yes, you will die from war, famine, and disease. None of you will escape the disaster I will bring upon you there.'

¹⁸"This is what the LORD of Heaven's Armies, the God of Israel, says: 'Just as my anger and fury have been poured out on the people of Jerusalem, so they will be poured out on you when you enter Egypt. You will be an object of damnation, horror, cursing, and mockery. And you will never see your homeland again.'

¹⁹"Listen, you remnant of Judah. The LORD has told you: 'Do not go to Egypt!' Don't forget this warning I have given you today. ²⁰For you were not being honest when you sent me to pray to the LORD your God for you. You said, 'Just tell us what the LORD our God says, and we will do it!' ²¹And today I have told you exactly what he said, but you will not obey the LORD your God any better now than you have in the past. ²²So you can be sure that you will die from war, famine, and disease in Egypt, where you insist on going."

43 JEREMIAH TAKEN TO EGYPT

When Jeremiah had finished giving this message from the LORD their God to all the people, ²Azariah son of Hoshaiah and Johanan son of Kareah and all the other proud men said to Jeremiah, "You lie! The LORD our God hasn't forbidden us to go to Egypt! ³Baruch son of Neriah has convinced you to say this, because he wants us to stay here and be killed by the Babylonians* or be carried off into exile."

⁴So Johanan and the other guerrilla leaders and all the people refused to obey the LORD's command to stay in Judah. ⁵Johanan and the other leaders took with them all the people who had returned from the nearby countries to which they had fled. ⁶In the crowd were men, women, and children, the king's daughters, and all those whom Nebuzaradan, the captain of the guard, had left with Gedaliah. The prophet Jeremiah and Baruch were also included. ⁷The people refused to obey the voice of the LORD and went to Egypt, going as far as the city of Tahpanhes.

⁸Then at Tahpanhes, the LORD gave another message to Jeremiah. He said, ⁹"While the people of Judah are watching, take some large rocks and bury them under the pavement stones at the entrance of Pharaoh's palace here in Tahpanhes. ¹⁰Then say to the people

---

41:18 Or *Chaldeans.* **42:1** Greek version reads *Azariah;* compare 43:2. **43:3** Or *Chaldeans.*

DON'T PRAY
(42:5-6) Johanan and his associates spoke their own curse; Jeremiah merely elaborated on it. It was a tragic mistake to ask for God's guidance with no intention of following it. Be sure never to ask God for something if you know in your heart that you do not want it. It is better not to pray than to pray deceptively. God cannot be deceived.

of Judah, 'This is what the LORD of Heaven's Armies, the God of Israel, says: I will certainly bring my servant Nebuchadnezzar,* king of Babylon, here to Egypt. I will set his throne over these stones that I have hidden. He will spread his royal canopy over them. ¹¹And when he comes, he will destroy the land of Egypt. He will bring death to those destined for death, captivity to those destined for captivity, and war to those destined for war. ¹²He will set fire to the temples of Egypt's gods; he will burn the temples and carry the idols away as plunder. He will pick clean the land of Egypt as a shepherd picks fleas from his cloak. And he himself will leave unharmed. ¹³He will break down the sacred pillars standing in the temple of the sun* in Egypt, and he will burn down the temples of Egypt's gods.'"

44 **JUDGMENT FOR IDOLATRY** This is the message Jeremiah received concerning the Judeans living in northern Egypt in the cities of Migdol, Tahpanhes, and Memphis,* and in southern Egypt* as well: ²"This is what the LORD of Heaven's Armies, the God of Israel, says: You saw the calamity I brought on Jerusalem and all the towns of Judah. They now lie deserted and in ruins. ³They provoked my anger with all their wickedness. They burned incense and worshiped other gods—gods that neither they nor you nor any of your ancestors had ever even known.

⁴"Again and again I sent my servants, the prophets, to plead with them, 'Don't do these horrible things that I hate so much.' ⁵But my people would not listen or turn back from their wicked ways. They kept on burning incense to these gods. ⁶And so my fury boiled over and fell like fire on the towns of Judah and into the streets of Jerusalem, and they are still a desolate ruin today.

....

REPEATING
(44:9-10) *The people of Judah failed to learn from mistakes made in the past. Your past is your school of experience. Mistakes are to be learned from, rather than ignored. When you don't learn from a mistake, you risk repeating it. Let your past mistakes point you to God's way.*

A CHANGE OF ATTITUDE AND ACTION
(44:14) *Through Jeremiah, God warned the people of Judah not to go to Egypt. But they ignored him. Only those who repented of going to Egypt and returned to their own land would escape judgment. God wanted both a change of attitude and some action. The same goes for us when we mess up. We need to (1) admit we have rebelled against God, (2) turn from whatever we've done wrong, and (3) seek to live as God instructs in his Word.*

⁷"And now the LORD God of Heaven's Armies, the God of Israel, asks you: Why are you destroying yourselves? For not one of you will survive—not a man, woman, or child among you who has come here from Judah, not even the babies in your arms. ⁸Why provoke my anger by burning incense to the idols you have made here in Egypt? You will only destroy yourselves and make yourselves an object of cursing and mockery for all the nations of the earth. ⁹Have you forgotten the sins of your ancestors, the sins of the kings and queens of Judah, and the sins you and your wives committed in Judah and Jerusalem? ¹⁰To this very hour you have shown no remorse or reverence. No one has chosen to follow my word and the decrees I gave to you and your ancestors before you.

¹¹"Therefore, this is what the LORD of Heaven's Armies, the God of Israel, says: I am determined to destroy every one of you! ¹²I will take this remnant of Judah—those who were determined to come here and live in Egypt—and I will consume them. They will fall here in Egypt, killed by war and famine. All will die, from the least to the greatest. They will be an object of damnation, horror, cursing, and mockery. ¹³I will punish them in Egypt just as I punished them in Jerusalem, by war, famine, and disease. ¹⁴Of that remnant who fled to Egypt, hoping someday to return to Judah, there will be no survivors. Even though they long to return home, only a handful will do so."

¹⁵Then all the women present and all the men who knew that their wives had burned incense to idols—a great crowd of all the Judeans living in northern Egypt and southern Egypt*—answered Jeremiah, ¹⁶"We will not listen to your messages from the LORD! ¹⁷We will do whatever we want. We will burn incense and pour out liquid offerings to the Queen of Heaven just as much as we like—just as we, and our ancestors, and our kings and officials have always done in the towns of Judah and in the streets of Jerusalem. For in those days we had plenty to eat, and we were well off and had no troubles! ¹⁸But ever since we quit burning incense to the Queen of Heaven and stopped worshiping her with liquid offerings, we have been in great trouble and have been dying from war and famine."

¹⁹"Besides," the women added, "do you suppose that we were burning incense and pouring out liquid offerings to the Queen of

43:10 Hebrew *Nebuchadrezzar,* a variant spelling of Nebuchadnezzar.   **43:13** Or *in Heliopolis.*   **44:1a** Hebrew *Noph.*   **44:1b** Hebrew *in Pathros.*   **44:15** Hebrew *in Egypt, in Pathros.*

Heaven, and making cakes marked with her image, without our husbands knowing it and helping us? Of course not!"

²⁰Then Jeremiah said to all of them, men and women alike, who had given him that answer, ²¹"Do you think the LORD did not know that you and your ancestors, your kings and officials, and all the people were burning incense to idols in the towns of Judah and in the streets of Jerusalem? ²²It was because the LORD could no longer bear all the disgusting things you were doing that he made your land an object of cursing—a desolate ruin without inhabitants—as it is today. ²³All these terrible things happened to you because you have burned incense to idols and sinned against the LORD. You have refused to obey him and have not followed his instructions, his decrees, and his laws."

²⁴Then Jeremiah said to them all, including the women, "Listen to this message from the LORD, all you citizens of Judah who live in Egypt. ²⁵This is what the LORD of Heaven's Armies, the God of Israel, says: 'You and your wives have said, "We will keep our promises to burn incense and pour out liquid offerings to the Queen of Heaven," and you have proved by your actions that you meant it. So go ahead and carry out your promises and vows to her!'

²⁶"But listen to this message from the LORD, all you Judeans now living in Egypt: 'I have sworn by my great name,' says the LORD, 'that my name will no longer be spoken by any of the Judeans in the land of Egypt. None of you may invoke my name or use this oath: "As surely as the Sovereign LORD lives." ²⁷For I will watch over you to bring you disaster and not good. Everyone from Judah who is now living in Egypt will suffer war and famine until all of you are dead. ²⁸Only a small number will escape death and return to Judah from Egypt. Then all those who came to Egypt will find out whose words are true—mine or theirs!

²⁹"'And this is the proof I give you,' says the LORD, 'that all I have threatened will happen to you and that I will punish you here.' ³⁰This is what the LORD says: 'I will turn Pharaoh Hophra, king of Egypt, over to his enemies who want to kill him, just as I turned King Zedekiah of Judah over to King Nebuchadnezzar* of Babylon.'"

44:30 Hebrew *Nebuchadrezzar,* a variant spelling of Nebuchadnezzar.   45:1 The fourth year of Jehoiakim's reign was 605 B.C.   46:2a This event occurred in 605 B.C., during the fourth year of Jehoiakim's reign (according to the calendar system in which the new year begins in the spring).   46:2b Hebrew *Nebuchadrezzar,* a variant spelling of Nebuchadnezzar; also in 46:13, 26.

45 **A MESSAGE FOR BARUCH** The prophet Jeremiah gave a message to Baruch son of Neriah in the fourth year of the reign of Jehoiakim son of Josiah,* after Baruch had written down everything Jeremiah had dictated to him. He said, ²"This is what the LORD, the God of Israel, says to you, Baruch: ³You have said, 'I am overwhelmed with trouble! Haven't I had enough pain already? And now the LORD has added more! I am worn out from sighing and can find no rest.'

⁴"Baruch, this is what the LORD says: 'I will destroy this nation that I built. I will uproot what I planted. ⁵Are you seeking great things for yourself? Don't do it! I will bring great disaster upon all these people; but I will give you your life as a reward wherever you go. I, the LORD, have spoken!'"

46 **MESSAGES FOR THE NATIONS** The following messages were given to Jeremiah the prophet from the LORD concerning foreign nations.

MESSAGES ABOUT EGYPT ²This message concerning Egypt was given in the fourth year of the reign of Jehoiakim son of Josiah, the king of Judah, on the occasion of the battle of Carchemish* when Pharaoh Neco, king of Egypt, and his army were defeated beside the Euphrates River by King Nebuchadnezzar* of Babylon.

³ "Prepare your shields,
    and advance into battle!
⁴ Harness the horses,
    and mount the stallions.
Take your positions.
    Put on your helmets.
Sharpen your spears,
    and prepare your armor.
⁵ But what do I see?
    The Egyptian army flees in terror.
The bravest of its fighting men run
    without a backward glance.
They are terrorized at every turn,"
    says the LORD.
⁶ "The swiftest runners cannot flee;

ALL ABOUT GOD
(46:1-28) In this chapter, we gain several insights about God and his plan for this world. (1) Although God chose Israel for a special purpose, he loves all people and wants them to come to him. (2) God is holy and will not tolerate sin. (3) God's judgments are not based on prejudice and a desire for revenge, but on fairness and justice. (4) God does not delight in judgment, but in salvation. (5) God is impartial—he judges everyone by the same standard. How do these insights affect your view of God?

the mightiest warriors cannot escape.
By the Euphrates River to the north,
they stumble and fall.

7 "Who is this, rising like the Nile at
floodtime,
overflowing all the land?
8 It is the Egyptian army,
overflowing all the land,
boasting that it will cover the earth like
a flood,
destroying cities and their people.
9 Charge, you horses and chariots;
attack, you mighty warriors of Egypt!
Come, all you allies from Ethiopia, Libya,
and Lydia*
who are skilled with the shield and bow!
10 For this is the day of the Lord, the LORD of
Heaven's Armies,
a day of vengeance on his enemies.
The sword will devour until it is satisfied,
yes, until it is drunk with your blood!
The Lord, the LORD of Heaven's Armies, will
receive a sacrifice today
in the north country beside the Euphrates
River.

11 "Go up to Gilead to get medicine,
O virgin daughter of Egypt!
But your many treatments
will bring you no healing.
12 The nations have heard of your shame.
The earth is filled with your cries of
despair.
Your mightiest warriors will run into each
other
and fall down together."

13 Then the LORD gave the prophet Jeremiah
this message about King Nebuchadnezzar's
plans to attack Egypt.

14 "Shout it out in Egypt!
Publish it in the cities of Migdol,
Memphis,* and Tahpanhes!
Mobilize for battle,
for the sword will devour everyone
around you.
15 Why have your warriors fallen?
They cannot stand, for the LORD has
knocked them down.
16 They stumble and fall over each other
and say among themselves,
'Come, let's go back to our people,
to the land of our birth.
Let's get away from the sword of the
enemy!'
17 There they will say,

'Pharaoh, the king of Egypt, is a
loudmouth
who missed his opportunity!'

18 "As surely as I live," says the King,
whose name is the LORD of Heaven's
Armies,
"one is coming against Egypt
who is as tall as Mount Tabor,
or as Mount Carmel by the sea!
19 Pack up! Get ready to leave for exile,
you citizens of Egypt!
The city of Memphis will be destroyed,
without a single inhabitant.
20 Egypt is as sleek as a beautiful young cow,
but a horsefly from the north is on its way!
21 Egypt's mercenaries have become like
fattened calves.
They, too, will turn and run,
for it is a day of great disaster for Egypt,
a time of great punishment.
22 Egypt flees, silent as a serpent gliding away.
The invading army marches in;
they come against her with axes like
woodsmen.
23 They will cut down her people like trees,"
says the LORD,
"for they are more numerous than
locusts.
24 Egypt will be humiliated;
she will be handed over to people from
the north."

25 The LORD of Heaven's Armies, the God of
Israel, says: "I will punish Amon, the god of
Thebes,* and all the other gods of Egypt. I will
punish its rulers and Pharaoh, too, and all who
trust in him. 26 I will hand them over to those
who want them killed—to King Nebuchadnezzar of Babylon and his army. But afterward the
land will recover from the ravages of war. I, the
LORD, have spoken!

27 "But do not be afraid, Jacob, my servant;
do not be dismayed, Israel.
For I will bring you home again from distant
lands,
and your children will return from their
exile.
Israel* will return to a life of peace and
quiet,
and no one will terrorize them.
28 Do not be afraid, Jacob, my servant,
for I am with you," says the LORD.
"I will completely destroy the nations to
which I have exiled you,

46:9 Hebrew from Cush, Put, and Lud.   46:14 Hebrew Noph; also
in 46:19.   46:25 Hebrew of No.   46:27 Hebrew Jacob. See note
on 5:20.

but I will not completely destroy you.
I will discipline you, but with justice;
I cannot let you go unpunished."

47 A MESSAGE ABOUT PHILISTIA This is the LORD's message to the prophet Jeremiah concerning the Philistines of Gaza, before it was captured by the Egyptian army. ²This is what the LORD says:

"A flood is coming from the north
to overflow the land.
It will destroy the land and everything in it—
cities and people alike.
People will scream in terror,
and everyone in the land will wail.
³ Hear the clatter of stallions' hooves
and the rumble of wheels as the chariots
rush by.
Terrified fathers run madly,
without a backward glance at their
helpless children.

⁴ "The time has come for the Philistines to be
destroyed,
along with their allies from Tyre and
Sidon.
Yes, the LORD is destroying the remnant of
the Philistines,
those colonists from the island of Crete.*
⁵ Gaza will be humiliated, its head shaved
bald;
Ashkelon will lie silent.
You remnant from the Mediterranean
coast,*
how long will you lament and mourn?

⁶ "Now, O sword of the LORD,
when will you be at rest again?
Go back into your sheath;
rest and be still.

⁷ "But how can it be still
when the LORD has sent it on a mission?
For the city of Ashkelon
and the people living along the sea
must be destroyed."

48 A MESSAGE ABOUT MOAB This message was given concerning Moab. This is what the LORD of Heaven's Armies, the God of Israel, says:

"What sorrow awaits the city of Nebo;
it will soon lie in ruins.

The city of Kiriathaim will be humiliated and
captured;
the fortress will be humiliated and broken
down.
² No one will ever brag about Moab again,
for in Heshbon there is a plot to destroy
her.
'Come,' they say, 'we will cut her off from
being a nation.'
The town of Madmen,* too, will be
silenced;
the sword will follow you there.
³ Listen to the cries from Horonaim,
cries of devastation and great
destruction.
⁴ All Moab is destroyed.
Her little ones will cry out.*
⁵ Her refugees weep bitterly,
climbing the slope to Luhith.
They cry out in terror,
descending the slope to Horonaim.
⁶ Flee for your lives!
Hide* in the wilderness!
⁷ Because you have trusted in your wealth
and skill,
you will be taken captive.
Your god Chemosh, with his priests and
officials,
will be hauled off to distant lands!

⁸ "All the towns will be destroyed,
and no one will escape—
either on the plateaus or in the valleys,
for the LORD has spoken.
⁹ Oh, that Moab had wings
so she could fly away,*
for her towns will be left empty,
with no one living in them.
¹⁰ Cursed are those who refuse to do the
LORD's work,
who hold back their swords from
shedding blood!

¹¹ "From his earliest history, Moab has lived
in peace,
never going into exile.

47:4 Hebrew from Caphtor.   47:5 Hebrew the plain.   48:2 Madmen sounds like the Hebrew word for "silence"; it should not be confused with the English word madmen.   48:4 Greek version reads Her cries are heard as far away as Zoar.   48:6 Or Hide like a wild donkey; or Hide like a juniper shrub; or Be like [the town of] Aroer. The meaning of the Hebrew is uncertain.   48:9 Or Put salt on Moab, / for she will be laid waste.

DON'T PUSH IT
(48–49:38) God is loving, merciful, and kind. But he is also just. Eventually, he will judge and punish those who do wrong. Check out God's words in the prophecies of Jeremiah as he speaks to the Moabites who trusted in their military might (48:1-47), the Ammonites who trusted in their wealth (49:1-6), the Edomites who trusted in their wisdom and secure location (49:7-22), and others. Yet many times people think they can "push their luck" by ignoring God until they're ready to be serious about him. The warnings in Jeremiah are a chilling reminder of the folly of playing with God.

He is like wine that has been allowed to
  settle.
  He has not been poured from flask to
    flask,
  and he is now fragrant and smooth.
¹² But the time is coming soon," says the
  LORD,
  "when I will send men to pour him from
    his jar.
  They will pour him out,
    then shatter the jar!
¹³ At last Moab will be ashamed of his idol
  Chemosh,
  as the people of Israel were ashamed
    of their gold calf at Bethel.*

¹⁴ "You used to boast, 'We are heroes,
  mighty men of war.'
¹⁵ But now Moab and his towns will be
  destroyed.
  His most promising youth are doomed
    to slaughter,"
  says the King, whose name is the LORD
    of Heaven's Armies.
¹⁶ "Destruction is coming fast for Moab;
  calamity threatens ominously.
¹⁷ You friends of Moab,
  weep for him and cry!
  See how the strong scepter is broken,
  how the beautiful staff is shattered!

¹⁸ "Come down from your glory
  and sit in the dust, you people of Dibon,
  for those who destroy Moab will shatter
    Dibon, too.
  They will tear down all your towers.
¹⁹ You people of Aroer,
  stand beside the road and watch.
  Shout to those who flee from Moab,
  'What has happened there?'

²⁰ "And the reply comes back,
  'Moab lies in ruins, disgraced;
    weep and wail!
  Tell it by the banks of the Arnon River:
  Moab has been destroyed!'
²¹ Judgment has been poured out on the
    towns of the plateau—
  on Holon and Jahaz* and Mephaath,
²² on Dibon and Nebo and Beth-diblathaim,
²³   on Kiriathaim and Beth-gamul and
    Beth-meon,
²⁴ on Kerioth and Bozrah—
  all the towns of Moab, far and near.

²⁵ "The strength of Moab has ended.
  His arm has been broken," says the LORD.
²⁶ "Let him stagger and fall like a drunkard,
  for he has rebelled against the LORD.

Moab will wallow in his own vomit,
  ridiculed by all.
²⁷ Did you not ridicule the people of Israel?
  Were they caught in the company of
    thieves
  that you should despise them as you do?

²⁸ "You people of Moab,
  flee from your towns and live in the caves.
  Hide like doves that nest
  in the clefts of the rocks.
²⁹ We have all heard of the pride of Moab,
  for his pride is very great.
  We know of his lofty pride,
  his arrogance, and his haughty heart.
³⁰ I know about his insolence,"
  says the LORD,
  "but his boasts are empty—
  as empty as his deeds.
³¹ So now I wail for Moab;
  yes, I will mourn for Moab.
  My heart is broken for the men of
    Kir-hareseth.*

³² "You people of Sibmah, rich in vineyards,
  I will weep for you even more than I did
    for Jazer.
  Your spreading vines once reached as far as
    the Dead Sea,*
  but the destroyer has stripped you bare!
  He has harvested your grapes and
    summer fruits.
³³ Joy and gladness are gone from fruitful
    Moab.
  The presses yield no wine.
  No one treads the grapes with shouts
    of joy.
  There is shouting, yes, but not of joy.

³⁴"Instead, their awful cries of terror can be
heard from Heshbon clear across to Elealeh
and Jahaz; from Zoar all the way to Horonaim
and Eglath-shelishiyah. Even the waters of
Nimrim are dried up now.

³⁵"I will put an end to Moab," says the LORD,
"for the people offer sacrifices at the pagan
shrines and burn incense to their false gods.
³⁶My heart moans like a flute for Moab and
Kir-hareseth, for all their wealth has disappeared. ³⁷The people shave their heads and
beards in mourning. They slash their hands
and put on clothes made of burlap. ³⁸There is
crying and sorrow in every Moabite home and
on every street. For I have smashed Moab like
an old, unwanted jar. ³⁹How it is shattered!

48:13 Hebrew *ashamed when they trusted in Bethel.*   48:21 Hebrew
Jahzah, a variant spelling of Jahaz.   48:31 Hebrew *Kir-heres,* a
variant spelling of Kir-hareseth; also in 48:36.   48:32 Hebrew *the
sea of Jazer.*

Hear the wailing! See the shame of Moab! It has become an object of ridicule, an example of ruin to all its neighbors."

⁴⁰This is what the LORD says:

"Look! The enemy swoops down like an
    eagle,
    spreading his wings over Moab.
⁴¹ Its cities will fall,
    and its strongholds will be seized.
Even the mightiest warriors will be in
    anguish
    like a woman in labor.
⁴² Moab will no longer be a nation,
    for it has boasted against the LORD.

⁴³ "Terror and traps and snares will be your lot,
    O Moab," says the LORD.
⁴⁴ "Those who flee in terror will fall into a trap,
    and those who escape the trap will step
        into a snare.
I will see to it that you do not get away,
    for the time of your judgment has come,"
    says the LORD.
⁴⁵ "The people flee as far as Heshbon
    but are unable to go on.
For a fire comes from Heshbon,
    King Sihon's ancient home,
to devour the entire land
    with all its rebellious people.

⁴⁶ "O Moab, they weep for you!
    The people of the god Chemosh are
        destroyed!
Your sons and your daughters
    have been taken away as captives.
⁴⁷ But I will restore the fortunes of Moab
    in days to come.
    I, the LORD, have spoken!"

This is the end of Jeremiah's prophecy concerning Moab.

49 **A MESSAGE ABOUT AMMON** This message was given concerning the Ammonites. This is what the LORD says:

"Are there no descendants of Israel
    to inherit the land of Gad?
Why are you, who worship Molech,*
    living in its towns?
² In the days to come," says the LORD,
    "I will sound the battle cry against your
        city of Rabbah.
It will become a desolate heap of ruins,
    and the neighboring towns will be
        burned.

49:1 Hebrew *Malcam,* a variant spelling of Molech; also in 49:3.
49:8 Hebrew *Esau;* also in 49:10.

Then Israel will take back the land
    you took from her," says the LORD.

³ "Cry out, O Heshbon,
    for the town of Ai is destroyed.
Weep, O people of Rabbah!
    Put on your clothes of mourning.
Weep and wail, hiding in the hedges,
    for your god Molech, with his priests and
        officials,
    will be hauled off to distant lands.
⁴ You are proud of your fertile valleys,
    but they will soon be ruined.
You trusted in your wealth,
    you rebellious daughter,
    and thought no one could ever harm you.
⁵ But look! I will bring terror upon you,"
    says the Lord, the LORD of Heaven's
        Armies.
"Your neighbors will chase you from your
    land,
    and no one will help your exiles as they
        flee.
⁶ But I will restore the fortunes of the
    Ammonites
    in days to come.
    I, the LORD, have spoken."

MESSAGES ABOUT EDOM ⁷This message was given concerning Edom. This is what the LORD of Heaven's Armies says:

"Is there no wisdom in Teman?
    Is no one left to give wise counsel?
⁸ Turn and flee!
    Hide in deep caves, you people of Dedan!
For when I bring disaster on Edom,*
    I will punish you, too!
⁹ Those who harvest grapes
    always leave a few for the poor.
If thieves came at night,
    they would not take everything.
¹⁰ But I will strip bare the land of Edom,
    and there will be no place left to hide.
Its children, its brothers, and its neighbors
    will all be destroyed,
    and Edom itself will be no more.
¹¹ But I will protect the orphans who remain
    among you.
    Your widows, too, can depend on me for
        help."

¹²And this is what the LORD says: "If the innocent must suffer, how much more must you! You will not go unpunished! You must drink this cup of judgment! ¹³For I have sworn by my own name," says the LORD, "that Bozrah will become an object of horror and a heap

of ruins; it will be mocked and cursed. All its towns and villages will be desolate forever."

14 I have heard a message from the LORD
  that an ambassador was sent to the
    nations to say,
  "Form a coalition against Edom,
    and prepare for battle!"

15 The LORD says to Edom,
  "I will cut you down to size among the
    nations.
  You will be despised by all.
16 You have been deceived
    by the fear you inspire in others
    and by your own pride.
  You live in a rock fortress
    and control the mountain heights.
  But even if you make your nest among the
    peaks with the eagles,
    I will bring you crashing down,"
    says the LORD.

17 "Edom will be an object of horror.
  All who pass by will be appalled
    and will gasp at the destruction they see
    there.
18 It will be like the destruction of Sodom and
    Gomorrah
  and their neighboring towns," says the
    LORD.
  "No one will live there;
    no one will inhabit it.
19 I will come like a lion from the thickets
    of the Jordan,
  leaping on the sheep in the pasture.
  I will chase Edom from its land,
    and I will appoint the leader of
    my choice.
  For who is like me, and who can
    challenge me?
    What ruler can oppose my will?"

20 Listen to the LORD's plans against Edom
    and the people of Teman.
  Even the little children will be dragged off
    like sheep,
    and their homes will be destroyed.
21 The earth will shake with the noise of
    Edom's fall,

and its cry of despair will be heard all the
    way to the Red Sea.*
22 Look! The enemy swoops down like an
    eagle,
  spreading his wings over Bozrah.
  Even the mightiest warriors will be in
    anguish
    like a woman in labor.

A MESSAGE ABOUT DAMASCUS 23This message was given concerning Damascus. This is what the LORD says:

  "The towns of Hamath and Arpad are struck
    with fear,
  for they have heard the news of their
    destruction.
  Their hearts are troubled
    like a wild sea in a raging storm.
24 Damascus has become feeble,
    and all her people turn to flee.
  Fear, anguish, and pain have gripped her
    as they grip a woman in labor.
25 That famous city, a city of joy,
    will be forsaken!
26 Her young men will fall in the streets
    and die.
  Her soldiers will all be killed,"
    says the LORD of Heaven's Armies.
27 "And I will set fire to the walls of Damascus
    that will burn up the palaces of
    Ben-hadad."

A MESSAGE ABOUT KEDAR AND HAZOR 28This message was given concerning Kedar and the kingdoms of Hazor, which were attacked by King Nebuchadnezzar* of Babylon. This is what the LORD says:

  "Advance against Kedar!
    Destroy the warriors from the East!
29 Their flocks and tents will be captured,
    and their household goods and camels
    will be taken away.
  Everywhere shouts of panic will be heard:
    'We are terrorized at every turn!'
30 Run for your lives," says the LORD.
    "Hide yourselves in deep caves, you
    people of Hazor,
  for King Nebuchadnezzar of Babylon has
    plotted against you
    and is preparing to destroy you.

31 "Go up and attack that complacent nation,"
    says the LORD.
  "Its people live alone in the desert
    without walls or gates.

SELF-CENTERED
(49:16) Edom was destroyed because of its pride. Pride can destroy individuals, relationships, churches, and nations. It makes us think we can take care of ourselves without God's help. Even serving God and others can lead us into pride. Why do you follow Christ? Why do you serve others? Check your motives. Ask God to point out and remove any self-centeredness.

49:21 Hebrew *sea of reeds.*   **49:28** Hebrew *Nebuchadrezzar,* a variant spelling of Nebuchadnezzar; also in 49:30.

32 Their camels and other livestock will all be
　　yours.
　　I will scatter to the winds these people
　　　who live in remote places.*
　I will bring calamity upon them
　　from every direction," says the Lord.
33 "Hazor will be inhabited by jackals,
　　and it will be desolate forever.
　No one will live there;
　　no one will inhabit it."

A MESSAGE ABOUT ELAM

34This message concerning Elam came to the prophet Jeremiah from the Lord at the beginning of the reign of King Zedekiah of Judah. 35This is what the Lord of Heaven's Armies says:

"I will destroy the archers of Elam—
　　the best of their forces.
36 I will bring enemies from all directions,
　　and I will scatter the people of Elam to the
　　　four winds.
　They will be exiled to countries around
　　the world.
37 I myself will go with Elam's enemies to
　　shatter it.
　In my fierce anger, I will bring great
　　disaster
　upon the people of Elam," says the Lord.
"Their enemies will chase them with the
　　sword
　until I have destroyed them completely.
38 I will set my throne in Elam," says the Lord,
　　"and I will destroy its king and officials.
39 But I will restore the fortunes of Elam
　　in days to come.
　I, the Lord, have spoken!"

50 A MESSAGE ABOUT BABYLON

The Lord gave Jeremiah the prophet this message concerning Babylon and the land of the Babylonians.* 2This is what the Lord says:

"Tell the whole world,
　　and keep nothing back.
　Raise a signal flag
　　to tell everyone that Babylon will fall!
　Her images and idols* will be shattered.
　　Her gods Bel and Marduk will be utterly
　　　disgraced.
3 For a nation will attack her from the north
　　and bring such destruction that no one
　　　will live there again.
　Everything will be gone;
　　both people and animals will flee.

HOPE FOR ISRAEL AND JUDAH

4 "In those coming days,"
　　says the Lord,
　"the people of Israel will return home
　　together with the people of Judah.
　They will come weeping
　　and seeking the Lord their God.
5 They will ask the way to Jerusalem*
　　and will start back home again.
　They will bind themselves to the Lord
　　with an eternal covenant that will never
　　　be forgotten.

6 "My people have been lost sheep.
　　Their shepherds have led them astray
　　and turned them loose in the mountains.
　They have lost their way
　　and can't remember how to get back to
　　　the sheepfold.
7 All who found them devoured them.
　　Their enemies said,
　'We did nothing wrong in attacking them,
　　for they sinned against the Lord,
　their true place of rest,
　　and the hope of their ancestors.'

8 "But now, flee from Babylon!
　　Leave the land of the Babylonians.
　Like male goats at the head of the flock,
　　lead my people home again.
9 For I am raising up an army
　　of great nations from the north.
　They will join forces to attack Babylon,
　　and she will be captured.
　The enemies' arrows will go straight to the
　　　mark;
　　they will not miss!
10 Babylonia* will be looted
　　until the attackers are glutted with loot.
　I, the Lord, have spoken!

BABYLON'S SURE FALL

11 "You rejoice and are glad,
　　you who plundered my chosen people.
　You frisk about like a calf in a meadow
　　and neigh like a stallion.
12 But your homeland* will be overwhelmed
　　with shame and disgrace.

．．．

A POWERFUL PAWN
(50:1-3) Babylon is another name for the nation of the Chaldeans. At the height of its power, this empire seemed unbeatable. Yet this powerful nation was just a pawn. When Babylon had finished serving God's purpose of punishing Judah for her sins, it would be punished and crushed for its own. Babylon was destroyed in 539 B.C. by the Medo-Persians (see Dan 5). Only God has real, lasting power.

49:32 Or who clip the corners of their hair.　50:1 Or Chaldeans; also in 50:8, 25, 35, 45.　50:2 The Hebrew term (literally round things) probably alludes to dung.　50:5 Hebrew Zion; also in 50:28.
50:10 Or Chaldea.　50:12 Hebrew your mother.

You will become the least of nations—
  a wilderness, a dry and desolate land.
¹³ Because of the LORD's anger,
  Babylon will become a deserted
    wasteland.
All who pass by will be horrified
  and will gasp at the destruction they see
    there.

¹⁴ "Yes, prepare to attack Babylon,
  all you surrounding nations.
Let your archers shoot at her; spare no
    arrows.
  For she has sinned against the LORD.
¹⁵ Shout war cries against her from every side.
  Look! She surrenders!
  Her walls have fallen.
It is the LORD's vengeance,
  so take vengeance on her.
  Do to her as she has done to others!
¹⁶ Take from Babylon all those who plant
    crops;
  send all the harvesters away.
Because of the sword of the enemy,
  everyone will run away and rush back to
    their own lands.

HOPE FOR GOD'S PEOPLE

¹⁷ "The Israelites are like sheep
  that have been scattered by lions.
First the king of Assyria ate them up.
  Then King Nebuchadnezzar* of Babylon
    cracked their bones."
¹⁸ Therefore, this is what the LORD of Heaven's
    Armies,
  the God of Israel, says:
"Now I will punish the king of Babylon and
    his land,
  just as I punished the king of Assyria.
¹⁹ And I will bring Israel home again to its own
    land,
  to feed in the fields of Carmel and
    Bashan,
and to be satisfied once more
  in the hill country of Ephraim and Gilead.
²⁰ In those days," says the LORD,
  "no sin will be found in Israel or in Judah,
  for I will forgive the remnant I preserve.

THE LORD'S JUDGMENT ON BABYLON

²¹ "Go up, my warriors, against the land of
    Merathaim
  and against the people of Pekod.
Pursue, kill, and completely destroy* them,
  as I have commanded you," says the
    LORD.
²² "Let the battle cry be heard in the land,
  a shout of great destruction.

²³ Babylon, the mightiest hammer in all the
    earth,
  lies broken and shattered.
  Babylon is desolate among the nations!
²⁴ Listen, Babylon, for I have set a trap for you.
  You are caught, for you have fought
    against the LORD.
²⁵ The LORD has opened his armory
  and brought out weapons to vent his fury.
The terror that falls upon the Babylonians
  will be the work of the Sovereign LORD of
    Heaven's Armies.
²⁶ Yes, come against her from distant lands.
  Break open her granaries.
Crush her walls and houses into heaps of
    rubble.
  Destroy her completely, and leave
    nothing!
²⁷ Destroy even her young bulls—
  it will be terrible for them, too!
Slaughter them all!
  For Babylon's day of reckoning has come.
²⁸ Listen to the people who have escaped from
    Babylon,
  as they tell in Jerusalem
how the LORD our God has taken vengeance
  against those who destroyed his Temple.

²⁹ "Send out a call for archers to come to
    Babylon.
  Surround the city so none can escape.
Do to her as she has done to others,
  for she has defied the LORD, the Holy One
    of Israel.
³⁰ Her young men will fall in the streets and
    die.
  Her soldiers will all be killed,"
    says the LORD.

³¹ "See, I am your enemy, you arrogant
    people,"
  says the Lord, the LORD of Heaven's
    Armies.
"Your day of reckoning has arrived—
  the day when I will punish you.
³² O land of arrogance, you will stumble and
    fall,
  and no one will raise you up.
For I will light a fire in the cities of Babylon
  that will burn up everything around them."

³³ This is what the LORD of Heaven's Armies
    says:
"The people of Israel and Judah have been
    wronged.

50:17 Hebrew *Nebuchadrezzar,* a variant spelling of
Nebuchadnezzar.   **50:21** The Hebrew term used here refers to
the complete consecration of things or people to the LORD, either
by destroying them or by giving them as an offering.

Their captors hold them and refuse to let
them go.
³⁴ But the one who redeems them is strong.
His name is the LORD of Heaven's Armies.
He will defend them
and give them rest again in Israel.
But for the people of Babylon
there will be no rest!

³⁵ "The sword of destruction will strike the
Babylonians,"
says the LORD.
"It will strike the people of Babylon—
her officials and wise men, too.
³⁶ The sword will strike her wise counselors,
and they will become fools.
The sword will strike her mightiest warriors,
and panic will seize them.
³⁷ The sword will strike her horses and chariots
and her allies from other lands,
and they will all become like women.
The sword will strike her treasures,
and they all will be plundered.
³⁸ The sword will even strike her water supply,
causing it to dry up.
And why? Because the whole land is filled
with idols,
and the people are madly in love with
them.

³⁹ "Soon Babylon will be inhabited by desert
animals and hyenas.
It will be a home for owls.
Never again will people live there;
it will lie desolate forever.
⁴⁰ I will destroy it as I* destroyed Sodom and
Gomorrah
and their neighboring towns," says the
LORD.
"No one will live there;
no one will inhabit it.

⁴¹ "Look! A great army is coming from the
north.
A great nation and many kings
are rising against you from far-off lands.
⁴² They are armed with bows and spears.
They are cruel and show no mercy.
As they ride forward on horses,
they sound like a roaring sea.
They are coming in battle formation,
planning to destroy you, Babylon.
⁴³ The king of Babylon has heard reports about
the enemy,
and he is weak with fright.

Pangs of anguish have gripped him,
like those of a woman in labor.
⁴⁴ "I will come like a lion from the thickets
of the Jordan,
leaping on the sheep in the pasture.
I will chase Babylon from its land,
and I will appoint the leader of my choice.
For who is like me, and who can
challenge me?
What ruler can oppose my will?"

⁴⁵ Listen to the LORD's plans against Babylon
and the land of the Babylonians.
Even the little children will be dragged off
like sheep,
and their homes will be destroyed.
⁴⁶ The earth will shake with the shout,
"Babylon has been taken!"
and its cry of despair will be heard around
the world.

51

¹This is what the LORD says:
"I will stir up a destroyer against
Babylon
and the people of Babylonia.*
² Foreigners will come and winnow her,
blowing her away as chaff.
They will come from every side
to rise against her in her day of trouble.
³ Don't let the archers put on their armor
or draw their bows.
Don't spare even her best soldiers!
Let her army be completely destroyed.*
⁴ They will fall dead in the land of the
Babylonians,*
slashed to death in her streets.
⁵ For the LORD of Heaven's Armies
has not abandoned Israel and Judah.
He is still their God,
even though their land was filled with sin
against the Holy One of Israel."

⁶ Flee from Babylon! Save yourselves!
Don't get trapped in her punishment!
It is the LORD's time for vengeance;
he will repay her in full.
⁷ Babylon has been a gold cup in the LORD's
hands,
a cup that made the whole earth drunk.

50:40 Hebrew as God. 51:1 Hebrew of Leb-kamai, a code name for Babylonia. 51:3 The Hebrew term used here refers to the complete consecration of things or people to the LORD, either by destroying them or by giving them as an offering. 51:4 Or Chaldeans; also in 51:54.

· ·

BLOWN AWAY
(51:2) Winnowers worked to separate the wheat from the chaff. When they threw the mixture into the air, the wind would blow away the worthless chaff while the wheat would settle to the ground. Babylon would be blown away like chaff in the wind. (See also Matthew 3:12 where John the Baptist says that Jesus will separate the wheat from the chaff.) Is there chaff in your life?

The nations drank Babylon's wine,
and it drove them all mad.
⁸ But suddenly Babylon, too, has fallen.
Weep for her.
Give her medicine.
Perhaps she can yet be healed.
⁹ We would have helped her if we could,
but nothing can save her now.
Let her go; abandon her.
Return now to your own land.
For her punishment reaches to the heavens;
it is so great it cannot be measured.
¹⁰ The LORD has vindicated us.
Come, let us announce in Jerusalem*
everything the LORD our God has done.

¹¹ Sharpen the arrows!
Lift up the shields!*
For the LORD has inspired the kings of the
Medes
to march against Babylon and destroy
her.
This is his vengeance against those
who desecrated his Temple.
¹² Raise the battle flag against Babylon!
Reinforce the guard and station the
watchmen.
Prepare an ambush,
for the LORD will fulfill all his plans
against Babylon.
¹³ You are a city by a great river,
a great center of commerce,
but your end has come.
The thread of your life is cut.
¹⁴ The LORD of Heaven's Armies has taken
this vow
and has sworn to it by his own name:
"Your cities will be filled with enemies,
like fields swarming with locusts,
and they will shout in triumph over you."

A HYMN OF PRAISE TO THE LORD

¹⁵ The LORD made the earth by his power,
and he preserves it by his wisdom.
With his own understanding
he stretched out the heavens.
¹⁶ When he speaks in the thunder,
the heavens are filled with water.
He causes the clouds to rise over the earth.
He sends the lightning with the rain
and releases the wind from his
storehouses.

¹⁷ The whole human race is foolish and has
no knowledge!
The craftsmen are disgraced by the idols
they make,
for their carefully shaped works are a fraud.

These idols have no breath or power.
¹⁸ Idols are worthless; they are ridiculous lies!
On the day of reckoning they will all be
destroyed.
¹⁹ But the God of Israel* is no idol!
He is the Creator of everything that exists,
including his people, his own special
possession.
The LORD of Heaven's Armies is his name!

BABYLON'S GREAT PUNISHMENT

²⁰ "You* are my battle-ax and sword,"
says the LORD.
"With you I will shatter nations
and destroy many kingdoms.
²¹ With you I will shatter armies—
destroying the horse and rider,
the chariot and charioteer.
²² With you I will shatter men and women,
old people and children,
young men and maidens.
²³ With you I will shatter shepherds and flocks,
farmers and oxen,
captains and officers.

²⁴ "I will repay Babylon
and the people of Babylonia*
for all the wrong they have done
to my people in Jerusalem," says the
LORD.

²⁵ "Look, O mighty mountain, destroyer of the
earth!
I am your enemy," says the LORD.
"I will raise my fist against you,
to knock you down from the heights.
When I am finished,
you will be nothing but a heap of burnt
rubble.
²⁶ You will be desolate forever.
Even your stones will never again be used
for building.
You will be completely wiped out,"
says the LORD.

²⁷ Raise a signal flag to the nations.
Sound the battle cry!
Mobilize them all against Babylon.
Prepare them to fight against her!
Bring out the armies of Ararat, Minni, and
Ashkenaz.
Appoint a commander,
and bring a multitude of horses like
swarming locusts!
²⁸ Bring against her the armies of the
nations—

51:10 Hebrew *Zion;* also in 51:24.   **51:11** Greek version reads *Fill up
the quivers.*   **51:19** Hebrew *the Portion of Jacob.* See note on 5:20.
51:20 Possibly Cyrus, whom God used to conquer Babylon.
Compare Isa 44:28; 45:1.   **51:24** Or *Chaldea;* also in 51:35.

led by the kings of the Medes
and all their captains and officers.

²⁹ The earth trembles and writhes in pain,
for everything the LORD has planned
against Babylon stands unchanged.
Babylon will be left desolate without a
single inhabitant.
³⁰ Her mightiest warriors no longer fight.
They stay in their barracks, their courage
gone.
They have become like women.
The invaders have burned the houses
and broken down the city gates.
³¹ The news is passed from one runner to the
next
as the messengers hurry to tell the king
that his city has been captured.
³² All the escape routes are blocked.
The marshes have been set aflame,
and the army is in a panic.

³³ This is what the LORD of Heaven's Armies,
the God of Israel, says:
"Babylon is like wheat on a threshing floor,
about to be trampled.
In just a little while
her harvest will begin."

³⁴ "King Nebuchadnezzar* of Babylon has
eaten and crushed us
and drained us of strength.
He has swallowed us like a great monster
and filled his belly with our riches.
He has thrown us out of our own country.
³⁵ Make Babylon suffer as she made us
suffer,"
say the people of Zion.
"Make the people of Babylonia pay for
spilling our blood,"
says Jerusalem.

THE LORD'S VENGEANCE ON BABYLON

³⁶This
is what the LORD says to Jerusalem:

"I will be your lawyer to plead your case,
and I will avenge you.
I will dry up her river,
as well as her springs,
³⁷ and Babylon will become a heap of ruins,
haunted by jackals.
She will be an object of horror and
contempt,
a place where no one lives.
³⁸ Her people will roar together like strong
lions.

They will growl like lion cubs.
³⁹ And while they lie inflamed with all their
wine,
I will prepare a different kind of feast for
them.
I will make them drink until they fall asleep,
and they will never wake up again,"
says the LORD.
⁴⁰ "I will bring them down
like lambs to the slaughter,
like rams and goats to be sacrificed.

⁴¹ "How Babylon* is fallen—
great Babylon, praised throughout the
earth!
Now she has become an object of horror
among the nations.
⁴² The sea has risen over Babylon;
she is covered by its crashing waves.
⁴³ Her cities now lie in ruins;
she is a dry wasteland
where no one lives or even passes by.
⁴⁴ And I will punish Bel, the god of Babylon,
and make him vomit up all he has eaten.
The nations will no longer come and
worship him.
The wall of Babylon has fallen!

A MESSAGE FOR THE EXILES

⁴⁵ "Come out, my people, flee from Babylon.
Save yourselves! Run from the LORD's
fierce anger.
⁴⁶ But do not panic; don't be afraid
when you hear the first rumor of
approaching forces.
For rumors will keep coming year by year.
Violence will erupt in the land
as the leaders fight against each other.
⁴⁷ For the time is surely coming
when I will punish this great city and all
her idols.
Her whole land will be disgraced,
and her dead will lie in the streets.
⁴⁸ Then the heavens and earth will rejoice,
for out of the north will come destroying
armies
against Babylon," says the LORD.
⁴⁹ "Just as Babylon killed the people of Israel
and others throughout the world,
so must her people be killed.
⁵⁰ Get out, all you who have escaped the
sword!
Do not stand and watch—flee while you
can!
Remember the LORD, though you are in a
far-off land,
and think about your home in Jerusalem."

51:34 Hebrew *Nebuchadrezzar*, a variant spelling of
Nebuchadnezzar.   51:41 Hebrew *Sheshach*, a code name for
Babylon.

51 "We are ashamed," the people say.
   "We are insulted and disgraced
because the LORD's Temple
   has been defiled by foreigners."

52 "Yes," says the LORD, "but the time is
   coming
when I will destroy Babylon's idols.
The groans of her wounded people
   will be heard throughout the land.

53 Though Babylon reaches as high as the
   heavens
   and makes her fortifications incredibly
   strong,
I will still send enemies to plunder her.
   I, the LORD, have spoken!

BABYLON'S COMPLETE DESTRUCTION

54 "Listen! Hear the cry of Babylon,
   the sound of great destruction from the
   land of the Babylonians.

55 For the LORD is destroying Babylon.
   He will silence her loud voice.
Waves of enemies pound against her;
   the noise of battle rings through the city.

56 Destroying armies come against Babylon.
   Her mighty men are captured,
   and their weapons break in their hands.
For the LORD is a God who gives just
   punishment;
   he always repays in full.

57 I will make her officials and wise men drunk,
   along with her captains, officers, and
   warriors.
They will fall asleep
   and never wake up again!"
says the King, whose name is
   the LORD of Heaven's Armies.

58 This is what the LORD of Heaven's Armies
   says:
   "The thick walls of Babylon will be leveled to
   the ground,
   and her massive gates will be burned.
The builders from many lands have worked
   in vain,
   for their work will be destroyed by fire!"

JEREMIAH'S MESSAGE SENT TO BABYLON

59 The prophet Jeremiah gave this message to
Seraiah son of Neriah and grandson of Mahseiah, a staff officer, when Seraiah went to
Babylon with King Zedekiah of Judah. This was
during the fourth year of Zedekiah's reign.* 60Jeremiah had recorded on a scroll all the
terrible disasters that would soon come upon
Babylon—all the words written here. 61He said
to Seraiah, "When you get to Babylon, read
aloud everything on this scroll. 62Then say,
'LORD, you have said that you will destroy Babylon so that neither people nor animals will remain here. She will lie empty and abandoned
forever.' 63When you have finished reading the
scroll, tie it to a stone and throw it into the Euphrates River. 64Then say, 'In this same way
Babylon and her people will sink, never again
to rise, because of the disasters I will bring
upon her.'"

This is the end of Jeremiah's messages.

52 THE FALL OF JERUSALEM Zedekiah
was twenty-one years old when he became king, and he reigned in Jerusalem eleven
years. His mother was Hamutal, the daughter
of Jeremiah from Libnah. 2But Zedekiah did
what was evil in the LORD's sight, just as Jehoiakim had done. 3These things happened because of the LORD's anger against the people
of Jerusalem and Judah, until he finally banished them from his presence and sent them
into exile.

Zedekiah rebelled against the king of Babylon. 4So on January 15,* during the ninth year
of Zedekiah's reign, King Nebuchadnezzar* of
Babylon led his entire army against Jerusalem.
They surrounded the city and built siege ramps
against its walls. 5Jerusalem was kept under
siege until the eleventh year of King Zedekiah's reign.

6By July 18 in the eleventh year of Zedekiah's
reign,* the famine in the city had become very
severe, and the last of the food was entirely
gone. 7Then a section of the city wall was broken down, and all the soldiers fled. Since the
city was surrounded by the Babylonians,* they
waited for nightfall. Then they slipped through
the gate between the two walls behind the
king's garden and headed toward the Jordan
Valley.*

....

51:59 The fourth year of Zedekiah's reign was 593 B.C.
52:4a Hebrew *on the tenth day of the tenth month*, of the ancient
Hebrew lunar calendar. A number of events in Jeremiah can be
cross-checked with dates in surviving Babylonian records and
related accurately to our modern calendar. This day was January 15,
588 B.C.   52:4b Hebrew *Nebuchadrezzar*, a variant spelling of
Nebuchadnezzar; also in 52:12, 28, 29, 30.   52:6 Hebrew *By the
ninth day of the fourth month* [in the eleventh year of Zedekiah's
reign]. This day was July 18, 586 B.C.; also see note on 52:4a.
52:7a Or *the Chaldeans*; similarly in 52:8, 17.   52:7b Hebrew *the
Arabah*.

JUDGMENT

*(51:60-64) In Jeremiah's last message, we find again the
twin themes of God's sovereignty and his judgment. Babylon had been allowed to torment the people of Israel, but
here God says that Babylon itself will be judged. Although
God brings good out of evil, he doesn't allow evil to
remain unpunished (see Ps 37 also).*

⁸But the Babylonian troops chased King Zedekiah and caught him on the plains of Jericho, for his men had all deserted him and scattered. ⁹They took him to the king of Babylon at Riblah in the land of Hamath. There the king of Babylon pronounced judgment upon Zedekiah. ¹⁰He made Zedekiah watch as they slaughtered his sons and all the other officials of Judah. ¹¹Then they gouged out Zedekiah's eyes, bound him in bronze chains, and led him away to Babylon. Zedekiah remained there in prison until the day of his death.

THE TEMPLE DESTROYED ¹²On August 17 of that year,* which was the nineteenth year of King Nebuchadnezzar's reign, Nebuzaradan, the captain of the guard and an official of the Babylonian king, arrived in Jerusalem. ¹³He burned down the Temple of the LORD, the royal palace, and all the houses of Jerusalem. He destroyed all the important buildings* in the city. ¹⁴Then he supervised the entire Babylonian* army as they tore down the walls of Jerusalem on every side. ¹⁵Nebuzaradan, the captain of the guard, then took as exiles some of the poorest of the people, the rest of the people who remained in the city, the defectors who had declared their allegiance to the king of Babylon, and the rest of the craftsmen. ¹⁶But Nebuzaradan allowed some of the poorest people to stay behind in Judah to care for the vineyards and fields.

¹⁷The Babylonians broke up the bronze pillars in front of the LORD's Temple, the bronze water carts, and the great bronze basin called the Sea, and they carried all the bronze away to Babylon. ¹⁸They also took all the ash buckets, shovels, lamp snuffers, basins, dishes, and all the other bronze articles used for making sacrifices at the Temple. ¹⁹Nebuzaradan, the captain of the guard, also took the small bowls, incense burners, basins, pots, lampstands, dishes, bowls used for liquid offerings, and all the other articles made of pure gold or silver.

²⁰The weight of the bronze from the two pillars, the Sea with the twelve bronze oxen beneath it, and the water carts was too great to be measured. These things had been made for the LORD's Temple in the days of King Solomon. ²¹Each of the pillars was 27 feet tall and 18 feet in circumference.* They were hollow, with walls 3 inches thick.* ²²The bronze capital on top of each pillar was 7½ feet* high and was decorated with a network of bronze pomegranates all the way around. ²³There were 96 pomegranates on the sides, and a total of 100 on the network around the top.

²⁴Nebuzaradan, the captain of the guard, took with him as prisoners Seraiah the high priest, Zephaniah the priest of the second rank, and the three chief gatekeepers. ²⁵And from among the people still hiding in the city, he took an officer who had been in charge of the Judean army; seven of the king's personal advisers; the army commander's chief secretary, who was in charge of recruitment; and sixty other citizens. ²⁶Nebuzaradan, the captain of the guard, took them all to the king of Babylon at Riblah. ²⁷And there at Riblah, in the land of Hamath, the king of Babylon had them all put to death. So the people of Judah were sent into exile from their land.

²⁸The number of captives taken to Babylon in the seventh year of Nebuchadnezzar's reign* was 3,023. ²⁹Then in Nebuchadnezzar's eighteenth year* he took 832 more. ³⁰In Nebuchadnezzar's twenty-third year* he sent Nebuzaradan, the captain of the guard, who took 745 more—a total of 4,600 captives in all.

HOPE FOR ISRAEL'S ROYAL LINE ³¹In the thirty-seventh year of the exile of King Jehoiachin of Judah, Evil-merodach ascended to the Babylonian throne. He was kind to* Jehoiachin and released him from prison on March 31 of that year.* ³²He spoke kindly to Jehoiachin and gave him a higher place than all the other exiled kings in Babylon. ³³He supplied Jehoiachin with new clothes to replace his prison garb and allowed him to dine in the king's presence for the rest of his life. ³⁴So the Babylonian king gave him a regular food allowance as long as he lived. This continued until the day of his death.

....

GOD'S VIEW OF SUCCESS
(52:34) In the world's eyes, Jeremiah looked like a total failure. He had no money, family, or friends. For over 40 years, he prophesied about the destruction of the nation, the capital city, and the Temple, but the political and religious leaders neither accepted nor followed his advice. The people of Judah ignored him, too. Yet to God, Jeremiah was a huge success. God measures our success with the yardsticks of obedience, faithfulness, and righteousness. If you are faithfully doing the work God gives you, you are successful in his eyes.

52:12 Hebrew *On the tenth day of the fifth month,* of the ancient Hebrew lunar calendar. This day was August 17, 586 B.C.; also see note on 52:4a. 52:13 Or *destroyed the houses of all the important people.* 52:14 Or *Chaldean.* 52:21a Hebrew *18 cubits* [8.1 meters] *tall and 12 cubits* [5.4 meters] *in circumference.* 52:21b Hebrew *4 fingers thick* [8 centimeters]. 52:22 Hebrew *5 cubits* [2.3 meters]. 52:28 This exile in the seventh year of Nebuchadnezzar's reign occurred in 597 B.C. 52:29 This exile in the eighteenth year of Nebuchadnezzar's reign occurred in 586 B.C. 52:30 This exile in the twenty-third year of Nebuchadnezzar's reign occurred in 581 B.C. 52:31a Hebrew *He raised the head of.* 52:31b Hebrew *on the twenty-fifth day of the twelfth month,* of the ancient Hebrew lunar calendar. This day was March 31, 561 B.C.; also see note on 52:4a.

LAMENTATIONS

After Susan broke up with Brad, depression filled his sad eyes for weeks. Tears streamed down Tamika's face as she gave a last hug to her best friend. She stood waving good-bye as the moving van pulled out of the drive. The night Michael lost the election, he cried himself to sleep. As the final seconds of the state tournament ticked away, the cheerleaders wept uncontrollably.

What breaks your heart? Losing a game? Saying good-bye? Being dumped or ignored? These are emotional experiences, and worthy of tears. But would you shed a tear over injustice, poverty, war, famine, or for people who don't know God and are bound for destruction?

Jeremiah would. As a prophet of God, he couldn't help seeing the mess people made of their lives as they disobeyed God. He cared about them and he cared about God. Seeing their sorrow and the destruction they had earned because of their choices made him weep. But he did more than just cry. He talked to God on their behalf.

As you read Lamentations, think about the people in your area or in other parts of the world. What breaks your heart about their situations? What will you do to help?

STATS

PURPOSE
To teach people that to disobey God is to invite disaster and to show that God suffers when his people suffer

AUTHOR
Jeremiah

ORIGINAL AUDIENCE
The people of Judah

DATE WRITTEN
Soon after the fall of Jerusalem in 586 B.C.

SETTING
Babylon destroyed Jerusalem and captured the people of Judah.

KEY PEOPLE
Jeremiah; the people of Judah

KEY PLACE
Jerusalem

SPECIAL FEATURES
Lamentations is written in the rhythm and style of ancient Jewish funeral songs or chants. It contains five poems in five chapters.

KEY POINTS

SIN'S CONSEQUENCES Lamentations is a requiem—sad funeral song—for Jerusalem, the great capital city of the Jews. The Temple had been destroyed, the king was gone, and the people were in exile. This chilling reminder of the consequences of wrong actions also is an invitation to make things right with God.

GOD'S MERCY God's compassion was at work even though the Israelites suffered in captivity. When we mess up and suffer the consequences, God's mercy seems like a dream. But he never forgets his people nor lets them suffer forever.

HOPE The fact that God spared the lives of the people of Judah gave them hope for better days. In the same way, Christ's death for us, his resurrection, and his promise to return provide the hope of a better life—eternal life with God.

1 * SORROW IN JERUSALEM

¹ Jerusalem, once so full of people,
    is now deserted.
She who was once great among the nations
    now sits alone like a widow.
Once the queen of all the earth,
    she is now a slave.

² She sobs through the night;
    tears stream down her cheeks.
Among all her lovers,
    there is no one left to comfort her.
All her friends have betrayed her
    and become her enemies.

³ Judah has been led away into captivity,
    oppressed with cruel slavery.
She lives among foreign nations
    and has no place of rest.
Her enemies have chased her down,
    and she has nowhere to turn.

⁴ The roads to Jerusalem* are in mourning,
    for crowds no longer come to celebrate
      the festivals.
The city gates are silent,
    her priests groan,
her young women are crying—
    how bitter is her fate!

⁵ Her oppressors have become her masters,
    and her enemies prosper,
for the LORD has punished Jerusalem
    for her many sins.
Her children have been captured
    and taken away to distant lands.

⁶ All the majesty of beautiful Jerusalem*
    has been stripped away.
Her princes are like starving deer
    searching for pasture.
They are too weak to run
    from the pursuing enemy.

⁷ In the midst of her sadness and wandering,
    Jerusalem remembers her ancient
      splendor.
But now she has fallen to her enemy,
    and there is no one to help her.

Her enemy struck her down
    and laughed as she fell.

⁸ Jerusalem has sinned greatly,
    so she has been tossed away like a filthy
      rag.
All who once honored her now despise her,
    for they have seen her stripped naked
      and humiliated.
All she can do is groan
    and hide her face.

⁹ She defiled herself with immorality
    and gave no thought to her future.
Now she lies in the gutter
    with no one to lift her out.
"LORD, see my misery," she cries.
    "The enemy has triumphed."

¹⁰ The enemy has plundered her completely,
    taking every precious thing she owns.
She has seen foreigners violate her sacred
      Temple,
the place the LORD had forbidden them
    to enter.

¹¹ Her people groan as they search for bread.
    They have sold their treasures for food to
      stay alive.
"O LORD, look," she mourns,
    "and see how I am despised.

¹² "Does it mean nothing to you, all you who
      pass by?
    Look around and see if there is any
      suffering like mine,
which the LORD brought on me
    when he erupted in fierce anger.

¹³ "He has sent fire from heaven that burns in
      my bones.
    He has placed a trap in my path and
      turned me back.
He has left me devastated,
    racked with sickness all day long.

¹⁴ "He wove my sins into ropes
    to hitch me to a yoke of captivity.
The Lord sapped my strength and turned me
      over to my enemies;
    I am helpless in their hands.

¹⁵ "The Lord has treated my mighty men
    with contempt.
At his command a great army has come
    to crush my young warriors.

....

TRUE FREEDOM
(1:1-14) *The people of Judah's captivity to sin led to their physical captivity. As with any addiction, the sin cycle grows gradually. Before we know it, we can't help doing wrong. Freedom from sin's captivity comes only from God. He gives us the freedom, not to do anything we want, but to do what he knows is best for us. Strange as it may seem, true freedom comes in obeying God—following his guidance so that we can receive his best.*

1 Each of the first four chapters of this book is an acrostic, laid out in the order of the Hebrew alphabet. The first word of each verse begins with a successive Hebrew letter. Chapters 1, 2, and 4 have one verse for each of the 22 Hebrew letters. Chapter 3 contains 22 stanzas of three verses each. Though chapter 5 has 22 verses, it is not an acrostic. **1:4** Hebrew *Zion;* also in 1:17. **1:6** Hebrew *of the daughter of Zion.*

The Lord has trampled his beloved city*
    like grapes are trampled in a winepress.

16 "For all these things I weep;
    tears flow down my cheeks.
No one is here to comfort me;
    any who might encourage me are far
        away.
My children have no future,
    for the enemy has conquered us."

17 Jerusalem reaches out for help,
    but no one comforts her.
Regarding his people Israel,*
    the LORD has said,
"Let their neighbors be their enemies!
    Let them be thrown away like a filthy rag!"

18 "The LORD is right," Jerusalem says,
    "for I rebelled against him.
Listen, people everywhere;
    look upon my anguish and despair,
for my sons and daughters
    have been taken captive to
        distant lands.

19 "I begged my allies for help,
    but they betrayed me.
My priests and leaders
    starved to death in the city,
even as they searched for food
    to save their lives.

20 "LORD, see my anguish!
    My heart is broken
and my soul despairs,
    for I have rebelled against you.
In the streets the sword kills,
    and at home there is only death.

21 "Others heard my groans,
    but no one turned to comfort me.
When my enemies heard about
       my troubles,
    they were happy to see what you
       had done.
Oh, bring the day you promised,
    when they will suffer as I have suffered.

22 "Look at all their evil deeds, LORD.
    Punish them,
as you have punished me
    for all my sins.
My groans are many,
    and I am sick at heart."

2 GOD'S ANGER AT SIN

1 The Lord in his anger
    has cast a dark shadow over beautiful
        Jerusalem.*
The fairest of Israel's cities lies in the dust,
    thrown down from the heights of heaven.
In his day of great anger,
    the Lord has shown no mercy even to his
        Temple.*

2 Without mercy the Lord has destroyed
    every home in Israel.*
In his anger he has broken down
    the fortress walls of beautiful Jerusalem.*
He has brought them to the ground,
    dishonoring the kingdom and its rulers.

3 All the strength of Israel
    vanishes beneath his fierce anger.
The Lord has withdrawn his protection
    as the enemy attacks.
He consumes the whole land of Israel
    like a raging fire.

4 He bends his bow against his people,
    as though he were their enemy.
His strength is used against them
    to kill their finest youth.
His fury is poured out like fire
    on beautiful Jerusalem.*

5 Yes, the Lord has vanquished Israel
    like an enemy.
He has destroyed her palaces
    and demolished her fortresses.
He has brought unending sorrow
    and tears
    upon beautiful Jerusalem.

6 He has broken down his Temple
    as though it were merely a garden shelter.
The LORD has blotted out all memory
    of the holy festivals and Sabbath days.

....

WEAK ALLIES
*(1:19) The allies of the people of Judah could not come
to their aid. Like Judah, they failed to seek God. Though
these allies appeared strong, they were actually weak,
because God was not with them. Dependable assistance
can come only from an ally whose power is from God.
When you need advice or other help, whom do you
depend on? Do your allies have God's seal of approval?*

TRUE WORSHIP
*(2:1-7) Although the people of Judah had a beautiful
Temple, their rejection of God made their worship a lie.
Where we worship is not as important to God as how we
worship. A church may be beautiful, but if its people don't
sincerely follow God, it decays from within. When you
worship, do you mean the words you say? How do your
actions show that you worship God wholeheartedly?*

1:15 Hebrew *the virgin daughter of Judah.*   1:17 Hebrew *Jacob.* The
names "Jacob" and "Israel" are often interchanged throughout the
Old Testament, referring sometimes to the individual patriarch and
sometimes to the nation.   2:1a Hebrew *the daughter of Zion;* also
in 2:8, 10, 18.   2:1b Hebrew *his footstool.*   2:2a Hebrew *Jacob;*
also in 2:3b. See note on 1:17.   2:2b Hebrew *the daughter of Judah;*
also in 2:5.   2:4 Hebrew *on the tent of the daughter of Zion.*

Kings and priests fall together
　before his fierce anger.

7 The Lord has rejected his own altar;
　he despises his own sanctuary.
He has given Jerusalem's palaces
　to her enemies.
They shout in the LORD's Temple
　as though it were a day of celebration.

8 The LORD was determined
　to destroy the walls of beautiful
　Jerusalem.
He made careful plans for their destruction,
　then did what he had planned.
Therefore, the ramparts and walls
　have fallen down before him.

9 Jerusalem's gates have sunk into the
　ground.
　He has smashed their locks and bars.
Her kings and princes have been exiled to
　distant lands;
　her law has ceased
　to exist.
Her prophets receive
　no more visions from the LORD.

10 The leaders of beautiful Jerusalem
　sit on the ground in silence.
They are clothed in burlap
　and throw dust on their heads.
The young women of Jerusalem
　hang their heads in shame.

11 I have cried until the tears no longer come;
　my heart is broken.
My spirit is poured out in agony
　as I see the desperate plight of my
　people.
Little children and tiny babies
　are fainting and dying in the streets.

12 They cry out to their mothers,
　"We need food and drink!"
Their lives ebb away in the streets
　like the life of a warrior wounded
　in battle.
They gasp for life
　as they collapse in their mothers' arms.

13 What can I say about you?
　Who has ever seen such sorrow?
O daughter of Jerusalem,
　to what can I compare your anguish?
O virgin daughter of Zion,
　how can I comfort you?
For your wound is as deep as the sea.
　Who can heal you?

14 Your prophets have said
　so many foolish things, false to the core.

They did not save you from exile
　by pointing out your sins.
Instead, they painted false pictures,
　filling you with false hope.

15 All who pass by jeer at you.
　They scoff and insult beautiful
　Jerusalem,* saying,
"Is this the city called 'Most Beautiful in All
　the World'
　and 'Joy of All the Earth'?"

16 All your enemies mock you.
　They scoff and snarl and say,
"We have destroyed her at last!
　We have long waited for this day,
　and it is finally here!"

17 But it is the LORD who did just as he
　planned.
He has fulfilled the promises of disaster
　he made long ago.
He has destroyed Jerusalem without mercy.
　He has caused her enemies to gloat over
　her
　and has given them power over her.

18 Cry aloud* before the Lord,
　O walls of beautiful Jerusalem!
Let your tears flow like a river
　day and night.
Give yourselves no rest;
　give your eyes no relief.

19 Rise during the night and cry out.
　Pour out your hearts like water to the Lord.
Lift up your hands to him in prayer,
　pleading for your children,
for in every street
　they are faint with hunger.

20 "O LORD, think about this!
　Should you treat your own people this
　way?
Should mothers eat their own children,
　those they once bounced on their knees?
Should priests and prophets be killed
　within the Lord's Temple?

21 "See them lying in the streets—
　young and old,
boys and girls,
　killed by the swords of the enemy.
You have killed them in your anger,
　slaughtering them without mercy.

22 "You have invited terrors from all around,
　as though you were calling them to a day
　of feasting.

2:15 Hebrew the daughter of Jerusalem.　2:18 Hebrew Their heart
cried.

In the day of the LORD's anger,
no one has escaped or survived.
The enemy has killed all the children
whom I carried and raised."

3 HOPE IN THE LORD'S FAITHFULNESS

1 I am the one who has seen the afflictions
that come from the rod of the LORD's
anger.
2 He has led me into darkness,
shutting out all light.
3 He has turned his hand against me
again and again, all day long.

4 He has made my skin and flesh grow old.
He has broken my bones.
5 He has besieged and surrounded me
with anguish and distress.
6 He has buried me in a dark place,
like those long dead.

7 He has walled me in, and I cannot escape.
He has bound me in heavy chains.
8 And though I cry and shout,
he has shut out my prayers.
9 He has blocked my way with a high stone
wall;
he has made my road crooked.

10 He has hidden like a bear or a lion,
waiting to attack me.
11 He has dragged me off the path and torn me
in pieces,
leaving me helpless and devastated.
12 He has drawn his bow
and made me the target for his arrows.

13 He shot his arrows
deep into my heart.

3:19 Or *is wormwood and gall.* **3:22** As in Syriac version; Hebrew
reads *of the LORD keeps us from destruction.*

14 My own people laugh at me.
All day long they sing their mocking
songs.
15 He has filled me with bitterness
and given me a bitter cup of sorrow to
drink.

16 He has made me chew on gravel.
He has rolled me in the dust.
17 Peace has been stripped away,
and I have forgotten what prosperity is.
18 I cry out, "My splendor is gone!
Everything I had hoped for from the LORD
is lost!"

19 The thought of my suffering and
homelessness
is bitter beyond words.*
20 I will never forget this awful time,
as I grieve over my loss.
21 Yet I still dare to hope
when I remember this:

22 The faithful love of the LORD never ends!*
His mercies never cease.
23 Great is his faithfulness;
his mercies begin afresh each morning.
24 I say to myself, "The LORD is my inheritance;
therefore, I will hope in him!"

25 The LORD is good to those who depend
on him,

....

GRACE

*(3:19-23) Jeremiah saw one ray of hope in Judah's sad
situation: The faithful love of the Lord never ends (3:22)!
Even when we mess up, God willingly responds with help
when we ask. God offers love and forgiveness even when
we don't deserve it. That's GRACE: God's Riches At Christ's
Expense. Need some? Don't be afraid to ask.*

CHOICES
advice

Sitting on an uncomfortable bench in the visitor's
area at a large juvenile correctional facility, Dylan is
somber and subdued. He claws unconsciously at the
handcuffs that bite into his bony wrists.

Who would imagine that this tiny 14-year-old, a
former A-student, is a convicted felon with a rap sheet
that includes car theft and armed robbery? How could
a young life go so wrong?

"I knew better," Dylan mutters. "My grandmother
was always on me to straighten up and do right. I did
for a while. I even sang in the church choir. But when

it came down to it, I picked my homeboys over church.
I chose the wrong thing, and from there it was all
downhill. I kept making bad decisions. I let my friends
tell me what to do. And, well, here I am.

"Every day I ask God to forgive me, but I don't know
if it does any good. I just don't know . . ."

The conversation continues for another twenty
minutes. At last the guards come in and usher Dylan
away. *Clang!*—just like that, the steel doors slam shut
and the little guy disappears from view.

*Jeremiah's diary—the book of Lamentations—is a similarly sad account of what happens when people neglect or
reject the Lord. His advice brought life; the advice and example of other nations brought trouble. Yet, despite the
book's generally depressing tone, we find a wonderful note of hope in 3:19-26. Check it out. If you had a chance
to talk to Dylan, what would you tell him about this passage or about seeking the right sources for advice?*

MY STORY: Kara

I had blown it again—my parents and I had another major argument. I ran to my room, slammed the door, and threw myself on the bed. Then I burst into tears, thinking, They're so unfair! And I can't do anything about it!

After I had cried for a while, I thought about our fight. I still thought my parents were wrong, but I also had to admit that I had said some pretty ugly things. The more I thought about it, the more I realized that I needed to apologize.

It took me a couple of hours. Finally, I came out and apologized for some of the hurtful things I had said. My mother's response was, "You think it's that easy? Just say you're sorry, and everything's okay? Well, it doesn't work that way."

I just turned and went back to my room and cried some more. I had said I was sorry, and I was. Why couldn't they just forgive me? It seemed as if they didn't really know much about forgiveness.

The next morning, still feeling bad, I picked up my Bible. I remembered reading a verse one time that I wanted to look up, something about God's mercies being new. A passage from a strange book in the Old Testament—Lamentations. "Yet I still dare to hope when I remember this: The faithful love of the Lord never ends! . . . Great is his faithfulness; his mercies begin afresh each morning" (3:21-23).

It was a new day. God had forgiven me; his love and mercy were fresh and new. I didn't have to carry my burdens by myself. Even if my parents didn't forgive me, God did. He knew I was sincere, and would help me to start again. And even if I didn't, he'd love me. His compassion would be there for me tomorrow, just like the sun coming up to warm me.

to those who search for him.
²⁶ So it is good to wait quietly
for salvation from the Lord.
²⁷ And it is good for people to submit at an
early age
to the yoke of his discipline:

²⁸ Let them sit alone in silence
beneath the Lord's demands.
²⁹ Let them lie face down in the dust,
for there may be hope at last.
³⁰ Let them turn the other cheek to those who
strike them
and accept the insults of their enemies.

³¹ For no one is abandoned
by the Lord forever.
³² Though he brings grief, he also shows
compassion

because of the greatness of his unfailing
love.
³³ For he does not enjoy hurting people
or causing them sorrow.

³⁴ If people crush underfoot
all the prisoners of the land,
³⁵ if they deprive others of their rights
in defiance of the Most High,
³⁶ if they twist justice in the courts—
doesn't the Lord see all these things?

³⁷ Who can command things to happen
without the Lord's permission?
³⁸ Does not the Most High
send both calamity and good?
³⁹ Then why should we, mere humans,
complain
when we are punished for our sins?

⁴⁰ Instead, let us test and examine our ways.
Let us turn back to the Lord.
⁴¹ Let us lift our hearts and hands
to God in heaven and say,
⁴² "We have sinned and rebelled,
and you have not forgiven us.

⁴³ "You have engulfed us with your anger,
chased us down,
and slaughtered us without mercy.

SUBMIT
(3:25-33) To "submit . . . to the yoke of his discipline" means to accept God's correction. It sometimes means letting go of your anger or disappointment because of your circumstances and paying attention to what God wants to teach you. Some attitudes of learning involve (1) humility, (2) self-control in the face of adversity, and (3) confident patience. God has several long-term and short-term lessons for you right now. Are you willing to learn?

44 You have hidden yourself in a cloud
    so our prayers cannot reach you.
45 You have discarded us as refuse and
    garbage
    among the nations.

46 "All our enemies
    have spoken out against us.
47 We are filled with fear,
    for we are trapped, devastated, and
    ruined."

48 Tears stream from my eyes
    because of the destruction of my people!

49 My tears flow endlessly;
    they will not stop
50 until the LORD looks down
    from heaven and sees.
51 My heart is breaking
    over the fate of all the women of
    Jerusalem.

52 My enemies, whom I have never harmed,
    hunted me down like a bird.
53 They threw me into a pit
    and dropped stones on me.
54 The water rose over my head,
    and I cried out, "This is the end!"

55 But I called on your name, LORD,
    from deep within the pit.
56 You heard me when I cried, "Listen to my
    pleading!
    Hear my cry for help!"
57 Yes, you came when I called;
    you told me, "Do not fear."

58 Lord, you are my lawyer! Plead my case!
    For you have redeemed my life.
59 You have seen the wrong they have done to
    me, LORD.
    Be my judge, and prove me right.
60 You have seen the vengeful plots
    my enemies have laid against me.

61 LORD, you have heard the vile names they
    call me.
    You know all about the plans they have
    made.
62 My enemies whisper and mutter
    as they plot against me all day long.
63 Look at them! Whether they sit or stand,
    I am the object of their mocking songs.

64 Pay them back, LORD,
    for all the evil they have done.
65 Give them hard and stubborn hearts,
    and then let your curse fall on them!

4:2 Hebrew precious sons of Zion.   4:6 Or punishment.
4:7 Hebrew like lapis lazuli.

GREAT (IS) HIS FAITHFULNESS; HIS MERCIES BEGIN AFRESH EACH MORNING.

LAMENTATIONS 3:23 ■■■■■■■

66 Chase them down in your anger,
    destroying them beneath the LORD's
    heavens.

4 GOD'S ANGER SATISFIED

1 How the gold has lost its luster!
    Even the finest gold has become dull.
The sacred gemstones
    lie scattered in the streets!

2 See how the precious children of Jerusalem,*
    worth their weight in fine gold,
are now treated like pots of clay
    made by a common potter.

3 Even the jackals feed their young,
    but not my people Israel.
They ignore their children's cries,
    like ostriches in the desert.

4 The parched tongues of their little ones
    stick to the roofs of their mouths in thirst.
The children cry for bread,
    but no one has any to give them.

5 The people who once ate the richest foods
    now beg in the streets for anything they
    can get.
Those who once wore the finest clothes
    now search the garbage dumps for food.

6 The guilt* of my people
    is greater than that of Sodom,
where utter disaster struck in a moment
    and no hand offered help.

7 Our princes once glowed with health—
    brighter than snow, whiter than milk.
Their faces were as ruddy as rubies,
    their appearance like fine jewels.*

BANKRUPT

(4:1-22) This chapter provides a view of Jerusalem
before and after the siege. The people of Judah had been
prosperous before; now they were poor. What they didn't
realize was that they were spiritually poor when they were
financially wealthy. How is your spiritual bank account
these days? Are you spiritually rich or overdrawn?

⁸ But now their faces are blacker than soot.
   No one recognizes them in the streets.
Their skin sticks to their bones;
   it is as dry and hard as wood.

⁹ Those killed by the sword are better off
   than those who die of hunger.
Starving, they waste away
   for lack of food from the fields.

¹⁰ Tenderhearted women
   have cooked their own children.
They have eaten them
   to survive the siege.

¹¹ But now the anger of the LORD is satisfied.
   His fierce anger has been poured out.
He started a fire in Jerusalem*
   that burned the city to its foundations.

¹² Not a king in all the earth—
   no one in all the world—
would have believed that an enemy
   could march through the gates of
    Jerusalem.

¹³ Yet it happened because of the sins of her
   prophets
   and the sins of her priests,
who defiled the city
   by shedding innocent blood.

¹⁴ They wandered blindly
   through the streets,
so defiled by blood
   that no one dared touch them.

¹⁵ "Get away!" the people shouted at them.
   "You're defiled! Don't touch us!"
So they fled to distant lands
   and wandered among foreign nations,
   but none would let them stay.

¹⁶ The LORD himself has scattered them,
   and he no longer helps them.
People show no respect for the priests
   and no longer honor the leaders.

¹⁷ We looked in vain for our allies
   to come and save us,
but we were looking to nations
   that could not help us.

¹⁸ We couldn't go into the streets
   without danger to our lives.
Our end was near; our days were numbered.
   We were doomed!

¹⁹ Our enemies were swifter than eagles
   in flight.
If we fled to the mountains, they
   found us.
If we hid in the wilderness,
   they were waiting for us there.

²⁰ Our king—the LORD's anointed, the very life
   of our nation—
was caught in their snares.
We had thought that his shadow
   would protect us against any nation on
    earth!

²¹ Are you rejoicing in the land of Uz,
   O people of Edom?
But you, too, must drink from the cup of the
   LORD's anger.
   You, too, will be stripped naked in your
    drunkenness.

²² O beautiful Jerusalem,* your punishment
   will end;
   you will soon return from exile.
But Edom, your punishment is just
   beginning;
   soon your many sins will be exposed.

5 PRAYER FOR RESTORATION

¹ LORD, remember what has happened to us.
   See how we have been disgraced!
² Our inheritance has been turned over to
   strangers,
   our homes to foreigners.
³ We are orphaned and fatherless.
   Our mothers are widowed.
⁴ We have to pay for water to drink,
   and even firewood is expensive.
⁵ Those who pursue us are at our heels;
   we are exhausted but are given no rest.
⁶ We submitted to Egypt and Assyria
   to get enough food to survive.
⁷ Our ancestors sinned, but they have died—
   and we are suffering the punishment they
    deserved!

⁸ Slaves have now become our masters;
   there is no one left to rescue us.
⁹ We hunt for food at the risk of our lives,
   for violence rules the countryside.
¹⁰ The famine has blackened our skin
   as though baked in an oven.

··

THE PROMISE OF RESTORATION
(5:1-22) A high calling flouted by low living results in deep suffering. The book of Lamentations is a portrait of the suffering experienced by the people of Judah as a consequence for sin. Every material goal they had lived for disappeared. Even though God allowed them to go through pain, he did not abandon them. He promised to restore them if they returned to him. He promises to do the same for us when we seek him.

4:11 Hebrew *in Zion.*   **4:22** Hebrew *O daughter of Zion.*

11 Our enemies rape the women in Jerusalem*
    and the young girls in all the towns of
        Judah.
12 Our princes are being hanged by their
        thumbs,
    and our elders are treated with contempt.
13 Young men are led away to work at
        millstones,
    and boys stagger under heavy loads of
        wood.
14 The elders no longer sit in the city gates;
    the young men no longer dance and sing.
15 Joy has left our hearts;
    our dancing has turned to mourning.
16 The garlands have* fallen from our heads.

5:11 Hebrew *in Zion*.   5:16 Or *The crown has*.   5:18 Hebrew
Mount Zion.

    Weep for us because we have sinned.
17 Our hearts are sick and weary,
    and our eyes grow dim with tears.
18 For Jerusalem* is empty and desolate,
    a place haunted by jackals.

19 But LORD, you remain the same forever!
    Your throne continues from generation
        to generation.
20 Why do you continue to forget us?
    Why have you abandoned us for
        so long?
21 Restore us, O LORD, and bring us back
        to you again!
    Give us back the joys we once had!
22 Or have you utterly rejected us?
    Are you angry with us still?

"Don't worry," Andrew chided his friend, Ben. "I can get away with anything. I'm my dad's favorite."

Andrew's dad was out of town, leaving his brand new convertible in the garage. Andrew was allowed to drive the family car, but not the convertible.

"Hey, dude, c'mon," he continued, "Dad'll never even know. Besides, it's got a killer sound system."

The drive to the movie was great. Girls honked and guys drooled at the car. Andrew and Ben loved the attention. "See," Andrew said. "No problem. It sure beats the other car!" Ben had to agree.

After the movie, they headed to the car. It was late, and the parking lot was no longer full. But they were shocked to find wires dangling from where the stereo used to be.

The book of Ezekiel was written to captive Jews in Babylon. They were "God's favorites." Like Andrew, they thought they could get away with anything. Ezekiel corrected their thinking. They were captives in Babylon because they had disobeyed God. God would not overlook sin just because they were his chosen people.

Ezekiel reminds us of the very real consequences of wrong actions. Just as God loves us, he also loves justice.

As you read Ezekiel, stand in awe of the God who judges all sin. Then thank him for providing a way (through Jesus) to escape the judgment that we all deserve.

KEY POINTS

RESPONSIBILITY Ezekiel warned the exiles of Israel that not only was the nation guilty of sin, each individual also was responsible. In the same way, each of us is responsible for the wrong things we do.

RESTORATION Ezekiel comforted the people with God's promise to restore them to their land. When life seems bleak for us, we can choose to focus on God's promises of restoration, peace, and eternal life with him.

ROGUE SHEPHERDS Ezekiel condemned the unfaithful priests and leaders ("shepherds") who led the people astray. By contrast, Ezekiel was a caring shepherd as he warned the people about their sin. Good leaders do whatever is necessary to care for the people under their charge.

REAL WORSHIP Although God's holy presence had left the Temple, one day the Lord would return and restore true worship. We too can look forward to the fulfillment of God's promises under the future rule of the Savior. Faithful followers will be brought back to perfect fellowship with God and with one another. We can prepare for that by walking closely with God today.

1 A VISION OF LIVING BEINGS

On July 31* of my thirtieth year,* while I was with the Judean exiles beside the Kebar River in Babylon, the heavens were opened and I saw visions of God. ²This happened during the fifth year of King Jehoiachin's captivity. ³(The LORD gave this message to Ezekiel son of Buzi, a priest, beside the Kebar River in the land of the Babylonians,* and he felt the hand of the LORD take hold of him.)

⁴As I looked, I saw a great storm coming from the north, driving before it a huge cloud that flashed with lightning and shone with brilliant light. There was fire inside the cloud, and in the middle of the fire glowed something like gleaming amber.* ⁵From the center of the cloud came four living beings that looked human, ⁶except that each had four faces and four wings. ⁷Their legs were straight, and their feet had hooves like those of a calf and shone like burnished bronze. ⁸Under each of their four wings I could see human hands. So each of the four beings had four faces and four wings. ⁹The wings of each living being touched the wings of the beings beside it. Each one moved straight forward in any direction without turning around.

¹⁰Each had a human face in the front, the face of a lion on the right side, the face of an ox on the left side, and the face of an eagle at the back. ¹¹Each had two pairs of outstretched wings—one pair stretched out to touch the wings of the living beings on either side of it, and the other pair covered its body. ¹²They went in whatever direction the spirit chose, and they moved straight forward in any direction without turning around.

¹³The living beings looked like bright coals of fire or brilliant torches, and lightning seemed to flash back and forth among them. ¹⁴And the living beings darted to and fro like flashes of lightning.

¹⁵As I looked at these beings, I saw four wheels touching the ground beside them, one wheel belonging to each. ¹⁶The wheels sparkled as if made of beryl. All four wheels looked alike and were made the same; each wheel had a second wheel turning crosswise within it. ¹⁷The beings could move in any of the four directions they faced, without turning as they moved. ¹⁸The rims of the four wheels were tall and frightening, and they were covered with eyes all around.

¹⁹When the living beings moved, the wheels moved with them. When they flew upward, the wheels went up, too. ²⁰The spirit of the living beings was in the wheels. So wherever the spirit went, the wheels and the living beings also went. ²¹When the beings moved, the wheels moved. When the beings stopped, the wheels stopped. When the beings flew upward, the wheels rose up, for the spirit of the living beings was in the wheels.

²²Spread out above them was a surface like the sky, glittering like crystal. ²³Beneath this surface the wings of each living being stretched out to touch the others' wings, and each had two wings covering its body. ²⁴As they flew, their wings sounded to me like waves crashing against the shore or like the voice of the Almighty* or like the shouting of a mighty army. When they stopped, they let down their wings. ²⁵As they stood with wings lowered, a voice spoke from beyond the crystal surface above them.

²⁶Above this surface was something that looked like a throne made of blue lapis lazuli. And on this throne high above was a figure whose appearance resembled a man. ²⁷From what appeared to be his waist up, he looked like gleaming amber, flickering like a fire. And from his waist down, he looked like a burning flame, shining with splendor. ²⁸All around him was a glowing halo, like a rainbow shining in the clouds on a rainy day. This is what the glory of the LORD looked like to me. When I saw it, I fell face down on the ground, and I heard someone's voice speaking to me.

IN AWE
(1:1-28) A bright light, a dazzling fire—that's what the glory of the Lord looked like to Ezekiel. He fell to the ground, overwhelmed by the holiness of God and his own sinfulness and insignificance. Eventually every person will kneel before God, either out of awe and gratitude for his mercy, or out of fear of his judgment. Based on the way you're living today, how will you respond?

TOUGH TALK
(2:1-8) Ezekiel was given the difficult responsibility of presenting God's messages to people who wouldn't listen to him. Sometimes we also are called to share our faith with people who react the same way the exiles did. Just as God told Ezekiel not to give up, he tells us not to give up either. Instead, we are to tell the Good News whether people listen or not (see 2 Tim 4:2). Are you willing?

2 EZEKIEL'S CALL AND COMMISSION

"Stand up, son of man," said the voice. "I want to speak with you." ²The Spirit came

---

1:1a Hebrew *On the fifth day of the fourth month,* of the ancient Hebrew lunar calendar. A number of dates in Ezekiel can be cross-checked with dates in surviving Babylonian records and related accurately to our modern calendar. This event occurred on July 31, 593 B.C. **1:1b** Or *in the thirtieth year.* **1:3** Or *Chaldeans.* **1:4** Or *like burnished metal;* also in 1:27. **1:24** Hebrew *Shaddai.*

into me as he spoke, and he set me on my feet. I listened carefully to his words. ³"Son of man," he said, "I am sending you to the nation of Israel, a rebellious nation that has rebelled against me. They and their ancestors have been rebelling against me to this very day. ⁴They are a stubborn and hard-hearted people. But I am sending you to say to them, 'This is what the Sovereign LORD says!' ⁵And whether they listen or refuse to listen—for remember, they are rebels—at least they will know they have had a prophet among them.

⁶"Son of man, do not fear them or their words. Don't be afraid even though their threats surround you like nettles and briers and stinging scorpions. Do not be dismayed by their dark scowls, even though they are rebels. ⁷You must give them my messages whether they listen or not. But they won't listen, for they are completely rebellious! ⁸Son of man, listen to what I say to you. Do not join them in their rebellion. Open your mouth, and eat what I give you."

⁹Then I looked and saw a hand reaching out to me. It held a scroll, ¹⁰which he unrolled. And I saw that both sides were covered with funeral songs, words of sorrow, and pronouncements of doom.

3 The voice said to me, "Son of man, eat what I am giving you—eat this scroll! Then go and give its message to the people of Israel." ²So I opened my mouth, and he fed me the scroll. ³"Fill your stomach with this," he said. And when I ate it, it tasted as sweet as honey in my mouth.

3:12 A possible reading for this verse is *Then the Spirit lifted me up, and as the glory of the LORD rose from its place, I heard a loud rumbling sound behind me.*

⁴Then he said, "Son of man, go to the people of Israel and give them my messages. ⁵I am not sending you to a foreign people whose language you cannot understand. ⁶No, I am not sending you to people with strange and difficult speech. If I did, they would listen! ⁷But the people of Israel won't listen to you any more than they listen to me! For the whole lot of them are hard-hearted and stubborn. ⁸But look, I have made you as obstinate and hard-hearted as they are. ⁹I have made your forehead as hard as the hardest rock! So don't be afraid of them or fear their angry looks, even though they are rebels."

¹⁰Then he added, "Son of man, let all my words sink deep into your own heart first. Listen to them carefully for yourself. ¹¹Then go to your people in exile and say to them, 'This is what the Sovereign LORD says!' Do this whether they listen to you or not."

¹²Then the Spirit lifted me up, and I heard a loud rumbling sound behind me. (May the glory of the LORD be praised in his place!)* ¹³It was the sound of the wings of the living beings as they brushed against each other and the rumbling of their wheels beneath them.

¹⁴The Spirit lifted me up and took me away. I went in bitterness and turmoil, but the LORD's hold on me was strong. ¹⁵Then I came to the colony of Judean exiles in Tel-abib, beside the Kebar River. I was overwhelmed and sat among them for seven days.

A WATCHMAN FOR ISRAEL ¹⁶After seven days the LORD gave me a message. He said, ¹⁷"Son of man, I have appointed you as a watchman

CHOICES confront

Chad's been hearing rumors about his friend Seth for a couple of weeks, rumors such as: "You should've seen Seth at Becca's party last weekend! Man, was he wasted!"

"I heard Seth popped Ecstasy at a party the other day. Didn't Seth used to be religious? He sure has changed!" Chad had heard some of these rumors before.

Tonight some of Chad's worst fears were confirmed. Driving through the school parking lot after a game, Chad happened to see Seth and Will, another guy from school, sitting in the back of a pickup truck, drinking tequila shots. Chad didn't stop, so he doesn't know whether or not Seth saw him.

Chad is concerned, but also confused. Here's his childhood friend starting to run with a pretty wild crowd. It seems Seth is headed for major-league trouble. Chad ponders what to do: *Should I talk to Seth or just keep my mouth shut? Should I tell my parents what's going on and get their advice? I mean, I want to do what's right, but if I speak up, Seth'll just laugh at me. Besides, who am I to tell him how to live?*

Do you agree or disagree with Chad? Why? When friends head for trouble, we have a God-given responsibility to pull them aside and help them get back on track. The question isn't how they may or may not respond—that's irrelevant. The real question is whether or not we love them enough to do what's right and confront them. Well? Do you? Check out Ezekiel 2:3-7. What do you think God is saying to you?

for Israel. Whenever you receive a message from me, warn people immediately. ¹⁸If I warn the wicked, saying, 'You are under the penalty of death,' but you fail to deliver the warning, they will die in their sins. And I will hold you responsible for their deaths. ¹⁹If you warn them and they refuse to repent and keep on sinning, they will die in their sins. But you will have saved yourself because you obeyed me.

²⁰"If righteous people turn away from their righteous behavior and ignore the obstacles I put in their way, they will die. And if you do not warn them, they will die in their sins. None of their righteous acts will be remembered, and I will hold you responsible for their deaths. ²¹But if you warn righteous people not to sin and they listen to you and do not sin, they will live, and you will have saved yourself, too."

²²Then the LORD took hold of me and said, "Get up and go out into the valley, and I will speak to you there." ²³So I got up and went, and there I saw the glory of the LORD, just as I had seen in my first vision by the Kebar River. And I fell face down on the ground.

²⁴Then the Spirit came into me and set me on my feet. He spoke to me and said, "Go to your house and shut yourself in. ²⁵There, son of man, you will be tied with ropes so you cannot go out among the people. ²⁶And I will make your tongue stick to the roof of your mouth so that you will be speechless and unable to rebuke them, for they are rebels. ²⁷But when I give you a message, I will loosen your tongue and let you speak. Then you will say to them, 'This is what the Sovereign LORD says!' Those who choose to listen will listen, but those who refuse will refuse, for they are rebels.

4 **A SIGN OF THE COMING SIEGE** "And now, son of man, take a large clay brick and set it down in front of you. Then draw a map of the city of Jerusalem on it. ²Show the city under siege. Build a wall around it so no one can escape. Set up the enemy camp, and surround the city with siege ramps and battering rams. ³Then take an iron griddle and place it between you and the city. Turn toward the city and demonstrate how harsh the siege will be

against Jerusalem. This will be a warning to the people of Israel.

⁴"Now lie on your left side and place the sins of Israel on yourself. You are to bear their sins for the number of days you lie there on your side. ⁵I am requiring you to bear Israel's sins for 390 days—one day for each year of their sin. ⁶After that, turn over and lie on your right side for 40 days—one day for each year of Judah's sin.

⁷"Meanwhile, keep staring at the siege of Jerusalem. Lie there with your arm bared and prophesy her destruction. ⁸I will tie you up with ropes so you won't be able to turn from side to side until the days of your siege have been completed.

⁹"Now go and get some wheat, barley, beans, lentils, millet, and emmer wheat, and mix them together in a storage jar. Use them to make bread for yourself during the 390 days you will be lying on your side. ¹⁰Ration this out to yourself, eight ounces* of food for each day, and eat it at set times. ¹¹Then measure out a jar* of water for each day, and drink it at set times. ¹²Prepare and eat this food as you would barley cakes. While all the people are watching, bake it over a fire using dried human dung as fuel and then eat the bread." ¹³Then the LORD said, "This is how Israel will eat defiled bread in the Gentile lands to which I will banish them!"

¹⁴Then I said, "O Sovereign LORD, must I be defiled by using human dung? For I have never been defiled before. From the time I was a child until now I have never eaten any animal that died of sickness or was killed by other animals. I have never eaten any meat forbidden by the law."

¹⁵"All right," the LORD said. "You may bake your bread with cow dung instead of human dung." ¹⁶Then he told me, "Son of man, I will make food very scarce in Jerusalem. It will be weighed out with great care and eaten fearfully. The water will be rationed out drop by drop, and the people will drink it with dismay. ¹⁷Lacking food and water, people will look at one another in terror, and they will waste away under their punishment.

5 **A SIGN OF THE COMING JUDGMENT** "Son of man, take a sharp sword and use it as a razor to shave your head and beard. Use a scale to weigh the hair into three equal parts. ²Place a third of it at the center of your map of Jerusalem. After acting out the siege, burn it

DETAILS
(4:1-17) Ezekiel dramatically enacted the siege and fall of Jerusalem before the actual events happened. God gave Ezekiel specific instructions about what to say and how to say it. Each detail had a special meaning. These days, some of the details of God's Word are ignored. Ever notice that? Some might think these details don't really matter. Like Ezekiel, are you willing to obey God completely, even down to the smallest detail?

4:10 Hebrew *20 shekels* [228 grams].   4:11 Hebrew *⅙ of a hin* [about 1 pint or 0.6 liters].

there. Scatter another third across your map and chop it with a sword. ³Scatter the last third to the wind, for I will scatter my people with the sword. ³Keep just a bit of the hair and tie it up in your robe. ⁴Then take some of these hairs out and throw them into the fire, burning them up. A fire will then spread from this remnant and destroy all of Israel.

⁵"This is what the Sovereign LORD says: This is an illustration of what will happen to Jerusalem. I placed her at the center of the nations, ⁶but she has rebelled against my regulations and decrees and has been even more wicked than the surrounding nations. She has refused to obey the regulations and decrees I gave her to follow.

⁷"Therefore, this is what the Sovereign LORD says: You people have behaved worse than your neighbors and have refused to obey my decrees and regulations. You have not even lived up to the standards of the nations around you. ⁸Therefore, I myself, the Sovereign LORD, am now your enemy. I will punish you publicly while all the nations watch. ⁹Because of your detestable idols, I will punish you like I have never punished anyone before or ever will again. ¹⁰Parents will eat their own children, and children will eat their parents. I will punish and scatter to the winds the few who survive.

¹¹"As surely as I live, says the Sovereign LORD, I will cut you off completely. I will show you no pity at all because you have defiled my Temple with your vile images and detestable sins. ¹²A third of your people will die in the city from disease and famine. A third of them will be slaughtered by the enemy outside the city walls. And I will scatter a third to the winds, chasing them with my sword. ¹³Then at last my anger will be spent, and I will be satisfied. And when my fury against them has subsided, all Israel will know that I, the LORD, have spoken to them in my jealous anger.

¹⁴"So I will turn you into a ruin, a mockery in the eyes of the surrounding nations and to all who pass by. ¹⁵You will become an object of mockery and taunting and horror. You will be a warning to all the nations around you. They will see what happens when the LORD punishes a nation in anger and rebukes it, says the LORD.

¹⁶"I will shower you with the deadly arrows of famine to destroy you. The famine will become more and more severe until every crumb of food is gone. ¹⁷And along with the famine,

6:4 The Hebrew term (literally *round things*) probably alludes to dung; also in 6:5, 6, 9, 13.

wild animals will attack you and rob you of your children. Disease and war will stalk your land, and I will bring the sword of the enemy against you. I, the LORD, have spoken!"

6 JUDGMENT AGAINST ISRAEL'S MOUNTAINS Again a message came to me from the LORD: ²"Son of man, turn and face the mountains of Israel and prophesy against them. ³Proclaim this message from the Sovereign LORD against the mountains of Israel. This is what the Sovereign LORD says to the mountains and hills and to the ravines and valleys: I am about to bring war upon you, and I will smash your pagan shrines. ⁴All your altars will be demolished, and your places of worship will be destroyed. I will kill your people in front of your idols.* ⁵I will lay your corpses in front of your idols and scatter your bones around your altars. ⁶Wherever you live there will be desolation, and I will destroy your pagan shrines. Your altars will be demolished, your idols will be smashed, your places of worship will be torn down, and all the religious objects you have made will be destroyed. ⁷The place will be littered with corpses, and you will know that I alone am the LORD.

⁸"But I will let a few of my people escape destruction, and they will be scattered among the nations of the world. ⁹Then when they are exiled among the nations, they will remember me. They will recognize how hurt I am by their unfaithful hearts and lustful eyes that long for their idols. Then at last they will hate themselves for all their detestable sins. ¹⁰They will know that I alone am the LORD and that I was

....

FOLLOW THROUGH

(5:1-13) Have you ever seen a parent try to discipline a child by saying, "If you do that one more time . . . "? If the parent never follows through on his or her threat, the child learns not to listen. Empty threats backfire. God planned to punish the Israelites for their blatant sins, and he wanted them to know that he would do what he said. The people learned the hard way that God always follows through on his word. Too many people ignore God's warnings that he will punish sin. But what God threatens, he does. What will you do to avoid learning this truth the hard way?

ONE AND ONLY

(6:7-14) The phrase "then they will know that I am the LORD" (or a variation of this phrase) occurs almost 70 times in the book of Ezekiel. God used the punishment method to remind the exiled people of Israel and Judah that he was the only God. Many people in Ezekiel's day worshiped human-made idols. Today money, sex, and power have become idols for many. God sometimes uses the difficulties of a person's life to remind him or her that he alone is God. Is he your only God?

serious when I said I would bring this calamity on them.

¹¹"This is what the Sovereign LORD says: Clap your hands in horror, and stamp your feet. Cry out because of all the detestable sins the people of Israel have committed. Now they are going to die from war and famine and disease. ¹²Disease will strike down those who are far away in exile. War will destroy those who are nearby. And anyone who survives will be killed by famine. So at last I will spend my fury on them. ¹³They will know that I am the LORD when their dead lie scattered among their idols and altars on every hill and mountain and under every green tree and every great shade tree—the places where they offered sacrifices to their idols. ¹⁴I will crush them and make their cities desolate from the wilderness in the south to Riblah* in the north. Then they will know that I am the LORD."

7 THE COMING OF THE END

Then this message came to me from the LORD: ²"Son of man, this is what the Sovereign LORD says to Israel:

"The end is here!
    Wherever you look—
east, west, north, or south—
    your land is finished.
³ No hope remains,
    for I will unleash my anger against you.
I will call you to account
    for all your detestable sins.
⁴ I will turn my eyes away and show no pity.
    I will repay you for all your detestable
        sins.
Then you will know that I am the LORD.

⁵ "This is what the Sovereign LORD says:
Disaster after disaster
    is coming your way!
⁶ The end has come.
    It has finally arrived.
    Your final doom is waiting!
⁷ O people of Israel, the day of your
        destruction is dawning.
    The time has come; the day of trouble
        is near.
Shouts of anguish will be heard on the
        mountains,
    not shouts of joy.
⁸ Soon I will pour out my fury on you
    and unleash my anger against you.
I will call you to account
    for all your detestable sins.
⁹ I will turn my eyes away and show no pity.
    I will repay you for all your detestable sins.

Then you will know that it is I, the LORD,
    who is striking the blow.

¹⁰ "The day of judgment is here;
    your destruction awaits!
The people's wickedness and pride
    have blossomed to full flower.
¹¹ Their violence has grown into a rod
    that will beat them for their wickedness.
None of these proud and wicked people will
        survive.
    All their wealth and prestige will be swept
        away.
¹² Yes, the time has come;
    the day is here!
Buyers should not rejoice over bargains,
    nor sellers grieve over losses,
for all of them will fall
    under my terrible anger.
¹³ Even if the merchants survive,
    they will never return to their business.
For what God has said applies to everyone—
    it will not be changed!
Not one person whose life is twisted by sin
    will ever recover.

THE DESOLATION OF ISRAEL

¹⁴ "The trumpet calls Israel's army to mobilize,
    but no one listens,
    for my fury is against them all.
¹⁵ There is war outside the city
    and disease and famine within.
Those outside the city walls
    will be killed by enemy swords.
Those inside the city
    will die of famine and disease.
¹⁶ The survivors who escape to the mountains
    will moan like doves, weeping for their
        sins.
¹⁷ Their hands will hang limp,
    their knees will be weak as water.
¹⁸ They will dress themselves in burlap;
    horror and shame will cover them.
They will shave their heads
    in sorrow and remorse.

¹⁹ "They will throw their money in the streets,
    tossing it out like worthless trash.
Their silver and gold won't save them
    on that day of the LORD's anger.
It will neither satisfy nor feed them,
    for their greed can only trip them up.
²⁰ They were proud of their beautiful jewelry
    and used it to make detestable idols and
        vile images.
Therefore, I will make all their wealth

6:14 As in some Hebrew manuscripts; most Hebrew manuscripts read *Diblah*.

disgusting to them.
²¹ I will give it as plunder to foreigners,
   to the most wicked of nations,
   and they will defile it.
²² I will turn my eyes from them
   as these robbers invade and defile my
      treasured land.

²³ "Prepare chains for my people,
   for the land is bloodied by terrible crimes.
   Jerusalem is filled with violence.
²⁴ I will bring the most ruthless of nations
   to occupy their homes.
   I will break down their proud fortresses
   and defile their sanctuaries.
²⁵ Terror and trembling will overcome my
      people.
   They will look for peace but not find it.
²⁶ Calamity will follow calamity;
   rumor will follow rumor.
   They will look in vain
   for a vision from the prophets.
   They will receive no teaching from the
      priests
   and no counsel from the leaders.
²⁷ The king and the prince will stand helpless,
      weeping in despair,
   and the people's hands
      will tremble with fear.
   I will bring on them
      the evil they have done to others,
   and they will receive the punishment
      they so richly deserve.
   Then they will know that I am the Lord."

8 IDOLATRY IN THE TEMPLE Then on September 17,* during the sixth year of King Jehoiachin's captivity, while the leaders of Judah were in my home, the Sovereign Lord took hold of me. ²I saw a figure that appeared to be a man. From what appeared to be his waist down, he looked like a burning flame. From the waist up he looked like gleaming amber.* ³He reached out what seemed to be a hand and took me by the hair. Then the Spirit lifted me up into the sky and transported me to Jerusalem in a vision from God. I was taken to the north gate of the inner courtyard of the Temple, where there is a large idol that has made the Lord very jealous. ⁴Suddenly, the glory of the God of Israel was there, just as I had seen it before in the valley.

⁵Then the Lord said to me, "Son of man, look toward the north." So I looked, and there

to the north, beside the entrance to the gate near the altar, stood the idol that had made the Lord so jealous.

⁶"Son of man," he said, "do you see what they are doing? Do you see the detestable sins the people of Israel are committing to drive me from my Temple? But come, and you will see even more detestable sins than these!" ⁷Then he brought me to the door of the Temple courtyard, where I could see a hole in the wall. ⁸He said to me, "Now, son of man, dig into the wall." So I dug into the wall and found a hidden doorway.

⁹"Go in," he said, "and see the wicked and detestable sins they are committing in there!" ¹⁰So I went in and saw the walls engraved with all kinds of crawling animals and detestable creatures. I also saw the various idols* worshiped by the people of Israel. ¹¹Seventy leaders of Israel were standing there with Jaazaniah son of Shaphan in the center. Each of them held an incense burner, from which a cloud of incense rose above their heads.

¹²Then the Lord said to me, "Son of man, have you seen what the leaders of Israel are doing with their idols in dark rooms? They are saying, 'The Lord doesn't see us; he has deserted our land!'" ¹³Then the Lord added, "Come, and I will show you even more detestable sins than these!"

¹⁴He brought me to the north gate of the Lord's Temple, and some women were sitting there, weeping for the god Tammuz. ¹⁵"Have you seen this?" he asked. "But I will show you even more detestable sins than these!"

¹⁶Then he brought me into the inner courtyard of the Lord's Temple. At the entrance to the sanctuary, between the entry room and the bronze altar, there were about twenty-five

8:1 Hebrew *on the fifth day of the sixth month,* of the ancient Hebrew lunar calendar. This event occurred on September 17, 592 B.C.; also see note on 1:1.   8:2 Or *like burnished metal.*   8:10 The Hebrew term (literally *round things*) probably alludes to dung.

MONEY
(7:19) Ezekiel prophesied that hard times would make money seem worthless. Money wouldn't buy them out of trouble. Have you ever thought of money as the ultimate deliverance from your problems? Many people do. It can pay for a lot of things. But it can also cause trouble if it stands between a person and God. That's why the apostle Paul later wrote that the love of money—not money itself—is the real problem (see 1 Tim 6:10). How ironic that we use wealth—a gift of God—to buy things that separate us from him. Is God your true source of satisfaction, or is money?

AN OPEN BOOK
(8:6) In scene after scene, God revealed to Ezekiel the moral downfall of the people of Judah. God's Spirit works with us in a similar way, convicting us of the wrong things we do. Our lives are like an open book to him. How comfortable would you feel if God revealed what's on the pages of your life today?

men with their backs to the sanctuary of the Lord. They were facing east, bowing low to the ground, worshiping the sun!

¹⁷"Have you seen this, son of man?" he asked. "Is it nothing to the people of Judah that they commit these detestable sins, leading the whole nation into violence, thumbing their noses at me, and provoking my anger? ¹⁸Therefore, I will respond in fury. I will neither pity nor spare them. And though they cry for mercy, I will not listen."

9 THE SLAUGHTER OF IDOLATERS Then the Lord thundered, "Bring on the men appointed to punish the city! Tell them to bring their weapons with them!" ²Six men soon appeared from the upper gate that faces north, each carrying a deadly weapon in his hand. With them was a man dressed in linen, who carried a writer's case at his side. They all went into the Temple courtyard and stood beside the bronze altar.

³Then the glory of the God of Israel rose up from between the cherubim, where it had rested, and moved to the entrance of the Temple. And the Lord called to the man dressed in linen who was carrying the writer's case. ⁴He said to him, "Walk through the streets of Jerusalem and put a mark on the foreheads of all who weep and sigh because of the detestable sins being committed in their city."

⁵Then I heard the Lord say to the other men, "Follow him through the city and kill everyone whose forehead is not marked. Show no mercy; have no pity! ⁶Kill them all—old and young, girls and women and little children. But do not touch anyone with the mark. Begin right here at the Temple." So they began by killing the seventy leaders.

⁷"Defile the Temple!" the Lord commanded. "Fill its courtyards with corpses. Go!" So they went and began killing throughout the city.

⁸While they were out killing, I was all alone. I fell face down on the ground and cried out, "O Sovereign Lord! Will your fury against Jerusalem wipe out everyone left in Israel?"

⁹Then he said to me, "The sins of the people of Israel and Judah are very, very great. The en-

tire land is full of murder; the city is filled with injustice. They are saying, 'The Lord doesn't see it! The Lord has abandoned the land!' ¹⁰So I will not spare them or have any pity on them. I will fully repay them for all they have done."

¹¹Then the man in linen clothing, who carried the writer's case, reported back and said, "I have done as you commanded."

10 THE LORD'S GLORY LEAVES THE TEMPLE In my vision I saw what appeared to be a throne of blue lapis lazuli above the crystal surface over the heads of the cherubim. ²Then the Lord spoke to the man in linen clothing and said, "Go between the whirling wheels beneath the cherubim, and take a handful of burning coals and scatter them over the city." He did this as I watched.

³The cherubim were standing at the south end of the Temple when the man went in, and the cloud of glory filled the inner courtyard. ⁴Then the glory of the Lord rose up from above the cherubim and went over to the door of the Temple. The Temple was filled with this cloud of glory, and the courtyard glowed brightly with the glory of the Lord. ⁵The moving wings of the cherubim sounded like the voice of God Almighty* and could be heard even in the outer courtyard.

⁶The Lord said to the man in linen clothing, "Go between the cherubim and take some burning coals from between the wheels." So the man went in and stood beside one of the wheels. ⁷Then one of the cherubim reached out his hand and took some live coals from the fire burning among them. He put the coals into the hands of the man in linen clothing, and the man took them and went out. ⁸(All the cherubim had what looked like human hands under their wings.)

⁹I looked, and each of the four cherubim had a wheel beside him, and the wheels sparkled like beryl. ¹⁰All four wheels looked alike and were made the same; each wheel had a second wheel turning crosswise within it. ¹¹The cherubim could move in any of the four directions they faced, without turning as they moved. They went straight in the direction they faced, never turning aside. ¹²Both the cherubim and the wheels were covered with eyes. The cherubim had eyes all over their bodies, including their hands, their backs, and their wings. ¹³I heard someone refer to the wheels as "the whirling wheels." ¹⁴Each of the four cherubim had four faces: the first was the face

10:5 Hebrew El-Shaddai.

of an ox,* the second was a human face, the third was the face of a lion, and the fourth was the face of an eagle.

¹⁵Then the cherubim rose upward. These were the same living beings I had seen beside the Kebar River. ¹⁶When the cherubim moved, the wheels moved with them. When they lifted their wings to fly, the wheels stayed beside them. ¹⁷When the cherubim stopped, the wheels stopped. When they flew upward, the wheels rose up, for the spirit of the living beings was in the wheels.

¹⁸Then the glory of the Lord moved out from the door of the Temple and hovered above the cherubim. ¹⁹And as I watched, the cherubim flew with their wheels to the east gate of the Lord's Temple. And the glory of the God of Israel hovered above them.

²⁰These were the same living beings I had seen beneath the God of Israel when I was by the Kebar River. I knew they were cherubim, ²¹for each had four faces and four wings and what looked like human hands under their wings. ²²And their faces were just like the faces of the beings I had seen at the Kebar, and they traveled straight ahead, just as the others had.

11 JUDGMENT ON ISRAEL'S LEADERS

Then the Spirit lifted me and brought me to the east gateway of the Lord's Temple, where I saw twenty-five prominent men of the city. Among them were Jaazaniah son of Azzur and Pelatiah son of Benaiah, who were leaders among the people.

²The Spirit said to me, "Son of man, these are the men who are planning evil and giving wicked counsel in this city. ³They say to the people, 'Is it not a good time to build houses? This city is like an iron pot. We are safe inside it like meat in a pot.*' ⁴Therefore, son of man, prophesy against them loudly and clearly."

⁵Then the Spirit of the Lord came upon me, and he told me to say, "This is what the Lord says to the people of Israel: I know what you are saying, for I know every thought that comes into your minds. ⁶You have murdered many in this city and filled its streets with the dead.

⁷"Therefore, this is what the Sovereign Lord says: This city is an iron pot all right, but the pieces of meat are the victims of your injustice. As for you, I will soon drag you from this pot. ⁸I will bring on you the sword of war you so greatly fear, says the Sovereign Lord. ⁹I will drive you out of Jerusalem and hand you over to foreigners, who will carry out my judgments

against you. ¹⁰You will be slaughtered all the way to the borders of Israel. I will execute judgment on you, and you will know that I am the Lord. ¹¹No, this city will not be an iron pot for you, and you will not be like meat safe inside it. I will judge you even to the borders of Israel, ¹²and you will know that I am the Lord. For you have refused to obey my decrees and regulations; instead, you have copied the standards of the nations around you."

¹³While I was still prophesying, Pelatiah son of Benaiah suddenly died. Then I fell face down on the ground and cried out, "O Sovereign Lord, are you going to kill everyone in Israel?"

HOPE FOR EXILED ISRAEL

¹⁴Then this message came to me from the Lord: ¹⁵"Son of man, the people still left in Jerusalem are talking about you and your relatives and all the people of Israel who are in exile. They are saying, 'Those people are far away from the Lord, so now he has given their land to us!'

¹⁶"Therefore, tell the exiles, 'This is what the Sovereign Lord says: Although I have scattered you in the countries of the world, I will be a sanctuary to you during your time in exile. ¹⁷I, the Sovereign Lord, will gather you back from the nations where you have been scattered, and I will give you the land of Israel once again.'

¹⁸"When the people return to their homeland, they will remove every trace of their vile images and detestable idols. ¹⁹And I will give them singleness of heart and put a new spirit within them. I will take away their stony, stubborn heart and give them a tender, responsive heart,* ²⁰so they will obey my decrees and regulations. Then they will truly be my people, and I will be their God. ²¹But as for those who long for vile images and detestable idols, I will repay them fully for their sins. I, the Sovereign Lord, have spoken!"

THE LORD'S GLORY LEAVES JERUSALEM

²²Then the cherubim lifted their wings and rose into the air with their wheels beside them, and

10:14 Hebrew *the face of a cherub;* compare 1:10.   11:3 Hebrew *This city is the pot, and we are the meat.*   11:19 Hebrew *a heart of flesh.*

··

CONSEQUENCES

(11:1-12) From the time they entered the Promised Land (see Joshua), the Israelites were warned not to copy the customs and religious practices of other nations. Both then and now, disobeying this command has always led to trouble. Following the crowd might save you the hassle of being ridiculed and might even make you popular temporarily. But it won't save you from the consequences of wrong. Is anything (popularity, a relationship with the person of your dreams, money) worth the price of your soul (see Matt 16:26)?

the glory of the God of Israel hovered above them. [23]Then the glory of the LORD went up from the city and stopped above the mountain to the east.

[24]Afterward the Spirit of God carried me back again to Babylonia,* to the people in exile there. And so ended the vision of my visit to Jerusalem. [25]And I told the exiles everything the LORD had shown me.

12 SIGNS OF THE COMING EXILE Again a message came to me from the LORD: [2]"Son of man, you live among rebels who have eyes but refuse to see. They have ears but refuse to hear. For they are a rebellious people.

[3]"So now, son of man, pretend you are being sent into exile. Pack the few items an exile could carry, and leave your home to go somewhere else. Do this right in front of the people so they can see you. For perhaps they will pay attention to this, even though they are such rebels. [4]Bring your baggage outside during the day so they can watch you. Then in the evening, as they are watching, leave your house as captives do when they begin a long march to distant lands. [5]Dig a hole through the wall while they are watching and go out through it. [6]As they watch, lift your pack to your shoulders and walk away into the night. Cover your face so you cannot see the land you are leaving. For I have made you a sign for the people of Israel."

[7]So I did as I was told. In broad daylight I brought my pack outside, filled with the things I might carry into exile. Then in the evening while the people looked on, I dug through the wall with my hands and went out into the night with my pack on my shoulder.

[8]The next morning this message came to me from the LORD: [9]"Son of man, these rebels, the people of Israel, have asked you what all this means. [10]Say to them, 'This is what the Sovereign LORD says: These actions contain a message for King Zedekiah in Jerusalem* and for all the people of Israel.' [11]Explain that your actions are a sign to show what will soon happen to them, for they will be driven into exile as captives.

[12]"Even Zedekiah will leave Jerusalem at

OUT OF TIME
(12:21-28) *These two short messages were warnings that God's words would come true—soon! Less than six years later, Jerusalem was destroyed. Ever think that you or someone you know has plenty of time to make things right with God? Judgment can sometimes come swiftly. Before you know it, you may be out of time.*

night through a hole in the wall, taking only what he can carry with him. He will cover his face, and his eyes will not see the land he is leaving. [13]Then I will throw my net over him and capture him in my snare. I will bring him to Babylon, the land of the Babylonians,* though he will never see it, and he will die there. [14]I will scatter his servants and warriors to the four winds and send the sword after them. [15]And when I scatter them among the nations, they will know that I am the LORD. [16]But I will spare a few of them from death by war, famine, or disease, so they can confess all their detestable sins to their captors. Then they will know that I am the LORD."

[17]Then this message came to me from the LORD: [18]"Son of man, tremble as you eat your food. Shake with fear as you drink your water. [19]Tell the people, 'This is what the Sovereign LORD says concerning those living in Israel and Jerusalem: They will eat their food with trembling and sip their water in despair, for their land will be stripped bare because of their violence. [20]The cities will be destroyed and the farmland made desolate. Then you will know that I am the LORD.'"

A NEW PROVERB FOR ISRAEL [21]Again a message came to me from the LORD: [22]"Son of man, you've heard that proverb they quote in Israel: 'Time passes, and prophecies come to nothing.' [23]Tell the people, 'This is what the Sovereign LORD says: I will put an end to this proverb, and you will soon stop quoting it.' Now give them this new proverb to replace the old one: 'The time has come for every prophecy to be fulfilled!'

[24]"There will be no more false visions and flattering predictions in Israel. [25]For I am the LORD! If I say it, it will happen. There will be no more delays, you rebels of Israel. I will fulfill my threat of destruction in your own lifetime. I, the Sovereign LORD, have spoken!"

[26]Then this message came to me from the LORD: [27]"Son of man, the people of Israel are saying, 'He's talking about the distant future. His visions won't come true for a long, long time.' [28]Therefore, tell them, 'This is what the Sovereign LORD says: No more delay! I will now do everything I have threatened. I, the Sovereign LORD, have spoken!'"

13 JUDGMENT AGAINST FALSE PROPHETS Then this message came to me from the LORD: [2]"Son of man, prophesy

11:24 Or *Chaldea.* 12:10 Hebrew *the prince in Jerusalem;* similarly in 12:12. 12:13 Or *Chaldeans.*

against the false prophets of Israel who are inventing their own prophecies. Say to them, 'Listen to the word of the LORD. ³This is what the Sovereign LORD says: What sorrow awaits the false prophets who are following their own imaginations and have seen nothing at all!'

⁴"O people of Israel, these prophets of yours are like jackals digging in the ruins. ⁵They have done nothing to repair the breaks in the walls around the nation. They have not helped it to stand firm in battle on the day of the LORD. ⁶Instead, they have told lies and made false predictions. They say, 'This message is from the LORD,' even though the LORD never sent them. And yet they expect him to fulfill their prophecies! ⁷Can your visions be anything but false if you claim, 'This message is from the LORD,' when I have not even spoken to you?

⁸"Therefore, this is what the Sovereign LORD says: Because what you say is false and your visions are a lie, I will stand against you, says the Sovereign LORD. ⁹I will raise my fist against all the prophets who see false visions and make lying predictions, and they will be banished from the community of Israel. I will blot their names from Israel's record books, and they will never again set foot in their own land. Then you will know that I am the Sovereign LORD.

¹⁰"This will happen because these evil prophets deceive my people by saying, 'All is peaceful' when there is no peace at all! It's as if the people have built a flimsy wall, and these prophets are trying to reinforce it by covering it with whitewash! ¹¹Tell these whitewashers that their wall will soon fall down. A heavy rainstorm will undermine it; great hailstones and mighty winds will knock it down. ¹²And when the wall falls, the people will cry out, 'What happened to your whitewash?'

¹³"Therefore, this is what the Sovereign LORD says: I will sweep away your whitewashed wall with a storm of indignation, with a great flood of anger, and with hailstones of fury. ¹⁴I will break down your wall right to its foundation, and when it falls, it will crush you. Then you will know that I am the LORD. ¹⁵At last my anger against the wall and those who covered it with whitewash will be satisfied. Then I will say to you: 'The wall and those who whitewashed it are both gone. ¹⁶They were lying prophets who claimed peace would come to Jerusalem when there was no peace. I, the Sovereign LORD, have spoken!'

14:3 The Hebrew term (literally *round things*) probably alludes to dung; also in 14:4, 5, 6, 7.

JUDGMENT AGAINST FALSE WOMEN PROPHETS

¹⁷"Now, son of man, speak out against the women who prophesy from their own imaginations. ¹⁸This is what the Sovereign LORD says: What sorrow awaits you women who are ensnaring the souls of my people, young and old alike. You tie magic charms on their wrists and furnish them with magic veils. Do you think you can trap others without bringing destruction on yourselves? ¹⁹You bring shame on me among my people for a few handfuls of barley or a piece of bread. By lying to my people who love to listen to lies, you kill those who should not die, and you promise life to those who should not live.

²⁰"This is what the Sovereign LORD says: I am against all your magic charms, which you use to ensnare my people like birds. I will tear them from your arms, setting my people free like birds set free from a cage. ²¹I will tear off the magic veils and save my people from your grasp. They will no longer be your victims. Then you will know that I am the LORD. ²²You have discouraged the righteous with your lies, but I didn't want them to be sad. And you have encouraged the wicked by promising them life, even though they continue in their sins. ²³Because of all this, you will no longer talk of seeing visions that you never saw, nor will you make predictions. For I will rescue my people from your grasp. Then you will know that I am the LORD."

14 THE IDOLATRY OF ISRAEL'S LEADERS

Then some of the leaders of Israel visited me, and while they were sitting with me, ²this message came to me from the LORD: ³"Son of man, these leaders have set up idols* in their hearts. They have embraced things that will make them fall into sin. Why should I listen to their requests? ⁴Tell them, 'This is what the Sovereign LORD says: The people of Israel have set up idols in their hearts and fallen into sin, and then they go to a prophet asking for a message. So I, the LORD, will give them the kind of answer their great idolatry deserves. ⁵I will do

....

A COMFORTABLE LIE
(13:1-3) The false prophets had a large following because they comforted the people and approved of their actions even while they were sinning. Lies often are attractive, and liars may have large followings. Today, for example, some leaders assure us that God wants everyone to have health and material success. This is comforting, but is it true? God's own Son did not have an easy life on earth. He didn't even have a home (Matt 8:20)! Are the messages you believe consistent with what God teaches in his Word?

this to capture the minds and hearts of all my people who have turned from me to worship their detestable idols.'

⁶"Therefore, tell the people of Israel, 'This is what the Sovereign LORD says: Repent and turn away from your idols, and stop all your detestable sins. ⁷I, the LORD, will answer all those, both Israelites and foreigners, who reject me and set up idols in their hearts and so fall into sin, and who then come to a prophet asking for my advice. ⁸I will turn against such people and make a terrible example of them, eliminating them from among my people. Then you will know that I am the LORD.

⁹"'And if a prophet is deceived into giving a message, it is because I, the LORD, have deceived that prophet. I will lift my fist against such prophets and cut them off from the community of Israel. ¹⁰False prophets and those who seek their guidance will all be punished for their sins. ¹¹In this way, the people of Israel will learn not to stray from me, polluting themselves with sin. They will be my people, and I will be their God. I, the Sovereign LORD, have spoken!'"

....

A FEW GOOD PEOPLE
(14:6-11) The nation of Judah, though eager to accept the messages of false prophets, considered the presence of a few godly people in the nation an insurance policy against disaster. But merely having godly people around didn't prevent the nation from being destroyed. In the same way, the godliness of a pastor or friends will not protect us from the consequences of our own wrong actions. Each person is responsible for his or her own relationship with God. How are you living?

THE CERTAINTY OF THE LORD'S JUDGMENT

¹²Then this message came to me from the LORD: ¹³"Son of man, suppose the people of a country were to sin against me, and I lifted my fist to crush them, cutting off their food supply and sending a famine to destroy both people and animals. ¹⁴Even if Noah, Daniel, and Job were there, their righteousness would save no one but themselves, says the Sovereign LORD.

¹⁵"Or suppose I were to send wild animals to invade the country, kill the people, and make the land too desolate and dangerous to pass through. ¹⁶As surely as I live, says the Sovereign LORD, even if those three men were there, they wouldn't be able to save their own sons or daughters. They alone would be saved, but the land would be made desolate.

¹⁷"Or suppose I were to bring war against the land, and I sent enemy armies to destroy both people and animals. ¹⁸As surely as I live, says the Sovereign LORD, even if those three men were there, they wouldn't be able to save their own sons or daughters. They alone would be saved.

¹⁹"Or suppose I were to pour out my fury by sending an epidemic into the land, and the disease killed people and animals alike. ²⁰As surely as I live, says the Sovereign LORD, even if Noah, Daniel, and Job were there, they wouldn't be able to save their own sons or daughters. They alone would be saved by their righteousness.

²¹"Now this is what the Sovereign LORD says: How terrible it will be when all four of these

I WONDER...

It doesn't seem like I'm making much progress as a Christian. It even seems like I'm going backward. What can I do to reverse my reversal?

Until about age 25, we grow physically. After that, we start to die. Fortunately, it usually takes another 50 to 60 years to complete the dying process!

Our spiritual life goes through a living-and-dying process, too. It either grows, or it gradually dies. It can't remain at the same level.

When you recognize that you've messed up, you're already at the beginning stage of spiritual growth.

The second stage is discovering what caused you to "die" spiritually. God confronted his people continually about this. Speaking through Ezekiel, he showed them that idols had taken God's place in their hearts (see Ezek 14:1-5).

Is there an "idol" (sports or other leisure activities,

a relationship, money and possessions) in your life—something you love more than God? If so, are you willing to give up the idol and be straight with God (see 1 Jn 1:9)?

The third stage is the one that many Christians forget—finding someone to hold us accountable. You need someone to encourage you, to ask tough questions, to kick you in the pants when you need it, and to pray for you. This could be a friend your own age who has a real desire to grow spiritually. It could be a Christian adult whom you like and respect—or anyone who is genuinely concerned for you, who won't give up on you and will always pull for you.

Ask God to send you such a person. This may be scary, but Christians who are growing have learned the secret of asking others to help them stay on track. Always seek out someone who will walk with you. It will help keep you from falling and provide you with close, lifelong friends.

dreadful punishments fall upon Jerusalem—war, famine, wild animals, and disease—destroying all her people and animals. ²²Yet there will be survivors, and they will come here to join you as exiles in Babylon. You will see with your own eyes how wicked they are, and then you will feel better about what I have done to Jerusalem. ²³When you meet them and see their behavior, you will understand that these things are not being done to Israel without cause. I, the Sovereign LORD, have spoken!"

15 JERUSALEM—A USELESS VINE Then this message came to me from the LORD: ²"Son of man, how does a grapevine compare to a tree? Is a vine's wood as useful as the wood of a tree? ³Can its wood be used for making things, like pegs to hang up pots and pans? ⁴No, it can only be used for fuel, and even as fuel, it burns too quickly. ⁵Vines are useless both before and after being put into the fire!

⁶"And this is what the Sovereign LORD says: The people of Jerusalem are like grapevines growing among the trees of the forest. Since they are useless, I have thrown them on the fire to be burned. ⁷And I will see to it that if they escape from one fire, they will fall into another. When I turn against them, you will know that I am the LORD. ⁸And I will make the land desolate because my people have been unfaithful to me. I, the Sovereign LORD, have spoken!"

16 JERUSALEM—AN UNFAITHFUL WIFE Then another message came to me from the LORD: ²"Son of man, confront Jerusalem with her detestable sins. ³Give her this message from the Sovereign LORD: You are nothing but a Canaanite! Your father was an Amorite and your mother a Hittite. ⁴On the day you were born, no one cared about you. Your umbilical cord was not cut, and you were never washed, rubbed with salt, and wrapped in cloth. ⁵No one had the slightest interest in you; no one pitied you or cared for you. On the day you were born, you were unwanted, dumped in a field and left to die.

⁶"But I came by and saw you there, helplessly kicking about in your own blood. As you lay there, I said, 'Live!' ⁷And I helped you to thrive like a plant in the field. You grew up and became a beautiful jewel. Your breasts became full, and your body hair grew, but you were still naked. ⁸And when I passed by again, I saw that you were old enough for love. So I wrapped my cloak around you to cover your nakedness and declared my marriage vows. I made a covenant with you, says the Sovereign LORD, and you became mine.

⁹"Then I bathed you and washed off your blood, and I rubbed fragrant oils into your skin. ¹⁰I gave you expensive clothing of fine linen and silk, beautifully embroidered, and sandals made of fine goatskin leather. ¹¹I gave you lovely jewelry, bracelets, beautiful necklaces, ¹²a ring for your nose, earrings for your ears, and a lovely crown for your head. ¹³And so you were adorned with gold and silver. Your clothes were made of fine linen and were beautifully embroidered. You ate the finest foods—choice flour, honey, and olive oil—and became more beautiful than ever. You looked like a queen, and so you were! ¹⁴Your fame soon spread throughout the world because of your beauty. I dressed you in my splendor and perfected your beauty, says the Sovereign LORD.

¹⁵"But you thought your fame and beauty were your own. So you gave yourself as a prostitute to every man who came along. Your beauty was theirs for the asking. ¹⁶You used the lovely things I gave you to make shrines for idols, where you played the prostitute. Unbelievable! How could such a thing ever happen? ¹⁷You took the very jewels and gold and silver ornaments I had given you and made statues of men and worshiped them. This is adultery against me! ¹⁸You used the beautifully embroidered clothes I gave you to dress your idols. Then you used my special oil and my incense

---

SPIRITUAL CHECKUP
(15:1-8) The messages given to Ezekiel in chapters 15 through 17 provided further evidence that God was going to destroy Jerusalem. The first message was about a grapevine, useless at first and even more useless after being burned. Since the people of Jerusalem were useless to God because of their idol worship, they would be destroyed and their cities burned (see also Jer 13:1-11). All of that could have been prevented with regular spiritual checkups. Just as a physical checkup is necessary for good health, a spiritual checkup is necessary for spiritual health. You can do that by regularly communicating with God and keeping a clean slate with him (1 Jn 1:9). Are you spiritually healthy?

SPECIAL PRIVILEGES
(16:8-16) The people of Israel were God's chosen people—the nation through whom his message of salvation would be communicated to the entire world. Israel had been privileged as a nation. But their resources and advantages became sources of pride that eventually destroyed them. Ever know someone who allowed his or her advantages (looks, money, grades, whatever) to go to his or her head? Pride always leads to a fall (Prov 16:18).

to worship them. ¹⁹Imagine it! You set before them as a sacrifice the choice flour, olive oil, and honey I had given you, says the Sovereign Lord.

²⁰"Then you took your sons and daughters—the children you had borne to me—and sacrificed them to your gods. Was your prostitution not enough? ²¹Must you also slaughter my children by sacrificing them to idols? ²²In all your years of adultery and detestable sin, you have not once remembered the days long ago when you lay naked in a field, kicking about in your own blood.

²³"What sorrow awaits you, says the Sovereign Lord. In addition to all your other wickedness, ²⁴you built a pagan shrine and put altars to idols in every town square. ²⁵On every street corner you defiled your beauty, offering your body to every passerby in an endless stream of prostitution. ²⁶Then you added lustful Egypt to your lovers, provoking my anger with your increasing promiscuity. ²⁷That is why I struck you with my fist and reduced your boundaries. I handed you over to your enemies, the Philistines, and even they were shocked by your lewd conduct. ²⁸You have prostituted yourself with the Assyrians, too. It seems you can never find enough new lovers! And after your prostitution there, you still were not satisfied. ²⁹You added to your lovers by embracing Babylonia,* the land of merchants, but you still weren't satisfied.

³⁰"What a sick heart you have, says the Sovereign Lord, to do such things as these, acting like a shameless prostitute. ³¹You build your pagan shrines on every street corner and your altars to idols in every square. In fact, you have been worse than a prostitute, so eager for sin that you have not even demanded payment. ³²Yes, you are an adulterous wife who takes in strangers instead of her own husband. ³³Prostitutes charge for their services—but not you! You give gifts to your lovers, bribing them to come and have sex with you. ³⁴So you are the opposite of other prostitutes. You pay your lovers instead of their paying you!

NOT AS BAD?

(16:46-58) The people of Judah might have believed they weren't as bad as the people of Sodom (see Gen 19) or of Samaria (the northern kingdom of Israel). But God cured them of that delusion. These days, we might think we're better than people who murder, steal, or commit sexual sins. But we conveniently forget about (or overlook) sins like pride, laziness, overeating, lying, and ignoring the needy. These sins may not seem as "bad" as the others to us. Yet all sins are equal in God's eyes, and they all separate us from him.

JUDGMENT ON JERUSALEM'S PROSTITUTION

³⁵"Therefore, you prostitute, listen to this message from the Lord! ³⁶This is what the Sovereign Lord says: Because you have poured out your lust and exposed yourself in prostitution to all your lovers, and because you have worshiped detestable idols,* and because you have slaughtered your children as sacrifices to your gods, ³⁷this is what I am going to do. I will gather together all your allies—the lovers with whom you have sinned, both those you loved and those you hated—and I will strip you naked in front of them so they can stare at you. ³⁸I will punish you for your murder and adultery. I will cover you with blood in my jealous fury. ³⁹Then I will give you to these many nations who are your lovers, and they will destroy you. They will knock down your pagan shrines and the altars to your idols. They will strip you and take your beautiful jewels, leaving you stark naked. ⁴⁰They will band together in a mob to stone you and cut you up with swords. ⁴¹They will burn your homes and punish you in front of many women. I will stop your prostitution and end your payments to your many lovers.

⁴²"Then at last my fury against you will be spent, and my jealous anger will subside. I will be calm and will not be angry with you anymore. ⁴³But first, because you have not remembered your youth but have angered me by doing all these evil things, I will fully repay you for all of your sins, says the Sovereign Lord. For you have added lewd acts to all your detestable sins. ⁴⁴Everyone who makes up proverbs will say of you, 'Like mother, like daughter.' ⁴⁵For your mother loathed her husband and her children, and so do you. And you are exactly like your sisters, for they despised their husbands and their children. Truly your mother was a Hittite and your father an Amorite.

⁴⁶"Your older sister was Samaria, who lived with her daughters in the north. Your younger sister was Sodom, who lived with her daughters in the south. ⁴⁷But you have not merely sinned as they did. You quickly surpassed them in corruption. ⁴⁸As surely as I live, says the Sovereign Lord, Sodom and her daughters were never as wicked as you and your daughters. ⁴⁹Sodom's sins were pride, gluttony, and laziness, while the poor and needy suffered outside her door. ⁵⁰She was proud and committed detestable sins, so I wiped her out, as you have seen.*

16:29 Or *Chaldea.* **16:36** The Hebrew term (literally *round things*) probably alludes to dung. **16:50** As in a few Hebrew manuscripts and Greek version; Masoretic Text reads *as I have seen.*

⁵¹"Even Samaria did not commit half your sins. You have done far more detestable things than your sisters ever did. They seem righteous compared to you. ⁵²Shame on you! Your sins are so terrible that you make your sisters seem righteous, even virtuous.

⁵³"But someday I will restore the fortunes of Sodom and Samaria, and I will restore you, too. ⁵⁴Then you will be truly ashamed of everything you have done, for your sins make them feel good in comparison. ⁵⁵Yes, your sisters, Sodom and Samaria, and all their people will be restored, and at that time you also will be restored. ⁵⁶In your proud days you held Sodom in contempt. ⁵⁷But now your greater wickedness has been exposed to all the world, and you are the one who is scorned—by Edom* and all her neighbors and by Philistia. ⁵⁸This is your punishment for all your lewdness and detestable sins, says the LORD.

⁵⁹"Now this is what the Sovereign LORD says: I will give you what you deserve, for you have taken your solemn vows lightly by breaking your covenant. ⁶⁰Yet I will remember the covenant I made with you when you were young, and I will establish an everlasting covenant with you. ⁶¹Then you will remember with shame all the evil you have done. I will make your sisters, Samaria and Sodom, to be your daughters, even though they are not part of our covenant. ⁶²And I will reaffirm my covenant with you, and you will know that I am the LORD. ⁶³You will remember your sins and cover your mouth in silent shame when I forgive you of all that you have done. I, the Sovereign LORD, have spoken!"

17 **A STORY OF TWO EAGLES** Then this message came to me from the LORD: ²"Son of man, give this riddle, and tell this story to the people of Israel. ³Give them this message from the Sovereign LORD:

"A great eagle with broad wings and long feathers,
    covered with many-colored plumage,
    came to Lebanon.
He seized the top of a cedar tree
⁴   and plucked off its highest branch.
He carried it away to a city filled with merchants.
    He planted it in a city of traders.
⁵ He also took a seedling from the land
    and planted it in fertile soil.
He placed it beside a broad river,

16:57 As in many Hebrew manuscripts and Syriac version; Masoretic Text reads Aram.

where it could grow like a willow tree.
⁶ It took root there
    and grew into a low, spreading vine.
Its branches turned up toward the eagle,
    and its roots grew down into the ground.
It produced strong branches
    and put out shoots.
⁷ But then another great eagle came
    with broad wings and full plumage.
So the vine now sent its roots and branches
    toward him for water,
⁸ even though it was already planted in good soil
    and had plenty of water
so it could grow into a splendid vine
    and produce rich leaves and luscious fruit.

⁹ "So now the Sovereign LORD asks:
Will this vine grow and prosper?
No! I will pull it up, roots and all!
I will cut off its fruit
    and let its leaves wither and die.
I will pull it up easily
    without a strong arm or a large army.
¹⁰ But when the vine is transplanted,
    will it thrive?
No, it will wither away
    when the east wind blows against it.
It will die in the same good soil
    where it had grown so well."

THE RIDDLE EXPLAINED ¹¹Then this message came to me from the LORD: ¹²"Say to these rebels of Israel: Don't you understand the meaning of this riddle of the eagles? The king of Babylon came to Jerusalem, took away her king and princes, and brought them to Babylon. ¹³He made a treaty with a member of the royal family and forced him to take an oath of loyalty. He also exiled Israel's most influential leaders, ¹⁴so Israel would not become strong again and revolt. Only by keeping her treaty with Babylon could Israel survive.

¹⁵"Nevertheless, this man of Israel's royal family rebelled against Babylon, sending

GOD'S MESSENGERS
(17:1-8) The first eagle in this chapter represents King Nebuchadnezzar of Babylon (see 17:12), who appointed or "planted" Zedekiah as king in Jerusalem. Zedekiah rebelled against this arrangement and tried to join with Egypt, the second eagle, to battle Babylon. At the same time that Ezekiel described these events from Babylon, Jeremiah, a prophet located in Judah, was also warning Zedekiah not to form this alliance (Jer 2:36-37). Though miles apart, the prophets had the same message because both spoke for God. God still directs his chosen people to speak his truth all around the world.

ambassadors to Egypt to request a great army and many horses. Can Israel break her sworn treaties like that and get away with it? ¹⁶No! For as surely as I live, says the Sovereign LORD, the king of Israel will die in Babylon, the land of the king who put him in power and whose treaty he disregarded and broke. ¹⁷Pharaoh and all his mighty army will fail to help Israel when the king of Babylon lays siege to Jerusalem again and destroys many lives. ¹⁸For the king of Israel disregarded his treaty and broke it after swearing to obey; therefore, he will not escape.

¹⁹"So this is what the Sovereign LORD says: As surely as I live, I will punish him for breaking my covenant and disregarding the solemn oath he made in my name. ²⁰I will throw my net over him and capture him in my snare. I will bring him to Babylon and put him on trial for this treason against me. ²¹And all his best warriors* will be killed in battle, and those who survive will be scattered to the four winds. Then you will know that I, the LORD, have spoken.

²²"This is what the Sovereign LORD says: I will take a branch from the top of a tall cedar, and I will plant it on the top of Israel's highest mountain. ²³It will become a majestic cedar, sending forth its branches and producing seed. Birds of every sort will nest in it, finding shelter in the shade of its branches. ²⁴And all the trees will know that it is I, the LORD, who cuts the tall tree down and makes the short tree grow tall. It is I who makes the green tree wither and gives the dead tree new life. I, the LORD, have spoken, and I will do what I said!"

18 THE JUSTICE OF A RIGHTEOUS GOD

Then another message came to me from the LORD: ²"Why do you quote this proverb concerning the land of Israel: 'The parents have eaten sour grapes, but their children's mouths pucker at the taste'? ³As surely as I live, says the Sovereign LORD, you will not quote this proverb anymore in Israel. ⁴For all people are mine to judge—both parents and children alike. And this is my rule: The person who sins is the one who will die.

⁵"Suppose a certain man is righteous and

does what is just and right. ⁶He does not feast in the mountains before Israel's idols* or worship them. He does not commit adultery or have intercourse with a woman during her menstrual period. ⁷He is a merciful creditor, not keeping the items given as security by poor debtors. He does not rob the poor but instead gives food to the hungry and provides clothes for the needy. ⁸He grants loans without interest, stays away from injustice, is honest and fair when judging others, ⁹and faithfully obeys my decrees and regulations. Anyone who does these things is just and will surely live, says the Sovereign LORD.

¹⁰"But suppose that man has a son who grows up to be a robber or murderer and refuses to do what is right. ¹¹And that son does all the evil things his father would never do—he worships idols on the mountains, commits adultery, ¹²oppresses the poor and helpless, steals from debtors by refusing to let them redeem their security, worships idols, commits detestable sins, ¹³and lends money at excessive interest. Should such a sinful person live? No! He must die and must take full blame.

¹⁴"But suppose that sinful son, in turn, has a son who sees his father's wickedness and decides against that kind of life. ¹⁵This son refuses to worship idols on the mountains and does not commit adultery. ¹⁶He does not exploit the poor, but instead is fair to debtors and does not rob them. He gives food to the hungry and provides clothes for the needy. ¹⁷He helps the poor,* does not lend money at interest, and obeys all my regulations and decrees. Such a person will not die because of his father's sins; he will surely live. ¹⁸But the father will die for his many sins—for being cruel, robbing people, and doing what was clearly wrong among his people.

¹⁹"'What?' you ask. 'Doesn't the child pay for the parent's sins?' No! For if the child does what is just and right and keeps my decrees, that child will surely live. ²⁰The person who sins is the one who will die. The child will not be punished for the parent's sins, and the parent will not be punished for the child's sins. Righteous people will be rewarded for their own righteous behavior, and wicked people will be punished for their own wickedness. ²¹But if wicked people turn away from all their sins and begin to obey my decrees and do what is just and right, they will surely live and not die. ²²All their past sins will be forgotten,

---

TRADITIONS

(18:14-18) *Family traditions were very important to the Jews, but God made it clear that people should not follow the tradition of wrongdoing. Although your family is a powerful influence in your life, your actions are not determined by the past behavior of family members. Worried about being the product of your environment? You can choose to start a new tradition of closely following God.*

17:21 Or *his fleeing warriors.* The meaning of the Hebrew is uncertain.   **18:6** The Hebrew term (literally *round things*) probably alludes to dung; also in 18:12, 15.   **18:17** Greek version reads *He refuses to do evil.*

and they will live because of the righteous things they have done.

²³"Do you think that I like to see wicked people die? says the Sovereign LORD. Of course not! I want them to turn from their wicked ways and live. ²⁴However, if righteous people turn from their righteous behavior and start doing sinful things and act like other sinners, should they be allowed to live? No, of course not! All their righteous acts will be forgotten, and they will die for their sins.

²⁵"Yet you say, 'The Lord isn't doing what's right!' Listen to me, O people of Israel. Am I the one not doing what's right, or is it you? ²⁶When righteous people turn from their righteous behavior and start doing sinful things, they will die for it. Yes, they will die because of their sinful deeds. ²⁷And if wicked people turn from their wickedness, obey the law, and do what is just and right, they will save their lives. ²⁸They will live because they thought it over and decided to turn from their sins. Such people will not die. ²⁹And yet the people of Israel keep saying, 'The Lord isn't doing what's right!' O people of Israel, it is you who are not doing what's right, not I.

³⁰"Therefore, I will judge each of you, O people of Israel, according to your actions, says the Sovereign LORD. Repent, and turn from your sins. Don't let them destroy you! ³¹Put all your rebellion behind you, and find yourselves a new heart and a new spirit. For why should you die, O people of Israel? ³²I don't want you to die, says the Sovereign LORD. Turn back and live!

19 A FUNERAL SONG FOR ISRAEL'S KINGS
"Sing this funeral song for the princes of Israel:

² "What is your mother?
    A lioness among lions!
She lay down among the young lions
    and reared her cubs.
³ She raised one of her cubs
    to become a strong young lion.
He learned to hunt and devour prey,
    and he became a man-eater.
⁴ Then the nations heard about him,
    and he was trapped in their pit.
They led him away with hooks
    to the land of Egypt.

⁵ "When the lioness saw
    that her hopes for him were gone,
she took another of her cubs
    and taught him to be a strong young lion.

19:7 As in Greek version; Hebrew reads *He knew widows.*

⁶ He prowled among the other lions
    and stood out among them in his
        strength.
He learned to hunt and devour prey,
    and he, too, became a man-eater.
⁷ He demolished fortresses*
    and destroyed their towns and cities.
Their farms were desolated,
    and their crops were destroyed.
The land and its people trembled in fear
    when they heard him roar.
⁸ Then the armies of the nations attacked
        him,
    surrounding him from every direction.
They threw a net over him
    and captured him in their pit.
⁹ With hooks, they dragged him into a cage
    and brought him before the king of
        Babylon.
They held him in captivity,
    so his voice could never again be heard
        on the mountains of Israel.

¹⁰ "Your mother was like a vine
    planted by the water's edge.
It had lush, green foliage
    because of the abundant water.
¹¹ Its branches became strong—
    strong enough to be a ruler's scepter.
It grew very tall,
    towering above all others.
It stood out because of its height
    and its many lush branches.
¹² But the vine was uprooted in fury
    and thrown down to the ground.
The desert wind dried up its fruit
    and tore off its strong branches,
so that it withered
    and was destroyed by fire.
¹³ Now the vine is transplanted to the
        wilderness,
    where the ground is hard and dry.

....

UNFAREFR?
(18:25-32) The exiled people of Israel accused God of being unjust for punishing them. A typical response to punishment is to say, "That's not fair!" Ever think that? In reality, God is fair, but we have broken the rules. God doesn't have to live up to our ideas of fairness; instead, we must live up to his. Looking for loopholes in God's law? Why not commit to live by it instead?

TRUE POWER
(19:11-14) Not even the political and military might of Judah's kings could save the nation. Like branches of a vine, they would be cut off and uprooted by "the desert wind"—the Babylonian army (19:12). What do you depend on most? Physical strength? Intelligence? Financial status? Popularity? Nothing can stand against the true power—or judgment—of almighty God.

¹⁴ A fire has burst out from its branches
   and devoured its fruit.
Its remaining limbs are not
   strong enough to be a ruler's scepter.

"This is a funeral song, and it will be used in a funeral."

20 **THE REBELLION OF ISRAEL** On August 14,* during the seventh year of King Jehoiachin's captivity, some of the leaders of Israel came to request a message from the LORD. They sat down in front of me to wait for his reply. ²Then this message came to me from the LORD: ³"Son of man, tell the leaders of Israel, 'This is what the Sovereign LORD says: How dare you come to ask me for a message? As surely as I live, says the Sovereign LORD, I will tell you nothing!'

⁴"Son of man, bring charges against them and condemn them. Make them realize how detestable the sins of their ancestors really were. ⁵Give them this message from the Sovereign LORD: When I chose Israel—when I revealed myself to the descendants of Jacob in Egypt—I took a solemn oath that I, the LORD, would be their God. ⁶I took a solemn oath that day that I would bring them out of Egypt to a land I had discovered and explored for them— a good land, a land flowing with milk and honey, the best of all lands anywhere. ⁷Then I said to them, 'Each of you, get rid of the vile images you are so obsessed with. Do not defile yourselves with the idols* of Egypt, for I am the LORD your God.'

⁸"But they rebelled against me and would not listen. They did not get rid of the vile images they were obsessed with, or forsake the idols of Egypt. Then I threatened to pour out my fury on them to satisfy my anger while they were still in Egypt. ⁹But I didn't do it, for I acted to protect the honor of my name. I would not allow shame to be brought on my name among the surrounding nations who saw me reveal myself by bringing the Israelites out of Egypt. ¹⁰So I brought them out of Egypt and led them into the wilderness. ¹¹There I gave them my decrees and regulations so they could find life by keeping them. ¹²And I gave them my Sabbath days of rest as a sign between them and me. It was to remind them that I am the LORD, who had set them apart to be holy.

¹³"But the people of Israel rebelled against me, and they refused to obey my decrees there in the wilderness. They wouldn't obey my regulations even though obedience would have given them life. They also violated my Sab-

bath days. So I threatened to pour out my fury on them, and I made plans to utterly consume them in the wilderness. ¹⁴But again I held back in order to protect the honor of my name before the nations who had seen my power in bringing Israel out of Egypt. ¹⁵But I took a solemn oath against them in the wilderness. I swore I would not bring them into the land I had given them, a land flowing with milk and honey, the most beautiful place on earth. ¹⁶For they had rejected my regulations, refused to follow my decrees, and violated my Sabbath days. Their hearts were given to their idols. ¹⁷Nevertheless, I took pity on them and held back from destroying them in the wilderness.

¹⁸"Then I warned their children not to follow in their parents' footsteps, defiling themselves with their idols. ¹⁹'I am the LORD your God,' I told them. 'Follow my decrees, pay attention to my regulations, ²⁰and keep my Sabbath days holy, for they are a sign to remind you that I am the LORD your God.'

²¹"But their children, too, rebelled against me. They refused to keep my decrees and follow my regulations, even though obedience would have given them life. And they also violated my Sabbath days. So again I threatened to pour out my fury on them in the wilderness. ²²Nevertheless, I withdrew my judgment against them to protect the honor of my name before the nations that had seen my power in bringing them out of Egypt. ²³But I took a solemn oath against them in the wilderness. I swore I would scatter them among all the nations ²⁴because they did not obey my regulations. They scorned my decrees by violating my Sabbath days and longing for the idols of their ancestors. ²⁵I gave them over to worthless decrees and regulations that would not lead to life. ²⁶I let them pollute themselves* with the very gifts I had given them, and I allowed them to give their firstborn children as offerings to their gods—so I might devastate them and remind them that I alone am the LORD.

JUDGMENT AND RESTORATION ²⁷"Therefore, son of man, give the people of Israel this message from the Sovereign LORD: Your ancestors continued to blaspheme and betray me, ²⁸for when I brought them into the land I had promised them, they offered sacrifices on every high hill and under every green tree they saw! They roused my fury as they offered up

20:1 Hebrew *In the fifth month, on the tenth day,* of the ancient Hebrew lunar calendar. This day was August 14, 591 B.C.; also see note on 1:1. 20:7 The Hebrew term (literally *round things*) probably alludes to dung; also in 20:8, 16, 18, 24, 31, 39. 20:25-26 Or *I gave them worthless decrees and regulations. . . . I polluted them.*

sacrifices to their gods. They brought their perfumes and incense and poured out their liquid offerings to them. ²⁹I said to them, 'What is this high place where you are going?' (This kind of pagan shrine has been called Bamah—'high place'—ever since.)

³⁰"Therefore, give the people of Israel this message from the Sovereign LORD: Do you plan to pollute yourselves just as your ancestors did? Do you intend to keep prostituting yourselves by worshiping vile images? ³¹For when you offer gifts to them and give your little children to be burned as sacrifices,* you continue to pollute yourselves with idols to this day. Should I allow you to ask for a message from me, O people of Israel? As surely as I live, says the Sovereign LORD, I will tell you nothing.

³²"You say, 'We want to be like the nations all around us, who serve idols of wood and stone.' But what you have in mind will never happen. ³³As surely as I live, says the Sovereign LORD, I will rule over you with an iron fist in great anger and with awesome power. ³⁴And in anger I will reach out with my strong hand and powerful arm, and I will bring you back* from the lands where you are scattered. ³⁵I will bring you into the wilderness of the nations, and there I will judge you face to face. ³⁶I will judge you there just as I did your ancestors in the wilderness after bringing them out of Egypt, says the Sovereign LORD. ³⁷I will examine you carefully and hold you to the terms of the covenant. ³⁸I will purge you of all those who rebel and revolt against me. I will bring them out of the countries where they are in exile, but they will never enter the land of Israel. Then you will know that I am the LORD.

³⁹"As for you, O people of Israel, this is what the Sovereign LORD says: Go right ahead and worship your idols, but sooner or later you will obey me and will stop bringing shame on my holy name by worshiping idols. ⁴⁰For on my holy mountain, the great mountain of Israel, says the Sovereign LORD, the people of Israel will someday worship me, and I will accept them. There I will require that you bring me all your offerings and choice gifts and sacrifices. ⁴¹When I bring you home from exile, you will be like a pleasing sacrifice to me. And I will display my holiness through you as all the nations watch. ⁴²Then when I have brought you home to the land I promised with a solemn oath to give to your ancestors, you will know

that I am the LORD. ⁴³You will look back on all the ways you defiled yourselves and will hate yourselves because of the evil you have done. ⁴⁴You will know that I am the LORD, O people of Israel, when I have honored my name by treating you mercifully in spite of your wickedness. I, the Sovereign LORD, have spoken!"

JUDGMENT AGAINST THE NEGEV ⁴⁵*Then this message came to me from the LORD: ⁴⁶"Son of man, turn and face the south* and speak out against it; prophesy against the brushlands of the Negev. ⁴⁷Tell the southern wilderness, 'This is what the Sovereign LORD says: Hear the word of the LORD! I will set you on fire, and every tree, both green and dry, will be burned. The terrible flames will not be quenched and will scorch everything from south to north. ⁴⁸And everyone in the world will see that I, the LORD, have set this fire. It will not be put out.'"

⁴⁹Then I said, "O Sovereign LORD, they are saying of me, 'He only talks in riddles!'"

21 THE LORD'S SWORD OF JUDGMENT

¹*Then this message came to me from the LORD: ²"Son of man, turn and face Jerusalem and prophesy against Israel and her sanctuaries. ³Tell her, 'This is what the LORD says: I am your enemy, O Israel, and I am about to unsheath my sword to destroy your people—the righteous and the wicked alike. ⁴Yes, I will cut off both the righteous and the wicked! I will draw my sword against everyone in the land from south to north. ⁵Everyone in the world will know that I am the LORD. My sword is in my hand, and it will not return to its sheath until its work is finished.'

⁶"Son of man, groan before the people! Groan before them with bitter anguish and

....

POLLUTION
(20:30-38) God told the people of Israel that worshiping idols made them polluted. Water containing contaminants is polluted. Likewise, our lives are polluted when we accept the contaminants—immoral values—of this world. If we love money, we become greedy. If we lust, we become sexually immoral. Remaining pure in a polluted world is difficult, to say the least. But a heart filled with God's Holy Spirit leaves little room for pollution (see Titus 1:15-16).

ALL OF ME
(20:39) The Israelites were worshiping idols and sacrificing to God at the same time! Some people think that some religion is better than none at all. While persisting in a life of sin, we may think, Well, at least I go to church. God will be pleased with this effort. But God wants all of a person's life, not just part of it. No amount of religious ritual or personal sacrifice can make up for continuing sinful practices.

20:31 Or *and make your little children pass through the fire.*
20:34 Greek version reads *I will welcome you.* Compare 2 Cor 6:17.
20:45 Verses 20:45-49 are numbered 21:1-5 in Hebrew text.
20:46 Hebrew *toward Teman.*   21:1 Verses 21:1-32 are numbered 21:6-37 in Hebrew text.

a broken heart. [7]When they ask why you are groaning, tell them, 'I groan because of the terrifying news I have heard. When it comes true, the boldest heart will melt with fear; all strength will disappear. Every spirit will faint; strong knees will become as weak as water. And the Sovereign LORD says: It is coming! It's on its way!'"

[8]Then the LORD said to me, [9]"Son of man, give the people this message from the Lord:

"A sword, a sword
    is being sharpened and polished.
[10] It is sharpened for terrible slaughter
    and polished to flash like lightning!
Now will you laugh?
    Those far stronger than you have fallen
        beneath its power!*
[11] Yes, the sword is now being sharpened and polished;
    it is being prepared for the executioner.

[12] "Son of man, cry out and wail;
    pound your thighs in anguish,
for that sword will slaughter my people and their leaders—
    everyone will die!
[13] It will put them all to the test.
    What chance do they have?*
    says the Sovereign LORD.

[14] "Son of man, prophesy to them
    and clap your hands.
Then take the sword and brandish it twice,
        even three times,
to symbolize the great massacre,
    the great massacre facing them on every side.
[15] Let their hearts melt with terror,
    for the sword glitters at every gate.
It flashes like lightning
    and is polished for slaughter!
[16] O sword, slash to the right,
    then slash to the left,
wherever you will,
    wherever you want.

[17] I, too, will clap my hands,
    and I will satisfy my fury.
I, the LORD, have spoken!"

OMENS FOR BABYLON'S KING [18]Then this message came to me from the LORD: [19]"Son of man, make a map and trace two routes on it for the sword of Babylon's king to follow. Put a signpost on the road that comes out of Babylon where the road forks into two—[20]one road going to Ammon and its capital, Rabbah, and the other to Judah and fortified Jerusalem. [21]The king of Babylon now stands at the fork, uncertain whether to attack Jerusalem or Rabbah. He calls his magicians to look for omens. They cast lots by shaking arrows from the quiver. They inspect the livers of animal sacrifices. [22]The omen in his right hand says, 'Jerusalem!' With battering rams his soldiers will go against the gates, shouting for the kill. They will put up siege towers and build ramps against the walls. [23]The people of Jerusalem will think it is a false omen, because of their treaty with the Babylonians. But the king of Babylon will remind the people of their rebellion. Then he will attack and capture them.

[24]"Therefore, this is what the Sovereign LORD says: Again and again you remind me of your sin and your guilt. You don't even try to hide it! In everything you do, your sins are obvious for all to see. So now the time of your punishment has come!

[25]"O you corrupt and wicked prince of Israel, your final day of reckoning is here! [26]This is what the Sovereign LORD says:

"Take off your jeweled crown,
    for the old order changes.
Now the lowly will be exalted,
    and the mighty will be brought down.
[27] Destruction! Destruction!
    I will surely destroy the kingdom.
And it will not be restored until the one appears
    who has the right to judge it.
Then I will hand it over to him.

A MESSAGE FOR THE AMMONITES [28]"And now, son of man, prophesy concerning the Ammonites and their mockery. Give them this message from the Sovereign LORD:

"A sword, a sword
    is drawn for your slaughter.
It is polished to destroy,
    flashing like lightning!

IN THE FIRE
(21:1-27) The short message in 20:45-48 introduces the four messages in chapter 21 about the judgments that would come upon Jerusalem. The city would be destroyed because it was corrupted or spiritually unclean. According to Jewish law, unclean objects were to be passed through fire in order to purify them (see Num 31:21-23). God's judgment is designed to purify; destruction often is a necessary part of that process. Hard times and discipline are the "fire" God uses to purify our hearts (Ps 66:10; Prov 17:3). Feeling the heat? Can you, like Job, say with confidence, "[God] knows where I am going. And when he tests me, I will come out as pure as gold" (Job 23:10)?

21:10 The meaning of the Hebrew is uncertain.   **21:13** The meaning of the Hebrew is uncertain.

²⁹ Your prophets have given false visions,
     and your fortune-tellers have told lies.
The sword will fall on the necks of the
     wicked
       for whom the day of final reckoning has
       come.

³⁰ "Now return the sword to its sheath,
     for in your own country,
the land of your birth,
     I will pass judgment upon you.
³¹ I will pour out my fury on you
     and blow on you with the fire of my
     anger.
I will hand you over to cruel men
     who are skilled in destruction.
³² You will be fuel for the fire,
     and your blood will be spilled in your
     own land.
You will be utterly wiped out,
     your memory lost to history,
     for I, the LORD, have spoken!"

22 **THE SINS OF JERUSALEM** Now this message came to me from the LORD: ²"Son of man, are you ready to judge Jerusalem? Are you ready to judge this city of murderers? Publicly denounce her detestable sins, ³and give her this message from the Sovereign LORD: O city of murderers, doomed and damned—city of idols,* filthy and foul— ⁴you are guilty because of the blood you have shed. You are defiled because of the idols you have made. Your day of destruction has come! You have reached the end of your years. I will make you an object of mockery throughout the world. ⁵O infamous city, filled with confusion, you will be mocked by people far and near.

⁶"Every leader in Israel who lives within your walls is bent on murder. ⁷Fathers and mothers are treated with contempt. Foreigners are forced to pay for protection. Orphans and widows are wronged and oppressed among you. ⁸You despise my holy things and violate my Sabbath days of rest. ⁹People accuse others falsely and send them to their death. You are filled with idol worshipers and people who do obscene things. ¹⁰Men sleep with their fathers' wives and have intercourse with women who are menstruating. ¹¹Within your walls live men who commit adultery with their neighbors' wives, who defile their daughters-in-law, or who rape their own sisters. ¹²There are hired murderers, loan racketeers, and extortioners

everywhere. They never even think of me and my commands, says the Sovereign LORD.

¹³"But now I clap my hands in indignation over your dishonest gain and bloodshed. ¹⁴How strong and courageous will you be in my day of reckoning? I, the LORD, have spoken, and I will do what I said. ¹⁵I will scatter you among the nations and purge you of your wickedness. ¹⁶And when I have been dishonored among the nations because of you,* you will know that I am the LORD."

THE LORD'S REFINING FURNACE ¹⁷Then this message came to me from the LORD: ¹⁸"Son of man, the people of Israel are the worthless slag that remains after silver is smelted. They are the dross that is left over—a useless mixture of copper, tin, iron, and lead. ¹⁹So tell them, 'This is what the Sovereign LORD says: Because you are all worthless slag, I will bring you to my crucible in Jerusalem. ²⁰Just as copper, iron, lead, and tin are melted down in a furnace, I will melt you down in the heat of my fury. ²¹I will gather you together and blow the fire of my anger upon you, ²²and you will melt like silver in fierce heat. Then you will know that I, the LORD, have poured out my fury on you.'"

THE SINS OF ISRAEL'S LEADERS ²³Again a message came to me from the LORD: ²⁴"Son of man, give the people of Israel this message: In the day of my indignation, you will be like a polluted land, a land without rain. ²⁵Your princes* plot conspiracies just as lions stalk their prey. They devour innocent people, seizing treasures and extorting wealth. They make many widows in the land. ²⁶Your priests have violated my instructions and defiled my holy things. They make no distinction between what is holy and what is not. And they do not teach my people the difference between what is ceremonially clean and unclean. They disregard my Sabbath days so that I am dishonored among them. ²⁷Your leaders are like wolves who tear apart their victims. They actually destroy people's lives for money! ²⁸And

....

LEADERS
(22:6-13) *The leaders were especially responsible for the moral climate of the nation because they had been chosen by God to lead. The same is true today (see Jas 3:1-2). Unfortunately, many of the sins mentioned here have been committed in recent years by Christian leaders. We are living in a time of unprecedented attacks by Satan. It is vital that we uphold our leaders in prayer, and it is vital for leaders to seek accountability and help in their walk with God.*

22:3 The Hebrew term (literally *round things*) probably alludes to dung; also in 22:4.   **22:16** Or *when you have been dishonored among the nations.*   **22:25** As in Greek version; Hebrew reads *prophets.*

your prophets cover up for them by announcing false visions and making lying predictions. They say, 'My message is from the Sovereign LORD,' when the LORD hasn't spoken a single word to them. ²⁹Even common people oppress the poor, rob the needy, and deprive foreigners of justice.

³⁰"I looked for someone who might rebuild the wall of righteousness that guards the land. I searched for someone to stand in the gap in the wall so I wouldn't have to destroy the land, but I found no one. ³¹So now I will pour out my fury on them, consuming them with the fire of my anger. I will heap on their heads the full penalty for all their sins. I, the Sovereign LORD, have spoken!"

23 THE ADULTERY OF TWO SISTERS This message came to me from the LORD:

²"Son of man, once there were two sisters who were daughters of the same mother. ³They became prostitutes in Egypt. Even as young girls, they allowed men to fondle their breasts. ⁴The older girl was named Oholah, and her sister was Oholibah. I married them, and they bore me sons and daughters. I am speaking of Samaria and Jerusalem, for Oholah is Samaria and Oholibah is Jerusalem.

⁵"Then Oholah lusted after other lovers instead of me, and she gave her love to the Assyrian officers. ⁶They were all attractive young men, captains and commanders dressed in handsome blue, charioteers driving their horses. ⁷And so she prostituted herself with the most desirable men of Assyria, worshiping their idols* and defiling herself. ⁸For when she left Egypt, she did not leave her spirit of prostitution behind. She was still as lewd as in her youth, when the Egyptians slept with her, fondled her breasts, and used her as a prostitute.

⁹"And so I handed her over to her Assyrian lovers, whom she desired so much. ¹⁰They stripped her, took away her children as their slaves, and then killed her. After she received her punishment, her reputation was known to every woman in the land.

¹¹"Yet even though Oholibah saw what had happened to Oholah, her sister, she followed right in her footsteps. And she was even more depraved, abandoning herself to her lust and prostitution. ¹²She fawned over all the Assyrian officers—those captains and commanders in handsome uniforms, those charioteers driving their horses—all of them attractive young men. ¹³I saw the way she was going, defiling herself just like her older sister.

¹⁴"Then she carried her prostitution even further. She fell in love with pictures that were painted on a wall—pictures of Babylonian* military officers, outfitted in striking red uniforms. ¹⁵Handsome belts encircled their waists, and flowing turbans crowned their heads. They were dressed like chariot officers from the land of Babylonia.* ¹⁶When she saw these paintings, she longed to give herself to them, so she sent messengers to Babylonia to invite them to come to her. ¹⁷So they came and committed adultery with her, defiling her in the bed of love. After being defiled, however, she rejected them in disgust.

¹⁸"In the same way, I became disgusted with Oholibah and rejected her, just as I had rejected her sister, because she flaunted herself before them and gave herself to satisfy their lusts. ¹⁹Yet she turned to even greater prostitution, remembering her youth when she was a prostitute in Egypt. ²⁰She lusted after lovers with genitals as large as a donkey's and emissions like those of a horse. ²¹And so, Oholibah, you relived your former days as a young girl in Egypt, when you first allowed your breasts to be fondled.

THE LORD'S JUDGMENT OF OHOLIBAH

²²"Therefore, Oholibah, this is what the Sovereign LORD says: I will send your lovers against you from every direction—those very nations from which you turned away in disgust. ²³For the Babylonians will come with all the Chaldeans from Pekod and Shoa and Koa. And all the Assyrians will come with them—handsome young captains, commanders, chariot officers, and other high-ranking officers, all riding their horses. ²⁴They will all come against you from the north* with chariots, wagons, and a great army prepared for attack. They will take up positions on every side, surrounding you with men armed with shields and helmets. And I will hand you over to them for punishment so they can do with you as they please. ²⁵I will turn my jealous anger against you, and they will deal harshly with you. They will cut off your nose and ears, and any survivors will then be slaughtered by the sword. Your children will be taken away as captives, and everything that is left will be burned. ²⁶They will strip you of your beautiful clothes and jewels. ²⁷In this way, I will put a stop to the lewdness and prostitution you brought from Egypt. You will never again cast longing eyes on those things or fondly remember your time in Egypt.

23:7 The Hebrew term (literally *round things*) probably alludes to dung; also in 23:30, 37, 39, 49.   **23:14** Or *Chaldean.*   **23:15** Or *Chaldea;* also in 23:16.   **23:24** As in Greek version; the meaning of the Hebrew is uncertain.

²⁸"For this is what the Sovereign LORD says: I will surely hand you over to your enemies, to those you loathe, those you rejected. ²⁹They will treat you with hatred and rob you of all you own, leaving you stark naked. The shame of your prostitution will be exposed to all the world. ³⁰You brought all this on yourself by prostituting yourself to other nations, defiling yourself with all their idols. ³¹Because you have followed in your sister's footsteps, I will force you to drink the same cup of terror she drank.

³²"Yes, this is what the Sovereign LORD says:

"You will drink from your sister's cup
    of terror,
  a cup that is large and deep.
It is filled to the brim
  with scorn and derision.
³³ Drunkenness and anguish will fill you,
  for your cup is filled to the brim with
    distress and desolation,
  the same cup your sister Samaria drank.
³⁴ You will drain that cup of terror
  to the very bottom.
Then you will smash it to pieces
  and beat your breast in anguish.
I, the Sovereign LORD, have spoken!

³⁵"And because you have forgotten me and turned your back on me, this is what the Sovereign LORD says: You must bear the consequences of all your lewdness and prostitution."

THE LORD'S JUDGMENT ON BOTH SISTERS

³⁶The LORD said to me, "Son of man, you must accuse Oholah and Oholibah of all their detestable sins. ³⁷They have committed both adultery and murder—adultery by worshiping idols and murder by burning as sacrifices the children they bore to me. ³⁸Furthermore, they have defiled my Temple and violated my Sabbath day! ³⁹On the very day that they sacrificed their children to their idols, they boldly came into my Temple to worship! They came in and defiled my house.

⁴⁰"You sisters sent messengers to distant lands to get men. Then when they arrived, you bathed yourselves, painted your eyelids, and put on your finest jewels for them. ⁴¹You sat with them on a beautifully embroidered couch and put my incense and my special oil on a table that was spread before you. ⁴²From your room came the sound of many men carousing. They were lustful men and drunkards* from the wilderness, who put bracelets on your

wrists and beautiful crowns on your heads. ⁴³Then I said, 'If they really want to have sex with old worn-out prostitutes like these, let them!' ⁴⁴And that is what they did. They had sex with Oholah and Oholibah, these shameless prostitutes. ⁴⁵But righteous people will judge these sister cities for what they really are—adulterers and murderers.

⁴⁶"Now this is what the Sovereign LORD says: Bring an army against them and hand them over to be terrorized and plundered. ⁴⁷For their enemies will stone them and kill them with swords. They will butcher their sons and daughters and burn their homes. ⁴⁸In this way, I will put an end to lewdness and idolatry in the land, and my judgment will be a warning to others not to follow their wicked example. ⁴⁹You will be fully repaid for all your prostitution—your worship of idols. Yes, you will suffer the full penalty. Then you will know that I am the Sovereign LORD."

24 THE SIGN OF THE COOKING POT

On January 15,* during the ninth year of King Jehoiachin's captivity, this message came to me from the LORD: ²"Son of man, write down today's date, because on this very day the king of Babylon is beginning his attack against Jerusalem. ³Then give these rebels an illustration with this message from the Sovereign LORD:

"Put a pot on the fire,
    and pour in some water.
⁴ Fill it with choice pieces of meat—
    the rump and the shoulder
    and all the most tender cuts.
⁵ Use only the best sheep from the flock,
    and heap fuel on the fire beneath the pot.
Bring the pot to a boil,
    and cook the bones along with the meat.

⁶ "Now this is what the Sovereign LORD says:
What sorrow awaits Jerusalem,
    the city of murderers!
She is a cooking pot
    whose corruption can't be cleaned out.
Take the meat out in random order,

DOUBLE-MINDED
(23:36-39) *The Israelites sacrificed their own children to idols and then sacrificed to the Lord on the same day. But God called them on their double-mindedness. As James 1:6 says, "A person with divided loyalty is as unsettled as a wave of the sea that is blown and tossed by the wind." We cannot praise God and willfully do wrong things at the same time! That would be like telling your crush that he or she's your one and only, but then going on a date with someone else. As Joshua once told the people of Israel, "Choose today whom you will serve" (Josh 24:15).*

23:42 Or *Sabeans.*   24:1 Hebrew *On the tenth day of the tenth month,* of the ancient Hebrew lunar calendar. This event occurred on January 15, 588 B.C.; also see note on 1:1.

for no piece is better than another.
7 For the blood of her murders
    is splashed on the rocks.
It isn't even spilled on the ground,
    where the dust could cover it!
8 So I will splash her blood on a rock
    for all to see,
an expression of my anger
    and vengeance against her.

9 "This is what the Sovereign LORD says:
What sorrow awaits Jerusalem,
    the city of murderers!
I myself will pile up the fuel beneath her.
10 Yes, heap on the wood!
Let the fire roar to make the pot boil.
Cook the meat with many spices,
    and afterward burn the bones.
11 Now set the empty pot on the coals.
    Heat it red hot!
Burn away the filth and corruption.
12 But it's hopeless;
    the corruption can't be cleaned out.
    So throw it into the fire.
13 Your impurity is your lewdness
    and the corruption of your idolatry.
I tried to cleanse you,
    but you refused.
So now you will remain in your filth
    until my fury against you has been
        satisfied.

14"I, the LORD, have spoken! The time has come, and I won't hold back. I will not change my mind, and I will have no pity on you. You will be judged on the basis of all your wicked actions, says the Sovereign LORD."

THE DEATH OF EZEKIEL'S WIFE 15Then this message came to me from the LORD: 16"Son of man, with one blow I will take away your dearest treasure. Yet you must not show any sorrow at her death. Do not weep; let there be no tears. 17Groan silently, but let there be no wailing at her grave. Do not uncover your head or take off your sandals. Do not perform the

usual rituals of mourning or accept any food brought to you by consoling friends."

18So I proclaimed this to the people the next morning, and in the evening my wife died. The next morning I did everything I had been told to do. 19Then the people asked, "What does all this mean? What are you trying to tell us?"

20So I said to them, "A message came to me from the LORD, 21and I was told to give this message to the people of Israel. This is what the Sovereign LORD says: I will defile my Temple, the source of your security and pride, the place your heart delights in. Your sons and daughters whom you left behind in Judah will be slaughtered by the sword. 22Then you will do as Ezekiel has done. You will not mourn in public or console yourselves by eating the food brought by friends. 23Your heads will remain covered, and your sandals will not be taken off. You will not mourn or weep, but you will waste away because of your sins. You will mourn privately for all the evil you have done. 24Ezekiel is an example for you; you will do just as he has done. And when that time comes, you will know that I am the Sovereign LORD."

25Then the LORD said to me, "Son of man, on the day I take away their stronghold—their joy and glory, their heart's desire, their dearest treasure—I will also take away their sons and daughters. 26And on that day a survivor from Jerusalem will come to you in Babylon and tell you what has happened. 27And when he arrives, your voice will suddenly return so you can talk to him, and you will be a symbol for these people. Then they will know that I am the LORD."

25 **A MESSAGE FOR AMMON** Then this message came to me from the LORD: 2"Son of man, turn and face the land of Ammon and prophesy against its people. 3Give the Ammonites this message from the Sovereign LORD: Hear the word of the Sovereign LORD! Because you cheered when my Temple was defiled, mocked Israel in her desolation, and laughed at Judah as she went away into exile, 4I will allow nomads from the eastern deserts to overrun your country. They will set up their camps among you and pitch their tents on your land. They will harvest all your fruit and drink the milk from your livestock. 5And I will turn the city of Rabbah into a pasture for camels, and all the land of the Ammonites into a resting place for sheep and goats. Then you will know that I am the LORD.

6"This is what the Sovereign LORD says: Because you clapped and danced and cheered

....

THE AGONY OF OBEDIENCE
(24:15-27) *Although Ezekiel's wife died, God told him not to do the usual public mourning rituals (loud crying, putting dust on the head, wearing sackcloth). Instead, he was to be silent to mirror the grief Israel would go through when Jerusalem was destroyed. Ezekiel was obedient even in the face of agonizing grief. Would you have done the same? Many times, we slip into disobedience mode when obedience seems too difficult. But "too difficult" is an excuse, really. When the going gets tough, are you willing to keep going in obedience?*

with glee at the destruction of my people, [7]I will raise my fist of judgment against you. I will give you as plunder to many nations. I will cut you off from being a nation and destroy you completely. Then you will know that I am the LORD.

A MESSAGE FOR MOAB

[8]"This is what the Sovereign LORD says: Because the people of Moab have said that Judah is just like all the other nations, [9]I will open up their eastern flank and wipe out their glorious frontier towns—Beth-jeshimoth, Baal-meon, and Kiriathaim. [10]And I will hand Moab over to nomads from the eastern deserts, just as I handed over Ammon. Yes, the Ammonites will no longer be counted among the nations. [11]In the same way, I will bring my judgment down on the Moabites. Then they will know that I am the LORD.

A MESSAGE FOR EDOM

[12]"This is what the Sovereign LORD says: The people of Edom have sinned greatly by avenging themselves against the people of Judah. [13]Therefore, says the Sovereign LORD, I will raise my fist of judgment against Edom. I will wipe out its people and animals with the sword. I will make a wasteland of everything from Teman to Dedan. [14]I will accomplish this by the hand of my people of Israel. They will carry out my vengeance with anger, and Edom will know that this vengeance is from me. I, the Sovereign LORD, have spoken!

A MESSAGE FOR PHILISTIA

[15]"This is what the Sovereign LORD says: The people of Philistia have acted against Judah out of bitter revenge and long-standing contempt. [16]Therefore, this is what the Sovereign LORD says: I will raise my fist of judgment against the land of the Philistines. I will wipe out the Kerethites and utterly destroy the people who live by the sea. [17]I will execute terrible vengeance against them to punish them for what they have done. And when I have inflicted my revenge, they will know that I am the LORD."

26 A MESSAGE FOR TYRE

On February 3, during the twelfth year of King Jehoiachin's captivity,* this message came to me from the LORD: [2]"Son of man, Tyre has rejoiced over the fall of Jerusalem, saying, 'Ha! She who

was the gateway to the rich trade r[...] the east has been broken, and I am th[...] Because she has been made desolate, I [...] become wealthy!'

[3]"Therefore, this is what the Sovereign LORD says: I am your enemy, O Tyre, and I will bring many nations against you, like the waves of the sea crashing against your shoreline. [4]They will destroy the walls of Tyre and tear down its towers. I will scrape away its soil and make it a bare rock! [5]It will be just a rock in the sea, a place for fishermen to spread their nets, for I have spoken, says the Sovereign LORD. Tyre will become the prey of many nations, [6]and its mainland villages will be destroyed by the sword. Then they will know that I am the LORD.

[7]"This is what the Sovereign LORD says: From the north I will bring King Nebuchadnezzar* of Babylon against Tyre. He is king of kings and brings his horses, chariots, charioteers, and great army. [8]First he will destroy your mainland villages. Then he will attack you by building a siege wall, constructing a ramp, and raising a roof of shields against you. [9]He will pound your walls with battering rams and demolish your towers with sledgehammers. [10]The hooves of his horses will choke the city with dust, and the noise of the charioteers and chariot wheels will shake your walls as they storm through your broken gates. [11]His horsemen will trample through every street in the city. They will butcher your people, and your strong pillars will topple.

[12]"They will plunder all your riches and merchandise and break down your walls. They will destroy your lovely homes and dump your stones and timbers and even your dust into the sea. [13]I will stop the music of your songs. No more will the sound of harps be heard among your people. [14]I will make your island a bare rock, a place for fishermen to spread

....

HE MEANS WHAT HE SAYS

(26:1-14) Through Ezekiel, God declared that Tyre would be destroyed and never rebuilt. After a 15-year siege, Nebuchadnezzar couldn't conquer the part of Tyre located on the island. Consequently, certain aspects of the description in 26:12-14 actually go beyond the damage done to Tyre by Nebuchadnezzar and predict what would happen to the island settlement later during the conquests of Alexander the Great. Alexander threw the rubble of the mainland city into the sea until it made a bridge to the island. Today, the island city is still a pile of rubble—a testimony to God's judgment.

What God says will happen will happen. He doesn't take pleasure in destruction. He would much rather save than destroy. This is why he often warned people what would happen if they chose to disobey. How seriously do you take God's warnings?

26:1 Hebrew *In the eleventh year, on the first day of the month*, of the ancient Hebrew lunar calendar year. Since an element is missing in the date formula here, scholars have reconstructed this probable reading: *In the eleventh [month of the twelfth] year, on the first day of the month*. This reading would put this message on February 3, 585 B.C.; also see note on 1:1. **26:7** Hebrew *Nebuchadrezzar*, a variant spelling of Nebuchadnezzar.

will never be rebuilt, for I, the ... en. Yes, the Sovereign LORD ...

... TYRE'S DESTRUCTION [15]"This ... the Sovereign LORD says to Tyre: The whole coastline will tremble at the sound of your fall, as the screams of the wounded echo in the continuing slaughter. [16]All the seaport rulers will step down from their thrones and take off their royal robes and beautiful clothing. They will sit on the ground trembling with horror at your destruction. [17]Then they will wail for you, singing this funeral song:

"O famous island city,
    once ruler of the sea,
    how you have been destroyed!
Your people, with their naval power,
    once spread fear around the world.
[18] Now the coastlands tremble at your fall.
    The islands are dismayed as you
        disappear.

[19]"This is what the Sovereign LORD says: I will make Tyre an uninhabited ruin, like many others. I will bury you beneath the terrible waves of enemy attack. Great seas will swallow you. [20]I will send you to the pit to join those who descended there long ago. Your city will lie in ruins, buried beneath the earth, like those in the pit who have entered the world of the dead. You will have no place of respect here in the land of the living. [21]I will bring you to a terrible end, and you will exist no more. You will be looked for, but you will never again be found. I, the Sovereign LORD, have spoken!"

27 **THE END OF TYRE'S GLORY** Then this message came to me from the LORD: [2]"Son of man, sing a funeral song for Tyre, [3]that mighty gateway to the sea, the trading center of the world. Give Tyre this message from the Sovereign LORD:

"You boasted, O Tyre,
    'My beauty is perfect!'
[4] You extended your boundaries into the sea.
    Your builders made your beauty perfect.
[5] You were like a great ship
    built of the finest cypress from Senir.*

DANGER SIGNAL
(27:3-4) The beauty of Tyre was the source of its pride, and Tyre's pride guaranteed its judgment. Pride in our own accomplishments should be a danger signal to us (see Jas 4:14-16). We must maintain a humble dependence upon God.

They took a cedar from Lebanon
    to make a mast for you.
[6] They carved your oars
    from the oaks of Bashan.
Your deck of pine from the coasts of Cyprus*
    was inlaid with ivory.
[7] Your sails were made of Egypt's finest linen,
    and they flew as a banner above you.
You stood beneath blue and purple awnings
    made bright with dyes from the coasts of
        Elishah.
[8] Your oarsmen came from Sidon and Arvad;
    your helmsmen were skilled men from
        Tyre itself.
[9] Wise old craftsmen from Gebal did the
        caulking.
    Ships from every land came with goods to
        barter for your trade.

[10]"Men from distant Persia, Lydia, and Libya* served in your great army. They hung their shields and helmets on your walls, giving you great honor. [11]Men from Arvad and Helech stood on your walls. Your towers were manned by men from Gammad. Their shields hung on your walls, completing your beauty.

[12]"Tarshish sent merchants to buy your wares in exchange for silver, iron, tin, and lead. [13]Merchants from Greece,* Tubal, and Meshech brought slaves and articles of bronze to trade with you.

[14]"From Beth-togarmah came riding horses, chariot horses, and mules, all in exchange for your goods. [15]Merchants came to you from Dedan.* Numerous coastlands were your captive markets; they brought payment in ivory tusks and ebony wood.

[16]"Syria* sent merchants to buy your rich variety of goods. They traded turquoise, purple dyes, embroidery, fine linen, and jewelry of coral and rubies. [17]Judah and Israel traded for your wares, offering wheat from Minnith, figs,* honey, olive oil, and balm.

[18]"Damascus sent merchants to buy your rich variety of goods, bringing wine from Helbon and white wool from Zahar. [19]Greeks from Uzal* came to trade for your merchandise. Wrought iron, cassia, and fragrant calamus were bartered for your wares.

[20]"Dedan sent merchants to trade their expensive saddle blankets with you. [21]The Arabians and the princes of Kedar sent merchants to trade lambs and rams and male

27:5 Or Hermon.   27:6 Hebrew Kittim.   27:10 Hebrew Paras, Lud, and Put.   27:13 Hebrew Javan.   27:15 Greek version reads Rhodes.   27:16 Hebrew Aram; some manuscripts read Edom.   27:17 The meaning of the Hebrew is uncertain.   27:19 Hebrew Vedan and Javan from Uzal. The meaning of the Hebrew is uncertain.

goats in exchange for your goods. ²²The merchants of Sheba and Raamah came with all kinds of spices, jewels, and gold in exchange for your wares.

²³"Haran, Canneh, Eden, Sheba, Asshur, and Kilmad came with their merchandise, too. ²⁴They brought choice fabrics to trade—blue cloth, embroidery, and multicolored carpets rolled up and bound with cords. ²⁵The ships of Tarshish were your ocean caravans. Your island warehouse was filled to the brim!

THE DESTRUCTION OF TYRE

²⁶ "But look! Your oarsmen
     have taken you into stormy seas!
 A mighty eastern gale
     has wrecked you in the heart of the sea!
²⁷ Everything is lost—
     your riches and wares,
 your sailors and pilots,
     your ship builders, merchants, and
         warriors.
 On the day of your ruin,
     everyone on board sinks into the depths
         of the sea.
²⁸ Your cities by the sea tremble
     as your pilots cry out in terror.
²⁹ All the oarsmen abandon their ships;
     the sailors and pilots on shore come to
         stand on the beach.
³⁰ They cry aloud over you
     and weep bitterly.
 They throw dust on their heads
     and roll in ashes.
³¹ They shave their heads in grief for you
     and dress themselves in burlap.
 They weep for you with bitter anguish
     and deep mourning.
³² As they wail and mourn over you,
     they sing this sad funeral song:
 'Was there ever such a city as Tyre,
     now silent at the bottom of the sea?
³³ The merchandise you traded
     satisfied the desires of many nations.
 Kings at the ends of the earth
     were enriched by your trade.
³⁴ Now you are a wrecked ship,
     broken at the bottom of the sea.
 All your merchandise and crew
     have gone down with you.
³⁵ All who live along the coastlands
     are appalled at your terrible fate.
 Their kings are filled with horror
     and look on with twisted faces.

³⁶ The merchants among the nations
     shake their heads at the sight of you,
 for you have come to a horrible end
     and will exist no more.'"

28

A MESSAGE FOR TYRE'S KING Then this message came to me from the LORD: ²"Son of man, give the prince of Tyre this message from the Sovereign LORD:

"In your great pride you claim, 'I am a god!
     I sit on a divine throne in the heart of the
         sea.'
 But you are only a man and not a god,
     though you boast that you are a god.
³ You regard yourself as wiser than Daniel
     and think no secret is hidden from you.
⁴ With your wisdom and understanding you
     have amassed great wealth—
 gold and silver for your treasuries.
⁵ Yes, your wisdom has made you very rich,
     and your riches have made you very
         proud.

⁶ "Therefore, this is what the Sovereign LORD
     says:
 Because you think you are as wise as a god,
⁷   I will now bring against you a foreign
         army,
     the terror of the nations.
 They will draw their swords against your
     marvelous wisdom
     and defile your splendor!
⁸ They will bring you down to the pit,
     and you will die in the heart of the sea,
     pierced with many wounds.
⁹ Will you then boast, 'I am a god!'
     to those who kill you?
 To them you will be no god
     but merely a man!
¹⁰ You will die like an outcast*
     at the hands of foreigners.
     I, the Sovereign LORD, have spoken!"

¹¹Then this further message came to me from the LORD: ¹²"Son of man, sing this funeral song for the king of Tyre. Give him this message from the Sovereign LORD:

"You were the model of perfection,
     full of wisdom and exquisite in beauty.
¹³ You were in Eden,
     the garden of God.
 Your clothing was adorned with every
     precious stone*—
 red carnelian, pale-green peridot, white
     moonstone,
 blue-green beryl, onyx, green jasper,

27:36 Hebrew *hiss at you.* 28:10 Hebrew *will die the death of the uncircumcised.* 28:13 The identification of some of these gemstones is uncertain.

zuli, turquoise, and
.fted for you
nest gold.
.ven to you
the day you were created.
I ordained and anointed you
as the mighty angelic guardian.*
You had access to the holy mountain of God
and walked among the stones of fire.

¹⁵ "You were blameless in all you did
from the day you were created
until the day evil was found in you.
¹⁶ Your rich commerce led you to violence,
and you sinned.
So I banished you in disgrace
from the mountain of God.
I expelled you, O mighty guardian,
from your place among the stones of fire.
¹⁷ Your heart was filled with pride
because of all your beauty.
Your wisdom was corrupted
by your love of splendor.
So I threw you to the ground
and exposed you to the curious gaze
of kings.
¹⁸ You defiled your sanctuaries
with your many sins and your dishonest
trade.
So I brought fire out from within you,
and it consumed you.
I reduced you to ashes on the ground
in the sight of all who were watching.
¹⁹ All who knew you are appalled at your fate.
You have come to a terrible end,
and you will exist no more."

A MESSAGE FOR SIDON ²⁰Then another
message came to me from the Lord: ²¹"Son
of man, turn and face the city of Sidon and
prophesy against it. ²²Give the people of Sidon
this message from the Sovereign Lord:

"I am your enemy, O Sidon,
and I will reveal my glory by what I do
to you.

- -

THE PROMISE REMAINS
*(28:24-26) The promise that God's people will live in
complete safety has yet to be fulfilled. Although many
Jews were allowed to return from exile under Zerubbabel,
Ezra, and Nehemiah, and the political nation is restored
today, the inhabitants do not yet "live safely in Israel"
(28:26). Therefore, this promise will have its ultimate
fulfillment when Christ sets up his eternal kingdom. Never
doubt God's promises. They will come true—if not now,
then in eternity. God is into long-range planning. Are you
willing to trust his plans for your life?*

When I bring judgment against you
and reveal my holiness among you,
everyone watching will know
that I am the Lord.
²³ I will send a plague against you,
and blood will be spilled in your streets.
The attack will come from every direction,
and your people will lie slaughtered
within your walls.
Then everyone will know
that I am the Lord.
²⁴ No longer will Israel's scornful neighbors
prick and tear at her like briers and
thorns.
For then they will know
that I am the Sovereign Lord.

RESTORATION FOR ISRAEL ²⁵"This is what
the Sovereign Lord says: The people of Israel will again live in their own land, the land
I gave my servant Jacob. For I will gather them
from the distant lands where I have scattered
them. I will reveal to the nations of the world
my holiness among my people. ²⁶They will live
safely in Israel and build homes and plant
vineyards. And when I punish the neighboring
nations that treated them with contempt, they
will know that I am the Lord their God."

29 **A MESSAGE FOR EGYPT** On January 7,*
during the tenth year of King Jehoiachin's captivity, this message came to me from
the Lord: ²"Son of man, turn and face Egypt
and prophesy against Pharaoh the king and all
the people of Egypt. ³Give them this message
from the Sovereign Lord:

"I am your enemy, O Pharaoh, king of
Egypt—
you great monster, lurking in the streams
of the Nile.
For you have said, 'The Nile River is mine;
I made it for myself.'
⁴ I will put hooks in your jaws
and drag you out on the land
with fish sticking to your scales.
⁵ I will leave you and all your fish
stranded in the wilderness to die.
You will lie unburied on the open ground,
for I have given you as food to the wild
animals and birds.
⁶ All the people of Egypt will know that I am
the Lord,
for to Israel you were just a staff made
of reeds.

28:14 Hebrew *guardian cherub*; similarly in 28:16. **29:1** Hebrew
On the twelfth day of the tenth month, of the ancient Hebrew lunar
calendar. This event occurred on January 7, 587 B.C.; also see note
on 1:1.

7 When Israel leaned on you,
    you splintered and broke
    and stabbed her in the armpit.
When she put her weight on you, you gave
        way,
    and her back was thrown out of joint.

8"Therefore, this is what the Sovereign LORD
says: I will bring an army against you, O Egypt,
and destroy both people and animals. 9The
land of Egypt will become a desolate wasteland, and the Egyptians will know that I am the
LORD.

"Because you said, 'The Nile River is mine; I
made it,' 10I am now the enemy of both you and
your river. I will make the land of Egypt a totally
desolate wasteland, from Migdol to Aswan, as
far south as the border of Ethiopia.* 11For forty
years not a soul will pass that way, neither
people nor animals. It will be completely uninhabited. 12I will make Egypt desolate, and it
will be surrounded by other desolate nations.
Its cities will be empty and desolate for forty
years, surrounded by other ruined cities. I will
scatter the Egyptians to distant lands.

13"But this is what the Sovereign LORD also
says: At the end of the forty years I will bring
the Egyptians home again from the nations to
which they have been scattered. 14I will restore
the prosperity of Egypt and bring its people
back to the land of Pathros in southern Egypt
from which they came. But Egypt will remain
an unimportant, minor kingdom. 15It will be the
lowliest of all the nations, never again great
enough to rise above its neighbors. 16"Then Israel will no longer be tempted to
trust in Egypt for help. Egypt's shattered con-
dition will remind Israel of how sinful she was
to trust Egypt in earlier days. Then Israel will
know that I am the Sovereign LORD."

NEBUCHADNEZZAR TO CONQUER EGYPT 17On
April 26, the first day of the new year,* during
the twenty-seventh year of King Jehoiachin's
captivity, this message came to me from the
LORD: 18"Son of man, the army of King Nebuchadnezzar* of Babylon fought so hard against
Tyre that the warriors' heads were rubbed bare
and their shoulders were raw and blistered. Yet
Nebuchadnezzar and his army won no plunder
to compensate them for all their work. 19There-

fore, this is what the Sovereign LORD say
give the land of Egypt to Nebuchadnezza
of Babylon. He will carry off its wealth, plund
ing everything it has so he can pay his arm
20Yes, I have given him the land of Egypt as a
reward for his work, says the Sovereign LORD,
because he was working for me when he destroyed Tyre.

21"And the day will come when I will cause
the ancient glory of Israel to revive,* and then,
Ezekiel, your words will be respected. Then
they will know that I am the LORD."

30 A SAD DAY FOR EGYPT This is another
message that came to me from the
LORD: 2"Son of man, prophesy and give this
message from the Sovereign LORD:

"Weep and wail
    for that day,
3 for the terrible day is almost here—
    the day of the LORD!
It is a day of clouds and gloom,
    a day of despair for the nations.
4 A sword will come against Egypt,
    and those who are slaughtered will cover
        the ground.
Its wealth will be carried away
    and its foundations destroyed.
The land of Ethiopia* will be ravished.
5   Ethiopia, Libya, Lydia, all Arabia,*
and all their other allies
    will be destroyed in that war.

6 "For this is what the LORD says:
All of Egypt's allies will fall,
    and the pride of her power will end.
From Migdol to Aswan*
    they will be slaughtered by the sword,
    says the Sovereign LORD.
7 Egypt will be desolate,
    surrounded by desolate nations,
and its cities will be in ruins,
    surrounded by other ruined cities.
8 And the people of Egypt will know that I am
        the LORD

29:10 Hebrew from Migdol to Syene as far as the border of Cush.
29:17 Hebrew On the first day of the first month, of the ancient
Hebrew lunar calendar. This event occurred on April 26, 571 B.C.;
also see note on 1:1. 29:18 Hebrew Nebuchadrezzar, a variant
spelling of Nebuchadnezzar; also in 29:19. 29:21 Hebrew I will
cause a horn to sprout for the house of Israel. 30:4 Hebrew Cush;
similarly in 30:9. 30:5 Hebrew Cush, Put, Lud, all Arabia, Cub. Cub
is otherwise unknown and may be another spelling for Lub (Libya).
30:6 Hebrew to Syene.

CREDIT WHERE CREDIT IS DUE
*(29:9-12) The Nile River was Egypt's pride and joy, a life-
giving river cutting through the middle of the desert.
Rather than thanking God, however, Egypt declared, "The
Nile is mine!" We do the same when we say, "This house
is mine." Or, "I owe all of my success to me, myself." Or,
"I did it by myself." Sometimes we take for granted what
God has given us, thinking we have made it ourselves. Of
course, we have put forth a lot of hard effort, but God supplied us with the resources, abilities, and opportunities
to make it happen. Tempted to pat yourself on the back?
Why not give God some praise instead?*

...et Egypt on fire
...all their allies.
...end swift messengers in
...
...the complacent Ethiopians.
...t panic will come upon them
on that day of Egypt's certain destruction.
Watch for it!
It is sure to come!

[10] "For this is what the Sovereign LORD says:
By the power of King Nebuchadnezzar* of
Babylon,
I will destroy the hordes of Egypt.
[11] He and his armies—the most ruthless
of all—
will be sent to demolish the land.
They will make war against Egypt
until slaughtered Egyptians cover the
ground.
[12] I will dry up the Nile River
and sell the land to wicked men.
I will destroy the land of Egypt and
everything in it
by the hands of foreigners.
I, the LORD, have spoken!

[13] "This is what the Sovereign LORD says:
I will smash the idols* of Egypt
and the images at Memphis.*
There will be no rulers left in Egypt;
terror will sweep the land.
[14] I will destroy southern Egypt,*
set fire to Zoan,
and bring judgment against Thebes.*
[15] I will pour out my fury on Pelusium,*
the strongest fortress of Egypt,
and I will stamp out
the hordes of Thebes.
[16] Yes, I will set fire to all Egypt!
Pelusium will be racked with pain;
Thebes will be torn apart;
Memphis will live in constant terror.
[17] The young men of Heliopolis and Bubastis*
will die in battle,
and the women* will be taken away as
slaves.

[18] When I come to break the proud strength of
Egypt,
it will be a dark day for Tahpanhes, too.
A dark cloud will cover Tahpanhes,
and its daughters will be led away as
captives.
[19] And so I will greatly punish Egypt,
and they will know that I am the LORD."

THE BROKEN ARMS OF PHARAOH [20]On April 29,* during the eleventh year of King Jehoiachin's captivity, this message came to me from the LORD: [21]"Son of man, I have broken the arm of Pharaoh, the king of Egypt. His arm has not been put in a cast so that it may heal. Neither has it been bound up with a splint to make it strong enough to hold a sword. [22]Therefore, this is what the Sovereign LORD says: I am the enemy of Pharaoh, the king of Egypt! I will break both of his arms—the good arm along with the broken one—and I will make his sword clatter to the ground. [23]I will scatter the Egyptians to many lands throughout the world. [24]I will strengthen the arms of Babylon's king and put my sword in his hand. But I will break the arms of Pharaoh, king of Egypt, and he will lie there mortally wounded, groaning in pain. [25]I will strengthen the arms of the king of Babylon, while the arms of Pharaoh fall useless to his sides. And when I put my sword in the hand of Babylon's king and he brings it against the land of Egypt, Egypt will know that I am the LORD. [26]I will scatter the Egyptians among the nations, dispersing them throughout the earth. Then they will know that I am the LORD."

31 **EGYPT COMPARED TO FALLEN ASSYRIA** On June 21,* during the eleventh year of King Jehoiachin's captivity, this message came to me from the LORD: [2]"Son of man, give this message to Pharaoh, king of Egypt, and all his hordes:

"To whom would you compare your
greatness?
[3] You are like mighty Assyria,
which was once like a cedar of Lebanon,
with beautiful branches that cast deep
forest shade
and with its top high among the clouds.

RUMORS OF WAR
(30:20-26) This prophecy was given to Ezekiel in 587 B.C. God ended Egypt's military superiority and passed the torch to Babylon. God allows nations to rise to power to accomplish a particular purpose, often beyond our immediate understanding. Sometimes wars happen as a result. Rumors of war or ongoing wars can inspire fear, but God is still in control. Besides praying for your military and government leaders, you could pray that God's greater purpose will be carried out "on earth, as it is in heaven" (Matt 6:10).

30:10 Hebrew *Nebuchadrezzar,* a variant spelling of Nebuchadnezzar. **30:13a** The Hebrew term (literally *round things*) probably alludes to dung. **30:13b** Hebrew *Noph;* also in 30:16. **30:14a** Hebrew *Pathros.* **30:14b** Hebrew *No;* also in 30:15, 16. **30:15** Hebrew *Sin;* also in 30:16. **30:17a** Hebrew *of Awen and Pi-beseth.* **30:17b** Or *and her cities.* **30:20** Hebrew *On the seventh day of the first month,* of the ancient Hebrew lunar calendar. This event occurred on April 29, 587 B.C.; also see note on 1:1. **31:1** Hebrew *On the first day of the third month,* of the ancient Hebrew lunar calendar. This event occurred on June 21, 587 B.C.; also see note on 1:1.

⁴ Deep springs watered it
   and helped it to grow tall and luxuriant.
The water flowed around it like a river,
   streaming to all the trees nearby.
⁵ This great tree towered high,
   higher than all the other trees around it.
It prospered and grew long thick branches
   because of all the water at its roots.
⁶ The birds nested in its branches,
   and in its shade all the wild animals gave
      birth.
All the great nations of the world
   lived in its shadow.
⁷ It was strong and beautiful,
   with wide-spreading branches,
for its roots went deep
   into abundant water.
⁸ No other cedar in the garden of God
   could rival it.
No cypress had branches to equal it;
   no plane tree had boughs to compare.
No tree in the garden of God
   came close to it in beauty.
⁹ Because I made this tree so beautiful,
   and gave it such magnificent foliage,
it was the envy of all the other trees of Eden,
   the garden of God.

¹⁰"Therefore, this is what the Sovereign LORD
says: Because Egypt* became proud and arrogant, and because it set itself so high above
the others, with its top reaching to the clouds,
¹¹I will hand it over to a mighty nation that will
destroy it as its wickedness deserves. I have
already discarded it. ¹²A foreign army—the
terror of the nations—has cut it down and left
it fallen on the ground. Its branches are scattered across the mountains and valleys and
ravines of the land. All those who lived in its
shadow have gone away and left it lying there.

¹³ "The birds roost on its fallen trunk,
   and the wild animals lie among its
      branches.
¹⁴ Let the tree of no other nation
   proudly exult in its own prosperity,
though it be higher than the clouds
   and it be watered from the depths.
For all are doomed to die,
   to go down to the depths of the earth.
They will land in the pit
   along with everyone else on earth.

¹⁵"This is what the Sovereign LORD says:
When Assyria went down to the grave,* I made

the deep springs mourn. I stopped its rivers
and dried up its abundant water. I clothed
Lebanon in black and caused the trees of the
field to wilt. ¹⁶I made the nations shake with
fear at the sound of its fall, for I sent it down
to the grave with all the others who descend
to the pit. And all the other proud trees of
Eden, the most beautiful and the best of Lebanon, the ones whose roots went deep into the
water, took comfort to find it there with them
in the depths of the earth. ¹⁷Its allies, too, were
all destroyed and had passed away. They had
gone down to the grave—all those nations that
had lived in its shade.

¹⁸"O Egypt, to which of the trees of Eden will
you compare your strength and glory? You, too,
will be brought down to the depths with all
these other nations. You will lie there among
the outcasts* who have died by the sword.
This will be the fate of Pharaoh and all his
hordes. I, the Sovereign LORD, have spoken!"

32 A WARNING FOR PHARAOH On
March 3,* during the twelfth year of
King Jehoiachin's captivity, this message came
to me from the LORD: ²"Son of man, mourn
for Pharaoh, king of Egypt, and give him this
message:

"You think of yourself as a strong young lion
   among the nations,
but you are really just a sea monster,
heaving around in your own rivers,
   stirring up mud with your feet.
³ Therefore, this is what the Sovereign LORD
      says:
I will send many people
   to catch you in my net
   and haul you out of the water.
⁴ I will leave you stranded on the land to die.
   All the birds of the heavens will land on
      you,
and the wild animals of the whole earth
   will gorge themselves on you.
⁵ I will scatter your flesh on the hills
   and fill the valleys with your bones.

....

THE CRASH
(31:1-18) *Ezekiel compared Egypt to Assyria, calling
Assyria a great cedar tree that had crashed to the ground.
The fall of the mighty nation of Assyria was to be an
example to the Egyptians of what would happen to them.
Just like Assyria, Egypt took pride in her strength and
beauty. Someday, however, Egypt would come crashing
down just like Assyria. Nothing—not even a great society
with magnificent culture and military power—lasts apart
from God. Even a person with a bank account the size of
Fort Knox or super model looks can still crash and burn
if God is ignored. In what do you trust?*

31:10 Hebrew *you.*   31:15 Hebrew *to Sheol;* also in 31:16, 17.
31:18 Hebrew *among the uncircumcised.*   32:1 Hebrew *On the first
day of the twelfth month,* of the ancient Hebrew lunar calendar. This
event occurred on March 3, 585 B.C.; also see note on 1:1.

⁶ I will drench the earth with your gushing
blood
all the way to the mountains,
filling the ravines to the brim.
⁷ When I blot you out,
I will veil the heavens and darken the
stars.
I will cover the sun with a cloud,
and the moon will not give you its light.
⁸ I will darken the bright stars overhead
and cover your land in darkness.
I, the Sovereign LORD, have spoken!

⁹"I will disturb many hearts when I bring
news of your downfall to distant nations you
have never seen. ¹⁰Yes, I will shock many
lands, and their kings will be terrified at your
fate. They will shudder in fear for their lives as
I brandish my sword before them on the day of
your fall. ¹¹For this is what the Sovereign LORD
says:

"The sword of the king of Babylon
will come against you.
¹² I will destroy your hordes with the swords
of mighty warriors—
the terror of the nations.
They will shatter the pride of Egypt,

and all its hordes will be destroyed.
¹³ I will destroy all your flocks and herds
that graze beside the streams.
Never again will people or animals
muddy those waters with their feet.
¹⁴ Then I will let the waters of Egypt become
calm again,
and they will flow as smoothly as olive oil,
says the Sovereign LORD.
¹⁵ And when I destroy Egypt
and strip you of everything you own
and strike down all your people,
then you will know that I am the LORD.
¹⁶ Yes, this is the funeral song
they will sing for Egypt.
Let all the nations mourn.
Let them mourn for Egypt and its hordes.
I, the Sovereign LORD, have spoken!"

EGYPT FALLS INTO THE PIT ¹⁷On March 17,*
during the twelfth year, another message
came to me from the LORD: ¹⁸"Son of man,

32:17 Hebrew *On the fifteenth day of the month*, presumably in the
twelfth month of the ancient Hebrew lunar calendar (see 32:1). This
would put this message at the end of King Jehoiachin's twelfth year
of captivity, on March 17, 585 B.C.; also see note on 1:1. Greek
version reads *On the fifteenth day of the first month*, which would
put this message on April 27, 586 B.C., at the beginning of Jehoiachin's twelfth year.

ULTIMATE ISSUES *WHO'S IN CHARGE?*

Many Christians throw around terms like free will and
sovereignty. Free will, of course, is freedom of choice.
But sovereignty means that God ultimately is in control of everything. So, is free will really possible?

The idea that God is in control goes against our
notions of fairness and individual choice. And yet, we
draw strength and comfort from the belief that God
is running the universe. (That's what "sovereignty"
means.) Which is right? Is God truly sovereign—is he
calling the shots—or are people free and ultimately
responsible for making their own decisions, even
those that have eternal consequences?

This question has perplexed people for thousands
of years. It raises itself here, in the account of Pharaoh in Ezekiel 32. It came up in the story of another
Pharaoh, too (Exod 3–15). Before he allowed Pharaoh
to rise to power, did God know that Pharaoh would
sin? Did God simply allow Pharaoh to follow his own
course of action? In other words, did God simply roll
the dice, placing this man in authority without knowing whether or not he would obey his command to
let his people go? If so, does that mean that since
Creation, God has been a spectator in human events,
allowing us total freedom and responsibility? Either
conclusion leads to some awesome implications.
These questions might lead some to think, *If God is
truly and completely sovereign, then I have no real*

*freedom, and I'm just a puppet. But if I'm truly free
to do whatever I want, then God isn't really in control
of the universe.*

What's really true?

The greatest minds of history have wrestled with
this issue, and quite frankly, it remains as impenetra-
ble today as ever. So if you were hoping this article
would resolve it, you're going to be disappointed. But
we can consider it from a slightly different angle.

Contemporary theologian J. I. Packer, one of the
greatest minds of our time, was once asked, "If God
is truly sovereign, in what sense are humans responsible? And if human beings are truly responsible, in
what sense is God sovereign?" Packer replied, "I think
that it is a 'mystery'. . . . The really surprising thing
would be if we really could understand God. Then
he wouldn't be any bigger than we are."

Sovereignty, responsibility, predestination, free
will . . . and mystery. The Bible teaches them all. The
modern American mind balks at accepting two truths
that seem to be contradictory. But when you think
about it, it makes sense that God is bigger than our
minds—big enough to encompass what seems to us
to be paradoxical.

If someone asks you whether you believe in God's
sovereignty or human freedom, the best answer
is yes. ∎

weep for the hordes of Egypt and for the other mighty nations.* For I will send them down to the world below in company with those who descend to the pit. ¹⁹Say to them,

'O Egypt, are you lovelier than the other nations?
No! So go down to the pit and lie there among the outcasts.*'

²⁰The Egyptians will fall with the many who have died by the sword, for the sword is drawn against them. Egypt and its hordes will be dragged away to their judgment. ²¹Down in the grave* mighty leaders will mockingly welcome Egypt and its allies, saying, 'They have come down; they lie among the outcasts, hordes slaughtered by the sword.'

²²"Assyria lies there surrounded by the graves of its army, those who were slaughtered by the sword. ²³Their graves are in the depths of the pit, and they are surrounded by their allies. They struck terror in the hearts of people everywhere, but now they have been slaughtered by the sword.

²⁴"Elam lies there surrounded by the graves of all its hordes, those who were slaughtered by the sword. They struck terror in the hearts of people everywhere, but now they have descended as outcasts to the world below. Now they lie in the pit and share the shame of those who have gone before them. ²⁵They have a resting place among the slaughtered, surrounded by the graves of all their hordes. Yes, they terrorized the nations while they lived, but now they lie in shame with others in the pit, all of them outcasts, slaughtered by the sword.

²⁶"Meshech and Tubal are there, surrounded by the graves of all their hordes. They once struck terror in the hearts of people everywhere. But now they are outcasts, all slaughtered by the sword. ²⁷They are not buried in honor like their fallen heroes, who went down to the grave* with their weapons—their shields covering their bodies* and their swords beneath their heads. Their guilt rests upon them because they brought terror to everyone while they were still alive.

²⁸"You too, Egypt, will lie crushed and broken among the outcasts, all slaughtered by the sword.

²⁹"Edom is there with its kings and princes. Mighty as they were, they also lie among those slaughtered by the sword, with the outcasts who have gone down to the pit.

³⁰"All the princes of the north and the Sidonians are there with others who have died. Once a terror, they have been put to shame. They lie there as outcasts with others who were slaughtered by the sword. They share the shame of all who have descended to the pit.

³¹"When Pharaoh and his entire army arrive, he will take comfort that he is not alone in having his hordes killed, says the Sovereign LORD. ³²Although I have caused his terror to fall upon all the living, Pharaoh and his hordes will lie there among the outcasts who were slaughtered by the sword. I, the Sovereign LORD, have spoken!"

33 EZEKIEL AS ISRAEL'S WATCHMAN

Once again a message came to me from the LORD: ²"Son of man, give your people this message: 'When I bring an army against a country, the people of that land choose one of their own to be a watchman. ³When the watchman sees the enemy coming, he sounds the alarm to warn the people. ⁴Then if those who hear the alarm refuse to take action, it is their own fault if they die. ⁵They heard the alarm but ignored it, so the responsibility is theirs. If they had listened to the warning, they could have saved their lives. ⁶But if the watchman sees

···

LIFE AFTER DEATH
(32:17-21) The people of Israel believed in an existence beyond the grave for all people, good and bad, in "the world below." Ezekiel's message assumed that other nations had already been sent "to the pit" (32:19) and that Egypt would soon follow. The Egyptians had a preoccupation with the afterlife; after all, the pyramids were built solely to ensure the pharaohs' comfort in the next life. Such human attempts are foolish. God alone controls what happens after death. But we can decide where we want to spend eternity: in heaven with God or in hell.

FAITHFUL
(33:1-6) This chapter shows a new direction for Ezekiel's prophecies. Up to this point, he had pronounced judgment on Judah (chs 1–24) and the surrounding nations (chs 25–32). After Jerusalem fell, his messages of doom turned to messages of hope for God's people (chs 33–48). Previously God appointed Ezekiel to be a watchman, warning the nation of coming judgment (see 3:16-21). Here God appointed him to be a watchman again, to preach a message of hope (see 34:11-16, 22-31; 36:8-38). Ezekiel still gave warnings (33:23–34:10, 17-21; 36:1-7), but these are part of the larger picture of hope.

God warns and comforts us today through the Bible and through messengers he appoints. Most, if we're honest, would say that we prefer God's words of comfort rather than his warnings. But both are needed. Are both heeded in your life? How willing are you to be a watchman—someone who warns people about spiritual issues?

32:18 The meaning of the Hebrew is uncertain.   **32:19** Hebrew *the uncircumcised;* also in 32:21, 24, 25, 26, 28, 29, 30, 32.
32:21 Hebrew *in Sheol.*   **32:27a** Hebrew *to Sheol.*   **32:27b** The meaning of the Hebrew is uncertain.

the enemy coming and doesn't sound the alarm to warn the people, he is responsible for their captivity. They will die in their sins, but I will hold the watchman responsible for their deaths.'

⁷"Now, son of man, I am making you a watchman for the people of Israel. Therefore, listen to what I say and warn them for me. ⁸If I announce that some wicked people are sure to die and you fail to tell them to change their ways, then they will die in their sins, and I will hold you responsible for their deaths. ⁹But if you warn them to repent and they don't repent, they will die in their sins, but you will have saved yourself.

THE WATCHMAN'S MESSAGE
¹⁰"Son of man, give the people of Israel this message: You are saying, 'Our sins are heavy upon us; we are wasting away! How can we survive?' ¹¹As surely as I live, says the Sovereign LORD, I take no pleasure in the death of wicked people. I only want them to turn from their wicked ways so they can live. Turn! Turn from your wickedness, O people of Israel! Why should you die?

¹²"Son of man, give your people this message: The righteous behavior of righteous people will not save them if they turn to sin, nor will the wicked behavior of wicked people destroy them if they repent and turn from their sins. ¹³When I tell righteous people that they will live, but then they sin, expecting their past righteousness to save them, then none of their righteous acts will be remembered. I will destroy them for their sins. ¹⁴And suppose I tell some wicked people that they will surely die, but then they turn from their sins and do what is just and right. ¹⁵For instance, they might give back a debtor's security, return what they have stolen, and obey my life-giving laws,

no longer doing what is evil. If they do this, then they will surely live and not die. ¹⁶None of their past sins will be brought up again, for they have done what is just and right, and they will surely live.

¹⁷"Your people are saying, 'The Lord isn't doing what's right,' but it is they who are not doing what's right. ¹⁸For again I say, when righteous people turn away from their righteous behavior and turn to evil, they will die. ¹⁹But if wicked people turn from their wickedness and do what is just and right, they will live. ²⁰O people of Israel, you are saying, 'The Lord isn't doing what's right.' But I judge each of you according to your deeds."

EXPLANATION OF JERUSALEM'S FALL
²¹On January 8,* during the twelfth year of our captivity, a survivor from Jerusalem came to me and said, "The city has fallen!" ²²The previous evening the LORD had taken hold of me and given me back my voice. So I was able to speak when this man arrived the next morning.

²³Then this message came to me from the LORD: ²⁴"Son of man, the scattered remnants of Judah living among the ruined cities keep saying, 'Abraham was only one man, yet he gained possession of the entire land. We are many; surely the land has been given to us as a possession.' ²⁵So tell these people, 'This is what the Sovereign LORD says: You eat meat with blood in it, you worship idols,* and you murder the innocent. Do you really think the land should be yours? ²⁶Murderers! Idolaters! Adulterers! Should the land belong to you?'

²⁷"Say to them, 'This is what the Sovereign LORD says: As surely as I live, those living in the ruins will die by the sword. And I will send wild animals to eat those living in the open fields. Those hiding in the forts and caves will die of disease. ²⁸I will completely destroy the land and demolish her pride. Her arrogant power will come to an end. The mountains of Israel will be so desolate that no one will even travel through them. ²⁹When I have completely destroyed the land because of their detestable sins, then they will know that I am the LORD.'

³⁰"Son of man, your people talk about you in their houses and whisper about you at the doors. They say to each other, 'Come on, let's go hear the prophet tell us what the LORD is saying!' ³¹So my people come pretending to be sincere and sit before you. They listen to your

FACE IT
(33:10-12) The exiles were discouraged by their past sins. They felt heavy guilt for living in rebellion against God for so many years. This was an important turning point. Elsewhere in Ezekiel the people had refused to admit their wrong. But God assured them of forgiveness if they were willing to change. God wants *everyone* to turn to him. He looks at what we are and will become, not what we have been. God gives every person the opportunity to turn to him. Desperately seeking change? You know where to turn.

IGNORED
(33:30-32) Even though the exiles ignored Ezekiel's messages, he kept delivering them anyway. When people make fun of you because of your faith or fail to take your advice, don't give up. You cannot make others accept your message; you can only be faithful in delivering it.

33:21 Hebrew *On the fifth day of the tenth month,* of the ancient Hebrew lunar calendar. This event occurred on January 8, 585 B.C.; also see note on 1:1. **33:25** The Hebrew term (literally *round things*) probably alludes to dung.

words, but they have no intention of doing what you say. Their mouths are full of lustful words, and their hearts seek only after money. [32]You are very entertaining to them, like someone who sings love songs with a beautiful voice or plays fine music on an instrument. They hear what you say, but they don't act on it! [33]But when all these terrible things happen to them—as they certainly will—then they will know a prophet has been among them."

34 THE SHEPHERDS OF ISRAEL Then this message came to me from the LORD: [2]"Son of man, prophesy against the shepherds, the leaders of Israel. Give them this message from the Sovereign LORD: What sorrow awaits you shepherds who feed yourselves instead of your flocks. Shouldn't shepherds feed their sheep? [3]You drink the milk, wear the wool, and butcher the best animals, but you let your flocks starve. [4]You have not taken care of the weak. You have not tended the sick or bound up the injured. You have not gone looking for those who have wandered away and are lost. Instead, you have ruled them with harshness and cruelty. [5]So my sheep have been scattered without a shepherd, and they are easy prey for any wild animal. [6]They have wandered through all the mountains and all the hills, across the face of the earth, yet no one has gone to search for them.

[7]"Therefore, you shepherds, hear the word of the LORD: [8]As surely as I live, says the Sovereign LORD, you abandoned my flock and left them to be attacked by every wild animal. And though you were my shepherds, you didn't search for my sheep when they were lost. You took care of yourselves and left the sheep to starve. [9]Therefore, you shepherds, hear the word of the LORD. [10]This is what the Sovereign LORD says: I now consider these shepherds my enemies, and I will hold them responsible for what has happened to my flock. I will take away their right to feed the flock, and I will stop them from feeding themselves. I will rescue my flock from their mouths; the sheep will no longer be their prey.

THE GOOD SHEPHERD [11]"For this is what the Sovereign LORD says: I myself will search and find my sheep. [12]I will be like a shepherd looking for his scattered flock. I will find my sheep and rescue them from all the places where they were scattered on that dark and cloudy day. [13]I will bring them back home to their own land of Israel from among the peoples and nations. I

EZEKIEL

Served as a prophet to the exiles in Babylon from 593 to 571 B.C.

CLIMATE OF THE TIMES
Ezekiel and his people are taken to Babylon as captives. The Jews become foreigners in a strange land ruled by an authoritarian government.

MAIN MESSAGE
God allowed the nation of Judah to be destroyed because of the people's sins, but there was still hope—God promised to restore the land to those who remained faithful to him.

IMPORTANCE OF MESSAGE
God never forgets those who faithfully seek to obey him. They have a glorious future ahead.

CONTEMPORARY PROPHETS
Daniel (605–536)
Habakkuk (612–588)
Jeremiah (627–586)

will feed them on the mountains of Israel and by the rivers and in all the places where people live. [14]Yes, I will give them good pastureland on the high hills of Israel. There they will lie down in pleasant places and feed in the lush pastures of the hills. [15]I myself will tend my sheep and give them a place to lie down in peace, says the Sovereign LORD. [16]I will search for my lost ones who strayed away, and I will bring them safely home again. I will bandage the injured and strengthen the weak. But I will destroy those who are fat and powerful. I will feed them, yes—feed them justice!

[17]"And as for you, my flock, this is what the Sovereign LORD says to his people: I will judge between one animal of the flock and another, separating the sheep from the goats. [18]Isn't it enough for you to keep the best of the pastures for yourselves? Must you also trample down

....

GOOD AND BAD SHEPHERDS
(34:1-16) God had hard words for the leaders of the people of Israel. He was angry because these leaders (the shepherds) didn't take care of his people (the sheep). The shepherds' actions (34:2-4) were just the opposite of God's (34:11-16; see also Ps 23).

A good spiritual leader points his or her "flock" toward God. In the New Testament, Jesus gives a warning to would-be spiritual leaders. "If you cause one of these little ones who trusts in me to fall into sin, it would be better for you to be thrown into the sea with a large millstone hung around your neck" (Mark 9:42). You don't have to be a pastor to be in a position of leadership. You're a leader anytime you work or hang out with anyone younger. How will you care for your "flock"?

the rest? Isn't it enough for you to drink clear water for yourselves? Must you also muddy the rest with your feet? ¹⁹Why must my flock eat what you have trampled down and drink water you have fouled?

²⁰"Therefore, this is what the Sovereign LORD says: I will surely judge between the fat sheep and the scrawny sheep. ²¹For you fat sheep pushed and butted and crowded my sick and hungry flock until you scattered them to distant lands. ²²So I will rescue my flock, and they will no longer be abused. I will judge between one animal of the flock and another. ²³And I will set over them one shepherd, my servant David. He will feed them and be a shepherd to them. ²⁴And I, the LORD, will be their God, and my servant David will be a prince among my people. I, the LORD, have spoken!

THE LORD'S COVENANT OF PEACE

²⁵"I will make a covenant of peace with my people and drive away the dangerous animals from the land. Then they will be able to camp safely in the wildest places and sleep in the woods without fear. ²⁶I will bless my people and their homes around my holy hill. And in the proper season I will send the showers they need. There will be showers of blessing. ²⁷The orchards and fields of my people will yield bumper crops, and everyone will live in safety. When I have broken their chains of slavery and rescued them from those who enslaved them, then they will know that I am the LORD. ²⁸They will no longer be prey for other nations, and wild animals will no longer devour them. They will live in safety, and no one will frighten them.

²⁹"And I will make their land famous for its crops, so my people will never again suffer from famines or the insults of foreign nations. ³⁰In this way, they will know that I, the LORD their God, am with them. And they will know that they, the people of Israel, are my people, says the Sovereign LORD. ³¹You are my flock, the sheep of my pasture. You are my people,

SYMBOLS OF PRIDE
(35:1-9) Ezekiel prophesied not only against the people of Edom, but also against their mountains and land. Mountains, usually symbols of strength and power, represented the pride of a nation who thought it could get away with evil. We have different symbols of pride these days. We take pride in our possessions or in being known as cool or popular. But neither money nor status can make a person invincible. What symbols of pride have you noticed around you? Which ones have you noticed in your own life? Anyone who takes a stand against God won't find a strong shelter in status or possessions.

and I am your God. I, the Sovereign LORD, have spoken!"

35 A MESSAGE FOR EDOM

Again a message came to me from the LORD: ²"Son of man, turn and face Mount Seir, and prophesy against its people. ³Give them this message from the Sovereign LORD:

"I am your enemy, O Mount Seir,
    and I will raise my fist against you
        to destroy you completely.
⁴ I will demolish your cities
    and make you desolate.
Then you will know that I am the LORD.

⁵"Your eternal hatred for the people of Israel led you to butcher them when they were helpless, when I had already punished them for all their sins. ⁶As surely as I live, says the Sovereign LORD, since you show no distaste for blood, I will give you a bloodbath of your own. Your turn has come! ⁷I will make Mount Seir utterly desolate, killing off all who try to escape and any who return. ⁸I will fill your mountains with the dead. Your hills, your valleys, and your ravines will be filled with people slaughtered by the sword. ⁹I will make you desolate forever. Your cities will never be rebuilt. Then you will know that I am the LORD.

¹⁰"For you said, 'The lands of Israel and Judah will be ours. We will take possession of them. What do we care that the LORD is there!' ¹¹Therefore, as surely as I live, says the Sovereign LORD, I will pay back your angry deeds with my own. I will punish you for all your acts of anger, envy, and hatred. And I will make myself known to Israel* by what I do to you. ¹²Then you will know that I, the LORD, have heard every contemptuous word you spoke against the mountains of Israel. For you said, 'They are desolate; they have been given to us as food to eat!' ¹³In saying that, you boasted proudly against me, and I have heard it all!

¹⁴"This is what the Sovereign LORD says: The whole world will rejoice when I make you desolate. ¹⁵You rejoiced at the desolation of Israel's territory. Now I will rejoice at yours! You will be wiped out, you people of Mount Seir and all who live in Edom! Then you will know that I am the LORD.

36 RESTORATION FOR ISRAEL

"Son of man, prophesy to Israel's mountains. Give them this message: O mountains of Israel, hear the word of the LORD! ²This is what the Sovereign LORD says: Your enemies have

35:11 Hebrew *to them;* Greek version reads *to you.*

OLD AND NEW COVENANTS

OLD COVENANT	NEW COVENANT
Placed upon stone	Placed upon people's hearts
Based on the law	Based on desire to love and serve God
Must be taught	Known by all
Legal relationship with God	Personal relationship with God

taunted you, saying, 'Aha! Now the ancient heights belong to us!' ³Therefore, son of man, give the mountains of Israel this message from the Sovereign LORD: Your enemies have attacked you from all directions, making you the property of many nations and the object of much mocking and slander. ⁴Therefore, O mountains of Israel, hear the word of the Sovereign LORD. He speaks to the hills and mountains, ravines and valleys, and to ruined wastes and long-deserted cities that have been destroyed and mocked by the surrounding nations. ⁵This is what the Sovereign LORD says: My jealous anger burns against these nations, especially Edom, because they have shown utter contempt for me by gleefully taking my land for themselves as plunder.

⁶"Therefore, prophesy to the hills and mountains, the ravines and valleys of Israel. This is what the Sovereign LORD says: I am furious that you have suffered shame before the surrounding nations. ⁷Therefore, this is what the Sovereign LORD says: I have taken a solemn oath that those nations will soon have their own shame to endure.

⁸"But the mountains of Israel will produce heavy crops of fruit for my people—for they will be coming home again soon! ⁹See, I care about you, and I will pay attention to you. Your ground will be plowed and your crops planted. ¹⁰I will greatly increase the population of Israel, and the ruined cities will be rebuilt and filled with people. ¹¹I will increase not only the people, but also your animals. O mountains of Israel, I will bring people to live on you once again. I will make you even more prosperous than you were before. Then you will know that I am the LORD. ¹²I will cause my people to walk on you once again, and you will be their territory. You will never again rob them of their children.

¹³"This is what the Sovereign LORD says: The other nations taunt you, saying, 'Israel is

a land that devours its own people and robs them of their children!' ¹⁴But you will never again devour your people or rob them of their children, says the Sovereign LORD. ¹⁵I will not let you hear those other nations insult you, and you will no longer be mocked by them. You will not be a land that causes its nation to fall, says the Sovereign LORD."

¹⁶Then this further message came to me from the LORD: ¹⁷"Son of man, when the people of Israel were living in their own land, they defiled it by the evil way they lived. To me their conduct was as unclean as a woman's menstrual cloth. ¹⁸They polluted the land with murder and the worship of idols,* so I poured out my fury on them. ¹⁹I scattered them to many lands to punish them for the evil way they had lived. ²⁰But when they were scattered among the nations, they brought shame on my holy name. For the nations said, 'These are the people of the LORD, but he couldn't keep them safe in his own land!' ²¹Then I was concerned for my holy name, on which my people brought shame among the nations.

²²"Therefore, give the people of Israel this message from the Sovereign LORD: I am bringing you back, but not because you deserve it. I am doing it to protect my holy name, on which you brought shame while you were scattered among the nations. ²³I will show how holy my great name is—the name on which you brought shame among the nations. And when I reveal my holiness through you before their very eyes, says the Sovereign LORD, then the nations will know that I am the LORD. ²⁴For I will

36:18 The Hebrew term (literally *round things*) probably alludes to dung; also in 36:25.

···

THE HONOR OF HIS NAME
(36:16-24) Why did God bring his people back to the land of Israel, even after their sin and idolatry? To protect his holy name—his reputation. Allowing his people to be destroyed by their enemies would lead other nations to believe their phony gods were victorious (Isa 48:11). Yet God also made it clear that the people of Israel had a responsibility to represent God properly to the rest of the world (see 36:25-38). Believers today have that same responsibility. What would people learn about God by watching you?

I WILL GIVE YOU A NEW HEART, AND
I WILL PUT A NEW SPIRIT IN YOU. { EZEKIEL 36:26 }
I WILL TAKE OUT YOUR STONY, STUBBORN HEART AND GIVE YOU A TENDER, RESPONSIVE HEART.

gather you up from all the nations and bring you home again to your land.

²⁵"Then I will sprinkle clean water on you, and you will be clean. Your filth will be washed away, and you will no longer worship idols. ²⁶And I will give you a new heart, and I will put a new spirit in you. I will take out your stony, stubborn heart and give you a tender, responsive heart.* ²⁷And I will put my Spirit in you so that you will follow my decrees and be careful to obey my regulations.

²⁸"And you will live in Israel, the land I gave your ancestors long ago. You will be my people, and I will be your God. ²⁹I will cleanse you of your filthy behavior. I will give you good crops of grain, and I will send no more famines on the land. ³⁰I will give you great harvests from your fruit trees and fields, and never again will the surrounding nations be able to scoff at your land for its famines. ³¹Then you will remember your past sins and despise yourselves for all the detestable things you did. ³²But remember, says the Sovereign LORD, I am not doing this because you deserve it. O my people of Israel, you should be utterly ashamed of all you have done!

³³"This is what the Sovereign LORD says: When I cleanse you from your sins, I will repopulate your cities, and the ruins will be rebuilt. ³⁴The fields that used to lie empty and desolate in plain view of everyone will again be

farmed. ³⁵And when I bring you back, people will say, 'This former wasteland is now like the Garden of Eden! The abandoned and ruined cities now have strong walls and are filled with people!' ³⁶Then the surrounding nations that survive will know that I, the LORD, have rebuilt the ruins and replanted the wasteland. For I, the LORD, have spoken, and I will do what I say.

³⁷"This is what the Sovereign LORD says: I am ready to hear Israel's prayers and to increase their numbers like a flock. ³⁸They will be as numerous as the sacred flocks that fill Jerusalem's streets at the time of her festivals. The ruined cities will be crowded with people once more, and everyone will know that I am the LORD."

37 **A VALLEY OF DRY BONES** The LORD took hold of me, and I was carried away by the Spirit of the LORD to a valley filled with bones. ²He led me all around among the bones that covered the valley floor. They were scattered everywhere across the ground and were completely dried out. ³Then he asked me, "Son of man, can these bones become living people again?"

"O Sovereign LORD," I replied, "you alone know the answer to that."

⁴Then he said to me, "Speak a prophetic message to these bones and say, 'Dry bones, listen to the word of the LORD! ⁵This is what the Sovereign LORD says: Look! I am going to put breath into you and make you live again! ⁶I will put flesh and muscles on you and cover you with skin. I will put breath into you, and you will come to life. Then you will know that I am the LORD.'"

⁷So I spoke this message, just as he told me. Suddenly as I spoke, there was a rattling noise all across the valley. The bones of each body came together and attached themselves as complete skeletons. ⁸Then as I watched, muscles and flesh formed over the bones. Then skin formed to cover their bodies, but they still had no breath in them.

⁹Then he said to me, "Speak a prophetic message to the winds, son of man. Speak a prophetic message and say, 'This is what the Sovereign LORD says: Come, O breath, from the four winds! Breathe into these dead bodies so they may live again.'"

¹⁰So I spoke the message as he commanded me, and breath came into their bodies. They all came to life and stood up on their feet—a great army.

¹¹Then he said to me, "Son of man, these

DRIED UP
(37:1-14) *The dry bones represented the people's spiritually dead condition. At some point or other, every Christian will probably feel spiritually dry. Sometimes this dryness is due to doubt. At other times, dryness is a result of wrong actions that haven't been confessed. But just as God promised to restore his nation, he can restore anyone, no matter how dry or dead that person may feel. Rather than give up, pray for God to restore you or someone else you know.*

36:26 Hebrew *a heart of flesh.*

bones represent the people of Israel. They are saying, 'We have become old, dry bones—all hope is gone. Our nation is finished.' ¹²Therefore, prophesy to them and say, 'This is what the Sovereign LORD says: O my people, I will open your graves of exile and cause you to rise again. Then I will bring you back to the land of Israel. ¹³When this happens, O my people, you will know that I am the LORD. ¹⁴I will put my Spirit in you, and you will live again and return home to your own land. Then you will know that I, the LORD, have spoken, and I have done what I said. Yes, the LORD has spoken!'"

REUNION OF ISRAEL AND JUDAH ¹⁵Again a message came to me from the LORD: ¹⁶"Son of man, take a piece of wood and carve on it these words: 'This represents Judah and its allied tribes.' Then take another piece and carve these words on it: 'This represents Ephraim and the northern tribes of Israel.'* ¹⁷Now hold them together in your hand as if they were one piece of wood. ¹⁸When your people ask you what your actions mean, ¹⁹say to them, 'This is what the Sovereign LORD says: I will take Ephraim and the northern tribes and join them to Judah. I will make them one piece of wood in my hand.'

²⁰"Then hold out the pieces of wood you have inscribed, so the people can see them. ²¹And give them this message from the Sovereign LORD: I will gather the people of Israel from among the nations. I will bring them home to their own land from the places where they have been scattered. ²²I will unify them into one nation on the mountains of Israel. One king will rule them all; no longer will they be divided into two nations or into two kingdoms. ²³They will never again pollute themselves with their idols* and vile images and rebellion, for I will save them from their sinful backsliding. I will cleanse them. Then they will truly be my people, and I will be their God.

²⁴"My servant David will be their king, and they will have only one shepherd. They will obey my regulations and be careful to keep my decrees. ²⁵They will live in the land I gave my servant Jacob, the land where their ancestors lived. They and their children and their grandchildren after them will live there forever, generation after generation. And my servant David will be their prince forever. ²⁶And I will

make a covenant of peace with them, an everlasting covenant. I will give them their land and increase their numbers,* and I will put my Temple among them forever. ²⁷I will make my home among them. I will be their God, and they will be my people. ²⁸And when my Temple is among them forever, the nations will know that I am the LORD, who makes Israel holy."

38
A MESSAGE FOR GOG This is another message that came to me from the LORD: ²"Son of man, turn and face Gog of the land of Magog, the prince who rules over the nations of Meshech and Tubal, and prophesy against him. ³Give him this message from the Sovereign LORD: Gog, I am your enemy! ⁴I will turn you around and put hooks in your jaws to lead you out with your whole army—your horses and charioteers in full armor and a great horde armed with shields and swords. ⁵Persia, Ethiopia, and Libya* will join you, too, with all their weapons. ⁶Gomer and all its armies will also join you, along with the armies of Beth-togarmah from the distant north, and many others.

⁷"Get ready; be prepared! Keep all the armies around you mobilized, and take command of them. ⁸A long time from now you will be called into action. In the distant future you will swoop down on the land of Israel, which will be enjoying peace after recovering from war and after its people have returned from many lands to the mountains of Israel. ⁹You and all your allies—a vast and awesome army—will roll down on them like a storm and cover the land like a cloud.

¹⁰"This is what the Sovereign LORD says: At that time evil thoughts will come to your mind, and you will devise a wicked scheme. ¹¹You will say, 'Israel is an unprotected land filled with unwalled villages! I will march against her and destroy these people who live in such confidence! ¹²I will go to those formerly desolate cities that are now filled with people who have returned from exile in many nations. I will capture vast amounts of plunder, for the people are rich with livestock and other possessions now. They think the whole world revolves around them!' ¹³But Sheba and Dedan and the merchants of Tarshish will ask, 'Do you really think the armies you have gathered can rob them of silver and gold? Do you think you can drive away their livestock and seize their goods and carry off plunder?'

¹⁴"Therefore, son of man, prophesy against Gog. Give him this message from the Sovereign LORD: When my people are living in peace

---

37:16 Hebrew *This is Ephraim's wood, representing Joseph and all the house of Israel.*   **37:23** The Hebrew term (literally *round things*) probably alludes to dung.   **37:26** Hebrew reads *I will give them and increase their numbers;* Greek version lacks the entire phrase. **38:5** Hebrew *Paras, Cush, and Put.*

in their land, then you will rouse yourself.* [15]You will come from your homeland in the distant north with your vast cavalry and your mighty army, [16]and you will attack my people Israel, covering their land like a cloud. At that time in the distant future, I will bring you against my land as everyone watches, and my holiness will be displayed by what happens to you, Gog. Then all the nations will know that I am the Lord.

[17]"This is what the Sovereign Lord asks: Are you the one I was talking about long ago, when I announced through Israel's prophets that in the future I would bring you against my people? [18]But this is what the Sovereign Lord says: When Gog invades the land of Israel, my fury will boil over! [19]In my jealousy and blazing anger, I promise a mighty shaking in the land of Israel on that day. [20]All living things—the fish in the sea, the birds of the sky, the animals of the field, the small animals that scurry along the ground, and all the people on earth—will quake in terror at my presence. Mountains will be thrown down; cliffs will crumble; walls will fall to the earth. [21]I will summon the sword against you on all the hills of Israel, says the Sovereign Lord. Your men will turn their swords against each other. [22]I will punish you and your armies with disease and bloodshed; I will send torrential rain, hailstones, fire, and burning sulfur! [23]In this way, I will show my greatness and holiness, and I will make myself known to all the nations of the world. Then they will know that I am the Lord.

39 THE SLAUGHTER OF GOG'S HORDES

"Son of man, prophesy against Gog. Give him this message from the Sovereign Lord: I am your enemy, O Gog, ruler of the nations of Meshech and Tubal. [2]I will turn you around and drive you toward the mountains of Israel, bringing you from the distant north. [3]I will knock the bow from your left hand and the arrows from your right hand, and I will leave you helpless. [4]You and your army and your allies will all die on the mountains. I will feed you to the vultures and wild animals. [5]You will fall in the open fields, for I have spoken, says the Sovereign Lord. [6]And I will rain down fire on Magog and on all your allies who live safely on the coasts. Then they will know that I am the Lord.

[7]"In this way, I will make known my holy name among my people of Israel. I will not let anyone bring shame on it. And the nations, too, will know that I am the Lord, the Holy One

of Israel. [8]That day of judgment will come, says the Sovereign Lord. Everything will happen just as I have declared it.

[9]"Then the people in the towns of Israel will go out and pick up your small and large shields, bows and arrows, javelins and spears, and they will use them for fuel. There will be enough to last them seven years! [10]They won't need to cut wood from the fields or forests, for these weapons will give them all the fuel they need. They will plunder those who planned to plunder them, and they will rob those who planned to rob them, says the Sovereign Lord.

[11]"And I will make a vast graveyard for Gog and his hordes in the Valley of the Travelers, east of the Dead Sea.* It will block the way of those who travel there, and they will change the name of the place to the Valley of Gog's Hordes. [12]It will take seven months for the people of Israel to bury the bodies and cleanse the land. [13]Everyone in Israel will help, for it will be a glorious victory for Israel when I demonstrate my glory on that day, says the Sovereign Lord.

[14]"After seven months, teams of men will be appointed to search the land for skeletons to bury, so the land will be made clean again. [15]Whenever bones are found, a marker will be set up so the burial crews will take them to be buried in the Valley of Gog's Hordes. [16](There will be a town there named Hamonah, which means 'horde.') And so the land will finally be cleansed.

[17]"And now, son of man, this is what the Sovereign Lord says: Call all the birds and wild animals. Say to them: Gather together for my great sacrificial feast. Come from far and near to the mountains of Israel, and there eat flesh and drink blood! [18]Eat the flesh of mighty men and drink the blood of princes as though they were rams, lambs, goats, and bulls—all fattened animals from Bashan! [19]Gorge yourselves with flesh until you are glutted; drink blood until you are drunk. This is the sacrificial feast I have prepared for you. [20]Feast at my banquet table—feast on horses and charioteers, on mighty men and all kinds of valiant warriors, says the Sovereign Lord.

[21]"In this way, I will demonstrate my glory to the nations. Everyone will see the punishment I have inflicted on them and the power of my fist when I strike. [22]And from that time on the people of Israel will know that I am the Lord their God. [23]The nations will then know why

38:14 As in Greek version; Hebrew reads *then you will know.*
39:11 Hebrew *the sea.*

Israel was sent away to exile—it was punishment for sin, for they were unfaithful to their God. Therefore, I turned away from them and let their enemies destroy them. ²⁴I turned my face away and punished them because of their defilement and their sins.

RESTORATION FOR GOD'S PEOPLE ²⁵"So now, this is what the Sovereign LORD says: I will end the captivity of my people*; I will have mercy on all Israel, for I jealously guard my holy reputation! ²⁶They will accept responsibility for* their past shame and unfaithfulness after they come home to live in peace in their own land, with no one to bother them. ²⁷When I bring them home from the lands of their enemies, I will display my holiness among them for all the nations to see. ²⁸Then my people will know that I am the LORD their God, because I sent them away to exile and brought them home again. I will leave none of my people behind. ²⁹And I will never again turn my face from them, for I will pour out my Spirit upon the people of Israel. I, the Sovereign LORD, have spoken!"

40 THE NEW TEMPLE AREA On April 28,* during the twenty-fifth year of our captivity—fourteen years after the fall of Jerusalem—the LORD took hold of me. ²In a vision from God he took me to the land of Israel and set me down on a very high mountain. From there I could see toward the south what appeared to be a city. ³As he brought me nearer, I saw a man whose face shone like bronze standing beside a gateway entrance. He was holding in his hand a linen measuring cord and a measuring rod.

⁴He said to me, "Son of man, watch and listen. Pay close attention to everything I show you. You have been brought here so I can show you many things. Then you will return to the

people of Israel and tell them everything you have seen."

THE EAST GATEWAY ⁵I could see a wall completely surrounding the Temple area. The man took a measuring rod that was 10½ feet* long and measured the wall, and the wall was 10½ feet* thick and 10½ feet high.

⁶Then he went over to the eastern gateway. He climbed the steps and measured the threshold of the gateway; it was 10½ feet front to back.* ⁷There were guard alcoves on each side built into the gateway passage. Each of these alcoves was 10½ feet square, with a distance between them of 8¾ feet* along the passage wall. The gateway's inner threshold, which led to the entry room at the inner end of the gateway passage, was 10½ feet front to back. ⁸He also measured the entry room of the gateway.* ⁹It was 14 feet* across, with supporting columns 3½ feet* thick. This entry room was at the inner end of the gateway structure, facing toward the Temple.

¹⁰There were three guard alcoves on each side of the gateway passage. Each had the same measurements, and the dividing walls separating them were also identical. ¹¹The man measured the gateway entrance, which was 17½ feet* wide at the opening and 22¾ feet* wide in the gateway passage. ¹²In front of each of the guard alcoves was a 21-inch* curb. The alcoves themselves were 10½ feet* on each side.

¹³Then he measured the entire width of the gateway, measuring the distance between the back walls of facing guard alcoves; this distance was 43¾ feet.* ¹⁴He measured the dividing walls all along the inside of the gateway up to the entry room of the gateway; this distance was 105 feet.* ¹⁵The full length of the gateway passage was 87½ feet* from one end to the other. ¹⁶There were recessed windows that narrowed inward through the walls of the guard alcoves and their dividing walls. There were also windows in the entry room. The surfaces of

39:25 Hebrew *of Jacob.* **39:26** A few Hebrew manuscripts read *They will forget.* **40:1** Hebrew *At the beginning of the year, on the tenth day of the month,* of the ancient Hebrew lunar calendar. This event occurred on April 28, 573 B.C.; also see note on 1:1. **40:5a** Hebrew *6 long cubits* [3.2 meters], *each being a cubit* [18 inches or 45 centimeters] *and a handbreadth* [3 inches or 8 centimeters] *in length.* **40:5b** Hebrew *1 rod* [3.2 meters]; also in 40:5c, 7. **40:6** As in Greek version, which reads *1 rod* [3.2 meters] *deep;* Hebrew reads *1 rod deep, and 1 threshold, 1 rod deep.* **40:7** Hebrew *5 cubits* [2.7 meters]; also in 40:48. **40:8** Many Hebrew manuscripts add *which faced inward toward the Temple; it was 1 rod* [10.5 feet or 3.2 meters] *deep.* ⁹*Then he measured the entry room of the gateway.* **40:9a** Hebrew *8 cubits* [4.2 meters]. **40:9b** Hebrew *2 cubits* [1.1 meters]. **40:11a** Hebrew *10 cubits* [5.3 meters]. **40:11b** Hebrew *13 cubits* [6.9 meters]. **40:12a** Hebrew *1 cubit* [53 centimeters]. **40:12b** Hebrew *6 cubits* [3.2 meters]. **40:13** Hebrew *25 cubits* [13.3 meters]; also in 40:21, 25, 29, 30, 33, 36. **40:14** Hebrew *60 cubits* [31.8 meters]. Greek version reads *20 cubits* [35 feet or 10.6 meters]. The meaning of the Hebrew in this verse is uncertain. **40:15** Hebrew *50 cubits* [26.5 meters]; also in 40:21, 25, 29, 33, 36.

....

RESTORED DREAMS
(40:1–42:20) Ezekiel saw a vision of a restored temple. After hearing about the destruction of the Temple, this vision probably comforted the grieving people of Israel. If you've ever suffered the loss of a dream, you can probably understand their need for hope. But sometimes God has something even bigger in mind for his people. Ezekiel saw a temple more beautiful than the one that had been destroyed. Are you hoping that God will restore a dream you once had? Maybe he has something bigger in mind for you.

the dividing walls were decorated with carved palm trees.

THE OUTER COURTYARD

¹⁷Then the man brought me through the gateway into the outer courtyard of the Temple. A stone pavement ran along the walls of the courtyard, and thirty rooms were built against the walls, opening onto the pavement. ¹⁸This pavement flanked the gates and extended out from the walls into the courtyard the same distance as the gateway entrance. This was the lower pavement. ¹⁹Then the man measured across the Temple's outer courtyard between the outer and inner gateways; the distance was 175 feet.*

THE NORTH GATEWAY

²⁰The man measured the gateway on the north just like the one on the east. ²¹Here, too, there were three guard alcoves on each side, with dividing walls and an entry room. All the measurements matched those of the east gateway. The gateway passage was 87½ feet long and 43¾ feet wide between the back walls of facing guard alcoves. ²²The windows, the entry room, and the palm tree decorations were identical to those in the east gateway. There were seven steps leading up to the gateway entrance, and the entry room was at the inner end of the gateway passage. ²³Here on the north side, just as on the east, there was another gateway leading to the Temple's inner courtyard directly opposite this outer gateway. The distance between the two gateways was 175 feet.

THE SOUTH GATEWAY

²⁴Then the man took me around to the south gateway and measured its various parts, and they were exactly the same as in the others. ²⁵It had windows along the walls as the others did, and there was an entry room where the gateway passage opened into the outer courtyard. And like the others, the gateway passage was 87½ feet long and 43¾ feet wide between the back walls of facing guard alcoves. ²⁶This gateway also had a stairway of seven steps leading up to it, and an entry room at the inner end, and palm tree decorations along the dividing walls. ²⁷And here again, directly opposite the outer gateway, was

another gateway that led into the inner courtyard. The distance between the two gateways was 175 feet.

GATEWAYS TO THE INNER COURTYARD

²⁸Then the man took me to the south gateway leading into the inner courtyard. He measured it, and it had the same measurements as the other gateways. ²⁹Its guard alcoves, dividing walls, and entry room were the same size as those in the others. It also had windows along its walls and in the entry room. And like the others, the gateway passage was 87½ feet long and 43¾ feet wide. ³⁰(The entry rooms of the gateways leading into the inner courtyard were 14 feet* across and 43¾ feet wide.) ³¹The entry room to the south gateway faced into the outer courtyard. It had palm tree decorations on its columns, and there were eight steps leading to its entrance.

³²Then he took me to the east gateway leading to the inner courtyard. He measured it, and it had the same measurements as the other gateways. ³³Its guard alcoves, dividing walls, and entry room were the same size as those of the others, and there were windows along the walls and in the entry room. The gateway passage measured 87½ feet long and 43¾ feet wide. ³⁴Its entry room faced into the outer courtyard. It had palm tree decorations on its columns, and there were eight steps leading to its entrance.

³⁵Then he took me around to the north gateway leading to the inner courtyard. He measured it, and it had the same measurements as the other gateways. ³⁶The guard alcoves, dividing walls, and entry room of this gateway had the same measurements as in the others and the same window arrangements. The gateway passage measured 87½ feet long and 43¾ feet wide. ³⁷Its entry room faced into the outer courtyard, and it had palm tree decorations on the columns. There were eight steps leading to its entrance.

ROOMS FOR PREPARING SACRIFICES

³⁸A door led from the entry room of one of the inner gateways into a side room, where the meat for sacrifices was washed. ³⁹On each side of this entry room were two tables, where the sacrificial animals were slaughtered for the burnt offerings, sin offerings, and guilt offerings. ⁴⁰Outside the entry room, on each side of the stairs going up to the north entrance, were two

40:19 Hebrew *100 cubits* [53 meters]; also in 40:23, 27, 47.
40:30 As in 40:9, which reads *8 cubits* [14 feet or 4.2 meters]; here the Hebrew reads *5 cubits* [8¾ feet or 2.7 meters]. Some Hebrew manuscripts and the Greek version lack this entire verse.

more tables. 41So there were eight tables in all—four inside and four outside—where the sacrifices were cut up and prepared. 42There were also four tables of finished stone for preparation of the burnt offerings, each 31½ inches square and 21 inches high.* On these tables were placed the butchering knives and other implements for slaughtering the sacrificial animals. 43There were hooks, each 3 inches* long, fastened to the foyer walls. The sacrificial meat was laid on the tables.

ROOMS FOR THE PRIESTS 44Inside the inner courtyard were two rooms,* one beside the north gateway, facing south, and the other beside the south* gateway, facing north. 45And the man said to me, "The room beside the north inner gate is for the priests who supervise the Temple maintenance. 46The room beside the south inner gate is for the priests in charge of the altar—the descendants of Zadok—for they alone of all the Levites may approach the LORD to minister to him."

THE INNER COURTYARD AND TEMPLE 47Then the man measured the inner courtyard, and it was a square, 175 feet wide and 175 feet across. The altar stood in the courtyard in front of the Temple. 48Then he brought me to the entry room of the Temple. He measured the walls on either side of the opening to the entry room, and they were 8¾ feet thick. The entrance itself was 24½ feet wide, and the walls on each side of the entrance were an additional 5¼ feet long.* 49The entry room was 35 feet* wide and 21 feet* deep. There were ten steps leading up to it, with a column on each side.

41 After that, the man brought me into the sanctuary of the Temple. He measured the walls on either side of its doorway, and they were 10½ feet* thick. 2The doorway was 17½ feet* wide, and the walls on each side of it were 8¾ feet* long. The sanctuary itself was 70 feet long and 35 feet wide.*

3Then he went beyond the sanctuary into the inner room. He measured the walls on either side of its entrance, and they were 3½ feet* thick. The entrance was 10½ feet wide, and the walls on each side of the entrance were 12¼ feet* long. 4The inner room of the sanctuary was 35 feet* long and 35 feet wide. "This," he told me, "is the Most Holy Place."

5Then he measured the wall of the Temple, and it was 10½ feet thick. There was a row of rooms along the outside wall; each room was 7 feet* wide. 6These side rooms were built in three levels, one above the other, with thirty rooms on each level. The supports for these side rooms rested on exterior ledges on the Temple wall; they did not extend into the wall. 7Each level was wider than the one below it, corresponding to the narrowing of the Temple wall as it rose higher. A stairway led up from the bottom level through the middle level to the top level.

8I saw that the Temple was built on a terrace, which provided a foundation for the side rooms. This terrace was 10½ feet* high. 9The outer wall of the Temple's side rooms was 8¾ feet thick. This left an open area between these side rooms 10and the row of rooms along the outer wall of the inner courtyard. This open area was 35 feet wide, and it went all the way around the Temple. 11Two doors opened from the side rooms into the terrace yard, which was 8¾ feet wide. One door faced north and the other south.

12A large building stood on the west, facing the Temple courtyard. It was 122½ feet wide and 157½ feet long, and its walls were 8¾ feet* thick. 13Then the man measured the Temple, and it was 175 feet* long. The courtyard around the building, including its walls, was an additional 175 feet in length. 14The inner courtyard to the east of the Temple was also 175 feet wide. 15The building to the west, including its two walls, was also 175 feet wide.

40:42 Hebrew 1½ cubits [80 centimeters] long and 1½ cubits wide and 1 cubit [53 centimeters] high.   40:43 Hebrew a handbreadth [8 centimeters].   40:44a As in Greek version; Hebrew reads rooms for singers.   40:44b As in Greek version; Hebrew reads east.
40:48 As in Greek version, which reads The entrance was 14 cubits [7.4 meters] wide, and the walls of the entrance were 3 cubits [1.6 meters] on each side; Hebrew lacks 14 cubits wide, and the walls of the entrance were.   40:49a Hebrew 20 cubits [10.6 meters].
40:49b As in Greek version, which reads 12 cubits [21 feet or 6.4 meters]; Hebrew reads 11 cubits [19¼ feet or 5.8 meters].
41:1 Hebrew 6 cubits [3.2 meters]; also in 41:3, 5.   41:2a Hebrew 10 cubits [5.3 meters].   41:2b Hebrew 5 cubits [2.7 meters]; also in 41:9, 11.   41:2c Hebrew 40 cubits [21.2 meters] long and 20 cubits [10.6 meters] wide.   41:3a Hebrew 2 cubits [1.1 meters].
41:3b Hebrew 7 cubits [3.7 meters].   41:4 Hebrew 20 cubits [10.6 meters]; also in 41:4b, 10.   41:5 Hebrew 4 cubits [2.1 meters].
41:8 Hebrew 1 rod, 6 cubits [3.2 meters].   41:12 Hebrew 70 cubits [37.1 meters] wide and 90 cubits [47.7 meters] long, and its walls were 5 cubits [2.7 meters] thick.   41:13 Hebrew 100 cubits [53 meters]; also in 41:13b, 14, 15.

....

THE MOST HOLY PLACE
(41:1-26) The Most Holy Place was the innermost room in the Temple (Exod 26:33-34). This was where the Ark of the Covenant was kept and where God's glory was said to dwell. It was entered only once a year by the High Priest, who would perform a ceremony to atone for the nation's sins. God's holiness is a central theme throughout both the Old and New Testaments. Today, because of Jesus, we can enter the Most Holy Place—not just once a year, but anytime (Hebrews 10:19). Enjoy your privilege today by spending time in God's presence.

The sanctuary, the inner room, and the entry room of the Temple [16]were all paneled with wood, as were the frames of the recessed windows. The inner walls of the Temple were paneled with wood above and below the windows. [17]The space above the door leading into the inner room, and its walls inside and out, were also paneled. [18]All the walls were decorated with carvings of cherubim, each with two faces, and there was a carving of a palm tree between each of the cherubim. [19]One face—that of a man—looked toward the palm tree on one side. The other face—that of a young lion—looked toward the palm tree on the other side. The figures were carved all along the inside of the Temple, [20]from the floor to the top of the walls, including the outer wall of the sanctuary.

[21]There were square columns at the entrance to the sanctuary, and the ones at the entrance of the Most Holy Place were similar. [22]There was an altar made of wood, 5¼ feet high and 3½ feet across.* Its corners, base, and sides were all made of wood. "This," the man told me, "is the table that stands in the LORD's presence."

[23]Both the sanctuary and the Most Holy Place had double doorways, [24]each with two swinging doors. [25]The doors leading into the sanctuary were decorated with carved cherubim and palm trees, just as on the walls. And there was a wooden roof at the front of the entry room to the Temple. [26]On both sides of the entry room were recessed windows decorated with carved palm trees. The side rooms along the outside wall also had roofs.

42 ROOMS FOR THE PRIESTS Then the man led me out of the Temple courtyard by way of the north gateway. We entered the outer courtyard and came to a group of rooms against the north wall of the inner courtyard. [2]This structure, whose entrance opened toward the north, was 175 feet* long and 87½ feet* wide. [3]One block of rooms overlooked the 35-foot* width of the inner courtyard. Another block of rooms looked out onto the pavement of the outer courtyard. The two blocks were built three levels high and stood across from each other. [4]Between the two blocks of rooms ran a walkway 17½ feet* wide. It extended the entire 175 feet of the complex,* and all the doors faced north. [5]Each of the two upper levels of rooms was narrower than the one beneath it because the upper levels had to allow space for walkways in front of them. [6]Since there were three levels and they did not

have supporting columns as in the courtyards, each of the upper levels was set back from the level beneath it. [7]There was an outer wall that separated the rooms from the outer courtyard; it was 87½ feet long. [8]This wall added length to the outer block of rooms, which extended for only 87½ feet, while the inner block—the rooms toward the Temple—extended for 175 feet. [9]There was an eastern entrance from the outer courtyard to these rooms.

[10]On the south* side of the Temple there were two blocks of rooms just south of the inner courtyard between the Temple and the outer courtyard. These rooms were arranged just like the rooms on the north. [11]There was a walkway between the two blocks of rooms just like the complex on the north side of the Temple. This complex of rooms was the same length and width as the other one, and it had the same entrances and doors. The dimensions of each were identical. [12]So there was an entrance in the wall facing the doors of the inner block of rooms, and another on the east at the end of the interior walkway.

[13]Then the man told me, "These rooms that overlook the Temple from the north and south are holy. Here the priests who offer sacrifices to the LORD will eat the most holy offerings. And because these rooms are holy, they will be used to store the sacred offerings—the grain offerings, sin offerings, and guilt offerings. [14]When the priests leave the sanctuary, they must not go directly to the outer courtyard. They must first take off the clothes they wore while ministering, because these clothes are holy. They must put on other clothes before entering the parts of the building complex open to the public."

[15]When the man had finished measuring the inside of the Temple area, he led me out through the east gateway to measure the entire perimeter. [16]He measured the east side with his measuring rod, and it was 875 feet long.* [17]Then he measured the north side, and it was also 875 feet. [18]The south side was also 875 feet, [19]and the west side was also 875 feet. [20]So the area was 875 feet on each side with a wall all around it to separate what was holy from what was common.

41:22 Hebrew 3 cubits [1.6 meters] high and 2 cubits [1.1 meters] across. 42:2a Hebrew 100 cubits [53 meters]; also in 42:8. 42:2b Hebrew 50 cubits [26.5 meters]; also in 42:7, 8. 42:3 Hebrew 20-cubit [10.6-meter]. 42:4a Hebrew 10 cubits [5.3 meters]. 42:4b As in Greek and Syriac versions, which read its length was 100 cubits [53 meters]; Hebrew reads and a passage 1 cubit [18 inches or 53 centimeters] wide. 42:10 As in Greek version; Hebrew reads east. 42:16 As in 45:2 and in Greek version at 42:17, which reads 500 cubits [265 meters]; Hebrew reads 500 rods [5,250 feet or 1,590 meters]; similarly in 42:17, 18, 19, 20.

43

THE LORD'S GLORY RETURNS After this, the man brought me back around to the east gateway. ²Suddenly, the glory of the God of Israel appeared from the east. The sound of his coming was like the roar of rushing waters, and the whole landscape shone with his glory. ³This vision was just like the others I had seen, first by the Kebar River and then when he came to destroy Jerusalem. I fell face down on the ground. ⁴And the glory of the LORD came into the Temple through the east gateway.

⁵Then the Spirit took me up and brought me into the inner courtyard, and the glory of the LORD filled the Temple. ⁶And I heard someone speaking to me from within the Temple, while the man who had been measuring stood beside me. ⁷The LORD said to me, "Son of man, this is the place of my throne and the place where I will rest my feet. I will live here forever among the people of Israel. They and their kings will not defile my holy name any longer by their adulterous worship of other gods or by honoring the relics of their kings who have died. ⁸They put their idol altars right next to mine with only a wall between them and me. They defiled my holy name by such detestable sin, so I consumed them in my anger. ⁹Now let them stop worshiping other gods and honoring the relics of their kings, and I will live among them forever.

¹⁰"Son of man, describe to the people of Israel the Temple I have shown you, so they will be ashamed of all their sins. Let them study its plan, ¹¹and they will be ashamed* of what they have done. Describe to them all the specifications of the Temple—including its entrances and exits—and everything else about it. Tell them about its decrees and laws. Write down all these specifications and decrees as they watch so they will be sure to remember and follow them. ¹²And this is the basic law of the Temple: absolute holiness! The entire top of the mountain where the Temple is built is holy. Yes, this is the basic law of the Temple.

THE ALTAR ¹³"These are the measurements of the altar*: There is a gutter all around the altar 21 inches deep and 21 inches wide,* with a

curb 9 inches* wide around its edge. And this is the height* of the altar: ¹⁴From the gutter the altar rises 3½ feet* to a lower ledge that surrounds the altar and is 21 inches* wide. From the lower ledge the altar rises 7 feet* to the upper ledge that is also 21 inches wide. ¹⁵The top of the altar, the hearth, rises another 7 feet higher, with a horn rising up from each of the four corners. ¹⁶The top of the altar is square, measuring 21 feet by 21 feet.* ¹⁷The upper ledge also forms a square, measuring 24½ feet by 24½ feet,* with a 21-inch gutter and a 10½-inch curb* all around the edge. There are steps going up the east side of the altar."

¹⁸Then he said to me, "Son of man, this is what the Sovereign LORD says: These will be the regulations for the burning of offerings and the sprinkling of blood when the altar is built. ¹⁹At that time, the Levitical priests of the family of Zadok, who minister before me, are to be given a young bull for a sin offering, says the Sovereign LORD. ²⁰You will take some of its blood and smear it on the four horns of the altar, the four corners of the upper ledge, and the curb that runs around that ledge. This will cleanse and make atonement for the altar. ²¹Then take the young bull for the sin offering and burn it at the appointed place outside the Temple area.

²²"On the second day, sacrifice as a sin offering a young male goat that has no physical defects. Then cleanse and make atonement for the altar again, just as you did with the young bull. ²³When you have finished the cleansing ceremony, offer another young bull that has no defects and a perfect ram from the flock. ²⁴You are to present them to the LORD, and the priests are to sprinkle salt on them and offer them as a burnt offering to the LORD.

²⁵"Every day for seven days a male goat, a young bull, and a ram from the flock will be sacrificed as a sin offering. None of these animals may have physical defects of any kind. ²⁶Do this each day for seven days to cleanse and make atonement for the altar, thus setting it apart for holy use. ²⁷On the eighth day, and on each day afterward, the priests will

....

RETURNING GLORY

(43:1-9) Ezekiel saw a vision of God's glory returning to the Temple—the ultimate sign of blessing for a nation. When we've blown it spiritually, we can't imagine God wanting to remain with us. Ever feel this way? Maybe you've wondered whether God plans to leave you forever because of something you did or said. But check out verse 7 again: "This is the place of my throne and the place where I will rest my feet. I will live here forever." If he won't give up on you, should you give up on him?

43:11 As in Greek version; Hebrew reads *if they are ashamed.*
43:13a Hebrew *measurements of the altar in long cubits, each being a cubit* [18 inches or 45 centimeters] *and a handbreadth* [3 inches or 8 centimeters] *in length.*   **43:13b** Hebrew *a cubit* [53 centimeters] *deep and a cubit wide.*   **43:13c** Hebrew *1 span* [23 centimeters].
43:13d As in Greek version; Hebrew reads *base.*   **43:14a** Hebrew *2 cubits* [1.1 meters].   **43:14b** Hebrew *1 cubit* [53 centimeters]; also in 43:14d.   **43:14c** Hebrew *4 cubits* [2.1 meters]; also in 43:15.
43:16 Hebrew *12 cubits* [6.4 meters] *long and 12 cubits wide.*
43:17a Hebrew *14 cubits* [7.4 meters] *long and 14 cubits wide.*
43:17b Hebrew *a gutter of 1 cubit* [53 centimeters] *and a curb of ½ a cubit* [27 centimeters].

sacrifice on the altar the burnt offerings and peace offerings of the people. Then I will accept you. I, the Sovereign LORD, have spoken!"

44 THE PRINCE, LEVITES, AND PRIESTS
Then the man brought me back to the east gateway in the outer wall of the Temple area, but it was closed. ²And the LORD said to me, "This gate must remain closed; it will never again be opened. No one will ever open it and pass through, for the LORD, the God of Israel, has entered here. Therefore, it must always remain shut. ³Only the prince himself may sit inside this gateway to feast in the LORD's presence. But he may come and go only through the entry room of the gateway."

⁴Then the man brought me through the north gateway to the front of the Temple. I looked and saw that the glory of the LORD filled the Temple of the LORD, and I fell face down on the ground.

⁵And the LORD said to me, "Son of man, take careful notice. Use your eyes and ears, and listen to everything I tell you about the regulations concerning the LORD's Temple. Take careful note of the procedures for using the Temple's entrances and exits. ⁶And give these rebels, the people of Israel, this message from the Sovereign LORD: O people of Israel, enough of your detestable sins! ⁷You have brought uncircumcised foreigners into my sanctuary—people who have no heart for God. In this way, you defiled my Temple even as you offered me my food, the fat and blood of sacrifices. In addition to all your other detestable sins, you have broken my covenant. ⁸Instead of safeguarding my sacred rituals, you have hired foreigners to take charge of my sanctuary.

⁹"So this is what the Sovereign LORD says: No foreigners, including those who live among the people of Israel, will enter my sanctuary if they have not been circumcised and have not surrendered themselves to the LORD. ¹⁰And the men of the tribe of Levi who abandoned me when Israel strayed away from me to worship idols* must bear the consequences of their unfaithfulness. ¹¹They may still be Temple guards and gatekeepers, and they may slaughter the animals brought for burnt offerings and be present to help the people. ¹²But they encouraged my people to worship idols, causing Israel to fall into deep sin. So I have taken a solemn oath that they must bear the consequences for their sins, says the Sovereign LORD. ¹³They may not approach me to minister as priests. They may not touch any of my holy things or the holy offerings, for they must bear the shame of all the detestable sins they have committed. ¹⁴They are to serve as the Temple caretakers, taking charge of the maintenance work and performing general duties.

¹⁵"However, the Levitical priests of the family of Zadok continued to minister faithfully in the Temple when Israel abandoned me for idols. These men will serve as my ministers. They will stand in my presence and offer the fat and blood of the sacrifices, says the Sovereign LORD. ¹⁶They alone will enter my sanctuary and approach my table to serve me. They will fulfill all my requirements.

¹⁷"When they enter the gateway to the inner courtyard, they must wear only linen clothing. They must wear no wool while on duty in the inner courtyard or in the Temple itself. ¹⁸They must wear linen turbans and linen undergarments. They must not wear anything that would cause them to perspire. ¹⁹When they return to the outer courtyard where the people are, they must take off the clothes they wear while ministering to me. They must leave them in the sacred rooms and put on other clothes so they do not endanger anyone by transmitting holiness to them through this clothing.

²⁰"They must neither shave their heads nor let their hair grow too long. Instead, they must trim it regularly. ²¹The priests must not drink wine before entering the inner courtyard. ²²They may choose their wives only from among the virgins of Israel or the widows of the priests. They may not marry other widows or divorced women. ²³They will teach my people the difference between what is holy and what is common, what is ceremonially clean and unclean.

²⁴"They will serve as judges to resolve any disagreements among my people. Their decisions must be based on my regulations. And the priests themselves must obey my instructions and decrees at all the sacred festivals, and see to it that the Sabbaths are set apart as holy days.

²⁵"A priest must not defile himself by being in the presence of a dead person unless it is his father, mother, child, brother, or unmarried sister. In such cases it is permitted. ²⁶Even then, he can return to his Temple duties only after being ceremonially cleansed and then waiting for seven days. ²⁷The first day he returns to work and enters the inner courtyard and the sanctuary, he must offer a sin offering for himself, says the Sovereign LORD.

44:10 The Hebrew term (literally *round things*) probably alludes to dung; also in 44:12.

28"The priests will not have any property or possession of land, for I alone am their special possession. 29Their food will come from the gifts and sacrifices brought to the Temple by the people—the grain offerings, the sin offerings, and the guilt offerings. Whatever anyone sets apart* for the LORD will belong to the priests. 30The first of the ripe fruits and all the gifts brought to the LORD will go to the priests. The first samples of each grain harvest and the first of your flour must also be given to the priests so the LORD will bless your homes. 31The priests may not eat meat from any bird or animal that dies a natural death or that dies after being attacked by another animal.

45 DIVISION OF THE LAND "When you divide the land among the tribes of Israel, you must set aside a section for the LORD as his holy portion. This piece of land will be 8⅓ miles long and 6⅔ miles wide.* The entire area will be holy. 2A section of this land, measuring 875 feet by 875 feet,* will be set aside for the Temple. An additional strip of land 87½ feet* wide is to be left empty all around it. 3Within the larger sacred area, measure out a portion of land 8⅓ miles long and 3⅓ miles wide.* Within it the sanctuary of the Most Holy Place will be located. 4This area will be holy, set aside for the priests who minister to the LORD in the sanctuary. They will use it for their homes, and my Temple will be located within it. 5The strip of sacred land next to it, also 8⅓ miles long and 3⅓ miles wide, will be a living area for the Levites who work at the Temple. It will be their possession and a place for their towns.*

6"Adjacent to the larger sacred area will be a section of land 8⅓ miles long and 1⅔ miles wide.* This will be set aside for a city where anyone in Israel can live.

7"Two special sections of land will be set apart for the prince. One section will share a border with the east side of the sacred lands and city, and the second section will share a border on the west side. Then the far eastern and western borders of the prince's lands will line up with the eastern and western boundaries of the tribal areas. 8These sections of land will be the prince's allotment. Then my princes will no longer oppress and rob my people; they will assign the rest of the land to the people, giving an allotment to each tribe.

RULES FOR THE PRINCES 9"For this is what the Sovereign LORD says: Enough, you princes of Israel! Stop your violence and oppression and do what is just and right. Quit robbing and cheating my people out of their land. Stop expelling them from their homes, says the Sovereign LORD. 10Use only honest weights and scales and honest measures, both dry and liquid.* 11The homer* will be your standard unit for measuring volume. The ephah and the bath* will each measure one-tenth of a homer. 12The standard unit for weight will be the silver shekel.* One shekel will consist of twenty gerahs, and sixty shekels will be equal to one mina.*

SPECIAL OFFERINGS AND CELEBRATIONS 13"You must give this tax to the prince: one bushel of wheat or barley for every 60* you harvest, 14one percent of your olive oil,* 15and one sheep or goat for every 200 in your flocks in Israel. These will be the grain offerings, burnt offerings, and peace offerings that will make atonement for the people who bring them, says the Sovereign LORD. 16All the people of Israel must join in bringing these offerings to the prince. 17The prince will be required to provide offerings that are given at the religious festivals, the new moon celebrations, the Sabbath days, and all other similar occasions. He will provide the sin offerings, burnt offerings, grain offerings, liquid offerings, and peace offerings to purify the people of Israel, making them right with the LORD.*

18"This is what the Sovereign LORD says: In

44:29 The Hebrew term used here refers to the complete consecration of things or people to the LORD, either by destroying them or by giving them as an offering. 45:1 As in Greek version, which reads 25,000 cubits [13.3 kilometers] long and 20,000 cubits [10.6 kilometers] wide; Hebrew reads 25,000 cubits long and 10,000 cubits [3⅓ miles or 5.3 kilometers] wide. Compare 45:3, 5; 48:9. 45:2a Hebrew 500 cubits [265 meters] by 500 cubits, a square. 45:2b Hebrew 50 cubits [26.5 meters]. 45:3 Hebrew 25,000 cubits [13.3 kilometers] long and 10,000 cubits [5.3 kilometers] wide; also in 45:5. 45:5 As in Greek version; Hebrew reads They will have as their possession 20 rooms. 45:6 Hebrew 25,000 cubits [13.3 kilometers] long and 5,000 cubits [2.65 kilometers] wide. 45:10 Hebrew use honest scales, an honest ephah, and an honest bath. 45:11a The homer measures about 40 gallons or 182 liters. 45:11b The ephah is a dry measure; the bath is a liquid measure. 45:12a The shekel weighs about 0.4 ounces or 11 grams. 45:12b Elsewhere the mina is equated to 50 shekels. 45:13 Hebrew ⅙ of an ephah from each homer of wheat and ⅙ of an ephah from each homer of barley. 45:14 Hebrew the portion of oil, measured by the bath, is 1⁄100 of a bath from each cor, which consists of 10 baths or 1 homer, for 10 baths are equivalent to a homer. 45:17 Or to make atonement for the people of Israel.

HONESTY
(45:7-12) Greed and extortion were two of the major social sins of the nation during this time (see also Amos 5:7-13). In the new economy, plenty of land would be available for the "princes" (45:7-8) and no longer any basis for greed. Therefore, the princes and the people were commanded to be fair and honest, especially in business transactions. Are fair and honest two words that describe you?

early spring, on the first day of each new year,* sacrifice a young bull with no defects to purify the Temple. ¹⁹The priest will take blood from this sin offering and put it on the doorposts of the Temple, the four corners of the upper ledge of the altar, and the gateposts at the entrance to the inner courtyard. ²⁰Do this also on the seventh day of the new year for anyone who has sinned through error or ignorance. In this way, you will purify* the Temple.

²¹"On the fourteenth day of the first month,* you must celebrate the Passover. This festival will last for seven days. The bread you eat during that time must be made without yeast. ²²On the day of Passover the prince will provide a young bull as a sin offering for himself and the people of Israel. ²³On each of the seven days of the feast he will prepare a burnt offering to the LORD, consisting of seven young bulls and seven rams without defects. A male goat will also be given each day for a sin offering. ²⁴The prince will provide a basket of flour as a grain offering and a gallon of olive oil* with each young bull and ram.

²⁵"During the seven days of the Festival of Shelters, which occurs every year in early autumn,* the prince will provide these same sacrifices for the sin offering, the burnt offering, and the grain offering, along with the required olive oil.

46 "This is what the Sovereign LORD says: The east gateway of the inner courtyard will be closed during the six workdays each week, but it will be open on Sabbath days and the days of new moon celebrations. ²The prince will enter the entry room of the gateway from the outside. Then he will stand by the gatepost while the priest offers his burnt offering and peace offering. He will bow down in worship inside the gateway passage and then go back out the way he came. The gateway will not be closed until evening. ³The common people will bow down and worship the LORD in front of this gateway on Sabbath days and the days of new moon celebrations.

....

RHYTHM
(46:1-15) Ezekiel continued to describe various aspects of daily worship. While allowing for diversity in worship, God prescribed order and continuity. This provided a healthy rhythm to the spiritual life of his people. Just as the goal of exercise is to maintain a healthy heart rhythm, the goal of keeping spiritually fit is to maintain a healthy spiritual rhythm. What's your spiritual routine? Do you set aside time with God each day? Each week? Each month? What do you need to do to maintain a healthy spiritual rhythm?

⁴"Each Sabbath day the prince will present to the LORD a burnt offering of six lambs and one ram, all with no defects. ⁵He will present a grain offering of a basket of choice flour to go with the ram and whatever amount of flour he chooses to go with each lamb, and he is to offer one gallon of olive oil* for each basket of flour. ⁶At the new moon celebrations, he will bring one young bull, six lambs, and one ram, all with no defects. ⁷With the young bull he must bring a basket of choice flour for a grain offering. With the ram he must bring another basket of flour. And with each lamb he is to bring whatever amount of flour he chooses to give. With each basket of flour he must offer one gallon of olive oil.

⁸"The prince must enter the gateway through the entry room, and he must leave the same way. ⁹But when the people come in through the north gateway to worship the LORD during the religious festivals, they must leave by the south gateway. And those who entered through the south gateway must leave by the north gateway. They must never leave by the same gateway they came in, but must always use the opposite gateway. ¹⁰The prince will enter and leave with the people on these occasions.

¹¹"So at the special feasts and sacred festivals, the grain offering will be a basket of choice flour with each young bull, another basket of flour with each ram, and as much flour as the prince chooses to give with each lamb. Give one gallon of olive oil with each basket of flour. ¹²When the prince offers a voluntary burnt offering or peace offering to the LORD, the east gateway to the inner courtyard will be opened for him, and he will offer his sacrifices as he does on Sabbath days. Then he will leave, and the gateway will be shut behind him.

¹³"Each morning you must sacrifice a one-year-old lamb with no defects as a burnt offering to the LORD. ¹⁴With the lamb, a grain offering must also be given to the LORD—about three quarts of flour with a third of a gallon of olive oil* to moisten the choice flour. This will be a permanent law for you. ¹⁵The

45:18 Hebrew *On the first day of the first month*, of the Hebrew calendar. This day in the ancient Hebrew lunar calendar occurred in March or April.   45:20 Or *will make atonement for.*   45:21 This day in the ancient Hebrew lunar calendar occurred in late March, April, or early May.   45:24 Hebrew *an ephah* [20 quarts or 22 liters] *of flour . . . and a hin* [3.8 liters] *of olive oil.*   45:25 Hebrew *the festival which begins on the fifteenth day of the seventh month* (see Lev 23:34). This day in the ancient Hebrew lunar calendar occurred in late September, October, or early November.   46:5 Hebrew *an ephah* [20 quarts or 22 liters] *of choice flour . . . a hin* [3.8 liters] *of olive oil;* similarly in 46:7, 11.   46:14 Hebrew *⅙ of an ephah* [3.7 liters] *of flour with ⅓ of a hin* [1.3 liters] *of olive oil.*

lamb, the grain offering, and the olive oil must be given as a daily sacrifice every morning without fail.

16"This is what the Sovereign LORD says: If the prince gives a gift of land to one of his sons as his inheritance, it will belong to him and his descendants forever. 17But if the prince gives a gift of land from his inheritance to one of his servants, the servant may keep it only until the Year of Jubilee, which comes every fiftieth year.* At that time the land will return to the prince. But when the prince gives gifts to his sons, those gifts will be permanent. 18And the prince may never take anyone's property by force. If he gives property to his sons, it must be from his own land, for I do not want any of my people unjustly evicted from their property."

THE TEMPLE KITCHENS 19In my vision, the man brought me through the entrance beside the gateway and led me to the sacred rooms assigned to the priests, which faced toward the north. He showed me a place at the extreme west end of these rooms. 20He explained, "This is where the priests will cook the meat from the guilt offerings and sin offerings and bake the flour from the grain offerings into bread. They will do it here to avoid carrying the sacrifices through the outer courtyard and endangering the people by transmitting holiness to them."

21Then he brought me back to the outer courtyard and led me to each of its four corners. In each corner I saw an enclosure. 22Each of these enclosures was 70 feet long and 52½ feet wide,* surrounded by walls. 23Along the inside of these walls was a ledge of stone with fireplaces under the ledge all the way around. 24The man said to me, "These are the kitchens to be used by the Temple assistants to boil the sacrifices offered by the people."

47 **THE RIVER OF HEALING** In my vision, the man brought me back to the entrance of the Temple. There I saw a stream flowing east from beneath the door of the Temple and passing to the right of the altar on its south side. 2The man brought me outside the wall through the north gateway and led me around to the eastern entrance. There I could see the water flowing out through the south side of the east gateway.

3Measuring as he went, he took me along the stream for 1,750 feet* and then led me across. The water was up to my ankles. 4He measured off another 1,750 feet and led me across again. This time the water was up to my knees. After another 1,750 feet, it was up to my waist. 5Then he measured another 1,750 feet, and the river was too deep to walk across. It was deep enough to swim in, but too deep to walk through.

6He asked me, "Have you been watching, son of man?" Then he led me back along the riverbank. 7When I returned, I was surprised by the sight of many trees growing on both sides of the river. 8Then he said to me, "This river flows east through the desert into the valley of the Dead Sea.* The waters of this stream will make the salty waters of the Dead Sea fresh and pure. 9There will be swarms of living things wherever the water of this river flows. Fish will abound in the Dead Sea, for its waters will become fresh. Life will flourish wherever this water flows. 10Fishermen will stand along the shores of the Dead Sea. All the way from En-gedi to En-eglaim, the shores will be covered with nets drying in the sun. Fish of every kind will fill the Dead Sea, just as they fill the Mediterranean.* 11But the marshes and swamps will not be purified; they will still be salty. 12Fruit trees of all kinds will grow along both sides of the river. The leaves of these trees will never turn brown and fall, and there will always be fruit on their branches. There will be a new crop every month, for they are watered by the river flowing from the Temple. The fruit will be for food and the leaves for healing."

BOUNDARIES FOR THE LAND 13This is what the Sovereign LORD says: "Divide the land in this way for the twelve tribes of Israel: The descendants of Joseph will be given two shares of land.* 14Otherwise each tribe will receive an equal share. I took a solemn oath and swore that I would give this land to your ancestors, and it will now come to you as your possession.

HEALING RIVER
(47:1-12) This river (or stream) is similar to the river mentioned in Revelation 22:1-2, both of which are associated with the river in the Garden of Eden (see Gen 2:10). It is a gentle, safe river that expands as it flows and brings life to all it touches. This is one of the images the Bible gives us of heaven: health and well-being for all who love God. When you or someone you know faces illness or other undeserved suffering, may this picture of God's healing power comfort you.

46:17 Hebrew until the Year of Release; see Lev 25:8-17. 46:22 Hebrew 40 cubits [21.2 meters] long and 30 cubits [15.9 meters] wide. 47:3 Hebrew 1,000 cubits [530 meters]; also in 47:4, 5. 47:8 Hebrew the sea. 47:10 Hebrew the Great Sea; also in 47:15, 17, 19, 20. 47:13 It was important to retain twelve portions of land. Since Levi had no portion, the descendants of Joseph's sons, Ephraim and Manasseh, received land as two tribes.

¹⁵"These are the boundaries of the land: The northern border will run from the Mediterranean toward Hethlon, then on through Lebo-hamath to Zedad; ¹⁶then it will run to Berothah and Sibraim, which are on the border between Damascus and Hamath, and finally to Hazer-hatticon, on the border of Hauran. ¹⁷So the northern border will run from the Mediterranean to Hazar-enan, on the border between Hamath to the north and Damascus to the south.

¹⁸"The eastern border starts at a point between Hauran and Damascus and runs south along the Jordan River between Israel and Gilead, past the Dead Sea* and as far south as Tamar.* This will be the eastern border.

¹⁹"The southern border will go west from Tamar to the waters of Meribah at Kadesh* and then follow the course of the Brook of Egypt to the Mediterranean. This will be the southern border.

²⁰"On the west side, the Mediterranean itself will be your border from the southern border to the point where the northern border begins, opposite Lebo-hamath.

²¹"Divide the land within these boundaries among the tribes of Israel. ²²Distribute the land as an allotment for yourselves and for the foreigners who have joined you and are raising their families among you. They will be like native-born Israelites to you and will receive an allotment among the tribes. ²³These foreigners are to be given land within the territory of the tribe with whom they now live. I, the Sovereign LORD, have spoken!

48 DIVISION OF THE LAND "Here is the list of the tribes of Israel and the territory each is to receive. The territory of Dan is in the extreme north. Its boundary line follows the Hethlon road to Lebo-hamath and then runs on to Hazar-enan on the border of Damascus, with Hamath to the north. Dan's territory extends all the way across the land of Israel from east to west.

²"Asher's territory lies south of Dan's and also extends from east to west. ³Naphtali's land lies south of Asher's, also extending from east to west. ⁴Then comes Manasseh south of Naphtali, and its territory also extends from east to west. ⁵South of Manasseh is Ephraim, ⁶and then Reuben, ⁷and then Judah, all of whose boundaries extend from east to west.

⁸"South of Judah is the land set aside for a special purpose. It will be 8⅓ miles* wide and will extend as far east and west as the tribal territories, with the Temple at the center.

⁹"The area set aside for the LORD's Temple will be 8⅓ miles long and 6⅔ miles wide.* ¹⁰For the priests there will be a strip of land measuring 8⅓ miles long by 3⅓ miles wide,* with the LORD's Temple at the center. ¹¹This area is set aside for the ordained priests, the descendants of Zadok who served me faithfully and did not go astray with the people of Israel and the rest of the Levites. ¹²It will be their special portion when the land is distributed, the most sacred land of all. Next to the priests' territory will lie the land where the other Levites will live.

¹³"The land allotted to the Levites will be the same size and shape as that belonging to the priests—8⅓ miles long and 3⅓ miles wide. Together these portions of land will measure 8⅓ miles long by 6⅔ miles wide.* ¹⁴None of this special land may ever be sold or traded or used by others, for it belongs to the LORD; it is set apart as holy.

¹⁵"An additional strip of land 8⅓ miles long by 1⅔ miles wide,* south of the sacred Temple area, will be allotted for public use—homes, pasturelands, and common lands, with a city at the center. ¹⁶The city will measure 1½ miles* on each side—north, south, east, and west. ¹⁷Open lands will surround the city for 150 yards* in every direction. ¹⁸Outside the city there will be a farming area that stretches 3⅓ miles to the east and 3⅓ miles to the west* along the border of the sacred area. This farmland will produce food for the people working

....

THE PRESENCE
(48:1-35) The book of Ezekiel begins by describing the holiness of God, which Israel had ignored. As a result, God's presence had departed from the Temple, the city, and the people. The book ends with a detailed vision of the new Temple, the new city, and the new people—all demonstrating God's holiness.

The concept of a holy God might seem prehistoric in the face of changing technology and constantly evolving ideas of right and wrong. Yet God never changes. He still wants his people to follow his ways, even if they clash with the ways of our society. Are you willing?

47:18a Hebrew *the eastern sea.*   **47:18b** As in Greek version; Hebrew reads *you will measure.*   **47:19** Hebrew *waters of Meribath-kadesh.*   **48:8** Hebrew *25,000 cubits* [13.3 kilometers].   **48:9** As in one Greek manuscript and the Greek reading in 45:1: *25,000 cubits* [13.3 kilometers] *long and 20,000 cubits* [10.6 kilometers] *wide;* Hebrew reads *25,000 cubits long and 10,000 cubits* [3⅓ miles or 5.3 kilometers] *wide.* Similarly in 48:13b. Compare 45:1-5; 48:10-13.   **48:10** Hebrew *25,000 cubits* [13.3 kilometers] *long by 10,000 cubits* [5.3 kilometers] *wide;* also in 48:13a.   **48:13** See note on 48:9.   **48:15** Hebrew *25,000 cubits* [13.3 kilometers] *long by 5,000 cubits* [2.65 kilometers] *wide.*   **48:16** Hebrew *4,500 cubits* [2.4 kilometers]; also in 48:30, 32, 33, 34.   **48:17** Hebrew *250 cubits* [133 meters].   **48:18** Hebrew *10,000 cubits* [5.3 kilometers] *to the east and 10,000 cubits to the west.*

in the city. ¹⁹Those who come from the various tribes to work in the city may farm it. ²⁰This entire area—including the sacred lands and the city—is a square that measures 8⅓ miles* on each side.

²¹"The areas that remain, to the east and to the west of the sacred lands and the city, will belong to the prince. Each of these areas will be 8⅓ miles wide, extending in opposite directions to the eastern and western borders of Israel, with the sacred lands and the sanctuary of the Temple in the center. ²²So the prince's land will include everything between the territories allotted to Judah and Benjamin, except for the areas set aside for the sacred lands and the city.

²³"These are the territories allotted to the rest of the tribes. Benjamin's territory lies just south of the prince's lands, and it extends across the entire land of Israel from east to west. ²⁴South of Benjamin's territory lies that of Simeon, also extending across the land from east to west. ²⁵Next is the territory of Issachar with the same eastern and western boundaries.

48:20 Hebrew *25,000 cubits* [13.3 kilometers]; also in 48:21.
48:28a Hebrew *waters of Meribath-kadesh.* **48:28b** Hebrew *the Great Sea.* **48:35a** Hebrew *18,000 cubits* [9.6 kilometers].
48:35b Hebrew *Yahweh Shammah.*

²⁶"Then comes the territory of Zebulun, which also extends across the land from east to west. ²⁷The territory of Gad is just south of Zebulun with the same borders to the east and west. ²⁸The southern border of Gad runs from Tamar to the waters of Meribah at Kadesh* and then follows the Brook of Egypt to the Mediterranean.*

²⁹"These are the allotments that will be set aside for each tribe's exclusive possession. I, the Sovereign LORD, have spoken!

THE GATES OF THE CITY ³⁰"These will be the exits to the city: On the north wall, which is 1½ miles long, ³¹there will be three gates, each one named after a tribe of Israel. The first will be named for Reuben, the second for Judah, and the third for Levi. ³²On the east wall, also 1½ miles long, the gates will be named for Joseph, Benjamin, and Dan. ³³The south wall, also 1½ miles long, will have gates named for Simeon, Issachar, and Zebulun. ³⁴And on the west wall, also 1½ miles long, the gates will be named for Gad, Asher, and Naphtali.

³⁵"The distance around the entire city will be 6 miles.* And from that day the name of the city will be 'The LORD Is There.'*"

DANIEL

Courage is . . . risking injury to help a friend . . . doing what's right against all odds . . . standing for the truth despite the consequences . . . living for God, no matter what.

Daniel had courage. While living in a foreign land, he stood up for what he believed and did what was right in the face of incredible pressure from society, from peers, and from the government.

Courage was Daniel's trademark throughout his life. Under the reign of four successive kings, he boldly interpreted dreams, rejected royal food and drink, and publicly lived his faith.

God still needs men and women of courage and faith. What kinds of risks or pressures do you face? How do you avoid giving in to the temptation to conform or to turn away from God?

As you read the book of Daniel, take note of any impressions you gain of the man who refused to give in or give up. Ask God to give you the courage to live out your faith, just as Daniel did, as you develop a stronger relationship with "the greatest of gods" (2:47).

KEY POINTS

GOD'S CONTROL God is the behind-the-scenes power behind world events. Although nations compete for world dominance now, one day Christ will rule.

UNCOMPROMISING Daniel and his three friends refused to give in to pressures from an ungodly society. Like Daniel and his friends, we can choose to avoid compromising, no matter what the consequences.

PERSEVERANCE For many decades and with many kings, Daniel persevered in his role as godly counselor. He was truthful, persistent in prayer, and humble. Persistence in prayer can help us hold fast to our commitment to God.

GOD'S FAITHFULNESS God's faithfulness could be seen as he rescued Daniel from enemies. Therefore, we can trust God to take us through any trial.

STATS

PURPOSE
To give a history of the faithful Jews living in captivity and to show God's control over heaven and earth, nature, nations, and his people

AUTHOR
Daniel

ORIGINAL AUDIENCE
The captives in Babylon

DATE WRITTEN
Around 535 B.C., recording events that occurred from about 605 to 535 B.C.

SETTING
Daniel had been taken captive and deported to Babylon by Nebuchadnezzar in 605 B.C. There he served in the government for about 60 years during the reigns of Nebuchadnezzar, Belshazzar, Darius, and Cyrus.

KEY PEOPLE
Daniel, Shadrach, Meshach, Abednego, Nebuchadnezzar, Belshazzar, Darius

KEY PLACES
Nebuchadnezzar's palace, the fiery furnace, Belshazzar's banquet, the den of lions

SPECIAL FEATURES
Daniel's apocalyptic visions (chs 7–12) provide a glimpse of God's plan for the ages, including information about the coming Messiah.

1 DANIEL IN NEBUCHADNEZZAR'S COURT

During the third year of King Jehoiakim's reign in Judah,* King Nebuchadnezzar of Babylon came to Jerusalem and besieged it. ²The Lord gave him victory over King Jehoiakim of Judah and permitted him to take some of the sacred objects from the Temple of God. So Nebuchadnezzar took them back to the land of Babylonia* and placed them in the treasure-house of his god.

³Then the king ordered Ashpenaz, his chief of staff, to bring to the palace some of the young men of Judah's royal family and other noble families, who had been brought to Babylon as captives. ⁴"Select only strong, healthy, and good-looking young men," he said. "Make sure they are well versed in every branch of learning, are gifted with knowledge and good judgment, and are suited to serve in the royal palace. Train these young men in the language and literature of Babylon.*" ⁵The king assigned them a daily ration of food and wine from his own kitchens. They were to be trained for three years, and then they would enter the royal service.

⁶Daniel, Hananiah, Mishael, and Azariah were four of the young men chosen, all from the tribe of Judah. ⁷The chief of staff renamed them with these Babylonian names:

Daniel was called Belteshazzar.
Hananiah was called Shadrach.
Mishael was called Meshach.
Azariah was called Abednego.

⁸But Daniel was determined not to defile himself by eating the food and wine given to them by the king. He asked the chief of staff for permission not to eat these unacceptable foods. ⁹Now God had given the chief of staff both respect and affection for Daniel. ¹⁰But he responded, "I am afraid of my lord the king, who has ordered that you eat this food and wine. If you become pale and thin compared to the other youths your age, I am afraid the king will have me beheaded."

¹¹Daniel spoke with the attendant who had been appointed by the chief of staff to look after Daniel, Hananiah, Mishael, and Azariah. ¹²"Please test us for ten days on a diet of vegetables and water," Daniel said. ¹³"At the end of the ten days, see how we look compared to the other young men who are eating the king's food. Then make your decision in light of what you see." ¹⁴The attendant agreed to Daniel's suggestion and tested them for ten days.

¹⁵At the end of the ten days, Daniel and his three friends looked healthier and better nourished than the young men who had been eating the food assigned by the king. ¹⁶So after that, the attendant fed them only vegetables instead of the food and wine provided for the others.

¹⁷God gave these four young men an unusual aptitude for understanding every aspect of literature and wisdom. And God gave Daniel the special ability to interpret the meanings of visions and dreams.

1:1 This event occurred in 605 B.C., during the third year of Jehoiakim's reign (according to the calendar system in which the new year begins in the spring).   1:2 Hebrew *the land of Shinar.*   1:4 Or *of the Chaldeans.*

··

WHERE DO YOU STAND?
(1:1-8) Resisting temptation can be easier if you've thought through your convictions well before the temptation arises. Since Daniel and his friends had made their decision to remain faithful to God's dietary laws (see Lev 11) before they were faced with the king's delicacies, they didn't hesitate to stick with their convictions. Sometimes we get into trouble because we failed to decide where to draw the line beforehand. Before such situations arise, make a decision about your beliefs. Then, when temptation comes, you'll be ready.

I WONDER...

Christians are really persecuted at my school. I've even heard some teachers speak critically of Christians. Is there a way to avoid compromising and not be thought of as ... well ... a freak?

Jesus once said, "No one can serve two masters." He was talking about God and money. But the same truth—you can only serve one master—applies here.

Sometimes God's desires and those approved by society are as different as night from day. Daniel and his friends understood that. When they were taken to Babylon as teens, they were plunged into a new culture. It was like being in a new school in a new town. Since they were handpicked to work for the king, the temptation to compromise probably was a daily occurrence. Yet they risked their lives to avoid compromising (see Dan 1, 3, 6). They valued God more than they valued their reputations or even their lives.

Instead of wondering how you can avoid looking like a "freak," or how you can be accepted by those around you and still be a Christian, why not ask God to give you the courage to please him, no matter what?

¹⁸When the training period ordered by the king was completed, the chief of staff brought all the young men to King Nebuchadnezzar. ¹⁹The king talked with them, and no one impressed him as much as Daniel, Hananiah, Mishael, and Azariah. So they entered the royal service. ²⁰Whenever the king consulted them in any matter requiring wisdom and balanced judgment, he found them ten times more capable than any of the magicians and enchanters in his entire kingdom.

²¹Daniel remained in the royal service until the first year of the reign of King Cyrus.*

2 NEBUCHADNEZZAR'S DREAM One night during the second year of his reign,* Nebuchadnezzar had such disturbing dreams that he couldn't sleep. ²He called in his magicians, enchanters, sorcerers, and astrologers,* and he demanded that they tell him what he had dreamed. As they stood before the king, ³he said, "I have had a dream that deeply troubles me, and I must know what it means."

⁴Then the astrologers answered the king in Aramaic,* "Long live the king! Tell us the dream, and we will tell you what it means."

⁵But the king said to the astrologers, "I am serious about this. If you don't tell me what my dream was and what it means, you will be torn limb from limb, and your houses will be turned into heaps of rubble! ⁶But if you tell me what I dreamed and what the dream means, I will give you many wonderful gifts and honors. Just tell me the dream and what it means!"

⁷They said again, "Please, Your Majesty. Tell us the dream, and we will tell you what it means."

⁸The king replied, "I know what you are doing! You're stalling for time because you know I am serious when I say, ⁹'If you don't tell me the dream, you are doomed.' So you have conspired to tell me lies, hoping I will change my mind. But tell me the dream, and then I'll know that you can tell me what it means."

¹⁰The astrologers replied to the king, "No one on earth can tell the king his dream! And no king, however great and powerful, has ever asked such a thing of any magician, enchanter, or astrologer! ¹¹The king's demand is impossible. No one except the gods can tell you your dream, and they do not live here among people."

¹²The king was furious when he heard this, and he ordered that all the wise men of Bab-

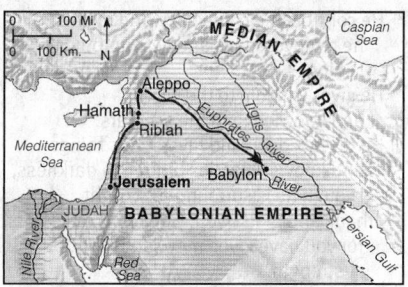

ylon be executed. ¹³And because of the king's decree, men were sent to find and kill Daniel and his friends.

¹⁴When Arioch, the commander of the king's guard, came to kill them, Daniel handled the situation with wisdom and discretion. ¹⁵He asked Arioch, "Why has the king issued such a harsh decree?" So Arioch told him all that had happened. ¹⁶Daniel went at once to see the king and requested more time to tell the king what the dream meant.

¹⁷Then Daniel went home and told his friends Hananiah, Mishael, and Azariah what had happened. ¹⁸He urged them to ask the God of heaven to show them his mercy by telling them the secret, so they would not be executed along with the other wise men of Babylon. ¹⁹That night the secret was revealed to Daniel in a vision. Then Daniel praised the God of heaven. ²⁰He said,

"Praise the name of God forever and ever,
for he has all wisdom and power.

··

CULTURE CLASH?
(1:17) Daniel and his friends learned all they could about their new culture so they could do their work with excellence. But while they learned, they remained faithful to God. So, does this mean you have to totally ignore pop culture and become a hermit? No. What you know about culture can aid in accomplishing God's purpose. We who follow God are free to be leaders in our culture, but God wants to be first in our lives.

DOING THE IMPOSSIBLE
(2:10-11) King Nebuchadnezzar's astrologers told him that no one could know the dreams of another person. But Daniel was able to explain the meaning of the king's dream because God worked through him. In daily life, we face many apparently impossible situations that would be hopeless if we had to handle them with limited human strength alone. But God specializes in the impossible.

1:21 Cyrus began his reign (over Babylon) in 539 B.C. 2:1 The second year of Nebuchadnezzar's reign was 603 B.C. 2:2 Or *Chaldeans;* also in 2:4, 5, 10. 2:4 The original text from this point through chapter 7 is in Aramaic.

²¹ He controls the course of world events;
he removes kings and sets up other
kings.
He gives wisdom to the wise
and knowledge to the scholars.
²² He reveals deep and mysterious things
and knows what lies hidden in darkness,
though he is surrounded by light.
²³ I thank and praise you, God of my ancestors,
for you have given me wisdom and
strength.
You have told me what we asked of you
and revealed to us what the king
demanded."

DANIEL INTERPRETS THE DREAM

²⁴Then Daniel went in to see Arioch, whom the king had ordered to execute the wise men of Babylon.

DUE CREDIT
(2:27-30) Before Daniel told the king anything else, he gave credit to God, explaining that he did not know the dream through his own wisdom but only because God had revealed it. How easily we take credit for what God does through us. This robs God of the honor that is due him.

Daniel said to him, "Don't kill the wise men. Take me to the king, and I will tell him the meaning of his dream."

²⁵Arioch quickly took Daniel to the king and said, "I have found one of the captives from Judah who will tell the king the meaning of his dream!"

²⁶The king said to Daniel (also known as Belteshazzar), "Is this true? Can you tell me what my dream was and what it means?"

²⁷Daniel replied, "There are no wise men, enchanters, magicians, or fortune-tellers who can reveal the king's secret. ²⁸But there is a God in heaven who reveals secrets, and he has shown King Nebuchadnezzar what will happen in the future. Now I will tell you your dream and the visions you saw as you lay on your bed.

²⁹"While Your Majesty was sleeping, you dreamed about coming events. He who reveals secrets has shown you what is going to happen. ³⁰And it is not because I am wiser than anyone else that I know the secret of your dream, but because God wants you to understand what was in your heart.

³¹"In your vision, Your Majesty, you saw

DANIEL

PERSONALITY PROFILE

HAVE YOU EVER NOTICED HOW OFTEN LIFE'S BIGGEST MISTAKES BEGIN WITH THIS THOUGHT: *I'd better do this because everybody else is doing it?* Sometimes we cave to the pressures to be like everyone else, simply to save face.

Even as a young man, Daniel refused to compromise. Adults can't help being impressed whenever a young person speaks and acts wisely. Those were Daniel's strongest personal traits—wise words and actions. He spoke the truth and did what was right, even when it looked as though he were the only one doing it.

One example of Daniel's wisdom is the way he held on to the habits and convictions that came from studying God's Word. Pleasing God was more important to Daniel than pleasing anyone else.

Daniel's convictions weren't just beliefs; they created positive actions in his life. For instance, he ate carefully and lived prayerfully. His position gave him all-you-can-eat privileges at the king's table, but Daniel chose a simpler menu, a choice that proved to be healthier.

While Daniel cut back on food (Dan 1), he cut loose in prayer. He felt comfortable talking to God because he did it all the time. Even lions couldn't come between him and his habit of prayer (Dan 6).

Where do your habits come from? What happens to your convictions when the pressure is on? Like Daniel, is prayer your lifeline? Notice, though, that prayer may not keep you from hard times like "lions' dens." Rather, prayer will keep you in touch with God even in the middle of problems or pain!

BOTTOM LINE: Wise words and actions often earn long-term respect.
God never promised to keep his people from hard times. He does promise to be with us as we go through hard times.
God has the power to deliver his people even from the worst situations.

Daniel's story is told in the book of Daniel. He is also mentioned in Matthew 24:15.

UPS:
• Remained true to his faith even though he was taken from his home at an early age
• Served as a counselor to two Babylonian kings and two Medo-Persian kings
• Was a man of prayer and a statesman with the gift of prophecy
• Survived the lions' den

STATS:
• Where: Judah and the courts of Babylon and Persia
• Occupation: A captive from Israel who became a counselor of kings
• Contemporaries: Hananiah (Shadrach), Mishael (Meshach), Azariah (Abednego), Nebuchadnezzar, Belshazzar, Darius, Cyrus

KEY VERSE: Daniel 5:12

standing before you a huge, shining statue of a man. It was a frightening sight. ³²The head of the statue was made of fine gold. Its chest and arms were silver, its belly and thighs were bronze, ³³its legs were iron, and its feet were a combination of iron and baked clay. ³⁴As you watched, a rock was cut from a mountain, but not by human hands. It struck the feet of iron and clay, smashing them to bits. ³⁵The whole statue was crushed into small pieces of iron, clay, bronze, silver, and gold. Then the wind blew them away without a trace, like chaff on a threshing floor. But the rock that knocked the statue down became a great mountain that covered the whole earth.

³⁶"That was the dream. Now we will tell the king what it means. ³⁷Your Majesty, you are the greatest of kings. The God of heaven has given you sovereignty, power, strength, and honor. ³⁸He has made you the ruler over all the inhabited world and has put even the wild animals and birds under your control. You are the head of gold.

³⁹"But after your kingdom comes to an end, another kingdom, inferior to yours, will rise to take your place. After that kingdom has fallen, yet a third kingdom, represented by bronze, will rise to rule the world. ⁴⁰Following that kingdom, there will be a fourth one, as strong as iron. That kingdom will smash and crush all previous empires, just as iron smashes and crushes everything it strikes. ⁴¹The feet and toes you saw were a combination of iron and baked clay, showing that this kingdom will be divided. Like iron mixed with clay, it will have some of the strength of iron. ⁴²But while some parts of it will be as strong as iron, other parts will be as weak as clay. ⁴³This mixture of iron and clay also shows that these kingdoms will try to strengthen themselves by forming alliances with each other through intermarriage. But they will not hold together, just as iron and clay do not mix.

⁴⁴"During the reigns of those kings, the God of heaven will set up a kingdom that will never be destroyed or conquered. It will crush all these kingdoms into nothingness, and it will stand forever. ⁴⁵That is the meaning of the rock cut from the mountain, though not by human hands, that crushed to pieces the statue of iron, bronze, clay, silver, and gold. The great God was showing the king what will happen in the future. The dream is true, and its meaning is certain."

NEBUCHADNEZZAR REWARDS DANIEL

⁴⁶Then King Nebuchadnezzar threw himself down before Daniel and worshiped him, and he commanded his people to offer sacrifices and burn sweet incense before him. ⁴⁷The king said to Daniel, "Truly, your God is the greatest of gods, the Lord over kings, a revealer of mysteries, for you have been able to reveal this secret."

⁴⁸Then the king appointed Daniel to a high position and gave him many valuable gifts. He made Daniel ruler over the whole province of Babylon, as well as chief over all his wise men. ⁴⁹At Daniel's request, the king appointed Shadrach, Meshach, and Abednego to be in charge of all the affairs of the province of Babylon, while Daniel remained in the king's court.

3 NEBUCHADNEZZAR'S GOLD STATUE

King Nebuchadnezzar made a gold statue ninety feet tall and nine feet wide* and set it up on the plain of Dura in the province of Babylon. ²Then he sent messages to the high officers, officials, governors, advisers, treasurers, judges, magistrates, and all the provincial officials to come to the dedication of the statue he had set up. ³So all these officials* came and stood before the statue King Nebuchadnezzar had set up.

⁴Then a herald shouted out, "People of all races and nations and languages, listen to the king's command! ⁵When you hear the sound of the horn, flute, zither, lyre, harp, pipes, and other musical instruments,* bow to the ground to worship King Nebuchadnezzar's gold statue. ⁶Anyone who refuses to obey will immediately be thrown into a blazing furnace."

⁷So at the sound of the musical instruments,* all the people, whatever their race or nation or language, bowed to the ground and worshiped the gold statue that King Nebuchadnezzar had set up.

⁸But some of the astrologers* went to the king and informed on the Jews. ⁹They said to King Nebuchadnezzar, "Long live the king! ¹⁰You issued a decree requiring all the people to bow down and worship the gold statue when they hear the sound of the horn, flute, zither, lyre, harp, pipes, and other musical instruments. ¹¹That decree also states that those who refuse to obey must be thrown into a blazing furnace. ¹²But there are some Jews—Shadrach, Meshach, and Abednego— whom you have put in charge of the province of Babylon. They pay no attention to you, Your

3:1 Aramaic *60 cubits* [27 meters] *tall and 6 cubits* [2.7 meters] *wide*.
3:3 Aramaic *the high officers, officials, governors, advisers, treasurers, judges, magistrates, and all the provincial officials*.
3:5 The identification of some of these musical instruments is uncertain.   **3:7** Aramaic *the horn, flute, zither, lyre, harp, and other musical instruments*.   **3:8** Aramaic *Chaldeans*.

Majesty. They refuse to serve your gods and do not worship the gold statue you have set up."

¹³Then Nebuchadnezzar flew into a rage and ordered that Shadrach, Meshach, and Abednego be brought before him. When they were brought in, ¹⁴Nebuchadnezzar said to them, "Is it true, Shadrach, Meshach, and Abednego, that you refuse to serve my gods or to worship the gold statue I have set up? ¹⁵I will give you one more chance to bow down and worship the statue I have made when you hear the sound of the musical instruments.* But if you refuse, you will be thrown immediately into the blazing furnace. And then what god will be able to rescue you from my power?"

¹⁶Shadrach, Meshach, and Abednego replied, "O Nebuchadnezzar, we do not need to defend ourselves before you. ¹⁷If we are thrown into the blazing furnace, the God whom we serve is able to save us. He will rescue us from your power, Your Majesty. ¹⁸But even if he doesn't, we want to make it clear to you, Your Majesty, that we will never serve your gods or worship the gold statue you have set up."

THE BLAZING FURNACE ¹⁹Nebuchadnezzar was so furious with Shadrach, Meshach, and Abednego that his face became distorted with rage. He commanded that the furnace be heated seven times hotter than usual. ²⁰Then he ordered some of the strongest men of his army to bind Shadrach, Meshach, and Abednego and throw them into the blazing furnace. ²¹So they tied them up and threw them into the

STAND OUT

(3:12-18) Why didn't Shadrach, Meshach, and Abednego just bow to the image and tell God that they didn't mean it? They had determined never to worship an idol, and they courageously took their stand. As a result, they were condemned to be executed. They didn't know whether or not they would be rescued from the fire; all they knew was that they wouldn't disobey God. Are you ready to take a stand for God no matter what? When you stand for God, you will stand out. Taking a stand is painful sometimes, and doesn't always have a happy ending. Are you, like Shadrach, Meshach, and Abednego, prepared to say, "Whether he rescues me or not, I will only serve God"? (see 3:17-18).

3:15 Aramaic *the horn, flute, zither, lyre, harp, pipes, and other musical instruments.*

SHADRACH, MESHACH, & ABEDNEGO
PERSONALITY PROFILE

HAVE YOU EVER WOUND UP TOO CLOSE TO A FIRE THAT SUDDENLY FLARED UP? If so, you know how powerful and frightening fire can be. But would you willingly walk into a blast furnace to prove your faith in God? Daniel's friends Shadrach, Meshach, and Abednego did.

Along with Daniel and the other people of Jerusalem, these three young men were taken into captivity by the Babylonians in 605 B.C. and forced to serve in the court of an enemy king, Nebuchadnezzar.

Although the king obviously respected and admired his young Jewish servants, he just as clearly did not understand the depth of their relationship with the one true God.

If you've read Daniel 3, you know the story. Shadrach, Meshach, and Abednego refused to bow to a statue built by order of Nebuchadnezzar. Disobedience meant a trip to the fiery furnace. Of course, with a choice like that, almost everyone obeyed . . . but not Shadrach, Meshach, and Abednego. They preferred to face the fire rather than offend God by worshiping a statue. Now, that's putting your faith on the line!

Shadrach, Meshach, and Abednego were three friends who probably encouraged each other to stick with God. They were a living example of Proverbs 27:17: "As iron sharpens iron, so a friend sharpens a friend." What also helped their friendship was a fourth friend: God. Do you have friends like that—friends who will encourage you to avoid compromising, even at the cost of your reputation? *Being* a friend like that is the start.

BOTTOM LINE: A real friend shares your convictions and is willing to take a stand with you when the going gets tough.

God can be trusted even when we can't predict the outcome of a trial.

The story of Shadrach (Hananiah), Meshach (Mishael), and Abednego (Azariah) is told in the book of Daniel.

UPS:
- *Like Daniel, refused to break the dietary laws of their people*
- *Shared a friendship that stood the tests of hardship, success, wealth, and threats of death*
- *Would not compromise their convictions even in the face of death*
- *Survived the fiery furnace*

STATS:
- *Where: Babylon*
- *Occupations: King's servants and counselors*
- *Contemporaries: Daniel, Nebuchadnezzar*

KEY VERSES: *Daniel 3:16-18*

furnace, fully dressed in their pants, turbans, robes, and other garments. ²²And because the king, in his anger, had demanded such a hot fire in the furnace, the flames killed the soldiers as they threw the three men in. ²³So Shadrach, Meshach, and Abednego, securely tied, fell into the roaring flames.

²⁴But suddenly, Nebuchadnezzar jumped up in amazement and exclaimed to his advisers, "Didn't we tie up three men and throw them into the furnace?"

"Yes, Your Majesty, we certainly did," they replied.

²⁵"Look!" Nebuchadnezzar shouted. "I see four men, unbound, walking around in the fire unharmed! And the fourth looks like a god*!"

²⁶Then Nebuchadnezzar came as close as he could to the door of the flaming furnace and shouted: "Shadrach, Meshach, and Abednego, servants of the Most High God, come out! Come here!"

So Shadrach, Meshach, and Abednego stepped out of the fire. ²⁷Then the high officers, officials, governors, and advisers crowded around them and saw that the fire had not touched them. Not a hair on their heads was singed, and their clothing was not scorched. They didn't even smell of smoke!

²⁸Then Nebuchadnezzar said, "Praise to the God of Shadrach, Meshach, and Abednego! He sent his angel to rescue his servants who trusted in him. They defied the king's command and were willing to die rather than serve or worship any god except their own God. ²⁹Therefore, I make this decree: If any people, whatever their race or nation or language, speak a word against the God of Shadrach, Meshach, and Abednego, they will be torn limb from limb, and their houses will be turned into heaps of rubble. There is no other god who can rescue like this!"

³⁰Then the king promoted Shadrach, Meshach, and Abednego to even higher positions in the province of Babylon.

4 NEBUCHADNEZZAR'S DREAM ABOUT A TREE

¹*King Nebuchadnezzar sent this message to the people of every race and nation and language throughout the world:

"Peace and prosperity to you!

²"I want you all to know about the miraculous signs and wonders the Most High God has performed for me.

3:25 Aramaic *like a son of the gods.* 4:1 Verses 4:1-3 are numbered 3:31-33 in Aramaic text. 4:4 Verses 4:4-37 are numbered 4:1-34 in Aramaic text. 4:7 Or *Chaldeans.* 4:13 Aramaic *a watcher;* also in 4:23. 4:17 Aramaic *the watchers.*

³ How great are his signs,
how powerful his wonders!
His kingdom will last forever,
his rule through all generations.

⁴*"I, Nebuchadnezzar, was living in my palace in comfort and prosperity. ⁵But one night I had a dream that frightened me; I saw visions that terrified me as I lay in my bed. ⁶So I issued an order calling in all the wise men of Babylon, so they could tell me what my dream meant. ⁷When all the magicians, enchanters, astrologers,* and fortune-tellers came in, I told them the dream, but they could not tell me what it meant. ⁸At last Daniel came in before me, and I told him the dream. (He was named Belteshazzar after my god, and the spirit of the holy gods is in him.)

⁹"I said to him, 'Belteshazzar, chief of the magicians, I know that the spirit of the holy gods is in you and that no mystery is too great for you to solve. Now tell me what my dream means.

¹⁰"'While I was lying in my bed, this is what I dreamed. I saw a large tree in the middle of the earth. ¹¹The tree grew very tall and strong, reaching high into the heavens for all the world to see. ¹²It had fresh green leaves, and it was loaded with fruit for all to eat. Wild animals lived in its shade, and birds nested in its branches. All the world was fed from this tree.

¹³"'Then as I lay there dreaming, I saw a messenger,* a holy one, coming down from heaven. ¹⁴The messenger shouted,

"Cut down the tree and lop off its branches!
Shake off its leaves and scatter its fruit!
Chase the wild animals from its shade
and the birds from its branches.
¹⁵ But leave the stump and the roots in the ground,
bound with a band of iron and bronze
and surrounded by tender grass.
Now let him be drenched with the dew of heaven,
and let him live with the wild animals among the plants of the field.
¹⁶ For seven periods of time,
let him have the mind of a wild animal instead of the mind of a human.
¹⁷ For this has been decreed by the messengers*;
it is commanded by the holy ones,
so that everyone may know

that the Most High rules over the
kingdoms of the world.
He gives them to anyone he chooses—
even to the lowliest of people."

[18] "'Belteshazzar, that was the dream that
I, King Nebuchadnezzar, had. Now tell me
what it means, for none of the wise men
of my kingdom can do so. But you can tell
me because the spirit of the holy gods is
in you.'

DANIEL EXPLAINS THE DREAM

[19] "Upon hearing this, Daniel (also known as Belteshazzar) was overcome for a time, frightened by the meaning of the dream. Then the king said to him, 'Belteshazzar, don't be alarmed by the dream and what it means.'

"Belteshazzar replied, 'I wish the events foreshadowed in this dream would happen to your enemies, my lord, and not to you! [20] The tree you saw was growing very tall and strong, reaching high into the heavens for all the world to see. [21] It had fresh green leaves and was loaded with fruit for all to

....

HARD TO FORGIVE
(4:19) When Daniel understood the meaning of Nebu-
chadnezzar's dream, he was stunned. How could he be so
deeply grieved at the fate of Nebuchadnezzar—the king
who was responsible for the destruction of his home and
the captivity of his people? One word: forgiveness. Often,
when we have been wronged by someone, we find it diffi-
cult to forget the past. We may even be glad if that person
suffers. Forgiving people means putting the past behind
us. Can you love someone who has hurt you? Ask God to
help you forgive, forget, and love. God may use you in an
extraordinary way in that person's life!

eat. Wild animals lived in its shade, and
birds nested in its branches. [22] That tree,
Your Majesty, is you. For you have grown
strong and great; your greatness reaches
up to heaven, and your rule to the ends of
the earth.

[23] "'Then you saw a messenger, a holy
one, coming down from heaven and saying,
"Cut down the tree and destroy it. But leave
the stump and the roots in the ground,
bound with a band of iron and bronze and
surrounded by tender grass. Let him be
drenched with the dew of heaven. Let him
live with the animals of the field for seven
periods of time."

[24] "'This is what the dream means, Your
Majesty, and what the Most High has
declared will happen to my lord the king.
[25] You will be driven from human society,
and you will live in the fields with the wild
animals. You will eat grass like a cow,
and you will be drenched with the dew of
heaven. Seven periods of time will pass
while you live this way, until you learn that
the Most High rules over the kingdoms of
the world and gives them to anyone he
chooses. [26] But the stump and roots of the
tree were left in the ground. This means that
you will receive your kingdom back again
when you have learned that heaven rules.

[27] "'King Nebuchadnezzar, please accept
my advice. Stop sinning and do what is
right. Break from your wicked past and be
merciful to the poor. Perhaps then you will
continue to prosper.'

THE DREAM'S FULFILLMENT

[28] "But all these things did happen to King
Nebuchadnezzar. [29] Twelve months later

CHOICES
friendship

Kennedy, Lola, and Montana are inseparable. Find
one and you'll find the other two. Besides a lot of
laughs and six years' worth of great memories, the
three-way friendship has helped keep the girls on
track with God all through high school. Whenever one
struggled in her faith, the other two were there to pick
her up. For instance:

• When Lola began dating a non-Christian, the other
  two girls confronted her and convinced her that
  she was making a mistake.
• When Montana's parents split up one winter and
  Montana wondered if God really cared, Kennedy
  and Lola showered their hurting friend with love.
• When Kennedy got so involved in extracurricular

school activities one semester that she quit coming
to Bible study, the other girls practically dragged
her back into the fold!
• When none of them were asked to the prom
  because of their stands against alcohol, they all
  dressed up and went to dinner instead.

Without such a strong Christ-centered friendship,
these teens might have wandered away from God
when the pressure became too intense. However, because they had a friendship like this to lean on, they
all were able to have a huge impact for Christ!

Do you have close Christian friends who constantly
challenge you to grow in Christ? Read in Daniel 3 about
three godly guys who braved some serious heat together.

he was taking a walk on the flat roof of the royal palace in Babylon. [30]As he looked out across the city, he said, 'Look at this great city of Babylon! By my own mighty power, I have built this beautiful city as my royal residence to display my majestic splendor.'

[31]"While these words were still in his mouth, a voice called down from heaven, 'O King Nebuchadnezzar, this message is for you! You are no longer ruler of this kingdom. [32]You will be driven from human society. You will live in the fields with the wild animals, and you will eat grass like a cow. Seven periods of time will pass while you live this way, until you learn that the Most High rules over the kingdoms of the world and gives them to anyone he chooses.'

[33]"That same hour the judgment was fulfilled, and Nebuchadnezzar was driven from human society. He ate grass like a cow, and he was drenched with the dew of heaven. He lived this way until his hair was as long as eagles' feathers and his nails were like birds' claws.

NEBUCHADNEZZAR PRAISES GOD [34]"After this time had passed, I, Nebuchadnezzar, looked up to heaven. My sanity returned, and I praised and worshiped the Most High and honored the one who lives forever.

His rule is everlasting,
    and his kingdom is eternal.
[35] All the people of the earth
    are nothing compared to him.
He does as he pleases
    among the angels of heaven
    and among the people of the earth.
No one can stop him or say to him,
    'What do you mean by doing these
        things?'

[36]"When my sanity returned to me, so did my honor and glory and kingdom. My advisers and nobles sought me out, and I was restored as head of my kingdom, with even greater honor than before. [37]Now I, Nebuchadnezzar, praise and glorify and honor the King of heaven. All his acts are just and true, and he is able to humble the proud."

5 **THE WRITING ON THE WALL** Many years later King Belshazzar gave a great feast for 1,000 of his nobles, and he drank wine with them. [2]While Belshazzar was drinking the

5:2 Aramaic *father;* also in 5:11, 13, 18.   5:7 Or *Chaldeans;* also in 5:11.

wine, he gave orders to bring in the gold and silver cups that his predecessor,* Nebuchadnezzar, had taken from the Temple in Jerusalem. He wanted to drink from them with his nobles, his wives, and his concubines. [3]So they brought these gold cups taken from the Temple, the house of God in Jerusalem, and the king and his nobles, his wives, and his concubines drank from them. [4]While they drank from them they praised their idols made of gold, silver, bronze, iron, wood, and stone.

[5]Suddenly, they saw the fingers of a human hand writing on the plaster wall of the king's palace, near the lampstand. The king himself saw the hand as it wrote, [6]and his face turned pale with fright. His knees knocked together in fear and his legs gave way beneath him.

[7]The king shouted for the enchanters, astrologers,* and fortune-tellers to be brought before him. He said to these wise men of Babylon, "Whoever can read this writing and tell me what it means will be dressed in purple robes of royal honor and will have a gold chain placed around his neck. He will become the third highest ruler in the kingdom!"

[8]But when all the king's wise men had come in, none of them could read the writing or tell him what it meant. [9]So the king grew even more alarmed, and his face turned pale. His nobles, too, were shaken.

[10]But when the queen mother heard what was happening, she hurried to the banquet hall. She said to Belshazzar, "Long live the king! Don't be so pale and frightened. [11]There is a man in your kingdom who has within him the spirit of the holy gods. During Nebuchadnezzar's reign, this man was found to have insight, understanding, and wisdom like that of the gods. Your predecessor, the king—your predecessor King Nebuchadnezzar—made

....

ACKNOWLEDGE GOD
(4:1-37) In 2:47, Nebuchadnezzar acknowledged that God revealed dreams to Daniel. In 3:28-29, he praised the God who delivered the three young men. Despite Nebuchadnezzar's recognition of God's power (4:2-3), in 4:30 we see that he still did not acknowledge God as his own ruler. What about you? Is God just a great God who performs miracles? Or, is he a great God whom you trust as your ruler?

UNBIASED
(5:1-17) The king offered Daniel beautiful gifts and great power if he would explain the writing on the wall. Daniel, however, refused them. He wanted the king to know that the interpretation of his dream was unbiased. Delivering a hard message from God isn't easy, especially when you have to talk to someone in authority. Like Daniel, you may be in a position to confront someone about a wrongdoing. Will their influence sway you or will God's?

him chief over all the magicians, enchanters, astrologers, and fortune-tellers of Babylon. ¹²This man Daniel, whom the king named Belteshazzar, has exceptional ability and is filled with divine knowledge and understanding. He can interpret dreams, explain riddles, and solve difficult problems. Call for Daniel, and he will tell you what the writing means."

DANIEL EXPLAINS THE WRITING ¹³So Daniel was brought in before the king. The king asked him, "Are you Daniel, one of the exiles brought from Judah by my predecessor, King Nebuchadnezzar? ¹⁴I have heard that you have the spirit of the gods within you and that you are filled with insight, understanding, and wisdom. ¹⁵My wise men and enchanters have tried to read the words on the wall and tell me their meaning, but they cannot do it. ¹⁶I am told that you can give interpretations and solve difficult problems. If you can read these words and tell me their meaning, you will be clothed in purple robes of royal honor, and you will have a gold chain placed around your neck. You will become the third highest ruler in the kingdom."

¹⁷Daniel answered the king, "Keep your gifts or give them to someone else, but I will tell you what the writing means. ¹⁸Your Majesty, the Most High God gave sovereignty, majesty, glory, and honor to your predecessor, Nebuchadnezzar. ¹⁹He made him so great that people of all races and nations and languages trembled before him in fear. He killed those he wanted to kill and spared those he wanted to spare. He honored those he wanted to honor and disgraced those he wanted to disgrace. ²⁰But when his heart and mind were puffed up with arrogance, he was brought down from his royal throne and stripped of his glory. ²¹He was driven from human society. He was given the mind of a wild animal, and he lived among the wild donkeys. He ate grass like a cow, and he

was drenched with the dew of heaven, until he learned that the Most High God rules over the kingdoms of the world and appoints anyone he desires to rule over them.

²²"You are his successor,* O Belshazzar, and you knew all this, yet you have not humbled yourself. ²³For you have proudly defied the Lord of heaven and have had these cups from his Temple brought before you. You and your nobles and your wives and concubines have been drinking wine from them while praising gods of silver, gold, bronze, iron, wood, and stone—gods that neither see nor hear nor know anything at all. But you have not honored the God who gives you the breath of life and controls your destiny! ²⁴So God has sent this hand to write this message.

²⁵"This is the message that was written: MENE, MENE, TEKEL, and PARSIN. ²⁶This is what these words mean:

> *Mene* means 'numbered'—God has
>   numbered the days of your reign and has
>   brought it to an end.
> ²⁷ *Tekel* means 'weighed'—you have been
>   weighed on the balances and have not
>   measured up.
> ²⁸ *Parsin** means 'divided'—your kingdom has
>   been divided and given to the Medes and
>   Persians."

²⁹Then at Belshazzar's command, Daniel was dressed in purple robes, a gold chain was hung around his neck, and he was proclaimed the third highest ruler in the kingdom.

³⁰That very night Belshazzar, the Babylonian* king, was killed.*

³¹*And Darius the Mede took over the kingdom at the age of sixty-two.

6 **DANIEL IN THE LIONS' DEN** ¹*Darius the Mede decided to divide the kingdom into 120 provinces, and he appointed a high officer to rule over each province. ²The king also chose Daniel and two others as administrators to supervise the high officers and protect the king's interests. ³Daniel soon proved himself more capable than all the other administrators and high officers. Because of Daniel's great ability, the king made plans to place him over the entire empire.

⁴Then the other administrators and high officers began searching for some fault in the way Daniel was handling government affairs,

DO IT NOW
(5:25-27) Belshazzar probably thought that his kingdom would last a lot longer than it did. But God ended it that night. God's time of judgment comes for all people. Yet many people believe that they have plenty of time to make things right with God. "I'll do it tomorrow," they say. Know anyone like that? The time to make things right is now.

RESPECT
(6:1-3) At this time, Daniel was in his eighties and was one of Darius's top three administrators. Yet Daniel was a cut above all of the other workers. Thus, Daniel earned the king's respect. One of the best ways to influence non-Christian employers is to work hard. Are you gainfully employed? How do you represent God to your employer?

5:22 Aramaic *son.*   **5:28** Aramaic *Peres,* the singular of *Parsin.*   **5:30a** Or *Chaldean.*   **5:30b** The Persians and Medes conquered Babylon in October 539 B.C.   **5:31** Verse 5:31 is numbered 6:1 in Aramaic text.   **6:1** Verses 6:1-28 are numbered 6:2-29 in Aramaic text.

but they couldn't find anything to criticize or condemn. He was faithful, always responsible, and completely trustworthy. [5]So they concluded, "Our only chance of finding grounds for accusing Daniel will be in connection with the rules of his religion."

[6]So the administrators and high officers went to the king and said, "Long live King Darius! [7]We are all in agreement—we administrators, officials, high officers, advisers, and governors—that the king should make a law that will be strictly enforced. Give orders that for the next thirty days any person who prays to anyone, divine or human—except to you, Your Majesty—will be thrown into the den of lions. [8]And now, Your Majesty, issue and sign this law so it cannot be changed, an official law of the Medes and Persians that cannot be revoked." [9]So King Darius signed the law.

[10]But when Daniel learned that the law had been signed, he went home and knelt down as usual in his upstairs room, with its windows open toward Jerusalem. He prayed three times a day, just as he had always done, giving thanks to his God. [11]Then the officials went together to Daniel's house and found him praying and asking for God's help. [12]So they went straight to the king and reminded him about his law. "Did you not sign a law that for the next thirty days any person who prays to anyone, divine or human—except to you, Your Majesty—will be thrown into the den of lions?"

"Yes," the king replied, "that decision stands; it is an official law of the Medes and Persians that cannot be revoked."

[13]Then they told the king, "That man Daniel, one of the captives from Judah, is ignoring you and your law. He still prays to his God three times a day."

[14]Hearing this, the king was deeply troubled, and he tried to think of a way to save Daniel. He spent the rest of the day looking for a way to get Daniel out of this predicament.

[15]In the evening the men went together to the king and said, "Your Majesty, you know that according to the law of the Medes and the Persians, no law that the king signs can be changed."

[16]So at last the king gave orders for Daniel to be arrested and thrown into the den of lions. The king said to him, "May your God, whom you serve so faithfully, rescue you."

[17]A stone was brought and placed over the mouth of the den. The king sealed the stone with his own royal seal and the seals of his nobles, so that no one could rescue Daniel. [18]Then the king returned to his palace and

DANIEL

Served as a prophet to exiles in Babylon from 605 to 536 B.C.

CLIMATE OF THE TIMES
The people of Judah were captives in a strange land, feeling hopeless.

MAIN MESSAGE
God is sovereign over all of human history, past, present, and future.

IMPORTANCE OF MESSAGE
We should spend less time wondering when future events will happen and more time learning how we should live now.

CONTEMPORARY PROPHETS
Jeremiah (627-586)
Habakkuk (612-588)

---

spent the night fasting. He refused his usual entertainment and couldn't sleep at all that night.

[19]Very early the next morning, the king got up and hurried out to the lions' den. [20]When he got there, he called out in anguish, "Daniel, servant of the living God! Was your God, whom you serve so faithfully, able to rescue you from the lions?"

[21]Daniel answered, "Long live the king! [22]My God sent his angel to shut the lions' mouths so that they would not hurt me, for I have been found innocent in his sight. And I have not wronged you, Your Majesty."

[23]The king was overjoyed and ordered that Daniel be lifted from the den. Not a scratch was found on him, for he had trusted in his God.

[24]Then the king gave orders to arrest the men who had maliciously accused Daniel. He had them thrown into the lions' den, along with their wives and children. The lions leaped on them and tore them apart before they even hit the floor of the den.

[25]Then King Darius sent this message to the people of every race and nation and language throughout the world:

....

CRITICS
(6:4-5) Since the jealous officials couldn't find anything about Daniel's life to criticize, they attacked his habit of prayer. If you face jealous critics because of your faith, be glad they're criticizing that part of your life. Perhaps they had to focus on your relationship with God as a last resort! As you consider your response, remember that God is in control, fighting this battle for you.

"Peace and prosperity to you!

²⁶"I decree that everyone throughout my kingdom should tremble with fear before the God of Daniel.

For he is the living God,
    and he will endure forever.
His kingdom will never be destroyed,
    and his rule will never end.
²⁷ He rescues and saves his people;
    he performs miraculous signs and
        wonders
    in the heavens and on earth.
He has rescued Daniel
    from the power of the lions."

²⁸So Daniel prospered during the reign of Darius and the reign of Cyrus the Persian.*

7 DANIEL'S VISION OF FOUR BEASTS

Earlier, during the first year of King Belshazzar's reign in Babylon,* Daniel had a dream and saw visions as he lay in his bed. He wrote down the dream, and this is what he saw.

²In my vision that night, I, Daniel, saw a great storm churning the surface of a great sea, with strong winds blowing from every direction. ³Then four huge beasts came up out of the water, each different from the others.

⁴The first beast was like a lion with eagles' wings. As I watched, its wings were pulled off,

and it was left standing with its two hind feet on the ground, like a human being. And it was given a human mind.

⁵Then I saw a second beast, and it looked like a bear. It was rearing up on one side, and it had three ribs in its mouth between its teeth. And I heard a voice saying to it, "Get up! Devour the flesh of many people!"

⁶Then the third of these strange beasts appeared, and it looked like a leopard. It had four bird's wings on its back, and it had four heads. Great authority was given to this beast.

⁷Then in my vision that night, I saw a fourth beast—terrifying, dreadful, and very strong. It devoured and crushed its victims with huge iron teeth and trampled their remains beneath its feet. It was different from any of the other beasts, and it had ten horns.

⁸As I was looking at the horns, suddenly another small horn appeared among them. Three of the first horns were torn out by the roots to make room for it. This little horn had eyes like human eyes and a mouth that was boasting arrogantly.

⁹ I watched as thrones were put in place
    and the Ancient One* sat down to
        judge.
His clothing was as white as snow,
    his hair like purest wool.
He sat on a fiery throne
    with wheels of blazing fire,
¹⁰ and a river of fire was pouring out,
    flowing from his presence.
Millions of angels ministered to him;
    many millions stood to attend him.
Then the court began its session,
    and the books were opened.

¹¹I continued to watch because I could hear the little horn's boastful speech. I kept watching until the fourth beast was killed and its body was destroyed by fire. ¹²The other three beasts had their authority taken from them, but they were allowed to live a while longer.*

¹³As my vision continued that night, I saw someone like a son of man* coming with the clouds of heaven. He approached the Ancient One and was led into his presence. ¹⁴He was given authority, honor, and sovereignty over all the nations of the world, so that people of every race and nation and language would obey him. His rule is eternal—it will never end. His kingdom will never be destroyed.

A FAITHFUL WITNESS

(6:25-27) Nebuchadnezzar learned about God through the faithfulness of Daniel and his friends (chs 2–3). Here Darius also was convinced of God's power after God rescued his faithful servant. Although Daniel was captive in a strange land, his devotion to God was a testimony to powerful rulers. If you find yourself in new surroundings, take the opportunity to tell about God's power and work in your life. Be faithful to God, so he can use you to reach others.

JUDGMENT DAY

(7:9-10) Daniel saw a vision of God judging millions of people as they stood before his throne. Someday, we'll all be judged by God for our actions. If God were to judge your life today, what would he say about it? Is the thought of God's judgment scary? If so, you can change that right now. Wondering how? Take the keys of your life and hand them over to Jesus. Let him "drive" it from now on. Feel better?

A MYSTERY

(7:1-15) If you feel as Daniel did about these prophecies—troubled (7:15)—recognize with him that these events have yet to come to pass. Some prophecies are mysteries that God has chosen not to fully reveal at this time. We may or may not know the whole story in this life. Yet the Bible presents some mysteries (for example, how God is three, yet one) that we may never fully understand. Are you content to believe, even if you don't fully understand?

6:28 Or of Darius, that is, the reign of Cyrus the Persian.   **7:1** The first year of Belshazzar's reign (who was co-regent with his father, Nabonidus) was 556 B.C. (or perhaps as late as 553 B.C.).
7:9 Aramaic an Ancient of Days; also in 7:13, 22.   **7:12** Aramaic for a season and a time.   **7:13** Or like a Son of Man.

THE VISION IS EXPLAINED ¹⁵I, Daniel, was troubled by all I had seen, and my visions terrified me. ¹⁶So I approached one of those standing beside the throne and asked him what it all meant. He explained it to me like this: ¹⁷"These four huge beasts represent four kingdoms that will arise from the earth. ¹⁸But in the end, the holy people of the Most High will be given the kingdom, and they will rule forever and ever."

¹⁹Then I wanted to know the true meaning of the fourth beast, the one so different from the others and so terrifying. It had devoured and crushed its victims with iron teeth and bronze claws, trampling their remains beneath its feet. ²⁰I also asked about the ten horns on the fourth beast's head and the little horn that came up afterward and destroyed three of the other horns. This horn had seemed greater than the others, and it had human eyes and a mouth that was boasting arrogantly. ²¹As I watched, this horn was waging war against God's holy people and was defeating them, ²²until the Ancient One—the Most High—came and judged in favor of his holy people. Then the time arrived for the holy people to take over the kingdom.

²³Then he said to me, "This fourth beast is the fourth world power that will rule the earth. It will be different from all the others. It will devour the whole world, trampling and crushing everything in its path. ²⁴Its ten horns are ten kings who will rule that empire. Then another king will arise, different from the other ten, who will subdue three of them. ²⁵He will defy the Most High and oppress the holy people of the Most High. He will try to change their sacred festivals and laws, and they will be placed under his control for a time, times, and half a time.

²⁶"But then the court will pass judgment, and all his power will be taken away and completely destroyed. ²⁷Then the sovereignty, power, and greatness of all the kingdoms under heaven will be given to the holy people of the Most High. His kingdom will last forever, and all rulers will serve and obey him."

²⁸That was the end of the vision. I, Daniel, was terrified by my thoughts and my face was pale with fear, but I kept these things to myself.

8 DANIEL'S VISION OF A RAM AND GOAT

¹*During the third year of King Belshazzar's reign, I, Daniel, saw another vision, fol-

lowing the one that had already appeared to me. ²In this vision I was at the fortress of Susa, in the province of Elam, standing beside the Ulai River.*

³As I looked up, I saw a ram with two long horns standing beside the river.* One of the horns was longer than the other, even though it had grown later than the other one. ⁴The ram butted everything out of his way to the west, to the north, and to the south, and no one could stand against him or help his victims. He did as he pleased and became very great.

⁵While I was watching, suddenly a male goat appeared from the west, crossing the land so swiftly that he didn't even touch the ground. This goat, which had one very large horn between its eyes, ⁶headed toward the two-horned ram that I had seen standing beside the river, rushing at him in a rage. ⁷The goat charged furiously at the ram and struck him, breaking off both his horns. Now the ram was helpless, and the goat knocked him down and trampled him. No one could rescue the ram from the goat's power.

⁸The goat became very powerful. But at the height of his power, his large horn was broken off. In the large horn's place grew four prominent horns pointing in the four directions of the earth. ⁹Then from one of the prominent horns came a small horn whose power grew very great. It extended toward the south and the east and toward the glorious land of Israel. ¹⁰Its power reached to the heavens, where it attacked the heavenly army, throwing some of the heavenly beings and some of the stars to the ground and trampling them. ¹¹It even challenged the Commander of heaven's army by canceling the daily sacrifices offered to him and by destroying his Temple. ¹²The army of heaven was restrained from responding to this rebellion. So the daily sacrifice was halted, and truth was overthrown. The horn succeeded in everything it did.*

¹³Then I heard two holy ones talking to each other. One of them asked, "How long will the events of this vision last? How long will the rebellion that causes desecration stop the daily sacrifices? How long will the Temple and heaven's army be trampled on?"

¹⁴The other replied, "It will take 2,300 evenings and mornings; then the Temple will be made right again."

GABRIEL EXPLAINS THE VISION ¹⁵As I, Daniel, was trying to understand the meaning of this vision, someone who looked like a man stood in front of me. ¹⁶And I heard a human voice

---

8:1 The original text from this point through chapter 12 is in Hebrew. See note at 2:4. **8:2** Or *the Ulai Gate;* also in 8:16. **8:3** Or *the gate;* also in 8:6. **8:11-12** The meaning of the Hebrew for these verses is uncertain.

calling out from the Ulai River, "Gabriel, tell this man the meaning of his vision."

¹⁷As Gabriel approached the place where I was standing, I became so terrified that I fell with my face to the ground. "Son of man," he said, "you must understand that the events you have seen in your vision relate to the time of the end."

¹⁸While he was speaking, I fainted and lay there with my face to the ground. But Gabriel roused me with a touch and helped me to my feet.

¹⁹Then he said, "I am here to tell you what will happen later in the time of wrath. What you have seen pertains to the very end of time. ²⁰The two-horned ram represents the kings of Media and Persia. ²¹The shaggy male goat represents the king of Greece,* and the large horn between his eyes represents the first king of the Greek Empire. ²²The four prominent horns that replaced the one large horn show that the Greek Empire will break into four kingdoms, but none as great as the first.

²³"At the end of their rule, when their sin is at its height, a fierce king, a master of intrigue, will rise to power. ²⁴He will become very strong, but not by his own power. He will cause a shocking amount of destruction and succeed in everything he does. He will destroy powerful leaders and devastate the holy people. ²⁵He

· ·

INVINCIBLE
(8:23-25) Daniel saw a vision of a battle between the "Prince of princes" (God) and "a master of intrigue." The master of intrigue was a seemingly invincible human ruler whom God defeated long after Daniel's death. Only God can truly be called invincible. Does this invincible God—the God who can defeat even the greatest evil—have your trust?

GOD-CENTERED PRAYER
(9:1-19) Daniel prayed, fasted, confessed his sins, and pleaded that God would reveal his will. Daniel's openness and faith that God would answer pleased God. Most of us, if we were honest, would admit that our prayers are more of a laundry list than communication that honors God. When you pray, how open are you to honoring God and seeing his will done? Daniel's prayer can inspire you to make your communication God-centered rather than you-centered.

TRUTH HURTS
(9:6) God had sent many prophets to speak to his people through the years, but their messages had been ignored. The truth was too painful to hear. God still speaks infallibly and authoritatively through the Bible, and he also speaks through preachers, teachers, and spiritually sensitive and concerned friends. Sometimes the truth hurts, and we would rather settle for a soothing falsehood. Don't settle for a comforting lie that will result in harsh judgment. Accept and obey God's truth, even though it may hurt.

will be a master of deception and will become arrogant; he will destroy many without warning. He will even take on the Prince of princes in battle, but he will be broken, though not by human power.

²⁶"This vision about the 2,300 evenings and mornings* is true. But none of these things will happen for a long time, so keep this vision a secret."

²⁷Then I, Daniel, was overcome and lay sick for several days. Afterward I got up and performed my duties for the king, but I was greatly troubled by the vision and could not understand it.

9 DANIEL'S PRAYER FOR HIS PEOPLE It was the first year of the reign of Darius the Mede, the son of Ahasuerus, who became king of the Babylonians.* ²During the first year of his reign, I, Daniel, learned from reading the word of the LORD, as revealed to Jeremiah the prophet, that Jerusalem must lie desolate for seventy years.* ³So I turned to the Lord God and pleaded with him in prayer and fasting. I also wore rough burlap and sprinkled myself with ashes.

⁴I prayed to the LORD my God and confessed:

"O Lord, you are a great and awesome God! You always fulfill your covenant and keep your promises of unfailing love to those who love you and obey your commands. ⁵But we have sinned and done wrong. We have rebelled against you and scorned your commands and regulations. ⁶We have refused to listen to your servants the prophets, who spoke on your authority to our kings and princes and ancestors and to all the people of the land.

⁷"Lord, you are in the right; but as you see, our faces are covered with shame. This is true of all of us, including the people of Judah and Jerusalem and all Israel, scattered near and far, wherever you have driven us because of our disloyalty to you. ⁸O LORD, we and our kings, princes, and ancestors are covered with shame because we have sinned against you. ⁹But the Lord our God is merciful and forgiving, even though we have rebelled against him. ¹⁰We have not obeyed the LORD our God, for we have not followed the instructions he gave us through his servants the prophets. ¹¹All Israel has disobeyed your instruction and turned away, refusing to listen to your voice.

8:21 Hebrew *of Javan.*   **8:26** Hebrew *about the evenings and mornings;* compare 8:14.   **9:1** Or *the Chaldeans.*   **9:2** See Jer 25:11-12; 29:10.

"So now the solemn curses and judgments written in the Law of Moses, the servant of God, have been poured down on us because of our sin. ¹²You have kept your word and done to us and our rulers exactly as you warned. Never has there been such a disaster as happened in Jerusalem. ¹³Every curse written against us in the Law of Moses has come true. Yet we have refused to seek mercy from the LORD our God by turning from our sins and recognizing his truth. ¹⁴Therefore, the LORD has brought upon us the disaster he prepared. The LORD our God was right to do all of these things, for we did not obey him.

¹⁵"O Lord our God, you brought lasting honor to your name by rescuing your people from Egypt in a great display of power. But we have sinned and are full of wickedness. ¹⁶In view of all your faithful mercies, Lord, please turn your furious anger away from your city Jerusalem, your holy mountain. All the neighboring nations mock Jerusalem and your people because of our sins and the sins of our ancestors.

¹⁷"O our God, hear your servant's prayer! Listen as I plead. For your own sake, Lord, smile again on your desolate sanctuary.

¹⁸"O my God, lean down and listen to me. Open your eyes and see our despair. See how your city—the city that bears your name—lies in ruins. We make this plea, not because we deserve help, but because of your mercy.

¹⁹"O Lord, hear. O Lord, forgive. O Lord, listen and act! For your own sake, do not delay, O my God, for your people and your city bear your name."

GABRIEL'S MESSAGE ABOUT THE ANOINTED ONE
²⁰I went on praying and confessing my sin and the sin of my people, pleading with the LORD my God for Jerusalem, his holy mountain. ²¹As I was praying, Gabriel, whom I had seen in the earlier vision, came swiftly to me at the time of the evening sacrifice. ²²He explained to me, "Daniel, I have come here to give you insight and understanding. ²³The moment you began praying, a command was given. And

now I am here to tell you what it was, for you are very precious to God. Listen carefully so that you can understand the meaning of your vision.

²⁴"A period of seventy sets of seven* has been decreed for your people and your holy city to finish their rebellion, to put an end to their sin, to atone for their guilt, to bring in everlasting righteousness, to confirm the prophetic vision, and to anoint the Most Holy Place.* ²⁵Now listen and understand! Seven sets of seven plus sixty-two sets of seven* will pass from the time the command is given to rebuild Jerusalem until a ruler—the Anointed One*—comes. Jerusalem will be rebuilt with streets and strong defenses,* despite the perilous times.

²⁶"After this period of sixty-two sets of seven,* the Anointed One will be killed, appearing to have accomplished nothing, and a ruler will arise whose armies will destroy the city and the Temple. The end will come with a flood, and war and its miseries are decreed from that time to the very end. ²⁷The ruler will make a treaty with the people for a period of one set of seven,* but after half this time, he will put an end to the sacrifices and offerings. And as a climax to all his terrible deeds,* he will set up a sacrilegious object that causes desecration,* until the fate decreed for this defiler is finally poured out on him."

10 DANIEL'S VISION OF A MESSENGER
In the third year of the reign of King Cyrus of Persia,* Daniel (also known as Belteshazzar) had another vision. He understood that the vision concerned events certain to happen in the future—times of war and great hardship.

²When this vision came to me, I, Daniel, had been in mourning for three whole weeks. ³All that time I had eaten no rich food. No meat or wine crossed my lips, and I used no fragrant lotions until those three weeks had passed.

⁴On April 23,* as I was standing on the bank of the great Tigris River, ⁵I looked up and saw a man dressed in linen clothing, with a belt of pure gold around his waist. ⁶His body looked like a precious gem. His face flashed like lightning, and his eyes flamed like torches. His arms and feet shone like polished bronze, and his voice roared like a vast multitude of people.

⁷Only I, Daniel, saw this vision. The men with me saw nothing, but they were suddenly terrified and ran away to hide. ⁸So I was left there all alone to see this amazing vision. My strength left me, my face grew deathly pale,

---

9:24a Hebrew *seventy sevens.*   **9:24b** Or *the Most Holy One.*
9:25a Hebrew *Seven sevens plus sixty-two sevens.*   **9:25b** Or *an anointed one;* similarly in 9:26. Hebrew reads *a messiah.*   **9:25c** Or *and a moat, or trenches.*   **9:26** Hebrew *After sixty-two sevens.*   **9:27a** Hebrew *for one seven.*   **9:27b** Hebrew *And on the wing of abominations;* the meaning of the Hebrew is uncertain.
9:27c Hebrew *an abomination of desolation.*   **10:1** The third year of Cyrus's reign was 536 B.C.   **10:4** Hebrew *On the twenty-fourth day of the first month,* of the ancient Hebrew lunar calendar. This date in the book of Daniel can be cross-checked with dates in surviving Persian records and can be related accurately to our modern calendar. This event occurred on April 23, 536 B.C.

and I felt very weak. ⁹Then I heard the man speak, and when I heard the sound of his voice, I fainted and lay there with my face to the ground.

¹⁰Just then a hand touched me and lifted me, still trembling, to my hands and knees. ¹¹And the man said to me, "Daniel, you are very precious to God, so listen carefully to what I have to say to you. Stand up, for I have been sent to you." When he said this to me, I stood up, still trembling.

¹²Then he said, "Don't be afraid, Daniel. Since the first day you began to pray for understanding and to humble yourself before your God, your request has been heard in heaven. I have come in answer to your prayer. ¹³But for twenty-one days the spirit prince* of the kingdom of Persia blocked my way. Then Michael, one of the archangels,* came to help me, and I left him there with the spirit prince of the kingdom of Persia.* ¹⁴Now I am here to explain what will happen to your people in the future, for this vision concerns a time yet to come."

¹⁵While he was speaking to me, I looked down at the ground, unable to say a word. ¹⁶Then the one who looked like a man* touched my lips, and I opened my mouth and began to speak. I said to the one standing in front of me, "I am filled with anguish because of the vision I have seen, my lord, and I am very weak. ¹⁷How can someone like me, your servant, talk to you, my lord? My strength is gone, and I can hardly breathe."

¹⁸Then the one who looked like a man touched me again, and I felt my strength returning. ¹⁹"Don't be afraid," he said, "for you are very precious to God. Peace! Be encouraged! Be strong!"

As he spoke these words to me, I suddenly felt stronger and said to him, "Please speak to me, my lord, for you have strengthened me."

²⁰He replied, "Do you know why I have come? Soon I must return to fight against the spirit prince of the kingdom of Persia, and after that the spirit prince of the kingdom of Greece* will come. ²¹Meanwhile, I will tell you what is written in the Book of Truth. (No one helps me against these spirit princes except Michael,

your spirit prince.* ¹¹:¹I have been standing beside Michael* to support and strengthen him since the first year of the reign of Darius the Mede.)

11 KINGS OF THE SOUTH AND NORTH

²"Now then, I will reveal the truth to you. Three more Persian kings will reign, to be succeeded by a fourth, far richer than the others. He will use his wealth to stir up everyone to fight against the kingdom of Greece.*

³"Then a mighty king will rise to power who will rule with great authority and accomplish everything he sets out to do. ⁴But at the height of his power, his kingdom will be broken apart and divided into four parts. It will not be ruled by the king's descendants, nor will the kingdom hold the authority it once had. For his empire will be uprooted and given to others.

⁵"The king of the south will increase in power, but one of his own officials will become more powerful than he and will rule his kingdom with great strength.

⁶"Some years later an alliance will be formed between the king of the north and the king of the south. The daughter of the king of the south will be given in marriage to the king of the north to secure the alliance, but she will lose her influence over him, and so will her father. She will be abandoned along with her supporters. ⁷But when one of her relatives* becomes king of the south, he will raise an army and enter the fortress of the king of the north and defeat him. ⁸When he returns to Egypt, he will carry back their idols with him, along with priceless articles of gold and silver. For some years afterward he will leave the king of the north alone.

⁹"Later the king of the north will invade the realm of the king of the south but will soon return to his own land. ¹⁰However, the sons of the king of the north will assemble a mighty army that will advance like a flood and carry the battle as far as the enemy's fortress.

¹¹"Then, in a rage, the king of the south will rally against the vast forces assembled by the king of the north and will defeat them. ¹²After the enemy army is swept away, the king of the south will be filled with pride and will execute

....

HIS STRENGTH

(10:10-19) Daniel was frightened by this vision, but the messenger's hand calmed his fears; Daniel felt weak, but the messenger's words strengthened him. God can heal when we are hurt, provide peace when we are troubled, and strengthen when we are weak. All we have to do is ask.

10:13a Hebrew *the prince;* also in 10:13c, 20.   10:13b Hebrew *the chief princes.*   10:13c As in one Greek version; Hebrew reads *and I was left there with the kings of Persia.* The meaning of the Hebrew is uncertain.   10:16 As in most manuscripts of the Masoretic Text; one manuscript of the Masoretic Text and one Greek version read *Then something that looked like a human hand.*   10:20 Hebrew *of Javan.*   10:21 Hebrew *against these except Michael, your prince.*   11:1 Hebrew *him.*   11:2 Hebrew *of Javan.*   11:7 Hebrew *a branch from her roots.*

many thousands of his enemies. But his success will be short lived.

¹³"A few years later the king of the north will return with a fully equipped army far greater than before. ¹⁴At that time there will be a general uprising against the king of the south. Violent men among your own people will join them in fulfillment of this vision, but they will not succeed. ¹⁵Then the king of the north will come and lay siege to a fortified city and capture it. The best troops of the south will not be able to stand in the face of the onslaught.

¹⁶"The king of the north will march onward unopposed; none will be able to stop him. He will pause in the glorious land of Israel,* intent on destroying it. ¹⁷He will make plans to come with the might of his entire kingdom and will form an alliance with the king of the south. He will give him a daughter in marriage in order to overthrow the kingdom from within, but his plan will fail.

¹⁸"After this, he will turn his attention to the coastland and conquer many cities. But a commander from another land will put an end to his insolence and cause him to retreat in shame. ¹⁹He will take refuge in his own fortresses but will stumble and fall and be seen no more.

²⁰"His successor will send out a tax collector to maintain the royal splendor. But after a very brief reign, he will die, though not from anger or in battle.

²¹"The next to come to power will be a despicable man who is not in line for royal succession. He will slip in when least expected and take over the kingdom by flattery and intrigue. ²²Before him great armies will be swept away, including a covenant prince. ²³With deceitful promises, he will make various alliances. He will become strong despite having only a handful of followers. ²⁴Without warning he will enter the richest areas of the land. Then he will distribute among his followers the plunder and wealth of the rich—something his predecessors had never done. He will plot the overthrow of strongholds, but this will last for only a short while.

²⁵"Then he will stir up his courage and raise a great army against the king of the south. The king of the south will go to battle with a mighty army, but to no avail, for there will be plots against him. ²⁶His own household will cause his downfall. His army will be swept away, and many will be killed. ²⁷Seeking nothing but each other's harm, these kings will plot against each other at the conference table, attempting to deceive each other. But it will make no difference, for the end will come at the appointed time.

²⁸"The king of the north will then return home with great riches. On the way he will set himself against the people of the holy covenant, doing much damage before continuing his journey.

²⁹"Then at the appointed time he will once again invade the south, but this time the result will be different. ³⁰For warships from western coastlands* will scare him off, and he will withdraw and return home. But he will vent his anger against the people of the holy covenant and reward those who forsake the covenant.

³¹"His army will take over the Temple fortress, pollute the sanctuary, put a stop to the daily sacrifices, and set up the sacrilegious object that causes desecration.* ³²He will flatter and win over those who have violated the covenant. But the people who know their God will be strong and will resist him.

³³"Wise leaders will give instruction to many, but these teachers will die by fire and sword, or they will be jailed and robbed. ³⁴During these persecutions, little help will arrive, and many who join them will not be sincere. ³⁵And some of the wise will fall victim to persecution. In this way, they will be refined and cleansed and made pure until the time of the end, for the appointed time is still to come.

³⁶"The king will do as he pleases, exalting himself and claiming to be greater than every god, even blaspheming the God of gods. He will succeed, but only until the time of wrath is completed. For what has been determined will surely take place. ³⁷He will have no respect for the gods of his ancestors, or for the god loved by women, or for any other god, for he will boast that he is greater than them all. ³⁸Instead of these, he will worship the god of fortresses—a god his ancestors never knew—and lavish on him gold, silver, precious stones, and expensive gifts. ³⁹Claiming this foreign god's help, he will attack the strongest fortresses. He will honor those who submit to

....

GET READY

(11:33-35) *Trying times remind us of our weaknesses and inability to cope. We reach out for answers, for leadership, for clear direction. God's Word begins to interest even those who, in better times, would never look at it. We who are believers can prepare ourselves for the opportunities God provides to share his Word in needy times. We also can prepare ourselves for persecution and rejection as we teach God's Word. Are you prepared?*

11:16 Hebrew *the glorious land.*   **11:30** Hebrew *from Kittim.*
11:31 Hebrew *the abomination of desolation.*

THOSE WHO ARE WISE WILL SHINE AS BRIGHT AS THE SKY, AND THOSE WHO LEAD MANY TO RIGHTEOUSNESS WILL SHINE LIKE THE STARS FOREVER. {DANIEL 12:3}

him, appointing them to positions of authority and dividing the land among them as their reward.*

⁴⁰"Then at the time of the end, the king of the south will attack the king of the north. The king of the north will storm out with chariots, charioteers, and a vast navy. He will invade various lands and sweep through them like a flood. ⁴¹He will enter the glorious land of Israel,* and many nations will fall, but Moab, Edom, and the best part of Ammon will escape. ⁴²He will conquer many countries, and even Egypt will not escape. ⁴³He will gain control over the gold, silver, and treasures of Egypt, and the Libyans and Ethiopians* will be his servants.

⁴⁴"But then news from the east and the north will alarm him, and he will set out in great anger to destroy and obliterate many. ⁴⁵He will stop between the glorious holy mountain and the sea and will pitch his royal tents. But while he is there, his time will suddenly run out, and no one will help him.

....

BE OPEN
(12:10) Daniel was told that to understand what is happening, people have to be open to instruction. Trials and persecutions make little sense when we're in the middle of them. But they can teach and strengthen us if we are willing to learn from them. After surviving a difficult time, seek to learn from it so that it can help you in the future.

A LEGACY OF FAITHFULNESS
(12:13) Daniel stands tall in the gallery of God's remarkable servants. Born of royal heritage, yet taken into exile when young, Daniel remained faithful to God in the land of his captivity. God chose Daniel to record events of his life and significant events concerning the future. As an old man, having always been faithful to God, Daniel was assured by God that he would be resurrected from the dead and receive his portion in God's eternal kingdom.

Consider your own "spiritual résumé." How are you adding to your legacy of faithfulness? Faithfulness to God has a rich reward, not necessarily in this life, but most certainly in the life to come.

12 THE TIME OF THE END "At that time Michael, the archangel* who stands guard over your nation, will arise. Then there will be a time of anguish greater than any since nations first came into existence. But at that time every one of your people whose name is written in the book will be rescued. ²Many of those whose bodies lie dead and buried will rise up, some to everlasting life and some to shame and everlasting disgrace. ³Those who are wise will shine as bright as the sky, and those who lead many to righteousness will shine like the stars forever. ⁴But you, Daniel, keep this prophecy a secret; seal up the book until the time of the end, when many will rush here and there, and knowledge will increase."

⁵Then I, Daniel, looked and saw two others standing on opposite banks of the river. ⁶One of them asked the man dressed in linen, who was now standing above the river, "How long will it be until these shocking events are over?"

⁷The man dressed in linen, who was standing above the river, raised both his hands toward heaven and took a solemn oath by the One who lives forever, saying, "It will go on for a time, times, and half a time. When the shattering of the holy people has finally come to an end, all these things will have happened."

⁸I heard what he said, but I did not understand what he meant. So I asked, "How will all this finally end, my lord?"

⁹But he said, "Go now, Daniel, for what I have said is kept secret and sealed until the time of the end. ¹⁰Many will be purified, cleansed, and refined by these trials. But the wicked will continue in their wickedness, and none of them will understand. Only those who are wise will know what it means.

¹¹"From the time the daily sacrifice is stopped and the sacrilegious object that causes desecration* is set up to be worshiped, there will be 1,290 days. ¹²And blessed are those who wait and remain until the end of the 1,335 days!

¹³"As for you, go your way until the end. You will rest, and then at the end of the days, you will rise again to receive the inheritance set aside for you."

11:39 Or *at a price.* **11:41** Hebrew *the glorious land.* **11:43** Hebrew *Cushites.* **12:1** Hebrew *the great prince.* **12:11** Hebrew *the abomination of desolation.*

HOSEA

"Oh," she whispered, "I love you, too!" Together the reunited lovers rode off into the sunset.

Isn't love wonderful? We've grown up believing love is a cure-all; someday we'll meet "Mr. Right" or "Miss Perfect." He or she will be totally hot, of course. He or she will also be free of emotional baggage. Is that your dream of love?

Hosea is a book about love, but with an unusual twist. Hosea was a prophet who was told to marry Gomer. But far from being "Miss Perfect," Gomer was a prostitute. In fact, after they were married, she was unfaithful to Hosea. But God told him to marry her anyway, knowing that she would be unfaithful.

The book of Hosea is a love story: Hosea and Gomer's and also that of God and his people, who were unfaithful like Gomer.

As you read this story, you'll learn a lot about God and what he expects of his followers. But look for yourself in the story, too. Are you like Hosea? Gomer? Israel? Then decide to have a true love relationship with God.

STATS

PURPOSE
To illustrate God's love for his sinful people

AUTHOR
Hosea, son of Beeri ("Hosea" means "salvation")

ORIGINAL AUDIENCE
Israel (the northern kingdom)

DATE WRITTEN
Around 715 B.C., recording events from about 753 to 715 B.C.

SETTING
Hosea ministered during the reign of Jeroboam II of Israel, a prosperous but morally declining time. Hosea prophesied until shortly after the fall of Israel's capital in 722 B.C.

KEY PEOPLE
Hosea, Gomer, their children

KEY PLACES
The northern kingdom (Israel), Samaria, Ephraim

SPECIAL FEATURES
Hosea employs many images from daily life. God is depicted as a husband, leopard, dew, moth, and others. Israel is pictured as a wife, a sick person, olive tree, woman in labor, oven, morning mist, and smoke, to name a few.

KEY POINTS

A NATION'S SIN Just as Hosea's wife Gomer was unfaithful to him, so the nation of Israel had been spiritually unfaithful to God. The temptations in this world (power, popularity, pleasure, or money) can lure us toward spiritual unfaithfulness. God wants his people to remain faithful to him.

GOD'S JUDGMENT Because Judah turned away from God, the nation experienced a devastating invasion and exile. Wrong actions still result in terrible consequences. Some may not happen right away.

GOD'S LOVE Just as Hosea went after his unfaithful wife to bring her back, so God pursues us with his unchanging and undying love.

RESTORATION God encouraged and restored those who repented. There's forgiveness and restoration for all who turn back to God.

1

The Lord gave this message to Hosea son of Beeri during the years when Uzziah, Jotham, Ahaz, and Hezekiah were kings of Judah, and Jeroboam son of Jehoash* was king of Israel.

HOSEA'S WIFE AND CHILDREN

²When the Lord first began speaking to Israel through Hosea, he said to him, "Go and marry a prostitute,* so that some of her children will be conceived in prostitution. This will illustrate how Israel has acted like a prostitute by turning against the Lord and worshiping other gods."

³So Hosea married Gomer, the daughter of Diblaim, and she became pregnant and gave Hosea a son. ⁴And the Lord said, "Name the child Jezreel, for I am about to punish King Jehu's dynasty to avenge the murders he committed at Jezreel. In fact, I will bring an end to Israel's independence. ⁵I will break its military power in the Jezreel Valley."

⁶Soon Gomer became pregnant again and gave birth to a daughter. And the Lord said to Hosea, "Name your daughter Lo-ruhamah— 'Not loved'—for I will no longer show love to the people of Israel or forgive them. ⁷But I will show love to the people of Judah. I will free them from their enemies—not with weapons and armies or horses and charioteers, but by my power as the Lord their God."

⁸After Gomer had weaned Lo-ruhamah, she again became pregnant and gave birth to a second son. ⁹And the Lord said, "Name him Lo-ammi—'Not my people'—for Israel is not my people, and I am not their God.

¹⁰*"Yet the time will come when Israel's people will be like the sands of the seashore— too many to count! Then, at the place where they were told, 'You are not my people,' it will be said, 'You are children of the living God.' ¹¹Then the people of Judah and Israel will unite together. They will choose one leader for themselves, and they will return from exile together. What a day that will be—the day of Jezreel*—when God will again plant his people in his land.

²:¹*"In that day you will call your brothers Ammi—'My people.' And you will call your sisters Ruhamah—'The ones I love.'

2

CHARGES AGAINST AN UNFAITHFUL WIFE

² "But now bring charges against Israel—your mother—
for she is no longer my wife,
and I am no longer her husband.
Tell her to remove the prostitute's makeup from her face
and the clothing that exposes her breasts.
³ Otherwise, I will strip her as naked as she was on the day she was born.
I will leave her to die of thirst,
as in a dry and barren wilderness.
⁴ And I will not love her children,
for they were conceived in prostitution.
⁵ Their mother is a shameless prostitute
and became pregnant in a shameful way.
She said, 'I'll run after other lovers
and sell myself to them for food and water,
for clothing of wool and linen,
and for olive oil and drinks.'

⁶ "For this reason I will fence her in with thornbushes.
I will block her path with a wall
to make her lose her way.
⁷ When she runs after her lovers,
she won't be able to catch them.
She will search for them
but not find them.
Then she will think,
'I might as well return to my husband,
for I was better off with him than I am now.'
⁸ She doesn't realize it was I who gave her everything she has—
the grain, the new wine, the olive oil;
I even gave her silver and gold.
But she gave all my gifts to Baal.

⁹ "But now I will take back the ripened grain and new wine
I generously provided each harvest season.
I will take away the wool and linen clothing
I gave her to cover her nakedness.
¹⁰ I will strip her naked in public,
while all her lovers look on.

1:1 Hebrew *Joash,* a variant spelling of Jehoash. 1:2 Or *a promiscuous woman.* 1:10 Verses 1:10-11 are numbered 2:1-2 in Hebrew text. 1:11 *Jezreel* means "God plants." 2:1 Verses 2:1-23 are numbered 2:3-25 in Hebrew text.

A DIFFICULT TASK
(1:1-3) It's hard to imagine Hosea's feelings when God told him to marry a woman who would be unfaithful to him. Although such a marriage was far from ideal, Hosea still obeyed. Other prophets like Jeremiah and Ezekiel also faced some difficult tasks. If God asks you to do something difficult, how will you respond? Will you obey him, trusting that he who knows everything has a special purpose for his request? Will you be satisfied with the knowledge that the pain involved in obedience may benefit those whom you serve, and not you personally?

No one will be able
    to rescue her from my hands.
[11] I will put an end to her annual festivals,
    her new moon celebrations, and her
        Sabbath days—
    all her appointed festivals.
[12] I will destroy her grapevines and fig trees,
    things she claims her lovers gave her.
I will let them grow into tangled thickets,
    where only wild animals will eat the fruit.
[13] I will punish her for all those times
    when she burned incense to her images
        of Baal,
when she put on her earrings and jewels
    and went out to look for her lovers
but forgot all about me,"
    says the LORD.

THE LORD'S LOVE FOR UNFAITHFUL ISRAEL

[14] "But then I will win her back once again.
    I will lead her into the desert
    and speak tenderly to her there.
[15] I will return her vineyards to her
    and transform the Valley of Trouble* into
        a gateway of hope.
She will give herself to me there,
    as she did long ago when she was young,
    when I freed her from her captivity
        in Egypt.
[16] When that day comes," says the LORD,
    "you will call me 'my husband'
    instead of 'my master.'*
[17] O Israel, I will wipe the many names of Baal
        from your lips,
    and you will never mention them again.
[18] On that day I will make a covenant
    with all the wild animals and the birds
        of the sky

and the animals that scurry along the
        ground
    so they will not harm you.
I will remove all weapons of war from
        the land,
    all swords and bows,
so you can live unafraid
    in peace and safety.
[19] I will make you my wife forever,
    showing you righteousness and justice,
    unfailing love and compassion.
[20] I will be faithful to you and make you mine,
    and you will finally know me as the LORD.

[21] "In that day, I will answer,"
    says the LORD.
"I will answer the sky as it pleads for
        clouds.
    And the sky will answer the earth
        with rain.
[22] Then the earth will answer the thirsty cries
    of the grain, the grapevines, and the
        olive trees.
And they in turn will answer,
    'Jezreel'—'God plants!'
[23] At that time I will plant a crop of Israelites
    and raise them for myself.
I will show love
    to those I called 'Not loved.'*
And to those I called 'Not my people,'*
    I will say, 'Now you are my people.'
And they will reply, 'You are our God!'"

2:15 Hebrew *valley of Achor.*   **2:16** Hebrew *'my baal.'*
2:23a Hebrew *Lo-ruhamah;* see 1:6.   **2:23b** Hebrew *Lo-ammi;*
see 1:9.

SIGNS OF SUCCESS
(2:8) *Material possessions are signs of success in most
societies. Although Israel was a wealthy nation at this
time, the people didn't recognize God as the Giver of
blessings. They used their possessions irresponsibly as
they worshiped other gods. How do you use your possessions? How could you honor God with your resources?*

CHOICES
adultery

Marianna still can't believe the news. Her mom has
decided to leave their family to live with someone
she claims to have fallen in love with. One day she
seemed fine. The next—boom! She's packing and
telling their family that she can no longer live a lie.

A lie? Marianna wonders. *Was her marriage to
Dad a lie? . . . I still don't believe it. I think there must
be some mistake.*

Yet, there are the suitcases by the door. Her father
had asked—demanded, actually—that Marianna's
mom leave. Not that she was reluctant to do so . . .

"You can come with me if you like," her mom says.
But her words are like a knife through Marianna's
heart. She doesn't want her mom to go. But she
doesn't want to leave her dad, either, or her friends.

Can you imagine how Marianna feels as the awful-
ness of adultery plays out in her life? But how many
Christians are guilty of spiritual adultery? We claim to
belong to God while we flirt with the world and spend
most of our time in other pursuits. Imagine how
rejected God must feel!

*Don't just imagine it. Read the startling book of Hosea for an intimate look at how unfaithfulness hurts God's heart. Chapter
2 is especially expressive as it depicts God as a wounded lover who desperately wants his people to return to him.*

3 HOSEA'S WIFE IS REDEEMED

Then the LORD said to me, "Go and love your wife again, even though she* commits adultery with another lover. This will illustrate that the LORD still loves Israel, even though the people have turned to other gods and love to worship them.*"

²So I bought her back for fifteen pieces of silver* and five bushels of barley and a measure of wine.* ³Then I said to her, "You must live in my house for many days and stop your prostitution. During this time, you will not have sexual relations with anyone, not even with me.*"

⁴This shows that Israel will go a long time without a king or prince, and without sacrifices, sacred pillars, priests,* or even idols! ⁵But afterward the people will return and devote themselves to the LORD their God and to David's descendant, their king.* In the last days, they will tremble in awe of the LORD and of his goodness.

4 THE LORD'S CASE AGAINST ISRAEL

¹ Hear the word of the LORD, O people
   of Israel!
   The LORD has brought charges against
      you, saying:
   "There is no faithfulness, no kindness,
      no knowledge of God in your land.
² You make vows and break them;
      you kill and steal and commit adultery.
   There is violence everywhere—
      one murder after another.
³ That is why your land is in mourning,
      and everyone is wasting away.
   Even the wild animals, the birds of the sky,
      and the fish of the sea are disappearing.

⁴ "Don't point your finger at someone else
      and try to pass the blame!
   My complaint, you priests,
      is with you.*
⁵ So you will stumble in broad daylight,
      and your false prophets will fall with you
         in the night.
   And I will destroy Israel, your mother.
⁶ My people are being destroyed

because they don't know me.
   Since you priests refuse to know me,
      I refuse to recognize you as my priests.
   Since you have forgotten the laws of
         your God,
      I will forget to bless your children.
⁷ The more priests there are,
      the more they sin against me.
   They have exchanged the glory of God
      for the shame of idols.*

⁸ "When the people bring their sin offerings,
         the priests get fed.
   So the priests are glad when the
         people sin!
⁹ 'And what the priests do, the people
         also do.'
   So now I will punish both priests
         and people
      for their wicked deeds.
¹⁰ They will eat and still be hungry.
      They will play the prostitute and gain
            nothing from it,
   for they have deserted the LORD
¹¹   to worship other gods.

"Wine has robbed my people
      of their understanding.
¹² They ask a piece of wood for advice!
      They think a stick can tell them the future!
   Longing after idols
      has made them foolish.
   They have played the prostitute,
      serving other gods and deserting
         their God.
¹³ They offer sacrifices to idols on the
         mountaintops.
      They go up into the hills to burn incense
         in the pleasant shade of oaks, poplars,
         and terebinth trees.

"That is why your daughters turn to
         prostitution,
   and your daughters-in-law commit
         adultery.
¹⁴ But why should I punish them
      for their prostitution and adultery?
   For your men are doing the same thing,
         sinning with whores and shrine
         prostitutes.
   O foolish people! You refuse to understand,
      so you will be destroyed.

··

ABSENT AND ISOLATED

(3:1-5) After this passage, Gomer is no longer mentioned by Hosea. Gomer's absence and isolation were signs of how God would deal with the constantly rebellious northern kingdom (5:6-15). The consequences of rebellion can be high. If God were ever to withdraw his love and mercy, we would be without hope. Is any act of rebellion worth that?

3:1a Or Go and love a woman who.   3:1b Hebrew love their raisin cakes.   3:2a Hebrew 15 shekels of silver, about 6 ounces or 171 grams in weight.   3:2b As in Greek version, which reads a homer of barley and a wineskin full of wine; Hebrew reads a homer [5 bushels or 182 liters] of barley and a lethech [2.5 bushels or 91 liters] of barley.   3:3 Or and I will live with you.   3:4 Hebrew ephod, the vest worn by the priest.   3:5 Hebrew to David their king. 4:4 Hebrew Your people are like those with a complaint against the priests.   4:7 As in Syriac version and an ancient Hebrew tradition; Masoretic Text reads I will turn their glory into shame.

THE SYMBOLIC NATURE OF MARRIAGE

While the prophet Hosea lived out his message regarding Israel's relationship with God, other prophets also used the symbol of marriage to describe God's love for his people.

HOSEA AND GOMER

God said to Hosea: "Go and marry a prostitute, so that some of her children will be conceived in prostitution. This will illustrate how Israel has acted like a prostitute by turning against the Lord and worshiping other gods." So Hosea married Gomer, the daughter of Diblaim, and she became pregnant and gave Hosea a son. *Hosea 1:2-3*

Then [Hosea] said to [Gomer, his wife], "You must live in my house for many days and stop your prostitution. During this time, you will not have sexual relations with anyone, not even with me." This shows that Israel will go a long time without a king or prince, and without sacrifices, sacred pillars, priests, or even idols! *Hosea 3:3-4*

God said to Hosea: "Go and love your wife again, even though she commits adultery with another lover. This will illustrate that the Lord still loves Israel, even though the people have turned to other gods and love to worship them." *Hosea 3:1*

God said to Hosea: "Afterward the people will return and devote themselves to the Lord their God and to David's descendant, their king. In the last days, they will tremble in awe of the Lord and of his goodness." *Hosea 3:5*

GOD AND ISRAEL

God said to Israel through Jeremiah: "I remember how eager you were to please me as a young bride long ago, how you loved me and followed me even through the barren wilderness." *Jeremiah 2:2*

God said to Israel through Ezekiel: "I wrapped my cloak around you . . . and declared my marriage vows. I made a covenant with you, says the Sovereign Lord, and you became mine." *Ezekiel 16:8*

God said to Israel through Jeremiah: "How can I pardon you? For even your children have turned from me. They have sworn by gods that are not gods at all! I fed my people until they were full. But they thanked me by committing adultery and lining up at the brothels." *Jeremiah 5:7*

God said to Israel through Ezekiel: "You thought your fame and beauty were your own. So you gave yourself as a prostitute to every man who came along. Your beauty was theirs for the asking." *Ezekiel 16:15*

God said to Israel through Jeremiah: "O Israel, my faithless people, come home to me again, for I am merciful. I will not be angry with you forever. Only acknowledge your guilt. Admit that you rebelled against the Lord your God and committed adultery against him by worshiping idols under every green tree. . . . Return home . . . for I am your master." *Jeremiah 3:12-14*

God said to Israel through Ezekiel: "I will remember the covenant I made with you when you were young, and I will establish an everlasting covenant with you." *Ezekiel 16:60*

---

15 "Though you, Israel, are a prostitute,
    may Judah avoid such guilt.
Do not join the false worship at Gilgal or
    Beth-aven,*
      even though they take oaths there in the
      Lord's name.
16 Israel is stubborn,
    like a stubborn heifer.
So should the Lord feed her
    like a lamb in a lush pasture?
17 Leave Israel* alone,
    because she is married to idolatry.

18 When the rulers of Israel finish their
    drinking,
    off they go to find some prostitutes.
    They love shame more than honor.*
19 So a mighty wind will sweep them away.
    Their sacrifices to idols will bring them
    shame.

5 THE FAILURE OF ISRAEL'S LEADERS

1 "Hear this, you priests.
    Pay attention, you leaders of Israel.
Listen, you members of the royal family.
    Judgment has been handed down
    against you.

4:15 *Beth-aven* means "house of wickedness"; it is being used as another name for Bethel, which means "house of God."
4:17 Hebrew *Ephraim,* referring to the northern kingdom of Israel.
4:18 As in Greek version; the meaning of the Hebrew is uncertain.

OH, THAT WE MIGHT KNOW THE LORD!

LET US PRESS ON TO KNOW HIM. HE WILL RESPOND TO US AS SURELY AS THE ARRIVAL OF DAWN OR THE COMING OF RAINS IN EARLY SPRING.

For you have led the people into a snare
  by worshiping the idols at Mizpah and
  Tabor.
² You have dug a deep pit to trap them at
  Acacia Grove.*
  But I will settle with you for what you
  have done.
³ I know what you are like, O Ephraim.
  You cannot hide yourself from me,
  O Israel.
You have left me as a prostitute leaves
  her husband;
  you are utterly defiled.
⁴ Your deeds won't let you return to your God.
  You are a prostitute through and through,
  and you do not know the LORD.

⁵ "The arrogance of Israel testifies
  against her;
  Israel and Ephraim will stumble under
  their load of guilt.
  Judah, too, will fall with them.
⁶ When they come with their flocks and herds
  to offer sacrifices to the LORD,
they will not find him,
  because he has withdrawn from them.
⁷ They have betrayed the honor of the LORD,
  bearing children that are not his.
Now their false religion will devour them
  along with their wealth.*

⁸ "Sound the alarm in Gibeah!
  Blow the trumpet in Ramah!
  Raise the battle cry in Beth-aven*!

Lead on into battle, O warriors
  of Benjamin!
⁹ One thing is certain, Israel*:
  On your day of punishment,
  you will become a heap of rubble.

¹⁰ "The leaders of Judah have become
  like thieves.*
  So I will pour my anger on them like
  a waterfall.
¹¹ The people of Israel will be crushed and
  broken by my judgment
  because they are determined to
  worship idols.*
¹² I will destroy Israel as a moth
  consumes wool.
  I will make Judah as weak as rotten wood.

¹³ "When Israel and Judah saw how sick
  they were,
  Israel turned to Assyria—
to the great king there—
  but he could neither help nor cure them.
¹⁴ I will be like a lion to Israel,
  like a strong young lion to Judah.
  I will tear them to pieces!
I will carry them off,
  and no one will be left to rescue them.
¹⁵ Then I will return to my place
  until they admit their guilt and turn to me.
For as soon as trouble comes,
  they will earnestly search for me."

6 A CALL TO REPENTANCE

¹ "Come, let us return to the LORD.
He has torn us to pieces;
  now he will heal us.
He has injured us;
  now he will bandage our wounds.
² In just a short time he will restore us,
  so that we may live in his presence.
³ Oh, that we might know the LORD!
  Let us press on to know him.
He will respond to us as surely as the arrival
  of dawn
  or the coming of rains in early spring."

5:2 Hebrew *at Shittim.* The meaning of the Hebrew for this sentence
is uncertain.   5:7 The meaning of the Hebrew is uncertain.
5:8 *Beth-aven* means "house of wickedness"; it is being used as
another name for Bethel, which means "house of God."
5:9 Hebrew *Ephraim,* referring to the northern kingdom of Israel;
also in 5:11, 12, 13, 14.   5:10 Hebrew *like those who move a
boundary marker.*   5:11 Or *determined to follow human commands.*
The meaning of the Hebrew is uncertain.

A DIET OF DISOBEDIENCE
(5:4) Hosea confronted the leaders of Israel about their
sinning habit. Their actions kept them from returning to
God. A constant diet of disobedience hardens a person's
heart and builds a solid path away from God. Each sin
makes the next one easier to commit. But even this hard
habit can begin to be broken by just three words, "Help
me, God." Know anyone who needs to say those words?
Do you need to say them?

REAL REGRET
(6:1-3) Ever hear someone say, "I'm sorry," but know that
person didn't mean those words? The people of Israel
claimed to be sorry about the wrong things they did. Yet
they didn't seem to understand or regret what they had
done. Basically, they were apologizing to stop God from
punishing them. In a sense they were saying, "I'm sorry
we were caught." Repentance is more than just saying,
"I'm sorry." It involves a sincere desire to change.

⁴ "O Israel* and Judah,
      what should I do with you?" asks
      the LORD.
  "For your love vanishes like the
      morning mist
      and disappears like dew in
      the sunlight.
⁵ I sent my prophets to cut you to pieces—
      to slaughter you with my words,
      with judgments as inescapable as light.
⁶ I want you to show love,*
      not offer sacrifices.
  I want you to know me*
      more than I want burnt offerings.
⁷ But like Adam,* you broke my covenant
      and betrayed my trust.

⁸ "Gilead is a city of sinners,
      tracked with footprints of blood.
⁹ Priests form bands of robbers,
      waiting in ambush for their victims.
  They murder travelers along the road to
      Shechem
      and practice every kind of sin.
¹⁰ Yes, I have seen something horrible in
      Ephraim and Israel:
      My people are defiled by prostituting
      themselves with other gods!

¹¹ "O Judah, a harvest of punishment is also
      waiting for you,
      though I wanted to restore the fortunes
      of my people.

7 ISRAEL'S LOVE FOR WICKEDNESS

¹ "I want to heal Israel,* but its sins are
      too great.
  Samaria is filled with liars.
  Thieves are on the inside
      and bandits on the outside!
² Its people don't realize
      that I am watching them.
  Their sinful deeds are all around them,
      and I see them all.

³ "The people entertain the king with their
      wickedness,
      and the princes laugh at their lies.
⁴ They are all adulterers,
      always aflame with lust.
  They are like an oven that is kept hot
      while the baker is kneading the dough.

---

⁵ On royal holidays, the princes get drunk
      with wine,
      carousing with those who mock them.
⁶ Their hearts are like an oven
      blazing with intrigue.
  Their plot smolders* through the night,
      and in the morning it breaks out like
      a raging fire.
⁷ Burning like an oven,
      they consume their leaders.
  They kill their kings one after another,
      and no one cries to me for help.

⁸ "The people of Israel mingle with godless
      foreigners,
      making themselves as worthless as
      a half-baked cake!
⁹ Worshiping foreign gods has sapped their
      strength,
      but they don't even know it.
  Their hair is gray,
      but they don't realize they're old
      and weak.
¹⁰ Their arrogance testifies against them,
      yet they don't return to the LORD their God
      or even try to find him.

¹¹ "The people of Israel have become like silly,
      witless doves,
      first calling to Egypt, then flying to Assyria
      for help.
¹² But as they fly about,
      I will throw my net over them
  and bring them down like a bird from
      the sky.
      I will punish them for all the evil they do.*

¹³ "What sorrow awaits those who have
      deserted me!
      Let them die, for they have rebelled
      against me.
  I wanted to redeem them,
      but they have told lies about me.
¹⁴ They do not cry out to me with sincere
      hearts.
      Instead, they sit on their couches
      and wail.
  They cut themselves,* begging foreign gods
      for grain and new wine,
      and they turn away from me.
¹⁵ I trained them and made them strong,
      yet now they plot evil against me.
¹⁶ They look everywhere except to the
      Most High.
  They are as useless as a crooked bow.
  Their leaders will be killed by their enemies
      because of their insolence toward me.
  Then the people of Egypt
      will laugh at them.

6:4 Hebrew *Ephraim,* referring to the northern kingdom of Israel.
6:6a Greek version translates this Hebrew term as *to show mercy.*
Compare Matt 9:13; 12:7.   6:6b Hebrew *to know God.*   6:7 Or *But
at Adam.*   7:1 Hebrew *Ephraim,* referring to the northern kingdom
of Israel; also in 7:8, 11.   7:6 Hebrew *Their baker sleeps.*
7:12 Hebrew *I will punish them because of what was reported
against them in the assembly.*   7:14 As in Greek version; Hebrew
reads *They gather together.*

8 ISRAEL HARVESTS THE WHIRLWIND

1 "Sound the alarm!
   The enemy descends like an eagle on the
      people of the LORD,
for they have broken my covenant
   and revolted against my law.
2 Now Israel pleads with me,
   'Help us, for you are our God!'
3 But it is too late.
The people of Israel have rejected what
      is good,
   and now their enemies will chase
      after them.
4 The people have appointed kings without
      my consent,
   and princes without my knowledge.
By making idols for themselves from their
      silver and gold,
   they have brought about their own
      destruction.

5 "O Samaria, I reject this calf—
   this idol you have made.
My fury burns against you.
   How long will you be incapable of
      innocence?
6 This calf you worship, O Israel,
   was crafted by your own hands!
It is not God!
   Therefore, it must be smashed
      to bits.

7 "They have planted the wind
   and will harvest the whirlwind.
The stalks of grain wither
   and produce nothing to eat.
And even if there is any grain,
   foreigners will eat it.
8 The people of Israel have been
      swallowed up;
   they lie among the nations like an old
      discarded pot.
9 Like a wild donkey looking for a mate,
   they have gone up to Assyria.
The people of Israel* have sold
      themselves—
   sold themselves to many lovers.

10 But though they have sold themselves
      to many allies,
   I will now gather them together
      for judgment.
Then they will writhe
   under the burden of the great king.

11 "Israel has built many altars to take
      away sin,
   but these very altars became places
      for sinning!
12 Even though I gave them all my laws,
   they act as if those laws don't apply
      to them.
13 The people of Israel love their rituals
      of sacrifice,
   but to me their sacrifices are all
      meaningless.
I will hold my people accountable for
      their sins,
   and I will punish them.
   They will return to Egypt.
14 Israel has forgotten its Maker and built
      great palaces,
   and Judah has fortified its cities.
Therefore, I will send down fire on
      their cities
   and will burn up their fortresses."

9 HOSEA ANNOUNCES ISRAEL'S PUNISHMENT

1 O people of Israel,
   do not rejoice as other nations do.
For you have been unfaithful to your God,
   hiring yourselves out like prostitutes,
   worshiping other gods on every
      threshing floor.
2 So now your harvests will be too small to
      feed you.
   There will be no grapes for making
      new wine.
3 You may no longer stay here in the
      LORD's land.
   Instead, you will return to Egypt,
and in Assyria you will eat food
   that is ceremonially unclean.
4 There you will make no offerings of wine
      to the LORD.
   None of your sacrifices there will
      please him.
They will be unclean, like food touched by
      a person in mourning.
   All who present such sacrifices will be
      defiled.
They may eat this food themselves,
   but they may not offer it to the LORD.

8:9 Hebrew *Ephraim*, referring to the northern kingdom of Israel;
also in 8:11.

APPLYING THE WORD
*(8:11-12) The Israelites applied God's laws to others but
not to themselves. We can easily listen to a sermon or
read a Bible passage and think of other people who need
this message. But applying God's Word to our own lives is
more difficult, mainly because doing so involves humility
most of the time. As you think of others who might benefit
from what you are hearing or reading, check to see if the
same application might fit you.*

⁵ What then will you do on festival days?
How will you observe the Lord's
festivals?
⁶ Even if you escape destruction from Assyria,
Egypt will conquer you, and Memphis*
will bury you.
Nettles will take over your treasures
of silver;
thistles will invade your ruined homes.
⁷ The time of Israel's punishment has come;
the day of payment is here.
Soon Israel will know this all too well.
Because of your great sin and hostility,
you say, "The prophets are crazy
and the inspired men are fools!"
⁸ The prophet is a watchman over Israel* for
my God,
yet traps are laid for him wherever
he goes.
He faces hostility even in the house
of God.
⁹ The things my people do are as depraved
as what they did in Gibeah long ago.
God will not forget.
He will surely punish them for
their sins.
¹⁰ The Lord says, "O Israel, when I first
found you,
it was like finding fresh grapes in the
desert.
When I saw your ancestors,
it was like seeing the first ripe figs of the
season.
But then they deserted me for Baal-peor,
giving themselves to that shameful idol.
Soon they became vile,
as vile as the god they worshiped.
¹¹ The glory of Israel will fly away like a bird,
for your children will not be born
or grow in the womb
or even be conceived.
¹² Even if you do have children who grow up,
I will take them from you.
It will be a terrible day when I turn away
and leave you alone.
¹³ I have watched Israel become as beautiful
as Tyre.
But now Israel will bring out her children
for slaughter."
¹⁴ O Lord, what should I request for your
people?
I will ask for wombs that don't give birth
and breasts that give no milk.

9:6 Memphis was the capital of northern Egypt.   9:8 Hebrew *Ephraim,* referring to the northern kingdom of Israel; also in 9:11, 13, 16.

HOSEA

Served as a prophet to Israel (the northern kingdom) from 753 to 715 B.C.

CLIMATE OF THE TIMES

Israel's last six kings were especially wicked; they promoted heavy taxes, oppression of the poor, idol worship, and total disregard for God. Israel was subjected to Assyria and was forced to pay tribute, which robbed its few remaining resources.

MAIN MESSAGE

The people of Israel had sinned against God as an adulterous woman sins against her husband. They were sure to be judged for living in total disregard for God and fellow humans. Hosea saw the nation fall to Assyria in 722 B.C.

IMPORTANCE OF MESSAGE

When we sin, we sever our relationship with God, which breaks our commitment to him. While all must answer to God for their sins, those who seek God's forgiveness are spared eternal judgment.

CONTEMPORARY PROPHETS

Jonah (793–753)
Amos (760–750)
Micah (742–687)
Isaiah (740–681)

---

¹⁵ The Lord says, "All their wickedness
began at Gilgal;
there I began to hate them.
I will drive them from my land
because of their evil actions.
I will love them no more
because all their leaders are rebels.
¹⁶ The people of Israel are struck down.
Their roots are dried up,
and they will bear no more fruit.
And if they give birth,
I will slaughter their beloved children."

¹⁷ My God will reject the people of Israel
because they will not listen or obey.
They will be wanderers,
homeless among the nations.

....

YOU ARE WHAT YOU WORSHIP
(9:10) Back in Numbers 22–24, Balaam, a prophet, was hired by King Balak of Moab to curse the Israelites. The Moabites enticed the Israelites into sexual sin and the worship of the Moabite god, Baal-peor (see Num 25:3). Before long, the people of Israel became as corrupt as the Moabites. People can take on the characteristics of whatever or whomever they love or worship. What do you worship? Are you becoming more like God, or are you becoming more like someone or something else?

10 THE LORD'S JUDGMENT AGAINST ISRAEL

¹ How prosperous Israel is—
a luxuriant vine loaded with fruit.
But the richer the people get,
the more pagan altars they build.
The more bountiful their harvests,
the more beautiful their sacred pillars.
² The hearts of the people are fickle;
they are guilty and must be punished.
The LORD will break down their altars
and smash their sacred pillars.
³ Then they will say, "We have no king
because we didn't fear the LORD.
But even if we had a king,
what could he do for us anyway?"
⁴ They spout empty words
and make covenants they don't intend
to keep.
So injustice springs up among them
like poisonous weeds in a farmer's field.

⁵ The people of Samaria tremble in fear
for what might happen to their calf idol
at Beth-aven.*
The people mourn and the priests wail,
because its glory will be stripped away.*
⁶ This idol will be carted away to Assyria,
a gift to the great king there.
Ephraim will be ridiculed and Israel will
be shamed,
because its people have trusted in
this idol.
⁷ Samaria and its king will be cut off;
they will float away like driftwood on an
ocean wave.
⁸ And the pagan shrines of Aven,* the place
of Israel's sin, will crumble.
Thorns and thistles will grow up around
their altars.
They will beg the mountains, "Bury us!"
and plead with the hills, "Fall on us!"

⁹ The LORD says, "O Israel, ever since Gibeah,
there has been only sin and more sin!
You have made no progress whatsoever.
Was it not right that the wicked men of
Gibeah were attacked?

¹⁰ Now whenever it fits my plan,
I will attack you, too.
I will call out the armies of the nations
to punish you for your multiplied sins.

¹¹ "Israel* is like a trained heifer treading out
the grain—
an easy job she loves.
But I will put a heavy yoke on her
tender neck.
I will force Judah to pull the plow
and Israel* to break up the hard ground.
¹² I said, 'Plant the good seeds of
righteousness,
and you will harvest a crop of love.
Plow up the hard ground of your hearts,
for now is the time to seek the LORD,
that he may come
and shower righteousness upon you.'

¹³ "But you have cultivated wickedness
and harvested a thriving crop of sins.
You have eaten the fruit of lies—
trusting in your military might,
believing that great armies
could make your nation safe.
¹⁴ Now the terrors of war
will rise among your people.
All your fortifications will fall,
just as when Shalman destroyed
Beth-arbel.
Even mothers and children
were dashed to death there.
¹⁵ You will share that fate, Bethel,
because of your great wickedness.
When the day of judgment dawns,
the king of Israel will be completely
destroyed.

11 THE LORD'S LOVE FOR ISRAEL

¹ "When Israel was a child, I loved him,
and I called my son out of Egypt.
² But the more I* called to him,
the farther he moved from me,
offering sacrifices to the images of Baal
and burning incense to idols.
³ I myself taught Israel* how to walk,
leading him along by the hand.
But he doesn't know or even care
that it was I who took care of him.

MORE AND MORE STUFF?
(10:1) Israel prospered under Jeroboam II, gaining military and economic strength. But the more prosperous the nation became, the more the people spent on sacrifices to idols. Are we any different? We want more and more stuff: more DVDs, a better car, a faster computer, a newer cell phone. God isn't against material possessions, but he grieves when people live only to acquire more and more stuff. As you prosper, consider where your money is going. Is it being used for God's purposes or your own?

10:5a Beth-aven means "house of wickedness"; it is being used as another name for Bethel, which means "house of God." **10:5b** Or will be taken away into exile. **10:8** Aven is a reference to Beth-aven; see 10:5a and the note there. **10:11a** Hebrew Ephraim, referring to the northern kingdom of Israel. **10:11b** Hebrew Jacob. The names "Jacob" and "Israel" are often interchanged throughout the Old Testament, referring sometimes to the individual patriarch and sometimes to the nation. **11:2** As in Greek version; Hebrew reads they. **11:3** Hebrew Ephraim, referring to the northern kingdom of Israel; also in 11:8, 9, 12.

4 I led Israel along
  with my ropes of kindness and love.
I lifted the yoke from his neck,
  and I myself stooped to feed him.

5 "But since my people refuse to return
    to me,
  they will return to Egypt
  and will be forced to serve Assyria.

6 War will swirl through their cities;
    their enemies will crash through
    their gates.
  They will destroy them,
    trapping them in their own evil plans.

7 For my people are determined to desert me.
  They call me the Most High,
    but they don't truly honor me.

8 "Oh, how can I give you up, Israel?
    How can I let you go?
  How can I destroy you like Admah
    or demolish you like Zeboiim?
  My heart is torn within me,
    and my compassion overflows.

9 No, I will not unleash my fierce anger.
  I will not completely destroy Israel,
  for I am God and not a mere mortal.
  I am the Holy One living among you,
    and I will not come to destroy.

10 For someday the people will follow me.
  I, the LORD, will roar like a lion.
  And when I roar,
    my people will return trembling from
    the west.

11 Like a flock of birds, they will come
    from Egypt.
  Trembling like doves, they will return
    from Assyria.
  And I will bring them home again,"
    says the LORD.

CHARGES AGAINST ISRAEL AND JUDAH

12 *Israel surrounds me with lies and deceit,
    but Judah still obeys God
    and is faithful to the Holy One.*

12

1 *The people of Israel* feed on
    the wind;
  they chase after the east wind all
    day long.
  They pile up lies and violence;
    they are making an alliance with Assyria

while sending olive oil to buy support
  from Egypt.

2 Now the LORD is bringing charges
    against Judah.
  He is about to punish Jacob* for all his
    deceitful ways,
  and pay him back for all he has done.

3 Even in the womb,
    Jacob struggled with his brother;
  when he became a man,
    he even fought with God.

4 Yes, he wrestled with the angel and won.
  He wept and pleaded for a blessing
    from him.
  There at Bethel he met God face to face,
    and God spoke to him*—

5 the LORD God of Heaven's Armies,
    the LORD is his name!

6 So now, come back to your God.
  Act with love and justice,
    and always depend on him.

7 But no, the people are like crafty merchants
    selling from dishonest scales—
    they love to cheat.

8 Israel boasts, "I am rich!
    I've made a fortune all by myself!
  No one has caught me cheating!
    My record is spotless!"

9 "But I am the LORD your God,
    who rescued you from slavery in Egypt.
  And I will make you live in tents again,
    as you do each year at the Festival of
    Shelters.*

10 I sent my prophets to warn you
    with many visions and parables."

11 But the people of Gilead are worthless
    because of their idol worship.
  And in Gilgal, too, they sacrifice bulls;
    their altars are lined up like the heaps
    of stone
  along the edges of a plowed field.

12 Jacob fled to the land of Aram,
    and there he* earned a wife by tending
    sheep.

....

REMEMBER
(12:1-10) Israel took credit for its own success. Many
successful people and nations today often claim that their
material success is due to their own hard work, initiative,
and intelligence. Because they have all they want, they
don't feel a need for God. Believing their riches are their
own, they feel they have the right to use them any way
they please. If you find yourself taking credit for all of your
accomplishments, remember that all your opportunities,
abilities, and resources come from God and that you hold
them in sacred trust for him.

11:12a Verse 11:12 is numbered 12:1 in Hebrew text.   11:12b Or *and
Judah is unruly against God, the faithful Holy One.* The meaning of
the Hebrew is uncertain.   12:1a Verses 12:1-14 are numbered
12:2-15 in Hebrew text.   12:1b Hebrew *Ephraim,* referring to the
northern kingdom of Israel; also in 12:8, 14.   12:2 *Jacob* sounds
like the Hebrew word for "deceiver."   12:4 As in Greek and Syriac
versions; Hebrew reads *to us.*   12:9 Hebrew *as in the days of your
appointed feast.*   12:12 Hebrew *Israel.* See note on 10:11b.

¹³ Then by a prophet
　　the LORD brought Jacob's descendants*
　　　　out of Egypt;
and by that prophet
　　they were protected.
¹⁴ But the people of Israel
　　have bitterly provoked the LORD,
so their Lord will now sentence them
　　　　to death
in payment for their sins.

13 THE LORD'S ANGER AGAINST ISRAEL

¹ When the tribe of Ephraim spoke,
　　the people shook with fear,
　　for that tribe was important in Israel.
But the people of Ephraim sinned by
　　　　worshiping Baal
　　and thus sealed their destruction.
² Now they continue to sin by making
　　　　silver idols,
　　images shaped skillfully with
　　　　human hands.
"Sacrifice to these," they cry,
　　"and kiss the calf idols!"
³ Therefore, they will disappear like the
　　　　morning mist,
　　like dew in the morning sun,

like chaff blown by the wind,
　　like smoke from a chimney.

⁴ "I have been the LORD your God
　　ever since I brought you out of Egypt.
You must acknowledge no God but me,
　　for there is no other savior.
⁵ I took care of you in the wilderness,
　　in that dry and thirsty land.
⁶ But when you had eaten and were satisfied,
　　you became proud and forgot me.
⁷ So now I will attack you like a lion,
　　like a leopard that lurks along the road.
⁸ Like a bear whose cubs have been
　　　　taken away,
　　I will tear out your heart.
I will devour you like a hungry lioness
　　and mangle you like a wild animal.

⁹ "You are about to be destroyed, O Israel—
　　yes, by me, your only helper.
¹⁰ Now where is* your king?
　　Let him save you!
Where are all the leaders of the land,
　　the king and the officials you demanded
　　　　of me?
¹¹ In my anger I gave you kings,
　　and in my fury I took them away.

12:13 Hebrew *brought Israel.* See note on 10:11b.　**13:10** As in Greek and Syriac versions and Latin Vulgate; Hebrew reads *I will be.*

I WONDER . . .

People around me don't act like they need God. How can I share my faith in Christ with them if they don't feel a need to know him?

Rarely will people want a relationship with someone whom they feel they don't need. The Bible is filled with stories of people who have actively rejected God, who felt no need for him because their lives were going so well. In Hosea 13:6, God confronted the people of Israel—his chosen people—for doing that very thing.

It's funny, though, that when things are rough, people quickly pin the blame on God. This makes as much sense as a six-year-old child hitting himself on the thumb with a hammer and then blaming his dad. "I saw you use your hammer once, Dad. I know you told me not to use it, but I did it anyway. You should have made sure I never hurt myself with it! So it's your fault I hurt myself!"

People do the same with God: "I'm going to take my life and run it the way I want to, God—but if things go wrong, it's your fault!"

You can't make someone need God, but here are some things you can do:

First, be ready to help your friends when they do have needs. Keep the friendship bridges strong so they will come to you for help. Then you can point them to Christ. Seek the help of a mature Christian friend for advice on how to do this best.

Second, look for people who are hurt already and share the Good News with them. Be sensitive when you do this. Don't make it sound as though you have all the answers, or as if having a relationship with God means you'll never go through bad times. Simply share how God has helped you, and what he means in your life.

Third, watch out for your own heart. The Bible warns us that some things can distract us from God: "Trust in your money and down you go! But the godly flourish like leaves in spring" (Prov 11:28), and "There is a path before each person that seems right, but it ends in death" (Prov 14:12).

Satan wants us to live the "easy" life, apart from (and even numb to) God. Be careful, the stakes are high. Being separated from God now affects where we spend eternity.

12 "Ephraim's guilt has been collected,
    and his sin has been stored up for
       punishment.
13 Pain has come to the people
    like the pain of childbirth,
    but they are like a child
       who resists being born.
    The moment of birth has arrived,
    but they stay in the womb!

14 "Should I ransom them from the grave*?
    Should I redeem them from death?
    O death, bring on your terrors!
    O grave, bring on your plagues!*
    For I will not take pity on them.
15 Ephraim was the most fruitful of all
       his brothers,
    but the east wind—a blast from
       the LORD—
    will arise in the desert.
    All their flowing springs will run dry,
    and all their wells will disappear.
    Every precious thing they own
    will be plundered and carried away.
16*The people of Samaria
    must bear the consequences of
       their guilt
    because they rebelled against
       their God.
    They will be killed by an invading army,
    their little ones dashed to death against
       the ground,
    their pregnant women ripped open
       by swords."

14 HEALING FOR THE REPENTANT

1*Return, O Israel, to the LORD your God,
    for your sins have brought you down.
2 Bring your confessions, and return to
       the LORD.
    Say to him,
    "Forgive all our sins and graciously
       receive us,
    so that we may offer you our praises.*
3 Assyria cannot save us,
    nor can our warhorses.
    Never again will we say to the idols we
       have made,
       'You are our gods.'

13:14a Hebrew *Sheol*; also in 13:14b. 13:14b Greek version reads
*O death, where is your punishment? / O grave [Hades], where is
your sting?* Compare 1 Cor 15:55. 13:16 Verse 16 is numbered 14:1
in Hebrew text. 14:1 Verses 14:1-9 are numbered 14:2-10 in Hebrew
text. 14:2 As in Greek and Syriac versions, which read *may repay
the fruit of our lips*; Hebrew reads *may repay the bulls of our lips.*
14:8 Hebrew *Ephraim*, referring to the northern kingdom of Israel.

No, in you alone
    do the orphans find mercy."

4 The LORD says,
    "Then I will heal you of your faithlessness;
    my love will know no bounds,
    for my anger will be gone forever.
5 I will be to Israel
    like a refreshing dew from heaven.
    Israel will blossom like the lily;
    it will send roots deep into the soil
    like the cedars in Lebanon.
6 Its branches will spread out like beautiful
       olive trees,
    as fragrant as the cedars of Lebanon.
7 My people will again live under my shade.
    They will flourish like grain and blossom
       like grapevines.
    They will be as fragrant as the wines
       of Lebanon.

8 "O Israel,* stay away from idols!
    I am the one who answers your prayers
       and cares for you.
    I am like a tree that is always green;
    all your fruit comes from me."

9 Let those who are wise understand
       these things.
    Let those with discernment listen
       carefully.
    The paths of the LORD are true and right,
    and righteous people live by walking
       in them.
    But in those paths sinners stumble
       and fall.

....

RESTORED
(14:1-2) *The people could return to God by asking him to
forgive them and turn their lives around. The same is true
for us: We can pray Hosea's prayer and know our sins are
forgiven because Christ paid the penalty for them on the
cross (John 3:16). Forgiveness begins when we admit our
need for it. We cannot save ourselves; our only hope is in
God's mercy. Is that what you believe?*

NEVER-FAILING
(14:4) *God declared his boundless love to Israel. When
our will is weak and our conscience is burdened with a
load of guilt, we can remind ourselves that God offers
forgiveness and boundless love. When friends and family
desert us or don't understand us, when we are tired of
being good, God's love knows no bounds. When we can't
see the way or hear God's voice, when we lack courage
to go on, when our shortcomings or an awareness of
our messed-up lives overwhelms us, God's love knows
no bounds. Regardless of how things seem or even how
you feel, you can rely on this truth: God's love knows no
bounds.*

JOEL

"Okay, people," Mr. Ortiz said, "your final papers are due. Anyone who fails to hand in a paper will receive a zero for 25 percent of this quarter's grade. Don't look startled! We discussed the penalty for late papers when I gave you this assignment."

Akiko considered Mr. Ortiz to be a good teacher; yet she knew that he was tough. She expected to get an A or a B in his class. Unfortunately, her paper wasn't ready. She'd meant to finish it last weekend but hadn't gotten around to it. Maybe if she talked to him. . . .

Akiko walked up to Mr. Ortiz's desk. "Mr. Ortiz," she began, "I know what you said about the paper being due, but I've been really busy. Can I hand it in next week?"

Mr. Ortiz frowned as he answered. "Akiko, you're one of my better students, but two months ago I told the class there would be only a few acceptable reasons for a late paper. Not having time isn't good enough. I can't extend the deadline for you. I'm sorry." Sadly, Akiko left the room.

Deadlines and penalties are a part of life. The book of Joel also is about a deadline, one for Judah to turn back to God. Joel called this deadline "the day of the Lord," (see 1:15) when God would judge people for their actions. The people of Judah had forgotten about God and were living their own way. Joel reminded them that those who ignored God would one day face God's wrath.

The book of Joel reminds us that a day will come when God will judge the actions of all people. What do you think he will say about your life?

STATS

PURPOSE
To warn Judah of God's impending judgment because of their sins and to urge them to turn back to God

AUTHOR
Joel, son of Pethuel

ORIGINAL AUDIENCE
The people of Judah, the southern kingdom

DATE WRITTEN
Probably during the time Joel prophesied, from about 835 to 796 B.C.

SETTING
The people of Judah had become prosperous and complacent. They were taking God for granted as they indulged in idol worship. Joel warned them that this kind of lifestyle would inevitably bring God's judgment.

KEY PEOPLE
Joel, the people of Judah

KEY PLACE
Jerusalem

KEY POINTS

PUNISHMENT Joel warned Judah of the coming "day of the Lord"—God's judgment for wrongdoing. All of us are accountable to God for our actions. One day he will judge both good and bad actions accordingly.

FORGIVENESS God offered to restore his people to a proper relationship with him. He offers the same forgiveness today. As long as life endures on earth, it's never too late to ask for God's forgiveness.

THE HOLY SPIRIT Joel predicted the time when God would pour out his Holy Spirit on all people. The Holy Spirit confirms God's love for us and convicts us when we do wrong.

1

The LORD gave this message to Joel son of Pethuel.

MOURNING OVER THE LOCUST PLAGUE

2 Hear this, you leaders of the people.
  Listen, all who live in the land.
In all your history,
  has anything like this happened before?
3 Tell your children about it in the years
    to come,
  and let your children tell their children.
  Pass the story down from generation to
    generation.
4 After the cutting locusts finished eating
    the crops,
  the swarming locusts took what was left!
After them came the hopping locusts,
  and then the stripping locusts,* too!

5 Wake up, you drunkards, and weep!
  Wail, all you wine-drinkers!
All the grapes are ruined,
  and all your sweet wine is gone.
6 A vast army of locusts* has invaded
    my land,
  a terrible army too numerous to count.
Its teeth are like lions' teeth,
  its fangs like those of a lioness.
7 It has destroyed my grapevines
  and ruined my fig trees,
stripping their bark and destroying it,
  leaving the branches white and bare.

8 Weep like a bride dressed in black,
  mourning the death of her husband.
9 For there is no grain or wine
  to offer at the Temple of the LORD.
So the priests are in mourning.
  The ministers of the LORD are weeping.
10 The fields are ruined,
  the land is stripped bare.
The grain is destroyed,
  the grapes have shriveled,
  and the olive oil is gone.

11 Despair, all you farmers!
  Wail, all you vine growers!

Weep, because the wheat and barley—
  all the crops of the field—are ruined.
12 The grapevines have dried up,
  and the fig trees have withered.
The pomegranate trees, palm trees, and
    apple trees—
  all the fruit trees—have dried up.
  And the people's joy has dried up
    with them.

13 Dress yourselves in burlap and weep,
    you priests!
  Wail, you who serve before the altar!
Come, spend the night in burlap,
  you ministers of my God.
For there is no grain or wine
  to offer at the Temple of your God.
14 Announce a time of fasting;
  call the people together for a solemn
    meeting.
Bring the leaders
  and all the people of the land
into the Temple of the LORD your God,
  and cry out to him there.
15 The day of the LORD is near,
  the day when destruction comes from
    the Almighty.
  How terrible that day will be!

16 Our food disappears before our very eyes.
  No joyful celebrations are held in the
    house of our God.
17 The seeds die in the parched ground,
  and the grain crops fail.
The barns stand empty,
  and granaries are abandoned.
18 How the animals moan with hunger!
  The herds of cattle wander about
    confused,
because they have no pasture.
  The flocks of sheep and goats bleat
    in misery.

19 LORD, help us!
The fire has consumed the wilderness
    pastures,
  and flames have burned up all the trees.
20 Even the wild animals cry out to you
  because the streams have dried up,
  and fire has consumed the wilderness
    pastures.

WAKE-UP CALL

(1:1-5) The people of Judah had become apathetic about their wrong actions. Joel wanted them to wake up before "the day of the LORD" (1:15) occurred. Otherwise, everything would be destroyed—even the grapes and wine that caused their drunkenness. Our times of peace and prosperity can lull us into thinking that everything's cool. But we must never let material abundance substitute for spiritual readiness. The only way to know that everything's cool is to check in with God regularly. If you stick with God (see John 15), you'll be cool with him.

2 LOCUSTS INVADE LIKE AN ARMY

1 Sound the alarm in Jerusalem*!
  Raise the battle cry on my holy mountain!

1:4 The precise identification of the four kinds of locusts mentioned here is uncertain. 1:6 Hebrew *A nation.* 2:1 Hebrew *Zion;* also in 2:15, 23.

Let everyone tremble in fear
    because the day of the LORD is upon us.
² It is a day of darkness and gloom,
    a day of thick clouds and deep blackness.
Suddenly, like dawn spreading across the
        mountains,
    a great and mighty army appears.
Nothing like it has been seen before
    or will ever be seen again.

³ Fire burns in front of them,
    and flames follow after them.
Ahead of them the land lies
    as beautiful as the Garden of Eden.
Behind them is nothing but desolation;
    not one thing escapes.
⁴ They look like horses;
    they charge forward like warhorses.*
⁵ Look at them as they leap along the
        mountaintops.
    Listen to the noise they make—like the
        rumbling of chariots,
like the roar of fire sweeping across a field
        of stubble,
    or like a mighty army moving into battle.

⁶ Fear grips all the people;
    every face grows pale with terror.
⁷ The attackers march like warriors
    and scale city walls like soldiers.
Straight forward they march,
    never breaking rank.
⁸ They never jostle each other;
    each moves in exactly the right position.
They break through defenses
    without missing a step.
⁹ They swarm over the city
    and run along its walls.
They enter all the houses,

2:4 Or *like charioteers.*

JOEL

Served as a prophet to Judah from 835 to 796 B.C.

CLIMATE OF THE TIMES
Wicked Queen Athaliah seized power in a bloody coup but was overthrown after a few years. Joash was crowned king, but he was only seven years old and in great need of spiritual guidance. Joash followed God in his early years, then turned away from him.

MAIN MESSAGE
A plague of locusts had come to discipline the nation. Joel called the people to turn back to God before an even greater judgment occurred.

IMPORTANCE OF MESSAGE
God judges all people for their sins but is merciful and offers eternal salvation to those who turn to him in repentance.

CONTEMPORARY PROPHETS
Elisha (848–797)
Jonah (793–753)

climbing like thieves through the
        windows.
¹⁰ The earth quakes as they advance,
    and the heavens tremble.
The sun and moon grow dark,
    and the stars no longer shine.

¹¹ The LORD is at the head of the column.
    He leads them with a shout.
This is his mighty army,
    and they follow his orders.
The day of the LORD is an awesome,
        terrible thing.
    Who can possibly survive?

CHOICES
forgiveness

After praying together, volunteers from The Shelter, an inner-city mission to troubled youth, hit the streets. The theater district will soon be teeming with teens—runaways, pimps, prostitutes (both male and female), dealers, you name it. These are kids on the edge; their goal is to make it through another night.

Making his rounds, Tom notices a strange face—a young boy who's new to the streets. When the youth leader approaches the youngster, the kid begins to sob. His name is Sean, and he hasn't eaten in three days. Tom takes Sean to The Shelter, gives him some food, and listens.

Sean tells him of an abusive father, an unstable

mother, and a history of personal failure. He describes his decision to run away a month ago, and the horrible things he has done to survive on the streets.

Tom nods knowingly and begins to tell Sean about the love of Christ and the unconditional forgiveness he offers. Sean can't believe it. "That's too good to be true," he says. "Nobody could ever love me—not after what I've done."

Maybe you can relate to Sean's feelings. Perhaps you feel hopelessly guilty due to your decisions and choices. Don't despair!

Consider the message of Joel 2:12-13: When people genuinely turn to God—no matter what kind of mess they've gotten into—he responds with love and forgiveness. No matter what.

A CALL TO REPENTANCE

¹² That is why the LORD says,
"Turn to me now, while there is time.
Give me your hearts.
Come with fasting, weeping, and
mourning.
¹³ Don't tear your clothing in your grief,
but tear your hearts instead."
Return to the LORD your God,
for he is merciful and compassionate,
slow to get angry and filled with
unfailing love.
He is eager to relent and not punish.
¹⁴ Who knows? Perhaps he will give you
a reprieve,
sending you a blessing instead of
this curse.
Perhaps you will be able to offer grain
and wine
to the LORD your God as before.

¹⁵ Blow the ram's horn in Jerusalem!
Announce a time of fasting;
call the people together
for a solemn meeting.
¹⁶ Gather all the people—
the elders, the children, and even the
babies.

Call the bridegroom from his quarters
and the bride from her private room.
¹⁷ Let the priests, who minister in the LORD's
presence,
stand and weep between the entry room
to the Temple and the altar.
Let them pray, "Spare your people, LORD!
Don't let your special possession become
an object of mockery.
Don't let them become a joke for
unbelieving foreigners who say,
'Has the God of Israel left them?'"

THE LORD'S PROMISE OF RESTORATION

¹⁸ Then the LORD will pity his people
and jealously guard the honor of
his land.
¹⁹ The LORD will reply,
"Look! I am sending you grain and new wine
and olive oil,
enough to satisfy your needs.
You will no longer be an object of mockery
among the surrounding nations.
²⁰ I will drive away these armies from
the north.
I will send them into the parched
wastelands.
Those in the front will be driven into the
Dead Sea,
and those at the rear into the
Mediterranean.*
The stench of their rotting bodies will rise
over the land."

PUT ON
*(2:13) Deep remorse often was shown by tearing one's
clothes. But God didn't want an outward display of
sorrow without true inward repentance (1 Sam 16:7; Matt
23:1-36). Be sure your attitude toward God is correct, not
just your outward actions.*

2:20 Hebrew *into the eastern sea, . . . into the western sea.*

I WONDER...

I wish God would do more "miracles" in my life. Why don't amazing things happen more often?

Miracles and "amazing things" are great, but the best miracle God could ever perform is the miracle of salvation.

The fact that God actually chose to forgive our sins and live inside us is an incredible miracle. We should thank him for that every day. But often we forget.

Some teachers of the law once came to Jesus and said, "We want you to show us a miraculous sign" (Matt 12:38). He answered that they wouldn't see any greater miracle than him being dead, buried in the ground three days, and then coming back to life! But they weren't satisfied.

The real question is, what kind of miracles do you want God to do in your life?

Do you want him to give you As in subjects you

haven't studied for? Let you score the winning touchdown? Perform some healing to "prove" that he's there? If so, you'll be disappointed. God doesn't do anything just to prove he exists—beyond, of course, what he has already done through Christ.

But if you want to see God perform miracles in your life and in the lives of those around you, stand back. That's the kind he specializes in.

God promised his followers that he would do wonderful things through them (see Joel 2:28-32). And you'll find that the most exciting miracles are when God uses you to lead someone else to him. Those miracles are better; they lead to something eternal!

The longer you follow Christ, the more you'll see things happen. When someone's eternal destiny is changed, and God used *you* to make it happen, you'll experience a "high" like you've never known.

So ask God to use you to perform the greatest miracle of all—to lead someone to Christ.

Surely the LORD has done great things!
²¹   Don't be afraid, my people.
      Be glad now and rejoice,
          for the LORD has done great things.
²² Don't be afraid, you animals of the field,
          for the wilderness pastures will soon
              be green.
      The trees will again be filled with fruit;
          fig trees and grapevines will be loaded
              down once more.
²³ Rejoice, you people of Jerusalem!
          Rejoice in the LORD your God!
      For the rain he sends demonstrates his
          faithfulness.
      Once more the autumn rains will come,
          as well as the rains of spring.
²⁴ The threshing floors will again be piled high
          with grain,
      and the presses will overflow with new
          wine and olive oil.

²⁵ The LORD says, "I will give you back what
          you lost
      to the swarming locusts, the hopping
          locusts,
      the stripping locusts, and the cutting
          locusts.*
      It was I who sent this great destroying
          army against you.
²⁶ Once again you will have all the food
          you want,
      and you will praise the LORD your God,
      who does these miracles for you.
      Never again will my people be disgraced.
²⁷ Then you will know that I am among my
          people Israel,
      that I am the LORD your God, and there is
          no other.
      Never again will my people be disgraced.

THE LORD'S PROMISE OF HIS SPIRIT

²⁸*"Then, after doing all those things,
      I will pour out my Spirit upon all people.
      Your sons and daughters will prophesy.
          Your old men will dream dreams,
          and your young men will see visions.
²⁹ In those days I will pour out my Spirit
          even on servants—men and women alike.
³⁰ And I will cause wonders in the heavens and
          on the earth—
          blood and fire and columns of smoke.
³¹ The sun will become dark,
          and the moon will turn blood red

THEN, AFTER DOING ALL THOSE THINGS, I WILL POUR OUT MY SPIRIT UPON ALL PEOPLE. YOUR SONS AND DAUGHTERS WILL PROPHESY. YOUR OLD MEN WILL DREAM DREAMS, AND YOUR YOUNG MEN WILL SEE VISIONS.

■ JOEL 2:28 ■

before that great and terrible* day of the
          LORD arrives.
³² But everyone who calls on the name
          of the LORD
      will be saved,
      for some on Mount Zion in Jerusalem
          will escape,
          just as the LORD has said.
      These will be among the survivors
          whom the LORD has called.

3 JUDGMENT AGAINST ENEMY NATIONS

¹*"At the time of those events," says
          the LORD,
      "when I restore the prosperity of Judah
          and Jerusalem,
² I will gather the armies of the world
          into the valley of Jehoshaphat.*
      There I will judge them
          for harming my people, my special
              possession,
      for scattering my people among the nations,
          and for dividing up my land.
³ They threw dice* to decide which of
          my people
          would be their slaves.
      They traded boys to obtain prostitutes
          and sold girls for enough wine to
              get drunk.

⁴"What do you have against me, Tyre and Sidon and you cities of Philistia? Are you trying
to take revenge on me? If you are, then watch
out! I will strike swiftly and pay you back for
everything you have done. ⁵You have taken my
silver and gold and all my precious treasures,
and have carried them off to your pagan temples. ⁶You have sold the people of Judah and
Jerusalem to the Greeks,* so they could take
them far from their homeland.

⁷"But I will bring them back from all the
places to which you sold them, and I will pay

2:25 The precise identification of the four kinds of locusts
mentioned here is uncertain.   2:28 Verses 2:28-32 are
numbered 3:1-5 in Hebrew text.   2:31 Greek version reads
glorious.   3:1 Verses 3:1-21 are numbered 4:1-21 in Hebrew text.
3:2 *Jehoshaphat* means "the LORD judges."   3:3 Hebrew *They
cast lots.*   3:6 Hebrew *to the peoples of Javan.*

you back for everything you have done. [8]I will sell your sons and daughters to the people of Judah, and they will sell them to the people of Arabia,* a nation far away. I, the LORD, have spoken!"

[9] Say to the nations far and wide:
  "Get ready for war!
Call out your best warriors.
  Let all your fighting men advance for
    the attack.
[10] Hammer your plowshares into swords
  and your pruning hooks into spears.
  Train even your weaklings to be warriors.
[11] Come quickly, all you nations everywhere.
  Gather together in the valley."

And now, O LORD, call out your warriors!

[12] "Let the nations be called to arms.
  Let them march to the valley of
    Jehoshaphat.
  There I, the LORD, will sit
    to pronounce judgment on them all.

....

FOR REAL
(3:14) Joel described the multitudes waiting in the "valley of decision" (the "valley of Jehoshaphat" of 3:2, 12). This is a description of judgment. Everyone who has ever lived will be judged. Look around you. See your friends, those with whom you work and live. Have they received God's forgiveness? Have they been warned about sin's consequences? If we really understood the severity of God's final judgment on the lost, we wouldn't want anyone to face it in their sins.

NOT TOO LATE
(3:21) The book of Joel begins with a prophecy about the destruction of the land and ends with a prophecy about its restoration. The prophet began by stressing the need for repentance and ended with the promise of forgiveness that repentance brings. Joel was trying to convince the people to wake up (1:5), get rid of their complacency, and realize the danger of living apart from God. His message is that we still have time; anyone who calls on God's name can be saved (2:12-14, 32). Those who do this will enjoy the blessings mentioned in Joel's prophecy; those who refuse to turn to God will face destruction at some point. Is God's forgiveness an offer you've accepted? If you haven't, it's not too late.

[13] Swing the sickle,
  for the harvest is ripe.*
Come, tread the grapes,
  for the winepress is full.
The storage vats are overflowing
  with the wickedness of these people."

[14] Thousands upon thousands are waiting
  in the valley of decision.
There the day of the LORD will soon arrive.
[15] The sun and moon will grow dark,
  and the stars will no longer shine.
[16] The LORD's voice will roar from Zion
  and thunder from Jerusalem,
  and the heavens and the earth will shake.
But the LORD will be a refuge for his people,
  a strong fortress for the people of Israel.

BLESSINGS FOR GOD'S PEOPLE

[17] "Then you will know that I, the LORD
    your God,
  live in Zion, my holy mountain.
Jerusalem will be holy forever,
  and foreign armies will never conquer
    her again.
[18] In that day the mountains will drip with
    sweet wine,
  and the hills will flow with milk.
Water will fill the streambeds of Judah,
  and a fountain will burst forth from the
    LORD's Temple,
  watering the arid valley of acacias.*
[19] But Egypt will become a wasteland
  and Edom will become a wilderness,
because they attacked the people of Judah
  and killed innocent people in their land.

[20] "But Judah will be filled with people forever,
  and Jerusalem will endure through all
    generations.
[21] I will pardon my people's crimes,
  which I have not yet pardoned;
and I, the LORD, will make my home
  in Jerusalem* with my people."

3:8 Hebrew *to the Sabeans.* **3:13** Greek version reads *for the harvest time has come.* Compare Mark 4:29. **3:18** Hebrew *valley of Shittim.* **3:21** Hebrew *Zion.*

AMOS

What makes your blood boil? Social injustice? Someone borrowing your stuff without asking? Failing a test? Being humiliated or mocked?

All of the above are anger-producing. Yet many people would agree that social injustice really gets under their skin. We all have a sense of fairness. We want to see justice done, especially when someone stronger bullies someone weaker. But how many of us would willingly charge into battle against an oppressor if doing so took us out of our comfort zone or caused us to lose status, a job, or even our lives? Sadly, we sometimes want to see justice done but at little cost to ourselves.

God has always had a passion for justice. As God's spokesman, Amos had the responsibility of speaking a message to the people of Judah. They had become complacent. Life was good for some. But for others—the ones being oppressed—life wasn't so good. God was outraged at the wealthier citizens' lack of compassion for the poor. Through Amos, he warned them that injustice would reap a harvest of judgment. God doesn't utter idle warnings—he carries out his threats. But first, he wanted to give his people the opportunity to change.

When was the last time you felt a sense of outrage on someone else's behalf? As you read Amos, perhaps you'll consider the plight of those around you. Who knows? Maybe you will be the catalyst for change in your community.

STATS

PURPOSE
To show God's judgment on Israel, the northern kingdom, for their idolatry and oppression of the poor

AUTHOR
Amos

ORIGINAL AUDIENCE
Israel, the northern kingdom

DATE WRITTEN
Probably during the reigns of Jeroboam II of Israel and Uzziah of Judah (about 760 to 750 B.C.)

SETTING
The wealthy people of Israel were complacent in their oppression of the poor. Soon, however, Israel would be conquered by Assyria, and the rich would become slaves.

KEY PEOPLE
Amos, Amaziah, Jeroboam II

KEY PLACES
Bethel, Samaria

KEY POINTS

JUDGMENT Through Amos, God announced that he would judge Judah and the surrounding nations. Someday God will judge all people for their actions.

COMPLACENCY Everyone was optimistic, business was booming, and people were happy (except for the poor and oppressed). With all the comfort and luxury came self-sufficiency and a false sense of security. But prosperity also brought corruption and destruction. A complacent present can lead to a disastrous future.

OPPRESSION The wealthy and powerful people of Samaria, the capital of Israel, had become prosperous, greedy, and indifferent toward the poor. God never tolerates injustice. He wants his people to take a stand against injustice and to care for those in need.

PHONY RELIGION Although many people in Israel and Judah had abandoned real faith in God, they still pretended to be religious. Merely participating in a ritual falls short of true faith. This leads to religion without relationship. God wants sincere obedience and commitment.

1 This message was given to Amos, a shepherd from the town of Tekoa in Judah. He received this message in visions two years before the earthquake, when Uzziah was king of Judah and Jeroboam II, the son of Jehoash,* was king of Israel.

²This is what he saw and heard:

> "The LORD's voice will roar from Zion
>   and thunder from Jerusalem!
> The lush pastures of the shepherds will
>   dry up;
>   the grass on Mount Carmel will wither
>   and die."

GOD'S JUDGMENT ON ISRAEL'S NEIGHBORS

³This is what the LORD says:

> "The people of Damascus have sinned
>   again and again,*
>   and I will not let them go unpunished!
> They beat down my people in Gilead
>   as grain is threshed with iron sledges.
> ⁴ So I will send down fire on King Hazael's
>   palace,
>   and the fortresses of King Ben-hadad will
>   be destroyed.
> ⁵ I will break down the gates of Damascus
>   and slaughter the people in the valley
>   of Aven.
> I will destroy the ruler in Beth-eden,
>   and the people of Aram will go as
>   captives to Kir,"
>   says the LORD.

⁶This is what the LORD says:

> "The people of Gaza have sinned again
>   and again,
>   and I will not let them go unpunished!
> They sent whole villages into exile,
>   selling them as slaves to Edom.
> ⁷ So I will send down fire on the walls of Gaza,
>   and all its fortresses will be destroyed.
> ⁸ I will slaughter the people of Ashdod
>   and destroy the king of Ashkelon.
> Then I will turn to attack Ekron,
>   and the few Philistines still left will
>   be killed,"
>   says the Sovereign LORD.

⁹This is what the LORD says:

> "The people of Tyre have sinned again
>   and again,
>   and I will not let them go unpunished!
> They broke their treaty of brotherhood
>   with Israel,
>   selling whole villages as slaves to Edom.
> ¹⁰ So I will send down fire on the walls of Tyre,
>   and all its fortresses will be destroyed."

¹¹This is what the LORD says:

> "The people of Edom have sinned again
>   and again,
>   and I will not let them go unpunished!
> They chased down their relatives, the
>   Israelites, with swords,
>   showing them no mercy.
> In their rage, they slashed them continually
>   and were unrelenting in their anger.
> ¹² So I will send down fire on Teman,
>   and the fortresses of Bozrah will be
>   destroyed."

¹³This is what the LORD says:

> "The people of Ammon have sinned again
>   and again,
>   and I will not let them go unpunished!
> When they attacked Gilead to extend their
>   borders,
>   they ripped open pregnant women with
>   their swords.
> ¹⁴ So I will send down fire on the walls of
>   Rabbah,
>   and all its fortresses will be destroyed.
> The battle will come upon them with shouts,
>   like a whirlwind in a mighty storm.
> ¹⁵ And their king* and his princes will go into
>   exile together,"
>   says the LORD.

2 This is what the LORD says:

> "The people of Moab have sinned again
>   and again,*
>   and I will not let them go unpunished!
> They desecrated the bones of Edom's king,
>   burning them to ashes.
> ² So I will send down fire on the land
>   of Moab,
>   and all the fortresses in Kerioth will
>   be destroyed.
> The people will fall in the noise of battle,

WORK
(1:1) All day long Amos took care of sheep—not a particularly "spiritual" job. Yet this ordinary man was chosen to do something extraordinary. Your job may not cause you to feel spiritual or successful, but it can be a vital work if you are in the place God wants you to be. God can work through you to do extraordinary things, no matter how ordinary your occupation.

1:1 Hebrew *Joash*, a variant spelling of Jehoash. **1:3** Hebrew *have committed three sins, even four;* also in 1:6, 9, 11, 13. **1:15** Hebrew *malcam*, possibly referring to their god Molech. **2:1** Hebrew *have committed three sins, even four;* also in 2:4, 6.

as the warriors shout and the ram's horn
　　sounds.
³ And I will destroy their king
　　and slaughter all their princes,"
　　says the LORD.

GOD'S JUDGMENT ON JUDAH AND ISRAEL

⁴This is what the LORD says:

"The people of Judah have sinned again
　　and again,
　　and I will not let them go unpunished!
They have rejected the instruction of
　　the LORD,
　　refusing to obey his decrees.
They have been led astray by the same lies
　　that deceived their ancestors.
⁵ So I will send down fire on Judah,
　　and all the fortresses of Jerusalem will
　　be destroyed."

⁶This is what the LORD says:

"The people of Israel have sinned again
　　and again,
　　and I will not let them go unpunished!
They sell honorable people for silver
　　and poor people for a pair of sandals.
⁷ They trample helpless people in the dust
　　and shove the oppressed out of the way.
Both father and son sleep with the same
　　woman,
　　corrupting my holy name.

2:8 Or *their God.*

⁸ At their religious festivals,
　　they lounge in clothing their debtors put
　　up as security.
In the house of their gods,*
　　they drink wine bought with unjust fines.

⁹ "But as my people watched,
　　I destroyed the Amorites,
though they were as tall as cedars
　　and as strong as oaks.
I destroyed the fruit on their branches
　　and dug out their roots.
¹⁰ It was I who rescued you from Egypt
　　and led you through the desert for forty
　　years,
　　so you could possess the land of the
　　Amorites.
¹¹ I chose some of your sons to be prophets
　　and others to be Nazirites.
Can you deny this, my people of Israel?"
　　asks the LORD.
¹² "But you caused the Nazirites to sin by
　　making them drink wine,

CARETAKERS
(2:6-7) Amos spoke to the upper class. Israel had no middle class—only the very rich and the very poor. The rich kept religious rituals. They gave extra tithes, went to places of worship, and offered sacrifices. But they were greedy and unjust, and they took advantage of the help-less. Be sure that you do not neglect the needs of the poor while you faithfully attend church and do religious things. God expects us to live out our faith, and that means responding to people in need.

I WONDER . . .

My friends do things that my conscience won't let me get away with; yet they never seem to get caught. Why do some people who do wrong never seem to get punished? Are there really consequences for what we do?

At the dentist, Novocain deadens the nerves in our mouth so we won't feel the drill. Repeated sin dead-ens the conscience, so the person no longer feels guilty about wrong behavior. But whether a person feels guilty or not, sin *does* have consequences. Some are immediate, like when the teacher catches you cheating on a test and gives you an *F.* Other con-sequences may be delayed, such as with people who cheat on their income tax return and seem to get away with it. Then they are audited and receive a hefty fine or even a prison sentence.

The prophet Amos told the people of Israel what would happen if they didn't shape up: they would be conquered (see 2:6-16). Though his predictions didn't immediately come to pass, they did prove to be right after many years. The Israelites were conquered by the Assyrians and were dragged away from their land.

Without a doubt, the Bible is clear about what will eventually happen to those who act contrary to God's way: "Don't be misled—you cannot mock the justice of God. You will always harvest what you plant. Those who live only to satisfy their own sinful nature will harvest decay and death from that sinful nature. But those who live to please the Spirit will harvest ever-lasting life from the Spirit" (Gal 6:7-8).

If we "sow" bad actions, we'll reap that kind of fruit. If we sow good things and genuinely try to follow God's instructions, God will use us, and we'll reap a wonderful harvest.

Yet sometimes we tire of always trying to be good, especially when so much bad surrounds us. That's when we have to remember God's promise of the eventual harvest: "Let's not get tired of doing what is good. At just the right time we will reap a harvest of blessing if we don't give up" (Gal 6:9).

and you commanded the prophets,
'Shut up!'

13 "So I will make you groan
like a wagon loaded down with sheaves
of grain.
14 Your fastest runners will not get away.
The strongest among you will become
weak.
Even mighty warriors will be unable to save
themselves.
15 The archers will not stand their ground.
The swiftest runners won't be fast enough
to escape.
Even those riding horses won't be able
to save themselves.
16 On that day the most courageous of your
fighting men
will drop their weapons and run for
their lives,"
says the Lord.

3
Listen to this message that the Lord has
spoken against you, O people of Israel
and Judah—against the entire family I rescued
from Egypt:

2 "From among all the families on the earth,
I have been intimate with you alone.
That is why I must punish you
for all your sins."

WITNESSES AGAINST GUILTY ISRAEL

3 Can two people walk together
without agreeing on the direction?
4 Does a lion ever roar in a thicket
without first finding a victim?
Does a young lion growl in its den
without first catching its prey?
5 Does a bird ever get caught in a trap
that has no bait?
Does a trap spring shut
when there's nothing to catch?
6 When the ram's horn blows a warning,
shouldn't the people be alarmed?
Does disaster come to a city
unless the Lord has planned it?

7 Indeed, the Sovereign Lord never does
anything

until he reveals his plans to his servants
the prophets.

8 The lion has roared—
so who isn't frightened?
The Sovereign Lord has spoken—
so who can refuse to proclaim his
message?
9 Announce this to the leaders of Philistia*
and to the great ones of Egypt:
"Take your seats now on the hills around
Samaria,
and witness the chaos and oppression
in Israel."

10 "My people have forgotten how to do right,"
says the Lord.
"Their fortresses are filled with wealth
taken by theft and violence.
11 Therefore," says the Sovereign Lord,
"an enemy is coming!
He will surround them and shatter their
defenses.
Then he will plunder all their fortresses."

12 This is what the Lord says:

"A shepherd who tries to rescue a sheep
from a lion's mouth
will recover only two legs or a piece
of an ear.
So it will be for the Israelites in Samaria
lying on luxurious beds,
and for the people of Damascus reclining
on couches.*

13 "Now listen to this, and announce it
throughout all Israel,*" says the Lord, the Lord
God of Heaven's Armies.

14 "On the very day I punish Israel for its sins,
I will destroy the pagan altars at Bethel.
The horns of the altar will be cut off
and fall to the ground.
15 And I will destroy the beautiful homes of the
wealthy—
their winter mansions and their summer
houses, too—
all their palaces filled with ivory,"
says the Lord.

· ·

MOVED TO HELP?
*(4:1-3) Israel's wealthy women were compared to the
cows of Bashan—pampered, sleek, and well-fed (see Ps
22:12). These selfish women pushed their husbands
to oppress the helpless in order to finance their lavish
lifestyles. Their behavior outraged God. Amos warned
them that their time of prosperity would soon be over.
Instead of harming others, God wants us to be moved to
help. Are you?*

4
ISRAEL'S FAILURE TO LEARN
1 Listen to me, you fat cows*
living in Samaria,
you women who oppress the poor

3:9 Hebrew *Ashdod.* 3:12 The meaning of the Hebrew in this
sentence is uncertain. 3:13 Hebrew *the house of Jacob.* The names
"Jacob" and "Israel" are often interchanged throughout the Old
Testament, referring sometimes to the individual patriarch and
sometimes to the nation. 4:1 Hebrew *you cows of Bashan.*

and crush the needy,
and who are always calling to your
husbands,
"Bring us another drink!"
² The Sovereign LORD has sworn this by
his holiness:
"The time will come when you will be
led away
with hooks in your noses.
Every last one of you will be dragged away
like a fish on a hook!
³ You will be led out through the ruins of
the wall;
you will be thrown from your fortresses,*"
says the LORD.

⁴ "Go ahead and offer sacrifices to the idols
at Bethel.
Keep on disobeying at Gilgal.
Offer sacrifices each morning,
and bring your tithes every three days.

4:3 Or *thrown out toward Harmon,* possibly a reference to Mount Hermon.

⁵ Present your bread made with yeast
as an offering of thanksgiving.
Then give your extra voluntary offerings
so you can brag about it everywhere!
This is the kind of thing you Israelites
love to do,"
says the Sovereign LORD.

⁶ "I brought hunger to every city
and famine to every town.
But still you would not return to me,"
says the LORD.

⁷ "I kept the rain from falling
when your crops needed it the most.
I sent rain on one town
but withheld it from another.
Rain fell on one field,
while another field withered away.
⁸ People staggered from town to town
looking for water,
but there was never enough.
But still you would not return to me,"
says the LORD.

ULTIMATE ISSUES DO THE RIGHT THING

"In Germany they came first for the Communists, and I didn't speak up because I wasn't a Communist. Then they came for the Jews, and I didn't speak up because I wasn't a Jew. Then they came for the trade unionists, and I didn't speak up because I wasn't a trade unionist. Then they came for the Catholics, and I didn't speak up because I was a Protestant. Then they came for me, and by that time no one was left to speak up."—Martin Niemoller

"No, O people, the LORD has told you what is good, and this is what he requires of you: to do what is right, to love mercy, and to walk humbly with your God" (Mic 6:8).

Justice. You can't read more than a chapter or two in any of the Minor Prophets without a cry for justice leaping off the pages. Not that it is a minor theme found only in these books—God has woven a broad thread of compassion for the oppressed throughout the tapestry of the Bible. But here in the books of the Minor Prophets, it becomes a central theme.

Check out Amos 5:24: "I want to see a mighty flood of justice, an endless river of righteous living."

Over and over, God told Israel that they were not to be like the other nations; they were to hold to a higher standard. The other nations took advantage of the poor, allowing the wealthy and powerful to grow fat off of their labor. God said that it was not to be like that in Israel: His people were to treat the less fortunate with compassion and fairness. In Proverbs 14:31, God even goes so far as to identify intimately with the plight of the poor: "Those who oppress the poor insult their Maker, but helping the poor honors him."

Other nations could treat foreigners like second-class people, but not Israel. "You must not mistreat or oppress foreigners in any way. Remember, you yourselves were once foreigners in the land of Egypt" (Exod 22:21). Other nations considered widows and orphans as little better than discarded property, but God said that in Israel, such people had rights and were to be treated with dignity. " 'I will put you on trial. . . . I will speak against those who . . . oppress widows and orphans . . .' says the LORD of Heaven's Armies" (Mal 3:5).

"This is what the LORD of Heaven's Armies says: Judge fairly, and show mercy and kindness to one another. Do not oppress widows, orphans, foreigners, and the poor. And do not scheme against each other" (Zech 7:9-10).

We are confronted today with a great many opportunities to do the right thing in the name of God. The plight of the homeless, the distress of our inner cities, the suffering of the hungry, questions of racial and economic fairness, the struggle for peace—these and countless other issues cry out for people of courage, compassion, and conviction to stand strong for justice in Jesus' name. God is vitally concerned for the widow, the orphan, the refugee, the crack baby—indeed, anyone who suffers and needs help.

Are you?

"I tell you the truth, when you did it to one of the least of these my brothers and sisters, you were doing it to me! . . . I tell you the truth, when you refused to help the least of these my brothers and sisters, you were refusing to help me" (Matt 25:40, 45). ∎

9 "I struck your farms and vineyards with
      blight and mildew.
   Locusts devoured all your fig and
      olive trees.
   But still you would not return to me,"
      says the LORD.

10 "I sent plagues on you
      like the plagues I sent on Egypt long ago.
   I killed your young men in war
      and led all your horses away.*
   The stench of death filled the air!
   But still you would not return to me,"
      says the LORD.

11 "I destroyed some of your cities,
      as I destroyed* Sodom and Gomorrah.
   Those of you who survived
      were like charred sticks pulled from a fire.
   But still you would not return to me,"
      says the LORD.

12 "Therefore, I will bring upon you all the
      disasters I have announced.
   Prepare to meet your God in judgment,
      you people of Israel!"

13 For the LORD is the one who shaped the
      mountains,
   stirs up the winds, and reveals his
      thoughts to mankind.
   He turns the light of dawn into darkness
      and treads on the heights of the earth.
   The LORD God of Heaven's Armies is
      his name!

5 A CALL TO REPENTANCE Listen, you
   people of Israel! Listen to this funeral
song I am singing:

2 "The virgin Israel has fallen,
      never to rise again!

   She lies abandoned on the ground,
      with no one to help her up."

3 The Sovereign LORD says:

   "When a city sends a thousand men to
      battle,
      only a hundred will return.
   When a town sends a hundred,
      only ten will come back alive."

4 Now this is what the LORD says to the family
of Israel:

   "Come back to me and live!
5   Don't worship at the pagan altars at Bethel;
      don't go to the shrines at Gilgal or
         Beersheba.
   For the people of Gilgal will be dragged off
      into exile,
      and the people of Bethel will be reduced
         to nothing."
6 Come back to the LORD and live!
   Otherwise, he will roar through Israel* like
      a fire,
      devouring you completely.
   Your gods in Bethel
      won't be able to quench the flames.
7 You twist justice, making it a bitter pill for
      the oppressed.
   You treat the righteous like dirt.

8 It is the LORD who created the stars,
      the Pleiades and Orion.
   He turns darkness into morning
      and day into night.
   He draws up water from the oceans
      and pours it down as rain on the land.
   The LORD is his name!
9 With blinding speed and power he destroys
      the strong,
      crushing all their defenses.

4:10 Or and slaughtered your captured horses. 4:11 Hebrew
as when God destroyed. 5:6 Hebrew the house of Joseph.

CHOICES
complacency

When Deepa joined the youth group at her church
three years ago, exciting events were always taking
place. One semester, some group members served in
a local retirement home. During Deepa's sophomore
year, the group developed an ongoing outreach to
homeless people. Each summer at least 30 or 40
teens went on some sort of short-term mission trip.

These days things are different. Most of the older
crowd has gone on to college. And for whatever reason, the younger kids in the group only seem to come
to "fun" activities—parties, cookouts, and so forth.

Deepa is concerned that youth group is becoming
more of a social club than a place of ministry.

During sharing time at youth group, she expresses
her concerns, explaining that she misses the commitment to ministry, and sharing stories of the real
joy and fun the group had experienced in the past
through serving others.

The group's reaction ranges from glares, to whispers, to yawns. One girl approaches Deepa after
the meeting and says, "Who do you think you are?
You act like you're so spiritual. What's wrong with
having fun?"

*Like Deepa, the prophet Amos had the unpleasant task of lighting a spiritual fire under complacent people.
Read Amos 5:21–6:8 and ask yourself: Am I more like Amos . . . or the people he addressed?*

¹⁰ How you hate honest judges!
   How you despise people who tell
      the truth!
¹¹ You trample the poor,
   stealing their grain through taxes and
      unfair rent.
   Therefore, though you build beautiful
      stone houses,
   you will never live in them.
   Though you plant lush vineyards,
      you will never drink wine from them.
¹² For I know the vast number of your sins
      and the depth of your rebellions.
   You oppress good people by
      taking bribes
   and deprive the poor of justice
      in the courts.
¹³ So those who are smart keep their
      mouths shut,
   for it is an evil time.

¹⁴ Do what is good and run from evil
      so that you may live!
   Then the LORD God of Heaven's Armies will
      be your helper,
   just as you have claimed.
¹⁵ Hate evil and love what is good;
      turn your courts into true halls of justice.
   Perhaps even yet the LORD God of Heaven's
      Armies
   will have mercy on the remnant of his
      people.*

¹⁶Therefore, this is what the Lord, the LORD God
of Heaven's Armies, says:

   "There will be crying in all the public
      squares
   and mourning in every street.
   Call for the farmers to weep with you,
      and summon professional mourners
      to wail.
¹⁷ There will be wailing in every vineyard,
      for I will destroy them all,"
   says the LORD.

WARNING OF COMING JUDGMENT

¹⁸ What sorrow awaits you who say,
   "If only the day of the LORD were here!"
   You have no idea what you are wishing for.
   That day will bring darkness, not light.
¹⁹ In that day you will be like a man who runs
      from a lion—
   only to meet a bear.
   Escaping from the bear, he leans his hand
      against a wall in his house—
   and he's bitten by a snake.

5:15 Hebrew *the remnant of Joseph.*

I WANT TO SEE A MIGHTY FLOOD OF JUSTICE, AN ENDLESS RIVER OF RIGHTEOUS LIVING.

AMOS 5:24

²⁰ Yes, the day of the LORD will be dark and
      hopeless,
   without a ray of joy or hope.

²¹ "I hate all your show and pretense—
      the hypocrisy of your religious festivals
      and solemn assemblies.
²² I will not accept your burnt offerings and
      grain offerings.
   I won't even notice all your choice peace
      offerings.
²³ Away with your noisy hymns of praise!
   I will not listen to the music of your harps.
²⁴ Instead, I want to see a mighty flood of
      justice,
   an endless river of righteous living.

²⁵"Was it to me you were bringing sacrifices
and offerings during the forty years in the wilderness, Israel? ²⁶No, you served your pagan

FREELY GIVE
(5:10-12) Why does God put so much emphasis on the
way we treat the poor? How we treat the rich—or those of
equal status too—often reflects what we hope to get from
them. But since the poor can give us nothing, how we
treat them reflects our true character (see Matt 5:43-48).
Do you, like Christ, give without thought of gain? We
should treat the poor as we would like God to treat us.

WARNINGS
(5:21-24) The Jews of Amos's day had lost sight of God's
love for them. The rich were carefree and comfortable,
and they refused to help those who were in need. They
observed their religious rituals in hopes of appeasing
God; yet they didn't truly love him. Amos announced
God's warnings of destruction for their wrong actions.
Likewise, we must not assume that going to church is
enough. God expects our belief in him to penetrate all
areas of our lives and conduct. May Amos's words inspire
us to live faithfully as God would have us live.

AMOS

Served as a prophet to Israel (the northern kingdom) from 760 to 750 B.C.

CLIMATE OF THE TIMES

Israel was enjoying prosperity and peace. But this had caused it to become a selfish, materialistic society. Those who were well off ignored the needs of those less fortunate. The people were self-centered and indifferent toward God.

MAIN MESSAGE

Amos spoke against those who exploited or ignored the needy.

IMPORTANCE OF MESSAGE

Believing in God is more than a personal matter. God calls all believers to work against injustices in society and to aid those less fortunate.

CONTEMPORARY PROPHETS

Jonah (793–753)
Hosea (753–715)

gods—Sakkuth your king god and Kaiwan your star god—the images you made for yourselves. ²⁷So I will send you into exile, to a land east of Damascus,*" says the LORD, whose name is the God of Heaven's Armies.

6 ¹What sorrow awaits you who lounge in luxury in Jerusalem,*
and you who feel secure in Samaria!
You are famous and popular in Israel,
and people go to you for help.
² But go over to Calneh
and see what happened there.
Then go to the great city of Hamath
and down to the Philistine city of Gath.
You are no better than they were,
and look at how they were destroyed.
³ You push away every thought of coming disaster,
but your actions only bring the day
of judgment closer.
⁴ How terrible for you who sprawl on ivory beds
and lounge on your couches,
eating the meat of tender lambs from the flock
and of choice calves fattened in the stall.
⁵ You sing trivial songs to the sound of the harp
and fancy yourselves to be great
musicians like David.
⁶ You drink wine by the bowlful

and perfume yourselves with fragrant lotions.
You care nothing about the ruin of your nation.*
⁷ Therefore, you will be the first to be led away as captives.
Suddenly, all your parties will end.

⁸The Sovereign LORD has sworn by his own name, and this is what he, the LORD God of Heaven's Armies, says:

"I despise the arrogance of Israel,*
and I hate their fortresses.
I will give this city
and everything in it to their enemies."

⁹(If there are ten men left in one house, they will all die. ¹⁰And when a relative who is responsible to dispose of the dead* goes into the house to carry out the bodies, he will ask the last survivor, "Is anyone else with you?" When the person begins to swear, "No, by . . . ," he will interrupt and say, "Stop! Don't even mention the name of the LORD.")

¹¹ When the LORD gives the command,
homes both great and small will be
smashed to pieces.

¹² Can horses gallop over boulders?
Can oxen be used to plow them?
But that's how foolish you are when you
turn justice into poison
and the sweet fruit of righteousness into
bitterness.
¹³ And you brag about your conquest of Lo-debar.*
You boast, "Didn't we take Karnaim* by
our own strength?"

¹⁴ "O people of Israel, I am about to bring an
enemy nation against you,"
says the LORD God of Heaven's Armies.
"They will oppress you throughout your land—
from Lebo-hamath in the north
to the Arabah Valley in the south."

7 **A VISION OF LOCUSTS** The Sovereign LORD showed me a vision. I saw him preparing to send a vast swarm of locusts over the land. This was after the king's share had been harvested from the fields and as the main crop

5:26-27 Greek version reads *No, you carried your pagan gods—the shrine of Molech, the star of your god Rephan, and the images you made for yourselves. So I will send you into exile, to a land east of Damascus.* Compare Acts 7:43.   **6:1** Hebrew *in Zion.*   **6:6** Hebrew *of Joseph.*   **6:8** Hebrew *Jacob.* See note on 3:13.   **6:10** Or *to burn the dead.* The meaning of the Hebrew is uncertain.   **6:13a** *Lo-debar* means "nothing."   **6:13b** *Karnaim* means "horns," a term that symbolizes strength.

was coming up. ²In my vision the locusts ate every green plant in sight. Then I said, "O Sovereign LORD, please forgive us or we will not survive, for Israel* is so small."

³So the LORD relented from this plan. "I will not do it," he said.

A VISION OF FIRE ⁴Then the Sovereign LORD showed me another vision. I saw him preparing to punish his people with a great fire. The fire had burned up the depths of the sea and was devouring the entire land. ⁵Then I said, "O Sovereign LORD, please stop or we will not survive, for Israel is so small."

⁶Then the LORD relented from this plan, too. "I will not do that either," said the Sovereign LORD.

A VISION OF A PLUMB LINE ⁷Then he showed me another vision. I saw the Lord standing beside a wall that had been built using a plumb line. He was using a plumb line to see if it was still straight. ⁸And the LORD said to me, "Amos, what do you see?"

I answered, "A plumb line."

And the Lord replied, "I will test my people with this plumb line. I will no longer ignore all their sins. ⁹The pagan shrines of your ancestors* will be ruined, and the temples of Israel will be destroyed; I will bring the dynasty of King Jeroboam to a sudden end."

AMOS AND AMAZIAH ¹⁰Then Amaziah, the priest of Bethel, sent a message to Jeroboam, king of Israel: "Amos is hatching a plot against you right here on your very doorstep! What he is saying is intolerable. ¹¹He is saying, 'Jeroboam will soon be killed, and the people of Israel will be sent away into exile.'"

¹²Then Amaziah sent orders to Amos: "Get out of here, you prophet! Go on back to the land of Judah, and earn your living by prophesying there! ¹³Don't bother us with your prophecies here in Bethel. This is the king's sanctuary and the national place of worship!"

¹⁴But Amos replied, "I'm not a professional prophet, and I was never trained to be one.* I'm just a shepherd, and I take care of sycamore-fig trees. ¹⁵But the LORD called me away from my flock and told me, 'Go and prophesy to my people in Israel.' ¹⁶Now then, listen to this message from the LORD:

"You say,
'Don't prophesy against Israel.
Stop preaching against my people.*'
¹⁷ But this is what the LORD says:
'Your wife will become a prostitute in
 this city,
 and your sons and daughters will be
 killed.
Your land will be divided up,
 and you yourself will die in
 a foreign land.
And the people of Israel will certainly
 become captives in exile,
 far from their homeland.'"

8

A VISION OF RIPE FRUIT Then the Sovereign LORD showed me another vision. In it I saw a basket filled with ripe fruit. ²"What do you see, Amos?" he asked.

I replied, "A basket full of ripe fruit."

Then the LORD said, "Like this fruit, Israel is ripe for punishment! I will not delay their punishment again. ³In that day the singing in the Temple will turn to wailing. Dead bodies will be scattered everywhere. They will be carried out of the city in silence. I, the Sovereign LORD, have spoken!"

⁴ Listen to this, you who rob the poor
 and trample down the needy!
⁵ You can't wait for the Sabbath day to
 be over
 and the religious festivals to end
 so you can get back to cheating the
 helpless.
You measure out grain with dishonest
 measures
 and cheat the buyer with dishonest
 scales.*
⁶ And you mix the grain you sell
 with chaff swept from the floor.
Then you enslave poor people
 for one piece of silver or a pair
 of sandals.

⁷ Now the LORD has sworn this oath
 by his own name, the Pride of Israel*:
"I will never forget
 the wicked things you have done!
⁸ The earth will tremble for your deeds,
 and everyone will mourn.

7:2 Hebrew *Jacob;* also in 7:5. See note on 3:13.   7:9 Hebrew *of Isaac.*   7:14 Or *I'm not a prophet nor the son of a prophet.*   7:16 Hebrew *against the house of Isaac.*   8:5 Hebrew *You make the ephah* [a unit for measuring grain] *small and the shekel* [a unit of weight] *great, and you deal falsely by using deceitful balances.*   8:7 Hebrew *the pride of Jacob.* See note on 3:13.

PRAYER POWER
(7:1-9) Twice Amos was shown a vision of Israel's impending punishment. His immediate response was to pray that God would spare Israel. Is that your prayer for this nation? Prayer is a powerful privilege, one not to be wasted.

The ground will rise like the Nile River at
    floodtime;
  it will heave up, then sink again.

9 "In that day," says the Sovereign LORD,
  "I will make the sun go down at noon
    and darken the earth while it is
    still day.
10 I will turn your celebrations into times
    of mourning
  and your singing into weeping.
  You will wear funeral clothes
    and shave your heads to show your
    sorrow—
  as if your only son had died.
  How very bitter that day will be!

11 "The time is surely coming," says the
    Sovereign LORD,
  "when I will send a famine on
    the land—
  not a famine of bread or water
    but of hearing the words of the LORD.
12 People will stagger from sea to sea
    and wander from border to border*
  searching for the word of the LORD,
    but they will not find it.
13 Beautiful girls and strong young men
    will grow faint in that day,
  thirsting for the LORD's word.
14 And those who swear by the shameful
    idols of Samaria—
  who take oaths in the name of the
    god of Dan
  and make vows in the name of the
    god of Beersheba*—
  they will all fall down,
    never to rise again."

AN APPETITE FOR ANSWERS
(8:11-14) The people had no appetite for God's messages when prophets like Amos delivered them.
Because of their apathy, God announced that he would
take away even the opportunity to hear his word. We
have God's Word, the Bible, but many people still look
for answers to life's problems everywhere except in
Scripture. Does that describe anyone you know? You
can help them by directing them to the Bible, showing
them the parts that speak to their special needs and
questions. God's Word is available to us. Our challenge
is to point people toward it.

SIGN OF LOVE
(9:8) Amos assured the Israelites that God would not
"completely destroy" Israel. In other words, the punishment would not be permanent or total. God wants to
redeem, not punish. But when punishment is necessary,
he doesn't withhold it. Like a loving father, God disciplines those whom he loves in order to correct them. If
he disciplines you, are you willing to accept it as a sign
of his love?

9 **A VISION OF GOD AT THE ALTAR** Then I
saw a vision of the Lord standing beside
the altar. He said,

  "Strike the tops of the Temple columns,
    so that the foundation will shake.
  Bring down the roof
    on the heads of the people below.
  I will kill with the sword those who survive.
    No one will escape!
2 "Even if they dig down to the place of the
    dead,*
  I will reach down and pull them up.
  Even if they climb up into the heavens,
    I will bring them down.
3 Even if they hide at the very top of Mount
    Carmel,
  I will search them out and capture them.
  Even if they hide at the bottom of the ocean,
    I will send the sea serpent after them to
    bite them.
4 Even if their enemies drive them into exile,
    I will command the sword to kill them
    there.
  I am determined to bring disaster upon
    them
    and not to help them."

5 The Lord, the LORD of Heaven's Armies,
    touches the land and it melts,
  and all its people mourn.
  The ground rises like the Nile River at
    floodtime,
    and then it sinks again.
6 The LORD's home reaches up to the
    heavens,
  while its foundation is on the earth.
  He draws up water from the oceans
    and pours it down as rain on the land.
    The LORD is his name!

7 "Are you Israelites more important to me
    than the Ethiopians?*" asks the LORD.
  "I brought Israel out of Egypt,
    but I also brought the Philistines
    from Crete*
  and led the Arameans out of Kir.

8 "I, the Sovereign LORD,
    am watching this sinful nation of Israel.
  I will destroy it
    from the face of the earth.
  But I will never completely destroy the
    family of Israel,*"
    says the LORD.

8:12 Hebrew *from north to east.* 8:14 Hebrew *the way of
Beersheba.* 9:2 Hebrew *to Sheol.* 9:7a Hebrew *the Cushites?*
9:7b Hebrew *Caphtor.* 9:8 Hebrew *the house of Jacob.* See note
on 3:13.

9 "For I will give the command
and will shake Israel along with the other
nations
as grain is shaken in a sieve,
yet not one true kernel will be lost.
10 But all the sinners will die by the sword—
all those who say, 'Nothing bad will
happen to us.'

A PROMISE OF RESTORATION

11 "In that day I will restore the fallen house*
of David.
I will repair its damaged walls.
From the ruins I will rebuild it
and restore its former glory.
12 And Israel will possess what is left of Edom
and all the nations I have called to
be mine.*"

9:11a Or *kingdom;* Hebrew reads *tent.*   **9:11b-12** Greek version
reads *and restore its former glory, / so that the rest of humanity,
including the Gentiles— / all those I have called to be mine—might
seek me.* Compare Acts 15:16-17.

The LORD has spoken,
and he will do these things.

13 "The time will come," says the LORD,
"when the grain and grapes will grow faster
than they can be harvested.
Then the terraced vineyards on the hills
of Israel
will drip with sweet wine!
14 I will bring my exiled people of Israel
back from distant lands,
and they will rebuild their ruined cities
and live in them again.
They will plant vineyards and gardens;
they will eat their crops and drink
their wine.
15 I will firmly plant them there
in their own land.
They will never again be uprooted
from the land I have given them,"
says the LORD your God.

"Let me tell you a joke!" Five-year-old Alice bubbled with excitement as she spoke. "Which do you want first, the bad news or the bad news?"

"You're silly," her brother Al retorted. "Don't you know anything? Those jokes are supposed to have good news and bad news, not just bad news."

"Not this one," answered Alice.

Most of life includes both good news and bad news. Some positive aspects have a downside. For example, you finally get your driver's license and discover that your parents want you to drive your younger brother everywhere. Meanwhile, some negative elements have a "silver lining" to give us hope.

The writings of the prophets (Isaiah—Malachi) have good and bad news. The bad news was that Jerusalem would be destroyed and its people taken away as captives to another land. The good news was that God would someday bring his people back from captivity and restore Israel's glory.

But one book is unique: It has no good news. That book is Obadiah. Written about Edom (a nearby nation), the prophet describes the utter ruin about to come. Why? Because Edom had rejoiced when Israel was taken captive and had taken advantage of Israel's plight.

God loves his children. He will deal harshly with those who attempt to hurt them.

If you are God's child, he will do the same for you (see Matt 18:6).

As you read Obadiah, see how God indeed is watching over his children.

KEY POINTS

JUSTICE Obadiah predicted that God would destroy Edom for their treachery in helping Babylon invade Judah. This story reminds us that God will judge and fiercely punish all who harm his people.

PRIDE Because of their seemingly invincible rock fortress, the Edomites were proud and self-confident. But God caused their nation to disappear from the face of the earth. Likewise, any nation that trusts in power, wealth, technology, or wisdom more than in God will be brought down. No one can escape God's justice.

This is the vision that the Sovereign LORD revealed to Obadiah concerning the land of Edom.

EDOM'S JUDGMENT ANNOUNCED

We have heard a message from the LORD
that an ambassador was sent to the
nations to say,
"Get ready, everyone!
Let's assemble our armies and attack
Edom!"

² The LORD says to Edom,
"I will cut you down to size among the
nations;
you will be greatly despised.
³ You have been deceived by your
own pride
because you live in a rock fortress
and make your home high in the
mountains.
'Who can ever reach us way up here?'
you ask boastfully.
⁴ But even if you soar as high as eagles
and build your nest among the stars,
I will bring you crashing down,"
says the LORD.

⁵ "If thieves came at night and robbed you
(what a disaster awaits you!),
they would not take everything.
Those who harvest grapes
always leave a few for the poor.

But your enemies will wipe you out
completely!
⁶ Every nook and cranny of Edom*
will be searched and looted.
Every treasure will be found and taken.

⁷ "All your allies will turn against you.
They will help to chase you from
your land.
They will promise you peace
while plotting to deceive and destroy you.
Your trusted friends will set traps for you,
and you won't even know about it.
⁸ At that time not a single wise person
will be left in the whole land of Edom,"
says the LORD.
"For on the mountains of Edom
I will destroy everyone who has
understanding.
⁹ The mightiest warriors of Teman
will be terrified,
and everyone on the mountains of Edom
will be cut down in the slaughter.

REASONS FOR EDOM'S PUNISHMENT

¹⁰ "Because of the violence you did
to your close relatives in Israel,*
you will be filled with shame
and destroyed forever.
¹¹ When they were invaded,
you stood aloof, refusing to help them.
Foreign invaders carried off their wealth
and cast lots to divide up Jerusalem,
but you acted like one of Israel's
enemies.

¹² "You should not have gloated
when they exiled your relatives to distant
lands.
You should not have rejoiced

TRUE SECURITY
(1:3) The Edomites felt secure, and they were proud of their might and land. But God warned them that they would be "cut down to size" (1:2). Is your security in objects, people, or your own abilities? Possessions, people, and some abilities can disappear in a moment. God, however, never changes. Only he is the source of true security. Is he your source? Depend on him.

6 Hebrew *Esau*; also in 8b, 9, 18, 19, 21. **10** Hebrew *your brother Jacob.* The names "Jacob" and "Israel" are often interchanged throughout the Old Testament, referring sometimes to the individual patriarch and sometimes to the nation.

CHOICES
arrogance

Henderson Heights is a basketball community. Between the two high schools there are at least a dozen good basketball players. Then there is Kyle. He is something special. Kyle will be able to play collegiate ball just about wherever he wants. Some people think that if he works hard enough, Kyle might have the skills to play in the NBA.

Kyle's 21 points-per-game scoring average is the good news. The bad news is his arrogant personality. Kyle talks a steady stream of trash out on the

court. Not only does he like to run up the score on his opponents, but he often goes out of his way to humiliate whoever happens to be guarding him. Even Kyle's own teammates sometimes get embarrassed by his showing off.

Last night Kyle came crashing back to reality. His team lost a game they were supposed to win easily. Kyle was thrown out late in the game for questioning a referee's call. He scored a grand total of seven points. And three college scouts were in the stands.

See what happened when a whole nation (Edom) had an arrogant attitude. Read Obadiah 1:2-10.

OBADIAH

Served as a prophet to Judah about 853 B.C.	**CLIMATE OF THE TIMES**	Edom was a constant thorn in Judah's side. It often participated in attacks initiated by other enemies.
	MAIN MESSAGE	God will judge Edom for its evil actions toward God's people.
	IMPORTANCE OF MESSAGE	Just as Edom was destroyed and disappeared as a nation, so God will destroy proud and wicked people.
	CONTEMPORARY PROPHETS	Elijah (875–848) Micaiah (865–853) Jehu (855–840?)

when the people of Judah suffered such
  misfortune.
You should not have spoken arrogantly
  in that terrible time of trouble.
¹³ You should not have plundered the land
  of Israel
  when they were suffering such calamity.
You should not have gloated over their
  destruction
  when they were suffering such calamity.
You should not have seized their wealth
  when they were suffering such calamity.
¹⁴ You should not have stood at the
  crossroads,
  killing those who tried to escape.
You should not have captured the survivors
  and handed them over in their terrible
  time of trouble.

EDOM DESTROYED, ISRAEL RESTORED

¹⁵ "The day is near when I, the LORD,
  will judge all godless nations!
As you have done to Israel,
  so it will be done to you.
All your evil deeds
  will fall back on your own heads.
¹⁶ Just as you swallowed up my people
  on my holy mountain,
so you and the surrounding nations
  will swallow the punishment I pour out
  on you.
Yes, all you nations will drink and stagger
  and disappear from history.

¹⁷ "But Jerusalem* will become a refuge for
  those who escape;

it will be a holy place.
And the people of Israel* will come back
  to reclaim their inheritance.
¹⁸ The people of Israel will be a raging fire,
  and Edom a field of dry stubble.
The descendants of Joseph will be a flame
  roaring across the field, devouring
  everything.
There will be no survivors in Edom.
  I, the LORD, have spoken!

¹⁹ "Then my people living in the Negev
  will occupy the mountains of Edom.
Those living in the foothills of Judah*
  will possess the Philistine plains
  and take over the fields of Ephraim and
  Samaria.
And the people of Benjamin
  will occupy the land of Gilead.
²⁰ The exiles of Israel will return to their land
  and occupy the Phoenician coast as far
  north as Zarephath.
The captives from Jerusalem exiled in the
  north*
  will return home and resettle the towns
  of the Negev.
²¹ Those who have been rescued* will go up
  to* Mount Zion in Jerusalem
  to rule over the mountains of Edom.
And the LORD himself will be king!"

17a Hebrew *Mount Zion.*   **17b** Hebrew *house of Jacob;* also in 18. See note on 10.   **19** Hebrew *the Shephelah.*   **20** Hebrew *in Sepharad.*   **21a** As in Greek and Syriac versions; Hebrew reads *Rescuers.*   **21b** Or *from.*

**WHEN THEY WERE INVADED,
YOU STOOD ALOOF,
REFUSING TO HELP THEM....
YOU SHOULD NOT HAVE
GLOATED....OBADIAH 1:11-12**

JONAH

"Don't get mad, get even." We've all heard or said that. Movies reflect the "get even" idea. We watch and cheer as the victim evens the score and the villains get what they deserve. We often live that way, too, sometimes without even knowing it. We do or say things to get back at those whom we think have offended us.

Jonah was like that. He's famous for being swallowed by a "great fish," but he ended up in that fish because of his get-even attitude.

God told Jonah to go to Assyria (Israel's greatest enemy) and warn the people of Nineveh (the capital) to change their ways or God would destroy them. Because Jonah thought Assyria should be destroyed (and he was afraid to go there), he ran in the other direction—straight into the fish. Finally, after Jonah cried out to God and was rescued, he preached God's message in Nineveh.

"Don't get mad, get even." Fortunately, God doesn't work that way. Instead, God is "a merciful and compassionate God, slow to get angry and filled with unfailing love" (4:2). He wants our attitude to reflect these qualities also. As you read Jonah, ask God to give you an attitude adjustment, to make yours more like his.

STATS

PURPOSE
To show the extent of God's grace—the message of salvation is for *all* people

AUTHOR
Jonah, son of Amittai

ORIGINAL AUDIENCE
The people of Israel

DATE WRITTEN
Approximately 785 to 760 B.C.

SETTING
Jonah ministered under Jeroboam II, Israel's most powerful king (793–753 B.C., see 2 Kgs 14:23-25). Nineveh was the capital of Assyria, Israel's greatest enemy. Assyria conquered Israel in 722 B.C.

KEY PEOPLE
Jonah, the ship's captain and crew

KEY PLACES
Joppa, Nineveh

SPECIAL FEATURES
Unlike other prophetic books, this one centers on the prophet, not his prophecies. The book of Jonah is a historical narrative. Jesus also mentioned the story of Jonah as a picture of his death and resurrection (Matt 12:38-41).

KEY POINTS

GOD'S SOVEREIGNTY Jonah tried to run, but couldn't hide from God. Through Jonah's experience, we can understand how saying no to God can lead to disaster. Saying yes, however, can bring new understanding of God and his purposes for us and for the world.

MISSIONARY MESSAGE God had given Jonah a purpose—to preach to the great Assyrian city of Nineveh. God wants his people to proclaim his love in words and actions to the whole world.

GOD'S COMPASSION Although the Assyrians didn't deserve it, God spared them when they repented. God loves each of us, even when we fail him. His love also transcends cultural backgrounds, races, or denominations.

MIRACLES IN THE BOOK OF JONAH

God caused a great storm 1:4	God arranged for a great fish to swallow Jonah 1:17	God ordered the fish to spit up Jonah 2:10	God made a plant to shade Jonah 4:6	God prepared a worm to eat the plant 4:7	God ordered a scorching wind to blow on Jonah 4:8

1 **JONAH RUNS FROM THE LORD** The LORD gave this message to Jonah son of Amittai: ²"Get up and go to the great city of Nineveh. Announce my judgment against it because I have seen how wicked its people are."

³But Jonah got up and went in the opposite direction to get away from the LORD. He went down to the port of Joppa, where he found a ship leaving for Tarshish. He bought a ticket and went on board, hoping to escape from the LORD by sailing to Tarshish.

⁴But the LORD hurled a powerful wind over the sea, causing a violent storm that threatened to break the ship apart. ⁵Fearing for their lives, the desperate sailors shouted to their gods for help and threw the cargo overboard to lighten the ship.

But all this time Jonah was sound asleep down in the hold. ⁶So the captain went down after him. "How can you sleep at a time like this?" he shouted. "Get up and pray to your god! Maybe he will pay attention to us and spare our lives."

⁷Then the crew cast lots to see which of them had offended the gods and caused the terrible storm. When they did this, the lots identified Jonah as the culprit. ⁸"Why has this awful storm come down on us?" they demanded. "Who are you? What is your line of work? What country are you from? What is your nationality?"

⁹Jonah answered, "I am a Hebrew, and I worship the LORD, the God of heaven, who made the sea and the land."

¹⁰The sailors were terrified when they heard this, for he had already told them he was running away from the LORD. "Oh, why did you do it?" they groaned. ¹¹And since the storm was getting worse all the time, they asked him, "What should we do to you to stop this storm?"

¹²"Throw me into the sea," Jonah said, "and it will become calm again. I know that this terrible storm is all my fault."

¹³Instead, the sailors rowed even harder to get the ship to the land. But the stormy sea was too violent for them, and they couldn't make it. ¹⁴Then they cried out to the LORD, Jonah's God. "O LORD," they pleaded, "don't make us die for this man's sin. And don't hold us responsible for his death. O LORD, you have sent this storm upon him for your own good reasons."

¹⁵Then the sailors picked Jonah up and threw him into the raging sea, and the storm stopped at once! ¹⁶The sailors were awestruck by the LORD's great power, and they offered him a sacrifice and vowed to serve him.

¹⁷*Now the LORD had arranged for a great fish to swallow Jonah. And Jonah was inside the fish for three days and three nights.

2 **JONAH'S PRAYER** ¹*Then Jonah prayed to the LORD his God from inside the fish. ²He said,

"I cried out to the LORD in my great trouble,
    and he answered me.
I called to you from the land of the dead,*
    and LORD, you heard me!
³ You threw me into the ocean depths,
    and I sank down to the heart of the sea.
The mighty waters engulfed me;
    I was buried beneath your wild and
      stormy waves.
⁴ Then I said, 'O LORD, you have driven me
    from your presence.
Yet I will look once more toward your
      holy Temple.'

RUNNING AWAY

(1:1-3) Jonah knew that God had a specific job for him, but he didn't want to do it. When God gives us directions through his Word, sometimes we run in fear, claiming that God is asking too much. Jonah ran, but he ran into worse trouble. Eventually, Jonah learned that it is best to do what God asks in the first place. Obeying from the start is far better. Instead of running, are you willing to trust that when God asks you to do a task, he has your best interests at heart?

IN A HARD PLACE

(2:1-10) While inside the fish, Jonah prayed, asking God to forgive him. Sometimes God places us in a hard place in order to gain our obedience. While we're there, we have two choices: to ask for help or to be angry and resentful toward God. Jonah chose the first one. Which will you choose?

1:17 Verse 1:17 is numbered 2:1 in Hebrew text.   **2:1** Verses 2:1-10 are numbered 2:2-11 in Hebrew text.   **2:2** Hebrew *from Sheol.*

JONAH

Served as a prophet to Israel and Assyria from 793 to 753 B.C.	**CLIMATE OF THE TIMES** While Nineveh was the most important city in Assyria and would soon become the capital of the huge Assyrian empire, it also was a very wicked city.
	MAIN MESSAGE Jonah, who hated the powerful and wicked Assyrians, was called by God to warn the Assyrians that they would receive judgment if they did not repent.
	IMPORTANCE OF MESSAGE Jonah didn't want to go to Nineveh, so he tried to run from God. But God has ways of teaching us to obey and follow him. When Jonah finally did preach, the people repented and God withheld his judgment. Even the most wicked will be saved if they truly repent of their sins and turn to God.
	CONTEMPORARY PROPHETS Joel (853–796?) Amos (760–750)

⁵ "I sank beneath the waves,
  and the waters closed over me.
  Seaweed wrapped itself around
    my head.
⁶ I sank down to the very roots of the
    mountains.
  I was imprisoned in the earth,
  whose gates lock shut forever.
  But you, O LORD my God,
    snatched me from the jaws of death!
⁷ As my life was slipping away,
  I remembered the LORD.
And my earnest prayer went out to you
  in your holy Temple.
⁸ Those who worship false gods
  turn their backs on all God's mercies.
⁹ But I will offer sacrifices to you with songs
    of praise,
  and I will fulfill all my vows.
  For my salvation comes from the
    LORD alone."

¹⁰Then the LORD ordered the fish to spit Jonah out onto the beach.

3 **JONAH GOES TO NINEVEH** Then the LORD spoke to Jonah a second time: ²"Get up and go to the great city of Nineveh, and deliver the message I have given you."

³This time Jonah obeyed the LORD's command and went to Nineveh, a city so large that it took three days to see it all.* ⁴On the day Jonah entered the city, he shouted to the crowds: "Forty days from now Nineveh will be

3:3 Hebrew *a great city to God, of three days' journey.*

destroyed!" ⁵The people of Nineveh believed God's message, and from the greatest to the least, they declared a fast and put on burlap to show their sorrow.

⁶When the king of Nineveh heard what Jonah was saying, he stepped down from his throne and took off his royal robes. He dressed himself in burlap and sat on a heap of ashes. ⁷Then the king and his nobles sent this decree throughout the city:

"No one, not even the animals from your herds and flocks, may eat or drink anything at all. ⁸People and animals alike must wear garments of mourning, and everyone must pray earnestly to God. They must turn from their evil ways and stop all their violence. ⁹Who can tell? Perhaps even yet God will change his mind and hold back his fierce anger from destroying us."

¹⁰When God saw what they had done and how they had put a stop to their evil ways, he

AS MY LIFE WAS SLIPPING AWAY,
I REMEMBERED THE LORD.
AND MY EARNEST PRAYER WENT OUT TO YOU IN YOUR HOLY TEMPLE.
■ ■ ■ ■ ■ ■ JONAH 2:7 ■ ■ ■ ■ ■ ■

changed his mind and did not carry out the destruction he had threatened.

4 JONAH'S ANGER AT THE LORD'S MERCY

This change of plans greatly upset Jonah, and he became very angry. ²So he complained to the LORD about it: "Didn't I say before I left home that you would do this, LORD? That is why I ran away to Tarshish! I knew that you are a merciful and compassionate God, slow to get angry and filled with unfailing love. You are eager to turn back from destroying people.

UNDESERVING
(4:1-2) Jonah revealed the reason for his reluctance to go to Nineveh (1:3): He wanted the Ninevites destroyed, not forgiven. Jonah didn't understand that the God of Israel is also the God of the world. Maybe there is someone you think is undeserving of God's forgiveness. Are you surprised when an unexpected person turns to God? Do you know a person to whom you're reluctant to extend forgiveness? Maybe your view is as narrow as Jonah's. News flash: No one deserves to be forgiven by God. But he's willing to forgive us anyway. Are you?

SPIRITUALLY SENSITIVE
(4:9) Jonah was angry at the death of the plant, but not over Nineveh's plight. Most of us have cried at the death of a pet or when an object with sentimental value is broken. But have we cried over a friend who does not know God? We can easily be more sensitive to our own interests than to the spiritual needs of people around us. The best way to start being sensitive is to find out what the needs are. So, what are the needs of the people in your area? What will you do about them?

³Just kill me now, LORD! I'd rather be dead than alive if what I predicted will not happen."

⁴The LORD replied, "Is it right for you to be angry about this?"

⁵Then Jonah went out to the east side of the city and made a shelter to sit under as he waited to see what would happen to the city. ⁶And the LORD God arranged for a leafy plant to grow there, and soon it spread its broad leaves over Jonah's head, shading him from the sun. This eased his discomfort, and Jonah was very grateful for the plant.

⁷But God also arranged for a worm! The next morning at dawn the worm ate through the stem of the plant so that it withered away. ⁸And as the sun grew hot, God arranged for a scorching east wind to blow on Jonah. The sun beat down on his head until he grew faint and wished to die. "Death is certainly better than living like this!" he exclaimed.

⁹Then God said to Jonah, "Is it right for you to be angry because the plant died?"

"Yes," Jonah retorted, "even angry enough to die!"

¹⁰Then the LORD said, "You feel sorry about the plant, though you did nothing to put it there. It came quickly and died quickly. ¹¹But Nineveh has more than 120,000 people living in spiritual darkness,* not to mention all the animals. Shouldn't I feel sorry for such a great city?"

4:11 Hebrew *people who don't know their right hand from their left.*

CHOICES attitudes

Stephanie's favorite TV show is a hot new drama, *Manhattan Nights*. It's really not new—just a shameless rip-off of the afternoon soaps and other nighttime dramas. The only difference is that the show is set in New York, and all the characters work on Wall Street.

Tonight Stephanie is dying to find out if Heather is pregnant with Dade's child. But just as the show gets underway, the local TV station breaks in with a special report about a natural gas explosion in a nearby community.

"At least 12 people are known dead and another 17 are en route to area hospitals," the shaken reporter explains, as fires rage out of control behind him. "Nine others are still missing."

"Great!" Stephanie yells. "Because of this *stupid* fire, I'm gonna miss my show! Why can't they wait until the regular news to report all this junk?"

Stephanie grabs her cell phone and texts her friend Ashley. "Can you *believe* they're doing this?" she types.

Stephanie has a major attitude problem. She's more concerned about some fictional characters on TV than she is about her real-life neighbors. As a child of God, she should know better.

Read about a prophet of God who also had some misplaced priorities: Jonah 3–4. What advice would you have for Stephanie, based on Jonah's experiences?

MICAH

Yesterday, at 2 A.M., our country officially surrendered. Realizing our situation was hopeless, generals from both sides agreed to end the bloodshed, provided we hand over all guns and ammunition. Morale is low. The most perplexing question yet unanswered is, "How could we have been overrun?"

Imagine reading that on the Internet. What a terrible thought! Yet history proves it's possible. That happened to both Israel (the northern ten tribes) and Judah (the southern tribes). They couldn't understand how they could have been defeated. After all, they were God's chosen people.

Although God had been faithful to his people, neither Israel nor Judah had been faithful to God. Micah wrote, "Why is this happening? Because of the rebellion of Israel—yes, the sins of the whole nation" (1:5). Israel and Judah were being judged for their sins. Instead of worshiping the true God, the people worshiped idols they had made. Those who were rich and influential harassed the poor. God was going to punish them all because no one was without guilt.

Micah presents lessons for us to learn. God's standards haven't changed. He also hasn't turned a blind eye to the wrong things people do. One day, he will judge the actions of all people.

As you read Micah, remember that we as individuals and as a nation are responsible before God for the way we live. Are you faithful to him?

KEY POINTS

FAKE FAITH God said that he would judge the false prophets, dishonest leaders, and selfish priests in Israel and Judah. While they publicly carried out religious ceremonies, they privately sought to gain money and influence. God desires the sincere worship of people publicly and privately.

OPPRESSION The upper classes oppressed and exploited the poor. Yet no one spoke out against such behavior. Nowadays, we sometimes ignore those who are needy and oppressed, or silently condone the actions of those who oppress them. Sharing God's love includes meeting the needs of those who are rejected and neglected by society.

PLEASING GOD Micah preached that God delighted in faith that produced fairness, love to others, and obedience to him. You can please God by showing these qualities at home, at school, or in your neighborhood.

MICAH

Served as a prophet to Judah from 742 to 687 B.C.	**CLIMATE OF THE TIMES**	King Ahaz set up heathen idols in the Temple and finally nailed the Temple door shut. Four different nations harassed Judah. When Hezekiah became king, the nation began a slow road to recovery and economic strength. Hezekiah probably heeded much of Micah's advice.
	MAIN MESSAGE	Predicted the fall of both the northern kingdom of Israel and the southern kingdom of Judah. Through his disciplining the people, God was actually showing how much he cared for them. Hezekiah's good reign helped postpone Judah's punishment.
	IMPORTANCE OF MESSAGE	Choosing to live a life apart from God is making a commitment to sin. Sin leads to judgment and death. God alone shows us the way to eternal peace. His discipline often keeps us on the right path.
	CONTEMPORARY PROPHETS	Hosea (753–715) Isaiah (740–681)

1 The LORD gave this message to Micah of Moresheth during the years when Jotham, Ahaz, and Hezekiah were kings of Judah. The visions he saw concerned both Samaria and Jerusalem.

GRIEF OVER SAMARIA AND JERUSALEM

² Attention! Let all the people of the world
    listen!
    Let the earth and everything in it hear.
The Sovereign LORD is making accusations
        against you;
    the Lord speaks from his holy Temple.
³ Look! The LORD is coming!
    He leaves his throne in heaven
    and tramples the heights of the earth.
⁴ The mountains melt beneath his feet
    and flow into the valleys
like wax in a fire,
    like water pouring down a hill.
⁵ And why is this happening?
    Because of the rebellion of Israel*—
    yes, the sins of the whole nation.
Who is to blame for Israel's rebellion?
    Samaria, its capital city!
Where is the center of idolatry in Judah?
    In Jerusalem, its capital!

⁶ "So I, the LORD, will make the city
        of Samaria
    a heap of ruins.
Her streets will be plowed up
    for planting vineyards.

I will roll the stones of her walls into the
        valley below,
    exposing her foundations.
⁷ All her carved images will be smashed.
    All her sacred treasures will be burned.
These things were bought with the money
        earned by her prostitution,
    and they will now be carried away
    to pay prostitutes elsewhere."

⁸ Therefore, I will mourn and lament.
    I will walk around barefoot and naked.
I will howl like a jackal
    and moan like an owl.
⁹ For my people's wound
    is too deep to heal.
It has reached into Judah,
    even to the gates of Jerusalem.

¹⁰ Don't tell our enemies in Gath*;
    don't weep at all.
You people in Beth-leaphrah,*
    roll in the dust to show your despair.
¹¹ You people in Shaphir,*
    go as captives into exile—naked and
        ashamed.
The people of Zaanan*
    dare not come outside their walls.
The people of Beth-ezel* mourn,

1:5 Hebrew *Jacob*; also in 1:5b. The names "Jacob" and "Israel" are often interchanged throughout the Old Testament, referring sometimes to the individual patriarch and sometimes to the nation.   **1:10a** *Gath* sounds like the Hebrew term for "tell."   **1:10b** *Beth-leaphrah* means "house of dust."   **1:11a** *Shaphir* means "pleasant."   **1:11b** *Zaanan* sounds like the Hebrew term for "come out."   **1:11c** *Beth-ezel* means "adjoining house."

for their house has no support.
12 The people of Maroth* anxiously wait
    for relief,
  but only bitterness awaits them
    as the LORD's judgment reaches
    even to the gates of Jerusalem.

13 Harness your chariot horses and flee,
    you people of Lachish.*
  You were the first city in Judah
    to follow Israel in her rebellion,
    and you led Jerusalem* into sin.

14 Send farewell gifts to Moresheth-gath*;
    there is no hope of saving it.
  The town of Aczib*
    has deceived the kings of Israel.

15 O people of Mareshah,*
    I will bring a conqueror to capture
    your town.
  And the leaders* of Israel
    will go to Adullam.

16 Oh, people of Judah, shave your heads
    in sorrow,
  for the children you love will be
    snatched away.
  Make yourselves as bald as a vulture,
    for your little ones will be exiled to
    distant lands.

2 JUDGMENT AGAINST WEALTHY OPPRESSORS

1 What sorrow awaits you who lie awake
    at night,
  thinking up evil plans.
  You rise at dawn and hurry to carry
    them out,
  simply because you have the power
    to do so.
2 When you want a piece of land,
    you find a way to seize it.
  When you want someone's house,
    you take it by fraud and violence.
  You cheat a man of his property,
    stealing his family's inheritance.

3 But this is what the LORD says:
  "I will reward your evil with evil;
    you won't be able to pull your neck
    out of the noose.
  You will no longer walk around proudly,
    for it will be a terrible time."

4 In that day your enemies will make fun
    of you
  by singing this song of despair about you:
  "We are finished,
    completely ruined!
  God has confiscated our land,
    taking it from us.
  He has given our fields
    to those who betrayed us.*"
5 Others will set your boundaries then,
    and the LORD's people will have no say
    in how the land is divided.

TRUE AND FALSE PROPHETS

6 "Don't say such things,"
    the people respond.*
  "Don't prophesy like that.
    Such disasters will never come
    our way!"

7 Should you talk that way, O family
    of Israel?*
  Will the LORD's Spirit have patience with
    such behavior?
  If you would do what is right,
    you would find my words comforting.
8 Yet to this very hour
    my people rise against me like an enemy!
  You steal the shirts right off the backs
    of those who trusted you,
  making them as ragged as men
    returning from battle.
9 You have evicted women from their
    pleasant homes
  and forever stripped their children of all
    that God would give them.
10 Up! Begone!
    This is no longer your land and home,
  for you have filled it with sin
    and ruined it completely.

....

FOLLOW ME?
(1:13) The people of Lachish (a fortress city in Judah)
influenced many to follow their bad example. You probably have heard or know people who do the same thing
today. Everyone has the opportunity to influence others
for good or bad. Regardless of whether or not you
consider yourself a leader, your actions and words are
observed by others more than you suspect. They may
choose to follow your example, whether you know it or
not. So, what kind of example are you setting?

IN YOUR DREAMS
(2:1-2) Micah spoke out against those who planned
evil deeds at night and rose at dawn to carry them out.
People's thoughts reflect their character. Evil thoughts
lead to evil deeds as surely as morning follows night.
What do you think about as you lie down to sleep? Is
Hebrews 10:24—"Let us think of ways to motivate one
another to acts of love and good works"—your motto?

1:12 *Maroth* sounds like the Hebrew term for "bitter."
1:13a *Lachish* sounds like the Hebrew term for "team of horses."
1:13b Hebrew *the daughter of Zion.*   1:14a *Moresheth* sounds like
the Hebrew term for "gift" or "dowry."   1:14b *Aczib* means
"deception."   1:15a *Mareshah* sounds like the Hebrew term for
"conqueror."   1:15b Hebrew *the glory.*   2:4 Or *to those who took
us captive.*   2:6 Or *the prophets respond;* Hebrew reads *they
prophesy.*   2:7 Hebrew *O house of Jacob?* See note on 1:5a.

¹¹ Suppose a prophet full of lies would say
to you,
"I'll preach to you the joys of wine and
alcohol!"
That's just the kind of prophet you
would like!

HOPE FOR RESTORATION

¹² "Someday, O Israel, I will gather you;
I will gather the remnant who are left.
I will bring you together again like sheep
in a pen,
like a flock in its pasture.
Yes, your land will again
be filled with noisy crowds!
¹³ Your leader will break out
and lead you out of exile,
out through the gates of the enemy cities,
back to your own land.
Your king will lead you;
the LORD himself will guide you."

3 JUDGMENT AGAINST ISRAEL'S LEADERS

¹ I said, "Listen, you leaders of Israel!
You are supposed to know right from
wrong,
² but you are the very ones
who hate good and love evil.
You skin my people alive
and tear the flesh from their bones.
³ Yes, you eat my people's flesh,
strip off their skin,
and break their bones.
You chop them up
like meat for the cooking pot.
⁴ Then you beg the LORD for help in times
of trouble!
Do you really expect him to answer?
After all the evil you have done,
he won't even look at you!"

⁵ This is what the LORD says:
"You false prophets are leading my
people astray!
You promise peace for those who give
you food,

but you declare war on those who refuse
to feed you.
⁶ Now the night will close around you,
cutting off all your visions.
Darkness will cover you,
putting an end to your predictions.
The sun will set for you prophets,
and your day will come to an end.
⁷ Then you seers will be put to shame,
and you fortune-tellers will be disgraced.
And you will cover your faces
because there is no answer from God."

⁸ But as for me, I am filled with power—
with the Spirit of the LORD.
I am filled with justice and strength
to boldly declare Israel's sin and
rebellion.
⁹ Listen to me, you leaders of Israel!
You hate justice and twist all that is right.
¹⁰ You are building Jerusalem
on a foundation of murder and
corruption.
¹¹ You rulers make decisions based on bribes;
you priests teach God's laws only for
a price;
you prophets won't prophesy unless you
are paid.
Yet all of you claim to depend on
the LORD.
"No harm can come to us," you say,
"for the LORD is here among us."
¹² Because of you, Mount Zion will be plowed
like an open field;
Jerusalem will be reduced to ruins!
A thicket will grow on the heights
where the Temple now stands.

4 THE LORD'S FUTURE REIGN

¹ In the last days, the mountain of the LORD's
house
will be the highest of all—
the most important place on earth.
It will be raised above the other hills,
and people from all over the world will
stream there to worship.
² People from many nations will come
and say,
"Come, let us go up to the mountain
of the LORD,
to the house of Jacob's God.
There he will teach us his ways,
and we will walk in his paths."
For the LORD's teaching will go out
from Zion;
his word will go out from Jerusalem.

3 The LORD will mediate between peoples
and will settle disputes between strong
nations far away.
They will hammer their swords into
plowshares
and their spears into pruning hooks.
Nation will no longer fight against nation,
nor train for war anymore.
4 Everyone will live in peace and prosperity,
enjoying their own grapevines and
fig trees,
for there will be nothing to fear.
The LORD of Heaven's Armies
has made this promise!
5 Though the nations around us follow
their idols,
we will follow the LORD our God forever
and ever.

ISRAEL'S RETURN FROM EXILE

6 "In that coming day," says the LORD,
"I will gather together those who are lame,
those who have been exiles,
and those whom I have filled with grief.
7 Those who are weak will survive as
a remnant;
those who were exiles will become
a strong nation.
Then I, the LORD, will rule from Jerusalem*
as their king forever."
8 As for you, Jerusalem,
the citadel of God's people,*
your royal might and power
will come back to you again.
The kingship will be restored
to my precious Jerusalem.

9 But why are you now screaming in terror?
Have you no king to lead you?
Have your wise people all died?
Pain has gripped you like a woman in
childbirth.
10 Writhe and groan like a woman in labor,
you people of Jerusalem,*
for now you must leave this city
to live in the open country.
You will soon be sent in exile
to distant Babylon.
But the LORD will rescue you there;
he will redeem you from the grip of your
enemies.
11 Now many nations have gathered
against you.
"Let her be desecrated," they say.

4:7 Hebrew *Mount Zion.* 4:8 Hebrew *As for you, Migdal-eder, / the
Ophel of the daughter of Zion.* 4:10 Hebrew *O daughter of Zion.*
4:11 Hebrew *of Zion.* 4:13 Hebrew *"Rise up and thresh, O daughter
of Zion."*

MY STORY: Krista

*It wasn't easy being a Christian at my high
school. One time, several of the more popular girls were putting down another girl,
Nicole, for being a Christian. I didn't think
it was right to remain silent, so I said, "So
what if she's a Christian? I am, too. Why does
that bother you?"*

*"Because it's weird," one of them said. "I
mean, you don't party; you don't fool around
with guys; you don't drink—you must lead a
pretty boring life." They all laughed.*

*"Why don't you try it yourself and see how
boring it is?" I suggested. They just laughed
and made fun of me.*

*A few days later, when I was walking down
the hall, one of the girls from that group
called out, "What are you gonna do for fun
today, Krista? Gonna pray on your knees for
a couple of hours?" Her friends laughed.
Other people heard and looked at me curi-
ously. I felt like a complete loser.*

*One day, Nicole told me to read Micah 4:6-
13. I did, and it helped me a lot. It reminded
me that even though these kids who rejected
me were considered "cool," they weren't
cool in God's eyes. This passage helped take
away the pain of being rejected, because
I stood up for someone else and for my
beliefs.*

"Let us see the destruction of
Jerusalem.*"
12 But they do not know the LORD's thoughts
or understand his plan.
These nations don't know
that he is gathering them together
to be beaten and trampled
like sheaves of grain on a threshing floor.
13 "Rise up and crush the nations,
O Jerusalem!"*
says the LORD.
"For I will give you iron horns and bronze
hooves,
so you can trample many nations to
pieces.
You will present their stolen riches to
the LORD,
their wealth to the LORD of all the earth."

5

¹*Mobilize! Marshal your troops!
  The enemy is laying siege to Jerusalem.
They will strike Israel's leader
  in the face with a rod.

A RULER FROM BETHLEHEM

²*But you, O Bethlehem Ephrathah,
  are only a small village among all the
  people of Judah.
Yet a ruler of Israel will come from you,
  one whose origins are from the
  distant past.

³ The people of Israel will be abandoned to
  their enemies
  until the woman in labor gives birth.
Then at last his fellow countrymen
  will return from exile to their own land.

⁴ And he will stand to lead his flock with the
  LORD's strength,
  in the majesty of the name of the LORD
  his God.
Then his people will live there undisturbed,
  for he will be highly honored around
  the world.

⁵ And he will be the source of peace.

When the Assyrians invade our land
  and break through our defenses,
we will appoint seven rulers to watch
  over us,
  eight princes to lead us.

⁶ They will rule Assyria with drawn swords
  and enter the gates of the land of Nimrod.
He will rescue us from the Assyrians
  when they pour over the borders to
  invade our land.

THE REMNANT PURIFIED

⁷ Then the remnant left in Israel*
  will take their place among the nations.
They will be like dew sent by the LORD
  or like rain falling on the grass,
which no one can hold back
  and no one can restrain.

⁸ The remnant left in Israel
  will take their place among the nations.

They will be like a lion among the animals
  of the forest,
  like a strong young lion among flocks
  of sheep and goats,
pouncing and tearing as they go
  with no rescuer in sight.

⁹ The people of Israel will stand up to
  their foes,
  and all their enemies will be wiped out.

¹⁰ "In that day," says the LORD,
  "I will slaughter your horses
  and destroy your chariots.

¹¹ I will tear down your walls
  and demolish your defenses.

¹² I will put an end to all witchcraft,
  and there will be no more fortune-tellers.

¹³ I will destroy all your idols and sacred
  pillars,
  so you will never again worship the work
  of your own hands.

¹⁴ I will abolish your idol shrines with their
  Asherah poles
  and destroy your pagan cities.

¹⁵ I will pour out my vengeance
  on all the nations that refuse to
  obey me."

6

THE LORD'S CASE AGAINST ISRAEL Listen
to what the LORD is saying:

"Stand up and state your case against me.
  Let the mountains and hills be called to
  witness your complaints.

² And now, O mountains,
  listen to the LORD's complaint!
He has a case against his people.
  He will bring charges against Israel.

³ "O my people, what have I done to you?
  What have I done to make you tired
  of me?
  Answer me!

⁴ For I brought you out of Egypt
  and redeemed you from slavery.
I sent Moses, Aaron, and Miriam to
  help you.

⁵ Don't you remember, my people,
  how King Balak of Moab tried to have
  you cursed
  and how Balaam son of Beor blessed
  you instead?
And remember your journey from Acacia
  Grove* to Gilgal,
  when I, the LORD, did everything I could
  to teach you about my faithfulness."

BORN IN BETHLEHEM
(5:2) *Micah pinpointed the birthplace of Jesus hundreds
of years before Jesus was born. Yet the promised Savior,
who was to be born through David's family line, already
existed: His "origins are from the distant past." Although
eternal, he entered human history as the man Jesus.
This prophecy and others in the Old Testament (Isa 7:14;
9:6) concerning the Savior show God's control over the
events of human history. They also show his faithfulness.
Knowing that God is faithful to keep his promises, are you
willing to trust him with your life?*

5:1 Verse 5:1 is numbered 4:14 in Hebrew text.   **5:2** Verses 5:2-15
are numbered 5:1-14 in Hebrew text.   **5:7** Hebrew *in Jacob;* also in
5:8. See note on 1:5a.   **6:5** Hebrew *Shittim.*

⁶ What can we bring to the LORD?
    What kind of offerings should we
        give him?
Should we bow before God
    with offerings of yearling calves?
⁷ Should we offer him thousands of rams
    and ten thousand rivers of olive oil?
Should we sacrifice our firstborn children
    to pay for our sins?

⁸ No, O people, the LORD has told you what
        is good,
    and this is what he requires of you:
to do what is right, to love mercy,
    and to walk humbly with your God.

ISRAEL'S GUILT AND PUNISHMENT

⁹ Fear the LORD if you are wise!
    His voice calls to everyone in Jerusalem:
    "The armies of destruction are coming;
        the LORD is sending them.*
¹⁰ What shall I say about the homes of the
        wicked
    filled with treasures gained by cheating?
What about the disgusting practice
    of measuring out grain with dishonest
        measures?*
¹¹ How can I tolerate your merchants
    who use dishonest scales and weights?
¹² The rich among you have become wealthy
    through extortion and violence.
Your citizens are so used to lying
    that their tongues can no longer tell
        the truth.
¹³ "Therefore, I will wound you!
    I will bring you to ruin for all your sins.
¹⁴ You will eat but never have enough.

6:9 Hebrew "Listen to the rod. / Who appointed it?"   6:10 Hebrew
of using the short ephah? The ephah was a unit for measuring grain.

Your hunger pangs and emptiness
    will remain.
And though you try to save your money,
    it will come to nothing in the end.
You will save a little,
    but I will give it to those who
        conquer you.
¹⁵ You will plant crops
    but not harvest them.
You will press your olives
    but not get enough oil to anoint
        yourselves.
You will trample the grapes
    but get no juice to make your wine.
¹⁶ You keep only the laws of evil King Omri;
    you follow only the example of wicked
        King Ahab!
Therefore, I will make an example of you,
    bringing you to complete ruin.
You will be treated with contempt,
    mocked by all who see you."

7 MISERY TURNED TO HOPE

¹ How miserable I am!
    I feel like the fruit picker after the harvest
        who can find nothing to eat.

EVERYBODY'S DOING IT?
*(7:1-4) Micah couldn't find a godly or fair-minded person
anywhere in the land. Ever share that feeling of despair?
When wrong actions are rationalized and we see Christians compromising, we can understand Micah's feelings.
Sadly, too often we convince ourselves that wrong actions
are okay, especially when "everyone else is doing it." But
our standards for behavior come from God, not society.
Are his standards yours?*

CHOICES honesty

Terrance needs some new basketball shoes. He's
got the perfect pair all picked out—an air-cushioned,
super-grip, lightweight model with reinforced ankle
supports—the exact shoe that all the best dunkers
in the NBA wear. The problem is that the shoes cost
about $200.

A few other guys in the neighborhood already
have the shoes. One guy who deals drugs has three
pairs. Another kid stole a pair from a locker at school.
A third guy shoplifted his pair. Terrance really wants
these new basketball shoes, but he would never
do something illegal or dishonest to get them . . . or
would he?

This afternoon, a guy from the neighborhood, who

is the assistant manager of a downtown shoe store,
came up with a foolproof plan. By marking certain
shoes defective, he can cut the price and then cover
it all up by juggling some figures.

"It's cool," a friend tells Terrance. "The store makes
money, you get your shoes cheap, and you're not
stealing."

Terrance thinks long and hard, then decides that
the plan is wrong. "It's hard to walk away from such
a good deal," Terrance says, "but those shoes aren't
worth doing something dishonest."

Meanwhile, all his friends are taking advantage
of the store's "defective" merchandise.

*Read Micah 7:1-4. Do you think Terrance might be feeling the way the prophet
Micah felt? How would you have handled this situation?*

ALL THE NATIONS OF THE WORLD WILL STAND AMAZED AT WHAT THE LORD WILL DO FOR YOU. { MICAH 7:16 }

Not a cluster of grapes or a single early fig
can be found to satisfy my hunger.
² The godly people have all disappeared;
not one honest person is left on the earth.
They are all murderers,
setting traps even for their own brothers.
³ Both their hands are equally skilled at
doing evil!
Officials and judges alike demand bribes.
The people with influence get what
they want,
and together they scheme to twist justice.
⁴ Even the best of them is like a brier;
the most honest is as dangerous as
a hedge of thorns.
But your judgment day is coming
swiftly now.
Your time of punishment is here, a time
of confusion.
⁵ Don't trust anyone—
not your best friend or even your wife!
⁶ For the son despises his father.
The daughter defies her mother.
The daughter-in-law defies her
mother-in-law.
Your enemies are right in your own
household!

⁷ As for me, I look to the LORD for help.
I wait confidently for God to save me,
and my God will certainly hear me.
⁸ Do not gloat over me, my enemies!
For though I fall, I will rise again.
Though I sit in darkness,
the LORD will be my light.
⁹ I will be patient as the LORD punishes me,
for I have sinned against him.
But after that, he will take up my case
and give me justice for all I have suffered
from my enemies.
The LORD will bring me into the light,
and I will see his righteousness.
¹⁰ Then my enemies will see that the LORD
is on my side.

They will be ashamed that they taunted
me, saying,
"So where is the LORD—
that God of yours?"
With my own eyes I will see their downfall;
they will be trampled like mud in the
streets.

¹¹ In that day, Israel, your cities will
be rebuilt,
and your borders will be extended.
¹² People from many lands will come and
honor you—
from Assyria all the way to the towns
of Egypt,
from Egypt all the way to the
Euphrates River,*
and from distant seas and mountains.
¹³ But the land* will become empty and
desolate
because of the wickedness of those who
live there.

THE LORD'S COMPASSION ON ISRAEL
¹⁴ O LORD, protect your people with your
shepherd's staff;
lead your flock, your special
possession.
Though they live alone in a thicket
on the heights of Mount Carmel,*
let them graze in the fertile pastures
of Bashan and Gilead
as they did long ago.

¹⁵ "Yes," says the LORD,
"I will do mighty miracles for you,
like those I did when I rescued you
from slavery in Egypt."

¹⁶ All the nations of the world will stand
amazed
at what the LORD will do for you.
They will be embarrassed
at their feeble power.
They will cover their mouths in
silent awe,
deaf to everything around them.
¹⁷ Like snakes crawling from their holes,
they will come out to meet the LORD
our God.
They will fear him greatly,
trembling in terror at his presence.

MERCY
*(7:18-20) The book of Micah ends with a message of
mercy. God delights in showing mercy. He doesn't forgive
grudgingly; he's truly glad when we admit that we need
his help to change. He offers forgiveness to all who come
back to him. Is that the kind of mercy you offer to those
who wrong you?*

7:12 Hebrew *the river.*   7:13 Or *earth.*   7:14 Or *surrounded by
a fruitful land.*

¹⁸ Where is another God like you,
    who pardons the guilt of the remnant,
    overlooking the sins of his
      special people?
  You will not stay angry with your people
    forever,
    because you delight in showing
      unfailing love.

¹⁹ Once again you will have compassion on us.
    You will trample our sins under your feet
    and throw them into the depths of
      the ocean!
²⁰ You will show us your faithfulness and
    unfailing love
    as you promised to our ancestors
      Abraham and Jacob long ago.

NAHUM

Oh no, thought Cullen, *we're gonna lose again. The Enforcer is on their side.* "The Enforcer" was Jamie, the best athlete in the school. Whichever team got the Enforcer always won.

Cullen usually rejoiced when his phys. ed. class played football—except when the Enforcer was on the other team. Cullen was good, but the Enforcer was great. He could outrun, outthrow, outcatch, outeverything *anyone.*

Nineveh, the Assyrian capital, was like the Enforcer. Not one nation had been able to stand against the Assyrians. The Assyrians had overthrown Israel (the northern kingdom of the divided nation); now their sights were on Judah. The people of Judah were afraid. How could they withstand such a terrible enemy?

Through Nahum, God brought words of comfort to Judah and words of doom to Assyria. Nahum said, "The Lord is a jealous God. . . . He takes revenge on all who oppose him and continues to rage against his enemies!" (1:2). God told Judah, "Now I will break the yoke of bondage from your neck and tear off the chains of Assyrian oppression" (1:13). But God told Assyria, "I am your enemy! . . . Your chariots will soon go up in smoke. Your young men will be killed in battle. Never again will you plunder conquered nations. The voices of your proud messengers will be heard no more" (2:13).

Such is the end of those who oppose the Lord and hurt his people. God loves his children and will protect them, at all costs. As you read Nahum, may this promise encourage you.

STATS

PURPOSE
To pronounce God's judgment on Assyria and to comfort Judah with this truth

AUTHOR
Nahum

ORIGINAL AUDIENCE
The people of Nineveh and Judah

DATE WRITTEN
Sometime during Nahum's prophetic ministry (probably between 663 and 612 B.C.)

SETTING
This particular prophecy takes place after the fall of Thebes in 663 B.C. (see 3:8-10).

KEY PLACE
Nineveh, the capital of Assyria

KEY POINTS

INVINCIBLE Although Assyria was the leading military power in the world, God would completely destroy this "invincible" nation. Only God is truly invincible. He has supreme power.

GOD RULES God rules over all the earth, even over those who don't acknowledge him. God is all-powerful—no one can thwart his plans. If you're impressed by or afraid of any weapons, armies, or powerful people, remember that God alone can truly rescue you from fear or oppression.

1
This message concerning Nineveh came as a vision to Nahum, who lived in Elkosh.

THE LORD'S ANGER AGAINST NINEVEH

² The LORD is a jealous God,
  filled with vengeance and rage.
He takes revenge on all who oppose him
  and continues to rage against his
    enemies!
³ The LORD is slow to get angry, but his power
    is great,
  and he never lets the guilty go unpunished.
He displays his power in the whirlwind and
    the storm.
  The billowing clouds are the dust beneath
    his feet.
⁴ At his command the oceans dry up,
  and the rivers disappear.
The lush pastures of Bashan and
    Carmel fade,
  and the green forests of Lebanon wither.
⁵ In his presence the mountains quake,
  and the hills melt away;
the earth trembles,
  and its people are destroyed.

⁶ Who can stand before his fierce anger?
  Who can survive his burning fury?
His rage blazes forth like fire,
  and the mountains crumble to dust in
    his presence.
⁷ The LORD is good,
  a strong refuge when trouble comes.
  He is close to those who trust in him.
⁸ But he will sweep away his enemies
  in an overwhelming flood.
He will pursue his foes
  into the darkness of night.
⁹ Why are you scheming against the LORD?
  He will destroy you with one blow;
  he won't need to strike twice!
¹⁰ His enemies, tangled like thornbushes
  and staggering like drunks,
    will be burned up like dry stubble in
    a field.
¹¹ Who is this wicked counselor of yours
  who plots evil against the LORD?

¹² This is what the LORD says:
"Though the Assyrians have many allies,
  they will be destroyed and disappear.
O my people, I have punished you before,
  but I will not punish you again.
¹³ Now I will break the yoke of bondage from
    your neck
  and tear off the chains of Assyrian
    oppression."

¹⁴ And this is what the LORD says concerning
    the Assyrians in Nineveh:
"You will have no more children to carry on
    your name.
  I will destroy all the idols in the temples
    of your gods.
I am preparing a grave for you
  because you are despicable!"

TIME'S UP

(1:1-8) Although God is slow to get angry, when he's ready to punish, even the earth trembles. Often people become angry with God because they think he is powerless over the evil in the world and hypocrites in the church. They don't realize that because God is slow to anger, he gives people the opportunity to seek his forgiveness. But judgment will come. God won't allow evil to go unchecked and unpunished forever. When people wonder why God doesn't punish evil immediately, you can remind them that if he did, none of us would be here. Thankfully, God gives people time to turn to him. But one day, God will call a time-out on evil.

CHOICES
vengeance

Rich is one angry guy—and rightly so. Before football practice yesterday, he confided in teammates Tony and Paul about his secret attraction to Danielle and how he wished he could get up the nerve to ask her to the winter formal.

Not only did Rich's confidants take that information, twist it, and spread embarrassing rumors all over the locker room, but Tony went home last night and called Danielle himself and asked her to the dance!

All day Rich has wanted to punch Tony out, or at the very least, knock his head off in practice that afternoon. He has been daydreaming of ways to get even. Mixed in with his rage is also a measure of hurt. *I thought those guys were my friends,* he tells himself over and over.

But at practice, Rich doesn't react at all. He doesn't yell or throw punches. He even passes up several prime opportunities to hit Tony and Paul with cheap shots and blindsides.

"Just because they were jerks doesn't mean I have to be one, too," he tells a surprised friend later.

When people wrong us, a natural response is to want to take revenge. But, like Rich, we can resist that powerful urge to get even!

Yet there is one who claims the right to take revenge. Check out Nahum 1:2-8. While you're at it, read Leviticus 19:18 and Deuteronomy 32:35. Why do you think revenge is off-limits for us but not for God?

¹⁵*Look! A messenger is coming over the
    mountains with good news!
  He is bringing a message of peace.
Celebrate your festivals, O people of Judah,
    and fulfill all your vows,
for your wicked enemies will never invade
    your land again.
  They will be completely destroyed!

2 THE FALL OF NINEVEH

¹*Your enemy is coming to crush you,
    Nineveh.
  Man the ramparts! Watch the roads!
  Prepare your defenses! Call out your
    forces!

² Even though the destroyer has destroyed
    Judah,
  the Lord will restore its honor.
Israel's vine has been stripped of branches,
  but he will restore its splendor.

³ Shields flash red in the sunlight!
  See the scarlet uniforms of the valiant
    troops!
Watch as their glittering chariots move into
    position,
  with a forest of spears waving above
    them.*

⁴ The chariots race recklessly along the streets
    and rush wildly through the squares.
They flash like firelight
  and move as swiftly as lightning.

⁵ The king shouts to his officers;
  they stumble in their haste,
  rushing to the walls to set up their
    defenses.

⁶ The river gates have been torn open!
  The palace is about to collapse!

⁷ Nineveh's exile has been decreed,
  and all the servant girls mourn its capture.
They moan like doves
  and beat their breasts in sorrow.

⁸ Nineveh is like a leaking water reservoir!
  The people are slipping away.
"Stop, stop!" someone shouts,
  but no one even looks back.

⁹ Loot the silver!
  Plunder the gold!
There's no end to Nineveh's treasures—
  its vast, uncounted wealth.

¹⁰ Soon the city is plundered, empty, and
    ruined.
  Hearts melt and knees shake.

1:15 Verse 1:15 is numbered 2:1 in Hebrew text.   2:1 Verses 2:1-13
are numbered 2:2-14 in Hebrew text.   2:3 Greek and Syriac
versions read *into position, / the horses whipped into a frenzy.*
2:13 Hebrew *young lions.*

The people stand aghast,
  their faces pale and trembling.

¹¹ Where now is that great Nineveh,
  that den filled with young lions?
It was a place where people—like lions
    and their cubs—
  walked freely and without fear.

¹² The lion tore up meat for his cubs
  and strangled prey for his mate.
He filled his den with prey,
  his caverns with his plunder.

¹³ "I am your enemy!"
  says the Lord of Heaven's Armies.
"Your chariots will soon go up in smoke.
  Your young men* will be killed in battle.
Never again will you plunder conquered
    nations.
  The voices of your proud messengers
    will be heard no more."

3 THE LORD'S JUDGMENT AGAINST NINEVEH

¹ What sorrow awaits Nineveh,
  the city of murder and lies!
She is crammed with wealth
  and is never without victims.

² Hear the crack of whips,
  the rumble of wheels!
Horses' hooves pound,
  and chariots clatter wildly.

³ See the flashing swords and glittering
    spears
  as the charioteers charge past!
There are countless casualties,
  heaps of bodies—
so many bodies that
  people stumble over them.

⁴ All this because Nineveh,
  the beautiful and faithless city,
mistress of deadly charms,
  enticed the nations with her beauty.
She taught them all her magic,
  enchanting people everywhere.

⁵ "I am your enemy!"
  says the Lord of Heaven's Armies.

....

TAKE A STAND
*(2:1–3:1) The major source of the Assyrians' wealth was
what they stole from other nations. The Assyrians took the
food of people they conquered to maintain their own luxurious standard of living. They deprived others to supply
their excesses. Does that sound familiar? Depriving poor
people to support the luxury of a few is a sin that angers
God. Are you ever tempted to take from someone so that
you can benefit or have more? God wants his people to
take a stand against this common but evil practice. What
are you willing to do in this fight for justice?*

NAHUM

	CLIMATE OF THE TIMES	

Served as a prophet to
Judah and Assyria from
663 to 654 B.C.

CLIMATE OF THE TIMES — Manasseh, one of Judah's most wicked kings, ruled the land. He openly defied God and persecuted God's people. Assyria, the world power at that time, made Judah one of its vassal states. The people of Judah wanted to be like the Assyrians, who seemed to have all the power and possessions they wanted.

MAIN MESSAGE — The mighty empire of Assyria, the oppressors of God's people, would tumble soon.

IMPORTANCE OF MESSAGE — Those who do evil and oppress others will one day meet a bitter end.

CONTEMPORARY PROPHET — Zephaniah (640–621)

"And now I will lift your skirts
    and show all the earth your nakedness
        and shame.
⁶ I will cover you with filth
    and show the world how vile you
        really are.
⁷ All who see you will shrink back and say,
        'Nineveh lies in ruins.
Where are the mourners?'
    Does anyone regret your destruction?"

⁸ Are you any better than the city of Thebes,*
    situated on the Nile River, surrounded
        by water?
She was protected by the river on all sides,
    walled in by water.
⁹ Ethiopia* and the land of Egypt
    gave unlimited assistance.
The nations of Put and Libya
    were among her allies.
¹⁰ Yet Thebes fell,
    and her people were led away as captives.
Her babies were dashed to death
    against the stones of the streets.
Soldiers threw dice* to get Egyptian officers
    as servants.
All their leaders were bound in chains.

¹¹ And you, Nineveh, will also stagger like
        a drunkard.
    You will hide for fear of the attacking
        enemy.
¹² All your fortresses will fall.
    They will be devoured like the ripe figs
        that fall into the mouths
    of those who shake the trees.
¹³ Your troops will be as weak
    and helpless as women.
The gates of your land will be opened wide
    to the enemy

and set on fire and burned.
¹⁴ Get ready for the siege!
    Store up water!
    Strengthen the defenses!
Go into the pits to trample clay,
    and pack it into molds,
    making bricks to repair the walls.

¹⁵ But the fire will devour you;
    the sword will cut you down.
The enemy will consume you like locusts,
    devouring everything they see.
There will be no escape,
    even if you multiply like swarming locusts.
¹⁶ Your merchants have multiplied
    until they outnumber the stars.
But like a swarm of locusts,
    they strip the land and fly away.
¹⁷ Your guards* and officials are also like
        swarming locusts
    that crowd together in the hedges on
        a cold day.
But like locusts that fly away when the sun
        comes up,
    all of them will fly away and disappear.

¹⁸ Your shepherds are asleep, O Assyrian king;
    your princes lie dead in the dust.
Your people are scattered across the
        mountains
    with no one to gather them together.
¹⁹ There is no healing for your wound;
    your injury is fatal.
All who hear of your destruction
    will clap their hands for joy.
Where can anyone be found
    who has not suffered from your continual
        cruelty?

3:8 Hebrew *No-amon;* also in 3:10.   **3:9** Hebrew *Cush.*
3:10 Hebrew *They cast lots.*   **3:17** Or *princes.*

HABAKKUK

Emma sat in Sunday school that week, hoping to get some questions answered. Each week the class had discussed questions that seemed to have no easy answers: If God is so good, why is there suffering in the world? If God controls everything, how can we truly have free will?

But Emma had her own question to ask. Finally, as the room settled down, Emma awkwardly raised her hand. She began, "Why does it seem like those who are trying to live the way Jesus would want them to are so often abused by those who don't care how they live? Doesn't God care? It doesn't seem fair!"

Many centuries ago, Habakkuk had similar thoughts. He looked over his own country, Judah, and saw wherever he looked "destruction and violence. . . . The wicked far outnumber the righteous" (1:3-4). He questioned God's concern for the people who really tried to please God. Those who did evil always seemed to get the upper hand.

God answered Habakkuk enough to satisfy his concerns. Habakkuk was inspired to reply, "I have heard all about you, LORD. I am filled with awe by your amazing works. In this time of our deep need, help us again as you did in years gone by. And in your anger, remember your mercy" (3:2).

As you read this book, take note of God's answer. It may surprise you. And then, like Habakkuk, you can resolve to trust God to care for you.

STATS

PURPOSE
To show that God is still in control of the world despite the apparent triumph of evil

AUTHOR
Habakkuk

ORIGINAL AUDIENCE
Judah (the southern kingdom)

DATE WRITTEN
Between 612 and 588 B.C.

SETTING
Babylon was becoming the dominant world power. Judah would soon feel Babylon's destructive force.

KEY PEOPLE
Habakkuk, the Chaldeans (Babylonians)

KEY PLACE
Judah

KEY POINTS

STRUGGLE AND DOUBT When Habakkuk cried out for answers in his time of struggle, God answered him with words of hope. God wants us to come to him with our struggles and doubts.

GOD'S SOVEREIGNTY God planned to use the Babylonians to punish his people. He would also punish the Babylonians after they had fulfilled his purpose. God is still in control of this world, despite the apparent triumph of evil. One day he will rule the whole earth with perfect justice.

HOPE Habakkuk ended his book on a note of hope as he praised God for strengthening him. We also can have confidence that God loves us and provides strength when we're weak.

1

This is the message that the prophet Habakkuk received in a vision.

HABAKKUK'S COMPLAINT

² How long, O Lord, must I call for help?
But you do not listen!
"Violence is everywhere!" I cry,
but you do not come to save.
³ Must I forever see these evil deeds?
Why must I watch all this misery?
Wherever I look,
I see destruction and violence.
I am surrounded by people
who love to argue and fight.
⁴ The law has become paralyzed,
and there is no justice in the courts.
The wicked far outnumber the righteous,
so that justice has become perverted.

THE LORD'S REPLY ⁵The Lord replied,

"Look around at the nations;
look and be amazed!*
For I am doing something in your own day,
something you wouldn't believe
even if someone told you about it.
⁶ I am raising up the Babylonians,*
a cruel and violent people.
They will march across the world
and conquer other lands.
⁷ They are notorious for their cruelty
and do whatever they like.
⁸ Their horses are swifter than cheetahs*
and fiercer than wolves at dusk.
Their charioteers charge from far away.
Like eagles, they swoop down to devour
their prey.

⁹ "On they come, all bent on violence.
Their hordes advance like a desert wind,
sweeping captives ahead of them
like sand.
¹⁰ They scoff at kings and princes
and scorn all their fortresses.
They simply pile ramps of earth
against their walls and capture them!
¹¹ They sweep past like the wind
and are gone.
But they are deeply guilty,
for their own strength is their god."

HABAKKUK'S SECOND COMPLAINT

¹² O Lord my God, my Holy One, you who
are eternal—
surely you do not plan to wipe us out?
O Lord, our Rock, you have sent these
Babylonians to correct us,
to punish us for our many sins.
¹³ But you are pure and cannot stand the sight
of evil.
Will you wink at their treachery?
Should you be silent while the wicked
swallow up people more righteous
than they?

¹⁴ Are we only fish to be caught and killed?
Are we only sea creatures that have no
leader?
¹⁵ Must we be strung up on their hooks
and caught in their nets while they rejoice
and celebrate?
¹⁶ Then they will worship their nets
and burn incense in front of them.
"These nets are the gods who have made
us rich!"
they will claim.
¹⁷ Will you let them get away with this
forever?
Will they succeed forever in their
heartless conquests?

2

¹ I will climb up to my watchtower
and stand at my guardpost.
There I will wait to see what the Lord says
and how he* will answer my complaint.

THE LORD'S SECOND REPLY ²Then the Lord said to me,

"Write my answer plainly on tablets,
so that a runner can carry the correct
message to others.
³ This vision is for a future time.
It describes the end, and it will be
fulfilled.

....

FORGOTTEN
(1:2-4) When circumstances become almost unbearable, we may wonder if God has forgotten us. We must remember that he is in control. God has a plan and will judge evildoers in his time. If we are truly humble, and willing to accept God's answers and timing.

WAIT FOR IT
(1:1–2:3) Often evil seems to have the upper hand in the world. Habakkuk complained vigorously to God about the evil he noticed. Like Habakkuk, Christians often feel angry and discouraged as they observe the injustices that take place. Can you relate? God's answer to his prophet is the same answer he would give us: "If it [the unfolding of God's plans] seems slow in coming, wait patiently, for it will surely take place" (2:3). Being patient isn't easy, but it helps to remember that God hates sin even more than we do. Trusting God fully means trusting him even when we don't understand why events occur as they do.

1:5 Greek version reads *Look, you mockers; / look and be amazed and die.* Compare Acts 13:41.   1:6 Or *Chaldeans.*   1:8 Or *leopards.*
2:1 As in Syriac version; Hebrew reads *I.*

If it seems slow in coming, wait patiently,
for it will surely take place.
It will not be delayed.

4 "Look at the proud!
They trust in themselves, and their lives
are crooked.
But the righteous will live by their
faithfulness to God.*

5 Wealth* is treacherous,
and the arrogant are never at rest.
They open their mouths as wide as the
grave,*
and like death, they are never satisfied.
In their greed they have gathered up many
nations
and swallowed many peoples.

6 "But soon their captives will taunt them.
They will mock them, saying,
'What sorrow awaits you thieves!
Now you will get what you deserve!
You've become rich by extortion,
but how much longer can this go on?'

7 Suddenly, your debtors will take action.
They will turn on you and take all
you have,
while you stand trembling
and helpless.

8 Because you have plundered
many nations,
now all the survivors will plunder you.
You committed murder throughout the
countryside
and filled the towns with violence.

9 "What sorrow awaits you who build big
houses
with money gained dishonestly!
You believe your wealth will buy security,
putting your family's nest beyond the
reach of danger.

10 But by the murders you committed,
you have shamed your name and
forfeited your lives.

11 The very stones in the walls cry out
against you,
and the beams in the ceilings echo the
complaint.

12 "What sorrow awaits you who
build cities
with money gained through murder
and corruption!

FOR AS THE WATERS FILL THE SEA, THE EARTH WILL BE FILLED WITH AN AWARENESS OF THE GLORY OF THE LORD. (HABAKKUK 2:14)

13 Has not the LORD of Heaven's Armies
promised
that the wealth of nations will turn
to ashes?
They work so hard,
but all in vain!

14 For as the waters fill the sea,
the earth will be filled with
an awareness
of the glory of the LORD.

15 "What sorrow awaits you who make your
neighbors drunk!
You force your cup on them
so you can gloat over their shameful
nakedness.

16 But soon it will be your turn to be disgraced.
Come, drink and be exposed!*
Drink from the cup of the LORD's judgment,
and all your glory will be turned to shame.

17 You cut down the forests of Lebanon.
Now you will be cut down.
You destroyed the wild animals,
so now their terror will be yours.
You committed murder throughout the
countryside
and filled the towns with violence.

18 "What good is an idol carved by man,
or a cast image that deceives you?
How foolish to trust in your own creation—
a god that can't even talk!

19 What sorrow awaits you who say to
wooden idols,
'Wake up and save us!'
To speechless stone images you say,
'Rise up and teach us!'
Can an idol tell you what to do?
They may be overlaid with gold and silver,
but they are lifeless inside.

20 But the LORD is in his holy Temple.
Let all the earth be silent before him."

···

2:3b-4 Greek version reads *If the vision is delayed, wait patiently, /
for it will surely come and not delay. / ⁴I will take no pleasure in
anyone who turns away. / But the righteous person will live by
my faith.* Compare Rom 1:17; Gal 3:11; Heb 10:37-38. 2:5a As in
Dead Sea Scroll 1QpHab; other Hebrew manuscripts read *Wine.*
2:5b Hebrew *as Sheol.* 2:16 Dead Sea Scrolls and Greek and
Syriac versions read *and stagger!*

LIVE BY FAITH
(2:4) The just (righteous) live by their faith and trust in
God. This verse has inspired countless Christians. Paul
refers to it in Romans 1:17 and quotes it in Galatians 3:11.
The writer of Hebrews quotes it in 10:38, just before the
famous chapter on faith. And it is helpful to all Christians
who live through difficult times. Those who live by faith
believe that God directs all things according to his purposes. Is that your belief?

HABAKKUK

Served as a prophet to Judah from 612 to 588 B.C.	**CLIMATE OF THE TIMES**	Judah's last four kings were wicked men who rejected God and oppressed their own people. Babylon invaded Judah twice before finally destroying it in 586. It was a time of fear, oppression, persecution, lawlessness, and immorality.
	MAIN MESSAGE	Habakkuk couldn't understand why God seemed to do nothing about the wickedness in society. Then he realized that faith in God alone would supply the answers to his questions.
	IMPORTANCE OF MESSAGE	Instead of questioning the ways of God, we should realize that he is totally just, and we should have faith that he is in control and that one day evil will be utterly destroyed.
	CONTEMPORARY PROPHETS	Jeremiah (627–586) Daniel (605–536) Ezekiel (593–571)

3 **HABAKKUK'S PRAYER** This prayer was sung by the prophet Habakkuk*:

² I have heard all about you, LORD.
 I am filled with awe by your amazing
 works.
In this time of our deep need,
 help us again as you did in years gone by.
And in your anger,
 remember your mercy.

³ I see God moving across the deserts from
 Edom,*
 the Holy One coming from Mount Paran.*
His brilliant splendor fills the heavens,
 and the earth is filled with his praise.

⁴ His coming is as brilliant as the sunrise.
 Rays of light flash from his hands,
 where his awesome power is hidden.
⁵ Pestilence marches before him;
 plague follows close behind.
⁶ When he stops, the earth shakes.
 When he looks, the nations tremble.
He shatters the everlasting mountains
 and levels the eternal hills.
 He is the Eternal One!
⁷ I see the people of Cushan in distress,
 and the nation of Midian trembling
 in terror.

3:1 Hebrew adds *according to shigionoth,* probably indicating the musical setting for the prayer.   **3:3a** Hebrew *Teman.*   **3:3b** Hebrew adds *selah*; also in 3:9, 13. The meaning of this Hebrew term is uncertain; it is probably a musical or literary term.

CHOICES
hard times

When people drive past the Hunter house, they almost always shake their heads and say, "I just don't understand why one family has had to undergo so much grief."

 "I know. They've had one crisis after another."
 "How do Sheila and her mom keep going? I don't know what I'd do if I were either one of them."
 Exaggerations? Not at all.

• Shane, the youngest son, committed suicide two years ago.
• Mr. Hunter had hepatitis, strokes, and serious back problems. Then he suddenly died last spring.
• The family has faced serious financial problems.

• Shannon, the 18-year-old daughter, has been rebellious and promiscuous. She just moved in with an older, married man.

 How *do* Sheila, the youngest daughter, and her mom keep going? Well, Sheila relies on her faith in God—a faith her mom has. Both cling to the promise that somehow, some way, God is in control. And in the dark and lonely nights of their ordeal, they hope that God will one day restore their shattered family.

 Habakkuk tackles the tough issue of "Where is God when my world is falling apart?" The situation facing the ancient Hebrew prophet was very different from the problems above—and probably from yours—but the words of 3:17-19 give hope to all who hurt.

⁸ Was it in anger, LORD, that you struck
      the rivers
   and parted the sea?
Were you displeased with them?
   No, you were sending your chariots of
      salvation!
⁹ You brandished your bow
   and your quiver of arrows.
   You split open the earth with flowing
      rivers.
¹⁰ The mountains watched and trembled.
   Onward swept the raging waters.
The mighty deep cried out,
   lifting its hands to the LORD.
¹¹ The sun and moon stood still in the sky
   as your brilliant arrows flew
   and your glittering spear flashed.

¹² You marched across the land in anger
   and trampled the nations in your fury.
¹³ You went out to rescue your chosen people,
   to save your anointed ones.
You crushed the heads of the wicked
   and stripped their bones from head
      to toe.
¹⁴ With his own weapons,
   you destroyed the chief of those
who rushed out like a whirlwind,
   thinking Israel would be easy prey.
¹⁵ You trampled the sea with your horses,
   and the mighty waters piled high.

¹⁶ I trembled inside when I heard this;
   my lips quivered with fear.

3:16 Hebrew *Decay entered my bones.*   **3:19** Or *He gives me the speed of a deer.*

My legs gave way beneath me,*
   and I shook in terror.
I will wait quietly for the coming day
   when disaster will strike the people who
      invade us.
¹⁷ Even though the fig trees have no blossoms,
   and there are no grapes on the vines;
even though the olive crop fails,
   and the fields lie empty and barren;
even though the flocks die in the fields,
   and the cattle barns are empty,
¹⁸ yet I will rejoice in the LORD!
   I will be joyful in the God of my salvation!
¹⁹ The Sovereign LORD is my strength!
   He makes me as surefooted as a deer,*
   able to tread upon the heights.

(For the choir director: This prayer is to be accompanied by stringed instruments.)

••

AMAZING STRENGTH
(3:17-19) Crop failure and the death of animals would
devastate Judah. But Habakkuk affirmed that even in
the midst of starvation, he would still rejoice in the
Lord. Habakkuk's feelings were not controlled by the
events around him, but by faith in God's ability to give
him strength. When nothing seems to make sense, and
when troubles seem more than you can handle, what do
you usually focus on—your difficulties or his deity? Like
Habakkuk, will you choose to rely on God?

CONFIDENCE
(3:19) Habakkuk had asked God why evil people prosper
while the righteous suffer. God's answer: In the long run,
they don't. Habakkuk saw his own limitations in contrast
to God's unlimited control of the world's events. God
still maintains that control. We cannot see all that God is
doing or will do. But we can be assured that he is God and
will do what is right. Do you believe that?

ZEPHANIAH

It was the day for grades to be handed out and parent-teacher meetings—probably the most dreaded day on the school calendar. No classes were held, but appointments were set between student, parents, homeroom teacher, and the most recent grade slips. What a deadly mix!

Most students hated the idea of such a grand gathering, especially those who were not doing well in school. It was one thing to get bad grades but quite another to sit in a room with three adults and talk about those grades. Parents were known to scream or cry or both. One never knew. At times, the teachers would get emotional, too. Even students who were doing well in school sometimes were reprimanded—they could be doing better. Not many students slept too well the night before meeting day.

When the school paper wrote about this day (affectionately termed "Death Day"), the reactions were varied. However, most of the student body agreed with one student who was quoted as saying, "I don't think Judgment Day could be any worse!"

Well, that student was wrong. Judgment Day will be much worse! God's prophet Zephaniah tells us about it in his book. Like "Death Day," it will be a day of reckoning—a time of terrible wrath and punishment. But it will also be a time of mercy.

As you read Zephaniah, perhaps you'll confront any fears you have about Judgment Day. If you're a believer, this is one day you won't have to fear. Isn't that comforting?

STATS

PURPOSE
To shake the people of Judah out of their complacency and urge them to return to God

AUTHOR
Zephaniah

ORIGINAL AUDIENCE
Judah and all nations

DATE WRITTEN
Probably near the end of Zephaniah's ministry (640–621 B.C.), when King Josiah's great reforms began

SETTING
King Josiah of Judah attempted to reverse the evil course set by the two previous kings—Manasseh and Amon (see 2 Kgs 21–23). Zephaniah's prophecy may have been the motivating factor in Josiah's reform. Zephaniah was a contemporary of Jeremiah.

KEY PLACE
Jerusalem

KEY POINTS

DAY OF JUDGMENT Destruction was coming because the people of Judah worshiped idols instead of God. God's warning was a strong hint for them to return to him. Likewise, God warns of a coming worldwide time of judgment. Those who trust in Jesus will not have to fear this judgment.

INDIFFERENCE TO GOD God's demands for righteous living seemed irrelevant to the people of Judah, whose security and wealth made them complacent. Complacency is a trap we can avoid by admitting our dependence on God, rather than on our resources.

DAY OF JOY The day of judgment will also be a day of joy. God will restore his people and give them hope. God promises to restore us whenever we confess our wrongs and seek his forgiveness.

1

The LORD gave this message to Zephaniah when Josiah son of Amon was king of Judah. Zephaniah was the son of Cushi, son of Gedaliah, son of Amariah, son of Hezekiah.

COMING JUDGMENT AGAINST JUDAH

² "I will sweep away everything
   from the face of the earth," says the LORD.
³ "I will sweep away people and animals
      alike.
   I will sweep away the birds of the sky and
      the fish in the sea.
   I will reduce the wicked to heaps of rubble,*
      and I will wipe humanity from the face of
      the earth," says the LORD.
⁴ "I will crush Judah and Jerusalem with
      my fist
      and destroy every last trace of their Baal
      worship.
   I will put an end to all the idolatrous priests,
      so that even the memory of them will
      disappear.
⁵ For they go up to their roofs
      and bow down to the sun, moon,
      and stars.
   They claim to follow the LORD,
      but then they worship Molech,* too.

··

SHORTSIGHTED

(1:1-18) The people of Judah were clearly warned by the highest authority of all—God. But they refused to listen, either because they doubted God's prophet (and thus did not believe the message was from God), or because they doubted God himself (and thus did not believe he would do what he said). Now that we have the whole Bible, we can see how shortsighted they were. The people of Judah were conquered by their enemies, just as Zephaniah prophesied. But we are equally shortsighted if we ignore the warnings in the Bible.

⁶ And I will destroy those who used to
      worship me
      but now no longer do.
   They no longer ask for the LORD's guidance
      or seek my blessings."

⁷ Stand in silence in the presence of the
      Sovereign LORD,
   for the awesome day of the LORD's
      judgment is near.
   The LORD has prepared his people for
      a great slaughter
      and has chosen their executioners.*
⁸ "On that day of judgment,"
      says the LORD,
   "I will punish the leaders and princes
      of Judah
      and all those following pagan customs.
⁹ Yes, I will punish those who participate in
      pagan worship ceremonies,
      and those who fill their masters' houses
      with violence and deceit.

¹⁰ "On that day," says the LORD,
      "a cry of alarm will come from the
      Fish Gate
   and echo throughout the New Quarter
      of the city.*
   And a great crash will sound from
      the hills.
¹¹ Wail in sorrow, all you who live in the
      market area,
      for all the merchants and traders will be
      destroyed.

¹² "I will search with lanterns in Jerusalem's
      darkest corners

1:3 The meaning of the Hebrew is uncertain.   1:5 Hebrew *Malcam*, a variant spelling of Molech; or it could possibly mean *their king*.
1:7 Hebrew *has prepared a sacrifice and sanctified his guests*.
1:10 Or *the Second Quarter*, a newer section of Jerusalem. Hebrew reads *the Mishneh*.

CHOICES
Judgment

The people of Crossroads Church sit in shocked silence as the guest preacher delivers his thundering message of moral decay and imminent judgment.

Point by point, he describes in gripping detail how "our nation has turned its back on God." He cites court decisions, humanistic trends, disturbing statistics, and alarming examples of Christians in this country who are being persecuted by the government.

Afterwards Joey, Luke, and Zoe are discussing the service over a large pepperoni pizza.

"Do you think that what that preacher said is true?"

"Pretty much."

"So you think this nation is going to be judged by God?"

"Probably so."

"But can't we do anything?"

"I guess if there was a nationwide revival or something like that, maybe God would hold back."

"What are the odds of a revival?"

"I don't know. Who knows what might happen if all the Christians in this town would really get right with God? Just think, if we all started praying and living right and loving people, maybe it would spread. Maybe then things would turn around."

Around 635 B.C. Zephaniah prophesied judgment on the nation of Judah. Read about the only alternative to national (as well as personal) disaster in 1:14–2:3.

to punish those who sit complacent
    in their sins.
They think the Lord will do nothing
    to them,
    either good or bad.
¹³ So their property will be plundered,
    their homes will be ransacked.
They will build new homes
    but never live in them.
They will plant vineyards
    but never drink wine from them.

¹⁴ "That terrible day of the Lord is near.
    Swiftly it comes—
a day of bitter tears,
    a day when even strong men will cry out.
¹⁵ It will be a day when the Lord's anger is
       poured out—
    a day of terrible distress and anguish,
a day of ruin and desolation,
    a day of darkness and gloom,
a day of clouds and blackness,
¹⁶   a day of trumpet calls and battle cries.
Down go the walled cities
    and the strongest battlements!

¹⁷ "Because you have sinned against
    the Lord,
    I will make you grope around like
      the blind.
Your blood will be poured into the dust,
    and your bodies will lie rotting on the
      ground."

¹⁸ Your silver and gold will not save you
    on that day of the Lord's anger.
For the whole land will be devoured
    by the fire of his jealousy.
He will make a terrifying end
    of all the people on earth.*

2   A CALL TO REPENTANCE

¹ Gather together—yes, gather together,
    you shameless nation.
² Gather before judgment begins,
    before your time to repent is blown away
      like chaff.
Act now, before the fierce fury of the
    Lord falls
    and the terrible day of the Lord's anger
      begins.
³ Seek the Lord, all who are humble,
    and follow his commands.
Seek to do what is right
    and to live humbly.
Perhaps even yet the Lord will protect you—

1:18 Or *the people living in the land.*   2:5 Hebrew *Kerethites.*

SEEK THE LORD, ALL WHO ARE HUMBLE, AND FOLLOW HIS COMMANDS. SEEK TO DO WHAT IS RIGHT AND TO LIVE HUMBLY.
ZEPHANIAH 2:3

    protect you from his anger on that day
      of destruction.

JUDGMENT AGAINST PHILISTIA

⁴ Gaza and Ashkelon will be abandoned,
    Ashdod and Ekron torn down.
⁵ And what sorrow awaits you Philistines*
    who live along the coast and in the land
      of Canaan,
    for this judgment is against you, too!
The Lord will destroy you
    until not one of you is left.
⁶ The Philistine coast will become
      a wilderness pasture,
    a place of shepherd camps
    and enclosures for sheep and goats.
⁷ The remnant of the tribe of Judah will
      pasture there.
They will rest at night in the abandoned
    houses in Ashkelon.
For the Lord their God will visit his people
    in kindness
    and restore their prosperity again.

JUDGMENT AGAINST MOAB AND AMMON

⁸ "I have heard the taunts of the Moabites
    and the insults of the Ammonites,
mocking my people
    and invading their borders.
⁹ Now, as surely as I live,"
    says the Lord of Heaven's Armies, the
      God of Israel,
    "Moab and Ammon will be destroyed—

COUNT ON IT
*(2:7) Although God promised that Judah would be
destroyed, he also promised to save a remnant. In this
way, he would keep his original covenant to preserve
Abraham's descendants (Gen 17:4-8; see also Jer 4:27).
God is holy and can't allow sin to continue; yet he also
keeps his promises. Feeling the heat of hard times? You
can still count on this promise from God: "I will never fail
you. I will never abandon you" (Heb 13:5).*

ZEPHANIAH

Served as a prophet to Judah from 640 to 621 B.C.	**CLIMATE OF THE TIMES**	Josiah was the last good king in Judah. His bold attempts to reform the nation and turn it back to God were probably influenced by Zephaniah.
	MAIN MESSAGE	A day will come when God, as Judge, will severely punish all nations. But after judgment, he will show mercy to all who have been faithful to him.
	IMPORTANCE OF MESSAGE	We will all be judged for our disobedience to God—but if we remain faithful to him, he will show us mercy.
	CONTEMPORARY PROPHET	Jeremiah (627–586)

destroyed as completely as Sodom and Gomorrah.
Their land will become a place of stinging nettles,
salt pits, and eternal desolation.
The remnant of my people will plunder them
and take their land."

¹⁰ They will receive the wages of their pride,
for they have scoffed at the people of the LORD of Heaven's Armies.
¹¹ The LORD will terrify them
as he destroys all the gods in the land.
Then nations around the world will worship the LORD,
each in their own land.

JUDGMENT AGAINST ETHIOPIA AND ASSYRIA
¹² "You Ethiopians* will also be slaughtered by my sword," says the LORD.

¹³ And the LORD will strike the lands of the north with his fist,
destroying the land of Assyria.
He will make its great capital, Nineveh,
a desolate wasteland,
parched like a desert.
¹⁴ The proud city will become a pasture for flocks and herds,

and all sorts of wild animals will settle there.
The desert owl and screech owl will roost on its ruined columns,
their calls echoing through the gaping windows.
Rubble will block all the doorways,
and the cedar paneling will be exposed to the weather.
¹⁵ This is the boisterous city,
once so secure.
"I am the greatest!" it boasted.
"No other city can compare with me!"
But now, look how it has become an utter ruin,
a haven for wild animals.
Everyone passing by will laugh in derision
and shake a defiant fist.

3 JERUSALEM'S REBELLION AND REDEMPTION
¹ What sorrow awaits rebellious, polluted Jerusalem,
the city of violence and crime!
² No one can tell it anything;
it refuses all correction.
It does not trust in the LORD
or draw near to its God.
³ Its leaders are like roaring lions
hunting for their victims.
Its judges are like ravenous wolves at evening time,
who by dawn have left no trace of their prey.
⁴ Its prophets are arrogant liars seeking their own gain.
Its priests defile the Temple by disobeying God's instructions.

···

CLOSED EARS
(3:1-2) The people of Judah had become too proud to listen to God's correction. Do you know people who refuse to listen when someone disagrees with their opinions? Those who are proud often refuse to listen to anything that contradicts their opinions. Some close their ears to the spiritual advice of others or from the Bible. But God has a way of opening closed ears. Sometimes he has to do it the hard way—through hard times. How willing are you to listen to spiritual advice? Does God have to get your attention the hard way?

2:12 Hebrew *Cushites.*

5 But the Lord is still there in the city,
　　and he does no wrong.
Day by day he hands down justice,
　　and he does not fail.
But the wicked know no shame.

6 "I have wiped out many nations,
　　devastating their fortress walls and
　　towers.
Their streets are now deserted;
　　their cities lie in silent ruin.
There are no survivors—
　　none at all.
7 I thought, 'Surely they will have reverence
　　for me now!
　Surely they will listen to my warnings.
Then I won't need to strike again,
　　destroying their homes.'
But no, they get up early
　　to continue their evil deeds.
8 Therefore, be patient," says the Lord.
　　"Soon I will stand and accuse these evil
　　nations.
For I have decided to gather the kingdoms
　　of the earth
　and pour out my fiercest anger and fury
　　on them.
All the earth will be devoured
　　by the fire of my jealousy.

9 "Then I will purify the speech of all people,
　　so that everyone can worship the
　　Lord together.
10 My scattered people who live beyond the
　　rivers of Ethiopia*
　　will come to present their offerings.
11 On that day you will no longer need to be
　　ashamed,
　for you will no longer be rebels
　　against me.
I will remove all proud and arrogant people
　　from among you.
There will be no more haughtiness on my
　　holy mountain.
12 Those who are left will be the lowly and
　　humble,
　for it is they who trust in the name
　　of the Lord.
13 The remnant of Israel will do no wrong;
　　they will never tell lies or deceive one
　　another.

3:10 Hebrew *Cush*.　3:17 Or *He will be silent in his love.* Greek and
Syriac versions read *He will renew you with his love.*　3:18 The
meaning of the Hebrew for this verse is uncertain.

They will eat and sleep in safety,
　　and no one will make them afraid."

14 Sing, O daughter of Zion;
　　shout aloud, O Israel!
Be glad and rejoice with all your heart,
　　O daughter of Jerusalem!
15 For the Lord will remove his hand
　　of judgment
　and will disperse the armies of your
　　enemy.
And the Lord himself, the King of Israel,
　　will live among you!
At last your troubles will be over,
　　and you will never again fear disaster.
16 On that day the announcement to Jerusalem
　　will be,
　"Cheer up, Zion! Don't be afraid!
17 For the Lord your God is living among you.
　　He is a mighty savior.
He will take delight in you with gladness.
　　With his love, he will calm all your fears.*
　　He will rejoice over you with joyful songs."

18 "I will gather you who mourn for the
　　appointed festivals;
　you will be disgraced no more.*
19 And I will deal severely with all who have
　　oppressed you.
　I will save the weak and helpless ones;
I will bring together
　　those who were chased away.
I will give glory and fame to my former
　　exiles,
　wherever they have been mocked and
　　shamed.
20 On that day I will gather you together
　　and bring you home again.
I will give you a good name, a name
　　of distinction,
　among all the nations of the earth,
as I restore your fortunes before their
　　very eyes.
　I, the Lord, have spoken!"

••

OPPOSED TO PRIDE
*(3:12) God is opposed to the proud and haughty of every
generation. But as Zephaniah prophesied, the lowly and
humble, both physically and spiritually, will be blessed
because they trust in God. The message of humility is
echoed throughout the Bible (see Prov 3:34; Jas 4:6; 1 Pet
5:5). Is it one you live by? Self-reliance and arrogance
have no place among God's people or in his kingdom.*

HAGGAI

Clay and Derek are camping. Actually, they're in Derek's back-
yard, but the backyard is huge. You can barely see the lights
in the house from their tent.

On "camping nights" Clay and Derek usually talk. This night is no
exception. In the past, they've often talked about girls, but sometimes
they've discussed other subjects.

"Derek," Clay asks, "if you had to give up everything but one thing
in your life, what would you keep?"

"I'd have to give up everything?" Derek responds.

"All but one thing. What's the most important thing to you?"

Derek thinks for a few seconds, before answering. "I can narrow it
down to three. I would keep my family and friends, Cassandra (the girl
he just started dating), and my wheels, of course."

"What about God?" Clay questions. "You would give him up for
Cassandra?"

"Oh," laughs Derek, "I didn't even think about God."

The Jews, who had returned from captivity, were like Derek—they
had forgotten about God. They'd let him slip from their life. So God sent
Haggai, a prophet, to remind them of what was really important in life.

God refuses to be forgotten. He demanded a higher priority in his
people's lives, and he wants top priority in our lives too. As you read the
book of Haggai, notice how God blesses those who make him number
one. Then ask God to help you live with him in first place.

KEY POINTS
....

RIGHT PRIORITIES God had given the formerly captive people of Israel the
task of finishing the Temple in Jerusalem. But after 15 years, they still had not
completed it. It's easy to make other activities more important than doing
God's work. But God wants following his commands to be a high priority in
his people's lives.

GOD'S ENCOURAGEMENT Haggai encouraged the people as they worked,
assuring them of the presence of the Holy Spirit, of final victory, and the future
reign of the Messiah. If God gives you a task, he will help you complete it. His
resources are infinite.

1 A CALL TO REBUILD THE TEMPLE

On August 29* of the second year of King Darius's reign, the LORD gave a message through the prophet Haggai to Zerubbabel son of Shealtiel, governor of Judah, and to Jeshua* son of Jehozadak, the high priest.

2"This is what the LORD of Heaven's Armies says: The people are saying, 'The time has not yet come to rebuild the house of the LORD.'"

3Then the LORD sent this message through the prophet Haggai: 4"Why are you living in luxurious houses while my house lies in ruins? 5This is what the LORD of Heaven's Armies says: Look at what's happening to you! 6You have planted much but harvest little. You eat but are not satisfied. You drink but are still thirsty. You put on clothes but cannot keep warm. Your wages disappear as though you were putting them in pockets filled with holes!

7"This is what the LORD of Heaven's Armies says: Look at what's happening to you! 8Now go up into the hills, bring down timber, and rebuild my house. Then I will take pleasure in it and be honored, says the LORD. 9You hoped for rich harvests, but they were poor. And when you brought your harvest home, I blew it away. Why? Because my house lies in ruins, says the LORD of Heaven's Armies, while all of you are busy building your own fine houses. 10It's because of you that the heavens withhold the dew and the earth produces no crops. 11I have called for a drought on your fields and hills—a drought to wither the grain and grapes and olive trees and all your other crops, a drought to starve you and your livestock and to ruin everything you have worked so hard to get."

OBEDIENCE TO GOD'S CALL

12Then Zerubbabel son of Shealtiel, and Jeshua son of Jehozadak, the high priest, and the whole remnant of God's people began to obey the message from the LORD their God. When they heard the words of the prophet Haggai, whom the LORD their God had sent, the people feared the LORD. 13Then Haggai, the LORD's messenger, gave the people this message from the LORD: "I am with you, says the LORD!"

14So the LORD sparked the enthusiasm of Zerubbabel son of Shealtiel, governor of Judah, and the enthusiasm of Jeshua son of Jehozadak, the high priest, and the enthusiasm of the whole remnant of God's people. They began to work on the house of their God, the LORD of Heaven's Armies, 15on September 21* of the second year of King Darius's reign.

2 THE NEW TEMPLE'S DIMINISHED SPLENDOR

Then on October 17 of that same year,* the LORD sent another message through the prophet Haggai. 2"Say this to Zerubbabel

1:1a Hebrew *On the first day of the sixth month,* of the ancient Hebrew lunar calendar. A number of dates in Haggai can be cross-checked with dates in surviving Persian records and related accurately to our modern calendar. This event occurred on August 29, 520 B.C.
1:1b Hebrew *Joshua,* a variant spelling of Jeshua; also in 1:12, 14.
1:15 Hebrew *on the twenty-fourth day of the sixth month,* of the ancient Hebrew lunar calendar. This event occurred on September 21, 520 B.C.; also see note on 1:1a. **2:1** Hebrew *on the twenty-first day of the seventh month,* of the ancient Hebrew lunar calendar. This event (in the second year of Darius's reign) occurred on October 17, 520 B.C.; also see note on 1:1a.

PRIORITIES

(1:1-9) The people of Judah had rebuilt their homes upon returning to Jerusalem. Yet the Temple—the house of God—still lay in ruins. Haggai reminded them that their priorities were mixed up. Sometimes our priorities (work, family, and God's work) are mixed up. Friends, possessions, and fun may be higher on our list of importance than God. What is most important to you? Where does God rank?

CHOICES
satisfaction

With nothing more demanding to do than catch rays at the Fairfield Swim Club in early August, 15-year-old Gabrielle is bored silly. She had been looking forward to summer ever since the first winter storm (and since her first day in algebra). She'd had big plans to relax, sleep late, hang out with friends, and just have fun—to enjoy three months of doing whatever she wanted.

Now here she sits, frustrated and unsatisfied. She has been involved in a ton of things in the last two months; yet summer hasn't been nearly as exciting as she had imagined it would be. *Something's missing,* she thinks, as she sips her diet soda and watches the clouds form shapes against the crystal blue sky.

Gabrielle picks up her cell phone and sighs. *Oh well. Guess I'll call Drina and see if she's as bored as me.*

Two thousand miles away, 14-year-old Greg is drenched in sweat. Along with nineteen other teens from his youth group, he's helping to build a church in a poor village near the US–Mexico border. It's backbreaking work, the living conditions are brutal, the food is . . . well, not exactly gourmet fare. Yet Greg and his friends are having a blast serving God and the community.

What a paradox! When we chase after satisfaction, we inevitably find frustration. When we stop trying to find personal fulfillment and give our life away in service to God, we find indescribable joy.

See Haggai 1 for another example of this truth. Based on this passage, what advice would you have for Gabrielle?

son of Shealtiel, governor of Judah, and to Jeshua* son of Jehozadak, the high priest, and to the remnant of God's people there in the land: ³'Does anyone remember this house—this Temple—in its former splendor? How, in comparison, does it look to you now? It must seem like nothing at all! ⁴But now the LORD says: Be strong, Zerubbabel. Be strong, Jeshua son of Jehozadak, the high priest. Be strong, all you people still left in the land. And now get to work, for I am with you, says the LORD of Heaven's Armies. ⁵My Spirit remains among you, just as I promised when you came out of Egypt. So do not be afraid.'

⁶"For this is what the LORD of Heaven's Armies says: In just a little while I will again shake the heavens and the earth, the oceans and the dry land. ⁷I will shake all the nations, and the treasures of all the nations will be brought to this Temple. I will fill this place with glory, says the LORD of Heaven's Armies. ⁸The silver is mine, and the gold is mine, says the LORD of Heaven's Armies. ⁹The future glory of this Temple will be greater than its past glory, says the LORD of Heaven's Armies. And in this place I will bring peace. I, the LORD of Heaven's Armies, have spoken!"

BLESSINGS PROMISED FOR OBEDIENCE
¹⁰On December 18* of the second year of King Darius's reign, the LORD sent this message to the prophet Haggai: ¹¹"This is what the LORD of Heaven's Armies says. Ask the priests this question about the law: ¹²'If one of you is carrying some meat from a holy sacrifice in his robes and his robe happens to brush against some bread or stew, wine or olive oil, or any other kind of food, will it also become holy?'"

The priests replied, "No."

¹³Then Haggai asked, "If someone becomes ceremonially unclean by touching a dead person and then touches any of these foods, will the food be defiled?"

And the priests answered, "Yes."

¹⁴Then Haggai responded, "That is how it is with this people and this nation, says the LORD. Everything they do and everything they offer is defiled by their sin. ¹⁵Look at what was happening to you before you began to lay the foundation of the LORD's Temple. ¹⁶When you hoped for a twenty-bushel crop, you harvested only ten. When you expected to draw

WHY ARE YOU LIVING IN LUXURIOUS HOUSES WHILE MY HOUSE LIES IN RUINS?

HAGGAI 1:4

fifty gallons from the winepress, you found only twenty. ¹⁷I sent blight and mildew and hail to destroy everything you worked so hard to produce. Even so, you refused to return to me, says the LORD.

¹⁸"Think about this eighteenth day of December, the day* when the foundation of the LORD's Temple was laid. Think carefully. ¹⁹I am giving you a promise now while the seed is still in the barn.* You have not yet harvested your grain, and your grapevines, fig trees, pomegranates, and olive trees have not yet produced their crops. But from this day onward I will bless you."

PROMISES FOR ZERUBBABEL
²⁰On that same day, December 18,* the LORD sent this second message to Haggai: ²¹"Tell Zerubbabel, the governor of Judah, that I am about to shake the heavens and the earth. ²²I will overthrow royal thrones and destroy the power of foreign kingdoms. I will overturn their chariots and riders. The horses will fall, and their riders will kill each other.

²³"But when this happens, says the LORD of Heaven's Armies, I will honor you, Zerubbabel son of Shealtiel, my servant. I will make you like a signet ring on my finger, says the LORD, for I have chosen you. I, the LORD of Heaven's Armies, have spoken!"

....

FREE FORGIVENESS
(2:10-14) Now that the people were beginning to obey God, he promised to bless them. But they needed to understand that performing activities in the Temple wouldn't earn them God's forgiveness or make them right with him. Only their repentance and acceptance of his forgiveness could do that. Many times, we think that by giving money or doing something nice for someone we can somehow erase the wrong things we've done and thereby earn God's forgiveness. Or, we may think we're somehow good on our own. Wrong. As Isaiah said, "When we display our righteous deeds, they are nothing but filthy rags" (64:6). Forgiveness is a free gift from God already paid for by Jesus. Is that a gift you've accepted?

CHOSEN
(2:23) God ended his message to Zerubbabel with this tremendous affirmation: "I have chosen you." Such a proclamation is ours as well. God chose each of us (Eph 1:4). This truth can help us see our value in God's eyes and motivate us to work for him. When you feel down, remind yourself, "God has chosen me!"

2:2 Hebrew *Joshua*, a variant spelling of Jeshua; also in 2:4.
2:10 Hebrew *On the twenty-fourth day of the ninth month*, of the ancient Hebrew lunar calendar (similarly in 2:18). This event occurred on December 18, 520 B.C.; also see note on 1:1a.
2:18 Or *On this eighteenth day of December, think about the day.*
2:19 Hebrew *Is the seed yet in the barn?*   2:20 Hebrew *On the twenty-fourth day of the [ninth] month*; see note on 2:10.

Ever wonder about the future? Almost everyone wants to know what the future holds. Some people fear the future, afraid of what evils might lurk around the corner. Others consult fortune-tellers, astrologers, and other future-telling charlatans who make a living providing personal prophecies.

But tomorrow's story is known only by God and by those special messengers, the prophets, to whom he has revealed a chapter or two. A prophet's job was to proclaim the word of the Lord, point out wrongdoings and their consequences, and direct men and women to God.

Nestled here among what are known as the Minor Prophets (the books starting with Hosea) is the book of Zechariah. As one of God's spokesmen, Zechariah preached to the small group of Jews who had returned to Judah to rebuild the Temple and the nation. Zechariah encouraged them, but his message went far beyond mere encouragement. Zechariah gave a spectacular and graphic prophecy of the Messiah, the one whom God would send to rescue his people and reign over the earth.

Zechariah is an important prophetic book because it gives detailed messianic references that have been clearly fulfilled in Jesus. Jesus is the Messiah, the promised deliverer of Israel, and the only hope for humankind.

God knows and controls the future. We may never see a moment ahead, but we can be secure if we trust him. Read Zechariah and strengthen your faith in God. He alone is your hope and security.

STATS

PURPOSE
To give hope to God's people by revealing God's future deliverance through the Messiah

AUTHOR
Zechariah

ORIGINAL AUDIENCE
The Jews in Jerusalem who had returned from their captivity in Babylon and God's people everywhere

DATE WRITTEN
Chapters 1–8 were written about 520 to 518 B.C. Chapters 9–14 were written around 480 B.C.

KEY PEOPLE
Zerubbabel, Joshua

KEY PLACE
Jerusalem

SPECIAL FEATURES
This book is the most apocalyptic and messianic of all the Minor Prophets.

KEY POINTS

GOD'S JEALOUSY Disobedience was the root of Judah's problems. God was jealous ("zealous") for his people's devotion. Likewise, God wants our complete loyalty.

REBUILDING THE TEMPLE The Jews were home from exile, but the Temple was not yet rebuilt. Zechariah encouraged them to get moving on the rebuilding. God would both protect his workmen and also empower them by his Holy Spirit to complete the rebuilding. God will empower us to do whatever we're assigned to do.

THE COMING KING Zechariah prophesied that the Messiah would come someday to rescue people from sin and to reign as King. Jesus already has fulfilled the first part of the prophecy. Someday, he will return to earth as a victorious King to usher in peace throughout the world.

GOD'S PROTECTION Zechariah prophesied future times of trouble. But God would protect his people. God cares for his people and will deliver them from all who oppress them.

1

A CALL TO RETURN TO THE LORD In November* of the second year of King Darius's reign, the LORD gave this message to the prophet Zechariah son of Berekiah and grandson of Iddo:

²"I, the LORD, was very angry with your ancestors. ³Therefore, say to the people, 'This is what the LORD of Heaven's Armies says: Return to me, and I will return to you, says the LORD of Heaven's Armies.' ⁴Don't be like your ancestors who would not listen or pay attention when the earlier prophets said to them, 'This is what the LORD of Heaven's Armies says: Turn from your evil ways, and stop all your evil practices.'

⁵"Where are your ancestors now? They and the prophets are long dead. ⁶But everything I said through my servants the prophets happened to your ancestors, just as I said. As a result, they repented and said, 'We have received what we deserved from the LORD of Heaven's Armies. He has done what he said he would do.'"

A MAN AMONG THE MYRTLE TREES

⁷Three months later, on February 15,* the LORD sent another message to the prophet Zechariah son of Berekiah and grandson of Iddo.

⁸In a vision during the night, I saw a man sitting on a red horse that was standing among some myrtle trees in a small valley. Behind him were riders on red, brown, and white horses. ⁹I asked the angel who was talking with me, "My lord, what do these horses mean?"

"I will show you," the angel replied.

¹⁰The rider standing among the myrtle trees then explained, "They are the ones the LORD has sent out to patrol the earth."

¹¹Then the other riders reported to the angel

of the LORD, who was standing among the myrtle trees, "We have been patrolling the earth, and the whole earth is at peace."

¹²Upon hearing this, the angel of the LORD prayed this prayer: "O LORD of Heaven's Armies, for seventy years now you have been angry with Jerusalem and the towns of Judah. How long until you again show mercy to them?"

¹³And the LORD spoke kind and comforting words to the angel who talked with me.

¹⁴Then the angel said to me, "Shout this message for all to hear: 'This is what the LORD of Heaven's Armies says: My love for Jerusalem and Mount Zion is passionate and strong. ¹⁵But I am very angry with the other nations that are now enjoying peace and security. I was only a little angry with my people, but the nations inflicted harm on them far beyond my intentions.

¹⁶"'Therefore, this is what the LORD says: I have returned to show mercy to Jerusalem. My Temple will be rebuilt, says the LORD of Heaven's Armies, and measurements will be taken for the reconstruction of Jerusalem.*'

¹⁷"Say this also: 'This is what the LORD of Heaven's Armies says: The towns of Israel will again overflow with prosperity, and the LORD will again comfort Zion and choose Jerusalem as his own.'"

FOUR HORNS AND FOUR BLACKSMITHS

¹⁸*Then I looked up and saw four animal horns. ¹⁹"What are these?" I asked the angel who was talking with me.

He replied, "These horns represent the nations that scattered Judah, Israel, and Jerusalem."

²⁰Then the LORD showed me four blacksmiths. ²¹"What are these men coming to do?" I asked.

The angel replied, "These four horns—these nations—scattered and humbled Judah. Now these blacksmiths have come to terrify those nations and throw them down and destroy them."

2

FUTURE PROSPERITY OF JERUSALEM ¹*When I looked again, I saw a man with a measuring line in his hand. ²"Where are you going?" I asked.

....

THE CHOICE IS YOURS

(1:2-4) The familiar phrase "Like father, like son" implies that children turn out like their parents. But God warned Israel not to be like their fathers who disobeyed him and reaped the consequences—his judgment. We are responsible before God for our actions. We aren't trapped by our heredity or environment, and we can't use these as excuses for our sins. We can choose to follow God or go our own way. What's your choice?

TURN BACK

(1:12-17) God's people had endured 70 years of exile as a punishment for hundreds of years of wrongdoing. But here God spoke words of comfort and kindness. He promised that their Temple would be rebuilt. Ever worry that the hard times you're going through will last forever? Maybe you've thought that God is angry because of something you did in the past and is bent on ruining your life forever. The same encouragement that God offered to his people is there for you—just for the asking.

1:1 Hebrew *In the eighth month.* A number of dates in Zechariah can be cross-checked with dates in surviving Persian records and related accurately to our modern calendar. This month of the ancient Hebrew lunar calendar occurred within the months of October and November 520 B.C. **1:7** Hebrew *On the twenty-fourth day of the eleventh month, the month of Shebat, in the second year of Darius.* This event occurred on February 15, 519 B.C.; also see note on 1:1. **1:16** Hebrew *and the measuring line will be stretched out over Jerusalem.* **1:18** Verses 1:18-21 are numbered 2:1-4 in Hebrew text. **2:1** Verses 2:1-13 are numbered 2:5-17 in Hebrew text.

He replied, "I am going to measure Jerusalem, to see how wide and how long it is."

³Then the angel who was with me went to meet a second angel who was coming toward him. ⁴The other angel said, "Hurry, and say to that young man, 'Jerusalem will someday be so full of people and livestock that there won't be room enough for everyone! Many will live outside the city walls. ⁵Then I, myself, will be a protective wall of fire around Jerusalem, says the LORD. And I will be the glory inside the city!'"

THE EXILES ARE CALLED HOME ⁶The LORD says, "Come away! Flee from Babylon in the land of the north, for I have scattered you to the four winds. ⁷Come away, people of Zion, you who are exiled in Babylon!"

⁸After a period of glory, the LORD of Heaven's Armies sent me* against the nations who plundered you. For he said, "Anyone who harms you harms my most precious possession.* ⁹I will raise my fist to crush them, and their own slaves will plunder them." Then you will know that the LORD of Heaven's Armies has sent me.

¹⁰The LORD says, "Shout and rejoice, O beautiful Jerusalem,* for I am coming to live among you. ¹¹Many nations will join themselves to the LORD on that day, and they, too, will be my people. I will live among you, and you will know that the LORD of Heaven's Armies sent me to you. ¹²The land of Judah will be the LORD's special possession in the holy land, and he will once again choose Jerusalem to be his own city. ¹³Be silent before the LORD, all humanity, for he is springing into action from his holy dwelling."

3 **CLEANSING FOR THE HIGH PRIEST** Then the angel showed me Jeshua* the high priest standing before the angel of the LORD. The Accuser, Satan,* was there at the angel's right hand, making accusations against Jeshua. ²And the LORD said to Satan, "I, the LORD, reject your accusations, Satan. Yes, the LORD, who has chosen Jerusalem, rebukes you. This man is like a burning stick that has been snatched from the fire."

³Jeshua's clothing was filthy as he stood there before the angel. ⁴So the angel said to the others standing there, "Take off his filthy clothes." And turning to Jeshua he said, "See,

IT IS NOT BY FORCE NOR BY STRENGTH, BUT BY MY SPIRIT,
SAYS THE LORD OF HEAVEN'S ARMIES.
■■■ ZECHARIAH 4:6 ■■■

I have taken away your sins, and now I am giving you these fine new clothes."

⁵Then I said, "They should also place a clean turban on his head." So they put a clean priestly turban on his head and dressed him in new clothes while the angel of the LORD stood by.

⁶Then the angel of the LORD spoke very solemnly to Jeshua and said, ⁷"This is what the LORD of Heaven's Armies says: If you follow my ways and carefully serve me, then you will be given authority over my Temple and its courtyards. I will let you walk among these others standing here.

⁸"Listen to me, O Jeshua the high priest, and all you other priests. You are symbols of things to come. Soon I am going to bring my servant, the Branch. ⁹Now look at the jewel I have set before Jeshua, a single stone with seven facets.* I will engrave an inscription on it, says the LORD of Heaven's Armies, and I will remove the sins of this land in a single day.

¹⁰"And on that day, says the LORD of Heaven's Armies, each of you will invite your neighbor to sit with you peacefully under your own grapevine and fig tree."

4 **A LAMPSTAND AND TWO OLIVE TREES** Then the angel who had been talking with me returned and woke me, as though I had been asleep. ²"What do you see now?" he asked.

I answered, "I see a solid gold lampstand with a bowl of oil on top of it. Around the bowl are seven lamps, each having seven spouts with wicks. ³And I see two olive trees, one on each side of the bowl." ⁴Then I asked the

----

2:8a The meaning of the Hebrew is uncertain. *2:8b* Hebrew *Anyone who touches you touches the pupil of his eye.* *2:10* Hebrew *O daughter of Zion.* *3:1a* Hebrew *Joshua,* a variant spelling of Jeshua; also in 3:3, 4, 6, 8, 9. *3:1b* Hebrew *The satan;* similarly in 3:2. *3:9* Hebrew *seven eyes.*

HELPING GOD
(2:8-9) God expressed his love for his people. Believers are precious to God (Ps 116:15); they're his children (Ps 103:13). Treating any believer unkindly is the same as treating God that way. As Jesus told his disciples, when we help others, we're really helping him; when we neglect them, we neglect him (Matt 25:34-46). Be careful, therefore, how you treat fellow believers—that is the way you are treating God.

angel, "What are these, my lord? What do they mean?"

5"Don't you know?" the angel asked.

"No, my lord," I replied.

6Then he said to me, "This is what the LORD says to Zerubbabel: It is not by force nor by strength, but by my Spirit, says the LORD of Heaven's Armies. 7Nothing, not even a mighty mountain, will stand in Zerubbabel's way; it will become a level plain before him! And when Zerubbabel sets the final stone of the Temple in place, the people will shout: 'May God bless it! May God bless it!'*"

8Then another message came to me from the LORD: 9"Zerubbabel is the one who laid the foundation of this Temple, and he will complete it. Then you will know that the LORD of Heaven's Armies has sent me. 10Do not despise these small beginnings, for the LORD rejoices to see the work begin, to see the plumb line in Zerubbabel's hand."

(The seven lamps* represent the eyes of the LORD that search all around the world.)

11Then I asked the angel, "What are these two olive trees on each side of the lampstand, 12and what are the two olive branches that pour out golden oil through two gold tubes?"

13"Don't you know?" he asked.

"No, my lord," I replied.

14Then he said to me, "They represent the two heavenly beings who stand in the court of the Lord of all the earth."

5 A FLYING SCROLL
I looked up again and saw a scroll flying through the air.

2"What do you see?" the angel asked.

"I see a flying scroll," I replied. "It appears to be about 30 feet long and 15 feet wide.*"

3Then he said to me, "This scroll contains

....

BY HIS SPIRIT
(4:6) Many people believe that to survive in this world a person must be strong and aggressive. But God says, "It is not by force nor by strength, but by my Spirit." The key words are "by my Spirit." It is only through God's Spirit that anything of lasting value is accomplished. The returned exiles were indeed weak—harassed by their enemies, tired, discouraged, and poor. But they had God on their side! Where is the bulk of your trust? In your own strength or abilities? Or in God?

WIPED OUT
(5:5-11) Zechariah saw a vision of wickedness (as represented by the woman in 5:8) being taken away from Israel. One day, that vision will come true. During Christ's future reign, all sin will be eliminated. People will live in safety and security. He has already removed sin's power and penalty by his death on the Cross. When we trust him to forgive us, he gives us the power to live a life that's pleasing to him.

the curse that is going out over the entire land. One side of the scroll says that those who steal will be banished from the land; the other side says that those who swear falsely will be banished from the land. 4And this is what the LORD of Heaven's Armies says: I am sending this curse into the house of every thief and into the house of everyone who swears falsely using my name. And my curse will remain in that house and completely destroy it—even its timbers and stones."

A WOMAN IN A BASKET 5Then the angel who was talking with me came forward and said, "Look up and see what's coming."

6"What is it?" I asked.

He replied, "It is a basket for measuring grain,* and it's filled with the sins* of everyone throughout the land."

7Then the heavy lead cover was lifted off the basket, and there was a woman sitting inside it. 8The angel said, "The woman's name is Wickedness," and he pushed her back into the basket and closed the heavy lid again.

9Then I looked up and saw two women flying toward us, gliding on the wind. They had wings like a stork, and they picked up the basket and flew into the sky.

10"Where are they taking the basket?" I asked the angel.

11He replied, "To the land of Babylonia,* where they will build a temple for the basket. And when the temple is ready, they will set the basket there on its pedestal."

6 FOUR CHARIOTS
Then I looked up again and saw four chariots coming from between two bronze mountains. 2The first chariot was pulled by red horses, the second by black horses, 3the third by white horses, and the fourth by powerful dappled-gray horses. 4"And what are these, my lord?" I asked the angel who was talking with me.

5The angel replied, "These are the four spirits* of heaven who stand before the Lord of all the earth. They are going out to do his work. 6The chariot with black horses is going north, the chariot with white horses is going west,* and the chariot with dappled-gray horses is going south."

7The powerful horses were eager to set out to patrol the earth. And the LORD said, "Go

4:7 Hebrew 'Grace, grace to it.' 4:10 Or The seven facets (see 3:9); Hebrew reads These seven. 5:2 Hebrew 20 cubits [9 meters] long and 10 cubits [4.5 meters] wide. 5:6a Hebrew an ephah [20 quarts or 22 liters]; also in 5:7, 8, 9, 10, 11. 5:6b As in Greek version; Hebrew reads the appearance. 5:11 Hebrew the land of Shinar. 6:5 Or the four winds. 6:6 Hebrew is going after them.

and patrol the earth!" So they left at once on their patrol.

⁸Then the Lord summoned me and said, "Look, those who went north have vented the anger of my Spirit* there in the land of the north."

THE CROWNING OF JESHUA ⁹Then I received another message from the Lord: ¹⁰"Heldai, Tobijah, and Jedaiah will bring gifts of silver and gold from the Jews exiled in Babylon. As soon as they arrive, meet them at the home of Josiah son of Zephaniah. ¹¹Accept their gifts, and make a crown* from the silver and gold. Then put the crown on the head of Jeshua* son of Jehozadak, the high priest. ¹²Tell him, 'This is what the Lord of Heaven's Armies says: Here is the man called the Branch. He will branch out from where he is and build the Temple of the Lord. ¹³Yes, he will build the Temple of the Lord. Then he will receive royal honor and will rule as king from his throne. He will also serve as priest from his throne,* and there will be perfect harmony between his two roles.'

¹⁴"The crown will be a memorial in the Temple of the Lord to honor those who gave it—Heldai,* Tobijah, Jedaiah, and Josiah* son of Zephaniah."

¹⁵People will come from distant lands to rebuild the Temple of the Lord. And when this happens, you will know that my messages have

6:8 Hebrew *have given my Spirit rest.*   6:11a As in Greek and Syriac versions; Hebrew reads *crowns.*   6:11b Hebrew *Joshua,* a variant spelling of Jeshua.   6:13 Or *There will be a priest by his throne.* 6:14a As in Syriac version (compare 6:10); Hebrew reads *Helem.* 6:14b As in Syriac version (compare 6:10); Hebrew reads *Hen.* 7:1 Hebrew *On the fourth day of the ninth month, the month of Kislev,* of the ancient Hebrew lunar calendar. This event occurred on December 7, 518 B.C.; also see note on 1:1.   7:2 Or *Bethel-sharezer had sent Regemmelech.*   7:3 Hebrew *mourn and fast in the fifth month.* The Temple had been destroyed in the fifth month of the ancient Hebrew lunar calendar (August 586 B.C.); see 2 Kgs 25:8. 7:5 Hebrew *fasted and mourned in the fifth and seventh months.* The fifth month of the ancient Hebrew lunar calendar usually occurs within the months of July and August. The seventh month usually occurs within the months of September and October; both the Day of Atonement and the Festival of Shelters were celebrated in the seventh month.   7:7 Hebrew *the Shephelah.*

been from the Lord of Heaven's Armies. All this will happen if you carefully obey what the Lord your God says.

7 **A CALL TO JUSTICE AND MERCY** On December 7* of the fourth year of King Darius's reign, another message came to Zechariah from the Lord. ²The people of Bethel had sent Sharezer and Regemmelech,* along with their attendants, to seek the Lord's favor. ³They were to ask this question of the prophets and the priests at the Temple of the Lord of Heaven's Armies: "Should we continue to mourn and fast each summer on the anniversary of the Temple's destruction,* as we have done for so many years?"

⁴The Lord of Heaven's Armies sent me this message in reply: ⁵"Say to all your people and your priests, 'During these seventy years of exile, when you fasted and mourned in the summer and in early autumn,* was it really for me that you were fasting? ⁶And even now in your holy festivals, aren't you eating and drinking just to please yourselves? ⁷Isn't this the same message the Lord proclaimed through the prophets in years past when Jerusalem and the towns of Judah were bustling with people, and the Negev and the foothills of Judah* were well populated?'"

⁸Then this message came to Zechariah from the Lord: ⁹"This is what the Lord of Heaven's Armies says: Judge fairly, and show mercy and kindness to one another. ¹⁰Do not oppress widows, orphans, foreigners, and the poor. And do not scheme against each other.

¹¹"Your ancestors refused to listen to this message. They stubbornly turned away and put their fingers in their ears to keep from hearing. ¹²They made their hearts as hard as stone, so they could not hear the instructions or the messages that the Lord of Heaven's

CHOICES
Justice

Christopher has a twisted sense of fairness: When a convenience store clerk gave him change for $20 instead of $10 (it was her first day on the job and she was nervous), he never said a word. He eagerly pocketed the extra bucks. "She shouldn't have been so stupid," he laughed.

• When he babysat his little brother last weekend, he locked the kid in a closet for about an hour.
• While keeping score for an intramural basketball

game, Christopher gave his favorite team three extra points.

But you can bet Christopher was not amused today when *he* was treated wrongly. He was docked an hour's pay just for being a measly five minutes late for work because of a wreck on the expressway!

"That's not fair!" he whined.

Like Christopher, we're quick to complain whenever we feel as though we've been treated unfairly. But check out Zechariah 7:8-14. Is this your idea of fairness? What would you say to Christopher based on this passage?

Armies had sent them by his Spirit through the earlier prophets. That is why the Lord of Heaven's Armies was so angry with them.

¹³"Since they refused to listen when I called to them, I would not listen when they called to me, says the Lord of Heaven's Armies. ¹⁴As with a whirlwind, I scattered them among the distant nations, where they lived as strangers. Their land became so desolate that no one even traveled through it. They turned their pleasant land into a desert."

8 PROMISED BLESSINGS FOR JERUSALEM
Then another message came to me from the Lord of Heaven's Armies: ²"This is what the Lord of Heaven's Armies says: My love for Mount Zion is passionate and strong; I am consumed with passion for Jerusalem!

³"And now the Lord says: I am returning to Mount Zion, and I will live in Jerusalem. Then Jerusalem will be called the Faithful City; the mountain of the Lord of Heaven's Armies will be called the Holy Mountain.

⁴"This is what the Lord of Heaven's Armies says: Once again old men and women will walk Jerusalem's streets with their canes and will sit together in the city squares. ⁵And the streets of the city will be filled with boys and girls at play.

⁶"This is what the Lord of Heaven's Armies says: All this may seem impossible to you now, a small remnant of God's people. But is it impossible for me? says the Lord of Heaven's Armies.

⁷"This is what the Lord of Heaven's Armies says: You can be sure that I will rescue my people from the east and from the west. ⁸I will bring them home again to live safely in Jerusalem. They will be my people, and I will be faithful and just toward them as their God.

⁹"This is what the Lord of Heaven's Armies says: Be strong and finish the task! Ever since the laying of the foundation of the Temple of the Lord of Heaven's Armies, you have heard what the prophets have been saying about completing the building. ¹⁰Before the work on the Temple began, there were no jobs and no money to hire people or animals. No traveler was safe from the enemy, for there were

enemies on all sides. I had turned everyone against each other.

¹¹"But now I will not treat the remnant of my people as I treated them before, says the Lord of Heaven's Armies. ¹²For I am planting seeds of peace and prosperity among you. The grapevines will be heavy with fruit. The earth will produce its crops, and the heavens will release the dew. Once more I will cause the remnant in Judah and Israel to inherit these blessings. ¹³Among the other nations, Judah and Israel became symbols of a cursed nation. But no longer! Now I will rescue you and make you both a symbol and a source of blessing. So don't be afraid. Be strong, and get on with rebuilding the Temple!

¹⁴"For this is what the Lord of Heaven's Armies says: I was determined to punish you when your ancestors angered me, and I did not change my mind, says the Lord of Heaven's Armies. ¹⁵But now I am determined to bless Jerusalem and the people of Judah. So don't be afraid. ¹⁶But this is what you must do: Tell the truth to each other. Render verdicts in your courts that are just and that lead to peace. ¹⁷Don't scheme against each other. Stop your love of telling lies that you swear are the truth. I hate all these things, says the Lord."

¹⁸Here is another message that came to me from the Lord of Heaven's Armies. ¹⁹"This is what the Lord of Heaven's Armies says: The traditional fasts and times of mourning you have kept in early summer, midsummer, autumn, and winter* are now ended. They will become festivals of joy and celebration for the people of Judah. So love truth and peace.

²⁰"This is what the Lord of Heaven's Armies says: People from nations and cities around the world will travel to Jerusalem. ²¹The people of one city will say to the people of another, 'Come with us to Jerusalem to ask the Lord to bless us. Let's worship the Lord of Heaven's Armies. I'm determined to go.' ²²Many peoples and powerful nations will come to Jerusalem to seek the Lord of Heaven's Armies and to ask for his blessing.

²³"This is what the Lord of Heaven's Armies says: In those days ten men from different nations and languages of the world will clutch at the sleeve of one Jew. And they will say, 'Please let us walk with you, for we have heard that God is with you.'"

GET GOING!
(8:9) God had to give the Temple workers a push. He as much as said, "Get going and finish the job! You've listened long enough!" Listen to what God says, but once he has shown you a course of action, get going and finish the job.

8:19 Hebrew *in the fourth, fifth, seventh, and tenth months.* The fourth month of the ancient Hebrew lunar calendar usually occurs within the months of June and July. The fifth month usually occurs within the months of July and August. The seventh month usually occurs within the months of September and October. The tenth month usually occurs within the months of December and January.

ZECHARIAH

Served as a prophet to Judah about 520 B.C., after the return from exile.	**CLIMATE OF THE TIMES**	The exiles had returned from captivity to rebuild their Temple. But work on the Temple had stalled, and the people were neglecting their service to God.
	MAIN MESSAGE	Zechariah, like Haggai, encouraged the people to finish rebuilding the Temple. His visions gave the people hope. He told the people of a future King who one day would establish an eternal kingdom.
	IMPORTANCE OF MESSAGE	Even in times of discouragement and despair, God is working out his plan. God protects and guides us; we must trust and follow him.
	CONTEMPORARY PROPHET	Haggai (about 520 B.C.)

9 JUDGMENT AGAINST ISRAEL'S ENEMIES

This is the message* from the LORD against the land of Aram* and the city of Damascus, for the eyes of humanity, including all the tribes of Israel, are on the LORD.

2 Doom is certain for Hamath,
    near Damascus,
and for the cities of Tyre and Sidon,
    though they are so clever.
3 Tyre has built a strong fortress
    and has made silver and gold
    as plentiful as dust in the streets!
4 But now the Lord will strip away Tyre's
        possessions
    and hurl its fortifications into the sea,
    and it will be burned to the ground.
5 The city of Ashkelon will see Tyre fall
    and will be filled with fear.
Gaza will shake with terror,
    as will Ekron, for their hopes will
        be dashed.
Gaza's king will be killed,
    and Ashkelon will be deserted.
6 Foreigners will occupy the city of Ashdod.
    I will destroy the pride of the Philistines.
7 I will grab the bloody meat from their
        mouths
    and snatch the detestable sacrifices
        from their teeth.
Then the surviving Philistines will worship
        our God
    and become like a clan in Judah.*
The Philistines of Ekron will join my people,
    as the ancient Jebusites once did.

8 I will guard my Temple
    and protect it from invading armies.
I am watching closely to ensure
    that no more foreign oppressors overrun
        my people's land.

ZION'S COMING KING

9 Rejoice, O people of Zion!*
    Shout in triumph, O people of Jerusalem!
Look, your king is coming to you.
    He is righteous and victorious,*
yet he is humble, riding on a donkey—
    riding on a donkey's colt.
10 I will remove the battle chariots from Israel*
    and the warhorses from Jerusalem.
I will destroy all the weapons used in battle,
    and your king will bring peace to the
        nations.
His realm will stretch from sea to sea
    and from the Euphrates River* to the ends
        of the earth.*
11 Because of the covenant I made with you,
        sealed with blood,
I will free your prisoners
    from death in a waterless dungeon.
12 Come back to the place of safety,
    all you prisoners who still have hope!
I promise this very day
    that I will repay two blessings for each of
        your troubles.
13 Judah is my bow,
    and Israel is my arrow.

....

9:1a Hebrew *An Oracle: The message.*   **9:1b** Hebrew *land of Hadrach.*   **9:7** Hebrew *and will become a leader in Judah.*
9:9a Hebrew *O daughter of Zion!*   **9:9b** Hebrew *and is being vindicated.*   **9:10a** Hebrew *Ephraim,* referring to the northern kingdom of Israel; also in 9:13.   **9:10b** Hebrew *the river.*   **9:10c** Or *the end of the land.*

PREDICTIONS
(9:9) Jesus' triumphal entry into Jerusalem (Matt 21:1-11) is predicted here, more than 500 years before the event happened. Just as this prophecy was fulfilled when Jesus came to earth, so the prophecies of his second coming are certain to come true. Are you ready for his return?

Jerusalem* is my sword,
and like a warrior, I will brandish it
against the Greeks.*

14 The LORD will appear above his people;
his arrows will fly like lightning!
The Sovereign LORD will sound the
ram's horn
and attack like a whirlwind from the
southern desert.

15 The LORD of Heaven's Armies will protect his
people,
and they will defeat their enemies by
hurling great stones.
They will shout in battle as though drunk
with wine.
They will be filled with blood like a bowl,
drenched with blood like the corners of
the altar.

16 On that day the LORD their God will rescue
his people,
just as a shepherd rescues his sheep.
They will sparkle in his land
like jewels in a crown.

17 How wonderful and beautiful they will be!
The young men will thrive on abundant
grain,
and the young women will flourish on
new wine.

10 THE LORD WILL RESTORE HIS PEOPLE

1 Ask the LORD for rain in the spring,
for he makes the storm clouds.

· ·

FOOLISH TRUST

(10:2) God warned the people not to trust in fortune-tellers or interpreters of dreams. Ever been tempted to consult a psychic or read a horoscope? Maybe you haven't, but some have. Psychic hotlines are big business. And many magazines, newspapers, and Internet sites carry horoscopes. People either want to know what's going to happen in the future or hope to find some direction for their lives in the present. Sadly, some place their trust in just a few lines of text written on the page of a magazine. If you want to trust a few lines of text, check out this promise: Proverbs 3:5-6.

SHEPHERDING THE SHEEP

(10:3–11:17) Zechariah prophesied against the leaders of Israel who failed to care for the people under their care. He also predicted that the coming Savior, "the good shepherd" (John 10:11), would be rejected by his own people. It is a great tragedy for God's people when their leaders fail to care for them adequately. God holds leaders particularly accountable for the condition of his people. The New Testament tells believers, "Not many of you should become teachers in the church, for we who teach will be judged more strictly" (Jas 3:1). If God puts you in a position of leadership, remember that it is also a place of great responsibility.

And he will send showers of rain
so every field becomes a lush pasture.

2 Household gods give worthless advice,
fortune-tellers predict only lies,
and interpreters of dreams pronounce
falsehoods that give no comfort.
So my people are wandering like lost sheep;
they are attacked because they have no
shepherd.

3 "My anger burns against your shepherds,
and I will punish these leaders.*
For the LORD of Heaven's Armies has arrived
to look after Judah, his flock.
He will make them strong and glorious,
like a proud warhorse in battle.

4 From Judah will come the cornerstone,
the tent peg,
the bow for battle,
and all the rulers.

5 They will be like mighty warriors in battle,
trampling their enemies in the mud under
their feet.
Since the LORD is with them as they fight,
they will overthrow even the enemy's
horsemen.

6 "I will strengthen Judah and save Israel*;
I will restore them because of my
compassion.
It will be as though I had never rejected
them,
for I am the LORD their God, who will hear
their cries.

7 The people of Israel* will become like
mighty warriors,
and their hearts will be made happy as
if by wine.
Their children, too, will see it and be glad;
their hearts will rejoice in the LORD.

8 When I whistle to them, they will come
running,
for I have redeemed them.
From the few who are left,
they will grow as numerous as they
were before.

9 Though I have scattered them like seeds
among the nations,
they will still remember me in distant
lands.
They and their children will survive
and return again to Israel.

10 I will bring them back from Egypt
and gather them from Assyria.
I will resettle them in Gilead and Lebanon

9:13a Hebrew *Zion.* 9:13b Hebrew *the sons of Javan.* 10:3 Or *these male goats.* 10:6 Hebrew *save the house of Joseph.* 10:7 Hebrew *of Ephraim.*

until there is no more room for them all.
¹¹ They will pass safely through the sea of
distress,*
for the waves of the sea will be held back,
and the waters of the Nile will dry up.
The pride of Assyria will be crushed,
and the rule of Egypt will end.
¹² By my power* I will make my people strong,
and by my authority they will go wherever
they wish.
I, the LORD, have spoken!"

11

¹ Open your doors, Lebanon,
so that fire may devour your cedar
forests.
² Weep, you cypress trees, for all the ruined
cedars;
the most majestic ones have fallen.
Weep, you oaks of Bashan,
for the thick forests have been cut down.
³ Listen to the wailing of the shepherds,
for their rich pastures are destroyed.
Hear the young lions roaring,
for their thickets in the Jordan Valley
are ruined.

THE GOOD AND EVIL SHEPHERDS ⁴This is
what the LORD my God says: "Go and care for
the flock that is intended for slaughter. ⁵The
buyers slaughter their sheep without remorse.
The sellers say, 'Praise the LORD! Now I'm rich!'
Even the shepherds have no compassion for
them. ⁶Likewise, I will no longer have pity on
the people of the land," says the LORD. "I will
let them fall into each other's hands and into
the hands of their king. They will turn the land
into a wilderness, and I will not rescue them."

⁷So I cared for the flock intended for slaughter—the flock that was oppressed. Then I took
two shepherd's staffs and named one Favor
and the other Union. ⁸I got rid of their three
evil shepherds in a single month.

But I became impatient with these sheep,
and they hated me, too. ⁹So I told them, "I
won't be your shepherd any longer. If you die,
you die. If you are killed, you are killed. And let
those who remain devour each other!"

¹⁰Then I took my staff called Favor and cut
it in two, showing that I had revoked the covenant I had made with all the nations. ¹¹That
was the end of my covenant with them. The
suffering flock was watching me, and they
knew that the LORD was speaking through my
actions.

10:11 Or the sea of Egypt, referring to the Red Sea.   10:12 Hebrew In
the LORD.   11:13 Syriac version reads into the treasury; also in
11:13b. Compare Matt 27:6-10.   11:16 Or the scattered.
12:1 Hebrew An Oracle: This.

¹²And I said to them, "If you like, give me my
wages, whatever I am worth; but only if you
want to." So they counted out for my wages
thirty pieces of silver.

¹³And the LORD said to me, "Throw it to the
potter*"—this magnificent sum at which they
valued me! So I took the thirty coins and threw
them to the potter in the Temple of the LORD.

¹⁴Then I took my other staff, Union, and cut
it in two, showing that the bond of unity between Judah and Israel was broken.

¹⁵Then the LORD said to me, "Go again and
play the part of a worthless shepherd. ¹⁶This illustrates how I will give this nation a shepherd
who will not care for those who are dying, nor
look after the young,* nor heal the injured, nor
feed the healthy. Instead, this shepherd will
eat the meat of the fattest sheep and tear off
their hooves.

¹⁷ "What sorrow awaits this worthless
shepherd
who abandons the flock!
The sword will cut his arm
and pierce his right eye.
His arm will become useless,
and his right eye completely blind."

12

**FUTURE DELIVERANCE FOR JERU-
SALEM** This* message concerning the
fate of Israel came from the LORD: "This message is from the LORD, who stretched out the
heavens, laid the foundations of the earth,
and formed the human spirit. ²I will make Jerusalem like an intoxicating drink that makes the
nearby nations stagger when they send their
armies to besiege Jerusalem and Judah. ³On
that day I will make Jerusalem an immovable
rock. All the nations will gather against it to try
to move it, but they will only hurt themselves.

⁴"On that day," says the LORD, "I will cause
every horse to panic and every rider to lose his
nerve. I will watch over the people of Judah,
but I will blind all the horses of their enemies.
⁵And the clans of Judah will say to themselves,
'The people of Jerusalem have found strength
in the LORD of Heaven's Armies, their God.'

⁶"On that day I will make the clans of Judah
like a flame that sets a woodpile ablaze or like
a burning torch among sheaves of grain. They

A GREAT DAY!
*(12:1-5) This prophecy speaks of a great future battle
against Jerusalem. Some say this battle is Armageddon—
the last great battle on earth. Those who go against God's
people will not prevail forever. One day all evil will be
abolished once and for all. What do you think the world
will be like without it?*

will burn up all the neighboring nations right and left, while the people living in Jerusalem remain secure.

⁷"The LORD will give victory to the rest of Judah first, before Jerusalem, so that the people of Jerusalem and the royal line of David will not have greater honor than the rest of Judah. ⁸On that day the LORD will defend the people of Jerusalem; the weakest among them will be as mighty as King David! And the royal descendants will be like God, like the angel of the LORD who goes before them! ⁹For on that day I will begin to destroy all the nations that come against Jerusalem.

¹⁰"Then I will pour out a spirit* of grace and prayer on the family of David and on the people of Jerusalem. They will look on me whom they have pierced and mourn for him as for an only son. They will grieve bitterly for him as for a firstborn son who has died. ¹¹The sorrow and mourning in Jerusalem on that day will be like the great mourning for Hadad-rimmon in the valley of Megiddo.

¹²"All Israel will mourn, each clan by itself, and with the husbands separate from their wives. The clan of David will mourn alone, as will the clan of Nathan, ¹³the clan of Levi, and the clan of Shimei. ¹⁴Each of the surviving clans from Judah will mourn separately, and with the husbands separate from their wives.

13 A FOUNTAIN OF CLEANSING

"On that day a fountain will be opened for the dynasty of David and for the people of Jerusalem, a fountain to cleanse them from all their sins and impurity.

²"And on that day," says the LORD of Heaven's Armies, "I will erase idol worship throughout the land, so that even the names of the idols will be forgotten. I will remove from the land both the false prophets and the spirit of impurity that came with them. ³If anyone continues to prophesy, his own father and mother will tell him, 'You must die, for you have prophesied lies in the name of the LORD.' And as he prophesies, his own father and mother will stab him.

⸳⸳⸳⸳⸳⸳⸳⸳⸳⸳⸳⸳⸳⸳⸳⸳⸳⸳⸳⸳⸳⸳⸳⸳⸳⸳⸳⸳⸳⸳⸳⸳⸳⸳

ANY MOMENT

(14:1-10) Zechariah warned the people of the coming "day of the LORD." Days of judgment are mentioned in a number of Old Testament passages (see Isa 13:6; Joel 1:15; 2:1; Mal 4:1). One day, the ultimate day of judgment will take place. Jesus will return as the king and judge of all people (see also Mark 13). What if you knew exactly when this judgment day would happen? What, if anything, would you do differently?

⁴"On that day people will be ashamed to claim the prophetic gift. No one will pretend to be a prophet by wearing prophet's clothes. ⁵He will say, 'I'm no prophet; I'm a farmer. I began working for a farmer as a boy.' ⁶And if someone asks, 'Then what about those wounds on your chest?*' he will say, 'I was wounded at my friends' house!'

THE SCATTERING OF THE SHEEP

⁷ "Awake, O sword, against my shepherd,
　　the man who is my partner,"
　　says the LORD of Heaven's Armies.
"Strike down the shepherd,
　　and the sheep will be scattered,
　　and I will turn against the lambs.
⁸ Two-thirds of the people in the land
　　will be cut off and die," says the LORD.
　　"But one-third will be left in the land.
⁹ I will bring that group through the fire
　　and make them pure.
I will refine them like silver
　　and purify them like gold.
They will call on my name,
　　and I will answer them.
I will say, 'These are my people,'
　　and they will say, 'The LORD is our God.'"

14 THE LORD WILL RULE THE EARTH

Watch, for the day of the LORD is coming when your possessions will be plundered right in front of you! ²I will gather all the nations to fight against Jerusalem. The city will be taken, the houses looted, and the women raped. Half the population will be taken into captivity, and the rest will be left among the ruins of the city.

³Then the LORD will go out to fight against those nations, as he has fought in times past. ⁴On that day his feet will stand on the Mount of Olives, east of Jerusalem. And the Mount of Olives will split apart, making a wide valley running from east to west. Half the mountain will move toward the north and half toward the south. ⁵You will flee through this valley, for it will reach across to Azal.* Yes, you will flee as you did from the earthquake in the days of King Uzziah of Judah. Then the LORD my God will come, and all his holy ones with him.*

⁶On that day the sources of light will no longer shine,* ⁷yet there will be continuous day! Only the LORD knows how this could happen. There will be no normal day and night, for at evening time it will still be light.

12:10 Or the Spirit.　**13:6** Hebrew wounds between your hands?　**14:5a** The meaning of the Hebrew is uncertain.　**14:5b** As in Greek version; Hebrew reads with you.　**14:6** Hebrew there will be no light, no cold or frost. The meaning of the Hebrew is uncertain.

⁸On that day life-giving waters will flow out from Jerusalem, half toward the Dead Sea and half toward the Mediterranean,* flowing continuously in both summer and winter.

⁹And the LORD will be king over all the earth. On that day there will be one LORD—his name alone will be worshiped.

¹⁰All the land from Geba, north of Judah, to Rimmon, south of Jerusalem, will become one vast plain. But Jerusalem will be raised up in its original place and will be inhabited all the way from the Benjamin Gate over to the site of the old gate, then to the Corner Gate, and from the Tower of Hananel to the king's winepresses. ¹¹And Jerusalem will be filled, safe at last, never again to be cursed and destroyed.

¹²And the LORD will send a plague on all the nations that fought against Jerusalem. Their people will become like walking corpses, their flesh rotting away. Their eyes will rot in their sockets, and their tongues will rot in their mouths. ¹³On that day they will be terrified, stricken by the LORD with great panic. They will fight their neighbors hand to hand. ¹⁴Judah, too, will be fighting at Jerusalem. The wealth of all the neighboring nations will be captured—great quantities of gold and silver and fine clothing. ¹⁵This same plague will strike the horses, mules, camels, donkeys, and all the other animals in the enemy camps.

¹⁶In the end, the enemies of Jerusalem who survive the plague will go up to Jerusalem each year to worship the King, the LORD of Heaven's Armies, and to celebrate the Festival of Shelters. ¹⁷Any nation in the world that refuses to come to Jerusalem to worship the King, the LORD of Heaven's Armies, will have no rain. ¹⁸If the people of Egypt refuse to attend the festival, the LORD will punish them with the same plague that he sends on the other nations who refuse to go. ¹⁹Egypt and the other nations will all be punished if they don't go to celebrate the Festival of Shelters.

²⁰On that day even the harness bells of the horses will be inscribed with these words: HOLY TO THE LORD. And the cooking pots in the Temple of the LORD will be as sacred as the basins used beside the altar. ²¹In fact, every cooking pot in Jerusalem and Judah will be holy to the LORD of Heaven's Armies. All who come to worship will be free to use any of these pots to boil their sacrifices. And on that day there will no longer be traders* in the Temple of the LORD of Heaven's Armies.

14:8 Hebrew *half toward the eastern sea and half toward the western sea.*   14:21 Hebrew *Canaanites.*

....

PROPHECY PANORAMA
(14:21) Zechariah spoke to a people who were enduring great hardships. They were harassed by neighbors and were discouraged over their small numbers and seemingly inadequate Temple. Consequently, their worship lacked energy and sincerity. Still God declared, "My love for Jerusalem and Mount Zion is passionate and strong" (1:14). He promised to restore their land, their city, and their Temple. Like other prophets, Zechariah blended prophecies of the present, near future, and the final days into one sweeping panorama. Through his message we learn that our hope is found in God, who is in complete control of the world.

MALACHI

"Mom, she did it again!" Sierra's angry voice echoed throughout the house. "Mom!"

Sierra had a little sister, Caitlin, who was five. She never seemed to listen to what she was told.

Because their house was small, Sierra and Caitlin shared a room . . . and a closet. Caitlin, had been told to keep out of Sierra's clothes. Yet Sierra or her mother often found Caitlin in the bedroom, sitting on the floor, surrounded by Sierra's shirts, jeans, shoes . . . Lectures hadn't helped; neither had time-outs. Nothing seemed to deter Caitlin from playing in Sierra's clothes. Sierra wondered if Caitlin ever would learn.

God must have thought the same thing about his people. God had warned them repeatedly that he would punish them if they did not stop sinning. When they refused to change, God punished them. Israel was taken into captivity, and some years later so was Judah. They hadn't learned.

Then God brought his people back. He forgave them and offered them a fresh start. Certainly, they must have learned.

But they hadn't. God's people, rather than learn from the mistakes of their ancestors, chose to repeat their actions. Because they hadn't learned, Malachi came to warn them that God was watching—and he cared.

As you read Malachi, consider the lessons you've learned the hard way over the years. Is there still something you need to learn?

KEY POINTS

REAL LOVE Malachi pointed out the hypocrisy of Israel's "love" for God. God hates hypocrisy and careless living. This kind of lifestyle denies him the relationship he wants to have with us. What we give and how we live reflects the sincerity of our love for God.

THE PRIESTS' SINS Malachi singled out the priests for condemnation. They knew what God required, yet they had a casual attitude toward worshiping God and meeting his standards. We all are leaders in some capacity. Neglect and insensitivity are acts of disobedience. God wants leaders who are faithful and sincere.

THE PEOPLE'S SINS The people had not learned from their exile, nor had they listened to the prophets. Men were callously divorcing their faithful wives to marry younger women from other nations. God deserves our total honor, respect, and faithfulness.

THE LORD'S COMING Malachi prophesied about the coming Messiah. The Messiah's purpose was, and is, to lead the people to the realization of all their fondest hopes. The day of his final coming will be a day of comfort and healing for a faithful few, and a day of judgment for those who reject him.

STATS

PURPOSE
To confront the people with their sins and to restore their relationship with God

AUTHOR
Malachi

ORIGINAL AUDIENCE
The Jews in Jerusalem

DATE WRITTEN
About 430 B.C.

SETTING
Malachi, Haggai, and Zechariah were post-exilic prophets to Judah (the southern kingdom). Haggai and Zechariah rebuked the people for their failure to rebuild the Temple. Malachi confronted them with their neglect of the Temple and their false and profane worship.

KEY PEOPLE
Malachi, the priests

KEY PLACES
Jerusalem, the Temple

SPECIAL FEATURES
Malachi's literary style displays a continual use of questions asked by God and his people (for example, see 3:7-8).

1

This is the message* that the LORD gave to Israel through the prophet Malachi.*

THE LORD'S LOVE FOR ISRAEL ²"I have always loved you," says the LORD.

But you retort, "Really? How have you loved us?"

And the LORD replies, "This is how I showed my love for you: I loved your ancestor Jacob, ³but I rejected his brother, Esau, and devastated his hill country. I turned Esau's inheritance into a desert for jackals."

⁴Esau's descendants in Edom may say, "We have been shattered, but we will rebuild the ruins."

But the LORD of Heaven's Armies replies, "They may try to rebuild, but I will demolish them again. Their country will be known as 'The Land of Wickedness,' and their people will be called 'The People with Whom the LORD Is Forever Angry.' ⁵When you see the destruction for yourselves, you will say, 'Truly, the LORD's greatness reaches far beyond Israel's borders!'"

UNWORTHY SACRIFICES ⁶The LORD of Heaven's Armies says to the priests: "A son honors his father, and a servant respects his master. If I am your father and master, where are the honor and respect I deserve? You have shown contempt for my name!

"But you ask, 'How have we ever shown contempt for your name?'

⁷"You have shown contempt by offering defiled sacrifices on my altar.

"Then you ask, 'How have we defiled the sacrifices?*'

"You defile them by saying the altar of the LORD deserves no respect. ⁸When you give blind animals as sacrifices, isn't that wrong? And isn't it wrong to offer animals that are crippled and diseased? Try giving gifts like that to your governor, and see how pleased he is!" says the LORD of Heaven's Armies.

⁹"Go ahead, beg God to be merciful to you! But when you bring that kind of offering, why should he show you any favor at all?" asks the LORD of Heaven's Armies.

¹⁰"How I wish one of you would shut the Temple doors so that these worthless sacrifices could not be offered! I am not pleased with you," says the LORD of Heaven's Armies, "and I will not accept your offerings. ¹¹But my

1:1a Hebrew *An Oracle: The message.*   1:1b *Malachi* means "my messenger."   1:7 As in Greek version; Hebrew reads *defiled you?*

***

LEFTOVERS
(1:6-14) God accused Israel of dishonoring him by offering imperfect sacrifices. If we give God only our leftover time, money, and energy, we repeat the same sin as these worshipers who didn't want to bring anything valuable to God. What we give to God reflects our attitude toward him. What have you given lately?

CHOSEN
(1:11) A theme that occurs throughout the Old Testament is affirmed in this book—"My name is honored by people of other nations. . . . My name is great among the nations." God planned to save and bless the world through his chosen people—the nation of Israel. Today God's chosen people include all who believe in Jesus—Jews and Gentiles. Does that include you? In what ways are you bringing honor to his name?

CHOICES
halfhearted worship

Last Sunday, Byron and John fidgeted their way through the morning worship service, mumbled their way through the songs, daydreamed their way through the prayers, and played games on their cell phones while the pastor delivered his message. In short, they went through the motions of worshiping God, but they never actually thought about the one they were in church to honor.

What a shame because the songs and sermon were powerful reminders of the greatness of God—to those whose hearts and minds were attentive.

That same Sunday afternoon, Byron and John headed to the mall to catch a new flick filled with car races, chases, and other action. For two hours they were mesmerized, and they emerged into the bright sunlight enthusiastically buzzing about what they had just witnessed on the screen.

Bored with God in the morning . . . enthralled with Hollywood in the afternoon. That's how Byron and John spent last Sunday.

So, what do Byron and John's Sunday activities tell you about where their hearts are? Why do we take worship so lightly? How can we be so moved by the things of this world and so unimpressed by the majesty of our God?

Read Malachi 1:6-14 to find out what God thinks about worthless worship and half-hearted devotion. What would you say to Byron and John?

I see the offering plate passed every Sunday. I'm only a kid. Am I supposed to be giving my money to the church?

In Malachi 3:8-10, God warns that refusing to give him tithes and offerings is actually stealing from him!

So, why should God care? After all, he doesn't need our money. He owns everything! But he knows what an idol money can be.

Maybe that's why Jesus talked about money more than he talked about anything else (see, for example, Matt 6:19-24). He knew that the love of money (rather than money itself) leads to all sorts of problems (1 Tim 6:10).

The best way to keep from idolizing money is to learn the joy of giving it away. Some people do this by tithing: taking 10 percent of their income right off the top and giving it to their local church or in support of a missionary. Others give by supporting a child overseas.

Remember, it doesn't matter how much you give. What matters is your attitude when you give. Read Luke 21:1-4 and 2 Corinthians 9:6-11.

---

name is honored* by people of other nations from morning till night. All around the world they offer* sweet incense and pure offerings in honor of my name. For my name is great among the nations," says the LORD of Heaven's Armies.

¹²"But you dishonor my name with your actions. By bringing contemptible food, you are saying it's all right to defile the Lord's table. ¹³You say, 'It's too hard to serve the LORD,' and you turn up your noses at my commands," says the LORD of Heaven's Armies. "Think of it! Animals that are stolen and crippled and sick are being presented as offerings! Should I accept from you such offerings as these?" asks the LORD.

¹⁴"Cursed is the cheat who promises to give a fine ram from his flock but then sacrifices a defective one to the Lord. For I am a great king," says the LORD of Heaven's Armies, "and my name is feared among the nations!

2 **A WARNING TO THE PRIESTS** "Listen, you priests—this command is for you! ²Listen to me and make up your minds to honor my name," says the LORD of Heaven's Armies, "or I will bring a terrible curse against you. I will curse even the blessings you receive. Indeed, I have already cursed them, because you have not taken my warning to heart. ³I will punish your descendants and splatter your faces with the manure from your festival sacrifices, and I will throw you on the manure pile. ⁴Then at last you will know it was I who sent you this warning so that my covenant with the Levites can continue," says the LORD of Heaven's Armies.

⁵"The purpose of my covenant with the Levites was to bring life and peace, and that

---

is what I gave them. This required reverence from them, and they greatly revered me and stood in awe of my name. ⁶They passed on to the people the truth of the instructions they received from me. They did not lie or cheat; they walked with me, living good and righteous lives, and they turned many from lives of sin.

⁷"The words of a priest's lips should preserve knowledge of God, and people should go to him for instruction, for the priest is the messenger of the LORD of Heaven's Armies. ⁸But you priests have left God's paths. Your instructions have caused many to stumble into sin. You have corrupted the covenant I made with the Levites," says the LORD of Heaven's Armies. ⁹"So I have made you despised and humiliated in the eyes of all the people. For you have not obeyed me but have shown favoritism in the way you carry out my instructions."

A CALL TO FAITHFULNESS ¹⁰Are we not all children of the same Father? Are we not all created by the same God? Then why do we betray each other, violating the covenant of our ancestors?

¹¹Judah has been unfaithful, and a detestable thing has been done in Israel and in Jerusalem. The men of Judah have defiled the LORD's beloved sanctuary by marrying women who worship idols. ¹²May the LORD cut off from the nation of Israel* every last man who has done this and yet brings an offering to the LORD of Heaven's Armies.

¹³Here is another thing you do. You cover the LORD's altar with tears, weeping and groaning because he pays no attention to your offerings and doesn't accept them with pleasure. ¹⁴You cry out, "Why doesn't the LORD accept my worship?" I'll tell you why! Because the LORD witnessed the vows you and your wife made when you were young. But you have been unfaithful

---

1:11a Or *will be honored.* **1:11b** Or *will offer.* **2:12** Hebrew *from the tents of Jacob.* The names "Jacob" and "Israel" are often interchanged throughout the Old Testament, referring sometimes to the individual patriarch and sometimes to the nation.

to her, though she remained your faithful partner, the wife of your marriage vows.

¹⁵Didn't the LORD make you one with your wife? In body and spirit you are his.* And what does he want? Godly children from your union. So guard your heart; remain loyal to the wife of your youth. ¹⁶"For I hate divorce!" says the LORD, the God of Israel. "To divorce your wife is to overwhelm her with cruelty,* says the LORD of Heaven's Armies. "So guard your heart; do not be unfaithful to your wife."

¹⁷You have wearied the LORD with your words. "How have we wearied him?" you ask.

You have wearied him by saying that all who do evil are good in the LORD's sight, and he is

pleased with them. You have wearied him by asking, "Where is the God of justice?"

3 THE COMING DAY OF JUDGMENT "Look! I am sending my messenger, and he will prepare the way before me. Then the Lord you are seeking will suddenly come to his Temple. The messenger of the covenant, whom you look for so eagerly, is surely coming," says the LORD of Heaven's Armies.

²"But who will be able to endure it when he comes? Who will be able to stand and face him

2:15 Or *Didn't the one LORD make us and preserve our life and breath?* or *Didn't the one LORD make her, both flesh and spirit?* The meaning of the Hebrew is uncertain. **2:16** Hebrew *to cover one's garment with violence.*

ULTIMATE ISSUES *DIVORCE*

Everyone knows how prevalent divorce is in our society today. Maybe you're no stranger to the trauma of divorce. Once divorce was considered a social stigma—sort of a "Scarlet Letter" for our time. Now it's so commonplace that we barely even react to the news that another couple is calling it quits.

Before we discuss divorce, let's consider a couple of basic truths about marriage. First, marriage was God's idea. At the beginning of human history, God declared, "It is not good for the man to be alone. I will make a helper who is just right for him" (Gen 2:18). God made Adam and Eve to be husband and wife—one man for one woman—thereby setting the parameters for marriage. Jesus added his stamp of approval by performing his first miracle at a wedding (John 2). Marriage is God's institution; it is "holy ground." No one should enter into it lightly, and no one should walk out of it lightly either.

Divorce, however, is a human invention. When asked why Moses allowed divorce, Jesus replied: "Moses permitted divorce only as a concession to your hard hearts, but it was not what God had originally intended" (Matt 19:8). Divorce was never "Plan A."

We are sinful, fallen people. God knows that we will make mistakes. We will "fall short of God's glorious standard" (Rom 3:23). Our fallen nature affects every area of our lives, including marriage. So God has allowed for divorce in some situations. (For more on the specifics of "biblical divorce," see Matthew 19 and 1 Corinthians 7.) Some marriage relationships become so badly damaged through sexual immorality, desertion, abuse, or betrayal that healing them becomes impossible. At those times God has allowed for divorce. Even so, a divorce is always painful and damaging. That's why, in Mala-

chi 2:16, God says, "I hate divorce!" Even when it is permissible it is terribly destructive to persons made in God's image—an image that takes a real beating from divorce.

If the thought of divorce makes you slightly hesitant about marriage—good. That is a healthy hesitation to have, not because you should be terrified to the point of being paralyzed, but because you shouldn't rush into marriage. If a fuller understanding of the awesome implications of "two becoming one" (see Gen 2:24) causes you to approach the altar with prayer, respect for the holiness of marriage, and a godly perspective on the marriage covenant—great! Marriage is a high calling and should be treated as such. Never approach marriage with the attitude, "Oh well, if it doesn't work out, there's always divorce." Such a mind-set is a formula for marital meltdown.

In 1519 the Spanish conquistadors, headed by Hernán Cortés, landed at Veracruz, Mexico. His army, consisting of 500 men and 16 horses, seemed no match for the thousands of Aztec warriors standing between them and their goal of conquering the Aztec empire. Upon landing, Cortés sent a few of his men to do what seemed like a very stupid thing: burn all 10 of the ships they had sailed over on. In so doing, the Spaniards got their leader's message: Conquer or die. There was no turning back.

When a man and woman say, "I do," they are in effect burning their boats. The two become one, and the only way to fully make that transition is by focusing on the goal ahead: a godly marriage. If either one is constantly looking for a way out, the relationship is in serious trouble. Divorce may provide a sometimes necessary escape hatch, but it is never God's first choice for his children. ∎

I AM THE LORD, AND I DO NOT CHANGE.
THAT IS WHY YOU DESCENDANTS OF JACOB ARE NOT ALREADY DESTROYED. (MALACHI 3:6)

when he appears? For he will be like a blazing fire that refines metal, or like a strong soap that bleaches clothes. ³He will sit like a refiner of silver, burning away the dross. He will purify the Levites, refining them like gold and silver, so that they may once again offer acceptable sacrifices to the LORD. ⁴Then once more the LORD will accept the offerings brought to him by the people of Judah and Jerusalem, as he did in the past.

⁵"At that time I will put you on trial. I am eager to witness against all sorcerers and adulterers and liars. I will speak against those who cheat employees of their wages, who oppress widows and orphans, or who deprive the foreigners living among you of justice, for these people do not fear me," says the LORD of Heaven's Armies.

A CALL TO REPENTANCE ⁶"I am the LORD, and I do not change. That is why you descendants of Jacob are not already destroyed. ⁷Ever since the days of your ancestors, you have scorned my decrees and failed to obey them. Now return to me, and I will return to you," says the LORD of Heaven's Armies.

"But you ask, 'How can we return when we have never gone away?'

⁸"Should people cheat God? Yet you have cheated me!

"But you ask, 'What do you mean? When did we ever cheat you?'

"You have cheated me of the tithes and offerings due to me. ⁹You are under a curse, for your whole nation has been cheating me. ¹⁰Bring all the tithes into the storehouse so there will be enough food in my Temple. If you do," says the LORD of Heaven's Armies, "I will open the windows of heaven for you. I will pour out a blessing so great you won't have enough room to take it in! Try it! Put me to the test! ¹¹Your crops will be abundant, for I will guard them from insects and disease.* Your grapes will not fall from the vine before they are ripe," says the LORD of Heaven's Armies. ¹²"Then all nations will call you blessed, for your land will be such a delight," says the LORD of Heaven's Armies.

¹³"You have said terrible things about me," says the LORD.

3:11 Hebrew *from the devourer.*   4:1 Verses 4:1-6 are numbered 3:19-24 in Hebrew text.

"But you say, 'What do you mean? What have we said against you?'

¹⁴"You have said, 'What's the use of serving God? What have we gained by obeying his commands or by trying to show the LORD of Heaven's Armies that we are sorry for our sins?' ¹⁵From now on we will call the arrogant blessed. For those who do evil get rich, and those who dare God to punish them suffer no harm.'"

THE LORD'S PROMISE OF MERCY ¹⁶Then those who feared the LORD spoke with each other, and the LORD listened to what they said. In his presence, a scroll of remembrance was written to record the names of those who feared him and always thought about the honor of his name.

¹⁷"They will be my people," says the LORD of Heaven's Armies. "On the day when I act in judgment, they will be my own special treasure. I will spare them as a father spares an obedient child. ¹⁸Then you will again see the difference between the righteous and the wicked, between those who serve God and those who do not."

4 **THE COMING DAY OF JUDGMENT** ¹*The LORD of Heaven's Armies says, "The day of judgment is coming, burning like a furnace. On that day the arrogant and the wicked will be burned up like straw. They will be consumed—roots, branches, and all.

²"But for you who fear my name, the Sun of Righteousness will rise with healing in his

···

HOLDING BACK
(3:6-12) Malachi urged the people not to hold back their gifts (tithes) to the priests. Tithing began during Moses' time (see Lev 27:30-34; Deut 14:22-25). The Levites received some of the tithes because they couldn't own land (Num 18:20-21). But during Malachi's day, since the tithes weren't given to support God's workers, the Levites had to go to work. God has given us everything. When we refuse to return to him a part of what he has given, we rob him. What are you willing to give to help advance God's kingdom?

WHY SERVE GOD?
(3:13-15) These verses deal with the people's arrogant attitude toward God. When we say, "What good does it do to serve God?" we are really saying, "What good does it do for me?" Our focus is selfish. Our real question should be, "What good does it do for God?" We must serve God just because he is God and deserves it.

MALACHI

Served as a prophet to Judah about 430 B.C. He was the last of the Old Testament prophets.

CLIMATE OF THE TIMES	The city of Jerusalem and the Temple had been rebuilt for almost a century, but the people had become complacent in their worship of God.
MAIN MESSAGE	The people's relationship with God was broken because of their sin, and they would soon be punished. But the few who repented would receive God's blessing, illustrated in his promise to send a Messiah.
IMPORTANCE OF MESSAGE	Hypocrisy, neglecting God, and careless living have devastating consequences. Service and worship of God must be the primary focus of our life, both now and in eternity.
CONTEMPORARY PROPHETS	None

COST OF COMMITMENT
(4:4) Malachi gives us practical guidelines about commitment to God. He deserves the best we have to offer (1:7-14). We must be willing to change any wrong attitudes or ways of living (2:1-2), make family a priority (2:13-16), submit to God's refining process (3:3), give of our resources (3:8-12), and put pride aside (3:13-15).

Malachi closes his message by pointing to the day of judgment. For those committed to God, it will be a day of joy, of ushering in eternity in God's presence. Those who have ignored God will be "straw" to be burned (4:1). To help people prepare for that day, God was to send a prophet (John the Baptist). At the beginning of the New Testament, we read about this prophet calling the people to turn from their sins and turn toward God. Such a commitment to God demands great sacrifice on our part. Is this a sacrifice you're prepared to make?

wings.* And you will go free, leaping with joy like calves let out to pasture. ³On the day when I act, you will tread upon the wicked as if they were dust under your feet," says the LORD of Heaven's Armies.

⁴"Remember to obey the Law of Moses, my servant—all the decrees and regulations that I gave him on Mount Sinai* for all Israel.

⁵"Look, I am sending you the prophet Elijah before the great and dreadful day of the LORD arrives. ⁶His preaching will turn the hearts of fathers to their children, and the hearts of children to their fathers. Otherwise I will come and strike the land with a curse."

4:2 Or *the sun of righteousness will rise with healing in its wings.*
4:4 Hebrew *Horeb,* another name for Sinai.

NEW TESTAMENT

MATTHEW

Who would you put on a list of the most influential people of all time? We're talking about the real "heavyweights of history." Men and women about whom we say, "Because of his (or her) presence, the world will never be the same."

Your list might feature leaders both good and bad: Julius Caesar, Martin Luther King, Jr., Napoleon, Abraham Lincoln, Genghis Khan, Mohammed, Alexander the Great, or Mohandas Gandhi. Or, maybe your list includes people who helped advance science and technology: Marie Curie, George Washington Carver, Henry Ford, Albert Einstein, Thomas Edison, Alexander Graham Bell, Bill Gates, or Steve Jobs.

Those people—and many others—deserve to be on such a list. But if you're looking for the one person who changed the world more than anyone, check out Jesus.

Two thousand years ago, Jesus of Nazareth launched a spiritual revolution that continues today. He has been the motivation behind more songs, sermons, and acts of charity, and is the object of more affection, than all of the other great figures of history combined. And don't forget the millions of lives that have been transformed by his timeless touch.

See for yourself how Jesus turned ancient Israel on its ear. In the Gospel of Matthew, you'll also begin to see why he still rocks the planet.

STATS

PURPOSE
To prove that Jesus is the Messiah, the eternal King

AUTHOR
Matthew (Levi)

ORIGINAL AUDIENCE
The Jewish People

DATE WRITTEN
Around A.D. 60–65

SETTING
Matthew was a Jewish tax collector who became one of Jesus' disciples. This Gospel connects the Old and New Testaments by emphasizing the fulfillment of prophecy.

KEY PEOPLE
Jesus, Mary, Joseph, John the Baptist, Jesus' disciples, Jewish religious leaders, Caiaphas, Pilate, Mary Magdalene

KEY PLACES
Bethlehem, Jerusalem, Capernaum, Galilee, Judea

KEY POINTS

JESUS CHRIST, THE KING Jesus is the King of kings. His miraculous birth, his life and teaching, his miracles, and his resurrection show us who he really is. He is the supreme ruler of time and eternity, heaven and earth, people and angels. We should give him his rightful place as King and Lord.

EXPECTATIONS ABOUT THE SAVIOR. Jesus was the Messiah, the deliverer for whom the Jews had waited for centuries. Many rejected him because he didn't fit their expectations. Likewise, our expectations of Jesus may need to be adjusted. God wants us to accept him as he is.

THE KINGDOM OF GOD Jesus preached about the Kingdom of God, and how people could belong to it through spiritual rebirth. We can belong to this Kingdom now through faith in Jesus.

TEACHINGS Jesus taught the people using sermons, illustrations, and parables. He illustrated true faith and warned against hypocrisy. As we follow Jesus, we prepare for life in his Kingdom.

RESURRECTION Jesus rose from the dead in power as the true King. The Resurrection shows that Jesus is all-powerful—even over death. People who believe in Jesus can hope for a resurrection like his. Our role is to live in that victory and share the message of his victory with those who do not yet know that "Jesus is alive!"

TIMELINE

6/5 B.C.
Jesus is born

5/4 B.C.
Jesus' family escapes to Egypt

4/3 B.C.
Jesus' family returns to Nazareth

6/7
Jesus visits the Temple as a boy

26/27
Jesus begins his ministry

28
Jesus chooses 12 disciples

29
Jesus feeds 5,000

30
Jesus is crucified, rises again, and ascends to heaven

The broken lines (—·—·—) indicate modern boundaries.

A MINISTRY ON THE MOVE
Jesus' earthly story begins in the town of Bethlehem in the Roman province of Judea (2:1). A threat to kill the infant King led Joseph to take his family to Egypt (2:14). When they returned, God led them to settle in Nazareth in Galilee (2:22-23). At about age 30, Jesus was baptized in the Jordan River (3:13) and was tempted by Satan in the Judean wilderness (4:1). He set up his base of operations in Capernaum (4:12-13) and from there ministered throughout Israel, telling parables, teaching about the Kingdom, and healing the sick. He traveled to the country of the Gadarenes and healed two demon-possessed men (8:28-34); fed over 5,000 people with five loaves of bread and two fish on the shores of Galilee near Bethsaida (14:13-21); healed the sick in Gennesaret (14:34-36); ministered to the Gentiles in Tyre and Sidon (15:21-28); visited Caesarea Philippi, where Peter declared him to be the Messiah (16:13-20); and taught in Perea, across the Jordan River (19:1). As he set out on his last journey to Jerusalem, he told the disciples what would happen to him there (20:17-19). He spent some time in Jericho (20:29), then stayed in Bethany at night as he went back and forth into Jerusalem during his last week (21:17). In Jerusalem, he would be crucified, but he would rise again.

1 THE ANCESTORS OF JESUS THE MESSIAH

This is a record of the ancestors of Jesus the Messiah, a descendant of David* and of Abraham:

² Abraham was the father of Isaac.
Isaac was the father of Jacob.
Jacob was the father of Judah and his brothers.

··

ORDINARY PEOPLE, EXTRAORDINARY GOD
(1:1-17) In the first 17 verses of Matthew we meet 46 people spanning 2,000 years. All were ancestors of Jesus, but they varied considerably in personality, spirituality, and experience. Some were well-known for their faith (Abraham, Isaac, Ruth, and David). Many were ordinary (Hezron, Ram, and Akim). Others had bad reputations (Manasseh and Abijah). God's work has never been limited by human failures. He works through ordinary people to accomplish extraordinary things. What has he accomplished through you?

³ Judah was the father of Perez and Zerah (whose mother was Tamar).
Perez was the father of Hezron.
Hezron was the father of Ram.*
⁴ Ram was the father of Amminadab.
Amminadab was the father of Nahshon.
Nahshon was the father of Salmon.
⁵ Salmon was the father of Boaz (whose mother was Rahab).
Boaz was the father of Obed (whose mother was Ruth).
Obed was the father of Jesse.
⁶ Jesse was the father of King David.
David was the father of Solomon (whose mother was Bathsheba, the widow of Uriah).
⁷ Solomon was the father of Rehoboam.
Rehoboam was the father of Abijah.

1:1 Greek *Jesus the Messiah, son of David.* **1:3** Greek *Aram*, a variant spelling of Ram; also in 1:4. See 1 Chr 2:9-10.

Abijah was the father of Asa.*
8 Asa was the father of Jehoshaphat.
Jehoshaphat was the father of Jehoram.*
Jehoram was the father* of Uzziah.
9 Uzziah was the father of Jotham.
Jotham was the father of Ahaz.
Ahaz was the father of Hezekiah.
10 Hezekiah was the father of Manasseh.
Manasseh was the father of Amon.*
Amon was the father of Josiah.
11 Josiah was the father of Jehoiachin* and
his brothers (born at the time of the exile
to Babylon).
12 After the Babylonian exile:
Jehoiachin was the father of Shealtiel.
Shealtiel was the father of Zerubbabel.
13 Zerubbabel was the father of Abiud.
Abiud was the father of Eliakim.
Eliakim was the father of Azor.
14 Azor was the father of Zadok.
Zadok was the father of Akim.
Akim was the father of Eliud.
15 Eliud was the father of Eleazar.
Eleazar was the father of Matthan.
Matthan was the father of Jacob.
16 Jacob was the father of Joseph, the
husband of Mary.
Mary gave birth to Jesus, who is called
the Messiah.

17All those listed above include fourteen generations from Abraham to David, fourteen from
David to the Babylonian exile, and fourteen
from the Babylonian exile to the Messiah.

THE BIRTH OF JESUS THE MESSIAH 18This is
how Jesus the Messiah was born. His mother,
Mary, was engaged to be married to Joseph.
But before the marriage took place, while
she was still a virgin, she became pregnant
through the power of the Holy Spirit. 19Joseph,
her fiancé, was a good man and did not want
to disgrace her publicly, so he decided to
break the engagement* quietly.

20As he considered this, an angel of the Lord
appeared to him in a dream. "Joseph, son of
David," the angel said, "do not be afraid to
take Mary as your wife. For the child within her
was conceived by the Holy Spirit. 21And she will
have a son, and you are to name him Jesus,*
for he will save his people from their sins."

AND SHE WILL HAVE A SON, AND YOU ARE TO NAME HIM JESUS, FOR HE WILL SAVE HIS PEOPLE FROM THEIR SINS.

MATTHEW 1:21

22All of this occurred to fulfill the Lord's message through his prophet:

23 "Look! The virgin will conceive a child!
She will give birth to a son,
and they will call him Immanuel,*
which means 'God is with us.'"

24When Joseph woke up, he did as the angel
of the Lord commanded and took Mary as his
wife. 25But he did not have sexual relations
with her until her son was born. And Joseph
named him Jesus.

2 VISITORS FROM THE EAST Jesus was born
in Bethlehem in Judea, during the reign of
King Herod. About that time some wise men*
from eastern lands arrived in Jerusalem, asking, 2"Where is the newborn king of the Jews?
We saw his star as it rose,* and we have come
to worship him."

3King Herod was deeply disturbed when he
heard this, as was everyone in Jerusalem. 4He
called a meeting of the leading priests and
teachers of religious law and asked, "Where is
the Messiah supposed to be born?"

5"In Bethlehem in Judea," they said, "for this
is what the prophet wrote:

6 'And you, O Bethlehem in the land of Judah,
are not least among the ruling cities*
of Judah,
for a ruler will come from you
who will be the shepherd for my people
Israel.'*"

....

UNSTOPPABLE
*(2:1-18) When told about the newborn King, Herod
devised a cruel plan to ensure he would keep his
throne (2:16-18). This sad event was prophesied
in Jeremiah 31:15.*

*But God protected his Son. Herod couldn't stop God's
plan. No one could. This fact is no less true today. Yet
because of the evil they see around them, many people
wonder if God is really all-powerful. Is that your belief?
The plans of a sovereign God—a God still in control—
cannot be stopped.*

1:7 Greek Asaph, a variant spelling of Asa; also in 1:8. See 1 Chr 3:10.
1:8a Greek Joram, a variant spelling of Jehoram; also in 1:8b. See
1 Kgs 22:50 and note at 1 Chr 3:11. 1:8b Or ancestor; also in 1:11.
1:10 Greek Amos, a variant spelling of Amon; also in 1:10b. See 1 Chr
3:14. 1:11 Greek Jeconiah, a variant spelling of Jehoiachin; also in
1:12. See 2 Kgs 24:6 and note at 1 Chr 3:16. 1:19 Greek to divorce
her. 1:21 Jesus means "The LORD saves." 1:23 Isa 7:14; 8:8, 10
(Greek version). 2:1 Or royal astrologers; Greek reads magi; also in
2:7, 16. 2:2 Or star in the east. 2:6a Greek the rulers. 2:6b Mic
5:2; 2 Sam 5:2.

7Then Herod called for a private meeting with the wise men, and he learned from them the time when the star first appeared. 8Then he told them, "Go to Bethlehem and search carefully for the child. And when you find him, come back and tell me so that I can go and worship him, too!"

9After this interview the wise men went their way. And the star they had seen in the east guided them to Bethlehem. It went ahead of them and stopped over the place where the child was. 10When they saw the star, they were filled with joy! 11They entered the house and saw the child with his mother, Mary, and they bowed down and worshiped him. Then they opened their treasure chests and gave him gifts of gold, frankincense, and myrrh.

12When it was time to leave, they returned to their own country by another route, for God had warned them in a dream not to return to Herod.

THE ESCAPE TO EGYPT

13After the wise men were gone, an angel of the Lord appeared to Joseph in a dream. "Get up! Flee to Egypt with the child and his mother," the angel said. "Stay there until I tell you to return, because Herod is going to search for the child to kill him."

14That night Joseph left for Egypt with the child and Mary, his mother, 15and they stayed there until Herod's death. This fulfilled what the Lord had spoken through the prophet: "I called my Son out of Egypt."*

16Herod was furious when he realized that the wise men had outwitted him. He sent soldiers to kill all the boys in and around Bethlehem who were two years old and under, based on the wise men's report of the star's first appearance. 17Herod's brutal action fulfilled what God had spoken through the prophet Jeremiah:

18 "A cry was heard in Ramah—
      weeping and great mourning.
    Rachel weeps for her children,
      refusing to be comforted,
        for they are dead."*

PROVE IT
(3:1-8) *According to John the Baptist, actions speak louder than words. As he told the people of Israel, "Prove by the way you live that you have repented of your sins and turned to God" (3:8). God looks beyond our words and "Christian" activities (going to church, reading the Bible, giving money) to see if the way we live backs up what we say. Do your actions agree with your words?*

THE RETURN TO NAZARETH

19When Herod died, an angel of the Lord appeared in a dream to Joseph in Egypt. 20"Get up!" the angel said. "Take the child and his mother back to the land of Israel, because those who were trying to kill the child are dead."

21So Joseph got up and returned to the land of Israel with Jesus and his mother. 22But when he learned that the new ruler of Judea was Herod's son Archelaus, he was afraid to go there. Then, after being warned in a dream, he left for the region of Galilee. 23So the family went and lived in a town called Nazareth. This fulfilled what the prophets had said: "He will be called a Nazarene."

3 JOHN THE BAPTIST PREPARES THE WAY

In those days John the Baptist came to the Judean wilderness and began preaching. His message was, 2"Repent of your sins and turn to God, for the Kingdom of Heaven is near.*" 3The prophet Isaiah was speaking about John when he said,

"He is a voice shouting in the wilderness,
  'Prepare the way for the LORD's coming!
    Clear the road for him!'"*

4John's clothes were woven from coarse camel hair, and he wore a leather belt around his waist. For food he ate locusts and wild honey. 5People from Jerusalem and from all of Judea and all over the Jordan Valley went out to see and hear John. 6And when they confessed their sins, he baptized them in the Jordan River.

7But when he saw many Pharisees and Sadducees coming to watch him baptize,* he denounced them. "You brood of snakes!" he exclaimed. "Who warned you to flee God's coming wrath? 8Prove by the way you live that you have repented of your sins and turned to God. 9Don't just say to each other, 'We're safe, for we are descendants of Abraham.' That means nothing, for I tell you, God can create children of Abraham from these very stones. 10Even now the ax of God's judgment is poised, ready to sever the roots of the trees. Yes, every tree that does not produce good fruit will be chopped down and thrown into the fire.

11"I baptize with* water those who repent of their sins and turn to God. But someone is coming soon who is greater than I am—so much greater that I'm not worthy even to be his slave and carry his sandals. He will baptize you with the Holy Spirit and with fire.* 12He

2:15 Hos 11:1.   **2:18** Jer 31:15.   **3:2** Or has come, or is coming soon.   **3:3** Isa 40:3 (Greek version).   **3:7** Or coming to be baptized.   **3:11a** Or in.   **3:11b** Or in the Holy Spirit and in fire.

is ready to separate the chaff from the wheat with his winnowing fork. Then he will clean up the threshing area, gathering the wheat into his barn but burning the chaff with never-ending fire."

THE BAPTISM OF JESUS [13]Then Jesus went from Galilee to the Jordan River to be baptized by John. [14]But John tried to talk him out of it. "I am the one who needs to be baptized by you," he said, "so why are you coming to me?"

[15]But Jesus said, "It should be done, for we must carry out all that God requires.*" So John agreed to baptize him.

[16]After his baptism, as Jesus came up out of the water, the heavens were opened* and he saw the Spirit of God descending like a dove and settling on him. [17]And a voice from heaven said, "This is my dearly loved Son, who brings me great joy."

4 **THE TEMPTATION OF JESUS** Then Jesus was led by the Spirit into the wilderness to be tempted there by the devil. [2]For forty days and forty nights he fasted and became very hungry.

[3]During that time the devil* came and said to him, "If you are the Son of God, tell these stones to become loaves of bread."

[4]But Jesus told him, "No! The Scriptures say,

'People do not live by bread alone,
    but by every word that comes from the
        mouth of God.'*"

[5]Then the devil took him to the holy city, Jerusalem, to the highest point of the Temple, [6]and said, "If you are the Son of God, jump off! For the Scriptures say,

'He will order his angels to protect you.
And they will hold you up with their hands
    so you won't even hurt your foot on a
        stone.'*"

[7]Jesus responded, "The Scriptures also say, 'You must not test the LORD your God.'*"

[8]Next the devil took him to the peak of a very high mountain and showed him all the kingdoms of the world and their glory. [9]"I will give it all to you," he said, "if you will kneel down and worship me."

[10]"Get out of here, Satan," Jesus told him. "For the Scriptures say,

'You must worship the LORD your God
    and serve only him.'*"

[11]Then the devil went away, and angels came and took care of Jesus.

THE MINISTRY OF JESUS BEGINS [12]When Jesus heard that John had been arrested, he left Judea and returned to Galilee. [13]He went first to Nazareth, then left there and moved to Capernaum, beside the Sea of Galilee, in the region of Zebulun and Naphtali. [14]This fulfilled what God said through the prophet Isaiah:

[15] "In the land of Zebulun and of Naphtali,
    beside the sea, beyond the Jordan River,
    in Galilee where so many Gentiles live,
[16] the people who sat in darkness
    have seen a great light.
And for those who lived in the land where
        death casts its shadow,
    a light has shined."*

[17]From then on Jesus began to preach, "Repent of your sins and turn to God, for the Kingdom of Heaven is near.*"

THE FIRST DISCIPLES [18]One day as Jesus was walking along the shore of the Sea of Galilee, he saw two brothers—Simon, also called Peter, and Andrew—throwing a net into the water, for they fished for a living. [19]Jesus called out to them, "Come, follow me, and I will show you how to fish for people!" [20]And they left their nets at once and followed him.

[21]A little farther up the shore he saw two other brothers, James and John, sitting in a boat with their father, Zebedee, repairing their nets. And he called them to come, too. [22]They immediately followed him, leaving the boat and their father behind.

CROWDS FOLLOW JESUS [23]Jesus traveled throughout the region of Galilee, teaching in the synagogues and announcing the Good News about the Kingdom. And he healed every kind of disease and illness. [24]News about him spread as far as Syria, and people soon began

<hr>

INTEGRITY

(3:11-15) Put yourself in John's shoes. Your work is going well; people are taking notice. But you know your work is to prepare people's hearts for someone else—the coming Savior (3:11; John 1:27-36). Now Jesus has arrived, and with him, the real test of your integrity. Will you be able to turn your followers over to him? John passed the test by publicly baptizing Jesus. Soon John would say, "He must become greater and greater, and I must become less and less" (John 3:30). Are you willing to say the same?

3:15 Or for we must fulfill all righteousness.   **3:16** Some manuscripts read opened to him.   **4:3** Greek the tempter.   **4:4** Deut 8:3.   **4:6** Ps 91:11-12.   **4:7** Deut 6:16.   **4:10** Deut 6:13.   **4:15-16** Isa 9:1-2 (Greek version).   **4:17** Or has come, or is coming soon.

bringing to him all who were sick. And whatever their sickness or disease, or if they were demon possessed or epileptic or paralyzed—he healed them all. ²⁵Large crowds followed him wherever he went—people from Galilee, the Ten Towns,* Jerusalem, from all over Judea, and from east of the Jordan River.

5 THE SERMON ON THE MOUNT

One day as he saw the crowds gathering, Jesus went up on the mountainside and sat down. His disciples gathered around him, ²and he began to teach them.

THE BEATITUDES

³ "God blesses those who are poor and
    realize their need for him,*
    for the Kingdom of Heaven is theirs.
⁴ God blesses those who mourn,
    for they will be comforted.
⁵ God blesses those who are humble,
    for they will inherit the whole earth.
⁶ God blesses those who hunger and thirst for
    justice,*

A "BLESSED" LIFE

(5:1-12) Jesus began his sermon with words that seem to contradict each other. After all, no one would think that someone facing persecution or death was "blessed"—in favor with God. But God's way of living usually contradicts the world's way. He wants his people to give when others take, to love when others hate, to help when others abuse. Is his way your way?

for they will be satisfied.
⁷ God blesses those who are merciful,
    for they will be shown mercy.
⁸ God blesses those whose hearts are pure,
    for they will see God.
⁹ God blesses those who work for peace,
    for they will be called the children of God.
¹⁰ God blesses those who are persecuted for
    doing right,
    for the Kingdom of Heaven is theirs.

¹¹"God blesses you when people mock you and persecute you and lie about you* and say all sorts of evil things against you because you are my followers. ¹²Be happy about it! Be very glad! For a great reward awaits you in heaven. And remember, the ancient prophets were persecuted in the same way.

TEACHING ABOUT SALT AND LIGHT

¹³"You are the salt of the earth. But what good is salt if it has lost its flavor? Can you make it salty again? It will be thrown out and trampled underfoot as worthless.

¹⁴"You are the light of the world—like a city on a hilltop that cannot be hidden. ¹⁵No one lights a lamp and then puts it under a basket. Instead, a lamp is placed on a stand, where it gives light to everyone in the house. ¹⁶In the same way, let your good deeds shine out for

4:25 Greek *Decapolis.*   **5:3** Greek *poor in spirit.*   **5:6** Or *for righteousness.*   **5:11** Some manuscripts do not include *and lie about you.*

I WONDER...

I'm trying to understand how the Old and New Testaments relate to each other. Which one is more important?

It's not that one is more important than the other. Instead, it's a question of timing.

Imagine being seven years old and your parents sitting you down and telling you all of the rules about driving a car. Not only would you have tuned them out after about two minutes, but ten years later when it came time to drive, you wouldn't have remembered anything they said.

Timing is everything. Wise parents have figured this out; that's why they didn't give you all their rules as soon as you could talk. They waited until you were ready so that you would want to listen, the rules would make sense to you, and you would remember what they said.

The Old Testament was given to us for several reasons. After explaining Creation, its main purpose was to show God's developing plan for rescuing humanity

from the power of sin. In Matthew 5:21-48, we see Jesus contrasting the Old and New Testaments. Romans 7:7 tells us that the Old Testament Law was good because it showed us what sin was, and thus, showed us our need for a Savior.

That's why the Old Testament points directly to Christ as the Savior we needed. There are dozens of verses that tell the exact place of Jesus' birth, his sinless life, his death on the Cross, his resurrection, and his return. Though the Old Testament was written from about 1460 to 430 B.C., it predicted minute details about the life of Jesus! This also serves to prove the inspiration of the Scriptures.

The Old Testament also helps the New Testament make sense. In Matthew 5:17, Jesus said he came to fulfill the law, not to abolish it. The Old Testament helps us understand why Jesus did what he did.

The Old Testament speaks of sacrifices (picturing Jesus as the ultimate sacrifice) and having faith in God's promise. This was how God prepared the way for Christ.

all to see, so that everyone will praise your heavenly Father.

TEACHING ABOUT THE LAW ¹⁷"Don't misunderstand why I have come. I did not come to abolish the law of Moses or the writings of the prophets. No, I came to accomplish their purpose. ¹⁸I tell you the truth, until heaven and earth disappear, not even the smallest detail of God's law will disappear until its purpose is achieved. ¹⁹So if you ignore the least commandment and teach others to do the same, you will be called the least in the Kingdom of Heaven. But anyone who obeys God's laws and teaches them will be called great in the Kingdom of Heaven.

²⁰"But I warn you—unless your righteousness is better than the righteousness of the teachers of religious law and the Pharisees, you will never enter the Kingdom of Heaven!

TEACHING ABOUT ANGER ²¹"You have heard that our ancestors were told, 'You must not murder. If you commit murder, you are subject to judgment.'* ²²But I say, if you are even angry with someone,* you are subject to judgment! If you call someone an idiot,* you are in danger of being brought before the court. And if you curse someone,* you are in danger of the fires of hell.*

²³"So if you are presenting a sacrifice* at the altar in the Temple and you suddenly remember that someone has something against you, ²⁴leave your sacrifice there at the altar. Go and be reconciled to that person. Then come and offer your sacrifice to God.

²⁵"When you are on the way to court with your adversary, settle your differences quickly. Otherwise, your accuser may hand you over to the judge, who will hand you over to an officer, and you will be thrown into prison. ²⁶And if that happens, you surely won't be free again until you have paid the last penny.*

TEACHING ABOUT ADULTERY ²⁷"You have heard the commandment that says, 'You must not commit adultery.'* ²⁸But I say, anyone who even looks at a woman with lust has already committed adultery with her in his heart. ²⁹So if your eye—even your good eye*—causes you to lust, gouge it out and throw it away. It is better for you to lose one part of your body

5:21 Exod 20:13; Deut 5:17.   **5:22a** Some manuscripts add *without cause.*   **5:22b** Greek uses an Aramaic term of contempt: *If you say to your brother, 'Raca.'*   **5:22c** Greek *if you say, 'You fool.'*   **5:22d** Greek *Gehenna;* also in 5:29, 30.   **5:23** Greek *gift;* also in 5:24.   **5:26** Greek *the last kodrantes* [i.e., quadrans].   **5:27** Exod 20:14; Deut 5:18.   **5:29** Greek *your right eye.*

MY STORY: Suzi

Who would've thought that during a soccer game I would apply Matthew 5:38-39 about "turning the other cheek" in a very real way?

I was captain of the team. The other team was really out for blood—they took cheap shots every chance they got, elbowing and kicking. The refs never saw any of it. People don't realize how dirty girls can play. My team started taking matters into their own hands.

One time I was passed the ball and managed to have a clear break—only one person stood in my way. But she decided to play rough. So, instead of scoring, I was injured and taken out of the game. I was angry, but I started praying about it.

By halftime the other girls on my team were really down. But I told them not to seek revenge—not to take the attitude of "an eye for eye," but to "offer the other cheek" as Matthew 5:39 says—in other words, to play fair. I told them that's what I planned to do.

I went back into the game and made sure I played clean. My team followed my example. I scored two goals late in the game and our team tied, 2–2.

The most important thing to me wasn't the score of that game, though. It was the fact that playing clean really was better. I think the whole team learned something that day. I know I did.

....

ANGER MANAGEMENT
(5:21-22) Jesus spoke about the wrongs that result from anger. Everyone would agree that murder is wrong. But anger? No way. Yet anger in this case refers to uncontrolled anger. This type of anger can lead to violence, emotional hurt, increased mental stress, and other destructive results.

Does this mean that anger is wrong? If you believe that, check out Jesus' actions in John 2:13-16 or the advice of Ephesians 4:26-27. The wise person practices self-control over thoughts and actions (see Gal 5:22-23; 2 Pet 1:6). Get control of anger before it controls you.

SEVEN REASONS NOT TO WORRY

1	2	3	4	5	6	7
The same God who created life in you can be trusted with the details of your life. 6:25	Worrying about the future hampers your efforts for today. 6:26	Worrying is more harmful than helpful. 6:27	God does not ignore those who depend on him. 6:28-30	Worry shows a lack of faith and understanding of God. 6:31-32	There are real challenges God wants us to pursue, and worrying keeps us from them. 6:33	Living one day at a time keeps us from being consumed with worry. 6:34

than for your whole body to be thrown into hell. ³⁰And if your hand—even your stronger hand*—causes you to sin, cut it off and throw it away. It is better for you to lose one part of your body than for your whole body to be thrown into hell.

TEACHING ABOUT DIVORCE ³¹"You have heard the law that says, 'A man can divorce his wife by merely giving her a written notice of divorce.'* ³²But I say that a man who divorces his wife, unless she has been unfaithful, causes her to commit adultery. And anyone who marries a divorced woman also commits adultery.

TEACHING ABOUT VOWS ³³"You have also heard that our ancestors were told, 'You must not break your vows; you must carry out the vows you make to the LORD.'* ³⁴But I say, do not make any vows! Do not say, 'By heaven!' because heaven is God's throne. ³⁵And do not say, 'By the earth!' because the earth is his footstool. And do not say, 'By Jerusalem!' for Jerusalem is the city of the great King. ³⁶Do not even say, 'By my head!' for you can't turn one hair white or black. ³⁷Just say a simple, 'Yes, I will,' or 'No, I won't.' Anything beyond this is from the evil one.

TEACHING ABOUT REVENGE ³⁸"You have heard the law that says the punishment must match the injury: 'An eye for an eye, and a tooth for a tooth.'* ³⁹But I say, do not resist an evil person! If someone slaps you on the right cheek, offer the other cheek also. ⁴⁰If you are sued in court and your shirt is taken from you, give your coat, too. ⁴¹If a soldier demands that you carry his gear for a mile,* carry it two miles. ⁴²Give to those who ask, and don't turn away from those who want to borrow.

TEACHING ABOUT LOVE FOR ENEMIES ⁴³"You have heard the law that says, 'Love your neighbor'* and hate your enemy. ⁴⁴But I say, love

your enemies!* Pray for those who persecute you! ⁴⁵In that way, you will be acting as true children of your Father in heaven. For he gives his sunlight to both the evil and the good, and he sends rain on the just and the unjust alike. ⁴⁶If you love only those who love you, what reward is there for that? Even corrupt tax collectors do that much. ⁴⁷If you are kind only to your friends,* how are you different from anyone else? Even pagans do that. ⁴⁸But you are to be perfect, even as your Father in heaven is perfect.

6 **TEACHING ABOUT GIVING TO THE NEEDY** "Watch out! Don't do your good deeds publicly, to be admired by others, for you will lose the reward from your Father in heaven. ²When you give to someone in need, don't do as the hypocrites do—blowing trumpets in the synagogues and streets to call attention to their acts of charity! I tell you the truth, they have received all the reward they will ever get. ³But when you give to someone in need, don't let your left hand know what your right hand is doing. ⁴Give your gifts in private, and your Father, who sees everything, will reward you.

TEACHING ABOUT PRAYER AND FASTING ⁵"When you pray, don't be like the hypocrites who love to pray publicly on street corners and in the synagogues where everyone can see them. I tell you the truth, that is all the reward they will ever get. ⁶But when you pray, go away by yourself, shut the door behind you, and pray to your Father in private. Then your Father, who sees everything, will reward you.

⁷"When you pray, don't babble on and on as people of other religions do. They think their prayers are answered merely by repeating their words again and again. ⁸Don't be like them, for

5:30 Greek *your right hand.*   **5:31** Deut 24:1.   **5:33** Num 30:2.
5:38 Greek *the law that says: 'An eye for an eye and a tooth for a tooth.'* Exod 21:24; Lev 24:20; Deut 19:21.   **5:41** Greek *milion* [4,854 feet or 1,478 meters].   **5:43** Lev 19:18.   **5:44** Some manuscripts add *Bless those who curse you. Do good to those who hate you.* Compare Luke 6:27-28.   **5:47** Greek *your brothers.*

your Father knows exactly what you need even before you ask him! ⁹Pray like this:

> Our Father in heaven,
> may your name be kept holy.
> ¹⁰ May your Kingdom come soon.
> May your will be done on earth,
> as it is in heaven.
> ¹¹ Give us today the food we need,*
> ¹² and forgive us our sins,
> as we have forgiven those who sin
> against us.
> ¹³ And don't let us yield to temptation,*
> but rescue us from the evil one.*

¹⁴"If you forgive those who sin against you, your heavenly Father will forgive you. ¹⁵But if you refuse to forgive others, your Father will not forgive your sins.

¹⁶"And when you fast, don't make it obvious, as the hypocrites do, for they try to look miserable and disheveled so people will admire them for their fasting. I tell you the truth, that is the only reward they will ever get. ¹⁷But when you fast, comb your hair and wash your face. ¹⁸Then no one will notice that you are fasting, except your Father, who knows what you do in private. And your Father, who sees everything, will reward you.

TEACHING ABOUT MONEY AND POSSESSIONS

¹⁹"Don't store up treasures here on earth, where moths eat them and rust destroys them, and where thieves break in and steal. ²⁰Store your treasures in heaven, where moths and rust cannot destroy, and thieves do not break in and steal. ²¹Wherever your treasure is, there the desires of your heart will also be.

²²"Your eye is a lamp that provides light for your body. When your eye is good, your whole body is filled with light. ²³But when your eye is bad, your whole body is filled with darkness. And if the light you think you have is actually darkness, how deep that darkness is!

²⁴"No one can serve two masters. For you will hate one and love the other; you will be devoted to one and despise the other. You cannot serve both God and money.

²⁵"That is why I tell you not to worry about everyday life—whether you have enough food and drink, or enough clothes to wear. Isn't life more than food, and your body more

than clothing? ²⁶Look at the birds. They don't plant or harvest or store food in barns, for your heavenly Father feeds them. And aren't you far more valuable to him than they are? ²⁷Can all your worries add a single moment to your life?

²⁸"And why worry about your clothing? Look at the lilies of the field and how they grow. They don't work or make their clothing, ²⁹yet Solomon in all his glory was not dressed as beautifully as they are. ³⁰And if God cares so wonderfully for wildflowers that are here today and thrown into the fire tomorrow, he will certainly care for you. Why do you have so little faith?

³¹"So don't worry about these things, saying, 'What will we eat? What will we drink? What will we wear?' ³²These things dominate the thoughts of unbelievers, but your heavenly Father already knows all your needs. ³³Seek the Kingdom of God* above all else, and live righteously, and he will give you everything you need.

³⁴"So don't worry about tomorrow, for tomorrow will bring its own worries. Today's trouble is enough for today.

7 DO NOT JUDGE OTHERS "Do not judge others, and you will not be judged. ²For you will be treated as you treat others.* The standard you use in judging is the standard by which you will be judged.*

³"And why worry about a speck in your friend's eye* when you have a log in your own? ⁴How can you think of saying to your friend,* 'Let me help you get rid of that speck in your eye,' when you can't see past the log in your own eye? ⁵Hypocrite! First get rid of the log in your own eye; then you will see well enough to deal with the speck in your friend's eye.

⁶"Don't waste what is holy on people who are unholy.* Don't throw your pearls to pigs! They will trample the pearls, then turn and attack you.

EFFECTIVE PRAYER ⁷"Keep on asking, and you will receive what you ask for. Keep on seeking,

6:11 Or *Give us today our food for the day*; or *Give us today our food for tomorrow.*   **6:13a** Or *And keep us from being tested.*   **6:13b** Or *from evil.* Some manuscripts add *For yours is the kingdom and the power and the glory forever. Amen.*   **6:33** Some manuscripts do not include *of God.*   **7:2a** Or *For God will judge you as you judge others.*   **7:2b** Or *The measure you give will be the measure you get back.*   **7:3** Greek *your brother's eye*; also in 7:5.   **7:4** Greek *your brother.*   **7:6** Greek *Don't give the sacred to dogs.*

MEANINGLESS REPETITION
(6:7-8) Jesus warned his followers against meaningless repetition in prayer. Meaningless repetition is not the same as persistence in prayer. Jesus encourages persistent prayer. Some people think that repeating the same words over and over ("O God, hear me; hear me, O God") will ensure that God will hear them. But God promises to listen to the prayers of his people (2 Chr 7:14; Jer 29:12). We can never pray too much if our prayers are honest and sincere. Before you start to pray, make sure you mean what you say.

ANYONE WHO LISTENS TO MY TEACHING AND FOLLOWS IT IS WISE,

MATTHEW 7:24

LIKE A PERSON WHO BUILDS A HOUSE ON SOLID ROCK.

and you will find. Keep on knocking, and the door will be opened to you. ⁸For everyone who asks, receives. Everyone who seeks, finds. And to everyone who knocks, the door will be opened.

⁹"You parents—if your children ask for a loaf of bread, do you give them a stone instead? ¹⁰Or if they ask for a fish, do you give them a snake? Of course not! ¹¹So if you sinful people know how to give good gifts to your children, how much more will your heavenly Father give good gifts to those who ask him.

THE GOLDEN RULE ¹²"Do to others whatever you would like them to do to you. This is the essence of all that is taught in the law and the prophets.

THE NARROW GATE ¹³"You can enter God's Kingdom only through the narrow gate. The highway to hell* is broad, and its gate is wide for the many who choose that way. ¹⁴But the gateway to life is very narrow and the road is difficult, and only a few ever find it.

THE TREE AND ITS FRUIT ¹⁵"Beware of false prophets who come disguised as harmless sheep but are really vicious wolves. ¹⁶You can identify them by their fruit, that is, by the way they act. Can you pick grapes from thornbushes, or figs from thistles? ¹⁷A good tree produces good fruit, and a bad tree produces bad fruit. ¹⁸A good tree can't produce bad fruit, and a bad tree can't produce good fruit. ¹⁹So every tree that does not produce good fruit is chopped down and thrown into the fire. ²⁰Yes, just as you can identify a tree by its fruit, so you can identify people by their actions.

TRUE DISCIPLES ²¹"Not everyone who calls out to me, 'Lord! Lord!' will enter the Kingdom of Heaven. Only those who actually do the will of my Father in heaven will enter. ²²On judgment day many will say to me, 'Lord! Lord! We prophesied in your name and cast out demons in your name and performed many miracles in your name.' ²³But I will reply, 'I never knew you. Get away from me, you who break God's laws.'

BUILDING ON A SOLID FOUNDATION ²⁴"Anyone who listens to my teaching and follows it is wise, like a person who builds a house on solid rock. ²⁵Though the rain comes in torrents and the floodwaters rise and the winds beat against that house, it won't collapse because it is built on bedrock. ²⁶But anyone who hears

7:13 Greek *The road that leads to destruction.*

I WONDER...

I've been praying that my dad would become a Christian for over six months. Why hasn't God answered my prayer?

You have certainly been persistent. And you're doing exactly what Matthew 7:7-11 is talking about. You're asking, seeking, and knocking.

God answers our prayers in three different ways: "Yes," "No," or "Wait." In our instant society, where everything happens when we want it, "Wait" answers are not the ones we're accustomed to hearing, especially when it seems as though the prayer is not being answered. Or is it?

God, in his perfect wisdom, knows the perfect time for people to respond to his call, turn from their sin, and come into a right relationship with him. If we try to manipulate circumstances apart from God's will, perhaps these people will say no instead of yes.

Your dad may have no one in his life right now who could help him grow. Maybe he has important questions still unanswered that would cause him to respond out of emotion rather than with his will. Perhaps he still harbors hurts or misconceptions about God and the church that need to be worked through before he can begin to examine God's love for him.

Whatever the reason, the best thing you can do is to keep praying for him. Also, ask a Christian friend if his or her father would be able to start a friendship with your dad.

Even persistence in prayer will not always change the heart that is hard toward God. People have a will that can say no to any openings God's love may try to penetrate. Just continue your persistent prayer. Never give up.

my teaching and doesn't obey it is foolish, like a person who builds a house on sand. 27When the rains and floods come and the winds beat against that house, it will collapse with a mighty crash."

28When Jesus had finished saying these things, the crowds were amazed at his teaching, 29for he taught with real authority—quite unlike their teachers of religious law.

8 JESUS HEALS A MAN WITH LEPROSY

Large crowds followed Jesus as he came down the mountainside. 2Suddenly, a man with leprosy approached him and knelt before him. "Lord," the man said, "if you are willing, you can heal me and make me clean."

3Jesus reached out and touched him. "I am willing," he said. "Be healed!" And instantly the leprosy disappeared. 4Then Jesus said to him, "Don't tell anyone about this. Instead, go to the priest and let him examine you. Take along the offering required in the law of Moses for those who have been healed of leprosy.* This will be a public testimony that you have been cleansed."

THE FAITH OF A ROMAN OFFICER

5When Jesus returned to Capernaum, a Roman officer* came and pleaded with him, 6"Lord, my young servant* lies in bed, paralyzed and in terrible pain."

7Jesus said, "I will come and heal him."

8But the officer said, "Lord, I am not worthy to have you come into my home. Just say the word from where you are, and my servant will be healed. 9I know this because I am under the authority of my superior officers, and I have authority over my soldiers. I only need to say, 'Go,' and they go, or 'Come,' and they come. And if I say to my slaves, 'Do this,' they do it."

10When Jesus heard this, he was amazed. Turning to those who were following him, he said, "I tell you the truth, I haven't seen faith like this in all Israel! 11And I tell you this, that many Gentiles will come from all over the world—from east and west—and sit down with Abraham, Isaac, and Jacob at the feast in the Kingdom of Heaven. 12But many Israelites—those for whom the Kingdom was prepared—will be thrown into outer darkness, where there will be weeping and gnashing of teeth."

13Then Jesus said to the Roman officer, "Go back home. Because you believed, it has happened." And the young servant was healed that same hour.

8:4 See Lev 14:2-32. 8:5 Greek *a centurion;* similarly in 8:8, 13. 8:6 Or *child;* also in 8:13. 8:17 Isa 53:4.

MY STORY: Laura

I used to struggle a lot with doubt. Was God real? Did he really care about me? Is the Bible relevant? Then someone challenged me to try to apply a passage from the Bible every day for two weeks and see if that made any difference. So, I did. I read some of the Psalms and found that they were wonderfully relevant. When I felt lonely and had no one to turn to, I found that David's words perfectly expressed my feelings.

When I came across Jesus' words in Matthew 7:24-27, I realized that only through obeying and applying God's Word can we know he's real. His Word is the only solid thing we have to build our lives on. The Matthew passage, and my two-week experiment, motivated me to try to live out what I read more and more every day.

JESUS HEALS MANY PEOPLE 14When Jesus arrived at Peter's house, Peter's mother-in-law was sick in bed with a high fever. 15But when Jesus touched her hand, the fever left her. Then she got up and prepared a meal for him.

16That evening many demon-possessed people were brought to Jesus. He cast out the evil spirits with a simple command, and he healed all the sick. 17This fulfilled the word of the Lord through the prophet Isaiah, who said,

> "He took our sicknesses
> and removed our diseases."*

THE COST OF FOLLOWING JESUS 18When Jesus saw the crowd around him, he instructed his disciples to cross to the other side of the lake.

19Then one of the teachers of religious law

....

A GOOD WAY TO HEAVEN
(8:10-12) The people of Israel thought that their good works would earn them a life in heaven. But after talking with a centurion, Jesus told the crowd that many of them would be excluded from the Kingdom of God because of their lack of faith in him. Like the Jews, many people today believe that their good actions will get them to heaven. But only faith in Jesus will. Are you relying on your good works or good decisions to earn a place in heaven? The best decision you can make is to trust that Jesus is your only ticket there.

said to him, "Teacher, I will follow you wherever you go."

²⁰But Jesus replied, "Foxes have dens to live in, and birds have nests, but the Son of Man* has no place even to lay his head."

²¹Another of his disciples said, "Lord, first let me return home and bury my father."

²²But Jesus told him, "Follow me now. Let the spiritually dead bury their own dead.*"

JESUS CALMS THE STORM

²³Then Jesus got into the boat and started across the lake with his disciples. ²⁴Suddenly, a fierce storm struck the lake, with waves breaking into the boat. But Jesus was sleeping. ²⁵The disciples went and woke him up, shouting, "Lord, save us! We're going to drown!"

²⁶Jesus responded, "Why are you afraid? You have so little faith!" Then he got up and rebuked the wind and waves, and suddenly there was a great calm.

²⁷The disciples were amazed. "Who is this man?" they asked. "Even the winds and waves obey him!"

JESUS HEALS TWO DEMON-POSSESSED MEN

²⁸When Jesus arrived on the other side of the lake, in the region of the Gadarenes,* two men who were possessed by demons met him. They lived in a cemetery and were so violent that no one could go through that area.

²⁹They began screaming at him, "Why are you interfering with us, Son of God? Have you come here to torture us before God's appointed time?"

³⁰There happened to be a large herd of pigs feeding in the distance. ³¹So the demons begged, "If you cast us out, send us into that herd of pigs."

³²"All right, go!" Jesus commanded them. So the demons came out of the men and entered the pigs, and the whole herd plunged down the steep hillside into the lake and drowned in the water.

³³The herdsmen fled to the nearby town, telling everyone what happened to the demon-possessed men. ³⁴Then the entire town came out to meet Jesus, but they begged him to go away and leave them alone.

9 JESUS HEALS A PARALYZED MAN

Jesus climbed into a boat and went back across the lake to his own town. ²Some people brought to him a paralyzed man on a mat. Seeing their faith, Jesus said to the paralyzed man, "Be encouraged, my child! Your sins are forgiven."

³But some of the teachers of religious law said to themselves, "That's blasphemy! Does he think he's God?"

⁴Jesus knew* what they were thinking, so he asked them, "Why do you have such evil thoughts in your hearts? ⁵Is it easier to say 'Your sins are forgiven,' or 'Stand up and walk'? ⁶So I will prove to you that the Son of Man* has the authority on earth to forgive sins." Then Jesus turned to the paralyzed man and said, "Stand up, pick up your mat, and go home!"

⁷And the man jumped up and went home! ⁸Fear swept through the crowd as they saw this happen. And they praised God for sending a man with such great authority.*

JESUS CALLS MATTHEW

⁹As Jesus was walking along, he saw a man named Matthew sitting at his tax collector's booth. "Follow me and be my disciple," Jesus said to him. So Matthew got up and followed him.

¹⁰Later, Matthew invited Jesus and his disciples to his home as dinner guests, along with many tax collectors and other disreputable sinners. ¹¹But when the Pharisees saw this, they asked his disciples, "Why does your teacher eat with such scum?*"

¹²When Jesus heard this, he said, "Healthy people don't need a doctor—sick people do." ¹³Then he added, "Now go and learn the meaning of this Scripture: 'I want you to show mercy, not offer sacrifices.'* For I have come to call not those who think they are righteous, but those who know they are sinners."

COUNT THE COST

(8:19-20) Following Jesus is not always easy or comfortable. Often it involves great cost and sacrifice, with no earthly rewards or security. For example, Jesus didn't have a place to call home. Following Jesus may cost you friendships, popularity, or treasured habits. But while the costs of being Christ's disciple may be high, the benefits last for eternity. Are you willing to pay the price?

CONCERN FOR ALL

(9:9-13) The Pharisees thought Jesus' association with tax collectors was the perfect opportunity to trap him. They were more concerned with criticism than encouragement and with their own appearance of holiness than in helping people. But God is concerned for all people, including those you've labeled as "losers" in society. Is there someone you've labeled as undeserving of help or unworthy to hear the Good News? According to God, no one is too low-down—or too "high up," for that matter—to experience his forgiveness.

8:20 "Son of Man" is a title Jesus used for himself. **8:22** Greek *Let the dead bury their own dead.* **8:28** Other manuscripts read *Gerasenes;* still others read *Gergesenes.* Compare Mark 5:1; Luke 8:26. **9:4** Some manuscripts read *saw.* **9:6** "Son of Man" is a title Jesus used for himself. **9:8** Greek *for giving such authority to human beings.* **9:11** Greek *with tax collectors and sinners?* **9:13** Hos 6:6 (Greek version).

A DISCUSSION ABOUT FASTING ¹⁴One day the disciples of John the Baptist came to Jesus and asked him, "Why don't your disciples fast* like we do and the Pharisees do?"

¹⁵Jesus replied, "Do wedding guests mourn while celebrating with the groom? Of course not. But someday the groom will be taken away from them, and then they will fast.

¹⁶"Besides, who would patch old clothing with new cloth? For the new patch would shrink and rip away from the old cloth, leaving an even bigger tear than before.

¹⁷"And no one puts new wine into old wineskins. For the old skins would burst from the pressure, spilling the wine and ruining the skins. New wine is stored in new wineskins so that both are preserved."

JESUS HEALS IN RESPONSE TO FAITH ¹⁸As Jesus was saying this, the leader of a synagogue came and knelt before him. "My daughter has just died," he said, "but you can bring her back to life again if you just come and lay your hand on her."

¹⁹So Jesus and his disciples got up and went with him. ²⁰Just then a woman who had

9:14 Some manuscripts read *fast often*.

suffered for twelve years with constant bleeding came up behind him. She touched the fringe of his robe, ²¹for she thought, "If I can just touch his robe, I will be healed."

²²Jesus turned around, and when he saw her he said, "Daughter, be encouraged! Your faith has made you well." And the woman was healed at that moment.

²³When Jesus arrived at the official's home, he saw the noisy crowd and heard the funeral music. ²⁴"Get out!" he told them. "The girl isn't dead; she's only asleep." But the crowd laughed at him. ²⁵After the crowd was put outside, however, Jesus went in and took the girl by the hand, and she stood up! ²⁶The report of this miracle swept through the entire countryside.

JESUS HEALS THE BLIND ²⁷After Jesus left the girl's home, two blind men followed along behind him, shouting, "Son of David, have mercy on us!"

²⁸They went right into the house where he was staying, and Jesus asked them, "Do you believe I can make you see?"

"Yes, Lord," they told him, "we do."

²⁹Then he touched their eyes and said,

PERSONALITY PROFILE

MATTHEW

UPS:
- Was one of Jesus' 12 disciples
- Responded immediately to Jesus' call to be his disciple
- Invited many friends to his home to meet Jesus
- Wrote the Gospel of Matthew
- Clarified for his Jewish audience Jesus' fulfillment of Old Testament prophecies

STATS:
- Where: Capernaum
- Occupation: Tax collector, disciple of Jesus
- Relatives: Alphaeus (father)
- Contemporaries: Jesus, Pilate, Herod, other disciples

KEY VERSE: Matthew 9:9

EVER WONDER WHETHER SOMEONE WITH A BAD REPUTATION could ever really change? Being a tax collector for the Romans had earned Matthew a bad rep. Now Jesus undoubtedly knew about Matthew's reputation; yet he called him anyway (see Matt 9:9-13).

Matthew's life totally changed when he decided to follow Jesus. First, he not only belonged to a new group (Jesus' disciples); he belonged to the Son of God. He was not just accepting a different way of life; he was now accepted as a person. For a despised tax collector, that change must have been wonderful! Second, Jesus gave Matthew a new purpose for his skills. When he followed Jesus, the only item from his past job that he carried with him was a writing tool. From the beginning, God had made him a record keeper. Jesus' call eventually allowed him to put his skills to their finest work. Matthew was a keen observer, and he must have mentally recorded what he saw going on around him. The Gospel that bears his name came as a result.

Matthew's experience reminds us that each person is a work in progress. Sometimes God trusts us with skills and abilities before we know what to do with them. He has made us each capable of being his servant. When we trust God to help us use what he has given us, we begin a life of real adventure.

Matthew couldn't have known beforehand that God would use the very skills he had sharpened as a tax collector to record the greatest story ever lived. And God has no less meaningful a purpose for each of us. Have you recognized Jesus's voice saying to you, "Follow me"? How have you responded?

BOTTOM LINE: Jesus consistently accepted people from every level of society.
God has the power to change any life for the better.
One sign of faith in Jesus is the desire to tell others about him.

Matthew's story is told in the Gospels. He also is mentioned in Acts 1:13.

"Because of your faith, it will happen." ³⁰Then their eyes were opened, and they could see! Jesus sternly warned them, "Don't tell anyone about this." ³¹But instead, they went out and spread his fame all over the region.

³²When they left, a demon-possessed man who couldn't speak was brought to Jesus. ³³So Jesus cast out the demon, and then the man began to speak. The crowds were amazed. "Nothing like this has ever happened in Israel!" they exclaimed.

³⁴But the Pharisees said, "He can cast out demons because he is empowered by the prince of demons."

THE NEED FOR WORKERS ³⁵Jesus traveled through all the towns and villages of that area, teaching in the synagogues and announcing the Good News about the Kingdom. And he healed every kind of disease and illness. ³⁶When he saw the crowds, he had compassion on them because they were confused and helpless, like sheep without a shepherd. ³⁷He said to his disciples, "The harvest is great, but the workers are few. ³⁸So pray to the Lord who is in charge of the harvest; ask him to send more workers into his fields."

10 **JESUS SENDS OUT THE TWELVE APOSTLES** Jesus called his twelve disciples together and gave them authority to cast out evil* spirits and to heal every kind of disease and illness. ²Here are the names of the twelve apostles:

first, Simon (also called Peter),
then Andrew (Peter's brother),
James (son of Zebedee),
John (James's brother),
³ Philip,
Bartholomew,
Thomas,
Matthew (the tax collector),
James (son of Alphaeus),
Thaddaeus,*
⁴ Simon (the zealot*),
Judas Iscariot (who later betrayed him).

⋯⋯⋯⋯⋯⋯⋯⋯⋯⋯⋯⋯⋯⋯⋯⋯⋯⋯⋯⋯⋯⋯⋯⋯⋯⋯

TESTING
(9:27-31) Jesus didn't respond immediately to the blind men's pleas. He waited to see how earnest they were. Not everyone who says he or she wants help really wants it badly enough to do something about it. Jesus may have waited and questioned these men to make their desire and faith stronger. If you believe that God is too slow in answering your prayers, consider the fact that he could be testing you as he did the blind men. Do you believe that God can help you? Do you really want his help?

⁵Jesus sent out the twelve apostles with these instructions: "Don't go to the Gentiles or the Samaritans, ⁶but only to the people of Israel—God's lost sheep. ⁷Go and announce to them that the Kingdom of Heaven is near.* ⁸Heal the sick, raise the dead, cure those with leprosy, and cast out demons. Give as freely as you have received!

⁹"Don't take any money in your money belts—no gold, silver, or even copper coins. ¹⁰Don't carry a traveler's bag with a change of clothes and sandals or even a walking stick. Don't hesitate to accept hospitality, because those who work deserve to be fed.

¹¹"Whenever you enter a city or village, search for a worthy person and stay in his home until you leave town. ¹²When you enter the home, give it your blessing. ¹³If it turns out to be a worthy home, let your blessing stand; if it is not, take back the blessing. ¹⁴If any household or town refuses to welcome you or listen to your message, shake its dust from your feet as you leave. ¹⁵I tell you the truth, the wicked cities of Sodom and Gomorrah will be better off than such a town on the judgment day.

¹⁶"Look, I am sending you out as sheep among wolves. So be as shrewd as snakes and harmless as doves. ¹⁷But beware! For you will be handed over to the courts and will be flogged with whips in the synagogues. ¹⁸You will stand trial before governors and kings because you are my followers. But this will be your opportunity to tell the rulers and other unbelievers about me.* ¹⁹When you are arrested, don't worry about how to respond or what to say. God will give you the right words at the right time. ²⁰For it is not you who will be speaking—it will be the Spirit of your Father speaking through you.

²¹"A brother will betray his brother to death, a father will betray his own child, and children will rebel against their parents and cause them to be killed. ²²And all nations will hate you because you are my followers.* But everyone who endures to the end will be saved. ²³When you are persecuted in one town, flee to the next. I tell you the truth, the Son of Man* will return before you have reached all the towns of Israel.

²⁴"Students* are not greater than their teacher, and slaves are not greater than their master. ²⁵Students are to be like their teacher,

10:1 Greek *unclean.* 10:3 Other manuscripts read *Lebbaeus;* still others read *Lebbaeus who is called Thaddaeus.* 10:4 Greek *the Cananean,* an Aramaic term for Jewish nationalists. 10:7 Or *has come, or is coming soon.* 10:18 Or *But this will be your testimony against the rulers and other unbelievers.* 10:22 Greek *on account of my name.* 10:23 "Son of Man" is a title Jesus used for himself. 10:24 Or *Disciples.*

and slaves are to be like their master. And since I, the master of the household, have been called the prince of demons,* the members of my household will be called by even worse names!

[26]"But don't be afraid of those who threaten you. For the time is coming when everything that is covered will be revealed, and all that is secret will be made known to all. [27]What I tell you now in the darkness, shout abroad when daybreak comes. What I whisper in your ear, shout from the housetops for all to hear!

[28]"Don't be afraid of those who want to kill your body; they cannot touch your soul. Fear only God, who can destroy both soul and body in hell.* [29]What is the price of two sparrows—one copper coin*? But not a single sparrow can fall to the ground without your Father knowing it. [30]And the very hairs on your head are all numbered. [31]So don't be afraid; you are more valuable to God than a whole flock of sparrows.

[32]"Everyone who acknowledges me publicly here on earth, I will also acknowledge before my Father in heaven. [33]But everyone who denies me here on earth, I will also deny before my Father in heaven.

[34]"Don't imagine that I came to bring peace to the earth! I came not to bring peace, but a sword.

[35] 'I have come to set a man against his father,
         a daughter against her mother,
     and a daughter-in-law against her
             mother-in-law.
[36]   Your enemies will be right in your own
             household!'*

10:25 Greek *Beelzeboul;* other manuscripts read *Beezeboul;* Latin version reads *Beelzebub.* 10:28 Greek *Gehenna.* 10:29 Greek *one assarion* [i.e., one "as," a Roman coin equal to 1/16 of a denarius]. 10:35-36 Mic 7:6.

VALUABLE
(10:29-31) Jesus said that God cares for the sparrows' every need. You are far more valuable to God than these little birds. Your worth was proven by the fact that God sent his only Son to die for you (John 3:16). Because God places such value on you, you need never fear personal threats or difficult trials. But don't think that because you're valuable to God, he will take away all of your troubles (see 10:16). Instead, he tests you to see how well you hold up under the wear, tear, and hassles of everyday life. Those who stand up for Christ in spite of their troubles will receive great rewards (see 5:11-12).

I WONDER...

My parents are quietly putting up with my new faith. Mom thinks it's "nice" and Dad won't talk to me about it. How do I make them see that Jesus is a real person?

The New Testament records many difficult sayings of Jesus. Matthew 10:34-39 is one of the toughest. What does Jesus mean when he says, "Your enemies will be right in your own household" (v 36)?

If you have faced pressure and opposition from friends because of your new faith, you realize that your decision for Christ causes people to make decisions about you. Some will stay with you and support your decision because they are your true friends. Others will leave because they don't understand or because your values no longer encourage their lifestyle.

We also may find opposition at home. In these verses, Jesus is not telling us to disobey parents or to try to cause problems at home. He simply means that a person with different goals and values may cause division in a household. Rarely will the only Christian in a family go unchallenged.

Though parents seldom become openly hostile toward someone in their home, some do. Put-downs can really hurt, especially if they come from someone you love.

The best course of action is to avoid trying to *make* your parents see anything. Instead, just live your life in obedience to them as the Bible commands: "Children, obey your parents because you belong to the Lord, for this is the right thing to do. 'Honor your father and mother.' This is the first commandment with a promise: If you honor your father and mother, 'things will go well for you, and you will have a long life on the earth'" (Eph 6:1-3).

Is it your job to make your parents change? Nope. Only the Holy Spirit can do that. Check it out: "And when he comes, he will convict the world of its sin, and of God's righteousness, and of the coming judgment" (John 16:8). You are simply to be God's representative in your home. Maybe someday you'll have the joy of seeing your family turn to Christ.

Don't neglect your family members because they do not yet accept your faith. But don't neglect the higher mission of keeping God as your number-one priority either.

Find some Christian friends who will pray for you and pray with you about your situation. Go to them for encouragement and when you need advice on how to respond as each difficult situation arises.

37"If you love your father or mother more than you love me, you are not worthy of being mine; or if you love your son or daughter more than me, you are not worthy of being mine. 38If you refuse to take up your cross and follow me, you are not worthy of being mine. 39If you cling to your life, you will lose it; but if you give up your life for me, you will find it.

40"Anyone who receives you receives me, and anyone who receives me receives the Father who sent me. 41If you receive a prophet as one who speaks for God,* you will be given the same reward as a prophet. And if you receive righteous people because of their righteousness, you will be given a reward like theirs. 42And if you give even a cup of cold water to one of the least of my followers, you will surely be rewarded."

11 **JESUS AND JOHN THE BAPTIST** When Jesus had finished giving these instructions to his twelve disciples, he went out to teach and preach in towns throughout the region.

2John the Baptist, who was in prison, heard about all the things the Messiah was doing. So he sent his disciples to ask Jesus, 3"Are you the Messiah we've been expecting,* or should we keep looking for someone else?"

4Jesus told them, "Go back to John and tell him what you have heard and seen—5the blind see, the lame walk, the lepers are cured, the deaf hear, the dead are raised to life, and the Good News is being preached to the poor. 6And tell him, 'God blesses those who do not turn away because of me.'*"

7As John's disciples were leaving, Jesus began talking about him to the crowds. "What kind of man did you go into the wilderness to see? Was he a weak reed, swayed by every breath of wind? 8Or were you expecting to see a man dressed in expensive clothes? No, people with expensive clothes live in palaces. 9Were you looking for a prophet? Yes, and he

· ·

DOUBTS
(11:1-6) *As John sat in prison, he began to doubt whether Jesus really was the Savior. John's purpose was to prepare people for the coming Messiah (3:3). If Jesus really was that Messiah, the Savior, he surmised, then why was John in prison instead of preaching to the crowds, preparing their hearts? Jesus answered John's doubts by reminding him of the acts that revealed his identity: healing the sick, raising the dead, and preaching the gospel to the poor. With so much evidence, Jesus' identity was obvious. Do you share John's doubt? Look at the evidence in Scripture and in your life. When you doubt, don't turn away from Christ, turn to him.*

is more than a prophet. 10John is the man to whom the Scriptures refer when they say,

'Look, I am sending my messenger ahead
    of you,
    and he will prepare your way before you.'*

11"I tell you the truth, of all who have ever lived, none is greater than John the Baptist. Yet even the least person in the Kingdom of Heaven is greater than he is! 12And from the time John the Baptist began preaching until now, the Kingdom of Heaven has been forcefully advancing,* and violent people are attacking it. 13For before John came, all the prophets and the law of Moses looked forward to this present time. 14And if you are willing to accept what I say, he is Elijah, the one the prophets said would come.* 15Anyone with ears to hear should listen and understand!

16"To what can I compare this generation? It is like children playing a game in the public square. They complain to their friends,

17 'We played wedding songs,
        and you didn't dance,
    so we played funeral songs,
        and you didn't mourn.'

18For John didn't spend his time eating and drinking, and you say, 'He's possessed by a demon.' 19The Son of Man,* on the other hand, feasts and drinks, and you say, 'He's a glutton and a drunkard, and a friend of tax collectors and other sinners!' But wisdom is shown to be right by its results."

JUDGMENT FOR THE UNBELIEVERS 20Then Jesus began to denounce the towns where he had done so many of his miracles, because they hadn't repented of their sins and turned to God. 21"What sorrow awaits you, Korazin and Bethsaida! For if the miracles I did in you had been done in wicked Tyre and Sidon, their people would have repented of their sins long ago, clothing themselves in burlap and throwing ashes on their heads to show their remorse. 22I tell you, Tyre and Sidon will be better off on judgment day than you.

23"And you people of Capernaum, will you be honored in heaven? No, you will go down to the place of the dead.* For if the miracles I did for you had been done in wicked Sodom, it would still be here today. 24I tell you, even Sodom will be better off on judgment day than you."

10:41 Greek *receive a prophet in the name of a prophet.* **11:3** Greek *Are you the one who is coming?* **11:6** Or *who are not offended by me.* **11:10** Mal 3:1. **11:12** Or *the Kingdom of Heaven has suffered from violence.* **11:14** See Mal 4:5. **11:19** "Son of Man" is a title Jesus used for himself. **11:23** Greek *to Hades.*

JESUS' PRAYER OF THANKSGIVING ²⁵At that time Jesus prayed this prayer: "O Father, Lord of heaven and earth, thank you for hiding these things from those who think themselves wise and clever, and for revealing them to the childlike. ²⁶Yes, Father, it pleased you to do it this way!

²⁷"My Father has entrusted everything to me. No one truly knows the Son except the Father, and no one truly knows the Father except the Son and those to whom the Son chooses to reveal him."

²⁸Then Jesus said, "Come to me, all of you who are weary and carry heavy burdens, and I will give you rest. ²⁹Take my yoke upon you. Let me teach you, because I am humble and gentle at heart, and you will find rest for your souls. ³⁰For my yoke is easy to bear, and the burden I give you is light."

12 A DISCUSSION ABOUT THE SABBATH

At about that time Jesus was walking through some grainfields on the Sabbath. His disciples were hungry, so they began breaking off some heads of grain and eating them. ²But some Pharisees saw them do it and protested, "Look, your disciples are breaking the law by harvesting grain on the Sabbath."

³Jesus said to them, "Haven't you read in the Scriptures what David did when he and his companions were hungry? ⁴He went into the house of God, and he and his companions broke the law by eating the sacred loaves of bread that only the priests are allowed to eat. ⁵And haven't you read in the law of Moses that the priests on duty in the Temple may work on the Sabbath? ⁶I tell you, there is one here who is even greater than the Temple! ⁷But you would not have condemned my innocent disciples if you knew the meaning of this Scripture: 'I want you to show mercy, not offer sacrifices.'* ⁸For the Son of Man* is Lord, even over the Sabbath!"

JESUS HEALS ON THE SABBATH ⁹Then Jesus went over to their synagogue, ¹⁰where he noticed a man with a deformed hand. The Pharisees asked Jesus, "Does the law permit a person to work by healing on the Sabbath?" (They were hoping he would say yes, so they could bring charges against him.)

¹¹And he answered, "If you had a sheep that fell into a well on the Sabbath, wouldn't you work to pull it out? Of course you would. ¹²And

how much more valuable is a person than a sheep! Yes, the law permits a person to do good on the Sabbath."

¹³Then he said to the man, "Hold out your hand." So the man held out his hand, and it was restored, just like the other one! ¹⁴Then the Pharisees called a meeting to plot how to kill Jesus.

JESUS, GOD'S CHOSEN SERVANT ¹⁵But Jesus knew what they were planning. So he left that area, and many people followed him. He healed all the sick among them, ¹⁶but he warned them not to reveal who he was. ¹⁷This fulfilled the prophecy of Isaiah concerning him:

¹⁸ "Look at my Servant, whom I have chosen.
He is my Beloved, who pleases me.
I will put my Spirit upon him,
and he will proclaim justice to the
nations.
¹⁹ He will not fight or shout
or raise his voice in public.
²⁰ He will not crush the weakest reed
or put out a flickering candle.
Finally he will cause justice to be
victorious.
²¹ And his name will be the hope
of all the world."*

JESUS AND THE PRINCE OF DEMONS ²²Then a demon-possessed man, who was blind and couldn't speak, was brought to Jesus. He healed the man so that he could both speak and see. ²³The crowd was amazed and asked, "Could it be that Jesus is the Son of David, the Messiah?"

²⁴But when the Pharisees heard about the miracle, they said, "No wonder he can cast out demons. He gets his power from Satan,* the prince of demons."

²⁵Jesus knew their thoughts and replied, "Any kingdom divided by civil war is doomed. A town or family splintered by feuding will fall apart. ²⁶And if Satan is casting out Satan, he is divided and fighting against himself. His own kingdom will not survive. ²⁷And if I am empowered by Satan, what about your own exorcists? They cast out demons, too, so they will condemn you for what you have said. ²⁸But if I am casting out demons by the Spirit of God, then the Kingdom of God has arrived among you. ²⁹For who is powerful enough to enter the house of a strong man like Satan and plunder his goods? Only someone even stronger—someone who could tie him up and then plunder his house.

12:7 Hos 6:6 (Greek version).   12:8 "Son of Man" is a title Jesus used for himself.   12:18-21 Isa 42:1-4 (Greek version for 42:4).   12:24 Greek *Beelzeboul;* also in 12:27. Other manuscripts read *Beezeboul;* Latin version reads *Beelzebub.*

THE PHARISEES AND SADDUCEES

The Pharisees and Sadducees were the two major religious groups in Israel at the time of Christ. The Pharisees were more religiously minded, while the Sadducees were more politically minded. Although the groups disliked and distrusted each other, they became allies in their common hatred for Jesus.

PHARISEES

Positive Characteristics

- Were committed to obeying all of God's Word
- Were admired by the common people for their apparent piety
- Believed in a bodily resurrection and eternal life
- Believed in angels and demons

Negative Characteristics

- Behaved as though their own religious rules were just as important as God's rules for living
- Were often hypocritical, forcing others to try to live up to standards they themselves could not live up to
- Believed that salvation came from perfect obedience to the law and was not based on forgiveness of sins
- Became so obsessed with obeying their legal interpretations in every detail that they completely ignored God's message of mercy and grace
- Were more concerned with appearing to be good than with obeying God

SADDUCEES

Positive Characteristics

- Showed great respect for the five books of Moses: Genesis through Deuteronomy
- Were more practically minded than the Pharisees

Negative Characteristics

- Relied on logic while placing little importance on faith
- Did not believe all the Old Testament was God's Word
- Did not believe in a bodily resurrection or eternal life
- Did not believe in angels or demons
- Were often willing to compromise their values with the Romans and others in order to maintain their status and influential positions

³⁰"Anyone who isn't with me opposes me, and anyone who isn't working with me is actually working against me.

³¹"So I tell you, every sin and blasphemy can be forgiven—except blasphemy against the Holy Spirit, which will never be forgiven. ³²Anyone who speaks against the Son of Man can be forgiven, but anyone who speaks against the Holy Spirit will never be forgiven, either in this world or in the world to come.

³³"A tree is identified by its fruit. If a tree is good, its fruit will be good. If a tree is bad, its fruit will be bad. ³⁴You brood of snakes! How could evil men like you speak what is good and right? For whatever is in your heart determines what you say. ³⁵A good person produces good things from the treasury of a good heart, and an evil person produces evil things from the treasury of an evil heart. ³⁶And I tell you this, you must give an account on judgment day for every idle word you speak. ³⁷The words you say will either acquit you or condemn you."

THE SIGN OF JONAH ³⁸One day some teachers of religious law and Pharisees came to Jesus and said, "Teacher, we want you to show us a miraculous sign to prove your authority."

³⁹But Jesus replied, "Only an evil, adulterous generation would demand a miraculous sign; but the only sign I will give them is the sign of the prophet Jonah. ⁴⁰For as Jonah was in the belly of the great fish for three days and three nights, so will the Son of Man be in the heart of the earth for three days and three nights.

⁴¹"The people of Nineveh will stand up against this generation on judgment day and condemn it, for they repented of their sins at the preaching of Jonah. Now someone greater than Jonah is here—but you refuse to repent. ⁴²The queen of Sheba* will also stand up

I NEED TO SEE A MIRACLE!
(12:38-42) The Pharisees wanted Jesus to prove his identity as Savior by showing them a miracle. But Jesus knew that the Pharisees didn't believe in him and that more miracles wouldn't change their minds. Like the Pharisees, many people have thought, I need to see a miracle in order to believe! But Jesus' death, resurrection, and ascension, plus the Bible and stories of believers around the world, all point to Jesus as the Savior. Instead of looking for additional evidence or miracles, are you willing to accept what God has already given and move forward? He may use your life as evidence to reach another person.

12:42 Greek *The queen of the south.*

against this generation on judgment day and condemn it, for she came from a distant land to hear the wisdom of Solomon. Now someone greater than Solomon is here—but you refuse to listen.

43"When an evil* spirit leaves a person, it goes into the desert, seeking rest but finding none. 44Then it says, 'I will return to the person I came from.' So it returns and finds its former home empty, swept, and in order. 45Then the spirit finds seven other spirits more evil than itself, and they all enter the person and live there. And so that person is worse off than before. That will be the experience of this evil generation."

THE TRUE FAMILY OF JESUS 46As Jesus was speaking to the crowd, his mother and brothers stood outside, asking to speak to him. 47Someone told Jesus, "Your mother and your brothers are outside, and they want to speak to you."*

48Jesus asked, "Who is my mother? Who are my brothers?" 49Then he pointed to his disciples and said, "Look, these are my mother and brothers. 50Anyone who does the will of my Father in heaven is my brother and sister and mother!"

13 PARABLE OF THE FARMER SCATTERING SEED Later that same day Jesus left the house and sat beside the lake. 2A large crowd soon gathered around him, so he got into a boat. Then he sat there and taught as the people stood on the shore. 3He told many stories in the form of parables, such as this one:

"Listen! A farmer went out to plant some seeds. 4As he scattered them across his field, some seeds fell on a footpath, and the birds came and ate them. 5Other seeds fell on

12:43 Greek *unclean*.　12:47 Some manuscripts do not include verse 47. Compare Mark 3:32 and Luke 8:20.　13:11 Greek *the mysteries*.

shallow soil with underlying rock. The seeds sprouted quickly because the soil was shallow. 6But the plants soon wilted under the hot sun, and since they didn't have deep roots, they died. 7Other seeds fell among thorns that grew up and choked out the tender plants. 8Still other seeds fell on fertile soil, and they produced a crop that was thirty, sixty, and even a hundred times as much as had been planted! 9Anyone with ears to hear should listen and understand."

10His disciples came and asked him, "Why do you use parables when you talk to the people?"

11He replied, "You are permitted to understand the secrets* of the Kingdom of Heaven, but others are not. 12To those who listen to my teaching, more understanding will be given, and they will have an abundance of knowledge. But for those who are not listening, even what little understanding they have will be taken away from them. 13That is why I use these parables,

> For they look, but they don't really see.
> They hear, but they don't really listen or
> understand.

14This fulfills the prophecy of Isaiah that says,

> 'When you hear what I say,
> you will not understand.
> When you see what I do,
> you will not comprehend.

....

SOWING SEEDS
(13:1-23) Although the farmer in this parable sowed good seed, not all of his sowing brought a high yield. Ever wonder whether the "good seed" you've planted by telling someone about Jesus will ever sprout? Don't be discouraged if no one seems to be listening to you as you faithfully talk about or teach the Word. Belief doesn't come through a formula. Rather, it is a miracle of God's Holy Spirit as he uses your words to move others to come to him.

CHOICES
mouth

Mrs. Rogers puts the groceries in the trunk, buckles four-year-old Richie in his seat, and heads for home. Soon Richie is holding his plastic airplane out the open window, watching its propeller spin. Mrs. Rogers notices the open window and quickly closes it.

Startled, the little boy drops the plane and mumbles a word that four-year-old boys have no business knowing.

Mrs. Rogers is shocked. "Richie! Where did you learn that word?"

"From Christi."

"Christi shouldn't say that word and neither should you!"

When Mrs. Rogers gets home, she marches into her 16-year-old daughter's bedroom. "Christi, Richie used some horrible language in the car today. . . . and he said he learned it from you. You want to explain?"

"Gee, Mom," Christi responds nervously. "No way. Not me. I don't know why he would say something like that."

Obviously Christi is caught up in lying as well as profanity. She needs to read Matthew 12:33-37.

¹⁵ For the hearts of these people are
    hardened,
    and their ears cannot hear,
    and they have closed their eyes—
        so their eyes cannot see,
    and their ears cannot hear,
        and their hearts cannot understand,
    and they cannot turn to me
        and let me heal them.'*

¹⁶"But blessed are your eyes, because they see; and your ears, because they hear. ¹⁷I tell you the truth, many prophets and righteous people longed to see what you see, but they didn't see it. And they longed to hear what you hear, but they didn't hear it.

¹⁸"Now listen to the explanation of the parable about the farmer planting seeds: ¹⁹The seed that fell on the footpath represents those who hear the message about the Kingdom and don't understand it. Then the evil one comes and snatches away the seed that was planted in their hearts. ²⁰The seed on the rocky soil represents those who hear the message and immediately receive it with joy. ²¹But since they don't have deep roots, they don't last long. They fall away as soon as they have problems or are persecuted for believing God's word. ²²The seed that fell among the thorns represents those who hear God's word, but all too quickly the message is crowded out by the worries of this life and the lure of wealth, so no fruit is produced. ²³The seed that fell on good soil represents those who truly hear and understand God's word and produce a harvest of thirty, sixty, or even a hundred times as much as had been planted!"

PARABLE OF THE WHEAT AND WEEDS ²⁴Here is another story Jesus told: "The Kingdom of Heaven is like a farmer who planted good seed in his field. ²⁵But that night as the workers slept, his enemy came and planted weeds among the wheat, then slipped away. ²⁶When the crop began to grow and produce grain, the weeds also grew.

²⁷"The farmer's workers went to him and said, 'Sir, the field where you planted that good seed is full of weeds! Where did they come from?'

²⁸"'An enemy has done this!' the farmer exclaimed.

"'Should we pull out the weeds?' they asked.

²⁹"'No,' he replied, 'you'll uproot the wheat if you do. ³⁰Let both grow together until the harvest. Then I will tell the harvesters to sort out the weeds, tie them into bundles, and burn them, and to put the wheat in the barn.'"

PARABLE OF THE MUSTARD SEED ³¹Here is another illustration Jesus used: "The Kingdom of Heaven is like a mustard seed planted in a field. ³²It is the smallest of all seeds, but it becomes the largest of garden plants; it grows into a tree, and birds come and make nests in its branches."

PARABLE OF THE YEAST ³³Jesus also used this illustration: "The Kingdom of Heaven is like the yeast a woman used in making bread. Even though she put only a little yeast in three measures of flour, it permeated every part of the dough."

³⁴Jesus always used stories and illustrations like these when speaking to the crowds. In fact, he never spoke to them without using such parables. ³⁵This fulfilled what God had spoken through the prophet:

"I will speak to you in parables.
    I will explain things hidden since the
        creation of the world.*"

PARABLE OF THE WHEAT AND WEEDS EXPLAINED ³⁶Then, leaving the crowds outside, Jesus went into the house. His disciples said, "Please explain to us the story of the weeds in the field."

³⁷Jesus replied, "The Son of Man* is the farmer who plants the good seed. ³⁸The field is the world, and the good seed represents the people of the Kingdom. The weeds are the people who belong to the evil one. ³⁹The enemy who planted the weeds among the wheat is the devil. The harvest is the end of the world,* and the harvesters are the angels.

⁴⁰"Just as the weeds are sorted out and burned in the fire, so it will be at the end of the world. ⁴¹The Son of Man will send his angels, and they will remove from his Kingdom everything that causes sin and all who do evil. ⁴²And the angels will throw them into the fiery furnace, where there will be weeping and gnash-

....

RESPONSES
(13:18-23) The four types of soil represent the different responses we can have to God's message. We respond differently because we are in different states of readiness. Some people are hardened, others are shallow. Distracting cares contaminate some, while some are receptive. How has God's Word taken root in your life? What kind of soil are you?

13:14-15 Isa 6:9-10 (Greek version). **13:35** Some manuscripts do not include *of the world*. Ps 78:2. **13:37** "Son of Man" is a title Jesus used for himself. **13:39** Or *the age*; also in 13:40, 49.

ing of teeth. ⁴³Then the righteous will shine like the sun in their Father's Kingdom. Anyone with ears to hear should listen and understand!

PARABLES OF THE HIDDEN TREASURE AND THE PEARL
⁴⁴"The Kingdom of Heaven is like a treasure that a man discovered hidden in a field. In his excitement, he hid it again and sold everything he owned to get enough money to buy the field.

⁴⁵"Again, the Kingdom of Heaven is like a merchant on the lookout for choice pearls. ⁴⁶When he discovered a pearl of great value, he sold everything he owned and bought it!

PARABLE OF THE FISHING NET
⁴⁷"Again, the Kingdom of Heaven is like a fishing net that was thrown into the water and caught fish of every kind. ⁴⁸When the net was full, they dragged it up onto the shore, sat down, and sorted the good fish into crates, but threw the bad ones away. ⁴⁹That is the way it will be at the end of the world. The angels will come and separate the wicked people from the righteous, ⁵⁰throwing the wicked into the fiery furnace, where there will be weeping and gnashing of teeth. ⁵¹Do you understand all these things?"

"Yes," they said, "we do."

⁵²Then he added, "Every teacher of religious law who becomes a disciple in the Kingdom of Heaven is like a homeowner who brings from his storeroom new gems of truth as well as old."

JESUS REJECTED AT NAZARETH
⁵³When Jesus had finished telling these stories and illustrations, he left that part of the country. ⁵⁴He returned to Nazareth, his hometown. When he taught there in the synagogue, everyone was amazed and said, "Where does he get this wisdom and the power to do miracles?" ⁵⁵Then they scoffed, "He's just the carpenter's son, and we know Mary, his mother, and his brothers—James, Joseph,* Simon, and Judas. ⁵⁶All his sisters live right here among us. Where did he learn all these things?" ⁵⁷And they were deeply offended and refused to believe in him.

Then Jesus told them, "A prophet is honored everywhere except in his own hometown and among his own family." ⁵⁸And so he did only a few miracles there because of their unbelief.

14 THE DEATH OF JOHN THE BAPTIST
When Herod Antipas, the ruler of Galilee,* heard about Jesus, ²he said to his advis-

ers, "This must be John the Baptist raised from the dead! That is why he can do such miracles."

³For Herod had arrested and imprisoned John as a favor to his wife Herodias (the former wife of Herod's brother Philip). ⁴John had been telling Herod, "It is against God's law for you to marry her." ⁵Herod wanted to kill John, but he was afraid of a riot, because all the people believed John was a prophet.

⁶But at a birthday party for Herod, Herodias's daughter performed a dance that greatly pleased him, ⁷so he promised with a vow to give her anything she wanted. ⁸At her mother's urging, the girl said, "I want the head of John the Baptist on a tray!" ⁹Then the king regretted what he had said; but because of the vow he had made in front of his guests, he issued the necessary orders. ¹⁰So John was beheaded in the prison, ¹¹and his head was brought on a tray and given to the girl, who took it to her mother. ¹²Later, John's disciples came for his body and buried it. Then they went and told Jesus what had happened.

JESUS FEEDS FIVE THOUSAND
¹³As soon as Jesus heard the news, he left in a boat to a remote area to be alone. But the crowds heard where he was headed and followed him on foot from many towns. ¹⁴Jesus saw the huge crowd as he stepped from the boat, and he had compassion on them and healed their sick.

¹⁵That evening the disciples came to him and said, "This is a remote place, and it's already getting late. Send the crowds away so they can go to the villages and buy food for themselves."

¹⁶But Jesus said, "That isn't necessary—you feed them."

¹⁷"But we have only five loaves of bread and two fish!" they answered.

¹⁸"Bring them here," he said. ¹⁹Then he told the people to sit down on the grass. Jesus took the five loaves and two fish, looked up toward heaven, and blessed them. Then, breaking the loaves into pieces, he gave the bread to the disciples, who distributed it to the people. ²⁰They all ate as much as they wanted, and

13:55 Other manuscripts read *Joses;* still others read *John.*
14:1 Greek *Herod the tetrarch.* Herod Antipas was a son of King Herod and was ruler over Galilee.

GIVING IN
(14:1-12) Although Herod didn't want to kill John the Baptist, he gave the order to avoid being embarrassed in front of his guests. Many of us say we would never make a similar decision. Yet, how often do we go along with what everyone else is doing just to avoid the "loser" label? Hanging on to your integrity might cost you some popularity points. But in the long run, you'll win far more than you lose.

afterward, the disciples picked up twelve baskets of leftovers. ²¹About 5,000 men were fed that day, in addition to all the women and children!

JESUS WALKS ON WATER ²²Immediately after this, Jesus insisted that his disciples get back into the boat and cross to the other side of the lake, while he sent the people home. ²³After sending them home, he went up into the hills by himself to pray. Night fell while he was there alone.

²⁴Meanwhile, the disciples were in trouble far away from land, for a strong wind had risen, and they were fighting heavy waves. ²⁵About three o'clock in the morning* Jesus came toward them, walking on the water. ²⁶When the disciples saw him walking on the water, they were terrified. In their fear, they cried out, "It's a ghost!"

²⁷But Jesus spoke to them at once. "Don't be afraid," he said. "Take courage. I am here!*"

²⁸Then Peter called to him, "Lord, if it's really you, tell me to come to you, walking on the water."

²⁹"Yes, come," Jesus said.

So Peter went over the side of the boat and walked on the water toward Jesus. ³⁰But when he saw the strong* wind and the waves, he was terrified and began to sink. "Save me, Lord!" he shouted.

³¹Jesus immediately reached out and grabbed him. "You have so little faith," Jesus said. "Why did you doubt me?"

³²When they climbed back into the boat, the wind stopped. ³³Then the disciples worshiped him. "You really are the Son of God!" they exclaimed.

³⁴After they had crossed the lake, they landed at Gennesaret. ³⁵When the people recognized Jesus, the news of his arrival spread quickly throughout the whole area, and soon

....

WALK OR SINK?
(14:28-33) Peter was not testing Jesus, something we are told not to do (4:7). Instead, he was the only one in the boat to react in faith. His impulsive request led him to experience a rather unusual demonstration of God's power. But then Peter started to sink because he took his eyes off Jesus and focused on the high waves around him. His faith wavered when he realized what he was doing. We may not walk on water, but we do walk through tough situations. If we focus on the waves of difficult circumstances around us without looking to Christ for help, we too may despair and sink. What tough situations are you facing now? Where is your focus: on the situation or on Jesus? To maintain your faith in the middle of difficulties, keep your eyes on Christ's power rather than on your inadequacies.

people were bringing all their sick to be healed. ³⁶They begged him to let the sick touch at least the fringe of his robe, and all who touched him were healed.

15 JESUS TEACHES ABOUT INNER PURITY

Some Pharisees and teachers of religious law now arrived from Jerusalem to see Jesus. They asked him, ²"Why do your disciples disobey our age-old tradition? For they ignore our tradition of ceremonial hand washing before they eat."

³Jesus replied, "And why do you, by your traditions, violate the direct commandments of God? ⁴For instance, God says, 'Honor your father and mother,'* and 'Anyone who speaks disrespectfully of father or mother must be put to death.'* ⁵But you say it is all right for people to say to their parents, 'Sorry, I can't help you. For I have vowed to give to God what I would have given to you.' ⁶In this way, you say they don't need to honor their parents.* And so you cancel the word of God for the sake of your own tradition. ⁷You hypocrites! Isaiah was right when he prophesied about you, for he wrote,

⁸ 'These people honor me with their lips,
　　but their hearts are far from me.
⁹ Their worship is a farce,
　　for they teach man-made ideas as
　　　commands from God.'*

¹⁰Then Jesus called to the crowd to come and hear. "Listen," he said, "and try to understand. ¹¹It's not what goes into your mouth that defiles you; you are defiled by the words that come out of your mouth."

¹²Then the disciples came to him and asked, "Do you realize you offended the Pharisees by what you just said?"

¹³Jesus replied, "Every plant not planted by my heavenly Father will be uprooted, ¹⁴so ignore them. They are blind guides leading the blind, and if one blind person guides another, they will both fall into a ditch."

¹⁵Then Peter said to Jesus, "Explain to us the parable that says people aren't defiled by what they eat."

¹⁶"Don't you understand yet?" Jesus asked. ¹⁷"Anything you eat passes through the stomach and then goes into the sewer. ¹⁸But the words you speak come from the heart—that's what defiles you. ¹⁹For from the heart come

14:25 Greek *In the fourth watch of the night.* **14:27** Or *The 'I AM' is here;* Greek reads *I am.* See Exod 3:14. **14:30** Some manuscripts do not include *strong.* **15:4a** Exod 20:12; Deut 5:16. **15:4b** Exod 21:17 (Greek version); Lev 20:9 (Greek version). **15:6** Greek *their father;* other manuscripts read *their father or their mother.* **15:8-9** Isa 29:13 (Greek version).

evil thoughts, murder, adultery, all sexual immorality, theft, lying, and slander. ²⁰These are what defile you. Eating with unwashed hands will never defile you."

THE FAITH OF A GENTILE WOMAN
²¹Then Jesus left Galilee and went north to the region of Tyre and Sidon. ²²A Gentile* woman who lived there came to him, pleading, "Have mercy on me, O Lord, Son of David! For my daughter is possessed by a demon that torments her severely."

²³But Jesus gave her no reply, not even a word. Then his disciples urged him to send her away. "Tell her to go away," they said. "She is bothering us with all her begging."

²⁴Then Jesus said to the woman, "I was sent only to help God's lost sheep—the people of Israel."

²⁵But she came and worshiped him, pleading again, "Lord, help me!"

²⁶Jesus responded, "It isn't right to take food from the children and throw it to the dogs."

²⁷She replied, "That's true, Lord, but even dogs are allowed to eat the scraps that fall beneath their masters' table."

²⁸"Dear woman," Jesus said to her, "your faith is great. Your request is granted." And her daughter was instantly healed.

JESUS HEALS MANY PEOPLE
²⁹Jesus returned to the Sea of Galilee and climbed a hill and sat down. ³⁰A vast crowd brought to him people who were lame, blind, crippled, those who couldn't speak, and many others. They laid them before Jesus, and he healed them all. ³¹The crowd was amazed! Those who hadn't been able to speak were talking, the crippled were made well, the lame were walking, and the blind could see again! And they praised the God of Israel.

JESUS FEEDS FOUR THOUSAND
³²Then Jesus called his disciples and told them, "I feel sorry for these people. They have been here with me for three days, and they have nothing left to eat. I don't want to send them away hungry, or they will faint along the way."

³³The disciples replied, "Where would we get enough food here in the wilderness for such a huge crowd?"

³⁴Jesus asked, "How much bread do you have?"

They replied, "Seven loaves, and a few small fish."

15:22 Greek *Canaanite.*   16:2-3 Several manuscripts do not include any of the words in 16:2-3 after *He replied.*   16:4 Greek *the sign of Jonah.*

³⁵So Jesus told all the people to sit down on the ground. ³⁶Then he took the seven loaves and the fish, thanked God for them, and broke them into pieces. He gave them to the disciples, who distributed the food to the crowd. ³⁷They all ate as much as they wanted. Afterward, the disciples picked up seven large baskets of leftover food. ³⁸There were 4,000 men who were fed that day, in addition to all the women and children. ³⁹Then Jesus sent the people home, and he got into a boat and crossed over to the region of Magadan.

16 LEADERS DEMAND A MIRACULOUS SIGN
One day the Pharisees and Sadducees came to test Jesus, demanding that he show them a miraculous sign from heaven to prove his authority.

²He replied, "You know the saying, 'Red sky at night means fair weather tomorrow; ³red sky in the morning means foul weather all day.' You know how to interpret the weather signs in the sky, but you don't know how to interpret the signs of the times!* ⁴Only an evil, adulterous generation would demand a miraculous sign, but the only sign I will give them is the sign of the prophet Jonah.*" Then Jesus left them and went away.

YEAST OF THE PHARISEES AND SADDUCEES
⁵Later, after they crossed to the other side of the lake, the disciples discovered they had forgotten to bring any bread. ⁶"Watch out!" Jesus warned them. "Beware of the yeast of the Pharisees and Sadducees."

⁷At this they began to argue with each other because they hadn't brought any bread. ⁸Jesus knew what they were saying, so he said, "You have so little faith! Why are you arguing with each other about having no bread? ⁹Don't you understand even yet? Don't you remember the 5,000 I fed with five loaves, and the baskets of leftovers you picked up? ¹⁰Or the 4,000 I fed with seven loaves, and the large baskets of leftovers you picked up? ¹¹Why can't you understand that I'm not talking about bread? So

....

MEETING THE NEEDS
(15:21-28) The disciples asked Jesus to get rid of the woman because she was bothering them with her begging. They showed no compassion for her or sensitivity to her needs. Ever respond that way when someone threatens to inconvenience you with a need? If honest, many would answer yes. It's possible to become so occupied with spiritual activities that we miss real spiritual needs right around us. What are the needs of the people around you? How willing are you to meet those needs, even if doing so means stepping out of your comfort zone?

again I say, 'Beware of the yeast of the Pharisees and Sadducees.'"

¹²Then at last they understood that he wasn't speaking about the yeast in bread, but about the deceptive teaching of the Pharisees and Sadducees.

PETER'S DECLARATION ABOUT JESUS ¹³When Jesus came to the region of Caesarea Philippi, he asked his disciples, "Who do people say that the Son of Man is?"*

¹⁴"Well," they replied, "some say John the Baptist, some say Elijah, and others say Jeremiah or one of the other prophets."

¹⁵Then he asked them, "But who do you say I am?"

¹⁶Simon Peter answered, "You are the Messiah,* the Son of the living God."

¹⁷Jesus replied, "You are blessed, Simon son of John,* because my Father in heaven has revealed this to you. You did not learn this from any human being. ¹⁸Now I say to you that you are Peter (which means 'rock'),* and upon this rock I will build my church, and all the powers of hell* will not conquer it. ¹⁹And I will give you the keys of the Kingdom of Heaven. Whatever you forbid* on earth will be forbidden in heaven, and whatever you permit* on earth will be permitted in heaven."

²⁰Then he sternly warned the disciples not to tell anyone that he was the Messiah.

16:13 "Son of Man" is a title Jesus used for himself.   **16:16** Or the Christ. Messiah (a Hebrew term) and Christ (a Greek term) both mean "the anointed one."   **16:17** Greek Simon bar-Jonah; see John 1:42; 21:15-17.   **16:18a** Greek that you are Peter.   **16:18b** Greek and the gates of Hades.   **16:19a** Or bind, or lock.   **16:19b** Or loose, or open.

ULTIMATE ISSUES — WHO IS JESUS?

Gorillas are amazingly bright animals. Researchers have even been able to teach some gorillas to communicate by using sign language. Koko, one of the best ape "students" ever trained, has an impressive sign vocabulary through which she is able to communicate a number of surprisingly complicated concepts. But she was unprepared for the day an earthquake shook the ground underneath her.

After it was over, one of her trainers asked Koko to describe what she had just experienced. Having no word in her vocabulary for "earthquake," Koko described it as best she could. Using sign language, she said, "Darn floor—big bite."

It's not entirely clear what she was trying to communicate with those words; perhaps the fear that the floor might open up and swallow her. She was trying to express something beyond her limited ability in the only way she knew.

People have struggled throughout history in a similar way with a different—and much more significant—problem: how to describe who God is and what he's like. (See the Ultimate Issue "Who Is God?" in Isaiah 1.) God communicated with humans in many ways in the past: talking freely with Adam and Eve, through the covenant sign of the rainbow, through a burning bush and columns of fire and smoke, through his Law, and through miracles and visions. Still, powerful and meaningful as all those were, they only gave a hint of the reality behind them. The people who witnessed those signs must have felt like Koko—overwhelmed by what they'd experienced but with no adequate way to express their feelings. That's why God saved the best way of revealing himself for last. He became one of us—the man called Jesus. He came with a nickname: Immanuel, which means "God with us" (Matt 1:23).

Understandably, the coming of Jesus was an explosive event. Nothing like it had ever happened before, nor has it happened since. God—in human form—walking the same ground with us! Breathing our air, sharing our pain, laughing and bleeding just like we do, entering into all the exhilaration—and the anguish—of being human. Before this revelation, God had given us hints, glimpses, and whispers of who he was. Then he came in all his fullness.

But Jesus was not what people expected. Even the Jewish authorities—the people who knew more about God than anyone—were totally unprepared for the way God came. They expected a strong political and military savior, one who would free his people from Rome. Instead, the Messiah came as a "suffering servant," proclaiming a Kingdom that was not of this world. Like so many others, the Jews were very confused as to who Jesus really was. Jesus himself knew that even his closest followers felt that uncertainty. He asked them point-blank: "Who do you say I am?" Peter's response to this question, given in Matthew 16:16, was simple, direct, and tremendously powerful: "The Messiah, the Son of the living God."

Peter's answer, simple though it was, set off shock waves that have rippled down through history. If Jesus was—and is—indeed the Messiah, the Son of the living God, then God had entered into human history in a way he had never done before, and life on this planet could never be the same again. Countless millions of lives since then give testimony that that is exactly what has happened. Jesus of Nazareth was, and is, the unique Son of God: fully God, fully human, Lord of lords, and King of kings.

That same question Jesus asked his disciples confronts each of us today: Who do you say Jesus is? Be careful how you answer. It makes all the difference in eternity. ∎

JESUS PREDICTS HIS DEATH ²¹From then on Jesus* began to tell his disciples plainly that it was necessary for him to go to Jerusalem, and that he would suffer many terrible things at the hands of the elders, the leading priests, and the teachers of religious law. He would be killed, but on the third day he would be raised from the dead.

²²But Peter took him aside and began to reprimand him* for saying such things. "Heaven forbid, Lord," he said. "This will never happen to you!"

²³Jesus turned to Peter and said, "Get away from me, Satan! You are a dangerous trap to me. You are seeing things merely from a human point of view, not from God's."

²⁴Then Jesus said to his disciples, "If any of you wants to be my follower, you must turn from your selfish ways, take up your cross, and follow me. ²⁵If you try to hang on to your life, you will lose it. But if you give up your life for my sake, you will save it. ²⁶And what do you benefit if you gain the whole world but lose your own soul?* Is anything worth more than your soul? ²⁷For the Son of Man will come with his angels in the glory of his Father and will judge all people according to their deeds. ²⁸And I tell you the truth, some standing here right now will not die before they see the Son of Man coming in his Kingdom."

17 **THE TRANSFIGURATION** Six days later Jesus took Peter and the two brothers, James and John, and led them up a high mountain to be alone. ²As the men watched, Jesus' appearance was transformed so that his face shone like the sun, and his clothes became as white as light. ³Suddenly, Moses and Elijah appeared and began talking with Jesus.

⁴Peter exclaimed, "Lord, it's wonderful for us to be here! If you want, I'll make three shelters as memorials*—one for you, one for Moses, and one for Elijah."

⁵But even as he spoke, a bright cloud overshadowed them, and a voice from the cloud said, "This is my dearly loved Son, who brings me great joy. Listen to him." ⁶The disciples were terrified and fell face down on the ground.

⁷Then Jesus came over and touched them. "Get up," he said. "Don't be afraid." ⁸And

when they looked up, Moses and Elijah were gone, and they saw only Jesus.

⁹As they went back down the mountain, Jesus commanded them, "Don't tell anyone what you have seen until the Son of Man* has been raised from the dead."

¹⁰Then his disciples asked him, "Why do the teachers of religious law insist that Elijah must return before the Messiah comes?*"

¹¹Jesus replied, "Elijah is indeed coming first to get everything ready. ¹²But I tell you, Elijah has already come, but he wasn't recognized, and they chose to abuse him. And in the same way they will also make the Son of Man suffer." ¹³Then the disciples realized he was talking about John the Baptist.

JESUS HEALS A DEMON-POSSESSED BOY ¹⁴At the foot of the mountain, a large crowd was waiting for them. A man came and knelt before Jesus and said, ¹⁵"Lord, have mercy on my son. He has seizures and suffers terribly. He often falls into the fire or into the water. ¹⁶So I brought him to your disciples, but they couldn't heal him."

¹⁷Jesus said, "You faithless and corrupt people! How long must I be with you? How long must I put up with you? Bring the boy here to me." ¹⁸Then Jesus rebuked the demon in the boy, and it left him. From that moment the boy was well.

¹⁹Afterward the disciples asked Jesus privately, "Why couldn't we cast out that demon?"

²⁰"You don't have enough faith," Jesus told them. "I tell you the truth, if you had faith even as small as a mustard seed, you could say to this mountain, 'Move from here to there,' and it would move. Nothing would be impossible.*"

JESUS AGAIN PREDICTS HIS DEATH ²²After they gathered again in Galilee, Jesus told them, "The Son of Man is going to be betrayed into the hands of his enemies. ²³He will be killed, but on the third day he will be raised from the dead." And the disciples were filled with grief.

16:21 Some manuscripts read *Jesus the Messiah.* **16:22** Or *began to correct him.* **16:26** Or *your self?* also in 16:26b. **17:4** Greek *three tabernacles.* **17:9** "Son of Man" is a title Jesus used for himself. **17:10** Greek *that Elijah must come first?* **17:20** Some manuscripts add verse 21, *But this kind of demon won't leave except by prayer and fasting.* Compare Mark 9:29.

HARMLESS ADVICE?
(16:21-22) Peter, Jesus' friend and devoted follower who had just eloquently proclaimed his Lord's true identity as the Christ (16:13-16), sought to protect Jesus from the suffering Jesus had to face. Great temptation can come from those who love us and seek to protect us from something we must experience. Be wary when a friend says, "This will never happen to you!" Although his or her motive is to prevent harm, this advice might cause more harm than good.

PAYMENT OF THE TEMPLE TAX   24On their arrival in Capernaum, the collectors of the Temple tax* came to Peter and asked him, "Doesn't your teacher pay the Temple tax?"

25"Yes, he does," Peter replied. Then he went into the house.

But before he had a chance to speak, Jesus asked him, "What do you think, Peter?* Do kings tax their own people or the people they have conquered?*"

26"They tax the people they have conquered," Peter replied.

∙∙

BELIEVE

(17:22-23) Jesus again predicted his death; but more important, he told of his resurrection. Unfortunately, the disciples heard only the first part and became discouraged. They couldn't understand why Jesus wanted to go back to Jerusalem when trouble awaited him there. The disciples didn't fully comprehend the purpose of Jesus' death and resurrection until Pentecost (Acts 2). Don't get upset at yourself if you are slow to understand everything about Jesus. After all, the disciples were with him, saw his miracles, and heard his words, and they still had difficulty understanding. Despite their questions and doubts, however, they believed. We can do no less.

"Well, then," Jesus said, "the citizens are free! 27However, we don't want to offend them, so go down to the lake and throw in a line. Open the mouth of the first fish you catch, and you will find a large silver coin.* Take it and pay the tax for both of us."

18 THE GREATEST IN THE KINGDOM About that time the disciples came to Jesus and asked, "Who is greatest in the Kingdom of Heaven?"

2Jesus called a little child to him and put the child among them. 3Then he said, "I tell you the truth, unless you turn from your sins and become like little children, you will never get into the Kingdom of Heaven. 4So anyone who becomes as humble as this little child is the greatest in the Kingdom of Heaven.

5"And anyone who welcomes a little child like this on my behalf* is welcoming me. 6But if you cause one of these little ones who trusts in me to fall into sin, it would be better for you

17:24 Greek *the two-drachma [tax]*; also in 17:24b. See Exod 30:13-16; Neh 10:32-33.   **17:25a** Greek *Simon?*   **17:25b** Greek *their sons or others?*   **17:27** Greek *a stater* [a Greek coin equivalent to four drachmas].   **18:5** Greek *in my name*.

I WONDER...

Is temptation a sin? If it is, I'm sinning all the time. It seems like thoughts are always coming into my mind to do things that are wrong.

If temptation were a sin, then Jesus was a sinner. Jesus was tempted by Satan in the wilderness (Matthew 4:1-11). But temptation is not a sin. According to Matthew 18:7-9, it's the natural consequence of living in this world.

Sin comes from following the path temptation wants us to take. If taken far enough, the path will cause us to think and do what is wrong.

Though temptation will always be present, we do not have to wave a white flag in surrender. We have the power to resist and defeat temptation because the Holy Spirit lives in us.

God's Word also reminds us how to overcome temptation. First Corinthians 10:13 says, "The temptations in your life are no different from what others experience. And God is faithful. He will not allow the temptation to be more than you can stand. When you are tempted, he will show you a way out so that you can endure."

Find the "way out" in this story:

At school a friend asks if you want to spend the night with some friends and watch DVDs. You check with your folks, assuring them there will be no R-rated movies. They give the okay. Everything is cool, so far.

Once you arrive, you look at the stack of DVDs and notice that half of them are R-rated. You get your friend alone and ask him what the deal is. He says the other guys picked out the DVDs. Besides, everyone (except you) has seen them before, so he didn't think you'd mind.

Do you stay and go along with the group, or do you keep your commitment to your parents?

Let's say you stay. The next day your dad asks what movies you watched. Now you have to lie to stay out of trouble. So you lie. Unfortunately, your mom spoke with the mom of one of your friends on the phone and found out there were R-rated movies at the sleepover. Now you're grounded until age 27!

Where were the escape hatches to the temptation to disobey your parents? When you found out that R-rated movies would be shown, you had two choices. You could have apologized to your friends, called your dad, and had him pick you up. Or you could have gone to a different part of the house and done something else.

God always provides a way out of every temptation. We choose whether to take his way out or to do things we know are wrong.

If we stay close to God, we'll be more likely to resist and do what is right. We don't have to give in.

to have a large millstone tied around your neck and be drowned in the depths of the sea.

⁷"What sorrow awaits the world, because it tempts people to sin. Temptations are inevitable, but what sorrow awaits the person who does the tempting. ⁸So if your hand or foot causes you to sin, cut it off and throw it away. It's better to enter eternal life with only one hand or one foot than to be thrown into eternal fire with both of your hands and feet. ⁹And if your eye causes you to sin, gouge it out and throw it away. It's better to enter eternal life with only one eye than to have two eyes and be thrown into the fire of hell.*

¹⁰"Beware that you don't look down on any of these little ones. For I tell you that in heaven their angels are always in the presence of my heavenly Father.*

PARABLE OF THE LOST SHEEP
¹²"If a man has a hundred sheep and one of them wanders away, what will he do? Won't he leave the ninety-nine others on the hills and go out to search for the one that is lost? ¹³And if he finds it, I tell you the truth, he will rejoice over it more than over the ninety-nine that didn't wander away! ¹⁴In the same way, it is not my heavenly Father's will that even one of these little ones should perish.

CORRECTING ANOTHER BELIEVER
¹⁵"If another believer* sins against you,* go privately and point out the offense. If the other person listens and confesses it, you have won that person back. ¹⁶But if you are unsuccessful, take one or two others with you and go back again, so that everything you say may be confirmed by two or three witnesses. ¹⁷If the person still refuses to listen, take your case to the church. Then if he or she won't accept the church's decision, treat that person as a pagan or a corrupt tax collector.

¹⁸"I tell you the truth, whatever you forbid* on earth will be forbidden in heaven, and whatever you permit* on earth will be permitted in heaven.

¹⁹"I also tell you this: If two of you agree here on earth concerning anything you ask, my Father in heaven will do it for you. ²⁰For where two or three gather together as my followers,* I am there among them."

PARABLE OF THE UNFORGIVING DEBTOR
²¹Then Peter came to him and asked, "Lord, how often should I forgive someone* who sins against me? Seven times?"

²²"No, not seven times," Jesus replied, "but seventy times seven!*

²³"Therefore, the Kingdom of Heaven can be compared to a king who decided to bring his accounts up to date with servants who had borrowed money from him. ²⁴In the process, one of his debtors was brought in who owed him millions of dollars.* ²⁵He couldn't pay, so his master ordered that he be sold—along with his wife, his children, and everything he owned—to pay the debt.

²⁶"But the man fell down before his master and begged him, 'Please, be patient with me, and I will pay it all.' ²⁷Then his master was filled with pity for him, and he released him and forgave his debt.

²⁸"But when the man left the king, he went to a fellow servant who owed him a few thousand dollars.* He grabbed him by the throat and demanded instant payment.

²⁹"His fellow servant fell down before him and begged for a little more time. 'Be patient with me, and I will pay it,' he pleaded. ³⁰But his creditor wouldn't wait. He had the man arrested and put in prison until the debt could be paid in full.

³¹"When some of the other servants saw this, they were very upset. They went to the king and told him everything that had happened. ³²Then the king called in the man he had forgiven and said, 'You evil servant! I forgave you that tremendous debt because you pleaded with me. ³³Shouldn't you have mercy on your fellow servant, just as I had mercy on you?' ³⁴Then the angry king sent the man to prison to be tortured until he had paid his entire debt.

··

LITTLE KIDS
(18:6) Children are trusting by nature. They trust adults, which helps them trust God. Parents and others who influence young children are held accountable by God for how they affect these little ones' ability to trust. Jesus warned that anyone who turns little children away from faith will receive severe punishment.

ALWAYS OPEN?
(18:21-33) The rabbis taught that Jews should forgive those who offend them up to three times. Peter, in trying to be especially generous, asked Jesus if forgiving someone for the same offense seven (the "perfect" number) times was good enough. But Jesus' reply hints that forgiveness is to be offered always (18:22). When it comes to forgiving others, are you like a convenience store—open 24/7—or like a store with limited hours?

18:9 Greek the Gehenna of fire.   18:10 Some manuscripts add verse 11, And the Son of Man came to save those who are lost. Compare Luke 19:10.   18:15a Greek If your brother.   18:15b Some manuscripts do not include against you.   18:18a Or bind, or lock.   18:18b Or loose, or open.   18:20 Greek gather together in my name.   18:21 Greek my brother.   18:22 Or seventy-seven times.   18:24 Greek 10,000 talents [375 tons or 340 metric tons of silver].   18:28 Greek 100 denarii. A denarius was equivalent to a laborer's full day's wage.

³⁵"That's what my heavenly Father will do to you if you refuse to forgive your brothers and sisters* from your heart."

19 DISCUSSION ABOUT DIVORCE AND MARRIAGE

When Jesus had finished saying these things, he left Galilee and went down to the region of Judea east of the Jordan River. ²Large crowds followed him there, and he healed their sick.

³Some Pharisees came and tried to trap him with this question: "Should a man be allowed to divorce his wife for just any reason?"

⁴"Haven't you read the Scriptures?" Jesus replied. "They record that from the beginning 'God made them male and female.'*" ⁵And he said, "'This explains why a man leaves his father and mother and is joined to his wife, and the two are united into one.'* ⁶Since they are no longer two but one, let no one split apart what God has joined together."

⁷"Then why did Moses say in the law that a man could give his wife a written notice of divorce and send her away?"* they asked.

⁸Jesus replied, "Moses permitted divorce only as a concession to your hard hearts, but it was not what God had originally intended. ⁹And I tell you this, whoever divorces his wife and marries someone else commits adultery—unless his wife has been unfaithful.*"

¹⁰Jesus' disciples then said to him, "If this is the case, it is better not to marry!"

¹¹"Not everyone can accept this statement," Jesus said. "Only those whom God helps. ¹²Some are born as eunuchs, some have been made eunuchs by others, and some choose not to marry* for the sake of the Kingdom of Heaven. Let anyone accept this who can."

JESUS BLESSES THE CHILDREN

¹³One day some parents brought their children to Jesus so he could lay his hands on them and pray for them. But the disciples scolded the parents for bothering him.

¹⁴But Jesus said, "Let the children come to me. Don't stop them! For the Kingdom of Heaven belongs to those who are like these children." ¹⁵And he placed his hands on their heads and blessed them before he left.

THE RICH MAN

¹⁶Someone came to Jesus with this question: "Teacher,* what good deed must I do to have eternal life?"

¹⁷"Why ask me about what is good?" Jesus replied. "There is only One who is good. But to answer your question—if you want to receive eternal life, keep* the commandments."

¹⁸"Which ones?" the man asked.

And Jesus replied: "'You must not murder. You must not commit adultery. You must not steal. You must not testify falsely. ¹⁹Honor your father and mother. Love your neighbor as yourself.'*"

²⁰"I've obeyed all these commandments," the young man replied. "What else must I do?"

²¹Jesus told him, "If you want to be perfect, go and sell all your possessions and give the money to the poor, and you will have treasure in heaven. Then come, follow me."

²²But when the young man heard this, he went away sad, for he had many possessions.

²³Then Jesus said to his disciples, "I tell you the truth, it is very hard for a rich person to enter the Kingdom of Heaven. ²⁴I'll say it

18:35 Greek your brother. **19:4** Gen 1:27; 5:2. **19:5** Gen 2:24. **19:7** See Deut 24:1. **19:9** Some manuscripts add And anyone who marries a divorced woman commits adultery. Compare Matt 5:32. **19:12** Greek and some make themselves eunuchs. **19:16** Some manuscripts read Good Teacher. **19:17** Some manuscripts read continue to keep. **19:18-19** Exod 20:12-16; Deut 5:16-20; Lev 19:18.

CHOICES
divorce

Annette and Liu are watching the evening soap opera "California Millionaires". In this particular episode, police are investigating a possible murder at the Stanwick estate, Lance and Natasha are having an affair, and Sutherland is still thinking about having a sex-change operation. But as wild as those events are, they still are not the main plot of this week's show. No, the most disturbing revelation is that Gabrielle and Miles Stanwick are divorcing.

"I can't believe it!" Annette laments as she clicks off the TV in disgust. "They were so perfect together. Now it's over."

"Yeah, I never thought we'd ever see them call it quits. I guess it just goes to show you that even the best marriages sometimes come to an end."

"Just like my aunt and uncle. They were married for 25 years and . . ."

"Ooh, don't tell me one of them had an affair?" Liu asks, an eager tone in her voice.

"No, they just grew apart over the years. . . ."

"That is so sad!" Liu says.

Liu is right. Divorce is sad. But what about her statement that even the best marriages sometimes come to an end? Does God sanction divorce for reasons of incompatibility or "Well, we just don't love each other anymore"?

Read Matthew 19:1-12 to see what Jesus thinks about marriage, commitment, and divorce.

again—it is easier for a camel to go through the eye of a needle than for a rich person to enter the Kingdom of God!"

²⁵The disciples were astounded. "Then who in the world can be saved?" they asked.

²⁶Jesus looked at them intently and said, "Humanly speaking, it is impossible. But with God everything is possible."

²⁷Then Peter said to him, "We've given up everything to follow you. What will we get?"

²⁸Jesus replied, "I assure you that when the world is made new* and the Son of Man* sits upon his glorious throne, you who have been my followers will also sit on twelve thrones, judging the twelve tribes of Israel. ²⁹And everyone who has given up houses or brothers or sisters or father or mother or children or property, for my sake, will receive a hundred times as much in return and will inherit eternal life. ³⁰But many who are the greatest now will be least important then, and those who seem least important now will be the greatest then.*

20 PARABLE OF THE VINEYARD WORKERS

"For the Kingdom of Heaven is like the landowner who went out early one morning to hire workers for his vineyard. ²He agreed to pay the normal daily wage* and sent them out to work.

³"At nine o'clock in the morning he was passing through the marketplace and saw some people standing around doing nothing. ⁴So he hired them, telling them he would pay them whatever was right at the end of the day. ⁵So they went to work in the vineyard. At noon and again at three o'clock he did the same thing.

⁶"At five o'clock that afternoon he was in town again and saw some more people standing around. He asked them, 'Why haven't you been working today?'

⁷"They replied, 'Because no one hired us.'

"The landowner told them, 'Then go out and join the others in my vineyard.'

⁸"That evening he told the foreman to call the workers in and pay them, beginning with the last workers first. ⁹When those hired at five o'clock were paid, each received a full day's wage. ¹⁰When those hired first came to get their pay, they assumed they would receive more. But they, too, were paid a day's wage. ¹¹When they received their pay, they protested to the owner, ¹²'Those people worked only one hour, and yet you've paid them just as much as you paid us who worked all day in the scorching heat.'

¹³"He answered one of them, 'Friend, I haven't been unfair! Didn't you agree to work all day for the usual wage? ¹⁴Take your money and go. I wanted to pay this last worker the same as you. ¹⁵Is it against the law for me to do what I want with my money? Should you be jealous because I am kind to others?'

¹⁶"So those who are last now will be first then, and those who are first will be last."

JESUS AGAIN PREDICTS HIS DEATH

¹⁷As Jesus was going up to Jerusalem, he took the twelve disciples aside privately and told them what was going to happen to him. ¹⁸"Listen," he said, "we're going up to Jerusalem, where the Son of Man* will be betrayed to the leading priests and the teachers of religious law. They will sentence him to die. ¹⁹Then they will hand him over to the Romans* to be mocked, flogged with a whip, and crucified. But on the third day he will be raised from the dead."

JESUS TEACHES ABOUT SERVING OTHERS

²⁰Then the mother of James and John, the sons of Zebedee, came to Jesus with her sons. She knelt respectfully to ask a favor. ²¹"What is your request?" he asked.

She replied, "In your Kingdom, please let my two sons sit in places of honor next to you, one on your right and the other on your left."

²²But Jesus answered by saying to them, "You don't know what you are asking! Are you able to drink from the bitter cup of suffering I am about to drink?"

"Oh yes," they replied, "we are able!"

•••

GOD'S GENEROSITY

(20:1-15) The parable of the vineyard is a story about grace—God's generosity. Those who trust Jesus will get the same reward—eternal life with him—regardless of whether they turn to him early in life or in their last moments of life. We shouldn't begrudge those who turn to God in the last moments of life because, in reality, no one deserves eternal life. Many people we don't expect to see in the Kingdom may be there. The criminal who repented as he was dying will be there, as well as the person who has believed and served God for many years (Luke 23:40-43). Do you resent God's gracious acceptance of the despised, the outcast, and the sinners who have turned to him for forgiveness? Are you ever jealous of what God has given to another person? Instead, focus on God's gracious benefits to you, and be thankful for what you have. This, also, is not an invitation to wait until the last minute to make up your mind about Jesus. After all, no one knows when the last minute of life will take place. God is generous to all. Are you cool with that?

19:28a Or *in the regeneration.* **19:28b** "Son of Man" is a title Jesus used for himself. **19:30** Greek *But many who are first will be last; and the last, first.* **20:2** Greek *a denarius,* the payment for a full day's labor; similarly in 20:9, 10, 13. **20:18** "Son of Man" is a title Jesus used for himself. **20:19** Greek *the Gentiles.*

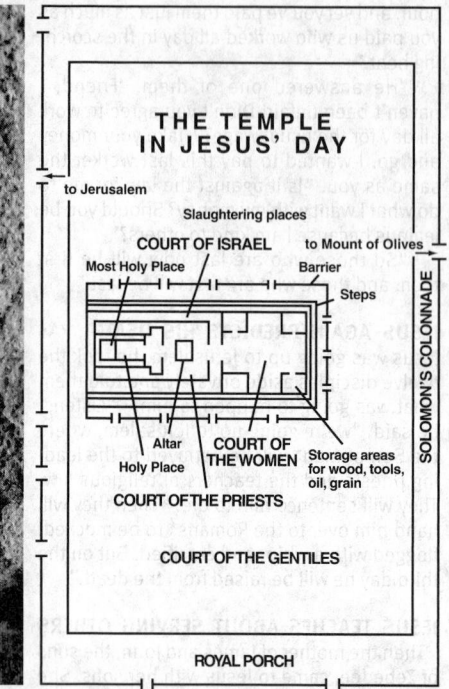

THE TEMPLE IN JESUS' DAY

to Jerusalem

Slaughtering places

COURT OF ISRAEL   to Mount of Olives

Most Holy Place   Barrier

                       Steps

                       SOLOMON'S COLONNADE

Altar   COURT OF
Holy Place THE WOMEN   Storage areas
                         for wood, tools,
COURT OF THE PRIESTS   oil, grain

COURT OF THE GENTILES

ROYAL PORCH

23Jesus told them, "You will indeed drink from my bitter cup. But I have no right to say who will sit on my right or my left. My Father has prepared those places for the ones he has chosen."

24When the ten other disciples heard what James and John had asked, they were indignant. 25But Jesus called them together and said, "You know that the rulers in this world lord it over their people, and officials flaunt their authority over those under them. 26But among you it will be different. Whoever wants to be a leader among you must be your servant, 27and whoever wants to be first among you must become your slave. 28For even the Son of Man came not to be served but to serve others and to give his life as a ransom for many."

JESUS HEALS TWO BLIND MEN 29As Jesus and the disciples left the town of Jericho, a large

crowd followed behind. 30Two blind men were sitting beside the road. When they heard that Jesus was coming that way, they began shouting, "Lord, Son of David, have mercy on us!"

31"Be quiet!" the crowd yelled at them.

But they only shouted louder, "Lord, Son of David, have mercy on us!"

32When Jesus heard them, he stopped and called, "What do you want me to do for you?"

33"Lord," they said, "we want to see!" 34Jesus felt sorry for them and touched their eyes. Instantly they could see! Then they followed him.

21 JESUS' TRIUMPHANT ENTRY As Jesus and the disciples approached Jerusalem, they came to the town of Bethphage on the Mount of Olives. Jesus sent two of them on ahead. 2"Go into the village over there," he said. "As soon as you enter it, you will see a donkey tied there, with its colt beside it. Untie them and bring them to me. 3If anyone asks what you are doing, just say, 'The Lord needs them,' and he will immediately let you take them."

4This took place to fulfill the prophecy that said,

5 "Tell the people of Jerusalem,*
     'Look, your King is coming to you.
   He is humble, riding on a donkey—
     riding on a donkey's colt.'"*

6The two disciples did as Jesus commanded. 7They brought the donkey and the colt to him and threw their garments over the colt, and he sat on it.*

8Most of the crowd spread their garments on the road ahead of him, and others cut branches from the trees and spread them on the road. 9Jesus was in the center of the procession, and the people all around him were shouting,

"Praise God* for the Son of David!
  Blessings on the one who comes in the
    name of the LORD!
  Praise God in highest heaven!"*

10The entire city of Jerusalem was in an uproar as he entered. "Who is this?" they asked.

11And the crowds replied, "It's Jesus, the prophet from Nazareth in Galilee."

JESUS CLEARS THE TEMPLE 12Jesus entered the Temple and began to drive out all the

---

LEADERS
(20:27) Jesus' description of leadership: Serve people; don't use them. Jesus served others and gave his life away. A real leader appreciates others and realizes that he or she is not above any job. Does something need to be done? Take the initiative and do it like a faithful servant.

21:5a Greek *Tell the daughter of Zion.* Isa 62:11. **21:5b** Zech 9:9. **21:7** Greek *over them, and he sat on them.* **21:9a** Greek *Hosanna,* an exclamation of praise that literally means "save now"; also in 21:9b, 15. **21:9b** Pss 118:25-26; 148:1.

people buying and selling animals for sacrifice. He knocked over the tables of the money changers and the chairs of those selling doves. [13]He said to them, "The Scriptures declare, 'My Temple will be called a house of prayer,' but you have turned it into a den of thieves!"*

[14]The blind and the lame came to him in the Temple, and he healed them. [15]The leading priests and the teachers of religious law saw these wonderful miracles and heard even the children in the Temple shouting, "Praise God for the Son of David."

But the leaders were indignant. [16]They asked Jesus, "Do you hear what these children are saying?"

"Yes," Jesus replied. "Haven't you ever read the Scriptures? For they say, 'You have taught children and infants to give you praise.'*" [17]Then he returned to Bethany, where he stayed overnight.

JESUS CURSES THE FIG TREE

[18]In the morning, as Jesus was returning to Jerusalem, he was hungry, [19]and he noticed a fig tree beside the road. He went over to see if there were any figs, but there were only leaves. Then he said to it, "May you never bear fruit again!" And immediately the fig tree withered up.

[20]The disciples were amazed when they saw this and asked, "How did the fig tree wither so quickly?"

[21]Then Jesus told them, "I tell you the truth, if you have faith and don't doubt, you can do things like this and much more. You can even say to this mountain, 'May you be lifted up and thrown into the sea,' and it will happen. [22]You can pray for anything, and if you have faith, you will receive it."

THE AUTHORITY OF JESUS CHALLENGED

[23]When Jesus returned to the Temple and began teaching, the leading priests and elders came up to him. They demanded, "By what authority are you doing all these things? Who gave you the right?"

[24]"I'll tell you by what authority I do these things if you answer one question," Jesus replied. [25]"Did John's authority to baptize come from heaven, or was it merely human?"

They talked it over among themselves. "If we say it was from heaven, he will ask us why we didn't believe John. [26]But if we say it was merely human, we'll be mobbed because the

people believe John was a prophet." [27]So they finally replied, "We don't know."

And Jesus responded, "Then I won't tell you by what authority I do these things."

PARABLE OF THE TWO SONS

[28]"But what do you think about this? A man with two sons told the older boy, 'Son, go out and work in the vineyard today.' [29]The son answered, 'No, I won't go,' but later he changed his mind and went anyway. [30]Then the father told the other son, 'You go,' and he said, 'Yes, sir, I will.' But he didn't go.

[31]"Which of the two obeyed his father?"

They replied, "The first."*

Then Jesus explained his meaning: "I tell you the truth, corrupt tax collectors and prostitutes will get into the Kingdom of God before you do. [32]For John the Baptist came and showed you the right way to live, but you didn't believe him, while tax collectors and prostitutes did. And even when you saw this happening, you refused to believe him and repent of your sins.

PARABLE OF THE EVIL FARMERS

[33]"Now listen to another story. A certain landowner planted a vineyard, built a wall around it, dug a pit for pressing out the grape juice, and built a lookout tower. Then he leased the vineyard to tenant farmers and moved to another country. [34]At the time of the grape harvest, he sent his servants to collect his share of the crop. [35]But the farmers grabbed his servants, beat one, killed one, and stoned another. [36]So the landowner sent a larger group of his servants to collect for him, but the results were the same.

....

ANYTHING WE WANT?
(21:21-22) Jesus made a startling statement about prayer and faith: "You can pray for anything, and if you have faith, you will receive it." Yet this statement is not a guarantee that we can get anything we want simply by asking for it. God wouldn't grant requests that violate his nature or will. He always responds in wisdom and love. So, what will you ask for?

FAKING IT
(21:28-32) In Jesus' parable, the son who said he would obey but didn't follow through represents the leaders of Israel who thought they were better than the tax collectors and other "sinners." Although they claimed to be obedient to God, their actions didn't match their words.

God always knows when a person is being phony. All of the "good" behavior in the world (perfect attendance at youth group, Bible reading, helping out in homeless shelters, going on a mission trip) can't hide a heart that's cold toward God. Feel like you're faking it sometimes? Relax. God doesn't expect you to fake being on fire for him. He just wants you to admit that your flame is a little low. Only he can turn up the flame.

21:13 Isa 56:7; Jer 7:11.   21:16 Ps 8:2 (Greek version).   21:29-31 Other manuscripts read *"The second."* In still other manuscripts the first son says "Yes" but does nothing, the second son says "No" but then repents and goes, and the answer to Jesus' question is that the second son obeyed his father.

37"Finally, the owner sent his son, thinking, 'Surely they will respect my son.'

38"But when the tenant farmers saw his son coming, they said to one another, 'Here comes the heir to this estate. Come on, let's kill him and get the estate for ourselves!' 39So they grabbed him, dragged him out of the vineyard, and murdered him.

40"When the owner of the vineyard returns," Jesus asked, "what do you think he will do to those farmers?"

41The religious leaders replied, "He will put the wicked men to a horrible death and lease the vineyard to others who will give him his share of the crop after each harvest."

42Then Jesus asked them, "Didn't you ever read this in the Scriptures?

'The stone that the builders rejected
    has now become the cornerstone.
This is the LORD's doing,
    and it is wonderful to see.'*

43I tell you, the Kingdom of God will be taken away from you and given to a nation that will produce the proper fruit. 44Anyone who stumbles over that stone will be broken to pieces, and it will crush anyone it falls on.*"

45When the leading priests and Pharisees heard this parable, they realized he was telling the story against them—they were the wicked farmers. 46They wanted to arrest him, but they were afraid of the crowds, who considered Jesus to be a prophet.

22 PARABLE OF THE GREAT FEAST Jesus also told them other parables. He said, 2"The Kingdom of Heaven can be illustrated by the story of a king who prepared a great wedding feast for his son. 3When the banquet was ready, he sent his servants to notify those who were invited. But they all refused to come!

4"So he sent other servants to tell them, 'The feast has been prepared. The bulls and fattened cattle have been killed, and everything is ready. Come to the banquet!' 5But the guests he had invited ignored them and went their own way, one to his farm, another to his

business. 6Others seized his messengers and insulted them and killed them.

7"The king was furious, and he sent out his army to destroy the murderers and burn their town. 8And he said to his servants, 'The wedding feast is ready, and the guests I invited aren't worthy of the honor. 9Now go out to the street corners and invite everyone you see.' 10So the servants brought in everyone they could find, good and bad alike, and the banquet hall was filled with guests.

11"But when the king came in to meet the guests, he noticed a man who wasn't wearing the proper clothes for a wedding. 12'Friend,' he asked, 'how is it that you are here without wedding clothes?' But the man had no reply. 13Then the king said to his aides, 'Bind his hands and feet and throw him into the outer darkness, where there will be weeping and gnashing of teeth.'

14"For many are called, but few are chosen."

TAXES FOR CAESAR 15Then the Pharisees met together to plot how to trap Jesus into saying something for which he could be arrested. 16They sent some of their disciples, along with the supporters of Herod, to meet with him. "Teacher," they said, "we know how honest you are. You teach the way of God truthfully. You are impartial and don't play favorites. 17Now tell us what you think about this: Is it right to pay taxes to Caesar or not?"

18But Jesus knew their evil motives. "You hypocrites!" he said. "Why are you trying to trap me? 19Here, show me the coin used for the tax.* " When they handed him a Roman coin,* 20he asked, "Whose picture and title are stamped on it?"

21"Caesar's," they replied.

"Well, then," he said, "give to Caesar what belongs to Caesar, and give to God what belongs to God."

22His reply amazed them, and they went away.

DISCUSSION ABOUT RESURRECTION 23That same day Jesus was approached by some Sadducees—religious leaders who say there is no resurrection from the dead. They posed this question: 24"Teacher, Moses said, 'If a man dies without children, his brother should marry the widow and have a child who will carry on the brother's name.'* 25Well, suppose there were seven brothers. The oldest one married

....

YOU'RE INVITED
(22:1-14) In this culture, two invitations were expected for a wedding banquet. The first one invited the guests to attend; the second announced that the feast was about to begin. Here the king—God—invited his guests three times. But each time they refused to come. God wants us to join him at his banquet, which will last for eternity. That's why he sends us invitations again and again. Have you accepted his invitation?

21:42 Ps 118:22-23.   **21:44** This verse is not included in some early manuscripts. Compare Luke 20:18.   **22:19** Greek *a denarius*.   **22:24** Deut 25:5-6.

and then died without children, so his brother married the widow. [26]But the second brother also died, and the third brother married her. This continued with all seven of them. [27]Last of all, the woman also died. [28]So tell us, whose wife will she be in the resurrection? For all seven were married to her."

[29]Jesus replied, "Your mistake is that you don't know the Scriptures, and you don't know the power of God. [30]For when the dead rise, they will neither marry nor be given in marriage. In this respect they will be like the angels in heaven.

[31]"But now, as to whether there will be a resurrection of the dead—haven't you ever read about this in the Scriptures? Long after Abraham, Isaac, and Jacob had died, God said,* [32]'I am the God of Abraham, the God of Isaac, and the God of Jacob.'* So he is the God of the living, not the dead."

[33]When the crowds heard him, they were astounded at his teaching.

THE MOST IMPORTANT COMMANDMENT
[34]But when the Pharisees heard that he had silenced the Sadducees with his reply, they met together to question him again. [35]One of them, an expert in religious law, tried to trap him with this question: [36]"Teacher, which is the most important commandment in the law of Moses?"

[37]Jesus replied, "'You must love the LORD your God with all your heart, all your soul, and all your mind.'* [38]This is the first and greatest commandment. [39]A second is equally important: 'Love your neighbor as yourself.'* [40]The entire law and all the demands of the prophets are based on these two commandments."

WHOSE SON IS THE MESSIAH?
[41]Then, surrounded by the Pharisees, Jesus asked them a question: [42]"What do you think about the Messiah? Whose son is he?"

They replied, "He is the son of David."

[43]Jesus responded, "Then why does David, speaking under the inspiration of the Spirit, call the Messiah 'my Lord'? For David said,

[44] 'The LORD said to my Lord,
Sit in the place of honor at my right hand

until I humble your enemies beneath your feet.'*

[45]Since David called the Messiah 'my Lord,' how can the Messiah be his son?"

[46]No one could answer him. And after that, no one dared to ask him any more questions.

23 JESUS CRITICIZES THE RELIGIOUS LEADERS
Then Jesus said to the crowds and to his disciples, [2]"The teachers of religious law and the Pharisees are the official interpreters of the law of Moses.* [3]So practice and obey whatever they tell you, but don't follow their example. For they don't practice what they teach. [4]They crush people with unbearable religious demands and never lift a finger to ease the burden.

[5]"Everything they do is for show. On their arms they wear extra wide prayer boxes with Scripture verses inside, and they wear robes with extra long tassels.* [6]And they love to sit at the head table at banquets and in the seats of honor in the synagogues. [7]They love to receive respectful greetings as they walk in the marketplaces, and to be called 'Rabbi.'*

[8]"Don't let anyone call you 'Rabbi,' for you have only one teacher, and all of you are equal as brothers and sisters.* [9]And don't address anyone here on earth as 'Father,' for only God in heaven is your spiritual Father. [10]And don't let anyone call you 'Teacher,' for you have only one teacher, the Messiah. [11]The greatest among you must be a servant. [12]But those who exalt themselves will be humbled, and those who humble themselves will be exalted.

[13]"What sorrow awaits you teachers of religious law and you Pharisees. Hypocrites! For you shut the door of the Kingdom of Heaven in people's faces. You won't go in yourselves, and you don't let others enter either.*

[15]"What sorrow awaits you teachers of religious law and you Pharisees. Hypocrites! For you cross land and sea to make one convert, and then you turn that person into twice the child of hell* you yourselves are!

....

22:31 Greek read about this? God said.   22:32 Exod 3:6.
22:37 Deut 6:5.   22:39 Lev 19:18.   22:44 Ps 110:1.   23:2 Greek and the Pharisees sit in the seat of Moses.   23:5 Greek They enlarge their phylacteries and lengthen their tassels.   23:7 Rabbi, from Aramaic, means "master" or "teacher."   23:8 Greek brothers.
23:13 Some manuscripts add verse 14, What sorrow awaits you teachers of religious law and you Pharisees. Hypocrites! You shamelessly cheat widows out of their property and then pretend to be pious by making long prayers in public. Because of this, you will be severely punished. Compare Mark 12:40 and Luke 20:47.
23:15 Greek of Gehenna; also in 23:33.

LIFE AFTER DEATH
(22:23-33) The Sadducees asked Jesus what marriage would be like in eternity. But Jesus knew that their question was more about eternity than it was about marriage. They didn't believe in life after death. Many people today share that opinion. Maybe you've heard people say things like, "The one who dies with the most toys wins!" or, "Might as well live it up now 'cause when you die, that's it!" Jesus would respond to both views with the same words he spoke to the Sadducees: "Your mistake is that you don't know the Scriptures." Do you?

¹⁶"Blind guides! What sorrow awaits you! For you say that it means nothing to swear 'by God's Temple,' but that it is binding to swear 'by the gold in the Temple.' ¹⁷Blind fools! Which is more important—the gold or the Temple that makes the gold sacred? ¹⁸And you say that to swear 'by the altar' is not binding, but to swear 'by the gifts on the altar' is binding. ¹⁹How blind! For which is more important—the gift on the altar or the altar that makes the gift sacred? ²⁰When you swear 'by the altar,' you are swearing by it and by everything on it. ²¹And when you swear 'by the Temple,' you are swearing by it and by God, who lives in it. ²²And when you swear 'by heaven,' you are swearing by the throne of God and by God, who sits on the throne.

²³"What sorrow awaits you teachers of religious law and you Pharisees. Hypocrites! For you are careful to tithe even the tiniest income from your herb gardens,* but you ignore the more important aspects of the law—justice, mercy, and faith. You should tithe, yes, but do not neglect the more important things. ²⁴Blind guides! You strain your water so you won't accidentally swallow a gnat, but you swallow a camel!*

²⁵"What sorrow awaits you teachers of religious law and you Pharisees. Hypocrites! For you are so careful to clean the outside of the cup and the dish, but inside you are filthy—full of greed and self-indulgence! ²⁶You blind Pharisee! First wash the inside of the cup and the dish,* and then the outside will become clean, too.

²⁷"What sorrow awaits you teachers of religious law and you Pharisees. Hypocrites! For you are like whitewashed tombs—beautiful on the outside but filled on the inside with dead people's bones and all sorts of impurity. ²⁸Outwardly you look like righteous people, but inwardly your hearts are filled with hypocrisy and lawlessness.

²⁹"What sorrow awaits you teachers of religious law and you Pharisees. Hypocrites! For you build tombs for the prophets your ancestors killed, and you decorate the monuments of the godly people your ancestors destroyed. ³⁰Then you say, 'If we had lived in the days of

our ancestors, we would never have joined them in killing the prophets.' ³¹"But in saying that, you testify against yourselves that you are indeed the descendants of those who murdered the prophets. ³²Go ahead and finish what your ancestors started. ³³Snakes! Sons of vipers! How will you escape the judgment of hell?

³⁴"Therefore, I am sending you prophets and wise men and teachers of religious law. But you will kill some by crucifixion, and you will flog others with whips in your synagogues, chasing them from city to city. ³⁵As a result, you will be held responsible for the murder of all godly people of all time—from the murder of righteous Abel to the murder of Zechariah son of Berekiah, whom you killed in the Temple between the sanctuary and the altar. ³⁶I tell you the truth, this judgment will fall on this very generation.

JESUS GRIEVES OVER JERUSALEM ³⁷"O Jerusalem, Jerusalem, the city that kills the prophets and stones God's messengers! How often I have wanted to gather your children together as a hen protects her chicks beneath her wings, but you wouldn't let me. ³⁸And now, look, your house is abandoned and desolate.* ³⁹For I tell you this, you will never see me again until you say, 'Blessings on the one who comes in the name of the LORD!'*"

24 **JESUS FORETELLS THE FUTURE** As Jesus was leaving the Temple grounds, his disciples pointed out to him the various Temple buildings. ²But he responded, "Do you see all these buildings? I tell you the truth, they will be completely demolished. Not one stone will be left on top of another!"

³Later, Jesus sat on the Mount of Olives. His disciples came to him privately and said, "Tell us, when will all this happen? What sign will signal your return and the end of the world?*"

⁴Jesus told them, "Don't let anyone mislead you, ⁵for many will come in my name, claiming, 'I am the Messiah.' They will deceive many. ⁶And you will hear of wars and threats of wars, but don't panic. Yes, these things must take place, but the end won't follow immediately. ⁷Nation will go to war against nation, and kingdom against kingdom. There will be famines and earthquakes in many parts of the world.

INSIDE
(23:25-28) Jesus condemned the Pharisees and religious leaders for appearing saintly and holy but remaining full of corruption and greed on the inside. Living our Christianity merely as a show for others is like washing a cup on the outside only. When we are clean on the inside, our cleanliness on the outside won't be phony.

23:23 Greek *tithe the mint, the dill, and the cumin.*   **23:24** See Lev 11:4, 23, where gnats and camels are both forbidden as food.   **23:26** Some manuscripts do not include *and the dish.*   **23:38** Some manuscripts do not include *and desolate.*   **23:39** Ps 118:26.   **24:3** Or *the age?*

⁸But all this is only the first of the birth pains, with more to come.

⁹"Then you will be arrested, persecuted, and killed. You will be hated all over the world because you are my followers.* ¹⁰And many will turn away from me and betray and hate each other. ¹¹And many false prophets will appear and will deceive many people. ¹²Sin will be rampant everywhere, and the love of many will grow cold. ¹³But the one who endures to the end will be saved. ¹⁴And the Good News about the Kingdom will be preached throughout the whole world, so that all nations* will hear it; and then the end will come.

¹⁵"The day is coming when you will see what Daniel the prophet spoke about—the sacrilegious object that causes desecration* standing in the Holy Place." (Reader, pay attention!) ¹⁶"Then those in Judea must flee to the hills. ¹⁷A person out on the deck of a roof must not go down into the house to pack. ¹⁸A person out in the field must not return even to get a coat. ¹⁹How terrible it will be for pregnant women and for nursing mothers in those days. ²⁰And pray that your flight will not be in winter or on the Sabbath. ²¹For there will be greater anguish than at any time since the world began. And it will never be so great again. ²²In fact, unless that time of calamity is shortened, not a single person will survive. But it will be shortened for the sake of God's chosen ones.

²³"Then if anyone tells you, 'Look, here is the Messiah,' or 'There he is,' don't believe it. ²⁴For false messiahs and false prophets will rise up and perform great signs and wonders so as to deceive, if possible, even God's chosen ones. ²⁵See, I have warned you about this ahead of time.

²⁶"So if someone tells you, 'Look, the Messiah is out in the desert,' don't bother to go and look. Or, 'Look, he is hiding here,' don't believe it! ²⁷For as the lightning flashes in the east and shines to the west, so it will be when the Son of Man* comes. ²⁸Just as the gathering of vultures shows there is a carcass nearby, so these signs indicate that the end is near.*

²⁹"Immediately after the anguish of those days,

the sun will be darkened,
the moon will give no light,
the stars will fall from the sky,

and the powers in the heavens will be shaken.*

³⁰And then at last, the sign that the Son of Man is coming will appear in the heavens, and there will be deep mourning among all the peoples of the earth. And they will see the Son of Man coming on the clouds of heaven with power and great glory.* ³¹And he will send out his angels with the mighty blast of a trumpet, and they will gather his chosen ones from all over the world*—from the farthest ends of the earth and heaven.

³²"Now learn a lesson from the fig tree. When its branches bud and its leaves begin to sprout, you know that summer is near. ³³In the same way, when you see all these things, you can know his return is very near, right at the door. ³⁴I tell you the truth, this generation* will not pass from the scene until all these things take place. ³⁵Heaven and earth will disappear, but my words will never disappear.

³⁶"However, no one knows the day or hour when these things will happen, not even the angels in heaven or the Son himself.* Only the Father knows.

³⁷"When the Son of Man returns, it will be like it was in Noah's day. ³⁸In those days before the flood, the people were enjoying banquets and parties and weddings right up to the time Noah entered his boat. ³⁹People didn't realize what was going to happen until the flood came and swept them all away. That is the way it will be when the Son of Man comes.

⁴⁰"Two men will be working together in the field; one will be taken, the other left. ⁴¹Two women will be grinding flour at the mill; one will be taken, the other left.

⁴²"So you, too, must keep watch! For you don't know what day your Lord is coming. ⁴³Understand this: If a homeowner knew exactly when a burglar was coming, he would keep watch and not permit his house to be broken

....

FRAUDS

(24:11, 23-26) Jesus warned the disciples that in the end times false prophets would spring up in the land and fool many people. The Old Testament frequently mentions false prophets (see 2 Kgs 3:13; Isa 44:25; Jer 23:16-17; Ezek 13:1-3; Mic 3:5-7; Zech 13:2-3). These prophets would claim to receive messages from God but really would be speaking for themselves and telling people what they wanted to hear.

These days, many people claim to speak for God, but not all have been sent by God. So, how can you tell a false prophet from a true one? A true prophet's words always agree with Scriptures. Check out 2 Corinthians 4:2; 1 John 4:1-4.

24:9 Greek *on account of my name.*   **24:14** Or *all peoples.*
24:15 Greek *the abomination of desolation.* See Dan 9:27; 11:31;
12:11.   **24:27** "Son of Man" is a title Jesus used for himself.
24:28 Greek *Wherever the carcass is, the vultures gather.*
24:29 See Isa 13:10; 34:4; Joel 2:10.   **24:30** See Dan 7:13.
24:31 Greek *from the four winds.*   **24:34** Or *this age,* or *this nation.*
24:36 Some manuscripts do not include *or the Son himself.*

into. ⁴⁴You also must be ready all the time, for the Son of Man will come when least expected.

⁴⁵"A faithful, sensible servant is one to whom the master can give the responsibility of managing his other household servants and feeding them. ⁴⁶If the master returns and finds that the servant has done a good job, there will be a reward. ⁴⁷I tell you the truth, the master will put that servant in charge of all he owns. ⁴⁸But what if the servant is evil and thinks, 'My master won't be back for a while,' ⁴⁹and he begins beating the other servants, partying, and getting drunk? ⁵⁰The master will return unannounced and unexpected, ⁵¹and he will cut the servant to pieces and assign him a place with the hypocrites. In that place there will be weeping and gnashing of teeth.

25 PARABLE OF THE TEN BRIDESMAIDS

"Then the Kingdom of Heaven will be like ten bridesmaids* who took their lamps and went to meet the bridegroom. ²Five of them were foolish, and five were wise. ³The five who were foolish didn't take enough olive oil for their lamps, ⁴but the other five were wise enough to take along extra oil. ⁵When the bridegroom was delayed, they all became drowsy and fell asleep.

⁶"At midnight they were roused by the shout, 'Look, the bridegroom is coming! Come out and meet him!'

⁷"All the bridesmaids got up and prepared their lamps. ⁸Then the five foolish ones asked the others, 'Please give us some of your oil because our lamps are going out.'

⁹"But the others replied, 'We don't have enough for all of us. Go to a shop and buy some for yourselves.'

¹⁰"But while they were gone to buy oil, the bridegroom came. Then those who were ready went in with him to the marriage feast, and the door was locked. ¹¹Later, when the other five bridesmaids returned, they stood outside, calling, 'Lord! Lord! Open the door for us!'

¹²"But he called back, 'Believe me, I don't know you!'

USE WHAT YOU'VE GOT
(25:14-30) The master divided the money among his servants according to their abilities. No one received more or less money than he could handle. If a servant failed in his master's assignment, his excuse could not be that he was overwhelmed. Failure could come only from laziness or hatred for the master. The money in this story represents any kind of resource we're given. God gives us time, abilities, and other resources to invest wisely until he returns. The issue is not how much we have, but what we do with what we have. How are you investing your resources?

¹³"So you, too, must keep watch! For you do not know the day or hour of my return.

PARABLE OF THE THREE SERVANTS ¹⁴"Again, the Kingdom of Heaven can be illustrated by the story of a man going on a long trip. He called together his servants and entrusted his money to them while he was gone. ¹⁵He gave five bags of silver* to one, two bags of silver to another, and one bag of silver to the last—dividing it in proportion to their abilities. He then left on his trip.

¹⁶"The servant who received the five bags of silver began to invest the money and earned five more. ¹⁷The servant with two bags of silver also went to work and earned two more. ¹⁸But the servant who received the one bag of silver dug a hole in the ground and hid the master's money.

¹⁹"After a long time their master returned from his trip and called them to give an account of how they had used his money. ²⁰The servant to whom he had entrusted the five bags of silver came forward with five more and said, 'Master, you gave me five bags of silver to invest, and I have earned five more.'

²¹"The master was full of praise. 'Well done, my good and faithful servant. You have been faithful in handling this small amount, so now I will give you many more responsibilities. Let's celebrate together!*'

²²"The servant who had received the two bags of silver came forward and said, 'Master, you gave me two bags of silver to invest, and I have earned two more.'

²³"The master said, 'Well done, my good and faithful servant. You have been faithful in handling this small amount, so now I will give you many more responsibilities. Let's celebrate together!'

²⁴"Then the servant with the one bag of silver came and said, 'Master, I knew you were a harsh man, harvesting crops you didn't plant and gathering crops you didn't cultivate. ²⁵I was afraid I would lose your money, so I hid it in the earth. Look, here is your money back.'

²⁶"But the master replied, 'You wicked and lazy servant! If you knew I harvested crops I didn't plant and gathered crops I didn't cultivate, ²⁷why didn't you deposit my money in the bank? At least I could have gotten some interest on it.'

²⁸"Then he ordered, 'Take the money from this servant, and give it to the one with the ten

25:1 Or *virgins;* also in 25:7, 11.   **25:15** Greek *talents;* also throughout the story. A talent is equal to 75 pounds or 34 kilograms. **25:21** Greek *Enter into the joy of your master* [or *your Lord*]; also in 25:23.

bags of silver. ²⁹To those who use well what they are given, even more will be given, and they will have an abundance. But from those who do nothing, even what little they have will be taken away. ³⁰Now throw this useless servant into outer darkness, where there will be weeping and gnashing of teeth.'

THE FINAL JUDGMENT

³¹"But when the Son of Man* comes in his glory, and all the angels with him, then he will sit upon his glorious throne. ³²All the nations* will be gathered in his presence, and he will separate the people as a shepherd separates the sheep from the goats. ³³He will place the sheep at his right hand and the goats at his left.

³⁴"Then the King will say to those on his right, 'Come, you who are blessed by my Father, inherit the Kingdom prepared for you from the creation of the world. ³⁵For I was hungry, and you fed me. I was thirsty, and you gave me a drink. I was a stranger, and you invited me into your home. ³⁶I was naked, and you gave me clothing. I was sick, and you cared for me. I was in prison, and you visited me.'

³⁷"Then these righteous ones will reply, 'Lord, when did we ever see you hungry and feed you? Or thirsty and give you something to drink? ³⁸Or a stranger and show you hospitality? Or naked and give you clothing? ³⁹When did we ever see you sick or in prison and visit you?'

⁴⁰"And the King will say, 'I tell you the truth, when you did it to one of the least of these my brothers and sisters,* you were doing it to me!'

⁴¹"Then the King will turn to those on the left and say, 'Away with you, you cursed ones, into the eternal fire prepared for the devil and his demons.* ⁴²For I was hungry, and you didn't feed me. I was thirsty, and you didn't give me a drink. ⁴³I was a stranger, and you didn't invite me into your home. I was naked, and you didn't give me clothing. I was sick and in prison, and you didn't visit me.'

⁴⁴"Then they will reply, 'Lord, when did we ever see you hungry or thirsty or a stranger or naked or sick or in prison, and not help you?'

⁴⁵"And he will answer, 'I tell you the truth, when you refused to help the least of these my brothers and sisters, you were refusing to help me.'

⁴⁶"And they will go away into eternal punishment, but the righteous will go into eternal life."

25:31 "Son of Man" is a title Jesus used for himself.   25:32 Or peoples.   25:40 Greek my brothers.   25:41 Greek his angels. 26:2 "Son of Man" is a title Jesus used for himself.   26:7 Or reclining.

26 THE PLOT TO KILL JESUS

When Jesus had finished saying all these things, he said to his disciples, ²"As you know, Passover begins in two days, and the Son of Man* will be handed over to be crucified."

³At that same time the leading priests and elders were meeting at the residence of Caiaphas, the high priest, ⁴plotting how to capture Jesus secretly and kill him. ⁵"But not during the Passover celebration," they agreed, "or the people may riot."

JESUS ANOINTED AT BETHANY

⁶Meanwhile, Jesus was in Bethany at the home of Simon, a man who had previously had leprosy. ⁷While he was eating,* a woman came in with a beautiful alabaster jar of expensive perfume and poured it over his head.

⁸The disciples were indignant when they saw this. "What a waste!" they said. ⁹"It could have been sold for a high price and the money given to the poor."

¹⁰But Jesus, aware of this, replied, "Why criticize this woman for doing such a good thing to me? ¹¹You will always have the poor among you, but you will not always have me. ¹²She has poured this perfume on me to prepare my body for burial. ¹³I tell you the truth, wherever the Good News is preached throughout the world, this woman's deed will be remembered and discussed."

JUDAS AGREES TO BETRAY JESUS

¹⁴Then Judas Iscariot, one of the twelve disciples, went to the leading priests ¹⁵and asked, "How much will you pay me to betray Jesus to you?" And they gave him thirty pieces of silver. ¹⁶From that time on, Judas began looking for an opportunity to betray Jesus.

THE LAST SUPPER

¹⁷On the first day of the Festival of Unleavened Bread, the disciples came to Jesus and asked, "Where do you want us to prepare the Passover meal for you?"

¹⁸"As you go into the city," he told them, "you will see a certain man. Tell him, 'The Teacher says: My time has come, and I will eat the Passover meal with my disciples at your

....

SEPARATING THE GOOD FROM THE BAAAAD
(25:31-46) God will separate his obedient followers (the sheep) from pretenders and unbelievers (the goats). What we do for others demonstrates what we really think about Jesus' words to us—feed the hungry, give the homeless a place to stay, visit the sick. How well do your actions separate you from pretenders and unbelievers?

house.'" [19]So the disciples did as Jesus told them and prepared the Passover meal there.

[20]When it was evening, Jesus sat down at the table* with the twelve disciples.* [21]While they were eating, he said, "I tell you the truth, one of you will betray me."

[22]Greatly distressed, each one asked in turn, "Am I the one, Lord?"

[23]He replied, "One of you who has just eaten from this bowl with me will betray me. [24]For the Son of Man must die, as the Scriptures declared long ago. But how terrible it will be for the one who betrays him. It would be far better for that man if he had never been born!"

[25]Judas, the one who would betray him, also asked, "Rabbi, am I the one?"

And Jesus told him, "You have said it."

[26]As they were eating, Jesus took some bread and blessed it. Then he broke it in pieces and gave it to the disciples, saying, "Take this and eat it, for this is my body."

[27]And he took a cup of wine and gave thanks to God for it. He gave it to them and said, "Each of you drink from it, [28]for this is my blood, which confirms the covenant* between God and his people. It is poured out as a sacrifice to forgive the sins of many. [29]Mark my words—I will not drink wine again until the day I drink it new with you in my Father's Kingdom."

[30]Then they sang a hymn and went out to the Mount of Olives.

JESUS PREDICTS PETER'S DENIAL [31]On the way, Jesus told them, "Tonight all of you will desert me. For the Scriptures say,

'God will strike* the Shepherd,
    and the sheep of the flock will be
        scattered.'

[32]But after I have been raised from the dead, I will go ahead of you to Galilee and meet you there."

[33]Peter declared, "Even if everyone else deserts you, I will never desert you."

[34]Jesus replied, "I tell you the truth, Peter—

this very night, before the rooster crows, you will deny three times that you even know me."

[35]"No!" Peter insisted. "Even if I have to die with you, I will never deny you!" And all the other disciples vowed the same.

JESUS PRAYS IN GETHSEMANE [36]Then Jesus went with them to the olive grove called Gethsemane, and he said, "Sit here while I go over there to pray." [37]He took Peter and Zebedee's two sons, James and John, and he became anguished and distressed. [38]He told them, "My soul is crushed with grief to the point of death. Stay here and keep watch with me."

[39]He went on a little farther and bowed with his face to the ground, praying, "My Father! If it is possible, let this cup of suffering be taken away from me. Yet I want your will to be done, not mine."

[40]Then he returned to the disciples and found them asleep. He said to Peter, "Couldn't you watch with me even one hour? [41]Keep watch and pray, so that you will not give in to temptation. For the spirit is willing, but the body is weak!"

[42]Then Jesus left them a second time and prayed, "My Father! If this cup cannot be taken away* unless I drink it, your will be done." [43]When he returned to them again, he found them sleeping, for they couldn't keep their eyes open.

[44]So he went to pray a third time, saying the same things again. [45]Then he came to the disciples and said, "Go ahead and sleep. Have your rest. But look—the time has come. The Son of Man is betrayed into the hands of sinners. [46]Up, let's be going. Look, my betrayer is here!"

JESUS IS BETRAYED AND ARRESTED [47]And even as Jesus said this, Judas, one of the twelve disciples, arrived with a crowd of men armed with swords and clubs. They had been sent by the leading priests and elders of the people. [48]The traitor, Judas, had given them a prearranged signal: "You will know which one to arrest when I greet him with a kiss." [49]So Judas came straight to Jesus. "Greetings, Rabbi!" he exclaimed and gave him the kiss.

[50]Jesus said, "My friend, go ahead and do what you have come for."

Then the others grabbed Jesus and arrested him. [51]But one of the men with Jesus pulled out his sword and struck the high priest's slave, slashing off his ear.

ALERT
(26:40-41) *Jesus used Peter's drowsiness to warn him about the kinds of temptation he would soon face (see 26:69-75). The way to overcome temptation is to be alert to it and pray. Being alert involves being aware of the possibilities of temptation, sensitive to the subtleties, and spiritually equipped to fight it. Because temptation strikes where we are most vulnerable, we can't resist it alone. Prayer is essential because God's strength can shore up our defenses and defeat Satan's power. (Check out 1 Corinthians 10:13; Ephesians 6:10-18.) Are you alert?*

26:20a Or *Jesus reclined.*   **26:20b** Some manuscripts read *the Twelve.*   **26:28** Some manuscripts read *the new covenant.*
26:31 Greek *I will strike.* Zech 13:7.   **26:42** Greek *If this cannot pass.*

52"Put away your sword," Jesus told him. "Those who use the sword will die by the sword. 53Don't you realize that I could ask my Father for thousands* of angels to protect us, and he would send them instantly? 54But if I did, how would the Scriptures be fulfilled that describe what must happen now?"

55Then Jesus said to the crowd, "Am I some dangerous revolutionary, that you come with swords and clubs to arrest me? Why didn't you arrest me in the Temple? I was there teaching every day. 56But this is all happening to fulfill the words of the prophets as recorded in the Scriptures." At that point, all the disciples deserted him and fled.

JESUS BEFORE THE COUNCIL 57Then the people who had arrested Jesus led him to the home of Caiaphas, the high priest, where the teachers of religious law and the elders had gathered. 58Meanwhile, Peter followed him at a distance and came to the high priest's courtyard. He went in and sat with the guards and waited to see how it would all end.

59Inside, the leading priests and the entire high council* were trying to find witnesses who would lie about Jesus, so they could put him to death. 60But even though they found many who agreed to give false witness, they could not use anyone's testimony. Finally, two men came forward 61who declared, "This man said, 'I am able to destroy the Temple of God and rebuild it in three days.'"

62Then the high priest stood up and said to Jesus, "Well, aren't you going to answer these charges? What do you have to say for yourself?" 63But Jesus remained silent. Then the high priest said to him, "I demand in the name of the living God—tell us if you are the Messiah, the Son of God."

64Jesus replied, "You have said it. And in the future you will see the Son of Man seated in the place of power at God's right hand* and coming on the clouds of heaven."*

65Then the high priest tore his clothing to show his horror and said, "Blasphemy! Why do we need other witnesses? You have all heard his blasphemy. 66What is your verdict?"

"Guilty!" they shouted. "He deserves to die!"

67Then they began to spit in Jesus' face and beat him with their fists. And some slapped him, 68jeering, "Prophesy to us, you Messiah! Who hit you that time?"

26:53 Greek *twelve legions.* 26:59 Greek *the Sanhedrin.*
26:64a Greek *seated at the right hand of the power.* See Ps 110:1.
26:64b See Dan 7:13. 26:71 Or *Jesus the Nazarene.*

PETER DENIES JESUS 69Meanwhile, Peter was sitting outside in the courtyard. A servant girl came over and said to him, "You were one of those with Jesus the Galilean."

70But Peter denied it in front of everyone. "I don't know what you're talking about," he said.

71Later, out by the gate, another servant girl noticed him and said to those standing around, "This man was with Jesus of Nazareth.*"

72Again Peter denied it, this time with an oath. "I don't even know the man," he said.

73A little later some of the other bystanders came over to Peter and said, "You must be one of them; we can tell by your Galilean accent."

74Peter swore, "A curse on me if I'm lying— I don't know the man!" And immediately the rooster crowed.

75Suddenly, Jesus' words flashed through Peter's mind: "Before the rooster crows, you will deny three times that you even know me." And he went away, weeping bitterly.

27 **JUDAS HANGS HIMSELF** Very early in the morning the leading priests and the elders of the people met again to lay plans for putting Jesus to death. 2Then they bound him, led him away, and took him to Pilate, the Roman governor.

3When Judas, who had betrayed him, realized that Jesus had been condemned to die, he was filled with remorse. So he took the thirty pieces of silver back to the leading priests and the elders. 4"I have sinned," he declared, "for I have betrayed an innocent man."

"What do we care?" they retorted. "That's your problem."

DENIAL
(26:69-75) When asked about the disciple with whom they most identify, most people would say Peter. And this is the passage that clinches it for them. As Jesus predicted, Peter denied him not once, but three times (see 26:31-35). Peter's denial has three stages. First, he acted confused and said he didn't know what the girl was talking about. Second, using an oath, he denied that he knew Jesus. Third, he began to curse and swear. Believers who deny Christ often begin doing so subtly by pretending not to know him. Then, when opportunities to discuss religious issues come up, they walk away or pretend they don't know the answers. With just a little more pressure, they can be induced to flatly deny their relationship with Christ. If you find yourself subtly avoiding occasions to talk about Christ, watch out. You may be on the road to denying him. Before his denial, Peter never could have imagined that he would do something so hurtful. Like Peter, have you ever denied that you could ever deny Jesus? Those of us who claim to be immune from denial are in denial.

⁵Then Judas threw the silver coins down in the Temple and went out and hanged himself. ⁶The leading priests picked up the coins. "It wouldn't be right to put this money in the Temple treasury," they said, "since it was payment for murder."* ⁷After some discussion they finally decided to buy the potter's field, and they made it into a cemetery for foreigners. ⁸That is why the field is still called the Field of Blood. ⁹This fulfilled the prophecy of Jeremiah that says,

"They took* the thirty pieces of silver—
    the price at which he was valued by the
        people of Israel,
¹⁰ and purchased the potter's field,
    as the LORD directed.*"

JESUS' TRIAL BEFORE PILATE ¹¹Now Jesus was standing before Pilate, the Roman governor. "Are you the king of the Jews?" the governor asked him.

Jesus replied, "You have said it."

¹²But when the leading priests and the elders made their accusations against him, Jesus remained silent. ¹³"Don't you hear all these charges they are bringing against you?" Pilate demanded. ¹⁴But Jesus made no response to any of the charges, much to the governor's surprise.

¹⁵Now it was the governor's custom each year during the Passover celebration to release one prisoner to the crowd—anyone they wanted. ¹⁶This year there was a notorious prisoner, a man named Barabbas.* ¹⁷As the crowds gathered before Pilate's house that morning, he asked them, "Which one do you want me to release to you—Barabbas, or Jesus who is called the Messiah?" ¹⁸(He knew very well that the religious leaders had arrested Jesus out of envy.)

¹⁹Just then, as Pilate was sitting on the judgment seat, his wife sent him this message: "Leave that innocent man alone. I suffered through a terrible nightmare about him last night."

²⁰Meanwhile, the leading priests and the el-

ders persuaded the crowd to ask for Barabbas to be released and for Jesus to be put to death. ²¹So the governor asked again, "Which of these two do you want me to release to you?"

The crowd shouted back, "Barabbas!"

²²Pilate responded, "Then what should I do with Jesus who is called the Messiah?"

They shouted back, "Crucify him!"

²³"Why?" Pilate demanded. "What crime has he committed?"

But the mob roared even louder, "Crucify him!"

²⁴Pilate saw that he wasn't getting anywhere and that a riot was developing. So he sent for a bowl of water and washed his hands before the crowd, saying, "I am innocent of this man's blood. The responsibility is yours!"

²⁵And all the people yelled back, "We will take responsibility for his death—we and our children!"*

²⁶So Pilate released Barabbas to them. He ordered Jesus flogged with a lead-tipped whip, then turned him over to the Roman soldiers to be crucified.

THE SOLDIERS MOCK JESUS ²⁷Some of the governor's soldiers took Jesus into their headquarters* and called out the entire regiment. ²⁸They stripped him and put a scarlet robe on him. ²⁹They wove thorn branches into a crown and put it on his head, and they placed a reed stick in his right hand as a scepter. Then they knelt before him in mockery and taunted, "Hail! King of the Jews!" ³⁰And they spit on him and grabbed the stick and struck him on the head with it. ³¹When they were finally tired of mocking him, they took off the robe and put his own clothes on him again. Then they led him away to be crucified.

THE CRUCIFIXION ³²Along the way, they came across a man named Simon, who was from Cyrene,* and the soldiers forced him to carry Jesus' cross. ³³And they went out to a place called Golgotha (which means "Place of the Skull"). ³⁴The soldiers gave him wine mixed with bitter gall, but when he had tasted it, he refused to drink it.

³⁵After they had nailed him to the cross, the soldiers gambled for his clothes by throwing dice.* ³⁶Then they sat around and kept guard

....

REGRETS
(27:3-4) Jesus' formal accuser wanted to drop his charges, but the religious leaders refused to halt the trial. When Judas first betrayed Jesus, perhaps he was trying to force Jesus' hand to get him to lead a revolt against Rome. This did not work, of course. Whatever his reason, Judas regretted his action, but it was too late. Many of the plans we set into motion cannot be reversed. It is best to think of the potential consequences before we launch into an action we may later regret.

27:6 Greek *since it is for the price for blood.* **27:9** Or *I took.* **27:9-10** Greek *as the LORD directed me.* Zech 11:12-13; Jer 32:6-9. **27:16** Some manuscripts read *Jesus Barabbas;* also in 27:17. **27:25** Greek *"His blood be on us and on our children."* **27:27** Or *into the Praetorium.* **27:32** *Cyrene* was a city in northern Africa. **27:35** Greek *by casting lots.* A few late manuscripts add *This fulfilled the word of the prophet: "They divided my garments among themselves and cast lots for my robe."* See Ps 22:18.

as he hung there. ³⁷A sign was fastened above Jesus' head, announcing the charge against him. It read: "This is Jesus, the King of the Jews." ³⁸Two revolutionaries* were crucified with him, one on his right and one on his left.

³⁹The people passing by shouted abuse, shaking their heads in mockery. ⁴⁰"Look at you now!" they yelled at him. "You said you were going to destroy the Temple and rebuild it in three days. Well then, if you are the Son of God, save yourself and come down from the cross!"

⁴¹The leading priests, the teachers of religious law, and the elders also mocked Jesus. ⁴²"He saved others," they scoffed, "but he can't save himself! So he is the King of Israel, is he? Let him come down from the cross right now, and we will believe in him! ⁴³He trusted God, so let God rescue him now if he wants him! For he said, 'I am the Son of God.'" ⁴⁴Even the revolutionaries who were crucified with him ridiculed him in the same way.

THE DEATH OF JESUS ⁴⁵At noon, darkness fell across the whole land until three o'clock. ⁴⁶At about three o'clock, Jesus called out with a loud voice, "Eli, Eli,* lema sabachthani?" which means "My God, my God, why have you abandoned me?"*

⁴⁷Some of the bystanders misunderstood and thought he was calling for the prophet Elijah. ⁴⁸One of them ran and filled a sponge with sour wine, holding it up to him on a reed stick so he could drink. ⁴⁹But the rest said, "Wait! Let's see whether Elijah comes to save him."*

⁵⁰Then Jesus shouted out again, and he released his spirit. ⁵¹At that moment the curtain in the sanctuary of the Temple was torn in two, from top to bottom. The earth shook, rocks split apart, ⁵²and tombs opened. The bodies of many godly men and women who had died were raised from the dead. ⁵³They left the cemetery after Jesus' resurrection, went into the holy city of Jerusalem, and appeared to many people.

⁵⁴The Roman officer* and the other soldiers at the crucifixion were terrified by the earthquake and all that had happened. They said, "This man truly was the Son of God!"

⁵⁵And many women who had come from Galilee with Jesus to care for him were watching from a distance. ⁵⁶Among them were Mary Magdalene, Mary (the mother of James and Joseph), and the mother of James and John, the sons of Zebedee.

THE BURIAL OF JESUS ⁵⁷As evening approached, Joseph, a rich man from Arimathea who had become a follower of Jesus, ⁵⁸went to Pilate and asked for Jesus' body. And Pilate issued an order to release it to him. ⁵⁹Joseph took the body and wrapped it in a long sheet of clean linen cloth. ⁶⁰He placed it in his own new tomb, which had been carved out of the rock. Then he rolled a great stone across the entrance and left. ⁶¹Both Mary Magdalene and the other Mary were sitting across from the tomb and watching.

THE GUARD AT THE TOMB ⁶²The next day, on the Sabbath,* the leading priests and Pharisees went to see Pilate. ⁶³They told him, "Sir, we remember what that deceiver once said while he was still alive: 'After three days I will rise from the dead.' ⁶⁴So we request that you seal the tomb until the third day. This will prevent his disciples from coming and stealing his body and then telling everyone he was raised from the dead! If that happens, we'll be worse off than we were at first."

⁶⁵Pilate replied, "Take guards and secure it the best you can." ⁶⁶So they sealed the tomb and posted guards to protect it.

28 **THE RESURRECTION** Early on Sunday morning,* as the new day was dawning, Mary Magdalene and the other Mary went out to visit the tomb.

²Suddenly there was a great earthquake! For

....

SEPARATION
(27:46) Jesus was not questioning God; he was quoting the first line of Psalm 22. Because Jesus died for every wrongdoing ever committed, he experienced what no one has yet experienced—complete separation from God. This was what Jesus dreaded as he prayed in the garden (26:39). The physical agony was horrible, but even worse was the period of spiritual separation from the Father. Although we may feel far away from God, we still have access to him. Jesus suffered so that we would never have to experience eternal separation from God.

CHOICES
(28:1-15) Jesus' resurrection caused a great stir in Jerusalem. A group of women moved quickly through the streets, looking for the disciples to tell them the amazing news that Jesus was alive. At the same time, a group of religious leaders were trying to cover up the Resurrection. The same two choices exist today: to believe that Jesus rose from the dead, or to be closed to the truth—denying it, ignoring it, or trying to explain it away. What's your choice?

27:38 Or criminals; also in 27:44. **27:46a** Some manuscripts read Eloi, Eloi. **27:46b** Ps 22:1. **27:49** Some manuscripts add And another took a spear and pierced his side, and out flowed water and blood. Compare John 19:34. **27:54** Greek The centurion. **27:62** Or On the next day, which is after the Preparation. **28:1** Greek After the Sabbath, on the first day of the week.

an angel of the Lord came down from heaven, rolled aside the stone, and sat on it. ³His face shone like lightning, and his clothing was as white as snow. ⁴The guards shook with fear when they saw him, and they fell into a dead faint.

⁵Then the angel spoke to the women. "Don't be afraid!" he said. "I know you are looking for Jesus, who was crucified. ⁶He isn't here! He is risen from the dead, just as he said would happen. Come, see where his body was lying. ⁷And now, go quickly and tell his disciples that he has risen from the dead, and he is going ahead of you to Galilee. You will see him there. Remember what I have told you."

⁸The women ran quickly from the tomb. They were very frightened but also filled with great joy, and they rushed to give the disciples the angel's message. ⁹And as they went, Jesus met them and greeted them. And they ran to him, grasped his feet, and worshiped him. ¹⁰Then

....

COMMISSIONED
(28:18-20) Jesus left the disciples with these last words of instruction: They were to make more disciples. Best of all, he promised to be with them always. Whereas in previous missions Jesus had sent his disciples only to the Jews (10:5-6), their mission from now on would be world-wide. Jesus is Lord of the earth, and he died for the sins of all those who trust him, everywhere.

The disciples' mission also is ours. We are to go— whether it is next door or to another country—and make disciples. Making disciples is not an option—it is a command to all who call Jesus Lord. As we obey, we have comfort in the knowledge that Jesus is always with us.

Jesus said to them, "Don't be afraid! Go tell my brothers to leave for Galilee, and they will see me there."

THE REPORT OF THE GUARD ¹¹As the women were on their way, some of the guards went into the city and told the leading priests what had happened. ¹²A meeting with the elders was called, and they decided to give the soldiers a large bribe. ¹³They told the soldiers, "You must say, 'Jesus' disciples came during the night while we were sleeping, and they stole his body.' ¹⁴If the governor hears about it, we'll stand up for you so you won't get in trouble." ¹⁵So the guards accepted the bribe and said what they were told to say. Their story spread widely among the Jews, and they still tell it today.

THE GREAT COMMISSION ¹⁶Then the eleven disciples left for Galilee, going to the mountain where Jesus had told them to go. ¹⁷When they saw him, they worshiped him—but some of them doubted!

¹⁸Jesus came and told his disciples, "I have been given all authority in heaven and on earth. ¹⁹Therefore, go and make disciples of all the nations,* baptizing them in the name of the Father and the Son and the Holy Spirit. ²⁰Teach these new disciples to obey all the commands I have given you. And be sure of this: I am with you always, even to the end of the age."

28:19 Or *all peoples.*

MARK

Has this ever happened to you?

Friends invite you to a just-released, critically acclaimed movie. "It's supposed to be great," they insist. "You'll like it. Trust us."

So you go—with high expectations. Only the movie isn't great. It drags on and on. As far as excitement goes, this particular film ranks right up there with reading the phone book.

You keep thinking, This has got to get better. *Surely there's a car chase, special effects, or some sort of surprise plot twist in the next scene.* But nothing happens—nothing at all. *The most adventurous moment of the film comes at the end when two of the actors go to a fancy French restaurant and eat snails. It's gross, but at least they're finally doing something.*

When the final credits roll, you leave the theater vowing, "Never again!"

Guess what? You don't have to spend your time with stale stories, boring characters, or lame plots! Instead, you can read one of the most exciting books in existence! And it's right here, on the next few pages.

You name it, and the Gospel of Mark has it—demons, death, and amazing special effects (also called miracles)—all served up in a swirling atmosphere of intrigue, jealousy, controversy, and murder. In short, this book is an action-packed biography of the most influential person in the history of the world.

KEY POINTS

MIRACLES Mark records more of Jesus' miracles than his sermons. Jesus was clearly a man of power and action, not just words. His example encourages us to be people of faith and action.

SPREADING THE GOSPEL Jesus directed his public ministry to the Jews first. But as he prepared to leave the earth, he commissioned the disciples to preach the gospel everywhere. Jesus' message of faith and forgiveness is for the whole world—not just a particular church, neighborhood, or nation. Like the disciples, we are called to take the message everywhere.

RESURRECTION When Jesus rose from the dead, he proved that he was God, that he could forgive sin, and that he has the power to change lives. By trusting in Christ for forgiveness, we can begin a new life with him.

STATS

PURPOSE
To present Jesus' person, work, and teachings

AUTHOR
John Mark. He accompanied Paul on his first missionary journey (Acts 12:25).

ORIGINAL AUDIENCE
Christians in Rome

DATE WRITTEN
Between A.D. 55 and 65

SETTING
The Roman Empire

KEY PEOPLE
Jesus, the 12 disciples, Pilate, the Jewish religious leaders

KEY PLACES
Capernaum, Nazareth, Caesarea Philippi, Jericho, Bethany, Mount of Olives, Jerusalem, Golgotha

SPECIAL FEATURES
Mark was the first Gospel written. Mark records more miracles than any other Gospel.

TIMELINE

37 B.C.
Herod the Great begins to rule
6/5 B.C.
Jesus is born
5/4 B.C.
Jesus' family escapes to Egypt
4 B.C.
Herod the Great dies
4/3 B.C.
Jesus' family returns to Nazareth
A.D. 6/7
Jesus visits the Temple as a boy
14
Tiberius Caesar becomes emperor
26
John the Baptist begins his ministry
26/27
Jesus begins his ministry
28
Jesus chooses 12 disciples
29
Jesus feeds 5,000
30
Jesus is crucified, rises again, and ascends to heaven

Sidon
LEBANON
N
Tyre · Caesarea Philippi
PHOENICIA
Mediterranean
Sea
GALILEE SYRIA
Capernaum
Gennesaret · Bethsaida
Dalmanutha Sea of
Galilee
Nazareth ·
DECAPOLIS
(Region of Ten Towns)
ISRAEL
SAMARIA
Jordan River
Jericho ·
Jerusalem · + Mount of Olives
Bethphage · · Bethany JORDAN
Dead
Sea
JUDEA
IDUMEA

0   20 Mi.
0   20 Km.

The broken lines (—·—·) indicate modern boundaries.

JESUS IN ACTION

Of the four Gospels, Mark's narrative is the most chronological—most of the stories are positioned in the order they actually occurred. Though the shortest of the four, the Gospel of Mark contains the most events; it is action-packed. Most of this action centers in Galilee, where Jesus began his ministry. Capernaum served as his base of operation (1:21; 2:1; 9:33), from which he would go out to cities like Bethsaida—where he healed a blind man (8:22-26); Gennesaret—where he performed many healings (6:53-56); Tyre and Sidon—where he cured many, cast out demons, and met the Syro-Phoenician woman (7:24-30); and Caesarea Philippi—where Peter declared him to be the Messiah (8:27-29). After his ministry in Galilee and the surrounding regions, Jesus headed south for Jerusalem (10:1). Before going there, Jesus told his disciples three times that he would be crucified there and then come back to life (8:31; 9:31; 10:33-34).

1 JOHN THE BAPTIST PREPARES THE WAY

This is the Good News about Jesus the Messiah, the Son of God.* It began ²just as the prophet Isaiah had written:

"Look, I am sending my messenger ahead
of you,
and he will prepare your way.*
³ He is a voice shouting in the wilderness,
'Prepare the way for the LORD's coming!
Clear the road for him!'*"

⁴This messenger was John the Baptist. He was in the wilderness and preached that people should be baptized to show that they had repented of their sins and turned to God to be forgiven. ⁵All of Judea, including all the people of Jerusalem, went out to see and hear John. And when they confessed their sins, he baptized them in the Jordan River. ⁶His clothes were woven from coarse camel hair, and he wore a leather belt around his waist. For food he ate locusts and wild honey.

⁷John announced: "Someone is coming soon who is greater than I am—so much greater that I'm not even worthy to stoop down like a slave and untie the straps of his sandals. ⁸I baptize you with* water, but he will baptize you with the Holy Spirit!"

THE BAPTISM AND TEMPTATION OF JESUS

⁹One day Jesus came from Nazareth in Galilee, and John baptized him in the Jordan River. ¹⁰As Jesus came up out of the water, he saw the heavens splitting apart and the Holy Spirit descending on him* like a dove. ¹¹And a voice from heaven said, "You are my dearly loved Son, and you bring me great joy."

1:1 Some manuscripts do not include *the Son of God.*   1:2 Mal 3:1.
1:3 Isa 40:3 (Greek version).   1:8 Or *in;* also in 1:8b.   1:10 Or
toward him, or *into him.*

¹²The Spirit then compelled Jesus to go into the wilderness, ¹³where he was tempted by Satan for forty days. He was out among the wild animals, and angels took care of him.

¹⁴Later on, after John was arrested, Jesus went into Galilee, where he preached God's Good News.* ¹⁵"The time promised by God has come at last!" he announced. "The Kingdom of God is near! Repent of your sins and believe the Good News!"

THE FIRST DISCIPLES ¹⁶One day as Jesus was walking along the shore of the Sea of Galilee, he saw Simon* and his brother Andrew throwing a net into the water, for they fished for a living. ¹⁷Jesus called out to them, "Come, follow me, and I will show you how to fish for people!" ¹⁸And they left their nets at once and followed him.

¹⁹A little farther up the shore Jesus saw Zebedee's sons, James and John, in a boat repairing their nets. ²⁰He called them at once, and they also followed him, leaving their father, Zebedee, in the boat with the hired men.

JESUS CASTS OUT AN EVIL SPIRIT ²¹Jesus and his companions went to the town of Capernaum. When the Sabbath day came, he went into the synagogue and began to teach. ²²The people were amazed at his teaching, for he taught with real authority—quite unlike the teachers of religious law.

²³Suddenly, a man in the synagogue who was possessed by an evil* spirit began shouting, ²⁴"Why are you interfering with us, Jesus of Nazareth? Have you come to destroy us? I know who you are—the Holy One of God!"

²⁵Jesus cut him short. "Be quiet! Come out of the man," he ordered. ²⁶At that, the evil spirit screamed, threw the man into a convulsion, and then came out of him.

²⁷Amazement gripped the audience, and they began to discuss what had happened. "What sort of new teaching is this?" they asked excitedly. "It has such authority! Even evil spirits obey his orders!" ²⁸The news about Jesus spread quickly throughout the entire region of Galilee.

JESUS HEALS MANY PEOPLE ²⁹After Jesus left the synagogue with James and John, they went to Simon and Andrew's home. ³⁰Now Simon's mother-in-law was sick in bed with a high fever. They told Jesus about her right away.

³¹So he went to her bedside, took her by the hand, and helped her sit up. Then the fever left her, and she prepared a meal for them.

³²That evening after sunset, many sick and demon-possessed people were brought to Jesus. ³³The whole town gathered at the door to watch. ³⁴So Jesus healed many people who were sick with various diseases, and he cast out many demons. But because the demons knew who he was, he did not allow them to speak.

JESUS PREACHES IN GALILEE ³⁵Before daybreak the next morning, Jesus got up and went out to an isolated place to pray. ³⁶Later Simon and the others went out to find him. ³⁷When they found him, they said, "Everyone is looking for you."

³⁸But Jesus replied, "We must go on to other towns as well, and I will preach to them, too. That is why I came." ³⁹So he traveled throughout the region of Galilee, preaching in the synagogues and casting out demons.

JESUS HEALS A MAN WITH LEPROSY ⁴⁰A man with leprosy came and knelt in front of Jesus, begging to be healed. "If you are willing, you can heal me and make me clean," he said.

⁴¹Moved with compassion,* Jesus reached out and touched him. "I am willing," he said. "Be healed!" ⁴²Instantly the leprosy disappeared, and the man was healed. ⁴³Then Jesus sent him on his way with a stern warning: ⁴⁴"Don't tell anyone about this. Instead, go to the priest and let him examine you. Take along the offering required in the law of Moses for those who have been healed of leprosy.* This will be a public testimony that you have been cleansed."

⁴⁵But the man went and spread the word,

THRILLS
(1:1) When you experience the excitement of a big event, you naturally want to tell someone. Telling the story can bring back that original thrill as you relive the experience. As you read Mark's first words, you can sense his excitement. Picture yourself in the crowd as Jesus heals and teaches. Imagine yourself as one of the disciples. Respond to Jesus' words of love and encouragement—and remember that he came for us who live today as well as for those who lived two thousand years ago.

THE PRIORITY OF PRAYER
(1:35) Jesus started his day with prayer. He considered his communication with his Father a necessary part of his day—one that he couldn't do without. How do you start your day? What are some activities you can't do without each day? We usually find the time to do whatever we really want to do. Is communicating with God a priority for you?

1:14 Some manuscripts read *the Good News of the Kingdom of God.* **1:16** *Simon* is called "Peter" in 3:16 and thereafter. **1:23** Greek *unclean;* also in 1:26, 27. **1:41** Some manuscripts read *Moved with anger.* **1:44** See Lev 14:2-32.

proclaiming to everyone what had happened. As a result, large crowds soon surrounded Jesus, and he couldn't publicly enter a town anywhere. He had to stay out in the secluded places, but people from everywhere kept coming to him.

2 JESUS HEALS A PARALYZED MAN

When Jesus returned to Capernaum several days later, the news spread quickly that he was back home. [2] Soon the house where he was staying was so packed with visitors that there was no more room, even outside the door. While he was preaching God's word to them, [3] four men arrived carrying a paralyzed man on a mat. [4] They couldn't bring him to Jesus because of the crowd, so they dug a hole through the roof above his head. Then they lowered the man on his mat, right down in front of Jesus. [5] Seeing their faith, Jesus said to the paralyzed man, "My child, your sins are forgiven."

[6] But some of the teachers of religious law who were sitting there thought to themselves, [7] "What is he saying? This is blasphemy! Only God can forgive sins!"

[8] Jesus knew immediately what they were thinking, so he asked them, "Why do you question this in your hearts? [9] Is it easier to say to the paralyzed man 'Your sins are forgiven,' or 'Stand up, pick up your mat, and walk'? [10] So I will prove to you that the Son of Man* has the authority on earth to forgive sins." Then Jesus turned to the paralyzed man and said, [11] "Stand up, pick up your mat, and go home!"

[12] And the man jumped up, grabbed his mat, and walked out through the stunned onlookers. They were all amazed and praised God, exclaiming, "We've never seen anything like this before!"

JESUS CALLS LEVI (MATTHEW)

[13] Then Jesus went out to the lakeshore again and taught the crowds that were coming to him. [14] As he walked along, he saw Levi son of Alphaeus sitting at his tax collector's booth. "Follow me and be my disciple," Jesus said to him. So Levi got up and followed him.

[15] Later, Levi invited Jesus and his disciples to his home as dinner guests, along with many tax collectors and other disreputable sinners. (There were many people of this kind among

SOMEONE YOU SHOULD KNOW

(2:14-17) On the day that Levi (also known as Matthew; see Matt 9:9-13) met Jesus, he held a meeting at his house to introduce his friends to Jesus. Levi didn't waste any time starting to witness! His excitement and gratitude toward Jesus were obvious. He didn't worry about whether his friends would laugh at him or reject him because of his new faith in Jesus. He just wanted them to know Jesus. Is that what you want? How eager are you to introduce others to the Savior?

2:10 "Son of Man" is a title Jesus used for himself.

I WONDER...

I partied a lot in clubs and stuff before I became a Christian. Should I give that up? Why or why not?

Let's talk about motives for a minute. Some people party simply to get drunk, take drugs, and pick up the opposite sex. Others party to be seen with cool people. Is that your motive? Maybe being with certain people made you feel accepted and even popular. But what if their acceptance comes with a price—for example, take a little "X" [ecstasy], have a few drinks?

Motive is key.

Now, let's talk about Jesus for a second. Jesus went to parties and was, in fact, the life of the party! But his motives were entirely different from the ones described above. He went to show people that he accepted them, to communicate truth about the character of God, and to celebrate life (see Mark 2:13-17; John 2:1-11).

Should you do the same? Perhaps, but here are a few questions to consider:

- Have you grown sufficiently in your faith that you will not be tempted when pressured to drink (or whatever)?
- Do you know someone who will go with you, so you can encourage each other to stay clean?
- Are you going as a light or as a hammer? That is, do you genuinely want to be a light in darkness (Matt 5:14-16), or do you want to pound on people to feel good about their "moral" lifestyle?
- Would you cause someone you've been talking to about Jesus to stumble (see 1 Cor 10:32-33) in the assumption that you probably were pressured to drink simply because you were present?
- Would you have to lie to someone (your parents or a guardian) about what'll happen at the party in order to go? If so, the advice of Romans 13:13 is for you. Need more advice? Check out Galatians 5:19-21.

Remember, motive is the key. But even with good motives, be cautious. The results of such activities, even with the best of motives, may be more than you can handle.

Jesus' followers.) ¹⁶But when the teachers of religious law who were Pharisees* saw him eating with tax collectors and other sinners, they asked his disciples, "Why does he eat with such scum?*"

¹⁷When Jesus heard this, he told them, "Healthy people don't need a doctor—sick people do. I have come to call not those who think they are righteous, but those who know they are sinners."

A DISCUSSION ABOUT FASTING ¹⁸Once when John's disciples and the Pharisees were fasting, some people came to Jesus and asked, "Why don't your disciples fast like John's disciples and the Pharisees do?"

¹⁹Jesus replied, "Do wedding guests fast while celebrating with the groom? Of course not. They can't fast while the groom is with them. ²⁰But someday the groom will be taken away from them, and then they will fast.

²¹"Besides, who would patch old clothing with new cloth? For the new patch would shrink and rip away from the old cloth, leaving an even bigger tear than before.

²²"And no one puts new wine into old wineskins. For the wine would burst the wineskins, and the wine and the skins would both be lost. New wine calls for new wineskins."

A DISCUSSION ABOUT THE SABBATH ²³One Sabbath day as Jesus was walking through some grainfields, his disciples began breaking off heads of grain to eat. ²⁴But the Pharisees said to Jesus, "Look, why are they breaking the law by harvesting grain on the Sabbath?"

²⁵Jesus said to them, "Haven't you ever read in the Scriptures what David did when he and his companions were hungry? ²⁶He went into the house of God (during the days when Abiathar was high priest) and broke the law by eating the sacred loaves of bread that only the priests are allowed to eat. He also gave some to his companions."

²⁷Then Jesus said to them, "The Sabbath was made to meet the needs of people, and not people to meet the requirements of the Sabbath. ²⁸So the Son of Man is Lord, even over the Sabbath!"

3 **JESUS HEALS ON THE SABBATH** Jesus went into the synagogue again and noticed a man with a deformed hand. ²Since it was the Sabbath, Jesus' enemies watched him closely. If he healed the man's hand, they planned to accuse him of working on the Sabbath.

³Jesus said to the man with the deformed hand, "Come and stand in front of everyone."* ⁴Then he turned to his critics and asked, "Does the law permit good deeds on the Sabbath, or is it a day for doing evil? Is this a day to save life or to destroy it?" But they wouldn't answer him.

⁵He looked around at them angrily and was deeply saddened by their hard hearts. Then he said to the man, "Hold out your hand." So the man held out his hand, and it was restored! ⁶At once the Pharisees went away and met with the supporters of Herod to plot how to kill Jesus.

CROWDS FOLLOW JESUS ⁷Jesus went out to the lake with his disciples, and a large crowd followed him. They came from all over Galilee, Judea, ⁸Jerusalem, Idumea, from east of the Jordan River, and even from as far north as Tyre and Sidon. The news about his miracles had spread far and wide, and vast numbers of people came to see him.

⁹Jesus instructed his disciples to have a boat ready so the crowd would not crush him. ¹⁰He had healed many people that day, so all the sick people eagerly pushed forward to touch him. ¹¹And whenever those possessed by evil* spirits caught sight of him, the spirits would throw them to the ground in front of him shrieking, "You are the Son of God!" ¹²But Jesus sternly commanded the spirits not to reveal who he was.

JESUS CHOOSES THE TWELVE APOSTLES ¹³Afterward Jesus went up on a mountain and called out the ones he wanted to go with him. And they came to him. ¹⁴Then he appointed twelve of them and called them his apostles.* They were to accompany him, and he would send them out to preach, ¹⁵giving them authority to cast out demons. ¹⁶These are the twelve he chose:

2:16a Greek *the scribes of the Pharisees.* 2:16b Greek *with tax collectors and sinners?* 3:11 Greek *unclean;* also in 3:30. 3:14 Some manuscripts do not include *and called them his apostles.*

USEFUL ANGER
(3:1-6) Jesus was angry about the Pharisees' callous attitude toward a man with a crippled hand. What makes you angry? Anger itself isn't wrong. It depends on what makes us angry and what we do with our anger. Too often anger is expressed in selfish and harmful ways. By contrast, Jesus expressed his anger by correcting a problem—healing the man's hand. Use your anger to find constructive solutions rather than to add to a problem by tearing people down.

Simon (whom he named Peter),
¹⁷ James and John (the sons of Zebedee,
   but Jesus nicknamed them "Sons of
   Thunder"*),
¹⁸ Andrew,
   Philip,
   Bartholomew,
   Matthew,
   Thomas,
   James (son of Alphaeus),
   Thaddaeus,
   Simon (the zealot*),
¹⁹ Judas Iscariot (who later betrayed him).

JESUS AND THE PRINCE OF DEMONS
²⁰One time Jesus entered a house, and the crowds began to gather again. Soon he and his disciples couldn't even find time to eat. ²¹When his family heard what was happening, they tried to take him away. "He's out of his mind," they said.

²²But the teachers of religious law who had arrived from Jerusalem said, "He's possessed by Satan,* the prince of demons. That's where he gets the power to cast out demons."

²³Jesus called them over and responded with an illustration. "How can Satan cast out Satan?" he asked. ²⁴"A kingdom divided by civil war will collapse. ²⁵Similarly, a family splintered by feuding will fall apart. ²⁶And if Satan is divided and fights against himself, how can he stand? He would never survive. ²⁷Let me illustrate this further. Who is powerful enough to enter the house of a strong man like Satan and plunder his goods? Only someone even

3:17 Greek *whom he named Boanerges, which means Sons of Thunder.* **3:18** Greek *the Cananean,* an Aramaic term for Jewish nationalists. **3:22** Greek *Beelzeboul;* other manuscripts read *Beezeboul;* Latin version reads *Beelzebub.*

JUDAS ISCARIOT   *PERSONALITY PROFILE*

SUPPOSE YOU KNEW AHEAD OF TIME that a friend would later betray you. Would you still let him or her hang out with you?

Jesus would.

It's easy to forget that Jesus chose Judas to be his disciple (see Mark 3:19). We may also miss the point that while Judas betrayed Jesus, all of the disciples abandoned him (Mark 14:50).

The disciples, including Judas, all had the wrong idea of Jesus' mission on earth. They expected Jesus to rescue them from Roman tyranny. But when he kept talking about dying, they probably all felt a mixture of anger, fear, and disappointment.

We don't know exactly why Judas betrayed Jesus. But we can see that Judas let his own desires become so important that Satan was able to control him.

He tried to undo the evil he had done by returning the money to the priests (Matt 27:3-5), but it was too late. How sad that Judas ended his life in despair without ever experiencing the forgiveness God could have supplied, even to him.

In betraying Jesus, Judas made one of the greatest mistakes in history. But just the fact that Jesus knew Judas would betray him doesn't mean that Judas was a puppet of God's will. Judas made the choice. God knew what that choice would be and made it part of the plan. Judas didn't lose his relationship with Jesus; rather, he had never found Jesus. Judas is called "the one headed for destruction" (John 17:12) because he was never saved.

Judas's life reminds us to think deeply about our commitment to God. Are we serious about following God, or just faking it? We can choose disobedience and death, or we can choose repentance, forgiveness, hope, and eternal life. Judas's betrayal sent Jesus to the Cross to guarantee that second choice, our only chance. Will we accept Christ's free gift, or—like Judas—betray him? Our eternal destiny hangs on that decision.

BOTTOM LINE: Evil plans and motives leave us open to being used by Satan for even greater evil.

The consequences of evil are so devastating that even small lies and little wrongdoings have serious results.

God's plan and purposes are worked out even in the worst possible events.

Judas's story is told in the Gospels. He is also mentioned in Acts 1:17-19.

UPS:
* Chosen as one of the 12 disciples; the only non-Galilean
* Kept the money bag for the expenses of the group
* Recognized the evil in his betrayal of Jesus

DOWNS:
* Was greedy (John 12:6)
* Betrayed Jesus
* Committed suicide instead of seeking forgiveness

STATS:
* Where: probably from the town of Kerioth
* Occupation: disciple of Jesus
* Relatives: Simon (father)
* Contemporaries: Jesus, Pilate, Herod, the other 11 disciples

KEY VERSES: *Luke 22:3-4*

stronger—someone who could tie him up and then plunder his house.

28"I tell you the truth, all sin and blasphemy can be forgiven, 29but anyone who blasphemes the Holy Spirit will never be forgiven. This is a sin with eternal consequences." 30He told them this because they were saying, "He's possessed by an evil spirit."

THE TRUE FAMILY OF JESUS 31Then Jesus' mother and brothers came to see him. They stood outside and sent word for him to come out and talk with them. 32There was a crowd sitting around Jesus, and someone said, "Your mother and your brothers* are outside asking for you."

33Jesus replied, "Who is my mother? Who are my brothers?" 34Then he looked at those around him and said, "Look, these are my mother and brothers. 35Anyone who does God's will is my brother and sister and mother."

4 PARABLE OF THE FARMER SCATTERING SEED Once again Jesus began teaching by the lakeshore. A very large crowd soon gathered around him, so he got into a boat. Then he sat in the boat while all the people remained on the shore. 2He taught them by telling many stories in the form of parables, such as this one:

3"Listen! A farmer went out to plant some seed. 4As he scattered it across his field, some of the seed fell on a footpath, and the birds came and ate it. 5Other seed fell on shallow soil with underlying rock. The seed sprouted quickly because the soil was shallow. 6But the plant soon wilted under the hot sun, and since it didn't have deep roots, it died. 7Other seed fell among thorns that grew up and choked out the tender plants so they produced no grain. 8Still other seeds fell on fertile soil, and they sprouted, grew, and produced a crop that was thirty, sixty, and even a hundred times as much as had been planted!" 9Then he said, "Anyone with ears to hear should listen and understand."

10Later, when Jesus was alone with the twelve disciples and with the others who were gathered around, they asked him what the parables meant.

11He replied, "You are permitted to understand the secret* of the Kingdom of God. But I use parables for everything I say to outsiders, 12so that the Scriptures might be fulfilled:

'When they see what I do,
    they will learn nothing.
When they hear what I say,
    they will not understand.
Otherwise, they will turn to me
    and be forgiven.'*"

13Then Jesus said to them, "If you can't understand the meaning of this parable, how will you understand all the other parables? 14The farmer plants seed by taking God's word to others. 15The seed that fell on the footpath represents those who hear the message, only to have Satan come at once and take it away. 16The seed on the rocky soil represents those who hear the message and immediately receive it with joy. 17But since they don't have deep roots, they don't last long. They fall away as soon as they have problems or are persecuted for believing God's word. 18The seed that fell among the thorns represents others who hear God's word, 19but all too quickly the message is crowded out by the worries of this life, the lure of wealth, and the desire for other things, so no fruit is produced. 20And the seed that fell on good soil represents those who hear and accept God's word and produce a harvest of thirty, sixty, or even a hundred times as much as had been planted!"

PARABLE OF THE LAMP 21Then Jesus asked them, "Would anyone light a lamp and then put it under a basket or under a bed? Of course not! A lamp is placed on a stand, where its light will shine. 22For everything that is hidden will

....

READY OR NOT?
(4:1-12) *The disciples didn't understand Jesus' parable. Some people don't understand God's truth because they're not ready for it. God reveals truth to people who will do something about it.*

Many people hesitate to tell others about God because they think they have to make them believe. But only God can help a person to understand truth and act on it. With whom have you been meaning to talk about God? Start with prayer first, asking for courage, for the opportunity, and for the Holy Spirit to help that person be ready to receive the truth.

RESPONSES
(4:14-20) *The four soils represent four different ways people respond to God's word. Usually we think Jesus was talking about four different kinds of people, but he may also have been talking about (1) different times or phases in a person's life, or (2) how we willingly receive God's message in some areas of our lives and resist it in others. For example, you may be open to God where your future is concerned but closed about the way you spend your money. You may respond like good soil to God's demand for worship but like rocky soil to his demand to give to those in need. What will you do to make every area of your life like the "good soil" mentioned in this passage?*

3:32 Some manuscripts add *and sisters.*   4:11 Greek *mystery.*
4:12 Isa 6:9-10 (Greek version).

eventually be brought into the open, and every secret will be brought to light. ²³Anyone with ears to hear should listen and understand."

²⁴Then he added, "Pay close attention to what you hear. The closer you listen, the more understanding you will be given*—and you will receive even more. ²⁵To those who listen to my teaching, more understanding will be given. But for those who are not listening, even what little understanding they have will be taken away from them."

PARABLE OF THE GROWING SEED ²⁶Jesus also said, "The Kingdom of God is like a farmer who scatters seed on the ground. ²⁷Night and day, while he's asleep or awake, the seed sprouts and grows, but he does not understand how it happens. ²⁸The earth produces the crops on its own. First a leaf blade pushes through, then the heads of wheat are formed, and finally the grain ripens. ²⁹And as soon as the grain is ready, the farmer comes and harvests it with a sickle, for the harvest time has come."

PARABLE OF THE MUSTARD SEED ³⁰Jesus said, "How can I describe the Kingdom of God? What story should I use to illustrate it? ³¹It is like a mustard seed planted in the ground. It is the smallest of all seeds, ³²but it becomes the largest of all garden plants; it grows long branches, and birds can make nests in its shade."

³³Jesus used many similar stories and illustrations to teach the people as much as they could understand. ³⁴In fact, in his public ministry he never taught without using parables; but afterward, when he was alone with his disciples, he explained everything to them.

JESUS CALMS THE STORM ³⁵As evening came, Jesus said to his disciples, "Let's cross to the other side of the lake." ³⁶So they took Jesus in the boat and started out, leaving the crowds behind (although other boats followed). ³⁷But soon a fierce storm came up. High waves were breaking into the boat, and it began to fill with water.

³⁸Jesus was sleeping at the back of the boat with his head on a cushion. The disciples woke him up, shouting, "Teacher, don't you care that we're going to drown?"

³⁹When Jesus woke up, he rebuked the wind and said to the waves, "Silence! Be still!" Suddenly the wind stopped, and there was a great calm. ⁴⁰Then he asked them, "Why are you afraid? Do you still have no faith?"

⁴¹The disciples were absolutely terrified. "Who is this man?" they asked each other. "Even the wind and waves obey him!"

5 **JESUS HEALS A DEMON-POSSESSED MAN** So they arrived at the other side of the lake, in the region of the Gerasenes.* ²When Jesus climbed out of the boat, a man possessed by an evil* spirit came out from a cemetery to meet him. ³This man lived among

4:24 Or *The measure you give will be the measure you get back.*
5:1 Other manuscripts read *Gadarenes;* still others read *Gergesenes.* See Matt 8:28; Luke 8:26. **5:2** Greek *unclean;* also in 5:8, 13.

I WONDER...

Now that I am a Christian, how should I act around my friends and family who are not believers?

The most important thing you have going for you in both sets of relationships is that you already have a "relational bridge." Your friends and family knew what your life was like before you met Christ. Now they will have the chance to see you afterward.

In Mark 5:1-20, Jesus recognized that this was the case with the man he had just cleansed from demon possession. So he sent him back to his home to tell his family everything Jesus had done for him.

Another passage calls us Christ's ambassadors to our world (2 Cor 5:18-20). This means we are his handpicked representatives! If people want to know what God is like, all they have to do is look at us.

God does not expect you to be perfect, but he does expect your faith to grow (Col 2:7), and he expects you to try to live more like Jesus Christ would (Rom 12:1-2).

The people around you will be able to relate to your progress, not to perfection. Progress may be slow at first, but eventually, as you give areas of your life to Christ's control, changes will become noticeable. You may find others starting to ask questions about your new faith.

When this happens, don't worry. Although you may feel inadequate answering some of their questions, your responsibility is only to share what God has done for you and what you have learned, not to be the Bible expert. Sharing and living your faith as a new Christian is just as important (and biblical!) as being more mature in the faith or being a Bible scholar. God is not limited by our lack of knowledge.

For those who know you well, *seeing* how following Christ is changing your life may have a much greater impact than any stranger's eloquent words.

the burial caves and could no longer be restrained, even with a chain. [4]Whenever he was put into chains and shackles—as he often was—he snapped the chains from his wrists and smashed the shackles. No one was strong enough to subdue him. [5]Day and night he wandered among the burial caves and in the hills, howling and cutting himself with sharp stones.

[6]When Jesus was still some distance away, the man saw him, ran to meet him, and bowed low before him. [7]With a shriek, he screamed, "Why are you interfering with me, Jesus, Son of the Most High God? In the name of God, I beg you, don't torture me!" [8]For Jesus had already said to the spirit, "Come out of the man, you evil spirit."

[9]Then Jesus demanded, "What is your name?"

And he replied, "My name is Legion, because there are many of us inside this man." [10]Then the evil spirits begged him again and again not to send them to some distant place.

[11]There happened to be a large herd of pigs feeding on the hillside nearby. [12]"Send us into those pigs," the spirits begged. "Let us enter them."

[13]So Jesus gave them permission. The evil spirits came out of the man and entered the pigs, and the entire herd of about 2,000 pigs plunged down the steep hillside into the lake and drowned in the water.

[14]The herdsmen fled to the nearby town and the surrounding countryside, spreading the news as they ran. People rushed out to see what had happened. [15]A crowd soon gathered around Jesus, and they saw the man who had been possessed by the legion of demons. He was sitting there fully clothed and perfectly sane, and they were all afraid. [16]Then those who had seen what happened told the others about the demon-possessed man and the pigs. [17]And the crowd began pleading with Jesus to go away and leave them alone.

[18]As Jesus was getting into the boat, the man who had been demon possessed begged to go with him. [19]But Jesus said, "No, go home to your family, and tell them everything the Lord has done for you and how merciful he has been." [20]So the man started off to visit the Ten Towns* of that region and began to proclaim the great things Jesus had done for him; and everyone was amazed at what he told them.

JESUS HEALS IN RESPONSE TO FAITH [21]Jesus got into the boat again and went back to the other side of the lake, where a large crowd

5:20 Greek *Decapolis.*

NO, GO HOME TO YOUR FAMILY, AND TELL THEM EVERYTHING THE LORD HAS DONE FOR YOU AND HOW MERCIFUL HE HAS BEEN.

■ ■ ■ ■ ■ MARK 5:19 ■ ■ ■ ■ ■

gathered around him on the shore. [22]Then a leader of the local synagogue, whose name was Jairus, arrived. When he saw Jesus, he fell at his feet, [23]pleading fervently with him. "My little daughter is dying," he said. "Please come and lay your hands on her; heal her so she can live."

[24]Jesus went with him, and all the people followed, crowding around him. [25]A woman in the crowd had suffered for twelve years with constant bleeding. [26]She had suffered a great deal from many doctors, and over the years she had spent everything she had to pay them, but she had gotten no better. In fact, she had gotten worse. [27]She had heard about Jesus, so she came up behind him through the crowd and touched his robe. [28]For she thought to herself, "If I can just touch his robe, I will be healed." [29]Immediately the bleeding stopped, and she could feel in her body that she had been healed of her terrible condition.

[30]Jesus realized at once that healing power had gone out from him, so he turned around in the crowd and asked, "Who touched my robe?"

[31]His disciples said to him, "Look at this crowd pressing around you. How can you ask, 'Who touched me?'"

[32]But he kept on looking around to see who had done it. [33]Then the frightened woman, trembling at the realization of what had happened to her, came and fell to her knees in front of him and told him what she had done. [34]And he said to her, "Daughter, your faith has made you well. Go in peace. Your suffering is over."

ENTHUSIASTIC
(5:18-20) This man who had been demon-possessed became a living example of Jesus' power. He wanted to go with Jesus, but Jesus told him to go home and share his story there. If you have experienced Jesus' power, you too are a living example. Are you, like this man, enthusiastic about sharing the Good News with those around you? Just as we would tell others about a doctor who cured a physical disease, we should tell about Christ, who cures our sin.

[35]While he was still speaking to her, messengers arrived from the home of Jairus, the leader of the synagogue. They told him, "Your daughter is dead. There's no use troubling the Teacher now."

[36]But Jesus overheard* them and said to Jairus, "Don't be afraid. Just have faith."

[37]Then Jesus stopped the crowd and wouldn't let anyone go with him except Peter, James, and John (the brother of James). [38]When they came to the home of the synagogue leader, Jesus saw much commotion and weeping and wailing. [39]He went inside and asked, "Why all this commotion and weeping? The child isn't dead; she's only asleep."

[40]The crowd laughed at him. But he made them all leave, and he took the girl's father and mother and his three disciples into the room where the girl was lying. [41]Holding her hand, he said to her, "Talitha koum," which means "Little girl, get up!" [42]And the girl, who was twelve years old, immediately stood up and walked around! They were overwhelmed and totally amazed. [43]Jesus gave them strict orders not to tell anyone what had happened, and then he told them to give her something to eat.

6 JESUS REJECTED AT NAZARETH Jesus left that part of the country and returned with his disciples to Nazareth, his hometown. [2]The next Sabbath he began teaching in the synagogue, and many who heard him were amazed. They asked, "Where did he get all this wisdom and the power to perform such miracles?" [3]Then they scoffed, "He's just a

∙∙

FAMILIARITY
(6:1-6) The old saying "Familiarity breeds contempt" is true in this case. Although Jesus taught effectively and wisely, the people of his hometown saw him only as a carpenter. They rejected his authority because he grew up in their town. They thought they knew him, but their preconceived notions about who he was made it impossible for them to accept his message. Ever have that reaction to someone? Sometimes, we reject the truth because we don't like or respect the source of it. But God's truth often comes in ways we don't expect. He might speak through a small child or through someone we've known forever. Are you open to his truth in whatever form it takes?

TEAMWORK
(6:7) The disciples were sent out in pairs. Individually, they could have reached more areas of the country, but this was not Jesus' plan. One advantage in traveling by twos was that they could strengthen and encourage each other, especially when they faced rejection. Likewise, God sometimes meets some of our needs through others. How has teamwork aided you as you worked to build God's Kingdom?

carpenter, the son of Mary* and the brother of James, Joseph,* Judas, and Simon. And his sisters live right here among us." They were deeply offended and refused to believe in him.

[4]Then Jesus told them, "A prophet is honored everywhere except in his own hometown and among his relatives and his own family." [5]And because of their unbelief, he couldn't do any miracles among them except to place his hands on a few sick people and heal them. [6]And he was amazed at their unbelief.

JESUS SENDS OUT THE TWELVE DISCIPLES
Then Jesus went from village to village, teaching the people. [7]And he called his twelve disciples together and began sending them out two by two, giving them authority to cast out evil* spirits. [8]He told them to take nothing for their journey except a walking stick—no food, no traveler's bag, no money.* [9]He allowed them to wear sandals but not to take a change of clothes.

[10]"Wherever you go," he said, "stay in the same house until you leave town. [11]But if any place refuses to welcome you or listen to you, shake its dust from your feet as you leave to show that you have abandoned those people to their fate."

[12]So the disciples went out, telling everyone they met to repent of their sins and turn to God. [13]And they cast out many demons and healed many sick people, anointing them with olive oil.

THE DEATH OF JOHN THE BAPTIST [14]Herod Antipas, the king, soon heard about Jesus, because everyone was talking about him. Some were saying,* "This must be John the Baptist raised from the dead. That is why he can do such miracles." [15]Others said, "He's the prophet Elijah." Still others said, "He's a prophet like the other great prophets of the past."

[16]When Herod heard about Jesus, he said, "John, the man I beheaded, has come back from the dead."

[17]For Herod had sent soldiers to arrest and imprison John as a favor to Herodias. She had been his brother Philip's wife, but Herod had married her. [18]John had been telling Herod, "It is against God's law for you to marry your brother's wife." [19]So Herodias bore a grudge against John and wanted to kill him. But without Herod's approval she was powerless, [20]for

5:36 Or *ignored.*   **6:3a** Some manuscripts read *He's just the son of the carpenter and of Mary.*   **6:3b** Most manuscripts read *Joses*; see Matt 13:55.   **6:7** Greek *unclean.*   **6:8** Greek *no copper coins in their money belts.*   **6:14** Some manuscripts read *He was saying.*

Herod respected John; and knowing that he was a good and holy man, he protected him. Herod was greatly disturbed whenever he talked with John, but even so, he liked to listen to him.

²¹Herodias's chance finally came on Herod's birthday. He gave a party for his high government officials, army officers, and the leading citizens of Galilee. ²²Then his daughter, also named Herodias,* came in and performed a dance that greatly pleased Herod and his guests. "Ask me for anything you like," the king said to the girl, "and I will give it to you." ²³He even vowed, "I will give you whatever you ask, up to half my kingdom!"

²⁴She went out and asked her mother, "What should I ask for?"

Her mother told her, "Ask for the head of John the Baptist!"

²⁵So the girl hurried back to the king and told him, "I want the head of John the Baptist, right now, on a tray!"

²⁶Then the king deeply regretted what he had said; but because of the vows he had made in front of his guests, he couldn't refuse her. ²⁷So he immediately sent an executioner to the prison to cut off John's head and bring it to him. The soldier beheaded John in the prison, ²⁸brought his head on a tray, and gave it to the girl, who took it to her mother. ²⁹When John's disciples heard what had happened, they came to get his body and buried it in a tomb.

JESUS FEEDS FIVE THOUSAND
³⁰The apostles returned to Jesus from their ministry tour and told him all they had done and taught. ³¹Then Jesus said, "Let's go off by ourselves to a quiet place and rest awhile." He said this because there were so many people coming and going that Jesus and his apostles didn't even have time to eat.

³²So they left by boat for a quiet place, where they could be alone. ³³But many people recognized them and saw them leaving, and people from many towns ran ahead along the shore and got there ahead of them. ³⁴Jesus saw the huge crowd as he stepped from the boat, and he had compassion on them because they were like sheep without a shepherd. So he began teaching them many things.

³⁵Late in the afternoon his disciples came to him and said, "This is a remote place, and it's already getting late. ³⁶Send the crowds away

so they can go to the nearby farms and villages and buy something to eat."

³⁷But Jesus said, "You feed them."

"With what?" they asked. "We'd have to work for months to earn enough money* to buy food for all these people!"

³⁸"How much bread do you have?" he asked. "Go and find out."

They came back and reported, "We have five loaves of bread and two fish."

³⁹Then Jesus told the disciples to have the people sit down in groups on the green grass. ⁴⁰So they sat down in groups of fifty or a hundred.

⁴¹Jesus took the five loaves and two fish, looked up toward heaven, and blessed them. Then, breaking the loaves into pieces, he kept giving the bread to the disciples so they could distribute it to the people. He also divided the fish for everyone to share. ⁴²They all ate as much as they wanted, ⁴³and afterward, the disciples picked up twelve baskets of leftover bread and fish. ⁴⁴A total of 5,000 men and their families were fed from those loaves!

JESUS WALKS ON WATER
⁴⁵Immediately after this, Jesus insisted that his disciples get back into the boat and head across the lake to Bethsaida, while he sent the people home. ⁴⁶After telling everyone good-bye, he went up into the hills by himself to pray.

⁴⁷Late that night, the disciples were in their boat in the middle of the lake, and Jesus was alone on land. ⁴⁸He saw that they were in serious trouble, rowing hard and struggling against the wind and waves. About three o'clock in the morning* Jesus came toward them, walking on the water. He intended to go past them, ⁴⁹but when they saw him walking on the water, they cried out in terror, thinking he was a ghost. ⁵⁰They were all terrified when they saw him.

But Jesus spoke to them at once. "Don't be afraid," he said. "Take courage! I am here!*" ⁵¹Then he climbed into the boat, and the wind stopped. They were totally amazed, ⁵²for they still didn't understand the significance of the miracle of the loaves. Their hearts were too hard to take it in.

⁵³After they had crossed the lake, they landed at Gennesaret. They brought the boat to shore ⁵⁴and climbed out. The people recognized Jesus at once, ⁵⁵and they ran throughout the whole area, carrying sick people on mats to wherever they heard he was. ⁵⁶Wherever he went—in villages, cities, or the countryside—they brought the sick out to the marketplaces.

6:22 Some manuscripts read *the daughter of Herodias herself.*
6:37 Greek *It would take 200 denarii.* A denarius was equivalent to a laborer's full day's wage.   6:48 Greek *About the fourth watch of the night.*   6:50 Or *The 'I AM' is here;* Greek reads *I am.* See Exod 3:14.

They begged him to let the sick touch at least the fringe of his robe, and all who touched him were healed.

7 JESUS TEACHES ABOUT INNER PURITY

One day some Pharisees and teachers of religious law arrived from Jerusalem to see Jesus. ²They noticed that some of his disciples failed to follow the Jewish ritual of hand washing before eating. ³(The Jews, especially the Pharisees, do not eat until they have poured water over their cupped hands,* as required by their ancient traditions. ⁴Similarly, they don't eat anything from the market until they immerse their hands* in water. This is but one of many traditions they have clung to—such as their ceremonial washing of cups, pitchers, and kettles.*)

⁵So the Pharisees and teachers of religious law asked him, "Why don't your disciples follow our age-old tradition? They eat without first performing the hand-washing ceremony."

⁶Jesus replied, "You hypocrites! Isaiah was right when he prophesied about you, for he wrote,

---

MONEY MATTERS

(7:1-13) The Pharisees used God as an excuse to avoid helping their families, especially their parents. They thought putting money in the Temple treasury was more important than helping their needy parents. But Jesus exposed their hypocrisy by reminding them of specific laws (see Exod 20:12; 21:17).

We often have the opposite problem. We would rather use our money to buy gifts for friends and family than to give it in church or to serve others. But helping those in need is one of the most important ways to honor God. How will you use your money to honor God?

'These people honor me with their lips,
  but their hearts are far from me.
⁷ Their worship is a farce,
  for they teach man-made ideas as
    commands from God.'*

⁸For you ignore God's law and substitute your own tradition."

⁹Then he said, "You skillfully sidestep God's law in order to hold on to your own tradition. ¹⁰For instance, Moses gave you this law from God: 'Honor your father and mother,'* and 'Anyone who speaks disrespectfully of father or mother must be put to death.'* ¹¹But you say it is all right for people to say to their parents, 'Sorry, I can't help you. For I have vowed to give to God what I would have given to you.'* ¹²In this way, you let them disregard their needy parents. ¹³And so you cancel the word of God in order to hand down your own tradition. And this is only one example among many others."

¹⁴Then Jesus called to the crowd to come and hear. "All of you listen," he said, "and try to understand. ¹⁵It's not what goes into your body that defiles you; you are defiled by what comes from your heart.*"

¹⁷Then Jesus went into a house to get away from the crowd, and his disciples asked him what he meant by the parable he had just used. ¹⁸"Don't you understand either?" he asked. "Can't you see that the food you put into your body cannot defile you? ¹⁹Food doesn't go into

7:3 Greek *have washed with the fist.* **7:4a** Some manuscripts read *sprinkle themselves.* **7:4b** Some manuscripts add *and dining couches.* **7:7** Isa 29:13 (Greek version). **7:10a** Exod 20:12; Deut 5:16. **7:10b** Exod 21:17 (Greek version); Lev 20:9 (Greek version). **7:11** Greek *'What I would have given to you is Corban' (that is, a gift).* **7:15** Some manuscripts add verse 16, *Anyone with ears to hear should listen and understand.* Compare 4:9, 23.

CHOICES
legalism

Perhaps you know someone like 17-year-old Neal. A very opinionated churchgoer, he has the Christian life all figured out, or so he thinks. For Neal, everything is black and white, cut-and-dried, no "gray areas." Certain deeds are expected, and most other activities simply are not acceptable for believers. And if you don't see things his way, Neal treats you like your relationship with the Lord is defective. Just look at some of his recent pronouncements:

- "Anybody who goes dancing is not walking with God."
- "How a girl who wears an outfit like that could call herself a Christian is beyond me!"
- "Going to a movie theater is no different than going into a bar. Both places are evil."

- "If you guys are serious about God, you'll be at youth group Wednesday night."

Is it any wonder that this outspoken junior has been nicknamed "Negative Neal"?

Legalism is the crazy idea that we can earn God's acceptance by strenuously following a lot of dos and don'ts. Legalistic people almost always feel either prideful ("I'm better than the people who do those things") or frustrated ("I can never measure up").

Is that what the Christian life is all about—a long list of rules and regulations? Not at all! Even if you don't know anyone as extreme as Neal, and even if you don't think you struggle with legalism, see what Jesus said in Mark 7:1-23.

your heart, but only passes through the stomach and then goes into the sewer." (By saying this, he declared that every kind of food is acceptable in God's eyes.)

²⁰And then he added, "It is what comes from inside that defiles you. ²¹For from within, out of a person's heart, come evil thoughts, sexual immorality, theft, murder, ²²adultery, greed, wickedness, deceit, lustful desires, envy, slander, pride, and foolishness. ²³All these vile things come from within; they are what defile you."

THE FAITH OF A GENTILE WOMAN

²⁴Then Jesus left Galilee and went north to the region of Tyre.* He didn't want anyone to know which house he was staying in, but he couldn't keep it a secret. ²⁵Right away a woman who had heard about him came and fell at his feet. Her little girl was possessed by an evil* spirit, ²⁶and she begged him to cast out the demon from her daughter.

Since she was a Gentile, born in Syrian Phoenicia, ²⁷Jesus told her, "First I should feed the children—my own family, the Jews.* It isn't right to take food from the children and throw it to the dogs."

²⁸She replied, "That's true, Lord, but even the dogs under the table are allowed to eat the scraps from the children's plates."

²⁹"Good answer!" he said. "Now go home, for the demon has left your daughter." ³⁰And when she arrived home, she found her little girl lying quietly in bed, and the demon was gone.

JESUS HEALS A DEAF MAN

³¹Jesus left Tyre and went up to Sidon before going back to the Sea of Galilee and the region of the Ten Towns.* ³²A deaf man with a speech impediment was brought to him, and the people begged Jesus to lay his hands on the man to heal him.

³³Jesus led him away from the crowd so they could be alone. He put his fingers into the man's ears. Then, spitting on his own fingers, he touched the man's tongue. ³⁴Looking up to heaven, he sighed and said, "Ephphatha," which means, "Be opened!" ³⁵Instantly the man could hear perfectly, and his tongue was freed so he could speak plainly!

³⁶Jesus told the crowd not to tell anyone, but the more he told them not to, the more they spread the news. ³⁷They were completely amazed and said again and again, "Everything he does is wonderful. He even makes the deaf

to hear and gives speech to those who cannot speak."

8 JESUS FEEDS FOUR THOUSAND

About this time another large crowd had gathered, and the people ran out of food again. Jesus called his disciples and told them, ²"I feel sorry for these people. They have been here with me for three days, and they have nothing left to eat. ³If I send them home hungry, they will faint along the way. For some of them have come a long distance."

⁴His disciples replied, "How are we supposed to find enough food to feed them out here in the wilderness?"

⁵Jesus asked, "How much bread do you have?"

"Seven loaves," they replied.

⁶So Jesus told all the people to sit down on the ground. Then he took the seven loaves, thanked God for them, and broke them into pieces. He gave them to his disciples, who distributed the bread to the crowd. ⁷A few small fish were found, too, so Jesus also blessed these and told the disciples to distribute them.

⁸They ate as much as they wanted. Afterward, the disciples picked up seven large baskets of leftover food. ⁹There were about 4,000 people in the crowd that day, and Jesus sent them home after they had eaten. ¹⁰Immediately after this, he got into a boat with his disciples and crossed over to the region of Dalmanutha.

PHARISEES DEMAND A MIRACULOUS SIGN

¹¹When the Pharisees heard that Jesus had arrived, they came and started to argue with him. Testing him, they demanded that he show them a miraculous sign from heaven to prove his authority.

¹²When he heard this, he sighed deeply in his spirit and said, "Why do these people keep demanding a miraculous sign? I tell you the truth, I will not give this generation any such sign." ¹³So he got back into the boat and left them, and he crossed to the other side of the lake.

....

HE KNOWS

(8:1-3) Do you ever feel that God is so busy with important concerns that he can't possibly be aware of your needs? Just as Jesus was concerned about a large crowd's need for food, he is concerned about our daily needs. After all, he's the one who said, "Your heavenly Father already knows all your needs" (Matt 6:32). Do you have concerns that you think would not interest God? No concern is too large for him to handle and no need too small to escape his interest.

7:24 Some manuscripts add *and Sidon.*   7:25 Greek *unclean.*
7:27 Greek *Let the children eat first.*   7:31 Greek *Decapolis.*

YEAST OF THE PHARISEES AND HEROD

[14]But the disciples had forgotten to bring any food. They had only one loaf of bread with them in the boat. [15]As they were crossing the lake, Jesus warned them, "Watch out! Beware of the yeast of the Pharisees and of Herod."

[16]At this they began to argue with each other because they hadn't brought any bread. [17]Jesus knew what they were saying, so he said, "Why are you arguing about having no bread? Don't you know or understand even yet? Are your hearts too hard to take it in? [18]You have eyes—can't you see? You have ears—can't you hear?* Don't you remember anything at all? [19]When I fed the 5,000 with five loaves of bread, how many baskets of leftovers did you pick up afterward?"

"Twelve," they said.

[20]"And when I fed the 4,000 with seven loaves, how many large baskets of leftovers did you pick up?"

"Seven," they said.

[21]"Don't you understand yet?" he asked them.

JESUS HEALS A BLIND MAN

[22]When they arrived at Bethsaida, some people brought a blind man to Jesus, and they begged him to touch the man and heal him. [23]Jesus took the blind man by the hand and led him out of the village. Then, spitting on the man's eyes, he laid his hands on him and asked, "Can you see anything now?"

[24]The man looked around. "Yes," he said, "I see people, but I can't see them very clearly. They look like trees walking around."

[25]Then Jesus placed his hands on the man's eyes again, and his eyes were opened. His sight was completely restored, and he could see everything clearly. [26]Jesus sent him away, saying, "Don't go back into the village on your way home."

PETER'S DECLARATION ABOUT JESUS

[27]Jesus and his disciples left Galilee and went up to the villages near Caesarea Philippi. As they were walking along, he asked them, "Who do people say I am?"

[28]"Well," they replied, "some say John the Baptist, some say Elijah, and others say you are one of the other prophets."

[29]Then he asked them, "But who do you say I am?"

Peter replied, "You are the Messiah.*"

[30]But Jesus warned them not to tell anyone about him.

JESUS PREDICTS HIS DEATH

[31]Then Jesus began to tell them that the Son of Man* must suffer many terrible things and be rejected by the elders, the leading priests, and the teachers of religious law. He would be killed, but three days later he would rise from the dead. [32]As he talked about this openly with his disciples, Peter took him aside and began to reprimand him for saying such things.*

[33]Jesus turned around and looked at his disciples, then reprimanded Peter. "Get away from me, Satan!" he said. "You are seeing things merely from a human point of view, not from God's."

[34]Then, calling the crowd to join his disciples, he said, "If any of you wants to be my follower, you must turn from your selfish ways, take up your cross, and follow me. [35]If you try to hang on to your life, you will lose it. But if you give up your life for my sake and for the sake of the Good News, you will save it. [36]And what do you benefit if you gain the whole world but lose your own soul?* [37]Is anything worth more than your soul? [38]If anyone is ashamed of me and my message in these adulterous and sinful days, the Son of Man will be ashamed of that person when he returns in the glory of his Father with the holy angels."

9 Jesus went on to say, "I tell you the truth, some standing here right now will not die before they see the Kingdom of God arrive in great power!"

THE TRANSFIGURATION

[2]Six days later Jesus took Peter, James, and John, and led them up a high mountain to be alone. As the men watched, Jesus' appearance was transformed, [3]and his clothes became dazzling white, far whiter than any earthly bleach could ever make them. [4]Then Elijah and Moses appeared and began talking with Jesus.

[5]Peter exclaimed, "Rabbi, it's wonderful for us to be here! Let's make three shelters as memorials*—one for you, one for Moses, and one for Elijah." [6]He said this because he didn't

8:18 Jer 5:21.   **8:29** Or *the Christ. Messiah* (a Hebrew term) and *Christ* (a Greek term) both mean "the anointed one."   **8:31** "Son of Man" is a title Jesus used for himself.   **8:32** Or *began to correct him.*   **8:36** Or *your self;* also in 8:37.   **9:5** Greek *three tabernacles.*

really know what else to say, for they were all terrified.

7Then a cloud overshadowed them, and a voice from the cloud said, "This is my dearly loved Son. Listen to him." 8Suddenly, when they looked around, Moses and Elijah were gone, and they saw only Jesus with them.

9As they went back down the mountain, he told them not to tell anyone what they had seen until the Son of Man* had risen from the dead. 10So they kept it to themselves, but they often asked each other what he meant by "rising from the dead."

11Then they asked him, "Why do the teachers of religious law insist that Elijah must return before the Messiah comes?*"

12Jesus responded, "Elijah is indeed coming first to get everything ready. Yet why do the Scriptures say that the Son of Man must suffer greatly and be treated with utter contempt? 13But I tell you, Elijah has already come, and they chose to abuse him, just as the Scriptures predicted."

JESUS HEALS A DEMON-POSSESSED BOY

14When they returned to the other disciples, they saw a large crowd surrounding them, and some teachers of religious law were arguing with them. 15When the crowd saw Jesus, they were overwhelmed with awe, and they ran to greet him.

16"What is all this arguing about?" Jesus asked.

17One of the men in the crowd spoke up and said, "Teacher, I brought my son so you could heal him. He is possessed by an evil spirit that won't let him talk. 18And whenever this spirit seizes him, it throws him violently to the ground. Then he foams at the mouth and grinds his teeth and becomes rigid.* So I asked your disciples to cast out the evil spirit, but they couldn't do it."

19Jesus said to them,* "You faithless people! How long must I be with you? How long must I put up with you? Bring the boy to me."

20So they brought the boy. But when the evil spirit saw Jesus, it threw the child into a violent convulsion, and he fell to the ground, writhing and foaming at the mouth. 21"How long has this been happening?" Jesus asked the boy's father.

He replied, "Since he was a little boy. 22The spirit often throws him into the fire or into

water, trying to kill him. Have mercy on us and help us, if you can."

23"What do you mean, 'If I can'?" Jesus asked. "Anything is possible if a person believes."

24The father instantly cried out, "I do believe, but help me overcome my unbelief!"

25When Jesus saw that the crowd of onlookers was growing, he rebuked the evil* spirit. "Listen, you spirit that makes this boy unable to hear and speak," he said. "I command you to come out of this child and never enter him again!"

26Then the spirit screamed and threw the boy into another violent convulsion and left him. The boy appeared to be dead. A murmur ran through the crowd as people said, "He's dead." 27But Jesus took him by the hand and helped him to his feet, and he stood up.

28Afterward, when Jesus was alone in the house with his disciples, they asked him, "Why couldn't we cast out that evil spirit?"

29Jesus replied, "This kind can be cast out only by prayer.*"

JESUS AGAIN PREDICTS HIS DEATH

30Leaving that region, they traveled through Galilee. Jesus didn't want anyone to know he was there, 31for he wanted to spend more time with his disciples and teach them. He said to them, "The Son of Man is going to be betrayed into the hands of his enemies. He will be killed, but three days later he will rise from the dead." 32They didn't understand what he was saying, however, and they were afraid to ask him what he meant.

THE GREATEST IN THE KINGDOM

33After they arrived at Capernaum and settled in a house, Jesus asked his disciples, "What were you discussing out on the road?" 34But they didn't answer, because they had been arguing about which of them was the greatest. 35He sat down, called the twelve disciples over to him, and said, "Whoever wants to be first must take last place and be the servant of everyone else."

36Then he put a little child among them. Taking the child in his arms, he said to them,

....

YOUR PRAYER, GOD'S POWER
(9:23) Jesus' words don't mean that we can automatically obtain anything we want if we just think positively. Jesus meant that anything is possible with faith because nothing is too difficult for God (see Gen 18:14; Luke 1:37). This is not a teaching on how to pray as much as a statement about God's power to overcome obstacles. Although we won't receive everything we pray for as if by magic, with faith we can have everything we need to serve God.

9:9 "Son of Man" is a title Jesus used for himself. 9:11 Greek *that Elijah must come first?* 9:18 Or *becomes weak.* 9:19 Or *said to his disciples.* 9:25 Greek *unclean.* 9:29 Some manuscripts read *by prayer and fasting.*

[37]"Anyone who welcomes a little child like this on my behalf* welcomes me, and anyone who welcomes me welcomes not only me but also my Father who sent me."

USING THE NAME OF JESUS   [38]John said to Jesus, "Teacher, we saw someone using your name to cast out demons, but we told him to stop because he wasn't in our group."

[39]"Don't stop him!" Jesus said. "No one who performs a miracle in my name will soon be able to speak evil of me. [40]Anyone who is not against us is for us. [41]If anyone gives you even a cup of water because you belong to the Messiah, I tell you the truth, that person will surely be rewarded.

[42]"But if you cause one of these little ones who trusts in me to fall into sin, it would be better for you to be thrown into the sea with a large millstone hung around your neck. [43]If your hand causes you to sin, cut it off. It's better to enter eternal life with only one hand than to go into the unquenchable fires of hell* with two hands.* [45]If your foot causes you to sin, cut it off. It's better to enter eternal life with only one foot than to be thrown into hell with two feet.* [47]And if your eye causes you to sin, gouge it out. It's better to enter the Kingdom of God with only one eye than to have two eyes and be thrown into hell, [48]'where the maggots never die and the fire never goes out.'*

[49]"For everyone will be tested with fire.*

....

CUT IT OUT
(9:43-48) Jesus used startling language to stress the importance of ridding our lives of bad habits. Giving up a relationship, job, or habit that causes you to disobey God may seem just as painful as cutting off a hand. What, if anything, are you willing to give up if God asks it of you?

[50]Salt is good for seasoning. But if it loses its flavor, how do you make it salty again? You must have the qualities of salt among yourselves and live in peace with each other."

10 DISCUSSION ABOUT DIVORCE AND MARRIAGE Then Jesus left Capernaum and went down to the region of Judea and into the area east of the Jordan River. Once again crowds gathered around him, and as usual he was teaching them.

[2]Some Pharisees came and tried to trap him with this question: "Should a man be allowed to divorce his wife?"

[3]Jesus answered them with a question: "What did Moses say in the law about divorce?"

[4]"Well, he permitted it," they replied. "He said a man can give his wife a written notice of divorce and send her away."*

[5]But Jesus responded, "He wrote this commandment only as a concession to your hard hearts. [6]But 'God made them male and female'* from the beginning of creation. [7]'This explains why a man leaves his father and mother and is joined to his wife,* [8]and the two are united into one.'* Since they are no longer two but one, [9]let no one split apart what God has joined together."

[10]Later, when he was alone with his disciples in the house, they brought up the subject again. [11]He told them, "Whoever divorces his wife and marries someone else commits adultery against her. [12]And if a woman divorces her husband and marries someone else, she commits adultery."

9:37 Greek *in my name.*   **9:43a** Greek *Gehenna;* also in 9:45, 47. **9:43b** Some manuscripts add verse 44, *'where the maggots never die and the fire never goes out.'* See 9:48.   **9:45** Some manuscripts add verse 46, *'where the maggots never die and the fire never goes out.'* See 9:48.   **9:48** Isa 66:24.   **9:49** Greek *salted with fire;* other manuscripts add *and every sacrifice will be salted with salt.* **10:4** See Deut 24:1.   **10:6** Gen 1:27; 5:2.   **10:7** Some manuscripts do not include *and is joined to his wife.*   **10:7-8** Gen 2:24.

CHOICES
success

You've heard of A Tale of Two Cities by Charles Dickens? Call this "A Tale of Two Sisters." Elisa, a senior, has a 4.0 grade point average and is practically guaranteed a scholarship. She is drop-dead gorgeous, president of her class, and both captain and number-one seed on the girls' tennis team. She also dates Miguel, the hottest guy at school. Together they were voted by their class as "the couple most likely to succeed." Elisa's ambition? To be the next American Idol and possibly marry Miguel.

If Elisa represents "the best of times," then to many, Alita, a sophomore, probably embodies "the worst of times." She struggles in school, making mostly Cs. She is not especially popular, nor is she very athletic. No, the truth is that Alita is painfully shy and sort of average looking. She's not going out with anyone (not yet anyway) nor has she been voted into office or had predictions of greatness bestowed upon her. Most of her free time goes to serving as a Big Sister to two kids in a housing project in her town. Her goal in life? To be a social worker.

Do you know anyone like Elisa? Like Alita? Which girl do you think is the most successful? By what standards does our society judge success and failure? What does Jesus say in Mark 9:33-37?

JESUS BLESSES THE CHILDREN ¹³One day some parents brought their children to Jesus so he could touch and bless them. But the disciples scolded the parents for bothering him.

¹⁴When Jesus saw what was happening, he was angry with his disciples. He said to them, "Let the children come to me. Don't stop them! For the Kingdom of God belongs to those who are like these children. ¹⁵I tell you the truth, anyone who doesn't receive the Kingdom of God like a child will never enter it." ¹⁶Then he took the children in his arms and placed his hands on their heads and blessed them.

THE RICH MAN ¹⁷As Jesus was starting out on his way to Jerusalem, a man came running up to him, knelt down, and asked, "Good Teacher, what must I do to inherit eternal life?"

¹⁸"Why do you call me good?" Jesus asked. "Only God is truly good. ¹⁹But to answer your question, you know the commandments: 'You must not murder. You must not commit adultery. You must not steal. You must not testify falsely. You must not cheat anyone. Honor your father and mother.'*"

²⁰"Teacher," the man replied, "I've obeyed all these commandments since I was young."

²¹Looking at the man, Jesus felt genuine love for him. "There is still one thing you haven't done," he told him. "Go and sell all your possessions and give the money to the poor, and you will have treasure in heaven. Then come, follow me."

²²At this the man's face fell, and he went away sad, for he had many possessions.

²³Jesus looked around and said to his disciples, "How hard it is for the rich to enter the Kingdom of God!" ²⁴This amazed them. But Jesus said again, "Dear children, it is very hard* to enter the Kingdom of God. ²⁵In fact, it is easier for a camel to go through the eye of a needle than for a rich person to enter the Kingdom of God!"

²⁶The disciples were astounded. "Then who in the world can be saved?" they asked.

²⁷Jesus looked at them intently and said, "Humanly speaking, it is impossible. But not with God. Everything is possible with God."

²⁸Then Peter began to speak up. "We've given up everything to follow you," he said.

²⁹"Yes," Jesus replied, "and I assure you that everyone who has given up house or brothers or sisters or mother or father or children or property, for my sake and for the Good News,

³⁰will receive now in return a hundred times as many houses, brothers, sisters, mothers, children, and property—along with persecution. And in the world to come that person will have eternal life. ³¹But many who are the greatest now will be least important then, and those who seem least important now will be the greatest then.*"

JESUS AGAIN PREDICTS HIS DEATH ³²They were now on the way up to Jerusalem, and Jesus was walking ahead of them. The disciples were filled with awe, and the people following behind were overwhelmed with fear. Taking the twelve disciples aside, Jesus once more began to describe everything that was about to happen to him. ³³"Listen," he said, "we're going up to Jerusalem, where the Son of Man* will be betrayed to the leading priests and the teachers of religious law. They will sentence him to die and hand him over to the Romans.* ³⁴They will mock him, spit on him, flog him with a whip, and kill him, but after three days he will rise again."

JESUS TEACHES ABOUT SERVING OTHERS ³⁵Then James and John, the sons of Zebedee, came over and spoke to him. "Teacher," they said, "we want you to do us a favor."

³⁶"What is your request?" he asked.

³⁷They replied, "When you sit on your glorious throne, we want to sit in places of honor next to you, one on your right and the other on your left."

³⁸But Jesus said to them, "You don't know what you are asking! Are you able to drink from the bitter cup of suffering I am about to drink? Are you able to be baptized with the baptism of suffering I must be baptized with?"

³⁹"Oh yes," they replied, "we are able!"

Then Jesus told them, "You will indeed drink from my bitter cup and be baptized with my baptism of suffering. ⁴⁰But I have no right to say who will sit on my right or my left. God has

···

BARRIERS
(10:17-23) This young man wanted to be sure he would get eternal life, so he asked what he could do. Jesus lovingly addressed him with a challenge that brought out his true motives: "Sell all your possessions and give the money to the poor." Here was the barrier that could keep this man out of the Kingdom: his love of money. Ironically, the young man's attitude kept him from keeping the first commandment—to let nothing be more important than God (Exod 20:3). He came to Jesus wondering what he could do; he left seeing what he was unable to do. What barriers, if any, are keeping you from turning your life completely over to Jesus?

10:19 Exod 20:12-16; Deut 5:16-20.   **10:24** Some manuscripts read *very hard for those who trust in riches.*   **10:31** Greek *But many who are first will be last; and the last, first.*   **10:33a** "Son of Man" is a title Jesus used for himself.   **10:33b** Greek *the Gentiles.*

MY STORY: Marita

In my school, people are popular only if they have the right looks and the right clothes, live in a certain neighborhood, play on the football team or are a cheerleader, or date a football player or cheerleader. The lines are pretty clearly drawn. And I'm on the other side of every one of those lines.

For a while it really bothered me. But when I tried to break into one of the cliques at school, I found myself acting phony, and I couldn't stand it. I couldn't seem to help it, though. I wanted people to like me. I wanted to be popular.

Then, slowly, my viewpoint changed when my youth group studied the book of Mark. I really related to the disciples in chapters 9 and 10. They were trying to see who was more popular with Jesus, who would be considered the greatest. And Jesus said, "Many who are the greatest now will be least important then [in the world to come], and those who seem least important now will be the greatest then" (Mark 10:31).

I realized that it didn't really matter whether kids in my school thought I was great; what matters is what God thinks of me. To please him, I have to stop being phony and try to be friends with all kinds of people.

I've started doing that. Now I have lots of friends. Although I'm not one of the "popular" people, I'm okay with that. I know I'm popular with the one person whose opinion really matters—God.

prepared those places for the ones he has chosen."

⁴¹When the ten other disciples heard what James and John had asked, they were indignant. ⁴²So Jesus called them together and said, "You know that the rulers in this world lord it over their people, and officials flaunt their authority over those under them. ⁴³But among you it will be different. Whoever wants to be a leader among you must be your servant, ⁴⁴and whoever wants to be first among you must be the slave of everyone else. ⁴⁵For even the Son of Man came not to be served but to serve others and to give his life as a ransom for many."

JESUS HEALS BLIND BARTIMAEUS ⁴⁶Then they reached Jericho, and as Jesus and his disciples left town, a large crowd followed him. A blind beggar named Bartimaeus (son of Timaeus) was sitting beside the road. ⁴⁷When Bartimaeus heard that Jesus of Nazareth was nearby, he began to shout, "Jesus, Son of David, have mercy on me!"

⁴⁸"Be quiet!" many of the people yelled at him.

But he only shouted louder, "Son of David, have mercy on me!"

⁴⁹When Jesus heard him, he stopped and said, "Tell him to come here."

So they called the blind man. "Cheer up," they said. "Come on, he's calling you!" ⁵⁰Bartimaeus threw aside his coat, jumped up, and came to Jesus.

⁵¹"What do you want me to do for you?" Jesus asked.

"My rabbi,*" the blind man said, "I want to see!"

⁵²And Jesus said to him, "Go, for your faith has healed you." Instantly the man could see, and he followed Jesus down the road.*

11 **JESUS' TRIUMPHANT ENTRY** As Jesus and his disciples approached Jerusalem, they came to the towns of Bethphage and Bethany on the Mount of Olives. Jesus sent two of them on ahead. ²"Go into that village over there," he told them. "As soon as you enter it, you will see a young donkey tied there that no one has ever ridden. Untie it and bring it here. ³If anyone asks, 'What are you doing?' just say, 'The Lord needs it and will return it soon.'"

⁴The two disciples left and found the colt standing in the street, tied outside the front door. ⁵As they were untying it, some bystanders demanded, "What are you doing, untying that colt?" ⁶They said what Jesus had told them to say, and they were permitted to take it. ⁷Then they brought the colt to Jesus and threw their garments over it, and he sat on it.

⁸Many in the crowd spread their garments on the road ahead of him, and others spread leafy branches they had cut in the fields. ⁹Jesus was in the center of the procession, and the people all around him were shouting,

"Praise God!*

10:51 Greek uses the Hebrew term *Rabboni*. **10:52** Or *on the way.* **11:9** Greek *Hosanna*, an exclamation of praise that literally means "save now"; also in 11:10.

Blessings on the one who comes in the
name of the LORD!
¹⁰ Blessings on the coming Kingdom of our
ancestor David!
Praise God in highest heaven!"*

¹¹So Jesus came to Jerusalem and went into
the Temple. After looking around carefully at
everything, he left because it was late in the
afternoon. Then he returned to Bethany with
the twelve disciples.

JESUS CURSES THE FIG TREE

¹²The next morn-
ing as they were leaving Bethany, Jesus was
hungry. ¹³He noticed a fig tree in full leaf a little
way off, so he went over to see if he could find
any figs. But there were only leaves because
it was too early in the season for fruit. ¹⁴Then
Jesus said to the tree, "May no one ever eat
your fruit again!" And the disciples heard him
say it.

JESUS CLEARS THE TEMPLE

¹⁵When they ar-
rived back in Jerusalem, Jesus entered the
Temple and began to drive out the people
buying and selling animals for sacrifices. He
knocked over the tables of the money changers and the chairs of those selling doves, ¹⁶and
he stopped everyone from using the Temple
as a marketplace.* ¹⁷He said to them, "The
Scriptures declare, 'My Temple will be called
a house of prayer for all nations,' but you have
turned it into a den of thieves."*

¹⁸When the leading priests and teachers
of religious law heard what Jesus had done,
they began planning how to kill him. But they
were afraid of him because the people were so
amazed at his teaching.

¹⁹That evening Jesus and the disciples left*
the city.

²⁰The next morning as they passed by the
fig tree he had cursed, the disciples noticed it
had withered from the roots up. ²¹Peter remembered what Jesus had said to the tree on the
previous day and exclaimed, "Look, Rabbi! The
fig tree you cursed has withered and died!"

²²Then Jesus said to the disciples, "Have
faith in God. ²³I tell you the truth, you can say
to this mountain, 'May you be lifted up and
thrown into the sea,' and it will happen. But
you must really believe it will happen and have
no doubt in your heart. ²⁴I tell you, you can pray
for anything, and if you believe that you've received it, it will be yours. ²⁵But when you are

11:9-10 Pss 118:25-26; 148:1. **11:16** Or *from carrying merchandise
through the Temple.* **11:17** Isa 56:7; Jer 7:11. **11:19** Greek *they left;*
other manuscripts read *he left.* **11:25** Some manuscripts add
verse 26, *But if you refuse to forgive, your Father in heaven will not
forgive your sins.* Compare Matt 6:15.

praying, first forgive anyone you are holding a
grudge against, so that your Father in heaven
will forgive your sins, too.*"

THE AUTHORITY OF JESUS CHALLENGED

²⁷Again they entered Jerusalem. As Jesus was
walking through the Temple area, the leading
priests, the teachers of religious law, and the
elders came up to him. ²⁸They demanded, "By
what authority are you doing all these things?
Who gave you the right to do them?"

²⁹"I'll tell you by what authority I do these
things if you answer one question," Jesus replied. ³⁰"Did John's authority to baptize come
from heaven, or was it merely human? Answer
me!"

³¹They talked it over among themselves. "If
we say it was from heaven, he will ask why
we didn't believe John. ³²But do we dare say
it was merely human?" For they were afraid of
what the people would do, because everyone
believed that John was a prophet. ³³So they finally replied, "We don't know."

And Jesus responded, "Then I won't tell you
by what authority I do these things."

12 PARABLE OF THE EVIL FARMERS

Then
Jesus began teaching them with stories: "A man planted a vineyard. He built a
wall around it, dug a pit for pressing out the
grape juice, and built a lookout tower. Then
he leased the vineyard to tenant farmers and
moved to another country. ²At the time of the
grape harvest, he sent one of his servants to
collect his share of the crop. ³But the farmers
grabbed the servant, beat him up, and sent
him back empty-handed. ⁴The owner then
sent another servant, but they insulted him
and beat him over the head. ⁵The next servant he sent was killed. Others he sent were
either beaten or killed, ⁶until there was only
one left—his son whom he loved dearly. The
owner finally sent him, thinking, 'Surely they
will respect my son.'

⁷"But the tenant farmers said to one another,
'Here comes the heir to this estate. Let's kill
him and get the estate for ourselves!' ⁸So they
grabbed him and murdered him and threw his
body out of the vineyard.

···

UPSET
*(11:15-17) Jesus became angry, but he did not sin in his
anger. There is a place for righteous indignation. Christians should be upset about sin and injustice and should
take a stand against them. Unfortunately, believers often
are passive about these important issues and get angry
over personal insults and petty irritations. Direct your
anger toward the right issues.*

WHAT JESUS SAID ABOUT LOVE

In Mark 12:28, a religious teacher asked Jesus which one of all the commandments was the most important to follow. Jesus mentioned two commandments, one from Deuteronomy 6:5, the other from Leviticus 19:18. Both had to do with love. Why is love so important? Jesus said that all of the commandments were given for two simple reasons—to help us love God and love others as we should.

What else did Jesus say about love?
God loves us. . . . John 3:16
We are to love God. . . . Matthew 22:37
Because God loves us, he cares for us. . . . Matthew 6:25-34
God wants everyone to know how much he loves them. . . . John 17:23
God loves even those who hate him, and we are to do the same. . . . Matthew 5:43-47; Luke 6:35
God seeks out even those most alienated from him. . . .Luke 15
God must be your first love. . . . Matthew 6:24; 10:37
You love God when you obey him. . . . John 14:21; 15:10
God loves Jesus, his Son. . . . John 5:20; 10:17
Those who reject Jesus don't have God's love. . . . John 5:41-44
Jesus loves us just as God loves Jesus. . . . John 15:9
Jesus proved his love for us by dying on the cross so that we could live eternally with him. . . . John 3:14-15; 15:13 14
The love between God and Jesus is the perfect example of how we are to love others. . . . John 17:21-26
We are to demonstrate our love for one another. . . . Matthew 5:40-42; 10:42; John 13:34-35
We are not to love anything — recognition, wealth, earthly belongings, or praise from others — more than God. . . . Matthew 23:6; Luke 16:13; Luke 16:19-31; John 12:43
Jesus' love extends to each individual. . . . Luke 15:1-7
Jesus wants us to love him through both the good and difficult times. . . . Matthew 26:31-35
Jesus wants our love to be genuine. . . . John 21:15-17

9"What do you suppose the owner of the vineyard will do?" Jesus asked. "I'll tell you— he will come and kill those farmers and lease the vineyard to others. 10Didn't you ever read this in the Scriptures?

'The stone that the builders rejected
    has now become the cornerstone.
11 This is the LORD's doing,
    and it is wonderful to see.'*"

12The religious leaders* wanted to arrest Jesus because they realized he was telling the story against them—they were the wicked farmers. But they were afraid of the crowd, so they left him and went away.

• •

IMAGE
(12:12-17) The Pharisees and supporters of Herod (a group of Jewish leaders who tried to keep on the Romans' good side) thought they had the perfect question to trap Jesus. But Jesus answered wisely, once again exposing their self-interest and wrong motives. Jesus said that the coin bearing the emperor's image should be given to the emperor. But whatever bears God's image— our life—belongs to God. Are you giving God all that's rightfully his?

TAXES FOR CAESAR 13Later the leaders sent some Pharisees and supporters of Herod to trap Jesus into saying something for which he could be arrested. 14"Teacher," they said, "we know how honest you are. You are impartial and don't play favorites. You teach the way of God truthfully. Now tell us—is it right to pay taxes to Caesar or not? 15Should we pay them, or shouldn't we?"

Jesus saw through their hypocrisy and said, "Why are you trying to trap me? Show me a Roman coin,* and I'll tell you." 16When they handed it to him, he asked, "Whose picture and title are stamped on it?"

"Caesar's," they replied.

17"Well, then," Jesus said, "give to Caesar what belongs to Caesar, and give to God what belongs to God."

His reply completely amazed them.

DISCUSSION ABOUT RESURRECTION 18Then Jesus was approached by some Sadducees— religious leaders who say there is no resurrection from the dead. They posed this question: 19"Teacher, Moses gave us a law that if a man

12:10-11 Ps 118:22-23.   **12:12** Greek *They.*   **12:15** Greek *a denarius.*

dies, leaving a wife without children, his brother should marry the widow and have a child who will carry on the brother's name.* ²⁰Well, suppose there were seven brothers. The oldest one married and then died without children. ²¹So the second brother married the widow, but he also died without children. Then the third brother married her. ²²This continued with all seven of them, and still there were no children. Last of all, the woman also died. ²³So tell us, whose wife will she be in the resurrection? For all seven were married to her."

²⁴Jesus replied, "Your mistake is that you don't know the Scriptures, and you don't know the power of God. ²⁵For when the dead rise, they will neither marry nor be given in marriage. In this respect they will be like the angels in heaven.

²⁶"But now, as to whether the dead will be raised—haven't you ever read about this in the writings of Moses, in the story of the burning bush? Long after Abraham, Isaac, and Jacob had died, God said to Moses,* 'I am the God of Abraham, the God of Isaac, and the God of Jacob.'* ²⁷So he is the God of the living, not the dead. You have made a serious error."

THE MOST IMPORTANT COMMANDMENT

²⁸One of the teachers of religious law was standing there listening to the debate. He realized that Jesus had answered well, so he asked, "Of all the commandments, which is the most important?"

²⁹Jesus replied, "The most important commandment is this: 'Listen, O Israel! The LORD our God is the one and only LORD. ³⁰And you must love the LORD your God with all your heart, all your soul, all your mind, and all your strength.'* ³¹The second is equally important: 'Love your neighbor as yourself.'* No other commandment is greater than these."

³²The teacher of religious law replied, "Well said, Teacher. You have spoken the truth by saying that there is only one God and no other. ³³And I know it is important to love him with all my heart and all my understanding and all my strength, and to love my neighbor as myself. This is more important than to offer all of the burnt offerings and sacrifices required in the law."

³⁴Realizing how much the man understood, Jesus said to him, "You are not far from the Kingdom of God." And after that, no one dared to ask him any more questions.

12:19 See Deut 25:5-6.   12:26a Greek in the story of the bush? God said to him.   12:26b Exod 3:6.   12:29-30 Deut 6:4-5.   12:31 Lev 19:18.   12:36 Ps 110:1.   12:42 Greek two lepta, which is a kodrantes [i.e., a quadrans].

WHOSE SON IS THE MESSIAH?

³⁵Later, as Jesus was teaching the people in the Temple, he asked, "Why do the teachers of religious law claim that the Messiah is the son of David? ³⁶For David himself, speaking under the inspiration of the Holy Spirit, said,

'The LORD said to my Lord,
Sit in the place of honor at my right hand
    until I humble your enemies beneath
      your feet.'*

³⁷Since David himself called the Messiah 'my Lord,' how can the Messiah be his son?" The large crowd listened to him with great delight.

³⁸Jesus also taught: "Beware of these teachers of religious law! For they like to parade around in flowing robes and receive respectful greetings as they walk in the marketplaces. ³⁹And how they love the seats of honor in the synagogues and the head table at banquets. ⁴⁰Yet they shamelessly cheat widows out of their property and then pretend to be pious by making long prayers in public. Because of this, they will be more severely punished."

THE WIDOW'S OFFERING

⁴¹Jesus sat down near the collection box in the Temple and watched as the crowds dropped in their money. Many rich people put in large amounts. ⁴²Then a poor widow came and dropped in two small coins.*

⁴³Jesus called his disciples to him and said, "I tell you the truth, this poor widow has given more than all the others who are making contributions. ⁴⁴For they gave a tiny part of their surplus, but she, poor as she is, has given everything she had to live on."

13 JESUS FORETELLS THE FUTURE

As Jesus was leaving the Temple that day, one of his disciples said, "Teacher, look at these magnificent buildings! Look at the impressive stones in the walls."

²Jesus replied, "Yes, look at these great buildings. But they will be completely demolished. Not one stone will be left on top of another!"

....

TWO SIMPLE RULES

(12:29-34) God's laws can be reduced to two simple rules for life: Love God and love others. These commands are from the Old Testament (Deut 6:5; Lev 19:18). When you love God completely and care for others as you care for yourself, then you have fulfilled the intent of the Ten Commandments and the other Old Testament laws. According to Jesus, these two rules summarize all God's laws. Do they rule your thoughts, decisions, and actions?

WHY DID JESUS HAVE TO DIE?

The Problem	We have all done things that are wrong, and we have failed to obey God's laws. Because of this, we have been separated from God our Creator and deserve death. By ourselves we can do nothing to be reunited with God.
Why Jesus Could Help	Jesus was not only a man, he was also God's unique Son. Because Jesus never disobeyed God and never sinned, he is the only one who can bridge the gap between the sinless God and sinful humanity.
The Solution	Jesus freely offered his life for us, dying on the cross in our place, taking all our wrongdoing upon himself, and saving us from the consequences of sin— including God's judgment and death. God in his love and his justice sent Jesus to take our place.
The Results	Jesus took our past, present, and future sins upon himself so that we could have new life. Because all our sins are forgiven, our relationship with God is restored. Furthermore, Jesus' resurrection from the dead is the proof that his sacrifice on the cross in our place was acceptable to God, and his resurrection has become the source of new life for those who believe that Jesus is the Son of God. All who believe in him may have new life and live it in union with him.

³Later, Jesus sat on the Mount of Olives across the valley from the Temple. Peter, James, John, and Andrew came to him privately and asked him, ⁴"Tell us, when will all this happen? What sign will show us that these things are about to be fulfilled?"

⁵Jesus replied, "Don't let anyone mislead you, ⁶for many will come in my name, claiming, 'I am the Messiah.'* They will deceive many. ⁷And you will hear of wars and threats of wars, but don't panic. Yes, these things must take place, but the end won't follow immediately. ⁸Nation will go to war against nation, and kingdom against kingdom. There will be earthquakes in many parts of the world, as well as famines. But this is only the first of the birth pains, with more to come.

⁹"When these things begin to happen, watch out! You will be handed over to the local councils and beaten in the synagogues. You will stand trial before governors and kings because you are my followers. But this will be your opportunity to tell them about me.* ¹⁰For the Good News must first be preached to all nations.* ¹¹But when you are arrested and stand trial, don't worry in advance about what to say. Just say what God tells you at that time, for it is not you who will be speaking, but the Holy Spirit.

¹²"A brother will betray his brother to death, a father will betray his own child, and children will rebel against their parents and cause them to be killed. ¹³And everyone will hate you because you are my followers.* But the one who endures to the end will be saved.

¹⁴"The day is coming when you will see the sacrilegious object that causes desecration* standing where he* should not be." (Reader, pay attention!) "Then those in Judea must flee to the hills. ¹⁵A person out on the deck of a roof must not go down into the house to pack. ¹⁶A person out in the field must not return even to get a coat. ¹⁷How terrible it will be for pregnant women and for nursing mothers in those days. ¹⁸And pray that your flight will not be in winter. ¹⁹For there will be greater anguish in those days than at any time since God created the world. And it will never be so great again. ²⁰In fact, unless the Lord shortens that time of calamity, not a single person will survive. But for the sake of his chosen ones he has shortened those days.

PERSECUTION

(13:9-13) *As the first-century church began to grow, most of the disciples experienced the kind of persecution Jesus described in this passage. Later, he promised that Christians could expect trouble of this kind (John 16:33). Since the time of Christ, Christians have been persecuted in their own lands and in foreign mission fields. Though you may be safe from persecution now, your vision of God's Kingdom must not be limited by what happens only to you. A quick look at a newspaper will show you that many Christians in other parts of the world daily face hardships. Although you might not experience persecution now, you might face it someday. Are you prepared to take a stand for Christ, even if doing so means trouble for you?*

13:6 Greek *claiming, 'I am.'*   **13:9** Or *But this will be your testimony against them.*   **13:10** Or *all peoples.*   **13:13** Greek *on account of my name.*   **13:14a** Greek *the abomination of desolation.* See Dan 9:27; 11:31; 12:11.   **13:14b** Or *it.*

²¹"Then if anyone tells you, 'Look, here is the Messiah,' or 'There he is,' don't believe it. ²²For false messiahs and false prophets will rise up and perform signs and wonders so as to deceive, if possible, even God's chosen ones. ²³Watch out! I have warned you about this ahead of time!

²⁴"At that time, after the anguish of those days,

the sun will be darkened,
    the moon will give no light,
²⁵ the stars will fall from the sky,
    and the powers in the heavens will be
      shaken.*

²⁶Then everyone will see the Son of Man* coming on the clouds with great power and glory.* ²⁷And he will send out his angels to gather his chosen ones from all over the world*—from the farthest ends of the earth and heaven.

²⁸"Now learn a lesson from the fig tree. When its branches bud and its leaves begin to sprout, you know that summer is near. ²⁹In the same way, when you see all these things taking place, you can know that his return is very near, right at the door. ³⁰I tell you the truth, this generation* will not pass from the scene before all these things take place. ³¹Heaven and earth will disappear, but my words will never disappear.

³²"However, no one knows the day or hour when these things will happen, not even the angels in heaven or the Son himself. Only the Father knows. ³³And since you don't know when that time will come, be on guard! Stay alert*!

³⁴"The coming of the Son of Man can be illustrated by the story of a man going on a long trip. When he left home, he gave each of his slaves instructions about the work they were to do, and he told the gatekeeper to watch for his return. ³⁵You, too, must keep watch! For you don't know when the master of the household will return—in the evening, at midnight, before dawn, or at daybreak. ³⁶Don't let him find you sleeping when he arrives without warning. ³⁷I say to you what I say to everyone: Watch for him!"

14 JESUS ANOINTED AT BETHANY It was
now two days before Passover and the Festival of Unleavened Bread. The leading

UPPER ROOM AND GETHSEMANE
Jesus and the disciples ate the traditional Passover meal in an upper room in Jerusalem and then went up on the Mount of Olives to a garden called Gethsemane. In the cool of the evening, Jesus prayed for strength to face the trial and suffering ahead.

priests and the teachers of religious law were still looking for an opportunity to capture Jesus secretly and kill him. ²"But not during the Passover celebration," they agreed, "or the people may riot."

³Meanwhile, Jesus was in Bethany at the home of Simon, a man who had previously had leprosy. While he was eating,* a woman came in with a beautiful alabaster jar of expensive perfume made from essence of nard. She broke open the jar and poured the perfume over his head.

⁴Some of those at the table were indignant. "Why waste such expensive perfume?" they asked. ⁵"It could have been sold for a year's wages* and the money given to the poor!" So they scolded her harshly.

⁶But Jesus replied, "Leave her alone. Why criticize her for doing such a good thing to me? ⁷You will always have the poor among you, and you can help them whenever you want to. But

....

HIGHEST LOVE
(14:1-9) *By his statements, Jesus was not saying that we should neglect the poor or be indifferent to them. He simply was praising Mary for her unselfish act of worship. The essence of worshiping Christ is to regard him with utmost love, respect, and devotion—and to be willing to sacrifice to him what is most precious. Is that the kind of love you have for him?*

13:24-25 See Isa 13:10; 34:4; Joel 2:10.   **13:26a** "Son of Man" is a title Jesus used for himself.   **13:26b** See Dan 7:13.   **13:27** Greek *from the four winds.*   **13:30** Or *this age,* or *this nation.*   **13:33** Some manuscripts add *and pray.*   **14:3** Or *reclining.*   **14:5** Greek *for 300 denarii.* A denarius was equivalent to a laborer's full day's wage.

JESUS' TRIAL
After his arrest in Gethsemane, Jesus' trial began at the home of Caiaphas, the high priest. He was then taken to Pilate, the Roman governor. Luke records that Pilate sent him to Herod, who was in Jerusalem. Herod sent him back to Pilate, who sentenced him to be crucified.

you will not always have me. ⁸She has done what she could and has anointed my body for burial ahead of time. ⁹I tell you the truth, wherever the Good News is preached throughout the world, this woman's deed will be remembered and discussed."

JUDAS AGREES TO BETRAY JESUS ¹⁰Then Judas Iscariot, one of the twelve disciples, went to the leading priests to arrange to betray Jesus to them. ¹¹They were delighted when they heard why he had come, and they promised to give him money. So he began looking for an opportunity to betray Jesus.

THE LAST SUPPER ¹²On the first day of the Festival of Unleavened Bread, when the Pass-

BETRAYAL
(14:19) Judas was at the table with the others. He had already determined to betray Jesus, but in cold-blooded hypocrisy he shared the fellowship of this meal. We can easily become enraged or shocked by what Judas did, yet when we profess commitment to Christ and then deny him with how we live, we also betray him. We deny Christ's truth because he taught us how to live, and we live otherwise. We deny Christ's love by not obeying him. And we deny Christ's deity by rejecting his authority. Do your words and actions match? If not, consider a change of mind and heart that will protect you from making a terrible mistake.

over lamb is sacrificed, Jesus' disciples asked him, "Where do you want us to go to prepare the Passover meal for you?"

¹³So Jesus sent two of them into Jerusalem with these instructions: "As you go into the city, a man carrying a pitcher of water will meet you. Follow him. ¹⁴At the house he enters, say to the owner, 'The Teacher asks: Where is the guest room where I can eat the Passover meal with my disciples?' ¹⁵He will take you upstairs to a large room that is already set up. That is where you should prepare our meal." ¹⁶So the two disciples went into the city and found everything just as Jesus had said, and they prepared the Passover meal there.

¹⁷In the evening Jesus arrived with the twelve disciples.* ¹⁸As they were at the table* eating, Jesus said, "I tell you the truth, one of you eating with me here will betray me."

¹⁹Greatly distressed, each one asked in turn, "Am I the one?"

²⁰He replied, "It is one of you twelve who is eating from this bowl with me. ²¹For the Son of Man* must die, as the Scriptures declared long ago. But how terrible it will be for the one who betrays him. It would be far better for that man if he had never been born!"

²²As they were eating, Jesus took some bread and blessed it. Then he broke it in pieces and gave it to the disciples, saying, "Take it, for this is my body."

²³And he took a cup of wine and gave thanks to God for it. He gave it to them, and they all drank from it. ²⁴And he said to them, "This is my blood, which confirms the covenant* between God and his people. It is poured out as a sacrifice for many. ²⁵I tell you the truth, I will not drink wine again until the day I drink it new in the Kingdom of God."

²⁶Then they sang a hymn and went out to the Mount of Olives.

JESUS PREDICTS PETER'S DENIAL ²⁷On the way, Jesus told them, "All of you will desert me. For the Scriptures say,

'God will strike* the Shepherd,
    and the sheep will be scattered.'

²⁸But after I am raised from the dead, I will go ahead of you to Galilee and meet you there."

²⁹Peter said to him, "Even if everyone else deserts you, I never will."

³⁰Jesus replied, "I tell you the truth, Peter— this very night, before the rooster crows

14:17 Greek *the Twelve.* **14:18** Or *As they reclined.* **14:21** "Son of Man" is a title Jesus used for himself. **14:24** Some manuscripts read *the new covenant.* **14:27** Greek *I will strike.* Zech 13:7.

twice, you will deny three times that you even know me."

[31]"No!" Peter declared emphatically. "Even if I have to die with you, I will never deny you!" And all the others vowed the same.

JESUS PRAYS IN GETHSEMANE

[32]They went to the olive grove called Gethsemane, and Jesus said, "Sit here while I go and pray." [33]He took Peter, James, and John with him, and he became deeply troubled and distressed. [34]He told them, "My soul is crushed with grief to the point of death. Stay here and keep watch with me."

[35]He went on a little farther and fell to the ground. He prayed that, if it were possible, the awful hour awaiting him might pass him by. [36]"Abba, Father,"* he cried out, "everything is possible for you. Please take this cup of suffering away from me. Yet I want your will to be done, not mine."

[37]Then he returned and found the disciples asleep. He said to Peter, "Simon, are you asleep? Couldn't you watch with me even one hour? [38]Keep watch and pray, so that you will not give in to temptation. For the spirit is willing, but the body is weak."

[39]Then Jesus left them again and prayed the same prayer as before. [40]When he returned to them again, he found them sleeping, for they couldn't keep their eyes open. And they didn't know what to say.

[41]When he returned to them the third time, he said, "Go ahead and sleep. Have your rest. But no—the time has come. The Son of Man is betrayed into the hands of sinners. [42]Up, let's be going. Look, my betrayer is here!"

JESUS IS BETRAYED AND ARRESTED

[43]And immediately, even as Jesus said this, Judas, one of the twelve disciples, arrived with a crowd of men armed with swords and clubs. They had been sent by the leading priests, the teachers of religious law, and the elders. [44]The traitor, Judas, had given them a prearranged signal: "You will know which one to arrest when I greet him with a kiss. Then you can take him away under guard." [45]As soon as they arrived, Judas walked up to Jesus. "Rabbi!" he exclaimed, and gave him the kiss.

[46]Then the others grabbed Jesus and arrested him. [47]But one of the men with Jesus pulled out his sword and struck the high priest's slave, slashing off his ear.

[48]Jesus asked them, "Am I some dangerous

14:36 *Abba* is an Aramaic term for "father."   **14:55** Greek *the Sanhedrin.*

JESUS' ROUTE TO GOLGOTHA
After being sentenced by Pilate, Jesus was taken from the governor's headquarters (the Praetorium) to Golgotha, a place outside of Jerusalem, for crucifixion.

revolutionary, that you come with swords and clubs to arrest me? [49]Why didn't you arrest me in the Temple? I was there among you teaching every day. But these things are happening to fulfill what the Scriptures say about me."

[50]Then all his disciples deserted him and ran away. [51]One young man following behind was clothed only in a long linen shirt. When the mob tried to grab him, [52]he slipped out of his shirt and ran away naked.

JESUS BEFORE THE COUNCIL

[53]They took Jesus to the high priest's home where the leading priests, the elders, and the teachers of religious law had gathered. [54]Meanwhile, Peter followed him at a distance and went right into the high priest's courtyard. There he sat with the guards, warming himself by the fire.

[55]Inside, the leading priests and the entire high council* were trying to find evidence against Jesus, so they could put him to death. But they couldn't find any. [56]Many false witnesses spoke against him, but they contradicted each other. [57]Finally, some men stood up and gave this false testimony: [58]"We heard him say, 'I will destroy this Temple made with human hands, and in three days I will build another, made without human hands.'" [59]But even then they didn't get their stories straight!

[60]Then the high priest stood up before the others and asked Jesus, "Well, aren't you

going to answer these charges? What do you have to say for yourself?" [61]But Jesus was silent and made no reply. Then the high priest asked him, "Are you the Messiah, the Son of the Blessed One?"

[62]Jesus said, "I AM.* And you will see the Son of Man seated in the place of power at God's right hand* and coming on the clouds of heaven.*"

[63]Then the high priest tore his clothing to show his horror and said, "Why do we need other witnesses? [64]You have all heard his blasphemy. What is your verdict?"

"Guilty!" they all cried. "He deserves to die!"

[65]Then some of them began to spit at him, and they blindfolded him and beat him with their fists. "Prophesy to us," they jeered. And the guards slapped him as they took him away.

PETER DENIES JESUS [66]Meanwhile, Peter was in the courtyard below. One of the servant girls who worked for the high priest came by [67]and noticed Peter warming himself at the fire. She looked at him closely and said, "You were one of those with Jesus of Nazareth.*"

[68]But Peter denied it. "I don't know what you're talking about," he said, and he went out into the entryway. Just then, a rooster crowed.*

....

ALL TO BLAME
(14:55-72) The members of the Jewish Sanhedrin are easy targets for our anger because of their injustice in condemning Jesus. Yet Peter and the rest of the disciples also contributed to Jesus' pain by deserting him and denying him (14:50, 66-72). We might shake our heads at their actions, thinking that we would never do such a thing. But how many of us deny Jesus by keeping silent about our Christianity or going along with actions that are contrary to God's word? Every wrong thing we do is a denial of Jesus. Tempted to point the finger at someone who messed up? Show them compassion by remembering that you've messed up too.

GUILTY
(15:15) Who was guilty of Jesus' death? In reality, everyone was at fault. The disciples deserted him in fear. Peter denied that he even knew Jesus. Judas betrayed him. The crowds who had cheered him stood by and did nothing. Pilate tried to blame the mob. The religious leaders actively promoted Jesus' death. The Roman soldiers tortured and crucified him. If you were there watching these trials, how would you have responded?

THE RIGHT THING
(15:15) Although Jesus was innocent according to Roman law, Pilate caved in under political pressure. He abandoned what he knew was right in his struggle to give a decision that would please everyone and keep himself safe. When we ignore God's statements of right and wrong and make decisions based on our audience, we compromise. God promises to honor those who do what's right, not those who make everyone happy.

[69]When the servant girl saw him standing there, she began telling the others, "This man is definitely one of them!" [70]But Peter denied it again.

A little later some of the other bystanders confronted Peter and said, "You must be one of them, because you are a Galilean."

[71]Peter swore, "A curse on me if I'm lying— I don't know this man you're talking about!" [72]And immediately the rooster crowed the second time.

Suddenly, Jesus' words flashed through Peter's mind: "Before the rooster crows twice, you will deny three times that you even know me." And he broke down and wept.

15 **JESUS' TRIAL BEFORE PILATE** Very early in the morning the leading priests, the elders, and the teachers of religious law—the entire high council*—met to discuss their next step. They bound Jesus, led him away, and took him to Pilate, the Roman governor.

[2]Pilate asked Jesus, "Are you the king of the Jews?"

Jesus replied, "You have said it."

[3]Then the leading priests kept accusing him of many crimes, [4]and Pilate asked him, "Aren't you going to answer them? What about all these charges they are bringing against you?" [5]But Jesus said nothing, much to Pilate's surprise.

[6]Now it was the governor's custom each year during the Passover celebration to release one prisoner—anyone the people requested. [7]One of the prisoners at that time was Barabbas, a revolutionary who had committed murder in an uprising. [8]The crowd went to Pilate and asked him to release a prisoner as usual.

[9]"Would you like me to release to you this 'King of the Jews'?" Pilate asked. [10](For he realized by now that the leading priests had arrested Jesus out of envy.) [11]But at this point the leading priests stirred up the crowd to demand the release of Barabbas instead of Jesus. [12]Pilate asked them, "Then what should I do with this man you call the king of the Jews?"

[13]They shouted back, "Crucify him!"

[14]"Why?" Pilate demanded. "What crime has he committed?"

But the mob roared even louder, "Crucify him!"

[15]So to pacify the crowd, Pilate released Bar-

14:62a Or *The 'I AM' is here; or I am the LORD.* See Exod 3:14.
14:62b Greek *seated at the right hand of the power.* See Ps 110:1.
14:62c See Dan 7:13.   **14:67** Or *Jesus the Nazarene.*   **14:68** Some manuscripts do not include *Just then, a rooster crowed.*   **15:1** Greek *the Sanhedrin;* also in 15:43.

EVIDENCE THAT JESUS ACTUALLY DIED AND ROSE AGAIN

This evidence demonstrates Jesus' uniqueness in history and proves that he is God's Son. No one else has ever been able to predict his own resurrection and then accomplish it.

PROPOSED EXPLANATIONS FOR EMPTY TOMB	EVIDENCE AGAINST THESE EXPLANATIONS	REFERENCES
Jesus was only unconscious and later revived	A Roman soldier told Pilate that Jesus was dead.	Mark 15:44-45
	The Roman soldiers did not break Jesus' legs because he had already died, and one of them pierced Jesus' side with a spear.	John 19:32-34
	Joseph of Arimathea and Nicodemus wrapped Jesus' body and placed it in the tomb.	John 19:38-40
The women made a mistake and went to the wrong tomb.	Mary Magdalene and Mary the mother of Jesus saw Jesus placed in the tomb.	Matthew 27:59-61 Mark 15:47 Luke 23:55
	On Sunday morning, Peter and John also went to the same tomb.	John 20:3-9
Unknown thieves stole Jesus' body.	The tomb was sealed and guarded by Roman soldiers.	Matthew 27:65-66
The disciples stole Jesus' body	The disciples were ready to die for their faith. Stealing Jesus' body would have been admitting their faith was meaningless.	Acts 12:2
	The tomb was guarded and sealed.	Matthew 27:65-66
The religious leaders stole Jesus' body to secure it.	If the religious leaders had taken Jesus' body, they would have produced it to stop the rumors of his resurrection.	None

abbas to them. He ordered Jesus flogged with a lead-tipped whip, then turned him over to the Roman soldiers to be crucified.

THE SOLDIERS MOCK JESUS ¹⁶The soldiers took Jesus into the courtyard of the governor's headquarters (called the Praetorium) and called out the entire regiment. ¹⁷They dressed him in a purple robe, and they wove thorn branches into a crown and put it on his head. ¹⁸Then they saluted him and taunted, "Hail! King of the Jews!" ¹⁹And they struck him on the head with a reed stick, spit on him, and dropped to their knees in mock worship. ²⁰When they were finally tired of mocking him, they took off the purple robe and put his own

15:21 *Cyrene* was a city in northern Africa.   15:24 Greek *cast lots.* See Ps 22:18.   15:27a Or *Two criminals.*   15:27b Some manuscripts add verse 28, *And the Scripture was fulfilled that said, "He was counted among those who were rebels."* See Isa 53:12; also compare Luke 22:37.

clothes on him again. Then they led him away to be crucified.

THE CRUCIFIXION ²¹A passerby named Simon, who was from Cyrene,* was coming in from the countryside just then, and the soldiers forced him to carry Jesus' cross. (Simon was the father of Alexander and Rufus.) ²²And they brought Jesus to a place called Golgotha (which means "Place of the Skull"). ²³They offered him wine drugged with myrrh, but he refused it.

²⁴Then the soldiers nailed him to the cross. They divided his clothes and threw dice* to decide who would get each piece. ²⁵It was nine o'clock in the morning when they crucified him. ²⁶A sign announced the charge against him. It read, "The King of the Jews." ²⁷Two revolutionaries* were crucified with him, one on his right and one on his left.*

²⁹The people passing by shouted abuse, shaking their heads in mockery. "Ha! Look at you now!" they yelled at him. "You said you were going to destroy the Temple and rebuild it in three days. ³⁰Well then, save yourself and come down from the cross!"

³¹The leading priests and teachers of religious law also mocked Jesus. "He saved others," they scoffed, "but he can't save himself! ³²Let this Messiah, this King of Israel, come down from the cross so we can see it and believe him!" Even the men who were crucified with Jesus ridiculed him.

• •

RIGHT AND LEFT

(15:27) *When James and John asked Jesus for the places of honor next to him in his Kingdom, Jesus told them that they didn't know what they were asking (10:35-39). Here, where Jesus was preparing to inaugurate his Kingdom through his death, the places on his right and on his left were taken by dying men—criminals. As Jesus explained to his two power-hungry disciples, a person who wants to be close to him must be prepared to suffer and die as he himself was doing.*

THE DEATH OF JESUS ³³At noon, darkness fell across the whole land until three o'clock. ³⁴Then at three o'clock Jesus called out with a loud voice, "Eloi, Eloi, lema sabachthani?" which means "My God, my God, why have you abandoned me?"*

³⁵Some of the bystanders misunderstood and thought he was calling for the prophet Elijah. ³⁶One of them ran and filled a sponge with sour wine, holding it up to him on a reed stick so he could drink. "Wait!" he said. "Let's see whether Elijah comes to take him down!"

³⁷Then Jesus uttered another loud cry and breathed his last. ³⁸And the curtain in the sanctuary of the Temple was torn in two, from top to bottom.

³⁹When the Roman officer* who stood facing him* saw how he had died, he exclaimed, "This man truly was the Son of God!"

⁴⁰Some women were there, watching from a distance, including Mary Magdalene, Mary

15:34 Ps 22:1.   **15:39a** Greek *the centurion;* similarly in 15:44, 45.
15:39b Some manuscripts add *heard his cry and.*

ULTIMATE ISSUES *THE RESURRECTION*

Often, when life seems bleak and hopeless, something happens that puts things in a new perspective.

Imagine what must have been going through the disciples' minds as they witnessed (or heard about) the crucifixion of their Master. All their hopes and expectations—lifeless as the corpse that Joseph of Arimathea took away and laid in his tomb. Dead! Broken and crushed . . . along with the dreams of the Twelve and many others who had truly believed that Jesus was the Messiah who would lead Israel to freedom. And now he lay rotting in a tomb.

If that were the end of the story, you would never have heard of Jesus or Christianity. Jesus' followers would have disappeared like the followers of dozens of other would-be messiahs. If that were the end, you wouldn't be holding this book in your hands, reading it as countless millions of others have, and basing your life on its principles. There would be no churches, nor any trace of this faith that has spread around the world. But Jesus' death was not the end. It was only the beginning.

You probably are familiar with the story of the Resurrection. The bare facts are that Jesus was put to death by crucifixion, his body was placed in a borrowed tomb, and his followers were scattered and dejected. But, as Mark 16 tells us, Jesus didn't stay dead. On the Sunday morning following his death, strange events unfolded around his grave.

The strangest of all was that the tomb was empty; Jesus had risen from the dead!

We have a tendency to take the resurrection story for granted—after all, we may have heard it dozens or even hundreds of times. But we need to remember that people didn't vacate their graves 2,000 years ago in Palestine any more than they do today. Dead people stayed dead back then, just like they do now.

Except for Jesus. Jesus' resurrection has made all the difference for countless Christians. When the early Christians, including the disciples, were called upon to defend their faith in Jesus as the Messiah, they didn't point to his great moral teachings and ethical principles. They didn't even refer to his miracles. They pointed to one rock-solid proof: his death and resurrection. If anyone had ever shown that it was science fiction—perhaps by getting one of the disciples to confess that it was a lie, or going to the tomb and showing that Jesus' body was still there—Christianity would have fizzled out on the spot. It hasn't fizzled out yet, and it never will, for the very same reason: Jesus Christ rose from the dead.

Because Jesus really came back from death, it stands to reason that the rest of what he told us is true: He is the way to the Father; anyone who puts his or her faith in Christ can live forever with him in heaven; and no matter how dark it looks right now, nothing can overpower the one who won the battle with the grave. ∎

(the mother of James the younger and of Joseph*), and Salome. [41]They had been followers of Jesus and had cared for him while he was in Galilee. Many other women who had come with him to Jerusalem were also there.

THE BURIAL OF JESUS
[42]This all happened on Friday, the day of preparation,* the day before the Sabbath. As evening approached, [43]Joseph of Arimathea took a risk and went to Pilate and asked for Jesus' body. (Joseph was an honored member of the high council, and he was waiting for the Kingdom of God to come.) [44]Pilate couldn't believe that Jesus was already dead, so he called for the Roman officer and asked if he had died yet. [45]The officer confirmed that Jesus was dead, so Pilate told Joseph he could have the body. [46]Joseph bought a long sheet of linen cloth. Then he took Jesus' body down from the cross, wrapped it in the cloth, and laid it in a tomb that had been carved out of the rock. Then he rolled a stone in front of the entrance. [47]Mary Magdalene and Mary the mother of Joseph saw where Jesus' body was laid.

16 THE RESURRECTION
Saturday evening, when the Sabbath ended, Mary Magdalene, Mary the mother of James, and Salome went out and purchased burial spices so they could anoint Jesus' body. [2]Very early on Sunday morning,* just at sunrise, they went to the tomb. [3]On the way they were asking each other, "Who will roll away the stone for us from the entrance to the tomb?" [4]But as they arrived, they looked up and saw that the stone, which was very large, had already been rolled aside.

[5]When they entered the tomb, they saw a young man clothed in a white robe sitting on the right side. The women were shocked, [6]but the angel said, "Don't be alarmed. You are looking for Jesus of Nazareth,* who was crucified. He isn't here! He is risen from the dead! Look, this is where they laid his body. [7]Now go and tell his disciples, including Peter,

that Jesus is going ahead of you to Galilee. You will see him there, just as he told you before he died."

[8]The women fled from the tomb, trembling and bewildered, and they said nothing to anyone because they were too frightened.*

[Shorter Ending of Mark]

Then they briefly reported all this to Peter and his companions. Afterward Jesus himself sent them out from east to west with the sacred and unfailing message of salvation that gives eternal life. Amen.

[Longer Ending of Mark]

[9]After Jesus rose from the dead early on Sunday morning, the first person who saw him was Mary Magdalene, the woman from whom he had cast out seven demons. [10]She went to the disciples, who were grieving and weeping, and told them what had happened. [11]But when she told them that Jesus was alive and she had seen him, they didn't believe her.

[12]Afterward he appeared in a different form to two of his followers who were walking from Jerusalem into the country. [13]They rushed back to tell the others, but no one believed them.

[14]Still later he appeared to the eleven disciples as they were eating together. He rebuked them for their stubborn unbelief because they refused to believe those who had seen him after he had been raised from the dead.*

....

15:40 Greek Joses; also in 15:47. See Matt 27:56.   15:42 Greek It was the day of preparation.   16:2 Greek on the first day of the week; also in 16:9.   16:6 Or Jesus the Nazarene.   16:8 The most reliable early manuscripts of the Gospel of Mark end at verse 8. Other manuscripts include various endings to the Gospel. A few include both the "shorter ending" and the "longer ending." The majority of manuscripts include the "longer ending" immediately after verse 8.   16:14 Some early manuscripts add: And they excused themselves, saying, "This age of lawlessness and unbelief is under Satan, who does not permit God's truth and power to conquer the evil [unclean] spirits. Therefore, reveal your justice now." This is what they said to Christ. And Christ replied to them, "The period of years of Satan's power has been fulfilled, but other dreadful things will happen soon. And I was handed over to death for those who have sinned, so that they may return to the truth and sin no more, and so they may inherit the spiritual, incorruptible, and righteous glory in heaven."

RISKY BUSINESS
(15:42-46) After Jesus died on the cross, Joseph of Arimathea buried his body in a new tomb. Although he was a member of the Jewish Sanhedrin, Joseph also was a secret disciple of Jesus. He risked his reputation to give Jesus a proper burial. In the same way, taking a stand for Jesus can be risky. But consider the outcome of Joseph's actions. He's mentioned in Bibles all over the world. How many of the other members of the Jewish Supreme Court (aside from Nicodemus; see John 3) are remembered?

OPPORTUNITIES
(15:40-16:8) The women at the tomb could do very little. They couldn't speak before the Sanhedrin in Jesus' defense; they couldn't appeal to Pilate; they couldn't stand against the crowds; they couldn't overpower the Roman guards. But they did what they could. They stayed at the Cross when the disciples had fled; they followed Jesus' body to its tomb; they prepared spices for his body. Because they used the opportunities they had, they were the first to witness the Resurrection. God blessed their devotion and diligence. As believers, we should take advantage of the opportunities we have and do what we can for Christ, instead of worrying about what we cannot do.

¹⁵And then he told them, "Go into all the world and preach the Good News to everyone. ¹⁶Anyone who believes and is baptized will be saved. But anyone who refuses to believe will be condemned. ¹⁷These miraculous signs will accompany those who believe: They will cast out demons in my name, and they will speak in new languages.* ¹⁸They will be able to handle snakes with safety, and if they drink anything poisonous, it won't hurt them. They will be able to place their hands on the sick, and they will be healed."

¹⁹When the Lord Jesus had finished talking with them, he was taken up into heaven and sat down in the place of honor at God's right hand. ²⁰And the disciples went everywhere and preached, and the Lord worked through them, confirming what they said by many miraculous signs.

16:17 Or *new tongues;* some manuscripts do not include *new.*

YOU'VE GOT THE POWER

(16:15) The risen Jesus gave his disciples a mission: Make more disciples. Their mission is also the mission of believers today. Christian disciples today are living in all parts of the world, telling this Good News to people who haven't heard it. The driving power that carries missionaries around the world and sets Christ's church in motion is the faith that comes from the Resurrection. Have you ever believed that you lack the skill or determination to do anything for God? Through the Holy Spirit, you've got the power. How will you use it?

LUKE

They were two kids in love. In fact, they were engaged. As in
"headed for the altar" and "marital bliss." M & J had big plans
and even bigger dreams. Then the roof caved in. M found out
she was pregnant. J was hurt, confused, and angry. After all,
he knew he wasn't the father. There was only one thing to do:
Call off the wedding.

But weird things started happening. M claimed she'd been visited
by a real-life angel, and that she'd been made pregnant by the Spirit
of God! J had heard some wild stories before, but angels? Divine
fertilization? Come on!

Then J started seeing angels! Surely it was all a dream . . . until the
angel said (in a serious tone and with a straight face), "Don't break
off the engagement! The child really is the Savior of the world." Soon
M could no longer hide her pregnancy. People stared. Rumors flew.
M and J purposely kept a low profile. Together they wondered what it
would be like to be parents—especially of such a special child.

Did M realize that her little baby would incite a king to slaughter
thousands of newborn infants? Did J know that the child would one
day speak such profound words or perform astounding miracles? Did
these two realize their precious boy would die a brutal death?

Even if they were able to grasp any of that, did they truly believe
that their murdered son would come back to life?

You can read about M & J and their son—mainly about their son—in
the following pages. The story is the Gospel of Luke. It's one you won't
forget.

KEY POINTS

THE PERFECT MAN, THE PERFECT SACRIFICE Jesus' divine nature, life,
and sacrifice uniquely qualify him to offer forgiveness to all who believe.

HISTORY Luke emphasized dates and details, connecting Jesus to events
and people in history. Luke's accuracy assures us of the reliability of the
history of Jesus' life.

CARING FOR PEOPLE Jesus was deeply interested in people and relationships. Jesus' love for people inspires us to show the same concern for others.

HOLY SPIRIT The Holy Spirit was present at Jesus' birth, baptism, ministry,
and resurrection. As a perfect example for us, Jesus lived in dependence on
the Holy Spirit. The Holy Spirit enables believers to live for Christ. By faith
we can have the Holy Spirit's presence and power to witness and to serve.

STATS

PURPOSE
To present an accurate
account of the life of Christ
and to present Christ as the
perfect man and Savior

AUTHOR
Luke, a Greek doctor (Col
4:14). He also wrote the book
of Acts and is the only known
Gentile author in the New
Testament. He was a close
friend and companion of Paul.

ORIGINAL AUDIENCE
Theophilus ("lover of God")
and Gentiles

DATE WRITTEN
About A.D. 60

SETTING
Luke wrote from either
Caesarea or Rome.

KEY PEOPLE
Jesus, the disciples, John
the Baptist, Mary, Mary
Magdalene

KEY PLACES
Bethlehem, Galilee, Judea,
Jerusalem

TIMELINE

37 B.C.
Herod the Great begins to rule
6/5 B.C.
Jesus is born
5/4 B.C.
Jesus' family escapes to Egypt
4 B.C.
Herod the Great dies
4/3 B.C.
**Jesus' family returns
to Nazareth**
A.D. 6/7
**Jesus visits the Temple
as a boy**
14
**Tiberius Caesar becomes
emperor**
26
**John the Baptist begins his
ministry**
26/27
Jesus begins his ministry
28
Jesus chooses 12 disciples
29
Jesus feeds 5,000
30
**Jesus is crucified, rises again,
and ascends to heaven**

THE PEOPLE AND PLACES
OF JESUS' MINISTRY

Luke's account begins in the Temple in Jerusalem, giving us the background for the birth of John the Baptist (1:5-25), and then moves on to the city of Nazareth and the story of Mary, chosen to be Jesus' mother (1:26-38). As a result of Caesar's call for a census, Mary and Joseph had to travel to Bethlehem, where Jesus was born in fulfillment of prophecy (2:1-20). Jesus grew up in Nazareth and began his earthly ministry by being baptized by John (3:21-22) and tempted by Satan (4:1-13). Much of his ministry focused on Galilee—he set up his "home base" in Capernaum (4:31), and from there he taught throughout the region (8:1-3). Later he visited the Gerasene country, where he healed a demon-possessed man from Gerasa (8:26-39). He fed more than 5,000 people with one lunch on the shores of the Sea of Galilee near Bethsaida (9:10-17). Jesus traveled to Jerusalem for the major feasts and enjoyed visiting friends in nearby Bethany (10:38-42). He healed 10 men with leprosy on the border between Galilee and Samaria (17:11-15) and helped a dishonest tax collector in Jericho turn his life around (19:1-10). The little villages of Bethphage and Bethany on the Mount of Olives were Jesus' resting places during his last days on earth. He was crucified outside Jerusalem's walls, but he would rise again. Two people on the road leading to Emmaus were among the first to see the resurrected Christ (24:13-34).

The broken lines (–·–·–) indicate modern boundaries.

1 INTRODUCTION
Many people have set out to write accounts about the events that have been fulfilled among us. ²They used the eyewitness reports circulating among us from the early disciples.* ³Having carefully investigated everything from the beginning, I also have decided to write a careful account for you, most honorable Theophilus, ⁴so you can be certain of the truth of everything you were taught.

THE BIRTH OF JOHN THE BAPTIST FORETOLD
⁵When Herod was king of Judea, there was a Jewish priest named Zechariah. He was a member of the priestly order of Abijah, and his wife, Elizabeth, was also from the priestly line of Aaron. ⁶Zechariah and Elizabeth were righteous in God's eyes, careful to obey all of the Lord's commandments and regulations. ⁷They

had no children because Elizabeth was unable to conceive, and they were both very old.

⁸One day Zechariah was serving God in the Temple, for his order was on duty that week. ⁹As was the custom of the priests, he was chosen by lot to enter the sanctuary of the Lord and burn incense. ¹⁰While the incense was being burned, a great crowd stood outside, praying.

¹¹While Zechariah was in the sanctuary, an angel of the Lord appeared to him, standing to the right of the incense altar. ¹²Zechariah was shaken and overwhelmed with fear when he saw him. ¹³But the angel said, "Don't be afraid, Zechariah! God has heard your prayer. Your wife, Elizabeth, will give you a son, and you are to name him John. ¹⁴You will have great joy and gladness, and many will rejoice at his birth,

1:2 Greek *from those who from the beginning were servants of the word.*

¹⁵for he will be great in the eyes of the Lord. He must never touch wine or other alcoholic drinks. He will be filled with the Holy Spirit, even before his birth.* ¹⁶And he will turn many Israelites to the Lord their God. ¹⁷He will be a man with the spirit and power of Elijah. He will prepare the people for the coming of the Lord. He will turn the hearts of the fathers to their children,* and he will cause those who are rebellious to accept the wisdom of the godly."

¹⁸Zechariah said to the angel, "How can I be sure this will happen? I'm an old man now, and my wife is also well along in years."

¹⁹Then the angel said, "I am Gabriel! I stand in the very presence of God. It was he who sent me to bring you this good news! ²⁰But now, since you didn't believe what I said, you will be silent and unable to speak until the child is born. For my words will certainly be fulfilled at the proper time."

²¹Meanwhile, the people were waiting for Zechariah to come out of the sanctuary, wondering why he was taking so long. ²²When he finally did come out, he couldn't speak to them. Then they realized from his gestures and his silence that he must have seen a vision in the sanctuary.

²³When Zechariah's week of service in the Temple was over, he returned home. ²⁴Soon afterward his wife, Elizabeth, became pregnant and went into seclusion for five months. ²⁵"How kind the Lord is!" she exclaimed. "He has taken away my disgrace of having no children."

THE BIRTH OF JESUS FORETOLD ²⁶In the sixth month of Elizabeth's pregnancy, God sent the angel Gabriel to Nazareth, a village in Galilee, ²⁷to a virgin named Mary. She was engaged to be married to a man named Joseph, a descendant of King David. ²⁸Gabriel appeared to her and said, "Greetings, favored woman! The Lord is with you!*"

²⁹Confused and disturbed, Mary tried to think what the angel could mean. ³⁰"Don't be afraid, Mary," the angel told her, "for you have found favor with God! ³¹You will conceive and give birth to a son, and you will name him Jesus. ³²He will be very great and will be called the Son of the Most High. The Lord God will give him the throne of his ancestor David. ³³And he will reign over Israel* forever; his Kingdom will never end!"

1:15 Or even from birth.   1:17 See Mal 4:5-6.   1:28 Some manuscripts add Blessed are you among women.   1:33 Greek over the house of Jacob.   1:37 Some manuscripts read For the word of God will never fail.

³⁴Mary asked the angel, "But how can this happen? I am a virgin."

³⁵The angel replied, "The Holy Spirit will come upon you, and the power of the Most High will overshadow you. So the baby to be born will be holy, and he will be called the Son of God. ³⁶What's more, your relative Elizabeth has become pregnant in her old age! People used to say she was barren, but she has conceived a son and is now in her sixth month. ³⁷For nothing is impossible with God.*"

³⁸Mary responded, "I am the Lord's servant. May everything you have said about me come true." And then the angel left her.

MARY VISITS ELIZABETH ³⁹A few days later Mary hurried to the hill country of Judea, to the town ⁴⁰where Zechariah lived. She entered the house and greeted Elizabeth. ⁴¹At the sound of Mary's greeting, Elizabeth's child leaped within her, and Elizabeth was filled with the Holy Spirit.

⁴²Elizabeth gave a glad cry and exclaimed to Mary, "God has blessed you above all women, and your child is blessed. ⁴³Why am I so honored, that the mother of my Lord should visit me? ⁴⁴When I heard your greeting, the baby in my womb jumped for joy. ⁴⁵You are blessed because you believed that the Lord would do what he said."

THE MAGNIFICAT: MARY'S SONG OF PRAISE ⁴⁶Mary responded,

"Oh, how my soul praises the Lord.
⁴⁷ How my spirit rejoices in God my Savior!
⁴⁸ For he took notice of his lowly servant girl,

ALL CHECKED OUT
(1:1-3) As a medical doctor, Luke knew the importance of a thorough checkup. He used his skills in observation and analysis to do a complete investigation of the stories about Jesus. His diagnosis? The gospel of Jesus Christ is true! You can read Luke's account of Jesus' life with confidence that it was written by a clear thinker and a thoughtful researcher. Because the gospel is founded on historical truth, our spiritual growth must involve careful, disciplined, thorough investigation of God's Word. If this kind of study is not part of your life, find a pastor, teacher, or book to help you get started and to guide you in this important part of Christian growth.

UNLIKELY
(1:26-55) Mary was young, poor, and female—all characteristics that, to the people of her day, would make her seem useless to God for any major task. But God chose Mary for one of the most important acts of obedience he has ever asked of anyone. Ever feel that your situation in life makes you an unlikely candidate for God's service? He can use you if you trust him. Do you?

and from now on all generations will call
me blessed.
49 For the Mighty One is holy,
and he has done great things for me.
50 He shows mercy from generation to
generation
to all who fear him.
51 His mighty arm has done tremendous
things!
He has scattered the proud and
haughty ones.
52 He has brought down princes from their
thrones
and exalted the humble.
53 He has filled the hungry with good things
and sent the rich away with empty hands.
54 He has helped his servant Israel
and remembered to be merciful.
55 For he made this promise to our ancestors,
to Abraham and his children forever."

56Mary stayed with Elizabeth about three
months and then went back to her own home.

THE BIRTH OF JOHN THE BAPTIST

57When it
was time for Elizabeth's baby to be born, she
gave birth to a son. 58And when her neighbors
and relatives heard that the Lord had been
very merciful to her, everyone rejoiced with
her.

59When the baby was eight days old, they
all came for the circumcision ceremony. They
wanted to name him Zechariah, after his father. 60But Elizabeth said, "No! His name is
John!"

61"What?" they exclaimed. "There is no one
in all your family by that name." 62So they
used gestures to ask the baby's father what he
wanted to name him. 63He motioned for a writing tablet, and to everyone's surprise he wrote,
"His name is John." 64Instantly Zechariah could
speak again, and he began praising God.

65Awe fell upon the whole neighborhood,
and the news of what had happened spread
throughout the Judean hills. 66Everyone who
heard about it reflected on these events and
asked, "What will this child turn out to be?" For

MARY
PERSONALITY PROFILE

MARY OF NAZARETH HAD BEEN UNIQUELY CHOSEN to be the mother of the Son
of God. Mary was the only human present at Jesus' birth who also witnessed
his death. She saw Jesus arrive as her baby son, and she watched him die as
her Savior.

Until Gabriel's surprise visit, Mary's life was going well. She had recently
become engaged to a local carpenter, Joseph, and was anticipating married life.
But God had additional plans for her.

Angels don't usually make appointments before visiting. They just show up.
The angel greeted Mary as if she were the winner of a contest she had never
entered. But Mary found the angel's greeting puzzling and his presence frightening. What she heard next was the news almost every woman in Israel hoped
to hear—that her child would be the Messiah, God's promised Savior. Mary
didn't doubt the message nor did she worry about how her pregnancy would
look to others. She just wondered how she could be pregnant without the
involvement of a man. Gabriel told her that the baby would be God's Son.

Mary's answer was one that God waits to hear from every person: "I am
the Lord's servant. May everything you have said about me come true" (Luke
1:38). Later, her song of joy to Elizabeth shows us how well Mary knew God. Her
thoughts were filled with his words from the Scriptures (1:46-55).

After Jesus' birth, he was taken to the Temple to be dedicated to God. A man
named Simeon had shocking words for Mary concerning the future: "And a
sword will pierce your very soul" (Luke 2:35).

We can imagine that even if she had known all that she would suffer as
Jesus' mother, Mary would have given the same response. Is your life as available to be used by God as Mary's was?

BOTTOM LINE: God's plans involve extraordinary events in the lives of ordinary
people.

A person's character is revealed by his or her response to the unexpected.

Mary's story is told throughout the Gospels. She also is mentioned in Acts 1:14.

UPS:
• *Mother of Jesus, the
Messiah*
• *The one person who knew
Jesus from birth to death*
• *Willing to be available
to God*
• *Knew and applied God's
Word*

STATS:
• *Where: Nazareth,
Bethlehem*
• *Occupation: Homemaker*
• *Relatives: Joseph
(husband); Zechariah
and Elizabeth (relatives);
Jesus, James, Joseph,
Judas, Simon, plus
daughters (children)*

KEY VERSE: *Luke 1:38*

the hand of the Lord was surely upon him in a special way.

ZECHARIAH'S PROPHECY 67Then his father, Zechariah, was filled with the Holy Spirit and gave this prophecy:

68 "Praise the Lord, the God of Israel,
      because he has visited and redeemed
            his people.
69 He has sent us a mighty Savior*
      from the royal line of his servant David,
70 just as he promised
      through his holy prophets long ago.
71 Now we will be saved from our enemies
      and from all who hate us.
72 He has been merciful to our ancestors
      by remembering his sacred covenant—
73 the covenant he swore with an oath
      to our ancestor Abraham.
74 We have been rescued from our enemies
      so we can serve God without fear,
75 in holiness and righteousness
      for as long as we live.

76 "And you, my little son,
      will be called the prophet of the
            Most High,
      because you will prepare the way for
            the Lord.
77 You will tell his people how to find salvation
      through forgiveness of their sins.
78 Because of God's tender mercy,
      the morning light from heaven is about to
            break upon us,*
79 to give light to those who sit in darkness
      and in the shadow of death,
      and to guide us to the path of peace."

80John grew up and became strong in spirit. And he lived in the wilderness until he began his public ministry to Israel.

2 **THE BIRTH OF JESUS** At that time the Roman emperor, Augustus, decreed that a census should be taken throughout the Roman Empire. 2(This was the first census taken when Quirinius was governor of Syria.) 3All returned to their own ancestral towns to register for this census. 4And because Joseph was a descendant of King David, he had to go to Bethlehem in Judea, David's ancient home. He traveled there from the village of Nazareth in Galilee. 5He took with him Mary, his fiancée, who was now obviously pregnant.

6And while they were there, the time came for her baby to be born. 7She gave birth to her first child, a son. She wrapped him snugly in strips of cloth and laid him in a manger, because there was no lodging available for them.

THE SHEPHERDS AND ANGELS 8That night there were shepherds staying in the fields nearby, guarding their flocks of sheep. 9Suddenly, an angel of the Lord appeared among them, and the radiance of the Lord's glory surrounded them. They were terrified, 10but the angel reassured them. "Don't be afraid!" he said. "I bring you good news that will bring great joy to all people. 11The Savior—yes, the Messiah, the Lord—has been born today in Bethlehem, the city of David! 12And you will recognize him by this sign: You will find a baby wrapped snugly in strips of cloth, lying in a manger."

13Suddenly, the angel was joined by a vast host of others—the armies of heaven—praising God and saying,

14 "Glory to God in highest heaven,
      and peace on earth to those with whom
            God is pleased."

15When the angels had returned to heaven, the shepherds said to each other, "Let's go to Bethlehem! Let's see this thing that has happened, which the Lord has told us about."

16They hurried to the village and found Mary and Joseph. And there was the baby, lying in the manger. 17After seeing him, the shepherds told everyone what had happened and what the angel had said to them about this child. 18All who heard the shepherds' story were astonished, 19but Mary kept all these things in her heart and thought about them often. 20The shepherds went back to their flocks, glorifying and praising God for all they had heard and seen. It was just as the angel had told them.

JESUS IS PRESENTED IN THE TEMPLE 21Eight days later, when the baby was circumcised, he was named Jesus, the name given him by the angel even before he was conceived.

··

GROW UP
(2:7) Although our first impression of Jesus is as a baby in a manger, it must not be our last. The Christ child in the manger makes a beautiful Christmas scene, but we cannot leave him there. This tiny, helpless baby lived an amazing life, died for us, ascended to heaven, and will return to earth as King of kings. He will rule the world and judge all people according to their decisions about him. Do you still picture Jesus as a baby in a manger—or is he your Lord? Make sure you don't underestimate Jesus. Let him grow up in your life.

1:69 Greek *has raised up a horn of salvation for us.* **1:78** Or the Morning Light from Heaven is about to visit us.

²²Then it was time for their purification offering, as required by the law of Moses after the birth of a child; so his parents took him to Jerusalem to present him to the Lord. ²³The law of the Lord says, "If a woman's first child is a boy, he must be dedicated to the Lord."* ²⁴So they offered the sacrifice required in the law of the Lord—"either a pair of turtledoves or two young pigeons."*

THE PROPHECY OF SIMEON
²⁵At that time there was a man in Jerusalem named Simeon. He was righteous and devout and was eagerly waiting for the Messiah to come and rescue Israel. The Holy Spirit was upon him ²⁶and had revealed to him that he would not die until he had seen the Lord's Messiah. ²⁷That day the Spirit led him to the Temple. So when Mary and Joseph came to present the baby Jesus to the Lord as the law required, ²⁸Simeon was there. He took the child in his arms and praised God, saying,

²⁹ "Sovereign Lord, now let your servant die
      in peace,
      as you have promised.
³⁰ I have seen your salvation,
³¹   which you have prepared for all people.
³² He is a light to reveal God to the nations,
      and he is the glory of your people Israel!"

³³Jesus' parents were amazed at what was being said about him. ³⁴Then Simeon blessed them, and he said to Mary, the baby's mother, "This child is destined to cause many in Israel to fall, but he will be a joy to many others. He has been sent as a sign from God, but many

....

ELDER WISDOM
(2:25-38) Although Simeon and Anna were very old, they still hoped to see the Messiah. Led by the Holy Spirit, they were among the first to proclaim the arrival of the Savior. Since elders were respected in the Jewish culture, Simeon's and Anna's prophecies carried extra weight. The opposite happens in our society. The opinions of youth often carry more weight, particularly with advertisers, than those of senior citizens. Think about the older people in your life or in your area. What have you learned from them? How can you encourage them through your friendship? You might be surprised at what you can teach each other!

GRIT AND SUBMIT?
(2:46-52) This is the first hint that Jesus realized he was God's Son. Even though Jesus knew his real Father, he didn't reject his earthly parents. Jesus went back to Nazareth with them and lived under their authority for another 18 years. Do you find yourself grumbling about your parents' authority sometimes? Consider this: The Son of God submitted to the authority of his parents. How do you show by your actions that you're willing to submit?

will oppose him. ³⁵As a result, the deepest thoughts of many hearts will be revealed. And a sword will pierce your very soul."

THE PROPHECY OF ANNA
³⁶Anna, a prophet, was also there in the Temple. She was the daughter of Phanuel from the tribe of Asher, and she was very old. Her husband died when they had been married only seven years. ³⁷Then she lived as a widow to the age of eighty-four.* She never left the Temple but stayed there day and night, worshiping God with fasting and prayer. ³⁸She came along just as Simeon was talking with Mary and Joseph, and she began praising God. She talked about the child to everyone who had been waiting expectantly for God to rescue Jerusalem.

³⁹When Jesus' parents had fulfilled all the requirements of the law of the Lord, they returned home to Nazareth in Galilee. ⁴⁰There the child grew up healthy and strong. He was filled with wisdom, and God's favor was on him.

JESUS SPEAKS WITH THE TEACHERS
⁴¹Every year Jesus' parents went to Jerusalem for the Passover festival. ⁴²When Jesus was twelve years old, they attended the festival as usual. ⁴³After the celebration was over, they started home to Nazareth, but Jesus stayed behind in Jerusalem. His parents didn't miss him at first, ⁴⁴because they assumed he was among the other travelers. But when he didn't show up that evening, they started looking for him among their relatives and friends.

⁴⁵When they couldn't find him, they went back to Jerusalem to search for him there. ⁴⁶Three days later they finally discovered him in the Temple, sitting among the religious teachers, listening to them and asking questions. ⁴⁷All who heard him were amazed at his understanding and his answers.

⁴⁸His parents didn't know what to think. "Son," his mother said to him, "why have you done this to us? Your father and I have been frantic, searching for you everywhere."

⁴⁹"But why did you need to search?" he asked. "Didn't you know that I must be in my Father's house?"* ⁵⁰But they didn't understand what he meant.

⁵¹Then he returned to Nazareth with them and was obedient to them. And his mother stored all these things in her heart.

⁵²Jesus grew in wisdom and in stature and in favor with God and all the people.

2:23 Exod 13:2. 2:24 Lev 12:8. 2:37 Or *She had been a widow for eighty-four years.* 2:49 Or *"Didn't you realize that I should be involved with my Father's affairs?"*

3 **JOHN THE BAPTIST PREPARES THE WAY** It was now the fifteenth year of the reign of Tiberius, the Roman emperor. Pontius Pilate was governor over Judea; Herod Antipas was ruler* over Galilee; his brother Philip was ruler* over Iturea and Traconitis; Lysanias was ruler over Abilene. ²Annas and Caiaphas were the high priests. At this time a message from God came to John son of Zechariah, who was living in the wilderness. ³Then John went from place to place on both sides of the Jordan River, preaching that people should be baptized to show that they had repented of their sins and turned to God to be forgiven. ⁴Isaiah had spoken of John when he said,

"He is a voice shouting in the wilderness,
'Prepare the way for the LORD's coming!
    Clear the road for him!
⁵ The valleys will be filled,
    and the mountains and hills made level.
The curves will be straightened,
    and the rough places made smooth.
⁶ And then all people will see
    the salvation sent from God.'"*

⁷When the crowds came to John for baptism, he said, "You brood of snakes! Who warned you to flee God's coming wrath? ⁸Prove by the way you live that you have repented of your sins and turned to God. Don't just say to each other, 'We're safe, for we are descendants of Abraham.' That means nothing, for I tell you, God can create children of Abraham from these very stones. ⁹Even now the ax of God's judgment is poised, ready to sever the roots of the trees. Yes, every tree that does not produce good fruit will be chopped down and thrown into the fire."

¹⁰The crowds asked, "What should we do?"

¹¹John replied, "If you have two shirts, give one to the poor. If you have food, share it with those who are hungry."

¹²Even corrupt tax collectors came to be baptized and asked, "Teacher, what should we do?"

¹³He replied, "Collect no more taxes than the government requires."

¹⁴"What should we do?" asked some soldiers. John replied, "Don't extort money or make false accusations. And be content with your pay."

¹⁵Everyone was expecting the Messiah to come soon, and they were eager to know whether John might be the Messiah. ¹⁶John answered their questions by saying, "I baptize you with* water; but someone is coming soon who is greater than I am—so much greater that I'm not even worthy to be his slave and untie the straps of his sandals. He will baptize you with the Holy Spirit and with fire.* ¹⁷He is ready to separate the chaff from the wheat with his winnowing fork. Then he will clean up the threshing area, gathering the wheat into his barn but burning the chaff with never-ending fire." ¹⁸John used many such warnings as he announced the Good News to the people.

¹⁹John also publicly criticized Herod Antipas, the ruler of Galilee,* for marrying Herodias, his brother's wife, and for many other wrongs he had done. ²⁰So Herod put John in prison, adding this sin to his many others.

THE BAPTISM OF JESUS ²¹One day when the crowds were being baptized, Jesus himself was baptized. As he was praying, the heavens opened, ²²and the Holy Spirit, in bodily form, descended on him like a dove. And a voice from heaven said, "You are my dearly loved Son, and you bring me great joy.*"

THE ANCESTORS OF JESUS ²³Jesus was about thirty years old when he began his public ministry.

Jesus was known as the son of Joseph.
Joseph was the son of Heli.
²⁴ Heli was the son of Matthat.
Matthat was the son of Levi.

....

ON YOUR OWN
(3:7-9) Many of John's hearers were shocked when he said that being Abraham's descendants was not enough. The religious leaders relied more on their family line than on their faith. They thought being descendants of Abraham automatically made them right with God. Many people today think that having parents who are Christians automatically makes them Christians too. But a relationship with God isn't handed down from parents to children. Everyone has to have his or her own relationship with God. As the old saying goes, God has children—not grandchildren. Are you relying on the faith of your family or your own?

TIMING
(3:23) Imagine the Savior of the world driving nails in some small-town carpenter's shop until he was 30 years old! Jesus patiently trusted the Father's timing for his life and ministry. Do you have the same level of trust? If you're a believer, God wants the final say in your decisions. Waiting on his timing means letting go of your right to run your life, and being patient when you want to run ahead of God.

3:1a Greek *Herod was tetrarch.* Herod Antipas was a son of King Herod. **3:1b** Greek *tetrarch;* also in 3:1c. **3:4-6** Isa 40:3-5 (Greek version). **3:16a** Or *in.* **3:16b** Or *in the Holy Spirit and in fire.* **3:19** Greek *Herod the tetrarch.* **3:22** Some manuscripts read *my Son, and today I have become your Father.*

Levi was the son of Melki.
Melki was the son of Jannai.
Jannai was the son of Joseph.
²⁵ Joseph was the son of Mattathias.
Mattathias was the son of Amos.
Amos was the son of Nahum.
Nahum was the son of Esli.
Esli was the son of Naggai.
²⁶ Naggai was the son of Maath.
Maath was the son of Mattathias.
Mattathias was the son of Semein.
Semein was the son of Josech.
Josech was the son of Joda.
²⁷ Joda was the son of Joanan.
Joanan was the son of Rhesa.
Rhesa was the son of Zerubbabel.
Zerubbabel was the son of Shealtiel.
Shealtiel was the son of Neri.
²⁸ Neri was the son of Melki.
Melki was the son of Addi.
Addi was the son of Cosam.
Cosam was the son of Elmadam.
Elmadam was the son of Er.
²⁹ Er was the son of Joshua.
Joshua was the son of Eliezer.
Eliezer was the son of Jorim.
Jorim was the son of Matthat.
Matthat was the son of Levi.
³⁰ Levi was the son of Simeon.
Simeon was the son of Judah.
Judah was the son of Joseph.
Joseph was the son of Jonam.
Jonam was the son of Eliakim.
³¹ Eliakim was the son of Melea.
Melea was the son of Menna.
Menna was the son of Mattatha.
Mattatha was the son of Nathan.
Nathan was the son of David.
³² David was the son of Jesse.
Jesse was the son of Obed.
Obed was the son of Boaz.
Boaz was the son of Salmon.*
Salmon was the son of Nahshon.
³³ Nahshon was the son of Amminadab.
Amminadab was the son of Admin.
Admin was the son of Arni.*
Arni was the son of Hezron.
Hezron was the son of Perez.

Perez was the son of Judah.
³⁴ Judah was the son of Jacob.
Jacob was the son of Isaac.
Isaac was the son of Abraham.
Abraham was the son of Terah.
Terah was the son of Nahor.
³⁵ Nahor was the son of Serug.
Serug was the son of Reu.
Reu was the son of Peleg.
Peleg was the son of Eber.
Eber was the son of Shelah.
³⁶ Shelah was the son of Cainan.
Cainan was the son of Arphaxad.
Arphaxad was the son of Shem.
Shem was the son of Noah.
Noah was the son of Lamech.
³⁷ Lamech was the son of Methuselah.
Methuselah was the son of Enoch.
Enoch was the son of Jared.
Jared was the son of Mahalalel.
Mahalalel was the son of Kenan.
³⁸ Kenan was the son of Enosh.*
Enosh was the son of Seth.
Seth was the son of Adam.
Adam was the son of God.

4 THE TEMPTATION OF JESUS

Then Jesus, full of the Holy Spirit, returned from the Jordan River. He was led by the Spirit in the wilderness,* ²where he was tempted by the devil for forty days. Jesus ate nothing all that time and became very hungry.

³Then the devil said to him, "If you are the Son of God, tell this stone to become a loaf of bread."

⁴But Jesus told him, "No! The Scriptures say, 'People do not live by bread alone.'*"

⁵Then the devil took him up and revealed to him all the kingdoms of the world in a moment of time. ⁶"I will give you the glory of these kingdoms and authority over them," the devil said, "because they are mine to give to anyone I please. ⁷I will give it all to you if you will worship me."

⁸Jesus replied, "The Scriptures say,

'You must worship the LORD your God
   and serve only him.'*"

⁹Then the devil took him to Jerusalem, to the highest point of the Temple, and said, "If you are the Son of God, jump off! ¹⁰For the Scriptures say,

VULNERABLE
(4:1-13) Jesus' defeat of Satan during his period of temptation was decisive but not final. Throughout his ministry, Jesus would confront Satan in many forms. Too often we see temptation as a once-and-for-all proposition. In reality, we need to be constantly on guard against the devil's ongoing attacks. What tempts you the most right now? How are you preparing to withstand it?

3:32 Greek *Sala*, a variant spelling of Salmon; also in 3:32b. See Ruth 4:20. **3:33** Some manuscripts read *Amminadab was the son of Aram. Arni* and *Aram* are alternate spellings of Ram. See 1 Chr 2:9-10. **3:38** Greek *Enos*, a variant spelling of Enosh; also in 3:38b. See Gen 5:6. **4:1** Some manuscripts read *into the wilderness*. **4:4** Deut 8:3. **4:8** Deut 6:13.

'He will order his angels to protect and guard you.

¹¹ And they will hold you up with their hands
so you won't even hurt your foot on
a stone.'*"

¹²Jesus responded, "The Scriptures also say, 'You must not test the Lord your God.'*"

¹³When the devil had finished tempting Jesus, he left him until the next opportunity came.

JESUS REJECTED AT NAZARETH ¹⁴Then Jesus returned to Galilee, filled with the Holy Spirit's power. Reports about him spread quickly through the whole region. ¹⁵He taught regularly in their synagogues and was praised by everyone.

¹⁶When he came to the village of Nazareth, his boyhood home, he went as usual to the synagogue on the Sabbath and stood up to read the Scriptures. ¹⁷The scroll of Isaiah the prophet was handed to him. He unrolled the scroll and found the place where this was written:

¹⁸ "The Spirit of the Lord is upon me,
for he has anointed me to bring Good
News to the poor.
He has sent me to proclaim that captives
will be released,
that the blind will see,
that the oppressed will be set free,
¹⁹ and that the time of the Lord's favor
has come.*"

²⁰He rolled up the scroll, handed it back to the attendant, and sat down. All eyes in the synagogue looked at him intently. ²¹Then he began to speak to them. "The Scripture you've just heard has been fulfilled this very day!"

²²Everyone spoke well of him and was amazed by the gracious words that came from his lips. "How can this be?" they asked. "Isn't this Joseph's son?"

²³Then he said, "You will undoubtedly quote me this proverb: 'Physician, heal yourself'—meaning, 'Do miracles here in your hometown like those you did in Capernaum.' ²⁴But I tell you the truth, no prophet is accepted in his own hometown.

²⁵"Certainly there were many needy widows in Israel in Elijah's time, when the heavens were closed for three and a half years, and a severe famine devastated the land. ²⁶Yet Elijah was not sent to any of them. He was sent

> ## "THE SPIRIT OF THE LORD IS UPON ME, FOR HE HAS ANOINTED ME TO BRING GOOD NEWS TO THE POOR....
>
> # THE TIME OF THE { LUKE 4:18-19 } LORD'S FAVOR HAS COME."

instead to a foreigner—a widow of Zarephath in the land of Sidon. ²⁷And there were many lepers in Israel in the time of the prophet Elisha, but the only one healed was Naaman, a Syrian."

²⁸When they heard this, the people in the synagogue were furious. ²⁹Jumping up, they mobbed him and forced him to the edge of the hill on which the town was built. They intended to push him over the cliff, ³⁰but he passed right through the crowd and went on his way.

JESUS CASTS OUT A DEMON ³¹Then Jesus went to Capernaum, a town in Galilee, and taught there in the synagogue every Sabbath day. ³²There, too, the people were amazed at his teaching, for he spoke with authority.

³³Once when he was in the synagogue, a man possessed by a demon—an evil* spirit—began shouting at Jesus, ³⁴"Go away! Why are you interfering with us, Jesus of Nazareth?

....

JESUS' EXAMPLE
(4:16) Jesus went to the synagogue "as usual." Even though he was the perfect Son of God, and his local synagogue left much to be desired, he attended services every week. Jesus' example makes most excuses for not attending church sound weak and self-serving. Make regular worship a part of your life.

4:10-11 Ps 91:11-12. **4:12** Deut 6:16. **4:18-19** Or *and to proclaim the acceptable year of the Lord.* Isa 61:1-2 (Greek version); 58:6. **4:33** Greek *unclean;* also in 4:36.

Have you come to destroy us? I know who you are—the Holy One of God!"

[35]Jesus cut him short. "Be quiet! Come out of the man," he ordered. At that, the demon threw the man to the floor as the crowd watched; then it came out of him without hurting him further.

[36]Amazed, the people exclaimed, "What authority and power this man's words possess! Even evil spirits obey him, and they flee at his command!" [37]The news about Jesus spread through every village in the entire region.

JESUS HEALS MANY PEOPLE
[38]After leaving the synagogue that day, Jesus went to Simon's home, where he found Simon's mother-in-law very sick with a high fever. "Please heal her," everyone begged. [39]Standing at her bedside, he rebuked the fever, and it left her. And she got up at once and prepared a meal for them.

[40]As the sun went down that evening, people throughout the village brought sick family members to Jesus. No matter what their diseases were, the touch of his hand healed every one. [41]Many were possessed by demons; and the demons came out at his command, shouting, "You are the Son of God!" But because they knew he was the Messiah, he rebuked them and refused to let them speak.

JESUS CONTINUES TO PREACH
[42]Early the next morning Jesus went out to an isolated place. The crowds searched everywhere for him, and when they finally found him, they begged him not to leave them. [43]But he replied, "I must preach the Good News of the Kingdom of God in other towns, too, because that is why I was sent." [44]So he continued to travel around, preaching in synagogues throughout Judea.*

5 **THE FIRST DISCIPLES** One day as Jesus was preaching on the shore of the Sea of Galilee,* great crowds pressed in on him to listen to the word of God. [2]He noticed two empty boats at the water's edge, for the fishermen had left them and were washing their nets. [3]Stepping into one of the boats, Jesus asked Simon,* its owner, to push it out into

the water. So he sat in the boat and taught the crowds from there.

[4]When he had finished speaking, he said to Simon, "Now go out where it is deeper, and let down your nets to catch some fish."

[5]"Master," Simon replied, "we worked hard all last night and didn't catch a thing. But if you say so, I'll let the nets down again." [6]And this time their nets were so full of fish they began to tear! [7]A shout for help brought their partners in the other boat, and soon both boats were filled with fish and on the verge of sinking.

[8]When Simon Peter realized what had happened, he fell to his knees before Jesus and said, "Oh, Lord, please leave me—I'm too much of a sinner to be around you." [9]For he was awestruck by the number of fish they had caught, as were the others with him. [10]His partners, James and John, the sons of Zebedee, were also amazed.

Jesus replied to Simon, "Don't be afraid! From now on you'll be fishing for people!" [11]And as soon as they landed, they left everything and followed Jesus.

JESUS HEALS A MAN WITH LEPROSY
[12]In one of the villages, Jesus met a man with an advanced case of leprosy. When the man saw Jesus, he bowed with his face to the ground, begging to be healed. "Lord," he said, "if you are willing, you can heal me and make me clean."

[13]Jesus reached out and touched him. "I am willing," he said. "Be healed!" And instantly the leprosy disappeared. [14]Then Jesus instructed him not to tell anyone what had happened. He said, "Go to the priest and let him examine you. Take along the offering required in the law of Moses for those who have been healed of leprosy.* This will be a public testimony that you have been cleansed."

[15]But despite Jesus' instructions, the report of his power spread even faster, and vast crowds came to hear him preach and to be healed of their diseases. [16]But Jesus often withdrew to the wilderness for prayer.

JESUS HEALS A PARALYZED MAN
[17]One day while Jesus was teaching, some Pharisees and teachers of religious law were sitting nearby. (It seemed that these men showed up from every village in all Galilee and Judea, as well as from Jerusalem.) And the Lord's healing power was strongly with Jesus.

BRING YOUR FRIENDS
(5:17-26) Jesus responded to the faith of four men by healing their paralyzed friend. For better or worse, our faith affects others. Although we can't make others follow Christ, we can do much through our words and actions to encourage them to respond positively. Like the four friends, you have a chance to bring your friends to Jesus. So, how about it? You might be amazed at how God responds to your faith.

4:44 Some manuscripts read *Galilee.* **5:1** Greek *Lake Gennesaret,* another name for the Sea of Galilee. **5:3** *Simon* is called "Peter" in 6:14 and thereafter. **5:14** See Lev 14:2-32.

¹⁸Some men came carrying a paralyzed man on a sleeping mat. They tried to take him inside to Jesus, ¹⁹but they couldn't reach him because of the crowd. So they went up to the roof and took off some tiles. Then they lowered the sick man on his mat down into the crowd, right in front of Jesus. ²⁰Seeing their faith, Jesus said to the man, "Young man, your sins are forgiven."

²¹But the Pharisees and teachers of religious law said to themselves, "Who does he think he is? That's blasphemy! Only God can forgive sins!"

²²Jesus knew what they were thinking, so he asked them, "Why do you question this in your hearts? ²³Is it easier to say 'Your sins are forgiven,' or 'Stand up and walk'? ²⁴So I will prove to you that the Son of Man* has the authority on earth to forgive sins." Then Jesus turned to the paralyzed man and said, "Stand up, pick up your mat, and go home!"

²⁵And immediately, as everyone watched, the man jumped up, picked up his mat, and went home praising God. ²⁶Everyone was gripped with great wonder and awe, and they praised God, exclaiming, "We have seen amazing things today!"

JESUS CALLS LEVI (MATTHEW) ²⁷Later, as Jesus left the town, he saw a tax collector named Levi sitting at his tax collector's booth. "Follow me and be my disciple," Jesus said to him. ²⁸So Levi got up, left everything, and followed him.

²⁹Later, Levi held a banquet in his home with Jesus as the guest of honor. Many of Levi's fellow tax collectors and other guests also ate with them. ³⁰But the Pharisees and their teachers of religious law complained bitterly to Jesus' disciples, "Why do you eat and drink with such scum?*"

³¹Jesus answered them, "Healthy people don't need a doctor—sick people do. ³²I have come to call not those who think they are righteous, but those who know they are sinners and need to repent."

A DISCUSSION ABOUT FASTING ³³One day some people said to Jesus, "John the Baptist's disciples fast and pray regularly, and so do the disciples of the Pharisees. Why are your disciples always eating and drinking?"

5:24 "Son of Man" is a title Jesus used for himself.   5:30 Greek with tax collectors and sinners.

PERSONALITY PROFILE **JAMES**

UPS:
- One of the 12 disciples
- One of a special inner circle of three with Peter and John
- First of the 12 disciples to be killed for his faith

DOWNS:
- Two outbursts indicate a struggle with his temper (Luke 9:54) and selfishness (Mark 10:37). Both times, he and his brother, John, spoke as one.

STATS:
- Where: Galilee
- Occupations: Fisherman, disciple
- Relatives: Zebedee (father), Salome (mother), John (brother)
- Contemporaries: Jesus, Pilate, Herod Agrippa, the other 11 disciples

KEY VERSES: Mark 10:35-37

WHO ARE YOUR CLOSEST FRIENDS? Of his 12 disciples, Jesus hung out the most with Peter, James, and James's brother John. Later, each played a key role among the first Christians. Peter became a great speaker. John became a great writer. But James became the first of the 12 disciples to die for his faith.

James was older than his brother, John. Zebedee, their father, owned a fishing business where they worked along with Peter and Andrew, who also became disciples of Jesus. While Peter, Andrew, and John spent some time with John the Baptist, James stayed with the boats and nets. Later, when Jesus chose them to be his disciples, James was as eager as his partners to follow.

Like all of the disciples, though, James had a limited view of Jesus' purpose. He hoped Jesus would start an earthly kingdom that would overthrow Rome and restore the nation of Israel. When that kingdom was established, he hoped to have a special position in it. More than anything, James wanted to be with Jesus. He didn't understand his leader, but he understood that Jesus was worth following. After Jesus died and rose from the grave, James finally understood Jesus' purpose—to provide new life for all.

Many years after Jesus' return to heaven, James was arrested and put to death (see Acts 12:1-2). He was willing to die because he knew that Jesus had conquered death. And he realized that death was only the doorway to eternal life.

Jesus promised eternal life to those willing to trust him. If we believe this promise, he'll give us the courage to stand for him even during dangerous times.

BOTTOM LINE: Many of Jesus' followers do not consider the loss of life too heavy a price to pay for following him.

James's story is told in the Gospels. He also is mentioned in Acts 1:13 and 12:2.

[34]Jesus responded, "Do wedding guests fast while celebrating with the groom? Of course not. [35]But someday the groom will be taken away from them, and then they will fast."

[36]Then Jesus gave them this illustration: "No one tears a piece of cloth from a new garment and uses it to patch an old garment. For then the new garment would be ruined, and the new patch wouldn't even match the old garment. [37]"And no one puts new wine into old wineskins. For the new wine would burst the wineskins, spilling the wine and ruining the skins. [38]New wine must be stored in new wineskins. [39]But no one who drinks the old wine seems to want the new wine. 'The old is just fine,' they say."

6 A DISCUSSION ABOUT THE SABBATH

One Sabbath day as Jesus was walking through some grainfields, his disciples broke off heads of grain, rubbed off the husks in their hands, and ate the grain. [2]But some Pharisees said, "Why are you breaking the law by harvesting grain on the Sabbath?"

[3]Jesus replied, "Haven't you read in the Scriptures what David did when he and his companions were hungry? [4]He went into the house of God and broke the law by eating the sacred loaves of bread that only the priests can eat. He also gave some to his companions." [5]And Jesus added, "The Son of Man* is Lord, even over the Sabbath."

JESUS HEALS ON THE SABBATH [6]On another Sabbath day, a man with a deformed right hand was in the synagogue while Jesus was teaching. [7]The teachers of religious law and the Pharisees watched Jesus closely. If he healed the man's hand, they planned to accuse him of working on the Sabbath.

[8]But Jesus knew their thoughts. He said to the man with the deformed hand, "Come and stand in front of everyone." So the man came forward. [9]Then Jesus said to his critics, "I have a question for you. Does the law permit good deeds on the Sabbath, or is it a day for doing evil? Is this a day to save life or to destroy it?"

[10]He looked around at them one by one and then said to the man, "Hold out your hand." So the man held out his hand, and it was restored! [11]At this, the enemies of Jesus were wild with rage and began to discuss what to do with him.

JESUS CHOOSES THE TWELVE APOSTLES [12]One day soon afterward Jesus went up on a mountain to pray, and he prayed to God all night. [13]At daybreak he called together all of his disciples and chose twelve of them to be apostles. Here are their names:

[14] Simon (whom he named Peter),
　Andrew (Peter's brother),
　James,
　John,
　Philip,
　Bartholomew,
[15] Matthew,
　Thomas,
　James (son of Alphaeus),
　Simon (who was called the zealot),
[16] Judas (son of James),
　Judas Iscariot (who later betrayed him).

CROWDS FOLLOW JESUS [17]When they came down from the mountain, the disciples stood with Jesus on a large, level area, surrounded by many of his followers and by the crowds. There were people from all over Judea and from Jerusalem and from as far north as the seacoasts of Tyre and Sidon. [18]They had come to hear him and to be healed of their diseases; and those troubled by evil* spirits were healed. [19]Everyone tried to touch him, because healing power went out from him, and he healed everyone.

THE BEATITUDES [20]Then Jesus turned to his disciples and said,

　"God blesses you who are poor,
　　for the Kingdom of God is yours.
[21] God blesses you who are hungry now,
　　for you will be satisfied.
　God blesses you who weep now,
　　for in due time you will laugh.

[22]What blessings await you when people hate you and exclude you and mock you and curse you as evil because you follow the Son of Man. [23]When that happens, be happy! Yes, leap for joy! For a great reward awaits you in heaven.

QUALIFIED

(6:13-16) Jesus chose ordinary men—not superheroes or famous people—to be his disciples. Do you think your pastor or a famous evangelist somehow has "secret powers" that you lack, thereby disqualifying you to serve God? Guess what? God still calls "ordinary" people to build his church. Alone we may feel unqualified to serve Christ well. But together, with the help of the Holy Spirit, we can serve God faithfully. Ask for patience to accept differences and to build on the variety of strengths in your group. Are you ready to serve?

6:5 "Son of Man" is a title Jesus used for himself.　**6:18** Greek *unclean.*

MY STORY: Daniel

Even before I became a Christian, the Bible amazed me. I remember being floored the first time I read Luke 6:27-38. That's the passage about loving your enemies. I wondered, How could anyone act like that?

A year later, just before my freshman year in high school, I became a Christian. And that year I had the chance to find out firsthand how someone can follow Jesus' words.

In shop class, I decided to make a small bookcase for my mother for Christmas. I designed it myself. I worked on it a lot in my spare time, finally getting to the point where I put final touches on it and left it in the finishing room, which was always locked.

After school, when I went back to get the bookcase, it was gone. The shop teacher did some investigating and finally discovered that a dude named Andy had stolen it. "We've had problems with Andy before," Mr. Petrako said. "Andy needs to learn a lesson. I've arranged to have him meet you after school to return your bookshelf." That's all he said, but I knew what he meant.

I didn't need any encouragement to "teach Andy a lesson." I was furious. And since I was a football player—y'know, kinda big—I wouldn't have any trouble beating someone up.

I waited for Andy, psyching myself up to face my enemy. Finally, he walked in.

Something happened to me when I saw him. I had expected someone tough, but what I saw was just a boy, smaller and younger than me, who was obviously afraid. When I saw Andy's scared face, all the hate just leaked out of me.

Andy said, "Here's your bookcase. I'm sorry." I had no words for him. I growled something, took the bookcase, and left.

That night I felt very confused. What happened? What took away my hate? As I thought about these things, I remembered the passage in Luke. I read it again: "Love your enemies. . . . When things are taken away from you, don't try to get them back" (6:27-30).

Father God, I thought, am I supposed to give the bookcase back to him? I can't! I made it for my mom! I felt like God was asking me to respond to what I read. But how? Suddenly, I knew. I went to school early the next morning and started work on an identical bookcase. For four days straight I stayed as long as shop was open.

When the bookcase was finished, I had Andy meet me after school in an empty shop class. I said, "Andy, I want to give you this. It's a gift from me to you, and from me to Jesus. I'd never be able to do this if it weren't for him."

That's all I could say then. I didn't know how to share my faith. All I knew was that Jesus had touched my life and I wanted Andy to know.

Well, after that I got to know Andy. Seeing his family situation (they were broke), I understood him better. I invited him to youth group on Thursday afternoons. When there was a retreat and Andy couldn't afford to go, my friends and I scraped up enough money for him. And at that retreat, Andy became a Christian.

It's hard to know who was more excited about God right then, me or Andy.

And remember, their ancestors treated the ancient prophets that same way.

SORROWS FORETOLD

24 "What sorrow awaits you who are rich,
for you have your only happiness now.
25 What sorrow awaits you who are fat and prosperous now,
for a time of awful hunger awaits you.
What sorrow awaits you who laugh now,
for your laughing will turn to mourning and sorrow.
26 What sorrow awaits you who are praised by the crowds,
for their ancestors also praised false prophets.

LOVE FOR ENEMIES

27"But to you who are willing to listen, I say, love your enemies! Do good to those who hate you. 28Bless those who curse you. Pray for those who hurt you. 29If someone slaps you on one cheek, offer the other cheek also. If someone demands your coat, offer your shirt also. 30Give to anyone who asks; and when things are taken away from you, don't try to get them back. 31Do to others as you would like them to do to you.

32"If you love only those who love you, why should you get credit for that? Even sinners love those who love them! 33And if you do good only to those who do good to you, why should you get credit? Even sinners do that much! 34And if you lend money only to those who can repay you, why should you get credit? Even sinners will lend to other sinners for a full return.

35"Love your enemies! Do good to them. Lend to them without expecting to be repaid. Then your reward from heaven will be very great, and you will truly be acting as children of the Most High, for he is kind to those who are unthankful and wicked. 36You must be compassionate, just as your Father is compassionate.

DO NOT JUDGE OTHERS

37"Do not judge others, and you will not be judged. Do not condemn others, or it will all come back against you. Forgive others, and you will be forgiven. 38Give, and you will receive. Your gift will return to you in full—pressed down, shaken together to make room for more, running over, and poured into your lap. The amount you give will determine the amount you get back.*"

TOUGH LOVE
(6:27-36) The Jews hated the Romans because the Romans oppressed them. But Jesus told them to love these enemies. What's your immediate reaction to Jesus' words? Many turned away from him because of these words. But Jesus wasn't talking about having affection for enemies; he was talking about an act of the will.

Loving our enemies means acting in their best interests. You can't "fall into" this kind of love—it takes conscious effort. But mainly, you need the help of God.

Jesus loved the whole world, even though the world rebelled against God. He asks us to follow his example by loving our enemies. Will you?

NO POINTING
(6:41-42) Jesus doesn't mean we should ignore wrongdoing, but we are not to be so worried about others' sins that we overlook our own. We often rationalize our sins by pointing out the same mistakes in others. What kinds of specks in others' eyes are the easiest for you to criticize? Remember your own logs when you feel like criticizing, and you may find you have less to say.

39Then Jesus gave the following illustration: "Can one blind person lead another? Won't they both fall into a ditch? 40Students* are not greater than their teacher. But the student who is fully trained will become like the teacher.

41"And why worry about a speck in your friend's eye* when you have a log in your own? 42How can you think of saying, 'Friend,* let me help you get rid of that speck in your eye,' when you can't see past the log in your own eye? Hypocrite! First get rid of the log in your own eye; then you will see well enough to deal with the speck in your friend's eye.

THE TREE AND ITS FRUIT

43"A good tree can't produce bad fruit, and a bad tree can't produce good fruit. 44A tree is identified by its fruit. Figs are never gathered from thornbushes, and grapes are not picked from bramble bushes. 45A good person produces good things from the treasury of a good heart, and an evil person produces evil things from the treasury of an evil heart. What you say flows from what is in your heart.

BUILDING ON A SOLID FOUNDATION

46"So why do you keep calling me 'Lord, Lord!' when you don't do what I say? 47I will show you what it's like when someone comes to me, listens to my teaching, and then follows it. 48It is like a person building a house who digs deep and lays the foundation on solid rock. When the floodwaters rise and break against that house, it stands firm because it is well built. 49But anyone who hears and doesn't obey is like a person who builds a house without a foundation. When the floods sweep down against that house, it will collapse into a heap of ruins."

7 THE FAITH OF A ROMAN OFFICER

When Jesus had finished saying all this to the people, he returned to Capernaum. 2At that time the highly valued slave of a Roman officer* was sick and near death. 3When the officer heard about Jesus, he sent some respected Jewish elders to ask him to come and heal his slave. 4So they earnestly begged Jesus to help the man. "If anyone deserves your help, he does," they said, 5"for he loves the Jewish people and even built a synagogue for us."

6So Jesus went with them. But just before they arrived at the house, the officer sent some friends to say, "Lord, don't trouble yourself by

6:38 Or *The measure you give will be the measure you get back.*
6:40 Or *Disciples.*   6:41 Greek *your brother's eye;* also in 6:42.
6:42 Greek *Brother.*   7:2 Greek *a centurion;* similarly in 7:6.

coming to my home, for I am not worthy of such an honor. [7]I am not even worthy to come and meet you. Just say the word from where you are, and my servant will be healed. [8]I know this because I am under the authority of my superior officers, and I have authority over my soldiers. I only need to say, 'Go,' and they go, or 'Come,' and they come. And if I say to my slaves, 'Do this,' they do it."

[9]When Jesus heard this, he was amazed. Turning to the crowd that was following him, he said, "I tell you, I haven't seen faith like this in all Israel!" [10]And when the officer's friends returned to his house, they found the slave completely healed.

JESUS RAISES A WIDOW'S SON [11]Soon afterward Jesus went with his disciples to the village of Nain, and a large crowd followed him. [12]A funeral procession was coming out as he approached the village gate. The young man who had died was a widow's only son, and a large crowd from the village was with her. [13]When the Lord saw her, his heart overflowed with compassion. "Don't cry!" he said. [14]Then he walked over to the coffin and touched it, and the bearers stopped. "Young man," he said, "I tell you, get up." [15]Then the dead boy sat up and began to talk! And Jesus gave him back to his mother.

[16]Great fear swept the crowd, and they praised God, saying, "A mighty prophet has risen among us," and "God has visited his people today." [17]And the news about Jesus spread throughout Judea and the surrounding countryside.

JESUS AND JOHN THE BAPTIST [18]The disciples of John the Baptist told John about everything Jesus was doing. So John called for two of his disciples, [19]and he sent them to the Lord to ask him, "Are you the Messiah we've been expecting,* or should we keep looking for someone else?"

[20]John's two disciples found Jesus and said to him, "John the Baptist sent us to ask, 'Are you the Messiah we've been expecting, or should we keep looking for someone else?'"

[21]At that very time, Jesus cured many people of their diseases, illnesses, and evil spirits, and he restored sight to many who were blind. [22]Then he told John's disciples, "Go back to John and tell him what you have seen and heard—the blind see, the lame walk, the lepers are cured, the deaf hear, the dead are

7:19 Greek *Are you the one who is coming?* Also in 7:20.   **7:23** Or *who are not offended by me.*   **7:27** Mal 3:1.   **7:29** Or *praised God for his justice.*

JESUS AND FORGIVENESS

Jesus not only taught frequently about forgiveness, he also demonstrated his own willingness to forgive. Here are several examples that should help us recognize his willingness to forgive us also.

JESUS FORGAVE . . .
the paralyzed man lowered on a mat through the roof . . . Luke 5:17-26
the woman caught in adultery . . . John 8:3-11
the woman who anointed his feet with oil . . . Luke 7:47-50
Peter, for denying he knew Jesus . . . John 18:15-18, 25-27; 21:15-19
the criminal on the cross . . . Luke 23:39-43
the people who crucified him . . . Luke 23:34

raised to life, and the Good News is being preached to the poor. [23]And tell him, 'God blesses those who do not turn away because of me.*'"

[24]After John's disciples left, Jesus began talking about him to the crowds. "What kind of man did you go into the wilderness to see? Was he a weak reed, swayed by every breath of wind? [25]Or were you expecting to see a man dressed in expensive clothes? No, people who wear beautiful clothes and live in luxury are found in palaces. [26]Were you looking for a prophet? Yes, and he is more than a prophet. [27]John is the man to whom the Scriptures refer when they say,

'Look, I am sending my messenger ahead of you,
    and he will prepare your way before you.'*

[28]I tell you, of all who have ever lived, none is greater than John. Yet even the least person in the Kingdom of God is greater than he is!"

[29]When they heard this, all the people—even the tax collectors—agreed that God's way was right,* for they had been baptized by John. [30]But the Pharisees and experts in religious law rejected God's plan for them, for they had refused John's baptism.

....

QUESTIONS
(7:18-23) While imprisoned, John's discouragement led him to wonder whether or not Jesus really was the Messiah (see also Matt 11:1-6). John's doubts were natural, and Jesus didn't condemn him for them. Instead, Jesus responded in a way that John would understand by explaining that he had in fact accomplished the things the Messiah was supposed to accomplish.

God can handle our doubts also. In fact, he welcomes our sincere questions. What questions, if any, do you have? Do you really want to know the answers?

³¹"To what can I compare the people of this generation?" Jesus asked. "How can I describe them? ³²They are like children playing a game in the public square. They complain to their friends,

'We played wedding songs,
    and you didn't dance,
so we played funeral songs,
    and you didn't weep.'

³³For John the Baptist didn't spend his time eating bread or drinking wine, and you say, 'He's possessed by a demon.' ³⁴The Son of Man,* on the other hand, feasts and drinks, and you say, 'He's a glutton and a drunkard, and a friend of tax collectors and other sinners!' ³⁵But wisdom is shown to be right by the lives of those who follow it.*"

JESUS ANOINTED BY A SINFUL WOMAN
³⁶One of the Pharisees asked Jesus to have dinner with him, so Jesus went to his home and sat down to eat.* ³⁷When a certain immoral woman from that city heard he was eating there, she brought a beautiful alabaster jar filled with expensive perfume. ³⁸Then she knelt behind him at his feet, weeping. Her tears fell on his feet, and she wiped them off with her hair. Then she kept kissing his feet and putting perfume on them.

³⁹When the Pharisee who had invited him saw this, he said to himself, "If this man were a prophet, he would know what kind of woman is touching him. She's a sinner!"

⁴⁰Then Jesus answered his thoughts. "Simon," he said to the Pharisee, "I have something to say to you."

"Go ahead, Teacher," Simon replied.

⁴¹Then Jesus told him this story: "A man loaned money to two people—500 pieces of silver* to one and 50 pieces to the other. ⁴²But neither of them could repay him, so he kindly forgave them both, canceling their debts. Who do you suppose loved him more after that?"

⁴³Simon answered, "I suppose the one for whom he canceled the larger debt."

"That's right," Jesus said. ⁴⁴Then he turned to the woman and said to Simon, "Look at this woman kneeling here. When I entered your home, you didn't offer me water to wash the dust from my feet, but she has washed them with her tears and wiped them with her hair. ⁴⁵You didn't greet me with a kiss, but from the time I first came in, she has not stopped kissing my feet. ⁴⁶You neglected the courtesy of olive oil to anoint my head, but she has anointed my feet with rare perfume.

⁴⁷"I tell you, her sins—and they are many—have been forgiven, so she has shown me much love. But a person who is forgiven little shows only little love." ⁴⁸Then Jesus said to the woman, "Your sins are forgiven."

⁴⁹The men at the table said among themselves, "Who is this man, that he goes around forgiving sins?"

⁵⁰And Jesus said to the woman, "Your faith has saved you; go in peace."

8 WOMEN WHO FOLLOWED JESUS Soon
afterward Jesus began a tour of the nearby towns and villages, preaching and announcing the Good News about the Kingdom of God. He took his twelve disciples with him, ²along with some women who had been cured of evil spirits and diseases. Among them were Mary Magdalene, from whom he had cast out seven demons; ³Joanna, the wife of Chuza, Herod's business manager; Susanna; and many others who were contributing from their own resources to support Jesus and his disciples.

PARABLE OF THE FARMER SCATTERING SEED
⁴One day Jesus told a story in the form of a parable to a large crowd that had gathered from many towns to hear him: ⁵"A farmer went out to plant his seed. As he scattered it across his field, some seed fell on a footpath, where it was stepped on, and the birds ate it. ⁶Other seed fell among rocks. It began to grow, but the plant soon wilted and died for lack of moisture. ⁷Other seed fell among thorns that grew up with it and choked out the tender plants. ⁸Still other seed fell on fertile soil. This seed grew and produced a crop that was a hundred times as much as had been planted!" When he had said this, he called out, "Anyone with ears to hear should listen and understand."

⁹His disciples asked him what this parable meant. ¹⁰He replied, "You are permitted to understand the secrets* of the Kingdom of God. But I use parables to teach the others so that the Scriptures might be fulfilled:

'When they look, they won't really see.
    When they hear, they won't understand.'*

¹¹"This is the meaning of the parable: The seed is God's word. ¹²The seeds that fell on the footpath represent those who hear the message, only to have the devil come and take it away from their hearts and prevent them from

7:34 "Son of Man" is a title Jesus used for himself.   7:35 Or *But wisdom is justified by all her children.*   7:36 Or *and reclined.*   7:41 Greek *500 denarii*. A denarius was equivalent to a laborer's full day's wage.   8:10a Greek *mysteries.*   8:10b Isa 6:9 (Greek version).

believing and being saved. ¹³The seeds on the rocky soil represent those who hear the message and receive it with joy. But since they don't have deep roots, they believe for a while, then they fall away when they face temptation. ¹⁴The seeds that fell among the thorns represent those who hear the message, but all too quickly the message is crowded out by the cares and riches and pleasures of this life. And so they never grow into maturity. ¹⁵And the seeds that fell on the good soil represent honest, good-hearted people who hear God's word, cling to it, and patiently produce a huge harvest.

PARABLE OF THE LAMP ¹⁶"No one lights a lamp and then covers it with a bowl or hides it under a bed. A lamp is placed on a stand, where its light can be seen by all who enter the house. ¹⁷For all that is secret will eventually be brought into the open, and everything that is concealed will be brought to light and made known to all.

¹⁸"So pay attention to how you hear. To those who listen to my teaching, more understanding will be given. But for those who are not listening, even what they think they understand will be taken away from them."

THE TRUE FAMILY OF JESUS ¹⁹Then Jesus' mother and brothers came to see him, but

8:26 Other manuscripts read *Gadarenes;* still others read *Gergesenes;* also in 8:37. See Matt 8:28; Mark 5:1.

they couldn't get to him because of the crowd. ²⁰Someone told Jesus, "Your mother and your brothers are outside, and they want to see you."

²¹Jesus replied, "My mother and my brothers are all those who hear God's word and obey it."

JESUS CALMS THE STORM ²²One day Jesus said to his disciples, "Let's cross to the other side of the lake." So they got into a boat and started out. ²³As they sailed across, Jesus settled down for a nap. But soon a fierce storm came down on the lake. The boat was filling with water, and they were in real danger.

²⁴The disciples went and woke him up, shouting, "Master, Master, we're going to drown!"

When Jesus woke up, he rebuked the wind and the raging waves. Suddenly the storm stopped and all was calm. ²⁵Then he asked them, "Where is your faith?"

The disciples were terrified and amazed. "Who is this man?" they asked each other. "When he gives a command, even the wind and waves obey him!"

JESUS HEALS A DEMON-POSSESSED MAN
²⁶So they arrived in the region of the Gerasenes,* across the lake from Galilee. ²⁷As Jesus was climbing out of the boat, a man who was possessed by demons came out to meet him. For a long time he had been homeless

I WONDER...

So many things in my life could pull me away from God. How can I make sure I will always be "good soil"?

Skyscrapers must be carefully planned in order for them not to topple when a stiff wind hits. First, a huge hole is dug deep in the ground. Thousands of tons of concrete are poured, steel girders are welded into place, and everything is made to fit according to exact specifications. If the foundation is strong and straight, a strong building can be built on it.

The rest of the structure, however, must also be built strong, with the right materials fitted together in the right way, at the right time.

In Luke 8:11-15, Jesus tells a parable about the Word of God. He compares it to a seed being planted. Like the skyscraper, seeds need to be planted in the right kind of soil, at the right time. So it is with the Word of God. Only God knows when and how to plant his Spirit and life within each of us.

The first phase in your new life began when you accepted Christ's forgiveness and became a Christian: "For no one can lay any foundation other than the one we already have—Jesus Christ" (1 Cor 3:11).

The second phase starts with the Word of God. If you study the Bible and have other Christians help you understand and apply it, your life in Christ will be strong. "Anyone who builds on that foundation may use a variety of material—gold, silver, jewels, wood, hay, or straw" (1 Cor 3:12). If you are exposed to teaching that downplays God's Word, that would be like building your life with wood, hay, and straw. It will collapse when problems or persecution from friends and family arise (see Matt 7:24-27).

To build a solid Christian life, you should make sure that all you're hearing is lining up with what the Bible really says. You can do this by praying for direction, asking questions, and finding people who believe as you do that the Bible is God's blueprint for building a strong life.

and naked, living in a cemetery outside the town.

[28]As soon as he saw Jesus, he shrieked and fell down in front of him. Then he screamed, "Why are you interfering with me, Jesus, Son of the Most High God? Please, I beg you, don't torture me!" [29]For Jesus had already commanded the evil* spirit to come out of him. This spirit had often taken control of the man. Even when he was placed under guard and put in chains and shackles, he simply broke them and rushed out into the wilderness, completely under the demon's power.

[30]Jesus demanded, "What is your name?"

"Legion," he replied, for he was filled with many demons. [31]The demons kept begging Jesus not to send them into the bottomless pit.*

[32]There happened to be a large herd of pigs feeding on the hillside nearby, and the demons begged him to let them enter into the pigs.

So Jesus gave them permission. [33]Then the demons came out of the man and entered the pigs, and the entire herd plunged down the steep hillside into the lake and drowned.

[34]When the herdsmen saw it, they fled to the nearby town and the surrounding countryside, spreading the news as they ran. [35]People rushed out to see what had happened. A crowd soon gathered around Jesus, and they saw the man who had been freed from the demons. He was sitting at Jesus' feet, fully clothed and perfectly sane, and they were all afraid. [36]Then those who had seen what happened told the others how the demon-possessed man had been healed. [37]And all the people in the region of the Gerasenes begged Jesus to go away and leave them alone, for a great wave of fear swept over them.

So Jesus returned to the boat and left, crossing back to the other side of the lake. [38]The man who had been freed from the demons begged to go with him. But Jesus sent him home, say-ing, [39]"No, go back to your family, and tell them everything God has done for you." So he went all through the town proclaiming the great things Jesus had done for him.

JESUS HEALS IN RESPONSE TO FAITH [40]On the other side of the lake the crowds welcomed Jesus, because they had been waiting for him. [41]Then a man named Jairus, a leader of the local synagogue, came and fell at Jesus' feet, pleading with him to come home with him. [42]His only daughter,* who was about twelve years old, was dying.

As Jesus went with him, he was surrounded by the crowds. [43]A woman in the crowd had suffered for twelve years with constant bleeding,* and she could find no cure. [44]Coming up behind Jesus, she touched the fringe of his robe. Immediately, the bleeding stopped.

[45]"Who touched me?" Jesus asked.

Everyone denied it, and Peter said, "Master, this whole crowd is pressing up against you."

[46]But Jesus said, "Someone deliberately touched me, for I felt healing power go out from me." [47]When the woman realized that she could not stay hidden, she began to tremble and fell to her knees in front of him. The whole crowd heard her explain why she had touched him and that she had been immediately healed. [48]"Daughter," he said to her, "your faith has made you well. Go in peace."

[49]While he was still speaking to her, a messenger arrived from the home of Jairus, the leader of the synagogue. He told him, "Your daughter is dead. There's no use troubling the Teacher now."

[50]But when Jesus heard what had happened, he said to Jairus, "Don't be afraid. Just have faith, and she will be healed."

[51]When they arrived at the house, Jesus wouldn't let anyone go in with him except Peter, John, James, and the little girl's father and mother. [52]The house was filled with people weeping and wailing, but he said, "Stop the weeping! She isn't dead; she's only asleep."

[53]But the crowd laughed at him because they all knew she had died. [54]Then Jesus took her by the hand and said in a loud voice, "My child, get up!" [55]And at that moment her life* returned, and she immediately stood up! Then Jesus told them to give her something to eat. [56]Her parents were overwhelmed, but Jesus insisted that they not tell anyone what had happened.

PIGS OR PEOPLE?
(8:26-37) When the demon-possessed pigs drowned, the herdsmen complained about their loss of money. But can pigs and money compare with a human life? A man had been freed from the devil's power, but the villagers thought only about the money they lost when the pigs died.

Throughout history many wars have been fought to protect economic interests. Much injustice and oppression, both at home and abroad, is the direct result of some individual's or company's goal to get rich. What's your goal? How do you show by your actions that you value people over "pigs" (money, possessions, etc.)?

8:29 Greek *unclean.*   **8:31** Or *the abyss,* or *the underworld.*
8:42 Or *His only child, a daughter.*   **8:43** Some manuscripts add *having spent everything she had on doctors.*   **8:55** Or *her spirit.*

9 JESUS SENDS OUT THE TWELVE DISCIPLES

One day Jesus called together his twelve disciples* and gave them power and authority to cast out all demons and to heal all diseases. ²Then he sent them out to tell everyone about the Kingdom of God and to heal the sick. ³"Take nothing for your journey," he instructed them. "Don't take a walking stick, a traveler's bag, food, money,* or even a change of clothes. ⁴Wherever you go, stay in the same house until you leave town. ⁵And if a town refuses to welcome you, shake its dust from your feet as you leave to show that you have abandoned those people to their fate."

⁶So they began their circuit of the villages, preaching the Good News and healing the sick.

HEROD'S CONFUSION

⁷When Herod Antipas, the ruler of Galilee,* heard about everything Jesus was doing, he was puzzled. Some were saying that John the Baptist had been raised from the dead. ⁸Others thought Jesus was Elijah or one of the other prophets risen from the dead.

⁹"I beheaded John," Herod said, "so who is this man about whom I hear such stories?" And he kept trying to see him.

JESUS FEEDS FIVE THOUSAND

¹⁰When the apostles returned, they told Jesus everything they had done. Then he slipped quietly away with them toward the town of Bethsaida. ¹¹But the crowds found out where he was going, and they followed him. He welcomed them and taught them about the Kingdom of God, and he healed those who were sick.

¹²Late in the afternoon the twelve disciples came to him and said, "Send the crowds away to the nearby villages and farms, so they can find food and lodging for the night. There is nothing to eat here in this remote place."

¹³But Jesus said, "You feed them."

"But we have only five loaves of bread and two fish," they answered. "Or are you expecting us to go and buy enough food for this whole crowd?" ¹⁴For there were about 5,000 men there.

Jesus replied, "Tell them to sit down in groups of about fifty each." ¹⁵So the people all sat down. ¹⁶Jesus took the five loaves and two fish, looked up toward heaven, and blessed them. Then, breaking the loaves into pieces, he kept giving the bread and fish to the disciples so they could distribute it to the people. ¹⁷They all ate as much as they wanted, and afterward, the disciples picked up twelve baskets of leftovers!

PETER'S DECLARATION ABOUT JESUS

¹⁸One day Jesus left the crowds to pray alone. Only his disciples were with him, and he asked them, "Who do people say I am?"

¹⁹"Well," they replied, "some say John the Baptist, some say Elijah, and others say you are one of the other ancient prophets risen from the dead."

²⁰Then he asked them, "But who do you say I am?"

Peter replied, "You are the Messiah* sent from God!"

JESUS PREDICTS HIS DEATH

²¹Jesus warned his disciples not to tell anyone who he was. ²²"The Son of Man* must suffer many terrible things," he said. "He will be rejected by the elders, the leading priests, and the teachers of religious law. He will be killed, but on the third day he will be raised from the dead."

²³Then he said to the crowd, "If any of you wants to be my follower, you must turn from your selfish ways, take up your cross daily, and follow me. ²⁴If you try to hang on to your life, you will lose it. But if you give up your life

....

TROUBLEMAKER OR THE SON OF GOD?

(9:7, 20) People couldn't accept Jesus for who he was, so they tried to come up with other answers. Many thought he was John the Baptist (see Matt 14:1-12) or another prophet who had come back to life. Some suggested he was Elijah, the great prophet who did not die but was taken to heaven in a whirlwind (2 Kgs 2:1-11). Few found the correct answer, as Peter did (Luke 9:20).

Many today find it no easier to accept Jesus as the fully human yet fully divine Son of God. They seek alternate explanations: He was a great prophet, a radical political leader, a self-deceived troublemaker. None of these explanations can account for Jesus' miracles or, especially, his glorious resurrection. In the end, the attempts to explain Jesus away are far more difficult to believe than the truth.

Who do you say that Jesus is?

ENDANGERED

(9:24-25) If this life is most important to you, you will do everything you can to protect it. You will not want to do anything that might endanger your safety, health, or comfort. By contrast, if following Jesus is most important, you may find yourself in some very unsafe, unhealthy, and uncomfortable places. You will risk death, but you will not fear it because you know Jesus will raise you to eternal life. The person who is concerned only with this life has no such assurance. His or her earthly life may be longer, but it will most likely be marred by feelings of boredom and worthlessness.

9:1 Greek *the Twelve;* other manuscripts read *the twelve apostles.* **9:3** Or *silver coins.* **9:7** Greek *Herod the tetrarch.* Herod Antipas was a son of King Herod and was ruler over Galilee. **9:20** Or *the Christ. Messiah* (a Hebrew term) and *Christ* (a Greek term) both mean "the anointed one." **9:22** "Son of Man" is a title Jesus used for himself.

for my sake, you will save it. ²⁵And what do you benefit if you gain the whole world but are yourself lost or destroyed? ²⁶If anyone is ashamed of me and my message, the Son of Man will be ashamed of that person when he returns in his glory and in the glory of the Father and the holy angels. ²⁷I tell you the truth, some standing here right now will not die before they see the Kingdom of God."

THE TRANSFIGURATION ²⁸About eight days later Jesus took Peter, John, and James up on a mountain to pray. ²⁹And as he was praying, the appearance of his face was transformed, and his clothes became dazzling white. ³⁰Suddenly, two men, Moses and Elijah, appeared and began talking with Jesus. ³¹They were glorious to see. And they were speaking about his exodus from this world, which was about to be fulfilled in Jerusalem.

³²Peter and the others had fallen asleep. When they woke up, they saw Jesus' glory and the two men standing with him. ³³As Moses and Elijah were starting to leave, Peter, not even knowing what he was saying, blurted out, "Master, it's wonderful for us to be here! Let's make three shelters as memorials*—one for you, one for Moses, and one for Elijah." ³⁴But even as he was saying this, a cloud overshadowed them, and terror gripped them as the cloud covered them.

³⁵Then a voice from the cloud said, "This is my Son, my Chosen One.* Listen to him." ³⁶When the voice finished, Jesus was there alone. They didn't tell anyone at that time what they had seen.

JESUS HEALS A DEMON-POSSESSED BOY ³⁷The next day, after they had come down the mountain, a large crowd met Jesus. ³⁸A man in the crowd called out to him, "Teacher, I beg you to look at my son, my only child. ³⁹An evil spirit keeps seizing him, making him scream. It throws him into convulsions so that he foams at the mouth. It batters him and hardly ever

leaves him alone. ⁴⁰I begged your disciples to cast out the spirit, but they couldn't do it."

⁴¹Jesus said, "You faithless and corrupt people! How long must I be with you and put up with you?" Then he said to the man, "Bring your son here."

⁴²As the boy came forward, the demon knocked him to the ground and threw him into a violent convulsion. But Jesus rebuked the evil* spirit and healed the boy. Then he gave him back to his father. ⁴³Awe gripped the people as they saw this majestic display of God's power.

JESUS AGAIN PREDICTS HIS DEATH While everyone was marveling at everything he was doing, Jesus said to his disciples, ⁴⁴"Listen to me and remember what I say. The Son of Man is going to be betrayed into the hands of his enemies." ⁴⁵But they didn't know what he meant. Its significance was hidden from them, so they couldn't understand it, and they were afraid to ask him about it.

THE GREATEST IN THE KINGDOM ⁴⁶Then his disciples began arguing about which of them was the greatest. ⁴⁷But Jesus knew their thoughts, so he brought a little child to his side. ⁴⁸Then he said to them, "Anyone who welcomes a little child like this on my behalf* welcomes me, and anyone who welcomes me also welcomes my Father who sent me. Whoever is the least among you is the greatest."

USING THE NAME OF JESUS ⁴⁹John said to Jesus, "Master, we saw someone using your name to cast out demons, but we told him to stop because he isn't in our group."

⁵⁰But Jesus said, "Don't stop him! Anyone who is not against you is for you."

OPPOSITION FROM SAMARITANS ⁵¹As the time drew near for him to ascend to heaven, Jesus resolutely set out for Jerusalem. ⁵²He sent messengers ahead to a Samaritan village to prepare for his arrival. ⁵³But the people of the village did not welcome Jesus because he was on his way to Jerusalem. ⁵⁴When James and John saw this, they said to Jesus, "Lord, should we call down fire from heaven to burn them up*?" ⁵⁵But Jesus turned and rebuked them.* ⁵⁶So they went on to another village.

....

RETREAT AND RETURN
(9:28-36) Peter, James, and John had such an amazing time with Jesus up on a mountain that they didn't want to leave. Ever been to a youth retreat or had a time with God that was so cool you didn't want it to end? Being away from the reality and problems of our daily life can seem inviting. But we can't stay "on top of a mountain" forever. Instead of becoming spiritual giants, we would soon become giants of self-centeredness. We need times of retreat and renewal, but only so we can return to help build up our family and friends. Our faith must make sense off the mountain as well as on it.

9:33 Greek *three tabernacles.*   **9:35** Some manuscripts read *This is my dearly loved Son.*   **9:42** Greek *unclean.*   **9:48** Greek *in my name.*   **9:54** Some manuscripts add *as Elijah did.*   **9:55** Some manuscripts add an expanded conclusion to verse 55 and an additional sentence in verse 56: *And he said, "You don't realize what your hearts are like. ⁵⁶For the Son of Man has not come to destroy people's lives, but to save them."*

THE COST OF FOLLOWING JESUS ⁵⁷As they were walking along, someone said to Jesus, "I will follow you wherever you go."

⁵⁸But Jesus replied, "Foxes have dens to live in, and birds have nests, but the Son of Man has no place even to lay his head."

⁵⁹He said to another person, "Come, follow me."

The man agreed, but he said, "Lord, first let me return home and bury my father."

⁶⁰But Jesus told him, "Let the spiritually dead bury their own dead!* Your duty is to go and preach about the Kingdom of God."

⁶¹Another said, "Yes, Lord, I will follow you, but first let me say good-bye to my family."

⁶²But Jesus told him, "Anyone who puts a hand to the plow and then looks back is not fit for the Kingdom of God."

10 JESUS SENDS OUT HIS DISCIPLES The Lord now chose seventy-two* other disciples and sent them ahead in pairs to all the towns and places he planned to visit. ²These were his instructions to them: "The harvest is great, but the workers are few. So pray to the Lord who is in charge of the harvest; ask him to send more workers into his fields. ³Now go, and remember that I am sending you out as lambs among wolves. ⁴Don't take any money with you, nor a traveler's bag, nor an extra pair of sandals. And don't stop to greet anyone on the road.

⁵Whenever you enter someone's home, first say, 'May God's peace be on this house.' ⁶If those who live there are peaceful, the bless-

ing will stand; if they are not, the blessing will return to you. ⁷Don't move around from home to home. Stay in one place, eating and drinking what they provide. Don't hesitate to accept hospitality, because those who work deserve their pay.

⁸"If you enter a town and it welcomes you, eat whatever is set before you. ⁹Heal the sick, and tell them, 'The Kingdom of God is near you now.' ¹⁰But if a town refuses to welcome you, go out into its streets and say, ¹¹"We wipe even the dust of your town from our feet to show that we have abandoned you to your fate. And know this—the Kingdom of God is near!' ¹²I assure you, even wicked Sodom will be better off than such a town on judgment day.

¹³"What sorrow awaits you, Korazin and Bethsaida! For if the miracles I did in you had been done in wicked Tyre and Sidon, their people would have repented of their sins long ago, clothing themselves in burlap and throwing ashes on their heads to show their remorse. ¹⁴Yes, Tyre and Sidon will be better off on judgment day than you. ¹⁵And you people of Capernaum, will you be honored in heaven? No, you will go down to the place of the dead.*"

¹⁶Then he said to the disciples, "Anyone who accepts your message is also accepting me. And anyone who rejects you is rejecting me. And anyone who rejects me is rejecting God, who sent me."

¹⁷When the seventy-two disciples returned, they joyfully reported to him, "Lord, even the demons obey us when we use your name!"

¹⁸"Yes," he told them, "I saw Satan fall from

9:60 Greek *Let the dead bury their own dead.*   **10:1** Some manuscripts read *seventy;* also in 10:17.   **10:15** Greek *to Hades.*

CHOICES
enemies

The situation:

Madison is driving home from Starbucks on a rainy night. As she rounds a curve in the road, she sees someone walking in the mud along the side of the road. It's Ginny. A hundred yards up the road, Madison sees Ginny's car in the ditch.

Should she stop and help?

Maybe that seems like a stupid question, but consider . . .

The background:

Ginny's life is like a fairy tale . . . no exaggeration:
• Her family has some major cash.
• She drives a brand-new BMW convertible.
• She always looks like she just stepped off the cover of a fashion magazine.
• She dates a really handsome college sophomore.

• She makes straight As.
• She has traveled all over the world.

As you might imagine, many people are jealous of Ginny's good fortune. Madison is right there among them. But Madison's feelings go beyond envy to include, shall we say, extreme dislike.

See, last year, Ginny always went out of her way to make Madison feel like an absolute loser. She has made some really rude remarks about Madison—behind her back. Not only that, Ginny absolutely humiliated Madison at a pep rally—right in front of everyone! The two haven't spoken since. When they're in the same room, everyone can feel the tension.

The solution:

Read Luke 10:25-37. Based on this passage, what do you think Madison should do? Why?

A COLLECTION OF ATTITUDES

The needs of others bring out various attitudes in us. Jesus used the story of the good but despised Samaritan (Luke 10:30-37) to make clear what attitude was acceptable to him. If we are honest, we often will find ourselves in the place of the lawyer, needing to learn again who our neighbor is. Note the variety of attitudes toward the wounded man:

To the **LAWYER**, the wounded man was a subject to discuss.

To the **INNKEEPER**, the wounded man was a customer to serve for a fee.

To the **BANDITS**, the wounded man was someone to use and exploit.

To the **RELIGIOUS MEN**, the wounded man was a problem to be avoided.

To the **SAMARITAN**, the wounded man was a human being worthy of care and love.

To **JESUS**, all of them—and all of us—were worth dying for.

heaven like lightning! [19]Look, I have given you authority over all the power of the enemy, and you can walk among snakes and scorpions and crush them. Nothing will injure you. [20]But don't rejoice because evil spirits obey you; rejoice because your names are registered in heaven."

JESUS' PRAYER OF THANKSGIVING [21]At that same time Jesus was filled with the joy of the Holy Spirit, and he said, "O Father, Lord of heaven and earth, thank you for hiding these things from those who think themselves wise and clever, and for revealing them to the childlike. Yes, Father, it pleased you to do it this way.

[22]"My Father has entrusted everything to me. No one truly knows the Son except the Father, and no one truly knows the Father except the Son and those to whom the Son chooses to reveal him."

[23]Then when they were alone, he turned to

the disciples and said, "Blessed are the eyes that see what you have seen. [24]I tell you, many prophets and kings longed to see what you see, but they didn't see it. And they longed to hear what you hear, but they didn't hear it."

THE MOST IMPORTANT COMMANDMENT [25]One day an expert in religious law stood up to test Jesus by asking him this question: "Teacher, what should I do to inherit eternal life?"

[26]Jesus replied, "What does the law of Moses say? How do you read it?"

[27]The man answered, "'You must love the LORD your God with all your heart, all your soul, all your strength, and all your mind.' And, 'Love your neighbor as yourself.'"*

[28]"Right!" Jesus told him. "Do this and you will live!"

[29]The man wanted to justify his actions, so he asked Jesus, "And who is my neighbor?"

PARABLE OF THE GOOD SAMARITAN [30]Jesus replied with a story: "A Jewish man was traveling from Jerusalem down to Jericho, and he was attacked by bandits. They stripped him of his clothes, beat him up, and left him half dead beside the road.

[31]"By chance a priest came along. But when he saw the man lying there, he crossed to the other side of the road and passed him by. [32]A Temple assistant* walked over and looked at him lying there, but he also passed by on the other side.

[33]"Then a despised Samaritan came along, and when he saw the man, he felt compassion for him. [34]Going over to him, the Samaritan soothed his wounds with olive oil and wine and bandaged them. Then he put the man on his own donkey and took him to an inn, where he took care of him. [35]The next day he handed the innkeeper two silver coins,* telling him, 'Take care of this man. If his bill runs higher than this, I'll pay you the next time I'm here.'

[36]"Now which of these three would you say was a neighbor to the man who was attacked by bandits?" Jesus asked.

[37]The man replied, "The one who showed him mercy."

Then Jesus said, "Yes, now go and do the same."

JESUS VISITS MARTHA AND MARY [38]As Jesus and the disciples continued on their way to Jerusalem, they came to a certain village where a

---

A GOOD NEIGHBOR
(10:27-37) The parable of the Good Samaritan teaches three principles about loving our neighbors: (1) Lack of love is often easy to justify. (2) Our neighbor is anyone of any race or social background who is in need. (3) Loving someone means acting to meet that person's need. Wherever you live, there are needy people close by. To whom will you be a "Good Samaritan"?

10:27 Deut 6:5; Lev 19:18.   **10:32** Greek *A Levite.*   **10:35** Greek *two denarii.* A denarius was equivalent to a laborer's full day's wage.

woman named Martha welcomed him into her home. [39]Her sister, Mary, sat at the Lord's feet, listening to what he taught. [40]But Martha was distracted by the big dinner she was preparing. She came to Jesus and said, "Lord, doesn't it seem unfair to you that my sister just sits here while I do all the work? Tell her to come and help me."

[41]But the Lord said to her, "My dear Martha, you are worried and upset over all these details! [42]There is only one thing worth being concerned about. Mary has discovered it, and it will not be taken away from her."

11 **TEACHING ABOUT PRAYER** Once Jesus was in a certain place praying. As he finished, one of his disciples came to him and said, "Lord, teach us to pray, just as John taught his disciples."

[2]Jesus said, "This is how you should pray:*

"Father, may your name be kept holy.
　　May your Kingdom come soon.
[3] Give us each day the food we need,*
[4] and forgive us our sins,
　　as we forgive those who sin against us.
　And don't let us yield to temptation.*"

[5]Then, teaching them more about prayer, he used this story: "Suppose you went to a friend's house at midnight, wanting to borrow three loaves of bread. You say to him, [6]'A friend of mine has just arrived for a visit, and I have nothing for him to eat.' [7]And suppose he calls out from his bedroom, 'Don't bother me. The door is locked for the night, and my family and I are all in bed. I can't help you.' [8]But I tell you this—though he won't do it for friendship's sake, if you keep knocking long enough, he will get up and give you whatever you need because of your shameless persistence.*

[9]"And so I tell you, keep on asking, and you will receive what you ask for. Keep on seeking, and you will find. Keep on knocking, and the door will be opened to you. [10]For everyone who asks, receives. Everyone who seeks, finds. And to everyone who knocks, the door will be opened.

[11]"You fathers—if your children ask* for a fish, do you give them a snake instead? [12]Or if they ask for an egg, do you give them a scorpion? Of course not! [13]So if you sinful people

know how to give good gifts to your children, how much more will your heavenly Father give the Holy Spirit to those who ask him."

JESUS AND THE PRINCE OF DEMONS [14]One day Jesus cast out a demon from a man who couldn't speak, and when the demon was gone, the man began to speak. The crowds were amazed, [15]but some of them said, "No wonder he can cast out demons. He gets his power from Satan,* the prince of demons." [16]Others, trying to test Jesus, demanded that he show them a miraculous sign from heaven to prove his authority.

[17]He knew their thoughts, so he said, "Any kingdom divided by civil war is doomed. A family splintered by feuding will fall apart. [18]You say I am empowered by Satan. But if Satan is divided and fighting against himself, how can his kingdom survive? [19]And if I am empowered by Satan, what about your own exorcists? They cast out demons, too, so they will condemn you for what you have said. [20]But if I am casting out demons by the power of God,* then the Kingdom of God has arrived among you. [21]For when a strong man like Satan is fully armed and guards his palace, his possessions are safe—[22]until someone even stronger attacks and overpowers him, strips him of his weapons, and carries off his belongings.

[23]"Anyone who isn't with me opposes me, and anyone who isn't working with me is actually working against me.

[24]"When an evil* spirit leaves a person, it goes into the desert, searching for rest. But when it finds none, it says, 'I will return to the person I came from.' [25]So it returns and finds that its former home is all swept and in order. [26]Then the spirit finds seven other spirits more evil than itself, and they all enter the person and live there. And so that person is worse off than before."

....

PRAYER OR SHOPPING LIST?
(11:1-4) Notice the order in this prayer. First Jesus praised God; then he made his requests. Praising God first puts us in the right frame of mind to tell him about our needs. Too often our prayers are more like shopping lists than conversations.

TEMPTATION
(11:4) In this verse Jesus is not implying that God leads us into temptation. He is simply asking for deliverance from Satan and his deceit. All Christians struggle with temptation. Sometimes a temptation is so subtle we don't even realize what's happening to us. God promised that he won't allow us to be tempted beyond our endurance (1 Cor 10:13). God can help you recognize temptation and overcome it.

11:2 Some manuscripts add additional phrases from the Lord's Prayer as it reads in Matt 6:9-13.　**11:3** Or *Give us each day our food for the day;* or *Give us each day our food for tomorrow.*　**11:4** Or *And keep us from being tested.*　**11:8** Or *in order to avoid shame,* or *so his reputation won't be damaged.*　**11:11** Some manuscripts add *for bread, do you give them a stone? Or [if they ask].*　**11:15** Greek *Beelzeboul;* also in 11:18, 19. Other manuscripts read *Beezeboul;* Latin version reads *Beelzebub.*　**11:20** Greek *by the finger of God.*　**11:24** Greek *unclean.*

²⁷As he was speaking, a woman in the crowd called out, "God bless your mother—the womb from which you came, and the breasts that nursed you!"

²⁸Jesus replied, "But even more blessed are all who hear the word of God and put it into practice."

THE SIGN OF JONAH ²⁹As the crowd pressed in on Jesus, he said, "This evil generation keeps asking me to show them a miraculous sign. But the only sign I will give them is the sign of Jonah. ³⁰What happened to him was a sign to the people of Nineveh that God had sent him. What happens to the Son of Man* will be a sign to these people that he was sent by God.

³¹"The queen of Sheba* will stand up against this generation on judgment day and condemn it, for she came from a distant land to hear the wisdom of Solomon. Now someone greater than Solomon is here—but you refuse to listen. ³²The people of Nineveh will also stand up against this generation on judgment day and condemn it, for they repented of their sins at the preaching of Jonah. Now someone greater than Jonah is here—but you refuse to repent.

•••

FOR OR AGAINST?
(11:23) Jesus' statement, "Anyone who isn't working with me is actually working against me," goes along with a statement made earlier: "Anyone who is not against you is for you" (9:50). People who are neutral toward Christians are actually helping them more than hurting them because they aren't setting up barriers. But no one can remain neutral forever. Sooner or later everyone must choose. If you aren't actively for Christ, you are against him. What's your choice?

MOTIVES
(11:37-54) Jesus had harsh words for the Pharisees, because they (1) washed their hands but not their hearts, (2) remembered to tithe but forgot justice, (3) loved people's praise, (4) made impossible religious demands, and (5) didn't accept the truth about Jesus and prevented others from believing it. They wrongly focused on outward appearances and ignored the condition of their hearts. We do the same when our service is motivated by a desire to be seen rather than coming from a pure heart and love for others. Others may be fooled, but God isn't. What motivates you to serve others?

RECEIVING THE LIGHT ³³"No one lights a lamp and then hides it or puts it under a basket.* Instead, a lamp is placed on a stand, where its light can be seen by all who enter the house.

³⁴"Your eye is a lamp that provides light for your body. When your eye is good, your whole body is filled with light. But when it is bad, your body is filled with darkness. ³⁵Make sure that the light you think you have is not actually darkness. ³⁶If you are filled with light, with no dark corners, then your whole life will be radiant, as though a floodlight were filling you with light."

JESUS CRITICIZES THE RELIGIOUS LEADERS
³⁷As Jesus was speaking, one of the Pharisees invited him home for a meal. So he went in and took his place at the table.* ³⁸His host was amazed to see that he sat down to eat without first performing the hand-washing ceremony required by Jewish custom. ³⁹Then the Lord said to him, "You Pharisees are so careful to clean the outside of the cup and the dish, but inside you are filthy—full of greed and wickedness! ⁴⁰Fools! Didn't God make the inside as well as the outside? ⁴¹So clean the inside by giving gifts to the poor, and you will be clean all over.

⁴²"What sorrow awaits you Pharisees! For you are careful to tithe even the tiniest income from your herb gardens,* but you ignore justice and the love of God. You should tithe, yes, but do not neglect the more important things.

⁴³"What sorrow awaits you Pharisees! For you love to sit in the seats of honor in the synagogues and receive respectful greetings as you walk in the marketplaces. ⁴⁴Yes, what sorrow awaits you! For you are like hidden graves in a field. People walk over them without knowing the corruption they are stepping on."

⁴⁵"Teacher," said an expert in religious law, "you have insulted us, too, in what you just said."

⁴⁶"Yes," said Jesus, "what sorrow also awaits you experts in religious law! For you crush people with unbearable religious demands, and you never lift a finger to ease the burden. ⁴⁷What sorrow awaits you! For you build monuments for the prophets your own ancestors killed long ago. ⁴⁸But in fact, you stand as witnesses who agree with what your ancestors did. They killed the prophets, and you join in their crime by building the monuments! ⁴⁹This is what God in his wisdom said

11:30 "Son of Man" is a title Jesus used for himself.   11:31 Greek *The queen of the south.*   11:33 Some manuscripts do not include *or puts it under a basket.*   11:37 Or *and reclined.*   11:42 Greek *tithe the mint, the rue, and every herb.*

about you:* 'I will send prophets and apostles to them, but they will kill some and persecute the others.'

⁵⁰"As a result, this generation will be held responsible for the murder of all God's prophets from the creation of the world—⁵¹from the murder of Abel to the murder of Zechariah, who was killed between the altar and the sanctuary. Yes, it will certainly be charged against this generation.

⁵²"What sorrow awaits you experts in religious law! For you remove the key to knowledge from the people. You don't enter the Kingdom yourselves, and you prevent others from entering."

⁵³As Jesus was leaving, the teachers of religious law and the Pharisees became hostile and tried to provoke him with many questions. ⁵⁴They wanted to trap him into saying something they could use against him.

12 A WARNING AGAINST HYPOCRISY

Meanwhile, the crowds grew until thousands were milling about and stepping on each other. Jesus turned first to his disciples and warned them, "Beware of the yeast of the Pharisees—their hypocrisy. ²The time is coming when everything that is covered up will be revealed, and all that is secret will be made known to all. ³Whatever you have said in the dark will be heard in the light, and what you have whispered behind closed doors will be shouted from the housetops for all to hear!

⁴"Dear friends, don't be afraid of those who want to kill your body; they cannot do any more to you after that. ⁵But I'll tell you whom to fear. Fear God, who has the power to kill you and then throw you into hell.* Yes, he's the one to fear.

⁶"What is the price of five sparrows—two copper coins*? Yet God does not forget a single one of them. ⁷And the very hairs on your head are all numbered. So don't be afraid; you are more valuable to God than a whole flock of sparrows.

⁸"I tell you the truth, everyone who acknowledges me publicly here on earth, the Son of Man* will also acknowledge in the presence of God's angels. ⁹But anyone who denies me here on earth will be denied before God's angels.

¹⁰Anyone who speaks against the Son of Man can be forgiven, but anyone who blasphemes the Holy Spirit will not be forgiven.

¹¹"And when you are brought to trial in the synagogues and before rulers and authorities, don't worry about how to defend yourself or what to say, ¹²for the Holy Spirit will teach you at that time what needs to be said."

PARABLE OF THE RICH FOOL ¹³Then someone called from the crowd, "Teacher, please tell my brother to divide our father's estate with me."

¹⁴Jesus replied, "Friend, who made me a judge over you to decide such things as that?" ¹⁵Then he said, "Beware! Guard against every kind of greed. Life is not measured by how much you own."

¹⁶Then he told them a story: "A rich man had a fertile farm that produced fine crops. ¹⁷He said to himself, 'What should I do? I don't have room for all my crops.' ¹⁸Then he said, 'I know! I'll tear down my barns and build bigger ones. Then I'll have room enough to store all my wheat and other goods. ¹⁹And I'll sit back and say to myself, "My friend, you have enough stored away for years to come. Now take it easy! Eat, drink, and be merry!"'

²⁰"But God said to him, 'You fool! You will die this very night. Then who will get everything you worked for?'

²¹"Yes, a person is a fool to store up earthly wealth but not have a rich relationship with God."

TEACHING ABOUT MONEY AND POSSESSIONS ²²Then, turning to his disciples, Jesus said, "That is why I tell you not to worry about everyday life—whether you have enough food to eat or enough clothes to wear. ²³For life is more than food, and your body more than clothing. ²⁴Look at the ravens. They don't plant or harvest or store food in barns, for God feeds them. And you are far more valuable to him than any birds! ²⁵Can all your worries add a single moment to your life? ²⁶And if worry can't accomplish a little thing like that, what's the use of worrying over bigger things?

²⁷"Look at the lilies and how they grow. They don't work or make their clothing, yet Solomon in all his glory was not dressed as beautifully as they are. ²⁸And if God cares so wonderfully

....

REAL VALUE
(12:13-21) When asked to give advice on how an estate should be split, Jesus gave a different answer than was expected: "Life is not measured by how much you own" (12:15). The parable he told (12:16-20) emphasized his point. Sadly, we often measure our worth or success by how much money or stuff we have. But as Jesus warned, a person with lots of stuff who lacks a relationship with God is poor indeed. Tempted to measure your life by your stuff? Don't.

11:49 Greek *Therefore, the wisdom of God said.*　12:5 Greek *Gehenna.*　12:6 Greek *two assaria* [Roman coins equal to ¹⁄₁₆ of a denarius].　12:8 "Son of Man" is a title Jesus used for himself.

for flowers that are here today and thrown into the fire tomorrow, he will certainly care for you. Why do you have so little faith?

²⁹"And don't be concerned about what to eat and what to drink. Don't worry about such things. ³⁰These things dominate the thoughts of unbelievers all over the world, but your Father already knows your needs. ³¹Seek the Kingdom of God above all else, and he will give you everything you need.

³²"So don't be afraid, little flock. For it gives your Father great happiness to give you the Kingdom.

³³"Sell your possessions and give to those in need. This will store up treasure for you in heaven! And the purses of heaven never get old or develop holes. Your treasure will be safe; no thief can steal it and no moth can destroy it. ³⁴Wherever your treasure is, there the desires of your heart will also be.

BE READY FOR THE LORD'S COMING ³⁵"Be dressed for service and keep your lamps burning, ³⁶as though you were waiting for your master to return from the wedding feast. Then you will be ready to open the door and let him in the moment he arrives and knocks. ³⁷The servants who are ready and waiting for his return will be rewarded. I tell you the truth, he himself will seat them, put on an apron, and serve them as they sit and eat! ³⁸He may come in the middle of the night or just before dawn.* But whenever he comes, he will reward the servants who are ready.

³⁹"Understand this: If a homeowner knew exactly when a burglar was coming, he would not permit his house to be broken into. ⁴⁰You also must be ready all the time, for the Son of Man will come when least expected."

⁴¹Peter asked, "Lord, is that illustration just for us or for everyone?"

⁴²And the Lord replied, "A faithful, sensible servant is one to whom the master can give the responsibility of managing his other household servants and feeding them. ⁴³If the master returns and finds that the servant has done a

good job, there will be a reward. ⁴⁴I tell you the truth, the master will put that servant in charge of all he owns. ⁴⁵But what if the servant thinks, 'My master won't be back for a while,' and he begins beating the other servants, partying, and getting drunk? ⁴⁶The master will return unannounced and unexpected, and he will cut the servant in pieces and banish him with the unfaithful.

⁴⁷"And a servant who knows what the master wants, but isn't prepared and doesn't carry out those instructions, will be severely punished. ⁴⁸But someone who does not know, and then does something wrong, will be punished only lightly. When someone has been given much, much will be required in return; and when someone has been entrusted with much, even more will be required.

JESUS CAUSES DIVISION ⁴⁹"I have come to set the world on fire, and I wish it were already burning! ⁵⁰I have a terrible baptism of suffering ahead of me, and I am under a heavy burden until it is accomplished. ⁵¹Do you think I have come to bring peace to the earth? No, I have come to divide people against each other! ⁵²From now on families will be split apart, three in favor of me, and two against—or two in favor and three against.

⁵³ 'Father will be divided against son
    and son against father;
mother against daughter
    and daughter against mother;
and mother-in-law against daughter-in-law
    and daughter-in-law against
        mother-in-law.'*"

⁵⁴Then Jesus turned to the crowd and said, "When you see clouds beginning to form in the west, you say, 'Here comes a shower.' And you are right. ⁵⁵When the south wind blows, you say, 'Today will be a scorcher.' And it is. ⁵⁶You fools! You know how to interpret the weather signs of the earth and sky, but you don't know how to interpret the present times.

⁵⁷"Why can't you decide for yourselves what is right? ⁵⁸When you are on the way to court with your accuser, try to settle the matter before you get there. Otherwise, your accuser may drag you before the judge, who will hand you over to an officer, who will throw you into prison. ⁵⁹And if that happens, you won't be free again until you have paid the very last penny.*"

. . . .

DIVIDED LOYALTIES
(12:51-53) Jesus revealed that his coming often results in conflict. There is no middle ground with Jesus. Close groups can be torn apart when some choose to follow him and others refuse to do so. Loyalties must be declared and commitments made, sometimes to the severing of other relationships. Life is easiest when a whole family believes in Christ; yet this often is not the case. Are you willing to risk your family's disapproval (if necessary) to take a stand for Jesus?

12:38 Greek *in the second or third watch.*   12:53 Mic 7:6.
12:59 Greek *last lepton* [the smallest Jewish coin].

13 A CALL TO REPENTANCE

About this time Jesus was informed that Pilate had murdered some people from Galilee as they were offering sacrifices at the Temple. ²"Do you think those Galileans were worse sinners than all the other people from Galilee?" Jesus asked. "Is that why they suffered? ³Not at all! And you will perish, too, unless you repent of your sins and turn to God. ⁴And what about the eighteen people who died when the tower in Siloam fell on them? Were they the worst sinners in Jerusalem? ⁵No, and I tell you again that unless you repent, you will perish, too."

PARABLE OF THE BARREN FIG TREE

⁶Then Jesus told this story: "A man planted a fig tree in his garden and came again and again to see if there was any fruit on it, but he was always disappointed. ⁷Finally, he said to his gardener, 'I've waited three years, and there hasn't been a single fig! Cut it down. It's just taking up space in the garden.'

⁸"The gardener answered, 'Sir, give it one more chance. Leave it another year, and I'll give it special attention and plenty of fertilizer. ⁹If we get figs next year, fine. If not, then you can cut it down.'"

JESUS HEALS ON THE SABBATH

¹⁰One Sabbath day as Jesus was teaching in a synagogue, ¹¹he saw a woman who had been crippled by an evil spirit. She had been bent double for eighteen years and was unable to stand up straight. ¹²When Jesus saw her, he called her over and said, "Dear woman, you are healed of your sickness!" ¹³Then he touched her, and instantly she could stand straight. How she praised God!

¹⁴But the leader in charge of the synagogue was indignant that Jesus had healed her on the Sabbath day. "There are six days of the week for working," he said to the crowd. "Come on those days to be healed, not on the Sabbath."

¹⁵But the Lord replied, "You hypocrites! Each of you works on the Sabbath day! Don't you untie your ox or your donkey from its stall on the Sabbath and lead it out for water? ¹⁶This dear woman, a daughter of Abraham, has been held in bondage by Satan for eighteen years. Isn't it right that she be released, even on the Sabbath?"

¹⁷This shamed his enemies, but all the people rejoiced at the wonderful things he did.

13:30 Greek *Some are last who will be first, and some are first who will be last.*

PARABLE OF THE MUSTARD SEED

¹⁸Then Jesus said, "What is the Kingdom of God like? How can I illustrate it? ¹⁹It is like a tiny mustard seed that a man planted in a garden; it grows and becomes a tree, and the birds make nests in its branches."

PARABLE OF THE YEAST

²⁰He also asked, "What else is the Kingdom of God like? ²¹It is like the yeast a woman used in making bread. Even though she put only a little yeast in three measures of flour, it permeated every part of the dough."

THE NARROW DOOR

²²Jesus went through the towns and villages, teaching as he went, always pressing on toward Jerusalem. ²³Someone asked him, "Lord, will only a few be saved?"

He replied, ²⁴"Work hard to enter the narrow door to God's Kingdom, for many will try to enter but will fail. ²⁵When the master of the house has locked the door, it will be too late. You will stand outside knocking and pleading, 'Lord, open the door for us!' But he will reply, 'I don't know you or where you come from.' ²⁶Then you will say, 'But we ate and drank with you, and you taught in our streets.' ²⁷And he will reply, 'I tell you, I don't know you or where you come from. Get away from me, all you who do evil.'

²⁸"There will be weeping and gnashing of teeth, for you will see Abraham, Isaac, Jacob, and all the prophets in the Kingdom of God, but you will be thrown out. ²⁹And people will come from all over the world—from east and west, north and south—to take their places in the Kingdom of God. ³⁰And note this: Some who seem least important now will be the greatest then, and some who are the greatest now will be least important then.*"

JESUS GRIEVES OVER JERUSALEM

³¹At that time some Pharisees said to him, "Get away from here if you want to live! Herod Antipas wants to kill you!"

³²Jesus replied, "Go tell that fox that I will keep on casting out demons and healing

NARROW-MINDED
(13:22-30) Maybe you've heard people talk about how "narrow-minded" Christians are. Well, they're right. Jesus declared that the way to heaven is narrow. In John 14:6, he talked more about this "narrow" way: He is the only way to heaven. For many, this narrow view is a stumbling block. They want more options. But those who seek other options will find the door to heaven closed to them (see 13:25). Want to get there? Jesus is your only option.

people today and tomorrow; and the third day I will accomplish my purpose. [33]Yes, today, tomorrow, and the next day I must proceed on my way. For it wouldn't do for a prophet of God to be killed except in Jerusalem!

[34]"O Jerusalem, Jerusalem, the city that kills the prophets and stones God's messengers! How often I have wanted to gather your children together as a hen protects her chicks beneath her wings, but you wouldn't let me. [35]And now, look, your house is abandoned. And you will never see me again until you say, 'Blessings on the one who comes in the name of the Lord!'*"

14 JESUS HEALS ON THE SABBATH One Sabbath day Jesus went to eat dinner in the home of a leader of the Pharisees, and the people were watching him closely. [2]There was a man there whose arms and legs were swollen.* [3]Jesus asked the Pharisees and experts in religious law, "Is it permitted in the law to heal people on the Sabbath day, or not?" [4]When they refused to answer, Jesus touched the sick man and healed him and sent him away. [5]Then he turned to them and said, "Which of you doesn't work on the Sabbath? If your son* or your cow falls into a pit, don't you rush to get him out?" [6]Again they could not answer.

JESUS TEACHES ABOUT HUMILITY [7]When Jesus noticed that all who had come to the dinner were trying to sit in the seats of honor near the head of the table, he gave them this advice: [8]"When you are invited to a wedding feast, don't sit in the seat of honor. What if someone who is more distinguished than you has also been invited? [9]The host will come and say, 'Give this person your seat.' Then you will be embarrassed, and you will have to take whatever seat is left at the foot of the table!

[10]"Instead, take the lowest place at the foot of the table. Then when your host sees you, he will come and say, 'Friend, we have a better

- -

HOW LOW WILL YOU GO?
(14:7-11) Jesus advised people not to rush for the best seats at a feast. Instead, he suggested, "Take the lowest place." In other words, go the humble route. Now, that advice is contrary to the "Look out for number one" philosophy. Taking the lowest place might involve helping someone less fortunate without making an announcement about doing so; letting someone else have the best seat in the movie theater, instead of racing to get it yourself; or even giving up something you want in order to let someone else have it. How "low" will you go?

place for you!' Then you will be honored in front of all the other guests. [11]For those who exalt themselves will be humbled, and those who humble themselves will be exalted."

[12]Then he turned to his host. "When you put on a luncheon or a banquet," he said, "don't invite your friends, brothers, relatives, and rich neighbors. For they will invite you back, and that will be your only reward. [13]Instead, invite the poor, the crippled, the lame, and the blind. [14]Then at the resurrection of the righteous, God will reward you for inviting those who could not repay you."

PARABLE OF THE GREAT FEAST [15]Hearing this, a man sitting at the table with Jesus exclaimed, "What a blessing it will be to attend a banquet* in the Kingdom of God!"

[16]Jesus replied with this story: "A man prepared a great feast and sent out many invitations. [17]When the banquet was ready, he sent his servant to tell the guests, 'Come, the banquet is ready.' [18]But they all began making excuses. One said, 'I have just bought a field and must inspect it. Please excuse me.' [19]Another said, 'I have just bought five pairs of oxen, and I want to try them out. Please excuse me.' [20]Another said, 'I now have a wife, so I can't come.'

[21]"The servant returned and told his master what they had said. His master was furious and said, 'Go quickly into the streets and alleys of the town and invite the poor, the crippled, the blind, and the lame.' [22]After the servant had done this, he reported, 'There is still room for more.' [23]So his master said, 'Go out into the country lanes and behind the hedges and urge anyone you find to come, so that the house will be full. [24]For none of those I first invited will get even the smallest taste of my banquet.'"

THE COST OF BEING A DISCIPLE [25]A large crowd was following Jesus. He turned around and said to them, [26]"If you want to be my disciple, you must hate everyone else by comparison—your father and mother, wife and children, brothers and sisters—yes, even your own life. Otherwise, you cannot be my disciple. [27]And if you do not carry your own cross and follow me, you cannot be my disciple.

[28]"But don't begin until you count the cost. For who would begin construction of a building without first calculating the cost to see if there is enough money to finish it? [29]Other-

13:35 Ps 118:26.   **14:2** Or *who had dropsy.*   **14:5** Some manuscripts read *donkey.*   **14:15** Greek *to eat bread.*

wise, you might complete only the foundation before running out of money, and then everyone would laugh at you. ³⁰They would say, 'There's the person who started that building and couldn't afford to finish it!'

³¹"Or what king would go to war against another king without first sitting down with his counselors to discuss whether his army of 10,000 could defeat the 20,000 soldiers marching against him? ³²And if he can't, he will send a delegation to discuss terms of peace while the enemy is still far away. ³³So you cannot become my disciple without giving up everything you own.

³⁴"Salt is good for seasoning. But if it loses its flavor, how do you make it salty again? ³⁵Flavorless salt is good neither for the soil nor for the manure pile. It is thrown away. Anyone with ears to hear should listen and understand!"

15 **PARABLE OF THE LOST SHEEP** Tax collectors and other notorious sinners often came to listen to Jesus teach. ²This made the Pharisees and teachers of religious law complain that he was associating with such sinful people—even eating with them!

³So Jesus told them this story: ⁴"If a man has a hundred sheep and one of them gets lost, what will he do? Won't he leave the ninety-nine others in the wilderness and go to search for the one that is lost until he finds it? ⁵And when he has found it, he will joyfully carry it home on his shoulders. ⁶When he arrives, he will call together his friends and neighbors, saying, 'Rejoice with me because I have found my lost sheep.' ⁷In the same way, there is more joy in heaven over one lost sinner who repents and returns to God than over ninety-nine others who are righteous and haven't strayed away!

PARABLE OF THE LOST COIN ⁸"Or suppose a woman has ten silver coins* and loses one. Won't she light a lamp and sweep the entire house and search carefully until she finds it? ⁹And when she finds it, she will call in her friends and neighbors and say, 'Rejoice with me because I have found my lost coin.' ¹⁰In the same way, there is joy in the presence of God's angels when even one sinner repents."

PARABLE OF THE LOST SON ¹¹To illustrate the point further, Jesus told them this story: "A man had two sons. ¹²The younger son told his

15:8 Greek *ten drachmas.* A drachma was the equivalent of a full day's wage.

MY STORY: Taylor

My mother and I sometimes had difficulty getting along. Often we would argue, sometimes over the stupidest things. After our fights, I'd feel real bad, but I didn't know what to do about it. I felt it was all her fault, she just didn't understand me, she was being totally unreasonable, etc.

Then I read the parable of the lost son (Luke 15:11-32). And I began to realize that the younger son felt he had every right to take his inheritance and go off on his own. But it didn't get him anywhere. He finally decided to go back home. But his father didn't say, "I told you so," or anything like that. Instead, he gave him a big welcome.

I got to thinking about my attitude toward my mom. I had to admit that I probably was at fault at least some of the time. As hard as it was, I had to apologize when I was wrong and ask forgiveness. (It was probably really hard for the lost son, too.)

I sat down and went over the past several arguments that weren't really resolved and wrote down the specifics on where I was wrong. Then I prayed hard that I could swallow my pride and ask my mom to forgive me.

I finally did. And my mom reacted very much like the father in the story; she was very forgiving. Since then, I've tried to concentrate more on my attitude than on my mom's. And, amazingly, we argue less. But even when we do argue, and I fall into the old patterns, I know that God will forgive me when I ask for it. (So does Mom—usually.)

SALTY

(14:34-35) Salt can lose its flavor. When it gets wet and then dries, nothing is left but a tasteless residue. When Christians blend into the world to avoid the cost of standing for Christ, they're like salt without flavor. Just as salt flavors and preserves food, Christians preserve the good in the world, keep it from spoiling, and bring new flavor to life. This requires planning, willing sacrifice, and unswerving commitment to Christ's Kingdom. Being "salty" isn't always easy, but if a Christian fails in this function, he or she fails to represent Christ in the world. How salty are you?

father, 'I want my share of your estate now before you die.' So his father agreed to divide his wealth between his sons.

¹³"A few days later this younger son packed all his belongings and moved to a distant land, and there he wasted all his money in wild living. ¹⁴About the time his money ran out, a great famine swept over the land, and he began to starve. ¹⁵He persuaded a local farmer to hire him, and the man sent him into his fields to feed the pigs. ¹⁶The young man became so hungry that even the pods he was feeding the pigs looked good to him. But no one gave him anything.

¹⁷"When he finally came to his senses, he said to himself, 'At home even the hired servants have food enough to spare, and here I am dying of hunger! ¹⁸I will go home to my father and say, "Father, I have sinned against both heaven and you, ¹⁹and I am no longer worthy of being called your son. Please take me on as a hired servant."'

²⁰"So he returned home to his father. And while he was still a long way off, his father saw him coming. Filled with love and compassion, he ran to his son, embraced him, and kissed him. ²¹His son said to him, 'Father, I have sinned against both heaven and you, and I am no longer worthy of being called your son.*'

²²"But his father said to the servants, 'Quick! Bring the finest robe in the house and put it on him. Get a ring for his finger and sandals for his feet. ²³And kill the calf we have been fattening. We must celebrate with a feast, ²⁴for this son of mine was dead and has now returned to life. He was lost, but now he is found.' So the party began.

²⁵"Meanwhile, the older son was in the fields working. When he returned home, he heard music and dancing in the house, ²⁶and he asked one of the servants what was going on. ²⁷'Your brother is back,' he was told, 'and your father has killed the fattened calf. We are celebrating because of his safe return.'

²⁸"The older brother was angry and wouldn't go in. His father came out and begged him, ²⁹but he replied, 'All these years I've slaved for you and never once refused to do a single thing you told me to. And in all that time you never gave me even one young goat for a feast with my friends. ³⁰Yet when this son of yours comes back after squandering your money on prostitutes, you celebrate by killing the fattened calf!'

³¹"His father said to him, 'Look, dear son, you have always stayed by me, and everything I have is yours. ³²We had to celebrate this happy day. For your brother was dead and has come back to life! He was lost, but now he is found!'"

16 PARABLE OF THE SHREWD MANAGER

Jesus told this story to his disciples: "There was a certain rich man who had a manager handling his affairs. One day a report came that the manager was wasting his employer's money. ²So the employer called him in and said, 'What's this I hear about you? Get your report in order, because you are going to be fired.'

³"The manager thought to himself, 'Now what? My boss has fired me. I don't have the strength to dig ditches, and I'm too proud to beg. ⁴Ah, I know how to ensure that I'll have plenty of friends who will give me a home when I am fired.'

⁵"So he invited each person who owed money to his employer to come and discuss the situation. He asked the first one, 'How much do you owe him?' ⁶The man replied, 'I owe him 800 gallons of olive oil.' So the manager told him, 'Take the bill and quickly change it to 400 gallons.*'

⁷"'And how much do you owe my employer?' he asked the next man. 'I owe him 1,000 bushels of wheat,' was the reply. 'Here,' the manager said, 'take the bill and change it to 800 bushels.*'

⁸"The rich man had to admire the dishonest rascal for being so shrewd. And it is true that the children of this world are more shrewd in dealing with the world around them than are the children of the light. ⁹Here's the lesson: Use your worldly resources to benefit others and make friends. Then, when your earthly

---

A FORGIVING RESPONSE
(15:11-32) In the story of the lost son, we find a contrast between the response of the father and that of the older brother (see 15:20-30). The father was forgiving and overjoyed. The brother was unforgiving and bitter. The father forgave because he was joyful, and the son refused to forgive because he was bitter. In fact, the older son didn't think his brother deserved forgiveness.

We sometimes base our decision to forgive someone on whether or not he or she deserves it. But lack of forgiveness reflects more on the attitude of the person who refuses to offer it than on the person who needs it. Which response will you choose when someone seeks your forgiveness?

15:21 Some manuscripts add *Please take me on as a hired servant.* **16:6** Greek *100 baths . . . 50 [baths].* **16:7** Greek *100 korous . . . 80 [korous].*

JESUS AND THE TEN COMMANDMENTS

THE TEN COMMANDMENTS SAID . . .	JESUS SAID . . .
You must not have any other god but me. *Exodus 20:3*	You must worship the LORD your God and serve only him. *Matthew 4:10*
You must not make for yourself an idol of any kind or an image of anything in the heavens or on the earth or in the sea. *Exodus 20:4*	No one can serve two masters. *Luke 16:13*
You must not misuse the name of the LORD your God. The LORD will not let you go unpunished if you misuse his name. *Exodus 20:7*	Do not make any vows! Do not say, "By heaven!" because heaven is God's throne. *Matthew 5:34*
Remember to observe the Sabbath day by keeping it holy. *Exodus 20:8*	The Sabbath was made to meet the needs of people, and not people to meet the requirements of the Sabbath. So the Son of Man is Lord, even over the Sabbath! *Mark 2:27-28*
Honor your father and mother. Then you will live a long, full life in the land the LORD your God is giving you. *Exodus 20:12*	If you love your father or mother more than you love me, you are not worthy of being mine; or if you love your son or daughter more than me, you are not worthy of being mine. *Matthew 10:37*
You must not murder. *Exodus 20:13*	If you are even angry with someone, you are subject to judgment! If you call someone an idiot, you are in danger of being brought before the court. And if you curse someone, you are in danger of the fires of hell. *Matthew 5:22*
You must not commit adultery. *Exodus 20:14*	Anyone who even looks at a woman with lust has already committed adultery with her in his heart. *Matthew 5:28*
You must not steal. *Exodus 20:15*	If you are sued in court and your shirt is taken from you, give your coat, too. *Matthew 5:40*
You must not testify falsely against your neighbor. *Exodus 20:16*	You must give an account on judgment day for every idle word you speak. The words you say will either acquit you or condemn you. *Matthew 12:36-37*
You must not covet your neighbor's house. You must not covet your neighbor's wife, male or female servant, ox or donkey, or anything else that belongs to your neighbor. *Exodus 20:17*	Guard against every kind of greed. Life is not measured by how much you own. *Luke 12:15*

possessions are gone, they will welcome you to an eternal home.*

¹⁰"If you are faithful in little things, you will be faithful in large ones. But if you are dishonest in little things, you won't be honest with greater responsibilities. ¹¹And if you are untrustworthy about worldly wealth, who will trust you with the true riches of heaven? ¹²And if you are not faithful with other people's things, why should you be trusted with things of your own?

¹³"No one can serve two masters. For you will hate one and love the other; you will be devoted to one and despise the other. You cannot serve both God and money."

¹⁴The Pharisees, who dearly loved their money, heard all this and scoffed at him. ¹⁵Then he said to them, "You like to appear righteous in public, but God knows your hearts. What this world honors is detestable in the sight of God.

¹⁶"Until John the Baptist, the law of Moses and the messages of the prophets were your guides. But now the Good News of the Kingdom of God is preached, and everyone is eager to get in.* ¹⁷But that doesn't mean that the law

16:9 Or *you will be welcomed into eternal homes.* **16:16** Or *everyone is urged to enter in.*

has lost its force. It is easier for heaven and earth to disappear than for the smallest point of God's law to be overturned.

¹⁸"For example, a man who divorces his wife and marries someone else commits adultery. And anyone who marries a woman divorced from her husband commits adultery."

PARABLE OF THE RICH MAN AND LAZARUS

¹⁹Jesus said, "There was a certain rich man who was splendidly clothed in purple and fine linen and who lived each day in luxury. ²⁰At his gate lay a poor man named Lazarus who was covered with sores. ²¹As Lazarus lay there longing for scraps from the rich man's table, the dogs would come and lick his open sores.

²²"Finally, the poor man died and was carried by the angels to be with Abraham.* The rich man also died and was buried, ²³and his soul went to the place of the dead.* There, in torment, he saw Abraham in the far distance with Lazarus at his side.

²⁴"The rich man shouted, 'Father Abraham, have some pity! Send Lazarus over here to dip the tip of his finger in water and cool my tongue. I am in anguish in these flames.'

²⁵"But Abraham said to him, 'Son, remember that during your lifetime you had everything you wanted, and Lazarus had nothing. So now he is here being comforted, and you are in anguish. ²⁶And besides, there is a great chasm separating us. No one can cross over to you from here, and no one can cross over to us from there.'

²⁷"Then the rich man said, 'Please, Father Abraham, at least send him to my father's home. ²⁸For I have five brothers, and I want him to warn them so they don't end up in this place of torment.'

²⁹"But Abraham said, 'Moses and the proph-

ets have warned them. Your brothers can read what they wrote.'

³⁰"The rich man replied, 'No, Father Abraham! But if someone is sent to them from the dead, then they will repent of their sins and turn to God.'

³¹"But Abraham said, 'If they won't listen to Moses and the prophets, they won't listen even if someone rises from the dead.'"

17 TEACHINGS ABOUT FORGIVENESS AND FAITH

One day Jesus said to his disciples, "There will always be temptations to sin, but what sorrow awaits the person who does the tempting! ²It would be better to be thrown into the sea with a millstone hung around your neck than to cause one of these little ones to fall into sin. ³So watch yourselves!

"If another believer* sins, rebuke that person; then if there is repentance, forgive. ⁴Even if that person wrongs you seven times a day and each time turns again and asks forgiveness, you must forgive."

⁵The apostles said to the Lord, "Show us how to increase our faith."

⁶The Lord answered, "If you had faith even as small as a mustard seed, you could say to this mulberry tree, 'May you be uprooted and thrown into the sea,' and it would obey you!

⁷"When a servant comes in from plowing or taking care of sheep, does his master say, 'Come in and eat with me'? ⁸No, he says, 'Prepare my meal, put on your apron, and serve me while I eat. Then you can eat later.' ⁹And does the master thank the servant for doing what he was told to do? Of course not. ¹⁰In the same way, when you obey me you should say, 'We are unworthy servants who have simply done our duty.'"

TEN HEALED OF LEPROSY

¹¹As Jesus continued on toward Jerusalem, he reached the border between Galilee and Samaria. ¹²As he entered a village there, ten lepers stood at a distance, ¹³crying out, "Jesus, Master, have mercy on us!"

¹⁴He looked at them and said, "Go show yourselves to the priests."* And as they went, they were cleansed of their leprosy.

¹⁵One of them, when he saw that he was healed, came back to Jesus, shouting, "Praise God!" ¹⁶He fell to the ground at Jesus' feet, thanking him for what he had done. This man was a Samaritan.

· ·

DIVORCE
(16:18) With today's high divorce rate, have you ever found yourself wondering whether God has changed his mind about divorce? Most religious leaders of Jesus' day permitted a man to divorce his wife for nearly any reason. Jesus' words about divorce (see also Matt 19:8-9) went beyond Moses' (Deut 24:1-4). Jesus says in unmistakable terms that marriage is a lifetime commitment. Is that your view of marriage?

LOVE AND TRUTH
(17:3-4) To "rebuke" or confront someone does not mean pointing out every fault that person has. It means caring enough to bring wrongdoing to a person's attention with the purpose of restoring him or her to God and mending relationships with others. When you feel you must rebuke another Christian for something he or she did wrong, check your attitude first. Will you, like Ephesians 4:15 says, "speak the truth in love"?

16:22 Greek *into Abraham's bosom.*   16:23 Greek *to Hades.*
17:3 Greek *If your brother.*   17:14 See Lev 14:2-32.

¹⁷Jesus asked, "Didn't I heal ten men? Where are the other nine? ¹⁸Has no one returned to give glory to God except this foreigner?" ¹⁹And Jesus said to the man, "Stand up and go. Your faith has healed you.*"

THE COMING OF THE KINGDOM
²⁰One day the Pharisees asked Jesus, "When will the Kingdom of God come?"

Jesus replied, "The Kingdom of God can't be detected by visible signs.* ²¹You won't be able to say, 'Here it is!' or 'It's over there!' For the Kingdom of God is already among you.*"

²²Then he said to his disciples, "The time is coming when you will long to see the day when the Son of Man returns,* but you won't see it. ²³People will tell you, 'Look, there is the Son of Man,' or 'Here he is,' but don't go out and follow them. ²⁴For as the lightning flashes and lights up the sky from one end to the other, so it will be on the day when the Son of Man comes. ²⁵But first the Son of Man must suffer terribly* and be rejected by this generation.

²⁶"When the Son of Man returns, it will be like it was in Noah's day. ²⁷In those days, the people enjoyed banquets and parties and weddings right up to the time Noah entered his boat and the flood came and destroyed them all.

²⁸"And the world will be as it was in the days of Lot. People went about their daily business—eating and drinking, buying and selling, farming and building—²⁹until the morning Lot left Sodom. Then fire and burning sulfur rained down from heaven and destroyed them all. ³⁰Yes, it will be 'business as usual' right up to the day when the Son of Man is revealed. ³¹On that day a person out on the deck of a roof must not go down into the house to pack. A person out in the field must not return home. ³²Remember what happened to Lot's wife! ³³If you cling to your life, you will lose it, and if you let your life go, you will save it. ³⁴That night two people will be asleep in one bed; one will be taken, the other left. ³⁵Two women will be grinding flour together at the mill; one will be taken, the other left.*"

³⁷"Where will this happen, Lord?"* the disciples asked.

Jesus replied, "Just as the gathering of vultures shows there is a carcass nearby, so these signs indicate that the end is near."*

18 PARABLE OF THE PERSISTENT WIDOW
One day Jesus told his disciples a story to show that they should always pray and never give up. ²"There was a judge in a certain city," he said, "who neither feared God nor cared about people. ³A widow of that city came to him repeatedly, saying, 'Give me justice in this dispute with my enemy.' ⁴The judge ignored her for a while, but finally he said to himself, 'I don't fear God or care about people, ⁵but this woman is driving me crazy. I'm going to see that she gets justice, because she is wearing me out with her constant requests!'"

⁶Then the Lord said, "Learn a lesson from this unjust judge. ⁷Even he rendered a just decision in the end. So don't you think God will surely give justice to his chosen people who cry out to him day and night? Will he keep putting them off? ⁸I tell you, he will grant justice to them quickly! But when the Son of Man* returns, how many will he find on the earth who have faith?"

PARABLE OF THE PHARISEE AND TAX COLLECTOR
⁹Then Jesus told this story to some who had great confidence in their own righteousness and scorned everyone else: ¹⁰"Two men went to the Temple to pray. One was a Pharisee, and the other was a despised tax collector. ¹¹The Pharisee stood by himself and prayed this prayer*: 'I thank you, God, that I am not a sinner like everyone else. For I don't cheat, I don't sin, and I don't commit adultery. I'm certainly not like that tax collector! ¹²I fast twice a week, and I give you a tenth of my income.'

¹³"But the tax collector stood at a distance and dared not even lift his eyes to heaven as he prayed. Instead, he beat his chest in sorrow, saying, 'O God, be merciful to me, for I am a sinner.' ¹⁴I tell you, this sinner, not the Pharisee, returned home justified before God. For those who exalt themselves will be humbled, and those who humble themselves will be exalted."

JESUS BLESSES THE CHILDREN
¹⁵One day some parents brought their little children to Jesus so he could touch and bless them. But when the disciples saw this, they scolded the parents for bothering him.

¹⁶Then Jesus called for the children and said to the disciples, "Let the children come to me.

17:19 Or *Your faith has saved you.*   **17:20** Or *by your speculations.*   **17:21** Or *is within you,* or *is in your grasp.*   **17:22** Or *long for even one day with the Son of Man.* "Son of Man" is a title Jesus used for himself.   **17:25** Or *suffer many things.*   **17:35** Some manuscripts add verse 36, *Two men will be working in the field; one will be taken, the other left.* Compare Matt 24:40.   **17:37a** Greek *"Where, Lord?"*   **17:37b** Greek *"Wherever the carcass is, the vultures gather."*   **18:8** "Son of Man" is a title Jesus used for himself.   **18:11** Some manuscripts read *stood and prayed this prayer to himself.*

Don't stop them! For the Kingdom of God belongs to those who are like these children. [17]I tell you the truth, anyone who doesn't receive the Kingdom of God like a child will never enter it."

THE RICH MAN [18]Once a religious leader asked Jesus this question: "Good Teacher, what should I do to inherit eternal life?"

[19]"Why do you call me good?" Jesus asked him. "Only God is truly good. [20]But to answer your question, you know the commandments: 'You must not commit adultery. You must not murder. You must not steal. You must not testify falsely. Honor your father and mother.'*"

[21]The man replied, "I've obeyed all these commandments since I was young."

[22]When Jesus heard his answer, he said,

· ·

A CHILDLIKE FAITH
(18:15-17) It was customary for parents to bring their children to a rabbi for a blessing. The disciples, however, thought the children were unworthy of the Master's time. But Jesus welcomed them because little children have the kind of faith needed to enter God's Kingdom. Is that the kind of faith you have?

GIVE AND GAIN
(18:28-30) Peter and the other disciples had paid a high price—leaving their homes and jobs—to follow Jesus. But Jesus reminded Peter that following him has its benefits as well as its sacrifices. Are you worried about what you have to give up in order to say yes to God? Any believer who has had to give up something to follow Christ will be paid back in this life as well as in the next. Whatever you give, you'll gain. Convinced?

"There is still one thing you haven't done. Sell all your possessions and give the money to the poor, and you will have treasure in heaven. Then come, follow me."

[23]But when the man heard this he became very sad, for he was very rich.

[24]When Jesus saw this,* he said, "How hard it is for the rich to enter the Kingdom of God! [25]In fact, it is easier for a camel to go through the eye of a needle than for a rich person to enter the Kingdom of God!"

[26]Those who heard this said, "Then who in the world can be saved?"

[27]He replied, "What is impossible for people is possible with God."

[28]Peter said, "We've left our homes to follow you."

[29]"Yes," Jesus replied, "and I assure you that everyone who has given up house or wife or brothers or parents or children, for the sake of the Kingdom of God, [30]will be repaid many times over in this life, and will have eternal life in the world to come."

JESUS AGAIN PREDICTS HIS DEATH [31]Taking the twelve disciples aside, Jesus said, "Listen, we're going up to Jerusalem, where all the predictions of the prophets concerning the Son of Man will come true. [32]He will be handed over to the Romans,* and he will be mocked, treated shamefully, and spit upon. [33]They will flog him

18:20 Exod 20:12-16; Deut 5:16-20.   **18:24** Some manuscripts read When Jesus saw how sad the man was.   **18:32** Greek the Gentiles.

I WONDER . . .

I've always been taught to be independent and self-sufficient. My youth leader says this isn't right. What's wrong about being proud about doing your best?

Have you ever known someone who thought he was so good in sports that he rarely listened to the coach? Although all coaches love to have players with great natural ability, most would settle for those with a few skills who are teachable. An athlete is much easier to mold than to motivate.

Being totally self-reliant is sort of like an athlete allowing the coach to give him advice only when he wants it. Before too long the athlete will start to develop sloppy technique. That's why advice from a coach is needed.

God wants us to always do our best. We should never do anything halfway. But there's a difference between doing our best and allowing God to do his best through us.

Taking the credit for everything we do is called pride. There is a good type of pride that comes from doing something that turned out great. Perhaps we've worked hard at something that turned out great. We feel good about ourselves—that's okay. The problem comes when we take all the credit. That's the wrong kind of pride.

God wants us to recognize that he gave us our lives and our talents. This shows humility and a deep respect for God.

The Pharisee in Jesus' parable (Luke 18:9-14) is a perfect example of someone with the wrong kind of pride. He was proud of his "holy" life. Although he acted like he was talking to God, he was really just talking to himself.

On the flip side is the tax collector. He had nothing to be proud of, especially as it related to his relationship with God. In humility, he asked God for mercy.

If we go through life with an I-can-make-it-by-myself attitude, we're really saying to God, "I don't need you." But God wants us to depend on him.

with a whip and kill him, but on the third day he will rise again."

³⁴But they didn't understand any of this. The significance of his words was hidden from them, and they failed to grasp what he was talking about.

JESUS HEALS A BLIND BEGGAR

³⁵As Jesus approached Jericho, a blind beggar was sitting beside the road. ³⁶When he heard the noise of a crowd going past, he asked what was happening. ³⁷They told him that Jesus the Nazarene* was going by. ³⁸So he began shouting, "Jesus, Son of David, have mercy on me!"

³⁹"Be quiet!" the people in front yelled at him.

But he only shouted louder, "Son of David, have mercy on me!"

⁴⁰When Jesus heard him, he stopped and ordered that the man be brought to him. As the man came near, Jesus asked him, ⁴¹"What do you want me to do for you?"

"Lord," he said, "I want to see!"

⁴²And Jesus said, "All right, receive your sight! Your faith has healed you." ⁴³Instantly the man could see, and he followed Jesus, praising God. And all who saw it praised God, too.

19

JESUS AND ZACCHAEUS

Jesus entered Jericho and made his way through the town. ²There was a man there named Zacchaeus. He was the chief tax collector in the region, and he had become very rich. ³He tried to get a look at Jesus, but he was too short to see over the crowd. ⁴So he ran ahead and climbed a sycamore-fig tree beside the road, for Jesus was going to pass that way.

⁵When Jesus came by, he looked up at Zacchaeus and called him by name. "Zacchaeus!" he said. "Quick, come down! I must be a guest in your home today."

⁶Zacchaeus quickly climbed down and took Jesus to his house in great excitement and joy. ⁷But the people were displeased. "He has gone to be the guest of a notorious sinner," they grumbled.

⁸Meanwhile, Zacchaeus stood before the Lord and said, "I will give half my wealth to the poor, Lord, and if I have cheated people on their taxes, I will give them back four times as much!"

⁹Jesus responded, "Salvation has come to this home today, for this man has shown him-

18:37 Or *Jesus of Nazareth.* 19:10 "Son of Man" is a title Jesus used for himself. 19:13 Greek *ten minas;* one mina was worth about three months' wages.

self to be a true son of Abraham. ¹⁰For the Son of Man* came to seek and save those who are lost."

PARABLE OF THE TEN SERVANTS

¹¹The crowd was listening to everything Jesus said. And because he was nearing Jerusalem, he told them a story to correct the impression that the Kingdom of God would begin right away. ¹²He said, "A nobleman was called away to a distant empire to be crowned king and then return. ¹³Before he left, he called together ten of his servants and divided among them ten pounds of silver,* saying, 'Invest this for me while I am gone.' ¹⁴But his people hated him and sent a delegation after him to say, 'We do not want him to be our king.'

¹⁵"After he was crowned king, he returned and called in the servants to whom he had given the money. He wanted to find out what their profits were. ¹⁶The first servant reported, 'Master, I invested your money and made ten times the original amount!'

¹⁷"'Well done!' the king exclaimed. 'You are a good servant. You have been faithful with the little I entrusted to you, so you will be governor of ten cities as your reward.'

¹⁸"The next servant reported, 'Master, I invested your money and made five times the original amount.'

¹⁹"'Well done!' the king said. 'You will be governor over five cities.'

²⁰"But the third servant brought back only the original amount of money and said, 'Master, I hid your money and kept it safe. ²¹I was afraid because you are a hard man to deal with, taking what isn't yours and harvesting crops you didn't plant.'

²²"'You wicked servant!' the king roared. 'Your own words condemn you. If you knew that I'm a hard man who takes what isn't mine and harvests crops I didn't plant, ²³why didn't you deposit my money in the bank? At least I could have gotten some interest on it.'

²⁴"Then, turning to the others standing nearby, the king ordered, 'Take the money

....

UNPOPULAR

(19:1-10) Tax collectors were among the most unpopular people in Israel. Jews who chose to work for Rome were considered traitors. Besides, it was common knowledge that tax collectors made themselves rich by gouging their fellow Jews. No wonder the crowds were displeased when Jesus went home with the tax collector Zacchaeus. But Jesus' love caused Zacchaeus to change. Who are the "Zacchaeuses" at your school or in your neighborhood? How can you, like Jesus, reach out to the "lost"?

from this servant, and give it to the one who has ten pounds.'

²⁵"'But, master,' they said, 'he already has ten pounds!'

²⁶"'Yes,' the king replied, 'and to those who use well what they are given, even more will be given. But from those who do nothing, even what little they have will be taken away. ²⁷And as for these enemies of mine who didn't want me to be their king—bring them in and execute them right here in front of me.'"

JESUS' TRIUMPHANT ENTRY ²⁸After telling this story, Jesus went on toward Jerusalem, walking ahead of his disciples. ²⁹As he came to the towns of Bethphage and Bethany on the Mount of Olives, he sent two disciples ahead. ³⁰"Go into that village over there," he told them. "As you enter it, you will see a young donkey tied there that no one has ever ridden. Untie it and bring it here. ³¹If anyone asks, 'Why are you untying that colt?' just say, 'The Lord needs it.'"

³²So they went and found the colt, just as Jesus had said. ³³And sure enough, as they were untying it, the owners asked them, "Why are you untying that colt?"

³⁴And the disciples simply replied, "The Lord needs it." ³⁵So they brought the colt to Jesus and threw their garments over it for him to ride on.

³⁶As he rode along, the crowds spread out their garments on the road ahead of him. ³⁷When he reached the place where the road started down the Mount of Olives, all of his followers began to shout and sing as they walked along, praising God for all the wonderful miracles they had seen.

³⁸ "Blessings on the King who comes in the
        name of the Lord!
    Peace in heaven, and glory in highest
        heaven!"*

³⁹But some of the Pharisees among the crowd said, "Teacher, rebuke your followers for saying things like that!"

⁴⁰He replied, "If they kept quiet, the stones along the road would burst into cheers!"

JESUS WEEPS OVER JERUSALEM ⁴¹But as he came closer to Jerusalem and saw the city ahead, he began to weep. ⁴²"How I wish today that you of all people would understand the way to peace. But now it is too late, and peace is hidden from your eyes. ⁴³Before long your enemies will build ramparts against your walls and encircle you and close in on you

from every side. ⁴⁴They will crush you into the ground, and your children with you. Your enemies will not leave a single stone in place, because you did not accept your opportunity for salvation."

JESUS CLEARS THE TEMPLE ⁴⁵Then Jesus entered the Temple and began to drive out the people selling animals for sacrifices. ⁴⁶He said to them, "The Scriptures declare, 'My Temple will be a house of prayer,' but you have turned it into a den of thieves."*

⁴⁷After that, he taught daily in the Temple, but the leading priests, the teachers of religious law, and the other leaders of the people began planning how to kill him. ⁴⁸But they could think of nothing, because all the people hung on every word he said.

20 **THE AUTHORITY OF JESUS CHALLENGED** One day as Jesus was teaching the people and preaching the Good News in the Temple, the leading priests, the teachers of religious law, and the elders came up to him. ²They demanded, "By what authority are you doing all these things? Who gave you the right?"

³"Let me ask you a question first," he replied. ⁴"Did John's authority to baptize come from heaven, or was it merely human?"

⁵They talked it over among themselves. "If we say it was from heaven, he will ask why we didn't believe John. ⁶But if we say it was merely human, the people will stone us because they are convinced John was a prophet." ⁷So they finally replied that they didn't know.

⁸And Jesus responded, "Then I won't tell you by what authority I do these things."

PARABLE OF THE EVIL FARMERS ⁹Now Jesus turned to the people again and told them this story: "A man planted a vineyard, leased it to tenant farmers, and moved to another country to live for several years. ¹⁰At the time of the grape harvest, he sent one of his servants to collect his share of the crop. But the farmers attacked the servant, beat him up, and sent him back empty-handed. ¹¹So the owner sent another servant, but they also insulted him, beat him up, and sent him away empty-handed. ¹²A third man was sent, and they wounded him and chased him away.

¹³"'What will I do?' the owner asked himself. 'I know! I'll send my cherished son. Surely they will respect him.'

¹⁴"But when the tenant farmers saw his son,

19:38 Pss 118:26; 148:1.   19:46 Isa 56:7; Jer 7:11.

they said to each other, 'Here comes the heir to this estate. Let's kill him and get the estate for ourselves!' ¹⁵So they dragged him out of the vineyard and murdered him.

"What do you suppose the owner of the vineyard will do to them?" Jesus asked. ¹⁶"I'll tell you—he will come and kill those farmers and lease the vineyard to others."

"How terrible that such a thing should ever happen," his listeners protested.

¹⁷Jesus looked at them and said, "Then what does this Scripture mean?

'The stone that the builders rejected
    has now become the cornerstone.'*

¹⁸Everyone who stumbles over that stone will be broken to pieces, and it will crush anyone it falls on."

¹⁹The teachers of religious law and the leading priests wanted to arrest Jesus immediately because they realized he was telling the story against them—they were the wicked farmers. But they were afraid of the people's reaction.

TAXES FOR CAESAR ²⁰Watching for their opportunity, the leaders sent spies pretending to be honest men. They tried to get Jesus to say something that could be reported to the Roman governor so he would arrest Jesus. ²¹"Teacher," they said, "we know that you speak and teach what is right and are not influenced by what others think. You teach the way of God truthfully. ²²Now tell us—is it right for us to pay taxes to Caesar or not?"

²³He saw through their trickery and said, ²⁴"Show me a Roman coin.* Whose picture and title are stamped on it?"

"Caesar's," they replied.

²⁵"Well then," he said, "give to Caesar what belongs to Caesar, and give to God what belongs to God."

²⁶So they failed to trap him by what he said in front of the people. Instead, they were amazed by his answer, and they became silent.

DISCUSSION ABOUT RESURRECTION ²⁷Then Jesus was approached by some Sadducees—religious leaders who say there is no resurrection from the dead. ²⁸They posed this question: "Teacher, Moses gave us a law that if a man dies, leaving a wife but no children, his brother should marry the widow and have

a child who will carry on the brother's name.* ²⁹Well, suppose there were seven brothers. The oldest one married and then died without children. ³⁰So the second brother married the widow, but he also died. ³¹Then the third brother married her. This continued with all seven of them, who died without children. ³²Finally, the woman also died. ³³So tell us, whose wife will she be in the resurrection? For all seven were married to her!"

³⁴Jesus replied, "Marriage is for people here on earth. ³⁵But in the age to come, those worthy of being raised from the dead will neither marry nor be given in marriage. ³⁶And they will never die again. In this respect they will be like angels. They are children of God and children of the resurrection.

³⁷"But now, as to whether the dead will be raised—even Moses proved this when he wrote about the burning bush. Long after Abraham, Isaac, and Jacob had died, he referred to the Lord* as 'the God of Abraham, the God of Isaac, and the God of Jacob.'* ³⁸So he is the God of the living, not the dead, for they are all alive to him."

³⁹"Well said, Teacher!" remarked some of the teachers of religious law who were standing there. ⁴⁰And then no one dared to ask him any more questions.

WHOSE SON IS THE MESSIAH? ⁴¹Then Jesus presented them with a question. "Why is it," he asked, "that the Messiah is said to be the son of David? ⁴²For David himself wrote in the book of Psalms:

'The LORD said to my Lord,
    Sit in the place of honor at my right hand
⁴³ until I humble your enemies,
        making them a footstool under your
        feet.'*

⁴⁴Since David called the Messiah 'Lord,' how can the Messiah be his son?"

⁴⁵Then, with the crowds listening, he turned to his disciples and said, ⁴⁶"Beware of these teachers of religious law! For they like to parade around in flowing robes and love to receive respectful greetings as they walk in the marketplaces. And how they love the seats of

20:17 Ps 118:22. 20:24 Greek *a denarius*. 20:28 See Deut 25:5-6. 20:37a Greek *when he wrote about the bush. He referred to the Lord*. 20:37b Exod 3:6. 20:42-43 Ps 110:1.

....

DUTY
(20:20-26) Jesus turned his enemies' attempt to trap him into a powerful lesson: God's followers have legitimate obligations to both God and the government. But keeping our priorities straight is important. When the two authorities conflict, our duty to God always comes before our duty to the government.

honor in the synagogues and the head table at banquets. ⁴⁷Yet they shamelessly cheat widows out of their property and then pretend to be pious by making long prayers in public. Because of this, they will be severely punished."

21 **THE WIDOW'S OFFERING** While Jesus was in the Temple, he watched the rich people dropping their gifts in the collection box. ²Then a poor widow came by and dropped in two small coins.*

³"I tell you the truth," Jesus said, "this poor widow has given more than all the rest of them. ⁴For they have given a tiny part of their surplus, but she, poor as she is, has given everything she has."

JESUS FORETELLS THE FUTURE ⁵Some of his disciples began talking about the majestic stonework of the Temple and the memorial decorations on the walls. But Jesus said, ⁶"The time is coming when all these things will be completely demolished. Not one stone will be left on top of another!"

⁷"Teacher," they asked, "when will all this

....

TROUBLE
(21:12-19) Jesus warned his followers to expect persecution. Christians of every age have had to face this possibility. Yet even when we feel completely abandoned, the Holy Spirit stays with us. He will comfort us, protect us, and give us the words we need to defend our faith (see also John 14:26; 16:7-15; Heb 13:5-6).

happen? What sign will show us that these things are about to take place?"

⁸He replied, "Don't let anyone mislead you, for many will come in my name, claiming, 'I am the Messiah,'* and saying, 'The time has come!' But don't believe them. ⁹And when you hear of wars and insurrections, don't panic. Yes, these things must take place first, but the end won't follow immediately." ¹⁰Then he added, "Nation will go to war against nation, and kingdom against kingdom. ¹¹There will be great earthquakes, and there will be famines and plagues in many lands, and there will be terrifying things and great miraculous signs from heaven.

¹²"But before all this occurs, there will be a time of great persecution. You will be dragged into synagogues and prisons, and you will stand trial before kings and governors because you are my followers. ¹³But this will be your opportunity to tell them about me.* ¹⁴So don't worry in advance about how to answer the charges against you, ¹⁵for I will give you the right words and such wisdom that none of your opponents will be able to reply or refute you! ¹⁶Even those closest to you—your parents, brothers, relatives, and friends—will betray you. They will even kill some of you. ¹⁷And everyone will hate you because you are my followers.* ¹⁸But not a hair of your head will perish! ¹⁹By standing firm, you will win your souls.

21:2 Greek *two lepta* [the smallest of Jewish coins].   21:8 Greek *claiming, 'I am.'*   21:13 Or *This will be your testimony against them.* 21:17 Greek *on account of my name.*

CHOICES
giving

The hot topic at Thurgood Marshall High School is what Kyla Whitfield will do with the huge inheritance she's getting as a result of her grandfather's death last week.

"How much do you think she'll end up getting?" Alexis asks.

"Well, everyone says old man Whitfield was worth at least nine million dollars," her friend Harmony replies.

"Kyla gets it all?"

"No, I think she'll have to split it with three other relatives. But everyone will wind up loaded."

"Oh my gosh! That's over two million dollars!"

"Well, she'll have to pay inheritance taxes on it first."

"But she'll still be a millionaire!"

"That's right."

"I know what I'd do if I had a boatload of money!"

"What would you do?"

"Spend most of it."

"On what?"

Alexis counts the items with her fingers as she speaks. "I would buy clothes, a new iPod, DVDs, a cool car, a new computer, a trip around the world, a flat-screen high-definition TV for my room, the latest games software, tuition at the best college in the world—whatever I wanted."

"What about giving?"

"What about it?"

"Would you give any of it away? You know, to other people, to your church, to charity?"

"Are you serious?"

That's a common response to the suggestion of giving. Unfortunately, even many Christians are that way.

What would you do if you were Kyla? What's your view of giving? (By the way, "I will when I'm rich like Kyla," is a lousy excuse!) Need a shot in the arm about giving? Check out Luke 21:1-4.

²⁰"And when you see Jerusalem surrounded by armies, then you will know that the time of its destruction has arrived. ²¹Then those in Judea must flee to the hills. Those in Jerusalem must get out, and those out in the country should not return to the city. ²²For those will be days of God's vengeance, and the prophetic words of the Scriptures will be fulfilled. ²³How terrible it will be for pregnant women and for nursing mothers in those days. For there will be disaster in the land and great anger against this people. ²⁴They will be killed by the sword or sent away as captives to all the nations of the world. And Jerusalem will be trampled down by the Gentiles until the period of the Gentiles comes to an end.

²⁵"And there will be strange signs in the sun, moon, and stars. And here on earth the nations will be in turmoil, perplexed by the roaring seas and strange tides. ²⁶People will be terrified at what they see coming upon the earth, for the powers in the heavens will be shaken. ²⁷Then everyone will see the Son of Man* coming on a cloud with power and great glory.* ²⁸So when all these things begin to happen, stand and look up, for your salvation is near!"

²⁹Then he gave them this illustration: "Notice the fig tree, or any other tree. ³⁰When the leaves come out, you know without being told that summer is near. ³¹In the same way, when you see all these things taking place, you can know that the Kingdom of God is near. ³²I tell you the truth, this generation will not pass from the scene until all these things have taken place. ³³Heaven and earth will disappear, but my words will never disappear.

³⁴"Watch out! Don't let your hearts be dulled by carousing and drunkenness, and by the worries of this life. Don't let that day catch you unaware, ³⁵like a trap. For that day will come upon everyone living on the earth. ³⁶Keep alert at all times. And pray that you might be strong enough to escape these coming horrors and stand before the Son of Man."

³⁷Every day Jesus went to the Temple to teach, and each evening he returned to spend the night on the Mount of Olives. ³⁸The crowds gathered at the Temple early each morning to hear him.

22 JUDAS AGREES TO BETRAY JESUS The Festival of Unleavened Bread, which is

also called Passover, was approaching. ²The leading priests and teachers of religious law were plotting how to kill Jesus, but they were afraid of the people's reaction.

³Then Satan entered into Judas Iscariot, who was one of the twelve disciples, ⁴and he went to the leading priests and captains of the Temple guard to discuss the best way to betray Jesus to them. ⁵They were delighted, and they promised to give him money. ⁶So he agreed and began looking for an opportunity to betray Jesus so they could arrest him when the crowds weren't around.

THE LAST SUPPER ⁷Now the Festival of Unleavened Bread arrived, when the Passover lamb is sacrificed. ⁸Jesus sent Peter and John ahead and said, "Go and prepare the Passover meal, so we can eat it together."

⁹"Where do you want us to prepare it?" they asked him.

¹⁰He replied, "As soon as you enter Jerusalem, a man carrying a pitcher of water will meet you. Follow him. At the house he enters, ¹¹say to the owner, 'The Teacher asks: Where is the guest room where I can eat the Passover meal with my disciples?' ¹²He will take you upstairs to a large room that is already set up. That is where you should prepare our meal." ¹³They went off to the city and found everything just as Jesus had said, and they prepared the Passover meal there.

¹⁴When the time came, Jesus and the apostles sat down together at the table.* ¹⁵Jesus said, "I have been very eager to eat this Passover meal with you before my suffering begins. ¹⁶For I tell you now that I won't eat this meal again until its meaning is fulfilled in the Kingdom of God."

¹⁷Then he took a cup of wine and gave thanks to God for it. Then he said, "Take this and share it among yourselves. ¹⁸For I will not drink wine again until the Kingdom of God has come."

¹⁹He took some bread and gave thanks to God for it. Then he broke it in pieces and gave it to the disciples, saying, "This is my body, which is given for you. Do this to remember me."

²⁰After supper he took another cup of wine and said, "This cup is the new covenant between God and his people—an agreement confirmed with my blood, which is poured out as a sacrifice for you.*

²¹"But here at this table, sitting among us as a friend, is the man who will betray me. ²²For it has been determined that the Son of Man*

21:27a "Son of Man" is a title Jesus used for himself.   **21:27b** See Dan 7:13.   **22:14** Or *reclined together.*   **22:19-20** Some manuscripts do not include 22:19b-20, *which is given for you . . . which is poured out as a sacrifice for you.*   **22:22** "Son of Man" is a title Jesus used for himself.

must die. But what sorrow awaits the one who betrays him." ²³The disciples began to ask each other which of them would ever do such a thing.

²⁴Then they began to argue among themselves about who would be the greatest among them. ²⁵Jesus told them, "In this world the kings and great men lord it over their people, yet they are called 'friends of the people.' ²⁶But among you it will be different. Those who are the greatest among you should take the lowest rank, and the leader should be like a servant. ²⁷Who is more important, the one who sits at the table or the one who serves? The one who sits at the table, of course. But not here! For I am among you as one who serves.

²⁸"You have stayed with me in my time of trial. ²⁹And just as my Father has granted me a Kingdom, I now grant you the right ³⁰to eat and drink at my table in my Kingdom. And you will sit on thrones, judging the twelve tribes of Israel.

JESUS PREDICTS PETER'S DENIAL
³¹"Simon, Simon, Satan has asked to sift each of you like wheat. ³²But I have pleaded in prayer for you, Simon, that your faith should not fail. So when you have repented and turned to me again, strengthen your brothers."

³³Peter said, "Lord, I am ready to go to prison with you, and even to die with you."

³⁴But Jesus said, "Peter, let me tell you something. Before the rooster crows tomorrow morning, you will deny three times that you even know me."

³⁵Then Jesus asked them, "When I sent you out to preach the Good News and you did not have money, a traveler's bag, or an extra pair of sandals, did you need anything?"

"No," they replied.

³⁶"But now," he said, "take your money and a traveler's bag. And if you don't have a sword, sell your cloak and buy one! ³⁷For the time has come for this prophecy about me to be fulfilled: 'He was counted among the reb-

els.'* Yes, everything written about me by the prophets will come true."

³⁸"Look, Lord," they replied, "we have two swords among us."

"That's enough," he said.

JESUS PRAYS ON THE MOUNT OF OLIVES
³⁹Then, accompanied by the disciples, Jesus left the upstairs room and went as usual to the Mount of Olives. ⁴⁰There he told them, "Pray that you will not give in to temptation."

⁴¹He walked away, about a stone's throw, and knelt down and prayed, ⁴²"Father, if you are willing, please take this cup of suffering away from me. Yet I want your will to be done, not mine." ⁴³Then an angel from heaven appeared and strengthened him. ⁴⁴He prayed more fervently, and he was in such agony of spirit that his sweat fell to the ground like great drops of blood.*

⁴⁵At last he stood up again and returned to the disciples, only to find them asleep, exhausted from grief. ⁴⁶"Why are you sleeping?" he asked them. "Get up and pray, so that you will not give in to temptation."

JESUS IS BETRAYED AND ARRESTED
⁴⁷But even as Jesus said this, a crowd approached, led by Judas, one of the twelve disciples. Judas walked over to Jesus to greet him with a kiss. ⁴⁸But Jesus said, "Judas, would you betray the Son of Man with a kiss?"

⁴⁹When the other disciples saw what was about to happen, they exclaimed, "Lord, should we fight? We brought the swords!" ⁵⁰And one of them struck at the high priest's slave, slashing off his right ear.

⁵¹But Jesus said, "No more of this." And he touched the man's ear and healed him.

⁵²Then Jesus spoke to the leading priests, the captains of the Temple guard, and the elders who had come for him. "Am I some dangerous revolutionary," he asked, "that you come with swords and clubs to arrest me? ⁵³Why didn't you arrest me in the Temple? I was there every day. But this is your moment, the time when the power of darkness reigns."

PETER DENIES JESUS
⁵⁴So they arrested him and led him to the high priest's home. And Peter followed at a distance. ⁵⁵The guards lit a fire in the middle of the courtyard and sat around it, and Peter joined them there. ⁵⁶A servant girl noticed him in the firelight and began staring at him. Finally she said, "This man was one of Jesus' followers!"

ALL WRAPPED UP
(22:24) Although the most important events in human history (Jesus' death and resurrection) were about to take place, the disciples were too focused on arguing about their prestige in the Kingdom! Looking back, we say, "This was no time to worry about status." But the disciples, wrapped up in their own concerns, didn't perceive what Jesus had been trying to tell them about his approaching death and resurrection. What are your major concerns today? Five years from now, will these worries look petty and inappropriate? What can you choose to focus on instead?

22:37 Isa 53:12.   22:43-44 Verses 43 and 44 are not included in many ancient manuscripts.

⁵⁷But Peter denied it. "Woman," he said, "I don't even know him!"

⁵⁸After a while someone else looked at him and said, "You must be one of them!"

"No, man, I'm not!" Peter retorted.

⁵⁹About an hour later someone else insisted, "This must be one of them, because he is a Galilean, too."

⁶⁰But Peter said, "Man, I don't know what you are talking about." And immediately, while he was still speaking, the rooster crowed.

⁶¹At that moment the Lord turned and looked at Peter. Suddenly, the Lord's words flashed through Peter's mind: "Before the rooster crows tomorrow morning, you will deny three times that you even know me." ⁶²And Peter left the courtyard, weeping bitterly.

⁶³The guards in charge of Jesus began mocking and beating him. ⁶⁴They blindfolded him and said, "Prophesy to us! Who hit you that time?" ⁶⁵And they hurled all sorts of terrible insults at him.

JESUS BEFORE THE COUNCIL ⁶⁶At daybreak all the elders of the people assembled, including the leading priests and the teachers of religious law. Jesus was led before this high council,* ⁶⁷and they said, "Tell us, are you the Messiah?"

But he replied, "If I tell you, you won't believe

22:66 Greek *before their Sanhedrin.*   **22:69** See Ps 110:1.

me. ⁶⁸And if I ask you a question, you won't answer. ⁶⁹But from now on the Son of Man will be seated in the place of power at God's right hand.*"

⁷⁰They all shouted, "So, are you claiming to be the Son of God?"

And he replied, "You say that I am."

⁷¹"Why do we need other witnesses?" they said. "We ourselves heard him say it."

23 JESUS' TRIAL BEFORE PILATE Then the entire council took Jesus to Pilate, the Roman governor. ²They began to state their case: "This man has been leading our people astray by telling them not to pay their taxes to the Roman government and by claiming he is the Messiah, a king."

A BITTER FAILURE

(22:62) Peter wept bitterly after realizing that he had denied his Lord. Although Peter had said he would never deny Christ (Matt 26:35), he went against all he had boldly promised. Unable to stand up for his Lord for even 12 hours, he had failed as a disciple and as a friend. We need to be aware of our own breaking points and not become overconfident or self-sufficient. When we fail, we must remember that Christ can use those who recognize their failure.

Like Peter, have you ever been afraid that God will never use you again because you've blown it somehow? After his failure, Peter learned much that would help him in the leadership responsibilities he soon would assume. So can you.

I WONDER...

There aren't very many Christians at my school, and I'm kind of embarrassed to admit that I'm one of them. Do I have to come out and let the whole world know I've become a Christian?

High school guys and girls wear letter jackets that tell the world they're athletes. Most people wear such jackets with pride. They have accomplished something, and they want other people to know it.

Identifying yourself as a Christian, however, isn't as popular. Peter found that out when he was confronted by the people who were trying to get warm around the fire (see Luke 22:54-62). Although he had been with Jesus for three years and was one of his best friends, Peter denied even knowing who Jesus was! He was afraid and embarrassed. But something happened during the next two months that convinced Peter that he would never be ashamed of Jesus again. (Read about Peter in the first four chapters of the book of Acts.)

As a new Christian, it is hard to identify yourself

with Christ because you don't know him very well. It's like striking up a friendship with the new kid at school. You want to be his friend, but you hold back because you aren't sure how popular he's going to be.

Jesus understands our fears. It can be tough to admit we're his followers. He will patiently wait until we are confident in our relationship with him before we begin to speak out for him.

Sometimes it takes new Christians awhile before they aren't embarrassed about admitting they're Christians. But at some point, something clicks that convinces them that Jesus Christ is alive. It could be the feeling of being forgiven, a miraculous answer to prayer, or a quiet realization that the Bible is accurate and everything Jesus said about himself is true!

However it happens, God doesn't expect you to get on the PA system at school and make the "big announcement." He just expects you to be prepared in case anyone asks you about your faith: "And if someone asks about your Christian hope, always be ready to explain it" (1 Pet 3:15).

³So Pilate asked him, "Are you the king of the Jews?"

Jesus replied, "You have said it."

⁴Pilate turned to the leading priests and to the crowd and said, "I find nothing wrong with this man!"

⁵Then they became insistent. "But he is causing riots by his teaching wherever he goes—all over Judea, from Galilee to Jerusalem!"

⁶"Oh, is he a Galilean?" Pilate asked. ⁷When they said that he was, Pilate sent him to Herod Antipas, because Galilee was under Herod's jurisdiction, and Herod happened to be in Jerusalem at the time.

⁸Herod was delighted at the opportunity to see Jesus, because he had heard about him and had been hoping for a long time to see him perform a miracle. ⁹He asked Jesus question after question, but Jesus refused to answer. ¹⁰Meanwhile, the leading priests and the teachers of religious law stood there shouting their accusations. ¹¹Then Herod and his soldiers began mocking and ridiculing Jesus. Finally, they put a royal robe on him and sent him back to Pilate. ¹²(Herod and Pilate, who had been enemies before, became friends that day.)

¹³Then Pilate called together the leading priests and other religious leaders, along with the people, ¹⁴and he announced his verdict. "You brought this man to me, accusing him of leading a revolt. I have examined him thoroughly on this point in your presence and find him innocent. ¹⁵Herod came to the same con-

ULTIMATE ISSUES WHY THE CROSS?

A youth pastor was talking to a group of junior highers about the Cross of Christ, explaining how Jesus' death had provided for their individual forgiveness and salvation. "It's personal," he said. "Jesus didn't just die for people in general. He died for you." The youth pastor paused to let the impact of the statement sink in. Suddenly, one seventh-grade girl blurted out: "So?"

"So?" As irreverent and inappropriate as that question seems, the seventh grader's response is sadly representative of how people think today. We know Jesus died on a cross for us; we just don't see the connection between that event 2,000 years ago and our lives today.

What is the Cross about? Why did Jesus have to die such a horrible death?

The Cross has inspired endless debates, wars, books, songs, and lives through the centuries. Hopefully this short note will help you gain some insight into why Jesus had to die and why he died in such a gruesome way.

The first reason is humanity's problem. All humans are sinners. We've broken God's laws, so we stand guilty before God and deserve to be punished. Sin has warped every aspect of human life; it has had such a radical effect on us that we stand in open rebellion and defiance of the God who made us and loves us. Think this is overstating the case? Consider this: God made himself vulnerable to human beings one time, and we murdered him.

Because of our sinful nature, we are incapable of pleasing God or doing anything on our own to change the situation. We are, as Paul writes in Ephesians 2:5 and Colossians 2:13, spiritually dead because of our sins—and dead people can't exactly help themselves. We desperately need help from someone who can please God, who can do something about the hopeless state of human souls. Jesus, by virtue of his sinless life, is that Someone. But helping us was a terribly painful process.

Again, we are guilty before God—we deserve his anger and punishment. But God took the wrath we deserve and poured it out on Jesus, on the cross. In some ways, this is beyond human understanding. Jesus took upon himself our sins—every mean, dishonest, disgusting thought or action—and was transformed from the perfect, holy, righteous Person he was into utter sin itself. Second Corinthians 5:21 tells us, "For God made Christ, who never sinned, to be the offering for our sin, so that we could be made right with God through Christ." On the cross, Jesus received the punishment that our sins deserve. As the perfect God-man, Jesus alone was in a position to do that. Jesus stood in the chasm between God and humanity, which was created by our sins, and brought us back together by his blood. As horrible as the physical agony must have been, the spiritual agony of this transformation and punishment was worse. No wonder he screamed out, "My God, my God, why have you abandoned me?" (Matt 27:46). Jesus was deserted by God so that you and I never have to be.

That's the second fact you need to know—it's personal. Jesus took your place on the cross and bore the terrible brunt of the sentence God could have imposed on you. He died for you. Take it personally.

It's still a mystery how the death of one righteous Man—the only righteous Man—pays for the sins of the world. Still, though we may not understand it, we can depend upon it for our salvation. This is the only way to peace with God and eternal life. It's fitting that God took the Cross of Christ—the single darkest hour in the history of humanity—and turned it into the way of redemption for all people everywhere. That's the kind of God the Bible talks about. A God who loves you so much he would even die on a cross for you. ∎

clusion and sent him back to us. Nothing this man has done calls for the death penalty. [16]So I will have him flogged, and then I will release him."*

[18]Then a mighty roar rose from the crowd, and with one voice they shouted, "Kill him, and release Barabbas to us!" [19](Barabbas was in prison for taking part in an insurrection in Jerusalem against the government, and for murder.) [20]Pilate argued with them, because he wanted to release Jesus. [21]But they kept shouting, "Crucify him! Crucify him!"

[22]For the third time he demanded, "Why? What crime has he committed? I have found no reason to sentence him to death. So I will have him flogged, and then I will release him."

[23]But the mob shouted louder and louder, demanding that Jesus be crucified, and their voices prevailed. [24]So Pilate sentenced Jesus to die as they demanded. [25]As they had requested, he released Barabbas, the man in prison for insurrection and murder. But he turned Jesus over to them to do as they wished.

THE CRUCIFIXION [26]As they led Jesus away, a man named Simon, who was from Cyrene,* happened to be coming in from the countryside. The soldiers seized him and put the cross on him and made him carry it behind Jesus. [27]A large crowd trailed behind, including many grief-stricken women. [28]But Jesus turned and said to them, "Daughters of Jerusalem, don't weep for me, but weep for yourselves and for your children. [29]For the days are coming when they will say, 'Fortunate indeed are the women who are childless, the wombs that have not borne a child and the breasts that have never nursed.' [30]People will beg the mountains, 'Fall on us,' and plead with the hills, 'Bury us.'* [31]For if these things are done when the tree is green, what will happen when it is dry?*"

[32]Two others, both criminals, were led out to be executed with him. [33]When they came to a place called The Skull,* they nailed him to the cross. And the criminals were also crucified—one on his right and one on his left.

[34]Jesus said, "Father, forgive them, for they don't know what they are doing."* And the

soldiers gambled for his clothes by throwing dice.*

[35]The crowd watched and the leaders scoffed. "He saved others," they said, "let him save himself if he is really God's Messiah, the Chosen One." [36]The soldiers mocked him, too, by offering him a drink of sour wine. [37]They called out to him, "If you are the King of the Jews, save yourself!" [38]A sign was fastened above him with these words: "This is the King of the Jews."

[39]One of the criminals hanging beside him scoffed, "So you're the Messiah, are you? Prove it by saving yourself—and us, too, while you're at it!"

[40]But the other criminal protested, "Don't you fear God even when you have been sentenced to die? [41]We deserve to die for our crimes, but this man hasn't done anything wrong." [42]Then he said, "Jesus, remember me when you come into your Kingdom."

[43]And Jesus replied, "I assure you, today you will be with me in paradise."

THE DEATH OF JESUS [44]By this time it was about noon, and darkness fell across the whole land until three o'clock. [45]The light from the sun was gone. And suddenly, the curtain in the sanctuary of the Temple was torn down the middle. [46]Then Jesus shouted, "Father, I entrust my spirit into your hands!"* And with those words he breathed his last.

[47]When the Roman officer* overseeing the execution saw what had happened, he worshiped God and said, "Surely this man was innocent.*" [48]And when all the crowd that came to see the crucifixion saw what had happened, they went home in deep sorrow.* [49]But

....

AN OFFER OF FORGIVENESS
(23:34) Jesus asked God to forgive the people who were putting him to death—Jewish leaders, Roman politicians and soldiers, and bystanders. God answered that prayer by opening up the way of salvation even to the people who put him to death. That includes us. Because of the wrong things we've done, we've played a part in crucifying Jesus. The Good News is that God is gracious. He still offers forgiveness through his Son. Have you taken him up on his offer?

NOT TOO LATE
(23:39-43) As one of the criminals next to Jesus was about to die, he turned to Jesus for forgiveness. This shows that it's never too late to turn to God. Even in his misery, Jesus had mercy on the man who decided to believe in him. Our life is much more useful and fulfilling if we turn to God early, but even those who turn to him at the very last moment will be with God in his Kingdom. (But don't use this as an excuse to wait until the last moment to turn to him! If you know the truth, why wait?)

23:16 Some manuscripts add verse 17, *Now it was necessary for him to release one prisoner to them during the Passover celebration.* Compare Matt 27:15; Mark 15:6; John 18:39. **23:26** *Cyrene* was a city in northern Africa. **23:30** Hos 10:8. **23:31** Or *If these things are done to me, the living tree, what will happen to you, the dry tree?* **23:33** Sometimes rendered *Calvary,* which comes from the Latin word for "skull." **23:34a** This sentence is not included in many ancient manuscripts. **23:34b** Greek *by casting lots.* See Ps 22:18. **23:46** Ps 31:5. **23:47a** Greek *the centurion.* **23:47b** Or *righteous.* **23:48** Greek *went home beating their breasts.*

Jesus' friends, including the women who had followed him from Galilee, stood at a distance watching.

THE BURIAL OF JESUS ⁵⁰Now there was a good and righteous man named Joseph. He was a member of the Jewish high council, ⁵¹but he had not agreed with the decision and actions of the other religious leaders. He was from the town of Arimathea in Judea, and he was waiting for the Kingdom of God to come. ⁵²He went to Pilate and asked for Jesus' body. ⁵³Then he took the body down from the cross and wrapped it in a long sheet of linen cloth and laid it in a new tomb that had been carved out of rock. ⁵⁴This was done late on Friday afternoon, the day of preparation,* as the Sabbath was about to begin.

⁵⁵As his body was taken away, the women from Galilee followed and saw the tomb where his body was placed. ⁵⁶Then they went home and prepared spices and ointments to anoint his body. But by the time they were finished the Sabbath had begun, so they rested as required by the law.

24 **THE RESURRECTION** But very early on Sunday morning* the women went to the tomb, taking the spices they had prepared. ²They found that the stone had been rolled away from the entrance. ³So they went in, but they didn't find the body of the Lord Jesus. ⁴As they stood there puzzled, two men

suddenly appeared to them, clothed in dazzling robes.

⁵The women were terrified and bowed with their faces to the ground. Then the men asked, "Why are you looking among the dead for someone who is alive? ⁶He isn't here! He is risen from the dead! Remember what he told you back in Galilee, ⁷that the Son of Man* must be betrayed into the hands of sinful men and be crucified, and that he would rise again on the third day."

⁸Then they remembered that he had said this. ⁹So they rushed back from the tomb to tell his eleven disciples—and everyone else— what had happened. ¹⁰It was Mary Magdalene, Joanna, Mary the mother of James, and several other women who told the apostles what had happened. ¹¹But the story sounded like nonsense to the men, so they didn't believe it. ¹²However, Peter jumped up and ran to the tomb to look. Stooping, he peered in and saw the empty linen wrappings; then he went home again, wondering what had happened.

THE WALK TO EMMAUS ¹³That same day two of Jesus' followers were walking to the village of Emmaus, seven miles* from Jerusalem. ¹⁴As they walked along they were talking about everything that had happened. ¹⁵As they talked and discussed these things, Jesus himself

23:54 Greek *It was the day of preparation.* **24:1** Greek *But on the first day of the week, very early in the morning.* **24:7** "Son of Man" is a title Jesus used for himself. **24:13** Greek *60 stadia* [11.1 kilometers].

I WONDER...

My church regularly does something called "Communion." What is it supposed to do for me?

Have you ever saved something from a special event because you wanted to remember how great that moment was? Odds are you have. And if you ask your parents to take you through their "nostalgia boxes" sometime, they'll probably say things like: "This is the varsity letter I won my senior year for swimming." Or, "Here is the ring box from the ring your father gave me the day he proposed."

Certain items help us remember special moments in our lives.

When Jesus was about to die, be resurrected, and return to heaven, he wanted to leave his followers something tangible to remember him by. He could have left a physical item like a robe or a cup. But people probably would begin to worship the object instead of God, and the object would be seen by just

a few. So instead, he left an "act," something we could do.

Communion (the Lord's Supper, Eucharist) is that act—a word picture of what Jesus did on the Cross. There, his body was broken and his blood was shed . . . for us. Luke 24:13-35 says that Jesus was recognized "as he was breaking the bread" (verse 35). Communion helps us recognize who Jesus is and that he is with us as we worship.

Because Communion is celebrated by believers throughout the world, it is a unifying act. And because we retell the message of Christ's death, we are reminded that he is going to return someday to take us to heaven (see 1 Cor 11:23-26).

Christians will always need those reminders. Life has too many distractions that cause us to lose our focus on what really matters in this life. Communion briefly reminds us that real life revolves not around us, but around one incredible act of love at a certain time in history.

suddenly came and began walking with them. [16]But God kept them from recognizing him.

[17]He asked them, "What are you discussing so intently as you walk along?"

They stopped short, sadness written across their faces. [18]Then one of them, Cleopas, replied, "You must be the only person in Jerusalem who hasn't heard about all the things that have happened there the last few days."

[19]"What things?" Jesus asked.

"The things that happened to Jesus, the man from Nazareth," they said. "He was a prophet who did powerful miracles, and he was a mighty teacher in the eyes of God and all the people. [20]But our leading priests and other religious leaders handed him over to be condemned to death, and they crucified him. [21]We had hoped he was the Messiah who had come to rescue Israel. This all happened three days ago.

[22]"Then some women from our group of his followers were at his tomb early this morning, and they came back with an amazing report. [23]They said his body was missing, and they had seen angels who told them Jesus is alive! [24]Some of our men ran out to see, and sure enough, his body was gone, just as the women had said."

[25]Then Jesus said to them, "You foolish people! You find it so hard to believe all that the prophets wrote in the Scriptures. [26]Wasn't it clearly predicted that the Messiah would have to suffer all these things before entering his glory?" [27]Then Jesus took them through the writings of Moses and all the prophets, explaining from all the Scriptures the things concerning himself.

[28]By this time they were nearing Emmaus and the end of their journey. Jesus acted as if he were going on, [29]but they begged him, "Stay the night with us, since it is getting late." So he went home with them. [30]As they sat down to eat,* he took the bread and blessed it. Then he broke it and gave it to them. [31]Suddenly, their eyes were opened, and they recognized him. And at that moment he disappeared!

[32]They said to each other, "Didn't our hearts burn within us as he talked with us on the road and explained the Scriptures to us?" [33]And within the hour they were on their way back to Jerusalem. There they found the eleven disciples and the others who had gathered with them, [34]who said, "The Lord has really risen! He appeared to Peter.*"

24:30 Or As they reclined. 24:34 Greek Simon. 24:47 Or all peoples.

JESUS APPEARS TO THE DISCIPLES

[35]Then the two from Emmaus told their story of how Jesus had appeared to them as they were walking along the road, and how they had recognized him as he was breaking the bread. [36]And just as they were telling about it, Jesus himself was suddenly standing there among them. "Peace be with you," he said. [37]But the whole group was startled and frightened, thinking they were seeing a ghost!

[38]"Why are you frightened?" he asked. "Why are your hearts filled with doubt? [39]Look at my hands. Look at my feet. You can see that it's really me. Touch me and make sure that I am not a ghost, because ghosts don't have bodies, as you see that I do." [40]As he spoke, he showed them his hands and his feet.

[41]Still they stood there in disbelief, filled with joy and wonder. Then he asked them, "Do you have anything here to eat?" [42]They gave him a piece of broiled fish, [43]and he ate it as they watched.

[44]Then he said, "When I was with you before, I told you that everything written about me in the law of Moses and the prophets and in the Psalms must be fulfilled." [45]Then he opened their minds to understand the Scriptures. [46]And he said, "Yes, it was written long ago that the Messiah would suffer and die and rise from the dead on the third day. [47]It was also written that this message would be proclaimed in the authority of his name to all the nations,* beginning in Jerusalem: 'There is forgiveness of sins for all who repent.' [48]You are witnesses of all these things.

[49]"And now I will send the Holy Spirit, just as my Father promised. But stay here in the city

....

SCRIPTURE
(24:25-27) After the two disciples told Jesus they were puzzled, he answered them by going to Scripture and applying it to his ministry. When we are puzzled by questions or problems, we, too, can go to Scripture and find authoritative help. If we, like these two disciples, do not understand what the Bible means, we can turn to other believers who know the Bible and have the wisdom to apply it to our situations.

INSIGHT
(24:45) In two instances Jesus helped his disciples understand Scriptures: while on the road to Emmaus (24:13-34) and at this time. The Holy Spirit provides this kind of help when we study the Bible. Have you ever wondered how to understand a difficult Bible passage? Besides reading surrounding passages, asking other people, and consulting reference works, you can pray that the Holy Spirit will open your mind to understand, giving you the needed insight to put God's Word into action in your life.

until the Holy Spirit comes and fills you with power from heaven."

THE ASCENSION [50]Then Jesus led them to Bethany, and lifting his hands to heaven, he blessed them. [51]While he was blessing them, he left them and was taken up to heaven. [52]So they worshiped him and then returned to Jerusalem filled with great joy. [53]And they spent all of their time in the Temple, praising God.

JOHN

Questions. Life is full of all kinds of them.

Dumb questions:

"If the plural of goose is geese, shouldn't the plural of moose be meese?"

"If God can do anything, can he make a rock so big that even he couldn't lift it?"

Mysterious questions:

"Why do toasters always have a setting that burns the toast to a crisp, which no one would eat anyway?"

Serious questions:

"If God really cares about us, why does he allow evil in the world?"

"What gives my life meaning?"

Everyone has ideas about where to find happiness or fulfillment—even people who don't (or won't) openly discuss serious issues. For example, Cameron's formula for fulfillment includes partying and sex. Ilsa thinks she'll find it in a 4.0 GPA and a college scholarship. Sebastian is banking on his athletic ability. Anna's relying on beauty and bucks.

Nagging questions:

"If the pursuit of sex, academic or athletic achievement, or money really makes people happy, why are so many people who pursue them so unhappy?"

"Why don't more people consider what Jesus had to say about the ingredients of a purpose-filled life?"

Personal questions:

"Have you ever really thought about Jesus' teachings in the Gospel of John?"

"What are you waiting for?"

KEY POINTS

ETERNAL LIFE Because Jesus is God, he can offer eternal life—unending life—to us. This personal, eternal relationship with him begins now and will continue after our lives end here on Earth.

MIRACLES John records specific signs or miracles that prove Jesus' identity as God's promised Savior. These signs encourage us to believe in him.

HOLY SPIRIT Jesus told his disciples that after he returned to heaven, the Holy Spirit would come. The Holy Spirit would guide and comfort all believers. The Holy Spirit draws us to Jesus in faith.

RESURRECTION On the third day after Jesus died, he rose from the dead. This reality changed the disciples from frightened deserters to dynamic leaders in the new church. The resurrection gives us hope for the future, which transforms our decisions for today.

STATS

PURPOSE
To prove that Jesus is the Son of God and that all who believe in him will have eternal life

AUTHOR
The apostle John, one of the "Sons of Thunder"

ORIGINAL AUDIENCE
Non-Christians and new Christians wanting to learn about Jesus

DATE WRITTEN
Probably between A.D. 85 and 90

SETTING
Written after the destruction of Jerusalem in A.D. 70 and before John's exile to the island of Patmos

KEY PEOPLE
Jesus, John the Baptist, the disciples, Mary, Martha, Lazarus, Jesus' mother Mary, Pilate, Mary Magdalene

KEY PLACES
Judean countryside, Samaria, Galilee, Bethany, Jerusalem

TIMELINE

37 B.C.
Herod the Great begins to rule

6/5 B.C.
Jesus is born

5/4 B.C.
Jesus' family escapes to Egypt

4 B.C.
Herod the Great dies

4/3 B.C.
Jesus' family returns to Nazareth

26/27
Jesus begins his ministry

27
Nicodemus comes to Jesus

28
Jesus chooses 12 disciples

29
Jesus feeds 5,000

30
Jesus is crucified, rises again, and ascends to heaven

FOLLOWING JESUS' JOURNEY
The Gospel of John begins with John the Baptist ministering near Bethany across the Jordan River (1:28). Jesus also began his ministry there, talking to some of the men who would later become his 12 disciples. Jesus' ministry in Galilee began with a visit to a wedding in Cana (2:1-11). Then he went to Capernaum, which became his new home (2:12). He journeyed to Jerusalem for the special feasts (2:13) and there met with Nicodemus, a religious leader (3:1-21). When he left Judea, he traveled through Samaria and ministered to the Samaritans (4:3-42). Jesus did miracles in Galilee (4:46-54) and Jerusalem (5:1-15). We follow him as he fed 5,000 near Bethsaida beside the Sea of Galilee (Sea of Tiberias) (6:1-15), walked on the water to his frightened disciples (6:16-21), preached throughout Galilee (7:1), returned to Jerusalem (7:10), preached across the Jordan in Perea (10:40), raised Lazarus from the dead in Bethany (11:1-44), and finally entered Jerusalem for the last time to celebrate the Passover with his disciples and give them key teachings about what was to come and how they should act. His last hours before his crucifixion were spent in the city (13–17), in the garden of Gethsemane (18:1-11), and finally in various buildings in Jerusalem during his trial (18:12–19:16). He would be crucified, but he would rise again as he had promised.

The broken lines (— · —·) indicate modern boundaries.

1 PROLOGUE: CHRIST, THE ETERNAL WORD

¹ In the beginning the Word already existed.
   The Word was with God,
   and the Word was God.
² He existed in the beginning with God.
³ God created everything through him,
   and nothing was created except
      through him.
⁴ The Word gave life to everything that was
      created,*
   and his life brought light to everyone.
⁵ The light shines in the darkness,
   and the darkness can never
      extinguish it.*

⁶God sent a man, John the Baptist,* ⁷to tell about the light so that everyone might believe because of his testimony. ⁸John himself was not the light; he was simply a witness to tell about the light. ⁹The one who is the true light, who gives light to everyone, was coming into the world.

¹⁰He came into the very world he created, but the world didn't recognize him. ¹¹He came to his own people, and even they rejected him. ¹²But to all who believed him and accepted him, he gave the right to become children of God. ¹³They are reborn—not with a physical birth resulting from human passion or plan, but a birth that comes from God.

SO COMPLEX
(1:3-5) Do you ever feel as though your life is so complex that God would never understand? Remember, God created the entire universe—nothing is too complex for him to understand. He created you, he is alive today, and his love is greater than any problem you may face.

1:3-4 Or and nothing that was created was created except through him. The Word gave life to everything. **1:5** Or and the darkness has not understood it. **1:6** Greek a man named John.

¹⁴So the Word became human* and made his home among us. He was full of unfailing love and faithfulness.* And we have seen his glory, the glory of the Father's one and only Son.

¹⁵John testified about him when he shouted to the crowds, "This is the one I was talking about when I said, 'Someone is coming after me who is far greater than I am, for he existed long before me.'"

¹⁶From his abundance we have all received one gracious blessing after another.* ¹⁷For the law was given through Moses, but God's unfailing love and faithfulness came through Jesus Christ. ¹⁸No one has ever seen God. But the unique One, who is himself God,* is near to the Father's heart. He has revealed God to us.

THE TESTIMONY OF JOHN THE BAPTIST ¹⁹This was John's testimony when the Jewish leaders sent priests and Temple assistants* from Jerusalem to ask John, "Who are you?" ²⁰He came right out and said, "I am not the Messiah."

²¹"Well then, who are you?" they asked. "Are you Elijah?"

"No," he replied.

"Are you the Prophet we are expecting?"*

"No."

²²"Then who are you? We need an answer for those who sent us. What do you have to say about yourself?"

²³John replied in the words of the prophet Isaiah:

"I am a voice shouting in the wilderness,
'Clear the way for the LORD's coming!'"*

²⁴Then the Pharisees who had been sent ²⁵asked him, "If you aren't the Messiah or Elijah or the Prophet, what right do you have to baptize?"

²⁶John told them, "I baptize with* water, but right here in the crowd is someone you do not recognize. ²⁷Though his ministry follows mine, I'm not even worthy to be his slave and untie the straps of his sandal."

²⁸This encounter took place in Bethany, an area east of the Jordan River, where John was baptizing.

JESUS, THE LAMB OF GOD ²⁹The next day John saw Jesus coming toward him and said, "Look! The Lamb of God who takes away the sin of

1:14a Greek *became flesh.* 1:14b Or *grace and truth;* also in 1:17. 1:16 Or *received grace upon grace.* 1:18 Some manuscripts read *But the one and only Son.* 1:19 Greek *and Levites.* 1:21 Greek *Are you the Prophet?* See Deut 18:15, 18; Mal 4:5-6. 1:23 Isa 40:3. 1:26 Or *in;* also in 1:31, 33.

MY STORY: Haley

It was a devastating weekend. A twister hit my town, and suddenly our house was ruined, my wrist was broken, and I lost my best friend.

I didn't know what to do, where to turn. It was too much to take in all at once. I felt depressed, then angry, then cheated. In all the confusion of adjusting to these disasters, I finally decided to open the Bible.

I started reading the Gospel of John. And as I thought about Jesus and all he gave up in heaven to come down to earth and live among us, my attitude started to change. I thought about verses 10-12 in the first chapter, how Jesus wasn't respected by the very people he came to help. If anybody had the right to feel self-pity, he did! But Jesus did everything for love, all for us.

The first 27 verses of chapter one opened my eyes to God's faithfulness and love. They made me realize that God would stand by me through everything, even this terrible time. I turned everything over to God and discovered a joy that was as incredible as everything that had happened to me in that one terrible weekend. I began to live the kind of Christian life I'd been missing so long when I was just going my own way.

The following weeks were the happiest I'd ever felt, even though I still had to deal with the sorrow over losing my friend and our home. I found that the love of God was so much more real. It gave me strength.

the world! ³⁰He is the one I was talking about when I said, 'A man is coming after me who is far greater than I am, for he existed long before me.' ³¹I did not recognize him as the Messiah, but I have been baptizing with water so that he might be revealed to Israel."

³²Then John testified, "I saw the Holy Spirit descending like a dove from heaven and resting upon him. ³³I didn't know he was the one, but when God sent me to baptize with water, he told me, 'The one on whom you see the Spirit descend and rest is the one who will baptize with the Holy Spirit.' ³⁴I saw this happen

to Jesus, so I testify that he is the Chosen One of God.*"

THE FIRST DISCIPLES ³⁵The following day John was again standing with two of his disciples. ³⁶As Jesus walked by, John looked at him and declared, "Look! There is the Lamb of God!" ³⁷When John's two disciples heard this, they followed Jesus.

³⁸Jesus looked around and saw them following. "What do you want?" he asked them.

They replied, "Rabbi" (which means "Teacher"), "where are you staying?"

³⁹"Come and see," he said. It was about four o'clock in the afternoon when they went with him to the place where he was staying, and they remained with him the rest of the day.

⁴⁰Andrew, Simon Peter's brother, was one of these men who heard what John said and then followed Jesus. ⁴¹Andrew went to find his brother, Simon, and told him, "We have found the Messiah" (which means "Christ"*).

⁴²Then Andrew brought Simon to meet Jesus. Looking intently at Simon, Jesus said, "Your name is Simon, son of John—but you will be called Cephas" (which means "Peter"*).

⁴³The next day Jesus decided to go to Galilee. He found Philip and said to him, "Come, follow me." ⁴⁴Philip was from Bethsaida, Andrew and Peter's hometown.

⁴⁵Philip went to look for Nathanael and told him, "We have found the very person Moses* and the prophets wrote about! His name is Jesus, the son of Joseph from Nazareth."

⁴⁶"Nazareth!" exclaimed Nathanael. "Can anything good come from Nazareth?"

"Come and see for yourself," Philip replied.

⁴⁷As they approached, Jesus said, "Now here is a genuine son of Israel—a man of complete integrity."

⁴⁸"How do you know about me?" Nathanael asked.

Jesus replied, "I could see you under the fig tree before Philip found you."

⁴⁹Then Nathanael exclaimed, "Rabbi, you are the Son of God—the King of Israel!"

⁵⁰Jesus asked him, "Do you believe this just because I told you I had seen you under the

fig tree? You will see greater things than this." ⁵¹Then he said, "I tell you the truth, you will all see heaven open and the angels of God going up and down on the Son of Man, the one who is the stairway between heaven and earth.*"

2 **THE WEDDING AT CANA** The next day* there was a wedding celebration in the village of Cana in Galilee. Jesus' mother was there, ²and Jesus and his disciples were also invited to the celebration. ³The wine supply ran out during the festivities, so Jesus' mother told him, "They have no more wine."

⁴"Dear woman, that's not our problem," Jesus replied. "My time has not yet come."

⁵But his mother told the servants, "Do whatever he tells you."

⁶Standing nearby were six stone water jars, used for Jewish ceremonial washing. Each could hold twenty to thirty gallons.* ⁷Jesus told the servants, "Fill the jars with water." When the jars had been filled, ⁸he said, "Now dip some out, and take it to the master of ceremonies." So the servants followed his instructions.

⁹When the master of ceremonies tasted the water that was now wine, not knowing where it had come from (though, of course, the servants knew), he called the bridegroom over. ¹⁰"A host always serves the best wine first," he said. "Then, when everyone has had a lot to drink, he brings out the less expensive wine. But you have kept the best until now!"

¹¹This miraculous sign at Cana in Galilee was the first time Jesus revealed his glory. And his disciples believed in him.

¹²After the wedding he went to Capernaum for a few days with his mother, his brothers, and his disciples.

JESUS CLEARS THE TEMPLE ¹³It was nearly time for the Jewish Passover celebration, so Jesus went to Jerusalem. ¹⁴In the Temple area he saw merchants selling cattle, sheep, and doves for sacrifices; he also saw dealers at tables exchanging foreign money. ¹⁵Jesus made a whip from some ropes and chased them all out of the Temple. He drove out the sheep and cattle, scattered the money changers' coins over the floor, and turned over their tables. ¹⁶Then, going over to the people who sold doves, he told them, "Get these things

---

HUMILITY
(1:30) Although John the Baptist was a well-known preacher and attracted large crowds, he was content for Jesus to take the higher place (see also 3:27-36). This is true humility, the basis for greatness in anything we do for God. When you are content to do what God wants you to do and let Jesus be honored for it, God will do great things through you.

1:34 Some manuscripts read *the Son of God.* **1:41** *Messiah* (a Hebrew term) and *Christ* (a Greek term) both mean "the anointed one." **1:42** The names *Cephas* (from Aramaic) and *Peter* (from Greek) both mean "rock." **1:45** Greek *Moses in the law.*
1:51 Greek *going up and down on the Son of Man;* see Gen 28:10-17. "Son of Man" is a title Jesus used for himself. **2:1** Greek *On the third day;* see 1:35, 43. **2:6** Greek *2 or 3 measures* [75 to 113 liters].

out of here. Stop turning my Father's house into a marketplace!"

[17]Then his disciples remembered this prophecy from the Scriptures: "Passion for God's house will consume me."*

[18]But the Jewish leaders demanded, "What are you doing? If God gave you authority to do this, show us a miraculous sign to prove it."

[19]"All right," Jesus replied. "Destroy this temple, and in three days I will raise it up."

[20]"What!" they exclaimed. "It has taken forty-six years to build this Temple, and you can rebuild it in three days?" [21]But when Jesus said "this temple," he meant his own body. [22]After he was raised from the dead, his disciples remembered he had said this, and they believed both the Scriptures and what Jesus had said.

JESUS AND NICODEMUS [23]Because of the miraculous signs Jesus did in Jerusalem at the Passover celebration, many began to trust in him. [24]But Jesus didn't trust them, because he knew human nature. [25]No one needed to tell him what mankind is really like.

3 There was a man named Nicodemus, a Jewish religious leader who was a Pharisee. [2]After dark one evening, he came to speak with Jesus. "Rabbi," he said, "we all know that God has sent you to teach us. Your miraculous signs are evidence that God is with you."

[3]Jesus replied, "I tell you the truth, unless you are born again,* you cannot see the Kingdom of God."

[4]"What do you mean?" exclaimed Nicodemus. "How can an old man go back into his mother's womb and be born again?"

[5]Jesus replied, "I assure you, no one can enter the Kingdom of God without being born of water and the Spirit.* [6]Humans can reproduce only human life, but the Holy Spirit gives birth to spiritual life.* [7]So don't be surprised when I say, 'You* must be born again.' [8]The wind blows wherever it wants. Just as you can hear the wind but can't tell where it comes from or where it is going, so you can't explain how people are born of the Spirit."

[9]"How are these things possible?" Nicodemus asked.

[10]Jesus replied, "You are a respected Jewish teacher, and yet you don't understand these things? [11]I assure you, we tell you what we

---

"FOR GOD LOVED THE WORLD SO MUCH THAT HE GAVE HIS ONE AND ONLY SON, SO THAT EVERYONE WHO BELIEVES IN HIM WILL NOT PERISH BUT HAVE ETERNAL LIFE."

JOHN 3:16

---

know and have seen, and yet you won't believe our testimony. [12]But if you don't believe me when I tell you about earthly things, how can you possibly believe if I tell you about heavenly things? [13]No one has ever gone to heaven and returned. But the Son of Man* has come down from heaven. [14]And as Moses lifted up the bronze snake on a pole in the wilderness, so the Son of Man must be lifted up, [15]so that everyone who believes in him will have eternal life.*

[16]"For God loved the world so much that he gave his one and only Son, so that everyone who believes in him will not perish but have eternal life. [17]God sent his Son into the world

....

ANGER
(2:15-16) Jesus obviously was angry with the merchants who conducted business in the Temple. Although there is a difference between uncontrolled rage and righteous indignation, both are called anger. How we use the powerful emotion of anger makes all the difference. Jesus used his anger for good instead of evil. Feeling angry? How can you use your anger to bring about positive changes?

GOD WITH US
(3:6) Jesus explained to Nicodemus that the Holy Spirit is involved in the spiritual rebirth of each person. Who is the Holy Spirit? God is three persons in one—the Father, the Son, and the Holy Spirit. God became a man in Jesus (God the Son) so that Jesus could die for our sins. Jesus rose from the dead to offer salvation to all who believe in him. When Jesus ascended into heaven, his physical presence left the earth, but he had promised to send the Holy Spirit so that his spiritual presence would still be among us and in us (see Luke 24:49). In Old Testament days, the Holy Spirit empowered specific individuals for specific purposes. Then came Pentecost (Acts 2), and now all believers have the power of the Holy Spirit available to them. For more on the Holy Spirit, read John 14:16-28; Romans 8:9; 1 Corinthians 12:13; and 2 Corinthians 1:22. If you're a believer, you're never alone. The Holy Spirit is with you.

2:17 Or *"Concern for God's house will be my undoing."* Ps 69:9. **3:3** Or *born from above;* also in 3:7. **3:5** Or *and spirit.* The Greek word for *Spirit* can also be translated *wind;* see 3:8. **3:6** Greek *what is born of the Spirit is spirit.* **3:7** The Greek word for *you* is plural; also in 3:12. **3:13** Some manuscripts add *who lives in heaven.* "Son of Man" is a title Jesus used for himself. **3:15** Or *everyone who believes will have eternal life in him.*

not to judge the world, but to save the world through him.

[18]"There is no judgment against anyone who believes in him. But anyone who does not believe in him has already been judged for not believing in God's one and only Son. [19]And the judgment is based on this fact: God's light came into the world, but people loved the darkness more than the light, for their actions were evil. [20]All who do evil hate the light and refuse to go near it for fear their sins will be exposed. [21]But those who do what is right come to the light so others can see that they are doing what God wants.*"

JOHN THE BAPTIST EXALTS JESUS

[22]Then Jesus and his disciples left Jerusalem and went into the Judean countryside. Jesus spent some time with them there, baptizing people.

[23]At this time John the Baptist was baptizing at Aenon, near Salim, because there was plenty of water there; and people kept coming to him for baptism. [24](This was before John was thrown into prison.) [25]A debate broke out between John's disciples and a certain Jew* over ceremonial cleansing. [26]So John's disciples came to him and said, "Rabbi, the man you met on the other side of the Jordan River, the one you identified as the Messiah, is also baptizing people. And everybody is going to him instead of coming to us."

[27]John replied, "No one can receive anything unless God gives it from heaven. [28]You your-

3:21 Or *can see God at work in what he is doing.*   **3:25** Some manuscripts read *some Jews.*

JOHN THE BAPTIST *PERSONALITY PROFILE*

MAYBE YOU HAVE A LIST OF PEOPLE whom you would consider odd. Judging by today's standards, John the Baptist would be called . . . well . . . odd. He wore unusual clothes, ate strange food, and preached an unusual message.

John really wasn't interested in how "unique" he was or whether or not people judged him based on his appearance. He was more concerned about his unique role: to tell the world that the Savior was on his way. John was totally committed to this purpose.

This wild-looking man stood face-to-face with people and told them to change their ways. He knew that the best way to get ready for the Savior was to be deeply sorry for their sins.

What's more, John didn't try to monopolize the spotlight once Jesus arrived. When some of his disciples complained that Jesus seemed more popular than John, John replied, "He must become greater and greater, and I must become less and less" (John 3:30).

John's message still applies today. We also need to prepare for the Savior's arrival in our lives (through the Holy Spirit) by first admitting that we need a Savior. Once we admit that need, we can choose to allow Jesus to become "greater and greater" in our lives—to be the one who calls the shots.

Today, we still need to hear John's favorite word—repent! If you don't know what it means, you may not have done it. Repenting means that you are not only deeply sorry for your sinfulness but are also serious in wanting God's help to live his way. Until you have repented, you won't experience God's forgiveness or the strength he offers to live a life of obedience. Repentance may be the most important thing you think about today.

BOTTOM LINE: God doesn't guarantee an easy or safe life to those who serve him.

Doing what God desires is the greatest possible life investment.

Standing for the truth might make you feel alone. But you aren't really alone—God is with you.

John's story is told in all four Gospels. His message and arrival are predicted in Isaiah 40:3 and Malachi 4:5-6. He also is mentioned in Acts 1:5, 22; 10:37; 11:16; 13:24-25; 18:25; 19:3-4.

UPS:
- *The God-appointed messenger who announced the arrival of Jesus*
- *A preacher who encouraged people to make things right with God*
- *A fearless confronter*
- *Known for his remarkable lifestyle*
- *Uncompromising*

DOWNS:
- *Was imprisoned and beheaded*
- *Faced doubts about who Jesus was*

STATS:
- *Where: Judea*
- *Occupation: Prophet*
- *Relatives: Zechariah (father); Elizabeth (mother); Jesus (distant cousin perhaps—see Luke 1:36)*
- *Contemporaries: Herod, Herodias*

KEY VERSE: *Matt 11:11*

selves know how plainly I told you, 'I am not the Messiah. I am only here to prepare the way for him.' ²⁹It is the bridegroom who marries the bride, and the best man is simply glad to stand with him and hear his vows. Therefore, I am filled with joy at his success. ³⁰He must become greater and greater, and I must become less and less.

³¹"He has come from above and is greater than anyone else. We are of the earth, and we speak of earthly things, but he has come from heaven and is greater than anyone else.* ³²He testifies about what he has seen and heard, but how few believe what he tells them! ³³Anyone who accepts his testimony can affirm that God is true. ³⁴For he is sent by God. He speaks God's words, for God gives him the Spirit without limit. ³⁵The Father loves his Son and has put everything into his hands. ³⁶And anyone who believes in God's Son has eternal life. Anyone who doesn't obey the Son will never experience eternal life but remains under God's angry judgment."

4 JESUS AND THE SAMARITAN WOMAN

Jesus* knew the Pharisees had heard that he was baptizing and making more disciples than John ²(though Jesus himself didn't baptize them—his disciples did). ³So he left Judea and returned to Galilee.

⁴He had to go through Samaria on the way. ⁵Eventually he came to the Samaritan village of Sychar, near the field that Jacob gave to his son Joseph. ⁶Jacob's well was there; and Jesus, tired from the long walk, sat wearily beside the well about noontime. ⁷Soon a Samaritan woman came to draw water, and Jesus said to her, "Please give me a drink." ⁸He was alone at the time because his disciples had gone into the village to buy some food.

⁹The woman was surprised, for Jews refuse to have anything to do with Samaritans.* She said to Jesus, "You are a Jew, and I am a Samaritan woman. Why are you asking me for a drink?"

¹⁰Jesus replied, "If you only knew the gift God has for you and who you are speaking to, you would ask me, and I would give you living water."

¹¹"But sir, you don't have a rope or a bucket," she said, "and this well is very deep. Where would you get this living water? ¹²And besides, do you think you're greater than our ancestor

Jacob, who gave us this well? How can you offer better water than he and his sons and his animals enjoyed?"

¹³Jesus replied, "Anyone who drinks this water will soon become thirsty again. ¹⁴But those who drink the water I give will never be thirsty again. It becomes a fresh, bubbling spring within them, giving them eternal life."

¹⁵"Please, sir," the woman said, "give me this water! Then I'll never be thirsty again, and I won't have to come here to get water."

¹⁶"Go and get your husband," Jesus told her.

¹⁷"I don't have a husband," the woman replied.

Jesus said, "You're right! You don't have a husband—¹⁸for you have had five husbands, and you aren't even married to the man you're living with now. You certainly spoke the truth!"

¹⁹"Sir," the woman said, "you must be a prophet. ²⁰So tell me, why is it that you Jews insist that Jerusalem is the only place of worship, while we Samaritans claim it is here at Mount Gerizim,* where our ancestors worshiped?"

²¹Jesus replied, "Believe me, dear woman, the time is coming when it will no longer matter whether you worship the Father on this mountain or in Jerusalem. ²²You Samaritans know very little about the one you worship, while we Jews know all about him, for salvation comes through the Jews. ²³But the time is coming—indeed it's here now—when true worshipers will worship the Father in spirit and in truth. The Father is looking for those who will worship him that way. ²⁴For God is Spirit, so those who worship him must worship in spirit and in truth."

²⁵The woman said, "I know the Messiah is coming—the one who is called Christ. When he comes, he will explain everything to us."

²⁶Then Jesus told her, "I AM the Messiah!"*

²⁷Just then his disciples came back. They were shocked to find him talking to a woman, but none of them had the nerve to ask, "What do you want with her?" or "Why are you talking to her?" ²⁸The woman left her water jar beside the well and ran back to the village, telling everyone, ²⁹"Come and see a man who told me

3:31 Some manuscripts do not include *and is greater than anyone else.*   4:1 Some manuscripts read *The Lord.*   4:9 Some manuscripts do not include this sentence.   4:20 Greek *on this mountain.*   4:26 Or *"The 'I AM' is here";* or *"I am the LORD";* Greek reads *"I am, the one speaking to you."* See Exod 3:14.

CROSSING BARRIERS

(4:7-9) This woman (1) was a Samaritan, a person of mixed heritage whom the Jews normally avoided, (2) had a bad reputation, and (3) was in a public place. No respectable Jewish man would talk to a woman under such circumstances. But Jesus didn't let these excuses stop him from talking to the woman. Would you have done the same? Is there someone you normally avoid for various reasons? Like Jesus, are you prepared to cross all barriers to share the Good News?

everything I ever did! Could he possibly be the Messiah?" ³⁰So the people came streaming from the village to see him.

³¹Meanwhile, the disciples were urging Jesus, "Rabbi, eat something."

³²But Jesus replied, "I have a kind of food you know nothing about."

³³"Did someone bring him food while we were gone?" the disciples asked each other.

³⁴Then Jesus explained: "My nourishment comes from doing the will of God, who sent me, and from finishing his work. ³⁵You know the saying, 'Four months between planting and harvest.' But I say, wake up and look around. The fields are already ripe* for harvest. ³⁶The harvesters are paid good wages, and the fruit they harvest is people brought to eternal life. What joy awaits both the planter and the harvester alike! ³⁷You know the saying, 'One plants and another harvests.' And it's true. ³⁸I sent you to harvest where you didn't plant; others had already done the work, and now you will get to gather the harvest."

READY
(4:35) *Sometimes Christians excuse themselves from witnessing by saying their family or friends aren't ready to believe. Jesus, however, makes it clear that around us a continual harvest waits to be reaped. Don't let Jesus find you making excuses. Look around. You will find people ready to hear God's Word.*

AN ACTIVE BELIEF
(4:46-54) *This nobleman not only believed that Jesus could heal, he also demonstrated his faith in Jesus by returning home. It isn't enough to say that we believe Jesus can take care of our problems. We need to act on that belief. When you pray about a need or a problem, do your actions show that you believe Jesus can do what he says?*

MANY SAMARITANS BELIEVE ³⁹Many Samaritans from the village believed in Jesus because the woman had said, "He told me everything I ever did!" ⁴⁰When they came out to see him, they begged him to stay in their village. So he stayed for two days, ⁴¹long enough for many more to hear his message and believe. ⁴²Then they said to the woman, "Now we believe, not just because of what you told us, but because we have heard him ourselves. Now we know that he is indeed the Savior of the world."

JESUS HEALS AN OFFICIAL'S SON ⁴³At the end of the two days, Jesus went on to Galilee. ⁴⁴He himself had said that a prophet is not honored in his own hometown. ⁴⁵Yet the Galileans welcomed him, for they had been in Jerusalem at the Passover celebration and had seen everything he did there.

⁴⁶As he traveled through Galilee, he came to Cana, where he had turned the water into wine. There was a government official in nearby Capernaum whose son was very sick. ⁴⁷When he heard that Jesus had come from Judea to Galilee, he went and begged Jesus to come to Capernaum to heal his son, who was about to die.

⁴⁸Jesus asked, "Will you never believe in me unless you see miraculous signs and wonders?"

⁴⁹The official pleaded, "Lord, please come now before my little boy dies."

⁵⁰Then Jesus told him, "Go back home. Your son will live!" And the man believed what Jesus said and started home.

⁵¹While the man was on his way, some of his servants met him with the news that his son was alive and well. ⁵²He asked them when the

4:35 Greek *white.*

CHOICES
prejudice

Ever think that prejudice is just related to race? If so, meet Jocelyn. She answers to Lyn, Jo, and Jay Bee, depending on her mood. Everybody thinks she's cool, and not because she plays the drums in her own band. She's also an excellent volleyball player, loves hanging out with her friends, and has more school spirit than anyone else at her high school.

So, what's the deal with Jocelyn? Check this out.

"No," Jocelyn says firmly. "I can't hang out with Brandi. She's so not cool. When I asked if she heard the latest cut from the Flea Bites' CD, I could tell she'd never heard of them. I was like, 'Where have you been for the last six months?' Who hasn't heard of the Flea Bites?"

"So, you're really not coming over tonight?" her friend Jessica asks. "I thought you said you wanted to hang out."

"With you, yes; with Brandi, no. I mean, Jess, why'd you invite her? Look at her clothes. Everybody at school thinks she's a complete loser."

"So, you're really not coming?"

"You already asked me that, Jess. I just can't. Sorry. Guess I'll see you at youth group on Thursday."

Check out John 4:1-42. The Jews treated the Samaritans the way that Jocelyn treated Brandi. Based on this passage, what advice would you have for Jocelyn?

boy had begun to get better, and they replied, "Yesterday afternoon at one o'clock his fever suddenly disappeared!" ⁵³Then the father realized that that was the very time Jesus had told him, "Your son will live." And he and his entire household believed in Jesus. ⁵⁴This was the second miraculous sign Jesus did in Galilee after coming from Judea.

5 JESUS HEALS A LAME MAN Afterward Jesus returned to Jerusalem for one of the Jewish holy days. ²Inside the city, near the Sheep Gate, was the pool of Bethesda,* with five covered porches. ³Crowds of sick people—blind, lame, or paralyzed—lay on the porches.* ⁵One of the men lying there had been sick for thirty-eight years. ⁶When Jesus saw him and knew he had been ill for a long time, he asked him, "Would you like to get well?"

⁷"I can't, sir," the sick man said, "for I have no one to put me into the pool when the water bubbles up. Someone else always gets there ahead of me."

⁸Jesus told him, "Stand up, pick up your mat, and walk!"

⁹Instantly, the man was healed! He rolled up his sleeping mat and began walking! But this miracle happened on the Sabbath, ¹⁰so the Jewish leaders objected. They said to the man who was cured, "You can't work on the Sabbath! The law doesn't allow you to carry that sleeping mat!"

¹¹But he replied, "The man who healed me told me, 'Pick up your mat and walk.'"

¹²"Who said such a thing as that?" they demanded.

¹³The man didn't know, for Jesus had disappeared into the crowd. ¹⁴But afterward Jesus found him in the Temple and told him, "Now you are well; so stop sinning, or something even worse may happen to you." ¹⁵Then the man went and told the Jewish leaders that it was Jesus who had healed him.

JESUS CLAIMS TO BE THE SON OF GOD ¹⁶So the Jewish leaders began harassing* Jesus for breaking the Sabbath rules. ¹⁷But Jesus replied, "My Father is always working, and so am I." ¹⁸So the Jewish leaders tried all the harder to find a way to kill him. For he not only broke the Sabbath, he called God his Father, thereby making himself equal with God.

5:2 Other manuscripts read Beth-zatha; still others read Bethsaida. 5:3 Some manuscripts add an expanded conclusion to verse 3 and all of verse 4: waiting for a certain movement of the water, ⁴for an angel of the Lord came from time to time and stirred up the water. And the first person to step in after the water was stirred was healed of whatever disease he had. 5:16 Or persecuting. 5:27 "Son of Man" is a title Jesus used for himself.

¹⁹So Jesus explained, "I tell you the truth, the Son can do nothing by himself. He does only what he sees the Father doing. Whatever the Father does, the Son also does. ²⁰For the Father loves the Son and shows him everything he is doing. In fact, the Father will show him how to do even greater works than healing this man. Then you will truly be astonished. ²¹For just as the Father gives life to those he raises from the dead, so the Son gives life to anyone he wants. ²²In addition, the Father judges no one. Instead, he has given the Son absolute authority to judge, ²³so that everyone will honor the Son, just as they honor the Father. Anyone who does not honor the Son is certainly not honoring the Father who sent him.

²⁴"I tell you the truth, those who listen to my message and believe in God who sent me have eternal life. They will never be condemned for their sins, but they have already passed from death into life.

²⁵"And I assure you that the time is coming, indeed it's here now, when the dead will hear my voice—the voice of the Son of God. And those who listen will live. ²⁶The Father has life in himself, and he has granted that same lifegiving power to his Son. ²⁷And he has given him authority to judge everyone because he is the Son of Man.* ²⁸Don't be so surprised! Indeed, the time is coming when all the dead in their graves will hear the voice of God's Son, ²⁹and they will rise again. Those who have done good will rise to experience eternal life, and those who have continued in evil will rise

....

TRAPPED
(5:6) Jesus' question to a sick man, "Would you like to get well?" might have seemed strange. Of course he would want to get well . . . wouldn't he? But after 38 years, this man's problem had become a way of life. He had no hope of ever being healed and no desire to help himself. Ever feel trapped like that? Many have. Unfortunately, a loss of hope has led some people to wonder if God cares at all. But God wants his people to keep on asking (Matt 7:7) and to be willing to stick with him (John 15:4-8). God may have special work for you to do in spite of your condition, or even because of it. Many have ministered effectively to hurting people because they have triumphed, with God's help, over their own hurts.

JUST LIKE HIM
(5:19-23) Jesus told a crowd of people that he did whatever he saw the Father do. In other words, he imitated the Father's actions. Many people imitate the actions of their parents. For example, some may play a musical instrument or have the ability to fix cars because their parents have done so or encouraged them to do so. But Jesus' example encourages us to imitate the actions of another parent—our heavenly Father. The questions "What would Jesus do?" and "What would Jesus have me do?" can help us make the right choices.

to experience judgment. ³⁰I can do nothing on my own. I judge as God tells me. Therefore, my judgment is just, because I carry out the will of the one who sent me, not my own will.

WITNESSES TO JESUS

³¹"If I were to testify on my own behalf, my testimony would not be valid. ³²But someone else is also testifying about me, and I assure you that everything he says about me is true. ³³In fact, you sent investigators to listen to John the Baptist, and his testimony about me was true. ³⁴Of course, I have no need of human witnesses, but I say these things so you might be saved. ³⁵John was like a burning and shining lamp, and you were excited for a while about his message. ³⁶But I have a greater witness than John—my teachings and my miracles. The Father gave me these works to accomplish, and they prove that he sent me. ³⁷And the Father who sent me has testified about me himself. You have never heard his voice or seen him face to face, ³⁸and you do not have his message in your hearts, because you do not believe me—the one he sent to you.

³⁹"You search the Scriptures because you think they give you eternal life. But the Scriptures point to me! ⁴⁰Yet you refuse to come to me to receive this life.

⁴¹"Your approval means nothing to me, ⁴²because I know you don't have God's love within you. ⁴³For I have come to you in my Father's name, and you have rejected me. Yet if others come in their own name, you gladly welcome them. ⁴⁴No wonder you can't believe! For you gladly honor each other, but you don't care about the honor that comes from the one who alone is God.*

⁴⁵"Yet it isn't I who will accuse you before the Father. Moses will accuse you! Yes, Moses, in whom you put your hopes. ⁴⁶If you really believed Moses, you would believe me, because he wrote about me. ⁴⁷But since you don't believe what he wrote, how will you believe what I say?"

6 JESUS FEEDS FIVE THOUSAND

After this, Jesus crossed over to the far side of the Sea of Galilee, also known as the Sea of Tiberias. ²A huge crowd kept following him

wherever he went, because they saw his miraculous signs as he healed the sick. ³Then Jesus climbed a hill and sat down with his disciples around him. ⁴(It was nearly time for the Jewish Passover celebration.) ⁵Jesus soon saw a huge crowd of people coming to look for him. Turning to Philip, he asked, "Where can we buy bread to feed all these people?" ⁶He was testing Philip, for he already knew what he was going to do.

⁷Philip replied, "Even if we worked for months, we wouldn't have enough money* to feed them!"

⁸Then Andrew, Simon Peter's brother, spoke up. ⁹"There's a young boy here with five barley loaves and two fish. But what good is that with this huge crowd?"

¹⁰"Tell everyone to sit down," Jesus said. So they all sat down on the grassy slopes. (The men alone numbered about 5,000.) ¹¹Then Jesus took the loaves, gave thanks to God, and distributed them to the people. Afterward he did the same with the fish. And they all ate as much as they wanted. ¹²After everyone was full, Jesus told his disciples, "Now gather the leftovers, so that nothing is wasted." ¹³So they picked up the pieces and filled twelve baskets with scraps left by the people who had eaten from the five barley loaves.

¹⁴When the people saw him* do this miraculous sign, they exclaimed, "Surely, he is the Prophet we have been expecting!"* ¹⁵When Jesus saw that they were ready to force him to be their king, he slipped away into the hills by himself.

JESUS WALKS ON WATER

¹⁶That evening Jesus' disciples went down to the shore to wait for him. ¹⁷But as darkness fell and Jesus still hadn't come back, they got into the boat and headed across the lake toward Capernaum. ¹⁸Soon a gale swept down upon them, and the sea grew very rough. ¹⁹They had rowed three or four miles* when suddenly they saw Jesus walking on the water toward the boat. They were terrified, ²⁰but he called out to them, "Don't be afraid. I am here!*" ²¹Then they were eager to let him in the boat, and immediately they arrived at their destination!

JESUS, THE BREAD OF LIFE

²²The next day the crowd that had stayed on the far shore saw that

···

RESOURCES

(6:8-9) The disciples are contrasted with the boy who offered his lunch to help feed the crowd. While the disciples offered little but doubt, the boy gave what little he had. But God can turn a little into a lot. What will you offer to God from your time, talents, and resources?

5:44 Some manuscripts read *from the only One.* **6:7** Greek *Two hundred denarii would not be enough.* A denarius was equivalent to a laborer's full day's wage. **6:14a** Some manuscripts read *Jesus.* **6:14b** See Deut 18:15, 18; Mal 4:5-6. **6:19** Greek *25 or 30 stadia* [4.6 or 5.5 kilometers]. **6:20** Or *The 'I Am' is here;* Greek reads *I am.* See Exod 3:14.

the disciples had taken the only boat, and they realized Jesus had not gone with them. ²³Several boats from Tiberias landed near the place where the Lord had blessed the bread and the people had eaten. ²⁴So when the crowd saw that neither Jesus nor his disciples were there, they got into the boats and went across to Capernaum to look for him. ²⁵They found him on the other side of the lake and asked, "Rabbi, when did you get here?"

²⁶Jesus replied, "I tell you the truth, you want to be with me because I fed you, not because you understood the miraculous signs. ²⁷But don't be so concerned about perishable things like food. Spend your energy seeking the eternal life that the Son of Man* can give you. For God the Father has given me the seal of his approval."

²⁸They replied, "We want to perform God's works, too. What should we do?"

²⁹Jesus told them, "This is the only work God wants from you: Believe in the one he has sent."

³⁰They answered, "Show us a miraculous sign if you want us to believe in you. What can you do? ³¹After all, our ancestors ate manna while they journeyed through the wilderness! The Scriptures say, 'Moses gave them bread from heaven to eat.'*"

³²Jesus said, "I tell you the truth, Moses didn't give you bread from heaven. My Father did. And now he offers you the true bread from heaven. ³³The true bread of God is the one who comes down from heaven and gives life to the world."

³⁴"Sir," they said, "give us that bread every day."

³⁵Jesus replied, "I am the bread of life. Whoever comes to me will never be hungry again. Whoever believes in me will never be thirsty. ³⁶But you haven't believed in me even though you have seen me. ³⁷However, those the Father has given me will come to me, and I will never reject them. ³⁸For I have come down from heaven to do the will of God who sent me, not to do my own will. ³⁹And this is the will of God, that I should not lose even one of all those he has given me, but that I should raise them up at the last day. ⁴⁰For it is my Father's will that all who see his Son and believe in him should have eternal life. I will raise them up at the last day."

⁴¹Then the people* began to murmur in disagreement because he had said, "I am the

bread that came down from heaven." ⁴²They said, "Isn't this Jesus, the son of Joseph? We know his father and mother. How can he say, 'I came down from heaven'?"

⁴³But Jesus replied, "Stop complaining about what I said. ⁴⁴For no one can come to me unless the Father who sent me draws them to me, and at the last day I will raise them up. ⁴⁵As it is written in the Scriptures,* 'They will all be taught by God.' Everyone who listens to the Father and learns from him comes to me. ⁴⁶(Not that anyone has ever seen the Father; only I, who was sent from God, have seen him.)

⁴⁷"I tell you the truth, anyone who believes has eternal life. ⁴⁸Yes, I am the bread of life! ⁴⁹Your ancestors ate manna in the wilderness, but they all died. ⁵⁰Anyone who eats the bread from heaven, however, will never die. ⁵¹I am the living bread that came down from heaven. Anyone who eats this bread will live forever; and this bread, which I will offer so the world may live, is my flesh."

⁵²Then the people began arguing with each other about what he meant. "How can this man give us his flesh to eat?" they asked.

⁵³So Jesus said again, "I tell you the truth, unless you eat the flesh of the Son of Man and drink his blood, you cannot have eternal life within you. ⁵⁴But anyone who eats my flesh and drinks my blood has eternal life, and I will raise that person at the last day. ⁵⁵For my flesh is true food, and my blood is true drink. ⁵⁶Anyone who eats my flesh and drinks my blood remains in me, and I in him. ⁵⁷I live because of the living Father who sent me; in the same way, anyone who feeds on me will live because of me. ⁵⁸I am the true bread that came down from heaven. Anyone who eats this bread will not die as your ancestors did (even though they ate the manna) but will live forever."

⁵⁹He said these things while he was teaching in the synagogue in Capernaum.

MANY DISCIPLES DESERT JESUS ⁶⁰Many of his disciples said, "This is very hard to understand. How can anyone accept it?"

⁶¹Jesus was aware that his disciples were complaining, so he said to them, "Does this offend you? ⁶²Then what will you think if you see

....

THE WAY
(6:26) Jesus knew that many of the people who followed him did so only because he fed them miraculously. Yet they weren't "hungry" for the truth. True believers follow Jesus simply because they know his way is the way to live. Is that why you follow him?

6:27 "Son of Man" is a title Jesus used for himself. 6:31 Exod 16:4; Ps 78:24. 6:41 Greek *Jewish people;* also in 6:52. 6:45 Greek *in the prophets.* Isa 54:13.

the Son of Man ascend to heaven again? 63The Spirit alone gives eternal life. Human effort accomplishes nothing. And the very words I have spoken to you are spirit and life. 64But some of you do not believe me." (For Jesus knew from the beginning which ones didn't believe, and he knew who would betray him.) 65Then he said, "That is why I said that people can't come to me unless the Father gives them to me."

66At this point many of his disciples turned away and deserted him. 67Then Jesus turned to the Twelve and asked, "Are you also going to leave?"

68Simon Peter replied, "Lord, to whom would we go? You have the words that give eternal life. 69We believe, and we know you are the Holy One of God.*"

70Then Jesus said, "I chose the twelve of you, but one is a devil." 71He was speaking of Judas, son of Simon Iscariot, one of the Twelve, who would later betray him.

7 JESUS AND HIS BROTHERS After this, Jesus traveled around Galilee. He wanted to stay out of Judea, where the Jewish leaders were plotting his death. 2But soon it was time for the Jewish Festival of Shelters, 3and Jesus' brothers said to him, "Leave here and go to Judea, where your followers can see your miracles! 4You can't become famous if you hide like this! If you can do such wonderful things, show yourself to the world!" 5For even his brothers didn't believe in him.

6Jesus replied, "Now is not the right time for me to go, but you can go anytime. 7The world can't hate you, but it does hate me because I accuse it of doing evil. 8You go on. I'm not going* to this festival, because my time has not yet come." 9After saying these things, Jesus remained in Galilee.

....

JESUS TEACHES OPENLY AT THE TEMPLE 10But after his brothers left for the festival, Jesus also went, though secretly, staying out of public view. 11The Jewish leaders tried to find him at the festival and kept asking if anyone had seen him. 12There was a lot of grumbling about him among the crowds. Some argued, "He's a good man," but others said, "He's nothing but a fraud who deceives the people." 13But no one had the courage to speak favorably about him in public, for they were afraid of getting in trouble with the Jewish leaders.

14Then, midway through the festival, Jesus went up to the Temple and began to teach. 15The people* were surprised when they heard him. "How does he know so much when he hasn't been trained?" they asked.

16So Jesus told them, "My message is not my own; it comes from God who sent me. 17Anyone who wants to do the will of God will know whether my teaching is from God or is merely my own. 18Those who speak for themselves want glory only for themselves, but a person who seeks to honor the one who sent him speaks truth, not lies. 19Moses gave you the law, but none of you obeys it! In fact, you are trying to kill me."

20The crowd replied, "You're demon possessed! Who's trying to kill you?"

21Jesus replied, "I did one miracle on the Sabbath, and you were amazed. 22But you work on the Sabbath, too, when you obey Moses' law of circumcision. (Actually, this tradition of circumcision began with the patriarchs, long before the law of Moses.) 23For if the correct time for circumcising your son falls on the Sabbath, you go ahead and do it so as not to break the law of Moses. So why should you be angry with me for healing a man on the Sabbath? 24Look beneath the surface so you can judge correctly."

IS JESUS THE MESSIAH? 25Some of the people who lived in Jerusalem started to ask each other, "Isn't this the man they are trying to kill? 26But here he is, speaking in public, and they say nothing to him. Could our leaders possibly believe that he is the Messiah? 27But how could he be? For we know where this man comes from. When the Messiah comes, he will simply appear; no one will know where he comes from."

28While Jesus was teaching in the Temple, he called out, "Yes, you know me, and you

6:69 Other manuscripts read *you are the Christ, the Holy One of God;* still others read *you are the Christ, the Son of God;* and still others read *you are the Christ, the Son of the living God.* **7:8** Some manuscripts read *not yet going.* **7:15** Greek *Jewish people.*

know where I come from. But I'm not here on my own. The one who sent me is true, and you don't know him. [29]But I know him because I come from him, and he sent me to you." [30]Then the leaders tried to arrest him; but no one laid a hand on him, because his time* had not yet come.

[31]Many among the crowds at the Temple believed in him. "After all," they said, "would you expect the Messiah to do more miraculous signs than this man has done?"

[32]When the Pharisees heard that the crowds were whispering such things, they and the leading priests sent Temple guards to arrest Jesus. [33]But Jesus told them, "I will be with you only a little longer. Then I will return to the one who sent me. [34]You will search for me but not find me. And you cannot go where I am going."

[35]The Jewish leaders were puzzled by this statement. "Where is he planning to go?" they asked. "Is he thinking of leaving the country and going to the Jews in other lands?* Maybe he will even teach the Greeks! [36]What does he mean when he says, 'You will search for me but not find me,' and 'You cannot go where I am going'?"

JESUS PROMISES LIVING WATER [37]On the last day, the climax of the festival, Jesus stood and shouted to the crowds, "Anyone who is thirsty may come to me! [38]Anyone who believes in me may come and drink! For the Scriptures declare, 'Rivers of living water will flow from his heart.'"* [39](When he said "living water," he was speaking of the Spirit, who would be given to everyone believing in him. But the Spirit had not yet been given,* because Jesus had not yet entered into his glory.)

DIVISION AND UNBELIEF [40]When the crowds heard him say this, some of them declared, "Surely this man is the Prophet we've been expecting."* [41]Others said, "He is the Messiah." Still others said, "But he can't be! Will the Messiah come from Galilee? [42]For the Scriptures clearly state that the Messiah will be born of the royal line of David, in Bethlehem, the village where King David was born."* [43]So the crowd was divided about him. [44]Some even wanted him arrested, but no one laid a hand on him.

[45]When the Temple guards returned without

having arrested Jesus, the leading priests and Pharisees demanded, "Why didn't you bring him in?"

[46]"We have never heard anyone speak like this!" the guards responded.

[47]"Have you been led astray, too?" the Pharisees mocked. [48]"Is there a single one of us rulers or Pharisees who believes in him? [49]This foolish crowd follows him, but they are ignorant of the law. God's curse is on them!"

[50]Then Nicodemus, the leader who had met with Jesus earlier, spoke up. [51]"Is it legal to convict a man before he is given a hearing?" he asked.

[52]They replied, "Are you from Galilee, too? Search the Scriptures and see for yourself—no prophet ever comes* from Galilee!"

[The most ancient Greek manuscripts do not include John 7:53–8:11.]

---

[53]Then the meeting broke up, and everybody went home.

8 A WOMAN CAUGHT IN ADULTERY
Jesus returned to the Mount of Olives, [2]but early the next morning he was back again at the Temple. A crowd soon gathered, and he sat down and taught them. [3]As he was speaking, the teachers of religious law and the Pharisees brought a woman who had been caught in the act of adultery. They put her in front of the crowd.

[4]"Teacher," they said to Jesus, "this woman was caught in the act of adultery. [5]The law of Moses says to stone her. What do you say?"

[6]They were trying to trap him into saying something they could use against him, but Jesus stooped down and wrote in the dust with his finger. [7]They kept demanding an answer, so he stood up again and said, "All right, but let the one who has never sinned throw the first stone!" [8]Then he stooped down again and wrote in the dust.

[9]When the accusers heard this, they slipped

···

DON'T JUMP!
(7:37-43) The crowd of people was divided in its reaction to Jesus. Some believed. Others were hostile. Still others disqualified Jesus as the Messiah because he was from Nazareth rather than Bethlehem as prophesied in Micah 5:2. (Jesus was born in Bethlehem; see Luke 2:1-7.) If they had looked more carefully or searched the Scriptures, they wouldn't have jumped to the wrong conclusions. What conclusions have you come to about Jesus? Are you willing to keep searching for answers if you're not sure what to believe?

7:30 Greek *his hour.*   **7:35** Or *the Jews who live among the Greeks?*
7:37-38 Or *"Let anyone who is thirsty come to me and drink. [38]For the Scriptures declare, 'Rivers of living water will flow from the heart of anyone who believes in me.'"*   **7:39** Some manuscripts read *But as yet there was no Spirit.* Still others read *But as yet there was no Holy Spirit.*   **7:40** See Deut 18:15, 18; Mal 4:5-6.   **7:42** See Mic 5:2.
7:52 Some manuscripts read *the prophet does not come.*

away one by one, beginning with the oldest, until only Jesus was left in the middle of the crowd with the woman. ¹⁰Then Jesus stood up again and said to the woman, "Where are your accusers? Didn't even one of them condemn you?"

¹¹"No, Lord," she said.

And Jesus said, "Neither do I. Go and sin no more."

JESUS, THE LIGHT OF THE WORLD
¹²Jesus spoke to the people once more and said, "I am the light of the world. If you follow me, you won't have to walk in darkness, because you will have the light that leads to life."

¹³The Pharisees replied, "You are making those claims about yourself! Such testimony is not valid."

¹⁴Jesus told them, "These claims are valid even though I make them about myself. For I know where I came from and where I am going, but you don't know this about me. ¹⁵You judge me by human standards, but I do not judge anyone. ¹⁶And if I did, my judgment would be correct in every respect because I am not alone. The Father* who sent me is with me. ¹⁷Your own law says that if two people agree about something, their witness is accepted as fact.* ¹⁸I am one witness, and my Father who sent me is the other."

¹⁹"Where is your father?" they asked.

....

JUDGE NOT
(8:9-11) *Jesus refused to condemn a woman caught in adultery. By this action, Jesus wasn't saying, "Adultery is okay" (see Exod 20:14). Actually, he was reacting to the hypocrisy of the Pharisees who wanted to condemn the woman.*

Judging someone else is always easier than judging our own actions. During his Sermon on the Mount, Jesus' warning to "judge not" included this advice: "Why worry about a speck in your friend's eye when you have a log in your own? How can you think of saying to your friend, 'Let me help you get rid of that speck in your eye,' when you can't see past the log in your own eye? Hypocrite! First get rid of the log in your own eye; then you will see well enough to deal with the speck in your friend's eye" (Matt 7:3-5). Tempted to judge someone else? Judge not.

FREE
(8:32-36) *Jesus spoke of the freedom he offered. What's your idea of freedom? Having wheels that can take you wherever you want to go? Being able to make your own choices? But some choices aren't good. In fact, making their own choices caused trouble for Adam and Eve (see Gen 3). Consequently, we were all born with a desire to do wrong. That's why Jesus said, "Everyone who sins is a slave of sin" (John 8:34). But the freedom Jesus offers is the freedom to choose not to do wrong. Are you free?*

Jesus answered, "Since you don't know who I am, you don't know who my Father is. If you knew me, you would also know my Father." ²⁰Jesus made these statements while he was teaching in the section of the Temple known as the Treasury. But he was not arrested, because his time* had not yet come.

THE UNBELIEVING PEOPLE WARNED
²¹Later Jesus said to them again, "I am going away. You will search for me but will die in your sin. You cannot come where I am going."

²²The people* asked, "Is he planning to commit suicide? What does he mean, 'You cannot come where I am going'?"

²³Jesus continued, "You are from below; I am from above. You belong to this world; I do not. ²⁴That is why I said that you will die in your sins; for unless you believe that I AM who I claim to be,* you will die in your sins."

²⁵"Who are you?" they demanded.

Jesus replied, "The one I have always claimed to be.* ²⁶I have much to say about you and much to condemn, but I won't. For I say only what I have heard from the one who sent me, and he is completely truthful." ²⁷But they still didn't understand that he was talking about his Father.

²⁸So Jesus said, "When you have lifted up the Son of Man on the cross, then you will understand that I AM he.* I do nothing on my own but say only what the Father taught me. ²⁹And the one who sent me is with me—he has not deserted me. For I always do what pleases him." ³⁰Then many who heard him say these things believed in him.

JESUS AND ABRAHAM
³¹Jesus said to the people who believed in him, "You are truly my disciples if you remain faithful to my teachings. ³²And you will know the truth, and the truth will set you free."

³³"But we are descendants of Abraham," they said. "We have never been slaves to anyone. What do you mean, 'You will be set free'?"

³⁴Jesus replied, "I tell you the truth, everyone who sins is a slave of sin. ³⁵A slave is not a permanent member of the family, but a son is part of the family forever. ³⁶So if the Son sets you free, you are truly free. ³⁷Yes, I realize that you are descendants of Abraham. And yet some of you are trying to kill me because

8:16 Some manuscripts read *The One.*   **8:17** See Deut 19:15.
8:20 Greek *his hour.*   **8:22** Greek *Jewish people;* also in 8:31, 48, 52, 57.   **8:24** Greek *unless you believe that I am.* See Exod 3:14.
8:25 Or *Why do I speak to you at all?*   **8:28** Greek *When you have lifted up the Son of Man, then you will know that I am.* "Son of Man" is a title Jesus used for himself.

there's no room in your hearts for my message. ³⁸I am telling you what I saw when I was with my Father. But you are following the advice of your father."

³⁹"Our father is Abraham!" they declared.

"No," Jesus replied, "for if you were really the children of Abraham, you would follow his example.* ⁴⁰Instead, you are trying to kill me because I told you the truth, which I heard from God. Abraham never did such a thing. ⁴¹No, you are imitating your real father."

They replied, "We aren't illegitimate children! God himself is our true Father."

⁴²Jesus told them, "If God were your Father, you would love me, because I have come to you from God. I am not here on my own, but he sent me. ⁴³Why can't you understand what I am saying? It's because you can't even hear me! ⁴⁴For you are the children of your father the devil, and you love to do the evil things he does. He has always hated the truth, because there is no truth in him. When he lies, it is consistent with his character; for he is a liar and the father of lies. ⁴⁵So when I tell the truth, you just naturally don't believe me! ⁴⁶Which of you can truthfully accuse me of sin? And since I am telling you the truth, why don't you believe me? ⁴⁷Anyone who belongs to God listens gladly to the words of God. But you don't listen because you don't belong to God."

⁴⁸The people retorted, "You Samaritan devil! Didn't we say all along that you were possessed by a demon?"

⁴⁹"No," Jesus said, "I have no demon in me. For I honor my Father—and you dishonor me. ⁵⁰And though I have no wish to glorify myself, God is going to glorify me. He is the true judge. ⁵¹I tell you the truth, anyone who obeys my teaching will never die!"

⁵²The people said, "Now we know you are possessed by a demon. Even Abraham and the prophets died, but you say, 'Anyone who obeys my teaching will never die!' ⁵³Are you greater than our father Abraham? He died, and so did the prophets. Who do you think you are?"

⁵⁴Jesus answered, "If I want glory for myself, it doesn't count. But it is my Father who will glorify me. You say, 'He is our God,'* ⁵⁵but you don't even know him. I know him. If I said

otherwise, I would be as great a liar as you! But I do know him and obey him. ⁵⁶Your father Abraham rejoiced as he looked forward to my coming. He saw it and was glad."

⁵⁷The people said, "You aren't even fifty years old. How can you say you have seen Abraham?*"

⁵⁸Jesus answered, "I tell you the truth, before Abraham was even born, I AM!*" ⁵⁹At that point they picked up stones to throw at him. But Jesus was hidden from them and left the Temple.

9 JESUS HEALS A MAN BORN BLIND As Jesus was walking along, he saw a man who had been blind from birth. ²"Rabbi," his disciples asked him, "why was this man born blind? Was it because of his own sins or his parents' sins?"

³"It was not because of his sins or his parents' sins," Jesus answered. "This happened so the power of God could be seen in him. ⁴We must quickly carry out the tasks assigned us by the one who sent us.* The night is coming, and then no one can work. ⁵But while I am here in the world, I am the light of the world."

⁶Then he spit on the ground, made mud with the saliva, and spread the mud over the blind man's eyes. ⁷He told him, "Go wash yourself in the pool of Siloam" (Siloam means "sent"). So the man went and washed and came back seeing!

⁸His neighbors and others who knew him as a blind beggar asked each other, "Isn't this the man who used to sit and beg?" ⁹Some said he was, and others said, "No, he just looks like him!"

But the beggar kept saying, "Yes, I am the same one!"

¹⁰They asked, "Who healed you? What happened?"

¹¹He told them, "The man they call Jesus made mud and spread it over my eyes and told me, 'Go to the pool of Siloam and wash

8:39 Some manuscripts read *if you are really the children of Abraham, follow his example.*   **8:54** Some manuscripts read *You say he is your God.*   **8:57** Some manuscripts read *How can you say Abraham has seen you?*   **8:58** Or *before Abraham was even born, I have always been alive;* Greek reads *before Abraham was, I am.* See Exod 3:14.   **9:4** Other manuscripts read *I must quickly carry out the tasks assigned me by the one who sent me;* still others read *We must quickly carry out the tasks assigned us by the one who sent me.*

....

SUFFERING
(9:1-3) A common belief in Jewish culture was that hardships were punishments for sins. But through the healing of the man born blind, Jesus revealed that some hardships were allowed as a means to glorify God.

We live in a world where good behavior is not always rewarded and bad behavior is not always punished; therefore, innocent people sometimes suffer. Regardless of the reasons for our suffering, Jesus has the power to help us deal with it. When hard times come, instead of asking, "Why did this happen to me?" or, "What did I do wrong?" consider asking God to strengthen you and offer you a deeper perspective on what's at stake.

yourself.' So I went and washed, and now I can see!"

¹²"Where is he now?" they asked.

"I don't know," he replied.

¹³Then they took the man who had been blind to the Pharisees, ¹⁴because it was on the Sabbath that Jesus had made the mud and healed him. ¹⁵The Pharisees asked the man all about it. So he told them, "He put the mud over my eyes, and when I washed it away, I could see!"

¹⁶Some of the Pharisees said, "This man Jesus is not from God, for he is working on the Sabbath." Others said, "But how could an ordinary sinner do such miraculous signs?" So there was a deep division of opinion among them.

¹⁷Then the Pharisees again questioned the man who had been blind and demanded, "What's your opinion about this man who healed you?"

The man replied, "I think he must be a prophet."

¹⁸The Jewish leaders still refused to believe the man had been blind and could now see, so they called in his parents. ¹⁹They asked them, "Is this your son? Was he born blind? If so, how can he now see?"

²⁰His parents replied, "We know this is our son and that he was born blind, ²¹but we don't know how he can see or who healed him. Ask him. He is old enough to speak for himself." ²²His parents said this because they were afraid of the Jewish leaders, who had announced that anyone saying Jesus was the Messiah would be expelled from the synagogue. ²³That's why they said, "He is old enough. Ask him."

²⁴So for the second time they called in the man who had been blind and told him, "God should get the glory for this,* because we know this man Jesus is a sinner."

²⁵"I don't know whether he is a sinner," the man replied. "But I know this: I was blind, and now I can see!"

²⁶"But what did he do?" they asked. "How did he heal you?"

²⁷"Look!" the man exclaimed. "I told you once. Didn't you listen? Why do you want to hear it again? Do you want to become his disciples, too?"

²⁸Then they cursed him and said, "You are his disciple, but we are disciples of Moses! ²⁹We know God spoke to Moses, but we don't even know where this man comes from."

³⁰"Why, that's very strange!" the man replied. "He healed my eyes, and yet you don't know where he comes from? ³¹We know that God doesn't listen to sinners, but he is ready to hear those who worship him and do his will. ³²Ever since the world began, no one has been able to open the eyes of someone born blind. ³³If this man were not from God, he couldn't have done it."

³⁴"You were born a total sinner!" they answered. "Are you trying to teach us?" And they threw him out of the synagogue.

SPIRITUAL BLINDNESS ³⁵When Jesus heard what had happened, he found the man and asked, "Do you believe in the Son of Man?*"

³⁶The man answered, "Who is he, sir? I want to believe in him."

³⁷"You have seen him," Jesus said, "and he is speaking to you!"

³⁸"Yes, Lord, I believe!" the man said. And he worshiped Jesus.

³⁹Then Jesus told him,* "I entered this world to render judgment—to give sight to the blind and to show those who think they see* that they are blind."

⁴⁰Some Pharisees who were standing nearby heard him and asked, "Are you saying we're blind?"

⁴¹"If you were blind, you wouldn't be guilty," Jesus replied. "But you remain guilty because you claim you can see.

10 THE GOOD SHEPHERD AND HIS SHEEP

"I tell you the truth, anyone who sneaks over the wall of a sheepfold, rather than going through the gate, must surely be a thief and a robber! ²But the one who enters through the gate is the shepherd of the sheep. ³The gatekeeper opens the gate for him, and the sheep recognize his voice and come to him. He calls his own sheep by name and leads them out. ⁴After he has gathered his own flock, he walks ahead of them, and they follow him because they know his voice. ⁵They won't follow a

---

PERSECUTION

(9:28-34) Because of his faith in Jesus, the man who had been born blind was thrown out of the synagogue. Jesus later told his disciples to expect this kind of persecution (16:1-4). If you're a follower of Jesus, you can expect to face some kind of persecution. Does that sound horrible? Maybe that's why Jesus also promised, "I have told you all this so that you may have peace in me. Here on earth you will have many trials and sorrows. But take heart, because I have overcome the world" (16:33).

9:24 Or *Give glory to God, not to Jesus;* Greek reads *Give glory to God.*   **9:35** Some manuscripts read *the Son of God?* "Son of Man" is a title Jesus used for himself.   **9:38-39a** Some manuscripts do not include *"Yes, Lord, I believe!" the man said. And he worshiped Jesus. Then Jesus told him.*   **9:39b** Greek *those who see.*

stranger; they will run from him because they don't know his voice."

[6]Those who heard Jesus use this illustration didn't understand what he meant, [7]so he explained it to them: "I tell you the truth, I am the gate for the sheep. [8]All who came before me* were thieves and robbers. But the true sheep did not listen to them. [9]Yes, I am the gate. Those who come in through me will be saved.* They will come and go freely and will find good pastures. [10]The thief's purpose is to steal and kill and destroy. My purpose is to give them a rich and satisfying life.

[11]"I am the good shepherd. The good shepherd sacrifices his life for the sheep. [12]A hired hand will run when he sees a wolf coming. He will abandon the sheep because they don't belong to him and he isn't their shepherd. And so the wolf attacks them and scatters the flock. [13]The hired hand runs away because he's working only for the money and doesn't really care about the sheep.

[14]"I am the good shepherd; I know my own sheep, and they know me, [15]just as my Father knows me and I know the Father. So I sacrifice my life for the sheep. [16]I have other sheep, too, that are not in this sheepfold. I must bring them also. They will listen to my voice, and there will be one flock with one shepherd.

[17]"The Father loves me because I sacrifice my life so I may take it back again. [18]No one can take my life from me. I sacrifice it voluntarily. For I have the authority to lay it down when I want to and also to take it up again. For this is what my Father has commanded."

[19]When he said these things, the people* were again divided in their opinions about him. [20]Some said, "He's demon possessed and out of his mind. Why listen to a man like that?" [21]Others said, "This doesn't sound like a man possessed by a demon! Can a demon open the eyes of the blind?"

JESUS CLAIMS TO BE THE SON OF GOD

[22]It was now winter, and Jesus was in Jerusalem at the time of Hanukkah, the Festival of Dedication. [23]He was in the Temple, walking through the section known as Solomon's Colonnade. [24]The people surrounded him and asked, "How long are you going to keep us in suspense? If you are the Messiah, tell us plainly."

[25]Jesus replied, "I have already told you, and you don't believe me. The proof is the work I do in my Father's name. [26]But you don't believe me because you are not my sheep. [27]My sheep listen to my voice; I know them, and they follow me. [28]I give them eternal life, and they will never perish. No one can snatch them away from me, [29]for my Father has given them to me, and he is more powerful than anyone else.* No one can snatch them from the Father's hand. [30]The Father and I are one."

[31]Once again the people picked up stones to kill him. [32]Jesus said, "At my Father's direction I have done many good works. For which one are you going to stone me?"

[33]They replied, "We're stoning you not for any good work, but for blasphemy! You, a mere man, claim to be God."

[34]Jesus replied, "It is written in your own Scriptures* that God said to certain leaders of the people, 'I say, you are gods!'* [35]And you know that the Scriptures cannot be altered. So if those people who received God's message were called 'gods,' [36]why do you call it blasphemy when I say, 'I am the Son of God'? After all, the Father set me apart and sent me into the world. [37]Don't believe me unless I carry out my Father's work. [38]But if I do his work, believe in the evidence of the miraculous works I have done, even if you don't believe me. Then you will know and understand that the Father is in me, and I am in the Father."

[39]Once again they tried to arrest him, but he got away and left them. [40]He went beyond the Jordan River near the place where John was first baptizing and stayed there awhile. [41]And many followed him. "John didn't perform miraculous signs," they remarked to one another, "but everything he said about this man has come true." [42]And many who were there believed in Jesus.

11 THE RAISING OF LAZARUS

A man named Lazarus was sick. He lived in Bethany with his sisters, Mary and Martha. [2]This is the Mary who later poured the expensive perfume on the Lord's feet and wiped them with her hair.* Her brother, Lazarus, was sick. [3]So the two sisters sent a message

---

10:8 Some manuscripts do not include *before me.*   10:9 Or *will find safety.*   10:19 Greek *Jewish people;* also in 10:24, 31.   10:29 Other manuscripts read *for what my Father has given me is more powerful than anything;* still others read *for regarding that which my Father has given me, he is greater than all.*   10:34a Greek *your own law.*   10:34b Ps 82:6.   11:2 This incident is recorded in chapter 12.

SPIRITUAL BLINDNESS
(10:24-29) *These leaders were waiting for the evidence they thought would convince them that Jesus was the Savior whom God had promised to send. Thus they couldn't accept the truth Jesus offered. Spiritual blindness like this still keeps people away from Jesus. They want him on their own terms—not his. Know anyone like that? Are you like that? Spiritual blindness has only one cure: a sincere desire to believe.*

to Jesus telling him, "Lord, your dear friend is very sick."

⁴But when Jesus heard about it he said, "Lazarus's sickness will not end in death. No, it happened for the glory of God so that the Son of God will receive glory from this." ⁵So although Jesus loved Martha, Mary, and Lazarus, ⁶he stayed where he was for the next two days. ⁷Finally, he said to his disciples, "Let's go back to Judea."

⁸But his disciples objected. "Rabbi," they said, "only a few days ago the people* in Judea were trying to stone you. Are you going there again?"

⁹Jesus replied, "There are twelve hours of daylight every day. During the day people can walk safely. They can see because they have the light of this world. ¹⁰But at night there is danger of stumbling because they have no light." ¹¹Then he said, "Our friend Lazarus has fallen asleep, but now I will go and wake him up."

11:8 Greek *Jewish people*; also in 11:19, 31, 33, 36, 45, 54.

RIGHT ON TIME

(11:5-7) Although Jesus knew that Lazarus was dying, he didn't rush over to help, as Mary and Martha had requested. Jesus' delay had a specific purpose—one that Mary and Martha didn't understand. Jesus' timing, especially his delays, may make us think he plans to ignore us or that he won't answer the way we want. But he will meet all of our needs (see Phil 4:19) according to his perfect schedule and purpose. Like David, can you say "I waited patiently for the LORD to help me"? If so, like David, you might also say, "He turned to me and heard my cry" (Ps 40:1).

I WONDER...

Bad things seem to happen all the time. Does God care about what is happening in the world?

Bad things happen; so do tragedies. At some time in life everyone will experience both of these. Let's cover them one at a time.

The guy who flunks a math test had something bad happen to him. Did he learn that it is important to keep up with assignments and study before a test? Hopefully.

A 10-year-old boy races out from behind a parked car and is almost hit by a driver. He is scared to death, realizing that he could have been killed! Did he learn a lesson about not darting into the street? He better have; he may not get another chance!

In each case the person probably was not happy about what happened. But each situation in life, good or bad, can be a learning experience.

Does God care that we learn important lessons about studying and safety? He cares very much!

Ask your folks about the five worst things that have happened to them. Next, ask what they learned from these bad experiences. Then, ask them if they were thankful that these occurred.

Going through tough times is bad only when you don't learn something when it's over.

Now let's discuss tragedy.

Unfortunately, no one is immune from what we believe is the ultimate tragedy—death. Even Jesus went through the loss of someone he loved (see John 11). It is the timing of death (especially when someone dies young), and how it occurs (like an innocent victim killed by a drunk driver), that makes us wonder if God really cares.

So, why are evil and death allowed in the world?

Ages ago, after losing a war with the angels of God, a group of fallen angels led by Satan left heaven (see Jude 1:6) and made earth their kingdom. They still exist and have only one purpose, to destroy. Their evil contrasts God's love and mercy. But even though God made people to be with him, he still allows people the freedom to choose between good and evil.

As a result of believing the lie of Satan, Adam and Eve disobeyed God in the Garden of Eden and were separated from him. (You know the story.) This incident also set in motion a new cycle of mortality: All people are born "spiritually dead" and die a bodily death.

Jesus' angry words to the Pharisees in John 8:44 describe the result of spiritual death: "You are the children of your father the devil, and you love to do the evil things he does. He was a murderer from the beginning. He has always hated the truth, because there is no truth in him. When he lies, it is consistent with his character; for he is a liar and the father of lies."

God knows that spiritual death is far worse than physical death. That's why he focused his attention on taking care of the real penalty for our sin—spiritual death (see Rom 6:23)! God also knows how tragedy can point us to him and his purposes: "We know that God causes everything to work together for the good of those who love God and are called according to his purpose for them" (Rom 8:28).

But there's good news: Jesus' death on the cross provides the antidote for spiritual death. Although we all will die eventually, a second life—eternal life—will begin.

So, although evil and death continue, God can use any situation for good. He loves you and wants to work out his purposes in your life.

[12]The disciples said, "Lord, if he is sleeping, he will soon get better!" [13]They thought Jesus meant Lazarus was simply sleeping, but Jesus meant Lazarus had died.

[14]So he told them plainly, "Lazarus is dead. [15]And for your sakes, I'm glad I wasn't there, for now you will really believe. Come, let's go see him."

[16]Thomas, nicknamed the Twin,* said to his fellow disciples, "Let's go, too—and die with Jesus."

[17]When Jesus arrived at Bethany, he was told that Lazarus had already been in his grave for four days. [18]Bethany was only a few miles* down the road from Jerusalem, [19]and many of the people had come to console Martha and Mary in their loss. [20]When Martha got word that Jesus was coming, she went to meet him. But Mary stayed in the house. [21]Martha said to Jesus, "Lord, if only you had been here, my brother would not have died. [22]But even now I know that God will give you whatever you ask."

[23]Jesus told her, "Your brother will rise again."

[24]"Yes," Martha said, "he will rise when everyone else rises, at the last day."

[25]Jesus told her, "I am the resurrection and the life.* Anyone who believes in me will live, even after dying. [26]Everyone who lives in me and believes in me will never ever die. Do you believe this, Martha?"

[27]"Yes, Lord," she told him. "I have always believed you are the Messiah, the Son of God, the one who has come into the world from God." [28]Then she returned to Mary. She called Mary aside from the mourners and told her, "The Teacher is here and wants to see you." [29]So Mary immediately went to him.

[30]Jesus had stayed outside the village, at the place where Martha met him. [31]When the people who were at the house consoling Mary saw her leave so hastily, they assumed she was going to Lazarus's grave to weep. So they followed her there. [32]When Mary arrived and saw Jesus, she fell at his feet and said, "Lord, if only you had been here, my brother would not have died."

[33]When Jesus saw her weeping and saw the other people wailing with her, a deep anger welled up within him,* and he was deeply troubled. [34]"Where have you put him?" he asked them.

They told him, "Lord, come and see." [35]Then Jesus wept. [36]The people who were standing nearby said, "See how much he loved him!" [37]But some said, "This man healed a blind man. Couldn't he have kept Lazarus from dying?"

[38]Jesus was still angry as he arrived at the tomb, a cave with a stone rolled across its entrance. [39]"Roll the stone aside," Jesus told them.

But Martha, the dead man's sister, protested, "Lord, he has been dead for four days. The smell will be terrible."

[40]Jesus responded, "Didn't I tell you that you would see God's glory if you believe?" [41]So they rolled the stone aside. Then Jesus looked up to heaven and said, "Father, thank you for hearing me. [42]You always hear me, but I said it out loud for the sake of all these people standing here, so that they will believe you sent me." [43]Then Jesus shouted, "Lazarus, come out!" [44]And the dead man came out, his hands and feet bound in graveclothes, his face wrapped in a headcloth. Jesus told them, "Unwrap him and let him go!"

THE PLOT TO KILL JESUS [45]Many of the people who were with Mary believed in Jesus when they saw this happen. [46]But some went to the Pharisees and told them what Jesus had done. [47]Then the leading priests and Pharisees called the high council* together. "What are we going to do?" they asked each other. "This man certainly performs many miraculous signs. [48]If we allow him to go on like this, soon everyone will believe in him. Then the Roman army will come and destroy both our Temple* and our nation."

[49]Caiaphas, who was high priest at that time,* said, "You don't know what you're talking about! [50]You don't realize that it's better for you that one man should die for the people than for the whole nation to be destroyed."

[51]He did not say this on his own; as high priest at that time he was led to prophesy that Jesus would die for the entire nation. [52]And not only for that nation, but to bring together and unite all the children of God scattered around the world.

11:16 Greek *Thomas, who was called Didymus.* 11:18 Greek *was about 15 stadia* [about 2.8 kilometers]. 11:25 Some manuscripts do not include *and the life.* 11:33 Or *he was angry in his spirit.* 11:47 Greek *the Sanhedrin.* 11:48 Or *our position;* Greek reads *our place.* 11:49 Greek *that year;* also in 11:51.

···

HE CARES
(11:33-38) This passage reveals a God who cares. This contrasts with the Greek concept of God that was popular in John's day—a God with no emotions and no messy involvement with humans. Here we see many of Jesus' emotions—compassion, indignation, sorrow, even frustration. Jesus often expressed deep emotion. Knowing that, are you willing to express your deepest emotions to him?

53So from that time on, the Jewish leaders began to plot Jesus' death. 54As a result, Jesus stopped his public ministry among the people and left Jerusalem. He went to a place near the wilderness, to the village of Ephraim, and stayed there with his disciples.

55It was now almost time for the Jewish Passover celebration, and many people from all over the country arrived in Jerusalem several days early so they could go through the purification ceremony before Passover began. 56They kept looking for Jesus, but as they stood around in the Temple, they said to each other, "What do you think? He won't come for Passover, will he?" 57Meanwhile, the leading priests and Pharisees had publicly ordered that anyone seeing Jesus must report it immediately so they could arrest him.

12 JESUS ANOINTED AT BETHANY Six days before the Passover celebration began, Jesus arrived in Bethany, the home of Lazarus—the man he had raised from the dead. 2A dinner was prepared in Jesus' honor. Martha served, and Lazarus was among those who ate* with him. 3Then Mary took a twelve-ounce jar* of expensive perfume made from essence of nard, and she anointed Jesus' feet with it, wiping his feet with her hair. The house was filled with the fragrance.

4But Judas Iscariot, the disciple who would soon betray him, said, 5"That perfume was worth a year's wages.* It should have been sold and the money given to the poor." 6Not that he cared for the poor—he was a thief, and since he was in charge of the disciples' money, he often stole some for himself.

7Jesus replied, "Leave her alone. She did this in preparation for my burial. 8You will always have the poor among you, but you will not always have me."

9When all the people* heard of Jesus' arrival, they flocked to see him and also to see Lazarus, the man Jesus had raised from the dead.

12:2 Or *who reclined.* **12:3** Greek *took 1 litra* [327 grams]. **12:5** Greek *worth 300 denarii.* A denarius was equivalent to a laborer's full day's wage. **12:9** Greek *Jewish people;* also in 12:11.

MARY & MARTHA
PERSONALITY PROFILE

ARE YOU THE KIND OF PERSON who loves to have people hang out at your house? Hospitality is an art. Making sure a guest is welcomed and well fed requires creativity, organization, and teamwork. Mary and Martha's ability to accomplish these makes them the best sister hospitality team in the Bible.

For Mary, hospitality meant giving more attention to the guest himself than to his needs. She was more interested in her guest's words than in how clean her house was or what time dinner was served. She let her sister Martha take care of those details. Mary was mainly a "responder." She prepared little, but participated a lot.

Unlike her sister, Martha worried about details. She wished to please, to serve, to do the right thing. Perhaps she was the oldest and felt responsible. So, she tried too hard to have everything perfect. Mary's lack of cooperation bothered Martha so much that she finally asked Jesus to tell Mary to help. Jesus gently pointed out that Mary was actually doing her part.

Each sister had her own lesson to learn. Mary needed to learn that action often is appropriate and necessary. The fact that she later anointed Jesus' feet (John 12:2-8) shows that she probably learned that lesson.

Martha learned that obedient service often goes unnoticed. The last time she appears in the Gospels she is again serving a meal to Jesus and the disciples—this time without complaint (John 12:2).

There may be times when you feel like Mary or Martha. How will you determine the "one thing worth being concerned about" (serving others or spending time with Jesus)?

BOTTOM LINE: Getting caught up in details can make us forget the main reasons for our actions.

There is a proper time to listen to Jesus and a proper time to work for him.

Mary and Martha's story is told in Luke 10:38-42 and John 11:1–12:8.

UPS:
• *Known for their hospitality*
• *Friends of Jesus*
• *Had a strong desire to do everything right (Martha)*
• *Had a deep concern for people's feelings (Mary)*

DOWNS:
• *Expected others to agree with her priorities (Martha)*
• *Overly concerned with details (Martha)*
• *Tended toward self-pity when her efforts were not recognized (Martha)*
• *Allowed others to do the work (Mary)*
• *Tended to respond, rather than prepare (Mary)*

STATS:
• *Where: Bethany*
• *Relative: Lazarus (brother)*

KEY VERSE: *Luke 10:40*

¹⁰Then the leading priests decided to kill Lazarus, too, ¹¹for it was because of him that many of the people had deserted them* and believed in Jesus.

JESUS' TRIUMPHANT ENTRY
¹²The next day, the news that Jesus was on the way to Jerusalem swept through the city. A large crowd of Passover visitors ¹³took palm branches and went down the road to meet him. They shouted,

"Praise God!*
Blessings on the one who comes in the
     name of the LORD!
Hail to the King of Israel!"*

¹⁴Jesus found a young donkey and rode on it, fulfilling the prophecy that said:

¹⁵ "Don't be afraid, people of Jerusalem.*
Look, your King is coming,
     riding on a donkey's colt."*

¹⁶His disciples didn't understand at the time that this was a fulfillment of prophecy. But after Jesus entered into his glory, they remembered what had happened and realized that these things had been written about him.

¹⁷Many in the crowd had seen Jesus call Lazarus from the tomb, raising him from the dead, and they were telling others* about it. ¹⁸That was the reason so many went out to meet him—because they had heard about this miraculous sign. ¹⁹Then the Pharisees said to each other, "There's nothing we can do. Look, everyone* has gone after him!"

JESUS PREDICTS HIS DEATH
²⁰Some Greeks who had come to Jerusalem for the Passover celebration ²¹paid a visit to Philip, who was from Bethsaida in Galilee. They said, "Sir, we want to meet Jesus." ²²Philip told Andrew about it, and they went together to ask Jesus.

²³Jesus replied, "Now the time has come for the Son of Man* to enter into his glory. ²⁴I tell you the truth, unless a kernel of wheat is planted in the soil and dies, it remains alone. But its death will produce many new kernels—a plentiful harvest of new lives. ²⁵Those who love their life in this world will lose it. Those who care nothing for their life in this world will keep it for eternity. ²⁶Anyone who wants to be my disciple must follow me, because my servants

must be where I am. And the Father will honor anyone who serves me.

²⁷"Now my soul is deeply troubled. Should I pray, 'Father, save me from this hour'? But this is the very reason I came! ²⁸Father, bring glory to your name."

Then a voice spoke from heaven, saying, "I have already brought glory to my name, and I will do so again." ²⁹When the crowd heard the voice, some thought it was thunder, while others declared an angel had spoken to him.

³⁰Then Jesus told them, "The voice was for your benefit, not mine. ³¹The time for judging this world has come, when Satan, the ruler of this world, will be cast out. ³²And when I am lifted up from the earth, I will draw everyone to myself." ³³He said this to indicate how he was going to die.

³⁴The crowd responded, "We understood from Scripture* that the Messiah would live forever. How can you say the Son of Man will die? Just who is this Son of Man, anyway?"

³⁵Jesus replied, "My light will shine for you just a little longer. Walk in the light while you can, so the darkness will not overtake you. Those who walk in the darkness cannot see where they are going. ³⁶Put your trust in the light while there is still time; then you will become children of the light."

After saying these things, Jesus went away and was hidden from them.

THE UNBELIEF OF THE PEOPLE
³⁷But despite all the miraculous signs Jesus had done, most of the people still did not believe in him.

....

LOOK BACK
(12:12-16) Although they traveled with Jesus for three years, the disciples didn't always understand him. After the Resurrection, Jesus' words and actions made more sense to the disciples. For example, they later understood how Jesus' entry into Jerusalem on the back of a donkey's colt was one of the ways he fulfilled Scripture (see Zech 9:9).

Reflect on the events of your life up to now. How has God led you to this point? As you grow older, you probably will look back and see God's involvement even more clearly than you do today.

REACH OUT
(12:37-38) Although Jesus had performed many miracles, most people still didn't believe in him. Likewise, many today refuse to believe despite all that God does. Have you ever felt discouraged because a friend refused to believe, even when you've shared your faith with him or her? You aren't responsible for your friend's lack of faith. After all, you can't make a person believe. Even God doesn't force faith on people. All you can do is reach out in faith and pray that God will reveal himself in a way that leads to belief. Salvation is God's work, not yours.

12:11 Or *had deserted their traditions;* Greek reads *had deserted.*
12:13a Greek *Hosanna,* an exclamation of praise adapted from a Hebrew expression that means "save now."   **12:13b** Ps 118:25-26; Zeph 3:15.   **12:15a** Greek *daughter of Zion.*   **12:15b** Zech 9:9.
12:17 Greek *were testifying.*   **12:19** Greek *the world.*   **12:23** "Son of Man" is a title Jesus used for himself.   **12:34** Greek *from the law.*

[38]This is exactly what Isaiah the prophet had predicted:

"LORD, who has believed our message?
To whom has the LORD revealed his
powerful arm?"*

[39]But the people couldn't believe, for as Isaiah also said,

[40] "The Lord has blinded their eyes
and hardened their hearts—
so that their eyes cannot see,
and their hearts cannot understand,
and they cannot turn to me
and have me heal them."*

[41]Isaiah was referring to Jesus when he said this, because he saw the future and spoke of the Messiah's glory. [42]Many people did believe in him, however, including some of the Jewish leaders. But they wouldn't admit it for fear that the Pharisees would expel them from the synagogue. [43]For they loved human praise more than the praise of God.

[44]Jesus shouted to the crowds, "If you trust me, you are trusting not only me, but also God who sent me. [45]For when you see me, you are seeing the one who sent me. [46]I have come as a light to shine in this dark world, so that all who put their trust in me will no longer remain in the dark. [47]I will not judge those who hear me but don't obey me, for I have come to save the world and not to judge it. [48]But all who reject me and my message will be judged on the day of judgment by the truth I have spoken. [49]I don't speak on my own authority. The Father who sent me has commanded me what to say and how to say it. [50]And I know his commands lead to eternal life; so I say whatever the Father tells me to say."

13 JESUS WASHES HIS DISCIPLES' FEET
Before the Passover celebration, Jesus knew that his hour had come to leave this world and return to his Father. He had loved his disciples during his ministry on earth, and now he loved them to the very end.* [2]It was time for supper, and the devil had already prompted Judas,* son of Simon Iscariot, to betray Jesus. [3]Jesus knew that the Father had given him authority over everything and that he had come from God and would return to God. [4]So he got up from the table, took off his robe, wrapped a towel around his waist, [5]and poured water into a basin. Then he began to wash the disciples' feet, drying them with the towel he had around him.

[6]When Jesus came to Simon Peter, Peter said to him, "Lord, are you going to wash my feet?"

[7]Jesus replied, "You don't understand now what I am doing, but someday you will."

[8]"No," Peter protested, "you will never ever wash my feet!"

Jesus replied, "Unless I wash you, you won't belong to me."

[9]Simon Peter exclaimed, "Then wash my hands and head as well, Lord, not just my feet!"

[10]Jesus replied, "A person who has bathed all over does not need to wash, except for the feet,* to be entirely clean. And you disciples are clean, but not all of you." [11]For Jesus knew who would betray him. That is what he meant when he said, "Not all of you are clean."

[12]After washing their feet, he put on his robe again and sat down and asked, "Do you understand what I was doing? [13]You call me 'Teacher' and 'Lord,' and you are right, because that's what I am. [14]And since I, your Lord and Teacher, have washed your feet, you ought to wash each other's feet. [15]I have given you an example to follow. Do as I have done to you. [16]I tell you the truth, slaves are not greater than their master. Nor is the messenger more important than the one who sends the message. [17]Now that you know these things, God will bless you for doing them.

JESUS PREDICTS HIS BETRAYAL [18]"I am not saying these things to all of you; I know the ones I have chosen. But this fulfills the Scripture that says, 'The one who eats my food has turned against me.'* [19]I tell you this beforehand, so that when it happens you will believe that I AM the Messiah.* [20]I tell you the truth, anyone who welcomes my messenger is welcoming me, and anyone who welcomes me is welcoming the Father who sent me."

[21]Now Jesus was deeply troubled,* and he exclaimed, "I tell you the truth, one of you will betray me!"

[22]The disciples looked at each other, wondering whom he could mean. [23]The disciple Jesus loved was sitting next to Jesus at the table.* [24]Simon Peter motioned to him to ask, "Who's he talking about?" [25]So that disciple leaned over to Jesus and asked, "Lord, who is it?"

[26]Jesus responded, "It is the one to whom I give the bread I dip in the bowl." And when

12:38 Isa 53:1.   12:40 Isa 6:10.   13:1 Or he showed them the full extent of his love.   13:2 Or the devil had already intended for Judas.
13:10 Some manuscripts do not include except for the feet.
13:18 Ps 41:9.   13:19 Or that the 'I AM' has come; or that I am the LORD; Greek reads that I am. See Exod 3:14.   13:21 Greek was troubled in his spirit.   13:23 Greek was reclining on Jesus' bosom. The "disciple Jesus loved" was probably John.

JESUS TOLD HIM, "I AM THE WAY, THE TRUTH, AND THE LIFE.

NO ONE CAN COME TO THE FATHER EXCEPT THROUGH ME." { JOHN 14:6 }

he had dipped it, he gave it to Judas, son of Simon Iscariot. [27]When Judas had eaten the bread, Satan entered into him. Then Jesus told him, "Hurry and do what you're going to do." [28]None of the others at the table knew what Jesus meant. [29]Since Judas was their treasurer, some thought Jesus was telling him to go and pay for the food or to give some money to the poor. [30]So Judas left at once, going out into the night.

JESUS PREDICTS PETER'S DENIAL [31]As soon as Judas left the room, Jesus said, "The time has come for the Son of Man* to enter into his glory, and God will be glorified because of him. [32]And since God receives glory because of the Son,* he will soon give glory to the Son. [33]Dear children, I will be with you only a little longer. And as I told the Jewish leaders, you will search for me, but you can't come where I am going. [34]So now I am giving you a new commandment: Love each other. Just as I have loved you, you should love each other. [35]Your love for one another will prove to the world that you are my disciples."

[36]Simon Peter asked, "Lord, where are you going?"

And Jesus replied, "You can't go with me now, but you will follow me later."

[37]"But why can't I come now, Lord?" he asked. "I'm ready to die for you."

[38]Jesus answered, "Die for me? I tell you the truth, Peter—before the rooster crows tomorrow morning, you will deny three times that you even know me.

14 **JESUS, THE WAY TO THE FATHER** "Don't let your hearts be troubled. Trust in God, and trust also in me. [2]There is more than enough room in my Father's home.* If this were not so, would I have told you that I am going to prepare a place for you?* [3]When

everything is ready, I will come and get you, so that you will always be with me where I am. [4]And you know the way to where I am going."

[5]"No, we don't know, Lord," Thomas said. "We have no idea where you are going, so how can we know the way?"

[6]Jesus told him, "I am the way, the truth, and the life. No one can come to the Father except through me. [7]If you had really known me, you would know who my Father is.* From now on, you do know him and have seen him!"

[8]Philip said, "Lord, show us the Father, and we will be satisfied."

[9]Jesus replied, "Have I been with you all this time, Philip, and yet you still don't know who I am? Anyone who has seen me has seen the Father! So why are you asking me to show him to you? [10]Don't you believe that I am in the Father and the Father is in me? The words I speak are not my own, but my Father who lives in me does his work through me. [11]Just believe that I am in the Father and the Father is in me. Or at least believe because of the work you have seen me do.

[12]"I tell you the truth, anyone who believes in me will do the same works I have done, and even greater works, because I am going to be with the Father. [13]You can ask for anything in my name, and I will do it, so that the Son can bring glory to the Father. [14]Yes, ask me for anything in my name, and I will do it!

JESUS PROMISES THE HOLY SPIRIT [15]"If you love me, obey* my commandments. [16]And I will ask the Father, and he will give you another Advocate,* who will never leave you. [17]He is the Holy Spirit, who leads into all truth. The world cannot receive him, because it isn't looking for him and doesn't recognize him.

13:31 "Son of Man" is a title Jesus used for himself.   13:32 Some manuscripts do not include *And since God receives glory because of the Son.*   14:2a Or *There are many rooms in my Father's house.*   14:2b Or *If this were not so, I would have told you that I am going to prepare a place for you.* Some manuscripts read *If this were not so, I would have told you. I am going to prepare a place for you.*   14:7 Some manuscripts read *If you have really known me, you will know who my Father is.*   14:15 Other manuscripts read *you will obey;* still others read *you should obey.*   14:16 Or *Comforter,* or *Encourager,* or *Counselor.* Greek reads *Paraclete;* also in 14:26.

ACTIVE LOVE
(13:34-35) Jesus told his disciples to love each other. Real love isn't warm fuzzies—it's an attitude that reveals itself in action. How can we love others as Christ loves us? By helping when it's not convenient, by giving when it hurts, by devoting energy to others' welfare rather than our own without complaining or seeking recognition for what we do (see 1 Cor 13). Although showing love isn't always easy, the impact is always noticeable. Is this the kind of love you show?

MY STORY: Zoë

One day I came home from school only to find a note saying that my mother had been rushed to the hospital! I called the hospital and discovered that she had a blood clot in her leg and would have to be hospitalized for a while.

Suddenly, our household was thrown into chaos. Nothing seemed normal without Mom. Plus, I was worried that this could be something serious, or lead to something serious.

Through this time, I read the Bible a lot. I memorized John 14:27: "I am leaving you with a gift—peace of mind and heart. And the peace I give is a gift the world cannot give. So don't be troubled or afraid." These words of Jesus' helped me not to freak out. Instead I gave the situation to God and trusted him to see me through it. Every time I started to worry, I repeated this verse to myself and felt calmer. Jesus understood what I was going through. Not only that, he was in control! The more I concentrated on this, the more peace I felt. It was strange to feel so peaceful even when there was plenty I could worry about. But I just kept reminding myself of this verse. It helped me get through that difficult time.

But you know him, because he lives with you now and later will be in you.* ¹⁸No, I will not abandon you as orphans—I will come to you. ¹⁹Soon the world will no longer see me, but you will see me. Since I live, you also will live. ²⁰When I am raised to life again, you will know that I am in my Father, and you are in me, and I am in you. ²¹Those who accept my commandments and obey them are the ones who love me. And because they love me, my Father will love them. And I will love them and reveal myself to each of them."

²²Judas (not Judas Iscariot, but the other disciple with that name) said to him, "Lord, why are you going to reveal yourself only to us and not to the world at large?"

²³Jesus replied, "All who love me will do what I say. My Father will love them, and we will come and make our home with each of them. ²⁴Anyone who doesn't love me will not obey me. And remember, my words are not my own. What I am telling you is from the Father who sent me. ²⁵I am telling you these things now while I am still with you. ²⁶But when the Father sends the Advocate as my representative—that is, the Holy Spirit—he will teach you everything and will remind you of everything I have told you.

²⁷"I am leaving you with a gift—peace of mind and heart. And the peace I give is a gift the world cannot give. So don't be troubled or afraid. ²⁸Remember what I told you: I am going away, but I will come back to you again. If you really loved me, you would be happy that I am going to the Father, who is greater than I am. ²⁹I have told you these things before they happen so that when they do happen, you will believe.

³⁰"I don't have much more time to talk to you, because the ruler of this world approaches. He has no power over me, ³¹but I will do what the Father requires of me, so that the world will know that I love the Father. Come, let's be going.

15 **JESUS, THE TRUE VINE** "I am the true grapevine, and my Father is the gardener. ²He cuts off every branch of mine that doesn't produce fruit, and he prunes the branches that do bear fruit so they will produce even more. ³You have already been pruned and purified by the message I have given you. ⁴Remain in me, and I will remain in you. For a branch cannot produce fruit if it is severed from the vine, and you cannot be fruitful unless you remain in me.

⁵"Yes, I am the vine; you are the branches. Those who remain in me, and I in them, will produce much fruit. For apart from me you can do nothing. ⁶Anyone who does not remain in me is thrown away like a useless branch and withers. Such branches are gathered into a pile to be burned. ⁷But if you remain in me and my words remain in you, you may ask for anything you want, and it will be granted! ⁸When you produce much fruit, you are my true disciples. This brings great glory to my Father.

⁹"I have loved you even as the Father has loved me. Remain in my love. ¹⁰When you obey my commandments, you remain in my love, just as I obey my Father's commandments and remain in his love. ¹¹I have told you these things so that you will be filled with my joy. Yes, your joy will overflow! ¹²This is my commandment: Love each other in the same way

14:17 Some manuscripts read *and is in you.*

I have loved you. ¹³There is no greater love than to lay down one's life for one's friends. ¹⁴You are my friends if you do what I command. ¹⁵I no longer call you slaves, because a master doesn't confide in his slaves. Now you are my friends, since I have told you everything the Father told me. ¹⁶You didn't choose me. I chose you. I appointed you to go and produce lasting fruit, so that the Father will give you whatever you ask for, using my name. ¹⁷This is my command: Love each other.

THE WORLD'S HATRED

¹⁸"If the world hates you, remember that it hated me first. ¹⁹The world would love you as one of its own if you belonged to it, but you are no longer part of the world. I chose you to come out of the world, so it hates you. ²⁰Do you remember what I told you? 'A slave is not greater than the master.' Since they persecuted me, naturally they will persecute you. And if they had listened to me, they would listen to you. ²¹They will do all this to you because of me, for they have rejected the one who sent me. ²²They would not be guilty if I had not come and spoken to them. But now they have no excuse for their sin. ²³Anyone who hates me also hates my Father. ²⁴If I hadn't done such miraculous signs among them that no one else could do, they would not be guilty. But as it is, they have seen everything I did, yet they still hate me and my Father. ²⁵This fulfills what is written in their Scriptures*: 'They hated me without cause.'

²⁶"But I will send you the Advocate*—the Spirit of truth. He will come to you from the Father and will testify all about me. ²⁷And you must also testify about me because you have been with me from the beginning of my ministry.

16

"I have told you these things so that you won't abandon your faith. ²For you will be expelled from the synagogues, and the time is coming when those who kill you will think they are doing a holy service for God. ³This is because they have never known the Father or me. ⁴Yes, I'm telling you these things now, so that when they happen, you will remember my warning. I didn't tell you earlier because I was going to be with you for a while longer.

THE WORK OF THE HOLY SPIRIT

⁵"But now I am going away to the one who sent me, and not one of you is asking where I am going. ⁶Instead, you grieve because of what I've told you. ⁷But in fact, it is best for you that I go away, because if I don't, the Advocate* won't come. If I do go away, then I will send him to you. ⁸And when he comes, he will convict the world of its sin, and of God's righteousness, and of the coming judgment. ⁹The world's sin is that it refuses to believe in me. ¹⁰Righteousness is available because I go to the Father, and you will see me no more. ¹¹Judgment will come because the ruler of this world has already been judged.

¹²"There is so much more I want to tell you, but you can't bear it now. ¹³When the Spirit of truth comes, he will guide you into all truth. He will not speak on his own but will tell you what he has heard. He will tell you about the future. ¹⁴He will bring me glory by telling you whatever he receives from me. ¹⁵All that belongs to the Father is mine; this is why I said, 'The Spirit will tell you whatever he receives from me.'

SADNESS WILL BE TURNED TO JOY

¹⁶"In a little while you won't see me anymore. But a little while after that, you will see me again."

¹⁷Some of the disciples asked each other, "What does he mean when he says, 'In a little while you won't see me, but then you will see me,' and 'I am going to the Father'? ¹⁸And what does he mean by 'a little while'? We don't understand."

¹⁹Jesus realized they wanted to ask him about it, so he said, "Are you asking yourselves what I meant? I said in a little while you won't see me, but a little while after that you will see me again. ²⁰I tell you the truth, you will weep

....

ACCURATE ACCOUNTS
(14:26) Jesus promised the disciples that the Holy Spirit would help them remember what they had learned from Jesus. This promise underscores the validity of the Gospels, as well as the rest of the New Testament. The disciples were eyewitnesses of Jesus' life and teachings. The Holy Spirit helped them remember Jesus' words without taking away their individual perspectives. We can be confident that the Gospels are accurate records of what Jesus taught and did (see also 1 Cor 2:10-16). How thoroughly have you investigated these records?

LAST-MINUTE WARNINGS
(16:1-16) In his last moments with his disciples, Jesus (1) warned them about further persecution, (2) told them where he was going, when he was leaving, and why, and (3) assured them they wouldn't be left alone—the Holy Spirit would come to stay with them. Although Jesus knew what lay ahead, he didn't want their faith shaken or destroyed. Likewise, God wants you to know that you aren't alone in the world. You have the Holy Spirit to comfort you, teach you truth, and help you.

15:25 Greek in their law. Pss 35:19; 69:4.   **15:26** Or Comforter, or Encourager, or Counselor. Greek reads Paraclete.   **16:7** Or Comforter, or Encourager, or Counselor. Greek reads Paraclete.

and mourn over what is going to happen to me, but the world will rejoice. You will grieve, but your grief will suddenly turn to wonderful joy. [21]It will be like a woman suffering the pains of labor. When her child is born, her anguish gives way to joy because she has brought a new baby into the world. [22]So you have sorrow now, but I will see you again; then you will rejoice, and no one can rob you of that joy. [23]At that time you won't need to ask me for anything. I tell you the truth, you will ask the Father directly, and he will grant your request because you use my name. [24]You haven't done this before. Ask, using my name, and you will receive, and you will have abundant joy.

[25]"I have spoken of these matters in figures of speech, but soon I will stop speaking figuratively and will tell you plainly all about the Father. [26]Then you will ask in my name. I'm not saying I will ask the Father on your behalf, [27]for the Father himself loves you dearly because you love me and believe that I came from God.* [28]Yes, I came from the Father into the world, and now I will leave the world and return to the Father."

[29]Then his disciples said, "At last you are speaking plainly and not figuratively. [30]Now we understand that you know everything, and there's no need to question you. From this we believe that you came from God."

[31]Jesus asked, "Do you finally believe? [32]But the time is coming—indeed it's here now—when you will be scattered, each one going his own way, leaving me alone. Yet I am not alone because the Father is with me. [33]I have told you all this so that you may have peace in me. Here on earth you will have many trials and sorrows. But take heart, because I have overcome the world."

17 THE PRAYER OF JESUS After saying all these things, Jesus looked up to heaven and said, "Father, the hour has come. Glorify your Son so he can give glory back to you. [2]For you have given him authority over everyone. He gives eternal life to each one you

have given him. [3]And this is the way to have eternal life—to know you, the only true God, and Jesus Christ, the one you sent to earth. [4]I brought glory to you here on earth by completing the work you gave me to do. [5]Now, Father, bring me into the glory we shared before the world began.

[6]"I have revealed you* to the ones you gave me from this world. They were always yours. You gave them to me, and they have kept your word. [7]Now they know that everything I have is a gift from you, [8]for I have passed on to them the message you gave me. They accepted it and know that I came from you, and they believe you sent me.

[9]"My prayer is not for the world, but for those you have given me, because they belong to you. [10]All who are mine belong to you, and you have given them to me, so they bring me glory. [11]Now I am departing from the world; they are staying in this world, but I am coming to you. Holy Father, you have given me your name;* now protect them by the power of your name so that they will be united just as we are. [12]During my time here, I protected them by the power of the name you gave me.* I guarded them so that not one was lost, except the one headed for destruction, as the Scriptures foretold.

[13]"Now I am coming to you. I told them many things while I was with them in this world so they would be filled with my joy. [14]I have given them your word. And the world hates them because they do not belong to the world, just as I do not belong to the world. [15]I'm not asking you to take them out of the world, but to keep them safe from the evil one. [16]They do not belong to this world any more than I do. [17]Make them holy by your truth; teach them your word, which is truth. [18]Just as you sent me into the world, I am sending them into the world. [19]And I give myself as a holy sacrifice for them so they can be made holy by your truth.

[20]"I am praying not only for these disciples but also for all who will ever believe in me through their message. [21]I pray that they will all be one, just as you and I are one—as you are in me, Father, and I am in you. And may they be in us so that the world will believe you sent me.

[22]"I have given them the glory you gave me, so they may be one as we are one. [23]I am in them and you are in me. May they experience such perfect unity that the world will know that

---

THE WORLD: IN IT BUT NOT OF IT
(17:15-18) Jesus didn't ask God to take believers out of the world but instead to use them in the world. In the same way, we're called to be salt and light (Matt 5:13-16)—to make a difference for Christ in the world. Some, however, would have to admit that we have no trouble blending into the world. In fact, we blend in so well that no one could distinguish our actions from those of non-Christians! If so, perhaps we could make Jesus' prayer ours: "Make [us] holy by your truth; teach [us] your word, which is truth."

16:27 Some manuscripts read *from the Father.*   **17:6** Greek *have revealed your name;* also in 17:26.   **17:11** Some manuscripts read *you have given me these [disciples].*   **17:12** Some manuscripts read *I protected those you gave me, by the power of your name.*

you sent me and that you love them as much as you love me. ²⁴Father, I want these whom you have given me to be with me where I am. Then they can see all the glory you gave me because you loved me even before the world began!

²⁵"O righteous Father, the world doesn't know you, but I do; and these disciples know you sent me. ²⁶I have revealed you to them, and I will continue to do so. Then your love for me will be in them, and I will be in them."

18 JESUS IS BETRAYED AND ARRESTED
After saying these things, Jesus crossed the Kidron Valley with his disciples and entered a grove of olive trees. ²Judas, the betrayer, knew this place, because Jesus had often gone there with his disciples. ³The leading priests and Pharisees had given Judas a contingent of Roman soldiers and Temple guards to accompany him. Now with blazing torches, lanterns, and weapons, they arrived at the olive grove.

⁴Jesus fully realized all that was going to happen to him, so he stepped forward to meet them. "Who are you looking for?" he asked.

⁵"Jesus the Nazarene,"* they replied.

"I Am he,"* Jesus said. (Judas, who betrayed him, was standing with them.) ⁶As Jesus said "I Am he," they all drew back and fell to the ground! ⁷Once more he asked them, "Who are you looking for?"

And again they replied, "Jesus the Nazarene."

⁸"I told you that I Am he," Jesus said. "And since I am the one you want, let these others go." ⁹He did this to fulfill his own statement: "I did not lose a single one of those you have given me."*

¹⁰Then Simon Peter drew a sword and slashed off the right ear of Malchus, the high priest's slave. ¹¹But Jesus said to Peter, "Put your sword back into its sheath. Shall I not drink from the cup of suffering the Father has given me?"

JESUS AT THE HIGH PRIEST'S HOUSE
¹²So the soldiers, their commanding officer, and the Temple guards arrested Jesus and tied him up. ¹³First they took him to Annas, the father-in-law of Caiaphas, the high priest at that time.* ¹⁴Caiaphas was the one who had told the other Jewish leaders, "It's better that one man should die for the people."

PETER'S FIRST DENIAL
¹⁵Simon Peter followed Jesus, as did another of the disciples. That other disciple was acquainted with the high priest, so he was allowed to enter the high priest's courtyard with Jesus. ¹⁶Peter had to stay outside the gate. Then the disciple who knew the high priest spoke to the woman watching at the gate, and she let Peter in. ¹⁷The woman asked Peter, "You're not one of that man's disciples, are you?"

"No," he said, "I am not."

¹⁸Because it was cold, the household servants and the guards had made a charcoal fire. They stood around it, warming themselves, and Peter stood with them, warming himself.

THE HIGH PRIEST QUESTIONS JESUS
¹⁹Inside, the high priest began asking Jesus about his followers and what he had been teaching them. ²⁰Jesus replied, "Everyone knows what I teach. I have preached regularly in the synagogues and the Temple, where the people* gather. I have not spoken in secret. ²¹Why are you asking me this question? Ask those who heard me. They know what I said."

²²Then one of the Temple guards standing nearby slapped Jesus across the face. "Is that the way to answer the high priest?" he demanded.

²³Jesus replied, "If I said anything wrong, you must prove it. But if I'm speaking the truth, why are you beating me?"

²⁴Then Annas bound Jesus and sent him to Caiaphas, the high priest.

PETER'S SECOND AND THIRD DENIALS
²⁵Meanwhile, as Simon Peter was standing by the fire warming himself, they asked him again, "You're not one of his disciples, are you?"

He denied it, saying, "No, I am not."

²⁶But one of the household slaves of the high priest, a relative of the man whose ear Peter had cut off, asked, "Didn't I see you out there in the olive grove with Jesus?" ²⁷Again Peter denied it. And immediately a rooster crowed.

....

GUILTY TOO
(18:22-27) *We can easily get angry at the members of the Jewish council for their injustice in condemning Jesus, but Peter and the rest of the disciples also contributed to Jesus' pain by deserting and denying him (see Matt 26:56). While most of us are not like the religious leaders, we all are like the disciples, for all of us have been guilty of denying Christ as Lord in vital areas of our lives. Don't excuse yourself by pointing at others whose sins seem worse than yours. Instead, come to Jesus for forgiveness and healing.*

18:5a Or *Jesus of Nazareth*; also in 18:7.   **18:5b** Or *"The 'I Am' is here"*; or *"I am the LORD"*; Greek reads *I am*; also in 18:6, 8. See Exod 3:14.   **18:9** See John 6:39 and 17:12.   **18:13** Greek *that year.*   **18:20** Greek *Jewish people*; also in 18:38.

JESUS' TRIAL BEFORE PILATE ²⁸Jesus' trial before Caiaphas ended in the early hours of the morning. Then he was taken to the headquarters of the Roman governor.* His accusers didn't go inside because it would defile them, and they wouldn't be allowed to celebrate the Passover. ²⁹So Pilate, the governor, went out to them and asked, "What is your charge against this man?"

³⁰"We wouldn't have handed him over to you if he weren't a criminal!" they retorted.

³¹"Then take him away and judge him by your own law," Pilate told them.

"Only the Romans are permitted to execute someone," the Jewish leaders replied. ³²(This fulfilled Jesus' prediction about the way he would die.*)

³³Then Pilate went back into his headquarters and called for Jesus to be brought to him. "Are you the king of the Jews?" he asked him.

³⁴Jesus replied, "Is this your own question, or did others tell you about me?"

³⁵"Am I a Jew?" Pilate retorted. "Your own people and their leading priests brought you to me for trial. Why? What have you done?"

³⁶Jesus answered, "My Kingdom is not an earthly kingdom. If it were, my followers would fight to keep me from being handed over to the Jewish leaders. But my Kingdom is not of this world."

³⁷Pilate said, "So you are a king?"

Jesus responded, "You say I am a king. Actually, I was born and came into the world to testify to the truth. All who love the truth recognize that what I say is true."

³⁸"What is truth?" Pilate asked. Then he went out again to the people and told them, "He is not guilty of any crime. ³⁹But you have a custom of asking me to release one prisoner each year at Passover. Would you like me to release this 'King of the Jews'?"

⁴⁰But they shouted back, "No! Not this man. We want Barabbas!" (Barabbas was a revolutionary.)

19 **JESUS SENTENCED TO DEATH** Then Pilate had Jesus flogged with a lead-tipped whip. ²The soldiers wove a crown of thorns and put it on his head, and they put a purple robe on him. ³"Hail! King of the Jews!" they mocked, as they slapped him across the face.

⁴Pilate went outside again and said to the people, "I am going to bring him out to you now, but understand clearly that I find him not guilty." ⁵Then Jesus came out wearing the crown of thorns and the purple robe. And Pilate said, "Look, here is the man!"

⁶When they saw him, the leading priests and Temple guards began shouting, "Crucify him! Crucify him!"

"Take him yourselves and crucify him," Pilate said. "I find him not guilty."

⁷The Jewish leaders replied, "By our law he ought to die because he called himself the Son of God."

⁸When Pilate heard this, he was more frightened than ever. ⁹He took Jesus back into the headquarters* again and asked him, "Where are you from?" But Jesus gave no answer. ¹⁰"Why don't you talk to me?" Pilate demanded. "Don't you realize that I have the power to release you or crucify you?"

¹¹Then Jesus said, "You would have no power over me at all unless it were given to you from above. So the one who handed me over to you has the greater sin."

¹²Then Pilate tried to release him, but the Jewish leaders shouted, "If you release this man, you are no 'friend of Caesar.'* Anyone who declares himself a king is a rebel against Caesar."

¹³When they said this, Pilate brought Jesus out to them again. Then Pilate sat down on the judgment seat on the platform that is called the Stone Pavement (in Hebrew, *Gabbatha*). ¹⁴It was now about noon on the day of preparation for the Passover. And Pilate said to the people,* "Look, here is your king!"

¹⁵"Away with him," they yelled. "Away with him! Crucify him!"

"What? Crucify your king?" Pilate asked.

"We have no king but Caesar," the leading priests shouted back.

¹⁶Then Pilate turned Jesus over to them to be crucified.

THE CRUCIFIXION So they took Jesus away. ¹⁷Carrying the cross by himself, he went to the place called Place of the Skull (in Hebrew, *Golgotha*). ¹⁸There they nailed him to the cross. Two others were crucified with him, one on either side, with Jesus between them. ¹⁹And Pilate posted a sign on the cross that read, "Jesus of Nazareth,* the King of the Jews." ²⁰The place where Jesus was crucified was near the city, and the sign was written in Hebrew, Latin, and Greek, so that many people could read it.

²¹Then the leading priests objected and said

18:28 Greek *to the Praetorium;* also in 18:33.   **18:32** See John 12:32-33.   **19:9** Greek *the Praetorium.*   **19:12** "Friend of Caesar" is a technical term that refers to an ally of the emperor.   **19:14** Greek *Jewish people;* also in 19:20.   **19:19** Or *Jesus the Nazarene.*

to Pilate, "Change it from 'The King of the Jews' to 'He said, I am King of the Jews.'"

²²Pilate replied, "No, what I have written, I have written."

²³When the soldiers had crucified Jesus, they divided his clothes among the four of them. They also took his robe, but it was seamless, woven in one piece from top to bottom. ²⁴So they said, "Rather than tearing it apart, let's throw dice* for it." This fulfilled the Scripture that says, "They divided my garments among themselves and threw dice for my clothing."* So that is what they did.

²⁵Standing near the cross were Jesus' mother, and his mother's sister, Mary (the wife of Clopas), and Mary Magdalene. ²⁶When Jesus saw his mother standing there beside the disciple he loved, he said to her, "Dear woman, here is your son." ²⁷And he said to this disciple, "Here is your mother." And from then on this disciple took her into his home.

THE DEATH OF JESUS ²⁸Jesus knew that his mission was now finished, and to fulfill Scripture he said, "I am thirsty."* ²⁹A jar of sour wine was sitting there, so they soaked a sponge in it, put it on a hyssop branch, and held it up to his lips. ³⁰When Jesus had tasted it, he said, "It is finished!" Then he bowed his head and released his spirit.

³¹It was the day of preparation, and the Jewish leaders didn't want the bodies hanging there the next day, which was the Sabbath (and a very special Sabbath, because it was the Passover). So they asked Pilate to hasten their deaths by ordering that their legs be broken. Then their bodies could be taken down. ³²So the soldiers came and broke the legs of the two men crucified with Jesus. ³³But when they came to Jesus, they saw that he was already dead, so they didn't break his legs. ³⁴One of the soldiers, however, pierced his side with a spear, and immediately blood and water flowed out. ³⁵(This report is from an eyewitness giving an accurate account. He speaks the truth so that you also can believe.*) ³⁶These things happened in fulfillment of the Scriptures that say, "Not one of his bones will be broken,"* ³⁷and "They will look on the one they pierced."*

THE BURIAL OF JESUS ³⁸Afterward Joseph of Arimathea, who had been a secret disciple of Jesus (because he feared the Jewish leaders), asked Pilate for permission to take down Jesus' body. When Pilate gave permission, Joseph came and took the body away. ³⁹With him came Nicodemus, the man who had come to Jesus at night. He brought about seventy-five pounds* of perfumed ointment made from myrrh and aloes. ⁴⁰Following Jewish burial custom, they wrapped Jesus' body with the spices in long sheets of linen cloth. ⁴¹The place of crucifixion was near a garden, where there was a new tomb, never used before. ⁴²And so, because it was the day of preparation for the Jewish Passover* and since the tomb was close at hand, they laid Jesus there.

20 **THE RESURRECTION** Early on Sunday morning,* while it was still dark, Mary Magdalene came to the tomb and found that the stone had been rolled away from the entrance. ²She ran and found Simon Peter and the other disciple, the one whom Jesus loved. She said, "They have taken the Lord's body out of the tomb, and we don't know where they have put him!"

³Peter and the other disciple started out for the tomb. ⁴They were both running, but the other disciple outran Peter and reached the tomb first. ⁵He stooped and looked in and saw the linen wrappings lying there, but he didn't go in. ⁶Then Simon Peter arrived and went inside. He also noticed the linen wrappings lying there, ⁷while the cloth that had covered Jesus' head was folded up and lying apart from the other wrappings. ⁸Then the disciple who had reached the tomb first also went in, and he saw and believed—⁹for until then they still hadn't understood the Scriptures that said Jesus must rise from the dead. ¹⁰Then they went home.

JESUS APPEARS TO MARY MAGDALENE ¹¹Mary was standing outside the tomb crying, and as she wept, she stooped and looked in. ¹²She saw two white-robed angels, one sitting at the head and the other at the foot of the place where the body of Jesus had been lying. ¹³"Dear woman, why are you crying?" the angels asked her.

"Because they have taken away my Lord,"

19:24a Greek *cast lots.*   **19:24b** Ps 22:18.   **19:28** See Pss 22:15; 69:21.   **19:35** Some manuscripts read *can continue to believe.*
19:36 Exod 12:46; Num 9:12; Ps 34:20.   **19:37** Zech 12:10.
19:39 Greek *100 litras* [32.7 kilograms].   **19:42** Greek *because of the Jewish day of preparation.*   **20:1** Greek *On the first day of the week.*

FAMILY
(19:25-27) Even while dying on the cross, Jesus was concerned about his mother. He instructed John to take care of Mary. What do you do to show your love for your family?

she replied, "and I don't know where they have put him."

¹⁴She turned to leave and saw someone standing there. It was Jesus, but she didn't recognize him. ¹⁵"Dear woman, why are you crying?" Jesus asked her. "Who are you looking for?"

She thought he was the gardener. "Sir," she said, "if you have taken him away, tell me where you have put him, and I will go and get him."

¹⁶"Mary!" Jesus said.

She turned to him and cried out, "Rabboni!" (which is Hebrew for "Teacher").

¹⁷"Don't cling to me," Jesus said, "for I haven't yet ascended to the Father. But go find my brothers and tell them, 'I am ascending to my Father and your Father, to my God and your God.'"

¹⁸Mary Magdalene found the disciples and told them, "I have seen the Lord!" Then she gave them his message.

JESUS APPEARS TO HIS DISCIPLES ¹⁹That Sunday evening* the disciples were meeting behind locked doors because they were afraid of the Jewish leaders. Suddenly, Jesus was standing there among them! "Peace be with you," he said. ²⁰As he spoke, he showed them the wounds in his hands and his side. They were filled with joy when they saw the Lord! ²¹Again he said, "Peace be with you. As the Father has sent me, so I am sending you." ²²Then he breathed on them and said, "Receive the Holy Spirit. ²³If you forgive anyone's sins, they are forgiven. If you do not forgive them, they are not forgiven."

JESUS APPEARS TO THOMAS ²⁴One of the twelve disciples, Thomas (nicknamed the Twin),* was not with the others when Jesus came. ²⁵They told him, "We have seen the Lord!"

But he replied, "I won't believe it unless I see the nail wounds in his hands, put my fingers into them, and place my hand into the wound in his side."

²⁶Eight days later the disciples were together again, and this time Thomas was with them. The doors were locked; but suddenly, as before, Jesus was standing among them. "Peace be with you," he said. ²⁷Then he said

20:19 Greek *In the evening of that day, the first day of the week.*
20:24 Greek *Thomas, who was called Didymus.*

I WONDER...

After I became a Christian, I was told to start reading the Bible, but it's bigger than any book I ever even attempted to read. Where do I start?

Unfortunately, at no place in the Bible does it say, "Start here," and then, "Read this next." Consequently, we need help.

When two people in love have to be separated for a while, they usually send streams of letters to each other. Intertwined with the boring facts about daily life is a story of love and devotion to the other person.

To find the "good stuff," you would have to wade through the details. If you wanted to find out how the relationship developed, you would need to go through those details.

Sometimes that's how it is with the Bible. The events that occurred so long ago don't seem to have any relevance to us today. But if your goal is to understand the relationship between God and his people, from Adam to Jesus, those details become essential information.

New Christians usually want the "good stuff." Later, as they grow in their faith, they will be more interested in the details that will help them put God's whole plan together.

So for now, consider these suggestions:

- Check out the Gospels to get to know Jesus. Listen to his words. Try to understand what each story is saying and watch how Jesus treats others. John tells us that he wrote his book "so that you may continue to believe that Jesus is the Messiah, the Son of God, and that by believing in him you will have life by the power of his name" (John 20:31). The first four books of the New Testament give four different perspectives on Jesus' life. Getting to know him should be your first priority.
- Next, read through some of the letters that Paul, Peter, and John wrote to the early churches. Most of the New Testament letters were written by Paul to guide those first believers.
- Try Proverbs next. You can read one chapter a day and finish the book in a month.
- After this, read books like Genesis, Exodus, Daniel, and Jonah. They offer stories of real people whose problems were not all that different from yours.

The Christian life has no shortcuts. We must be disciplined enough to dig into the Bible to find all the buried treasure that God wants to give those who will dig deep enough. Many people read through the Bible in a year. By reading the whole Bible, you can see how God's plan came about over the centuries.

JESUS' APPEARANCES AFTER HIS RESURRECTION

The truth of Christianity rests heavily on the Resurrection. If Jesus rose from the grave, who saw him? How trustworthy were the witnesses? Those who claimed to have seen the risen Jesus went on to turn the world upside down. Most of them also died for being followers of Christ. People rarely die for halfhearted beliefs. These are the people who saw Jesus risen from the grave:

Mary Magdalene	Mark 16:9-11; John 20:11-18
Other women at the tomb	Matthew 28:8-10
Peter in Jerusalem	Luke 24:34; 1 Corinthians 15:5
Two travelers on the road to Emmaus	Mark 16:12-13; Luke 24:13-35
Ten disciples behind closed doors	Luke 24:36-43; John 20:19-25
All the disciples, including Thomas (except Judas Iscariot)	Mark 16:14; John 20:26-31; 1 Corinthians 15:5
Seven disciples while fishing	John 21:1-14
Eleven disciples on the mountain	Matthew 28:16-20
A crowd of more than 500	1 Corinthians 15:6
Jesus' brother James	1 Corinthians 15:7
Those who watched Jesus ascend into heaven	Luke 24:33, 50-51; Acts 1:3-14

to Thomas, "Put your finger here, and look at my hands. Put your hand into the wound in my side. Don't be faithless any longer. Believe!"

[28]"My Lord and my God!" Thomas exclaimed.

[29]Then Jesus told him, "You believe because you have seen me. Blessed are those who believe without seeing me."

PURPOSE OF THE BOOK [30]The disciples saw Jesus do many other miraculous signs in addition to the ones recorded in this book. [31]But these are written so that you may continue to believe* that Jesus is the Messiah, the Son of God, and that by believing in him you will have life by the power of his name.

21 **EPILOGUE: JESUS APPEARS TO SEVEN DISCIPLES** Later, Jesus appeared again to the disciples beside the Sea of Galilee.* This is how it happened. [2]Several of the disciples were there—Simon Peter, Thomas (nicknamed the Twin),* Nathanael from Cana in Galilee, the sons of Zebedee, and two other disciples.

[3]Simon Peter said, "I'm going fishing."

"We'll come, too," they all said. So they went out in the boat, but they caught nothing all night.

[4]At dawn Jesus was standing on the beach, but the disciples couldn't see who he was. [5]He called out, "Fellows,* have you caught any fish?"

"No," they replied.

[6]Then he said, "Throw out your net on the right-hand side of the boat, and you'll get some!" So they did, and they couldn't haul in the net because there were so many fish in it.

[7]Then the disciple Jesus loved said to Peter, "It's the Lord!" When Simon Peter heard that it was the Lord, he put on his tunic (for he had stripped for work), jumped into the water, and headed to shore. [8]The others stayed with the boat and pulled the loaded net to the shore, for they were only about a hundred yards* from shore. [9]When they got there, they found breakfast waiting for them—fish cooking over a charcoal fire, and some bread.

[10]"Bring some of the fish you've just caught," Jesus said. [11]So Simon Peter went aboard and dragged the net to the shore. There were 153 large fish, and yet the net hadn't torn.

20:31 Some manuscripts read *that you may believe.*   **21:1** Greek *Sea of Tiberias,* another name for the Sea of Galilee.   **21:2** Greek *Thomas, who was called Didymus.*   **21:5** Greek *Children.*   **21:8** Greek *200 cubits* [90 meters].

PROOF
(20:29-31) Some people think they would believe in Jesus if they could see something miraculous. But Jesus says we're blessed if we believe without seeing. We have all the proof we need in the words of the Bible and the testimony of believers. How has this proof influenced your faith?

¹²"Now come and have some breakfast!" Jesus said. None of the disciples dared to ask him, "Who are you?" They knew it was the Lord. ¹³Then Jesus served them the bread and the fish. ¹⁴This was the third time Jesus had appeared to his disciples since he had been raised from the dead.

¹⁵After breakfast Jesus asked Simon Peter, "Simon son of John, do you love me more than these?*"

"Yes, Lord," Peter replied, "you know I love you."

"Then feed my lambs," Jesus told him.

¹⁶Jesus repeated the question: "Simon son of John, do you love me?"

"Yes, Lord," Peter said, "you know I love you."

"Then take care of my sheep," Jesus said.

¹⁷A third time he asked him, "Simon son of John, do you love me?"

Peter was hurt that Jesus asked the question a third time. He said, "Lord, you know everything. You know that I love you."

Jesus said, "Then feed my sheep.

¹⁸"I tell you the truth, when you were young, you were able to do as you liked; you dressed yourself and went wherever you wanted to go. But when you are old, you will stretch out your hands, and others* will dress you and take you where you don't want to go." ¹⁹Jesus said this to let him know by what kind of death he would glorify God. Then Jesus told him, "Follow me."

²⁰Peter turned around and saw behind them the disciple Jesus loved—the one who had leaned over to Jesus during supper and asked, "Lord, who will betray you?" ²¹Peter asked Jesus, "What about him, Lord?"

²²Jesus replied, "If I want him to remain alive until I return, what is that to you? As for

21:15 Or *more than these others do?* **21:18** Some manuscripts read *and another one.*

THOMAS
PERSONALITY PROFILE

WHAT ARE YOU KNOWN FOR? Being cool? Being a troublemaker? Inspiring others? Throughout the ages, Thomas mainly has been known for doubting the resurrection of Jesus. Yet Thomas expressed doubt because he really wanted to know the truth. He didn't hang on to his doubts but humbly believed when they were answered. Expressing doubts is a good way to clarify the truth.

Although the Bible doesn't tell us much about Thomas, the brief glimpses of his life are consistent. He tried hard to be faithful to what he knew, even though faithfulness seemed costly. For example, when it was clear to everyone that Jesus' life would be in danger if he went to Jerusalem, only Thomas put into words what the other disciples probably felt: "Let's go, too—and die with Jesus" (John 11:16). But even though he expressed this fear, he didn't hesitate to follow Jesus.

We don't know why Thomas was missing the first time Jesus appeared to the disciples after the Resurrection (see John 20:19-24). Whatever the reason, Thomas was reluctant to believe that Jesus was alive (20:25). Even 10 friends couldn't change his mind! But Jesus' appearance soon changed his doubts to belief (20:28-29).

We can doubt without living a doubting way of life. Doubts help us clarify what we believe. They also encourage us to ask good questions, seek answers, and push for decisions. But doubt was never meant to be a permanent condition. Doubt is one foot lifted, poised to step forward or back. There is no motion until the foot comes down.

When you experience doubt, take encouragement from Thomas. He didn't remain doubtful. Instead, he allowed Jesus to help him toward belief. Take encouragement also from the fact that countless other followers of Christ have struggled with doubts. The answers God gave them may be of great help. Don't settle into doubt—move beyond it to decision and belief.

BOTTOM LINE: Jesus doesn't condemn doubts that are honest and directed toward belief.

Doubting out loud is better than disbelieving in silence.

Thomas's story is told in the Gospels. He also is mentioned in Acts 1:13.

UPS:
- *One of Jesus' 12 disciples*
- *Intense, both in doubt and belief*
- *Was a loyal and honest man*

DOWNS:
- *Along with the others, abandoned Jesus after his arrest*
- *Refused to believe the others' claims to have seen the risen Jesus*
- *Struggled with a pessimistic outlook*

STATS:
- *Where: Galilee, Judea, Samaria*
- *Occupation: Disciple of Jesus*
- *Contemporaries: Jesus, other disciples, Herod, Pilate*

KEY VERSES: *John 20:27-28*

you, follow me." ²³So the rumor spread among the community of believers* that this disciple wouldn't die. But that isn't what Jesus said at all. He only said, "If I want him to remain alive until I return, what is that to you?"

²⁴This disciple is the one who testifies to

21:23 Greek *the brothers.*

these events and has recorded them here. And we know that his account of these things is accurate.

²⁵Jesus also did many other things. If they were all written down, I suppose the whole world could not contain the books that would be written.

ACTS

Assemble nine very different people:

- *The class clown who makes everything funny*
- *The heir with the expensive cell phone permanently glued to his ear and a car that costs more than the principal makes in a year*
- *The hipster wannabes who look with contempt on anyone who's not down with their music*
- *The brainiac who just built her own computer*
- *The mammoth football player who loves to bash things—especially quarterbacks*
- *The student whose recent "achievements" read like a sleazy novel*
- *The school druggie who's not exactly headed for a career in molecular biology*
- *The campus philosopher/political activist who loves to argue and hates shallow people*
- *The quiet classmate who, for whatever reasons, never fits in*

Now, give this diverse crowd a simple task to do . . . together. What do you think would happen?

Even if you could get them all in the same room, they'd never complete the assignment. What they'd most likely produce is nonstop arguing, bickering, and chaos! If they functioned as a team at all, it would be bumpy and very brief.

So, how do we explain the first-century church? How did several hundred radically different people accomplish the complicated and time-consuming project of taking Jesus' story all over the world? How did they handle conflicts? What kept them going when hard times hit? What is it that those first Christians had that is lacking among believers today?

If you'd like the answers to those questions (and you'd like to see how you can help improve your own church), dive into the book of Acts.

KEY POINTS

CHURCH BEGINNINGS The community of believers was unified by faith in the risen Christ. Through faith in Jesus and in the power of the Holy Spirit, the church can be a vibrant agent for change in the world.

HOLY SPIRIT The disciples were empowered by the Holy Spirit, the Counselor sent by Jesus. By faith, any believer can experience the Holy Spirit's power to serve God.

WITNESSING Peter, John, Philip, Paul, Barnabas, and thousands more boldly told others about their faith in Christ. Their lives encourage us to pass on the truth of Christ to the world.

OPPOSITION Although the first-century Christians experienced persecution, this opposition was a catalyst for the spread of Christianity. God can work through any obstacle to accomplish his purposes.

Modern names and boundaries are shown in gray.

KEY PLACES
The apostle Paul traveled tremendous distances as he tirelessly spread the gospel across much of the Roman Empire. His combined trips, by land and ship, total more than 13,000 miles, probably more, given the circuitous land routes he walked.

❶ JUDEA
Jesus ascended to heaven from the Mount of Olives outside Jerusalem, and his followers returned to the city to await the coming of the Holy Spirit, which occurred at Pentecost. Peter gave a powerful sermon that was heard by Jews from across the empire. The Jerusalem church grew, but Stephen was martyred for his faith by Jewish leaders who did not believe in Jesus (1:1–7:59).

❷ SAMARIA
After Stephen's death, persecution of Christians intensified, but it caused the believers to leave Jerusalem and spread the gospel to other cities in the empire. Philip took the gospel into Samaria and even to a man from Ethiopia (8:1–40).

❸ SYRIA
Paul began as a persecutor of Christians, only to be met by Jesus himself on the road to Damascus. Barnabas sought out Paul and brought him to the church in Antioch in Syria, where they worked together. Meanwhile, Peter had received a vision that led him to Caesarea, where he presented the gospel

to a Gentile family, who became believers (9:1–12:25).

❹ CYPRUS AND GALATIA
The church in Antioch in Syria dedicated Paul and Barnabas for God's work of spreading the gospel to other cities. They set off on their first missionary journey through Cyprus and Galatia (13:1–14:28).

❺ JERUSALEM
Controversy between Jewish Christians and Gentile Christians over keeping the law led to a special council, with delegates meeting in Jerusalem. Together they resolved the conflict (15:1–35).

❻ MACEDONIA
Barnabas traveled to Cyprus while Paul took a second missionary journey. He revisited Galatia and headed toward Ephesus, but the Holy Spirit said no. He then turned north toward Bithynia and Pontus, but again was told not to go. He then followed the Spirit's direction to the cities in Macedonia (15:36–17:14).

❼ ACHAIA
Paul traveled from Macedonia to Athens and Corinth in Achaia,

then by ship to Ephesus before returning to Caesarea, Jerusalem, and finally Antioch (17:15–18:22).

❽ EPHESUS
Paul's third missionary journey took him back through Cilicia and Galatia, and then to Ephesus in Asia. He visited other cities in Asia before going back to Macedonia and Achaia. He returned to Jerusalem by ship, despite knowing that arrest awaited him there (18:23–23:30).

❾ CAESAREA
Paul was arrested and imprisoned in Jerusalem, then taken to Caesarea under Roman guard. Paul took advantage of any opportunity to share the gospel, and he did so before many Gentile leaders. But when Paul appealed to Caesar, he began the long journey to Rome (23:31–26:32).

❿ ROME
After storms, layovers in Crete, and a shipwreck on Malta, Paul arrived in Sicily, and finally Italy, where he traveled under guard, to his long-awaited destination, Rome, the capital of the empire (27:1–28:31).

1 THE PROMISE OF THE HOLY SPIRIT

In my first book* I told you, Theophilus, about everything Jesus began to do and teach ²until the day he was taken up to heaven after giving his chosen apostles further instructions through the Holy Spirit. ³During the forty days after his crucifixion, he appeared to the apostles from time to time, and he proved to them in many ways that he was actually alive. And he talked to them about the Kingdom of God.

⁴Once when he was eating with them, he commanded them, "Do not leave Jerusalem until the Father sends you the gift he promised, as I told you before. ⁵John baptized with* water, but in just a few days you will be baptized with the Holy Spirit."

THE ASCENSION OF JESUS

⁶So when the apostles were with Jesus, they kept asking him, "Lord, has the time come for you to free Israel and restore our kingdom?"

⁷He replied, "The Father alone has the authority to set those dates and times, and they are not for you to know. ⁸But you will receive power when the Holy Spirit comes upon you. And you will be my witnesses, telling people about me everywhere—in Jerusalem, throughout Judea, in Samaria, and to the ends of the earth."

⁹After saying this, he was taken up into a cloud while they were watching, and they could no longer see him. ¹⁰As they strained to see him rising into heaven, two white-robed men suddenly stood among them. ¹¹"Men of Galilee," they said, "why are you standing here staring into heaven? Jesus has been taken from you into heaven, but someday he will return from heaven in the same way you saw him go!"

MATTHIAS REPLACES JUDAS

¹²Then the apostles returned to Jerusalem from the Mount of Olives, a distance of half a mile.* ¹³When they arrived, they went to the upstairs room of the house where they were staying.

Here are the names of those who were present: Peter, John, James, Andrew, Philip, Thomas, Bartholomew, Matthew, James (son of Alphaeus), Simon (the Zealot), and Judas (son of James). ¹⁴They all met together and were constantly united in prayer, along with Mary the mother of Jesus, several other women, and the brothers of Jesus.

¹⁵During this time, when about 120 believers* were together in one place, Peter stood up and addressed them. ¹⁶"Brothers," he said,

"BUT YOU WILL RECEIVE POWER WHEN THE HOLY SPIRIT COMES UPON YOU. AND YOU WILL BE MY WITNESSES, TELLING PEOPLE ABOUT ME EVERYWHERE—IN JERUSALEM, THROUGHOUT JUDEA, IN SAMARIA, AND TO THE ENDS OF THE EARTH." { ACTS 1:8 }

"the Scriptures had to be fulfilled concerning Judas, who guided those who arrested Jesus. This was predicted long ago by the Holy Spirit, speaking through King David. ¹⁷Judas was one of us and shared in the ministry with us."

¹⁸(Judas had bought a field with the money he received for his treachery. Falling headfirst there, his body split open, spilling out all his intestines. ¹⁹The news of his death spread to all the people of Jerusalem, and they gave the place the Aramaic name *Akeldama,* which means "Field of Blood.")

²⁰Peter continued, "This was written in the book of Psalms, where it says, 'Let his home become desolate, with no one living in it.' It also says, 'Let someone else take his position.'*

²¹"So now we must choose a replacement for Judas from among the men who were with us the entire time we were traveling with the Lord Jesus—²²from the time he was baptized by John until the day he was taken from us. Whoever is chosen will join us as a witness of Jesus' resurrection."

²³So they nominated two men: Joseph called Barsabbas (also known as Justus) and Matthias. ²⁴Then they all prayed, "O Lord, you know every heart. Show us which of these men you

··

CHANGED
(1:3-4) Today some people still doubt that Jesus rose from the dead. But Jesus appeared to the apostles on many occasions after his resurrection, proving that he was alive. Look at the change the Resurrection made in the disciples' lives. When Jesus was arrested, tried, and executed, they scattered. They were disillusioned and they feared for their lives. But after seeing the resurrected Christ, they grew fearless and risked everything to spread the Good News about him around the world. They faced imprisonment, beatings, rejection, and martyrdom, yet they never compromised their mission. These men would not have risked their lives for something they knew was a fraud. They knew Jesus was raised from the dead, and the early church was fired with their enthusiasm to tell others.

1:1 The reference is to the Gospel of Luke. **1:5** Or *in;* also in 1:5b. **1:12** Greek *a Sabbath day's journey.* **1:15** Greek *brothers.* **1:20** Pss 69:25; 109:8.

have chosen [25]as an apostle to replace Judas in this ministry, for he has deserted us and gone where he belongs." [26]Then they cast lots, and Matthias was selected to become an apostle with the other eleven.

CHOOSE WELL
(1:21-26) The apostles had to choose a replacement for Judas Iscariot. They outlined specific criteria for making the choice. When the "finalists" had been chosen, the apostles prayed, asking God to guide the selection process. In that way, they knew they had chosen well. What is your usual way of making decisions? This gives us a good example of how to proceed when we are making important decisions: Set up criteria consistent with the Bible, examine the alternatives, and pray for wisdom and guidance to reach a wise decision.

2 **THE HOLY SPIRIT COMES** On the day of Pentecost* all the believers were meeting together in one place. [2]Suddenly, there was a sound from heaven like the roaring of a mighty windstorm, and it filled the house where they were sitting. [3]Then, what looked like flames or tongues of fire appeared and settled on each of them. [4]And everyone present was filled with the Holy Spirit and began speaking in other languages,* as the Holy Spirit gave them this ability.

[5]At that time there were devout Jews from every nation living in Jerusalem. [6]When they heard the loud noise, everyone came running,

2:1 The Festival of Pentecost came 50 days after Passover (when Jesus was crucified). **2:4** Or *in other tongues.*

ULTIMATE ISSUES *THE HOLY SPIRIT*

Author Sheldon Vanauken describes a scene in which the characters in a drama sit around and discuss their play. The playwright's name is Smith. Some of the characters believe Smith exists; some don't. One of them recalls an earlier scene where a character named Smithson claimed that he was Smith, and that he had written himself into the play. After considerable debate over the likelihood of that happening, another character speaks:

"Look, do you know what's so impressive about all this? It's the idea of a sort of a trinity: Smith outside writing the play; and inside as a character; and inside each of us, too. I don't know whether it's true, but it's exactly the way it would be if it were. . . . This thing has the feel of something true. A sort of rightness."

No one can truly understand—much less explain—the Trinity, God in three persons. But Vanauken's analogy is a good attempt: an Author who writes characters into existence, then writes himself in as one of the players, and also is somehow in each of his characters.

Historically, Christians have believed that God exists in three persons: the Father, Son, and Holy Spirit. How this works, no one knows. This is one of the mysteries that the Bible mentions.

If we were to take a poll, we might find that the Holy Spirit is probably the least understood member of the Trinity. So just who is the Holy Spirit? What does he do?

- First of all, the New Testament always refers to the Holy Spirit as "he," not "it." The Spirit is personal, not merely a "force" or instrument. Just as God the Father and God the Son represent distinct personalities within the Trinity, so does the Spirit. We don't have any real point of reference to help us understand this since we don't know anyone else who is pure spirit. Still, it is true: The Holy Spirit is a person

with intellect, feelings, will, and other personal characteristics.

- Second, the Holy Spirit is not in any way inferior to the Father or the Son. He is equal to them. One of the clearest statements of this reality is found in Matthew 28:19, where Jesus tells the disciples: "Go and make disciples of all the nations, baptizing them in the name of the Father and the Son and the Holy Spirit" (see also John 14:16-26 and 15:26-27; 2 Cor 3:17 and 13:14). The classic description of the Trinity is "one in essence, three in persons." The Holy Spirit is the third person described here, and he is just as much God as are the Father and the Son.

- Third, the Spirit acts in many powerful ways. Here are just a few: he anoints and serves alongside the Messiah (Isa 48:16; 61:1; Luke 4:18-19); he ushers in the "last days" (Joel 2:28-32; Acts 2:14-36); he unifies believers and helps them grow and serve others (1 Cor 12:4-11; Gal 5:22-25; Eph 4:1-16;); he gives new life (John 3:5-8); he helps us own up to what we've done and to change (John 16:8); he is our teacher and advocate (John 14:26); he guides us into truth (John 16:13-15); he bears fruit in us (Gal 5:22-25); he gives us supernatural gifts (1 Cor 12–14); he prays for us (Rom 8:26); he is present in all Christians (Rom 8:9-11; 1 Cor 6:19-20). His arrival in Acts 2 completely changed the lives of all of the believers.

Jesus described the Holy Spirit as the "Advocate" (John 15:26). Unlike a high school guidance counselor, the Holy Spirit is with you 24/7. He is your unseen adviser—one who will never steer you wrong.

As characters in a divine drama, it is comforting for us to know that an Author knows and loves the people he created so much that he "wrote himself into the play." And that now, having left the visible stage, he remains behind in an unseen—but no less real—way, guiding and strengthening his people. ■

and they were bewildered to hear their own languages being spoken by the believers.

[7]They were completely amazed. "How can this be?" they exclaimed. "These people are all from Galilee, [8]and yet we hear them speaking in our own native languages! [9]Here we are—Parthians, Medes, Elamites, people from Mesopotamia, Judea, Cappadocia, Pontus, the province of Asia, [10]Phrygia, Pamphylia, Egypt, and the areas of Libya around Cyrene, visitors from Rome [11](both Jews and converts to Judaism), Cretans, and Arabs. And we all hear these people speaking in our own languages about the wonderful things God has done!" [12]They stood there amazed and perplexed. "What can this mean?" they asked each other.

[13]But others in the crowd ridiculed them, saying, "They're just drunk, that's all!"

PETER PREACHES TO THE CROWD

[14]Then Peter stepped forward with the eleven other apostles and shouted to the crowd, "Listen carefully, all of you, fellow Jews and residents of Jerusalem! Make no mistake about this. [15]These people are not drunk, as some of you are assuming. Nine o'clock in the morning is much too early for that. [16]No, what you see was predicted long ago by the prophet Joel:

[17] 'In the last days,' God says,
   'I will pour out my Spirit upon all people.
Your sons and daughters will prophesy.
   Your young men will see visions,
   and your old men will dream dreams.
[18] In those days I will pour out my Spirit
   even on my servants—men and women
      alike—
   and they will prophesy.
[19] And I will cause wonders in the heavens
      above
   and signs on the earth below—
   blood and fire and clouds of smoke.
[20] The sun will become dark,
   and the moon will turn blood red
   before that great and glorious day
      of the LORD arrives.
[21] But everyone who calls on the name
      of the LORD
   will be saved.'*

[22]"People of Israel, listen! God publicly endorsed Jesus the Nazarene* by doing powerful miracles, wonders, and signs through him, as you well know. [23]But God knew what would happen, and his prearranged plan was carried

out when Jesus was betrayed. With the help of lawless Gentiles, you nailed him to a cross and killed him. [24]But God released him from the horrors of death and raised him back to life, for death could not keep him in its grip. [25]King David said this about him:

'I see that the LORD is always with me.
   I will not be shaken, for he is right
      beside me.
[26] No wonder my heart is glad,
   and my tongue shouts his praises!
   My body rests in hope.
[27] For you will not leave my soul among
      the dead*
   or allow your Holy One to rot in the grave.
[28] You have shown me the way of life,
   and you will fill me with the joy of your
      presence.'*

[29]"Dear brothers, think about this! You can be sure that the patriarch David wasn't referring to himself, for he died and was buried, and his tomb is still here among us. [30]But he was a prophet, and he knew God had promised with an oath that one of David's own descendants would sit on his throne. [31]David was looking into the future and speaking of the Messiah's resurrection. He was saying that God would not leave him among the dead or allow his body to rot in the grave.

[32]"God raised Jesus from the dead, and we are all witnesses of this. [33]Now he is exalted to the place of highest honor in heaven, at God's right hand. And the Father, as he had promised, gave him the Holy Spirit to pour out upon us, just as you see and hear today. [34]For David himself never ascended into heaven, yet he said,

'The LORD said to my Lord,
   "Sit in the place of honor at my right hand
[35] until I humble your enemies,
   making them a footstool under
      your feet."'*

[36]"So let everyone in Israel know for certain that God has made this Jesus, whom you crucified, to be both Lord and Messiah!"

[37]Peter's words pierced their hearts, and they said to him and to the other apostles, "Brothers, what should we do?"

[38]Peter replied, "Each of you must repent of your sins and turn to God, and be baptized in the name of Jesus Christ for the forgiveness of your sins. Then you will receive the gift of the Holy Spirit. [39]This promise is to you, and to your children, and even to the Gentiles*—all who have been called by the Lord our God." [40]Then Peter continued preaching for a long time,

2:17-21 Joel 2:28-32. 2:22 Or Jesus of Nazareth. 2:27 Greek in Hades; also in 2:31. 2:25-28 Ps 16:8-11 (Greek version). 2:34-35 Ps 110:1. 2:39 Or and to people far in the future; Greek reads and to those far away.

strongly urging all his listeners, "Save your-selves from this crooked generation!"

⁴¹Those who believed what Peter said were baptized and added to the church that day—about 3,000 in all.

THE BELIEVERS FORM A COMMUNITY ⁴²All the believers devoted themselves to the apostles' teaching, and to fellowship, and to sharing in meals (including the Lord's Supper*), and to prayer.

⁴³A deep sense of awe came over them all, and the apostles performed many miraculous signs and wonders. ⁴⁴And all the believers met together in one place and shared everything they had. ⁴⁵They sold their property and pos-sessions and shared the money with those in need. ⁴⁶They worshiped together at the Temple each day, met in homes for the Lord's Supper, and shared their meals with great joy and generosity*—⁴⁷all the while prais-ing God and enjoying the goodwill of all the people. And each day the Lord added to their fellowship those who were being saved.

3 **PETER HEALS A CRIPPLED BEGGAR** Peter and John went to the Temple one afternoon to take part in the three o'clock prayer service. ²As they approached the Temple, a man lame from birth was being carried in. Each day he was put beside the Temple gate, the one called the Beautiful Gate, so he could beg from the people going into the Temple. ³When he saw Peter and John about to enter, he asked them for some money.

2:42 Greek *the breaking of bread*; also in 2:46. **2:46** Or *and sincere hearts.*

....

WE'RE IN THIS TOGETHER
(2:44-47) Recognizing the other believers as brothers and sisters in the family of God, the Christians in Jeru-salem shared all they had so that all could benefit from God's blessings. Sometimes having lots of money and possessions can tempt people to isolate themselves from others, each enjoying his or her own little piece of the world. But as part of God's spiritual family, we have a responsibility to help one another in every way possible. God's family works best when its members work together.

I WONDER...

My mom has said some pretty bad things to me over the years. Now that I'm a Christian, I know I should forgive her, but I can't. What should I do?

The gap between knowing you need to forgive some-one and actually being able to do it often seems like a vast canyon. You can see the other side, but getting there seems impossible.

Ever seen a shower drain plugged up with a two-month accumulation of hair? The water slowly seeps through the molding mass of greasy, soapy gunk. No amount of plunging can bring the glob up because it's too deep.

The next solution usually is to burn away the clog by applying something like Drano. Sometimes this works if the buildup is not too severe. The last resort, of course, is to call a plumber. The plumber will bring a narrow, hard, yet flexible piece of metal called a snake and drill through the clog until the water is flowing freely.

Unforgiveness is like a clogged drain. Sometimes it is fairly easy to unclog. Someone hurts us. We let the person know how we feel, and the person says that he or she is sorry. We forgive him or her, and the whole episode is forgotten. But when unforgiveness collects from years of hurt, the situation becomes similar to what a drain would look like after years of bathing your cat in the sink without cleaning out the drain! You might as well buy a new sink.

Likewise, our sin can collect and become a gross, yucky mass that eventually clogs our relationship with God. Until it is removed, we can't really receive anything meaningful from him. Jesus came to "unclog our pipes" so God's love and forgiveness could flow to us freely. He did nothing wrong—we were the transgressors—yet he died to open the way for that flow of love.

From what you wrote, your mom's sin against you has clogged your relationship. You may have every right not to forgive your mom, but you must put aside that right for a greater goal—you must "die" and open yourself to learning how you and your mom can love each other. Otherwise, the clog will only get worse.

God took the initiative with us by humbling him-self and forgiving all of our sin. (To see the com-parison of how much God has forgiven us and how much we must forgive others, see Matthew 18:21-34.) You must do the same with the person who has wronged you.

The forgiveness must be from your heart and must not be dependent upon whether she feels sorry for what she has done. Forgiving someone is a gift only you can offer. You can't make someone take a free gift; they must reach out and receive it. Though the canyon looks deep and treacherous, the reward on the other side is a clear conscience, times of wonder-ful refreshment (see Acts 3:19-20), and—hopefully—a renewed relationship.

[4] Peter and John looked at him intently, and Peter said, "Look at us!" [5] The lame man looked at them eagerly, expecting some money. [6] But Peter said, "I don't have any silver or gold for you. But I'll give you what I have. In the name of Jesus Christ the Nazarene,* get up and* walk!"

[7] Then Peter took the lame man by the right hand and helped him up. And as he did, the man's feet and ankles were instantly healed and strengthened. [8] He jumped up, stood on his feet, and began to walk! Then, walking, leaping, and praising God, he went into the Temple with them.

[9] All the people saw him walking and heard him praising God. [10] When they realized he was the lame beggar they had seen so often at the Beautiful Gate, they were absolutely astounded! [11] They all rushed out in amazement to Solomon's Colonnade, where the man was holding tightly to Peter and John.

PETER PREACHES IN THE TEMPLE [12] Peter saw his opportunity and addressed the crowd. "People of Israel," he said, "what is so surprising about this? And why stare at us as though we had made this man walk by our own power or godliness? [13] For it is the God of Abraham, Isaac, and Jacob—the God of all our ancestors—who has brought glory to his servant Jesus by doing this. This is the same Jesus whom you handed over and rejected before Pilate, despite Pilate's decision to release him. [14] You rejected this holy, righteous one and instead demanded the release of a murderer. [15] You killed the author of life, but God raised him from the dead. And we are witnesses of this fact!

[16] "Through faith in the name of Jesus, this man was healed—and you know how crippled he was before. Faith in Jesus' name has healed him before your very eyes.

[17] "Friends,* I realize that what you and your leaders did to Jesus was done in ignorance. [18] But God was fulfilling what all the prophets had foretold about the Messiah—that he must suffer these things. [19] Now repent of your sins and turn to God, so that your sins may be wiped away. [20] Then times of refreshment will come from the presence of the Lord, and he will again send you Jesus, your appointed Messiah. [21] For he must remain in heaven until the time for the final restoration of all things, as God promised long ago through his holy prophets. [22] Moses said, 'The Lord your God will raise up for you a Prophet like me from among your own people. Listen carefully to everything he tells you.'* [23] Then Moses said, 'Anyone who will not listen to that Prophet will be completely cut off from God's people.'*

[24] "Starting with Samuel, every prophet spoke about what is happening today. [25] You are the children of those prophets, and you are included in the covenant God promised to your ancestors. For God said to Abraham, 'Through your descendants* all the families on earth will be blessed.' [26] When God raised up his servant, Jesus, he sent him first to you people of Israel, to bless you by turning each of you back from your sinful ways."

4 PETER AND JOHN BEFORE THE COUNCIL
While Peter and John were speaking to the people, they were confronted by the priests, the captain of the Temple guard, and some of the Sadducees. [2] These leaders were very disturbed that Peter and John were teaching the people that through Jesus there is a resurrection of the dead. [3] They arrested them and, since it was already evening, put them in jail until morning. [4] But many of the people who heard their message believed it, so the number of believers now totaled about 5,000 men, not counting women and children.*

[5] The next day the council of all the rulers and elders and teachers of religious law met in Jerusalem. [6] Annas the high priest was there, along with Caiaphas, John, Alexander, and other relatives of the high priest. [7] They brought in the two disciples and demanded, "By what power, or in whose name, have you done this?"

····································

BETTER
(3:1-8) The lame beggar asked for something that would have offered him temporary help—money. Instead, Peter gave him something much better and more permanent— the use of his legs. Often our requests are for items that will help us temporarily. But God always has the big picture in mind when he answers our prayers. When we ask God for help, he may say, "I've got something even better for you." Are you willing to trust that he knows what's best?

REFRESHED
(3:19-20) Peter advised the crowd to change their ways. When we turn from a bad habit (for example, lying, stealing, looking at porn, and so forth) and agree to change, God promises not only to wipe away that mark against us but also to bring spiritual refreshment. Breaking a bad habit may seem painful at first, but God will give you a better way. As Hosea promised, "Let us press on to know him. He will respond to us as surely as the arrival of dawn or the coming of rains in early spring" (Hos 6:3). Do you feel a need to be refreshed?

3:6a Or *Jesus Christ of Nazareth.*   **3:6b** Some manuscripts do not include *get up and.*   **3:17** Greek *Brothers.*   **3:22** Deut 18:15.
3:23 Deut 18:19; Lev 23:29.   **3:25** Greek *your seed;* see Gen 12:3; 22:18.   **4:4** Greek *5,000 adult males.*

[8]Then Peter, filled with the Holy Spirit, said to them, "Rulers and elders of our people, [9]are we being questioned today because we've done a good deed for a crippled man? Do you want to know how he was healed? [10]Let me clearly state to all of you and to all the people of Israel that he was healed by the powerful name of Jesus Christ the Nazarene,* the man you crucified but whom God raised from the dead. [11]For Jesus is the one referred to in the Scriptures, where it says,

'The stone that you builders rejected
    has now become the cornerstone.'*

[12]There is salvation in no one else! God has given no other name under heaven by which we must be saved."

[13]The members of the council were amazed when they saw the boldness of Peter and John, for they could see that they were ordinary men with no special training in the Scriptures. They also recognized them as men who had been

with Jesus. [14]But since they could see the man who had been healed standing right there among them, there was nothing the council could say. [15]So they ordered Peter and John out of the council chamber* and conferred among themselves.

[16]"What should we do with these men?" they asked each other. "We can't deny that they have performed a miraculous sign, and everybody in Jerusalem knows about it. [17]But to keep them from spreading their propaganda any further, we must warn them not to speak to anyone in Jesus' name again." [18]So they called the apostles back in and commanded them never again to speak or teach in the name of Jesus.

[19]But Peter and John replied, "Do you think God wants us to obey you rather than him? [20]We cannot stop telling about everything we have seen and heard."

[21]The council then threatened them further,

4:10 Or *Jesus Christ of Nazareth.*   **4:11** Ps 118:22.   **4:15** Greek *the Sanhedrin.*

ULTIMATE ISSUES — WHAT ABOUT THOSE WHO NEVER HEAR THE GOSPEL?

Ever wonder whether or not God would send someone to hell who has never heard of him? How about a tribesman in a South American jungle? What about the millions of Hindus and Buddhists who are good, moral people but have never heard the gospel—God couldn't possibly send them to hell, could he?

If you've been following Jesus for very long, you've probably had a couple of discussions that deal with questions like these. What does God do with those who've never heard of Jesus?

For starters, God doesn't send anyone anywhere. Each person has a choice. Concerning that question, however, the Bible doesn't deal with it directly. Instead, it talks about Jesus in rather exclusive terms. Take a look at Acts 4:12: "There is salvation in no one else! God has given no other name under heaven [other than Jesus Christ] by which we must be saved." Because the Bible doesn't talk directly about the problem, we must proceed with humility and caution. Still, we aren't left totally in the dark.

First, remember that God doesn't owe anyone a break. He would be entirely justified in condemning everyone, for "everyone has sinned; we all fall short of God's glorious standard" (Rom 3:23). But Jesus offers forgiveness to all. That's grace—we get what we don't deserve, instead of what we do. Even if God arbitrarily chose whom to save and whom to condemn, he could not be accused of being unjust or unmerciful.

Second, Romans 1 (especially verses 18-20) makes it clear that God has created everyone with the knowl-

edge of the Creator. This truth is evident in other passages as well. Check out Psalm 19:1-2: "The heavens proclaim the glory of God. The skies display his craftsmanship. Day after day they continue to speak; night after night they make him known." Yet many people suppress that knowledge. Every person ever born has an innate knowledge that a Creator exists, someone bigger, smarter, and more powerful than we are, who put us here in this universe. Those who do not hear the message about Jesus are responsible for how they respond to the knowledge they do have about God.

So, for anyone who has heard the Good News—that God came to earth as a man named Jesus of Nazareth, and that Jesus lived, died, and rose again so that through him we could have forgiveness of sins and eternal life—salvation comes through faith in Jesus. For the person who has never heard of Jesus, his love and work, salvation comes based on the knowledge of our loving Creator and responding to that knowledge with love, obedience, and worship. For all people, Christ is the only one who has opened the way for us to be restored to God. It is his death on the Cross and his resurrection that enable any of us to approach our holy and all-righteous God.

We don't have all the answers to all the questions that confuse us about life and death, heaven and hell, and so on. But we can know the one who not only knows the truth, but is the Truth—and we know that he is loving, kind, and merciful. We don't decide who will be saved and who won't, God does. And he will do what is right. ∎

but they finally let them go because they didn't know how to punish them without starting a riot. For everyone was praising God ²²for this miraculous sign—the healing of a man who had been lame for more than forty years.

THE BELIEVERS PRAY FOR COURAGE ²³As soon as they were freed, Peter and John returned to the other believers and told them what the leading priests and elders had said. ²⁴When they heard the report, all the believers lifted their voices together in prayer to God: "O Sovereign Lord, Creator of heaven and earth, the sea, and everything in them—²⁵you spoke long ago by the Holy Spirit through our ancestor David, your servant, saying,

'Why were the nations so angry?
    Why did they waste their time with futile
        plans?
²⁶ The kings of the earth prepared for battle;
    the rulers gathered together
against the Lord
    and against his Messiah.'*

²⁷"In fact, this has happened here in this very city! For Herod Antipas, Pontius Pilate the governor, the Gentiles, and the people of Israel were all united against Jesus, your holy servant, whom you anointed. ²⁸But everything they did was determined beforehand according to your will. ²⁹And now, O Lord, hear their threats, and give us, your servants, great boldness in preaching your word. ³⁰Stretch out your hand with healing power; may miraculous signs and wonders be done through the name of your holy servant Jesus."

³¹After this prayer, the meeting place shook, and they were all filled with the Holy Spirit. Then they preached the word of God with boldness.

THE BELIEVERS SHARE THEIR POSSESSIONS
³²All the believers were united in heart and mind. And they felt that what they owned was not their own, so they shared everything they had. ³³The apostles testified powerfully to the resurrection of the Lord Jesus, and God's great blessing was upon them all. ³⁴There were no needy people among them, because those who owned land or houses would sell them ³⁵and bring the money to the apostles to give to those in need.

³⁶For instance, there was Joseph, the one the apostles nicknamed Barnabas (which means "Son of Encouragement"). He was from the tribe of Levi and came from the island of

4:25-26 Or *his anointed one;* or *his Christ.* Ps 2:1-2.

MY STORY: Kenneth

It's hard for me to talk to people about God, ya know? I haven't memorized a lot of verses. I'm still working my way through the Bible. It's easy to tell myself that I can wait until I know more.

But when I read Acts 4:13, I realized I was kidding myself. The verse talks about the boldness of Peter and John, and says that the Jewish council noticed that they were uneducated and nonprofessionals. But they knew Jesus. In other words, a person doesn't have to know the whole Bible or go to seminary to be able to share the faith. The main thing is to know Jesus and share what I know with other people. I'm finding that he gives me the boldness to open my mouth if I ask him.

Cyprus. ³⁷He sold a field he owned and brought the money to the apostles.

5 **ANANIAS AND SAPPHIRA** But there was a certain man named Ananias who, with his wife, Sapphira, sold some property. ²He brought part of the money to the apostles, claiming it was the full amount. With his wife's consent, he kept the rest.

³Then Peter said, "Ananias, why have you let Satan fill your heart? You lied to the Holy Spirit, and you kept some of the money for yourself. ⁴The property was yours to sell or not sell, as you wished. And after selling it, the money was also yours to give away. How could you do a thing like this? You weren't lying to us but to God!"

⁵As soon as Ananias heard these words, he fell to the floor and died. Everyone who heard about it was terrified. ⁶Then some young men got up, wrapped him in a sheet, and took him out and buried him.

⁷About three hours later his wife came in, not knowing what had happened. ⁸Peter asked

....

STRENGTH
(4:24-30) *Notice how the believers prayed. They praised God, told him their problem, and asked for his help. They didn't ask God to remove the problem. Instead, they asked for help to deal with it. God doesn't always remove problems from our lives. Many times he provides the strength to deal with them.*

her, "Was this the price you and your husband received for your land?"

"Yes," she replied, "that was the price."

⁹And Peter said, "How could the two of you even think of conspiring to test the Spirit of the Lord like this? The young men who buried your husband are just outside the door, and they will carry you out, too."

¹⁰Instantly, she fell to the floor and died. When the young men came in and saw that she was dead, they carried her out and buried her beside her husband. ¹¹Great fear gripped the entire church and everyone else who heard what had happened.

THE APOSTLES HEAL MANY ¹²The apostles were performing many miraculous signs and wonders among the people. And all the believers were meeting regularly at the Temple in the area known as Solomon's Colonnade. ¹³But no one else dared to join them, even though all the people had high regard for them. ¹⁴Yet more and more people believed and were brought to the Lord—crowds of both men and women. ¹⁵As a result of the apostles' work, sick people were brought out into the streets on beds and mats so that Peter's shadow might fall across some of them as he went by. ¹⁶Crowds came from the villages around Jerusalem, bringing their sick and those possessed by evil* spirits, and they were all healed.

THE APOSTLES MEET OPPOSITION ¹⁷The high priest and his officials, who were Sadducees, were filled with jealousy. ¹⁸They arrested the apostles and put them in the public jail. ¹⁹But an angel of the Lord came at night, opened the gates of the jail, and brought them out. Then

he told them, ²⁰"Go to the Temple and give the people this message of life!"

²¹So at daybreak the apostles entered the Temple, as they were told, and immediately began teaching.

When the high priest and his officials arrived, they convened the high council*—the full assembly of the elders of Israel. Then they sent for the apostles to be brought from the jail for trial. ²²But when the Temple guards went to the jail, the men were gone. So they returned to the council and reported, ²³"The jail was securely locked, with the guards standing outside, but when we opened the gates, no one was there!"

²⁴When the captain of the Temple guard and the leading priests heard this, they were perplexed, wondering where it would all end. ²⁵Then someone arrived with startling news: "The men you put in jail are standing in the Temple, teaching the people!"

²⁶The captain went with his Temple guards and arrested the apostles, but without violence, for they were afraid the people would stone them. ²⁷Then they brought the apostles before the high council, where the high priest confronted them. ²⁸"Didn't we tell you never again to teach in this man's name?" he demanded. "Instead, you have filled all Jerusalem with your teaching about him, and you want to make us responsible for his death!"

²⁹But Peter and the apostles replied, "We must obey God rather than any human authority. ³⁰The God of our ancestors raised Jesus from the dead after you killed him by hanging him on a cross.* ³¹Then God put him in the place of honor at his right hand as Prince and Savior. He did this so the people of Israel would repent of their sins and be forgiven. ³²We are witnesses of these things and so is the Holy Spirit, who is given by God to those who obey him."

³³When they heard this, the high council was furious and decided to kill them. ³⁴But one member, a Pharisee named Gamaliel, who was an expert in religious law and respected by all the people, stood up and ordered that the men be sent outside the council chamber for a while. ³⁵Then he said to his colleagues, "Men of Israel, take care what you are planning to do to these men! ³⁶Some time ago there was that fellow Theudas, who pretended to be someone great. About 400 others joined him, but he was killed, and all his followers went their various ways. The whole movement came to nothing.

ATTRACTIONS
(5:14) What makes Christianity attractive? We can easily be drawn to churches because of exciting programs, good speakers, beautiful facilities, or friendly people. Believers were attracted to the early church by God's power and miracles; the generosity, sincerity, honesty, and unity of the members; and the character of the leaders. We must be careful that our standards don't slip. God wants to add to his Church, not just to programs or congregations.

THIS MEANS WAR
(5:17-21) The high priest and other leaders reacted negatively to the apostles' bold preaching and miracles. Negative reactions like these can remind us that we're in a war. As Ephesians 6:12 says, "We are not fighting against flesh-and-blood enemies, but against evil rulers and authorities of the unseen world, against mighty powers in this dark world, and against evil spirits in the heavenly places." When you share your faith, you might experience what the apostles experienced. "But take heart," Jesus said, "because I have overcome the world" (John 16:33).

5:16 Greek *unclean.*   **5:21** Greek *Sanhedrin;* also in 5:27, 41.
5:30 Greek *on a tree.*

37After him, at the time of the census, there was Judas of Galilee. He got people to follow him, but he was killed, too, and all his followers were scattered.

38"So my advice is, leave these men alone. Let them go. If they are planning and doing these things merely on their own, it will soon be overthrown. 39But if it is from God, you will not be able to overthrow them. You may even find yourselves fighting against God!"

40The others accepted his advice. They called in the apostles and had them flogged. Then they ordered them never again to speak in the name of Jesus, and they let them go.

41The apostles left the high council rejoicing that God had counted them worthy to suffer disgrace for the name of Jesus.* 42And every day, in the Temple and from house to house, they continued to teach and preach this message: "Jesus is the Messiah."

6 SEVEN MEN CHOSEN TO SERVE But as the believers* rapidly multiplied, there were rumblings of discontent. The Greek-speaking believers complained about the Hebrew-speaking believers, saying that their widows were being discriminated against in the daily distribution of food.

2So the Twelve called a meeting of all the believers. They said, "We apostles should spend our time teaching the word of God, not running a food program. 3And so, brothers, select seven men who are well respected and are full of the Spirit and wisdom. We will give them this responsibility. 4Then we apostles can spend our time in prayer and teaching the word."

5Everyone liked this idea, and they chose the following: Stephen (a man full of faith and the Holy Spirit), Philip, Procorus, Nicanor, Timon, Parmenas, and Nicolas of Antioch (an earlier convert to the Jewish faith). 6These seven were presented to the apostles, who prayed for them as they laid their hands on them.

7So God's message continued to spread. The number of believers greatly increased in Jerusalem, and many of the Jewish priests were converted, too.

STEPHEN IS ARRESTED
8Stephen, a man full of God's grace and power, performed amazing miracles and signs among the people. 9But one day some men from the Synagogue of Freed Slaves, as it was called, started to debate with him. They were Jews from Cyrene, Alexandria,

Cilicia, and the province of Asia. 10None of them could stand against the wisdom and the Spirit with which Stephen spoke.

11So they persuaded some men to lie about Stephen, saying, "We heard him blaspheme Moses, and even God." 12This roused the people, the elders, and the teachers of religious law. So they arrested Stephen and brought him before the high council.*

13The lying witnesses said, "This man is always speaking against the holy Temple and against the law of Moses. 14We have heard him say that this Jesus of Nazareth* will destroy the Temple and change the customs Moses handed down to us."

15At this point everyone in the high council stared at Stephen, because his face became as bright as an angel's.

7 STEPHEN ADDRESSES THE COUNCIL Then the high priest asked Stephen, "Are these accusations true?"

2This was Stephen's reply: "Brothers and fathers, listen to me. Our glorious God appeared to our ancestor Abraham in Mesopotamia before he settled in Haran.* 3God told him, 'Leave your native land and your relatives, and come into the land that I will show you.'* 4So Abraham left the land of the Chaldeans and lived in Haran until his father died. Then God brought him here to the land where you now live.

5"But God gave him no inheritance here, not even one square foot of land. God did promise, however, that eventually the whole land would belong to Abraham and his descendants—even though he had no children yet. 6God also told him that his descendants would live in a foreign land, where they would be oppressed

....

THE WAVE
(6:7) The gospel spread like ripples on a pond where, from a single center, each wave touched the next, spreading wider and farther. The gospel still spreads this way today. You don't have to change the world single-handedly. Being part of the wave, touching those around you, is enough. They in turn will touch others until all have felt the movement. Are you part of the wave?

ACCUSED
(6:8–7:60) When accused of the crime of speaking against the Temple and the law of Moses, Stephen took the offensive, seizing the opportunity to summarize the history of the Jewish people. This history helped point the accusing finger back at the religious leaders. They failed to obey the laws they prided themselves in following so meticulously. Before his death, Jesus had leveled the same charge against the Pharisees (see Matt 23).

Like Stephen, we don't need to be on the defensive when we witness for Jesus. The truth of Christ is its own defense.

5:41 Greek *for the name.*   6:1 Greek *disciples;* also in 6:2, 7.
6:12 Greek *Sanhedrin;* also in 6:15.   6:14 Or *Jesus the Nazarene.*
7:2 *Mesopotamia* was the region now called Iraq. *Haran* was a city in what is now called Syria.   7:3 Gen 12:1.

as slaves for 400 years. ⁷'But I will punish the nation that enslaves them,' God said, 'and in the end they will come out and worship me here in this place.'*

⁸"God also gave Abraham the covenant of circumcision at that time. So when Abraham became the father of Isaac, he circumcised him on the eighth day. And the practice was continued when Isaac became the father of Jacob, and when Jacob became the father of the twelve patriarchs of the Israelite nation.

⁹"These patriarchs were jealous of their brother Joseph, and they sold him to be a slave in Egypt. But God was with him ¹⁰and rescued him from all his troubles. And God gave him favor before Pharaoh, king of Egypt. God also gave Joseph unusual wisdom, so that Pharaoh appointed him governor over all of Egypt and put him in charge of the palace.

¹¹"But a famine came upon Egypt and Canaan. There was great misery, and our ancestors ran out of food. ¹²Jacob heard that there was still grain in Egypt, so he sent his sons— our ancestors—to buy some. ¹³The second time they went, Joseph revealed his identity to his brothers,* and they were introduced to Pharaoh. ¹⁴Then Joseph sent for his father, Jacob, and all his relatives to come to Egypt, seventy-five persons in all. ¹⁵So Jacob went to Egypt. He died there, as did our ancestors. ¹⁶Their bodies were taken to Shechem and buried in the tomb Abraham had bought for a certain price from Hamor's sons in Shechem.

¹⁷"As the time drew near when God would fulfill his promise to Abraham, the number of our people in Egypt greatly increased. ¹⁸But then a new king came to the throne of Egypt who knew nothing about Joseph. ¹⁹This king exploited our people and oppressed them, forcing parents to abandon their newborn babies so they would die.

²⁰"At that time Moses was born—a beautiful child in God's eyes. His parents cared for him at home for three months. ²¹When they had to abandon him, Pharaoh's daughter adopted him and raised him as her own son. ²²Moses was taught all the wisdom of the Egyptians, and he was powerful in both speech and action.

²³"One day when Moses was forty years old, he decided to visit his relatives, the people of Israel. ²⁴He saw an Egyptian mistreating an Israelite. So Moses came to the man's defense and avenged him, killing the Egyptian. ²⁵Moses assumed his fellow Israelites would realize that God had sent him to rescue them, but they didn't.

²⁶"The next day he visited them again and saw two men of Israel fighting. He tried to be a peacemaker. 'Men,' he said, 'you are brothers. Why are you fighting each other?'

²⁷"But the man in the wrong pushed Moses aside. 'Who made you a ruler and judge over us?' he asked. ²⁸'Are you going to kill me as you killed that Egyptian yesterday?' ²⁹When Moses heard that, he fled the country and lived as a foreigner in the land of Midian. There his two sons were born.

³⁰"Forty years later, in the desert near Mount Sinai, an angel appeared to Moses in the flame of a burning bush. ³¹When Moses saw it, he was amazed at the sight. As he went to take a closer look, the voice of the LORD called out to him, ³²'I am the God of your ancestors—the God of Abraham, Isaac, and Jacob.' Moses shook with terror and did not dare to look.

³³"Then the LORD said to him, 'Take off your sandals, for you are standing on holy ground. ³⁴I have certainly seen the oppression of my people in Egypt. I have heard their groans and have come down to rescue them. Now go, for I am sending you back to Egypt.'*

³⁵"So God sent back the same man his people had previously rejected when they demanded, 'Who made you a ruler and judge over us?' Through the angel who appeared to him in the burning bush, God sent Moses to be their ruler and savior. ³⁶And by means of many wonders and miraculous signs, he led them out of Egypt, through the Red Sea, and through the wilderness for forty years.

³⁷"Moses himself told the people of Israel, 'God will raise up for you a Prophet like me from among your own people.'* ³⁸Moses was with our ancestors, the assembly of God's people in the wilderness, when the angel spoke to him at Mount Sinai. And there Moses received life-giving words to pass on to us.*

³⁹"But our ancestors refused to listen to Moses. They rejected him and wanted to return to Egypt. ⁴⁰They told Aaron, 'Make us some gods who can lead us, for we don't know what has become of this Moses, who brought us out of Egypt.' ⁴¹So they made an idol shaped like a calf, and they sacrificed to it and celebrated over this thing they had made. ⁴²Then God turned away from them and abandoned them to serve the stars of heaven as their gods! In the book of the prophets it is written,

'Was it to me you were bringing sacrifices
    and offerings

7:5-7 Gen 12:7; 15:13-14; Exod 3:12.   **7:13** Other manuscripts read *Joseph was recognized by his brothers.*   **7:31-34** Exod 3:5-10.
7:37 Deut 18:15.   **7:38** Some manuscripts read *to you.*

during those forty years in the wilderness, Israel?

43 No, you carried your pagan gods—
the shrine of Molech,
the star of your god Rephan,
and the images you made to worship them.
So I will send you into exile
as far away as Babylon.'*

44"Our ancestors carried the Tabernacle* with them through the wilderness. It was constructed according to the plan God had shown to Moses. 45Years later, when Joshua led our ancestors in battle against the nations that God drove out of this land, the Tabernacle was taken with them into their new territory. And it stayed there until the time of King David.

46"David found favor with God and asked for

the privilege of building a permanent Temple for the God of Jacob.* 47But it was Solomon who actually built it. 48However, the Most High doesn't live in temples made by human hands. As the prophet says,

49 'Heaven is my throne,
and the earth is my footstool.
Could you build me a temple as good as that?'
asks the LORD.
'Could you build me such a resting place?
50   Didn't my hands make both heaven and earth?'*

51"You stubborn people! You are heathen* at heart and deaf to the truth. Must you forever resist the Holy Spirit? That's what your ancestors did, and so do you! 52Name one prophet your ancestors didn't persecute! They even killed the ones who predicted the coming of the Righteous One—the Messiah whom you

7:42-43 Amos 5:25-27 (Greek version).   7:44 Greek *the tent of witness.*   7:46 Some manuscripts read *the house of Jacob.*
7:49-50 Isa 66:1-2.   7:51 Greek *uncircumcised.*

PERSONALITY PROFILE · STEPHEN

UPS:
• One of seven leaders chosen to supervise food distribution to the needy in the early church
• Known for his spiritual qualities of faith, wisdom, grace, and power, and for the Spirit's presence in his life
• Outstanding leader, teacher, and debater
• The first to be martyred for his faith

STATS:
• Occupation: Deacon
• Contemporaries: Paul, Caiaphas, Gamaliel, the apostles

KEY VERSES: Acts 7:59-60

HOW SERIOUS ARE YOU ABOUT YOUR FAITH IN JESUS? Would you give your life for it?

Stephen did. The book you hold in your hand is here today because thousands of Christians throughout history have given their lives to carry the gospel around the world. They died for the Good News. It is important for us to remember, though, that a person cannot give his life for the gospel until he has learned to live his life for the gospel. Stephen was just that kind of person.

One way God trains his servants is to have them do jobs that don't seem very important or glamorous. We first meet Stephen when he was chosen along with six others to manage the distribution of food among Christians in Jerusalem. Because many people lost jobs and belongings when they became Christians, other Christians had to share what they had with each other. Stephen and the other leaders were asked to make sure that the available food was handed out fairly. This probably was a job with more headaches than thank-yous.

Stephen also was a powerful speaker. When he was harassed in the Temple about his faith, he responded calmly and clearly. His logic devastated their arguments.

Consequently, Stephen was hauled before the official religious court, where he used a summary of the Jews' own history to show that Jesus was the Savior. Since the court was unable to answer him, they decided to silence him for good. They stoned him to death while he prayed for their forgiveness.

Stephen's final words show how much he had become like Jesus in a short time. His death had a lasting effect on a young man named Saul, who would later change from fiercely destroying the growing church to radically defending it.

How many risks do you take as a follower of Jesus? Would you die for him? Do you live for him? Consider Stephen an example.

BOTTOM LINE: Striving for excellence in small assignments prepares a person for greater responsibilities.

Real understanding of God always leads to practical and compassionate actions.

Stephen's story is told in Acts 6:1–8:2. He also is mentioned in Acts 11:19; 22:20.

betrayed and murdered. ⁵³You deliberately disobeyed God's law, even though you received it from the hands of angels."

⁵⁴The Jewish leaders were infuriated by Stephen's accusation, and they shook their fists at him in rage.* ⁵⁵But Stephen, full of the Holy Spirit, gazed steadily into heaven and saw the glory of God, and he saw Jesus standing in the place of honor at God's right hand. ⁵⁶And he told them, "Look, I see the heavens opened and the Son of Man standing in the place of honor at God's right hand!"

⁵⁷Then they put their hands over their ears and began shouting. They rushed at him ⁵⁸and dragged him out of the city and began to stone him. His accusers took off their coats and laid them at the feet of a young man named Saul.*

⁵⁹As they stoned him, Stephen prayed, "Lord Jesus, receive my spirit." ⁶⁰He fell to his knees, shouting, "Lord, don't charge them with this sin!" And with that, he died.

8 Saul was one of the witnesses, and he agreed completely with the killing of Stephen.

PERSECUTION SCATTERS THE BELIEVERS A great wave of persecution began that day, sweeping over the church in Jerusalem; and all the believers except the apostles were scattered through the regions of Judea and Samaria. ²(Some devout men came and buried Stephen with great mourning.) ³But Saul was going everywhere to destroy the church. He went from house to house, dragging out both men and women to throw them into prison.

PHILIP PREACHES IN SAMARIA ⁴But the believers who were scattered preached the Good

News about Jesus wherever they went. ⁵Philip, for example, went to the city of Samaria and told the people there about the Messiah. ⁶Crowds listened intently to Philip because they were eager to hear his message and see the miraculous signs he did. ⁷Many evil* spirits were cast out, screaming as they left their victims. And many who had been paralyzed or lame were healed. ⁸So there was great joy in that city.

⁹A man named Simon had been a sorcerer there for many years, amazing the people of Samaria and claiming to be someone great. ¹⁰Everyone, from the least to the greatest, often spoke of him as "the Great One—the Power of God." ¹¹They listened closely to him because for a long time he had astounded them with his magic.

¹²But now the people believed Philip's message of Good News concerning the Kingdom of God and the name of Jesus Christ. As a result, many men and women were baptized. ¹³Then Simon himself believed and was baptized. He began following Philip wherever he went, and he was amazed by the signs and great miracles Philip performed.

¹⁴When the apostles in Jerusalem heard that the people of Samaria had accepted God's message, they sent Peter and John there. ¹⁵As soon as they arrived, they prayed for these new believers to receive the Holy Spirit. ¹⁶The Holy Spirit had not yet come upon any of them, for they had only been baptized in the name of the Lord Jesus. ¹⁷Then Peter and John laid their hands upon these believers, and they received the Holy Spirit.

¹⁸When Simon saw that the Spirit was given when the apostles laid their hands on people, he offered them money to buy this power. ¹⁹"Let me have this power, too," he exclaimed, "so that when I lay my hands on people, they will receive the Holy Spirit!"

²⁰But Peter replied, "May your money be destroyed with you for thinking God's gift can be bought! ²¹You can have no part in this, for your heart is not right with God. ²²Repent of your wickedness and pray to the Lord. Perhaps he will forgive your evil thoughts, ²³for I can see that you are full of bitter jealousy and are held captive by sin."

²⁴"Pray to the Lord for me," Simon exclaimed, "that these terrible things you've said won't happen to me!"

²⁵After testifying and preaching the word of the Lord in Samaria, Peter and John returned to

· ·

PRODUCTIVE DISCOMFORT
(8:4) Although persecuted believers were forced to move out of their homes in Jerusalem, the gospel was spread as a result. God can sometimes accomplish his purposes through the uncomfortable situations of our lives. Tempted to complain about uncomfortable or painful circumstances? Maybe God is preparing you for a special task.

THE WHOLE PACKAGE
(8:18-24) Simon wanted the power of the Holy Spirit, but not the Holy Spirit himself. Having the Holy Spirit would have meant giving up the right to run his own life. Likewise, many people want the gifts of God (the peace, power, or other provisions), but not the giver of those gifts. In other words, they don't want the whole package. Or, they want just a part of God: his love and his grace but not his judgment or discipline. How much do you want of God? Do you want the whole package or just a part? With God, it's all or nothing.

7:54 Greek *they were grinding their teeth against him.*   **7:58** *Saul* is later called Paul; see 13:9.   **8:7** Greek *unclean.*

Jerusalem. And they stopped in many Samaritan villages along the way to preach the Good News.

PHILIP AND THE ETHIOPIAN EUNUCH ²⁶As for Philip, an angel of the Lord said to him, "Go south* down the desert road that runs from Jerusalem to Gaza." ²⁷So he started out, and he met the treasurer of Ethiopia, a eunuch of great authority under the Kandake, the queen of Ethiopia. The eunuch had gone to Jerusalem to worship, ²⁸and he was now returning. Seated in his carriage, he was reading aloud from the book of the prophet Isaiah.

²⁹The Holy Spirit said to Philip, "Go over and walk along beside the carriage."

³⁰Philip ran over and heard the man reading from the prophet Isaiah. Philip asked, "Do you understand what you are reading?"

³¹The man replied, "How can I, unless someone instructs me?" And he urged Philip to come up into the carriage and sit with him.

³²The passage of Scripture he had been reading was this:

"He was led like a sheep to the slaughter.
     And as a lamb is silent before the
          shearers,
     he did not open his mouth.
³³ He was humiliated and received no justice.
     Who can speak of his descendants?
     For his life was taken from the earth."*

8:26 Or *Go at noon.*   **8:32-33** Isa 53:7-8 (Greek version).
8:36 Some manuscripts add verse 37, *"You can,"* Philip answered, *"if you believe with all your heart." And the eunuch replied, "I believe that Jesus Christ is the Son of God."*   **9:1** Greek *disciples.*

³⁴The eunuch asked Philip, "Tell me, was the prophet talking about himself or someone else?" ³⁵So beginning with this same Scripture, Philip told him the Good News about Jesus.

³⁶As they rode along, they came to some water, and the eunuch said, "Look! There's some water! Why can't I be baptized?"* ³⁸He ordered the carriage to stop, and they went down into the water, and Philip baptized him.

³⁹When they came up out of the water, the Spirit of the Lord snatched Philip away. The eunuch never saw him again but went on his way rejoicing. ⁴⁰Meanwhile, Philip found himself farther north at the town of Azotus. He preached the Good News there and in every town along the way until he came to Caesarea.

9 **SAUL'S CONVERSION** Meanwhile, Saul was uttering threats with every breath and was eager to kill the Lord's followers.* So he went to the high priest. ²He requested letters addressed to the synagogues in Damascus, asking for their cooperation in the arrest of any followers of the Way he found there. He wanted

....

REACHING THE UNREACHABLE
(9:1-16) Ananias had trouble believing that Saul, the persecutor of Christians, was now a believer. Yet Saul had met the risen Christ in a dramatic way. Have you ever doubted that someone really believes in Jesus? Or, maybe you've thought that some people are impossible to reach for Christ. They're too hard, too stubborn, too whatever (fill in your own adjective) for God to change. With God, nothing is impossible (Gen 18:14; Luke 1:37). He can reach even the "unreachable."

I WONDER...

Some kids at school (and even some teachers) give Christians a pretty tough time. This makes me not want to let anyone know I'm a believer. What should I do?

Rejection comes with being a Christian because our lives and beliefs go against the flow of the rest of the world. Growing closer to God will naturally make you grow farther away from the world.

   Read Acts 7:54-60. Stephen took a stand for Christ that cost him much more than rejection from a few friends. It cost him his life. Read further, and in Acts 8 and 9 you will see what the results of a fearless faith can be.

   Imagine being able to see all of history from beginning to end. You would understand so much more because you could see the whole picture. But only God can do that—so we have to trust him. We have to live on this earth without being able to see the future.

If Stephen had known what his death would accomplish, he would have died smiling. A man named Paul (Saul) was one of the foremost persecutors of Christians. But Paul's life was turned around, and he became a follower of Christ. Paul had heard Stephen speak—and he had watched him die.

   Paul didn't just become a church-only, pew-sitter type of follower. He traveled throughout the world, sharing the Good News about Christ. He also wrote nearly half of the books of the New Testament! Stephen's rejection helped bring Paul to Christ.

   People are watching you and other Christians at school. They are seeing how you respond to rejection and verbal abuse. Within those crowded halls are people who want to believe in something true, something worth living for no matter what the cost. And when they find it, they may make an incredible impact in their world for Christ.

   What do they learn from watching you?

to bring them—both men and women—back to Jerusalem in chains.

³As he was approaching Damascus on this mission, a light from heaven suddenly shone down around him. ⁴He fell to the ground and heard a voice saying to him, "Saul! Saul! Why are you persecuting me?"

⁵"Who are you, lord?" Saul asked.

And the voice replied, "I am Jesus, the one you are persecuting! ⁶Now get up and go into the city, and you will be told what you must do."

⁷The men with Saul stood speechless, for they heard the sound of someone's voice but saw no one! ⁸Saul picked himself up off the ground, but when he opened his eyes he was blind. So his companions led him by the hand to Damascus. ⁹He remained there blind for three days and did not eat or drink.

¹⁰Now there was a believer* in Damascus named Ananias. The Lord spoke to him in a vision, calling, "Ananias!"

"Yes, Lord!" he replied.

¹¹The Lord said, "Go over to Straight Street, to the house of Judas. When you get there, ask for a man from Tarsus named Saul. He is praying to me right now. ¹²I have shown him in a vision of a man named Ananias coming in and laying hands on him so he can see again."

¹³"But Lord," exclaimed Ananias, "I've heard many people talk about the terrible things this man has done to the believers* in Jerusalem! ¹⁴And he is authorized by the leading priests to arrest everyone who calls upon your name."

¹⁵But the Lord said, "Go, for Saul is my chosen instrument to take my message to the Gentiles and to kings, as well as to the people of Israel. ¹⁶And I will show him how much he must suffer for my name's sake."

¹⁷So Ananias went and found Saul. He laid his hands on him and said, "Brother Saul, the Lord Jesus, who appeared to you on the road, has sent me so that you might regain your sight and be filled with the Holy Spirit." ¹⁸Instantly something like scales fell from Saul's eyes, and he regained his sight. Then he got up and was baptized. ¹⁹Afterward he ate some food and regained his strength.

SAUL IN DAMASCUS AND JERUSALEM
Saul stayed with the believers* in Damascus for a few days. ²⁰And immediately he began preaching about Jesus in the synagogues, saying, "He is indeed the Son of God!"

²¹All who heard him were amazed. "Isn't this the same man who caused such devastation among Jesus' followers in Jerusalem?" they asked. "And didn't he come here to arrest them and take them in chains to the leading priests?"

²²Saul's preaching became more and more powerful, and the Jews in Damascus couldn't refute his proofs that Jesus was indeed the Messiah. ²³After a while some of the Jews plotted together to kill him. ²⁴They were watching for him day and night at the city gate so they could murder him, but Saul was told about their plot. ²⁵So during the night, some of the other believers* lowered him in a large basket through an opening in the city wall.

²⁶When Saul arrived in Jerusalem, he tried to meet with the believers, but they were all afraid of him. They did not believe he had truly become a believer! ²⁷Then Barnabas brought him to the apostles and told them how Saul had seen the Lord on the way to Damascus and how the Lord had spoken to Saul. He also told them that Saul had preached boldly in the name of Jesus in Damascus.

²⁸So Saul stayed with the apostles and went all around Jerusalem with them, preaching boldly in the name of the Lord. ²⁹He debated with some Greek-speaking Jews, but they tried to murder him. ³⁰When the believers* heard about this, they took him down to Caesarea and sent him away to Tarsus, his hometown.

³¹The church then had peace throughout Judea, Galilee, and Samaria, and it became stronger as the believers lived in the fear of the Lord. And with the encouragement of the Holy Spirit, it also grew in numbers.

PETER HEALS AENEAS AND RAISES DORCAS
³²Meanwhile, Peter traveled from place to place, and he came down to visit the believers in the town of Lydda. ³³There he met a man named Aeneas, who had been paralyzed and bedridden for eight years. ³⁴Peter said to him, "Aeneas, Jesus Christ heals you! Get up, and roll up your sleeping mat!" And he was healed instantly. ³⁵Then the whole population of Lydda and Sharon saw Aeneas walking around, and they turned to the Lord.

³⁶There was a believer in Joppa named Tabitha (which in Greek is Dorcas*). She was always doing kind things for others and helping the poor. ³⁷About this time she became ill and died. Her body was washed for burial and laid in an upstairs room. ³⁸But the believers had heard that Peter was nearby at Lydda, so they sent two men to beg him, "Please come as soon as possible!"

9:10 Greek *disciple;* also in 9:26, 36. 9:13 Greek *God's holy people;* also in 9:32, 41. 9:19 Greek *disciples;* also in 9:26, 38. 9:25 Greek *his disciples.* 9:30 Greek *brothers.* 9:36 The names *Tabitha* in Aramaic and *Dorcas* in Greek both mean "gazelle."

³⁹So Peter returned with them; and as soon as he arrived, they took him to the upstairs room. The room was filled with widows who were weeping and showing him the coats and other clothes Dorcas had made for them. ⁴⁰But Peter asked them all to leave the room; then he knelt and prayed. Turning to the body he said, "Get up, Tabitha." And she opened her eyes! When she saw Peter, she sat up! ⁴¹He gave her his hand and helped her up. Then he called in the widows and all the believers, and he presented her to them alive.

⁴²The news spread through the whole town, and many believed in the Lord. ⁴³And Peter stayed a long time in Joppa, living with Simon, a tanner of hides.

10:1 Greek *a centurion*; similarly in 10:22.

10 CORNELIUS CALLS FOR PETER In Caesarea there lived a Roman army officer* named Cornelius, who was a captain of the Italian Regiment. ²He was a devout, God-fearing man, as was everyone in his household. He gave generously to the poor and prayed regularly to God. ³One afternoon about three o'clock, he had a vision in which he saw an

KINDNESS
(9:36-42) *Dorcas never preached a sermon like Peter or Paul. Yet she had an enormous impact on her community by "doing kind things for others and helping the poor." When she died, the room was filled with mourners, people she had helped. Do you have this kind of impact on your community? Kindness is one "fruit" that all believers can have (see Gal 5:22).*

PERSONALITY PROFILE PAUL

UPS:
- *Transformed by God from a persecutor of Christians to a preacher for Christ*
- *Preached for Christ throughout the Roman Empire on three missionary journeys*
- *Wrote letters to various churches; those letters were collected and became part of the New Testament*
- *Was never afraid to face an issue head-on and deal with it*
- *Was sensitive to God's leading and, despite his strong personality, always did as God directed*
- *Is often called the apostle to the Gentiles*

DOWNS:
- *Witnessed and approved of Stephen's stoning*
- *Set out to destroy Christianity by persecuting Christians*

STATS:
- *Where: Born in Tarsus, but became a world traveler for Christ*
- *Occupations: Trained as a Pharisee; learned the tentmaking trade; served as a missionary*
- *Contemporaries: Gamaliel, Stephen, the apostles, Luke, Barnabas, Timothy*

KEY VERSES: *Phil 1:21-24*

HAVE YOU EVER THOUGHT YOU WERE TOTALLY RIGHT ABOUT SOMETHING, but wound up being totally wrong? That was Paul in a nutshell.

Paul—or Saul, the Hebrew version of his name—was a leader in the frenzied persecution of Christians following Stephen's death. Eventually, Paul met Christ personally, and his life was changed. Paul never lost his energy and intensity, however; instead, they were redirected to spread the gospel. No person, apart from Jesus himself, shaped the history of Christianity as much as the apostle Paul.

Paul was an expert on the Old Testament and was a member of the Jewish council. Since he was convinced that Christianity was dangerous to Judaism, Paul hated the Christian faith and persecuted Christians without mercy. At one point, Paul received permission from the high priest to travel to Damascus to arrest Christians and bring them back to Jerusalem. His plans would have resulted in the death of many believers, but God had other plans. After an encounter with the risen Christ on the road to Damascus, Paul's life changed forever.

He became God's ambassador to the Gentiles. Until Paul was converted, little had been done to carry Christ's message to non-Jewish people. Paul and his missionary teams eventually carried the gospel across the Roman Empire.

Although Paul worked hard to convince the Jews that Gentiles were acceptable to God, he spent even more time convincing Gentiles themselves that they were acceptable to God. People were changed and challenged by meeting Christ through Paul.

God used everything that made up Paul's life—his background, his training, his citizenship, his mind, and even his weaknesses—to add people to the church, the body of Christ. Are you willing to let God do the same for you? You'll never know what he can do with you until you allow him to have all that you are!

BOTTOM LINE: The Good News is that forgiveness and eternal life are a gift of God's grace received by faith in Christ and available to all people.

Obedience results from a relationship with God, but obedience will never create or earn that relationship.

God will use our past and present so that we may serve him with our future.

Paul's story is told in Acts 7:58–28:31 and throughout his New Testament letters.

angel of God coming toward him. "Cornelius!" the angel said.

⁴Cornelius stared at him in terror. "What is it, sir?" he asked the angel.

And the angel replied, "Your prayers and gifts to the poor have been received by God as an offering! ⁵Now send some men to Joppa, and summon a man named Simon Peter. ⁶He is staying with Simon, a tanner who lives near the seashore."

⁷As soon as the angel was gone, Cornelius called two of his household servants and a devout soldier, one of his personal attendants. ⁸He told them what had happened and sent them off to Joppa.

PETER VISITS CORNELIUS

⁹The next day as Cornelius's messengers were nearing the town, Peter went up on the flat roof to pray. It was about noon, ¹⁰and he was hungry. But while a meal was being prepared, he fell into a trance. ¹¹He saw the sky open, and something like a large sheet was let down by its four corners. ¹²In the sheet were all sorts of animals, reptiles, and birds. ¹³Then a voice said to him, "Get up, Peter; kill and eat them."

¹⁴"No, Lord," Peter declared. "I have never eaten anything that our Jewish laws have declared impure and unclean.*"

¹⁵But the voice spoke again: "Do not call something unclean if God has made it clean." ¹⁶The same vision was repeated three times. Then the sheet was suddenly pulled up to heaven.

¹⁷Peter was very perplexed. What could the vision mean? Just then the men sent by Cornelius found Simon's house. Standing outside the gate, ¹⁸they asked if a man named Simon Peter was staying there.

¹⁹Meanwhile, as Peter was puzzling over the vision, the Holy Spirit said to him, "Three men have come looking for you. ²⁰Get up, go downstairs, and go with them without hesitation. Don't worry, for I have sent them."

²¹So Peter went down and said, "I'm the man you are looking for. Why have you come?"

²²They said, "We were sent by Cornelius, a Roman officer. He is a devout and God-fearing man, well respected by all the Jews. A holy angel instructed him to summon you to his house so that he can hear your message." ²³So Peter invited the men to stay for the night. The next day he went with them, accompanied by some of the brothers from Joppa.

²⁴They arrived in Caesarea the following day. Cornelius was waiting for them and had called together his relatives and close friends. ²⁵As

Peter entered his home, Cornelius fell at his feet and worshiped him. ²⁶But Peter pulled him up and said, "Stand up! I'm a human being just like you!" ²⁷So they talked together and went inside, where many others were assembled.

²⁸Peter told them, "You know it is against our laws for a Jewish man to enter a Gentile home like this or to associate with you. But God has shown me that I should no longer think of anyone as impure or unclean. ²⁹So I came without objection as soon as I was sent for. Now tell me why you sent for me."

³⁰Cornelius replied, "Four days ago I was praying in my house about this same time, three o'clock in the afternoon. Suddenly, a man in dazzling clothes was standing in front of me. ³¹He told me, 'Cornelius, your prayer has been heard, and your gifts to the poor have been noticed by God! ³²Now send messengers to Joppa, and summon a man named Simon Peter. He is staying in the home of Simon, a tanner who lives near the seashore.' ³³So I sent for you at once, and it was good of you to come. Now we are all here, waiting before God to hear the message the Lord has given you."

THE GENTILES HEAR THE GOOD NEWS

³⁴Then Peter replied, "I see very clearly that God shows no favoritism. ³⁵In every nation he accepts those who fear him and do what is right. ³⁶This is the message of Good News for the people of Israel—that there is peace with God through Jesus Christ, who is Lord of all. ³⁷You know what happened throughout Judea, beginning in Galilee, after John began preaching his message of baptism. ³⁸And you know that God anointed Jesus of Nazareth with the Holy Spirit and with power. Then Jesus went around doing good and healing all who were oppressed by the devil, for God was with him.

³⁹"And we apostles are witnesses of all he did throughout Judea and in Jerusalem. They put him to death by hanging him on a cross,* ⁴⁰but God raised him to life on the third day. Then God allowed him to appear, ⁴¹not to the general public,* but to us whom God had chosen in advance to be his witnesses. We were those who ate and drank with him after he rose from the dead. ⁴²And he ordered us to preach everywhere and to testify that Jesus is the one appointed by God to be the judge of all—the living and the dead. ⁴³He is the one all the prophets testified about, saying that

10:14 Greek *anything common and unclean.* 10:39 Greek *on a tree.*
10:41 Greek *the people.*

everyone who believes in him will have their sins forgiven through his name."

THE GENTILES RECEIVE THE HOLY SPIRIT

⁴⁴Even as Peter was saying these things, the Holy Spirit fell upon all who were listening to the message. ⁴⁵The Jewish believers* who came with Peter were amazed that the gift of the Holy Spirit had been poured out on the Gentiles, too. ⁴⁶For they heard them speaking in other tongues* and praising God.

Then Peter asked, ⁴⁷"Can anyone object to their being baptized, now that they have received the Holy Spirit just as we did?" ⁴⁸So he gave orders for them to be baptized in the name of Jesus Christ. Afterward Cornelius asked him to stay with them for several days.

11 PETER EXPLAINS HIS ACTIONS Soon the news reached the apostles and other believers* in Judea that the Gentiles had received the word of God. ²But when Peter arrived back in Jerusalem, the Jewish believers* criticized him. ³"You entered the home of Gentiles* and even ate with them!" they said.

⁴Then Peter told them exactly what had happened. ⁵"I was in the town of Joppa," he said, "and while I was praying, I went into a trance and saw a vision. Something like a large sheet was let down by its four corners from the sky. And it came right down to me. ⁶When I looked inside the sheet, I saw all sorts of tame and wild animals, reptiles, and birds. ⁷And I heard a voice say, 'Get up, Peter; kill and eat them.'

⁸"'No, Lord,' I replied. 'I have never eaten anything that our Jewish laws have declared impure or unclean.*'

⁹"But the voice from heaven spoke again: 'Do not call something unclean if God has made it clean.' ¹⁰This happened three times before the sheet and all it contained was pulled back up to heaven.

¹¹"Just then three men who had been sent from Caesarea arrived at the house where we were staying. ¹²The Holy Spirit told me to go with them and not to worry that they were Gentiles. These six brothers here accompanied me, and we soon entered the home of the man who had sent for us. ¹³He told us how an angel had appeared to him in his home and had told him, 'Send messengers to Joppa, and summon a man named Simon Peter. ¹⁴He will

tell you how you and everyone in your household can be saved!'

¹⁵"As I began to speak," Peter continued, "the Holy Spirit fell on them, just as he fell on us at the beginning. ¹⁶Then I thought of the Lord's words when he said, 'John baptized with* water, but you will be baptized with the Holy Spirit.' ¹⁷And since God gave these Gentiles the same gift he gave us when we believed in the Lord Jesus Christ, who was I to stand in God's way?"

¹⁸When the others heard this, they stopped objecting and began praising God. They said, "We can see that God has also given the Gentiles the privilege of repenting of their sins and receiving eternal life."

THE CHURCH IN ANTIOCH OF SYRIA

¹⁹Meanwhile, the believers who had been scattered during the persecution after Stephen's death traveled as far as Phoenicia, Cyprus, and Antioch of Syria. They preached the word of God, but only to Jews. ²⁰However, some of the believers who went to Antioch from Cyprus and Cyrene began preaching to the Gentiles* about the Lord Jesus. ²¹The power of the Lord was with them, and a large number of these Gentiles believed and turned to the Lord.

²²When the church at Jerusalem heard what had happened, they sent Barnabas to Antioch. ²³When he arrived and saw this evidence of God's blessing, he was filled with joy, and he encouraged the believers to stay true to the Lord. ²⁴Barnabas was a good man, full of the Holy Spirit and strong in faith. And many people were brought to the Lord.

²⁵Then Barnabas went on to Tarsus to look for Saul. ²⁶When he found him, he brought him back to Antioch. Both of them stayed there with

10:45 Greek *The faithful ones of the circumcision.* 10:46 Or *in other languages.* 11:1 Greek *brothers.* 11:2 Greek *those of the circumcision.* 11:3 Greek *of uncircumcised men.* 11:8 Greek *anything common or unclean.* 11:16 Or *in;* also in 11:16b. 11:20 Greek *the Hellenists* (i.e., those who speak Greek); other manuscripts read *the Greeks.*

EAGER
(10:48) Cornelius wanted Peter to stay with him for several days. As a new believer, Cornelius realized his need for teaching and fellowship. Are you that eager to learn more about Christ? Recognize your need to be with more mature Christians, and then learn from them.

THE WHOLE STORY
(11:1-18) When Peter brought the news of Cornelius's conversion back to Jerusalem, the believers were shocked that he had eaten with Gentiles. Why were they shocked? Because Peter risked being contaminated by foods that were "unclean" under Jewish law (see Lev 11). After they heard the whole story, however, they began praising God (11:18). Their reactions teach us how to handle disagreements with other Christians. Before judging the behavior of fellow believers, we need to hear them out. The Holy Spirit may be using them to teach us something important.

THINK ABOUT THE PEOPLE WHO REALLY MATTER IN YOUR LIFE. Odds are that many of them are encouragers who have found ways to help you keep going. Good friends can tell when you're doing well and when you need to try harder. Mostly, they never give up on you! Everyone needs that kind of encouragement.

Among the first Christians, a man named Joseph was such an encourager that other believers nicknamed him "Son of Encouragement," or "Barnabas" (Acts 4:36). Barnabas had an unusual ability to find people he could help. Whenever Barnabas encouraged Christians, the result was that others became believers!

Barnabas's actions were crucial to the early church. In a way, we can thank him for most of the New Testament. God used Barnabas's relationship with Paul at one point and with Mark at another to help these two men when either might have failed. Barnabas did wonders with encouragement.

We're surrounded by people we can encourage. Think about this: are you faster at encouraging others or criticizing them? Although showing people where they're wrong may be important at times, we'll be of greater help in the long run if we encourage people. How will you encourage others today?

BOTTOM LINE: Encouragement is one of the most effective ways to help others.

Sooner or later, true obedience to God will involve risk.

There is always someone who needs encouragement.

Barnabas's story is told in Acts 4:36-37; 9:27; 11:25-30; 12:25–15:39. He also is mentioned in 1 Corinthians 9:6; Galatians 2:1, 9-13; Colossians 4:10.

UPS:
- One of the first to sell his possessions to help the Christians in Jerusalem
- Paul's first missionary partner
- Was an encourager, as his nickname shows, and thus one of the most quietly influential people in the early days of Christianity
- Called an apostle, although not one of the original Twelve

DOWNS:
- Temporarily stayed aloof from Gentile believers until Paul corrected him

STATS:
- Where: Cyprus, Jerusalem, Antioch
- Occupation: Missionary, teacher
- Relatives: Mary (sister); John Mark (cousin)
- Contemporaries: Peter, Silas, Paul, Herod Agrippa I

KEY VERSES: Acts 11:23-24

---

the church for a full year, teaching large crowds of people. (It was at Antioch that the believers* were first called Christians.)

²⁷During this time some prophets traveled from Jerusalem to Antioch. ²⁸One of them named Agabus stood up in one of the meetings and predicted by the Spirit that a great famine was coming upon the entire Roman world. (This was fulfilled during the reign of Claudius.) ²⁹So the believers in Antioch decided to send relief to the brothers and sisters* in Judea, everyone giving as much as they could. ³⁰This they did, entrusting their gifts to Barnabas and Saul to take to the elders of the church in Jerusalem.

12 **JAMES IS KILLED AND PETER IS IMPRISONED** About that time King Herod Agrippa* began to persecute some believers in the church. ²He had the apostle James (John's

ANSWERS
(12:5-15) *The prayers of the little group of believers were answered, even as they prayed. But when the answer arrived at the door, they didn't believe it. Sometimes the answer to a prayer might be staring us in the face. When you pray, believe you'll get an answer. When the answer comes, don't be surprised!*

brother) killed with a sword. ³When Herod saw how much this pleased the Jewish people, he also arrested Peter. (This took place during the Passover celebration.*) ⁴Then he imprisoned him, placing him under the guard of four squads of four soldiers each. Herod intended to bring Peter out for public trial after the Passover. ⁵But while Peter was in prison, the church prayed very earnestly for him.

PETER'S MIRACULOUS ESCAPE FROM PRISON
⁶The night before Peter was to be placed on trial, he was asleep, fastened with two chains between two soldiers. Others stood guard at the prison gate. ⁷Suddenly, there was a bright light in the cell, and an angel of the Lord stood before Peter. The angel struck him on the side to awaken him and said, "Quick! Get up!" And the chains fell off his wrists. ⁸Then the angel told him, "Get dressed and put on your sandals." And he did. "Now put on your coat and follow me," the angel ordered.

⁹So Peter left the cell, following the angel. But all the time he thought it was a vision. He

11:26 Greek *disciples;* also in 11:29.   **11:29** Greek *the brothers.*
12:1 Greek *Herod the king.* He was the nephew of Herod Antipas and a grandson of Herod the Great.   **12:3** Greek *the days of unleavened bread.*

didn't realize it was actually happening. ¹⁰They passed the first and second guard posts and came to the iron gate leading to the city, and this opened for them all by itself. So they passed through and started walking down the street, and then the angel suddenly left him.

¹¹Peter finally came to his senses. "It's really true!" he said. "The Lord has sent his angel and saved me from Herod and from what the Jewish leaders* had planned to do to me!"

¹²When he realized this, he went to the home of Mary, the mother of John Mark, where many were gathered for prayer. ¹³He knocked at the door in the gate, and a servant girl named Rhoda came to open it. ¹⁴When she recognized Peter's voice, she was so overjoyed that, instead of opening the door, she ran back inside and told everyone, "Peter is standing at the door!"

¹⁵"You're out of your mind!" they said. When she insisted, they decided, "It must be his angel."

¹⁶Meanwhile, Peter continued knocking. When they finally opened the door and saw him, they were amazed. ¹⁷He motioned for them to quiet down and told them how the Lord had led him out of prison. "Tell James and the other brothers what happened," he said. And then he went to another place.

¹⁸At dawn there was a great commotion among the soldiers about what had happened to Peter. ¹⁹Herod Agrippa ordered a thorough search for him. When he couldn't be found, Herod interrogated the guards and sentenced them to death. Afterward Herod left Judea to stay in Caesarea for a while.

12:11 Or the Jewish people.   12:25 Or mission, they returned to Jerusalem. Other manuscripts read mission, they returned from Jerusalem; still others read mission, they returned from Jerusalem to Antioch.   13:1a Greek who was called Niger.   13:1b Greek Herod the tetrarch.

THE DEATH OF HEROD AGRIPPA ²⁰Now Herod was very angry with the people of Tyre and Sidon. So they sent a delegation to make peace with him because their cities were dependent upon Herod's country for food. The delegates won the support of Blastus, Herod's personal assistant, ²¹and an appointment with Herod was granted. When the day arrived, Herod put on his royal robes, sat on his throne, and made a speech to them. ²²The people gave him a great ovation, shouting, "It's the voice of a god, not of a man!"

²³Instantly, an angel of the Lord struck Herod with a sickness, because he accepted the people's worship instead of giving the glory to God. So he was consumed with worms and died.

²⁴Meanwhile, the word of God continued to spread, and there were many new believers.

²⁵When Barnabas and Saul had finished their mission to Jerusalem, they returned,* taking John Mark with them.

13 **BARNABAS AND SAUL ARE COMMISSIONED** Among the prophets and teachers of the church at Antioch of Syria were Barnabas, Simeon (called "the black man"*), Lucius (from Cyrene), Manaen (the childhood companion of King Herod Antipas*), and Saul. ²One day as these men were worshiping the Lord and fasting, the Holy Spirit said, "Dedicate Barnabas and Saul for the special work

THREAD
(13:1) What variety there is in the church! The only common thread among these five men was their deep faith in Christ. We must never exclude anyone whom Christ has called to follow him.

CHOICES
pride

Seventeen-year-old Leslie loves music and has always wanted to sing, and not just in the youth choir at church or the high school choir. She wants to be an "American Idol," performing in an auditorium packed with cheering fans.

Leslie is talented and practices a lot. Every now and then she gets to do solos at church. But last night, she finally got the big break she's been hoping for. She sang three songs at a huge youth rally (with over 2,000 teens) in a city 250 miles away. There she was in the spotlight on a big stage, using professional sound equipment managed by top-notch technicians. For that she was paid $500! We're talking "big time"!

Well, it went great. The audience loved her. Afterward, a handful of youth pastors asked her, "Can I book you to sing for my group?" People complimented her like crazy, tossing around words and phrases like "wonderful," "beautiful," and "going places." Some even asked when her first CD would be out. The killer was the group of younger kids who asked Leslie to autograph their Bibles!

The day after, Leslie is still basking in her sudden success. She barely wants to talk to her friends, who suddenly don't seem as successful.

Why is success or admiration/adulation so difficult to handle sometimes? Where do our talents come from? What happens if we forget God and snatch all of the glory for ourselves? Check out Acts 12:20-23. What would you say to Leslie based on this passage?

to which I have called them." ³So after more fasting and prayer, the men laid their hands on them and sent them on their way.

PAUL'S FIRST MISSIONARY JOURNEY

⁴So Barnabas and Saul were sent out by the Holy Spirit. They went down to the seaport of Seleucia and then sailed for the island of Cyprus. ⁵There, in the town of Salamis, they went to the Jewish synagogues and preached the word of God. John Mark went with them as their assistant.

⁶Afterward they traveled from town to town across the entire island until finally they reached Paphos, where they met a Jewish sorcerer, a false prophet named Bar-Jesus. ⁷He had attached himself to the governor, Sergius Paulus, who was an intelligent man. The governor invited Barnabas and Saul to visit him, for he wanted to hear the word of God. ⁸But Elymas, the sorcerer (as his name means in Greek), interfered and urged the governor to pay no attention to what Barnabas and Saul said. He was trying to keep the governor from believing.

⁹Saul, also known as Paul, was filled with the Holy Spirit, and he looked the sorcerer in the eye. ¹⁰Then he said, "You son of the devil, full of every sort of deceit and fraud, and enemy of all that is good! Will you never stop perverting the true ways of the Lord? ¹¹Watch now, for the Lord has laid his hand of punishment upon you, and you will be struck blind. You will not see the sunlight for some time." Instantly mist and darkness came over the man's eyes, and he began groping around begging for someone to take his hand and lead him.

¹²When the governor saw what had happened, he became a believer, for he was astonished at the teaching about the Lord.

JOHN MARK
PERSONALITY PROFILE

WHAT DID YOU LEARN FROM YOUR LAST MISTAKE? Mistakes can be effective teachers because the consequences have a way of making lessons painfully clear. But those who learn from their mistakes gain wisdom.

John Mark, with the help of some time and encouragement, became a wise learner. Although he was eager to do what was right, he had trouble staying on task. In his Gospel, Mark mentions a young man (probably himself) who fled in such fear during Jesus' arrest that he left his clothes behind (Mark 14:50-52). This tendency to run showed up again later in Mark's life when Paul and Barnabas took him as their assistant on their first missionary journey. Early in the trip, Mark left them and returned to Jerusalem (see Acts 12:25–13:13).

Paul didn't appreciate Mark's desertion. Two years later, Paul wouldn't even consider letting Mark try again. As a result, the team split up (Acts 15:36-39). Barnabas took his cousin Mark as his traveling companion, while Paul chose Silas.

Barnabas was patient with Mark, and the young man turned out to be a good investment. In fact, Paul and Mark were later reunited and the older apostle became a close friend of the young disciple (see 2 Tim 4:11).

Mark was able to watch closely the lives of three Christian leaders— Barnabas, Paul, and Peter. Peter probably provided much of the information in Mark's Gospel. As his helper, Mark had a chance to hear Peter's stories of the years with Jesus over and over. Mark became one of the first to put Jesus' life into writing.

Barnabas played a key role in Mark's life. He stood beside the young man in his failure, giving him patient encouragement. Mark's experience can remind us to learn from our mistakes and to appreciate the patience of others. Who is the Barnabas or Peter in your life? How has he or she encouraged you?

BOTTOM LINE: Maturity comes as a result of learning from mistakes, not the absence of them.

Effective living is not measured by what we accomplish as much as it is by what we overcome in order to accomplish our goals.

Encouragement can change a person's life.

John Mark's story is told in Acts 12:25–13:13 and 15:36-39. He also is mentioned in Colossians 4:10; 2 Timothy 4:11; Philemon 1:24; and 1 Peter 5:13.

UPS:
- *Wrote the Gospel of Mark*
- *Allowed his home to be used as one of the main meeting places for Christians in Jerusalem*
- *Persisted beyond his youthful mistakes*
- *Was an assistant and traveling companion to three of the greatest early missionaries*

DOWNS:
- *Probably the nameless young man described in the Gospel of Mark who fled in panic when Jesus was arrested*
- *Left Paul and Barnabas during the first missionary journey*

STATS:
- *Where: Jerusalem*
- *Occupation: Missionary-in-training, Gospel writer, traveling companion*
- *Relatives: Mary (mother); Barnabas (cousin)*
- *Contemporaries: Paul, Peter, Timothy, Luke, Silas*

KEY VERSE: *2 Tim 4:11*

PAUL PREACHES IN ANTIOCH OF PISIDIA

¹³Paul and his companions then left Paphos by ship for Pamphylia, landing at the port town of Perga. There John Mark left them and returned to Jerusalem. ¹⁴But Paul and Barnabas traveled inland to Antioch of Pisidia.*

On the Sabbath they went to the synagogue for the services. ¹⁵After the usual readings from the books of Moses* and the prophets, those in charge of the service sent them this message: "Brothers, if you have any word of encouragement for the people, come and give it."

¹⁶So Paul stood, lifted his hand to quiet them, and started speaking. "Men of Israel," he said, "and you God-fearing Gentiles, listen to me.

¹⁷"The God of this nation of Israel chose our ancestors and made them multiply and grow strong during their stay in Egypt. Then with a powerful arm he led them out of their slavery. ¹⁸He put up with them* through forty years of wandering in the wilderness. ¹⁹Then he destroyed seven nations in Canaan and gave their land to Israel as an inheritance. ²⁰All this took about 450 years.

"After that, God gave them judges to rule until the time of Samuel the prophet. ²¹Then the people begged for a king, and God gave them Saul son of Kish, a man of the tribe of Benjamin, who reigned for forty years. ²²But God removed Saul and replaced him with David, a man about whom God said, 'I have found David son of Jesse, a man after my own heart. He will do everything I want him to do.'*

²³"And it is one of King David's descendants, Jesus, who is God's promised Savior of Israel! ²⁴Before he came, John the Baptist preached that all the people of Israel needed to repent of their sins and turn to God and be baptized. ²⁵As John was finishing his ministry he asked, 'Do you think I am the Messiah? No, I am not! But he is coming soon—and I'm not even worthy to be his slave and untie the sandals on his feet.'

²⁶"Brothers—you sons of Abraham, and also you God-fearing Gentiles—this message of salvation has been sent to us! ²⁷The people in Jerusalem and their leaders did not recognize Jesus as the one the prophets had spoken about. Instead, they condemned him, and in doing this they fulfilled the prophets' words

that are read every Sabbath. ²⁸They found no legal reason to execute him, but they asked Pilate to have him killed anyway.

²⁹"When they had done all that the prophecies said about him, they took him down from the cross* and placed him in a tomb. ³⁰But God raised him from the dead! ³¹And over a period of many days he appeared to those who had gone with him from Galilee to Jerusalem. They are now his witnesses to the people of Israel.

³²"And now we are here to bring you this Good News. The promise was made to our ancestors, ³³and God has now fulfilled it for us, their descendants, by raising Jesus. This is what the second psalm says about Jesus:

'You are my Son.
Today I have become your Father.*'

³⁴For God had promised to raise him from the dead, not leaving him to rot in the grave. He said, 'I will give you the sacred blessings I promised to David.'* ³⁵Another psalm explains it more fully: 'You will not allow your Holy One to rot in the grave.'* ³⁶This is not a reference to David, for after David had done the will of God in his own generation, he died and was buried with his ancestors, and his body decayed. ³⁷No, it was a reference to someone else—someone whom God raised and whose body did not decay.

³⁸*"Brothers, listen! We are here to proclaim that through this man Jesus there is forgiveness for your sins. ³⁹Everyone who believes in him is declared right with God—something the law of Moses could never do. ⁴⁰Be careful! Don't let the prophets' words apply to you. For they said,

⁴¹ 'Look, you mockers,
    be amazed and die!
For I am doing something in your own day,
    something you wouldn't believe
    even if someone told you about it.'*"

⁴²As Paul and Barnabas left the synagogue that day, the people begged them to speak about these things again the next week. ⁴³Many Jews and devout converts to Judaism followed Paul and Barnabas, and the two men urged them to continue to rely on the grace of God.

....

FROM JEALOUSY TO JOY
(13:42-45) Although the Jewish leaders brought theological arguments against Paul and Barnabas, jealousy was the real reason behind their denunciation. When we see others succeeding where we haven't or receiving the glory that we want, we may feel envy instead of feeling happy for them. Is that your response? With God's help, we can rise above envy or jealousy and rejoice.

13:13-14 *Pamphylia* and *Pisidia* were districts in what is now Turkey. **13:15** Greek *from the law.* **13:18** Some manuscripts read *He cared for them;* compare Deut 1:31. **13:22** 1 Sam 13:14. **13:29** Greek *from the tree.* **13:33** Or *Today I reveal you as my Son.* Ps 2:7. **13:34** Isa 55:3. **13:35** Ps 16:10. **13:38** English translations divide verses 38 and 39 in various ways. **13:41** Hab 1:5 (Greek version).

PAUL'S FIRST MISSIONARY JOURNEY (ACTS 13:1—14:28)

PAUL TURNS TO THE GENTILES ⁴⁴The following week almost the entire city turned out to hear them preach the word of the Lord. ⁴⁵But when some of the Jews saw the crowds, they were jealous; so they slandered Paul and argued against whatever he said.

⁴⁶Then Paul and Barnabas spoke out boldly and declared, "It was necessary that we first preach the word of God to you Jews. But since you have rejected it and judged yourselves unworthy of eternal life, we will offer it to the Gentiles. ⁴⁷For the Lord gave us this command when he said,

'I have made you a light to the Gentiles,
    to bring salvation to the farthest corners
        of the earth.'*"

⁴⁸When the Gentiles heard this, they were very glad and thanked the Lord for his message; and all who were chosen for eternal life became believers. ⁴⁹So the Lord's message spread throughout that region.

⁵⁰Then the Jews stirred up the influential religious women and the leaders of the city, and they incited a mob against Paul and Barnabas and ran them out of town. ⁵¹So they shook the dust from their feet as a sign of rejection and went to the town of Iconium. ⁵²And the believers* were filled with joy and with the Holy Spirit.

14 PAUL AND BARNABAS IN ICONIUM

The same thing happened in Iconium.* Paul and Barnabas went to the Jewish synagogue and preached with such power that a great number of both Jews and Greeks became believers. ²Some of the Jews, however, spurned God's message and poisoned the minds of the Gentiles against Paul and Barnabas. ³But the apostles stayed there a long time, preaching boldly about the grace of the Lord. And the Lord proved their message was true by giving them power to do miraculous signs and wonders. ⁴But the people of the town were divided in their opinion about them. Some sided with the Jews, and some with the apostles.

⁵Then a mob of Gentiles and Jews, along with their leaders, decided to attack and stone them. ⁶When the apostles learned of it, they fled to the region of Lycaonia—to the towns of Lystra and Derbe and the surrounding area. ⁷And there they preached the Good News.

PAUL AND BARNABAS IN LYSTRA AND DERBE
⁸While they were at Lystra, Paul and Barnabas came upon a man with crippled feet. He had been that way from birth, so he had never walked. He was sitting ⁹and listening as Paul

13:47 Isa 49:6.   13:52 Greek *the disciples.*   14:1 *Iconium,* as well as *Lystra* and *Derbe* (14:6), were towns in what is now Turkey.

preached. Looking straight at him, Paul realized he had faith to be healed. ¹⁰So Paul called to him in a loud voice, "Stand up!" And the man jumped to his feet and started walking.

¹¹When the crowd saw what Paul had done, they shouted in their local dialect, "These men are gods in human form!" ¹²They decided that Barnabas was the Greek god Zeus and that Paul was Hermes, since he was the chief speaker. ¹³Now the temple of Zeus was located just outside the town. So the priest of the temple and the crowd brought bulls and wreaths of flowers to the town gates, and they prepared to offer sacrifices to the apostles.

¹⁴But when the apostles Barnabas and Paul heard what was happening, they tore their clothing in dismay and ran out among the people, shouting, ¹⁵"Friends,* why are you doing this? We are merely human beings—just like you! We have come to bring you the Good News that you should turn from these worthless things and turn to the living God, who made heaven and earth, the sea, and everything in them. ¹⁶In the past he permitted all the nations to go their own ways, ¹⁷but he never left them without evidence of himself and his goodness. For instance, he sends you rain and good crops and gives you food and joyful hearts." ¹⁸But even with these words, Paul and Barnabas could scarcely restrain the people from sacrificing to them.

¹⁹Then some Jews arrived from Antioch and Iconium and won the crowds to their side. They stoned Paul and dragged him out of town, thinking he was dead. ²⁰But as the believers* gathered around him, he got up and went back into the town. The next day he left with Barnabas for Derbe.

PAUL AND BARNABAS RETURN TO ANTIOCH OF SYRIA ²¹After preaching the Good News in Derbe and making many disciples, Paul and Barnabas returned to Lystra, Iconium, and Antioch of Pisidia, ²²where they strengthened the believers. They encouraged them to continue in the faith, reminding them that we must suffer many hardships to enter the Kingdom of God. ²³Paul and Barnabas also appointed elders in every church. With prayer and fasting, they turned the elders over to the care of the Lord, in whom they had put their trust. ²⁴Then they traveled back through Pisidia to Pamphylia. ²⁵They preached the word in Perga, then went down to Attalia.

²⁶Finally, they returned by ship to Antioch of Syria, where their journey had begun. The believers there had entrusted them to the grace of God to do the work they had now completed. ²⁷Upon arriving in Antioch, they called the church together and reported everything God had done through them and how he had opened the door of faith to the Gentiles, too. ²⁸And they stayed there with the believers for a long time.

15 **THE COUNCIL AT JERUSALEM** While Paul and Barnabas were at Antioch of Syria, some men from Judea arrived and began to teach the believers*: "Unless you are circumcised as required by the law of Moses, you cannot be saved." ²Paul and Barnabas disagreed with them, arguing vehemently. Finally, the church decided to send Paul and Barnabas to Jerusalem, accompanied by some local believers, to talk to the apostles and elders about this question. ³The church sent the delegates to Jerusalem, and they stopped along the way in Phoenicia and Samaria to visit the believers. They told them—much to everyone's joy—that the Gentiles, too, were being converted.

⁴When they arrived in Jerusalem, Barnabas and Paul were welcomed by the whole church, including the apostles and elders. They reported everything God had done through them. ⁵But then some of the believers who belonged to the sect of the Pharisees stood up and insisted, "The Gentile converts must be circumcised and required to follow the law of Moses."

⁶So the apostles and elders met together to resolve this issue. ⁷At the meeting, after a long discussion, Peter stood and addressed them as follows: "Brothers, you all know that God chose me from among you some time ago to preach to the Gentiles so that they could hear the Good News and believe. ⁸God knows people's hearts, and he confirmed that he accepts Gentiles by giving them the Holy Spirit, just as he did to us. ⁹He made no distinction between us and them, for he cleansed their

....

EVIDENCE
(14:1-18) Responding to the people of Lystra, Paul and Barnabas reminded them that God always provided "evidence of himself and his goodness." Rain and crops, for example, demonstrate God's goodness, as does the health people enjoy because they have the food they need. Later, Paul wrote that this evidence in nature and in people's lives left people without an excuse for unbelief (Rom 1:20). Ever feel like you have to prove that God exists? Look around. You'll see plenty of evidence that he's at work in our world.

14:15 Greek Men. 14:20 Greek disciples; also in 14:22, 28.
15:1 Greek brothers; also in 15:3, 23, 32, 33, 36, 40.

PAUL'S SECOND MISSIONARY JOURNEY (ACTS 15:36—18:22)

hearts through faith. ¹⁰So why are you now challenging God by burdening the Gentile believers* with a yoke that neither we nor our ancestors were able to bear? ¹¹We believe that we are all saved the same way, by the undeserved grace of the Lord Jesus."

¹²Everyone listened quietly as Barnabas and Paul told about the miraculous signs and wonders God had done through them among the Gentiles.

¹³When they had finished, James stood and said, "Brothers, listen to me. ¹⁴Peter* has told you about the time God first visited the Gentiles to take from them a people for himself. ¹⁵And this conversion of Gentiles is exactly what the prophets predicted. As it is written:

¹⁶ 'Afterward I will return
　　and restore the fallen house* of David.
　　I will rebuild its ruins

and restore it,
¹⁷ so that the rest of humanity might seek
　　the Lord,
　　including the Gentiles—
　　all those I have called to be mine.
　The Lord has spoken—
¹⁸ 　he who made these things known
　　so long ago.'*

¹⁹"And so my judgment is that we should not make it difficult for the Gentiles who are turning to God. ²⁰Instead, we should write and tell them to abstain from eating food offered to idols, from sexual immorality, from eating the meat of strangled animals, and from consuming blood. ²¹For these laws of Moses have been preached in Jewish synagogues in every city on every Sabbath for many generations."

THE LETTER FOR GENTILE BELIEVERS ²²Then the apostles and elders together with the whole church in Jerusalem chose delegates, and they sent them to Antioch of Syria with Paul and Barnabas to report on this decision. The men chosen were two of the church leaders*—Judas (also called Barsabbas) and Silas. ²³This is the letter they took with them:

....

YOUR ATTITUDE
(15:23-29) This letter answered their questions and brought great joy to the Gentile Christians in Antioch (15:31). Beautifully written, it appeals to the Holy Spirit's guidance and explains what should be done as though the readers already knew it. It is helpful when people learn to be careful not only in what they say, but also in how they say it. We may be correct in our content, but we can lose our audience by our tone of voice or attitude.

15:10 Greek *disciples.* **15:14** Greek *Symeon.* **15:16** Or *kingdom;* Greek reads *tent.* **15:16-18** Amos 9:11-12 (Greek version); Isa 45:21. **15:22** Greek *were leaders among the brothers.*

"This letter is from the apostles and elders, your brothers in Jerusalem. It is written to the Gentile believers in Antioch, Syria, and Cilicia. Greetings!

²⁴"We understand that some men from here have troubled you and upset you with their teaching, but we did not send them! ²⁵So we decided, having come to complete agreement, to send you official representatives, along with our beloved Barnabas and Paul, ²⁶who have risked their lives for the name of our Lord Jesus Christ. ²⁷We are sending Judas and Silas to confirm what we have decided concerning your question.

²⁸"For it seemed good to the Holy Spirit and to us to lay no greater burden on you than these few requirements: ²⁹You must abstain from eating food offered to idols, from consuming blood or the meat of strangled animals, and from sexual immorality. If you do this, you will do well. Farewell."

³⁰The messengers went at once to Antioch, where they called a general meeting of the believers and delivered the letter. ³¹And there was great joy throughout the church that day as they read this encouraging message.

³²Then Judas and Silas, both being prophets, spoke at length to the believers, encouraging and strengthening their faith. ³³They stayed for a while, and then the believers sent them back to the church in Jerusalem with a blessing of peace.* ³⁵Paul and Barnabas stayed in Antioch. They and many others taught and preached the word of the Lord there.

PAUL AND BARNABAS SEPARATE ³⁶After some time Paul said to Barnabas, "Let's go back and visit each city where we previously preached the word of the Lord, to see how the new believers are doing." ³⁷Barnabas agreed and wanted to take along John Mark. ³⁸But Paul disagreed strongly, since John Mark had deserted them in Pamphylia and had not continued with them in their work. ³⁹Their disagreement was so sharp that they separated. Barnabas took John Mark with him and sailed for Cyprus. ⁴⁰Paul chose Silas, and as he left, the believers entrusted him to the Lord's gracious care. ⁴¹Then he traveled throughout Syria and Cilicia, strengthening the churches there.

15:33 Some manuscripts add verse 34, *But Silas decided to stay there.*   16:2 Greek *brothers;* also in 16:40.   16:6-7 *Phrygia, Galatia, Asia, Mysia,* and *Bithynia* were all districts in what is now Turkey.   16:10 Luke, the writer of this book, here joined Paul and accompanied him on his journey.

16 PAUL'S SECOND MISSIONARY JOURNEY
Paul went first to Derbe and then to Lystra, where there was a young disciple named Timothy. His mother was a Jewish believer, but his father was a Greek. ²Timothy was well thought of by the believers* in Lystra and Iconium, ³so Paul wanted him to join them on their journey. In deference to the Jews of the area, he arranged for Timothy to be circumcised before they left, for everyone knew that his father was a Greek. ⁴Then they went from town to town, instructing the believers to follow the decisions made by the apostles and elders in Jerusalem. ⁵So the churches were strengthened in their faith and grew larger every day.

A CALL FROM MACEDONIA ⁶Next Paul and Silas traveled through the area of Phrygia and Galatia, because the Holy Spirit had prevented them from preaching the word in the province of Asia at that time. ⁷Then coming to the borders of Mysia, they headed north for the province of Bithynia,* but again the Spirit of Jesus did not allow them to go there. ⁸So instead, they went on through Mysia to the seaport of Troas.

⁹That night Paul had a vision: A man from Macedonia in northern Greece was standing there, pleading with him, "Come over to Macedonia and help us!" ¹⁰So we* decided to leave for Macedonia at once, having concluded that God was calling us to preach the Good News there.

LYDIA OF PHILIPPI BELIEVES IN JESUS ¹¹We boarded a boat at Troas and sailed straight across to the island of Samothrace, and the

....

BARRIERS
(16:1-3) Timothy was the son of a Jewish mother and a Greek father. Consequently, Paul asked Timothy to be circumcised because he knew that some of the Jewish believers would have trouble accepting him if he hadn't been circumcised. Although this act wasn't required (the Jerusalem council had voted against the necessity of it—see chapter 15), Timothy voluntarily did so to overcome barriers to his witness for Christ. Going beyond the minimum requirements is sometimes necessary to avoid giving anyone a reason to reject what we say about God.

HOW GOD SPEAKS
(16:6) We don't know how the Holy Spirit told Paul that he and his men were not to go into Asia. He may have spoken through a prophet, a vision, an inner conviction, or some other circumstance. Are you wondering what God is telling you to do? He often speaks through (1) well-chosen verses in the Bible; (2) the advice of mature Christians; (3) opportunities he provides; (4) prayer. Are you listening?

UNSUNG HEROES IN ACTS

When we think of the success of the early church, we often think of the work of the apostles. But the church could have died if it hadn't been for the "unsung" heroes, the men and women who moved the church forward through small but committed acts.

HERO	REFERENCE	HEROIC ACTION
LAME BEGGAR	3:9-10	After his healing, he praised God. With the crowds gathering to see what happened, Peter used the opportunity to tell many about Jesus.
FIVE DEACONS	6:2-5	Everyone knows Stephen, and many people know Philip, but there were five other men chosen to be deacons. They not only laid the foundation for service in the church, but their hard work gave the apostles more time to preach the gospel.
ANANIAS	9:10-19	He had the responsibility of being the first to demonstrate Christ's love to Saul (Paul) after his conversion.
CORNELIUS	10:30-35	His example showed Peter that the gospel was for all people, Jews and Gentiles.
RHODA	12:13-15	Her persistence brought Peter inside Mary's home, where he would be safe.
JAMES	15:13-21	He took command of the Jerusalem council and had the courage and discernment to make a decision that would affect literally millions of Christians over many generations.
LYDIA	16:13-15	She opened her home to Paul, from which he led many to Christ and founded a church in Philippi.
JASON	17:5-9	He risked his life for the gospel by allowing Paul to stay in his home. He stood up for what was true and right, even though he faced persecution for it.
PAUL'S NEPHEW	23:16-24	He saved Paul's life by telling officials of a plot to murder Paul.
JULIUS	27:1, 43	He spared Paul's life when the other soldiers wanted to kill him.

next day we landed at Neapolis. ¹²From there we reached Philippi, a major city of that district of Macedonia and a Roman colony. And we stayed there several days.

¹³On the Sabbath we went a little way outside the city to a riverbank, where we thought people would be meeting for prayer, and we sat down to speak with some women who had gathered there. ¹⁴One of them was Lydia from

••

A GODLY RESPONSE
(16:16-34) While in Philippi, Paul and Silas were beaten and placed in stocks in a dungeon. Instead of grumbling about how unfairly they had been treated, they sang praise songs to God while the other prisoners listened. Later, the jailer and his whole family became believers because of Paul and Silas's example.

How do you respond to unfair circumstances? Do you grumble or praise? Like Paul and Silas, you never know who might be listening. God may use your Christlike reaction to lead someone to him.

Thyatira, a merchant of expensive purple cloth, who worshiped God. As she listened to us, the Lord opened her heart, and she accepted what Paul was saying. ¹⁵She was baptized along with other members of her household, and she asked us to be her guests. "If you agree that I am a true believer in the Lord," she said, "come and stay at my home." And she urged us until we agreed.

PAUL AND SILAS IN PRISON ¹⁶One day as we were going down to the place of prayer, we met a demon-possessed slave girl. She was a fortune-teller who earned a lot of money for her masters. ¹⁷She followed Paul and the rest of us, shouting, "These men are servants of the Most High God, and they have come to tell you how to be saved."

¹⁸This went on day after day until Paul got so exasperated that he turned and said to

the demon within her, "I command you in the name of Jesus Christ to come out of her." And instantly it left her.

¹⁹Her masters' hopes of wealth were now shattered, so they grabbed Paul and Silas and dragged them before the authorities at the marketplace. ²⁰"The whole city is in an uproar because of these Jews!" they shouted to the city officials. ²¹"They are teaching customs that are illegal for us Romans to practice."

²²A mob quickly formed against Paul and Silas, and the city officials ordered them stripped and beaten with wooden rods. ²³They were severely beaten, and then they were thrown into prison. The jailer was ordered to make sure they didn't escape. ²⁴So the jailer put them into the inner dungeon and clamped their feet in the stocks.

²⁵Around midnight Paul and Silas were praying and singing hymns to God, and the other prisoners were listening. ²⁶Suddenly, there was a massive earthquake, and the prison was shaken to its foundations. All the doors immediately flew open, and the chains of every prisoner fell off! ²⁷The jailer woke up to see the prison doors wide open. He assumed the prisoners had escaped, so he drew his sword to kill himself. ²⁸But Paul shouted to him, "Stop! Don't kill yourself! We are all here!"

²⁹The jailer called for lights and ran to the dungeon and fell down trembling before Paul and Silas. ³⁰Then he brought them out and asked, "Sirs, what must I do to be saved?"

³¹They replied, "Believe in the Lord Jesus and you will be saved, along with everyone in your household." ³²And they shared the word of the Lord with him and with all who lived in his household. ³³Even at that hour of the night, the jailer cared for them and washed their wounds. Then he and everyone in his household were immediately baptized. ³⁴He brought them into his house and set a meal before them, and he and his entire household rejoiced because they all believed in God.

³⁵The next morning the city officials sent the police to tell the jailer, "Let those men go!" ³⁶So the jailer told Paul, "The city officials have said you and Silas are free to leave. Go in peace."

³⁷But Paul replied, "They have publicly beaten us without a trial and put us in prison—and we are Roman citizens. So now they want us to leave secretly? Certainly not! Let them come themselves to release us!"

³⁸When the police reported this, the city

PERSONALITY PROFILE SILAS

UPS:
- *A leader in the Jerusalem church*
- *Represented the church in carrying the "acceptance letter" prepared by the Jerusalem council to the Gentile believers in Antioch*
- *Was closely associated with Paul from the second missionary journey onward*
- *When imprisoned with Paul in Philippi, sang songs of praise to God*
- *Worked as a secretary for both Paul and Peter, using "Silvanus" as his pen name*

STATS:
- *Where: Roman citizen living in Jerusalem*
- *Occupation: One of the first career missionaries*
- *Contemporaries: Paul, Timothy, Peter, Mark, Barnabas*

KEY VERSES: *Acts 15:25-27*

ONE WORD THAT DOESN'T FIT IN THE LIVES OF THE FIRST CHRISTIANS IS BORING. Too many exciting things happened. Christian missionaries took hazardous journeys over land and sea. Even preaching the gospel was sometimes dangerous, since resistance and hatred of the message often occurred.

Right in the middle of all the excitement was a young man named Silas. We first meet Silas when he acted as one of the representatives from Jerusalem to spread the official news that Gentiles did not have to be circumcised before they became Christians (see Acts 15). This was an important mission.

Later, Silas joined Paul and Timothy's ministry team. Life continued to be exciting. Paul and Silas spent a night singing in prison in Philippi after being severely beaten. Another time, they were almost beaten in Thessalonica but were able to pull off a daring escape in the night. Then after Paul left, Silas and Timothy continued to encourage the young believers in the Berean church.

We don't know what eventually happened to Silas. He spent some time with Peter and is acknowledged in 1 Peter. He continued to live the same faithful life that had made him a good choice to represent the church in Jerusalem. Though he never sought the spotlight, his humility and consistency caused him to be remembered.

BOTTOM LINE: Partnership is a significant part of effective ministry.

God never said that his servants would not suffer. In fact, he guarantees that they will.

Obedience to God may mean giving up what makes us feel secure.

Silas's story is told in Acts 15:22–19:10. He also is mentioned in 2 Corinthians 1:19; 1 Thessalonians 1:1; 2 Thessalonians 1:1; 1 Peter 5:12.

officials were alarmed to learn that Paul and Silas were Roman citizens. [39]So they came to the jail and apologized to them. Then they brought them out and begged them to leave the city. [40]When Paul and Silas left the prison, they returned to the home of Lydia. There they met with the believers and encouraged them once more. Then they left town.

17 PAUL PREACHES IN THESSALONICA

Paul and Silas then traveled through the towns of Amphipolis and Apollonia and came to Thessalonica, where there was a Jewish synagogue. [2]As was Paul's custom, he went to the synagogue service, and for three Sabbaths in a row he used the Scriptures to reason with the people. [3]He explained the prophecies and proved that the Messiah must suffer and rise from the dead. He said, "This Jesus I'm telling you about is the Messiah." [4]Some of the Jews who listened were persuaded and joined Paul and Silas, along with many God-fearing Greek men and quite a few prominent women.*

[5]But some of the Jews were jealous, so they gathered some troublemakers from the marketplace to form a mob and start a riot. They attacked the home of Jason, searching for Paul and Silas so they could drag them out to the crowd.* [6]Not finding them there, they dragged out Jason and some of the other believers* instead and took them before the city council.

••

COMPARE

(17:11) The people in Berea studied the Scriptures to verify or disprove the messages Paul and Silas preached. Do you take the time to evaluate the messages you hear? You can know what's true by comparing what you hear to what's in the Bible (see John 8:32; 2 Tim 2:15; see also the "I Wonder" question).

"Paul and Silas have caused trouble all over the world," they shouted, "and now they are here disturbing our city, too. [7]And Jason has welcomed them into his home. They are all guilty of treason against Caesar, for they profess allegiance to another king, named Jesus."

[8]The people of the city, as well as the city council, were thrown into turmoil by these reports. [9]So the officials forced Jason and the other believers to post bond, and then they released them.

PAUL AND SILAS IN BEREA   [10]That very night the believers sent Paul and Silas to Berea. When they arrived there, they went to the Jewish synagogue. [11]And the people of Berea were more open-minded than those in Thessalonica, and they listened eagerly to Paul's message. They searched the Scriptures day after day to see if Paul and Silas were teaching the truth. [12]As a result, many Jews believed, as did many of the prominent Greek women and men.

[13]But when some Jews in Thessalonica learned that Paul was preaching the word of God in Berea, they went there and stirred up trouble. [14]The believers acted at once, sending Paul on to the coast, while Silas and Timothy remained behind. [15]Those escorting Paul went with him all the way to Athens; then they returned to Berea with instructions for Silas and Timothy to hurry and join him.

PAUL PREACHES IN ATHENS   [16]While Paul was waiting for them in Athens, he was deeply troubled by all the idols he saw everywhere in the city. [17]He went to the synagogue to reason with the Jews and the God-fearing Gentiles,

17:4 Some manuscripts read *quite a few of the wives of the leading men.*   **17:5** Or *the city council.*   **17:6** Greek *brothers;* also in 17:10, 14.

I WONDER...

I'm not the kind of person who can take everything at face value. I have to have more proof. Is it wrong to want to seek answers to questions I have about the Bible?

The Christians in Berea were complimented by Luke, the author of Acts, because "they searched the Scriptures day after day to see if Paul and Silas were teaching the truth" (Acts 17:11).

Because being a Christian means accepting Christ's forgiveness by faith, some think we must believe everything just because another Christian said it. But getting your questions answered by studying the Bible is an important part of being a Christian.

Although not every question can be answered, most of them can.

Some people are natural skeptics. They challenge everything in the Bible simply because they're looking for an argument, rather than answers. If, however, you really want answers, God will help you find them. "Keep on asking, and you will receive what you ask for. Keep on seeking, and you will find. Keep on knocking, and the door will be opened to you. For everyone who asks, receives. Everyone who seeks, finds. And to everyone who knocks, the door will be opened" (Matt 7:7-8).

Keep asking your questions and looking for answers.

and he spoke daily in the public square to all who happened to be there.

[18]He also had a debate with some of the Epicurean and Stoic philosophers. When he told them about Jesus and his resurrection, they said, "What's this babbler trying to say with these strange ideas he's picked up?" Others said, "He seems to be preaching about some foreign gods."

[19]Then they took him to the high council of the city.* "Come and tell us about this new teaching," they said. [20]"You are saying some rather strange things, and we want to know what it's all about." [21](It should be explained that all the Athenians as well as the foreigners in Athens seemed to spend all their time discussing the latest ideas.)

[22]So Paul, standing before the council,* addressed them as follows: "Men of Athens, I notice that you are very religious in every way, [23]for as I was walking along I saw your many shrines. And one of your altars had this inscription on it: 'To an Unknown God.' This God, whom you worship without knowing, is the one I'm telling you about.

[24]"He is the God who made the world and everything in it. Since he is Lord of heaven and earth, he doesn't live in man-made temples, [25]and human hands can't serve his needs—for he has no needs. He himself gives life and breath to everything, and he satisfies every need. [26]From one man* he created all the nations throughout the whole earth. He decided beforehand when they should rise and fall, and he determined their boundaries.

[27]"His purpose was for the nations to seek after God and perhaps feel their way toward him and find him—though he is not far from any one of us. [28]For in him we live and move and exist. As some of your* own poets have said, 'We are his offspring.' [29]And since this is true, we shouldn't think of God as an idol designed by craftsmen from gold or silver or stone.

[30]"God overlooked people's ignorance about these things in earlier times, but now he commands everyone everywhere to repent of their sins and turn to him. [31]For he has set a day for judging the world with justice by the man he has appointed, and he proved to everyone who this is by raising him from the dead."

[32]When they heard Paul speak about the resurrection of the dead, some laughed in contempt, but others said, "We want to hear more about this later." [33]That ended Paul's discussion with them, [34]but some joined him and became believers. Among them were Dionysius, a member of the council,* a woman named Damaris, and others with them.

18

PAUL MEETS PRISCILLA AND AQUILA IN CORINTH

Then Paul left Athens and went to Corinth.* [2]There he became acquainted with a Jew named Aquila, born in Pontus, who had recently arrived from Italy with his wife, Priscilla. They had left Italy when Claudius Caesar deported all Jews from Rome. [3]Paul lived and worked with them, for they were tentmakers* just as he was.

[4]Each Sabbath found Paul at the synagogue, trying to convince the Jews and Greeks alike. [5]And after Silas and Timothy came down from Macedonia, Paul spent all his time preaching the word. He testified to the Jews that Jesus was the Messiah. [6]But when they opposed and insulted him, Paul shook the dust from his clothes and said, "Your blood is upon your own heads—I am innocent. From now on I will go preach to the Gentiles."

[7]Then he left and went to the home of Titius Justus, a Gentile who worshiped God and lived next door to the synagogue. [8]Crispus, the leader of the synagogue, and everyone in his household believed in the Lord. Many others in Corinth also heard Paul, became believers, and were baptized.

[9]One night the Lord spoke to Paul in a vision and told him, "Don't be afraid! Speak out! Don't be silent! [10]For I am with you, and no one will attack and harm you, for many people in this city belong to me." [11]So Paul stayed there for the next year and a half, teaching the word of God.

[12]But when Gallio became governor of Achaia, some Jews rose up together against Paul and brought him before the governor for judgment. [13]They accused Paul of "persuading people to worship God in ways that are contrary to our law."

[14]But just as Paul started to make his defense, Gallio turned to Paul's accusers and

---

17:19 Or *the most learned society of philosophers in the city.* Greek reads *the Areopagus.* **17:22** Traditionally rendered *standing in the middle of Mars Hill;* Greek reads *standing in the middle of the Areopagus.* **17:26** Greek *From one;* other manuscripts read *From one blood.* **17:28** Some manuscripts read *our.* **17:34** Greek *an Areopagite.* **18:1** *Athens* and *Corinth* were major cities in Achaia, the region in the southern portion of the Greek peninsula. **18:3** Or *leatherworkers.*

WORTH IT
(17:22-34) Paul's speech received a mixed reaction: some people laughed, some kept searching for more information, and a few believed. As you tell others about Jesus, you might have this kind of mixed response. But the belief of only a few is still worth the effort.

PAUL'S THIRD MISSIONARY JOURNEY (ACTS 18:23—21:16)

said, "Listen, you Jews, if this were a case involving some wrongdoing or a serious crime, I would have a reason to accept your case. ¹⁵But since it is merely a question of words and names and your Jewish law, take care of it yourselves. I refuse to judge such matters." ¹⁶And he threw them out of the courtroom.

¹⁷The crowd* then grabbed Sosthenes, the leader of the synagogue, and beat him right there in the courtroom. But Gallio paid no attention.

PAUL RETURNS TO ANTIOCH OF SYRIA ¹⁸Paul stayed in Corinth for some time after that, then said good-bye to the brothers and sisters* and went to nearby Cenchrea. There he shaved his head according to Jewish custom, marking the end of a vow. Then he set sail for Syria, taking Priscilla and Aquila with him.

¹⁹They stopped first at the port of Ephesus, where Paul left the others behind. While he was there, he went to the synagogue to reason with the Jews. ²⁰They asked him to stay longer, but he declined. ²¹As he left, however, he said, "I will come back later,* God willing." Then he set sail from Ephesus. ²²The next stop was at the port of Caesarea. From there he went up and visited the church at Jerusalem* and then went back to Antioch.

²³After spending some time in Antioch, Paul went back through Galatia and Phrygia, visiting and strengthening all the believers.*

APOLLOS INSTRUCTED AT EPHESUS ²⁴Meanwhile, a Jew named Apollos, an eloquent speaker who knew the Scriptures well, had arrived in Ephesus from Alexandria in Egypt. ²⁵He had been taught the way of the Lord, and he taught others about Jesus with an enthusiastic spirit* and with accuracy. However, he knew only about John's baptism. ²⁶When Priscilla and Aquila heard him preaching boldly in the

- -

A REASONABLE ARGUMENT
(18:24-28) Apollos was from Alexandria in Egypt, the second largest city in the Roman Empire. He was a scholar as well as an eloquent speaker. After his knowledge about Christ was more complete, God greatly used his gifts to strengthen the church. Reason is a powerful tool in the right hands and the right situation. Apollos used his reasoning ability to convince many in Greece of the truth of the gospel. You don't have to turn off your mind when you turn to Christ. You can use your reasoning skills to bring others to God.

18:17 Greek *Everyone;* other manuscripts read *All the Greeks.*
18:18 Greek *brothers;* also in 18:27.   18:21 Some manuscripts read *"I must by all means be at Jerusalem for the upcoming festival, but I will come back later."*   18:22 Greek *the church.*   18:23 Greek *disciples;* also in 18:27.   18:25 Or *with enthusiasm in the Spirit.*

synagogue, they took him aside and explained the way of God even more accurately.

27Apollos had been thinking about going to Achaia, and the brothers and sisters in Ephesus encouraged him to go. They wrote to the believers in Achaia, asking them to welcome him. When he arrived there, he proved to be of great benefit to those who, by God's grace, had believed. 28He refuted the Jews with powerful arguments in public debate. Using the Scriptures, he explained to them that Jesus was the Messiah.

19 PAUL'S THIRD MISSIONARY JOURNEY

While Apollos was in Corinth, Paul traveled through the interior regions until he reached Ephesus, on the coast, where he found several believers.* 2"Did you receive the Holy Spirit when you believed?" he asked them.

"No," they replied, "we haven't even heard that there is a Holy Spirit."

3"Then what baptism did you experience?" he asked.

And they replied, "The baptism of John."

4Paul said, "John's baptism called for repentance from sin. But John himself told the people to believe in the one who would come later, meaning Jesus."

5As soon as they heard this, they were baptized in the name of the Lord Jesus. 6Then when Paul laid his hands on them, the Holy Spirit came on them, and they spoke in other tongues* and prophesied. 7There were about twelve men in all.

PAUL MINISTERS IN EPHESUS 8Then Paul went to the synagogue and preached boldly for the next three months, arguing persuasively about the Kingdom of God. 9But some became stubborn, rejecting his message and publicly speaking against the Way. So Paul left the synagogue and took the believers with him. Then he held daily discussions at the lecture hall of Tyrannus. 10This went on for the next two years, so that people throughout the province of Asia—both Jews and Greeks—heard the word of the Lord.

11God gave Paul the power to perform unusual miracles. 12When handkerchiefs or aprons that had merely touched his skin were placed on sick people, they were healed of their diseases, and evil spirits were expelled.

13A group of Jews was traveling from town to town casting out evil spirits. They tried to use the name of the Lord Jesus in their incantation,

19:1 Greek *disciples;* also in 19:9, 30.   **19:6** Or *in other languages.*

MY STORY: Riley

At my high school we have a Christian Bible study group called Saints' Battalion. A while ago, some kids on our campus formed a group called Young Satanists of America. Before their group meetings, which are held on the same day as ours, they come into our meetings and bother us in any way they can. In their meetings they put down Christianity and exalt Satanism as a "philosophy."

Since our group has to be open to all, we can't ban them from coming to our meetings. They still remain a problem—one that our group and my church continue to pray about. A passage that has really encouraged us is Acts 19:13-20. It talks about the power in the name of Jesus to cast out evil spirits, and about how lots of people who heard about Christ burned their witchcraft books and turned to God. This passage reminds us of the power of Jesus. Also, we pray that many of the Young Satanists who come to our meetings will hear God's Word and turn to Christ.

saying, "I command you in the name of Jesus, whom Paul preaches, to come out!" 14Seven sons of Sceva, a leading priest, were doing this. 15But one time when they tried it, the evil spirit replied, "I know Jesus, and I know Paul, but who are you?" 16Then the man with the evil spirit leaped on them, overpowered them, and attacked them with such violence that they fled from the house, naked and battered.

17The story of what happened spread quickly all through Ephesus, to Jews and Greeks alike. A solemn fear descended on the city, and the name of the Lord Jesus was greatly honored. 18Many who became believers confessed their sinful practices. 19A number of them who had been practicing sorcery brought their

....

THE POWER OF HIS NAME
(19:13-20) The sons of Sceva were impressed by Paul, whose power to cast out demons came from the Holy Spirit. This power obviously was greater than theirs. But they discovered the hard way that Jesus' name could not be used like a magic charm. No person can control or duplicate God's power. Only through a relationship with Jesus—one sealed by the presence of the Holy Spirit—can one experience the power of God.

ncantation books and burned them at a public bonfire. The value of the books was several million dollars.* ²⁰So the message about the Lord spread widely and had a powerful effect.

²¹Afterward Paul felt compelled by the Spirit* to go over to Macedonia and Achaia before going to Jerusalem. "And after that," he said, "I must go on to Rome!" ²²He sent his two assistants, Timothy and Erastus, ahead to Macedonia while he stayed awhile longer in the province of Asia.

THE RIOT IN EPHESUS ²³About that time, serious trouble developed in Ephesus concerning the Way. ²⁴It began with Demetrius, a silversmith who had a large business manufacturing silver shrines of the Greek goddess Artemis.* He kept many craftsmen busy. ²⁵He called them together, along with others employed in similar trades, and addressed them as follows:

"Gentlemen, you know that our wealth comes from this business. ²⁶But as you have

seen and heard, this man Paul has persuaded many people that handmade gods aren't really gods at all. And he's done this not only here in Ephesus but throughout the entire province! ²⁷Of course, I'm not just talking about the loss of public respect for our business. I'm also concerned that the temple of the great goddess Artemis will lose its influence and that Artemis—this magnificent goddess worshiped throughout the province of Asia and all around the world—will be robbed of her great prestige!"

²⁸At this their anger boiled, and they began shouting, "Great is Artemis of the Ephesians!" ²⁹Soon the whole city was filled with confusion. Everyone rushed to the amphitheater, dragging along Gaius and Aristarchus, who were Paul's traveling companions from Macedonia. ³⁰Paul wanted to go in, too, but the believers wouldn't let him. ³¹Some of the offi-

19:19 Greek *50,000 pieces of silver,* each of which was the equivalent of a day's wage.   **19:21** Or *decided in his spirit.* **19:24** *Artemis* is otherwise known as Diana.

AQUILA & PRISCILLA
PERSONALITY PROFILE

SOME COUPLES KNOW HOW TO MAKE THE MOST OF LIFE. They fit together, let each do his or her best, and form an effective team. Their combined efforts affect those around them. Aquila and Priscilla were such a couple. They are never mentioned apart from one another in the Bible. Together, they loved God and people.

Priscilla and Aquila met Paul in Corinth while he was on his second missionary journey. They had just left Rome. Their home was as movable as the tents they made in their business. They invited Paul to stay with them, and he joined them in making tents. Paul helped them by sharing his wisdom about God.

Priscilla and Aquila made good use of what they learned from Paul. They listened and evaluated what they heard. For instance, when another preacher, Apollos, came to town, they listened to what he had to say. They realized he was a good speaker, but that he had much more to learn. Instead of correcting Apollos in public, they quietly took him home with them and shared with him what he needed to know. Apollos had been preaching John the Baptist's message of repentance. Priscilla and Aquila told Apollos about Jesus' life, death, and resurrection, and how God's Spirit wanted to live in us. Apollos then used his great ability to tell the whole story!

This couple continued to use their home as a place for training and worship. Later, back in Rome, one of the churches met in their house. (The first Christians did not meet in church buildings, but in the homes of believers.) We can easily imagine that anywhere Aquila and Priscilla lived would be a place of fellowship.

BOTTOM LINE: Couples can have an effective ministry together. The home is a valuable tool for evangelism and teaching.

Priscilla and Aquila's story is told in Acts 18. They are also mentioned in Romans 16:3-5; 1 Corinthians 16:19; 2 Timothy 4:19.

UPS:
- Outstanding husband-wife team who ministered in the early church
- Supported themselves by making tents while serving Christ
- Close friends of Paul
- Explained the full message of Christ to Apollos

STATS:
- Where: Originally from Rome; moved to Corinth, then Ephesus
- Occupation: Tentmakers
- Contemporaries: Emperor Claudius, Paul, Timothy, Apollos

KEY VERSES: Rom 16:3-5

cials of the province, friends of Paul, also sent a message to him, begging him not to risk his life by entering the amphitheater.

³²Inside, the people were all shouting, some one thing and some another. Everything was in confusion. In fact, most of them didn't even know why they were there. ³³The Jews in the crowd pushed Alexander forward and told him to explain the situation. He motioned for silence and tried to speak. ³⁴But when the crowd realized he was a Jew, they started shouting again and kept it up for about two hours: "Great is Artemis of the Ephesians! Great is Artemis of the Ephesians!"

³⁵At last the mayor was able to quiet them down enough to speak. "Citizens of Ephesus," he said. "Everyone knows that Ephesus is the official guardian of the temple of the great Artemis, whose image fell down to us from heaven. ³⁶Since this is an undeniable fact, you should stay calm and not do anything rash. ³⁷You have brought these men here, but they have stolen nothing from the temple and have not spoken against our goddess.

³⁸"If Demetrius and the craftsmen have a case against them, the courts are in session and the officials can hear the case at once. Let them make formal charges. ³⁹And if there are complaints about other matters, they can be settled in a legal assembly. ⁴⁰I am afraid we are in danger of being charged with rioting by the Roman government, since there is no cause for all this commotion. And if Rome demands an explanation, we won't know what to say." ⁴¹*Then he dismissed them, and they dispersed.

20 PAUL GOES TO MACEDONIA AND GREECE

When the uproar was over, Paul sent for the believers* and encouraged them. Then he said good-bye and left for Macedonia. ²While there, he encouraged the believers in all the towns he passed through. Then he traveled down to Greece, ³where he stayed for three months. He was preparing to sail back to Syria when he discovered a plot by some Jews against his life, so he decided to return through Macedonia.

⁴Several men were traveling with him. They were Sopater son of Pyrrhus from Berea; Aristarchus and Secundus from Thessalonica; Gaius from Derbe; Timothy; and Tychicus and

Trophimus from the province of Asia. ⁵They went on ahead and waited for us at Troas. ⁶After the Passover* ended, we boarded a ship at Philippi in Macedonia and five days later joined them in Troas, where we stayed a week.

PAUL'S FINAL VISIT TO TROAS ⁷On the first day of the week, we gathered with the local believers to share in the Lord's Supper.* Paul was preaching to them, and since he was leaving the next day, he kept talking until midnight. ⁸The upstairs room where we met was lighted with many flickering lamps. ⁹As Paul spoke on and on, a young man named Eutychus, sitting on the windowsill, became very drowsy. Finally, he fell sound asleep and dropped three stories to his death below. ¹⁰Paul went down, bent over him, and took him into his arms. "Don't worry," he said, "he's alive!" ¹¹Then they all went back upstairs, shared in the Lord's Supper,* and ate together. Paul continued talking to them until dawn, and then he left. ¹²Meanwhile, the young man was taken home unhurt, and everyone was greatly relieved.

PAUL MEETS THE EPHESIAN ELDERS ¹³Paul went by land to Assos, where he had arranged for us to join him, while we traveled by ship. ¹⁴He joined us there, and we sailed together to Mitylene. ¹⁵The next day we sailed past the island of Kios. The following day we crossed to the island of Samos, and* a day later we arrived at Miletus.

¹⁶Paul had decided to sail on past Ephesus, for he didn't want to spend any more time in the province of Asia. He was hurrying to get to Jerusalem, if possible, in time for the Festival of Pentecost. ¹⁷But when we landed at Miletus, he sent a message to the elders of the church at Ephesus, asking them to come and meet him.

¹⁸When they arrived he declared, "You know that from the day I set foot in the province of Asia until now ¹⁹I have done the Lord's work humbly and with many tears. I have endured the trials that came to me from the plots of the Jews. ²⁰I never shrank back from telling you what you needed to hear, either publicly or in your homes. ²¹I have had one message for Jews and Greeks alike—the necessity of repenting from sin and turning to God, and of having faith in our Lord Jesus.

²²"And now I am bound by the Spirit* to go to Jerusalem. I don't know what awaits me, ²³except that the Holy Spirit tells me in city after city that jail and suffering lie ahead. ²⁴But my life is worth nothing to me unless I use it for

19:41 Some translations include verse 41 as part of verse 40. 20:1 Greek *disciples.* 20:6 Greek *the days of unleavened bread.* 20:7 Greek *to break bread.* 20:11 Greek *broke the bread.* 20:15 Some manuscripts read *and having stayed at Trogyllium.* 20:22 Or *by my spirit,* or *by an inner compulsion;* Greek reads *by the spirit.*

finishing the work assigned me by the Lord Jesus—the work of telling others the Good News about the wonderful grace of God.

²⁵"And now I know that none of you to whom I have preached the Kingdom will ever see me again. ²⁶I declare today that I have been faithful. If anyone suffers eternal death, it's not my fault,* ²⁷for I didn't shrink from declaring all that God wants you to know.

²⁸"So guard yourselves and God's people. Feed and shepherd God's flock—his church, purchased with his own blood*—over which the Holy Spirit has appointed you as elders.* ²⁹I know that false teachers, like vicious wolves, will come in among you after I leave, not sparing the flock. ³⁰Even some men from your own group will rise up and distort the truth in order to draw a following. ³¹Watch out! Remember the three years I was with you—my constant watch and care over you night and day, and my many tears for you.

³²"And now I entrust you to God and the message of his grace that is able to build you up and give you an inheritance with all those he has set apart for himself.

³³"I have never coveted anyone's silver or gold or fine clothes. ³⁴You know that these hands of mine have worked to supply my own needs and even the needs of those who were with me. ³⁵And I have been a constant example of how you can help those in need by working hard. You should remember the words of the Lord Jesus: 'It is more blessed to give than to receive.'"

³⁶When he had finished speaking, he knelt and prayed with them. ³⁷They all cried as they embraced and kissed him good-bye. ³⁸They were sad most of all because he had said that they would never see him again. Then they escorted him down to the ship.

. . . .

REAL SATISFACTION
(20:24-34) These days many people believe they won't be satisfied in life unless there's something in it for them: glory, fun, money, or popularity. Yet Paul was satisfied with whatever he had, wherever he was, as long as he could do God's work. Is that your definition of satisfaction?

THE WAY OF PAIN
(21:10-14) Paul knew that he would be imprisoned in Jerusalem. Although his friends pleaded with him not to go, Paul knew that God wanted him there. Although none of us wants to face hardship or pain, obedience to God sometimes involves suffering. Jesus' life is proof of this. Like Paul's friends, are you willing to say "The Lord's will be done," no matter what the circumstances?

21 **PAUL'S JOURNEY TO JERUSALEM** After saying farewell to the Ephesian elders, we sailed straight to the island of Cos. The next day we reached Rhodes and then went to Patara. ²There we boarded a ship sailing for Phoenicia. ³We sighted the island of Cyprus, passed it on our left, and landed at the harbor of Tyre, in Syria, where the ship was to unload its cargo.

⁴We went ashore, found the local believers,* and stayed with them a week. These believers prophesied through the Holy Spirit that Paul should not go on to Jerusalem. ⁵When we returned to the ship at the end of the week, the entire congregation, including women* and children, left the city and came down to the shore with us. There we knelt, prayed, ⁶and said our farewells. Then we went aboard, and they returned home.

⁷The next stop after leaving Tyre was Ptolemais, where we greeted the brothers and sisters* and stayed for one day. ⁸The next day we went on to Caesarea and stayed at the home of Philip the Evangelist, one of the seven men who had been chosen to distribute food. ⁹He had four unmarried daughters who had the gift of prophecy.

¹⁰Several days later a man named Agabus, who also had the gift of prophecy, arrived from Judea. ¹¹He came over, took Paul's belt, and bound his own feet and hands with it. Then he said, "The Holy Spirit declares, 'So shall the owner of this belt be bound by the Jewish leaders in Jerusalem and turned over to the Gentiles.'" ¹²When we heard this, we and the local believers all begged Paul not to go on to Jerusalem.

¹³But he said, "Why all this weeping? You are breaking my heart! I am ready not only to be jailed at Jerusalem but even to die for the sake of the Lord Jesus." ¹⁴When it was clear that we couldn't persuade him, we gave up and said, "The Lord's will be done."

PAUL ARRIVES AT JERUSALEM ¹⁵After this we packed our things and left for Jerusalem. ¹⁶Some believers from Caesarea accompanied us, and they took us to the home of Mnason, a man originally from Cyprus and one of the early believers. ¹⁷When we arrived, the brothers and sisters in Jerusalem welcomed us warmly.

¹⁸The next day Paul went with us to meet with James, and all the elders of the Jerusalem church were present. ¹⁹After greeting them, Paul

20:26 Greek *I am innocent of the blood of all.* **20:28a** Or *with the blood of his own [Son].* **20:28b** Greek *overseers.* **21:4** Greek *disciples;* also in 21:16. **21:5** Or *wives.* **21:7** Greek *brothers;* also in 21:17.

PAUL'S JOURNEY TO ROME   (ACTS 21:17—28:31)

gave a detailed account of the things God had accomplished among the Gentiles through his ministry.

²⁰After hearing this, they praised God. And then they said, "You know, dear brother, how many thousands of Jews have also believed, and they all follow the law of Moses very seriously. ²¹But the Jewish believers here in Jerusalem have been told that you are teaching all the Jews who live among the Gentiles to turn their backs on the laws of Moses. They've heard that you teach them not to circumcise their children or follow other Jewish customs. ²²What should we do? They will certainly hear that you have come.

²³"Here's what we want you to do. We have four men here who have completed their vow. ²⁴Go with them to the Temple and join them in the purification ceremony, paying for them to have their heads ritually shaved. Then everyone will know that the rumors are all false and that you yourself observe the Jewish laws. ²⁵"As for the Gentile believers, they should do what we already told them in a letter: They should abstain from eating food offered to idols, from consuming blood or the meat of strangled animals, and from sexual immorality."

21:28 Greek *Greeks*.   **21:29** Greek *Trophimus, the Ephesian.*
21:32 Greek *centurions*.

PAUL IS ARRESTED   ²⁶So Paul went to the Temple the next day with the other men. They had already started the purification ritual, so he publicly announced the date when their vows would end and sacrifices would be offered for each of them.

²⁷The seven days were almost ended when some Jews from the province of Asia saw Paul in the Temple and roused a mob against him. They grabbed him, ²⁸yelling, "Men of Israel, help us! This is the man who preaches against our people everywhere and tells everybody to disobey the Jewish laws. He speaks against the Temple—and even defiles this holy place by bringing in Gentiles.*" ²⁹(For earlier that day they had seen him in the city with Trophimus, a Gentile from Ephesus,* and they assumed Paul had taken him into the Temple.)

³⁰The whole city was rocked by these accusations, and a great riot followed. Paul was grabbed and dragged out of the Temple, and immediately the gates were closed behind him. ³¹As they were trying to kill him, word reached the commander of the Roman regiment that all Jerusalem was in an uproar. ³²He immediately called out his soldiers and officers* and ran down among the crowd. When the mob saw the commander and the troops coming, they stopped beating Paul.

³³Then the commander arrested him and ordered him bound with two chains. He asked the crowd who he was and what he had done. ³⁴Some shouted one thing and some another. Since he couldn't find out the truth in all the uproar and confusion, he ordered that Paul be taken to the fortress. ³⁵As Paul reached the stairs, the mob grew so violent the soldiers had to lift him to their shoulders to protect him. ³⁶And the crowd followed behind, shouting, "Kill him, kill him!"

PAUL SPEAKS TO THE CROWD ³⁷As Paul was about to be taken inside, he said to the commander, "May I have a word with you?"

"Do you know Greek?" the commander asked, surprised. ³⁸"Aren't you the Egyptian who led a rebellion some time ago and took 4,000 members of the Assassins out into the desert?"

³⁹"No," Paul replied, "I am a Jew and a citizen of Tarsus in Cilicia, which is an important city. Please, let me talk to these people." ⁴⁰The commander agreed, so Paul stood on the stairs and motioned to the people to be quiet. Soon a deep silence enveloped the crowd, and he addressed them in their own language, Aramaic.*

22 "Brothers and esteemed fathers," Paul said, "listen to me as I offer my defense." ²When they heard him speaking in their own language,* the silence was even greater.

³Then Paul said, "I am a Jew, born in Tarsus, a city in Cilicia, and I was brought up and educated here in Jerusalem under Gamaliel. As his student, I was carefully trained in our Jewish laws and customs. I became very zealous to honor God in everything I did, just like all of you today. ⁴And I persecuted the followers of the Way, hounding some to death, arresting both men and women and throwing them in prison. ⁵The high priest and the whole council of elders can testify that this is so. For I received letters from them to our Jewish brothers in Damascus, authorizing me to bring the

Christians from there to Jerusalem, in chains, to be punished.

⁶"As I was on the road, approaching Damascus about noon, a very bright light from heaven suddenly shone down around me. ⁷I fell to the ground and heard a voice saying to me, 'Saul, Saul, why are you persecuting me?'

⁸"'Who are you, lord?' I asked.

"And the voice replied, 'I am Jesus the Nazarene,* the one you are persecuting.' ⁹The people with me saw the light but didn't understand the voice speaking to me.

¹⁰"I asked, 'What should I do, Lord?'

"And the Lord told me, 'Get up and go into Damascus, and there you will be told everything you are to do.'

¹¹"I was blinded by the intense light and had to be led by the hand to Damascus by my companions. ¹²A man named Ananias lived there. He was a godly man, deeply devoted to the law, and well regarded by all the Jews of Damascus. ¹³He came and stood beside me and said, 'Brother Saul, regain your sight.' And that very moment I could see him!

¹⁴"Then he told me, 'The God of our ancestors has chosen you to know his will and to see the Righteous One and hear him speak. ¹⁵For you are to be his witness, telling everyone what you have seen and heard. ¹⁶What are you waiting for? Get up and be baptized. Have your sins washed away by calling on the name of the Lord.'

¹⁷"After I returned to Jerusalem, I was praying in the Temple and fell into a trance. ¹⁸I saw a vision of Jesus* saying to me, 'Hurry! Leave Jerusalem, for the people here won't accept your testimony about me.'

¹⁹"'But Lord,' I argued, 'they certainly know that in every synagogue I imprisoned and beat those who believed in you. ²⁰And I was in complete agreement when your witness Stephen was killed. I stood by and kept the coats they took off when they stoned him.'

²¹"But the Lord said to me, 'Go, for I will send you far away to the Gentiles!'"

²²The crowd listened until Paul said that word. Then they all began to shout, "Away with such a fellow! He isn't fit to live!" ²³They yelled, threw off their coats, and tossed handfuls of dust into the air.

PAUL REVEALS HIS ROMAN CITIZENSHIP
²⁴The commander brought Paul inside and ordered him lashed with whips to make him confess his crime. He wanted to find out why

---

SOMETHING IN COMMON
(22:1-5) Before launching into a full-scale defense of Christianity, Paul usually tried to find something in common with his audience. By revealing that he too had persecuted Christian leaders in the past, Paul was saying that he was as zealous for God as any of his listeners, and acknowledging their sincere motives in trying to kill him. Like Paul, are you ready to defend your faith? People are much more likely to listen if they feel they have something in common with you.

21:40 Or *Hebrew.*   **22:2** Greek *in Aramaic,* or *in Hebrew.*   **22:8** Or *Jesus of Nazareth.*   **22:18** Greek *him.*

the crowd had become so furious. ²⁵When they tied Paul down to lash him, Paul said to the officer* standing there, "Is it legal for you to whip a Roman citizen who hasn't even been tried?"

²⁶When the officer heard this, he went to the commander and asked, "What are you doing? This man is a Roman citizen!"

²⁷So the commander went over and asked Paul, "Tell me, are you a Roman citizen?"

"Yes, I certainly am," Paul replied.

²⁸"I am, too," the commander muttered, "and it cost me plenty!"

Paul answered, "But I am a citizen by birth!"

²⁹The soldiers who were about to interrogate Paul quickly withdrew when they heard he was a Roman citizen, and the commander was frightened because he had ordered him bound and whipped.

PAUL BEFORE THE HIGH COUNCIL ³⁰The next day the commander ordered the leading priests into session with the Jewish high council.* He wanted to find out what the trouble was all about, so he released Paul to have him stand before them.

23 Gazing intently at the high council,* Paul began: "Brothers, I have always lived before God with a clear conscience!"

²Instantly Ananias the high priest commanded those close to Paul to slap him on the mouth. ³But Paul said to him, "God will slap you, you corrupt hypocrite!* What kind of judge are you to break the law yourself by ordering me struck like that?"

⁴Those standing near Paul said to him, "Do you dare to insult God's high priest?"

⁵"I'm sorry, brothers. I didn't realize he was the high priest," Paul replied, "for the Scriptures say, 'You must not speak evil of any of your rulers.'*"

⁶Paul realized that some members of the high council were Sadducees and some were Pharisees, so he shouted, "Brothers, I am a Pharisee, as were my ancestors! And I am on trial because my hope is in the resurrection of the dead!"

⁷This divided the council—the Pharisees against the Sadducees—⁸for the Sadducees say there is no resurrection or angels or spirits, but the Pharisees believe in all of these. ⁹So there was a great uproar. Some of the teachers of religious law who were Pharisees jumped up and began to argue forcefully. "We see nothing wrong with him," they shouted. "Perhaps a spirit or an angel spoke to him." ¹⁰As the conflict grew more violent, the commander was afraid they would tear Paul apart. So he ordered his soldiers to go and rescue him by force and take him back to the fortress.

¹¹That night the Lord appeared to Paul and said, "Be encouraged, Paul. Just as you have been a witness to me here in Jerusalem, you must preach the Good News in Rome as well."

THE PLAN TO KILL PAUL ¹²The next morning a group of Jews* got together and bound themselves with an oath not to eat or drink until they had killed Paul. ¹³There were more than forty of them in the conspiracy. ¹⁴They went to the leading priests and elders and told them, "We have bound ourselves with an oath to eat nothing until we have killed Paul. ¹⁵So you and the high council should ask the commander to bring Paul back to the council again. Pretend you want to examine his case more fully. We will kill him on the way."

¹⁶But Paul's nephew—his sister's son—heard of their plan and went to the fortress and told Paul. ¹⁷Paul called for one of the Roman officers* and said, "Take this young man to the commander. He has something important to tell him."

¹⁸So the officer did, explaining, "Paul, the prisoner, called me over and asked me to bring this young man to you because he has something to tell you."

¹⁹The commander took his hand, led him aside, and asked, "What is it you want to tell me?"

²⁰Paul's nephew told him, "Some Jews are going to ask you to bring Paul before the high council tomorrow, pretending they want to get some more information. ²¹But don't do it! There are more than forty men hiding along the way ready to ambush him. They have vowed not to eat or drink anything until they have killed him. They are ready now, just waiting for your consent."

··

AMAZING!
(23:12-24) The Roman commander ordered Paul to be sent to Caesarea. Jerusalem was the seat of Jewish government, but Caesarea was the area's Roman headquarters. God works in amazing and amusing ways. He could have gotten Paul to Caesarea by a variety of means, but he chose to use the Roman army to deliver Paul from his enemies. God's ways are not ours—we are limited, he is not. Don't ask him to respond your way. When God intervenes, anything can happen—often much more and much better than you could ever anticipate.

22:25 Greek *the centurion;* also in 22:26.   22:30 Greek *Sanhedrin.*
23:1 Greek *Sanhedrin;* also in 23:6, 15, 20, 28.   23:3 Greek *you whitewashed wall.*   23:5 Exod 22:28.   23:12 Greek *the Jews.*
23:17 Greek *centurions;* also in 23:23.

²²"Don't let anyone know you told me this," the commander warned the young man.

PAUL IS SENT TO CAESAREA
²³Then the commander called two of his officers and ordered, "Get 200 soldiers ready to leave for Caesarea at nine o'clock tonight. Also take 200 spearmen and 70 mounted troops. ²⁴Provide horses for Paul to ride, and get him safely to Governor Felix." ²⁵Then he wrote this letter to the governor:

²⁶"From Claudius Lysias, to his Excellency, Governor Felix: Greetings!

²⁷"This man was seized by some Jews, and they were about to kill him when I arrived with the troops. When I learned that he was a Roman citizen, I removed him to safety. ²⁸Then I took him to their high council to try to learn the basis of the accusations against him. ²⁹I soon discovered the charge was something regarding their religious law—certainly nothing worthy of imprisonment or death. ³⁰But when I was informed of a plot to kill him, I immediately sent him on to you. I have told his accusers to bring their charges before you."

³¹So that night, as ordered, the soldiers took Paul as far as Antipatris. ³²They returned to the fortress the next morning, while the mounted troops took him on to Caesarea. ³³When they arrived in Caesarea, they presented Paul and the letter to Governor Felix. ³⁴He read it and then asked Paul what province he was from. "Cilicia," Paul answered.

³⁵"I will hear your case myself when your accusers arrive," the governor told him. Then the governor ordered him kept in the prison at Herod's headquarters.*

24 PAUL APPEARS BEFORE FELIX
Five days later Ananias, the high priest, arrived with some of the Jewish elders and the lawyer* Tertullus, to present their case against Paul to the governor. ²When Paul was called in, Tertullus presented the charges against Paul in the following address to the governor:

"You have provided a long period of peace for us Jews and with foresight have enacted reforms for us. ³For all of this, Your Excellency, we are very grateful to you. ⁴But I don't want to bore you, so please give me your attention for only a moment. ⁵We have found this man to be a troublemaker who is constantly stirring up riots among the Jews all over the world. He is a ringleader of the cult known as the Nazarenes.

⁶Furthermore, he was trying to desecrate the Temple when we arrested him.* ⁸You can find out the truth of our accusations by examining him yourself." ⁹Then the other Jews chimed in, declaring that everything Tertullus said was true.

¹⁰The governor then motioned for Paul to speak. Paul said, "I know, sir, that you have been a judge of Jewish affairs for many years, so I gladly present my defense before you. ¹¹You can quickly discover that I arrived in Jerusalem no more than twelve days ago to worship at the Temple. ¹²My accusers never found me arguing with anyone in the Temple, nor stirring up a riot in any synagogue or on the streets of the city. ¹³These men cannot prove the things they accuse me of doing.

¹⁴"But I admit that I follow the Way, which they call a cult. I worship the God of our ancestors, and I firmly believe the Jewish law and everything written in the prophets. ¹⁵I have the same hope in God that these men have, that he will raise both the righteous and the unrighteous. ¹⁶Because of this, I always try to maintain a clear conscience before God and all people.

¹⁷"After several years away, I returned to Jerusalem with money to aid my people and to offer sacrifices to God. ¹⁸My accusers saw me in the Temple as I was completing a purification ceremony. There was no crowd around me and no rioting. ¹⁹But some Jews from the province of Asia were there—and they ought to be here to bring charges if they have anything against me! ²⁰Ask these men here what crime the Jewish high council* found me guilty of, ²¹except for the one time I shouted out, 'I am on trial before you today because I believe in the resurrection of the dead!'"

²²At that point Felix, who was quite familiar with the Way, adjourned the hearing and said, "Wait until Lysias, the garrison commander, arrives. Then I will decide the case." ²³He ordered an officer* to keep Paul in custody but to give him some freedom and allow his friends to visit him and take care of his needs.

²⁴A few days later Felix came back with his wife, Drusilla, who was Jewish. Sending for Paul, they listened as he told them about faith in Christ Jesus. ²⁵As he reasoned with them about righteousness and self-control and the coming day of judgment, Felix became fright-

23:35 Greek Herod's Praetorium.   24:1 Greek some elders and an orator.   24:6 Some manuscripts add an expanded conclusion to verse 6, all of verse 7, and an additional phrase in verse 8: We would have judged him by our law, ⁷but Lysias, the commander of the garrison, came and violently took him away from us, ⁸commanding his accusers to come before you.   24:20 Greek Sanhedrin.   24:23 Greek a centurion.

ened. "Go away for now," he replied. "When it is more convenient, I'll call for you again." [26]He also hoped that Paul would bribe him, so he sent for him quite often and talked with him.

[27]After two years went by in this way, Felix was succeeded by Porcius Festus. And because Felix wanted to gain favor with the Jewish people, he left Paul in prison.

25 **PAUL APPEARS BEFORE FESTUS** Three days after Festus arrived in Caesarea to take over his new responsibilities, he left for Jerusalem, [2]where the leading priests and other Jewish leaders met with him and made their accusations against Paul. [3]They asked Festus as a favor to transfer Paul to Jerusalem (planning to ambush and kill him on the way). [4]But Festus replied that Paul was at Caesarea and he himself would be returning there soon. [5]So he said, "Those of you in authority can return with me. If Paul has done anything wrong, you can make your accusations."

[6]About eight or ten days later Festus returned to Caesarea, and on the following day he took his seat in court and ordered that Paul be brought in. [7]When Paul arrived, the Jewish leaders from Jerusalem gathered around and made many serious accusations they couldn't prove.

[8]Paul denied the charges. "I am not guilty of any crime against the Jewish laws or the Temple or the Roman government," he said.

[9]Then Festus, wanting to please the Jews, asked him, "Are you willing to go to Jerusalem and stand trial before me there?"

[10]But Paul replied, "No! This is the official Roman court, so I ought to be tried right here. You know very well I am not guilty of harming the Jews. [11]If I have done something worthy of death, I don't refuse to die. But if I am innocent, no one has a right to turn me over to these men to kill me. I appeal to Caesar!"

[12]Festus conferred with his advisers and then replied, "Very well! You have appealed to Caesar, and to Caesar you will go!"

[13]A few days later King Agrippa arrived with his sister, Bernice,* to pay their respects to Festus. [14]During their stay of several days, Festus discussed Paul's case with the king. "There is a prisoner here," he told him, "whose case was left for me by Felix. [15]When I was in Jerusalem, the leading priests and Jewish elders pressed charges against him and asked me to condemn him. [16]I pointed out to them that Roman law does not convict people without a trial. They must be given an oppor-

25:13 Greek *Agrippa the king and Bernice arrived.*

tunity to confront their accusers and defend themselves.

[17]"When his accusers came here for the trial, I didn't delay. I called the case the very next day and ordered Paul brought in. [18]But the accusations made against him weren't any of the crimes I expected. [19]Instead, it was something about their religion and a dead man named Jesus, who Paul insists is alive. [20]I was at a loss to know how to investigate these things, so I asked him whether he would be willing to stand trial on these charges in Jerusalem. [21]But Paul appealed to have his case decided by the emperor. So I ordered that he be held in custody until I could arrange to send him to Caesar."

[22]"I'd like to hear the man myself," Agrippa said.

And Festus replied, "You will—tomorrow!"

PAUL SPEAKS TO AGRIPPA [23]So the next day Agrippa and Bernice arrived at the auditorium with great pomp, accompanied by military officers and prominent men of the city. Festus ordered that Paul be brought in. [24]Then Festus said, "King Agrippa and all who are here, this is the man whose death is demanded by all the Jews, both here and in Jerusalem. [25]But in my opinion he has done nothing deserving

"I ALWAYS TRY TO MAINTAIN A **CLEAR CONSCIENCE** BEFORE GOD AND ALL PEOPLE." ■ ■ ■ ■ ■ ACTS 24:16 ■ ■ ■ ■ ■

· ·

A LIFE-CHANGING MESSAGE
(24:24-25) Paul's talk with Felix became so personal that Felix felt convicted. Felix, like Herod Antipas (Mark 6:17-18), had taken another man's wife. Paul's words were interesting until they focused on "righteousness and self-control and the coming day of judgment." Like Felix, many people are glad to talk about the Bible or God as long as they don't have to change in any way. When truth hits home, they resist. But the gospel is all about God's power to change lives. Sometimes the truth hurts. How have you responded to the truth you've heard?

OPPORTUNITIES
(25:23) Paul was in prison, but that didn't stop him from making the most of his situation. Military officers and prominent city leaders met in the palace room with Agrippa to hear this case. Paul saw this new audience as yet another opportunity to present the gospel. Rather than complain about your present situation, look for opportunities to serve God and share him with others. Problems may be opportunities in disguise.

death. However, since he appealed his case to the emperor, I have decided to send him to Rome.

²⁶"But what shall I write the emperor? For there is no clear charge against him. So I have brought him before all of you, and especially you, King Agrippa, so that after we examine him, I might have something to write. ²⁷For it makes no sense to send a prisoner to the emperor without specifying the charges against him!"

26

Then Agrippa said to Paul, "You may speak in your defense."

So Paul, gesturing with his hand, started his defense: ²"I am fortunate, King Agrippa, that you are the one hearing my defense today against all these accusations made by the Jewish leaders, ³for I know you are an expert on all Jewish customs and controversies. Now please listen to me patiently!

⁴"As the Jewish leaders are well aware, I was given a thorough Jewish training from my earliest childhood among my own people and in Jerusalem. ⁵If they would admit it, they know that I have been a member of the Pharisees, the strictest sect of our religion. ⁶Now I am on trial because of my hope in the fulfillment of God's promise made to our ancestors. ⁷In fact, that is why the twelve tribes of Israel zealously worship God night and day, and they share the same hope I have. Yet, Your Majesty, they accuse me for having this hope! ⁸Why does it seem incredible to any of you that God can raise the dead?

⁹"I used to believe that I ought to do everything I could to oppose the very name of Jesus the Nazarene.* ¹⁰Indeed, I did just that in Jerusalem. Authorized by the leading priests, I caused many believers* there to be sent to prison. And I cast my vote against them when they were condemned to death. ¹¹Many times I had them punished in the synagogues to get them to curse Jesus.* I was so violently opposed to them that I even chased them down in foreign cities.

....

FACTS

(26:26) When he defended the gospel message, Paul mentioned facts. People were still alive who had heard Jesus and seen his miracles. The empty tomb could still be seen. And the Christian message was having an effect "all over the world" (17:6). Likewise, we can study the evidence that the Bible presents concerning Jesus' life as well as historical and archaeological records of the early church. Examine the events and facts as verified by many witnesses. Reconfirm your faith with the truth of these accounts.

¹²"One day I was on such a mission to Damascus, armed with the authority and commission of the leading priests. ¹³About noon, Your Majesty, as I was on the road, a light from heaven brighter than the sun shone down on me and my companions. ¹⁴We all fell down, and I heard a voice saying to me in Aramaic,* 'Saul, Saul, why are you persecuting me? It is useless for you to fight against my will.*'

¹⁵"'Who are you, lord?' I asked.

"And the Lord replied, 'I am Jesus, the one you are persecuting. ¹⁶Now get to your feet! For I have appeared to you to appoint you as my servant and witness. You are to tell the world what you have seen and what I will show you in the future. ¹⁷And I will rescue you from both your own people and the Gentiles. Yes, I am sending you to the Gentiles ¹⁸to open their eyes, so they may turn from darkness to light and from the power of Satan to God. Then they will receive forgiveness for their sins and be given a place among God's people, who are set apart by faith in me.'

¹⁹"And so, King Agrippa, I obeyed that vision from heaven. ²⁰I preached first to those in Damascus, then in Jerusalem and throughout all Judea, and also to the Gentiles, that all must repent of their sins and turn to God—and prove they have changed by the good things they do. ²¹Some Jews arrested me in the Temple for preaching this, and they tried to kill me. ²²But God has protected me right up to this present time so I can testify to everyone, from the least to the greatest. I teach nothing except what the prophets and Moses said would happen— ²³that the Messiah would suffer and be the first to rise from the dead, and in this way announce God's light to Jews and Gentiles alike."

²⁴Suddenly, Festus shouted, "Paul, you are insane. Too much study has made you crazy!"

²⁵But Paul replied, "I am not insane, Most Excellent Festus. What I am saying is the sober truth. ²⁶And King Agrippa knows about these things. I speak boldly, for I am sure these events are all familiar to him, for they were not done in a corner! ²⁷King Agrippa, do you believe the prophets? I know you do—"

²⁸Agrippa interrupted him. "Do you think you can persuade me to become a Christian so quickly?"*

²⁹Paul replied, "Whether quickly or not, I pray to God that both you and everyone here in this audience might become the same as I am, except for these chains."

26:9 Or *Jesus of Nazareth.*   **26:10** Greek *many of God's holy people.*   **26:11** Greek *to blaspheme.*   **26:14a** Or *Hebrew.*   **26:14b** Greek *It is hard for you to kick against the oxgoads.*   **26:28** Or *"A little more, and your arguments would make me a Christian."*

[30]Then the king, the governor, Bernice, and all the others stood and left. [31]As they went out, they talked it over and agreed, "This man hasn't done anything to deserve death or imprisonment."

[32]And Agrippa said to Festus, "He could have been set free if he hadn't appealed to Caesar."

27 PAUL SAILS FOR ROME When the time came, we set sail for Italy. Paul and several other prisoners were placed in the custody of a Roman officer* named Julius, a captain of the Imperial Regiment. [2]Aristarchus, a Macedonian from Thessalonica, was also with us. We left on a ship whose home port was Adramyttium on the northwest coast of the province of Asia;* it was scheduled to make several stops at ports along the coast of the province.

[3]The next day when we docked at Sidon, Julius was very kind to Paul and let him go ashore to visit with friends so they could provide for his needs. [4]Putting out to sea from there, we encountered strong headwinds that made it difficult to keep the ship on course, so we sailed north of Cyprus between the island and the mainland. [5]Keeping to the open sea, we passed along the coast of Cilicia and Pamphylia, landing at Myra, in the province of Lycia. [6]There the commanding officer found an Egyptian ship from Alexandria that was bound for Italy, and he put us on board.

[7]We had several days of slow sailing, and after great difficulty we finally neared Cnidus. But the wind was against us, so we sailed across to Crete and along the sheltered coast of the island, past the cape of Salmone. [8]We struggled along the coast with great difficulty and finally arrived at Fair Havens, near the town of Lasea. [9]We had lost a lot of time. The weather was becoming dangerous for sea travel because it was so late in the fall,* and Paul spoke to the ship's officers about it.

[10]"Men," he said, "I believe there is trouble ahead if we go on—shipwreck, loss of cargo, and danger to our lives as well." [11]But the officer in charge of the prisoners listened more to the ship's captain and the owner than to Paul. [12]And since Fair Havens was an exposed harbor—a poor place to spend the winter—most of the crew wanted to go on to Phoenix, farther up the coast of Crete, and spend the winter there. Phoenix was a good harbor with only a southwest and northwest exposure.

THE STORM AT SEA [13]When a light wind began blowing from the south, the sailors thought they could make it. So they pulled up anchor and sailed close to the shore of Crete. [14]But the weather changed abruptly, and a wind of typhoon strength (called a "northeaster") burst across the island and blew us out to sea. [15]The sailors couldn't turn the ship into the wind, so they gave up and let it run before the gale.

[16]We sailed along the sheltered side of a small island named Cauda,* where with great difficulty we hoisted aboard the lifeboat being towed behind us. [17]Then the sailors bound ropes around the hull of the ship to strengthen it. They were afraid of being driven across to the sandbars of Syrtis off the African coast, so they lowered the sea anchor to slow the ship and were driven before the wind.

[18]The next day, as gale-force winds continued to batter the ship, the crew began throwing the cargo overboard. [19]The following day they even took some of the ship's gear and threw it overboard. [20]The terrible storm raged for many days, blotting out the sun and the stars, until at last all hope was gone.

[21]No one had eaten for a long time. Finally, Paul called the crew together and said, "Men, you should have listened to me in the first place and not left Crete. You would have avoided all this damage and loss. [22]But take courage! None of you will lose your lives, even though the ship will go down. [23]For last night an angel of the God to whom I belong and whom I serve stood beside me, [24]and he said, 'Don't be afraid, Paul, for you will surely stand trial before Caesar! What's more, God in his goodness has granted safety to everyone sailing with you.' [25]So take courage! For I believe God. It will be just as he said. [26]But we will be shipwrecked on an island."

....

EVEN BETTER
(27:1–28:24) *One of Paul's most important journeys was to Rome. He didn't get there in quite the way he had expected, however. His journey turned out to be more of a legal one than a missionary journey, thanks to a series of trials and transactions. These events resulted in Paul being delivered to Rome, where he shared the gospel message in places like the emperor's palace.*

Ever feel frustrated because your plans didn't work out the way you wanted them to? Just think: God is never out of control! He knows how to work things out so that the results are even better than we expected. Trusting God with your plans is a surefire plan for success!

27:1 Greek *centurion;* similarly in 27:6, 11, 31, 43.   **27:2** *Asia* was a Roman province in what is now western Turkey.   **27:9** Greek *because the fast was now already gone by.* This fast was associated with the Day of Atonement (*Yom Kippur*), which occurred in late September or early October.   **27:16** Some manuscripts read *Clauda.*

THE SHIPWRECK [27]About midnight on the fourteenth night of the storm, as we were being driven across the Sea of Adria,* the sailors sensed land was near. [28]They dropped a weighted line and found that the water was 120 feet deep. But a little later they measured again and found it was only 90 feet deep.* [29]At this rate they were afraid we would soon be driven against the rocks along the shore, so they threw out four anchors from the back of the ship and prayed for daylight.

[30]Then the sailors tried to abandon the ship; they lowered the lifeboat as though they were going to put out anchors from the front of the ship. [31]But Paul said to the commanding officer and the soldiers, "You will all die unless the sailors stay aboard." [32]So the soldiers cut the ropes to the lifeboat and let it drift away.

[33]Just as day was dawning, Paul urged everyone to eat. "You have been so worried that you haven't touched food for two weeks," he said. [34]"Please eat something now for your own good. For not a hair of your heads will perish." [35]Then he took some bread, gave thanks to God before them all, and broke off a piece and ate it. [36]Then everyone was encouraged and began to eat—[37]all 276 of us who were on board. [38]After eating, the crew lightened the ship further by throwing the cargo of wheat overboard.

[39]When morning dawned, they didn't recognize the coastline, but they saw a bay with a beach and wondered if they could get to shore by running the ship aground. [40]So they cut off the anchors and left them in the sea. Then they lowered the rudders, raised the foresail, and headed toward shore. [41]But they hit a shoal and ran the ship aground too soon. The bow of the ship stuck fast, while the stern was repeatedly smashed by the force of the waves and began to break apart.

[42]The soldiers wanted to kill the prisoners to make sure they didn't swim ashore and escape. [43]But the commanding officer wanted to spare Paul, so he didn't let them carry out their plan. Then he ordered all who could swim to jump overboard first and make for land. [44]The others held on to planks or debris from the broken ship.* So everyone escaped safely to shore.

28 **PAUL ON THE ISLAND OF MALTA** Once we were safe on shore, we learned that we were on the island of Malta. [2]The people of the island were very kind to us. It was cold and rainy, so they built a fire on the shore to welcome us.

[3]As Paul gathered an armful of sticks and was laying them on the fire, a poisonous snake, driven out by the heat, bit him on the hand. [4]The people of the island saw it hanging from his hand and said to each other, "A murderer, no doubt! Though he escaped the sea, justice will not permit him to live." [5]But Paul shook off the snake into the fire and was unharmed. [6]The people waited for him to swell up or suddenly drop dead. But when they had waited a long time and saw that he wasn't harmed, they changed their minds and decided he was a god.

[7]Near the shore where we landed was an estate belonging to Publius, the chief official of the island. He welcomed us and treated us kindly for three days. [8]As it happened, Publius's father was ill with fever and dysentery. Paul went in and prayed for him, and laying his hands on him, he healed him. [9]Then all the other sick people on the island came and were healed. [10]As a result we were showered with honors, and when the time came to sail, people supplied us with everything we would need for the trip.

PAUL ARRIVES AT ROME [11]It was three months after the shipwreck that we set sail on another ship that had wintered at the island—an Alexandrian ship with the twin gods* as its figurehead. [12]Our first stop was Syracuse,* where we stayed three days. [13]From there we sailed across to Rhegium.* A day later a south wind began blowing, so the following day we sailed up the coast to Puteoli. [14]There we found some believers,* who invited us to spend a week with them. And so we came to Rome.

[15]The brothers and sisters* in Rome had heard we were coming, and they came to meet us at the Forum* on the Appian Way. Others joined us at The Three Taverns.* When Paul saw them, he was encouraged and thanked God.

[16]When we arrived in Rome, Paul was permitted to have his own private lodging, though he was guarded by a soldier.

PAUL PREACHES AT ROME UNDER GUARD
[17]Three days after Paul's arrival, he called

27:27 The *Sea of Adria* includes the central portion of the Mediterranean.   27:28 Greek *20 fathoms . . . 15 fathoms* [37 meters . . . 27 meters].   27:44 Or *or were helped by members of the ship's crew.*   28:11 The *twin gods* were the Roman gods Castor and Pollux.   28:12 *Syracuse* was on the island of Sicily. 28:13 *Rhegium* was on the southern tip of Italy.   28:14 Greek *brothers.*   28:15a Greek *brothers.*   28:15b The *Forum* was about 43 miles (70 kilometers) from Rome.   28:15c The *Three Taverns* was about 35 miles (57 kilometers) from Rome.

together the local Jewish leaders. He said to them, "Brothers, I was arrested in Jerusalem and handed over to the Roman government, even though I had done nothing against our people or the customs of our ancestors. ¹⁸The Romans tried me and wanted to release me, because they found no cause for the death sentence. ¹⁹But when the Jewish leaders protested the decision, I felt it necessary to appeal to Caesar, even though I had no desire to press charges against my own people. ²⁰I asked you to come here today so we could get acquainted and so I could explain to you that I am bound with this chain because I believe that the hope of Israel—the Messiah—has already come."

²¹They replied, "We have had no letters from Judea or reports against you from anyone who has come here. ²²But we want to hear what you believe, for the only thing we know about this movement is that it is denounced everywhere."

²³So a time was set, and on that day a large number of people came to Paul's lodging. He explained and testified about the Kingdom of God and tried to persuade them about Jesus from the Scriptures. Using the law of Moses and the books of the prophets, he spoke to them from morning until evening. ²⁴Some were persuaded by the things he said, but others did not believe. ²⁵And after they had argued back and forth among themselves, they left with this final word from Paul: "The Holy Spirit was right when he said to your ancestors through Isaiah the prophet,

²⁶ 'Go and say to this people:
When you hear what I say,
    you will not understand.
When you see what I do,
    you will not comprehend.
²⁷ For the hearts of these people are
        hardened,
    and their ears cannot hear,
    and they have closed their eyes—
so their eyes cannot see,
    and their ears cannot hear,
    and their hearts cannot understand,
and they cannot turn to me
    and let me heal them.'*

²⁸So I want you to know that this salvation from God has also been offered to the Gentiles, and they will accept it."*

³⁰For the next two years, Paul lived in Rome at his own expense.* He welcomed all who visited him, ³¹boldly proclaiming the Kingdom of God and teaching about the Lord Jesus Christ. And no one tried to stop him.

....

CHURCH HISTORY
(28:31) The book of Acts shows the history of the Christian church and its expansion in ever-widening circles to Jerusalem, Antioch, Ephesus, and Rome—the most influential cities in the western world. Acts also presents the stories of the members of the early church—people like Peter, Stephen, James, and Paul as well as ordinary people like merchants, slaves, jailers, church leaders, men, women, Gentiles, and Jews—who acted through the power of the Holy Spirit.

Many unsung heroes of the faith continued the acts of the Holy Spirit, changing the world with a changeless message: Jesus Christ is Savior and Lord for all who call upon him. Today we can take part in the continuing story of the spread of the gospel, bringing that same message to our world so that others may hear and believe.

28:26-27 Isa 6:9-10 (Greek version). 28:28 Some manuscripts add verse 29, *And when he had said these words, the Jews departed, greatly disagreeing with each other.* 28:30 Or *in his own rented quarters.*

Imagine you're out one evening, when you happen upon your dream car. As you admire its beauty, you notice a key in the ignition . . . and unlocked doors. You glance around. The street is deserted.

For an agonizingly long moment the inner voices battle. But that would be stealing! *your conscience protests.* No way! *another voice whispers.* You're not going to keep it. *Then adventure wins out. Your heart pounds as you slide into the driver's seat and the engine hums to life.*

You slip the car into gear for one slow trip around the block—but one glance at the speedometer's 160-mph top speed has a better idea. You head for the open road.

Everything is a blur. You remember the exhilaration of 143 mph, then flashing blue lights, cold steel handcuffs, being in court, and the judge's gavel pounding out a guilty verdict. The sentence: twenty thousand dollars and a six-month jail term. You deserve punishment, but that's a severe penalty!

Then the judge does something curious. He removes his robe, pulls out his checkbook, and pays your fine! Next he announces he will serve your jail sentence. Then he looks you in the eyes and says, "I love you."

This analogy isn't perfect, but it does help explain how God deals with sinful humanity. The very penalty he demands, he provided. The penalty is death, and Christ dies instead. If you'd like an even better explanation of God's perfect justice and his intense love for you, read the book of Romans.

KEY POINTS

SIN All of us were born with a desire to do wrong—a desire that comes with a consequence: death.

SALVATION Although we don't deserve it, God in his kindness reaches out to love and forgive us. Christ's death paid the penalty for our sin.

GROWTH The Holy Spirit provides freedom from the demands of the law and from the fear of God's judgment. Because we are free from sin's control and the fear of God's punishment, we can grow in our relationship with Christ.

SOVEREIGNTY Throughout the ages, God shaped events to bring about his plan to save humans. Although God ultimately has control over all aspects of life, he still allows people to choose to accept or reject his forgiveness.

SERVICE God gives spiritual gifts to each member of the body of Christ. These gifts enable believers to serve God and to be loving and sensitive to others. By actively and vigorously building up other believers, Christians grow in unity and can be a symphony of service to God.

1 **GREETINGS FROM PAUL** This letter is from Paul, a slave of Christ Jesus, chosen by God to be an apostle and sent out to preach his Good News. [2]God promised this Good News long ago through his prophets in the holy Scriptures. [3]The Good News is about his Son. In his earthly life he was born into King David's family line, [4]and he was shown to be* the Son of God when he was raised from the dead by the power of the Holy Spirit.* He is Jesus Christ our Lord. [5]Through Christ, God has given us the privilege* and authority as apostles to tell Gentiles everywhere what God has done for them, so that they will believe and obey him, bringing glory to his name.

[6]And you are included among those Gentiles who have been called to belong to Jesus Christ. [7]I am writing to all of you in Rome who are loved by God and are called to be his own holy people.

May God our Father and the Lord Jesus Christ give you grace and peace.

GOD'S GOOD NEWS [8]Let me say first that I thank my God through Jesus Christ for all of you, because your faith in him is being talked about all over the world. [9]God knows how often I pray for you. Day and night I bring you and your needs in prayer to God, whom I serve with all my heart* by spreading the Good News about his Son.

[10]One of the things I always pray for is the opportunity, God willing, to come at last to see you. [11]For I long to visit you so I can bring you some spiritual gift that will help you grow strong in the Lord. [12]When we get together, I want to encourage you in your faith, but I also want to be encouraged by yours.

[13]I want you to know, dear brothers and sisters,* that I planned many times to visit you, but I was prevented until now. I want to work among you and see spiritual fruit, just as I have seen among other Gentiles. [14]For I have

1:4a Or *and was designated.*   **1:4b** Or *by the Spirit of holiness; or in the new realm of the Spirit.*   **1:5** Or *the grace.*   **1:9** Or *in my spirit.*   **1:13** Greek *brothers.*

ULTIMATE ISSUES HOMOSEXUALITY

Is the gay lifestyle really wrong? Shows like *Will & Grace*, *Boy Meets Boy*, and *Queer Eye for the Straight Guy* would say no. Instead, they would argue that homosexuality is "an alternative lifestyle"—one that you hear about more and more on TV and also in the courts.

For example, in 2003 the Massachusetts Supreme Judicial Court decided that denying same-sex couples the right to marriage was unconstitutional. They also decided that the definition of marriage needed to change from union of a man and a woman to the "voluntary union of two persons as spouses, to the exclusion of all others."

By now, you might wonder what the real scoop is. In the face of changing legislation, has God's view of homosexuality also changed?

Here's the short answer: No.

Now here's a longer one: in Romans 1:18-32, the apostle Paul argues that all people everywhere are without excuse in knowing that there is a God. Proclaiming that nature itself reveals its Creator, Paul then begins a scathing rebuke against people who deny God and his plan for creation. Paul has particularly harsh words for those who engage in the sins of idolatry and homosexuality. These people, he writes, go against God's design for human sexuality, and in so doing realize drastic consequences for their behavior. Men and women who practice homosexuality experience tremendous opposition—socially, emotionally, physically, and spiritually. Yet

they ignore all these warning signs. And sooner or later they will crash and burn.

Two important messages need to be given on the subject of homosexuality. One is for our society, where biblical notions of right and wrong are sometimes viewed as outdated. That message is that some lifestyles are not acceptable "alternatives." Some lifestyles—such as alcoholism or materialism . . . or homosexuality—are wrong; they are sinful. Those who engage in such behaviors should come to God in confession and repentance and ask for his forgiveness and healing.

The second message is for Christians. While homosexuality is sin, it is not the unforgivable sin (see Mark 3:29). God loves homosexuals just as much as he loves other people who do wrong. Jesus' death on the Cross paid for the sin of homosexuality, just as it paid for the sins of lying, greed, lust, hate, and pride. Someone has said—and it is true—that the church is a hospital for sinners, not a showcase for saints. It is a place where those caught in the sin of homosexuality can come to be freed and forgiven. It is a place where believers who have committed the sins of hatred, prejudice, and self-righteousness toward homosexuals need to go to ask the Lord for forgiveness and healing.

Homosexuals, like all sinners, stand guilty before God. If that were the whole story, we would have no hope. The great message of Romans—and of the entire Bible—is that Jesus Christ can set us free, regardless of what we've done wrong. ∎

THE GOSPEL GOES TO ROME
When Paul wrote his letter to the church in Rome he had not yet been there, but he had taken the gospel "from Jerusalem all the way to Illyricum" (15:19). He planned to visit and preach in Rome one day, and hoped to continue to take the gospel farther west—even to Spain.

a great sense of obligation to people in both the civilized world and the rest of the world,* to the educated and uneducated alike. ¹⁵So I am eager to come to you in Rome, too, to preach the Good News.

¹⁶For I am not ashamed of this Good News about Christ. It is the power of God at work, saving everyone who believes—the Jew first and also the Gentile.* ¹⁷This Good News tells us how God makes us right in his sight. This is accomplished from start to finish by faith. As the Scriptures say, "It is through faith that a righteous person has life."*

GOD'S ANGER AT SIN ¹⁸But God shows his anger from heaven against all sinful, wicked people who suppress the truth by their wickedness.* ¹⁹They know the truth about God because he has made it obvious to them. ²⁰For ever since the world was created, people have seen the earth and sky. Through everything God made, they can clearly see his invisible qualities—his eternal power and divine nature. So they have no excuse for not knowing God.

²¹Yes, they knew God, but they wouldn't wor-

1:14 Greek *to Greeks and barbarians.* **1:16** Greek *also the Greek.* **1:17** Or *"The righteous will live by faith."* Hab 2:4. **1:18** Or *who, by their wickedness, prevent the truth from being known.*

ship him as God or even give him thanks. And they began to think up foolish ideas of what God was like. As a result, their minds became dark and confused. ²²Claiming to be wise, they instead became utter fools. ²³And instead of worshiping the glorious, ever-living God, they worshiped idols made to look like mere people and birds and animals and reptiles.

²⁴So God abandoned them to do whatever shameful things their hearts desired. As a result, they did vile and degrading things

·····························

GOOD NEWS
(1:16-17) Paul was not ashamed because his message was Good News. It was powerful, it was for everyone, and it was part of God's revealed plan. When you are tempted to be ashamed, remember what the Good News is all about. If you focus on God and on what he is doing in the world rather than on your own inadequacy, your embarrassment will soon disappear.

NO EXCUSE
(1:18-20) Paul answers a common question: How could a loving God condemn someone to hell who has never heard the Good News of Christ? In fact, says Paul, God has revealed himself to all people. Although everyone knows what God requires, no one lives up to his standards. That's why Jesus died. But if people suppress God's truth in order to live their own way, they have no excuse. (See also the Ultimate Issue "What About Those Who Never Hear the Gospel?" in Acts.)

with each other's bodies. 25They traded the truth about God for a lie. So they worshiped and served the things God created instead of the Creator himself, who is worthy of eternal praise! Amen. 26That is why God abandoned them to their shameful desires. Even the women turned against the natural way to have sex and instead indulged in sex with each other. 27And the men, instead of having normal sexual relations with women, burned with lust for each other. Men did shameful things with other men, and as a result of this sin, they suffered within themselves the penalty they deserved.

28Since they thought it foolish to acknowledge God, he abandoned them to their foolish thinking and let them do things that should never be done. 29Their lives became full of every kind of wickedness, sin, greed, hate, envy, murder, quarreling, deception, malicious behavior, and gossip. 30They are backstabbers, haters of God, insolent, proud, and boastful. They invent new ways of sinning, and they disobey their parents. 31They refuse to understand, break their promises, are heartless, and have no mercy. 32They know God's justice requires that those who do these things deserve to die, yet they do them anyway. Worse yet, they encourage others to do them, too.

2 GOD'S JUDGMENT OF SIN
You may think you can condemn such people, but you are just as bad, and you have no excuse! When you say they are wicked and should be punished, you are condemning yourself, for you who judge others do these very same things. 2And we know that God, in his justice, will punish anyone who does such things. 3Since you judge others for doing these things, why do you think you can avoid God's judgment when you do the same things? 4Don't you see how wonderfully kind, tolerant, and patient God is with you? Does this mean nothing to you? Can't you see that his kindness is intended to turn you from your sin?

5But because you are stubborn and refuse to turn from your sin, you are storing up terrible punishment for yourself. For a day of anger is coming, when God's righteous judgment will be revealed. 6He will judge everyone according to what they have done. 7He will give eternal life to those who keep on doing good, seeking after the glory and honor and immortality that God offers. 8But he will pour out his anger and wrath on those who live for themselves, who refuse to obey the truth and instead live lives of wickedness. 9There will be trouble and calamity for everyone who keeps on doing what is evil—for the Jew first and also for the Gentile.* 10But there will be glory and honor and peace from God for all who do good—for the Jew first and also for the Gentile. 11For God does not show favoritism.

12When the Gentiles sin, they will be destroyed, even though they never had God's written law. And the Jews, who do have God's law, will be judged by that law when they fail to obey it. 13For merely listening to the law doesn't make us right with God. It is obeying the law that makes us right in his sight. 14Even Gentiles, who do not have God's written law, show that they know his law when they instinctively obey it, even without having heard it. 15They demonstrate that God's law is written in their hearts, for their own conscience and thoughts either accuse them or tell them

2:9 Greek also for the Greek; also in 2:10.

CHOICES
alternatives

James and Kristy are watching a popular afternoon talk show. Today's topic is "Should homosexual marriage be legalized?" Most of the guests, as well as members of the studio audience, are gay and lesbian activists who are "tired of being treated like second-class citizens."

Says the most outspoken member of the panel: "Why can't people just accept us as we are? We didn't choose to be homosexual. We were born this way. We don't condemn straight people for acting on their natural desires. Why condemn us for being the way God made us?"

With each statement like this, the talk show host nods approvingly and the audience cheers loudly.

All, that is, except the one guy on the panel who is a minister. He is trying patiently (and lovingly) to point out why homosexuality is not acceptable behavior, but the others keep interrupting him and describing him as "backwards," "narrow-minded," and a "religious extremist."

By the end of the show, James and Kristy feel a little bit differently. They aren't ready to accept everything about the homosexual lifestyle, but they do wonder if maybe they haven't been a bit intolerant in their views.

What do you think? Is homosexuality just "an alternative lifestyle"? Is it really okay? See what God says about it in Romans 1:24-28.

MY STORY: Lisa

During my freshman and sophomore years in high school, I led something of a double life. At home and at church, I was a "good Christian kid." I read my Bible, helped with Sunday school, and went to youth group. I really wanted to live a committed Christian life, but at school I was embarrassed to make it known that I was a Christian. I guess I was afraid of what people would think of me if they knew. When people said, "Come on, let's party," I'd feel torn. I loved God and knew he didn't approve of their idea of "party," but too often I just couldn't stand up to these people. I'd give in, and then feel bad about myself for compromising what I knew was right.

The summer before my junior year, I knew things would have to change. That's when I read Romans 2:6-8. Verse 6 says God "will judge everyone according to what they have done." When I thought about what I'd done, I realized how self-seeking I was. Yet I really did want to please God. So I decided right then to make my goal the eternal life that God promises "to those who keep on doing good" (2:7).

So I memorized that passage and decided to let people at school know I'm a Christian. It has made a big difference. For one thing, I've met other Christians who were there all the time, but whom I hadn't bothered to get to know before. The last two years have been much better than the first two. I found that taking a stand against certain things didn't really cost me friends. In fact, because I've found other friends who know what friendship is about, I actually have more and better friends than I had before. But most of all I have a clear conscience. I know I'm trying to do God's will every day, at school as well as at church.

they are doing right. ¹⁶And this is the message I proclaim—that the day is coming when God, through Christ Jesus, will judge everyone's secret life.

THE JEWS AND THE LAW ¹⁷You who call yourselves Jews are relying on God's law, and you boast about your special relationship with him. ¹⁸You know what he wants; you know what is right because you have been taught his law. ¹⁹You are convinced that you are a guide for the blind and a light for people who are lost in darkness. ²⁰You think you can instruct the ignorant and teach children the ways of God. For you are certain that God's law gives you complete knowledge and truth.

²¹Well then, if you teach others, why don't you teach yourself? You tell others not to steal, but do you steal? ²²You say it is wrong to commit adultery, but do you commit adultery? You condemn idolatry, but do you use items stolen from pagan temples?* ²³You are so proud of knowing the law, but you dishonor God by breaking it. ²⁴No wonder the Scriptures say, "The Gentiles blaspheme the name of God because of you."*

²⁵The Jewish ceremony of circumcision has value only if you obey God's law. But if you don't obey God's law, you are no better off than an uncircumcised Gentile. ²⁶And if the Gentiles obey God's law, won't God declare them to be his own people? ²⁷In fact, uncircumcised Gentiles who keep God's law will condemn you Jews who are circumcised and possess God's law but don't obey it.

²⁸For you are not a true Jew just because you were born of Jewish parents or because you have gone through the ceremony of circumcision. ²⁹No, a true Jew is one whose heart is right with God. And true circumcision is not merely obeying the letter of the law; rather, it is a change of heart produced by God's Spirit. And a person with a changed heart seeks praise* from God, not from people.

3 **GOD REMAINS FAITHFUL** Then what's the advantage of being a Jew? Is there any value in the ceremony of circumcision? ²Yes, there are great benefits! First of all, the Jews were entrusted with the whole revelation of God.*

³True, some of them were unfaithful; but just because they were unfaithful, does that mean God will be unfaithful? ⁴Of course not! Even if everyone else is a liar, God is true. As the Scriptures say about him,

2:22 Greek *do you steal from temples?* **2:24** Isa 52:5 (Greek version). **2:29** Or *receives praise.* **3:2** Greek *the oracles of God.*

"You will be proved right in what you say,
　　and you will win your case in court."*

⁵"But," some might say, "our sinfulness serves a good purpose, for it helps people see how righteous God is. Isn't it unfair, then, for him to punish us?" (This is merely a human point of view.) ⁶Of course not! If God were not entirely fair, how would he be qualified to judge the world? ⁷"But," someone might still argue, "how can God condemn me as a sinner if my dishonesty highlights his truthfulness and brings him more glory?" ⁸And some people even slander us by claiming that we say, "The more we sin, the better it is!" Those who say such things deserve to be condemned.

ALL PEOPLE ARE SINNERS ⁹Well then, should we conclude that we Jews are better than others? No, not at all, for we have already shown that all people, whether Jews or Gentiles,* are under the power of sin. ¹⁰As the Scriptures say,

"No one is righteous—
　　not even one.
¹¹ No one is truly wise;
　　no one is seeking God.
¹² All have turned away;
　　all have become useless.
No one does good,
　　not a single one."*
¹³ "Their talk is foul, like the stench from
　　an open grave.
　　Their tongues are filled with lies."
"Snake venom drips from their lips."*
¹⁴ 　"Their mouths are full of cursing and
　　bitterness."*
¹⁵ "They rush to commit murder.
¹⁶ 　Destruction and misery always
　　follow them.
¹⁷ They don't know where to find peace."*
¹⁸ 　"They have no fear of God at all."*

¹⁹Obviously, the law applies to those to whom it was given, for its purpose is to keep people from having excuses, and to show that

- -

A HARD TRUTH
(3:23) Paul revealed a hard truth: All people have blown it in some way. Some actions might seem "worse" than others because their obvious consequences are much more serious. Murder, for example, seems much worse than hatred; adultery seems worse than lust. But this does not mean we can get away with some sins and not with others. All sin cuts us off from our holy God. All sin, therefore, leads to death (see Rom 6:23). Thanks to Christ, forgiveness is offered for all. See why they call it "Good News"?

the entire world is guilty before God. ²⁰For no one can ever be made right with God by doing what the law commands. The law simply shows us how sinful we are.

CHRIST TOOK OUR PUNISHMENT ²¹But now God has shown us a way to be made right with him without keeping the requirements of the law, as was promised in the writings of Moses* and the prophets long ago. ²²We are made right with God by placing our faith in Jesus Christ. And this is true for everyone who believes, no matter who we are.

²³For everyone has sinned; we all fall short of God's glorious standard. ²⁴Yet God, with undeserved kindness, declares that we are righteous. He did this through Christ Jesus when he freed us from the penalty for our sins. ²⁵For God presented Jesus as the sacrifice for sin. People are made right with God when they believe that Jesus sacrificed his life, shedding his blood. This sacrifice shows that God was being fair when he held back and did not punish those who sinned in times past, ²⁶for he was looking ahead and including them in what he would do in this present time. God did this to demonstrate his righteousness, for he himself is fair and just, and he declares sinners to be right in his sight when they believe in Jesus.

²⁷Can we boast, then, that we have done anything to be accepted by God? No, because our acquittal is not based on obeying the law. It is based on faith. ²⁸So we are made right with God through faith and not by obeying the law.

²⁹After all, is God the God of the Jews only? Isn't he also the God of the Gentiles? Of course he is. ³⁰There is only one God, and he makes people right with himself only by faith, whether they are Jews or Gentiles.* ³¹Well then, if we emphasize faith, does this mean that we can forget about the law? Of course not! In fact, only when we have faith do we truly fulfill the law.

4 **THE FAITH OF ABRAHAM** Abraham was, humanly speaking, the founder of our Jewish nation. What did he discover about being made right with God? ²If his good deeds had made him acceptable to God, he would have had something to boast about. But that was not God's way. ³For the Scriptures tell us, "Abraham believed God, and God counted him as righteous because of his faith."*

3:4 Ps 51:4 (Greek version). **3:9** Greek *or Greeks.* **3:10-12** Pss 14:1-3; 53:1-3 (Greek version). **3:13** Pss 5:9 (Greek version); 140:3. **3:14** Ps 10:7 (Greek version). **3:15-17** Isa 59:7-8. **3:18** Ps 36:1. **3:21** Greek *in the law.* **3:30** Greek *whether they are circumcised or uncircumcised.* **4:3** Gen 15:6.

⁴When people work, their wages are not a gift, but something they have earned. ⁵But people are counted as righteous, not because of their work, but because of their faith in God who forgives sinners. ⁶David also spoke of this when he described the happiness of those who are declared righteous without working for it:

⁷ "Oh, what joy for those
   whose disobedience is forgiven,
   whose sins are put out of sight.
⁸ Yes, what joy for those
   whose record the LORD has cleared
      of sin."*

⁹Now, is this blessing only for the Jews, or is it also for uncircumcised Gentiles?* Well, we have been saying that Abraham was counted as righteous by God because of his faith. ¹⁰But how did this happen? Was he counted as righteous only after he was circumcised, or was it before he was circumcised? Clearly, God accepted Abraham before he was circumcised!

¹¹Circumcision was a sign that Abraham already had faith and that God had already accepted him and declared him to be righteous—even before he was circumcised. So Abraham is the spiritual father of those who have faith but have not been circumcised. They are counted as righteous because of their faith. ¹²And Abraham is also the spiritual father of those who have been circumcised, but only if they have the same kind of faith Abraham had before he was circumcised.

¹³Clearly, God's promise to give the whole earth to Abraham and his descendants was based not on his obedience to God's law, but on a right relationship with God that comes by faith. ¹⁴If God's promise is only for those who obey the law, then faith is not necessary and the promise is pointless. ¹⁵For the law always brings punishment on those who try to obey it. (The only way to avoid breaking the law is to have no law to break!)

¹⁶So the promise is received by faith. It is given as a free gift. And we are all certain to receive it, whether or not we live according to the law of Moses, if we have faith like Abraham's. For Abraham is the father of all who believe. ¹⁷That is what the Scriptures mean when God told him, "I have made you the father of many nations."* This happened because Abraham believed in the God who brings the dead

back to life and who creates new things out of nothing.

¹⁸Even when there was no reason for hope, Abraham kept hoping—believing that he would become the father of many nations. For God had said to him, "That's how many descendants you will have!"* ¹⁹And Abraham's faith did not weaken, even though, at about 100 years of age, he figured his body was as good as dead—and so was Sarah's womb.

²⁰Abraham never wavered in believing God's promise. In fact, his faith grew stronger, and in this he brought glory to God. ²¹He was fully convinced that God is able to do whatever he promises. ²²And because of Abraham's faith, God counted him as righteous. ²³And when God counted him as righteous, it wasn't just for Abraham's benefit. It was recorded ²⁴for our benefit, too, assuring us that God will also count us as righteous if we believe in him, the one who raised Jesus our Lord from the dead. ²⁵He was handed over to die because of our sins, and he was raised to life to make us right with God.

5 **FAITH BRINGS JOY** Therefore, since we have been made right in God's sight by faith, we have peace with God because of what Jesus Christ our Lord has done for us. ²Because of our faith, Christ has brought us into this place of undeserved privilege where we now stand, and we confidently and joyfully look forward to sharing God's glory.

³We can rejoice, too, when we run into problems and trials, for we know that they help us develop endurance. ⁴And endurance develops strength of character, and character strengthens our confident hope of salvation. ⁵And this

....

A GIFT
(4:4-5) When some people learn that all can be saved through faith in Christ, they start to worry: "Do I have enough faith?" "Is my faith strong enough to save me?" But they miss the point. Jesus Christ, rather than our feelings or actions, saves us. He offers us forgiveness because he loves us, not because we earned it through our powerful faith. What, then, is the role of faith? Faith enables us to accept God's forgiveness. Have you accepted this gift?

OVERCOME
(5:2-4) Paul tells us what we will become in the future. Until then we must overcome. This means we will experience difficulties that could help us grow. Problems we face will help develop our patience, which will strengthen our character, deepen our trust in God, and give us greater confidence about the future. As you find your patience tested in some way every day, how will you respond to these opportunities to grow? Check out James 1:2-4 and 1 Peter 1:6-7 for some advice.

4:7-8 Ps 32:1-2 (Greek version).   **4:9** Greek *is this blessing only for the circumcised, or is it also for the uncircumcised?*   **4:17** Gen 17:5.
4:18 Gen 15:5.

SALVATION'S FREEWAY

Everyone has sinned. (Romans 3:23)	The penalty for our sin is death. (Romans 6:23)	Jesus Christ died for sin. (Romans 5:8)	To be forgiven for our sins, we must believe and confess that Jesus is Lord. Salvation comes through Jesus Christ. (Romans 10:8-10)

hope will not lead to disappointment. For we know how dearly God loves us, because he has given us the Holy Spirit to fill our hearts with his love.

⁶When we were utterly helpless, Christ came at just the right time and died for us sinners. ⁷Now, most people would not be willing to die for an upright person, though someone might perhaps be willing to die for a person who is especially good. ⁸But God showed his great love for us by sending Christ to die for us while we were still sinners. ⁹And since we have been made right in God's sight by the blood of Christ, he will certainly save us from God's condemnation. ¹⁰For since our friendship with God was restored by the death of his Son while we were still his enemies, we will certainly be saved through the life of his Son. ¹¹So now we can rejoice in our wonderful new relationship with God because our Lord Jesus Christ has made us friends of God.

ADAM AND CHRIST CONTRASTED ¹²When Adam sinned, sin entered the world. Adam's sin brought death, so death spread to everyone, for everyone sinned. ¹³Yes, people sinned even before the law was given. But it was not counted as sin because there was not yet any law to break. ¹⁴Still, everyone died—from the time of Adam to the time of Moses—even those who did not disobey an explicit commandment of God, as Adam did. Now Adam is a symbol, a representation of Christ, who was yet to come. ¹⁵But there is a great difference between Adam's sin and God's gracious gift. For the sin of this one man, Adam, brought death to many. But even greater is God's wonderful grace and his gift of forgiveness to many through this other man, Jesus Christ.

··

BEFORE
(5:8) While we were still sinners—these are amazing words. God sent Jesus to die for us, not because we were good enough, but because he loved us so much. Whenever you feel uncertain about God's love for you, remember that God loved you even before you turned to him.

¹⁶And the result of God's gracious gift is very different from the result of that one man's sin. For Adam's sin led to condemnation, but God's free gift leads to our being made right with God, even though we are guilty of many sins. ¹⁷For the sin of this one man, Adam, caused death to rule over many. But even greater is God's wonderful grace and his gift of righteousness, for all who receive it will live in triumph over sin and death through this one man, Jesus Christ.

¹⁸Yes, Adam's one sin brings condemnation for everyone, but Christ's one act of righteousness brings a right relationship with God and new life for everyone. ¹⁹Because one person disobeyed God, many became sinners. But because one other person obeyed God, many will be made righteous.

²⁰God's law was given so that all people could see how sinful they were. But as people sinned more and more, God's wonderful grace became more abundant. ²¹So just as sin ruled over all people and brought them to death, now God's wonderful grace rules instead, giving us right standing with God and resulting in eternal life through Jesus Christ our Lord.

6 **SIN'S POWER IS BROKEN** Well then, should we keep on sinning so that God can show us more and more of his wonderful grace? ²Of course not! Since we have died to sin, how can we continue to live in it? ³Or have you forgotten that when we were joined with Christ Jesus in baptism, we joined him in his death? ⁴For we died and were buried with Christ by baptism. And just as Christ was raised from the dead by the glorious power of the Father, now we also may live new lives.

⁵Since we have been united with him in his death, we will also be raised to life as he was. ⁶We know that our old sinful selves were crucified with Christ so that sin might lose its power in our lives. We are no longer slaves to sin. ⁷For when we died with Christ we were set free from the power of sin. ⁸And since we died with Christ, we know we will also live with him. ⁹We are sure of this because Christ was raised from

the dead, and he will never die again. Death no longer has any power over him. ¹⁰When he died, he died once to break the power of sin. But now that he lives, he lives for the glory of God. ¹¹So you also should consider yourselves to be dead to the power of sin and alive to God through Christ Jesus.

¹²Do not let sin control the way you live;* do not give in to sinful desires. ¹³Do not let any part of your body become an instrument of evil to serve sin. Instead, give yourselves completely to God, for you were dead, but now you have new life. So use your whole body as an instrument to do what is right for the glory of God. ¹⁴Sin is no longer your master, for you no longer live under the requirements of the law. Instead, you live under the freedom of God's grace.

¹⁵Well then, since God's grace has set us free from the law, does that mean we can go on sinning? Of course not! ¹⁶Don't you realize that you become the slave of whatever you choose to obey? You can be a slave to sin, which leads to death, or you can choose to obey God, which leads to righteous living. ¹⁷Thank God! Once you were slaves of sin, but now you wholeheartedly obey this teaching we have given you. ¹⁸Now you are free from your slavery to sin, and you have become slaves to righteous living.

¹⁹Because of the weakness of your human nature, I am using the illustration of slavery to help you understand all this. Previously, you let yourselves be slaves to impurity and lawlessness, which led ever deeper into sin. Now you must give yourselves to be slaves to righteous living so that you will become holy.

²⁰When you were slaves to sin, you were free from the obligation to do right. ²¹And what was the result? You are now ashamed of the things you used to do, things that end in eternal doom. ²²But now you are free from the power of sin and have become slaves of God. Now you do those things that lead to holiness and result in eternal life. ²³For the wages of sin is death, but the free gift of God is eternal life through Christ Jesus our Lord.

7 NO LONGER BOUND TO THE LAW Now, dear brothers and sisters*—you who are familiar with the law—don't you know that the law applies only while a person is living? ²For example, when a woman marries, the law binds her to her husband as long as he is

6:12 Or Do not let sin reign in your body, which is subject to death.
7:1 Greek brothers; also in 7:4.   7:5 Greek When we were in the flesh.   7:7 Exod 20:17; Deut 5:21.

FOR THE WAGES (OF) SIN IS DEATH, BUT THE FREE GIFT OF GOD IS ETERNAL LIFE THROUGH CHRIST JESUS OUR LORD.

ROMANS 6:23

alive. But if he dies, the laws of marriage no longer apply to her. ³So while her husband is alive, she would be committing adultery if she married another man. But if her husband dies, she is free from that law and does not commit adultery when she remarries.

⁴So, my dear brothers and sisters, this is the point: You died to the power of the law when you died with Christ. And now you are united with the one who was raised from the dead. As a result, we can produce a harvest of good deeds for God. ⁵When we were controlled by our old nature,* sinful desires were at work within us, and the law aroused these evil desires that produced a harvest of sinful deeds, resulting in death. ⁶But now we have been released from the law, for we died to it and are no longer captive to its power. Now we can serve God, not in the old way of obeying the letter of the law, but in the new way of living in the Spirit.

GOD'S LAW REVEALS OUR SIN ⁷Well then, am I suggesting that the law of God is sinful? Of course not! In fact, it was the law that showed me my sin. I would never have known that coveting is wrong if the law had not said, "You must not covet."* ⁸But sin used this command to arouse all kinds of covetous desires within me! If there were no law, sin would not have that power. ⁹At one time I lived without understanding the law. But when I learned the command not to covet, for instance, the

....

WHY THE LAW?
(7:9-11) If people feel fine without the law, why did God give it? Because sin is real and dangerous. Imagine a sunny day at the beach. You have just plunged into the surf and you've never felt better. Suddenly you notice a sign on the pier: No swimming: Sharks in water. Your day is ruined. Is the sign responsible? Are you angry with the people who put it up? Of course not. The law is like the sign. It's essential, and we're grateful for it. But it isn't a solution for the sharks!

power of sin came to life, ¹⁰and I died. So I discovered that the law's commands, which were supposed to bring life, brought spiritual death instead. ¹¹Sin took advantage of those commands and deceived me; it used the commands to kill me. ¹²But still, the law itself is holy, and its commands are holy and right and good.

¹³But how can that be? Did the law, which is good, cause my death? Of course not! Sin used what was good to bring about my condemnation to death. So we can see how terrible sin really is. It uses God's good commands for its own evil purposes.

STRUGGLING WITH SIN ¹⁴So the trouble is not with the law, for it is spiritual and good. The trouble is with me, for I am all too human, a slave to sin. ¹⁵I don't really understand myself, for I want to do what is right, but I don't do it. Instead, I do what I hate. ¹⁶But if I know that what I am doing is wrong, this shows that I

agree that the law is good. ¹⁷So I am not the one doing wrong; it is sin living in me that does it.

¹⁸And I know that nothing good lives in me, that is, in my sinful nature.* I want to do what is right, but I can't. ¹⁹I want to do what is good, but I don't. I don't want to do what is wrong, but I do it anyway. ²⁰But if I do what I don't want to do, I am not really the one doing wrong; it is sin living in me that does it.

²¹I have discovered this principle of life—that when I want to do what is right, I inevitably do what is wrong. ²²I love God's law with all my heart. ²³But there is another power* within me that is at war with my mind. This power makes me a slave to the sin that is still within me. ²⁴Oh, what a miserable person I am! Who will free me from this life that is dominated by sin and death? ²⁵Thank God! The answer is in Jesus Christ our Lord. So you see how it is: In my mind I really want to obey God's law, but because of my sinful nature I am a slave to sin.

8 **LIFE IN THE SPIRIT** So now there is no condemnation for those who belong to Christ Jesus. ²And because you belong to him, the power* of the life-giving Spirit has freed you* from the power of sin that leads to death. ³The law of Moses was unable to save us because of the weakness of our sinful nature.* So God did what the law could not do. He sent his own

7:18 Greek *my flesh;* also in 7:25.   7:23 Greek *law;* also in 7:23b.
8:2a Greek *the law;* also in 8:2b.   8:2b Some manuscripts read *me.*
8:3 Greek *our flesh;* similarly in 8:4, 5, 6, 7, 8, 9, 12.

A DESPERATE STRUGGLE

(7:15) This is more than the cry of one desperate man—it describes the experience of any Christian struggling against a wrong desire. We must never underestimate the power of sin. While Satan is a crafty tempter, we also have a great ability to make excuses. Instead of trying to overcome sin with human willpower, we have access to the tremendous power of Christ through the Holy Spirit. And when we fall, God lovingly reaches out to us and helps us get up again.

I WONDER...

Ever since I became a Christian, I keep fighting against certain thoughts and habits that I used to never give a second thought about. Why is this happening?

Picture your life as a door. Before you became a Christian, wrong actions were like nails being pounded into the door and left there. When you asked Christ to forgive you, all of the nails you had collected were removed! Unfortunately, what was left was a door full of holes—not very pleasant to look at and not very useful.

But God began patching up the holes! More accurately, he began to heal the scars left by sin, making your life into a door that will look unscarred after years of constant pounding. We truly can become a new creation (see 2 Cor 5:17).

That is why it is so important for people to come to know Christ's forgiveness early in life. Because we inherited a sinful nature from Adam (Rom 5:12), time

and wrong choices can pound some pretty large nails into our life. And those scars may take longer to heal. Paul knew this all too well, as you can see if you read his words in Romans 7:15–8:2. Like Paul, we're all tempted to give in to our sin nature, our desire to do wrong, but our new nature moves us to resist.

So what you are experiencing is a new sensitivity to sin. Since sin wants to "drive a hole" in you, and Christ wants to keep you unscarred by the effects of sin, it is no longer comfortable to ignore the constant pounding. Confessing your sin will always remove the nail. Your new sensitivity means two things. First, it's a sign that the Spirit of God has truly entered your life (Rom 8:9). Otherwise, you would still be numb to the nails (sin) if you had rejected Christ's forgiveness. Second, it means that God is reminding you of his love for you (Rom 8:38-39). He doesn't want you to be left scarred by the consequences of wrong actions, so he begins at the source of it—your thoughts.

Son in a body like the bodies we sinners have. And in that body God declared an end to sin's control over us by giving his Son as a sacrifice for our sins. 4He did this so that the just requirement of the law would be fully satisfied for us, who no longer follow our sinful nature but instead follow the Spirit.

5Those who are dominated by the sinful nature think about sinful things, but those who are controlled by the Holy Spirit think about things that please the Spirit. 6So letting your sinful nature control your mind leads to death. But letting the Spirit control your mind leads to life and peace. 7For the sinful nature is always hostile to God. It never did obey God's laws, and it never will. 8That's why those who are still under the control of their sinful nature can never please God.

9But you are not controlled by your sinful nature. You are controlled by the Spirit if you have the Spirit of God living in you. (And remember that those who do not have the Spirit of Christ living in them do not belong to him at all.) 10And Christ lives within you, so even though your body will die because of sin, the Spirit gives you life* because you have been made right with God. 11The Spirit of God, who raised Jesus from the dead, lives in you. And just as God raised Christ Jesus from the dead, he will give life to your mortal bodies by this same Spirit living within you.

12Therefore, dear brothers and sisters,* you have no obligation to do what your sinful nature urges you to do. 13For if you live by its dictates, you will die. But if through the power of the Spirit you put to death the deeds of your sinful nature,* you will live. 14For all who are led by the Spirit of God are children* of God.

15So you have not received a spirit that makes you fearful slaves. Instead, you received God's Spirit when he adopted you as his own children.* Now we call him, "Abba, Father."* 16For his Spirit joins with our spirit to affirm that we are God's children. 17And since we are his children, we are his heirs. In fact, together with Christ we are heirs of God's glory. But if we are to share his glory, we must also share his suffering.

THE FUTURE GLORY 18Yet what we suffer now is nothing compared to the glory he will reveal to us later. 19For all creation is waiting eagerly

for that future day when God will reveal who his children really are. 20Against its will, all creation was subjected to God's curse. But with eager hope, 21the creation looks forward to the day when it will join God's children in glorious freedom from death and decay. 22For we know that all creation has been groaning as in the pains of childbirth right up to the present time. 23And we believers also groan, even though we have the Holy Spirit within us as a foretaste of future glory, for we long for our bodies to be released from sin and suffering. We, too, wait with eager hope for the day when God will give us our full rights as his adopted children,* including the new bodies he has promised us. 24We were given this hope when we were saved. (If we already have something, we don't need to hope* for it. 25But if we look forward to something we don't yet have, we must wait patiently and confidently.)

26And the Holy Spirit helps us in our weakness. For example, we don't know what God wants us to pray for. But the Holy Spirit prays for us with groanings that cannot be expressed in words. 27And the Father who knows all hearts knows what the Spirit is saying, for the Spirit pleads for us believers* in harmony with God's own will. 28And we know that God causes everything to work together* for the good of those who love God and are called according to his purpose for them. 29For God knew his people in advance, and he chose them to become like his Son, so that his Son would be the firstborn* among many brothers and sisters. 30And having chosen them, he called them to come to him. And having called them, he gave them right standing with himself. And having given them right standing, he gave them his glory.

NOTHING CAN SEPARATE US FROM GOD'S LOVE 31What shall we say about such wonderful things as these? If God is for us, who can ever be against us? 32Since he did not spare

....

THE GREATER GOOD
(8:28) God works in "everything"—not just isolated incidents—for our good. This doesn't mean that all that happens to us is good. Although evil is prevalent in the world, God is able to turn it around for our long-range good. Note that God is not working to make us happy but to fulfill his purpose. Note also that this promise is not for everybody—it is for those who love God and are called by him. Such people have a new perspective, a new mindset. They trust God, not their intellect or bank account. They look to their security in heaven, not on earth. They learn to accept pain and persecution rather than resent it, because it brings them closer to God.

8:10 Or your spirit is alive.   8:12 Greek brothers; also in 8:29.
8:13 Greek deeds of the body.   8:14 Greek sons; also in 8:19.
8:15a Greek you received a spirit of sonship.   8:15b Abba is an Aramaic term for "father."   8:23 Greek wait anxiously for sonship.
8:24 Some manuscripts read wait.   8:27 Greek for God's holy people.   8:28 Some manuscripts read And we know that everything works together.   8:29 Or would be supreme.

even his own Son but gave him up for us all, won't he also give us everything else? ³³Who dares accuse us whom God has chosen for his own? No one—for God himself has given us right standing with himself. ³⁴Who then will condemn us? No one—for Christ Jesus died for us and was raised to life for us, and he is sitting in the place of honor at God's right hand, pleading for us.

³⁵Can anything ever separate us from Christ's love? Does it mean he no longer loves us if we have trouble or calamity, or are persecuted, or hungry, or destitute, or in danger, or threatened with death? ³⁶(As the Scriptures say, "For your sake we are killed every day; we are being slaughtered like sheep."*) ³⁷No, despite all these things, overwhelming victory is ours through Christ, who loved us.

³⁸And I am convinced that nothing can ever separate us from God's love. Neither death nor life, neither angels nor demons,* neither our fears for today nor our worries about tomorrow—not even the powers of hell can separate us from God's love. ³⁹No power in the sky above or in the earth below—indeed, nothing in all creation will ever be able to separate us from the love of God that is revealed in Christ Jesus our Lord.

9 GOD'S SELECTION OF ISRAEL With Christ as my witness, I speak with utter truthfulness. My conscience and the Holy Spirit confirm it. ²My heart is filled with bitter sorrow and unending grief ³for my people, my Jewish brothers and sisters.* I would be willing to be forever cursed—cut off from Christ!—if that would save them. ⁴They are the people of Israel, chosen to be God's adopted children.* God revealed his glory to them. He made covenants with them and gave them his law. He gave them the privilege of worshiping him and receiving his wonderful promises. ⁵Abraham, Isaac, and Jacob are their ancestors, and Christ himself was an Israelite as far as his human nature is concerned. And he is God, the one who rules over everything and is worthy of eternal praise! Amen.*

⁶Well then, has God failed to fulfill his promise to Israel? No, for not all who are born into the nation of Israel are truly members of God's people! ⁷Being descendants of Abraham doesn't make them truly Abraham's children. For the Scriptures say, "Isaac is the son through whom your descendants will be counted,"* though Abraham had other children, too. ⁸This means that Abraham's physical descendants are not necessarily children

of God. Only the children of the promise are considered to be Abraham's children. ⁹For God had promised, "I will return about this time next year, and Sarah will have a son."*

¹⁰This son was our ancestor Isaac. When he married Rebekah, she gave birth to twins.* ¹¹But before they were born, before they had done anything good or bad, she received a message from God. (This message shows that God chooses people according to his own purposes; ¹²he calls people, but not according to their good or bad works.) She was told, "Your older son will serve your younger son."* ¹³In the words of the Scriptures, "I loved Jacob, but I rejected Esau."*

¹⁴Are we saying, then, that God was unfair? Of course not! ¹⁵For God said to Moses,

"I will show mercy to anyone I choose,
    and I will show compassion to anyone I
    choose."*

¹⁶So it is God who decides to show mercy. We can neither choose it nor work for it.

¹⁷For the Scriptures say that God told Pharaoh, "I have appointed you for the very purpose of displaying my power in you and to spread my fame throughout the earth."* ¹⁸So you see, God chooses to show mercy to some, and he chooses to harden the hearts of others so they refuse to listen.

¹⁹Well then, you might say, "Why does God blame people for not responding? Haven't they simply done what he makes them do?"

²⁰No, don't say that. Who are you, a mere human being, to argue with God? Should the thing that was created say to the one who created it, "Why have you made me like this?" ²¹When a potter makes jars out of clay, doesn't he have a right to use the same lump of clay to make one jar for decoration and another to throw garbage into? ²²In the same way, even though God has the right to show his anger and his power, he is very patient with those on whom his anger falls, who are destined for destruction. ²³He does this to make the riches of his glory shine even brighter on those to whom he shows mercy, who were prepared in advance for glory. ²⁴And we are among those whom he selected, both from the Jews and from the Gentiles.

²⁵Concerning the Gentiles, God says in the prophecy of Hosea,

8:36 Ps 44:22.   **8:38** Greek *nor rulers.*   **9:3** Greek *my brothers.*
9:4 Greek *chosen for sonship.*   **9:5** Or *May God, the one who rules over everything, be praised forever. Amen.*   **9:7** Gen 21:12.
9:9 Gen 18:10, 14.   **9:10** Greek *she conceived children through this one man.*   **9:12** Gen 25:23.   **9:13** Mal 1:2-3.   **9:15** Exod 33:19.
9:17 Exod 9:16 (Greek version).

"Those who were not my people,
    I will now call my people.
And I will love those
    whom I did not love before."*

²⁶And,

"Then, at the place where they were told,
    'You are not my people,'
there they will be called
    'children of the living God.'"*

²⁷And concerning Israel, Isaiah the prophet
cried out,

"Though the people of Israel are as
        numerous as the sand of the seashore,
    only a remnant will be saved.
²⁸ For the LORD will carry out his sentence
        upon the earth
    quickly and with finality."*

²⁹And Isaiah said the same thing in another
place:

"If the LORD of Heaven's Armies
    had not spared a few of our children,
we would have been wiped out like Sodom,
    destroyed like Gomorrah."*

NOTHING
IN ALL CREATION
WILL EVER
BE ABLE TO ······
SEPARATE
US FROM THE
LOVE OF GOD
THAT IS REVEALED IN
CHRIST JESUS OUR LORD.
■ ■ ■ ■ ROMANS 8:39 ■ ■ ■ ■

ISRAEL'S UNBELIEF ³⁰What does all this
mean? Even though the Gentiles were not
trying to follow God's standards, they were
made right with God. And it was by faith that
this took place. ³¹But the people of Israel, who
tried so hard to get right with God by keeping
the law, never succeeded. ³²Why not? Because
they were trying to get right with God by keeping the law* instead of by trusting in him. They
stumbled over the great rock in their path.
³³God warned them of this in the Scriptures
when he said,

"I am placing a stone in Jerusalem* that
        makes people stumble,
    a rock that makes them fall.
But anyone who trusts in him
    will never be disgraced."*

10 Dear brothers and sisters,* the longing of my heart and my prayer to God
is for the people of Israel to be saved. ²I know
what enthusiasm they have for God, but it is
misdirected zeal. ³For they don't understand
God's way of making people right with himself. Refusing to accept God's way, they cling
to their own way of getting right with God by

trying to keep the law. ⁴For Christ has already
accomplished the purpose for which the law
was given.* As a result, all who believe in him
are made right with God.

SALVATION IS FOR EVERYONE ⁵For Moses
writes that the law's way of making a person
right with God requires obedience to all of its
commands.* ⁶But faith's way of getting right
with God says, "Don't say in your heart, 'Who
will go up to heaven?' (to bring Christ down to
earth). ⁷And don't say, 'Who will go down to the
place of the dead?' (to bring Christ back to life
again)." ⁸In fact, it says,

"The message is very close at hand;
    it is on your lips and in your heart."*

And that message is the very message about
faith that we preach: ⁹If you confess with your
mouth that Jesus is Lord and believe in your
heart that God raised him from the dead, you

···

FOREVER TRYING
(9:31-33) The people of Israel tried to get right with God
by keeping his laws. In the same way, we may think that
activities like church work, giving offerings, and being
nice will make us right with God. After all, we've played
by the rules, haven't we? But as Paul explains, no one can
earn God's favor (see also Isa 64:6-7; Rom 11:6-7). Only
by putting our faith in what Christ has done will we be
saved. Because of Jesus, we "will never be disgraced."

9:25 Hos 2:23.   **9:26** Greek *sons of the living God.* Hos 1:10.
9:27-28 Isa 10:22-23 (Greek version).   **9:29** Isa 1:9 (Greek version).
9:32 Greek *by works.*   **9:33a** Greek *in Zion.*   **9:33b** Isa 8:14; 28:16
(Greek version).   **10:1** Greek *Brothers.*   **10:4** Or *For Christ is the end
of the law.*   **10:5** See Lev 18:5.   **10:6-8** Deut 30:12-14.

will be saved. ¹⁰For it is by believing in your heart that you are made right with God, and it is by confessing with your mouth that you are saved. ¹¹As the Scriptures tell us, "Anyone who trusts in him will never be disgraced."* ¹²Jew and Gentile* are the same in this respect. They have the same Lord, who gives generously to all who call on him. ¹³For "Everyone who calls on the name of the Lord will be saved."*

¹⁴But how can they call on him to save them unless they believe in him? And how can they believe in him if they have never heard about him? And how can they hear about him unless someone tells them? ¹⁵And how will anyone go and tell them without being sent? That is why the Scriptures say, "How beautiful are the feet of messengers who bring good news!"*

¹⁶But not everyone welcomes the Good News, for Isaiah the prophet said, "Lord, who has believed our message?"* ¹⁷So faith comes from hearing, that is, hearing the Good News about Christ. ¹⁸But I ask, have the people of Israel actually heard the message? Yes, they have:

"The message has gone throughout the earth,
　and the words to all the world."*

¹⁹But I ask, did the people of Israel really understand? Yes, they did, for even in the time of Moses, God said,

"I will rouse your jealousy through people
　who are not even a nation.
I will provoke your anger through the
　foolish Gentiles."*

²⁰And later Isaiah spoke boldly for God, saying,

"I was found by people who were not
　looking for me.
I showed myself to those who were not
　asking for me."*

²¹But regarding Israel, God said,

"All day long I opened my arms to them,
　but they were disobedient and
　　rebellious."*

....

FREE
(11:6) This great truth can be hard to grasp. Do you think it's easier for God to love you when you're good? Do you secretly suspect God chose you because you deserved to be chosen? Do you think some people's behavior is so bad that God couldn't possibly save them? If you ever think this way, you don't entirely understand the Good News that salvation is a free gift. It cannot be earned, in whole or in part; it can only be accepted with thankfulness and praise.

11 **GOD'S MERCY ON ISRAEL** I ask, then, has God rejected his own people, the nation of Israel? Of course not! I myself am an Israelite, a descendant of Abraham and a member of the tribe of Benjamin.

²No, God has not rejected his own people, whom he chose from the very beginning. Do you realize what the Scriptures say about this? Elijah the prophet complained to God about the people of Israel and said, ³"Lord, they have killed your prophets and torn down your altars. I am the only one left, and now they are trying to kill me, too."*

⁴And do you remember God's reply? He said, "No, I have 7,000 others who have never bowed down to Baal!"*

⁵It is the same today, for a few of the people of Israel* have remained faithful because of God's grace—his undeserved kindness in choosing them. ⁶And since it is through God's kindness, then it is not by their good works. For in that case, God's grace would not be what it really is—free and undeserved.

⁷So this is the situation: Most of the people of Israel have not found the favor of God they are looking for so earnestly. A few have—the ones God has chosen—but the hearts of the rest were hardened. ⁸As the Scriptures say,

"God has put them into a deep sleep.
To this day he has shut their eyes so they
　do not see,
　and closed their ears so they do not
　　hear."*

⁹Likewise, David said,

"Let their bountiful table become a snare,
　a trap that makes them think all is well.
Let their blessings cause them to stumble,
　and let them get what they deserve.
¹⁰ Let their eyes go blind so they cannot see,
　and let their backs be bent forever."*

¹¹Did God's people stumble and fall beyond recovery? Of course not! They were disobedient, so God made salvation available to the Gentiles. But he wanted his own people to become jealous and claim it for themselves. ¹²Now if the Gentiles were enriched because the people of Israel turned down God's offer of salvation, think how much greater a blessing the world will share when they finally accept it. ¹³I am saying all this especially for you Gen-

10:11 Isa 28:16 (Greek version). 10:12 Greek *and Greek.* 10:13 Joel 2:32. 10:15 Isa 52:7. 10:16 Isa 53:1. 10:18 Ps 19:4. 10:19 Deut 32:21. 10:20 Isa 65:1 (Greek version). 10:21 Isa 65:2 (Greek version). 11:3 1 Kgs 19:10, 14. 11:4 1 Kgs 19:18. 11:5 Greek *for a remnant.* 11:8 Isa 29:10; Deut 29:4. 11:9-10 Ps 69:22-23 (Greek version).

tiles. God has appointed me as the apostle to the Gentiles. I stress this, ¹⁴for I want somehow to make the people of Israel jealous of what you Gentiles have, so I might save some of them. ¹⁵For since their rejection meant that God offered salvation to the rest of the world, their acceptance will be even more wonderful. It will be life for those who were dead! ¹⁶And since Abraham and the other patriarchs were holy, their descendants will also be holy—just as the entire batch of dough is holy because the portion given as an offering is holy. For if the roots of the tree are holy, the branches will be, too.

¹⁷But some of these branches from Abraham's tree—some of the people of Israel—have been broken off. And you Gentiles, who were branches from a wild olive tree, have been grafted in. So now you also receive the blessing God has promised Abraham and his children, sharing in the rich nourishment from the root of God's special olive tree. ¹⁸But you must not brag about being grafted in to replace the branches that were broken off. You are just a branch, not the root.

¹⁹"Well," you may say, "those branches were broken off to make room for me." ²⁰Yes, but remember—those branches were broken off because they didn't believe in Christ, and you are there because you do believe. So don't think highly of yourself, but fear what could happen. ²¹For if God did not spare the original branches, he won't* spare you either.

²²Notice how God is both kind and severe. He is severe toward those who disobeyed, but kind to you if you continue to trust in his kindness. But if you stop trusting, you also will be cut off. ²³And if the people of Israel turn from their unbelief, they will be grafted in again, for God has the power to graft them back into the tree. ²⁴You, by nature, were a branch cut from a wild olive tree. So if God was willing to do something contrary to nature by grafting you into his cultivated tree, he will be far more eager to graft the original branches back into the tree where they belong.

GOD'S MERCY IS FOR EVERYONE ²⁵I want you

to understand this mystery, dear brothers and sisters,* so that you will not feel proud about yourselves. Some of the people of Israel have hard hearts, but this will last only until the full number of Gentiles comes to Christ. ²⁶And so all Israel will be saved. As the Scriptures say,

"The one who rescues will come from
    Jerusalem,*
  and he will turn Israel* away from
    ungodliness.
²⁷ And this is my covenant with them,
  that I will take away their sins."*

²⁸Many of the people of Israel are now enemies of the Good News, and this benefits you Gentiles. Yet they are still the people he loves because he chose their ancestors Abraham, Isaac, and Jacob. ²⁹For God's gifts and his call can never be withdrawn. ³⁰Once, you Gentiles were rebels against God, but when the people of Israel rebelled against him, God was merciful to you instead. ³¹Now they are the rebels, and God's mercy has come to you so that they, too, will share* in God's mercy. ³²For God has imprisoned everyone in disobedience so he could have mercy on everyone.

³³Oh, how great are God's riches and wisdom and knowledge! How impossible it is for us to understand his decisions and his ways!

³⁴ For who can know the LORD's thoughts?
    Who knows enough to give him advice?*
³⁵ And who has given him so much
    that he needs to pay it back?*

³⁶For everything comes from him and exists by his power and is intended for his glory. All glory to him forever! Amen.

12 A LIVING SACRIFICE TO GOD And so, dear brothers and sisters,* I plead with you to give your bodies to God because of all

....

A RENEWED MIND
(12:2) "The behavior and customs of this world" are usually selfish and often corrupting. Many Christians, therefore, wisely decide that such behavior is off-limits for them. Yet it is possible to avoid most worldly customs and still be proud, covetous, selfish, stubborn, and arrogant. That's why our refusal to conform to the world must go even deeper than the level of behavior and customs—it must become a mind-set. Only when our mind is renewed by the new attitude Christ gives us are we truly transformed.

GIFTS
(12:4-8) God gives us spiritual gifts to use to build up his church. To use them effectively, we must (1) realize that all gifts and abilities come from God and that the Holy Spirit works through us as we use them; (2) understand that not everyone has the same gifts; (3) know who we are and what we do best; (4) dedicate our gifts to God's service and not to our personal success; (5) be willing to spend our gifts generously, not holding back anything from God's service. (See also 1 Corinthians 12–14.)

11:21 Some manuscripts read *perhaps he won't.* 11:25 Greek *brothers.* 11:26a Greek *from Zion.* 11:26b Greek *Jacob.* 11:26-27 Isa 59:20-21; 27:9 (Greek version). 11:31 Other manuscripts read *will now share;* still others read *will someday share.* 11:34 Isa 40:13 (Greek version). 11:35 See Job 41:11. 12:1a Greek *brothers.*

MY STORY: Yvonne

My boyfriend and I didn't have a very good relationship. We couldn't communicate much. So, I decided that we should break up. I tried to be as tactful as I could—I didn't want to hurt his feelings. His reaction was to call me a couple of names that were hurtful, demeaning, and completely untrue. Not only did he say these things to me, he said them to other people.

That enraged me! I immediately thought of different ways to get even. But then I thought about Romans 12:19: "Dear friends, never take revenge. Leave that to the righteous anger of God. For the Scriptures say, 'I will take revenge; I will pay them back,' says the Lord." This helped me to remove any thoughts of revenge from my mind and to concentrate instead on forgiving him and praying for him. As I do this, concern for his spiritual life overshadows my feelings of anger and hurt.

he has done for you. Let them be a living and holy sacrifice—the kind he will find acceptable. This is truly the way to worship him.* ²Don't copy the behavior and customs of this world, but let God transform you into a new person by changing the way you think. Then you will learn to know God's will for you, which is good and pleasing and perfect.

³Because of the privilege and authority* God has given me, I give each of you this warning: Don't think you are better than you really are. Be honest in your evaluation of yourselves, measuring yourselves by the faith God has given us.* ⁴Just as our bodies have many parts and each part has a special function, ⁵so it is with Christ's body. We are many parts of one body, and we all belong to each other.

⁶In his grace, God has given us different gifts for doing certain things well. So if God has given you the ability to prophesy, speak out with as much faith as God has given you. ⁷If your gift is serving others, serve them well. If you are a teacher, teach well. ⁸If your gift is to encourage others, be encouraging. If it is giving, give generously. If God has given you leadership ability, take the responsibility seriously. And if you have a gift for showing kindness to others, do it gladly.

⁹Don't just pretend to love others. Really love them. Hate what is wrong. Hold tightly to what is good. ¹⁰Love each other with genuine affection,* and take delight in honoring each other. ¹¹Never be lazy, but work hard and serve the Lord enthusiastically.* ¹²Rejoice in our confident hope. Be patient in trouble, and keep on praying. ¹³When God's people are in need, be ready to help them. Always be eager to practice hospitality.

¹⁴Bless those who persecute you. Don't curse them; pray that God will bless them. ¹⁵Be happy with those who are happy, and weep with those who weep. ¹⁶Live in harmony with each other. Don't be too proud to enjoy the company of ordinary people. And don't think you know it all!

¹⁷Never pay back evil with more evil. Do things in such a way that everyone can see you are honorable. ¹⁸Do all that you can to live in peace with everyone.

¹⁹Dear friends, never take revenge. Leave that to the righteous anger of God. For the Scriptures say,

"I will take revenge;
    I will pay them back,"*
    says the Lord.

²⁰Instead,

"If your enemies are hungry, feed them.
    If they are thirsty, give them something
        to drink.
In doing this, you will heap
    burning coals of shame on their heads."*

²¹Don't let evil conquer you, but conquer evil by doing good.

13 **RESPECT FOR AUTHORITY** Everyone must submit to governing authorities. For all authority comes from God, and those in positions of authority have been placed there by God. ²So anyone who rebels against authority is rebelling against what God has instituted, and they will be punished. ³For the authorities do not strike fear in people who are doing right, but in those who are doing wrong. Would you like to live without fear of the authorities? Do what is right, and they will honor you. ⁴The authorities are God's servants, sent for your good. But if you are doing wrong, of course you should be afraid, for they have the power to

12:1b Or *This is your spiritual worship;* or *This is your reasonable service.* 12:3a Or *Because of the grace;* compare 1:5. 12:3b Or *by the faith God has given you;* or *by the standard of our God-given faith.* 12:10 Greek *with brotherly love.* 12:11 Or *but serve the Lord with a zealous spirit;* or *but let the Spirit excite you as you serve the Lord.* 12:19 Deut 32:35. 12:20 Prov 25:21-22.

punish you. They are God's servants, sent for the very purpose of punishing those who do what is wrong. [5]So you must submit to them, not only to avoid punishment, but also to keep a clear conscience.

[6]Pay your taxes, too, for these same reasons. For government workers need to be paid. They are serving God in what they do. [7]Give to everyone what you owe them: Pay your taxes and government fees to those who collect them, and give respect and honor to those who are in authority.

LOVE FULFILLS GOD'S REQUIREMENTS [8]Owe nothing to anyone—except for your obligation to love one another. If you love your neighbor, you will fulfill the requirements of God's law. [9]For the commandments say, "You must not commit adultery. You must not murder. You must not steal. You must not covet."* These— and other such commandments—are summed up in this one commandment: "Love your neighbor as yourself."* [10]Love does no wrong to others, so love fulfills the requirements of God's law.

[11]This is all the more urgent, for you know how late it is; time is running out. Wake up, for our salvation is nearer now than when we first believed. [12]The night is almost gone; the day of salvation will soon be here. So remove your dark deeds like dirty clothes, and put on the shining armor of right living. [13]Because we belong to the day, we must live decent lives for all to see. Don't participate in the darkness of wild parties and drunkenness, or in sexual

13:9a Exod 20:13-15, 17.   **13:9b** Lev 19:18.

promiscuity and immoral living, or in quarreling and jealousy. [14]Instead, clothe yourself with the presence of the Lord Jesus Christ. And don't let yourself think about ways to indulge your evil desires.

14 THE DANGER OF CRITICISM Accept other believers who are weak in faith, and don't argue with them about what they think is right or wrong. [2]For instance, one person believes it's all right to eat anything. But another believer with a sensitive conscience will eat only vegetables. [3]Those who feel free to eat anything must not look down on those who don't. And those who don't eat certain foods must not condemn those who do, for God has accepted them. [4]Who are you to condemn

....

IN DEBT
(13:8) Why is love for others called a debt? We are permanently in debt to Christ for the love he lavished on us. The only way we can even begin to repay this debt is by loving others in turn. Because Christ's love will always be infinitely greater than ours, we will always have the obligation to love our neighbors. In what ways do you pay your debt?

SELF-INVENTORY
(14:1) Who is weak in faith and who is strong? We are all weak in some areas and strong in others. Our faith is strong in an area where we consistently avoid giving into temptation. It's weak if we must avoid certain activities or places in order to protect our spiritual life. We need to take a self-inventory to find our weaknesses and strengths. What are your weaknesses? Your strengths? Regardless of your weaknesses, you can always count on God. Where you are weak, he is strong (2 Cor 12:9-10).

CHOICES
authority

"What a stupid law!" Logan complains. "How can they—?"

"I know," Gabriel interrupts. "Can you believe it? An 11 o'clock curfew!"

"And," chimes in Abbie, "all because some losers from across town crashed a party and trashed a house. It's not fair!"

"Well," Logan concludes, "I don't know about you guys, but I'm not gonna let a bunch of 80-year-olds at city hall tell me what to do."

"What?" Abbie and Gabriel say together, as if they had rehearsed it.

"I mean, I'm gonna pretend like the dumb curfew doesn't exist. I'll be 18 in less than two months anyways."

"What are your parents gonna say?" Abbie asks. "Won't they freak?"

"Aw, they're cool. They know I'm not gonna go out and make a big scene. See, we should keep doing what we're doing—just be quiet about it. The cops'll never even know."

Abbie nods. "I can understand the law for those people who really get out of hand. But we're not like that."

"Right," Gabriel agrees. "What's wrong with some Christian friends having a low-key party on the weekend—ya know, listening to some music or watching a few DVDs?"

"Nothin'!" Logan yells.

"Then, we're all agreed?" Abbie asks.

"Yep," Gabriel responds. "We ignore the curfew."

"What curfew?" Logan quips.

Everyone smiles.

For an eye-opening look at how we should respond to our civil authorities, read Romans 13:1-7.

someone else's servants? Their own master will judge whether they stand or fall. And with the Lord's help, they will stand and receive his approval.

⁵In the same way, some think one day is more holy than another day, while others think every day is alike. You should each be fully convinced that whichever day you choose is acceptable. ⁶Those who worship the Lord on a special day do it to honor him. Those who eat any kind of food do so to honor the Lord, since they give thanks to God before eating. And those who refuse to eat certain foods also want to please the Lord and give thanks to God. ⁷For we don't live for ourselves or die for ourselves. ⁸If we live, it's to honor the Lord. And if we die, it's to honor the Lord. So whether we live or die, we belong to the Lord. ⁹Christ died and rose again for this very purpose—to be Lord both of the living and of the dead.

¹⁰So why do you condemn another believer*? Why do you look down on another believer? Remember, we will all stand before the judgment seat of God. ¹¹For the Scriptures say,

"'As surely as I live,' says the LORD,
'every knee will bend to me,
   and every tongue will confess and give
      praise to God.*'"

¹²Yes, each of us will give a personal account to God. ¹³So let's stop condemning each other. Decide instead to live in such a way that you will not cause another believer to stumble and fall.

¹⁴I know and am convinced on the authority of the Lord Jesus that no food, in and of itself, is wrong to eat. But if someone believes it is wrong, then for that person it is wrong. ¹⁵And if another believer is distressed by what you eat, you are not acting in love if you eat it. Don't let your eating ruin someone for whom Christ died. ¹⁶Then you will not be criticized for doing something you believe is good. ¹⁷For the Kingdom of God is not a matter of what we eat or drink, but of living a life of goodness and peace and joy in the Holy Spirit. ¹⁸If you serve Christ with this attitude, you will please God, and others will approve of you, too. ¹⁹So then, let us aim

for harmony in the church and try to build each other up.

²⁰Don't tear apart the work of God over what you eat. Remember, all foods are acceptable, but it is wrong to eat something if it makes another person stumble. ²¹It is better not to eat meat or drink wine or do anything else if it might cause another believer to stumble. ²²You may believe there's nothing wrong with what you are doing, but keep it between yourself and God. Blessed are those who don't feel guilty for doing something they have decided is right. ²³But if you have doubts about whether or not you should eat something, you are sinning if you go ahead and do it. For you are not following your convictions. If you do anything you believe is not right, you are sinning.

15 LIVING TO PLEASE OTHERS

We who are strong must be considerate of those who are sensitive about things like this. We must not just please ourselves. ²We should help others do what is right and build them up in the Lord. ³For even Christ didn't live to please himself. As the Scriptures say, "The insults of those who insult you, O God, have fallen on me."* ⁴Such things were written in the Scriptures long ago to teach us. And the Scriptures give us hope and encouragement as we wait patiently for God's promises to be fulfilled.

⁵May God, who gives this patience and encouragement, help you live in complete harmony with each other, as is fitting for followers of Christ Jesus. ⁶Then all of you can join together with one voice, giving praise and glory to God, the Father of our Lord Jesus Christ.

⁷Therefore, accept each other just as Christ has accepted you so that God will be given glory. ⁸Remember that Christ came as a servant to the Jews* to show that God is true to the promises he made to their ancestors. ⁹He also came so that the Gentiles might give glory to God for his mercies to them. That is what the psalmist meant when he wrote:

"For this, I will praise you among the
      Gentiles;
   I will sing praises to your name."*

¹⁰And in another place it is written,

"Rejoice with his people,
   you Gentiles."*

SILENCE
(14:23–15:6) We try to steer clear of actions forbidden by Scripture, of course. But when Scripture is silent, we should follow our conscience. When God shows us something is wrong for us, we should avoid it—but we should not look down on other Christians who exercise their freedom in those areas.

14:10 Greek *your brother;* also in 14:10b, 13, 15, 21.   **14:11** Or *confess allegiance to God.* Isa 49:18; 45:23 (Greek version).
15:3 Greek *who insult you have fallen on me.* Ps 69:9.   **15:8** Greek *servant of circumcision.*   **15:9** Ps 18:49.   **15:10** Deut 32:43.

[11]And yet again,

"Praise the LORD, all you Gentiles.
Praise him, all you people of the earth."*

[12]And in another place Isaiah said,

"The heir to David's throne* will come,
and he will rule over the Gentiles.
They will place their hope on him."*

[13]I pray that God, the source of hope, will fill you completely with joy and peace because you trust in him. Then you will overflow with confident hope through the power of the Holy Spirit.

PAUL'S REASON FOR WRITING [14]I am fully convinced, my dear brothers and sisters,* that you are full of goodness. You know these things so well you can teach each other all about them. [15]Even so, I have been bold enough to write about some of these points, knowing that all you need is this reminder. For by God's grace, [16]I am a special messenger from Christ Jesus to you Gentiles. I bring you the Good News so that I might present you as an acceptable offering to God, made holy by the Holy Spirit. [17]So I have reason to be enthusiastic about all Christ Jesus has done through me in my service to God. [18]Yet I dare not boast about anything except what Christ has done through me, bringing the Gentiles to God by my message and by the way I worked among them. [19]They were convinced by the power of miraculous signs and wonders and by the power of God's Spirit.* In this way, I have fully presented the Good News of Christ from Jerusalem all the way to Illyricum.*

[20]My ambition has always been to preach the Good News where the name of Christ has never been heard, rather than where a church has already been started by someone else. [21]I have been following the plan spoken of in the Scriptures, where it says,

"Those who have never been told about him
will see,
and those who have never heard of him
will understand."*

[22]In fact, my visit to you has been delayed so long because I have been preaching in these places.

15:11 Ps 117:1.   15:12a Greek *The root of Jesse.* David was the son of Jesse.   15:12b Isa 11:10 (Greek version).   15:14 Greek *brothers;* also in 15:30.   15:19a Other manuscripts read *the Spirit;* still others read *the Holy Spirit.*   15:19b *Illyricum* was a region northeast of Italy.   15:21 Isa 52:15 (Greek version).   15:25 Greek *God's holy people;* also in 15:26, 31.   15:26 *Macedonia* and *Achaia* were the northern and southern regions of Greece.   15:31 Greek *the ministry;* other manuscripts read *the gift.*   15:33 Some manuscripts do not include *Amen.* One very early manuscript places 16:25-27 here.

PAUL'S TRAVEL PLANS [23]But now I have finished my work in these regions, and after all these long years of waiting, I am eager to visit you. [24]I am planning to go to Spain, and when I do, I will stop off in Rome. And after I have enjoyed your fellowship for a little while, you can provide for my journey.

[25]But before I come, I must go to Jerusalem to take a gift to the believers* there. [26]For you see, the believers in Macedonia and Achaia* have eagerly taken up an offering for the poor among the believers in Jerusalem. [27]They were glad to do this because they feel they owe a real debt to them. Since the Gentiles received the spiritual blessings of the Good News from the believers in Jerusalem, they feel the least they can do in return is to help them financially. [28]As soon as I have delivered this money and completed this good deed of theirs, I will come to see you on my way to Spain. [29]And I am sure that when I come, Christ will richly bless our time together.

[30]Dear brothers and sisters, I urge you in the name of our Lord Jesus Christ to join in my struggle by praying to God for me. Do this because of your love for me, given to you by the Holy Spirit. [31]Pray that I will be rescued from those in Judea who refuse to obey God. Pray also that the believers there will be willing to accept the donation* I am taking to Jerusalem. [32]Then, by the will of God, I will be able to come to you with a joyful heart, and we will be an encouragement to each other.

[33]And now may God, who gives us his peace, be with you all. Amen.*

....

GOD'S WORK
(15:17) *Paul wasn't proud of what he had done but of what God had done through him. Being proud of God's work isn't a sin—it's an act of worship. If you aren't sure whether your pride is selfish or holy, ask this question: Are you just as proud of what God is doing through other people as you are of what he's doing through you?*

A BOND OF LOVE
(15:23-29) *In Paul's day, Rome was the world's political, religious, social, and economic center. The major governmental decisions were made in Rome, and it was from Rome that the gospel spread to the ends of the earth. Because the church in Rome was a mixture of Jews, Gentiles, slaves, free people, men, women, Roman citizens, and world travelers, it had potential for great influence and great conflict. But the Holy Spirit was the "glue" that held all of these believers together in a bond of love.*

We also live in a world full of different kinds of people. Like the Roman Christians, we have the potential for widespread influence and terrible conflict. Yet the same God who unified the Roman Christians also unites us through his love. It is this love that causes us to influence others.

16 PAUL GREETS HIS FRIENDS

I commend to you our sister Phoebe, who is a deacon in the church in Cenchrea. ²Welcome her in the Lord as one who is worthy of honor among God's people. Help her in whatever she needs, for she has been helpful to many, and especially to me.

³Give my greetings to Priscilla and Aquila, my co-workers in the ministry of Christ Jesus. ⁴In fact, they once risked their lives for me. I am thankful to them, and so are all the Gentile churches. ⁵Also give my greetings to the church that meets in their home.

Greet my dear friend Epenetus. He was the first person from the province of Asia to become a follower of Christ. ⁶Give my greetings to Mary, who has worked so hard for your benefit. ⁷Greet Andronicus and Junia,* my fellow Jews,* who were in prison with me. They are highly respected among the apostles and became followers of Christ before I did. ⁸Greet Ampliatus, my dear friend in the Lord. ⁹Greet Urbanus, our co-worker in Christ, and my dear friend Stachys.

¹⁰Greet Apelles, a good man whom Christ approves. And give my greetings to the believers from the household of Aristobulus. ¹¹Greet Herodion, my fellow Jew.* Greet the Lord's people from the household of Narcissus. ¹²Give my greetings to Tryphena and Tryphosa, the Lord's workers, and to dear Persis, who has worked so hard for the Lord. ¹³Greet Rufus, whom the Lord picked out to be his very own; and also his dear mother, who has been a mother to me.

¹⁴Give my greetings to Asyncritus, Phlegon, Hermes, Patrobas, Hermas, and the brothers and sisters* who meet with them. ¹⁵Give my greetings to Philologus, Julia, Nereus and his sister, and to Olympas and all the believers* who meet with them. ¹⁶Greet each other in Christian love.* All the churches of Christ send you their greetings.

PAUL'S FINAL INSTRUCTIONS

¹⁷And now I make one more appeal, my dear brothers and sisters. Watch out for people who cause divisions and upset people's faith by teaching things contrary to what you have been taught. Stay away from them. ¹⁸Such people are not serving Christ our Lord; they are serving their own personal interests. By smooth talk and glowing words they deceive innocent people. ¹⁹But everyone knows that you are obedient to the Lord. This makes me very happy. I want you to be wise in doing right and to stay innocent of any wrong. ²⁰The God of peace will soon crush Satan under your feet. May the grace of our Lord Jesus* be with you.

²¹Timothy, my fellow worker, sends you his greetings, as do Lucius, Jason, and Sosipater, my fellow Jews.

²²I, Tertius, the one writing this letter for Paul, send my greetings, too, as one of the Lord's followers.

²³Gaius says hello to you. He is my host and also serves as host to the whole church. Erastus, the city treasurer, sends you his greetings, and so does our brother Quartus.*

²⁵Now all glory to God, who is able to make you strong, just as my Good News says. This message about Jesus Christ has revealed his plan for you Gentiles, a plan kept secret from the beginning of time. ²⁶But now as the prophets* foretold and as the eternal God has commanded, this message is made known to all Gentiles everywhere, so that they too might believe and obey him. ²⁷All glory to the only wise God, through Jesus Christ, forever. Amen.

···

CHECK

(16:17-20) When we read books or listen to sermons, we should check the content of what is written or said and not be fooled by smooth style. Christians who study God's Word don't need to be fooled, even if superficial listeners are easily taken in. For an example of believers who carefully checked God's Word, see Acts 17:10-12.

16:7a *Junia* is a feminine name. Some late manuscripts accent the word so it reads *Junias,* a masculine name; still others read *Julia* (feminine). **16:7b** Or *compatriots;* also in 16:21. **16:11** Or *compatriot.* **16:14** Greek *brothers;* also in 16:17. **16:15** Greek *all of God's holy people.* **16:16** Greek *with a sacred kiss.* **16:20** Some manuscripts read *Lord Jesus Christ.* **16:23** Some manuscripts add verse 24, *May the grace of our Lord Jesus Christ be with you all. Amen.* Still others add this sentence after verse 27. **16:26** Greek *the prophetic writings.*

1 CORINTHIANS

Rob recently accepted Christ. Yesterday, he watched in total disbelief as two of the "leaders" of his church got into a shouting match after Sunday services. Rob asks you why supposedly "mature" Christians act that way. What do you say?

Kim has discovered that a man and woman who are active in the church aren't married, but are living together. "Isn't that supposed to be wrong?" she asks you, puzzled. "Why doesn't the pastor talk to them? Isn't that a sin?" What would you tell her?

Imelda knows, as a Christian, that certain activities—drunkenness, premarital sex, lying, stealing—are wrong. But what about all those "gray areas" that God's Word doesn't directly address? Is it okay to hang out in clubs? "I would just go to dance," she reminds you. What about watching her favorite music videos on the Internet or listening to songs on the radio? And how does God feel about the movies she's seen recently?

"I want to do what's right," she tells you, "but sometimes it's hard to know what I should do. Aren't there some guidelines from the Bible that can help?" How do you answer?

These questions are far from new. Christians (and churches) have struggled with immaturity, division, and immorality from the beginning. Fortunately, the apostle Paul has some real and practical answers in his first letter to the Corinthians. Got questions? Keep reading.

STATS

PURPOSE
To identify and resolve conflicts in the Corinthian church, and to teach the believers how to live for Christ in a Christ-less society

AUTHOR
Paul

ORIGINAL AUDIENCE
The church in Corinth, largely made up of Gentiles

DATE WRITTEN
About A.D. 55, during Paul's third missionary journey

SETTING
The city of Corinth was a major city, seaport, and center of trade. It was the most important city in Achaia and also one of the most pagan. Paul had established this church during his second missionary journey.

KEY PEOPLE
Paul, Timothy, members of Chloe's household

KEY PLACES
Worship meetings in Corinth

KEY POINTS

LOYALTIES The Corinthians' loyalties to various church leaders and teachers—Peter, Paul, and Apollos—led to intellectual pride, which divided the church. We must guard against the division caused by misguided loyalty or pride in human wisdom.

IMMORALITY Paul used tough love to deal with an incident of sexual sin in the church at Corinth. Paul's advice encourages us to avoid compromising, even if others seem to disagree with our moral stance.

FREEDOM Paul taught freedom of choice on practices not expressly forbidden in Scripture. Although Jesus makes us free (see John 8:32, 36), we don't have the right to abuse that freedom by encouraging others to do wrong.

WORSHIP Paul addressed disorder in worship. Worship must be carried out properly and orderly. Everything we do to worship God should be done in a manner worthy of his high honor.

LIFE AFTER DEATH Some people denied that Jesus rose from the dead. Others believed that people would not be physically resurrected after death. Jesus' resurrection assures us that each of us will have a new, living body after we die.

1 GREETINGS FROM PAUL This letter is from Paul, chosen by the will of God to be an apostle of Christ Jesus, and from our brother Sosthenes.

²I am writing to God's church in Corinth,* to you who have been called by God to be his own holy people. He made you holy by means of Christ Jesus,* just as he did for all people everywhere who call on the name of our Lord Jesus Christ, their Lord and ours.

³May God our Father and the Lord Jesus Christ give you grace and peace.

PAUL GIVES THANKS TO GOD ⁴I always thank my God for you and for the gracious gifts he has given you, now that you belong to Christ Jesus. ⁵Through him, God has enriched your church in every way—with all of your eloquent words and all of your knowledge. ⁶This confirms that what I told you about Christ is true. ⁷Now you have every spiritual gift you need as you eagerly wait for the return of our Lord Jesus Christ. ⁸He will keep you strong to the end so that you will be free from all blame on the day when our Lord Jesus Christ returns. ⁹God will do this, for he is faithful to do what he says, and he has invited you into partnership with his Son, Jesus Christ our Lord.

DIVISIONS IN THE CHURCH ¹⁰I appeal to you, dear brothers and sisters,* by the authority of our Lord Jesus Christ, to live in harmony with each other. Let there be no divisions in the church. Rather, be of one mind, united in thought and purpose. ¹¹For some members of Chloe's household have told me about your quarrels, my dear brothers and sisters. ¹²Some of you are saying, "I am a follower of Paul." Others are saying, "I follow Apollos," or "I follow Peter,*" or "I follow only Christ."

¹³Has Christ been divided into factions? Was I, Paul, crucified for you? Were any of you baptized in the name of Paul? Of course not! ¹⁴I thank God that I did not baptize any of you except Crispus and Gaius, ¹⁵for now no one can say they were baptized in my name. ¹⁶(Oh yes, I also baptized the household of Stephanas, but I don't remember baptizing anyone else.) ¹⁷For Christ didn't send me to baptize, but to preach

1:2a *Corinth* was the capital city of Achaia, the southern region of the Greek peninsula. **1:2b** Or *because you belong to Christ Jesus.* **1:10** Greek *brothers;* also in 1:11, 26. **1:12** Greek *Cephas.*

USEFUL
(1:1) Paul was chosen by God to be a missionary. Likewise, each Christian has a task to do. Although some tasks may seem more spectacular than others, all are necessary to carry out God's greater plans for the world. How will you use your abilities in his service? (Check out 1 Corinthians 12–14 for more on these abilities.)

I WONDER...

I want to grow in my faith, but my Christian friends are dragging me down. How can I grow as a Christian without their support?

Because God is the one who "invited you into partnership with his Son (1 Cor 1:9), he will make sure that you are able to grow in your faith. He has no intention of abandoning you.

Often, a growing faith develops by having good role models to imitate. It makes sense, then, that having friends who are modeling a strong faith can really help.

The role models in our lives have a big impact on us—positive or negative. Kids of divorced parents are often determined to make sure that their own marriage is a success. They seek out positive role models to observe, and they pore over numerous resources to learn how to build a strong marriage. But the opposite also can be true. Kids who grow up without a good model of what a family is supposed to look like can easily repeat their parents' mistakes.

Because your friends are acting as if they have "divorced God," you are faced with a choice. Will you learn from their mistakes and search out people to help you succeed in your relationship with Christ? Or will you follow their lead and turn your back on God as well? If you're serious about giving God every chance to make himself real in your life, consider these suggestions:

First, pray for your friends and for an opportunity to talk to them about the situation. Don't worry about how much you've blown it by participating in whatever they've done. Thinking about your future is more important than dwelling on the past. Next, go to one of your Christian friends, perhaps the leader of the group, and say something like: "I really want to give God a shot. I need your help. Can I count on you?" If this person says yes, it worked! If not, go to another friend and tell him the same thing. If no one responds, wait a week or two and start the process again, trusting that God has been working in their hearts. Or find some new friends you can count on. Maybe that's the answer God has for you.

Remember, God is faithful. He knows that you need friends and a group to hang around with. Be persistent in prayer and reaching out to others, and see how God provides.

CORINTH AND EPHESUS
Paul wrote this letter to Corinth during his three-year visit in Ephesus during his third missionary journey. The two cities sat across from each other on the Aegean Sea—both were busy and important ports. Titus may have carried this letter from Ephesus to Corinth (2 Cor 12:18).

the Good News—and not with clever speech, for fear that the cross of Christ would lose its power.

THE WISDOM OF GOD [18]The message of the cross is foolish to those who are headed for destruction! But we who are being saved know it is the very power of God. [19]As the Scriptures say,

"I will destroy the wisdom of the wise
    and discard the intelligence of the
        intelligent."*

[20]So where does this leave the philosophers, the scholars, and the world's brilliant debaters? God has made the wisdom of this world look foolish. [21]Since God in his wisdom saw to it that the world would never know him through human wisdom, he has used our foolish preaching to save those who believe. [22]It is foolish to the Jews, who ask for signs from heaven. And it is foolish to the Greeks, who seek human wisdom. [23]So when we preach that Christ was crucified, the Jews are offended and the Gentiles say it's all nonsense. [24]But to those called by God to salvation,

both Jews and Gentiles,* Christ is the power of God and the wisdom of God. [25]This foolish plan of God is wiser than the wisest of human plans, and God's weakness is stronger than the greatest of human strength.

[26]Remember, dear brothers and sisters, that few of you were wise in the world's eyes or powerful or wealthy* when God called you. [27]Instead, God chose things the world considers foolish in order to shame those who think they are wise. And he chose things that are powerless to shame those who are powerful. [28]God chose things despised by the world,* things counted as nothing at all, and used them to bring to nothing what the world considers important. [29]As a result, no one can ever boast in the presence of God.

[30]God has united you with Christ Jesus. For our benefit God made him to be wisdom itself.

1:19 Isa 29:14.   1:24 Greek and Greeks.   1:26 Or high born.
1:28 Or God chose those who are low born.

••

SIMPLE FAITH
(1:18-31) Paul explained that faith in Jesus is the key to forgiveness and eternal life with God. God planned it this way so that no one could boast that his achievements helped him secure eternal life (see also Eph 2:8-10). Good intentions or actions do not make us acceptable to God. Instead, God accepts us when we put our faith in what Jesus has already done for us. Have you?

Christ made us right with God; he made us pure and holy, and he freed us from sin. [31]Therefore, as the Scriptures say, "If you want to boast, boast only about the LORD."*

2 **PAUL'S MESSAGE OF WISDOM** When I first came to you, dear brothers and sisters,* I didn't use lofty words and impressive wisdom to tell you God's secret plan.* [2]For I decided that while I was with you I would forget everything except Jesus Christ, the one who was crucified. [3]I came to you in weakness—timid and trembling. [4]And my message and my preaching were very plain. Rather than

using clever and persuasive speeches, I relied only on the power of the Holy Spirit. [5]I did this so you would trust not in human wisdom but in the power of God.

[6]Yet when I am among mature believers, I do speak with words of wisdom, but not the kind of wisdom that belongs to this world or to the rulers of this world, who are soon forgotten. [7]No, the wisdom we speak of is the mystery of God*—his plan that was previously hidden, even though he made it for our ultimate glory before the world began. [8]But the rulers of this world have not understood it; if they had, they would not have crucified our glorious Lord. [9]That is what the Scriptures mean when they say,

"No eye has seen, no ear has heard,
    and no mind has imagined
what God has prepared
    for those who love him."*

1:31 Jer 9:24.   2:1a Greek *brothers.*   2:1b Greek *God's mystery;* other manuscripts read *God's testimony.*   2:7 Greek *But we speak God's wisdom in a mystery.*   2:9 Isa 64:4.

WHAT'S IN STORE?
(2:9) Paul quoted a promise in Isaiah concerning the amazing things that God has in store for his people in this life and for eternity. He will create a new heaven and a new earth (Isa 65:17; Rev 21:1), and we will live with him forever. Until then, his Holy Spirit comforts and guides us. This promise of an amazing future can give us hope and courage to press on in this life, even through hardship. Even when life seems at its most hopeless, we still have hope.

I WONDER . . .

I hear a lot about the New Age movement. Some of my friends say they are in it. How is this different from what I believe as a Christian?

The most convenient religion is one you create yourself, and that is what the New Age movement does for people. It allows them to create their own rules concerning God, their behavior, and how to make it to the next life.

Because of this, New Age is impossible to define! But, generally, here is what most New-Agers believe:

- They believe that God is everywhere and in everybody. Because we are humans, we all have a unity of spirit that allows us to be brothers and sisters no matter what. God is not good or bad. In fact, each person is a god. He or she is the center of the universe. Since God isn't seen as either good or bad, morality isn't important. But the mind and intellect are very important, because supposedly, a person has to think deep thoughts to understand these concepts.
- They believe that "salvation" comes through reincarnation. This means coming back to life again in the form of someone or something else, again and again, until you get it right. (Reincarnation is a lie; the Bible is very clear on this point. See Hebrews 9:27.)

The New Age movement has so many strains that outlining them all would be impossible. But at the center is the belief that no personal God exists, humans are not sinful, and the next life is assured in some form, no matter what a person has done. This is a very convenient religion if people just want to do their own thing.

But listen to God: "Cursed are those who put their trust in mere humans, who rely on human strength and turn their hearts away from the LORD" (Jer 17:5). When people set their own beliefs and thoughts up as more important than what God thinks, they are actually being cursed by him!

Nearly every belief within the New Age movement allows you to become your own god. Eve was told by Satan that she would become like God if she ate of the fruit of the tree (Gen 3:1-6). People are being told they can be god of their life if they would just look away from the one, true God.

The Bible must be our authority on what we believe about God, ourselves as humans, and what it takes to be saved from our sin. If it isn't, then anyone can create a religion to suit his or her own desires. Unfortunately, that religion will lead to destruction. Don't believe it? Just take a look at 1 Corinthians 1:19: "I will destroy the wisdom of the wise and discard the intelligence of the intelligent."

Only one place has the real answers to who God is and what he's about: his holy Word, the Bible.

¹⁰But* it was to us that God revealed these things by his Spirit. For his Spirit searches out everything and shows us God's deep secrets. ¹¹No one can know a person's thoughts except that person's own spirit, and no one can know God's thoughts except God's own Spirit. ¹²And we have received God's Spirit (not the world's spirit), so we can know the wonderful things God has freely given us.

¹³When we tell you these things, we do not use words that come from human wisdom. Instead, we speak words given to us by the Spirit, using the Spirit's words to explain spiritual truths.* ¹⁴But people who aren't spiritual* can't receive these truths from God's Spirit. It all sounds foolish to them and they can't understand it, for only those who are spiritual can understand what the Spirit means. ¹⁵Those who are spiritual can evaluate all things, but they themselves cannot be evaluated by others. ¹⁶For,

"Who can know the LORD's thoughts?
    Who knows enough to teach him?"*

But we understand these things, for we have the mind of Christ.

3 **PAUL AND APOLLOS, SERVANTS OF CHRIST** Dear brothers and sisters,* when I was with you I couldn't talk to you as I would to spiritual people.* I had to talk as though you belonged to this world or as though you were infants in the Christian life.* ²I had to feed you with milk, not with solid food, because you weren't ready for anything stronger. And you still aren't ready, ³for you are still controlled by your sinful nature. You are jealous of one another and quarrel with each other. Doesn't that prove you are controlled by your sinful nature? Aren't you living like people of the world? ⁴When one of you says, "I am a follower of Paul," and another says, "I follow Apollos," aren't you acting just like people of the world?

⁵After all, who is Apollos? Who is Paul? We are only God's servants through whom you believed the Good News. Each of us did the work the Lord gave us. ⁶I planted the seed in your hearts, and Apollos watered it, but it was God who made it grow. ⁷It's not important who does the planting, or who does the watering. What's important is that God makes the seed grow. ⁸The one who plants and the one who waters work together with the same purpose. And both will be rewarded for their own hard work. ⁹For we are both God's workers. And you are God's field. You are God's building.

¹⁰Because of God's grace to me, I have laid the foundation like an expert builder. Now others are building on it. But whoever is building on this foundation must be very careful. ¹¹For no one can lay any foundation other than the one we already have—Jesus Christ.

¹²Anyone who builds on that foundation may use a variety of materials—gold, silver, jewels, wood, hay, or straw. ¹³But on the judgment day, fire will reveal what kind of work each builder has done. The fire will show if a person's work has any value. ¹⁴If the work survives, that builder will receive a reward. ¹⁵But if the work is burned up, the builder will suffer great loss. The builder will be saved, but like someone barely escaping through a wall of flames.

¹⁶Don't you realize that all of you together are the temple of God and that the Spirit of God lives in* you? ¹⁷God will destroy anyone who destroys this temple. For God's temple is holy, and you are that temple.

¹⁸Stop deceiving yourselves. If you think you are wise by this world's standards, you need to become a fool to be truly wise. ¹⁹For the wisdom of this world is foolishness to God. As the Scriptures say,

"He traps the wise
    in the snare of their own cleverness."*

²⁰And again,

"The LORD knows the thoughts of the wise;
    he knows they are worthless."*

²¹So don't boast about following a particular human leader. For everything belongs to you—²²whether Paul or Apollos or Peter,* or the world, or life and death, or the present and the future. Everything belongs to you, ²³and you belong to Christ, and Christ belongs to God.

4 **PAUL'S RELATIONSHIP WITH THE CORINTHIANS** So look at Apollos and me as mere servants of Christ who have been put in charge of explaining God's mysteries. ²Now, a

....

DESIRES
(3:1-9) *Paul called the Corinthians "infants" in the Christian life because they were not yet spiritually healthy and mature. The proof was that they quarreled like children. Baby Christians are controlled by their own desires, while mature believers are controlled by God's desires. Are your desires the same as God's?*

2:10 Some manuscripts read *For*.   2:13 Or *explaining spiritual truths in spiritual language,* or *explaining spiritual truths to spiritual people*.   2:14 Or *who don't have the Spirit;* or *who have only physical life*.   2:16 Isa 40:13 (Greek version).   3:1a Greek *Brothers*.   3:1b Or *to people who have the Spirit*.   3:1c Greek *in Christ*.   3:16 Or *among*.   3:19 Job 5:13.   3:20 Ps 94:11.   3:22 Greek *Cephas*.

person who is put in charge as a manager must be faithful. ³As for me, it matters very little how I might be evaluated by you or by any human authority. I don't even trust my own judgment on this point. ⁴My conscience is clear, but that doesn't prove I'm right. It is the Lord himself who will examine me and decide.

⁵So don't make judgments about anyone ahead of time—before the Lord returns. For he will bring our darkest secrets to light and will reveal our private motives. Then God will give to each one whatever praise is due.

⁶Dear brothers and sisters,* I have used Apollos and myself to illustrate what I've been saying. If you pay attention to what I have quoted from the Scriptures,* you won't be proud of one of your leaders at the expense of another. ⁷For what gives you the right to make such a judgment? What do you have that God hasn't given you? And if everything you have is from God, why boast as though it were not a gift?

⁸You think you already have everything you need. You think you are already rich. You have begun to reign in God's kingdom without us! I wish you really were reigning already, for then we would be reigning with you. ⁹Instead, I sometimes think God has put us apostles on display, like prisoners of war at the end of a victor's parade, condemned to die. We have become a spectacle to the entire world—to people and angels alike.

¹⁰Our dedication to Christ makes us look like fools, but you claim to be so wise in Christ! We are weak, but you are so powerful! You are honored, but we are ridiculed. ¹¹Even now we go hungry and thirsty, and we don't have enough clothes to keep warm. We are often beaten and have no home. ¹²We work wearily with our own hands to earn our living. We bless those who curse us. We are patient with those who abuse us. ¹³We appeal gently when evil things are said about us. Yet we are treated like the world's garbage, like everybody's trash—right up to the present moment.

¹⁴I am not writing these things to shame you, but to warn you as my beloved children. ¹⁵For even if you had ten thousand others to teach

you about Christ, you have only one spiritual father. For I became your father in Christ Jesus when I preached the Good News to you. ¹⁶So I urge you to imitate me.

¹⁷That's why I have sent Timothy, my beloved and faithful child in the Lord. He will remind you of how I follow Christ Jesus, just as I teach in all the churches wherever I go.

¹⁸Some of you have become arrogant, thinking I will not visit you again. ¹⁹But I will come—and soon—if the Lord lets me, and then I'll find out whether these arrogant people just give pretentious speeches or whether they really have God's power. ²⁰For the Kingdom of God is not just a lot of talk; it is living by God's power. ²¹Which do you choose? Should I come with a rod to punish you, or should I come with love and a gentle spirit?

5 PAUL CONDEMNS SPIRITUAL PRIDE I can hardly believe the report about the sexual immorality going on among you—something that even pagans don't do. I am told that a man in your church is living in sin with his step-mother.* ²You are so proud of yourselves, but you should be mourning in sorrow and shame. And you should remove this man from your fellowship.

³Even though I am not with you in person, I am with you in the Spirit.* And as though I were there, I have already passed judgment on this man ⁴in the name of the Lord Jesus. You must call a meeting of the church.* I will be present with you in spirit, and so will the power of our Lord Jesus. ⁵Then you must throw this man out and hand him over to Satan so that his sinful nature will be destroyed* and he himself* will be saved on the day the Lord* returns.

⁶Your boasting about this is terrible. Don't you realize that this sin is like a little yeast that spreads through the whole batch of dough? ⁷Get rid of the old "yeast" by removing this wicked person from among you. Then you will be like a fresh batch of dough made without yeast, which is what you really are. Christ, our Passover Lamb, has been sacrificed for us.* ⁸So let us celebrate the festival, not with the old bread* of wickedness and evil, but with the new bread* of sincerity and truth.

⁹When I wrote to you before, I told you not to associate with people who indulge in sexual

---

JUDGING
(4:1-7) Paul warned the Corinthian believers to avoid judging one leader's performance by another's. Have you ever judged another person about the quality or sincerity of his or her relationship with God? Maybe you've even heard someone express skepticism as to whether or not someone really is a Christian. Only God has the perfect insight to correctly judge.

4:6a Greek *Brothers.*　　**4:6b** Or *If you learn not to go beyond "what is written."*　　**5:1** Greek *his father's wife.*　　**5:3** Or *in spirit.*　　**5:4** Or *In the name of the Lord Jesus, you must call a meeting of the church.*　　**5:5a** Or *so that his body will be destroyed;* Greek reads *for the destruction of the flesh.*　　**5:5b** Greek *and the spirit.*　　**5:5c** Other manuscripts read *the Lord Jesus;* still others read *our Lord Jesus Christ.*　　**5:7** Greek *has been sacrificed.*　　**5:8a** Greek *not with old leaven.*　　**5:8b** Greek *but with unleavened [bread].*

sin. ¹⁰But I wasn't talking about unbelievers who indulge in sexual sin, or are greedy, or cheat people, or worship idols. You would have to leave this world to avoid people like that. ¹¹I meant that you are not to associate with anyone who claims to be a believer* yet indulges in sexual sin, or is greedy, or worships idols, or is abusive, or is a drunkard, or cheats people. Don't even eat with such people.

¹²It isn't my responsibility to judge outsiders, but it certainly is your responsibility to judge those inside the church who are sinning. ¹³God will judge those on the outside; but as the Scriptures say, "You must remove the evil person from among you."*

6 AVOIDING LAWSUITS WITH CHRISTIANS

When one of you has a dispute with another believer, how dare you file a lawsuit and ask a secular court to decide the matter instead of taking it to other believers*! ²Don't you realize that someday we believers will judge the world? And since you are going to judge the world, can't you decide even these little things among yourselves? ³Don't you realize that we will judge angels? So you should surely be able to resolve ordinary disputes in this life. ⁴If you have legal disputes about such matters, why go to outside judges who are not respected by the church? ⁵I am saying this to shame you. Isn't there anyone in all the church who is wise enough to decide these issues? ⁶But instead, one believer* sues another— right in front of unbelievers!

⁷Even to have such lawsuits with one another is a defeat for you. Why not just accept the injustice and leave it at that? Why not let yourselves be cheated? ⁸Instead, you yourselves are

the ones who do wrong and cheat even your fellow believers.*

⁹Don't you realize that those who do wrong will not inherit the Kingdom of God? Don't fool yourselves. Those who indulge in sexual sin, or who worship idols, or commit adultery, or are male prostitutes, or practice homosexuality, ¹⁰or are thieves, or greedy people, or drunkards, or are abusive, or cheat people— none of these will inherit the Kingdom of God. ¹¹Some of you were once like that. But you were cleansed; you were made holy; you were made right with God by calling on the name of the Lord Jesus Christ and by the Spirit of our God.

AVOIDING SEXUAL SIN

¹²You say, "I am allowed to do anything"—but not everything is good for you. And even though "I am allowed to do anything," I must not become a slave to anything. ¹³You say, "Food was made for the stomach, and the stomach for food." (This is true, though someday God will do away with both of them.) But you can't say that our bodies were made for sexual immorality. They were made for the Lord, and the Lord cares about our bodies. ¹⁴And God will raise us from the dead by his power, just as he raised our Lord from the dead.

¹⁵Don't you realize that your bodies are actually parts of Christ? Should a man take his

....

WARNING!
(6:13-20) Next on Paul's list of warnings was one on sexual immorality. Such a warning may seem old-fashioned in light of what's regularly seen in movies and on television. But God's standards haven't changed. He doesn't forbid sex outside of marriage just to be difficult. He wants to prevent us from hurting ourselves and others.

5:11 Greek *a brother.*   5:13 Deut 17:7.   6:1 Greek *God's holy people; also in 6:2.*   6:6 Greek *one brother.*   6:8 Greek *even the brothers.*

CHOICES drugs

Scene 1: Lyle is having a massive argument with his parents. They've just discovered a small amount of marijuana in his coat pocket.

"Lighten up, okay? It's no big deal! It's just a little grass."

"'No big deal'? Listen here, that grass is illegal! You could go to jail for that grass!"

"Lyle, how could you do this to your father and me?"

"What? I'm not doing anything to you! It's my life!"

"That's right. It's your life. But you're gonna cut it short if you fill your body with drugs."

"Aw, come off it! I don't 'fill my body with drugs.' I smoke a little harmless grass."

Scene 2: Gary looks nervously over his shoulder. No one is watching, so he pulls a pill bottle—containing anabolic steroids—out of his locker.

Quickly he turns and heads for the gym. Time to pump some serious iron.

Scene 3: With her parents out for the evening, Staci and her friend Kimberly search the workshop and garage for gas, paint thinner, or anything else with the right kind of fumes to get them high.

Drugs, no matter what kind, damage the human body. If you're a Christian, your body doesn't belong to you. God owns it, and he tells you to take care of it.

For that reason alone, you must resist the temporary thrill of a chemical high. See 1 Corinthians 6:19-20.

body, which is part of Christ, and join it to a prostitute? Never! [16]And don't you realize that if a man joins himself to a prostitute, he becomes one body with her? For the Scriptures say, "The two are united into one."* [17]But the person who is joined to the Lord is one spirit with him.

[18]Run from sexual sin! No other sin so clearly affects the body as this one does. For sexual immorality is a sin against your own body. [19]Don't you realize that your body is the temple of the Holy Spirit, who lives in you and was given to you by God? You do not belong to yourself, [20]for God bought you with a high price. So you must honor God with your body.

TO MARRY OR NOT

(7:1-9) Because many new believers in Corinth thought that everyone should remain celibate, some engaged couples had decided not to get married. But Paul advised the couples who wanted to marry that they should not deny their normal sexual drives by avoiding marriage. This does not mean, however, that people who have trouble controlling their thoughts should marry the first person who comes along. It is better to deal with the pressure of sexual desire than to deal with an unhappy marriage.

7 **INSTRUCTION ON MARRIAGE** Now regarding the questions you asked in your letter. Yes, it is good to abstain from sexual relations.* [2]But because there is so much sexual immorality, each man should have his own wife, and each woman should have her own husband.

[3]The husband should fulfill his wife's sexual needs, and the wife should fulfill her husband's needs. [4]The wife gives authority over her body

6:16 Gen 2:24. 7:1 Or *to live a celibate life;* Greek reads *It is good for a man not to touch a woman.*

ULTIMATE ISSUES *AIDS: WHAT WOULD JESUS DO?*

During the last several decades, AIDS has been a topic of concern in America and throughout the world. Some have claimed that AIDS is God's judgment on certain groups of sinners. Others scream just as loudly that this is a medical issue, not a moral one. Who's right? And how should Christians respond to this overwhelming problem?

In one sense, AIDS (Acquired Immune Deficiency Syndrome) is primarily a medical issue. The AIDS virus attacks the body's immune system, making the body defenseless against the diseases a healthy person's immune system would destroy. AIDS is an "equal opportunity" nightmare—it affects everyone: young, old, male, female, gay, or straight.

If AIDS isn't a punishment from God, why has it hit the male gay community and IV drug abusers so hard? The answer is that gay men and IV drug abusers participate in activities that pass the virus from person to person. God hasn't singled out particular groups for special judgment; rather, those people engage in activities that are particularly risky in regard to the transmission of AIDS.

God created the universe to run in accordance with natural laws, like gravity, inertia, and so forth. When you try to defy those laws, you lose. You may not like the law of gravity, but jump off a building and you will—like it or not—encounter it. Certain natural laws govern human behavior, too. One such law is that your body is not made for sexual promiscuity. Violate that law and you risk contracting AIDS or other sexually transmitted diseases. Likewise, your body was not made to handle large amounts of drugs. Continually inject them into your veins and you will experience physical problems, and AIDS may be contracted if dirty needles are used.

So it's not that God is using AIDS to "get" certain kinds of people. AIDS simply is a natural—though terrifying—result of human behavior that goes against God's design for our lives. Those who believe AIDS is a special divine judgment simply don't understand the reality of their own sin. As Psalm 143:1-2 exclaims, "Hear my prayer, O LORD; listen to my plea! Answer me because you are faithful and righteous. Don't put your servant on trial, for no one is innocent before you."

A cure for AIDS is still years away; but even if it weren't, the only reasonable, Christian response is to follow God's standards for sexual morality. Sex is made for marriage only—to be kept in the context of a faithful, monogamous relationship between husband and wife. Likewise, we must reaffirm God's ownership of our body by not abusing it with drugs. Paul writes in 1 Corinthians 6:19-20, "Don't you realize that your body is the temple of the Holy Spirit, who lives in you and was given to you by God? You do not belong to yourself, for God bought you with a high price. So you must honor God with your body." Where we have failed to live up to this, we need to confess our sins, repent, and ask for God's forgiveness.

Many Christians also need to confess their judgmental attitudes toward persons with AIDS. There is no room in Christianity for feelings of superiority or self-righteousness. Jesus had strong words for those who were guilty of spiritual pride, of thinking they were better than others. Our response toward anyone with this terrible disease should be concern, compassion, and a hand reaching out to ease his or her pain and distress.

Isn't that how Jesus deals with us all, regardless of our sins? ∎

to her husband, and the husband gives authority over his body to his wife.

⁵Do not deprive each other of sexual relations, unless you both agree to refrain from sexual intimacy for a limited time so you can give yourselves more completely to prayer. Afterward, you should come together again so that Satan won't be able to tempt you because of your lack of self-control. ⁶I say this as a concession, not as a command. ⁷But I wish everyone were single, just as I am. Yet each person has a special gift from God, of one kind or another.

⁸So I say to those who aren't married and to widows—it's better to stay unmarried, just as I am. ⁹But if they can't control themselves, they should go ahead and marry. It's better to marry than to burn with lust.

¹⁰But for those who are married, I have a command that comes not from me, but from the Lord.* A wife must not leave her husband. ¹¹But if she does leave him, let her remain single or else be reconciled to him. And the husband must not leave his wife.

¹²Now, I will speak to the rest of you, though I do not have a direct command from the Lord. If a Christian man* has a wife who is not a believer and she is willing to continue living with him, he must not leave her. ¹³And if a Christian woman has a husband who is not a believer and he is willing to continue living with her, she must not leave him. ¹⁴For the Christian wife brings holiness to her marriage, and the Christian husband* brings holiness to his marriage. Otherwise, your children would not be holy, but now they are holy. ¹⁵(But if the husband or wife who isn't a believer insists on leaving, let them go. In such cases the Christian husband or wife* is no longer bound to the other, for God has called you* to live in peace.) ¹⁶Don't you wives realize that your husbands might be saved because of you? And don't you husbands realize that your wives might be saved because of you?

¹⁷Each of you should continue to live in whatever situation the Lord has placed you, and remain as you were when God first called you. This is my rule for all the churches. ¹⁸For instance, a man who was circumcised before he became a believer should not try to reverse it. And the man who was uncircumcised when he became a believer should not be circumcised now. ¹⁹For it makes no difference whether or not a man has been circumcised. The important thing is to keep God's commandments.

²⁰Yes, each of you should remain as you were when God called you. ²¹Are you a slave? Don't let that worry you—but if you get a chance to be free, take it. ²²And remember, if you were a slave when the Lord called you, you are now free in the Lord. And if you were free when the Lord called you, you are now a slave of Christ. ²³God paid a high price for you, so don't be enslaved by the world.* ²⁴Each of you, dear brothers and sisters,* should remain as you were when God first called you.

²⁵Now regarding your question about the young women who are not yet married. I do not have a command from the Lord for them. But the Lord in his mercy has given me wisdom that can be trusted, and I will share it with you. ²⁶Because of the present crisis,* I think it is best to remain as you are. ²⁷If you have a wife, do not seek to end the marriage. If you do not have a wife, do not seek to get married. ²⁸But if you do get married, it is not a sin. And if a young woman gets married, it is not a sin. However, those who get married at this time will have troubles, and I am trying to spare you those problems.

²⁹But let me say this, dear brothers and sisters: The time that remains is very short. So from now on, those with wives should not focus only on their marriage. ³⁰Those who

7:10 See Matt 5:32; 19:9; Mark 10:11-12; Luke 16:18.   7:12 Greek *a brother.*   7:14 Greek *the brother.*   7:15a Greek *the brother or sister.* 7:15b Some manuscripts read *us.*   7:23 Greek *don't become slaves of people.*   7:24 Greek *brothers*; also in 7:29.   7:26 Or *the pressures of life.*

··

BE CONTENT

(7:17-24) Have you ever had a bad case of the "If only blues"? These are the feelings you get when you think that life would be complete if only you had what you want. "Life would be perfect if only I had someone to go out with." "I would be successful if only I weren't stuck in the family I'm in." Paul advised the believers to "live in whatever situation the Lord has placed [them]." In other words, be content. Does this mean you have to pretend that you're happy to be single when you don't really feel glad? Nope. It does mean accepting where you are instead of blaming God or demanding that he change your situation right now.

NO PROBLEMS?

(7:29-40) Many people think that finding the right boyfriend/girlfriend or getting married will solve all their problems. Having someone special in your life is cool. But no relationship—even a marriage—is a "cure for whatever ails you"! For example, here are a few of the problems marriage won't solve: (1) loneliness (some married people are really lonely), (2) sexual temptation, (3) satisfaction of one's deepest emotional needs, (4) elimination of life's difficulties. Marriage alone does not hold two people together, but commitment does—commitment to Christ and to each other despite conflicts and problems. Marriage can be great, but it isn't the solution to problems. There is only one reliable solution for anyone: Trust God to solve your problems.

weep or who rejoice or who buy things should not be absorbed by their weeping or their joy or their possessions. ³¹Those who use the things of the world should not become attached to them. For this world as we know it will soon pass away.

³²I want you to be free from the concerns of this life. An unmarried man can spend his time doing the Lord's work and thinking how to please him. ³³But a married man has to think about his earthly responsibilities and how to please his wife. ³⁴His interests are divided. In the same way, a woman who is no longer married or has never been married can be devoted to the Lord and holy in body and in spirit.

But a married woman has to think about her earthly responsibilities and how to please her husband. ³⁵I am saying this for your benefit, not to place restrictions on you. I want you to do whatever will help you serve the Lord best, with as few distractions as possible.

³⁶But if a man thinks that he's treating his fiancée improperly and will inevitably give in to his passion, let him marry her as he wishes. It is not a sin. ³⁷But if he has decided firmly not to marry and there is no urgency and he can control his passion, he does well not to marry. ³⁸So the person who marries his fiancée does well, and the person who doesn't marry does even better.

ULTIMATE ISSUES *MARRIAGE*

Maria was 23 years old, bright, attractive—and headed for divorce. She and Danny had been married two years. Now she sat in her former youth pastor's office and dissolved into tears.

"It's not working out," she choked out between sobs. "I don't know what happened. We were really in love, but we've lost something. I don't think we're going to make it . . ."

Tragically, this scene is repeated over and over. Why is it that two people who are "made for each other" so often end up looking for the escape hatch labeled "divorce"? Maybe a better question is: What does it take to keep a marriage from becoming a casualty?

If marriage were just another human institution—like a corporation or a university—then getting out of it would be no more significant or painful than changing jobs or switching schools. Indeed, many people have tried to treat marriage that way, as something to enjoy when it's good or helpful and to terminate when it isn't. But those who have experienced a divorce will attest that a failed marriage is infinitely more painful. There's more to marriage than the human dimension.

Marriage was God's holy and sacred idea. He performed "the first wedding" in the Garden of Eden (see Gen 2:18-25), thus setting up guidelines for all people to follow: Marriage is for one man and one woman for life. There are valid reasons for sometimes breaking this pattern (for example, death or adultery). But the intended pattern is one man, one woman, for life. Unfortunately, in a fallen world, submitting to God's standards is often difficult, especially since his standards do not change.

Marriage is a covenant between a husband and wife. A covenant is an agreement between two people (or groups) that has benefits for keeping the arrangement and penalties for breaking it. Our relationship to God is described in covenant language throughout Scripture. The marriage relationship is described as a covenant (Mal 2:14-15) and is used as an illustration of our relationship with God (Hos 1:2; Eph 5:22-33). Just as our relationship with God is built on his steadfast, unchanging love and commitment toward us, so a marriage relationship is designed to be solid, faithful, and committed. Therein lies another extremely important—but often overlooked—principle for a successful marriage: commitment.

Marriage is based on commitment, not emotions. The emotional rush two people experience when they "fall in love" and when they decide to marry is wonderful. It also is a terribly inadequate basis for marriage. That "rush," as powerful and enjoyable as it may be, will undoubtedly wear off at some point. If that's what the relationship is based on—physical attraction, romantic ideals, passion—the flame may burn brightly, but it will not burn for long.

Romance, sexual attraction, and passion are tremendous God-given elements of a love relationship. But do not mistake them for the foundation of a lifelong commitment. They are like icing on a cake. Icing makes the cake much sweeter, but a diet of 100 percent refined sugar doesn't make for good health.

To survive the pressure and temptations that attack a marriage, both husband and wife have to be totally committed to making it work. Even when the romance is gone (as it sometimes will be in any marriage), when the money is tight, or when the urge to run out is overwhelming, Christians must stand strong on the commitment they have made. Instead of allowing the stresses to divide them, they must cling that much more tightly together. "What God has joined together, let no one"—and no thing—"separate."

Marriage, when seen from God's perspective, can be one of his greatest gifts to his children. It can also, as Maria and millions of others have unfortunately discovered, be a source of deepest pain.

Whether or not to marry—and what happens if you do marry—is up to you. ∎

³⁹A wife is bound to her husband as long as he lives. If her husband dies, she is free to marry anyone she wishes, but only if he loves the Lord.* ⁴⁰But in my opinion it would be better for her to stay single, and I think I am giving you counsel from God's Spirit when I say this.

8 FOOD SACRIFICED TO IDOLS

Now regarding your question about food that has been offered to idols. Yes, we know that "we all have knowledge" about this issue. But while knowledge makes us feel important, it is love that strengthens the church. ²Anyone who claims to know all the answers doesn't really know very much. ³But the person who loves God is the one whom God recognizes.*

⁴So, what about eating meat that has been offered to idols? Well, we all know that an idol is not really a god and that there is only one God. ⁵There may be so-called gods both in heaven and on earth, and some people actually worship many gods and many lords. ⁶But we know that there is only one God, the Father, who created everything, and we live for him. And there is only one Lord, Jesus Christ, through whom God made everything and through whom we have been given life.

⁷However, not all believers know this. Some are accustomed to thinking of idols as being real, so when they eat food that has been offered to idols, they think of it as the worship of real gods, and their weak consciences are violated. ⁸It's true that we can't win God's approval by what we eat. We don't lose anything if we don't eat it, and we don't gain anything if we do.

⁹But you must be careful so that your freedom does not cause others with a weaker conscience to stumble. ¹⁰For if others see you—with your "superior knowledge"—eating in the temple of an idol, won't they be encouraged to violate their conscience by eating food that has been offered to an idol? ¹¹So because of your superior knowledge, a weak believer* for whom Christ died will be destroyed. ¹²And when you sin against other believers* by encouraging them to do something they believe is wrong, you are sinning against Christ. ¹³So if what I eat causes another believer to sin, I will never eat meat again as long as I live—for I don't want to cause another believer to stumble.

7:39 Greek but only in the Lord.   8:3 Some manuscripts read the person who loves has full knowledge.   8:11 Greek brother; also in 8:13.   8:12 Greek brothers.   9:3 Greek those who examine me.   9:5 Greek Cephas.

MAKING CHOICES ON SENSITIVE ISSUES

All of us make hundreds of choices every day. Most choices have no right or wrong attached to them—like what to wear or what to eat. But we always face decisions that carry a little more weight. We don't want to do wrong, and we don't want to cause others to do wrong. So how can we make right decisions?

IF I CHOOSE ONE COURSE OF ACTION . . .

. . .is it against a specific command in Scripture and thus will cause me to sin? (6:9-10)

. . .will it help my witness for Christ? (9:19-22)

. . .am I motivated by a desire to help others know Christ? (9:23; 10:33)

. . .will it help me do my best? (9:25)

. . .will it be best and helpful? (10:23, 33)

. . .will I be thinking only of myself or do I truly care about the other person? (10:24)

. . .will I be acting lovingly or selfishly? (10:28-31; Rom 14:15)

. . .will it glorify God? (10:31)

. . .will it compel someone else to sin? (10:28; Rom 14:13, 21)

9 PAUL GIVES UP HIS RIGHTS

Am I not as free as anyone else? Am I not an apostle? Haven't I seen Jesus our Lord with my own eyes? Isn't it because of my work that you belong to the Lord? ²Even if others think I am not an apostle, I certainly am to you. You yourselves are proof that I am the Lord's apostle.

³This is my answer to those who question my authority.* ⁴Don't we have the right to live in your homes and share your meals? ⁵Don't we have the right to bring a Christian wife with us as the other apostles and the Lord's brothers do, and as Peter* does? ⁶Or is it only Barnabas and I who have to work to support ourselves?

⁷What soldier has to pay his own expenses? What farmer plants a vineyard and doesn't

....

FREEDOM
(8:1-13) You may have heard people talk about legalism and freedom in Christ. Although Paul doesn't mention the word legalism, he implies it in his message to the Corinthians. On one side is the freedom that Jesus offers through his forgiveness of sins. On the other side is legalism, which is all about keeping every rule in order to look "good" or to earn God's favor. Jesus often reprimanded the Pharisees for their love of rules rather than people.

Still, with freedom comes responsibility. Some actions may be perfectly all right for us but may harm someone new to the faith. As Paul warned, "You must be careful so that your freedom does not cause others with a weaker conscience to stumble."

MY STORY: Brooke

For many years I had a problem with gossip. I knew it was wrong, but I kept giving in to temptation. I prayed about it a lot. Then the Lord gave me two Scriptures that have helped me begin to conquer this habit.

The first was 1 Corinthians 10:13. That verse says that God will always provide a way to escape temptation's power. So I reminded myself of this whenever I felt the temptation to pass on some juicy bit of news that came my way. Although it helped somewhat, I still gave in more often than I wanted to.

Then God gave me another verse that's helped me even more. It's Psalm 141:3: "Take control of what I say, O LORD, and guard my lips." That's the prayer I pray whenever I'm tempted to gossip. This prayer-verse has become my way to escape the temptation. Whenever I take the time to pray it, I find I can keep my mouth shut. But I have to take a moment to refocus my thoughts on the prayer rather than on the temptation to say something. Otherwise, I find myself giving in to temptation.

This experience has shown me just how practical the Bible can be. With God's power I can conquer anything!

have the right to eat some of its fruit? What shepherd cares for a flock of sheep and isn't allowed to drink some of the milk? [8]Am I expressing merely a human opinion, or does the law say the same thing? [9]For the law of Moses says, "You must not muzzle an ox to keep it from eating as it treads out the grain."* Was God thinking only about oxen when he said this? [10]Wasn't he actually speaking to us? Yes, it was written for us, so that the one who plows and the one who threshes the grain might both expect a share of the harvest.

[11]Since we have planted spiritual seed among you, aren't we entitled to a harvest of physical food and drink? [12]If you support others who preach to you, shouldn't we have an even greater right to be supported? But we have never used this right. We would rather put up with anything than be an obstacle to the Good News about Christ.

[13]Don't you realize that those who work in the temple get their meals from the offerings brought to the temple? And those who serve at the altar get a share of the sacrificial offerings. [14]In the same way, the Lord ordered that those who preach the Good News should be supported by those who benefit from it. [15]Yet I have never used any of these rights. And I am not writing this to suggest that I want to start now. In fact, I would rather die than lose my right to boast about preaching without charge. [16]Yet preaching the Good News is not something I can boast about. I am compelled by God to do it. How terrible for me if I didn't preach the Good News!

[17]If I were doing this on my own initiative, I would deserve payment. But I have no choice, for God has given me this sacred trust. [18]What then is my pay? It is the opportunity to preach the Good News without charging anyone. That's why I never demand my rights when I preach the Good News.

[19]Even though I am a free man with no master, I have become a slave to all people to bring many to Christ. [20]When I was with the Jews, I lived like a Jew to bring the Jews to Christ. When I was with those who follow the Jewish law, I too lived under that law. Even though I am not subject to the law, I did this so I could bring to Christ those who are under the law. [21]When I am with the Gentiles who do not follow the Jewish law,* I too live apart from that law so I can bring them to Christ. But I do not ignore the law of God; I obey the law of Christ.

[22]When I am with those who are weak, I share their weakness, for I want to bring the weak to Christ. Yes, I try to find common ground with everyone, doing everything I can to save some. [23]I do everything to spread the Good News and share in its blessings.

[24]Don't you realize that in a race everyone runs, but only one person gets the prize? So run to win! [25]All athletes are disciplined in their training. They do it to win a prize that will fade away, but we do it for an eternal prize. [26]So I run with purpose in every step. I am not just shadowboxing. [27]I discipline my body like an athlete, training it to do what it should. Otherwise, I fear that after preaching to others I myself might be disqualified.

10 LESSONS FROM ISRAEL'S IDOLATRY

I don't want you to forget, dear brothers and sisters,* about our ancestors in the wilderness long ago. All of them were guided

9:9 Deut 25:4.   9:21 Greek *those without the law.*   10:1 Greek *brothers.*

by a cloud that moved ahead of them, and all of them walked through the sea on dry ground. ²In the cloud and in the sea, all of them were baptized as followers of Moses. ³All of them ate the same spiritual food, ⁴and all of them drank the same spiritual water. For they drank from the spiritual rock that traveled with them, and that rock was Christ. ⁵Yet God was not pleased with most of them, and their bodies were scattered in the wilderness.

⁶These things happened as a warning to us, so that we would not crave evil things as they did, ⁷or worship idols as some of them did. As the Scriptures say, "The people celebrated with feasting and drinking, and they indulged in pagan revelry."* ⁸And we must not engage in sexual immorality as some of them did, causing 23,000 of them to die in one day.

⁹Nor should we put Christ* to the test, as some of them did and then died from snakebites. ¹⁰And don't grumble as some of them did, and then were destroyed by the angel of death. ¹¹These things happened to them as examples for us. They were written down to warn us who live at the end of the age.

¹²If you think you are standing strong, be careful not to fall. ¹³The temptations in your life are no different from what others experience. And God is faithful. He will not allow the temptation to be more than you can stand. When you are tempted, he will show you a way out so that you can endure.

¹⁴So, my dear friends, flee from the worship of idols. ¹⁵You are reasonable people. Decide for yourselves if what I am saying is true. ¹⁶When we bless the cup at the Lord's Table, aren't we sharing in the blood of Christ? And when we break the bread, aren't we sharing in the body of Christ? ¹⁷And though we are many, we all eat from one loaf of bread, showing that we are one body. ¹⁸Think about the people of Israel. Weren't they united by eating the sacrifices at the altar?

¹⁹What am I trying to say? Am I saying that food offered to idols has some significance, or that idols are real gods? ²⁰No, not at all. I am saying that these sacrifices are offered to demons, not to God. And I don't want you to participate with demons. ²¹You cannot drink from the cup of the Lord and from the cup of demons, too. You cannot eat at the Lord's Table and at the table of demons, too. ²²What? Do we dare to rouse the Lord's jealousy? Do you think we are stronger than he is?

GOD IS FAITHFUL. HE WILL NOT ALLOW THE TEMPTATION TO BE MORE THAN YOU CAN STAND.

=== 1 CORINTHIANS 10:13 ===

²³You say, "I am allowed to do anything"*— but not everything is good for you. You say, "I am allowed to do anything"—but not everything is beneficial. ²⁴Don't be concerned for your own good but for the good of others.

²⁵So you may eat any meat that is sold in the marketplace without raising questions of conscience. ²⁶For "the earth is the LORD's, and everything in it."*

²⁷If someone who isn't a believer asks you home for dinner, accept the invitation if you want to. Eat whatever is offered to you without raising questions of conscience. ²⁸(But suppose someone tells you, "This meat was offered to an idol." Don't eat it, out of consideration for the conscience of the one who told you. ²⁹It might not be a matter of conscience for you, but it is for the other person.) For why should my freedom be limited by what someone else thinks? ³⁰If I can thank God for the food and enjoy it, why should I be condemned for eating it?

³¹So whether you eat or drink, or whatever you do, do it all for the glory of God. ³²Don't give offense to Jews or Gentiles* or the church of God. ³³I, too, try to please everyone in everything I do. I don't just do what is best for me; I do what is best for others so that many may be saved. ¹¹:¹And you should imitate me, just as I imitate Christ.

11 INSTRUCTIONS FOR PUBLIC WORSHIP
²I am so glad that you always keep me in your thoughts, and that you are following the teachings I passed on to you. ³But there is

TEMPTATION
(10:13) In a culture filled with moral depravity and pressures, Paul gave strong encouragement to the Corinthians about temptation. (1) Wrong desires and temptations happen to everyone, so don't feel you've been singled out. (2) Others have resisted temptation, and so can you. (3) Any temptation can be resisted because God will help you resist it. As with the Corinthian believers, God helps you resist temptation by first helping you to recognize it. He then gives you the courage to run from anything you know is wrong and to seek friends who love God and can offer help in times of temptation. Running from a tempting situation is the first step to victory (see 2 Tim 2:22).

10:7 Exod 32:6. **10:9** Some manuscripts read *the Lord*.
10:23 Greek *All things are lawful*; also in 10:23b. **10:26** Ps 24:1.
10:32 Greek *or Greeks*.

HIGHLIGHTS OF 1 CORINTHIANS

The Meaning of the Cross,
1:18–2:16. Be considerate of one another because of what Christ has done for us. There is no place for pride or a know-it-all attitude. We are to have the mind of Christ.

The Story of the Lord's Supper, 11:23-34. The Lord's Supper is a time of reflection on Christ's final words to his disciples before he died on the cross. We must celebrate this in an orderly and correct manner.

The Poem of Love,
13:1-13. Love is to guide all we do. We have different gifts, abilities, likes, dislikes—but we are called, without exception, to love.

The Christian's Destiny, 15:42-58. We are promised by Christ, who died for us, that, just as he came back to life after death, our perishable bodies will be exchanged for heavenly bodies. Then we will live and reign with Christ.

one thing I want you to know: The head of every man is Christ, the head of woman is man, and the head of Christ is God.* ⁴A man dishonors his head* if he covers his head while praying or prophesying. ⁵But a woman dishonors her head* if she prays or prophesies without a covering on her head, for this is the same as shaving her head. ⁶Yes, if she refuses to wear a head covering, she should cut off all her hair! But since it is shameful for a woman to have her hair cut or her head shaved, she should wear a covering.*

⁷A man should not wear anything on his head when worshiping, for man is made in God's image and reflects God's glory. And woman reflects man's glory. ⁸For the first man

didn't come from woman, but the first woman came from man. ⁹And man was not made for woman, but woman was made for man. ¹⁰For this reason, and because the angels are watching, a woman should wear a covering on her head to show she is under authority.*

¹¹But among the Lord's people, women are not independent of men, and men are not independent of women. ¹²For although the first woman came from man, every other man was born from a woman, and everything comes from God.

¹³Judge for yourselves. Is it right for a woman to pray to God in public without covering her head? ¹⁴Isn't it obvious that it's disgraceful for a man to have long hair? ¹⁵And isn't long hair a woman's pride and joy? For it has been given to her as a covering. ¹⁶But if anyone wants to argue about this, I simply say that we have no other custom than this, and neither do God's other churches.

ORDER AT THE LORD'S SUPPER ¹⁷But in the following instructions, I cannot praise you. For it sounds as if more harm than good is done when you meet together. ¹⁸First, I hear that there are divisions among you when you meet as a church, and to some extent I believe it. ¹⁹But, of course, there must be divisions among you so that you who have God's approval will be recognized!

²⁰When you meet together, you are not really interested in the Lord's Supper. ²¹For some of you hurry to eat your own meal without sharing with others. As a result, some go hungry while others get drunk. ²²What? Don't you have your own homes for eating and drinking? Or do you really want to disgrace God's church and

THE BEST
(10:33) Paul's criterion for making choices was not what he liked best but what was best for those around him. We can have several hurtful attitudes toward others: (1) being insensitive and doing what we want, no matter who is hurt by our actions; (2) being oversensitive and doing nothing, for fear that someone may be displeased; (3) being a "yes person" by going along with everything, trying to gain approval from people rather than from God. In this age of "me first" and "looking out for number one," Paul's startling statement is a good standard. When we make the good of others our primary goal, we develop a servant's heart.

EQUALS
(11:3) Submission is a key element in the smooth functioning of any business, government, or family. God ordained submission in certain relationships to prevent chaos. We must understand, however, that submission is not surrender, withdrawal, apathy, or inferiority. Since God created all people in his image, all have equal value. Submission, therefore, involves mutual commitment and cooperation.

Thus, God calls for submission among equals. Although Jesus Christ was equal with God the Father, he submitted to the Father for the good of all. Likewise, although equal to man under God, a woman is called to submit to her husband for the sake of their marriage and family. Submission between equals is submission by choice, not force. In what ways do you submit to others?

11:3 Or to know: The source of every man is Christ, the source of woman is man, and the source of Christ is God. Or to know: Every man is responsible to Christ, a woman is responsible to her husband, and Christ is responsible to God. **11:4** Or dishonors Christ. **11:5** Or dishonors her husband. **11:6** Or should have long hair. **11:10** Greek should have an authority on her head.

shame the poor? What am I supposed to say? Do you want me to praise you? Well, I certainly will not praise you for this!

²³For I pass on to you what I received from the Lord himself. On the night when he was betrayed, the Lord Jesus took some bread ²⁴and gave thanks to God for it. Then he broke it in pieces and said, "This is my body, which is given for you.* Do this to remember me." ²⁵In the same way, he took the cup of wine after supper, saying, "This cup is the new covenant between God and his people—an agreement confirmed with my blood. Do this to remember me as often as you drink it." ²⁶For every time you eat this bread and drink this cup, you are announcing the Lord's death until he comes again.

²⁷So anyone who eats this bread or drinks this cup of the Lord unworthily is guilty of sinning against* the body and blood of the Lord. ²⁸That is why you should examine yourself before eating the bread and drinking the cup. ²⁹For if you eat the bread or drink the cup without honoring the body of Christ,* you are eating and drinking God's judgment upon yourself. ³⁰That is why many of you are weak and sick and some have even died.

³¹But if we would examine ourselves, we would not be judged by God in this way. ³²Yet when we are judged by the Lord, we are being disciplined so that we will not be condemned along with the world.

³³So, my dear brothers and sisters,* when you gather for the Lord's Supper, wait for each other. ³⁴If you are really hungry, eat at home so you won't bring judgment upon yourselves when you meet together. I'll give you instructions about the other matters after I arrive.

12
SPIRITUAL GIFTS Now, dear brothers and sisters,* regarding your question about the special abilities the Spirit gives us. I don't want you to misunderstand this. ²You know that when you were still pagans, you were led astray and swept along in worshiping speechless idols. ³So I want you to know that no one speaking by the Spirit of God will curse Jesus, and no one can say Jesus is Lord, except by the Holy Spirit.

⁴There are different kinds of spiritual gifts, but the same Spirit is the source of them all. ⁵There are different kinds of service, but we serve the same Lord. ⁶God works in different ways, but it is the same God who does the work in all of us.

⁷A spiritual gift is given to each of us so we can help each other. ⁸To one person the Spirit gives the ability to give wise advice*; to another the same Spirit gives a message of special knowledge.* ⁹The same Spirit gives great faith to another, and to someone else the one Spirit gives the gift of healing. ¹⁰He gives one person the power to perform miracles, and another the ability to prophesy. He gives someone else the ability to discern whether a message is from the Spirit of God or from another spirit. Still another person is given the ability to speak in unknown languages,* while another is given the ability to interpret what is being said. ¹¹It is the one and only Spirit who distributes all these gifts. He alone decides which gift each person should have.

ONE BODY WITH MANY PARTS ¹²The human body has many parts, but the many parts make up one whole body. So it is with the body of Christ. ¹³Some of us are Jews, some are Gentiles,* some are slaves, and some are free. But we have all been baptized into one body by one Spirit, and we all share the same Spirit.*

¹⁴Yes, the body has many different parts, not just one part. ¹⁵If the foot says, "I am not a part of the body because I am not a hand," that does not make it any less a part of the body. ¹⁶And if the ear says, "I am not part of the body because I am not an eye," would that make it any less a part of the body? ¹⁷If the whole body were an eye, how would you hear? Or if your whole body were an ear, how would you smell anything?

¹⁸But our bodies have many parts, and God

....

TEST THEM
(12:3) Anyone can claim to speak for God, and the world is full of false teachers. Paul gives us a test to help us discern whether or not a messenger is really from God: Does he or she confess Christ as Lord? Don't naively accept the words of all who claim to speak for God. Test their credentials by finding what they teach about Christ.

THE BODY
(12:4-31) Using the analogy of the human body, Paul emphasized the importance of each church member. The Holy Spirit gives each person an ability to use to serve others and to help build God's kingdom. Some believe that certain spiritual gifts are more important than others. Yet no ability is insignificant. Check out the list of gifts in this passage. What are your spiritual gifts? How are you using them to build up the body?

11:24 Greek *which is for you;* other manuscripts read *which is broken for you.* **11:27** Or *is responsible for.* **11:29** Greek *the body;* other manuscripts read *the Lord's body.* **11:33** Greek *brothers.* **12:1** Greek *brothers.* **12:8a** Or *gives a word of wisdom.* **12:8b** Or *gives a word of knowledge.* **12:10** Or *in various tongues;* also in 12:28, 30. **12:13a** Greek *some are Greeks.* **12:13b** Greek *we were all given one Spirit to drink.*

has put each part just where he wants it. [19]How strange a body would be if it had only one part! [20]Yes, there are many parts, but only one body. [21]The eye can never say to the hand, "I don't need you." The head can't say to the feet, "I don't need you."

[22]In fact, some parts of the body that seem weakest and least important are actually the most necessary. [23]And the parts we regard as less honorable are those we clothe with the greatest care. So we carefully protect these parts that should not be seen, [24]while the more honorable parts do not require this special care. So God has put the body together such that extra honor and care are given to those parts that have less dignity. [25]This makes for harmony among the members, so that all the members care for each other. [26]If one part suffers, all the parts suffer with it, and if one part is honored, all the parts are glad.

[27]All of you together are Christ's body, and each of you is a part of it. [28]Here are some of the parts God has appointed for the church:

first are apostles,
second are prophets,
third are teachers,
then those who do miracles,
those who have the gift of healing,
those who can help others,
those who have the gift of leadership,
those who speak in unknown languages.

ULTIMATE ISSUES THE CHURCH

Please check the appropriate box:

The church is: a building where religious people go on Sunday; a place where you're told all the things you should not do; where a nice, respectable person tells a bunch of nice, respectable people to be nicer and more respectable (with apologies to Mark Twain); the people of God all over the world, those who follow Jesus and proclaim him as Lord.

Okay, you probably figured out that the last response is the best. But most of us probably feel there is some truth to the other statements as well. In Matthew 16:18 we have the first biblical use of the term church. Many misconceptions exist about what the church is; here is an attempt to clear up at least a few.

Misconception #1: The church is a building. While most local churches in America own buildings, the church and the building are not one and the same. The church is people—God's covenant people called to follow him in faith and action—not the structures where they meet. When we say, "I'm going to church," we're not simply talking about driving to, entering, and sitting down in a building. We mean we are meeting together as God's people, gathered in one place for the purposes of worship, fellowship, instruction, etc.

In many parts of the world, congregations often do not own property. They meet in homes, stores, schools, prisons, and other creative locations. The earliest Christians met in secret, in caves and other hidden places, for fear of persecution and death. (Even today, in some places it's dangerous to be a follower of Jesus.) But it's not where the meeting is held, it's who holds it. Wherever Christians gather, there is the church.

Misconception #2: The church is where good people go to do religious things. Let's make it very plain: No "good" people exist. (If you're unclear on this concept, read Romans, particularly chapter 3.) There are simply sinners who are forgiven and sinners who are not forgiven. The church isn't for "good" people; it's for sinners who know they've been forgiven and who come together regularly to celebrate God and the unbelievable love he has for us. Someone has put it this way: The church is not a showcase for saints; it's a hospital for sinners.

We come together, not just because that's what religious people do on certain days. We come together to praise and worship our God, to thank him for all he has done for us. We thank and honor him for who he is—God and Creator of all, the One who loved us enough to let his Son die for our sins. We praise God with our attendance, our prayers, our music, the preaching of the Word, our money, our fellowship, and countless other ways.

Misconception #3: The church is a human institution. Due to the way many Christians behave, it is sometimes difficult to see any difference between the church and other organizations. But the church is God's own institution, called into being as his instrument on this planet. It is the church that proclaims the Good News (gospel) of Jesus Christ; seeks justice for the poor, rejected, and suffering; tries to influence society for the good of all people and the glory of God; and lifts up the name of God the Father, God the Son, and God the Holy Spirit before an unbelieving world. In other words, we exist for God's pleasure and purposes before our own. As Psalm 100:3 says, "Acknowledge that the LORD is God! He made us, and we are his. We are his people, the sheep of his pasture." No, there are no perfect churches. Made up of sinful humans, how could any church be perfect? But the church is made up of God's people, called into existence by Jesus himself, and built on the rock-solid foundation of his promise that "all the powers of hell will not conquer it." ■

²⁹Are we all apostles? Are we all prophets? Are we all teachers? Do we all have the power to do miracles? ³⁰Do we all have the gift of healing? Do we all have the ability to speak in unknown languages? Do we all have the ability to interpret unknown languages? Of course not! ³¹So you should earnestly desire the most helpful gifts.

But now let me show you a way of life that is best of all.

13 LOVE IS THE GREATEST

If I could speak all the languages of earth and of angels, but didn't love others, I would only be a noisy gong or a clanging cymbal. ²If I had the gift of prophecy, and if I understood all of God's secret plans and possessed all knowledge, and if I had such faith that I could move mountains, but didn't love others, I would be nothing. ³If I gave everything I have to the poor and even sacrificed my body, I could boast about it;* but if I didn't love others, I would have gained nothing.

⁴Love is patient and kind. Love is not jealous or boastful or proud ⁵or rude. It does not demand its own way. It is not irritable, and it keeps no record of being wronged. ⁶It does not rejoice about injustice but rejoices whenever the truth wins out. ⁷Love never gives up, never loses faith, is always hopeful, and endures through every circumstance.

⁸Prophecy and speaking in unknown languages* and special knowledge will become useless. But love will last forever! ⁹Now our knowledge is partial and incomplete, and even the gift of prophecy reveals only part of the whole picture! ¹⁰But when the time of perfection comes, these partial things will become useless.

¹¹When I was a child, I spoke and thought and reasoned as a child. But when I grew up, I put away childish things. ¹²Now we see things imperfectly, like puzzling reflections in a mirror, but then we will see everything with perfect clarity.* All that I know now is partial and incomplete, but then I will know everything completely, just as God now knows me completely.

¹³Three things will last forever—faith, hope, and love—and the greatest of these is love.

14 TONGUES AND PROPHECY

Let love be your highest goal! But you should

13:3 Some manuscripts read *sacrificed my body to be burned.* **13:8** Or *in tongues.* **13:12** Greek *see face to face.* **14:2a** Or *in unknown languages;* also in 14:4, 5, 13, 14, 18, 22, 26, 27, 28, 39. **14:2b** Or *speaking in your spirit.* **14:6a** Greek *brothers;* also in 14:20, 26, 39. **14:6b** Or *in tongues;* also in 14:19, 23.

MY STORY: Sam

After a bad dating experience, I decided to find out what God wanted a dating relationship to be. I talked to my youth pastor and studied Scripture. This time, when I felt ready to date again, I made sure I went out with a Christian.

Jenny and I talked about God's will right from the beginning and adopted 1 Corinthians 13 as the basis for our relationship. Even though Jenny and I didn't stay together forever, our relationship was a very positive experience. We both tried to let verses 4-7 guide all our thoughts and actions toward each other, even when we broke up. I learned a lot from that. God's way really is so much better than any other way of running your life—or of having a relationship.

also desire the special abilities the Spirit gives—especially the ability to prophesy. ²For if you have the ability to speak in tongues,* you will be talking only to God, since people won't be able to understand you. You will be speaking by the power of the Spirit,* but it will all be mysterious. ³But one who prophesies strengthens others, encourages them, and comforts them. ⁴A person who speaks in tongues is strengthened personally, but one who speaks a word of prophecy strengthens the entire church.

⁵I wish you could all speak in tongues, but even more I wish you could all prophesy. For prophecy is greater than speaking in tongues, unless someone interprets what you are saying so that the whole church will be strengthened.

⁶Dear brothers and sisters,* if I should come to you speaking in an unknown language,* how would that help you? But if I bring you a revelation or some special knowledge or prophecy or teaching, that will be helpful.

REAL LOVE

(13:4-7) Most people are pretty sure they know what real love is. Think about the last movie, song, or TV show where someone talked about love. How was love defined? More than likely, the described love was pretty conditional. "I love what you do for me." "I love the way you look." But when a change occurs, "love" disappears. Now check out this passage. What similarities or differences do you notice between what you've heard recently and what you read here? Is this the kind of love you have for others?

[7]Even lifeless instruments like the flute or the harp must play the notes clearly, or no one will recognize the melody. [8]And if the bugler doesn't sound a clear call, how will the soldiers know they are being called to battle?

[9]It's the same for you. If you speak to people in words they don't understand, how will they know what you are saying? You might as well be talking into empty space.

[10]There are many different languages in the world, and every language has meaning. [11]But if I don't understand a language, I will be a foreigner to someone who speaks it, and the one who speaks it will be a foreigner to me. [12]And the same is true for you. Since you are so eager to have the special abilities the Spirit gives, seek those that will strengthen the whole church.

[13]So anyone who speaks in tongues should pray also for the ability to interpret what has been said. [14]For if I pray in tongues, my spirit is praying, but I don't understand what I am saying.

[15]Well then, what shall I do? I will pray in the spirit,* and I will also pray in words I understand. I will sing in the spirit, and I will also sing in words I understand. [16]For if you praise God only in the spirit, how can those who don't understand you praise God along with you? How can they join you in giving thanks when they don't understand what you are saying? [17]You will be giving thanks very well, but it won't strengthen the people who hear you.

[18]I thank God that I speak in tongues more than any of you. [19]But in a church meeting I would rather speak five understandable words to help others than ten thousand words in an unknown language.

[20]Dear brothers and sisters, don't be childish in your understanding of these things. Be innocent as babies when it comes to evil, but mature in understanding matters of this kind. [21]It is written in the Scriptures*:

"I will speak to my own people
through strange languages
and through the lips of foreigners.
But even then, they will not listen to me,"*
says the LORD.

....

REAL WORSHIP

(14:26) Everything done in worship services must be beneficial to the worshipers. This principle touches every aspect—singing, preaching, and the exercise of spiritual gifts. Those contributing to the service (singers, speakers, readers) must have love as their chief motivation, giving useful words or help that will strengthen the faith of other believers.

[22]So you see that speaking in tongues is a sign, not for believers, but for unbelievers. Prophecy, however, is for the benefit of believers, not unbelievers. [23]Even so, if unbelievers or people who don't understand these things come into your church meeting and hear everyone speaking in an unknown language, they will think you are crazy. [24]But if all of you are prophesying, and unbelievers or people who don't understand these things come into your meeting, they will be convicted of sin and judged by what you say. [25]As they listen, their secret thoughts will be exposed, and they will fall to their knees and worship God, declaring, "God is truly here among you."

A CALL TO ORDERLY WORSHIP [26]Well, my brothers and sisters, let's summarize. When you meet together, one will sing, another will teach, another will tell some special revelation God has given, one will speak in tongues, and another will interpret what is said. But everything that is done must strengthen all of you.

[27]No more than two or three should speak in tongues. They must speak one at a time, and someone must interpret what they say. [28]But if no one is present who can interpret, they must be silent in your church meeting and speak in tongues to God privately.

[29]Let two or three people prophesy, and let the others evaluate what is said. [30]But if someone is prophesying and another person receives a revelation from the Lord, the one who is speaking must stop. [31]In this way, all who prophesy will have a turn to speak, one after the other, so that everyone will learn and be encouraged. [32]Remember that people who prophesy are in control of their spirit and can take turns. [33]For God is not a God of disorder but of peace, as in all the meetings of God's holy people.*

[34]Women should be silent during the church meetings. It is not proper for them to speak. They should be submissive, just as the law says. [35]If they have any questions, they should ask their husbands at home, for it is improper for women to speak in church meetings.*

[36]Or do you think God's word originated with you Corinthians? Are you the only ones to whom it was given? [37]If you claim to be a prophet or think you are spiritual, you should recognize that what I am saying is a command from the Lord himself. [38]But if you do

14:15 Or *in the Spirit;* also in 14:15b, 16.   **14:21a** Greek *in the law.* **14:21b** Isa 28:11-12.   **14:33** The phrase *as in all the meetings of God's holy people* could instead be joined to the beginning of 14:34. **14:35** Some manuscripts place verses 34-35 after 14:40.

not recognize this, you yourself will not be recognized.*

³⁹So, my dear brothers and sisters, be eager to prophesy, and don't forbid speaking in tongues. ⁴⁰But be sure that everything is done properly and in order.

15 THE RESURRECTION OF CHRIST Let me now remind you, dear brothers and sisters,* of the Good News I preached to you before. You welcomed it then, and you still stand firm in it. ²It is this Good News that saves you if you continue to believe the message I told you—unless, of course, you believed something that was never true in the first place.*

³I passed on to you what was most important and what had also been passed on to me. Christ died for our sins, just as the Scriptures said. ⁴He was buried, and he was raised from the dead on the third day, just as the Scriptures said. ⁵He was seen by Peter* and then by the Twelve. ⁶After that, he was seen by more than 500 of his followers* at one time, most of whom are still alive, though some have died. ⁷Then he was seen by James and later by all the apostles. ⁸Last of all, as though I had been born at the wrong time, I also saw him. ⁹For I am the least of all the apostles. In fact, I'm not even worthy to be called an apostle after the way I persecuted God's church.

¹⁰But whatever I am now, it is all because God poured out his special favor on me—and not without results. For I have worked harder than any of the other apostles; yet it was not I but God who was working through me by his grace. ¹¹So it makes no difference whether I preach or they preach, for we all preach the same message you have already believed.

THE RESURRECTION OF THE DEAD ¹²But tell me this—since we preach that Christ rose from the dead, why are some of you saying there will be no resurrection of the dead? ¹³For if there is no resurrection of the dead, then Christ has not been raised either. ¹⁴And if Christ has not been raised, then all our preaching is useless, and your faith is useless. ¹⁵And we apostles would all be lying about God—for we have said that God raised Christ from the grave. But that can't be true if there is no resurrection of the dead. ¹⁶And if there is no resurrection of the dead, then Christ has not been raised. ¹⁷And if Christ has not been raised, then your faith is useless and you are still guilty of your sins. ¹⁸In that case, all who have died believing in Christ are lost! ¹⁹And if our hope in Christ is only for this life, we are more to be pitied than anyone in the world.

²⁰But in fact, Christ has been raised from the dead. He is the first of a great harvest of all who have died.

²¹So you see, just as death came into the world through a man, now the resurrection from the dead has begun through another man. ²²Just as everyone dies because we all belong to Adam, everyone who belongs to Christ will be given new life. ²³But there is an order to this resurrection: Christ was raised as the first of the harvest; then all who belong to Christ will be raised when he comes back.

²⁴After that the end will come, when he will turn the Kingdom over to God the Father, having destroyed every ruler and authority and power. ²⁵For Christ must reign until he humbles all his enemies beneath his feet. ²⁶And the last enemy to be destroyed is death. ²⁷For the Scriptures say, "God has put all things under his authority."* (Of course, when it says "all things are under his authority," that does not include God himself, who gave Christ his authority.) ²⁸Then, when all things are under his authority, the Son will put himself under God's authority, so that God, who gave his Son authority over all things, will be utterly supreme over everything everywhere.

²⁹If the dead will not be raised, what point is there in people being baptized for those who are dead? Why do it unless the dead will someday rise again?

³⁰And why should we ourselves risk our lives hour by hour? ³¹For I swear, dear brothers and sisters, that I face death daily. This is as certain as my pride in what Christ Jesus our Lord has done in you. ³²And what value was there in fighting wild beasts—those people of Ephesus*—if there will be no resurrection from the dead? And if there is no resurrection, "Let's feast and drink, for tomorrow we die!"* ³³Don't be fooled by those who say such things, for "bad company corrupts good character."

....

PROOF

(15:4-8) *There will always be people who will say that Jesus didn't rise from the dead. Paul assures us that many people saw Jesus after his resurrection, including more than 500 Christian believers. The Resurrection is a historical fact. Don't be discouraged by doubters who deny the Resurrection. Be filled with hope by the knowledge that one day you, and they, will stand before the living proof when Christ returns.*

14:38 Some manuscripts read *If you are ignorant of this, stay in your ignorance.* **15:1** Greek *brothers;* also in 15:31, 50, 58. **15:2** Or *unless you never believed it in the first place.* **15:5** Greek *Cephas.* **15:6** Greek *the brothers.* **15:27** Ps 8:6. **15:32a** Greek *fighting wild beasts in Ephesus.* **15:32b** Isa 22:13.

34Think carefully about what is right, and stop sinning. For to your shame I say that some of you don't know God at all.

THE RESURRECTION BODY

35But someone may ask, "How will the dead be raised? What kind of bodies will they have?" 36What a foolish question! When you put a seed into the ground, it doesn't grow into a plant unless it dies first. 37And what you put in the ground is not the plant that will grow, but only a bare seed of wheat or whatever you are planting. 38Then God gives it the new body he wants it to have. A different plant grows from each kind of seed. 39Similarly there are different kinds of flesh—one kind for humans, another for animals, another for birds, and another for fish.

40There are also bodies in the heavens and bodies on the earth. The glory of the heavenly bodies is different from the glory of the earthly bodies. 41The sun has one kind of glory, while the moon and stars each have another kind. And even the stars differ from each other in their glory.

42It is the same way with the resurrection of the dead. Our earthly bodies are planted in the ground when we die, but they will be raised to live forever. 43Our bodies are buried in brokenness, but they will be raised in glory. They are buried in weakness, but they will be raised in strength. 44They are buried as natural human bodies, but they will be raised as spiritual bodies. For just as there are natural bodies, there are also spiritual bodies.

45The Scriptures tell us, "The first man, Adam, became a living person."* But the last Adam—that is, Christ—is a life-giving Spirit. 46What comes first is the natural body, then the spiritual body comes later. 47Adam, the first man, was made from the dust of the earth, while Christ, the second man, came from heaven. 48Earthly people are like the earthly man, and heavenly people are like the heavenly man. 49Just as we are now like the earthly man, we will someday be like* the heavenly man.

50What I am saying, dear brothers and sisters, is that our physical bodies cannot inherit the Kingdom of God. These dying bodies cannot inherit what will last forever.

51But let me reveal to you a wonderful secret. We will not all die, but we will all be transformed! 52It will happen in a moment, in the blink of an eye, when the last trumpet is blown. For when the trumpet sounds, those who have died will be raised to live forever. And we who are living will also be transformed. 53For our dying bodies must be transformed into bodies that will never die; our mortal bodies must be transformed into immortal bodies.

54Then, when our dying bodies have been transformed into bodies that will never die,* this Scripture will be fulfilled:

"Death is swallowed up in victory.*
55 O death, where is your victory?
O death, where is your sting?*"

56For sin is the sting that results in death, and the law gives sin its power. 57But thank God! He gives us victory over sin and death through our Lord Jesus Christ.

58So, my dear brothers and sisters, be strong and immovable. Always work enthusiastically for the Lord, for you know that nothing you do for the Lord is ever useless.

16 THE COLLECTION FOR JERUSALEM

Now regarding your question about the money being collected for God's people in Jerusalem. You should follow the same procedure I gave to the churches in Galatia. 2On the first day of each week, you should each put aside a portion of the money you have earned. Don't wait until I get there and then try to collect it all at once. 3When I come, I will write letters of recommendation for the messengers you choose to deliver your gift to Jerusalem. 4And if it seems appropriate for me to go along, they can travel with me.

PAUL'S FINAL INSTRUCTIONS

5I am coming to visit you after I have been to Macedonia,* for I am planning to travel through Macedonia. 6Perhaps I will stay awhile with you, possibly all winter, and then you can send me on my way to my next destination. 7This time I don't want to make just a short visit and then go right on. I want to come and stay awhile, if the Lord will let me. 8In the meantime, I will be staying here at Ephesus until the Festival of Pentecost.

RESULTS

(15:58) *Ever hesitate to tell someone about Jesus because you haven't seen what good that does? Because of the Resurrection, nothing we do is useless. Yet in this lifetime, we might not see all of the good that results from our efforts. Don't let discouragement over an apparent lack of results keep you from working. Do the good that you have opportunity to do, knowing that your work will have eternal results.*

15:45 Gen 2:7.   **15:49** Some manuscripts read *let us be like.*
15:54a Some manuscripts add *and our mortal bodies have been transformed into immortal bodies.*   **15:54b** Isa 25:8.   **15:55** Hos 13:14 (Greek version).   **16:5** *Macedonia* was in the northern region of Greece.

[9]There is a wide-open door for a great work here, although many oppose me.

[10]When Timothy comes, don't intimidate him. He is doing the Lord's work, just as I am. [11]Don't let anyone treat him with contempt. Send him on his way with your blessing when he returns to me. I expect him to come with the other believers.*

[12]Now about our brother Apollos—I urged him to visit you with the other believers, but he was not willing to go right now. He will see you later when he has the opportunity.

[13]Be on guard. Stand firm in the faith. Be courageous.* Be strong. [14]And do everything with love.

[15]You know that Stephanas and his household were the first of the harvest of believers in Greece,* and they are spending their lives in service to God's people. I urge you, dear brothers and sisters,* [16]to submit to them and others like them who serve with such devotion. [17]I am very glad that Stephanas, Fortuna-

16:11 Greek with the brothers; also in 16:12.　16:13 Greek Be men.
16:15a Greek in Achaia, the southern region of the Greek peninsula.
16:15b Greek brothers; also in 16:20.　16:19a Asia was a Roman province in what is now western Turkey.　16:19b Greek Prisca.
16:20 Greek with a sacred kiss.　16:22 From Aramaic, Marana tha. Some manuscripts read Maran atha, "Our Lord has come."
16:24 Some manuscripts add Amen.

tus, and Achaicus have come here. They have been providing the help you weren't here to give me. [18]They have been a wonderful encouragement to me, as they have been to you. You must show your appreciation to all who serve so well.

PAUL'S FINAL GREETINGS [19]The churches here in the province of Asia* send greetings in the Lord, as do Aquila and Priscilla* and all the others who gather in their home for church meetings. [20]All the brothers and sisters here send greetings to you. Greet each other with Christian love.*

[21]HERE IS MY GREETING IN MY OWN HANDWRITING—PAUL.

[22]If anyone does not love the Lord, that person is cursed. Our Lord, come!*

[23]May the grace of the Lord Jesus be with you.

[24]My love to all of you in Christ Jesus.*

••

GRAND FINALE
(16:22) Paul ended his letter with his hope for Jesus' swift return. To Paul, this was a glad hope, the best he could look forward to. He wasn't afraid of seeing Christ—he could hardly wait! Do you share Paul's eager anticipation? Those who love Jesus look forward to "that wonderful day" (Titus 2:13).

2 CORINTHIANS

Ministry . . . or Madness? A Quiz Just for You.

1. While you are helping at Vacation Bible School, a kid throws up on you and a six-year-old complains for 90 minutes *about watery punch.* Do you: (a) Dump the watery punch on the obnoxious kid? (b) Clean yourself up, then *dump the punch on the obnoxious kid?* (c) Retire from your VBS career? (d) Pray (really hard!) for patience and kindness?

2. Your youth group gives 400 dollars to a family whose house just burned down. The family never even acknowledges the gift! Do you: (a) Get on your soapbox about the importance of gratitude? (b) Think of all the ways you could have used the cash? (c) Ask for the money back? (d) Trust that God is in control?

3. During a church mission trip, some older teens surround you, call you names, and push you around. Do you: (a) Introduce them to your kung fu moves? (b) Imagine the day you'll be able to push others around? (c) Vow never to stand up for Christ again? (d) Consider it an honor to suffer for Christ?

4. Second Corinthians discusses: (a) Living for the Lord when nothing seems to go right. (b) Why serving God and others *is worth it (no matter what happens).* (c) The amazing truth that we can't outgive God. (d) The importance of telling others about Jesus Christ. (e) All of the above.

At times, being Christ's ambassador may seem as crazy as the above quiz, and much more difficult. When you're faced with hard times, are you tempted to give up? Second Corinthians is just what you need.

STATS

PURPOSE
To affirm Paul's own ministry, defend his authority as an apostle, and disprove the false teachers in Corinth

AUTHOR
Paul

ORIGINAL AUDIENCE
The church in Corinth

DATE WRITTEN
About A.D. 55-57, from Macedonia

SETTING
Paul is writing to defend his authority and his motives. Paul had already written three letters to the Corinthians, including 1 Corinthians and two lost letters.

KEY PEOPLE
Paul, Timothy, Titus, false teachers

KEY PLACES
Corinth, Jerusalem

KEY POINTS

TRIALS Paul depended on God to help him through some extremely difficult times. Likewise, we can look to God for comfort during trials. As he comforts us, we learn to comfort others.

CHURCH DISCIPLINE As Paul explained, the church was to be neither too lax nor too severe in administering discipline. The goal of discipline in the church should be correction, not vengeance. An effective church confronts and solves problems, rather than ignoring them.

HOPE Paul encouraged the Corinthians as they faced trials by reminding them that they would receive new bodies in heaven. This would be a great victory in contrast to their present suffering. We share that same hope.

GENEROSITY Paul organized a collection of funds for the poor in the Jerusalem church. Our giving must be generous, sacrificial, according to a plan, and based on need. Generosity helps the needy, enabling them to thank God.

1 GREETINGS FROM PAUL

This letter is from Paul, chosen by the will of God to be an apostle of Christ Jesus, and from our brother Timothy.

I am writing to God's church in Corinth and to all of his holy people throughout Greece.*

²May God our Father and the Lord Jesus Christ give you grace and peace.

GOD OFFERS COMFORT TO ALL

³All praise to God, the Father of our Lord Jesus Christ. God is our merciful Father and the source of all comfort. ⁴He comforts us in all our troubles so that we can comfort others. When they are troubled, we will be able to give them the same comfort God has given us. ⁵For the more we suffer for Christ, the more God will shower us with his comfort through Christ. ⁶Even when we are weighed down with troubles, it is for your comfort and salvation! For when we ourselves are comforted, we will certainly comfort you. Then you can patiently endure the same things we suffer. ⁷We are confident that as you share in our sufferings, you will also share in the comfort God gives us.

⁸We think you ought to know, dear brothers and sisters,* about the trouble we went through in the province of Asia. We were crushed and overwhelmed beyond our ability to endure, and we thought we would never live through it. ⁹In fact, we expected to die. But as a result, we stopped relying on ourselves and learned to rely only on God, who raises the dead. ¹⁰And he did rescue us from mortal danger, and he will rescue us again. We have placed our confidence in him, and he will continue to rescue us. ¹¹And you are helping us by praying for us. Then many people will give thanks because God has graciously answered so many prayers for our safety.

PAUL'S CHANGE OF PLANS

¹²We can say with confidence and a clear conscience that we have lived with a God-given holiness* and sincerity in all our dealings. We have depended on God's grace, not on our own human wisdom. That is how we have conducted ourselves before the world, and especially toward you. ¹³Our letters have been straightforward, and there is nothing written between the lines and nothing you can't understand. I hope someday you will fully understand us, ¹⁴even if you don't understand us now. Then on the day when the Lord Jesus* returns, you will be proud of us in the same way we are proud of you.

¹⁵Since I was so sure of your understanding and trust, I wanted to give you a double blessing by visiting you twice—¹⁶first on my way to Macedonia and again when I returned from Macedonia.* Then you could send me on my way to Judea.

¹⁷You may be asking why I changed my plan. Do you think I make my plans carelessly? Do you think I am like people of the world who say "Yes" when they really mean "No"? ¹⁸As

---

COMFORT

(1:3-7) Many people believe that when God comforts us, our hardships go away. If that were so, people would turn to God only to be relieved of pain and not out of love for him. Real comfort can also mean receiving the strength to deal with our hardships. The more we suffer, the more comfort God gives us (1:5). If you're feeling overwhelmed, allow God to comfort you. Remember, every trial you endure will later become an opportunity to help someone who suffers a similar hardship.

1:1 Greek *Achaia,* the southern region of the Greek peninsula. 1:8 Greek *brothers.* 1:12 Some manuscripts read *honesty.* 1:14 Some manuscripts read *our Lord Jesus.* 1:16 *Macedonia* was in the northern region of Greece.

I WONDER...

My grandma has been a Christian for 40 years. Her life has been hard, though. Why would God allow so much trouble to come into one person's life?

Do you or someone you know work out with weights? If so, you know that the goal of weight training is to develop the muscles and make them stronger. At first, the strain of lifting causes the person to feel weak. Eventually, however, it makes the lifter strong.

Like a muscle, faith grows stronger when it is exercised (see Jas 1:2-4). The book of Hebrews is all about faith—how to strengthen it, how it can help you endure.

One of God's goals for us is to learn to trust him more. When a Christian asks God for more faith, he or she is really asking for more trials. God knows that our faith can only be strengthened when we exercise it.

Another benefit of hardships can be found in 2 Corinthians 1:3-5. Suffering helps us develop the compassion to help others. Our endurance through trials is very important to God. It allows him to use us to pass along comfort and encouragement to others.

Some Christians are glad that they have few problems. (Can you relate?) But our response to hardships and troubles helps us to grow.

surely as God is faithful, our word to you does not waver between "Yes" and "No." [19]For Jesus Christ, the Son of God, does not waver between "Yes" and "No." He is the one whom Silas,* Timothy, and I preached to you, and as God's ultimate "Yes," he always does what he says. [20]For all of God's promises have been fulfilled in Christ with a resounding "Yes!" And through Christ, our "Amen" (which means "Yes") ascends to God for his glory.

[21]It is God who enables us, along with you, to stand firm for Christ. He has commissioned us, [22]and he has identified us as his own by placing the Holy Spirit in our hearts as the first installment that guarantees everything he has promised us.

[23]Now I call upon God as my witness that I am telling the truth. The reason I didn't return to Corinth was to spare you from a severe rebuke. [24]But that does not mean we want to dominate you by telling you how to put your faith into practice. We want to work together with you so you will be full of joy, for it is by your own faith that you stand firm.

2 So I decided that I would not bring you grief with another painful visit. [2]For if I cause you grief, who will make me glad? Certainly not someone I have grieved. [3]That is why I wrote to you as I did, so that when I do come, I won't be grieved by the very ones who ought to give me the greatest joy. Surely you all know that my joy comes from your being joyful. [4]I wrote that letter in great anguish, with a troubled heart and many tears. I didn't want to grieve you, but I wanted to let you know how much love I have for you.

FORGIVENESS FOR THE SINNER [5]I am not overstating it when I say that the man who caused all the trouble hurt all of you more than he hurt me. [6]Most of you opposed him, and that was punishment enough. [7]Now, however, it is time to forgive and comfort him. Otherwise he may be overcome by discouragement. [8]So I urge you now to reaffirm your love for him.

[9]I wrote to you as I did to test you and see if you would fully comply with my instructions. [10]When you forgive this man, I forgive him, too. And when I forgive whatever needs to be forgiven, I do so with Christ's authority for your benefit, [11]so that Satan will not outsmart us. For we are familiar with his evil schemes.

[12]When I came to the city of Troas to preach the Good News of Christ, the Lord opened a door of opportunity for me. [13]But I had no

1:19 Greek *Silvanus*.

MY STORY: Lily

Last year, I went through a very difficult time for a whole month. One thing after another happened. I wasn't sure I could take any more. Although God saw me through that time, I still had lots of unresolved questions about why those things had to happen to me.

Not long afterward, my friend's sister had a leukemia relapse. When I found out, I prayed and cried for a while. Then I decided to write her a note of encouragement. Later that night, I read 2 Corinthians 1:3-7. It was like God was speaking tender words of comfort right to me. I realized that there was a reason for the pain I had gone through not long before—so that I could relate to the pain of other people and offer true encouragement.

I was not only able to offer my friend's sister some sincere encouragement, but also my nagging questions over why God let me go through pain were answered. Since then, whenever something painful happens to me, it's much easier for me to believe that there's a good reason for it.

peace of mind because my dear brother Titus hadn't yet arrived with a report from you. So I said good-bye and went on to Macedonia to find him.

MINISTERS OF THE NEW COVENANT [14]But thank God! He has made us his captives and continues to lead us along in Christ's triumphal procession. Now he uses us to spread the knowledge of Christ everywhere, like a sweet perfume. [15]Our lives are a Christ-like fragrance rising up to God. But this fragrance is perceived differently by those who are being saved and by those who are perishing. [16]To those who are perishing, we are a dreadful smell of death and doom. But to those who

SEAL OF APPROVAL
(1:21-22) When we become believers, God provides the Holy Spirit as a guarantee that we belong to him (see also Eph 1:13-14). With the privilege of belonging to God comes the responsibility of identifying ourselves as faithful representatives and servants of our master. How do you let others know you are his?

PAUL SEARCHES FOR TITUS
Paul had searched for Titus, hoping to meet him in Troas and receive news about the Corinthian church. When he did not find Titus in Troas, Paul went on to Macedonia (2:13), most likely to Philippi, where he found Titus.

are being saved, we are a life-giving perfume. And who is adequate for such a task as this?

¹⁷You see, we are not like the many hucksters* who preach for personal profit. We preach the word of God with sincerity and with Christ's authority, knowing that God is watching us.

3 Are we beginning to praise ourselves again? Are we like others, who need to bring you letters of recommendation, or who ask you to write such letters on their behalf? Surely not! ²The only letter of recommendation we need is you yourselves. Your lives are a letter written in our* hearts; everyone can read it and recognize our good work among you. ³Clearly, you are a letter from Christ showing the result of our ministry among you. This "letter" is written not with pen and ink, but with the Spirit of the living God. It is carved not on tablets of stone, but on human hearts.

⁴We are confident of all this because of our great trust in God through Christ. ⁵It is not that we think we are qualified to do anything on our own. Our qualification comes from God. ⁶He has enabled us to be ministers of his new covenant. This is a covenant not of written laws, but of the Spirit. The old written covenant ends in death; but under the new covenant, the Spirit gives life.

THE GLORY OF THE NEW COVENANT ⁷The old way,* with laws etched in stone, led to death, though it began with such glory that the people of Israel could not bear to look at Moses' face. For his face shone with the glory of God, even though the brightness was already fading away. ⁸Shouldn't we expect far greater glory under the new way, now that the Holy Spirit is giving life? ⁹If the old way, which brings condemnation, was glorious, how much more glorious is the new way, which makes us right with God! ¹⁰In fact, that first glory was not glorious at all compared with the overwhelming glory of the new way. ¹¹So if the old way, which has been replaced, was glorious, how much more glorious is the new, which remains forever!

¹²Since this new way gives us such confidence, we can be very bold. ¹³We are not like Moses, who put a veil over his face so the people of Israel would not see the glory, even though it was destined to fade away. ¹⁴But the people's minds were hardened, and to this day

2:17 Some manuscripts read *the rest of the hucksters.*   **3:2** Some manuscripts read *your.*   **3:7** Or *ministry;* also in 3:8, 9, 10, 11, 12.

whenever the old covenant is being read, the same veil covers their minds so they cannot understand the truth. And this veil can be removed only by believing in Christ. ¹⁵Yes, even today when they read Moses' writings, their hearts are covered with that veil, and they do not understand.

¹⁶But whenever someone turns to the Lord, the veil is taken away. ¹⁷For the Lord is the Spirit, and wherever the Spirit of the Lord is, there is freedom. ¹⁸So all of us who have had that veil removed can see and reflect the glory of the Lord. And the Lord—who is the Spirit—makes us more and more like him as we are changed into his glorious image.

4 **TREASURE IN FRAGILE CLAY JARS** Therefore, since God in his mercy has given us this new way,* we never give up. ²We reject all shameful deeds and underhanded methods. We don't try to trick anyone or distort the word of God. We tell the truth before God, and all who are honest know this.

³If the Good News we preach is hidden behind a veil, it is hidden only from people who are perishing. ⁴Satan, who is the god of this world, has blinded the minds of those who don't believe. They are unable to see the glorious light of the Good News. They don't understand this message about the glory of Christ, who is the exact likeness of God.

⁵You see, we don't go around preaching about ourselves. We preach that Jesus Christ is Lord, and we ourselves are your servants for Jesus' sake. ⁶For God, who said, "Let there be light in the darkness," has made this light shine in our hearts so we could know the glory of God that is seen in the face of Jesus Christ.

⁷We now have this light shining in our hearts, but we ourselves are like fragile clay jars containing this great treasure.* This makes it clear that our great power is from God, not from ourselves.

⁸We are pressed on every side by troubles, but we are not crushed. We are perplexed, but not driven to despair. ⁹We are hunted down, but never abandoned by God. We get knocked down, but we are not destroyed. ¹⁰Through suffering, our bodies continue to share in the death of Jesus so that the life of Jesus may also be seen in our bodies.

¹¹Yes, we live under constant danger of death because we serve Jesus, so that the life of Jesus will be evident in our dying bodies. ¹²So we live

in the face of death, but this has resulted in eternal life for you.

¹³But we continue to preach because we have the same kind of faith the psalmist had when he said, "I believed in God, so I spoke."* ¹⁴We know that God, who raised the Lord Jesus,* will also raise us with Jesus and present us to himself together with you. ¹⁵All of this is for your benefit. And as God's grace reaches more and more people, there will be great thanksgiving, and God will receive more and more glory.

¹⁶That is why we never give up. Though our bodies are dying, our spirits are* being renewed every day. ¹⁷For our present troubles are small and won't last very long. Yet they produce for us a glory that vastly outweighs them and will last forever! ¹⁸So we don't look at the troubles we can see now; rather, we fix our gaze on things that cannot be seen. For the things we see now will soon be gone, but the things we cannot see will last forever.

5 **NEW BODIES** For we know that when this earthly tent we live in is taken down (that is, when we die and leave this earthly body), we will have a house in heaven, an eternal body made for us by God himself and not by human hands. ²We grow weary in our present bodies, and we long to put on our heavenly bodies like new clothing. ³For we will put on heavenly bodies; we will not be spirits without bodies.* ⁴While we live in these earthly bodies, we groan and sigh, but it's not that we want to

....

LIKE HIM
(3:17-18) The glory that the Spirit imparts to the believer is greater both in quality and longevity than that which Moses experienced (see Exod 34:33-35). The glory gradually makes the believer more like Christ. Becoming Christ-like is a progressive experience (see Rom 8:29; Gal 4:19; Phil 1:6; 1 Jn 3:2-3). The more closely we relate to Jesus, the more we will be like him.

FOCUS
(4:5) The focus of Paul's preaching was Christ, not himself. When you witness, tell people about what Christ has done rather than about your abilities and accomplishments. People must be introduced to Jesus, not to you. Beware of people who preach about themselves or their ideas rather than Christ—the Bible calls them false teachers.

THE PURPOSE OF PROBLEMS
(4:8-18) As Paul realized, our suffering has a purpose. Problems and human limitations have several benefits. (1) They help us remember Christ's suffering for us. (2) They help keep us humble. (3) They help us look beyond this brief life. (4) They prove our faith to others. (5) They give God the opportunity to demonstrate his great power. Problems getting you down? Don't give up!

4:1 Or *ministry.*   **4:7** Greek *We now have this treasure in clay jars.*
4:13 Ps 116:10.   **4:14** Some manuscripts read *who raised Jesus.*
4:16 Greek *our inner being is.*   **5:3** Greek *we will not be naked.*

THIS MEANS THAT ANYONE WHO BELONGS TO CHRIST HAS BECOME A NEW PERSON.

THE OLD LIFE IS GONE; A NEW LIFE HAS BEGUN!

2 CORINTHIANS 5:17

die and get rid of these bodies that clothe us. Rather, we want to put on our new bodies so that these dying bodies will be swallowed up by life. ⁵God himself has prepared us for this, and as a guarantee he has given us his Holy Spirit.

⁶So we are always confident, even though we know that as long as we live in these bodies we are not at home with the Lord. ⁷For we live by believing and not by seeing. ⁸Yes, we are fully confident, and we would rather be away from these earthly bodies, for then we will be at home with the Lord. ⁹So whether we are here in this body or away from this body, our goal is to please him. ¹⁰For we must all stand before Christ to be judged. We will each receive whatever we deserve for the good or evil we have done in this earthly body.

WE ARE GOD'S AMBASSADORS ¹¹Because we understand our fearful responsibility to the Lord, we work hard to persuade others. God knows we are sincere, and I hope you know this, too. ¹²Are we commending ourselves to you again? No, we are giving you a reason to be proud of us,* so you can answer those who brag about having a spectacular ministry rather than having a sincere heart. ¹³If it seems we are crazy, it is to bring glory to God. And if we are in our right minds, it is for your benefit. ¹⁴Either way, Christ's love controls us.* Since we believe that Christ died for all, we also believe that we have all died to our old life.* ¹⁵He died for everyone so that those who receive his new life will no longer live for themselves. Instead, they will live for Christ, who died and was raised for them.

¹⁶So we have stopped evaluating others from a human point of view. At one time we thought of Christ merely from a human point of view. How differently we know him now! ¹⁷This means that anyone who belongs to Christ has become a new person. The old life is gone; a new life has begun!

¹⁸And all of this is a gift from God, who brought us back to himself through Christ. And God has given us this task of reconciling people to him. ¹⁹For God was in Christ, reconciling the world to himself, no longer counting people's sins against them. And he gave us this wonderful message of reconciliation. ²⁰So we are Christ's ambassadors; God is making his appeal through us. We speak for Christ when we plead, "Come back to God!" ²¹For God made Christ, who never sinned, to be the offering for our sin,* so that we could be made right with God through Christ.

5:12 Some manuscripts read *proud of yourselves.* **5:14a** Or *urges us on.* **5:14b** Greek *Since one died for all, then all died.* **5:21** Or *to become sin itself.*

MADE NEW
(5:16-17) Christians are brand-new people on the inside. The Holy Spirit gives believers new life. Having new life isn't the same as being reformed or reeducated. Those who trust Christ learn to adjust to a new attitude and a new boss: God. Are you feeling like there's nothing really new under the sun? There is: you.

CHOICES
serving god

"Tom, maybe you've got the dates mixed up," Austin says.

"No way!" Tom replies. "The prison outreach is the same weekend."

"But what about Ethan's ski party?"

"I guess I'll have to miss it."

"Dude, you can't! Everybody will be at Ethan's—including the hottest girls in the whole sophomore class! It's the party of the year, man!"

"Look, I wish I could go. But I promised to sing with the group at this prison thing."

"Can't you get out of it?"

Tom shakes his head. "Austin, you just don't understand."

"Well, I say you're making a huge mistake. You'll regret it if you miss Ethan's party."

Two weeks later the big weekend has come and gone. Ethan's party was every bit as fun as advertised. Great weather, great skiing—it was a certified blast!

And the prison outreach? By comparison, it didn't seem as successful. The prisoners showered Tom's group with verbal abuse during the concert. Afterward, during a meal stop on the way home, someone broke into the church van and stole the sound equipment!

Does serving the Lord really pay? Is the hardship encountered worth all the effort? Take it from the apostle Paul, a guy who should know. Although he endured unbelievable difficulties (see 2 Cor 4:8-10; 6:4-10; 11:23-33), he remained faithful to the end of his life. How do you respond to the difficulties you face?

169/196

6 As God's partners,* we beg you not to accept this marvelous gift of God's kindness and then ignore it. ²For God says,

"At just the right time, I heard you.
On the day of salvation, I helped you."*

Indeed, the "right time" is now. Today is the day of salvation.

PAUL'S HARDSHIPS ³We live in such a way that no one will stumble because of us, and no one will find fault with our ministry. ⁴In everything we do, we show that we are true ministers of God. We patiently endure troubles and hardships and calamities of every kind. ⁵We have been beaten, been put in prison, faced angry mobs, worked to exhaustion, endured sleepless nights, and gone without food. ⁶We prove ourselves by our purity, our understanding, our patience, our kindness, by the Holy Spirit within us,* and by our sincere love. ⁷We faithfully preach the truth. God's power is working in us. We use the weapons of righteousness in the right hand for attack and the left hand for defense. ⁸We serve God whether people honor us or despise us, whether they slander us or praise us. We are honest, but they call us impostors. ⁹We are ignored, even though we are well known. We live close to death, but we are still alive. We have been beaten, but we have not been killed. ¹⁰Our hearts ache, but we always have joy. We are poor, but we give spiritual riches to others. We own nothing, and yet we have everything.

¹¹Oh, dear Corinthian friends! We have spoken honestly with you, and our hearts are open to you. ¹²There is no lack of love on our part, but you have withheld your love from us. ¹³I am asking you to respond as if you were my own children. Open your hearts to us!

THE TEMPLE OF THE LIVING GOD ¹⁴Don't team up with those who are unbelievers. How can righteousness be a partner with wickedness? How can light live with darkness? ¹⁵What harmony can there be between Christ and the devil*? How can a believer be a partner with an unbeliever? ¹⁶And what union can there be between God's temple and idols? For we are the temple of the living God. As God said:

"I will live in them
and walk among them.
I will be their God,
and they will be my people.*
¹⁷ Therefore, come out from among
unbelievers,
and separate yourselves from them, says
the LORD.
Don't touch their filthy things,
and I will welcome you.*
¹⁸ And I will be your Father,
and you will be my sons and daughters,
says the LORD Almighty.*"

7 Because we have these promises, dear friends, let us cleanse ourselves from everything that can defile our body or spirit. And let us work toward complete holiness because we fear God.

²Please open your hearts to us. We have not

6:1 Or *As we work together.* **6:2** Isa 49:8 (Greek version). **6:6** Or *by our holiness of spirit.* **6:15** Greek *Beliar;* various other manuscripts render this proper name of the devil as *Belian, Beliab,* or *Belial.* **6:16** Lev 26:12; Ezek 37:27. **6:17** Isa 52:11; Ezek 20:34 (Greek version). **6:18** 2 Sam 7:14.

done wrong to anyone, nor led anyone astray, nor taken advantage of anyone. ³I'm not saying this to condemn you. I said before that you are in our hearts, and we live or die together with you. ⁴I have the highest confidence in you, and I take great pride in you. You have greatly encouraged me and made me happy despite all our troubles.

PAUL'S JOY AT THE CHURCH'S REPENTANCE

⁵When we arrived in Macedonia, there was no rest for us. We faced conflict from every direction, with battles on the outside and fear on the inside. ⁶But God, who encourages those who are discouraged, encouraged us by the arrival of Titus. ⁷His presence was a joy, but so was the news he brought of the encouragement he received from you. When he told us how much you long to see me, and how sorry you are for what happened, and how loyal you are to me, I was filled with joy!

⁸I am not sorry that I sent that severe letter to you, though I was sorry at first, for I know it was painful to you for a little while. ⁹Now I am glad I sent it, not because it hurt you, but because the pain caused you to repent and change your ways. It was the kind of sorrow God wants his people to have, so you were not harmed by us in any way. ¹⁰For the kind of sorrow God wants us to experience leads us away from sin and results in salvation. There's no regret for that kind of sorrow. But worldly sorrow, which lacks repentance, results in spiritual death.

¹¹Just see what this godly sorrow produced in you! Such earnestness, such concern to clear yourselves, such indignation, such alarm, such longing to see me, such zeal, and such a readiness to punish wrong. You showed that you have done everything necessary to make

things right. ¹²My purpose, then, was not to write about who did the wrong or who was wronged. I wrote to you so that in the sight of God you could see for yourselves how loyal you are to us. ¹³We have been greatly encouraged by this.

In addition to our own encouragement, we were especially delighted to see how happy Titus was about the way all of you welcomed him and set his mind* at ease. ¹⁴I had told him how proud I was of you—and you didn't disappoint me. I have always told you the truth, and now my boasting to Titus has also proved true! ¹⁵Now he cares for you more than ever when he remembers the way all of you obeyed him and welcomed him with such fear and deep respect. ¹⁶I am very happy now because I have complete confidence in you.

8 **A CALL TO GENEROUS GIVING** Now I want you to know, dear brothers and sisters,* what God in his kindness has done through the churches in Macedonia. ²They are being tested by many troubles, and they are very poor. But they are also filled with abundant joy, which has overflowed in rich generosity.

³For I can testify that they gave not only what they could afford, but far more. And they did it of their own free will. ⁴They begged us again and again for the privilege of sharing in the gift for the believers in Jerusalem.* ⁵They even did more than we had hoped, for their first action was to give themselves to the Lord and to us, just as God wanted them to do.

⁶So we have urged Titus, who encouraged your giving in the first place, to return to you and encourage you to finish this ministry of giving. ⁷Since you excel in so many ways—in your faith, your gifted speakers, your knowledge, your enthusiasm, and your love from us*—I want you to excel also in this gracious act of giving.

⁸I am not commanding you to do this. But I am testing how genuine your love is by comparing it with the eagerness of the other churches.

⁹You know the generous grace of our Lord Jesus Christ. Though he was rich, yet for your sakes he became poor, so that by his poverty he could make you rich.

¹⁰Here is my advice: It would be good for you to finish what you started a year ago. Last year you were the first who wanted to give, and you were the first to begin doing it. ¹¹Now you should finish what you started. Let the eagerness you showed in the beginning be matched

---

ADMIT IT

(7:11) Paul praised the Corinthians for clearing up an especially troublesome situation. How do you deal with correction for a fault? Do you tend to be defensive when confronted? Don't let pride keep you from admitting when you're wrong. Confrontation can be a tool for growth.

THE POINT OF GIVING

(8:1-2) While on his third missionary journey, Paul was collecting money for the impoverished believers in Jerusalem. The churches in Macedonia—Philippi, Thessalonica, and Berea—had given money even though they were also poor, and they had given more than Paul had expected. This was sacrificial giving; they were poor themselves, but they wanted to help. The point of giving is not the amount we give, but why and how we give. God wants us to give as these churches did—out of dedication to him, love for fellow believers, the joy of helping those in need, and because it is right to do so. How does your giving measure up?

7:13 Greek his spirit.   8:1 Greek brothers.   8:4 Greek for God's holy people.   8:7 Some manuscripts read your love for us.

now by your giving. Give in proportion to what you have. ¹²Whatever you give is acceptable if you give it eagerly. And give according to what you have, not what you don't have. ¹³Of course, I don't mean your giving should make life easy for others and hard for yourselves. I only mean that there should be some equality. ¹⁴Right now you have plenty and can help those who are in need. Later, they will have plenty and can share with you when you need it. In this way, things will be equal. ¹⁵As the Scriptures say,

> "Those who gathered a lot had nothing
>> left over,
>> and those who gathered only a little
>> had enough."*

TITUS AND HIS COMPANIONS ¹⁶But thank God! He has given Titus the same enthusiasm for you that I have. ¹⁷Titus welcomed our request that he visit you again. In fact, he himself was very eager to go and see you. ¹⁸We are also sending another brother with Titus. All the churches praise him as a preacher of the Good News. ¹⁹He was appointed by the churches to accompany us as we take the offering to Jerusalem*—a service that glorifies the Lord and shows our eagerness to help.

²⁰We are traveling together to guard against any criticism for the way we are handling this generous gift. ²¹We are careful to be honorable before the Lord, but we also want everyone else to see that we are honorable.

²²We are also sending with them another of our brothers who has proven himself many times and has shown on many occasions how eager he is. He is now even more enthusiastic because of his great confidence in you. ²³If anyone asks about Titus, say that he is my partner who works with me to help you. And the brothers with him have been sent by the churches,* and they bring honor to Christ. ²⁴So show them your love, and prove to all the churches that our boasting about you is justified.

9 **THE COLLECTION FOR CHRISTIANS IN JERUSALEM** I really don't need to write to you about this ministry of giving for the believers in Jerusalem.* ²For I know how eager you are to help, and I have been boasting to the churches in Macedonia that you in Greece* were ready to send an offering a year ago. In fact, it was your enthusiasm that stirred up

PRINCIPLES OF CONFRONTATION IN 2 CORINTHIANS

Sometimes rebuke is necessary, but it must be used with caution. The purpose of any rebuke, confrontation, or discipline is to help people, not hurt them.

Be firm. (7:8-10)

Affirm the good that you see. (7:4)

Be accurate and honest. (4:2; 6:11; 7:14; 8:21)

Communicate love. (2:4)

Follow up after the confrontation. (2:5-8; 7:13; 12:14)

Be gentle after being firm. (2:5-8; 7:15; 13:11-13)

Speak words that reflect Christ's message, not your own ideas. (5:16; 10:3, 12-13; 12:19)

Use discipline only when all else fails. (13:2)

---

many of the Macedonian believers to begin giving.

³But I am sending these brothers to be sure you really are ready, as I have been telling them, and that your money is all collected. I don't want to be wrong in my boasting about you. ⁴We would be embarrassed—not to mention your own embarrassment—if some Macedonian believers came with me and found that you weren't ready after all I had told them! ⁵So I thought I should send these brothers ahead of me to make sure the gift you promised is ready. But I want it to be a willing gift, not one given grudgingly.

⁶Remember this—a farmer who plants only a few seeds will get a small crop. But the one who plants generously will get a generous crop. ⁷You must each decide in your heart how much to give. And don't give reluctantly or in response to pressure. "For God loves a person who gives cheerfully."* ⁸And God will generously provide all you need. Then you will always have everything you need and plenty left over to share with others. ⁹As the Scriptures say,

....

MORE TO GIVE
(9:6-15) God gives us resources to use and invest for him. Paul used the illustration of seeds to explain that the resources God gives us are not to be hidden, foolishly devoured, or thrown away. Instead, they should be used to help others (see also 8:1-5). When we invest what God has given us in his work, he will provide us with even more to give. What has God given you lately? How will you use what you've been given?

8:15 Exod 16:18.   **8:19** See 1 Cor 16:3-4.   **8:23** Greek *are apostles of the churches.*   **9:1** Greek *about the offering for God's holy people.* **9:2** Greek *in Achaia,* the southern region of the Greek peninsula. *Macedonia* was in the northern region of Greece.   **9:7** See footnote on Prov 22:8.

"They share freely and give generously to
the poor.
Their good deeds will be remembered
forever."*

¹⁰For God is the one who provides seed for the
farmer and then bread to eat. In the same way,
he will provide and increase your resources
and then produce a great harvest of generosity* in you.

¹¹Yes, you will be enriched in every way so
that you can always be generous. And when we
take your gifts to those who need them, they
will thank God. ¹²So two good things will result
from this ministry of giving—the needs of the
believers in Jerusalem* will be met, and they
will joyfully express their thanks to God.

¹³As a result of your ministry, they will give
glory to God. For your generosity to them and
to all believers will prove that you are obedient to the Good News of Christ. ¹⁴And they will
pray for you with deep affection because of
the overflowing grace God has given to you.
¹⁵Thank God for this gift* too wonderful for
words!

10 **PAUL DEFENDS HIS AUTHORITY** Now
I, Paul, appeal to you with the gentleness and kindness of Christ—though I realize
you think I am timid in person and bold only
when I write from far away. ²Well, I am begging
you now so that when I come I won't have to be
bold with those who think we act from human
motives.

³We are human, but we don't wage war as humans do. ⁴*We use God's mighty weapons, not
worldly weapons, to knock down the strongholds of human reasoning and to destroy false
arguments. ⁵We destroy every proud obstacle
that keeps people from knowing God. We capture their rebellious thoughts and teach them
to obey Christ. ⁶And after you have become fully
obedient, we will punish everyone who remains
disobedient.

⁷Look at the obvious facts.* Those who say
they belong to Christ must recognize that we
belong to Christ as much as they do. ⁸I may
seem to be boasting too much about the au-

thority given to us by the Lord. But our authority
builds you up; it doesn't tear you down. So I
will not be ashamed of using my authority.
⁹I'm not trying to frighten you by my letters.
¹⁰For some say, "Paul's letters are demanding
and forceful, but in person he is weak, and
his speeches are worthless!" ¹¹Those people
should realize that our actions when we arrive
in person will be as forceful as what we say in
our letters from far away.

¹²Oh, don't worry; we wouldn't dare say that
we are as wonderful as these other men who
tell you how important they are! But they are
only comparing themselves with each other,
using themselves as the standard of measurement. How ignorant!

¹³We will not boast about things done outside
our area of authority. We will boast only about
what has happened within the boundaries of
the work God has given us, which includes our
working with you. ¹⁴We are not reaching beyond
these boundaries when we claim authority over
you, as if we had never visited you. For we were
the first to travel all the way to Corinth with the
Good News of Christ.

¹⁵Nor do we boast and claim credit for
the work someone else has done. Instead,
we hope that your faith will grow so that the
boundaries of our work among you will be
extended. ¹⁶Then we will be able to go and
preach the Good News in other places far beyond you, where no one else is working. Then
there will be no question of our boasting about
work done in someone else's territory. ¹⁷As the
Scriptures say, "If you want to boast, boast
only about the LORD."*

¹⁸When people commend themselves, it
doesn't count for much. The important thing is
for the Lord to commend them.

11 **PAUL AND THE FALSE APOSTLES**
I hope you will put up with a little more
of my foolishness. Please bear with me. ²For
I am jealous for you with the jealousy of God
himself. I promised you as a pure bride* to
one husband—Christ. ³But I fear that somehow
your pure and undivided devotion to Christ
will be corrupted, just as Eve was deceived by
the cunning ways of the serpent. ⁴You happily
put up with whatever anyone tells you, even
if they preach a different Jesus than the one
we preach, or a different kind of Spirit than the
one you received, or a different kind of gospel
than the one you believed.

- -

WHICH WAY?
*(10:3-6) In some situations, Christians must choose
between two strategies: God's or humans'. Paul assures
us that God's mighty weapons—prayer, faith, hope, love,
his Word, the Holy Spirit—are powerful and effective
(see Eph 6:10-18)! When dealing with the pride that
keeps people from a relationship with Christ, we may be
tempted to use our own methods. But nothing can break
down Satan's barriers like God's weapons.*

9:9 Ps 112:9.   **9:10** Greek *righteousness.*   **9:12** Greek *of God's holy
people.*   **9:15** Greek *his gift.*   **10:4** English translations divide
verses 4 and 5 in various ways.   **10:7** Or *You look at things only on
the basis of appearance.*   **10:17** Jer 9:24.   **11:2** Greek *a virgin.*

⁵But I don't consider myself inferior in any way to these "super apostles" who teach such things. ⁶I may be unskilled as a speaker, but I'm not lacking in knowledge. We have made this clear to you in every possible way.

⁷Was I wrong when I humbled myself and honored you by preaching God's Good News to you without expecting anything in return? ⁸I "robbed" other churches by accepting their contributions so I could serve you at no cost. ⁹And when I was with you and didn't have enough to live on, I did not become a financial burden to anyone. For the brothers who came from Macedonia brought me all that I needed. I have never been a burden to you, and I never will be. ¹⁰As surely as the truth of Christ is in me, no one in all of Greece* will ever stop me from boasting about this. ¹¹Why? Because I don't love you? God knows that I do.

¹²But I will continue doing what I have always done. This will undercut those who are looking for an opportunity to boast that their work is just like ours. ¹³These people are false apostles. They are deceitful workers who disguise themselves as apostles of Christ. ¹⁴But I am not surprised! Even Satan disguises himself as an angel of light. ¹⁵So it is no wonder that his servants also disguise themselves as servants of righteousness. In the end they will get the punishment their wicked deeds deserve.

PAUL'S MANY TRIALS ¹⁶Again I say, don't think that I am a fool to talk like this. But even if you do, listen to me, as you would to a foolish person, while I also boast a little. ¹⁷Such boasting is not from the Lord, but I am acting like a fool. ¹⁸And since others boast about their human achievements, I will, too. ¹⁹After all, you think you are so wise, but you enjoy putting up with fools! ²⁰You put up with it when someone enslaves you, takes everything you have, takes advantage of you, takes control of everything, and slaps you in the face. ²¹I'm ashamed to say that we've been too "weak" to do that!

But whatever they dare to boast about— I'm talking like a fool again—I dare to boast about it, too. ²²Are they Hebrews? So am I. Are they Israelites? So am I. Are they descendants of Abraham? So am I. ²³Are they servants of Christ? I know I sound like a madman, but I have served him far more! I have worked harder, been put in prison more often, been whipped times without number, and faced death again and again. ²⁴Five different times the Jewish leaders gave me thirty-nine lashes. ²⁵Three times I was beaten with rods. Once I was stoned. Three times I was shipwrecked. Once I spent a whole night and a day adrift at sea. ²⁶I have traveled on many long journeys. I have faced danger from rivers and from robbers. I have faced danger from my own people, the Jews, as well as from the Gentiles. I have faced danger in the cities, in the deserts, and on the seas. And I have faced danger from men who claim to be believers but are not.* ²⁷I worked hard and long, enduring many sleepless nights. I have been hungry and thirsty and have often gone without food. I have shivered in the cold, without enough clothing to keep me warm.

²⁸Then, besides all this, I have the daily burden of my concern for all the churches. ²⁹Who is weak without my feeling that weakness? Who is led astray, and I do not burn with anger?

³⁰If I must boast, I would rather boast about the things that show how weak I am. ³¹God, the Father of our Lord Jesus, who is worthy of eternal praise, knows I am not lying. ³²When I was in Damascus, the governor under King Aretas kept guards at the city gates to catch me. ³³I had to be lowered in a basket through a window in the city wall to escape from him.

12 **PAUL'S VISION AND HIS THORN IN THE FLESH** This boasting will do no good, but I must go on. I will reluctantly tell about visions and revelations from the Lord. ²I* was caught up to the third heaven fourteen years ago. Whether I was in my body or out of

11:10 Greek *Achaia,* the southern region of the Greek peninsula. 11:26 Greek *from false brothers.* 12:2 Greek *I know a man in Christ who.*

SMOOTH TALK
(11:3-4) The Corinthian believers fell for messages that sounded good and seemed to make sense. Yet these messages were false teaching. Today there are many false messages that seem to make sense. Don't believe anyone simply because he or she sounds like an authority or says things you like to hear. Search the Bible and check people's words against God's Word (see Acts 17:11).

WHEN GOD SAYS NO
(12:1-10) God said no to Paul's request for healing. What is your expectation when you pray? That God will always answer yes? Many believe that Jesus' invitation to "keep on asking" (Matt 7:7) is a guaranteed yes. But sometimes, God says no.

Let's face it: A "no" can sometimes seem harsh. Think about how you would feel if someone turned you down for a date. But with God, a "no" could be the best answer you could receive. In Paul's case, "no" meant that he would experience more of God's strength. Has God said no to you recently? Like Paul, do you believe that he still has your best interests at heart?

I AM GLAD TO BOAST ABOUT MY WEAKNESSES,
SO THAT THE POWER OF CHRIST CAN WORK THROUGH ME.
2 CORINTHIANS 12:9

my body, I don't know—only God knows. ³Yes, only God knows whether I was in my body or outside my body. But I do know ⁴that I was caught up* to paradise and heard things so astounding that they cannot be expressed in words, things no human is allowed to tell.

⁵That experience is worth boasting about, but I'm not going to do it. I will boast only about my weaknesses. ⁶If I wanted to boast, I would be no fool in doing so, because I would be telling the truth. But I won't do it, because I don't want anyone to give me credit beyond what they can see in my life or hear in my message, ⁷even though I have received such wonderful revelations from God. So to keep me from becoming proud, I was given a thorn in my flesh, a messenger from Satan to torment me and keep me from becoming proud.

⁸Three different times I begged the Lord to take it away. ⁹Each time he said, "My grace is all you need. My power works best in weakness." So now I am glad to boast about my weaknesses, so that the power of Christ can work through me. ¹⁰That's why I take pleasure in my weaknesses, and in the insults, hardships, persecutions, and troubles that I suffer for Christ. For when I am weak, then I am strong.

PAUL'S CONCERN FOR THE CORINTHIANS
¹¹You have made me act like a fool—boasting like this.* You ought to be writing commendations for me, for I am not at all inferior to these "super apostles," even though I am nothing at all. ¹²When I was with you, I certainly gave you proof that I am an apostle. For I patiently did many signs and wonders and miracles among you. ¹³The only thing I failed to do, which I do in the other churches, was to become a financial burden to you. Please forgive me for this wrong!

¹⁴Now I am coming to you for the third time, and I will not be a burden to you. I don't want what you have—I want you. After all, children don't provide for their parents. Rather, parents

provide for their children. ¹⁵I will gladly spend myself and all I have for you, even though it seems that the more I love you, the less you love me.

¹⁶Some of you admit I was not a burden to you. But others still think I was sneaky and took advantage of you by trickery. ¹⁷But how? Did any of the men I sent to you take advantage of you? ¹⁸When I urged Titus to visit you and sent our other brother with him, did Titus take advantage of you? No! For we have the same spirit and walk in each other's steps, doing things the same way.

¹⁹Perhaps you think we're saying these things just to defend ourselves. No, we tell you this as Christ's servants, and with God as our witness. Everything we do, dear friends, is to strengthen you. ²⁰For I am afraid that when I come I won't like what I find, and you won't like my response. I am afraid that I will find quarreling, jealousy, anger, selfishness, slander, gossip, arrogance, and disorderly behavior. ²¹Yes, I am afraid that when I come again, God will humble me in your presence. And I will be grieved because many of you have not given up your old sins. You have not repented of your impurity, sexual immorality, and eagerness for lustful pleasure.

13 PAUL'S FINAL ADVICE This is the third time I am coming to visit you (and as the Scriptures say, "The facts of every case must be established by the testimony of two or three witnesses"*). ²I have already warned those who had been sinning when I was there on my second visit. Now I again warn them and all others, just as I did before, that next time I will not spare them.

³I will give you all the proof you want that Christ speaks through me. Christ is not weak when he deals with you; he is powerful among you. ⁴Although he was crucified in weakness, he now lives by the power of God. We, too, are weak, just as Christ was, but when we deal with you we will be alive with him and will have God's power.

⁵Examine yourselves to see if your faith is genuine. Test yourselves. Surely you know that Jesus Christ is among you*; if not, you have

---

EXAMS
(13:5) Just as we get physical examinations, Paul urges us to give ourselves spiritual examinations. We can do this by asking ourselves one question: Am I becoming more Christlike? If we're not taking active steps to grow closer to God, we're moving away from him.

12:3-4 Greek *But I know such a man,* ⁴*that he was caught up.*
12:11 Some manuscripts do not include *boasting like this.*
13:1 Deut 19:15.   13:5 Or *in you.*

failed the test of genuine faith. [6]As you test yourselves, I hope you will recognize that we have not failed the test of apostolic authority.

[7]We pray to God that you will not do what is wrong by refusing our correction. I hope we won't need to demonstrate our authority when we arrive. Do the right thing before we come— even if that makes it look like we have failed to demonstrate our authority. [8]For we cannot oppose the truth, but must always stand for the truth. [9]We are glad to seem weak if it helps show that you are actually strong. We pray that you will become mature.

13:11 Greek *Brothers.* 13:12 Greek *with a sacred kiss.* 13:14 Some English translations include verse 13 as part of verse 12, and then verse 14 becomes verse 13.

[10]I am writing this to you before I come, hoping that I won't need to deal severely with you when I do come. For I want to use the authority the Lord has given me to strengthen you, not to tear you down.

PAUL'S FINAL GREETINGS [11]Dear brothers and sisters,* I close my letter with these last words: Be joyful. Grow to maturity. Encourage each other. Live in harmony and peace. Then the God of love and peace will be with you.

[12]Greet each other with Christian love.* [13]All of God's people here send you their greetings.

[14]*May the grace of the Lord Jesus Christ, the love of God, and the fellowship of the Holy Spirit be with you all.

GALATIANS

Ever known a church like Luis's? Words like different *and* strict
*don't even begin to tell the story. Maybe Luis's best friend
Esteban gave the best description. He attended Luis's church
for several months—then quit. Luis wanted to know why.*

"I just don't like it, okay?" Esteban finally said. "It's the 'don't church.'
There's like about fifty million rules, man. Don't wear certain clothes.
Don't go to parties. Don't be friends with non-Christians. And the list just
keeps going. Who could keep up with them? Besides, some people there
act like they're better than everyone else."

"But you said you liked our youth pastor and some of the messages
you heard."

"I guess I did—at first. But I came home feeling more and more guilty.
Sorry, tipo [dude], but if following all those rules is how I'm supposed
to get close to God I might as well forget it. . . . Hey, I want to be a good
Christian—but I'll never be that good."

Almost 2,000 years ago another "don't church" tried to earn God's
acceptance by following rules. That's what Paul's letter to the Galatians
is all about. If you think that being a Christian is all about what you do
or don't do, check out Galatians.

STATS

PURPOSE
To refute the Judaizers
(who taught that
Gentile believers must
obey the Jewish law
to be saved), and to
remind Christians
about faith and
freedom in Christ

AUTHOR
Paul

ORIGINAL AUDIENCE
The churches in
southern Galatia
(including Iconium,
Lystra, Derbe)

DATE WRITTEN
About A.D. 49

SETTING
The early church
disagreed over whether
believers, especially
Gentiles, had to follow
the Jewish laws. Paul
wrote a letter from
Antioch to address
the issue (see also
Acts 15).

KEY PEOPLE
Paul, Peter, Barnabas,
Titus, false teachers

KEY PLACES
Galatia, Jerusalem

KEY POINTS

SAVED BY WORKS? Paul opposed a group of Jewish teachers who insisted that
Gentile believers obey Jewish laws in order to be saved. Rules and good works
can't save anyone. Only Jesus can.

FREEDOM Paul explained the freedom that believers have through Christ. Yet
freedom is a privilege that comes with responsibilities.

THE WORK OF THE HOLY SPIRIT IN BELIEVERS The Holy Spirit instructs us,
guides us, leads us, and empowers us. When the Holy Spirit controls us, he
produces his fruit (love, joy, peace, and so on) in us.

1 GREETINGS FROM PAUL

This letter is from Paul, an apostle. I was not appointed by any group of people or any human authority, but by Jesus Christ himself and by God the Father, who raised Jesus from the dead.

²All the brothers and sisters* here join me in sending this letter to the churches of Galatia.

³May God our Father and the Lord Jesus Christ* give you grace and peace. ⁴Jesus gave his life for our sins, just as God our Father planned, in order to rescue us from this evil world in which we live. ⁵All glory to God forever and ever! Amen.

THERE IS ONLY ONE GOOD NEWS

⁶I am shocked that you are turning away so soon from God, who called you to himself through the loving mercy of Christ.* You are following a different way that pretends to be the Good News ⁷but is not the Good News at all. You are being fooled by those who deliberately twist the truth concerning Christ.

⁸Let God's curse fall on anyone, including us or even an angel from heaven, who preaches a different kind of Good News than the one we preached to you. ⁹I say again what we have said before: If anyone preaches any other Good News than the one you welcomed, let that person be cursed.

¹⁰Obviously, I'm not trying to win the approval of people, but of God. If pleasing people were my goal, I would not be Christ's servant.

PAUL'S MESSAGE COMES FROM CHRIST

¹¹Dear brothers and sisters, I want you to understand that the gospel message I preach is not based on mere human reasoning. ¹²I received

my message from no human source, and no one taught me. Instead, I received it by direct revelation from Jesus Christ.*

¹³You know what I was like when I followed the Jewish religion—how I violently persecuted God's church. I did my best to destroy it. ¹⁴I was far ahead of my fellow Jews in my zeal for the traditions of my ancestors.

¹⁵But even before I was born, God chose me and called me by his marvelous grace. Then it pleased him ¹⁶to reveal his Son to me* so that I would proclaim the Good News about Jesus to the Gentiles.

When this happened, I did not rush out to consult with any human being.* ¹⁷Nor did I go up to Jerusalem to consult with those who were apostles before I was. Instead, I went away into Arabia, and later I returned to the city of Damascus.

¹⁸Then three years later I went to Jerusalem to get to know Peter,* and I stayed with him for fifteen days. ¹⁹The only other apostle I met at that time was James, the Lord's brother. ²⁰I declare before God that what I am writing to you is not a lie.

²¹After that visit I went north into the provinces of Syria and Cilicia. ²²And still the Christians in the churches in Judea didn't know me personally. ²³All they knew was that people were saying, "The one who used to persecute us is now preaching the very faith he tried to destroy!" ²⁴And they praised God because of me.

2 THE APOSTLES ACCEPT PAUL

Then fourteen years later I went back to Jerusalem again, this time with Barnabas; and Titus came along, too. ²I went there because God revealed to me that I should go. While I was there I met privately with those considered to be leaders of the church and shared with them the message I had been preaching to the Gentiles. I wanted to make sure that we were in agreement, for fear that all my efforts had been wasted and I was running the race for nothing. ³And they supported me and did not even demand that my companion Titus be circumcised, though he was a Gentile.*

⁴Even that question came up only because of some so-called Christians there—false ones, really*—who were secretly brought in. They sneaked in to spy on us and take away the freedom we have in Christ Jesus. They wanted to enslave us and force us to follow their Jewish

---

TWISTED TRUTH

(1:6-7) Twisted truth is sometimes more difficult to spot than outright lies. The Judaizers twisted the truth about Christ because they believed that all believers had to follow Jewish laws in order to be saved. Although these people claimed to follow Jesus, they denied that his death was sufficient for salvation.

There will always be people who twist the Good News. Either they don't understand what the Bible teaches, or they're uncomfortable with the truth as it stands. How can we tell when people are twisting the truth? Find out what they teach about Jesus Christ. If what they say doesn't match the truth in God's Word, then they're wrong.

A BIG CHANGE

(1:13-24) Paul's changed life brought many comments from people who saw or heard of him. They praised God because only he could have turned this zealous persecutor of Christians into a believer. Although we may not have had as dramatic a change as Paul had, our new life should be noticeable. When people look at you, do they recognize that God has made changes in you?

1:2 Greek *brothers;* also in 1:11.   1:3 Some manuscripts read *God the Father and our Lord Jesus Christ.*   1:6 Some manuscripts read *through loving mercy.*   1:12 Or *by the revelation of Jesus Christ.*   1:16a Or *in me.*   1:16b Greek *with flesh and blood.*   1:18 Greek *Cephas.*   2:3 Greek *a Greek.*   2:4 Greek *some false brothers.*

CITIES IN GALATIA
Paul visited several cities in Galatia on each of his three missionary journeys. On his first journey he went through Antioch in Pisidia, Iconium, Lystra, and Derbe, then retraced his steps. On his second journey he went by land from Antioch in Syria through the four cities in Galatia. On his third journey he also went through those cities on the main route to Ephesus.

regulations. ⁵But we refused to give in to them for a single moment. We wanted to preserve the truth of the gospel message for you.

⁶And the leaders of the church had nothing to add to what I was preaching. (By the way, their reputation as great leaders made no difference to me, for God has no favorites.) ⁷Instead, they saw that God had given me the responsibility of preaching the gospel to the Gentiles, just as he had given Peter the responsibility of preaching to the Jews. ⁸For the same God who worked through Peter as the apostle to the Jews also worked through me as the apostle to the Gentiles.

⁹In fact, James, Peter,* and John, who were known as pillars of the church, recognized the gift God had given me, and they accepted Barnabas and me as their co-workers. They encouraged us to keep preaching to the Gentiles, while they continued their work with the Jews. ¹⁰Their only suggestion was that we keep on helping the poor, which I have always been eager to do.

PAUL CONFRONTS PETER ¹¹But when Peter came to Antioch, I had to oppose him to his

2:9 Greek *Cephas*; also in 2:11, 14.

face, for what he did was very wrong. ¹²When he first arrived, he ate with the Gentile Christians, who were not circumcised. But afterward, when some friends of James came, Peter wouldn't eat with the Gentiles anymore. He was afraid of criticism from these people who insisted on the necessity of circumcision. ¹³As a result, other Jewish Christians followed Peter's hypocrisy, and even Barnabas was led astray by their hypocrisy.

¹⁴When I saw that they were not following the truth of the gospel message, I said to Peter in front of all the others, "Since you, a Jew by birth, have discarded the Jewish laws and living like a Gentile, why are you now trying to make these Gentiles follow the Jewish traditions?

CONCERN FOR THOSE IN NEED
(2:10) Here the apostles were referring to the poor people of Jerusalem. While many Gentile believers were financially comfortable, the Jerusalem church was suffering from a severe famine (see Acts 11:28-30). Much of Paul's time was spent gathering funds for the Jewish Christians (Acts 24:17; Rom 15:25-29; 1 Cor 16:1-4; 2 Cor 8). Believers caring for the poor is a constant theme of Scripture. Both in your own city and across the oceans, there are people who need help. What can you do to show your concern for those in need?

¹⁵"You and I are Jews by birth, not 'sinners' like the Gentiles. ¹⁶Yet we know that a person is made right with God by faith in Jesus Christ, not by obeying the law. And we have believed in Christ Jesus, so that we might be made right with God because of our faith in Christ, not because we have obeyed the law. For no one will ever be made right with God by obeying the law."*

¹⁷But suppose we seek to be made right with God through faith in Christ and then we are found guilty because we have abandoned the law. Would that mean Christ has led us into sin? Absolutely not! ¹⁸Rather, I am a sinner if I rebuild the old system of law I already tore down. ¹⁹For when I tried to keep the law, it condemned me. So I died to the law—I stopped trying to meet all its requirements—so that I might live for God. ²⁰My old self has been crucified with Christ.* It is no longer I who live, but Christ lives in me. So I live in this earthly body by trusting in the Son of God, who loved me and gave himself for me. ²¹I do not treat the grace of God as meaningless. For if keeping the law could make us right with God, then there was no need for Christ to die.

3 **THE LAW AND FAITH IN CHRIST** Oh, foolish Galatians! Who has cast an evil spell on you? For the meaning of Jesus Christ's death was made as clear to you as if you had seen a picture of his death on the cross. ²Let me ask you this one question: Did you receive the Holy Spirit by obeying the law of Moses? Of course not! You received the Spirit because you believed the message you heard about Christ. ³How foolish can you be? After starting your Christian lives in the Spirit, why are you now trying to become perfect by your own human effort? ⁴Have you experienced* so much for nothing? Surely it was not in vain, was it?

⁵I ask you again, does God give you the Holy Spirit and work miracles among you because you obey the law? Of course not! It is because you believe the message you heard about Christ.

⁶In the same way, "Abraham believed God, and God counted him as righteous because of his faith."* ⁷The real children of Abraham, then, are those who put their faith in God.

⁸What's more, the Scriptures looked forward to this time when God would declare the Gentiles to be righteous because of their faith. God proclaimed this good news to Abraham long ago when he said, "All nations will be blessed through you."* ⁹So all who put their faith in Christ share the same blessing Abraham received because of his faith.

¹⁰But those who depend on the law to make them right with God are under his curse, for the Scriptures say, "Cursed is everyone who does not observe and obey all the commands that are written in God's Book of the Law."* ¹¹So it is clear that no one can be made right with God by trying to keep the law. For the Scriptures say, "It is through faith that a righteous person has life."* ¹²This way of faith is very different from the way of law, which says, "It is through obeying the law that a person has life."*

¹³But Christ has rescued us from the curse pronounced by the law. When he was hung on the cross, he took upon himself the curse for our wrongdoing. For it is written in the Scriptures, "Cursed is everyone who is hung on a tree."* ¹⁴Through Christ Jesus, God has blessed the Gentiles with the same blessing he promised to Abraham, so that we who are believers might receive the promised* Holy Spirit through faith.

THE LAW AND GOD'S PROMISE ¹⁵Dear brothers and sisters,* here's an example from everyday life. Just as no one can set aside or amend an irrevocable agreement, so it is in this case. ¹⁶God gave the promises to Abraham and his child.* And notice that the Scripture doesn't say "to his children,*" as if it meant many descendants. Rather, it says "to his child"—and that, of course, means Christ. ¹⁷This is what I am trying to say: The agreement God made with Abraham could not be canceled 430 years later when God gave the law to Moses. God would be breaking his promise. ¹⁸For if the inheritance could be received by keeping the law, then it would not be the result of accepting God's promise. But God graciously gave it to Abraham as a promise.

¹⁹Why, then, was the law given? It was given alongside the promise to show people their sins. But the law was designed to last only until the coming of the child who was promised. God gave his law through angels to Moses, who was the mediator between God and the people. ²⁰Now a mediator is helpful if more than one party must reach an agreement. But God, who is one, did not use a mediator when he gave his promise to Abraham.

²¹Is there a conflict, then, between God's law and God's promises?* Absolutely not! If the law

---

2:16 Some translators hold that the quotation extends through verse 14; others through verse 16; and still others through verse 21. **2:20** Some English translations put this sentence in verse 19. **3:4** Or *Have you suffered.* **3:6** Gen 15:6. **3:8** Gen 12:3; 18:18; 22:18. **3:10** Deut 27:26. **3:11** Hab 2:4. **3:12** Lev 18:5. **3:13** Deut 21:23 (Greek version). **3:14** Some manuscripts read *the blessing of the.* **3:15** Greek *Brothers.* **3:16a** Greek *seed;* also in 3:16c, 19. See notes on Gen 12:7 and 13:15. **3:16b** Greek *seeds.* **3:21** Some manuscripts read *and the promises?*

WHAT IS THE LAW?

Part of the Jewish law included those laws found in the Old Testament. In the Old Testament there were three categories of law: ceremonial laws, civil laws, and moral laws. When Paul says that non-Jews (Gentiles) are no longer bound by these laws, he is not saying that the Old Testament laws do not apply to us today. He is saying certain types of laws may not apply to us.

CEREMONIAL LAW	CIVIL LAW	MORAL LAW
This kind of law relates specifically to Israel's worship (for example, see Lev 1:1-13). Its primary purpose was to point forward to Jesus Christ. Therefore, these laws were no longer necessary after Jesus' death and resurrection. While we are no longer bound by ceremonial laws, the principles behind them—to worship and love a holy God—still apply. The Jewish Christians often accused the Gentile Christians of violating the ceremonial law.	This type of law dictated Israel's daily living (for example, see Deut 24:10-11). Because modern society and culture are so radically different, some of these guidelines cannot be followed specifically. But the principles behind the commands should guide our conduct. At times, Paul asked Gentile Christians to follow some of these laws, not because they had to, but to promote unity.	This sort of law is the direct command of God—for example, the Ten Commandments (Exod 20:1-17). It requires strict obedience. It reveals the nature and will of God, and it still applies to us today. We are to obey this moral law, not to obtain salvation, but to live in ways pleasing to God.

could give us new life, we could be made right with God by obeying it. ²²But the Scriptures declare that we are all prisoners of sin, so we receive God's promise of freedom only by believing in Jesus Christ.

GOD'S CHILDREN THROUGH FAITH ²³Before the way of faith in Christ was available to us, we were placed under guard by the law. We were kept in protective custody, so to speak, until the way of faith was revealed.

²⁴Let me put it another way. The law was our guardian until Christ came; it protected us until we could be made right with God through faith. ²⁵And now that the way of faith has come, we no longer need the law as our guardian.

²⁶For you are all children* of God through faith in Christ Jesus. ²⁷And all who have been united with Christ in baptism have put on Christ, like putting on new clothes.* ²⁸There is no longer Jew or Gentile,* slave or free, male and female. For you are all one in Christ Jesus. ²⁹And now that you belong to Christ, you are the true children* of Abraham. You are his heirs, and God's promise to Abraham belongs to you.

4 Think of it this way. If a father dies and leaves an inheritance for his young children, those children are not much better off than slaves until they grow up, even though they actually own everything their father had.

²They have to obey their guardians until they reach whatever age their father set. ³And that's the way it was with us before Christ came. We were like children; we were slaves to the basic spiritual principles* of this world.

⁴But when the right time came, God sent his Son, born of a woman, subject to the law. ⁵God sent him to buy freedom for us who were slaves to the law, so that he could adopt us as his very own children.* ⁶And because we* are his children, God has sent the Spirit of his Son into our hearts, prompting us to call out, "Abba, Father."* ⁷Now you are no longer a slave but God's own child.* And since you are his child, God has made you his heir.

PAUL'S CONCERN FOR THE GALATIANS ⁸Before you Gentiles knew God, you were slaves to so-called gods that do not even exist. ⁹So now that you know God (or should I say, now that

3:26 Greek sons. 3:27 Greek have put on Christ. 3:28 Greek Jew or Greek. 3:29 Greek seed. 4:3 Or powers; also in 4:9. 4:5 Greek sons; also in 4:6. 4:6a Greek you. 4:6b Abba is an Aramaic term for "father." 4:7 Greek son; also in 4:7b.

DIFFERENCES
(3:28) Age, gender, race, and social or economic status make no difference to God—all people are welcome. Yet these differences have often been the means of dividing us. In what ways do you show your belief in the unity of all believers in Christ? Is your faith not only color-blind, but also blind to status or age as well?

CORRECTED
(4:1-16) Paul didn't become popular after he criticized the Galatians for turning away from their first faith in Christ (see also 1:6-7). Human nature hasn't changed much. We still get angry when we're scolded. How do you usually react when challenged? Are you willing to receive the correction with humility and to carefully think it over?

God knows you), why do you want to go back again and become slaves once more to the weak and useless spiritual principles of this world? [10]You are trying to earn favor with God by observing certain days or months or seasons or years. [11]I fear for you. Perhaps all my hard work with you was for nothing. [12]Dear brothers and sisters,* I plead with you to live as I do in freedom from these things, for I have become like you Gentiles—free from those laws.

You did not mistreat me when I first preached to you. [13]Surely you remember that I was sick when I first brought you the Good News. [14]But even though my condition tempted you to reject me, you did not despise me or turn me away. No, you took me in and cared for me as though I were an angel from God or even Christ Jesus himself. [15]Where is that joyful and grateful spirit you felt then? I am sure you would have taken out your own eyes and given them to me if it had been possible. [16]Have I now become your enemy because I am telling you the truth?

[17]Those false teachers are so eager to win your favor, but their intentions are not good. They are trying to shut you off from me so that you will pay attention only to them. [18]If someone is eager to do good things for you, that's all right; but let them do it all the time, not just when I'm with you.

[19]Oh, my dear children! I feel as if I'm going through labor pains for you again, and they will continue until Christ is fully developed in your lives. [20]I wish I were with you right now so I could change my tone. But at this distance I don't know how else to help you.

ABRAHAM'S TWO CHILDREN

[21]Tell me, you who want to live under the law, do you know what the law actually says? [22]The Scriptures say that Abraham had two sons, one from his slave wife and one from his freeborn wife.* [23]The son of the slave wife was born in a human attempt to bring about the fulfillment of God's promise. But the son of the freeborn wife was born as God's own fulfillment of his promise.

[24]These two women serve as an illustration of God's two covenants. The first woman, Hagar, represents Mount Sinai where people received the law that enslaved them. [25]And now Jerusalem is just like Mount Sinai in Arabia,* because she and her children live in slavery to the law. [26]But the other woman, Sarah, represents the heavenly Jerusalem. She is the free woman, and she is our mother. [27]As Isaiah said,

"Rejoice, O childless woman,
    you who have never given birth!
Break into a joyful shout,
    you who have never been in labor!
For the desolate woman now has more
        children
    than the woman who lives with her
        husband!"*

[28]And you, dear brothers and sisters, are children of the promise, just like Isaac. [29]But you are now being persecuted by those who want you to keep the law, just as Ishmael, the child born by human effort, persecuted Isaac, the child born by the power of the Spirit.

[30]But what do the Scriptures say about that? "Get rid of the slave and her son, for the son of

4:12 Greek brothers; also in 4:28, 31.   4:22 See Gen 16:15; 21:2-3.
4:25 Greek And Hagar, which is Mount Sinai in Arabia, is now like Jerusalem; other manuscripts read And Mount Sinai in Arabia is now like Jerusalem.   4:27 Isa 54:1.

CHOICES
freedom

Hope storms upstairs, slams her bedroom door, and flings herself onto the bed. Burying her face in a pillow, she lets out a yell of disgust.

Rolling over, she stares at the ceiling and begins thinking:

Ooooh. I can't believe them! They're like the Gestapo! Why don't they just go ahead and put bars around my room? They don't let me do anything. They ask me six million questions about everything. They hate all my friends. They try to make me dress like a loser.

Hope glances at the calendar above her desk.

Nine more months—then I can go to college and do whatever I want. I'll be totally free. If I don't want to go to church, I won't go. If I want to trash my room and leave it that way the whole semester, I can. I'll be able to hang out whenever I want with whoever I want without Mom and Bill totally humiliating me. She shakes her head at the thought of her mother and stepfather.

Oh, gosh, that is gonna be so great. I can't wait to leave! No more missing out on life. There'll be parties, tons of hot guys, and . . .

Hope's daydream is shattered by a voice yelling: "Hope! Come pick up your shoes from out of the middle of the living room floor—now!"

Hope groans and heads downstairs, mumbling, "Enjoy it now, Mother. Because in nine months, I'm so outta here!"

What's Hope's definition of freedom? Check out Galatians 5:16-25. Can freedom have limits? Why or why not?

the slave woman will not share the inheritance with the free woman's son."* ³¹So, dear brothers and sisters, we are not children of the slave woman; we are children of the free woman.

5 **FREEDOM IN CHRIST** So Christ has truly set us free. Now make sure that you stay free, and don't get tied up again in slavery to the law.

²Listen! I, Paul, tell you this: If you are counting on circumcision to make you right with God, then Christ will be of no benefit to you. ³I'll say it again. If you are trying to find favor with God by being circumcised, you must obey every regulation in the whole law of Moses. ⁴For if you are trying to make yourselves right with God by keeping the law, you have been cut off from Christ! You have fallen away from God's grace.

⁵But we who live by the Spirit eagerly wait to receive by faith the righteousness God has promised to us. ⁶For when we place our faith in Christ Jesus, there is no benefit in being circumcised or being uncircumcised. What is important is faith expressing itself in love.

⁷You were running the race so well. Who has held you back from following the truth? ⁸It certainly isn't God, for he is the one who called you to freedom. ⁹This false teaching is like a little yeast that spreads through the whole batch of dough! ¹⁰I am trusting the Lord to keep you from believing false teachings. God will judge that person, whoever he is, who has been confusing you.

¹¹Dear brothers and sisters,* if I were still preaching that you must be circumcised—as some say I do—why am I still being persecuted? If I were no longer preaching salvation through the cross of Christ, no one would be offended. ¹²I just wish that those troublemakers who want to mutilate you by circumcision would mutilate themselves.*

¹³For you have been called to live in freedom, my brothers and sisters. But don't use your freedom to satisfy your sinful nature. Instead, use your freedom to serve one another in love. ¹⁴For the whole law can be summed up in this one command: "Love your neighbor as yourself."* ¹⁵But if you are always biting and devouring one another, watch out! Beware of destroying one another.

LIVING BY THE SPIRIT'S POWER ¹⁶So I say, let the Holy Spirit guide your lives. Then you won't be doing what your sinful nature craves. ¹⁷The

4:30 Gen 21:10.   5:11 Greek *Brothers;* similarly in 5:13.   5:12 Or *castrate themselves,* or *cut themselves off from you;* Greek reads *cut themselves off.*   5:14 Lev 19:18.

THE HOLY SPIRIT PRODUCES...
FRUIT IN OUR LIVES:
LOVE, JOY, PEACE, PATIENCE, KINDNESS, GOODNESS, FAITHFULNESS, GENTLENESS, AND SELF-CONTROL.

GALATIANS 5:22-23

sinful nature wants to do evil, which is just the opposite of what the Spirit wants. And the Spirit gives us desires that are the opposite of what the sinful nature desires. These two forces are constantly fighting each other, so you are not free to carry out your good intentions. ¹⁸But when you are directed by the Spirit, you are not under obligation to the law of Moses.

¹⁹When you follow the desires of your sinful nature, the results are very clear: sexual immorality, impurity, lustful pleasures, ²⁰idolatry, sorcery, hostility, quarreling, jealousy, outbursts of anger, selfish ambition, dissension, division, ²¹envy, drunkenness, wild parties, and other sins like these. Let me tell you again, as I have before, that anyone living that sort of life will not inherit the Kingdom of God.

²²But the Holy Spirit produces this kind of fruit in our lives: love, joy, peace, patience,

· ·

LOVE
(5:14-15) *When we are not motivated by love, we become critical of others. We stop looking for good in them and see only their faults. Soon the unity of believers becomes broken. Have you talked behind someone's back? Have you focused on others' short-comings instead of their strengths? Remind yourself of Jesus' command to love others as we love ourselves (Matt 22:39). When you begin to feel critical of someone, make a list of that person's positive qualities. And don't say anything behind the person's back that you wouldn't say to his or her face.*

FRUIT
(5:22-23) *The Holy Spirit produces character traits, not specific actions. We can't go out and do these things, and we can't obtain them by trying to get them. If we want the fruit of the Holy Spirit to develop within us, we must recognize that all of these characteristics are found in Christ. The way to develop them is to first develop a relationship with him (see John 15:4-5). As a result, we will fulfill the intended purpose of the law—loving God and people (Gal 5:14). Which of the qualities in this passage most needs further development in your life?*

kindness, goodness, faithfulness, [23]gentleness, and self-control. There is no law against these things!

[24]Those who belong to Christ Jesus have nailed the passions and desires of their sinful nature to his cross and crucified them there. [25]Since we are living by the Spirit, let us follow the Spirit's leading in every part of our lives. [26]Let us not become conceited, or provoke one another, or be jealous of one another.

6 WE HARVEST WHAT WE PLANT Dear brothers and sisters, if another believer* is overcome by some sin, you who are godly* should gently and humbly help that person back onto the right path. And be careful not to fall into the same temptation yourself. [2]Share each other's burdens, and in this way obey the law of Christ. [3]If you think you are too important to help someone, you are only fooling yourself. You are not that important.

[4]Pay careful attention to your own work, for

· ·

EVERY PART
(5:25) God is interested in all aspects of our lives, not just the spiritual part. As we live by the Holy Spirit's power, we need to submit every aspect of our lives—emotional, physical, social, intellectual, and vocational—to God. This is a process that requires perseverance. How much of your life does God control?

LOOK AT JESUS
(6:4) When you do your very best, you feel good about the results. Consequently, you don't need to compare yourself with others. Yet people make comparisons for many reasons. Some point out others' flaws in order to feel better about themselves. Others simply want reassurance that they are doing well. When you're tempted to compare, look at Jesus Christ. His example will inspire you to do your very best. His loving acceptance will comfort you when you fall short of your goals.

then you will get the satisfaction of a job well done, and you won't need to compare yourself to anyone else. [5]For we are each responsible for our own conduct.

[6]Those who are taught the word of God should provide for their teachers, sharing all good things with them.

[7]Don't be misled—you cannot mock the justice of God. You will always harvest what you plant. [8]Those who live only to satisfy their own sinful nature will harvest decay and death from that sinful nature. But those who live to please the Spirit will harvest everlasting life from the Spirit. [9]So let's not get tired of doing what is good. At just the right time we will reap a harvest of blessing if we don't give up. [10]Therefore, whenever we have the opportunity, we should do good to everyone—especially to those in the family of faith.

PAUL'S FINAL ADVICE [11]NOTICE WHAT LARGE LETTERS I USE AS I WRITE THESE CLOSING WORDS IN MY OWN HANDWRITING.

[12]Those who are trying to force you to be circumcised want to look good to others. They don't want to be persecuted for teaching that the cross of Christ alone can save. [13]And even those who advocate circumcision don't keep the whole law themselves. They only want you to be circumcised so they can boast about it and claim you as their disciples.

[14]As for me, may I never boast about anything except the cross of our Lord Jesus Christ. Because of that cross,* my interest in this world has been crucified, and the world's interest in me has also died. [15]It doesn't matter whether we have been circumcised or not. What counts

6:1a Greek *Brothers, if a man.*   **6:1b** Greek *spiritual.*   **6:14** Or *Because of him.*

I WONDER...

I know that taking drugs is wrong, but the Bible doesn't talk about them. What should I say to someone who asks me about drugs?

Some topics the Bible doesn't mention directly. For example, you won't find a Scripture that discusses CDs with explicit lyrics. Maybe you would naturally avoid them or maybe you wouldn't, depending on what music you or your friends like. But you will find Scriptures on wisdom and the value of positive words.

You won't find a Scripture on drug usage (the illegal kind). But other Scriptures imply that this behavior is wrong.

In Galatians 5:21, Christians are warned against "envy, drunkenness, wild parties, and other sins like

these." In other words, any situation that causes you to lose control—whether through drugs or alcohol—is dangerous.

In health class and on TV commercials, you've heard that drugs can cause permanent damage to the human body. For that reason alone, resisting the temporary thrill of a chemical high is wise. That's just common sense. But drug abuse doesn't always mean the illegal kind. Many people have become addicted to prescription drugs and have had a tough time kicking the habit.

The Bible *is* specific about the best kind of control to be under: the Holy Spirit's control. Check out Galatians 5:22-23. See also Romans 12:1-2; 1 Corinthians 6:19-20; and 3 John 1:2.

is whether we have been transformed into a new creation. ¹⁶May God's peace and mercy be upon all who live by this principle; they are the new people of God.*

6:16 Greek *this principle, and upon the Israel of God.* **6:18** Greek *Brothers.*

¹⁷From now on, don't let anyone trouble me with these things. For I bear on my body the scars that show I belong to Jesus.

¹⁸Dear brothers and sisters,* may the grace of our Lord Jesus Christ be with your spirit. Amen.

EPHESIANS

An argument with a friend

   A hug from Mom

   A drive with Dad

   A note in your locker

   A prayer of thanks

Every event of every day underlines this fundamental fact: Life is made up of relationships. *We relate in a "horizontal" way to other people, and we relate in a "vertical" manner to our Creator. Pretty basic stuff, right?*

But here's where things get profound: Our problems, at every level, are due to broken relationships. *We fail to relate properly to God and to each other. We lie, cheat, steal, murder, divorce, have premarital sex, fight wars, pollute, ignore the needy, commit suicide, and do all the other wrong things we do.*

So, what's the remedy? In a nutshell: Jesus Christ can repair our broken relationships!

First, Jesus pardons our sins, bringing us into a right relationship with God. (Get this—by faith in Christ we are adopted into God's family! We become his children . . . forever!) Then Christ gives us the wisdom and the power to build stronger horizontal ties—with parents, friends, bosses . . . even enemies!

Can your relationships stand a little improving? Check out Ephesians. The first three chapters explain how Jesus made knowing God in a personal way possible for us. The rest of the book provides practical tips for getting along with people.

Hey, it just might change your life!

STATS

PURPOSE
To strengthen the faith of the believers in Ephesus by explaining the nature and purpose of the church—the body of Christ

AUTHOR
Paul

ORIGINAL AUDIENCE
The church at Ephesus

DATE WRITTEN
About A.D. 60

SETTING
The letter was not written to confront any heresy or problem. Paul wrote this letter from Rome during his imprisonment there and sent it with Tychicus (see Acts 20:4; Eph 6:21) to encourage the church in Ephesus. Paul spent over three years with the believers at Ephesus; he was very close to them. His last meeting with the Ephesian elders was at Miletus (Acts 20:17-38)—a meeting filled with great sadness since Paul was leaving them forever. This letter contains no specific references to people or problems in the Ephesian church, so Paul may have intended it to be read to all the area churches.

KEY PEOPLE
Paul, Tychicus

KEY POINTS

CHRIST, THE CENTER Jesus is the focus of history as well as the head of his body, the church. Because Christ is central to everything, his priorities must be central to us.

NEW FAMILY Because God through Christ paid our penalty for sin and forgave us, we have been reconciled to him. Being united with Christ means that we are one family in Christ. Because we all belong to him, we have the responsibility of living together in harmony.

CHRISTIAN CONDUCT Paul encourages all Christians to make wise decisions. With that goal in mind, God provides his Holy Spirit to enable us to live his way.

LOCATION OF EPHESUS
Ephesus was a strategic city, ranking in importance with Alexandria in Egypt and Antioch in Syria as a port. It lay on the westernmost edge of Asia Minor (modern-day Turkey), and was the most important port on the Aegean Sea on the main route from Rome to the east.

1

GREETINGS FROM PAUL This letter is from Paul, chosen by the will of God to be an apostle of Christ Jesus.

I am writing to God's holy people in Ephesus,* who are faithful followers of Christ Jesus.

² May God our Father and the Lord Jesus Christ give you grace and peace.

SPIRITUAL BLESSINGS ³ All praise to God, the Father of our Lord Jesus Christ, who has blessed us with every spiritual blessing in the heavenly realms because we are united with Christ. ⁴ Even before he made the world, God loved us and chose us in Christ to be holy and without fault in his eyes. ⁵ God decided in advance to adopt us into his own family by bringing us to himself through Jesus Christ. This is what he wanted to do, and it gave him great pleasure.

⁶ So we praise God for the glorious grace he has poured out on us who belong to his dear Son.* ⁷ He is so rich in kindness and grace that he purchased our freedom with the blood of his Son and forgave our sins. ⁸ He has showered his kindness on us, along with all wisdom and understanding.

⁹ God has now revealed to us his mysterious plan regarding Christ, a plan to fulfill his own good pleasure. ¹⁰ And this is the plan: At the right time he will bring everything together under the authority of Christ—everything in heaven and on earth. ¹¹ Furthermore, because we are united with Christ, we have received an inheritance from God,* for he chose us in advance, and he makes everything work out according to his plan.

¹² God's purpose was that we Jews who were the first to trust in Christ would bring praise and glory to God. ¹³ And now you Gentiles have also heard the truth, the Good News that God saves you. And when you believed in Christ, he identified you as his own* by giving you the Holy Spirit, whom he promised long ago. ¹⁴ The Spirit is God's guarantee that he will give us

UNSOLVED MYSTERY?
(1:3-5) Paul's declaration that God "chose us in Christ" emphasizes that God made forgiveness possible. We didn't influence God's decision to save us; he did it according to his plan (see also 2:10). The mystery of salvation originated in the timeless mind of God long before we existed. Because of Christ, we are "holy and without fault in his eyes." This is one mystery you don't have to solve—just believe.

1:1 The most ancient manuscripts do not include *in Ephesus.*
1:6 Greek *to us in the beloved.*   1:11 Or *we have become God's inheritance.*   1:13 Or *he put his seal on you.*

OUR LIFE BEFORE AND AFTER CHRIST

BEFORE	AFTER
Under God's curse	Loved by God
Doomed because of our sins	Shown God's mercy and given salvation
Went along with the crowd	Stand for Christ and truth
God's enemies	God's children
Enslaved to Satan	Free to love and serve Christ
Followed our evil thoughts and passions	Created anew to do good things
Under God's anger	Given undeserved favor
Spiritually dead	Given new spiritual life in Christ

the inheritance he promised and that he has purchased us to be his own people. He did this so we would praise and glorify him.

PAUL'S PRAYER FOR SPIRITUAL WISDOM
¹⁵Ever since I first heard of your strong faith in the Lord Jesus and your love for God's people everywhere,* ¹⁶I have not stopped thanking God for you. I pray for you constantly, ¹⁷asking God, the glorious Father of our Lord Jesus Christ, to give you spiritual wisdom* and insight so that you might grow in your knowledge of God. ¹⁸I pray that your hearts will be flooded with light so that you can understand the confident hope he has given to those he called—his holy people who are his rich and glorious inheritance.*

¹⁹I also pray that you will understand the incredible greatness of God's power for us who believe him. This is the same mighty power ²⁰that raised Christ from the dead and seated him in the place of honor at God's right hand in the heavenly realms. ²¹Now he is far above any ruler or authority or power or leader or anything else—not only in this world but also in the world to come. ²²God has put all things under the authority of Christ and has made him head over all things for the benefit of the church. ²³And the church is his body; it is made full and complete by Christ, who fills all things everywhere with himself.

2 **MADE ALIVE WITH CHRIST** Once you were dead because of your disobedience and your many sins. ²You used to live in sin, just like the rest of the world, obeying the devil—

the commander of the powers in the unseen world.* He is the spirit at work in the hearts of those who refuse to obey God. ³All of us used to live that way, following the passionate desires and inclinations of our sinful nature. By our very nature we were subject to God's anger, just like everyone else.

⁴But God is so rich in mercy, and he loved us so much, ⁵that even though we were dead because of our sins, he gave us life when he raised Christ from the dead. (It is only by God's grace that you have been saved!) ⁶For he raised us from the dead along with Christ and seated us with him in the heavenly realms because we are united with Christ Jesus. ⁷So God can point to us in all future ages as examples of the incredible wealth of his grace and kindness toward us, as shown in all he has done for us who are united with Christ Jesus.

⁸God saved you by his grace when you believed. And you can't take credit for this; it is a gift from God. ⁹Salvation is not a reward for the good things we have done, so none of us can boast about it. ¹⁰For we are God's masterpiece. He has created us anew in Christ Jesus, so we can do the good things he planned for us long ago.

ONENESS AND PEACE IN CHRIST
¹¹Don't forget that you Gentiles used to be outsiders. You were called "uncircumcised heathens" by the Jews, who were proud of their circumcision,

1:15 Some manuscripts read your faithfulness to the Lord Jesus and to God's people everywhere.   1:17 Or to give you the Spirit of wisdom.   1:18 Or called, and the rich and glorious inheritance he has given to his holy people.   2:2 Greek obeying the commander of the power of the air.

SPIRITUAL PRIDE
(2:11-13) Jews and Gentiles alike could be guilty of spiritual pride: Jews for thinking their ceremonies elevated them above everyone else; Gentiles for forgetting the hopelessness of their condition apart from Christ. Spiritual pride blinds us to our faults and magnifies the faults of others. Humility is the only cure for spiritual pride.

even though it affected only their bodies and not their hearts. [12]In those days you were living apart from Christ. You were excluded from citizenship among the people of Israel, and you did not know the covenant promises God had made to them. You lived in this world without God and without hope. [13]But now you have been united with Christ Jesus. Once you were far away from God, but now you have been brought near to him through the blood of Christ.

[14]For Christ himself has brought peace to us. He united Jews and Gentiles into one people when, in his own body on the cross, he broke down the wall of hostility that separated us. [15]He did this by ending the system of law with its commandments and regulations. He made peace between Jews and Gentiles by creating in himself one new people from the two groups. [16]Together as one body, Christ reconciled both groups to God by means of his death on the cross, and our hostility toward each other was put to death.

[17]He brought this Good News of peace to you Gentiles who were far away from him, and peace to the Jews who were near. [18]Now all of us can come to the Father through the same Holy Spirit because of what Christ has done for us.

A TEMPLE FOR THE LORD   [19]So now you Gentiles are no longer strangers and foreigners. You are citizens along with all of God's holy people. You are members of God's family. [20]Together, we are his house, built on the foundation of the apostles and the prophets. And the cornerstone is Christ Jesus himself. [21]We are care-

fully joined together in him, becoming a holy temple for the Lord. [22]Through him you Gentiles are also being made part of this dwelling where God lives by his Spirit.

3 GOD'S MYSTERIOUS PLAN REVEALED
When I think of all this, I, Paul, a prisoner of Christ Jesus for the benefit of you Gentiles* . . . [2]assuming, by the way, that you know God gave me the special responsibility of extending his grace to you Gentiles. [3]As I briefly wrote earlier, God himself revealed his mysterious plan to me. [4]As you read what I have written, you will understand my insight into this plan regarding Christ. [5]God did not reveal it to previous generations, but now by his Spirit he has revealed it to his holy apostles and prophets.

[6]And this is God's plan: Both Gentiles and Jews who believe the Good News share equally in the riches inherited by God's children. Both are part of the same body, and both enjoy the promise of blessings because they belong to Christ Jesus.* [7]By God's grace and mighty power, I have been given the privilege of serving him by spreading this Good News.

[8]Though I am the least deserving of all God's people, he graciously gave me the privilege of telling the Gentiles about the endless treasures available to them in Christ. [9]I was chosen to explain to everyone* this mysterious plan that God, the Creator of all things, had kept secret from the beginning.

[10]God's purpose in all this was to use the

3:1 Paul resumes this thought in verse 14: "When I think of all this, I fall to my knees and pray to the Father."   **3:6** Or *because they are united with Christ Jesus.*   **3:9** Some manuscripts do not include *to everyone.*

I WONDER . . .

What does it mean to "grow as a Christian"?

Spiritual growth is a lot like physical growth. To stay healthy and grow physically, we must eat the right foods, exercise, and get plenty of rest. You've heard that since you were a child. According to Scripture, especially passages like Ephesians 4:14-15, growing spiritually involves the same formula.

Christians must eat the right "spiritual food": God's Word. Yet many Christians try to survive on spiritual "fast food." That is, they watch Christian shows on TV, read Christian magazines, and listen to Christian music, while cutting the Bible out of their diet. But nothing builds the body—the body of Christ—like the Bible. Everything else is supplementary.

Exercise is another body builder. Christians

exercise through resisting temptation, enduring trials, serving others, and telling others about their faith. Temptation and problems test our character; serving others stretches our faith; telling people about Christ strengthens our love for him.

Christians rest through worship. Our world has a tendency to pull us in different directions like a rubber band stretched to the limit. We need sleep, rest, and times of vacation to get our physical batteries recharged. In the same way, we need worship to keep us spiritually renewed.

Spiritual growth takes time—a lifetime! This means growing in a relationship, not just changing our behavior. Growing a strong Christian life means learning how to love Jesus more each day, staying close to him, and getting to know him better.

church to display his wisdom in its rich variety to all the unseen rulers and authorities in the heavenly places. [11]This was his eternal plan, which he carried out through Christ Jesus our Lord.

[12]Because of Christ and our faith in him,* we can now come boldly and confidently into God's presence. [13]So please don't lose heart because of my trials here. I am suffering for you, so you should feel honored.

PAUL'S PRAYER FOR SPIRITUAL GROWTH

[14]When I think of all this, I fall to my knees and pray to the Father,* [15]the Creator of everything in heaven and on earth.* [16]I pray that from his glorious, unlimited resources he will empower you with inner strength through his Spirit. [17]Then Christ will make his home in your hearts as you trust in him. Your roots will grow down into God's love and keep you strong. [18]And may you have the power to understand, as all God's people should, how wide, how long, how high, and how deep his love is. [19]May you experience the love of Christ, though it is too great to understand fully. Then you will be made complete with all the fullness of life and power that comes from God.

[20]Now all glory to God, who is able, through his mighty power at work within us, to accomplish infinitely more than we might ask or think. [21]Glory to him in the church and in Christ Jesus through all generations forever and ever! Amen.

4 **UNITY IN THE BODY** Therefore I, a prisoner for serving the Lord, beg you to lead a life worthy of your calling, for you have been called by God. [2]Always be humble and gentle. Be patient with each other, making allowance for each other's faults because of your love. [3]Make every effort to keep yourselves united in the Spirit, binding yourselves together with peace. [4]For there is one body and one Spirit, just as you have been called to one glorious hope for the future. [5]There is one Lord, one faith, one baptism, [6]and one God and Father, who is over all and in all and living through all.

[7]However, he has given each one of us a special gift* through the generosity of Christ. [8]That is why the Scriptures say,

> "When he ascended to the heights,
>   he led a crowd of captives
>   and gave gifts to his people."*

3:12 Or *Because of Christ's faithfulness.*   3:14 Some manuscripts read *the Father of our Lord Jesus Christ.*   3:15 Or *from whom every family in heaven and on earth takes its name.*   4:7 Greek *a grace.*
4:8 Ps 68:18.   4:9 Or *to the lowest parts of the earth.*

> THEN WE WILL NO LONGER BE IMMATURE LIKE CHILDREN. WE WON'T BE TOSSED AND BLOWN ABOUT BY EVERY WIND OF NEW TEACHING. WE WILL NOT BE INFLUENCED WHEN PEOPLE TRY TO TRICK US WITH LIES SO CLEVER THEY SOUND LIKE THE TRUTH. {EPHESIANS 4:14}

[9]Notice that it says "he ascended." This clearly means that Christ also descended to our lowly world.* [10]And the same one who descended is the one who ascended higher than all the heavens, so that he might fill the entire universe with himself.

[11]Now these are the gifts Christ gave to the church: the apostles, the prophets, the evangelists, and the pastors and teachers. [12]Their responsibility is to equip God's people to do his work and build up the church, the body of Christ. [13]This will continue until we all come to such unity in our faith and knowledge of God's Son that we will be mature in the Lord, measuring up to the full and complete standard of Christ.

[14]Then we will no longer be immature like children. We won't be tossed and blown about by every wind of new teaching. We will not be influenced when people try to trick us with lies so clever they sound like the truth. [15]Instead, we will speak the truth in love, growing in every way more and more like Christ, who is the head of his body, the church. [16]He makes the whole body fit together perfectly. As each part does its own special work, it helps the other parts grow, so that the whole body is healthy and growing and full of love.

LIVING AS CHILDREN OF LIGHT

[17]With the Lord's authority I say this: Live no longer as the Gentiles do, for they are hopelessly confused. [18]Their minds are full of darkness; they wander far from the life God gives because they have closed their minds and hardened their hearts against him. [19]They have no sense of shame.

....

LITTLE BY LITTLE
(4:17-24) Paul encouraged the Ephesians to leave behind their old life of sin now that they were followers of Christ. The Christian life is a process. Despite our new nature in Christ, we don't automatically have all good thoughts and attitudes. Yet little by little, the Holy Spirit begins to change us.

As you look over the past year, do you see a process of change for the better in your thoughts, attitudes, and actions? Although change may be slow, it comes about if you trust God to change you. For more about our new nature as believers see Romans 6:6; 8:9; 2 Corinthians 5:17; Galatians 5:16-26; and Colossians 3:3-15.

IF YOU HONOR YOUR FATHER ᴬᴺᴰ MOTHER, "THINGS WILL GO WELL FOR YOU, AND YOU WILL HAVE A LONG LIFE ON THE EARTH." {EPHESIANS 6:3}

They live for lustful pleasure and eagerly practice every kind of impurity.

²⁰But that isn't what you learned about Christ. ²¹Since you have heard about Jesus and have learned the truth that comes from him, ²²throw off your old sinful nature and your former way of life, which is corrupted by lust and deception. ²³Instead, let the Spirit renew your thoughts and attitudes. ²⁴Put on your new nature, created to be like God—truly righteous and holy.

²⁵So stop telling lies. Let us tell our neighbors the truth, for we are all parts of the same body. ²⁶And "don't sin by letting anger control you."* Don't let the sun go down while you are still angry, ²⁷for anger gives a foothold to the devil.

²⁸If you are a thief, quit stealing. Instead, use your hands for good hard work, and then give generously to others in need. ²⁹Don't use foul

or abusive language. Let everything you say be good and helpful, so that your words will be an encouragement to those who hear them.

³⁰And do not bring sorrow to God's Holy Spirit by the way you live. Remember, he has identified you as his own,* guaranteeing that you will be saved on the day of redemption.

³¹Get rid of all bitterness, rage, anger, harsh words, and slander, as well as all types of evil behavior. ³²Instead, be kind to each other, tenderhearted, forgiving one another, just as God through Christ has forgiven you.

5 **LIVING IN THE LIGHT** Imitate God, therefore, in everything you do, because you are his dear children. ²Live a life filled with love, following the example of Christ. He loved us* and offered himself as a sacrifice for us, a pleasing aroma to God.

³Let there be no sexual immorality, impurity, or greed among you. Such sins have no place among God's people. ⁴Obscene stories, foolish talk, and coarse jokes—these are not for you. Instead, let there be thankfulness to God. ⁵You can be sure that no immoral, impure, or greedy person will inherit the Kingdom of Christ and of God. For a greedy person is an idolater, worshiping the things of this world.

⁶Don't be fooled by those who try to excuse these sins, for the anger of God will fall on all who disobey him. ⁷Don't participate in the things these people do. ⁸For once you were full of darkness, but now you have light from the Lord. So live as people of light! ⁹For this light within you produces only what is good and right and true.

¹⁰Carefully determine what pleases the Lord. ¹¹Take no part in the worthless deeds of evil and darkness; instead, expose them. ¹²It is shameful even to talk about the things that ungodly

4:26 Ps 4:4. 4:30 Or has put his seal on you. 5:2 Some manuscripts read loved you.

SPEAK OUT
(5:10-14) Paul advised the Ephesians to expose "worthless deeds of evil and darkness." That advice is for us as well. Often our silence is interpreted as approval. God needs people who will take a stand for what's right. Are you willing?

CHOICES
dating

Michelle met Greg at a party during the holidays, and they've been going out ever since. She fell in love with his quick wit, and he fell right into her bright brown eyes.

In some ways, theirs is a really positive relationship. Both have trusted Christ as their Savior. They share a lot of the same interests and goals. They even attend a campus Bible study together.

But the "Michelle-n-Greg" romance also has some negative aspects. For instance, on the weekends the two have gradually gotten into the habit of watching whatever movies happen to be on cable TV, which

usually means a large dose of skin, sex, and raw language. At the same time, Michelle has noticed that four-letter words that she never used to say are slipping out of her mouth with increasing frequency. And, as if that weren't enough to deal with, Michelle and Greg suddenly seem powerless to resist the constant sexual pressures they feel. They haven't gone all the way, but they've come awfully close.

"What's happened to us?" Michelle asks. "It's like we've thrown our standards out the window!"

What would you do in Michelle's situation? Find help in Ephesians 5:3-11.

people do in secret. 13But their evil intentions will be exposed when the light shines on them, 14for the light makes everything visible. This is why it is said,

"Awake, O sleeper,
    rise up from the dead,
    and Christ will give you light."

LIVING BY THE SPIRIT'S POWER 15So be careful how you live. Don't live like fools, but like those who are wise. 16Make the most of every opportunity in these evil days. 17Don't act thoughtlessly, but understand what the Lord wants you to do. 18Don't be drunk with wine, because that will ruin your life. Instead, be filled with the Holy Spirit, 19singing psalms and hymns and spiritual songs among yourselves, and making music to the Lord in your hearts. 20And give thanks for everything to God the Father in the name of our Lord Jesus Christ.

SPIRIT-GUIDED RELATIONSHIPS: WIVES AND HUSBANDS 21And further, submit to one another out of reverence for Christ.

22For wives, this means submit to your husbands as to the Lord. 23For a husband is the head of his wife as Christ is the head of the church. He is the Savior of his body, the church. 24As the church submits to Christ, so you wives should submit to your husbands in everything.

25For husbands, this means love your wives, just as Christ loved the church. He gave up his life for her 26to make her holy and clean, washed by the cleansing of God's word.* 27He did this to present her to himself as a glorious church without a spot or wrinkle or any other blemish. Instead, she will be holy and without fault. 28In the same way, husbands ought to love their wives as they love their own bodies. For a man who loves his wife actually shows love for himself. 29No one hates his own body but feeds and cares for it, just as Christ cares for the church. 30And we are members of his body.

31As the Scriptures say, "A man leaves his father and mother and is joined to his wife, and the two are united into one."* 32This is a great mystery, but it is an illustration of the way Christ and the church are one. 33So again I say, each man must love his wife as he loves himself, and the wife must respect her husband.

5:26 Greek washed by water with the word.   5:31 Gen 2:24.   6:1 Or Children, obey your parents who belong to the Lord; some manuscripts read simply Children, obey your parents.   6:2-3 Exod 20:12; Deut 5:16.

MY STORY: Connor

"Connor, what've you decided about going to the college we talked about? The deadline is coming up, isn't it?"

Though my dad was trying to be casual, I could tell he wanted an answer.

"Yeah, I've decided I don't want to go to that school. But you won't take that for an answer," I said.

"Connor," Dad began, but I could tell by his tone what he was going to say. We'd been through this too many times before. I didn't want to go; he wanted me to. His pressuring me just made me angry.

I talked to my youth pastor about it the next day. "What do you think the Bible says about your situation?" Les asked me.

"Well, I know I'm not supposed to be angry at my dad, but I can't stand him pressuring me."

"Read Ephesians and let me know what you discover," Les suggested. So I did, and I began to understand that I can't always do what I want. Loving God means wanting to do his will, not mine.

When I read Ephesians 6:1-3, I realized that God often chooses to work through my earthly parents. So, I tried to think through all the reasons why Dad wanted me to go to that particular college and why I didn't want to go. Finally, I decided to trust God and believe that he was leading me there.

Now I'm glad I attend this college. I'm really growing in my faith here.

6 **CHILDREN AND PARENTS** Children, obey your parents because you belong to the Lord,* for this is the right thing to do. 2"Honor your father and mother." This is the first commandment with a promise: 3If you honor your father and mother, "things will go well for you, and you will have a long life on the earth."*

4Fathers, do not provoke your children to anger by the way you treat them. Rather, bring them up with the discipline and instruction that comes from the Lord.

SLAVES AND MASTERS 5Slaves, obey your earthly masters with deep respect and fear.

Serve them sincerely as you would serve Christ. [6]Try to please them all the time, not just when they are watching you. As slaves of Christ, do the will of God with all your heart. [7]Work with enthusiasm, as though you were working for the Lord rather than for people. [8]Remember that the Lord will reward each one of us for the good we do, whether we are slaves or free.

[9]Masters, treat your slaves in the same way. Don't threaten them; remember, you both have the same Master in heaven, and he has no favorites.

THE WHOLE ARMOR OF GOD

[10]A final word: Be strong in the Lord and in his mighty power. [11]Put on all of God's armor so that you will be able to stand firm against all strategies of the devil. [12]For we* are not fighting against flesh-and-blood enemies, but against evil rulers and authorities of the unseen world, against mighty powers in this dark world, and against evil spirits in the heavenly places.

[13]Therefore, put on every piece of God's armor so you will be able to resist the enemy in the time of evil. Then after the battle you will still be standing firm. [14]Stand your ground, putting on the belt of truth and the body armor of God's righteousness. [15]For shoes, put on the peace that comes from the Good News so that you will be fully prepared.* [16]In addition to all of these, hold up the shield of faith to stop the fiery arrows of the devil.* [17]Put on salvation as your helmet, and take the sword of the Spirit, which is the word of God.

[18]Pray in the Spirit at all times and on every

6:12 Some manuscripts read *you.*　**6:15** Or *For shoes, put on the readiness to preach the Good News of peace with God.*　**6:16** Greek *the evil one.*

ULTIMATE ISSUES *THE ENEMY*

April 1989—Matamoros, Mexico: Police unearthed thirteen bodies, all showing signs of torture and mutilation. The cause? The murders were part of satanic sacrificial rites.

Forget about what you've heard about in horror movies or in novels. Satan—the enemy of Christians—is real. The Bible has many names for him: the devil, Satan, the deceiver, the evil one, and the tempter. And today, interest in Satan and occult activities are on the rise. What does the Bible teach about this being and those under his command?

In the Old Testament, the Hebrew word from which we get "Satan" primarily means "adversary." Passages such as 1 Chronicles 21:1, Job 1–2, and Zechariah 3 portray Satan as an accuser of God's people. It is historically believed that Satan was behind the serpent that deceived Eve in Genesis 3. Many interpret Isaiah 14:12 (the beginning of a prophecy about the "king of Babylon") as a reference to Satan: "How you are fallen from heaven, O shining star, son of the morning! You have been thrown down to the earth, you who destroyed the nations of the world."

Turning to the New Testament, Matthew 4:1-11 and Mark 1:12-13 describe Jesus' temptation by Satan. In Matthew 12:25-29, Jesus describes Satan as a powerful ruler over a demonic kingdom. John quotes Jesus as referring to Satan as "the ruler of this world" (John 12:31; 14:30; 16:11). Passages such as Matthew 13:19, 2 Corinthians 4:4, and Ephesians 6:16 show that Satan's goal is to keep people from understanding and believing God's Word and the good news of salvation through Christ. Ultimately, Satan wants to destroy us: "Stay alert! Watch out for your great enemy, the devil. He prowls around like a roaring lion, looking for someone to devour" (1 Pet 5:8; see also 2 Thes 2:1-12 and Rev 13).

Okay. That's the bad news. Now here's the good news: God has already defeated this enemy. Satan is a powerful enemy, but the universe is not a cosmic tug-of-war contest between God and Satan. For all Satan's power and cunning, he is not God's equal; he is one of God's creatures, given some freedom to cause evil for a period of time. We can't really understand why God allows Satan this freedom, but we can be certain that God is still in control. Satan is like a mean dog on a leash. If you get close to him he can hurt you; but his Master can always rein him in. (Just turn to the last book of the Bible, Revelation, to see how the battle turns out.)

But even a defeated enemy still has claws. From time to time you'll find yourself in a skirmish with this enemy. But God doesn't leave you defenseless. That's the message of Ephesians 6:10-18. "Put on all of God's armor so that you will be able to stand firm against all strategies of the devil" (6:11). The rest of the passage talks about what you can do to defend yourself against an attack. Over 50 years ago, in *The Screwtape Letters*, C. S. Lewis wrote: "There are two equal and opposite errors into which our race can fall about the devils. One is to disbelieve in their existence. The other is to believe, and to feel an excessive and unhealthy interest in them. They themselves are equally pleased by both errors."

The Bible clearly teaches that a literal, personal evil being called Satan exists. He is not to be taken lightly, but neither does the Christian need to be afraid. If you're a believer, you have the power of God behind you. We know the one who holds Satan's leash securely in his nail-scarred hands. ∎

GOD'S ARMOR FOR US

We are engaged in a spiritual battle—all believers find themselves subject to Satan's attacks because they are no longer on Satan's side. Thus, Paul tells us in Ephesians 6:10-17 to use every piece of God's armor to resist Satan's attacks and to stand true to God in the midst of them.

PIECE OF ARMOR	USE	APPLICATION
BELT	Truth	Satan fights with lies, and sometimes his lies sound like truth; but believers have God's truth, which can defeat Satan's lies.
BODY ARMOR	God's righteousness	Satan often attacks our heart—the seat of our emotions, self-worth, and trust. God's righteousness is the breastplate that protects our heart and ensures his approval. He approves of us because we have trusted Christ to save us and cleanse our hearts from sin.
SHOES	The peace that comes from the Good News	Satan wants us to think that telling others the Good News is a worthless and hopeless task—the size of the task is too big, and the negative responses are too much to handle. But the "shoes" God gives us are the true peace that is available in God, which prepares us to share the news with others.
SHIELD	Faith	The shield of faith protects us from Satan's fiery darts in the form of insults, setbacks, and temptations. With God's perspective, we can see beyond our circumstances and know that ultimate victory is ours.
HELMET	Salvation	Satan wants to make us doubt God, Jesus, and our salvation. The helmet protects our mind from doubting God's saving work for us.
SWORD	The Word of God	The sword is the only weapon of offense in this list of armor. There are times when we need to take the offensive against Satan. When we are tempted, we need to trust in the truth of God's Word.

occasion. Stay alert and be persistent in your prayers for all believers everywhere.*

¹⁹And pray for me, too. Ask God to give me the right words so I can boldly explain God's mysterious plan that the Good News is for Jews and Gentiles alike.* ²⁰I am in chains now, still preaching this message as God's ambassador. So pray that I will keep on speaking boldly for him, as I should.

6:18 Greek *all of God's holy people.*   6:19 Greek *explain the mystery of the Good News;* some manuscripts read simply *explain the mystery.*   6:23 Greek *brothers.*

FINAL GREETINGS ²¹To bring you up to date, Tychicus will give you a full report about what I am doing and how I am getting along. He is a beloved brother and faithful helper in the Lord's work. ²²I have sent him to you for this very purpose—to let you know how we are doing and to encourage you.

²³Peace be with you, dear brothers and sisters,* and may God the Father and the Lord Jesus Christ give you love with faithfulness. ²⁴May God's grace be eternally upon all who love our Lord Jesus Christ.

PHILIPPIANS

Time for a little daydreaming:

Scenario #1—A high-powered attorney calls to inform you that a distant relative has left you her entire estate worth several million bucks!

Scenario #2—You ace all of your midterm exams.

Scenario #3—In the biggest game of the year, you score with one second left to give your school an upset victory.

Scenario #4—You learn that the most attractive member of the opposite sex (in your whole school!) likes you.

Some dreams, huh? So, do you think you could get excited about those situations? Okay, let's daydream some more:

Scenario #5—While using the computer, your dad accidentally deletes your term paper—the one you worked on for over a month that's due today.

Scenario #6—You develop a huge zit on the end of your nose on the night before the most important date of your life.

Scenario #7—You've trained for months for track team tryouts. On the way to school, you get in a wreck and break your ankle.

Scenario #8—Your latest crush dumps you for your best friend!

All right, so these are more like nightmares. Is it possible to be joyful in bad situations like these?

Believe it or not, it is possible to be content—even in the middle of horrible circumstances.

Facing problems or trials? Get a fresh perspective. Read Philippians, Paul's letter to the Christians in Philippi. The message is clear: Joy and contentment really can be ours . . . as long as we keep trusting God even when bad times hit.

KEY POINTS

HUMILITY Christ showed true humility when he laid aside his rights and privileges as God to become human. Laying aside self-interest is essential to all our relationships. When we give up the need to receive credit and praise, we'll be able to serve with joy, love, and kindness.

UNITY Paul encouraged the Philippians to agree with one another, to stop complaining, and to work together. In every church, in every generation, there are issues, loyalties, and conflicts that divide people. However, the love of Christ unites all believers.

CHRISTIAN LIVING Paul provides tips for living a successful Christian life. Developing as a mature Christian requires discipline, obedience, and perseverance.

JOY Believers can experience contentment and peace no matter what happens. This joy comes from knowing Christ personally and from depending on his strength rather than on our own.

LOCATION OF PHILIPPI
Philippi sat on the Egnatian Way, the main transportation route in Macedonia, an extension of the Appian Way, which joined the eastern portion of the Roman Empire with Italy.

1

GREETINGS FROM PAUL This letter is from Paul and Timothy, slaves of Christ Jesus.

I am writing to all of God's holy people in Philippi who belong to Christ Jesus, including the elders* and deacons.

²May God our Father and the Lord Jesus Christ give you grace and peace.

PAUL'S THANKSGIVING AND PRAYER ³Every time I think of you, I give thanks to my God. ⁴Whenever I pray, I make my requests for all of you with joy, ⁵for you have been my partners in spreading the Good News about Christ from the time you first heard it until now. ⁶And I am certain that God, who began the good work within you, will continue his work until it is finally finished on the day when Christ Jesus returns.

⁷So it is right that I should feel as I do about all of you, for you have a special place in my heart. You share with me the special favor of God, both in my imprisonment and in defending and confirming the truth of the Good News. ⁸God knows how much I love you and long for you with the tender compassion of Christ Jesus.

⁹I pray that your love will overflow more and more, and that you will keep on growing in knowledge and understanding. ¹⁰For I want you to understand what really matters, so that you may live pure and blameless lives until the day of Christ's return. ¹¹May you always be filled with the fruit of your salvation—the righteous character produced in your life by Jesus Christ*—for this will bring much glory and praise to God.

PAUL'S JOY THAT CHRIST IS PREACHED ¹²And I want you to know, my dear brothers and sisters,* that everything that has happened to me here has helped to spread the Good News. ¹³For everyone here, including the whole palace guard,* knows that I am in chains because of Christ. ¹⁴And because of my imprisonment,

....

JOY SOURCE
(1:4-5) This is the first of many times Paul uses the word joy in his letter. Here he wrote that the Philippians were a source of joy when he prayed. By helping Paul, they were helping to spread the gospel. Paul knew that the Philippians were willing to be used by God for whatever task he had in store for them. Have others ever commented that you're a source of joy for them? In what ways do you show a willingness to do whatever God wants?

1:1 Or *overseers;* or *bishops.*   1:11 Greek *with the fruit of righteousness through Jesus Christ.*   1:12 Greek *brothers.*
1:13 Greek *including all the Praetorium.*

most of the believers* here have gained confidence and boldly speak God's message* without fear.

¹⁵It's true that some are preaching out of jealousy and rivalry. But others preach about Christ with pure motives. ¹⁶They preach because they love me, for they know I have been appointed to defend the Good News. ¹⁷Those others do not have pure motives as they preach about Christ. They preach with selfish ambition, not sincerely, intending to make my chains more painful to me. ¹⁸But that doesn't matter. Whether their motives are false or genuine, the message about Christ is being preached either way, so I rejoice. And I will continue to rejoice. ¹⁹For I know that as you pray for me and the Spirit of Jesus Christ helps me, this will lead to my deliverance.

PAUL'S LIFE FOR CHRIST ²⁰For I fully expect and hope that I will never be ashamed, but that I will continue to be bold for Christ, as I have been in the past. And I trust that my life will bring honor to Christ, whether I live or die. ²¹For to me, living means living for Christ, and dying is even better. ²²But if I live, I can do more fruitful work for Christ. So I really don't know which is better. ²³I'm torn between two desires: I long to go and be with Christ, which would be far better for me. ²⁴But for your sakes, it is better that I continue to live.

²⁵Knowing this, I am convinced that I will remain alive so I can continue to help all of you grow and experience the joy of your faith. ²⁶And when I come to you again, you will have even more reason to take pride in Christ Jesus because of what he is doing through me.

LIVE AS CITIZENS OF HEAVEN ²⁷Above all, you must live as citizens of heaven, conducting yourselves in a manner worthy of the Good News about Christ. Then, whether I come and see you again or only hear about you, I will know that you are standing together with one spirit and one purpose, fighting together for the faith, which is the Good News. ²⁸Don't be intimidated in any way by your enemies. This will be a sign to them that they are going to be destroyed, but that you are going to be saved, even by God himself. ²⁹For you have been given not only the privilege of trusting in Christ but also the privilege of suffering for him. ³⁰We are in this struggle together. You have seen my

struggle in the past, and you know that I am still in the midst of it.

2 **HAVE THE ATTITUDE OF CHRIST** Is there any encouragement from belonging to Christ? Any comfort from his love? Any fellowship together in the Spirit? Are your hearts tender and compassionate? ²Then make me truly happy by agreeing wholeheartedly with each other, loving one another, and working together with one mind and purpose.

³Don't be selfish; don't try to impress others. Be humble, thinking of others as better than yourselves. ⁴Don't look out only for your own interests, but take an interest in others, too.

⁵You must have the same attitude that Christ Jesus had.

⁶ Though he was God,*
   he did not think of equality with God
   as something to cling to.
⁷ Instead, he gave up his divine privileges*;
   he took the humble position of a slave*
   and was born as a human being.
When he appeared in human form,*
⁸   he humbled himself in obedience to God
   and died a criminal's death on a cross.

⁹ Therefore, God elevated him to the place
      of highest honor
   and gave him the name above all other
      names,
¹⁰ that at the name of Jesus every knee
      should bow,
   in heaven and on earth and under the
      earth,
¹¹ and every tongue confess that Jesus Christ
      is Lord,
   to the glory of God the Father.

SHINE BRIGHTLY FOR CHRIST ¹²Dear friends, you always followed my instructions when I was with you. And now that I am away, it is even more important. Work hard to show the results of your salvation, obeying God with deep

1:14a Greek *brothers in the Lord.*   **1:14b** Some manuscripts read *speak the message.*   **2:6** Or *Being in the form of God.*   **2:7a** Greek *he emptied himself.*   **2:7b** Or *the form of a slave.*   **2:7c** Some English translations put this phrase in verse 8.

SUFFERING
(1:29-30) *Suffering, in and of itself, is not a privilege. But when we suffer because we faithfully represent Christ, we know that our message and example are having an effect and that God considers us worthy to represent him (see Acts 5:41). Suffering has these additional benefits: (1) It takes us out of our comfort zone. (2) It weeds out those who are only half-serious about God. (3) It strengthens the faith of those who endure. (4) It serves as an example to others who may follow us. Suffering for our faith doesn't mean we've done something wrong. In fact, the opposite is often true—it may verify that we have been faithful.*

reverence and fear. [13]For God is working in you, giving you the desire and the power to do what pleases him.

[14]Do everything without complaining and arguing, [15]so that no one can criticize you. Live clean, innocent lives as children of God, shining like bright lights in a world full of crooked and perverse people. [16]Hold firmly to the word of life; then, on the day of Christ's return, I will be proud that I did not run the race in vain and that my work was not useless. [17]But I will rejoice even if I lose my life, pouring it out like a liquid offering to God,* just like your faithful service is an offering to God. And I want all of you to share that joy. [18]Yes, you should rejoice, and I will share your joy.

PAUL COMMENDS TIMOTHY [19]If the Lord Jesus is willing, I hope to send Timothy to you soon for a visit. Then he can cheer me up by telling me how you are getting along. [20]I have no one else like Timothy, who genuinely cares about your welfare. [21]All the others care only for themselves and not for what matters to Jesus Christ. [22]But you know how Timothy has proved himself. Like a son with his father, he has served with me in preaching the Good News. [23]I hope to send him to you just as soon as I find out what is going to happen to me here. [24]And I have confidence from the Lord that I myself will come to see you soon.

PAUL COMMENDS EPAPHRODITUS [25]Meanwhile, I thought I should send Epaphroditus back to you. He is a true brother, co-worker, and fellow soldier. And he was your messenger to help me in my need. [26]I am sending him because he has been longing to see you, and he was very distressed that you heard he was ill. [27]And he certainly was ill; in fact, he almost died. But God had mercy on him—and also on me, so that I would not have one sorrow after another.

[28]So I am all the more anxious to send him back to you, for I know you will be glad to see him, and then I will not be so worried about you. [29]Welcome him with Christian love* and with great joy, and give him the honor that people like him deserve. [30]For he risked his life for the work of Christ, and he was at the point of death while doing for me what you couldn't do from far away.

3 **THE PRICELESS VALUE OF KNOWING CHRIST** Whatever happens, my dear brothers and sisters,* rejoice in the Lord. I never get tired of telling you these things, and I do it to safeguard your faith.

[2]Watch out for those dogs, those people who do evil, those mutilators who say you must be circumcised to be saved. [3]For we who worship by the Spirit of God* are the ones who are truly circumcised. We rely on what Christ Jesus has done for us. We put no confidence in human effort, [4]though I could have confidence in my own effort if anyone could. Indeed, if others have reason for confidence in their own efforts, I have even more!

[5]I was circumcised when I was eight days old. I am a pure-blooded citizen of Israel and a member of the tribe of Benjamin—a real Hebrew if there ever was one! I was a member of the Pharisees, who demand the strictest obedience to the Jewish law. [6]I was so zealous that I harshly persecuted the church. And as for righteousness, I obeyed the law without fault.

[7]I once thought these things were valuable,

2:17 Greek *I will rejoice even if I am to be poured out as a liquid offering.* **2:29** Greek *in the Lord.* **3:1** Greek *brothers;* also in 3:13, 17. **3:3** Some manuscripts read *worship God in spirit;* one early manuscript reads *worship in spirit.*

CHOICES
self

Marie's favorite topic for discussion, her major concern, the number one thing on her mind is . . . Marie. Seriously, when we say she's stuck on herself, we're talking really stuck—super-glue style.

Just look:
- When Beth was really upset at not being asked to Homecoming, Marie responded by going on and on about her date.
- When anyone asks, "How was your weekend?" Marie gives a twenty-minute discourse. (Funny how she never asks anyone else that question.)

- When her favorite daytime TV show was interrupted last summer by a live news report about a four-alarm apartment fire, Marie got emotional. Not at the fact that people were dying and losing their homes, but at the fact that she had to miss her program.
- When Marie's neighbor called, desperately needing a babysitter at the last minute, Marie wouldn't go, even though she had no other plans. She ended up going to work out at the health club.
- Whenever Marie gets her allowance or paycheck, or any other unexpected cash, she immediately goes to the mall and buys something for herself.

Do you know anyone like Marie? Are you like Marie? See Philippians 2:3-11 for a better way.

but now I consider them worthless because of what Christ has done. [8]Yes, everything else is worthless when compared with the infinite value of knowing Christ Jesus my Lord. For his sake I have discarded everything else, counting it all as garbage, so that I could gain Christ [9]and become one with him. I no longer count on my own righteousness through obeying the law; rather, I become righteous through faith in Christ.* For God's way of making us right with himself depends on faith. [10]I want to know Christ and experience the mighty power that raised him from the dead. I want to suffer with him, sharing in his death, [11]so that one way or another I will experience the resurrection from the dead!

PRESSING TOWARD THE GOAL [12]I don't mean to say that I have already achieved these things or that I have already reached perfection. But I press on to possess that perfection for which Christ Jesus first possessed me. [13]No, dear brothers and sisters, I have not achieved it,* but I focus on this one thing: Forgetting the past and looking forward to what lies ahead, [14]I press on to reach the end of the race and receive the heavenly prize for which God, through Christ Jesus, is calling us.

[15]Let all who are spiritually mature agree on these things. If you disagree on some point, I believe God will make it plain to you. [16]But we must hold on to the progress we have already made.

[17]Dear brothers and sisters, pattern your lives after mine, and learn from those who follow our example. [18]For I have told you often before, and I say it again with tears in my eyes, that there are many whose conduct shows they are really enemies of the cross of Christ. [19]They are headed for destruction. Their god is their appetite, they brag about shameful things, and they think only about this life here on earth. [20]But we are citizens of heaven, where the Lord Jesus Christ lives. And we are eagerly waiting for him to return as our Savior. [21]He will take our weak mortal bodies and change them into glorious bodies like his own, using the same power with which he will bring everything under his control.

4 Therefore, my dear brothers and sisters,* stay true to the Lord. I love you and long to see you, dear friends, for you are my joy and the crown I receive for my work.

3:9 Or *through the faithfulness of Christ.* 3:13 Some manuscripts read *not yet achieved it.* 4:1 Greek *brothers;* also in 4:8. 4:3 Or *loyal Syzygus.*

MY STORY: Jeff

My grandmother was in the hospital. I heard my mom telling someone on the phone that the doctors weren't sure whether Grandma would make it; things looked pretty serious.

I went to my room feeling agitated. As far as I knew, Grandma didn't know that Jesus died for her sins. I had always wanted to tell her, but how would I do it? I felt so unsure of myself. What would I say? Would she even listen to me?

I prayed about this for quite a while. I knew God would want my grandmother to hear that God loves her and wants to save her for eternity. I tried to think through what I could say to her. Then I started reading my Bible. As I read Philippians, the thirteenth verse in chapter 4 leaped out at me: "I can do everything through Christ, who gives me strength." I believed that God was assuring me that I would know what to say to my grandmother.

I went to the hospital and told my grandmother about Jesus. She listened and later accepted Christ as her Lord and Savior!

One week later, she died. But I know she is with the Lord now.

WORDS OF ENCOURAGEMENT [2]Now I appeal to Euodia and Syntyche. Please, because you belong to the Lord, settle your disagreement. [3]And I ask you, my true partner,* to help these two women, for they worked hard with me in telling others the Good News. They worked along with Clement and the rest of my co-workers, whose names are written in the Book of Life.

[4]Always be full of joy in the Lord. I say it again—rejoice! [5]Let everyone see that you are considerate in all you do. Remember, the Lord is coming soon.

[6]Don't worry about anything; instead, pray about everything. Tell God what you need, and thank him for all he has done. [7]Then you will

NO WORRIES
(4:6-18) Imagine never being worried about anything! That seems impossible. But Paul's advice is to turn our worries into prayers. Do you want to worry less? Then pray more! Whenever you start to worry, stop and pray.

FOR I CAN DO EVERYTHING THROUGH CHRIST, WHO GIVES ME STRENGTH. PHILIPPIANS 4:13

experience God's peace, which exceeds anything we can understand. His peace will guard your hearts and minds as you live in Christ Jesus.

⁸And now, dear brothers and sisters, one final thing. Fix your thoughts on what is true, and honorable, and right, and pure, and lovely, and admirable. Think about things that are excellent and worthy of praise. ⁹Keep putting into practice all you learned and received from me—everything you heard from me and saw me doing. Then the God of peace will be with you.

PAUL'S THANKS FOR THEIR GIFTS ¹⁰How I praise the Lord that you are concerned about me again. I know you have always been concerned for me, but you didn't have the chance to help me. ¹¹Not that I was ever in need, for I have learned how to be content with whatever I have. ¹²I know how to live on almost nothing or with everything. I have learned the secret of living in every situation, whether it is with a full stomach or empty, with plenty or little. ¹³For I

can do everything through Christ,* who gives me strength. ¹⁴Even so, you have done well to share with me in my present difficulty.

¹⁵As you know, you Philippians were the only ones who gave me financial help when I first brought you the Good News and then traveled on from Macedonia. No other church did this. ¹⁶Even when I was in Thessalonica you sent help more than once. ¹⁷I don't say this because I want a gift from you. Rather, I want you to receive a reward for your kindness.

¹⁸At the moment I have all I need—and more! I am generously supplied with the gifts you sent me with Epaphroditus. They are a sweet-smelling sacrifice that is acceptable and pleasing to God. ¹⁹And this same God who takes care of me will supply all your needs from his glorious riches, which have been given to us in Christ Jesus.

²⁰Now all glory to God our Father forever and ever! Amen.

PAUL'S FINAL GREETINGS ²¹Give my greetings to each of God's holy people—all who belong to Christ Jesus. The brothers who are with me send you their greetings. ²²And all the rest of God's people send you greetings, too, especially those in Caesar's household.

²³May the grace of the Lord Jesus Christ be with your spirit.

4:13 Greek through the one.

COOPERATION SECRET

(4:23) In many ways the church in Philippi was a model congregation made up of different kinds of people who had learned to work together. The whole church—the body of Christ—has a similar makeup. Want to know the secret to cooperation? Imitate Christ. By focusing on Christ we experience unity, humility, joy, and peace.

COLOSSIANS

Will the real Jesus please stand up?

Sometimes it's hard to know what to think about Jesus Christ.

Some believers call him God with skin on—the second person of the Trinity and the carpenter from Nazareth all rolled into one. But some nonbelievers insist that he was nothing more than just a good man. Still others regard Jesus as a troublesome politician with a messiah complex, who ended up being executed. Then there is the Hollywood Jesus—weak, wishy-washy, misguided, filled with contradictions, and surrounded by controversy.

How about the popular New Age Jesus who is but one of many ways to God? And don't forget some cults who claim that Christ is living on the earth now in the person of their leader!

So, was Jesus just a good man or a great moral teacher? Or was he, as Islam teaches, a prophet like Moses, Buddha, and Mohammed? Was he just one of many gods? Was he truly divine, or was he simply one manifestation of a divine, universal force?

Hundreds of conflicting ideas are floating around about who Jesus is. But only one of the views can be true—which makes the others wrong . . . and extremely dangerous!

Wondering what's true about Jesus? Check out the letter to the Colossians. See for yourself why the apostle Paul considered him to be "supreme over all creation" (1:15).

STATS

PURPOSE
To combat errors in the church and to show that believers have everything they need in Christ

AUTHOR
Paul

ORIGINAL AUDIENCE
The churches at Colosse (and Laodicea) in Asia Minor

DATE WRITTEN
About A.D. 60

SETTING
Paul had never visited Colosse. Evidently Epaphras and other converts from Paul's missionary travels had founded the church. The church, however, had been infiltrated by religious relativism with some believers attempting to combine elements of heathenism and secular philosophy with Christian doctrine. Writing from Rome, where he was imprisoned, Paul confronted these false teachings and affirmed the sufficiency of Christ.

KEY PEOPLE
Paul, Timothy, Tychicus, Onesimus, Aristarchus, Mark, Epaphras

KEY PLACES
Colosse, Laodicea

KEY POINTS

GOD WITH US Jesus is the exact reflection of the invisible God. He is eternal, preexistent, all-powerful, and equal with the Father. To recognize Jesus as God means to allow him to call the shots in our lives.

HEAD OF THE CHURCH Christ is the founder and leader of the church and the highest authority on earth. To acknowledge Christ as our leader, we must welcome his leadership in all we do or think.

UNITED WITH CHRIST Jesus' death, burial, and resurrection make forgiveness possible. Because our sin has been forgiven and we have been reconciled to God, we have a union with Christ that can never be broken.

MAN-MADE RELIGION False teachers promoted the need to follow man-made rules. We must not let our hunger for a more fulfilling Christian experience cause us to trust in a teacher, group, or system of thought more than in Christ himself. Christ is our hope and our true source of wisdom.

LOCATION OF COLOSSE
Paul had undoubtedly been through Laodicea on his third missionary journey because it lay on the main route to Ephesus, but he had never been to Colosse. Though a large city with a significant population, Colosse was smaller and less important than the nearby cities of Laodicea and Hierapolis.

1 GREETINGS FROM PAUL

This letter is from Paul, chosen by the will of God to be an apostle of Christ Jesus, and from our brother Timothy.

²We are writing to God's holy people in the city of Colosse, who are faithful brothers and sisters* in Christ.

May God our Father give you grace and peace.

PAUL'S THANKSGIVING AND PRAYER

³We always pray for you, and we give thanks to God, the Father of our Lord Jesus Christ. ⁴For we have heard of your faith in Christ Jesus and your love for all of God's people, ⁵which come from your confident hope of what God has reserved for you in heaven. You have had this expectation ever since you first heard the truth of the Good News.

⁶This same Good News that came to you is going out all over the world. It is bearing fruit everywhere by changing lives, just as it changed your lives from the day you first heard and understood the truth about God's wonderful grace.

⁷You learned about the Good News from Epaphras, our beloved co-worker. He is Christ's faithful servant, and he is helping us on your behalf.* ⁸He has told us about the love for others that the Holy Spirit has given you.

⁹So we have not stopped praying for you since we first heard about you. We ask God to give you complete knowledge of his will and to give you spiritual wisdom and understanding. ¹⁰Then the way you live will always honor and please the Lord, and your lives will produce every kind of good fruit. All the while, you will grow as you learn to know God better and better.

¹¹We also pray that you will be strengthened

CHANGED
(1:6) Wherever Paul went, he preached the gospel—to Gentile audiences, to hostile Jewish leaders, and even to his Roman guards. Whenever people believed in the message he spoke, they were changed. God's Word is not just for our information; it is for our transformation! Becoming a Christian means beginning a whole new relationship with God, not just turning over a new leaf or determining to do right. New believers have a changed purpose, direction, attitude, and behavior. They no longer seek to serve themselves but to serve God. In what areas has God's Word changed your life? What areas still need changing?

1:2 Greek *faithful brothers.* **1:7** Or *he is ministering on your behalf;* some manuscripts read *he is ministering on our behalf.*

with all his glorious power so you will have all the endurance and patience you need. May you be filled with joy,* [12] always thanking the Father. He has enabled you to share in the inheritance that belongs to his people, who live in the light. [13] For he has rescued us from the kingdom of darkness and transferred us into the Kingdom of his dear Son, [14] who purchased our freedom* and forgave our sins.

CHRIST IS SUPREME

[15] Christ is the visible image of the
    invisible God.
    He existed before anything was created
      and is supreme over all creation,*
[16] for through him God created everything
      in the heavenly realms and on earth.
    He made the things we can see
    and the things we can't see—
    such as thrones, kingdoms, rulers, and
      authorities in the unseen world.
    Everything was created through him and
      for him.
[17] He existed before anything else,
    and he holds all creation together.
[18] Christ is also the head of the church,
    which is his body.
    He is the beginning,
      supreme over all who rise from the dead.*
    So he is first in everything.
[19] For God in all his fullness
    was pleased to live in Christ,
[20] and through him God reconciled
      everything to himself.
    He made peace with everything in heaven
      and on earth
    by means of Christ's blood on the cross.

[21] This includes you who were once far away from God. You were his enemies, separated from him by your evil thoughts and actions. [22] Yet now he has reconciled you to himself through the death of Christ in his physical body. As a result, he has brought you into his own presence, and you are holy and blameless as you stand before him without a single fault.

[23] But you must continue to believe this truth and stand firmly in it. Don't drift away from the assurance you received when you heard the Good News. The Good News has been preached all over the world, and I, Paul, have been appointed as God's servant to proclaim it.

PAUL'S WORK FOR THE CHURCH [24] I am glad when I suffer for you in my body, for I am participating in the sufferings of Christ that continue for his body, the church. [25] God has given me the responsibility of serving his church by proclaiming his entire message to you. [26] This message was kept secret for centuries and generations past, but now it has been revealed to God's people. [27] For God wanted them to know that the riches and glory of Christ are for you Gentiles, too. And this is the secret: Christ lives in you. This gives you assurance of sharing his glory.

[28] So we tell others about Christ, warning everyone and teaching everyone with all the wisdom God has given us. We want to present them to God, perfect* in their relationship to Christ. [29] That's why I work and struggle so hard, depending on Christ's mighty power that works within me.

2 I want you to know how much I have agonized for you and for the church at Laodicea, and for many other believers who have never met me personally. [2] I want them to be encouraged and knit together by strong ties of love. I want them to have complete confidence that they understand God's mysterious plan, which is Christ himself. [3] In him lie hidden all the treasures of wisdom and knowledge.

[4] I am telling you this so no one will deceive you with well-crafted arguments. [5] For though I am far away from you, my heart is with you. And I rejoice that you are living as you should and that your faith in Christ is strong.

FREEDOM FROM RULES AND NEW LIFE IN CHRIST [6] And now, just as you accepted Christ Jesus as your Lord, you must continue to follow him. [7] Let your roots grow down into him, and let your lives be built on him. Then your faith will grow strong in the truth you were taught, and you will overflow with thankfulness.

[8] Don't let anyone capture you with empty philosophies and high-sounding nonsense

1:11 Or all the patience and endurance you need with joy.
1:14 Some manuscripts add with his blood.   1:15 Or He is the firstborn of all creation.   1:18 Or the firstborn from the dead.
1:28 Or mature.

HOW TO PRAY
(1:9-14) *Sometimes we wonder how to pray for missionaries and other leaders we have never met. Although Paul had never met the Colossians, he faithfully prayed for them. His prayers remind us to pray for others, whether we know them or not. All believers have a need to grow spiritually. You can pray for someone to understand God's will, gain wisdom and spiritual understanding, honor God, bear fruit (love, joy, peace, patience, etc.), appreciate God in a deeper way, be filled with God's strength, stay full of Christ's joy, and always be thankful.*

I have been a Christian for about two months and I feel so far behind spiritually, compared to friends who have been Christians for a lot longer. Sometimes it gets pretty discouraging. How do I catch up?

Have you ever planted a seed in a clear plastic cup? If the seed was planted close enough to the edge, you would see that the roots would grow downward first; then a few days later a plant would appear above the dirt. It's miraculous!

When you took the first step of faith to trust Christ with your life, that was like the seed being planted. From this point it's up to you and God to nourish the seed and let the roots grow deep (see Col 2:6-7).

The only difference between you and your friends is that they have had more time to spread their roots down deep. They have let their "roots grow down into

him" and their lives "be built on him" for a longer period of time. Getting to know Jesus happens by spending time with him. As with any relationship, time together helps you to appreciate God's character and will lead to a greater love for him (2 Pet 3:18).

Remember, too, that God doesn't compare one Christian to another. So you shouldn't, either. That would be like a father wanting his two-year-old son to throw a baseball as well as his nine-year-old. He can't!

As Christians, we never get to a point where we are totally mature. Our love and appreciation for God can always grow deeper as he shows us new areas in our life with which to trust him.

Enjoy these beginning stages of your faith by taking in all of the spiritual nourishment you can handle. Remember, the stronger and deeper your roots grow below the surface, the more beautiful and fruitful you will be as a Christian (see John 15:4-5).

---

that come from human thinking and from the spiritual powers* of this world, rather than from Christ. [9]For in Christ lives all the fullness of God in a human body.* [10]So you also are complete through your union with Christ, who is the head over every ruler and authority.

[11]When you came to Christ, you were "circumcised," but not by a physical procedure. Christ performed a spiritual circumcision—the cutting away of your sinful nature.* [12]For you were buried with Christ when you were baptized. And with him you were raised to new life because you trusted the mighty power of God, who raised Christ from the dead.

[13]You were dead because of your sins and because your sinful nature was not yet cut away. Then God made you alive with Christ, for he forgave all our sins. [14]He canceled the record of the charges against us and took it away by nailing it to the cross. [15]In this way, he disarmed* the spiritual rulers and authorities. He shamed them publicly by his victory over them on the cross.

[16]So don't let anyone condemn you for what you eat or drink, or for not celebrating certain holy days or new moon ceremonies or Sabbaths. [17]For these rules are only shadows of the reality yet to come. And Christ himself is that reality. [18]Don't let anyone condemn you by insisting on pious self-denial or the worship of angels,* saying they have had visions about these things. Their sinful minds have made them proud, [19]and they are not connected to Christ, the head of the body. For he holds the

whole body together with its joints and ligaments, and it grows as God nourishes it.

[20]You have died with Christ, and he has set you free from the spiritual powers of this world. So why do you keep on following the rules of the world, such as, [21]"Don't handle! Don't taste! Don't touch!"? [22]Such rules are mere human teachings about things that deteriorate as we use them. [23]These rules may seem wise because they require strong devotion, pious self-denial, and severe bodily discipline. But they provide no help in conquering a person's evil desires.

3 **LIVING THE NEW LIFE** Since you have been raised to new life with Christ, set your sights on the realities of heaven, where Christ sits in the place of honor at God's right hand. [2]Think about the things of heaven, not the things of earth. [3]For you died to this life, and your real life is hidden with Christ in God. [4]And when Christ, who is your* life, is revealed to the whole world, you will share in all his glory.

[5]So put to death the sinful, earthly things lurking within you. Have nothing to do with sexual immorality, impurity, lust, and evil desires. Don't be greedy, for a greedy person is an idolater, worshiping the things of this world. [6]Because of these sins, the anger of God is coming.* [7]You used to do these things when your life was still part of this world. [8]But now is

2:8 Or *the spiritual principles;* also in 2:20. **2:9** Or *in him dwells all the completeness of the Godhead bodily.* **2:11** Greek *the cutting away of the body of the flesh.* **2:15** Or *he stripped off.* **2:18** Or *or worshiping with angels.* **3:4** Some manuscripts read *our.* **3:6** Some manuscripts read *is coming on all who disobey him.*

the time to get rid of anger, rage, malicious behavior, slander, and dirty language. 9Don't lie to each other, for you have stripped off your old sinful nature and all its wicked deeds. 10Put on your new nature, and be renewed as you learn to know your Creator and become like him. 11In this new life, it doesn't matter if you are a Jew or a Gentile,* circumcised or uncircumcised, barbaric, uncivilized,* slave, or free. Christ is all that matters, and he lives in all of us.

12Since God chose you to be the holy people he loves, you must clothe yourselves with tenderhearted mercy, kindness, humility, gentleness, and patience. 13Make allowance for each other's faults, and forgive anyone who offends you. Remember, the Lord forgave you, so you must forgive others. 14Above all, clothe yourselves with love, which binds us all together in perfect harmony. 15And let the peace that comes from Christ rule in your hearts. For as members of one body you are called to live in peace. And always be thankful.

16Let the message about Christ, in all its richness, fill your lives. Teach and counsel each other with all the wisdom he gives. Sing psalms and hymns and spiritual songs to God with thankful hearts. 17And whatever you do or say, do it as a representative of the Lord Jesus, giving thanks through him to God the Father.

INSTRUCTIONS FOR CHRISTIAN HOUSEHOLDS

18Wives, submit to your husbands, as is fitting for those who belong to the Lord.

19Husbands, love your wives and never treat them harshly.

20Children, always obey your parents, for this pleases the Lord. 21Fathers, do not aggravate your children, or they will become discouraged.

22Slaves, obey your earthly masters in everything you do. Try to please them all the time,

3:11a Greek *a Greek.*   **3:11b** Greek *Barbarian, Scythian.*   **3:24** Or *and serve Christ as your Master.*

WORK WILLINGLY AT WHATEVER YOU DO,

AS THOUGH YOU WERE WORKING FOR THE LORD RATHER THAN FOR PEOPLE.

COLOSSIANS 3:23

not just when they are watching you. Serve them sincerely because of your reverent fear of the Lord. 23Work willingly at whatever you do, as though you were working for the Lord rather than for people. 24Remember that the Lord will give you an inheritance as your reward, and that the Master you are serving is Christ.* 25But if you do what is wrong, you will be paid back for the wrong you have done. For God has no favorites.

....

CHANGES FOR THE BETTER
(3:1-17) People should be able to see a difference between the way Christians and non-Christians live. Still, we should not expect instant maturity of new Christians. The Christian life is a process. Although we have a new nature, we don't automatically have all good thoughts and attitudes when we become new people in Christ. If we keep listening to God, however, we will grow toward maturity. As you think about the events of the past year, what changes for the better have you noticed in your thoughts and attitudes? Change may be slow, but your life will change significantly if you trust God to work within you.

PEACE RULES
(3:15) The word rule comes from athletics: Paul tells us to let God's peace be the "umpire" in our hearts. A person's heart is the center of conflict because that's where feelings and desires clash. How can we deal with these constant conflicts and live as God wants? Paul explains that we must decide between conflicting elements on the basis of peace. Ask yourself which choice will promote peace in your soul, your family, and your church.

CHOICES lust

Last year, thirteen-year-old Danny found a secret stash of pornographic magazines in his older brother's bedroom. Since then, he has developed a system. Each time his brother goes out for the evening, Danny sneaks one of the magazines into his own bedroom. There he'll stay for long hours fantasizing about being with each of the beautiful models. After a few days, he smuggles the much-studied magazine back into its place, whereupon he takes another one and repeats the process.

Each time he yields to these lustful temptations, Danny is overcome by a wave of guilt. After the short-term pleasure, Danny experiences only feelings of

emptiness and loneliness. Even so, he rationalizes it this way:

"It's better to do what I'm doing than to be like my friends and actually go out and have sex! At least this way, I don't get myself or anybody else in trouble. Besides, I can't help it if I have a healthy sex drive. And anyway, I'm not sure I can stop."

What about Danny's ideas on lust? Are they sound arguments? Is it okay to stare at pictures, or real people, and imagine having sex with them? Take a look at Colossians 3:5 for God's thoughts on the issue.

MY STORY: Blake

For a couple of years in high school, I didn't get along very well with my dad. I'm not sure why, now. It just seemed like everything he said irritated me. Dad seemed old-fashioned, too restrictive. I began to rebel, not openly, but more in my heart and on the sly. For instance, I'd say yes when he asked me to do something, but then I'd never get around to doing what he asked. Then when he'd get angry, I'd tune him out. Or, I would tell Dad I was going somewhere that I knew he'd approve of. But I would really hang out with friends he didn't like very much.

I knew things weren't great between us, but I didn't think much about it until our youth group did a study on relationships. When we talked about parents, we studied Colossians 3:20 and Ephesians 6:1-3. We talked about why we should obey our parents, and what obedience means.

I felt cut to the heart, knowing how hurtful I had been to my dad. Suddenly I understood that his rules were his way of showing that he loved me. If I was honest with myself, a lot of his rules made sense. I was being disobedient and rebellious. I cried some, knowing that I had been hurting my dad for a long time.

That evening I asked Dad to forgive me for all the ways I'd gone against him. Apologizing was hard, but it cleared the air. Dad took my apology well. He even admitted to some areas where he might have been too hard on me. That was the start of a much better father-son relationship, which has continued.

4 Masters, be just and fair to your slaves. Remember that you also have a Master—in heaven.

AN ENCOURAGEMENT FOR PRAYER
²Devote yourselves to prayer with an alert mind and a thankful heart. ³Pray for us, too, that God will give us many opportunities to speak about his mysterious plan concerning Christ. That is why I am here in chains. ⁴Pray that I will proclaim this message as clearly as I should.

⁵Live wisely among those who are not believers, and make the most of every opportunity.

PERSIST
(4:2) Have you ever grown tired of praying for something or someone? Paul says, "Devote yourselves to prayer with an alert mind and a thankful heart." Vigilance demonstrates our faith that God answers our prayers. Faith shouldn't die if the answers don't come immediately. The delay may be God's way of working his will in your life. When you feel weary in your prayers, know that God is present, always listening, always acting.

LIFELONG
(4:2-8) The Christian is in a continuing education program. The more we know of Christ and his work, the more we will be changed to be like him. Because this process is lifelong, we must never stop learning and obeying. This should not be a justification for drifting along, but an incentive to find the rich treasures of growing in Christ. It takes practice, review, patience, and concentration to stay in line with his will.

⁶Let your conversation be gracious and attractive* so that you will have the right response for everyone.

PAUL'S FINAL INSTRUCTIONS AND GREETINGS
⁷Tychicus will give you a full report about how I am getting along. He is a beloved brother and faithful helper who serves with me in the Lord's work. ⁸I have sent him to you for this very purpose—to let you know how we are doing and to encourage you. ⁹I am also sending Onesimus, a faithful and beloved brother, one of your own people. He and Tychicus will tell you everything that's happening here.

¹⁰Aristarchus, who is in prison with me, sends you his greetings, and so does Mark, Barnabas's cousin. As you were instructed before, make Mark welcome if he comes your way. ¹¹Jesus (the one we call Justus) also sends his greetings. These are the only Jewish believers among my co-workers; they are working with me here for the Kingdom of God. And what a comfort they have been!

¹²Epaphras, a member of your own fellowship and a servant of Christ Jesus, sends you his greetings. He always prays earnestly for you, asking God to make you strong and perfect, fully confident that you are following the whole will of God. ¹³I can assure you that he prays hard

4:6 Greek *and seasoned with salt.*

for you and also for the believers in Laodicea and Hierapolis.

¹⁴Luke, the beloved doctor, sends his greetings, and so does Demas. ¹⁵Please give my greetings to our brothers and sisters* at Laodicea, and to Nympha and the church that meets in her house.

¹⁶After you have read this letter, pass it on to the church at Laodicea so they can read it, too. And you should read the letter I wrote to them.

¹⁷And say to Archippus, "Be sure to carry out the ministry the Lord gave you."

4:15 Greek *brothers.*

¹⁸HERE IS MY GREETING IN MY OWN HANDWRITING—PAUL.

Remember my chains.

May God's grace be with you.

....

THE SOURCE
(4:18) *The Colossian church was swayed by false teachers who promised a deeper spiritual life through secret knowledge. But Paul made it clear in Colossians that Christ alone is the source of true spiritual maturity. He is the head of the body, the Lord of all. The path to deeper spiritual life is not through spiritual duties, special knowledge, or secrets; it is only through a clear connection with the Lord Jesus Christ. We must never let anything come between us and our Savior.*

1 THESSALONIANS

Phobias are fascinating phenomena. Psychiatrists and psychologists have catalogued hundreds of them. Check out this list:

Anthophobia—fear of flowers

Belonophobia—fear of pins and needles

Decidophobia—fear of making decisions

Mysophobia—fear of dirt

Trichophobia/trichopathophobia—fear of hair

Would you believe that some people are even terrified about peanut butter sticking to the roof of their mouth? *That's called* arachibutyrophobia.

Okay, maybe you don't have these fears. Perhaps your worries are more about the concerns you hear about on the Internet or on the news. For example: Is the environment damaged beyond repair? Will researchers ever find a cure for AIDS and other deadly diseases? Are we on the brink of a worldwide economic collapse? How are we going to deal with a generation of drug-addicted babies? Can we confront and correct our country's epidemic of violent crimes? How has war affected our lives? Will there ever be lasting peace in the Middle East?

These are scary issues. Yet Christians can have real hope and genuine peace even in uncertain times.

That's the message of this letter: Be comforted, for no matter what happens God is with us. Rest in the reassuring truth that Jesus Christ is coming back soon to. . . .

Well, you'll just have to read 1 Thessalonians for yourself to find out!

STATS

PURPOSE
To strengthen the faith of Christians in Thessalonica and to pass on the assurance of Christ's return

AUTHOR
Paul

ORIGINAL AUDIENCE
The church at Thessalonica

DATE WRITTEN
About A.D. 51 from Corinth; this is one of Paul's earliest letters

SETTING
The church at Thessalonica had been established only two or three years before this letter was written. The Christians needed to mature in their faith. Also, there was a misunderstanding about Jesus' second coming. Some thought he would return immediately. Others wondered if the dead would experience a bodily resurrection at his return.

KEY PEOPLE
Paul, Timothy, Silas

KEY PLACE
Thessalonica

KEY POINTS

PERSECUTION Paul and the new Christians at Thessalonica experienced persecution because of their faith in Christ. We can expect trials and troubles as well. The Holy Spirit helps our faith to remain strong even when we are persecuted.

PAUL'S MINISTRY Paul expressed his concern for this church even when some of the members slandered him. Paul's commitment to share the gospel even through difficult times is an example for us to follow.

BE PREPARED Paul encouraged believers to live as though they expected Jesus to return at any moment. No one knows when Jesus will return. While we wait, we are to remain faithful to God.

LOCATION OF THESSALONICA
Paul visited Thessalonica on his second and third missionary journeys. It was a seaport and trade center located on the Egnatian Way, a busy international highway. Paul probably wrote his two letters to the Thessalonians from Corinth.

1 **GREETINGS FROM PAUL** This letter is from Paul, Silas,* and Timothy.

We are writing to the church in Thessalonica, to you who belong to God the Father and the Lord Jesus Christ.

May God give you grace and peace.

THE FAITH OF THE THESSALONIAN BELIEVERS ²We always thank God for all of you and pray for you constantly. ³As we pray to our God and Father about you, we think of your faithful work, your loving deeds, and the enduring hope you have because of our Lord Jesus Christ.

⁴We know, dear brothers and sisters,* that God loves you and has chosen you to be his own people. ⁵For when we brought you the Good News, it was not only with words but also with power, for the Holy Spirit gave you full assurance* that what we said was true. And you know of our concern for you from the way we lived when we were with you. ⁶So you received the message with joy from the Holy Spirit in spite of the severe suffering it brought you. In this way, you imitated both us and the Lord. ⁷As a result, you have become an example to all the believers in Greece—throughout both Macedonia and Achaia.*

⁸And now the word of the Lord is ringing out from you to people everywhere, even beyond Macedonia and Achaia, for wherever we go we find people telling us about your faith in God. We don't need to tell them about it, ⁹for they keep talking about the wonderful welcome you gave us and how you turned away from idols to serve the living and true God. ¹⁰And they speak of how you are looking forward to the coming of God's Son from heaven—Jesus, whom God raised from the dead. He is the one who has rescued us from the terrors of the coming judgment.

2 **PAUL REMEMBERS HIS VISIT** You yourselves know, dear brothers and sisters,* that our visit to you was not a failure. ²You know how badly we had been treated at Philippi just before we came to you and how much we suffered there. Yet our God gave us the courage to declare his Good News to you boldly, in spite of great opposition. ³So you can see we were not preaching with any deceit or impure motives or trickery.

⁴For we speak as messengers approved

1:1 Greek *Silvanus,* the Greek form of the name.   1:4 Greek *brothers.*   1:5 Or *with the power of the Holy Spirit, so you can have full assurance.*   1:7 *Macedonia* and *Achaia* were the northern and southern regions of Greece.   2:1 Greek *brothers;* also in 2:9, 14, 17.

by God to be entrusted with the Good News. Our purpose is to please God, not people. He alone examines the motives of our hearts. ⁵Never once did we try to win you with flattery, as you well know. And God is our witness that we were not pretending to be your friends just to get your money! ⁶As for human praise, we have never sought it from you or anyone else.

⁷As apostles of Christ we certainly had a right to make some demands of you, but instead we were like children* among you. Or we were like a mother feeding and caring for her own children. ⁸We loved you so much that we shared with you not only God's Good News but our own lives, too.

⁹Don't you remember, dear brothers and sisters, how hard we worked among you? Night and day we toiled to earn a living so that we would not be a burden to any of you as we preached God's Good News to you. ¹⁰You yourselves are our witnesses—and so is God—that we were devout and honest and faultless toward all of you believers. ¹¹And you know that we treated each of you as a father treats his own children. ¹²We pleaded with you, encouraged you, and urged you to live your lives in a way that God would consider worthy. For he called you to share in his Kingdom and glory.

¹³Therefore, we never stop thanking God that when you received his message from us, you didn't think of our words as mere human ideas. You accepted what we said as the very word of God—which, of course, it is. And this word continues to work in you who believe.

¹⁴And then, dear brothers and sisters, you suffered persecution from your own countrymen. In this way, you imitated the believers in

2:7 Some manuscripts read we were gentle.

God's churches in Judea who, because of their belief in Christ Jesus, suffered from their own people, the Jews. ¹⁵For some of the Jews killed the prophets, and some even killed the Lord Jesus. Now they have persecuted us, too. They fail to please God and work against all humanity ¹⁶as they try to keep us from preaching the Good News of salvation to the Gentiles. By doing this, they continue to pile up their sins. But the anger of God has caught up with them at last.

TIMOTHY'S GOOD REPORT ABOUT THE CHURCH ¹⁷Dear brothers and sisters, after we were separated from you for a little while (though our hearts never left you), we tried very hard to come back because of our intense longing to see you again. ¹⁸We wanted very much to come to you, and I, Paul, tried again and again, but Satan prevented us. ¹⁹After all, what gives us hope and joy, and what will be our proud reward and crown as we stand before our Lord Jesus when he returns? It is you! ²⁰Yes, you are our pride and joy.

3 Finally, when we could stand it no longer, we decided to stay alone in Athens, ²and

....

OPPOSED
(2:14) Just as the Jewish Christians in Jerusalem were persecuted by their own people, so the Gentile Christians in Thessalonica were persecuted by their fellow Gentiles. Persecution is discouraging, especially when it comes from family or friends. But taking a stand for Christ usually leads to persecution. Are you still willing to declare your faith even if doing so may lead to being harassed, opposed, or even hurt?

CHOICES
sex

Melanie is confused about sex—not how (she learned that a long time ago), but when. Her mom tells her to wait. Her youth director gives her the same advice. But everywhere else the message is clearly, "Go for it!" Or, "If you're still a virgin, you're a total loser!"

- Friends at school tell her how great it is and how experienced they are.
- All the glamorous stars in TV shows and movies seem to be hopping from bed to bed—both on- and off-screen.
- In a health class lecture on birth control two weeks ago, the teacher stated, "Now, most normal young people are sexually active. I'm assuming you all are normal, so . . ."

- Melanie's boyfriend keeps telling her how much sex will strengthen their relationship.
- Almost every ad and billboard Melanie sees has a sexual twist or theme.
- A talk show featured live-in lovers talking about their "great" lifestyle.

"What am I supposed to think?" Melanie asks. "I feel like everybody else in the world is enjoying this really fantastic experience . . . and I'm like a nun or something. I want to wait, at least I think I do. Tell me, is it really worth saving yourself till marriage?"

The Bible says it's definitely wiser to wait until marriage for sex. Think hard about the message in 1 Thessalonians 4:1-8.

we sent Timothy to visit you. He is our brother and God's co-worker* in proclaiming the Good News of Christ. We sent him to strengthen you, to encourage you in your faith, ³and to keep you from being shaken by the troubles you were going through. But you know that we are destined for such troubles. ⁴Even while we were with you, we warned you that troubles would soon come—and they did, as you well know. ⁵That is why, when I could bear it no longer, I sent Timothy to find out whether your faith was still strong. I was afraid that the tempter had gotten the best of you and that our work had been useless.

⁶But now Timothy has just returned, bringing us good news about your faith and love. He reports that you always remember our visit with joy and that you want to see us as much as we want to see you. ⁷So we have been greatly encouraged in the midst of our troubles and suffering, dear brothers and sisters,* because you have remained strong in your faith. ⁸It gives us new life to know that you are standing firm in the Lord.

⁹How we thank God for you! Because of you we have great joy as we enter God's presence. ¹⁰Night and day we pray earnestly for you, asking God to let us see you again to fill the gaps in your faith.

¹¹May God our Father and our Lord Jesus bring us to you very soon. ¹²And may the Lord make your love for one another and for all people grow and overflow, just as our love for you overflows. ¹³May he, as a result, make your hearts strong, blameless, and holy as you stand before God our Father when our Lord Jesus comes again with all his holy people. Amen.

4 LIVE TO PLEASE GOD Finally, dear brothers and sisters,* we urge you in the name of the Lord Jesus to live in a way that pleases God, as we have taught you. You live this way already, and we encourage you to do so even more. ²For you remember what we taught you by the authority of the Lord Jesus.

³God's will is for you to be holy, so stay away from all sexual sin. ⁴Then each of you will control his own body* and live in holiness and honor—⁵not in lustful passion like the pagans who do not know God and his ways. ⁶Never harm or cheat a Christian brother in this matter by violating his wife,* for the Lord avenges all such sins, as we have solemnly warned you before. ⁷God has called us to live holy lives, not impure lives. ⁸Therefore, anyone who refuses to live by these rules is not disobeying human teaching but is rejecting God, who gives his Holy Spirit to you.

⁹But we don't need to write to you about

3:2 Other manuscripts read *and God's servant;* still others read *and a co-worker,* or *and a servant and co-worker for God,* or *and God's servant and our co-worker.* **3:7** Greek *brothers.* **4:1** Greek *brothers;* also in 4:10, 13. **4:4** Or *will know how to take a wife for himself;* or *will learn to live with his own wife;* Greek reads *will know how to possess his own vessel.* **4:6** Greek *Never harm or cheat a brother in this matter.*

I WONDER . . .

Even though I know I'm going to heaven, I'm still afraid of dying. How can I quit being so afraid of death?

Extreme fear of the unknown can cripple a person. Unfortunately, death is an unknown for everyone, even for Christians.

What will we find on the other side? How is God going to take me? Will the people left behind be able to adjust? What if I die before I have a chance to get married or experience what I want to experience?

Many questions don't have concrete answers, and we can find that to be frustrating. Someone once said that trying to explain to another person what God and heaven are like is similar to one dog telling another dog what being a human is like. It's impossible!

But death is not something that Christians have to fear, because—for them—death is not the end of the story. It is the gateway to a place of indescribable joy and beauty. Death marks the beginning of a new life!

Fear is a learned response. Through the years we learned to fear certain things. Little kids aren't afraid of death because they don't understand it. Yet as they grow and see the response of adults and the media to death, they learn that it's something to be avoided at all costs.

After we become Christians, we need to go through a relearning process about death. Paul, the author of much of the New Testament, said this about death: "For to me, living means living for Christ, and dying is even better" (Phil 1:21).

Paul had learned that death would actually put an end to the struggles he faced on earth. He looked forward to the day when he could see Jesus face-to-face. In the meantime, though, he had work to do: winning people to Christ. Life wasn't a chore—it was a privilege!

Fear of dying doesn't disappear instantly. But as you spend time in the Bible and with other Christians who have the same hope you do, you will grow to realize that death is only a door to an eternity far better than your wildest dreams (see 1 Thes 4:13-14).

NEVER STOP PRAYING.

the importance of loving each other,* for God himself has taught you to love one another. [10]Indeed, you already show your love for all the believers* throughout Macedonia. Even so, dear brothers and sisters, we urge you to love them even more.

[11]Make it your goal to live a quiet life, minding your own business and working with your hands, just as we instructed you before. [12]Then people who are not Christians will respect the way you live, and you will not need to depend on others.

THE HOPE OF THE RESURRECTION [13]And now, dear brothers and sisters, we want you to know what will happen to the believers who have died* so you will not grieve like people who have no hope. [14]For since we believe that Jesus died and was raised to life again, we also believe that when Jesus returns, God will bring back with him the believers who have died.

[15]We tell you this directly from the Lord: We who are still living when the Lord returns will not meet those ahead of those who have died.* [16]For the Lord himself will come down from heaven with a commanding shout, with the voice of the archangel, and with the trumpet call of God. First, the Christians who have died* will rise from their graves. [17]Then, together with them, we who are still alive and remain on the earth will be caught up in the clouds to meet the Lord in the air. Then we will be with the Lord forever. [18]So encourage each other with these words.

5 Now concerning how and when all this will happen, dear brothers and sisters,* we don't really need to write you. [2]For you know quite well that the day of the Lord's return will come unexpectedly, like a thief in the night. [3]When people are saying, "Everything is peaceful and secure," then disaster will fall on them as suddenly as a pregnant woman's labor pains begin. And there will be no escape.

[4]But you aren't in the dark about these things, dear brothers and sisters, and you won't be surprised when the day of the Lord comes like a thief.* [5]For you are all children of the light and of the day; we don't belong to darkness and night. [6]So be on your guard, not asleep like the others. Stay alert and be clearheaded. [7]Night is the time when people sleep and drinkers get drunk. [8]But let us who live in the light be clearheaded, protected by the armor of faith and love, and wearing as our helmet the confidence of our salvation.

[9]For God chose to save us through our Lord Jesus Christ, not to pour out his anger on us. [10]Christ died for us so that, whether we are dead or alive when he returns, we can live with him forever. [11]So encourage each other and build each other up, just as you are already doing.

PAUL'S FINAL ADVICE [12]Dear brothers and sisters, honor those who are your leaders in the Lord's work. They work hard among you and give you spiritual guidance. [13]Show them great respect and wholehearted love because of their work. And live peacefully with each other.

[14]Brothers and sisters, we urge you to warn those who are lazy. Encourage those who are timid. Take tender care of those who are weak. Be patient with everyone.

[15]See that no one pays back evil for evil, but always try to do good to each other and to all people.

[16]Always be joyful. [17]Never stop praying. [18]Be thankful in all circumstances, for this is God's will for you who belong to Christ Jesus.

[19]Do not stifle the Holy Spirit. [20]Do not scoff at prophecies, [21]but test everything that is said. Hold on to what is good. [22]Stay away from every kind of evil.

....

THE FINISH LINE
(5:9-11) As you near the end of a foot race, your legs ache, your throat burns, and your whole body cries out for you to stop. This is when friends and fans are most valuable. Their encouragement helps you push through the pain and reach the finish line. In the same way, Christians are to encourage one another. A word of encouragement offered at the right moment can mean the difference between finishing well and collapsing along the way. Look around. Who needs your encouragement?

4:9 Greek *about brotherly love.* **4:10** Greek *the brothers.* **4:13** Greek *those who have fallen asleep;* also in 4:14. **4:15** Greek *those who have fallen asleep.* **4:16** Greek *the dead in Christ.* **5:1** Greek *brothers;* also in 5:4, 12, 14, 25, 26, 27. **5:4** Some manuscripts read *comes upon you as if you were thieves.*

PAUL'S FINAL GREETINGS ²³Now may the God of peace make you holy in every way, and may your whole spirit and soul and body be kept blameless until our Lord Jesus Christ comes again. ²⁴God will make this happen, for he who calls you is faithful.

²⁵Dear brothers and sisters, pray for us.

²⁶Greet all the brothers and sisters with Christian love.*

²⁷I command you in the name of the Lord to read this letter to all the brothers and sisters.

²⁸May the grace of our Lord Jesus Christ be with you.

5:26 Greek with a holy kiss.

IN CONTROL

(5:23) The spirit, soul, and body are integral parts of a person. This expression is Paul's way of saying that God must be involved in every aspect of our lives. We can't separate our spiritual life from everything else. Christ must control all of us, not just the part we give him on Sundays. How much of your life have you given to God?

2 THESSALONIANS

A prominent author's best-selling new book has predicted that Christ is coming back in a few days.

Anne: "It's supposed to happen this weekend."

Shelby: "I guess I'm ready, but if it does happen, I'll never get my license—and I'll never get to . . . well, you know."

(Everyone but Faith giggles.)

Jade: "I think it's great. I've got a huge trig test on Monday that I can't possibly pass. Now I can just relax and forget about it."

Shelby: "Right, and no more abuse from Garrett Hampton and his atheist friends!"

Anne: "Omigosh, I never even thought about that. That will be the best!"

Faith: "You guys cannot be serious! You talk like you actually believe that stuff!"

Anne: "Of course we do! It all fits together, and it's in the Bible, Faith. It's going to be this weekend, so you better get ready."

Jesus is coming back. And his return will radically change things. But that doesn't mean we should start picking dates or sit around waiting. The prospect of Christ's return should motivate us to action, not laziness.

That's the message of 2 Thessalonians. Yes, the world can be messy. Yes, the Christian life can be hard. But Christ is returning soon to make everything right. So keep watching, waiting—and working.

(And by all means, study for your trig exam!)

KEY POINTS
. . . .

PERSECUTION Paul encouraged the believers to have patience in spite of persecution. That encouragement is for us as well. Suffering for our faith can strengthen us to serve Christ.

CHRIST'S RETURN Christ will return and bring total victory to all who trust in him. If we stand firm and keep working, we'll be ready. If we're ready, we don't have to be concerned about when he'll return.

THE GREAT REBELLION Before Jesus' return, there will be a great rebellion against God led by the man of lawlessness (the Antichrist). We don't have to fear when we see evil increase. God is in control, no matter how much evil infects the world.

DON'T QUIT Paul had harsh words for believers who stopped working and became disorderly. We must never get so tired of doing right that we quit. Instead, we are to persevere in the use of our time and talents.

1

GREETINGS FROM PAUL This letter is from Paul, Silas,* and Timothy.

We are writing to the church in Thessalonica, to you who belong to God our Father and the Lord Jesus Christ.

²May God our Father* and the Lord Jesus Christ give you grace and peace.

ENCOURAGEMENT DURING PERSECUTION

³Dear brothers and sisters,* we can't help but thank God for you, because your faith is flourishing and your love for one another is growing. ⁴We proudly tell God's other churches about your endurance and faithfulness in all the persecutions and hardships you are suffering. ⁵And God will use this persecution to show his justice and to make you worthy of his Kingdom, for which you are suffering. ⁶In his justice he will pay back those who persecute you.

⁷And God will provide rest for you who are being persecuted and also for us when the Lord Jesus appears from heaven. He will come with his mighty angels, ⁸in flaming fire, bringing judgment on those who don't know God and on those who refuse to obey the Good News of our Lord Jesus. ⁹They will be punished with eternal destruction, forever separated from the Lord and from his glorious power. ¹⁰When he comes on that day, he will receive glory from his holy people—praise from all who believe. And this includes you, for you believed what we told you about him.

¹¹So we keep on praying for you, asking our God to enable you to live a life worthy of his call. May he give you the power to accomplish all the good things your faith prompts you to do. ¹²Then the name of our Lord Jesus will be honored because of the way you live, and you will be honored along with him. This is all made possible because of the grace of our God and Lord, Jesus Christ.*

2

EVENTS PRIOR TO THE LORD'S SECOND COMING Now, dear brothers and sisters,* let us clarify some things about the coming of our Lord Jesus Christ and how we will be gathered to meet him. ²Don't be so easily shaken or alarmed by those who say that the day of the Lord has already begun. Don't believe them, even if they claim to have had a spiritual vision, a revelation, or a letter supposedly from us. ³Don't be fooled by what they say. For that day will not come until there is a great rebellion against God and the man of lawlessness* is revealed—the one who brings destruction.* ⁴He will exalt himself and defy everything that people call god and every object of worship. He will even sit in the temple of God, claiming that he himself is God.

⁵Don't you remember that I told you about all this when I was with you? ⁶And you know what is holding him back, for he can be revealed only when his time comes. ⁷For this lawlessness is already at work secretly, and it will remain secret until the one who is holding it back steps out of the way. ⁸Then the man of lawlessness will be revealed, but the Lord Jesus will kill him with the breath of his mouth and destroy him by the splendor of his coming.

⁹This man will come to do the work of Satan with counterfeit power and signs and miracles. ¹⁰He will use every kind of evil deception to fool those on their way to destruction, because they refuse to love and accept the truth that would save them. ¹¹So God will cause them to be greatly deceived, and they will believe these lies. ¹²Then they will be condemned for enjoying evil rather than believing the truth.

BELIEVERS SHOULD STAND FIRM

¹³As for us, we can't help but thank God for you, dear brothers and sisters loved by the Lord. We are always thankful that God chose you to be among the first* to experience salvation—a salvation that came through the Spirit who makes you holy and through your belief in the truth. ¹⁴He called you to salvation when we told you the Good News; now you can share in the glory of our Lord Jesus Christ.

¹⁵With all these things in mind, dear brothers and sisters, stand firm and keep a strong grip on the teaching we passed on to you both in person and by letter.

¹⁶Now may our Lord Jesus Christ himself and God our Father, who loved us and by his grace gave us eternal comfort and a wonderful hope, ¹⁷comfort you and strengthen you in every good thing you do and say.

TROUBLES

(1:5) As we live for Christ, we will experience trouble. Some say that hardships are a result of sin or lack of faith. Paul, however, teaches that they may be a part of God's plan for believers. Our problems help us look upward and forward, not inward (Mark 13:35-36); help build strong character (Rom 5:3-4); and help us to be sensitive to others (2 Cor 1:3-5).

1:1 Greek *Silvanus,* the Greek form of the name.   **1:2** Some manuscripts read *God the Father.*   **1:3** Greek *Brothers.*   **1:12** Or *of our God and our Lord Jesus Christ.*   **2:1** Greek *brothers;* also in 2:13, 15.   **2:3a** Some manuscripts read *the man of sin.*   **2:3b** Greek *the son of destruction.*   **2:13** Some manuscripts read *chose you from the very beginning.*

3 PAUL'S REQUEST FOR PRAYER Finally,

dear brothers and sisters,* we ask you to pray for us. Pray that the Lord's message will spread rapidly and be honored wherever it goes, just as when it came to you. ²Pray, too, that we will be rescued from wicked and evil people, for not everyone is a believer. ³But the Lord is faithful; he will strengthen you and guard you from the evil one.* ⁴And we are confident in the Lord that you are doing and will continue to do the things we commanded you. ⁵May the Lord lead your hearts into a full understanding and expression of the love of God and the patient endurance that comes from Christ.

AN EXHORTATION TO PROPER LIVING ⁶And now, dear brothers and sisters, we give you this command in the name of our Lord Jesus Christ: Stay away from all believers* who live idle lives and don't follow the tradition they received* from us. ⁷For you know that you ought to imitate us. We were not idle when we were with you. ⁸We never accepted food from anyone without paying for it. We worked hard day and night so we would not be a burden to any of you. ⁹We certainly had the right to ask you to feed us, but we wanted to give you an example to follow. ¹⁰Even while we were with you, we gave you this command: "Those unwilling to work will not get to eat."

¹¹Yet we hear that some of you are living idle lives, refusing to work and meddling in other people's business. ¹²We command such people and urge them in the name of the Lord Jesus Christ to settle down and work to earn their own living. ¹³As for the rest of you, dear brothers and sisters, never get tired of doing good.

¹⁴Take note of those who refuse to obey what we say in this letter. Stay away from them so they will be ashamed. ¹⁵Don't think of them as enemies, but warn them as you would a brother or sister.*

BUT THE LORD IS FAITHFUL; HE WILL STRENGTHEN YOU AND GUARD YOU FROM THE EVIL ONE.
■ ■ 2 THESSALONIANS 3:3 ■ ■

3:1 Greek brothers; also in 3:6, 13.　3:3 Or from evil.　3:6a Greek from every brother.　3:6b Some manuscripts read you received.　3:15 Greek as a brother.

SPIRITUAL ATTACKS
(3:1-3) Aside from the routine of daily life, a spiritual battle is taking place. Attacks from the forces of evil (discouragement, depression, and so forth) can be devastating. But we're not without help! We have prayer and the Word of God (see also Eph 6:10-19).
The following guidelines can help you prepare for and survive satanic attacks: (1) Take the threat of spiritual attack seriously. (2) Pray for strength and help from God. (3) Study the Bible to recognize Satan's tactics. (4) Memorize Scripture. (5) Associate with those who speak the truth. (6) Practice what you have been taught.

WORK AND PLAY?
(3:6-15) Paul advised the Christians of Thessalonica to avoid lazy believers. A great difference stands between leisure and laziness. Relaxation and recreation provide a necessary and much needed balance to the workday schedule. Yet Christians are still responsible to work. Do you have a balance between your work schedule and your free time? Too much of one or the other can be hazardous.

CHOICES laziness

Luke walks in the door, drops his backpack on the couch, and heads straight for the kitchen. Opening the pantry, he scans the shelves and scowls. "How come there's never anything to eat in this stupid house?" he mutters to no one in particular.

Grabbing a banana, he settles on the floor in front of the TV for a quick game of Motorist Mayhem. A "quick game" usually lasts five hours.

The phone rings. Luke doesn't budge.

"Luke, can you get the phone? I've got shaving cream all over my hands!" his dad suddenly yells from the bathroom.

It'll stop soon, Luke thinks. He continues playing the game.

The phone continues to ring. The voice from the rear of the house gets louder. "Luke! Answer the phone!"

Just as the mystery caller gives up, Luke's mom staggers through the door, her arms loaded with grocery bags.

Luke watches her struggle from his easy chair and greets her by saying, "I hope you bought something decent to eat."

"Maybe if you help me carry the bags in, you'll find out," his mother quips.

"Sheesh!" Luke exclaims, as he grudgingly leaves his comfortable throne. "Why do I always have to do everything around here? You and Dad treat me like a slave!"

Check out 2 Thessalonians 3:6-13. What would you say to Luke?

PAUL'S FINAL GREETINGS [16]Now may the Lord of peace himself give you his peace at all times and in every situation. The Lord be with you all.

[17]HERE IS MY GREETING IN MY OWN HAND-WRITING—PAUL. I DO THIS IN ALL MY LETTERS TO PROVE THEY ARE FROM ME.

[18]May the grace of our Lord Jesus Christ be with you all.

1 TIMOTHY

What does it take to be a leader? Super intelligence? Good looks?
A magnetic personality? The ability to speak persuasively?
A ruthless obsession for power? That's what the world says.

The world is wrong. Leadership has nothing to do with impressive resumes or rousing speeches or physical attractiveness. Leadership is far more than being highly educated or multitalented. Jesus defined leadership as servanthood. It involves compassion, courage, and conviction.

So, here's the shocker: Anyone who takes the time to develop those qualities can be a leader.

Even you.

"Who? Me?! You must be kidding! I don't have any special talents. Besides, I'm young and kind of shy. I could never lead anyone."

Funny you should say that. A young man by the name of Timothy once felt the same way. He found himself facing big responsibilities and even bigger challenges. He wondered what to do and whether he could really be a leader.

Then he received the following letter from his friend and mentor, Paul. More than a mere letter, the Epistle of 1 Timothy is also an essay on leadership.

Hey, you may never be a major politician or the CEO of a big company. But you'll always have friends, relatives, neighbors, and acquaintances that you can influence for Christ.

So read about the character, compassion, courage, and conviction that leadership involves. Then give it a try. Be a leader.

STATS

PURPOSE
To encourage and instruct Timothy

AUTHOR
Paul

ORIGINAL AUDIENCE
Timothy, a young church leader

DATE WRITTEN
About A.D. 64, from Rome or Macedonia (possibly Philippi), probably just prior to Paul's final imprisonment in Rome

SETTING
Timothy was one of Paul's closest companions. Paul had sent him to the church at Ephesus to counter the false teaching that had arisen there (1 Tim 1:3-4). Timothy probably served for a time as a leader in the church at Ephesus. Paul hoped to visit Timothy (3:14-15; 4:13). In the meantime, he wrote this letter to give Timothy practical advice for the ministry.

KEY PEOPLE
Paul, Timothy

KEY PLACE
Ephesus

KEY POINTS

TEACH AND MODEL Paul instructed Timothy to preserve the Christian faith by correctly teaching the foundational truths of the Scriptures and modeling right living. Likewise, we must know the truth in order to defend it. We can know the truth by studying the Bible.

PUBLIC WORSHIP Paul provided guidelines for conducting worship services. Christian character must be evident in every aspect of worship. We must rid ourselves of any attitudes that might disrupt worship or damage church unity.

CHURCH LEADERSHIP Paul gave specific instructions concerning the qualifications for church leaders. These qualifications haven't changed. When church leaders live up to these standards, God is honored.

A LIFE OF DISCIPLINE Timothy, like all church leaders, had to guard his motives, serve faithfully, and live a disciplined life. We can gain discipline by consistently studying God's Word and obeying it.

A CARING CHURCH Paul wrote about the church's responsibility to care for the needs of all of its members, especially the sick, the poor, and the widowed. Caring for the family of believers demonstrates our Christlike attitude and genuine love.

1 GREETINGS FROM PAUL

This letter is from Paul, an apostle of Christ Jesus, appointed by the command of God our Savior and Christ Jesus, who gives us hope.

²I am writing to Timothy, my true son in the faith.

May God the Father and Christ Jesus our Lord give you grace, mercy, and peace.

WARNINGS AGAINST FALSE TEACHINGS

³When I left for Macedonia, I urged you to stay there in Ephesus and stop those whose teaching is contrary to the truth. ⁴Don't let them waste their time in endless discussion of myths and spiritual pedigrees. These things only lead to meaningless speculations,* which don't help people live a life of faith in God.*

⁵The purpose of my instruction is that all believers would be filled with love that comes from a pure heart, a clear conscience, and genuine faith. ⁶But some people have missed this whole point. They have turned away from these things and spend their time in meaningless discussions. ⁷They want to be known as teachers of the law of Moses, but they don't know what they are talking about, even though they speak so confidently.

⁸We know that the law is good when used correctly. ⁹For the law was not intended for people who do what is right. It is for people who are lawless and rebellious, who are ungodly and sinful, who consider nothing sacred and defile what is holy, who kill their father or mother or commit other murders. ¹⁰The law is for people who are sexually immoral, or who practice homosexuality, or are slave traders,* liars, promise breakers, or who do anything else that contradicts the wholesome teaching ¹¹that comes from the glorious Good News entrusted to me by our blessed God.

PAUL'S GRATITUDE FOR GOD'S MERCY

¹²I thank Christ Jesus our Lord, who has given me strength to do his work. He considered me trustworthy and appointed me to serve him, ¹³even though I used to blaspheme the name of Christ. In my insolence, I persecuted his people. But God had mercy on me because I did it in ignorance and unbelief. ¹⁴Oh, how generous and gracious our Lord was! He filled me with the faith and love that come from Christ Jesus.

¹⁵This is a trustworthy saying, and everyone should accept it: "Christ Jesus came into the world to save sinners"—and I am the worst of them all. ¹⁶But God had mercy on me so that Christ Jesus could use me as a prime example of his great patience with even the worst sinners. Then others will realize that they, too, can believe in him and receive eternal life. ¹⁷All honor and glory to God forever and ever! He is the eternal King, the unseen one who never dies; he alone is God. Amen.

TIMOTHY'S RESPONSIBILITY

¹⁸Timothy, my son, here are my instructions for you, based on the prophetic words spoken about you earlier. May they help you fight well in the Lord's battles. ¹⁹Cling to your faith in Christ, and keep your conscience clear. For some people have deliberately violated their consciences; as a result, their faith has been shipwrecked. ²⁰Hymenaeus and Alexander are two examples. I threw them out and handed them over to Satan so they might learn not to blaspheme God.

2 INSTRUCTIONS ABOUT WORSHIP

I urge you, first of all, to pray for all people. Ask God to help them; intercede on their behalf, and give thanks for them. ²Pray this way for kings and all who are in authority so that we can live peaceful and quiet lives marked by godliness and dignity. ³This is good and pleases God our Savior, ⁴who wants everyone to be saved and to understand the truth. ⁵For there is only one God and one Mediator who can reconcile God and humanity—the man Christ Jesus. ⁶He gave his life to purchase freedom for everyone. This is the message God gave to the world at just the right time. ⁷And I have been chosen as a preacher and apostle

---

FALSE TEACHING

(1:3-11) Paul urged Timothy to put a stop to those who spread false information about God or the Scriptures. False teaching usually has these characteristics: (1) It stirs up questions and arguments instead of helping people come to Jesus (1:4). (2) It often is promoted by teachers whose motivation is to make a name for themselves (1:7). (3) It differs from what's taught in the Scriptures (1:6-7; 4:1-3). The best way to avoid being hurt by false teaching is to have a firm grasp on what's really true.

CLEAR CONSCIENCE

(1:19) How can you "keep your conscience clear"? Treasure your faith in Christ more than anything else and do what you know is right. Each time you deliberately ignore your conscience, you're hardening your heart. Your capacity to tell right from wrong slowly erodes. But when you stay close to God, he reminds you of what's right. Feeling the tug of your conscience? Don't ignore it!

1:4a Greek in myths and endless genealogies, which cause speculation. 1:4b Greek a stewardship of God in faith. 1:10 Or kidnappers.

to teach the Gentiles this message about faith and truth. I'm not exaggerating—just telling the truth.

8In every place of worship, I want men to pray with holy hands lifted up to God, free from anger and controversy.

9And I want women to be modest in their appearance.* They should wear decent and appropriate clothing and not draw attention to themselves by the way they fix their hair or by wearing gold or pearls or expensive clothes. 10For women who claim to be devoted to God should make themselves attractive by the good things they do.

11Women should learn quietly and submissively. 12I do not let women teach men or have authority over them.* Let them listen quietly. 13For God made Adam first, and afterward he made Eve. 14And it was not Adam who was deceived by Satan. The woman was deceived, and sin was the result. 15But women will be saved through childbearing,* assuming they continue to live in faith, love, holiness, and modesty.

3 **LEADERS IN THE CHURCH** This is a trustworthy saying: "If someone aspires to be an elder,* he desires an honorable position." 2So an elder must be a man whose life is above reproach. He must be faithful to his wife.* He must exercise self-control, live wisely, and have a good reputation. He must enjoy having guests in his home, and he must be able to teach. 3He must not be a heavy drinker* or be violent. He must be gentle, not quarrelsome, and not love money. 4He must manage his own family well, having children who respect and obey him. 5For if a man cannot manage his own household, how can he take care of God's church?

6An elder must not be a new believer, because he might become proud, and the devil would cause him to fall.* 7Also, people outside the church must speak well of him so that he will not be disgraced and fall into the devil's trap.

8In the same way, deacons must be well respected and have integrity. They must not be heavy drinkers or dishonest with money. 9They

must be committed to the mystery of the faith now revealed and must live with a clear conscience. 10Before they are appointed as deacons, let them be closely examined. If they pass the test, then let them serve as deacons.

11In the same way, their wives* must be respected and must not slander others. They must exercise self-control and be faithful in everything they do.

12A deacon must be faithful to his wife, and he must manage his children and household well. 13Those who do well as deacons will be rewarded with respect from others and will have increased confidence in their faith in Christ Jesus.

THE TRUTHS OF OUR FAITH 14I am writing these things to you now, even though I hope to be with you soon, 15so that if I am delayed, you will know how people must conduct themselves in the household of God. This is the church of the living God, which is the pillar and foundation of the truth.

16Without question, this is the great mystery of our faith*:

Christ* was revealed in a human body
    and vindicated by the Spirit.*
He was seen by angels
    and announced to the nations.
He was believed in throughout the world
    and taken to heaven in glory.

4 **WARNINGS AGAINST FALSE TEACHERS** Now the Holy Spirit tells us clearly that in the last times some will turn away from the true faith; they will follow deceptive spirits and teachings that come from demons. 2These people are hypocrites and liars, and their consciences are dead.*

3They will say it is wrong to be married and wrong to eat certain foods. But God created those foods to be eaten with thanks by faithful

....

MAKE PEACE
(2:8) Besides being displeasing to God, it is difficult to pray when we have sinned or when we feel angry and resentful. That is why Jesus told us to interrupt worship, if necessary, to make peace with others (Matt 5:23-24). Our goal is to have a right relationship with God and also with others.

GREAT EXPECTATIONS
(3:1-13) The word elder can refer to a pastor, church leader, or presiding elder. Paul stressed the high standards for spiritual leaders. Do you hold a position of spiritual leadership? Maybe you're a mentor for a younger teen or are a peer counselor in some way. Check yourself against Paul's standard of excellence. Those with great responsibility must meet high expectations.

2:9 Or *to pray in modest apparel.* 2:12 Or *teach men or usurp their authority.* 2:15 Or *will be saved by accepting their role as mothers,* or *will be saved by the birth of the Child.* 3:1 Or *an overseer,* or *a bishop;* also in 3:2, 6. 3:2 Or *must have only one wife,* or *must be married only once;* Greek reads *must be the husband of one wife;* also in 3:12. 3:3 Greek *must not drink too much wine;* similarly in 3:8. 3:6 Or *he might fall into the same judgment as the devil.* 3:11 Or *the women deacons.* The Greek word can be translated *women* or *wives.* 3:16a Or *of godliness.* 3:16b Greek *He who;* other manuscripts read *God.* 3:16c Or *in his spirit.* 4:2 Greek *are seared.*

{1 TIMOTHY 4:12} **DON'T LET ANYONE THINK LESS OF YOU BECAUSE YOU ARE YOUNG.**

BE AN EXAMPLE TO ALL BELIEVERS.

people who know the truth. ⁴Since everything God created is good, we should not reject any of it but receive it with thanks. ⁵For we know it is made acceptable* by the word of God and prayer.

A GOOD SERVANT OF CHRIST JESUS ⁶If you explain these things to the brothers and sisters,* Timothy, you will be a worthy servant of Christ Jesus, one who is nourished by the message of faith and the good teaching you have followed. ⁷Do not waste time arguing over godless ideas and old wives' tales. Instead, train yourself to be godly. ⁸"Physical training is good, but training for godliness is much better, promising benefits in this life and in the life to come." ⁹This is a trustworthy saying, and everyone should accept it. ¹⁰This is why we work hard and continue to struggle,* for our hope is in the living God, who is the Savior of all people and particularly of all believers.

¹¹Teach these things and insist that everyone learn them. ¹²Don't let anyone think less of you because you are young. Be an example to all believers in what you say, in the way you live, in your love, your faith, and your purity. ¹³Until I get there, focus on reading the Scriptures to

the church, encouraging the believers, and teaching them.

¹⁴Do not neglect the spiritual gift you received through the prophecy spoken over you when the elders of the church laid their hands on you. ¹⁵Give your complete attention to these matters. Throw yourself into your tasks so that everyone will see your progress. ¹⁶Keep a close watch on how you live and on your teaching. Stay true to what is right for the sake of your own salvation and the salvation of those who hear you.

5 **ADVICE ABOUT WIDOWS, ELDERS, AND SLAVES** Never speak harshly to an older man,* but appeal to him respectfully as you would to your own father. Talk to younger men as you would to your own brothers. ²Treat older women as you would your mother, and treat younger women with all purity as you would your own sisters.

³Take care of* any widow who has no one else to care for her. ⁴But if she has children or grandchildren, their first responsibility is to show godliness at home and repay their parents by taking care of them. This is something that pleases God.

⁵Now a true widow, a woman who is truly alone in this world, has placed her hope in God. She prays night and day, asking God for his help. ⁶But the widow who lives only for pleasure is spiritually dead even while she lives. ⁷Give these instructions to the church so that no one will be open to criticism.

⁸But those who won't care for their relatives, especially those in their own household, have

4:5 Or *made holy.* 4:6 Greek *brothers.* 4:10 Some manuscripts read *continue to suffer.* 5:1 Or *an elder.* 5:3 Or *Honor.*

CHOICES
materialism

Jeremy and his girlfriend Bianca (whom he calls Bee) can hardly wait until next Saturday. That's the day when the winning numbers in the state lottery will be announced. Everybody is buzzing about the jackpot—now more than 170 million dollars!

"Just think what we could do if we won," Jeremy says. "We'd be able—"

"I'm not gonna even think about it," Bianca interrupts. "I'll just get my hopes up, and then I'll be all disappointed."

"C'mon, Bee, why do you always have to be so negative? We've got as much of a chance as anyone else. In fact, we've got 10 chances to win. It's gotta happen to someone—might as well be us. And if we

do win, just think of all the stuff we could do, of all the things we could buy!"

"It *would* be great to be rich," Bianca admits. "Imagine going into the mall and picking up whatever you want and not even having to look at the price tag."

"Yeah, or going to any car dealership, walking over to the car you want, and saying, 'I'll take it.' Imagine that!"

"That'd be awesome!" Bianca exclaims.

The two dreamers sit thinking quietly for a few minutes. Finally Bianca breaks the silence. "Jeremy, I still can't help feeling like we just poured 10 dollars down the drain!"

"Bee!"

Ever felt like Bianca and Jeremy? See what God's Word says about the desire to get rich quick—1 Timothy 6:9-10.
Why do you think Paul stressed this message?

I WONDER...

Trying to be good and not sin seems like a full-time job. How can anyone stay pure? Why would anyone want to?

In 1 Timothy 6:11, Paul encouraged Timothy to "pursue righteousness and a godly life." In other words, keep doing what's right. But some try to seem holier than others in order to be admired or to earn their way to heaven.

Jesus talked a lot about the Pharisees. These men had created long lists of rules that they followed. They wanted to be admired for their discipline.

However, in Matthew 5:20, Jesus made an incredible statement: "I warn you—unless your righteousness is better than the righteousness of the teachers of religious law and the Pharisees, you will never enter the Kingdom of Heaven!" In other words, you have to have more than just correct behavior. You have to be pure on the inside. This inner purity begins by accepting Christ's death on the cross as punishment for our sins. When we do this, we take on Christ's purity. In God's eyes, we are worthy of eternity in heaven! Now that's a pretty good deal!

It doesn't stop there, of course. God wants us to be like Jesus. This is a lifelong process of allowing God to change us (see John 15:1-17; 1 Tim 6:11-12). It happens by staying close to Christ and living like he wants us to. It's what keeps the Christian life fun, interesting, and challenging.

Christians who are really alive realize that their eternity is settled. But they also genuinely want to be more like the one who paid such a high price for their souls—Jesus. Their motivation—and yours—should not be to parade goodness in front of others but rather to please God.

Staying pure and growing as a Christian is a "full-time job," but it is also a natural by-product of staying close to Christ.

---

denied the true faith. Such people are worse than unbelievers.

⁹A widow who is put on the list for support must be a woman who is at least sixty years old and was faithful to her husband.* ¹⁰She must be well respected by everyone because of the good she has done. Has she brought up her children well? Has she been kind to strangers and served other believers humbly?* Has she helped those who are in trouble? Has she always been ready to do good?

¹¹The younger widows should not be on the list, because their physical desires will overpower their devotion to Christ and they will want to remarry. ¹²Then they would be guilty of breaking their previous pledge. ¹³And if they are on the list, they will learn to be lazy and will spend their time gossiping from house to house, meddling in other people's business and talking about things they shouldn't. ¹⁴So I advise these younger widows to marry again, have children, and take care of their own homes. Then the enemy will not be able to say anything against them. ¹⁵For I am afraid that some of them have already gone astray and now follow Satan.

¹⁶If a woman who is a believer has relatives who are widows, she must take care of them and not put the responsibility on the church. Then the church can care for the widows who are truly alone.

¹⁷Elders who do their work well should be re-spected and paid well,* especially those who work hard at both preaching and teaching. ¹⁸For the Scripture says, "You must not muzzle an ox to keep it from eating as it treads out the grain." And in another place, "Those who work deserve their pay!"*

¹⁹Do not listen to an accusation against an elder unless it is confirmed by two or three witnesses. ²⁰Those who sin should be reprimanded in front of the whole church; this will serve as a strong warning to others.

²¹I solemnly command you in the presence of God and Christ Jesus and the highest angels to obey these instructions without taking sides or showing favoritism to anyone.

²²Never be in a hurry about appointing a church leader.* Do not share in the sins of others. Keep yourself pure.

²³Don't drink only water. You ought to drink a little wine for the sake of your stomach because you are sick so often.

²⁴Remember, the sins of some people are obvious, leading them to certain judgment. But there are others whose sins will not be revealed until later. ²⁵In the same way, the good deeds of some people are obvious. And the good deeds done in secret will someday come to light.

....

YOUR FAMILY
(5:8) Paul spoke out against those who refused to take care of their families. Almost everyone has relatives. According to Paul, people who neglect their family responsibilities have denied the faith. Are you doing your part to meet the needs of those in your family circle—even your little brothers and sisters?

5:9 Greek *was the wife of one husband.* **5:10** Greek *and washed the feet of God's holy people?* **5:17** Greek *should be worthy of double honor.* **5:18** Deut 25:4; Luke 10:7. **5:22** Greek *about the laying on of hands.*

6 All slaves should show full respect for their masters so they will not bring shame on the name of God and his teaching. ²If the masters are believers, that is no excuse for being disrespectful. Those slaves should work all the harder because their efforts are helping other believers* who are well loved.

FALSE TEACHING AND TRUE RICHES Teach these things, Timothy, and encourage every-one to obey them. ³Some people may contradict our teaching, but these are the wholesome teachings of the Lord Jesus Christ. These teachings promote a godly life. ⁴Anyone who teaches something different is arrogant and lacks understanding. Such a person has an unhealthy desire to quibble over the meaning of words. This stirs up arguments ending in jealousy, division, slander, and evil suspicions. ⁵These people always cause trouble. Their minds are corrupt, and they have turned their backs on the truth. To them, a show of godliness is just a way to become wealthy.

⁶Yet true godliness with contentment is itself great wealth. ⁷After all, we brought nothing with us when we came into the world, and we can't take anything with us when we leave it. ⁸So if we have enough food and clothing, let us be content.

⁹But people who long to be rich fall into

MONEY CYCLE
(6:6-21) Despite almost overwhelming evidence to the contrary, some people still believe that money brings happiness. Rich people craving greater riches can be caught in an endless cycle that only ends in ruin and desperation. How can you avoid the love of money? Paul gives us some principles: (1) Realize that one day riches will all be gone (6:7, 17). (2) Be content with what you have (6:8). (3) Avoid compromising your principles just to gain money (6:9-10). (4) Love people and God's work more than money (6:11). (5) Freely share what you have with others (6:18). (See also Proverbs 30:7-9.)

6:2 Greek *brothers.*

TIMOTHY
PERSONALITY PROFILE

EVER STRUGGLE WITH SHYNESS or know someone who does? Real leadership abilities are sometimes buried under a person's shyness. Yet a friend with understanding and patience can uncover those strengths. That's what happened between the apostle Paul and a young man named Timothy.

Timothy probably became a Christian when Paul visited his hometown of Lystra during his first missionary journey (Acts 14:8-20). Timothy's Jewish mother and grandmother had prepared him by teaching him from the Old Testament. By the time Paul visited Lystra again, Timothy was a growing Christian. When invited, Timothy jumped at the chance to travel with Paul and Silas.

Away from home, Timothy struggled with shyness. Unfortunately, shy people are often written off as being unable to carry much responsibility. But Paul chose to give Timothy important responsibilities in the ministry. Paul even made Timothy his personal representative on several occasions. Although Timothy sometimes failed, Paul never gave up on him.

Timothy was like a son to Paul, which is evident throughout 1 and 2 Timothy. The letters were intended to encourage and direct Timothy in Ephesus, where Paul had left him in charge of a young church (1 Tim 1:3-4). These letters also have encouraged countless other "Timothys" through the centuries. Are you a "Timothy"? Be encouraged!

When you face a challenge that seems beyond your abilities, you can find encouragement in 1 and 2 Timothy.

BOTTOM LINE: Those who are young can have a great influence on others through the power of God.

Our inadequacies and inabilities should not keep us from being available to God.

Timothy's story is told in Acts, starting in chapter 16. He also is mentioned in Romans 16:21; 1 Corinthians 4:17; 16:10-11; 2 Corinthians 1:1, 19; Philippians 1:1; 2:19-23; Colossians 1:1; 1 Thessalonians 1:1-10; 2:3-4; 3:1-6; 1 and 2 Timothy; Philemon 1:1; Hebrews 13:23.

UPS:
- *Became a believer after Paul's first missionary journey and joined him for two more journeys*
- *Was a respected Christian in his hometown*
- *Was Paul's special representative on several occasions*
- *Received two personal letters from Paul*
- *Probably knew Paul better than any other person, becoming like a son to him*

DOWNS:
- *Struggled with a timid and reserved nature*
- *Was disrespected because of his youthfulness*
- *Was apparently unable to correct some of the problems in the church at Ephesus when Paul sent him there*

STATS:
- *Where: Originally from Lystra; served in Ephesus*
- *Occupations: Missionary, church leader*
- *Relatives: Eunice (mother); Lois (grandmother); Greek father*
- *Contemporaries: Paul, Silas, Luke, Mark, Peter, Barnabas*

KEY VERSES: *Philippians 2:20-22*

temptation and are trapped by many foolish and harmful desires that plunge them into ruin and destruction. ¹⁰For the love of money is the root of all kinds of evil. And some people, craving money, have wandered from the true faith and pierced themselves with many sorrows.

PAUL'S FINAL INSTRUCTIONS ¹¹But you, Timothy, are a man of God; so run from all these evil things. Pursue righteousness and a godly life, along with faith, love, perseverance, and gentleness. ¹²Fight the good fight for the true faith. Hold tightly to the eternal life to which God has called you, which you have confessed so well before many witnesses. ¹³And I charge you before God, who gives life to all, and before Christ Jesus, who gave a good testimony before Pontius Pilate, ¹⁴that you obey this command without wavering. Then no one can find fault with you from now until our Lord Jesus Christ comes again. ¹⁵For at just the right time Christ will be revealed from heaven by the blessed and only almighty God, the King of all kings and Lord of all lords. ¹⁶He alone can never die, and he lives in light so brilliant that no human can approach him. No human eye has ever seen him, nor ever will. All honor and power to him forever! Amen.

¹⁷Teach those who are rich in this world not to be proud and not to trust in their money, which is so unreliable. Their trust should be in God, who richly gives us all we need for our enjoyment. ¹⁸Tell them to use their money to do good. They should be rich in good works and generous to those in need, always being ready to share with others. ¹⁹By doing this they will be storing up their treasure as a good foundation for the future so that they may experience true life.

²⁰Timothy, guard what God has entrusted to you. Avoid godless, foolish discussions with those who oppose you with their so-called knowledge. ²¹Some people have wandered from the faith by following such foolishness.

May God's grace be with you all.

YOU'RE RICH
(6:17-19) Ephesus was a wealthy city, and the church there probably had many wealthy members. Paul advised Timothy to deal with a potential problem by teaching that the possession of riches carries great responsibility. Those who have money must be generous, not arrogant. They must be careful not to put their trust in money instead of in the living God. Even if we don't have material wealth, we can be rich in good works toward others. No matter how poor we are, we have something to share with someone.

2 TIMOTHY

Trivia includes information that's often interesting but doesn't really matter much. For instance, did you know that . . .

- *Grasshoppers are more nutritious than steak?*
- *The record for the most bowling balls stacked vertically without glue or tape is ten?*
- *France's King Louis XIV probably bathed only twice in his life?*
- *Benjamin Franklin invented swim fins and the rocking chair?*
- *Mozart wrote the tune "Twinkle, Twinkle, Little Star" when he was five?*
- *Eating too many carrots can turn your skin yellow?*
- *Nine hundred and twenty-eight average size fleas will fit inside a Ping-Pong ball?*

Though amusing—and helpful for filling the silence in an awkward conversation—the facts just cited are worthless. They won't change your life. They're trivia. Trivial trivia.

Not so the book of 2 Timothy.

The apostle Paul's second letter to Timothy is serious stuff. History says that these were Paul's last words; he died shortly after penning them.

Perhaps the aged missionary recognized that his time was running out. If so, it's not surprising that he talked about important matters. Consider carefully Paul's final thoughts. He is, after all, one of the most influential individuals in church history. And Paul's challenge to Timothy is just as appropriate 2,000 years later.

The bottom line? Second Timothy is no trivial pursuit!

KEY POINTS

BOLDNESS In the face of opposition and persecution, Paul told Timothy to carry out his ministry unashamed and unafraid of the earthly consequences. To get over our fear of what people might say or do, we must take our eyes off people and look only to God.

FAITHFULNESS Paul urged Timothy to maintain not only a firm knowledge of what's true, but also to be steadfast. As we trust Christ, he counts us worthy to suffer and will give us the strength and endurance we need.

PREACHING AND TEACHING Paul encouraged Timothy not only to carry the torch of truth but also to train others, passing on to them his knowledge of the Scriptures and his enthusiasm for serving God's kingdom. Likewise, each of us can look for ways to become better equipped to serve, as well as for ways to teach others what we have learned.

ERROR In the final days before Christ returns, there will be false teachers, spiritual dropouts, and heresy. Therefore, we must be disciplined and ready to reject error. Knowing the Bible is a sure defense against error and confusion.

1

GREETINGS FROM PAUL This letter is from Paul, chosen by the will of God to be an apostle of Christ Jesus. I have been sent out to tell others about the life he has promised through faith in Christ Jesus.

²I am writing to Timothy, my dear son.

May God the Father and Christ Jesus our Lord give you grace, mercy, and peace.

ENCOURAGEMENT TO BE FAITHFUL
³Timothy, I thank God for you—the God I serve with a clear conscience, just as my ancestors did. Night and day I constantly remember you in my prayers. ⁴I long to see you again, for I remember your tears as we parted. And I will be filled with joy when we are together again.

⁵I remember your genuine faith, for you share the faith that first filled your grandmother Lois and your mother, Eunice. And I know that same faith continues strong in you. ⁶This is why I remind you to fan into flames the spiritual gift God gave you when I laid my hands on you. ⁷For God has not given us a spirit of fear and timidity, but of power, love, and self-discipline.

⁸So never be ashamed to tell others about our Lord. And don't be ashamed of me, either, even though I'm in prison for him. With the strength God gives you, be ready to suffer with me for the sake of the Good News. ⁹For God saved us and called us to live a holy life. He did this, not because we deserved it, but because that was his plan from before the beginning of time—to show us his grace through Christ Jesus. ¹⁰And now he has made all of this plain to us by the appearing of Christ Jesus, our Savior. He broke the power of death and illuminated the way to life and immortality through the Good News. ¹¹And God chose me to be a preacher, an apostle, and a teacher of this Good News.

¹²That is why I am suffering here in prison.

But I am not ashamed of it, for I know the one in whom I trust, and I am sure that he is able to guard what I have entrusted to him* until the day of his return.

¹³Hold on to the pattern of wholesome teaching you learned from me—a pattern shaped by the faith and love that you have in Christ Jesus. ¹⁴Through the power of the Holy Spirit who lives within us, carefully guard the precious truth that has been entrusted to you.

¹⁵As you know, everyone from the province of Asia has deserted me—even Phygelus and Hermogenes.

¹⁶May the Lord show special kindness to Onesiphorus and all his family because he often visited and encouraged me. He was never ashamed of me because I was in chains. ¹⁷When he came to Rome, he searched everywhere until he found me. ¹⁸May the Lord show him special kindness on the day of Christ's return. And you know very well how helpful he was in Ephesus.

2

A GOOD SOLDIER OF CHRIST JESUS Timothy, my dear son, be strong through the grace that God gives you in Christ Jesus. ²You have heard me teach things that have been confirmed by many reliable witnesses. Now teach these truths to other trustworthy people who will be able to pass them on to others.

³Endure suffering along with me, as a good soldier of Christ Jesus. ⁴Soldiers don't get tied up in the affairs of civilian life, for then they cannot please the officer who enlisted them. ⁵And athletes cannot win the prize unless they follow the rules. ⁶And hardworking farmers should be the first to enjoy the fruit of their labor. ⁷Think about what I am saying. The Lord will help you understand all these things.

⁸Always remember that Jesus Christ, a descendant of King David, was raised from the dead. This is the Good News I preach. ⁹And because I preach this Good News, I am suffering and have been chained like a criminal. But the word of God cannot be chained. ¹⁰So I am willing to endure anything if it will bring salvation and eternal glory in Christ Jesus to those God has chosen.

¹¹This is a trustworthy saying:

If we die with him,
    we will also live with him.
¹² If we endure hardship,
    we will reign with him.
If we deny him,
    he will deny us.

BE BOLD
(1:6-8) Timothy was experiencing great opposition to his message and to himself as a leader. Timothy's youth, his association with Paul, and his leadership had come under fire. But Paul urged Timothy to be bold. When we allow people to intimidate us, we neutralize our effectiveness for God. The power of the Holy Spirit can help us overcome our fear of what some might say or do to us so we can continue to do God's work.

CHOSEN
(2:10) We are free to choose between life and death, yet God has chosen us. This is a mystery our finite minds cannot easily grasp. But even if we do not completely understand it, we can still choose Jesus and be grateful that he has chosen us.

1:12 Or *what has been entrusted to me.*

¹³ If we are unfaithful,
  he remains faithful,
  for he cannot deny who he is.

¹⁴Remind everyone about these things, and command them in God's presence to stop fighting over words. Such arguments are useless, and they can ruin those who hear them.

AN APPROVED WORKER ¹⁵Work hard so you can present yourself to God and receive his approval. Be a good worker, one who does not need to be ashamed and who correctly explains the word of truth. ¹⁶Avoid worthless, foolish talk that only leads to more godless behavior. ¹⁷This kind of talk spreads like cancer,* as in the case of Hymenaeus and Philetus. ¹⁸They have left the path of truth, claiming that the resurrection of the dead has already occurred; in this way, they have turned some people away from the faith.

¹⁹But God's truth stands firm like a foundation stone with this inscription: "The Lord knows those who are his,"* and "All who belong to the Lord must turn away from evil."*

²⁰In a wealthy home some utensils are made of gold and silver, and some are made of wood and clay. The expensive utensils are used for special occasions, and the cheap ones are for everyday use. ²¹If you keep yourself pure, you will be a special utensil for honorable use. Your life will be clean, and you will be ready for the Master to use you for every good work.

²²Run from anything that stimulates youthful lusts. Instead, pursue righteous living, faithfulness, love, and peace. Enjoy the companionship of those who call on the Lord with pure hearts.

2:17 Greek *gangrene.*   **2:19a** Num 16:5.   **2:19b** See Isa 52:11.
3:6 Greek *and take captive.*

²³Again I say, don't get involved in foolish, ignorant arguments that only start fights. ²⁴A servant of the Lord must not quarrel but must be kind to everyone, be able to teach, and be patient with difficult people. ²⁵Gently instruct those who oppose the truth. Perhaps God will change those people's hearts, and they will learn the truth. ²⁶Then they will come to their senses and escape from the devil's trap. For they have been held captive by him to do whatever he wants.

3 **THE DANGERS OF THE LAST DAYS** You should know this, Timothy, that in the last days there will be very difficult times. ²For people will love only themselves and their money. They will be boastful and proud, scoffing at God, disobedient to their parents, and ungrateful. They will consider nothing sacred. ³They will be unloving and unforgiving; they will slander others and have no self-control. They will be cruel and hate what is good. ⁴They will betray their friends, be reckless, be puffed up with pride, and love pleasure rather than God. ⁵They will act religious, but they will reject the power that could make them godly. Stay away from people like that!

⁶They are the kind who work their way into people's homes and win the confidence of*

....

RUN!
(2:22) Paul warned Timothy to run from anything that produces evil thoughts. Running away is sometimes considered cowardly. But wise people realize that removing themselves physically from temptation is often very wise. Perhaps you've experienced a temptation that seems difficult to resist. Knowing when to run is as important in a spiritual battle as knowing when and how to fight (see also 1 Tim 6:11).

CHOICES music

It's guaranteed to be the most spectacular concert tour ever. The members of Last Champion are getting back together for one last show.

People begin lining up a week in advance for tickets! Among the L.C. faithful are three teens who happen to be Christians. Let's ask Emily (Em), Noah, and Angel a few questions.

"So you guys are pretty hyped, huh?"

Noah: "Oh, yeah! This is gonna be awesome! I saw Last Champion on their last tour, and they were unbelievable. During the last song, the guitarist shattered nine guitars!"

"Isn't he the same guy who pulls the ears off rabbits?"

Em: "Only once . . . and he apologized later. I'd give anything for a front row seat. I want to see what he wears."

"You mean almost wears?" (Em and the guys laugh.)

"Does it bother you that these guys constantly brag about how many women they've slept with?"

Angel: "Naw, man. I just like their music."

"But should Christians support people who laugh at our beliefs and values?"

Em: "Chill, dude! It's just a concert!"

What's your view? Does the band's behavior outside of the auditorium really matter? Read 2 Timothy 3:1-5, noting especially the end of verse 5. How would this advice affect your choice of music?

ALL SCRIPTURE IS INSPIRED BY GOD AND IS USEFUL TO TEACH US WHAT IS TRUE AND TO MAKE US REALIZE WHAT IS WRONG IN OUR LIVES.

||||||||||||| 2 TIMOTHY 3:16 |||||||||||||

vulnerable women who are burdened with the guilt of sin and controlled by various desires. 7(Such women are forever following new teachings, but they are never able to understand the truth.) 8These teachers oppose the truth just as Jannes and Jambres opposed Moses. They have depraved minds and a counterfeit faith. 9But they won't get away with this for long. Someday everyone will recognize what fools they are, just as with Jannes and Jambres.

PAUL'S CHARGE TO TIMOTHY 10But you, Timothy, certainly know what I teach, and how I live, and what my purpose in life is. You know my faith, my patience, my love, and my endurance. 11You know how much persecution and suffering I have endured. You know all about how I was persecuted in Antioch, Iconium, and Lystra—but the Lord rescued me from all of it.

....

DIVINE INSPIRATION
(3:16) The Bible is not a collection of stories, fables, myths, or merely human ideas about God. Through the Holy Spirit, God revealed himself and his plan to godly men, who wrote down God's message for his people (see 2 Pet 1:20-21). This process is known as inspiration. The writers wrote from their own personal, historical, and cultural contexts. Yet, though they used their own minds, talents, languages, and styles, they wrote what God wanted them to write. Scripture is completely trustworthy because God was in control of its writing. How does this truth affect your view of the Bible?

12Yes, and everyone who wants to live a godly life in Christ Jesus will suffer persecution. 13But evil people and impostors will flourish. They will deceive others and will themselves be deceived.

14But you must remain faithful to the things you have been taught. You know they are true, for you know you can trust those who taught you. 15You have been taught the holy Scriptures from childhood, and they have given you the wisdom to receive the salvation that comes by trusting in Christ Jesus. 16All Scripture is inspired by God and is useful to teach us what is true and to make us realize what is wrong in our lives. It corrects us when we are wrong and teaches us to do what is right. 17God uses it to prepare and equip his people to do every good work.

4 I solemnly urge you in the presence of God and Christ Jesus, who will someday judge the living and the dead when he appears to set up his Kingdom: 2Preach the word of God. Be prepared, whether the time is favorable or not. Patiently correct, rebuke, and encourage your people with good teaching.

3For a time is coming when people will no longer listen to sound and wholesome teaching. They will follow their own desires and will look for teachers who will tell them whatever their itching ears want to hear. 4They will reject the truth and chase after myths.

5But you should keep a clear mind in every situation. Don't be afraid of suffering for the Lord. Work at telling others the Good News, and fully carry out the ministry God has given you.

6As for me, my life has already been poured out as an offering to God. The time of my death is near. 7I have fought the good fight, I have

I WONDER...

A friend of mine stopped coming to church because he said that God had stopped answering his prayers. How do I answer him?

Like Demas, who deserted Paul (see 2 Tim 4:10), many Christians have a what-have-you-done-for-me-lately type of faith in God. Oh, they're willing to trust him in the good times. When trouble hits, however, they figure God has "checked out" on them—so they "check out" on God.

Because we live in a society where we often can get what we want when we want it, we may begin to think

that God's only purpose is to meet our needs. When something doesn't work out or we think that God hasn't come through for us, we turn away from him.

God is in the business of molding our character. One way he does this is by allowing us to go through tough times. When Paul wrote 2 Timothy, the church was going through intense persecution. Demas got tired of it and left. He wanted his comforts more than he wanted God's will.

Encourage your friend to change the what-have-you-done-for-me-lately attitude. Help him realize that God wants to build his character. His goal is not to make us feel good, but to help us mature.

finished the race, and I have remained faithful. ⁸And now the prize awaits me—the crown of righteousness, which the Lord, the righteous Judge, will give me on the day of his return. And the prize is not just for me but for all who eagerly look forward to his appearing.

PAUL'S FINAL WORDS

⁹Timothy, please come as soon as you can. ¹⁰Demas has deserted me because he loves the things of this life and has gone to Thessalonica. Crescens has gone to Galatia, and Titus has gone to Dalmatia. ¹¹Only Luke is with me. Bring Mark with you when you come, for he will be helpful to me in my ministry. ¹²I sent Tychicus to Ephesus. ¹³When you come, be sure to bring the coat I left with Carpus at Troas. Also bring my books, and especially my papers.*

¹⁴Alexander the coppersmith did me much harm, but the Lord will judge him for what he has done. ¹⁵Be careful of him, for he fought against everything we said.

¹⁶The first time I was brought before the judge, no one came with me. Everyone abandoned me. May it not be counted against them. ¹⁷But the Lord stood with me and gave me strength so that I might preach the Good News in its entirety for all the Gentiles to hear. And he rescued me from certain death.* ¹⁸Yes, and the Lord will deliver me from every evil attack and will bring me safely into his heavenly Kingdom. All glory to God forever and ever! Amen.

PAUL'S FINAL GREETINGS

¹⁹Give my greetings to Priscilla and Aquila and those living in the household of Onesiphorus. ²⁰Erastus stayed at Corinth, and I left Trophimus sick at Miletus.

²¹Do your best to get here before winter. Eubulus sends you greetings, and so do Pudens, Linus, Claudia, and all the brothers and sisters.*

²²May the Lord be with your spirit. And may his grace be with all of you.

....

4:13 Greek *especially the parchments.* 4:17 Greek *from the mouth of a lion.* 4:21 Greek *brothers.*

THIS LIFE
(4:10) *Demas had been one of Paul's co-workers (Col 4:14; Phlm 1:24). Yet he deserted Paul because Demas loved "the things of this life." Do you love what the world has to offer—wealth, power, pleasure—even if gaining it means hurting people and neglecting the work God has given you to do? If so, the apostle John has this advice: "Do not love this world nor the things it offers you, for when you love the world, you do not have the love of the Father in you" (1 Jn 2:15).*

TITUS

In many of life's situations—whether from natural instinct, repeated instruction, or unpleasant experience—you know precisely what to do.

For instance:

- *If your clothing catches on fire, drop to the ground and roll.*
- *In case of emergency, call 9-1-1.*
- *Never stare at the sun during an eclipse.*
- *Always wash your hands after using the restroom and before eating.*
- *On a first date, never order pizza with extra garlic and onions.*
- *Don't run while carrying sharp objects.*
- *Never swim right after eating.*
- *When attacked by a bear, fall face down and play dead.*
- *Look both ways before crossing a street.*
- *Make certain you know the price of an object before you agree to buy it.*
- *Never sign anything until you read the fine print.*

You've probably heard these rules before; no doubt you could handle each situation with ease. But what about the millions of other situations where you aren't sure what to do?

Now you see why Paul's epistle to Titus is so important. Through it you'll gain plenty of practical advice for living a pure life in an impure world. Wondering about commitment, discipline, self-control, purity, solid relationships, or civic duties? Dive on into this dynamic little letter—it's all here.

STATS

PURPOSE
To advise Titus in his responsibility of supervising the churches on the island of Crete

AUTHOR
Paul

ORIGINAL AUDIENCE
Titus, a Greek convert, who had become Paul's special representative to the island of Crete

DATE WRITTEN
About A.D. 64, around the same time 1 Timothy was written; probably from Macedonia in between Paul's periods of imprisonment in Rome

SETTING
Paul had left Titus on Crete to organize and oversee the churches there. This letter tells him how to do the job.

KEY PEOPLE
Paul, Titus

KEY PLACES
Crete

SPECIAL FEATURE
Titus is very similar to 1 Timothy with its instructions to church leaders.

KEY POINTS

A GOOD LIFE Paul gave Titus advice on living "the good life." This life consists of a belief in Jesus, along with the commitment and discipline to serve others.

CHARACTER Titus's responsibility on Crete was to appoint church leaders (elders) to maintain proper organization and discipline. Their qualifications—self-control and integrity—are important qualities for all Christians.

CHURCH RELATIONSHIPS Older Christians were to teach and be examples to younger men and women. Every age and group has a lesson to learn and a role to play.

CITIZENSHIP Christians must be good citizens in society, not just in church. Believers must obey the government and work honestly. How you fulfill your civic duties is a witness to the watching world.

TITUS GOES TO CRETE
Tradition says that after Paul was released from prison in Rome, he and Titus traveled together for a while. They stopped in Crete. When it was time for Paul to go, he left Titus behind to help the churches there.

1 **GREETINGS FROM PAUL** This letter is from Paul, a slave of God and an apostle of Jesus Christ. I have been sent to proclaim faith to* those God has chosen and to teach them to know the truth that shows them how to live godly lives. ²This truth gives them confidence that they have eternal life, which God—who does not lie—promised them before the world began. ³And now at just the right time he has revealed this message, which we announce to everyone. It is by the command of God our Savior that I have been entrusted with this work for him.

⁴I am writing to Titus, my true son in the faith that we share.

May God the Father and Christ Jesus our Savior give you grace and peace.

TITUS'S WORK IN CRETE ⁵I left you on the island of Crete so you could complete our work there and appoint elders in each town as I instructed you. ⁶An elder must live a blameless life. He must be faithful to his wife,* and his children must be believers who don't have a reputation for being wild or rebellious. ⁷An elder* is a manager of God's household, so he must live a blameless life. He must not be arrogant or quick-tempered; he must not be a heavy drinker,* violent, or dishonest with money.

⁸Rather, he must enjoy having guests in his home, and he must love what is good. He must live wisely and be just. He must live a devout and disciplined life. ⁹He must have a strong belief in the trustworthy message he was taught; then he will be able to encourage others with wholesome teaching and show those who oppose it where they are wrong.

¹⁰For there are many rebellious people who engage in useless talk and deceive others. This is especially true of those who insist on circumcision for salvation. ¹¹They must be silenced, because they are turning whole families away from the truth by their false teaching. And they do it only for money. ¹²Even one of their own men, a prophet from Crete, has said

----

THE FOUNDATION OF FAITH
(1:1-2) As Paul explained, the foundation of a believer's faith is trust in God's character. Because he is the source of all truth, he cannot lie. The eternal life he has promised will be ours because he keeps his promises. Is your faith built on that foundation?

1:1 Or *to strengthen the faith of.* **1:6** Or *must have only one wife,* or *must be married only once;* Greek reads *must be the husband of one wife.* **1:7a** Or *An overseer,* or *A bishop.* **1:7b** Greek *must not drink too much wine.*

about them, "The people of Crete are all liars, cruel animals, and lazy gluttons."* [13]This is true. So reprimand them sternly to make them strong in the faith. [14]They must stop listening to Jewish myths and the commands of people who have turned away from the truth.

[15]Everything is pure to those whose hearts are pure. But nothing is pure to those who are corrupt and unbelieving, because their minds and consciences are corrupted. [16]Such people claim they know God, but they deny him by the way they live. They are detestable and disobedient, worthless for doing anything good.

2 PROMOTE RIGHT TEACHING As for you, Titus, promote the kind of living that reflects wholesome teaching. [2]Teach the older men to exercise self-control, to be worthy of respect, and to live wisely. They must have sound faith and be filled with love and patience.

[3]Similarly, teach the older women to live in a way that honors God. They must not slander others or be heavy drinkers.* Instead, they should teach others what is good. [4]These older women must train the younger women to love their husbands and their children, [5]to live wisely and be pure, to work in their homes,* to do good, and to be submissive to their husbands. Then they will not bring shame on the word of God.

[6]In the same way, encourage the young men to live wisely. [7]And you yourself must be an example to them by doing good works of every kind. Let everything you do reflect the integrity

1:12 This quotation is from Epimenides of Knossos. 2:3 Greek be enslaved to much wine. 2:5 Some manuscripts read to care for their homes.

and seriousness of your teaching. [8]Teach the truth so that your teaching can't be criticized. Then those who oppose us will be ashamed and have nothing bad to say about us.

[9]Slaves must always obey their masters and do their best to please them. They must not talk back [10]or steal, but must show themselves to be entirely trustworthy and good. Then they will make the teaching about God our Savior attractive in every way.

[11]For the grace of God has been revealed, bringing salvation to all people. [12]And we are instructed to turn from godless living and sinful pleasures. We should live in this evil world with wisdom, righteousness, and devotion to God, [13]while we look forward with hope to that wonderful day when the glory of our great God and Savior, Jesus Christ, will be revealed. [14]He gave his life to free us from every kind of sin, to cleanse us, and to make us his very own people, totally committed to doing good deeds.

[15]You must teach these things and encourage the believers to do them. You have the authority to correct them when necessary, so don't let anyone disregard what you say.

....

BE AN EXAMPLE
(2:6-8) Paul urged Titus to be a good example to those around him so that others might see his good works and imitate him. Titus's life would give his words greater impact. If you want someone to act a certain way, be sure to live that way yourself. You then will earn the right to be heard.

CHOICES
integrity

When Dawn sticks her head into her youth leader's office, it's plain to see that she's troubled. "Evangeline, can I talk to you?" she asks.

"Sure, Dawn. Come in."

"It's this whole youth group leadership team thing. I feel bad saying anything. . . ."

"What do you mean?"

"Well, you know Kelly, the girl who's been coming with me to church the last few weeks?"

"Yeah."

"Well, she told me that she wants to be on the team. She wants to be in charge of publicity for the youth group."

"That's great. We've been looking for someone to fill that—"

"No, that's not great! You don't know Kelly. She's pretty wild . . . I mean, she's not exactly living like a Christian."

"I see."

"Don't get me wrong. I really love Kelly, and I'm trying to be a good influence on her and everything. I just don't think it's a very good idea to have her out there in charge of publicizing our group. At least not while she's living like she is. People might get the wrong idea, you know?"

"I agree. So, are you going to talk to her?"

"Oh, I guess so. Any advice?"

"Sure. If I were you, I'd . . ."

Christians in leadership positions are expected to be people of integrity. Read Titus 1:5-8; 2:11–3:8 for a quick glimpse at the qualities Christian leaders must possess.

{ TITUS 2:12 } WE ARE INSTRUCTED TO TURN
FROM GODLESS LIVING AND SINFUL PLEASURES.

WE SHOULD LIVE IN THIS EVIL WORLD WITH WISDOM, RIGHTEOUSNESS, ᴬᴺᴰDEVOTION TO GOD.

3 **DO WHAT IS GOOD** Remind the believers to submit to the government and its officers. They should be obedient, always ready to do what is good. ²They must not slander anyone and must avoid quarreling. Instead, they should be gentle and show true humility to everyone.

³Once we, too, were foolish and disobedient. We were misled and became slaves to many

lusts and pleasures. Our lives were full of evil and envy, and we hated each other.

⁴But—"When God our Savior revealed his kindness and love, ⁵he saved us, not because of the righteous things we had done, but because of his mercy. He washed away our sins, giving us a new birth and new life through the Holy Spirit.* ⁶He generously poured out the Spirit upon us through Jesus Christ our Savior. ⁷Because of his grace he declared us righteous and gave us confidence that we will inherit eternal life." ⁸This is a trustworthy saying, and I want you to insist on these teachings so that all who trust in God will devote themselves to doing good. These teachings are good and beneficial for everyone.

⁹Do not get involved in foolish discussions about spiritual pedigrees* or in quarrels and fights about obedience to Jewish laws. These things are useless and a waste of time. ¹⁰If people are causing divisions among you, give a first and second warning. After that, have nothing more to do with them. ¹¹For people like that have turned away from the truth, and their own sins condemn them.

··

SLAVE TO SIN
(3:3) Following a life of pleasure and giving in to every desire leads to slavery. Many think freedom consists of doing anything they want. But this path leads to an addiction to gratification. A person is no longer free, but is a slave to what his or her body dictates (2 Pet 2:19). But Jesus frees us from the desires and control of sin. Have you been released?

AVOIDING ARGUMENTS
(3:9-11) Paul warns Titus, as he warned Timothy, not to get involved in foolish and unprofitable disputes (2 Tim 2:14). This does not mean that we should refuse to study or discuss different interpretations of difficult Bible passages. Paul warned against petty quarrels, rather than honest discussions that lead to wisdom. You can stop an argument by turning the discussion back in a direction that leads to a deeper understanding of the passage.

PAUL'S FINAL REMARKS AND GREETINGS

¹²I am planning to send either Artemas or Tychicus to you. As soon as one of them arrives, do your best to meet me at Nicopolis, for I have decided to stay there for the winter. ¹³Do everything you can to help Zenas the lawyer and Apollos with their trip. See that they are given everything they need. ¹⁴Our people must learn to do good by meeting the urgent needs of others; then they will not be unproductive.

¹⁵Everybody here sends greetings. Please give my greetings to the believers—all who love us.

May God's grace be with you all.

3:5 Greek *He saved us through the washing of regeneration and renewing of the Holy Spirit.*   **3:9** Or *spiritual genealogies.*

PHILEMON

"I could never forgive her!"

"He'll never get serious about God!"

"I wish things would work out, but they won't. My situation is impossible!"

Ever heard—or made—statements like those? If so, take this hint! Never say never. Many of the hard-to-believe things we declare "impossible!" eventually do come to pass . . . right before our embarrassed eyes.

Consider the Munich elementary school teacher who told ten-year-old Albert Einstein that he would never amount to very much.

Or the doctors who wanted to amputate the feet of track star Gail Devers. Devers suffered from Graves' disease, a thyroid disorder. Her doctors were sure that she would never run again. But Devers not only recovered, she went on to win the gold medal in the 100-meter dash in not one but two consecutive Olympics (1992 and 1996). She also won gold medals in the 100-meter hurdles.

Or the misguided executive with the Decca Recording Company in the early '60s who decided not to offer a contract to an obscure musical group called The Beatles.

And you can be sure Simon Newcomb is red-faced in his grave. He's the guy who asserted in the 1800s that "flight by machines heavier than air is . . . utterly impossible."

Never say never. Don't end that friendship or relationship just because you've been wronged. Don't give up on that friend who claims to be an atheist. Don't throw in the towel on your dream. Don't write off your future just because you've made some bad choices in the past.

Never say never. The Gospel of Matthew states that same principle: "With God everything is possible" (Matt 19:26). The book of Philemon illustrates it with the story of how a poor slave and his rich master ended up as Christian brothers. You're about to read a story of betrayal and forgiveness and of how Jesus Christ breaks down all barriers.

So before you say, "That's impossible!" or, "That could never happen!" take five minutes to read Paul's postcard to Philemon.

STATS

PURPOSE
To convince Philemon to forgive—and accept as a brother in the faith—his runaway slave, Onesimus

AUTHOR
Paul

ORIGINAL AUDIENCE
Philemon, who probably was a wealthy member of the church in Colosse

DATE WRITTEN
About A.D. 60, during Paul's first imprisonment in Rome, at about the same time that the Epistles to the Ephesians and Colossians were written

SETTING
Slavery was very common in the Roman Empire. Evidently, some Christians had slaves.

KEY PEOPLE
Paul, Philemon, Onesimus

KEY PLACES
Colosse, Rome

KEY POINTS

FORGIVENESS Paul asked Philemon not to punish Onesimus for his infractions, but to forgive and restore him as a new Christian brother. In the same way, forgiving those who have wronged you is the appropriate response to Christ's forgiveness of you.

BARRIERS While slavery was a barrier between people, Paul declared Onesimus, a slave, to be Philemon's brother in Christ. Paul stressed that Christian love and fellowship could overcome cultural barriers. Although similar social and economic barriers still exist today, in Christ we are one family. Racial, economic, or political differences should not separate believers.

RESPECT Paul had the authority as an apostle to tell Philemon what to do. Yet Paul chose to appeal to his friend in Christian love rather than order him to do what he wished. Like Paul, we can choose to use tactful persuasion when dealing with people. Tact often accomplishes a great deal more than commands.

GREETINGS FROM PAUL This letter is from Paul, a prisoner for preaching the Good News about Christ Jesus, and from our brother Timothy.

I am writing to Philemon, our beloved co-worker, ²and to our sister Apphia, and to our fellow soldier Archippus, and to the church that meets in your* house.

³May God our Father and the Lord Jesus Christ give you grace and peace.

PAUL'S THANKSGIVING AND PRAYER ⁴I always thank my God when I pray for you, Philemon, ⁵because I keep hearing about your faith in the Lord Jesus and your love for all of God's people. ⁶And I am praying that you will

HE IS NO LONGER LIKE A SLAVE TO YOU.... HE IS A BELOVED BROTHER.... NOW HE WILL MEAN MUCH MORE TO YOU.

■ ■ ■ ■ PHILEMON 1:16 ■ ■ ■ ■

put into action the generosity that comes from your faith as you understand and experience all the good things we have in Christ. ⁷Your love has given me much joy and comfort, my brother, for your kindness has often refreshed the hearts of God's people.

PAUL'S APPEAL FOR ONESIMUS ⁸That is why I am boldly asking a favor of you. I could demand it in the name of Christ because it is the right thing for you to do. ⁹But because of our love, I prefer simply to ask you. Consider this as a request from me—Paul, an old man and now also a prisoner for the sake of Christ Jesus.*

¹⁰I appeal to you to show kindness to my child, Onesimus. I became his father in the faith while here in prison. ¹¹Onesimus* hasn't been of much use to you in the past, but now he is very useful to both of us. ¹²I am sending him back to you, and with him comes my own heart.

¹³I wanted to keep him here with me while I am in these chains for preaching the Good News, and he would have helped me on your behalf. ¹⁴But I didn't want to do anything without your consent. I wanted you to help because you were willing, not because you

2 Throughout this letter, *you* and *your* are singular except in verses 3, 22, and 25.   9 Or *a prisoner of Christ Jesus.*   11 *Onesimus* means "useful."

DEALING WITH CONFLICT
(1:8-9) Because Paul was an elder and an apostle, he could have used his authority with Philemon, commanding his friend to deal kindly with his runaway slave. But Paul based his request not on his own authority, but on Philemon's Christian commitment. Paul wanted Philemon's heartfelt obedience.

When you know something is right and you have the power to demand it, do you appeal to your authority or the other person's commitment? Here Paul provides a good example of how to deal with a possible conflict between Christian friends.

FORGIVEN
(1:10, 16) Paul asked Philemon not only to forgive his runaway slave who had become a Christian, but to accept him as a brother. As Christians, we have the responsibility of forgiving as we have been forgiven (Matt 6:12; Eph 4:31-32). True forgiveness means that we treat the person we've forgiven as we would want to be treated. Is there someone you say you have forgiven, but who still needs your kindness?

CHOICES
reconciliation

As roommates (and total opposites), college freshmen Arwen and Morgan had a very awkward relationship:

- Morgan was totally into sports; Arwen preferred activities that didn't involve sweat.
- Morgan was loud; Arwen was quiet.
- Morgan had to get a scholarship since her family couldn't afford to send her to college; Arwen came from a family with money.
- Morgan was a night owl; Arwen was a morning person.
- Morgan was not a Christian; Arwen was.

At the end of the fall semester, Arwen moved out of the dorm into an apartment. Right about that same time, she couldn't find her diamond earrings.

Although she suspected Morgan, she never said a word.

The following summer, Arwen received a letter from Morgan. The first part of the letter told how Morgan had come to Christ during a beach outreach. The second half was a confession. Morgan had indeed taken the earrings and pawned them for some needed cash. She pleaded for forgiveness and promised to pay back the money.

Arwen immediately wrote back, welcoming Morgan to the family of God, granting the requested forgiveness, and suggesting that they get together first thing in the fall.

Could you have responded to Morgan as Arwen did? Their story isn't a fairy tale. Read Philemon to see for yourself the amazing reconciliation that Jesus makes possible.

were forced. [15]It seems you lost Onesimus for a little while so that you could have him back forever. [16]He is no longer like a slave to you. He is more than a slave, for he is a beloved brother, especially to me. Now he will mean much more to you, both as a man and as a brother in the Lord.

[17]So if you consider me your partner, welcome him as you would welcome me. [18]If he has wronged you in any way or owes you anything, charge it to me. [19]I, Paul, write this with my own hand: I will repay it. And I won't mention that you owe me your very soul!

[20]Yes, my brother, please do me this favor* for the Lord's sake. Give me this encouragement in Christ.

[21]I am confident as I write this letter that you will do what I ask and even more! [22]One more thing—please prepare a guest room for me, for I am hoping that God will answer your prayers and let me return to you soon.

PAUL'S FINAL GREETINGS [23]Epaphras, my fellow prisoner in Christ Jesus, sends you his greetings. [24]So do Mark, Aristarchus, Demas, and Luke, my co-workers.

[25]May the grace of the Lord Jesus Christ be with your spirit.

20 Greek *onaimen*, a play on the name Onesimus.

EQUALS

(1:13-16) What a difference Onesimus's status as a Christian made in his relationship to Philemon. He was no longer merely a servant, he was also a brother. Now both Onesimus and Philemon were members of God's family—equals in Christ. A Christian's status as a member of God's family transcends all other distinctions among believers. Do you look down on any fellow Christians? Remember, they are your brothers and sisters, your equals before Christ (Gal 3:28). How you treat your brothers and sisters in Christ's family reflects your true Christian commitment.

IN THE FAMILY

(1:16) Paul urged Philemon to be reconciled to his slave, receiving him as a brother and fellow member of God's family. Reconciliation means reestablishing a relationship. Christ has reconciled us to God and to others. Many barriers come between people—race, social status, sex, personality differences—but Christ can break down these barriers. Jesus Christ changed Onesimus's relationship to Philemon from slave to brother. Only in Christ can our most hopeless relationships be transformed into something wonderful.

HEBREWS

Would you . . .

- *wear a diaper to school and suck on a pacifier during all of your classes?*

- *treat yourself to a lunch of jars of baby food: strained carrots, creamed spinach, and milk (out of a baby bottle, of course)?*

- *drool all over yourself in front of everyone?*

- *crawl from class to class?*

- *kick your legs, flail your arms, and cry uncontrollably anytime anything doesn't go your way?*

You wouldn't do any of the above, would you? Such behavior is totally inappropriate and uncool for a teen. We expect this kind of immature behavior from babies. Sadly, we sometimes see these kinds of responses from fellow believers. Some remain "baby Christians" all of their lives.

In the same way that little kids grow physically, "baby" Christians need to grow in their relationship with Christ. The Epistle of Hebrews is all about spiritual maturity. You should know up front that Hebrews contains some tough challenges. It's a risky book to read—especially if you apply it. Are you up for the challenge?

KEY POINTS

JESUS' SUPERIORITY Hebrews affirms Jesus' identity as God. The testimonies in the Scriptures can help us conclude that he is greater than any religion or any angel, and superior to any Jewish leader (such as Abraham, Moses, or Joshua) or priest.

HIGH PRIEST In the Old Testament, the high priest represented the Jews before God. As the ultimate High Priest, Jesus guarantees our access to God the Father.

SACRIFICE Jesus' sacrifice was the ultimate fulfillment of all that the Old Testament sacrifices represented—God's forgiveness for sin. But we must accept this sacrifice for us. By believing in him we are declared "not guilty" and reconciled to God.

MATURITY THROUGH ENDURANCE Faith enables Christians to face trials. Genuine faith includes the commitment to stay true to God when we are under fire. Endurance builds character and leads to victory.

STATS

PURPOSE
To present Christ's superiority to angels and the great prophets of the Old Testament

AUTHOR
Unknown. Paul, Luke, Barnabas, Apollos, Silas, Philip, Priscilla, and others have been suggested as possible authors. This unknown author refers to Timothy as a "brother" (13:23).

ORIGINAL AUDIENCE
Hebrew Christians who may have considered a return to Judaism, perhaps because of their lack of understanding of biblical truths. They probably were "second-generation" Christians (2:3).

DATE WRITTEN
Probably before the destruction of the Temple in Jerusalem in A.D. 70; sacrifices and ceremonies are referred to, while the Temple's destruction is not.

SETTING
Jewish Christians probably were experiencing persecution, socially and physically, from fellow Jews and from Romans. The believers needed to be reassured that Christianity was true and that Jesus was the Messiah.

KEY PEOPLE
Old Testament men and women of faith (chapter 11)

1 JESUS CHRIST IS GOD'S SON

Long ago God spoke many times and in many ways to our ancestors through the prophets. ²And now in these final days, he has spoken to us through his Son. God promised everything to the Son as an inheritance, and through the Son he created the universe. ³The Son radiates God's own glory and expresses the very character of God, and he sustains everything by the mighty power of his command. When he had cleansed us from our sins, he sat down in the place of honor at the right hand of the majestic God in heaven. ⁴This shows that the Son is far greater than the angels, just as the name God gave him is greater than their names.

THE SON IS GREATER THAN THE ANGELS

⁵For God never said to any angel what he said to Jesus:

"You are my Son.
Today I have become your Father.*"

God also said,

"I will be his Father,
and he will be my Son."*

⁶And when he brought his supreme* Son into the world, God said,*

"Let all of God's angels worship him."*

⁷Regarding the angels, he says,

"He sends his angels like the winds,
his servants like flames of fire."*

⁸But to the Son he says,

"Your throne, O God, endures forever
and ever.
You rule with a scepter of justice.
⁹ You love justice and hate evil.
Therefore, O God, your God has
anointed you,

pouring out the oil of joy on you more
than on anyone else."*

¹⁰He also says to the Son,

"In the beginning, Lord, you laid the
foundation of the earth
and made the heavens with your hands.
¹¹ They will perish, but you remain forever.
They will wear out like old clothing.
¹² You will fold them up like a cloak
and discard them like old clothing.
But you are always the same;
you will live forever."*

¹³And God never said to any of the angels,

"Sit in the place of honor at my right hand
until I humble your enemies,
making them a footstool under
your feet."*

¹⁴Therefore, angels are only servants—spirits sent to care for people who will inherit salvation.

2 A WARNING AGAINST DRIFTING AWAY

So we must listen very carefully to the truth we have heard, or we may drift away from it. ²For the message God delivered through angels has always stood firm, and every violation of the law and every act of disobedience was punished. ³So what makes us think we can escape if we ignore this great salvation that was first announced by the Lord Jesus himself and then delivered to us by those who heard him speak? ⁴And God confirmed the message by giving signs and wonders and various miracles and gifts of the Holy Spirit whenever he chose.

JESUS, THE MAN

⁵And furthermore, it is not angels who will control the future world we are talking about. ⁶For in one place the Scriptures say,

"What are mere mortals that you should
think about them,
or a son of man* that you should care
for him?
⁷ Yet you made them only a little lower than
the angels
and crowned them with glory and honor.*
⁸ You gave them authority over all things."*

GOD REVEALED
(1:2-3) Not only is Jesus God's exact representation, he is God himself. Christ is eternal; he worked with the Father in creating the world (John 1:3; Col 1:16). He is the full revelation of God. You can have no clearer view of God than by looking at him. Jesus Christ is the complete expression of God in a human body.

STILL IN CONTROL
(2:8-9) Christ has authority over everything. His authority is sometimes not apparent, especially when evil actions take place on a daily basis. These actions cause many to wonder whether or not God has totally abandoned the earth. Ever feel this way? But as this passage states, Jesus still is in control. Someday he will return to reign as King. Do you believe that?

1:5a Or *Today I reveal you as my Son.* Ps 2:7.   **1:5b** 2 Sam 7:14.   **1:6a** Or *firstborn.*   **1:6b** Or *when he again brings his supreme Son* [or *firstborn Son*] *into the world, God will say.*   **1:6c** Deut 32:43.   **1:7** Ps 104:4 (Greek version).   **1:8-9** Ps 45:6-7.   **1:10-12** Ps 102:25-27.   **1:13** Ps 110:1.   **2:6** Or *the Son of Man.*   **2:7** Some manuscripts add *You gave them charge of everything you made.*   **2:6-8** Ps 8:4-6 (Greek version).

Now when it says "all things," it means nothing is left out. But we have not yet seen all things put under their authority. [9]What we do see is Jesus, who was given a position "a little lower than the angels"; and because he suffered death for us, he is now "crowned with glory and honor." Yes, by God's grace, Jesus tasted death for everyone. [10]God, for whom and through whom everything was made, chose to bring many children into glory. And it was only right that he should make Jesus, through his suffering, a perfect leader, fit to bring them into their salvation.

[11]So now Jesus and the ones he makes holy have the same Father. That is why Jesus is not ashamed to call them his brothers and sisters.* [12]For he said to God,

> "I will proclaim your name to my brothers and sisters.
> I will praise you among your assembled people."*

[13]He also said,

> "I will put my trust in him,"
> that is, "I and the children God has given me."*

[14]Because God's children are human beings—made of flesh and blood—the Son also became flesh and blood. For only as a human being could he die, and only by dying could he break the power of the devil, who had* the power of death. [15]Only in this way could he set

---

SINCE HE HIMSELF HAS GONE THROUGH SUFFERING AND TESTING,

HE IS ABLE TO HELP US

WHEN WE ARE BEING TESTED.

HEBREWS 2:18

---

free all who have lived their lives as slaves to the fear of dying.

[16]We also know that the Son did not come to help angels; he came to help the descendants of Abraham. [17]Therefore, it was necessary for him to be made in every respect like us, his brothers and sisters,* so that he could be our merciful and faithful High Priest before God. Then he could offer a sacrifice that would take away the sins of the people. [18]Since he himself has gone through suffering and testing, he is able to help us when we are being tested.

3 **JESUS IS GREATER THAN MOSES** And so, dear brothers and sisters who belong to God and* are partners with those called to heaven, think carefully about this Jesus whom we declare to be God's messenger* and High Priest. [2]For he was faithful to God, who appointed him, just as Moses served faithfully when he was entrusted with God's entire* house.

2:11 Greek *brothers;* also in 2:12.   **2:12** Ps 22:22.   **2:13** Isa 8:17-18.   **2:14** Or *has.*   **2:17** Greek *like the brothers.*   **3:1a** Greek *And so, holy brothers who.*   **3:1b** Greek *God's apostle.*   **3:2** Some manuscripts do not include *entire.*

I WONDER...

I've heard so many different opinions on what God is really like that I'm beginning to wonder if anyone really knows. How can we know God?

Have you ever assembled a complicated jigsaw puzzle? If so, you know how important the picture on the box is. As you put the puzzle together, you use the picture as a reference, your guide.

But what if you had the wrong box top, and the picture didn't match the puzzle? The puzzle would be nearly impossible to assemble (at least until you realized the mistake).

People throughout the world are trying to put the "God puzzle" together. But often they're trying to match the pieces to the wrong picture!

God isn't trying to hide. As Hebrews 1:1-3 tells us, God has clearly shown the world what he is

like—through nature, through the Bible, and especially through Christ.

When Jesus was asked point-blank by Philip, he was straightforward in his reply. "Anyone who has seen me has seen the Father!" (John 14:9; see also John 10:30).

It doesn't get more obvious than that! To know what God is like, all you have to do is look at Jesus.

People get their God-pictures from media preachers; friends who say they believe in God, but never act like it; religious relatives; coaches who pray before games and then swear the paint off the walls at halftime; and so forth. But these aren't accurate pictures of God.

No wonder they can't put the puzzle together.

If you want to know what God is like, you don't have to settle for hearsay. Instead, look at the right picture—look at Christ.

³But Jesus deserves far more glory than Moses, just as a person who builds a house deserves more praise than the house itself. ⁴For every house has a builder, but the one who built everything is God.

⁵Moses was certainly faithful in God's house as a servant. His work was an illustration of the truths God would reveal later. ⁶But Christ, as the Son, is in charge of God's entire house. And we are God's house, if we keep our courage and remain confident in our hope in Christ.*

⁷That is why the Holy Spirit says,

"Today when you hear his voice,
⁸   don't harden your hearts
as Israel did when they rebelled,
    when they tested me in
        the wilderness.

⁹ There your ancestors tested and tried my
        patience,
    even though they saw my miracles for
        forty years.
¹⁰ So I was angry with them, and I said,
    'Their hearts always turn away from me.
    They refuse to do what I tell them.'
¹¹ So in my anger I took an oath:
    'They will never enter my place of rest.'"*

¹²Be careful then, dear brothers and sisters.* Make sure that your own hearts are not evil and unbelieving, turning you away from the living God. ¹³You must warn each other every day, while it is still "today," so that none of you will be deceived by sin and hardened against God. ¹⁴For if we are faithful to the end, trusting God

3:6 Some manuscripts add *faithful to the end.*   **3:7-11** Ps 95:7-11.
3:12 Greek *brothers.*

ULTIMATE ISSUES PRAYER

Imagine you were about to meet someone famous— maybe the lead singer of your favorite band or an actor or politician you admire. Chances are you'd be nervous, wondering what to say and how to act. You wouldn't want to make a fool of yourself by doing or saying something inappropriate.

Now imagine you're just sitting around gabbing with your best friend. You don't worry about what to say or do. You can just be yourself. The talk flows freely.

These two situations illustrate something about the nature of prayer. On the one hand, prayer brings you into the presence of the King of the universe, the Lord and Creator of everything (see Heb 4:16). That's fairly intimidating! No wonder people feel tongue-tied when they pray. On the other hand, prayer is simply talking with your heavenly Father, the person who knows you better and loves you more than anyone else does. He is, in a very real way, your best friend; you can talk with him openly and honestly—about anything.

Prayer has inspired countless books, debates, songs, poems, and lives. Though there is little that is new to be said about prayer, consider the following perspectives:

Prayer is simply communication with God. Christianity talks about a personal God, not a force, concept, or abstract idea. God is a person—we can know him. Imagine that! Small, limited, finite human beings are invited to know God in a personal way. When you want to get to know a person, there really is only one way to do it: spend time together. The same is true of God.

What happens when we spend time with God? Basically, three things:

First, we can tell God what is on our mind: our worries, joys, pains, fears, hopes—everything. Nothing is too big or too trivial to tell him. He is a loving Father, and good fathers want to hear what is on the hearts and minds of their children. We can be ourselves with God; we don't need to change how we talk when we talk with him, or use words like "thee," "thou," and "beseech." We can speak to God the way we would to our most trusted friend.

Second, in prayer we can hear what God has to say to us. Listening to God requires more patience and practice than talking to him. That shouldn't be surprising—most of us are better talkers than listeners—but listening to God can be a very rewarding experience. It is one more way God can give us guidance as we seek his will (other ways include the Bible, the counsel of other Christians, and knowing our own particular gifts and limitations). One caution: if you ever feel God is telling you to do something contrary to Scripture, you have misunderstood. God never contradicts himself or his inspired Word. Seek counsel from your parents, your pastor, your youth leader, or other Christians when this happens.

Third, when we pray we are in the presence of God. Prayer brings us into the throne room of God (Heb 4:16), where we may present our praise, confessions, and requests. This time spent in the presence of God will begin to have an effect on us: we will begin to become more like him. Have you ever noticed that when two people spend a lot of time together, they begin to talk, act, and even think alike? The same principle applies to our relationship with God. The more we're with him, the more we become like him.

Prayer is more than simply asking God to give us what we want. It's living, active, and powerful communication with the Lord of all. ∎

just as firmly as when we first believed, we will share in all that belongs to Christ. [15]Remember what it says:

"Today when you hear his voice,
 don't harden your hearts
 as Israel did when they rebelled."*

[16]And who was it who rebelled against God, even though they heard his voice? Wasn't it the people Moses led out of Egypt? [17]And who made God angry for forty years? Wasn't it the people who sinned, whose corpses lay in the wilderness? [18]And to whom was God speaking when he took an oath that they would never enter his rest? Wasn't it the people who disobeyed him? [19]So we see that because of their unbelief they were not able to enter his rest.

4 PROMISED REST FOR GOD'S PEOPLE
God's promise of entering his rest still stands, so we ought to tremble with fear that some of you might fail to experience it. [2]For this good news—that God has prepared this rest—has been announced to us just as it was to them. But it did them no good because they didn't share the faith of those who listened to God.* [3]For only we who believe can enter his rest. As for the others, God said,

"In my anger I took an oath:
 'They will never enter my place of rest,'"*

even though this rest has been ready since he made the world. [4]We know it is ready because of the place in the Scriptures where it mentions the seventh day: "On the seventh day God rested from all his work."* [5]But in the other passage God said, "They will never enter my place of rest."*

[6]So God's rest is there for people to enter, but those who first heard this good news failed to enter because they disobeyed God. [7]So God set another time for entering his rest, and that time is today. God announced this through David much later in the words already quoted:

"Today when you hear his voice,
 don't harden your hearts."*

[8]Now if Joshua had succeeded in giving them this rest, God would not have spoken about another day of rest still to come. [9]So there is a special rest* still waiting for the people of God. [10]For all who have entered into God's rest have rested from their labors, just as God did after creating the world. [11]So let us do our best to

3:15 Ps 95:7-8.   4:2 Some manuscripts read they didn't combine what they heard with faith.   4:3 Ps 95:11.   4:4 Gen 2:2.   4:5 Ps 95:11.   4:7 Ps 95:7-8.   4:9 Or a Sabbath rest.

enter that rest. But if we disobey God, as the people of Israel did, we will fall.

[12]For the word of God is alive and powerful. It is sharper than the sharpest two-edged sword, cutting between soul and spirit, between joint and marrow. It exposes our innermost thoughts and desires. [13]Nothing in all creation is hidden from God. Everything is naked and exposed before his eyes, and he is the one to whom we are accountable.

CHRIST IS OUR HIGH PRIEST [14]So then, since we have a great High Priest who has entered heaven, Jesus the Son of God, let us hold firmly to what we believe. [15]This High Priest of ours understands our weaknesses, for he faced all of the same testings we do, yet he did not sin. [16]So let us come boldly to the throne of our gracious God. There we will receive his mercy, and we will find grace to help us when we need it most.

5 Every high priest is a man chosen to represent other people in their dealings with God. He presents their gifts to God and offers sacrifices for their sins. [2]And he is able to deal gently with ignorant and wayward people because he himself is subject to the same weaknesses. [3]That is why he must offer sacrifices for his own sins as well as theirs.

[4]And no one can become a high priest simply because he wants such an honor. He must be called by God for this work, just as Aaron was. [5]That is why Christ did not honor himself by assuming he could become High Priest. No, he was chosen by God, who said to him,

> SO LET US COME BOLDLY TO THE THRONE OF OUR GRACIOUS GOD. THERE WE WILL RECEIVE HIS MERCY, AND WE WILL FIND GRACE TO HELP US WHEN WE NEED IT MOST.
> { HEBREWS 4:16 }

....

TRUE REST
(4:1-3) In this passage rest *refers to a belief in Jesus, whose death makes forgiveness possible. Some of the Jewish Christians who received this letter may have been on the verge of turning back from their promised rest in Christ, just as the people in Moses' day turned back from the Promised Land.*

In both cases, the difficulties of the present moment overshadowed the reality of God's promise. Therefore, the people stopped believing that God was able to fulfill his promises. When we trust our own efforts instead of Christ, we too are in danger of turning back. Our own efforts are never adequate; only Christ can see us through.

"You are my Son.
Today I have become your Father.*"

⁶And in another passage God said to him,

"You are a priest forever in the order of
Melchizedek."*

⁷While Jesus was here on earth, he offered prayers and pleadings, with a loud cry and tears, to the one who could rescue him from death. And God heard his prayers because of his deep reverence for God. ⁸Even though Jesus was God's Son, he learned obedience from the things he suffered. ⁹In this way, God qualified him as a perfect High Priest, and he became the source of eternal salvation for all those who obey him. ¹⁰And God designated him to be a High Priest in the order of Melchizedek.

A CALL TO SPIRITUAL GROWTH ¹¹There is much more we would like to say about this, but it is difficult to explain, especially since you are spiritually dull and don't seem to listen. ¹²You have been believers so long now that you ought to be teaching others. Instead, you need someone to teach you again the basic things about God's word.* You are like babies who need milk and cannot eat solid food. ¹³For someone who lives on milk is still an infant and doesn't know how to do what is right. ¹⁴Solid food is for those who are mature, who through training have the skill to recognize the difference between right and wrong.

6 So let us stop going over the basic teachings about Christ again and again. Let us go on instead and become mature in our understanding. Surely we don't need to start again with the fundamental importance of repenting from evil deeds* and placing our faith in God. ²You don't need further instruction about baptisms, the laying on of hands, the resurrection of the dead, and eternal judgment. ³And so, God willing, we will move forward to further understanding.

⁴For it is impossible to bring back to repen-

....

PRUNING
(6:7-8) Land that produces a good crop receives loving care, but land that produces thorns and briers has to be burned off so that the farmer can start over. In the same way, God prunes branches that haven't produced fruit, in order to encourage fruit to grow (see John 15:1-8). Although we aren't saved by works or conduct, what we do is the evidence of our faith. Being productive for Christ is serious business. How serious are you about your productivity?

tance those who were once enlightened— those who have experienced the good things of heaven and shared in the Holy Spirit, ⁵who have tasted the goodness of the word of God and the power of the age to come—⁶and who then turn away from God. It is impossible to bring such people back to repentance; by rejecting the Son of God, they themselves are nailing him to the cross once again and holding him up to public shame.

⁷When the ground soaks up the falling rain and bears a good crop for the farmer, it has God's blessing. ⁸But if a field bears thorns and thistles, it is useless. The farmer will soon condemn that field and burn it.

⁹Dear friends, even though we are talking this way, we really don't believe it applies to you. We are confident that you are meant for better things, things that come with salvation. ¹⁰For God is not unjust. He will not forget how hard you have worked for him and how you have shown your love to him by caring for other believers,* as you still do. ¹¹Our great desire is that you will keep on loving others as long as life lasts, in order to make certain that what you hope for will come true. ¹²Then you will not become spiritually dull and indifferent. Instead, you will follow the example of those who are going to inherit God's promises because of their faith and endurance.

GOD'S PROMISES BRING HOPE ¹³For example, there was God's promise to Abraham. Since there was no one greater to swear by, God took an oath in his own name, saying:

¹⁴ "I will certainly bless you,
and I will multiply your descendants
beyond number."*

¹⁵Then Abraham waited patiently, and he received what God had promised.

¹⁶Now when people take an oath, they call on someone greater than themselves to hold them to it. And without any question that oath is binding. ¹⁷God also bound himself with an oath, so that those who received the promise could be perfectly sure that he would never change his mind. ¹⁸So God has given both his promise and his oath. These two things are unchangeable because it is impossible for God to lie. Therefore, we who have fled to him for refuge can have great confidence as we hold to the hope that lies before us. ¹⁹This hope is a strong and trustworthy anchor for

5:5 Or *Today I reveal you as my Son.* Ps 2:7. 5:6 Ps 110:4. 5:12 Or *about the oracles of God.* 6:1 Greek *from dead works.* 6:10 Greek *for God's holy people.* 6:14 Gen 22:17.

our souls. It leads us through the curtain into God's inner sanctuary. 20Jesus has already gone in there for us. He has become our eternal High Priest in the order of Melchizedek.

7 MELCHIZEDEK IS GREATER THAN ABRAHAM

This Melchizedek was king of the city of Salem and also a priest of God Most High. When Abraham was returning home after winning a great battle against the kings, Melchizedek met him and blessed him. 2Then Abraham took a tenth of all he had captured in battle and gave it to Melchizedek. The name Melchizedek means "king of justice," and king of Salem means "king of peace." 3There is no record of his father or mother or any of his ancestors—no beginning or end to his life. He remains a priest forever, resembling the Son of God.

4Consider then how great this Melchizedek was. Even Abraham, the great patriarch of Israel, recognized this by giving him a tenth of what he had taken in battle. 5Now the law of Moses required that the priests, who are descendants of Levi, must collect a tithe from the rest of the people of Israel,* who are also descendants of Abraham. 6But Melchizedek, who was not a descendant of Levi, collected a tenth from Abraham. And Melchizedek placed a blessing upon Abraham, the one who had already received the promises of God. 7And without question, the person who has the power to give a blessing is greater than the one who is blessed.

8The priests who collect tithes are men who die, so Melchizedek is greater than they are, because we are told that he lives on. 9In addition, we might even say that these Levites—the ones who collect the tithe—paid a tithe to Melchizedek when their ancestor Abraham paid a tithe to him. 10For although Levi wasn't born yet, the seed from which he came was in Abraham's body when Melchizedek collected the tithe from him.

11So if the priesthood of Levi, on which the law was based, could have achieved the perfection God intended, why did God need to establish a different priesthood, with a priest in the order of Melchizedek instead of the order of Levi and Aaron?* 12And if the priesthood is changed, the law must also be changed to permit it. 13For the priest we are talking about belongs to a different tribe, whose members have never served

at the altar as priests. 14What I mean is, our Lord came from the tribe of Judah, and Moses never mentioned priests coming from that tribe.

JESUS IS LIKE MELCHIZEDEK

15This change has been made very clear since a different priest, who is like Melchizedek, has appeared. 16Jesus became a priest, not by meeting the physical requirement of belonging to the tribe of Levi, but by the power of a life that cannot be destroyed. 17And the psalmist pointed this out when he prophesied,

"You are a priest forever in the order
    of Melchizedek."*

18Yes, the old requirement about the priesthood was set aside because it was weak and useless. 19For the law never made anything perfect. But now we have confidence in a better hope, through which we draw near to God.

20This new system was established with a solemn oath. Aaron's descendants became priests without such an oath, 21but there was an oath regarding Jesus. For God said to him,

"The LORD has taken an oath and will not
    break his vow:
    'You are a priest forever.'"*

22Because of this oath, Jesus is the one who guarantees this better covenant with God.

23There were many priests under the old system, for death prevented them from remaining in office. 24But because Jesus lives forever, his priesthood lasts forever. 25Therefore he is able, once and forever, to save* those who come to God through him. He lives forever to intercede with God on their behalf.

26He is the kind of high priest we need because he is holy and blameless, unstained by sin. He has been set apart from sinners and has been given the highest place of honor in heaven.* 27Unlike those other high priests, he does not need to offer sacrifices every day. They did this for their own sins first and then for the sins of the people. But Jesus did this once for all when he offered himself as the sacrifice

....

PAID IN FULL
(7:25) The fact that Jesus "is able, once and forever, to save those who come to God through him" is staggering. No one else can add to what Jesus did to save us. Jesus is with the Father as a sign that every sin we could ever commit is already forgiven (see also 9:24-28). This, however, is not an encouragement for us to make bad choices simply because we can be forgiven. After all, our actions have consequences. Instead, we can do the same thing we do whenever we receive a great gift: say thank you.

7:5 Greek from their brothers.   7:11 Greek the order of Aaron?
7:17 Ps 110:4.   7:21 Ps 110:4.   7:25 Or is able to save completely.
7:26 Or has been exalted higher than the heavens.

for the people's sins. ²⁸The law appointed high priests who were limited by human weakness. But after the law was given, God appointed his Son with an oath, and his Son has been made the perfect High Priest forever.

8 **CHRIST IS OUR HIGH PRIEST** Here is the main point: We have a High Priest who sat down in the place of honor beside the throne of the majestic God in heaven. ²There he ministers in the heavenly Tabernacle,* the true place of worship that was built by the Lord and not by human hands.

³And since every high priest is required to offer gifts and sacrifices, our High Priest must make an offering, too. ⁴If he were here on earth, he would not even be a priest, since there already are priests who offer the gifts required by the law. ⁵They serve in a system of worship that is only a copy, a shadow of the real one in heaven. For when Moses was getting ready to build the Tabernacle, God gave him this warning: "Be sure that you make everything according to the pattern I have shown you here on the mountain."*

⁶But now Jesus, our High Priest, has been given a ministry that is far superior to the old priesthood, for he is the one who mediates for us a far better covenant with God, based on better promises.

⁷If the first covenant had been faultless, there would have been no need for a second covenant to replace it. ⁸But when God found fault with the people, he said:

"The day is coming, says the LORD,
    when I will make a new covenant
    with the people of Israel and Judah.
⁹ This covenant will not be like the one
    I made with their ancestors
when I took them by the hand
    and led them out of the land of Egypt.
They did not remain faithful to my covenant,
    so I turned my back on them, says
      the LORD.
¹⁰ But this is the new covenant I will make
    with the people of Israel on that day,*
      says the LORD:
I will put my laws in their minds,
    and I will write them on their hearts.
I will be their God,
    and they will be my people.
¹¹ And they will not need to teach their
    neighbors,
    nor will they need to teach their relatives,*
    saying, 'You should know the LORD.'
For everyone, from the least to the greatest,

will know me already.
¹² And I will forgive their wickedness,
    and I will never again remember
      their sins."*

¹³When God speaks of a "new" covenant, it means he has made the first one obsolete. It is now out of date and will soon disappear.

9 **OLD RULES ABOUT WORSHIP** That first covenant between God and Israel had regulations for worship and a place of worship here on earth. ²There were two rooms in that Tabernacle.* In the first room were a lampstand, a table, and sacred loaves of bread on the table. This room was called the Holy Place. ³Then there was a curtain, and behind the curtain was the second room* called the Most Holy Place. ⁴In that room were a gold incense altar and a wooden chest called the Ark of the Covenant, which was covered with gold on all sides. Inside the Ark were a gold jar containing manna, Aaron's staff that sprouted leaves, and the stone tablets of the covenant. ⁵Above the Ark were the cherubim of divine glory, whose wings stretched out over the Ark's cover, the place of atonement. But we cannot explain these things in detail now.

⁶When these things were all in place, the priests regularly entered the first room* as they performed their religious duties. ⁷But only the high priest ever entered the Most Holy Place, and only once a year. And he always offered blood for his own sins and for the sins the people had committed in ignorance. ⁸By these regulations the Holy Spirit revealed that the entrance to the Most Holy Place was not freely open as long as the Tabernacle* and the system it represented were still in use.

⁹This is an illustration pointing to the present time. For the gifts and sacrifices that the priests offer are not able to cleanse the consciences of the people who bring them. ¹⁰For that old system deals only with food and drink and various cleansing ceremonies— physical regulations that were in effect only until a better system could be established.

CHRIST IS THE PERFECT SACRIFICE ¹¹So Christ has now become the High Priest over all the good things that have come.* He has entered that greater, more perfect Tabernacle in heaven, which was not made by human

8:2 Or *tent*; also in 8:5.   **8:5** Exod 25:40; 26:30.   **8:10** Greek *after those days.*   **8:11** Greek *their brother.*   **8:8-12** Jer 31:31-34.   **9:2** Or *tent*; also in 9:11, 21.   **9:3** Greek *second tent.*   **9:6** Greek *first tent.*   **9:8** Or *the first room*; Greek reads *the first tent.*   **9:11** Some manuscripts read *that are about to come.*

hands and is not part of this created world. [12]With his own blood—not the blood of goats and calves—he entered the Most Holy Place once for all time and secured our redemption forever.

[13]Under the old system, the blood of goats and bulls and the ashes of a young cow could cleanse people's bodies from ceremonial impurity. [14]Just think how much more the blood of Christ will purify our consciences from sinful deeds* so that we can worship the living God. For by the power of the eternal Spirit, Christ offered himself to God as a perfect sacrifice for our sins. [15]That is why he is the one who mediates a new covenant between God and people, so that all who are called can receive the eternal inheritance God has promised them. For Christ died to set them free from the penalty of the sins they had committed under that first covenant.

[16]Now when someone leaves a will,* it is necessary to prove that the person who made it is dead.* [17]The will goes into effect only after the person's death. While the person who made it is still alive, the will cannot be put into effect.

[18]That is why even the first covenant was put into effect with the blood of an animal. [19]For after Moses had read each of God's commandments to all the people, he took the blood of calves and goats,* along with water, and sprinkled both the book of God's law and all the people, using hyssop branches and scarlet wool. [20]Then he said, "This blood confirms the covenant God has made with you."* [21]And in the same way, he sprinkled blood on the Tabernacle and on everything used for worship. [22]In fact, according to the law of Moses, nearly everything was purified with blood. For without the shedding of blood, there is no forgiveness.

[23]That is why the Tabernacle and everything in it, which were copies of things in heaven, had to be purified by the blood of animals. But the real things in heaven had to be purified with far better sacrifices than the blood of animals.

[24]For Christ did not enter into a holy place made with human hands, which was only a copy of the true one in heaven. He entered into heaven itself to appear now before God on our behalf. [25]And he did not enter heaven to offer himself again and again, like the high priest here on earth who enters the Most Holy Place year after year with the blood of an animal. [26]If that had been necessary, Christ would have had to die again and again, ever since the world began. But now, once for all time, he has appeared at the end of the age* to remove sin by his own death as a sacrifice.

[27]And just as each person is destined to die once and after that comes judgment, [28]so also Christ died once for all time as a sacrifice to take away the sins of many people. He will come again, not to deal with our sins, but to bring salvation to all who are eagerly waiting for him.

10 CHRIST'S SACRIFICE ONCE FOR ALL

The old system under the law of Moses was only a shadow, a dim preview of the good things to come, not the good things themselves. The sacrifices under that system were repeated again and again, year after year, but they were never able to provide perfect cleansing for those who came to worship. [2]If they could have provided perfect cleansing, the sacrifices would have stopped, for the worshipers would have been purified once for all time, and their feelings of guilt would have disappeared.

[3]But instead, those sacrifices actually reminded them of their sins year after year. [4]For it is not possible for the blood of bulls and goats to take away sins. [5]That is why, when Christ* came into the world, he said to God,

"You did not want animal sacrifices or sin offerings.
But you have given me a body to offer.
[6] You were not pleased with burnt offerings or other offerings for sin.

....

UNLOAD
(9:9-14) Though you know Christ, you may still be trying to make yourself good enough for God. But rules and rituals have never cleansed people's hearts. By Jesus' blood alone: (1) Our conscience is cleared. (2) We are freed from death and can live to serve God. (3) We are freed from sin's power. If you are carrying a load of guilt because you can't be good enough for God, take another look at Jesus' death and what it means for you.

VALUE
(9:15) Value, in our human way of thinking, is not measured by how many people can have something good, but by how few. "Limited edition" means "valuable" because only a few can have it. Eternal life, however, is dramatically different. Although it's the most valuable of all treasures, it is available to all. The more who have it, and the more they express their thankfulness for it, the greater its value! Got faith in God? How do your actions show its value to you?

9:14 Greek from dead works.   9:16a Or covenant; also in 9:17.
9:16b Or Now when someone makes a covenant, it is necessary to ratify it with the death of a sacrifice.   9:19 Some manuscripts do not include and goats.   9:20 Exod 24:8.   9:26 Greek the ages.
10:5 Greek he; also in 10:8.

7 Then I said, 'Look, I have come to do your
   will, O God—
      as is written about me in the
      Scriptures.'"*

8First, Christ said, "You did not want animal
sacrifices or sin offerings or burnt offerings or
other offerings for sin, nor were you pleased
with them" (though they are required by the
law of Moses). 9Then he said, "Look, I have
come to do your will." He cancels the first covenant in order to put the second into effect.
10For God's will was for us to be made holy by
the sacrifice of the body of Jesus Christ, once
for all time.

11Under the old covenant, the priest stands
and ministers before the altar day after day,
offering the same sacrifices again and again,
which can never take away sins. 12But our
High Priest offered himself to God as a single
sacrifice for sins, good for all time. Then he
sat down in the place of honor at God's right
hand. 13There he waits until his enemies are
humbled and made a footstool under his feet.
14For by that one offering he forever made perfect those who are being made holy.

15And the Holy Spirit also testifies that this is
so. For he says,

··

KEEP MEETING!
(10:25) *When we neglect meeting with other Christians
(for example, going to church), we lose out on the blessing of their encouragement and help. We come together
as believers to share our faith and strengthen each other
in the Lord. As we get closer to the time of Christ's return,
we may face many spiritual struggles. We'll need to pull
together, just as any family needs to do in a crisis. (See
also the "I Wonder" note on this topic.)*

16 "This is the new covenant I will make
   with my people on that day,* says
      the LORD:
   I will put my laws in their hearts,
      and I will write them on their minds."*

17Then he says,

   "I will never again remember
      their sins and lawless deeds."*

18And when sins have been forgiven, there is
no need to offer any more sacrifices.

A CALL TO PERSEVERE 19And so, dear brothers and sisters,* we can boldly enter heav-
en's Most Holy Place because of the blood of
Jesus. 20By his death,* Jesus opened a new
and life-giving way through the curtain into
the Most Holy Place. 21And since we have a
great High Priest who rules over God's house,
22let us go right into the presence of God with
sincere hearts fully trusting him. For our guilty
consciences have been sprinkled with Christ's
blood to make us clean, and our bodies have
been washed with pure water.

23Let us hold tightly without wavering to the
hope we affirm, for God can be trusted to keep
his promise. 24Let us think of ways to motivate
one another to acts of love and good works.
25And let us not neglect our meeting together,
as some people do, but encourage one another, especially now that the day of his return
is drawing near.

26Dear friends, if we deliberately continue
sinning after we have received knowledge of
the truth, there is no longer any sacrifice that

10:5-7 Ps 40:6-8 (Greek version).   10:16a Greek *after those days.*
10:16b Jer 31:33a.   10:17 Jer 31:34b.   10:19 Greek *brothers.*
10:20 Greek *Through his flesh.*

I WONDER...

*I like the idea about having a personal
faith in God. I just don't like having to go to
church. It seems boring and a waste of time.
I've been to churches, and they all seem the
same. Why can't there be a church with just
kids my own age?*

Imagine growing up without a family. It's tough to
think of life without at least one parent who really
cares.

Now imagine growing up with just brothers and
sisters in the house and no parents at all! For a day
or two it might seem like heaven, but very soon you
would see that it is chaos! Eventually you would
miss not having someone take care of your basic
needs.

Families are designed to take care of your daily
needs and to give you the continual love and guidance you need as you are growing up. Because Mom
and Dad have been around longer, they often know
what to do when a tough circumstance comes up (as
much as you may hate to admit it!).

In Hebrews 10:24-25, we're warned against
neglecting our church meetings. The body of Christ is
our spiritual family. If we stay away from church gatherings, we are left to try to survive by ourselves.

The church, like the family, can often be underval-
ued for the role it plays in our spiritual growth. Some
Christians don't recognize the positive influence of
other Christians until years later. At that point, they
realize that they would still be spiritual babies without the church's influence and love.

will cover these sins. ²⁷There is only the terrible expectation of God's judgment and the raging fire that will consume his enemies. ²⁸For anyone who refused to obey the law of Moses was put to death without mercy on the testimony of two or three witnesses. ²⁹Just think how much worse the punishment will be for those who have trampled on the Son of God, and have treated the blood of the covenant, which made us holy, as if it were common and unholy, and have insulted and disdained the Holy Spirit who brings God's mercy to us. ³⁰For we know the one who said,

"I will take revenge.
     I will pay them back."*

He also said,

"The LORD will judge his own people."*

³¹It is a terrible thing to fall into the hands of the living God.

³²Think back on those early days when you first learned about Christ.* Remember how you remained faithful even though it meant terrible suffering. ³³Sometimes you were exposed to public ridicule and were beaten, and sometimes you helped others who were suffering the same things. ³⁴You suffered along with those who were thrown into jail, and when all you owned was taken from you, you accepted it with joy. You knew there were better things waiting for you that will last forever.

³⁵So do not throw away this confident trust in the Lord. Remember the great reward it brings you! ³⁶Patient endurance is what you need now, so that you will continue to do God's will. Then you will receive all that he has promised.

³⁷ "For in just a little while,
     the Coming One will come and not delay.
³⁸ And my righteous ones will live by faith.*
     But I will take no pleasure in anyone who
          turns away."*

³⁹But we are not like those who turn away from God to their own destruction. We are the faithful ones, whose souls will be saved.

11 GREAT EXAMPLES OF FAITH
Faith is the confidence that what we hope for will actually happen; it gives us assurance about things we cannot see. ²Through their faith, the people in days of old earned a good reputation.

³By faith we understand that the entire universe was formed at God's command, that what we now see did not come from anything that can be seen.

⁴It was by faith that Abel brought a more acceptable offering to God than Cain did. Abel's offering gave evidence that he was a righteous man, and God showed his approval of his gifts. Although Abel is long dead, he still speaks to us by his example of faith.

⁵It was by faith that Enoch was taken up to heaven without dying—"he disappeared, because God took him."* For before he was taken up, he was known as a person who pleased God. ⁶And it is impossible to please God without faith. Anyone who wants to come to him must believe that God exists and that he rewards those who sincerely seek him.

⁷It was by faith that Noah built a large boat to save his family from the flood. He obeyed God, who warned him about things that had never happened before. By his faith Noah condemned the rest of the world, and he received the righteousness that comes by faith.

⁸It was by faith that Abraham obeyed when God called him to leave home and go to another land that God would give him as his inheritance. He went without knowing where he was going. ⁹And even when he reached the land God promised him, he lived there by faith—for he was like a foreigner, living in tents. And so did Isaac and Jacob, who inherited the same promise. ¹⁰Abraham was confidently looking forward to a city with eternal foundations, a city designed and built by God.

¹¹It was by faith that even Sarah was able to have a child, though she was barren and was too old. She believed* that God would keep his promise. ¹²And so a whole nation came from this one man who was as good as dead—a nation with so many people that, like the stars in the sky and the sand on the seashore, there is no way to count them.

¹³All these people died still believing what God had promised them. They did not receive

....

FAITHFUL
(11:13-16) Although the people of faith listed here died without receiving all that God had promised, they still believed that God would keep his promises. Many Christians become frustrated and defeated because their needs, wants, expectations, and demands are not immediately met when they believe in Christ. They become impatient and want to quit. Are you discouraged because you're still waiting for a promise to be fulfilled? Take courage from these heroes of faith who lived and died without seeing the fruit of their faith on earth, yet continued to believe.

10:30a Deut 32:35.   10:30b Deut 32:36.   10:32 Greek *when you were first enlightened.*   10:38 Or *My righteous ones will live by their faithfulness;* Greek reads *my righteous one will live by faith.*
10:37-38 Hab 2:3-4.   11:5 Gen 5:24.   11:11 Or *It was by faith that he [Abraham] was able to have a child, even though Sarah was barren and he was too old. He believed.*

what was promised, but they saw it all from a distance and welcomed it. They agreed that they were foreigners and nomads here on earth. ¹⁴Obviously people who say such things are looking forward to a country they can call their own. ¹⁵If they had longed for the country they came from, they could have gone back. ¹⁶But they were looking for a better place, a heavenly homeland. That is why God is not ashamed to be called their God, for he has prepared a city for them.

¹⁷It was by faith that Abraham offered Isaac as a sacrifice when God was testing him. Abraham, who had received God's promises, was ready to sacrifice his only son, Isaac, ¹⁸even though God had told him, "Isaac is the son through whom your descendants will be counted."* ¹⁹Abraham reasoned that if Isaac died, God was able to bring him back to life again. And in a sense, Abraham did receive his son back from the dead.

²⁰It was by faith that Isaac promised blessings for the future to his sons, Jacob and Esau.

²¹It was by faith that Jacob, when he was old and dying, blessed each of Joseph's sons and bowed in worship as he leaned on his staff.

²²It was by faith that Joseph, when he was about to die, said confidently that the people of Israel would leave Egypt. He even commanded them to take his bones with them when they left.

²³It was by faith that Moses' parents hid him for three months when he was born. They saw that God had given them an unusual child, and they were not afraid to disobey the king's command.

²⁴It was by faith that Moses, when he grew up, refused to be called the son of Pharaoh's daughter. ²⁵He chose to share the oppression of God's people instead of enjoying the fleeting pleasures of sin. ²⁶He thought it was better to suffer for the sake of Christ than to own the treasures of Egypt, for he was looking ahead to his great reward. ²⁷It was by faith that Moses left the land of Egypt, not fearing the king's anger. He kept right on going because he kept his eyes on the one who is invisible. ²⁸It was by faith that Moses commanded the people of Israel to keep the Passover and to sprinkle blood on the doorposts so that the angel of death would not kill their firstborn sons.

²⁹It was by faith that the people of Israel went right through the Red Sea as though they were on dry ground. But when the Egyptians tried to follow, they were all drowned.

³⁰It was by faith that the people of Israel marched around Jericho for seven days, and the walls came crashing down.

³¹It was by faith that Rahab the prostitute was not destroyed with the people in her city who refused to obey God. For she had given a friendly welcome to the spies.

³²How much more do I need to say? It would take too long to recount the stories of the faith of Gideon, Barak, Samson, Jephthah, David, Samuel, and all the prophets. ³³By faith these people overthrew kingdoms, ruled with justice, and received what God had promised them. They shut the mouths of lions, ³⁴quenched the flames of fire, and escaped death by the edge of the sword. Their weakness was turned to strength. They became strong in battle and put whole armies to flight. ³⁵Women received their loved ones back again from death.

But others were tortured, refusing to turn from God in order to be set free. They placed their hope in a better life after the resurrection. ³⁶Some were jeered at, and their backs were cut open with whips. Others were chained in prisons. ³⁷Some died by stoning, some were sawed in half,* and others were killed with the sword. Some went about wearing skins of sheep and goats, destitute and oppressed and mistreated. ³⁸They were too good for this world, wandering over deserts and mountains, hiding in caves and holes in the ground.

³⁹All these people earned a good reputation because of their faith, yet none of them received all that God had promised. ⁴⁰For God had something better in mind for us, so that they would not reach perfection without us.

12 GOD'S DISCIPLINE PROVES HIS LOVE

Therefore, since we are surrounded by such a huge crowd of witnesses to the life of faith, let us strip off every weight that slows us down, especially the sin that so easily trips us up. And let us run with endurance the race God has set before us. ²We do this by keeping our eyes on Jesus, the champion who initiates and perfects our faith.* Because of the joy* awaiting him, he endured the cross, disregarding its shame. Now he is seated in the place of honor beside God's throne. ³Think of all the hostility he endured from sinful people;* then you won't become weary and give up. ⁴After all, you have not yet given your lives in your struggle against sin.

⁵And have you forgotten the encouraging

11:18 Gen 21:12.   11:37 Some manuscripts add *some were tested.*
12:2a Or *Jesus, the originator and perfecter of our faith.*   12:2b Or *Instead of the joy.*   12:3 Some manuscripts read *Think of how people hurt themselves by opposing him.*

words God spoke to you as his children?* He said,

"My child,* don't make light of the LORD's discipline,
   and don't give up when he corrects you.
6 For the LORD disciplines those he loves,
   and he punishes each one he accepts
      as his child."*

7As you endure this divine discipline, remember that God is treating you as his own children. Who ever heard of a child who is never disciplined by its father? 8If God doesn't discipline you as he does all of his children, it means that you are illegitimate and are not really his children at all. 9Since we respected our earthly fathers who disciplined us, shouldn't we submit even more to the discipline of the Father of our spirits, and live forever?*

10For our earthly fathers disciplined us for a few years, doing the best they knew how. But God's discipline is always good for us, so that we might share in his holiness. 11No discipline is enjoyable while it is happening—it's painful! But afterward there will be a peaceful harvest of right living for those who are trained in this way.

12So take a new grip with your tired hands and strengthen your weak knees. 13Mark out a straight path for your feet so that those who are weak and lame will not fall but become strong.

A CALL TO LISTEN TO GOD 14Work at living in peace with everyone, and work at living a holy life, for those who are not holy will not see the Lord. 15Look after each other so that none of you fails to receive the grace of God. Watch out that no poisonous root of bitterness grows up

to trouble you, corrupting many. 16Make sure that no one is immoral or godless like Esau, who traded his birthright as the firstborn son for a single meal. 17You know that afterward, when he wanted his father's blessing, he was rejected. It was too late for repentance, even though he begged with bitter tears.

18You have not come to a physical mountain,* to a place of flaming fire, darkness, gloom, and whirlwind, as the Israelites did at Mount Sinai. 19For they heard an awesome trumpet blast and a voice so terrible that they begged God to stop speaking. 20They staggered back under God's command: "If even an animal touches the mountain, it must be stoned to death."* 21Moses himself was so frightened at the sight that he said, "I am terrified and trembling."*

22No, you have come to Mount Zion, to the city of the living God, the heavenly Jerusalem, and to countless thousands of angels in a joyful gathering. 23You have come to the assembly of God's firstborn children, whose names are written in heaven. You have come to God himself, who is the judge over all things. You have come to the spirits of the righteous ones in heaven who have now been made perfect. 24You have come to Jesus, the one who mediates the new covenant between God and people, and to the sprinkled blood, which speaks of forgiveness instead of crying out for vengeance like the blood of Abel.

· ·

OUR COACH
(12:12-13) God is not only a disciplining parent, he also is a coach who sometimes pushes us beyond our comfort zone in order to help us excel. Although we may not feel strong enough to push on to victory, we "can do everything through Christ, who gives [us] strength" (Phil 4:13). We can use this strength to help those around us who are struggling.

12:5a Greek sons; also in 12:7, 8.   **12:5b** Greek son; also in 12:6, 7.
12:5-6 Prov 3:11-12 (Greek version).   **12:9** Or and really live?
12:18 Greek to something that can be touched.   **12:20** Exod 19:13.
12:21 Deut 9:19.

CHOICES
consistency

Follow for six months the paths of Will and Jackson, two guys who made commitments to Christ in August at youth camp:

September: Both guys begin attending a midweek Bible study sponsored by a local church.

October: Both guys make a commitment to spend time with God and start digging into his Word.

November: Will shares his newfound faith in Christ with two friends on the football team. Jackson, claiming a busy schedule, begins skipping Bible study.

December: Will begins to be mentored by an "older

brother" in the faith—his cousin Richard. Jackson no longer reads his Bible.

January: Will has signed up to go to a Christian discipleship conference over spring break. Jackson doesn't want to go to the conference. Also, he acts weird whenever Will tries to talk to him about spiritual matters.

February: Will leads his girlfriend to Christ. Jackson's girlfriend is pregnant and planning to get an abortion.

Why do you think Will was so consistent while Jackson fell away? For a possible answer, read Hebrews 12:1-4.

²⁵Be careful that you do not refuse to listen to the One who is speaking. For if the people of Israel did not escape when they refused to listen to Moses, the earthly messenger, we will certainly not escape if we reject the One who speaks to us from heaven! ²⁶When God spoke from Mount Sinai his voice shook the earth, but now he makes another promise: "Once again I will shake not only the earth but the heavens also."* ²⁷This means that all of creation will be shaken and removed, so that only unshakable things will remain.

²⁸Since we are receiving a Kingdom that is unshakable, let us be thankful and please God by worshiping him with holy fear and awe. ²⁹For our God is a devouring fire.

13 **CONCLUDING WORDS** Keep on loving each other as brothers and sisters.* ²Don't forget to show hospitality to strangers, for some who have done this have entertained angels without realizing it! ³Remember those in prison, as if you were there yourself. Remember also those being mistreated, as if you felt their pain in your own bodies.

⁴Give honor to marriage, and remain faithful to one another in marriage. God will surely judge people who are immoral and those who commit adultery.

···

UNCHANGING
(13:8) You change classes every day. Friendships begin and end. Someday you will leave your present school. Life seems to be in a constant state of change. Yet, there are some constants. Jesus "is the same yesterday, today, and forever." We must keep our eyes on Christ, our ultimate leader, who, unlike human leaders, will never change. He has been and will be the same forever. In a changing world we can trust our unchanging Lord.

⁵Don't love money; be satisfied with what you have. For God has said,

"I will never fail you.
    I will never abandon you."*

⁶So we can say with confidence,

"The Lᴏʀᴅ is my helper,
    so I will have no fear.
What can mere people do to me?"*

⁷Remember your leaders who taught you the word of God. Think of all the good that has come from their lives, and follow the example of their faith.

⁸Jesus Christ is the same yesterday, today, and forever. ⁹So do not be attracted by strange, new ideas. Your strength comes from God's grace, not from rules about food, which don't help those who follow them.

¹⁰We have an altar from which the priests in the Tabernacle* have no right to eat. ¹¹Under the old system, the high priest brought the blood of animals into the Holy Place as a sacrifice for sin, and the bodies of the animals were burned outside the camp. ¹²So also Jesus suffered and died outside the city gates to make his people holy by means of his own blood. ¹³So let us go out to him, outside the camp, and bear the disgrace he bore. ¹⁴For this world is not our permanent home; we are looking forward to a home yet to come.

¹⁵Therefore, let us offer through Jesus a continual sacrifice of praise to God, proclaiming our allegiance to his name. ¹⁶And don't forget to do good and to share with those in need. These are the sacrifices that please God.

¹⁷Obey your spiritual leaders, and do what they say. Their work is to watch over your souls,

12:26 Hag 2:6.   **13:1** Greek *Continue in brotherly love.*   **13:5** Deut 31:6, 8.   **13:6** Ps 118:6.   **13:10** Or *tent.*

CHOICES
reputation

A time-out has been called, and the varsity cheerleaders are building a pyramid at mid-court. Their complicated stunt, however, is not the most fascinating thing taking place in Butler Gymnasium.

Far more interesting are the thoughts that fill the minds of those in the student section. What if you could crawl through each set of watching eyes into each churning brain? What would you discover?

Well, you'd find that most of the students, when they glance at Tammy (the girl at the apex of the pyramid), are thinking words like *conceited, snotty, snob, fake,* and *back-stabber.* Her reputation is, frankly, not the best.

Meanwhile the girl doing the splits out in front of the others, Amy, is regarded by almost everyone in the stands as "sweet," "nice," "friendly," "fun to be with," and "likable."

Three quick questions:

1. Why would you suppose there is such a sharp contrast in reputations?
2. Do you know any people like Tammy and Amy?
3. How do other people regard you?

Read Hebrews 13 for a fast lesson in reputation-making.

MY STORY: Katie

Money and material things used to be very important to me. I cared a lot about the clothes I wore. I liked it that my parents had a nice home and nice cars—and I wasn't very interested in people who didn't have nice clothes or nice things. I just didn't think I had much in common with people who didn't have as much money as I did.

Then I met Delaney. Even though she attended my school, I didn't know her because we hung out with different groups. I got to know her at a Christian camp. She and I were worlds apart in lots of ways. Her parents didn't have much money, and she didn't care about fashion at all. Yet Delaney was the most caring person I had ever met. She knew how to listen, and that summer she turned out to be a good friend to me as I went through a rough time. Some other kids at the camp spread some untrue rumors about me, which hurt me a lot. But Delaney was always there to listen and encourage.

That fall when we returned to school, I began to see how shallow some of my other friendships were compared to what I'd experienced with Delaney. I began to do more things with her and her friends, and I found that I liked her friends, even though they weren't "cool." My old friends started making fun of me for hanging around Delaney, but that only showed me more that those people weren't true friends.

I asked Delaney why she didn't seem to care about money. She said, "Sometimes I do care that I don't have nice clothes like you. But I found a Bible verse that says we're not to love money. Instead, we should be satisfied with what we have. I try to do that." She showed me the verse: Hebrews 13:5. What struck me was that she seemed to be more satisfied with what she had than I was, even though she owned much less. I knew she had something that I was just beginning to appreciate: the sense that God really was with her.

My attitude toward money and toward people started to change as I prayed that God would help me to be satisfied with what I had and not care so much about externals. I saw that God—and true friends—look on the heart, not on whether you wear the latest fashions.

and they are accountable to God. Give them reason to do this with joy and not with sorrow. That would certainly not be for your benefit.

[18]Pray for us, for our conscience is clear and we want to live honorably in everything we do. [19]And especially pray that I will be able to come back to you soon.

[20] Now may the God of peace—
who brought up from the dead our
Lord Jesus,
the great Shepherd of the sheep,
and ratified an eternal covenant with
his blood—
[21] may he equip you with all you need
for doing his will.
May he produce in you,*
through the power of Jesus Christ,
every good thing that is pleasing
to him.

All glory to him forever
and ever! Amen.

[22]I urge you, dear brothers and sisters,* to pay attention to what I have written in this brief exhortation.

[23]I want you to know that our brother Timothy has been released from jail. If he comes here soon, I will bring him with me to see you. [24]Greet all your leaders and all the believers there.* The believers from Italy send you their greetings.

[25]May God's grace be with you all.

....

13:21 Some manuscripts read *in us.*   **13:22** Greek *brothers.*
13:24 Greek *all of God's holy people.*

MATURITY
(13:15-25) Hebrews is a call to Christian maturity. Although this book was addressed to first-century Jewish Christians, it applies to Christians of any age or background. The road to Christian maturity begins when we make Christ the beginning and end of our faith. To mature, we have to be willing to submit our plans to him, rather than call our own shots.

JAMES

You've been feeling strange all week. At first you had trouble sleeping. Then came the headaches. Yesterday your teeth hurt and your fingernails turned blue for several hours. This morning you realized it was time to consult your family doctor when, after a morning jog, your mom asked if you'd been sprayed by a skunk.

The doctor tries to hold her breath as she asks you questions. She nods knowingly as you tick off your symptoms. After looking in your eyes and noting your swollen eardrums, she orders some lab work.

A few hours later she returns to tell you, "Just what I suspected—you have an extremely high number of antibiomolecularsucrothyamin microbes in your liver."

"Huh?" you gulp.

"Oh, don't worry. You have a common ailment we call odoramonia. We'll put you on an antibiotic and get you eating a balanced diet, and you'll be fine."

Aren't doctors amazing? By examining us and noting our symptoms, they're usually able to diagnose our physical ailments and prescribe the proper treatment.

God does the same thing for us spiritually.

By looking at our actions (or lack of action) God can tell us exactly what attitudes and desires need healing. His Word gives detailed prescriptions for curing wrong behavior patterns.

Is your spiritual life on the sick side? Are you fighting worldly infections or possibly even the disease of disobedience?

Follow the advice of the Great Physician. No matter what your ailment, the Epistle of James has the cure.

STATS

PURPOSE
To expose unethical practices and to teach right Christian behavior

AUTHOR
James, Jesus' brother, a leader in the Jerusalem church

ORIGINAL AUDIENCE
First-century Jewish Christians residing in Gentile communities outside Palestine

DATE WRITTEN
Probably A.D. 49, prior to the Jerusalem council held in A.D. 50

SETTING
This letter expresses James's concern for persecuted Christians who were once part of the Jerusalem church.

KEY POINTS

TRIALS James, the brother of Jesus, warned believers about the inevitability of trials and temptations in life. Successfully overcoming these adversities produces maturity and strong character.

LIVING FAITH James contrasted empty faith ("claims without conduct") with faith that works. Commitment to love and to serve is evidence of true faith.

LAW OF LOVE James reminded believers of the "law of love"—the debt of love owed to others, as Jesus commanded (see also Matt 19:19). Keeping the law of love shows that our faith is vital and real.

WISE SPEECH James explained how God offers wisdom to control the tongue. This wisdom is shown by the way a person controls his or her speech.

WEALTH James warned Christians not to compromise with worldly attitudes about wealth. Because the glory of wealth fades, Christians are encouraged to store up heavenly treasures through sincere, impartial service.

1 GREETINGS FROM JAMES
This letter is from James, a slave of God and of the Lord Jesus Christ.

I am writing to the "twelve tribes"—Jewish believers scattered abroad.

Greetings!

FAITH AND ENDURANCE
2Dear brothers and sisters,* when troubles come your way, consider it an opportunity for great joy. 3For you know that when your faith is tested, your endurance has a chance to grow. 4So let it grow, for when your endurance is fully developed, you will be perfect and complete, needing nothing.

5If you need wisdom, ask our generous God, and he will give it to you. He will not rebuke you for asking. 6But when you ask him, be sure that your faith is in God alone. Do not waver, for a person with divided loyalty is as unsettled as a wave of the sea that is blown and tossed by the wind. 7Such people should not expect to receive anything from the Lord. 8Their loyalty is divided between God and the world, and they are unstable in everything they do.

9Believers who are* poor have something to boast about, for God has honored them. 10And those who are rich should boast that God has humbled them. They will fade away like a little flower in the field. 11The hot sun rises and the grass withers; the little flower droops and falls, and its beauty fades away. In the same way, the rich will fade away with all of their achievements.

12God blesses those who patiently endure testing and temptation. Afterward they will receive the crown of life that God has promised to those who love him. 13And remember, when you are being tempted, do not say, "God is tempting me." God is never tempted to do wrong,* and he never tempts anyone else. 14Temptation comes from our own desires, which entice us and drag us away. 15These desires give birth to sinful actions. And when sin is allowed to grow, it gives birth to death.

16So don't be misled, my dear brothers and sisters. 17Whatever is good and perfect comes down to us from God our Father, who created all the lights in the heavens.* He never changes or casts a shifting shadow.* 18He chose to give birth to us by giving us his true word. And we, out of all creation, became his prized possession.*

LISTENING AND DOING
19Understand this, my dear brothers and sisters: You must all be quick to listen, slow to speak, and slow to get angry. 20Human anger* does not produce the righteousness* God desires. 21So get rid of all the filth and evil in your lives, and humbly accept the word God has planted in your hearts, for it has the power to save your souls.

22But don't just listen to God's word. You must do what it says. Otherwise, you are only

---

SNOWBALL
(1:12-15) Temptation begins with a thought. It becomes sin when we dwell on the thought and allow it to become an action. Like a snowball rolling downhill, sin's destruction grows the more we let that thought have its way. The best time to stop a snowball is at the top of the hill, before it's too big or moving too fast to control. In the same way, we can escape the destruction of bad choices by not giving in to temptation in the first place (see Matt 4:1-11; 1 Cor 10:13; and 2 Tim 2:22 for more about escaping temptation).

1:2 Greek *brothers;* also in 1:16, 19.   1:9 Greek *The brother who is.*   1:13 Or *God should not be put to a test by evil people.*   1:17a Greek *from above, from the Father of lights.*   1:17b Some manuscripts read *He never changes, as a shifting shadow does.*   1:18 Greek *we became a kind of firstfruit of his creatures.*   1:20a Greek *A man's anger.*   1:20b Or *the justice.*

CHOICES
obedience

The First Church youth group has just heard a great talk about the importance of serving others. On the way home, three friends discuss the meeting:

"Ray is a great speaker! He's so funny! Don't you think so, dude?"

"¡Por supuesto! [Of course!] His talk was awesome."

"I'm sayin'! I feel so convicted. I never do anything for my mama or my pops."

"His suggestion about getting involved with the after-school tutoring program is good."

"Yeah, I'm stoked about that. We should do that sometime."

Now, let's listen in on the conversation a few minutes later:

"So, what's up for this weekend?"

"Probably the same ol' stuff—go somewhere and hang out."

"Man, there's nothin' around here for us to do. I'm as bored as a board."

"I agree!"

What's wrong with that conversation? Anything? Check out James 1:21-27. Based on this passage, what would you suggest to the three friends?

fooling yourselves. ²³For if you listen to the word and don't obey, it is like glancing at your face in a mirror. ²⁴You see yourself, walk away, and forget what you look like. ²⁵But if you look carefully into the perfect law that sets you free, and if you do what it says and don't forget what you heard, then God will bless you for doing it.

²⁶If you claim to be religious but don't control your tongue, you are fooling yourself, and your religion is worthless. ²⁷Pure and genuine religion in the sight of God the Father means caring for orphans and widows in their distress and refusing to let the world corrupt you.

2 **A WARNING AGAINST PREJUDICE** My dear brothers and sisters,* how can you claim to have faith in our glorious Lord Jesus Christ if you favor some people over others?

²For example, suppose someone comes into your meeting* dressed in fancy clothes and expensive jewelry, and another comes in who is poor and dressed in dirty clothes. ³If you give special attention and a good seat to the rich person, but you say to the poor one, "You can stand over there, or else sit on the floor"—well, ⁴doesn't this discrimination show that your judgments are guided by evil motives?

⁵Listen to me, dear brothers and sisters. Hasn't God chosen the poor in this world to be rich in faith? Aren't they the ones who will inherit the Kingdom he promised to those who love him? ⁶But you dishonor the poor! Isn't it the rich who oppress you and drag you into court? ⁷Aren't they the ones who slander Jesus Christ, whose noble name* you bear?

⁸Yes indeed, it is good when you obey the royal law as found in the Scriptures: "Love your neighbor as yourself."* ⁹But if you favor some people over others, you are committing a sin. You are guilty of breaking the law.

¹⁰For the person who keeps all of the laws except one is as guilty as a person who has broken all of God's laws. ¹¹For the same God who said, "You must not commit adultery," also said, "You must not murder."* So if you murder someone but do not commit adultery, you have still broken the law.

¹²So whatever you say or whatever you do, remember that you will be judged by the law that sets you free. ¹³There will be no mercy for those who have not shown mercy to others. But

2:1 Greek *brothers*; also in 2:5, 14.   2:2 Greek *your synagogue*.
2:7 Greek *slander the noble name*.   2:8 Lev 19:18.   2:11 Exod 20:13-14; Deut 5:17-18.   2:19 Some manuscripts read *that God is one*; see Deut 6:4.   2:23a Gen 15:6.   2:23b See Isa 41:8.   2:26 Or *without spirit*.   3:1 Greek *brothers*; also in 3:10.

UNDERSTAND THIS, MY DEAR BROTHERS AND SISTERS:

YOU MUST ALL BE QUICK TO LISTEN, SLOW TO SPEAK, AND SLOW TO GET ANGRY.

■ ■ ■ ■ ■ ■ JAMES 1:19 ■ ■ ■ ■ ■ ■

if you have been merciful, God will be merciful when he judges you.

FAITH WITHOUT GOOD DEEDS IS DEAD

¹⁴What good is it, dear brothers and sisters, if you say you have faith but don't show it by your actions? Can that kind of faith save anyone? ¹⁵Suppose you see a brother or sister who has no food or clothing, ¹⁶and you say, "Goodbye and have a good day; stay warm and eat well"—but then you don't give that person any food or clothing. What good does that do?

¹⁷So you see, faith by itself isn't enough. Unless it produces good deeds, it is dead and useless.

¹⁸Now someone may argue, "Some people have faith; others have good deeds." But I say, "How can you show me your faith if you don't have good deeds? I will show you my faith by my good deeds."

¹⁹You say you have faith, for you believe that there is one God.* Good for you! Even the demons believe this, and they tremble in terror. ²⁰How foolish! Can't you see that faith without good deeds is useless?

²¹Don't you remember that our ancestor Abraham was shown to be right with God by his actions when he offered his son Isaac on the altar? ²²You see, his faith and his actions worked together. His actions made his faith complete. ²³And so it happened just as the Scriptures say: "Abraham believed God, and God counted him as righteous because of his faith."* He was even called the friend of God.* ²⁴So you see, we are shown to be right with God by what we do, not by faith alone.

²⁵Rahab the prostitute is another example. She was shown to be right with God by her actions when she hid those messengers and sent them safely away by a different road. ²⁶Just as the body is dead without breath,* so also faith is dead without good works.

3 **CONTROLLING THE TONGUE** Dear brothers and sisters,* not many of you should become teachers in the church, for we who teach will be judged more strictly. ²Indeed, we all make many mistakes. For if we could control our tongues, we would be perfect and could also control ourselves in every other way.

³We can make a large horse go wherever we want by means of a small bit in its mouth. ⁴And a small rudder makes a huge ship turn wherever the pilot chooses to go, even though the winds are strong. ⁵In the same way, the tongue is a small thing that makes grand speeches.

But a tiny spark can set a great forest on fire. ⁶And the tongue is a flame of fire. It is a whole world of wickedness, corrupting your entire body. It can set your whole life on fire, for it is set on fire by hell itself.*

⁷People can tame all kinds of animals, birds, reptiles, and fish, ⁸but no one can tame the tongue. It is restless and evil, full of deadly poison. ⁹Sometimes it praises our Lord and Father, and sometimes it curses those who have been made in the image of God. ¹⁰And so blessing and cursing come pouring out of the same mouth. Surely, my brothers and sisters, this is not right! ¹¹Does a spring of water bubble out with both fresh water and bitter water? ¹²Does a fig tree produce olives, or a grapevine produce figs? No, and you can't draw fresh water from a salty spring.*

TRUE WISDOM COMES FROM GOD ¹³If you are wise and understand God's ways, prove it by living an honorable life, doing good works with the humility that comes from wisdom. ¹⁴But if you are bitterly jealous and there is selfish

ambition in your heart, don't cover up the truth with boasting and lying. ¹⁵For jealousy and self-ishness are not God's kind of wisdom. Such things are earthly, unspiritual, and demonic. ¹⁶For wherever there is jealousy and selfish ambition, there you will find disorder and evil of every kind.

¹⁷But the wisdom from above is first of all pure. It is also peace loving, gentle at all times, and willing to yield to others. It is full of mercy and good deeds. It shows no favoritism and is always sincere. ¹⁸And those who are peace-makers will plant seeds of peace and reap a harvest of righteousness.*

4 DRAWING CLOSE TO GOD

What is caus-ing the quarrels and fights among you? Don't they come from the evil desires at war within you? ²You want what you don't have, so you scheme and kill to get it. You are jealous of what others have, but you can't get it, so you fight and wage war to take it away from them. Yet you don't have what you want because you don't ask God for it. ³And even when you ask, you don't get it because your motives are all wrong—you want only what will give you pleasure.

⁴You adulterers!* Don't you realize that friendship with the world makes you an enemy of God? I say it again: If you want to be a friend of the world, you make yourself an enemy of God. ⁵What do you think the Scriptures mean when they say that the spirit God has placed within us is filled with envy?* ⁶But he gives us even more grace to stand against such evil de-sires. As the Scriptures say,

"God opposes the proud
    but favors the humble."*

⁷So humble yourselves before God. Resist the devil, and he will flee from you. ⁸Come close to God, and God will come close to you. Wash your hands, you sinners; purify your hearts, for your loyalty is divided between God and the world. ⁹Let there be tears for what you have done. Let there be sorrow and deep grief. Let there be sadness instead of laughter, and gloom instead of joy. ¹⁰Humble yourselves be-fore the Lord, and he will lift you up in honor.

WARNING AGAINST JUDGING OTHERS ¹¹Don't speak evil against each other, dear brothers and sisters.* If you criticize and judge each

---

SAY WHAT?
(3:1-12) According to James, "The tongue is a small thing that makes grand speeches. But a tiny spark can set a great forest on fire." Thus, what you say and what you don't say are both important. Proper speech is not only saying the right words at the right time but also controlling your desire to say what you shouldn't. Examples of wrongly using the tongue include gossiping, putting others down, bragging, manipulating, false teaching, exaggerating, complaining, flattering, and lying. Before you speak, you might ask, "Is it true, is it necessary, and is it kind?"

BUILD UP
(4:10-12) Jesus summarized the law as loving God and your neighbor (Matt 22:37-40), and Paul said that love demonstrated toward a neighbor fully satisfies the law (Rom 13:8-10). When we fail to love, we break God's law. Examine your attitude and actions. Do you build people up or tear them down? Instead of criticizing someone, remember God's law of love and say something good instead. If you make this a habit, your tendency to find fault with others will decrease and your ability to obey God will increase.

3:6 Or for it will burn in hell (Greek Gehenna).   **3:12** Greek from salt.   **3:18** Or of good things, or of justice.   **4:4** Greek You adulteresses!   **4:5** Or that God longs jealously for the human spirit he has placed within us? or that the Holy Spirit, whom God has placed within us, opposes our envy?   **4:6** Prov 3:34 (Greek version).   **4:11** Greek brothers.

other, then you are criticizing and judging God's law. But your job is to obey the law, not to judge whether it applies to you. ¹²God alone, who gave the law, is the Judge. He alone has the power to save or to destroy. So what right do you have to judge your neighbor?

WARNING ABOUT SELF-CONFIDENCE ¹³Look here, you who say, "Today or tomorrow we are going to a certain town and will stay there a year. We will do business there and make a profit." ¹⁴How do you know what your life will be like tomorrow? Your life is like the morning fog—it's here a little while, then it's gone. ¹⁵What you ought to say is, "If the Lord wants us to, we will live and do this or that." ¹⁶Otherwise you are boasting about your own plans, and all such boasting is evil.

¹⁷Remember, it is sin to know what you ought to do and then not do it.

5 **WARNING TO THE RICH** Look here, you rich people: Weep and groan with anguish because of all the terrible troubles ahead of you. ²Your wealth is rotting away, and your fine clothes are moth-eaten rags. ³Your gold and silver have become worthless. The very wealth you were counting on will eat away your flesh like fire. This treasure you have accumulated will stand as evidence against you on the day of judgment. ⁴For listen! Hear the cries of the field workers whom you have cheated of their pay. The wages you held back cry out against you. The cries of those who harvest your fields have reached the ears of the LORD of Heaven's Armies.

⁵You have spent your years on earth in luxury, satisfying your every desire. You have fattened yourselves for the day of slaughter.

....

GOALS
(4:13-16) James cautioned against making plans without seeking God's opinion. Although goals are great to have, goals can disappoint us if we leave God out of them. God wants some say in the plans of his people. What would you like to be doing ten years from now? One year from now? Tomorrow? How would you react if God were to step in and rearrange your plans? Plan ahead but hang on to your plans lightly. If you put God's desires at the center of your planning, you will not be disappointed.

TODAY!
(4:14) Life is short no matter how long we live. Don't be deceived into thinking that you have lots of time to live for Christ, to enjoy your loved ones, or to do what you know you should. Live for God today! Then, no matter when your life ends, you will have fulfilled God's plan for you.

I WONDER . . .

I feel guilty more often now that I'm a Christian. Sometimes the guilt comes on for just little stuff that I used to never give a second thought about. When do I need to ask God for forgiveness?

God's goal is not to overwhelm us with our sin so that we become discouraged. He knows when to point out sin in our lives.

Some people are basically pretty "good" people when they come to faith in Christ. They don't have many destructive habits to overcome, and their parents have tried to teach them right from wrong. Others come with a lot of sin "baggage."

Although each person is unique, we're the same when it comes to our nature—we're sinners. In fact, we were each born with a sinful nature. This is called "original sin." And throughout our lives, we do all sorts of things that are wrong.

When we accept Christ as Savior, God declares us "not guilty." But this doesn't mean that we're perfect and don't sin anymore. Daily we must deal with sin while we're still alive on earth. It's part of being human. Christians, like everyone, have two types of sin to deal with: past sins and present sins.

When we become Christians, all of our past sins are wiped away. "[God] has removed our sins as far from us as the east is from the west" (Ps 103:12). That distance can't be measured!

Ideally, having past sins removed should also take away our guilt feelings. We can put the past behind us. We're forgiven!

But what about present sin? One of the roles of the Holy Spirit is to remind us when we sin. He doesn't do this to condemn us, but to prompt us to confess the sin, forsake it, and move on. God has forgiven us for these present sins, too. We confess them to him to keep the communication channels open and to keep the relationship close. So we should talk to God about our lives, and confess, whenever we need to. And remember, sins aren't limited to doing what is wrong. They also include not doing what is right.

The passage in James 4:17 is plain: "It is sin to know what you ought to do and then not do it."

If we know we should help someone stop gossiping; give our parents the whole truth, instead of only part of it; turn off the TV and spend time with God . . . and don't do it—we sin!

Let God, not others, do the convicting in your life and you'll be glad to confess your sins to him. He's eager to clear away the barriers between you and himself and start fresh.

[6]You have condemned and killed innocent people,* who do not resist you.*

PATIENCE AND ENDURANCE [7]Dear brothers and sisters,* be patient as you wait for the Lord's return. Consider the farmers who patiently wait for the rains in the fall and in the spring. They eagerly look for the valuable harvest to ripen. [8]You, too, must be patient. Take courage, for the coming of the Lord is near.

[9]Don't grumble about each other, brothers and sisters, or you will be judged. For look—the Judge is standing at the door!

[10]For examples of patience in suffering, dear brothers and sisters, look at the prophets who spoke in the name of the Lord. [11]We give great honor to those who endure under suffering. For instance, you know about Job, a man of great endurance. You can see how the Lord was kind to him at the end, for the Lord is full of tenderness and mercy.

[12]But most of all, my brothers and sisters, never take an oath, by heaven or earth or any-thing else. Just say a simple yes or no, so that you will not sin and be condemned.

THE POWER OF PRAYER [13]Are any of you suffering hardships? You should pray. Are any of you happy? You should sing praises. [14]Are any of you sick? You should call for the elders of the church to come and pray over you, anointing you with oil in the name of the Lord. [15]Such a prayer offered in faith will heal the sick, and the Lord will make you well. And if you have committed any sins, you will be forgiven.

[16]Confess your sins to each other and pray for each other so that you may be healed. The earnest prayer of a righteous person has great power and produces wonderful results. [17]Elijah was as human as we are, and yet when he prayed earnestly that no rain would fall, none fell for three and a half years! [18]Then, when he prayed again, the sky sent down rain and the earth began to yield its crops.

RESTORE WANDERING BELIEVERS [19]My dear brothers and sisters, if someone among you wanders away from the truth and is brought back, [20]you can be sure that whoever brings the sinner back will save that person from death and bring about the forgiveness of many sins.

5:6a Or killed the Righteous One.   **5:6b** Or Don't they resist you? or Doesn't God oppose you? or Aren't they now accusing you before God?   **5:7** Greek brothers; also in 5:9, 10, 12, 19.

GREAT RESULTS
(5:16-18) Prayer is a Christian's most powerful resource. The results often are greater than we thought were possible. Sadly, some people see prayer as a last resort when all else fails. This is backward; prayer should come first. Because God's power is infinitely greater than our own, it only makes sense to rely on it, especially because God encourages us to do so. Do you?

1 PETER

Each year a few individuals compete in what may be the most grueling athletic competition of all: a bicycle race across the U.S. Consider the obstacles: blazing deserts, towering mountain ranges, inclement weather, 18- to 20-hour stretches of pedaling, flat tires, potholes, skin-scraping spills, inconsiderate motorists, and sheer fatigue. It's amazing *anyone ever finishes*. The fact that some complete the 2,000-plus mile trip in just over a week is downright unbelievable!

How do they do it?

With the help of carefully trained support teams. These support teams follow the cyclists in specially equipped vehicles and provide whatever they need—food, water, bike repairs, replacement bikes, medical attention, a rubdown, a place to nap, coaching, or a few shouts of encouragement. These support teams make an otherwise impossible trip very possible.

The Christian life is similar to that grueling bicycle marathon. The occasional joys of gliding downhill are obscured by the more frequent times of having to churn our way up steep mountain peaks. We get weary. We feel like quitting. The finish line seems far, far away.

Fortunately God has given us a first-rate support team to help us go the distance. With the Holy Spirit, the Word of God, and other believers to encourage us, we can not only finish the race, we can win!

Find out more about your spiritual support team in the letter that follows, the letter called 1 Peter.

But don't wait too long. The race has already started!

STATS

PURPOSE
To offer encouragement to suffering Christians

AUTHOR
Peter

ORIGINAL AUDIENCE
Jewish Christians who had been driven out of Jerusalem and scattered throughout Asia Minor

DATE WRITTEN
About A.D. 62 to 64, from Rome

SETTING
Peter was probably in Rome when the great persecution under Emperor Nero began. (Peter eventually was executed during this time of persecution.) Throughout the Roman Empire, Christians were tortured and killed for their faith. Because of this persecution, the church in Jerusalem was scattered throughout the Mediterranean world.

KEY PEOPLE
Peter, Silas (Silvanus), Mark

KEY PLACES
Jerusalem, Rome, and the regions of Pontus, Galatia, Cappadocia, Asia Minor, and Bithynia

KEY POINTS

GRATITUDE ATTITUDE Because of Jesus, forgiveness and reconciliation with God are possible. Our hope in him motivates us to serve Christ even more.

PERSECUTION Peter encouraged believers to persevere through persecution. Persecution makes us stronger because it refines our faith. We can face persecution victoriously as Christ did, if we rely on him.

GOD'S FAMILY Believers are privileged to belong to God's family—a community with Christ as the Founder and Foundation. Through obedience, we show that we belong to this family.

FAMILY LIFE Peter encouraged all family members to treat each other with sympathy, love, tenderness, and humility. Likewise, we must treat our family members lovingly. Relationships with parents, brothers and sisters, and spouses are important aspects of Christian discipleship.

JUDGMENT God will judge everyone with perfect justice. He will punish evildoers; those who love God will be rewarded with life forever in his presence. Because all are accountable to God, we are free to avoid judging others.

THE CHURCHES OF PETER'S LETTER
Peter addressed his letter to the churches located throughout Bithynia, Pontus, Asia, Galatia, and Cappadocia. Paul had evange-lized many of these areas; others had churches that were begun by the Jews who were in Jerusalem on the day of Pentecost and had heard Peter's powerful sermon (see Acts 2:9-11).

1 **GREETINGS FROM PETER** This letter is from Peter, an apostle of Jesus Christ.

I am writing to God's chosen people who are living as foreigners in the provinces of Pontus, Galatia, Cappadocia, Asia, and Bithynia.* 2God the Father knew you and chose you long ago, and his Spirit has made you holy. As a result, you have obeyed him and have been cleansed by the blood of Jesus Christ.

May God give you more and more grace and peace.

THE HOPE OF ETERNAL LIFE 3All praise to God, the Father of our Lord Jesus Christ. It is by his great mercy that we have been born again, be-cause God raised Jesus Christ from the dead. Now we live with great expectation, 4and we have a priceless inheritance—an inheritance

LIVE IN HOPE
(1:3-6) Do you need encouragement? Peter's words offer joy and hope in times of trouble. He based his confidence on what God has done for us through Jesus. We're called into a living hope of eternal life (1:3). Our hope is not only for the future; eternal life begins when we believe in God and join his family. The eternal life we now have gives us hope and enables us to live with confidence in God.

that is kept in heaven for you, pure and unde-filed, beyond the reach of change and decay. 5And through your faith, God is protecting you by his power until you receive this salvation, which is ready to be revealed on the last day for all to see.

6So be truly glad.* There is wonderful joy ahead, even though you have to endure many trials for a little while. 7These trials will show that your faith is genuine. It is being tested as fire tests and purifies gold—though your faith is far more precious than mere gold. So when your faith remains strong through many trials, it will bring you much praise and glory and honor on the day when Jesus Christ is revealed to the whole world.

8You love him even though you have never seen him. Though you do not see him now, you trust him; and you rejoice with a glorious, inex-pressible joy. 9The reward for trusting him will be the salvation of your souls.

10This salvation was something even the prophets wanted to know more about when they prophesied about this gracious salvation prepared for you. 11They wondered what time

1:1 *Pontus, Galatia, Cappadocia, Asia,* and *Bithynia* were Roman provinces in what is now Turkey. **1:6** Or *So you are truly glad.*

BUT THE WORD ᴼᶠ ᴛʜᴇ LORD REMAINS FOREVER.
=== 1 PETER 1:25 ===

or situation the Spirit of Christ within them was talking about when he told them in advance about Christ's suffering and his great glory afterward.

¹²They were told that their messages were not for themselves, but for you. And now this Good News has been announced to you by those who preached in the power of the Holy Spirit sent from heaven. It is all so wonderful that even the angels are eagerly watching these things happen.

A CALL TO HOLY LIVING ¹³So think clearly and exercise self-control. Look forward to the gracious salvation that will come to you when Jesus Christ is revealed to the world. ¹⁴So you must live as God's obedient children. Don't slip back into your old ways of living to satisfy your own desires. You didn't know any better then. ¹⁵But now you must be holy in everything you do, just as God who chose you is holy. ¹⁶For the Scriptures say, "You must be holy because I am holy."*

¹⁷And remember that the heavenly Father to whom you pray has no favorites. He will judge or reward you according to what you do. So you must live in reverent fear of him during your time as "foreigners in the land." ¹⁸For you know that God paid a ransom to save you from the empty life you inherited from your ancestors. And the ransom he paid was not mere gold or silver. ¹⁹It was the precious blood of Christ, the

1:16 Lev 11:44-45; 19:2; 20:7. **1:22a** Greek *must have brotherly love.* **1:22b** Some manuscripts read *with a pure heart.*

sinless, spotless Lamb of God. ²⁰God chose him as your ransom long before the world began, but he has now revealed him to you in these last days.

²¹Through Christ you have come to trust in God. And you have placed your faith and hope in God because he raised Christ from the dead and gave him great glory.

²²You were cleansed from your sins when you obeyed the truth, so now you must show sincere love to each other as brothers and sisters.* Love each other deeply with all your heart.*

²³For you have been born again, but not to a life that will quickly end. Your new life will last forever because it comes from the eternal, living word of God. ²⁴As the Scriptures say,

"People are like grass;
  their beauty is like a flower in the field.
The grass withers and the flower fades.

···

BE HOLY
(1:13-16) Peter tells us to be like our heavenly Father—holy in everything we do. Holiness means being totally devoted or dedicated to God, set aside for his special use and set apart from sin and its influence. We're not supposed to blend in with the crowd; yet at the same time we don't need to try to be different just to be different. The fruit God develops in our lives—his characteristics in us—automatically make us different. Our focus and priorities must be his. All of this is in direct contrast to our old ways (1:14). Since we can't become holy on our own, God gives us his Holy Spirit to help us. He can turn an excuse like "I couldn't help it" into "I can do everything through Christ, who gives me strength" (Phil 4:13).

I WONDER . . .

It's hard to believe in something you can't see. Why has God made it so difficult for people who would believe in him if they could only see him?

God is big, strong, and powerful, and could appear to anyone anyway he wants. But if he suddenly appeared, most people would feel forced or intimidated into following him rather than loved into it. God wants us to respond out of love for him, not fear!

The truth is that people *can* see God . . . through the eyes of faith. This means taking God at his word—opening ourselves up to him. Some people say, "Seeing is believing." The truth is that "believing is seeing."

All of us believe in people or things we've never seen: for example, people in history, gravity, or the wind. Everyone has the capacity to believe things that aren't seen. The bottom line for most who say, "I can't believe in something I haven't seen," is "I won't believe in God because I want to run my own life." God doesn't work that way. Each person must trust in Christ, acknowledging him as his or her Savior.

Peter said that loving God, even though we have never seen him, will bring us "a glorious, inexpressible joy" (1 Pet 1:8). Jesus said, "Blessed are those who believe without seeing me" (John 20:29; see also Heb 11:1).

"We live by believing and not by seeing". (2 Cor 5:7).

[25] But the word of the Lord remains
forever."*

And that word is the Good News that was
preached to you.

2 So get rid of all evil behavior. Be done
with all deceit, hypocrisy, jealousy, and
all unkind speech. [2]Like newborn babies, you
must crave pure spiritual milk so that you will
grow into a full experience of salvation. Cry out
for this nourishment, [3]now that you have had a
taste of the Lord's kindness.

LIVING STONES FOR GOD'S HOUSE [4]You are
coming to Christ, who is the living cornerstone
of God's temple. He was rejected by people,
but he was chosen by God for great honor.

[5]And you are living stones that God is building into his spiritual temple. What's more, you
are his holy priests.* Through the mediation of
Jesus Christ, you offer spiritual sacrifices that
please God. [6]As the Scriptures say,

"I am placing a cornerstone in Jerusalem,*
    chosen for great honor,
and anyone who trusts in him
    will never be disgraced."*

[7]Yes, you who trust him recognize the honor
God has given him. But for those who reject
him,

"The stone that the builders rejected
    has now become the cornerstone."*

[8]And,

"He is the stone that makes people
    stumble,
the rock that makes them fall."*

They stumble because they do not obey God's
word, and so they meet the fate that was
planned for them.

[9]But you are not like that, for you are a chosen people. You are royal priests,* a holy nation, God's very own possession. As a result,
you can show others the goodness of God, for
he called you out of the darkness into his wonderful light.

[10] "Once you had no identity as a people;
    now you are God's people.
Once you received no mercy;
    now you have received
        God's mercy."*

[11]Dear friends, I warn you as "temporary
residents and foreigners" to keep away from
worldly desires that wage war against your
very souls. [12]Be careful to live properly among
your unbelieving neighbors. Then even if they
accuse you of doing wrong, they will see your
honorable behavior, and they will give honor
to God when he judges the world.*

RESPECTING PEOPLE IN AUTHORITY [13]For
the Lord's sake, respect all human authority—
whether the king as head of state, [14]or the officials he has appointed. For the king has sent
them to punish those who do wrong and to
honor those who do right.

[15]It is God's will that your honorable lives
should silence those ignorant people who
make foolish accusations against you. [16]For
you are free, yet you are God's slaves, so don't
use your freedom as an excuse to do evil.
[17]Respect everyone, and love your Christian
brothers and sisters.* Fear God, and respect
the king.

SLAVES [18]You who are slaves must accept the
authority of your masters with all respect.* Do
what they tell you—not only if they are kind
and reasonable, but even if they are cruel. [19]For
God is pleased with you when you do what you
know is right and patiently endure unfair treatment. [20]Of course, you get no credit for being
patient if you are beaten for doing wrong. But
if you suffer for doing good and endure it patiently, God is pleased with you.

[21]For God called you to do good, even if it
means suffering, just as Christ suffered* for
you. He is your example, and you must follow
in his steps.

[22] He never sinned,
    nor ever deceived anyone.*
[23] He did not retaliate when he was insulted,
    nor threaten revenge when he suffered.
He left his case in the hands of God,
    who always judges fairly.
[24] He personally carried our sins
    in his body on the cross
so that we can be dead to sin
    and live for what is right.
By his wounds
    you are healed.
[25] Once you were like sheep
    who wandered away.
But now you have turned to
    your Shepherd,
        the Guardian of your souls.

1:24-25 Isa 40:6-8.   **2:5** Greek *holy priesthood*.   **2:6a** Greek *in
Zion*.   **2:6b** Isa 28:16 (Greek version).   **2:7** Ps 118:22.   **2:8** Isa
8:14.   **2:9** Greek *a royal priesthood*.   **2:10** Hos 1:6, 9; 2:23.
2:12 Or *on the day of visitation*.   **2:17** Greek *love the brotherhood*.
2:18 Or *because you fear God*.   **2:21** Some manuscripts read *died*.
2:22 Isa 53:9.

MY STORY: Jenny

I attended a Christian school during junior high and the first year of high school. But after three years at Christian schools, I felt like God wanted me to go back to a public school. I talked it over in depth with my parents. They supported me, but reminded me of how difficult it could be because of all the pressures to live for oneself, not for God.

They were right—the pressures and temptations were greater. I didn't know quite how to be a Christian in that atmosphere. I was afraid people would make fun of me once they found out I was a Christian, yet I was determined not to hide my faith. After all, I knew Jesus, the one person in this life who will never let me down. I wanted to share my faith with the new friends I was making.

I decided to take to heart the message of 1 Peter 3:15. It shows me how to live my life in that setting, among people who really need to hear some Good News. This verse keeps me in line in difficult situations. For instance, if I'm at a party and drinking only Coke, often someone will ask me why I'm not drinking any alcohol. I usually tell them that I don't need alcohol to have a good time. Jesus helps me to enjoy life and people just as they are. Most people respect me when I say that. Even when they don't, as it says in 1 Peter 3:16-17, it's better that they mock me for doing something right than for making a fool of myself by getting drunk.

First Peter 3:15 reminds me of my purpose for being in a public school: to be ready to tell people of the hope I have in Jesus.

3 **WIVES** In the same way, you wives must accept the authority of your husbands. Then, even if some refuse to obey the Good News, your godly lives will speak to them without any words. They will be won over ²by observing your pure and reverent lives.

³Don't be concerned about the outward beauty of fancy hairstyles, expensive jewelry, or beautiful clothes. ⁴You should clothe yourselves instead with the beauty that comes from within, the unfading beauty of a gentle and quiet spirit, which is so precious to God. ⁵This is how the holy women of old made themselves beautiful. They trusted God and accepted the authority of their husbands. ⁶For instance, Sarah obeyed her husband, Abraham, and called him her master. You are her daughters when you do what is right without fear of what your husbands might do.

HUSBANDS ⁷In the same way, you husbands must give honor to your wives. Treat your wife with understanding as you live together. She may be weaker than you are, but she is your equal partner in God's gift of new life. Treat her as you should so your prayers will not be hindered.

ALL CHRISTIANS ⁸Finally, all of you should be of one mind. Sympathize with each other.

3:8 Greek *Show brotherly love.* **3:10-12** Ps 34:12-16.

Love each other as brothers and sisters.* Be tenderhearted, and keep a humble attitude. ⁹Don't repay evil for evil. Don't retaliate with insults when people insult you. Instead, pay them back with a blessing. That is what God has called you to do, and he will bless you for it. ¹⁰For the Scriptures say,

"If you want to enjoy life
 and see many happy days,
keep your tongue from speaking evil
 and your lips from telling lies.
¹¹ Turn away from evil and do good.
 Search for peace, and work to maintain it.
¹² The eyes of the Lord watch over those who
 do right,
 and his ears are open to their prayers.
But the Lord turns his face
 against those who do evil."*

SUFFERING FOR DOING GOOD ¹³Now, who will want to harm you if you are eager to do good? ¹⁴But even if you suffer for doing what is right,

....

AN ALTERNATIVE TO REVENGE
(3:8-12) Remembering Jesus' teaching to turn the other cheek (Matt 5:39-45), Peter encouraged his readers to pay back wrongs by praying for the offenders. In our society, tearing people down verbally or getting revenge is acceptable. In God's kingdom, revenge and insults are both unacceptable. Want to rise above revenge or rudeness? Pray for those who hurt you.

God will reward you for it. So don't worry or be afraid of their threats. [15]Instead, you must worship Christ as Lord of your life. And if someone asks about your Christian hope, always be ready to explain it. [16]But do this in a gentle and respectful way.* Keep your conscience clear. Then if people speak against you, they will be ashamed when they see what a good life you live because you belong to Christ. [17]Remember, it is better to suffer for doing good, if that is what God wants, than to suffer for doing wrong!

[18]Christ suffered* for our sins once for all time. He never sinned, but he died for sinners to bring you safely home to God. He suffered physical death, but he was raised to life in the Spirit.*

[19]So he went and preached to the spirits in prison—[20]those who disobeyed God long ago when God waited patiently while Noah was building his boat. Only eight people were saved from drowning in that terrible flood.* [21]And that water is a picture of baptism, which now saves you, not by removing dirt from your body, but as a response to God from* a clean conscience. It is effective because of the resurrection of Jesus Christ.

··

SPEAK UP

(3:15) *Some Christians believe that faith is a personal matter and should be kept to oneself. Although we shouldn't be boisterous or obnoxious in sharing our faith, we should be ready at all times to answer—gently and respectfully—when asked about our beliefs, our lifestyle, or our Christian perspective (see also 2 Tim 4:2). Are you ready to share?*

[22]Now Christ has gone to heaven. He is seated in the place of honor next to God, and all the angels and authorities and powers accept his authority.

4 LIVING FOR GOD

So then, since Christ suffered physical pain, you must arm yourselves with the same attitude he had, and be ready to suffer, too. For if you have suffered physically for Christ, you have finished with sin.* [2]You won't spend the rest of your lives chasing your own desires, but you will be anxious to do the will of God. [3]You have had enough in the past of the evil things that godless people enjoy—their immorality and lust, their feasting and drunkenness and wild parties, and their terrible worship of idols.

[4]Of course, your former friends are surprised when you no longer plunge into the flood of wild and destructive things they do. So they slander you. [5]But remember that they will have to face God, who will judge everyone, both the living and the dead. [6]That is why the Good News was preached to those who are now dead*—so although they were destined to die like all people,* they now live forever with God in the Spirit.*

[7]The end of the world is coming soon. Therefore, be earnest and disciplined in your prayers. [8]Most important of all, continue to show deep love for each other, for love covers a multitude of sins. [9]Cheerfully share your

3:16 Some English translations put this sentence in verse 15.   **3:18a** Some manuscripts read *died.*   **3:18b** Or *in spirit.*   **3:20** Greek *saved through water.*   **3:21** Or *as an appeal to God for.*   **4:1** Or *For the one* [or *One*] *who has suffered physically has finished with sin.*   **4:6a** Greek *preached even to the dead.*   **4:6b** Or *so although people had judged them worthy of death.*   **4:6c** Or *in spirit.*

CHOICES
parties

It's prom time, and Courtney and Samantha are getting nervous. Their problem? Getting their dates, Costa and Patrick, to forget the idea of an unchaperoned party in a hotel suite after the prom.

Maybe that situation seems simple to solve, but consider the facts:

- The girls are sophomores. Their dates are seniors and are expected at the hotel.
- The party will feature an open bar and available beds.
- Costa and Patrick each have already kicked in $150 to pay for this private affair.
- A similar party last year featured some unbelievably wild activities.

"What are we gonna do?" Courtney asks.

"Well, we could just tell our parents and let them get us out of this," Samantha says, not really believing that herself.

"Oh, right, Samantha! And get laughed out of school? We can't do that!"

"Okay, what if we fake like we're sick or something?"

"Samantha!! And miss the prom? It's our first one—and I don't want it to be our last. Look, this whole mess isn't our fault. Let's just pray about it. Maybe God wants us to go and be good examples or something."

"Okay," Samantha agrees.

The girls bow their heads.

Do Courtney and Samantha need to pray about such a decision? What would you do in this situation? Check out 1 Peter 4:3-6 and Galatians 5:19-21. How would either passage help Courtney and Samantha with their decision?

home with those who need a meal or a place to stay.

¹⁰God has given each of you a gift from his great variety of spiritual gifts. Use them well to serve one another. ¹¹Do you have the gift of speaking? Then speak as though God himself were speaking through you. Do you have the gift of helping others? Do it with all the strength and energy that God supplies. Then everything you do will bring glory to God through Jesus Christ. All glory and power to him forever and ever! Amen.

SUFFERING FOR BEING A CHRISTIAN ¹²Dear friends, don't be surprised at the fiery trials you are going through, as if something strange were happening to you. ¹³Instead, be very glad—for these trials make you partners with Christ in his suffering, so that you will have the wonderful joy of seeing his glory when it is revealed to all the world.

¹⁴So be happy when you are insulted for being a Christian,* for then the glorious Spirit of God* rests upon you.* ¹⁵If you suffer, however, it must not be for murder, stealing, making trouble, or prying into other people's affairs. ¹⁶But it is no shame to suffer for being a Christian. Praise God for the privilege of being called by his name! ¹⁷For the time has come for judgment, and it must begin with God's household. And if judgment begins with us, what terrible fate awaits those who have never obeyed God's Good News? ¹⁸And also,

"If the righteous are barely saved,
    what will happen to godless sinners?"*

¹⁹So if you are suffering in a manner that pleases God, keep on doing what is right, and trust your lives to the God who created you, for he will never fail you.

5 **ADVICE FOR ELDERS AND YOUNG MEN** And now, a word to you who are elders in the churches. I, too, am an elder and a witness to the sufferings of Christ. And I, too, will share in his glory when he is revealed to the whole world. As a fellow elder, I appeal to you: ²Care for the flock that God has entrusted to you. Watch over it willingly, not grudgingly—not for what you will get out of it, but because you

are eager to serve God. ³Don't lord it over the people assigned to your care, but lead them by your own good example. ⁴And when the Great Shepherd appears, you will receive a crown of never-ending glory and honor.

⁵In the same way, you younger men must accept the authority of the elders. And all of you, serve each other in humility, for

"God opposes the proud
    but favors the humble."*

⁶So humble yourselves under the mighty power of God, and at the right time he will lift you up in honor. ⁷Give all your worries and cares to God, for he cares about you.

⁸Stay alert! Watch out for your great enemy, the devil. He prowls around like a roaring lion, looking for someone to devour. ⁹Stand firm against him, and be strong in your faith. Remember that your Christian brothers and sisters* all over the world are going through the same kind of suffering you are.

¹⁰In his kindness God called you to share in his eternal glory by means of Christ Jesus. So after you have suffered a little while, he will restore, support, and strengthen you, and he will place you on a firm foundation. ¹¹All power to him forever! Amen.

PETER'S FINAL GREETINGS ¹²I have written and sent this short letter to you with the help of Silas,* whom I commend to you as a faithful brother. My purpose in writing is to encourage you and assure you that what you are experiencing is truly part of God's grace for you. Stand firm in this grace.

¹³Your sister church here in Babylon* sends you greetings, and so does my son Mark. ¹⁴Greet each other with Christian love.*

Peace be with all of you who are in Christ.

··

SUFFERING
(4:16) Suffering for being a Christian isn't shameful. When Peter and the other apostles were persecuted for preaching the Good News, they rejoiced because such persecution was a mark of God's approval of their work (Acts 5:41). Don't seek out suffering, and don't try to avoid it. Instead, keep on doing what is right regardless of the suffering your actions might bring.

DIFFERENT SEASONS OF LIFE, SAME ADVICE
(5:5) Pride sometimes keeps older people from trying to understand younger people and vice versa. Peter advised both young and old to be humble and to serve each other. Young men should follow the leadership of older men, who should lead by example. What have you learned from someone older? What has someone older learned from you?

4:14a Greek *for the name of Christ.*   **4:14b** Or *for the glory of God, which is his Spirit.*   **4:14c** Some manuscripts add *On their part he is blasphemed, but on your part he is glorified.*   **4:18** Prov 11:31 (Greek version).   **5:5** Prov 3:34 (Greek version).   **5:9** Greek *your brothers.*   **5:12** Greek *Silvanus.*   **5:13** Greek *The elect one in Babylon.* Babylon was probably symbolic for Rome.   **5:14** Greek *with a kiss of love.*

2 PETER

We've all come face-to-face with life's ironies. One man, noting the regularity (and certainty) of these quirks, decided to make a list. The result? The famous "Murphy's Laws." Additions to the list have been added over the years.

Some of the more interesting observations on this list include:

- If anything can go wrong, it will.
- "Broken" gadgets will operate perfectly in the presence of a repairman.
- Saying "Watch this!" guarantees that the behavior you want others to witness will not happen.
- A poorly thrown Frisbee will always come to rest under the exact center of a parked car.
- Stored objects are never needed . . . until immediately after they are discarded.
- The bowl that breaks is never the one that was already chipped.
- The other line always moves faster.
- If you put a napkin in your lap you will not spill; failure to use a napkin ensures spillage.
- You will only be forced to wait when you do not have time to wait.

We nod and smile at those "laws" because we've lived them. They're amazingly true to life. How about some other laws of life? Perhaps these are not as humorous, but they're just as true—and much more life-changing:

- Spiritual growth only happens when we get to know God and make an effort to serve him.
- The world is full of people who will try to lead you astray.
- Jesus Christ is coming back.

Would you like to know more about these critical principles? They're all contained in the letter known as 2 Peter.

STATS

PURPOSE
To warn Christians about false teachers and to encourage them to grow in their faith and knowledge of Christ

AUTHOR
Peter

ORIGINAL AUDIENCE
The church at large

DATE WRITTEN
About A.D. 67, three years after 1 Peter was written, possibly from Rome

SETTING
Since Peter knew that his time on earth was limited (1:13-15), he wrote what was on his heart, warning believers of what would happen after he was gone. Peter especially wanted to warn them about false teachers and to remind them of the unchanging truth of the gospel.

KEY PEOPLE
Peter, Paul

SPECIAL FEATURES
The date and destination are uncertain, and the authorship has been disputed. Because of this, 2 Peter was the last epistle admitted to the canon of the New Testament. There are similarities between 2 Peter and Jude.

KEY POINTS

DILIGENCE Peter encouraged believers to grow spiritually. Growth begins with faith and results in love for others. To keep growing, we need to be diligent in our relationship with God and remember what he taught us.

FALSE TEACHERS Peter advised the church to beware of false teachers. God provides discernment through the Holy Spirit and his Word to recognize false teaching. The truth is our best defense.

JESUS' RETURN One day Jesus will return to earth. But with his return comes his judgment on all who refuse to believe. The cure for unbelief, complacency, lawlessness, and heresy is found in the confident assurance that Jesus will return.

MY STORY: Joel

I didn't want to break up with my girlfriend. But the more I prayed about the relationship, the more I saw that it was interfering with my relationship with God. My girlfriend wasn't a Christian; her values were completely different from mine. I cared about her, but it came down to a choice: either her or God.

The clincher came when I read 2 Peter 1:5-8. The last part of it says: "The more you grow like this [in following Jesus' example], the more productive and useful you will be in your knowledge of our Lord Jesus Christ."

I didn't need any more guidance. I knew I had to break up with Cate and concentrate on strengthening my relationship with the Lord. Though I felt bad after breaking up with her, I was confident that I had done the right thing and that the Lord still cared about me and my decisions.

I also was encouraged. God showed me that I was slowly but surely becoming stronger spiritually. Every verse of that passage fit a part of my life. As I put God first and determined to obey him, I could see times when I put aside my own desires and how I was becoming more patient, etc.

Yes, breaking up was hard. But knowing that I did it to obey God made all the difference.

1 **GREETINGS FROM PETER** This letter is from Simon* Peter, a slave and apostle of Jesus Christ.

I am writing to you who share the same precious faith we have. This faith was given to you because of the justice and fairness* of Jesus Christ, our God and Savior. ²May God give you more and more grace and peace as you grow in your knowledge of God and Jesus our Lord.

GROWING IN FAITH ³By his divine power, God has given us everything we need for living a godly life. We have received all of this by coming to know him, the one who called us to himself by means of his marvelous glory and excellence. ⁴And because of his glory and excellence, he has given us great and precious promises. These are the promises that enable you to share his divine nature and escape the world's corruption caused by human desires. ⁵In view of all this, make every effort to re-

spond to God's promises. Supplement your faith with a generous provision of moral excellence, and moral excellence with knowledge, ⁶and knowledge with self-control, and self-control with patient endurance, and patient endurance with godliness, ⁷and godliness with brotherly affection, and brotherly affection with love for everyone.

⁸The more you grow like this, the more productive and useful you will be in your knowledge of our Lord Jesus Christ. ⁹But those who fail to develop in this way are shortsighted or blind, forgetting that they have been cleansed from their old sins.

¹⁰So, dear brothers and sisters,* work hard to prove that you really are among those God has called and chosen. Do these things, and you will never fall away. ¹¹Then God will give you a grand entrance into the eternal Kingdom of our Lord and Savior Jesus Christ.

PAYING ATTENTION TO SCRIPTURE ¹²Therefore, I will always remind you about these things—even though you already know them and are standing firm in the truth you have been taught. ¹³And it is only right that I should keep on reminding you as long as I live.* ¹⁴For our Lord Jesus Christ has shown me that I must soon leave this earthly life,* ¹⁵so I will work hard to make sure you always remember these things after I am gone.

BE ALL THAT YOU CAN BE

(1:5-11) Faith must be more than belief in certain facts; it must result in action, growth in Christian character, and discipline, or it will die (Jas 2:14-17). Peter lists several actions of faith, including learning to know God better, developing endurance and godliness, and loving others. These actions don't come automatically; they require hard work. They're also not optional; all must be a continual part of the Christian life. We need to work on them all together, not one at a time. But here's the good news: God will help you be all that you can be.

1:1a Greek *Symeon.* **1:1b** Or *to you in the righteousness.* **1:10** Greek *brothers.* **1:13** Greek *as long as I am in this tent [or tabernacle].* **1:14** Greek *I must soon put off my tent [or tabernacle].*

¹⁶For we were not making up clever stories when we told you about the powerful coming of our Lord Jesus Christ. We saw his majestic splendor with our own eyes ¹⁷when he received honor and glory from God the Father. The voice from the majestic glory of God said to him, "This is my dearly loved Son, who brings me great joy."* ¹⁸We ourselves heard that voice from heaven when we were with him on the holy mountain.

¹⁹Because of that experience, we have even greater confidence in the message proclaimed by the prophets. You must pay close attention to what they wrote, for their words are like a lamp shining in a dark place—until the Day dawns, and Christ the Morning Star shines* in your hearts. ²⁰Above all, you must realize that no prophecy in Scripture ever came from the prophet's own understanding,* ²¹or from human initiative. No, those prophets were moved by the Holy Spirit, and they spoke from God.

2 THE DANGER OF FALSE TEACHERS But there were also false prophets in Israel, just as there will be false teachers among you. They will cleverly teach destructive heresies and even deny the Master who bought them. In this way, they will bring sudden destruction on themselves. ²Many will follow their evil teaching and shameful immorality. And because of these teachers, the way of truth will be slandered. ³In their greed they will make up clever lies to get hold of your money. But God

1:17 Matt 17:5; Mark 9:7; Luke 9:35. 1:19 Or rises. 1:20 Or is a matter of one's own interpretation. 2:4a Greek Tartarus. 2:4b Some manuscripts read in chains of gloom. 2:10 Greek at glorious ones, which are probably evil angels. 2:11 Other manuscripts read to the Lord; still others do not include this phrase at all.

condemned them long ago, and their destruction will not be delayed.

⁴For God did not spare even the angels who sinned. He threw them into hell,* in gloomy pits of darkness,* where they are being held until the day of judgment. ⁵And God did not spare the ancient world—except for Noah and the seven others in his family. Noah warned the world of God's righteous judgment. So God protected Noah when he destroyed the world of ungodly people with a vast flood. ⁶Later, God condemned the cities of Sodom and Gomorrah and turned them into heaps of ashes. He made them an example of what will happen to ungodly people. ⁷But God also rescued Lot out of Sodom because he was a righteous man who was sick of the shameful immorality of the wicked people around him. ⁸Yes, Lot was a righteous man who was tormented in his soul by the wickedness he saw and heard day after day. ⁹So you see, the Lord knows how to rescue godly people from their trials, even while keeping the wicked under punishment until the day of final judgment. ¹⁰He is especially hard on those who follow their own twisted sexual desire, and who despise authority.

These people are proud and arrogant, daring even to scoff at supernatural beings* without so much as trembling. ¹¹But the angels, who are far greater in power and strength, do not dare to bring from the Lord* a charge of blasphemy against those supernatural beings.

¹²These false teachers are like unthinking animals, creatures of instinct, born to be caught and destroyed. They scoff at things they do not understand, and like animals, they will be destroyed. ¹³Their destruction is their reward for

CHOICES cults

A month ago, while on a city bus, Hannah picked up a discarded leaflet advertising a free music festival and complimentary vegetarian meal. She called her friend Jasmine to go with her to check it out.

Throughout the afternoon Jasmine kept whispering, "Let's get out of here. This is weird!" But Hannah kept replying, "Chill, Jas! You're too intense."

On the way home, Jasmine made it clear what she thought. "Look, I don't care what you say. That group is some kind of cult or something."

"Why? Name one thing they did or said that was bad," Hannah challenged.

"Well, I dunno. . . . They just gave me the creeps, that's all!"

"Aw, I think you're paranoid. Who knows? I just might go to one of their classes."

Hannah returned on the following week. And now she's a full-fledged member of the "church"—The Society of Enlightened Minds. The members accept her and make her feel special.

Jasmine's parents did some checking. Hannah's "church" doesn't accept the Bible or the belief that Christ is God. It teaches that each of us is a god and that together we can recreate the world—or so they believe.

With their popular, feel-good philosophies, many cults have captured millions of hungry hearts and uncritical minds. No wonder we're told in 2 Peter 2:12-22 to carefully consider the ideas that we hear every day. Do you? What would you say to Hannah?

THE DAY OF THE LORD WILL COME
AS UNEXPECTEDLY AS A THIEF. {2 PETER 3:10}

the harm they have done. They love to indulge in evil pleasures in broad daylight. They are a disgrace and a stain among you. They delight in deception* even as they eat with you in your fellowship meals. ¹⁴They commit adultery with their eyes, and their desire for sin is never satisfied. They lure unstable people into sin, and they are well trained in greed. They live under God's curse. ¹⁵They have wandered off the right road and followed the footsteps of Balaam son of Beor,* who loved to earn money by doing wrong. ¹⁶But Balaam was stopped from his mad course when his donkey rebuked him with a human voice.

¹⁷These people are as useless as dried-up springs or as mist blown away by the wind. They are doomed to blackest darkness. ¹⁸They brag about themselves with empty, foolish boasting. With an appeal to twisted sexual desires, they lure back into sin those who have barely escaped from a lifestyle of deception. ¹⁹They promise freedom, but they themselves are slaves of sin and corruption. For you are a slave to whatever controls you. ²⁰And when people escape from the wickedness of the world by knowing our Lord and Savior Jesus Christ and then get tangled up and enslaved by sin again, they are worse off than before. ²¹It would be better if they had never known the way to righteousness than to know it and then reject the command they were given to live a holy life. ²²They prove the truth of this proverb: "A dog returns to its vomit."* And another says, "A washed pig returns to the mud."

3 **THE DAY OF THE LORD IS COMING** This is my second letter to you, dear friends, and

....

FREEDOM
(2:19) Peter warned that false teachers promised a freedom that in reality led to slavery. Ever wish that you didn't have to follow so many rules—that you could live however you wanted to live? Many people would define freedom that way. But if we continually follow our own desires, we'll eventually become enslaved to those desires. If we submit to Christ, however, he'll free us from slavery to wrong desires (see also Titus 3:3). Is that the kind of freedom you want? It's yours for the asking.

ANY DAY NOW
(3:14) Peter warned believers not to become complacent simply because Christ has not yet returned. Instead, believers are encouraged to live each day in the eager expectation of his coming. What would you like to be doing when Christ returns? Is that the way you're living now?

in both of them I have tried to stimulate your wholesome thinking and refresh your memory. ²I want you to remember what the holy prophets said long ago and what our Lord and Savior commanded through your apostles.

³Most importantly, I want to remind you that in the last days scoffers will come, mocking the truth and following their own desires. ⁴They will say, "What happened to the promise that Jesus is coming again? From before the times of our ancestors, everything has remained the same since the world was first created."

⁵They deliberately forget that God made the heavens by the word of his command, and he brought the earth out from the water and surrounded it with water. ⁶Then he used the water to destroy the ancient world with a mighty flood. ⁷And by the same word, the present heavens and earth have been stored up for fire. They are being kept for the day of judgment, when ungodly people will be destroyed.

⁸But you must not forget this one thing, dear friends: A day is like a thousand years to the Lord, and a thousand years is like a day. ⁹The Lord isn't really being slow about his promise, as some people think. No, he is being patient for your sake. He does not want anyone to be destroyed, but wants everyone to repent. ¹⁰But the day of the Lord will come as unexpectedly as a thief. Then the heavens will pass away with a terrible noise, and the very elements themselves will disappear in fire, and the earth and everything on it will be found to deserve judgment.*

¹¹Since everything around us is going to be destroyed like this, what holy and godly lives you should live, ¹²looking forward to the day of God and hurrying it along. On that day, he will set the heavens on fire, and the elements will melt away in the flames. ¹³But we are looking forward to the new heavens and new earth he has promised, a world filled with God's righteousness.

¹⁴And so, dear friends, while you are waiting for these things to happen, make every effort to be found living peaceful lives that are pure and blameless in his sight.

¹⁵And remember, our Lord's patience gives people time to be saved. This is what our be-

2:13 Some manuscripts read *in fellowship meals.*   **2:15** Some manuscripts read *Bosor.*   **2:22** Prov 26:11.   **3:10** Other manuscripts read *will be burned up;* one early manuscript reads *will be found destroyed.*

loved brother Paul also wrote to you with the wisdom God gave him—[16]speaking of these things in all of his letters. Some of his comments are hard to understand, and those who are ignorant and unstable have twisted his letters to mean something quite different, just as they do with other parts of Scripture. And this will result in their destruction.

PETER'S FINAL WORDS [17]I am warning you ahead of time, dear friends. Be on guard so that you will not be carried away by the errors of these wicked people and lose your own secure footing. [18]Rather, you must grow in the grace and knowledge of our Lord and Savior Jesus Christ.

All glory to him, both now and forever! Amen.

Love.

We can't touch it, count it, bottle it, or even see it. But who among us would argue that love isn't real?

Love.

It makes sane people do and say crazy things. It prompts selfish people to do noble things. It turns boring people into exciting, unpredictable creatures. What else on earth has that kind of power?

Love.

It can hurt like nothing else in the world. And yet, paradoxically, not *loving is much more painful.*

Love.

The most talked-about, sung-about, and thought-about theme in the world—as well as the most misunderstood.

Love.

Would you like to know more about it and see it in a brand-new light? Then read 1 John, the most eloquent description of love ever penned.

Love.

It's not everything you think it is. It's more . . . much, much more.

KEY POINTS

FORGIVENESS John encouraged believers to confess their wrongdoings to God and receive his forgiveness. Although our wrong actions are our fault, we don't have to solve this problem on our own. Jesus offers forgiveness.

LOVE Jesus commands us to love others as he did. Love means showing others we care, not just saying it.

THE FAMILY OF GOD We become God's children by believing in Christ. How we treat others shows who our Father is.

TRUTH AND ERROR False teachers encouraged believers to do whatever they wanted to do. As a result, many people became indifferent to sin. Believers need to know what's true to avoid being fooled by false teachers.

ASSURANCE God is in control of heaven and earth. Because God's Word is true, we have an assurance of eternal life and victory over sin.

STATS

PURPOSE
To reassure Christians in their faith and to counter false teachings

AUTHOR
The apostle John

ORIGINAL AUDIENCE
Several Gentile congregations

DATE WRITTEN
Probably between A.D. 85 and 90 from Ephesus

SETTING
John was an older man—perhaps the only surviving apostle at this time. He had not yet been exiled to the island of Patmos. As an eyewitness of Christ, he wrote authoritatively to encourage a new generation of believers in their faith.

KEY PEOPLE
John, Jesus

SPECIAL FEATURES
The topic of love is mentioned throughout this letter. This letter has a number of similarities in vocabulary, style, and main ideas to John's Gospel. John uses brief statements and simple words and includes sharp contrasts—light and darkness, truth and error, God and Satan, life and death, love and hate.

1 INTRODUCTION

We proclaim to you the one who existed from the beginning,* whom we have heard and seen. We saw him with our own eyes and touched him with our own hands. He is the Word of life. ²This one who is life itself was revealed to us, and we have seen him. And now we testify and proclaim to you that he is the one who is eternal life. He was with the Father, and then he was revealed to us. ³We proclaim to you what we ourselves have actually seen and heard so that you may have fellowship with us. And our fellowship is with the Father and with his Son, Jesus Christ. ⁴We are writing these things so that you may fully share our joy.*

LIVING IN THE LIGHT

⁵This is the message we heard from Jesus* and now declare to you: God is light, and there is no darkness in him at all. ⁶So we are lying if we say we have fellowship with God but go on living in spiritual darkness; we are not practicing the truth. ⁷But if we are living in the light, as God is in the light, then we have fellowship with each other, and the blood of Jesus, his Son, cleanses us from all sin.

⁸If we claim we have no sin, we are only fooling ourselves and not living in the truth. ⁹But if we confess our sins to him, he is faithful and just to forgive us our sins and to cleanse us from all wickedness. ¹⁰If we claim we have not sinned, we are calling God a liar and showing that his word has no place in our hearts.

2 My dear children, I am writing this to you so that you will not sin. But if anyone does sin, we have an advocate who pleads our case before the Father. He is Jesus Christ, the one who is truly righteous. ²He himself is the sacrifice that atones for our sins—and not only our sins but the sins of all the world.

³And we can be sure that we know him if we obey his commandments. ⁴If someone claims, "I know God," but doesn't obey God's commandments, that person is a liar and is not living in the truth. ⁵But those who obey God's word truly show how completely they love him. That is how we know we are living in him. ⁶Those who say they live in God should live their lives as Jesus did.

A NEW COMMANDMENT

⁷Dear friends, I am not writing a new commandment for you; rather it is an old one you have had from the very beginning. This old commandment—to love one another—is the same message you heard before. ⁸Yet it is also new. Jesus lived the truth of this commandment, and you also are living it. For the darkness is disappearing, and the true light is already shining.

⁹If anyone claims, "I am living in the light," but hates a Christian brother or sister,* that person is still living in darkness. ¹⁰Anyone who loves another brother or sister* is living in the light and does not cause others to stumble. ¹¹But anyone who hates another brother or sister is still living and walking in darkness. Such a person does not know the way to go, having been blinded by the darkness.

¹² I am writing to you who are God's children
  because your sins have been forgiven
    through Jesus.*
¹³ I am writing to you who are mature in
    the faith*
  because you know Christ, who existed
    from the beginning.
  I am writing to you who are young in
    the faith
  because you have won your battle with
    the evil one.
¹⁴ I have written to you who are God's children
  because you know the Father.
  I have written to you who are mature in
    the faith
  because you know Christ, who existed
    from the beginning.

OVER AND OVER

(1:9) God offers forgiveness when we own up to what we've done wrong. Yet some Christians feel guilty because they've confessed the same actions over and over. Others believe that if they were to die with unconfessed sins, they would be lost forever. But God wants to forgive us. He allowed his beloved Son to die so that he could forgive us. We don't need to fear that God will reject us if we have to keep telling him about what we have done wrong. He won't. Instead, he offers forgiveness and the strength to defeat the temptation the next time it appears.

A CHOICE

(2:9-11) Ever fear that if you dislike someone, you're not really a Christian? These verses are not talking about disliking a disagreeable Christian brother or sister. We will always know people that we won't like as well as others. John's words focus on the attitude that causes us to ignore or despise others—to treat them as irritants, competitors, or enemies. But love is not so much a feeling as a choice. We can choose to be concerned about the welfare of others and to treat them with respect, whether or not we feel affection toward them. If we choose to love others, God will give us the strength to express his love.

1:1 Greek *What was from the beginning.* **1:4** Or *so that our joy may be complete;* some manuscripts read *your joy.* **1:5** Greek *from him.* **2:9** Greek *hates his brother;* similarly in 2:11. **2:10** Greek *loves his brother.* **2:12** Greek *through his name.* **2:13** Or *to you fathers;* also in 2:14.

MY STORY: Trish

I was the master of rationalization—at least in some areas of my life. When I got into an argument with my parents, I always knew they were totally wrong. If I talked about someone behind her back, I told myself that I wasn't gossiping—I was providing information that person needed to know. When my boyfriend and I started having sex, I rationalized that it was okay because we loved each other, and didn't the Bible say that love was what it was all about?

Then I heard my pastor preach on 1 John 1:8-10, and I suddenly knew that I was just fooling myself. I never fooled God though. He called these things—rebelliousness toward my parents, gossip, premarital sex—sins. I was kidding myself, but not God. The preacher said we are calling God a liar when we don't acknowledge our sins! That really shook me up.

I reread the passage after church, when I was alone in my room, and I cried, not only because I'd been lying to myself and to God, but because this passage also talks about how willing God is to forgive us and cleanse us.

Before God that day, I owned up to the sins I had rationalized. It was hard to do because I knew I had to be willing to change, not just to say "I'm sorry." Change would be hard, particularly in my relationship with my boyfriend. But verse 9 encouraged me that God wouldn't just forgive me, but he'd also give me the strength to make a new start.

I ended up breaking up with my boyfriend. Our physical relationship made starting over impossible. The breakup hurt a lot. But underneath the pain, something felt very good, very right: I was no longer lying to myself or to God. A new, clear conscience is helping me through the pain of change.

I have written to you who are young
  in the faith
   because you are strong.
God's word lives in your hearts,
  and you have won your battle with
   the evil one.

DO NOT LOVE THIS WORLD ¹⁵Do not love this world nor the things it offers you, for when you love the world, you do not have the love of the Father in you. ¹⁶For the world offers only a craving for physical pleasure, a craving for everything we see, and pride in our achievements and possessions. These are not from the Father, but are from this world. ¹⁷And this world is fading away, along with everything that people crave. But anyone who does what pleases God will live forever.

WARNING ABOUT ANTICHRISTS ¹⁸Dear children, the last hour is here. You have heard that the Antichrist is coming, and already many such antichrists have appeared. From this we know that the last hour has come. ¹⁹These people left our churches, but they never really

belonged with us; otherwise they would have stayed with us. When they left, it proved that they did not belong with us.

²⁰But you are not like that, for the Holy One has given you his Spirit,* and all of you know the truth. ²¹So I am writing to you not because you don't know the truth but because you know the difference between truth and lies. ²²And who is a liar? Anyone who says that Jesus is not the Christ.* Anyone who denies the Father and the Son is an antichrist.* ²³Anyone who denies the Son doesn't have the Father, either. But anyone who acknowledges the Son has the Father also.

²⁴So you must remain faithful to what you have been taught from the beginning. If you do, you will remain in fellowship with the Son and with the Father. ²⁵And in this fellowship we enjoy the eternal life he promised us.

²⁶I am writing these things to warn you about those who want to lead you astray. ²⁷But you have received the Holy Spirit,* and he lives within you, so you don't need anyone to teach you what is true. For the Spirit* teaches you everything you need to know, and what he teaches is true—it is not a lie. So just as he has taught you, remain in fellowship with Christ.

2:20 Greek *But you have an anointing from the Holy One.* **2:22a** Or *not the Messiah.* **2:22b** Or *the antichrist.* **2:27a** Greek *the anointing from him.* **2:27b** Greek *the anointing.*

SEE HOW VERY MUCH OUR FATHER LOVES US, FOR HE CALLS US HIS CHILDREN, AND THAT IS WHAT WE ARE!

■ ■ ■ ■ ■ 1 JOHN 3:1 ■ ■ ■ ■ ■

LIVING AS CHILDREN OF GOD ²⁸And now, dear children, remain in fellowship with Christ so that when he returns, you will be full of courage and not shrink back from him in shame.

²⁹Since we know that Christ is righteous, we also know that all who do what is right are God's children.

3 See how very much our Father loves us, for he calls us his children, and that is what we are! But the people who belong to this world don't recognize that we are God's children because they don't know him. ²Dear friends, we are already God's children, but he has not yet shown us what we will be like when Christ appears. But we do know that we will be like him, for we will see him as he really is. ³And all who have this eager expectation will keep themselves pure, just as he is pure.

⁴Everyone who sins is breaking God's law, for all sin is contrary to the law of God. ⁵And you know that Jesus came to take away our sins, and there is no sin in him. ⁶Anyone who continues to live in him will not sin. But anyone who keeps on sinning does not know him or understand who he is.

⁷Dear children, don't let anyone deceive you about this: When people do what is right, it shows that they are righteous, even as Christ is righteous. ⁸But when people keep on sinning, it shows that they belong to the devil, who has been sinning since the beginning. But the Son of God came to destroy the works of the devil. ⁹Those who have been born into God's family do not make a practice of sinning, because God's life* is in them. So they can't keep on sinning, because they are children of God. ¹⁰So now we can tell who are children of God and who are children of the devil. Anyone

3:9 Greek *because his seed.*

CAIN *PERSONALITY PROFILE*

THINK ABOUT THE LAST TIME you felt angry. What caused your anger? How did you deal with it?

Cain grew angry when God seemed to reject his offering but accepted that of his brother Abel. Although God warned Cain about his attitude, Cain didn't listen. Cain was angry at God, but he took it out on his brother. Instead of making things right with God by changing his attitude, he chose to kill his brother. As a result, he became an outcast.

Anger is a powerful reaction. When something happens to us that we don't expect, we get angry! Although anger is not a sin, uncontrolled anger can be. Beginning like a small flame on dry grass, anger can destroy a great deal unless it is snuffed out quickly. Cain's anger got out of control, but he wasn't in trouble until he acted on his anger in a wrong way. His attitude could have been corrected, but his actions couldn't. When we get angry, we're in the same danger.

Cain missed the opportunity to correct his attitude. We don't have to.

Our anger may not result in murder, but we still act like Cain. We get angry. We see that we have a choice to make between right and wrong. And we often choose wrong. Anger can remind us that we need God's help. Asking for his help to do the right thing may keep us from making mistakes we can't correct.

BOTTOM LINE: Anger is not sin. What we do with our anger can be sinful.

What we offer to God must be from the heart—the best that we are and have.

Sometimes the consequences of sin last a lifetime.

Cain's story is told in Genesis 4:1-17. He also is mentioned in Hebrews 11:4 and Jude 1:11.

UPS:
• *Was the first human child and the first to follow in his father's profession (farming)*

DOWNS:
• *When disappointed, reacted out of anger and discouragement*
• *Took the negative choice even when a positive one was offered*
• *Was the first murderer*

STATS:
• *Where: Near Eden, which was probably located in the area of modern-day Iraq or Iran*
• *Occupation: Farmer*
• *Relatives: Adam and Eve (parents); Abel, Seth, and other siblings not mentioned by name; son (Enoch)*

KEY VERSE: *1 John 3:12*

who does not live righteously and does not love other believers* does not belong to God.

LOVE ONE ANOTHER ¹¹This is the message you have heard from the beginning: We should love one another. ¹²We must not be like Cain, who belonged to the evil one and killed his brother. And why did he kill him? Because Cain had been doing what was evil, and his brother had been doing what was righteous. ¹³So don't be surprised, dear brothers and sisters,* if the world hates you.

¹⁴If we love our Christian brothers and sisters,* it proves that we have passed from death to life. But a person who has no love is still dead. ¹⁵Anyone who hates another brother or sister* is really a murderer at heart. And you know that murderers don't have eternal life within them.

¹⁶We know what real love is because Jesus gave up his life for us. So we also ought to give up our lives for our brothers and sisters. ¹⁷If someone has enough money to live well and sees a brother or sister* in need but shows no compassion—how can God's love be in that person?

¹⁸Dear children, let's not merely say that we love each other; let us show the truth by our actions. ¹⁹Our actions will show that we belong to the truth, so we will be confident when we stand before God. ²⁰Even if we feel guilty, God is greater than our feelings, and he knows everything.

²¹Dear friends, if we don't feel guilty, we can come to God with bold confidence. ²²And we will receive from him whatever we ask because we obey him and do the things that please him.

²³And this is his commandment: We must believe in the name of his Son, Jesus Christ, and love one another, just as he commanded us. ²⁴Those who obey God's commandments remain in fellowship with him, and he with them. And we know he lives in us because the Spirit he gave us lives in us.

4 DISCERNING FALSE PROPHETS Dear friends, do not believe everyone who claims to speak by the Spirit. You must test them to see if the spirit they have comes from God. For there are many false prophets in the world. ²This is how we know if they have the Spirit of God: If a person claiming to be a prophet* acknowledges that Jesus Christ

came in a real body, that person has the Spirit of God. ³But if someone claims to be a prophet and does not acknowledge the truth about Jesus, that person is not from God. Such a person has the spirit of the Antichrist, which you heard is coming into the world and indeed is already here.

MY STORY: Virginia

On a short-term mission trip, our group studied 1 John. When I read chapter 4, verses 20 and 21, I felt stunned. God was speaking straight to me. I had a problem: I claimed to love God but I hated my mother. This verse clearly says that we can't love God and keep hating another person. All of a sudden I felt like the biggest hypocrite in the world.

I started to pray that God would work on my attitude. First John 4:19 and other verses in this book helped me. I concentrated a lot on how much God loves me even though I don't deserve it. I felt like my mom didn't deserve my love because she drank and was wrecking our family. Yet because God loved me even though I often wronged others, I must love my mother in spite of her sins.

I can't say that everything is perfect yet in that relationship. I still struggle to be loving toward my mother. But I have found that as I concentrate on how much God loves me, and ask him to love my mother through me, it gets a little easier. I try to act lovingly toward my mother as an expression of my love for God. Whenever I feel my attitude slipping, I remind myself of how much God has forgiven me and how much he loves me. Studying 1 John opened my eyes to this important area of my life where I need to obey God.

DON'T GIVE IN!
(3:8-10) John warned believers against allowing Satan—the enemy of Christians—to tempt them to wrong actions. We all have areas where we feel especially tempted. This passage is not about people who are working to overcome a particular sin, however; it refers to people who constantly try to justify wrong actions. That attitude comes from the enemy. The Holy Spirit gives us the power to avoid giving in to temptation. But he won't force us to use his temptation escape route. We must choose to do so. Will you?

3:10 Greek *does not love his brother.* 3:13 Greek *brothers.* 3:14 Greek *the brothers;* similarly in 3:16. 3:15 Greek *hates his brother.* 3:17 Greek *sees his brother.* 4:2 Greek *If a spirit;* similarly in 4:3.

⁴But you belong to God, my dear children. You have already won a victory over those people, because the Spirit who lives in you is greater than the spirit who lives in the world. ⁵Those people belong to this world, so they speak from the world's viewpoint, and the world listens to them. ⁶But we belong to God, and those who know God listen to us. If they do not belong to God, they do not listen to us. That is how we know if someone has the Spirit of truth or the spirit of deception.

LOVING ONE ANOTHER ⁷Dear friends, let us continue to love one another, for love comes from God. Anyone who loves is a child of God and knows God. ⁸But anyone who does not love does not know God, for God is love.

⁹God showed how much he loved us by sending his one and only Son into the world so that we might have eternal life through him. ¹⁰This is real love—not that we loved God, but that he loved us and sent his Son as a sacrifice to take away our sins.

¹¹Dear friends, since God loved us that much, we surely ought to love each other. ¹²No one has ever seen God. But if we love each other, God lives in us, and his love is brought to full expression in us.

¹³And God has given us his Spirit as proof

that we live in him and he in us. ¹⁴Furthermore, we have seen with our own eyes and now testify that the Father sent his Son to be the Savior of the world. ¹⁵All who confess that Jesus is the Son of God have God living in them, and they live in God. ¹⁶We know how much God loves us, and we have put our trust in his love.

God is love, and all who live in love live in God, and God lives in them. ¹⁷And as we live in God, our love grows more perfect. So we will not be afraid on the day of judgment, but we can face him with confidence because we live like Jesus here in this world.

¹⁸Such love has no fear, because perfect love expels all fear. If we are afraid, it is for fear of punishment, and this shows that we have not fully experienced his perfect love. ¹⁹We love each other* because he loved us first.

²⁰If someone says, "I love God," but hates a Christian brother or sister,* that person is a liar; for if we don't love people we can see, how can we love God, whom we cannot see? ²¹And he has given us this command: Those who love God must also love their Christian brothers and sisters.*

5 **FAITH IN THE SON OF GOD** Everyone who believes that Jesus is the Christ* has become a child of God. And everyone who loves the Father loves his children, too. ²We know we love God's children if we love God and obey his commandments. ³Loving God means keeping his commandments, and his commandments are not burdensome. ⁴For every child of God defeats this evil world, and we achieve this victory through our faith. ⁵And who can win

4:19 Greek *We love.* Other manuscripts read *We love God;* still others read *We love him.* **4:20** Greek *hates his brother.* **4:21** Greek *The one who loves God must also love his brother.* **5:1** Or *the Messiah.*

A TEST
(4:20-21) Saying we love God is easy when it doesn't cost us anything more than weekly attendance at a church service. But the real test of our love for God is how we treat the people right in front of us—our family members, fellow believers, and even enemies. We cannot truly love God while neglecting to love those who are created in his image.

CHOICES
love

Just as Alondra leaves the school cafeteria one day, she suddenly slips on a discarded French fry and a glob of gelatin and winds up sprawled on the floor. Not only does she hear laughter from every corner of the room, much of it comes from her two best friends. Neither asks whether or not she's okay. (She is, by the way.)

Guess how Alondra feels?
(a) Angry
(b) Sad
(c) Hurt
(d) Totally humiliated
(e) All of the above
You guessed it: (e) describes *exactly* how she feels. Guess what Alondra wants to do?

(a) Go home immediately and beg her parents to enroll her in a different school
(b) Sarcastically tell her friends, "Hope you enjoyed the show, traitors!"
(c) Continue lying on the floor, pretending to be unconscious
(d) Cry
(e) All of the above
That's right: (e) again. You are *so* smart!
So what does Alondra *actually* do? Here's the shocker: She prays and asks the Lord to give her the strength to continue loving her friends instead of holding a grudge. Later, when she has the chance to get back at them, she refuses.

Check out 1 John 4:7-21. How does Alondra's attitude reflect this passage? Is this your attitude?

I WONDER...

I became a Christian at a big youth rally last fall. Afterwards, I felt great for a few days—I knew that having a relationship with God was something I wanted—but my good feelings soon went away. Did I lose God? Why didn't the good feelings stay around?

Picture yourself meeting your favorite celebrity face-to-face. That would be an experience you would likely never forget. Yet over time you would forget the intensity of the emotion you once felt. But would that mean you didn't actually meet this person? Of course not! It shows that our feelings often come and go based on current experience.

Asking Jesus Christ into your life is far better than meeting another human, famous or not! You've begun a lifelong relationship with the God who created everything!

In John 14:23, Jesus says, "All who love me will do what I say. My Father will love them, and we will come and make our home with each of them." God wants to come into your life and make something extraordinary out of it. God has begun a process of molding your character to become more like that of Jesus Christ. Within this lifelong process will be some good feelings, but more often we won't have—or want—a continual, intense excitement.

The wonder of getting to know someone as loving and forgiving as Jesus Christ has similarities to other relationships you enjoy. There is the initial experience of meeting a person, followed by months and years of growing to appreciate his or her friendship and influence. (Anything worthwhile takes time.)

First John 5:12 assures us that "whoever has the Son has life." Once you've genuinely chosen to follow Jesus Christ, you can never lose him. As Jesus once said, "No one can snatch them away from me" (John 10:28). *Them* includes you. He'll always be there to guide and love you, even in hard times. Knowing this truth should outweigh your tendency to base your relationship with God on your up-and-down feelings.

---

this battle against the world? Only those who believe that Jesus is the Son of God.

[6]And Jesus Christ was revealed as God's Son by his baptism in water and by shedding his blood on the cross*—not by water only, but by water and blood. And the Spirit, who is truth, confirms it with his testimony. [7]So we have these three witnesses*—[8]the Spirit, the water, and the blood—and all three agree. [9]Since we believe human testimony, surely we can believe the greater testimony that comes from God. And God has testified about his Son. [10]All who believe in the Son of God know in their hearts that this testimony is true. Those who don't believe this are actually calling God a liar because they don't believe what God has testified about his Son.

[11]And this is what God has testified: He has given us eternal life, and this life is in his Son. [12]Whoever has the Son has life; whoever does not have God's Son does not have life.

CONCLUSION [13]I have written this to you who believe in the name of the Son of God, so that you may know you have eternal life. [14]And we are confident that he hears us whenever we ask for anything that pleases him. [15]And since we know he hears us when we make our requests, we also know that he will give us what we ask for.

[16]If you see a Christian brother or sister* sinning in a way that does not lead to death, you should pray, and God will give that person life. But there is a sin that leads to death, and I am not saying you should pray for those who commit it. [17]All wicked actions are sin, but not every sin leads to death.

[18]We know that God's children do not make a practice of sinning, for God's Son holds them securely, and the evil one cannot touch them. [19]We know that we are children of God and that the world around us is under the control of the evil one.

[20]And we know that the Son of God has come, and he has given us understanding so that we can know the true God.* And now we live in fellowship with the true God because we live in fellowship with his Son, Jesus Christ. He is the only true God, and he is eternal life.

[21]Dear children, keep away from anything that might take God's place in your hearts.*

5:6 Greek *This is he who came by water and blood.*   **5:7** A few very late manuscripts add *in heaven—the Father, the Word, and the Holy Spirit, and these three are one. And we have three witnesses on earth.*   **5:16** Greek *a brother.*   **5:20** Greek *the one who is true.*   **5:21** Greek *keep yourselves from idols.*

YOU KNOW IT!
(5:13) Some people hope they will spend eternity with God. John says that we can know we will. Our certainty is based on God's promise that he has given us eternal life through his Son. This is true whether you feel close to God or distant from him. Eternal life is not based on feelings, but on facts. You can know you have eternal life if you believe God's truth. If you lack assurance about your future destination, ask yourself whether or not you've honestly committed your life to Christ as your Savior and Lord. If so, by faith you know where you'll be—with your Father.

2 JOHN

Ever played a practical joke on someone? Playing practical jokes on celebrities was the whole point of the MTV show Punk'd.

It's fun to fool people—or even to be fooled. Many people have tried shocking or embarrassing someone with a joy buzzer or a whoopee cushion. Others have short-sheeted beds or crank-called neighbors. Perhaps you've attempted a more complicated stunt—turning a friend's dresser drawers upside down or freezing your brother's underwear.

Some enterprising university pals once lined a dorm mate's room with plastic and turned it into a giant aquarium—complete with a shark!

As long as no one gets hurt, no laws are broken, and no property is damaged, pranks are no big deal—except in the spiritual dimension. There we can't afford to be deceived because our enemy, the devil, packs his pranks with disaster!

One of Satan's favorite methods of suckering us is to get us to listen to false teaching. That's what the Epistle of 2 John is all about. This can come in many different forms, some of which might seem to make sense. But no matter how valid it may seem, false teaching is always deadly. And that's no joke.

The book of 2 John warns us against false teaching. That's a warning we need to heed because the enemy's tricks aren't just for amusement—they're meant for destruction!

STATS

PURPOSE
To emphasize the basics of following Christ—truth and love—and to warn against the false teachers who had infiltrated the church

AUTHOR
The apostle John

ORIGINAL AUDIENCE
"The chosen lady and her children" (which could refer to a local church)

DATE WRITTEN
About the same time as 1 John, around A.D. 90, from Ephesus

SETTING
Evidently this woman and her family were involved in one of the churches under John's leadership. They had developed a strong friendship.

KEY PEOPLE
John, the chosen lady, and her children

KEY POINTS

KNOW THE WORD Following God's Word, the Bible, is essential to Christian living. A careful, consistent study of the Bible will help a believer to grow spiritually as well as provide the tools to recognize and counter false teaching.

LOVE John repeated Jesus' command to his followers: love others. Helping, giving, and meeting needs puts love into practice. Love in deed is love indeed.

FALSE LEADERS John warned the recipient of his letter to beware of false teachers. We must be wary of religious leaders who are not true to Christ's teachings. We should not give them a platform to spread false teachings. Don't encourage those who are contrary to Christ. Politely remove yourself from association with false leaders. Be aware of what's being taught in the church.

GREETINGS This letter is from John, the elder.*

I am writing to the chosen lady and to her children,* whom I love in the truth—as does everyone else who knows the truth—²because the truth lives in us and will be with us forever.

³Grace, mercy, and peace, which come from God the Father and from Jesus Christ—the Son of the Father—will continue to be with us who live in truth and love.

LIVE IN THE TRUTH ⁴How happy I was to meet some of your children and find them living according to the truth, just as the Father commanded.

⁵I am writing to remind you, dear friends,* that we should love one another. This is not a new commandment, but one we have had from the beginning. ⁶Love means doing what God has commanded us, and he has commanded us to love one another, just as you heard from the beginning.

⁷I say this because many deceivers have gone out into the world. They deny that Jesus Christ came* in a real body. Such a person is a deceiver and an antichrist. ⁸Watch out that you do not lose what we* have worked so hard to achieve. Be diligent so that you receive your full reward. ⁹Anyone who wanders away from this teaching has no relationship with God. But anyone who remains in the teaching of Christ has a relationship with both the Father and the Son.

¹⁰If anyone comes to your meeting and does not teach the truth about Christ, don't invite that person into your home or give any kind of encouragement. ¹¹Anyone who encourages such people becomes a partner in their evil work.

CONCLUSION ¹²I have much more to say to you, but I don't want to do it with paper and ink. For I hope to visit you soon and talk with you face to face. Then our joy will be complete.

¹³Greetings from the children of your sister,* chosen by God.

1a Greek *From the elder.* **1b** *Or the church God has chosen and its members.* **5** Greek *I urge you, lady.* **7** *Or will come.* **8** Some manuscripts read *you.* **13** *Or from the members of your sister church.*

....

KNOW THE TRUTH!
(1:7-11) John wrote this letter as a warning against false teachers. There are so many false teachings in our world today that we might be tempted to take them lightly. And some might fool us that really are false. Knowing what's true is usually an antidote to false teaching. A careful study of the Word can help you build up an "immunity" to false teaching. The Bible—it's what the doctor ordered.

ULTIMATE ISSUES

Mexico City is a fascinating place. Besides being one of the largest cities in the world, it's filled with interesting historical sights.

At the very center of the city, in the historical district known as the Zocalo, you'll find a huge square plaza surrounded by magnificent buildings. On the north side of the square is the beautiful Cathedral Metropolitana, which was begun in the late sixteenth century and dedicated in 1667 by the conquering Spaniards. Additions were added in the nineteenth century. It is stunning, inside and out.

For many years the cathedral had a slight problem: it sloped to the right. The cathedral wasn't built that way—the Spaniards had built it straight. Unfortunately, however, they had built it on a dry lake bed (formerly Lake Texcoco). The church had been sinking into the soft ground, little by little, year after year. But a restoration project has kept it from collapsing. If that action had not been taken, sooner or later the cathedral would have cracked and crumbled into rubble, just like so many of the Aztec ruins nearby.

Do you wonder why John placed so much emphasis on knowing the Bible? Well, he's not alone—many biblical authors stress the importance of knowing God's Word.

In Psalm 119, the longest chapter in the Bible, all but three of the 176 verses mention God's Word. Throughout the chapter, the psalm writer uses various synonyms for *Scriptures* interchangeably; words such as *law, instructions, rules*—not exactly favorites for any of us. Likewise, John refers to *the truth*—which comes only from God's Word—throughout this short letter. Why is it so important to know the Bible? And what in the world does this have to do with Mexico City's cathedral?

Just this: Like any structure, your life needs a foundation. The bigger the structure, the stronger the foundation has to be. To build a skyscraper or a massive cathedral, you must build on a deep, lasting, rock-solid foundation. If you just want to pitch a tent or throw together a wooden shack, it doesn't really matter where you build. Any place will do.

On the contrary, if you want to build a life that reflects God's glory, you need a firm base from which to start. You can gain that through time spent in the Word of God. It is the only platform that will never buckle under the pressure of living for Christ in a very non-Christian world. When you spend time reading, studying, and applying the Bible—even when you don't feel like it—you're building a solid foundation, one that won't sink (see Matt 7:24-27). ∎

3 JOHN

"It was over before it got started!" "Blink and you'll miss it."

"Short, sweet, and to the point."

Those are just some of the expressions you might use to describe:

- *The 1896 war between the United Kingdom and Zanzibar. (It lasted a mere 38 minutes!)*
- *Boxer Al Couture's 1946 knockout of opponent Ralph Walton in only 10.5 seconds (and that included a 10-second count by the referee)!*
- *The 20-minute reign of King Dom Luis III of Portugal in 1908.*
- *Montana's Roe River. (Its length? A measly 200 feet!)*
- *The 17-foot-long (or should we say "17-foot-short") McKinley Street in Bellefontaine, Ohio.*

But just because things are brief or small or short doesn't mean they're unimportant.

Take 3 John for instance. With only 15 verses, it is one of the shortest books of the Bible—a quick contrast between godly living and worldly behavior.

In fact, this introduction is about as long as the book itself! So go ahead and read this warm, personal note from the apostle John to his friend Gaius.

When you do, another familiar expression may come to mind:

"Good things come in small packages."

STATS

PURPOSE
To commend Gaius for his hospitality and to encourage him in his Christian life

AUTHOR
The apostle John

ORIGINAL AUDIENCE
Gaius, a prominent Christian in one of the churches known to John

DATE WRITTEN
About A.D. 90, from Ephesus

SETTING
Church leaders traveled from town to town helping to establish new congregations. They depended on the hospitality of fellow believers. Gaius welcomed them into his home.

KEY PEOPLE
John, Gaius, Diotrephes, Demetrius

KEY POINTS

HOSPITALITY John wrote to encourage the believers who showed hospitality to others. Genuine hospitality for traveling Christian workers was needed then and is still important.

PRIDE John planned to reprimand Diotrephes for his pride and lack of hospitality. Pride is a disrupter of fellowship. Servanthood is the best defense against pride.

FAITHFULNESS Gaius and Demetrius were commended for their faithful work in the church. Their examples of faithfulness are an encouragement for believers today.

GREETINGS

This letter is from John, the elder.*

I am writing to Gaius, my dear friend, whom I love in the truth.

²Dear friend, I hope all is well with you and that you are as healthy in body as you are strong in spirit. ³Some of the traveling teachers* recently returned and made me very happy by telling me about your faithfulness and that you are living according to the truth. ⁴I could have no greater joy than to hear that my children are following the truth.

CARING FOR THE LORD'S WORKERS

⁵Dear friend, you are being faithful to God when you care for the traveling teachers who pass through, even though they are strangers to you. ⁶They have told the church here of your loving friendship. Please continue providing for such teachers in a manner that pleases God. ⁷For they are traveling for the Lord,* and they accept nothing from people who are not believers.* ⁸So we ourselves should support them so that we can be their partners as they teach the truth.

⁹I wrote to the church about this, but Diotrephes, who loves to be the leader, refuses to have anything to do with us. ¹⁰When I come, I will report some of the things he is doing and the evil accusations he is making against us.

1 Greek *From the elder.* 3 Greek *the brothers;* also in verses 5 and 10. 7a Greek *They went out on behalf of the Name.* 7b Greek *from Gentiles.*

ULTIMATE ISSUES *THE NEW AGE MOVEMENT*

Following Christ isn't easy. Consider John's words: "Dear friend, don't let this bad example influence you. Follow only what is good. Remember that those who do good prove that they are God's children, and those who do evil prove that they do not know God" (1:11). Now take a look at Luke 9:23-24, where Jesus tells us, "If any of you wants to be my follower, you must turn from your selfish ways, take up your cross daily, and follow me. . . . If you give up your life for my sake, you will save it." That's quite a price tag for following Jesus! Isn't there an easier path to God—one that doesn't make such tough demands on us?

Yes! At least, that's what those in the "New Age" movement say. And lots of people are listening.

New religions researchers Bob and Gretchen Passantino describe the New Age movement as "the fastest-growing alternative belief system" in the U.S. Alternative to what? To the Jewish-Christian tradition that most Americans have been raised in. J. Gordon Melton, another new religions expert, defines New Age as "a vision of a world transformed, a heaven on earth, a society in which the problems of today are overcome and a new existence emerges." New Agers believe that we stand on the threshold of a new era, a "new age," a major transitional shift into humanity's next evolutionary stage.

The overriding philosophy of the New Age movement is the belief that "all is one." There is no distinction between right or wrong, male or female, good or bad. There isn't even a division between God and man. Everything is divine.

This philosophy isn't new. It has been around for thousands of years and is called "pantheism." Pantheism is the basis for all Eastern mystical religions (Hinduism, Buddhism, Confucianism, and so forth). But New Agers differ from these religions in that they see this unity from a positive and optimistic view. The New Age is kind of an "Eastern-religion-meets-American-positive-thinking."

This blend of exotic religious thought and popular psychology attracts many people to New Age teachings. But there's a catch. A big one.

If all is one, then no difference exists between right and wrong—or God and humans. If there's no difference between God and humans, the next logical step is that humans *are* god. No one can tell me "no"; I can do whatever I want. After all, I'm god. (Sound far-fetched? That's exactly what actress Shirley MacLaine, the "high priestess" of the New Age movement, claims in her autobiography, *Out On a Limb.* And she is not alone.)

The New Age movement is growing rapidly. The belief in the oneness of all things (along with things like ecological harmony, reincarnation, unlimited human potential) appeals to modern "enlightened" people. The idea that I can be my own god is very seductive. However, history is littered with the atrocities committed by people who thought they answered to no one—Hitler, Stalin, Pol Pot, Idi Amin, Saddam Hussein. In fact, this was Lucifer's sin, which resulted in his expulsion from heaven.

Don't be deceived. Only one true God exists—the God of Abraham, Moses, David, Peter, James, and John. He will not share his throne with anyone, and he has certain demands for his followers, like carrying your cross and losing your life for his sake. This is a high price, but Jesus promises that it is worth it. And he is worthy of our sacrificial commitment.

The god of the New Age—the god that looks like us—doesn't ask anything of us. But that kind of god can't deliver us from our sins, show us how to love, or die on a cross for us. That god isn't real—he's a lie.

Someone has said, "History is filled with men who would be gods; but only one God who would be man."

His name is Jesus. Take up your cross and follow him. ∎

DON'T LET THIS BAD EXAMPLE INFLUENCE YOU.

FOLLOW ONLY WHAT IS GOOD.

3 JOHN 1:11

Not only does he refuse to welcome the traveling teachers, he also tells others not to help them. And when they do help, he puts them out of the church.

¹¹Dear friend, don't let this bad example influence you. Follow only what is good. Remember that those who do good prove that they are God's children, and those who do evil prove that they do not know God.*

¹²Everyone speaks highly of Demetrius, as does the truth itself. We ourselves can say the same for him, and you know we speak the truth.

11 Greek *they have not seen God.*   **15** Some English translations combine verses 14 and 15 into verse 14.

CONCLUSION ¹³I have much more to say to you, but I don't want to write it with pen and ink. ¹⁴For I hope to see you soon, and then we will talk face to face.

¹⁵*Peace be with you.

Your friends here send you their greetings. Please give my personal greetings to each of our friends there.

. . . .

OPEN HOUSE
(1:5) In the church's early days, traveling prophets, evangelists, and teachers were helped on their way by people like Gaius who housed and fed them. Hospitality is a lost art in many churches today. We would do well to invite more people into our homes for meals—fellow church members, young and old, traveling missionaries, those in need, visitors. This is an active and much appreciated way to show your love. In fact, hospitality probably is more important today than ever because of our individualistic, self-centered society. Many lonely people wonder if anyone cares whether they live or die. If you find such a lonely person, show him or her that you care! To whom will you show hospitality?

JUDE

Could your faith withstand a spiritual battle?

What would you say if the school agnostic called the resurrection of Christ a myth? What if a minister you respect admitted that he believes the Bible contains errors and contradictions?

What if your favorite teacher announced, "It's insensitive and downright wrong for one group of people to try to force its views on another group! Who really knows what's true?"

Imagine meeting someone full of joy and peace, a person seemingly very much in touch with God. As you converse, this person tells you that she is content and fulfilled because of daily yoga exercises, meditation, and also because of an experience she recently had in which she journeyed back through her previous incarnations. She nods when you mention Jesus Christ and says, "If that works for you, great! But I found the truth another way."

If you haven't already had encounters like those just described, just wait. Your time is definitely coming!

The fact of the matter is that our world is full of confused people who eagerly spread their confusing ideas.

Don't get caught off-guard! You can get in battle readiness by understanding what you believe and why. There's no better place to start your Bible boot camp training than by reading the Epistle to Jude.

STATS

PURPOSE
To remind the church of the need for constant vigilance in order to keep strong in the faith and to defend it against false ideas about God and Scriptures

AUTHOR
Jude, James's brother and Jesus' half brother

ORIGINAL AUDIENCE
Jewish Christians and other believers

DATE WRITTEN
About A.D. 65

SETTING
From the first century on, heresy and false teaching have threatened the church.

KEY PEOPLE
Jude, James, Jesus

KEY POINTS

FALSE TEACHERS Jude warned believers about false teachers and leaders who reject the lordship of Christ, undermine the faith of others, and lead people astray. Genuine servants of God will faithfully portray Christ in their words and conduct.

APOSTASY Jude also warned against apostasy—turning away from Christ. We must be careful not to drift away from a firm commitment to Christ.

GREETINGS FROM JUDE This letter is from Jude, a slave of Jesus Christ and a brother of James.

I am writing to all who have been called by God the Father, who loves you and keeps you safe in the care of Jesus Christ.*

²May God give you more and more mercy, peace, and love.

THE DANGER OF FALSE TEACHERS ³Dear friends, I had been eagerly planning to write to you about the salvation we all share. But now I find that I must write about something else, urging you to defend the faith that God has entrusted once for all time to his holy people. ⁴I say this because some ungodly people have wormed their way into your churches, saying that God's marvelous grace allows us to live immoral lives. The condemnation of such people was recorded long ago, for they have denied our only Master and Lord, Jesus Christ.

WHAT'S TRUE
(1:4) Like the apostle John, Jude stressed the importance of knowing what's true about God and his Word. This is the only way to recognize false teaching. Because people think theology is dry, they avoid studying the Bible. Those who refuse to learn correct doctrine, however, are susceptible to false teaching because they are not fully grounded in God's truth. We must understand the basic doctrines of our faith so that we can recognize false doctrines and prevent them from hurting us and others. So, how do you know what's true? Study the Word.

WATCH OUT!
(1:8-10) False teachers were claiming to possess secret knowledge that gave them authority. Their "knowledge" of God was mystical and beyond human understanding. In reality, we can never fully know everything there is to know about God. But God in his grace has chosen to reveal himself to us through his Word and through Jesus. Beware of those who claim to have all of the answers and who belittle what they don't understand.

⁵So I want to remind you, though you already know these things, that Jesus* first rescued the nation of Israel from Egypt, but later he destroyed those who did not remain faithful. ⁶And I remind you of the angels who did not stay within the limits of authority God gave them but left the place where they belonged. God has kept them securely chained in prisons of darkness, waiting for the great day of judgment. ⁷And don't forget Sodom and Gomorrah and their neighboring towns, which were filled with immorality and every kind of sexual perversion. Those cities were destroyed by fire and serve as a warning of the eternal fire of God's judgment.

⁸In the same way, these people—who claim authority from their dreams—live immoral lives, defy authority, and scoff at supernatural beings.* ⁹But even Michael, one of the mightiest of the angels,* did not dare accuse the devil of blasphemy, but simply said, "The Lord rebuke you!" (This took place when Michael was arguing with the devil about Moses' body.) ¹⁰But these people scoff at things they do not understand. Like unthinking animals, they do whatever their instincts tell them, and so they bring about their own destruction. ¹¹What sorrow awaits them! For they follow in the footsteps of Cain, who killed his brother. Like Balaam, they deceive people for money. And like Korah, they perish in their rebellion.

¹²When these people eat with you in your fellowship meals commemorating the Lord's love, they are like dangerous reefs that can shipwreck you.* They are like shameless shepherds who care only for themselves. They are like clouds blowing over the land without giving any rain. They are like trees in autumn that

1 Or *keeps you for Jesus Christ.* 5 As in the best manuscripts; various other manuscripts read *[the] Lord,* or *God,* or *Christ;* one reads *God Christ.* 8 Greek *at glorious ones,* which are probably evil angels. 9 Greek *Michael, the archangel.* 12 Or *they are contaminants among you;* or *they are stains.*

CHOICES
perseverance

Erin and Arianna met way back in eighth grade. Not only did they become fast friends, but Erin had helped Arianna to become a Christian by the end of the school year. Throughout high school Erin always did her best to help Arianna grow in faith. She practically dragged Arianna to retreats and youth group events.

Had you known them in those years, you probably would've predicted that Erin would do great things for God. And you would have seriously doubted the long-term stability of Arianna's faith.

Boy, would you have been wrong!

During their first year of college, Erin got too physically involved with her boyfriend, a non-Christian. When she got pregnant, she married the guy and dropped out of sight. Meanwhile, Arianna has continued to mature in her walk with God. She's the one with the dynamic ministry on campus.

Baseball great Yogi Berra once said, "It ain't over till it's over." Another sports figure once quipped, "The opera isn't over until the fat lady sings." The point? The Christian life is a long, long race. Are you willing to go the distance? Read about perseverance in the Epistle of Jude.

are doubly dead, for they bear no fruit and have been pulled up by the roots. [13]They are like wild waves of the sea, churning up the foam of their shameful deeds. They are like wandering stars, doomed forever to blackest darkness.

[14]Enoch, who lived in the seventh generation after Adam, prophesied about these people. He said, "Listen! The Lord is coming with countless thousands of his holy ones [15]to execute judgment on the people of the world. He will convict every person of all the ungodly things they have done and for all the insults that ungodly sinners have spoken against him."*

[16]These people are grumblers and complainers, living only to satisfy their desires. They brag loudly about themselves, and they flatter others to get what they want.

A CALL TO REMAIN FAITHFUL   [17]But you, my dear friends, must remember what the apostles of our Lord Jesus Christ said. [18]They told you that in the last times there would be scoffers whose purpose in life is to satisfy their ungodly desires. [19]These people are the ones who are creating divisions among you. They follow their natural instincts because they do not have God's Spirit in them.

[20]But you, dear friends, must build each other up in your most holy faith, pray in the power of the Holy Spirit,* [21]and await the mercy

C JUDE 1:24]

NOW ALL GLORY TO GOD, WHO IS ABLE TO KEEP YOU FROM FALLING AWAY AND WILL BRING YOU WITH GREAT JOY INTO HIS GLORIOUS PRESENCE WITHOUT A SINGLE FAULT.

of our Lord Jesus Christ, who will bring you eternal life. In this way, you will keep yourselves safe in God's love.

[22]And you must show mercy to* those whose faith is wavering. [23]Rescue others by snatching them from the flames of judgment. Show mercy to still others,* but do so with great caution, hating the sins that contaminate their lives.*

A PRAYER OF PRAISE   [24]Now all glory to God, who is able to keep you from falling away and will bring you with great joy into his glorious presence without a single fault. [25]All glory to him who alone is God, our Savior through Jesus Christ our Lord. All glory, majesty, power, and authority are his before all time, and in the present, and beyond all time! Amen.

....

14-15 The quotation comes from intertestamental literature: 1 Enoch 1:9.   **20** Greek *pray in the Holy Spirit.*   **22** Some manuscripts read *must reprove.*   **22-23a** Some manuscripts have only two categories of people: (1) those whose faith is wavering and therefore need to be snatched from the flames of judgment, and (2) those who need to be shown mercy.   **23b** Greek *with fear, hating even the clothing stained by the flesh.*

DON'T SLIP
(1:23) Jude warned his readers to avoid compromising when trying to help others. In trying to find something in common with the people we talk to about Jesus, we also must be careful not to fall into the quicksand of compromise. Be careful not to become so much like non-Christians that no one can tell who you are or what you believe. We are to influence others for Christ, rather than be influenced to make a bad choice!

REVELATION

*Fairy tales always end perfectly. The frog turns into a prince,
the unloved stepsister becomes a beloved bride, and mean and
greedy people get paid back for the rotten things they've done.*

*Unfortunately, fairy tales aren't true. "Happily ever after"? No way! The
real world doesn't work that way.*

Or does it?

*Here at the end of the Bible we find a book of prophecy: the book of
Revelation. This strange vision received by the apostle John is one of
the most discussed, mysterious, and controversial books ever written.
Labeled "prophecy" and "theology," it reads like a fairy tale.*

*Don't look so surprised! According to Revelation, those who have
become God's children by faith in Christ will have the happiest of all
endings: being in the very presence of God, enjoying an existence
untouched by sorrow or death.*

*And every evil being (including the devil himself) will "face the
music." All injustices will be righted; all unforgiven sin will be judged.
That, in a nutshell, is the message of Revelation: happiness and reward
for the people of God; punishment and justice for all the guilty. A picture-
perfect ending.*

*You must admit that ending does sound like a fairy tale. There is, how-
ever, one important difference: this too-good-to-be-true story is truer
than anything that ever existed. It is going to happen.*

You can count on it.

STATS

PURPOSE
To reveal the full
identity of Christ and to
warn and provide hope
to believers

AUTHOR
The apostle John

ORIGINAL AUDIENCE
Seven Asian churches

DATE WRITTEN
About A.D. 95, from the
island of Patmos

SETTING
Most scholars believe
that the seven
churches of Asia to
whom John wrote
had experienced
persecution under the
emperor, Domitian
(A.D. 90–95). Appar-
ently the Roman
authorities had exiled
John to the island
of Patmos (off the
coast of Asia). John,
an eyewitness of the
incarnate Christ, had
a vision of the glorified
Christ. God also
revealed to him what
would take place in the
future: judgment and
the ultimate triumph
of God over evil.

KEY PEOPLE
John, Jesus

KEY PLACES
The island of Patmos,
the seven churches,
the New Jerusalem

KEY POINTS

GOD'S SOVEREIGNTY God is greater than any power in the universe. Knowing
this can prevent us from despair when evil seems to increase.

CHRIST'S RETURN Jesus came to earth as a "Lamb," the symbol of his perfect
sacrifice for our sin. He will return as King and Judge. Because no one knows
when he will appear, we must be ready at all times.

GOD'S FAITHFUL PEOPLE God's people, the church, should be devoted only to
Christ. We should be faithfully following Christ, ready for his soon return.

JUDGMENT God's final judgment will put an end to evil and injustice. We must
be certain of our commitment to Jesus if we want to escape this great final judgment. All who belong to him will receive their full reward.

HOPE FOR THE FUTURE One day God will create a new heaven and a new
earth. All believers will live with God forever in perfect peace and security. If we
have confidence in our final destination, we will follow Christ with unwavering
dedication no matter what trials we must face.

THE SEVEN CHURCHES
The seven churches were located on a major Roman road. A letter carrier would leave the island of Patmos (where John was exiled), arriving first at Ephesus. He would travel north to Smyrna and Pergamum (Pergamos), turn southeast to Thyatira, and continue on to Sardis, Philadelphia, and Laodicea—in the exact order in which the letters were dictated.

1 **PROLOGUE** This is a revelation from* Jesus Christ, which God gave him to show his servants the events that must soon* take place. He sent an angel to present this revelation to his servant John, ²who faithfully reported everything he saw. This is his report of the word of God and the testimony of Jesus Christ.

³God blesses the one who reads the words of this prophecy to the church, and he blesses all who listen to its message and obey what it says, for the time is near.

JOHN'S GREETING TO THE SEVEN CHURCHES
⁴This letter is from John to the seven churches in the province of Asia.*

....

INDESCRIBABLE?
(1:1) Jesus gave his message to John in a vision, allowing John to see and record certain future events as an encouragement to all believers. The vision includes many signs and symbols to effectively show what will happen. What John saw, in most cases, was indescribable, so he used illustrations to show what an event or item was like. When reading this symbolic language, don't stress yourself by trying to understand every detail. After all, John didn't fully understand what he saw! But one thing you can understand: Christ is the glorious, victorious Lord of all.

Grace and peace to you from the one who is, who always was, and who is still to come; from the sevenfold Spirit* before his throne; ⁵and from Jesus Christ. He is the faithful witness to these things, the first to rise from the dead, and the ruler of all the kings of the world.

All glory to him who loves us and has freed us from our sins by shedding his blood for us. ⁶He has made us a Kingdom of priests for God his Father. All glory and power to him forever and ever! Amen.

⁷ Look! He comes with the clouds of heaven.
    And everyone will see him—
    even those who pierced him.
And all the nations of the world
    will mourn for him.
Yes! Amen!

⁸"I am the Alpha and the Omega—the beginning and the end,"* says the Lord God. "I am the one who is, who always was, and who is still to come—the Almighty One."

VISION OF THE SON OF MAN ⁹I, John, am your brother and your partner in suffering and in

1:1a Or *of.* 1:1b Or *suddenly,* or *quickly.* 1:4a *Asia* was a Roman province in what is now western Turkey. 1:4b Greek *the seven spirits.* 1:8 Greek *I am the Alpha and the Omega,* referring to the first and last letters of the Greek alphabet.

God's Kingdom and in the patient endurance to which Jesus calls us. I was exiled to the island of Patmos for preaching the word of God and for my testimony about Jesus. [10]It was the Lord's Day, and I was worshiping in the Spirit.* Suddenly, I heard behind me a loud voice like a trumpet blast. [11]It said, "Write in a book* everything you see, and send it to the seven churches in the cities of Ephesus, Smyrna, Pergamum, Thyatira, Sardis, Philadelphia, and Laodicea."

[12]When I turned to see who was speaking to me, I saw seven gold lampstands. [13]And standing in the middle of the lampstands was someone like the Son of Man.* He was wearing a long robe with a gold sash across his chest. [14]His head and his hair were white like wool, as white as snow. And his eyes were like flames of fire. [15]His feet were like polished bronze refined in a furnace, and his voice thundered like mighty ocean waves. [16]He held seven stars in his right hand, and a sharp two-edged sword came from his mouth. And his face was like the sun in all its brilliance.

[17]When I saw him, I fell at his feet as if I were dead. But he laid his right hand on me and said, "Don't be afraid! I am the First and the Last. [18]I am the living one. I died, but look—

I am alive forever and ever! And I hold the keys of death and the grave.*

[19]"Write down what you have seen—both the things that are now happening and the things that will happen.* [20]This is the meaning of the mystery of the seven stars you saw in my right hand and the seven gold lampstands: The seven stars are the angels* of the seven churches, and the seven lampstands are the seven churches.

2 THE MESSAGE TO THE CHURCH IN EPHESUS "Write this letter to the angel* of the church in Ephesus. This is the message from the one who holds the seven stars in his right hand, the one who walks among the seven gold lampstands:

[2]"I know all the things you do. I have seen your hard work and your patient endurance. I know you don't tolerate evil people. You have examined the claims of those who say they are apostles but are not. You have discovered they are liars. [3]You have patiently suffered for me without quitting.

[4]"But I have this complaint against you. You don't love me or each other as you did at first!* [5]Look how far you have fallen! Turn back to me and do the works you did at first. If you don't repent, I will come and remove your lampstand from its place among the churches. [6]But this is in your favor: You hate the evil deeds of the Nicolaitans, just as I do.

1:10 Or *in spirit.*   **1:11** Or *on a scroll.*   **1:13** Or *like a son of man.* See Dan 7:13. "Son of Man" is a title Jesus used for himself.   **1:18** Greek *and Hades.*   **1:19** Or *what you have seen and what they mean—the things that have already begun to happen.*   **1:20** Or *the messengers.*   **2:1** Or *the messenger;* also in 2:8, 12, 18.   **2:4** Greek *You have lost your first love.*

I WONDER...

Because of my shyness and my family situation, I find it difficult to let people get close to me—even God. As a Christian, I hear all the time how much God loves me. How involved in my life does God want to be?

As involved as you'll let him.

Although God knows everything about us, he still wants to be a Father to us. Isn't that amazing?

King David wrote about how much God thinks of us. "How precious are your thoughts about me, O God. They cannot be numbered! I can't even count them; they outnumber the grains of sand! And when I wake up, you are still with me!" (Ps 139:17-18).

Knowing how much God thinks about us (especially in light of how little we think of him) should give us an incredible feeling of worth. Our response to God's constant attentiveness, however, should never be out of obligation. God doesn't want us

to hang out with him only because we feel we have to.

Revelation 2:4 warns us to avoid allowing our love for God to lessen or end. God wants us to grow beyond our initial commitment to him, just like in a marriage where love continues to grow. Unfortunately, this doesn't always happen. Many people who become Christians are really excited about their new relationship with God. But as problems come up, the excitement often wears off (just like what happens in some marriages).

To maintain a growing relationship with God, the key word is time: daily time with him, time with others who know him, and time (in years) to grow to appreciate his love for us.

God is anxious for an intimate relationship with us. With each day we live, we can better understand what loving him really means. Someday we will know this love completely (1 Cor 13:12). And what a wonderful day that will be!

7"Anyone with ears to hear must listen to the Spirit and understand what he is saying to the churches. To everyone who is victorious I will give fruit from the tree of life in the paradise of God.

THE MESSAGE TO THE CHURCH IN SMYRNA
8"Write this letter to the angel of the church in Smyrna. This is the message from the one who is the First and the Last, who was dead but is now alive:

9"I know about your suffering and your poverty—but you are rich! I know the blasphemy of those opposing you. They say they are Jews, but they are not, because their synagogue belongs to Satan. 10Don't be afraid of what you are about to suffer. The devil will throw some of you into prison to test you. You will suffer for ten days. But if you remain faithful even when facing death, I will give you the crown of life.

11"Anyone with ears to hear must listen to the Spirit and understand what he is saying to the churches. Whoever is victorious will not be harmed by the second death.

THE MESSAGE TO THE CHURCH IN PERGAMUM
12"Write this letter to the angel of the church in Pergamum. This is the message from the one with the sharp two-edged sword:

13"I know that you live in the city where Satan has his throne, yet you have remained loyal to me. You refused to deny me even when Antipas, my faithful witness, was martyred among you there in Satan's city. 14"But I have a few complaints against you. You tolerate some among you whose teaching is like that of Balaam, who showed Balak how to trip up the people of Israel. He taught them to sin by eating food offered to idols and by committing sexual sin. 15In

a similar way, you have some Nicolaitans among you who follow the same teaching. 16Repent of your sin, or I will come to you suddenly and fight against them with the sword of my mouth.

17"Anyone with ears to hear must listen to the Spirit and understand what he is saying to the churches. To everyone who is victorious I will give some of the manna that has been hidden away in heaven. And I will give to each one a white stone, and on the stone will be engraved a new name that no one understands except the one who receives it.

THE MESSAGE TO THE CHURCH IN THYATIRA
18"Write this letter to the angel of the church in Thyatira. This is the message from the Son of God, whose eyes are like flames of fire, whose feet are like polished bronze:

19"I know all the things you do. I have seen your love, your faith, your service, and your patient endurance. And I can see your constant improvement in all these things.

20"But I have this complaint against you. You are permitting that woman—that Jezebel who calls herself a prophet—to lead my servants astray. She teaches them to commit sexual sin and to eat food offered to idols. 21I gave her time to repent, but she does not want to turn away from her immorality.

22"Therefore, I will throw her on a bed of suffering,* and those who commit adultery with her will suffer greatly unless they repent and turn away from her evil deeds. 23I will strike her children dead. Then all the churches will know that I am the one who searches out the thoughts and intentions of every person. And I will give to each of you whatever you deserve.

24"But I also have a message for the rest of you in Thyatira who have not followed this false teaching ('deeper truths,' as they call them—depths of Satan, actually). I will ask nothing more of you 25except that you hold tightly to what you have until I come. 26To all who are victorious, who obey me to the very end,

To them I will give authority over all
    the nations.
27 They will rule the nations with
    an iron rod
    and smash them like clay pots.*

A SERIOUS PROBLEM
(2:20) Why is sexual immorality serious? Because it *always hurts someone. It hurts God because it shows that we prefer to follow our own desires instead of God's Word. It hurts others because it violates the commitment so necessary to a marriage relationship. It hurts us because it often brings disease to our body and harms our personality. Sexual sin has tremendous power to destroy families, communities, and even nations because it destroys the relationships upon which these institutions are built. God wants to protect us from hurting ourselves and others, so we should have no part in sexual immorality, even if our society says it's all right.*

2:22 Greek *a bed.*   2:26-27 Ps 2:8-9 (Greek version).

[28]They will have the same authority I received from my Father, and I will also give them the morning star!

[29]"Anyone with ears to hear must listen to the Spirit and understand what he is saying to the churches.

3 THE MESSAGE TO THE CHURCH IN SARDIS

"Write this letter to the angel* of the church in Sardis. This is the message from the one who has the sevenfold Spirit* of God and the seven stars:

"I know all the things you do, and that you have a reputation for being alive—but you are dead. [2]Wake up! Strengthen what little remains, for even what is left is almost dead. I find that your actions do not meet the requirements of my God. [3]Go back to what you heard and believed at first; hold to it firmly. Repent and turn to me again. If you don't wake up, I will come to you suddenly, as unexpected as a thief.

[4]"Yet there are some in the church in Sardis who have not soiled their clothes with evil. They will walk with me in white, for they are worthy. [5]All who are victorious will be clothed in white. I will never erase their names from the Book of Life, but I will announce before my Father and his angels that they are mine.

[6]"Anyone with ears to hear must listen to the Spirit and understand what he is saying to the churches.

THE MESSAGE TO THE CHURCH IN PHILADELPHIA

[7]"Write this letter to the angel of the church in Philadelphia.

3:1a Or *the messenger;* also in 3:7, 14.   **3:1b** Greek *the seven spirits.* **3:7** Isa 22:22.   **3:11** Or *suddenly,* or *quickly.*   **3:14** Or *the ruler,* or *the source.*

This is the message from the one who is holy and true, the one who has the key of David. What he opens, no one can close; and what he closes, no one can open:*

[8]"I know all the things you do, and I have opened a door for you that no one can close. You have little strength, yet you obeyed my word and did not deny me. [9]Look, I will force those who belong to Satan's synagogue—those liars who say they are Jews but are not—to come and bow down at your feet. They will acknowledge that you are the ones I love.

[10]"Because you have obeyed my command to persevere, I will protect you from the great time of testing that will come upon the whole world to test those who belong to this world. [11]I am coming soon.* Hold on to what you have, so that no one will take away your crown. [12]All who are victorious will become pillars in the Temple of my God, and they will never have to leave it. And I will write on them the name of my God, and they will be citizens in the city of my God—the new Jerusalem that comes down from heaven from my God. And I will also write on them my new name.

[13]"Anyone with ears to hear must listen to the Spirit and understand what he is saying to the churches.

THE MESSAGE TO THE CHURCH IN LAODICEA

[14]"Write this letter to the angel of the church in Laodicea. This is the message from the one who is the Amen—the faithful and true witness, the beginning* of God's new creation:

CHOICES — seek the truth

"*Dana, are you still planning* to talk to Rhonda?"

"I've got to. Those people she's been hanging around are weird. My mom even thinks they're a cult!"

"So why don't her parents say something? I mean, my folks would kill me if I came home spouting all that junk!"

"Oh, Mr. and Mrs. Jordan don't care what she does. He's all wrapped up in his business, and she has some pretty strange religious ideas herself. Their basic attitude is, 'Whatever makes you happy, Rhonda.'"

"What do you think she'll say?"

"I don't know."

"What are *you* going to say?"

"I'm going to tell her that what she's been hearing from those people isn't true. I'll show her what the Bible says about false teachers. And I'll challenge her to quit seeking some kind of ooey-gooey feeling and start seeking the truth."

We need more people like Dana—people who cling doggedly to the truth and who encourage others to do the same. Would you have the courage to confront a friend who was caught up in a false religion? Would you know what to say?

As you read Revelation, notice the constant emphasis on seeking the truth.

> "I STAND AT THE DOOR AND KNOCK.
>
> IF YOU HEAR MY VOICE AND OPEN
>
> THE DOOR, I WILL COME IN, AND
>
> WE WILL SHARE A MEAL TOGETHER
>
> AS FRIENDS." { REVELATION 3:20 }

[15]"I know all the things you do, that you are neither hot nor cold. I wish that you were one or the other! [16]But since you are like lukewarm water, neither hot nor cold, I will spit you out of my mouth! [17]You say, 'I am rich. I have everything I want. I don't need a thing!' And you don't realize that you are wretched and miserable and poor and blind and naked. [18]So I advise you to buy gold from me—gold that has been purified by fire. Then you will be rich. Also buy white garments from me so you will not be shamed by your nakedness, and ointment for your eyes so you will be able to see. [19]I correct and discipline everyone I love. So be diligent and turn from your indifference.

[20]"Look! I stand at the door and knock. If you hear my voice and open the door, I will come in, and we will share a meal together as friends. [21]Those who are victorious will sit with me on my throne, just as I was victorious and sat with my Father on his throne.

[22]"Anyone with ears to hear must listen to the Spirit and understand what he is saying to the churches."

4 **WORSHIP IN HEAVEN** Then as I looked, I saw a door standing open in heaven, and the same voice I had heard before spoke to me like a trumpet blast. The voice said, "Come up here, and I will show you what must happen after this." [2]And instantly I was in the Spirit,* and I saw a throne in heaven and someone sitting on it. [3]The one sitting on the throne was as brilliant as gemstones—like jasper and carnelian. And the glow of an emerald circled his throne like a rainbow. [4]Twenty-four thrones surrounded him, and twenty-four elders sat on them. They were all clothed in white and had gold crowns on their heads. [5]From the throne came flashes of lightning and the rumble of thunder. And in front of the throne were seven torches with burning flames. This is the sevenfold Spirit* of God. [6]In front of the throne was a shiny sea of glass, sparkling like crystal.

In the center and around the throne were four living beings, each covered with eyes, front and back. [7]The first of these living beings was like a lion; the second was like an ox; the third had a human face; and the fourth was like an eagle in flight. [8]Each of these living beings had six wings, and their wings were covered all over with eyes, inside and out. Day after day and night after night they keep on saying,

> "Holy, holy, holy is the Lord God, the
>   Almighty—
>   the one who always was, who is, and who
>   is still to come."

[9]Whenever the living beings give glory and honor and thanks to the one sitting on the throne (the one who lives forever and ever), [10]the twenty-four elders fall down and worship the one sitting on the throne (the one who lives forever and ever). And they lay their crowns before the throne and say,

> [11] "You are worthy, O Lord our God,
>   to receive glory and honor and power.
> For you created all things,
>   and they exist because you created what
>   you pleased."

5 **THE LAMB OPENS THE SCROLL** Then I saw a scroll* in the right hand of the one who was sitting on the throne. There was writing on the inside and the outside of the scroll, and it was sealed with seven seals. [2]And I saw

....

YOUR CHOICE
(3:20) Think back to the days when you were a little kid in Sunday school. Were you ever shown a picture of Jesus standing at a door knocking? Jesus knocks on the door of our hearts every time we sense that we should turn to him. This means he wants to hang out with us. He patiently and persistently knocks, rather than breaking and entering. He allows us to decide whether or not to open our lives to him. Have you?

NO FEAR
(4–5) Chapters 4 and 5 are a glimpse of the glory that Christ shares with God the Father. Here we see into the throne room of heaven as God orchestrates the events that John records. Ever think that life seems out of control or that the forces of evil seem to be winning? God is never out of control. He will carry out his plans as Jesus initiates the final battle with the forces of evil—one that Jesus will win. John shows us heaven before showing us earth so we won't be frightened by future events.

4:2 Or *in spirit.*   **4:5** Greek *They are the seven spirits.*   **5:1** Or *book;* also in 5:2, 3, 4, 5, 7, 8, 9.

a strong angel, who shouted with a loud voice: "Who is worthy to break the seals on this scroll and open it?" ³But no one in heaven or on earth or under the earth was able to open the scroll and read it.

⁴Then I began to weep bitterly because no one was found worthy to open the scroll and read it. ⁵But one of the twenty-four elders said to me, "Stop weeping! Look, the Lion of the tribe of Judah, the heir to David's throne,* has won the victory. He is worthy to open the scroll and its seven seals."

⁶Then I saw a Lamb that looked as if it had been slaughtered, but it was now standing between the throne and the four living beings and among the twenty-four elders. He had seven horns and seven eyes, which represent the sevenfold Spirit* of God that is sent out into every part of the earth. ⁷He stepped forward and took the scroll from the right hand of the one sitting on the throne. ⁸And when he took the scroll, the four living beings and the twenty-four elders fell down before the Lamb. Each one had a harp, and they held gold bowls filled with incense, which are the prayers of God's people. ⁹And they sang a new song with these words:

> "You are worthy to take the scroll
> and break its seals and open it.
> For you were slaughtered, and your blood
> has ransomed people for God
> from every tribe and language and
> people and nation.
> ¹⁰ And you have caused them to become
> a Kingdom of priests for our God.
> And they will reign* on the earth."

¹¹Then I looked again, and I heard the voices of thousands and millions of angels around the throne and of the living beings and the elders. ¹²And they sang in a mighty chorus:

> "Worthy is the Lamb who was
> slaughtered—
> to receive power and riches
> and wisdom and strength
> and honor and glory and blessing."

¹³And then I heard every creature in heaven and on earth and under the earth and in the sea. They sang:

> "Blessing and honor and glory and power
> belong to the one sitting on the throne
> and to the Lamb forever and ever."

5:5 Greek *the root of David.* See Isa 11:10. **5:6** Greek *which are the seven spirits.* **5:10** Some manuscripts read *they are reigning.* **6:1** Or *book.*

THE NAMES OF JESUS

Scattered among the vivid images of the book of Revelation is a large collection of names for Jesus. Each one tells something of his character and highlights a particular aspect of his role within God's plan of redemption.

JESUS' NAME	REFERENCE
Son of Man	1:13
The First and the Last	1:17
Son of God	2:18
Witness	3:14
Lion of the Tribe of Judah	5:5
Heir to David's Throne	5:5
Lamb	5:6
Shepherd	7:17
Christ	12:10
Faithful and True	19:11
The Word of God	19:13
King of All Kings	19:16
Lord of All Lords	19:16
The Alpha and the Omega / The Beginning and the End	22:13
The Bright Morning Star	22:16

¹⁴And the four living beings said, "Amen!" And the twenty-four elders fell down and worshiped the Lamb.

6 THE LAMB BREAKS THE FIRST SIX SEALS

As I watched, the Lamb broke the first of the seven seals on the scroll.* Then I heard one of the four living beings say with a voice like thunder, "Come!" ²I looked up and saw a white horse standing there. Its rider carried a bow, and a crown was placed on his head. He rode out to win many battles and gain the victory.

³When the Lamb broke the second seal, I heard the second living being say, "Come!" ⁴Then another horse appeared, a red one. Its rider was given a mighty sword and the

ALL TYPES
(5:9-10) People from every nation are praising God before his throne. The gospel is not limited to a specific culture, race, or country. Anyone who comes in repentance and faith is accepted by God and will be part of his kingdom. Don't allow prejudice or bias to stop you from sharing Christ with others. Christ welcomes all types of people into his Kingdom.

authority to take peace from the earth. And there was war and slaughter everywhere.

⁵When the Lamb broke the third seal, I heard the third living being say, "Come!" I looked up and saw a black horse, and its rider was holding a pair of scales in his hand. ⁶And I heard a voice from among the four living beings say, "A loaf of wheat bread or three loaves of barley will cost a day's pay.* And don't waste* the olive oil and wine."

⁷When the Lamb broke the fourth seal, I heard the fourth living being say, "Come!" ⁸I looked up and saw a horse whose color was pale green. Its rider was named Death, and his companion was the Grave.* These two were given authority over one-fourth of the earth, to kill with the sword and famine and disease* and wild animals.

⁹When the Lamb broke the fifth seal, I saw under the altar the souls of all who had been martyred for the word of God and for being faithful in their testimony. ¹⁰They shouted to the Lord and said, "O Sovereign Lord, holy and true, how long before you judge the people who belong to this world and avenge our blood for what they have done to us?" ¹¹Then a white robe was given to each of them. And they were told to rest a little longer until the full number of their brothers and sisters*—their fellow servants of Jesus who were to be martyred—had joined them.

¹²I watched as the Lamb broke the sixth seal, and there was a great earthquake. The sun became as dark as black cloth, and the moon became as red as blood. ¹³Then the stars of the sky fell to the earth like green figs falling from a tree shaken by a strong wind. ¹⁴The sky was rolled up like a scroll, and all of the mountains and islands were moved from their places.

¹⁵Then everyone—the kings of the earth, the rulers, the generals, the wealthy, the powerful, and every slave and free person—all hid themselves in the caves and among the rocks of the mountains. ¹⁶And they cried to the mountains and the rocks, "Fall on us and hide us from the face of the one who sits on the throne and from the wrath of the Lamb. ¹⁷For the great day

of their wrath has come, and who is able to survive?"

7 GOD'S PEOPLE WILL BE PRESERVED Then I saw four angels standing at the four corners of the earth, holding back the four winds so they did not blow on the earth or the sea, or even on any tree. ²And I saw another angel coming up from the east, carrying the seal of the living God. And he shouted to those four angels, who had been given power to harm land and sea, ³"Wait! Don't harm the land or the sea or the trees until we have placed the seal of God on the foreheads of his servants."

⁴And I heard how many were marked with the seal of God—144,000 were sealed from all the tribes of Israel:

⁵ from Judah	12,000
from Reuben	12,000
from Gad	12,000
⁶ from Asher	12,000
from Naphtali	12,000
from Manasseh	12,000
⁷ from Simeon	12,000
from Levi	12,000
from Issachar	12,000
⁸ from Zebulun	12,000
from Joseph	12,000
from Benjamin	12,000

PRAISE FROM THE GREAT CROWD ⁹After this I saw a vast crowd, too great to count, from every nation and tribe and people and language, standing in front of the throne and before the Lamb. They were clothed in white robes and held palm branches in their hands. ¹⁰And they were shouting with a great roar,

"Salvation comes from our God who sits on the throne
and from the Lamb!"

¹¹And all the angels were standing around the throne and around the elders and the four living beings. And they fell before the throne with their faces to the ground and worshiped God. ¹²They sang,

"Amen! Blessing and glory and wisdom
and thanksgiving and honor
and power and strength belong to our God
forever and ever! Amen."

¹³Then one of the twenty-four elders asked me, "Who are these who are clothed in white? Where did they come from?"

GOD'S TIME
(6:9-11) Although the martyrs are eager for God to bring justice to the earth, they are told to wait. Those who suffer and die for their faith won't be forgotten, nor are their deaths in vain. Rather, God will single them out for special honor. Like these martyrs, we may wish for justice immediately. Yet we must be patient. Although God works on his own timetable, he promises justice. No suffering for the sake of God's Kingdom is wasted effort.

6:6a Greek A choinix [1 quart or 1 liter] of wheat for a denarius, and 3 choinix of barley for a denarius. A denarius was equivalent to a laborer's full day's wage.   **6:6b** Or harm.   **6:8a** Greek was Hades.   **6:8b** Greek death.   **6:11** Greek their brothers.

¹⁴And I said to him, "Sir, you are the one who knows."

Then he said to me, "These are the ones who died in* the great tribulation.* They have washed their robes in the blood of the Lamb and made them white.

¹⁵ "That is why they stand in front of God's throne
and serve him day and night in his Temple.
And he who sits on the throne
will give them shelter.
¹⁶ They will never again be hungry or thirsty;
they will never be scorched by the heat of the sun.
¹⁷ For the Lamb on the throne*
will be their Shepherd.
He will lead them to springs of life-giving water.
And God will wipe every tear from their eyes."

8 THE LAMB BREAKS THE SEVENTH SEAL

When the Lamb broke the seventh seal on the scroll,* there was silence throughout heaven for about half an hour. ²I saw the seven angels who stand before God, and they were given seven trumpets.

³Then another angel with a gold incense burner came and stood at the altar. And a great amount of incense was given to him to mix with the prayers of God's people as an offering on the gold altar before the throne. ⁴The smoke of the incense, mixed with the prayers of God's holy people, ascended up to God from the altar where the angel had poured them out. ⁵Then the angel filled the incense burner with fire from the altar and threw it down upon the earth; and thunder crashed, lightning flashed, and there was a terrible earthquake.

THE FIRST FOUR TRUMPETS ⁶Then the seven angels with the seven trumpets prepared to blow their mighty blasts.

⁷The first angel blew his trumpet, and hail and fire mixed with blood were thrown down on the earth. One-third of the earth was set on fire, one-third of the trees were burned, and all the green grass was burned.

⁸Then the second angel blew his trumpet, and a great mountain of fire was thrown into the sea. One-third of the water in the sea became blood, ⁹one-third of all things living in the

7:14a Greek *who came out of.* 7:14b Or *the great suffering.*
7:17 Greek *on the center of the throne.* 8:1 Or *book.* 8:11 Greek
Wormwood. 9:1 Or *the abyss,* or *the underworld;* also in 9:11.

sea died, and one-third of all the ships on the sea were destroyed.

¹⁰Then the third angel blew his trumpet, and a great star fell from the sky, burning like a torch. It fell on one-third of the rivers and on the springs of water. ¹¹The name of the star was Bitterness.* It made one-third of the water bitter, and many people died from drinking the bitter water.

¹²Then the fourth angel blew his trumpet, and one-third of the sun was struck, and one-third of the moon, and one-third of the stars, and they became dark. And one-third of the day was dark, and also one-third of the night.

¹³Then I looked, and I heard a single eagle crying loudly as it flew through the air, "Terror, terror, terror to all who belong to this world because of what will happen when the last three angels blow their trumpets."

9 THE FIFTH TRUMPET BRINGS THE FIRST TERROR

Then the fifth angel blew his trumpet, and I saw a star that had fallen to earth from the sky, and he was given the key to the shaft of the bottomless pit.* ²When he opened it, smoke poured out as though from a huge furnace, and the sunlight and air turned dark from the smoke.

³Then locusts came from the smoke and descended on the earth, and they were given power to sting like scorpions. ⁴They were told not to harm the grass or plants or trees, but only the people who did not have the seal of God on their foreheads. ⁵They were told not to kill them but to torture them for five months with pain like the pain of a scorpion sting. ⁶In those days people will seek death but will not find it. They will long to die, but death will flee from them!

⁷The locusts looked like horses prepared for battle. They had what looked like gold crowns

....

THE ONLY WAY
(7:10) People try many methods to remove the guilt of sin—good works, intellectual pursuits, and even placing blame on others. The crowd in heaven, however, praises God, declaring that salvation comes from him and from the Lamb. Salvation from sin's penalty can only come through Jesus Christ. Have you had the guilt of sin removed in the only way possible?

MAKE SURE
(8:6) A trumpet blast is usually a rallying call. These trumpet blasts have three purposes: (1) to warn that judgment is certain, (2) to call the forces of good and evil to battle, and (3) to announce the return of the King, the Messiah. These warnings urge us to make sure our faith is firmly fixed on Christ. Is that where your faith is?

on their heads, and their faces looked like human faces. [8]They had hair like women's hair and teeth like the teeth of a lion. [9]They wore armor made of iron, and their wings roared like an army of chariots rushing into battle. [10]They had tails that stung like scorpions, and for five months they had the power to torment people. [11]Their king is the angel from the bottomless pit; his name in Hebrew is *Abaddon,* and in Greek, *Apollyon*—the Destroyer.

[12]The first terror is past, but look, two more terrors are coming!

THE SIXTH TRUMPET BRINGS THE SECOND TERROR

[13]Then the sixth angel blew his trumpet, and I heard a voice speaking from the four horns of the gold altar that stands in the presence of God. [14]And the voice said to the sixth angel who held the trumpet, "Release the four angels who are bound at the great Euphrates River." [15]Then the four angels who had been prepared for this hour and day and month and year were turned loose to kill one-third of all the people on earth. [16]I heard the size of their army, which was 200 million mounted troops.

[17]And in my vision, I saw the horses and the riders sitting on them. The riders wore armor that was fiery red and dark blue and yellow. The horses had heads like lions, and fire and smoke and burning sulfur billowed from their mouths. [18]One-third of all the people on earth were killed by these three plagues—by the fire and smoke and burning sulfur that came from the mouths of the horses. [19]Their power was in

their mouths and in their tails. For their tails had heads like snakes, with the power to injure people.

[20]But the people who did not die in these plagues still refused to repent of their evil deeds and turn to God. They continued to worship demons and idols made of gold, silver, bronze, stone, and wood—idols that can neither see nor hear nor walk! [21]And they did not repent of their murders or their witchcraft or their sexual immorality or their thefts.

10 THE ANGEL AND THE SMALL SCROLL

Then I saw another mighty angel coming down from heaven, surrounded by a cloud, with a rainbow over his head. His face shone like the sun, and his feet were like pillars of fire. [2]And in his hand was a small scroll* that had been opened. He stood with his right foot on the sea and his left foot on the land. [3]And he gave a great shout like the roar of a lion. And when he shouted, the seven thunders answered.

[4]When the seven thunders spoke, I was about to write. But I heard a voice from heaven saying, "Keep secret* what the seven thunders said, and do not write it down."

[5]Then the angel I saw standing on the sea and on the land raised his right hand toward heaven. [6]He swore an oath in the name of the one who lives forever and ever, who created the heavens and everything in them, the earth and everything in it, and the sea and everything in it. He said, "There will be no more delay. [7]When the seventh angel blows his trumpet, God's mysterious plan will be fulfilled. It will happen just as he announced it to his servants the prophets.

[8]Then the voice from heaven spoke to me again: "Go and take the open scroll from the hand of the angel who is standing on the sea and on the land."

[9]So I went to the angel and told him to give me the small scroll. "Yes, take it and eat it," he said. "It will be sweet as honey in your mouth, but it will turn sour in your stomach!" [10]So I took the small scroll from the hand of the angel, and I ate it! It was sweet in my mouth, but when I swallowed it, it turned sour in my stomach.

[11]Then I was told, "You must prophesy again about many peoples, nations, languages, and kings."

11 THE TWO WITNESSES

Then I was given a measuring stick, and I was told, "Go

COMPLETELY ENTANGLED
(9:20-21) *These people were so hard-hearted that even plagues couldn't drive them to God. People don't usually fall into immorality and evil suddenly—they slip into it a little at a time until they are completely entangled. Temptation entertained today can become a habit that eventually leads to separation from God forever (see Jas 1:15). To think you could never become this evil is the first step toward a hard heart. Do you feel yourself slipping? You know where to run: to God.*

LIVE NOW
(10:4) *Throughout history people have wanted to know what would happen in the future. God reveals some future events in this book. But some events he chooses not to reveal. John was prevented from writing about certain parts of his vision. During Old Testament times, an angel also told the prophet Daniel that some things he saw were not to be described to everyone at that time (Dan 12:9). Hundreds of years later, Jesus told his disciples that only God knows what will happen during the end times (Mark 13:32-33).*

God has revealed all we need to know in order to live for him now. In our desire to be ready for the end, we must not place more emphasis on what will happen during the last days than on living for God while we wait.

10:2 Or *book;* also in 10:8, 9, 10.   **10:4** Greek *Seal up.*

and measure the Temple of God and the altar, and count the number of worshipers. ²But do not measure the outer courtyard, for it has been turned over to the nations. They will trample the holy city for 42 months. ³And I will give power to my two witnesses, and they will be clothed in burlap and will prophesy during those 1,260 days."

⁴These two prophets are the two olive trees and the two lampstands that stand before the Lord of all the earth. ⁵If anyone tries to harm them, fire flashes from their mouths and consumes their enemies. This is how anyone who tries to harm them must die. ⁶They have power to shut the sky so that no rain will fall for as long as they prophesy. And they have the power to turn the rivers and oceans into blood, and to strike the earth with every kind of plague as often as they wish.

⁷When they complete their testimony, the beast that comes up out of the bottomless pit* will declare war against them, and he will conquer them and kill them. ⁸And their bodies will lie in the main street of Jerusalem,* the city that is figuratively called "Sodom" and "Egypt," the city where their Lord was crucified. ⁹And for three and a half days, all peoples, tribes, languages, and nations will stare at their bodies. No one will be allowed to bury them. ¹⁰All the people who belong to this world will gloat over them and give presents to each other to celebrate the death of the two prophets who had tormented them.

¹¹But after three and a half days, God breathed life into them, and they stood up! Terror struck all who were staring at them. ¹²Then a loud voice from heaven called to the two prophets, "Come up here!" And they rose to heaven in a cloud as their enemies watched.

¹³At the same time there was a terrible earthquake that destroyed a tenth of the city. Seven thousand people died in that earthquake, and everyone else was terrified and gave glory to the God of heaven.

¹⁴The second terror is past, but look, the third terror is coming quickly.

THE SEVENTH TRUMPET BRINGS THE THIRD TERROR   ¹⁵Then the seventh angel blew his trumpet, and there were loud voices shouting in heaven:

> "The world has now become the Kingdom
>   of our Lord and of his Christ,*
>   and he will reign forever and ever."

11:7 Or *the abyss,* or *the underworld.*   **11:8** Greek *the great city.*
11:15 Or *his Messiah.*

¹⁶The twenty-four elders sitting on their thrones before God fell with their faces to the ground and worshiped him. ¹⁷And they said,

> "We give thanks to you, Lord God, the
>   Almighty,
>   the one who is and who always was,
> for now you have assumed your great power
>   and have begun to reign.
> ¹⁸ The nations were filled with wrath,
>   but now the time of your wrath has come.
> It is time to judge the dead
>   and reward your servants the prophets,
>   as well as your holy people,
> and all who fear your name,
>   from the least to the greatest.
> It is time to destroy
>   all who have caused destruction
>   on the earth."

¹⁹Then, in heaven, the Temple of God was opened and the Ark of his covenant could be seen inside the Temple. Lightning flashed, thunder crashed and roared, and there was an earthquake and a terrible hailstorm.

12 THE WOMAN AND THE DRAGON   Then I witnessed in heaven an event of great significance. I saw a woman clothed with the sun, with the moon beneath her feet, and a crown of twelve stars on her head. ²She was pregnant, and she cried out because of her labor pains and the agony of giving birth.

³Then I witnessed in heaven another significant event. I saw a large red dragon with seven heads and ten horns, with seven crowns on his heads. ⁴His tail swept away one-third of the stars in the sky, and he threw them to the earth. He stood in front of the woman as she was about to give birth, ready to devour her baby as soon as it was born.

⁵She gave birth to a son who was to rule all nations with an iron rod. And her child was snatched away from the dragon and was caught up to God and to his throne. ⁶And the woman fled into the wilderness, where God had prepared a place to care for her for 1,260 days.

⁷Then there was war in heaven. Michael and his angels fought against the dragon and his angels. ⁸And the dragon lost the battle, and he and his angels were forced out of heaven. ⁹This great dragon—the ancient serpent called the devil, or Satan, the one deceiving the whole world—was thrown down to the earth with all his angels.

¹⁰Then I heard a loud voice shouting across the heavens,

"It has come at last—
salvation and power
and the Kingdom of our God,
and the authority of his Christ.*
For the accuser of our brothers and sisters*
has been thrown down to earth—
the one who accuses them
before our God day and night.
[11] And they have defeated him by the blood
of the Lamb
and by their testimony.
And they did not love their lives so much
that they were afraid to die.
[12] Therefore, rejoice, O heavens!
And you who live in the heavens, rejoice!
But terror will come on the earth and
the sea,
for the devil has come down to you in
great anger,
knowing that he has little time."

[13]When the dragon realized that he had been thrown down to the earth, he pursued the woman who had given birth to the male child. [14]But she was given two wings like those of a great eagle so she could fly to the place prepared for her in the wilderness. There she would be cared for and protected from the dragon* for a time, times, and half a time.

[15]Then the dragon tried to drown the woman with a flood of water that flowed from his mouth. [16]But the earth helped her by opening its mouth and swallowing the river that gushed out from the mouth of the dragon. [17]And the dragon was angry at the woman and declared war against the rest of her children—all who keep God's commandments and maintain their testimony for Jesus.

[18]Then the dragon took his stand* on the shore beside the sea.

13 THE BEAST OUT OF THE SEA Then I saw a beast rising up out of the sea.

....

TERRIBLE TRIO

(13:1-18) Satan (the dragon) has two evil accomplices: the beast out of the sea and the beast out of the earth. Together, the three form an unholy trinity in direct opposition to the holy Trinity of God the Father, God the Son, and God the Holy Spirit. Their goal: to overthrow God. But there's good news. God will someday defeat them. Check out Revelation 19:19–20:10.

You may have problems that seem like an "unholy trinity." Maybe you're facing tons of homework, conflicts at home, and a constant state of "empty wallet." When problems come in bunches, we sometimes feel discouraged. But consider what God has in store for the unholy three described above. A God with that kind of power can solve any problem you face.

It had seven heads and ten horns, with ten crowns on its horns. And written on each head were names that blasphemed God. [2]This beast looked like a leopard, but it had the feet of a bear and the mouth of a lion! And the dragon gave the beast his own power and throne and great authority.

[3]I saw that one of the heads of the beast seemed wounded beyond recovery—but the fatal wound was healed! The whole world marveled at this miracle and gave allegiance to the beast. [4]They worshiped the dragon for giving the beast such power, and they also worshiped the beast. "Who is as great as the beast?" they exclaimed. "Who is able to fight against him?"

[5]Then the beast was allowed to speak great blasphemies against God. And he was given authority to do whatever he wanted for forty-two months. [6]And he spoke terrible words of blasphemy against God, slandering his name and his dwelling—that is, those who dwell in heaven.* [7]And the beast was allowed to wage war against God's holy people and to conquer them. And he was given authority to rule over every tribe and people and language and nation. [8]And all the people who belong to this world worshiped the beast. They are the ones whose names were not written in the Book of Life before the world was made—the Book that belongs to the Lamb who was slaughtered.*

[9] Anyone with ears to hear
should listen and understand.
[10] Anyone who is destined for prison
will be taken to prison.
Anyone destined to die by the sword
will die by the sword.

This means that God's holy people must endure persecution patiently and remain faithful.

THE BEAST OUT OF THE EARTH [11]Then I saw another beast come up out of the earth. He had two horns like those of a lamb, but he spoke with the voice of a dragon. [12]He exercised all the authority of the first beast. And he required all the earth and its people to worship the first beast, whose fatal wound had been healed. [13]He did astounding miracles, even making fire flash down to earth from the sky while everyone was watching. [14]And with all the miracles he was allowed to perform on behalf of the first

12:10a Or his Messiah.   **12:10b** Greek brothers.   **12:14** Greek the serpent; also in 12:15. See 12:9.   **12:18** Greek Then he took his stand; some manuscripts read Then I took my stand. Some translations put this entire sentence into 13:1.   **13:6** Some manuscripts read and his dwelling and all who dwell in heaven. **13:8** Or not written in the Book of Life that belongs to the Lamb who was slaughtered before the world was made.

beast, he deceived all the people who belong to this world. He ordered the people to make a great statue of the first beast, who was fatally wounded and then came back to life. ¹⁵He was then permitted to give life to this statue so that it could speak. Then the statue of the beast commanded that anyone refusing to worship it must die.

¹⁶He required everyone—small and great, rich and poor, free and slave—to be given a mark on the right hand or on the forehead. ¹⁷And no one could buy or sell anything without that mark, which was either the name of the beast or the number representing his name. ¹⁸Wisdom is needed here. Let the one with understanding solve the meaning of the number of the beast, for it is the number of a man.* His number is 666.*

14 THE LAMB AND THE 144,000 Then I saw the Lamb standing on Mount Zion, and with him were 144,000 who had his name and his Father's name written on their foreheads. ²And I heard a sound from heaven like the roar of mighty ocean waves or the rolling of loud thunder. It was like the sound of many harpists playing together.

³This great choir sang a wonderful new song in front of the throne of God and before the four living beings and the twenty-four elders. No one could learn this song except the 144,000 who had been redeemed from the earth. ⁴They have kept themselves as pure as virgins,* following the Lamb wherever he goes. They have been purchased from among the people on the earth as a special offering* to God and to the Lamb. ⁵They have told no lies; they are without blame.

THE THREE ANGELS ⁶And I saw another angel flying through the sky, carrying the eternal Good News to proclaim to the people who belong to this world—to every nation, tribe, language, and people. ⁷"Fear God," he shouted. "Give glory to him. For the time has come when he will sit as judge. Worship him who made the heavens, the earth, the sea, and all the springs of water."

⁸Then another angel followed him through the sky, shouting, "Babylon is fallen—that great city is fallen—because she made all the nations of the world drink the wine of her passionate immorality."

⁹Then a third angel followed them, shout-

13:18a Or *of humanity.* 13:18b Some manuscripts read *616.*
14:4a Greek *They are virgins who have not defiled themselves with women.* 14:4b Greek *as firstfruits.* 14:14 Or *like a son of man.* See Dan 7:13. "Son of Man" is a title Jesus used for himself.

MY STORY: Spring

I struggle with apathy. Maybe that's how one of the churches John talks about in Revelation 3 felt. I guess you can say I'm not very disciplined. This affects both my schoolwork and my Christian life. I have trouble applying myself to what I need to do if I don't feel like doing it at the moment.

In my youth group we studied 2 Timothy. One verse—2:15—has really challenged me directly. It says, "Work hard so you can present yourself to God and receive his approval. Be a good worker, one who does not need to be ashamed and who correctly explains the word of truth." These words remind me that my actions and attitudes are significant. Someday, I'll have to answer to God for them (Rev 14:7). Knowing this helps me make an extra effort to do the right thing, whether it's reading my Bible regularly or turning off the TV and opening a textbook.

ing, "Anyone who worships the beast and his statue or who accepts his mark on the forehead or on the hand ¹⁰must drink the wine of God's anger. It has been poured full strength into God's cup of wrath. And they will be tormented with fire and burning sulfur in the presence of the holy angels and the Lamb. ¹¹The smoke of their torment will rise forever and ever, and they will have no relief day or night, for they have worshiped the beast and his statue and have accepted the mark of his name."

¹²This means that God's holy people must endure persecution patiently, obeying his commands and maintaining their faith in Jesus.

¹³And I heard a voice from heaven saying, "Write this down: Blessed are those who die in the Lord from now on. Yes, says the Spirit, they are blessed indeed, for they will rest from their hard work; for their good deeds follow them!"

THE HARVEST OF THE EARTH ¹⁴Then I saw a white cloud, and seated on the cloud was someone like the Son of Man.* He had a gold crown on his head and a sharp sickle in his hand.

¹⁵Then another angel came from the Temple and shouted to the one sitting on the cloud, "Swing the sickle, for the time of harvest has

come; the crop on earth is ripe." ¹⁶So the one sitting on the cloud swung his sickle over the earth, and the whole earth was harvested.

¹⁷After that, another angel came from the Temple in heaven, and he also had a sharp sickle. ¹⁸Then another angel, who had power to destroy with fire, came from the altar. He shouted to the angel with the sharp sickle, "Swing your sickle now to gather the clusters of grapes from the vines of the earth, for they are ripe for judgment." ¹⁹So the angel swung his sickle over the earth and loaded the grapes into the great winepress of God's wrath. ²⁰The grapes were trampled in the winepress outside the city, and blood flowed from the winepress in a stream about 180 miles* long and as high as a horse's bridle.

15 THE SONG OF MOSES AND OF THE LAMB

Then I saw in heaven another marvelous event of great significance. Seven angels were holding the seven last plagues, which would bring God's wrath to completion. ²I saw before me what seemed to be a glass sea mixed with fire. And on it stood all the people who had been victorious over the beast and his statue and the number representing his name. They were all holding harps that God had given them. ³And they were singing the song of Moses, the servant of God, and the song of the Lamb:

"Great and marvelous are your works,
    O Lord God, the Almighty.
Just and true are your ways,
    O King of the nations.*
⁴ Who will not fear you, Lord,
    and glorify your name?
    For you alone are holy.
All nations will come and worship before
    you,
    for your righteous deeds have been
        revealed."

THE SEVEN BOWLS OF THE SEVEN PLAGUES

⁵Then I looked and saw that the Temple in

heaven, God's Tabernacle, was thrown wide open. ⁶The seven angels who were holding the seven plagues came out of the Temple. They were clothed in spotless white linen* with gold sashes across their chests. ⁷Then one of the four living beings handed each of the seven angels a gold bowl filled with the wrath of God, who lives forever and ever. ⁸The Temple was filled with smoke from God's glory and power. No one could enter the Temple until the seven angels had completed pouring out the seven plagues.

16 Then I heard a mighty voice from the Temple say to the seven angels, "Go your ways and pour out on the earth the seven bowls containing God's wrath."

²So the first angel left the Temple and poured out his bowl on the earth, and horrible, malignant sores broke out on everyone who had the mark of the beast and who worshiped his statue.

³Then the second angel poured out his bowl on the sea, and it became like the blood of a corpse. And everything in the sea died.

⁴Then the third angel poured out his bowl on the rivers and springs, and they became blood. ⁵And I heard the angel who had authority over all water saying,

"You are just, O Holy One, who is and who
    always was,
    because you have sent these judgments.
⁶ Since they shed the blood
    of your holy people and your prophets,
you have given them blood to drink.
    It is their just reward."

⁷And I heard a voice from the altar,* saying,

"Yes, O Lord God, the Almighty,
    your judgments are true and just."

⁸Then the fourth angel poured out his bowl on the sun, causing it to scorch everyone with its fire. ⁹Everyone was burned by this blast of heat, and they cursed the name of God, who had control over all these plagues. They did not repent of their sins and turn to God and give him glory.

¹⁰Then the fifth angel poured out his bowl on the throne of the beast, and his kingdom was plunged into darkness. His subjects ground their teeth in anguish, ¹¹and they cursed the God of heaven for their pains and sores. But

....

JUDGMENT

(14:14-20) *Jesus separating the faithful from the unfaithful—like a farmer harvesting his crops—is an image of judgment. This will be a time of joy for the Christians who have been persecuted and martyred. At last they will receive their long-awaited reward. For this reason, Christians don't have to fear the last judgment. We have this assurance from Jesus: "Those who listen to my message and believe in God who sent me have eternal life. They will never be condemned for their sins, but they have already passed from death into life" (John 5:24).*

14:20 Greek *1,600 stadia* [296 kilometers].   **15:3** Some manuscripts read *King of the ages.*   **15:6** Other manuscripts read *white stone;* still others read *white [garments] made of linen.* **16:7** Greek *I heard the altar.*

they did not repent of their evil deeds and turn to God.

¹²Then the sixth angel poured out his bowl on the great Euphrates River, and it dried up so that the kings from the east could march their armies toward the west without hindrance. ¹³And I saw three evil* spirits that looked like frogs leap from the mouths of the dragon, the beast, and the false prophet. ¹⁴They are demonic spirits who work miracles and go out to all the rulers of the world to gather them for battle against the Lord on that great judgment day of God the Almighty.

¹⁵"Look, I will come as unexpectedly as a thief! Blessed are all who are watching for me, who keep their clothing ready so they will not have to walk around naked and ashamed."

¹⁶And the demonic spirits gathered all the rulers and their armies to a place with the Hebrew name *Armageddon.**

¹⁷Then the seventh angel poured out his bowl into the air. And a mighty shout came from the throne in the Temple, saying, "It is finished!" ¹⁸Then the thunder crashed and rolled, and lightning flashed. And a great earthquake struck—the worst since people were placed on the earth. ¹⁹The great city of Babylon split into three sections, and the cities of many nations fell into heaps of rubble. So God remembered all of Babylon's sins, and he made her drink the cup that was filled with the wine of his fierce wrath. ²⁰And every island disappeared, and all the mountains were leveled. ²¹There was a terrible hailstorm, and hailstones weighing as much as seventy-five pounds* fell from the sky onto the people below. They cursed God because of the terrible plague of the hailstorm.

17 THE GREAT PROSTITUTE One of the seven angels who had poured out the seven bowls came over and spoke to me. "Come with me," he said, "and I will show you the judgment that is going to come on the great prostitute, who rules over many waters. ²The kings of the world have committed adultery with her, and the people who belong to this world have been made drunk by the wine of her immorality."

³So the angel took me in the Spirit* into the wilderness. There I saw a woman sitting on a scarlet beast that had seven heads and ten horns, and blasphemies against God were written all over it. ⁴The woman wore purple and scarlet clothing and beautiful jewelry made of gold and precious gems and pearls. In her hand she held a gold goblet full of obscenities and the impurities of her immorality. ⁵A mysterious name was written on her forehead: "Babylon the Great, Mother of All Prostitutes and Obscenities in the World." ⁶I could see that she was drunk—drunk with the blood of God's holy people who were witnesses for Jesus. I stared at her in complete amazement.

⁷"Why are you so amazed?" the angel asked. "I will tell you the mystery of this woman and of the beast with seven heads and ten horns on which she sits. ⁸The beast you saw was once alive but isn't now. And yet he will soon come up out of the bottomless pit* and go to eternal destruction. And the people who belong to this world, whose names were not written in the Book of Life before the world was made, will be amazed at the reappearance of this beast who had died.

⁹"This calls for a mind with understanding: The seven heads of the beast represent the seven hills where the woman rules. They also represent seven kings. ¹⁰Five kings have already fallen, the sixth now reigns, and the seventh is yet to come, but his reign will be brief.

¹¹"The scarlet beast that was, but is no longer, is the eighth king. He is like the other seven, and he, too, is headed for destruction. ¹²The ten horns of the beast are ten kings who have not yet risen to power. They will be appointed to their kingdoms for one brief moment to reign with the beast. ¹³They will all agree to give him their power and authority. ¹⁴Together they will go to war against the Lamb, but the Lamb will defeat them because he is Lord of all lords and King of all kings. And his called and chosen and faithful ones will be with him."

¹⁵Then the angel said to me, "The waters where the prostitute is ruling represent masses of people of every nation and language. ¹⁶The scarlet beast and his ten horns all hate the prostitute. They will strip her naked, eat her flesh, and burn her remains with fire. ¹⁷For God has put a plan into their minds, a plan that will carry out his purposes. They will agree to give

16:13 Greek *unclean.*   16:16 Or *Harmagedon.*   16:21 Greek *1 talent* [34 kilograms].   17:3 Or *in spirit.*   17:8 Or *the abyss,* or *the underworld.*

....

READY OR NOT?
(16:15) Since Jesus will return unexpectedly (see 1 Thes 5:1-6), we must be ready when he returns. We can prepare ourselves by resisting temptation and by being committed to God's standards. In what ways does your life show your readiness for Christ's return?

their authority to the scarlet beast, and so the words of God will be fulfilled. [18]And this woman you saw in your vision represents the great city that rules over the kings of the world."

18 THE FALL OF BABYLON After all this I saw another angel come down from heaven with great authority, and the earth grew bright with his splendor. [2]He gave a mighty shout:

"Babylon is fallen—that great city is fallen!
  She has become a home for demons.
She is a hideout for every foul* spirit,
  a hideout for every foul vulture
  and every foul and dreadful animal.*
[3] For all the nations have fallen*
  because of the wine of her passionate
    immorality.
The kings of the world
  have committed adultery with her.
Because of her desires for extravagant
   luxury,
  the merchants of the world have
   grown rich."

[4]Then I heard another voice calling from heaven,

"Come away from her, my people.
  Do not take part in her sins,
  or you will be punished with her.
[5] For her sins are piled as high as heaven,
  and God remembers her evil deeds.
[6] Do to her as she has done to others.
  Double her penalty* for all her evil deeds.
She brewed a cup of terror for others,
  so brew twice as much* for her.
[7] She glorified herself and lived in luxury,
  so match it now with torment and sorrow.
She boasted in her heart,
  'I am queen on my throne.

. . . .

IN CHARGE
(17:17) No matter what happens, we can still trust that God is in charge and that his plans will come to pass just as he promised. God's control is shown in how he sometimes uses people opposed to him to carry out his will. Although God allows evil to filter through this present world, he will completely abolish evil someday.

GREED GUARD
(18:11-19) John foresaw the eventual destruction of those caught up in greed. Recognize any similarities between this society and ours? Many people fall into the obsession of owning more and more. Their motto is "Whoever dies with the most toys wins!" But no one has yet been able to take anything from this life into the next.

Many years before this vision, Jesus gave this warning: "Guard against every kind of greed. Life is not measured by how much you own" (Luke 12:15). Is that your motto?

I am no helpless widow,
  and I have no reason to mourn.'
[8] Therefore, these plagues will overtake her
  in a single day—
  death and mourning and famine.
She will be completely consumed by fire,
  for the Lord God who judges her is
   mighty."

[9]And the kings of the world who committed adultery with her and enjoyed her great luxury will mourn for her as they see the smoke rising from her charred remains. [10]They will stand at a distance, terrified by her great torment. They will cry out,

"How terrible, how terrible for you,
  O Babylon, you great city!
In a single moment
  God's judgment came on you."

[11]The merchants of the world will weep and mourn for her, for there is no one left to buy their goods. [12]She bought great quantities of gold, silver, jewels, and pearls; fine linen, purple, silk, and scarlet cloth; things made of fragrant thyine wood, ivory goods, and objects made of expensive wood; and bronze, iron, and marble. [13]She also bought cinnamon, spice, incense, myrrh, frankincense, wine, olive oil, fine flour, wheat, cattle, sheep, horses, chariots, and bodies—that is, human slaves.

[14] "The fancy things you loved so much
  are gone," they cry.
"All your luxuries and splendor
  are gone forever,
  never to be yours again."

[15]The merchants who became wealthy by selling her these things will stand at a distance, terrified by her great torment. They will weep and cry out,

[16] "How terrible, how terrible for that great city!
  She was clothed in finest purple and
   scarlet linens,
  decked out with gold and precious stones
   and pearls!
[17] In a single moment
  all the wealth of the city is gone!"

And all the captains of the merchant ships and their passengers and sailors and crews will stand at a distance. [18]They will cry out as they watch the smoke ascend, and they will say, "Where is there another city as great as this?"

18:2a Greek *unclean;* also in each of the two following phrases. **18:2b** Some manuscripts condense the last two lines to read *a hideout for every foul [unclean] and dreadful vulture.* **18:3** Some manuscripts read *have drunk.* **18:6a** Or *Give her an equal penalty.* **18:6b** Or *brew just as much.*

¹⁹And they will weep and throw dust on their heads to show their grief. And they will cry out,

> "How terrible, how terrible for that great city!
> The shipowners became wealthy
> by transporting her great wealth on
> the seas.
> In a single moment it is all gone."

²⁰ Rejoice over her fate, O heaven
> and people of God and apostles
> and prophets!
> For at last God has judged her
> for your sakes.

²¹Then a mighty angel picked up a boulder the size of a huge millstone. He threw it into the ocean and shouted,

> "Just like this, the great city Babylon
> will be thrown down with violence
> and will never be found again.
> ²² The sound of harps, singers, flutes,
> and trumpets
> will never be heard in you again.
> No craftsmen and no trades
> will ever be found in you again.
> The sound of the mill
> will never be heard in you again.
> ²³ The light of a lamp
> will never shine in you again.
> The happy voices of brides and grooms
> will never be heard in you again.
> For your merchants were the greatest
> in the world,
> and you deceived the nations with your
> sorceries.
> ²⁴ In your* streets flowed the blood of the
> prophets and of God's holy people
> and the blood of people slaughtered
> all over the world."

19 SONGS OF VICTORY IN HEAVEN After this, I heard what sounded like a vast crowd in heaven shouting,

> "Praise the Lord!*
> Salvation and glory and power belong
> to our God.
> ² His judgments are true and just.
> He has punished the great prostitute
> who corrupted the earth with her
> immorality.
> He has avenged the murder of his
> servants."

18:24 Greek *her.*   19:1 Greek *Hallelujah;* also in 19:3, 4, 6. *Hallelujah* is the transliteration of a Hebrew term that means "Praise the Lord."   19:6 Some manuscripts read *the Lord God.* 19:10a Greek *brothers.*   19:10b Or *is the message confirmed by Jesus.*

³And again their voices rang out:

> "Praise the Lord!
> The smoke from that city ascends forever
> and ever!"

⁴Then the twenty-four elders and the four living beings fell down and worshiped God, who was sitting on the throne. They cried out, "Amen! Praise the Lord!"

⁵And from the throne came a voice that said,

> "Praise our God,
> all his servants,
> all who fear him,
> from the least to the greatest."

⁶Then I heard again what sounded like the shout of a vast crowd or the roar of mighty ocean waves or the crash of loud thunder:

> "Praise the Lord!
> For the Lord our God,* the Almighty,
> reigns.
> ⁷ Let us be glad and rejoice,
> and let us give honor to him.
> For the time has come for the wedding feast
> of the Lamb,
> and his bride has prepared herself.
> ⁸ She has been given the finest of pure white
> linen to wear."
> For the fine linen represents the good
> deeds of God's holy people.

⁹And the angel said to me, "Write this: Blessed are those who are invited to the wedding feast of the Lamb." And he added, "These are true words that come from God."

¹⁰Then I fell down at his feet to worship him, but he said, "No, don't worship me. I am a servant of God, just like you and your brothers and sisters* who testify about their faith in Jesus. Worship only God. For the essence of prophecy is to give a clear witness for Jesus.*"

THE RIDER ON THE WHITE HORSE ¹¹Then I saw heaven opened, and a white horse was standing there. Its rider was named Faithful and True, for he judges fairly and wages a righteous war. ¹²His eyes were like flames of fire, and on his head were many crowns. A name was written on him that no one understood

---

TRUE WORSHIP
(19:1-10) Praise is the heartfelt response to God by those who love him. The more you get to know God and realize what he's done, the more you will respond with praise. Praise is at the heart of true worship. Let your praise to God flow out of your realization of who he is and how much he loves you.

THE BEGINNING AND THE END

The Bible records for us the beginning of the world and the end of the world. The story of humanity, from beginning to end—from the fall into sin to the redemption of Christ and God's ultimate victory over evil—is found in
the pages of the Bible.

GENESIS	REVELATION
The sun is created.	The sun is not needed.
Satan is victorious.	Satan is defeated.
Sin enters the human race.	Sin is banished.
People run and hide from God.	People are invited to live with God forever.
People are cursed.	The curse is removed.
Tears are shed, with sorrow for sin.	No more sin, no more tears or sorrow.
The garden and earth are cursed.	God's city is glorified; the earth is made new.
The fruit from the tree of life is not to be eaten.	God's people may eat from the tree of life.
Paradise is lost.	Paradise is regained.
People are doomed to death.	Death is defeated; believers live forever with God.

except himself. ¹³He wore a robe dipped in blood, and his title was the Word of God. ¹⁴The armies of heaven, dressed in the finest of pure white linen, followed him on white horses. ¹⁵From his mouth came a sharp sword to strike down the nations. He will rule them with an iron rod. He will release the fierce wrath of God, the Almighty, like juice flowing from a winepress. ¹⁶On his robe at his thigh* was written this title: King of all kings and Lord of all lords.

¹⁷Then I saw an angel standing in the sun, shouting to the vultures flying high in the sky: "Come! Gather together for the great banquet God has prepared. ¹⁸Come and eat the flesh of kings, generals, and strong warriors; of horses and their riders; and of all humanity, both free and slave, small and great."

¹⁹Then I saw the beast and the kings of the world and their armies gathered together to fight against the one sitting on the horse and his army. ²⁰And the beast was captured, and with him the false prophet who did mighty miracles on behalf of the beast—miracles that deceived all who had accepted the mark of the beast and who worshiped his statue. Both the beast and his false prophet were thrown alive into the fiery lake of burning sulfur. ²¹Their entire army was killed by the sharp sword that came from the mouth of the one riding the white horse. And the vultures all gorged themselves on the dead bodies.

20 THE THOUSAND YEARS Then I saw an angel coming down from heaven with the key to the bottomless pit* and a heavy chain in his hand. ²He seized the dragon—that old serpent, who is the devil, Satan—and bound him in chains for a thousand years. ³The angel threw him into the bottomless pit, which he then shut and locked so Satan could not deceive the nations anymore until the thousand years were finished. Afterward he must be released for a little while.

⁴Then I saw thrones, and the people sitting on them had been given the authority to judge. And I saw the souls of those who had been beheaded for their testimony about Jesus and for proclaiming the word of God. They had not worshiped the beast or his statue, nor accepted his mark on their foreheads or their hands. They all came to life again, and they reigned with Christ for a thousand years.

⁵This is the first resurrection. (The rest of the dead did not come back to life until the thousand years had ended.) ⁶Blessed and holy are those who share in the first resurrection. For them the second death holds no power, but they will be priests of God and of Christ and will reign with him a thousand years.

THE DEFEAT OF SATAN ⁷When the thousand years come to an end, Satan will be let out of his prison. ⁸He will go out to deceive the nations—called Gog and Magog—in every corner of the earth. He will gather them together for battle—a mighty army, as numberless as sand along the seashore. ⁹And I saw them as they went up on the broad plain of the earth and surrounded God's people and the beloved city.

19:16 Or *On his robe and thigh.* **20:1** Or *the abyss,* or *the underworld;* also in 20:3.

But fire from heaven came down on the attacking armies and consumed them.

¹⁰Then the devil, who had deceived them, was thrown into the fiery lake of burning sulfur, joining the beast and the false prophet. There they will be tormented day and night forever and ever.

THE FINAL JUDGMENT ¹¹And I saw a great white throne and the one sitting on it. The earth and sky fled from his presence, but they found no place to hide. ¹²I saw the dead, both great and small, standing before God's throne. And the books were opened, including the Book of Life. And the dead were judged according to what they had done, as recorded in the books. ¹³The sea gave up its dead, and death and the grave* gave up their dead. And all were judged according to their deeds. ¹⁴Then death and the grave were thrown into the lake of fire. This lake of fire is the second death. ¹⁵And anyone whose name was not found recorded in the Book of Life was thrown into the lake of fire.

21 **THE NEW JERUSALEM** Then I saw a new heaven and a new earth, for the old heaven and the old earth had disappeared. And the sea was also gone. ²And I saw the holy city, the new Jerusalem, coming down from God out of heaven like a bride beautifully dressed for her husband.

³I heard a loud shout from the throne, saying, "Look, God's home is now among his people! He will live with them, and they will be his people. God himself will be with them.* ⁴He will wipe every tear from their eyes, and there will be no more death or sorrow or crying or pain. All these things are gone forever."

⁵And the one sitting on the throne said, "Look, I am making everything new!" And then he said to me, "Write this down, for what I tell you is trustworthy and true." ⁶And he also said, "It is finished! I am the Alpha and the Omega—the Beginning and the End. To all who are thirsty I will give freely from the springs of the water of life. ⁷All who are victorious will inherit all these blessings, and I will be their God, and they will be my children.

⁸"But cowards, unbelievers, the corrupt, murderers, the immoral, those who practice witchcraft, idol worshipers, and all liars—their fate is in the fiery lake of burning sulfur. This is the second death."

⁹Then one of the seven angels who held the

20:13 Greek *and Hades;* also in 20:14.   **21:3** Some manuscripts read *God himself will be with them, their God.*   **21:10** Or *in spirit.*   **21:16** Greek *12,000 stadia* [2,220 kilometers].

I HEARD A LOUD SHOUT FROM THE THRONE, SAYING, "LOOK, GOD'S HOME IS NOW AMONG HIS PEOPLE! HE WILL LIVE WITH THEM, AND THEY WILL BE HIS PEOPLE. GOD HIMSELF WILL BE WITH THEM."

REVELATION 21:3

seven bowls containing the seven last plagues came and said to me, "Come with me! I will show you the bride, the wife of the Lamb."

¹⁰So he took me in the Spirit* to a great, high mountain, and he showed me the holy city, Jerusalem, descending out of heaven from God. ¹¹It shone with the glory of God and sparkled like a precious stone—like jasper as clear as crystal. ¹²The city wall was broad and high, with twelve gates guarded by twelve angels. And the names of the twelve tribes of Israel were written on the gates. ¹³There were three gates on each side—east, north, south, and west. ¹⁴The wall of the city had twelve foundation stones, and on them were written the names of the twelve apostles of the Lamb.

¹⁵The angel who talked to me held in his hand a gold measuring stick to measure the city, its gates, and its wall. ¹⁶When he measured it, he found it was a square, as wide as it was long. In fact, its length and width and height were each 1,400 miles.* ¹⁷Then he measured the walls

NO CONTEST
(20:7-10) *This is not a typical battle where the outcome is in doubt during the heat of the conflict. We already know the outcome. Two mighty forces of evil—those of the beast (19:19) and of Satan (20:7-8)—unite to do battle against God. The Bible uses just two small passages to describe each battle. Here is the play-by-play: the evil beast and his forces are captured and thrown into the lake of fire and completely destroyed (19:20-21); fire from heaven consumes Satan's armies while Satan is thrown into the lake of fire (20:9-10). Believers will have no doubt, worry, or second thoughts about whether they have chosen the right side. If you choose God, you will experience a tremendous victory with Christ.*

and found them to be 216 feet thick* (according to the human standard used by the angel).

¹⁸The wall was made of jasper, and the city was pure gold, as clear as glass. ¹⁹The wall of the city was built on foundation stones inlaid with twelve precious stones:* the first was jasper, the second sapphire, the third agate, the fourth emerald, ²⁰the fifth onyx, the sixth carnelian, the seventh chrysolite, the eighth beryl, the ninth topaz, the tenth chrysoprase, the eleventh jacinth, the twelfth amethyst. ²¹The twelve gates were made of pearls—each gate from a single pearl! And the main street was pure gold, as clear as glass.

²²I saw no temple in the city, for the Lord God Almighty and the Lamb are its temple. ²³And the city has no need of sun or moon, for the glory of God illuminates the city, and the Lamb is its light. ²⁴The nations will walk in its light, and the kings of the world will enter the city in all their glory. ²⁵Its gates will never be closed at the end of day because there is no night there. ²⁶And all the nations will bring their glory and honor into the city. ²⁷Nothing evil* will be allowed to enter, nor anyone who practices shameful idolatry and dishonesty—but only those whose names are written in the Lamb's Book of Life.

22 Then the angel showed me a river with the water of life, clear as crystal, flowing from the throne of God and of the Lamb. ²It flowed down the center of the main street. On each side of the river grew a tree of life, bearing twelve crops of fruit,* with a fresh crop each month. The leaves were used for medicine to heal the nations.

³No longer will there be a curse upon anything. For the throne of God and of the Lamb will be there, and his servants will worship him. ⁴And they will see his face, and his name will be written on their foreheads. ⁵And there will be no night there—no need for lamps or sun—for the Lord God will shine on them. And they will reign forever and ever.

⁶Then the angel said to me, "Everything you have heard and seen is trustworthy and true. The Lord God, who inspires his prophets,* has sent his angel to tell his servants what will happen soon.*"

JESUS IS COMING ⁷"Look, I am coming soon! Blessed are those who obey the words of prophecy written in this book.*"

⁸I, John, am the one who heard and saw all these things. And when I heard and saw them, I fell down to worship at the feet of the angel who showed them to me. ⁹But he said, "No, don't worship me. I am a servant of God, just like you and your brothers the prophets, as well as all who obey what is written in this book. Worship only God!"

¹⁰Then he instructed me, "Do not seal up the prophetic words in this book, for the time is near. ¹¹Let the one who is doing harm continue to do harm; let the one who is vile continue to be vile; let the one who is righteous continue to live righteously; let the one who is holy continue to be holy."

21:17 Greek *144 cubits* [65 meters]. **21:19** The identification of some of these gemstones is uncertain. **21:27** Or *ceremonially unclean.* **22:2** Or *twelve kinds of fruit.* **22:6a** Or *The Lord, the God of the spirits of the prophets.* **22:6b** Or *suddenly,* or *quickly;* also in 22:7, 12, 20. **22:7** Or *scroll;* also in 22:9, 10, 18, 19.

EYEWITNESS
(22:8-9) *Hearing or reading an eyewitness account is the next best thing to seeing the event yourself. John witnessed the events reported in Revelation and recorded them so we could "see" and believe as he did. If you have read this far, you have "seen." Have you also believed?*

CHOICES
despair

Blood, violence, murder, mayhem, images of doom and gloom. What have we got here? Some kind of horror movie?

No, just another edition of the nightly news.

With smiling faces and playful banter, the Channel 2 news anchors recite one horror story after another: the ongoing drug war, tensions in the Middle East, killer flus, tragic accidents, a psychotic killer on the loose, alarming new predictions about AIDS, a devastating flood in India, the growing nightmare of pollution, plus a host of other stories.

As Jeremiah turns off the TV, he sighs, then mutters to himself, "This world's messed up! What's the point? I mean, what do I have to live for? The way things are going, I won't even make it to age 30."

Is it any wonder this dude's depressed? The human race does seem bent on self-destruction. Is there any hope in a world that seems to be spinning out of control?

Yes! One of the greatest, most encouraging passages in the whole Bible is found right at the end. Read Revelation 21 and 22 for a fascinating and faith-building look at what the future holds for those who know Christ. (If you don't know Christ as your Savior, now is a perfect time to ask him to forgive your sins and to accept his offer of eternal life. So, what're you waiting for?)

¹²"Look, I am coming soon, bringing my reward with me to repay all people according to their deeds. ¹³I am the Alpha and the Omega, the First and the Last, the Beginning and the End."

¹⁴Blessed are those who wash their robes. They will be permitted to enter through the gates of the city and eat the fruit from the tree of life. ¹⁵Outside the city are the dogs—the sorcerers, the sexually immoral, the murderers, the idol worshipers, and all who love to live a lie.

¹⁶"I, Jesus, have sent my angel to give you this message for the churches. I am both the source of David and the heir to his throne.* I am the bright morning star."

¹⁷The Spirit and the bride say, "Come." Let anyone who hears this say, "Come." Let anyone who is thirsty come. Let anyone who desires drink freely from the water of life. ¹⁸And I solemnly declare to everyone who hears the words of prophecy written in this book: If anyone adds anything to what is written here, God will add to that person the plagues described in this book. ¹⁹And if anyone removes any of the words from this book of prophecy, God will remove that person's share in the tree of life and in the holy city that are described in this book.

22:16 Greek *I am the root and offspring of David.*   22:21 Other manuscripts read *be with all;* still others read *be with all of God's holy people.* Some manuscripts add *Amen.*

²⁰He who is the faithful witness to all these things says, "Yes, I am coming soon!"

Amen! Come, Lord Jesus!

²¹May the grace of the Lord Jesus be with God's holy people.*

....

YOU'RE INVITED
(22:17) When Jesus met the Samaritan woman at the well, he told her of the living water that he could supply (John 4:10-15). This image is used again as Jesus invites anyone to come and drink of the water of life. The gospel is unlimited in scope—all people, everywhere, may come. Salvation cannot be earned; God gives it freely. We live in a world desperately thirsty for living water, and many are dying of thirst. Who will you invite to come and drink?

GOD WINS!
(22:12-21) Revelation closes human history as Genesis opened it—in paradise. But there is one distinct difference: in Revelation, evil is gone forever. Genesis describes Adam and Eve walking and talking with God; Revelation describes people worshiping him face-to-face. Genesis describes a garden with an evil serpent; Revelation describes a perfect city with no evil.

The book of Revelation ends with an urgent request: "Come, Lord Jesus!" In a world of problems, persecution, evil, and immorality, Christ calls us to endure in our faith. Our efforts to better our world are important, but their results cannot compare with the transformation Jesus will bring about when he returns. He alone controls human history and forgives sin. Someday, he will recreate the earth and bring lasting peace.

Revelation is above all a book of hope. It shows that no matter what happens on earth, God is in control. It promises that evil will not last forever, and it depicts the wonderful reward that is waiting for all those who believe in Jesus Christ as Savior and Lord.

"Come, Lord Jesus!"

LIFE CHOICES INDEX

Need answers to nagging questions? Check out the Scriptures under each topic.

ABILITIES *Selected passages*
A misuse of strength...................................Judges 15:3-8.....................0280
Giving God credit for an ability.................Daniel 2:19-30....................0921
Using abilities wisely...............................Matthew 25:14-30.................1062
Gifted people have great responsibility.........Luke 12:48.......................1124
Using abilities to build up the body of Christ.....Romans 12:6-21;...............1240
   Ephesians 4:7-16................1295
Discover your spiritual gifts....................1 Corinthians 12.................1259
Use gifts and abilities for God.................1 Timothy 4:14-16................1328

Notes
"From Ordinary to Extraordinary"...............Exodus 4:2-4......................0069
"The Ways God Blesses"...........................Deuteronomy 33:6-25..............0226
"Special Privileges"............................Ezekiel 16:8-16..................0879
"Use What You've Got"...........................Matthew 25:14-30.................1062
"Kindness"......................................Acts 9:36-42.....................1195
"Gifts"...Romans 12:4-8....................1239
"Useful"..1 Corinthians 1:1................1246
"The Body"......................................1 Corinthians 12:4-31............1259
(See also POTENTIAL)

ABORTION *Selected passages*
Made in God's image.............................Genesis 1:26-27..................0005
Murder is the same before or after birth.......Exodus 20:13.....................0090
Alive and loved in the womb....................Psalm 139........................0664
Called and known by God........................Isaiah 49:1, 5...................0773
Formed by God in the womb......................Jeremiah 1:5.....................0792
Welcome children, welcome Christ...............Mark 9:36-37.....................1083
Jesus welcomed children........................Luke 18:15-17....................1131

Notes
Ultimate Issues: Abortion......................2 Chronicles 28:3................0496
Ultimate Issues: Made in the Image of God......Psalm 8..........................0591
Choices: Abortion..............................Psalm 139:13-18..................0665

ACHIEVEMENTS *(See ABILITIES, POTENTIAL, SUCCESS)*

ADDICTION *(See ALCOHOL, DRUGS)*

ADVICE *Selected passages*
Jethro's advice................................Exodus 18........................0087
God's guidance.................................Psalm 16:7-8.....................0595
A plea for guidance............................Psalm 25:4-7.....................0600
Guidance from God's Word.......................Psalm 119:105....................0657
A father's advice..............................Proverbs 3.......................0674
A need for advice..............................Proverbs 13:10, 13.........0682, 0683
Guided to a new life...........................Acts 8:26-39.....................1193

Notes
"Obstacles" .... Exodus 13:17-18 0081
"In the Right Spot" .... Numbers 9:23 0159
Choices: Astrology .... Deuteronomy 4:19; 17:2-5 0196
"Decisions" .... 1 Samuel 23:2 0323
"Directions" .... 1 Samuel 28:15 0328
"Battles" .... 2 Samuel 5:17-25 0338
"Seek God First" .... 1 Kings 1:49-50 0367
"Ask God First" .... 1 Chronicles 14:10 0452
"Already Prepared" .... Psalm 27:1-14 0601
"The Guide" .... Psalm 48:14 0614
My Story .... Isaiah 41:10 0764
"Too Young to Serve?" .... Jeremiah 1:1-8 0792
"Submit" .... Lamentations 3:25-33 0862
"False Teaching" .... 1 Timothy 1:3-11 1326
"Run!" .... 2 Timothy 2:22 1335
(See also BELIEVING IN GOD, FUTURE, GOD'S WILL, PRAYER)

ALCOHOL *Selected passages*
Being drunk leads to trouble .... Genesis 19:31-33 0024
Consequences of decisions made while drunk .... Esther 1:10–2:1 0542
Drinking ruins lives .... Proverbs 23:29-35 0693
The dangers of drinking .... Proverbs 31:4-6 0700
Don't get drunk .... Romans 13:11-14 1241
Instead of being drunk, be filled with the Spirit ... Ephesians 5:18 1297

Notes
Choices: Drinking .... Proverbs 23:29-35 0692
"The Sting of Drinking" .... Proverbs 23:29-35 0693
I Wonder .... Galatians 5:21 1288
(See also PARTYING)

ANGER *Selected passages*
Anger can lead to murder .... Genesis 4:6-8 0009
Pride often causes anger .... Numbers 22:29 0174
Anger can lead to hatred and revenge .... 1 Kings 21:4-10 0395
The wise person controls anger .... Proverbs 12:16 0682
Unjust anger can lead to eternal consequences ... Matthew 5:21-26 1033
Express anger by correcting the problem .... Mark 3:5-6 1073
Anger against sin .... John 2:13-17 1148
God's anger .... Romans 1:18-32 1227
The dangers of words spoken in anger .... James 3:5-6 1366

Notes
Choices: Anger .... Numbers 20:1-12 0171
"Righteous Anger" .... Numbers 25:6-11 0177
"Appropriate Anger" .... 1 Samuel 11:6 0308
My Story .... Psalm 13 0593
"Anger Management" .... Matthew 5:21-22 1033
"Useful Anger" .... Mark 3:1-6 1073
(See also HATRED, REVENGE, CONFLICT/CONFRONTATION)

APPEARANCE *Selected passages*
Beauty in a spouse .... Genesis 24:14-28 0029
Attractive on the inside .... Proverbs 19:22 0689
Don't worry about clothing .... Matthew 6:25-34 1035
Clothed in righteousness .... Matthew 22:11-12 1058

Develop inner beauty . . . . 1 Timothy 2:8-10 1327
Inner beauty . . . . 1 Peter 3:1-5 1373

Notes
"Inner Beauty" . . . . Genesis 24:15-16 0029
"Sex Roles" . . . . Deuteronomy 22:5 0214
"What Really Counts" . . . . 1 Samuel 16:7 0315
"Character" . . . . 1 Samuel 31:3-4 0330
Ultimate Issues: Looking for a Perfect 10 . . . . Proverbs 31 0701
"Self-Centered Thinking" . . . . Isaiah 3:16-26 0727

APPROVAL *Selected passages*
God doesn't approve of sin . . . . Joshua 23:12-14 0255
Having God's approval . . . . Matthew 10:32-33 1041
Seeking God's approval . . . . John 5:41 1154
Seeking God's praise . . . . John 7:18 1156
Approval from God or people? . . . . Acts 5:29 1188

Notes
"Consequences" . . . . Joshua 23:12-16 0255
"Wanting What He Wants" . . . . Psalm 97:10 0642
I Wonder . . . . Daniel 1, 3, 6 0920

ARGUMENTS *(See ANGER, REVENGE, CONFLICT/CONFRONTATION)*

ASTROLOGY/HOROSCOPES *(See OCCULT, THE)*

ATTITUDES *Selected passages*
Gaining a positive attitude . . . . Exodus 14:11-14 0082
The consequences of a negative attitude . . . . Numbers 13:25–14:38 0162
Negative attitudes make things worse . . . . Numbers 16:41-50 0167
Attitudes determine life . . . . Proverbs 15:13-15 0685
Life-giving attitudes . . . . Matthew 5:3-12 1032
In the world or out of it? . . . . 1 John 2:15-17 1385

Notes
"Positive Attitude" . . . . Genesis 39:21-23 0051
"Listening" . . . . 1 Samuel 3:1-15 0300
"A Change of Perspective" . . . . 1 Samuel 17:26-37 0317
Choices: Complacency . . . . Amos 5:21–6:8 0962
Choices: Arrogance . . . . Obadiah 1:1-10 0970
"Attitudes" . . . . Jonah 3–4 0976
Choices: Hard Times . . . . Habakkuk 3:17-19 0994
"Leftovers" . . . . Malachi 1:6-14 1020
My Story . . . . Revelation 3; 14:7 1413
(See also LIFESTYLE, THANKFULNESS)

AUTHORITY *Selected passages*
The problem of following your own way . . . . Judges 21:23-25 0288
Using authority well . . . . Esther 10:3 0551
God's authority . . . . Proverbs 21:1 0690
Jesus' authority in heaven and on earth . . . . Matthew 28:18 1068
Government authority . . . . Mark 12:13-17 1088
Jesus was under authority . . . . John 8:39-42 1159
Obey the authorities . . . . Romans 13:1-7 1240
Authority in marriage . . . . Ephesians 5:22-32 1297
Parents' authority . . . . Ephesians 6:1-3 1297
Honor church leaders . . . . 1 Thessalonians 5:12-13 1319

Notes
"Respect"... 1 Samuel 24:5-7................... 0324
"Selective or Thorough?" .... 1 Chronicles 6:49............... 0444
Ultimate Issues: Who's in Charge?............. Ezekiel 32..................... 0898
Choices: Authority .... Romans 13:1-7 1241
"Dealing with Conflict" .... Philemon 1:8-9 1344
(See also MARRIAGE, PARENTS)

BELIEVING IN GOD *Selected passages*
Abram believes God .... Genesis 15:6 0019
Belief leads to obedience...................... 2 Kings 5:13-15................ 0407
Jesus honors belief in him .... Luke 12:8-9 1123
Believing in what we cannot see............... John 20:24-31 1174
No excuse for unbelief .... Romans 1:18-20................. 1227
Believe and be saved .... Romans 10:9-10................. 1237

Notes
"Great Expectations" .... Deuteronomy 10:12-13 0203
Ultimate Issues: Covenants..................... Deuteronomy 11:26-32 0204
"Help!".. 1 Samuel 2:2 0298
"An Ingredient or the Source?".................. 1 Samuel 6:9 0303
Ultimate Issues: Miracles .... 2 Kings 5...................... 0404
"First Priority"................................. 2 Kings 15:34-35 0421
"Take Him Seriously" .... 1 Chronicles 28:1-10 0465
"Amazing Grace"................................. 2 Chronicles 6:18 0475
"Battles" .... 2 Chronicles 20:1-15 0486
"Never Enough Knowledge" .... Job 36:26 0580
"Shield"... Psalm 18:30 0597
"In God We Trust?".............................. Psalm 33:4 0605
My Story .... Psalm 34. 0606
"Wholehearted" .... Psalm 86:11-12 0636
"Family Name" .... Psalm 99:3. 0643
Ultimate Issues: Who is God? .... Isaiah 6. 0730
My Story .... Isaiah 41:10 0764
"Ridiculed" .... Isaiah 51:7 0776
Ultimate Issues: Modern-Day Idols .... Jeremiah 10 0808
"Changed"....................................... Acts 1:3-4 1181
"The Whole Package"............................ Acts 8:18-24.................. 1192
I Wonder.. Acts 17:11 1208
I Wonder.. Hebrews 1:1-3 1349
I Wonder.. 1 Peter 1:8. 1371
I Wonder.. Revelation 2:4 1403
(See also ADVICE, BIBLE, ETERNAL LIFE/SALVATION, EXPECTATIONS, GOD'S WILL,
OBEDIENCE, PRAYER, TIME WITH GOD)

BIBLE *Selected passages*
How to benefit from Bible reading .... Deuteronomy 17:18-20 0210
The value of God's Word........................ 2 Kings 22 0429
The Bible can guide your life .... Psalm 119 0654
The Word helps you resist temptation .... Matthew 4:1-11 1031
The Gospels were written to help people
    believe in Jesus............................ John 20:30-31 1175
The Bible is good news......................... Romans 1:16-17................. 1227
The wise follower studies the Bible .... 2 Timothy 2:15................. 1335
Inspired by the Holy Spirit .... 2 Peter 1:16-21 1379
The Bible has practical advice................. 1 John 2:1-17. 1384
Don't change or add to the Bible.............. Revelation 22:18-19 1421

Notes
Ultimate Issues: Absolute Answers . . . . Exodus 20 0090
Ultimate Issues: The Law . . . . Leviticus 19 0133
Ultimate Issues: Covenants . . . . Deuteronomy 11 0204
"Harmful Hearsay" . . . . 1 Kings 13:7-32 0383
"Gotta Read It" . . . . 2 Chronicles 34:31 0505
"Act On It" . . . . Nehemiah 8:1-14 0531
"Truth Hurts" . . . . Nehemiah 9:1-3 0532
"Medicine for Life" . . . . Psalm 119:125 0657
My Story . . . . Ecclesiastes 5:1-7 0707
"Deceit" . . . . Isaiah 36:7 0758
"God's Word" . . . . Jeremiah 36:21-32 0836
"Faithful" . . . . Ezekiel 33:1-6 0899
"An Appetite for Answers" . . . . Amos 8:11-14 0966
I Wonder . . . . Matthew 5:17 1032
"All Checked Out" . . . . Luke 1:1-3 1101
I Wonder . . . . Acts 17:11 1208
"Smooth Talk" . . . . 2 Corinthians 11:3-4 1277
"Twisted Truth" . . . . Galatians 1:6-7 1282
"Divine Inspiration" . . . . 2 Timothy 3:16 1336
Ultimate Issues: Foundational Truths . . . . 2 John 1392
(See also ADVICE, GODLY LIVING, GOD'S WILL, TIME WITH GOD)

BLAME *(See EXCUSES, JUDGING OTHERS)*

BLESSINGS *Selected passages*
Thanking God for what he has given . . . . 2 Samuel 7:18-27 0340
Gratitude is a depression fighter . . . . 2 Samuel 22:47-51 0359
A prayer for blessings . . . . 1 Chronicles 4:9-10 0441
Be thankful . . . . Psalm 95:2 0641
Thankful for what God gives . . . . Psalm 103 0644

Notes
"Curses and Blessings" . . . . Deuteronomy 27:15-26 0218
"The Blessing of Trouble" . . . . Jeremiah 24:1-10 0822
"God's Generosity" . . . . Matthew 20:1-15 1055
(See also THANKFULNESS)

CHANGE *Selected passages*
A drastic change . . . . Genesis 6:3 0011
Prayer can change things . . . . Exodus 32:9-14 0102
God's mercy outlasts the seasons of life . . . . Psalm 103:15-18 0645
God doesn't change . . . . James 1:17 1364

Notes
"Changed Life" . . . . Genesis 44:16-34 0057
"One Step at a Time" . . . . Deuteronomy 7:21-24 0201
"Progress" . . . . Joshua 11:16-23 0243
"Real Regret" . . . . Hosea 6:1-3 0942
"A Life-Changing Message" . . . . Acts 24:24-25 1219
"A Big Change" . . . . Galatians 1:13-24 1282
I Wonder . . . . Ephesians 4:14-15 1294
"Changes for the Better" . . . . Colossians 3:1-17 1311

CHARACTER *(See INTEGRITY, LIFESTYLE, VALUES)*

CHEATING *Selected passages*
God hates cheating.................................... Proverbs 11:1 0680
Don't cheat the poor................................ Amos 8:4-7......................... 0965
Don't cheat God..................................... Malachi 3:8-10.....................1023

Notes
Choices: Cheating.................................... Proverbs 11:1 0681

CHOICES *Selected passages*
The consequences of making the wrong choice ... Genesis 3:1-11 0007
A life or death choice .... Deuteronomy 30:15-20........... 0222
Choose whom you will serve.................... Joshua 24:14-28 0256
Obeying God requires consistency.............. 1 Samuel 15 0313
A wise choice .... Proverbs 8:1-21 0678
Choose to accept constructive criticism......... Proverbs 15:31-32 0685
Deciding to love Jesus above everyone .... Matthew 10:34-39..................1041
Deciding to be for Jesus or against him .... Matthew 12:30......................1044
A choice of heaven or hell .... Matthew 13:47-52 1047
Jesus prayed before making decisions.......... Luke 6:12 1110
Use wisdom when making decisions .... James 1:5 1364

Notes
"Conflict".. Numbers 20:14-21................. 0171
"Evil Seeds"... Deuteronomy 29:18 0221
"A Costly Decision"................................. 2 Chronicles 25:5-10 0493
"Decisions"... Esther 1:10-11..................... 0542
Choices: Taking a Stand .... Esther 3–4 0546
"Motives".. Proverbs 21:2...................... 0690
"Choices"... Isaiah 8:5-15 0733
Choices: Advice..................................... Lamentations 3:19-26............. 0861
I Wonder... Daniel 1, 3, 6 0920
"Just Like Him" .... John 5:19-23 1153
"Choose Well"...................................... Acts 1:21-26 1182
Choices: Serving God .... 2 Corinthians 4:8-10;
                                                  6:4-10; 11:23-33....................1272
My Story.. 2 Peter 1:5-8.......................1378
(See also FREEDOM)

CHURCH (THE BODY OF CHRIST; INVOLVEMENT IN A LOCAL CHURCH)
Selected passages
Jesus' habit of attending the synagogue .... Luke 4:16 1107
The birth of the church............................ Acts 2 1182
How the church works .... Romans 12:3-21....................1240
Spiritual gifts of the church .... 1 Corinthians 12 1259

Notes
Ultimate Issues: Worship.......................... 1 Samuel 1 0298
I Wonder... 2 Chronicles 20:20-22 0487
"True Worship" .... Isaiah 58:1-14 0781
"True Worship" .... Lamentations 2:1-7 0859
"Dried Up" .... Ezekiel 37:1-14.................... 0904
"The Presence" .... Ezekiel 48:1-35.................... 0916
Choices: Halfhearted Worship..................... Malachi 1:6-14 1020
Ultimate Issues: The Church .... 1 Corinthians 12...................1260
"Keep Meeting!".................................... Hebrews 10:25 1356
I Wonder... Hebrews 10:24-25 1356

COMMITMENT *Selected passages*
Commit all you do to the Lord . . . . Psalm 37:1-11 0607
Being committed to Christ . . . . Matthew 10:32-33 1041
Being committed to Christ in tough times . . . . Matthew 13:18-23 1046
Commitment to witness . . . . Matthew 28:19-20 1068
Commitment to living right . . . . Acts 24:16 .1218

Notes
"Passing the Test" . . . . Genesis 22:1-2 0027
Choices: Commitment . . . . Ruth 1:1-18 0290
I Wonder . . . . 1 Samuel 8:7 0305
"A Bold Response" . . . . Ezra 5:3-11 0514
"Committed" . . . . Nehemiah 10:28-39 0534
"Tough Times" . . . . Jeremiah 12:1-6 0808
I Wonder . . . . Jeremiah 29:11-13 0827
Choices: Complacency . . . . Amos 5:21–6:8 0962
Choices: Judgment . . . . Zephaniah 1:14–2:3 0998
"Count the Cost" . . . . Matthew 8:19-20 1038
"Cut It Out" . . . . Mark 9:43-48 1084
"Give and Gain" . . . . Luke 18:28-30 1132
My Story . . . . Romans 2:6-8 1229
"No Problems?" . . . . 1 Corinthians 7:29-40 1253
(See also MARRIAGE)

COMMUNICATION *Selected passages*
Three steps in communication . . . . Deuteronomy 5:1 0197
Listen to wise instruction . . . . Proverbs 10:8; 13:18 . . . . 0679, 0683
The problem of gossip . . . . Proverbs 11:13 0681
Communication to avoid . . . . Ephesians 4:31 1429
Swift to hear; slow to speak . . . . James 1:19 .1364
The dangers of the tongue . . . . James 3 1365

Notes
"Compliments" . . . . Numbers 10:29-32 0160
"The Whole Story" . . . . Acts 11:1-18 1197
(See also CRITICISM, GOSSIP, TALKING ABOUT GOD)

COMMUNION *Selected passages*
Jesus starts a new tradition . . . . Matthew 26:26-30; 1064
                                                            Mark 14:22-26 1092

COMPARISONS *Selected passages*
Actions of believers and unbelievers compared . . . Matthew 25:31-46 1063
What the kingdom of God is like . . . . Luke 13:18-20 1125
Avoid comparisons . . . . 2 Corinthians 10:12 1276
Don't compare yourself with others . . . . Galatians 6:4 1288
Jesus' glory and humility compared . . . . Philippians 2:5-11 1303

Notes
"Judging" . . . . 1 Corinthians 4:1-7 1250
"The Body" . . . . 1 Corinthians 12:4-31 1259
I Wonder . . . . Colossians 2:6-7 1310
(See also JEALOUSY, PRIDE)

COMPASSION *Selected passages*
God has compassion for Hagar and Ishmael . . . . . . Genesis 16:7-14; 21:8-21 . . . . . . 0021, 0025
God promises to show compassion . . . . Exodus 33:19 0104
David needs compassion in sorrow . . . . Psalm 51:1-12 0615

Jesus shows compassion .... Matthew 9:36-38 1040
Compassion can involve taking a risk .... Mark 3:1-6 1073
We are to be compassionate .... Luke 10:25-37 1120
Compassion rewarded .... Acts 9:36-42 1194

Notes
"Strangers" .... Exodus 22:21 0092
"Poverty" .... Deuteronomy 15:7-11 0208
"Fresh Start" .... Deuteronomy 30:1-6 0222
"Still Involved .... 1 Samuel 1:6-28 0297
"Kindness" .... 1 Samuel 30:11-15 0329
"Silent Comfort" .... Job 2:11-13 0555
"Comfort 101" .... Job 16:1-5 0566
"Greater Results" .... Job 26:1-4 0572
"Reaching Out to Those in Need" .... Psalm 72:12-14 0627
"Consequences" .... Isaiah 22:4 0744
"Magnificent Love" .... Jeremiah 31:3 0829
"Grace" .... Lamentations 3:19-23 0861
"Concern for All" .... Matthew 9:9-13 1038
"Concern for Those in Need" .... Galatians 2:10 1283
"The Finish Line" .... 1 Thessalonians 5:9-11 1319
Choices: Obedience .... James 1:21-27 1364
(See also SERVING OTHERS)

COMPLAINING Selected passages

Complaints of the Israelites .... Exodus 16–17 0084
The consequences of complaining .... Numbers 12 0161
Envy can lead to complaints .... Matthew 20:1-16 1055
Do everything without complaining .... Philippians 2:14-16 1304

Notes
"Get Moving!" .... Exodus 14:15 0082
"Complaints" .... Numbers 21:5 0172
"Abandoned or Just Inactive?" .... 1 Samuel 7:2-3 0303
"Grit or Submit?" .... Luke 2:46-52 1104
"Productive Discomfort" .... Acts 8:4 1192
(See also CONTENTMENT)

CONFESSION Selected passages

We must confess our sins .... Psalm 51 0615
God listens when we confess .... Psalm 66:13-20 0623
The need to confess .... Luke 3:4-18 1105
Confess to other believers .... James 5:16 1368
God forgives when we confess .... 1 John 1:8-10 1384

Notes
"Cleaning House" .... 1 Chronicles 21:1-16 0458
"Far Away" .... 2 Chronicles 6:21-39 0475
"Steps to Forgiveness" .... 2 Chronicles 7:12-22 0476
"From Sorrow to Action" .... Ezra 10:1-11 0519
"Intentions" .... Proverbs 28:9 0697
"Isolated" .... Isaiah 1:1-9 0724
"Stains" .... Isaiah 1:18 0724
"Downplay It?" .... Jeremiah 3:1-5 0796
"Refreshed" .... Acts 3:19-20 1185
(See also FORGIVENESS)

CONFLICT/CONFRONTATION *Selected passages*
Aaron and Miriam criticize Moses . . . . Numbers 12 0161
The people rebel at the report of the 12 spies. . . . . Numbers 14 0163
God confronts Moses . . . . Numbers 20:1-12 0170
Nathan confronts David . . . . 2 Samuel 12:1-14 0344
Elijah confronts Ahab . . . . 1 Kings 21:17-29 0396
Jesus confronts the Pharisees . . . . Matthew 15:1-20; 23 . . . . 1048, 1049

Notes
"Conflict" . . . . Numbers 20:14-21 0171
Choices: Confront . . . . Ezekiel 2:3-7 0869
"Useful Anger" . . . . Mark 3:1-6 1073
"Dealing with Conflict" . . . . Philemon 1:8-9 1344

CONFIDENCE *Selected passages*
Confidence comes from God . . . . 2 Kings 18:5-6 0423
Confidence in God . . . . Proverbs 3:26 0674
Confidence in talking to others about God . . . . . . Acts 5:19-32 .1188

Notes
"A Secret Weapon" . . . . "Deuteronomy 3:21-22 0195
"God's Victory Equation" . . . . Deuteronomy 20:1 0212
"A War Already Won" . . . . Joshua 6:2-5 0236
"Confidence" . . . . Psalm 46:1-3 0612
My Story . . . . Matthew 5:38-39 1033

CONFORMITY *Selected passages*
The dangers of conformity . . . . Exodus 32:1-10 0102
Don't follow those who reject God . . . . Leviticus 18:3 0132
Daniel refused to conform . . . . Daniel 6 0928
What to do instead of conforming . . . . 1 Peter 1:13-14 1371

Notes
"Copying" . . . . 2 Kings 17:7-17 0422
"Consequences" . . . . Ezekiel 11:1-12 0875
"Salty" . . . . Luke 14:34-35 1127
"A Renewed Mind" . . . . Romans 12:2 .1239
(See also PEER PRESSURE, POPULARITY)

CONSCIENCE *Selected passages*
Job's clear conscience . . . . Job 27:6 0573
Ignoring one's conscience . . . . Romans 1:18-25 1227
Keeping a clean conscience . . . . 1 Timothy 1:18-20 1326
                                                        1 Peter 3:15-16 1374

Notes
"Clear Conscience" . . . . Job 27:1-6 0573
"A Diet of Disobedience" . . . . Hosea 5:4 0942
"Clear Conscience" . . . . 1 Timothy 1:19 1326

CONSEQUENCES *Selected passages*
Sin has consequences . . . . Genesis 3:14-19 0008
Consequences of sin are passed on . . . . Exodus 34:7 .0104
Disobedience brings consequences . . . . Leviticus 26:14-33 0143
God warns us of consequences . . . . Deuteronomy 27:15-26 0218
Consequences of intentional sin . . . . 1 Samuel 2:23-25 0299
Consequences of David's sin . . . . 2 Samuel 11:1–12:18 0343
Consequences of denying Christ . . . . Matthew 10:32-33 1041
Each of us will stand before God . . . . 2 Corinthians 5:10 1272

Notes
"Impulse Buying" .... Genesis 25:29-33 0032
"What's Right?" .... Genesis 30:1-12 0039
"Sin's Consequences" .... Genesis 35:22 0046
"Self-Destruction" .... Leviticus 20:22-23 0136
"No Small Thing" .... Joshua 7:20-25 0238
"Consequences" .... 1 Chronicles 5:1 0442
"Not Indifferent" .... 2 Chronicles 21:6-11 0489
"Consequences" .... Ezekiel 11:1-12 0875
I Wonder .... Amos 2:6-16 0959

CONTENTMENT *Selected passages*
Satan tries to ruin contentment .... Genesis 3:1-10 0007
Doing what's right can lead to contentment ..... Psalm 17:15 0596
Humility brings contentment .... Psalm 131 0661
Be content with what you have .... Matthew 6:25 1035
Contentment .... Philippians 4:10-14 1306

Notes
"Bitterness" .... Genesis 33:1-11 0044
"Best Interests" .... Psalm 23:1-3 0600
"All We Need" .... Psalm 34:9-10 0605
"Real Satisfaction" .... Acts 20:24-34 1214
"Be Content" .... 1 Corinthians 7:17-24 1523
My Story .... Hebrews 13:5 1361
(See also GREED)

CREATION *Selected passages*
God created all things .... Genesis 1 0005
God created us like himself .... Genesis 5:1-2 0011
Less than the angels .... Psalm 8:4-5 0591
God spoke all things into existence .... Psalm 33:4-11 0604

Notes
Ultimate Issues: The Origin of Humanity .... Genesis 1 0006

CRITICISM/JUDGING OTHERS *Selected passages*
Blame hurts others .... Genesis 16:1-6 0020
Dealing with unjust criticism .... 1 Samuel 1:6-28 0297
Accept helpful criticism .... Psalm 141:5 0666
Learn from criticism .... Proverbs 9:7-9 0679
Be fair .... Zechariah 7:9 1011
Reasons to avoid criticizing others .... Matthew 7:1-5 1035

Notes
"Be Prepared" .... Psalm 79:10 0633
"Blame" .... Isaiah 8:21-22 0733
"Take Truth to Heart" .... Jeremiah 20:1-3 0816
"The Truth Hurts" .... Jeremiah 28:1-17 0826
"All to Blame" .... Mark 14:55-72 1094
"The Right Thing" .... Mark 15:15 1094
"Judge Not" .... John 8:9-11 1158
(See also COMMUNICATION, EXCUSES)

DEATH *Selected passages*
Death ends only earthly life .... Ecclesiastes 9:10 0710
Life after death .... 1 Corinthians 15 1263
Life after death .... 2 Corinthians 5:8 1272

A blessing to those who love Jesus.............. Philippians 1:21-24 1303
Death of a believer or an unbeliever............. 1 Thessalonians 4:13-14 1319
Everyone will die............................... Hebrews 9:27....................1355
We don't have to fear death..................... 1 John 4:17 1388
The end of death .... Revelation 20:14 1419

Notes
"Grief" .... 2 Samuel 1:1-12 0333
Ultimate Issues: Suicide .... Jeremiah 20:14, 18 0817
I Wonder....................................... John 8; 11 1162
I Wonder....................................... 1 Thessalonians 4:13-14 1318

DECISIONS *(See CHOICES, FREEDOM)*

DEPRESSION/DISCOURAGEMENT *Selected passages*

Discouragement over the past .... Exodus 6:6-9 0072
How God dealt with Elijah's depression.......... 1 Kings 19 0392
Depression over problems...................... Job 3 0555
When you feel like giving up .... Psalm 23........................0600
Hope during times of discouragement........... Psalm 42:5-11...................0611
The hope of God's Word........................ Psalm 119:25 0655
A cause for depression......................... Proverbs 15:13 0685
Physical consequences of depression .... Proverbs 17:22...................0687
Help for the weary and discouraged............. Isaiah 40:28-31 0763
Discouraged by persecution .... Matthew 10:16-31 1040
What to do when discouragement strikes .... John 16:33 1170
Discouragement during troubled times .... Romans 8:35-39 1236
Never get tired of doing right .... Galatians 6:9-10 1288
Don't give up during hard times .... 2 Timothy 2:3-13 1334

Notes
"A Small Fight against Evil"..................... Exodus 2:1-3....................0067
"Don't Give Up!" .... Exodus 9:1......................0076
"From a High to a Low"......................... 1 Kings 19:3-4...................0393
"A Cure for Discouragement" .... Nehemiah 4:10-14...............0527
"Struggles" .... Job 6:8-13 0558
"How Unfair!" .... Job 10:1........................0561
My Story....................................... Psalm 6:3.......................0590
"Depression"................................... Psalm 42:1-11...................0611
Ultimate Issues: Down in the Dumps .... Psalm 73........................0628
"The Meaning of Life" .... Ecclesiastes 1:8-11..............0704
Ultimate Issues: Suicide .... Jeremiah 20:14, 18 0817
Choices: Hard Times........................... Habakkuk 3:17-19 0994
"Amazing Strength"............................ Habakkuk 3:17-19 0995
"Results" .... 1 Corinthians 15:58 1264
"Spiritual Attacks"............................. 2 Thessalonians 3:1-3...........1323
Choices: Despair............................... Revelation 21–22 1420
(See also SUFFERING)

DISCIPLINE *Selected passages*

Punishment should fit the crime................ Deuteronomy 25:1-3 0216
Discipline shows love.......................... Proverbs 13:24..................0683
Judgment day will be too late for unbelievers ..... Matthew 7:22-23................1036
Steps in church discipline .... Matthew 18:15-17 1053
A good way to correct behavior................. Ephesians 6:4 1297
God disciplines his children .... Hebrews 12:5-7 1358

Notes
"Human Idols" .... Isaiah 5:1-13 0728
"Real Regret" .... Hosea 6:1-3 0942
"Sign of Love" .... Amos 9:8 0966
"Completely Entangled" .... Revelation 9:20-21 1410
(See also CONSEQUENCES)

DOUBT *Selected passages*
Don't doubt .... Genesis 17:15-21 0021
How Jesus helped remove John's doubts .... Matthew 11:1-6 1042
Removing Thomas's doubts .... John 20:24-31 1174
Don't let doubt ruin your faith .... James 1:5-8 1364

Notes
My Story .... Psalm 6:3 0590
My Story .... Matthew 7:24-27 1036
"Doubts" .... Matthew 11:1-6 1042
Thomas's profile .... John 20 1176
"Evidence" .... Acts 14:1-18 1203
"Facts" .... Acts 26:26 1220
(See also FAITH, TRUST)

DRINKING *(See ALCOHOL, PARTYING)*

DRUGS *Selected passages*
Resist pressure from others to do wrong .... Proverbs 1:7-19 0672
Use God's wisdom to battle evil .... Proverbs 2 0673
Your body is the home of the Holy Spirit .... 1 Corinthians 6:19-20 1252

Notes
I Wonder .... Galatians 5:21 1288
(See also PARTYING)

ENEMIES *Selected passages*
On the run from an enemy .... 1 Samuel 20–27 0320
When enemies seem numerous .... Psalm 3 0589
God's resources in the face of enemies .... Psalm 23:4-5 0600
God's protection from enemies .... Psalm 31:4 0603
Living in peace with enemies .... Proverbs 16:7 0685
Enemies in the family .... Micah 7:1-7 0983
Loving enemies .... Matthew 5:43-48 1034
Treat others the way you want to be treated ...... Luke 6:31 1112
Enemies of God .... Romans 5:10 1232

Notes
My Story .... Luke 6:27-38 1111
Choices: Enemies .... Luke 10:25-37 1119
(See also HATRED)

ETERNAL LIFE/SALVATION *Selected passages*
The narrow way to eternal life .... Matthew 7:13-14 1036
How to gain eternal life .... John 3:16 1149
Why we can have eternal life with God .... Romans 5–6 1231
The gift of eternal life .... Ephesians 2:8-10 1293
Who will have eternal life .... Revelation 3:5 1405

Notes
"God's Mercy"..................................... Deuteronomy 9:1-6 0202
"God on Our Side" .... 1 Chronicles 18:1-14 0456
"Unending Life" .... Job 14:1-15 0564
"Good Deeds"..................................... Isaiah 57:12-13...................... 0781
"Life after Death" .... Ezekiel 32:17-21 0899
"Life after Death" .... Matthew 22:23-33 1059
"On Your Own" .... Luke 3:7-9 1105
"Narrow-Minded".............................. Luke 13:22-30 1125
"Simple Faith"................................... 1 Corinthians 1:18-31............. 1247
"Unsolved Mystery?" .... Ephesians 1:3-5 1292
"Paid in Full" .... Hebrews 7:25........................ 1353
I Wonder.. James 4:17 1367
"You Know It!".................................. 1 John 5:13 1389
"You're Invited".................................. Revelation 22:17 1421
(See also FAITH, FORGIVENESS, FUTURE, HEAVEN)

EXCUSES *Selected passages*
Excuses made as a result of a wrong action ...... Genesis 3:8-13.................... 0007
Excuses to avoid a feast........................ Luke 14:16-24...................... 1126
Knowledge of God leaves a person without
   an excuse.................................... Romans 1:20 1227
There is no excuse when we sin .... James 1:13-16...................... 1364

Notes
"Excuses, Excuses"............................... 1 Samuel 13:8-13 0309
"No Excuse"...................................... Ezekiel 9:9-10 0874
"Money Matters" .... Mark 7:1-13 1080
"A Desperate Struggle" .... Romans 7:15......................... 1234
My Story.. 1 John 1:8-10 1385
(See also CRITICISM/JUDGING OTHERS)

EXPECTATIONS *Selected passages*
Job's expectations .... Job 6 0558
You can't expect to be saved by your strength .... Psalm 33:17-18.................... 0605
What you can expect when you trust God .... Isaiah 49:23........................ 0774
Jesus addresses John's and others'
   expectations about the Savior .... Matthew 11:1-15.................... 1042
Expect Jesus to return at any moment .... Matthew 24:42-50.................. 1061

Notes
I Wonder.. Genesis 4 0008
"Great Expectations" .... Deuteronomy 10:12-13 0203

FAILURE *(See DEPRESSION, MAKING MISTAKES)*

FAITH *Selected passages*
Abram's faith.................................... Genesis 15:6 0019
Faith of a centurion............................ Matthew 8:5-13 1037
Miracles as a result of faith .... Matthew 9:18-30................... 1039
Even small faith is valuable .... Luke 17:6 1130
Faith in Jesus is rewarded .... Luke 18:35-43 1133
Result of faith in God .... Romans 4:3-5........................ 1230
A list of faithful people....................... Hebrews 11.......................... 1357

Notes
"When the Going Gets Tough" .... Joshua 19:47-48 0251
I Wonder.. 2 Samuel 15 0350

"God's Help" . . . . 1 Kings 18:36-38 0392
"Empty Jars, Full Faith" . . . . 2 Kings 4:1-7 0405
"The Power of One" . . . . 2 Kings 20:1-11 0427
I Wonder . . . . 1 Chronicles 28:9 0467
"The Remnant" . . . . Isaiah 10:20-22 0735
"Live by Faith" . . . . Habakkuk 2:4 0993
"Unstoppable" . . . . Matthew 2:1-18 1029
"Walk or Sink?" . . . . Matthew 14:28-33 1048
"A Gift" . . . . Romans 4:4-5 1231
"Forever Trying" . . . . Romans 9:31-33 1237
"Self-Inventory" . . . . Romans 14:1 1241
"Simple Faith" . . . . 1 Corinthians 1:18-31 1247
"Faithful" . . . . Hebrews 11:13-16 1357
My Story . . . . 1 Peter 3:15-17 1373
(See also DOUBTS, TRUST)

FAMILY *Selected passages*

Family love . . . . Proverbs 5:15-17 0676
Avoid family feuds . . . . Proverbs 11:29 0681
Adopted into God's family . . . . John 1:12 1146
Jesus' family didn't always understand him . . . . . . John 7:1-10 1156
Paul pleads for unity in the family of God . . . . 1 Corinthians 1:10-13 1246
Caring for the family . . . . 1 Timothy 5:8 1328
Share Christ with your family . . . . 2 Timothy 1:5-8 1334

Notes

"Family Time" . . . . 1 Kings 5:13-14 0372
"Traditions" . . . . Ezekiel 18:14-18 0882
"Grit and Submit?" . . . . Luke 2:46-52 1104
"Divided Loyalties" . . . . Luke 12:51-53 1124
"Family" . . . . John 19:25-27 1173
(See also MARRIAGE, PARENTS)

FEAR *Selected passages*

Two reasons not to fear . . . . Genesis 15:1 0019
Antidotes to fear . . . . Joshua 1:6-9; Psalm 27 . . . . 0231, 0601
The best fear to have . . . . Psalm 25:12-14 0601
Why we don't have to fear when trouble comes . . . Psalm 46 0613
Don't fear people . . . . Proverbs 29:25 0699

Notes

"Frantic with Fear" . . . . Genesis 32:6-12 0043
"Strange Places" . . . . Genesis 46:1-4 0058
"Fear or Focus on God?" . . . . Numbers 13:25-29 0162
My Story . . . . Joshua 1:9 0232
"Have No Fear!" . . . . Nehemiah 2:3 0524
"Constant Love" . . . . Psalm 44:22-26 0612
"Confidence" . . . . Psalm 46:1-3 0612
"Fearless" . . . . Psalm 112:1, 7-8 0652
My Story . . . . Psalm 140 0666
My Story . . . . Proverbs 29:25 0698
"Running Away" . . . . Jonah 1:1-3 0974
"Unstoppable" . . . . Matthew 2:1-18 1029
(See also WORRY/STRESS)

FORGIVENESS *Selected passages*

The cleansing power of forgiveness . . . . Isaiah 1:18 0724
God promises to forgive his people . . . . Ezekiel 36:25-27 0904

Forgive as we have been forgiven . . . . Matthew 18:15-35 1053
God's offer of forgiveness . . . . Luke 3:3 1105
Jesus forgives . . . . Acts 13:38-39 1201
How to be forgiven . . . . Romans 10:9-10. 1237
Jesus died so we could be forgiven. . . . . Hebrews 9:22-28. 1356
We can ask for forgiveness . . . . 1 John 1:8-9 1384

Notes
"Forgiven" . . . . 2 Samuel 22:22-24 0358
"Stains" . . . . Isaiah 1:18 0724
I Wonder. . . . . Jeremiah 17:9. 0814
My Story. . . . . Lamentations 3:21-23 0862
"Face It" . . . . Ezekiel 33:10-12. 0900
"Hard to Forgive" . . . . Daniel 4:19. 0926
"Real Regret". . . . . Hosea 6:1-3 0942
"Restored". . . . . Hosea 14:1-2 0949
"Always Open?" . . . . Matthew 18:21-33 1053
"A Forgiving Response" . . . . Luke 15:11-32 1128
Choices: Reconciliation . . . . Philemon 1344
"Forgiven" . . . . Philemon 1:10, 16 1344
I Wonder. . . . . James 1:22-27; 2:14-26. 1367
(See also CONFESSION)

FREEDOM *Selected passages*

Freedom from the power of sin . . . . John 8:30-36; 1158
                                                              Romans 8:1-11 1234
Don't mislead others . . . . Romans 14:1-16 .1241
Jesus gives us freedom. . . . . Galatians 5:1-6. 1287

Notes
Ultimate Issues: Other Religions . . . . Judges 2 0263
"Freedom" . . . . Psalm 2:3 0588
"True Freedom". . . . . Lamentations 1:1-14 0858
"Freedom" . . . . 1 Corinthians 8:1-13. 1255
Choices: Freedom . . . . Galatians 5:16-25 1286
"Freedom" . . . . 2 Peter 2:19 1380
(See also CHOICES)

FRIENDSHIP *Selected passages*

Moses—the friend of God . . . . Exodus 33:11 0103
Ruth's loyalty to Naomi . . . . Ruth 1 0290
David and Jonathan's friendship. . . . . 1 Samuel 18:1-4 .0318
Friendship advice . . . . Proverbs 17:17; 18:24 . . . . 0687, 0688
The value of loyalty. . . . . Proverbs 19:22. 0689
More friendship advice . . . . Proverbs 27:6, 9-10. 0696
Friendship with Jesus . . . . John 15:11-17 1168
Barnabas befriends Paul . . . . Acts 9:26-29 1194

Notes
"A True Friendship" . . . . 1 Samuel 18:1-4 .0318
"Friends" . . . . 1 Samuel 23:16-18. 0323
Choices: Friendship . . . . Psalm 1. 0588
"Fake Friendship" . . . . Psalm 28:3-5 0602
"Real Friends". . . . . Psalm 55:12-14. 0618
"True Friendship" . . . . Proverbs 18:24. 0688
"Choosing Friends" . . . . Proverbs 22:24-25. 0692
My Story. . . . . Ecclesiastes 10:12. 0710
Choices: Friendship . . . . Daniel 3 0926

I Wonder. . . . . 2 Corinthians 5:18-20 1273
My Story. . . . . Philippians 2:3-4. 1305
(See also PEER PRESSURE, POPULARITY)

FUTURE *Selected passages*

The future is in God's hands . . . . Psalm 31:15 0604
Wisdom can ensure a bright future. . . . . Proverbs 24:14. 0694
God's plans for your future . . . . Jeremiah 29:11. 0827
Our future in heaven. . . . . John 3:16 1149
Don't give up your future in heaven . . . . 2 Timothy 2:11-13. 1334

Notes

"Good Will Triumph". . . . . 1 Samuel 22:18-19. 0323
"The Future" . . . . Isaiah 41:4 0764
"Star Charts". . . . . Jeremiah 10:1-5 0806
"Time's Up" . . . . Nahum 1:1-8. 0988
"Predictions". . . . . Zechariah 9:9. 1013
"A Great Day!" . . . . Zechariah 12:1-5 1015
"What's in Store?" . . . . 1 Corinthians 2:9 1248
"Live Now" . . . . Revelation 10:4 1410
(See also ADVICE, ETERNAL LIFE/SALVATION)

GIFTS, SPIRITUAL *(See ABILITIES)*

GIVING *Selected passages*

An offering that pleased God. . . . . Genesis 4:4 0009
What to give. . . . . Deuteronomy 14:22-23. 0208
Generous to the poor . . . . Deuteronomy 15:7-11. 0208
Contributions for the Temple. . . . . Nehemiah 7:70-72. 0529
What generosity brings . . . . Proverbs 22:9 0691
Robbing God . . . . Malachi 3:8-10. 1023
A plea for generosity. . . . . 2 Corinthians 8–9 1274

Notes

"Joyful Giving". . . . . 1 Chronicles 26:27. 0464
"Generosity" . . . . 2 Chronicles 31:4-12 0500
Choices: Giving . . . . Luke 21:1-4. 1136
"More to Give" . . . . 2 Corinthians 9:6-15 1275
(See also GOD'S WILL)

GOALS *Selected passages*

God can help you achieve your goals . . . . Psalm 20:4; 37:5 . . . . .0598, 0607
Make God's goals your goals. . . . . Psalm 97:10 0642
The ultimate goal in life . . . . Ecclesiastes 12:13-14 0713
Keep focusing on your goals . . . . Philippians 3:12-20 1305
Make goals with God . . . . James 4:13-16 1366

Notes

"Going for the Goal?". . . . . Genesis 27:5-10. 0034
"Sharing the Vision". . . . . Nehemiah 2:16-18. 0525
(See also SUCCESS)

GODLY LIVING *Selected passages*

Having the favor of God and people . . . . 1 Samuel 2:26 0299
Jesus was honored by God and people . . . . Luke 2:40, 52. 1104
Your body belongs to God . . . . Romans 6:12-14. 1233
Guidelines for living . . . . Romans 13:9-14. 1241

Improving attitudes and thoughts . . . . Ephesians 4:17-24 1295
Christians have new lives . . . . Colossians 3:8-17 1310
(See also ATTITUDES, BELIEVING IN GOD, VALUES)

GOD'S WILL *Selected passages*
Commandments to keep . . . . Exodus 20 0089
What God wants you to do . . . . Micah 6:8 0983
The most important commandments to follow . . . . Matthew 22:37-40 1059
Why Paul was a missionary . . . . 2 Corinthians 1:1 1268
Advice about following God's will . . . . 1 Peter 4:1-3 .1374

Notes
I Wonder . . . . Genesis 4 0008
My Story . . . . Genesis 4 0011
"Your Life, His Design" . . . . 1 Samuel 9:1–10:16 0304
"When God Says No" . . . . 2 Samuel 7:1-16 0340
"God's Unstoppable Will" . . . . 2 Chronicles 18:1-32 0484
"Confidence" . . . . Habakkuk 3:19 0995
"Unstoppable" . . . . Matthew 2:1-18 1029
"How God Speaks" . . . . Acts 16:6 1205
(See also BELIEVING IN GOD, BIBLE, EXPECTATIONS, ADVICE, PRAYER)

GOSSIP *Selected passages*
The problem of false reports . . . . Exodus 23:1; Leviticus 19:16 . . 0093, 0134
Gossip hurts others . . . . Proverbs 11:13; 25:13 . . . . 0681, 0695
Gossip problem . . . . 1 Timothy 5:13 1329
Unkind words . . . . Titus 3:2 1342

Notes
"Gossip" . . . . Exodus 23:1-3 0093
"Lying" . . . . Proverbs 25:18 0695
My Story . . . . 1 Corinthians 10:13 1256
(See also COMMUNICATION, HONESTY, LYING)

GRATITUDE *(See THANKFULNESS)*

GREED *Selected passages*
Greed can be disguised as ambition . . . . Numbers 16:8-10 0166
Greed causes fighting . . . . Proverbs 28:22, 25 0698
God's anger over greed . . . . Isaiah 56:9-12 0780
Beware of greed . . . . Luke 12:15 .1123
What the greedy won't inherit . . . . Ephesians 5:5 1296

Notes
"A Selfish Ambition" . . . . Numbers 16:1-10 0166
"Blind Greed" . . . . Numbers 22:20-23 0174
Choices: Giving . . . . Luke 21:1-4 .1136
"Greed Guard" . . . . Revelation 18:11-19 1416
(See also GIVING, MONEY AND POSSESSIONS)

GROWING AS A CHRISTIAN *(See SPIRITUAL GROWTH)*

GUIDANCE *(See ADVICE)*

GUILT *Selected passages*
A high priest's wrongs brought guilt
   on everyone . . . . Leviticus 4:3 0115
How to remove guilt . . . . Psalm 19:12-13 0598
Forgiveness: the antidote to guilt . . . . Psalm 51 0615

Guilt of the world .... John 15:21-22 1169
Freedom from guilt .... Acts 13:38-39 1201
Getting rid of guilt .... Romans 3:21-24 1230

Notes
"Salvaged" .... Judges 16:28-30 0282
"Beyond Forgiveness?" .... 2 Chronicles 33:1-13 0503
(See also CONFESSION, FORGIVENESS)

HATRED *Selected passages*

Hatred is destructive .... Genesis 37 0047
Don't hate your family .... Leviticus 19:17 0134
Hatred can consume a person................... Esther 5:9-14 0547
Hate evil, but love people .... Psalm 139:21-24 0665
What God hates................................. Proverbs 6:16-19 0677
Hatred starts trouble .... Proverbs 10:12 0680
When to hate .... Ecclesiastes 3:8...................0705
The world will hate believers.................. John 15:18-25 1169

Notes
"Seeing Good Instead of Evil".................. 2 Samuel 1:17-27 0333
"Traces of God" .... Psalm 74:1-8 0628
My Story.. Luke 6:27-38 1111
Choices: Enemies .... Luke 10:25-37.................... 1119
(See also ANGER, ENEMIES, REVENGE)

HEAVEN *Selected passages*

Death will be gone forever..................... Isaiah 25:8 0747
Actions on earth affect the future .... Matthew 5:18-20 1033
The only way to heaven .... Matthew 7:13-14 1036
All believers will be in heaven.................. Luke 13:29 1125
Preparing a home in heaven .... John 14:1-7 1167
Let your actions count for eternity .... Colossians 3:1-6 1310
New heaven..................................... Revelation 21–22 1419

Notes
"The Only Way".................................. Revelation 7:10 1409
(See also ETERNAL LIFE/SALVATION)

HELL *Selected passages*

The way to hell .... Matthew 7:13-14 1036
Hell is real .... Luke 16:19-31 1130
How to escape from hell........................ John 14:6 1167
Punishment for unbelievers .... Romans 2:1-9......................1228
Hell is eternal separation from God .... 2 Thessalonians 1:7-9.............1322
Jesus holds the keys to hell.................... Revelation 1:17-18 1403
Hell is described as a lake of fire............... Revelation 20:14 1419

Notes
"No Excuse"..................................... Romans 1:18-20....................1227
"Terrible Trio" .... Revelation 13:1-18 1412

HOLY SPIRIT *Selected passages*

The Holy Spirit's involvement in the lives of
    Old Testament people .... Judges 3:10; 1 Samuel 16:13... 0264, 0315
Sinning against the Holy Spirit .... Matthew 12:31-32 1044
The Holy Spirit produces new life .... John 3:6-8 1149
Promise of the Holy Spirit .... John 14:26; 16:5-15 1168

Arrival of the Holy Spirit . . . . Acts 2:1-4 1182
The Holy Spirit frees us . . . . Romans 8:2 1234
The Holy Spirit makes us new . . . . 2 Corinthians 5:16-17 1272

Notes
"Holy Spirit" . . . . 1 Chronicles 12:18 0451
I Wonder. . . . . Psalm 51 0616
"Spirit Power" . . . . Micah 3:8 0980
"Insight" . . . . Luke 24:45 1143
"God with Us" . . . . John 3:6 1149
"Accurate Accounts". . . . . John 14:26 1169
"Last Minute Warnings". . . . . John 16:1-16 1169
Ultimate Issues: The 411 on the Holy Spirit . . . . . Acts 2 1182
"Every Part" . . . . Galatians 5:25 1288
"Be Bold" . . . . 2 Timothy 1:6-8 1334

HOMOSEXUALITY *Selected passages*
God forbids homosexual practices . . . . Leviticus 18:22. 0133
Homosexual practices are not God's design . . . . . Romans 1:26-27. 1228

Notes
Ultimate Issues: Homosexuality . . . . Romans 1:18-32 1227

HONESTY *Selected passages*
Honesty helps you enter God's presence. . . . . Psalm 24:1-6 0600
God hates dishonesty . . . . Proverbs 6:16-17 0677
The value of honesty. . . . . Proverbs 19:1; 28:6 . . . . .0688, 0697
Be honest in your evaluation of yourself . . . . Romans 12:3 .1240

Notes
"Warning!". . . . . Genesis 27:11-12 0035
Choices: Confront . . . . Ezekiel 2:3-7. 0869
"Honesty" . . . . Ezekiel 45:7-12. 0913
Choices: Honesty . . . . Micah 7:1-4. 0983
(See also INTEGRITY, LYING)

HONOR (RESPECT OR PRAISE) *Selected passages*
A command to honor parents . . . . Deuteronomy 5:16. 0198
Any honor we enjoy comes from God . . . . Ezra 7:27-28. .0517
Honoring God . . . . Psalm 29:1-2 0602
Delight in honoring others. . . . . Romans 12:10 1240
Honor your church leaders. . . . . 1 Thessalonians 5:12-13 1319

Notes
"God's Name" . . . . Exodus 20:7 0089
"Honoring Parents" . . . . Exodus 20:12 0090

HOPE *Selected passages*
Hope in God. . . . . Psalm 42:5-11. 0611
Hope because of Jesus . . . . 1 Corinthians 15:51-58. 1264
The hope of Jesus' return . . . . Revelation 22:12-21. 1421

Notes
"Growth" . . . . Leviticus 26:40-45. 0144
"Hope for the Future" . . . . Joshua 10:25 0241
"Hope". . . . . Isaiah 22:13-14 0745
"Restored Dreams". . . . . Ezekiel 40:1–42:20 0907
"Trapped" . . . . John 5:6 1153
"Live in Hope" . . . . 1 Peter 1:3-6 .1370
(See also FAITH)

HUMILITY *Selected passages*

Humility brings contentment..................... Psalm 131........................ 0661
Humility leads to wisdom...................... Proverbs 11:2...................... 0680
Who is the greatest?.......................... Matthew 20:20-28 1055
Jesus teaches about humility .... Luke 14:7-11.......................1126
Jesus' glory and humility compared .... Philippians 2:5-11 1303
God's greatness .... James 4:10 1375
Be humble and serve others .... 1 Peter 5:5........................1375

Notes
"A Humble Response" .... 1 Chronicles 17:16-27 0456
"Running the Show"......................... 2 Chronicles 30:1-9.............. 0499
"How Low Will You Go?"..................... Luke 14:7-11.......................1126
"Humility" .... John 1:30 1148
"Corrected" .... Galatians 4:1-16..................1285
"Different Seasons of Life, Same Advice" .... 1 Peter 5:5.......................1375
(See also SELF-CENTEREDNESS)

HYPOCRISY *Selected passages*
The problem of criticizing someone when
   you're also doing wrong .... Matthew 7:1-5 1035
Jesus' warnings about hypocrisy .... Matthew 7:21-23; 23 .... 1036, 1059
Avoid hypocrisy............................. Luke 12:1-5........................1123
Getting rid of hypocrisy .... 1 Peter 2:1........................1372

Notes
"Hypocrisy"................................ Isaiah 29:13-14 0752
"Faking It" .... Matthew 21:28-32 1057
My Story.................................. Mark 9–10 1086
"Motives"................................. Luke 11:37-54.....................1122
"Freedom" .... 1 Corinthians 8:1-13..............1255

INFERIORITY *Selected passages*
God created you .... Psalm 139:13-18................... 0664
What you're worth to God .... Matthew 10:29-30..................1041
The worth of your soul .... Mark 8:37.........................1082
We can move forward in spite of our
   shortcomings .... Philippians 3:12-14 1305

Notes
"True Worth" .... Genesis 1:1-26.................... 0005
"What's Wrong with Murder?" .... Genesis 9:5-6.....................0014
Ultimate Issue: Made in the Image of God........ Psalm 8..........................0591
"Chosen" .... Haggai 2:23 1005
"Valuable" .... Matthew 10:29-31 1041
"Real Value".............................. Luke 12:11-21 1123
(See also SELF-WORTH)

INTEGRITY *Selected passages*
Ruth's reputation .... Ruth 2:1-13 0291
Job's promise of integrity.................. Job 31:1..........................0575
Love good and hate evil .... Psalm 101:3-8 0643
A person of integrity doesn't compromise........ Psalm 119:113-117 0657
How to gain a good reputation .... Proverbs 3:1-4 0674
Respect for God is part of integrity............ Proverbs 8:13..................... 0678
Character is shown through actions........... Proverbs 20:11.................... 0689
A wife with a good reputation .... Proverbs 31:10-31 0702
Do what you say you'll do .... Matthew 5:33-37 1034

God recognizes good character............... Matthew 6:1-4 1034
Money and integrity .... Luke 16:8-13....................... 1128
Character is developed as you respond
    to problems .... Romans 5:3-4....................... 1231
Be an example to others .... Philippians 3:17................... 1305
Integrity in words .... James 5:12 1368

Notes
"God's Ambassador" .... Exodus 7:1 0073
"A New Role"............................... Joshua 2:1 0232
"Promise Keeper"........................... Joshua 14:6-13 0246
"Reputation".............................. 1 Chronicles 2:3.................. 0439
"Inner Beauty" .... Proverbs 19:22.................... 0689
"An Ideal Woman" .... Proverbs 31:10-31 0702
"Double-Minded"........................... Ezekiel 23:36-39 0889
"Risky Business" .... Mark 15:42-43 1097
"Fruit"................................... Galatians 5:22-23 1287
Choices: Integrity .... Titus 1:5-8; 2:11–3:8 1341
(See also HONESTY, LEADERSHIP, LYING)

JEALOUSY/ENVY *Selected passages*

The problem of jealousy.................... Genesis 37 0047
God's kind of jealousy .... Deuteronomy 5:9................... 0198
Physical effects of jealousy .... Proverbs 14:30.................... 0684
Long-lasting jealousy .... Song of Songs 8:6................. 0721
More of God's kind of jealousy .... 2 Corinthians 11:1-2.............. 1276
The outcome of sinful desires .... Galatians 5:19-20 1287

Notes
"Jealousy" .... Genesis 26:12-16.................. 0033
"Ugly Rage" .... Genesis 37:19-20.................. 0048
"From Jealousy to Joy" .... Acts 13:42-45..................... 1201
(See also COMPARISONS)

JUDGING OTHERS *(See CRITICISM/JUDGING OTHERS)*

JUSTICE *Selected passages*

Be just .... Psalm 58. 0619
Be fair in business....................... Proverbs 16:11.................... 0685
Life isn't always fair .... Ecclesiastes 9:11................. 0710
God will punish injustice .... Isaiah 3.......................... 0726

Notes
Choices: Injustice .... Psalm 73.......................... 0629
"Fair Treatment" .... Isaiah 11:1-5..................... 0736
"Promises" .... Isaiah 33:1....................... 0756
"Unfair?" .... Ezekiel 18:25-32 0883
Choices: Justice........................... Zechariah 7:8-14 1011

LAZINESS *Selected passages*

Laziness ruins a life .... Proverbs 6:6-11 0676
Laziness leads to poverty................. Proverbs 10:4-5;.................. 0679
                                           12:24; 28:19.............. 0682, 0698
Avoiding laziness .... 2 Thessalonians 3:6-15............ 1323

Notes
My Story.................................. Proverbs 6:6-11 0676
"Wasted Time" .... Proverbs 10:4-5 0679

"Laziness" .... Proverbs 26:13-16 0696
Choices: Laziness .... 2 Thessalonians 3:6-13............ 1323

LEADERSHIP *Selected passages*
How God prepared Moses for leadership .... Exodus 3:1–4:17 0069
Let God lead................................. Jeremiah 17:7-8 0814
Leaders must be servants .... Matthew 20:20-28 1055
An example of leadership .... John 13:1-17 1166
The gift of leadership .... Romans 12:8 1240
Qualities of church leaders .... 1 Timothy 3...................... 1327
Qualifications of a good leader.............. Titus 1:7-9...................... 1326

Notes
"Leadership Qualities" .... Deuteronomy 1:13-18 0192
"Priorities"................................. Judges 9:7-21 0272
My Story..................................... 2 Kings 14...................... 0418
"Integrity" .... 2 Chronicles 19:5-10 0486

LIFESTYLE *Selected passages*
A lifestyle chosen by God.................... Leviticus 18:1-5 0132
A godly lifestyle............................ Psalm 1......................... 0588
Following God's advice....................... Psalm 16:11 0595
Live to give glory to God.................... 1 Corinthians 6:20.............. 1252
A lifestyle change .... Ephesians 4:17-32............... 1295

Notes
"A Holy Reminder"............................ Leviticus 10:2.................. 0122
"Holy Design" .... Leviticus 11:44-45.............. 0124
"All Talk, No Action"........................ Psalm 78........................ 0631
Choices: Music .... 2 Timothy 3:1-5................. 1335
"Be an Example".............................. Titus 2:6-8..................... 1341
(See also REPUTATION)

LONELINESS *Selected passages*
What God does for the lonely .... Psalm 68:6...................... 0623
Hope in God.................................. Psalm 71:5 0626
Helping others can cure your loneliness ..... Proverbs 18:24.................. 0688
Never alone .... Hebrews 13:5 1360

Notes
"Keep on Praying" .... Psalm 10:1 0592
"Thinking of You" .... Psalm 115:12 0653
"True Friendship" .... Proverbs 18:24.................. 0688
My Story..................................... Ecclesiastes 2:11............... 0705
My Story..................................... Isaiah 46:4..................... 0770
"No Problems?" .... 1 Corinthians 7:29-40 1253

LOVE *Selected passages*
God's everlasting love .... Jeremiah 31:3................... 0829
Loving enemies .... Matthew 5:43-48................. 1034
The greatest commandment .... Matthew 22:37-40................ 1059
God's love for the world..................... John 3:16 1149
Never separated from God's love .... Romans 8:31-39.................. 1235
Love demands that we give of ourselves ...... Romans 12:9-21.................. 1240
Real love.................................... 1 Corinthians 13:4-7............ 1261

Notes
"Love vs Lust" .... 2 Samuel 13:1-15 0345
"Priceless Love" .... Song of Songs 8:6-7 0721

"Two Simple Rules" .... Mark 12:29-34 1089
"Tough Love" .... Luke 6:27-36 1112
My Story .... Luke 6:27-38 1111
"Active Love" .... John 13:34-35 1167
"In Debt" .... Romans 13:8 1241
Ultimate Issues: Marriage .... 1 Corinthians 7 1254
"Real Love" .... 1 Corinthians 13:4-7 1261
"A Choice" .... 1 John 2:9-11 1384
"A Test" .... 1 John 4:20-21 1388

LYING *Selected passages*
Lying only makes problems worse .... Genesis 12:11-20 0017
God commands us not to lie .... Exodus 20:16 0090
God hates lying .... Proverbs 6:12-19 0676
Lying comes from the heart .... Matthew 15:16-20 1048

Notes
"Lying" .... Genesis 18:10-15 0022
Choices: Lying .... 1 Samuel 15:1-23 0313
"Lying" .... 1 Samuel 21:2 0321
"Lying Lips" .... Psalm 12:2-4 0593
"Lying" .... Proverbs 25:18 0695
"A Comfortable Lie" .... Ezekiel 13:1-3 0877
(See also COMMUNICATION, HONESTY, INTEGRITY)

MAKING MISTAKES *Selected passages*
The sin that led to all sin .... Genesis 3 0007
Unresolved anger leads to bigger problems .... Genesis 4:3-12 0009
Failure as a result of sin .... Joshua 7 0237
Israel messes up .... Judges 2:17-19 0262
A king messes up .... 1 Kings 11:1-11 0379
God's rules and temptation .... Psalm 119:11 0654
Refusing to help .... Matthew 25:45-46 1062
Recognize and learn from failures .... Luke 22:55-62 1138
We've all blown it .... Romans 3:23 1230
Rescued from a mess .... Romans 5:8-21 1232
The price of sin .... Romans 6:23 1233
Can't help making mistakes? .... Romans 7:15-25 1234
Avoiding what's right .... James 4:17 1375

Notes
"Big Mistake" .... Genesis 4:3-10 0009
"No Small Thing" .... Joshua 7:11 0238
"Defective Government" .... Judges 19:30 0285
"Failure" .... 1 Samuel 15:13-14 0313
"Learning from Mistakes" .... 1 Kings 16:1-7 0387
Choices: Pornography .... Job 31:1 0577
"Stolen Food" .... Proverbs 9:1-17 0679
"Repeating" .... Jeremiah 44:9-10 0842
"God's View of Success" .... Jeremiah 52:34 0855
I Wonder .... Ezekiel 14:1-5 0875
"A Bitter Failure" .... Luke 22:62 1139
(See also CONSCIENCE, CONSEQUENCES, EXCUSES, TEMPTATION)

MARRIAGE *Selected passages*
Marriage joins a man and woman .... Genesis 2:18-24 0007
Scenes from a marriage .... Genesis 29 0036
Newlyweds need a strong start .... Deuteronomy 24:5 0216

Adultery is destructive . . . . Proverbs 6:32-35 0677
Characteristics of a good wife . . . . Proverbs 31:10-31 0702
Marriage advice. . . . . 1 Corinthians 7 1252
Submission in marriage . . . . Ephesians 5:21-24. 1297
Characteristics of a good husband . . . . Ephesians 5:25-30. 1297
How Jesus' relationship with the church
  is like a marriage . . . . 2 Corinthians 11:2; 1276
                                                         Ephesians 5:25-30. 1297

Notes
"Marriage". . . . . Genesis 2:18-24. 0007
"Marriage Laws" . . . . Ezra 9:1-15 0518
Choices: Adultery . . . . Hosea 2 0939
Ultimate Issues: Divorce . . . . Malachi 2:16 .1022
"Divorce" . . . . Luke 16:18 1130
Ultimate Issues: Marriage . . . . 1 Corinthians 7 1254
"To Marry or Not" . . . . 1 Corinthians 7:1-9. 1252
"No Problems?" . . . . 1 Corinthians 7:29-40 1253
"Real Love" . . . . 1 Corinthians 13:4-7. 1261
(See also FAMILY, SEXUALITY)

MATERIALISM *(See GREED, MONEY AND POSSESSIONS)*

MEANING/PURPOSE *Selected passages*

Meaninglessness . . . . Ecclesiastes 1 0704
A search for meaning . . . . Ecclesiastes 2 0704
The purpose Jesus gives. . . . . John 10:10 1161
Freedom gives new meaning to life . . . . Galatians 3:28-29 1285
Serving others provides gives life meaning . . . . . Galatians 5:13 1287
The believer's purpose. . . . . 1 Thessalonians 2:4 1316

Notes
Choices: Living for the Moment . . . . 2 Samuel 11–12 0343
"The Meaning of Life" . . . . Ecclesiastes 1:8-11. 0704
My Story. . . . . Ecclesiastes 2:11 0705
"An Endless Party?" . . . . Ecclesiastes 2:24-26. 0705
I Wonder. . . . . Ecclesiastes 11:9–12:8 0711
Ultimate Issues: Is There Meaning to Life? . . . . . . Ecclesiastes 12:13 0712
"At Ease" . . . . Isaiah 32:9-13 0755

MONEY AND POSSESSIONS *Selected passages*

An abundance of possessions can cause pride. . . . Deuteronomy 8:11-20 0201
All good things come from God. . . . . 1 Chronicles 29:10-17 0467
Money gotten dishonestly causes pain . . . . Proverbs 15:27. 0685
Choosing between God and money . . . . Matthew 6:19-24. 1035
A hard choice. . . . . Matthew 19:16-30; 1054
                                                         Mark 10:17-31. 1085
Life is more than what you own. . . . . Luke 12:13-32. 1123
Sharing possessions . . . . Acts 2:42-47. .1184
The cure for love of money. . . . . 1 Timothy 6:10-19 1331
Favoritism for the wealthy . . . . James 2:1-9 1365

Notes
"Dividing the Spoils" . . . . Numbers 31:25-30. 0185
"What's More Important: Gain or God?" . . . . 2 Kings 5:20-27 0407
My Story. . . . . Ecclesiastes 2:11 0705
"Money Matters" . . . . Ecclesiastes 10:19 0711
"Money". . . . . Ezekiel 7:19 0873
"More and More Stuff?". . . . . Hosea 10:1 0946

I Wonder..................................... Malachi 3:8-10...................1021
"Barriers"................................... Mark 10:17-23...................1085
"Money Cycle".............................. 1 Timothy 6:6-21 1330
Choices: Materialism .... 1 Timothy 6:9-10 1328
My Story.................................... Hebrews 13:5....................1361
(See also GREED)

OBEDIENCE *Selected passages*

Noah obeyed God .... Genesis 6:9-22 0012
What God expects............................ Exodus 23:13....................0093
A will to obey.............................. Psalm 119:115 0657
The wise are obedient .... Proverbs 28:7....................0697
Obedience is a sign of friendship with Jesus...... John 15:9-17 1168
Obey leaders .... Romans 13:1;....................1240
                                            Hebrews 13:17...................1360
Peter's advice .... 1 Peter 1:14.....................1371
Obedience is seen through actions .... 1 John 2:3-11....................1384

Notes

I Wonder................................... Genesis 4........................0008
"Willing to Go" .... Genesis 12:2.....................0017
"Passing the Test"......................... Genesis 22:1-2 0027
My Story................................... Leviticus 26 0143
"Know It and Apply It" .... 1 Kings 11:1-12 0379
"Lip Service".............................. 2 Kings 10:30-31 0414
"Foundation of Obedience"................. 2 Kings 22:1-2 0430
"In Pursuit" .... 1 Chronicles 10:13-14 0449
"Exact Instructions"...................... 1 Chronicles 15:13-15............0453
"Conviction" .... Esther 3:2.......................0545
"The Courage to Stand Alone" .... Jeremiah 38:9-13.................0837
"A Difficult Task"......................... Hosea 1:1-3......................0938
"Faking It" .... Matthew 21:28-32................1057
(See also AUTHORITY, BELIEVING IN GOD)

OCCULT, THE *Selected passages*

No to witchcraft........................... Leviticus 19:26..................0134
Bad results of the occult................... Leviticus 20:6-8.................0135
God forbids occult practices .... Deuteronomy 18:9-14 0211
Saul consults a witch..................... 1 Samuel 28:3-19.................0328
Horoscopes are worthless .... Jeremiah 10:2-3 0806
Ephesians burn witchcraft books .... Acts 19:11-20 1211

Notes

"Just Say No to the Occult" .... Leviticus 20:6...................0135
Choices: Astrology .... Deuteronomy 4:19; 17:2-5 0196
"A Dangerous Fascination" .... Deuteronomy 18:9-14 0210
My Story................................... Deuteronomy 18:9-14 0211
"Knowing and Doing What's Right" .... 1 Samuel 28:3-25 0328
"Occult".................................... 2 Kings 21:1-18..................0428
I Wonder................................... Isaiah 47:12-15..................0771
"The Power of His Name".................... Acts 19:13-19 1211
My Story................................... Acts 19:13-20 1211
I Wonder................................... Galatians 5:21 1288

PARENTS *Selected passages*

A commandment with a promise .... Exodus 20:12....................0090
Result of cursing parents.................. Leviticus 20:9 0135

Accepting discipline from parents . . . . Proverbs 13:1; 15:5. 0628
Family relations. . . . . Ephesians 6:1-4. 1297

Notes
"Parents and Choices". . . . . Genesis 26:34-35 0026
"Honoring Parents" . . . . Exodus 20:12. 0090
"A Parent's Advice" . . . . Numbers 30:3-5. 0183
My Story. . . . . Deuteronomy 5:16. 0198
"Listen Up!". . . . . Proverbs 6:20-24. 0677
I Wonder. . . . . Matthew 10:34-39 1041
My Story. . . . . Luke 15:11-32 1127
My Story. . . . . Ephesians 6:1-3. 1297
My Story. . . . . Colossians 3:20. 1312
(See also AUTHORITY, HONOR)

PARTYING *Selected passages*
God sees everything. . . . . Proverbs 5:21. 0676
Advice concerning wild parties . . . . Romans 13:13-14 1241
Honor God in all you do . . . . 1 Corinthians 10:31. 1257
Out of control behavior . . . . Galatians 5:19-21. 1287
Putting wild parties in the past. . . . . 1 Peter 4:1-3 1374

Notes
My Story. . . . . Isaiah 7:9 0732
I Wonder. . . . . Mark 2:13-17. 1072
My Story. . . . . Romans 2:6-8 1229
Choices: PARTIES . . . . 1 Peter 4:3-6. .1374
(See also DRINKING, PEER PRESSURE)

PATIENCE *Selected passages*
Consequences of lacking patience . . . . 1 Samuel 13:8-14. 0309
One of the fruit of the Spirit. . . . . Galatians 5:22-23 1287
Put on patience . . . . Colossians 3:12 1311
Patient endurance of suffering . . . . James 5:10-11. 1368
How patience develops . . . . 2 Peter 1:5-9. .1378

Notes
"Worth the Wait". . . . . Genesis 29:20-28 0038
"Patience" . . . . 2 Samuel 5:4-5. 0337
"God's Timing" . . . . Psalm 75:2 0630
"Wait for It" . . . . Habakkuk 1:1–2:3 0992
"Overcome". . . . . Romans 5:2-4. 1231
"God's Time" . . . . Revelation 6:9-11. 1408

PEACE *Selected passages*
God's gift of peace . . . . Psalm 29:11; 0603
. . . . Galatians 5:22-23 1287
Jesus promises peace. . . . . John 14:27 1168
Why we have peace . . . . Romans 5:1. 1231
Live in peace with others . . . . Romans 12:18 1240
Steps to gaining peace. . . . . Philippians 4:6-7. 1305
Peace of Christ. . . . . Colossians 3:15 1311

Notes
"Best Interests" . . . . Psalm 23:1-3 0600
"Praying for Others". . . . . Psalm 122:6-9 0659

PEER PRESSURE *Selected passages*
When you're feeling pressured . . . . Psalm 119:143 0658
Some friendships are destructive. . . . . Proverbs 18:24. 0688

When you take a stand .... Luke 6:22-23 1110
Don't copy the world. .... Romans 12:1-2 1239
Develop faith, not just appearance. .... Colossians 2:23 1310
Life's pressures can strengthen us .... James 1:2-4 1364

Notes
Choices: Peer Pressure. .... Exodus 23:2 0093
"Molder or Molded?" .... Leviticus 18:3. 0132
"Peer Pressure". .... Judges 2:11-15 0262
"Peers". .... 2 Chronicles 10:1-14 0479
Choices: Opposition .... Nehemiah 4 0527
I Wonder. .... Proverbs 1:10 0672
My Story. .... Isaiah 7:9 0732
"Giving In" .... Matthew 14:1-12 1047
(See also CONFORMITY, POPULARITY, TEMPTATION)

PERSECUTION *(See SUFFERING)*

PERSEVERANCE/PERSISTENCE *Selected passages*
Keep living for God .... 1 Corinthians 9:24-27 1256
Persist in doing right .... Galatians 6:9-10 1288
Keep working toward your potential. .... Philippians 3:12-14 1305
Be persistent in prayer. .... Colossians 4:2 1312
Persist in prayer and joyfulness .... 1 Thessalonians 5:16-18 1319
Persevering through suffering .... 1 Peter 5:10. 1375
How you can endure .... 2 Peter 1:5-9. 1378

Notes
"The Diligence Payoff" .... Genesis 31:38-42. 0041
"Keep Talking" .... Exodus 5:1-3. 0071
"Stubborn" .... 2 Samuel 2:21-24 0334
"Don't Quit!" .... Jeremiah 25:1-6 0822
"Tough Talk" .... Ezekiel 2:1-8. 0868
Choices: Perseverance .... Jude. 1398
(See also POTENTIAL, PRAYER)

POPULARITY *Selected passages*
The meaninglessness of chasing
    after popularity .... Ecclesiastes 4:13-16 0707
Gaining and losing .... Mark 8:36-38. 1082
Persecution or popularity—a choice. .... John 15:18-25 1169
Result of friendship with the world. .... James 4:4 1366
Some things won't last forever .... 1 John 2:15-17 1385

Notes
"Warnings" .... Leviticus 26:1. 0143
"Popularity". .... 1 Samuel 18:5-18 0318
"The Public Eye" .... 2 Samuel 8:15 0341
"Fame" .... 1 Chronicles 11:9 0449
My Story. .... Mark 9–10 1086
(See also CONFORMITY, PEER PRESSURE)

PORNOGRAPHY

Notes
Choices: Pornography .... Job 31:1. 0577
(See also SEXUAL SIN)

POSSESSIONS *(See GREED, MONEY AND POSSESSIONS)*

POTENTIAL *Selected passages*
Samson wasted his potential . . . . Judges 13:2–16:21 0277
God looks at the heart . . . . 1 Samuel 16:7 0314
God helps you reach your potential . . . . Philippians 1:6 1303
What you can do through Christ . . . . Philippians 4:13 .1306

Notes
"Unlikely" . . . . Luke 1:26-55 1101
(See also ABILITIES)

PRAYER *Selected passages*
Praying for help . . . . Psalm 3 0589
God listens . . . . Psalm 4:3 0589
Effective prayer takes persistence . . . . Matthew 7:7-12 .1035
God hears your prayers . . . . Matthew 21:21-22 1057
How to pray . . . . Luke 11:1-13 1121
Persist in prayer and joyfulness . . . . 1 Thessalonians 5:16-18 1319
What prayer does . . . . James 5:16-18 1368

Notes
"Prayer Power" . . . . Exodus 32:9-14 .0102
"Get Ready" . . . . Leviticus 16:1-25 0130
"Directions" . . . . 1 Samuel 28:15 0328
I Wonder . . . . 1 Kings 3:3-14 0369
"Prayer Requests" . . . . 1 Kings 8:54-61 .0377
"Pure Motives" . . . . 2 Kings 2:9 0402
"Prayer" . . . . 2 Kings 19:1-37 0426
"He Always Listens" . . . . Psalm 4:1-3 0589
"Panic and Praise" . . . . Psalm 70:1-4 0626
"The Answer" . . . . Isaiah 37:8-10 0759
"Radical Change" . . . . Isaiah 38:1-8 0761
"God-Centered Prayer" . . . . Daniel 9:1-19 0932
"Anything We Want?" . . . . Matthew 21:21-22 1057
"Your Prayer, God's Power" . . . . Mark 9:23 1083
"Strength" . . . . Acts 4:24-30 1187
"How God Speaks" . . . . Acts 16:6 1205
"How to Pray" . . . . Colossians 1:9-14 1309
I Wonder . . . . 2 Timothy 4:10 .1336
Ultimate Issues: Prayer . . . . Hebrews 4:16 1350
(See also ADVICE, CHOICES)

PREJUDICE *Selected passages*
Pride causes prejudice . . . . Esther 3:1-6 0545
Prejudging someone makes us blind
 to God's truth . . . . Mark 6:1-6 1078
Helping someone from another culture . . . . Luke 10:25-37 1120
God shows no partiality . . . . Acts 10:34-43 1196
We are all the same before God . . . . Galatians 3:28-29 1285
Let Christ take away prejudice . . . . Ephesians 2:11-16 1293

Notes
Choices: Prejudice . . . . John 4:1-42 1152
"Crossing Barriers" . . . . John 4:7-9 1151
"Differences" . . . . Galatians 3:28 1285
"The Only Way" . . . . Revelation 7:10 .1409
(See also HATRED)

PRIDE *Selected passages*
God hates pride..................................... Proverbs 6:16-17; 16:5 .... 0677, 0685
Pride ends in shame................................ Proverbs 11:2 0680
Pride starts arguments and ruins friendships..... Proverbs 13:10 0682
Pride ends in destruction.......................... Proverbs 18:12; 29:23.........0688, 0699
Avoid pride about leaders .... 1 Corinthians 3:20-21 1249

Notes
"Towering Pride"................................... Genesis 11:4...................... 0016
"Vanity" .... 2 Samuel 17:11................... .0352
"The Pull of Pride" .... 2 Chronicles 26:1-16 0494
"The Problem of Pride" .... Isaiah 9:8-10 0734
"Credit Where Credit Is Due" .... Ezekiel 29:9-12 0895
"Closed Ears" .... Zephaniah 3:1-2................... 1000
I Wonder: Can I be proud of doing my best? ...... Luke 18 1132
Choices: Pride .... Acts 12:20-23.....................1199
"Judging".. 1 Corinthians 4:1-6 1250
"Admit It" .... 2 Corinthians 7:11 1274
(See also COMPARISONS, HUMILITY)

PRIORITIES *(See VALUES)*

PURITY *Selected passages*
Blessings of a pure life........................... Psalm 1:1-3....................... 0588
Asking for purity .... Psalm 86:11 0636
How to stay pure .... Psalm 119:9-20 0654
Purity starts in the heart .... Matthew 5:27-30 1033
How to gain purity................................. John 17:17........................1170
Work toward purity .... 2 Corinthians 7:1 1273
Hindrances to purity .... Philippians 3:7-11 1304

Notes
"Why Wait?" .... Song of Songs 4:12 0718
"Pollution".. Ezekiel 20:30-38 0885
I Wonder.. 1 Timothy 6:11-12.................1326
(See also MARRIAGE, SEXUAL SIN)

REJECTION *Selected passages*
Suffering unfair rejection......................... Judges 11:1-2 0274
When abandoned by parents, count on God ...... Psalm 27:10 0602
God won't reject his people........................ Psalm 94:14....................... .0641
Jesus' rejection foretold.......................... Isaiah 53..........................0777
A prophet is rejected in his hometown........... Matthew 13:53-58 1047
Those who reject believers reject Jesus .... Luke 10:16 1119

Notes
"Rejection" .... Judges 11:1-29 0275
My Story.. Micah 4:6-13 0981
"This Means War" .... Acts 5:17-21 1188

RELATIONSHIPS *Selected passages*
Avoiding an unequal relationship................. 2 Corinthians 6:14-18 1273
Ask God for wisdom .... James 1:5 1364

Notes
Ultimate Issues: Date Rape .... 2 Samuel 13 0346
Choices: Dating.................................. 1 Kings 11:1-13 0380
My Story.. Romans 12:19 1240

My Story . . . . 1 Corinthians 13:4-7 1261
My Story . . . . 2 Peter 1:5-8 1378
My Story . . . . 1 John 1:8-10 1385

RELIGIONS *Selected passages*

How to know that a message is from God . . . . Deuteronomy 18:20-22 0212
The problems of false prophets . . . . Jeremiah 23:9-10 0820
How God deals with false teachers . . . . Ezekiel 13:1-9 0876
Beware of false prophets . . . . Matthew 7:15 1036
Wise people evaluate the messages
    they hear . . . . 1 Thessalonians 5:21-23; 1319
                                                 1 John 4:1-6 1387
Compare new ideas with God's Word . . . . 2 Timothy 3:6-7 1335
False teachers deceive people . . . . 2 John 1392

Notes
Ultimate Issues: Other Religions . . . . Judges 2 0263
Choices: Cults . . . . 2 Peter 2:12-22 1379
"Know the Truth!" . . . . 2 John 7-11 1392
(See also BELIEVING IN GOD, BIBLE)

REPUTATION *(See INTEGRITY, LIFESTYLE)*

RESPONSIBILITY *Selected passages*

Christians are responsible to light up
    a dark world . . . . Matthew 5:13-16 1032
Use resources responsibly . . . . Matthew 25:14-30 1062
Responsibilities toward other Christians . . . . Romans 14 1241
Responsibilities of church leaders . . . . 1 Timothy 3 1326

Notes
"Full Responsibility" . . . . Genesis 43:8-9 0055
"Righting Wrongs" . . . . Exodus 22:1-15 0092
Choices: Responsibility . . . . Joshua 1:5-9 0231
"Hide and Seek" . . . . 1 Samuel 10:22-24 0307
"Basic Training" . . . . Psalm 78:71-72 0633

REVENGE *Selected passages*

Don't seek revenge . . . . Leviticus 19:18 0134
How to help others avoid revenge . . . . 1 Samuel 25:23-33 0325
Let God fight your battles for you . . . . Psalm 35:1-10 0606
Christians should pay back evil with good . . . . Matthew 5:38-48 1034
Don't bear a grudge . . . . Mark 11:25 1087
Avoid payback . . . . Romans 12:17-18 1240

Notes
"Set Things Right" . . . . Numbers 5:5-8 0153
"Revenge" . . . . Numbers 16:22-27 0167
"Boomerang" . . . . Judges 15:1-20 0279
"Revenge" . . . . Psalm 7:1-6 0590
Choices: Vengeance . . . . Nahum 1:2-8 0988
My Story . . . . Matthew 5:38-39 1033
My Story . . . . Romans 12:19 1240
"An Alternative to Revenge" . . . . 1 Peter 3:8-12 1373
(See also ANGER, HATRED)

SALVATION *(See BELIEVING IN GOD, ETERNAL LIFE, FAITH, FORGIVENESS)*

SELF-CONTROL *Selected passages*
Discipline and commitment.................... Luke 14:25-33..................1126
Discipline yourself for endurance............. 1 Corinthians 9:24-27 1256

Notes
"Follow Through" .... Ezekiel 5:1-13 0871
"Sign of Love"......................... Amos 9:8 0966
Choices: Consistency .... Hebrews 12:1-4 1359
"Fruit"................................ Galatians 5:22-23 1287
My Story.............................. Revelation 3; 14:7 1413

SELF-WORTH *Selected passages*
Made in God's image .... Genesis 1:26-27................. 0005
A little lower than the angels............. Psalm 8:3-5 0591
Your worth to God .... Luke 12:7 1123
God gave his Son for you .... John 3:16 1149
Nothing can separate you from God's love .... Romans 8:35-39 1236

Notes
"True Worth" .... Genesis 1:1-26 0005
"What's Wrong with Murder?" .... Genesis 9:5-6...................0014
Ultimate Issues: Made in the Image of God....... Psalm 8........................0591
"Chosen"............................... Haggai 2:23 1005
"Valuable"............................. Matthew 10:29-31...............1044
"Real Value"............................ Luke 12:13-21 1123
(See also INFERIORITY)

SERVING GOD AND OTHERS *Selected passages*
Serve God .... Joshua 24:14 0256
Serve as Christ served .... Matthew 20:28 1056
Helping a neighbor...................... Luke 10:25-37..................1120
An example of service.................... John 13:1-17 1166
Undistracted service..................... 1 Corinthians 7:35 1254
Serving others......................... Galatians 5:13 1287

Notes
"Separating the Good from the Baaaad"........ Matthew 25:31-46 1063
"Equals"............................... 1 Corinthians 11:3-4...............1258
(See also COMPASSION)

SEXUAL SIN *Selected passages*
Rape.................................. Genesis 34; 1 Samuel 13...... 0044, 0309
Judah's injustice .... Genesis 38.................... 0049
How Joseph avoided sexual temptation......... Genesis 39:6-12 0051
David and Bathsheba..................... 2 Samuel 11–12 0343
How to avoid it .... Proverbs 2:16-19; 5 .... 0673, 0675
The price of sexual sin .... Romans 1:18-32 1227
Don't give in........................... Ephesians 5:3;..................1296
                                        Colossians 3:5; 1310
                                        1 Thessalonians 4:3-5.............1318

Notes
"Passion"............................... Genesis 34:1-4..................0044
"Sex Roles" .... Deuteronomy 22:5 0214
"The Purpose for Sex" .... Deuteronomy 23:17-18 0215
Ultimate Issues: Date Rape .... 2 Samuel 13 0346
Choices: Compromise.................... Judges 16 0282
Ultimate Issues: Sexual Morality .... Ruth 3 0293
Choices: Pornography .... Job 31:1.......................0577

My Story . . . . Psalm 13 0593
The Real Truth about Sex . . . . Song of Songs 7:1-2 0721
Choices: Adultery . . . . Hosea 2 0939
"Warning!" . . . . 1 Corinthians 6:13-20 1251
My Story . . . . 1 John 1:8-10 1385
"A Serious Problem" . . . . Revelation 2:20 1404
*(See also DATING, EXCUSES, HOMOSEXUALITY, MAKING MISTAKES, MARRIAGE, PEER
PRESSURE, PURITY, TEMPTATION)*

SPIRITUAL GIFTS *(See ABILITIES)*

SPIRITUAL GROWTH *Selected passages*
Learn God's commands . . . . Deuteronomy 11:16-21 0204
Listening to advice can cause you to grow . . . . Proverbs 13:14 0682
Growth involves discipline. Lamentations 3:27-33 0862
Sticking with Jesus causes growth . . . . John 15 1168
Grow in faith . . . . Colossians 2:7 1309
Grow in knowledge of God . . . . 1 Peter 2:2; 2 Peter 3:18 . . . . 1372, 1381

Notes
"Growth" . . . . 1 Samuel 16:19-21 0315
My Story . . . . Ecclesiastes 5:1-7 0707
I Wonder. . . . . Ezekiel 14:1-11 0878
"Compare" . . . . Acts 17:11 1208
"A Reasonable Argument" . . . . Acts 18:24-28 1210
"Overcome" . . . . Romans 5:2-4 1231
I Wonder . . . . Ephesians 4:14-15 1295
"Little by Little" . . . . Ephesians 4:17-24 1295
I Wonder . . . . 2 Timothy 4:10 1336
(See also BIBLE, DISCIPLINE)

STEALING *Selected passages*
Don't steal . . . . Exodus 20:15 0090
                                                           Leviticus 19:11 0133
Stealing from God . . . . Malachi 3:8-10 1023
Work instead of stealing. . . . . Ephesians 4:28 1296

Notes
Choices: Stealing . . . . Leviticus 19 .0136

STRESS *(See SUFFERING, WORRY/STRESS)*

SUCCESS *Selected passages*
Achievements without God can end in disaster . . . Genesis 11:1-9 0016
Good advice can bring success . . . . Proverbs 15:22 0685
Commit all your work to the Lord . . . . Proverbs 16:3 0685
Be humble and respect God . . . . Proverbs 22:4. 0691
Admit your mistakes. . . . . Proverbs 28:13. 0697
God is the source of power and success . . . . 2 Corinthians 3:5 1270

Notes
"Two Simple Commands" . . . . Leviticus 19:18 0134
"From Failure to Success" . . . . Deuteronomy 34:10-12 0228
"Successful Failures" . . . . 1 Chronicles 5:23-26 0443
"Project Follow-Up" . . . . Nehemiah 7:1-4 0529
"False Security" . . . . Psalm 30:6-7 0603
My Story . . . . Ecclesiastes 2:11 0705
"God's View of Success" . . . . Jeremiah 52:34 0855
"Remember" . . . . Hosea 12:1-10 0947

"By His Spirit" .... Zechariah 4:6 1010
Choices: Success .... Mark 9:33-37 1084
(See also GOALS, THANKFULNESS)

SUFFERING Selected passages
Be an encouragement to those who
    are suffering .... Job 16:1-6 0566
God is our hope .... Psalm 3 0589
Getting rest from your troubles .... Matthew 11:28-30 1043
Jesus' followers will suffer .... John 16:33; 1170
    Philippians 1:29-30 1303
God can bring good from any problem .... Romans 8:28 1235
Suffering can bring you closer to God .... Philippians 3:7-11 1305
Respond to suffering as Christ did .... 1 Peter 4:1-2 1374
Persevering through suffering .... 1 Peter 5:10 1375

Notes
"Runaway" .... Genesis 16:6-14 0021
"Stressed Out" .... Exodus 16:1-3 0084
"Punishment" .... Judges 10:7-10 0274
"The Truth Hurts" .... 1 Samuel 5:1-7 0302
"Outnumbered" .... 1 Samuel 14:1-6 0311
"Trusting God" .... 2 Chronicles 32:1-8 0501
"How Unfair!" .... Job 10:1 0561
"Deep Purposes" .... Job 23:8-14 0571
Ultimate Issues: Suffering and Evil .... Job 18–41 0560
I Wonder .... Psalms 5, 6, 10, 13, 88 0594
"Short-/Long-Term Rewards" .... Psalm 37:1-40 0607
My Story .... Psalm 46:10 0613
"Be Prepared" .... Psalm 79:10 0633
"A Shelter" .... Psalm 91:1-16 0640
"Troubles" .... Psalm 106:40-42 0648
"Fix Your Eyes" .... Isaiah 26:3 0747
"Strength" .... Isaiah 40:29-31 0763
"Justice for the Suffering" .... Isaiah 61:1-3 0784
My Story .... John 1:10-12 1147
"Suffering" .... John 9:1-3 1159
"Persecution" .... John 9:28-34 1160
My Story .... John 14:27 1168
"Accused" .... Acts 6:8–7:60 1189
"Productive Discomfort" .... Acts 8:4 1192
"Comfort" .... 2 Corinthians 1:3-7 1268
My Story .... 2 Corinthians 1:3-7 1269
"The Purpose of Problems" .... 2 Corinthians 4:8-18 1271
"Suffering" .... Philippians 1:29-30 1303
"Troubles" .... 2 Thessalonians 1:5 1322
"Suffering" .... 1 Peter 4:16 1375
(See also DEPRESSION/DISCOURAGEMENT, TRUST)

SUICIDE (See DEPRESSION)

TALKING ABOUT GOD Selected passages
Believers provide light .... Matthew 5:14-16 1032
Commanded to spread the gospel .... Matthew 28:19-20 1068
    Mark 16:15 1098
The Holy Spirit helps you know what to say .... John 14:26 1168
Not ashamed of the gospel .... Romans 1:16 1227

Find common ground with others . . . . 1 Corinthians 9:22 1256
Tell others about Jesus . . . . 2 Timothy 4:1-8 1336

Notes
"Chameleon or Champion for God?" . . . . Genesis 19:14 0023
"Opportunity" . . . . Genesis 40:8 0051
My Story . . . . Exodus 5–11 .0071
Choices: Outspoken . . . . 2 Kings 6:24–7:11 0408
I Wonder . . . . 2 Kings 7:3-15 .0410
My Story . . . . Proverbs 29:25 0698
"God through Your Eyes" . . . . Isaiah 43:10-11 0766
I Wonder . . . . Hosea 13:6 0948
"Commissioned" . . . . Matthew 28:18-20 1068
"Someone You Should Know" . . . . Mark 2:14-17 1072
I Wonder . . . . Mark 5:1-20 1076
"Reach Out" . . . . John 12:37-38 1165
My Story . . . . Acts 4:13 1187
"Accused" . . . . Acts 6:8–7:60 1189
"Worth It" . . . . Acts 17:22-34 .1209
"Something in Common" . . . . Acts 22:1-5 1216
My Story . . . . 1 Peter 4 1373
(See also COMMUNICATION, BELIEVING IN GOD)

TEMPTATION *Selected passages*

A prayer to avoid temptation . . . . Psalm 19:13 0598
How to avoid temptation . . . . Proverbs 7:1-5 0677
Using the Word to combat temptation . . . . Matthew 4:1-11 1031
God will not allow temptations you
    cannot withstand . . . . 1 Corinthians 10:13 1257
Run from temptation . . . . 2 Timothy 2:22 .1335
Jesus helps during times of temptation . . . . Hebrews 2:16-18 1349
Jesus understands our weakness . . . . Hebrews 4:14-16 1351
God is not the cause of temptation . . . . James 1:12-16 1364

Notes
Choices: Peer Pressure . . . . Exodus 23:2 0093
"Keep Away" . . . . Leviticus 11:8 0123
"Stay Alert" . . . . Judges 8:31 0272
"Temptation" . . . . 2 Samuel 11:1-4 0343
"Be Prepared" . . . . 2 Chronicles 14:1-8 0482
"An Isolated Incident?" . . . . Psalm 51:4 0615
"Where Do You Stand?" . . . . Daniel 1:1-8 0920
"Alert" . . . . Matthew 26:40 .1064
I Wonder . . . . Romans 7:15–8:2 1234
"Temptation" . . . . 1 Corinthians 10:13 1257
My Story . . . . 1 Corinthians 10:13 1256
"Snowball" . . . . James 1:12-15 1364
"Don't Give In!" . . . . 1 John 3:8-10 1387
(See also MAKING MISTAKES, SEXUAL SIN)

THANKFULNESS *Selected passages*

A way to say thanks . . . . Psalm 100 0643
Jesus teaches by example to be thankful . . . . Mark 8:6 1081
Gratitude for a miracle . . . . Luke 17:11-19 .1130
A reason to thank God . . . . Ephesians 2:4-10 1293
Songs of gratitude . . . . Colossians 3:16-17 1311
Always be thankful . . . . 1 Thessalonians 5:18 1319

Notes
"Gratitude Attitude" .... Numbers 11:1-6 0160
"Thank You" .... 1 Chronicles 16:7-36 0454
"Praise List" .... Psalm 103:3-18 0644
"God at Work" .... Isaiah 38:9-20 0761
(See also BLESSINGS)

TIME WITH GOD *Selected passages*
Seeking God .... Psalm 63 0621
Jesus spent time in prayer .... Mark 1:35 1071
Stay joined to Jesus .... John 15:7 1168

Notes
"A Time Out with God" .... Exodus 16:23 0086
"Refresher Course" .... Joshua 8:33-35 0239
My Story .... Ecclesiastes 5:1-7 0707

TRUST *Selected passages*
David trusted God .... 1 Samuel 17:34-37 0317
Trust God to free you from fear and worry .... Psalm 34:4 0605
In God we trust .... Psalm 56:3-4, 11 0618
Trusting instead of doubting .... John 20:24-31 1174
We trust because God loves us .... 1 John 4:16 1388

Notes
"Wait for God" .... Genesis 30:22-24 0039
"Reliable" .... Genesis 50:5-6 0063
"Promises" .... Numbers 30:1-2 0183
"Why Me?" .... Job 1:1 0554
"A Right Attitude" .... Job 21:22 0570
My Story .... Psalm 57:1 0619
"Power" .... Isaiah 47:1-9 0771
"Trust" .... Jeremiah 32:6-12 0831
"Even Better" .... Acts 27:1–28:24 1221
"The Greater Good" .... Romans 8:28 1235
(See also DOUBTS, FAITH)

VALUES *Selected passages*
Valuing God's Word .... Psalm 119:111, 162 .... 0657, 0658
What you treasure .... Matthew 6:21 1035
A valuable pearl .... Matthew 13:45-46 1047

Notes
My Story .... Exodus 20 0089
"Idols" .... Exodus 32:1-10 0102
"Warnings" .... Leviticus 26:1 0143
"Stand Firm" .... 2 Samuel 3:7-11 0335
Choices: Living for the Moment .... 2 Samuel 11–12 0343
Choices: American Idols .... 2 Chronicles 34 0505
Choices: Absolutes .... Ezra 7:10 0516
"Idols" .... Isaiah 31:7 0755
Choices: Priorities .... Jeremiah 9:23-24 0805
Ultimate Issues: Modern-Day Idols .... Jeremiah 10 0808
"Culture Clash?" .... Daniel 1:17 0921
"Stand Out" .... Daniel 3:12-18 0924
"Priorities" .... Haggai 1:1-9 1004
My Story .... 2 Peter 1:5-8 1378
(See also GODLY LIVING, CHOICES)

WISDOM *Selected passages*
Solomon asks for wisdom . . . . 1 Kings 3:3-14 0369
Gain wisdom through studying the Bible . . . . Psalm 119:98-104 0656
Wisdom is available to you . . . . Proverbs 2–4; 8 0673
Love wisdom . . . . Proverbs 19:8 0688
Believe that God will give you wisdom . . . . James 1:5-8 1364

Notes
"Wise Guy" . . . . 1 Kings 3:5-9 0369
"Wise without God?" . . . . Job 28:1-28 0573
"Choices" . . . . Proverbs 2:9-10 0673
"Elder Wisdom" . . . . Luke 2:25-38 1104

WITNESSING *(See TALKING ABOUT GOD)*

WORRY/STRESS *Selected passages*
Why worry? . . . . Matthew 6:25-34 1035
. . . . Luke 12:22-34 1123
Don't worry about defending yourself . . . . Matthew 10:19-20 1040
How to have peace instead of worrying . . . . Philippians 4:6-19 1305

Notes
"Why Worry?" . . . . Genesis 7:15-16 0012
My Story . . . . Psalm 34 0606
"No Worries" . . . . Philippians 4:6-18 1305
(See also FEAR, SUFFERING)

WORSHIP *Selected passages*
Worship only God . . . . Exodus 20:3-5 0089
Ways to worship God . . . . Psalms 29:1-2; 150 . . . . .0602, 0670
Fake worship . . . . Matthew 15:9 1048
Worshiping Jesus . . . . Matthew 15:25 1049
An attitude of worship . . . . Ephesians 5:19-20 1297
Worship in heaven . . . . Revelation 14:3-7 1413

Notes
Ultimate Issues: Worship . . . . 1 Samuel 1 0298
"Panic" . . . . Psalm 70:1-4 0626
"Holidays" . . . . Psalm 81:1-5 0634
"True Worship" . . . . Isaiah 58:1-14 0781
"True Worship" . . . . Lamentations 2:1-7 0859
Choices: Halfhearted Worship . . . . Malachi 1:6-14 1020
(See also BELIEVING IN GOD, HONOR, THANKFULNESS)

FEATURES INDEX

CHOICES

Abortion Psalm 139 0664	**Laziness** 2 Thessalonians 3 1323
Absolutes Ezra 7 0516	**Legalism** Mark 7 1080
Adultery Hosea 2 0939	**Living for the Moment**
Advice Lamentations 3 0861	2 Samuel 11–12 0343
Alternatives Romans 1 1228	**Love** 1 John 4 1388
American Idol 2 Chronicles 34 0505	**Lust** Colossians 3 1311
Anger Numbers 20 0171	**Lying** 1 Samuel 15 0313
Arrogance Obadiah verses 2-10 0970	**Materialism** 1 Timothy 6 1328
Astrology Deuteronomy 4 0196	**Mouth** Matthew 12 1045
Attitudes Jonah 3–4 0976	**Music** 2 Timothy 3 1335
Authority Romans 13 1241	**Obedience** James 1 1364
Boss, The 1 Chronicles 28 0466	**Opposition** Nehemiah 4 0527
Cheating Proverbs 11 0681	**Outspoken** 2 Kings 6 0408
Commitment Ruth 1 0290	**Parties** 1 Peter 4 1374
Complacency Amos 5–6 0962	**Peer Pressure** Exodus 23 0093
Compromise Judges 16 0282	**Perseverance** Jude 1398
Confront Ezekiel 2 0869	**Pleasure** Ecclesiastes 1 0706
Consistency Hebrews 12 1359	**Pornography** Job 31 0577
Cults 2 Peter 2 1379	**Prejudice** John 4 1152
Dating 1 Kings 11; Ephesians 5 . . . 0380, 1296	**Pride** Acts 12 1199
Despair Revelation 21–22 1420	**Priorities** Jeremiah 9 0805
Divorce Matthew 19 1054	**Reconciliation** Philemon 1344
Drinking Proverbs 23 0692	**Reputation** Hebrews 13 1360
Drugs 1 Corinthians 6 1251	**Responsibility** Joshua 1 0231
Enemies Luke 10 1119	**Satisfaction** Haggai 1 1004
Forgiveness Joel 2 0953	**Seek the Truth** Revelation 3 1405
Freedom Galatians 5 1286	**Self** Philippians 2 1304
Friendship Psalm 1 0588	**Serving God** 2 Corinthians 4 1272
Friendship Daniel 3 0926	**Sex** 1 Thessalonians 4 1317
Giving Luke 21 .1136	**So Religious** Isaiah 1 0725
Halfhearted Worship Malachi 1 1020	**Stealing** Leviticus 19 0136
Hard Times Habakkuk 3 0994	**Success** Mark 9 1084
Honesty Micah 7 0983	**Taking a Stand** Esther 3–4 0546
Injustice Psalm 73 0629	**Vengeance** Nahum 1 0988
Integrity Titus 1–3 1341	**Violence** Genesis 6 0014
Judgment Zephaniah 1–2 0998	**Virginity** Song of Songs 4 0718
Justice Zechariah 7 1011	

I WONDER

How do science and the Bible relate? Genesis 3 0008
What God expects Genesis 22 0027
Does God care about the world? Genesis 48 0061
Letting people know I'm a Christian Exodus 4 0070
Are body piercing and tattoos okay? Leviticus 19 0134
Why is the Old Testament in the Bible? Deuteronomy 12 0206
Freedom of choice and God's plan Joshua 24 0256
Different religions Judges 8 0271

Who wrote the Bible? Ruth 2 0292
How much of my time does God want? 1 Samuel 8 0305
When others make fun of my faith 2 Samuel 15 0350
How to pray 1 Kings 3 0369
Living and telling my faith 2 Kings 7 0410
Developing my own faith 1 Chronicles 28 0467
The point of church rituals 2 Chronicles 20 0487
Can I get into heaven by being good? Psalm 14 0594
The sin that God cannot forgive Psalm 51 0616
Peer pressure Proverbs 1 0672
Has God already planned out my future? Proverbs 16 0686
Can Christians have fun? Ecclesiastes 11 0711
Hypocrisy and Christians Isaiah 29 0751
Horoscopes Isaiah 47 0771
Giving God more attention Jeremiah 2 0794
Can God forgive all my sins? Jeremiah 17 0814
Giving my life to God Jeremiah 29 0827
I keep blowing it Ezekiel 14 0878
Persecution Daniel 1, 3, 6 0920
Sharing my faith with people who don't seem to need God Hosea 13 0948
Why doesn't God do more miracles for me? Joel 2 0954
Why do some people never get punished? Amos 2 0959
Why do I have to give money to the church? Malachi 3 1021
Relating the Old and New Testaments Matthew 5 1032
Why hasn't God answered my prayer? Matthew 7 1036
Getting my parents to take my faith seriously Matthew 10 1041
Is temptation a sin? Matthew 18 1052
Are parties bad? Mark 2 1072
Fear of ridicule because of faith Mark 5 1076
Building a solid Christian life Luke 8 1115
Can I be proud of doing my best? Luke 18 1132
I'm worried about telling people I'm a Christian Luke 22 1139
What does Communion do for me? Luke 24 1142
Why does God allow evil and death in the world? John 11 1162
Where do I start reading the Bible? John 20 1174
How do I forgive people who have hurt me? Acts 3 1184
Persecution Acts 7 1193
Is it wrong to seek answers about the Bible? Acts 17 1208
Struggling with bad thoughts and habits Romans 7–8 1234
Finding Christian support from other people 1 Corinthians 1 1246
The New Age movement 1 Corinthians 1 1248
Why does God let Christians have so many problems? 2 Corinthians 1 1268
Keeping my non-Christian friends 2 Corinthians 6 1273
What about drugs? Galatians 5 1288
Growing as a Christian Ephesians 4 1294
My Christian maturity Colossians 2 1310
Fear of dying 1 Thessalonians 4 1318
How can I stay pure? 1 Timothy 6 1329
Talking to a friend who deserted God 2 Timothy 4 1336
What is God really like? Hebrews 1 1349
Why go to church? Hebrews 10 1356
How should Christians deal with their own guilt and sin? James 4 1367
Is seeing believing? 1 Peter 1 1371
Why don't I always have good feelings about my relationship
   with God? 1 John 5 1389
Closeness to God Revelation 2 1403

ULTIMATE ISSUES

Abortion 2 Chronicles 28 0496
Absolute Answers Exodus 20 0090
AIDS: What Would Jesus Do?
    1 Corinthians 7 1252
Church, The 1 Corinthians 1260
Covenants Deuteronomy 11 0204
Date Rape 2 Samuel 13 0346
Divorce Malachi 2 1022
Do the Right Thing Amos 5 0961
Down in the Dumps Psalm 73 0628
Terrible Trio Revelation 13:1-18 1298
Foundational Truths 2 John 1392
God's Chosen People Joshua 5 0235
Heard the Good News? Acts 4 1186
Holy Spirit, The Acts 2 1182
Holy War? Numbers 31 0184
Homosexuality Romans 1 1226
Is There Meaning to Life?
    Ecclesiastes 11 .0712
Law, The Leviticus 19 0133
Looking for a Perfect 10 Proverbs 31 . . . 0701
Made in the Image of God Psalm 8 0591

Marriage 1 Corinthians 7 1254
Miracles 2 Kings 5 0404
Modern-Day Idols Jeremiah 10–11 0808
New Age Movement, The 3 John 1394
Origin of Humanity, The
    Genesis 1–2 0006
Other Religions Judges 2 0263
Prayer Hebrews 4 1350
Prophets, The 1 Kings 16 0388
Resurrection, The Mark 16 1096
Sex, The Real Truth about
    Song of Songs 7 .0721
Sexual Abuse Jeremiah 38 0838
Sexual Morality Ruth 3 0293
Suffering and Evil Job 38–41 0560
Suicide Jeremiah 20 0817
Who Is God? Isaiah 6 0730
Who Is Jesus? Matthew 16 1050
Who's in Charge? Ezekiel 32 0898
Why the Cross? Luke 23 1140
Women of the Bible Esther 4 0547
Worship 1 Samuel 1 0298

CHARTS

Alliances Today Isaiah 29 0753
Amos Amos 6 0964
Appeal of Idols, The 1 Kings 1 0382
Attitudes, A Collection of Luke 10 1720
Beginning and the End, The Revelation 20 1418
Careful Obedience 2 Chronicles 3 0495
Daniel Daniel 3 0929
Days of Creation Genesis 2–5 0007
Evidence That Jesus Actually Died and Rose Again Mark 15 .1095
Ezekiel Ezekiel 7 0901
Famous Songs in the Bible Exodus 15 0085
Festivals, The Leviticus 23 0139
God or Idols 2 Kings 6 0415
God Uses Common People Judges 11 0275
God's Armor for Us Ephesians 6 1299
Habakkuk Habakkuk 3 0994
Hebrew Calendar, The Exodus 13 0080
Highlights of 1 Corinthians 1 Corinthians 11 1258
Highs and Lows of David's Life 2 Samuel 5 0337
Hosea Hosea 4 0945
How God Is Described in Proverbs Proverbs 30 0700
How God Works in the World Esther 4 0548
How Suffering Affects Us Job 14 0564
Isaiah Isaiah 18 0728
Israel's Complaining Numbers 14 0163
Jeremiah Jeremiah 6 0797
Jesus and Forgiveness Luke 5 1113
Jesus and the 10 Commandments Luke 16 1129
Jesus' Appearances after His Resurrection John 19 1175
Joel Joel 3 0953
Jonah Jonah 4 0975

Judges of Israel, The Judges 7 0270
Law, What Is the Galatians 3 1285
Love, What Jesus Said about Mark 12 1088
Making Choices on Sensitive Issues 1 Corinthians 9 1255
Malachi Malachi 3 1024
Marriage, The Symbolic Nature of Hosea 13 0941
Marriage, What the Bible Says about Genesis 24 0029
Micah Micah 1 0978
Miracles in the Book of Jonah Jonah 4 0974
Music in Bible Times 1 Chronicles 16 0455
Nahum Nahum 3 0990
Names for Messiah Isaiah 9 0734
Names of Jesus, The Revelation 7 1407
Obadiah Obadiah 0971
Obedience Deuteronomy 8 0201
Offerings, The Leviticus 3 0116
Old/New System of Sacrifice Leviticus 15 0129
Old and New Covenants Ezekiel 35 0903
Our Life before and after Christ Ephesians 2 1293
Pharisees and Sadducees, The Matthew 12 1044
Plagues, The Exodus 7 0074
Principles of Confrontation in 2 Corinthians 2 Corinthians 7 1275
Principles to Live By 1 Chronicles 26 0464
Prophets—False and True 1 Kings 18 0391
Reasons to Read Psalms Psalm 17 0595
Salvation's Freeway Romans 3 1232
Satan's Plan Genesis 4 0009
Simple Objects 1 Samuel 17 0316
Strategy for Effective Living Proverbs 20 0690
Temple in Jesus' Day, The Matthew 21 1056
Today's Idolatry Isaiah 44 0768
Unsung Heroes in Acts Acts 16 1206
Variety in Worship Deuteronomy 32 0225
Where to Get Help in the Book of Psalms Psalm 134 0662
Why Did Jesus Have to Die? Mark 14 0662
Women in Jesus' Family Tree Genesis 38 0050
Worry, Seven Reasons Not to Matthew 6 1034
Zechariah Zechariah 8 1013
Zephaniah Zephaniah 3 1000

PERSONALITY PROFILES

Abel Genesis 4 0010
Abraham Genesis 15 0020
Absalom 2 Samuel 14 0348
Adam and Eve Genesis 3 0009
Ahab 1 Kings 16 0387
Aquila and Priscilla Acts 18 1212
Barnabas Acts 13 1198
Cain 1 John 3 1386
Daniel Daniel 2 0922
David 1 Samuel 17 0310
David's Mighty Men 2 Samuel 23 0360
Delilah Judges 16 0281
Elijah 1 Kings 18 0390
Elisha 2 Kings 2 0402
Esau Genesis 27 0034
Esther Esther 2 0544

Gideon Judges 6 0267
Hezekiah 2 Kings 18 0425
Isaac Genesis 22 0028
Ishmael 1 Chronicles 1 0438
Jacob Genesis 28 0037
James Luke 5 1109
Jehoshaphat 2 Chronicles 17 0488
Joash 2 Chronicles 23 0490
Job Job 2 0556
John Mark Acts 13 1200
John the Baptist John 1 1150
Jonathan 1 Samuel 14 0318
Joseph Genesis 41 0053
Joshua Joshua 6 0236
Josiah 2 Kings 22 0429
Judah Genesis 38 0049

Judas Iscariot Mark 3 1074
Lot Genesis 19 0018
Manasseh 2 Chronicles 33 0502
Mary Luke 1........................1102
Mary and Martha John 11 1164
Matthew Matthew 9................. 1039
Michal 2 Samuel 6 0339
Miriam Exodus 15...................0084
Moses Exodus 2 0068
Noah Genesis 6 0013
Paul Acts 9 1195
Rachel Genesis 30 0038
Rahab Joshua 2 0233
Rebekah Genesis 24 0031

Reuben Genesis 39 0040
Ruth and Naomi Ruth 3 0294
Samson Judges 13 0278
Samuel 1 Samuel 3................. 0300
Sarah Genesis 21 0024
Saul 1 Samuel 9................... 0306
Shadrach, Meshach, and Abednego
   Daniel 3 0924
Silas Acts 16 1207
Solomon 1 Kings 3 0366
Stephen Acts 6.....................1191
Thomas John 20 1176
Timothy 1 Timothy 6...............1330

MAPS

A Ministry on the Move Matthew 1..... 1028
Abraham's Trip to Mount Moriah
   Genesis 20...................... 0025
Assyrian Empire, The
   2 Chronicles 28................. 0497
Babylon, Taken to Daniel 1 0921
Borders of the Promised Land, The
   Numbers 35..................... 0188
Churches of Peter's Letter, The
   1 Peter 1 1370
Colosse, Location of Colossians 1 1308
Conquered Land, The Joshua 13....... 0244
Corinth and Ephesus 1 Corinthians 1....1247
Ephesus, Location of Ephesians 2 1292
Events in Deuteronomy
   Deuteronomy 1 0192
Exile to Babylon 2 Chronicles 35 0507
Following Jesus' Journey John 1 1146
Galatia, Cities in Galatians 2......... 1283
Israel Taken Captive 2 Kings 17....... 0423
Israelites at Mount Sinai, The
   Leviticus 1 0114
Jesus in Action Mark 1 1070
Jesus' Route to Golgotha Mark 14 1093
Jesus' Trial Mark 14 1094
Joseph Goes to Meet His Brothers
   Genesis 37..................... 0047
Judah Exiled 2 Kings 24............. 0433
Key Places in 1 Chronicles
   1 Chronicles 1.................. 0436
Key Places in 2 Chronicles
   2 Chronicles 1 0470
Key Places in 1 Kings 1 Kings 1 0364

Key Places in 2 Kings 2 Kings 1........ 0400
Key Places in 1 Samuel 1 Samuel 1..... 0296
Key Places in 2 Samuel 2 Samuel 1 0332
Key Places Acts 1 1180
Key Places in Exodus Exodus 1........0066
Key Places in Genesis Genesis 1.......0004
Key Places in Joshua Joshua 1........0230
Key Places in Judges Judges 1........0260
Key Places in Numbers Numbers 1.....0148
Medo-Persian Empire, The Ezra 2 0510
Nehemiah Goes to Jerusalem
   Nehemiah 2..................... 0525
Paul Searches for Titus
   2 Corinthians 2 1270
Paul's First Missionary Journey
   Acts 13 1202
Paul's Second Missionary Journey
   Acts 15 1204
Paul's Third Missionary Journey
   Acts 18 1210
Paul's Journey to Rome Acts 27 1215
Philippi, Location of Philippians 1 1302
Rome, The Gospel Goes to Romans 1....1227
Ruth (Setting for the Story) Ruth 1..... 0290
Seven Churches, The Revelation 1..... 1402
The People and Places of Jesus' Ministry
   Luke 1........................1100
Thessalonica, Location of
   1 Thessalonians 1 1316
Titus Goes to Crete Titus 1............ 1340
Upper Room and Gethsemane
   Mark 14........................1091
World of Esther's Day, The Esther 1 0542

MY STORY

Submitting to God's will Genesis 4 0011
Convincing others of God's truth
   Exodus 5–11.................... 0071
A balanced life Exodus 20............0089
Obedience Leviticus 26.............. 0143

Honoring parents Deuteronomy 5 0198
Dabbling in the occult Deuteronomy 18 .0211
When you're afraid Joshua 1.......... 0232
God gives you strength 2 Samuel 22... 0358
How to be a leader 2 Kings 0418

Feeling depressed and confused
  Psalm 6 0590
Angry at God Psalm 13. 0593
Dealing with worry Psalm 34 0606
Keeping faith in bad times Psalm 46. . . 0613
Trusting that God is in control
  Psalm 57. 0619
God can protect from fear Psalm 140. . . 0666
Procrastination and laziness
  Proverbs 6 0676
Afraid to talk about God Proverbs 29. . . 0698
Starting over; living for the moment
  Ecclesiastes 2 0705
Spending time with God every day
  Ecclesiastes 5 0707
Healing broken friendships
  Ecclesiastes 10 0710
Dealing with peer pressure Isaiah 7 . . . 0732
Needing advice at a new school
  Isaiah 41 0764
Loneliness in a new country
  Isaiah 46 0770
Abortion Jeremiah 1. 0793
God forgives Lamentations 3 0862
Rejected for being a Christian
  Micah 4 0981
When you'd like to get revenge
  Matthew 5 1033
Doubts about God Matthew 7. 1037
Acting phony Mark 9 1086

Hatred Luke 6 1111
Disagreement with a parent Luke 15 1127
When disaster strikes John 1 1147
A parent's illness John 14 1168
Being bold in witnessing Acts 4 1187
Power of God versus the power of Satan
  Acts 19 1211
Leading a double life Romans 2 1229
When you're hurt and want revenge
  Romans 12 1240
A problem with gossiping
  1 Corinthians 10. 1256
Dating 1 Corinthians 13 1261
Why do bad things happen to you?
  2 Corinthians 1. 1269
Disagreeing with parents
  Ephesians 6. 1297
Talking to someone about God
  Philippians 4 1305
Getting along with parents
  Colossians 3 1312
Being satisfied with what you have
  Hebrews 13 1361
Not hiding faith 1 Peter 3. 1373
Ending a relationship 2 Peter 1. 1378
Making excuses for sin 1 John 1 1385
Learning to love 1 John 4 1387
Struggling with apathy
  Revelation 3; 14. . . . . .1405, 1413

WHERE TO FIND IT

STORY

Adam and Eve Genesis 2:1–4:25 0006
Balaam's donkey speaks Numbers 22:21-35 0174
Beatitudes Matthew 5:1-12, Luke 6:20-23 .... 1032, 1110
Bronze snake Numbers 21:4-9 0172
Burning bush Exodus 3 0069
Cain and Abel Genesis 4 0009
Creation Genesis 1:1–2:7 0005
Daniel in the lions' den Daniel 6 0928
David and Bathsheba 2 Samuel 11–12:25 0343
David and Goliath 1 Samuel 17 0315
Elijah on Mt. Carmel 1 Kings 18:16-46 0391
Elijah is taken to heaven 2 Kings 2:1-12 0401
Esau sells his birthright Genesis 25:27-34 0032
Exodus from Egypt Exodus 12:31-15 0079
Faith chapter Hebrews 11 1357
Fiery furnace Daniel 3 0923
First Passover Exodus 12:1-30 0078
First sin Genesis 3 0007
Fruit of the Spirit Galatians 5:22-23 1287
Garden of Eden Genesis 2:4–3:24 0006
Gideon and the fleece Judges 6 0267
Gideon battles the Midianites Judges 7 0269
Golden calf Exodus 32 0102
Golden rule Matthew 7:12; Luke 6:31 .... 1036, 1112
Great Commission Matthew 28:18-20 1068
Holy Spirit comes at Pentecost Acts 2:1-21 1182
Isaac almost sacrificed Genesis 22 0026
Jacob wrestles the angel Genesis 32:22-32 0043
Jericho (Battle of) Joshua 6 0236
Jesus is the Bread of Life John 6:35 1155
Jesus is the Gate for the sheep John 10:7 1161
Jesus is the Good Shepherd John 10:11-16 1161
Jesus is the Light of the World John 8:12 1158
Jesus is the Vine John 15:1 1168
Jesus is the Way, Truth, and Life John 14:6 1167
Jesus' baptism Matthew 3:13-17; Mark 1:9-11; Luke 3:21-22;
  John 1:31-34 .... 1031, 1070, 0105, 1147
Jesus' birth Matthew 1:18–2:12; Luke 2:1-20 .... 1029, 1103
Jesus' temptation by Satan Matthew 4:1-11; Mark 1:12-13; Luke 4:1-13 .... 1031, 1071, 1106
Jesus' transfiguration Matthew 17:1-13; Mark 9:2-13; Luke 9:28-36 .... 1051, 1082, 1118
John the Baptist killed Matthew 14:1-12; Mark 6:14-29 .... 1047, 1078
Jonah and the fish Jonah 1:1–2 0974
Jordan River parts Joshua 3 0233
Joseph sent to Egypt Genesis 37 0047
Lazarus raised from the dead John 11 1161
Lord's Prayer Matthew 6:9-13; Luke 11:2-4 .... 1035, 1121
Lot's wife turns to salt Genesis 19:12-26 0023
Love chapter 1 Corinthians 13 1261

Moses protected as a baby Exodus 2:1-10 0067
Moses' sin (water from the rock) Numbers 20:1-13 0170
Naaman is healed of leprosy 2 Kings 5 0406
Nicodemus talks with Jesus John 3:1-21 1149
Noah and the Flood Genesis 6:9–9 0012
Paul and Silas in prison Acts 16:16-40. 1206
Paul's (Saul's) conversion Acts 9:1-19 1193
Paul's shipwreck Acts 27–28:10 1221
Peter's escape from prison Acts 12:1-19 1198
Plagues on Egypt Exodus 7–11 0073
Rainbow after the Flood Genesis 9:8-17 0014
Red Sea parts Exodus 14:5-31. 0081
Samson and Delilah Judges 16:4-22 0280
Sermon on the Mount Matthew 5–7; Luke 6:17-49 .... 1032, 1110
Sodom and Gomorrah Genesis 19:1-29 0023
Stoning of Stephen Acts 6:8–7:60. 1189
Sun stands still Joshua 10:1-15. 0240
Ten Commandments Exodus 20:1-17 0089
Tower of Babel Genesis 11:1-9 0016
Wise men visit Jesus Matthew 2:1-12. 1029
Zacchaeus meets Jesus Luke 19:1-10. 1133

TEACHING PARABLES

About the Kingdom of God
The Soils Matthew 13:3-8, 18-23; Mark 4:3-8, 14-20; Luke 8:5-8, 11-15 .... 1045, 1075, 1114
The Weeds Matthew 13:24-30, 36-43. 1046
The Mustard Seed Matthew 13:31-32; Mark 4:30-32; Luke 13:18-19 ....1046, 1076, 1125
The Yeast (Leaven) Matthew 13:33; Luke 13:20-21 ....1046, 1125
The Treasure Matthew 13:44. 1047
The Pearl Matthew 13:45-46 1047
The Fishing Net Matthew 13:47-50. 1047
The Growing Seed Mark 4:26-29 1076

About Service and Obedience
The Workers in the Vineyard Matthew 20:1-16 1055
The Loaned Money Matthew 25:14-30; Luke 19:11-27 ....1062, 1133
The Servant's Role Luke 17:7-10. 1130

About Prayer
The Friend at Midnight Luke 11:5-8 1121
The Persistent Widow/Unjust Judge Luke 18:1-8 1131

About Neighbors
The Good Samaritan Luke 10:30-37. 1120

About Humility
The Lowest Seat Luke 14:7-14. 1126
The Proud Pharisee and the Corrupt Tax Collector Luke 18:9-14 1131

About Wealth
The Wealthy Fool Luke 12:16-21 1123
The Great Feast Luke 14:16-24 1126
The Shrewd Manager Luke 16:1-9 1128

GOSPEL PARABLES

About God's Love
The Lost Sheep Matthew 18:12-14; Luke 15:3-7 ....1053, 1127
The Lost Coin Luke 15:8-10 1127
The Lost Son Luke 15:11-32 1127

About Thankfulness
The Forgiven Loans Luke 7:41-43 1114

PARABLES OF JUDGMENT AND THE FUTURE

About Christ's Return
The Ten Virgins Matthew 25:1-13 1062
The Wise and Faithful Servant Matthew 24:45-51; Luke 12:42-48 . . . . .1062, 1124
The Traveling Boss Mark 13:34-37 1091

About God's Values
The Two Sons Matthew 21:28-32 1057
The Evil Tenants Matthew 21:33-44; Mark 12:1-11; Luke 20:9-16 . . . . 1057, 1087, 1134
The Unproductive Fig Tree Luke 13:6-9 1125
The Marriage Feast Matthew 22:1-14 1058
The Unforgiving Servant Matthew 18:23-35 1053

JESUS' MIRACLES

Five thousand people are fed Matthew 14:15-21; Mark 6:35-44;
  Luke 9:12-17; John 6:5-14 . . . . .1047, 1079, 1117, 1154
Stilling the storm Matthew 8:23-27; Mark 4:35-41; Luke 8:22-25 . . . . .1038, 1076, 1115
Demons sent into the pigs Matthew 8:28-34; Mark 5:1-20;
  Luke 8:26-39 . . . . .1038, 1076, 1115
Jairus's daughter raised from dead Matthew 9:18-26;
  Mark 5:22-24, 35-43; Luke 8:41-42, 49-56 . . . . 1039, 1077, 1116
Diseased woman healed Matthew 9:20-22; Mark 5:25-34;
  Luke 8:43-48 . . . . 1039, 1077, 1116
Jesus heals a paralyzed man Matthew 9:1-8; Mark 2:1-12;
  Luke 5:17-26 . . . . 1038, 1072, 1108
A leper is healed Matthew 8:1-4; Mark 1:40-45;
  Luke 5:12-15 . . . . 1037, 1071, 1108
Peter's mother-in-law healed Matthew 8:14-15; Mark 1:29-31;
  Luke 4:38-39 . . . . 1037, 1071, 1108
A deformed hand is restored Matthew 12:9-14; Mark 3:1-6;
  Luke 6:6-11 . . . . .1043, 1073, 1110
A demon-possessed boy is cured Matthew 17:14-21; Mark 9:14-29;
  Luke 9:37-43 . . . . 1051, 1083, 1118
Jesus walks on the sea Matthew 14:22-33; Mark 6:45-52;
  John 6:16-21 . . . . .1048, 1079, 1154
Blind Bartimaeus receives sight Matthew 20:29-34; Mark 10:46-52;
  Luke 18:35-43 . . . . 1056, 1086, 1133
A girl is freed from a demon Matthew 15:21-28; Mark 7:24-30 . . . . .1049, 1081
Four thousand are fed Matthew 15:29-38; Mark 8:1-9 . . . . .1049, 1081
Cursing the fig tree Matthew 21:18-22; Mark 11:12-14, 20-24 . . . . .1057, 1087
A centurion's servant is healed Matthew 8:5-13; Luke 7:1-10 . . . . 1037, 1112
A demon is sent out of a man Mark 1:23-28; Luke 4:33-37 . . . . 1071, 1107
A mute demon-possessed man is healed Matthew 12:22-23; Luke 11:14 . . . . 1043, 1121
Two blind men find sight Matthew 9:27-31 1039
Jesus heals the mute man Matthew 9:32-34 1040
A coin in a fish's mouth Matthew 17:24-27 1052
A deaf and dumb man is healed Mark 7:31-37 1081
A blind man sees at Bethsaida Mark 8:22-26 1082
The first miraculous catch of fish Luke 5:1-11 1108
The widow of Nain's son is raised from the dead Luke 7:11-17 1113
A handicapped woman is healed Luke 13:10-17 1125
Jesus cures a sick man Luke 14:1-6 1126
Ten lepers are cured Luke 17:11-19 1130
Jesus restores a man's ear Luke 22:49-51 1138

Jesus turns water into wine John 2:1-11 1148
A nobleman's son is healed at Cana John 4:46-54 1152
A lame man is cured John 5:1-15 1153
Jesus heals a man born blind John 9:1-34 1159
Lazarus is raised from the dead John 11 1161
The second miraculous catch of fish John 21:1-14 1175

WORLD OF THE PATRIARCHS

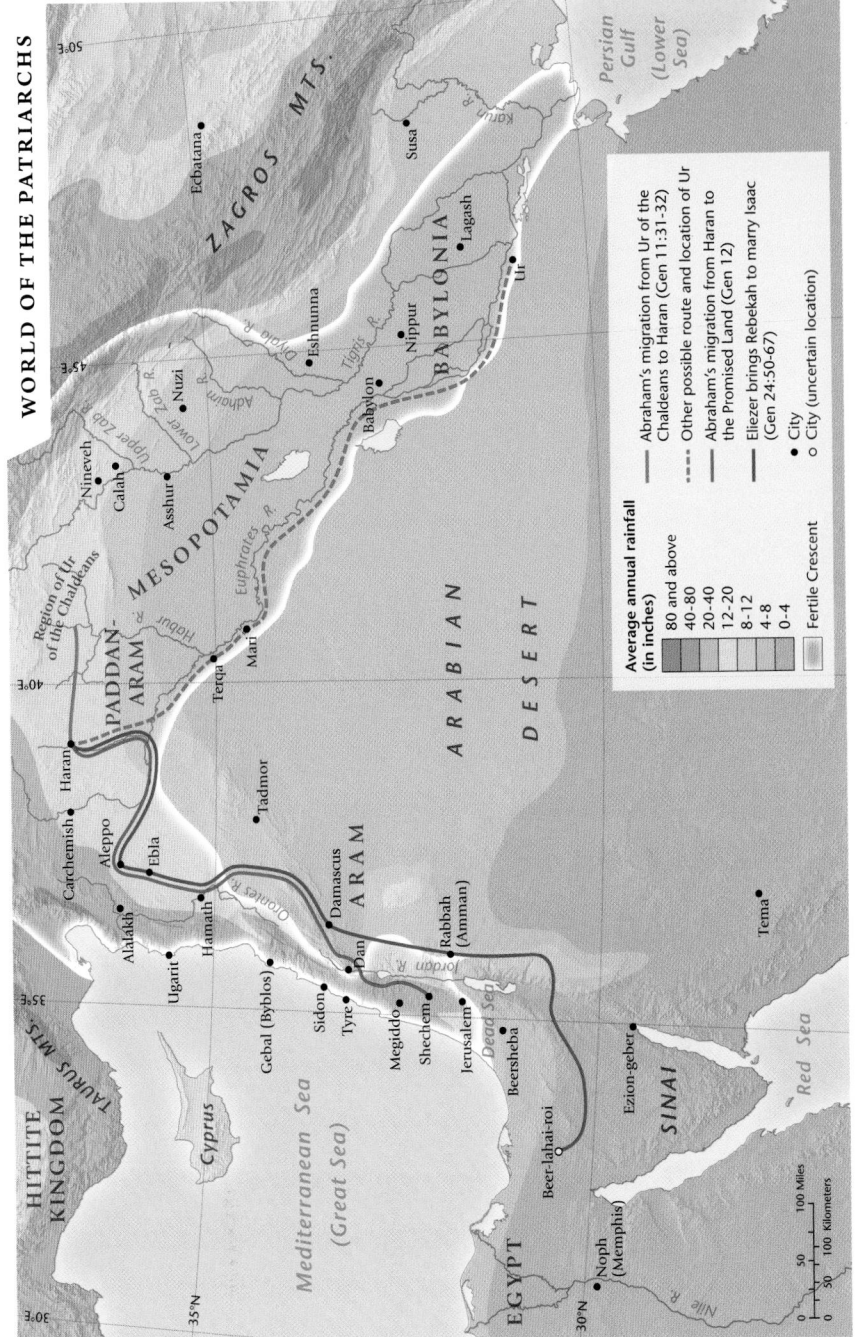

Average annual rainfall (in inches)
- 80 and above
- 40-80
- 20-40
- 12-20
- 8-12
- 4-8
- 0-4
- Fertile Crescent

— Abraham's migration from Ur of the Chaldeans to Haran (Gen 11:31-32)
--- Other possible route and location of Ur
— Abraham's migration from Haran to the Promised Land (Gen 12)
— Eliezer brings Rebekah to marry Isaac (Gen 24:50-67)
- City
○ City (uncertain location)

EXODUS FROM EGYPT

Legend:

- City
- ○ City (modern name)
- ▲ Mountain peak (possible sites of Mt. Sinai)

- ⇧⇧ Route from Egypt to Mt. Sinai
- ⇧⇧ Route from Mt. Sinai to Kadesh-barnea
- ⇧⇧ Route from Kadesh-barnea to Acacia Grove
- – – – Annual bird migration path
- —— Ancient roadway

UNITED KINGDOM

Map labels (United Kingdom map): 40 Miles / 40 Kilometers · Aleppo · YAMHAD · Tiphsah · Euphrates R. · Cyprus · Hamath · HAMATH · Arvad · Tadmor · Gebal (Byblos) · Lebo-hamath · 34°N · Mediterranean Sea (Great Sea) · Damascus · PHOENICIA · Tyre · Dan · ARAM · Hazor · Sea of Galilee (Kinnereth) · EASTERN DESERT · Dor · Megiddo · Shechem · Joppa · AMMON · 32°N · Gezer · Rabbah (Amman) · Jerusalem · PHILISTIA · Gaza · Dead Sea (Salt Sea) · Raphia · MOAB · Beersheba · AMALEK · EDOM · Kadesh-barnea · Petra · SINAI · Ezion-geber · Gulf of Aqaba

Legend: Kingdom of Saul · Kingdom of David · Solomon's Expansion

KINGDOMS OF ISRAEL

The United Kingdom of Israel came into being at the coronation of Saul, grew in size and influence under David, and reached its height during Solomon's reign. Solomon inherited a powerful kingdom from his father, David, covering the entire area inhabited by the 12 tribes of Israel. Throughout Solomon's reign, his power and influence increased as he also gained control over many of the surrounding nations.

After the death of Solomon, the kingdom of Israel divided. Solomon's son Rehoboam remained king of the southern kingdom of Judah, with Jerusalem as its capital. Jeroboam became the king of the northern kingdom of Israel and rebuilt Shechem as his capital. He also built new worship centers in Bethel and Dan, influencing his people to stay away from Jerusalem and its annual religious festivals. The division of the kingdom of Israel began a downward spiral into idolatry and godless leadership for both nations, eventually leading to the exile of the northern kingdom to Assyria and the southern kingdom to Babylon.

DIVIDED KINGDOM

Map labels (Divided Kingdom map): 20 Miles / 20 Kilometers · AMURRU · Great Trunk Road · Coastal Road · HAMATH · Hamath · Qatna · Arvad · Kadesh · Sadad · Mediterranean Sea (Great Sea) · Gebal (Byblos) · Lebo-hamath · 34°N · Berothai · PHOENICIA · Sidon · Great Trunk Road · Damascus · Tyre · Dan · ARAM · Kedesh · Ashtaroth · Acco · Hazor · Sea of Galilee (Kinnereth) · Dor · Megiddo · Salecah · Beth-shan · Ramoth-gilead · ISRAEL · Shechem · Joppa · AMMON · 32°N · Bethel · Gezer · Gibeah · Rabbah (Amman) · Ashdod · Gath · Jerusalem · Medeba · Gaza · Lachish · Hebron · Aroer · King's Highway · Raphia · Beersheba · MOAB · PHILISTIA · JUDAH · Kir-hareseth (Kir-moab) · NEGEV · Kadesh-barnea · Bozrah · EDOM · Brook of Egypt · Territory periodically contested by Edom and Judah · Petra · EASTERN DESERT · WILDERNESS OF ZIN · 30°N · SINAI · Ezion-geber · Gulf of Aqaba

ASSYRIAN AND BABYLONIAN EMPIRES

Assyria around 700 B.C.

Babylonia around 600 B.C.

Black Sea

Byzantium

LYDIA

URARTU

Moxes R.

Caspian Sea

40°N

Lake *Lake Van*

Lake Urmia

Tarsus

KUE

Carchemish

Haran

Nineveh

Calah

MEDIA

Aleppo

Asshur

Arrapha

Riblah

Tadmor

Ecbatana

Mediterranean Sea *(Great Sea)*

Cyprus

Tyre

Damascus

Sippar

Samaria

Babylon

Nippur

Susa

Jerusalem

KEDAR

Erech (Uruk)

Ur

ELAM

30°N

Memphis

Ezion-geber

Dumah

PERSIA

SAHARA DESERT

ARABIAN DESERT

Persian Gulf

0   100   200 Miles

0   100 200 Kilometers

30°E

40°E

Tema

50°E

Red Sea

GREEK EMPIRE

Danube R.

MACEDONIA

Black Sea

CAUCASUS MTS.

Caspian Sea

Pella

THRACE

Sinope

40°N

Moxes R.

ARMENIA

HELLAS

Athens

ASIA

Lake Tuz

Lake Van

Lake Urmia

Sparta

Ephesus

Tarsus

Carchemish

Haran

Gaugamela

Crete

Aleppo

Arbela

MEDIA

Cyrene

Mediterranean Sea *(Great Sea)*

Cyprus

Tadmor

Euphrates R.

BABYLONIA

Opis

Ecbatana

LIBYA

Tyre

Damascus

Babylon

Susa

Alexandria

Jerusalem

NABATEA

Erech (Uruk)

Ur

30°N

EGYPT

Memphis

Ezion-geber

Nile R.

SAHARA DESERT

ARABIAN DESERT

Extent of Alexandrian empire

Ptolemaic realm

Seleucid realm

Antigonid realm

Minor Hellenistic provinces

0   100   200 Miles

0   100 200 Kilometers

30°E

40°E

Thebes

Red Sea

ROMAN DIVISION OF PALESTINE

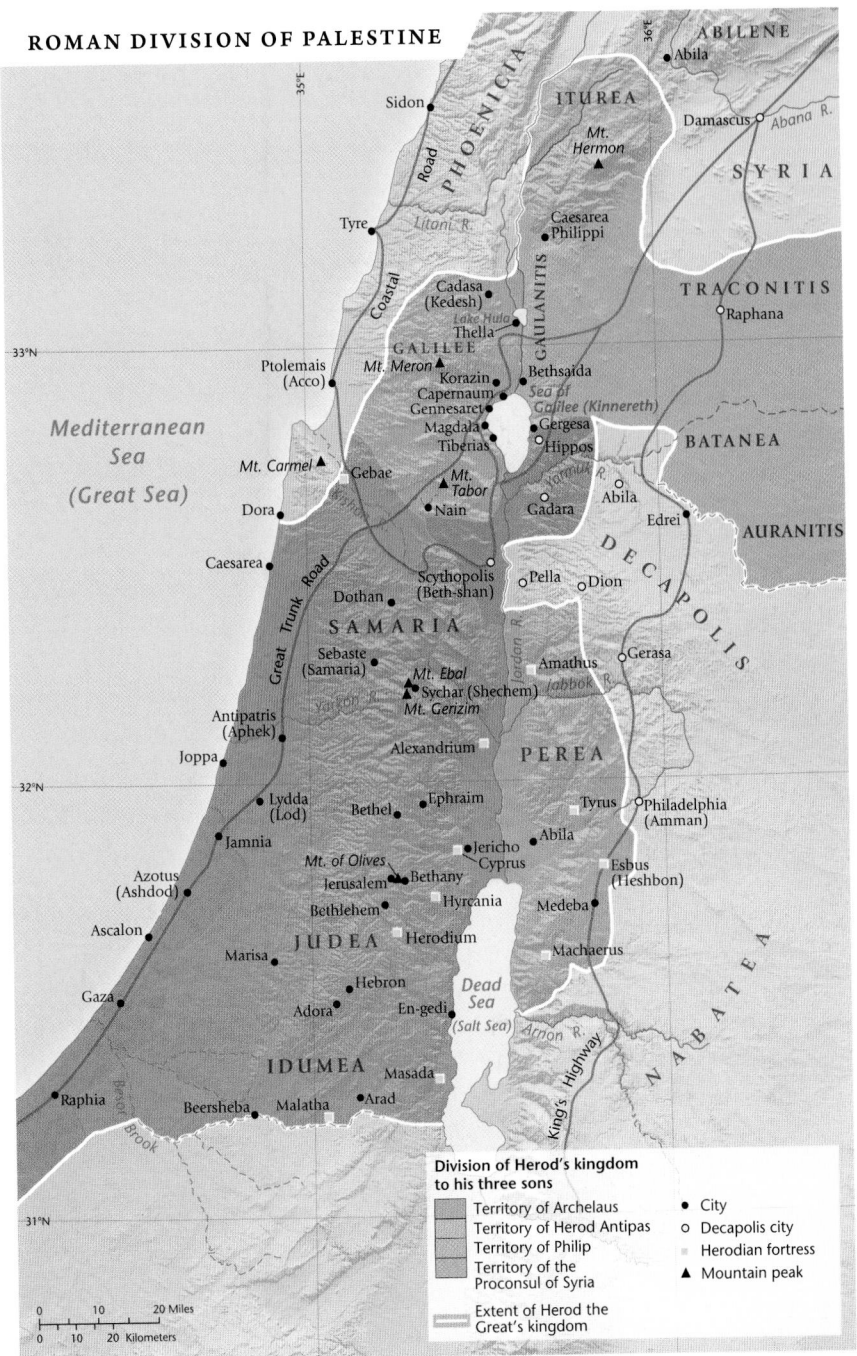

Mediterranean Sea (Great Sea)

PHOENICIA · **ITUREA** · **ABILENE** · **SYRIA** · **TRACONITIS** · **GAULANITIS** · **GALILEE** · **BATANEA** · **DECAPOLIS** · **AURANITIS** · **SAMARIA** · **PEREA** · **JUDEA** · **NABATEA** · **IDUMEA**

Abila · Damascus · Abana R. · Sidon · Mt. Hermon · Caesarea Philippi · Raphana · Tyre · Litani R. · Coastal Road · Cadasa (Kedesh) · Lake Hula · Thella · Ptolemais (Acco) · Mt. Meron · Korazin · Bethsaida · Capernaum · Sea of Galilee (Kinnereth) · Gennesaret · Magdala · Gergesa · Tiberias · Hippos · Mt. Carmel · Gebae · Mt. Tabor · Yarmuk R. · Dora · Nain · Gadara · Abila · Edrei · Caesarea · Scythopolis (Beth-shan) · Pella · Dion · Dothan · Sebaste (Samaria) · Mt. Ebal · Amathus · Gerasa · Sychar (Shechem) · Mt. Gerizim · Jordan R. · Jabbok R. · Great Trunk Road · Yarkon R. · Antipatris (Aphek) · Alexandrium · Joppa · Lydda (Lod) · Bethel · Ephraim · Tyrus · Philadelphia (Amman) · Jamnia · Abila · Azotus (Ashdod) · Jericho · Cyprus · Esbus (Heshbon) · Ascalon · Mt. of Olives · Bethany · Jerusalem · Hyrcania · Medeba · Bethlehem · Herodium · Machaerus · Marisa · Dead Sea (Salt Sea) · Gaza · Hebron · En-gedi · Adora · Arnon R. · King's Highway · Masada · Besor Brook · Raphia · Beersheba · Malatha · Arad

Division of Herod's kingdom to his three sons

- Territory of Archelaus
- Territory of Herod Antipas
- Territory of Philip
- Territory of the Proconsul of Syria
- Extent of Herod the Great's kingdom

- ● City
- ○ Decapolis city
- ▪ Herodian fortress
- ▲ Mountain peak

0   10   20 Miles
0 10 20 Kilometers

MINISTRY OF JESUS

Chronologically speaking, it is not possible to sequentially arrange the events in the life of Christ in any definitive way; none of the New Testament Gospels follows an overtly chronological pattern. Accordingly, the arrangement here follows a geographic order, basically proceeding from north to south on the map. Because the Gospel of Matthew most frequently contains information cited here, and because it is the most geographically particularistic Gospel, synoptic passages are keyed to the book of Matthew, except where they are unattested there or where more pertinent information about the event cited is available in another Gospel.

(A) Region of Phoenicia: Gentile woman's daughter healed (Mt 15:21-28)

(B) Caesarea Philippi: Peter's great declaration (Mt 16:13-20)

(C) Mt. Meron/Mt. Tabor/Mt. Hermon: (1) possible location of Transfiguration (Mt 17:1-13); (2) demon-possessed boy healed nearby (Mt 17:14-21)

(D) Cana of Galilee: (1) water changed to wine (Jn 2:1-11); (2) Capernaum official's son healed (Jn 4:46-54)

(E) Gennesaret: (1) possible location of feeding of multitudes (Mt 14:13-21; 15:32-39); (2) many healings (Mk 6:53-56)

(F) Area of Korazin: (1) judgment pronounced on the cities of Korazin, Bethsaida, and Capernaum (Mt 11:20-24); (2) possible area of Sermon on the Mount (Mt 5-7)

(G) Capernaum: (1) catch of fish (Lk 5:1-11); (2) evil spirit cast out (Mk 1:21-28); (3) Sermon on the Mount (Mt 5-7); (4) Peter's mother-in-law healed (Mt 8:14-15); (5) Roman officer's servant healed (Mt 8:5-13); (6) paralyzed man healed (Mt 2:1-12); (7) woman with a hemorrhage healed (Mk 5:25-34); (8) Jairus's daughter raised (Mt 9:32-34); (9) two blind men healed (Mt 9:27-31); (10) a mute, demon-possessed man healed (Mt 9:32-34); (11) the twelve apostles sent out (Mt 10:1-15); (12) man with deformed hand healed (Mt 12:9-13); (13) another demon-possessed man healed (Mt 12:22-37); (14) Temple tax provided (Mt 17:24-27); (15) Bread of Life discourse (Jn 6:22-59)

(H) Bethsaida: (1) possible location of feeding of multitudes (Mt 14:13-21; 15:32-39); (2) blind man healed (Mk 8:22-26)

(I) Sea of Galilee near Bethsaida: walking on water (Mt 14:22-33)

(J) Sea of Galilee: storm quieted (Mt 8:23-27)

(K) Gergesa/Gadara: possible location of casting out demons, which enter pigs; the pigs then rush down a steep bank and drown (Lk 8:26-39)

(L) Nazareth: (1) childhood home (Mt 2:19-23); (2) rejected by townspeople (Lk 4:16-30)

(M) Nain: widow's son raised (Lk 7:11-17)

(N) Region of Galilee: (1) leper cleansed (Mk 1:40-45); (2) post-resurrection appearances to the disciples (Mt 28:16-20)

(O) Decapolis (Region of Ten Towns): many healings (Mt 15:29-31; Mk 7:31-37)

(P) Region between Galilee and Samaria: (1) refused entry into village (Lk 9:51-56); (2) ten lepers healed (Lk 17:11-19)

(Q) Sychar: woman at the well of Samaria (Jn 4:1-42)

(R) Ephraim: enters into seclusion with the disciples (Jn 11:54)

(S) Region of Perea: (1) teaching on marriage (Mt 19:1-12); (2) possible location of healing of woman with infirmity (Lk 13:10-13); (3) possible location of healing of man with swollen limbs (Lk 14:1-6); (4) possible location of the rich young ruler (Lk 18:18-30)

(T) Jericho: (1) Bartimaeus healed (Mk 10:46-52); (2) Zacchaeus converted (Lk 19:1-10)

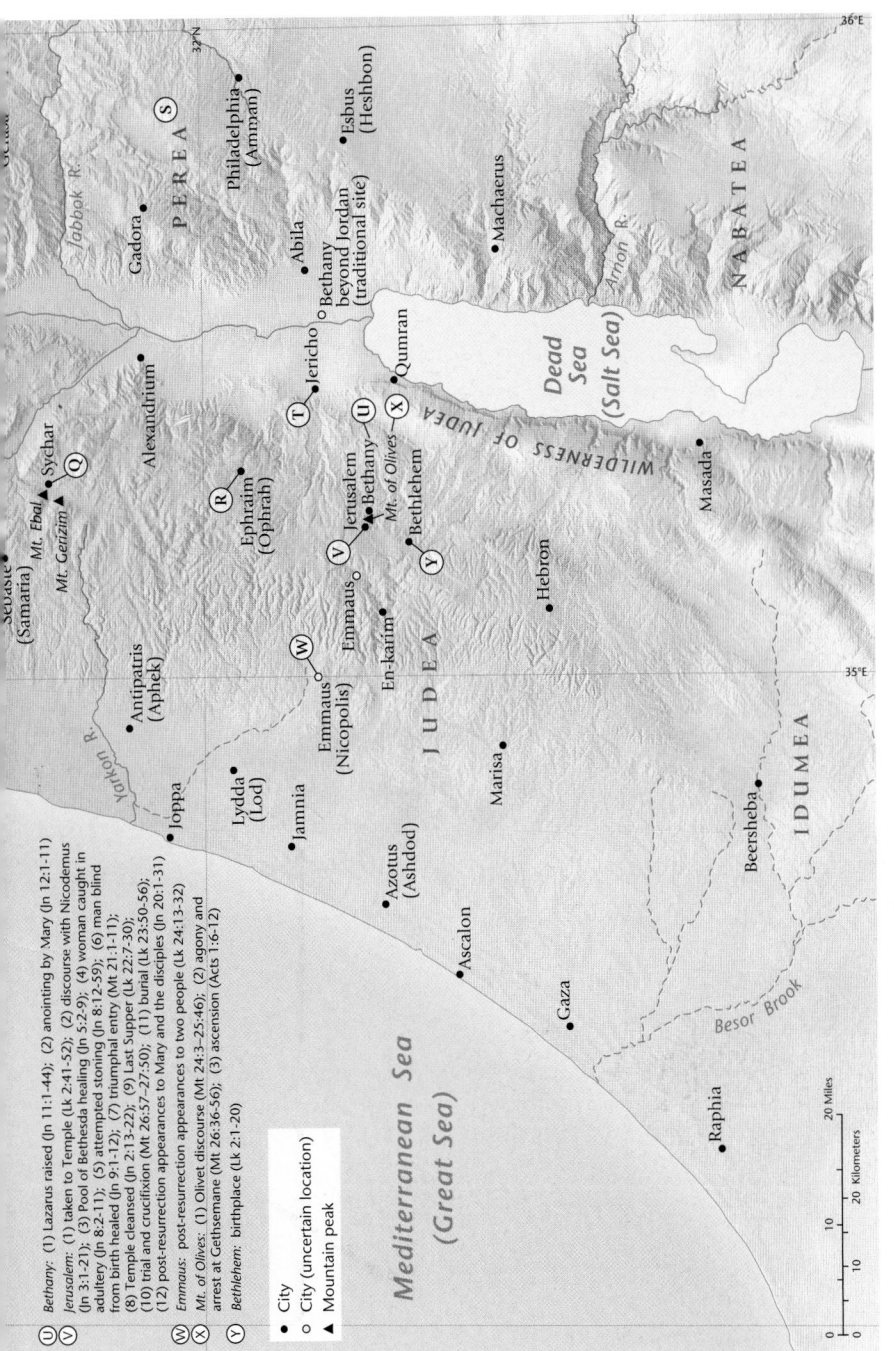

Ⓤ *Bethany:* (1) Lazarus raised (Jn 11:1-44); (2) anointing by Mary (Jn 12:1-11)

Ⓥ *Jerusalem:* (1) taken to Temple (Lk 2:41-52); (2) discourse with Nicodemus (Jn 3:1-21); (3) Pool of Bethesda healing (Jn 5:2-9); (4) woman caught in adultery (Jn 8:2-11); (5) attempted stoning (Jn 8:12-59); (6) man blind from birth healed (Jn 9:1-12); (7) triumphal entry (Mt 21:1-11); (8) Temple cleansed (Jn 2:13-22); (9) Last Supper (Lk 22:7-30); (10) trial and crucifixion (Mt 26:57–27:50); (11) burial (Lk 23:50-56); (12) post-resurrection appearances to Mary and the disciples (Jn 20:1-31)

Ⓦ *Emmaus:* post-resurrection appearances to two people (Lk 24:13-32)

Ⓧ *Mt. of Olives:* (1) Olivet discourse (Mt 24:3–25:46); (2) agony and arrest at Gethsemane (Mt 26:36-56); (3) ascension (Acts 1:6-12)

Ⓨ *Bethlehem:* birthplace (Lk 2:1-20)

• City

○ City (uncertain location)

▲ Mountain peak

COPYRIGHT © 2018 TYNDALE HOUSE PUBLISHERS

PAUL'S MISSIONARY JOURNEYS

Legend:
- Cilician Gates
- First journey (outbound)
- First journey (inbound)
- Second journey (outbound)
- Second journey (inbound)
- Third journey (outbound)
- Third journey (inbound)
- Journey to Rome

PAUL'S JOURNEY TO ROME